Presented on behalf of the Governors of Cathedral School and the Diocese of Wakefield to welcome you to our School and Christian Community.

Cathedral School Mission Statement

At Cathedral School, you are expected to:

- Learn through the teaching of Jesus and have respect for the beliefs and ways of other people
- Improve your skills, knowledge and qualifications to the highest level possible
- Show that you know the difference between right and wrong and be responsible for your own actions
- Show by the way you behave that you care for all the other people in school
- Live your life in an active and healthy way

WORKING TOGETHER THROUGHOUT GOD'S WORLD

Signed:

Sue Parton, Chair of Governors

Signed:

Paul West, Headteacher

Signed:

Reverend Canon Ian Wildey, Diocesan Director of Education

December 2008

YOUTH BIBLE

presented to

by

on

YOUTH BIBLE

Authentic

YOUTH BIBLE

First edition published 1993
Lifefiles updated and revised 2000, 2007

The preliminary research and development on the New Century Version was done by the World Bible Translation Centre, Inc., Fort Worth, Texas 76182.

Original devotional and study materials were developed by Group Publishing, Inc., Loveland, CO 80539, and adapted for UK use by Authentic Media.

Sunburst Hardback ISBN: 978-1-86024-614-2
Sunburst Paperback ISBN: 978-1-86024-615-9
Lightning Hardback ISBN: 978-1-86024-617-3
Worship Hardback ISBN: 978-1-86024-620-3
Purple Hardback ISBN: 978-1-86024-640-1

Published by Authentic Media, 9 Holdom Avenue, Bletchley, Milton Keynes, MK1 1QR.
Authentic Media is a division of IBS-STL UK, a company limited by guarantee (registered charity no.270162).
Typesetting and Print Management by Adare Ltd, Wellington Gate, Silverthorne Way, Waterlooville, Hampshire, PO7 7XY.
Printed and bound in Great Britain by William Clowes Ltd, Beccles, Suffolk.

Contents

Old Testament

New Testament

Start Here

(Mainly for ministers and youth leaders, but worth reading anyway)

The Bible is God's message to humanity. He has spoken to all peoples and all generations. Of course, God first did this by directly addressing his people, the Israelites, in the Old Testament and the young church in the New Testament, in a language they could understand.

The original text of the Bible was written in Hebrew, Aramaic and Greek – languages of the people. Since God intends to speak to all people of all ages through his Word, each generation and language group must translate the Bible into its own language.

These facts, that the Bible is God's message and that it is ultimately addressed to all people in every age, require that a translation be both accurate and clear. These are the two overarching principles that stand behind the *New Century Version*.

An Accurate Translation

The first concern of the *New Century Version* is that the translation be faithful to the manuscripts in the original languages. A team composed of the World Bible Translation Centre and fifty additional, highly qualified and experienced Bible scholars and translators was assembled. This team included people with experience on the *New International Version*, the *New American Standard Bible*, and the *New King James Version*. The scholars came from a variety of theological colleges, universities, and seminaries in the United States, Canada, Australia, and Great Britain. These translators recognise that the most accurate translations are those which pay close attention to the meanings of words in their broader context, rather than those which simply treat words as isolated entities. They understand that a contemporary English translation must sometimes depart from the word order of the original languages to reflect accurately the meaning of God's Word to a modern English-speaking audience.

Further, it is true that translation involves interpretive decisions. With this in mind, it is important to note that the breadth of scholarship which stands behind the *New Century Version* ensures an unbiased translation.

Last, it should be mentioned that the best available Hebrew and Greek texts were used, principally the third edition of the United Bible Societies' Greek text and the latest edition of the Biblia Hebraica, along with the Septuagint.

A Clear Translation

The second concern was to make the language clear enough for all people to read the Bible and understand it for themselves. In maintaining clear language, several guidelines were followed. Vocabulary choice has been based upon *The Living Word Vocabulary* by Dr Edgar Dale and Dr Joseph O'Rourke (Worldbook-Childcraft International, 1981), which is the standard used by the editors of *The World Book Encyclopedia* to determine appropriate vocabulary. For difficult words that have no simpler synonyms, footnotes and dictionary references are provided. Footnotes appear at the bottom of the page and are indicated in the text by a raised letter (n) for "note". The dictionary/topical concordance is located at the back of the Bible with references indicated in the text by a raised letter (d).

The *New Century Version* aids understanding by using contemporary references for measurements and geographical locations when it is feasible. For instance, terms such as "shekels", "cubits", "omer" and "hin" have been converted to modern equivalents. Where geographical references are identical, the modern name has been used, such as the "Mediterranean Sea" instead of "Great Sea" or "Western Sea". Also, to minimise confusion, the most familiar name for a place is used consistently, instead of using variant names for the same place. "Lake Galilee" is used throughout rather than its variant forms, "Sea of Kinnereth", "Lake Gennesaret" and "Sea of Tiberias".

Ancient customs are often unfamiliar to modern readers. Customs such as shaving a man's beard to shame him or ritually walking between the halves of a dead animal to seal an agreement are meaningless to many modern-day readers. So these are clarified either in the text or in a footnote.

Since **meanings** of words change with time, care has been taken to avoid potential misunderstandings. To do so, the *New Century Version* uses contemporary language in place of the archaic language often found in translations. Frequently in the Old Testament God tells his people to "devote" something to him, as when he tells the Israelites to devote Jericho and everything in it to him. While we might understand this to mean he is telling them to keep it safe and holy, the exact opposite is true. He is telling them to destroy it totally as an offering to him. The *New Century Version* communicates the idea clearly by translating "devoted", in these situations, as "destroyed as an offering to the Lord".

Where there was potential for confusion, **rhetorical questions** have been stated according to their implied answer. The psalmist's question, "Who, O God, is like you?" has been stated more directly as, "God, there is no one like you."

Figures of speech have been translated according to their meanings. For instance, the expression, "the Virgin Daughter of Zion", which is frequently used in the Old Testament, is simply and accurately translated "the people of Jerusalem" so that the meaning is not obscured by the figure of speech.

Idiomatic expressions of the biblical languages are translated to communicate the same meaning to today's reader that would have been understood by the original audience. For example, the Hebrew idiom "he rested with his fathers" is translated by its meaning – "he died".

Obscure terms have been clarified. Terms are often obscure in the Bible because they are part of the ancient culture which God directly addressed in his revelation. In the Old Testament, for instance, God frequently condemns the people for their "high places" and "Asherah poles". The *New Century Version* translates these according to their meanings, which would have been understood by the Hebrews. "High places" is translated "places where gods were worshipped" and "Asherah poles" is translated "Asherah idols".

Gender language has also been translated with a concern for clarity. To avoid the misconception that "man", "mankind" and "he" are exclusively masculine when they are being used in a generic sense, this translation has chosen to use less ambiguous language, such as "people", "humans" and "human beings", and has carefully worked throughout to choose gender language that would accurately convey the intent of the original writers. Specifically and exclusively masculine and feminine references in the text have been retained.

Following in the tradition of other English versions, the *New Century Version* indicates the divine name YHWH, the Tetragrammaton, by putting LORD, and sometimes GOD, in capital letters. This is to distinguish it from Adonai, another Hebrew word that is translated "Lord".

Every attempt has been made to maintain proper English style, while clarifying concepts and communication. The beauty of Hebrew parallelism in poetry has been retained, and the images of the ancient languages have been captured in equivalent English images wherever possible, but in all cases, clarity of communication with the modern reader has taken precedence over preservation of the ancient form.

Study Aids

Other features to enhance understanding of the text include maps of Bible lands, subject headings throughout to identify speakers and topics, book introductions to give a summary of each book's theme, a dictionary/topical concordance of biblical words and concepts, and footnotes identifying Old Testament quotations in the New Testament.

Our Prayer

It is with great humility and prayerfulness that this Bible is presented. We acknowledge the infallibility of God's Word and yet our own human frailty. We pray that God has worked through us as his vessels so that we all might better learn his truth for ourselves and that it might richly grow in our lives. It is to his glory that this Bible is given.

The Publisher

Using the Youth Bible with Groups

- **Why is it that the Bible ends up on so many shelves – unopened, unread and covered in a thick coat of dust?** Many young people say that they find the Bible dull, boring, remote and difficult to understand. Numbers of the teenagers we work with have heard it all hundreds of times before. On the other hand we all deal with people from an unchurched background. They don't understand church "lingo" and struggle to see how the Bible and God are in any way relevant to their lives. It's our task to bring the Bible to life for both those who've never heard it and those who have grown tired of listening. So what can you do?

- **Keep your eyes on the real goal.** Jesus asked us to make disciples not academics. Sadly Bible study has often been more about learning Bible history than helping young people understand what God's Word is really saying about contemporary life. The *Youth Bible* is all about challenging this approach. Bible background is important but needs to be kept in the background which is why the **Sidelights** are short. The goal of Bible study is to help young people grow in their friendship with Jesus and discover more about how important that friendship is to everyday life. This is why the **Life Files** have been developed, with their focus on relating the unchanging truth of the Bible to rapidly changing culture. And it is why they take up so much of the book.

- **Make quality time for preparation.** Start by praying and asking for God's help – after all he inspired the Bible's authors in the first place and he can do the same for you. Then read and re-read the Bible passage that you are going to study. Try and summarise the main points in your own words to get hold of what you think the text is actually saying. Now use the **Topical Concordance and Dictionary** at the back of the *Youth Bible* to get a highly focused view. Use a full-scale concordance or commentaries to get the broader picture. Use a book on Bible study methods to give you ideas on how to present your material. Do pinch ideas from books and magazines but adapt them rather than just swallowing them whole.

- **Use active learning approaches.** Outdated teaching methods have sometimes created a roadblock to making disciples and Bible studies based around a lecture will result in little Bible understanding and even less ability to apply it. The best learning methods are those that help your young people to discover the Bible's truths for themselves. Each **Life File** includes two active learning ideas under the heading "CONSIDER".

The Right Environment

- Use the smallest comfortable room. But remember 30 people in a crowded front room may make concentrating very difficult.
- Ensure that the phone will not ring at a vital moment.
- Never use a room which is being used for another activity at the same time.
- Avoid using a room which is on a through route to somewhere else.
- Use low chairs or cushions so people can put their bits on the floor.
- Get the temperature right. A stuffy room does not create a relaxed learning atmosphere.
- Leave space for latecomers so they don't feel awkward.
- Don't overrun and make sure people can get home on time.

- **See yourself as a facilitator rather than a lecturer.** Your aim should be to actively involve every group member. Let people express their thoughts and feelings. Having got healthy discussion going, your job is to occasionally steer it to keep it on target and moving, and to help group members to think through the implications of what they are discovering. You need to practise your listening as well as your speaking skills.
- **Questions are your basic tool to get the group thinking about the Bible passage.** Each **Life File** includes two questions to get the group going. Use extra questions that are clear and brief. Break long points down into a number of short statements and only then ask your question. Don't insult your group's intelligence by asking the obvious. Try to make your questions provocative to stir up reaction.
- **Bridge the cultural gap.** "The effective Christian is someone who holds the Bible in one hand, the newspaper in the other and reads both!" Use the newspaper or a video of the news to highlight issues like faith, drugs, alcohol, depression, death and poverty – the sort of subjects in the **Life File Guide** (starting on page 12). Get your youth group talking about what they think of the issue and introduce your biblical material from there.
- **Tie in to real-life experience.** The Bible is a practical guide to life today. Do things that encourage your members to put the Bible into practice, like visiting a prison or a soup kitchen or many of the other suggestions in the **Life Files**.
- **Always give page numbers.** Encourage people to use the list of contents to show where the books are. Don't give the impression that using the list of contents is second-rate.
- **Don't assume that all members of the group can read or write.** The *New Century Version* used in the *Youth Bible* is one of the most readable translations around (see **Start Here** p.6). But still be very careful before asking any group member to read aloud. You will never help people enjoy the Bible by intimidating or picking on them.

Using Life Files

- Always try and match the Life File to the situation of your group. Avoid using stories that are "too close for comfort".
- Ask the group whether they know of stories like the one that has been read.
- If you are working on a topic for an evening or at a weekend, break up into small groups each working on a different Life File.
- Dramatise the Life File stories.
- Get people to write alternative endings to the stories where appropriate. Have the group vote on the best/most realistic/most dramatic ending.
- Where the stories involve conflict, get people to role-play the characters and put them on trial as a way of discussing different points of view.
- Use stories as an opportunity to pray for people in situations like those in the story.
- Clip your own Life Files from newspapers, teen magazines or soap operas.

Getting to Know Your Bible

At times the Bible can feel like the most hard-going, difficult, confusing and boring book that has ever been written. The problem is that the Bible is very complicated.

- It isn't really a single book at all. The word "Bible" means "library" and that's exactly what it is – 66 books in all: 39 in the first section and 27 in the second.
- It was written by about 40 authors over a time period spanning more than 1,000 years and it contains 750,000 words. And if that's not enough, the Old Testament was written in Hebrew and the New Testament in Greek!

So why bother?

In a world where magazines, TV, radio, newspapers and other books bombard us with so many conflicting ideas about life, the Bible claims to be directly inspired by God himself – it's the Creator's message to his world. If that's true it means that the Bible is in a completely different league from any other advice you can find. If the Bible is God's guidebook to life, it makes sense to take it very, very seriously.

So, how do you make friends with the Bible and get the most out of reading it?

Here are ten dos and don'ts:

1. Do use a modern translation. It's very important that you read a version which captures the depth of the original language at the same time as expressing its truth in a clear up to date way. That's where the Youth Bible scores. See the notes down below.

2. Don't rush – read slowly. Think about what you are reading. Quality comes before quantity. Read it more than once. You'll find that you'll notice all sorts of things you missed first time round. Remember that it's better to understand one verse than read a whole chapter and forget the lot!

3. Do pray first. Ask God to speak to you. You might just pray, "Help me, God, to discover you and your will as I read my Bible." After you've finished reading it pray and talk to God about the things that he has said to you or if you have found it hard to understand, be honest with him about it.

Where The Youth Bible Scores

- It uses the *New Century Version* – a new translation, designed to be readable and reliable at the same time and the book itself is packed with all sorts of information that makes it user-friendly.
- If there is a particular problem or topic that you are thinking about you can look it up in the **Life File Guide** which lists over 400 topics on 80 important issues. Each **Life File** picks up on what the Bible has to say on that particular subject and then gives you a passage to read through or think about. Other relevant parts of the Bible are listed and because each reference comes with a page number beside it, you don't have to know where all those obscure books like Malachi, Jude and Esther are!
- Each individual book has a **Book Opener** – a short introduction to help you understand its purpose, with time charts and, in most cases, maps as well.
- **Sidelights** give you even more information about life in Bible times and the Bible itself.

4. Don't use it as a lucky dip. Don't open it at random and expect some magic word or phrase to leap out and solve all your problems. If you do, you are almost bound to end up getting confused. And don't try and read it from cover to cover right away. As we've already said it is a big and complicated book. Like with all other guidebooks the most sensible thing to do is to go to the issue you are thinking about at the time. Use a reading plan or the **Life File Guide** at the front of the Bible.

5. Do read it regularly. Just like food and exercise, "little and often" is best. If you can, set aside a short time every day to read a passage from the Bible and think it through. If your routine changes at the weekend, do something different then. Re-read what you have looked at during the week or talk it over with a friend. But remember that there is no right way to read the Bible. It's up to you to work out what suits you best.

6. Don't feel guilty if you miss a day. Why? Firstly, because everyone does. So you aren't odd. Life doesn't always work out quite according to plan for anybody. Secondly, the important point isn't to have your daily dose of Bible once every 24 hours but to take in its message.

7. Do ask yourself lots of questions. It's your job to find out what it's really saying rather than inventing your own meanings. Only when you have got to grips with its original meaning can you go on to discover what it's saying to you now. The box on this page gives you two sets of questions to ask your Bible passage. Copy them out onto a card or refer back to this page when you are reading.

8. Don't be put off when you have a boring week or more! It happens to everyone and you are probably gaining far more than you realise – though of course that will be easier to see looking back than at the time. The secret is to be disciplined and just keep on going.

9. Do read it responsibly. Having a time when you read the Bible each day isn't an end in itself, it is only a means to an end – understanding more about Jesus Christ, your Lord and friend, boss and brother. The biggest question isn't "How much have I read?" but "How much have I done about what I have read?" Once we have heard what God is saying about something we have a responsibility to act on it.

10. Don't be worried if you don't understand something. If you come across a difficult passage or anything that confuses you, get help. If you have a Bible commentary, concordance or Bible Dictionary, check it out there. If you can't solve it, ask your youth leader, minister or a friend – someone that you trust – to help you understand it.

What it meant then

(Use the **Sidelights** and **Book Openers** to help with these questions)

1. Who was the author and when and why was it written?
2. What kind of writing is it? Is it story or poetry and is the writer using symbols and pictures? If so, what do they mean?
3. Why did the author put it like this?
4. Was it written for a particular person or group of people?
5. What would the first readers have understood from these words?

What it means now

1. What is God saying to me through this passage?
2. What should I do?
3. What does it say about me or my situation?
4. What does it say about my relationships with God and with others?
5. Is there any special command, promise, warning or example that I should take notice of?

Life File Guide

This guide helps you find topics that interest or concern you. Refer to it when you are dealing with a particular problem or issue, or use it as a topical reading plan. Simply decide what topic you want to study and then read one Life File each day on that topic until you have read all the stories, thought about the issues and, most importantly, read the Bible passage.

Life File Guide (13)

Life File Guide (14)

Life File Guide (16)

Life File Guide (17)

Life File Guide (18)

Where do I find . . . ?

Have you ever known what you were looking for but didn't know where to find it in the Bible? A great event? A famous passage? A favourite story? Use this guide to help you find stories you remember but don't know where to find. The descriptions listed here are the common descriptions and are not always exactly the same as the descriptions in this Bible translation.

OLD
Testament

Genesis

Why Read This Book:

- Reflect on the beauty and wonder of God's creation (Genesis 1—2).
- Learn how God responds to rebellion against him (Genesis 3—11).
- Discover how God keeps his promises (Genesis 12—24).
- See how God works for good even during bad times (Genesis 37—50).

When?

Time Line:

Creation, the Flood, the Tower

- *2000 BC* — Abraham lived
- Joseph was sold into slavery
- *1500 BC* — The Israelites escaped from Egypt
- *1000 BC*
- *500 BC*
- *BC/AD* — Jesus was born

Behind the Scenes:

For weeks, you work tediously in art class creating a clay sculpture. You carefully shape the soft clay. One Friday, you leave the almost-finished sculpture to harden. On Monday you return. You find your clay twisted into a chaotic, unrecognisable blob. Rage and sadness swell up in you. You must begin the painstaking work all over again.

Genesis tells a similar story. It's the story of God's loving care in creating the world. But the story has a dark, twisted side. Genesis tells of human rebellion, murder and other human evil as people rebel against God.

Genesis falls naturally into two parts. Chapters 1—11 talk about the beginnings of the world. Here you'll read the famous stories of Adam and Eve, Cain and Abel, Noah and the tower of Babel. Each story shows how people often twist and destroy the gifts that God has given them.

Then chapters 12—50 talk specifically about the beginnings of the Hebrew people, later known as Israelites. You'll read about Abraham, the father of the nation, and his sons. And the book concludes with the story of Joseph, who God was able to use for great things even after his brothers had sold him into slavery.

Genesis is one of the most important books in the Bible. Not only does the rest of the Bible build on the foundation laid in this book, but the book shows how, from the beginning, God has used special people to play important roles in his world.

Where?

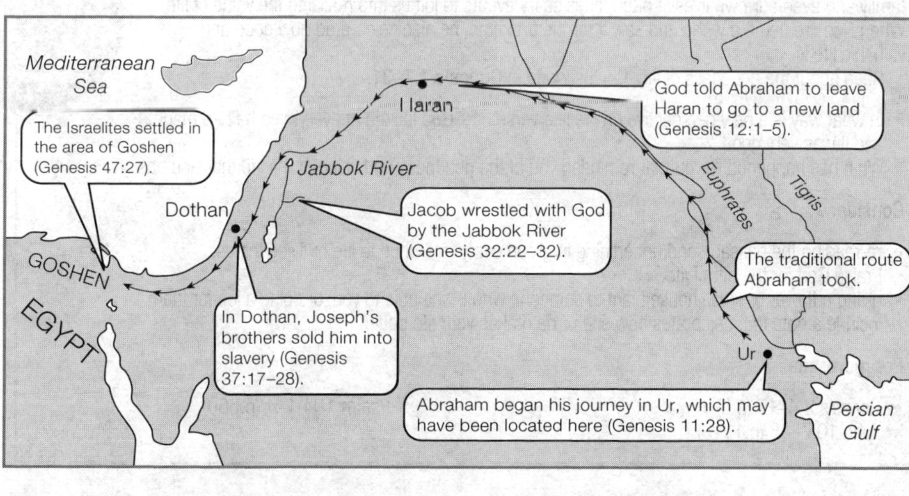

The Beginning of the World

1 In the beginning God created the sky and
the earth. 2The earth was empty and had no
form. Darkness covered the ocean, and God's
Spirit [d] was moving over the water.
3Then God said, "Let there be light," and there
was light. 4God saw that the light was good, so
he divided the light from the darkness. 5God
named the light "day" and the darkness "night".
Evening passed, and morning came. This was
the first day.
6Then God said, "Let there be something to
divide the water in two." 7So God made the air
and placed some of the water above the air and
some below it. 8God named the air "sky". Evening
passed, and morning came. This was the second
day.
9Then God said, "Let the water under the sky
be gathered together so the dry land will appear."
And it happened. 10God named the dry land
"earth" and the water that was gathered together
"seas". God saw that this was good.
11Then God said, "Let the earth produce
plants—some to make grain for seeds and others
to make fruits with seeds in them. Every seed
will produce more of its own kind of plant."
And it happened. 12The earth produced plants
with grain for seeds, and trees that made fruits
with seeds in them. Each seed grew its own
kind of plant. God saw that all this was good.

LIFE

The Value of Life

After two terrifying days at sea, John Howes' eyes were filled with fear when he was rescued after a heroic swim ashore by his friend Peter Wells. Peter, fifteen, had been given up as dead along with his two companions after a 1,000 square kilometre search. The rescue team had eventually been called off because of stormy weather and because the three boys were probably already dead.

Two days of stormy seas and low night temperatures meant that the odds were stacked against the boys' survival. But Peter had managed to push back the levels of his endurance and had chosen to swim away from their boat and head for the shore. After his successful night swim, he scrabbled up a cliff-face and broke a window to get into an empty cottage, where he found a phone and rang 999. In a hoarse voice he told the emergency services what had happened and where his friend could be found and rescued too.

Prayers had gone up as the headmaster of their school asked God to return the boys. Peter's phone call showed that their prayers had already been answered.

True stories like this show us how fragile our hold on life is. They leave us reeling and stunned at what happens and can happen.

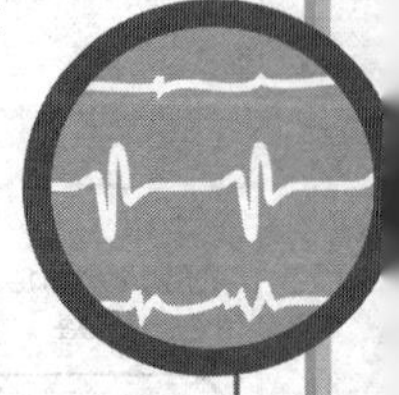

When we realise how temporary our lives are, it is hard to take things for granted – friends, family and even our own lives. It often takes scary events to jolt us into realising the value of life. When God created the world and saw it for the first time, he also celebrated how good and valuable life is.

Read about the goodness of life and the world in **Genesis 1:1–31**.

- In what way is a new perspective on life like verse 31: "God looked at everything he had made, and it was very good"?
- What has happened to you that reminded you of the goodness and value of the life that God has given you?

Consider . . .

- re-reading the passage and underlining in green every reference to life or living things. Praise God for the gift of life.
- giving a flower or small house plant to someone who is valuable to you, or doing a job for them. Include a note that celebrates how she or he makes your life better.

For more, see . . .

- Genesis 2:4–17 (p.3)
- John 10:7–18 (p.1113)
- Psalm 104:1–4 (p.560)

13Evening passed, and morning came. This was
the third day.
14Then God said, "Let there be lights in the sky
to separate day from night. These lights will be
used for signs, seasons, days and years. 15They
will be in the sky to give light to the earth." And
it happened.
16So God made the two large lights. He made
the brighter light to rule the day and the smaller
light to rule the night. He also made the stars.
17God put all these in the sky to shine on the
earth, 18to rule over the day and over the night,
and to separate the light from the darkness. God
saw that all these things were good. 19Evening
passed, and morning came. This was the
fourth day.
20Then God said, "Let the water be filled with
living things, and let birds fly in the air above the
earth."
21So God created the large sea animals and ev-
ery living thing that moves in the sea. The sea is
filled with these living things, with each one pro-
ducing more of its own kind. He also made every
bird that flies, and each bird produced more of its
own kind. God saw that this was good. 22God
blessed them and said, "Have many young ones
so that you may grow in number. Fill the water
of the seas, and let the birds grow in number on
the earth." 23Evening passed, and morning came.
This was the fifth day.
24Then God said, "Let the earth be filled with
animals, each producing more of its own kind.
Let there be tame animals and small crawling
animals and wild animals, and let each produce
more of its kind." And it happened.
25So God made the wild animals, the tame ani-
mals, and all the small crawling animals to pro-
duce more of their own kind. God saw that this
was good.
26Then God said, "Let us make human beings
in our image and likeness. And let them rule over
the fish in the sea and the birds in the sky, over the
tame animals, over all the earth, and over all the
small crawling animals on the earth."
27So God created human beings in his image.
In the image of God he created them. He created
them male and female. 28God blessed them and
said, "Have many children and grow in number.
Fill the earth and be its master. Rule over the fish
in the sea and over the birds in the sky and over
every living thing that moves on the earth."
29God said, "Look, I have given you all the
plants that have grain for seeds and all the trees
whose fruits have seeds in them. They will be
food for you. 30I have given all the green plants as
food for every wild animal, every bird of the air,
and every small crawling animal." And it hap-
pened. 31God looked at everything he had made,
and it was very good. Evening passed, and morn-
ing came. This was the sixth day.

The Seventh Day—Rest

2 So the sky, the earth, and all that filled them
were finished. 2By the seventh day God fin-
ished the work he had been doing, so he rested
from all his work. 3God blessed the seventh day
and made it a holy day, because on that day he
rested from all the work he had done in creating
the world.

The First People

4This is the story of the creation of the sky and
the earth. When the LORD God[d] first made the
earth and the sky, 5there were still no plants on
the earth. Nothing was growing in the fields be-
cause the LORD God had not yet made it rain on
the land. And there was no person to care for the
ground, 6but a mist would rise up from the earth
and water all the ground.
7Then the LORD God took dust from the ground
and formed a man from it. He breathed the
breath of life into the man's nose, and the man
became a living person. 8Then the LORD God
planted a garden in the east, in a place called
Eden, and put the man he had formed into it.
9The LORD God caused every beautiful tree and
every tree that was good for food to grow out of
the ground. In the middle of the garden, God
put the tree that gives life and also the tree that
gives the knowledge of good and evil.
10A river flowed through Eden and watered the
garden. From there the river branched out to be-
come four rivers. 11The first river, named Pishon,
flows around the whole land of Havilah, where
there is gold. 12The gold of that land is excellent.
Bdellium and onyx[n] are also found there. 13The
second river, named Gihon, flows around the
whole land of Cush. 14The third river, named
Tigris, flows out of Assyria towards the east. The
fourth river is the Euphrates.
15The LORD God put the man in the garden of
Eden to care for it and work it. 16The LORD God
commanded him, "You may eat the fruit from
any tree in the garden, 17but you must not eat the
fruit from the tree which gives the knowledge of
good and evil. If you ever eat fruit from that tree,
you will die!"

The First Woman

18Then the LORD God said, "It is not good for
the man to be alone. I will make a helper who is
right for him."

bdellium and onyx Bdellium is an expensive, sweet-smelling resin like myrrh, and onyx is a gem.

19From the ground God formed every wild
animal and every bird in the sky, and he brought
them to the man so the man could name them.
Whatever the man called each living thing, that

Sidelight Did Adam and Eve really eat an apple in the garden of Eden? The answer is probably not! The Bible never says. It is only described as "the fruit from the tree which gives the knowledge of good and evil" (Genesis 2:17). This does not sound too much like an ordinary apple!

became its name. 20The man gave names to all
the tame animals, to the birds in the sky, and to
all the wild animals. But Adam[n] did not find a
helper that was right for him. 21So the LORD God
caused the man to sleep very deeply, and while
he was asleep, God removed one of the man's
ribs. Then God closed up the man's skin at the
place where he took the rib. 22The LORD God used
the rib from the man to make a woman, and then
he brought the woman to the man.
23And the man said,

"Now, this is someone whose bones came
from my bones,
whose body came from my body.
I will call her 'woman',
because she was taken out of man."

24So a man will leave his father and mother
and be united with his wife, and the two will
become one body.
25The man and his wife were naked, but they
were not ashamed.

Adam This is the name of the first man. It also means "humans", including men and women.

CREATION

Will We Ever Learn?

More than five hundred years ago, Christopher Columbus wrote about the forests on the Haitian island of La Gonave. He described "thousands of kinds of trees so tall that they seem to be scratching heaven". Today, its mountains are almost barren. When the rain comes, the rich topsoil is eroded away, causing floods.

One year, 33 people in the town of Anse-à-Galets on La Gonave died in a flood. Three years later, the people were ready for the flooding. No one died, but two churches, four homes, and a drinking-water system were destroyed.

Some say the floods are natural disasters. But they happen, in part, because the people don't care for the land. They cut down trees to make charcoal to cook with or to sell. It's the only way they know to survive.

But it hurts them. Without trees, the highlands aren't protected. When rainfall comes, the good soil washes away, and the lowlands flood. So cutting trees to survive actually makes survival more difficult.

The people of La Gonave are experiencing the problems that come when people don't take care of the environment. Read **Genesis 2:4–17**, particularly verse 15, to see how God expects us to care for his world.

- How well do you think the people of La Gonave are fulfilling the responsibility of caring for God's garden?
- In what ways have you taken responsibility for caring for the world or garden God has given you?

Consider . . .

- noting everything you throw away in a day or week. Decide which item you could avoid throwing away by recycling, reusing, or not purchasing.
- contributing to or getting involved with an organisation that plants trees to repair damage people have caused by cutting them down.

For more, see . . .

- Leviticus 25:1–7 (p.124)
- Colossians 1:15–20 (p.1290)
- Psalm 8:1–9 (p.503)

The Beginning of Sin

3 Now the snake was the most clever of all the
wild animals the LORD God had made. One
day the snake said to the woman, "Did God really
say that you must not eat fruit from any tree in
the garden?"
2The woman answered the snake, "We may
eat fruit from the trees in the garden. 3But God
told us, 'You must not eat fruit from the tree that
is in the middle of the garden. You must not even
touch it, or you will die.' "
4But the snake said to the woman, "You will
not die. 5God knows that if you eat the fruit from
that tree, you will learn about good and evil and
you will be like God!"
6The woman saw that the tree was beautiful,
that its fruit was good to eat, and that it would
make her wise. So she took some of its fruit and
ate it. She also gave some of the fruit to her hus-
band, and he ate it.
7Then, it was as if their eyes were opened.
They realised they were naked, so they sewed fig
leaves together and made something to cover
themselves.
8Then they heard the LORD God walking in the
garden during the cool part of the day, and the
man and his wife hid from the LORD God among
the trees in the garden. 9But the LORD God called
to the man and said, "Where are you?"
10The man answered, "I heard you walking in
the garden, and I was afraid because I was naked,
so I hid."
11God asked, "Who told you that you were
naked? Did you eat fruit from the tree from
which I commanded you not to eat?"
12The man said, "You gave this woman to
me and she gave me fruit from the tree, so I
ate it."
13Then the LORD God said to the woman, "How
could you have done such a thing?"
She answered, "The snake tricked me, so I ate
the fruit."

MARRIAGE

So Lonely

Geoff and Samantha had been married for three years. They were mainly happy but Samantha's mother was an overbearing presence. Nothing could be decided outside the one-hour weekly phone call between Samantha and her mother. Geoff felt he had no power or authority to contribute to decisions in the relationship between him and Samantha. Things always needed her mum's approval, however obviously right they were. Samantha herself didn't seem to like this very much either, but she loved her mum who was very special to her – she was an only child. She didn't want to leave her mum out of things.

Geoff became frustrated and withdrawn. He had married Sam, not her mother, but somehow he never felt completely married to her. Then one day they took, jointly, a decision for themselves. Geoff's mother-in-law couldn't influence it because she was away travelling in India for a month. She couldn't be reached. Not that they tried that hard.

And it was a great decision – baby Alex is proof of that. And maybe Grandma sounds better than Mother-In-law does.

Marriage is about leaving as well as cleaving (joining).

Read **Genesis 2:18–24**. The story tells us that a human friend is the only cure for loneliness.

- What do you think this part of the creation story is trying to say about the relationship between God, man and woman?
- Does this passage teach us that the only answer to loneliness is a marriage partner?

Consider . . .

- what you are looking for in a life partner.
- listing, in order, all the things that would be important to you if you got married.

For more, see . . .

- Mark 10:7–8 (p.1016)
- Ephesians 5:21–33 (p.1275)

14The Lord God said to the snake,
"Because you did this,
a curse will be put on you.
You will be cursed as no other animal,
tame or wild, will ever be.
You will crawl on your stomach,
and you will eat dust all the days of your life.
15I will make you and the woman
enemies of each other.
Your descendants[d] and her descendants
will be enemies.
One of her descendants will crush your head,
and you will bite his heel."

16Then God said to the woman,
"I will cause you to have much trouble
when you are pregnant,
and when you give birth to children,
you will have great pain.
You will greatly desire your husband,
but he will rule over you."

17Then God said to the man, "You listened to
what your wife said, and you ate fruit from the
tree from which I commanded you not to eat.
"So I will put a curse on the ground,
and you will have to work very hard for
your food.
In pain you will eat its food
all the days of your life.
18The ground will produce thorns and weeds
for you,
and you will eat the plants of the field.
19You will sweat and work hard

SIN

An Expensive CD

Colin pulled the compact disc out from under his jacket as he sauntered out of the shopping centre. His cool exterior disguised his excitement. A track from the album had been at the top of the charts for five weeks now, and he couldn't get it out of his head. He'd never wanted a recording this much, and now he had it. He couldn't wait to listen to it.

Suddenly, a hand came down hard on the back of his neck and stopped him in his tracks. "Back inside, you," the security guard growled, as Colin turned to face him. "I'll take that CD, thank you."

Colin felt humiliated as the guard escorted him back to the manager's office in the music store. Then he sat awkwardly while the manager finished talking to the police on the phone.

"A police officer will be here in a few minutes," he said as he put the receiver down. "I won't press charges if you're a first-timer, but I need your home phone number. Your mum or dad will have to come and get you."

Colin dictated the number as the manager dialled. "And, young man," the manager said as the phone rang, "I never want to see you in my shop again."

Colin dreaded seeing his mum. She'd be so disappointed. Her eyes would be glassy-wet and red. She wouldn't look at him. That was the hardest part. He laid his head back and waited.

Colin experienced shame as Adam and Eve experienced shame when God caught them disobeying him. Read **Genesis 3:8–24** to learn what happened.

- How does the shop manager's punishment for shoplifting compare with God's punishment of Adam and Eve? What resulted from Adam and Eve's sin? Was Colin's punishment – and Adam and Eve's – appropriate?
- In what ways do you, like Adam and Eve, try to hide from God when you disobey him?

Consider . . .

- interrupting the "blame chain" ("somebody else made me do it") by accepting responsibility for things you do.
- talking to someone you trust about a sin you've been hiding inside, then confessing the sin to God. Discover how the confession affects you.

For more, see . . .

- Psalm 119:9–16 (p.571)
- 1 John 1:5–10 (p.1371)
- John 8:1–11 (p.1109)

for your food.
Later you will return to the ground,
because you were taken from it.
You are dust,
and when you die, you will return to the
dust."
[20]The man named his wife Eve,[n] because she
is the mother of everyone who has ever lived.
[21]The LORD God made clothes from animal
skins for the man and his wife and dressed them.
[22]Then the LORD God said, "The man has be-
come like one of us; he knows good and evil. We
must keep him from eating some of the fruit from
the tree of life, or he will live for ever." [23]So the
LORD God forced the man out of the garden of Eden
to work the ground from which he was taken.
[24]After God forced the man out of the garden, he
placed angels and a sword of fire that flashed
around in every direction on its eastern border.
This kept people from getting to the tree of life.

The First Family

4 Adam had sexual relations with his wife Eve,
and she became pregnant and gave birth to
Cain.[n] Eve said, "With the LORD's[d] help, I have
given birth to a man." [2]After that, Eve gave birth
to Cain's brother, Abel. Abel took care of flocks,
and Cain became a farmer.
[3]Later, Cain brought some food from the
ground as a gift to God. [4]Abel brought the best
parts from some of the firstborn[d] of his flock. The
LORD accepted Abel and his gift, [5]but he did not
accept Cain and his gift. So Cain became very
angry and felt rejected.
[6]The LORD asked Cain, "Why are you angry?
Why do you look so unhappy? [7]If you do things
well, I will accept you, but if you do not do them
well, sin is ready to attack you. Sin wants you,
but you must rule over it."
[8]Cain said to his brother Abel, "Let's go out
into the field." While they were out in the field,
Cain attacked his brother Abel and killed him.
[9]Later, the LORD said to Cain, "Where is your
brother Abel?"
Cain answered, "I don't know. Is it my job to
take care of my brother?"
[10]Then the LORD said, "What have you done?
Your brother's blood is crying out to me from the
ground. [11]And now you will be cursed in your
work with the ground, the same ground where
your brother's blood fell and where your hands
killed him. [12]You will work the ground, but it will
not grow good crops for you any more, and you
will wander around on the earth."
[13]Then Cain said to the LORD, "This punish-
ment is more than I can stand! [14]Today you have
forced me to stop working the ground, and now
I must hide from you. I must wander around on
the earth, and anyone who meets me can kill me."
[15]The LORD said to Cain, "No! If anyone kills
you, I will punish that person seven times more."
Then the LORD put a mark on Cain warning any-
one who met him not to kill him.

Cain's Family

[16]So Cain went away from the LORD and lived
in the land of Nod,[n] east of Eden. [17]He had
sexual relations with his wife, and she became
pregnant and gave birth to Enoch. At that time
Cain was building a city, which he named after
his son Enoch. [18]Enoch had a son named Irad,
Irad had a son named Mehujael, Mehujael had a
son named Methushael and Methushael had a
son named Lamech.
[19]Lamech married two women, Adah and
Zillah. [20]Adah gave birth to Jabal, who became
the first person to live in tents and raise cattle.
[21]Jabal's brother was Jubal, the first person to
play the harp and flute. [22]Zillah gave birth to
Tubal-Cain, who made tools out of bronze and
iron. The sister of Tubal-Cain was Naamah.
[23]Lamech said to his wives:
"Adah and Zillah, hear my voice!
You wives of Lamech, listen to what I say.
I killed a man for wounding me,
a young man for hitting me.
[24]If Cain's killer is punished seven times,
then Lamech's killer will be punished 77
times."

> **Sidelight** If one wife is a good idea, then two wives must be doubly wonderful, that is, twice as good. That's what Lamech thought (Genesis 4:19). The idea really caught on, and by the time it reached King Solomon, he ended up with seven hundred wives (1 Kings 11:3, p.325).

Adam and Eve Have a New Son

[25]Adam had sexual relations with his wife Eve
again, and she gave birth to a son. She named
him Seth[n] and said, "God has given me another
child. He will take the place of Abel, who was
killed by Cain." [26]Seth also had a son, and they
named him Enosh. At that time people began to
pray to the LORD.

Eve This name sounds like the Hebrew word for "alive".
Cain This name sounds like the Hebrew word for "I have given birth".
Nod This name sounds like the Hebrew word for "wander".
Seth This name sounds like the Hebrew word for "to give".

Adam's Family History

5 This is the family history of Adam. When
God created human beings, he made them
in his own likeness. 2He created them male and
female, and on that day he blessed them and
named them human beings.
3When Adam was 130 years old, he became
the father of another son in his likeness and im-
age, and Adam named him Seth. 4After Seth was
born, Adam lived 800 years and had other sons
and daughters. 5So Adam lived a total of 930
years, and then he died.
6When Seth was 105 years old, he had a son
named Enosh. 7After Enosh was born, Seth lived
807 years and had other sons and daughters. 8So
Seth lived a total of 912 years, and then he died.
9When Enosh was 90 years old, he had a son
named Kenan. 10After Kenan was born, Enosh
lived 815 years and had other sons and daugh-
ters. 11So Enosh lived a total of 905 years, and
then he died.
12When Kenan was 70 years old, he had a son
named Mahalalel. 13After Mahalalel was born,
Kenan lived 840 years and had other sons and
daughters. 14So Kenan lived a total of 910 years,
and then he died.
15When Mahalalel was 65 years old, he had a
son named Jared. 16After Jared was born, Mahala-
lel lived 830 years and had other sons and daugh-
ters. 17So Mahalalel lived a total of 895 years, and
then he died.
18When Jared was 162 years old, he had a
son named Enoch. 19After Enoch was born, Jared
lived 800 years and had other sons and daugh-
ters. 20So Jared lived a total of 962 years, and
then he died.
21When Enoch was 65 years old, he had a son
named Methuselah. 22After Methuselah was
born, Enoch walked with God 300 years more
and had other sons and daughters. 23So Enoch
lived a total of 365 years. 24Enoch walked with
God; one day Enoch could not be found, because
God took him.
25When Methuselah was 187 years old, he had
a son named Lamech. 26After Lamech was born,
Methuselah lived 782 years and had other sons
and daughters. 27So Methuselah lived a total of
969 years, and then he died.
28When Lamech was 182, he had a son. 29La-
mech named his son Noah[n] and said, "He will
comfort us in our work, which comes from the
ground the LORD has cursed." 30After Noah was
born, Lamech lived 595 years and had other sons
and daughters. 31So Lamech lived a total of 777
years, and then he died.
32After Noah was 500 years old, he became
the father of Shem, Ham and Japheth.

Sidelight If you think older adults tell too many stories about "When I was your age . . . " imagine what Methuselah's children must have thought. Genesis 5:27 says that he lived to be 969 years old. That means that, if he were born when Christopher Columbus discovered the Americas in 1492, he would only be middle-aged today!

The Human Race Becomes Evil

6 The number of people on earth began to
grow, and daughters were born to them.
2When the sons of God saw that these girls were
beautiful, they married any of them they chose.
3The LORD said, "My Spirit[d] will not remain in
human beings for ever, because they are flesh.
They will live only 120 years."
4The Nephilim[d] were on the earth in those
days and also later. That was when the sons of
God had sexual relations with the daughters of
human beings. These women gave birth to chil-
dren, who became famous and were the mighty
warriors of long ago.
5The LORD saw that the human beings on the
earth were very wicked and that everything they
thought about was evil. 6He was sorry he had
made human beings on the earth, and his heart
was filled with pain. 7So the LORD said, "I will
destroy all human beings that I made on the
earth. And I will destroy every animal and every-
thing that crawls on the earth and the birds of the
air, because I am sorry I have made them." 8But
Noah pleased the LORD.

Noah and the Great Flood

9This is the family history of Noah. Noah was
a good man, the most innocent man of his time,
and he walked with God. 10He had three sons:
Shem, Ham and Japheth.
11People on earth did what God said was evil,
and violence was everywhere. 12When God saw
that everyone on the earth did only evil, 13he said
to Noah, "Because people have made the earth
full of violence, I will destroy all of them from the
earth. 14Build a boat of cypress wood for yourself.
Make rooms in it and cover it inside and outside
with tar. 15This is how big I want you to build the
boat: 150 metres long, 25 metres wide and 15
metres high. 16Make an opening around the top
of the boat that is 50 centimetres high from the

Noah This name sounds like the Hebrew word for "rest".

edge of the roof down. Put a door in the side of
the boat. Make an upper, middle and lower deck
in it. [17]I will bring a flood of water on the earth
to destroy all living things that live under the sky,
including everything that has the breath of life.
Everything on the earth will die. [18]But I will
make an agreement with you—you, your sons,
your wife and your sons' wives will all go into the
boat. [19]Also, you must bring into the boat two
of every living thing, male and female. Keep
them alive with you. [20]Two of every kind of bird,
animal and crawling thing will come to you to be
kept alive. [21]Also, gather some of every kind of
food and store it on the boat as food for you and
the animals."
[22]Noah did everything that God commanded
him.

Sidelight Noah's boat described in Genesis 6:15 would have been huge for its time – about 108 metres long, the length of one and a half football fields. That's five times as long as the Mayflower in which the pilgrims sailed to North America in 1620. And it's more than half as long as a modern 206-metre ocean liner.

The Flood Begins

7 Then the LORD said to Noah, "I have seen
that you are the best person among the peo-
ple of this time, so you and your family can go
into the boat. [2]Take with you seven pairs, each
male with its female, of every kind of clean[d] ani-
mal; and take one pair, each male with its female,
of every kind of unclean animal. [3]Take seven
pairs of all the birds of the sky, each male with its
female. This will allow all these animals to con-
tinue living on the earth after the flood. [4]Seven
days from now I will send rain on the earth. It
will rain 40 days and 40 nights, and I will wipe
from the earth every living thing that I have
made."

EVIL

Quiet Cancer

The symptoms don't seem too serious at first. You start to feel tired and short of breath. Your blood doesn't clot as well as it should, and you bruise easily.

But these minor problems can be symptoms of leukaemia, a deadly cancer.

Although the outward signs don't seem all that bad, inside the body is under attack. Cancer has invaded the bone marrow and bloodstream. The body no longer produces enough healthy white blood cells, taking away its ability to fight off infections. Suddenly, the body feels sick and needs immediate medical attention. Untreated, a person can die within six weeks. Treatment can involve injections of drugs that kill the cancer, but also kill normal cells.

The hope is that healthy cells will grow again after treatment, and that cancerous ones won't.

Like leukaemia, evil can spread without people really noticing it. Yet it's deadly and difficult to get rid of. See how God feels about evil in the world by reading **Genesis 6:5—7:24**.

- What similarities do you see between leukaemia and the evil described in the passage? How is God's response to that evil like the treatment for cancer?
- What kinds of evil described in the passage still exist today? How is God working in the world today to stop the spread of evil?

Consider . . .

- identifying a potential evil in your life and then talking to a parent or other trusted adult about how you can stop it before it grows into a bigger problem.
- cutting out newspaper articles that show evil in the world. Each day this week, pray for people who are trapped by that evil.

For more, see . . .

- Psalm 43:1–5 (p.525)
- 1 John 5:18–20 (p.1377)
- Romans 1:28–32 (p.1185)

5Noah did everything the LORD commanded him.

6Noah was 600 years old when the flood came. 7He and his wife and his sons and their wives went into the boat to escape the waters of the flood. 8The clean animals, the unclean animals, the birds and everything that crawls on the ground 9came to Noah. They went into the boat in groups of two, male and female, just as God had commanded Noah. 10Seven days later the flood started.

11When Noah was 600 years old, the flood started. On the seventeenth day of the second month of that year the underground springs split open, and the clouds in the sky poured out rain. 12The rain fell on the earth for 40 days and 40 nights.

13On that same day Noah and his wife, his sons Shem, Ham and Japheth, and their wives went into the boat. 14They had every kind of wild and tame animal, every kind of animal that crawls on the earth and every kind of bird. 15Every creature that had the breath of life came to Noah in the boat in groups of two. 16One male and one female of every living thing came, just as God had commanded Noah. Then the LORD closed the door behind them.

17Water flooded the earth for 40 days, and as it rose it lifted the boat off the ground. 18The water continued to rise, and the boat floated on it above the earth. 19The water rose so much that even the highest mountains under the sky were covered by it. 20It continued to rise until it was more than 7 metres above the mountains.

21All living things that moved on the earth died. This included all the birds, tame animals, wild animals and creatures that swarm on the earth, as well as all human beings. 22So everything on dry land that had the breath of life in it died. 23God destroyed from the earth every living thing that was on the land—every man, animal, crawling thing and bird of the sky. All that was left was Noah and what was there with him in the boat. 24And the waters continued to cover the earth for 150 days.

The Flood Ends

8 But God remembered Noah and all the wild and tame animals with him in the boat. He made a wind blow over the earth, and the water went down. 2The underground springs stopped flowing, and the clouds in the sky stopped pouring down rain. 3–4The water that covered the earth began to go down. After 150 days it had gone down so much that the boat touched land again. It came to rest on one of the mountains of Ararat[n] on the seventeenth day of the seventh month. 5The water continued to go down so that by the first day of the tenth month the tops of the mountains could be seen.

6Forty days later Noah opened the window he had made in the boat, and 7he sent out a raven. It flew here and there until the water had dried up from the earth. 8Then Noah sent out a dove to find out if the water had dried up from the ground. 9The dove could not find a place to land because water still covered the earth, so it came back to the boat. Noah reached out his hand and took the bird and brought it back into the boat.

10After seven days Noah again sent out the dove from the boat, 11and that evening it came back to him with a fresh olive leaf in its mouth. Then Noah knew that the ground was almost dry. 12Seven days later he sent the dove out again, but this time it did not come back.

13When Noah was 601 years old, in the first day of the first month of that year, the water was dried up from the land. Noah removed the covering of the boat and saw that the land was dry. 14By the twenty-seventh day of the second month the land was completely dry.

15Then God said to Noah, 16"You and your wife, your sons and their wives should go out of the boat. 17Bring every animal out of the boat with you—the birds, animals and everything that crawls on the earth. Let them have many young ones so that they might grow in number."

18So Noah went out with his sons, his wife and his sons' wives. 19Every animal, everything that crawls on the earth and every bird went out of the boat by families.

20Then Noah built an altar to the LORD. He took some of all the clean[d] birds and animals, and he burned them on the altar as offerings to God. 21The LORD was pleased with these sacrifices and said to himself, "I will never again curse the ground because of human beings. Their thoughts are evil even when they are young, but I will never again destroy every living thing on the earth as I did this time.

22"As long as the earth continues,
planting and harvest,
cold and hot,
summer and winter,
day and night
will not stop."

The New Beginning

9 Then God blessed Noah and his sons and said to them, "Have many children; grow in number and fill the earth. 2Every animal on earth, every bird in the sky, every animal that

Ararat The ancient land of Urartu, an area in eastern Turkey.

crawls on the ground and every fish in the sea
will respect and fear you. I have given them to
you.
3"Everything that moves, everything that is
alive, is yours for food. Earlier I gave you the
green plants, but now I give you everything for
food. 4But you must not eat meat that still has
blood in it, because blood gives life. 5I will de-
mand blood for life. I will demand the life of any
animal that kills a person, and I will demand the
life of anyone who takes another person's life.

6"Whoever kills a human being
  will be killed by a human being,
because God made humans
  in his own image.

7"As for you, Noah, I want you and your family
to have many children, to grow in number on the
earth, and to become many."
8Then God said to Noah and his sons. 9"Now
I am making my agreement with you and your
people who will live after you, 10and with every
living thing that is with you—the birds, the tame
and the wild animals, and with everything that
came out of the boat with you—with every living
thing on earth. 11I make this agreement with you:
I will never again destroy all living things by a
flood. A flood will never again destroy the earth."
12And God said, "This is the sign of the agree-
ment between me and you and every living crea-
ture that is with you. 13I am putting my rainbow
in the clouds as the sign of the agreement be-
tween me and the earth. 14When I bring clouds
over the earth and a rainbow appears in them, 15I
will remember my agreement between me and
you and every living thing. Floods will never
again destroy all life on the earth. 16When the
rainbow appears in the clouds, I will see it and I will
remember the agreement that continues for ever
between me and every living thing on the earth."
17So God said to Noah, "The rainbow is a sign
of the agreement that I made with all living
things on earth."

Noah and His Sons

18The sons of Noah who came out of the boat

FUTURE

A Hope-Filled Dream

The future looked bleak for Miguel Rodriquez. Friends in his Brooklyn, New York neighbourhood used drugs, spent time in jail and dropped out of school. For them life seemed hopeless and the future bleak.

But Miguel had a friend who believed in him – Phill Carlos Archbold, his youth leader. Phill Carlos encouraged and supported Miguel, helped him with his homework and invited him over for meals. Sometimes he would even pay Miguel's bus fare so that he could get to school.

"He was a father-figure to me," Miguel says. "He was – and still is – always there for me." Phill Carlos' support and encouragement gave Miguel hope for the future. Though his friends dropped out of school, he completed his exams and went on to get a degree.

Because of Phill Carlos, Miguel looked forward to a bright future. God's promise to Noah also pointed to a bright future. Read about it in **Genesis 9:8–17**.

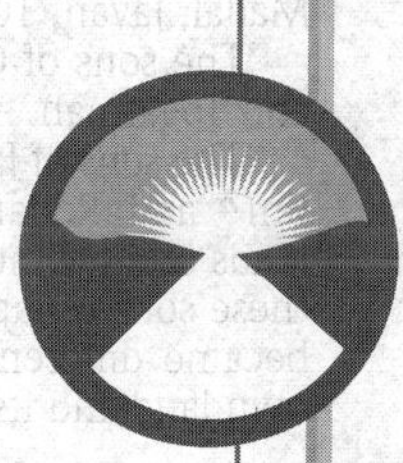

- How do you think God's promise to Noah gave him hope? How is that hope similar to the hope that Phill Carlos gave to Miguel?
- What signs – like the rainbow for Noah – do you see that give you hope and courage for the future?

Consider . . .

- drawing a rainbow on paper and putting it up where you can see it. Whenever something happens during the week that encourages you about your future, write it on the paper.
- watching the evening news to look for signs of hope. Thank God for those people who are working for a more positive future.

For more, see . . .

- Jeremiah 29:11 (p.749)
- 2 Corinthians 4:16–18 (p.1244)
- Matthew 6:25–34 (p.948)

with him were Shem, Ham and Japheth. (Ham was the father of Canaan.) [19]These three men were Noah's sons, and all the people on earth came from these three sons.

[20]Noah became a farmer and planted a vineyard. [21]When he drank wine made from his grapes, he became drunk and lay naked in his tent. [22]Ham, the father of Canaan, looked at his naked father and told his brothers outside. [23]Then Shem and Japheth got a coat and, carrying it on both their shoulders, they walked backwards into the tent and covered their father. They turned their faces away so that they did not see their father's nakedness.

[24]Noah was sleeping because of the wine. When he woke up and learned what his youngest son, Ham, had done to him, [25]he said,

"May there be a curse on Canaan!
May he be the lowest slave to his
brothers."

[26]Noah also said,

"May the LORD, the God of Shem, be praised!
May Canaan be Shem's slave.
[27]May God give more land to Japheth.
May Japheth live in Shem's tents,
and may Canaan be their slave."

[28]After the flood Noah lived 350 years. [29]He lived a total of 950 years, and then he died.

Nations Grow and Spread

10 This is the family history of Shem, Ham and Japheth, the sons of Noah. After the flood these three men had sons.

Japheth's Sons

[2]The sons of Japheth were Gomer, Magog, Madai, Javan, Tubal, Meshech and Tiras.

[3]The sons of Gomer were Ashkenaz, Riphath and Togarmah.

[4]The sons of Javan were Elishah, Tarshish, Kittim[n] and Rodanim. [5]Those who lived in the lands around the Mediterranean Sea came from these sons of Japheth. All the families grew and became different nations, each nation with its own land and its own language.

Ham's Sons

[6]The sons of Ham were Cush, Mizraim,[n] Put and Canaan.

[7]The sons of Cush were Seba, Havilah, Sabtah, Raamah and Sabteca.

The sons of Raamah were Sheba and Dedan.

[8]Cush also had a descendant[d] named Nimrod, who became a very powerful man on earth. [9]He was a great hunter before the LORD, which is why people say someone is "like Nimrod, a great hunter before the LORD." [10]At first Nimrod's kingdom covered Babylon, Erech, Akkad and Calneh in the land of Babylonia. [11]From there he went to Assyria, where he built the cities of Nineveh, Rehoboth Ir and Calah. [12]He also built Resen, the great city between Nineveh and Calah.

[13]Mizraim was the father of the Ludites, Anamites, Lehabites, Naphtuhites, [14]Pathrusites, Casluhites and the people of Crete. (The Philistines came from the Casluhites.)

[15]Canaan was the father of Sidon, his first son, and of Heth. [16]He was also the father of the Jebusites, Amorites, Girgashites, [17]Hivites, Arkites, Sinites, [18]Arvadites, Zemarites and Hamathites. The families of the Canaanites scattered. [19]Their land reached from Sidon to Gerar as far as Gaza and then to Sodom, Gomorrah, Admah and Zeboiim, as far as Lasha.

[20]All these people were the sons of Ham and all these families had their own languages, their own lands, and their own nations.

Shem's Sons

[21]Shem, Japheth's older brother, also had sons. One of his descendants[d] was the father of all the sons of Eber.

[22]The sons of Shem were Elam, Asshur, Arphaxad, Lud and Aram.

[23]The sons of Aram were Uz, Hul, Gether and Meshech.

[24]Arphaxad was the father of Shelah, who was the father of Eber. [25]Eber was the father of two sons—one named Peleg,[n] because the earth was divided during his life, and the other was named Joktan.

[26]Joktan was the father of Almodad, Sheleph, Hazarmaveth, Jerah, [27]Hadoram, Uzal, Diklah, [28]Obal, Abimael, Sheba, [29]Ophir, Havilah and Jobab. All these people were the sons of Joktan. [30]They lived in the area between Mesha and Sephar in the hill country in the east.

[31]These are the people from the family of Shem, arranged by families, languages, countries and nations.

[32]This is the list of the families from the sons of Noah, arranged according to their nations. From these families came all the nations who spread across the earth after the flood.

The Languages Confused

11 At this time the whole world spoke one language, and everyone used the same words. [2]As people moved from the east,

Kittim His descendants were the people of Cyprus.
Mizraim This is another name for Egypt.
Peleg This name sounds like the Hebrew word for "divided".

they found a plain in the land of Babylonia and
settled there.
3They said to each other, "Let's make bricks
and bake them to make them hard." So they used
bricks instead of stones, and tar instead of mortar.
4Then they said to each other, "Let's build a city
and a tower for ourselves, whose top will reach
high into the sky. We will become famous. Then
we will not be scattered over all the earth."
5The LORD came down to see the city and the
tower that the people had built. 6The LORD said,
"Now, these people are united, all speaking the
same language. This is only the beginning of what
they will do. They will be able to do anything
they want. 7Come, let us go down and confuse
their language so they will not be able to under-
stand each other."
8So the LORD scattered them from there over all
the earth, and they stopped building the city.
9The place is called Babel[n] since that is where
the LORD confused the language of the whole
world. So the LORD caused them to spread out
from there over the whole world.

Babel This name sounds like the Hebrew word for "confused".

> **Sidelight**
>
> The tower described in Genesis 11:1–9 was probably a ziggurat – a multi-storied temple built to worship Babylonian gods. The "temple towers", which looked like staircase pyramids, were built in most major Babylonian cities.

The Story of Shem's Family

10This is the family history of Shem. Two years
after the flood, when Shem was 100 years
old, his son Arphaxad was born. 11After that,
Shem lived 500 years and had other sons and
daughters.

BOASTING

Pride Hurts

Everyone was sure Susan would get the lead role of Maria in the spring musical, *West Side Story*, especially Susan. She kept reminding everyone of her experience – having been in every production since she had started at the college.

"I can make Maria come to life on the stage," she proclaimed. "Besides, this is my last show. Lots of people will be disappointed if I'm not cast as Maria."

Audition day came, and Susan was ready.
She confidently sang, danced and acted. It felt great. "I was really good," she told her best friend Debbie on the phone that evening. "It's a great part. It'll really stretch me."

Next morning, Susan rushed to the drama room to see the cast list and confirm what she already knew. But she stared at the list in disbelief. Her name wasn't next to Maria. It was way down the page – a little part with just a few lines in Act Two. Humiliated, Susan left in tears.

Susan's problem was pride. And it was at the heart of the events in **Genesis 11:1–9**, where the people built a tower in disobedience to God.

- How did Susan's pride hurt her like pride hurt the tower builders?
- What "towers" of pride are you building in your own life?

Consider . . .

- giving a compliment to another person when you're tempted to boast about yourself.
- listing everything about yourself that makes you proud. Then put ticks beside items you think are appropriate forms of pride, and crosses beside those that aren't. Decide how you'll begin overcoming one of the crosses this week.

For more, see . . .

- Proverbs 16:18–19 (p.603)
- Philippians 2:1–11 (p.1282)
- Hosea 5:5–6 (p.854)

12When Arphaxad was 35 years old, his son Shelah was born. 13After that, Arphaxad lived 403 years and had other sons and daughters.
14When Shelah was 30 years old, his son Eber was born. 15After that, Shelah lived 403 years and had other sons and daughters.
16When Eber was 34 years old, his son Peleg was born. 17After that, Eber lived 430 years and had other sons and daughters.
18When Peleg was 30 years old, his son Reu was born. 19After that, Peleg lived 209 years and had other sons and daughters.
20When Reu was 32 years old, his son Serug was born. 21After that, Reu lived 207 years and had other sons and daughters.
22When Serug was 30 years old, his son Nahor was born. 23After that, Serug lived 200 years and had other sons and daughters.
24When Nahor was 29 years old, his son Terah was born. 25After that, Nahor lived 119 years and had other sons and daughters.
26After Terah was 70 years old, his sons Abram, Nahor and Haran were born.

The Story of Terah's Family

27This is the family history of Terah. Terah was the father of Abram, Nahor and Haran. Haran was the father of Lot. 28While his father, Terah, was still alive, Haran died in Ur in Babylonia, where he was born. 29Abram and Nahor both married. Abram's wife was named Sarai, and Nahor's wife was named Milcah. She was the daughter of Haran, who was the father of both Milcah and Iscah. 30Sarai was not able to have children.
31Terah took his son Abram, his grandson Lot (Haran's son), and his daughter-in-law Sarai (Abram's wife) and moved out of Ur of Babylonia. They had planned to go to the land of Canaan, but when they reached the city of Haran, they settled there.
32Terah lived to be 205 years old, and then he died in Haran.

God Calls Abram

12 The LORD said to Abram,[n] "Leave your country, your relatives and your father's family, and go to the land I will show you.
2I will make you a great nation,
and I will bless you.
I will make you famous,
and you will be a blessing to others.
3I will bless those who bless you,
and I will place a curse on those who
harm you.
And all the people on earth
will be blessed through you."
4So Abram left Haran as the LORD had told him, and Lot went with him. At this time Abram was 75 years old. 5He took his wife Sarai, his nephew Lot, and everything they owned, as well as all the servants they had gained in Haran. They set out from Haran, planning to go to the land of Canaan, and in time they arrived there.

Sidelight When Abram left Egypt, he lived in tents. It would have been a real change in lifestyle. They were probably made from animal skins and quite heavy, like those of modern Bedouins.

6Abram travelled through that land as far as the great tree of Moreh at Shechem. The Canaanites were living in the land at that time. 7The LORD appeared to Abram and said, "I will give this land to your descendants."[d] So Abram built an altar there to the LORD, who had appeared to him. 8Then he travelled from Shechem to the mountain east of Bethel and set up his tent there. Bethel was to the west, and Ai was to the east. There Abram built another altar to the LORD and worshipped him. 9After this, he travelled on towards southern Canaan.

Abram Goes to Egypt

10At this time there was not much food in the land, so Abram went down to Egypt to live because there was so little food. 11Just before they arrived in Egypt, he said to his wife Sarai,[n] "I know you are a very beautiful woman. 12When the Egyptians see you, they will say, 'This woman is his wife.' Then they will kill me but let you live. 13Tell them you are my sister so that things will go well with me and I may be allowed to live because of you."
14When Abram came to Egypt, the Egyptians saw that Sarai was very beautiful. 15The Egyptian officers saw her and told the king of Egypt how beautiful she was. They took her to the king's palace, and 16the king was kind to Abram because he thought Abram was her brother. He gave Abram sheep, cattle, male and female donkeys, male and female servants and camels.
17But the LORD sent terrible diseases on the king and all the people in his house because of Abram's wife Sarai. 18So the king sent for Abram

Abram This name means "honoured father".
Sarai An Aramaic name meaning "princess".

and said, "What have you done to me? Why didn't you tell me Sarai was your wife? 19 Why did you say, 'She is my sister' so that I made her my wife? Now, here is your wife. Take her and leave!" 20 Then the king commanded his men to make Abram leave Egypt; so Abram and his wife left with everything they owned.

Abram and Lot Separate

13 So Abram, his wife and Lot left Egypt, taking everything they owned, and travelled to southern Canaan. 2 Abram was very rich in cattle, silver and gold.

3 He left southern Canaan and went back to Bethel where he had camped before, between Bethel and Ai, 4 and where he had built an altar. So he worshipped the LORD there.

5 During this time Lot was travelling with Abram, and Lot also had flocks, herds and tents. 6 Abram and Lot had so many animals that the land could not support both of them together, 7 so Abram's herdsmen and Lot's herdsmen began to argue. The Canaanites and the Perizzites were living in the land at this time.

8 Abram said to Lot, "There should be no arguing between you and me, or between your herdsmen and mine, because we are brothers. 9 We should separate. The whole land is there in front of you. If you go to the left, I will go to the right. If you go to the right, I will go to the left."

GOD'S WILL

Unknown Outcomes

Although it was the 1950s, the Auca Indians of Ecuador, South America, were still a violent, Stone Age tribe.

But Jim Elliot felt God calling him to Ecuador to share the Gospel with the Aucas. Only one missionary had ever gone: a Jesuit priest who, in 1667, was murdered at his jungle outpost.

Jim didn't let history stop him from what he knew God wanted. "My going to Ecuador is God's counsel," Jim wrote in his diary.

So Jim and four other missionaries left their families and boarded the ship for Ecuador. They built a camp in Auca territory and began trying to befriend the Aucas. They would fly over their village in a small aeroplane, drop gifts and call out to the Indians in the Auca language.

On 6 January 1956, they finally befriended one Auca, a young man they called "George". Now, they hoped, they could make more contact with the tribe.

That weekend, the Aucas attacked, killing all the missionaries, including Jim Elliot.

But that wasn't the end of the story. Jim's wife, Elisabeth, refused to let the murder of her husband keep her from following God's call to Ecuador. She and other missionaries returned to Auca territory.

Less than three years later, Elisabeth wrote: "Today I sit in a tiny leaf-thatched hut . . . In another leaf house, just three metres away, sit two of the seven men who killed my husband."

Jim Elliot followed God's will, with seemingly tragic consequences. But God was at work even when his plan was difficult to see. And the missionary effort, started by Jim Elliot and continued by Elisabeth, prospered. Abram also left everything he knew to follow God to an unknown place. Read about his faith in **Genesis 12:1–9**.

- In what ways was Jim Elliot's call similar to Abram's call in the passage?
- Have you ever sensed that God wanted you to do something without your knowing what the result would be? How did you respond?

Consider . . .

- taking a step of faith by doing something you believe God wants you to do, such as sharing your faith with a friend or working on a bad habit.
- making a bookmark for your Bible with two big eyes on it to remind you to look for God's will as you read.

For more, see . . .

- Genesis 45:1–8 (p.51)
- James 4:13–17 (p.1352)
- Matthew 8:18–22 (p.952)

10Lot looked all around and saw the whole Jor-
dan Valley and that there was much water there.
It was like the LORD's garden, like the land of
Egypt in the direction of Zoar. (This was before
the LORD destroyed Sodom and Gomorrah.) 11So
Lot chose to move east and live in the Jordan
Valley. In this way Abram and Lot separated.
12Abram lived in the land of Canaan, but Lot lived
among the cities in the Jordan Valley, very near
to Sodom. 13Now the people of Sodom were very
evil and were always sinning against the LORD.
14After Lot left, the LORD said to Abram, "Look
all around you—to the north and south and east
and west. 15All this land that you see I will give
to you and your descendants[d] for ever. 16I will
make your descendants as many as the dust of
the earth. If anyone could count the dust on the
earth, he could count your people. 17Get up!
Walk through all this land because I am now
giving it to you."
18So Abram moved his tents and went to live
near the great trees of Mamre at the city of Heb-
ron. There he built an altar to the LORD.

Lot is Captured

14 Now Amraphel was king of Babylonia,
Arioch was king of Ellasar, Kedorlaomer
was king of Elam and Tidal was king of Goiim.
2All these kings went to war against several other
kings: Bera, king of Sodom, Birsha, king of Go-
morrah, Shinab, king of Admah, Shemeber, king
of Zeboiim and the king of Bela. (Bela is also
called Zoar.)
3These kings who were attacked united their
armies in the Valley of Siddim (now the Dead
Sea[d]). 4They had served Kedorlaomer for twelve
years, but in the thirteenth year, they all turned
against him. 5Then in the fourteenth year, Kedor-
laomer and the kings with him came and de-
feated the Rephaites[d] in Ashteroth Karnaim, the
Zuzites in Ham and the Emites in Shaveh Kiria-
thaim. 6They also defeated the Horites in the
mountains of Edom to El Paran (near the desert).
7Then they turned back and went to En Mishpat
(that is, Kadesh). They defeated all the Amalek-
ites, as well as the Amorites who lived in Haza-
zon Tamar.
8At that time the kings of Sodom, Gomorrah,
Admah, Zeboiim and Bela went out to fight in
the Valley of Siddim. (Bela is called Zoar.) 9They
fought against Kedorlaomer, king of Elam, Tidal,
king of Goiim, Amraphel, king of Babylonia and
Arioch, king of Ellasar—four kings fighting
against five. 10There were many tar pits in the
Valley of Siddim. When the kings of Sodom and
Gomorrah and their armies ran away, some of the
soldiers fell into the tar pits, but the others ran
away to the mountains.
11Now Kedorlaomer and his armies took every-
thing the people of Sodom and Gomorrah owned,
including their food. 12They took Lot, Abram's
nephew, who was living in Sodom, and every-
thing he owned. Then they left. 13One of the men
who was not captured went to Abram, the Heb-
rew, and told him what had happened. At that
time Abram was camped near the great trees of
Mamre the Amorite. Mamre was a brother of
Eshcol and Aner, and they had all made an agree-
ment to help Abram.

Abram Rescues Lot

14When Abram learned that Lot had been cap-
tured, he called out his 318 trained men who had
been born in his camp. He led the men and
chased the enemy all the way to the town of Dan.
15That night he divided his men into groups, and
they made a surprise attack against the enemy.
They chased them all the way to Hobah, north of
Damascus. 16Then Abram brought back every-
thing the enemy had stolen, the women and the
other people and Lot and everything Lot owned.
17After defeating Kedorlaomer and the kings
who were with him, Abram went home. As he
was returning, the king of Sodom came out to
meet him in the Valley of Shaveh (now called
King's Valley).
18Melchizedek, king of Salem, brought out
bread and wine. He was a priest for God Most
High 19and blessed Abram, saying,

"Abram, may you be blessed by God Most
High,
the God who made heaven and earth.
20And we praise God Most High,
who has helped you to defeat your
enemies."

Then Abram gave Melchizedek a tenth of every-
thing he had brought back from the battle.
21The king of Sodom said to Abram, "You may
keep all these things for yourself. Just give me my
people who were captured."
22But Abram said to the king of Sodom, "I
make a promise to the LORD, the God Most High,
who made heaven and earth. 23I promise that I
will not keep anything that is yours. I will not
keep even a thread or a sandal strap so that you
cannot say, 'I made Abram rich.' 24I will keep
nothing but the food my young men have eaten.
But give Aner, Eshcol and Mamre their share of
what we won, because they went with me into
battle."

God's Agreement with Abram

15 After these things happened, the LORD
spoke his word to Abram in a vision:
"Abram, don't be afraid. I will defend you, and I
will give you a great reward."

[2]But Abram said, "Lord GOD,[d] what can you
give me? I have no son, so my slave Eliezer from
Damascus will get everything I own after I die."
[3]Abram said, "Look, you have given me no son,
so a slave born in my house will inherit every-
thing I have."
[4]Then the LORD spoke his word to Abram: "He
will not be the one to inherit what you have. You
will have a son of your own who will inherit
what you have."
[5]Then God led Abram outside and said, "Look
at the sky. There are so many stars you cannot
count them. Your descendants[d] also will be too
many to count."
[6]Abram believed the LORD. And the LORD ac-
cepted Abram's faith, and that faith made him
acceptable to God.
[7]God said to Abram, "I am the LORD who led
you out of Ur of Babylonia so that I could give
you this land to own."
[8]But Abram said, "Lord GOD, how can I be sure
that I will own this land?"
[9]The LORD said to Abram, "Bring me a three-
year-old cow, a three-year-old goat, a three-year-
old ram, a dove and a young pigeon."
[10]Abram brought them all to God. Then Abram
killed the animals and cut each of them into two
pieces, laying each half opposite the other half.
But he did not cut the birds in half. [11]Later, large
birds flew down to eat the animals, but Abram
chased them away.
[12]As the sun was going down, Abram fell into
a deep sleep. While he was asleep, a very terrible
darkness came. [13]Then the LORD said to Abram,
"You can be sure that your descendants will be
strangers and travel in a land they don't own. The
people there will make them slaves and be cruel
to them for 400 years. [14]But I will punish the
nation where they are slaves. Then your descend-
ants will leave that land, taking great wealth with

DISCOURAGEMENT

Counting

Thomas wanted to create something to store electricity. Time after time – in fact, 50,000 times – he failed. But he kept trying, and eventually he succeeded. He had invented the first battery.

Someone asked him, "Don't you get discouraged when you have to try 50,000 experiments before you get any results?"

"Results?" Thomas replied. "Why, I've got lots of results. I now know 50,000 things that won't work."

Thomas didn't get discouraged when he didn't get instant results. Perhaps that's why Thomas Edison is credited with almost 1,300 inventions, including record players, films, microphones, light bulbs, and the transmitter that made telephones possible.

Just as Thomas Edison didn't expect instant results, so Abram also waited for God's promises to come true. Read **Genesis 15:1–6** to see how he didn't give in to discouragement.

- What kept Thomas Edison from giving in to discouragement? What kept Abram from giving in? What's similar and different about the two situations?
- When have you been discouraged and tempted to give up on God as Abram was tempted? What happened?

Consider . . .

- writing a letter of encouragement to yourself, then sealing the letter in an envelope to keep in your Bible. Open the letter and read it sometime when you're discouraged.
- visiting a hospital's physiotherapy department. Ask a therapist what characteristics keep people from getting discouraged in recovery. Apply those characteristics in your own life.

For more, see . . .

- Psalm 77:1–15 (p.545)
- Hebrews 6:13–19 (p.1335)
- Isaiah 40:27–31 (p.680)

them. 15And you, Abram, will die in peace and
will be buried at an old age. 16After your great-
great-grandchildren are born, your people will
come to this land again. It will take that long,
because I am not yet going to punish the Amor-
ites for their evil behaviour."
17After the sun went down, it was very dark.
Suddenly a smoking firepot and a blazing torch
passed between the halves of the dead animals.[n]
18So on that day the LORD made an agreement
with Abram and said, "I will give to your des-
cendants the land between the river of Egypt and
the great river Euphrates. 19This is the land of the
Kenites, Kenizzites, Kadmonites, 20Hittites, Periz-
zites, Rephaites,[d] 21Amorites, Canaanites, Girga-
shites and Jebusites."

Ishmael is Born

16 Sarai, Abram's wife, had no children, but
she had a slave girl from Egypt named
Hagar. 2Sarai said to Abram, "Look, the LORD has
not allowed me to have children, so have sexual
relations with my slave girl. If she has a child,
maybe I can have my own family through her."
Abram did what Sarai said. 3It was after he had
lived ten years in Canaan that Sarai gave Hagar to
her husband Abram. (Hagar was her slave girl
from Egypt.)
4Abram had sexual relations with Hagar, and
she became pregnant. When Hagar learned she
was pregnant, she began to treat her mistress Sa-
rai badly. 5Then Sarai said to Abram, "This is your
fault. I gave my slave girl to you, and when she
became pregnant, she began to treat me badly.
Let the LORD decide who is right—you or me."
6But Abram said to Sarai, "You are Hagar's mis-
tress. Do anything you want to her." Then Sarai
ill-treated Hagar, and Hagar ran away.
7The angel of the LORD found Hagar beside a
spring of water in the desert, by the road to Shur.
8The angel said, "Hagar, Sarai's slave girl, where
have you come from? Where are you going?"
Hagar answered, "I am running away from my
mistress Sarai."
9The angel of the LORD said to her, "Go home
to your mistress and obey her." 10The angel also
said, "I will give you so many descendants[d] they
will be too many to count."
11The angel added,
"You are now pregnant,
and you will have a son.
You will name him Ishmael,[n]
because the LORD has heard your cries.
12Ishmael will be like a wild donkey.
He will be against everyone,
and everyone will be against him.
He will attack all his brothers."
13The slave girl gave a name to the LORD who
spoke to her: "You are 'God who sees me,'" be-
cause she said to herself, "Have I really seen God
who sees me?" 14So the well there, between Ka-
desh and Bered, was called Beer Lahai Roi.[n]
15Hagar gave birth to a son for Abram, and
Abram named him Ishmael. 16Abram was 86
years old when Hagar gave birth to Ishmael.

Proof of the Agreement

17 When Abram was 99 years old, the LORD
appeared to him and said, "I am God
Almighty. Obey me and do what is right. 2I will
make an agreement between us, and I will make
you the ancestor of many people."
3Then Abram bowed face down on the
ground. God said to him, 4"I am making my
agreement with you: I will make you the father of
many nations. 5I am changing your name from
Abram[n] to Abraham[n] because I am making you
a father of many nations. 6I will give you many
descendants.[d] New nations will be born from
you, and kings will come from you. 7And I will
make an agreement between me and you and all
your descendants from now on: I will be your God
and the God of all your descendants. 8You live in
the land of Canaan now as a stranger, but I will
give you and your descendants all this land for
ever. And I will be the God of your descendants."
9Then God said to Abraham, "You and your
descendants must keep this agreement from now
on. 10This is my agreement with you and all your
descendants, which you must obey: every male
among you must be circumcised.[d] 11Cut away
your foreskin to show that you are prepared to
follow the agreement between me and you.
12From now on when a baby boy is eight days
old, you will circumcise him. This includes any
boy born among your people or any who is your

Sidelight

In the Bible, a change of name had great significance. That was certainly true when God changed Abram's name to Abraham (Genesis 17:5). Abram means "exalted father" in Hebrew, but Abraham means "father of a multitude" – a sign of God's promise.

passed . . . animals This showed that God sealed the agreement between himself and Abram.
Ishmael The Hebrew words for "Ishmael" and "has heard" sound similar.
Beer Lahai Roi This means "the well of the Living One who sees me".
Abram This name means "honoured father".
Abraham The end of the Hebrew word for "Abraham" sounds like the beginning of the Hebrew word for "many".

slave, who is not one of your descendants. 13 Cir-
cumcise every baby boy whether he is born in
your family or bought as a slave. Your bodies will
be marked to show that you are part of my agree-
ment that lasts for ever. 14 Any male who is not
circumcised will be cut off from his people,
because he has broken my agreement."

Isaac—the Promised Son

15 God said to Abraham, "I will change the
name of Sarai,[n] your wife, to Sarah.[n] 16 I will
bless her and give her a son, and you will be the
father. She will be the mother of many nations.
Kings of nations will come from her."
17 Abraham bowed face down on the ground
and laughed. He said to himself, "Can a man have
a child when he is 100 years old? Can Sarah give
birth to a child when she is 90?" 18 Then Abraham
said to God, "Please let Ishmael be the son you
promised."
19 God said, "No, Sarah your wife will have a
son, and you will name him Isaac.[n] I will make
my agreement with him to be an agreement that
continues for ever with all his descendants.[d]
20 "As for Ishmael, I have heard you. I will bless
him and give him many descendants. And I will
cause their numbers to grow greatly. He will be the
father of twelve great leaders, and I will make him
into a great nation. 21 But I will make my agree-
ment with Isaac, the son whom Sarah will have at
this same time next year." 22 After God finished
talking with Abraham, God rose and left him.
23 Then Abraham gathered Ishmael, all the
males born in his camp, and the slaves he had

Sarai An Aramaic name meaning "princess".
Sarah A Hebrew name meaning "princess".
Isaac The Hebrew words for "he laughed" (v.17) and "Isaac" sound the same.

PROMISES

Silent Symbols

A wedding ring may just appear to be a little band of metal round someone's finger, but there's so much more to it than that.

Have you ever wondered why wedding rings are traditionally worn on the third finger of the left hand? It originates from the Egyptians who believed that the vein of that finger travelled directly to the heart. This belief was taken up by the Greeks when they conquered Egypt, and from them passed onto the Romans, who called this vein the *vena amoris*, which is Latin for "the vein of love". So, by wearing rings on the fourth finger of their left hands, a married couple symbolically declare their eternal love for each other.

Of course, every ring will symbolise something very individual from person to person. Who the ring was given by, the memories it triggers, how beautiful it is . . . all these things add up to making the humble wedding ring a very symbolic item. So, you can understand why the exchanging of the rings in a marriage service is such a big deal. When a man and woman promise before God to love one another, they want the rings to represent the relationship they'll have.

Read **Genesis 17:1–10**. God is talking about a promise between him and Abraham and all his descendants. God also asks Abraham to do something as a symbol of the promise between them.

- What was God asking the Israelites to do to symbolise their part of the promise?
- Why does it help to physically do something or have a symbol for a promise you've made?

Consider . . .

- what simple practical thing you could do to help you remember a promise God has made you.
- whenever you find promises in the Bible from God that apply to you, writing them down one side of a piece of paper. Then, when you want to commit to that promise, write your response down the other side.

For more, see . . .

- Numbers 23:19 (p.152)
- Matthew 28:16–20 (p.995)
- Joshua 4:15–24 (p.205)

bought. So that day Abraham circumcised every
man and boy in his camp as God had told him
to do. 24 Abraham was 99 years old when he was
circumcised. 25 And Ishmael, his son, was thirteen
years old when he was circumcised. 26 Abraham
and his son were circumcised on the same day.
27 Also on that day all the men in Abraham's camp
were circumcised, including all those born in his
camp and all the slaves he had bought from
other nations.

The Three Visitors

18 Later, the LORD again appeared to Abra-
ham near the great trees of Mamre.
Abraham was sitting at the entrance of his tent
during the hottest part of the day. 2 He looked up
and saw three men standing near him. When
Abraham saw them, he ran from his tent to meet
them. He bowed face down on the ground before
them 3 and said, "Sir, if you think well of me,
please stay awhile with me, your servant. 4 I will
bring some water so all of you can wash your
feet. You may rest under the tree, 5 and I will
get some bread for you so you can regain your
strength. Then you may continue your journey."

The three men said, "That is fine. Do as you
said."

6 Abraham hurried to the tent where Sarah was
and said to her, "Hurry, prepare 22 litres of fine
flour, and make it into loaves of bread." 7 Then
Abraham ran to his herd and took one of his best
calves. He gave it to a servant, who hurried to kill
it and to prepare it for food. 8 Abraham gave the
three men the calf that had been cooked, milk
curds and milk. While they ate, he stood under
the tree near them.

9 The men asked Abraham, "Where is your
wife, Sarah?"

"There, in the tent," said Abraham.

10 Then the LORD said, "I will certainly return to
you about this time a year from now. At that time
your wife Sarah will have a son."

Sarah was listening at the entrance of the tent
which was behind him. 11 Abraham and Sarah

DOUBT

Did God Really Say . . . ?

Craig was sure that God had told him that he was to move to Africa and tell people about Jesus. Only problem was, he didn't have the money to pay for the fare there or to live off! The more he prayed about it, the more he was convinced it was the right thing to do. He also believed God had said not to worry about the money because he would provide.

However, after just a few days, Craig began to doubt if he had really heard God. Maybe he had just been hoping that God would provide and God hadn't really spoken. Besides, why would God want to use someone like him anyway? Craig decided to try to find the money himself. He tried to get a personal loan, but the company refused. He even thought about selling some of his possessions, but in the end gave up. He'd obviously misheard God.

The next day Craig got a letter through the post from a great aunt he'd met once when he was a baby. He wasn't even sure if she was a Christian. She said in her letter that even though she didn't know what Craig was up to, she believed God had told her to give some of her savings to Craig to enable him to serve God as a missionary abroad. She sent Craig enough money to travel to Africa and to live off for three years!

Read **Genesis 17:15–19**.

- What do you think Craig and Abraham learnt from their experiences?
- Has God ever said something to you that seemed impossible? How did you react to it?

Consider . . .

- talking and praying through your doubts with someone whose friendship you respect.
- asking older Christians how they hear God.

For more, see . . .

- Matthew 21:18–22 (p.977)
- John 20:24–29 (p.1134)

were very old. Since Sarah was past the age when
women normally have children, 12she laughed to
herself, "My husband and I are too old to have a
baby."
13Then the LORD said to Abraham, "Why did
Sarah laugh? Why did she say, 'I am too old to
have a baby'? 14Is anything too hard for the
LORD? No! I will return to you at the right time a
year from now, and Sarah will have a son."
15Sarah was afraid, so she lied and said, "I
didn't laugh."
But the LORD said, "No. You did laugh."
16Then the men got up to leave and started out
towards Sodom. Abraham walked along with
them for a short time to send them on their way.

Abraham's Bargain with God

17The LORD said, "Should I tell Abraham what
I am going to do now? 18Abraham's children will
certainly become a great and powerful nation,
and all nations on earth will be blessed through
him. 19I have chosen him so he would command
his children and his descendants[d] to live the way
the LORD wants them to, to live right and be
fair. Then I, the LORD, will give Abraham what I
promised him."
20Then the LORD said, "I have heard many
complaints against the people of Sodom and
Gomorrah. They are very evil. 21I will go down
and see if they are as bad as I have heard. If not,
I will know."
22So the men turned and went towards
Sodom, but Abraham stood there before the LORD.
23Then Abraham approached him and asked, "Do
you plan to destroy the good people along with
the evil ones? 24What if there are 50 good people
in that city? Will you still destroy it? Surely you
will save the city for the 50 good people living
there. 25Surely you will not destroy the good peo-
ple along with the evil ones; then they would be
treated the same. You are the judge of all the
earth. Won't you do what is right?"

SERVICE

Gift For a Stranger

Unlike other leaders in India in the 1940s, V. P. Menon didn't have a university degree. He wasn't from a well-to-do or respected family. The oldest of thirteen children, he had to leave school at the age of thirteen to work in coal mines and factories.

As a young man, he went to Delhi to get a government job. On the way, everything he had – including his money and identification – was stolen at the railway station.

In desperation, he went to an elderly man standing nearby, explained his situation, and asked for a loan of fifteen rupees to buy food until he could get a job. The man gave him the money. Menon asked for his address so he could repay the loan, but the man said Menon didn't owe the debt to him, but to any stranger in need.

Menon never forgot his debt, and his life was marked by constant generosity to those in need. The day before Menon died, a beggar came to the family home asking for money to buy new sandals. Menon asked his daughter to take fifteen rupees out of his wallet to give to the man.

V. P. Menon served strangers selflessly, just as Abraham provided food for strangers in **Genesis 18:1–16**. Read how that incident affected Abraham.

- What attitudes cause people to share the way Menon and Abraham did?
- How do you need to become more like Abraham and Sarah? When have you served God by serving people you didn't know?

Consider . . .

- inviting someone who's new at your school, home to your house.
- trying V. P. Menon's approach. Give two pounds to a stranger in need, and ask that he or she repay it to another stranger in need.

For more, see . . .

- 1 Kings 17:10–16 (p.332)
- James 2:1–13 (p.1348)
- Hebrews 13:2 (p.1345)

26 The LORD said, "If I find 50 good people in
the city of Sodom, I will save the whole city
because of them."
27 Then Abraham said, "Though I am only dust
and ashes, I have been brave to speak to the Lord.
28 What if there are only 45 good people in the
city? Will you destroy the whole city for the lack
of five good people?"
The LORD said, "If I find 45 there, I will not
destroy the city."
29 Again Abraham said to him, "If you find only
40 good people there, will you destroy the city?"
The LORD said, "If I find 40, I will not des-
troy it."
30 Then Abraham said, "Lord, please don't be
angry with me, but let me ask you this. If you
find only 30 good people in the city, will you
destroy it?"
He said, "If I find 30 good people there, I will
not destroy the city."
31 Then Abraham said, "I have been brave to
speak to the Lord. But what if there are 20 good
people in the city?"
He answered, "If I find 20 there, I will not
destroy the city."
32 Then Abraham said, "Lord, please don't
be angry with me, but let me bother you this one
last time. What if you find ten there?"
He said, "If I find ten there, I will not des-
troy it."
33 When the LORD finished speaking to Abra-
ham, he left, and Abraham returned home.

GOD'S LOVE

A Second Chance

Most girls would love to have Amy's looks. Her face. Her hair. Her figure. You would think she had it made.

But her good looks haven't kept her life from being a mess. At home, her alcoholic mum either neglected her or screamed at her. So she avoided home and hung about on street corners with other kids who didn't fit in.

At thirteen, Amy ran away from home for the fourth time and ended up being taken into care. It was then that she decided to turn her life round and make something of herself – to give herself a second chance.

When she returned to school, things went well. She made new friends who didn't drink or go to wild parties. Her life seemed to be coming together. But then a rumour started. "Amy sleeps around," people whispered at school. Nothing Amy said or did made any difference, and the rumour stuck. One by one, her new friends ditched her. Except Helen.

"I don't believe the rumour," she told Amy. "Besides, you deserve a second chance."

But Amy still felt rejected, so she went back to her old friends. She started dating Tim, who gave her expensive gifts bought with drug money. "I love you," he would tell Amy. But she soon discovered that he was only saying it to get her to have sex with him. When she wouldn't, he dropped her.

But Amy wasn't friendless. She still had Helen, and Helen's family took her in so that she would have a place to live. Now, three years later, she feels like part of the family. She knows what it's like to have a second chance.

Like Amy, the people of Sodom and Gomorrah were given a second chance. Read how they responded to it in **Genesis 18:20–19:25**.

- How are Amy's friend Helen and Abraham similar? different?
- If you were Abraham, when would you have given up begging for the lives of the people?

Consider . . .

- giving a friend a second chance when he or she does something that hurts you.
- keeping track of all the times when people give you second chances. Thank them by baking a cake or running an errand – and learning from your mistake.

For more, see . . .

- Joel 2:12–13 (p.865)
- Acts 26:9–18 (p.1179)
- Zephaniah 3:14–20 (p.914)

Lot Leaves Sodom

19 The two angels came to Sodom in the evening as Lot was sitting near the city gate. When he saw them, he got up and went to them and bowed face down on the ground. 2 Lot said, "Sirs, please come to my house and spend the night. There you can wash your feet, and then tomorrow you may continue your journey."

The angels answered, "No, we will spend the night in the city's public square."

3 But Lot begged them to come, so they agreed and went to his house. Then Lot prepared a meal for them. He baked bread without yeast, and they ate it.

4 Before bedtime, men both young and old and from every part of Sodom surrounded Lot's house. 5 They called to Lot, "Where are the two men who came to you tonight? Bring them out to us so we can have sexual relations with them."

6 Lot went outside to them, closing the door behind him. 7 He said, "No, my brothers! Do not do this evil thing. 8 Look! I have two daughters who have never slept with a man. I will give them to you, and you may do anything you want with them. But please don't do anything to these men. They have come to my house, and I must protect them."

9 The men around the house answered, "Move out of the way!" Then they said to each other, "This man Lot came to our city as a stranger, and now he wants to tell us what to do!" They said to Lot, "We will do worse things to you than to them." They started pushing him back and were ready to break down the door.

10 But the two men staying with Lot opened the door, pulled him back inside the house, and then closed the door. 11 They struck those outside the door with blindness, so the men, both young and old, could not find the door.

12 The two men said to Lot, "Do you have any other relatives in this city? Do you have any sons-in-law, sons, daughters or any other relatives? If you do, tell them to leave now, 13 because we are about to destroy this city. The LORD has heard of all the evil that is here, so he has sent us to destroy it."

14 So Lot went out and said to his future sons-in-law who were pledged to marry his daughters, "Hurry and leave this city! The LORD is about to destroy it!" But they thought Lot was joking.

15 At dawn the next morning, the angels begged Lot to hurry. They said, "Go! Take your wife and your two daughters with you so you will not be destroyed when the city is punished."

16 But Lot delayed. So the two men took the hands of Lot, his wife and his two daughters and led them safely out of the city. So the LORD was merciful to Lot and his family. 17 After they brought them out of the city, one of the men said, "Run for your lives! Don't look back or stop anywhere in the valley. Run to the mountains, or you will be destroyed."

18 But Lot said to one of them, "Sir, please don't force me to go so far! 19 You have been merciful and kind to me and have saved my life. But I can't run to the mountains. The disaster will catch me, and I will die. 20 Look, that little town over there is not too far away. Let me run there. It's really just a little town, and I'll be safe there."

21 The angel said to Lot, "Very well, I will allow you to do this also. I will not destroy that town. 22 But run there fast, because I cannot destroy Sodom until you are safely in that town." (That town is named Zoar,[n] because it is little.)

Sodom and Gomorrah are Destroyed

23 The sun had already come up when Lot entered Zoar. 24 The LORD sent a rain of burning sulphur down from the sky on Sodom and Gomorrah 25 and destroyed those cities. He also destroyed the whole Jordan Valley, everyone living in the cities, and even all the plants.

26 At that point Lot's wife looked back. When she did, she became a pillar of salt.

27 Early the next morning, Abraham got up and went to the place where he had stood before the LORD. 28 He looked down towards Sodom and Gomorrah and all the Jordan Valley and saw smoke rising from the land, like smoke from a furnace.

29 God destroyed the cities in the valley, but he remembered what Abraham had asked. So God saved Lot's life, but he destroyed the city where Lot had lived.

Lot and His Daughters

30 Lot was afraid to continue living in Zoar, so he and his two daughters went to live in the mountains in a cave. 31 One day the older daughter said to the younger, "Our father is old. Everywhere on the earth women and men marry, but there are no men around here for us to marry. 32 Let's get our father drunk and have sexual relations with him. We can use him to have children and continue our family."

Sidelight

When God destroyed the cities of Sodom and Gomorrah (Genesis 19:23–29), he made sure they weren't built again. Archaeologists believe the two cities are now under water in a shallow part of the Dead Sea. The waters may have risen because of an earthquake around 2000 BC.

Zoar This name sounds like the Hebrew word for "little".

33That night the two girls got their father
drunk, and the older daughter went and had
sexual relations with him. But Lot did not know
when she lay down or when she got up.
34The next day the older daughter said to the
younger, “Last night I had sexual relations with
my father. Let’s get him drunk again tonight so
you can go and have sexual relations with him,
too. In this way we can use our father to have
children to continue our family.” 35So that night
they got their father drunk again, and the youn-
ger daughter went and had sexual relations with
him. Again, Lot did not know when she lay down
or when she got up.
36So both of Lot’s daughters became pregnant
by their father. 37The older daughter gave birth to
a son and named him Moab. He is the ancestor of
all the Moabite people who are still living today.
38The younger daughter also gave birth to a son
and named him Ben-Ammi. He is the father of all
the Ammonite people who are still living today.

Abraham Tricks Abimelech

20 Abraham left Hebron and travelled to
southern Canaan where he stayed
awhile between Kadesh and Shur. When he
moved to Gerar, 2he told people that his wife
Sarah was his sister. Abimelech, king of Gerar,
heard this, so he sent some servants to take her.
3But one night God spoke to Abimelech in a
dream and said, “You will die. The woman you
took is married.”
4But Abimelech had not gone near Sarah, so
he said, “Lord, would you destroy an innocent
nation? 5Abraham himself told me, ‘This
woman is my sister,’ and she also said, ‘He is my
brother.’ I am innocent. I did not know I was
doing anything wrong.”
6Then God said to Abimelech in the dream,
“Yes, I know you did not realise what you were
doing. So I did not allow you to sin against me
and touch her. 7Give Abraham his wife back. He
is a prophet.[d] He will pray for you, and you will
not die. But if you do not give Sarah back, you
and all your family will surely die.”
8So early the next morning, Abimelech called
all his officers and told them everything that had
happened in the dream. They were very afraid.
9Then Abimelech called Abraham to him and
said, “What have you done to us? What wrong
did I do against you? Why did you bring this
trouble to my kingdom? You should not have
done these things to me. 10What were you think-
ing that caused you to do this?”
11Then Abraham answered, “I thought no one
in this place respected God and that someone
would kill me to get Sarah. 12And it is true that
she is my sister. She is the daughter of my father,
but she is not the daughter of my mother.
13When God told me to leave my father’s house
and wander in many different places, I told Sarah,
‘You must do a special favour for me. Everywhere
we go, tell people I am your brother.’ ”
14Then Abimelech gave Abraham some sheep,
cattle and male and female slaves. He also gave
Sarah, Abraham’s wife, back to him 15and said,
“Look around you at my land. You may live any-
where you want.”
16Abimelech said to Sarah, “I gave your brother
Abraham 1,000 pieces of silver to make up for
any wrong that people may think about you. I
want everyone to know that you are innocent.”
17Then Abraham prayed to God, and God
healed Abimelech, his wife and his servant girls
so they could have children. 18The LORD had kept
all the women in Abimelech’s house from having
children as a punishment to Abimelech for taking
Abraham’s wife, Sarah.

A Baby for Sarah

21 The LORD cared for Sarah as he had said,
and did for her what he had promised.
2Sarah became pregnant and gave birth to a son
for Abraham in his old age. Everything happened
at the time God had said it would. 3Abraham
named his son Isaac, the son Sarah gave birth to.
4He circumcised[d] Isaac when he was eight days
old as God had commanded.
5Abraham was 100 years old when his son
Isaac was born. 6And Sarah said, “God has made
me laugh.[n] Everyone who hears about this will
laugh with me. 7No one thought that I would be
able to have Abraham’s child, but even though
Abraham is old I have given him a son.”

Hagar and Ishmael Leave

8Isaac grew, and when he became old enough
to eat food, Abraham gave a great feast. 9But
Sarah saw Ishmael making fun of Isaac. (Ishmael
was the son of Abraham by Hagar, Sarah’s
Egyptian slave.) 10So Sarah said to Abraham,
“Throw out this slave woman and her son. Her
son should not inherit anything; my son Isaac
should receive it all.”
11This troubled Abraham very much because
Ishmael was also his son. 12But God said to
Abraham, “Don’t be troubled about the boy and
the slave woman. Do whatever Sarah tells you.
The descendants[d] I promised you will be from
Isaac. 13I will also make the descendants of
Ishmael into a great nation because he is your
son, too.”

laugh The Hebrew words for “he laughed” and “Isaac” sound the same.

14Early the next morning Abraham took some
food and a leather bag full of water. He gave
them to Hagar and sent her away. Carrying these
things and her son, Hagar went and wandered in
the desert of Beersheba.
15Later, when all the water was gone from the
bag, Hagar put her son under a bush. 16Then she
went away a short distance and sat down. She
thought, "My son will die, and I cannot watch
this happen." She sat there and began to cry.
17God heard the boy crying, and God's angel
called to Hagar from heaven. He said, "What is
wrong, Hagar? Don't be afraid! God has heard
the boy crying there. 18Help him up and take him
by the hand. I will make his descendants into a
great nation."
19Then God showed Hagar a well of water. So
she went to the well and filled her bag with water
and gave the boy a drink.
20God was with the boy as he grew up. Ish-
mael lived in the desert and became an archer.
21He lived in the Desert of Paran, and his mother
found a wife for him in Egypt.

Abraham's Bargain with Abimelech

22Then Abimelech came with Phicol, the com-
mander of his army, and said to Abraham, "God
is with you in everything you do. 23So make a
promise to me here before God that you will be
fair with me and my children and my descend-
ants.[d] Be kind to me and to this land where you
have lived as a stranger—as kind as I have been
to you."
24And Abraham said, "I promise." 25Then
Abraham complained to Abimelech about Abime-
lech's servants who had seized a well of water.
26But Abimelech said, "I don't know who did
this. You never told me about this before today."
27Then Abraham gave Abimelech some sheep
and cattle, and they made an agreement. 28Abra-
ham also put seven female lambs in front of
Abimelech.
29Abimelech asked Abraham, "Why did you
put these seven female lambs by themselves?"
30Abraham answered, "Accept these lambs
from me to prove that you believe I dug this well."
31So that place was called Beersheba[n] because
they made a promise to each other there.
32After Abraham and Abimelech made the
agreement at Beersheba, Abimelech and Phicol,
the commander of his army, went back to the
land of the Philistines.
33Abraham planted a tamarisk tree at Beer-
sheba and prayed to the LORD, the God who lives
for ever. 34And Abraham lived as a stranger in the
land of the Philistines for a long time.

God Tests Abraham

22 After these things God tested Abraham's
faith. God said to him, "Abraham!"
And he answered, "Here I am."
2Then God said, "Take your only son, Isaac, the
son you love, and go to the land of Moriah. Kill
him there and offer him as a whole burnt offering
on one of the mountains I will tell you about."
3Abraham got up early in the morning and sad-
dled his donkey. He took Isaac and two servants
with him. After he cut the wood for the sacrifice,
they went to the place to which God had told
them to go. 4On the third day Abraham looked up
and saw the place in the distance. 5He said to his
servants, "Stay here with the donkey. My son
and I will go over there and worship, and then
we will come back to you."
6Abraham took the wood for the sacrifice and
gave it to his son to carry, but he himself took the
knife and the fire. So he and his son went on
together.
7Isaac said to his father Abraham, "Father!"
Abraham answered, "Yes, my son."
Isaac said, "We have the fire and the wood, but
where is the lamb we will burn as a sacrifice?"
8Abraham answered, "God will give us the
lamb for the sacrifice, my son."
So Abraham and his son went on together 9and
came to the place God had told him about. Abra-
ham built an altar there. He laid the wood on it
and then tied up his son Isaac and laid him on the
wood on the altar. 10Then Abraham took his knife
and was about to kill his son.
11But the angel of the LORD called to him from
heaven and said, "Abraham! Abraham!"
Abraham answered, "Yes."
12The angel said, "Don't kill your son or hurt
him in any way. Now I can see that you trust God
and that you have not kept your son, your only
son, from me."
13Then Abraham looked up and saw a ram
caught in a bush by its horns. So Abraham went
and took the ram and killed it. He offered it as a
whole burnt offering to God, and his son was
saved. 14So Abraham named that place The LORD
Provides. Even today people say, "On the moun-
tain of the LORD it will be provided."
15The angel of the LORD called to Abraham
from heaven a second time 16and said, "The
LORD says, 'Because you did not keep back your
son, your only son, from me, I make you this
promise by my own name: 17I will surely bless
you and give you many descendants.[d] They will
be as many as the stars in the sky and the sand
on the seashore, and they will capture the cities
of their enemies. 18Through your descendants all

Beersheba This name means "well of the promise" or "well of seven".

the nations on the earth will be blessed, because
you obeyed me.' "
19Then Abraham returned to his servants. They
all travelled back to Beersheba and Abraham
stayed there.
20After these things happened, someone told
Abraham: "Your brother Nahor and his wife
Milcah have children now. 21The first son is Uz,
and the second is Buz. The third son is Kemuel
(the father of Aram). 22Then there are Kesed,
Hazo, Pildash, Jidlaph and Bethuel." 23Bethuel
became the father of Rebekah. Milcah was the
mother of these eight sons, and Nahor, Abra-
ham's brother, was the father. 24Also Nahor had
four other sons by his slave woman, *d* Reumah.
Their names were Tebah, Gaham, Tahash and
Maacah.

Sarah Dies

23 Sarah lived to be 127 years old. 2She
died in Kiriath Arba (that is, Hebron) in

Sidelight If his name matches his sleeping habits, you probably wouldn't want to spend the night at Nahor's. His name means "snorer" (Genesis 22:23–24).

the land of Canaan. Abraham was very sad and
cried because of her. 3After a while he got up
from the side of his wife's body and went to talk
to the Hittites. He said, 4"I am only a stranger

PRIORITIES

Worth a Sacrifice

John couldn't sleep. He tossed restlessly in bed, wondering what to do. He had been planning to take a summer job at a local firm. The pay and hours looked great.

But then, last week at school, he had seen a poster about a camp for disabled children that needed someone to teach swimming. He loved water sports, and his youth leader had encouraged him to consider volunteering to help at the camp.

John wasn't prepared for the reaction when he mentioned the idea to his dad. "Why do you want to work for nothing when you could get paid?" his dad fumed. "It's not as if you're wealthy. And then you'll come running to me to pay your university fees."

His dad had a point, John reasoned as he stared up at the dark bedroom ceiling. But no matter how hard he tried, he couldn't forget about the camp – or those kids.

When John's alarm woke him the next morning, he knew what he had to do. "Dad," he explained at breakfast, "some things are worth sacrificing for. Helping at that camp is important to me." His dad didn't understand, but he agreed to let John stick with his priorities. So John phoned the camp organisers. Like John, Abraham had difficult decisions, but he also stuck with what he believed was right. Read **Genesis 22:1–18** to see what happened.

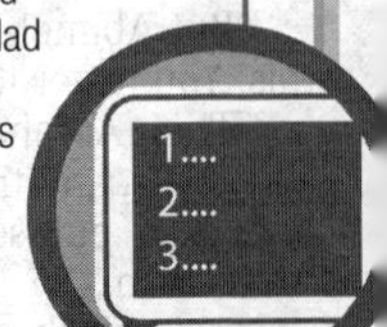

- What do John's and Abraham's decisions say about their priorities?
- When have you, like Abraham, had to make a difficult decision because of what you believed God wanted? What happened?

Consider . . .

- writing out the issues involved in a difficult decision. Keep the list by your bed or on your desk for a few days. Whenever you think of an option, benefit, or disadvantage, write it on the paper. Pray about your decision through the week and then make the decision, sticking to what you know to be right.
- having a "what if" discussion over lunch with friends in the school cafeteria. Brainstorm together several situations that test your priorities. Then discuss what you would do if you were in a particular situation.

For more, see . . .

- Proverbs 3 (p.592)
- Matthew 6:19–24 (p.948)
- Daniel 3:8–30 (p.835)

and a foreigner here. Sell me some of your land
so that I can bury my dead wife."
5The Hittites answered Abraham, 6"Sir, you are
a great leader among us. You may have the best
place we have to bury your dead. You may have
any of our burying places that you want, and none
of us will stop you from burying your dead wife."
7Abraham rose and bowed to the people of the
land, the Hittites. 8He said to them, "If you truly
want to help me bury my dead wife here, speak
to Ephron, the son of Zohar, for me. 9Ask him to
sell me the cave of Machpelah at the edge of his
field. I will pay him the full price. You can be the
witnesses that I am buying it as a burial place."
10Ephron was sitting among the Hittites at the
city gate. He answered Abraham, 11"No, sir. I will
give you the land and the cave that is in it, with
these people as witnesses. Bury your dead wife."
12Then Abraham bowed down before the Hit-
tites. 13He said to Ephron before all the people,
"Please let me pay you the full price for the field.
Accept my money, and I will bury my dead there."
14Ephron answered Abraham, 15"Sir, the land
is worth 400 pieces of silver, but I won't argue
with you over the price. Take the land, and bury
your dead wife."
16Abraham agreed and paid Ephron in front of
the Hittite witnesses. He weighed out the full
price, 400 pieces of silver, and they counted the
weight as the traders normally did.
17-18So Ephron's field in Machpelah, east of
Mamre, was sold. Abraham became the owner of
the field, the cave in it, and all the trees that were
in the field. The sale was made at the city gate,
with the Hittites as witnesses. 19After this, Abra-
ham buried his wife Sarah in the cave in the field
of Machpelah, near Mamre. (Mamre was later
called Hebron in the land of Canaan.) 20So Abra-
ham bought the field and the cave in it from the
Hittites to use as a burying place.

A Wife for Isaac

24 Abraham was now very old, and the LORD
had blessed him in every way. 2Abraham
said to his oldest servant, who was in charge of
everything he owned, "Put your hand under my
leg.[n] 3Make a promise to me before the LORD,
the God of heaven and earth. Don't get a wife for
my son from the Canaanite girls who live around
here. 4Instead, go back to my country, to the land
of my relatives, and get a wife for my son Isaac."
5The servant said to him, "What if this woman
does not want to return with me to this land?
Then, should I take your son with me back to
your homeland?"
6Abraham said to him, "No! Don't take my
son back there. 7The LORD, the God of heaven,
brought me from the home of my father and the
land of my relatives. And he promised me, 'I will
give this land to your descendants.'[d] The LORD
will send his angel before you to help you get a
wife for my son there. 8If the girl won't come
back with you, you will be free from this promise.
But you must not take my son back there." 9So
the servant put his hand under his master's leg
and made a promise to Abraham about this.
10The servant took ten of Abraham's camels
and left, carrying with him many different kinds
of beautiful gifts. He went to North West Meso-
potamia, to Nahor's city. 11In the evening, when
the women come out to get water, he made the
camels kneel down at the well outside the city.
12The servant said, "LORD, God of my master
Abraham, allow me to find a wife for his son
today. Please show this kindness to my master
Abraham. 13Here I am, standing by the spring,
and the girls from the city are coming out to get
water. 14I will say to one of them, 'Please put
your jar down so I can drink.' Then let her say,
'Drink, and I will also give water to your camels.'
If that happens, I will know she is the right one
for your servant Isaac and that you have shown
kindness to my master."
15Before the servant had finished praying, Re-
bekah, the daughter of Bethuel, came out of the
city. (Bethuel was the son of Milcah and Nahor,
Abraham's brother.) Rebekah was carrying her
water jar on her shoulder. 16She was very pretty,
a virgin;[d] she had never had sexual relations with
a man. She went down to the spring and filled
her jar, then came back up. 17The servant ran to
her and said, "Please give me a little water from
your jar."
18Rebekah said, "Drink, sir." She quickly low-
ered the jar from her shoulder and gave him a
drink. 19After he finished drinking, Rebekah said,
"I will also pour some water for your camels."
20So she quickly poured all the water from her jar
into the drinking trough for the camels. Then she
kept running to the well until she had given all
the camels enough to drink.

Sidelight

Making a promise is a serious business when God is involved; there is no conning him! "Deep down in me I knowed it was a lie, and he knowed it. You can't pray a lie – I found that out." Mark Twain – Huckleberry Finn.

Put . . . leg This showed that a person would keep a promise.

21The servant quietly watched her. He wanted
to be sure the LORD had made his trip successful.
22After the camels had finished drinking, he gave
Rebekah a gold ring weighing 5 grammes and
two gold arm bracelets weighing about 110
grammes each. 23He asked, "Who is your father?
Is there a place in his house for me and my men
to spend the night?"

24Rebekah answered, "My father is Bethuel,
the son of Milcah and Nahor." 25Then she said,
"And, yes, we have straw for your camels and a
place for you to spend the night."

26The servant bowed and worshipped the LORD
27and said, "Blessed is the LORD, the God of my
master Abraham. The LORD has been kind and
truthful to him and has led me to my master's
relatives."

28Then Rebekah ran and told her mother's fam-
ily about all these things. 29She had a brother
named Laban, who ran out to Abraham's servant,
who was still at the spring. 30Laban had heard
what she had said and had seen the ring and the
bracelets on his sister's arms. So he ran out to
the well, and there was the man standing by the
camels at the spring. 31Laban said, "Sir, you are
welcome to come in; you don't have to stand
outside. I have prepared the house for you and
also a place for your camels."

32So Abraham's servant went into the house.
After Laban unloaded the camels and gave them
straw and food, he gave water to Abraham's ser-
vant so he and the men with him could wash
their feet. 33Then Laban gave the servant food,
but the servant said, "I will not eat until I have
told you why I came."

So Laban said, "Then tell us."

34He said, "I am Abraham's servant. 35The
LORD has greatly blessed my master in everything,
and he has become a rich man. The LORD has
given him many flocks of sheep, herds of cattle,
silver and gold, male and female servants, camels
and horses. 36Sarah, my master's wife, gave birth
to a son when she was old, and my master has
given everything he owns to that son. 37My mas-
ter had me make a promise to him and said,
'Don't get a wife for my son from the Canaanite
girls who live around here. 38Instead, you must
go to my father's people and to my family. There
you must get a wife for my son.' 39I said to my
master, 'What if the woman will not come back
with me?' 40But he said, 'I serve the LORD, who
will send his angel with you and will help you.
You will get a wife for my son from my family and
my father's people. 41Then you will be free from
the promise. But if they will not give you a wife
for my son, you will be free from this promise.'

42"Today I came to this spring. I said, 'LORD,
God of my master Abraham, please make my trip
successful. 43I am standing by this spring. I will
wait for a young woman to come out to get wa-
ter, and I will say, "Please give me water from
your jar to drink." 44Then let her say, "Drink this
water, and I will also get water for your camels."
By this I will know the LORD has chosen her for
my master's son.'

45"Before I finished my silent prayer, Rebekah
came out of the city with her water jar on her
shoulder. She went down to the spring and got
water. I said to her, 'Please give me a drink.' 46She
quickly lowered the jar from her shoulder and said,
'Drink this. I will also get water for your camels.'
So I drank, and she gave water to my camels too.
47When I asked her, 'Who is your father?' she an-
swered, 'My father is Bethuel son of Milcah and
Nahor.' Then I put the ring in her nose and the
bracelets on her arms, 48and I bowed my head and
thanked the LORD. I praised the LORD, the God of
my master Abraham, because he led me on the
right road to get the granddaughter of my master's
brother for his son. 49Now, tell me, will you be
kind and truthful to my master? And if not, tell me
so. Then I will know what I should do."

50Laban and Bethuel answered, "This is clearly
from the LORD, and we cannot change what must
happen. 51Rebekah is yours. Take her and go.
Let her marry your master's son as the LORD has
commanded."

52When Abraham's servant heard these words,
he bowed face down on the ground before the
LORD. 53Then he gave Rebekah gold and silver
jewellery and clothes. He also gave expensive gifts
to her brother and mother. 54The servant and the
men with him ate and drank and spent the night
there. When they got up the next morning, the
servant said, "Now let me go back to my master."

55Rebekah's mother and her brother said, "Let
Rebekah stay with us at least ten days. After that
she may go."

56But the servant said to them, "Do not make
me wait, because the LORD has made my trip suc-
cessful. Now let me go back to my master."

57Rebekah's brother and mother said, "We will
call Rebekah and ask her what she wants to do."
58They called her and asked her, "Do you want to
go with this man now?"

She said, "Yes, I do."

59So they allowed Rebekah and her nurse to
go with Abraham's servant and his men. 60They
blessed Rebekah and said,

"Our sister, may you be the mother of
thousands of people,
and may your descendants[d] capture the
cities of their enemies."

61Then Rebekah and her servant girls got on
the camels and followed the servant and his men.
So the servant took Rebekah and left.

62 At this time Isaac had left Beer Lahai Roi and
was living in southern Canaan. 63 One evening
when he went out to the field to think, he looked
up and saw camels coming. 64 Rebekah also
looked and saw Isaac. Then she jumped down
from the camel 65 and asked the servant, "Who is
that man walking in the field to meet us?"
The servant answered, "That is my master." So
Rebekah covered her face with her veil.
66 The servant told Isaac everything that had
happened. 67 Then Isaac brought Rebekah into the
tent of Sarah, his mother, and she became his
wife. Isaac loved her very much, and so he was
comforted after his mother's death.

Abraham's Family

25 Abraham married again, and his new
wife was Keturah. 2 She gave birth to
Zimran, Jokshan, Medan, Midian, Ishbak and
Shuah. 3 Jokshan was the father of Sheba and De-
dan. Dedan's descendants[d] were the people of
Assyria, Letush and Leum. 4 The sons of Midian
were Ephah, Epher, Hanoch, Abida and Eldaah.
All these were descendants of Keturah. 5 Abraham
left everything he owned to Isaac. 6 But before
Abraham died, he did give gifts to the sons of his
other wives, then sent them to the east to be
away from Isaac.
7 Abraham lived to be 175 years old. 8 He
breathed his last breath and died at an old age,
after a long and satisfying life. 9 His sons Isaac and
Ishmael buried him in the cave of Machpelah in
the field of Ephron east of Mamre. (Ephron was
the son of Zohar the Hittite.) 10 So Abraham was
buried with his wife Sarah in the same field that
he had bought from the Hittites. 11 After Abraham
died, God blessed his son Isaac. Isaac was now
living at Beer Lahai Roi.
12 This is the family history of Ishmael, Abra-
ham's son. (Hagar, Sarah's Egyptian servant, was
Ishmael's mother.) 13 These are the names of Ish-
mael's sons in the order they were born: Neba-
ioth, the first son, then Kedar, Adbeel, Mibsam,
14 Mishma, Dumah, Massa, 15 Hadad, Tema, Jetur,

FAMILY

Teen Rivalry

According to the American Chicle Youth Poll, most teenagers have one brother and one sister. Only 8 per cent of teenagers have no brothers or sisters. But 12 per cent have three or more brothers and sisters.

So how do they get along with their brothers and sisters? Only 62 per cent of young people in the poll say they're happy with their relationships with their brothers and sisters. It's the area of home life they're least satisfied with.

About 40 per cent say getting along better with their brothers and sisters would improve their home life more than anything else. Only 15 per cent of teenagers say they can talk about their problems with their brothers. And only 19 per cent say they can talk about their problems with their sisters.

Some tension between brothers and sisters is normal. Relationships have been tough for a long time. **Genesis 25:19–34** describes fierce rivalry between Esau and Jacob. Read how it made life difficult for them.

- If someone asked Jacob and Esau to respond to a survey about relationships, what do you think the two of them would say?
- How is your relationship with your brother and/or sister like or unlike the relationship between Jacob and Esau? Which of the two brothers do you most closely identify with?

Consider . . .

- sending your brother or sister a note – through the post – giving a compliment for something he or she did recently.
- asking a trusted adult for some help with your family conflicts.

For more, see . . .

- Judges 9:1–6 (p.235)
- 1 John 3:11–18 (p.1374)
- Luke 10:38–42 (p.1058)

Naphish and Kedemah. 16These were Ishmael's
sons, and these are the names of the tribal leaders
listed according to their settlements and camps.
17Ishmael lived for 137 years and then breathed
his last breath and died. 18His descendants lived
from Havilah to Shur, which is east of Egypt
stretching towards Assyria. They often attacked
the descendants of his brothers.

Isaac's Family

19This is the family history of Isaac. 20When
Abraham's son, Isaac, was 40 years old, he mar-
ried Rebekah, who came from North West Meso-
potamia. She was Bethuel's daughter and the
sister of Laban the Aramean. 21Isaac's wife could
not have children, so Isaac prayed to the LORD for
her. The LORD heard Isaac's prayer, and Rebekah
became pregnant.

22While she was pregnant, the babies struggled
inside her. She asked, "Why is this happening to
me?" Then she went to get an answer from the
LORD.

23The LORD said to her,

"Two nations are in your body,
and two groups of people will be taken
from you.
One group will be stronger than the other,
and the older will serve the younger."

24When the time came, Rebekah gave birth to
twins. 25The first baby was born red. Since his
skin was like a hairy robe, he was named Esau.[n]
26When the second baby was born, he was holding
on to Esau's heel, so that baby was named Jacob.[n]
Isaac was 60 years old when they were born.

27When the boys grew up, Esau became a
skilled hunter. He loved to be out in the fields.
But Jacob was a quiet man and stayed among the
tents. 28Isaac loved Esau because he hunted the
wild animals that Isaac enjoyed eating. But Re-
bekah loved Jacob.

29One day Jacob was boiling a pot of vegetable
soup. Esau came in from hunting in the fields,
weak from hunger. 30So Esau said to Jacob, "Let
me eat some of that red soup, because I am weak
with hunger." (That is why people call him
Edom.[n])

31But Jacob said, "You must sell me your
rights as the firstborn son."[n]

32Esau said, "I am almost dead from hunger.
If I die, all of my father's wealth will not help
me."

33But Jacob said, "First, promise me that you
will give it to me." So Esau made a promise to
Jacob and sold his part of their father's wealth to
Jacob. 34Then Jacob gave Esau bread and veg-
etable soup, and he ate and drank, and then left.
So Esau showed how little he cared about his
rights as the firstborn son.

Isaac Lies to Abimelech

26 Now there was a time of hunger in the
land, besides the time of hunger that
happened during Abraham's life. So Isaac went
to the town of Gerar to see Abimelech king of
the Philistines. 2The LORD appeared to Isaac and
said, "Don't go down to Egypt, but live in the
land where I tell you to live. 3Stay in this land,
and I will be with you and bless you. I will give
you and your descendants[d] all these lands, and I
will keep the oath I made to Abraham your fa-
ther. 4I will give you many descendants, as hard
to count as the stars in the sky, and I will give
them all these lands. Through your descendants
all the nations on the earth will be blessed. 5I
will do this because your father Abraham obeyed
me. He did what I said and obeyed my com-
mands, my teachings and my rules."

6So Isaac stayed in Gerar. 7His wife Rebekah
was very beautiful, and the men of that place
asked Isaac about her. Isaac said, "She is my sis-
ter," because he was afraid to tell them she was
his wife. He thought they might kill him so they
could have her.

8Isaac lived there a long time. One day as
Abimelech king of the Philistines looked out of
his window, he saw Isaac holding his wife Re-
bekah tenderly. 9Abimelech called for Isaac and
said, "This woman is your wife. Why did you say
she was your sister?"

Isaac said to him, "I was afraid you would kill
me so you could have her."

10Abimelech said, "What have you done to
us? One of our men might have had sexual rela-
tions with your wife. Then we would have been
guilty of a great sin."

11So Abimelech warned everyone, "Anyone
who touches this man or his wife will be put to
death."

Isaac Becomes Rich

12Isaac planted seed in that land, and that year
he gathered a great harvest. The LORD blessed

Esau This name may mean "hairy".
Jacob This name sounds like the Hebrew word for "heel". "Holding on to someone's heel" is a Hebrew saying for tricking someone.
Edom This name sounds like the Hebrew word for "red".
rights . . . son Usually the firstborn son had a high rank in the family. The firstborn son usually became the new head of the family

him very much, 13and he became rich. He gath-
ered more wealth until he became a very rich
man. 14He had so many slaves and flocks and
herds that the Philistines envied him. 15So they
stopped up all the wells the servants of Isaac's fa-
ther Abraham had dug. (They had dug them
when Abraham was alive.) The Philistines filled
those wells with earth. 16And Abimelech said to
Isaac, "Leave our country because you have be-
come much more powerful than we are."
17So Isaac left that place and camped in the
Valley of Gerar and lived there. 18Long before
this time Abraham had dug many wells, but after
he died, the Philistines filled them with earth. So
Isaac dug those wells again and gave them the
same names his father had given them. 19Isaac's
servants dug a well in the valley, from which a
spring of water flowed. 20But the herdsmen of
Gerar argued with them and said, "This water is
ours." So Isaac named that well Argue because
they argued with him. 21Then his servants dug
another well. When the people also argued
about it, Isaac named that well Fight. 22He
moved from there and dug another well. No one
argued about this one, so he named it Room
Enough. Isaac said, "Now the LORD has made
room for us, and we will be successful in this
land."
23From there Isaac went to Beersheba. 24The
LORD appeared to him that night and said, "I am
the God of your father Abraham. Don't be afraid,
because I am with you. I will bless you and
give you many descendants[d] because of my
servant Abraham." 25So Isaac built an altar and

HONESTY

Getting Away With It

In sixties America, when it came to selling a particular make of television called RCA, one shop excelled. Everyone in the country town where the store was based who owned a TV owned that brand. A huge RCA store in Chicago was so impressed they sent one of their chief salesmen to find out if they could learn anything from the owners of the store about how to sell TVs.

When he arrived at the store in the late morning the salesman couldn't see anyone there. The salesman noticed a sign that said, "If you see a TV you like, take it home and try it out." Another sign instructed people bringing in a TV for repair to write down what was wrong with it and put the paper on the TV. Another sign said, "If you brought your TV in for repair and you see it here, it is fixed. The repair cost is on the tag. Leave the money in the box."

About an hour later, a customer from the town walked into the store. The Chicago salesman asked the customer where the store owners were.

The man replied, "Oh, they're out harvesting wheat. They should be back by 8 or 9 p.m. to close the store for the night."

The salesman realised with sadness that this type of honesty and trust wouldn't work back in his big city store.

Read **Genesis 26:1–11**.

- The salesman, like Isaac, wanted to get the best out of the situation. Both of them learned the value of honesty. Have you ever had to learn the hard way that "honesty is the best policy"?
- Read the passage and consider what God's reaction to Isaac's dishonesty might have been?

Consider . . .

- talking to a parent or trusted adult friend about situations when you might be tempted not to be honest. Ask what he or she would do in that situation.
- starting an honesty piggy bank. Each time you are honest when it's tough, put in a pound. Every time you are dishonest or tell a lie, take out a pound. Try to improve your "bank balance".

For more, see . . .

- Genesis 20:1–13 (p.24)
- Acts 5:1–11 (p.1145)
- Proverbs 3:3–4 (p.592)

worshipped the LORD there. He also made a
camp there, and his servants dug a well.
26 Abimelech came from Gerar to see Isaac. He
brought with him Ahuzzath, who advised him, and
Phicol, the commander of his army. 27 Isaac asked
them, "Why have you come to see me? You were
my enemy and forced me to leave your country."
28 They answered, "Now we know that the
LORD is with you. Let us swear an oath to each
other. Let us make an agreement with you 29 that
since we did not hurt you, you will not hurt us.
We were good to you and sent you away in
peace. Now the LORD has blessed you."
30 So Isaac prepared food for them, and they all
ate and drank. 31 Early the next morning the men
swore an oath to each other. Then Isaac sent
them away, and they left in peace.
32 That day Isaac's servants came and told him
about the well they had dug, saying, "We found
water in that well." 33 So Isaac named it Shibah[n]
and that city is called Beersheba even now.
34 When Esau was 40 years old, he married two
Hittite women—Judith daughter of Beeri and
Basemath daughter of Elon. 35 These women
brought much sorrow to Isaac and Rebekah.

Jacob Tricks Isaac

27 When Isaac was old, his eyes were poor,
so he could not see clearly. One day he
called his older son Esau to him and said, "Son."
Esau answered, "Here I am."
2 Isaac said, "I am old and don't know when I
might die. 3 So take your bow and arrows and go
hunting in the field for an animal for me to eat.
4 When you prepare the tasty food that I love, bring
it to me, and I will eat. Then I will bless you before
I die." 5 So Esau went out in the field to hunt.
Rebekah was listening as Isaac said this to his
son Esau. 6 She said to her son Jacob, "Listen, I
heard your father saying to your brother Esau,
7 'Kill an animal and prepare some tasty food for
me to eat. Then I will bless you in the presence
of the LORD before I die.' 8 So obey me, my son,
and do what I tell you. 9 Go out to our goats and
bring me two of the best young ones. I will pre-
pare them just the way your father likes them.
10 Then you will take the food to your father, and
he will bless you before he dies."
11 But Jacob said to his mother Rebekah, "My
brother Esau is a hairy man, and I am smooth! 12 If
my father touches me, he will know I am not
Esau. Then he will not bless me but will place a
curse on me because I tried to trick him."
13 So Rebekah said to him, "If your father puts
a curse on you, I will accept the blame. Just do
what I said and go, get the goats for me."
14 So Jacob went out and got two goats and
brought them to his mother, and she cooked
them in the special way Isaac enjoyed. 15 She took
the best clothes of her older son Esau that were
in the house and put them on the younger son
Jacob. 16 She also took the skins of the goats and put
them on Jacob's hands and neck. 17 Then she gave
Jacob the tasty food and the bread she had made.

Sidelight

Jacob was the world's first con man. With some help from his mother, Rebekah, and with the aid of goat skins, he fooled his father, Isaac, into thinking he was the older brother, Esau (Genesis 27:14–29). By mistakenly blessing Jacob instead of Esau, Isaac fulfilled God's promise to Rebekah in Genesis 25:23 (p.30).

18 Jacob went in to his father and said,
"Father."
And his father said, "Yes, my son. Who are you?"
19 Jacob said to him, "I am Esau, your first son.
I have done what you told me. Now sit up and
eat some meat of the animal I hunted for you.
Then bless me."
20 But Isaac asked his son, "How did you find
and kill the animal so quickly?"
Jacob answered, "Because the LORD your God
helped me to find it."
21 Then Isaac said to Jacob, "Come near so I can
touch you, my son. Then I will know if you are
really my son Esau."
22 So Jacob came near to Isaac his father. Isaac
touched him and said, "Your voice sounds like
Jacob's voice, but your hands are hairy like the
hands of Esau." 23 Isaac did not know it was Ja-
cob, because his hands were hairy like Esau's
hands, so Isaac blessed him. 24 Isaac asked, "Are
you really my son Esau?"
Jacob answered, "Yes, I am."
25 Then Isaac said, "Bring me the food, and I
will eat it and bless you." So Jacob gave him the
food, and he ate. Jacob gave him wine, and he
drank. 26 Then Isaac said to him, "My son, come
near and kiss me." 27 So Jacob went to his father
and kissed him. When Isaac smelled Esau's
clothes, he blessed him and said,
"The smell of my son
is like the smell of the field
that the LORD has blessed.
28 May God give you plenty of rain
and good soil
so that you will have plenty of grain and
new wine.

Shibah This name sounds like the Hebrew words for "seven" and "promise".

29May nations serve you
and peoples bow down to you.
May you be master over your brothers,
and may your mother's sons bow down
to you.
May everyone who curses you be cursed,
and may everyone who blesses you be
blessed."
30Isaac finished blessing Jacob. Then, just as
Jacob left his father Isaac, Esau came in from
hunting. 31He also prepared some tasty food and
brought it to his father. He said, "Father, rise and
eat the food that your son killed for you and then
bless me."
32Isaac asked, "Who are you?"
He answered, "I am your son—your firstborn[d]
son—Esau."
33Then Isaac trembled greatly and said, "Then
who was it that hunted the animals and brought
me food before you came? I ate it, and I blessed
him, and it is too late now to take back my
blessing."
34When Esau heard the words of his father, he
let out a loud and bitter cry. He said to his father,
"Bless me—me, too, my father!"
35But Isaac said, "Your brother came and
tricked me. He has taken your blessing."
36Esau said, "Jacob[n] is the right name for him.
He has tricked me these two times. He took away
my share of everything you own, and now he
has taken away my blessing." Then Esau asked,
"Haven't you saved a blessing for me?"
37Isaac answered, "I gave Jacob the power to
be master over you, and all his brothers will be
his servants. And I kept him strong with grain
and new wine. There is nothing left to give you,
my son."
38But Esau continued, "Do you have only one
blessing, Father? Bless me, too, Father!" Then
Esau began to cry out loud.
39Isaac said to him,
"You will live far away from the best land,
far from the rain.
40You will live by using your sword,
and you will be a slave to your brother.
But when you struggle,
you will break free from him."
41After that Esau hated Jacob because of the
blessing from Isaac. He thought to himself, "My
father will soon die, and I will be sad for him.
Then I will kill Jacob."
42Rebekah heard about Esau's plan to kill Ja-
cob. So she sent for Jacob and said to him, "Lis-
ten, your brother Esau is comforting himself by
planning to kill you. 43So, my son, do what I say.
My brother Laban is living in Haran. Go to him
at once! 44Stay with him for a while, until your
brother is not so angry. 45In time, your brother
will not be angry, and he will forget what you did
to him. Then I will send a servant to bring you
back. I don't want to lose both of my sons on the
same day."
46Then Rebekah said to Isaac, "I am tired of
Hittite women. If Jacob marries one of these Hit-
tite women here in this land, I want to die."

Jacob Searches for a Wife

28 Isaac called Jacob and blessed him and
commanded him, "You must not marry a
Canaanite woman. 2Go to the house of Bethuel,
your mother's father, in North West Mesopota-
mia. Laban, your mother's brother, lives there.
Marry one of his daughters. 3May God Almighty
bless you and give you many children, and may
you become a group of many peoples. 4May he
give you and your descendants[d] the blessing of
Abraham so that you may own the land where
you are now living as a stranger, the land God
gave to Abraham." 5So Isaac sent Jacob to North
West Mesopotamia, to Laban the brother of Re-
bekah. Bethuel the Aramean was the father of
Laban and Rebekah, and Rebekah was the
mother of Jacob and Esau.
6Esau learned that Isaac had blessed Jacob and
sent him to North West Mesopotamia to find a
wife there. He also learned that Isaac had com-
manded Jacob not to marry a Canaanite woman
7and that Jacob had obeyed his father and mother
and had gone to North West Mesopotamia. 8So
Esau saw that his father Isaac did not want his
sons to marry Canaanite women. 9Now Esau al-
ready had wives, but he went to Ishmael son of
Abraham and he married Mahalath, Ishmael's
daughter. Mahalath was the sister of Nebaioth.

Jacob's Dream at Bethel

10Jacob left Beersheba and set out for Haran.
11When he came to a place, he spent the night
there because the sun had set. He found a stone
and laid his head on it to go to sleep. 12Jacob
dreamed that there was a ladder resting on the
earth and reaching up into heaven, and he saw
angels of God going up and coming down the
ladder. 13Then Jacob saw the LORD standing above
the ladder, and he said, "I am the LORD, the God
of Abraham your grandfather, and the God of
Isaac. I will give you and your descendants[d] the
land on which you are now sleeping. 14Your des-
cendants will be as many as the dust of the earth.
They will spread west and east, north and south,
and all the families of the earth will be blessed
through you and your descendants. 15I am with

Jacob This name sounds like the Hebrew word for "heel". "Holding on to someone's heel" is a Hebrew saying for tricking someone.

you and will protect you everywhere you go and
will bring you back to this land. I will not leave
you until I have done what I have promised
you."
16Then Jacob woke from his sleep and said,
"Surely the LORD is in this place, but I did not
know it." 17He was afraid and said, "This place
frightens me! It is surely the house of God and
the gate of heaven."
18Jacob rose early in the morning and took the
stone he had slept on and set it up on its end.
Then he poured olive oil on the top of it. 19At
first, the name of that city was Luz, but Jacob
named it Bethel. [n]
20Then Jacob made a promise. He said, "I want
God to be with me and to protect me on this
journey. I want him to give me food to eat and
clothes to wear 21so I will be able to return in
peace to my father's house. If the LORD does these
things, he will be my God. 22This stone which I
have set up on its end will be the house of God.
And I will give God one-tenth of all he gives me."

Jacob Arrives in North West Mesopotamia

29 Then Jacob continued his journey and
came to the land of the people of the
East. 2He looked and saw a well in the field and
three flocks of sheep lying nearby, because they
drank water from this well. A large stone covered
the mouth of the well. 3When all the flocks gath-
ered there, the shepherds would roll the stone
away from the well and water the sheep. Then
they would put the stone back in its place.
4Jacob said to the shepherds there, "My broth-
ers, where are you from?"
They answered, "We are from Haran."
5Then Jacob asked, "Do you know Laban,
grandson of Nahor?"
They answered, "We know him."
6Then Jacob asked, "How is he?"
They answered, "He is well. Look, his daugh-
ter Rachel is coming now with his sheep."
7Jacob said, "But look, it is still the middle of
the day. It is not time for the sheep to be gathered
for the night, so give them water and let them go
back into the pasture."
8But they said, "We cannot do that until all the
flocks are gathered. Then we will roll away
the stone from the mouth of the well and water
the sheep."
9While Jacob was talking with the shepherds,
Rachel came with her father's sheep, because it
was her job to care for the sheep. 10When Jacob
saw Laban's daughter Rachel and Laban's sheep,
he went to the well and rolled the stone from its
mouth and watered Laban's sheep. Now Laban
was the brother of Rebekah, Jacob's mother.
11Then Jacob kissed Rachel and cried. 12He told
her that he was from her father's family and that
he was the son of Rebekah. So Rachel ran home
and told her father.
13When Laban heard the news about his sis-
ter's son Jacob, he ran to meet him. Laban
hugged him and kissed him and brought him to
his house, where Jacob told Laban everything
that had happened.
14Then Laban said, "You are my own flesh and
blood."

Jacob is Tricked

Jacob stayed there a month. 15Then Laban said
to Jacob, "You are my relative, but it is not right
for you to work for me without pay. What would
you like me to pay you?"
16Now Laban had two daughters. The older
was Leah, and the younger was Rachel. 17Leah
had weak eyes, but Rachel was very beautiful.
18Jacob loved Rachel, so he said to Laban, "Let
me marry your younger daughter Rachel. If you
will, I will work seven years for you."
19Laban said, "It would be better for her to
marry you than someone else, so stay here with
me." 20So Jacob worked for Laban seven years so
he could marry Rachel. But they seemed like just
a few days to him because he loved Rachel very
much.
21After seven years Jacob said to Laban, "Give
me Rachel so that I may marry her. The time I
promised to work for you is over."
22So Laban gave a feast for all the people there.
23That evening he brought his daughter Leah to
Jacob, and they had sexual relations. 24(Laban
gave his slave girl Zilpah to his daughter to be her
servant.) 25In the morning when Jacob saw that
he had had sexual relations with Leah, he said to
Laban, "What have you done to me? I worked
hard for you so that I could marry Rachel! Why
did you trick me?"
26Laban said, "In our country we do not allow
the younger daughter to marry before the older
daughter. 27But complete the full week of the

Sidelight If you think it's hard to go out with the right boy or girl, imagine how Jacob felt. He worked for seven years to marry Rachel, only to be tricked into marrying her "weak-eyed" sister Leah. Then Jacob was given Rachel too, but he had to work for seven more years (Genesis 29:16–30). Jacob might have been fooled because the bride was brought to the wedding festivities wearing a veil.

Bethel This name means "house of God".

marriage ceremony with Leah, and I will give you
Rachel to marry also. But you must serve me an-
other seven years."
28 So Jacob did this, and when he had comple-
ted the week with Leah, Laban gave him his
daughter Rachel as a wife. 29 (Laban gave his slave
girl Bilhah to his daughter Rachel to be her ser-
vant.) 30 So Jacob had sexual relations with Rachel
also, and Jacob loved Rachel more than Leah.
Jacob worked for Laban for another seven years.

Jacob's Family Grows

31 When the LORD saw that Jacob loved Rachel
more than Leah, he made it possible for Leah to
have children, but not Rachel. 32 Leah became
pregnant and gave birth to a son. She named him
Reuben,[n] because she said, "The LORD has seen my
troubles. Surely now my husband will love me."
33 Leah became pregnant again and gave birth
to another son. She named him Simeon[n] and
said, "The LORD has heard that I am not loved, so
he has given me this son."
34 Leah became pregnant again and gave birth
to another son. She named him Levi[n] and said,
"Now, surely my husband will be close to me,
because I have given him three sons."
35 Then Leah gave birth to another son. She
named him Judah,[n] because she said, "Now I
will praise the LORD." Then Leah stopped having
children.

30 When Rachel saw that she was not hav-
ing children for Jacob, she envied her sis-
ter Leah. She said to Jacob, "Give me children,
or I'll die!"
2 Jacob became angry with her and said, "Can
I do what only God can do? He is the one who
has kept you from having children."
3 Then Rachel said, "Here is my slave girl Bil-
hah. Have sexual relations with her so she can
give birth to a child for me. Then I can have my
own family through her."
4 So Rachel gave Bilhah, her slave girl, to Jacob
as a wife, and he had sexual relations with her.
5 She became pregnant and gave Jacob a son. 6 Ra-
chel said, "God has judged me innocent. He has
listened to my prayer and has given me a son," so
she named him Dan.[n]
7 Bilhah became pregnant again and gave Jacob
a second son. 8 Rachel said, "I have struggled hard
with my sister, and I have won." So she named
that son Naphtali.[n]
9 Leah saw that she had stopped having chil-
dren, so she gave her slave girl Zilpah to Jacob as
a wife. 10 When Zilpah had a son, 11 Leah said, "I
am lucky," so she named him Gad.[n] 12 Zilpah
gave birth to another son, 13 and Leah said, "I am
very happy! Now women will call me happy," so
she named him Asher.[n]
14 During the wheat harvest Reuben went into
the field and found some mandrake[n] plants and
brought them to his mother Leah. But Rachel
said to Leah, "Please give me some of your son's
mandrakes."
15 Leah answered, "You have already taken
away my husband, and now you are trying to
take away my son's mandrakes."
But Rachel answered, "If you will give me
your son's mandrakes, you may sleep with Jacob
tonight."
16 When Jacob came in from the field that
night, Leah went out to meet him. She
said, "You will have sexual relations with me
tonight because I have paid for you with my
son's mandrakes." So Jacob slept with her that
night.
17 Then God answered Leah's prayer, and
she became pregnant again. She gave birth
to a fifth son 18 and said, "God has given me
what I paid for, because I gave my slave girl
to my husband." So Leah named her son Is-
sachar.[n]
19 Leah became pregnant again and gave birth
to a sixth son. 20 She said, "God has given me a
fine gift. Now surely Jacob will honour me, be-
cause I have given him six sons," so she named
him Zebulun.[n]
21 Later Leah gave birth to a daughter and
named her Dinah.
22 Then God remembered Rachel and answered
her prayer, making it possible for her to have
children. 23 When she became pregnant and gave
birth to a son, she said, "God has taken away my
shame," 24 and she named him Joseph.[n] Rachel
said, "I wish the LORD would give me another
son."

Reuben This name sounds like the Hebrew word for "he has seen my troubles".
Simeon This name sounds like the Hebrew word for "has heard".
Levi This name sounds like the Hebrew word for "be close to".
Judah This name sounds like the Hebrew word for "praise".
Dan This name means "he has judged".
Naphtali This name sounds like the Hebrew word for "my struggle".
Gad This name may mean "lucky".
Asher This name may mean "happy".
mandrake A plant which was believed to cause a woman to become pregnant.
Issachar This name sounds like the Hebrew word for "paid for".
Zebulun This name sounds like the Hebrew word for "honour".
Joseph This name sounds like the Hebrew word for "he adds".

Jacob Tricks Laban

25After the birth of Joseph, Jacob said to Laban,
"Now let me go to my own home and country.
26Give me my wives and my children and let me
go. I have earned them by working for you, and
you know that I have served you well."
27Laban said to him, "If I have pleased you,
please stay. I know the LORD has blessed me be-
cause of you. 28Tell me what I should pay you,
and I will give it to you."
29Jacob answered, "You know that I have
worked hard for you, and your flocks have grown
while I cared for them. 30When I came, you had
little, but now you have much. Every time I did
something for you, the LORD blessed you. But
when will I be able to do something for my own
family?"
31Laban asked, "Then what should I give
you?"
Jacob answered, "I don't want you to give me
anything. Just do this one thing, and I will come
back and take care of your flocks. 32Today let me
go through all your flocks. I will take every speck-
led or spotted sheep, every black lamb and ev-
ery spotted or speckled goat. That will be my
pay. 33In the future you can easily see if I am
honest. When you come to look at my flocks,
if I have any goat that isn't speckled or spotted
or any lamb that isn't black, you will know I
stole it."
34Laban answered, "Agreed! We will do what
you ask." 35But that day Laban took away all the
male goats that had streaks or spots, all the speck-
led and spotted female goats (all those that had
white on them), and all the black sheep. He told
his sons to watch over them. 36Then he took
these animals to a place that was three days' jour-
ney away from Jacob. Jacob took care of all the
flocks that were left.
37So Jacob cut green branches from poplar, al-
mond and plane trees, and peeled off some of the
bark so that the branches had white stripes on
them. 38He put the branches in front of the flocks
at the watering places. When the animals came
to drink, they also mated there, 39so the flocks
mated in front of the branches. Then the young
that were born were streaked, speckled or spot-
ted. 40Jacob separated the young animals from the
others, and he made them face the streaked and
dark animals in Laban's flock. Jacob kept his ani-
mals separate from Laban's. 41When the stronger
animals in the flock were mating, Jacob put the
branches before their eyes so they would mate
near the branches. 42But when the weaker
animals mated, Jacob did not put the branches
there. So the animals born from the weaker ani-
mals were Laban's, and those born from the
stronger animals were Jacob's. 43In this way
Jacob became very rich. He had large flocks,
many male and female servants, camels and
donkeys.

Jacob Runs Away

31 One day Jacob heard Laban's sons talk-
ing. They said, "Jacob has taken every-
thing our father owned, and in this way he has
become rich." 2Then Jacob noticed that Laban
was not as friendly as he had been before. 3The
LORD said to Jacob, "Go back to the land where
your ancestors lived, and I will be with you."
4So Jacob told Rachel and Leah to meet him in
the field where he kept his flocks. 5He said to
them, "I have seen that your father is not as
friendly with me as he used to be, but the God of
my father has been with me. 6You both know
that I have worked as hard as I could for your
father, 7but he cheated me and changed my pay
ten times. But God has not allowed your father to
harm me. 8When Laban said, 'You can have all
the speckled animals as your pay,' all the animals
gave birth to speckled young ones. But when he
said, 'You can have all the streaked animals as
your pay,' all the flocks gave birth to streaked
babies. 9So God has taken the animals away from
your father and has given them to me.
10"I had a dream during the season when the
flocks were mating. I saw that the only male
goats who were mating were streaked, speckled
or spotted. 11The angel of God spoke to me in
that dream and said, 'Jacob!' I answered, 'Yes!'
12The angel said, 'Look! Only the streaked, speck-
led or spotted male goats are mating. I have seen
all the wrong things Laban has been doing to you.
13I am the God who appeared to you at Bethel,
where you poured olive oil on the stone you set
up on end and where you made a promise to me.
Now I want you to leave here and go back to the
land where you were born.' "
14Rachel and Leah answered Jacob, "Our
father has nothing to give us when he dies. 15He
has treated us like strangers. He sold us to you,
and then he spent all of the money you paid for
us. 16God took all this wealth from our father,
and now it belongs to us and our children. So do
whatever God has told you to do."
17So Jacob put his children and his wives on
camels, 18and they began their journey back to
Isaac, his father, in the land of Canaan. All the
flocks of animals that Jacob owned walked ahead
of them. He carried everything with him that he
had gained while he lived in North West
Mesopotamia.
19While Laban was gone to cut the wool from
his sheep, Rachel stole the idols that belonged
to him. 20And Jacob tricked Laban the Aramean
by not telling him he was leaving. 21Jacob and
his family left quickly, crossed the Euphrates

River, and travelled towards the mountains of
Gilead.
22Three days later Laban learned that Jacob
had run away, 23so he gathered his relatives and
began to chase him. After seven days Laban
found him in the mountains of Gilead. 24That
night God came to Laban the Aramean in a
dream and said, "Be careful! Do not say anything
to Jacob, good or bad."

The Search for the Stolen Idols

25So Laban caught up with Jacob. Now Jacob
had made his camp in the mountains, so Laban
and his relatives set up their camp in the moun-
tains of Gilead. 26Laban said to Jacob, "What have
you done? You cheated me and took my daugh-
ters as if you had captured them in a war. 27Why
did you run away secretly and trick me? Why
didn't you tell me? Then I could have sent you
away with joy and singing and with the music of
tambourines [d] and harps. 28You did not even let
me kiss my grandchildren and my daughters
goodbye. You were very foolish to do this! 29I
have the power to harm you, but last night the
God of your father spoke to me and warned me
not to say anything to you, good or bad. 30I know
you want to go back to your home, but why did
you steal my idols?"
31Jacob answered Laban, "I left without telling
you because I was afraid you would take your
daughters away from me. 32If you find anyone
here who has taken your idols, that person will be
killed! Your relatives will be my witnesses. You
may look for anything that belongs to you and
take anything that is yours." (Now Jacob did not
know that Rachel had stolen Laban's idols.)
33So Laban looked in Jacob's tent, in Leah's
tent, and in the tent where the two slave women
stayed, but he did not find his idols. When he left
Leah's tent, he went into Rachel's tent. 34Rachel
had hidden the idols inside her camel's saddle and
was sitting on them. Although Laban looked
through the whole tent, he did not find them.
35Rachel said to her father, "Father, don't be
angry with me. I am not able to stand up before
you because I am having my monthly period." So
Laban looked through the camp, but he did not
find his idols.
36Then Jacob became very angry and said,
"What wrong have I done? What law have I bro-
ken to cause you to chase me? 37You have looked
through everything I own, but you have found
nothing that belongs to you. If you have found
anything, show it to everyone. Put it in front of
your relatives and my relatives, and let them de-
cide which one of us is right. 38I have worked for
you now for 20 years. During all that time none
of the lambs and kids died during birth, and I
have not eaten any of the rams from your flocks.
39Any time an animal was killed by wild beasts, I
did not bring it to you, but made up for the loss
myself. You made me pay for any animal that was
stolen during the day or night. 40In the daytime
the sun took away my strength, and at night I was
cold and could not sleep. 41I worked like a slave
for you for 20 years—the first fourteen to get your
two daughters and the last six to earn your flocks.
During that time you changed my pay ten times.
42But the God of my father, the God of Abraham
and the God of Isaac, was with me. Otherwise,
you would have sent me away with nothing. But
he saw the trouble I had and the hard work I did,
and last night he corrected you."

Jacob and Laban's Agreement

43Laban said to Jacob, "These girls are my
daughters. Their children belong to me, and
these flocks are mine. Everything you see here
belongs to me, but I can do nothing to keep my
daughters and their children. 44Let us make an
agreement, and let us set up a pile of stones to
remind us of it."
45So Jacob took a large rock and set it up on its
end. 46He told his relatives to gather rocks, so
they took the rocks and piled them up; then they
ate beside the pile. 47Laban named that place in
his language A Pile to Remind Us, and Jacob gave
the place the same name in Hebrew.
48Laban said to Jacob, "This pile of rocks will
remind us of the agreement between us." That is
why the place was called A Pile to Remind Us.
49It was also called Mizpah, [n] because Laban
said, "Let the LORD watch over us while we are
separated from each other. 50Remember that God
is our witness even if no one else is around us. He
will know if you harm my daughters or marry
other women. 51Here is the pile of rocks that I
have put between us and here is the rock I set up
on end. 52This pile of rocks and this rock set on
end will remind us of our agreement. I will never
go past this pile to hurt you, and you must never
come to my side of them to hurt me. 53Let the
God of Abraham, who is the God of Nahor and
the God of their fathers, punish either of us if we
break this agreement."
So Jacob made a promise in the name of the
God whom his father Isaac worshipped. 54Then
Jacob killed an animal and offered it as a sacrifice
on the mountain, and he invited his relatives to
share in the meal. After they finished eating, they
spent the night on the mountain. 55Early the next
morning Laban kissed his grandchildren and his
daughters and blessed them, and then he left to
return home.

Mizpah This name sounds like the Hebrew word for "watch".

Jacob Meets Esau

32 When Jacob also went his way, the
angels of God met him. [2]When he saw
them, he said, "This is the camp of God!" So he
named that place Mahanaim.[n]
[3]Jacob's brother Esau was living in the area
called Seir in the country of Edom. Jacob sent
messengers to Esau, [4]telling them, "Give this
message to my master Esau: 'This is what Jacob,
your servant, says: I have lived with Laban
and have remained there until now. [5]I have
cattle, donkeys, flocks and male and female
servants. I send this message to you and ask you
to accept us.'"
[6]The messengers returned to Jacob and said,
"We went to your brother Esau. He is coming to
meet you and has 400 men with him."
[7]Then Jacob was very afraid and worried. He
divided the people who were with him and all
the flocks, herds and camels into two camps. [8]Ja-
cob thought, "Esau might come and destroy one
camp, but the other camp can run away and be
saved."
[9]Then Jacob said, "God of my father Abraham!
God of my father Isaac! LORD, you told me to
return to my country and my family. You said
that you would treat me well. [10]I am not worthy
of the kindness and continual goodness you have
shown me. The first time I travelled across the
Jordan River, I had only my walking stick, but
now I own enough to have two camps. [11]Please
save me from my brother Esau. I am afraid he will
come and kill all of us, even the mothers with the
children. [12]You said to me, 'I will treat you well

Mahanaim This name means "two camps".

SPIRITUAL GROWTH

Smackdown: Wrestling With God

Steve's relationship with his parents wasn't always plain sailing during his teenage years, but now in his twenties it was good. Then one Sunday afternoon the phone rang and everything changed. It was Steve's brother: "It's Mum . . . she collapsed and has been rushed to hospital."

The next day, Steve drove to the hospital thinking he'd do his sonly duty, give the obligatory bunch of flowers and then tomorrow she'll be home. But something was wrong. Steve's mum grabbed his arm and said with tears in her eyes, "I want you to know that I love you very much . . . they've found out I've got an aneurysm, and I could die unless I have a brain operation tomorrow . . . and even then, the operation's really risky and there's a good chance I won't make it."

Steve's mind flooded with a million questions and fears. In tears, Steve cried out to God in prayer all night. He finally reached the point where he could leave it all in the Lord's hands and say, "Lord, even if you allow her to die, I'll still trust you."

The operation was a success. Thanks to God, after a long recovery period, she left hospital and life continued as it always had, only somehow better. Steve was now able to comfort others going through similar situations, as he understood their heartache.

In **Genesis 32:22–32** we read about how God took hold of Jacob and wrestled with him, reminding him that his life was in God's hands and not his own.

- Why did God pick a wrestling match with Jacob and then let him win?
- Some people say that it is never God's will for his people to be ill, or have struggles, or pain, or poverty. How does this passage show that isn't true?

Consider . . .

- whether you are persistent in prayer or give up too easily if nothing seems to be happening? Maybe God wants you to patiently keep praying, in order to develop your faith.
- making a list of any tough times you've had recently. Now think how God may have used them to make you stronger and trust him more.

For more, see . . .

- Job 1:8–22 (p.469)
- Philippians 3:7–16 (p.1283)
- Romans 8:18–28 (p.1195)
- James 1:2–8 (p.1348)

and will make your children as many as the sand of the seashore. There will be too many to count.' "

13Jacob stayed there for the night and prepared a gift for Esau from what he had with him: 14200 female goats and 20 male goats, 200 female sheep and 20 rams, 1530 female camels and their young, 40 cows and 10 bulls, 20 female donkeys and 10 male donkeys. 16Jacob gave each separate flock of animals to one of his servants and said to them, "Go ahead of me and keep some space between each herd." 17Jacob gave them their orders. To the servant with the first group of animals he said, "My brother Esau will come to you and ask, 'Whose servant are you? Where are you going and whose animals are these?' 18Then you will answer, 'They belong to your servant Jacob. He sent them as a gift to you, my master Esau, and he also is coming behind us.' "

19Jacob ordered the second servant, the third servant, and all the other servants to do the same thing. He said, "Say the same thing to Esau when you meet him. 20Say, 'Your servant Jacob is coming behind us.' " Jacob thought, "If I send these gifts ahead of me, maybe Esau will forgive me. Then when I see him, perhaps he will accept me." 21So Jacob sent the gifts to Esau, but he himself stayed that night in the camp.

Jacob Wrestles with God

22During the night Jacob rose and crossed the Jabbok River at the crossing, taking with him his two wives, his two slave girls and his eleven sons. 23He sent his family and everything he had across the river. 24So Jacob was alone, and a man came and wrestled with him until the sun came up. 25When the man saw he could not defeat Jacob, he struck Jacob's hip and put it out of joint. 26Then he said to Jacob, "Let me go. The sun is coming up."

But Jacob said, "I will let you go if you will bless me."

27The man said to him, "What is your name?"

And he answered, "Jacob."

28Then the man said, "Your name will no longer be Jacob. Your name will now be Israel,[n] because you have wrestled with God and with people, and you have won."

29Then Jacob asked him, "Please tell me your name."

But the man said, "Why do you ask my name?" Then he blessed Jacob there.

30So Jacob named that place Peniel,[n] saying, "I have seen God face to face, but my life was saved." 31Then the sun rose as he was leaving that place, and Jacob was limping because of his leg. 32So even today the people of Israel do not eat the muscle that is on the hip joint of animals, because Jacob was touched there.

Sidelight The first wrestling match in the Bible was more than a three-minute bout. It lasted all night. Jacob's opponent had supernatural strength, but Jacob still finished the fight undefeated – although he did sustain a sports-related injury and was given a fighter's name, Israel, which means "he wrestles with God" (Genesis 32:22–32).

Jacob Shows His Bravery

33 Jacob looked up and saw Esau coming, and with him were 400 men. So Jacob divided his children among Leah, Rachel and the two slave girls. 2Jacob put the slave girls with their children first, then Leah and her children behind them, and Rachel and Joseph last. 3Jacob himself went out in front of them and bowed down flat on the ground seven times as he was walking towards his brother.

4But Esau ran to meet Jacob and put his arms around him and hugged him. Then Esau kissed him, and they both cried. 5When Esau looked up and saw the women and children, he asked, "Who are these people with you?"

Jacob answered, "These are the children God has given me. God has been good to me, your servant."

6Then the two slave girls and their children came up to Esau and bowed down flat on the earth before him. 7Leah and her children also came up to Esau and also bowed down flat on the earth. Last of all, Joseph and Rachel came up to Esau, and they, too, bowed down flat before him.

8Esau said, "I saw many herds as I was coming here. Why did you bring them?"

Jacob answered, "They were to please you, my master."

9But Esau said, "I already have enough, my brother. Keep what you have."

10Jacob said, "No! Please! If I have pleased you, then accept the gift I give you. I am very happy to see your face again. It is like seeing the face of God, because you have accepted me. 11So I beg you to accept the gift I give you. God has been very good to me, and I have more than I need." And because Jacob begged, Esau accepted the gift.

Israel This name means "he wrestles with God".
Peniel This name means "the face of God".

12Then Esau said, "Let us be going. I will travel with you."

13But Jacob said to him, "My master, you know that the children are weak. And I must be careful with my flocks and their young ones. If I force them to go too far in one day, all the animals will die. 14So, my master, you go on ahead of me, your servant. I will follow you slowly and let the animals and the children set the speed at which we travel. I will meet you, my master, in Edom."

15So Esau said, "Then let me leave some of my people with you."

"No, thank you," said Jacob. "I only want to please you, my master." 16So that day Esau started back to Edom. 17But Jacob went to Succoth, where he built a house for himself and shelters for his animals. That is why the place was named Succoth.[n]

18Jacob left North West Mesopotamia and arrived safely at the city of Shechem in the land of Canaan. There he camped east of the city. 19He bought a part of the field where he had camped from the sons of Hamor, father of Shechem, for 100 pieces of silver. 20He built an altar there and named it after God, the God of Israel.

Dinah is Attacked

34 At this time Dinah, the daughter of Leah and Jacob, went out to visit the women of the land. 2When Shechem, son of Hamor the Hivite, the ruler of the land, saw her, he took her and forced her to have sexual relations with him. 3Shechem fell in love with Dinah, and he spoke kindly to her. 4He told his father, Hamor, "Please get this girl for me so I can marry her."

5Jacob learned how Shechem had disgraced his daughter, but since his sons were out in the field with the cattle, Jacob said nothing until they came home. 6While he waited, Hamor, father of Shechem, went to talk with Jacob.

7When Jacob's sons heard what had happened, they came in from the field. They were very angry that Shechem had done such a wicked thing to Israel. It was wrong for him to have sexual relations with Jacob's daughter; a thing like this should not be done.

8But Hamor talked to Dinah's brothers and said, "My son Shechem is deeply in love with Dinah. Please let him marry her. 9Marry our people. Give your women to our men as wives and take our women for your men as wives. 10You can live in the same land with us. You will be free to own land and to trade here."

11Shechem also talked to Jacob and to Dinah's brothers and said, "Please accept my offer. I will give anything you ask. 12Ask as much as you want for the payment for the bride, and I will give it to you. Just let me marry Dinah."

13Jacob's sons answered Shechem and his father with lies, because Shechem had disgraced their sister Dinah. 14The brothers said to them, "We cannot allow you to marry our sister, because you are not circumcised.[d] That would be a disgrace to us. 15But we will allow you to marry her if you do this one thing: every man in your town must be circumcised like us. 16Then your men can marry our women, and our men can marry your women, and we will live in your land and become one people. 17If you refuse to be circumcised, we will take Dinah and leave."

18What they asked seemed fair to Hamor and Shechem. 19So Shechem quickly went to be circumcised because he loved Jacob's daughter.

Now Shechem was the most respected man in his family. 20So Hamor and Shechem went to the gate of their city and spoke to the men of their city, saying, 21"These people want to be friends with us. So let them live in our land and trade here. There is enough land for all of us. Let us marry their women, and we can let them marry our women. 22But we must agree to one thing: all our men must be circumcised as they are. Then they will agree to live in our land, and we will be one people. 23If we do this, their cattle and their animals will belong to us. Let us do what they say, and they will stay in our land." 24All the people who had come to the city gate heard this. They agreed with Hamor and Shechem and every man was circumcised.

25Three days later the men who were circumcised were still in pain. Two of Jacob's sons, Simeon and Levi (Dinah's brothers), took their swords and made a surprise attack on the city, killing all the men there. 26They killed Hamor and his son Shechem and then took Dinah out of Shechem's house and left. 27Jacob's sons came upon the dead bodies and stole everything that was in the city, to pay them back for what Shechem had done to their sister. 28So the brothers took the flocks, herds and donkeys, and everything in the city and in the fields. 29They took every valuable thing the people owned, even their wives and children and everything in the houses.

30Then Jacob said to Simeon and Levi, "You have caused me a lot of trouble. Now the Canaanites and the Perizzites who live in the land will hate me. Since there are only a few of us, if they join together to attack us, my people and I will be destroyed."

31But the brothers said, "We will not allow our sister to be treated like a prostitute."[d]

Succoth This name means "shelters"

Jacob in Bethel

35 God said to Jacob, "Go to the city of Bethel and live there. Make an altar to the God who appeared to you there when you were running away from your brother Esau."

2So Jacob said to his family and to all who were with him, "Put away the foreign gods you have, and make yourselves clean,[d] and change your clothes. 3We will leave here and go to Bethel. There I will build an altar to God, who has helped me during my time of trouble. He has been with me everywhere I have gone." 4So they gave Jacob all the foreign gods they had, and the earrings they were wearing, and he hid them under the great tree near the town of Shechem. 5Then Jacob and his sons left there. But God caused the people in the nearby cities to be afraid, so they did not follow them. 6And Jacob and all the people who were with him went to Luz, which is now called Bethel, in the land of Canaan. 7There Jacob built an altar and named the place Bethel, after God, because God had appeared to him there when he was running from his brother.

8Deborah, Rebekah's nurse, died and was buried under the oak tree at Bethel, so they named that place Oak of Crying.

Jacob's New Name

9When Jacob came back from North West Mesopotamia, God appeared to him again and blessed him. 10God said to him, "Your name is Jacob, but you will not be called Jacob any longer. Your new name will be Israel." So he called him Israel. 11God said to him, "I am God Almighty. Have many children and grow in number as a nation. You will be the ancestor of many nations and kings. 12The same land I gave to Abraham and Isaac I will give to you and your descendants."[d] 13Then God left him. 14Jacob set up a stone on edge in that place where God had talked to him, and he poured a drink offering and olive oil on it to make it special for God. 15And Jacob named the place Bethel.

Rachel Dies Giving Birth

16Jacob and his group left Bethel. Before they came to Ephrath, Rachel began giving birth to her baby, 17but she was having much trouble. When Rachel's nurse saw this, she said, "Don't be afraid, Rachel. You are giving birth to another son." 18Rachel gave birth to the son, but she herself died. As she lay dying, she named the boy Son of My Suffering, but Jacob called him Benjamin.[n]

19Rachel was buried on the road to Ephrath, a district of Bethlehem, 20and Jacob set up a rock on her grave to honour her. That rock is still there. 21Then Israel[n] continued his journey and camped just south of Migdal Eder.

22While Israel was there, Reuben had sexual relations with Israel's slave woman[d] Bilhah and Israel heard about it.

The Family of Israel

Jacob had twelve sons. 23He had six sons by his wife Leah: Reuben, his first son, then Simeon, Levi, Judah, Issachar and Zebulun.

24He had two sons by his wife Rachel: Joseph and Benjamin.

25He had two sons by Rachel's slave girl Bilhah: Dan and Naphtali.

26And he had two sons by Leah's slave girl Zilpah: Gad and Asher.

These are Jacob's sons who were born in North West Mesopotamia.

27Jacob went to his father Isaac at Mamre near Hebron, where Abraham and Isaac had lived. 28Isaac lived for 180 years. 29So Isaac breathed his last breath and died when he was very old, and his sons Esau and Jacob buried him.

Esau's Family

36 This is the family history of Esau (also called Edom).

2Esau married women from the land of Canaan: Adah daughter of Elon the Hittite; and Oholibamah daughter of Anah, the son of Zibeon the Hivite; 3and Basemath, Ishmael's daughter, the sister of Nebaioth.

4Adah gave birth to Eliphaz for Esau. Basemath gave him Reuel, 5and Oholibamah gave him Jeush, Jalam and Korah. These were Esau's sons who were born in the land of Canaan.

6Esau took his wives, his sons, his daughters and all the people who lived with him, his herds and other animals and all the belongings he had gained in Canaan, and he went to a land away from his brother Jacob. 7Esau's and Jacob's belongings were becoming too many for them to live in the same land. The land where they had lived could not support both of them, because they had too many herds. 8So Esau lived in the mountains of Edom. (Esau is also named Edom.)

Benjamin This name means "right-hand son" or "favourite son".
Israel Also called Jacob.

9This is the family history of Esau. He is the ancestor of the Edomites, who live in the mountains of Edom.

10Esau's sons were Eliphaz, son of Adah and Esau, and Reuel, son of Basemath and Esau.

11Eliphaz had five sons: Teman, Omar, Zepho, Gatam and Kenaz. 12Eliphaz also had a slave woman[d] named Timna, and Timna and Eliphaz gave birth to Amalek. These were Esau's grandsons by his wife Adah.

13Reuel had four sons: Nahath, Zerah, Shammah and Mizzah. These were Esau's grandsons by his wife Basemath.

14Esau's third wife was Oholibamah the daughter of Anah. (Anah was the son of Zibeon.) Esau and Oholibamah gave birth to Jeush, Jalam and Korah.

15These were the leaders that came from Esau: Esau's first son was Eliphaz. From him came these leaders: Teman, Omar, Zepho, Kenaz, 16Korah, Gatam and Amalek. These were the leaders that came from Eliphaz in the land of Edom. They were the grandsons of Adah.

17Esau's son Reuel was the father of these leaders: Nahath, Zerah, Shammah and Mizzah. These were the leaders that came from Reuel in the land of Edom. They were the grandsons of Esau's wife Basemath.

18Esau's wife Oholibamah gave birth to these leaders: Jeush, Jalam and Korah. These are the leaders that came from Esau's wife Oholibamah the daughter of Anah. 19These were the sons of Esau (also called Edom), and these were their leaders.

20These were the sons of Seir the Horite, who were living in the land: Lotan, Shobal, Zibeon, Anah, 21Dishon, Ezer and Dishan. These sons of Seir were the leaders of the Horites in Edom.

22The sons of Lotan were Hori and Homam. (Timna was Lotan's sister.)

23The sons of Shobal were Alvan, Manahath, Ebal, Shepho and Onam.

24The sons of Zibeon were Aiah and Anah. Anah is the man who found the hot springs in the desert while he was caring for his father's donkeys.

25The children of Anah were Dishon and Oholibamah, daughter of Anah.

26The sons of Dishon were Hemdan, Eshban, Ithran and Keran.

27The sons of Ezer were Bilhan, Zaavan and Akan.

28The sons of Dishan were Uz and Aran.

29These were the names of the Horite leaders: Lotan, Shobal, Zibeon, Anah, 30Dishon, Ezer and Dishan.

These men were the leaders of the Horite families who lived in the land of Edom.

31These are the kings who ruled in the land of Edom before the Israelites ever had a king:

32Bela son of Beor was the king of Edom. He came from the city of Dinhabah.

33When Bela died, Jobab son of Zerah became king. Jobab was from Bozrah.

34When Jobab died, Husham became king. He was from the land of the Temanites.

35When Husham died, Hadad son of Bedad, who had defeated Midian in the country of Moab, became king. Hadad was from the city of Avith.

36When Hadad died, Samlah became king. He was from Masrekah.

37When Samlah died, Shaul became king. He was from Rehoboth on the Euphrates River.

38When Shaul died, Baal-Hanan son of Acbor became king.

39When Baal-Hanan son of Acbor died, Hadad became king. He was from the city of Pau. His wife's name was Mehetabel, daughter of Matred, who was the daughter of Me-Zahab.

40These Edomite leaders, listed by their families and regions, came from Esau. Their names were Timna, Alvah, Jetheth, 41Oholibamah, Elah, Pinon, 42Kenaz, Teman, Mibzar, 43Magdiel and Iram. They were the leaders of Edom. (Esau was the father of the Edomites.) The area where each of these families lived was named after that family.

Joseph the Dreamer

37 Jacob lived in the land of Canaan, where his father had lived. 2This is the family history of Jacob:

Joseph was a young man, seventeen years old. He and his brothers, the sons of Bilhah and Zilpah, his father's wives, cared for the flocks. Joseph gave his father bad reports about his brothers. 3Since Joseph was born when his father Israel[n] was old, Israel loved him more than his other sons. He made Joseph a special robe with long sleeves. 4When Joseph's brothers saw that their father loved him more than he loved them, they hated their brother and could not speak to him politely.

5One time Joseph had a dream, and when he told his brothers about it, they hated him even more. 6Joseph said, "Listen to the dream I had. 7We were in the field tying bundles of wheat together. My bundle stood up, and your bundles of wheat gathered around it and bowed down to it."

8His brothers said, "Do you really think you will be king over us? Do you truly think you will rule over us?" His brothers hated him even more because of his dreams and what he had said.

Israel Also called Jacob

9Then Joseph had another dream, and he told
his brothers about it also. He said, "Listen, I had
another dream. I saw the sun, moon and eleven
stars bowing down to me."

> **Sidelight** Joseph's "coat of many colours" was probably a long robe with sleeves. Labourers wore shorter garments that allowed full use of their arms and legs. The coat upset Joseph's brothers as it signified that Joseph was special and didn't have to do any manual labour.

10Joseph also told his father about this dream,
but his father scolded him, saying, "What kind of
dream is this? Do you really believe that your
mother, your brothers and I will bow down to
you?" 11Joseph's brothers were jealous of him,
but his father thought about what all these things
could mean.
12One day Joseph's brothers went to Shechem
to herd their father's flocks. 13Israel said to Jo-
seph, "Go to Shechem where your brothers are
herding the flocks."
Joseph answered, "I will go."
14His father said, "Go and see if your brothers
and the flocks are all right. Then come back and
tell me." So Joseph's father sent him from the
Valley of Hebron.
When Joseph came to Shechem, 15a man
found him wandering in the field and asked him,
"What are you looking for?"

FAMILY

Family Feud

Another fight was brewing between Hannah and her sister. Usually Hannah was home from college for an hour or so before the anger boiled over. This time she hadn't even got her bag unpacked.

"How could you ruin my best jacket!" Hannah screamed as soon as she opened her wardrobe to hang up her clothes.

"I didn't fall off my bike on purpose," Naomi yelled from her room. "A car almost hit me. It's not my fault!"

"But you took my jacket," Hannah hissed, storming into her sister's room.

"Mum said I could wear anything in your wardrobe," Naomi retorted hotly.

"But you should've known I'd never let you wear this," Hannah shot back.

"It's just a stupid jacket," Naomi sneered sarcastically.

Hannah threw the torn jacket onto Naomi's bed. "Mum lets you get away with everything," she said, seething with anger. "But not this time. You're going to pay for this." And she stormed out of the room.

Naomi sat down on the bed, and her anger turned to tears. "Why do I have so much trouble with my sister?" she asked herself.

Naomi and Hannah's constant clashes are a lot like the clashes between Joseph and his brothers. Read **Genesis 37:1–36** to see what their bad relationship led to.

- What problems do you see in Hannah and Naomi's relationship that also show up in the relationship between Joseph and his brothers?
- Are you more like Joseph (the one who gets picked on) or his brothers (the ones who become jealous)?

Consider . . .

- writing an "I'm sorry" or "I forgive you" note to a family member and taping it to a mirror he or she uses.
- starting a "something nice" jar to collect notes about nice things other family members do for you. Look through the notes when you're angry at another family member.

For more, see . . .

- Genesis 27:1–41 (p.32)
- 1 John 2:9–11 (p.1372)
- Luke 10:38–41 (p.1058)

[16]Joseph answered, "I am looking for my brothers. Can you tell me where they are grazing the flocks?"

[17]The man said, "They have already gone. I heard them say they were going to Dothan." So Joseph went to look for his brothers and found them in Dothan.

Joseph Sold into Slavery

[18]Joseph's brothers saw him coming from far away. Before he reached them, they made a plan to kill him. [19]They said to each other, "Here comes that dreamer. [20]Let's kill him and throw his body into one of the wells. We can tell our father that a wild animal killed him. Then we will see what will become of his dreams."

[21]But Reuben heard their plan and saved Joseph, saying, "Let's not kill him. [22]Don't spill any blood. Throw him into this well here in the desert, but don't hurt him!" Reuben planned to save Joseph later and send him back to his father. [23]So when Joseph came to his brothers, they pulled off his robe with long sleeves [24]and threw him into the well. It was empty, and there was no water in it.

[25]While Joseph was in the well, the brothers sat down to eat. When they looked up, they saw a group of Ishmaelites travelling from Gilead to Egypt. Their camels were carrying spices, balm [d] and myrrh. [d]

[26]Then Judah said to his brothers, "What will we gain if we kill our brother and hide his death? [27]Let's sell him to these Ishmaelites. Then we will not be guilty of killing our own brother. After all, he is our brother, our own flesh and blood." And the other brothers agreed. [28]So when the Midianite traders came by, the brothers took Joseph out of the well and sold him to the Ishmaelites for 20 pieces of silver. And the Ishmaelites took him to Egypt.

[29]When Reuben came back to the well and Joseph was not there, he tore his clothes to show he was sad. [30]Then he went back to his brothers and said, "The boy is not there! What shall I do?" [31]The brothers killed a goat and dipped Joseph's robe in its blood. [32]Then they brought the long-sleeved robe to their father and said, "We found this robe. Look it over carefully and see if it is your son's robe."

[33]Jacob looked it over and said, "It is my son's robe! Some savage animal has eaten him. My son Joseph has been torn to pieces!" [34]Then Jacob tore his clothes and put on rough cloth to show that he was sad, and he continued to be sad about his son for a long time. [35]All of his sons and daughters tried to comfort him, but he could not be comforted. He said, "I will be sad about my son until the day I die." So Jacob cried for his son Joseph.

> **Sidelight** Joseph's jealous brothers sold him to Midianite slave merchants. For centuries a trade route called the King's Highway went from Egypt, east of the Jordan and through Damascus. Egyptian records list many slaves and soldiers who, like Joseph, had come from the area around Palestine.

[36]Meanwhile the Midianites who had bought Joseph had taken him to Egypt. There they sold him to Potiphar, an officer to the king of Egypt, and captain of the palace guard.

Judah and Tamar

38 About that time, Judah left his brothers and went to stay with a man named Hirah in the town of Adullam. [2]There Judah met a Canaanite girl, the daughter of a man named Shua and married her. Judah had sexual relations with her, [3]and she became pregnant and gave birth to a son, whom Judah named Er. [4]Later she gave birth to another son and named him Onan. [5]Still later she had another son and named him Shelah. She was at Kezib when this third son was born.

[6]Judah chose a girl named Tamar to be the wife of his first son Er. [7]But Er, Judah's oldest son, did what the LORD said was evil, so the LORD killed him. [8]Then Judah said to Er's brother Onan, "Go and have sexual relations with your dead brother's wife. [n] It is your duty to provide children for your brother in this way."

[9]But Onan knew that the children would not belong to him, so when he was supposed to have sexual relations with Tamar he did not complete the sex act. This made it impossible for Tamar to become pregnant and for Er to have descendants. [d] [10]The LORD was displeased by this wicked thing Onan had done, so the LORD killed Onan also. [11]Then Judah said to his daughter-in-law Tamar, "Go back to live in your father's house, and don't marry until my young son Shelah grows up." Judah was afraid that Shelah also would die like his brothers. So Tamar returned to her father's home.

[12]After a long time Judah's wife, the daughter of Shua, died. After Judah had got over his sorrow, he went to Timnah to his men who were cutting

Go . . . wife It was a custom in Israel that if a man died without children, one of his brothers would marry the widow. If a child was born, it would be considered the dead man's child.

the wool from his sheep. His friend Hirah
from Adullam went with him. 13Tamar learned
that Judah, her father-in-law, was going to
Timnah to cut the wool from his sheep. 14So she
took off the clothes that showed she was a
widow and covered her face with a veil to
hide who she was. Then she sat down by the
gate of Enaim on the road to Timnah. She did
this because Judah's younger son Shelah had
grown up, but Judah had not made plans for
her to marry him.
15When Judah saw her, he thought she was a
prostitute,[d] because she had covered her face
with a veil. 16So Judah went to her and said, "Let
me have sexual relations with you." He did not
know that she was Tamar, his daughter-in-law.
She asked, "What will you give me if I let you
have sexual relations with me?"
17Judah answered, "I will send you a young
goat from my flock."
She answered, "First give me something to
keep as a deposit until you send the goat."
18Judah asked, "What do you want me to give
you as a deposit?"
Tamar answered, "Give me your seal and its
cord,[n] and give me your walking stick." So Ju-
dah gave these things to her. Then Judah and
Tamar had sexual relations, and Tamar became
pregnant. 19When Tamar went home, she took
off the veil that covered her face and put on the
clothes that showed she was a widow.
20Judah sent his friend Hirah with the young
goat to find the woman and get back his seal and
the walking stick he had given her, but Hirah
could not find her. 21He asked some of the people
at the town of Enaim, "Where is the prostitute
who was here by the road?"
They answered, "There has never been a pros-
titute here."
22So he went back to Judah and said, "I could not
find the woman, and the people who lived there
said, 'There has never been a prostitute here.' "
23Judah said, "Let her keep the things. I don't
want people to laugh at us. I sent her the goat as
I promised, but you could not find her."
24About three months later someone told Ju-
dah, "Tamar, your daughter-in-law, is guilty of
acting like a prostitute, and now she is pregnant."
Then Judah said, "Bring her out and let her be
burned to death."
25When the people went to bring Tamar out,
she sent a message to her father-in-law that said,
"The man who owns these things has made me
pregnant. Look at this seal and its cord and this
walking stick, and tell me whose they are."
26Judah recognised them and said, "She is
more in the right than I. She did this because I
did not give her to my son Shelah as I promised."
And Judah did not have sexual relations with her
again.
27When the time came for Tamar to give birth,
there were twins in her body. 28While she was
giving birth, one baby put his hand out. The
nurse tied a red string on his hand and said, "This
baby came out first." 29But he pulled his hand
back in, so the other baby was born first. The
nurse said, "So you are able to break out first,"
and they named him Perez.[n] 30After this, the
baby with the red string on his hand was born,
and they named him Zerah.

Joseph is Sold to Potiphar

39 Now Joseph had been taken down to
Egypt. An Egyptian named Potiphar was
an officer to the king of Egypt and the captain of
the palace guard. He bought Joseph from the Ish-
maelites who had brought him down there. 2The
LORD was with Joseph, and he became a success-
ful man. He lived in the house of his master,
Potiphar the Egyptian.
3Potiphar saw that the LORD was with Joseph
and that the LORD made Joseph successful
in everything he did. 4So Potiphar was very
happy with Joseph and allowed him to be
his personal servant. He put Joseph in charge of
the house, trusting him with everything he
owned. 5When Joseph was put in charge of the
house and everything Potiphar owned, the
LORD blessed the people in Potiphar's house
because of Joseph. And the LORD blessed every-
thing that belonged to Potiphar, both in the
house and in the field. 6So Potiphar left Joseph in
charge of everything he owned and was not
concerned about anything except the food he
ate.

Joseph is Put into Prison

Now Joseph was well built and handsome.
7After some time the wife of Joseph's master began
to desire Joseph, and one day she said to him,
"Have sexual relations with me."
8But Joseph refused and said to her, "My mas-
ter trusts me with everything in his house. He has
put me in charge of everything he owns. 9There

seal . . . cord A seal was used like a rubber stamp, and people ran a string through it to tie around the neck. They wrote a contract, folded it, put wax or clay on the contract and pressed the seal onto it as a signature.
Perez This name means "breaking out".

is no one in his house greater than I. He has not kept anything from me except you, because you are his wife. How can I do such an evil thing? It is a sin against God."

10The woman talked to Joseph every day, but he refused to have sexual relations with her or even spend time with her.

11One day Joseph went into the house to do his work as usual and was the only man in the house at that time. 12His master's wife grabbed his coat and said to him, "Come and have sexual relations with me." But Joseph left his coat in her hand and ran out of the house.

13When she saw that Joseph had left his coat in her hands and had run outside, 14she called to the servants in her house and said, "Look! This Hebrew slave was brought here to shame us. He came in and tried to have sex with me, but I screamed. 15My scream scared him and he ran away, but he left his coat with me." 16She kept his coat until her husband came home, 17and she told him the same story. She said, "This Hebrew slave you brought here came in to shame me! 18When he came near me, I screamed. He ran away, but he left his coat."

19When Joseph's master heard what his wife said Joseph had done, he became very angry. 20So Potiphar arrested Joseph and put him into the prison where the king's prisoners were put. And Joseph stayed there in the prison.

21But the LORD was with Joseph and showed him kindness and caused the prison warden to like Joseph. 22The prison warden chose Joseph to take care of all the prisoners, and he was responsible for whatever was done in the prison. 23The warden paid no attention to anything that was in Joseph's care because the LORD was with Joseph and made him successful in everything he did.

Joseph Interprets Two Dreams

40 After these things happened, two of the king's officers displeased the king—the man who served wine to the king, and the king's baker. 2The king became angry with his officer who served him wine and his baker, 3so he put them in the prison of the captain of the guard, the same prison where Joseph was kept. 4The captain of the guard put the two prisoners in Joseph's care, and they stayed in prison for some time.

5One night both the king's officer who served him wine and the baker had a dream. Each had his own dream with its own meaning. 6When Joseph came to them the next morning, he saw they were worried. 7He asked the king's officers who were with him, "Why do you look so unhappy today?"

8The two men answered, "We both had dreams last night, but no one can explain their meaning to us."

Joseph said to them, "God is the only one who can explain the meaning of dreams. Tell me your dreams."

9So the man who served wine to the king told Joseph his dream. He said, "I dreamed I saw a vine, and 10on the vine were three branches. I watched the branches bud and blossom, and then the grapes ripened. 11I was holding the king's cup, so I took the grapes and squeezed the juice into the cup. Then I gave it to the king."

12Then Joseph said, "I will explain the dream to you. The three branches stand for three days. 13Before the end of three days the king will free you, and he will allow you to return to your work. You will serve the king his wine just as you did before. 14But when you are free, remember me. Be kind to me, and tell the king about me so I can get out of this prison. 15I was taken by force from the land of the Hebrews, and I have done nothing here to deserve being put in prison."

16The baker saw that Joseph's explanation of the dream was good, so he said to him, "I also had a dream. I dreamed there were three bread baskets on my head. 17In the top basket were all kinds of baked food for the king, but the birds were eating this food out of the basket on my head."

18Joseph answered, "I will tell you what the dream means. The three baskets stand for three days. 19Before the end of three days, the king will cut off your head! He will hang your body on a pole, and the birds will eat your flesh."

20Three days later, on his birthday, the king gave a feast for all his officers. In front of his officers, he released from prison the chief officer who served his wine and the chief baker. 21The king gave his chief officer who served wine his old position, and once again he put the king's cup of wine into the king's hand. 22But the king hanged the baker on a pole. Everything happened just as Joseph had said it would, 23but the officer who served wine did not remember Joseph. He forgot all about him.

The King's Dreams

41 Two years later the king dreamed he was standing on the bank of the Nile River. 2He saw seven fat and beautiful cows come up out of the river, and they stood there, eating the grass. 3Then seven more cows came up out of the river, but they were thin and ugly. They stood beside the seven beautiful cows on the bank of the Nile. 4The seven thin and ugly cows ate the seven beautiful fat cows. Then the king woke up.

5The king slept again and dreamed a second time.
In his dream he saw seven full and good heads of
grain growing on one stalk. 6After that, seven
more heads of grain sprang up, but they were
thin and burned by the hot east wind. 7The thin
heads of grain ate the seven full and good heads.
Then the king woke up again, and he realised it
was only a dream. 8The next morning the king
was troubled about these dreams, so he sent for
all the magicians and wise men of Egypt. The
king told them his dreams, but no one could ex-
plain their meaning to him.

9Then the chief officer who served wine to the
king said to him, "Now I remember something I
promised to do, but I forgot about it. 10There was
a time when you were angry with the baker and
me, and you put us in prison in the house of the
captain of the guard. 11In prison we each had a
dream on the same night, and each dream had a
different meaning. 12A young Hebrew man, a ser-
vant of the captain of the guard, was in the prison
with us. When we told him our dreams, he ex-
plained their meanings to us. He told each man
the meaning of his dream, and 13things happened
exactly as he said they would: I was given back
my old position, and the baker was hanged."

14So the king called for Joseph. The guards
quickly brought him out of the prison, and he
shaved, put on clean clothes and went before the
king.

15The king said to Joseph, "I have had a dream,
but no one can explain its meaning to me. I have
heard that you can explain a dream when some-
one tells it to you."

16Joseph answered the king, "I am not able to
explain the meaning of dreams, but God will do
this for the king."

17Then the king said to Joseph, "In my dream I
was standing on the bank of the Nile River. 18I saw
seven fat and beautiful cows that came up out of
the river and ate the grass. 19Then I saw seven
more cows come out of the river that were thin
and lean and ugly—the worst looking cows I have
seen in all the land of Egypt. 20And these thin and
ugly cows ate the first seven fat cows, 21but after
they had eaten the seven cows, no one could tell
they had eaten them. They looked just as thin and
ugly as they did in the beginning. Then I woke up.

22"I had another dream. I saw seven full and
good heads of grain growing on one stalk.
23Then seven more heads of grain sprang up
after them, but these heads were thin and ugly
and were burned by the hot east wind. 24Then
the thin heads ate the seven good heads. I told
this dream to the magicians, but no one could
explain its meaning to me."

Joseph Tells the Dreams' Meaning

25Then Joseph said to the king, "Both of these
dreams mean the same thing. God is telling you
what he is about to do. 26The seven good cows
stand for seven years, and the seven good heads
of grain stand for seven years. Both dreams mean
the same thing. 27The seven thin and ugly cows
stand for seven years, and the seven thin heads
of grain burned by the hot east wind stand for
seven years of hunger. 28This will happen as I told
you. God is showing the king what he is about
to do. 29You will have seven years of good crops
and plenty to eat in all the land of Egypt. 30But
after those seven years, there will come seven
years of hunger, and all the food that grew in the
land of Egypt will be forgotten. The time of
hunger will eat up the land. 31People will forget
what it was like to have plenty of food, because
the hunger that follows will be so great. 32You
had two dreams which mean the same thing.
This shows that God has firmly decided that this
will happen, and he will make it happen soon.

33"So let the king choose a man who is very
wise and understanding and set him over the
land of Egypt. 34And let the king also appoint
officers over the land, who should take one-fifth
of all the food that is grown during the seven
good years. 35They should gather all the food
that is produced during the good years that are
coming, and under the king's authority they
should store the grain in the cities and guard it.
36That food should be saved to use during the
seven years of hunger that will come on the land
of Egypt. Then the people in Egypt will not die
during the seven years of hunger."

Joseph is Made Ruler Over Egypt

37This seemed like a very good idea to the king,
and all his officers agreed. 38And the king asked
them, "Can we find a better man than Joseph to
take this job? God's Spirit is truly in him!"

39So the king said to Joseph, "God has shown
you all this. There is no one as wise and under-
standing as you are, so 40I will put you in charge
of my palace. All the people will obey your
orders, and only I will be greater than you."

41Then the king said to Joseph, "Look! I have
put you in charge of all the land of Egypt." 42Then
the king took off from his own finger his ring with
the royal seal on it, and he put it on Joseph's
finger. He gave Joseph fine linen clothes to wear,
and he put a gold chain around Joseph's neck.
43The king had Joseph ride in the second royal
chariot, and people walked ahead of his chariot
calling, "Bow down!" By doing these things, the
king put Joseph in charge of all of Egypt.

44The king said to him, "I am the king, and I say that no one in all the land of Egypt may lift a hand or a foot without your permission." 45The king gave Joseph the name Zaphenath-Paneah. He also gave Joseph a wife named Asenath, who was the daughter of Potiphera, priest of On. So Joseph travelled through all the land of Egypt.

> **Sidelight** In Old Testament times, Middle Easterners depended on rainfall to grow crops. If rain didn't come, people often went to Egypt, because the Nile River flooded each year, making the ground moist and rich. So famine in Egypt could mean disaster. That's why Joseph's prediction of seven years of famine was taken so seriously (Genesis 41:25–43).

46Joseph was 30 years old when he began serving the king of Egypt. And he left the king's court and travelled through all the land of Egypt. 47During the seven good years, the crops in the land grew well. 48And Joseph gathered all the food which was produced in Egypt during those seven years of good crops and stored the food in the cities. In every city he stored grain that had been grown in the fields around that city. 49Joseph stored much grain, as much as the sand of the seashore—so much that he could not measure it.

50Joseph's wife was Asenath, daughter of Potiphera, the priest of On. Before the years of hunger came, Joseph and Asenath had two sons. 51Joseph named the first son Manasseh[n] and said, "God has made me forget all the troubles I have had and all my father's family." 52Joseph named the second son Ephraim[n] and said, "God has given me children in the land of my troubles."

53The seven years of good crops came to an end in the land of Egypt. 54Then the seven years of hunger began, just as Joseph had said. In all the lands people had nothing to eat, but in Egypt there was food. 55The time of hunger became terrible in all of Egypt, and the people cried to the king for food. He said to all the Egyptians, "Go to Joseph and do whatever he tells you."

56The hunger was everywhere in that part of the world. And Joseph opened the storehouses and sold grain to the people of Egypt, because the time of hunger became terrible in Egypt. 57And all the people in that part of the world came to Joseph in Egypt to buy grain because the hunger was terrible everywhere in that part of the world.

The Dreams Come True

42 Jacob learned that there was grain in Egypt, so he said to his sons, "Why are you just sitting here looking at one another? 2I have heard that there is grain in Egypt. Go down there and buy grain for us to eat, so that we will live and not die."

3So ten of Joseph's brothers went down to buy grain from Egypt. 4But Jacob did not send Benjamin, Joseph's brother, with them, because he was afraid that something terrible might happen to him. 5Along with many other people, the sons of Israel[n] went to Egypt to buy grain, because the people in the land of Canaan were also hungry.

6Now Joseph was governor over Egypt. He was the one who sold the grain to people who came to buy it. So Joseph's brothers came to him and bowed face down on the ground before him. 7When Joseph saw his brothers, he knew who they were, but he acted as if he didn't know them. He asked unkindly, "Where do you come from?"

They answered, "We have come from the land of Canaan to buy food."

8Joseph knew they were his brothers, but they did not know who he was. 9And Joseph remembered his dreams about his brothers bowing to him. He said to them, "You are spies! You came to learn where the nation is weak!"

10But his brothers said to him, "No, my master. We come as your servants just to buy food. 11We are all sons of the same father. We are honest men, not spies."

12Then Joseph said to them, "No! You have come to learn where this nation is weak!"

13And they said, "We are ten of twelve brothers, sons of the same father, and we live in the land of Canaan. Our youngest brother is there with our father right now, and our other brother is gone."

14But Joseph said to them, "I can see I was right! You are spies! 15But I will give you a way to prove you are telling the truth. As surely as the king lives, you will not leave this place until your youngest brother comes here. 16One of you must go and get your brother. The rest of you will stay here in prison. We will see if you are telling the truth. If not, as surely as the king lives, you are spies." 17Then Joseph put them all in prison for three days.

18On the third day Joseph said to them, "I am a God-fearing man. Do this and I will let you live: 19if you are honest men, let one of your brothers stay here in prison while the rest of you go and

Manasseh This name sounds like the Hebrew word for "made me forget".
Ephraim This name sounds like the Hebrew word for "given me children".
Israel Also called Jacob.

carry grain back to feed your hungry families.
20Then bring your youngest brother back here to
me. If you do this, I will know you are telling the
truth, and you will not die."

The brothers agreed to this. 21They said to each
other, "We are being punished for what we did to
our brother. We saw his trouble, and he begged
us to save him, but we refused to listen. That is
why we are in this trouble now."

22Then Reuben said to them, "I told you not to
harm the boy, but you refused to listen to me. So
now we are being punished for what we did
to him."

23When Joseph talked to his brothers, he used
an interpreter, so they did not know that Joseph
understood what they were saying. 24Then Jo-
seph left them and cried. After a short time he
went back and spoke to them. He took Simeon
and tied him up while the other brothers
watched. 25Joseph told his servants to fill his
brothers' bags with grain and to put the money
the brothers had paid for the grain back in their
bags. The servants were also to give them what
they would need for their trip back home. And
the servants did this.

26So the brothers put the grain on their don-
keys and left. 27When they stopped for the night,
one of the brothers opened his sack to get food for
his donkey. Then he saw his money in the top of
the sack. 28He said to the other brothers, "The
money I paid for the grain has been put back.
Here it is in my sack!"

The brothers were very frightened. They said
to each other, "What has God done to us?"

The Brothers Return to Jacob

29The brothers went to their father Jacob in the
land of Canaan and told him everything that had
happened. 30They said, "The master of that land
spoke unkindly to us. He accused us of spying on
his country, 31but we told him that we were hon-
est men, not spies. 32We told him that we were
ten of twelve brothers—sons of one father. We
said that one of our brothers was gone and that
our youngest brother was with our father in
Canaan.

33"Then the master of the land said to us, 'Here
is a way I can know you are honest men: leave
one of your brothers with me, and take grain to
feed your hungry families, and go. 34And bring
your youngest brother to me so I will know you
are not spies but honest men. Then I will give
you back your brother whom you leave with me,
and you can move about freely in our land.' "

35As the brothers emptied their sacks, each of
them found his money in his sack. When they
and their father saw it, they were afraid.

36Their father Jacob said to them, "You are rob-
bing me of all my children. Joseph is gone, Sim-
eon is gone, and now you want to take Benjamin
away, too. Everything is against me."

37Then Reuben said to his father, "You may
put my two sons to death if I don't bring Benja-
min back to you. Trust him to my care, and I will
bring him back to you."

38But Jacob said, "I will not allow Benjamin to
go with you. His brother is dead, and he is the
only son left from my wife Rachel. I am afraid
something terrible might happen to him during
the trip to Egypt. Then I would be sad until the
day I die."

The Brothers Go Back to Egypt

43 Still no food grew in the land of Canaan.
2When Jacob's family had eaten all the
grain they had brought from Egypt, Jacob said to
them, "Go to Egypt again and buy a little more
grain for us to eat."

3But Judah said to Jacob, "The governor of that
country strongly warned us, 'If you don't bring
your brother back with you, you will not be al-
lowed to see me.' 4If you will send Benjamin with
us, we will go down and buy food for you. 5But
if you refuse to send Benjamin, we will not go.
The governor of that country warned us that we
would not see him if we didn't bring Benjamin
with us."

6Israel[n] said, "Why did you tell the man you
had another brother? You have caused me a lot of
trouble."

7The brothers answered, "He questioned us
carefully about ourselves and our family. He
asked us, 'Is your father still alive? Do you have
another brother?' We just answered his ques-
tions. How could we know he would ask us to
bring our other brother to him?"

8Then Judah said to his father Jacob, "Send
Benjamin with me, and we will go at once so that
we, you, and our children may live and not die.
9I will guarantee you that he will be safe, and I
will be personally responsible for him. If I don't
bring him back to you, you can blame me all my
life. 10If we had not wasted all this time, we could
have already made two trips."

11Then their father Jacob said to them,
"If it has to be that way, then do this: take some
of the best foods in our land in your packs. Give
them to the man as a gift: some balm,[d] some
honey, spices, myrrh,[d] pistachio nuts and

Israel Also called Jacob.

almonds. [12]Take twice as much money with you
this time, and take back the money that was re-
turned to you in your sacks last time. Maybe it
was a mistake. [13]And take Benjamin with you.
Now leave and go to the man. [14]I pray that God
Almighty will cause the governor to be merciful
to you and that he will allow Simeon and Ben-
jamin to come back with you. If I am robbed of
my children, then I am robbed of them!"

[15]So the brothers took the gifts. They also took
twice as much money as they had taken the first
time, and they took Benjamin. They hurried
down to Egypt and stood before Joseph.

[16]When Joseph saw Benjamin with them, he
said to the servant in charge of his house, "Bring
those men into my house. Kill an animal and
prepare a meal. Those men will eat with me to-
day at noon." [17]The servant did as Joseph told
him and brought the men to Joseph's house.

[18]The brothers were afraid when they were
brought to Joseph's house and thought, "We were
brought here because of the money that was put
in our sacks on the first trip. He wants to attack us,
make us slaves, and take our donkeys." [19]So the
brothers went to the servant in charge of Joseph's
house and spoke to him at the door of the house.
[20]They said, "Master, we came here once before
to buy food. [21]While we were going home, we
stopped for the night and when we opened our
sacks each of us found all his money in his sack.
We brought that money with us to give it back to
you. [22]And we have brought more money to pay
for the food we want to buy this time. We don't
know who put that money in our sacks."

[23]But the servant answered, "It's all right.
Don't be afraid. Your God, the God of your
father, must have put the money in your sacks. I
got the money you paid me for the grain last time."
Then the servant brought Simeon out to them.

[24]The servant led the men into Joseph's house
and gave them water, and they washed their feet.
Then he gave their donkeys food to eat. [25]The
men prepared their gift to give to Joseph when he
arrived at noon, because they had heard they
were going to eat with him there.

[26]When Joseph came home, the brothers gave
him the gift they had brought into the house and
bowed down to the ground in front of him. [27]Jo-
seph asked them how they were. He said, "How
is your aged father you told me about? Is he still
alive?"

[28]The brothers answered, "Your servant, our
father, is well. He is still alive." And they bowed
low before Joseph to show him respect.

[29]When Joseph saw his brother Benjamin, who
had the same mother as he, Joseph asked, "Is this
your youngest brother you told me about?" Then
he said to Benjamin, "God be good to you, my
son!" [30]Then Joseph hurried off because he had to
hold back the tears when he saw his brother Ben-
jamin. So Joseph went into his room and cried
there. [31]Then he washed his face and came out.
He controlled himself and said, "Serve the meal."

[32]So they served Joseph at one table, his broth-
ers at another table, and the Egyptians who ate
with him at another table. This was because
Egyptians did not like Hebrews and never ate
with them. [33]Joseph's brothers were seated in
front of him in order of their ages, from oldest to
youngest. They looked at each other because they
were so amazed. [34]Food from Joseph's table was
taken to them, but Benjamin was given five times
more food than the others. Joseph's brothers ate
and drank freely with him.

Joseph Sets a Trap

44 Then Joseph gave a command to the ser-
vant in charge of his house. He said, "Fill
the men's sacks with as much grain as they can
carry, and put each man's money into his sack
with the grain. [2]Put my silver cup in the sack of
the youngest brother, along with his money for
the grain." The servant did what Joseph told him.

[3]At dawn the brothers were sent away with
their donkeys. [4]They were not far from the city
when Joseph said to the servant in charge of his
house, "Go after the men. When you catch up
with them, say, 'Why have you paid back evil for
good? [5]The cup you have stolen is the one my
master uses for drinking and for explaining
dreams. You have done a very wicked thing!' "

[6]So the servant caught up with the brothers
and said to them what Joseph had told him
to say.

[7]But the brothers said to the servant, "Why do
you say these things? We would not do anything
like that! [8]We brought back to you from the land
of Canaan the money we found in our sacks. So
surely we would not steal silver or gold from your
master's house. [9]If you find that silver cup in the
sack of one of us, then let him die, and we will
be your slaves."

[10]The servant said, "We will do as you say, but
only the man who has taken the cup will become
my slave. The rest of you may go free."

[11]Then every brother quickly lowered his sack
to the ground and opened it. [12]The servant
searched the sacks, going from the oldest brother
to the youngest, and found the cup in Benjamin's
sack. [13]The brothers tore their clothes to show
they were afraid. Then they put their sacks back
on the donkeys and returned to the city.

[14]When Judah and his brothers went back to
Joseph's house, Joseph was still there, so the
brothers bowed face down on the ground before
him. [15]Joseph said to them, "What have you

done? Didn't you know that a man like me can learn things by signs and dreams?"

[16]Judah said, "Master, what can we say? And how can we show we are not guilty? God has uncovered our guilt, so all of us will be your slaves, not just Benjamin."

[17]But Joseph said, "I will not make you all slaves! Only the man who stole the cup will be my slave. The rest of you may go back safely to your father."

[18]Then Judah went to Joseph and said, "Master, please let me speak plainly to you, and please don't be angry with me. I know that you are as powerful as the king of Egypt himself. [19]When we were here before, you asked us, 'Do you have a father or a brother?' [20]And we answered you, 'We have an old father. And we have a younger brother, who was born when our father was old. This youngest son's brother is dead, so he is the only one of his mother's children left alive, and our father loves him very much.' [21]Then you said to us, 'Bring that brother to me. I want to see him.' [22]And we said to you, 'That young boy cannot leave his father, because if he leaves him, his father would die.' [23]But you said to us, 'If you don't bring your youngest brother, you will not be allowed to see me again.' [24]So we went back to our father and told him what you had said.

[25]"Later, our father said, 'Go again and buy us a little more food.' [26]We said to our father, 'We cannot go without our youngest brother. Without our youngest brother, we will not be allowed to see the governor.' [27]Then my father said to us, 'You know that my wife Rachel gave me two sons. [28]When one son left me, I thought, "Surely he has been torn apart by a wild animal," and I haven't seen him since. [29]Now you want to take this son away from me also. But something terrible might happen to him, and I would be miserable until the day I die.' [30]Now what will happen if we go home to our father without our youngest brother? He is so important in our father's life that [31]when our father sees the young boy is not with us, he will die. And it will be our fault. We will cause the great sorrow that kills our father.

[32]"I gave my father a guarantee that the young boy would be safe. I said to my father, 'If I don't bring him back to you, you can blame me all my life.' [33]So now, please allow me to stay here and be your slave, and let the young boy go back home with his brothers. [34]I cannot go back to my father if the boy is not with me. I couldn't stand to see my father that sad."

Joseph Reveals Who He Is

45 Joseph could not control himself in front of his servants any longer, so he cried out, "Have everyone leave me." When only the brothers were left with Joseph, he told them who he was. [2]Joseph cried so loudly that the Egyptians heard him, and the people in the king's palace heard about it. [3]He said to his brothers, "I am Joseph. Is my father still alive?" But the brothers could not answer him, because they were very afraid of him.

[4]So Joseph said to them, "Come close to me." When the brothers came close to him, he said to them, "I am your brother Joseph, whom you sold as a slave to go to Egypt. [5]Now don't be worried or angry with yourselves because you sold me here. God sent me here ahead of you to save people's lives. [6]No food has grown on the land for two years now, and there will be five more years without planting or harvest. [7]So God sent me here ahead of you to make sure you have some descendants[d] left on earth and to keep you alive in an amazing way. [8]So it was not you who sent me here, but God. God has made me the highest officer of the king of Egypt. I am in charge of his palace, and I am the master of all the land of Egypt.

[9]"So leave quickly and go to my father. Tell him, 'Your son Joseph says: God has made me master over all Egypt. Come down to me quickly. [10]Live in the land of Goshen where you will be near me. Your children, your grandchildren, your flocks and herds, and all that you have will also be near me. [11]I will care for you during the next five years of hunger so that you and your family and all that you have will not starve.'

[12]"Now you can see for yourselves, and so can my brother Benjamin, that the one speaking to you is really Joseph. [13]So tell my father about how powerful I have become in Egypt. Tell him about everything you have seen. Now hurry and bring him back to me." [14]Then Joseph hugged his brother Benjamin and cried, and Benjamin cried also. [15]And Joseph kissed all his brothers and cried as he hugged them. After this, his brothers talked with him.

[16]When the king of Egypt and his officers learned that Joseph's brothers had come, they were very happy. [17]So the king said to Joseph, "Tell your brothers to load their animals and go back to the land of Canaan [18]and bring their father and their families back here to me. I will give them the best land in Egypt, and they will eat the best food we have here. [19]Tell them to take some wagons from Egypt for their children and their wives and to bring their father back also. [20]Tell them not to worry about bringing any of their things with them, because we will give them the best of what we have in Egypt."

[21]So the sons of Israel did this. Joseph gave them wagons as the king had ordered and food

for their trip. 22He gave each brother a change of
clothes, but he gave Benjamin five changes of
clothes and about 300 pieces of silver. 23Joseph
also sent his father ten donkeys loaded with the
best things from Egypt and ten female donkeys
loaded with grain, bread and other food for his
father on his trip back. 24Then Joseph told his
brothers to go. As they were leaving, he said to
them, "Don't quarrel on the way home."
25So the brothers left Egypt and went to their
father Jacob in the land of Canaan. 26They told
him, "Joseph is still alive and is the ruler over all
the land of Egypt." Their father was shocked and
did not believe them. 27But when the brothers
told him everything Joseph had said, and when
Jacob saw the wagons Joseph had sent to carry
him back to Egypt, he felt better. 28Israel [n] said,
"Now I believe you. My son Joseph is still alive,
and I will go and see him before I die."

Jacob Goes to Egypt

46 So Israel [n] took all he had and started his
trip. He went to Beersheba, where he
offered sacrifices to the God of his father Isaac.
2During the night God spoke to Israel in a vision
and said, "Jacob, Jacob."
And Jacob answered, "Here I am."
3Then God said, "I am God, the God of your
father. Don't be afraid to go to Egypt, because I
will make your descendants [d] a great nation there.
4I will go to Egypt with you, and I will bring you
out of Egypt again. Joseph's own hands will close
your eyes when you die."
5Then Jacob left Beersheba. The sons of Israel
loaded their father, their children and their
wives in the wagons the king of Egypt had sent.
6They also took their farm animals and every-
thing they had gained in Canaan. So Jacob went
to Egypt with all his descendants— 7his sons

Israel Also called Jacob.

REVENGE

Was it Worth it?

"Just good friends, right?" Anna smiled. Andrew and Anna had been going out through most of school, but now she had dumped him!

Everything suddenly became clear two weeks later when Andrew discovered that his best friend Neil was seeing Anna. He wasn't prepared to simply forgive and forget and he was going to get even!

He waited impatiently outside the main school gates that afternoon. When he saw Neil, he took a deep breath and threw a punch to his face.

"That's for taking Anna," he said, then turned and walked away. He smiled to himself. He had carried out his revenge quickly and effectively.

Gradually, it dawned on him that he had now not only lost his girlfriend, but also his best friend. Revenge had tasted sweet at first, but now it had turned bitter.

- Andrew's motive for revenge seemed fine in the heat of the moment. In **Genesis 45:3–8**, Joseph also had the motive and the opportunity to take revenge. Read about the different way he reacted.
- What difference can you see between the attitudes of Andrew and Joseph? How did their attitudes affect their responses?

Consider . . .

- thinking of how many people have done something to you out of revenge. Decide how you will respond to them the next time they get under your skin.
- how many films you have seen which rely on revenge to carry the plot. How would the story develop differently if the characters acted a little more like Joseph?

For more, see . . .

- Joshua 20:1–6 (p.218)
- Acts 7:51–60 (p.1149)
- Luke 6:27–36 (p.1048)

and grandsons, his daughters and granddaugh-
ters. He took all his family to Egypt with him.

Jacob's Family

8Now these are the names of the children of
Israel who went into Egypt (Jacob and his des-
cendants[d]).
Reuben was Jacob's first son. 9Reuben's sons
were Hanoch, Pallu, Hezron and Carmi.
10Simeon's sons were Jemuel, Jamin, Ohad, Ja-
kin, Zohar and Shaul (Simeon's son by a Canaan-
ite woman).
11Levi's sons were Gershon, Kohath and Merari.
12Judah's sons were Er, Onan, Shelah, Perez
and Zerah (but Er and Onan had died in the
land of Canaan). Perez's sons were Hezron and
Hamul.
13Issachar's sons were Tola, Puah, Jashub and
Shimron.
14Zebulun's sons were Sered, Elon and Jahleel.
15These are the sons of Leah and Jacob born
in North West Mesopotamia, in addition to his
daughter Dinah. There were 33 persons in this
part of Jacob's family.
16Gad's sons were Zephon, Haggi, Shuni, Ez-
bon, Eri, Arodi and Areli.
17Asher's sons were Imnah, Ishvah, Ishvi and
Beriah, and their sister was Serah. Beriah's sons
were Heber and Malkiel.
18These are Jacob's sons by Zilpah, the slave
girl whom Laban gave to his daughter Leah.
There were sixteen persons in this part of Jacob's
family.
19The sons of Jacob's wife Rachel were Joseph
and Benjamin. 20In Egypt, Joseph became the
father of Manasseh and Ephraim by his wife Ase-
nath, the daughter of Potiphera, priest of On.
21Benjamin's sons were Bela, Beker, Ashbel,
Gera, Naaman, Ehi, Rosh, Muppim, Huppim
and Ard.
22These are the sons of Jacob by his wife Ra-
chel. There were fourteen persons in this part of
Jacob's family.
23Dan's son was Hushim.
24Naphtali's sons were Jahziel, Guni, Jezer and
Shillem.
25These are Jacob's sons by Bilhah, the slave
girl whom Laban gave to his daughter Rachel.
There were seven persons in this part of Jacob's
family.
26So the total number of Jacob's direct des-
cendants who went to Egypt was 66, not count-
ing the wives of Jacob's sons. 27Joseph had two
sons born in Egypt, so the total number in the
family of Jacob in Egypt was 70.

Jacob Arrives in Egypt

28Jacob sent Judah ahead of him to see Joseph
in Goshen. When Jacob and his people came into
the land of Goshen, 29Joseph prepared his chariot
and went to meet his father Israel in Goshen. As
soon as Joseph saw his father, he hugged him,
and cried there for a long time.
30Then Israel said to Joseph, "Now I am ready
to die, because I have seen your face and I know
you are still alive."
31Joseph said to his brothers and his father's
family, "I will go and tell the king you are here.
I will say, 'My brothers and my father's family
have left the land of Canaan and have come here
to me. 32They are shepherds and take care of farm
animals, and they have brought their flocks and
their herds and everything they own with them.'
33When the king calls you, he will ask, 'What
work do you do?' 34This is what you should tell
him: 'We, your servants, have taken care of farm
animals all our lives. Our ancestors did the same
thing.' Then the king will allow you to settle in
the land of Goshen, away from the Egyptians,
because they don't like to be near shepherds."

Jacob Settles in Goshen

47 Joseph went in to the king and said, "My
father and my brothers have arrived from
Canaan with their flocks and herds and every-
thing they own. They are now in the land of
Goshen." 2Joseph chose five of his brothers to
introduce to the king.
3The king said to the brothers, "What work do
you do?"
And they said to him, "We, your servants, are
shepherds, just as our ancestors were." 4They
said to the king, "We have come to live in this
land, because there is no grass in the land of
Canaan for our animals to eat, and the hunger is
terrible there. So please allow us to live in the
land of Goshen."
5Then the king said to Joseph, "Your father and
your brothers have come to you, 6and you may
choose any place in Egypt for them to live. Give
your father and your brothers the best land; let
them live in the land of Goshen. And if any of
them are skilled shepherds, put them in charge of
my sheep and cattle."
7Then Joseph brought in his father Jacob and
introduced him to the king, and Jacob blessed the
king.
8Then the king said to Jacob, "How old are
you?"
9Jacob said to him, "My life has been spent
wandering from place to place. It has been short
and filled with trouble—only 130 years. My an-
cestors lived much longer than I." 10Then Jacob
blessed the king and left.
11Joseph obeyed the king and gave his father
and brothers the best land in Egypt, near the city
of Rameses. 12And Joseph gave his father, his

brothers and everyone who lived with them the
food they needed.

Joseph Buys Land for the King

[13]The hunger became worse, and since there
was no food anywhere in the land, Egypt and
Canaan became very poor. [14]Joseph collected all
the money that was to be found in Egypt and
Canaan. People paid for the grain they were
buying, and he brought that money to the king's
palace. [15]After some time, when the people in
Egypt and Canaan had no money left, they went
to Joseph and said, "Please give us food. Our
money is gone, and if we don't eat, we will die
here in front of you."

[16]Joseph answered, "Since you have no
money, give me your farm animals, and I will
give you food in return." [17]So people brought
their farm animals to Joseph, and he gave them
food in exchange for their horses, sheep, goats,
cattle and donkeys. And he kept them alive by
trading food for their farm animals that year.

[18]The next year the people came to Joseph
and said, "You know we have no money left, and
all our animals belong to you. We have nothing
left except our bodies and our land. [19]Surely
both we and our land will die here in front of
you. Buy us and our land in exchange for food,
and we will be slaves to the king, together with
our land. Give us seed to plant so that we will
live and not die, and the land will not become a
desert."

[20]So Joseph bought all the land in Egypt for the
king. Every Egyptian sold Joseph his field, be-
cause the hunger was very great. So the land
became the king's, [21]and Joseph made the people
slaves from one end of Egypt to the other. [22]The
only land he did not buy was the land the priests
owned. They did not need to sell their land
because the king paid them for their work. So
they had money to buy food.

[23]Joseph said to the people, "Now I have
bought you and your land for the king, so I will
give you seed and you can plant your fields. [24]At
harvest time you must give one-fifth to the king.
You may keep four-fifths for yourselves to use as
seed for the field and as food for yourselves, your
families and your children."

[25]The people said, "You have saved our lives.
If you like, we will become slaves of the king."

[26]So Joseph made a law in Egypt, which
continues today: one-fifth of everything from the
land belongs to the king. The only land the king
did not get was the priests' land.

"Don't Bury Me in Egypt"

[27]The Israelites continued to live in the land of
Goshen in Egypt. There they gained possessions
and had many children and grew in number.

[28]Jacob[n] lived in Egypt seventeen years, so he
lived to be 147 years old. [29]When Israel knew he
soon would die, he called his son Joseph to him
and said to him, "If you love me, put your hand
under my leg.[n] Promise me you will not bury me
in Egypt. [30]When I die, carry me out of Egypt,
and bury me where my ancestors are buried."

Joseph answered, "I will do as you say."

[31]Then Jacob said, "Promise me." And Joseph
promised him that he would do this. Then Israel
worshipped as he leaned on the top of his
walking stick.

Blessings for Manasseh and Ephraim

48 Some time later Joseph learned that his
father was very sick, so he took his two
sons Manasseh and Ephraim and went to his
father. [2]When Joseph arrived, someone told
Jacob,[n] "Your son Joseph has come to see you."
Jacob was weak, so he used all his strength and
sat up on his bed.

[3]Then Jacob said to Joseph, "God Almighty
appeared to me at Luz in the land of Canaan and
blessed me there. [4]He said to me, 'I will give you
many children. I will make you the father of
many peoples, and I will give your descendants[d]
this land for ever.' [5]Your two sons, who were
born here in Egypt before I came, will be counted
as my own sons. Ephraim and Manasseh will be
my sons just as Reuben and Simeon are my sons.
[6]But if you have other children, they will be your
own, and their land will be part of the land given
to Ephraim and Manasseh. [7]When I came from
North West Mesopotamia, Rachel died in the
land of Canaan, as we were travelling towards
Ephrath. This made me very sad, and I buried her
there beside the road to Ephrath." (Today Eph-
rath is Bethlehem.)

[8]Then Israel saw Joseph's sons and said, "Who
are these boys?"

[9]Joseph said to his father, "They are my sons
that God has given me here in Egypt."

Israel said, "Bring your sons to me so I may
bless them."

[10]At this time Israel's eyesight was bad because
he was old. So Joseph brought the boys close to
him, and Israel kissed the boys and put his arms
around them. [11]He said to Joseph, "I thought I
would never see you alive again, and now God
has let me see you and also your children."

Jacob Also called Israel.
put . . . leg This showed that a person would keep a promise

12Then Joseph moved his sons off Israel's lap and
bowed face down to the ground. 13He put
Ephraim on his right side and Manasseh on
his left. (So Ephraim was near Israel's left hand,
and Manasseh was near Israel's right hand.)
Joseph brought the boys close to Israel. 14But
Israel crossed his arms and put his right hand on
the head of Ephraim, who was younger. He put
his left hand on the head of Manasseh, the first-
born[d] son. 15And Israel blessed Joseph and said,

"My ancestors Abraham and Isaac served
our God,
and like a shepherd God has led me all my
life.
16He was the Angel who saved me from all my
troubles.

Now I pray that he will bless these boys.
May my name be known through these boys,
and may the names of my ancestors
Abraham and Isaac be known through
them.
May they have many descendants[d]
on the earth."

17When Joseph saw that his father put his right
hand on Ephraim's head, he didn't like it. So he
took hold of his father's hand, wanting to move
it from Ephraim's head to Manasseh's head. 18Jo-
seph said to his father, "You are doing it wrong,
Father. Manasseh is the firstborn son. Put your
right hand on his head."
19But his father refused and said, "I know, my
son, I know. Manasseh will be great and have
many descendants. But his younger brother will
be greater, and his descendants will be enough to
make a nation."
20So Israel blessed them that day and said,

"When a blessing is given in Israel, they
will say:
'May God make you like Ephraim and
Manasseh.' "

In this way he made Ephraim greater than
Manasseh.
21Then Israel said to Joseph, "Look at me; I am
about to die. But God will be with you and will
take you back to the land of your fathers. 22I have
given you something that I did not give your
brothers—the land of Shechem that I took from
the Amorite people with my sword and
my bow."

Sidelight If you have older brothers and sisters and think they always get the best deal, take some comfort in Genesis 48:13–14. Though Israel blessed both Manasseh, the oldest, and Ephraim, the youngest, he crossed his hands and blessed Ephraim with his right hand. That made Ephraim's blessing more important.

Jacob Blesses His Sons

49 Then Jacob called his sons to him. He
said, "Come here to me, and I will tell
you what will happen to you in the future.

2"Come together and listen, sons of Jacob.
Listen to Israel, your father.

3"Reuben, my first son, you are my strength.
Your birth showed I could be a father.
You have the highest position among my
sons,
and you are the most powerful.
4But you are uncontrolled like water,
so you will no longer lead your brothers.
This is because you got into your father's bed
and shamed me by having sexual relations
with my slave girl.

5"Simeon and Levi are brothers
who used their swords to do violence.
6I will not join their secret talks,
and I will not meet with them to plan evil.
They killed men because they were angry,
and they crippled oxen just for fun.
7May their anger be cursed, because it is too
violent.
May their violence be cursed, because it is
too cruel.
I will divide them up among the tribes[d] of
Jacob
and scatter them through all the tribes of
Israel.

8"Judah, your brothers will praise you.
You will grab your enemies by the neck,
and your brothers will bow down to you.
9Judah is like a young lion.
You have returned from killing, my son.
Like a lion, he stretches out and lies down to
rest,
and no one is brave enough to wake him.
10Kings will come from Judah's family;
someone from Judah will always be on the
throne.
Judah will rule until Shiloh comes,
and the nations will obey him.
11He ties his donkey to a grapevine,
his young donkey to the best branch.
He can afford to use wine to wash his
clothes
and the best wine to wash his robes.
12His eyes are dark like the colour of wine,
and his teeth are as white as the colour of
milk.

13"Zebulun will live near the sea.
His shore will be a safe place for ships,
and his land will reach as far as Sidon.

14"Issachar is like a strong donkey
who lies down while carrying his load.
15When he sees his resting place is good
and how pleasant his land is,
he will put his back to the load
and become a slave.

16"Dan will rule his own people
like the other tribes in Israel.
17Dan will be like a snake by the side of the
road,
a dangerous snake lying near the path.
That snake bites a horse's leg,
and the rider is thrown off backwards.

18"LORD, I wait for your salvation.

19"Robbers will attack Gad,
but he will defeat them and drive them
away.

20"Asher's land will grow much good food;
he will grow food fit for a king.

21"Naphtali is like a female deer that runs free,
that has beautiful fawns.

22"Joseph is like a grapevine that produces
much fruit,
a healthy vine watered by a spring,
whose branches grow over the wall.
23Archers attack him violently
and shoot at him angrily,
24but he aims his bow well.
His arms are made strong.
He gets his power from the Mighty God of
Jacob
and his strength from the Shepherd, the
Rock [d] of Israel.
25Your father's God helps you.
God Almighty blesses you.
He blesses you with rain from above,
with water from springs below,
with many babies born to your wives,
and many young ones born to your
animals.
26The blessings of your father are greater
than the blessings of the oldest mountains,
greater than the good things of the
long-lasting hills.
May these blessings rest on the head of
Joseph,
on the forehead of the one who was
separated from his brothers.

27"Benjamin is like a hungry wolf.
In the morning he eats what he has caught,
and in the evening he divides what he has
taken."

28These are the twelve tribes of Israel, and this
is what their father said to them. He gave each
son the blessing that was right for him. 29Then
Israel gave them a command and said, "I am
about to die. Bury me with my ancestors in the
cave in the field of Ephron the Hittite. 30That cave
is in the field of Machpelah, east of Mamre, in the
land of Canaan. Abraham bought the field and
cave from Ephron the Hittite for a burying place.
31Abraham and Sarah his wife are buried there.
Isaac and Rebekah his wife are buried there, and
I buried my wife Leah there. 32The field and the
cave in it were bought from the Hittite people."
33After Jacob finished talking to his sons, he lay
down. He put his feet back on the bed, took his
last breath and died.

Jacob's Burial

50 When Jacob died, Joseph hugged his
father and cried over him and kissed
him. 2He commanded the doctors who served
him to prepare his father's body, so the doctors
prepared Jacob's body to be buried. 3It took the
doctors 40 days to prepare his body (the usual
time it took). And the Egyptians had a time of
sorrow for Jacob that lasted 70 days.
4When this time of sorrow had ended, Joseph
spoke to the king's officers and said, "If you think
well of me, please tell this to the king: 5'When my
father was near death, I made a promise to him
that I would bury him in a cave in the land of
Canaan, in a burial place that he cut out for
himself. So please let me go and bury my father,
and then I will return.' "
6The king answered, "Keep your promise. Go
and bury your father."
7So Joseph went to bury his father. All the
king's officers, the elders and all the leading men
of Egypt went with Joseph. 8Everyone who lived
with Joseph and his brothers went with him, as
well as everyone who lived with his father. They
left only their children, their flocks and their
herds in the land of Goshen. 9They went with
Joseph in chariots and on horses. It was a very
large group.
10When they came to the threshing [d] floor of
Atad, near the Jordan River, they cried loudly and
bitterly for his father. Joseph's time of sorrow
continued for seven days. 11The people that lived
in Canaan saw the sadness at the threshing floor
of Atad and said, "Those Egyptians are showing
great sorrow!" So now that place is named
Sorrow of the Egyptians.
12So Jacob's sons did as their father com-
manded. 13They carried his body to the land
of Canaan and buried it in the cave in the field of
Machpelah near Mamre. Abraham had bought
this cave and field from Ephron the Hittite to use

as a burial place. 14After Joseph buried his father,
he returned to Egypt, along with his brothers
and everyone who had gone with him to bury
his father.

The Brothers Fear Joseph

15After Jacob died, Joseph's brothers said,
"What if Joseph is still angry with us? We did
many wrong things to him. What if he plans
to pay us back?" 16So they sent a message
to Joseph that said, "Your father gave this
command before he died. 17He said to us, 'You
have done wrong and have sinned and done
evil to Joseph. Tell Joseph to forgive you, his
brothers.' So now, Joseph, we beg you to forgive
our wrong. We are the servants of the God
of your father." When Joseph received the
message, he cried.
18And his brothers went to him and bowed
low before him and said, "We are your slaves."
19Then Joseph said to them, "Don't be afraid.
Can I do what only God can do? 20You meant
to hurt me, but God turned your evil into
good to save the lives of many people, which
is being done. 21So don't be afraid. I will take
care of you and your children." So Joseph
comforted his brothers and spoke kind words
to them.
22Joseph continued to live in Egypt with all his
father's family. He died when he was 110 years
old. 23During Joseph's lifetime Ephraim had
children and grandchildren, and Joseph's son
Manasseh had a son named Makir. Joseph
accepted Makir's children as his own.

The Death of Joseph

24Joseph said to his brothers, "I am about to
die, but God will take care of you. He will lead
you out of this land to the land he promised to
Abraham, Isaac and Jacob." 25Then Joseph had
the sons of Israel make a promise. He said,
"Promise me that you will carry my bones with
you out of Egypt."
26Joseph died when he was 110 years old.
Doctors prepared his body for burial, and then
they put him in a coffin in Egypt.

Exodus

Why Read This Book:

- Discover how God works in miraculous ways to set people free (Exodus 1—18).
- Learn guidelines for living as they are described in the Ten Commandments (Exodus 20).
- Compare ancient worship practices with worship today (Exodus 25—31, 35—40).

When?

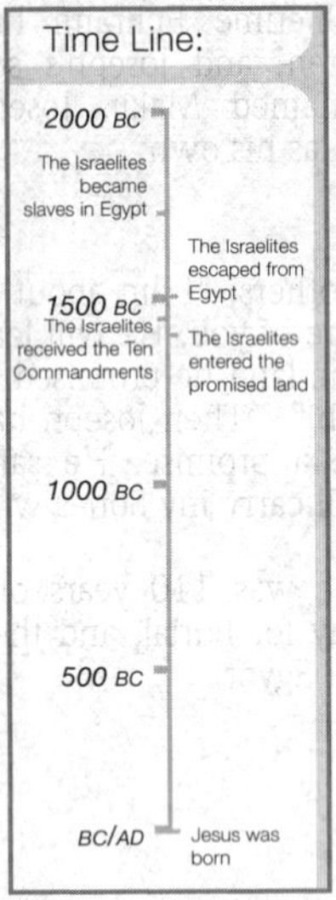

Behind the Scenes:

"Free at last, free at last; thank God Almighty, we are free at last."

This song celebrated freedom from slavery. And it became an important song in the American civil rights struggle in the 1950s and 1960s. But the song could also have been sung by the Israelites as they escaped from Egypt with Moses as their leader.

The Israelites had settled in Egypt about 400 years earlier when Joseph arranged for them to be Egypt's guests (see Genesis 47:1–12, p.53). But, in time, Egypt's rulers died, and the new rulers turned the Israelites into slaves.

The Israelites longed for freedom from the horrific slavery.

Exodus tells how God took the Hebrew people – descendants of Abraham – and shaped them into the free nation of Israel.

The book begins with the story of Moses being saved from death. Rescued by the king's daughter, Moses grew up in the king's palace. When Moses became an adult, God called him to lead the Israelites to freedom.

Though filled with uncertainty, Moses answered God's call and argued with the Egyptian king. ▷

Where?

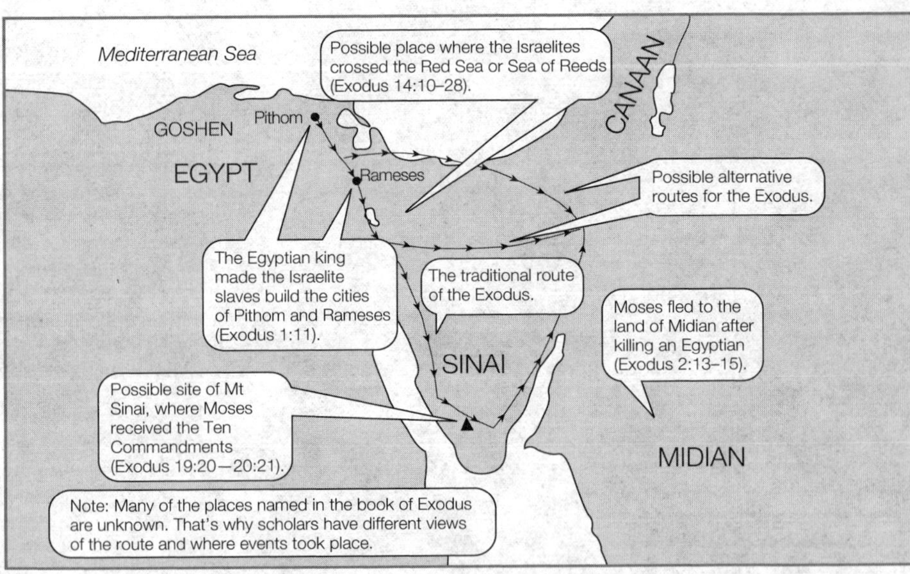

Behind the Scenes (cont.): Again and again the king resisted, but God's miraculous power eventually convinced him to let Israel go. In excited celebration, the Israelites left for the promised land, Canaan, only to be chased by the king's army. God's deliverance of Israel at the Red Sea is known as the Exodus.

Before reaching the promised land, however, the Israelites spent 40 years in the wilderness. There they learned more about what God wanted them to do and be, as people and as a nation.

In Exodus 3:14, God reveals his name to Moses: I AM WHO I AM or YAHWEH. It means "The One Who Is Always Present". And, indeed, God was always with Moses and the Israelites in the desert. And he is always with us today.

Jacob's Family Grows Strong

1 When Jacob[n] went to Egypt, he took his
sons, and each son took his own family with
him. These are the names of the sons of Israel:
2Reuben, Simeon, Levi, Judah, 3Issachar, Zebu-
lun, Benjamin, 4Dan, Naphtali, Gad and Asher.
5There was a total of 70 people who were des-
cendants[d] of Jacob. Jacob's son Joseph was al-
ready in Egypt.
6Some time later, Joseph and his brothers died,
along with all the people who had lived at that
same time. 7But the people of Israel had many
children, and their number grew greatly. They
became very strong, and the country of Egypt
was filled with them.

Trouble for the People of Israel

8Then a new king began to rule Egypt, who did
not know who Joseph was. 9This king said to his
people, "Look! The people of Israel are too many
and too strong for us to handle! 10If we don't
make plans against them, the number of their
people will grow even more. Then if there is a
war, they might join our enemies and fight us and
escape from the country!"
11So the Egyptians made life hard for the Israel-
ites. They put slave masters over them, who
forced the Israelites to build the cities Pithom and
Rameses as supply centres for the king. 12But the
harder the Egyptians forced the Israelites to work,
the more the Israelites grew in number and
spread out. So the Egyptians became very afraid
of them 13and demanded even more of them.
14They made their lives bitter. They forced the
Israelites to work hard to make bricks and mortar
and to do all kinds of work in the fields. The
Egyptians were not merciful to them in all their
painful work.

Sidelight

Making bricks in Egypt was a slow process for the Israelites (Exodus 1:14). Egyptian records show that a person could make about 65 bricks a day. A modern brickmaker turns out about 3,500 bricks daily.

15Two Hebrew nurses, named Shiphrah and
Puah, helped the Israelite women give birth to
their babies. The king of Egypt said to the nurses,
16"When you are helping the Hebrew women
give birth to their babies, watch! If the baby is a
girl, let her live, but if it is a boy, kill him!" 17But
the nurses feared God, so they did not do as the
king told them; they let all the boy babies live.
18Then the king of Egypt sent for the nurses and
said, "Why did you do this? Why did you let the
boys live?"
19The nurses said to him, "The Hebrew
women are much stronger than the Egyptian
women. They give birth to their babies before we
can get there." 20God was good to the nurses.
And the Hebrew people continued to grow in
number, so they became even stronger. 21Be-
cause the nurses feared God, he gave them famil-
ies of their own.
22So the king commanded all his people, "Ev-
ery time a boy is born to the Hebrews, you must
throw him into the Nile River, but let all the girl
babies live."

Baby Moses

2 Now a man from the family of Levi married
a woman who was also from the family of
Levi. 2She became pregnant and gave birth to a
son. When she saw how wonderful the baby was,

Jacob Also called Israel.

she hid him for three months. 3But after three
months she was not able to hide the baby any
longer, so she got a basket and covered it with tar
so that it would float. She put the baby in the
basket. Then she put the basket among the tall
stalks of grass at the edge of the Nile River. 4The
baby's sister stood a short distance away to see
what would happen to him.
5Then the daughter of the king of Egypt came
to the river to take a bath, and her servant girls
were walking beside the river. When she saw the
basket in the tall grass, she sent her slave girl to
get it. 6The king's daughter opened the basket
and saw the baby boy. He was crying, so she felt
sorry for him and said, "This is one of the Hebrew
babies."

Sidelight

If you think waterbeds are something new, read Exodus 2:3, where Moses is given the first waterbed in the Bible. The tall grass he was placed in was probably papyrus, which the Egyptians used for making paper.

7Then the baby's sister asked the king's daugh-
ter, "Would you like me to go and find a Hebrew

SUFFERING

Running For His Life

Sydney Maree felt as though he didn't fit anywhere. A black in South Africa, he lived under harsh apartheid laws that restricted blacks in virtually all areas of life. He and his family could only live in black townships, and many things were denied them.

Sydney only felt at peace when he ran. There was something about running that gave him a sense of power in a world where he felt powerless because of unjust government. He'd run to school. He'd run more than a mile to the shop. He'd run everywhere he went.

When Sydney was sixteen, the high school athletics coach noticed his speed, and got him involved in running. Sydney trained tirelessly. "He was running for revenge," his trainer recalls, "running for liberation."

In 1976, his liberation began. He entered a major race in South Africa, with the help of a white businessman. The only high-schooler and the only black in the race, he won – and set a record for the fastest time ever by a high-schooler.

Sydney's life changed that day. He became a national hero and then went to school in the USA. He set records for his university and joined the US team in the 1984 Olympics.

The white businessman who helped Sydney to start racing in South Africa came to his college graduation. "Sydney started to tell me how he could never thank me enough," the supporter said. "I stopped him and said, 'No, it is I who must thank you.' Before I met him I'd only known blacks as people who did gardening for me. Now I know . . . that they too have goals and aspirations and can be like sons in my home."

Like Sydney, the Israelites faced extreme persecution as slaves in Egypt. Read about their situation in **Exodus 1:6—2:10**.

- How was Sydney's world like the world of the enslaved Israelites?
- How would you react if you faced the suffering the Israelites faced? How do you react to people suffering around you?

Consider . . .

- writing a story that describes a time you experienced suffering. Thank God for getting you through that tough time.
- talking to someone who has been through tremendous suffering (such as a refugee or a war veteran). What helped him or her survive?

For more, see . . .

- Psalm 57:1–11 (p.533)
- 1 John 3:16–18 (p.1374)
- Philippians 4:14–19 (p.1286)

woman to nurse the baby for you?"

8 The king's daughter said, "Go!" So the girl went and got the baby's own mother.

9 The king's daughter said to the woman, "Take this baby and nurse him for me, and I will pay you." So the woman took her baby and nursed him. 10 When the child grew older, the woman took him to the king's daughter, and she adopted the baby as her own son. The king's daughter named him Moses,[n] because she had pulled him out of the water.

Moses Tries to Help

11 Moses grew and became a man. One day he visited his people and saw that they were forced to work very hard. He saw an Egyptian beating a Hebrew man, one of Moses' own people. 12 Moses looked all around and saw that no one was watching, so he killed the Egyptian and hid his body in the sand.

13 The next day Moses returned and saw two Hebrew men fighting each other. He said to the one that was in the wrong, "Why are you hitting one of your own people?"

14 The man answered, "Who made you our ruler and judge? Are you going to kill me as you killed the Egyptian?"

Moses was afraid and thought, "Now everyone knows what I did."

15 When the king heard what Moses had done, he tried to kill him. But Moses ran away from the king and went to live in the land of Midian. There he sat down near a well.

Moses in Midian

16 There was a priest in Midian who had seven daughters. His daughters went to that well to get water to fill the water troughs for their father's flock. 17 Some shepherds came and chased the girls away, but Moses defended the girls and watered their flock.

18 When they went back to their father Reuel,[n] he asked them, "Why have you come home early today?"

19 The girls answered, "The shepherds chased us away, but an Egyptian defended us. He got water for us and watered our flock."

20 He asked his daughters, "Where is this man? Why did you leave him? Invite him to eat with us."

21 Moses agreed to stay with Jethro, and he gave his daughter Zipporah to Moses to be his wife. 22 Zipporah gave birth to a son. Moses named him Gershom,[n] because Moses was a stranger in a land that was not his own.

23 After a long time, the king of Egypt died. The people of Israel groaned, because they were forced to work very hard. When they cried for help, God heard them. 24 God heard their cries, and he remembered the agreement he had made with Abraham, Isaac and Jacob. 25 He saw the troubles of the people of Israel, and he was concerned about them.

The Burning Bush

3 One day Moses was taking care of Jethro's flock. (Jethro was the priest of Midian and also Moses' father-in-law.) When Moses led the flock to the west side of the desert, he came to Sinai, the mountain of God. 2 There the angel of the LORD appeared to him in flames of fire coming out of a bush. Moses saw that the bush was on fire, but it was not burning up. 3 So he said, "I will go closer to this strange thing. How can a bush continue burning without burning up?"

4 When the LORD saw Moses was coming to look at the bush, God called to him from the bush, "Moses, Moses!"

And Moses said, "Here I am."

5 Then God said, "Do not come any closer. Take off your sandals, because you are standing on holy ground. 6 I am the God of your ancestors—the God of Abraham, the God of Isaac and the God of Jacob." Moses covered his face because he was afraid to look at God.

7 The LORD said, "I have seen the troubles my people have suffered in Egypt, and I have heard their cries when the Egyptian slave masters hurt them. I am concerned about their pain, 8 and I have come down to save them from the Egyptians. I will bring them out of that land and lead them to a good land with lots of room—a fertile land. It is the land of the Canaanites, Hittites, Amorites, Perizzites, Hivites and Jebusites. 9 I have heard the cries of the people of Israel, and I have seen the way the Egyptians have made life hard for them. 10 So now I am sending you to the king of Egypt. Go! Bring my people, the Israelites, out of Egypt!"

11 But Moses said to God, "I am not a great man! How can I go to the king and lead the Israelites out of Egypt?"

12 God said, "I will be with you. This will be the proof that I am sending you: after you lead the people out of Egypt, all of you will worship me on this mountain."

13 Moses said to God, "When I go to the Israelites, I will say to them, 'The God of your fathers sent me to you.' What if the people say, 'What is his name?' What should I tell them?"

Moses The name Moses sounds like the Hebrew word for "to pull out".

Reuel He was also called Jethro.

Gershom This name sounds like the Hebrew word for "a stranger there".

14Then God said to Moses, "I AM WHO I AM.[n]
When you go to the people of Israel, tell them, 'I
AM sent me to you.'"

Sidelight

In Exodus 3:14, God first chooses to say his name – I AM WHO I AM – YAHWEH, in the original Hebrew. Yahweh is the most used name for God in the Old Testament, appearing about 6,800 times in the original language. Most modern Bibles translate it as LORD.

15God also said to Moses, "This is what you
should tell the people: 'The LORD is the God of
your ancestors—the God of Abraham, the God of
Isaac and the God of Jacob. He sent me to you.'
This will always be my name, by which people
from now on will know me.
16"Go and gather the elders and tell them this:
'The LORD, the God of your ancestors Abraham,
Isaac and Jacob, has appeared to me. He said, I
care about you, and I have seen what has hap-
pened to you in Egypt. 17I promised I would take
you out of your troubles in Egypt. I will lead you
to the land of the Canaanites, Hittites, Amorites,
Perizzites, Hivites and Jebusites—a fertile land.'
18"The elders will listen to you. And then you
and the elders of Israel will go to the king of
Egypt and tell him, 'The LORD, the God of the
Hebrews, appeared to us. Let us travel three days
into the desert to offer sacrifices to the LORD
our God.'

I . . . I AM The Hebrew words are like the name "Yahweh". This Hebrew name for God, usually called "LORD", shows that God always lives and is always with his people.

LEADERSHIP

Phone-a-Friend

The late 1980s saw a serious increase in cases of child abuse. Children of all ages were being abused emotionally and physically. The abuse took many forms, from school bullying to incest, and there seemed to be no one for desperate children to turn to for help.

Esther Rantzen, the British television presenter, enthusiastically volunteered to spearhead the launch of ChildLine – an organisation that exists to help children in desperate circumstances. All the victims have to do is to phone a special free telephone number for a friend to talk to – usually a professional counsellor who can arrange immediate help if necessary.

The ChildLine switchboard was jammed with calls as soon as it was officially opened. Children all over the country rang to get help and advice. Since then, ChildLine has firmly established itself as a helping hand – available to any child in need.

Because Esther saw the very real problem of child abuse in the United Kingdom, she took steps towards setting up an organisation which could help those in need. In a similar way, Moses heard about the Israelites' persecution in Egypt, and followed God's call to lead them to freedom.

See **Exodus 3**.

- What are the differences between Esther's action and Moses' call to leadership?
- Have you, like Moses, felt called by God to take a leading role in fighting a particular problem? How have you responded to that call?

Consider . . .

- reading through a newspaper and identifying leaders and organisations who are fighting against suffering and injustice in the world. Pray for those leaders and organisations.
- making a list of the problems faced by the people around you – problems in your school, church, neighbourhood and country. Now think how you could help to solve one of those problems by taking a position of leadership.

For more, see . . .

- Psalm 22:1–12 (p.512)
- Luke 4:16–21 (p.1045)
- Micah 2:6–13 (p.892)

19“But I know that the king of Egypt will not
let you go. Only a great power will force him to
let you go, 20so I will use my great power against
Egypt. I will strike Egypt with all the miracles[d]
that will happen in that land. After I do that, he
will let you go. 21I will cause the Egyptians to
think well of the Israelites. So when you leave,
they will give gifts to your people. 22Each
woman should ask her Egyptian neighbour and
any Egyptian woman living in her house for
gifts—silver, gold and clothing. You should put
those gifts on your children when you leave
Egypt. In this way you will take with you the
riches of the Egyptians.”

Proof for Moses

4 Then Moses answered, “What if the people
of Israel do not believe me or listen to me?
What if they say, ‘The LORD did not appear to
you?’ ”

2The LORD said to him, “What is that in your
hand?”

Moses answered, “It's my walking stick.”

3The LORD said, “Throw it on the ground.”

So Moses threw it on the ground, and it be-
came a snake. Moses ran from the snake, 4but the
LORD said to him, “Reach out and grab the snake
by its tail.” When Moses reached out and took
hold of the snake, it again became a stick in his
hand. 5The LORD said, “This is so that the Israel-
ites will believe that the LORD appeared to you. I
am the God of their ancestors, the God of Abra-
ham, the God of Isaac and the God of Jacob.”

6Then the LORD said to Moses, “Put your hand
inside your coat.” So Moses put his hand inside
his coat. When he took it out, it was white with
a skin disease.

7Then he said, “Now put your hand inside
your coat again.” So Moses put his hand inside
his coat again. When he took it out, his hand
was healthy again, like the rest of his skin.

8Then the LORD said, “If the people do not be-
lieve you or pay attention to the first miracle,[d]
they may believe you when you show them this
second miracle. 9After these two miracles, if they
still do not believe or listen to you, take some
water from the Nile River and pour it on the dry
ground. The water will become blood when it
touches the ground.”

10But Moses said to the LORD, “Please, Lord, I
have never been a skilled speaker. Even now,
after talking to you, I cannot speak well. I speak
slowly and can't find the best words.”

11Then the LORD said to him, “Who made a
person's mouth? And who makes someone deaf
or not able to speak? Or who gives a person sight
or blindness? It is I, the LORD. 12Now go! I will
help you speak, and I will teach you what to say.”

13But Moses said, “Please, Lord, send some-
one else.”

14The LORD became angry with Moses and
said, “Your brother Aaron, from the family of
Levi, is a skilled speaker. He is already coming to
meet you, and he will be happy when he sees
you. 15You will speak to Aaron and tell him what
to say. I will help both of you to speak and will
teach you what to do. 16Aaron will speak to the
people for you. You will tell him what God says,
and he will speak for you. 17Take your walking
stick with you, and use it to do the miracles.”

Moses Returns to Egypt

18Moses went back to Jethro, his father-in-law,
and said to him, “Let me go back to my people in
Egypt. I want to see if they are still alive.”

Jethro said to Moses, “Go! I wish you well.”

19While Moses was still in Midian, the LORD
said to him, “Go back to Egypt, because the
men who wanted to kill you are dead now.”

20So Moses took his wife and his sons, put
them on a donkey, and started back to Egypt. He
took with him the walking stick of God.

21The LORD said to Moses, “When you get
back to Egypt, do all the miracles[d] I have given
you the power to do. Show them to the king of
Egypt. But I will make the king very stubborn,
and he will not let the people go. 22Then say to
the king, ‘This is what the LORD says: Israel is
my firstborn[d] son. 23I told you to let my son go
so he may worship me. But you refused to let
Israel go, so I will kill your firstborn son.’ ”

24As Moses was on his way to Egypt, he
stopped at a resting place for the night. The
LORD met him there and tried to kill him. 25But
Zipporah took a flint knife and circumcised[d] her
son. Taking the skin, she touched Moses' feet
with it and said to him, “You are a bridegroom
of blood to me.” 26She said, “You are a bride-
groom of blood,” because she had to circumcise
her son. So the LORD let Moses alone.

27Meanwhile the LORD said to Aaron, “Go
out into the desert to meet Moses.” When
Aaron went, he met Moses at Sinai, the moun-
tain of God, and kissed him. 28Moses told
Aaron everything the LORD had said to him
when he sent him to Egypt. He also told him
about the miracles which the LORD had com-
manded him to do.

29Moses and Aaron gathered all the elders of
the Israelites, 30and Aaron told them everything
that the LORD had told Moses. Then Moses did
the miracles for all the people to see, 31and the
Israelites believed. When they heard that the
LORD was concerned about them and had seen
their troubles, they bowed down and wor-
shipped him.

Moses and Aaron Before the King

5 After Moses and Aaron talked to the people, they went to the king of Egypt and said, "This is what the LORD, the God of Israel, says: 'Let my people go so they may hold a feast for me in the desert.' "

[2]But the king of Egypt said, "Who is the LORD? Why should I obey him and let Israel go? I do not know the LORD, and I will not let Israel go."

[3]Then Aaron and Moses said, "The God of the Hebrews has met with us. Now let us travel three days into the desert to offer sacrifices to the LORD our God. If we don't do this, he may kill us with a disease or in war."

[4]But the king said to them, "Moses and Aaron, why are you taking the people away from their work? Go back to your work! [5]There are very many Hebrews, and now you want them to stop working!"

[6]That same day the king gave a command to the slave masters and foremen. [7]He said, "Don't give the people straw to make bricks as you used to do. Let them gather their own straw. [8]But they must still make the same number of bricks as they did before. Do not accept fewer. They have become lazy, and that is why they are asking me, 'Let us go to offer sacrifices to our God.' [9]Make these people work harder and keep them busy; then they will not have time to listen to the lies of Moses."

[10]So the slave masters and foremen went to the Israelites and said, "This is what the king says: 'I will no longer give you straw. [11]Go and get your own straw wherever you can find it. But you must make as many bricks as you made before.' " [12]So the people went everywhere in Egypt looking for dry stalks to use for straw. [13]The slave masters kept forcing the people to work harder. They said, "You must make just as many bricks as you did when you were given straw." [14]The king's slave masters had made the Israelite foremen responsible for the work the people did. The Egyptian slave masters beat these men and asked them, "Why aren't you making as many bricks as you made in the past?"

[15]Then the Israelite foremen went to the king and complained, "Why are you treating us, your servants, this way? [16]You give us no straw, but we are commanded to make bricks. Our slave masters beat us, but it is your own people's fault."

[17]The king answered, "You are lazy! You don't want to work! That is why you ask to leave here and make sacrifices to the LORD. [18]Now, go back to work! We will not give you any straw, but you must make just as many bricks as you did before."

[19]The Israelite foremen knew they were in trouble, because the king had told them, "You must make just as many bricks each day as you did before." [20]As they were leaving the meeting with the king, they met Moses and Aaron, who were waiting for them. [21]So they said to Moses and Aaron, "May the LORD punish you. You caused the king and his officers to hate us. You have given them an excuse to kill us."

Moses Complains to God

[22]Then Moses returned to the LORD and said, "Lord, why have you brought this trouble on your people? Is this why you sent me here? [23]I went to the king and said what you told me to say, but ever since that time he has made the people suffer. And you have done nothing to save them."

6 Then the LORD said to Moses, "Now you will see what I will do to the king of Egypt. I will use my great power against him, and he will let my people go. Because of my power, he will force them out of his country."

[2]Then God said to Moses, "I am the LORD. [3]I appeared to Abraham, Isaac and Jacob by the name God Almighty, but they did not know me by my name, the LORD. [4]I also made my agreement with them to give them the land of Canaan. They lived in that land, but it was not their own. [5]Now I have heard the cries of the Israelites, whom the Egyptians are treating as slaves, and I remember my agreement. [6]So tell the people of Israel that I say to them, 'I am the LORD. I will save you from the hard work the Egyptians force you to do. I will make you free, so you will not be slaves to the Egyptians. I will free you by my great power, and I will punish the Egyptians terribly. [7]I will make you my own people, and I will be your God. You will know that I am the LORD your God, the One who saves you from the hard work the Egyptians force you to do. [8]I will lead you to the land that I promised to Abraham, Isaac and Jacob, and I will give you that land to own. I am the LORD.' "

[9]So Moses told this to the Israelites, but they would not listen to him. They were discouraged, and their slavery was hard.

[10]Then the LORD said to Moses, [11]"Go and tell the king of Egypt that he must let the Israelites leave his land."

[12]But Moses answered, "The Israelites will not listen to me, so surely the king will not listen to me either. I am not a good speaker."

[13]But the LORD spoke to Moses and Aaron and gave them orders about the Israelites and the king of Egypt. He commanded them to lead the Israelites out of Egypt.

Families of Israel

[14]These are the leaders of the families of Israel:

Israel's first son, Reuben, had four sons: Ha-
noch, Pallu, Hezron and Carmi. These are the
family groups of Reuben.
15 Simeon's sons were Jemuel, Jamin, Ohad, Ja-
kin, Zohar and Shaul, the son of a Canaanite
woman. These are the family groups of Simeon.
16 Levi lived 137 years. These are the names of
his sons according to their family history: Ger-
shon, Kohath and Merari.
17 Gershon had two sons, Libni and Shimei,
with their families.
18 Kohath lived for 133 years. The sons of Ko-
hath were Amram, Izhar, Hebron and Uzziel.
19 The sons of Merari were Mahli and Mushi.
These are the family groups of Levi, according
to their family history.
20 Amram married his father's sister Jochebed,
who gave birth to Aaron and Moses. Amram lived
for 137 years.
21 Izhar's sons were Korah, Nepheg and Zicri.
22 Uzziel's sons were Mishael, Elzaphan and
Sithri.
23 Aaron married Elisheba, the daughter of Am-
minadab and the sister of Nahshon. Elisheba gave
birth to Nadab, Abihu, Eleazar and Ithamar.
24 The sons of Korah were Assir, Elkanah and
Abiasaph. These are the family groups of the Ko-
rahites.
25 Eleazar, son of Aaron, married a daughter of
Putiel and she gave birth to Phinehas.
These are the leaders of the family groups of
the Levites.
26 This was the Aaron and Moses to whom the
LORD said, "Lead the people of Israel out of Egypt
by their divisions." 27 Aaron and Moses are the
ones who talked to the king of Egypt and told him
to let the Israelites leave Egypt.

God Repeats His Call to Moses

28 The LORD spoke to Moses in the land of Egypt
29 and said, "I am the LORD. Tell the king of Egypt
everything I tell you."
30 But Moses answered, "I am not a good
speaker. The king will not listen to me."

7 The LORD said to Moses, "I have made you
like God to the king of Egypt, and your
brother Aaron will be like a prophet[d] for you.
2 Tell Aaron your brother everything that I com-
mand you, and let him tell the king of Egypt
to let the Israelites leave his country. 3 But I
will make the king stubborn. I will do many
miracles[d] in Egypt, 4 but he will still refuse to
listen. So then I will punish Egypt terribly, and I
will lead my divisions, my people the Israelites,
out of that land. 5 I will punish Egypt with my
power, and I will bring the Israelites out of that
land. Then they will know I am the LORD."
6 Moses and Aaron did just as the LORD had
commanded them. 7 Moses was 80 years old and
Aaron was 83 when they spoke to the king.

Aaron's Walking Stick Becomes a Snake

8 The LORD said to Moses and Aaron, 9 "Moses,
when the king asks you to do a miracle,[d] tell
Aaron to throw his walking stick down in front of
the king, and it will become a snake."
10 So Moses and Aaron went to the king as the
LORD had commanded. Aaron threw his walking
stick down in front of the king and his officers,
and it became a snake.
11 So the king called in his wise men and his
magicians, and with their tricks the Egyptian ma-
gicians were able to do the same thing. 12 They
threw their walking sticks on the ground, and
their sticks became snakes. But Aaron's stick
swallowed theirs. 13 Still the king was stubborn
and refused to listen to Moses and Aaron, just as
the LORD had said.

The Water Becomes Blood

14 Then the LORD said to Moses, "The king is
being stubborn and refuses to let the people go.
15 In the morning the king will go out to the Nile
River. Go and meet him by the edge of the river,
and take with you the walking stick that became
a snake. 16 Tell him: the LORD, the God of the
Hebrews, sent me to you. He said, 'Let my people
go and worship me in the desert.' Until now you
have not listened. 17 This is what the LORD says:
'This is how you will know that I am the LORD. I
will strike the water of the Nile River with this
stick in my hand, and the water will change into
blood. 18 Then the fish in the Nile will die, and the
river will begin to stink. The Egyptians will not be
able to drink the water from the Nile.' "
19 The LORD said to Moses, "Tell Aaron: 'Take the
walking stick in your hand and stretch your hand
over the rivers, canals, ponds and pools in Egypt.'
The water will become blood everywhere in Egypt,
both in wooden buckets and in stone jars."
20 So Moses and Aaron did just as the LORD had
commanded. In front of the king and his officers,
Aaron raised his walking stick and struck the
water in the Nile River. So all the water in the
Nile changed into blood. 21 The fish in the Nile
died, and the river began to stink, so the Egyp-
tians could not drink water from it. Blood was
everywhere in the land of Egypt.
22 Using their tricks, the magicians of Egypt did
the same thing. So the king was stubborn and
refused to listen to Moses and Aaron, just as the
LORD had said. 23 The king turned and went into
his palace and ignored what Moses and Aaron
had done. 24 The Egyptians could not drink the

water from the Nile, so all of them dug along the bank of the river, looking for water to drink.

The Frogs

[25]Seven days passed after the LORD changed the Nile River into blood.

8 Then the LORD told Moses, "Go to the king of Egypt and tell him, 'This is what the LORD says: let my people go to worship me. [2]If you refuse, I will punish Egypt with frogs. [3]The Nile River will be filled with frogs. They will come up into your palace, into your bedroom, on your bed, into the houses of your officers and onto your people. They will come into your ovens and into your baking pans. [4]The frogs will jump all over you, your people and your officers.' "

[5]Then the LORD said to Moses, "Tell Aaron to hold his walking stick in his hand over the rivers, canals and ponds. Make frogs come up out of the water onto the land of Egypt."

[6]So Aaron held his hand over all the waters of Egypt, and the frogs came up out of the water and covered the land of Egypt. [7]The magicians used their tricks to do the same thing, so even more frogs came up onto the land of Egypt.

[8]The king called for Moses and Aaron and said, "Pray to the LORD to take the frogs away from me and my people. I will let your people go to offer sacrifices to the LORD."

[9]Moses said to the king, "Please set the time when I should pray for you, your people and your officers. Then the frogs will leave you and your houses and will remain only in the Nile."

[10]The king answered, "Tomorrow."

Moses said, "What you want will happen. By this you will know that there is no one like the LORD our God. [11]The frogs will leave you, your houses, your officers and your people. They will remain only in the Nile."

[12]After Moses and Aaron left the king, Moses asked the LORD about the frogs he had sent to the king. [13]And the LORD did as Moses asked. The frogs died in the houses, in the yards and in the fields. [14]The Egyptians put them in piles, and the whole country began to stink. [15]But when the king saw that they were free of the frogs, he became stubborn again. He did not listen to Moses and Aaron, just as the LORD had said.

The Gnats

[16]Then the LORD said to Moses, "Tell Aaron to raise his walking stick and strike the dust on the ground. Then everywhere in Egypt the dust will change into gnats." [17]They did this, and when Aaron raised the walking stick that was in his hand and struck the dust on the ground, everywhere in Egypt the dust changed into gnats. The gnats got on the people and animals. [18]Using their tricks, the magicians tried to do the same thing, but they could not make the dust change into gnats. The gnats remained on the people and animals. [19]So the magicians told the king that the power of God had done this. But the king was stubborn and refused to listen to them, just as the LORD had said.

The Flies

[20]The LORD told Moses, "Get up early in the morning, and meet the king of Egypt as he goes out to the river. Tell him, 'This is what the LORD says: let my people go so they can worship me. [21]If you don't let them go, I will send swarms of flies into your houses. The flies will be on you, your officers and your people. The houses of Egypt will be full of flies, and they will be all over the ground, too. [22]But I will not treat the Israelites the same as the Egyptian people. There will not be any flies in the land of Goshen, where my people live. By this you will know that I, the LORD, am in this land. [23]I will treat my people differently from your people. This miracle[d] will happen tomorrow.' "

[24]So the LORD did as he had said, and great swarms of flies came into the king's palace and his officers' houses. All over Egypt flies were ruining the land. [25]The king called for Moses and Aaron and told them, "Offer sacrifices to your God here in this country."

[26]But Moses said, "It wouldn't be right to do that, because the Egyptians hate the sacrifices we offer to the LORD our God. If they see us offering sacrifices they hate, they will throw stones at us and kill us. [27]Let us make a three-day journey into the desert. We must offer sacrifices to the LORD our God there, as the LORD told us to do."

[28]The king said, "I will let you go so that you may offer sacrifices to the LORD your God in the desert, but you must not go very far away. Now go and pray for me."

[29]Moses said, "I will leave and pray to the LORD, and he will take the flies away from you, your officers and your people tomorrow. But do not try to trick us again. Do not stop the people from going to offer sacrifices to the LORD."

[30]So Moses left the king and prayed to the LORD, [31]and the LORD did as he asked. He removed the flies from the king, his officers and his people so that not one fly was left. [32]But the king became stubborn again and did not let the people go.

The Disease on the Farm Animals

9 Then the LORD told Moses, "Go to the king of Egypt and tell him, 'This is what the LORD, the God of the Hebrews, says: let my people go to worship me. [2]If you refuse to let them go and continue to hold them, [3]the LORD will punish you.

He will send a terrible disease on your farm
animals that are in the fields. He will cause your
horses, donkeys, camels, cattle, goats and sheep
to become sick. 4But the LORD will treat Israel's
animals differently from the animals of Egypt.
None of the animals that belong to the Israelites
will die. 5The LORD has set tomorrow as the time
he will do this in the land.' " 6The next day the
LORD did as he promised. All the farm animals in
Egypt died, but none of the animals belonging to
the Israelites died. 7The king sent people to see
what had happened to the animals of Israel, and
they found that not one of them had died. But the
king was still stubborn and did not let the
people go.

The Boils

8The LORD said to Moses and Aaron, "Fill your
hands with ashes from a furnace. Moses, throw
the ashes into the air in front of the king of Egypt.
9The ashes will spread like dust through all the
land of Egypt. They will cause boils to break out
and become sores on the skin of people and
animals everywhere in the land."

10So Moses and Aaron took ashes from a
furnace and went and stood before the king.
Moses threw ashes into the air, which caused
boils to break out and become sores on people
and animals. 11The magicians could not stand
before Moses, because all the Egyptians had
boils, even the magicians. 12But the LORD made
the king stubborn, so he refused to listen to
Moses and Aaron, just as the LORD had said.

The Hail

13Then the LORD said to Moses, "Get up early
in the morning and go to the king of Egypt. Tell
him, 'This is what the LORD, the God of the Heb-
rews, says: let my people go to worship me. 14If
you don't, this time I will punish you, your offi-
cers and your people, with all my power. Then
you will know there is no one in the whole land
like me. 15By now I could have used my power
and caused a terrible disease that would have
destroyed you and your people from the earth.
16But I have let you live for this reason: to show
you my power so that my name will be talked
about in all the earth. 17You are still against my
people and do not want to let them go. 18So at
this time tomorrow, I will send a terrible hail-
storm, the worst in Egypt since it became a na-
tion. 19Now send for your animals and whatever
you have in the fields, and bring them into a safe
place. The hail will fall on every person or animal
that is still in the fields. If they have not been
brought in, they will die.' " 20Some of the king's
officers respected the word of the LORD and
hurried to bring their slaves and animals inside.
21But others ignored the LORD's message and left
their slaves and animals in the fields.

22The LORD told Moses, "Raise your hand to-
wards the sky. Then the hail will start falling in all
the land of Egypt. It will fall on people, animals
and on everything that grows in the fields of
Egypt." 23When Moses raised his walking stick
towards the sky, the LORD sent thunder and hail,
and lightning flashed down to the earth. So he
caused hail to fall upon the land of Egypt. 24There
was hail, and lightning flashed as it hailed—the
worst hailstorm in Egypt since it had become a
nation. 25The hail destroyed all the people and
animals that were in the fields in all the land of
Egypt. It also destroyed everything that grew in
the fields and broke all the trees in the fields.
26The only place it did not hail was in the land of
Goshen, where the Israelites lived.

27The king sent for Moses and Aaron and told
them, "This time I have sinned. The LORD is in the
right, and I and my people are in the wrong.
28Pray to the LORD. We have had enough of God's
thunder and hail. I will let you go; you do not
have to stay here any longer."

29Moses told the king, "When I leave the city,
I will raise my hands to the LORD in prayer, and
the thunder and hail will stop. Then you will
know that the earth belongs to the LORD. 30But I
know that you and your officers do not yet fear
the LORD God."

31The flax was in bloom, and the barley had
ripened, so these crops were destroyed. 32But
both wheat crops ripen later, so they were not
destroyed.

33Moses left the king and went outside the
city. He raised his hands to the LORD, and the
thunder and hail stopped. The rain also stopped
falling to the ground. 34When the king saw that
the rain, hail and thunder had stopped, he sinned
again, and he and his officers became stubborn.
35So the king became stubborn and refused to let
the Israelites go, just as the LORD had said through
Moses.

The Locusts

10 The LORD said to Moses, "Go to the king
of Egypt. I have made him and his offi-
cers stubborn so I could show them my powerful
miracles.[d] 2I also did this so you could tell your
children and your grandchildren how I was hard
on the Egyptians. Tell them about the miracles I
did among them so that all of you will know that
I am the LORD."

3So Moses and Aaron went to the king and told
him, "This is what the LORD, the God of the Heb-
rews, says: 'How long will you refuse to be sorry
for what you have done? Let my people go to
worship me. 4If you refuse to let my people go,

tomorrow I will bring locusts[d] into your country.
5They will cover the land so that no one will be
able to see the ground. They will eat anything
that was left from the hailstorm and the leaves
from every tree growing in the field. 6They will
fill your palaces and all your officers' houses, as
well as the houses of all the Egyptians. There will
be more locusts than your fathers or ancestors
have ever seen—more than there have been
since people began living in Egypt.' " Then Moses
turned and walked away from the king.

7The king's officers asked him, "How long will
this man make trouble for us? Let the Israelites go
to worship the LORD their God. Don't you know
that Egypt is ruined?"

8So Moses and Aaron were brought back to the
king. He said to them, "Go and worship the LORD
your God. But tell me, just who is going?"

9Moses answered, "We will go with our young
and old people, our sons and daughters, and our
flocks and herds, because we are going to have a
feast to honour the LORD."

10The king said to them, "The LORD will really
have to be with you if ever I let you and all of
your children leave Egypt. See, you are planning
something evil! 11No! Only the men may go and
worship the LORD, which is what you have been
asking for." Then the king forced Moses and
Aaron out of his palace.

12The LORD told Moses, "Raise your hand over
the land of Egypt, and the locusts will come. They
will spread all over the land of Egypt and will eat
all the plants the hail did not destroy."

13So Moses raised his walking stick over the
land of Egypt, and the LORD caused a strong
wind to blow from the east. It blew across the
land all that day and night, and when morning
came, the east wind had brought the locusts.
14Swarms of locusts covered all the land of Egypt
and settled everywhere. There were more locusts
than ever before or after, 15and they covered the
whole land so that it was black. They ate every-
thing that was left after the hail—every plant in
the field and all the fruit on the trees. Nothing
green was left on any tree or plant anywhere in
Egypt.

16The king quickly called for Moses and Aaron.
He said, "I have sinned against the LORD your God
and against you. 17Now forgive my sin this time.
Pray to the LORD your God, and ask him to stop
this punishment that kills."

18Moses left the king and prayed to the LORD.
19So the LORD changed the wind. He made a very
strong wind blow from the west, and it blew the
locusts away into the Red Sea.[d] Not one locust
was left anywhere in Egypt. 20But the LORD
caused the king to be stubborn again, and he did
not let the Israelites go.

The Darkness

21Then the LORD told Moses, "Raise your hand
towards the sky, and darkness will cover the land
of Egypt. It will be so dark you will be able to feel
it." 22Moses raised his hand towards the sky, and
total darkness was everywhere in Egypt for three
days. 23No one could see anyone else, and no one
could go anywhere for three days. But the Israel-
ites had light where they lived.

24Again the king of Egypt called for Moses. He
said, "All of you may go and worship the LORD.
You may take your women and children with you,
but you must leave your flocks and herds here."

25Moses said, "You must let us have animals to
use as sacrifices and burnt offerings, because we
have to offer them to the LORD our God. 26So we
must take our animals with us; not a hoof will be
left behind. We have to use some of the animals
to worship the LORD our God. We won't know
exactly what we will need to worship the LORD
until we get there."

27But the LORD made the king stubborn again,
so he refused to let them go. 28Then he told
Moses, "Get out of here, and don't come again!
The next time you see me, you will die."

29Then Moses told the king, "I'll do what you
say. I will not come to see you again."

The Death of the Firstborn

11 Now the LORD had told Moses, "I have
one more way to punish the king and
the people of Egypt. After this, the king will send
all of you away from Egypt. When he does, he
will force you to leave completely. 2Tell the men
and women of Israel to ask their neighbours for
things made of silver and gold." 3The LORD had
caused the Egyptians to respect the Israelites, and
both the king's officers and the Egyptian people
considered Moses to be a great man.

4So Moses said to the king, "This is what the
LORD says: 'About midnight tonight I will go
through all Egypt. 5Every firstborn[d] son in the
land of Egypt will die—from the firstborn son of
the king, who sits on his throne, to the firstborn
of the slave girl grinding grain. Also the firstborn
farm animals will die. 6There will be loud crying
everywhere in Egypt, worse than at any time be-
fore or after this. 7But not even a dog will bark at
the Israelites or their animals.' Then you will know
that the LORD treats Israel differently from Egypt.
8All your officers will come to me. They will bow
face down to the ground before me and say, 'Leave
and take all your people with you.' After that, I will
leave." Then Moses very angrily left the king.

9The LORD had told Moses, "The king will not
listen to you and Aaron so that I may do many
miracles[d] in the land of Egypt." 10Moses and

Aaron did all these great miracles in front of the
king. But the LORD made him stubborn, and the
king would not let the Israelites leave his country.

The First Passover

12 The LORD spoke to Moses and Aaron in
the land of Egypt: 2"This month will be
the beginning of months, the first month of the
year for you. 3Tell the whole community of Israel
that on the tenth day of this month each man
must get one lamb for the people in his house. 4If
there are not enough people in his house to eat a
whole lamb, he must share it with his closest
neighbour, considering the number of people.
There must be enough lamb for everyone to eat.
5The lamb must be a one-year-old male that has
nothing wrong with it. This animal can be either
a young sheep or a young goat. 6Take care of the
animals until the fourteenth day of the month.
On that day all the people of the community of
Israel will kill them in the evening before dark.
7The people must take some of the blood and put
it on the sides and tops of the doorframes of the
houses where they eat the lambs. 8On this night
they must roast the lamb over a fire. They must
eat it with bitter herbs and bread made without
yeast. 9Do not eat the lamb raw or boiled in wa-
ter. Roast the whole lamb over a fire—with its
head, legs and inner organs. 10You must not leave
any of it until morning, but if any of it is left over
until morning, you must burn it with fire.
11"This is the way you must eat it: you must be
fully dressed as if you were going on a trip. You
must have your sandals on and your walking stick

GOD'S LOVE

Waiting For Miracles

When the children in George Muller's orphanage in Bristol ate dinner, they didn't know that the food on their plates was the only food in the orphanage. There was no food or money left for next morning's breakfast. George prayed that something would arrive that evening, but nothing did. He went to bed, committing the need to God.

The next morning, George went out for his early morning walk and prayer. For some reason, he took a different route from usual, and a friend saw him. "I'm glad to see you," his friend said. "Please accept five pounds for the orphans."

"Thank you," George said graciously, never mentioning that the money would provide the children's food for several days. "God bless you."

Because of his faith, George fed hundreds of homeless children in Bristol in the 1800s. But he never made public appeals for funds.

When the food ran out at the orphanage, George told no one but God. And, miraculously, God supplied it time and time again. When George was low on funds, only God knew. And the money arrived when George needed it.

George Muller would never have been able to help hundreds of orphans without God's love to provide for them. In the same way, the Israelites would never have escaped from Egypt without God's love to protect them. Read **Exodus 12:1–14** to see how God's love delivered them during the Passover.

- What similarities do you see between God's provision for George Muller's orphanages and his protection of the Israelites during the Passover?
- Has God's love helped you through a situation you could never have survived on your own? How did the experience make you feel about God?

Consider . . .

- thanking God for his love that has delivered you in the past from difficult situations.
- writing on a card a difficult situation you are experiencing. Put the card in a place where you will find it in a week or so to see how God has helped you through that difficult time.

For more, see . . .

- Psalm 34 (p.519)
- Romans 5:1–11 (p.1190)
- Hosea 14:1–8 (p.860)

in your hand. You must eat it in a hurry; this is
the LORD's Passover.[d]
12“That night I will go through the land of
Egypt and kill all the firstborn[d] animals and peo-
ple in the land of Egypt. I will also punish all the
gods of Egypt. I am the LORD. 13But the blood will
be a sign on the houses where you are. When I
see the blood, I will pass over you. Nothing terri-
ble will hurt you when I punish the land of Egypt.
14“You are always to remember this day and
celebrate it with a feast to the LORD. Your des-
cendants[d] are to honour the LORD with this feast
from now on. 15For this feast you must eat bread
made without yeast for seven days. On the first
day, you are to remove all the yeast from your
houses. No one should eat any yeast for the full
seven days of the feast, or that person will be cut
off from Israel. 16You are to have holy meetings
on the first and last days of the feast. You must
not do any work on these days; the only work
you may do is to prepare your meals. 17You must
celebrate the Feast[d] of Unleavened Bread, be-
cause on this very day I brought your divisions of
people out of Egypt. So all of your descendants
must celebrate this day. This is a law that will last
from now on. 18In the first month of the year you
are to eat bread made without yeast, from the
evening of the fourteenth day until the evening of
the twenty-first day. 19For seven days there must
not be any yeast in your houses. Anybody who
eats yeast during this time, either an Israelite or
non-Israelite, must be cut off from the commu-
nity of Israel. 20During this feast you must not eat
anything made with yeast. You must eat only
bread made without yeast wherever you live.”
21Then Moses called all the elders of Israel to-
gether and told them, “Get the animals for your
families and kill the lamb for the Passover. 22Take
a branch of the hyssop plant, dip it into the bowl
filled with blood, and then wipe the blood on the
sides and tops of the doorframes. No one may
leave that house until morning. 23When the LORD
goes through Egypt to kill the Egyptians, he will
see the blood on the sides and tops of the door-
frames, and he will pass over that house. He will
not let the one who brings death come into your
houses and kill you.
24“You must keep this command as a law for
you and your descendants from now on. 25Do
this when you go to the land the LORD has prom-
ised to give you. 26When your children ask you,
‘Why are we doing these things?’ 27you will say,
‘This is the Passover sacrifice to honour the LORD.
When we were in Egypt, the LORD passed over
the houses of Israel, and when he killed the Egyp-
tians, he saved our homes.’ ” Then the people
bowed down and worshipped the LORD. 28They
did just as the LORD commanded Moses and Aaron.

29At midnight the LORD killed all the firstborn
sons in the land of Egypt—from the firstborn of
the king who sat on the throne to the firstborn of
the prisoner in jail. Also, all the firstborn farm
animals died. 30The king, his officers and all the
Egyptians got up during the night because some-
one had died in every house. So there was a loud
outcry everywhere in Egypt.

Israel Leaves Egypt

31During the night the king called for Moses
and Aaron and said, “Get up and leave my peo-
ple. You and your people may do as you have
asked; go and worship the LORD. 32Take all of your
flocks and herds as you have asked, and go. And
also bless me.” 33The Egyptians also asked the
Israelites to hurry and leave, saying, “If you don't
leave, we will all die!”
34So the people took their dough before the
yeast was added. They wrapped the bowls for
making dough in clothing and carried them on
their shoulders. 35The Israelites did what Moses
told them to do and asked their Egyptian neigh-
bours for things made of silver and gold and for
clothing. 36The LORD caused the Egyptians to
think well of them, and the Egyptians gave the
people everything they asked for. So the Israelites
took rich gifts from them.
37The Israelites travelled from Rameses to Suc-
coth. There were about 600,000 men walking,
not including the women and children. 38Many
other people who were not Israelites went with
them, as well as a large number of sheep, goats
and cattle. 39The Israelites used the dough they
had brought out of Egypt to bake loaves of bread
without yeast. The dough had no yeast in it, be-
cause they had been rushed out of Egypt and had
no time to get food ready for their trip.
40The people of Israel had lived in Egypt for
430 years; 41on the very day the 430 years ended,
the LORD's divisions of people left Egypt. 42That
night the LORD kept watch to bring them out of
Egypt, and so on this same night the Israelites are
to keep watch to honour the LORD from now on.
43The LORD told Moses and Aaron, “Here are
the rules for Passover:[d] no foreigner is to eat the
Passover. 44If someone buys a slave and circum-
cises[d] him, the slave may eat the Passover. 45But
neither a person who lives for a short time in your
country nor a hired worker may eat it.
46“The meal must be eaten inside a house; take
none of the meat outside the house. Don't break
any of the bones. 47The whole community of Is-
rael must take part in this feast. 48A foreigner who
lives with you may share in the LORD's Passover if
all the males in his house become circumcised.
Then, since he will be like a citizen of Israel, he
may share in the meal. But a man who is not

circumcised may not eat the Passover meal. 49The
same rules apply to an Israelite born in the coun-
try or to a foreigner living there."
50So all the Israelites did just as the LORD had
commanded Moses and Aaron. 51On that same
day the LORD led the Israelites out of Egypt by
their divisions.

The Law of the Firstborn

13 Then the LORD said to Moses, 2"Give
every firstborn [d] male to me. Every first-
born male among the Israelites belongs to me,
whether human or animal."
3Moses said to the people, "Remember this
day, the day you left Egypt. You were slaves in
that land, but the LORD with his great power
brought you out of it. You must not eat bread
made with yeast. 4Today, in the month of Abib, [d]
you are leaving Egypt. 5The LORD will lead you to
the land of the Canaanites, Hittites, Amorites, Hi-
vites and Jebusites. This is the land he promised
your ancestors he would give you, a fertile land.
There you must celebrate this feast during the
first month of every year. 6For seven days you
must eat bread made without yeast, and on the
seventh day there will be a feast to honour the
LORD. 7So for seven days you must not eat any
bread made with yeast. There must be no bread
made with yeast anywhere in your land. 8On that
day you should tell your son: 'We are having this
feast because of what the LORD did for me when
I came out of Egypt.' 9This feast will help you
remember, like a mark on your hand or a re-
minder on your forehead. This feast will remind
you to speak the LORD's teachings, because the
LORD used his great power to bring you out of
Egypt. 10So celebrate this feast every year at the
right time.
11"And when the LORD takes you into the land
of the Canaanites, the land he promised to give
you and your ancestors, 12you must give him ev-
ery firstborn male. Also every firstborn male ani-
mal must be given to the LORD. 13Buy back every
firstborn donkey by offering a lamb. But if you
don't want to buy the donkey back, then break its
neck. You must buy back from the LORD every
firstborn of your sons.
14"From now on when your son asks you,
'What does this mean?' you will answer, 'With
his great power, the LORD brought us out
from Egypt, the land where we were slaves.
15The king of Egypt was stubborn and refused
to let us leave. But the LORD killed every
firstborn male in Egypt, both human and animal.
That is why I sacrifice every firstborn male
animal to the LORD, and that is why I buy back
each of my firstborn sons from the LORD.' 16This
feast is like a mark on your hand and a reminder
on your forehead to help you remember that the
LORD brought us out of Egypt with his great
power."

The Way Out of Egypt

17When the king sent the people out of Egypt,
God did not lead them on the road through the
Philistine country, though that was the shortest
way. God said, "If they have to fight, they might
change their minds and go back to Egypt." 18So
God led them through the desert towards the Red
Sea. [d] The Israelites were dressed for fighting
when they left the land of Egypt.
19Moses carried the bones of Joseph with him,
because before Joseph died, he had made the Is-
raelites promise to do this. He had said, "When
God saves you, remember to carry my bones with
you out of Egypt."
20The Israelites left Succoth and camped at
Etham, on the edge of the desert. 21The LORD
showed them the way; during the day he went
ahead of them in a pillar of cloud, and during the
night he was in a pillar of fire to give them light.
In this way they could travel during the day or
night. 22The pillar of cloud was always with them
during the day, and the pillar of fire was always
with them at night.

14 Then the LORD said to Moses, 2"Tell the
Israelites to turn back to Pi Hahiroth and
to camp between Migdol and the Red Sea. Camp
across from Baal Zephon, on the shore of the sea.
3The king will think, 'The Israelites are lost,
trapped by the desert.' 4I will make the king stub-
born again so he will chase after them, but I will
defeat the king and his army. This will bring hon-
our to me, and the Egyptians will know that I am
the LORD." The Israelites did just as they were
told.

The King Chases the Israelites

5When the king of Egypt was told that the Is-
raelites had left, he and his officers changed their
minds about them. They said, "What have we
done? We have let the Israelites leave. We have
lost our slaves!" 6So the king prepared his war
chariot and took his army with him. 7He took
600 of his best chariots, together with all the
other chariots of Egypt, each with an officer in it.
8The LORD made the king of Egypt stubborn, so he
chased the Israelites, who were leaving victor-
iously. 9The Egyptians—with all the king's
horses, chariot drivers and army—chased the Is-
raelites. They caught up with them while they
were camped by the Red Sea, [d] near Pi Hahiroth
and Baal Zephon.
10When the Israelites saw the king and his
army coming after them, they were very fright-
ened and cried to the LORD for help. 11They said

to Moses, "What have you done to us? Why did
you bring us out of Egypt to die in the desert?
There were plenty of graves for us in Egypt. 12We
told you in Egypt, 'Let us alone; we will stay and
serve the Egyptians.' Now we will die in the
desert."
13But Moses answered, "Don't be afraid! Stand
still and you will see the LORD save you today. You
will never see these Egyptians again after today.
14You only need to remain calm; the LORD will
fight for you."
15Then the LORD said to Moses, "Why are you
crying out to me? Command the Israelites to start
moving. 16Raise your walking stick and hold it
over the sea so that the sea will split and the
people can cross it on dry land. 17I will make the
Egyptians stubborn so they will chase the Israel-
ites, but I will be honoured when I defeat the
king and all of his chariot drivers and chariots.
18When I defeat the king, his chariot drivers and
chariots, the Egyptians will know that I am the
LORD."
19Now the angel of God who usually travelled
in front of Israel's army moved behind them.
Also, the pillar of cloud moved from in front of
the people and stood behind them. 20So the cloud
came between the Egyptians and the Israelites.
This made it dark for the Egyptians but gave light
to the Israelites. So the cloud kept the two armies
apart all night.
21Then Moses held his hand over the sea. All
that night the LORD drove back the sea with a
strong east wind, making the sea become dry
ground. The water was split, 22and the Israelites
went through the sea on dry land, with a wall of
water on their right and on their left.
23Then all the king's horses, chariots and cha-
riot drivers followed them into the sea. 24When
morning came, the LORD looked down from the
pillar of cloud and fire at the Egyptian army and

FREEDOM

A Place to Call Home

The hot August night made it too stuffy to sleep. Elizabeth looked at her four children lying in the boxes in the back of her old car – the family's only home. She felt trapped with nowhere to go and no one to turn to.

"Oh God, my God," she cried and prayed silently. "Where are you, God? Have you forsaken me?" And she fell into a restless sleep.

For the next week, she went from hostel to hostel, hoping to find a place to live. One shelter took only children, and her four children wanted to be with their mum. When a hostel finally had room for all of them, it still wasn't a home.

Then a Christian friend gave Elizabeth hope. She arranged for the family to rent a house without having to pay a deposit first – and the first month was free. "God has told me to help you," the owner explained.

The new home gave Elizabeth a freedom from poverty that she had never known. "As a family, we've never been more secure," she says. "God solved my problem by using his people."

Elizabeth experienced new freedom from poverty and hopelessness as God worked through his people. The Israelites gained freedom from slavery in Egypt through Moses' leadership and God's work. Read about how they gained their freedom in **Exodus 14:19–31**.

- What feelings do you think Elizabeth would have if she read the story of the Israelites' new freedom? What parts would be most meaningful to her?
- As God led the Israelites to freedom, when has he freed you from a difficult situation? How did you celebrate?

Consider . . .

- finding someone in your school or church who's trapped by poverty, prejudice, or some other form of captivity. Talk to the person to find a way you can help him or her gain freedom.
- contacting a branch of Shelter in your area and volunteering to help repair homes.

For more, see . . .

- Exodus 15:1–11 (p.73)
- Galatians 5:1–15 (p.1263)
- John 8:31–38 (p.1110)

made them panic. 25 He kept the wheels of the
chariots from turning, making it hard to drive the
chariots. The Egyptians shouted, "Let's get away
from the Israelites! The LORD is fighting for them
and against Egypt."
26 Then the LORD told Moses, "Hold your hand
over the sea so that the water will come back
over the Egyptians, their chariots and chariot
drivers." 27 So Moses raised his hand over the sea,
and at dawn the sea returned to its place. The
Egyptians tried to run from it, but the LORD swept
them away into the sea. 28 The water returned,
covering the chariots, chariot drivers and all the
king's army that had followed the Israelites into
the sea. Not one of them survived.
29 But the Israelites crossed the sea on dry land,
with a wall of water on their right and on their
left. 30 So that day the LORD saved the Israelites
from the Egyptians, and the Israelites saw the
Egyptians lying dead on the seashore. 31 When the
Israelites saw the great power the LORD had used
against the Egyptians, they feared the LORD, and
they trusted him and his servant Moses.

The Song of Moses

15 Then Moses and the Israelites sang this song to the LORD:

"I will sing to the LORD,
because he is worthy of great honour.
He has thrown the horse and its rider
into the sea.
2 The LORD gives me strength and makes me
sing;
he has saved me.
He is my God,
and I will praise him.
He is the God of my fathers,
and I will honour him.
3 The LORD is a warrior;
the LORD is his name.
4 The chariots and soldiers of the king of Egypt
he has thrown into the sea.
The king's best officers
are drowned in the Red Sea.[d]
5 The deep waters covered them,
and they sank to the bottom like a rock.
6 Your right hand, LORD,
is amazingly strong.
LORD, your right hand
broke the enemy to pieces.
7 In your great victory
you destroyed those who were against you.
Your anger destroyed them,
like fire burning straw.
8 Just a blast of your breath,
and the waters piled up.
The moving waters stood like a wall;
the deep waters became solid in the middle
of the sea.
9 "The enemy boasted,
'I'll chase them and catch them.
I'll take all their riches;
I'll take all I want.
I'll pull out my sword,
and my hand will destroy them.'
10 But you blew on them with your breath
and covered them with the sea.
They sank like lead
in the raging water.

11 "Are there any gods like you, LORD?
There are no gods like you.
You are wonderfully holy,
amazingly powerful,
a worker of miracles.[d]
12 You reached out with your right hand,
and the earth swallowed our enemies.
13 You keep your loving promise
and lead the people you have saved.
With your strength you will guide them
to your holy place.

14 "The other nations will hear this and tremble
with fear;
terror will take hold of the Philistines.
15 The leaders of the tribes[d] of Edom will be
very frightened;
the powerful men of Moab will shake with fear;
the people of Canaan will lose all their
courage.
16 Terror and fear will fall on them.
When they see your strength,
they will be as still as a rock.
They will be still until your people pass by, LORD.
They will be still until the people you have
taken as your own pass by.
17 You will lead your people and place them
on your very own mountain,
the place that you, LORD, made for yourself to
live,
the temple, Lord, that your hands have made.
18 The LORD will be king for ever!"

19 The horses, chariot drivers and chariots of
the king of Egypt went into the sea, and the LORD
covered them with water from the sea. But the
Israelites walked through the sea on dry land.
20 Then Aaron's sister, Miriam, a prophetess,[d]
took a tambourine[d] in her hand. All the women
followed her, playing tambourines and dancing.
21 Miriam told them:
"Sing to the LORD,
because he is worthy of great honour;
he has thrown the horse and its rider
into the sea."

Bitter Water Becomes Good

22Moses led the Israelites away from the Red
Sea[d] into the Desert of Shur. They travelled for
three days in the desert but found no water.
23Then they came to Marah, where there was
water, but they could not drink it because it was
too bitter. (That is why the place was named
Marah.[n]) 24The people grumbled to Moses and
asked, "What will we drink?"
25So Moses cried out to the LORD, and the
LORD showed him a tree. When Moses threw the
tree into the water, the water became good to
drink.
There the LORD gave the people a rule and a
law to live by, and there he tested their loyalty to
him. 26He said, "You must obey the LORD your
God and do what he says is right. If you obey all
his commands and keep his rules, I will not bring
on you any of the sicknesses I brought on the
Egyptians. I am the LORD who heals you."
27Then the people travelled to Elim, where
there were twelve springs of water and 70 palm
trees. So the people camped there near the water.

The People Demand Food

16 The whole Israelite community left Elim
and came to the Desert of Sin, which
was between Elim and Sinai; they arrived there
on the fifteenth day of the second month after
they had left Egypt. 2Then the whole Israelite
community grumbled to Moses and Aaron in the
desert. 3They said to them, "It would have been

Marah This name means "bitter".

WORRYING

A Little Hope

Jimmy, fifteen, has a lot to worry about. Born with cystic fibrosis, a lung disease, he has been in hospital five or six times a year since he was six. Every day he takes 25 pills and spends 20 minutes in physiotherapy.

Whenever he has a cold, he has to have injections. And if he feels a little sick, he has to go to the hospital immediately. As a result, he misses 50 to 60 days of school each year.

"My body is a bit like a car that everyone wants to keep in tip-top shape," he explains.

Jimmy also has a future to worry about. "I have to realise that, no matter what, I'll never be totally independent," he says. "There's always going to have to be someone there for me."

Yet Jimmy doesn't worry. "There are some things in life you have choices about and there are things you don't," he explains. "God will take care of whatever is going to happen."

So instead of worrying, Jimmy has hope and faith in God. "You always have to have a little hope," he says, "because if you run out of that, there's nothing worth anything. You might as well give up right then and there."

Jimmy has learned how faith helps us to overcome worries. In contrast, the Israelites in the desert worried about how to find food. Read **Exodus 16:2–15** to learn how God took care of their worries.

- How does Jimmy's faith in God contrast with the Israelites' worries about how to survive?
- What in the passage comforts you in an area of life that's had you worried lately?

Consider . . .

- asking someone with a disability how God has helped him or her overcome the worries that come with the disability.
- writing a list of your worries about the future. Then fold the sheet in half and write one of the Bible verses below on the back. Keep the sheet in your Bible as a reminder of God's promises.

For more, see . . .

- Joshua 1:9 (p.203)
- James 4:13–15 (p.1352)
- Luke 12:22–31 (p.1064)

better if the LORD had killed us in the land of
Egypt. There we had meat to eat and all the food
we wanted. But you have brought us into this
desert to starve us to death."

[4]Then the LORD said to Moses, "I will cause
food to fall like rain from the sky for all of you.
Every day the people must go out and gather
what they need for that day. I want to see if the
people will do what I teach them. [5]On the sixth
day of each week, they are to gather twice as
much as they gather on other days. Then they
are to prepare it."

[6]So Moses and Aaron said to all the Israelites:
"This evening you will know that the LORD is the
one who brought you out of Egypt. [7]Tomorrow
morning you will see the glory of the LORD, be-
cause he has heard you grumble against him. We
are nothing, so you are not grumbling against us,
but against the LORD." [8]And Moses said, "Each
evening the LORD will give you meat to eat, and
every morning he will give you all the bread you
want, because he has heard you grumble against
him. You are not grumbling against Aaron and
me, because we are nothing; you are grumbling
against the LORD."

[9]Then Moses said to Aaron, "Speak to the
whole community of the Israelites, and say to
them, 'Meet together in the presence of the LORD,
because he has heard your grumblings.' "

[10]While Aaron was speaking to the whole com-
munity of the Israelites, they looked towards the
desert. There the glory of the LORD appeared in a
cloud.

[11]The LORD said to Moses, [12]"I have heard the
grumblings of the people of Israel. So tell them,
'At twilight you will eat meat, and every morning
you will eat all the bread you want. Then you
will know I am the LORD your God.' "

[13]That evening quail came and covered the
camp, and in the morning dew lay around the
camp. [14]When the dew was gone, thin flakes like
frost were on the desert ground. [15]When the Is-
raelites saw it, they asked each other, "What is
it?" because they did not know what it was.

So Moses told them, "This is the bread the LORD
has given you to eat. [16]The LORD has commanded,
'Each one of you must gather what he needs,
about 2 litres for every person in your family.' "

[17]So the people of Israel did this; some people
gathered much, and some gathered little. [18]Then
they measured it. The person who gathered more
did not have too much, nor did the person who
gathered less have too little. Each person gath-
ered just as much as he needed.

[19]Moses said to them, "Don't keep any of it to
eat the next day." [20]But some of the people did
not listen to Moses and kept part of it to eat the
next morning. It became full of worms and began
to stink, so Moses was angry with those people.

[21]Every morning each person gathered as
much food as he needed, but when the sun be-
came hot, it melted away.

[22]On the sixth day the people gathered twice as
much food—4 litres for every person. When all
the leaders of the community came and told this to
Moses, [23]he said to them, "This is what the LORD
commanded, because tomorrow is the Sabbath,[d]
the LORD's holy day of rest. Bake what you want to
bake, and boil what you want to boil today. Save
the rest of the food until tomorrow morning."

[24]So the people saved it until the next morn-
ing, as Moses had commanded, and none of it
began to stink or have worms in it. [25]Moses told
the people, "Eat the food you gathered yesterday.
Today is a Sabbath, the LORD's day of rest; you
will not find any out in the field today. [26]You
should gather the food for six days, but the sev-
enth day is a Sabbath day. On that day there will
not be any food on the ground."

[27]On the seventh day some of the people went
out to gather food, but they couldn't find any.
[28]Then the LORD said to Moses, "How long will
you people refuse to obey my commands and
teachings? [29]Look, the LORD has made the Sab-
bath a day of rest for you. So on the sixth day he
will give you enough food for two days, but on
the seventh day each of you must stay where you
are. Do not go anywhere." [30]So the people rested
on the seventh day.

[31]The people of Israel called the food manna.[d]
It was like small white seeds and tasted like wa-
fers made with honey.

[32]Then Moses said, "The LORD said, 'Save 2
litres of this food for your descendants.[d] Then
they can see the food I gave you to eat in the
desert when I brought you out of Egypt.' "

[33]Moses told Aaron, "Take a jar and fill it with
2 litres of manna. Then place it before the LORD,
and save it for your descendants." [34]So Aaron did
what the LORD had commanded Moses. He put
the jar of manna in front of the Agreement to
keep it safe. [35]The Israelites ate manna for 40
years, until they came to the land where they
settled—the edge of the land of Canaan. [36]The
measure they used for the manna was about 2
litres, or one-tenth of an ephah.[n]

Water from a Rock

17 The whole Israelite community left the
Desert of Sin and travelled from place to
place, as the LORD commanded. They camped at
Rephidim, but there was no water there for the

ephah An ephah was a measure that equalled 20 litres.

people to drink. 2So they quarrelled with Moses
and said, "Give us water to drink."
Moses said to them, "Why do you quarrel with
me? Why are you testing the LORD?"
3But the people were very thirsty for water, so
they grumbled against Moses. They said, "Why
did you bring us out of Egypt? Was it to kill us,
our children and our farm animals with thirst?"
4So Moses cried to the LORD, "What can I do
with these people? They are almost ready to
stone me to death."
5The LORD said to Moses, "Go ahead of the
people, and take some of the elders of Israel with
you. Carry with you the walking stick that you
used to strike the Nile River. Now go! 6I will
stand in front of you on a rock at Mount Sinai. Hit
that rock with the stick, and water will come out
of it so that the people can drink." Moses did
these things as the elders of Israel watched. 7He
named that place Massah,[n] because the Israelites
tested the LORD when they asked, "Is the LORD
with us or not?" He also named it Meribah,[n]
because they quarrelled.

The Amalekites Fight Israel

8At Rephidim the Amalekites came and fought
the Israelites. 9So Moses said to Joshua, "Choose
some men and go and fight the Amalekites. To-
morrow I will stand on the top of the hill, holding
the walking stick of God in my hands."

Massah This name is the Hebrew word for "testing".
Meribah This name is the Hebrew word for "quarrel".

PATIENCE

A Lesson in Trust

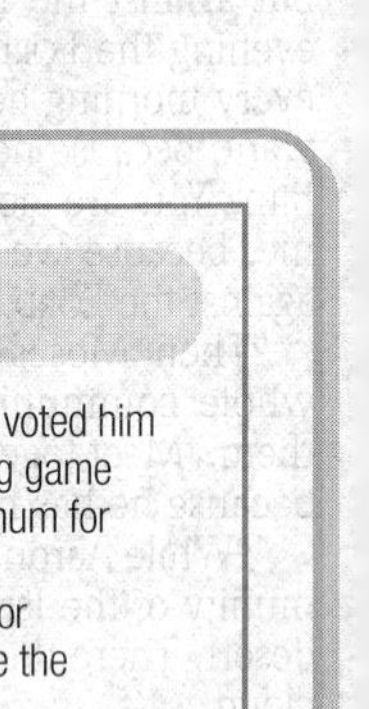

Dave had become captain of the football team. He couldn't believe it when all his team mates had voted him in; he was so honoured to lead the team in the year of the Schools Cup. Saturday was their first big game and, as captain, he was to provide the oranges at half time. The night before, Dave reminded his mum for the tenth time.

The next morning Dave was at school bright and early to make sure everything was organised for their first big game. He gave his team the carefully prepared speech and reached in his bag to give the oranges to his coach. The only thing Dave could find were his spare socks!

Dave couldn't believe it; he was furious. He couldn't believe his mum could forget on the very first game he had as captain. He rang her.

"Mum, the game starts in ten minutes and I have no oranges! I reminded you last night; I can't believe you forgot. I'm the captain and it's our first big game. I'm so embarrassed."

While Dave paused for breath, his mum asked if he had checked his lunch bag.

"No. Why?" he replied.

His mum sighed, "Because the oranges are in there."

Dave became very impatient when he needed the oranges for his game and in **Exodus 17:1–7** we see the Israelites responding in the same way when they need water.

- How hard would it have been for the Israelites to be patient when they were thirsty and needed water in the desert?
- Should the Israelites have trusted God to provide for them, just as Dave should've trusted his mum?

Consider . . .

- ways in which you could be more patient? Trusting God may be difficult sometimes but we know that when we do he always provides for us.
- trying to talk to God more about the things that you struggle with and praying first before chatting with others.

For more, see . . .

- Proverbs 3:5–6 (p.592)
- Matthew 7:7–11 (p.950)
- Proverbs 14:29 (p.602)
- Luke 12:22–31 (p.1064)

10Joshua obeyed Moses and went to fight the
Amalekites, while Moses, Aaron and Hur went to
the top of the hill. 11As long as Moses held his hands
up, the Israelites were winning the fight, but when
Moses put his hands down, the Amalekites were
winning. 12Later, when Moses' arms became tired,
the men put a large rock under him, and he sat on
it. Then Aaron and Hur held up Moses' hands—
Aaron on one side and Hur on the other. They kept
his hands steady until the sun went down. 13So
Joshua defeated the Amalekites in this battle.
14Then the LORD said to Moses, "Write about
this battle in a book so people will remember.
And be sure to tell Joshua, because I will com-
pletely destroy the Amalekites from the earth."
15Then Moses built an altar and named it The

> **Sidelight**
> Have you ever done the Mexican wave at a large event? Every time Moses raised his hands, God's power helped the Israelites to win the battle.

LORD is my Banner. 16Moses said, "I lifted my
hands towards the LORD's throne. The LORD will
fight against the Amalekites for ever."

Jethro Visits Moses

18 Jethro, Moses' father-in-law, was the
priest of Midian. He heard about every-
thing that God had done for Moses and his peo-
ple, the Israelites, and how the LORD had led the
Israelites out of Egypt. 2Now Moses had sent his
wife Zipporah to Jethro, his father-in-law, 3along
with his two sons. The first son was named Ger-
shom,[n] because when he was born, Moses said,
"I am a stranger in a foreign country." 4The other
son was named Eliezer,[n] because when he was
born, Moses said, "The God of my father is my
help. He saved me from the king of Egypt."
5So Jethro, Moses' father-in-law, took Moses'
wife and his two sons and went to Moses. He was
camped in the desert near the mountain of God.

> **Sidelight**
> The book of Exodus is quoted 250 times in the New Testament, making it the fourth most quoted book. Only Isaiah, Psalms and Genesis are quoted more.

6Jethro had sent a message ahead to Moses that
said, "I, Jethro, your father-in-law, am coming to
you with your wife and her two sons."
7So Moses went out to meet his father-in-law
and bowed down and kissed him. After the two
men asked about each other's health, they went
into Moses' tent. 8Moses told his father-in-law
everything the LORD had done to the king and
the Egyptians to help Israel. He told about all the
problems they had faced along the way and how
the LORD had saved them.
9Jethro was very happy to hear all the good
things the LORD had done for Israel when he
had saved them from the Egyptians. 10He said,
"Praise the LORD. He has saved you from the
Egyptians and their king, and he has saved the
people from the power of the Egyptians. 11Now
I know the LORD is greater than all gods, because
he did this to those who looked down on
Israel." 12Then Jethro, Moses' father-in-law, gave a
whole burnt offering and other sacrifices to
God. Aaron and all the elders of Israel came to
Moses' father-in-law to eat the holy meal together
before God.
13The next day Moses solved disagreements
among the people, and the people stood around
him from morning until night. 14When Moses'
father-in-law saw all that Moses was doing
for the people, he asked, "What is all this you are
doing for the people? Why are you the only
one to solve disagreements? All the people are
standing around you from morning until night!"
15Then Moses said to his father-in-law, "It is
because the people come to me for God's help in
solving their disagreements. 16When people
have a disagreement, they come to me, and I
decide who is right. I tell them God's laws and
teachings."
17Moses' father-in-law said to him, "You are
not doing this right. 18You and the people
who come to you will get too tired. This is too
much work for you; you can't do it by yourself.
19Now listen to me, and I will give you some
advice. I want God to be with you. You must
speak to God for the people and tell him about
their disagreements. 20Tell them about the
laws and teachings, and teach them the right way
to live and what they should do. 21But choose
some capable men from among the
people—men who respect God, who can be
trusted, and who will not change their decisions
for money. Make these men officers over
the people, to rule over groups of thousands,
hundreds, fifties and tens. 22Let these officers
solve the disagreements among the people all
the time. They can bring the hard cases to
you, but they can decide the simple cases them-
selves. That will make it easier for you, because

Gershom This name sounds like the Hebrew word for "a stranger there".
Eliezer This name sounds like the Hebrew words "My God is my help".

they will share the work with you. 23If you do
this as God commands you, then you will be able
to do your job, and all the people will go home
with their disagreements solved."
24So Moses listened to his father-in-law and
did everything he said. 25He chose capable men
from all the Israelites and made them leaders
over the people; they were officers over groups
of thousands, hundreds, fifties and tens. 26These
officers solved disagreements among the people all
the time. They brought the hard cases to Moses,
but they decided the simple cases themselves.
27So Moses sent his father-in-law on his way,
and Jethro went back to his own home.

Israel Camps at Sinai

19 Exactly three months after the Israelites
had left Egypt, they reached the Desert
of Sinai. 2When they left Rephidim, they came to
the Desert of Sinai and camped in the desert in
front of the mountain. 3Then Moses went up on
the mountain to God. The LORD called to him
from the mountain and said, "Say this to the fam-
ily of Jacob, and tell the people of Israel: 4'Every
one of you has seen what I did to the people of
Egypt. You saw how I carried you out of Egypt,
as if on eagle's wings. And I brought you here to
me. 5So now if you obey me and keep my agree-
ment, you will be my own possession, chosen

FOLLOWING GOD

A Trusted Leader

The whole drama class sniggered when it was announced that Adrian would be the student director for the spring production of *How to Succeed in Business*.

Adrian? He was a tall, thin student with a squeaky voice. The only reason classmates liked him was because he was a natural clown. He was hardly someone they would look up to.

But no matter. Mr Hall would be directing, and having Adrian as the assistant wouldn't hurt.

Then one evening the cast arrived for rehearsal to find Adrian sitting in Mr Hall's chair. "Mr Hall is ill," Adrian announced. "He'll be all right, but he won't be back for a couple of weeks."

Groans echoed across the stage. "There goes our big hit," someone on stage laughed. "Kiss that Oscar goodbye." And everyone laughed.

The rehearsal was a disaster. People joked with their lines, missed their entrances, and talked to Adrian with mock respect.

Suddenly, he threw his clipboard on the stage. "All right," he said. "I know I'm just a second-year, and I know you lot don't think I can do this. But we've got to do it together – for Mr Hall."

Surprised by his honesty, the cast started paying attention, and they discovered Adrian was a natural. In his quiet way, he turned the school play into a big success.

The cast members began following Adrian when they realised that he could lead them. The Israelites made a bigger commitment and trusted God because they had seen his work before. Read about their agreement to follow God in **Exodus 19:1–8**.

- What similarities and differences do you see between Adrian's speech to the cast and God's declaration to Moses? Which parts of what they said provide the most motivation?
- How does God's leadership of the Israelites give you faith that you too can follow God?

Consider . . .

- finding a calendar from the past month and writing ways God was with you through the month. Keep the calendar handy to remind you of God's guidance when you have trouble following him.
- memorising Exodus 19:4 to boost your faith when you're discouraged.

For more, see . . .

- Jeremiah 2:1–11 (p.717)
- John 9:1–25 (p.1111)
- Ezekiel 16:59–63 (p.800)

from all nations. Even though the whole earth is
mine, 6you will be my kingdom of priests and a
holy nation.' You must tell the Israelites these
words."
7So Moses went down and called the elders of
the people together. He told them all the words
the LORD had commanded him to say. 8All the
people answered together, "We will do every-
thing he has said." Then Moses took their an-
swer back to the LORD.
9And the LORD said to Moses, "I will come
to you in a thick cloud and speak to you. The
people will hear me speaking with you and will
always trust you." Then Moses told the LORD
what the people had said.
10The LORD said to Moses, "Go to the people
and have them spend today and tomorrow
preparing themselves. They must wash their
clothes 11and be ready by the day after tomorrow.
On that day I, the LORD, will come down on
Mount Sinai, and all the people will see me. 12But
you must set a limit around the mountain that
the people are not to cross. Tell them not to go up
on the mountain and not to touch the foot of it.
Anyone who touches the mountain must be put
to death 13with stones or shot with arrows. No
one is allowed to touch him. Whether it is a
person or an animal, he will not live. But the
trumpet will make a long blast, and only then
may the people go up on the mountain."
14After Moses went down from the mountain
to the people, he made them prepare them-
selves for service to God, and they washed their
clothes. 15Then Moses said to the people, "Be
ready in three days. Do not have sexual rela-
tions during this time."
16On the morning of the third day, there was
thunder and lightning with a thick cloud on the
mountain. There was a very loud blast from a
trumpet, and all the people in the camp trem-
bled. 17Then Moses led the people out of the
camp to meet God, and they stood at the foot of
the mountain. 18Mount Sinai was covered with
smoke, because the LORD came down on it in
fire. The smoke rose from the mountain like
smoke from a furnace, and the whole mountain
shook wildly. 19The sound from the trumpet be-
came louder. Then Moses spoke, and the voice
of God answered him.
20When the LORD came down on top of
Mount Sinai, he called Moses to come up to the
top of the mountain, and Moses went up. 21The
LORD said to Moses, "Go down and warn the
people that they must not force their way
through to see me. If they do, many of them will
die. 22Even the priests, who may come near
me, must first prepare themselves. If they don't,
I, the LORD, will punish them."
23Moses told the LORD, "The people cannot
come up on Mount Sinai, because you yourself
told us, 'Set a limit around the mountain, and
set it apart as holy.' "
24The LORD said to him, "Go down and bring
Aaron up with you, but don't allow the priests
or the people to force their way through. They
must not come up to the LORD, or I will punish
them."
25So Moses went down to the people and told
them these things.

The Ten Commandments

20 Then God spoke all these words:
2"I am the LORD your God, who
brought you out of the land of Egypt where you
were slaves.
3"You must not have any other gods ex-
cept me.
4"You must not make for yourselves an idol
that looks like anything in the sky above or on
the earth below or in the water below the land.
5You must not worship or serve any idol, because
I, the LORD your God, am a jealous God. If you
hate me, I will punish your children, and even
your grandchildren and great-grandchildren. 6But
I show kindness to thousands who love me and
obey my commands.
7"You must not use the name of the LORD
your God thoughtlessly; the LORD will punish
anyone who misuses his name.
8"Remember to keep the Sabbath[d] holy.
9Work and get everything done during six days
each week, 10but the seventh day is a day of rest
to honour the LORD your God. On that day no
one may do any work: not you, your son or
daughter, your male or female slaves, your ani-
mals, or the foreigners living in your cities.
11The reason is that in six days the LORD made
everything—the sky, the earth, the sea and
everything in them. On the seventh day he
rested. So the LORD blessed the Sabbath day and
made it holy.
12"Honour your father and your mother so
that you will live a long time in the land that the
LORD your God is going to give you.
13"You must not murder anyone.
14"You must not be guilty of adultery.[d]
15"You must not steal.

Sidelight The Ten Commandments (Exodus 20:2–17) are twice as easy to find as most famous Bible passages. They're also listed in Deuteronomy 5:6–21 (p.170), with only slight variations.

16“You must not tell lies about your neighbour.
17“You must not want to take your neighbour's
house. You must not want his wife or his male or
female slaves, or his ox or his donkey, or anything
that belongs to your neighbour.”
18When the people heard the thunder and the
trumpet, and when they saw the lightning and
the smoke rising from the mountain, they shook
with fear and stood far away from the mountain.
19Then they said to Moses, “Speak to us yourself,
and we will listen. But don't let God speak to us,
or we will die.”
20Then Moses said to the people, “Don't be
afraid, because God has come to test you. He
wants you to respect him so you will not sin.”
21The people stood far away from the moun-
tain while Moses went near the dark cloud where
God was. 22Then the LORD told Moses to say these
things to the Israelites: “You yourselves have seen
that I talked with you from heaven. 23You must
not use gold or silver to make idols for yourselves;
do not worship these gods in addition to me.
24“Make an altar of earth for me, and sacrifice
on it your whole burnt offerings and fellowship
offerings, your sheep and your cattle. Worship me
in every place that I choose, and I will come and
bless you. 25If you use stones to make an altar for
me, don't use stones that you have shaped with
tools. When you use any tools on them, you
make them unsuitable for use in worship. 26And
you must not go up to my altar on steps, or peo-
ple will be able to see under your clothes.”

Laws for Living

21 Then God said to Moses, “These are the
laws for living that you will give to the
Israelites:
2“If you buy a Hebrew slave, he will serve you
for six years. In the seventh year you are to set
him free, and he will have to pay nothing. 3If he
is not married when he becomes your slave, he
must leave without a wife. But if he is married
when he becomes your slave, he may take his
wife with him. 4If the slave's master gives him a

GOD'S WILL

Picture This

At a large football game, a man arrived to find a large piece of card by his seat. He'd been asked to hold up the card to show the crowd. “That's ridiculous,” the man thought, “it's a white card. There's nothing on it, no picture, nothing worth showing to anyone. I won't do it.” And he threw the card away.

At the appropriate time, the crowd were told to raise their cards. The entire side of the stadium held up their piece of the image, revealing an enormous picture of a face – the star player. The man hadn't realised his card was just one piece of a giant jigsaw. Suddenly the supporters in the other stand began to laugh. There was a gap, right in the middle of the smile. The handsome star player suddenly had a tooth missing. All because one man didn't recognise his part.

Read **Exodus 20:1–20**. God can see the bigger picture, and we've all got a role to play. We've got a choice as to whether we do as we're asked, lift our card and become part of the bigger picture, or throw it away. By disobeying God's rules, you're telling him he doesn't know what's best and that you will do it your own way.

God does know what's best. He's no spoilsport – he created fun and laughter. God's rules are just an instruction manual on how to get the absolute best out of life.

- Look at the Ten Commandments: can you think of good reasons why God would make each one?
- Which of the commandments do you think are most important and why?

Consider . . .

- how you can know what God's will for your life is. Discuss this with your friends.
- whether you are following God's will or his best plan for you. If not, what will you do about this?

For more, see . . .

- Psalm 139:16 (p.582)
- 1 John 5:14 (p.1376)
- Proverbs 2:3–5 (p.590)

wife, and she gives birth to sons or daughters, the woman and her children will belong to the master. When the slave is set free, only he may leave.
5“But if the slave says, ‘I love my master, my wife and my children, and I don’t want to go free,’ 6then the slave’s master must take him to God. The master is to take him to a door or doorframe and punch a hole through the slave’s ear using a sharp tool. Then the slave will serve that master all his life.
7“If a man sells his daughter as a slave, the rules for setting her free are different from the rules for setting the male slaves free. 8If the master wants to marry her but then decides he is not pleased with her, he must let one of her close relatives buy her back. He has no right to sell her to foreigners, because he has treated her unfairly. 9If the man who bought her promises to let the woman marry his son, he must treat her as a daughter. 10If the man who bought her marries another woman, he must not keep his first wife from having food or clothing or sexual relations. 11If he does not give her these three things, she may go free, and she owes him no money.

Laws About Injuries

12“Anyone who hits a person and kills him must be put to death. 13But if a person kills someone accidentally, God allowed that to happen, so the person must go to a place I will choose. 14But if someone plans and murders another person on purpose, put him to death, even if he has run to my altar for safety.
15“Anyone who hits his father or his mother must be put to death.
16“Anyone who kidnaps someone and either sells him as a slave or still has him when he is caught must be put to death.
17“Anyone who says cruel things to his father or mother must be put to death.
18“If two men argue, and one hits the other with a rock or with his fist, the one who is hurt but not killed might have to stay in bed. 19Later if he is able to get up and walk around outside with his walking stick, the one who hit him is not to be punished. But he must pay the injured man for the loss of his time, and he must support the injured man until he is completely healed.

Sidelight God gave Israel not only the Ten Commandments, but also laws to tell them how to get on with each other and indeed with himself, God. The Israelites were soon to become a nation, and rules of living can be found in Exodus, Leviticus and Deuteronomy.

20“If a man beats his male or female slave with a stick, and the slave dies on the spot, the owner must be punished. 21But if the slave gets well after a day or two, the owner will not be punished since the slave belongs to him.
22“Suppose two men are fighting and hit a pregnant woman, causing the baby to come out. If there is no further injury, the man who caused the accident must pay money—whatever amount the woman’s husband says and the court allows. 23But if there is further injury, then the punishment that must be paid is life for life, 24eye for eye, tooth for tooth, hand for hand, foot for foot, 25burn for burn, wound for wound and bruise for bruise.
26“If a man hits his male or female slave in the eye, and the eye is blinded, the man is to free the slave to pay for the eye. 27If a master knocks out a tooth of his male or female slave, the man is to free the slave to pay for the tooth.
28“If a man’s bull kills a man or woman, you must kill that bull by throwing stones at it, and you should not eat the bull. But the owner of the bull is not guilty. 29However, suppose the bull has hurt people in the past and the owner, though warned, did not keep it in a pen. Then if it kills a man or woman, the bull must be stoned to death, and the owner must also be put to death. 30But if the family of the dead person accepts money, the one who owned the bull may buy back his life, but he must pay whatever is demanded. 31Use this same law if the bull kills a person’s son or daughter. 32If the bull kills a male or female slave, the owner must pay the master the price for a new slave, or 30 pieces of silver, and the bull must also be stoned to death.
33“If a man takes the cover off a pit, or digs a pit and does not cover it, and another man’s ox or donkey comes and falls into it, 34the owner of the pit must pay the owner of the animal for the loss. The dead animal will belong to the one who pays.
35“If a man’s bull kills another man’s bull, they must sell the bull that is alive. Both men will get half of the money and half of the bull that was killed. 36But if a person’s bull has hurt other animals in the past and the owner did not keep it in a pen, that owner must pay bull for bull, and the dead animal is his.

Property Laws

22 “If a man steals a bull or a sheep and kills or sells it, he must pay back five bulls for the one bull he stole and four sheep for the one sheep he stole.

2–4“The robber who is caught must pay back
what he stole. If he owns nothing, he must be sold
as a slave to pay for what he stole. If the stolen
animal is found alive with the robber, he must
give the owner two animals for every animal he
stole, whether it was a bull, donkey or sheep.

“If a thief is killed while breaking into a house
at night, the one who killed him is not guilty of
murder. But if this happens during the day, he is
guilty of murder.

5“If a man lets his farm animal graze in his field
or vineyard, and it wanders into another man’s
field or vineyard, the owner of the animal must
pay back the loss from the best of his crop.

6“Suppose a man starts a fire that spreads
through the thorn bushes to his neighbour’s field.
If the fire burns his neighbour’s growing grain or
grain that has been stacked, or if it burns his
whole field, the person who started the fire must
pay for what was burned.

7“Suppose a man gives his neighbour money
or other things to keep for him and those things
are stolen from the neighbour’s house. If the
thief is caught, he must pay back twice as much
as he stole. 8But if the thief is never found, the
owner of the house must make a promise before
God that he has not stolen his neighbour’s
things.

9“Suppose two men disagree about who owns
something—whether ox, donkey, sheep, cloth-
ing or something else that is lost. If each says,
‘This is mine,’ each man must bring his case to
God. God’s judges will decide who is guilty, and
that person must pay the other man twice as
much as the object is worth.

10“Suppose a man asks his neighbour to keep
his donkey, ox, sheep or some other animal for
him, and that animal dies, gets hurt or is taken
away, without anyone seeing what happened.
11That neighbour must promise before the LORD
that he did not harm or kill the other man’s ani-
mal, and the owner of the animal must accept his
promise made before God. The neighbour does
not have to pay the owner for the animal. 12But
if the animal was stolen from the neighbour, he
must pay the owner for it. 13If wild animals killed
it, the neighbour must bring the body as proof,
and he will not have to pay for the animal that
was killed.

14“If a man borrows an animal from his neigh-
bour, and it gets hurt or dies while the owner is
not there, the one who borrowed it must pay the
owner for the animal. 15But if the owner is with
the animal, the one who borrowed it does not
have to pay. If the animal was rented, the rental
price covers the loss.

Laws and Relationships

16“Suppose a man finds a woman who is not
pledged to be married and has never had sexual
relations with a man. If he tricks her into having
sexual relations with him, he must give her
family the payment to marry her and she will be-
come his wife. 17But if her father refuses to allow
his daughter to marry him, the man must still
give the usual payment for a bride who has
never had sexual relations.

18“Put to death any woman who does evil
magic.

19“Put to death anyone who has sexual rela-
tions with an animal.

20“Destroy completely any person who makes
a sacrifice to any god except the LORD.

21“Do not cheat or hurt a foreigner, because
you were foreigners in the land of Egypt.

22“Do not cheat a widow or an orphan. 23If you
do, and they cry out to me for help, I certainly
will hear their cry. 24And I will be very angry and
kill you in war. Then your wives will become
widows, and your children will become orphans.

25“If you lend money to one of my people who
is poor, do not treat him as a moneylender would.
Charge him nothing for using your money. 26If
your neighbour gives you his coat as a promise for
the money he owes you, you must give it back to
him by sunset, 27because it is the only cover to
keep his body warm. He has nothing else to sleep
in. If he cries out to me for help, I will listen,
because I am merciful.

28“You must not speak against God or curse a
leader of your people.

29“Do not hold back your offering from the first
of your harvest and the first wine that you make.
Also, you must give me your firstborn[d] sons.
30You must do the same with your bulls and your
sheep. Let the firstborn males stay with their
mothers for seven days, and on the eighth day
you must give them to me.

31“You are to be my holy people. You must not
eat the meat of any animal that has been killed by
wild animals. Instead, give it to the dogs.

Laws About Fairness

23 “You must not tell lies. If you are a wit-
ness in court, don’t help a wicked person
by telling lies.

2“You must not do wrong just because every-
one else is doing it. If you are a witness in court,
you must not ruin a fair trial. You must not tell
lies just because everyone else does. 3If a poor
person is in court, you must not take his side just
because he is poor.

4"If you see your enemy's ox or donkey wandering away, you must return it to him. 5If you see that your enemy's donkey has fallen because its load is too heavy, do not leave it there. You must help your enemy get the donkey back on its feet.

6"You must not be unfair to a poor person when he is in court. 7You must not lie when you accuse someone in court. Never allow an innocent or honest person to be put to death as punishment, because I will not treat guilty people as if they were innocent.

8"You must not accept money from a person who wants you to lie in court, because such money will not let you see what is right. Such money makes good people tell lies.

9"You must not mistreat a foreigner. You know how it feels to be a foreigner, because you were foreigners in Egypt.

Laws for the Sabbath

10"For six years you are to plant and harvest crops on your land. 11Then during the seventh year, do not plough or plant your land. If any food grows there, allow the poor people to have it, and let the wild animals eat what is left. You should do the same with your vineyards and your orchards of olive trees.

12"You should work six days a week, but on the seventh day you must rest. This lets your ox and your donkey rest, and it also lets the slave born in your house and the foreigner be refreshed.

13"Be sure to do all that I have said to you. You must not even say the names of other gods; those names must not come out of your mouth.

Three Yearly Feasts

14"Three times each year you must hold a feast to honour me. 15You must celebrate the Feast[d] of Unleavened Bread in the way I commanded you. For seven days you must eat bread that is made without yeast at the set time during the month of Abib,[d] the month when you came out of Egypt. No one is to come to worship me without bringing an offering.

16"You must celebrate the Feast[d] of Weeks. Offer to God the first things you harvest from the crops you planted in your fields.

"You must celebrate the Feast[d] of Shelters in the autumn, when you gather all the crops from your fields.

17"So three times during every year all your males must come to worship the LORD God.

18"You must not offer animal blood along with anything that has yeast in it.

"You must not save any of the fat from the sacrifice for the next day.

19"You must bring the best of the firstfruits[d] of your land to the Holy Tent[n] of the LORD your God.

"You must not cook a young goat in its mother's milk.

God Will Help Israel

20"I am sending an angel ahead of you, who will protect you as you travel. He will lead you to the place I have prepared. 21Pay attention to the angel and obey him. Do not turn against him; he will not forgive such turning against him because my power is in him. 22If you listen carefully to all he says and do everything that I tell you, I will be an enemy to your enemies. I will fight all who fight against you. 23My angel will go ahead of you and take you into the land of the Amorites, Hittites, Perizzites, Canaanites, Hivites and Jebusites, and I will destroy them.

24"You must not bow down to their gods or worship them. You must not live in the way those people live. You must destroy their idols, breaking into pieces the stone pillars they use in worship. 25If you worship the LORD your God, I will bless your bread and your water. I will take away sickness from you. 26None of your women will have her baby die before it is born, and all women will have children. I will allow you to live long lives.

27"I will make your enemies afraid of me. I will confuse any people you fight against, and I will make all your enemies run away from you. 28I will send terror ahead of you that will force the Hivites, Canaanites and Hittites out of your way. 29But I will not force all those people out in only one year. If I did, the land would become a desert and the wild animals would become too many for you. 30Instead, I will force those people out slowly, until there are enough of you to take over the land.

31"I will give you the land from the Red Sea to the Mediterranean Sea, and from the desert to the Euphrates River. I will give you power over the people who now live in the land, and you will force them out ahead of you. 32You must not make an agreement with those people or with their gods. 33You must not let them live in your land, or they will make you sin against me. If you worship their gods, you will be caught in a trap."

Holy Tent Literally, "house of the LORD your God". See Exodus 25:9.

God and Israel Make Their Agreement

24 The LORD told Moses, "You, Aaron, Na-
dab, Abihu and 70 of the elders of Israel
must come up to me and worship me from a
distance. [2]Then Moses alone must come near me;
the others must not come near. The rest of the
people must not come up the mountain with
Moses."
[3]Moses told the people all the LORD's words
and laws for living. Then all of the people an-
swered out loud together, "We will do all the
things the LORD has said." [4]So Moses wrote down
all the words of the LORD. And he got up early the
next morning and built an altar near the bottom
of the mountain. He set up twelve stones, one
stone for each of the twelve tribes[d] of Israel.
[5]Then Moses sent young Israelite men to offer
whole burnt offerings and to sacrifice young bulls
as fellowship offerings to the LORD. [6]Moses put
half of the blood of these animals in bowls, and
he sprinkled the other half of the blood on the
altar. [7]Then he took the Book of the Agreement
and read it so the people could hear him. And
they said, "We will do everything that the LORD
has said; we will obey."
[8]Then Moses took the blood from the bowls
and sprinkled it on the people, saying, "This is the
blood that begins the Agreement, the Agreement
which the LORD has made with you about all
these words."
[9]Moses, Aaron, Nadab, Abihu and 70 of the
elders of Israel went up the mountain [10]and saw
the God of Israel. Under his feet was a surface
that looked as if it were paved with blue sapphire
stones and it was as clear as the sky! [11]These
leaders of the Israelites saw God, but God did not
destroy them. Then they ate and drank together.

God Promises Moses the Stone Tablets

[12]The LORD said to Moses, "Come up the
mountain to me. Wait there, and I will give you
two stone tablets. On these are the teachings
and the commands I have written to teach the
people."
[13]So Moses and his helper Joshua set out, and
Moses went up to Sinai, the mountain of God.
[14]Moses said to the elders, "Wait here for us until
we come back to you. Aaron and Hur are with
you, and anyone who has a disagreement with
others can take it to them."

Moses Meets with God

[15]When Moses went up on the mountain, the
cloud covered it. [16]The glory of the LORD came
down on Mount Sinai, and the cloud covered
it for six days. On the seventh day the LORD
called to Moses from inside the cloud. [17]To the
Israelites the glory of the LORD looked like a fire
burning on top of the mountain. [18]Then Moses
went into the cloud and went higher up the
mountain. He was on the mountain for 40 days
and 40 nights.

Gifts for the LORD

25 The LORD said to Moses, [2]"Tell the Israel-
ites to bring me gifts. Receive for me the
gifts each person wants to give. [3]These are the
gifts that you should receive from them: gold,
silver and bronze; [4]blue, purple and red thread;
fine linen, goat hair and [5]rams' skins that are
dyed red; fine leather; acacia wood; [6]olive oil to
burn in the lamps; spices for sweet-smelling in-
cense,[d] and the special olive oil poured on a per-
son's head to make him a priest; and [7]onyx stones
and other jewels to be put on the holy robe[d] and
the chest covering.
[8]"The people must build a holy place for me so
that I can live among them. [9]Build this Holy
Tent[d] and everything in it by the plan I will
show you.

The Ark of the Agreement

[10]"Use acacia wood and build an Ark[d] 110
centimetres long, 70 centimetres wide and 70
centimetres high. [11]Cover the Ark inside and out
with pure gold, and put a gold strip all around it.
[12]Make four gold rings for the Ark and attach
them to its four feet, two rings on each side.
[13]Then make poles from acacia wood and cover
them with gold. [14]Put the poles through the rings
on the sides of the Ark, and use these poles to
carry it. [15]These poles must always stay in the
rings of the Ark. Do not take them out. [16]Then
put in the Ark the Agreement which I will make
with you.
[17]"Then make a lid of pure gold for the Ark;
this is the mercy seat.[d] Make it 110 centimetres
long and 70 centimetres wide. [18]Then hammer
gold to make two creatures with wings, and put
one on each end of the lid. [19]Attach one creature
on one end of the lid and the other creature on
the other end. Make them to be one piece with
the lid at the ends. [20]The creatures' wings should
be spread upwards, covering the lid, and the
creatures are to face each other across the lid.
[21]Put this lid on top of the Ark, and put in the
Ark the Agreement which I will make with you.
[22]I will meet with you there, above the lid
between the two winged creatures on the Ark
of the Agreement. There I will give you all my
commands for the Israelites.

The Table

[23]"Make a table out of acacia wood, 90
centimetres long, 50 centimetres wide and 70
centimetres high. [24]Cover it with pure gold, and

put a gold strip around it. 25Make a frame 8 cen-
timetres high that stands up all around the edge,
and put a gold strip around it. 26Then make four
gold rings. Attach them to the four corners of the
table where the four legs are. 27Put the rings close
to the frame around the top of the table, because
they will hold the poles for carrying it. 28Make
the poles out of acacia wood, cover them with
gold, and carry the table with these poles. 29Make
the plates and bowls for the table, as well as the
jars and cups, out of pure gold. They will be used
for pouring out the drink offerings. 30On this table
put the bread that shows you are in my presence
so that it is always there in front of me.

The Lampstand

31"Hammer pure gold to make a lampstand. Its
base, stand, flower-like cups, buds and petals
must all be joined together in one piece. 32The
lampstand must have six branches going out
from its sides—three on one side and three on
the other. 33Each branch must have three cups
shaped like almond flowers on it. Each cup must
have a bud and a petal. Each of the six branches
going out from the lampstand must be the
same. 34And there must be four more cups made
like almond flowers on the lampstand itself.
These cups must also have buds and petals. 35Put
a bud under each pair of branches that goes
out from the lampstand. Each of the six branches
going out from the lampstand must be the
same. 36The branches, buds and lampstand must
be made of one piece, hammered out of pure
gold.

37"Then make seven small oil lamps and put
them on the lampstand so that they give light to
the area in front of it. 38The wick trimmers and
trays must be made of pure gold. 39Use 34 kilo-
grammes of pure gold to make the lampstand and
everything with it. 40Be very careful to make
them by the plan I showed you on the mountain.

The Holy Tent

26 "Make for the Holy Tent[d] ten curtains
of fine linen and blue, purple and red
thread. Have a skilled craftsman sew designs of
creatures with wings on the pieces of cloth.
2Make each curtain the same size—14 metres
long and 2 metres wide. 3Sew five curtains to-
gether for one set, and sew the other curtains
together for the second set. 4Make loops of blue
cloth on the edge of the end curtain of one set,
and do the same for the end curtain of the other
set. 5Make 50 loops on the end curtain of the first
set and 50 loops on the end curtain of the second
set. These loops must be opposite each other.
6And make 50 gold hooks to join the two sets of
curtains so that the Holy Tent is one piece.

7"Then make another tent that will cover the
Holy Tent, using eleven curtains made from goat
hair. 8All these curtains must be the same size—
15 metres long and 2 metres wide. 9Sew five of
the curtains together into one set. Then sew the
other six curtains together into the second set.
Fold the sixth curtain double over the front of the
Tent. 10Make 50 loops down the edge of the end
curtain of one set, and do the same for the end
curtain of the other set. 11Then make 50 bronze
hooks and put them in the loops to join the tent
together so that the covering is one piece. 12Let
the extra half piece of cloth hang over the back of
the Holy Tent. 13There will be 50 centimetres
hanging over the sides of the Holy Tent, to pro-
tect it. 14Make a covering for the Holy Tent from
ram's skins coloured red, and over that make a
covering from fine leather.

15"Use acacia wood to make upright frames for
the Holy Tent. 16Each frame must be 5 metres
long and 70 centimetres wide, 17with two pegs
side by side. Every frame must be made in this
way. 18Make 20 frames for the south side of the
Holy Tent. 19Each frame must have two silver
bases to go under it, a peg fitting into each base.
You must make 40 silver bases for the frames.
20Make 20 more frames for the north side of the
Holy Tent 21and 40 silver bases for them—two
bases for each frame. 22You must make six frames
for the rear or west end of the Holy Tent 23and
two frames for each corner at the rear. 24The two
frames are to be doubled at the bottom and joined
at the top with a metal ring. Both corner frames
must be made in this way. 25So there will be a
total of eight frames at the rear of the Tent, and
there will be sixteen silver bases—two bases un-
der each frame.

26"Make crossbars of acacia wood to connect
the upright frames of the Holy Tent. Make five
crossbars to hold the frames together on one side
27and five to hold the frames together on the
other side. Also make five crossbars to hold the
frames together on the west end, at the rear.
28The middle crossbar is to be set halfway up the
frames, and it is to run along the entire length of
each side and rear. 29Make gold rings on the sides
of the frames to hold the crossbars, and cover
the frames and the crossbars with gold. 30Set up
the Holy Tent by the plan shown to you on the
mountain.

31"Make a curtain of fine linen and blue, pur-
ple and red thread, and have a skilled craftsman
sew designs of creatures with wings on it. 32Hang
the curtain by gold hooks on four posts of acacia
wood that are covered with gold, and set them in
four silver bases. 33Hang the curtain from the
hooks in the roof, and put the Ark[d] of the Agree-
ment containing the two flat stones behind it.

This curtain will separate the Holy Place from the Most Holy Place. 34Put the lid on the Ark of the Agreement in the Most Holy Place.

35“Outside the curtain, put the table on the north side of the Holy Tent. Put the lampstand on the south side of the Holy Tent across from the table.

The Entrance of the Holy Tent

36“Then, for the entrance of the Tent,[d] make a curtain with fine linen and blue, purple and red thread. Someone who can sew well is to sew designs on it. 37Make five posts of acacia wood covered with gold. Make gold hooks for them on which to hang the curtain, and make five bronze bases for them.

The Altar for Burnt Offerings

27 “Make an altar of acacia wood, 1.5 metres high. It should be square—2.5 metres long and 2.5 metres wide. 2Make each of the four corners of the altar stick out like a horn, in such a way that the corners with their horns are all one piece. Then cover the whole altar with bronze.

3“Use bronze to make all the tools and dishes that will be used on the altar: the pots to remove the ashes, the shovels, the bowls for sprinkling blood, the meat forks and the pans for carrying the burning wood.

4“Make a large bronze screen to hold the burning wood, and put a bronze ring at each of the four corners of it. 5Put the screen inside the altar, under its rim, halfway up from the bottom.

6“Make poles of acacia wood for the altar, and cover them with bronze. 7Put the poles through the rings on both sides of the altar to carry it. 8Make the altar out of boards and leave the inside hollow. Make it as you were shown on the mountain.

The Courtyard of the Holy Tent

9“Make a wall of curtains to form a courtyard around the Holy Tent.[d] The south side should have a wall of fine linen curtains 50 metres long. 10Hang the curtains with silver hooks and bands on 20 bronze posts with 20 bronze bases. 11The north side must also be 50 metres long. Hang its curtains on silver hooks and bands on 20 bronze posts with 20 bronze bases.

12“The west end of the courtyard must have a wall of curtains 25 metres long, with ten posts and ten bases on that wall. 13The east end of the courtyard must also be 25 metres long. 14On one side of the entry, there is to be a wall of curtains 7.5 metres long, held up by three posts on three bases. 15On the other side of the entry, there is also to be a wall of curtains 7.5 metres long, held up by three posts on three bases.

16“The entry to the courtyard is to be a curtain 10 metres wide, made of fine linen with blue, purple and red thread. Someone who can sew well is to sew designs on it. It is to be held up by four posts on four bases. 17All the posts around the courtyard must have silver bands and hooks and bronze bases. 18The courtyard must be 50 metres long and 25 metres wide, with a wall of curtains around it 2.5 metres high, made of fine linen. The bases in which the posts are set must be bronze. 19All the things used in the Holy Tent and all the tent pegs for the Holy Tent and the wall around the courtyard must be made of bronze.

Oil for the Lamp

20“Command the people of Israel to bring you pure olive oil, made from pressed olives, to keep the lamps on the lampstand burning. 21Aaron and his sons must keep the lamps burning before the LORD from evening till morning. This will be in the Meeting Tent,[d] outside the curtain which is in front of the Ark.[d] The Israelites and their descendants[d] must obey this rule from now on.

Clothes for the Priests

28 “Tell your brother Aaron to come to you, along with his sons Nadab, Abihu, Eleazar and Ithamar. Separate them from the other Israelites to serve me as priests. 2Make holy clothes for your brother Aaron to give him honour and beauty. 3Tell all the skilled craftsmen to whom I have given wisdom to make special clothes for Aaron—clothes to show that he belongs to me so that he may serve me as a priest. 4These are the clothes they must make: a chest covering, a holy robe,[d] an outer robe, a woven inner robe, a turban and a cloth belt. The craftsmen must make these holy clothes for your brother Aaron and his sons. Then they may serve me as priests. 5The craftsmen must use gold and blue, purple and red thread, and fine linen.

The Holy Robe

6“Use gold and blue, purple and red thread, and fine linen to make the holy robe;[d] skilled craftsmen are to make it. 7At each top corner of this holy robe there will be a pair of shoulder straps tied together over each shoulder.

8“The craftsmen will very carefully weave a belt on the holy robe that is made with the same materials—gold and blue, purple and red thread, and fine linen.

9“Take two onyx stones and write the names of the twelve sons of Israel on them, 10six on one

stone and six on the other. Write the names in
order, from the oldest son to the youngest.
11Carve the names of the sons of Israel on these
stones in the same way that a person carves
words and designs on a seal. [d] Put gold around
the stones to hold them on the holy robe. 12Then
put the two stones on the two straps of the holy
robe as reminders of the twelve sons of Israel.
Aaron is to wear their names on his shoulders in
the presence of the LORD as reminders of the sons
of Israel. 13Make two gold pieces to hold the
stones 14and two chains of pure gold, twisted to-
gether like a rope. Attach the chains to the two
gold pieces that hold the stones.

The Chest Covering

15"Make a chest covering to help in making
decisions. The craftsmen should make it as they
made the holy robe, [d] using gold and blue, purple
and red thread, and fine linen. 16The chest cover-
ing must be square—23 centimetres long and 23
centimetres wide—and folded double to make a
pocket. 17Put four rows of beautiful gems on the
chest covering: the first row must have a ruby, a
topaz and a yellow quartz; 18the second must
have turquoise, a sapphire and an emerald; 19the
third must have a jacinth, an agate and an ameth-
yst; 20the fourth must have a chrysolite, an onyx
and a jasper. Put gold around these jewels to at-
tach them to the chest covering. 21There must be
twelve jewels on the chest covering—one jewel
for each of the names of the sons of Israel. Carve
the name of one of the twelve tribes [d] on each of
the stones as you would carve a seal. [d]

22"Make chains of pure gold, twisted together
like rope, for the chest covering. 23Make two gold
rings and put them on the two upper corners of
the chest covering. 24Attach the two gold chains
to the two rings at the upper corners of the chest
covering. 25Attach the other ends of the two
chains to the two gold pieces on the shoulder
straps in the front of the holy robe.

26"Make two gold rings and put them at the
two lower corners of the chest covering, on the
inside edge next to the holy robe. 27Make two
more gold rings and attach them to the bottom of
the shoulder straps in the front of the holy robe.
Put them close to the seam above the woven belt
of the holy robe. 28Join the rings of the chest
covering to the rings of the holy robe with blue
ribbon, connecting it to the woven belt so the
chest covering will not swing out from the holy
robe.

29"When Aaron enters the Holy Place, he will
wear the names of the sons of Israel over his
heart, on the chest covering that helps in making
decisions. This will be a continual reminder be-
fore the LORD. 30And put the Urim and Thummim [d]
inside the chest covering so that they will be
on Aaron's heart when he goes before the
LORD. They will help in making decisions for the
Israelites. So Aaron will always carry them with
him when he is before the LORD.

31"Make the outer robe to be worn under the
holy robe, using only blue cloth. 32Make a hole in
the centre for Aaron's head, with a woven collar
around the hole so it will not tear. 33Make balls
like pomegranates [d] of blue, purple and red
thread, and hang them around the bottom of the
outer robe with gold bells between them. 34All
around the bottom of the outer robe there should
be a gold bell and a pomegranate ball, a gold bell
and a pomegranate ball. 35Aaron must wear this
robe when he serves as priest. The ringing of the
bells will be heard when he enters and leaves the
Holy Place before the LORD so that Aaron will
not die.

36"Make a strip of pure gold and carve these
words on it as you would carve a seal: [d] 'Holy to
the LORD'. 37Use blue ribbon to tie it to the turban;
put it on the front of the turban. 38Aaron must
wear this on his forehead. In this way, he will be
blamed if anything is wrong with the gifts of
the Israelites. Aaron must always wear this on
his head so the LORD will accept the gifts of the
people.

39"Make the woven inner robe of fine linen,
and make the turban of fine linen also. Make the
cloth belt with designs sewn on it. 40Also make
woven inner robes, cloth belts and headbands for
Aaron's sons, to give them honour and beauty.
41Put these clothes on your brother Aaron and his
sons, and pour olive oil on their heads to appoint
them as priests. Make them belong to me so they
may serve me as priests.

42"Make for them linen underclothes to cover
them from the waist to the upper parts of the
legs. 43Aaron and his sons must wear these un-
derclothes when they enter the Meeting Tent [d]
and whenever they come near the altar to serve
as priests in the Holy Place. If they do not wear
these clothes, they will be guilty of wrong, and
they will die. This will be a law that will last from
now on for Aaron and all his descendants. [d]

Appointing the Priests

29 "This is what you must do to appoint
Aaron and his sons to serve me as priests.
Take one young bull and two rams that have
nothing wrong with them. 2Use fine wheat flour
without yeast to make bread, cakes mixed with
olive oil, and wafers brushed with olive oil. 3Put
these in one basket, and bring them along with
the bull and two rams. 4Bring Aaron and his sons
to the entrance of the Meeting Tent [d] and wash
them with water. 5Take the clothes and dress

Aaron in the inner robe and the outer robe of the
holy robe.[d] Then put on him the holy robe and
the chest covering, and tie the holy robe on him
with its skilfully woven belt. 6Put the turban on
his head, and put the holy crown on the turban.
7Take the special olive oil and pour it on his head
to make him a priest.

8"Then bring his sons and put the inner robes
on them. 9Put the headbands on their heads, and
tie cloth belts around their waists. Aaron and his
descendants[d] will be priests in Israel, according
to a rule that will continue from now on. This
is how you will appoint Aaron and his sons as
priests.

10"Bring the bull to the front of the Meeting
Tent, and Aaron and his sons must put their
hands on the bull's head. 11Then kill the bull be-
fore the LORD at the entrance to the Meeting Tent.
12Use your finger to put some of the bull's blood
on the corners of the altar, and then pour the
blood that is left at the bottom of the altar. 13Take
all the fat that covers the inner organs, as well as
the best part of the liver, both kidneys and the fat
around them, and burn them on the altar. 14Take
the bull's meat, skin and intestines, and burn
them outside the camp. This is an offering to take
away sin.

15"Take one of the rams, and have Aaron and
his sons put their hands on its head. 16Kill it, and
take its blood and sprinkle it on all four sides of
the altar. 17Then cut it into pieces and wash its
inner organs and its legs, putting them with its
head and its other pieces. 18Burn the whole ram
on the altar; it is a burnt offering made by fire to
the LORD. Its smell is pleasing to the LORD.

19"Take the other ram, and have Aaron and his
sons put their hands on its head. 20Kill it and take
some of its blood. Put the blood on the bottom of
the right ears of Aaron and his sons and on the
thumbs of their right hands and on the big toes
of their right feet. Then sprinkle the rest of the
blood against all four sides of the altar. 21Take
some of the blood from the altar, and mix it with
the special oil used in appointing priests. Sprinkle
this on Aaron and his clothes, and on his sons
and their clothes. This will show that Aaron
and his sons and their clothes are given to my
service.

22"Then take the fat from the rams, the fat tail
and the fat that covers the inner organs. In addi-
tion, take the best part of the liver, both kidneys,
and the fat around them, and the right thigh.
(This is the ram to be used in appointing priests.)

23"Then take the basket of bread that you
made without yeast, which you put before the
LORD. From it take a loaf of bread, a cake made
with olive oil and a wafer. 24Put all these in the
hands of Aaron and his sons, and tell them to
present them as an offering to the LORD. 25Then
take them from their hands and burn them on the
altar with the whole burnt offering. This is an
offering made by fire to the LORD; its smell is
pleasing to the LORD. 26Then take the breast of the
ram used to appoint Aaron as priest, and present
it before the LORD as an offering. This part of the
animal will be your share. 27Set aside the breast
and the thigh of the sheep that were used to
appoint Aaron and his sons as priests. These parts
belong to them. 28They are to be the regular share
which the Israelites will always give to Aaron
and his sons. It is the gift the Israelites must give to
the LORD from their fellowship offerings.

29"The holy clothes made for Aaron will belong
to his descendants so that they can wear these
clothes when they are appointed as priests.
30Aaron's son, who will become high priest after
Aaron, will come to the Meeting Tent to serve in
the Holy Place. He is to wear these clothes for
seven days.

31"Take the ram used to appoint priests and
boil its meat in a place that is holy. 32Then at the
entrance of the Meeting Tent, Aaron and his sons
must eat the meat of the ram and the bread that
is in the basket. 33They should eat these offerings
that were used to remove their sins and to make
them holy when they were made priests. But no
one else is to eat them, because they are holy
things. 34If any of the meat from that sheep or any
of the bread is left the next morning, it must be
burned. It must not be eaten, because it is holy.

35"Do all these things that I commanded you to
do to Aaron and his sons, and spend seven days
appointing them. 36Each day you are to offer a
bull to remove the sins of Aaron and his sons so
they will be given for service to the LORD. Make
the altar ready for service to the LORD, and pour
oil on it to make it holy. 37Spend seven days mak-
ing the altar ready for service to God and making
it holy. Then the altar will become very holy, and
anything that touches it must be holy.

The Daily Sacrifices

38"Every day from now on, offer on the altar
two lambs that are one year old. 39Offer one lamb
in the morning and the other in the evening be-
fore dark. 40In the morning, when you offer the
first lamb, offer also two litres of fine flour mixed
with one litre of oil from pressed olives. Pour out
one litre of wine as a drink offering. 41Offer the
second lamb in the evening with the same grain
offering and drink offering as you did in the morn-
ing. This is an offering made by fire to the LORD,
and its smell is pleasing to him.

42"You must burn these things as an offering to
the LORD every day, from now on, at the entrance
of the Meeting Tent[d] before the LORD. When you

make the offering, I, the LORD, will meet you there and speak to you. 43I will meet with the people of Israel there, and that place will be holy because of my glory.

44"So I will make the Meeting Tent and the altar holy; I will also make Aaron and his sons holy so they may serve me as priests. 45I will live with the people of Israel and be their God. 46And they will know that I am the LORD their God who led them out of Egypt so that I could live with them. I am the LORD their God.

The Altar for Burning Incense

30 "Make an altar out of acacia wood for burning incense.[d] 2Make it square—50 centimetres long and 50 centimetres wide—and make it 90 centimetres high. The corners that stick out like horns must be one piece with the altar. 3Cover its top, its sides and its corners with pure gold, and put a gold strip all around the altar. 4Make two gold rings beneath the gold strip on opposite sides of the altar, and slide poles through them to carry the altar. 5Make the poles from acacia wood and cover them with gold. 6Put the altar of incense in front of the curtain that is near the Ark[d] of the Agreement, in front of the lid that covers that Ark. There I will meet with you.

7"Aaron must burn sweet-smelling incense on the altar every morning when he comes to take care of the oil lamps. 8He must burn incense again in the evening when he lights the lamps, so incense will burn before the LORD every day from now on. 9Do not use this altar for offering any other incense or burnt offering, or any kind of grain offering or drink offering. 10Once a year Aaron must make the altar ready for service to God by putting blood on its corners—the blood of the animal offered to remove sins. He is to do this once a year from now on. This altar belongs completely to the LORD's service."

The Tax for the Meeting Tent

11The LORD said to Moses, 12"When you count the people of Israel, every person must buy back his life from the LORD so that no terrible things will happen to the people when you number them. 13Every person who is counted must pay 6 grammes of silver. (This is set by using a half of the Holy Place measure, which weighs 11.5 grammes.) This amount is a gift to the LORD. 14Every person who is counted and is 20 years old or older must give this amount to the LORD. 15A rich person must not give more than 6 grammes, and a poor person must not give less. You are paying this to the LORD to buy back your lives. 16Gather from the people of Israel this money paid to buy back their lives, and spend it on things for the service in the Meeting Tent.[d] This payment will remind the LORD that the Israelites' lives have been bought back."

The Bronze Bowl

17The LORD said to Moses, 18"Make a bronze bowl, on a bronze stand, for washing. Put the bowl and stand between the Meeting Tent[d] and the altar, and put water in the bowl. 19Aaron and his sons must wash their hands and feet with the water from this bowl. 20Each time they enter the Meeting Tent they must wash with water so they will not die. Each time they approach the altar to serve as priests and offer a sacrifice to the LORD by fire, 21they must wash their hands and their feet so that they will not die. This is a rule which Aaron and his descendants[d] are to keep from now on."

Oil for Appointing

22Then the LORD said to Moses, 23"Take the finest spices: 6 kilogrammes of liquid myrrh,[d] half that amount (that is, 3 kilogrammes) of sweet-smelling cinnamon, 3 kilogrammes of sweet-smelling cane 24and 6 kilogrammes of cassia.[d] Weigh all these by the Holy Place measure. Also take 4 litres of olive oil, 25and mix all these things like a perfume to make a holy olive oil. This special oil must be put on people and things to make them ready for service to God. 26Put this oil on the Meeting Tent[d] and the Ark[d] of the Agreement, 27on the table and all its dishes, on the lampstand and all its tools, and on the incense[d] altar. 28Also, put the oil on the altar for burnt offerings and on all its tools, as well as on the bowl and the stand under the bowl. 29You will prepare all these things for service to God, and they will be very holy. Anything that touches these things must be holy.

30"Put the oil on Aaron and his sons to give them for service to me, that they may serve me as priests. 31Tell the Israelites, 'This is to be my holy olive oil from now on. It is to be put on people and things to make them ready for service to God. 32Do not pour it on the bodies of ordinary people, and do not make perfume in the same way that you make this oil. It is holy, and you must treat it as holy. 33If anyone makes perfume like it or puts it on someone who is not a priest, that person must be cut off from his people.' "

Incense

34Then the LORD said to Moses, "Take these sweet-smelling spices: resin, onycha, galbanum and pure frankincense.[d] Be sure that you have equal amounts of each. 35Make incense[d] as a person who makes perfume would do. Add salt to it

to keep it pure and holy. 36Beat some of the in-
cense into a fine powder, and put it in front of the
Ark[d] of the Agreement in the Meeting Tent,[d]
where I will meet with you. You must use this
incense powder only for its very special purpose.
37Do not make incense for yourselves in the same
way that you make this incense. Treat it as holy
to the LORD. 38Whoever makes incense like this to
use as perfume must be cut off from his people."

Sidelight Kentucky Fried Chicken isn't the first company to have a secret recipe. In ancient Israel, priests had a secret recipe for the spices in the holy incense (Exodus 30:34–38). Three of the ingredients – resin, galbanum and frankincense – were extracted from plants or trees. Onycha came from a shellfish in the Red Sea.

Bezalel and Oholiab Help

31 Then the LORD said to Moses, 2"See, I
have chosen Bezalel, son of Uri, from the
tribe[d] of Judah. (Uri was the son of Hur.) 3I have
filled Bezalel with the Spirit[d] of God and have
given him the skill, ability and knowledge to do
all kinds of work. 4He is able to design pieces to
be made from gold, silver and bronze, 5to cut
jewels and put them in metal, to carve wood, and
to do all kinds of work. 6I have also chosen Oho-
liab, son of Ahisamach, from the tribe of Dan to
work with Bezalel. I have given skills to all the
craftsmen, and they will be able to make all these
things I have commanded you: 7the Meeting
Tent,[d] the Ark[d] of the Agreement, the lid that
covers the Ark, and everything in the Tent. 8This
includes the table and everything on it, the pure
gold lampstand and everything with it, the altar
of incense,[d] 9the altar for burnt offerings and
everything used with it, and the bowl and the
stand under it. 10They will make the woven
clothes and the holy clothes for Aaron and the
clothes for his sons to wear when they serve as
priests. 11They will also make the special olive oil
used in appointing people and things to the ser-
vice of the LORD, and the sweet-smelling incense
for the Holy Place.

"These workers will make all these things just
as I have commanded you."

The Day of Rest

12Then the LORD said to Moses, 13"Tell the Is-
raelites, 'You must keep the rules about my Sab-
baths,[d] because they will be a sign between you
and me from now on. In this way you will know
that I, the LORD, make you holy.

14" 'Make the Sabbath a holy day. If anyone
treats the Sabbath like any other day, that person
must be put to death; anyone who works on the
Sabbath day must be cut off from his people.
15There are six days for working, but the seventh
day is a day of rest, a day holy for the LORD.
Anyone who works during the Sabbath day must
be put to death. 16The Israelites must remember
the Sabbath day as an agreement between them
and me that will continue from now on. 17The
Sabbath day will be a sign between me and the
Israelites for ever, because in six days I, the LORD,
made the sky and the earth. On the seventh day
I did not work: I rested.' "

18When the LORD finished speaking to Moses
on Mount Sinai, he gave him the two stone tablets
with the Agreement written on them, written by
the finger of God.

The People Make a Gold Calf

32 The people saw that a long time had
passed and Moses had not come down
from the mountain. So they gathered around
Aaron and said, "Moses led us out of Egypt, but
we don't know what has happened to him. Make
us gods who will lead us."

2Aaron said to the people, "Take off the gold
earrings that your wives, sons and daughters are
wearing, and bring them to me." 3So all the peo-
ple took their gold earrings and brought them to
Aaron. 4He took the gold from the people and
formed it with a tool and made a statue of a calf.
Then the people said, "Israel, these are your gods
who brought you out of the land of Egypt!"

5When Aaron saw all this, he built an altar
before the calf and announced, "Tomorrow there
will be a special feast to honour the LORD." 6The
people got up early the next morning and offered
whole burnt offerings and fellowship offerings.
They sat down to eat and drink, and then they
got up and sinned sexually.

7Then the LORD said to Moses, "Go down from
this mountain, because your people, the people
you brought out of the land of Egypt, have ruined
themselves. 8They have quickly turned away
from the things I commanded them to do. They
have made for themselves a calf covered with
gold, and they have worshipped it and offered
sacrifices to it. They have said, 'Israel, these are
your gods who brought you out of Egypt.' "

9The LORD said to Moses, "I have seen these
people, and I know that they are very stubborn.
10So now do not stop me. I am so angry with
them that I am going to destroy them. Then I will
make you and your descendants[d] a great nation."

11But Moses begged the LORD his God and said,
"LORD, don't let your anger destroy your people,
whom you brought out of Egypt with your great

power and strength. 12Don't let the people of
Egypt say, 'The LORD brought the Israelites out of
Egypt for an evil purpose. He planned to kill them
in the mountains and destroy them from the
earth.' So stop being angry, and don't destroy
your people. 13Remember the men who served
you—Abraham, Isaac and Israel. You promised
with an oath to them and said, 'I will make your
descendants as many as the stars in the sky. I will
give your descendants all this land that I have
promised them, and it will be theirs for ever.'"
14So the LORD changed his mind and did not des-
troy the people as he had said he might.
15Then Moses went down the mountain, and
in his hands he had the two stone tablets with the
Agreement on them. The commands were written
on both sides of each stone, front and back. 16God
himself had made the tablets, and God himself
had written the commands on the tablets.
17When Joshua heard the sound of the people
shouting, he said to Moses, "It sounds like war
down in the camp."
18Moses answered:

"It is not a shout of victory;
it is not a cry of defeat.
It is the sound of singing that I hear."

19When Moses came close to the camp, he saw
the gold calf and the dancing, and he became
very angry. He threw down the stone tablets that
he was carrying and broke them at the bottom
of the mountain. 20Then he took the calf that
the people had made and melted it in the fire.

SIN

I Told You So

Peter carefully laid the extra pillows on his bed, fluffing them up to make them look bigger. Then he covered them with the sheets and bedspread. "That should do it," he whispered as he switched the light off.

He slipped over to the window and opened it carefully. Climbing out, he stretched his legs to reach the porch roof below, tiptoed to the edge and climbed down the trellis, carefully avoiding the climbing roses.

Chris and Ben were waiting in the car around the corner. "No problem," Peter said, hopping into the back seat. "They'll never know I've gone. Let's go."

The three friends didn't plan to stay at Sam's too long, but they didn't want to miss his end-of-exams party altogether. Peter had tried to get permission to go, but his parents wouldn't give him a later curfew. So he decided to go without them knowing.

It would have worked, except that the trellis wasn't as strong as he thought. When he returned home four hours later, it gave way beneath his foot, and he yelled with pain as he tumbled into the roses.

When the light came on in his parents' room, Peter knew he was in trouble. What would happen now? he wondered as he sat on the lawn and waited for his dad to appear.

Peter knew what he was doing was wrong, but he did it anyway. In the same way, the Israelites knew that they shouldn't build an idol to worship.

Read **Exodus 32:1–14** to see what happened when they did it anyway.

- What lesson might Peter have learned from the passage if he had read it before climbing out of the window?
- When have you, like the Israelites, doubted God's leadership and disobeyed him? What did you learn about trusting God from that experience?

Consider . . .

- praying that God will give you strength next time you're tempted to do something you know is wrong.
- listening to popular songs on the radio to find out what things people trust instead of God. How is their misplaced trust sinful?

For more, see . . .

- Deuteronomy 32:15–22 (p.196)
- Romans 6:1–7 (p.1191)
- 1 Kings 18:22–39 (p.334)

He ground it into powder. Then he threw the
powder into the water and forced the Israelites
to drink it.
21Moses said to Aaron, "What did these people
do to you? Why did you cause them to do such a
terrible sin?"
22Aaron answered, "Don't be angry, master.
You know that these people are always ready to
do wrong. 23The people said to me, 'Moses led us
out of Egypt, but we don't know what has hap-
pened to him. Make us gods who will lead us.'
24So I told the people, 'Take off your gold jewel-
lery.' When they gave me the gold, I threw it into
the fire and out came this calf!"
25Moses saw that the people were acting
wildly. Aaron had let them get out of control and
become fools in front of their enemies. 26So
Moses stood at the entrance to the camp and
said, "Let anyone who wants to follow the LORD
come to me." And all the people from the family
of Levi gathered around Moses.
27Then Moses said to them, "The LORD, the
God of Israel, says this: 'Every man must put on
his sword and go through the camp from one end
to the other. Each man must kill his brother, his
friend and his neighbour.' " 28The people from
the family of Levi obeyed Moses, and that day
about 3,000 of the Israelites died. 29Then Moses
said, "Today you have been given for service to
the LORD. You were willing to kill your own sons
and brothers, and God has blessed you for this."
30The next day Moses told the people, "You
have done a terrible sin. But now I will go up to
the LORD. Maybe I can do something so your sins
will be removed." 31So Moses went back to the
LORD and said, "How terribly these people have
sinned! They have made for themselves gods
from gold. 32Now, please forgive them this sin. If
you will not, then erase my name from the book
in which you have written the names of your
people."
33But the LORD told Moses, "I will erase from
my book the names of the people who sin against
me. 34So now, go. Lead the people where I have
told you, and my angel will lead you. When the
time comes to punish, I will punish them for
their sin."
35So the LORD caused terrible things to happen
to the people because of what they did with the
calf Aaron had made.

33 Then the LORD said to Moses, "You and
the people you brought out of Egypt
must leave this place. Go to the land that I prom-
ised with an oath to give to Abraham, Isaac and
Jacob when I said, 'I will give that land to your
descendants.' 2I will send an angel to lead you,
and I will force these people out of the land: the
Canaanites, Amorites, Hittites, Perizzites, Hivites
and Jebusites. 3Go up to a fertile land. But I will
not go with you, because I might destroy you on
the way, since you are such a stubborn people."
4When the people heard this bad news, they
became very sad, and none of them put on jewel-
lery. 5This was because the LORD had said to
Moses, "Tell the Israelites, 'You are a stubborn
people. If I were to go with you even for a mo-
ment, I would destroy you. So take off all your
jewellery, and I will decide what to do with
you.' " 6So the people of Israel took off their jew-
ellery at Mount Sinai.

The Meeting Tent

7Moses used to take a tent and set it up a long
way outside the camp; he called it the "Meeting
Tent".[d] Anyone who wanted to ask the LORD
about something would go to the Meeting Tent
outside the camp. 8Whenever Moses went out to
the Tent, all the people would rise and stand at
the entrances of their tents, watching him until
he entered the Meeting Tent. 9When Moses
went into the Tent, the pillar of cloud would al-
ways come down and stay at the entrance of the
Tent while the LORD spoke with Moses. 10When-
ever the people saw the pillar of cloud at the
entrance of the Tent, they stood and worshipped,
each person at the entrance of his own tent.
11The LORD spoke to Moses face to face as a
man speaks with his friend. Then Moses would
return to the camp, but Moses' young helper,
Joshua son of Nun, did not leave the Tent.
12Moses said to the LORD, "You have told me to
lead these people, but you did not say whom you
would send with me. You have said to me, 'I
know you very well, and I am pleased with you.'
13If I have truly pleased you, show me your plans
so that I may know you and continue to please
you. Remember that this nation is your people."
14The LORD answered, "I myself will go with
you, and I will give you victory."
15Then Moses said to him, "If you yourself
don't go with us, then don't send us away from
this place. 16If you don't go with us, no one will
know that you are pleased with me and with
your people. These people and I will be no differ-
ent from any other people on earth."
17Then the LORD said to Moses, "I will do what
you ask, because I know you very well, and I am
pleased with you."

Moses Sees God's Glory

18Then Moses said, "Now, please show me your
glory."
19The LORD answered, "I will cause all
my goodness to pass in front of you, and I will
announce my name, the LORD, so you can
hear it. I will show kindness to anyone to whom

I want to show kindness, and I will show mercy
to anyone to whom I want to show mercy. 20But
you cannot see my face, because no one can see
me and live.
21"There is a place near me where you may
stand on a rock. 22When my glory passes that
place, I will put you in a large crack in the rock
and cover you with my hand until I have passed
by. 23Then I will take away my hand, and you
will see my back. But my face must not be seen."

Moses Gets New Stone Tablets

34 The LORD said to Moses, "Cut two more
stone tablets like the first two, and I will
write the same words on them that were on the
first two stones which you broke. 2Be ready to-
morrow morning, and then come up on Mount
Sinai. Stand before me there on the top of the
mountain. 3No one may come with you or even
be seen anywhere on the mountain. Not even the
flocks or herds may eat grass near that mountain."
4So Moses cut two stone tablets like the first
ones. Then early the next morning he went up
Mount Sinai, just as the LORD had commanded
him, carrying the two stone tablets with him.
5Then the LORD came down in the cloud and
stood there with Moses, and the LORD called out
his name: the LORD.
6The LORD passed in front of Moses and said, "I
am the LORD. The LORD is a God who shows

FORGIVENESS

Sharing the Blame

It was the end of lunch-break at school and Paula's class were in their classroom waiting for the teacher to come and take registration. The game they played whilst waiting had become something of a ritual. The girls had to try and get from one side of the classroom to the other, without the boys catching them. If they got caught they were pelted with rolled up paper and left-over sandwiches. It was a stupid game, but one that they all enjoyed as it secretly gave the boys and girls a chance to seek out their favourites . . .

This particular time, Paula had been caught and was just in the throes of getting a bag of crisps emptied down her neck. The boys were laughing and chanting and the whole scene was quite chaotic. Unfortunately, Mrs Kendon chose that moment to walk through the door.

She blew a fuse! The result being that all the boys got detention. She left the room and went to report the whole incident to the headmaster.

While she was gone, the room became quiet and then one of the girls said: "That's not entirely fair. We were as much to blame as the boys."

The other girls agreed, and as one body, they ran to the headmaster's room and explained that they should be punished too. The head was amazed at the honesty of their confession, but, although he was delighted, he had no alternative but to write out a detention notice for the girls too!

The girls felt strangely relieved. The next day at school, the boys presented the girls with a huge box of chocolates to show their appreciation.

Confession really is good for the soul, read about it in **Exodus 34:4–8**.

- What happens when people confess their guilt, according to verse 7?
- When was the last time you owned up to something to defend someone else?

Consider . . .

- making a chart that shows the consequences of a particular sin, put the sin at the top and then list below it, everything that happens as a result. How does forgiving help the consequences?
- asking God's forgiveness for something you have done, while also asking him to guide you as you deal responsibly with the consequences.

For more, see . . .

- 2 Chronicles 6:24–31 (p.405)
- Luke 17:1–4 (p.1076)
- Psalm 51:1–13 (p.530)

mercy, who is kind, who doesn't become angry
quickly, who has great love and faithfulness 7and
is kind to thousands of people. The LORD forgives
people for evil, for sin and for turning against
him, but he does not forget to punish guilty
people. He will punish not only the guilty peo-
ple, but also their children, their grandchildren,
their great-grandchildren and their great-great-
grandchildren."
8Then Moses quickly bowed to the ground and
worshipped. 9He said, "Lord, if you are pleased
with me, please go with us. I know that these are
stubborn people, but forgive our evil and our sin.
Take us as your own people."
10Then the LORD said, "I am making this agree-
ment with you. I will do miracles[d] in front of all
your people—things that have never before been
done for any other nation on earth—and the peo-
ple with you will see my work. I, the LORD, will
do wonderful things for you. 11Obey the things I
command you today, and I will force out the Am-
orites, Canaanites, Hittites, Perizzites, Hivites
and Jebusites ahead of you. 12Be careful that you
don't make an agreement with the people who
live in the land where you are going, because
it will bring you trouble. 13Destroy their altars,
break their stone pillars and cut down their Ashe-
rah[d] idols. 14Don't worship any other god, be-
cause I, the LORD, the Jealous One, am a jealous
God.
15"Be careful that you don't make an agree-
ment with the people who live in that land.
When they worship their gods, they will invite
you to join them. Then you will eat their sacri-
fices. 16If you choose some of their daughters as
wives for your sons and those daughters worship
gods, they will lead your sons to do the same
thing.
17"Do not make gods of melted metal.
18"Celebrate the Feast[d] of Unleavened Bread.
For seven days you must eat bread made without
yeast as I commanded you. Do this during the
month I have chosen, the month of Abib,[d] be-
cause in that month you came out of Egypt.
19"The firstborn[d] of every mother belongs to
me, including every firstborn male animal that is
born in your flocks and herds. 20You may buy
back a donkey by paying for it with a lamb, but
if you don't want to buy back a donkey, you must
break its neck. You must buy back all your first-
born sons.
"No one is to come before me without a gift.
21"You must work for six days, but on the sev-
enth day you must rest—even during the plant-
ing season and the harvest season.
22"Celebrate the Feast[d] of Weeks when you
gather the first grain of the wheat harvest. And
celebrate the Feast[d] of Shelters in the autumn.
23"Three times each year all your males must
come before the Lord GOD, the God of Israel. 24I
will force out nations ahead of you and expand
the borders of your land. You will go before
the LORD your God three times each year, and at
that time no one will try to take your land from
you.
25"Do not offer the blood of a sacrifice to me
with anything containing yeast, and do not leave
any of the sacrifice of the Feast[d] of Passover until
the next morning.
26"Bring the best first crops that you harvest
from your ground to the Tent[d] of the LORD
your God.
"You must not cook a young goat in its
mother's milk."
27Then the LORD said to Moses, "Write down
these words, because with these words I have
made an agreement with you and Israel."
28Moses stayed there with the LORD 40 days
and 40 nights, and during that time he did not eat
food or drink water. And Moses wrote the words
of the Agreement—the Ten Commandments—
on the stone tablets.

The Face of Moses Shines

29Then Moses came down from Mount Sinai,
carrying the two stone tablets of the Agreement
in his hands. But he did not know that his face
was shining because he had talked with the LORD.
30When Aaron and all the people of Israel saw
that Moses' face was shining, they were afraid to
go near him. 31But Moses called to them, so
Aaron and all the leaders of the people returned
to Moses, and he talked with them. 32After that,
all the people of Israel came near him, and he
gave them all the commands that the LORD had
given him on Mount Sinai.
33When Moses finished speaking to the peo-
ple, he put a covering over his face. 34Whenever
Moses went before the LORD to speak with him,
Moses took off the covering until he came out.
Then Moses would come out and tell the Israel-
ites what the LORD had commanded. 35They
would see that Moses' face was shining. So he
would cover his face again until the next time he
went in to speak with the LORD.

Rules About the Sabbath

35 Moses gathered all the Israelite commu-
nity together and said to them, "These
are the things the LORD has commanded you to
do. 2You are to work for six days, but the seventh
day will be a holy day, a Sabbath[d] of rest to hon-
our the LORD. Anyone who works on that day
must be put to death. 3On the Sabbath day you
must not light a fire in any of your houses."

4Moses said to all the Israelites, "This is what
the LORD has commanded: 5From what you have,
take an offering for the LORD. Let everyone who is
willing bring this offering to the LORD: gold, silver,
bronze, 6blue, purple and red thread, and fine
linen, goat hair 7and rams' skins that are coloured
red. They may also bring fine leather, acacia
wood, 8olive oil for the lamps, spices for the spe-
cial olive oil used for appointing priests and for
the sweet-smelling incense,[d] 9onyx stones and
other jewels to be put on the holy robe[d] and
chest covering of the priests.
10"Let all the skilled workers come and make
everything the LORD commanded: 11the Holy
Tent,[d] its outer tent and its covering, the hooks,
frames, crossbars, posts and bases; 12the Ark[d] of
the Agreement, its poles, lid and the curtain in
front of it; 13the table and its poles, all the things
that go with the table, and the bread that shows
we are in God's presence; 14the lampstand for the
light and all the things that go with it, the lamps
and olive oil for the light; 15the altar of incense
and its poles, the special oil and the sweet-
smelling incense, the curtain for the entrance of
the Meeting Tent; 16the altar of burnt offering
and its bronze screen, its poles and all its tools,
the bronze bowl and its base; 17the curtains
around the courtyard, their posts and bases, and
the curtain at the entrance to the courtyard; 18the
pegs of the Holy Tent and of the courtyard and
their ropes; 19the special clothes that the priest
will wear in the Holy Place. These are the holy
clothes for Aaron the priest and his sons to wear
when they serve as priests."
20Then all the people of Israel went away from
Moses. 21Everyone who wanted to give, came
and brought a gift to the LORD for making the
Meeting Tent, all the things in the Tent, and the
special clothes. 22All the men and women who
wanted to give, brought gold jewellery of all
kinds—pins, earrings, rings and bracelets. They
all presented their gold to the LORD. 23Everyone
who had blue, purple and red thread, and fine
linen, and anyone who had goat hair or ram's
skins coloured red or fine leather brought them to
the LORD. 24Everyone who could give silver or
bronze brought that as a gift to the LORD, and
everyone who had acacia wood to be used in the
work brought it. 25Every skilled woman used her
hands to make the blue, purple and red thread,
and fine linen, and they brought what they had
made. 26All the women who were skilled and
wanted to help made thread of the goat hair.
27The leaders brought onyx stones and other jew-
els to put on the holy robe and chest covering for
the priest. 28They also brought spices and olive oil
for the sweet-smelling incense, the special oil,
and the oil to burn in the lamps. 29All the men
and women of Israel who wanted to help brought
gifts to the LORD for all the work the LORD had
commanded Moses and the people to do.
30Then Moses said to the Israelites, "Look, the
LORD has chosen Bezalel, son of Uri, the son of
Hur, from the tribe[d] of Judah. 31The LORD has
filled Bezalel with the Spirit[d] of God and has
given him the skill, ability and knowledge to do
all kinds of work. 32He is able to design pieces
to be made of gold, silver and bronze, 33to cut
stones and jewels and put them in metal, to carve
wood, and to do all kinds of work. 34Also, the
LORD has given Bezalel and Oholiab, the son of
Ahisamach from the tribe of Dan, the ability to
teach others. 35The LORD has given them the skill
to do all kinds of work. They are able to cut
designs in metal and stone. They can plan and
sew designs in the fine linen with the blue, pur-
ple and red thread. And they are also able to
36 weave things. 1So Bezalel, Oholiab and
every skilled person will do the work the
LORD has commanded, because he gave them the
wisdom and understanding to do all the skilled
work needed to build the Holy Tent."
2Then Moses called Bezalel, Oholiab and all
the other skilled people to whom the LORD had
given skills, and they came because they wanted
to help with the work. 3They received from
Moses everything the people of Israel had
brought as gifts to build the Holy Tent. The peo-
ple continued to bring gifts each morning because
they wanted to. 4So all the skilled workers left the
work they were doing on the Holy Tent, 5and
they said to Moses, "The people are bringing
more than we need to do the work the LORD
commanded."
6Then Moses sent this command throughout
the camp: "No man or woman should make any-
thing else as a gift for the Holy Tent." So the
people were kept from giving more, 7because
what they had was already more than enough to
do all the work.

The Holy Tent

8Then the skilled workers made the Holy
Tent.[d] They made the ten curtains of blue, purple
and red cloth, and they sewed designs of crea-
tures with wings on the curtains. 9Each curtain
was the same size—14 metres long and 2 metres
wide. 10Five of the curtains were fastened to-
gether to make one set, and the other five were
fastened together to make another set. 11Then
they made loops of blue cloth along the edge of
the end curtain on the first set of five, and they
did the same thing with the other set of five.
12There were 50 loops on one curtain and 50
loops on the other curtain, with the loops oppo-
site each other. 13They made 50 gold hooks to join

the two curtains together so that the Holy Tent was joined together as one piece.

[14]Then the workers made another tent of eleven curtains made of goat hair, to put over the Holy Tent. [15]All eleven curtains were the same size—15 metres long and 2 metres wide. [16]The workers sewed five curtains together into one set and six together into another set. [17]They made 50 loops along the edge of the outside curtain of one set and 50 loops along the edge of the outside curtain of the other set. [18]Then they made 50 bronze rings to join the two sets of cloth together and make the tent one piece. [19]They made two more coverings for the outer tent—one made of ram's skins coloured red and the other made of fine leather.

> **Sidelight**
>
> Goat hair was good material for building the Holy Tent (Exodus 36:14–19). When it's dry, it's open and airy, making it cooler inside. But when it rains, the goat hairs expand and keep the moisture out.

[20]Then they made upright frames of acacia wood for the Holy Tent. [21]Each frame was 5 metres tall and 70 centimetres wide, [22]and there were two pegs side by side on each one. Every frame of the Holy Tent was made in this way. [23]They made 20 frames for the south side of the Tent, [24]and they made 40 silver bases that went under the 20 frames. There were two bases for every frame—one for each peg of each frame. [25]They also made 20 frames for the north side of the Holy Tent [26]and 40 silver bases—two to go under each frame. [27]They made six frames for the rear or west end of the Holy Tent [28]and two frames for the corners at the rear of the Holy Tent. [29]These two frames were doubled at the bottom and joined at the top with a metal ring. They did this for each of these corners. [30]So there were eight frames and sixteen silver bases—two bases under each frame.

[31]Then they made crossbars of acacia wood to connect the upright frames of the Holy Tent. Five crossbars held the frames together on one side of the Tent, [32]and five held the frames together on the other side. Also, five crossbars held the frames together on the west end, at the rear of the Tent. [33]They made the middle crossbar run along the entire length of each side and rear of the Tent. It was set halfway up the frames. [34]They made gold rings on the sides of the frames to hold the crossbars, and they covered the frames and the crossbars with gold.

[35]Then they made the curtain of blue, purple and red thread, and fine linen. A skilled craftsman sewed designs of creatures with wings on it. [36]They made four posts of acacia wood for it and covered them with gold. Then they made gold hooks for the posts, as well as four silver bases in which to set the posts. [37]For the entrance to the Tent, they made a curtain of blue, purple and red thread, and fine linen. A person who sewed well, sewed designs on it. [38]Then they made five posts and hooks for it. They covered the tops of the posts and their bands with gold, and they made five bronze bases for the posts.

The Ark of the Agreement

37 Bezalel made the Ark[d] of acacia wood; it was 110 centimetres long, 70 centimetres wide and 70 centimetres high. [2]He covered it, both inside and out, with pure gold, and he put a gold strip around it. [3]He made four gold rings for it and attached them to its four feet, with two rings on each side. [4]Then he made poles of acacia wood and covered them with gold. [5]He put the poles through the rings on each side of the Ark to carry it. [6]Then he made a lid of pure gold that was 110 centimetres long and 70 centimetres wide. [7]Then Bezalel hammered gold to make two creatures with wings and attached them to each end of the lid. [8]He made one creature on one end of the lid and the other creature on the other end. He attached them to the lid so that it would be one piece. [9]The creatures' wings were spread upwards, covering the lid, and the creatures faced each other across the lid.

The Table

[10]Then he made the table of acacia wood; it was 90 centimetres long, 50 centimetres wide and 70 centimetres high. [11]He covered it with pure gold and put a gold strip around it. [12]He made a frame 8 centimetres high that stood up all around the edge, and he put a gold strip around it. [13]Then he made four gold rings for the table and attached them to the four corners of the table where the four legs were. [14]The rings were put close to the frame around the top of the table, because they held the poles for carrying it. [15]The poles for carrying the table were made of acacia wood and were covered with gold. [16]He made of pure gold all the things that were used on the table: the plates, bowls, cups and jars used for pouring the drink offerings.

The Lampstand

[17]Then he made the lampstand of pure gold, hammering out its base and stand. Its flower-like cups, buds and petals were joined together in one piece with the base and stand. [18]Six branches

went out from the sides of the lampstand—three on one side and three on the other. 19Each branch had three cups shaped like almond flowers, and each cup had a bud and a petal. Each of the six branches going out from the lampstand was the same. 20There were four more cups shaped like almond flowers on the lampstand itself, each with its buds and petals. 21Three pairs of branches went out from the lampstand. A bud was under the place where each pair was attached to the lampstand. Each of the six branches going out from the lampstand was the same. 22The buds, branches and lampstand were all one piece of pure, hammered gold. 23He made seven pure gold lamps for this lampstand, and he made pure gold wick trimmers and trays. 24He used about 35 kilogrammes of pure gold to make the lampstand and all the things that went with it.

The Altar for Burning Incense

25Then he made the altar of incense[d] out of acacia wood. It was square—50 centimetres long and 50 centimetres wide—and it was 90 centimetres high. Each corner that stuck out like a horn was joined into one piece with the altar. 26He covered the top and all the sides and the corners with pure gold, and he put gold trim around the altar. 27He made two gold rings and put them below the trim on opposite sides of the altar; these rings held the poles for carrying it. 28He made the poles of acacia wood and covered them with gold.

29Then he made the holy olive oil for appointing the priests and the pure, sweet-smelling incense. He made them like a person who mixes perfumes.

The Altar for Burnt Offerings

38 Then he built the altar for burnt offerings out of acacia wood. The altar was square—2.5 metres long and 2.5 metres wide—and it was 1.5 metres high. 2He made each corner stick out like a horn so that the horns and the altar were joined together in one piece. Then he covered the altar with bronze. 3He made all the tools of bronze to use on the altar: the pots, shovels, bowls for sprinkling blood, meat forks and pans for carrying the fire. 4He made a large bronze screen to hold the burning wood for the altar and put it inside the altar, under its rim, halfway up from the bottom. 5He made bronze rings to hold the poles for carrying the altar, and he put them at the four corners of the screen. 6Then he made poles of acacia wood and covered them with bronze. 7He put the poles through the rings on both sides of the altar, to carry it. He made the altar of boards and left the inside hollow.

The Bronze Bowl

8He made the bronze bowl for washing, and he built it on a bronze stand. He used the bronze from mirrors that belonged to the women who served at the entrance to the Meeting Tent.[d]

The Courtyard of the Holy Tent

9Then he made a wall of curtains to form a courtyard around the Holy Tent.[d] On the south side the curtains were 50 metres long and were made of fine linen. 10The curtains hung on silver hooks and bands, placed on 20 bronze posts with 20 bronze bases. 11On the north side the wall of curtains was also 50 metres long, and it hung on silver hooks and bands on 20 posts with 20 bronze bases.

12On the west side of the courtyard, the wall of curtains was 25 metres long. It was held up by silver hooks and bands on ten posts with ten bases. 13The east side was also 25 metres long. 14On one side of the entry there was a wall of curtains 7.5 metres long, held up by three posts and three bases. 15On the other side of the entry there was also a wall of curtains 7.5 metres long, held up by three posts and three bases. 16All the curtains around the courtyard were made of fine linen. 17The bases for the posts were made of bronze. The hooks and the bands on the posts were made of silver, and the tops of the posts were covered with silver also. All the posts in the courtyard had silver bands.

18The curtain for the entrance of the courtyard was made of blue, purple and red thread, and fine linen, sewn by a person who could sew well. The curtain was 10 metres long and 2.5 metres high, the same height as the curtains around the courtyard. 19It was held up by four posts and four bronze bases. The hooks and bands on the posts were made of silver, and the tops on the posts were covered with silver. 20All the tent pegs for the Holy Tent and for the curtains around the courtyard were made of bronze.

21This is a list of the materials used to make the Holy Tent, where the Agreement was kept. Moses ordered the Levites to make this list, and Ithamar, son of Aaron, was in charge of keeping it. 22Bezalel, son of Uri, the son of Hur, of the tribe[d] of Judah, made everything the LORD commanded Moses. 23Oholiab, son of Ahisamach, of the tribe of Dan, helped him. He could cut designs into metal and stone; he was a designer and also skilled at sewing the blue, purple and red thread, and fine linen.

24The total amount of gold used to build the Holy Tent was presented to the LORD. It weighed about a tonne, as set by the Holy Place measure.

25The silver was given by the members of the community who were counted. It weighed 3.5 tonnes, as set by the Holy Place measure. 26All the men 20 years old or older were counted. There were 603,550 men, and each man had to pay 6 grammes of silver, as set by the Holy Place measure. 27Of this silver, 3.5 tonnes were used to make the 100 bases for the Holy Tent and for the curtain—35 kilogrammes of silver in each base. 28They used 20 kilogrammes of silver to make the hooks for the posts and to cover the tops of the posts and to make the bands on them.

29The bronze which was presented to the LORD weighed about 2.5 tonnes. 30They used the bronze to make the bases at the entrance of the Meeting Tent, to make the altar and the bronze screen, and to make all the tools for the altar. 31This bronze was also used to make bases for the wall of curtains around the courtyard and bases for curtains at the entry to the courtyard, as well as to make the tent pegs for the Holy Tent and the curtains that surrounded the courtyard.

Clothes for the Priests

39 They used blue, purple and red thread to make woven clothes for the priests to wear when they served in the Holy Place. They made the holy clothes for Aaron as the LORD had commanded Moses.

2They made the holy robe[d] of gold and blue, purple and red thread, and fine linen. 3They hammered the gold into sheets and then cut it into long, thin strips. They worked the gold into the blue, purple and red thread, and fine linen. This was done by skilled craftsmen. 4They made the shoulder straps for the holy robe, which were attached to the top corners of the robe and tied together over each shoulder. 5The skilfully woven belt was made in the same way; it was joined to the holy robe as one piece. It was made of gold and blue, purple and red thread, and fine linen, in the way the LORD commanded Moses.

6They put gold around the onyx stones and then wrote the names of the sons of Israel on these gems, as a person carves words and designs on a seal.[d] 7Then they attached the gems on the shoulder straps of the holy robe, as reminders of the twelve sons of Israel. This was done just as the LORD had commanded Moses.

8The skilled craftsmen made the chest covering like the holy robe; it was made of gold and blue, purple and red thread, and fine linen. 9The chest covering was square—23 centimetres long and 23 centimetres wide—and it was folded double to make a pocket. 10Then they put four rows of beautiful jewels on it: in the first row there was a ruby, a topaz and a yellow quartz; 11in the second there was a turquoise, a sapphire and an emerald; 12in the third there was a jacinth, an agate and an amethyst; 13in the fourth there was a chrysolite, an onyx and a jasper. Gold was put around these jewels to attach them to the chest covering, 14and the names of the sons of Israel were carved on these twelve jewels as a person carves a seal. Each jewel had the name of one of the twelve tribes[d] of Israel.

15They made chains of pure gold, twisted together like a rope, for the chest covering. 16The workers made two gold pieces and two gold rings. They put the two gold rings on the two upper corners of the chest covering. 17Then they put two gold chains in the two rings at the ends of the chest covering, 18and they fastened the other two ends of the chains to the two gold pieces. They attached these gold pieces to the two shoulder straps in the front of the holy robe. 19They made two gold rings and put them at the lower corners of the chest covering on the inside edge next to the holy robe. 20They made two more gold rings on the bottom of the shoulder straps in front of the holy robe, near the seam, just above the woven belt of the holy robe. 21They used a blue ribbon and tied the rings of the chest covering to the rings of the holy robe, connecting it to the woven belt. So that the chest covering would not swing out from the holy robe. They did all these things in the way the LORD commanded.

22Then they made the outer robe to be worn under the holy robe. It was woven only of blue cloth. 23They made a hole in the centre of the outer robe, with a woven collar sewn around it so it would not tear. 24Then they made balls like pomegranates[d] of blue, purple and red thread, and fine linen, and hung them around the bottom of the outer robe. 25They also made bells of pure gold and hung these around the bottom of the outer robe between the balls. 26So around the bottom of the outer robe there was a bell and a pomegranate ball, a bell and a pomegranate ball. The priest wore this outer robe when he served as priest, just as the LORD had commanded Moses.

27They wove inner robes of fine linen for Aaron and his sons, 28and they made turbans, headbands and underclothes of fine linen. 29Then they made the cloth belt of fine linen, and blue, purple and red thread, and designs were sewn onto it, just as the LORD had commanded Moses.

30They made a strip of pure gold, which is the holy crown, and carved these words in the gold, as one might carve on a seal: "Holy to the LORD". 31Then they tied this flat piece to the turban with a blue ribbon, as the LORD had commanded Moses.

32So all the work on the Meeting Tent[d] was finished. The Israelites did everything just as the

LORD had commanded Moses. [33]Then they brought the Holy Tent to Moses: the Tent and all its furniture, hooks, frames, crossbars, posts and bases; [34]the covering made of rams' skins coloured red, the covering made of fine leather and the curtain that covered the entrance to the Most Holy Place; [35]the Ark[d] of the Agreement, its poles and lid; [36]the table, all its containers, and the bread that showed they were in God's presence; [37]the pure gold lampstand with its lamps in a row, all its tools and the olive oil for the light; [38]the gold altar, the special olive oil used for appointing priests, the sweet-smelling incense,[d] and the curtain that covered the entrance to the Tent; [39]the bronze altar and its screen, its poles and all its tools, the bowl and its stand; and [40]the curtains for the courtyard with their posts and bases, the curtain that covered the entrance to the courtyard, the cords, pegs, and all the things in the Meeting Tent. [41]They brought the clothes for the priests to wear when they served in the Holy Tent—the holy clothes for Aaron the priest and the clothes for his sons, which they wore when they served as priests.

[42]The Israelites had done all this work just as the LORD had commanded Moses. [43]Moses looked closely at all the work and saw they had done it just as the LORD had commanded. So Moses blessed them.

Setting Up the Holy Tent

40 Then the LORD said to Moses: [2]"On the first day of the first month, set up the Holy Tent,[d] which is the Meeting Tent. [3]Put the Ark[d] of the Agreement in it and hang the curtain in front of the Ark. [4]Bring in the table and arrange everything on the table that should be there. Then bring in the lampstand and set up its lamps. [5]Put the gold altar for burning incense[d] in front of the Ark of the Agreement, and put the curtain at the entrance to the Holy Tent.

[6]"Put the altar of burnt offerings in front of the entrance of the Holy Tent, the Meeting Tent. [7]Put the bowl between the Meeting Tent and the altar, and put water in it. [8]Set up the courtyard around the Holy Tent, and put the curtain at the entrance to the courtyard.

[9]"Use the special olive oil and pour it on the Holy Tent and everything in it, in order to give the Tent and all that is in it for service to the LORD. They will be holy. [10]Pour the special oil on the altar for burnt offerings and on all its tools. Give the altar for service to God, and it will be very holy. [11]Then pour the special olive oil on the bowl and the base under it so that they will be given for service to God.

[12]"Bring Aaron and his sons to the entrance of the Meeting Tent, and wash them with water. [13]Then put the holy clothes on Aaron. Pour the special oil on him, and give him for service to God so that he may serve me as a priest. [14]Bring Aaron's sons and put the inner robes on them. [15]Pour the special oil on them in the same way that you appointed their father as priest, so that they may also serve me as priests. Pouring oil on them will make them a family of priests, they and their descendants[d] from now on." [16]Moses did everything that the LORD commanded him.

[17]So the Holy Tent was set up on the first day of the first month during the second year after they left Egypt. [18]When Moses set up the Holy Tent, he put the bases in place, and he put the frames on the bases. Next he put the crossbars through the rings of the frames and set up the posts. [19]After that, Moses spread the cloth over the Holy Tent and put the covering over it, just as the LORD commanded.

[20]Moses put the stone tablets that had the Agreement written on them into the Ark. He put the poles through the rings of the Ark and put the lid on it. [21]Next he brought the Ark into the Tent and hung the curtain to cover the Ark, just as the LORD commanded him.

[22]Moses put the table in the Meeting Tent on the north side of the Holy Tent in front of the curtain. [23]Then he put the bread on the table before the LORD, just as the LORD commanded him. [24]Moses put the lampstand in the Meeting Tent on the south side of the Holy Tent across from the table. [25]Then he put the lamps on the lampstand before the LORD, just as the LORD commanded him.

[26]Moses put the gold altar for burning incense in the Meeting Tent in front of the curtain. [27]Then he burned sweet-smelling incense on it, just as the LORD commanded him. [28]Then he hung the curtain at the entrance to the Holy Tent.

[29]He put the altar for burnt offerings at the entrance to the Holy Tent, the Meeting Tent, and offered a whole burnt offering and grain offerings on it, just as the LORD commanded him. [30]Moses put the bowl between the Meeting Tent and the altar for burnt offerings, and he put water in it for washing. [31]Moses, Aaron and Aaron's sons used this water to wash their hands and feet. [32]They washed themselves every time they entered the Meeting Tent and every time they went near the altar for burnt offerings, just as the LORD commanded Moses.

[33]Then Moses set up the courtyard around the Holy Tent and the altar, and he put up the curtain at the entrance to the courtyard. So Moses finished the work.

The Cloud Over the Holy Tent

34Then the cloud covered the Meeting Tent,[d]
and the glory of the LORD filled the Holy Tent.
35Moses could not enter the Meeting Tent,
because the cloud had settled on it, and the glory
of the LORD filled the Holy Tent.

36When the cloud rose from the Holy Tent, the
Israelites would begin to travel, 37but as long as
the cloud stayed on the Holy Tent, they did not
travel. They stayed in that place until the cloud
rose. 38So the cloud of the LORD was over the Holy
Tent during the day, and there was a fire in the
cloud at night. So all the Israelites could see the
cloud while they travelled.

Leviticus

When?

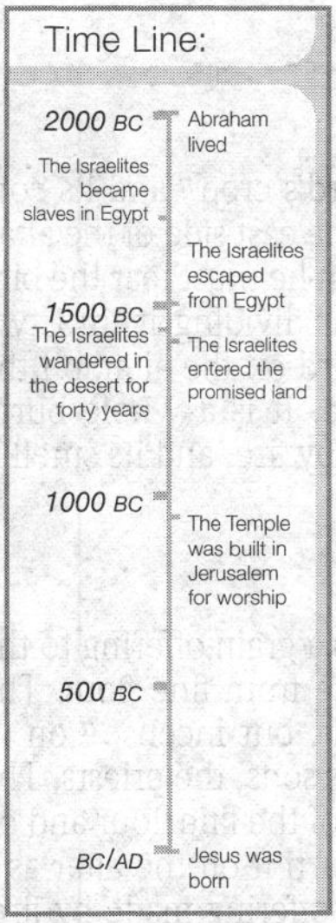

Why Read This Book:

- Discover how worshipping God today is different from how it used to be (Leviticus 1 – 7).
- Learn ancient laws people followed to obey God (Leviticus 18 – 20).
- Find out how people used to be punished for disobeying God's laws (Leviticus 24 – 26).

Behind the Scenes:

If you were a boy in ancient Israel and your great-great-great-grandfather was named Levi, you would be born with your career already planned. You would know where to live, what to wear, and exactly how to do your job. That's because the descendants of Levi – the Levites – were Israel's original priests. And Leviticus was the manual that they followed in leading people in worship.

The priests were the religious leaders in the Old Testament. They served God by preparing sacrifices to God from the people. People offered sacrifices to thank God and to ask for forgiveness for sins.

Priests were also responsible for maintaining the meeting place or "tabernacle". Many of the regulations in Leviticus deal with worship in the Meeting Tent – a portable sanctuary used as the Israelites wandered in the wilderness after being freed from slavery in Egypt. The worship regulations also applied to the Temple when it was built in Jerusalem about 350 years later.

This book is sometimes difficult for us to follow. It's filled with detailed (sometimes repulsive) instructions about animal sacrifices, building the Temple, and celebrating various religious festivals. It also contains explicit guidelines for all people about diet, sexuality, personal relationships and other areas of life. ▷

Where?

Where different worship acts took place in the Meeting Tent.

Behind the Scenes (cont.): Many of the guidelines seem irrelevant to us today. But behind all the details are themes that help us to understand what it means to follow God today. God wants a relationship with us, but we must first admit our sins and accept God's forgiveness. And God expects believers to live their lives in ways that are pleasing to him. As Leviticus 19:2 says: "I am the LORD your God. You must be holy because I am holy."

The Burnt Offering

1 The LORD called to Moses and spoke to him from the Meeting Tent,[d] saying, 2"Tell the people of Israel: 'When you bring an offering to the LORD, bring as your offering an animal from the herd or flock.

3" 'If the offering is a whole burnt offering from the herd, it must be a male that has nothing wrong with it. The person must take the animal to the entrance of the Meeting Tent so that the LORD will accept the offering. 4He must put his hand on the animal's head, and the LORD will accept it to remove the person's sin so that he will once again belong to God. 5He must kill the young bull before the LORD, and Aaron's sons, the priests, must bring its blood and sprinkle it on all sides of the altar at the entrance to the Meeting Tent. 6After that he will skin the animal and cut it into pieces. 7The priests, when they have put wood and fire on the altar, 8are to lay the head, the fat and other pieces on the wood that is on the fire of the altar. 9The animal's inner organs and legs must be washed with water. Then the priest must burn all the animal's parts on the altar. It is a whole burnt offering, an offering made by fire, and its smell is pleasing to the LORD.

10" 'If the burnt offering is a sheep or a goat from the flock, it must be a male that has nothing wrong with it. 11The person must kill the animal on the north side of the altar before the LORD, and Aaron's sons, the priests, must sprinkle its blood on all sides of the altar. 12The person must cut the animal into pieces, and the priest must lay them, with the head and fat, on the wood that is on the fire of the altar. 13The person must wash the animal's inner organs and legs with water, and then the priest must burn all its parts on the altar. It is a whole burnt offering, an offering made by fire, and its smell is pleasing to the LORD.

14" 'If the whole burnt offering for the LORD is a bird, it must be a dove or a young pigeon. 15The priest will bring it to the altar and pull off its head, which he will burn on the altar; the bird's blood must be drained out on the side of the altar. 16The priest must remove the bird's crop[n] and its contents and throw them on the east side of the altar, where the ashes are. 17Then he must tear the bird open by its wings without dividing it into two parts. He must burn the bird on the altar, on the wood which is on the fire. It is a whole burnt offering, an offering made by fire, and its smell is pleasing to the LORD.

The Grain Offering

2 " 'When anyone offers a grain offering to the LORD, it must be made from fine flour. The person must pour oil on it, put incense[d] on it, 2and then take it to Aaron's sons, the priests. The priest must take a handful of the fine flour and oil and all the incense, and burn it on the altar as a memorial portion. It is an offering made by fire, and its smell is pleasing to the LORD. 3The rest of the grain offering will belong to Aaron and the priests; it is a most holy part of the offerings made by fire to the LORD.

4" 'If you bring a grain offering that was baked in the oven, it must be made from fine flour. It may be loaves made without yeast and mixed with oil, or it may be wafers made without yeast that have oil poured over them. 5If your grain offering is cooked on a griddle, it must be made, without yeast, of fine flour mixed with oil. 6Crumble it and pour oil over it; it is a grain offering. 7If your grain offering is cooked in a pan, it must be made from fine flour and oil. 8Bring the grain offering made of these things to the LORD. Give it to the priest, and he will take it to the altar. 9He will take out the memorial portion from the grain offering and burn it on the altar, as an offering made by fire. Its smell is pleasing to the LORD. 10The rest of the grain offering belongs to Aaron and the priests. It is a most holy part of the offerings made to the LORD by fire.

11" 'Every grain offering you bring to the LORD must be made without yeast, because you must not burn any yeast or honey in an offering made by fire to the LORD. 12You may bring yeast and honey to the LORD as an offering from the first

crop A small bag inside a bird's throat. When a bird eats, its food goes into this part first. There, the food is made soft before it goes into the stomach.

harvest, but they must not be burned on the altar
as a pleasing smell. 13You must also put salt on all
your grain offerings. Salt stands for your agree-
ment with God that will last for ever; do not
leave it out of your grain offering. You must add
salt to all your offerings.
14" 'If you bring a grain offering from the first
harvest to the LORD, bring crushed heads of new
grain roasted in the fire. 15Put oil and incense on
it; it is a grain offering. 16The priest will burn the
memorial portion of the crushed grain and oil,
with the incense on it. It is an offering by fire to
the LORD.

The Fellowship Offering

3 " 'If a person's fellowship offering to the
LORD is from the herd, it may be a male or
female, but it must have nothing wrong with it.
2The person must put his hand on the animal's
head and kill it at the entrance to the Meeting
Tent.[d] Then Aaron's sons, the priests, must
sprinkle the blood on all sides of the altar. 3From
the fellowship offering he must make a sacrifice
by fire to the LORD. He must offer the fat of the
animal's inner organs (both the fat that is in them
and that covers them), 4both kidneys with the fat
that is on them near the lower back muscle, and
the best part of the liver, which he will remove
with the kidneys. 5Then the priests will burn
these parts on the altar, on the whole burnt offer-
ing that is on the wood of the fire. It is an offering
made by fire, and its smell is pleasing to the LORD.
6" 'If a person's fellowship offering to the LORD
is a lamb or a goat, it may be a male or female,
but it must have nothing wrong with it. 7If he
offers a lamb, he must bring it before the LORD
8and put his hand on its head. Then he must kill
the animal in front of the Meeting Tent, and the
priests must sprinkle its blood on all sides of the
altar. 9From the fellowship offering the person
must make a sacrifice by fire to the LORD. He must
bring the fat, the whole fat tail cut off close to the
backbone, the fat of the inner organs (both the fat
that is in them and that covers them), 10both kid-
neys with the fat that is on them, near the lower
back muscle, and the best part of the liver, which
he will remove with the kidneys. 11Then the
priest will burn these parts on the altar as food; it
will be an offering made by fire to the LORD.
12" 'If a person's offering is a goat, he must
offer it before the LORD 13and put his hand on its
head. Then he must kill it in front of the Meeting
Tent, and the priests must sprinkle its blood on all
sides of the altar. 14From this offering the person
must make a sacrifice by fire to the LORD. He must
offer all the fat of the goat's inner organs (both
the fat that is in them and that covers them),
15both kidneys with the fat that is on them near
the lower back muscle, and the best part of the
liver, which he will remove with the kidneys.
16The priest will burn these parts on the altar as
food. It is an offering made by fire, and its smell
is pleasing to the LORD. All the fat belongs to the
LORD.
17" 'This law will continue for people from
now on, wherever you live: you must not eat any
fat or blood.' "

The Sin Offering

4 The LORD said to Moses, 2"Tell the people of
Israel this: 'When a person sins by accident
and does some things the LORD has commanded
not to be done, that person must do these things:
3" 'If the appointed priest sins so that he brings
guilt on the people, then he must offer a young
bull to the LORD, one that has nothing wrong with
it, as a sin offering for the sin he has done. 4He
will bring the bull to the entrance of the Meeting
Tent[d] in front of the LORD, put his hand on its
head, and kill it before the LORD. 5Then the ap-
pointed priest must bring some of the bull's blood
into the Meeting Tent. 6The priest is to dip his
finger into the blood and sprinkle it seven times
before the LORD in front of the curtain of the Most
Holy Place. 7The priest must also put some of the
blood on the corners of the altar of incense[d] that
stands before the LORD in the Meeting Tent. The
rest of the blood he must pour out at the bottom
of the altar of burnt offering, which is at the en-
trance of the Meeting Tent. 8He must remove all
the fat from the bull of the sin offering—the fat
on and around the inner organs, 9both kidneys
with the fat that is on them near the lower back
muscle, and the best part of the liver which he
will remove with the kidneys. 10(He must do this
in the same way that the fat is removed from the
bull of the fellowship offering.) Then the priest
must burn the animal parts on the altar of burnt
offering. 11But the priest must carry off the skin of
the bull and all its meat, along with the rest of the
bull—its head, legs, intestines and other inner
organs. 12He must take it outside the camp to the
special clean[d] place where the ashes are poured
out. He must burn it on a wood fire on the pile
of ashes.

Sidelight

Collecting the church offering these days is simple compared with the offerings described in Leviticus 4:4–12. Imagine removing livers, kidneys, intestines and other inner organs from a sacrificed bull. Other animals sacrificed were sheep, goats, doves and pigeons.

13" 'If the whole nation of Israel sins accidentally without knowing it and does something the LORD has commanded not to be done, they are guilty. 14When they learn about the sin they have done, they must offer a young bull as a sin offering and bring it before the Meeting Tent. 15The elders of the group of people must put their hands on the bull's head before the LORD, and it must be killed before the LORD. 16Then the appointed priest must bring some of the bull's blood into the Meeting Tent. 17Dipping his finger in the blood, he must sprinkle it seven times before the LORD in front of the curtain. 18Then he must put some of the blood on the corners of the altar that is before the LORD in the Meeting Tent. The priest must pour out the rest of the blood at the bottom of the altar of burnt offering, which is at the entrance to the Meeting Tent. 19He must remove all the fat from the animal and burn it on the altar; 20he will do the same thing with this bull that he did with the first bull of the sin offering. In this way the priest removes the sins of the people so they will belong to the LORD and be forgiven. 21Then the priest must carry the bull outside the camp and burn it, just as he did with the first bull. This is the sin offering for the whole community.

22" 'If a ruler sins by accident and does something the LORD his God has commanded must not be done, he is guilty. 23When he learns about his sin, he must bring a male goat that has nothing wrong with it as his offering. 24The ruler must put his hand on the goat's head and kill it in the place where they kill the whole burnt offering before the LORD; it is a sin offering. 25The priest must take some of the blood of the sin offering on his finger and put it on the corners of the altar of burnt offering. He must pour out the rest of the blood at the bottom of the altar of burnt offering. 26He must burn all the goat's fat on the altar in the same way that he burns the fat of the fellowship offerings. In this way the priest removes the ruler's sin so that he belongs to the LORD, and the LORD will forgive him.

27" 'If any person in the community sins by accident and does something which the LORD has commanded must not be done, he is guilty. 28When the person learns about his sin, he must bring a female goat that has nothing wrong with it as an offering for his sin. 29He must put his hand on the animal's head and kill it at the place of the whole burnt offering. 30Then the priest must take some of the goat's blood on his finger and put it on the corners of the altar of burnt offering. He must pour out the rest of the goat's blood at the bottom of the altar. 31Then the priest must remove all the goat's fat in the same way the fat is removed from the fellowship offerings. He must burn it on the altar as a smell pleasing to the LORD. In this way the priest will remove that person's sin so he will belong to the LORD, and the LORD will forgive him.

32" 'If this person brings a lamb as his offering for sin, he must bring a female that has nothing wrong with it. 33He must put his hand on the animal's head and kill it as a sin offering in the place where the whole burnt offering is killed. 34The priest must take some of the blood from the sin offering on his finger and put it on the corners of the altar of burnt offering. He must pour out the rest of the lamb's blood at the bottom of the altar. 35Then the priest must remove all the lamb's fat in the same way that the lamb's fat is removed from the fellowship offerings. He must burn the pieces on the altar on top of the offerings made by fire to the LORD. In this way the priest will remove that person's sins so he will belong to the LORD, and the LORD will forgive him.

Special Types of Accidental Sins

5 " 'If a person is ordered to tell in court what he has seen or what he knows and he does not tell the court, he is guilty of sin.

2" 'Or someone might touch something unclean,[d] such as the dead body of an unclean wild animal or an unclean farm animal or an unclean crawling animal. Even if he does not know that he touched it, he will still be unclean and guilty of sin.

3" 'Someone might touch human uncleanness—anything that makes someone unclean—and not know it. But when he learns about it, he will be guilty.

4" 'Or someone might make a promise before the LORD without thinking. It might be a promise to do something bad or something good; it might be about anything. Even if he forgets about it, when he remembers, he will be guilty.

5" 'When anyone is guilty of any of these things, he must tell how he sinned. 6He must bring an offering to the LORD as a penalty for sin; it must be a female lamb or goat from the flock. The priest will perform the acts to remove that person's sin so that he will once again belong to the LORD.

7" 'But if the person cannot afford a lamb, he must bring two doves or two young pigeons to the LORD as the penalty for his sin. One bird must be for a sin offering, and the other must be for a whole burnt offering. 8He must bring them to the priest, who will first offer the one for the sin offering. He will pull the bird's head from its neck, but he will not pull it completely off. 9He must sprinkle the blood from the sin offering on the side of the altar, and then he must pour the rest of the blood at the bottom of the altar; it is a sin offering. 10Then the priest must offer the second bird as a whole burnt offering, as the law says. In this way the priest will remove the person's sin so he will belong to the LORD, and the LORD will forgive him.

11“ ‘If the person cannot afford two doves or two pigeons, he must bring about 2 litres of fine flour as an offering for sin. He must not put oil or incense[d] on the flour, because it is a sin offering. 12He must bring the flour to the priest. The priest will take a handful of the flour as a memorial offering and burn it on the altar on top of the offerings made by fire to the LORD; it is a sin offering. 13In this way the priest will remove the person's sins so that he will belong to the LORD, and the LORD will forgive him. What is left of the sin offering belongs to the priest, like the grain offering.' ”

The Penalty Offering

14The LORD said to Moses, 15“If a person accidentally sins and does something against the holy things of the LORD, he must bring from the flock a ram that has nothing wrong with it. This will be his penalty offering to the LORD. Its value in silver must be correct as set by the Holy Place measure. It is a penalty offering. 16That person must pay for the sin he did against the holy thing, adding one-fifth to its value. Then he must give it all to the priest. In this way the priest will remove the person's sin so he will belong to the LORD, by using the ram as the penalty offering. And the LORD will forgive the person.

17“If a person sins and does something the LORD has commanded not to be done, even if he does not know it, he is still guilty. He is responsible for his sin. 18He must bring the priest a ram from the flock, one that has nothing wrong with it and that is worth the correct amount. It will be a penalty offering. Though the person sinned without knowing it, with this offering the priest will remove the sin so that the person will belong to the LORD, and the LORD will forgive him. 19The person is guilty of doing wrong, so he must give the penalty offering to the LORD.”

6 The LORD said to Moses, 2“A person might sin against the LORD by doing one of these sins: he might lie about what happened to something he was taking care of for someone else, or he might lie about a promise he made. He might steal something or cheat someone. 3He might find something that had been lost and then lie about it. He might make a promise before the LORD about something and not mean it, or he might do some other sin. 4If he does any of these things, he is guilty of sin. He must bring back whatever he stole or whatever he took by cheating. He must bring back the thing he took care of for someone else. He must bring back what he found and lied about 5or what he made a false promise about. He must pay the full price plus an extra one-fifth of the value of what he took. He must give the money to the true owner on the day he brings his penalty offering. 6He must bring his penalty to the priest—a ram from the flock, one that does not have anything wrong with it and that is worth the correct amount. It will be a penalty offering to the LORD. 7Then the priest will perform the acts to remove that person's sin so that he will belong to the LORD, and the LORD will forgive him for the sins that made him guilty.”

The Whole Burnt Offering

8The LORD said to Moses, 9“Give this command to Aaron and the priests: ‘These are the teachings about the whole burnt offering: the burnt offering must stay on the altar all night until morning, and the altar's fire must be kept burning. 10The priest must put on his linen robe and linen underclothes next to his body. Then he will remove the ashes from the burnt offering on the altar and put them beside the altar. 11Then he must take off those clothes and put on others and carry the ashes outside the camp to a special clean[d] place. 12But the fire must be kept burning on the altar; it must not be allowed to go out. The priest must put more firewood on the altar every morning, place the whole burnt offering on the fire, and burn the fat of the fellowship offerings. 13The fire must be kept burning on the altar all the time; it must not go out.

The Grain Offering

14“ ‘These are the teachings about the grain offering: the priests must bring it to the LORD in front of the altar. 15The priest must take a handful of fine flour, with the oil and all of the incense[d] on it, and burn the grain offering on the altar as a memorial offering to the LORD. Its smell is pleasing to him. 16Aaron and the priests may eat what is left, but it must be eaten without yeast in a holy place. They must eat it in the courtyard of the Meeting Tent.[d] 17It must not be cooked with yeast. I have given it as their share of the offerings made to me by fire; it is most holy, like the sin offering and the penalty offering. 18Any male descendant[d] of Aaron may eat it as his share of the offerings made to the LORD by fire, and this will continue from now on. Whatever touches these offerings shall become holy.' ”

19The LORD said to Moses, 20“This is the offering Aaron and the priests must bring to the LORD on the day they appoint Aaron as high priest: they must bring 2 litres of fine flour for a continual grain offering, half of it in the morning and half in the evening. 21The fine flour must be mixed with oil and cooked on a griddle. Bring it when it is well mixed. Present the grain offering that is broken into pieces, and it will be a smell that is pleasing to the LORD. [22]One of the priests appointed to take Aaron's place as high priest must make the grain offering. It is a rule for ever that the grain offering must be completely burned to the LORD. [23]Every grain offering made by a priest must be completely burned; it must not be eaten."

The Sin Offering

[24]The LORD said to Moses, [25]"Tell Aaron and the priests: 'These are the teachings about the sin offering: the sin offering must be killed in front of the LORD in the same place that the whole burnt offering is killed; it is most holy. [26]The priest who offers the sin offering must eat it in a holy place, in the courtyard of the Meeting Tent.[d] [27]Whatever touches the meat of the sin offering must be holy, and if the blood is sprinkled on any clothes, you must wash them in a holy place. [28]The clay pot the meat is cooked in must be broken, or if a bronze pot is used, it must be scrubbed and rinsed with water. [29]Any male in a priest's family may eat the offering; it is most holy. [30]But if the blood of the sin offering is taken into the Meeting Tent and used to remove sin in the Holy Place, that sin offering must be burned with fire. It must not be eaten.

The Penalty Offering

7 " 'These are the teachings about the penalty offering, which is most holy: [2]the penalty offering must be killed where the whole burnt offering is killed. Then the priest must sprinkle its blood on all sides of the altar. [3]He must offer all the fat from the penalty offering—the fat tail, the fat that covers the inner organs, [4]both kidneys with the fat that is on them near the lower back muscle, and the best part of the liver, which is to be removed with the kidneys. [5]The priest must burn all these things on the altar as an offering made by fire to the LORD. It is a penalty offering. [6]Any male in a priest's family may eat it. It is most holy, so it must be eaten in a holy place.

[7]" 'The penalty offering is like the sin offering in that the teachings are the same for both. The priest who offers the sacrifice to remove sins will get the meat for food. [8]The priest who offers the burnt offering may also have the skin from it. [9]Every grain offering that is baked in an oven, cooked on a griddle or baked in a dish belongs to the priest who offers it. [10]Every grain offering, either dry or mixed with oil, belongs to the priests, and all priests will share alike.

The Fellowship Offering

[11]" 'These are the teachings about the fellowship offering a person may offer to the LORD: [12]if he brings the fellowship offering to show his thanks, he should also bring loaves of bread made without yeast that are mixed with oil, wafers made without yeast that have oil poured over them, and loaves of fine flour that are mixed with oil. [13]He must also offer loaves of bread made with yeast along with his fellowship offering, which he gives to show thanks. [14]One of each kind of offering will be for the LORD; it will be given to the priest who sprinkles the blood of the fellowship offering. [15]When the fellowship offering is given to thank the LORD, the meat from it must be eaten the same day it is offered; none of it must be left until morning.

[16]" 'If a person brings a fellowship offering just to give a gift to God or because of a special promise to him, the sacrifice should be eaten the same day he offers it. If there is any left, it may be eaten the next day. [17]If any meat from this sacrifice is left on the third day, it must be burned up. [18]Any meat of the fellowship offering eaten on the third day will not be accepted, nor will the sacrifice count for the person who offered it. It will become unclean,[d] and anyone who eats the meat will be guilty of sin.

[19]" 'People must not eat meat that touches anything unclean; they must burn this meat with fire. Anyone who is clean may eat other meat. [20]But if anyone is unclean and eats the meat from the fellowship offering that belongs to the LORD, he must be cut off from his people.

[21]" 'If anyone touches something unclean—uncleanness that comes from people, from an animal or from some hated thing—touching it will make him unclean. If he then eats meat from the fellowship offering that belongs to the LORD, he must be cut off from his people.' "

[22]The LORD said to Moses, [23]"Tell the people of Israel: 'You must not eat any of the fat from cattle, sheep or goats. [24]If an animal is found dead or torn by wild animals, you may use its fat for other things, but you must not eat it. [25]If someone eats fat from an animal offering made by fire to the LORD, he must be cut off from his people. [26]No matter where you live, you must not eat blood from any bird or animal. [27]Anyone who eats blood must be cut off from his people.' "

The Priests' Share

[28]The LORD said to Moses, [29]"Tell the people of Israel: 'If someone brings a fellowship offering to the LORD, he must give part of it as his sacrifice to the LORD. [30]He must carry that part of the gift in his own hands as an offering made by fire to the

LORD. He must bring the fat and the breast of the animal to the priest, to be presented to the LORD as the priests' share. 31Then the priest must burn the fat on the altar, but the breast of the animal will belong to Aaron and the priests. 32You must also give the right thigh from the fellowship offering to the priest as a gift; 33it will belong to the priest who offers the blood and fat of the fellowship offering. 34I have taken the breast and the thigh from the fellowship offerings of the Israelites, and I have given these parts to Aaron and the priests as their share for all time from the Israelites.' "

35This is the portion that belongs to Aaron and his sons from the offerings made by fire to the LORD. They were given this share on the day they were presented to the LORD as priests. 36On the day the LORD appointed the priests, he commanded Israel to give this share to them, and it is to be given to the priests as their share from now on.

37These are the teachings about the whole burnt offering, the grain offering, the sin offering, the penalty offering, the offering for the appointment of priests and the fellowship offering. 38The LORD gave these teachings to Moses on Mount Sinai on the day he commanded the Israelites to bring their offerings to the LORD in the Sinai Desert.

Aaron and His Sons Appointed

8 The LORD said to Moses, 2"Bring Aaron and his sons and their clothes, the special olive oil used in appointing people and things to the service of the LORD, the bull of the sin offering and the two rams, and the basket of bread made without yeast. 3Then gather the people together at the entrance to the Meeting Tent." [d] 4Moses did as the LORD commanded him, and the people met together at the entrance to the Meeting Tent.

5Then Moses spoke to the people and said, "This is what the LORD has commanded to be done." 6Bringing Aaron and his sons forwards, Moses washed them with water. 7He put the inner robe on Aaron and tied the cloth belt around him. Then Moses put the outer robe on him and placed the holy robe [d] on him. He tied the skilfully woven belt around him so that the holy robe was tied to Aaron. 8Then Moses put the chest covering on him and put the Urim and the Thummim [d] in the chest covering. 9He also put the turban on Aaron's head. He put the strip of gold, the holy crown, on the front of the turban, as the LORD commanded him to do.

10Then Moses put the special oil on the Holy Tent [d] and everything in it, making them holy for the LORD. 11He sprinkled some oil on the altar seven times, sprinkling the altar and all its tools and the large bowl and its base. In this way he made them holy for the LORD. 12He poured some of the special oil on Aaron's head to make Aaron holy for the LORD. 13Then Moses brought Aaron's sons forwards. He put the inner robes on them, tied cloth belts around them, and put headbands on them, as the LORD had commanded him.

14Then Moses brought the bull for the sin offering, and Aaron and his sons put their hands on its head. 15Moses killed the bull, took the blood, and with his finger put some of it on all the corners of the altar, to make it pure. Then he poured out the rest of the blood at the bottom of the altar. In this way he made it holy and ready for service to God. 16Moses took all the fat from the inner organs of the bull, the best part of the liver, and both kidneys with the fat that is on them, and he burned them on the altar. 17But he took the bull's skin, its meat and its intestines and burned them in a fire outside the camp, as the LORD had commanded him.

18Next Moses brought the ram of the burnt offering, and Aaron and his sons put their hands on its head. 19Then Moses killed it and sprinkled the blood on all sides of the altar. 20He cut the ram into pieces and burned the head, the pieces and the fat. 21He washed the inner organs and legs with water and burned the whole ram on the altar as a burnt offering made by fire to the LORD; its smell was pleasing to the LORD. Moses did these things as the LORD had commanded him.

22Then Moses brought the other ram, the one used in appointing Aaron and his sons as priests, and Aaron and his sons put their hands on its head. 23Then Moses killed the sheep and put some of its blood on the bottom of Aaron's right ear, some on the thumb of Aaron's right hand, and some on the big toe of his right foot. 24Then Moses brought Aaron's sons close to the altar. He put some of the blood on the bottom of their right ears, some on the thumbs of their right hands, and some on the big toes of their right feet. Then he sprinkled blood on all sides of the altar. 25He took the fat, the fat tail, all the fat on the inner organs, the best part of the liver, both kidneys with their fat and the right thigh. 26From the basket of bread made without yeast that is put before the LORD each day, Moses took a loaf of bread, a loaf made with oil and a wafer. He put these pieces of bread on the fat and right thigh of the ram. 27All these things he put in the hands of Aaron and his sons and presented them as an offering before the LORD. 28Then Moses took them from their hands and burned them on the altar on top of the burnt offering. So this was the offering for appointing Aaron and his sons as priests. It was an offering made by fire to the LORD, and its smell was pleasing to him. 29Moses also took the breast and presented it as an offering before the LORD. It was Moses' share of the ram used in appointing the priests, as the LORD had commanded him.

30Moses took some of the special oil and some of the blood which was on the altar, and he sprinkled them on Aaron and Aaron's clothes, and on Aaron's sons and their clothes. In this way Moses made Aaron, his clothes, his sons and their clothes holy for the LORD.

31Then Moses said to Aaron and his sons, "I gave you a command, saying, 'Aaron and his sons will eat these things.' So take the meat and basket of bread from the offering for appointing priests. Boil the meat at the door of the Meeting Tent, and eat it there with the bread. 32If any of the meat or bread is left, burn it. 33The time of appointing will last seven days; you must not go outside the entrance of the Meeting Tent until that time is up. Stay there until the time of your appointing is finished. 34The LORD commanded the things that were done today to remove your sins so you will belong to him. 35You must stay at the entrance of the Meeting Tent day and night for seven days. If you don't obey the LORD's commands, you will die. The LORD has given me these commands."

36So Aaron and his sons did everything the LORD had commanded through Moses.

Aaron and His Sons Offer Sacrifices

9 On the eighth day after the time of appointing, Moses called for Aaron and his sons and for the elders of Israel. 2He said to Aaron, "Take a bull calf and a ram that have nothing wrong with them, and offer them to the LORD. The calf will be a sin offering, and the ram will be a whole burnt offering. 3Tell the people of Israel, 'Take a male goat for a sin offering and a calf and a lamb for a whole burnt offering; each must be one year old, and it must have nothing wrong with it. 4Also take a bull and a ram for fellowship offerings, along with a grain offering mixed with oil. Offer all these things to the LORD, because the LORD will appear to you today.' "

5So all the people came to the front of the Meeting Tent,[d] bringing the things Moses had commanded them to bring, and they stood before the LORD. 6Moses said, "You have done what the LORD commanded, so you will see the LORD's glory."

7Then Moses told Aaron, "Go to the altar and offer sin offerings and whole burnt offerings. Do this to remove your sins and the people's sins so you will belong to God. Offer the sacrifices for the people and perform the acts to remove their sins for them so they will belong to the LORD, as the LORD has commanded."

8So Aaron went to the altar and killed the bull calf as a sin offering for himself. 9Then his sons brought the blood to him, and he dipped his finger in the blood and put it on the corners of the altar. He poured out the rest of the blood at the bottom of the altar. 10Aaron took the fat, the kidneys and the best part of the liver from the sin offering and burned them on the altar, in the way the LORD had commanded Moses. 11The meat and skin he burned outside the camp.

12Then Aaron killed the animal for the whole burnt offering. His sons brought the blood to him, and he sprinkled it on all sides of the altar. 13As they gave him the pieces and head of the burnt offering, Aaron burned them on the altar. 14He also washed the inner organs and the legs of the burnt offering and burned them on top of the burnt offering on the altar.

15Then Aaron brought the offering that was for the people. He took the goat of the people's sin offering and killed it and offered it for the sin offering, just as he had done for the first sin offering.

16Then Aaron brought the whole burnt offering and offered it in the way that the LORD had commanded. 17He also brought the grain offering to the altar. He took a handful of the grain and burned it on the altar, in addition to the morning's burnt offering.

18Aaron also killed the bull and the ram as the fellowship offerings for the people. His sons brought him the blood, and he sprinkled it on all sides of the altar. 19Aaron's sons also brought to Aaron the fat of the bull and the ram—the fat tail, the fat covering the inner organs, the kidneys and the best part of the liver. 20Aaron's sons put them on the breasts of the bull and the sheep. Then Aaron burned these fat parts on the altar. 21He presented the breasts and the right thigh before the LORD as the priests' share of the offering, as Moses had commanded.

22Then Aaron lifted his hands towards the people and blessed them. When he had finished offering the sin offering, the burnt offering and the fellowship offering, he stepped down from the altar.

23Moses and Aaron went into the Meeting Tent. Then they came out and blessed the people, and the LORD's glory came to all the people. 24Fire came out from the LORD and burned up the burnt offering and fat on the altar. When the people saw this, they shouted with joy and bowed face down on the ground.

God Destroys Nadab and Abihu

10 Aaron's sons Nadab and Abihu took their pans for burning incense,[d] put fire in them, and added incense; but they did not use

the special fire Moses had commanded them to use in the presence of the LORD. 2So fire came down from the LORD and destroyed Nadab and Abihu, and they died in front of the LORD. 3Then Moses said to Aaron, "This is what the LORD was speaking about when he said,

'I must be respected as holy
  by those who come near me;
before all the people
  I must be given honour.' "

So Aaron did not say anything about the death of his sons.

4Aaron's uncle Uzziel had two sons named Mishael and Elzaphan. Moses said to them, "Come here and pick up your cousins' bodies. Carry them outside the camp away from the front of the Holy Place." 5So Mishael and Elzaphan obeyed Moses and carried the bodies of Nadab and Abihu, still clothed in the special priest's inner robes, outside the camp.

6Then Moses said to Aaron and his other sons, Eleazar and Ithamar, "Don't show sadness by tearing your clothes or leaving your hair uncombed. If you do, you will die, and the LORD will be angry with all the people. All the people of Israel, your relatives, may cry loudly about the LORD burning Nadab and Abihu, 7but you must not even leave the Meeting Tent.[d] If you go out of the entrance, you will die, because the LORD has appointed you to his service." So Aaron, Eleazar and Ithamar obeyed Moses.

8Then the LORD said to Aaron, 9"You and your sons must not drink wine or beer when you go into the Meeting Tent. If you do, you will die. This law will continue from now on. 10You must keep what is holy separate from what is not holy; you must keep what is clean[d] separate from what is unclean. 11You must teach the people all the laws that the LORD gave to them through Moses."

12Moses said to Aaron and his remaining sons, Eleazar and Ithamar, "Eat the part of the grain offering that is left from the sacrifices offered by fire to the LORD, but do not add yeast to it. Eat it near the altar because it is most holy. 13You must eat it in a holy place, because this part of the offering made by fire to the LORD belongs to you and your sons. I have been commanded to tell you this. 14"Also, you and your sons and daughters may eat the breast and thigh of the fellowship offering that was presented to the LORD. You must eat them in a clean place; they are your share of the fellowship offerings given by the Israelites. 15The people must bring the fat from their animals that was part of the offering made by fire, and they must present it to the LORD along with the thigh and the breast of the fellowship offering. They will be the regular share of the offerings for you and your children, as the LORD has commanded."

16Moses locked for the goat of the sin offering, but it had already been burned up. So he became very angry with Eleazar and Ithamar, Aaron's remaining sons. He said, 17"Why didn't you eat that goat in a holy place? It is most holy, and the LORD gave it to you to take away the guilt of the people, to remove their sins so that they will belong to the LORD. 18You didn't bring the goat's blood inside the Holy Place. You were supposed to eat the goat in a holy place, as I commanded!"

19But Aaron said to Moses, "Today they brought their sin offering and burnt offering before the LORD, but these terrible things have still happened to me! Do you think the LORD would be any happier if I ate the sin offering today?" 20When Moses heard this, he was satisfied.

Rules About What May Be Eaten

11 The LORD said to Moses and Aaron, 2"Tell the Israelites this: 'These are the land animals you may eat: 3you may eat any animal that has split hoofs completely divided and that chews the cud.[d]

4" 'Some animals only chew the cud or only have split hoofs, and you must not eat them. The camel chews the cud but does not have a split hoof; it is unclean[d] for you. 5The rock badger chews the cud but does not have a split hoof; it is unclean for you. 6The rabbit chews the cud but does not have a split hoof; it is unclean for you. 7Now the pig has a split hoof that is completely divided, but it does not chew the cud; it is unclean for you. 8You must not eat the meat from these animals or even touch their dead bodies; they are unclean for you.

9" 'Of the animals that live in the sea or in a river, if the animal has fins and scales, you may eat it. 10But whatever lives in the sea or in a river and does not have fins and scales—including the things that fill the water and all other things that live in it—you should hate. 11You must not eat any meat from them or even touch their dead bodies, because you should hate them. 12You must hate any animal in the water that does not have fins and scales.

13" 'Also, these are the birds you are to hate. They are hateful and should not be eaten. You must not eat eagles, vultures, black vultures, 14kites, any kind of falcon, 15any kind of raven, 16horned owls, screech owls, sea gulls, any kind of hawk, 17little owls, cormorants, great owls, 18white owls, desert owls, ospreys, 19storks, any kind of heron, hoopoes or bats.

20" 'Don't eat insects that have wings and walk on all four feet; they also are to be hated.

21" 'But you may eat certain insects that have wings and walk on four feet. You may eat those that have legs with joints above their feet so that they can jump. [22]These are the insects you may eat: all kinds of locusts, winged locusts, crickets and grasshoppers. [23]But all other insects that have wings and walk on four feet you are to hate. [24]Those insects will make you unclean, and anyone who touches the dead body of one of these insects will become unclean until evening. [25]Anyone who picks up one of these dead insects must wash his clothes and be unclean until evening.

[26]" 'Some animals have split hoofs, but the hoofs are not completely divided; others do not chew the cud. They are unclean for you, and anyone who touches the dead body of one of these animals will become unclean. [27]Of all the animals that walk on four feet, the animals that walk on their paws are unclean for you. Anyone who touches the dead body of one of these animals will become unclean until evening. [28]Anyone who picks up their dead bodies must wash his clothes and be unclean until evening; these animals are unclean for you.

[29]" 'These crawling animals are unclean for you: moles, rats, all kinds of great lizards,

Sidelight The Israelites' dietary law forbade eating moles, rats, lizards, crocodiles, chameleons and other reptiles (Leviticus 11:29–30). It seems to have been a sign to show that Israel was chosen and holy. Scholars have given health reasons as to which animals were clean and which transmitted disease, but above all the laws proved that God had the right to tell his people exactly what to eat.

[30]geckos, crocodiles, lizards, sand reptiles and chameleons. [31]These crawling animals are unclean for you; anyone who touches their dead bodies will be unclean until evening.

[32]" 'If an unclean animal dies and falls on something, that thing will also become unclean. This includes anything made from wood, cloth, leather or rough cloth, regardless of its use. Whatever the animal falls on must be washed with water and be unclean until evening; then it will become clean again. [33]If the dead, unclean animal falls into a clay bowl, anything in the bowl will become unclean, and you must break the bowl. [34]If water from the unclean clay bowl gets on any food, that food will become unclean. [35]If any dead, unclean animal falls on something, it becomes unclean. If it is a clay oven or a clay baking pan, it must be broken into pieces. These things will be unclean; they are unclean for you.

[36]" 'A spring or well that collects water will stay clean, but anyone who touches the dead body of any unclean animal will become unclean. [37]If a dead, unclean animal falls on a seed to be planted, that seed is still clean. [38]But if you put water on some seeds and a dead, unclean animal falls on them, they are unclean for you.

[39]" 'Also, if an animal which you use for food dies, anyone who touches its body will be unclean until evening. [40]Anyone who eats meat from this animal's dead body must wash his clothes and be unclean until evening. Anyone who picks up the animal's dead body must wash his clothes and be unclean until evening.

[41]" 'Every animal that crawls on the ground is to be hated; it must not be eaten. [42]You must not eat any of the animals that crawl on the ground, including those that crawl on their stomachs, that walk on all four feet, or on many feet. They are to be hated. [43]Do not make yourself unclean by these animals; you must not become unclean by them. [44]I am the LORD your God. Keep yourselves holy for me because I am holy. Don't make yourselves unclean with any of these crawling animals. [45]I am the LORD who brought you out of Egypt to be your God; you must be holy because I am holy.

[46]" 'These are the teachings about all of the cattle, birds and other animals on earth, as well as the animals in the sea and those that crawl on the ground. [47]These teachings help people know the difference between unclean animals and clean animals; they help people know which animals may be eaten and which ones must not be eaten.' "

Rules for New Mothers

12 The LORD said to Moses, [2]"Tell the people of Israel this: 'If a woman gives birth to a son, she will become unclean [d] for seven days, as she is unclean during her monthly period. [3]On the eighth day the boy must be circumcised. [d] [4]Then it will be 33 days before she becomes clean from her loss of blood. She must not touch anything that is holy or enter the Holy Tent until her time of cleansing is finished. [5]But if she gives birth to a daughter, the mother will be unclean for two weeks, as she is unclean during her monthly period. It will be 66 days before she becomes clean from her loss of blood.

[6]" 'After she has a son or daughter and her days of cleansing are over, the new mother must bring certain sacrifices to the Meeting Tent. [d] She must give the priest at the entrance a year-old lamb for a burnt offering and a dove or young pigeon for a sin offering. [7]He will offer them before the LORD to make her clean so she will belong to the LORD again; then she will be clean from her loss of blood. These are the teachings for a woman who gives birth to a boy or girl.

8“ ‘If she cannot afford a lamb, she is to bring
two doves or two young pigeons, one for a burnt
offering and one for a sin offering. In this way the
priest will make her clean so she will belong to
the LORD again, and she will be clean.’ ”

Rules About Skin Diseases

13 The LORD said to Moses and Aaron,
2“Someone might have on his skin a
swelling or a sore or a bright spot. If the sore
looks like a harmful skin disease, the person must
be brought to Aaron, the priest, or to one of
Aaron’s sons, the priests. 3The priest must look at
the sore on the person’s skin. If the hair in the
sore has become white, and the sore seems
deeper than the person’s skin, it is a harmful skin
disease. When he has finished looking at the per-
son, the priest must announce that the person is
unclean.[d]
4“If there is a white spot on a person’s skin, but
the spot does not seem deeper than the skin, and
if the hair from the spot has not turned white, the
priest must separate that person from other peo-
ple for seven days. 5On the seventh day the priest
must look at the person again. If he sees that the
sore has not changed and it has not spread on the
skin, the priest must keep the person separated
for seven more days. 6On the seventh day the
priest must look at the person again. If the sore
has faded and has not spread on the skin, the
priest must announce that the person is clean.
The sore is only a rash. The person must wash his
clothes, and he will become clean again.
7“But if the sore spreads again after the priest
has announced him clean, the person must come
again to the priest. 8The priest must look at him,
and if the rash has spread on the skin, the priest
must announce that the person is unclean; it is a
harmful skin disease.
9“If a person has a harmful skin disease, he
must be brought to the priest, 10and the priest
must look at him. If there is a white swelling in
the skin, and the hair has become white, and the
skin looks raw in the swelling, 11it is a harmful
skin disease. It is one he has had for a long time.
The priest must announce that the person is un-
clean. He will not need to separate that person
from other people, because everyone already
knows that the person is unclean.
12“If the skin disease spreads all over a person’s
body, covering his skin from his head to his feet,
as far as the priest can see, the priest must look
at the person’s whole body. 13If the priest sees
that the disease covers the whole body and has
turned all of the person’s skin white, he must
announce that the person is clean.
14“But when the person has an open sore, he
is unclean. 15When the priest sees the open sore,
he must announce that the person is unclean.
The open sore is not clean; it is a harmful skin
disease. 16If the open sore becomes white again,
the person must come to the priest. 17The priest
must look at him, and if the sores have become
white, the priest must announce that the person
with the sores is clean. Then he will be clean.
18“Someone may have a boil on his skin that is
healed. 19If in the place where the boil was, there
is a white swelling or a bright red spot, this place
on the skin must be shown to the priest. 20And
the priest must look at it. If the spot seems deeper
than the skin and the hair on it has become
white, the priest must announce that the person
is unclean. The spot is a harmful skin disease that
has broken out from inside the boil. 21But if the
priest looks at the spot and there are no white
hairs in it and the spot is not deeper than the skin
and it has faded, the priest must separate the per-
son from other people for seven days. 22If the spot
spreads on the skin, the priest must announce
that the person is unclean; it is a disease that will
spread. 23But if the bright spot does not spread or
change, it is only the scar from the old boil. Then
the priest must announce that the person is clean.
24“When a person gets a burn on his skin, if the
open sore becomes white or red, 25the
priest must look at it. If the white spot seems
deeper than the skin and the hair at that spot
has become white, it is a harmful skin disease.
The disease has broken out in the burn, and
the priest must announce that the person is
unclean. It is a harmful skin disease. 26But if the
priest looks at the spot and there is no white hair
in the bright spot, and the spot is no deeper
than the skin and has faded, the priest must
separate the person from other people for seven
days. 27On the seventh day the priest must look
at him again. If the spot has spread on the skin,
the priest must announce that the person is
unclean. It is a harmful skin disease. 28But if the
bright spot has not spread on the skin but has
faded, it is the swelling from the burn. The priest
must announce that the person is clean, because
the spot is only a scar from the burn.
29“When a man or a woman gets a sore on the
scalp or on the chin, 30a priest must look at the
sore. If it seems deeper than the skin and the hair
around it is thin and yellow, the priest must an-
nounce that the person is unclean. It is an itch, a
harmful skin disease of the head or chin. 31But if
the priest looks at it and it does not seem deeper
than the skin and there is no black hair in it, the
priest must separate the person from other people
for seven days. 32On the seventh day the priest
must look at the sore. If it has not spread, and
there are no yellow hairs growing in it, and the
sore does not seem deeper than the skin, 33the

person must shave himself, but he must not shave the sore place. The priest must separate that person from other people for seven more days. [34]On the seventh day the priest must look at the sore. If it has not spread on the skin and it does not seem deeper than the skin, the priest must announce that the person is clean. So the person must wash his clothes and become clean. [35]But if the sore spreads on the skin after the person has become clean, [36]the priest must look at him again. If the sore has spread on the skin, the priest doesn't need to look for the yellowish hair; the person is unclean. [37]But if the priest thinks the sore has stopped spreading, and black hair is growing in it, the sore has healed. The person is clean, and the priest must announce that he is clean.

[38]"When a man or a woman has white spots on the skin, [39]a priest must look at them. If the spots on the skin are dull white, the disease is only a harmless rash. That person is clean.

[40]"When anyone loses hair from his head and is bald, he is clean. [41]If he loses hair from the front of his head and has a bald forehead, he is clean. [42]But if there is a red-white sore on his bald head or forehead, it is a skin disease breaking out in those places. [43]A priest must look at that person. If the swelling of the sore on his bald head or forehead is red-white, like a skin disease that spreads, [44]that person has a skin disease. He is unclean. The priest must announce that the person is unclean because of the sore on his head.

[45]"If a person has a skin disease that spreads, he must warn other people by shouting, 'Unclean, unclean!' His clothes must be torn at the seams, he must let his hair stay uncombed, and he must cover his mouth. [46]That person will remain unclean while he has the disease; he is unclean. He must live alone outside the camp.

Rules About Mildew

[47]"Clothing might have mildew [d] on it. It might be clothing made of linen or wool [48](either woven or knitted), or of leather, or something made from leather. [49]If the mildew in the clothing, leather or woven or knitted material is green or red, it is a spreading mildew. It must be shown to the priest. [50]The priest must look at the mildew, and he must put that piece of clothing in a separate place for seven days. [51]On the seventh day he must look at the mildew again. If the mildew has spread on the cloth (either woven or knitted) or the leather, no matter what the leather was used for, it is a mildew that destroys; it is unclean. [52]The priest must burn the clothing. It does not matter if it is woven or knitted, wool or linen, or made of leather, because the mildew is spreading. It must be burned.

[53]"If the priest sees that the mildew has not spread in the cloth (either knitted or woven) or leather, [54]he must order the people to wash that piece of leather or cloth. Then he must separate the clothing for seven more days. [55]After the piece with the mildew has been washed, the priest must look at it again. If the mildew still looks the same, the piece is unclean, [d] even if the mildew has not spread. You must burn it in fire; it does not matter if the mildew is on one side or the other.

[56]"But when the priest looks at that piece of leather or cloth, the mildew might have faded after the piece has been washed. Then the priest must tear the mildew out of the piece of leather or cloth (either woven or knitted). [57]But if the mildew comes back to that piece of leather or cloth (either woven or knitted), the mildew is spreading. And whatever has the mildew must be burned with fire. [58]When the cloth (either woven or knitted) or the leather is washed and the mildew is gone, it must be washed again; then it will be clean.

[59]"These are the teachings about mildew on pieces of cloth (either woven or knitted) or leather, to decide if they are clean or unclean."

Rules for Cleansing from Skin Diseases

14 The LORD said to Moses, [2]"These are the teachings for the time at which people who had a harmful skin disease are made clean. [d]

"The person shall be brought to the priest, [3]and the priest must go outside the camp and look at the one who had the skin disease. If the skin disease is healed, [4]the priest will command that two living, clean birds, a piece of cedar wood, a piece of red string and a hyssop plant be brought for cleansing the person with the skin disease.

[5]"The priest must order one bird to be killed in a clay bowl containing fresh water. [6]Then he will take the living bird, the piece of cedar wood, the red string and the hyssop; all these he will dip into the blood of the bird that was killed over the fresh water. [7]The priest will sprinkle the blood seven times on the person being cleansed from the skin disease. He must announce that the person is clean and then go to an open field and let the living bird go free.

[8]"The person to be cleansed must wash his clothes, shave off all his hair, and bathe in water. Then he will be clean and may go into the camp, though he must stay outside his tent for the first seven days. [9]On the seventh day he must shave off all his hair—the hair from his head, his beard, his eyebrows and the rest of his hair. He must wash his clothes and bathe his body in water, and he will be clean.

10"On the eighth day the person who had the skin disease must take two male lambs that have nothing wrong with them and a year-old female lamb that has nothing wrong with it. He must also take 7 litres of fine flour mixed with oil for a grain offering and a third of a litre of olive oil. 11The priest who is to announce that the person is clean must bring him and his sacrifices before the LORD at the entrance of the Meeting Tent.*d* 12The priest will take one of the male lambs and offer it with the olive oil as a penalty offering; he will present them before the LORD as an offering. 13Then he will kill the male lamb in the holy place, where the sin offering and the whole burnt offering are killed. The penalty offering is like the sin offering—it belongs to the priest and it is most holy.

14"The priest will take some of the blood of the penalty offering and put it on the bottom of the right ear of the person to be made clean. He will also put some of it on the thumb of the person's right hand and on the big toe of the person's right foot. 15Then the priest will take some of the oil and pour it into his own left hand. 16He will dip a finger of his right hand into the oil that is in his left hand, and with his finger he will sprinkle some of the oil seven times before the LORD. 17The priest will put some oil from his hand on the bottom of the right ear of the person to be made clean, some on the thumb of the person's right hand, and some on the big toe of the person's right foot. The oil will go on these places on top of the blood for the penalty offering. 18He will put the rest of the oil that is in his left hand on the head of the person to be made clean. In this way the priest will make that person clean so he can belong to the LORD again.

19"Next the priest will offer the sin offering to make that person clean so he can belong to the LORD again. After this the priest will kill the animal for the whole burnt offering, 20and he will offer the burnt offering and grain offering on the altar. In this way he will make that person clean so he can belong to the LORD again.

21"But if the person is poor and unable to afford these offerings, he must take one male lamb for a penalty offering. It will be presented to the LORD to make him clean so he can belong to the LORD again. The person must also take 2.2 litres of fine flour mixed with oil for a grain offering. He must also take 0.3 litres of olive oil 22and two doves or two young pigeons, which he can afford. One bird is for a sin offering and the other for a whole burnt offering. 23On the eighth day the person will bring them for his cleansing to the priest at the entrance of the Meeting Tent, before the LORD. 24The priest will take the lamb for the penalty offering and the oil, and he will present them as an offering before the LORD. 25Then he will kill the lamb of the penalty offering, take some of its blood, and put it on the bottom of the right ear of the person to be made clean. The priest will put some of this blood on the thumb of the person's right hand and some on the big toe of the person's right foot. 26He will also pour some of the oil into his own left hand. 27Then with a finger of his right hand, he will sprinkle some of the oil from his left hand seven times before the LORD. 28The priest will take some of the oil from his hand and put it on the bottom of the right ear of the person to be made clean. He will also put some of it on the thumb of the person's right hand and some on the big toe of the person's right foot. The oil will go on these places on top of the blood from the penalty offering. 29The priest must put the rest of the oil that is in his hand on the head of the person to be made clean, to make him clean so that he can belong to the LORD again. 30Then the priest will offer one of the doves or young pigeons, which the person can afford. 31He must offer one of the birds for a sin offering and the other for a whole burnt offering, along with the grain offering. In this way the priest will make the person clean so that he can belong to the LORD again; he will become clean.

32"These are the teachings for making a person clean after he has had a skin disease, if he cannot afford the regular sacrifices for becoming clean."

Rules for Cleaning Mildew

33The LORD also said to Moses and Aaron, 34"I am giving the land of Canaan to your people. When they enter that land, if I cause mildew*d* to grow in someone's house in that land, 35the owner of that house must come and tell the priest. He should say, 'I have seen something like mildew in my house.' 36Then the priest must order the people to empty the house before he goes in to look at the mildew. This is so he will not have to say that everything in the house is unclean.*d* After this, the priest will go in to look at it. 37He will look at the mildew, and if the mildew on the walls of the house is green or red and goes into the walls' surfaces, 38he must go out and close up the house for seven days. 39On the seventh day the priest must come back and check the house. If the mildew has spread on the walls of the house, 40the priest must order the people to tear out the stones with the mildew on them. They should throw them away, at a certain unclean place outside the city. 41Then the priest must have all the inside of the house scraped. The people must throw away the plaster they scraped off the walls, at a certain unclean place outside the city. [42]Then the owner must put new stones in the walls, and he must cover the walls with new clay plaster.

[43]"Suppose a person has taken away the old stones and plaster and put in new stones and plaster. If mildew again appears in his house, [44]the priest must come back and check the house again. If the mildew has spread in the house, it is a mildew that destroys things; the house is unclean. [45]Then the owner must tear down the house, remove all its stones, plaster and wood, and take them to the unclean place outside the city. [46]Anyone who goes into that house while it is closed up will be unclean until evening. [47]Anyone who eats in that house or lies down there must wash his clothes.

> **Sidelight**
> The bathroom's dirty, and it's your turn to clean it. But you cannot find the cleaning fluid. Leviticus 14:33–45 gives detailed instructions for cleaning mildew. You may find, however, that your parents are none too happy when you start tearing out all the mildewy bricks.

[48]"Suppose after new stones and plaster have been put in a house, the priest checks it again and the mildew has not spread. Then the priest will announce that the house is clean, because the mildew is gone.

[49]"Then, to make the house clean, the priest must take two birds, a piece of cedar wood, a piece of red string and a hyssop plant. [50]He will kill one bird in a clay bowl containing fresh water. [51]Then he will take the bird that is still alive, the cedar wood, the hyssop and the red string, and he will dip them into the blood of the bird that was killed over the fresh water. The priest will sprinkle the blood on the house seven times. [52]He will use the bird's blood, the fresh water, the live bird, the cedar wood, the hyssop and the red string to make the house clean. [53]He will then go to an open field outside the city and let the living bird go free. This is how the priest makes the house clean and ready for service to the LORD."

[54]These are the teachings about any kind of skin disease, [55]mildew on pieces of cloth or in a house, [56]swellings, rashes or bright spots on the skin; [57]they help people decide when things are unclean and when they are clean. These are the teachings about all these kinds of diseases.

Rules About a Person's Body

15 The LORD also said to Moses and Aaron, [2]"Say to the people of Israel: 'When a fluid comes from a person's body, the fluid is unclean.[d] [3]It doesn't matter if the fluid flows freely or if it is blocked from flowing; the fluid will make him unclean. This is the way the fluid makes him unclean:

[4]" 'If the person who discharges the body fluid lies on a bed, that bed becomes unclean, and everything he sits on becomes unclean. [5]Anyone who touches his bed must wash his clothes and bathe in water, and the person will be unclean until evening. [6]Whoever sits on something that the person who discharges the fluid sat on must wash his clothes and bathe in water; he will be unclean until evening. [7]Anyone who touches the person who discharges the body fluid must wash his clothes and bathe in water; he will be unclean until evening.

[8]" 'If the person who discharges the body fluid spits on someone who is clean, that person must wash his clothes and bathe in water; he will be unclean until evening. [9]Everything on which the person who is unclean sits when riding will become unclean. [10]Anyone who touches something that was under him will be unclean until evening. And anyone who carries these things must wash his clothes and bathe in water; he will be unclean until evening.

[11]" 'If the person who discharges a body fluid has not washed his hands in water and touches another person, that person must wash his clothes and bathe in water; he will be unclean until evening.

[12]" 'If a person who discharges a body fluid touches a clay bowl, that bowl must be broken. If he touches a wooden bowl, that bowl must be washed in water.

[13]" 'When a person who discharges a body fluid is made clean, he must count seven days for himself for his cleansing. He must wash his clothes and bathe his body in fresh water, and he will be clean. [14]On the eighth day he must take two doves or two young pigeons before the LORD at the entrance of the Meeting Tent.[d] He will give the two birds to the priest. [15]The priest will offer the birds, one for a sin offering and the other for a burnt offering. And the priest will make that person clean so he can belong to the LORD again.

[16]" 'If semen[n] goes out from a man, he must bathe in water; he will be unclean until evening. [17]If the fluid gets on any clothing or leather, it must be washed with water; it will be unclean until evening.

semen A man's body fluid by which he can make a woman pregnant.

18“ ‘If a man has sexual relations with a
woman and semen comes out, both people must
bathe in water; they will be unclean until evening.

Rules About a Woman’s Body

19“ ‘When a woman has her monthly period,
she is unclean[d] for seven days; anyone who
touches her will be unclean until evening. 20Any-
thing she lies on during this time will be unclean,
and everything she sits on during this time will be
unclean. 21Anyone who touches her bed must
wash his clothes and bathe in water; that person
will be unclean until evening. 22Anyone who
touches something she has sat on must wash his
clothes and bathe in water; that person will be
unclean until evening. 23It does not matter if the
person touched the woman’s bed or something
she sat on; he will be unclean until evening.

24“ ‘If a man has sexual relations with a
woman and her monthly period touches him, he
will be unclean for seven days; every bed he lies
on will be unclean.

25“ ‘If a woman has a loss of blood for many
days and it is not during her regular monthly
period, or if she continues to have a loss of
blood after her regular period, she will be un-
clean, as she is during her monthly period. She
will be unclean for as long as she continues to
bleed. 26Any bed she lies on during all the time
of her bleeding will be like her bed during
her regular monthly period. Everything she
sits on will be unclean, as during her regular
monthly period.

27“ ‘Whoever touches those things will be un-
clean and must wash his clothes and bathe in
water; he will be unclean until evening. 28When
the woman becomes clean from her bleeding, she
must wait seven days, and after this she will be
clean. 29Then on the eighth day she must take
two doves or two young pigeons and bring them
to the priest at the entrance of the Meeting
Tent.[d] 30The priest must offer one bird for a sin
offering and the other for a whole burnt offering.
In this way the priest will make her clean so she
can belong to the LORD again.

31“ ‘So you must warn the people of Israel to
stay separated from things that make them un-
clean. If you don’t warn the people, they might
make my Holy Tent[d] unclean, and then they
would have to die!’ ”

32These are the teachings for the person who
discharges a body fluid and for the man who be-
comes unclean from semen[n] coming out of his
body. 33These are the teachings for the woman
who becomes unclean from her monthly period,
for a man or woman who has a discharge, and for
a man who becomes unclean by having sexual
relations with a woman who is unclean.

The Day of Cleansing

16 Now two of Aaron’s sons had died while
offering incense[d] to the LORD, and after
that time the LORD spoke to Moses. 2The LORD said
to him, “Tell your brother Aaron that there are
times when he cannot go behind the curtain into
the Most Holy Place where the Ark[d] is. If he goes
in when I appear in a cloud over the lid on the
Ark, he will die.

3“This is how Aaron may enter the Most Holy
Place: before he enters, he must offer a bull for a
sin offering and a ram for a whole burnt offering.
4He must put on the holy linen inner robe, with
the linen underclothes next to his body. His belt
will be the cloth belt, and he will wear the linen
turban. These are holy clothes, so he must bathe
his body in water before he puts them on.

5“Aaron must take from the people of Israel
two male goats for a sin offering and one ram for
a burnt offering. 6Then he will offer the bull for
the sin offering for himself to remove sins from
him and his family so that they will belong to the
LORD.

7“Next Aaron will take the two goats and bring
them before the LORD at the entrance to the Meet-
ing Tent.[d] 8He will throw lots[d] for the two
goats—one will be for the LORD and the other for
the goat that removes sin. 9Then Aaron will take
the goat that was chosen for the LORD by throw-
ing the lot, and he will offer it as a sin offering.
10The other goat, which was chosen by lot to
remove the sin, must be brought alive before the
LORD. The priest will use it to perform the acts
that remove Israel’s sin so that they will belong
to the LORD. Then this goat will be sent out into the
desert as a goat that removes sin.

11“Then Aaron will offer the bull as a sin offer-
ing for himself, to remove the sins from him and
his family so they will belong to the LORD; he will
kill the bull for the sin offering for himself. 12Then
he must take a pan full of burning coals from the
altar before the LORD and two handfuls of sweet
incense that has been ground into powder. He
must bring it into the room behind the curtain.
13He must put the incense on the fire before the
LORD so that the cloud of incense will cover
the lid on the Ark. Then, when Aaron comes in, he
will not die. 14Also, he must take some of the
blood from the bull and sprinkle it with his finger
on the front of the lid; with his finger he will
sprinkle the blood seven times in front of the lid.

15“Then Aaron must kill the goat of the sin
offering for the people and bring its blood into

semen A man’s body fluid by which he can make a woman pregnant.

the room behind the curtain. He must do with the goat's blood as he did with the bull's blood, sprinkling it on the lid and in front of the lid. 16Because the people of Israel have been unclean,[d] Aaron will perform the acts to make the Most Holy Place ready for service to the LORD. Then it will be clean from the sins and crimes of the Israelites. He must also do this for the Meeting Tent, because it stays in the middle of unclean people. 17When Aaron makes the Most Holy Place ready for service to the LORD, no one is allowed in the Meeting Tent until he comes out. So Aaron will perform the acts to remove sins from himself, his family and all the people of Israel, so that they will belong to the LORD. 18Afterwards he will go out to the altar that is before the LORD and will make it ready for service to the LORD. Aaron will take some of the bull's blood and some of the goat's blood and put it on the corners of the altar on all sides. 19Then, with his finger, he will sprinkle some of the blood on the altar seven times to make the altar holy for the LORD and clean from all the sins of the Israelites.

20"When Aaron has finished making the Most Holy Place, the Meeting Tent and the altar ready for service to the LORD, he will offer the living goat. 21He will put both his hands on the head of the living goat, and he will confess over it all the sins and crimes of Israel. In this way Aaron will put the people's sins on the goat's head. Then he will send the goat away into the desert, and a man who has been appointed will lead the goat away. 22So the goat will carry on itself all the people's sins to a lonely place in the desert. The man who leads the goat will let it loose there.

23"Then Aaron will enter the Meeting Tent and take off the linen clothes he had put on before he went into the Most Holy Place; he must leave these clothes there. 24He will bathe his body in water in a holy place and put on his regular clothes. Then he will come out and offer the whole burnt offering for himself and for the people, to remove sins from himself and the people so they will belong to the LORD. 25Then he will burn the fat of the sin offering on the altar.

26"The person who led the goat, the goat to remove sins, into the desert must wash his clothes and bathe his body in water. After that, he may come back into the camp.

27"The bull and the goat for the sin offerings, whose blood was brought into the Most Holy Place to make it ready for service to the LORD, must be taken outside the camp; the animals' skins, bodies and intestines will be burned in the fire. 28Then the one who burns them must wash his clothes and bathe his body in water. After that, he may come back into the camp.

29"This law will always continue for you: on the tenth day of the seventh month, you must not eat and you must not do any work. The travellers or foreigners living with you must not work either. 30It is on this day that the priests will make you clean so you will belong to the LORD again. All your sins will be removed. 31This is a very important day of rest for you, and you must not eat. This law will continue for ever.

32"The priest appointed to take his father's place, on whom the oil was poured, will perform the acts for making things ready for service to the LORD. He must put on the holy linen clothes 33and make the Most Holy Place, the Meeting Tent and the altar ready for service to the LORD. He must also remove the sins of the priests and all the people of Israel so that they will belong to the LORD. 34That law for removing the sins of the Israelites so they will belong to the LORD will continue for ever. You will do these things once a year."

So they did the things the LORD had commanded Moses.

Offering Sacrifices

17 The LORD said to Moses, 2"Speak to Aaron, his sons and all the people of Israel. Tell them: 'This is what the LORD has commanded. 3If an Israelite kills an ox, a lamb or a goat either inside the camp or outside it, 4when he should have brought the animal to the entrance of the Meeting Tent[d] as a gift to the LORD in front of the LORD's Holy Tent, he is guilty of killing. He has killed, and he must be cut off from the people. 5This rule is so people will bring their sacrifices, which they have been sacrificing in the open fields, to the LORD. They must bring those animals to the LORD at the entrance of the Meeting Tent; they must bring them to the priest and offer them as fellowship offerings. 6Then the priest will sprinkle the blood from those animals on the LORD's altar near the entrance of the Meeting Tent. And he will burn the fat from those animals on the altar, as a smell pleasing to the LORD. 7They must not offer any more sacrifices to their goat idols, which they have chased like prostitutes.[d] These rules will continue for people from now on.'

8"Tell the people this: 'If any citizen of Israel or foreigner living with you offers a burnt offering or sacrifice, 9that person must take his sacrifice to the entrance of the Meeting Tent to offer it to the LORD. If he does not do this, he must be cut off from the people.

10" 'I will be against any citizen of Israel or foreigner living with you who eats blood. I will cut off that person from the people. 11This is because the life of the body is in the blood, and I have given you rules for pouring that blood on the altar to remove your sins so that you will

belong to the LORD. It is the blood that removes
the sins, because it is life. 12So I tell the people of
Israel this: "None of you may eat blood, and no
foreigner living among you may eat blood."
13" 'If any citizen of Israel or foreigner living
among you catches a wild animal or bird that
can be eaten, that person must pour the blood
on the ground and cover it with earth. 14If blood
is still in the meat, the animal's life is still in it. So
I give this command to the people of Israel:
"Don't eat meat that still has blood in it, because
the animal's life is in its blood. Anyone who eats
blood must be cut off."
15" 'If a person, either a citizen or a foreigner,
eats an animal that died by itself or was killed
by another animal, he must wash his clothes
and bathe in water. He will be unclean until
evening; then he will be clean. 16If he does not
wash his clothes and bathe his body, he will be
guilty of sin.' "

Rules About Sexual Relations

18 The LORD said to Moses 2"Tell the
people of Israel: 'I am the LORD your God.
3In the past you lived in Egypt, but you must not
do what was done in that country. And you must
not do as they do in the land of Canaan, where
I am bringing you. Do not follow their customs.
4You must obey my rules and follow them. I am
the LORD your God. 5Obey my laws and rules;
a person who obeys them will live because of
them. I am the LORD.
6" 'You must never have sexual relations with
your close relatives. I am the LORD.
7" 'You must not shame your father by having
sexual relations with your mother. She is your
mother; do not have sexual relations with her.
8You must not have sexual relations with your
father's wife; that would shame your father.
9" 'You must not have sexual relations with
your sister, either the daughter of your father or

HOMOSEXUALITY

Be Holy As I Am Holy

Duncan was part of a group of guys who grew up together at school. As they grew older, he became aware that they were increasingly taking the mickey out of homosexual people. They would constantly use the word "gay" to describe something they didn't like or that was bad, and started abusing a few other guys they knew who were openly homosexual. While he didn't agree with homosexuality, Duncan didn't think it was right to pick on others or bully them.

He thought about what he had heard at church, but all they seemed to say was that homosexuality is wrong, without saying what that meant practically. In the end, he decided that Jesus wouldn't agree with picking on other people. He would have shown them love – the love that God shows everyone. So he stopped getting involved in the abuse and started trying to show glimpses of God's love to the homosexual guys.

Leviticus 18:1–24 warns the Israelites several times not to behave like the nations who occupied Canaan before them. The fundamental reason for this is simply stated: "I am the Lord your God". They are called to be holy because the Lord himself is holy.

The context of this is very similar to the modern world that we live in today. The ancient Near East was a world in which the practice of homosexuality was well known. Set against that background, the Old Testament laws are very striking. These laws ban every type of homosexual activity – not just rape as the Assyrians did, or sex with young people as the Egyptians did.

- Why should you obey the laws in Leviticus 18?
- How can you respond to God's challenge to be sexually pure?

Consider . . .

- how you would react if your best friend confessed to being homosexual.
- how you can reflect God's perfect love to homosexual people.

For more, see . . .

- Romans 1:18–27 (p.1185)
- 1 Thessalonians 4:1–8 (p.1298)
- 1 Corinthians 6 (p.1220)

your mother. It doesn't matter if she was born in your house or somewhere else.

10“ ‘You must not have sexual relations with your son's daughter or your daughter's daughter; that would bring shame on you.

11“ ‘If your father and his wife have a daughter, she is your sister. You must not have sexual relations with her.

12“ ‘You must not have sexual relations with your father's sister; she is your father's close relative. 13You must not have sexual relations with your mother's sister; she is your mother's close relative. 14You must not have sexual relations with the wife of your father's brother, because this would shame him. She is your aunt.

15“ ‘You must not have sexual relations with your daughter-in-law; she is your son's wife. Do not have sexual relations with her.

16“ ‘You must not have sexual relations with your brother's wife. That would shame your brother.

17“ ‘You must not have sexual relations with both a woman and her daughter. And do not have sexual relations with this woman's granddaughter, either the daughter of her son or her daughter; they are her close relatives. It is evil to do this.

18“ ‘While your wife is still living, you must not take her sister as another wife. Do not have sexual relations with her.

19“ ‘You must not go near a woman to have sexual relations with her during her monthly period, when she is unclean.[d]

20“ ‘You must not have sexual relations with your neighbour's wife and make yourself unclean with her.

21“ ‘You must not give any of your children to be sacrificed to Molech,[d] because this would show that you do not respect your God. I am the LORD.

22“ ‘You must not have sexual relations with a man as you would a woman. That is a hateful sin.

23“ ‘You must not have sexual relations with an animal and make yourself unclean with it. Also a woman must not have sexual relations with an animal; it is not natural.

24“ ‘Don't make yourself unclean by any of these wrong things. I am forcing nations out of their countries because they did these sins, and I am giving their land to you. 25The land has become unclean, and I punished it for its sins, so the land is throwing out those people who live there.

26“ ‘You must obey my laws and rules, and you must not do any of these hateful sins. These rules are for the citizens of Israel and for the people who live with you. 27The people who lived in the land before you did all these hateful things and made the land unclean. 28If you do these things, you will also make the land unclean, and it will throw you out as it threw out the nations before you. 29Anyone who does these hateful sins must be cut off from the people. 30Keep my command not to do these hateful sins that were done by the people who lived in the land before you. Don't make yourself unclean by doing them. I am the LORD your God.’ ”

Other Laws

19 The LORD said to Moses, 2“Tell all the people of Israel: ‘I am the LORD your God. You must be holy because I am holy.

3“ ‘You must respect your mother and father, and you must keep my Sabbaths.[d] I am the LORD your God.

4“ ‘Do not worship idols or make statues or gods for yourselves. I am the LORD your God.

5“ ‘When you sacrifice a fellowship offering to the LORD, offer it in such a way that it will be accepted. 6You may eat it on the same day you offer it or on the next day. But if any is left on the third day, you must burn it up. 7If any of it is eaten on the third day, it is unclean,[d] and it will not be accepted. 8Anyone who eats it then will be guilty of sin, because he did not respect the holy things that belong to the LORD. He must be cut off from the people.

9“ ‘When you harvest your crops on your land, do not harvest all the way to the corners of your fields. If grain falls onto the ground, don't gather it up. 10Don't pick all the grapes in your vineyards, and don't pick up the grapes that fall to the ground. You must leave those things for poor people and for people travelling through your country. I am the LORD your God.

Sidelight They may not have had social security programmes to help the poor in Old Testament times, but the Israelites were careful to take care of the poor. Farmers were told to leave grain in their field so that poor people and travellers would have something to eat (Leviticus 19:9–10). The story of Ruth (Ruth 2:2–9, p.250) illustrates a time when someone used this law that provided for outsiders.

11“ ‘You must not steal. You must not cheat people, and you must not lie to each other. 12You must not make a false promise by my name, or you will show that you don't respect your God. I am the LORD.

13“ ‘You must not cheat your neighbour or rob him. You must not keep a hired worker's salary all night until morning. 14You must not curse a deaf person or put something in front of a blind person to make him fall. But you must respect your God. I am the LORD.

15“ ‘Be fair in your judging. You must not show special favour to poor people or great people, but be fair when you judge your neighbour. 16You must not spread false stories against other people, and you must not do anything that would put your neighbour’s life in danger. I am the LORD.

17“ ‘You must not hate your fellow citizen in your heart. If your neighbour does something wrong, tell him about it, or you will be partly to blame. 18Forget about the wrong things people do to you, and do not try to get even. Love your neighbour as you love yourself. I am the LORD.

19“ ‘Obey my laws. You must not mate two different kinds of cattle or sow your field with two different kinds of seed. You must not wear clothing made from two different kinds of material mixed together.

20“ ‘If a man has sexual relations with a slave girl of another man, but this slave girl has not been bought or given her freedom, there must be punishment. But they are not to be put to death, because the woman was not free. 21The man must bring a ram as his penalty offering to the LORD at the entrance to the Meeting Tent. [d] 22The priest will offer the ram as a penalty offering before the LORD for the man’s sin, to remove the sins of the man so that he will belong to the LORD. Then he will be forgiven for his sin.

23“ ‘In the future, when you enter your country, you will plant many kinds of trees for food. After planting a tree, wait three years before using its fruit. 24In the fourth year the fruit from the tree will be the LORD’s, a holy offering of praise to him. 25Then in the fifth year, you may eat the fruit from the tree. The tree will then produce more fruit for you. I am the LORD your God.

26“ ‘You must not eat anything with the blood in it.

“ ‘You must not try to tell the future by signs or black magic.

27“ ‘You must not cut the hair on the sides of your heads or cut the edges of your beard. 28You must not cut your body to show sadness for

HONESTY

Help Yourself

“Don’t take that!” Kerry was practically screaming at Michelle now.

“But my brother wants it for his room,” came the reply as Michelle inched a little bit further up the pole. Michelle’s target was the top of a crossing sign, one of the ones that beep and flash when it’s safe to walk across the road.

“Just catch this,” said Michelle as she pulled it from the top of the steel pole. ‘No one will miss it, and they’ll put a new one up. And anyway, my dad pays his taxes; it’s not like real stealing.’ Deep down, though, Michelle knew that Kerry thought it was wrong, and maybe she realised that too.

As Michelle dropped the sign, Kerry reached out her hands and caught it. It was broken now, no use – so they might as well take it. It wasn’t as if they could fix it.

But after she left Michelle, Kerry began to think again. Why did they put those signs up? And then she remembered – it was so that people could cross the road safely, even those who are deaf or blind.

Like the council in Kerry’s town, God put laws in place to make sure that people were protected. **Leviticus 19:1–18** shows us some of the rules that God wrote to protect people.

- Which parts of the passage can you see relate to what Kerry and Michelle were up to?
- Why do you think God put those rules in place? What happens when we break them?

Consider . . .

- going to a friend or family member and coming clean about something you’ve lied or misled others about.
- people less fortunate than you. How can you help them, as God says we should in verses 9 and 10?

For more, see . . .

- Proverbs 11:1–3 (p.599)
- Acts 5:1–11 (p.1145)
- Proverbs 24:26 (p.611)

someone who died or put tattoo marks on your-
selves. I am the LORD.
29“ ‘Do not dishonour your daughter by mak-
ing her become a prostitute.[d] If you do this, the
country will be filled with all kinds of sin.
30“ ‘Obey the laws about Sabbaths, and respect
my Most Holy Place. I am the LORD.
31“ ‘Do not go to mediums[d] or fortune-tellers
for advice, or you will become unclean. I am the
LORD your God.
32“ ‘Show respect to old people; stand up in
their presence. Show respect also to your God. I
am the LORD.
33“ ‘Do not mistreat foreigners living in your
country, 34but treat them just as you treat your
own citizens. Love foreigners as you love your-
selves, because you were once foreigners in
Egypt. I am the LORD your God.
35“ ‘Do not cheat when you measure the
length or weight or amount of something. 36Your
weights and balances should weigh correctly,
with your weighing baskets the right size and
your jars holding the right amount of liquid. I am
the LORD your God. I brought you out of the land
of Egypt.
37“ ‘Remember all my laws and rules, and obey
them. I am the LORD.’ ”

Warnings About Various Sins

20 The LORD said to Moses, 2“You must also
tell the people of Israel these things: ‘If
a person in your country gives one of his
children to Molech,[d] that person must be killed.
It doesn’t matter if he is a citizen or a foreigner
living in Israel; you must throw stones at him and
kill him. 3I will be against him and cut him off
from his people, because he gave his children
to Molech. He showed that he did not respect my
holy name, and he made my Holy Place
unclean.[d] 4The people of the community might
ignore that person and not kill the one who gave
his children to Molech. 5But I will be against him
and his family, and I will cut him off from
his people. I will do this to anyone who follows
him in being unfaithful to me by worshipping
Molech.
6“ ‘I will be against anyone who goes to me-
diums[d] and fortune-tellers for advice, because
that person is being unfaithful to me. So I will cut
him off from his people.
7“ ‘Be my holy people. Be holy because I am
the LORD your God. 8Remember and obey
my laws. I am the LORD, and I have made you
holy.
9“ ‘Anyone who curses his father or mother
must be put to death. He has cursed his father
or mother, so he has brought his own death on
himself.

Punishments for Sexual Sins

10“ ‘If a man has sexual relations with his
neighbour’s wife, both the man and the woman
are guilty of adultery[d] and must be put to death.
11If a man has sexual relations with his father’s
wife, he has shamed his father, and both the man
and his father’s wife must be put to death. They
have brought it on themselves.
12“ ‘If a man has sexual relations with his
daughter-in-law, both of them must be put to
death. What they have done is not natural. They
have brought their own deaths on themselves.
13“ ‘If a man has sexual relations with another
man as a man does with a woman, these two
men have done a hateful sin. They must be put
to death. They have brought it on themselves.
14“ ‘If a man has sexual relations with both a
woman and her mother, this is evil. The people
must burn that man and the two women in fire
so that your people will not be evil.
15“ ‘If a man has sexual relations with an ani-
mal, he must be put to death. You must also kill
the animal. 16If a woman approaches an animal
and has sexual relations with it, you must kill the
woman and the animal. They must be put to
death. They have brought it on themselves.
17“ ‘It is shameful for a brother to marry his
sister, the daughter of either his father or his
mother, and to have sexual relations with her. In
front of everyone they must both be cut off from
their people. The man has shamed his sister, and
he is guilty of sin.
18“ ‘If a man has sexual relations with a
woman during her monthly period, both the
woman and the man must be cut off from their
people. They have sinned because they have
showed the source of her blood.
19“ ‘Do not have sexual relations with your
mother’s sister or your father’s sister, because
that would shame a close relative. Both of you are
guilty of this sin.
20“ ‘If a man has sexual relations with his un-
cle’s wife, he has shamed his uncle. That man
and his uncle’s wife will die without children;
they are guilty of sin.
21“ ‘It is unclean for a man to marry his
brother’s wife. That man has shamed his brother,
and they will have no children.
22“ ‘Remember all my laws and rules, and obey
them. I am leading you to your own land, and if
you obey my laws and rules, that land will not
throw you out. 23I am forcing out ahead of you
the people who live there. Because they did all
these sins, I have hated them. Do not live the
way those people lived.
24“ ‘I have told you that you will get their land,
which I will give to you as your very own; it is a
fertile land. I am the LORD your God, and I have

set you apart from other people and made you my own. 25So you must treat clean animals and birds differently from unclean animals and birds. Do not make yourselves unclean by any of these unclean birds or animals or things that crawl on the ground, which I have made unclean for you. 26So you must be holy to me because I, the LORD, am holy, and I have set you apart from other people to be my own.

27" 'A man or woman who is a medium[d] or a fortune-teller must be put to death. You must stone them to death; they have brought it on themselves.' "

How Priests Must Behave

21 The LORD said to Moses, "Tell these things to Aaron's sons, the priests: 'A priest must not make himself unclean[d] by touching a dead person. 2But if the dead person was one of his close relatives, he may touch him. The priest may make himself unclean if the dead person is his mother or father, son or daughter, brother or 3unmarried sister who is close to him because she has no husband. The priest may make himself unclean for her if she dies. 4But a priest must not make himself unclean if the dead person was only related to him by marriage.

5" 'Priests must not shave their heads, or shave off the edges of their beards, or cut their bodies. 6They must be holy to their God and show respect for God's name, because they present the offerings made by fire to the LORD, which is the food of their God. So they must be holy.

7" 'A priest must not marry an unclean prostitute[d] or a divorced woman, because he is holy to his God. 8Treat him as holy, because he offers up the food of your God. Think of him as holy; I am the LORD who makes you holy, and I am holy.

9" 'If a priest's daughter makes herself unclean by becoming a prostitute, she shames her father. She must be burned with fire.

10" 'The high priest, who was chosen from among his brothers, had the special olive oil poured on his head. He was also appointed to wear the priestly clothes. So he must not show his sadness by letting his hair go uncombed or tearing his clothes. 11He must not go into a house where there is a dead body. He must not make himself unclean, even if it is for his own father or mother. 12The high priest must not go out of the Holy Place, because if he does and becomes unclean, he will make God's Holy Place unclean. The special oil used in appointing priests was poured on his head to separate him from the rest of the people. I am the LORD.

13" 'The high priest must marry a woman who is a virgin.[d] 14He must not marry a widow, a divorced woman or a prostitute. He must marry a virgin from his own people 15so the people will respect his children as his own. I am the LORD. I have set the high priest apart for his special job.' "

16The LORD said to Moses, 17"Tell Aaron: 'If any of your descendants[d] have something wrong with them, they must never come near to offer the special food of their God. 18Anyone who has something wrong with him must not come near: blind men, crippled men, men with damaged faces, deformed men, 19men with a crippled foot or hand, 20hunchbacks, dwarfs, men who have something wrong with their eyes, men who have an itching disease or a skin disease or men who have damaged sex glands.

21" 'If one of Aaron's descendants[d] has something wrong with him, he cannot come near to make the offerings made by fire to the LORD. He has something wrong with him; he cannot offer the food of his God. 22He may eat the most holy food and also the holy food. 23But he may not go through the curtain into the Most Holy Place, and he may not go near the altar, because he has something wrong with him. He must not make my Holy Place unfit. I am the LORD who makes these places holy.' "

24So Moses told these things to Aaron, Aaron's sons and all the people of Israel.

22 The LORD said to Moses, 2"Tell Aaron and his sons: 'The people of Israel will give offerings to me. These offerings are holy, and they are mine, so you must respect them to show that you respect my holy name. I am the LORD. 3Say to them: if any one of your descendants[d] from now on is unclean[d] and comes near the offerings that the Israelites made holy for me, that person must be cut off from appearing before me. I am the LORD.

4" 'If one of Aaron's descendants has a harmful skin disease, or if he discharges a body fluid, he cannot eat the holy offerings until he becomes clean. He could also become unclean from touching a dead body, from his own semen,[n] 5from touching any unclean crawling animal or from touching an unclean person (no matter what made the person unclean). 6Anyone who touches those things will become unclean until evening. That person must not eat the holy offerings unless he washes with water. 7He will be clean only after the sun goes down. Then he may eat the holy offerings; the offerings are his food.

8" 'If a priest finds an animal that died by itself or that was killed by some other animal, he must

semen A man's body fluid by which he can make a woman pregnant.

not eat it. If he does, he will become unclean. I am the LORD.

9“ ‘If the priests keep all the rules I have given, they will not become guilty; if they are careful, they will not die. I am the LORD who has made them holy. 10Only people in a priest’s family may eat the holy offering. A visitor staying with the priest or a hired worker must not eat it. 11But if the priest buys a slave with his own money, that slave may eat the holy offerings; slaves who were born in his house may also eat his food. 12If a priest’s daughter marries a person who is not a priest, she must not eat any of the holy offerings. 13But if the priest’s daughter becomes widowed or divorced, with no children to support her, and if she goes back to her father’s house where she lived as a child, she may eat some of her father’s food. But only people from a priest’s family may eat this food.

14“ ‘If someone eats some of the holy offering by mistake, that person must pay back the priest for that holy food, adding another one-fifth of the price of that food.

15“ ‘When the Israelites give their holy offerings to the LORD, the priest must not treat these holy things as though they were not holy. 16The priests must not allow those who are not priests to eat the holy offerings. If they do, they cause the ones who eat the holy offerings to become guilty, and they will have to pay for it. I am the LORD, who makes them holy.’ ”

17The LORD said to Moses, 18“Tell Aaron and his sons and all the people of Israel: ‘A citizen of Israel or a foreigner living in Israel might want to bring a whole burnt offering, either for some special promise he has made or for a special gift he wants to give to the LORD. 19If he does, he must bring a male animal that has nothing wrong with it—a bull, a sheep or a goat—so it might be accepted for him. 20He must not bring an animal that has something wrong with it, or it will not be accepted for him.

21“ ‘If someone brings a fellowship offering to the LORD, either as payment for a special promise the person has made or as a special gift the person wants to give the LORD, it might be from the herd or from the flock. But it must be healthy, with nothing wrong with it, so that it will be accepted. 22You must not offer to the LORD any animal that is blind, that has broken bones or is crippled, that has running sores or any sort of skin disease. You must not offer any animals like these on the altar as an offering by fire to the LORD.

23“ ‘If an ox or lamb is smaller than normal or is not perfectly formed, you may give it as a special gift to the LORD; it will be accepted. But it will not be accepted as payment for a special promise you have made.

24“ ‘If an animal has bruised, crushed, torn or cut sex glands, you must not offer it to the LORD. You must not do this in your own land, 25and you must not take such animals from foreigners as sacrifices to the LORD. Because the animals have been hurt in some way and have something wrong with them, they will not be accepted for you.’ ”

26The LORD said to Moses, 27“When an ox, a sheep or a goat is born, it must stay seven days with its mother. But from the eighth day on, this animal will be accepted as a sacrifice by fire to the LORD. 28But you must not kill the animal and its mother on the same day, either an ox or a sheep.

29“If you want to offer some special offering of thanks to the LORD, you must do it in a way that pleases him. 30You must eat the whole animal that same day and not leave any of the meat for the next morning. I am the LORD.

31“Remember my commands and obey them; I am the LORD. 32Show respect for my holy name. You Israelites must remember that I am holy; I am the LORD, who has made you holy. 33I brought you out of Egypt to be your God. I am the LORD.”

Special Holidays

23 The LORD said to Moses, 2“Tell the people of Israel: ‘You will announce the LORD’s appointed feasts as holy meetings. These are my special feasts.

The Sabbath

3“ ‘There are six days for you to work, but the seventh day will be a special day of rest. It is a day for a holy meeting; you must not do any work. It is a Sabbath[d] to the LORD in all your homes.

The Passover and Unleavened Bread

4“ ‘These are the LORD’s appointed feasts, the holy meetings, which you will announce at the times set for them. 5The LORD’s Passover[d] is on the fourteenth day of the first month, beginning at twilight. 6The Feast[d] of Unleavened Bread begins on the fifteenth day of the same month. You will eat bread made without yeast for seven days. 7On the first day of this feast you will have a holy meeting, and you must not do any work. 8For seven days you will bring an offering made by fire to the LORD. There will be a holy meeting on the seventh day, and on that day you must not do any regular work.’ ”

The First of the Harvest

9The LORD said to Moses, 10“Tell the people of Israel: ‘You will enter the land I will give you and gather its harvest. At that time you must bring the first bundle of grain from your harvest to the priest. 11The priest will present the bundle before the LORD, and it will be accepted for you; he will present the bundle on the day after the Sabbath.[d]

12" 'On the day when you present the bundle of grain, offer a male lamb, one year old, that has nothing wrong with it, as a burnt offering to the LORD. 13You must also offer a grain offering—4 litres of fine flour mixed with olive oil as an offering made by fire to the LORD; its smell will be pleasing to him. You must also offer a litre of wine as a drink offering. 14Until the day you bring your offering to your God, do not eat any new grain, roasted grain or bread made from new grain. This law will always continue for people from now on, wherever you live.

The Feast of Weeks

15" 'Count seven full weeks from the morning after the Sabbath.[d] (This is the Sabbath on which you bring the bundle of grain to present as an offering.) 16On the fiftieth day, the first day after the seventh week, you will bring a new grain offering to the LORD. 17On that day bring two loaves of bread from your homes to be presented as an offering. Use yeast and 4 litres of flour to make those loaves of bread; they will be your gift to the LORD from the first wheat of your harvest.

18" 'Offer with the bread one young bull, two rams and seven male lambs that are one year old and have nothing wrong with them. Offer them with their grain offerings and drink offerings, as a burnt offering to the LORD. They will be an offering made by fire, and the smell will be pleasing to the LORD. 19You must also offer one male goat for a sin offering and two male, one-year-old lambs as a fellowship offering.

20" 'The priest will present the two lambs as an offering before the LORD, along with the bread from the first wheat of the harvest. They are holy to the LORD, and they will belong to the priest. 21On that same day you will call a holy meeting; you must not do any work on that day. This law will continue for you from now on, wherever you live.

22" 'When you harvest your crops on your land, do not harvest all the way to the corners of your field. If grain falls onto the ground, don't gather it up. Leave it for poor people and foreigners in your country. I am the LORD your God.' "

The Feast of Trumpets

23Again the LORD said to Moses, 24"Tell the people of Israel: 'On the first day of the seventh month you must have a special day of rest, a holy meeting, when you blow the trumpet for a special time of remembering. 25Do not do any work, and bring an offering made by fire to the LORD.' "

The Day of Cleansing

26The LORD said to Moses, 27"The Day of Cleansing will be on the tenth day of the seventh month. There will be a holy meeting, and you will give up eating and bring an offering made by fire to the LORD. 28Do not do any work on that day, because it is the Day of Cleansing. On that day the priests will go before the LORD and perform the acts to make you clean[d] so that you will belong to the LORD.

29"Anyone who refuses to give up food on this day must be cut off from the people. 30If anyone works on this day, I will destroy that person from among the people. 31You must not do any work at all; this law will continue for people from now on wherever you live. 32It will be a special day of rest for you, and you must not eat. You will start this special day of rest on the evening after the ninth day of the month, and it will continue from that evening until the next evening.'

The Feast of Shelters

33Again the LORD said to Moses, 34"Tell the people of Israel: 'On the fifteenth day of the seventh month is the Feast[d] of Shelters. This feast to the LORD will continue for seven days. 35There will be a holy meeting on the first day; do not do any work. 36You will bring an offering made by fire to the LORD each day for seven days. On the eighth day you will have another holy meeting, and you will bring an offering made by fire to the LORD. This will be a holy meeting; do not do any work.

37(" 'These are the LORD's special feasts, when there will be holy meetings and when you bring offerings made by fire to the LORD. You will bring whole burnt offerings, grain offerings, sacrifices and drink offerings—each at the right time. 38These offerings are in addition to those for the LORD's Sabbath[d] days, in addition to offerings you give as payment for special promises, and in addition to special offerings you want to give to the LORD.)

39" 'So on the fifteenth day of the seventh month, after you have gathered in the crops of the land, celebrate the LORD's festival for seven days. You must rest on the first day and the eighth day. 40On the first day you will take good fruit from the fruit trees, as well as branches from palm trees, poplars and other leafy trees. You will celebrate before the LORD your God for seven days. 41Celebrate this festival to the LORD for seven days each year. This law will continue from now on; you will celebrate it in the seventh month. 42Live in shelters for seven days. All the people born in Israel must live in shelters 43so that all your descendants[d] will know I made Israel live in shelters during the time I brought them out of Egypt. I am the LORD your God.' "

44So Moses told the people of Israel about all of the LORD's appointed feast days.

The Lampstand and the Holy Bread

24 The LORD said to Moses, 2"Command the people of Israel to bring you pure oil from crushed olives. That oil is for the lamps so that these lamps may never go out. 3Aaron will keep the lamps burning in the Meeting Tent[d] from evening until morning before the LORD; this is in front of the curtain of the Ark[d] of the Agreement. This law will continue from now on. 4Aaron must always keep the lamps burning on the lampstands of pure gold before the LORD.

5"Take fine flour and bake twelve loaves of bread with it, using 4 litres of flour for each loaf. 6Put them in two rows on the golden table before the LORD, six loaves in each row. 7Put pure incense[d] on each row as the memorial portion to take the place of the bread. It is an offering made by fire to the LORD. 8Every Sabbath[d] day Aaron will put the bread in order before the LORD, as an agreement with the people of Israel that will continue for ever. 9That bread will belong to Aaron and his sons. They will eat it in a holy place, because it is a most holy part of the offerings made by fire to the LORD. That bread is their share for ever."

The Man Who Cursed God

10Now there was a son of an Israelite woman and an Egyptian father who was walking among the Israelites. A fight broke out in the camp between him and an Israelite. 11The son of the Israelite woman began cursing and speaking against the LORD, so the people took him to Moses. (The mother's name was Shelomith, the daughter of Debri from the family of Dan.) 12The people held him as a prisoner while they waited for the LORD's command to be made clear to them.

13Then the LORD said to Moses, 14"Take the one who spoke against me outside the camp. Then all the people who heard him must put their hands on his head, and all the people must throw stones at him and kill him. 15Tell the people of Israel this: 'If anyone curses his God, he is guilty of sin. 16Anyone who speaks against the LORD must be put to death; all the people must kill him by throwing stones at him. Foreigners must be punished just like the people born in Israel; if they speak against the LORD, they must be put to death.

17" 'Whoever kills another person must be put to death. 18Whoever kills an animal that belongs to another person must give that person another animal to take its place. 19And whoever causes an injury to a neighbour must receive the same kind of injury in return: 20broken bone for broken bone, eye for eye, tooth for tooth. Anyone who injures another person must be injured in the same way in return. 21Whoever kills another person's animal must give that person another animal to take its place. But whoever kills another person must be put to death.

22" 'The law will be the same for the foreigner as for those from your own country. I am the LORD your God.' "

23Then Moses spoke to the people of Israel, and they took the person who had cursed outside the camp and killed him by throwing stones at him. So the people of Israel did as the LORD had commanded Moses.

The Time of Rest for the Land

25 The LORD said to Moses at Mount Sinai, 2"Tell the people of Israel this: 'When you enter the land I will give you, let it have a special time of rest, to honour the LORD. 3You may plant seed in your field for six years, and you may trim your vineyards for six years and bring in their fruits. 4But during the seventh year, you must let the land rest. This will be a special time to honour the LORD. You must not plant seed in your field or trim your vineyards. 5You must not cut the crops that grow by themselves after harvest, or gather the grapes from your vines that are not trimmed. The land will have a year of rest.

6" 'You may eat whatever the land produces during that year of rest. It will be food for your men and women servants, for your hired workers and for the foreigners living in your country. 7It will also be food for your cattle and the wild animals of your land. Whatever the land produces may be eaten.

The Year of Jubilee

8" 'Count off seven groups of seven years, or 49 years. During that time there will be seven years of rest for the land. 9On the Day of Cleansing,[d] you must blow the horn of a ram; this will be on the tenth day of the seventh month. You must blow the horn through the whole country. 10Make the fiftieth year a special year, and announce freedom for all the people living in your country. This time will be called Jubilee.[n] You will each go back to your own property, each to your own family and family group. 11The fiftieth year will be a special time for you to celebrate. Don't plant seeds, or harvest the crops that grow

Jubilee This word comes from the Hebrew word for a horn of a ram.

by themselves, or gather grapes from the vines
that are not trimmed. 12That year is Jubilee;
it will be a holy time for you. You may eat only
the crops that come from the field. 13In the year
of Jubilee you each must go back to your own
property.
14“ ‘If you sell your land to your neighbour, or
if you buy land from your neighbour, don’t cheat
each other. 15If you want to buy your neighbour’s
land, count the number of years since the last
Jubilee, and use that number to decide the right
price. If your neighbour sells the land to you,
count the number of years left for harvesting
crops, and use that number to decide the right
price. 16If there are many years, the price will be
high. But if there are only a few years, lower the
price, because your neighbour is really selling
only a few crops to you. 17You must not cheat
each other, but you must respect your God. I am
the LORD your God.
18“ ‘Remember my laws and rules, and obey
them so that you will live safely in the land. 19The
land will give good crops to you, and you will eat
as much as you want and live safely in the land.

Sidelight The start of the year of Jubilee fell once every 50 years. Debts and grievances were forgiven and prisoners released in that year. Christ’s birth signified a new age of Jubilee in which, when we call on his name, our debts and sins are cancelled and we can declare a new birth of caring, forgiveness and freedom – a lifetime of Jubilee.

20“ ‘But you might ask, “If we don’t plant seeds
or gather crops, what will we eat during the sev-
enth year?” 21I will send you such a great blessing
during the sixth year that the land will produce
enough crops for three years. 22When you plant
in the eighth year, you will still be eating from the
old crop; you will eat the old crop until the har-
vest of the ninth year.

Property Laws

23“ ‘The land really belongs to me, so you can’t
sell it for all time. You are only foreigners and
travellers living for a while on my land. 24People
might sell their land, but it must always be possi-
ble for the family to get its land back. 25If a per-
son in your country becomes very poor and sells
some land, then close relatives must come and
buy it back. 26If there is not a close relative to buy
the land back, but if the person makes enough
money to be able to buy it back, 27the years must
be counted since the land was sold. That number
must be used to decide how much the first owner
should pay back the one who bought it. Then the
land will belong to the first owner again. 28But if
there is not enough money to buy it back, the one
who bought it will keep it until the year of Jubi-
lee.[d] During that celebration, the land will go
back to the first owner’s family.
29“ ‘If someone sells a home in a walled city,
for a full year after it is sold the person has the
right to buy it back. 30But if the owner does not
buy back the house before a full year has passed,
it will belong to the one who bought it and to his
future sons. The house will not go back to the
first owner at Jubilee. 31But houses in small towns
without walls are like open country; they can be
bought back, and they must be returned to their
first owner at Jubilee.
32“ ‘The Levites may always buy back their
houses in the cities that belong to them. 33If
someone buys a house from a Levite, that
house in the Levites’ city will again belong to the
Levites in the Jubilee. This is because houses in
Levite cities belong to the people of Levi; the
Israelites gave these cities to them. 34Also the
fields and pastures around the Levites’ cities
cannot be sold, because those fields belong to the
Levites for ever.

Rules for Slave Owners

35“ ‘If anyone from your country becomes too
poor to support himself, help him to live among
you as you would a stranger or foreigner. 36Do
not charge him any interest on money you loan
to him, but respect your God; let the poor live
among you. 37Don’t lend him money for interest,
and don’t try to make a profit from the food he
buys. 38I am the LORD your God, who brought you
out of the land of Egypt to give the land of Ca-
naan to you and to become your God.
39“ ‘If anyone from your country becomes very
poor and sells himself as a slave to you, you must
not make him work like a slave. 40He will be like
a hired worker and a visitor with you until the
year of Jubilee.[d] 41Then he may leave you, take
his children, and go back to his family and the
land of his ancestors. 42This is because the Israel-
ites are my servants, and I brought them out of
slavery in Egypt. They must not become slaves
again. 43You must not rule this person cruelly, but
you must respect your God.
44“ ‘Your men and women slaves must come
from other nations around you; from them you
may buy slaves. 45Also you may buy as slaves
children from the families of foreigners living in
your land. These child slaves will belong to you,
46and you may even pass them on to your chil-
dren after you die; you can make them slaves for
ever. But you must not rule cruelly over your
own people, the Israelites.

47“ ‘Suppose a foreigner or visitor among you
becomes rich. If someone in your country be-
comes so poor that he has to sell himself as a
slave to the foreigner living among you or to a
member of the foreigner’s family, 48the poor per-
son has the right to be bought back and become
free. One of his relatives may buy him back: 49His
uncle, his uncle’s son, or any one of his close
relatives may buy him back. Or, if he gets enough
money, he may pay the money to free himself.

50“ ‘He and the one who bought him must
count the time from when he sold himself up to
the next year of Jubilee. Use that number to de-
cide the price, because the person really only
hired himself out for a certain number of years.
51If there are still many years before the year of
Jubilee, the person must pay back a large part of
the price. 52If there are only a few years left until
Jubilee, the person must pay a small part of the
first price. 53But he will live like a hired person
with the foreigner every year; don’t let the
foreigner rule cruelly over him.

54“ ‘Even if no one buys him back, at the year
of Jubilee, he and his children will become free.
55This is because the people of Israel are servants
to me. They are my servants, whom I brought out
of Egypt. I am the LORD your God.

Rewards for Obeying God

26 “ ‘Don’t make idols for yourselves or set
up statues or memorials. Don’t put stone
statues in your land to bow down to, because I
am the LORD your God.

2“ ‘Remember my Sabbaths,[d] and respect my
Holy Place. I am the LORD.

3“ ‘If you remember my laws and commands
and obey them, 4I will give you rains at the right
season; the land will produce crops, and the trees
of the field will produce their fruit. 5Your thresh-
ing[d] will continue until the grape harvest, and
your grape harvest will continue until it is time to
plant. Then you will have plenty to eat and live
safely in your land. 6I will give peace to your
country; you will lie down in peace, and no one
will make you afraid. I will keep harmful animals
out of your country, and armies will not pass
through it.

7“ ‘You will chase your enemies and defeat
them, killing them with your sword. 8Five of
you will chase 100 men; 100 of you will chase
10,000 men. You will defeat your enemies and
kill them with your sword.

9“ ‘Then I will show kindness to you and let
you have many children; I will keep my agree-
ment with you. 10You will have enough crops to
last for more than a year. When you harvest the
new crops, you will have to throw out the old
ones to make room for them. 11Also I will place
my Holy Tent[d] among you, and I will not turn
away from you. 12I will walk with you and be
your God, and you will be my people. 13I am the
LORD your God, who brought you out of Egypt,
where you were slaves. I broke the heavy weights
that were on your shoulders and let you walk
proudly again.

Punishment for Not Obeying God

14“ ‘But if you do not obey me and keep all my
commands, 15and if you turn away from my rules
and hate my laws, refusing to obey all my com-
mands, you have broken our agreement. 16As a
result, I will do this to you: I will cause terrible
things to happen to you. I will cause you to have
disease and fever that will destroy your eyes and
slowly kill you. You will not have success when
you plant your seed, and your enemy will eat
your crops. 17I will be against you, and your en-
emies will defeat you. These people who hate you
will rule over you, and you will run away even
when no one is chasing you.

18“ ‘If after all this you still do not obey me, I
will punish you seven times more for your sins.
19I will break your great pride, and I will make
the sky like iron and the earth like bronze.[n]
20You will work hard, but it will not help. Your
land will not grow any crops, and your trees will
not give their fruit.

21“ ‘If you still turn against me and refuse to
obey me, I will beat you seven times harder. The
more you sin, the more you will be punished. 22I
will send wild animals to attack you, and they
will take your children away from you and des-
troy your cattle. They will make you so few in
number the roads will be empty.

23“ ‘If you don’t learn your lesson after all these
things, and if you still turn against me, 24I will
also turn against you. I will punish you seven
more times for your sins. 25You broke my agree-
ment, and I will punish you. I will bring armies
against you, and if you go into your cities for
safety, I will cause diseases to spread among you
so that your enemy will defeat you. 26There will
be very little bread to eat; ten women will be able
to cook all your bread in one oven. They will
measure each piece of bread, and you will eat,
but you will still be hungry.

27“ ‘If you still refuse to listen to me and still
turn against me, 28I will show my great anger; I
will punish you seven more times for your sins.
29You will eat the bodies of your sons and daugh-
ters. 30I will destroy your places where gods are
worshipped and cut down your incense[d] altars.

sky . . . bronze This means the sky will give no rain and the earth will produce no crops.

I will pile your dead bodies on the lifeless forms of your idols. I will hate you. 31I will destroy your cities and make your holy places empty, and I will not smell the pleasing smell of your offerings. 32I will make the land empty so that your enemies who come to live in it will be shocked at it. 33I will scatter you among the nations, and I will pull out my sword and destroy you. Your land will become empty, your cities a waste. 34When you are taken to your enemy's country, your land will finally get its rest. It will enjoy its time of rest all the time it lies empty. 35During the time the land is empty, it will have the rest you should have given it while you lived in it.

36" 'Those of you who are left alive will lose their courage in the land of their enemies. They will be frightened by the sound of a leaf being blown by the wind. They will run as if someone were chasing them with a sword, and they will fall even when no one is chasing them. 37They will fall over each other, as if someone were chasing them with a sword, even though no one is chasing them. You will not be strong enough to stand up against your enemies. 38You will die among other nations and disappear in your enemies' countries. 39So those who are left alive will rot away in their enemies' countries because of their sins. They will also rot away because of their ancestors' sins.

There is Always Hope

40" 'But perhaps the people will confess their sins and the sins of their ancestors; maybe they will admit they turned against me and sinned against me, 41which made me turn against them and send them into the land of their enemies. If these disobedient people are sorry for what they did and accept punishment for their sin, 42I will remember my agreement with Jacob, my agreement with Isaac and my agreement with Abraham, and I will remember the land. 43The land will be left empty by its people, and it will enjoy its time of rest as it lies bare without them. Then those who are left alive will accept the punishment for their sins. They will learn that they were punished because they hated my laws and refused to obey my rules. 44But even though this is true, I will not turn away from them when they are in the land of their enemies. I will not hate them so much that I completely destroy them and break my agreement with them, because I am the LORD their God. 45For their good I will remember the agreement with their ancestors, whom I brought out of the land of Egypt so I could become their God; the other nations saw these things. I am the LORD.' "

46These are the laws, rules and teachings the LORD made between himself and the Israelites through Moses at Mount Sinai.

Promises are Important

27 The LORD said to Moses, 2"Speak to the people of Israel and tell them: 'If someone makes a special promise to give a person as a servant to the LORD by paying a price that is the same value as that person, 3the price for a man 20 to 60 years old is about 50 pieces of silver. (You must use the measure as set by the Holy Place.) 4The price for a woman 20 to 60 years old is about 30 pieces of silver. 5The price for a man five to 20 years old is about 20 pieces of silver; for a woman it is about 10 pieces of silver. 6The price for a baby boy one month to five years old is about 5 pieces of silver; for a baby girl the price is about 3 pieces of silver. 7The price for a man 60 years old or older is about 15 pieces of silver; for a woman it is about 10 pieces of silver.

8" 'If anyone is too poor to pay the price, bring him to the priest, and the priest will set the price. The priest will decide how much money the person making the vow can afford to pay.

Gifts to the LORD

9" 'Some animals may be used as sacrifices to the LORD. If someone promises to bring one of these to the LORD, it will become holy. 10That person must not try to put another animal in its place or exchange it, a good animal for a bad one, or a bad animal for a good one. If this happens, both animals will become holy.

11" 'Unclean[d] animals cannot be offered as sacrifices to the LORD, and if someone brings one of them to the LORD, that animal must be brought to the priest. 12The priest will decide a price for the animal, according to whether it is good or bad; as the priest decides, that is the price for the animal. 13If the person wants to buy back the animal, an additional one-fifth must be added to the price.

Value of a House

14" 'If a person gives a house as holy to the LORD, the priest must decide its value, according to whether the house is good or bad; as the priest decides, that is the price for the house. 15But if the person who gives the house wants to buy it back, an additional one-fifth must be added to the price. Then the house will belong to that person again.

Value of Land

16" 'If a person gives some family property to the LORD, the value of the fields will depend on how much seed is needed to plant them. It will cost about 50 pieces of silver for each 100 kilogrammes of barley seed needed. 17If the person gives a field at the year of Jubilee,[d] its value will stay at what the priest has decided. 18But if the person gives the field after the Jubilee, the priest must decide the exact price by counting the number of years to the next year of Jubilee. Then he will subtract that number from its value. 19If the person who gave the field wants to buy it back, one-fifth must be added to that price, and the field will belong to the first owner again.

20“ ‘If the person does not buy back the field, or if it is sold to someone else, the first person cannot ever buy it back. 21When the land is released at the year of Jubilee, it will become holy to the LORD, like land specially given to him. It will become the property of the priests.

22“ ‘If someone gives to the LORD a field he has bought, which is not a part of his family land, 23the priest must count the years to the next Jubilee. He must decide the price for the land, and the price must be paid on that day. Then that land will be holy to the LORD. 24At the year of Jubilee, the land will go back to its first owner, to the family who sold the land.

25“ ‘You must use the measure as set by the Holy Place in paying these prices; it weighs 11.5 grammes.

Value of Animals

26“ ‘If an animal is the first one born to its parent, it already belongs to the LORD, so people may not give it again. If it is a cow or a sheep, it is the LORD's. 27If the animal is unclean, [d] the person must buy it back for the price set by the priest, and the person must add one-fifth to that price. If it is not bought back, the priest must sell it for the price he had decided.

28“ ‘There is a special kind of gift that people set apart to give to the LORD; it may be a person, animal or field from the family property. That gift cannot be bought back or sold. Every special kind of gift is most holy to the LORD.

29“ ‘If anyone is given for the purpose of being destroyed, he cannot be bought back; he must be put to death.

30“ ‘One-tenth of all crops belongs to the LORD, including the crops from fields and the fruit from trees. That one-tenth is holy to the LORD. 31If a person wants to get back that tenth, one-fifth must be added to its price.

32“ ‘The priest will take every tenth animal from a person's herd or flock, and it will be holy to the LORD. 33The owner should not pick out the good animals from the bad or exchange one animal for another. If that happens, both animals will become holy; they cannot be bought back.’ ”

34These are the commands the LORD gave to Moses at Mount Sinai for the people of Israel.

Numbers

Why Read This Book:

- Learn what can happen when you don't trust God's power (Numbers 13—14).
- See that God plans to be good to his people (Numbers 22—24).
- Read about the first equal rights for women (Numbers 27:1–11).

When?

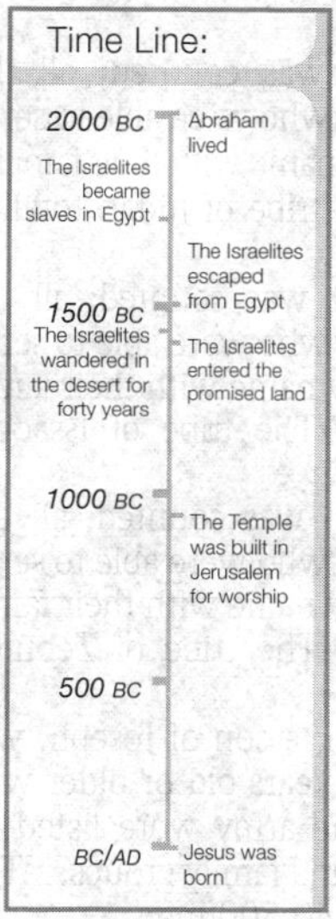

Behind the Scenes:

It's an important rugby match and there is just the chance for a try. You go for it and lose the ball. Within seconds the opposition are another five points up. Your discouraged team faces a long struggle if they are to turn the score in their favour.

On a far greater scale, the book of Numbers tells a similar story. The Hebrew people had been delivered from slavery in Egypt and were on their way to God's promised land. But they disobeyed God and spent 40 years wandering a hostile desert.

Numbers tells how God punished his people who had lost faith both in themselves and in him. It teaches us the importance of obeying and following God with all of our heart, and shows how God patiently and persistently disciplines his stubborn children.

Numbers gets its name from the census taken both at the beginning and at the end of the book. However, its original name "In the Desert" is more accurate.

Where?

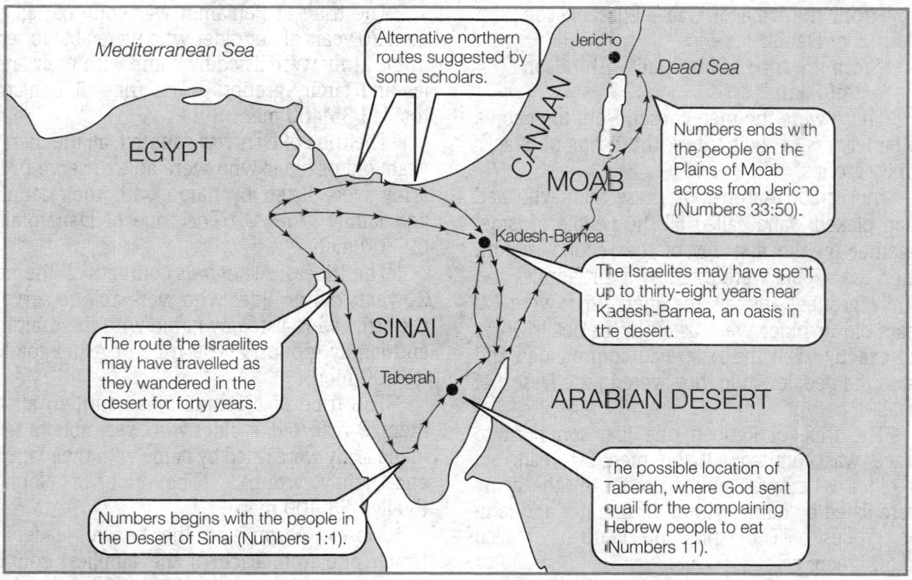

The People of Israel are Counted

1 The LORD spoke to Moses in the Meeting Tent in the Desert of Sinai. This was on the first day of the second month in the second year after the Israelites left Egypt. He said to Moses: 2“You and Aaron must count all the people of Israel by families and family groups, listing the name of each man. 3You and Aaron must count every man 20 years old or older who will serve in the army of Israel, and list them by their divisions. 4One man from each tribe, the leader of his family, will help you. 5These are the names of the men who will help you:

from the tribe of Reuben—Elizur son of Shedeur;
6from the tribe of Simeon—Shelumiel son of Zurishaddai;
7from the tribe of Judah—Nahshon son of Amminadab;
8from the tribe of Issachar—Nethanel son of Zuar;
9from the tribe of Zebulun—Eliab son of Helon;
10from the tribe of Ephraim son of Joseph—Elishama son of Ammihud;
from the tribe of Manasseh son of Joseph—Gamaliel son of Pedahzur;
11from the tribe of Benjamin—Abidan son of Gideoni;
12from the tribe of Dan—Ahiezer son of Ammishaddai;
13from the tribe of Asher—Pagiel son of Ocran;
14from the tribe of Gad—Eliasaph son of Deuel;
15from the tribe of Naphtali—Ahira son of Enan.”

16These were the men chosen from the people to be leaders of their tribes, the heads of Israel’s family groups.

17Moses and Aaron took these men who had been picked 18and called all the people of Israel together on the first day of the second month. Then the people were listed by their families and family groups, and all the men who were 20 years old or older were listed by name. 19Moses did exactly what the LORD had commanded and listed the people while they were in the Desert of Sinai.

20The tribe of Reuben, the first son born to Israel, was counted; all the men 20 years old or older who were able to serve in the army were listed by name with their families and family groups. 21The tribe of Reuben totalled 46,500 men.

22The tribe of Simeon was counted; all the men 20 years old or older who were able to serve in the army were listed by name with their families and family groups. 23The tribe of Simeon totalled 59,300 men.

24The tribe of Gad was counted; all the men 20 years old or older who were able to serve in the army were listed by name with their families and family groups. 25The tribe of Gad totalled 45,650 men.

26The tribe of Judah was counted; all the men 20 years old or older who were able to serve in the army were listed by name with their families and family groups. 27The tribe of Judah totalled 74,600 men.

28The tribe of Issachar was counted; all the men 20 years old or older who were able to serve in the army were listed by name with their families and family groups. 29The tribe of Issachar totalled 54,400 men.

30The tribe of Zebulun was counted; all the men 20 years old or older who were able to serve in the army were listed by name with their families and family groups. 31The tribe of Zebulun totalled 57,400 men.

32The tribe of Ephraim, a son of Joseph, was counted; all the men 20 years old or older who were able to serve in the army were listed by name with their families and family groups. 33The tribe of Ephraim totalled 40,500 men.

34The tribe of Manasseh, also a son of Joseph, was counted; all the men 20 years old or older who were able to serve in the army were listed by name with their families and family groups. 35The tribe of Manasseh totalled 32,200 men.

36The tribe of Benjamin was counted; all the men 20 years old or older who were able to serve in the army were listed by name with their families and family groups. 37The tribe of Benjamin totalled 35,400 men.

38The tribe of Dan was counted; all the men 20 years old or older who were able to serve in the army were listed by name with their families and family groups. 39The tribe of Dan totalled 62,700 men.

40The tribe of Asher was counted; all the men 20 years old or older who were able to serve in the army were listed by name with their families and family groups. 41The tribe of Asher totalled 41,500 men.

42The tribe of Naphtali was counted; all the men 20 years old or older who were able to serve in the army were listed by name with their families and family groups. 43The tribe of Naphtali totalled 53,400 men.

44Moses, Aaron and the twelve leaders of Israel, one from each of the families, counted these men. 45Every man of Israel 20 years old or older who was able to serve in the army was counted and listed with his family. 46The total number of men was 603,550.

47The families from the tribe of Levi were not listed with the others, because 48the LORD had told Moses: 49"Do not count the tribe of Levi or include them with the other Israelites. 50Instead put the Levites in charge of the Holy Tent[d] of the Agreement and everything that is with it. They must carry the Holy Tent and everything in it, and they must take care of it and make their camp around it. 51Any time the Holy Tent is moved, the Levites must take it down, and any time it is set up, the Levites must do it. Anyone else who goes near the Holy Tent will be put to death. 52The Israelites will make their camps in separate divisions, each family near its flag. 53But the Levites must make their camp around the Holy Tent of the Agreement so that I will not be angry with the Israelites. The Levites will take care of the Holy Tent of the Agreement."

54So the Israelites did everything just as the LORD commanded Moses.

Sidelight Imagine the entire population of Wales – more than two million people – marching into London. That would be roughly the number of Israelites that some scholars say escaped from Egypt and wandered in the desert, according to the figures given in Numbers 1:45–46.

The Camp Arrangement

2 The LORD said to Moses and Aaron: 2"The Israelites should make their camps around the Meeting Tent,[d] but they should not camp too close to it. They should camp under their family flag and banners."

3The camp of Judah will be on the east side, where the sun rises, and they will camp by divisions there under their flag. The leader of the people of Judah is Nahshon son of Amminadab. 4There are 74,600 men in his division.

5Next to them the tribe[d] of Issachar will camp. The leader of the people of Issachar is Nethanel son of Zuar. 6There are 54,400 men in his division.

7Next is the tribe of Zebulun. The leader of the people of Zebulun is Eliab son of Helon. 8There are 57,400 men in his division.

9There are a total of 186,400 men in the camps of Judah and its neighbours, in all their divisions. They will be the first to march out of camp.

10The divisions of the camp of Reuben will be on the south side, where they will camp under their flag. The leader of the people of Reuben is Elizur son of Shedeur. 11There are 46,500 men in his division.

12Next to them the tribe of Simeon will camp. The leader of the people of Simeon is Shelumiel son of Zurishaddai. 13There are 59,300 men in his division.

14Next is the tribe of Gad. The leader of the people of Gad is Eliasaph son of Deuel. 15There are 45,650 men in his division.

16There are a total of 151,450 men in the camps of Reuben and its neighbours, in all their divisions. They will be the second group to march out of camp.

17When the Levites march out with the Meeting Tent, they will be in the middle of the other camps. The tribes will march out in the same order as they camp, each in its place under its flag.

18The divisions of the camp of Ephraim will be on the west side, where they will camp under their flag. The leader of the people of Ephraim is Elishama son of Ammihud. 19There are 40,500 men in his division.

20Next to them the tribe of Manasseh will camp. The leader of the people of Manasseh is Gamaliel son of Pedahzur. 21There are 32,200 men in his division.

22Next is the tribe of Benjamin. The leader of the people of Benjamin is Abidan son of Gideoni. 23There are 35,400 men in his division.

24There are a total of 108,100 men in the camps of Ephraim and its neighbours, in all their divisions. They will be the third group to march out of camp.

25The divisions of the camp of Dan will be on the north side, where they will camp under their flag. The leader of the people of Dan is Ahiezer son of Ammishaddai. 26There are 62,700 men in his division.

27Next to them the tribe of Asher will camp. The leader of the people of Asher is Pagiel son of Ocran. 28There are 41,500 men in his division.

29Next is the tribe of Naphtali. The leader of the people of Naphtali is Ahira son of Enan. 30There are 53,400 men in his division.

31There are 157,600 men in the camps of Dan and its neighbours. They will be the last to march out of camp, and they will travel under their own flag.

32These are the Israelites who were counted by families. The total number of Israelites in the camps, counted by divisions, is 603,550. 33Moses obeyed the LORD and did not count the Levites among the other people of Israel.

34So the Israelites obeyed everything the LORD commanded Moses. They camped under their flags and marched out by families and family groups.

Aaron's Family, the Priests

3 This is the family history of Aaron and Moses at the time the LORD talked to Moses on Mount Sinai.

2Aaron had four sons: Nadab, the oldest, Abihu, Eleazar and Ithamar. 3These were the names of Aaron's sons, who were appointed to serve as priests. 4But Nadab and Abihu died in the presence of the LORD when they offered the wrong kind of fire before the LORD in the Desert of Sinai. They had no sons. So Eleazar and Ithamar served as priests during the lifetime of their father Aaron.

5The LORD said to Moses, 6"Bring the tribe[d] of Levi and present them to Aaron the priest to help him. 7They will help him and all the Israelites at the Meeting Tent,[d] doing the work in the Holy Tent. 8The Levites must take care of everything in the Meeting Tent and serve the people of Israel by doing the work in the Holy Tent. 9Give the Levites to Aaron and his sons; of all the Israelites, the Levites are given completely to him. 10Appoint Aaron and his sons to serve as priests, but anyone else who comes near the holy things must be put to death."

11The LORD also said to Moses, 12"I am choosing the Levites from all the Israelites to take the place of all the firstborn[d] children of Israel. The Levites will be mine, 13because the firstborn are mine. When you were in Egypt, I killed all the firstborn children of the Egyptians and took all the firstborn of Israel to be mine, both animals and children. They are mine. I am the LORD."

14The LORD again said to Moses in the Desert of Sinai, 15"Count the Levites by families and family groups. Count every male one month old or older." 16So Moses obeyed the LORD and counted them all.

17Levi had three sons, whose names were Gershon, Kohath and Merari.

18The Gershonite family groups were Libni and Shimei.

19The Kohathite family groups were Amram, Izhar, Hebron and Uzziel.

20The Merarite family groups were Mahli and Mushi.

These were the family groups of the Levites.

21The family groups of Libni and Shimei belonged to Gershon; they were the Gershonite family groups. 22The number that was counted was 7,500 males one month old or older. 23The Gershonite family groups camped on the west side, behind the Holy Tent. 24The leader of the families of Gershon was Eliasaph son of Lael. 25In the Meeting Tent the Gershonites were in charge of the Holy Tent, its covering, the curtain at the entrance to the Meeting Tent, 26the curtains in the courtyard, the curtain at the entrance to the courtyard around the Holy Tent and the altar, the ropes and all the work connected with these things.

27The family groups of Amram, Izhar, Hebron and Uzziel belonged to Kohath; they were the Kohathite family groups. 28They had 8,600 males one month old or older, and they were responsible for taking care of the Holy Place. 29The Kohathite family groups camped south of the Holy Tent. 30The leader of the Kohathite families was Elizaphan son of Uzziel. 31They were responsible for the Ark,[d] the table, the lampstand, the altars, the tools of the Holy Place which they were to use, the curtain and all the work connected with these things. 32The main leader of the Levites was Eleazar son of Aaron, the priest, who was in charge of all those responsible for the Holy Place.

33The family groups of Mahli and Mushi belonged to Merari; they were the Merarite family groups. 34The number that was counted was 6,200 males one month old or older. 35The leader of the Merari families was Zuriel son of Abihail, and they were to camp north of the Holy Tent. 36The Merarites were responsible for the frames of the Holy Tent, the braces, the posts, the bases and all the work connected with these things. 37They were also responsible for the posts in the courtyard around the Holy Tent and their bases, tent pegs and ropes.

38Moses, Aaron and his sons camped east of the Holy Tent, towards the sunrise, in front of the Meeting Tent. They were responsible for the Holy Place for the Israelites. Anyone else who came near the Holy Place was to be put to death.

39Moses and Aaron counted the Levite men by their families, as the LORD commanded, and there were 22,000 males one month old or older.

Levites Take the Place of the Firstborn Sons

40The LORD said to Moses, "Count all the firstborn[d] sons in Israel one month old or older, and list their names. 41Take the Levites for me instead of the firstborn sons of Israel; take the animals of the Levites instead of the firstborn animals from the rest of Israel. I am the LORD."

42So Moses did what the LORD commanded and counted all the firstborn sons of the Israelites. 43When he listed all the firstborn sons one month old or older, there were 22,273 names.

44The LORD also said to Moses, 45"Take the Levites instead of all the firstborn sons of the Israelites, and take the animals of the Levites instead of the animals of the other people. The Levites are mine. I am the LORD. 46Since there are 273 more firstborn sons than Levites, 47collect 5 pieces of silver for each of the 273 sons. Use the measure as set by the Holy Place, which is 11.5 grammes. 48Give the silver to Aaron and his sons as the payment for the 273 Israelites."

49So Moses collected the money for the people the Levites could not replace. 50From the firstborn of the Israelites, he collected 1,365 pieces of silver, using the measure set by the Holy Place. 51Moses obeyed the command of the LORD and gave the silver to Aaron and his sons.

The Jobs of the Kohath Family

4 The LORD said to Moses and Aaron, 2"Count the Kohathites among the Levites by family groups and families. 3Count the men from 30 to 50 years old, all who come to serve in the Meeting Tent.[d]

4"The Kohathites are responsible for the most holy things in the Meeting Tent. 5When the Israelites are ready to move, Aaron and his sons must go into the Holy Tent, take down the curtain, and cover the Ark[d] of the Agreement with it. 6Over this they must put a covering made from fine leather, then spread the solid blue cloth over that, and put the poles in place.

7"Then they must spread a blue cloth over the table for the bread that shows a person is in God's presence. They must put the plates, pans, bowls and the jars for drink offerings on the table; they must leave the bread that is always there on the table. 8Then they must put a red cloth over all of these things, cover everything with fine leather, and put the poles in place.

9"With a blue cloth they must cover the lampstand, its lamps, its wick trimmers, its trays and all the jars for the oil used in the lamps. 10Then they must wrap everything in fine leather and put all these things on a frame for carrying them.

11"They must spread a blue cloth over the gold altar, cover it with fine leather and put the poles in place.

12"They must gather all the things used for serving in the Holy Place and wrap them in a blue cloth. Then they must cover that with fine leather and put these things on a frame for carrying them.

13"They must clean the ashes off the bronze altar and spread a purple cloth over it. 14They must gather all the things used for serving at the altar—the pans for carrying the fire, the meat forks, the shovels and the bowls—and put them on the bronze altar. Then they must spread a covering of fine leather over it and put the poles in place.

15"When the Israelites are ready to move, and when Aaron and his sons have covered the holy furniture and all the holy things, the Kohathites may go in and carry them away. In this way they won't touch the holy things and die. It is the Kohathites' job to carry the things that are in the Meeting Tent.

16"Eleazar son of Aaron, the priest, will be responsible for the Holy Tent and for everything in it, for all the holy things it has: the oil for the lamp, the sweet-smelling incense,[d] the continual grain offering and the oil used to appoint priests and things to the LORD's service."

17The LORD said to Moses and Aaron, 18"Don't let the Kohathites be cut off from the Levites. 19Do this for the Kohathites so that they may go near the Most Holy Place and not die: Aaron and his sons must go in and show each Kohathite what to do and what to carry. 20The Kohathites must not enter and look at the holy things, even for a second, or they will die."

The Jobs of the Gershon Family

21The LORD said to Moses, 22"Count the Gershonites by families and family groups. 23Count the men from 30 to 50 years old, all who have a job to do in the Meeting Tent.[d]

24"This is what the Gershonite family groups must do and what they must carry. 25They must carry the curtains of the Holy Tent,[d] the Meeting Tent, its covering and its outer covering made from fine leather. They must also carry the curtains for the entrance to the Meeting Tent, 26the curtains of the courtyard that go around the Holy Tent and the altar, the curtain for the entrance to the courtyard, the ropes and all the things used with the curtains. They must do everything connected with these things. 27Aaron and his sons are in charge of what the Gershonites do or carry; you tell them what they are responsible for carrying. 28This is the work of the Gershonite family group at the Meeting Tent. Ithamar son of Aaron, the priest, will direct their work.

The Jobs of the Merari Family

29"Count the Merarite families and family groups. 30Count the men from 30 to 50 years old, all who work at the Meeting Tent.[d] 31It is their job to carry the following as they serve in the Meeting Tent: the frames of the Holy Tent, the crossbars, the posts and bases, 32in addition to the posts that go around the courtyard, their bases, tent pegs, ropes and everything that is used with the poles around the courtyard. Tell each man exactly what to carry. 33This is the work the Merarite family group will do for the Meeting Tent. Ithamar son of Aaron, the priest, will direct their work."

The Levite Families

34Moses, Aaron and the leaders of Israel counted the Kohathites by families and family groups,

35the men from 30 to 50 years old who were to work at the Meeting Tent.[d] 36There were 2,750 men in the family groups. 37This was the total of the Kohath family groups who worked at the Meeting Tent, whom Moses and Aaron counted as the LORD had commanded Moses.

38Also, the Gershonites were counted by families and family groups, 39the men from 30 to 50 years old who were given work at the Meeting Tent. 40The families and family groups had 2,630 men. 41This was the total of the Gershon family groups who worked at the Meeting Tent, whom Moses and Aaron counted as the LORD had commanded.

42Also, the men in the families and family groups of the Merari family were counted, 43the men from 30 to 50 years old who were to work at the Meeting Tent. 44The family groups had 3,200 men. 45This was the total of the Merari family groups, whom Moses and Aaron counted as the LORD had commanded Moses.

46So Moses, Aaron and the leaders of Israel counted all the Levites by families and family groups. 47They counted the men from 30 to 50 years old who were given work at the Meeting Tent and who carried the Tent. 48The total number of these men was 8,580. 49Each man was counted as the LORD had commanded Moses; each man was given his work and told what to carry as the LORD had commanded Moses.

Rules About Cleanliness

5 The LORD said to Moses, 2"Command the Israelites to send away from camp anyone with a harmful skin disease. Send away anyone who gives off body fluid or who has become unclean by touching a dead body. 3Send both men and women outside the camp so that they won't spread the disease there, where I am living among you." 4So Israel obeyed the LORD's command and sent those people outside the camp. They did just as the LORD had told Moses.

Paying for Doing Wrong

5The LORD said to Moses, 6"Tell the Israelites: 'When a man or woman does something wrong to another person, that is really sinning against the LORD. That person is guilty 7and must admit the wrong that has been done. The person must fully pay for the wrong that has been done, adding one-fifth to it, and giving it to the person who was wronged. 8But if that person is dead and does not have any close relatives to receive the payment, the one who did wrong owes the LORD and must pay the priest. In addition, the priest must sacrifice a ram to remove the wrong so that the person will belong to the LORD. 9When an Israelite brings a holy gift, it should be given to the priest. 10No one has to give these holy gifts, but if someone does give them, they belong to the priest.' "

Suspicious Husbands

11Then the LORD said to Moses, 12"Tell the Israelites: 'A man's wife might be unfaithful to him 13and have sexual relations with another man. Her sin might be kept hidden from her husband so that he does not know about the wrong she did. Perhaps no one saw it, and she wasn't caught. 14But if her husband has feelings of jealousy and suspects she has sinned—whether she has or not— 15he should take her to the priest. The husband must also take an offering for her of 2 litres of barley flour. He must not pour oil or incense[d] on it, because this is a grain offering for jealousy, an offering of remembrance. It is to find out if she is guilty.

16" 'The priest will bring in the woman and make her stand before the LORD. 17He will take some holy water in a clay jar, and he will put some earth from the floor of the Holy Tent into the water. 18The priest will make the woman stand before the LORD, and he will loosen her hair. He will hand her the offering of remembrance, the grain offering for jealousy; he will hold the bitter water that brings a curse. 19The priest will make her take an oath and ask her, "Has another man had sexual relations with you? Have you been unfaithful to your husband? If you haven't, this bitter water that brings a curse won't hurt you. 20But if you have been unfaithful to your husband and have had sexual relations with a man besides him"— 21the priest will then put on her the curse that the oath will bring—"the LORD will make the people curse and reject you. He will make your stomach get big, and he will make your body unable to give birth to another baby. 22This water that brings a curse will go inside you and make your body unable to give birth to another baby."

" 'The woman must say, "I agree."

23" 'The priest should write these curses on a scroll, wash the words off into the bitter water, 24and make the woman drink the bitter water that brings a curse. If she is guilty, the water will make her sick. 25Then the priest will take the grain offering for jealousy from her. He will present it before the LORD and bring it to the altar. 26He will take a handful of the grain, which is a memorial offering, and burn it on the altar. After that he will make the woman drink the water 27to see if she is not pure and if she has sinned against her husband. When it goes into her, if her stomach gets big so that she is not able to have another baby, her people will reject her. 28But if the woman has not sinned, she is pure. She is not guilty, and she will be able to have babies.

29“ ‘So this is the teaching about jealousy. This is what to do when a woman does wrong and is unfaithful while she is married to her husband. 30It also should be done if the man gets jealous because he suspects his wife. The priest will have her stand before the LORD, and he will do all these things, just as the teaching commands. 31In this way the husband can be proven correct, and the woman will suffer if she has done wrong.’ ”

Rules for the Nazirites

6 The LORD said to Moses, 2“Tell the Israelites: ‘If men or women want to promise to belong to the LORD in a special way, they will be called Nazirites. 3During this time, they must not drink wine or beer, or vinegar made from wine or beer. They must not even drink grape juice or eat grapes or raisins. 4While they are Nazirites, they must not eat anything that comes from the grapevine, even the seeds or the skin.

5“ ‘During the time they have promised to belong to the LORD, they must not cut their hair. They must be holy until this special time is over. They must let their hair grow long. 6During their special time of belonging to the LORD, Nazirites must not go near a dead body. 7Even if their own father, mother, brother or sister dies, they must not touch them, or they will become unclean.[d] They must still keep their promise to belong to God in a special way. 8While they are Nazirites, they belong to the LORD in a special way.

Sidelight

What do you call a person who grows a beard, watches what he eats, and never cuts his hair? A Nazirite. Nazirites were men who took a special vow to dedicate their lives to God (Numbers 6:2–8). Samson, whose story is in Judges 13—16 (p.239), was probably the most famous of these Nazirites.

9“ ‘If they are next to someone who dies suddenly, their hair, which was part of their promise, has been made unclean. So they must shave their head seven days later to be clean. 10Then on the eighth day, they must bring two doves or two young pigeons to the priest at the entrance to the Meeting Tent.[d] 11The priest will offer one as a sin offering and the other as a burnt offering. This removes sin so they will belong to the LORD. (They had sinned because they were near a dead body.) That same day they will again promise to let their hair grow 12and give themselves to the LORD for another special time. They must bring a male lamb a year old as a penalty offering. The days of the special time before don’t count, because they became unclean during their first special time.

13“ ‘This is the teaching for the Nazirites. When the promised time is over, they must go to the entrance of the Meeting Tent[d] 14and give their offerings to the LORD. They must offer a year-old male lamb that has nothing wrong with it, as a burnt offering, a year-old female lamb that has nothing wrong with it, as a sin offering, and a ram that has nothing wrong with it, for a fellowship offering. 15They must also bring the grain offerings and drink offerings that go with them. And they must bring a basket of bread made without yeast, loaves made with fine flour mixed with oil, and wafers made without yeast, spread with oil.

16“ ‘The priest will give these offerings to the LORD and make the sin offering and the burnt offering. 17Then he will kill the ram as a fellowship offering to the LORD; along with it, he will present the basket of bread made without yeast, the grain offering and the drink offering.

18“ ‘The Nazirites must go to the entrance of the Meeting Tent and shave off their hair that they grew for their promise. The hair will be put in the fire that is under the sacrifice of the fellowship offering.

19“ ‘After the Nazirites cut off their hair, the priest will give them a boiled shoulder from the ram. From the basket he will also give a loaf and a wafer, both made without yeast. 20Then the priest will present them to the LORD. They are holy and belong to the priest. Also, he is to present the breast and the thigh from the ram. After that, the Nazirites may drink wine.

21“ ‘This is the teaching for the Nazirites who make a promise. Everyone who makes the Nazirite promise must give all these gifts to the LORD. If they promised to do more, they must keep their promise, according to the teaching of the Nazirites.’ ”

The Priests’ Blessings

22The LORD said to Moses, 23“Tell Aaron and his sons, ‘This is how you should bless the Israelites. Say to them:

24“May the LORD bless you and keep you.
25May the LORD show you his kindness
and have mercy on you.
26May the LORD watch over you
and give you peace.” ’

27“So Aaron and his sons will bless the Israelites with my name, and I will bless them.”

The Holy Tent

7 When Moses finished setting up the Holy Tent,[d] he gave it for service to the LORD by

pouring olive oil on the Tent and on everything used in it. He also poured oil on the altar and all its tools to prepare them for service to the LORD. 2Then the leaders of Israel made offerings. These were the heads of the families, the leaders of each tribe[d] who counted the people. 3They brought to the LORD six covered carts and twelve oxen—each leader giving an ox, and every two leaders giving a cart. They brought these to the Holy Tent.

4The LORD said to Moses, 5"Accept these gifts from the leaders and use them in the work of the Meeting Tent. Give them to the Levites as they need them."

6So Moses accepted the carts and the oxen and gave them to the Levites. 7He gave two carts and four oxen to the Gershonites, which they needed for their work. 8Then Moses gave four carts and eight oxen to the Merarites, which they needed for their work. Ithamar son of Aaron, the priest, directed the work of all of them. 9Moses did not give any oxen or carts to the Kohathites, because their job was to carry the holy things on their shoulders.

10When the oil was poured on the altar, the leaders brought their offerings to it to give it to the LORD's service; they presented them in front of the altar. 11The LORD told Moses, "Each day one leader must bring his gift to make the altar ready for service to me."

12–83Each of the twelve leaders brought these gifts. Each leader brought one silver plate that weighed about 1,500 grammes, and one silver bowl that weighed about 800 grammes. These weights were set by the Holy Place measure. The bowl and the plate were filled with fine flour mixed with oil for a grain offering. Each leader also brought a large gold dish that weighed about 110 grammes and was filled with incense.[d]

In addition, each of the leaders brought one young bull, one ram and one male lamb a year old for a burnt offering; one male goat for a sin offering; and two oxen, five rams, five male goats and five male lambs a year old for a fellowship offering.

On the first day Nahshon son of Amminadab brought his gifts. He was the leader of the tribe of Judah.

PEACE

An Unlikely Gift

Adam, twenty-five, lives in a home with six handicapped people and four assistants. He can't speak, walk, or eat without help. His back is deformed, his movements are uncoordinated, and seizures grip his body daily.

But Adam's dependence on others has taught valuable lessons to those who know him. As people help Adam with things he can't do alone, they discover that Adam never hurries or worries. Without ever speaking, Adam communicates inner peace.

Some people would consider Adam worthless. But after being with Adam, people feel affected by that inner peace. As people help him, they are touched with a sense of affection that's much deeper than words. Though totally dependent on them, his gift is simply to be there with them. The peace Adam shares by his being with others far outweighs anything Adam can't do.

Adam shows that peace is a gift from God that's deeper than the things we do. Consider the source of Adam's peace as you read **Numbers 6:22–27**.

- How is the peace talked about in this passage like the peace that Adam shows in his life?
- Are you experiencing these things in your life? If not, how can you begin to experience them?

Consider . . .

- reading dictionary definitions of peace. Write the ones that apply to God's peace on a postcard and place it where you can see it every day.
- sitting silently for ten minutes in prayer, inviting God to give you inner peace. Think about how the experience affects the rest of your day.

For more, see . . .

- Psalm 119:165 (p.574)
- Romans 12:14–21 (p.1205)
- John 14:27 (p.1124)

On the second day Nethanel son of Zuar brought his gifts. He was the leader of the tribe of Issachar.

On the third day Eliab son of Helon brought his gifts. He was the leader of the tribe of Zebulun.

On the fourth day Elizur son of Shedeur brought his gifts. He was the leader of the tribe of Reuben.

On the fifth day Shelumiel son of Zurishaddai brought his gifts. He was the leader of the tribe of Simeon.

On the sixth day Eliasaph son of Deuel brought his gifts. He was the leader of the tribe of Gad.

On the seventh day Elishama son of Ammihud brought his gifts. He was the leader of the tribe of Ephraim.

On the eighth day Gamaliel son of Pedahzur brought his gifts. He was the leader of the tribe of Manasseh.

On the ninth day Abidan son of Gideoni brought his gifts. He was the leader of the tribe of Benjamin.

On the tenth day Ahiezer son of Ammishaddai brought his gifts. He was the leader of the tribe of Dan.

On the eleventh day Pagiel son of Ocran brought his gifts. He was the leader of the tribe of Asher.

On the twelfth day Ahira son of Enan brought his gifts. He was the leader of the tribe of Naphtali.

84So these were the gifts from the Israelite
leaders when oil was poured on the altar and it
was given for service to the LORD: twelve silver
plates, twelve silver bowls and twelve gold
dishes. 85Each silver plate weighed about 1,500
grammes, and each bowl weighed about 800
grammes. All the silver plates and silver bowls
together weighed about 27 kilogrammes accord-
ing to a weight set by the Holy Place measure.
86The twelve gold dishes filled with incense
weighed 110 grammes each, according to the
weight set by the Holy Place measure. Together
the gold dishes weighed about 1,400 grammes.
87The total number of animals for the burnt offer-
ing was twelve bulls, twelve rams and twelve
male lambs a year old. There was also a grain
offering, and there were twelve male goats for a
sin offering. 88The total number of animals for the
fellowship offering was 24 bulls, 60 rams, 60 male
goats and 60 male lambs a year old. All these
offerings were for giving the altar to the service
of the LORD after the oil had been poured on it.

89When Moses went into the Meeting Tent to
speak with the LORD, he heard the LORD speaking
to him. The voice was coming from between the
two gold creatures with wings that were above
the lid of the Ark[d] of the Agreement. In this way
the LORD spoke with him.

The Lampstand

8 The LORD said to Moses, 2"Speak to Aaron
and tell him, 'Put the seven lamps where
they can light the area in front of the lamp-
stand.' "

3Aaron did this, placing the lamps so that they
lighted the area in front of the lampstand; he
obeyed the command the LORD gave Moses. 4The
lampstand was made from hammered gold, from
its base to the flowers. It was made in exactly the
way the LORD had showed Moses.

The Levites are Given to God

5The LORD said to Moses, 6"Take the Levites
away from the other Israelites and make them
clean.[d] 7This is what you should do to make
them clean: sprinkle the cleansing water on
them, and make them shave their bodies and
wash their clothes so that they are clean. 8They
must take a young bull and the grain offering of
flour mixed with oil that goes with it. Then take
a second young bull for a sin offering. 9Bring the
Levites to the front of the Meeting Tent,[d] and
gather all the Israelites around. 10When you bring
the Levites before the LORD, the Israelites should
put their hands on them.[n] 11Aaron will present
the Levites before the LORD as an offering pre-
sented from the Israelites. Then the Levites will
be ready to do the work of the LORD.

12"The Levites will put their hands on the
bulls' heads—one bull will be a sin offering to the
LORD, and the other will be a burnt offering, to
remove the sins of the Levites so they will belong
to the LORD. 13Make the Levites stand in front of
Aaron and his sons and present the Levites as an
offering to the LORD. 14In this way you must set
apart the Levites from the other Israelites; the
Levites will be mine.

15"Make the Levites pure, and present them as
an offering so that they may come to work at the
Meeting Tent. 16They will be given completely to
me from the Israelites; I have taken them for my-
self instead of the firstborn[d] of every Israelite
woman. 17All the firstborn in Israel—people or
animals—are mine. When I killed all the first-
born in Egypt, I set the firstborn in Israel aside for
myself. 18But I have taken the Levites instead of
all the firstborn in Israel. 19From all the Israelites
I have given the Levites to Aaron and his sons so
that they may serve the Israelites at the Meeting
Tent. They will help remove the Israelites' sins
so that they belong to the LORD and so that no

put . . . them This showed that the people had a part in giving the Levites their special work.

disaster strikes the Israelites when they approach the Holy Place."

[20]So Moses, Aaron and all the Israelites obeyed and did with the Levites what the LORD commanded Moses. [21]The Levites made themselves clean and washed their clothes. Then Aaron presented them as an offering to the LORD. He also removed their sins so they would be pure. [22]After that, the Levites came to the Meeting Tent to work, and Aaron and his sons told them what to do. They did with the Levites what the LORD commanded Moses.

[23]The LORD said to Moses, [24]"This command is for the Levites. Everyone 25 years old or older must come to the Meeting Tent, because they all have jobs to do there. [25]At the age of 50, they must retire from their jobs and not work again. [26]They may help their fellow Levites with their work at the Meeting Tent, but they must not do the work themselves. This is how you are to give the Levites their jobs."

The Passover is Celebrated

9 The LORD spoke to Moses in the Desert of Sinai in the first month of the second year after the Israelites left Egypt. He said, [2]"Tell the Israelites to celebrate the Passover[d] at the appointed time. [3]That appointed time is the fourteenth day of this month at twilight; they must obey all the rules about it."

[4]So Moses told the Israelites to celebrate the Passover, [5]and they did; it was in the Desert of Sinai at twilight on the fourteenth day of the first month. The Israelites did everything just as the LORD commanded Moses.

[6]But some of the people could not celebrate the Passover on that day because they were unclean[d] from touching a dead body. So they went to Moses and Aaron that day and [7]said to Moses, "We are unclean because of touching a dead body. But why should we be kept from offering gifts to the LORD at this appointed time? Why can't we join the other Israelites?"

[8]Moses said to them, "Wait, and I will find out what the LORD says about you."

[9]Then the LORD said to Moses, [10]"Tell the Israelites this: 'If you or your descendants[d] become unclean because of a dead body, or if you are away on a trip during the Passover, you must still celebrate the LORD's Passover. [11]But celebrate it at twilight on the fourteenth day of the second month. Eat the lamb with bitter herbs and bread made without yeast. [12]Don't leave any of it until the next morning or break any of its bones. When you celebrate the Passover, follow all the rules. [13]Anyone who is clean and is not away on a trip but does not eat the Passover must be cut off from the people. That person did not give an offering to the LORD at the appointed time and must be punished for the sin.

[14]" 'Foreigners among you may celebrate the LORD's Passover, but they must follow all the rules. You must have the same rules for foreigners as you have for yourselves.' "

The Cloud Above the Tent

[15]On the day the Holy Tent,[d] the Tent of the Agreement, was set up, a cloud covered it. From dusk until dawn the cloud above the Tent looked like fire. [16]The cloud stayed above the Tent, and at night it looked like fire. [17]When the cloud moved from its place over the Tent, the Israelites moved, and wherever the cloud stopped, the Israelites camped. [18]So the Israelites moved at the LORD's command, and they camped at his command. While the cloud stayed over the Tent, they remained camped. [19]Sometimes the cloud stayed over the Tent for a long time, but the Israelites obeyed the LORD and did not move. [20]Sometimes the cloud was over it only a few days. At the LORD's command the people camped, and at his command they moved. [21]Sometimes the cloud stayed only from dusk until dawn; when the cloud lifted the next morning, the people moved. When the cloud lifted, day or night, the people moved. [22]The cloud might stay over the Tent for two days, a month or a year. As long as it stayed, the people camped, but when it lifted, they moved. [23]At the LORD's command the people camped, and at his command they moved. They obeyed the LORD's order that he commanded through Moses.

The Silver Trumpets

10 The LORD said to Moses, [2]"Make two trumpets of hammered silver, and use them to call the people together and to march out of camp. [3]When both trumpets are blown, the people should gather before you at the entrance to the Meeting Tent.[d] [4]If you blow only one trumpet, the leaders, the heads of the family groups of Israel, should meet before you. [5]When you loudly blow the trumpets, the tribes[d] camping on the east should move. [6]When you loudly blow them again, the tribes camping on the south should move; the loud sound will tell them to move. [7]When you want to gather the people, blow the trumpets, but don't blow them as loudly.

[8]"Aaron's sons, the priests, should blow the trumpets. This is a law for you and your descendants[d] from now on. [9]When you are fighting an enemy who attacks you in your own land, blow the trumpets loudly. The LORD your God will take notice of you and will save you from your enemies. [10]Also blow your trumpets at happy times and

during your feasts and at New Moon[d] festivals.
Blow them over your burnt offerings and fellowship offerings, because they will help you remember your God. I am the LORD your God."

The Israelites Move Camp

11The cloud lifted from the Tent[d] of the Agreement on the twentieth day of the second month
of the second year. 12So the Israelites moved from
the Desert of Sinai and continued until the cloud
stopped in the Desert of Paran. 13This was their
first time to move, and they did it as the LORD had commanded Moses.

14The divisions from the camp of Judah moved first under their flag. Nahshon son of Amminadab
was the commander. 15Nethanel son of Zuar was
over the division of the tribe[d] of Issachar. 16Eliab
son of Helon was over the division of the tribe of
Zebulun. 17Then the Holy Tent was taken down, and the Gershonites and Merarites, who carried it, moved next.

18Then came the divisions from the camp of Reuben under their flag, and Elizur son of Shedeur was the commander. 19Shelumiel son of Zurishaddai was over the division of the tribe of
Simeon. 20Eliasaph son of Deuel was over the
division of the tribe of Gad. 21Then came the
Kohathites, who carried the holy things; the Holy Tent was to be set up before they arrived.

22Next came the divisions from the camp of Ephraim under their flag, and Elishama son of
Ammihud was the commander. 23Gamaliel son
of Pedahzur was over the division of the tribe
of Manasseh, 24and Abidan son of Gideoni was
over the division of the tribe of Benjamin.

25The last ones were the rearguard for all the tribes. These were the divisions from the camp of Dan under their flag, and Ahiezer son of Ammishaddai was the commander. 26Pagiel son of
Ocran was over the division of the tribe of Asher;
27Ahira son of Enan was over the division of the
tribe of Naphtali. 28This was the order the Israelite divisions marched in when they moved.

29Hobab was the son of Reuel the Midianite,[n] who was Moses' father-in-law. Moses said to Hobab, "We are moving to the land the LORD promised to give us. Come with us and we will be good to you, because the LORD has promised good things to Israel."

30But Hobab answered, "No, I will not go. I will go back to my own land where I was born."

31But Moses said, "Please don't leave us. You know where we can camp in the desert, and you
can be our guide. 32Come with us. We will share
with you all the good things the LORD gives us."
33So they left the mountain of the LORD and travelled for three days. The Ark[d] of the LORD's Agreement went in front of the people for those three days, as they looked for a place to camp.
34The LORD's cloud was over them during the day when they left their camp.

35When the Ark left the camp, Moses said,
"Rise up, LORD!
Scatter your enemies:
make those who hate you run from you."

36And when the Ark was set down, Moses said,
"Return, LORD,
to the thousands of people of Israel."

Fire from the LORD

11 Now the people complained to the LORD about their troubles, and when he heard them, he became angry. Then fire from the LORD burned among the people at the edge of the
camp. 2The people cried out to Moses, and when
he prayed to the LORD, the fire stopped burning.
3So that place was called Taberah,[n] because the LORD's fire had burned among them.

Seventy Elders Help Moses

4Some troublemakers among them wanted better food, and soon all the Israelites began
complaining. They said, "We want meat! 5We remember the fish we ate for free in Egypt. We also
had cucumbers, melons, leeks, onions and garlic.
6But now we have lost our appetite; we never see anything but this manna!"

7The manna was like small white seeds. 8The
people would go to gather it, and then grind it in handmills, or crush it between stones. After they cooked it in a pot or made cakes with it, it tasted
like bread baked with olive oil. 9When the dew
fell on the camp each night, so did the manna.

10Moses heard every family crying as they stood in the entrances of their tents. Then the LORD became very angry, and Moses got upset.
11He asked the LORD, "Why have you brought me, your servant, this trouble? What have I done wrong that you made me responsible for all these
people? 12I am not the father of all these people, and I didn't give birth to them. So why do you make me carry them to the land you promised to our ancestors? Must I carry them in my arms as
a nurse carries a baby? 13Where can I get meat for
all these people? They keep crying to me, 'We
want meat!' 14I can't take care of all these people
alone. It's too much for me. 15If you are going to
continue doing this to me, then kill me now.

Reuel the Midianite Also called Jethro.
Taberah This name means "burning".

If you care about me, put me to death, and then
I won't have any more troubles."
16 The LORD said to Moses, "Bring me 70 of
Israel's elders, men that you know are leaders
among the people. Bring them to the Meeting
Tent,[d] and have them stand there with you. 17 I will
come down and speak with you there. I will take
some of the Spirit[d] that is in you, and I will give
it to them. They will help you care for the people
so that you will not have to care for them alone.
18 "Tell the people this: 'Make yourselves holy
for tomorrow, and you will eat meat. You cried to
the LORD, "We want meat! We were better off in
Egypt!" So now the LORD will give you meat to
eat. 19 You will eat it not for just one, two, five,
ten or even twenty days, 20 but you will eat that
meat for a whole month. You will eat it until it
comes out your nose, and you will grow to hate
it. This is because you have rejected the LORD,
who is with you. You have cried to him, saying,
"Why did we ever leave Egypt?"'"
21 Moses said, "LORD, here are 600,000 people
standing around me, and you say, 'I will give
them enough meat to eat for a month!' 22 If we
killed all the flocks and herds, that would not be
enough. If we caught all the fish in the sea, that
would not be enough."
23 But the LORD said to Moses, "Do you think
I'm weak? Now you will see if I can do what
I say."
24 So Moses went out to the people and told
them what the LORD had said. He gathered 70 of
the elders together and had them stand around
the Tent. 25 Then the LORD came down in the
cloud and spoke to Moses. The LORD took some
of the Spirit Moses had, and he gave it to the
70 leaders. With the Spirit in them, they prophes-
ied,[d] but just that one time.

STRESS

Exam Stress

Claire was very stressed. Her GCSEs were later that summer and her parents were fighting all the time now. They had all stopped going to church. There was nowhere calm for her to revise. Her parents finally agreed that she could go to a friend's house to stay, just until the exams were over.

Poor Claire was so wound up and worried that from the start things went horribly wrong. The first exam was her French oral. Claire was dreading it but hoped she would remember what she'd written down about her hobbies and interests. It started off well enough. Mrs Hixon asked Claire to tell her about the things she liked to do, and Claire began to say what she'd memorised. But suddenly she stopped. Her mind was a total blank. She froze in horror, completely forgetting what she was supposed to say. Mrs Hixon tried to help by asking her something in French, but Claire couldn't understand and started to get upset. She begged Mrs Hixon to turn off the tape and help her, but when Mrs Hixon replied in French, Claire blew up.

It was all a blur from then on, but Claire remembers swearing at her teacher, kicking her chair over and running from the room in tears, slamming the door behind her. Everything had got on top of her and she just couldn't cope.

In **Numbers 11:10–15** Moses got very upset too. But Moses asked God to help him with his stress so that he wouldn't react in a way he would regret.

- How do you think God wants us to deal with stress?
- When do you think you should ask for God's help – right at the beginning or just before you're about to lose it? Why?

Consider . . .

- when you have exams coming up, asking God to help you all the way through – from your coursework, to the revision, and the exam itself.
- giving your stressful situations to God and asking him to fill you with his peace and patience.

For more, see . . .

- Matthew 11:28–30 (p.960)
- 1 Peter 5:7 (p.1362)
- Galatians 5:22–23 (p.1264)

26Two men named Eldad and Medad were also
listed as leaders, but they did not go to the Tent.
They stayed in the camp, but the Spirit was also
given to them, and they prophesied in the camp.
27A young man ran to Moses and said, "Eldad and
Medad are prophesying in the camp."
28Joshua son of Nun said, "Moses, my master,
stop them!" (Ever since he was a young boy,
Joshua had been Moses' assistant.)
29But Moses answered, "Are you jealous for
me? I wish all the LORD's people could prophesy.
I wish the LORD would give his Spirit to all of
them!" 30Then Moses and the leaders of Israel
went back to the camp.

The LORD Sends Quail

31The LORD sent a strong wind from the sea,
and it blew quail into the area all around the
camp. The quail were about a metre deep on the
ground, and there were quail a day's walk in any
direction. 32The people went out and gathered
quail all that day, that night and the next day.
Everyone gathered at least a tonne, and they

> **Sidelight**
>
> If you get sick of Christmas leftovers, try to imagine having 180 turkeys left over! That's roughly the number of quail that each Israelite gathered after complaining that God hadn't provided them with meat in the desert (Numbers 11:31–32).

spread them around the camp. 33But the LORD
became very angry, and he gave the people a
terrible sickness that came while the meat was
still in their mouths. 34So the people named that
place Kibroth Hattaavah,[n] because there they
buried those who wanted other food.
35From Kibroth Hattaavah the people went to
stay at Hazeroth.

Miriam and Aaron Speak Against Moses

12 Miriam and Aaron began to talk against
Moses because of his Cushite wife (he
had married a Cushite). 2They said, "Is Moses the
only one the LORD speaks through? Doesn't he
also speak through us?" And the LORD heard this.
3(Now Moses was very humble. He was the
least proud person on earth.)
4So the LORD suddenly spoke to Moses, Aaron
and Miriam and said, "All three of you come to
the Meeting Tent."[d] So they went. 5The LORD
came down in a pillar of cloud and stood at the
entrance to the Tent. He called to Aaron and
Miriam, and they both came near. 6He said, "Lis-
ten to my words:

When a prophet[d] is among you,
I, the LORD, will show myself to him in visions;
I will speak to him in dreams.
7But this is not true with my servant Moses.
I trust him to lead all my people.
8I speak face to face with him—
clearly, not with hidden meanings.
He has even seen the form of the LORD.
You should be afraid
to speak against my servant Moses."

9The LORD was very angry with them, and he
left.
10When the cloud lifted from the Tent and
Aaron turned towards Miriam, she was as white
as snow; she had a skin disease. 11Aaron said to
Moses, "Please, my master, forgive us for our
foolish sin. 12Don't let her be like a baby who is
born dead. (Sometimes a baby is born with half of
its flesh eaten away.)"
13So Moses cried out to the LORD, "God, please
heal her!"
14The LORD answered Moses, "If her father had
spat in her face, she would have been shamed for
seven days, so put her outside the camp for seven
days. After that, she may come back." 15So Mir-
iam was put outside the camp for seven days, and
the people did not move on until she came back.
16After that, the people left Hazeroth and
camped in the Desert of Paran.

The Spies Explore Canaan

13 The LORD said to Moses, 2"Send men to
explore the land of Canaan, which I will
give to the Israelites. Send one leader from each
tribe."[d]
3So Moses obeyed the LORD's command and
sent the Israelite leaders out from the Desert of
Paran. 4These are their names: from the tribe of
Reuben, Shammua son of Zaccur; 5from the tribe
of Simeon, Shaphat son of Hori; 6from the tribe of
Judah, Caleb son of Jephunneh; 7from the tribe of
Issachar, Igal son of Joseph; 8from the tribe
of Ephraim, Hoshea son of Nun; 9from the tribe
of Benjamin, Palti son of Raphu; 10from the
tribe of Zebulun, Gaddiel son of Sodi; 11from the
tribe of Manasseh (a tribe of Joseph), Gaddi son
of Susi; 12from the tribe of Dan, Ammiel son of
Gemalli; 13from the tribe of Asher, Sethur son of
Michael; 14from the tribe of Naphtali, Nahbi son
of Vophsi; 15from the tribe of Gad, Geuel son of
Maki.

Kibroth Hattaavah This name in Hebrew means "graves of wanting".

16These are the names of the men Moses sent to explore the land. (Moses gave Hoshea son of Nun the new name Joshua.)

17Moses sent them to explore Canaan and said, "Go through southern Canaan and then into the mountains. 18See what the land looks like. Are the people who live there strong or weak? Are there a few or many? 19What kind of land do they live in? Is it good or bad? What about the towns they live in—are they open like camps, or do they have walls? 20What about the soil? Is it fertile or poor? Are there trees there? Try to bring back some of the fruit from that land." (It was the season for the first grapes.)

21So they went up and explored the land, from the Desert of Zin all the way to Rehob by Lebo Hamath. 22They went through the southern area to Hebron, where Ahiman, Sheshai and Talmai, the descendants[d] of Anak lived.[d] (The city of Hebron had been built seven years before Zoan in Egypt.) 23In the Valley of Eshcol, they cut off a branch of a grapevine that had one bunch of grapes on it and carried that branch on a pole between two of them. They also got some pomegranates[d] and figs. 24That place was called the Valley of Eshcol,[n] because the Israelites cut off the bunch of grapes there. 25After 40 days of exploring the land, the men returned to the camp.

26They came back to Moses and Aaron and all the Israelites at Kadesh, in the Desert of Paran. The men reported to them and showed everybody the fruit from the land. 27They told Moses, "We went to the land where you sent us, and it is a fertile land! Here is some of its fruit. 28But the people who live there are strong. Their cities are walled and very large. We even saw some Anakites there. 29The Amalekites live in the southern area; the Hittites, Jebusites and Amorites live in the mountains; and the Canaanites live near the sea and along the Jordan River."

30Then Caleb told the people near Moses to be quiet, and he said, "We should certainly go up and take the land for ourselves. We can certainly do it."

31But the men who had gone with him said, "We can't attack those people; they are stronger than we are." 32And those men gave the Israelites a bad report about the land they explored, saying, "The land that we explored is too large to conquer. All the people we saw are very tall. 33We saw the Nephilim[d] people there. (The Anakites come from the Nephilim people.) We felt like grasshoppers, and we looked like grasshoppers to them."

The People Complain Again

14 That night all the people in the camp began crying loudly. 2All the Israelites complained against Moses and Aaron, and all the people said to them, "We wish we had died in Egypt or in this desert. 3Why is the LORD bringing us to this land to be killed with swords? Our wives and children will be taken away. We would be better off going back to Egypt." 4They said to each other, "Let's choose a leader and go back to Egypt."

5Then Moses and Aaron bowed face down in front of all the Israelites gathered there. 6Joshua son of Nun and Caleb son of Jephunneh, who had explored the land, tore their clothes. 7They said to all of the Israelites, "The land we explored is very good. 8If the LORD is pleased with us, he will lead us into that land and give us that fertile land. 9Don't turn against the LORD! Don't be afraid of the people in that land! We will chew them up. They have no protection, but the LORD is with us. So don't be afraid of them."

10Then all the people talked about killing them with stones. But the glory of the LORD appeared at the Meeting Tent[d] to all the Israelites. 11The LORD said to Moses, "How long will these people ignore me? How long will they not believe me in spite of the miracles[d] I have done among them? 12I will give them a terrible sickness and get rid of them. But I will make you into a great nation that will be stronger than they are."

13Then Moses said to the LORD, "The Egyptians will hear about it! You brought these people from there by your great power, 14and the Egyptians will tell this to those who live in this land. They have already heard about you, LORD. They know that you are with your people and that you were seen face to face. They know that your cloud stays over your people and that you lead your people with that cloud during the day and with fire at night. 15If you put these people to death all at once, the nations who have heard about your power will say, 16'The LORD was not able to bring them into the land he promised them. So he killed them in the desert.'

17"So show your strength now, Lord. Do what you said: 18'The LORD doesn't become angry quickly, but he has great love. He forgives sin and law breaking. But the LORD never forgets to punish guilty people. When parents sin, he will also punish their children, their grandchildren, their great-grandchildren and their great-great-grandchildren.' 19By your great love, forgive these people's sin, just as you have forgiven them from the time they left Egypt until now."

Eshcol This name in Hebrew means "bunch".

20The LORD answered, "I have forgiven them as you asked. 21But, as surely as I live and as surely as my glory fills the whole earth, I make this promise: 22all these men saw my glory and the miracles I did in Egypt and in the desert, but they disobeyed me and tested me ten times. 23So not one of them will see the land I promised to their ancestors. No one who rejected me will see that land. 24But my servant Caleb thinks differently and follows me completely. So I will bring him into the land he has already seen, and his children will own that land. 25Since the Amalekites and the Canaanites are living in the valleys, leave tomorrow and follow the desert road towards the Red Sea."

The LORD Punishes the People

26The LORD said to Moses and Aaron, 27"How long will these evil people complain about me? I have heard the grumbling and complaining of these Israelites. 28So tell them, 'This is what the LORD says. I heard what you said, and as surely as I live, I will do those very things to you: 29you will die in this desert. Every one of you who is 20 years old or older and who was counted with the people—all of you who complained against me—will die. 30Not one of you will enter the land where I promised you would live; only Caleb son of Jephunneh and Joshua son of Nun will go in. 31You said that your children would be taken away, but I will bring them into the land to enjoy what you refused. 32As for you, you will die in this desert. 33Your children will be shepherds here for 40 years. Because you were not loyal, they will suffer until you lie dead in the desert. 34For 40 years you will suffer for your sins—a year for each of the 40 days you explored the land. You will know me as your enemy.' 35I, the LORD, have spoken, and I will certainly do these things to all these evil people who have come together against me. So they will all die here in this desert."

36The men Moses had sent to explore the land had returned and spread complaints among all the people. They had given a bad report about the land. 37The men who gave a very bad report died; the LORD killed them with a terrible sickness. 38Only two of the men who explored the land did not die—Joshua son of Nun and Caleb son of Jephunneh.

39When Moses told these things to all the Israelites, they were very sad. 40Early the next morning they started to go towards the top of the mountains, saying, "We have sinned. We will go where the LORD told us."

41But Moses said, "Why are you disobeying the LORD's command? You will not win! 42Don't go, because the LORD is not with you and you will be beaten by your enemies. 43You will run into the Amalekites and Canaanites, who will kill you with swords. You have turned away from the LORD, so the LORD will not be with you."

44But they were proud. They went towards the top of the mountains, but Moses and the Ark[d] of the Agreement with the LORD did not leave the camp. 45The Amalekites and the Canaanites who lived in those mountains came down and attacked the Israelites and beat them back all the way to Hormah.

Rules About Sacrifices

15 The LORD said to Moses, 2"Speak to the Israelites and say to them: 'When you enter the land that I am giving you as a home, 3give the LORD offerings made by fire. These may be from your herds or flocks, as a smell pleasing to the LORD. These may be burnt offerings or sacrifices for special promises, or as gifts to him, or as festival offerings. 4The one who brings the offering shall also give the LORD a grain offering. It should be 2 litres of fine flour mixed with 1 litre of olive oil. 5Each time you offer a lamb as a burnt offering or sacrifice, also prepare 1 litre of wine as a drink offering.

6" 'If you are giving a ram, also prepare a grain offering of 4 litres of fine flour mixed with one and a half litres of olive oil. 7Also prepare one and a half litres of wine as a drink offering. Its smell will be pleasing to the LORD.

8" 'If you prepare a young bull as a burnt offering or sacrifice, whether it is for a special promise or a fellowship offering to the LORD, 9bring a grain offering with the bull. It should be 7 litres of fine flour mixed with 2 litres of olive oil. 10Also bring 2 litres of wine as a drink offering. This offering is made by fire, and its smell will be pleasing to the LORD. 11Prepare each bull or ram, lamb or young goat in this way. 12Do this for every one of the animals you bring.

13" 'All citizens must do these things in this way, and the smell of their offerings by fire will be pleasing to the LORD. 14From now on if foreigners who live among you want to make offerings by fire so the smell will be pleasing to the LORD, they must offer them in the same way that you do. 15The law is the same for you and for foreigners, and it will be from now on; you and the foreigners are alike before the LORD. 16The teachings and rules are the same for you and for the foreigners among you.' "

17The LORD said to Moses, 18"Tell the Israelites: 'You are going to another land, where I am taking you. 19When you eat the food there, offer part of it to the LORD. 20Offer a loaf of bread from the first of your grain, which will be your offering from

the threshing[d] floor. 21From now on offer to the
LORD the first part of your grain.
22" 'Now what if you forget to obey any of
these commands the LORD gave Moses? 23These
are the LORD's commands given to you through
Moses, which began the day the LORD gave them
to you and will continue from now on. 24If the
people forget to obey one of these commands, all
the people must offer a young bull as a burnt
offering, a smell pleasing to the LORD. By law you
must also give the grain offering and the drink
offering with it, and you must bring a male goat
as a sin offering.
25" 'The priest will remove that sin for all the
Israelites so they will belong to the LORD. They are
forgiven, because they didn't know they were
sinning. For the wrong they did they brought
offerings to the LORD, an offering by fire and a sin
offering. 26So all of the people of Israel and the
foreigners living among them will be forgiven. No
one meant to do wrong.
27" 'If just one person sins without meaning to,
a year-old female goat must be brought for a sin
offering. 28The priest will remove the sin of the
person who sinned accidentally. He will remove
it before the LORD, and the person will be for-
given. 29The same teaching is for everyone who
sins accidentally—for those born Israelites and
for foreigners living among you.
30" 'But anyone who sins on purpose is against
the LORD and must be cut off from the people,
whether it is someone born among you or a
foreigner. 31That person has turned against the
LORD's word and has not obeyed his commands.
Such a person must surely be cut off from the
others. He is guilty.' "

A Man Worked on the Sabbath

32When the Israelites were still in the desert,
they found a man gathering wood on the Sab-
bath[d] day. 33Those who found him gathering
wood brought him to Moses and Aaron and all
the people. 34They held the man under guard,
because they did not know what to do with him.
35Then the LORD said to Moses, "The man must
surely die. All the people must kill him by throw-
ing stones at him outside the camp." 36So all the
people took him outside the camp and stoned
him to death, as the LORD commanded Moses.

The Tassels

37The LORD said to Moses, 38"Speak to the Is-
raelites and tell them this: 'Tie several pieces of
thread together and attach them to the corners of
your clothes. Put a blue thread in each one
of these tassels. Wear them from now on. 39You
will have these tassels to look at to remind you of
all the LORD's commands. Then you will obey
them and not be disloyal by following what your
bodies and eyes want. 40Then you will remember
to obey all my commands, and you will be God's
holy people. 41I am the LORD your God, who
brought you out of Egypt to be your God. I am
the LORD your God.' "

Korah, Dathan, Abiram and On

16 Korah, Dathan, Abiram and On turned
against Moses. (Korah was the son of
Izhar, the son of Kohath, the son of Levi; Dathan
and Abiram were brothers, the sons of Eliab; and
On was the son of Peleth; Dathan, Abiram and
On were from the tribe[d] of Reuben.) 2These men
gathered 250 other Israelite men, well-known
leaders chosen by the community, and chal-
lenged Moses. 3They came as a group to speak to
Moses and Aaron and said, "You have gone too
far. All the people are holy, every one of them,
and the LORD is among them. So why do you put
yourselves above all the people of the LORD?"
4When Moses heard this, he bowed face
down. 5Then he said to Korah and all his follow-
ers: "Tomorrow morning the LORD will show who
belongs to him. He will bring the one who is holy
near to him; he will bring to himself the person
he chooses. 6So Korah, you and all your followers
do this: get some pans for burning incense.[d] 7To-
morrow put fire and incense in them and take
them before the LORD. He will choose the man
who is holy. You Levites have gone too far."
8Moses also said to Korah, "Listen, you Levites.
9The God of Israel has separated you from the
rest of the Israelites. He brought you near to him-
self to do the work in the LORD's Holy Tent[d] and
to stand before all the Israelites and serve them.
Isn't that enough? 10He has brought you and all
your fellow Levites near to himself, yet now you
want to be priests. 11You and your followers have
joined together against the LORD. Your complaint
is not against Aaron."
12Then Moses called Dathan and Abiram, the
sons of Eliab, but they said, "We will not come!
13You have brought us out of a fertile land to this
desert to kill us, and now you want to order us
around. 14You haven't brought us into a fertile
land; you haven't given us any land with fields
and vineyards. Will you put out the eyes of these
men? No! We will not come!"
15Then Moses became very angry and said to
the LORD, "Don't accept their gifts. I have not
taken anything from them, not even a donkey,
and I have not done wrong to any of them."
16Then Moses said to Korah, "You and all your
followers must stand before the LORD tomorrow.
And Aaron will stand there with you and them.

17Each of you must take your pan and put incense
in it; present these 250 pans before the LORD. You
and Aaron must also present your pans." 18So
each man got his pan and put burning incense in
it and stood with Moses and Aaron at the en-
trance to the Meeting Tent. 19Korah gathered all
his followers who were against Moses and Aaron,
and they stood at the entrance to the Meeting
Tent. Then the glory of the LORD appeared to
everyone.
20The LORD said to Moses and Aaron, 21"Move
away from these men so I can destroy them
quickly."
22But Moses and Aaron bowed face down and
cried out, "God, you are the God over the spirits
of all people. Please don't be angry with this
whole group. Only one man has really sinned."
23Then the LORD said to Moses, 24"Tell every-
one to move away from the tents of Korah, Da-
than and Abiram."
25Moses stood and went to Dathan and Abi-
ram; the elders of Israel followed him. 26Moses
warned the people, "Move away from the tents of
these evil men! Don't touch anything of theirs, or
you will be destroyed because of their sins." 27So
they moved away from the tents of Korah, Da-
than and Abiram. Dathan and Abiram were
standing outside their tents with their wives, chil-
dren and little babies.
28Then Moses said, "Now you will know that
the LORD has sent me to do all these things; it was
not my idea. 29If these men die a normal death—
the way men usually die—then the LORD did not
really send me. 30But if the LORD does something
new, you will know they have insulted the LORD.
The ground will open and swallow them. They
will be buried alive and will go to the place of the
dead, and everything that belongs to them will go
with them."
31When Moses finished saying these things,
the ground under the men split open. 32The earth
opened and swallowed them and all their famil-
ies. All Korah's men and everything they owned
went down. 33They were buried alive, going to
the place of the dead, and everything they owned
went with them. Then the earth covered them.
They died and were gone from the community.
34The people of Israel around them heard their
screams and ran away, saying, "The earth will
swallow us, too!"
35Then a fire came down from the LORD and
destroyed the 250 men who had presented the
incense.
36The LORD said to Moses, 37"Tell Eleazar son
of Aaron, the priest, to take all the incense pans
out of the fire. Have him scatter the coals a long
distance away. But the incense pans are still holy.
38Take the pans of these men who sinned and lost
their lives, and hammer them into flat sheets that
will be used to cover the altar. They are holy,
because they were presented to the LORD, and
they will be a sign to the Israelites."
39So Eleazar the priest gathered all the bronze
pans that had been brought by the men who
were burned up. He had the pans hammered into
flat sheets to put on the altar, 40as the LORD had
commanded him through Moses. These sheets
were to remind the Israelites that only descend-
ants[d] of Aaron should burn incense before the
LORD. Anyone else would die like Korah and his
followers.

Aaron Saves the People

41The next day all the Israelites complained
against Moses and Aaron and said, "You have
killed the LORD's people."
42When the people gathered to complain
against Moses and Aaron, they turned towards
the Meeting Tent,[d] and the cloud covered it. The
glory of the LORD appeared. 43Then Moses and
Aaron went in front of the Meeting Tent.
44The LORD said to Moses, 45"Move away from
these people so I can destroy them quickly." So
Moses and Aaron bowed face down.
46Then Moses said to Aaron, "Get your pan,
and put fire from the altar and incense[d] in it.
Hurry to the people and remove their sin. The
LORD is angry with them; the sickness has already
started." 47So Aaron did as Moses said. He ran to
the middle of the people, where the sickness had
already started among them. So Aaron offered the
incense to remove their sin. 48He stood between
the dead and the living, and the sickness stopped
there. 49But 14,700 people died from that sick-
ness, in addition to those who died because of
Korah. 50Then Aaron went back to Moses at the
entrance to the Meeting Tent. The terrible sick-
ness had been stopped.

Aaron's Walking Stick Buds

17 The LORD said to Moses, 2"Speak to the
people of Israel and get twelve walking
sticks from them—one from the leader of each
tribe.[d] Write the name of each man on his stick,
and 3on the stick from Levi, write Aaron's name.
There must be one stick for the head of each
tribe. 4Put them in the Meeting Tent[d] in front of
the Ark[d] of the Agreement, where I meet with
you. 5I will choose one man whose walking stick
will begin to grow leaves; in this way I will
stop the Israelites from always complaining
against you."
6So Moses spoke to the Israelites. Each of the
twelve leaders gave him a walking stick—one

from each tribe—and Aaron's walking stick was among them. 7Moses put them before the LORD in the Tent of the Agreement.

8The next day, when Moses entered the Tent, he saw that Aaron's stick (which stood for the family of Levi) had grown leaves. It had even budded, blossomed and produced almonds. 9So Moses brought out to the Israelites all the walking sticks from the LORD's presence. They all looked, and each man took back his stick.

10Then the LORD said to Moses, "Put Aaron's walking stick back in front of the Ark of the Agreement. It will remind these people who are always turning against me to stop their complaining against me so they won't die." 11So Moses obeyed what the LORD commanded him.

12The people of Israel said to Moses, "We are going to die! We are destroyed. We are all destroyed! 13Anyone who even comes near the Holy Tent of the LORD will die. Will we all die?"

The Work of the Priests and Levites

18 The LORD said to Aaron, "You, your sons and your family are now responsible for any wrongs done against the Holy Place; you and your sons are responsible for any wrongs done against the priests. 2Bring with you your fellow Levites from your tribe,[d] and they will help you and your sons serve in the Tent[d] of the Agreement. 3They are under your control, to do all the work that needs to be done in the Tent. But they must not go near the things in the Holy Place or near the altar. If they do, both you and they will die. 4They will join you in taking care of the Meeting Tent. They must do the work at the Tent, and no one else may come near you.

5"You must take care of the Holy Place and the altar so that I won't become angry with the Israelites again. 6I myself chose your fellow Levites from among the Israelites as a gift given for you to the LORD, to work at the Meeting Tent. 7But only you and your sons may serve as priests. Only you may serve at the altar or go behind the curtain. I am giving you this gift of serving as a priest, and anyone else who comes near the Holy Place will be put to death."

8Then the LORD said to Aaron, "I myself make you responsible for the offerings given to me. All the holy offerings that the Israelites give to me, I give to you and your sons as your share, your continual portion. 9Your share of the holy offerings is that part which is not burned. When the people bring me gifts as most holy offerings, whether they are grain or sin or penalty offerings, they will be set apart for you and your sons. 10You must eat the offering in a most holy place. Any male may eat it, but you must respect it as holy.

11"I also give you the offerings the Israelites present to me. I give these to you and your sons and daughters as your continual share. Anyone in your family who is clean[d] may eat it.

12"And I give you all the best olive oil and all the best new wine and grain. This is what the Israelites give to me, the LORD, from the first crops they harvest. 13When they bring to the LORD all the first things they harvest, they will be yours. Anyone in your family who is clean may eat these things.

14"Everything in Israel that is given to the LORD is yours. 15The first one born to any family, whether people or animals, will be offered to the LORD. And that will be yours. But you must make a payment for every firstborn[d] child and every firstborn animal that is unclean. 16When they are one month old, you must make a payment for them of 5 pieces of silver, as set by the Holy Place measure.

> **Sidelight** Your parents may say you're priceless, but the ancient Hebrews knew exactly how much a baby was worth. Numbers 18:15–16 tells how parents had to offer their child to God and then buy it back for about 60 grammes of silver when the baby was a month old.

17"But you must not make a payment for the firstborn ox or sheep or goat. Those animals are holy. Sprinkle their blood on the altar and burn their fat as an offering made by fire. The smell is pleasing to the LORD. 18But the meat will be yours, just as the breast that is presented and the right thigh will be yours. 19Anything the Israelites present as holy gifts I, the LORD, give to you, your sons and daughters as your continual portion. This is a lasting agreement of salt[n] before the LORD for you and your children for ever."

20The LORD also said to Aaron, "You will not inherit any of the land, and you will not own any land among the other people. I will be yours. Out of all the Israelites, only you will inherit me.

21"When the people of Israel give me a tenth of what they make, I will give that tenth to the Levites. This is their payment for the work they do serving at the Meeting Tent. 22But the other Israelites must never go near the Meeting Tent, or they will die for their sin. 23Only the Levites

agreement of salt The meaning is not clear, but Leviticus 2:13 says, "Salt stands for your agreement with God that will last for ever."

should work in the Meeting Tent and be responsible for any sins against it. This is a rule from now on. The Levites will not inherit any land among the other Israelites, 24but when the Israelites give a tenth of everything they make to me, I will give that tenth to the Levites as a reward. That is why I said about the Levites: 'They will not inherit any land among the Israelites.' "

25The LORD said to Moses, 26"Speak to the Levites and tell them: 'You will receive a tenth of everything the Israelites make, which I will give to you. But you must give a tenth of that back to the LORD. 27I will accept your offering just as much as I accept the offerings from others, who give new grain or new wine. 28In this way you will present an offering to the LORD as the other Israelites do. When you receive a tenth from the Israelites, you will give a tenth of that to Aaron, the priest, as the LORD's share. 29Choose the best and holiest part from what you are given as the portion you must give to the LORD.'

30"Say to the Levites: 'When you present the best, it will be accepted as much as the grain and wine from the other people. 31You and your families may eat all that is left anywhere, because it is your pay for your work in the Meeting Tent. 32And if you always give the best part to the LORD, you will never be guilty. If you do not sin against the holy offerings of the Israelites, you will not die.' "

The Offering for Cleansing

19 The LORD said to Moses and Aaron, 2"These are the teachings that the LORD commanded. Tell the Israelites to get a young red cow that does not have anything wrong with it and that has never been worked. 3Give the cow to Eleazar the priest; he will take it outside the camp and kill it. 4Then Eleazar the priest must put some of its blood on his finger and sprinkle it seven times towards the front of the Meeting Tent.[d] 5The whole cow must be burned while he watches; the skin, the meat, the blood and the intestines must all be burned. 6Then the priest must take a cedar stick, a hyssop branch and a red string and throw them onto the burning cow. 7After the priest has washed himself and his clothes with water, he may come back into the camp, but he will be unclean[d] until evening. 8The man who burns the cow must wash himself and his clothes in water; he will be unclean until evening.

9"Then someone who is clean will collect the ashes from the cow and put them in a clean place outside the camp. The Israelites will keep these ashes to use in the cleansing water, in a special ceremony to cleanse away sin. 10The man who collected the cow's ashes must wash his clothes and be unclean until evening. This is a lasting rule for the Israelites and for the foreigners among them.

11"Those who touch a dead person's body will be unclean for seven days. 12They must wash themselves with the cleansing water on the third day and on the seventh day; then they will be clean. But if they do not wash themselves on the third day and the seventh day, they cannot be clean. 13If those who touch a dead person's body stay unclean and go to the LORD's Holy Tent, it becomes unclean; they must be cut off from Israel. If the cleansing water is not sprinkled on them, they are unclean and will stay unclean.

14"This is the teaching about someone who dies in a tent: anyone in the tent or anyone who enters it will be unclean for seven days. 15And every open jar or pot without a cover becomes unclean. 16If anyone is outside and touches someone who was killed by a sword or who died a natural death, or if anyone touches a human bone or a grave, that person will be unclean for seven days.

17"So you must use the ashes from the burnt offering to make that person clean again. Pour fresh water over the ashes into a jar. 18A clean person must take a hyssop branch and dip it into the water, and then he must sprinkle it over the Tent and all its objects. He must also sprinkle the people who were there, as well as anyone who touched a bone, or the body of someone who was killed, or a dead person, or a grave. 19The person who is clean must sprinkle this water on the unclean people on the third day and on the seventh day. On the seventh day they will become clean. They must wash their clothes and take a bath, and they will be clean that evening. 20If any who are unclean do not become clean, they must be cut off from the community. Since they were not sprinkled with the cleansing water, they stay unclean, and they could make the LORD's Holy Tent unclean. 21This is a lasting rule. Those who sprinkle the cleansing water must also wash their clothes, and anyone who touches the water will be unclean until evening. 22Anything an unclean person touches becomes unclean, and whoever touches it will be unclean until evening."

Moses Disobeys God

20 In the first month all the people of Israel arrived at the Desert of Zin, and they stayed at Kadesh. There Miriam died and was buried. 2There was no water for the people, so they came together against Moses and Aaron. 3They argued with Moses and said, "We should have died in front of the LORD as our brothers did. 4Why did you bring the LORD's people into this desert? Are we and our animals to die here?

5Why did you bring us from Egypt to this terrible place? It has no grain, figs, grapevines or pomegranates,[d] and there's no water to drink!"

6So Moses and Aaron left the people and went to the entrance of the Meeting Tent.[d] There they bowed face down, and the glory of the LORD appeared to them. 7The LORD said to Moses, 8"Take your walking stick, and you and your brother Aaron should gather the people. Speak to that rock in front of them so that its water will flow from it. When you bring the water out from that rock, give it to the people and their animals."

9So Moses took the stick from in front of the LORD, as he had said. 10Moses and Aaron gathered the people in front of the rock, and Moses said, "Now listen to me, you who turn against God! Do you want us to bring water out of this rock?" 11Then Moses lifted his hand and hit the rock twice with his stick. Water began pouring out, and the people and their animals drank it.

12But the LORD said to Moses and Aaron, "Because you did not believe me, and because you did not honour me as holy before the people, you will not lead them into the land I will give them."

13These are the waters of Meribah,[n] where the Israelites argued with the LORD and where he showed them he was holy.

Edom will Not Let Israel Pass

14From Kadesh, Moses sent messengers to the king of Edom. He said, "Your brothers, the Israelites, say to you: you know about all the troubles we have had, 15how our ancestors went down into Egypt and we lived there for many years. The people of Egypt were cruel to us and our ancestors, 16but when we cried out to the LORD, he heard us and sent us an angel to bring us out of Egypt.

"Now we are here at Kadesh, a town on the edge of your land. 17Please let us pass through your country. We will not touch any fields of grain or vineyards, and will not drink water from the wells. We will travel only along the king's road, not turning right or left until we have passed through your country."

18But the king of Edom answered: "You may not pass through here. If you try, I will come and meet you with swords."

19The Israelites answered: "We will go along the main road, and if we or our animals drink any of your water, we will pay for it. We only want to walk through. That's all."

20But he answered: "You may not pass through here."

Then the Edomites went out to meet the Israelites with a large and powerful army. 21The Edomites refused to let them pass through their country, so the Israelites turned back.

Aaron Dies

22All the Israelites moved from Kadesh to Mount Hor, 23near the border of Edom. There the LORD said to Moses and Aaron, 24"Aaron will die. He will not enter the land that I'm giving to the Israelites, because you both acted against my command at the waters of Meribah. 25Take Aaron and his son Eleazar up on Mount Hor, 26and take off Aaron's special clothes and put them on his son Eleazar. Aaron will die there; he will join his ancestors."

27Moses obeyed the LORD's command. They climbed up Mount Hor, and all the people saw them go. 28Moses took off Aaron's clothes and put them on Aaron's son Eleazar. Then Aaron died there on top of the mountain. Moses and Eleazar came back down the mountain, 29and when all the people learned that Aaron was dead, everyone in Israel cried for him for 30 days.

War with the Canaanites

21 The Canaanite king of Arad lived in the southern area. When he heard that the Israelites were coming on the road to Atharim, he attacked them and captured some of them. 2Then the Israelites made this promise to the LORD: "If you will help us defeat these people, we will completely destroy their cities." 3The LORD listened to the Israelites, and he let them defeat the Canaanites. The Israelites completely destroyed the Canaanites and their cities, so the place was named Hormah.[n]

The Bronze Snake

4The Israelites left Mount Hor and went on the road towards the Red Sea, in order to go around the country of Edom. But the people became impatient on the way 5and grumbled at God and Moses. They said, "Why did you bring us out of Egypt to die in this desert? There is no bread and no water, and we hate this terrible food!"

6So the LORD sent them poisonous snakes; they bit the people, and many of the Israelites died. 7The people came to Moses and said, "We sinned when we grumbled at you and the LORD. Pray that the LORD will take away these snakes." So Moses prayed for the people.

8The LORD said to Moses, "Make a bronze snake, and put it on a pole. When anyone who is

Meribah This name in Hebrew means "argument".
Hormah This name in Hebrew means "completely destroyed".

bitten looks at it, that person will live." 9So Moses
made a bronze snake and put it on a pole. Then
when a snake bit anyone, that person looked at
the bronze snake and lived.

The Journey to Moab

10The Israelites went and camped at Oboth.
11They went from Oboth to Iye Abarim, in the
desert east of Moab. 12From there they went and
camped in the Zered Valley. 13From there they
went and camped across the Arnon, in the desert
just inside the Amorite country. The Arnon is the
border between the Moabites and the Amorites.
14That is why the Book of the Wars of the LORD
says:

". . . and Waheb in Suphah, and the ravines,
the Arnon, 15and the slopes of the ravines
that lead to the settlement of Ar.
These places are at the border of Moab."

16The Israelites went from there to Beer; a well
is there where the LORD said to Moses, "Gather
the people and I will give them water."
17Then the Israelites sang this song:

"Pour out water, well!
Sing about it.
18Princes dug this well.
Important men made it.
With their sceptres *d* and poles, they
dug it."

The people went from the desert to Mattanah.
19From Mattanah they went to Nahaliel and on
to Bamoth. 20From Bamoth they went to the valley
of Moab where the top of Mount Pisgah looks
over the desert

Israel Kills Sihon and Og

21The Israelites sent messengers to Sihon, king
of the Amorites, saying, 22"Let us pass through

DISCOURAGEMENT

Keep Your Chin Up

People can be very annoying. Just when you are feeling your absolute worst, one really insensitive comment from a friend can leave you even more discouraged than you were before they tried to help! But comments like "Keep your chin up!" from well-meaning mates probably speak a lot more truth and wisdom than we may be willing to admit or even accept.

The Israelites were getting fed up with wandering around in the desert (**Numbers 21:4–9**). Despite the fact that God was providing all they needed, they were getting really discouraged. They were finding it hard to see the positive side of life and then, when they thought it couldn't get any worse, they were plagued by poisonous snakes!

But Moses offered them, and us, a simple God-inspired suggestion: "Keep your chin up!" By looking up at the bronze snake, the poison from the snakebites would be stopped and their bites would be healed. However, it wasn't so much the act of looking at a bronze snake on a pole that was important. It was the act of looking up to God – the encourager – that brought healing.

Feeling down about life can be a poison too. As the venom of depression, hurtful comments or stress hits, it might be worth listening to the advice of your mates and of Moses: "Keep your chin up!"

- What are the snakebite-type problems that are getting at you at the moment?
- What could the "keep your chin up" approach to your problems do to change the way you deal with the tough stuff life throws at you?

Consider . . .

- making a list of all the things that are getting you down at the moment. Now play the "Glad Game". For every thing you have listed that is getting you down, match it with something that is positive in your life.
- finding ways to support someone who is worse off than you.

For more, see . . .

- Psalm 56 (p.532)
- Hebrews 12:2–3 (p.1343)
- Philippians 4:8 (p.1286)

your country. We will not go through any fields
of grain or vineyards, or drink water from the
wells. We will travel only along the king's road
until we have passed through your country."
23But King Sihon would not let the Israelites
pass through his country. He gathered his whole
army together, and they marched out to meet
Israel in the desert. At Jahaz they fought the Is-
raelites. 24Israel killed the king and captured his
land from the Arnon River to the Jabbok River.
They took the land as far as the Ammonite bor-
der, which was strongly defended. 25Israel cap-
tured all the Amorite cities and lived in them,
taking Heshbon and all the towns around it.
26Heshbon was the city where Sihon, the Amorite
king, lived. In the past he had fought with the
king of Moab and had taken all the land as far as
the Arnon.
27That is why the poets say:

"Come to Heshbon
and rebuild it;
rebuild Sihon's city.
28A fire began in Heshbon;
flames came from Sihon's city.
It destroyed Ar in Moab,
and it burned the Arnon highlands.
29How terrible for you, Moab!
The people of Chemosh[d] are ruined.
His sons ran away
and his daughters were captured
by Sihon, king of the Amorites.
30But we defeated those Amorites.
We ruined their towns from Heshbon to
Dibon,
and we destroyed them as far as Nophah,
near Medeba."

31So Israel lived in the land of the Amorites.
32After Moses sent spies to the town of Jazer,
they captured the towns around it, forcing out
the Amorites who lived there.
33Then the Israelites went up the road towards
Bashan. Og king of Bashan and his whole army
marched out to meet the Israelites, and they
fought at Edrei.
34The LORD said to Moses, "Don't be afraid of
him. I will hand him, his whole army and his land
over to you. Do to him what you did to Sihon, the
Amorite king who lived in Heshbon."
35So the Israelites killed Og and his sons and all
his army; no one was left alive. And they took his
land.

Balak Sends for Balaam

22 Then the people of Israel went to the
plains of Moab, and they camped near
the Jordan River across from Jericho.
2Balak son of Zippor saw everything the Israel-
ites had done to the Amorites. 3And Moab was
scared of so many Israelites; truly, Moab was ter-
rified by them.
4The Moabites said to the elders of Midian,
"These people will take everything around us like
an ox eating grass."
Balak son of Zippor was the king of Moab at
this time. 5He sent messengers to Balaam son of
Beor at Pethor, near the Euphrates River in his
native land. Balak said, "A nation has come out of
Egypt that covers the land. They have camped
next to me, 6and they are too powerful for me. So
come and put a curse on them. Maybe then I can
defeat them and make them leave the area. I
know that if you bless someone, the blessings
happen, and if you put a curse on someone, it
happens."
7The elders of Moab and Midian went with
payment in their hands. When they found Ba-
laam, they told him what Balak had said.
8Balaam said to them, "Stay here for the night,
and I will tell you what the LORD tells me." So the
Moabite leaders stayed with him.
9God came to Balaam and asked, "Who are
these men with you?"
10Balaam said to God, "The king of Moab, Ba-
lak son of Zippor, sent them to me with this mes-
sage: 11'A nation has come out of Egypt that
covers the land. So come and put a curse on them,
and maybe I can fight them and force them out
of my land.' "
12But God said to Balaam, "Do not go with
them. Don't put a curse on those people, because
I have blessed them."
13The next morning Balaam awoke and said to
Balak's leaders, "Go back to your own country;
the LORD has refused to let me go with you."
14So the Moabite leaders went back to Balak
and said, "Balaam refused to come with us."
15So Balak sent other leaders—this time there
were more of them, and they were more import-
ant. 16They went to Balaam and said, "Balak son
of Zippor says this: Please don't let anything stop
you from coming to me. 17I will pay you very
well, and I will do what you say. Come and put
a curse on these people for me."
18But Balaam answered Balak's servants, "King
Balak could give me his palace full of silver and
gold, but I cannot disobey the LORD my God in
anything, great or small. 19You stay here tonight
as the other men did, and I will find out what
more the LORD tells me."
20That night God came to Balaam and said,
"These men have come to ask you to go with
them. Go, but only do what I tell you."

Balaam's Donkey Speaks

21Balaam got up the next morning and put a
saddle on his donkey. Then he went with the

Moabite leaders. 22But God became angry because Balaam went, so the angel of the LORD stood in the road to stop Balaam. Balaam was riding his donkey, and he had two servants with him. 23When the donkey saw the angel of the LORD standing in the road with a sword in his hand, the donkey left the road and went into the field. Balaam hit the donkey to force her back on the road.

24Later, the angel of the LORD stood on a narrow path between two vineyards, with walls on both sides. 25Again the donkey saw the angel of the LORD, and she walked close to one wall, crushing Balaam's foot against it. So he hit her again.

26The angel of the LORD went ahead again and stood at a narrow place, too narrow to turn left or right. 27When the donkey saw the angel of the LORD, she lay down under Balaam. This made him so angry that he hit her with his stick. 28Then the LORD made the donkey talk, and she said to Balaam, "What have I done to make you hit me three times?"

29Balaam answered the donkey, "You have made me look foolish! I wish I had a sword in my hand! I would kill you right now!"

30But the donkey said to Balaam, "I am your very own donkey, which you have ridden for years. Have I ever done this to you before?"

"No," Balaam said.

Sidelight When pets talk, people listen. At least, Balaam listened when his donkey talked (Numbers 22:21–30). And it's good that he listened, because the donkey's advice kept him out of some serious trouble. But Balaam later led the Israelites to sin (Numbers 31:16, p.159), which is why Bible writers consider him evil (see, for example, 2 Peter 2:15–16, p.1366, and Revelation 2:14, p.1390).

31Then the LORD let Balaam see the angel of the LORD, who was standing in the road with his sword drawn. Then Balaam bowed face down on the ground.

32The angel of the LORD asked Balaam, "Why have you hit your donkey three times? I have stood here to stop you, because what you are doing is wrong. 33The donkey saw me and turned away from me three times. If she had not turned away, I would have killed you by now, but I would have let her live."

34Then Balaam said to the angel of the LORD, "I have sinned; I did not know you were standing in the road to stop me. If I am wrong, I will go back."

35The angel of the LORD said to Balaam, "Go with these men, but say only what I tell you." So Balaam went with Balak's leaders.

36When Balak heard that Balaam was coming, he went out to meet him at Ar in Moab, which was beside the Arnon, at the edge of his country. 37Balak said to Balaam, "I had asked you before to come quickly. Why didn't you come to me? I am able to reward you well."

38But Balaam answered, "I have come to you now, but I can't say just anything. I can only say what God tells me to say."

39Then Balaam went with Balak to Kiriath Huzoth. 40Balak offered cattle and sheep as a sacrifice and gave some meat to Balaam and the leaders with him.

41The next morning Balak took Balaam to Bamoth Baal; from there he could see the edge of the Israelite camp.

Balaam's First Message

23 Balaam said to Balak, "Build me seven altars here, and prepare seven bulls and seven rams for me." 2Balak did what Balaam asked, and they offered a bull and a ram on each of the altars.

3Then Balaam said to Balak, "Stay here beside your burnt offering and I will go. If the LORD comes to me, I will tell you whatever he shows me." Then Balaam went to a higher place.

4God came to Balaam there, and Balaam said to him, "I have prepared seven altars, and I have offered a bull and a ram on each altar."

5The LORD told Balaam what he should say. Then the LORD said, "Go back to Balak and give him this message."

6So Balaam went back to Balak. Balak and all the leaders of Moab were still standing beside his burnt offering 7when Balaam gave them this message:

"Balak brought me here from Aram;
the king of Moab brought me from the eastern mountains.
Balak said, 'Come, put a curse on the people of Jacob for me.
Come, call down evil on the people of Israel.'
8But God has not cursed them,
so I cannot curse them.
The LORD has not called down evil on them,
so I cannot call down evil on them.
9I see them from the top of the mountains;
I see them from the hills.
I see a people who live alone,
who think they are different from other nations.
10No one can number the many people of Jacob,

and no one can count a fourth of Israel.
Let me die like good men,
and let me end up like them!"
11 Balak said to Balaam, "What have you done
to me? I brought you here to curse my enemies,
but you have only blessed them!"
12 But Balaam answered, "I must say what the
LORD tells me to say."

Balaam's Second Message

13 Then Balak said to him, "Come with me to
another place, where you can also see the people.
But you can only see part of them, not all of
them. Curse them for me from there." 14 So Balak
took Balaam to the field of Zophim, on top of
Mount Pisgah. There Balak built seven altars and
offered a bull and a ram on each altar.
15 So Balaam said to Balak, "Stay here by your
burnt offering, and I will meet with God over
there."
16 So the LORD came to Balaam and told him
what to say. Then he said, "Go back to Balak and
say such and such."
17 So Balaam went to Balak, where he and the
leaders of Moab were standing beside his burnt
offering. Balak asked him, "What did the
LORD say?"
18 Then Balaam gave this message:
"Stand up, Balak, and listen.
Hear me, son of Zippor.
19 God is not a human being, and he will
not lie.
He is not a human, and he does not
change his mind.
What he says he will do, he does.
What he promises, he makes come true.
20 He told me to bless them,
so I cannot change the blessing.
21 He has found no wrong in the people of
Jacob;
he saw no fault in Israel.
The LORD their God is with them,
and they praise their King.
22 God brought them out of Egypt;
they are as strong as a wild ox.
23 No tricks will work on the people of Jacob,
and no magic will work against Israel.
People now say about them,
'Look what God has done for Israel!'
24 The people rise up like a lioness;
they get up like a lion.
Lions don't rest until they have eaten,
until they have drunk their enemies'
blood."
25 Then Balak said to Balaam, "You haven't
cursed these people, so at least, don't bless
them!"
26 Balaam answered Balak, "I told you before
that I can only do what the LORD tells me."

Balaam's Third Message

27 Then Balak said to Balaam, "Come, I will
take you to another place. Maybe God will be
pleased to let you curse them from there." 28 So
Balak took Balaam to the top of Peor, the moun-
tain that looks over the desert.
29 Balaam told Balak, "Build me seven altars
here and prepare for me seven bulls and seven
rams." 30 Balak did what Balaam asked, and he
offered a bull and a ram on each altar.

24 Balaam saw that the LORD wanted to
bless Israel, so he did not try to use any
magic but looked towards the desert. 2 When Ba-
laam saw the Israelites camped in their tribes,[d]
the Spirit[d] of God took control of him, 3 and he
gave this message:
"This is the message of Balaam son of Beor,
the message of a man who sees clearly;
4 this is the message of a man who hears the
words of God.
I see a vision from the Almighty,
and my eyes are open as I fall before him.
5 Your tents are beautiful, people of Jacob!
So are your homes, Israel!
6 Your tents spread out like valleys,
like gardens beside a river.
They are like spices planted by the LORD,
like cedar trees growing by the water.
7 Israel's water buckets will always be full,
and their crops will have plenty of water.
Their king will be greater than Agag;
their kingdom will be very great.
8 God brought them out of Egypt;
they are as strong as a wild ox.
They will defeat their enemies
and break their enemies' bones;
they will shoot them with arrows.
9 Like a lion, they lie waiting to attack;
like a lioness, no one would be brave
enough to wake them.
Anyone who blesses you will be blessed,
and anyone who curses you will be cursed."
10 Then Balak was angry with Balaam, and he
pounded his fist. He said to Balaam, "I called you
here to curse my enemies, but you have contin-
ued to bless them three times. 11 Now go home!
I said I would pay you well, but the LORD has
made you lose your reward."
12 Balaam said to Balak, "When you sent mes-
sengers to me, I told them, 13 'Balak could give me
his palace filled with silver and gold, but I still
cannot go against the LORD's commands. I could
not do anything, good or bad, on my own, but I
must say what the LORD says.' 14 Now I am going

back to my own people, but I will tell you what
these people will do to your people in the future."

Balaam's Final Message

15Then Balaam gave this message:
"This is the message of Balaam son of Beor,
the message of a man who sees clearly;
16this is the message of a man who hears the
words of God.
I know well the Most High God.
I see a vision from the Almighty,
and my eyes are open as I fall before him.
17I see someone who will come some day,
someone who will come, but not soon.
A star will come from Jacob;
a ruler will rise from Israel.
He will crush the heads of the Moabites
and smash the skulls of the sons of Sheth.
18Edom will be conquered;
his enemy Edom will be conquered,
but Israel will grow wealthy.
19A ruler will come from the descendants[d] of
Jacob
and will destroy those left in the city."

20Then Balaam saw Amalek and gave this
message:
"Amalek was the most important nation,
but Amalek will be destroyed at last."

21Then Balaam saw the Kenites and gave this
message:
"Your home is safe,
like a nest on a cliff.
22But you Kenites will be burned up;
Assyria will keep you captive."

23Then Balaam gave this message:
"No one can live when God does this.
24 Ships will sail from the shores of Cyprus
and defeat Assyria and Eber,
but they will also be destroyed."

25Then Balaam got up and returned home, and
Balak also went on his way.

Israel Worships Baal at Peor

25 While the people of Israel were still
camped at Acacia, the men began sin-
ning sexually with Moabite women. 2The women
invited them to their sacrifices to their gods, and
the Israelites ate food there and worshipped these
gods. 3So the Israelites began to worship Baal[d] of
Peor, and the LORD was very angry with them.
4The LORD said to Moses, "Get all the leaders
of the people and kill them in open daylight in the
presence of the LORD. Then the LORD will not be
angry with the people of Israel."
5So Moses said to Israel's judges, "Each of you
must put to death your people who have become
worshippers of Baal of Peor."
6Moses and the Israelites were gathered at the
entrance to the Meeting Tent,[d] crying there.
Then an Israelite man brought a Midianite
woman to his brothers in plain sight of Moses and
all the people. 7Phinehas son of Eleazar, the son
of Aaron, the priest, saw this, so he left the meet-
ing and got his spear. 8He followed the Israelite
into his tent and drove his spear through both the
Israelite man and the Midianite woman. Then
the terrible sickness among the Israelites stopped.
9This sickness had killed 24,000 people.
10The LORD said to Moses, 11"Phinehas son of
Eleazar, the son of Aaron, the priest, has saved
the Israelites from my anger. He hates sin as
much as I do. Since he tried to save my honour
among them, I will not kill them. 12So tell
Phinehas that I am making my peace agreement
with him. 13He and his descendants[d] will always
be priests, because he had great concern for the
honour of his God. He removed the sins of the
Israelites so that they would belong to God."
14The Israelite man who was killed with the
Midianite woman was named Zimri son of Salu.
He was the leader of a family in the tribe[d] of
Simeon. 15And the name of the Midianite woman
who was put to death was Cozbi daughter of Zur,
who was the chief of a Midianite family.
16The LORD said to Moses, 17"The Midianites
are your enemies, and you should kill them.
18They have already made you their enemies, be-
cause they tricked you at Peor and because of
their sister Cozbi, the daughter of a Midianite
leader. She was the woman who was killed when
the sickness came because the people sinned at
Peor."

The People are Counted

26 After the great sickness, the LORD said to
Moses and Eleazar son of Aaron, the
priest, 2"Count all the people of Israel by families.
Count all the men who are 20 years old or older
who will serve in the army of Israel." 3Moses and
Eleazar the priest spoke to the people on the
plains of Moab near the Jordan River, across from
Jericho. They said, 4"Count the men 20 years old
or older, as the LORD commanded Moses."
Here are the Israelites who came out of Egypt:
5The tribe[d] of Reuben, the first son born to
Israel, was counted. From Hanoch came the Ha-
nochite family group; from Pallu came the Palluite
family group; 6from Hezron came the Hezronite
family group; from Carmi came the Carmite family
group. 7These were the family groups of Reuben,
and the total number of men was 43,730.

[8]The son of Pallu was Eliab, [9]and Eliab's sons were Nemuel, Dathan and Abiram. Dathan and Abiram were the leaders who turned against Moses and Aaron and followed Korah when he turned against the LORD. [10]The earth opened up and swallowed them and Korah; they died at the same time the fire burned up the 250 men. This was a warning, [11]but the children of Korah did not die.

[12]These were the family groups in the tribe of Simeon: from Nemuel came the Nemuelite family group; from Jamin came the Jaminite family group; from Jakin came the Jakinite family group; [13]from Zerah came the Zerahite family group; from Shaul came the Shaulite family group. [14]These were the family groups of Simeon, and the total number of men was 22,200.

[15]These were the family groups in the tribe of Gad: from Zephon came the Zephonite family group; from Haggi came the Haggite family group; from Shuni came the Shunite family group; [16]from Ozni came the Oznite family group; from Eri came the Erite family group; [17]from Arodi came the Arodite family group; from Areli came the Arelite family group. [18]These were the family groups of Gad, and the total number of men was 40,500.

[19]Two of Judah's sons, Er and Onan, died in Canaan.

[20]These were the family groups in the tribe of Judah: from Shelah came the Shelanite family group; from Perez came the Perezite family group; from Zerah came the Zerahite family group. [21]These were the family groups from Perez: from Hezron came the Hezronite family group; from Hamul came the Hamulite family group. [22]These were the family groups of Judah, and the total number of men was 76,500.

[23]These were the family groups in the tribe of Issachar: from Tola came the Tolaite family group; from Puah came the Puthite family group; [24]from Jashub came the Jashubite family group; from Shimron came the Shimronite family group. [25]These were the family groups of Issachar, and the total number of men was 64,300.

[26]These were the family groups in the tribe of Zebulun: from Sered came the Seredite family group; from Elon came the Elonite family group; from Jahleel came the Jahleelite family group. [27]These were the family groups of Zebulun, and the total number of men was 60,500.

[28]These were the family groups of Joseph through Manasseh and Ephraim.

[29]These were the family groups of Manasseh: from Makir came the Makirite family group (Makir was the father of Gilead); from Gilead came the Gileadite family group. [30]These were the family groups that came from Gilead: from Iezer came the Iezerite family group; from Helek came the Helekite family group; [31]from Asriel came the Asrielite family group; from Shechem came the Shechemite family group; [32]from Shemida came the Shemidaite family group; from Hepher came the Hepherite family group. [33](Zelophehad son of Hepher had no sons; he had only daughters, and their names were Mahlah, Noah, Hoglah, Milcah and Tirzah.) [34]These were the family groups of Manasseh, and the total number of men was 52,700.

[35]These were the family groups in the tribe of Ephraim: from Shuthelah came the Shuthelahite family group; from Beker came the Bekerite family group; from Tahan came the Tahanite family group. [36]This was the family group from Shuthelah: from Eran came the Eranite family group. [37]These were the family groups of Ephraim, and the total number of men was 32,500. These are the family groups that came from Joseph.

[38]These were the family groups in the tribe of Benjamin: from Bela came the Belaite family group; from Ashbel came the Ashbelite family group; from Ahiram came the Ahiramite family group; [39]from Shupham came the Shuphamite family group; from Hupham came the Huphamite family group. [40]These were the family groups from Bela through Ard and Naaman: from Ard came the Ardite family group; from Naaman came the Naamite family group. [41]These were the family groups of Benjamin, and the total number of men was 45,600.

[42]This was the family group in the tribe of Dan: from Shuham came the Shuhamite family group. That was the family of Dan, [43]and the total number of men in the Shuhamite family group of Dan was 64,400.

[44]These were the family groups in the tribe of Asher: from Imnah came the Imnite family group; from Ishvi came the Ishvite family group; from Beriah came the Beriite family group. [45]These were the family groups that came from Beriah: from Heber came the Heberite family group; from Malkiel came the Malkielite family group. [46](Asher also had a daughter named Serah.) [47]These were the family groups of Asher, and the total number of men was 53,400.

[48]These were the family groups in the tribe of Naphtali: from Jahzeel came the Jahzeelite family group; from Guni came the Gunite family group; [49]from Jezer came the Jezerite family group; from Shillem came the Shillemite family group. [50]These were the family groups of Naphtali, and the total number of men was 45,400.

[51]So the total number of the men of Israel was 601,730.

[52]The LORD said to Moses, [53]"Divide the land among these people by the number of names.

54A large tribe will get more land, and a small tribe
will get less land; the amount of land each tribe
gets will depend on the number of its people.
55Divide the land by drawing lots,[d] and the land
each tribe gets will be named after that tribe.
56Divide the land between large and small groups
by drawing lots."
57The tribe of Levi was also counted. These
were the family groups of Levi: from Gershon
came the Gershonite family group; from Kohath
came the Kohathite family group; from Merari
came the Merarite family group. 58These also
were Levite family groups: the Libnite family
group, the Hebronite family group, the Mahlite
family group, the Mushite family group and the
Korahite family group. (Kohath was the ancestor
of Amram, 59whose wife was named Jochebed.
She was from the tribe of Levi and she was born
in Egypt. She and Amram had two sons, Aaron
and Moses, and their sister Miriam. 60Aaron was
the father of Nadab, Abihu, Eleazar and Ithamar.
61But Nadab and Abihu died because they made
an offering before the LORD with the wrong kind
of fire.)
62The total number of male Levites one month
old or older was 23,000. But these men were not
counted with the other Israelites, because they
were not given any of the land among the other
Israelites.
63Moses and Eleazar the priest counted all
these people. They counted the Israelites on the
plains of Moab across the Jordan River from Jer-
icho. 64Moses and Aaron the priest had counted
the Israelites in the Desert of Sinai, but no one
Moses counted on the plains of Moab was in the
first counting. 65The LORD had told the Israelites
they would all die in the desert, and the only two
left were Caleb son of Jephunneh and Joshua son
of Nun.

Zelophehad's Daughters

27 Then the daughters of Zelophehad came
near. Zelophehad was the son of Hepher,
the son of Gilead, the son of Makir, the son of
Manasseh. Zelophehad's daughters belonged to
the family groups of Manasseh son of Joseph. The
daughters' names were Mahlah, Noah, Hoglah,
Milcah and Tirzah. 2They went to the entrance of
the Meeting Tent[d] and stood before Moses, Elea-
zar the priest, the leaders and all the people. They
said, 3"Our father died in the desert. He was not
one of Korah's followers who came together
against the LORD, but he died because of his own
sin, and he had no sons. 4Our father's name will
die out because he had no sons. Give us property
among our father's relatives."
5So Moses brought their case to the LORD,
6and the LORD said to him, 7"The daughters of
Zelophehad are right; they should certainly get
what their father owned. Give them property
among their father's relatives.
8"Tell the Israelites, 'If a man dies and has no
son, then everything he owned should go to his
daughter. 9If he has no daughter, then everything
he owned should go to his brothers. 10If he has no
brothers, then everything he owned should go to
his father's brothers. 11And if his father had no
brothers, then everything he owned should go
to the nearest relative in his family group. This
should be a rule among the people of Israel, as the
LORD has given this command to Moses.' "

Joshua is the New Leader

12Then the LORD said to Moses, "Climb this
mountain in the Abarim Mountains, and look at
the land I have given to the Israelites. 13After you
have seen it, you will die and join your ancestors
as your brother Aaron did, 14because you both
acted against my command in the Desert of Zin.
You did not honour me as holy before the people
at the waters of Meribah." (This was at Meribah
in Kadesh in the Desert of Zin.)
15Moses said to the LORD, 16"The LORD is the
God of the spirits of all people. May he choose a
leader for these people, 17who will go in and out
before them. He must lead them out like sheep
and bring them in; the LORD's people must not be
like sheep without a shepherd."
18So the LORD said to Moses, "Take Joshua son
of Nun, because my Spirit[d] is in him. Put your
hand on him, 19and have him stand before Elea-
zar the priest and all the people. Then give him
his orders as they watch. 20Let him share your
honour so that all the Israelites will obey him.
21He must stand before Eleazar the priest, and
Eleazar will get advice from the LORD by using
the Urim.[d] At his command all the Israelites
will go out, and at his command they will all
come in."
22Moses did what the LORD told him. He took
Joshua and had him stand before Eleazar the
priest and all the people, 23and he put his hands
on him and gave him orders, just as the LORD had
told him.

Daily Offerings

28 The LORD said to Moses, 2"Give this com-
mand to the Israelites. Tell them: 'Bring
me food offerings made by fire, for a smell that is
pleasing to me, and be sure to bring them at the
right time.' 3Say to them, 'These are the offerings
you must bring to the LORD: two male lambs, a
year old, as a burnt offering each day. They must
have nothing wrong with them. 4Offer one lamb
in the morning and the other lamb at twilight.

5Also bring a grain offering of 2 litres of fine flour,
mixed with 1 litre of oil from pressed olives.
6This is the daily burnt offering which began at
Mount Sinai; its smell is pleasing to the LORD. 7Offer
1 litre of wine with each lamb as a drink offering;
pour it out to the LORD at the Holy Place. 8Offer
the second lamb at twilight. As in the morning,
also give a grain offering and a drink offering. This
offering is made by fire, and its smell is pleasing
to the LORD.

Sabbath Offerings

9" 'On the Sabbath[d] day you must give two
male lambs, a year old, that have nothing wrong
with them. Also give a drink offering and a grain
offering; the grain offering must be 4 litres of fine
flour mixed with olive oil. 10This is the burnt
offering for every Sabbath, in addition to the daily
burnt offering and drink offering.

Monthly Offerings

11" 'On the first day of each month bring a
burnt offering to the LORD. This will be two young
bulls, one ram and seven male lambs a year old,
and they must have nothing wrong with them.
12Give a grain offering with each bull of 6.6 litres
of fine flour mixed with olive oil. Also give a grain
offering with the ram. It must be 4 litres of fine
flour mixed with olive oil. 13And give a grain
offering with each lamb of 2 litres of fine flour
mixed with olive oil. This is a burnt offering, and
its smell is pleasing to the LORD. 14The drink offer-
ing with each bull will be 2 litres of wine, with
the ram it will be one and a half litres, and with
each lamb it will be 1 litre of wine. This is the
burnt offering that must be offered each month of
the year. 15Besides the daily burnt offerings and
drink offerings, bring a sin offering of one goat to
the LORD.

LEADERSHIP

Taking the Stage

"Sam is in hospital," Mr Taylor told his class of drama students.

"But what about the play? Tonight's the first performance! What are we going to do?"

That was the question that was on the mind of everyone in the cast. For months Sam had been rehearsing his lead role. Without him the play would have to be cancelled.

"Someone will have to take Sam's place," Mr Taylor told them. "Someone who knows his lines off by heart."

The students looked at each other. "There's no one," they told him.

"I've got it!" Katie screamed excitedly. "What about Daniel?"

Daniel was one of Sam's closest friends and had accompanied him to all the rehearsals. It was Daniel who had helped Sam to learn his lines.

Daniel swallowed nervously, then nodded slowly. "OK," he said, "I'll do it."

Sam had prepared the way to making the play a success, but it was Daniel who had to perform on stage in the end.

Similarly, when Moses died, it was Joshua who had to step in and face the next challenge. Read about him in **Numbers 27:12–23**.

- How was Daniel's training similar to the 40 years of preparation that Joshua went through?
- According to the passage, what is the best way to become a leader? How could you do it?

Consider . . .

- asking your parents what skills they have that they would like to teach you, then decide together how to go about it.
- talking to a leader in your church or fellowship and asking how they got to be in their position. Then write a short biography of that leader in your church newsletter.

For more, see . . .

- Judges 6:11–16 (p.231)
- 2 Timothy 2:1–7 (p.1317)
- John 21:15–22 (p.1134)

The Passover

16“ ‘The LORD’s Passover[d] will be on the fourteenth day of the first month. 17The Feast[d] of Unleavened Bread begins on the fifteenth day of that month. For seven days, you may eat only bread made without yeast. 18Have a holy meeting on the first day of the festival, and don’t work that day. 19Bring to the LORD an offering made by fire, a burnt offering of two young bulls, one ram and seven male lambs a year old. They must have nothing wrong with them. 20With each bull give a grain offering of 6 litres of fine flour mixed with olive oil. With the ram it must be 4 litres of fine flour mixed with oil. 21With each of the seven lambs, it must be 2 litres of fine flour mixed with oil. 22Bring one goat as a sin offering, to remove your sins so you will belong to God. 23Bring these offerings in addition to the burnt offerings you give every morning. 24So bring food for the offering made by fire each day for seven days, for a smell that is pleasing to the LORD. Do it in addition to the daily burnt offering and its drink offering. 25On the seventh day have a holy meeting, and don’t work that day.

The Feast of Weeks

26“ ‘On the day of firstfruits[d] when you bring new grain to the LORD during the Feast[d] of Weeks, have a holy meeting. Don’t work that day. 27Bring this burnt offering to the LORD: two young bulls, one ram and seven male lambs a year old. This smell is pleasing to the LORD. 28Also, with each bull give a grain offering of 6 litres of fine flour mixed with oil. With the ram, it must be 4 litres of flour, 29and with each of the seven lambs offer 2 litres of flour. 30Offer one male goat to remove your sins so that you will belong to God. 31Bring these offerings and their drink offerings in addition to the daily burnt offering and its grain offering. The animals must have nothing wrong with them.

The Feast of Trumpets

29 “ ‘Have a holy meeting on the first day of the seventh month, and don’t work on that day. That is the day you blow the trumpets. 2Bring these burnt offerings as a smell pleasing to the LORD: one young bull, one ram and seven male lambs a year old. They must have nothing wrong with them. 3With the bull give a grain offering of 7 litres of fine flour mixed with oil. With the ram offer 4 litres, 4and with each of the seven lambs offer 2 litres. 5Offer one male goat for a sin offering to remove your sins so that you will belong to God. 6These offerings are in addition to the monthly and daily burnt offerings. Their grain offerings and drink offerings must be done as you have been told. These offerings are made by fire to the LORD, and their smell is pleasing to him.

The Day of Cleansing

7“ ‘Have a holy meeting on the tenth day of the seventh month. On that day do not eat and do not work. 8Bring these burnt offerings as a smell pleasing to the LORD: one young bull, one ram and seven male lambs a year old. They must have nothing wrong with them. 9With the bull give a grain offering of 7 litres of fine flour mixed with oil. With the ram it must be 4 litres, 10and with each of the seven lambs it must be 2 litres. 11Offer one male goat as a sin offering. This will be in addition to the sin offering which removes your sins, the daily burnt offering with its grain offering and the drink offerings.

The Feast of Shelters

12“ ‘Have a holy meeting on the fifteenth day of the seventh month, and do not work on that day. Celebrate a festival to the LORD for seven days. 13Bring these burnt offerings, made by fire, as a smell pleasing to the LORD: thirteen young bulls, two rams and fourteen male lambs a year old. They must have nothing wrong with them. 14With each of the thirteen bulls offer a grain offering of 7 litres of fine flour mixed with oil. With each of the two rams it must be 4 litres, 15and with each of the fourteen lambs it must be 2 litres. 16Offer one male goat as a sin offering in addition to the daily burnt offering with its grain and drink offerings.

17“ ‘On the second day of this festival give an offering of twelve bulls, two rams and fourteen male lambs a year old. They must have nothing wrong with them. 18Bring the grain and drink offerings for the bulls, rams and lambs, according to the number required. 19Offer one male goat as a sin offering, in addition to the daily burnt offering with its grain and drink offerings.

20“ ‘On the third day offer eleven bulls, two rams and fourteen male lambs a year old. They must have nothing wrong with them. 21Bring the grain and drink offerings for the bulls, rams and lambs, according to the number required. 22Offer one male goat as a sin offering, in addition to the daily burnt offering with its grain and drink offerings.

23“ ‘On the fourth day offer ten bulls, two rams and fourteen male lambs a year old. They must have nothing wrong with them. 24Bring the grain and drink offerings for the bulls, rams and lambs, according to the number required. 25Offer one male goat as a sin offering, in addition to the daily burnt offering with its grain and drink offerings.

26“ ‘On the fifth day offer nine bulls, two rams and fourteen male lambs a year old. They must have nothing wrong with them. 27Bring the grain and drink offerings for the bulls, rams and lambs, according to the number required. 28Offer one male goat as a sin offering, in addition to the daily burnt offering with its grain and drink offerings.

29“ ‘On the sixth day offer eight bulls, two rams and fourteen male lambs a year old. They must have nothing wrong with them. 30Bring the grain and drink offerings for the bulls, rams and lambs, according to the number required. 31Offer one male goat as a sin offering, in addition to the daily burnt offering with its grain and drink offerings.

32“ ‘On the seventh day offer seven bulls, two rams and fourteen male lambs a year old. They must have nothing wrong with them. 33Bring the grain and drink offerings for the bulls, rams and lambs, according to the number required. 34Offer one male goat as a sin offering, in addition to the daily burnt offering with its grain and drink offerings.

35“ ‘On the eighth day have a closing meeting and do not work on that day. 36Bring an offering made by fire, a burnt offering, as a smell pleasing to the LORD. Offer one bull, one ram and seven male lambs a year old. They must have nothing wrong with them. 37Bring the grain and drink offerings for the bull, the rams and the lambs, according to the number required. 38Offer one male goat as a sin offering, in addition to the daily burnt offering with its grain and drink offerings.

39“ ‘At your festivals you should bring these to the LORD: your burnt offerings, grain offerings, drink offerings and fellowship offerings. These are in addition to other promised offerings and special gifts you want to give to the LORD.’ ”

40Moses told the Israelites everything the LORD had commanded him.

Rules About Special Promises

30 Moses spoke with the leaders of the Israelite tribes.[d] He told them these commands from the LORD.

2“If a man makes a promise to the LORD or says he will do something special, he must keep his promise. He must do what he said. 3If a young woman still living at home makes a promise to the LORD or pledges to do something special, 4and if her father hears about the promise or pledge and says nothing, she must do what she promised. She must keep her pledge. 5But if her father hears about the promise or pledge and does not allow it, then the promise or pledge does not have to be kept. Her father would not allow it, so the LORD will free her from her promise.

6“If a woman makes a pledge or a careless promise and then gets married, 7and if her husband hears about it and says nothing, she must keep her promise or the pledge she made. 8But if her husband hears about it and does not allow it, he cancels her pledge or the careless promise she made. The LORD will free her from keeping it.

9“If a widow or divorced woman makes a promise, she must do whatever she promised.

10“If a woman makes a promise or pledge while she is married, 11and if her husband hears about it but says nothing and does not stop her, she must keep her promise or pledge. 12But if her husband hears about it and cancels it, she does not have to do what she said. Her husband has cancelled it, so the LORD will free her from it. 13A woman's husband may make her keep or cancel any promise or pledge she has made. 14If he says nothing to her about it for several days, she must keep her promises. If he hears about them and says nothing, she must keep her promises. 15But if he cancels them long after he heard about them, he is responsible if she breaks her promise.”

16These are commands that the LORD gave to Moses for husbands and wives, and for fathers with daughters living at home.

Israel Attacks the Midianites

31 The LORD spoke to Moses and said, 2“Pay back the Midianites for what they did to the Israelites; after that you will die.”

3So Moses said to the people, “Get some men ready for war. The LORD will use them to pay back the Midianites. 4Send to war 1,000 men from each of the tribes[d] of Israel.” 5So 12,000 men got ready for war, 1,000 men from each tribe. 6Moses sent those men to war; Phinehas son of Eleazar the priest was with them. He took with him the holy things and the trumpets for giving the alarm. 7They fought the Midianites as the LORD had commanded Moses, and they killed every Midianite man. 8Among those they killed were Evi, Rekem, Zur, Hur and Reba, who were the five kings of Midian. They also killed Balaam son of Beor with a sword.

9The Israelites captured the Midianite women and children, and they took all their flocks, herds and goods. 10They burned all the Midianite towns where they had settled and all their camps, 11but they took all the people and animals and goods. 12Then they brought the captives, the animals and the goods back to Moses and Eleazar the priest and all the Israelites. Their camp was on the plains of Moab near the Jordan River, across from Jericho.

13Moses, Eleazar the priest, and all the leaders of the people went outside the camp to meet them. 14Moses was angry with the army officers, the commanders over 1,000 men and those over 100 men, who returned from war.

15He asked them, "Why did you let the women live? 16They were the ones who followed Balaam's advice and turned the Israelites from the LORD at Peor. Then a terrible sickness struck the LORD's people. 17Kill all the Midianite boys, and kill all the Midianite women who have had sexual relations. 18But save for yourselves the girls who have not had sexual relations with a man.

19"All you men who killed anyone or touched a dead body must stay outside the camp for seven days. On the third and seventh days you and your captives must make yourselves clean.[d] 20You must clean all your clothes and anything made of leather, goat hair or wood."

21Then Eleazar the priest said to the soldiers who had gone to war, "These are the teachings that the LORD gave to Moses. 22Put any gold, silver, bronze, iron, tin or lead— 23anything that will not burn—into the fire, and then it will be clean. But also purify those things with the cleansing water. Then they will be clean. If something cannot stand the fire, wash it with the water. 24On the seventh day wash your clothes, and you will be clean. After that you may come into the camp."

Dividing the Goods

25The LORD said to Moses, 26"You, Eleazar the priest, and the leaders of the family groups should take a count of the goods, the men and the animals that were taken. 27Then divide those possessions between the soldiers who went to war and the rest of the people. 28From the soldiers who went to war, take a tax for the LORD of one thing out of every 500. This includes people, cattle, donkeys or sheep. 29Take it from the soldiers' half, and give it to Eleazar the priest as the LORD's share. 30And from the people's half, take one thing out of every 50. This includes people, cattle, donkeys, sheep or other animals. Give that to the Levites, who take care of the LORD's Holy Tent."[d] 31So Moses and Eleazar did as the LORD commanded Moses.

32There remained from what the soldiers had taken 675,000 sheep, 3372,000 cattle, 3461,000 donkeys 35and 32,000 women who had not had sexual relations with a man. 36The soldiers who went to war got 337,500 sheep 37and they gave 675 of them to the LORD. 38They got 36,000 cattle and they gave 72 of them to the LORD. 39They got 30,500 donkeys and they gave 61 of them to the LORD. 40They got 16,000 people, and they gave 32 of them to the LORD. 41Moses gave the LORD's share to Eleazar the priest, as the LORD had commanded him.

42Moses separated the people's half from the soldiers' half. 43The people got 337,500 sheep, 4436,000 cattle, 4530,500 donkeys 46and 16,000 people. 47From the people's half Moses took one thing out of every 50 for the LORD. This included the animals and the people. Then he gave them to the Levites, who took care of the LORD's Holy Tent. This was what the LORD had commanded Moses.

48Then the officers of the army, the commanders of 1,000 men and commanders of 100 men, came to Moses. 49They told Moses, "We, your servants, have counted our soldiers under our command, and not one of them is missing. 50So we have brought the LORD a gift of the gold things that each of us found: arm bands, bracelets, signet[d] rings, earrings and necklaces. These are to remove our sins so we will belong to the LORD."

51So Moses and Eleazar the priest took the gold from them, which had been made into all kinds of objects. 52The commanders of 1,000 men and the commanders of 100 men gave the LORD the gold, and all of it together weighed about 190 kilogrammes; 53each soldier had taken something for himself. 54Moses and Eleazar the priest took the gold from the commanders of 1,000 men and the commanders of 100 men. Then they put it in the Meeting Tent[d] as a memorial before the LORD for the people of Israel.

The Tribes East of the Jordan

32 The people of Reuben and Gad had large flocks and herds. When they saw that the lands of Jazer and Gilead were good for the animals, 2they came to Moses, Eleazar the priest and the leaders of the people. 3–4They said, "We, your servants, have flocks and herds. The LORD has captured for the Israelites a land that is good for animals—the land around Ataroth, Dibon, Jazer, Nimrah, Heshbon, Elealeh, Sebam, Nebo and Beon. 5If it pleases you, we would like this land to be given to us. Don't make us cross the Jordan River."

6Moses told the people of Gad and Reuben, "Shall your brothers go to war while you stay behind? 7You will discourage the Israelites from going over to the land the LORD has given them. 8Your ancestors did the same thing. I sent them from Kadesh Barnea to look at the land. 9They went as far as the Valley of Eshcol, and when they saw the land, they discouraged the Israelites from going into the land the LORD had given them. 10The LORD became very angry that day

and made this promise: [11]'None of the people who
came from Egypt and who are 20 years old or
older will see the land that I promised to Abra-
ham, Isaac and Jacob. These people have not
followed me completely. [12]Only Caleb son of Je-
phunneh the Kenizzite and Joshua son of Nun
followed the LORD completely.'

[13]"The LORD was angry with Israel, so he made
them wander in the desert for 40 years. Finally all
the people who had sinned against the LORD died,
[14]and now you are acting just like your ancestors!
You sinful people are making the LORD even more
angry with Israel. [15]If you stop following him, it
will add to their stay in the desert, and you will
destroy all these people."

[16]Then the Reubenites and Gadites came up to
Moses and said, "We will build pens for our ani-
mals and cities for our children here. [17]Then our
children will be in fortified cities, safe from the
people who live in this land. Then we will pre-
pare for war. We will help the other Israelites get
their land, [18]and we will not return home until
every Israelite has received his land. [19]We won't
take any of the land west of the Jordan River; our
part of the land is east of the Jordan."

[20]So Moses told them, "You must do these
things. You must go before the LORD into battle
[21]and cross the Jordan River armed, until the LORD
forces out the enemy. [22]After the LORD helps us
take the land, you may return home. You will
have done your duty to the LORD and Israel, and
you may have this land as your own.

[23]"But if you don't do these things, you will be
sinning against the LORD; know for sure that you
will be punished for your sin. [24]Build cities for
your children and pens for your animals, but then
you must do what you promised."

[25]The Gadites and Reubenites said to Moses,
"We are your servants, and we will do what you,
our master, command. [26]Our children, wives and
all our cattle will stay in the cities of Gilead, [27]but
we, your servants, will prepare for battle. We will
go over and fight for the LORD, as you, our master,
have said."

[28]So Moses gave orders about them to Eleazar
the priest, to Joshua son of Nun, and to the lead-
ers of the tribes[d] of Israel. [29]Moses said to them,
"If the Gadites and Reubenites prepare for battle
and cross the Jordan River with you, to go before
the LORD and help you take the land, give them
the land of Gilead for their own. [30]But if they do
not go over armed, they will not receive it; their
land will be in Canaan with you."

[31]The Gadites and Reubenites answered, "We
are your servants, and we will do as the LORD said.
[32]We will cross over into Canaan and go before
the LORD ready for battle. But our land will be east
of the Jordan River."

[33]So Moses gave that land to the tribes of Gad,
Reuben and East Manasseh. (Manasseh was Jo-
seph's son.) That land had been the kingdom of
Sihon, king of the Amorites, and the kingdom of
Og, king of Bashan, as well as all the cities and
the land around them.

[34]The Gadites rebuilt the cities of Dibon, Ata-
roth, Aroer, [35]Atroth Shophan, Jazer, Jogbehah,
[36]Beth Nimrah and Beth Haran. These were forti-
fied cities. And they built sheep pens.

[37]The Reubenites rebuilt Heshbon, Elealeh,
Kiriathaim, [38]Nebo, Baal Meon and Sibmah. They
renamed Nebo and Baal Meon when they rebuilt
them.

[39]The descendants[d] of Makir son of Manasseh
went and captured Gilead and forced out the Am-
orites who were there. [40]So Moses gave Gilead to
the family of Makir son of Manasseh and they
settled there. [41]Jair son of Manasseh went out
and captured the small towns there, and he called
them the Towns of Jair. [42]Nobah went and cap-
tured Kenath and the small towns around it; then
he named it Nobah after himself.

Israel's Journey from Egypt

33 These are the places where the Israelites
went as Moses and Aaron led them out
of Egypt in divisions. [2]At the LORD's command
Moses recorded the places where they went, and
these are the places they went.

[3]On the fifteenth day of the first month, the
day after the Passover,[d] the Israelites left Rameses
and marched out boldly in front of all the Egyp-
tians. [4]The Egyptians were burying their first-
born[d] sons, whom the LORD had killed; the LORD
showed that the gods of Egypt were false.

[5]The Israelites left Rameses and camped at
Succoth.

[6]They left Succoth and camped at Etham, at
the edge of the desert.

[7]They left Etham and went back to Pi Hahi-
roth, to the east of Baal Zephon, and camped near
Migdol.

[8]They left Pi Hahiroth and walked through
the sea into the desert. After going three days
through the Desert of Etham, they camped at
Marah.

[9]They left Marah and went to Elim; there were
twelve springs of water and 70 palm trees where
they camped.

[10]They left Elim and camped near the Red Sea.[d]

[11]They left the Red Sea and camped in the
Desert of Sin.

[12]They left the Desert of Sin and camped at
Dophkah.

[13]They left Dophkah and camped at Alush.

[14]They left Alush and camped at Rephidim,
where the people had no water to drink.

15They left Rephidim and camped in the Desert
of Sinai.
16They left the Desert of Sinai and camped at
Kibroth Hattaavah.
17They left Kibroth Hattaavah and camped at
Hazeroth.
18They left Hazeroth and camped at Rithmah.
19They left Rithmah and camped at Rimmon
Perez.
20They left Rimmon Perez and camped at
Libnah.
21They left Libnah and camped at Rissah.
22They left Rissah and camped at Kehelathah.
23They left Kehelathah and camped at Mount
Shepher.
24They left Mount Shepher and camped at
Haradah.
25They left Haradah and camped at Makheloth.
26They left Makheloth and camped at Tahath.
27They left Tahath and camped at Terah.
28They left Terah and camped at Mithcah.
29They left Mithcah and camped at Hashmonah.
30They left Hashmonah and camped at
Moseroth.
31They left Moseroth and camped at Bene
Berak Jaakan.
32They left Bene Berak Jaakan and camped at
Hor Haggidgad.
33They left Hor Haggidgad and camped at
Jotbathah.
34They left Jotbathah and camped at Abronah.
35They left Abronah and camped at Ezion Geber.
36They left Ezion Geber and camped at Kadesh
in the Desert of Zin.
37They left Kadesh and camped at Mount
Hor, on the border of Edom. 38Aaron the priest
obeyed the LORD and went up Mount Hor. There
he died on the first day of the fifth month in
the fortieth year after the Israelites left Egypt.
39Aaron was 123 years old when he died on
Mount Hor.
40The Canaanite king of Arad, who lived in the
southern area of Canaan, heard that the Israelites
were coming.
41The people left Mount Hor and camped at
Zalmonah.
42They left Zalmonah and camped at Punon.
43They left Punon and camped at Oboth.
44They left Oboth and camped at Iye Abarim,
on the border of Moab.
45They left Iye Abarim and camped at Dibon
Gad.
46They left Dibon Gad and camped at Almon
Diblathaim.
47They left Almon Diblathaim and camped in
the mountains of Abarim, near Nebo.
48They left the mountains of Abarim and
camped on the plains of Moab near the Jordan
River across from Jericho. 49They camped along
the Jordan on the plains of Moab, and their camp
went from Beth Jeshimoth to Abel Acacia.
50On the plains of Moab by the Jordan River
across from Jericho, the LORD spoke to Moses. He
said, 51"Speak to the Israelites and tell them,
'When you cross the Jordan River and go into
Canaan, 52force out all the people who live there.
Destroy all of their carved statues and metal idols.
Wreck all of their places of worship. 53Take over
the land and settle there, because I have given
this land to you to own. 54Throw lots[d] to divide
up the land by family groups, giving larger por-
tions to larger family groups and smaller portions
to smaller family groups. The land will be given
as the lots decide; each tribe[d] will get its own
land.
55" 'But if you don't force those people out of
the land, they will bring you trouble. They will be
like sharp hooks in your eyes and thorns in your
sides. They will bring trouble to the land where
you live. 56Then I will punish you as I had
planned to punish them.' "

The Borders of Canaan

34 The LORD said to Moses, 2"Give this com-
mand to the people of Israel: 'You will
soon enter Canaan and it will be yours. These
shall be the borders: 3On the south you will get
part of the Desert of Zin near the border of Edom.
On the east side your southern border will start at
the south end of the Dead Sea,[d] 4cross south of
Scorpion Pass, and go through the Desert of Zin
and south of Kadesh Barnea. Then it will go to
Hazar Addar and over to Azmon. 5From Azmon
it will go to the brook of Egypt, and it will end at
the Mediterranean Sea.
6" 'Your western border will be the Mediter-
ranean Sea.
7" 'Your northern border will begin at the
Mediterranean Sea and go to Mount Hor. 8From
Mount Hor it will go to Lebo Hamath, and on to
Zedad. 9Then the border will go to Ziphron, and
it will end at Hazar Enan. This will be your north-
ern border.
10" 'Your eastern border will begin at Hazar
Enan and go to Shepham. 11From Shepham the
border will go east of Ain to Riblah and along the
hills east of Lake Galilee. 12Then the border will
go down along the Jordan River and end at the
Dead Sea.
" 'These are the borders around your country.' "
13So Moses gave this command to the Israel-
ites: "This is the land you will receive. Throw
lots[d] to divide it among the nine and a half
tribes,[d] because the LORD commanded that it
should be theirs. 14The tribes of Reuben, Gad and
East Manasseh have already received their land.

15These two and a half tribes received land east of the Jordan River, across from Jericho."

16Then the LORD said to Moses, 17"These are the men who will divide the land: Eleazar the priest and Joshua son of Nun. 18Also take one leader from each tribe to help divide the land. 19These are the names of the leaders: from the tribe of Judah, Caleb son of Jephunneh; 20from the tribe of Simeon, Shemuel son of Ammihud; 21from the tribe of Benjamin, Elidad son of Kislon; 22from the tribe of Dan, Bukki son of Jogli; 23from the tribe of Manasseh son of Joseph, Hanniel son of Ephod; 24from the tribe of Ephraim son of Joseph, Kemuel son of Shiphtan; 25from the tribe of Zebulun, Elizaphan son of Parnach; 26from the tribe of Issachar, Paltiel son of Azzan; 27from the tribe of Asher, Ahihud son of Shelomi; 28from the tribe of Naphtali, Pedahel son of Ammihud."

29The LORD commanded these men to divide the land of Canaan among the Israelites.

The Levites' Towns

35 The LORD spoke to Moses on the plains of Moab across from Jericho by the Jordan River. He said, 2"Command the Israelites to give the Levites cities to live in from the land they receive. Also give the Levites the pastureland around these cities. 3Then the Levites will have cities where they may live and pastureland for their cattle, flocks and other animals. 4The pastureland you give the Levites will extend 500 metres from the city wall. 5Also measure 1,000 metres in each direction outside the city wall—1,000 metres east of the city, 1,000 metres south of the city, 1,000 metres west of the city and 1,000 metres north of the city, with the city in the centre. This will be pastureland for the Levites' cities.

Cities of Safety

6"Six of the cities you give the Levites will be cities of safety.[d] A person who accidentally kills someone may run to one of those cities for safety. You must also give 42 other cities to the Levites; 7give the Levites a total of 48 cities and their pastures. 8The larger tribes[d] of Israel must give more cities, and the smaller tribes must give fewer cities. Each tribe must give some of its cities to the Levites, but the number of cities they give will depend on the size of their land."

9Then the LORD said to Moses, 10"Tell the Israelites these things: 'When you cross the Jordan River and go into Canaan, 11you must choose cities to be cities of safety, so that a person who accidentally kills someone may run to them for safety. 12There the person will be safe from the dead person's relative who has the duty of punishing the killer. He will not die before he receives a fair trial in court. 13The six cities you give will be cities of safety. 14Give three cities east of the Jordan River and three cities in Canaan as cities of safety. 15These six cities will be places of safety for citizens of Israel, as well as for foreigners and other people living with you. Any of these people who accidentally kills someone may run to one of these cities.

16" 'Anyone who uses an iron weapon to kill someone is a murderer. He must be put to death. 17Anyone who takes a rock and kills a person with it is a murderer. He must be put to death. 18Anyone who picks up a piece of wood and kills someone with it is a murderer. He must be put to death. 19A relative of the dead person must put the murderer to death; when they meet, the relative must kill the murderer. 20A person might shove someone or throw something at someone and cause death. 21Or a person might hit someone with his hand and cause death. If it were done from hate, the person is a murderer and must be put to death. A relative of the dead person must kill the murderer when they meet.

22" 'But a person might suddenly push someone, and not from hatred. Or a person might accidentally throw something and hit someone. 23Or a person might drop a rock on someone he couldn't see and kill that person. There was no plan to hurt anyone and no hatred for the one who was killed. 24If that happens, the community must judge between the relative of the dead person and the killer, according to these rules. 25They must protect the killer from the dead person's relative, sending the killer back to the original city of safety, to stay there until the high priest dies (the high priest had the holy oil poured on him).

Sidelight Today, if a person kills someone, a trial is held. In Old Testament times, such a person could be killed by the victim's family. To protect people who accidentally killed someone, Numbers 35:6–28 tells of six cities of safety, where someone could go to be safe. But if the killer left the city, the dead person's family could take revenge.

26" 'Such a person must never go outside the limits of the city of safety. 27If a relative of the dead person finds the killer outside the city, the relative may kill that person and not be guilty of murder. 28The killer must stay in the city of safety until the high priest dies. After the high priest dies, the killer may go home.

29" 'These laws are for you from now on, wherever you live.

30" 'If anyone kills a person, the murderer may
be put to death only if there are witnesses. No
one may be put to death with only one witness.
31" 'Don't take money to spare the life of a
murderer who should be put to death. A mur-
derer must be put to death.
32" 'If someone has run to a city of safety, don't
take money to let the person go back home be-
fore the high priest dies.
33" 'Don't let murder spoil your land. The only
way to remove the sin of killing an innocent per-
son is for the murderer to be put to death. 34I am
the LORD, and I live among the Israelites. I live
in that land with you, so do not spoil it with
murder.' "

Land for Zelophehad's Daughters

36 The leaders of Gilead's family group
went to talk to Moses and the leaders of
the families of Israel. (Gilead was the son of Ma-
kir, the son of Manasseh, the son of Joseph.)
2They said, "The LORD commanded you, our mas-
ter, to give the land to the Israelites by throwing
lots,[d] and the LORD commanded you to give the
land of Zelophehad, our brother, to his daughters.
3But if his daughters marry men from other
tribes[d] of Israel, then that land will leave our
family, and the people of the other tribes will get
that land. So we will lose some of our land. 4When
the time of Jubilee[d] comes for the Israelites,
their land will go to the tribes of the people they
marry; their land will be taken away from us, the
land we received from our fathers."
5Then Moses gave the Israelites this command
from the LORD: "These men from the tribe of Jo-
seph are right. 6This is the LORD's command to
Zelophehad's daughters: you may marry anyone
you wish, as long as the person is from your own
tribe. 7In this way the Israelites' land will not pass
from tribe to tribe, and each Israelite will keep
the land in the tribe that belonged to his ances-
tors. 8A woman who inherits her father's land
may marry, but she must marry someone from
her own tribe. In this way every Israelite will
keep the land that belonged to his ancestors. 9The
land must not pass from tribe to tribe, and each
Israelite tribe will keep the land it received from
its ancestors."
10Zelophehad's daughters obeyed the LORD's
command to Moses.
11So Zelophehad's daughters—Mahlah, Tir-
zah, Hoglah, Milcah and Noah—married their
cousins, their father's relatives. 12Their husbands
were from the tribe of Manasseh son of Joseph, so
their land stayed in their father's family group and
tribe.
13These were the laws and commands that the
LORD gave to the Israelites through Moses on the
plains of Moab by the Jordan River, across from
Jericho.

Deuteronomy

Why Read This Book:

- Be reminded of all the good things that God has done for his people (Deuteronomy 1—4).
- Find out what God requires of people because of his special relationship with them (Deuteronomy 5—28).
- See what God has in store for his people, when they do right and when they do wrong (Deuteronomy 29—30).

When?

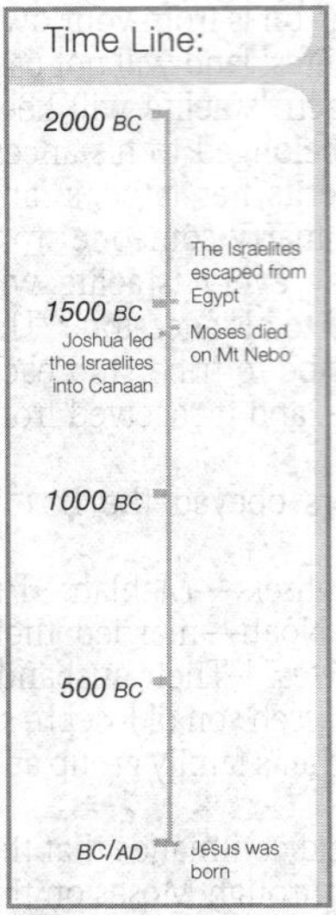

Behind the Scenes:

You've spent months reading books, listening in lessons and doing homework. You have learned lots of important information that will help you in the future. Then the week before the final exam, your teacher goes over what you've learned and urges you to remember everything that has happened.

The book of Deuteronomy is a lot like that final revision week. The Israelites, after wandering around the desert for 40 years, were preparing for the "final test" – about to enter God's promised land. But before that happened, their leader, Moses, made a point of delivering three "revision lesson" sermons.

In these sermons, Moses reminded God's people of all that he had done for them, and warned them against turning away from him as they entered the new land. ▷

Where?

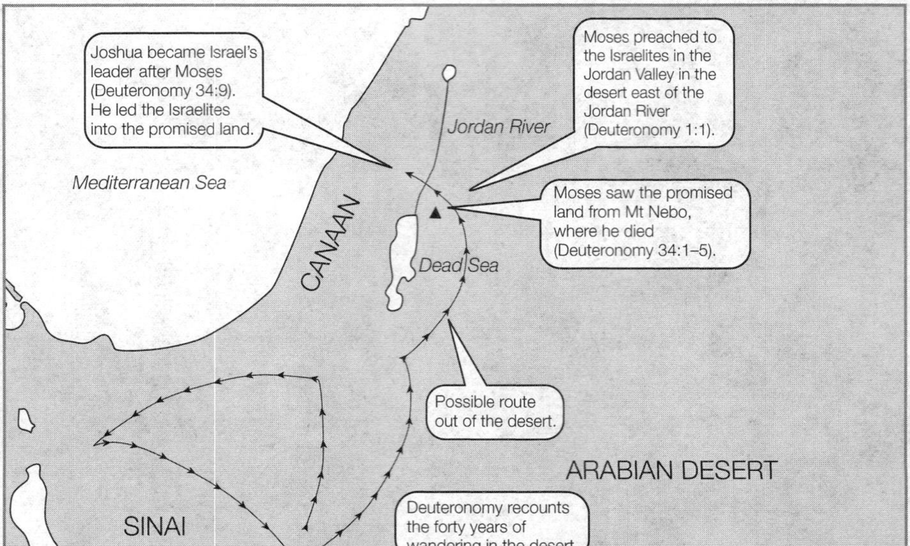

Behind the Scenes (cont.): The name "Deuteronomy" means "second law". It summarises the laws which the Israelites received during their time in the desert.

Moses encourages God's people to obey the laws – not because of some empty sense of "duty", but out of gratitude for God's unlimited love.

Moses Talks to the Israelites

1 This is the message Moses gave to all the people of Israel in the desert east of the Jordan River. They were in the desert area near Suph, between Paran and the towns of Tophel, Laban, Hazeroth and Dizahab.

2(The trip from Mount Sinai to Kadesh Barnea on the Mount Seir road takes eleven days.) 340 years after the Israelites had left Egypt, on the first day of the eleventh month, Moses told the people of Israel everything the LORD had commanded him to tell them. 4This was after the LORD had defeated Sihon and Og. Sihon was king of the Amorite people and lived in Heshbon. Og was king of Bashan and lived in Ashteroth and Edrei.

5Now the Israelites were east of the Jordan River in the land of Moab, and there Moses began to explain what God had commanded. He said:

6The LORD our God spoke to us at Mount Sinai and said, "You have stayed long enough at this mountain. 7Get ready, and go to the mountain country of the Amorites, and to all the places around there—the Jordan Valley, the mountains, the western hills, the southern area, the sea coast, the land of Canaan and Lebanon. Go as far as the great river, the Euphrates. 8See, I have given you this land, so go in and take it for yourselves. The LORD promised it to your ancestors—Abraham, Isaac and Jacob and their descendants." [d]

Moses Appoints Leaders

9At that time I said, "I am not able to take care of you by myself. 10The LORD your God has made you grow in number so that there are as many of you as there are stars in the sky. 11I pray that the LORD, the God of your ancestors, will give you a thousand times more people and do all the wonderful things he promised. 12But I cannot take care of your problems, your troubles and your arguments by myself. 13So choose some men from each tribe [d]—wise men who have understanding and experience—and I will make them leaders over you."

14And you said, "That's a good thing to do."

15So I took the wise and experienced leaders of your tribes, and I made them your leaders. I appointed commanders over 1,000 people, over 100 people, over 50 people and over ten people and made them officers over your tribes. 16Then I told your leaders, "Listen to the arguments between your people. Judge fairly between two Israelites or between an Israelite and a foreigner. 17When you judge, be fair to everyone; don't act as if one person is more important than another, and don't be afraid of anyone, because your decision comes from God. Bring the hard cases to me, and I will judge them." 18At that time I told you everything you must do.

Spies Enter the Land

19Then, as the LORD our God commanded us, we left Mount Sinai and went towards the mountain country of the Amorite people. We went through that large and terrible desert you saw, and then we came to Kadesh Barnea. 20I said to you, "You have now come to the mountain country of the Amorites, to the land the LORD our God will give us. 21Look, here it is! Go up and take it. The LORD, the God of your ancestors, told you to do this, so don't be afraid and don't worry."

22Then all of you came to me and said, "Let's send men before us to spy out the land. They can come back and tell us about the way we should go and the cities we will find."

23I thought that was a good idea, so I chose twelve of your men, one for each tribe. [d] 24They left and went up to the mountains, and when they came to the Valley of Eshcol they explored it. 25They took some of the fruit from that land and brought it down to us, saying, "It is a good land that the LORD our God is giving us."

Israel Refuses to Enter

26But you refused to go. You would not obey the command of the LORD your God, 27but grumbled in your tents, saying, "The LORD hates us. He brought us out of Egypt just to give us to the Amorites, who will destroy us. 28Where can we go now? The spies we sent have made us afraid, because they said, 'The people there are stronger and taller than we are. The cities are big, with walls up to the sky. And we saw the Anakites [d] there!' "

29Then I said to you, "Don't be frightened;
don't be afraid of those people. 30The LORD your
God will go ahead of you and fight for you as he
did in Egypt; you saw him do it. 31And in the
desert you saw how the LORD your God carried
you, as one carries a child. And he has brought
you safely all the way to this place."

32But you still did not trust the LORD your God,
even though 33he had always gone before you to
find places for you to camp. In a fire at night and
in a cloud during the day, he showed you which
way to go.

34When the LORD heard what you said, he was
angry and made an oath, saying, 35"I promised a
good land to your ancestors, but none of you evil
people will see it. 36Only Caleb son of Jephunneh
will see it. I will give him and his descendants [d]
the land he walked on, because he followed the
LORD completely."

37Because of you, the LORD was also angry with
me and said, "You won't enter the land either,
38but your assistant, Joshua son of Nun, will enter
it. Encourage him, because he will lead Israel to
take the land for their own.

39"Your little children that you said would be
captured, who do not know right from wrong at
this time, will go into the land. I will give the land
to them, and they will take it for their own. 40But
you must turn round and follow the desert road
towards the Red Sea."

41Then you said to me, "We have sinned
against the LORD, but now we will go up and fight,
as the LORD our God commanded us." Then all of
you put on weapons, thinking it would be easy to
go into the mountains.

42But the LORD said to me, "Tell the people,
'You must not go up there and fight. I will not be
with you, and your enemies will defeat you.' "

43So I told you, but you would not listen. You
would not obey the LORD's command. You were
proud, so you went on up into the mountains,
44and the Amorites who lived in those mountains
came out and fought you. They chased you like
bees and defeated you from Edom to Hormah.
45So you came back and cried before the LORD,
but the LORD did not listen to you; he refused to
pay attention to you. 46So you stayed in Kadesh a
long time.

Israel Wanders in the Desert

2 Then we turned round, and we travelled on
the desert road towards the Red Sea, as the
LORD had told me to do. We travelled through the
mountains of Edom for many days.

2Then the LORD said to me, 3"You have trav-
elled through these mountains long enough. Turn
north 4and give the people this command: 'You
will soon go through the land that belongs to your
relatives, the descendants [d] of Esau who live in
Edom. They will be afraid of you, but be very
careful. 5Do not go to war against them. I will not
give you any of their land—not even a foot of
it—because I have given the mountains of Edom
to Esau as his own. 6You must pay them in silver
for any food you eat or water you drink.' "

7The LORD your God has blessed everything
you have done; he has protected you while you
travelled through this great desert. The LORD your
God has been with you for the past 40 years, and
you have had everything you needed.

8So we passed by our relatives, the descend-
ants of Esau who lived in Edom. We turned off
the Jordan Valley road that comes from the towns
of Elath and Ezion Geber and travelled along the
desert road to Moab.

The Land of Ar

9Then the LORD said to me, "Don't bother the
people of Moab. Don't go to war against them,
because I will not give you any of their land as
your own; I have given Ar to the descendants [d] of
Lot as their own." 10(The Emites, who lived in Ar
before, were strong people, and there were many
of them. They were very tall, like the Anakites. [d]
11The Emites were thought to be Rephaites, [d] like
the Anakites, but the Moabite people called them
Emites. 12The Horites also lived in Edom before,
but the descendants of Esau forced them out and
destroyed them, taking their place as Israel did in
the land the LORD gave them as their own.)

13And the LORD said to me, "Now get up and
cross the Zered Valley." So we crossed the valley.
14It had been 38 years from the time we left Ka-
desh Barnea until we crossed the Zered Valley. By
then, all the fighting men from that time had
died, as the LORD had promised would happen.
15The LORD continued to work against them to
remove them from the camp until they were all
dead.

16When the last of those fighting men had
died, 17the LORD said to me, 18"Today you will
pass by Ar, on the border of Moab. 19When you
come near the people of Ammon, don't bother
them or go to war against them, because I will
not give you any of their land as your own. I have
given it to the descendants of Lot for their own."

20(That land was also thought to be a land of
the Rephaites, because those people used to live
there, but the Ammonites called them Zam-
zummites. 21They were strong people, and there
were many of them; they were very tall, like the
Anakites. The LORD destroyed the Zam-
zummites and the Ammonites forced them out
of the land and took their place. 22The LORD did
the same thing for the descendants of Esau, who
lived in Edom, when he destroyed the Horites.

The Edomites forced them out of the land and took their place, and they live there to this day. 23The Cretan people came from Crete and destroyed the Avvites, who lived in towns all the way to Gaza; the Cretan people destroyed them and took their place.)

Fighting the Amorites

24The LORD said, "Get up and cross the Arnon Ravine. See, I am giving you the power to defeat Sihon the Amorite, king of Heshbon, and I am giving you his land. So fight against him and begin taking his land. 25Today I will begin to make all the people in the world afraid of you. When they hear reports about you, they will shake with fear, and they will be terrified of you."

26I sent messengers from the desert of Kedemoth to Sihon king of Heshbon. They offered him peace, saying, 27"If you let us pass through your country, we will stay on the road and not turn right or left. 28We will pay you in silver for any food we eat or water we drink. We only want to walk through your country. 29The descendants[d] of Esau in Edom let us go through their land, and so did the Moabites in Ar. We want to cross the Jordan River into the land the LORD our God has given us." 30But Sihon king of Heshbon would not let us pass, because the LORD your God had made him stubborn. The LORD wanted you to defeat Sihon, and now this has happened.

31The LORD said to me, "See, I have begun to give Sihon and his country to you. Begin taking the land as your own."

32Then Sihon and all his army came out and fought us at Jahaz, 33but the LORD our God gave Sihon to us. We defeated him, his sons and all his army. 34We captured all his cities at that time and completely destroyed them, as well as the men, women and children. We left no one alive. 35But we kept the cattle and valuable things from the cities for ourselves. 36We defeated Aroer on the edge of the Arnon Ravine, and we defeated the town in the ravine, and even as far as Gilead. No town was too strong for us; the LORD our God gave us all of them. 37But you did not go near the land of the Ammonites, on the shores of the Jabbok River, or the towns in the mountains, as the LORD our God had commanded.

The Battle at Bashan

3 When we turned and went up the road towards Bashan, Og king of Bashan and all his army came out to fight us at Edrei. 2The LORD said to me, "Don't be afraid of Og, because I will hand him, his whole army and his land over to you. Do to him what you did to Sihon king of the Amorites, who ruled in Heshbon."

3So the LORD our God gave us Og king of Bashan and all his army; we defeated them and left no one alive. 4Then we captured all of Og's cities, all 60 of them, and took the whole area of Argob, Og's kingdom in Bashan. 5All these were strong cities, with high walls and gates with bars. And there were also many small towns with no walls. 6We completely destroyed them, just like the cities of Sihon king of Heshbon. We killed all the men, women and children, 7but we kept all the cattle and valuable things from the cities for ourselves.

8So at that time we took the land east of the Jordan River, from the Arnon Ravine to Mount Hermon, from these two Amorite kings. 9(Hermon is called Sirion by the Sidonian people, but the Amorites call it Senir.) 10We captured all the cities on the high plain and all of Gilead, and we took all of Bashan as far as Salecah and Edrei, towns in Og's kingdom of Bashan. 11(Only Og king of Bashan was left of the few Rephaites.[d] His bed was made of iron, and it was more than 4 metres long and 2 metres wide! It is still in the Ammonite city of Rabbah.)

The Land is Divided

12At that time we took this land to be our own. I gave the people of Reuben and Gad the land from Aroer by the Arnon Ravine, as well as half of the mountain country of Gilead and the cities in it. 13To the people of East Manasseh I gave the rest of Gilead and all of Bashan, the kingdom of Og. (The area of Argob in Bashan was called the land of the Rephaites.[d] 14Jair, a descendant[d] of Manasseh, took the whole area of Argob, all the way to the border of the Geshurites and Maacathites. So that land was named for Jair, and even today Bashan is called the Towns of Jair.) 15I gave Gilead to Makir. 16I gave the Reubenites and the Gadites the land that begins at Gilead and goes from the Arnon Ravine (the middle of the Arnon is the border) to the Jabbok River, which is the Ammonite border. 17The border on the west was the Jordan River in the Jordan Valley, and it goes from Lake Galilee to the Dead Sea[d] west of Mount Pisgah.

18At that time I gave you this command: "The LORD your God has given you this land as your own. Now your fighting men must take their weapons, and you must lead the other Israelites across the river. 19Your wives, your young children and your cattle may stay here. I know you have many cattle, and they may stay here in the cities I have given you, 20until the LORD also gives your Israelite relatives a place to rest. They will receive the land the LORD your God has given them on the other side of the Jordan River. After that, you may each return to the land I have given you."

21Then I gave this command to Joshua: "You have seen for yourself all that the LORD your God has done to these two kings. The LORD will do the same thing to all the kingdoms where you are going. 22Don't be afraid of them, because the LORD your God will fight for you."

Moses Cannot Enter the Land

23Then I begged the LORD: 24"Lord GOD, you have begun to show me, your servant, how great you are. You have great strength, and no other god in heaven or on earth can do the powerful things you do. There is no other god like you. 25Please let me cross the Jordan River so that I may see the good land by the Jordan. I want to see the beautiful mountains and Lebanon."

26But the LORD was angry with me because of you, and he would not listen to me. The LORD said to me, "That's enough. Don't talk to me any more about it. 27Climb to the top of Mount Pisgah and look west, north, south and east. You can look at the land, but you will not cross the Jordan River. 28Appoint Joshua and help him be brave and strong. He will lead the people across the river and give them the land that they are to inherit, but you can only look at it." 29So we stayed in the valley opposite Beth Peor.

Moses Tells Israel to Obey

4 Now, Israel, listen to the laws and commands I will teach you. Obey them so that you will live and so that you will go over and take the land the LORD, the God of your ancestors, is giving to you. 2Don't add to these commands, and don't leave anything out, but obey the commands of the LORD your God that I give you.

3You have seen for yourselves what the LORD did at Baal Peor, how the LORD your God destroyed everyone among you who followed Baal[d] in Peor. 4But all of you who continued following the LORD your God are still alive today.

5Look, I have taught you the laws and rules the LORD my God commanded me. Now you can obey the laws in the land you are entering, in the land you will take. 6Obey these laws carefully, in order to show the other nations that you have wisdom and understanding. When they hear about these laws, they will say, "This great nation of Israel is wise and understanding." 7No other nation is as great as we are. Their gods do not come near them, but the LORD our God comes near when we pray to him. 8And no other nation has such good teachings and commands as those I am giving to you today.

9But be careful! Watch out and don't forget the things you have seen. Don't forget them as long as you live, but teach them to your children and grandchildren. 10Remember the day you stood before the LORD your God at Mount Sinai. He said to me, "Bring the people together so I can tell them what I have to say. Then they will respect me as long as they live in the land, and they will teach these things to their children." 11When you came and stood at the bottom of the mountain, it blazed with fire that reached to the sky, and black clouds made it very dark. 12The LORD spoke to you from the fire. You heard the sound of words, but you did not see him; there was only a voice. 13The LORD told you about his Agreement, the Ten Commandments. He told you to obey them, and he wrote them on two stone tablets. 14Then the LORD commanded me to teach you the laws and rules that you must obey in the land you will take when you cross the Jordan River.

Laws About Idols

15Since the LORD spoke to you from the fire at Mount Sinai, but you did not see him, watch yourselves carefully! 16Don't sin by making idols of any kind, and don't make statues—of men or women, 17of animals on earth or birds that fly in the air, 18of anything that crawls on the ground or of fish in the water below. 19When you look up at the sky, you see the sun, moon and stars and everything in the sky. But don't bow down and worship them, because the LORD your God has made these things for all people everywhere. 20But the LORD brought you out of Egypt, which tested you like a furnace for melting iron, and he made you his very own people, as you are now.

21The LORD was angry with me because of you, and he swore that I would not cross the Jordan River to go into the good land the LORD your God is giving you as your own. 22I will die here in this land and not cross the Jordan, but you will soon go across and take that good land. 23Be careful. Don't forget the Agreement of the LORD your God that he made with you, and don't make any idols for yourselves, as the LORD your God has commanded you not to do. 24The LORD your God is a jealous God, like a fire that burns things up.

25Even after you have lived in the land a long time and have had children and grandchildren, don't do evil things. Don't make any kind of idol, and don't do what the LORD your God says is evil, because that will make him angry. 26If you do, I ask heaven and earth to speak against you this day that you will quickly be removed from this land that you are crossing the Jordan River to take. You will not live there long after that, but you will be completely destroyed. 27The LORD will scatter you among the other nations. Only a few of you will be left alive, and those few will

be in other nations where the LORD will send
you. [28]There you will worship gods made by peo-
ple, gods made of wood and stone, that cannot
see, hear, eat or smell. [29]But even there you can
look for the LORD your God, and you will find him
if you look for him with your whole being. [30]It
will be hard when all these things happen to you.
But after that you will come back to the LORD your
God and obey him, [31]because the LORD your God
is a merciful God. He will not leave you or des-
troy you. He will not forget the Agreement with
your ancestors, which he swore to them.

The LORD is Great

[32]Nothing like this has ever happened before!
Look at the past, long before you were even born.
Go all the way back to when God made man on
the earth, and look from one end of heaven to the
other. Nothing like this has ever been heard of!
[33]No other people have ever heard God speak
from a fire and have still lived. But you have.
[34]No other god has ever taken for himself one
nation out of another. But the LORD your God did
this for you in Egypt, right before your own eyes.
He did it with tests, signs, miracles,[d] war and
great sights, by his great power and strength.
[35]He showed you things so you would know
that the LORD is God, and there is no other God
besides him. [36]He spoke to you from heaven to
teach you. He showed you his great fire on earth,
and you heard him speak from the fire. [37]Because
the LORD loved your ancestors, he chose you,
their descendants,[d] and he brought you out of
Egypt himself by his great strength. [38]He forced

GOD'S LOVE

Persistent Love

According to most people, Martha Henry should have hated Edward Henderson. After all, he had shot her son Calvin twice – once between the eyes and once in the neck.

Martha got the details of the shooting from Edward, who said he had intended to fire warning shots over the car, not into the car. He called the hospital almost every hour to see how Calvin was doing. Calvin died five days after the shooting, never having regained consciousness.

Martha believed Edward when he said the shooting was accidental. But the court didn't; he was sentenced to life in prison without any chance of being let out.

Then Martha felt God nudging her to share God's love with Edward. "I had a lot to think about while the Lord was pushing me to love Edward and not hold any bitterness against him," Martha says. "But, I'd learned from experience that when God tells you to do something, he means what he says."

On Martha's first visit, Edward was suspicious of her motives and didn't want to see her again. "I'm praying for you," she told him as she left. But each succeeding visit helped him open up. Eventually, he committed his life to Christ and began calling Martha "Mother Henry".

When Edward began appealing for parole, Martha pleaded his case. Though he hasn't been released, Martha believes he eventually will be. "He's not staying in there for ever," she says confidently. "The Lord has things for him to do!"

Martha reached out to Edward and believed he had a special role to play. God also reached out to the Israelites and chose them for a special role, revealing his incredible love in **Deuteronomy 4:32–40**.

- According to the passage, how were the Israelites like Edward?
- How did God make himself known to the Israelites? How are the reasons God worked in them similar to the reasons he has worked in you?

Consider . . .

- writing a love letter to God, thanking him for the many things he's done for you.
- becoming a pen pal with a prison inmate. Offer God's love and encouragement in your letters.

For more, see . . .

- Psalm 91:14–16 (p.555)
- Romans 5:6–8 (p.1190)
- Isaiah 43:1–4 (p.683)

nations out of their land ahead of you, nations that were bigger and stronger than you were. The LORD did this so he could bring you into their land and give it to you as your own, and this land is yours today.

[39]Know and believe today that the LORD is God. He is God in heaven above and on the earth below. There is no other god! [40]Obey his laws and commands that I am giving you today so that things will go well for you and your children. Then you will live a long time in the land that the LORD your God is giving to you for ever.

Cities of Safety

[41]Moses chose three cities east of the Jordan River, [42]where a person who accidentally killed someone could go. If the person was not killed because of hatred, the murderer's life could be saved by running to one of these cities. [43]These were the cities: Bezer in the desert high plain was for the Reubenites; Ramoth in Gilead was for the Gadites; and Golan in Bashan was for the Manassites.

The Laws Moses Gave

[44]These are the teachings Moses gave to the people of Israel. [45]They are the rules, commands and laws he gave them when they came out of Egypt. [46]They were in the valley near Beth Peor, east of the Jordan River, in the land of Sihon. Sihon king of the Amorites ruled in Heshbon and was defeated by Moses and the Israelites as they came out of Egypt. [47]The Israelites took his land and the land of Og king of Bashan, the two Amorite kings east of the Jordan River. [48]This land went from Aroer, on the edge of the Arnon Ravine, to Mount Hermon. [49]It included all the Jordan Valley east of the Jordan River, and it went as far as the Dead Sea[d] below Mount Pisgah.

The Ten Commandments

5 Moses called all the people of Israel together and said: Listen, Israel, to the commands and laws I am giving you today. Learn them and obey them carefully. [2]The LORD our God made an Agreement with us at Mount Sinai. [3]He did not make this Agreement with our ancestors, but he made it with us, with all of us who are alive here today. [4]The LORD spoke to you face to face from the fire on the mountain. [5](At that time I stood between you and the LORD in order to tell you what the LORD said; you were afraid of the fire, so you would not go up on the mountain.) The LORD said:

[6]"I am the LORD your God; I brought you out of the land of Egypt where you were slaves.

[7]"You must not have any other gods except me.

[8]"You must not make for yourselves any idols or anything to worship that looks like something in the sky above or on the earth below or in the water below the land. [9]You must not worship or serve any idol, because I, the LORD your God, am a jealous God. If people sin against me and hate me, I will punish their children, even their grandchildren and great-grandchildren. [10]But I will be very kind for 1,000 lifetimes to those who love me and obey my commands.

[11]"You must not use the name of the LORD your God thoughtlessly, because the LORD will punish anyone who uses his name in this way.

[12]"Keep the Sabbath[d] as a holy day, as the LORD your God has commanded you. [13]You may work and get everything done during six days each week, [14]but the seventh day is a day of rest to honour the LORD your God. On that day no one may do any work: not you, your son or daughter, your male or female slaves, your ox, your donkey or any of your animals, or the foreigners living in your cities. That way your servants may rest as you do. [15]Remember that you were slaves in Egypt and that the LORD your God brought you out of there by his great power and strength. So the LORD your God has commanded you to rest on the Sabbath day.

[16]"Honour your father and your mother as the LORD your God has commanded you. Then you will live a long time, and things will go well for you in the land that the LORD your God is going to give you.

[17]"You must not murder anyone.

[18]"You must not be guilty of adultery.[d]

[19]"You must not steal.

[20]"You must not tell lies about your neighbour.

[21]"You must not want to take your neighbour's wife. You must not want to take your neighbour's house or land, his male or female slaves, his ox or his donkey, or anything that belongs to your neighbour."

[22]The LORD spoke these commands to all of you on the mountain in a loud voice out of the fire, the cloud and the deep darkness; he did not say anything else. Then he wrote them on two stone tablets, and he gave them to me.

[23]When you heard the voice from the darkness, as the mountain was blazing with fire, all your elders and leaders of your tribes[d] came to me. [24]And you said, "The LORD our God has shown us his glory and majesty, and we have heard his voice from the fire. Today we have seen that a person can live even if God speaks to him. [25]But now, we will die! This great fire will burn us up, and we will die if we hear the LORD our God speak any more. [26]No human being has ever heard the living God speaking from a fire and still lived, but we have. [27]Moses, you go near and listen to everything the LORD our God says. Then

you tell us what the LORD our God tells you, and
we will listen and obey."
28The LORD heard what you said to me, and he
said to me, "I have heard what the people said to
you. Everything they said was good. 29I wish
their hearts would always respect me and that
they would always obey my commands so that
things would go well for them and their children
for ever!
30"Go and tell the people to return to their
tents, 31but you stay here with me so that I may
give you all the commands, rules and laws that
you must teach the people to obey in the land I
am giving them as their own."
32So be careful to do what the LORD your God
has commanded you, and follow the commands
exactly. 33Live the way the LORD your God has
commanded you so that you may live and have
what is good and have a long life in the land you
will take.

The Command to Love God

6 These are the commands, rules and laws
that the LORD your God told me to teach you
to obey in the land you are crossing the Jordan
River to take. 2You, your children and your
grandchildren must respect the LORD your God as
long as you live. Obey all his rules and commands
I give you so that you will live a long time.
3Listen, Israel, and carefully obey these laws.
Then all will go well for you, and you will
become a great nation in a fertile land, just as the
LORD, the God of your ancestors, has promised
you.

FOLLOWING GOD

Walk and Talk

Peter was a birdwatcher. Some may say that's a very boring hobby, but he was an expert. When you went out with him, he made you aware of birds you'd never seen.

"Stand still," he'd say. "Now, listen."

Somewhere in the distance you heard a small cry.

"A Stone Curlew!" he would remark in triumph.

And before you knew what was happening, you were following him through bracken and long grass, getting scratched to pieces until suddenly, there in front of you was the bird in question. It made you feel almost as good as him.

Peter and his wife Miranda often felt that they should start a Bird Reserve. Somewhere where people could enjoy watching the beautiful creatures that God had made.

So they made their home in the Algarve, Portugal. A magnificent place for birdwatching. Gradually people came to stay at the A Rocha Reserve, and Peter took them out into the wilds and showed them Bee Eaters up close. It was the most natural thing for him to remark, "Isn't God fantastic? Just look at the colours on that one!" And as the sun came down, he would say, "The Lord seems to make a different sunset every night, have you noticed?"

Without really knowing it, Peter was doing exactly what it says in Deuteronomy 6:7. Talking about the Lord at home and walking down the road.

Deuteronomy 6:1–9 tells us about God's laws and how following them results in a better life.

- What promises did God give in this passage? How would they affect Peter's life?
- What could you do in your life to help fulfil these commands?

Consider . . .

- taking some time out to talk to God whilst enjoying a walk in the park or on the beach, appreciating God's creation.
- re-writing what Deuteronomy 6:5 means to you, in your own words.

For more, see . . .

- Deuteronomy 10:12–22 (p.175)
- Philippians 3:12–16 (p.1284)
- Psalm 119:9–16 (p.571)

4Listen, people of Israel! The LORD our God is
the only LORD. 5Love the LORD your God with all
your heart, all your soul and all your strength.
6Always remember these commands I give you
today. 7Teach them to your children, and talk
about them when you sit at home and walk along

> **Sidelight** Deuteronomy 6:4–9 is as important to the Jews as the Lord's Prayer (Matthew 6:9–13, p.948) is to Christians. The Deuteronomy passage is the basis for the Jewish Shema, which is recited morning and evening by many Jews. This classic declaration of faith is also recited just before death and in times of martyrdom.

the road, when you lie down and when you get
up. 8Write them down and tie them to your hands
as a sign. Tie them on your forehead to remind
you, 9and write them on your doors and gates.
10The LORD your God will bring you into the
land he promised to your ancestors, to Abraham,
Isaac and Jacob, and he will give it to you. The
land has large, growing cities you did not build,
11houses full of good things you did not buy, wells
you did not dig and vineyards and olive trees you
did not plant. You will eat as much as you want.
12But be careful! Do not forget the LORD, who
brought you out of the land of Egypt where you
were slaves.
13Respect the LORD your God. You must wor-
ship him and make your promises only in his
name. 14Do not worship other gods as the people
around you do, 15because the LORD your God is a
jealous God. He is present with you, and if you
worship other gods, he will become angry with
you and destroy you from the earth. 16Do not test
the LORD your God as you did at Massah. 17Be
sure to obey the commands of the LORD your God
and the rules and laws he has given you. 18Do
what the LORD says is good and right so that
things will go well for you. Then you may go in
and take the good land the LORD promised to your
ancestors. 19He will force all your enemies out as
you go in, as the LORD has said.
20In the future when your children ask you,
"What is the meaning of the laws, commands and
rules the LORD our God gave us?" 21tell them,
"We were slaves to the king of Egypt, but the
LORD brought us out of Egypt by his great power.
22The LORD showed us great and terrible signs and
miracles,[d] which he did to Egypt, the king and his
whole family. 23The LORD brought us out of Egypt
to lead us here and to give us the land he prom-
ised our ancestors. 24The LORD ordered us to obey
all these commands and to respect the LORD our
God so that we will always do well and stay alive,
as we are today. 25The right thing for us to do is
this: obey all these rules in the presence of the
LORD our God, as he has commanded."

You are God's People

7 The LORD your God will bring you into the
land that you are entering and that you will
have as your own. As you go in, he will force out
these nations: the Hittites, Girgashites, Amorites,
Canaanites, Perizzites, Hivites and Jebusites—
seven nations that are stronger than you. 2The
LORD your God will hand these nations over to
you, and when you defeat them, you must des-
troy them completely. Do not make a peace
treaty with them or show them any mercy. 3Do
not marry any of them, or let your daughters
marry their sons, or let your sons marry their
daughters. 4If you do, those people will turn your
children away from me, to begin serving other
gods. Then the LORD will be very angry with you,
and he will quickly destroy you. 5This is what you
must do to those people: tear down their altars,
smash their holy stone pillars, cut down their
Asherah[d] idols and burn their idols in the fire.
6You are holy people who belong to the LORD your
God. He has chosen you from all the people on
earth to be his very own.
7The LORD did not care for you and choose you
because there were many of you—you are the
smallest nation of all. 8But the LORD chose you
because he loved you, and he kept his promise to
your ancestors. So he brought you out of Egypt by
his great power and freed you from the land of
slavery, from the power of the king of Egypt. 9So
know that the LORD your God is God, the faithful
God. He will keep his agreement of love for
1,000 lifetimes for people who love him and obey
his commands. 10But he will pay back those peo-
ple who hate him. He will destroy them, and he
will not be slow to pay back those who hate him.
11So be careful to obey the commands, rules and
laws I give you today.
12If you pay attention to these laws and obey
them carefully, the LORD your God will keep his
agreement and show his love to you, as he prom-
ised your ancestors. 13He will love and bless you.
He will make the number of your people grow;
he will bless you with children. He will bless your
fields with good crops and will give you grain,
new wine and oil. He will bless your herds with
calves and your flocks with lambs in the land
he promised your ancestors he would give you.
14You will be blessed more than any other people.
Every husband and wife will have children, and
all your cattle will have calves. 15The LORD will
take away all disease from you; you will not have
the terrible diseases that were in Egypt, but he

will give them to all the people who hate you. 16You must destroy all the people the LORD your God hands over to you. Do not feel sorry for them, and do not worship their gods, or they will trap you.

17You might say to yourselves, "Because these nations are stronger than we are, we can't force them out." 18But don't be afraid of them. Remember what the LORD your God did to all of Egypt and its king. 19You saw for yourselves the troubles, signs and miracles[d] he did, how the LORD's great power and strength brought you out of Egypt. The LORD your God will do the same thing to all the nations you now fear. 20The LORD your God will also send terror among them so that even those who are alive and hiding from you will die. 21Don't be afraid of them, because the LORD your God is with you; he is a great God and people are afraid of him. 22When the LORD your God forces those nations out of the land, he will do it little by little ahead of you. You won't be able to destroy them all at once; otherwise, the wild animals will grow too many in number. 23But the LORD your God will hand those nations over to you, confusing them until they are destroyed. 24The LORD will help you defeat their kings, and the world will forget who they were. No one will be able to stop you; you will destroy them all. 25Burn up their idols in the fire. Do not wish for the silver and gold they have, and don't take it for yourselves, or you will be trapped by it. The LORD your God hates it. 26Do not bring one of those hateful things into your house, or you will be completely destroyed along with it. Hate and reject those things; they must be completely destroyed.

Remember the LORD

8 Carefully obey every command I give you today. Then you will live and grow in number, and you will enter and take the land the LORD promised your ancestors. 2Remember how the LORD your God has led you in the desert for these 40 years, taking away your pride and testing you, because he wanted to know what was in your heart. He wanted to know if you would obey his commands. 3He took away your pride when he let you get hungry, and then he fed you with manna,[d] which neither you nor your ancestors had ever seen. This was to teach you that a person does not live by eating only bread, but by everything the LORD says. 4During these 40 years, your clothes did not wear out, and your feet did not swell. 5Know in your heart that the LORD your God corrects you as a parent corrects a child.

6Obey the commands of the LORD your God, living as he has commanded you, and respect him. 7The LORD your God is bringing you into a good land, a land with rivers and pools of water, with springs that flow in the valleys and hills, 8a land that has wheat and barley, vines, fig trees, pomegranates,[d] olive oil and honey. 9It is a land where you will have plenty of food, where you will have everything you need, where the rocks are iron, and where you can dig copper out of the hills.

Sidelight Most Christians pray or say grace before they eat a meal. But the ancient Israelites didn't just pray before they ate. They prayed afterwards as well (Deuteronomy 8:10).

10When you have all you want to eat, then praise the LORD your God for giving you a good land. 11Be careful not to forget the LORD your God so that you fail to obey his commands, laws and rules that I am giving to you today. 12When you eat all you want and build nice houses and live in them, 13when your herds and flocks grow large and your silver and gold increase, when you have more of everything, 14then your heart will become proud. You will forget the LORD your God, who brought you out of the land of Egypt, where you were slaves. 15He led you through the large and terrible desert that was dry and had no water, and that had poisonous snakes and stinging insects. He gave you water from a solid rock 16and manna to eat in the desert. Manna was something your ancestors had never seen. He did this to take away your pride and to test you, so things would go well for you in the end. 17You might say to yourself, "I am rich because of my own power and strength," 18but remember the LORD your God! It is he who gives you the power to become rich, keeping the agreement he promised to your ancestors, as it is today.

19If you ever forget the LORD your God and follow other gods and worship them and bow down to them, I warn you today that you will be destroyed. 20Just as the LORD destroyed the other nations for you, you can be destroyed if you do not obey the LORD your God.

The LORD Will be With Israel

9 Listen, Israel. You will soon cross the Jordan River to go in and force out nations that are bigger and stronger than you. They have large cities with walls up to the sky. 2The people there are Anakites,[d] who are strong and tall. You know about them, and you have heard it said: "No one can stop the Anakites." 3But today remember that

the LORD your God goes in before you to destroy
them like a fire that burns things up. He will
defeat them ahead of you, and you will force
them out and destroy them quickly, just as the
LORD has said.
4After the LORD your God has forced those na-
tions out ahead of you, don't say to yourself, "The
LORD brought me here to take this land because I
am so good." No! It is because these nations are
evil that the LORD will force them out ahead of
you. 5You are going in to take the land, not be-
cause you are good and honest, but because these
nations are evil. That is why the LORD your God
will force them out ahead of you, to keep his
promise to your ancestors, to Abraham, Isaac and
Jacob. 6The LORD your God is giving you this good
land to take as your own. But know this: it is not
because you are good; you are a stubborn people.

Remember the LORD's Anger

7Remember this and do not forget it: you made
the LORD your God angry in the desert. You
would not obey the LORD from the day you left
Egypt until you arrived here. 8At Mount Sinai you
made the LORD angry—angry enough to destroy
you. 9When I went up on the mountain to re-
ceive the stone tablets, the tablets with the Agree-
ment the LORD had made with you, I stayed on
the mountain for 40 days and 40 nights; I did not
eat bread or drink water. 10The LORD gave me two
stone tablets, which God had written on with his
own finger. On them were all the commands that
the LORD gave to you on the mountain out of the
fire, on the day you were gathered there.
11When the 40 days and 40 nights were over,
the LORD gave me the two stone tablets, the tab-
lets with the Agreement on them. 12Then the

THANKFULNESS

Cinderella Story

Beth had grown up being passed from one foster home to the next. More often than not, she was sharing a room with at least one other child. Finally, when she was eighteen, a middle-aged couple called Rita and Paul agreed to adopt her permanently. She had a room of her own, clothes that were bought for her and not just cast-offs and, most importantly for her, Beth had people who loved her unconditionally and who were willing to accept her just as she was.

When college finished, her employers took her on full time, and by working hard Beth slowly but surely climbed her way up until she got the point where she was earning enough to buy her own place and provide for herself.

Things were amazing for a while, until one day she got a phone call from the hospital saying that her adoptive mum, Rita, had suffered a serious fall. She would be in hospital for a few weeks and then would need help around the house for a while.

Knowing that Rita's husband Paul wouldn't be able to cope by himself, Beth did as much as she could for the couple who had provided for her over the years. She also went to visit Rita in hospital every day until she was allowed to go home.

Read **Deuteronomy 8:10–18**.

- In what way is Beth's story similar to that of the Israelites mentioned in this passage?
- What pitfalls mentioned in this passage did Beth manage to avoid?

Consider . . .

- whether there are any situations where you didn't express proper thankfulness.
- making a list of all the things you have which you have to be thankful for. Take time to thank God properly for them – write a song, do it in prayer, etc.

For more, see . . .

- Psalm 92:1–5 (p.555)
- 2 Corinthians 9:6–15 (p.1248)
- Psalm 106:1–3 (p.562)

LORD told me, "Get up and go down quickly from
here, because the people you brought out from
Egypt are ruining themselves. They have quickly
turned away from what I commanded and have
made an idol for themselves."
13The LORD said to me, "I have watched these
people, and they are very stubborn! 14Get away
so that I may destroy them and make the whole
world forget who they are. Then I will make an-
other nation from you that will be bigger and
stronger than they are."
15So I turned and came down the mountain
that was burning with fire and the two stone
tablets with the Agreement were in my hands.
16When I looked, I saw you had sinned against
the LORD your God and had made an idol in
the shape of a calf. You had quickly turned away
from what the LORD had told you to do. 17So I
took the two stone tablets and threw them
down, breaking them into pieces right in front
of you.
18Then I again bowed face down on the
ground before the LORD for 40 days and 40 nights;
I did not eat bread or drink water. You had
sinned by doing what the LORD said was evil, and
you made him angry. 19I was afraid of the LORD's
anger and rage, because he was angry enough
with you to destroy you, but the LORD listened to
me again. 20And the LORD was angry enough with
Aaron to destroy him, but then I prayed for Aaron
too. 21I took that sinful calf idol you had made
and burned it in the fire. I crushed it into a pow-
der like dust and threw the dust into a stream
that flowed down the mountain.
22You also made the LORD angry at Taberah,
Massah and Kibroth Hattaavah.
23Then the LORD sent you away from Kadesh
Barnea and said, "Go up and take the land I have
given you." But you rejected the command of the
LORD your God. You did not trust him or obey
him. 24You have refused to obey the LORD as long
as I have known you.
25The LORD had said he would destroy you, so
I threw myself down in front of him for those 40
days and 40 nights. 26I prayed to the LORD and
said, "Lord GOD, do not destroy your people, your
own people, whom you freed and brought out of
Egypt by your great power and strength. 27Re-
member your servants Abraham, Isaac and Jacob.
Don't look at how stubborn these people are, and
don't look at their sin and evil. 28Otherwise,
Egypt will say, 'It was because the LORD was not
able to take his people into the land he promised
them, and it was because he hated them that he
took them into the desert to kill them.' 29But they
are your people, LORD, your own people, whom
you brought out of Egypt with your great power
and strength."

New Stone Tablets

10 At that time the LORD said to me, "Cut two
stone tablets like the first ones and come
up to me on the mountain. Also make a wooden
Ark.[d] 2I will write on the tablets the same words
that were on the first tablets, which you broke,
and you will put the new tablets in the Ark."
3So I made the Ark out of acacia wood, and I
cut out two stone tablets like the first ones. Then
I went up on the mountain with the two tablets
in my hands. 4The LORD wrote the same things on
these tablets he had written before—the Ten
Commandments that he had told you on the
mountain from the fire, on the day you were
gathered there. And the LORD gave them to me.
5Then I turned and came down the mountain; I
put the tablets in the Ark I had made, as the LORD
had commanded, and they are still there.
6(The people of Israel went from the wells of
the Jaakanites to Moserah. Aaron died there and
was buried; his son Eleazar became priest in his
place. 7From Moserah they went to Gudgodah,
and from Gudgodah they went to Jotbathah, a
place with streams of water. 8At that time the
LORD chose the tribe[d] of Levi to carry the Ark of
the Agreement with the LORD. They were to serve
the LORD and to bless the people in his name,
which they still do today. 9That is why the Le-
vites did not receive any land of their own; in-
stead, they received the LORD himself as their gift,
as the LORD your God told them.)
10I stayed on the mountain 40 days and 40
nights just like the first time, and the LORD lis-
tened to me this time also. He did not want to
destroy you. 11The LORD said to me, "Go and lead
the people so that they will go in and take the
land I promised their ancestors."

What the LORD Wants You to Do

12Now, Israel, this is what the LORD your God
wants you to do: respect the LORD your God, and
do what he has told you to do. Love him. Serve
the LORD your God with your whole being, 13and
obey the LORD's commands and laws that I am
giving you today for your own good.
14The LORD owns the world and everything in
it—the heavens, even the highest heavens, are
his. 15But the LORD cared for and loved your an-
cestors, and he chose you, their descendants,[d]
over all the other nations, just as it is today.
16Give yourselves completely to serving him, and
do not be stubborn any longer. 17The LORD your
God is God of all gods and Lord of all lords. He
is the great God, who is strong and wonderful.
He does not take sides, and he will not be talked
into doing evil. 18He helps orphans and widows,
and he loves foreigners and gives them food and

clothes. 19You also must love foreigners, because you were foreigners in Egypt. 20Respect the LORD your God and serve him. Be loyal to him and make your promises in his name. 21He is the one you should praise; he is your God, who has done great and wonderful things for you, which you have seen with your own eyes. 22There were only 70 of your ancestors when they went down to Egypt, and now the LORD your God has made you as many as the stars in the sky.

Great Things Israel Saw

11 Love the LORD your God and always obey his orders, rules, laws and commands. 2Remember today it was not your children who saw and felt the correction of the LORD your God. They did not see his majesty, his power, his strength 3or his signs and the things he did in Egypt to the king and his whole country. 4They did not see what he did to the Egyptian army, its horses and chariots, when he drowned them in the Red Sea[d] as they were chasing you. The LORD ruined them for ever. 5They did not see what he did for you in the desert until you arrived here. 6They did not see what he did to Dathan and Abiram, the sons of Eliab the Reubenite, when the ground opened up and swallowed them, their families, their tents and everyone who stood with them in Israel. 7It was you who saw all these great things the LORD has done.

8So obey all the commands I am giving you today so that you will be strong and can go in and take the land you are going to take as your own. 9Then you will live a long time in the land that the LORD promised to give to your ancestors and their descendants,[d] a fertile land. 10The land you are going to take is not like Egypt, where you were. There you had to plant your seed and water it, like a vegetable garden, by using your feet. 11But the land that you will soon cross the Jordan River to take is a land of hills and valleys, a land that drinks rain from heaven. 12It is a land the LORD your God cares for. His eyes are on it continually, and he watches it from the beginning of the year to the end.

13If you carefully obey the commands I am giving you today and love the LORD your God and serve him with your whole being, 14then he will send rain on your land at the right time, in the autumn and spring, and you will be able to gather your grain, new wine and oil. 15He will put grass in the fields for your cattle, and you will have plenty to eat.

16Be careful, or you will be fooled and will turn away to serve and worship other gods. 17If you do, the LORD will become angry with you and will shut the heavens so it will not rain. Then the land will not grow crops, and you will soon die in the good land the LORD is giving you. 18Remember my words with your whole being. Write them down and tie them to your hands as a sign; tie them on your foreheads to remind you. 19Teach them well to your children, talking about them when you sit at home and walk along the road, when you lie down and when you get up. 20Write them on your doors and gates 21so that both you and your children will live a long time in the land the LORD promised your ancestors, as long as the skies are above the earth.

Sidelight If you have trouble remembering scripture passages, you are not alone. The Israelites apparently did too. So God told his people to write down his words and tie them to their hands so that they wouldn't forget them (Deuteronomy 11:18). This might get heavy if you memorised the whole Bible!

22If you are careful to obey every command I am giving you to follow, and love the LORD your God, and do what he has told you to do, and are loyal to him, 23then the LORD will force all those nations out of the land ahead of you, and you will take the land from nations that are bigger and stronger than you. 24Everywhere you step will be yours. Your land will go from the desert to Lebanon and from the Euphrates River to the Mediterranean Sea. 25No one will be able to stop you. The LORD your God will do what he promised and will make the people afraid everywhere you go.

26See, today I am letting you choose a blessing or a curse. 27You will be blessed if you obey the commands of the LORD your God that I am giving you today. 28But you will be cursed if you disobey the commands of the LORD your God. So do not disobey the commands I am giving you today, and do not worship other gods you do not know. 29When the LORD your God brings you into the land you will take as your own, you are to announce the blessings from Mount Gerizim and the curses from Mount Ebal. 30(These mountains are on the other side of the Jordan River, to the west, towards the sunset. They are near the great trees of Moreh in the land of the Canaanites who live in the Jordan Valley opposite Gilgal.) 31You will soon cross the Jordan River to enter and take the land the LORD your God is giving you. When you take it over and live there, 32be careful to obey all the commands and laws I am giving you today.

The Place for Worship

12 These are the commands and laws you must carefully obey in the land the LORD, the God of your ancestors, is giving you. Obey them as long as you live in the land. 2When you inherit the lands of these nations, you must completely destroy all the places where they serve their gods, on high mountains and hills and under every green tree. 3Tear down their altars, smash their holy stone pillars and burn their Asherah[d] idols in the fire. Cut down their idols and destroy their names from those places.

4Don't worship the LORD your God that way, 5but look for the place the LORD your God will choose—a place among your tribes[d] where he is to be worshipped. Go there, 6and bring to that place your burnt offerings and sacrifices; bring a tenth of what you gain and your special gifts; bring what you have promised and the special gifts you want to give the LORD, and bring the first animals born to your herds and flocks.

7There you will be together with the LORD your God. There you and your families will eat, and you will enjoy all the good things for which you have worked, because the LORD your God has blessed you.

8Do not worship the way we have been doing today, each person doing what he thinks is right. 9You have not yet come to a resting place, to the land the LORD your God will give you as your own. 10But soon you will cross the Jordan River to live in the land the LORD your God is giving you as your own, where he will give you rest from all your enemies and you will live in safety. 11Then the LORD your God will choose a place where he is to be worshipped. To that place you must bring everything I tell you: your burnt offerings and sacrifices, your offerings of a tenth of what you gain, your special gifts and all your best things you promised to the LORD. 12There rejoice before the LORD your God. Everyone should rejoice: you, your sons and daughters, your male and female servants and the Levites from your towns who have no land of their own. 13Be careful that you don't sacrifice your burnt offerings just anywhere you please. 14Offer them only in the place the LORD will choose. He will choose a place in one of your tribes, and there you must do everything I am commanding you.

15But you may kill your animals in any of your towns and eat as much of the meat as you want, as if it were a deer or a gazelle; this is the blessing the LORD your God is giving you. Anyone, clean[d] or unclean, may eat this meat, 16but do not eat the blood. Pour it out on the ground like water. 17Do not eat in your own towns what belongs to the LORD: one-tenth of your grain, new wine or oil; the first animals born to your herds or flocks; whatever you have promised to give; the special gifts you want to give to the LORD, or any other gifts. 18Eat these things when you are together with the LORD your God, in the place the LORD your God chooses to be worshipped. Everyone must do this: you, your sons and daughters, your male and female servants and the Levites from your towns. Rejoice in the LORD your God's presence about the things you have worked for. 19Be careful not to forget the Levites as long as you live in the land.

20When the LORD your God enlarges your country as he has promised, and you want some meat so you say, "I want some meat," you may eat as much meat as you want. 21If the LORD your God chooses a place where he is to be worshipped that is too far away from you, you may kill animals from your herds and flocks, which the LORD has given to you. I have commanded that you may do this. You may eat as much of them as you want in your own towns, 22as you would eat gazelle or deer meat. Both clean and unclean people may eat this meat, 23but be sure you don't eat the blood, because the life is in the blood. Don't eat the life with the meat. 24Don't eat the blood, but pour it out on the ground like water. 25If you don't eat it, things will go well for you and your children, because you will be doing what the LORD says is right.

26Take your holy things and the things you have promised to give, and go to the place the LORD will choose. 27Present your burnt offerings on the altar of the LORD your God, both the meat and the blood. The blood of your sacrifices should be poured beside the altar of the LORD your God, but you may eat the meat. 28Be careful to obey all the rules I am giving you so that things will always go well for you and your children, and you will be doing what the LORD your God says is good and right.

29You will enter the land and take it away from the nations that the LORD your God will destroy ahead of you. When you force them out and live in their land, 30they will be destroyed for you, but be careful not to be trapped by asking about their gods. Don't say, "How do these nations worship? I will do the same." 31Don't worship the LORD your God that way, because the LORD hates the evil ways they worship their gods. They even burn their sons and daughters as sacrifices to their gods!

32Be sure to do everything I have commanded you. Do not add anything to it, and do not take anything away from it.

False Prophets

13 Prophets[d] or those who tell the future with dreams might come to you and say they will show you a miracle[d] or a sign. 2The miracle or sign might even happen, and then they might say, "Let's serve other gods" (gods you have not known) "and let's worship them." 3But you must not listen to those prophets or dreamers. The LORD your God is testing you, to find out if you love him with your whole being. 4Serve only the LORD your God. Respect him, keep his commands and obey him. Serve him and be loyal to him. 5The prophets or dreamers must be killed, because they said you should turn against the LORD your God, who brought you out of Egypt and saved you from the land where you were slaves. They tried to turn you from doing what the LORD your God commanded you to do. You must get rid of the evil among you.

6Someone might try to lead you to serve other gods—it might be your brother, your son or daughter, the wife you love or a close friend. The person might say, "Let's go and worship other gods." (These are gods that neither you nor your ancestors have known, 7gods of the people who live around you, either nearby or far away, from one end of the land to the other.) 8Do not give in to such people. Do not listen or feel sorry for them, and do not let them go free or protect them. 9You must put them to death. You must be the first one to start to kill them, and then everyone else must join in. 10You must throw stones at them until they die, because they tried to turn you away from the LORD your God, who brought you out of the land of Egypt, where you were slaves. 11Then everyone in Israel will hear about this and be afraid, and no one among you will ever do such an evil thing again.

Cities to Destroy

12The LORD your God is giving you cities in which to live, and you might hear something about one of them. Someone might say 13that evil people have moved in among you. And they might lead the people of that city away from God, saying, "Let's go and worship other gods." (These are gods you have not known.) 14Then you must ask about it, looking into the matter and checking carefully whether it is true. If it is proved that a hateful thing has happened among you, 15you must kill with a sword everyone who lives in that city. Destroy the city completely and kill everyone in it, as well as the animals, with a sword. 16Gather up everything those people owned, and put it in the middle of the city square. Then completely burn the city and everything they owned as a burnt offering to the LORD your God. That city should never be rebuilt; let it be ruined for ever. 17Don't keep for yourselves any of the things found in that city, so the LORD will not be angry any more. He will give you mercy and feel sorry for you, and he will make your nation grow larger, as he promised to your ancestors. 18You will have obeyed the LORD your God by keeping all his commands that I am giving to you today, and you will be doing what the LORD says is right.

God's Special People

14 You are the children of the LORD your God. When someone dies, do not cut yourselves or shave your heads to show your sadness. 2You are holy people, who belong to the LORD your God. He has chosen you from all the people on earth to be his very own.

3Do not eat anything the LORD hates. 4These are the animals you may eat: oxen, sheep, goats, 5deer, gazelle, roe deer, wild goats, ibex, antelope and mountain sheep. 6You may eat any animal that has a split hoof and chews the cud,[d] 7but you may not eat camels, rabbits or rock badgers. These animals chew the cud, but they do not have split hoofs, so they are unclean[d] for you. 8Pigs are also unclean for you; they have split hoofs, but they do not chew the cud. Do not eat their meat or touch their dead bodies.

9There are many things that live in the water. You may eat anything that has fins and scales, 10but do not eat anything that does not have fins and scales. It is unclean for you.

11You may eat any clean bird. 12But do not eat these birds: eagles, vultures, black vultures, 13red kites, falcons, any kind of kite, 14any kind of raven, 15horned owls, screech owls, sea gulls, any kind of hawk, 16little owls, great owls, white owls, 17desert owls, ospreys, cormorants, 18storks, any kind of heron, the hoopoes or bats.

19All insects with wings are unclean for you; do not eat them. 20Other things with wings are clean, and you may eat them.

21Do not eat anything you find that is already dead. You may give it to a foreigner living in your town, and he may eat it, or you may sell it to a foreigner. But you are holy people, who belong to the LORD your God.

Do not cook a baby goat in its mother's milk.

Sidelight Throughout the Old Testament God is rarely spoken of as "Father" – in fact there are only fourteen such times. Mostly God is referred to as the Creator with a special relationship with Israel, his special people.

Giving One-Tenth

22Be sure to save one-tenth of all your crops
each year. 23Take it to the place the LORD your
God will choose where he is to be worshipped.
There, where you will be together with the LORD,
eat the tenth of your grain, new wine and oil, and
eat the animals born first to your herds and
flocks. Do this so that you will learn to respect
the LORD your God always. 24But if the place the
LORD will choose to be worshipped is too far away
and he has blessed you so much you cannot carry
a tenth, 25exchange your one-tenth for silver.
Then take the silver with you to the place the
LORD your God shall choose. 26Use the silver to
buy anything you wish—cattle, sheep, wine,
beer or anything you wish. Then you and your
family will eat and celebrate there before the LORD
your God. 27Do not forget the Levites in your
town, because they have no land of their own
among you.

28At the end of every third year, everyone
should bring one-tenth of that year's crop and store
it in your towns. 29This is for the Levites so they
may eat and be full. (They have no land of
their own among you.) It is also for strangers,
orphans and widows who live in your towns so
that all of them may eat and be full. Then the LORD
your God will bless you and all the work you do.

The Special Seventh Year

15 At the end of every seven years, you
must tell those who owe you anything
that they do not have to pay you back. 2This is
how you must do it: everyone who has loaned
money must cancel the loan and not make a
neighbour or relative pay it back. This is the
LORD's time for cancelling what people owe. 3You
may make a foreigner pay what is owed to you,
but you must not collect what another Israelite
owes you. 4But there should be no poor people
among you, because the LORD your God will
richly bless you in the land he is giving you as
your own. 5He will bless you if you obey the LORD
your God completely, but you must be careful to
obey all the commands I am giving you today.
6The LORD your God will bless you as he prom-
ised, and you will lend to other nations, but you
will not need to borrow from them. You will rule
over many nations, but none will rule over you.

7If there are poor among you, in one of the
towns of the land the LORD your God is giving
you, do not be selfish or greedy towards them.
8But give freely to them, and freely lend them
whatever they need. 9Beware of evil thoughts.
Don't think, "The seventh year is near, the year
to cancel what people owe." You might be mean
to the needy and not give them anything. Then
they will complain to the LORD about you, and he
will find you guilty of sin. 10Give freely to the
poor person, and do not wish that you didn't
have to give. The LORD your God will bless your
work and everything you touch. 11There will al-
ways be poor people in the land, so I command
you to give freely to your neighbours and to the
poor and needy in your land.

Letting Slaves Go Free

12If one of your own people sells himself to
you as a slave, whether it is a Hebrew man or
woman, that person will serve you for six years.
But in the seventh year you must let the slave go
free. 13When you let slaves go, don't send them
away without anything. 14Give them some of
your flock, your grain and your wine, giving to
them as the LORD has given to you. 15Remember
that you were slaves in Egypt, and the LORD your
God saved you. That is why I give you this com-
mand today.

16But if your slave says to you, "I don't want to
leave you," because he loves you and your fam-
ily and has a good life with you, 17stick an awl[n]
through his ear into the door; he will be your
slave for life. Also do this to a female slave.

18Do not think of it as a hard thing when you
let your slaves go free. After all, they served you
six years and did twice the work of a hired per-
son. The LORD your God will bless you in every-
thing you do.

Rules About Firstborn Animals

19Save all the first male animals born to your
herds and flocks. They are for the LORD your God.
Do not work the first calf born to your oxen, and
do not cut off the wool from the first lamb born
to your sheep. 20Each year you and your family
are to eat these animals in the presence of the
LORD your God, in the place he will choose to be
worshipped. 21If an animal is crippled or blind or
has something else wrong, do not sacrifice it to
the LORD your God. 22But you may eat that animal
in your own town. Both clean[d] and unclean peo-
ple may eat it, as they would eat a gazelle or a
deer. 23But don't eat its blood; pour it out on the
ground like water.

The Passover

16 Celebrate the Passover[c] of the LORD
your God during the month of Abib,[d] be-
cause it was during Abib that he brought you out

awl A tool like a big needle with a handle at one end.

of Egypt at night. 2As the sacrifice for the Passover to the LORD your God, offer an animal from your flock or herd at the place the LORD will choose to be worshipped. 3Do not eat it with bread made with yeast. But for seven days eat bread made without yeast, the bread of suffering, because you left Egypt in a hurry. So all your life you will remember the time you left Egypt. 4There must be no yeast anywhere in your land for seven days. Offer the sacrifice on the evening of the first day, and eat all the meat before morning; do not leave it overnight.

5Do not offer the Passover sacrifice in just any town the LORD your God gives you, 6but offer it in the place he will choose to be worshipped. Offer it in the evening as the sun goes down, which is when you left Egypt. 7Roast the meat and eat it at the place the LORD your God will choose. The next morning go back to your tents. 8Eat bread made without yeast for six days. On the seventh day have a special meeting for the LORD your God, and do not work that day.

The Feast of Weeks

9Count seven weeks from the time you begin to harvest the grain, 10and then celebrate the Feast[d] of Weeks for the LORD your God. Bring an offering as a special gift to him, giving to him just as he has blessed you. 11Rejoice before the LORD your God at the place he will choose to be worshipped. Everybody should rejoice: you, your sons and daughters, your male and female servants, the Levites in your town, the strangers, orphans and widows living among you. 12Remember that you were slaves in Egypt, and carefully obey all these laws.

The Feast of Shelters

13Celebrate the Feast[d] of Shelters for seven days, after you have gathered your harvest from the threshing[d] floor and winepress.[d] 14Everybody should rejoice at your Feast: you, your sons and daughters, your male and female servants, the Levites, strangers, orphans and widows who live in your towns. 15Celebrate the Feast to the LORD your God for seven days at the place he will choose, because the LORD your God will bless all your harvest and all the work you do, and you will be completely happy.

16All your men must come before the LORD three times a year to the place he will choose. They must come at these times: the Feast[d] of Unleavened Bread, the Feast[d] of Weeks and the Feast of Shelters. No man should come before the LORD without a gift. 17Each of you must bring a gift that will show how much the LORD your God has blessed you.

Judges for the People

18Appoint judges and officers for your tribes[d] in every town the LORD your God is giving you; they must judge the people fairly. 19Do not judge unfairly or take sides. Do not let people pay you to make wrong decisions, because that kind of payment makes wise people seem blind, and it changes the words of good people. 20Always do what is right so that you will live and always have the land the LORD your God is giving you.

God Hates Idols

21Do not set up a wooden Asherah[d] idol next to the altar you build for the LORD your God, 22and do not set up holy stone pillars. The LORD your God hates them.

17 If an ox or sheep has something wrong with it, do not offer it as a sacrifice to the LORD your God. He would hate that.

2A man or woman in one of the towns the LORD gave you might be found doing something evil and breaking the Agreement. 3That person may have served other gods and bowed down to them or to the sun or moon or stars of the sky, which I have commanded should not be done. 4If someone has told you about it, you must look into the matter carefully. If it is true that such a hateful thing has happened in Israel, 5take the man or woman who has done the evil thing to the city gates and throw stones at that person until he dies. 6There must be two or three witnesses that it is true before the person is put to death; if there is only one witness, the person should not be put to death. 7The witnesses must be the first to throw stones at the person, and then everyone else will follow. You must get rid of the evil among you.

Courts of Law

8Some cases that come before you, such as murder, quarrelling or attack, may be too difficult to judge. Take these cases to the place the LORD your God will choose. 9Go to the priests who are Levites and to the judge who is on duty at that time. Ask them about the case, and they will decide. 10You must follow the decision they give you at the place the LORD your God will choose. Be careful to do everything they tell you. 11Follow the teachings they give you, and do whatever they decide, exactly as they tell you. 12The person who does not show respect for the judge or priest who is there serving the LORD your God must be put to death. You must get rid of that evil from Israel. 13Then everyone will hear about this and will be afraid, and they will not show disrespect any more.

Choosing a King

14When you enter the land the LORD your God is giving you, taking it as your own and living in it, you will say, "Let's appoint a king over us like the nations all around us." 15Be sure to appoint over you the king the LORD your God chooses. He must be one of your own people. Do not appoint as your king a foreigner who is not a fellow Israelite. 16The king must not have too many horses for himself, and he must not send people to Egypt to get more horses, because the LORD has told you, "Don't return that way again." 17The king must not have many wives, or his heart will be led away from God. He must not have too much silver and gold.

18When he becomes king, he should write a copy of the teachings on a scroll for himself, a copy taken from the priests and Levites. 19He should keep it with him all the time and read from it every day of his life. Then he will learn to respect the LORD his God, and he will obey all the teachings and commands. 20He should not think he is better than his fellow Israelites, and he must not stop obeying the law in any way so that he and his descendants[d] may rule the kingdom for a long time.

Shares for Priests and Levites

18 The priests are from the tribe[d] of Levi, and that tribe will not receive a share of the land with the Israelites. They will eat the offerings made to the LORD by fire, which is their share. 2They will not inherit any of the land like their brothers, but they will inherit the LORD himself, as he has promised them.

3When you offer a bull or sheep as a sacrifice, you must share with the priests, giving them the shoulder, the cheeks and the inner organs. 4Give them the first of your grain, new wine and oil, as well as the first wool you cut from your sheep. 5The LORD your God has chosen the priests and their descendants[d] out of all your tribes to stand and serve the LORD always.

6If a Levite moves from one of your towns anywhere in Israel where he lives and comes to the place the LORD will choose, because he wants to serve the LORD there, 7he may serve the LORD his God. He will be like his fellow Levites who serve there before the LORD. 8They all will have an equal share of the food. That is separate from what he has received from the sale of family possessions.

Do Not Follow Other Nations

9When you enter the land the LORD your God is giving you, don't learn to do the hateful things the other nations do. 10Don't let anyone among you offer a son or daughter as a sacrifice in the fire. Don't let anyone use magic or witchcraft,[d] or try to explain the meaning of signs. 11Don't let anyone try to control others with magic, and don't let them be mediums[d] or try to talk with the spirits of dead people. 12The LORD hates anyone who does these things. Because the other nations do these things, the LORD your God will force them out of the land ahead of you. 13But you must be innocent in the presence of the LORD your God.

The LORD's Special Prophet

14The nations you will force out listen to people who use magic and witchcraft,[d] but the LORD your God will not let you do those things. 15The LORD your God will give you a prophet[d] like me, who is one of your own people. Listen to him. 16This is what you asked the LORD your God to do when you were gathered at Mount Sinai. You said, "Don't make us listen to the voice of the LORD our God again, and don't make us look at this terrible fire any more, or we will die."

17So the LORD said to me, "What they have said is good. 18So I will give them a prophet like you, who is one of their own people. I will tell him what to say, and he will tell them everything I command. 19This prophet will speak for me; anyone who does not listen when he speaks will answer to me. 20But if a prophet says something I did not tell him to say as though he were speaking for me, or if a prophet speaks in the name of other gods, that prophet must be killed."

21You might be thinking, "How can we know if a message is not from the LORD?" 22If what a prophet says in the name of the LORD does not happen, it is not the LORD's message. That prophet was speaking his own ideas. Don't be afraid of him.

Cities of Safety

19 When the LORD your God gives you land that belongs to the other nations, nations that he will destroy, you will force them out and live in their cities and houses. 2Then choose three cities in the middle of the land the LORD your God is giving you as your own. 3Build roads to these cities, and divide the land the LORD is giving you into three parts so that someone who kills another person may run to these cities.

4This is the rule for someone who kills another person and runs to one of these cities in order to save his life. But the person must have killed a neighbour without meaning to, not out of hatred.

5For example, suppose someone goes into the
forest with a neighbour to cut wood and swings
an axe to cut down a tree. If the axe head flies off
the handle, hitting and killing the neighbour, the
one who killed him may run to one of these
cities to save his life. 6Otherwise, the dead per-
son's relative who has the duty of punishing a
murderer might be angry and chase him. If the
city is far away, the relative might catch and kill
the person, even though he should not be killed
because there was no intent to kill his neighbour.
7This is why I command you to choose these
three cities.
8–9Carefully obey all these laws I'm giving you
today. Love the LORD your God, and always do
what he wants you to do. Then the LORD your
God will enlarge your land as he promised your
ancestors, giving you the whole land he prom-
ised to them. After that, choose three more cities
of safety 10so that innocent people will not be
killed in your land, the land that the LORD your
God is giving you as your own. By doing this you
will not be guilty of allowing the death of inno-
cent people.
11But if a person hates his neighbour and, after
hiding and waiting, attacks and kills him and
then runs to one of these cities for safety, 12the
elders of his own city should send for the mur-
derer. They should bring the person back from
the city of safety and hand him over to the rela-
tive who has the duty of punishing the murderer.
13Show no mercy. You must remove from Israel

LEADERSHIP

Standing For Right

George Fox had a message from God, and he was not going to let anyone stop him from preaching it. In the 1600s, he urged people to listen to Christ, to be honest in business, and to care for the poor. He believed in religious liberty and that God worked through individual people, not just through the established church.

Though many people believed him and were converted, others opposed him. On many occasions, he was thrown down church steps or beaten. Once he was put in prison for six months. But he would not change his beliefs and so was sentenced to six more months as a result. "Truth can live in the jails," he wrote. "Be valiant for Truth upon the earth and tread upon deceit."

Despite the government's efforts to stop him from challenging the official church, Fox's message got through to people because of his conviction and honesty. Within eight years of beginning his ministry, 50,000 people had heard his message and had become followers.

Young followers, known as "the valiant 60", joined Fox in preaching at fairs, in markets, in fields, in prisons, and in courts.

When he died in 1691, about 100,000 people had joined Fox's movement, which became known as the Society of Friends. Today the Friends (or Quakers) span the world, spreading a message of peace, holiness, service, and religious liberty.

George Fox's ministry had a long-term impact because his message was a true message from God. In his farewell speech, Moses urged the Israelites to listen carefully to prophets' messages to learn if they are true or not. Read **Deuteronomy 18:15–20** to see the guidelines he established.

- In what ways did George Fox's message fit with the message of the prophets as described in this passage?
- How can this passage help you evaluate messages you hear from people who have leadership roles?

Consider . . .

- choosing key words from this passage to make a checklist for evaluating leaders. Use it whenever you wonder whether to believe what someone tells you.
- praying for Christian leaders around the world who sometimes have to risk their lives to speak God's truth.

For more, see . . .

- Jeremiah 37:1–21 (p.760)
- Hebrews 11:32–40 (p.1342)
- Luke 4:23–30 (p.1046)

the guilt of murdering innocent people so that things will go well for you.

14Do not move the stone that marks the border of your neighbour's land, which people long ago set in place. It marks what you inherit in the land the LORD your God is giving you as your own.

Rules About Witnesses

15One witness is not enough to accuse a person of a crime or sin. A case must be proved by two or three witnesses.

16If a witness lies and accuses a person of a crime, 17the two people who are arguing must stand in the presence of the LORD before the priests and judges who are on duty. 18The judges must check the matter carefully. The witness who is a liar, lying about a fellow Israelite, 19must be punished. He must be punished in the same way the other person would have been punished. You must get rid of the evil among you. 20The rest of the people will hear about this and be afraid, and no one among you will ever do such an evil thing again. 21Show no mercy. A life must be paid for a life, an eye for an eye, a tooth for a tooth, a hand for a hand, a foot for a foot.

Laws for War

20 When you go to war against your enemies and you see horses and chariots and an army that is bigger than yours, don't be afraid of them. The LORD your God, who brought you out of Egypt, will be with you. 2The priest must come and speak to the army before you go into battle. 3He will say, "Listen, Israel! Today you are going into battle against your enemies. Don't lose your courage or be afraid. Don't panic or be frightened, 4because the LORD your God goes with you, to fight for you against your enemies and to save you."

5The officers should say to the army, "Has anyone built a new house but not given it to God? He may go home, because he might die in battle and someone else would get to give his house to God. 6Has anyone planted a vineyard and not begun to enjoy it? He may go home, because he might die in battle and someone else would enjoy his vineyard. 7Is any man engaged to a woman and not yet married to her? He may go home, because he might die in battle and someone else would marry her." 8Then the officers should also say, "Is anyone here afraid? Has anyone lost his courage? He may go home so that he will not cause others to lose their courage too." 9When the officers finish speaking to the army, they should appoint commanders to lead it.

10When you march up to attack a city, first make them an offer of peace. 11If they accept your offer and open their gates to you, all the people of that city will become your slaves and work for you. 12But if they do not make peace with you and fight you in battle, you should surround that city. 13The LORD your God will give it to you. Then kill all the men with your swords, 14and you may take everything else in the city for yourselves. Take the women, children and animals, and you may use these things the LORD your God gives you from your enemies. 15Do this to all the cities that are far away, that do not belong to the nations nearby.

16But leave nothing alive in the cities of the land the LORD your God is giving you. 17Completely destroy these people: the Hittites, Amorites, Canaanites, Perizzites, Hivites and Jebusites, as the LORD your God has commanded. 18Otherwise, they will teach you what they do for their gods, and if you do these hateful things, you will sin against the LORD your God.

19If you surround and attack a city for a long time, trying to capture it, do not destroy its trees with an axe. You can eat the fruit from the trees, but do not cut them down. These trees are not the enemy, so don't make war against them. 20But you may cut down trees that you know are not fruit trees and use them to build devices to attack the city walls, until the city is captured.

A Person Found Murdered

21 Suppose someone is found murdered, lying in a field in the land the LORD your God is giving you as your own, and no one knows who killed the person. 2Your elders and judges should go to where the body was found, and they should measure how far it is to the nearby cities. 3The elders of the city nearest the body must take a young cow that has never worked or worn a yoke,[d] 4and they must lead her down to a valley that has never been ploughed or planted, with a stream flowing through it. There they must break the young cow's neck. 5The priests, the sons of Levi, should come forward, because they have been chosen by the LORD your God to serve him and to give blessings in the LORD's name. They are the ones who decide cases of quarrelling and attacks. 6Then all the elders of the city nearest the murdered person should wash their hands over

Sidelight If the army in the Old Testament had had chaplains they would not have needed to conduct weddings. That's because engaged men did not have to serve in the army (Deuteronomy 20:7). Newly married men were also exempt from duty for a year (Deuteronomy 24:5).

the young cow whose neck was broken in the
valley. 7They should declare: "We did not kill this
person, and we did not see it happen. 8LORD, re-
move this sin from your people Israel, whom you
have saved. Don't blame your people, the Israel-
ites, for the murder of this innocent person." And
so the murder will be paid for. 9Then you will
have removed from yourselves the guilt of mur-
dering an innocent person, because you will be
doing what the LORD says is right.

Captive Women as Wives

10When you go to war against your enemies,
the LORD will help you defeat them so that you
will take them captive. 11If you see a beautiful
woman among the captives and are attracted to
her, you may take her as your wife. 12Bring her
into your home, where she must shave her head
and cut her nails 13and change the clothes she
was wearing when you captured her. After she
has lived in your house and cried for her parents
for a month, you may marry her. You will be her
husband, and she will be your wife. 14But if you
are not pleased with her, you must let her go
anywhere she wants. You must not sell her for
money or make her a slave, because you have
taken away her honour.

The Oldest Son

15A man might have two wives, one he loves
and one he doesn't. Both wives might have sons
by him. If the older son belongs to the wife he
does not love, 16when that man wills his property
to his sons he must not give the son of the wife
he loves what belongs to the older son, the son of
the wife he does not love. 17He must agree to give
the older son two shares of everything he owns,
even though the older son is from the wife he
does not love. That son was the first to prove his
father could have children, so he has the rights
that belong to the older son.

Sons Who Refuse to Obey

18If someone has a son who is stubborn, who
turns against his father and mother and doesn't
obey them or listen when they correct him, 19his
parents must take him to the elders at the city
gate. 20They will say to the leaders, "Our son is
stubborn and turns against us. He will not obey
us. He eats too much, and he is always drunk."
21Then all the men in his town must throw stones
at him until he dies. Get rid of the evil among
you, because then all the people of Israel will hear
about this and be afraid.

Other Laws

22If someone is guilty of a sin worthy of death,
he must be put to death and his body displayed
on a tree. 23But don't leave his body hanging on
the tree overnight; be sure to bury him that same
day, because anyone whose body is displayed
on a tree is cursed by God. You must not ruin
the land the LORD your God is giving you as
your own.

22 If you see your fellow Israelite's ox or
sheep wandering away, don't ignore it.
Take it back to its owner. 2If the owner does not
live close to you, or if you do not know who the
owner is, take the animal home with you. Keep
it until the owner comes looking for it; then give
it back. 3Do the same thing if you find a donkey
or coat or anything someone lost. Don't just
ignore it.
4If you see your fellow Israelite's donkey or ox
fallen on the road, don't ignore it. Help the owner
get it up.
5A woman must not wear men's clothes, and
a man must not wear women's clothes. The LORD
your God hates anyone who does that.
6If you find a bird's nest by the road, either in
a tree or on the ground, and the mother bird is
sitting on the young birds or eggs, do not take the
mother bird with the young birds. 7You may take
the young birds, but you must let the mother bird
go free. Then things will go well for you, and you
will live a long time.
8When you build a new house, build a low
wall around the edge of the roof [n] so you will not
be guilty if someone falls off the roof.
9Don't plant two different kinds of seeds in your
vineyard. Otherwise, both crops will be ruined.
10Don't plough with an ox and a donkey tied
together.
11Don't wear clothes made of wool and linen
woven together.
12Tie several pieces of thread together; then
put these tassels on the four corners of your coat.

Marriage Laws

13If a man marries a girl and has sexual rela-
tions with her but then decides he does not like
her, 14he might talk badly about her and give
her a bad name. He might say, "I married this
woman, but when I had sexual relations with
her, I did not find that she was a virgin." [d] 15Then
the girl's parents must bring proof that she was a
virgin to the elders at the city gate. 16The girl's
father will say to the leaders, "I gave my daughter
to this man to be his wife, but now he does not
want her. 17This man has told lies about my

roof In Bible times houses were built with flat roofs. The roof was used for drying things such as flax and fruit. And it was used as an extra room, as a place for worship and as a place to sleep in the summer.

daughter. He has said, 'I did not find your daugh-
ter to be a virgin,' but here is the proof that my
daughter was a virgin." Then her parents are to
show the sheet to the city leaders, [18]and the
leaders must take the man and punish him.
[19]They must make him pay about a kilogramme
of silver to the girl's father, because the man has
given an Israelite virgin a bad name. The girl will
continue to be the man's wife, and he may not
divorce her as long as he lives.
[20]But if the things the husband said about his
wife are true, and there is no proof that she was
a virgin, [21]the girl must be brought to the door of
her father's house. Then the men of the town
must put her to death by throwing stones at her.
She has done a disgraceful thing in Israel by
having sexual relations before she was married.
You must get rid of the evil among you.
[22]If a man is found having sexual relations with
another man's wife, both the woman and the
man who had sexual relations with her must die.
Get rid of this evil from Israel.
[23]If a man meets a virgin in a city and has
sexual relations with her, but she is engaged to
another man, [24]you must take both of them to the
city gate and put them to death by throwing
stones at them. Kill the girl, because she was in
a city and did not scream for help. And
kill the man for having sexual relations with
another man's wife. You must get rid of the evil
among you.
[25]But if a man meets an engaged girl out in the
country and forces her to have sexual relations
with him, only the man who had sexual relations
with her must be put to death. [26]Don't do any-
thing to the girl, because she has not done a sin
worthy of death. This is like the person who at-
tacks and murders a neighbour; [27]the man found
the engaged girl in the country and she screamed,
but no one was there to save her.

PARENTS

Seaside Trouble

Rachel had her armbands on and was ready for action; it was perfect swimming conditions. She was only six, but as far as she was concerned, she was brilliant at swimming and would win medals when she was older! She was told by her parents not to swim out to sea – only to paddle. But she stomped off away from them. What did they know?

She waded in past her waist, and then launched out – doggy-paddling away.

After a while she turned back, and couldn't believe what she saw – everyone was very small and getting smaller. The current was taking her out to sea.

Thankfully, someone swam out to rescue Rachel and brought her safely to shore. As they stood on the beach, she caught sight of her mum – she looked so worried and upset. At that moment, Rachel realised two things – that her swimming career would have to wait for a bit and that next time she would listen to her parents.

Read **Deuteronomy 21:18–21**.

- Rachel was determined not to listen to her parents, but what was behind their rule and the ones in the Bible passage?
- The Bible passage seems pretty harsh about disobedience. Why do you think that is?

Consider . . .

- whether you need to say sorry to your parents if you know that you have had a bad attitude towards them.
- looking at baby photos of yourself. See how much effort it has taken for your parents to bring you up. Does this help you understand some of the rules they make for you?

For more, see . . .

- Exodus 20:12 (p.79)
- Luke 15:11–32 (p.1071)
- Proverbs 3:11–18 (p.592)

28 If a man meets a virgin who is not engaged to be married and forces her to have sexual relations with him and people find out about it, 29 the man must pay the girl's father about 50 pieces of silver. He must also marry the girl, because he has dishonoured her, and he may never divorce her for as long as he lives.

30 A man must not marry his father's wife; he must not dishonour his father in this way.

The LORD's People

23 No man who has had part of his sex organ cut off may come into the meeting to worship the LORD.

2 No one born to parents who were forbidden by law to marry may come into the meeting to worship the LORD. The descendants for ten generations may not come in either.

3 No Ammonite or Moabite may come into the meeting to worship the LORD, and none of their descendants for ten generations may come in. 4 This is because the Ammonites and Moabites did not give you bread and water when you came out of Egypt. And they hired Balaam son of Beor, from Pethor in North West Mesopotamia, to put a curse on you. 5 But the LORD your God would not listen to Balaam. He turned the curse into a blessing for you, because the LORD your God loves you. 6 Don't wish for their peace or success as long as you live.

7 Don't hate Edomites; they are your close relatives. Don't hate Egyptians, because you were foreigners in their country. 8 The great-grandchildren of these two peoples may come into the meeting to worship the LORD.

Keeping the Camp Clean

9 When you are camped in time of war, keep away from unclean [d] things. 10 If a man becomes unclean during the night, he must go outside the camp and not come back. 11 But when evening comes, he must wash himself, and at sunset he may come back into the camp.

12 Choose a place outside the camp where people may go to relieve themselves. 13 Carry a tent peg with you, and when you relieve yourself, dig a hole and cover up your dung. 14 The LORD your God moves around through your camp to protect you and to defeat your enemies for you, so the camp must be holy. He must not see anything unclean among you so that he will not leave you.

Other Laws

15 If an escaped slave comes to you, do not hand over the slave to his master. 16 Let the slave live with you anywhere he likes, in any town he chooses. Do not mistreat him.

17 No Israelite man or woman must ever become a temple prostitute. [d] 18 Do not bring a male or female prostitute's pay to the Temple [d] of the LORD your God to pay what you have promised to the LORD, because the LORD your God hates prostitution.

19 If you loan your fellow Israelites money or food or anything else, don't make them pay back more than you loaned them. 20 You may charge foreigners, but not fellow Israelites. Then the LORD your God will bless everything you do in the land you are entering to take as your own.

21 If you make a promise to give something to the LORD your God, do not be slow to pay it, because the LORD your God demands it from you. Do not be guilty of sin. 22 But if you do not make the promise, you will not be guilty. 23 You must do whatever you say you will do, because you chose to make the promise to the LORD your God.

24 If you go into your neighbour's vineyard, you may eat as many grapes as you wish, but do not put any grapes into your basket. 25 If you go into your neighbour's grainfield, you may pick grain with your hands, but you must not cut down your neighbour's grain with your sickle.

24 A man might marry a woman but later decide she doesn't please him because he has found something bad about her. He writes out divorce papers for her, gives them to her and sends her away from his house. 2 After she leaves his house, she goes and marries another man, 3 but her second husband does not like her either. So he writes out divorce papers for her, gives them to her and sends her away from his house. Or the second husband might die. 4 In either case, her first husband who divorced her must not marry her again, because she has become unclean. [d] The LORD would hate this. Don't bring this sin into the land the LORD your God is giving you as your own.

5 A man who has just married must not be sent to war or be given any other duty. He should be free to stay home for a year to make his new wife happy.

6 If someone owes you something, do not take his two stones for grinding grain—not even the upper one—in place of what he owes, because this is how the person makes a living.

7 If someone kidnaps a fellow Israelite, either to make him a slave or sell him, the kidnapper must be killed. You must get rid of the evil among you.

8 Be careful when someone has a skin disease. Do exactly what the priests, the Levites, teach you, being careful to do what I have commanded them. 9 Remember what the LORD your God did to Miriam on your way out of Egypt.

10When you make a loan to your neighbours, don't go into their homes to get something in place of it. 11Stay outside and let them go in and get what they promised you. 12If a poor person gives you a coat to show he will pay the loan back, don't keep it overnight. 13Give the coat back at sunset, because your neighbour needs that coat to sleep in, and he will thank you. And the LORD your God will see that you have done a good thing.

14Don't cheat hired servants who are poor and needy, whether they are fellow Israelites or foreigners living in one of your towns. 15Pay them each day before sunset, because they are poor and need the money. Otherwise, they may complain to the LORD about you, and you will be guilty of sin.

16Parents must not be put to death if their children do wrong, and children must not be put to death if their parents do wrong. Each person must die for his own sin.

17Do not be unfair to a foreigner or an orphan. Don't take a widow's coat to make sure she pays you back. 18Remember that you were slaves in Egypt, and the LORD your God saved you from there. That is why I am commanding you to do this.

19When you are gathering your harvest in the field and leave behind a bundle of grain, don't go back and get it. Leave it there for foreigners, orphans and widows so that the LORD your God can bless everything you do. 20When you beat your olive trees to knock the olives off, don't beat the trees a second time. Leave what is left for foreigners, orphans and widows. 21When you harvest the grapes in your vineyard, don't pick the vines a second time. Leave what is left for foreigners, orphans and widows. 22Remember that you were slaves in Egypt; that is why I am commanding you to do this.

25 If two people have an argument and go to court, the judges will decide the case. They will declare one person right and the other guilty. 2If the guilty person has to be punished with a beating, the judge will make that person lie down and be beaten in front of him. The number of lashes should match the crime. 3But don't hit a person more than 40 times, because more than that would disgrace him before others.

4When an ox is working in the grain, do not cover its mouth to keep it from eating.

5If two brothers are living together, and one of them dies without having a son, his widow must not marry someone outside her husband's family. Her husband's brother must marry her, which is his duty to her as a brother-in-law. 6The first son she has counts as the son of the dead brother so that his name will not be forgotten in Israel.

> **Sidelight** This chapter shows how to respect and treat other people. It is wrong to humiliate or take advantage of others – even when they are family. The law about marrying a brother-in-law's widow helped make sure she was looked after (Deuteronomy 25:5–9).

7But if a man does not want to marry his brother's widow, she should go to the elders at the town gate. She should say, "My brother-in-law will not carry on his brother's name in Israel. He refuses to do his duty for me."

8Then the elders of the town must call for the man and talk to him. But if he is stubborn and says, "I don't want to marry her," 9the woman must go up to him in front of the elders. She must take off one of his sandals and spit in his face and say, "This is for the man who won't continue his brother's family!" 10Then that man's family shall be known in Israel as the Family of the Unsandalled.

11If two men are fighting and one man's wife comes to save her husband from his attacker, grabbing the attacker by his sex organs, 12you must cut off her hand. Show her no mercy.

13Don't carry two sets of weights with you, one heavy and one light. 14Don't have two different sets of measures in your house, one large and one small. 15You must have true and honest weights and measures so that you will live a long time in the land the LORD your God is giving you. 16The LORD your God hates anyone who is dishonest and uses dishonest measures.

17Remember what the Amalekites did to you when you came out of Egypt. 18When you were tired and worn out, they met you on the road and attacked all those lagging behind. They were not afraid of God. 19When the LORD your God gives you rest from all the enemies around you in the land he is giving you as your own, you shall destroy any memory of the Amalekites on the earth. Do not forget!

The First Harvest

26 When you go into the land the LORD your God is giving you as your own, to take it over and live in it, 2you must take some of the first harvest of crops that grow from the land the

LORD your God is giving you. Put the food in a
basket and go to the place where the LORD your
God will choose to be worshipped. 3Say to the
priest on duty at that time, "Today I declare be-
fore the LORD your God that I have come into the
land the LORD promised our ancestors that he
would give us." 4The priest will take your basket
and set it down in front of the altar of the LORD
your God. 5Then you shall announce before the
LORD your God: "My father was a wandering Ara-
mean. He went down to Egypt with only a few
people, but they became a great, powerful and
large nation there. 6But the Egyptians were cruel
to us, making us suffer and work very hard. 7So
we prayed to the LORD, the God of our ancestors,
and he heard us. When he saw our trouble, hard
work and suffering, 8the LORD brought us out of
Egypt with his great power and strength, using
great terrors, signs and miracles.[d] 9Then he
brought us to this place and gave us this fertile
land. 10Now I bring part of the first harvest from
this land that you, LORD, have given me." Place
the basket before the LORD your God and bow
down before him. 11Then you and the Levites and
foreigners among you should rejoice, because the
LORD your God has given good things to you and
your family.

12Bring a tenth of all your harvest the third year
(the year to give a tenth of your harvest). Give it
to the Levites, foreigners, orphans and widows so
that they may eat in your towns and be full.
13Then say to the LORD your God, "I have taken
out of my house the part of my harvest that be-
longs to God, and I have given it to the Levites,
foreigners, orphans and widows. I have done
everything you commanded me; I have not bro-
ken your commands, and I have not forgotten
any of them. 14I have not eaten any of the holy
part while I was in sorrow. I have not removed
any of it while I was unclean,[d] and I have not

GIVING

First Harvest

Sue had never had so much money in her life. A distant relative had died and left £2,500 to Sue and each of her three brothers. Matthew was planning to buy a new guitar. Simon was a full-time youth worker. He wanted to buy a notebook computer and printer. Her youngest brother, Luke, had bought a set of drums. But as he was only thirteen, their parents had said that the rest had to be put into the bank.

Sue had lots of plans for her money, too. In a year she would be going to university. It would give her a "safety net". The money from her Saturday job never seemed to go far enough. She might even be able to buy a small car.

However, before any of those things she needed to decide how she was going to give away some of her legacy. There were so many needs. A friend was going to work for a mission and needed support. Sue was committed to a project for homeless young people.

The needs were limitless. But she knew that there was some way she could give – to share her "harvest" with others and show her thankfulness to God.

In **Deuteronomy 26:1–11** the Israelites were challenged to give to God because of all that he had given to them.

- Compare Sue's actions with the encouragement to give in the passage.
- What can you bring to God from your "first harvest" as a thank-offering?

Consider . . .

- participating in a project at your church as a way of giving back to God part of the love and time that he has given to you.
- taking 10 per cent of the money in your purse or wallet and giving it to God as a "tithe".

For more, see . . .

- Genesis 28:22 (p.34)
- Luke 11:42 (p.1062)
- Malachi 3:8–10 (p.930)

offered it for dead people. I have obeyed you, the LORD my God, and have done everything you commanded me. 15So look down from heaven, your holy home. Bless your people Israel and bless the land you have given us, which you promised to our ancestors—a fertile land."

Obey the LORD's Commands

16Today the LORD your God commands you to obey all these rules and laws; be careful to obey them with your whole being. 17Today you have said that the LORD is your God, and you have promised to do what he wants you to do—to keep his rules, commands and laws. You have said you will obey him. 18And today the LORD has said that you are his very own people, as he has promised you. But you must obey his commands. 19He will make you greater than all the other nations he made. He will give you praise, fame and honour, and you will be a holy people to the LORD your God, as he has said.

The Law Written on Stones

27 Then Moses, along with the elders of Israel, commanded the people, saying, "Keep all the commands I have given you today. 2Soon you will cross the Jordan River to go into the land the LORD your God is giving you. On that day set up some large stones and cover them with plaster. 3When you cross over, write all the words of these teachings on them. Then you may enter the land the LORD your God is giving you, a fertile land, just as the LORD, the God of your ancestors, promised. 4After you have crossed the Jordan River, set up these stones on Mount Ebal, as I command you today, and cover them with plaster. 5Build an altar of stones there to the LORD your God, but don't use any iron tool to cut the stones; 6build the altar of the LORD your God with stones from the field. Offer burnt offerings on it to the LORD your God, 7and offer fellowship offerings there, and eat them and rejoice before the LORD your God. 8Then write clearly all the words of these teachings on the stones."

Curses of the Law

9Then Moses and the Levites who were priests spoke to all Israel and said, "Be quiet, Israel. Listen! Today you have become the people of the LORD your God. 10Obey the LORD your God, and keep his commands and laws that I give you today."

11That day Moses also gave the people this command:

12When you cross the Jordan River, these tribes[d] must stand on Mount Gerizim to bless the people: Simeon, Levi, Judah, Issachar, Joseph and Benjamin. 13And these tribes must stand on Mount Ebal to announce the curses: Reuben, Gad, Asher, Zebulun, Dan and Naphtali.

14The Levites will say to all the people of Israel in a loud voice:

15"Anyone will be cursed who makes an idol or statue and secretly sets it up, because the LORD hates the idols people make."

Then all the people will say, "Amen!"

16"Anyone will be cursed who dishonours his father or mother."

Then all the people will say, "Amen!"

17"Anyone will be cursed who moves the stone that marks a neighbour's border."

Then all the people will say, "Amen!"

18"Anyone will be cursed who sends a blind person down the wrong road."

Then all the people will say, "Amen!"

19"Anyone will be cursed who is unfair to foreigners, orphans or widows."

Then all the people will say, "Amen!"

20"A man will be cursed who has sexual relations with his father's wife, because it is a dishonour to his father."

Then all the people will say, "Amen!"

21"Anyone will be cursed who has sexual relations with an animal."

Then all the people will say, "Amen!"

22"A man will be cursed who has sexual relations with his sister, whether she is his father's daughter or his mother's daughter."

Then all the people will say, "Amen!"

23"A man will be cursed who has sexual relations with his mother-in-law."

Then all the people will say, "Amen!"

24"Anyone will be cursed who kills a neighbour secretly."

Then all the people will say, "Amen!"

25"Anyone will be cursed who takes money to murder an innocent person."

Then all the people will say, "Amen!"

26"Anyone will be cursed who does not agree with the words of these teachings and does not obey them."

Then all the people will say, "Amen!"

Blessings for Obeying

28 You must completely obey the LORD your God, and you must carefully follow all his commands I am giving you today. Then the LORD your God will make you greater than any other nation on earth. 2Obey the LORD your God so that all these blessings will come and stay with you:

3You will be blessed in the city and blessed in the country.

4Your children will be blessed, as well as your crops; your herds will be blessed with calves and your flocks with lambs.

5Your basket and your kitchen will be blessed.

6You will be blessed when you come in and when you go out.

7The LORD will help you defeat the enemies that come to fight you. They will attack you from one direction, but they will run from you in seven directions.

8The LORD your God will bless you with full barns, and he will bless everything you do. He will bless the land he is giving you.

9The LORD will make you his holy people, as he promised. But you must obey his commands and do what he wants you to do. 10Then everyone on earth will see that you are the LORD's people, and they will be afraid of you. 11The LORD will make you rich: you will have many children, your animals will have many young, and your land will give good crops. It is the land that the LORD promised your ancestors he would give to you.

12The LORD will open up his heavenly storehouse so that the skies send rain on your land at the right time, and he will bless everything you do. You will lend to other nations, but you will not need to borrow from them. 13The LORD will make you like the head and not like the tail; you will be on top and not on the bottom. But you must obey the commands of the LORD your God that I am giving you today, being careful to keep them. 14Do not disobey anything I command you today. Do exactly as I command, and do not follow other gods or serve them.

Curses for Disobeying

15But if you do not obey the LORD your God and carefully follow all his commands and laws I am giving you today, all these curses will come upon you and stay:

16You will be cursed in the city and cursed in the country.

17Your basket and your kitchen will be cursed.

18Your children will be cursed, as well as your crops; the calves of your herds and the lambs of your flocks will be cursed.19You will be cursed when you go in and when you go out.

20The LORD will send you curses, confusion and punishment in everything you do. You will be destroyed and suddenly ruined because you did wrong when you left him. 21The LORD will give you terrible diseases and destroy you from the land you are going to take. 22The LORD will punish you with disease, fever, swelling, heat, lack of rain, plant diseases and mildew,[d] until you die. 23The sky above will be like bronze, and the ground below will be like iron.[n] 24The LORD will turn the rain into dust and sand, which will fall from the skies until you are destroyed.

25The LORD will help your enemies defeat you. You will attack them from one direction, but you will run from them in seven directions. And you will become a thing of horror among all the kingdoms on earth. 26Your dead bodies will be food for all the birds and wild animals, and there will be no one to scare them away. 27The LORD will punish you with boils like those the Egyptians had. You will have bad growths, sores and itches that can't be cured. 28The LORD will give you madness, blindness and a confused mind. 29You will have to feel around in the daylight like a blind person. You will fail in everything you do. People will hurt you and steal from you every day, and no one will save you.

30You will be engaged to a woman, but another man will force her to have sexual relations with him. You will build a house, but you will not live in it. You will plant a vineyard, but you will not get its grapes. 31Your ox will be killed before your eyes, but you will not eat any of it. Your donkey will be taken away from you, and it will not be brought back. Your sheep will be given to your enemies, and no one will save you. 32Your sons and daughters will be given to another nation, and you will grow tired looking for them every day, but there will be nothing you can do. 33People you don't know will eat the crops your land and hard work have produced. You will be mistreated and abused all your life. 34The things you see will cause you to go mad. 35The LORD will give you sore boils on your knees and legs that cannot be cured, and they will go from the soles of your feet to the tops of your heads.

36The LORD will send you and your king away to a nation neither you nor your ancestors know, where you will serve other gods made of wood and stone. 37You will become a hated thing to the nations where the LORD sends you; they will laugh at you and make fun of you.

38You will plant much seed in your field, but your harvest will be small, because locusts[d] will eat the crop. 39You will plant vineyards and work hard in them, but you will not pick the grapes or drink the wine, because the worms will eat them. 40You will have olive trees in all your land, but you will not get any olive oil, because the olives will drop off the trees. 41You will have sons and daughters, but you will not be able to keep them, because they will be taken captive. 42Locusts will destroy all your trees and crops.

43The foreigners who live among you will get stronger and stronger, and you will get weaker and weaker. 44Foreigners will lend money to you, but you will not be able to lend to them. They will be like the head, and you will be like the tail.

sky . . . iron This means the sky will give no rain and the earth will produce no crops.

45All these curses will come upon you. They will chase you and catch you and destroy you, because you did not obey the LORD your God and keep the commands and laws he gave you. 46The curses will be signs and miracles[d] to you and your descendants[d] for ever. 47You had plenty of everything, but you did not serve the LORD your God with joy and a pure heart, 48so you will serve the enemies the LORD sends against you. You will be hungry, thirsty, naked and poor, and the LORD will put a load on you until he has destroyed you.

The Curse of an Enemy Nation

49The LORD will bring a nation against you from far away, from the end of the world, and it will swoop down like an eagle. You won't understand their language, 50and they will look fierce. They will not respect old people or feel sorry for the young. 51They will eat the calves from your herds and the harvest of your field, and you will be destroyed. They will not leave you any grain, new wine or oil, or any calves from your herds or lambs from your flocks. You will be ruined. 52That nation will surround and attack all your cities. You trust in your high, strong walls, but they will fall down. That nation will surround all your cities everywhere in the land the LORD your God is giving you.

53Your enemy will surround you. Those people will make you starve so that you will eat your own babies, the bodies of the sons and daughters the LORD your God gave you. 54Even the most gentle and kind man among you will become cruel to his brother, his wife whom he loves and his children who are still alive. 55He will not even give them any of the flesh of his children he is eating, because it will be all he has left. Your enemy will surround you and make you starve in all your cities. 56The most gentle and kind woman among you, so gentle and kind she would hardly even walk on the ground, will be cruel to her husband whom she loves and to her son and daughter. 57She will give birth to a baby, but she will plan to eat the baby and what comes after the birth itself. She will eat them secretly while the enemy surrounds the city. Those people will make you starve in all your cities.

58Be careful to obey everything in these teachings that are written in this book. You must respect the glorious and wonderful name of the LORD your God, 59or the LORD will give terrible diseases to you and your descendants.[d] You will have long and serious diseases, and long and miserable sicknesses. 60He will give you all the diseases of Egypt that you dread, and the diseases will stay with you. 61The LORD will also give you every disease and sickness not written in this Book of the Teachings, until you are destroyed. 62You people may have outnumbered the stars, but only a few of you will be left, because you did not obey the LORD your God. 63Just as the LORD was once happy with you and gave you good things and made you grow in number, so then the LORD will be happy to ruin and destroy you, and you will be removed from the land you are entering to take as your own.

64Then the LORD will scatter you among the nations—from one end of the earth to the other. There you will serve other gods of wood and stone, gods that neither you nor your ancestors have known. 65You will have no rest among those nations and no place that is yours. The LORD will make your mind worried, your sight weak and your soul sad. 66You will live with danger and be afraid night and day. You will not be sure that you will live. 67In the morning you will say, "I wish it were evening," and in the evening you will say, "I wish it were morning." Terror will be in your heart, and the things you have seen will scare you. 68The LORD will send you back to Egypt in ships, even though I, Moses, said you would never go back to Egypt. And there you will try to sell yourselves as slaves to your enemies, but no one will buy you.

The Agreement in Moab

29 The LORD commanded Moses to make an agreement with the Israelites in Moab in addition to the agreement he had made with them at Mount Sinai. These are the words of that agreement.

2Moses called all the Israelites together and said to them:

You have seen everything the LORD did before your own eyes to the king of Egypt and to the king's leaders and to the whole country. 3With your own eyes you saw the great troubles, signs and miracles.[d] 4But to this day the LORD has not given you a mind that understands; you don't really understand what you see with your eyes or hear with your ears. 5I led you through the desert for 40 years, and during that time neither your clothes nor sandals wore out. 6You ate no bread and drank no wine or beer. This was so you would understand that I am the LORD your God.

7When you came to this place, Sihon king of Heshbon and Og king of Bashan came out to fight us, but we defeated them. 8We captured their land and gave it to the tribes[d] of Reuben, Gad and East Manasseh to be their own.

9You must carefully obey everything in this agreement so that you will succeed in everything you do. 10Today you are all standing here before the LORD your God—your leaders and important men, your elders, officers and all the other men of Israel, 11your wives and children and the foreigners who live among you, who chop your wood and carry your water. 12You are all here to enter into an agreement and a promise with the LORD your God, an agreement the LORD your God is making with you today. 13This will make you today his own people. He will be your God, as he told you and as he promised your ancestors Abraham, Isaac and Jacob. 14But I am not just making this agreement and its promises with you 15who are standing here before the LORD your God today, but also with those who are not here today.

16You know how we lived in Egypt and how we passed through the countries when we came here. 17You saw their hateful idols made of wood, stone, silver and gold. 18Make sure no man, woman, family group or tribe among you leaves the LORD our God to go and serve the gods of those nations. They would be to you like a plant that grows bitter, poisonous fruit.

19These are the kind of people who hear these curses but bless themselves, thinking, "We will be safe even though we continue doing what we want to do." Those people may destroy all of your land, both wet and dry. 20The LORD will not forgive them. His anger will be like a burning fire against those people, and all the curses written in this book will come on them. The LORD will destroy any memory of them on the earth. 21He will separate them from all the tribes of Israel for punishment. All the curses of the Agreement that are written in this Book of the Teachings will happen to them.

22Your children who will come after you, as well as foreigners from faraway lands, will see the disasters that come to this land and the diseases the LORD will send on it. They will say, 23"The land is nothing but burning cinders and salt. Nothing is planted, nothing grows and nothing blooms. It is like Sodom and Gomorrah, and Admah and Zeboiim, which the LORD destroyed because he was very angry." 24All the other nations will ask, "Why has the LORD done this to the land? Why is he so angry?"

25And the answer will be, "It is because the people broke the Agreement of the LORD, the God of their ancestors, which he made with them when he brought them out of Egypt. 26They went and served other gods and bowed down to gods they did not even know. The LORD did not allow that, 27so he became very angry at the land and brought all the curses on it that are written in this book. 28Since the LORD became angry and furious with them, he took them out of their land and put them in another land where they are today."

29There are some things the LORD our God has kept secret, but there are some things he has let us know. These things belong to us and our children for ever so that we will do everything in these teachings.

The Israelites Will Return

30 When all these blessings and curses I have described happen to you, and the LORD your God has sent you away to other nations, think about these things. 2Then you and your children will return to the LORD your God, and you will obey him with your whole being in everything I am commanding you today. 3Then the LORD your God will give you back your freedom. He will feel sorry for you, and he will bring you back again from the nations where he scattered you. 4He may send you to the ends of the earth, but he will gather you and bring you back from there, 5back to the land that belonged to your ancestors. It will be yours. He will give you success, and there will be more of you than there were of your ancestors. 6The LORD your God will prepare you and your descendants[d] to love him with your whole being so that you will live. 7The LORD your God will put all these curses on your enemies, who hate you and are cruel to you. 8And you will again obey the LORD, keeping all his commands that I give you today. 9The LORD your God will make you successful in everything you do. You will have many children, your cattle will have many calves, and your fields will produce good crops, because the LORD will again be happy with you, just as he was with your ancestors. 10But you must obey the LORD your God by keeping all his commands and rules that are written in this Book of the Teachings. You must return to the LORD your God with your whole being.

Choose Life or Death

11This command I give you today is not too hard for you; it is not beyond what you can do. 12It is not up in heaven. You do not have to ask, "Who will go up to heaven and get it for us so we can obey it and keep it?" 13It is not on the other side of the sea. You do not have to ask, "Who will go across the sea and get it? Who will tell it to us so we can keep it?" 14No, the word is very near you. It is in your mouth and in your heart so you may obey it.

15Look, today I offer you life and success, death and destruction. 16I command you today to love the LORD your God, to do what he wants you to do, and to keep his commands, his rules and his laws. Then you will live and grow in number, and the LORD your God will bless you in the land you are entering to take as your own.

17But if you turn away from the LORD and do not obey him, if you are led to bow and serve other gods, 18I tell you today that you will surely be destroyed. And you will not live long in the

land you are crossing the Jordan River to enter
and take as your own.
19Today I ask heaven and earth to be
witnesses. I am offering you life or death, bless-
ings or curses. Now, choose life! Then you and
your children may live. 20To choose life is to love
the LORD your God, obey him and stay close to
him. He is your life, and he will let you live many
years in the land, the land he promised to give
your ancestors Abraham, Isaac and Jacob.

Joshua Takes Moses' Place

31 Then Moses went and spoke these words
to all the Israelites: 2"I am now 120 years
old, and I cannot lead you any more. The LORD
told me I would not cross the Jordan River; 3the
LORD your God will lead you across himself. He
will destroy those nations for you, and you will
take over their land. Joshua will also lead you
across, as the LORD has said. 4The LORD will do to
those nations what he did to Sihon and Og, the
kings of the Amorites, when he destroyed them
and their land. 5The LORD will give those nations to
you; do to them everything I told you. 6Be strong
and brave. Don't be afraid of them and don't be
frightened, because the LORD your God will go
with you. He will not leave you or forget you."
7Then Moses called Joshua and said to him in
front of the people, "Be strong and brave, because
you will lead these people into the land the LORD
promised to give their ancestors, and help them
take it as their own. 8The LORD himself will go
before you. He will be with you; he will not leave
you or forget you. Don't be afraid and don't
worry."

Moses Writes the Teachings

9So Moses wrote down these teachings and
gave them to the priests and all the elders of
Israel. (The priests are the sons of Levi, who carry
the Ark[d] of the Agreement with the LORD.)
10–11Then Moses commanded them: "Read these
teachings for all Israel to hear at the end of every
seven years, which is the year to cancel what

DECISION MAKING

Living With Deadlines

Luke had never kissed a girl – until he met Rachel at youth camp. It was love at first sight. Rachel and Luke were good for each other, and they encouraged each other in their faith.

But there was Eve to think about – Luke's girlfriend back home. She was cynical about the church, and she made fun of Luke's efforts to grow in his faith. Luke decided that he needed to end this unhealthy relationship.

When Luke got back home at the end of July, he had mixed emotions. It was hard breaking away from the past. So he decided that he would go back to his old girlfriend if he didn't get a letter from Rachel by 15 August. Each day, he checked his post. No letters.

On 15 August, he nervously flipped through the post. Nothing.

So he phoned Eve.

On 16 August, Rachel's letter came, but Luke had already made his choice.

Luke had to decide what to do. In the same way, the Israelites had a choice to make in **Deuteronomy 30:11–20**. Theirs was a much more important choice: whether or not to follow God.

- With this passage in mind, how would you advise Luke if he came to you for advice about his dilemma?
- What principles from this passage can help you to make wise choices?

Consider . . .

- circling the things in the passage that God asks people to do. Underline the "not to do" items.
- writing out an important decision you face. List all the pros and cons of your choices. Then circle any reasons that fit the scripture passage. Cross out any that contradict it. Your decision may be easier now.

For more, see . . .

- Genesis 39:6–23 (p.45)
- Matthew 25:1–13 (p.985)
- Joshua 24:14–15 (p.222)

people owe. Do it during the Feast *d* of Shelters,
when all the Israelites will come to appear before
the LORD your God and stand at the place he
will choose. 12Gather all the people: the men,
women, children and foreigners living in your
towns so that they can listen and learn to respect
the LORD your God and carefully obey everything
in this law. 13Since their children do not know
this law, they must hear it. They must learn to
respect the LORD your God for as long as they live
in the land you are crossing the Jordan River to
take for your own."

The Lord Calls Moses and Joshua

14The LORD said to Moses, "Soon you will die.
Get Joshua and come to the Meeting Tent *d* so
that I may command him." So Moses and Joshua
went to the Meeting Tent.
15The LORD appeared at the Meeting Tent in a
cloud; the cloud stood over the entrance of the
Tent. 16And the LORD said to Moses, "You will
soon die. Then these people will not be loyal to
me but will worship the foreign gods of the land
they are entering. They will leave me, breaking
the Agreement I made with them. 17Then I will

ABORTION

Choose Life

When Clarissa was asked to talk to the girls at her local High School, she assumed they wanted her to give a testimony. After all, it was an RE lesson and she was the local youth leader of her church.

However, when she arrived, the teacher Mrs Holloway had other ideas.

"My girls have been looking at the whole issue of 'life', what it's worth, etc. and they still have many questions they need to discuss. We have looked at the sacrifice that Jesus made in dying for the world and now they want to make the whole thing a bit more personal, I hope you don't mind. It's a bit like being thrown to the lions I'm afraid." Mrs Holloway smiled hopefully and Clarissa nodded and followed her down the hallway.

When she arrived in the room she was met by a sea of girls' faces. They looked at her quizzically as their teacher introduced her. The questions started almost immediately: "Would you die for anybody?" "Why do undeserving people die so young?"

Everything was fine, Clarissa managed to answer clearly, until she was asked:

"If you were raped, would you keep the baby?"

"Yes," replied Clarissa. There was a stunned silence and a wave of horror.

"How could you?" asked the same girl.

It was the youth leader's turn to look puzzled. "Well, it's hardly the baby's fault is it?" she answered. There were hushed whispers as most of the girls took in what was being said.

"But how could you keep a reminder of a rape?" asked another girl.

Clarissa looked at them with understanding. "I've never been raped, so I don't have an experienced answer. All I know is that I would value the life of the child above the horror of the crime. I couldn't condemn an innocent baby to death."

Slowly the girls accepted her answer and a new respect shone in their eyes.

Deuteronomy 30:15–20 offers the choices of life or death.

- How was Clarissa's answer similar to the words in this passage?
- What instructions could the girls have learnt from reading this passage?

Consider . . .

- the value of human life. How does that affect your views on abortion?
- talking to a Christian counsellor or minister if you have emotionally upsetting feelings after experiencing an abortion.

For more, see . . .

- Psalm 139:13–16 (p.581)
- 1 Peter 5:7 (p.1362)
- Isaiah 44:1–4 (p.685)

become very angry at them, and I will leave
them. I will turn away from them, and they will
be destroyed. Many terrible things will happen to
them. Then they will say, 'It is because God is not
with us that these terrible things are happening.'
18 I will surely turn away from them then, because
they have done wrong and have turned to other
gods.
19 "Now write down this song and teach it to
the Israelites. Then have them sing it, because it
will be my witness against them. 20 When I bring
them into the land I promised to their ancestors,
a fertile land, they will eat as much as they want
and get fat. Then they will turn to other gods and
serve them. They will reject me and break my
Agreement. 21 Then when many troubles and
terrible things happen to them, this song will
testify against them, because the song will not be
forgotten by their descendants.[d] I know what
they plan to do, even before I take them into
the land I promised them." 22 So Moses wrote
down the song that day, and he taught it to the
Israelites.
23 Then the LORD gave this command to Joshua
son of Nun: "Be strong and brave, because you
will lead the people of Israel to the land
I promised them, and I will be with you."
24 After Moses finished writing all the words of
the teachings in a book, 25 he gave a command to
the Levites, who carried the Ark[d] of the Agree-
ment with the LORD. 26 He said, "Take this Book
of the Teachings and put it beside the Ark of the
Agreement with the LORD your God. It must stay
there as a witness against you. 27 I know how
stubborn and disobedient you are. You have
disobeyed the LORD while I am alive and with
you, and you will disobey even more after I die!
28 Gather all the elders of your tribes[d] and all your
officers to me so that I may say these things for
them to hear, and so that I may ask heaven and
earth to testify against them. 29 I know that after
I die you will become completely evil. You will
turn away from the commands I have given you.
Terrible things will happen to you in the future
when you do what the LORD says is evil, and you
will make him angry with the idols you have
made."

Moses' Song

30 And Moses spoke this whole song for all the
people of Israel to hear:

32

Hear, heavens, and I will speak.
Listen, earth, to what I say.
2 My teaching will drop like rain;
my words will fall like dew.
They will be like showers on the grass;
they will pour down like rain on young plants.
3 I will announce the name of the LORD.
Praise God because he is great!
4 He is like a rock; what he does is perfect,
and he is always fair.
He is a faithful God who does no wrong,
who is right and fair.

5 They have done evil against him.
To their shame they are no longer his children;
they are an evil and lying people.
6 This is not the way to repay the LORD,
you foolish and unwise people.
He is your Father and Maker,
who made you and formed you.

7 Remember the old days.
Think of the years already passed.
Ask your father and he will tell you;
ask your elders and they will inform you.
8 God Most High gave the nations their lands,
dividing up the human race.
He set up borders for the people
and even numbered the Israelites.
9 The LORD took his people as his share,
the people of Jacob as his very own.

10 He found them in a desert,
a windy, empty land.
He surrounded them and brought them up,
guarding them as those he loved very much.
11 He was like an eagle building its nest
that flutters over its young.
It spreads its wings to catch them
and carries them on its feathers.
12 The LORD alone led them,
and there was no foreign god helping him.

13 The LORD brought them to the heights of the land

Sidelight

Have you ever found that an important book is out of print? Bible scholars often have that problem. The Bible mentions several books that no longer exist. Deuteronomy 31:26 mentions the "Book of the Teachings". Others include: the "Book of the Wars of the Lord" (Numbers 21:14–15, p.149), and the "Book of Jashar" (Joshua 10:13, p.210). Fortunately, they don't affect the contents of our Bible.

and fed them the fruit of the fields.
He gave them honey from the rocks,
bringing oil from the solid rock.
14There were milk curds from the cows and milk from the flock;
there were fat sheep and goats.
There were rams and goats from Bashan
and the best of the wheat.
You drank the juice of grapes.

15Israel grew fat and kicked;
they were fat and full and firm.
They left the God who made them
and rejected the Rock[d] who saved them.
16They made God jealous with foreign gods
and angry with hateful idols.
17They made sacrifices to demons,[d] not God,
to gods they had never known,
new gods from nearby,
gods your ancestors did not fear.

18You left God who is the Rock, your Father,
and you forgot the God who gave you birth.

19The LORD saw this and rejected them;
his sons and daughters had made him angry.
20He said, "I will turn away from them
and see what will happen to them.
They are evil people,
unfaithful children.
21They used things that are not gods to make me jealous
and worthless idols to make me angry.
So I will use those who are not a nation to make them jealous;
I will use a nation that does not understand to make them angry.
22My anger has started a fire
that burns down to the place of the dead.

ENVIRONMENT

On Yer Bike!

Steve was a good minister and he tried hard to encompass the whole of God's teaching in his church. Lately, he had been concerned about the environment. He was aware that when God made the earth it was perfect, and that gradually so many things were being destroyed.

So, when one of the young people spoke to him on that very issue, he was all ears. Matthew's plan was that just for one Sunday, as many people as possible should come to church on bikes instead of in their cars. Some might even go as far as to walk instead!

Steve thought it was a great idea and announced it in church the following week. He let Matthew explain to the congregation that the air was getting so badly polluted by petrol fumes amongst a great deal of other things, that it would be good to do something about it. Things were far from the way God had made them.

The people were very enthusiastic and a few weeks later a very amusing sight hit the local town. Church members ranging from eight years to eighty years came whistling down the road on bicycles! They were wearing an assortment of shorts and coloured tops and the church looked very different.

Matthew's idea was a great success, and some of the people at his church still come on their bikes instead of cars, and others are more aware that sharing a car is better than nothing.

Deuteronomy 32:1–6 reminds us that we need to be wise with our world.

- How did Matthew's idea help to repay the Lord?
- What is our responsibility to God and to his creation?

Consider . . .

- whether you have done things to help reverse the pollution problem such as walking or cycling if your journey is less than two kilometres.
- making a list of plants and animals you see in your garden. Thank God for what he has made.

For more, see . . .

- Genesis 1:6–8 (p.2)
- Psalm 104 (p.560)

It will burn up the ground and its crops,
and it will set fire to the base of the mountains.

23"I will pile troubles upon them
and shoot my arrows at them.
24They will be starved and sick,
destroyed by terrible diseases.
I will send them vicious animals
and gliding, poisonous snakes.
25In the streets the sword will kill;
in their homes there will be terror.
Young men and women will die,
and so will babies and grey-haired men.
26I will scatter them as I said,
and no one will remember them.
27But I didn't want their enemy to boast;
their enemy might misunderstand
and say, 'We have won!
The LORD has done none of this.' "

28Israel has no sense;
they do not understand.
29I wish they were wise and understood this;
I wish they could see what will happen to them.
30One person cannot chase 1,000 people,
and two people cannot fight 10,000
unless their Rock has sold them,
unless the LORD has given them up.
31The rock of these people is not like our Rock;
our enemies agree to that.
32Their vine comes from Sodom,
and their fields are like Gomorrah.
Their grapes are full of poison;
their bunches of grapes are bitter.

GOD'S POWER

Stronger Than Hatred

Andrew was livid. He had come to pick up his son Rob from church camp. While waiting for the last session to end, he had overheard his son telling other campers how he hated his dad because of abuse. But Christ had changed Rob's life that week. "And I know Christ can change my dad, too," he had concluded.

Andrew stormed to camp director Ivor's office and verbally abused the director for what he had overheard.

Ivor calmed Andrew down and responded, "If your son is worse because of this camp experience, call me. I'll personally apologise. But, if your son is better, write to thank me."

Andrew picked up his son, still steaming with anger. The two drove silently in the car listening to the radio. About a hundred miles from camp, Rob's dad pulled into a service area. As they looked at the view, Rob awkwardly put his arms around his dad and said, "Dad, I've hated you ever since I can remember. Will you forgive me?"

Two hours later, Ivor found Rob's dad back at the camp. "Christ made my son better," he told Ivor. "Can he do it in my life too?"

That day, Rob's father began the long process of healing and recovery.

It was not easy for either Rob or his father to let go of the feelings of anger and hatred. But, in the process, they discovered God's power in the world and in their own lives. Read a description of God's power in **Deuteronomy 32:36–33:4**.

- How might Rob's father have responded to this passage in the first part of the story? How might he have responded at the end?
- What characteristic of God in the passage helps you to understand God's power the most? What comfort do you gain from knowing that power?

Consider . . .

- confessing a way in which you've tried to escape from God (such as making decisions for selfish reasons), then letting God's power work in that area of your life.
- sharing your faith in God's power with someone who has no hope.

For more, see . . .

- Job 9:4–10 (p.475)
- Ephesians 1:19–22 (p.1270)
- Isaiah 46:8–12 (p.689)

33Their wine is like snake poison,
like the deadly poison of cobras.

34"I have been saving this,
and I have it locked in my storehouses.
35I will punish those who do wrong; I will
repay them.
Soon their foot will slip,
because their day of trouble is near,
and their punishment will come quickly."

36The LORD will defend his people
and have mercy on his servants.
He will see that their strength is gone,
that nobody is left, slaves or free.
37Then he will say, "Where are their gods?
Where is the rock they trusted?
38Who ate the fat from their sacrifices,
and who drank the wine of their drink
offerings?
Let those gods come to help you!
Let them protect you!

39"Now you will see that I am the one God!
There is no god but me.
I send life and death;
I can hurt, and I can heal.
No one can escape from me.
40I raise my hand towards heaven and make
this promise:
As surely as I live for ever,
41I will sharpen my flashing sword,
and I will take it in my hand to judge.
I will punish my enemies
and pay back those who hate me.
42My arrows will be covered with their blood;
my sword will eat their flesh.
The blood will flow from those who are
killed and the captives.
The heads of the enemy leaders will be
cut off."

43Be happy, nations, with his people,
because he will repay you for the blood of
his servants.
He will punish his enemies,
and he will remove the sin of his land and
people.

44Moses came with Joshua son of Nun, and
they spoke all the words of this song for the peo-
ple to hear. 45When Moses finished speaking
these words to all Israel, 46he said to them: "Pay
careful attention to all the words I have said to
you today, and command your children to obey
carefully everything in these teachings. 47These
should not be unimportant words for you, but
rather they mean life for you! By these words you
will live a long time in the land you are crossing
the Jordan River to take as your own."

Moses Goes Up to Mount Nebo

48The LORD spoke to Moses again that same day
and said, 49"Go up the Abarim Mountains, to
Mount Nebo in the country of Moab, across from
Jericho. Look at the land of Canaan that I am
giving to the Israelites as their own. 50On that
mountain that you climb, you will die and join
your ancestors, just as your brother Aaron died
on Mount Hor and joined his ancestors. 51You
both sinned against me at the waters of Meribah
Kadesh in the Desert of Zin, and you did not
honour me as holy there among the Israelites.
52So now you will only look at the land from far
away. You will not enter the land I am giving the
people of Israel."

Moses Blesses the People

33 Moses, the man of God, gave this bless-
ing to the Israelites before he died. 2He
said:

"The LORD came from Mount Sinai
and rose like the sun from Edom;
he showed his greatness from Mount Paran.
He came with thousands of angels
from the southern mountains.
3The LORD surely loves his people
and takes care of all those who belong to him.
They bow down at his feet,
and they are taught by him.
4Moses gave us the teachings
that belong to the people of Jacob.
5The LORD became king of Israel
when the leaders of the people gathered,
when the tribes [d] of Israel came together.

6"Let the people of Reuben live and not die,
but let the people be few."

7Moses said this about the people of Judah:
"LORD, listen to Judah's prayer;
bring them back to their people.
They defend themselves with their hands.
Help them fight their enemies!"

8Moses said this about the people of Levi:
"LORD, your Thummim and Urim [d] belong
to Levi, whom you love.
LORD, you tested him at Massah
and argued with him at the waters of
Meribah.
9He said about his father and mother,
'I don't care about them.'
He did not treat his brothers as favourites
or give special favours to his children,
but he protected your word
and guarded your agreement.
10He teaches your laws to the people of Jacob
and your teachings to the people of Israel.
He burns incense [d] before you

and makes whole burnt offerings on your
altar.
11LORD, make them strong;
be pleased with the work they do.
Defeat those who attack them,
and don't let their enemies rise up again."

12Moses said this about the people of Benjamin:
"The LORD's loved ones will lie down in
safety,
because he protects them all day long.
The ones he loves rest with him."

13Moses said this about the people of Joseph:
"May the LORD bless their land with
wonderful dew from heaven,
with water from the springs below,
14with the best fruits that the sun brings,
and with the best fruits that the moon
brings.
15Let the old mountains give the finest crops,
and let the everlasting hills give the best
fruits.
16Let the full earth give the best fruits,
and let the LORD who lived in the burning
bush be pleased.
May these blessings rest on the head of Joseph,
on the forehead of the one who was
blessed among his brothers.
17Joseph has the majesty of a firstborn [d] bull;
he is as strong as a wild ox.
He will stab other nations,
even those nations far away.
These are the ten thousands of Ephraim,
and these are the thousands of Manasseh."

18Moses said this about the people of Zebulun:
"Be happy when you go out, Zebulun,
and be happy in your tents, Issachar.
19They will call the people to the mountain,
and there they will offer the right sacrifices.
They will do well from all that is in the sea,

DEATH

Breaking the Mould

"One Michael Owen! There's only one Michael Owen!" The England Football fans sang this at the top of their voices. The flags were raised high and scarves were waved from end to end of the stadium. And they were right. There is only one Michael Owen. We are all unique in God's eyes.

People often say, when talking of someone great – "God broke the mould after he made him!" And it's true! No two people are the same.

When we look back on the life of a friend who has died, we remember all the good things, all the unique things about that person and we realise that there will never be another person quite like them. When we understand this, we can start to understand how precious we are to God.

It makes the loss of a friend even more poignant as we realise we will never hear that voice or see that smile, for a long long time. It's an empty time, because no one will fill that space in the same way ever again. That's what grieving is all about. We need time to remember and mourn.

In **Deuteronomy 34:1–12** we find the same predicament.

- How did the Israelites grieve over Moses?
- When have you experienced the loss of someone close? How was your experience like that of the Israelites?

Consider . . .

- talking to a friend and a family member about times when they lost someone close. Ask what emotions they felt and how long they grieved.
- comforting someone who's facing death or grieving, by making a phone call, sending a card, visiting, or giving a hug.

For more, see . . .

- 2 Samuel 1:17–27 (p.284)
- Revelation 21:1–4 (p.1403)
- John 11:28–44 (p.1116)

and they will do well from the treasures
hidden in the sand on the shore."

20 Moses said this about the people of Gad:
"Praise God who gives Gad more land!
Gad lives there like a lion,
who tears off arms and heads.
21 They chose the best land for themselves.
They received a large share, like that given
to an officer.
When the leaders of the people gathered,
the people of Gad did what the LORD
said was right,
and they judged Israel fairly."

22 Moses said this about the people of Dan:
"Dan is like a lion's cub,
who jumps out of Bashan."

23 Moses said this about the people of Naphtali:
"Naphtali enjoys special kindnesses,
and they are full of the LORD's blessings.
Take as your own the west and south."

24 Moses said this about the people of Asher:
"Asher is the most blessed of the sons;
let him be his brothers' favourite.
Let him bathe his feet in olive oil.
25 Your gates will have locks of iron and
bronze,
and you will be strong as long as you live.

26 "There is no one like the God of Israel,
who rides through the skies to help you,
who rides on the clouds in his majesty.
27 The everlasting God is your place of safety,
and his arms will hold you up for ever.
He will force your enemy out ahead of you,
saying, "Destroy the enemy!'
28 The people of Israel will lie down in safety.
Jacob's spring is theirs alone.
Theirs is a land full of grain and new wine,
where the skies drop their dew.
29 Israel, you are blessed!
No one else is like you,
because you are a people saved by the
LORD.
He is your shield and helper,
your glorious sword.
Your enemies will be afraid of you,
and you will walk all over their holy places."

Moses Dies

34 Then Moses climbed Mount Nebo from
the plains of Moab to the top of Mount
Pisgah, across from Jericho. From there the LORD
showed him all the land from Gilead to Dan, 2 all
of Naphtali and the lands of Ephraim and Manas-
seh, all the land of Judah as far as the Mediter-
ranean Sea, 3 as well as the southern desert and
the whole Valley of Jericho up to Zoar. (Jericho is
called the city of palm trees.) 4 Then the LORD said
to Moses, "This is the land I promised to Abra-
ham, Isaac and Jacob when I said to them, 'I will
give this land to your descendants.'[d] I have let
you look at it, Moses, but you will not cross over
there."

5 Then Moses, the servant of the LORD, died
there in Moab, as the LORD had said. 6 He buried
Moses in Moab in the valley opposite Beth Peor,
but even today no one knows where his grave is.
7 Moses was 120 years old when he died. His eyes
were not weak, and he was still strong. 8 The
Israelites cried for Moses for 30 days, staying in
the plains of Moab until the time of sadness was
over.

9 Joshua son of Nun was then filled with wis-
dom, because Moses had put his hands on him.
So the Israelites listened to Joshua, and they did
what the LORD had commanded Moses.

10 There has never been another prophet[d] in
Israel like Moses. The LORD knew Moses face to
face 11 and sent him to do signs and miracles[d] in
Egypt—to the king, to all his officers and to the
whole land of Egypt. 12 Moses had great power,
and he did great and wonderful things for all the
Israelites to see.

Joshua

Why Read This Book:

- See how God leads people to victory when they are faithful (Joshua 1—12).
- Learn how God takes care of people's needs (Joshua 13—21).
- Be challenged to stay faithful to God (Joshua 22—24).

When?

Time Line:

- 2000 BC
- 1500 BC — Joshua led the Israelites into Canaan — The Israelites escaped from Egypt
- 1000 BC — David was Israel's king
- 500 BC
- BC/AD — Jesus was born

Behind the Scenes:

The book of Joshua could be a great script for an action-packed film. It's filled with spies, surprise attacks, warfare, leaders and unusual battles.

The central hero is Joshua, a creative military mind with great organisational skills. But above all, he's absolutely loyal to and dependent on God.

The plot tells how the Israelites conquered land that God promised to their ancestor Abram (Genesis 12:7, p.14). Their parents had escaped from Egypt but had not followed God.

So the whole generation that left Egypt had died in the desert, leaving the children – under Joshua's leadership – to conquer the land of Canaan.

Canaan consisted of many independent cities, each with its own king and army, and many had strong, high walls. So the Israelites had to defeat the cities one by one, beginning with the famous battle of Jericho (Joshua 6).

The books shows how God works through people and why obedience matters.

Where?

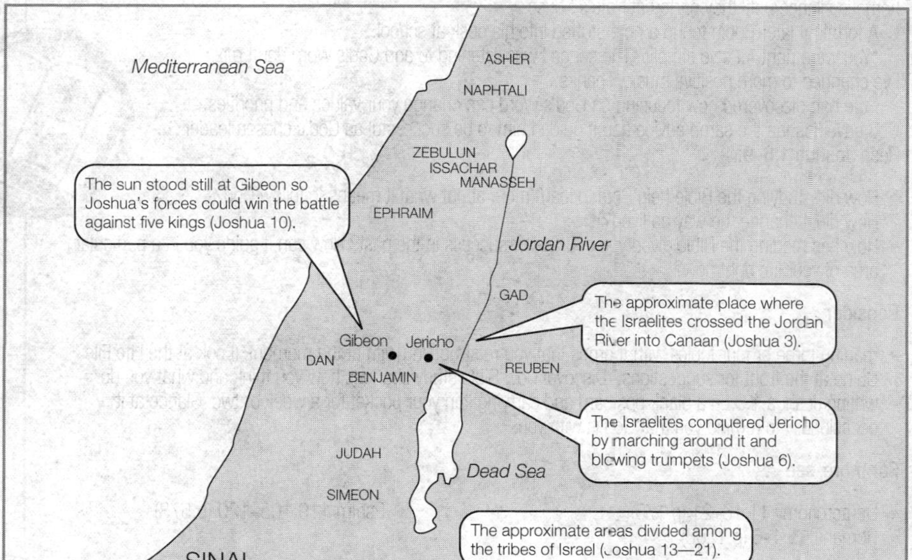

God's Command to Joshua

1 After Moses, the servant of the LORD, died,
the LORD spoke to Joshua son of Nun, Moses'
assistant. 2The LORD said, "My servant Moses is
dead. Now you and all these people go across
the Jordan River into the land I am giving to the Is-
raelites. 3I promised Moses I would give you this
land, so I will give you every place you go in the
land. 4All the land from the desert in the south to
Lebanon in the north will be yours. All the land
from the great river, the Euphrates, in the east, to
the Mediterranean Sea in the west will be yours
too, including the land of the Hittites. 5No one
will be able to defeat you all your life. Just as I
was with Moses, so I will be with you. I will not
leave you or forget you.
6"Joshua, be strong and brave! You must lead
these people so they can take the land that I prom-
ised their fathers I would give them. 7Be strong
and brave. Be sure to obey all the teachings my
servant Moses gave you. If you follow them ex-
actly, you will be successful in everything you do.

Sidelight The Hebrew name for Joshua means "The Lord saves". It's a more famous name than you might think. When you translate it into English, it's Jesus.

BIBLE STUDY

Where's the Focus?

Robin was appalled when he saw the CDs in his friend Pete's room.

"How can you listen to this rubbish?" he asked as he read the sexually explicit song titles.

"Give me a break," Pete shot back. "Who cares about the words?"

The conversation came back to Robin the next Wednesday night in Bible study. The group read the Bible and tried to apply its principles to their lives. They focused on how being a Christian shapes your priorities and interests in life and how it affects everything you do.

Robin was challenged by the discussion and wanted to talk about it with Pete. On the way home from the Bible study, they talked about friendships and being honest. Then Robin asked, "What does all this say about your music, Pete?"

Pete was furious. "Nothing. It's fine!" he shouted, hoping Robin would back off. Which he did. They walked home in silence until they parted at Pete's house.

A fortnight later Robin found a note stuffed into his desk at school.

"You were right," it said simply. "The songs I was listening to and God's Word don't mix. I've changed to more positive music. Thanks."

Pete had discovered how focusing on God's Word can change your values and priorities. God gave Joshua the same advice and it guided him to be successful as God's chosen leader. Read **Joshua 1:6–9**.

- How did studying the Bible help Pete to learn more about what it means to follow God? How did it change the way he lived?
- How has reading the Bible given you courage or success in the past? How can it guide you in a particular area of your life right now?

Consider . . .

- reading three or four topics with themes that you're struggling with at the moment. (Look at the Life File Guide at the front for suggestions.) Discover how Bible study changes how you think and what you do.
- writing Joshua 1:9 on a blank postcard and carrying it in your pocket for a week or two. Glance at it occasionally to remind you that God is with you.

For more, see . . .

- Deuteronomy 11:16–21 (p.176)
- Romans 15:4–6 (p.1208)
- Psalm 119:105–120 (p.573)

8Always remember what is written in the Book of the Teachings. Study it day and night to be sure to obey everything that is written there. If you do this, you will be wise and successful in everything. 9Remember that I commanded you to be strong and brave. Don't be afraid, because the LORD your God will be with you everywhere you go."

Joshua's Orders to the People

10Then Joshua gave orders to the officers of the people: 11"Go through the camp and tell the people, 'Get your supplies ready. Three days from now you will cross the Jordan River and take the land the LORD your God is giving you.'"

12Then Joshua said to the people of Reuben, Gad and East Manasseh, 13"Remember what Moses, the servant of the LORD, told you. He said the LORD your God would give you rest and would give you this land. 14Now the LORD has given you this land east of the Jordan River. Your wives, children and animals may stay here, but your fighting men must dress for war and cross the Jordan River ahead of your brothers to help them. 15The LORD has given you a place to rest and will do the same for your brothers. But you must help them until they take the land the LORD their God is giving them. Then you may return to your own land east of the Jordan River, the land that Moses, the servant of the LORD, gave you."

16Then the people answered Joshua, "Whatever you command us to do, we will do. Wherever you send us, we will go. 17Just as we fully obeyed Moses, we will obey you. We ask only that the LORD your God be with you just as he was with Moses. 18Whoever refuses to obey your commands or turns against you will be put to death. Just be strong and brave!"

Spies Sent to Jericho

2 Joshua son of Nun secretly sent out two spies from Acacia and said to them, "Go and look at the land, particularly at the city of Jericho."

So the men went to Jericho and stayed at the house of a prostitute[d] named Rahab.

2Someone told the king of Jericho, "Some men from Israel have come here tonight to spy out the land."

3So the king of Jericho sent this message to Rahab: "Bring out the men who came to you and entered your house. They have come to spy out our whole land."

4But the woman had hidden the two men. She said, "They did come here, but I didn't know where they came from. 5In the evening, when it was time to close the city gate, they left. I don't know where they went, but if you go quickly, maybe you can catch them." 6(The woman had taken the men up to the roof[n] and had hidden them there under stalks of flax[d] that she had spread out.) 7So the king's men went out looking for the spies on the road that leads to the crossings of the Jordan River. The city gate was closed just after the king's men left the city.

8Before the spies went to sleep for the night, Rahab went up to the roof. 9She said to them, "I know the LORD has given this land to your people. You frighten us very much. Everyone living in this land is terribly afraid of you 10because we have heard how the LORD dried up the Red Sea[d] when you came out of Egypt. We have heard how you destroyed Sihon and Og, two Amorite kings who lived east of the Jordan. 11When we heard this, we were very frightened. Now our men are afraid to fight you because the LORD your God rules the heavens above and the earth below! 12So now, promise me before the LORD that you will show kindness to my family just as I showed kindness to you. Give me some proof that you will do this. 13Allow my father, mother, brothers, sisters and all of their families to live. Save us from death."

14The men agreed and said, "It will be our lives for your lives if you don't tell anyone what we are doing. When the LORD gives us the land, we will be kind and true to you."

15The house Rahab lived in was built on the city wall, so she used a rope to let the men down through a window. 16She said to them, "Go into the hills so the king's men will not find you. Hide there for three days. After the king's men return, you may go on your way."

17The men said to her, "You must do as we say. If not, we cannot be responsible for keeping this oath you have made us swear. 18When we return to this land, you must tie this red rope in the window through which you let us down. Bring your father, mother, brothers and all your family into your house. 19If anyone leaves your house and is killed, it is his own fault. We cannot be responsible for him. If anyone in your house is hurt, we will be responsible. 20But if you tell anyone about this, we will be free from the oath you made us swear."

21Rahab answered, "I agree to this." So she sent them away, and they left. Then she tied the red rope in the window.

22The men left and went into the hills where they stayed for three days. The king's men looked for them all along the road, but after three days, they returned to the city without finding them.

roof In Bible times houses were built with flat roofs. The roof was used for drying things such as flax and fruit. And it was used as an extra room, as a place for worship and as a place to sleep in the summer.

23Then the two men started back. They left the hills and crossed the river and came to Joshua son of Nun and told him everything that had happened to them. 24They said, "The LORD surely has given us all of the land. All the people in that land are terribly afraid of us."

> **Sidelight**
> This is an unusually detailed scene for an Old Testament writer. Did you notice all the little details that help you imagine the spies talking to Rahab? We were even told the colour of rope that Rahab used to help the spies escape.

Crossing the Jordan

3 Early the next morning Joshua and all the Israelites left Acacia. They travelled to the Jordan River and camped there before crossing it. 2After three days the officers went through the camp 3and gave orders to the people: "When you see the priests and Levites carrying the Ark[d] of the Agreement with the LORD your God, leave where you are and follow it. 4That way you will know which way to go since you have never been here before. But do not follow too closely. Stay about a kilometre behind the Ark."

5Then Joshua told the people, "Make yourselves holy, because tomorrow the LORD will do amazing things among you."

6Joshua said to the priests, "Take the Ark of the Agreement and go ahead of the people." So the priests lifted the Ark and carried it ahead of the people.

7Then the LORD said to Joshua, "Today I will begin to make you great in the opinion of all the Israelites so the people will know I am with you just as I was with Moses. 8Tell the priests who carry the Ark of the Agreement to go to the edge of the Jordan River and stand in the water."

9Then Joshua said to the Israelites, "Come here and listen to the words of the LORD your God. 10Here is proof that the living God is with you and that he will force out the Canaanites, Hittites, Hivites, Perizzites, Girgashites, Amorites and Jebusites. 11The Ark of the Agreement with the Lord of the whole world will go ahead of you into the Jordan River. 12Now choose twelve men from among you, one from each of the twelve tribes[d] of Israel. 13The priests will carry the Ark of the LORD, the Master of the whole world, into the Jordan ahead of you. When they step into the water, it will stop. The river will stop flowing and will stand up in a heap."

14So the people left the place where they had camped, and they followed the priests who carried the Ark of the Agreement across the Jordan River. 15During harvest the Jordan overflows its banks. When the priests carrying the Ark came to the edge of the river and stepped into the water, 16the water a great distance away stopped flowing. It stood up in a heap a great distance away at Adam, a town near Zarethan. The water flowing down to the Sea of Arabah (the Dead Sea[d]) was completely cut off. So the people crossed the river near Jericho. 17The priests carried the Ark of the Agreement with the LORD to the middle of the river and stood there on dry ground. They waited there while all the people of Israel walked across the Jordan River on dry land.

Rocks to Remind the People

4 After all the people had finished crossing the Jordan, the LORD said to Joshua, 2"Choose twelve men from among the people, one from each tribe.[d] 3Tell them to get twelve rocks from the middle of the river, from where the priests stood. Carry the rocks and put them down where you stay tonight."

4So Joshua chose one man from each tribe. Then he called the twelve men together 5and said to them, "Go out into the river where the Ark[d] of the LORD your God is. Each of you bring back one rock, one for each tribe of Israel, and carry it on your shoulder. 6They will be a sign among you. In the future your children will ask you, 'What do these rocks mean?' 7Tell them the water stopped flowing in the Jordan when the Ark of the Agreement with the LORD crossed the river. These rocks will always remind the Israelites of this."

8So the Israelites obeyed Joshua and carried twelve rocks from the middle of the Jordan River, one rock for each of the twelve tribes of Israel, just as the LORD had commanded Joshua. They carried the rocks with them and put them down where they made their camp. 9Joshua also put twelve rocks in the middle of the Jordan River where the priests had stood while carrying the Ark of the Agreement. These rocks are still there today.

10The priests carrying the Ark continued standing in the middle of the river until everything was done that the LORD had commanded Joshua to tell the people, just as Moses had told Joshua. The people hurried across the river. 11After they finished crossing the river, the priests carried the Ark of the LORD to the other side as the people watched. 12The men from the tribes of Reuben, Gad and East Manasseh obeyed what Moses had told them. They were dressed for war, and they crossed the river ahead of the other people. 13About 40,000 soldiers, prepared for war, passed before the LORD as they marched across the river, going towards the plains of Jericho.

14That day the LORD made Joshua great in the
opinion of all the Israelites. They respected Jo-
shua all his life, just as they had respected Moses.
15Then the LORD said to Joshua, 16"Command
the priests to bring the Ark of the Agreement out
of the river."
17So Joshua commanded the priests, "Come up
out of the Jordan."
18Then the priests carried the Ark of the Agree-
ment with the LORD out of the river. As soon as
their feet touched dry land, the water began flow-
ing again. The river again overflowed its banks,
just as it had before they crossed.
19The people crossed the Jordan on the tenth
day of the first month and camped at Gilgal, east
of Jericho. 20They carried with them the twelve
rocks taken from the Jordan, and Joshua set them
up at Gilgal. 21Then he spoke to the Israelites: "In
the future your children will ask you, 'What do
these rocks mean?' 22Tell them, 'Israel crossed
the Jordan River on dry land. 23The LORD your
God caused the water to stop flowing until you
finished crossing it, just as the LORD did to the Red
Sea.[d] He stopped the water until we crossed it.
24The LORD did this so all people would know he
has great power and so you would always respect
the LORD your God.'"

5 All the kings of the Amorites west of the
Jordan and the Canaanite kings living by the
Mediterranean Sea heard that the LORD dried up
the Jordan River until the Israelites had crossed it.
After that they were scared and too afraid to face
the Israelites.

The Israelites are Circumcised

2At that time the LORD said to Joshua, "Make
knives from flint stones and circumcise[d] the Israel-
ites." 3So Joshua made knives from flint stones
and circumcised the Israelites at Gibeath Haaraloth.
4This is why Joshua circumcised the men: after
the Israelites left Egypt, all the men old enough to
serve in the army died in the desert on the way
out of Egypt. 5The men who had come out of
Egypt had been circumcised, but none of those
who were born in the desert on the trip from
Egypt had been circumcised. 6The Israelites had
moved about in the desert for 40 years. During
that time all the fighting men who had left Egypt
had died because they had not obeyed the LORD.
So the LORD swore they would not see the land he
had promised their ancestors to give them, a fer-
tile land. 7Their sons took their places. But none
of the sons born on the trip from Egypt had been
circumcised, so Joshua circumcised them. 8After
all the Israelites had been circumcised, they
stayed in camp until they were healed.
9Then the LORD said to Joshua, "As slaves
in Egypt you were ashamed, but today I have
removed that shame." So Joshua named that
place Gilgal, which it is still named today.
10The people of Israel were camped at Gilgal
on the plains of Jericho. It was there, on the eve-
ning of the fourteenth day of the month, they
celebrated the Passover[d] Feast. 11The day after
the Passover, the people ate food grown on that
land: bread made without yeast and roasted
grain. 12The day they ate this food, the manna[d]
stopped coming. The Israelites no longer got the
manna from heaven. They ate the food grown in
the land of Canaan that year.
13Joshua was near Jericho when he looked up
and saw a man standing in front of him with a
sword in his hand. Joshua went to him and asked,
"Are you a friend or an enemy?"
14The man answered, "I am neither. I have
come as the commander of the LORD's army."
Then Joshua bowed face down on the ground
and asked, "Does my master have a command for
me, his servant?"
15The commander of the LORD's army an-
swered, "Take off your sandals, because the place
where you are standing is holy." So Joshua did.

The Fall of Jericho

6 The people of Jericho were afraid because
the Israelites were near. They closed the city
gates and guarded them. No one went into the
city, and no one came out.
2Then the LORD said to Joshua, "Look, I have
given you Jericho, its king, and all its fighting
men. 3March around the city with your army
once a day for six days. 4Have seven priests carry
trumpets made from horns of rams and have
them march in front of the Ark.[d] On the seventh
day march around the city seven times and have
the priests blow the trumpets as they march.
5They will make one long blast on the trumpets.
When you hear that sound, have all the people
give a loud shout. Then the walls of the city will
fall so the people can go straight into the city."
6So Joshua son of Nun called the priests to-
gether and said to them, "Carry the Ark of the
Agreement. Tell seven priests to carry trumpets
and march in front of it." 7Then Joshua ordered
the people, "Now go! March around the city. The
soldiers with weapons should march in front of
the Ark of the Agreement with the LORD."
8When Joshua finished speaking to the people,
the seven priests began marching before the LORD.
They carried the seven trumpets and blew them
as they marched. The priests carrying the Ark of
the Agreement with the LORD followed them.
9Soldiers with weapons marched in front of the
priests, and armed men walked behind the Ark.
The priests were blowing their trumpets. 10But
Joshua had told the people not to give a war cry.

He said, "Don't shout. Don't say a word until the
day I tell you. Then shout." 11So Joshua had the
Ark of the LORD carried around the city once.
Then they went back to camp for the night.
12Early the next morning Joshua got up, and
the priests carried the Ark of the LORD again.
13The seven priests carried the seven trumpets
and marched in front of the Ark of the LORD,
blowing their trumpets. Soldiers with weapons
marched in front of them, and other soldiers
walked behind the Ark of the LORD. All this time
the priests were blowing their trumpets. 14So on
the second day they marched around the city
once and then went back to camp. They did this
every day for six days.
15On the seventh day they got up at dawn
and marched around the city, just as they
had on the days before. But on that day they
marched around the city seven times. 16The
seventh time around the priests blew their
trumpets. Then Joshua gave the command:
"Now, shout! The LORD has given you this
city! 17The city and everything in it are to
be destroyed as an offering to the LORD.
Only Rahab the prostitute[d] and everyone in
her house should remain alive. They must
not be killed, because Rahab hid the two
spies we sent out. 18Don't take any of the things
that are to be destroyed as an offering to the
LORD. If you take them and bring them into

MUSIC

God's Powerful Gift

Music has huge power – it can divide or unite people. It is one of the biggest ways in which people nowadays are defined, be it liking rap, alternative, dance, rock, pop, indie, classical, metal, experimental or punk to name a few. This can lead to whole sub-cultures being created – fashion styles, places to hang out, and other activities, such as skating, are all tied to genres of music. It can even lead to tensions between the sub-cultures – over the years, many different gangs have grown from these groups.

However, music is also often part of bringing people together. It has played a large part in many of the big campaigns for justice and peace alongside annual events such as Comic Relief and Children in Need. Several of the campaigns have used concerts with huge impact, both in the amount of money they raised to help deal with issues such as famine and starvation in Africa, and in the way that it brought those issues to our attention.

A number of music stars use their fame to encourage others to make a difference. They may support a particular charity, organisation or cause, and use their music and status to help provide funding and publicity for that cause.

In **Joshua 6:2–5** we read how God brought the Israelites together and showed how music truly is a powerful gift – one that can make huge physical differences – even knocking down a city's walls!

- Has the power of creativity, especially music, had an impact on your life?
- How could you and your friends use music to make a difference for God?

Consider . . .

- writing a paraphrase of some of the old hymns that you know. Take the lyrics and try to rewrite them in everyday language. Spend time looking at the meaning of the words you sing in church and be blessed by the creativity of the poetic words. Some good songs to look at include "Praise My Soul the King of Heaven", "To God Be the Glory", and "Tell Out My Soul".
- going to your music collection and listening to the lyrics of your secular music. Check out the themes within the lyrics.

For more, see . . .

- 2 Chronicles 5:12–14 (p.404)
- Psalm 147:1 (p.586)
- Psalm 81:2–4 (p.549)

our camp, you yourselves will be destroyed,
and you will bring trouble to all of Israel. 19 All
the silver and gold and things made from
bronze and iron belong to the LORD and must
be saved for him."

> **Sidelight** Jericho (Joshua 6:1–19) has been called "the oldest walled town in the world". Many archaeologists believe it was settled as early as 10,000 BC, and walls were built by 8,000 BC. After it was destroyed, it wasn't rebuilt for about 400 years. Today the ancient city of Jericho is a 23-metre high mound near the modern city of Jericho in Israel.

20 When the priests blew the trumpets, the
people shouted. At the sound of the trumpets and
the people's shout, the walls fell, and everyone
ran straight into the city. So the Israelites de-
feated that city. 21 They completely destroyed
with the sword every living thing in the city—
men and women, young and old, cattle, sheep
and donkeys.
22 Joshua said to the two men who had spied
out the land, "Go into the prostitute's house.
Bring her out and bring out those who are with
her, because of the promise you made to her."
23 So the two men went into the house and
brought out Rahab, her father, mother, brothers
and all those with her. They put all of her family
in a safe place outside the camp of Israel.
24 Then Israel burned the whole city and every-
thing in it, but they did not burn the things made
from silver, gold, bronze and iron. These were
saved for the LORD. 25 Joshua saved Rahab the
prostitute, her family and all who were with her,
because Rahab had helped the men he had sent
to spy out Jericho. Rahab still lives among the
Israelites today.
26 Then Joshua made this oath:
"Anyone who tries to rebuild this city of
Jericho
will be cursed by the LORD.
The one who lays the foundation of this city
will lose his oldest son,
and the one who sets up the gates
will lose his youngest son."
27 So the LORD was with Joshua, and Joshua be-
came famous through all the land.

The Sin of Achan

7 But the Israelites did not obey the LORD.
There was a man from the tribe[d] of Judah
named Achan. (He was the son of Carmi and
grandson of Zabdi, who was the son of Zerah.)
Because Achan kept some of the things that were
to be given to the LORD, the LORD became very
angry at the Israelites.
2 Joshua sent some men from Jericho to Ai,
which was near Beth Aven, east of Bethel. He
told them, "Go to Ai and spy out the area." So the
men went to spy on Ai.
3 Later they came back to Joshua and said,
"There are only a few people in Ai, so we will not
need all our people to defeat them. Send only
2,000 to 3,000 men to fight. There is no need to
send all of our people." 4 So about 3,000 men
went up to Ai, but the people of Ai beat them
badly. 5 The people of Ai killed about 36 Israelites
and then chased the rest from the city gate all the
way down to the quarry, killing them as they
went down the hill. When the Israelites saw this,
they lost their courage.
6 Then Joshua tore his clothes in sorrow. He
bowed face down on the ground before the Ark[d]
of the LORD and stayed there until evening. The
elders of Israel did the same thing. They also
threw dust on their heads to show their sorrow.
7 Then Joshua said, "Lord GOD, you brought our
people across the Jordan River. Why did you
bring us this far and then let the Amorites destroy
us? We would have been happy to stay on the
other side of the Jordan. 8 Lord, there is nothing I
can say now. Israel has been beaten by the en-
emy. 9 The Canaanites and all the other people in
this country will hear about this and will sur-
round and kill us all! Then what will you do for
your own great name?"
10 The LORD said to Joshua, "Stand up! Why are
you down on your face? 11 The Israelites have
sinned; they have broken the agreement I com-
manded them to obey. They took some of the
things I commanded them to destroy. They have
stolen and lied and have taken those things for
themselves. 12 That is why the Israelites cannot
face their enemies. They turn away from the fight
and run, because I have commanded that they be
destroyed. I will not help you any more unless
you destroy everything as I commanded you.
13 "Now go! Make the people holy. Tell them,
'Set yourselves apart to the LORD for tomorrow.
The LORD, the God of Israel, says some of you are
keeping things he commanded you to destroy.
You will never defeat your enemies until you
throw away those things.
14 " 'Tomorrow morning you must be present
with your tribes. The LORD will choose one tribe
to stand alone before him. Then the LORD will
choose one family group from that tribe to stand
before him. Then the LORD will choose one family
from that family group to stand before him,
person by person. 15 The one who is keeping
what should have been destroyed will himself be
destroyed by fire. Everything he owns will be

destroyed with him. He has broken the agreement with the LORD and has done a disgraceful thing among the people of Israel!' "

16Early the next morning Joshua led all of Israel to present themselves in their tribes, and the LORD chose the tribe of Judah. 17So the family groups of Judah presented themselves, and the LORD then chose the family group of Zerah. When all the families of Zerah presented themselves, the family of Zabdi was chosen. 18And Joshua told all the men in that family to present themselves. The LORD chose Achan son of Carmi. (Carmi was the son of Zabdi, who was the son of Zerah.)

19Then Joshua said to Achan, "My son, tell the truth. Confess to the LORD, the God of Israel. Tell me what you did, and don't try to hide anything from me."

20Achan answered, "It is true! I have sinned against the LORD, the God of Israel. This is what I did: 21among the things I saw was a beautiful coat from Babylonia and about 2 kilogrammes of silver and more than half a kilogramme of gold. I wanted these things very much for myself, so I took them. You will find them buried in the ground under my tent, with the silver underneath."

22So Joshua sent men who ran to the tent and found the things hidden there, with the silver. 23The men brought them out of the tent, took them to Joshua and all the Israelites, and spread them out on the ground before the LORD. 24Then Joshua and all the people led Achan son of Zerah to the Valley of Trouble. They also took the silver, the coat, the gold, Achan's sons, daughters, cattle, donkeys, sheep, tent and everything he owned. 25Joshua said, "I don't know why you caused so much trouble for us, but now the LORD will bring trouble to you." Then all the people threw stones at Achan and his family until they died. Then the people burned them. 26They piled rocks over Achan's body, and they are still there today. That is why it is called the Valley of Trouble. After this the LORD was no longer angry.

Ai is Destroyed

8 Then the LORD said to Joshua, "Don't be afraid or give up. Lead all your fighting men to Ai. I will help you defeat the king of Ai, his people, his city and his land. 2You will do to Ai and its king what you did to Jericho and its king. Only this time you may take all the wealth and keep it for yourselves. Now tell some of your soldiers to set up an ambush behind the city."

3So Joshua led his whole army towards Ai. Then he chose 30,000 of his best fighting men and sent them out at night. 4Joshua gave them these orders: "Listen carefully. You must set up an ambush behind the city. Don't go far from it, but continue to watch and be ready. 5I and the men who are with me will march towards the city, and the men in the city will come out to fight us, just as they did before. Then we will turn and run away from them. 6They will chase us away from the city, thinking we are running away from them as we did before. When we run away, 7come out from your ambush and take the city. The LORD your God will give you the power to win. 8After you take the city, burn it. See to it! You have your orders."

9Then Joshua sent them to wait in ambush between Bethel and Ai, to the west of Ai. But Joshua stayed the night with his people.

10Early the next morning Joshua gathered his men together. He and the elders of Israel led them up to Ai. 11All of the soldiers who were with Joshua marched up to Ai and stopped in front of the city and made camp north of it. There was a valley between them and the city. 12Then Joshua chose about 5,000 men and set them in ambush in the area west of the city between Bethel and Ai. 13So the people took their positions; the main camp was north of the city, and the other men were hiding to the west. That night Joshua went down into the valley.

14Now when the king of Ai saw the army of Israel, he and his people got up early the next morning and hurried out to fight them. They went out to a place east of the city, but the king did not know soldiers were waiting in ambush behind the city. 15Joshua and all the men of Israel let the army of Ai push them back. Then they ran towards the desert. 16The men in Ai were called to chase Joshua and his men, so they left the city and went after them. 17All the men of Ai and Bethel chased the army of Israel. The city was left open; not a man stayed to protect it.

18Then the LORD said to Joshua, "Hold your spear towards Ai, because I will give you that city." So Joshua held his spear towards the city of Ai. 19When the Israelites who were in ambush saw this, they quickly came out of their hiding place and hurried towards the city. They entered the city, took control of it, and quickly set it on fire.

20When the men of Ai looked back, they saw smoke rising from their city. At the same time the Israelites stopped running and turned against the men of Ai, who could not escape in any direction. 21When Joshua and all his men saw that the army had taken control of the city and saw the smoke rising from it, they stopped running and turned to fight the men of Ai. 22The men who were in ambush also came out of the city to help with the fight. So the men of Ai were caught between the armies of Israel. None of the enemy escaped. The Israelites fought until not one of the men of Ai was left alive, except 23the king of Ai, and they brought him to Joshua.

A Review of the Fighting

24During the fighting the army of Israel chased the men of Ai into the fields and desert and killed all of them. Then they went back to Ai and killed everyone there. 25All the people of Ai died that day, 12,000 men and women. 26Joshua had held his spear towards Ai, as a sign to destroy the city, and did not draw it back until all the people of Ai were destroyed. 27The people of Israel kept for themselves the animals and the other things the people of Ai had owned, as the LORD had commanded Joshua to do.

28Then Joshua burned the city of Ai and made it a pile of ruins. And it is still like that today. 29Joshua hanged the king of Ai on a tree and left him there until evening. At sunset Joshua told his men to take the king's body down from the tree and to throw it down at the city gate. Then they covered it with a pile of rocks, which is still there today.

30Joshua built an altar for the LORD, the God of Israel, on Mount Ebal, as 31Moses, the LORD's servant, had commanded. Joshua built the altar as it was explained in the Book of the Teachings of Moses. It was made from uncut stones; no tool was ever used on them. On that altar the Israelites offered burnt offerings to the LORD and fellowship offerings. 32There Joshua wrote the teachings of Moses on stones for all the people of Israel to see. 33The elders, officers, judges and all the Israelites were there; Israelites and non-Israelites were all standing around the Ark[d] of the Agreement with the LORD in front of the priests, the Levites who had carried the Ark. Half of the people stood in front of Mount Ebal, and half stood in front of Mount Gerizim. This was the way the LORD's servant Moses had earlier commanded the people to be blessed.

34Then Joshua read all the words of the teachings, the blessings and the curses, exactly as they were written in the Book of the Teachings. 35All the Israelites were gathered together—men, women and children—along with the non-Israelites who lived among them. Joshua read every command that Moses had given.

The Gibeonite Trickery

9 All the kings west of the Jordan River heard about these things: the kings of the Hittites, Amorites, Canaanites, Perizzites, Hivites and Jebusites. They lived in the mountains and on the western hills and along the whole Mediterranean Sea coast. 2So all these kings gathered to fight Joshua and the Israelites.

3When the people of Gibeon heard how Joshua had defeated Jericho and Ai, 4they decided to trick the Israelites. They gathered old sacks and old leather wine bags that were cracked and mended, and they put them on the backs of their donkeys. 5They put old sandals on their feet and wore old clothes, and they took some dry, mouldy bread. 6Then they went to Joshua in the camp near Gilgal.

The men said to Joshua and the Israelites, "We have travelled from a faraway country. Make a peace agreement with us."

7The Israelites said to these Hivites, "Maybe you live near us. How can we make a peace agreement with you?"

8The Hivites said to Joshua, "We are your servants."

But Joshua asked, "Who are you? Where do you come from?"

9The men answered, "We are your servants who have come from a far country, because we heard of the fame of the LORD your God. We heard about what he has done and everything he did in Egypt. 10We heard that he defeated the two kings of the Amorites from the east side of the Jordan River—Sihon king of Heshbon and Og king of Bashan who ruled in Ashtaroth. 11So our elders and our people said to us, 'Take food for your journey and go and meet the Israelites. Tell them, "We are your servants. Make a peace agreement with us." '

12"Look at our bread. On the day we left home to come to you it was warm and fresh, but now it is dry and mouldy. 13Look at our leather wine bags. They were new and filled with wine, but now they are cracked and old. Our clothes and sandals are worn out from the long journey."

14The men of Israel tasted the bread, but they did not ask the LORD what to do. 15So Joshua agreed to make peace with the Gibeonites and to let them live. And the leaders of the Israelites swore an oath to keep the agreement.

16Three days after they had made the agreement, the Israelites learned that the Gibeonites lived nearby. 17So the Israelites went to where they lived and on the third day came to their cities: Gibeon, Kephirah, Beeroth and Kiriath Jearim. 18But the Israelites did not attack those cities, because they had made a promise to them before the LORD, the God of Israel.

All the Israelites grumbled against the leaders. 19But the leaders answered, "We have given our promise before the LORD, the God of Israel, so we cannot attack them now. 20This is what we must do. We must let them live. Otherwise, God's anger will be against us for breaking the oath we swore to them. 21So let them live, but they will cut wood and carry water for our people." So the leaders kept their promise to them.

22Joshua called for the Gibeonites and asked, "Why did you lie to us? Your land was near our camp, but you told us you were from a far country. 23Now, you will be placed under a curse to be our slaves. You will have to cut wood and carry water for the house of my God."

24The Gibeonites answered Joshua, "We lied to you because we were afraid you would kill us. We heard that the LORD your God commanded his servant Moses to give you all of this land and to kill all the people who lived in it. That is why we did this. 25Now you can decide what to do with us, whatever you think is right."

26So Joshua saved their lives by not allowing the Israelites to kill them, 27but he made the Gibeonites slaves. They cut wood and carried water for the Israelites, and they did it for the altar of the LORD—wherever he chose it to be. They are still doing this today.

The Sun Stands Still

10 At this time Adoni-Zedek king of Jerusalem heard that Joshua had defeated Ai and completely destroyed it, as he had also done to Jericho and its king. The king also learned that the Gibeonites had made a peace agreement with Israel and that they lived nearby. 2Adoni-Zedek and his people were very afraid because of this. Gibeon was not a little town like Ai; it was a large city, as big as a city that had a king, and all its men were good fighters. 3So Adoni-Zedek king of Jerusalem sent a message to Hoham king of Hebron, Piram king of Jarmuth, Japhia king of Lachish and Debir king of Eglon. He begged them, 4"Come with me and help me attack Gibeon, which has made a peace agreement with Joshua and the Israelites."

5Then these five Amorite kings—the kings of Jerusalem, Hebron, Jarmuth, Lachish and Eglon—gathered their armies, went to Gibeon, surrounded it and attacked it.

6The Gibeonites sent this message to Joshua in his camp at Gilgal: "Don't let us, your servants, be destroyed. Come quickly and help us! Save us! All the Amorite kings from the mountains have joined their armies and are fighting against us."

7So Joshua marched out of Gilgal with his whole army, including his best fighting men. 8The LORD said to Joshua, "Don't be afraid of those armies, because I will hand them over to you. None of them will be able to stand against you."

9Joshua and his army marched all night from Gilgal for a surprise attack. 10The LORD confused those armies when Israel attacked, so Israel defeated them in a great victory at Gibeon. They chased them along the road going up to Beth Horon and killed men all the way to Azekah and Makkedah. 11As they chased the enemy down the Beth Horon Pass to Azekah, the LORD threw large hailstones on them from the sky and killed them. More people were killed by the hailstones than by the Israelites' swords.

12On the day that the LORD gave up the Amorites to the Israelites, Joshua stood before all the people of Israel and said to the LORD:

"Sun, stand still over Gibeon.
Moon, stand still over the Valley of
Aijalon."
13So the sun stood still,
and the moon stopped
until the people defeated their enemies.

These words are written in the Book of Jashar.[d]

The sun stopped in the middle of the sky and waited to go down for a full day. 14That has never happened at any time before that day or since. That was the day the LORD listened to a human being. Truly the LORD was fighting for Israel!

15After this, Joshua and his army went back to the camp at Gilgal.

16During the fight the five kings ran away and hid in a cave near Makkedah, 17but someone found them hiding in the cave at Makkedah and told Joshua. 18So he said, "Cover the opening of the cave with large rocks. Put some men there to guard it, 19but don't stay there yourselves. Continue chasing the enemy and attacking them from behind. Don't let them get to their cities, because the LORD your God will hand them over to you."

20So Joshua and the Israelites killed the enemy, but a few were able to get back to their fortified cities. 21After the fighting, Joshua's men came back safely to him at Makkedah. No one was brave enough to say a word against the Israelites.

22Joshua said, "Move the rocks that are covering the opening of the cave and bring those five kings out to me." 23So Joshua's men brought the five kings out of the cave—the kings of Jerusalem, Hebron, Jarmuth, Lachish and Eglon. 24When they brought the five kings out to Joshua, he called for all his men. He said to the commanders of his army, "Come here! Put your feet on the necks of these kings." So they came close and put their feet on their necks.

25Joshua said to his men, "Be strong and brave! Don't be afraid, because I will show you what the LORD will do to the enemies you will fight in the future." 26Then Joshua killed the five kings and hung their bodies on five trees, where he left them until evening.

27At sunset Joshua told his men to take the bodies down from the trees. Then they threw them into the same cave where they had been

hiding and covered the opening of the cave with
large rocks, which are still there today.
28That day Joshua defeated Makkedah. He
killed the king and completely destroyed all the
people in that city as an offering to the LORD; no
one was left alive. He did the same thing to the
king of Makkedah that he had done to the king
of Jericho.

Defeating Southern Cities

29Joshua and all the Israelites travelled from
Makkedah to Libnah and attacked it. 30The LORD
handed over the city and its king. They killed
every person in the city; no one was left alive.
And they did the same thing to that king that they
had done to the king of Jericho.
31Then Joshua and all the Israelites left Libnah
and went to Lachish, which they surrounded and
attacked. 32The LORD handed over Lachish on the
second day. The Israelites killed everyone in that
city just as they had done to Libnah. 33During this
same time Horam king of Gezer came to help
Lachish, but Joshua also defeated him and his
army; no one was left alive.
34Then Joshua and all the Israelites went from
Lachish to Eglon. They surrounded Eglon, at-
tacked it and 35captured it the same day. They
killed all its people and completely destroyed
everything in it as an offering to the LORD, just as
they had done to Lachish.
36Then Joshua and the Israelites went from Eg-
lon to Hebron and attacked it, 37capturing it and
all the little towns near it. The Israelites killed
everyone in Hebron; no one was left alive there.
Just as they had done to Eglon, they completely
destroyed the city and all its people as an offering
to the LORD.
38Then Joshua and the Israelites went back to
Debir and attacked it. 39They captured that city,
its king and all the little towns near it, completely
destroying everyone in Debir as an offering to the
LORD; no one was left alive there. Israel did to
Debir and its king just as they had done to Libnah
and its king, just as they had done to Hebron.

GOD'S POWER

The Ability and the Authority

The cars on the roads today are much more powerful than they used to be. Advances in aerodynamics and turbocharging mean that the speed limits which were set forty years ago don't seem to make much sense any more. But drivers still cannot drive down the motorway at 100 mph unless they have a flashing blue light and a shiny badge that says "Police". You see, there are two kinds of power: ability and authority.

It works the other way round too. That same policeman might be patrolling the community on a mountain bike when he comes across an armed robbery in progress. He has the power (authority) to arrest the criminal but doesn't have the power (ability) in his legs to chase the getaway car on his bike.

Read **Joshua 10:5–14** with this in mind. Can you see how both kinds of power are at work?

The people of Israel who were being led by Joshua understood God by giving him various names. One of their favourites was "El-Shaddai", which means "All-Powerful God". They had seen loads of amazing things taking place, things that made it clear to them that with God, nothing is impossible.

- Who can call themselves God's chosen people now? (You'll find clues in John 15:16, Colossians 3:12 and 1 Peter 2:9.)
- And now, in what ways might God's power – the ability and the authority – be made available?

Consider . . .

- doing some more study into the different names of God and what they reveal about his character.
- in what everyday situations you might need ability and authority.

For more, see . . .

- John 17:1–3 (p.1128)
- Colossians 1:15–17 (p.1290)
- Acts 2:1–4 (p.1138)

40So Joshua defeated all the kings of the cities of these areas: the mountains, southern Canaan, the western hills and the slopes. The LORD, the God of Israel, had told Joshua to completely destroy all the people as an offering to the LORD, so he left no one alive in those places. 41Joshua captured all the cities from Kadesh Barnea to Gaza, and from Goshen to Gibeon. 42He captured all these cities and their kings on one trip, because the LORD, the God of Israel, was fighting for Israel.

43Then Joshua and all the Israelites returned to their camp at Gilgal.

Defeating Northern Kings

11 When Jabin king of Hazor heard about all that had happened, he sent messages to Jobab king of Madon, to the king of Shimron and to the king of Achshaph. 2He sent messages to the kings in the northern mountains and also to the kings in the Jordan Valley south of Lake Galilee and in the western hills. He sent a message to the king of Naphoth Dor in the west 3and to the kings of the Canaanites in the east and in the west. He sent messages to the Amorites, Hittites, Perizzites and Jebusites in the mountains. Jabin also sent one to the Hivites, who lived below Mount Hermon in the area of Mizpah. 4So the armies of all these kings came together with their horses and chariots. There were as many soldiers as grains of sand on the seashore.

5All of these kings met together at the waters of Merom, joined their armies together into one camp, and made plans to fight against the Israelites.

6Then the LORD said to Joshua, "Don't be afraid of them, because at this time tomorrow I will give them to you. You will cripple their horses and burn all their chariots."

7So Joshua and his whole army surprised the enemy by attacking them at the waters of Merom. 8The LORD handed them over to Israel. They chased them to Greater Sidon, Misrephoth Maim and the Valley of Mizpah in the east. Israel fought until none of the enemy was left alive. 9Joshua did what the LORD said to do: he crippled their horses and burned their chariots.

10Then Joshua went back and captured the city of Hazor and killed its king. (Hazor had been the leader of all the kingdoms that fought against Israel.) 11Israel killed everyone in Hazor, completely destroying them; no one was left alive. Then they burned Hazor itself.

12Joshua captured all of these cities, killed all of their kings, and completely destroyed everything in these cities. He did this just as Moses, the servant of the LORD, had commanded. 13But the Israelites did not burn any cities that were built on their hills, except Hazor; only that city was burned by Joshua. 14The people of Israel kept for themselves everything they found in the cities,

Sidelight Joshua's victory over Hazor was remarkable, considering that the city was huge for its day (Joshua 11:10). It had 40,000 residents, and its walls were about seventeen metres high – roughly four or five storeys. But despite the city's size and strength, it was never rebuilt after Israel destroyed it.

including all the animals. But they killed all the people there; they left no one alive. 15Long ago the LORD had commanded his servant Moses to

Sidelight Joshua 11:13 tells us "the Israelites did not burn any cities that were built on their mounds". These mounds formed after war had destroyed a city – the people never cleared away the rubble, simply rebuilding on top of it. Soon the cities looked as if they were built on mounds. As many as 5,000 of these hills (which archeologists call "tells") exist today.

do this, and then Moses had commanded Joshua to do it. Joshua did everything the LORD had commanded Moses.

16So Joshua defeated all the people in the land. He had control of the mountains and the area of southern Canaan, all the areas of Goshen, the western hills and the Jordan Valley. He controlled the mountains of Israel and all the hills near them. 17Joshua controlled all the land from Mount Halak near Edom to Baal Gad in the Valley of Lebanon, below Mount Hermon. Joshua also captured all the kings in the land and killed them. 18He fought against them for many years. 19The people of only one city in all the land had made a peace agreement with Israel—the Hivites living in Gibeon. All the other cities were defeated in war. 20The LORD made those people stubborn so they would fight against Israel and he could completely destroy them without mercy. This is what the LORD had commanded Moses to do.

21Now Joshua fought the Anakites[d] who lived in the mountains of Hebron, Debir, Anab, Judah and Israel, and he completely destroyed them and their towns. 22There were no Anakites left living in the land of the Israelites and only a few were left in Gaza, Gath and Ashdod. 23Joshua took control of all the land of Israel as the LORD had told Moses to do long ago. He gave the land to Israel, because he had promised it to them. Then Joshua divided the land among the tribes[d] of Israel, and there was peace in the land.

Kings Defeated by Israel

12 The Israelites took control of the land east of the Jordan River from the Arnon Ravine to Mount Hermon and all the land along the eastern side of the Jordan Valley. These lands belonged to the kings whom the Israelites defeated.

[2]Sihon king of the Amorites lived in the city of Heshbon and ruled the land from Aroer at the Arnon Ravine to the Jabbok River. His land started in the middle of the ravine, which was their border with the Ammonites. Sihon ruled over half the land of Gilead [3]and over the eastern side of the Jordan Valley from Lake Galilee to the Dead Sea.[d] And he ruled from Beth Jeshimoth south to the slopes of Pisgah.

[4]Og king of Bashan was one of the last of the Rephaites.[d] He ruled the land in Ashtaroth and Edrei. [5]He ruled over Mount Hermon, Salecah and all the area of Bashan up to where the people of Geshur and Maacah lived. Og also ruled half the land of Gilead up to the border of Sihon king of Heshbon.

[6]The LORD's servant Moses and the Israelites defeated all these kings, and Moses gave that land to the tribes[d] of Reuben and Gad and to East Manasseh as their own.

[7]Joshua and the Israelites also defeated kings in the land west of the Jordan River. He gave the people the land and divided it among the twelve tribes to be their own. It was between Baal Gad in the Valley of Lebanon and Mount Halak near Edom. [8]This included the mountains, the western hills, the Jordan Valley, the slopes, the desert and southern Canaan. This was the land where the Hittites, Amorites, Canaanites, Perizzites, Hivites and Jebusites had lived. The Israelites defeated the king of each of the following cities: [9]Jericho, Ai (near Bethel), [10]Jerusalem, Hebron, [11]Jarmuth, Lachish, [12]Eglon, Gezer, [13]Debir, Geder, [14]Hormah, Arad, [15]Libnah, Adullam, [16]Makkedah, Bethel, [17]Tappuah, Hepher, [18]Aphek, Lasharon, [19]Madon, Hazor, [20]Shimron Meron, Achshaph, [21]Taanach, Megiddo, [22]Kedesh, Jokneam in Carmel, [23]Dor (in Naphoth Dor), Goyim in Gilgal and [24]Tirzah.

The total number of kings was 31.

Land Still to be Taken

13 When Joshua was very old, the LORD said to him, "Joshua, you have grown old, but there is still much land for you to take. [2]This is what is left: the regions of Geshur and of the Philistines; [3]the area from the Shihor River at the border of Egypt to Ekron in the north, which belongs to the Canaanites; the five Philistine leaders at Gaza, Ashdod, Ashkelon, Gath and Ekron; the Avvites, [4]who live south of the Canaanite land; [5]the Gebalites, and the area of Lebanon east of Baal Gad below Mount Hermon to Lebo Hamath.

[6]"The Sidonians are living in the hill country from Lebanon to Misrephoth Maim, but I will force all of them out ahead of the Israelites. Be sure to remember this land when you divide the land among the Israelites, as I told you.

[7]"Now divide the land among the nine tribes[d] and West Manasseh."

Dividing the Land

[8]East Manasseh and the tribes of Reuben and Gad had received their land. The LORD's servant Moses had given them the land east of the Jordan River. [9]Their land started at Aroer at the Arnon Ravine and continued to the town in the middle of the ravine, and it included the whole plain from Medeba to Dibon. [10]All the towns ruled by Sihon king of the Amorites, who ruled in the city of Heshbon, were in that land. The land continued to the area where the Ammonites lived. [11]Gilead was also there, as well as the area where the people of Geshur and Maacah lived, and all of Mount Hermon and Bashan as far as Salecah. [12]All the kingdom of Og king of Bashan was in the land. Og was one of the last of the Rephaites, and in the past he had ruled in Ashtaroth and Edrei. Moses had defeated them and had taken their land. [13]Because the Israelites did not force out the people of Geshur and Maacah, they still live among the Israelites today.

[14]The tribe of Levi was the only one that did not get any land. Instead, they were given all the burned sacrifices made to the LORD, the God of Israel, as he had promised them.

[15]Moses had given each family group from the tribe of Reuben some land: [16]theirs was the land from Aroer near the Arnon Ravine to the town of Medeba, including the whole plain and the town in the middle of the ravine; [17]Heshbon and all the towns on the plain: Dibon, Bamoth Baal and Beth Baal Meon, [18]Jahaz, Kedemoth, Mephaath, [19]Kiriathaim, Sibmah, Zereth Shahar on the hill in the valley, [20]Beth Peor, the hills of Pisgah and Beth Jeshimoth. [21]So that land included all the towns on the plain and all the area that Sihon king of the Amorites had ruled from the town of Heshbon. Moses had defeated him along with the leaders of the Midianites, including Evi, Rekem, Zur, Hur and Reba. All these leaders fought together with Sihon and lived in that country. [22]The Israelites

killed many people during the fighting, including Balaam of Beor, who tried to use magic to tell the future. 23The land given to Reuben stopped at the shore of the Jordan River. So the land given to the family groups of Reuben included all these towns and their villages that were listed.

24This is the land Moses gave to the tribe of Gad, to all its family groups: 25the land of Jazar and all the towns of Gilead; half the land of the Ammonites that went as far as Aroer near Rabbah; 26the area from Heshbon to Ramath Mizpah and Betonim; the area from Mahanaim to the land of Debir; 27in the valley, Beth Haram, Beth Nimrah, Succoth and Zaphon with the other land that Sihon king of Heshbon had ruled east of the Jordan River and continuing to the end of Lake Galilee. 28All this land went to the family groups of Gad, including all these towns and their villages.

29This is the land Moses had given to East Manasseh. Half of all the family groups in the tribe of Manasseh were given this land: 30the land started at Mahanaim and included all of Bashan and the land ruled by Og king of Bashan; all the towns of Jair in Bashan, 60 cities in all; 31half of Gilead, Ashtaroth and Edrei, the cities where Og king of Bashan had ruled. All this went to the family of Makir son of Manasseh, and half of all his sons were given this land.

32Moses had given this land to these tribes on the plains of Moab across the Jordan River east of Jericho. 33But Moses had given no land to the tribe of Levi because the LORD, the God of Israel, promised that he himself would be the gift for the Levites.

14 Eleazar the priest, Joshua son of Nun, and the leaders of all the tribes of Israel decided what land to give to the people in the land of Canaan. 2The LORD had commanded Moses long ago how he wanted the people to choose their land. The people of the nine-and-a-half tribes threw lots [d] to decide which land they would receive. 3Moses had already given the two-and-a-half tribes their land east of the Jordan River. But the tribe of Levi was not given any land like the others. 4The sons of Joseph had divided into two tribes—Manasseh and Ephraim. The tribe of Levi was not given any land. It was given only some towns in which to live and pastures for its animals. 5The LORD had told Moses how to give the land to the tribes of Israel, and the Israelites divided the land.

Caleb's Land

6One day some men from the tribe [d] of Judah went to Joshua at Gilgal. Among them was Caleb son of Jephunneh the Kenizzite. He said to Joshua, "You remember what the LORD said at Kadesh Barnea when he was speaking to the prophet Moses about you and me. 7Moses, the LORD's servant, sent me to look at the land where we were going. I was 40 years old then. When I came back, I told Moses what I thought about the land. 8The other men who went with me frightened the people, but I fully believed the LORD would allow us to take the land. 9So that day Moses promised me, 'The land where you went will become your land, and your children will own it for ever. I will give you that land because you fully believed in the LORD, my God.'

10"Now then, the LORD has kept his promise. He has kept me alive for 45 years from the time he said this to Moses during the time we all wandered in the desert. Now here I am, 85 years old. 11I am still as strong today as I was the day Moses sent me out, and I am just as ready to fight now as I was then. 12So give me the mountain country the LORD promised me that day long ago. Back then you heard that the Anakite [d] people lived there and the cities were large and well protected. But now with the LORD helping me, I will force them out, just as the LORD said."

13Joshua blessed Caleb son of Jephunneh and gave him the city of Hebron as his own. 14Hebron still belongs to the family of Caleb son of Jephunneh the Kenizzite because he had faith and obeyed the LORD, the God of Israel. 15(In the past it was called Kiriath Arba, named after Arba, the greatest man among the Anakites.)

After this there was peace in the land.

Land for Judah

15 The land that was given to the tribe [d] of Judah was divided among all the family groups. It went all the way to the Desert of Zin in the far south, at the border of Edom.

2The southern border of Judah's land started at the south end of the Dead Sea [d] 3and went south of Scorpion Pass to Zin. From there it passed to the south of Kadesh Barnea and continued past Hezron to Addar. From Addar it turned and went to Karka. 4It continued to Azmon, the brook of Egypt, and then to the Mediterranean Sea. This was the southern border.

5The eastern border was the shore of the Dead Sea, as far as the mouth of the Jordan River.

The northern border started at the shore of the sea at the mouth of the Jordan River. 6Then it went to Beth Hoglah and continued north of Beth Arabah to the stone of Bohan son of Reuben. 7Then the northern border went through the Valley of Achor to Debir where it turned towards the north and went to Gilgal. Gilgal is across from the road that goes through Adummim Pass, on the south side of the ravine. The border continued to the waters of En Shemesh and stopped at En Rogel. 8Then it went through the Valley of Ben Hinnom, next to the southern side of the Jebusite city (which is called Jerusalem). There the border went to the top of the hill on the west side of Hinnom Valley, at the northern end of the Valley of Giants. 9From there it went to the spring of the waters of Nephtoah and then it went to the cities near Mount Ephron. There it turned and went towards Baalah, which is called Kiriath Jearim. 10At Baalah the border turned west and went towards Mount Seir. It continued along the north side of Mount Jearim (also called Kesalon) and came to Beth Shemesh. From there it went past Timnah 11to the hill north of Ekron. Then it turned towards Shikkeron and went past Mount Baalah and continued on to Jabneel, ending at the sea.

12The Mediterranean Sea was the western border. Inside these borders lived the family groups of Judah.

13The LORD had commanded Joshua to give Caleb son of Jephunneh part of the land in Judah, so he gave Caleb the town of Kiriath Arba, also called Hebron. (Arba was the father of Anak.[d]) 14Caleb forced out the three Anakite families living in Hebron: Sheshai, Ahiman and Talmai, the descendants[d] of Anak. 15Then he left there and went to fight against the people living in Debir. (In the past Debir had been called Kiriath Sepher.) 16Caleb said, "I will give Achsah, my daughter, as a wife to the man who attacks and captures the city of Kiriath Sepher." 17Othniel son of Kenaz, Caleb's brother, captured the city, so Caleb gave his daughter Achsah to Othniel to be his wife. 18When Achsah came to Othniel, she told him to ask her father for a field.

So Achsah went to her father. When she got down from her donkey, Caleb asked her, "What do you want?"

19Achsah answered, "Do me a special favour. Since you have given me land in southern Canaan, also give me springs of water." So Caleb gave her the upper and lower springs.

20The tribe of Judah got the land God had promised them. Each family group got part of the land.

21The tribe of Judah got all these towns in the southern part of Canaan near the border of Edom: Kabzeel, Eder, Jagur, 22Kinah, Dimonah, Adadah, 23Kedesh, Hazor, Ithnan, 24Ziph, Telem, Bealoth, 25Hazor Hadattah, Kerioth Hezron (also called Hazor), 26Amam, Shema, Moladah, 27Hazar Gaddah, Heshmon, Beth Pelet, 28Hazar Shual, Beersheba, Biziothiah, 29Baalah, Iim, Ezem, 30Eltolad, Kesil, Hormah, 31Ziklag, Madmannah, Sansannah, 32Lebaoth, Shilhim, Ain and Rimmon. There were 29 towns and their villages.

33The tribe of Judah got these towns in the western hills: Eshtaol, Zorah, Ashnah, 34Zanoah, En Gannim, Tappuah, Enam, 35Jarmuth, Adullam, Socoh, Azekah, 36Shaaraim, Acithaim and Gederah (also called Gederothaim). There were fourteen towns and their villages.

37Judah was also given these towns in the western hills: Zenan, Hadashah, Migdal Gad, 38Dilean, Mizpah, Joktheel, 39Lachish, Bozkath, Eglon, 40Cabbon, Lahmas, Kitlish, 41Gederoth, Beth Dagon, Naamah and Makkedah. There were sixteen towns and their villages.

42Judah was also given these towns in the western hills: Libnah, Ether, Ashan, 43Iphtah, Ashnah, Nezib, 44Keilah, Achzib and Mareshah. There were nine towns and their villages.

45The tribe of Judah was also given these towns: Ekron and all the small towns and villages near it; 46the area west of Ekron and all the villages and small towns near Ashdod; 47Ashdod and the small towns and villages around it; the villages and small towns around Gaza as far as the brook of Egypt and along the coast of the Mediterranean Sea.

48The tribe of Judah was also given these towns in the mountains: Shamir, Jattir, Socoh, 49Dannah, Kiriath Sannah (also called Debir), 50Anab, Eshtemoh, Anim, 51Goshen, Holon and Giloh. There were eleven towns and their villages.

52They were also given these towns in the mountains: Arab, Dumah, Eshan, 53Janim, Beth Tappuah, Aphekah, 54Humtah, Kiriath Arba (also called Hebron) and Zior. There were nine towns and their villages.

55Judah was also given these towns in the mountains: Maon, Carmel, Ziph, Juttah, 56Jezreel, Jokdeam, Zanoah, 57Kain, Gibeah and Timnah. There were ten towns and their villages.

58They were also given these towns in the mountains: Halhul, Beth Zur, Gedor, 59Maarath, Beth Anoth and Eltekon. There were six towns and their villages.

60The people of Judah were also given the two towns of Rabbah and Kiriath Baal (also called Kiriath Jearim) and their villages.

61Judah was given these towns in the desert: Beth Arabah, Middin, Secacah, 62Nibshan, the City of Salt and En Gedi. There were six towns and all their villages.

63The army of Judah was not able to force out the Jebusites living in Jerusalem, so the Jebusites still live among the people of Judah to this day.

Land for Ephraim and Manasseh

16 This is the land the tribe [d] of Joseph re-
ceived. It started at the Jordan River near
Jericho and continued to the waters of Jericho,
just east of the city. The border went up from
Jericho to the mountains of Bethel. [2]Then it con-
tinued from Bethel (also called Luz) to the Arkite
border at Ataroth. [3]From there it went west to
the border of the Japhletites and continued to the
area of the Lower Beth Horon. Then it went to
Gezer and ended at the sea.

[4]So Manasseh and Ephraim, sons of Joseph,
received their land.

[5]This is the land that was given to the family
groups of Ephraim: their border started at Ataroth
Addar in the east, went to Upper Beth Horon,
[6]and then to the sea. From Micmethath it turned
eastwards towards Taanath Shiloh and continued
eastwards to Janoah. [7]Then it went down from
Janoah to Ataroth and to Naarah. It continued
until it touched Jericho and stopped at the Jordan
River. [8]The border went from Tappuah west to
Kanah Ravine and ended at the sea. This is all the
land that was given to each family group in the
tribe of the Ephraimites. [9]Many of the towns
were actually within Manasseh's borders, but the
people of Ephraim got those towns and their vil-
lages. [10]The Ephraimites could not force the Ca-
naanites to leave Gezer, so the Canaanites still
live among the Ephraimites today, but they be-
came slaves of the Ephraimites.

17 Then land was given to the tribe of Ma-
nasseh, Joseph's first son. Manasseh's
first son was Makir, the father of Gilead. Makir
was a great soldier, so the lands of Gilead and
Bashan were given to his family. [2]Land was also
given to the other family groups of Manasseh—
Abiezer, Helek, Asriel, Shechem, Hepher and
Shemida. These were all the other sons of Manas-
seh son of Joseph.

[3]Zelophehad was the son of Hepher, who was
the son of Gilead, who was the son of Makir,
who was the son of Manasseh. Zelophehad had
no sons, but he had five daughters, named Mah-
lah, Noah, Hoglah, Milcah and Tirzah. [4]They
went to Eleazar the priest and to Joshua son of
Nun and all the leaders. They said, "The LORD
told Moses to give us land like the men re-
ceived." So Eleazar obeyed the LORD and gave the
daughters some land, just like the brothers of
their father. [5]So the tribe of Manasseh had ten
sections of land west of the Jordan River and two
more sections, Gilead and Bashan, on the east
side of the Jordan River. [6]The daughters of Ma-
nasseh received land just as the sons did. Gilead
was given to the rest of the families of Manasseh.

[7]The lands of Manasseh were in the area be-
tween Asher and Micmethath, near Shechem.
The border went south to the En Tappuah area,
[8]which belonged to Manasseh, except for the
town of Tappuah. It was along the border of
Manasseh's land and belonged to the sons of
Ephraim. [9]The border of Manasseh continued
south to Kanah Ravine. The cities in this area of
Manasseh belonged to Ephraim. Manasseh's bor-
der was on the north side of the ravine and went
to the sea. [10]The land to the south belonged to
Ephraim, and the land to the north belonged to
Manasseh. The Mediterranean Sea was the west-
ern border. The border touched Asher's land on
the north and Issachar's land on the east.

[11]In the areas of Issachar and Asher, the people
of Manasseh owned these towns: Beth Shan and
its small towns; Ibleam and its small towns; the
people who lived in Dor and its small towns; the
people in Naphoth Dor and its small towns;
the people who lived in Taanach and its small
towns; the people in Megiddo and its small
towns. [12]Manasseh was not able to defeat those
cities, so the Canaanites continued to live there.
[13]When the Israelites grew strong, they forced
the Canaanites to work for them, although they
did not force them to leave the land.

Sidelight When we think of nations, we think of united territory. But when the Israelites conquered Canaan, they really only conquered parts of it at first. So they divided the land among the twelve tribes before they really controlled it (Joshua 17:11–13). Later, individual tribes would conquer cities to unite their areas.

[14]The people from the tribes of Joseph said to
Joshua, "You gave us only one area of land, but
we are many people. Why did you give us only
one part of all the land the LORD gave his people?"

[15]And Joshua answered them, "If you have too
many people, go up to the forest and make a
place for yourselves to live there in the land of the
Perizzites and the Rephaites. [d] The mountain
country of Ephraim is too small for you."

[16]The people of Joseph said, "It is true. The
mountain country of Ephraim is not enough for
us, but the land where the Canaanites live is dan-
gerous. They are skilled fighters. They have pow-
erful weapons in Beth Shan and all the small
towns in that area, and they are also in the Valley
of Jezreel."

[17]Then Joshua said to the people of Joseph—to
Ephraim and Manasseh, "There are many of you,
and you have great power. You should be given
more than one share of land. [18]You also will have
the mountain country. It is a forest, but you can

cut down the trees and make it a good place to live. You will own all of it because you will force the Canaanites to leave the land even though they have powerful weapons and are strong."

The Rest of the Land Divided

18 All of the Israelites gathered together at Shiloh where they set up the Meeting Tent.[d] The land was now under their control. 2But there were still seven tribes[d] of Israel that had not yet received their land.

3So Joshua said to the Israelites: "Why do you wait so long to take your land? The LORD, the God of your ancestors, has given this land to you. 4Choose three men from each tribe, and I will send them out to study the land. They will describe in writing the land their tribe wants as its share, and then they will come back to me. 5They will divide the land into seven parts. The people of Judah will keep their land in the south, and the people of Joseph will keep their land in the north. 6You should describe the seven parts of land in writing and bring what you have written to me. Then I will throw lots[d] in the presence of the LORD our God. 7But the Levites do not get any part of these lands, because they are priests, and their work is to serve the LORD. Gad, Reuben and East Manasseh have received the land promised to them, which is east of the Jordan River. Moses, the servant of the LORD, gave it to them."

8So the men who were chosen to map the land started out. Joshua told them, "Go and study the land and describe it in writing. Then come back to me, and I will throw lots in the presence of the LORD here in Shiloh." 9So the men left and went into the land. They described in a scroll each town in the seven parts of the land. Then they came back to Joshua, who was still at the camp at Shiloh. 10There Joshua threw lots in the presence of the LORD to choose the lands that should be given to each tribe.

Land for Benjamin

11The first part of the land was given to the tribe[d] of Benjamin. Each family group received some land between the land of Judah and the land of Joseph. This is the land chosen for Benjamin: 12the northern border started at the Jordan River and went along the northern edge of Jericho, and then it went west into the mountains. That boundary continued until it was just east of Beth Aven. 13From there it went south to Luz (also called Bethel) and then down to Ataroth Addar, which is on the hill south of Lower Beth Horon.

14At the hill to the south of Beth Horon, the border turned and went south near the western side of the hill. It went to Kiriath Baal (also called Kiriath Jearim), a town where people of Judah lived. This was the western border.

15The southern border started near Kiriath Jearim and went west to the waters of Nephtoah. 16Then it went down to the bottom of the hill, which was near the Valley of Ben Hinnom, on the north side of the Valley of Rephaim. The border continued down the Hinnom Valley just south of the Jebusite city to En Rogel. 17There it turned north and went to En Shemesh. It continued to Geliloth near the Adummim Pass. Then it went down to the great Stone of Bohan son of Reuben. 18The border continued to the northern part of Beth Arabah and went down into the Jordan Valley. 19From there it went to the northern part of Beth Hoglah and ended at the north shore of the Dead Sea,[d] where the Jordan River flows into the sea. This was the southern border.

20The Jordan River was the border on the eastern side. So this was the land given to the family groups of Benjamin with the borders on all sides.

21The family groups of Benjamin received these cities: Jericho, Beth Hoglah, Emek Keziz, 22Beth Arabah, Zemaraim, Bethel, 23Avvim, Parah, Ophrah, 24Kephar Ammoni, Ophni and Geba. There were twelve towns and all their villages.

25The tribe of Benjamin also received Gibeon, Ramah, Beeroth, 26Mizpah, Kephirah, Mozah, 27Rekem, Irpeel, Taralah, 28Zelah, Haeleph, the Jebusite city (Jerusalem), Gibeah and Kiriath. There were fourteen towns and their villages. All these areas are the lands the family groups of Benjamin were given.

Land for Simeon

19 The second part of the land was given to the tribe[d] of Simeon. Each family group received some of the land inside the area of Judah. 2They received Beersheba (also called Sheba), Moladah, 3Hazar Shual, Balah, Ezem, 4Eltolad, Bethul, Hormah, 5Ziklag, Beth Marcaboth, Hazar Susah, 6Beth Lebaoth and Sharuhen. There were thirteen towns and their villages.

7They received the towns of Ain, Rimmon, Ether and Ashan, four towns and their villages. 8They also received all the very small areas with people living in them as far as Baalath Beer (this is the same as Ramah in southern Canaan). So these were the lands given to the family groups in the tribe of Simeon. 9The land of the Simeonites was taken from part of the land of Judah. Since Judah had much more land than they needed, the Simeonites received part of their land.

Land for Zebulun

10The third part of the land was given to the tribe[d] of Zebulun. Each family group of Zebulun received some of the land. The border of Zebulun

went as far as Sarid. [11]Then it went west to Mara-
lah and came near Dabbesheth and then near
Jokneam. [12]Then it turned to the east. It went
from Sarid to the area of Kisloth Tabor and on to
Daberath and to Japhia. [13]It continued eastwards
to Gath Hepher and Eth Kazin, ending at Rim-
mon. There the border turned and went towards
Neah. [14]At Neah it turned again and went to the
north to Hannathon and continued to the Valley
of Iphtah El. [15]Inside this border were the cities
of Kattath, Nahalal, Shimron, Idalah and Bethle-
hem. There were twelve towns and their villages.
[16]So these are the towns and the villages that
were given to the family groups of Zebulun.

Land for Issachar

[17]The fourth part of the land was given to the
tribe [d] of Issachar. Each family group of Issachar
received some of the land. [18]Their land included
Jezreel, Kesulloth, Shunem, [19]Hapharaim, Shion,
Anaharath, [20]Rabbith, Kishion, Ebez, [21]Remeth,
En Gannim, En Haddah and Beth Pazzez.
[22]The border of their land touched the area
called Tabor, Shahazumah and Beth Shemesh
and stopped at the Jordan River. There were six-
teen towns and their villages.
[23]These cities and towns were part of the land
that was given to the family groups of Issachar.

Land for Asher

[24]The fifth part of the land was given to the
tribe [d] of Asher. Each family group of Asher re-
ceived some of the land. [25]Their land included
Helkath, Hali, Beten, Achshaph, [26]Allammelech,
Amad and Mishal.
The western border touched Mount Carmel
and Shihor Libnath. [27]Then it turned east and
went to Beth Dagon, touching Zebulun and the
Valley of Iphtah El. Then it went north of Beth
Emek and Neiel and passed north to Cabul.
[28]From there it went to Abdon, Rehob, Hammon
and Kanah and continued to Greater Sidon.
[29]Then the border went back south towards Ra-
mah and continued to the fortified city of Tyre.
There it turned and went towards Hosah, ending
at the sea. This was in the area of Achzib, [30]Um-
mah, Aphek and Rehob. There were 22 towns
and their villages.
[31]These cities and their villages were part of
the land that was given to the family groups of
Asher.

Land for Naphtali

[32]The sixth part of the land was given to the
tribe [d] of Naphtali. Each family group of Naphtali
received some of the land. [33]The border of their
land started at the large tree in Zaanannim,
which is near Heleph. Then it went through Ad-
ami Nekeb and Jabneel, as far as Lakkum, and
ended at the Jordan River. [34]Then it went to the
west through Aznoth Tabor and stopped at Huk-
kok. It went to the area of Zebulun on the south,
Asher on the west, and Judah, at the Jordan
River, on the east. [35]The fortified cities inside
these borders were called Ziddim, Zer, Hammath,
Rakkath, Kinnereth, [36]Adamah, Ramah, Hazor,
[37]Kedesh, Edrei, En Hazor, [38]Iron, Migdal El,
Horem, Beth Anath and Beth Shemesh. There
were nineteen towns and all their villages.
[39]The towns and the villages around them
were in the land that was given to the family
groups of Naphtali.

Land for Dan

[40]The seventh part of the land was given to the
tribe [d] of Dan. Each family group of Dan received
some of the land. [41]Their land included Zorah,
Eshtaol, Ir Shemesh, [42]Shaalabbin, Aijalon, Ithlah,
[43]Elon, Timnah, Ekron, [44]Eltekeh, Gibbethon,
Baalath, [45]Jehud, Bene Berak, Gath Rimmon,
[46]Me Jarkon, Rakkon and the area near Joppa.
[47](But the Danites had trouble taking their
land. They went and fought against Leshem, de-
feated it, and killed the people who lived there.
So the Danites moved into the town of Leshem
and changed its name to Dan, because he was the
father of their tribe.) [48]All of these towns and
villages were given to the family groups of Dan.

Land for Joshua

[49]After the leaders finished dividing the land
and giving it to the different tribes, [d] the Israelites
gave Joshua son of Nun his land also. [50]They gave
Joshua the town he asked for, Timnath Serah in
the mountains of Ephraim, just as the LORD com-
manded. He built up the town and lived there.
[51]So these lands were given to the different
tribes of Israel. Eleazar the priest, Joshua son of
Nun and the leaders of each tribe divided up the
land by lots at Shiloh. They met in the presence
of the LORD at the entrance to the Meeting Tent. [d]
Now they had finished dividing the land.

Cities of Safety

20 Then the LORD said to Joshua: [2]"Tell the
Israelites to choose the special cities of
safety, [n] as I had Moses command you to do. [3]If
a person kills someone accidentally and without
meaning to kill him, that person may go to a city
of safety [n] to hide. There the killer will be safe
from the relative who has the duty of punishing
a murderer.

cities of safety A person who had accidentally killed someone could go to one of the six cities of safety to receive protection and a fair trial.

4“When the killer runs to one of those cities,
he must stop at the entrance gate, stand there,
and tell the elders of the people what happened.
Then that person will be allowed to enter the city
and will be given a place to live among them.
5But if the one who is chasing him follows him to
that city, the leaders of the city must not hand
over the killer. It was an accident. He did not
hate him beforehand or kill him on purpose. 6The
killer must stay in the city until a court comes to
a decision and until the high priest dies. Then he
may go back home to the town from which he
ran away.”

7So the Israelites chose these cities to be cities
of safety: Kedesh in Galilee in the mountains of
Naphtali; Shechem in the mountains of Ephraim;
Kiriath Arba (also called Hebron) in the moun-
tains of Judah; 8Bezer on the east side of the Jor-
dan River near Jericho in the desert in the land of
Reuben; Ramoth in Gilead in the land of Gad;
and Golan in Bashan in the land of Manasseh.
9Any Israelite or anyone living among them who
killed someone accidentally was to be allowed to
run to one of these cities of safety. There he
would not be killed, before he was judged, by
the relative who had the duty of punishing a
murderer.

Towns for the Levites

21 The heads of the Levite families went to
talk to Eleazar the priest, to Joshua son of
Nun and to the heads of the families of all the
tribes[d] of Israel. 2At Shiloh in the land of Canaan,
the heads of the Levite families said to them,
“The LORD commanded Moses that you give us
towns where we may live and pastures for our
animals.” 3So the Israelites obeyed this command
of the LORD and gave the Levite people these
towns and pastures for their own land: 4the
Kohath family groups were part of the tribe of
Levi. Some of the Levites in the Kohath family
groups were from the family of Aaron the priest.
To these Levites were given thirteen towns in
the areas of Judah, Simeon and Benjamin. 5The
other family groups of Kohath were given ten
towns in the areas of Ephraim, Dan and West
Manasseh.

6The people from the Gershon family groups
were given thirteen towns in the land of Issachar,
Asher, Naphtali and East Manasseh in Bashan.

7The family groups of Merari were given
twelve towns in the areas of Reuben, Gad and
Zebulun.

8So the Israelites gave the Levites these towns
and the pastures around them, just as the LORD
had commanded Moses.

9These are the names of the towns that came
from the lands of Judah and Simeon. 10The first
choice of towns was given to the Kohath family
groups of the Levites. 11They gave them Kiriath
Arba, also called Hebron, and all its pastures in
the mountains of Judah. (Arba was the father of
Anak.[d]) 12But the fields and the villages around
Kiriath Arba had been given to Caleb son of
Jephunneh.

13So they gave the city of Hebron to the des-
cendants[d] of Aaron (Hebron was a city of
safety[n]). They also gave them the towns of Lib-
nah, 14Jattir, Eshtemoa, 15Holon, Debir, 16Ain,
Juttah and Beth Shemesh, and all the pastures
around them. Nine towns were given from these
two tribes.

17They also gave the people of Aaron these cit-
ies that belonged to the tribe of Benjamin: Gib-
eon, Geba, 18Anathoth and Almon. They gave
them these four towns and the pastures around
them.

19So these thirteen towns with their pastures
were given to the priests, who were from the
family of Aaron.

20The other Kohathite family groups of the Le-
vites were given these towns from the tribe of
Ephraim: 21Shechem in the mountains of
Ephraim (which was a city of safety), Gezer,
22Kibzaim and Beth Horon. There were four
towns and their pastures.

23The tribe of Dan gave them Eltekeh, Gibbe-
thon, 24Aijalon and Gath Rimmon. There were
four towns and their pastures.

25West Manasseh gave them Taanach and Gath
Rimmon and the pastures around these two towns.

26So these ten towns and the pastures around
them were given to the rest of the Kohathite fam-
ily groups.

27The Gershonite family groups of the Levite
tribe were given these towns: East Manasseh
gave them Golan in Bashan, which was a city of
safety, and Be Eshtarah, and the pastures around
these two towns.

28The tribe of Issachar gave them Kishion, Dab-
erath, 29Jarmuth and En Gannim, and the pas-
tures around these four towns.

30The tribe of Asher gave them Mishal, Abdon,
31Helkath and Rehob, and the pastures around
these four towns.

32The tribe of Naphtali gave them Kedesh in
Galilee (a city of safety[n]), Hammoth Dor and Kar-
tan, and the pastures around these three towns.

33So the Gershonite family groups received
thirteen towns and the pastures around them.

34The Merarite family groups (the rest of the
Levites) were given these towns: the tribe of

cities of safety A person who had accidentally killed someone could go to one of the six cities of safety to receive protection and a fair trial.

Zebulun gave them Jokneam, Kartah, [35]Dimnah and Nahalal, and the pastures around these four towns.

[36]The tribe of Reuben gave them Bezer, Jahaz, [37]Kedemoth and Mephaath, along with the pastures around these four towns.

[38]The tribe of Gad gave them Ramoth in Gilead (a city of safety[n]), Mahanaim, [39]Heshbon and Jazer, and the pastures around these four towns.

[40]So the total number of towns given to the Merarite family groups was twelve.

[41]A total of 48 towns with their pastures in the land of Israel were given to the Levites. [42]Each town had pastures around it.

[43]So the LORD gave the people all the land he had promised their ancestors. The people took the land and lived there. [44]The LORD gave them peace on all sides, as he had promised their ancestors. None of their enemies defeated them; the LORD handed all their enemies over to them. [45]He kept every promise he had made to the Israelites; each one came true.

Three Tribes Go Home

22 Then Joshua called a meeting of all the people from the tribes[d] of Reuben, Gad and East Manasseh. [2]He said to them, "You have done everything Moses, the LORD's servant, told you to do. You have also obeyed all my commands. [3]For a long time you have supported the other Israelites. You have been careful to obey the commands the LORD your God gave you. [4]The LORD your God promised to give the Israelites peace, and he has kept his promise. Now you may go back to your homes, to the land that Moses, the LORD's servant, gave you, on the east side of the Jordan River. [5]But be careful to obey the teachings and laws Moses, the LORD's servant, gave you: to love the LORD your God and obey his commands, to continue to follow him and serve him the very best you can."

[6]Then Joshua said goodbye to them, and they left and went away to their homes. [7]Moses had given the land of Bashan to East Manasseh. Joshua gave land on the west side of the Jordan River to West Manasseh. And he sent them to their homes and he blessed them. [8]He said, "Go back to your homes and your riches. You have many animals, silver, gold, bronze and iron, and many beautiful clothes. Also, you have taken many things from your enemies that you should divide among yourselves."

[9]So the people from the tribes of Reuben, Gad and East Manasseh left the other Israelites at Shiloh in Canaan and went back to Gilead. It was their own land, given to them by Moses as the LORD had commanded.

[10]The people of Reuben, Gad and East Manasseh went to Geliloth, near the Jordan River in the land of Canaan. There they built a beautiful altar. [11]The other Israelites still at Shiloh heard about the altar these three tribes built at the border of Canaan at Geliloth, near the Jordan River on Israel's side. [12]All the Israelites became very angry at these three tribes, so they met together and decided to fight them.

[13]The Israelites sent Phinehas son of Eleazar the priest to Gilead to talk to the people of Reuben, Gad and East Manasseh. [14]They also sent one leader from each of the ten tribes at Shiloh. Each of them was a leader of his family group of Israelites.

[15]These leaders went to Gilead to talk to the people of Reuben, Gad and East Manasseh. They said: [16]"All the Israelites ask you: "Why did you turn against the God of Israel by building an altar for yourselves? You know that this is against God's law. [17]Remember what happened at Peor? We still suffer today because of that sin, for which God made many Israelites very sick. [18]And now are you turning against the LORD and refusing to follow him?

" 'If you don't stop what you're doing today, the LORD will be angry with everyone in Israel tomorrow. [19]If your land is unclean,[d] come over into our land where the LORD's Tent is. Share it with us. But don't turn against the LORD and us by building another altar for the LORD our God. [20]Remember how Achan son of Zerah refused to obey the command about what must be completely destroyed. That one man broke God's law, but all the Israelites were punished. Achan died because of his sin, but others also died.' "

[21]The people from Reuben, Gad and East Manasseh answered, [22]"The LORD is God of gods! The LORD is God of gods! God knows, and we want you to know also. If we have done something wrong, you may kill us. [23]If we broke God's law, we ask the LORD himself to punish us. We did not build this altar to offer burnt offerings or grain and fellowship offerings.

[24]"We did not build it for that reason. We feared that some day your people would not accept us as part of your nation. Then they might say, 'You cannot worship the LORD, the God of Israel. [25]The LORD made the Jordan River a border between us and you people of Reuben and Gad. You cannot worship the LORD.' So we feared that your children might make our children stop worshipping the LORD.

cities of safety A person who had accidentally killed someone could go to one of the six cities of safety to receive protection and a fair trial.

26"That is why we decided to build this altar.
But it is not for burnt offerings and sacrifices.
27This altar is proof to you and us and to all our
children who will come after us that we worship
the LORD with our whole burnt offerings, grain
and fellowship offerings. This was so your
children would not say to our children, "You are
not the LORD's.'
28"In the future if your children say that, our
children can say, 'See the altar made by our
ancestors. It is exactly like the LORD's altar, but
we do not use it for sacrifices. It shows that we
are part of Israel.'
29"Truly, we don't want to be against the LORD
or to stop following him by building an altar for
burnt offerings, grain offerings or sacrifices. We
know the only true altar to the LORD our God is
in front of the Holy Tent."[d]
30When Phinehas the priest and the ten
leaders heard the people of Reuben, Gad and
East Manasseh, they were pleased. 31So Phine-
has, son of Eleazar the priest, said, "Now we
know the LORD is with us and that you didn't
turn against him. Now the Israelites will not be
punished by the LORD."

Sidelight Today we may worship God wherever we want. But that hasn't always been the case. In Joshua's time, Israel only presented its sacrifices at the Tabernacle. When three tribes built an altar by the Jordan River, the other tribes thought they might make sacrifices to a pagan God. They almost went to war, but talked through their differences instead (Joshua 22:9–34).

32Then Phinehas and the leaders left the peo-
ple of Reuben and Gad in Gilead and went back
to Canaan where they told the Israelites what
had happened. 33They were pleased and thanked
God. So they decided not to fight the people of
Reuben and Gad and destroy those lands.
34And the people of Reuben and Gad named
the altar Proof that We Believe the LORD Is
God.

The Last Words of Joshua

23 The LORD gave Israel peace from their en-
emies around them. Many years passed,
and Joshua grew very old. 2He called a meeting of
all the elders, heads of families, judges and offi-
cers of Israel. He said, "I am now very old. 3You
have seen what the LORD has done to our enemies
to help us. The LORD your God fought for you.
4Remember that your people have been given
their land between the Jordan River and the
Mediterranean Sea in the west, the land I prom-
ised to give you. 5The LORD your God will force
out the people living there. The LORD will push
them out ahead of you. And you will own the
land, as he has promised you.
6"Be strong. You must be careful to obey
everything commanded in the Book of the
Teachings of Moses. Do exactly as it says. 7Don't
become friends with the people living among us
who are not Israelites. Don't say the names of
their gods or make anyone swear by them. Don't
serve or worship them. 8You must continue to
follow the LORD your God, as you have done in
the past.
9"The LORD has forced many great and power-
ful nations to leave ahead of you. No nation has
been able to defeat you. 10With his help, one
Israelite could defeat 1,000, because the LORD
your God fights for you, as he promised to do.
11So you must be careful to love the LORD your
God.
12"If you turn away from the way of the LORD
and become friends with these people who are
not part of Israel and marry them, 13the LORD your
God will not help you defeat your enemies. They
will be like traps for you, like whips on your back
and thorns in your eyes, and none of you will be
left in this good land the LORD your God has
given you.
14"It's almost time for me to die. You know
and fully believe that the LORD has done great
things for you. You know that he has not failed to
keep any of his promises. 15Every good promise
that the LORD your God made has come true, and
in the same way, his other promises will come
true. He promised that evil will come to you and
that he will destroy you from this good land that
he gave you. 16This will happen if you don't keep
your agreement with the LORD your God. If you
go and serve other gods and worship them, the
LORD will become very angry with you. Then
none of you will be left in this good land he has
given you."

24 Joshua gathered all the tribes[d] of Israel
together at Shechem. He called the el-
ders, heads of families, judges and officers of Is-
rael to stand before God.
2Then Joshua said to all the people, "Here's
what the LORD, the God of Israel, says to you: "A
long time ago your ancestors lived on the other
side of the Euphrates River. Terah, the father
of Abraham and Nahor, worshipped other gods.
3But I, the LORD, took your ancestor Abraham
from the other side of the river and led him
through the land of Canaan. And I gave him many
children, including his son Isaac. 4I gave Isaac two

sons named Jacob and Esau. I gave the land around the mountains of Edom to Esau, but Jacob and his sons went down to Egypt. 5Then I sent Moses and Aaron to Egypt, where I brought many disasters on the Egyptians. Afterwards I brought you out. 6When I brought your ancestors out of Egypt, they came to the Red Sea,[d] and the Egyptians chased them with chariots and men on horses. 7So the people called out to the LORD. And I brought darkness between you and the Egyptians and created the sea to cover them. You yourselves saw what I did to the army of Egypt. After that, you lived in the desert for a long time.

8" 'Then I brought you to the land of the Amorites, east of the Jordan River. They fought against you, but I handed them over to you. I destroyed them before you, and you took control of that land. 9But the king of Moab, Balak son of Zippor, prepared to fight against the Israelites. The king sent for Balaam son of Beor to curse you, 10but I refused to listen to Balaam. So he asked for good things to happen to you! I saved you and brought you out of his power.

11" 'Then you crossed the Jordan River and came to Jericho, where the people of Jericho fought against you. Also, the Amorites, Perizzites, Canaanites, Hittites, Girgashites, Hivites and Jebusites fought against you. But I handed them over to you. 12I sent terror ahead of you to force out two Amorite kings. You took the land without using swords and bows. 13I gave you that land where you did not have to work. I gave you cities that you did not have to build. And now you live in that land and in those cities, and you eat from vineyards and olive trees that you did not plant.' "

14Then Joshua said to the people, "Now respect the LORD and serve him fully and sincerely. Throw away the gods that your ancestors worshipped on the other side of the Euphrates River and in Egypt. Serve the LORD. 15But if you don't want to serve the LORD, you must choose for yourselves today whom you will serve. You may serve the gods that your ancestors worshipped when they lived on the other side of the Euphrates River, or you may serve the gods of the Amorites who lived in this land. As for me and my family, we will serve the LORD."

16Then the people answered, "We will never stop following the LORD to serve other gods! 17It was the LORD our God who brought our ancestors out of Egypt. We were slaves in that land, but the LORD did great things for us there. He brought us out and protected us while we travelled through other lands. 18Then he forced out all the people living in these lands, even the Amorites. So we will serve the LORD, because he is our God."

19Then Joshua said, "You are not able to serve the LORD, because he is a holy God and a jealous God. If you turn against him and sin, he will not forgive you. 20If you leave the LORD and serve other gods, he will send you great trouble. The LORD may have been good to you, but if you turn against him, he will destroy you."

21But the people said to Joshua, "No! We will serve the LORD."

22Then Joshua said, "You are your own witnesses that you have chosen to serve the LORD."

The people said, "Yes, we are."

23Then Joshua said, "Now throw away the gods that you have. Love the LORD, the God of Israel, with all your heart."

24Then the people said to Joshua, "We will serve the LORD our God, and we will obey him."

25On that day at Shechem, Joshua made an agreement for the people. He made rules and laws for them to follow. 26Joshua wrote these things in the Book of the Teachings of God. Then he took a large stone and set it up under the oak tree near the LORD's Holy Tent.[d]

27Joshua said to all the people, "See this stone! It will remind you of what we did today. It was here the LORD spoke to us today. It will remind you of what happened so you will not turn against your God."

Joshua Dies

28Then Joshua sent the people back to their land.

29After that, Joshua son of Nun died at the age of 110. 30They buried him in his own land at Timnath Serah, in the mountains of Ephraim, north of Mount Gaash.

> **Sidelight**
>
> When Joseph's bones were buried (Joshua 24:32), the people didn't dig a grave as we do today. Rather, the bones were probably placed in a family cave or a tomb cut from rock, large enough for several family members.

31The Israelites served the LORD during the lifetime of Joshua and during the lifetimes of the elders who lived after Joshua who had seen what the LORD had done for Israel.

Joseph Comes Home

32When the Israelites left Egypt, they carried the bones of Joseph with them. They buried them at Shechem, in the land Jacob had bought for 100 pieces of silver from the sons of Hamor (Hamor was the father of Shechem). This land now belonged to Joseph's children.

33 And Eleazar son of Aaron died and was bur-
ied at Gibeah in the mountains of Ephraim,
which had been given to Eleazar's son Phinehas.

Judges

When?

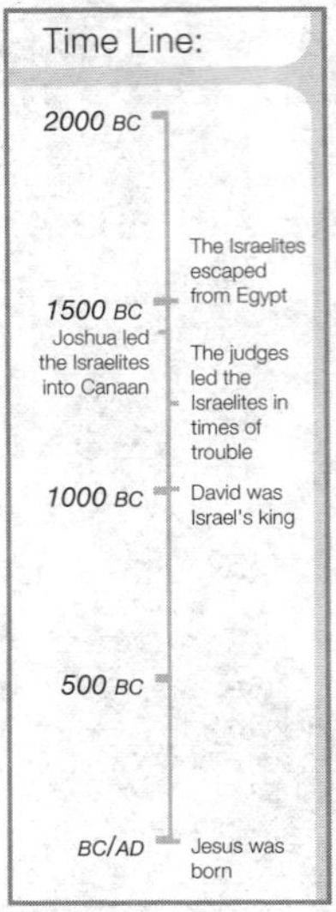

Why Read This Book:

- See how God does not want his people to follow the crowd (Judges 1—2).
- Discover how sin can capture people, but how God can set them free if they ask for forgiveness (Judges 3—16).
- Understand how people can become corrupt when they don't follow God (Judges 17—21).

Behind the Scenes:

Working in a fast food restaurant can be a disaster if the work isn't organised. Fries aren't ready when the burgers are done. The whipped ice cream runs empty. Customers receive the wrong orders. During the dinner-hour rush, lettuce can fly, mayonnaise can spill, and tempers flare as each person tries frantically to catch up.

The chaos of an unorganised fast food restaurant is similar to the chaos in Israel during the book of Judges. The last verse of the book summarises what it was like: "In those days Israel did not have a king. Everyone did what seemed right" (Judges 21:25).

Under the leadership of Joshua (see the book of Joshua, p.201), the Israelites had conquered major Canaanite cities and divided the land among the twelve Israelite tribes. But many Canaanites and other people still remained. They didn't believe in God, but worshipped idols and pagan gods.

These other people threatened the Israelites in two ways. First, they wanted the land back that the Israelites had taken away. So the Israelites had constantly to defend themselves. ▷

Where?

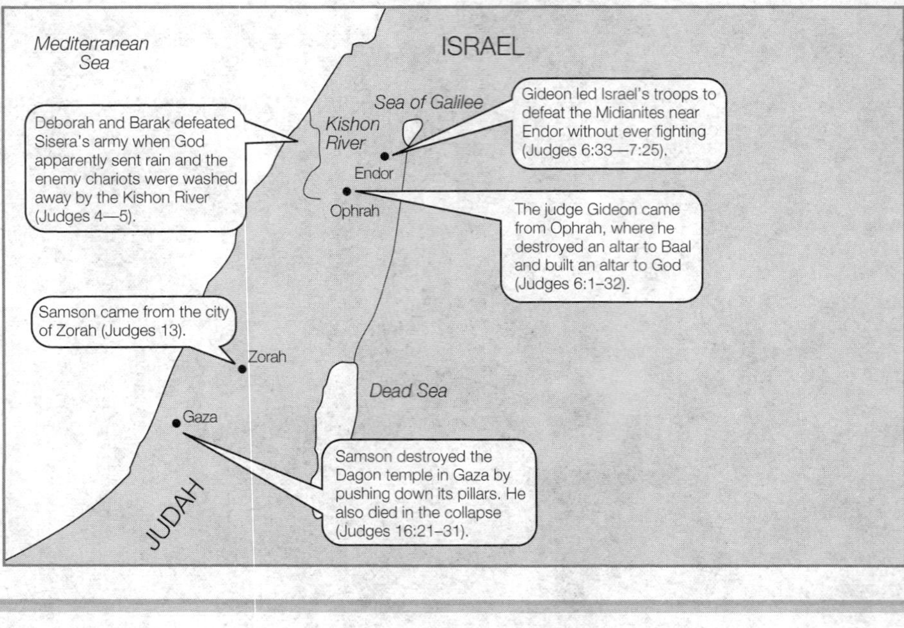

Behind the Scenes (cont.):

Second, the Israelites married Canaanites, which God had said not to do; then they accepted the Canaanites' religious practices, forgetting God.

Like workers in fast food restaurants, the Israelites needed leaders to organise them and keep them on track. So in times of crisis, God chose different judges to bring the twelve tribes together to fight their enemies. These judges – such as Deborah, Samson and Gideon – became national heroes for the Israelites.

Judges illustrates a common theme in the Old Testament. When a judge or leader was faithful to God, the people remained loyal to God and prospered. But when the judge died, the people sinned and were conquered. Then in their suffering, they confessed their sin and God called a new judge to deliver them.

Judges reminds us of the importance of always following God – and the dangers of ignoring God. At the same time, it shows that God is always willing to forgive us when we come back to him.

Judah Fights the Canaanites

1 After Joshua died, the Israelites asked the
LORD, "Who will be first to go and fight for
us against the Canaanites?"
2The LORD said to them, "The tribe [d] of Judah
will go. I have handed the land over to them."
3The men of Judah said to the men of Simeon,
their relatives, "Come and help us fight the Ca-
naanites for our land. If you do, we will go and
help you fight for your land." So the men of Sim-
eon went with them.
4When Judah attacked, the LORD handed over
the Canaanites and the Perizzites to them, and
they defeated 10,000 men at the city of Bezek.
5There they found Adoni-Bezek, the ruler of the
city, and fought him. The men of Judah defeated
the Canaanites and the Perizzites, 6but Adoni-
Bezek ran away. The men of Judah chased him,
and when they caught him, they cut off his
thumbs and big toes.
7Adoni-Bezek said, "Seventy kings whose
thumbs and big toes had been cut off used to eat
scraps that fell from my table. Now God has paid
me back for what I did to them." The men of
Judah took Adoni-Bezek to Jerusalem, and he
died there.
8Then the men of Judah fought against Jeru-
salem and captured it. They attacked with their
swords and burned the city.
9Later, they went down to fight the Canaanites
who lived in the mountains, in the dry country to
the south and in the western hills. 10The men of
Judah went to fight against the Canaanites in the
city of Hebron (which used to be called Kiriath
Arba). And they defeated Sheshai, Ahiman and
Talmai.

Caleb and His Daughter

11Then they left there and went to fight against
the people living in Debir. (In the past Debir had
been called Kiriath Sepher.) 12Before attacking
the city, Caleb said, "I will give Achsah, my
daughter, as a wife to the man who attacks and
captures the city of Kiriath Sepher." 13Othniel son
of Kenaz, Caleb's younger brother, captured the
city, so Caleb gave his daughter Achsah to Oth-
niel to be his wife. 14When Achsah came to Oth-
niel, she told him to ask her father for a field.
When she got down from her donkey, Caleb
asked her, "What do you want?"
15Achsah answered him, "Do me a special fa-
vour. Since you have given me land in southern
Canaan, also give me springs of water." So Caleb
gave her the upper and lower springs.

Fights with the Canaanites

16The Kenite people, who were from the family
of Moses' father-in-law, left Jericho, the city of
palm trees. They went with the men of Judah to
the Desert of Judah to live with them there in
southern Judah near the city of Arad.
17The men of Judah and the men of Simeon,
their relatives, defeated the Canaanites who lived
in Zephath. They completely destroyed the city,
so they called it Hormah. [n] 18The men of Judah

Hormah Hormah sounds like the Hebrew word meaning "to destroy completely".

captured Gaza, Ashkelon, Ekron and the lands
around them.
[19]The LORD was with the men of Judah. They
took the land in the mountains, but they could
not force out the people living on the plain, be-
cause they had iron chariots. [20]As Moses had
promised, Hebron was given to Caleb, and Caleb
forced out the three sons of Anak.[d] [21]But the
people of Benjamin could not make the Jebusite
people leave Jerusalem. Since that time the Jebus-
ites have lived with the people of Benjamin in
Jerusalem.
[22]The men of Joseph went to fight against the
city of Bethel, and the LORD was with them.
[23]They sent some spies to Bethel (which used to
be called Luz). [24]The spies saw a man coming out
of the city and said to him, "Show us a way into
the city, and we will be kind to you." [25]So the
man showed them the way into the city. The
men of Joseph attacked with swords the people in
Bethel, but they let the man and his family go
free. [26]He went to the land where the Hittites
lived and built a city. He named it Luz, which it
is called even today.
[27]There were Canaanites living in the cities of
Beth Shan, Taanach, Dor, Ibleam, Megiddo and
the small towns around them. The people of Ma-
nasseh did not force those people out of their
towns, because the Canaanites were determined
to stay there. [28]Later, the Israelites grew strong
and forced the Canaanites to work as slaves, but
they did not make all the Canaanites leave their
land. [29]The people of Ephraim did not force out
all of the Canaanites living in Gezer. So the Ca-
naanites continued to live in Gezer with the peo-
ple of Ephraim. [30]The people of Zebulun did not
force out the Canaanites living in the cities of
Kitron and Nahalol. They stayed and lived with
the people of Zebulun, but Zebulun made them
work as slaves.
[31]The people of Asher did not force the Ca-
naanites from the cities of Acco, Sidon, Ahlab,
Achzib, Helbah, Aphek and Rehob. [32]Since the
people of Asher did not force them out, the Ca-
naanites continued to live with them. [33]The peo-
ple of Naphtali did not force out the people of the
cities of Beth Shemesh and Beth Anath. So they
continued to live with the Canaanites in those
cities, and the Canaanites worked as slaves. [34]The
Amorites forced the Danites back into the moun-
tains and would not let them come down to live
in the plain. [35]The Amorites were determined to
stay in Mount Heres, Aijalon and Shaalbim. But
when the Israelites grew stronger, they made the
Amorites work as slaves. [36]The land of the Amo-
rites was from Scorpion Pass to Sela and beyond.

The Angel of the LORD at Bokim

2 The angel of the LORD went up from Gilgal
to Bokim[n] and said, "I brought you up from
Egypt and led you to the land I promised to give
your ancestors. I said, 'I will never break my
agreement with you. [2]But you must not make an
agreement with the people who live in this land.
You must destroy their altars.' But you did not
obey me. How could you do this? [3]Now I tell
you, 'I will not force out the people in this land.
They will be your enemies, and their gods will be
a trap for you.' "
[4]After the angel gave Israel this message from
the LORD, they cried loudly. [5]So they named the
place Bokim. There they offered sacrifices to the
LORD.

Joshua Dies

[6]Then Joshua sent the people back to their
land. [7]The people served the LORD during the life-
time of Joshua and during the lifetimes of the
elders who lived after Joshua and who had seen
what great things the LORD had done for Israel.
[8]Joshua son of Nun, the servant of the LORD, died
at the age of 110. [9]They buried him in his own
land at Timnath Serah in the mountains of
Ephraim, north of Mount Gaash.

The People Disobey

[10]After those people had died, their children
grew up and did not know the LORD or what he
had done for Israel. [11]So they did what the LORD
said was wrong, and they worshipped the Baal[d]
idols. [12]They stopped following the LORD, the God
of their ancestors who had brought them out of
Egypt. They began to worship the gods of the
people who lived around them, and that made
the LORD angry. [13]The Israelites stopped following
the LORD and worshipped Baal and Ashtoreth.[d]
[14]The LORD was angry with the people of Israel, so
he handed them over to robbers who took their
possessions. He let their enemies who lived
around them defeat them; they could not protect

Sidelight The Israelites sinned when they worshipped Baal (Judges 2:11), not only because Baal was a false god, but also because of the religion's worship practices. Archaeologists have found that the Canaanites practised infant sacrifice and prostitution in their temples. Baal worship included sexual elements intended to make the gods bring rain and fertility.

Bokim This name means "crying".

themselves. 15When the Israelites went out to fight, they always lost, because the LORD was not with them. The LORD had sworn to them this would happen. So the Israelites suffered very much.

Sidelight Judges in the Old Testament wouldn't fit in well with today's court systems. Instead of studying for years, they were leaders in battle and heroes for the people (Judges 2:16). It made sense when there was no official way of choosing judges.

God Chooses Judges

16Then the LORD chose leaders called judges,[n] who saved the Israelites from the robbers. 17But the Israelites did not listen to their judges. They were not faithful to God but worshipped other gods instead. Their ancestors had obeyed the LORD's commands, but they quickly turned away and did not obey. 18When their enemies hurt them, the Israelites cried for help. So the LORD felt sorry for them and sent judges to save them from their enemies. The LORD was with those judges all their lives. 19But when the judges died, the Israelites again sinned and worshipped other gods. They became worse than their ancestors. The Israelites were very stubborn and refused to change their evil ways.

20So the LORD became angry with the Israelites. He said, "These people have broken the agreement I made with their ancestors. They have not listened to me. 21I will no longer defeat the nations who were left when Joshua died. 22I will use them to test Israel, to see if Israel will keep the LORD's commands as their ancestors did." 23In the past the LORD had permitted those nations to stay in the land. He did not quickly force them out or help Joshua's army defeat them.

3 These are the nations the LORD did not force to leave. He wanted to test the Israelites who had not fought in the wars of Canaan. 2(The only reason the LORD left those nations in the land was to teach the descendants[d] of the Israelites who had not fought in those wars how to fight.) 3These are the nations: the five rulers of the Philistines, all the Canaanites, the people of Sidon and the Hivites who lived in the Lebanon mountains from Mount Baal Hermon to Lebo Hamath. 4Those nations were in the land to test the Israelites—to see if they would obey the commands the LORD had given to their ancestors by Moses.

5The people of Israel lived with the Canaanites, Hittites, Amorites, Perizzites, Hivites and Jebusites. 6The Israelites began to marry the daughters of those people, and they allowed their daughters to marry the sons of those people. Israel also served their gods.

Othniel, the First Judge

7The Israelites did what the LORD said was wrong. They forgot about the LORD their God and served the idols of Baal[d] and Asherah.[d] 8So the LORD was angry with Israel and allowed Cushan-Rishathaim king of North West Mesopotamia to rule over the Israelites for eight years. 9When Israel cried to the LORD, the LORD sent someone to save them. Othniel son of Kenaz, Caleb's younger brother, saved the Israelites. 10The Spirit[d] of the LORD entered Othniel, and he became Israel's judge. When he went to war, the LORD handed over to him Cushan-Rishathaim, king of North West Mesopotamia. 11So the land was at peace for 40 years. Then Othniel son of Kenaz died.

Ehud, the Judge

12Again the people of Israel did what the LORD said was wrong. So the LORD gave Eglon king of Moab power to defeat Israel because of the evil Israel did. 13Eglon got the Ammonites and the Amalekites to join him. Then he attacked Israel and took Jericho, the city of palm trees. 14So the people of Israel were ruled by Eglon king of Moab for eighteen years.

15When the people cried to the LORD, he sent someone to save them. He was Ehud, son of Gera from the people of Benjamin, who was left-handed. Israel sent Ehud to give Eglon king of Moab the payment he demanded. 16Ehud made himself a sword with two edges, about half a metre long, and he tied it to his right hip under his clothes. 17Ehud gave Eglon king of Moab the payment he demanded. Now Eglon was a very fat man. 18After he had given Eglon the payment, Ehud sent away the people who had carried it. 19When he passed the statues near Gilgal, he turned around and said to Eglon, "I have a secret message for you, King Eglon."

The king said, "Be quiet!" Then he sent all of his servants out of the room. 20Ehud went to King Eglon, as he was sitting alone in the room above his summer palace.

Ehud said, "I have a message from God for you." As the king stood up from his chair, 21Ehud reached with his left hand and took out the sword that was tied to his right hip. Then he stabbed the sword deep into the king's belly! 22Even the handle sank in, and the blade came out of his back. The king's fat covered the whole sword, so Ehud left the sword in Eglon. 23Then

Judges They were not judges in courts of law, but leaders of the people in times of emergency.

he went out of the room and closed and locked
the doors behind him.
24When the servants returned just after Ehud
left, they found the doors to the room locked.
So they thought the king was relieving himself.
25They waited for a long time. Finally they
became worried because he still had not opened
the doors. So they got the key and unlocked
them and saw their king lying dead on the floor!
26While the servants were waiting, Ehud had
escaped. He passed by the statues and went to
Seirah. 27When he reached the mountains of
Ephraim he blew the trumpet. The people of Is-
rael heard it and went down from the hills with
Ehud leading them.
28He said to them, "Follow me! The LORD has
helped you to defeat your enemies, the Moab-
ites." So Israel followed Ehud and captured the
crossings of the Jordan River. They did not allow
the Moabites to cross the Jordan River. 29Israel
killed about 10,000 strong and able men from
Moab; not one escaped. 30So that day Moab was
forced to be under the rule of Israel, and there
was peace in the land for 80 years.

Shamgar, the Judge

31After Ehud, Shamgar son of Anath saved Is-
rael. Shamgar killed 600 Philistines with a sharp
stick used to guide oxen.

Deborah, the Woman Judge

4 After Ehud died, the Israelites again did
what the LORD said was wrong. 2So he let
Jabin, a king of Canaan who ruled in the city of
Hazor, defeat Israel. Sisera, who lived in Haro-
sheth Haggoyim, was the commander of Jabin's
army. 3Because he had 900 iron chariots and was
very cruel to the people of Israel for 20 years,
they cried to the LORD for help.
4A prophetess[d] named Deborah, the wife of
Lappidoth, was judge of Israel at that time. 5Deb-
orah would sit under the Palm Tree of Deborah,
which was between the cities of Ramah and
Bethel, in the mountains of Ephraim. And the
people of Israel would come to her to settle their
arguments.
6Deborah sent a message to Barak son of Abin-
oam. Barak lived in the city of Kedesh, which is in
the area of Naphtali. Deborah said to Barak, "The

LEADERSHIP

Pass the Paintbrush

Leonardo da Vinci was one of the greatest artists who has ever lived. Almost six hundred years ago he came up with designs for a flying machine and other inventions, as well as his famous painting and sculpture.

One day a student walked into da Vinci's studio to find the master working on a huge canvas. He had chosen the subject and begun work. Then, suddenly, he stopped and asked the student to finish the painting.

The student protested, saying he could never do justice to the great painter's work. He felt he was unworthy to complete such an important job.

Da Vinci cut him off. "Will not what I have done inspire you to do your best?" he asked.

In the same way that da Vinci hoped to encourage his student, Deborah wanted to motivate Barak and the Israelites in battle. Read how she challenged Barak in **Judges 4:4–16**.

- How was da Vinci's challenge similar to Deborah's challenge to Barak?
- How can you use God's power to help you inspire others the way Deborah inspired Barak?

Consider . . .

- asking someone you admire for help to deal with a challenge you're facing.
- sending a thank-you note to someone – a parent, a friend, someone at church – who has inspired you in your faith in recent months.

For more, see . . .

- Judges 5:1–31 (p.229)
- Hebrews 12:1–3 (p.1343)
- 1 Corinthians 1:10–17 (p.1215)

LORD, the God of Israel, commands you: 'Go and
gather 10,000 men of Naphtali and Zebulun
and lead them to Mount Tabor. 7 I will make
Sisera, the commander of Jabin's army, and his
chariots, and his army meet you at the Kishon
River. I will hand Sisera over to you.' "
8 Then Barak said to Deborah, "I will go if you
will go with me, but if you won't go with me, I
won't go."
9 "Of course I will go with you," Deborah
answered, "but you will not get credit for the
victory. The LORD will let a woman defeat Sisera."
So Deborah went with Barak to Kedesh. 10 At
Kedesh, Barak called the people of Zebulun and
Naphtali together. From them, he gathered
10,000 men to follow him, and Deborah went
with him also.
11 Now Heber the Kenite had left the other
Kenites, the descendants[d] of Hobab, Moses'
brother-in-law. Heber had put up his tent by the
great tree in Zaanannim, near Kedesh.
12 When Sisera was told that Barak son of
Abinoam had gone to Mount Tabor, 13 Sisera
gathered his 900 iron chariots and all the men
with him, from Harosheth Haggoyim to the
Kishon River.
14 Then Deborah said to Barak, "Get up!
Today is the day the LORD will hand over Sisera.
The LORD has already cleared the way for you."
So Barak led 10,000 men down Mount Tabor.
15 As Barak approached, the LORD confused
Sisera and his army and chariots. The LORD de-
feated them with the sword, but Sisera left his
chariot and ran away on foot. 16 Barak and his
men chased Sisera's chariots and army to
Harosheth Haggoyim. With their swords they
killed all of Sisera's men; not one of them was
left alive.
17 But Sisera himself ran away to the tent where
Jael lived. She was the wife of Heber, one of the
Kenite family groups. Heber's family was at peace
with Jabin king of Hazor. 18 Jael went out to meet
Sisera and said to him, "Come into my tent, mas-
ter! Come in. Don't be afraid." So Sisera went
into Jael's tent, and she covered him with a rug.
19 Sisera said to Jael, "I am thirsty. Please give
me some water to drink." So she opened a leather
bag of milk and gave him a drink. Then she
covered him up.
20 He said to her, "Go and stand at the entrance
to the tent. If anyone comes and asks you, 'Is
anyone here?' say, 'No.' "
21 But Jael, the wife of Heber, took a tent peg
and a hammer and quietly went to Sisera. Since
he was very tired, he was in a deep sleep. She
hammered the tent peg through the side of
Sisera's head and into the ground. And so Sisera
died.
22 At that very moment Barak came by Jael's
tent, chasing Sisera. Jael went out to meet him
and said, "Come. I will show you the man you are
looking for." So Barak entered her tent, and there
Sisera lay dead, with the tent peg in his head.
23 On that day God defeated Jabin king of
Canaan in the sight of Israel.
24 Israel became stronger and stronger against
Jabin king of Canaan until finally they des-
troyed him.

The Song of Deborah

5 On that day Deborah and Barak son of
Abinoam sang this song:

2 "The leaders led Israel.
The people volunteered to go to battle.
Praise the LORD!
3 Listen, kings.
Pay attention, rulers!
I myself will sing to the LORD.
I will make music to the LORD, the God of
Israel.

4 "LORD, when you came from Edom,
when you marched from the land of Edom,
the earth shook,
the skies rained,
and the clouds dropped water.
5 The mountains shook before the LORD, the
God of Mount Sinai,
before the LORD, the God of Israel!

6 "In the days of Shamgar son of Anath,
in the days of Jael, the main roads were
empty.
Travellers went on the back roads.
7 There were no warriors in Israel
until I, Deborah, arose,
until I arose to be a mother to Israel.
8 At that time they chose to follow new gods.
Because of this, enemies fought us at our
city gates.
No one could find a shield or a spear
among the 40,000 people of Israel.
9 My heart is with the commanders of Israel.
They volunteered freely from among the
people.
Praise the LORD!

Sidelight

When Jael gave Sisera milk to drink, it probably wasn't ice-cold (Judges 4:19). Because of the hot climate, people often curdled milk to preserve it. The nutritious result (known as kefir) is similar to yogurt. Unfortunately, you couldn't get it with strawberries and bananas mixed in.

10"You who ride on white donkeys
and sit on saddle blankets,
and you who walk along the road, listen!
11Listen to the sound of the singers
at the watering holes.
There they tell about the victories of the LORD,
the victories of the LORD's warriors in Israel.
Then the LORD's people went down to the
city gates.

12"Wake up, wake up, Deborah!
Wake up, wake up, sing a song!
Get up, Barak!
Go and capture your enemies, son of
Abinoam!
13"Then those who were left came down to the
important leaders.
The LORD's people came down to me with
strong men.
14They came from Ephraim in the mountains of
Amalek.
Benjamin was among the people who
followed you.
From the family group of Makir, the
commanders came down.
And from Zebulun came those who lead.
15The princes of Issachar were with Deborah.
The people of Issachar were loyal to Barak
and followed him into the valley.
The Reubenites thought hard
about what they would do.
16Why did you stay by the sheepfold?
Was it to hear the music played for your
sheep?
The Reubenites thought hard
about what they would do.
17The people of Gilead stayed east of the
Jordan River.
People of Dan, why did you stay by the
ships?
The people of Asher stayed at the seashore,
at their safe harbours.

MUSIC

Which Came First?

"I have this great tune running round in my head, but I'm just hopeless at lyrics," said James sadly to his music teacher.

"That's because you're concentrating on the music all the time," Mr Bradley replied.

"But the music's so much easier, listen to this . . . " James played some chords on his guitar. He started to sing "Yeah, yeah, I know it. Yeah yeah."

"But what are you trying to say?" asked his teacher.

"What do you mean?" James was puzzled.

"Well, if you want to write a song, first you must know what you want to sing about. Is it a love song? Is it a sad song? Is it about personal feelings?" he asked.

"First you have to write down how you feel. Then put those words into a form of a poem and then say them out loud until you can hear a melody or a rhythm."

James grinned. "You're a good teacher you know. That sounds like an excellent idea!"

Many songs have wonderful melodies and hopeless words.

Judges 5:2–5 talks of making music.

- How do the words of the song in Judges compare with the word James was singing?
- When was the last time you felt inspired to worship God with a song?

Consider . . .

- writing out a favourite Bible passage in your own words. Find a musical friend to help you compose some music for it.
- praying for your church musicians, thanking God for the talent he has given them.

For more, see . . .

- Exodus 15:1–8 (p.73)
- Revelation 15:3–4 (p.1399)
- Psalm 33:1–3 (p.519)

18But the people of Zebulun risked their lives,
as did the people of Naphtali on the
battlefield.

19"The kings came, and they fought.
At that time the kings of Canaan fought
at Taanach, by the waters of Megiddo.
But they took away no silver or possessions
of Israel.
20The stars fought from heaven;
from their paths, they fought Sisera.
21The Kishon River swept Sisera's men away,
that old river, the Kishon River.
March on, my soul, with strength!
22Then the horses' hoofs beat the ground.
Galloping, galloping go Sisera's mighty
horses.
23'May the town of Meroz be cursed,' said the
angel of the LORD.
'Bitterly curse its people,
because they did not come to help the LORD.
They did not fight the strong enemy.'
24"May Jael, the wife of Heber the Kenite,
be blessed above all women who live in
tents.
25Sisera asked for water,
but Jael gave him milk.
In a bowl fit for a ruler,
she brought him cream.
26Jael reached out and took the tent peg.
Her right hand reached for the workman's
hammer.
She hit Sisera! She smashed his head!
She crushed and pierced the side of
his head!
27At Jael's feet he sank.
He fell, and he lay there.
At her feet he sank. He fell.
Where Sisera sank, there he fell, dead!

28"Sisera's mother looked out through the window.
She looked through the curtains and cried
out,
'Why is Sisera's chariot so late in coming?
Why are sounds of his chariots' horses
delayed?'
29The wisest of her servant ladies answer her,
and Sisera's mother says to herself,
30'Surely they are robbing the people they
defeated!
Surely they are dividing those things among
themselves!
Each soldier is given a girl or two.
Maybe Sisera is taking pieces of dyed cloth.
Maybe they are even taking
pieces of dyed, embroidered cloth for the
necks of the victors!'

31"Let all your enemies die this way, LORD!
But let all the people who love you
be as strong as the rising sun!"

Then there was peace in the land for 40 years.

The Midianites Attack Israel

6 Again the Israelites did what the LORD said
was wrong. So for seven years the LORD
handed them over to Midian. 2Because the
Midianites were very powerful and were cruel to
Israel, the Israelites made hiding places in the
mountains, in caves and in safe places. 3Whenever the Israelites planted crops, the Midianites,
Amalekites and other peoples from the east
would come and attack them. 4They camped in
the land and destroyed the crops that the
Israelites had planted as far away as Gaza. They
left nothing for Israel to eat, and no sheep, cattle
or donkeys. 5The Midianites came with their
tents and their animals like swarms of locusts [d]
to ruin the land. There were so many people and
camels they could not be counted. 6Israel became very poor because of the Midianites, so
they cried out to the LORD.

7When the Israelites cried out to the LORD
against the Midianites, 8the LORD sent a prophet [d]
to them. He said, "This is what the LORD, the God
of Israel, says: I brought you out of Egypt, the
land of slavery. 9I saved you from the Egyptians
and from all those who were against you. I forced
the Canaanites out of their land and gave it to
you. 10Then I said to you, 'I am the LORD your
God. Live in the land of the Amorites, but do not
worship their gods.' But you did not obey me."

The Angel of the LORD Visits Gideon

11The angel of the LORD came and sat down
under the oak tree at Ophrah that belonged to
Joash, one of the Abiezrite people. Gideon,
Joash's son, was separating some wheat from the
chaff [d] in a winepress [d] to keep the wheat from the
Midianites. 12The angel of the LORD appeared to
Gideon and said, "The LORD is with you, mighty
warrior!"

13Then Gideon said, "Sir, if the LORD is with
us, why are we having so much trouble? Where
are the miracles [d] our ancestors told us he did
when the LORD brought them out of Egypt? But
now he has left us and has handed us over to the
Midianites."

14The LORD turned to Gideon and said, "Go
with your strength and save Israel from the Midianites. I am the one who is sending you."

15But Gideon answered, "Lord, how can I save
Israel? My family group is the weakest in Manasseh, and I am the least important member of my
family."

16The LORD answered him, "I will be with you. It will seem as if the Midianites you are fighting are only one man."

17Then Gideon said to the LORD, "If you are pleased with me, give me proof that it is really you talking with me. 18Please wait here until I come back to you. Let me bring my offering and set it in front of you."

And the LORD said, "I will wait until you return."

19So Gideon went in and cooked a young goat, and with 10 kilogrammes of flour, made bread without yeast. Then he put the meat into a basket and the broth into a pot. He brought them out and gave them to the angel under the oak tree.

20The angel of God said to Gideon, "Put the meat and the bread without yeast on that rock over there. Then pour the broth on them." And Gideon did as he was told. 21The angel of the LORD touched the meat and the bread with the end of the stick that was in his hand. Then fire jumped up from the rock and completely burned up the meat and the bread! And the angel of the LORD disappeared! 22Then Gideon understood he had been talking to the angel of the LORD. So Gideon cried out, "Lord GOD! I have seen the angel of the LORD face to face!"

23But the LORD said to Gideon, "Calm down! Don't be afraid! You will not die!"

24So Gideon built an altar there to worship the LORD and named it The LORD Is Peace. It still stands at Ophrah, where the Abiezrites live.

Gideon Tears Down the Altar of Baal

25That same night the LORD said to Gideon, "Take the bull that belongs to your father and a second bull seven years old. Pull down your father's altar to Baal,[d] and cut down the Asherah[d] idol beside it. 26Then build an altar to the LORD your God with its stones in the right order on this high ground. Kill and burn a second bull on this altar, using the wood from the Asherah idol."

27So Gideon got ten of his servants and did what the LORD had told him to do. But Gideon was afraid that his family and the men of the city might see him, so he did it at night, not in the daytime.

28When the men of the city got up the next morning, they saw that the altar for Baal had been destroyed and that the Asherah idol beside it had been cut down! They also saw the altar Gideon had built and the second bull that had been sacrificed on it. 29The men of the city asked each other, "Who did this?"

After they asked many questions, someone told them, "Gideon son of Joash did this."

30So they said to Joash, "Bring your son out. He has pulled down the altar of Baal and cut down the Asherah idol beside it. He must die!"

31But Joash said to the angry crowd around him, "Are you going to take Baal's side? Are you going to defend him? Anyone who takes Baal's side will be killed by morning! If Baal is a god, let him fight for himself. It's his altar that has been pulled down." 32So on that day Gideon got the name Jerub-Baal, which means "let Baal fight against him," because Gideon pulled down Baal's altar.

Gideon Defeats Midian

33All the Midianites, the Amalekites and other peoples from the east joined together and came across the Jordan River and camped in the Valley of Jezreel. 34But the Spirit[d] of the LORD entered Gideon, and he blew a trumpet to call the Abiezrites to follow him. 35He sent messengers to all of Manasseh, calling them to follow him. He also sent messengers to the people of Asher, Zebulun and Naphtali. So they also went up to meet Gideon and his men.

36Then Gideon said to God, "You said you would help me save Israel. 37I will put some wool on the threshing[d] floor. If there is dew only on the wool but all of the ground is dry, then I will know that you will use me to save Israel, as you said." 38And that is just what happened. When Gideon got up early the next morning and squeezed the wool, he got a full bowl of water from it.

39Then Gideon said to God, "Don't be angry with me if I ask just one more thing. Please let me make one more test. Let only the wool be dry while the ground around it gets wet with dew." 40That night God did that very thing. Just the wool was dry, but the ground around it was wet with dew.

7 Early in the morning Jerub-Baal (also called Gideon) and all his men set up their camp at the spring of Harod. The Midianites were camped north of them in the valley at the bottom of the hill called Moreh. 2Then the LORD said to Gideon, "You have too many men to defeat the Midianites. I don't want the Israelites to boast that they saved themselves. 3So now, announce to the people, 'Anyone who is afraid may leave Mount Gilead and go back home.'" So 22,000 men returned home, but 10,000 remained.

4Then the LORD said to Gideon, "There are still too many men. Take the men down to the water, and I will test them for you there. If I say, 'This man will go with you,' he will go. But if I say, 'That one will not go with you,' he will not go."

5So Gideon led the men down to the water.
There the LORD said to him, "Separate them into
those who drink water by lapping it up like a dog
and those who bend down to drink." 6There
were 300 men who used their hands to bring
water to their mouths, lapping it as a dog does.
All the rest got down on their knees to drink.
7Then the LORD said to Gideon, "Using the 300
men who lapped the water, I will save you and
hand Midian over to you. Let all the others go
home." 8So Gideon sent the rest of Israel to their
homes. But he kept the 300 men and took the
jars and the trumpets of those who left.
Now the camp of Midian was in the valley
below Gideon. 9That night the LORD said to Gid-
eon, "Get up. Go down and attack the camp of
the Midianites, because I will give them to you.
10But if you are afraid to go down, take your servant
Purah with you. 11When you come to the camp
of Midian, you will hear what they are saying.
Then you will not be afraid to attack the camp."

Gideon is Encouraged

So Gideon and his servant Purah went down to
the edge of the enemy camp. 12The Midianites,
the Amalekites and all the peoples from the east
were camped in that valley. There were so many
of them they seemed like locusts. [d] Their camels
could not be counted because they were as many
as the grains of sand on the seashore!
13When Gideon came to the enemy camp, he
heard a man telling his friend about a dream. He
was saying, "I dreamed that a loaf of barley bread
rolled into the camp of Midian. It hit the tent so
hard that the tent turned over and fell flat!"
14The man's friend said, "Your dream is about
the sword of Gideon son of Joash, a man of Israel.
God will hand Midian and the whole army over
to him!"
15When Gideon heard about the dream and
what it meant, he worshipped God. Then Gideon
went back to the camp of Israel and called out to
them, "Get up! The LORD has handed the army

DOUBT

Doubting David

The big story of the 2002 football World Cup was David Beckham's metatarsal injury. Just one month before the biggest tournament in world football, England's golden boy and captain slid into a tackle and . . . snap . . . he'd broken a tiny bone in his foot. Things looked decidedly dodgy as to his participation.

To every football fan's delight, David made an amazingly swift recovery. The medical team duly announced he was fit to play and the good wishes of a nation were behind him.

It was pretty obvious, however, as the tournament progressed, that David himself was a little more doubtful about his recovery. Rather than his usual gutsy commitment, he was jumping out of tackles seemingly to protect his foot. One such missed challenge led to Brazil scoring a winner against England in the quarter finals.

In some ways, this is not unlike the story of Gideon in **Judges 6:33–40**. Gideon had all the promises – not from the England medical team but from the Lord himself – that he was a mighty man of valour and that he was going to defeat the Midianites. Yet he still wasn't convinced and doubted the Lord, looking for more signs from his fleeces on the ground.

- How did the doubt Gideon felt affect his behaviour?
- Was Gideon right to test God? Why did God not mind?

Consider . . .

- when it is and when it is not a good idea to test the Lord over his direction for our lives.
- whether there have ever been times when you have wanted to test God before trusting him. If so, what happened?

For more, see . . .

- Genesis 18:1–15 (p.20)
- John 20:24–29 (p.1134)
- Matthew 14 22–33 (p.966)

of Midian over to you!" 16Gideon divided the 300 men into three groups. He gave each man a trumpet and an empty jar with a burning torch inside.

17Gideon told the men, "Watch me and do what I do. When I get to the edge of the camp, do what I do. 18Surround the enemy camp. When I and everyone with me blow our trumpets, you blow your trumpets too. Then shout, 'For the LORD and for Gideon!' "

Midian is Defeated

19So Gideon and the 100 men with him came to the edge of the enemy camp just after they had changed guards. It was during the middle watch of the night. Then Gideon and his men blew their trumpets and smashed their jars. 20All three groups of Gideon's men blew their trumpets and smashed their jars. They held the torches in their left hands and the trumpets in their right hands. Then they shouted, "A sword for the LORD and for Gideon!" 21Each of Gideon's men stayed in his place around the camp, but the Midianites began shouting and running to escape.

22When Gideon's 300 men blew their trumpets, the LORD made all the Midianites fight each other with their swords! The enemy army ran away to the city of Beth Shittah towards Zererah. They ran as far as the border of Abel Meholah, near the city of Tabbath. 23Then men of Israel from Naphtali, Asher and all of Manasseh were called out to chase the Midianites. 24Gideon sent messengers through all the mountains of Ephraim, saying, "Come down and attack the Midianites. Take control of the Jordan River as far as Beth Barah before the Midianites can get to it."

So they called out all the men of Ephraim, who took control of the Jordan River as far as Beth Barah. 25The men of Ephraim captured two princes of Midian named Oreb and Zeeb. They killed Oreb at the rock of Oreb and Zeeb at the winepress[d] of Zeeb, and they continued chasing the Midianites. They brought the heads of Oreb and Zeeb to Gideon, who was east of the Jordan River.

8 The men of Ephraim asked Gideon, "Why did you treat us this way? Why didn't you call us when you went to fight against Midian?" They argued angrily with Gideon.

2But he answered them, "I have not done as well as you! The small part you did was better than all that my people of Abiezer did. 3God let you capture Oreb and Zeeb, the princes of Midian. How can I compare what I did with what you did?" When the men of Ephraim heard Gideon's answer, they were not as angry any more.

Gideon Captures Two Kings

4When Gideon and his 300 men came to the Jordan River, they were tired, but they chased the enemy across to the other side. 5Gideon said to the men of Succoth, "Please give my soldiers some bread because they are very tired. I am chasing Zebah and Zalmunna, the kings of Midian."

6But the leaders of Succoth said, "Why should we give your soldiers bread? You haven't caught Zebah and Zalmunna yet."

7Then Gideon said, "The LORD will surrender Zebah and Zalmunna to me. After that, I will whip your skin with thorns and briers from the desert."

8Gideon left Succoth and went to the city of Peniel and asked them for food. But the people of Peniel gave him the same answer as the people of Succoth. 9So Gideon said to the men of Peniel, "After I win the victory, I will return and pull down this tower."

10Zebah and Zalmunna and their army were in the city of Karkor. About 15,000 men were left of the armies of the peoples of the east. Already 120,000 soldiers had been killed. 11Gideon went up the road of those who live in tents east of Nobah and Jogbehah, and he attacked the enemy army when they did not expect it. 12Zebah and Zalmunna, the kings of Midian, ran away, but Gideon chased and captured them and frightened away their army.

13Then Gideon son of Joash returned from the battle by the Pass of Heres. 14Gideon captured a young man from Succoth and asked him some questions. So the young man wrote down for Gideon the names of 77 officers and elders of Succoth.

Gideon Punishes Succoth

15When Gideon came to Succoth, he said to the people of that city, "Here are Zebah and Zalmunna. You made fun of me by saying, 'Why should we give bread to your tired men? You have not caught Zebah and Zalmunna yet.' " 16So Gideon took the elders of the city and punished them with thorns and briers from the desert. 17He also pulled down the tower of Peniel and killed the people in that city.

18Gideon asked Zebah and Zalmunna, "What were the men like that you killed on Mount Tabor?"

They answered, "They were like you. Each one of them looked like a prince."

19Gideon said, "Those were my brothers, my mother's sons. As surely as the LORD lives, I would not kill you if you had spared them." 20Then Gideon said to Jether, his oldest son, "Kill them." But Jether was only a boy and was afraid, so he did not take out his sword.

21Then Zebah and Zalmunna said to Gideon, "Come on. Kill us yourself. As the saying goes, 'It takes a man to do a man's job.'" So Gideon got up and killed Zebah and Zalmunna and took the decorations off their camels' necks.

Gideon Makes an Idol

22The people of Israel said to Gideon, "You saved us from the Midianites. Now, we want you and your son and your grandson to rule over us."

23But Gideon told them, "The LORD will be your ruler. I will not rule over you, nor will my son rule over you." 24He said, "I want you to do this one thing for me. I want each of you to give me a gold earring from the things you took in the fighting." (The Ishmaelites [n] wore gold earrings.)

25They said, "We will gladly give you what you want." So they spread out a coat, and everyone threw down an earring from what he had taken. 26The gold earrings weighed about 20 kilogrammes. This did not include the decorations, necklaces and purple robes worn by the kings of Midian, nor the chains from the camels' necks. 27Gideon used the gold to make a holy robe, which he put in his home town of Ophrah. But all the Israelites were unfaithful to God and worshipped it, so it became a trap for Gideon and his family.

> **Sidelight** People today wear earrings for decoration, but that has not always been the only reason. Three thousand years ago, people also wore earrings because they thought that they had magical power – which may be one reason why the Israelites took away the Ishmaelites' earrings in battle (Judges 8:23–27).

The Death of Gideon

28So Midian was under the rule of Israel; they did not cause trouble any more. And the land had peace for 40 years, as long as Gideon was alive.

29Gideon [n] son of Joash went to his home to live. 30He had 70 sons of his own, because he had many wives. 31He had a slave woman [d] who lived in Shechem, and he had a son by her, whom he named Abimelech. 32So Gideon son of Joash died at a good old age. He was buried in the tomb of Joash, his father, in Ophrah, where the Abiezrites live.

33As soon as Gideon died, the people of Israel were again unfaithful to God and followed the Baals. [d] They made Baal-of-the-Agreement their god. 34The Israelites did not remember the LORD their God, who had saved them from all their enemies living all around them. 35And they were not kind to the family of Jerub-Baal, also called Gideon, for all the good he had done for Israel.

Abimelech Becomes King

9 Abimelech son of Gideon [n] went to his uncles in the city of Shechem. He said to his uncles and all of his mother's family group, 2"Ask the leaders of Shechem, 'Is it better for the 70 sons of Gideon to rule over you or for one man to rule?' Remember, I am your relative."

3Abimelech's uncles spoke to all the leaders of Shechem about this. And they decided to follow Abimelech, because they said, "He is our relative." 4So the leaders of Shechem gave Abimelech about 70 pieces of silver from the temple of the god Baal-of-the-Agreement. Abimelech used the silver to hire some worthless, reckless men, who followed him wherever he went. 5He went to Ophrah, the home town of his father, and murdered his 70 brothers, the sons of Gideon. He killed them all on one stone. But Gideon's youngest son, Jotham, hid from Abimelech and escaped. 6Then all of the leaders of Shechem and Beth Millo gathered beside the great tree standing in Shechem. There they made Abimelech their king.

Jotham's Story

7When Jotham heard this, he went and stood on the top of Mount Gerizim. He shouted to the people: "Listen to me, you leaders of Shechem, so that God will listen to you! 8One day the trees decided to appoint a king to rule over them. They said to the olive tree, 'You be king over us!'

9"But the olive tree said, 'Men and gods are honoured by my oil. Should I stop making it and go and sway over the other trees?'

10"Then the trees said to the fig tree, 'Come and be king over us!'

11"But the fig tree answered, 'Should I stop making my sweet and good fruit and go and sway over the other trees?'

12"Then the trees said to the vine, 'Come and be king over us!'

Ishmaelites Another name for the Midianites. See Genesis 37:25–28.
Gideon Also called Jerub-Baal.

13"But the vine answered, 'My new wine makes men and gods happy. Should I stop making it and go and sway over the trees?'

14"Then all the trees said to the thornbush, 'Come and be king over us.'

15"But the thornbush said to the trees, 'If you really want to appoint me king over you, come and find shelter in my shade! But if not, let fire come out of the thornbush and burn up the cedars of Lebanon!'

16"Now, were you completely honest and sincere when you made Abimelech king? Have you been fair to Gideon[n] and his family? Have you treated Gideon as you should? 17Remember, my father fought for you and risked his life to save you from the power of the Midianites. 18But now you have turned against my father's family and have killed his 70 sons on one stone. You have made Abimelech, the son of my father's slave girl, king over the leaders of Shechem just because he is your relative! 19So then, if you have been honest and sincere to Gideon and his family today, be happy with Abimelech as your king. And may he be happy with you! 20But if not, may fire come out of Abimelech and completely burn you leaders of Shechem and Beth Millo! Also may fire come out of the leaders of Shechem and Beth Millo and burn up Abimelech!"

21Then Jotham ran away and escaped to the city of Beer. He lived there because he was afraid of his brother Abimelech.

Abimelech Fights Against Shechem

22Abimelech ruled Israel for three years. 23Then God sent an evil spirit to make trouble between Abimelech and the leaders of Shechem so that the leaders of Shechem turned against him. 24Abimelech had killed Gideon's[n] 70 sons, his own brothers, and the leaders of Shechem had helped him. So God sent the evil spirit to punish them. 25The leaders of Shechem were against Abimelech then. They put men on the hilltops in ambush who robbed everyone going by. And Abimelech was told.

26A man named Gaal son of Ebed and his brothers moved into Shechem, and the leaders of Shechem trusted him. 27They went out to the vineyards to pick grapes, and they squeezed the grapes. Then they had a feast in the temple of their god, where they ate and drank and cursed Abimelech. 28Gaal son of Ebed said, "We are the men of Shechem. Who is Abimelech that we should serve him? Isn't he one of Gideon's sons, and isn't Zebul his officer? We should serve the men of Hamor, Shechem's father. Why should we serve Abimelech? 29If you made me commander of these people, I would get rid of Abimelech. I would say to him, 'Get your army ready and come out to battle.' "

30Now when Zebul, the ruler of Shechem, heard what Gaal son of Ebed said, he was very angry. 31He sent secret messengers to Abimelech, saying, "Gaal son of Ebed and Gaal's brothers have come to Shechem, and they are turning the city against you! 32You and your men should get up during the night and hide in the fields outside the city. 33As soon as the sun comes up in the morning, attack the city. When Gaal and his men come out to fight you, do what you can to them."

34So Abimelech and all his soldiers got up during the night and hid near Shechem in four groups. 35Gaal son of Ebed went out and was standing at the entrance to the city gate. As he was standing there, Abimelech and his soldiers came out of their hiding places.

36When Gaal saw the soldiers, he said to Zebul, "Look! There are people coming down from the mountains!"

But Zebul said, "You are seeing the shadows of the mountains. The shadows just look like people."

37But again Gaal said, "Look, there are people coming down from the centre of the land, and there is a group coming from the fortune-tellers' tree!"

38Zebul said to Gaal, "Where is your boasting now? You said, 'Who is Abimelech that we should serve him?' You made fun of these men. Now go out and fight them."

39So Gaal led the men of Shechem out to fight Abimelech. 40Abimelech and his men chased them, and many of Gaal's men were killed before they could get back to the city gate. 41While Abimelech stayed at Arumah, Zebul forced Gaal and his brothers to leave Shechem.

42The next day the people of Shechem went out to the fields. When Abimelech was told about it, 43he separated his men into three groups and hid them in the fields. When he saw the people coming out of the city, he jumped up and attacked them. 44Abimelech and his group ran to the entrance gate to the city. The other two groups ran out to the people in the fields and struck them down. 45Abimelech and his men fought the city of Shechem all day until they captured it and killed its people. Then he tore it down and threw salt[n] over the ruins.

Gideon Also called Jerub-Baal.
salt The salt would stop crops from growing there.

The Tower of Shechem Burns

46When the leaders who were in the Tower of
Shechem heard what had happened to Shechem,
they gathered in the safest room of the temple of
El Berith. 47Abimelech heard that all the leaders
of the Tower of Shechem had gathered there.
48So he and all his men went up Mount Zalmon,
near Shechem. Abimelech took an axe and cut
some branches and put them on his shoulders.
He said to all those with him, "Hurry! Do what
I have done!" 49So all those men cut branches
and followed Abimelech and piled them against
the safest room of the temple. Then they set them
on fire and burned the people inside. So all the
people who were at the Tower of Shechem also
died—about 1,000 men and women.

Abimelech's Death

50Then Abimelech went to the city of Thebez.
He surrounded the city, attacked it and captured
it. 51But inside the city was a strong tower, so all
the men, women and leaders of that city ran to
the tower. When they got inside, they locked the
door behind them. Then they climbed up to the
roof of the tower. 52Abimelech came to the tower
to attack it. He approached the door of the tower
to set it on fire, 53but as he came near, a woman
dropped a grinding stone on his head, crushing
his skull.

54He quickly called to the officer who carried
his armour and said, "Take out your sword and
kill me. I don't want people to say, 'A woman
killed Abimelech.' " So the officer stabbed Abime-
lech, and he died. 55When the people of Israel
saw Abimelech was dead, they all returned
home.

56In that way God punished Abimelech for all
the evil he had done to his father by killing his 70
brothers. 57God also punished the men of She-
chem for the evil they had done. So the curse
spoken by Jotham, the youngest son of Gideon, [n]
came true.

Tola, the Judge

10 After Abimelech died, another judge came
to save Israel. He was Tola son of Puah,
the son of Dodo. Tola was from the people of Is-
sachar and lived in the city of Shamir in the moun-
tains of Ephraim. 2Tola was a judge for Israel for 23
years. Then he died and was buried in Shamir.

Jair, the Judge

3After Tola died, Jair from the region of Gilead
became judge. He was a judge for Israel for 22
years. 4Jair had 30 sons, who rode 30 donkeys.
These 30 sons controlled 30 towns in Gilead,
which are called the Towns of Jair to this day.
5Jair died and was buried in the city of Kamon.

The Ammonites Trouble Israel

6Again the Israelites did what the LORD said was
wrong. They worshipped Baal [d] and Ashtoreth, [d]
the gods of Aram, Sidon, Moab and Ammon, and
the gods of the Philistines. The Israelites left the
LORD and stopped serving him. 7So the LORD was
angry with them and handed them over to the
Philistines and the Ammonites. 8In the same year
those people destroyed the Israelites who lived
east of the Jordan River in the region of Gilead,
where the Amorites lived. So the Israelites suf-
fered for eighteen years. 9The Ammonites then
crossed the Jordan River to fight the people of
Judah, Benjamin and Ephraim, causing much
trouble to the people of Israel. 10So the Israelites
cried out to the LORD, "We have sinned against
you. We left our God and worshipped the Baal
idols."

11The LORD answered the Israelites, "When the
Egyptians, Amorites, Ammonites, Philistines, 12Si-
donians, Amalekites and Maonites were cruel to
you, you cried out to me, and I saved you. 13But
now you have left me again and have worshipped
other gods. So I refuse to save you again. 14You
have chosen those gods. So go and call to them
for help. Let them save you when you are in
trouble."

15But the people of Israel said to the LORD, "We
have sinned. Do to us whatever you want, but
please save us today!" 16Then the Israelites threw
away the foreign gods among them, and they
worshipped the LORD again. So he felt sorry for
them when he saw their suffering.

17The Ammonites gathered for war and
camped in Gilead. The Israelites gathered and
camped at Mizpah. 18The leaders of the people of
Gilead said, "Who will lead us to attack the Am-
monites? He will become the head of all those
who live in Gilead."

Jephthah Is Chosen as Leader

11 Jephthah was a strong soldier from Gil-
ead. His father was named Gilead, and
his mother was a prostitute. [d] 2Gilead's wife had
several sons. When they grew up, they forced
Jephthah to leave his home, saying to him, "You
will not get any of our father's property, because
you are the son of another woman." 3So Jephthah
ran away from his brothers and lived in the land
of Tob. There some worthless men began to fol-
low him.

Gideon Also called Jerub-Baal.

4After a time the Ammonites fought against Israel. 5When the Ammonites made war against Israel, the elders of Gilead went to Jephthah to bring him back from Tob. 6They said to him, "Come and lead our army so we can fight the Ammonites."

7But Jephthah said to them, "Didn't you hate me? You forced me to leave my father's house. Why are you coming to me now that you are in trouble?"

8The elders of Gilead said to Jephthah, "It is because of those troubles that we come to you now. Please come with us and fight against the Ammonites. You will be the ruler over everyone who lives in Gilead."

9Then Jephthah answered, "If you take me back to Gilead to fight the Ammonites and the LORD helps me win, I will be your ruler."

10The elders of Gilead said to him, "The LORD is listening to everything we are saying. We promise to do all that you tell us to do." 11So Jephthah went with the elders of Gilead, and the people made him their leader and commander of their army. Jephthah repeated all of his words in front of the LORD at Mizpah.

Jephthah Sends Messengers to the Ammonite King

12Jephthah sent messengers to the king of the Ammonites, asking, "What have you got against Israel? Why have you come to attack our land?"

13The king of the Ammonites answered the messengers of Jephthah, "We are fighting Israel because you took our land when you came up from Egypt. You took our land from the Arnon River to the Jabbok River to the Jordan River. Now give our land back to us peacefully."

14Jephthah sent the messengers to the Ammonite king again. 15They said:

"This is what Jephthah says: Israel did not take the land of the people of Moab or Ammon. 16When the Israelites came out of Egypt, they went into the desert to the Red Sea and then to Kadesh. 17Israel sent messengers to the king of Edom, saying, 'Let the people of Israel go across your land.' But the king of Edom refused. We sent the same message to the king of Moab, but he also refused. So the Israelites stayed at Kadesh.

18"Then the Israelites went into the desert around the borders of the lands of Edom and Moab. Israel went east of the land of Moab and camped on the other side of the Arnon River, the border of Moab. They did not cross it to go into the land of Moab.

19"Then Israel sent messengers to Sihon king of the Amorites, king of the city of Heshbon, asking, 'Let the people of Israel pass through your land to go to our land.' 20But Sihon did not trust the Israelites to cross his land. So he gathered all of his people and camped at Jahaz and fought with Israel.

21"But the LORD, the God of Israel, handed Sihon and his army over to Israel. All the land of the Amorites became the property of Israel. 22So Israel took all the land of the Amorites from the Arnon River to the Jabbok River, from the desert to the Jordan River.

23"It was the LORD, the God of Israel, who forced out the Amorites ahead of the people of Israel. So do you think you can make them leave? 24Take the land that your god Chemosh[d] has given you. We will live in the land the LORD our God has given us!

25"Are you any better than Balak son of Zippor, king of Moab? Did he ever quarrel or fight with the people of Israel? 26For 300 years the Israelites have lived in Heshbon and Aroer and the towns around them and in all the cities along the Arnon River. Why have you not taken these cities back in all that time? 27I have not sinned against you, but you are sinning against me by making war on me. May the LORD, the Judge, decide whether the Israelites or the Ammonites are right."

28But the king of the Ammonites ignored this message from Jephthah.

Jephthah's Promise

29Then the Spirit[d] of the LORD entered Jephthah. Jephthah passed through Gilead and Manasseh and the city of Mizpah in Gilead to the land of the Ammonites. 30Jephthah made a promise to the LORD, saying, "If you will hand over the Ammonites to me, 31I will give you as a burnt offering the first thing that comes out of my house to meet me when I return from the victory. It will be the LORD's."

32Then Jephthah went over to fight the Ammonites, and the LORD handed them over to him. 33In a great defeat Jephthah struck them down from the city of Aroer to the area of Minnith, and 20 cities as far as the city of Abel Keramim. So the Ammonites were defeated by the Israelites.

34When Jephthah returned to his home in Mizpah, his daughter was the first one to come out to meet him, playing a tambourine[d] and dancing. She was his only child; he had no other sons or daughters. 35When Jephthah saw his daughter, he tore his clothes to show his sorrow. He said, "My daughter! You have made me so sad because I made a promise to the LORD, and I cannot break it!"

36Then his daughter said, "Father, you made a promise to the LORD. So do to me just what you promised, because the LORD helped you defeat your enemies, the Ammonites." 37She also said, "But let me do one thing. Let me be alone for two months to go to the mountains. Since I will never marry, let me and my friends go and cry together."

38Jephthah said, "Go." So he sent her away for two months. She and her friends stayed in the mountains and cried for her because she would never marry. 39After two months she returned to her father, and Jephthah did to her what he had promised. Jephthah's daughter never had a husband.

> **Sidelight** Have you ever made a promise you later regretted? Judge Jephthah did. He promised to sacrifice the first thing that came out of his house after battle. Jephthah may have expected to see an animal, since houses in that day often included space for cattle. But when his only daughter appeared, he tore his clothes in sorrow (Judges 11:30–40).

From this came a custom in Israel that 40every year the young women of Israel would go out for four days to remember the daughter of Jephthah from Gilead.

Jephthah and Ephraim

12 The men of Ephraim called all their soldiers together and crossed the river to the town of Zaphon. They said to Jephthah, "Why didn't you call us to help you fight the Ammonites? We will burn your house down with you in it."

2Jephthah answered them, "My people and I fought a great battle against the Ammonites. I called you, but you didn't come to help me. 3When I saw that you would not help me, I risked my own life and went against the Ammonites. The LORD handed them over to me. So why have you come to fight against me today?"

4Then Jephthah called the men of Gilead together and fought the men of Ephraim. The men of Gilead struck them down because the Ephraimites had said, "You men of Gilead are nothing but deserters from Ephraim—living between Ephraim and Manasseh." 5The men of Gilead captured the crossings of the Jordan River that led to the country of Ephraim. A person from Ephraim trying to escape would say, "Let me cross the river." Then the men of Gilead would ask him, "Are you from Ephraim?" If he replied "No," 6they would say to him, "Say the word 'Shibboleth'." The men of Ephraim could not say that word correctly. So if the person from Ephraim said, "Sibboleth," the men of Gilead would kill him at the crossing. So 42,000 people from Ephraim were killed at that time.

7Jephthah was a judge for Israel for six years. Then Jephthah, the man from Gilead, died and was buried in a town in Gilead.

Ibzan, the Judge

8After Jephthah died, Ibzan from Bethlehem was a judge for Israel. 9He had 30 sons and 30 daughters. He let his daughters marry men who were not in his family group, and he brought 30 women who were not in his tribe[d] to be wives for his sons. Ibzan judged Israel for seven years. 10Then he died and was buried in Bethlehem.

Elon, the Judge

11After Ibzan died, Elon from the tribe[d] of Zebulun was a judge for Israel. He judged Israel for ten years. 12Then Elon, the man of Zebulun, died and was buried in the city of Aijalon in the land of Zebulun.

Abdon, the Judge

13After Elon died, Abdon son of Hillel from the city of Pirathon was a judge for Israel. 14He had 40 sons and 30 grandsons, who rode on 70 donkeys. He judged Israel for eight years. 15Then Abdon son of Hillel died and was buried in Pirathon in the land of Ephraim, in the mountains where the Amalekites lived.

The Birth of Samson

13 Again the people of Israel did what the LORD said was wrong. So he handed them over to the Philistines for 40 years.

2There was a man named Manoah from the tribe[d] of Dan, who lived in the city of Zorah. He had a wife, but she could not have children. 3The angel of the LORD appeared to Manoah's wife and said, "You have not been able to have children, but you will become pregnant and give birth to a son. 4Be careful not to drink wine or beer or eat anything that is unclean,[d] 5because you will become pregnant and have a son. You must never cut his hair, because he will be a Nazirite,[d] given to God from birth. He will begin to save Israel from the power of the Philistines."

6Then Manoah's wife went to him and told him what had happened. She said, "A man from God came to me. He looked like an angel from God; his appearance was frightening. I didn't ask him where he was from, and he didn't tell me his name. 7But he said to me, 'You will become pregnant and will have a son. Don't drink wine or beer or eat anything that is unclean, because the boy will be a Nazirite to God from his birth until the day of his death.' "

8Then Manoah prayed to the LORD: "Lord, I beg you to let the man of God come to us again. Let him teach us what we should do for the boy who will be born to us."

9God heard Manoah's prayer, and the angel of God came to Manoah's wife again while she was sitting in the field. But her husband Manoah was not with her. 10So she ran to tell him, "He is here! The man who appeared to me the other day is here!"

11Manoah got up and followed his wife. When he came to the man, he said, "Are you the man who spoke to my wife?"

The man said, "I am."

12So Manoah asked, "When what you say happens, what kind of life should the boy live? What should he do?"

13The angel of the LORD said, "Your wife must be careful to do everything I told her to do. 14She must not eat anything that grows on a grapevine, or drink any wine or beer, or eat anything that is unclean. She must do everything I have commanded her."

15Manoah said to the angel of the LORD, "We would like you to stay awhile so we can cook a young goat for you."

16The angel of the LORD answered, "Even if I stay awhile, I would not eat your food. But if you want to prepare something, offer a burnt offering to the LORD." (Manoah did not understand that the man was really the angel of the LORD.)

17Then Manoah asked the angel of the LORD, "What is your name? Then we will honour you when what you have said really happens."

18The angel of the LORD said, "Why do you ask my name? It is too amazing for you to understand." 19So Manoah sacrificed a young goat on a rock and offered some grain as a gift to the LORD. Then an amazing thing happened as Manoah and his wife watched. 20The flames went up to the sky from the altar. As the fire burned, the angel of the LORD went up to heaven in the flame. When Manoah and his wife saw that, they bowed face down on the ground. 21The angel of the LORD did not appear to them again. Then Manoah understood that the man was really the angel of the LORD. 22Manoah said, "We have seen God, so we will surely die."

23But his wife said to him, "If the LORD wanted to kill us, he would not have accepted our burnt offering or grain offering. He would not have shown us all these things or told us all this."

24So the woman gave birth to a boy and named him Samson. He grew, and the LORD blessed him. 25The Spirit[d] of the LORD began to work in Samson while he was in the city of Mahaneh Dan, between the cities of Zorah and Eshtaol.

Samson's First Marriage

14 Samson went down to the city of Timnah where he saw a Philistine woman. 2When he returned home, he said to his father and mother, "I saw a Philistine woman in Timnah. I want you to get her for me so I can marry her."

3His father and mother answered, "Surely there is a woman from Israel you can marry. Do you have to marry a woman from the Philistines, who are not circumcised?"[d]

But Samson said, "Get that woman for me! She is the one I want!" 4(Samson's parents did not know that the LORD wanted this to happen because he was looking for a way to challenge the Philistines, who were ruling over Israel at this time.) 5Samson went down with his father and mother to Timnah, as far as the vineyard near there. Suddenly, a young lion came roaring towards Samson! 6The Spirit[d] of the LORD entered Samson with great power, and he tore the lion apart with his bare hands. For him it was as easy as tearing apart a young goat. But Samson did not tell his father or mother what he had done. 7Then he went down to the city and talked to the Philistine woman, and he liked her.

8Several days later Samson went back to marry her. On his way he went over to look at the body of the dead lion and found a swarm of bees and honey in it. 9Samson got some of the honey with his hands and walked along eating it. When he came to his parents, he gave some to them. They ate it, too, but Samson did not tell them he had taken the honey from the body of the dead lion.

10Samson's father went down to see the Philistine woman. And Samson gave a feast, as was the custom for the bridegroom. 11When the people saw him, they sent 30 friends to be with him.

Samson's Riddle

12Samson said to them, "Let me tell you a riddle. Try to find the answer during the seven days of the feast. If you can, I will give you 30 linen shirts and 30 changes of clothes. 13But if you can't, you must give me 30 linen shirts and 30 changes of clothes."

So they said, "Tell us your riddle so we can hear it."

14Samson said,

"Out of the eater comes something to eat.
Out of the strong comes something sweet."

After three days, they had not found the answer.

15On the fourth[n] day they said to Samson's wife, "Did you invite us here to make us poor?

fourth The Hebrew word is "seventh". Some old translations say "fourth", which fits the order of events better.

Trick your husband into telling us the answer to
the riddle. If you don't, we will burn you and
everyone in your father's house."
16So Samson's wife went to him, crying, and
said, "You hate me! You don't really love me!
You told my people a riddle, but you won't tell
me the answer."
Samson said, "I haven't even told my father or
mother. Why should I tell you?"
17Samson's wife cried for the rest of the seven
days of the feast. So he finally gave her the answer
on the seventh day, because she kept bothering
him. Then she told her people the answer to the
riddle.
18Before sunset on the seventh day of the feast,
the Philistine men had the answer. They came to
Samson and said,

"What is sweeter than honey?
What is stronger than a lion?"

Then Samson said to them,

"If you had not ploughed with my young cow,
you would not have solved my riddle!"

19Then the Spirit [d] of the LORD entered Sam-
son and gave him great power. Samson went
down to the city of Ashkelon and killed 30 of its
men and took all that they had and gave the
clothes to the men who had answered his riddle.
Then he went to his father's house very angry.
20And Samson's wife was given to his best man.

Samson Troubles the Philistines

15 At the time of the wheat harvest, Sam-
son went to visit his wife, taking a young
goat with him. He said, "I'm going to my wife's
room," but her father would not let him go in.
2He said to Samson, "I thought you really
hated your wife, so I gave her to your best man.
Her younger sister is more beautiful. Take her
instead."
3But Samson said to them, "This time no one
will blame me for hurting you Philistines!" 4So
Samson went out and caught 300 foxes. He took
two foxes at a time, tied their tails together and
then tied a torch to the tails of each pair of foxes.
5After he lit the torches, he let the foxes loose in
the grain fields of the Philistines so that he
burned up their standing grain, the piles of grain,
their vineyards and their olive trees.
6The Philistines asked, "Who did this?"
Someone told them, "Samson, the son-in-law
of the man from Timnah, did because his father-
in-law gave his wife to his best man."
So the Philistines burned Samson's wife and
her father to death. 7Then Samson said to the
Philistines, "Since you did this, I won't stop until
I pay you back!" 8Samson attacked the Philistines

> **Sidelight**
> Samson was strong because he was made that way. But he was a fighter – not a successful spiritual leader. If he had followed the rules God gave his parents and controlled himself as well as he controlled the Philistines, the story might have been very different.

and killed many of them. Then he went down
and stayed in a cave in the rock of Etam.
9The Philistines went up and camped in the
land of Judah, near a place named Lehi. 10The
men of Judah asked them, "Why have you come
here to fight us?"
They answered, "We have come to make Sam-
son our prisoner, to pay him back for what he did
to our people."
11Then 3,000 men of Judah went to the cave
in the rock of Etam and said to Samson, "What
have you done to us? Don't you know that the
Philistines rule over us?"
Samson answered, "I only paid them back for
what they did to me."
12Then they said to him, "We have come to tie
you up and to hand you over to the Philistines."
Samson said to them, "Promise me you will
not hurt me yourselves."
13The men from Judah said, "We agree. We
will just tie you up and give you to the Philistines.
We will not kill you." So they tied Samson with
two new ropes and led him up from the cave in
the rock. 14When Samson came to the place
named Lehi, the Philistines came to meet him,
shouting for joy. Then the Spirit [d] of the LORD en-
tered Samson and gave him great power. The
ropes on him weakened like burned strings and
fell off his hands! 15Samson found the jawbone of
a dead donkey, took it, and killed 1,000 men
with it!
16Then Samson said,

"With a donkey's jawbone
I made donkeys out of them.
With a donkey's jawbone
I killed 1,000 men!"

17When he finished speaking, he threw away the
jawbone. So that place was named Ramath
Lehi. [n]
18Samson was very thirsty, so he cried out to
the LORD, "You gave me, your servant, this great
victory. Do I have to die of thirst now? Do I have
to be captured by people who are not circum-
cised?" [d] 19Then God opened up a hole in the
ground at Lehi, and water came out. When Sam-
son drank, he felt better; he felt strong again.

Ramnath Lehi This name means "Jawbone Hill".

So he named that spring Caller's Spring, which is still in Lehi.

20Samson judged Israel for 20 years in the days of the Philistines.

Samson Goes to the City of Gaza

16 One day Samson went to Gaza and saw a prostitute *d* there. He went in to spend the night with her. 2When the people of Gaza heard, "Samson has come here!" they surrounded the place and waited for him near the city gate all night. They said to each other, "When dawn comes, we will kill Samson!"

3But Samson only stayed with the prostitute until midnight. Then he got up and took hold of the doors and the two posts of the city gate and tore them loose, along with the bar. He put them on his shoulders and carried them to the top of the hill that faces the city of Hebron.

Samson and Delilah

4After this, Samson fell in love with a woman named Delilah, who lived in the Valley of Sorek. 5The Philistine rulers went to Delilah and said, "Find out what makes Samson so strong. Trick him into telling you how we can overpower him, capture him and tie him up. If you do this, each one of us will give you 1,100 pieces of silver."

6So Delilah said to Samson, "Tell me why you are so strong. How can someone tie you up and capture you?"

7Samson answered, "Someone would have to tie me up with seven new bowstrings that have not been dried. Then I would be as weak as any other man."

8The Philistine rulers brought Delilah seven new bowstrings that had not been dried, and she tied Samson with them. 9Some men were hiding in another room. Delilah said to him, "Samson, the Philistines are here!" But Samson broke the bowstrings like pieces of burned string. So the Philistines did not find out the secret of Samson's strength.

10Then Delilah said to Samson, "You made a fool of me. You lied to me. Now tell me how someone can tie you up."

11Samson said, "They would have to tie me with new ropes that have not been used before. Then I would become as weak as any other man."

12So Delilah took new ropes and tied Samson. Some men were hiding in another room. She called out to him, "Samson, the Philistines are here!" But he broke the ropes as easily as if they were threads.

13Then Delilah said to Samson, "Again you have made a fool of me. You lied to me. Tell me how someone can tie you up."

He said, "Using the loom, *n* weave the seven plaits of my hair into the cloth, and tighten it with a pin. Then I will be as weak as any other man."

While Samson slept, Delilah wove the seven plaits of his hair into the cloth. 14Then she fastened it with a pin.

Again she said to him, "Samson, the Philistines are here!" Samson woke up and pulled out the pin and the loom with the cloth.

15Then Delilah said to him, "How can you say, 'I love you,' when you don't even trust me? This is the third time you have made a fool of me. You haven't told me the secret of your great strength." 16She kept bothering Samson about his secret day after day until he felt he was going to die!

17So he told her everything. He said, "I have never had my hair cut, because I have been set apart to God as a Nazirite *d* since I was born. If someone shaved my head, I would lose my strength and be as weak as any other man."

18When Delilah saw that he had told her everything sincerely, she sent a message to the Philistine rulers. She said, "Come back one more time, because he has told me everything." So the Philistine rulers came back to Delilah and brought the silver with them. 19Delilah got Samson to sleep, lying in her lap. Then she called in a man to shave off the seven plaits of Samson's hair. In this way she began to make him weak, and his strength left him.

20Then she said, "Samson, the Philistines are here!"

He woke up and thought, "I'll leave as I did before and shake myself free." But he did not know that the LORD had left him.

Sidelight When Samson was forced to grind grain as a prisoner, the punishment was severe (Judges 16:21). The millstone he would have turned was probably made of limestone and was at least 60 centimetres across with a hole in the middle. Only large animals and extremely strong people could operate the grinding mills.

21Then the Philistines captured Samson and tore out his eyes. They took him down to Gaza, where they put bronze chains on him and made him grind grain in the prison. 22But his hair began to grow again.

loom A machine for making cloth from thread.

Samson Dies

23The Philistine rulers gathered to celebrate
and to offer a great sacrifice to their god Dagon.[d]
They said, "Our god has handed Samson our
enemy over to us." 24When the people saw him,
they praised their god, saying,

"This man destroyed our country.
He killed many of us!
But our god handed over
our enemy to us."

25While the people were enjoying the celebra-
tion, they said, "Bring Samson out to perform for
us." So they brought Samson from the prison, and
he performed for them. They made him stand
between the pillars. 26Samson said to the servant
holding his hand, "Let me feel the pillars that
hold up the temple so I can lean against them."
27Now the temple was full of men and women.
All the Philistine rulers were there, and about
3,000 men and women were on the roof[n]
watching Samson perform. 28Then Samson
prayed to the LORD, "Lord GOD, remember me.
God, please give me strength one more time so I
can pay these Philistines back for putting out my
two eyes!" 29Then Samson turned to the two cen-
tre pillars that supported the whole temple. He
braced himself between the two pillars, with his
right hand on one and his left hand on the other.
30Samson said, "Let me die with these Philis-
tines!" Then he pushed as hard as he could, caus-
ing the temple to fall on the rulers and all the
people in it. So Samson killed more of the Philis-
tines when he died than when he was alive.

31Samson's brothers and his whole family went
down to get his body. They brought him back and
buried him in the tomb of Manoah, his father,
between the cities of Zorah and Eshtaol. Samson
was a judge for the people of Israel for 20 years.

Micah's Idols

17 There was a man named Micah who
lived in the mountains of Ephraim. 2He
said to his mother, "I heard you speak a curse
about the 1,100 pieces of silver that were taken
from you. I have the silver with me; I took it."

His mother said, "The LORD bless you, my son!"
3Micah gave the 1,100 pieces of silver to his
mother. Then she said, "I will give this silver to
the LORD. I will have my son make an idol and a
statue. So I will give the silver back to you."

4When he gave the silver back to his mother,
she took about 200 pieces and gave it to a
silversmith. With it he made an idol and a statue,
which stood in Micah's house. 5Micah had a
special holy place, and he made a holy robe[d] and
some household idols. Then Micah chose one of
his sons to be his priest. 6At that time Israel did not
have a king, so everyone did what seemed right.

7There was a young man who was a Levite[n]
from the city of Bethlehem in Judah who was
from the people of Judah. 8He left Bethlehem to
look for another place to live, and on his way
he came to Micah's house in the mountains of
Ephraim. 9Micah asked him, "Where are you
from?"

He answered, "I'm a Levite from Bethlehem in
Judah. I'm looking for a place to live."

10Micah said to him, "Live with me and be my
father and my priest. I will give you 10 pieces
of silver each year and clothes and food." So
the Levite went in. 11He agreed to live with
Micah and became like one of Micah's own
sons. 12Micah made him a priest, and he lived
in Micah's house. 13Then Micah said, "Now
I know the LORD will be good to me, because I
have a Levite as my priest."

Dan's Family Captures Laish

18 At that time Israel did not have a king.
And at that time the tribe[d] of Dan was
still looking for a land where they could live, a
land of their own. The Danites had not yet been
given their own land among the tribes of Israel.
2So, from their family groups, they chose five sol-
diers from the cities of Zorah and Eshtaol to spy
out and explore the land. They were told, "Go,
explore the land."

They came to the mountains of Ephraim, to
Micah's house, where they spent the night.
3When they came near Micah's house, they rec-
ognised the voice of the young Levite.[n] So they
stopped there and asked him, "Who brought you
here? What are you doing here? Why are you
here?"

4He told them what Micah had done for him,
saying, "He hired me. I am his priest."

5They said to him, "Please ask God if our
journey will be successful."

6The priest said to them, "Go in peace. The
LORD is pleased with your journey."

7So the five men left. When they came to the
city of Laish, they saw that the people there lived
in safety, like the people of Sidon. They thought
they were safe and had plenty of everything.
They lived a long way from the Sidonians and
had no dealings with anyone else.

roof In Bible times houses were built with flat roofs. The roof was used for drying things such as flax and fruit. And it was used as an extra room, as a place for worship and as a place to sleep in the summer.

Levite The Levites were the only ones God had appointed as priests.

8When the five men returned to Zorah and Eshtaol, their relatives asked them, "What did you find?"

9They answered, "We have seen the land, and it is very good. We should attack them. Aren't you going to do something? Don't wait! Let's go and take that land! 10When you go, you will see there is plenty of land—plenty of everything! The people are not expecting an attack. Surely God has handed that land over to us!"

11So 600 Danites left Zorah and Eshtaol ready for war. 12On their way they set up camp near the city of Kiriath Jearim in Judah. That is why the place west of Kiriath Jearim is named Mahaneh Dan[n] to this day. 13From there they travelled on to the mountains of Ephraim. Then they came to Micah's house.

14The five men who had explored the land around Laish said to their relatives, "Do you know, in one of these houses there are a holy robe,[d] household gods, an idol and a statue? You know what to do." 15So they stopped at the Levite's house, which was also Micah's house, and greeted the Levite. 16The 600 Danites stood at the entrance gate, wearing their weapons of war. 17The five spies went into the house and took the idol, the holy robe, the household idols and the statue. The priest and the 600 men armed for war stood by the entrance gate.

18When the spies went into Micah's house and took the image, the holy robe, the household idols and the statue, the priest asked them, "What are you doing?"

19They answered, "Be quiet! Don't say a word. Come with us and be our father and priest. Is it better for you to be a priest for one man's house or for a tribe and family group in Israel?" 20This made the priest happy. So he took the holy robe, the household idols and the idol and went with the Danites. 21They left Micah's house, putting their little children, their animals and everything they owned in front of them.

22When they had gone a little way from Micah's house, the men who lived near Micah were called out and caught up with them. 23The men with Micah shouted at the Danites, who turned round and said to Micah, 'What's the matter with you? Why have you been called out to fight?"

24Micah answered, "You took my gods that I made and my priest. What do I have left? How can you ask me, 'What's the matter?' "

25The Danites answered, "You should not argue with us. Some of our angry men might attack you, killing you and your family." 26Then the Danites went on their way. Micah knew they were too strong for him, so he turned and went back home.

27Then the Danites took what Micah had made and his priest and went on to Laish. They attacked those peaceful people and killed them with their swords and then burned the city. 28There was no one to save the people of Laish. They lived too far from Sidon, and they had no dealings with anyone else. Laish was in a valley near Beth Rehob.

The people of Dan rebuilt the city and lived there. 29They changed the name of Laish to Dan, naming it after their ancestor Dan, one of the sons of Israel.

30The people of Dan set up the idols in the city of Dan. Jonathan son of Gershom, Moses' son, and his sons served as priests for the tribe of Dan until the land was captured. 31The people of Dan set up the idols Micah had made as long as the Holy Tent[d] of God was in Shiloh.

A Levite and His Servant

19 At that time Israel did not have a king. There was a Levite who lived in the faraway mountains of Ephraim. He had taken a slave woman[d] from the city of Bethlehem in the land of Judah to live with him, 2but she was unfaithful to him. She left him and went back to her father's house in Bethlehem in Judah and stayed there for four months. 3Then her husband went to ask her to come back to him, taking with him his servant and two donkeys. When the Levite came to her father's house, she invited him to come in, and her father was happy to see him. 4The father-in-law, the young woman's father, asked him to stay. So he stayed for three days and ate, drank and slept there.

5On the fourth day they got up early in the morning. The Levite was getting ready to leave, but the woman's father said to his son-in-law, "Refresh yourself by eating something. Then go." 6So the two men sat down to eat and drink together. After that, the father said to him, "Please stay tonight. Relax and enjoy yourself." 7When the man got up to go, his father-in-law asked him to stay. So he stayed again that night. 8On the fifth day the man got up early in the morning to leave. The woman's father said, "Refresh yourself. Wait until this afternoon." So the two men ate together.

9When the Levite, his slave woman, and his servant got up to leave, the father-in-law, the young woman's father, said, "It's almost night. The day is almost gone. Spend the night here and enjoy yourself. Tomorrow morning you can get up early and go home." 10But the Levite did not

Mahaneh Dan This name means "the camp of Dan".

want to stay another night. So he took his two saddled donkeys and his slave woman and travelled towards the city of Jebus (also called Jerusalem).

[11]As the day was almost over, they came near Jebus. So the servant said to his master, "Let's stop at this city of the Jebusites, and spend the night here."

[12]But his master said, "No. We won't go inside a foreign city. Those people are not Israelites. We will go on to the city of Gibeah." [13]He said, "Come on. Let's try to make it to Gibeah or Ramah so we can spend the night in one of those cities." [14]So they went on. The sun went down as they came near Gibeah, which belongs to the tribe[d] of Benjamin. [15]They stopped there to spend the night. They came to the public square of the city and sat down, but no one invited them home to spend the night.

[16]Late in the evening an old man came in from his work in the fields. His home was in the mountains of Ephraim, but now he was living in Gibeah. (The people of Gibeah were from the tribe of Benjamin.) [17]He saw the traveller in the public square and asked, "Where are you going? Where did you come from?"

[18]The Levite answered, "We are travelling from Bethlehem in Judah to my home in the mountains of Ephraim. I have been to Bethlehem in Judah, but now I am going to the Holy Tent[d] of the LORD. No one has invited me to stay in his house. [19]We already have straw and food for our donkeys and bread and wine for me, the young woman and my servant. We don't need anything."

[20]The old man said, "You are welcome to stay at my house. Let me give you anything you need, but don't spend the night in the public square." [21]So the old man took the Levite into his house, and he fed their donkeys. They washed their feet and had something to eat and drink.

[22]While they were enjoying themselves, some wicked men of the city surrounded the house and beat on the door. They shouted to the old man who owned the house, "Bring out the man who came to your house. We want to have sexual relations with him."

[23]The owner of the house went outside and said to them, "No, my friends. Don't be so evil. This man is a guest in my house. Don't do this terrible thing! [24]Look, here is my daughter, who has never had sexual relations before, and also the man's slave woman. I will bring them out to you now. Do anything you want with them, but don't do such a terrible thing to this man."

[25]But the men would not listen to him. So the Levite took his slave woman and sent her outside to them. They forced her to have sexual relations with them, and they abused her all night long. Then, at dawn, they let her go. [26]She came back to the house where her master was staying and fell down at the door and lay there until daylight.

[27]In the morning when the Levite got up, he opened the door of the house and went outside to go on his way. But his slave woman was lying at the doorway of the house, with her hands on the doorsill. [28]The Levite said to her, "Get up; let's go." But she did not answer. So he put her on his donkey and went home.

[29]When the Levite got home, he took a knife and cut his slave woman into twelve parts, limb by limb. Then he sent a part to each area of Israel. [30]Everyone who saw this said, "Nothing like this has ever happened before, not since the people of Israel came out of Egypt. Think about it. Tell us what to do."

The War Between Israel and Benjamin

20 So all the Israelites from Dan to Beersheba,[r] including the land of Gilead, joined together before the LORD in the city of Mizpah. [2]The leaders of all the tribes[d] of Israel took their places in the meeting of the people of God. There were 400,000 soldiers with swords. [3](The people of Benjamin heard that the Israelites had gone up to Mizpah.) Then the Israelites said to the Levite, "Tell us how this evil thing happened."

[4]So the husband of the murdered woman answered, "My slave woman[d] and I came to Gibeah in Benjamin to spend the night. [5]During the night the men of Gibeah came after me. They surrounded the house and wanted to kill me. They forced my slave woman to have sexual relations and she died. [6]I took her and cut her into parts and sent one part to each area of Israel because the people of Benjamin did this wicked and terrible thing in Israel. [7]Now, all you Israelites, speak up. What is your decision?"

[8]Then all the people stood up at the same time, saying, "None of us will go home. Not one of us will go back to his house! [9]Now this is what we will do to Gibeah. We will throw lots.[d] [10]That way we will choose ten men from every 100 men from all the tribes of Israel, and we will choose 100 men from every 1,000, and 1,000 men from every 10,000. These will find supplies for the army. Then the army will go to the city of Gibeah of Benjamin to repay them for the terrible thing they have done in Israel." [11]So all the men of Israel were united and gathered against the city.

Dan to Beersheba Dan was the city farthest north in Israel and Beersheba was the city farthest south. So this means all the people of Israel.

12The tribes of Israel sent men throughout the
tribe of Benjamin demanding, "What is this evil
thing some of your men have done? 13Hand over
the wicked men in Gibeah so that we can put
them to death. We must remove this evil from
Israel."

But the Benjaminites would not listen to their
fellow Israelites. 14The Benjaminites left their
own cities and met at Gibeah to fight the Israel-
ites. 15In only one day the Benjaminites got
26,000 soldiers together who were trained with
swords. They also had 700 chosen men from Gib-
eah. 16Seven hundred of these trained soldiers
were left-handed, each of whom could sling a
stone at a hair and not miss!

Sidelight

Looking for a left-handed bowler? Try Judges 20:16 which tells how people with unusual skills were important in the Benjaminite army. They could hit a hair with a stone, and would have earned their place in anybody's cricket team.

17The Israelites, except for the Benjaminites,
gathered 400,000 soldiers with swords.

18The Israelites went up to the city of Bethel
and asked God, "Which tribe shall be first to
attack the Benjaminites?"

The LORD answered, "Judah shall go first."

19The next morning the Israelites got up and
made a camp near Gibeah. 20The men of Israel
went out to fight the Benjaminites and took their
battle position at Gibeah. 21Then the Benjamin-
ites came out of Gibeah and killed 22,000 Israel-
ites during the battle that day. 22–23The Israelites
went before the LORD and cried until evening.
They asked the LORD, "Shall we go to fight our
relatives, the Benjaminites, again?"

The LORD answered, "Go up and fight them."
The men of Israel encouraged each other. So they
took the same battle positions as they had taken
on the first day.

24The Israelites came to fight the Benjaminites
on the second day. 25The Benjaminites came out
of Gibeah to attack the Israelites. This time, the
Benjaminites killed 18,000 Israelites, all of whom
carried swords.

26Then the Israelites went up to Bethel. There
they sat down and cried to the LORD and went
without food all day until evening. They also
brought burnt offerings and fellowship offerings
to the LORD. 27The Israelites asked the LORD a
question. (In those days the Ark[d] of the Agree-
ment with God was there at Bethel. 28A priest
named Phinehas son of Eleazar, the son of
Aaron, served before the Ark of the Agreement.)
They asked, "Shall we go to fight our rela-
tives, the Benjaminites, again, or shall we stop
fighting?"

The LORD answered, "Go, because tomorrow I
will hand them over to you."

29Then the Israelites set up ambushes all
around Gibeah. 30They went to fight against the
Benjaminites at Gibeah on the third day, getting
into position for battle as they had done before.
31When the Benjaminites came out to fight them,
the Israelites backed up and led the Benjaminites
away from the city. The Benjaminites began to
kill some of the Israelites as they had done before.
About 30 Israelites were killed—some in the
fields and some on the roads leading to Bethel
and to Gibeah.

32The Benjaminites said, "We are winning as
before!"

But the Israelites said, "Let's run. Let's trick
them into going farther away from their city and
onto the roads."

33All the Israelites moved from their places and
got into battle positions at a place named Baal
Tamar. Then the Israelites ran out from their hid-
ing places west of Gibeah. 34Ten thousand of the
best trained soldiers from all of Israel attacked
Gibeah. The battle was very hard. The Benjamin-
ites did not know disaster was about to come to
them. 35The LORD used the Israelites to defeat the
Benjaminites. On that day the Israelites killed
25,100 Benjaminites, all armed with swords.
36Then the Benjaminites saw that they were
defeated.

The Israelites had moved back because they
were depending on the surprise attack they had
set up near Gibeah. 37The men in hiding rushed
into Gibeah, spread out and killed everyone in
the city with their swords. 38Now the Israelites
had set up a signal with the men in hiding. The
men in the surprise attack were to send up a
cloud of smoke from the city. 39Then the army of
Israel turned round in the battle.

The Benjaminites had killed about 30 Israel-
ites. They were saying, "We are winning, as
in the first battle!" 40But then a cloud of smoke
began to rise from the city. The Benjaminites
turned round and saw that the whole city
was going up in smoke. 41Then the Israelites
turned and began to fight. The Benjaminites
were terrified because they knew that disaster
was coming to them. 42So the Benjaminites ran
away from the Israelites towards the desert, but
they could not escape the battle. And the
Israelites who came out of the cities killed
them. 43They surrounded the Benjaminites and
chased them and caught them in the area
east of Gibeah. 44So 18,000 brave Benjaminite

fighters were killed. 45The Benjaminites ran towards the desert to the rock of Rimmon, but the Israelites killed 5,000 Benjaminites along the roads. They chased them as far as Gidom and killed 2,000 more Benjaminites there.

46On that day 25,000 Benjaminites were killed, all of whom had fought bravely with swords. 47But 600 Benjaminites ran to the rock of Rimmon in the desert, where they stayed for four months. 48Then the Israelites went back to the land of Benjamin and killed the people in every city and also the animals and everything they could find. And they burned every city they found.

Wives for the Men of Benjamin

21 At Mizpah the men of Israel had sworn, "Not one of us will let his daughter marry a man from the tribe[d] of Benjamin."

2The people went to the city of Bethel and sat before God until evening, crying loudly. 3They said, "LORD, God of Israel, why has this terrible thing happened to us so that one tribe of Israel is missing today?"

4Early the next day the people built an altar and put burnt offerings and fellowship offerings to God on it.

5Then the Israelites asked, "Did any tribe of Israel not come here to meet with us in the presence of the LORD?" They asked this question because they had sworn that anyone who did not meet with them at Mizpah would be killed.

6The Israelites felt sorry for their relatives, the Benjaminites. They said, "Today one tribe has been cut off from Israel. 7We swore before the LORD that we would not allow our daughters to marry a Benjaminite. How can we make sure that the remaining men of Benjamin will have wives?" 8Then they asked, "Which one of the tribes of Israel did not come here to Mizpah?" They found that no one from the city of Jabesh Gilead had come. 9The people of Israel counted everyone, but there was no one from Jabesh Gilead.

10So the whole group of Israelites sent 12,000 soldiers to Jabesh Gilead to kill the people with their swords, even the women and children.

11"This is what you must do," they said. "Kill every man in Jabesh Gilead and every married woman." 12The soldiers found 400 young unmarried women in Jabesh Gilead, so they brought them to the camp at Shiloh in Canaan.

13Then the whole group of Israelites sent a message to the men of Benjamin, who were at the rock of Rimmon, offering to make peace with them. 14So the men of Benjamin came back at that time. The Israelites gave them the women from Jabesh Gilead who had not been killed, but there were not enough women.

15The people of Israel felt sorry for the Benjaminites because the LORD had separated the tribes of Israel. 16The elders of the Israelites said, "The women of Benjamin have been killed. Where can we get wives for the men of Benjamin who are still alive? 17These men must have children to continue their families so a tribe in Israel will not die out. 18But we cannot allow our daughters to marry them, because we swore, 'Anyone who gives a wife to a man of Benjamin is cursed.' 19We have an idea! There is a yearly festival of the LORD at Shiloh, which is north of the city of Bethel, east of the road that goes from Bethel to Shechem, and south of the city of Lebonah."

20So the elders told the men of Benjamin, "Go and hide in the vineyards. 21Watch for the young women from Shiloh to come out to join the dancing. Then run out from the vineyards and take one of the young Shiloh women and return to the land of Benjamin. 22If their fathers or brothers come to us and complain, we will say: 'Be kind to the men of Benjamin. We did not get wives for Benjamin during the war, and you did not give the women to the men from Benjamin. So you are not guilty.'"

23So that is what the Benjaminites did. While the young women were dancing, each man caught one of them, took her away and married her. Then they went back to the land God had given them and rebuilt their cities and lived there.

24Then the Israelites went home to their own tribes and family groups, to their own land that God had given them.

25In those days Israel did not have a king. Everyone did what seemed right.

Ruth

Why Read This Book:

- See how relationships grow strong (Ruth 1—2).
- Discover the importance of keeping agreements (Ruth 3—4).

When?

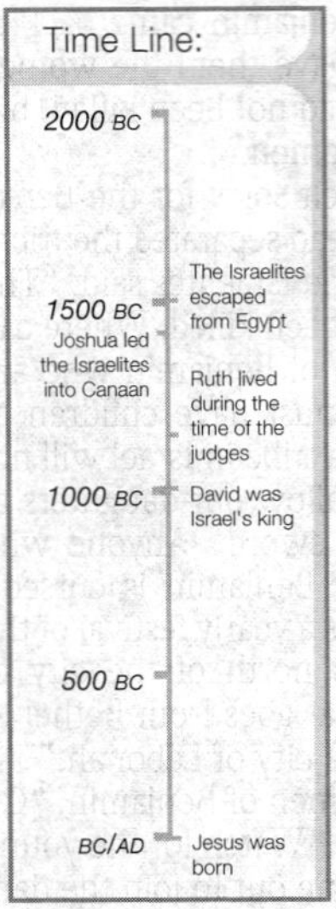

Behind the Scenes:

The story of Ruth would never have made the evening news. There are no wars, no twisted plots, no villains. In fact, much more "important" things were happening at the time. The story took place during the period of the judges (see Judges, p.224), and Israel faced moral decline, foreign attacks and national chaos.

But in the midst of other seemingly important events, the Bible tells the simple, beautiful story of Ruth. It's a story of loyalty and faithfulness, a story of how ordinary people kept following God even when the nation of Israel was abandoning God.

The story opens in Moab, a non-Jewish area, where Naomi had gone to live. Her son had married a Moabite woman, Ruth. After only ten years, Ruth's husband died. Even though Naomi could have left Ruth, she took her in, and the two became close friends.

Then Ruth and Naomi moved to Israel, Naomi's homeland, where Ruth was a foreigner. There Ruth met Boaz, who married her so that Ruth's family name could continue. Years later, one of Ruth's descendants, David, became the greatest king of Israel. ▷

Where?

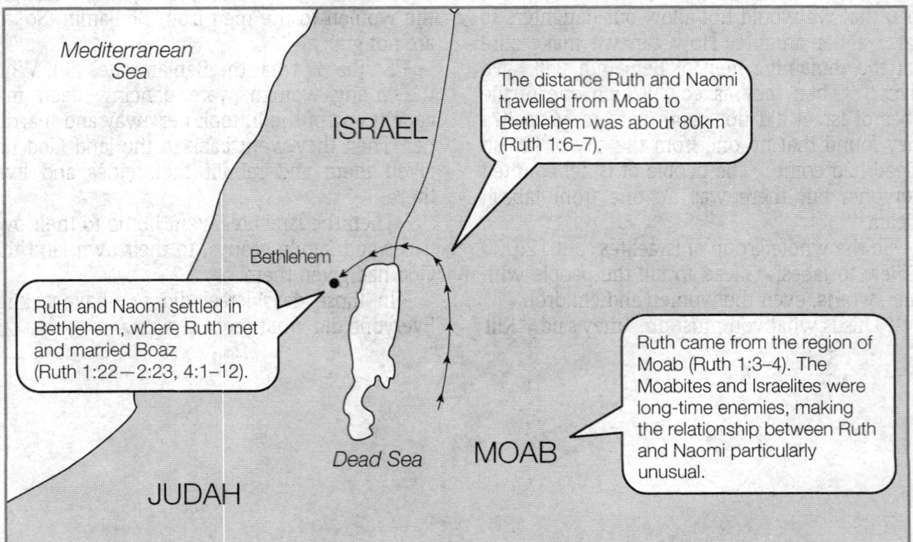

Behind the Scenes (cont.): Even more important, because of her marriage Ruth was included in the family of Jesus Christ (see Matthew 1:5, p.936).

The story of Ruth emphasises the importance of faithfulness and loyalty – of one person to another and to God. Each main character – Ruth, Naomi, Boaz – shows a loyalty beyond what's required.

The story also reminds us that we don't have to be famous or do great things to be important to God. What is most important to God is that people are faithful in whatever they do, whether or not they are famous.

---

1 1-2 Long ago when the judges[n] ruled Israel, there was a shortage of food in the land. So a man named Elimelech left the town of Bethlehem in Judah to live in the country of Moab with his wife and his two sons. His wife was named Naomi, and his two sons were named Mahlon and Kilion. They were from the Ephrathah district from Bethlehem in Judah. When they came to Moab, they settled there.

3 Then Naomi's husband, Elimelech, died, and she was left with her two sons. 4 These sons married women from Moab. One was named Orpah and the other was named Ruth. Naomi and her sons had lived in Moab about ten years 5 when Mahlon and Kilion also died. So Naomi was left alone without her husband or her two sons.

6 While Naomi was in Moab, she heard that the LORD had come to help his people and had given them food again. So she and her daughters-in-law got ready to leave Moab and return home. 7 Naomi and her daughters-in-law left the place where they had lived and started back to the land of Judah. 8 But Naomi said to her two daughters-in-law, "Go back home, each of you to your own mother's house. May the LORD be as kind to you as you have been to me and my sons who are now dead. 9 May the LORD give you another happy home and a new husband."

When Naomi kissed the women goodbye, they began to cry out loud. 10 They said to her, "No, we want to go with you to your people."

11 But Naomi said, "My daughters, return to your own homes. Why do you want to go with me? I cannot give birth to more sons to give you new husbands; 12 go back, my daughters, to your own homes. I am too old to have another husband. Even if I told myself, 'I still have hope' and had another husband tonight, and even if I had more sons, 13 should you wait until they were grown into men? Should you live for so many years without husbands? Don't do that, my daughters. My life is much too sad for you to share, because the LORD has been against me!"

14 The women cried together out loud again. Then Orpah kissed her mother-in-law Naomi goodbye, but Ruth held on to her tightly.

15 Naomi said to Ruth, "Look, your sister-in-law is going back to her own people and her own gods. Go back with her."

Ruth Stays with Naomi

16 But Ruth said, "Don't beg me to leave you or to stop following you. Where you go, I will go. Where you live, I will live. Your people will be my people, and your God will be my God. 17 And where you die, I will die, and there I will be buried. I ask the LORD to punish me terribly if I do not keep this promise: not even death will separate us."

18 When Naomi saw that Ruth had firmly made up her mind to go with her, she stopped arguing with her. 19 So Naomi and Ruth went on until they came to the town of Bethlehem. When they entered Bethlehem, all the people became very excited. The women of the town said, "Is this really Naomi?"

20 Naomi answered the people, "Don't call me Naomi.[n] Call me Mara,[n] because the Almighty has made my life very sad. 21 When I left, I had all I wanted, but now, the LORD has brought me home with nothing. Why should you call me Naomi when the LORD has spoken against me and the Almighty has given me so much trouble?"

22 So Naomi and her daughter-in-law Ruth, the Moabite, returned from Moab and arrived at Bethlehem at the beginning of the barley harvest.

Ruth Meets Boaz

2 Now Naomi had a rich relative named Boaz, from Elimelech's family.

---

judges They were not judges in courts of law, but leaders of the people in times of emergency.
Naomi This name means "happy" or "pleasant".
Mara This name means "bitter" or "sad".

2One day Ruth, the Moabite, said to Naomi, "I
am going to the fields. Maybe someone will be
kind enough to let me gather the grain he leaves
behind."
Naomi said, "Go, my daughter."
3So Ruth went to the fields and gathered the
grain that the workers cutting the grain had left
behind. It just so happened that the field be-
longed to Boaz, from Elimelech's family.

Sidelight When Ruth went to Boaz's field to harvest barley (Ruth 2:1–3), she wasn't stealing. Deuteronomy 24:19–21 (p.187) commanded farmers to leave some of the grain in the field so that the poor could harvest it.

4Soon Boaz came from Bethlehem and greeted
his workers, "The LORD be with you!"
And the workers answered, "May the LORD
bless you!"
5Then Boaz asked his servant in charge of the
workers, "Whose girl is that?"
6The servant answered, "She is the young
Moabite woman who came back with Naomi
from the country of Moab. 7She said, 'Please let
me follow the workers cutting grain and gather
what they leave behind.' She came and has re-
mained here, from morning until just now. She
has stopped only a few moments to rest in the
shelter."
8Then Boaz said to Ruth, "Listen, my daughter.
Don't go to gather grain for yourself in another
field. Don't even leave this field at all, but con-
tinue following closely behind my women work-
ers. 9Watch to see into which fields they go to cut
grain and follow them. I have warned the young
men not to bother you. When you are thirsty, you
may go and drink from the water jugs that the
young men have filled."
10Then Ruth bowed low with her face to the
ground and said to him, "I am not an Israelite.
Why have you been so kind to notice me?"
11Boaz answered her, "I know about all the
help you have given your mother-in-law after
your husband died. You left your father and
mother and your own country to come to a na-
tion where you did not know anyone. 12May the

FRIENDS

A Little Encouragement

Bruce would lie awake at night waiting to hear the sound of a car driving up. When he did, he would run to the front door to unlock it. Then he would cry with fear as his stepfather stumbled in, reeking of alcohol. Doors slammed. Dishes broke in the kitchen. The horrible yelling at his mother made Bruce wish his alcoholic stepfather would die.

Bruce might have gone mad if it hadn't been for friends like Tom. Tom was a year older than Bruce. The two laughed a lot together, and Tom taught Bruce how to fix cars. Whenever Tom gave Bruce a lift somewhere, he would end the trip by saying, "Stay cool, Bruce." Bruce knew he meant, "Hang on in there."

Those were hard times for Bruce, but he survived because of his friends – people like Tom.

Ruth and Naomi also faced hard times. Both lost their husbands, and Naomi also lost both her sons. But because of their friendship with each other, they got through it all. Read about their relationship in **Ruth 1:1–19**.

- How were Bruce's and Ruth's situations made better by friends?
- How can Ruth's example help you be a more committed friend?

Consider . . .

- befriending a newcomer at school or someone with a different background from you.
- being a committed friend to someone who is facing hard times by letting him or her talk openly about their problems.

For more, see . . .

- Leviticus 19:9–10 (p.118)
- 1 John 3:11–18 (p.1374)
- 1 Samuel 20:11–17 (p.274)

LORD reward you for all you have done. May your
wages be paid in full by the LORD, the God of
Israel, under whose wings you have come for
shelter."
13Then Ruth said, "I hope I can continue to
please you, sir. You have said kind and encour-
aging words to me, your servant, though I am not
one of your servants."
14At mealtime Boaz told Ruth, "Come here.
Eat some of our bread and dip it in our vinegar."
So Ruth sat down beside the workers. Boaz
handed her some roasted grain, and she ate until
she was full; she even had some food left over.
15When Ruth rose and went back to work, Boaz
commanded his workers, "Let her gather even
around the piles of cut grain. Don't tell her to go
away. 16In fact, drop some full heads of grain for
her from what you have in your hands, and let
her gather them. Don't tell her to stop."
17So Ruth gathered grain in the field until eve-
ning. Then she separated the grain from the
chaff,[d] and there was about 10 kilogrammes of
barley. 18Ruth carried the grain into town, and
her mother-in-law saw how much she had gath-
ered. Ruth also took out the food that was left
over from lunch and gave it to Naomi.
19Naomi asked her, "Where did you gather all
this grain today? Where did you work? Blessed be
whoever noticed you!"
Ruth told her mother-in-law whose field she
had worked in. She said, "The man I worked
with today is named Boaz."
20Naomi told her daughter-in-law, "The LORD
bless him! He continues to be kind to us—both
the living and the dead!" Then Naomi told Ruth,
"Boaz is one of our close relatives,[n] one who
should take care of us."
21Then Ruth, the Moabite, said, "Boaz also told
me, 'Keep close to my workers until they have
finished my whole harvest.' "
22But Naomi said to her daughter-in-law Ruth,
"It is better for you to continue working with his
women workers. If you work in another field,
someone might hurt you." 23So Ruth continued
working closely with the workers of Boaz, gather-
ing grain until the barley harvest and the wheat
harvest were finished. And she continued to live
with Naomi, her mother-in-law.

Naomi's Plan

3 Then Naomi, Ruth's mother-in-law, said to
her, "My daughter, I must find a suitable
home for you, one that will be good for you.
2Now Boaz, whose young women you worked
with, is our close relative.[n] Tonight he will be
working at the threshing[d] floor. 3Wash yourself,
put on perfume, change your clothes and go
down to the threshing floor. But don't let him
know you're there until he has finished his din-
ner. 4Watch him so you will know where he lies
down to sleep. When he lies down, go and lift the
cover off his feet[n] and lie down. He will tell you
what you should do."
5Then Ruth answered, "I will do everything
you say."
6So Ruth went down to the threshing floor and
did all her mother-in-law told her to do. 7After
his evening meal, Boaz felt good and went to
sleep lying beside the pile of grain. Ruth went to
him quietly and lifted the cover from his feet and
lay down.
8About midnight Boaz was startled and rolled
over. There was a woman lying near his feet!
9Boaz asked, "Who are you?"
She said, "I am Ruth, your servant girl. Spread
your cover over me, because you are a relative
who is supposed to take care of me."[n]
10Then Boaz said, "The LORD bless you, my
daughter. This act of kindness is greater than the
kindness you showed to Naomi in the beginning.
You didn't look for a young man to marry, either
rich or poor. 11Now, my daughter, don't be
afraid. I will do everything you ask, because all
the people in our town know you are a good
woman. 12It is true that I am a relative who is to
take care of you, but you have a closer relative
than I. 13Stay here tonight, and in the morning
we will see if he will take care of you. If he
decides to take care of you, that is fine. But if he
refuses, I will take care of you myself, as surely as
the LORD lives. So stay here until morning."
14So Ruth stayed near his feet until morning
but got up while it was still too dark to recognise
anyone. Boaz thought, "People in town must not
know that the woman came here to the threshing
floor." 15So Boaz said to Ruth, "Bring me your
shawl and hold it open."
So Ruth held her shawl open, and Boaz poured
six portions of barley into it. Boaz then put it on
her head and went back to the city.
16When Ruth went back to her mother-in-law,
Naomi asked, "How did you do, my daughter?"
Ruth told Naomi everything that Boaz did for
her. 17She said, "Boaz gave me these six portions
of barley, saying, 'You must not go home without
a gift for your mother-in-law.' "

close relatives In Bible times the closest relative could marry a widow without children so she could have children. He would care for this family, but they and their property would not belong to him. They would belong to the dead husband.
lift . . . feet This showed Ruth was asking him to be her husband.
Spread . . . me By this, Ruth was asking Boaz to marry her.

18Naomi answered, "Ruth, my daughter, wait
here until you see what happens. Boaz will not
rest until he has finished doing what he should do
today."

Boaz Marries Ruth

4 Boaz went to the city gate and sat there until
the close relative he had mentioned passed
by. Boaz called to him, "Come here, friend, and
sit down." So the man came over and sat down.
2Boaz gathered ten of the elders of the city and
told them, "Sit down here!" So they sat down.
3Then Boaz said to the close relative, "Naomi,
who has come back from the country of Moab,
wants to sell the piece of land that belonged to
our relative Elimelech. 4So I decided to tell you
about it. If you want to buy back the land, then
buy it in front of the people who are sitting here
and in front of the elders of my people. But if you
don't want to buy it, tell me, because you are the
only one who can buy it, and I am next after
you."
The close relative answered, "I will buy back
the land."
5Then Boaz explained, "When you buy the
land from Naomi, you must also marry Ruth, the
Moabite, the dead man's wife. That way, the land
will stay in the dead man's name."
6The close relative answered, "I can't buy back
the land. If I did, I might harm what I can pass
on to my own sons. I cannot buy the land back, so
buy it yourself."
7Long ago in Israel when people traded or
bought back something, one person took off his
sandal and gave it to the other person. This was
the proof of purchase in Israel.
8So the close relative said to Boaz, "Buy the
land yourself," and he took off his sandal.

MARRIAGE

What a Drag!

Fran was nervous – she always was when she was watching her fiancé Andrew prepare for a race. It wasn't that he was a bad driver – but even some of the best drag racers had been killed. All she could do was to watch and pray.

His team closed the cockpit of the dragster and Andrew nudged it forwards to the starting line. The flag came down and his foot slammed down hard on the accelerator. A drag race only lasted a few seconds, so there was never any time to think about anything.

And then it happened. Fran screamed as Andrew's car flipped over and rolled under the crash barrier. The emergency team ran to the overturned racer and helped Andrew out; he was badly shaken, but not hurt. Fran ran to him, with tears running down her face, relieved that he was all right.

Andrew removed his helmet and took a hard look, first at his wrecked racer, and then at his fiancée. Taking a breath he said, "This is no good. I hate seeing you hurt so much every time I race. I've decided to quit. If nothing else, it will show you how much you mean to me."

Andrew showed his commitment to Fran by giving up the sport that he loved. When Boaz married Ruth, he also demonstrated his commitment to her. Read all about it in **Ruth 4:7–17**.

- How did Boaz demonstrate his commitment to Ruth? How does this compare with the way Andrew showed his commitment to Fran?
- What can you learn from this passage about what is most important when choosing a husband or wife?

Consider . . .

- writing a list of characteristics that you would hope to find in a marriage partner. Review this list, bearing in mind your faith and commitments.
- asking a married couple that you know about their commitment to each other and how it maintains a strong relationship.

For more, see . . .

- Genesis 29:15–30 (p.34)
- Ephesians 5:21–33 (p.1275)
- Matthew 19:4–6 (p.974)

9Then Boaz said to the elders and to all the people, "You are witnesses today. I am buying from Naomi everything that belonged to Elimelech and Kilion and Mahlon. 10I am also taking Ruth, the Moabite who was the wife of Mahlon, as my wife. I am doing this so her dead husband's property will stay in his name and his name will not be separated from his family and his home town. You are witnesses today."

11So all the people and elders who were at the city gate said, "We are witnesses. May the LORD make this woman, who is coming into your home, like Rachel and Leah, who had many children and built up the people of Israel. May you become powerful in the district of Ephrathah and famous in Bethlehem. 12As Tamar gave birth to Judah's son Perez,[n] may the LORD give you many children through Ruth. May your family be great like his."

Sidelight Once Ruth had chosen God (Ruth 1:16) and remained faithful to him, her life changed – from having nothing in Chapter 1, she slowly reaped God's blessings. Once she was married to Boaz, she came to be the great-grandmother of King David and an ancestor of Jesus.

13So Boaz took Ruth home as his wife and had sexual relations with her. The LORD let her become pregnant, and she gave birth to a son. 14The women told Naomi, "Praise the LORD who gave you this grandson. May he become famous in Israel. 15He will give you new life and will take care of you in your old age because of your daughter-in-law who loves you. She is better for you than seven sons, because she has given birth to your grandson."

16Naomi took the boy, held him in her arms and cared for him. 17The neighbours gave the boy his name, saying, "This boy was born for Naomi." They named him Obed. Obed was the father of Jesse, and Jesse was the father of David.

18This is the family history of Perez, the father of Hezron. 19Hezron was the father of Ram, who was the father of Amminadab. 20Amminadab was the father of Nahshon, who was the father of Salmon. 21Salmon was the father of Boaz, who was the father of Obed. 22Obed was the father of Jesse, and Jesse was the father of David.

Perez One of Boaz's ancestors.

1 Samuel

Why Read This Book:

- See how God uses great leaders (1 Samuel 1—7).
- Discover what can happen when leaders don't obey God (1 Samuel 8—15).
- Find out how God can unite a nation under a holy leader (1 Samuel 16—31).

When?

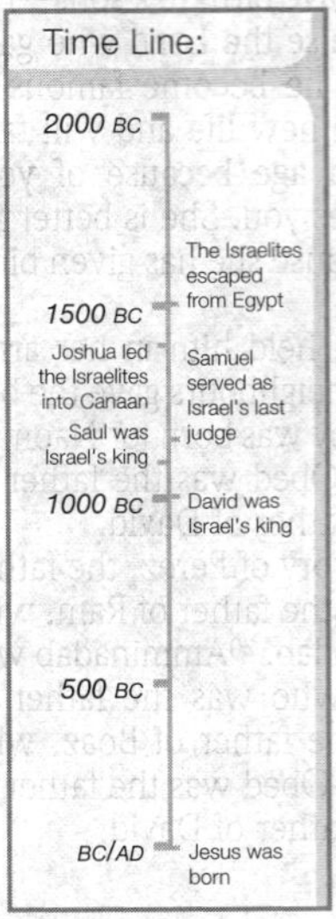

Behind the Scenes:

The pupils of the comprehensive school didn't get along very well with the pupils from the neighbouring school. There wasn't any reason for their dislike. The simple fact was that they preferred to keep themselves to themselves.

But when the local council announced that it was going to close the nearby sports centre, the pupils forgot their differences and united to fight the closure. The sports centre was an important facility which both schools used on a regular basis, and so the pupils got together and organised a protest march. A week later, the local council announced that they had changed their minds about the sports centre, and reassured both schools that it would remain open for their use.

At the time of Samuel, the Israelites lived in a similar situation. The twelve tribes existed independently, but always in fear of the Philistines who possessed superior iron weapons and controlled the fertile plains along the Mediterranean Sea – but wanted more. They wanted to conquer the Israelites and take their land too. ▷

Where?

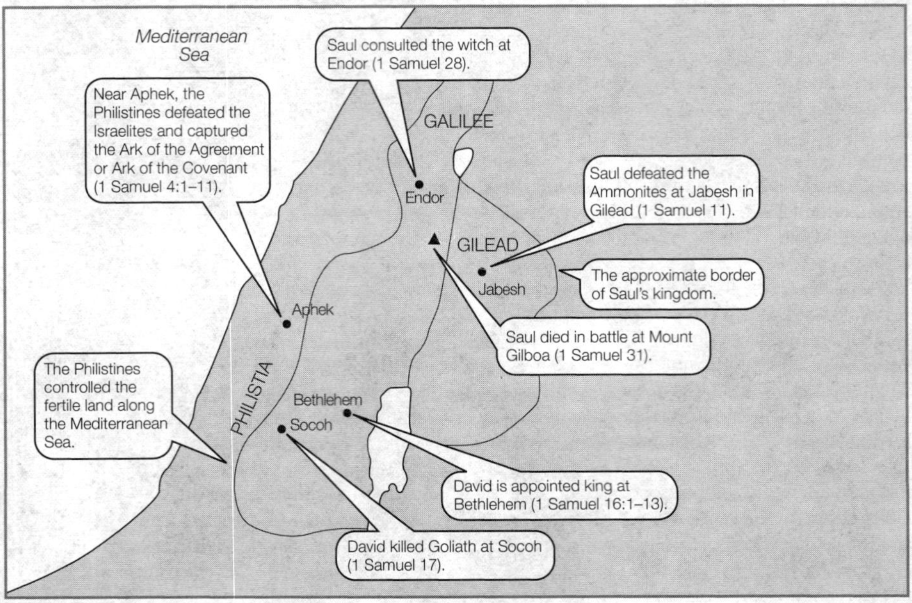

Behind the Scenes (cont.): In order to survive, the twelve tribes united and elected Samuel as their common leader. Samuel changed Israel's history. He stopped the Philistines from advancing, and then went on to appoint srael's first two kings: King Saul and King David.

1 Samuel contains some of the most exciting stories in the Bible, including Saul's spectacular victories over the Philistines, David's famous battle with Goliath, and David's friendship with Jonathan. Through the stories 1 Samuel teaches us about the importance of having leaders who follow God.

Samuel's Birth

1 There was a man named Elkanah son of
Jeroham from Ramathaim in the mountains
of Ephraim. Elkanah was from the family of Zuph.
(Jeroham was Elihu's son. Elihu was Tohu's son,
and Tohu was the son of Zuph from the family
group of Ephraim.) [2]Elkanah had two wives named
Hannah and Peninnah. Peninnah had children,
but Hannah had none.

> **Sidelight** 1 and 2 Samuel were originally one book. The prophet Samuel – after whom the books were named – doesn't actually appear in 2 Samuel.

[3]Every year Elkanah left his town of Ramah
and went up to Shiloh to worship the LORD All-
powerful [d] and to offer sacrifices to him. Shiloh
was where Hophni and Phinehas, the sons of Eli,
served as priests of the LORD. [4]When Elkanah of-
fered sacrifices, he always gave a share of the
meat to his wife Peninnah and to her sons and
daughters. [5]But Elkanah always gave a special
share of the meat to Hannah, because he loved
Hannah and because the LORD had kept her from
having children. [6]Peninnah would tease Hannah
and upset her, because the LORD had made her
unable to have children. [7]This happened every
year when they went up to the house of the LORD
at Shiloh. Peninnah would upset Hannah until
Hannah would cry and not eat anything. [8]Her
husband Elkanah would say to her, "Hannah,
why are you crying and why won't you eat? Why
are you sad? Don't I mean more to you than ten
sons?"
[9]Once, after they had eaten their meal in
Shiloh, Hannah got up. Now Eli the priest was
sitting on a chair near the entrance to the LORD's
house. [10]Hannah was so sad that she cried and
prayed to the LORD. [11]She made a promise, saying,
"LORD All-powerful, see how sad I am. Remember
me and don't forget me. If you will give me a son,
I will give him back to you all his life, and no one
will ever cut his hair with a razor."[n]
[12]While Hannah kept praying, Eli watched her
mouth. [13]She was praying in her heart so her lips
moved, but her voice was not heard. Eli thought
she was drunk [14]and said to her, "Stop getting
drunk! Throw away your wine!"
[15]Hannah answered, "No, sir, I have not drunk
any wine or beer. I am a deeply troubled woman,
and I was telling the LORD about all my problems.
[16]Don't think I am an evil woman. I have been
praying because I have many troubles and am
very sad."
[17]Eli answered, "Go! I wish you well. May
the God of Israel give you what you asked of
him."
[18]Hannah said, "May I always please you."
When she left and ate something, she was not
sad any more.
[19]Early the next morning Elkanah's family got
up and worshipped the LORD. Then they went
back home to Ramah. Elkanah had sexual rela-
tions with his wife Hannah, and the LORD remem-
bered her. [20]So Hannah became pregnant, and in
time she gave birth to a son. She named him
Samuel, [n] saying, "His name is Samuel because I
asked the LORD for him."

Hannah Gives Samuel to God

[21]Every year Elkanah went with his whole
family to Shiloh to offer sacrifices and to keep the
promise he had made to God. [22]But one year
Hannah did not go with him. She told him,
"When the boy is old enough to eat solid food, I
will take him to Shiloh. Then I will give him to
the LORD, and he will always live there."

cut . . . razor People who made special promises not to cut their hair or to drink wine or beer were called Nazirites. These people gave a specific time in their lives, or sometimes their entire lives, to the LORD. See Numbers 6:1–5.
Samuel This name sounds like the Hebrew word for "God heard".

23Elkanah, Hannah's husband, said to her, "Do
what you think is best. You may stay home until
the boy is old enough to eat. May the LORD do
what you have said." So Hannah stayed at home
to nurse her son until he was old enough to eat.
24When Samuel was old enough to eat, Han-
nah took him to the house of the LORD at Shiloh,
along with a three-year-old bull, ten kilogrammes
of flour, and a leather bag filled with wine. 25After
they had killed the bull for the sacrifice, Hannah
brought Samuel to Eli. 26She said to Eli, "As
surely as you live, sir, I am the same woman who
stood near you praying to the LORD. 27I prayed for
this child, and the LORD answered my prayer and
gave him to me. 28Now I give him back to the
LORD. He will belong to the LORD all his life." And
he worshipped the LORD there.

Hannah Gives Thanks

2 Hannah prayed:

"The LORD has filled my heart with joy;
I feel very strong in the LORD.
I can laugh at my enemies;
I am glad because you have helped me!

2"There is no one holy like the LORD.
There is no God but you;
there is no Rock[d] like our God.

3"Don't continue boasting,
don't speak proud words.
The LORD is a God who knows everything,
and he judges what people do.

4"The bows of warriors break,
but weak people become strong.
5Those who once had plenty of food now
must work for food,
but people who were hungry are hungry no
more.
The woman who could not have children
now has seven,
but the woman who had many children
now is sad.

BOASTING

She Spoke Too Soon

Elaine knew she was good looking. Stylish hair. Perfect complexion. Long eyelashes. Flawless figure. Whenever she had a chance, she would point out her own beauty and ridicule the "plain" girls. "Don't you care how you look?" she would say if someone's hair wasn't carefully curled or if make-up didn't hide every spot. "You really should take care of yourself . . . like I do."

When it was time for the local beauty contest, everyone knew Elaine would enter. And Elaine knew she would win. "Who round here can compete with me?" she would sneer.

As it turned out, Laura could. Laura entered the pageant because she wanted extra cash to eke out her college grant. And although she wasn't as strikingly beautiful as Elaine, her personality and smile gave her the edge.

When Laura was crowned, Elaine didn't even congratulate her. She burst into tears and stormed off the stage. "The judges are just stupid!" she cried, alone in the dressing room. "This whole thing is stupid!"

Elaine discovered how dangerous and humiliating boasting can be. Read **1 Samuel 2:1–10** to see what God thinks of people who boast.

- How does the passage describe what happened to Elaine? What does it say about Laura?
- What caution about events like beauty contests do you see?

Consider . . .

- stopping yourself next time you're tempted to boast about a high score or success. Instead, use your gifts to help others.
- thanking God for the gifts you have, instead of boasting about them.

For more, see . . .

- Proverbs 16:18–20 (p.603)
- Luke 1:46–55 (p.1037)
- Jeremiah 9:23–24 (p.728)

6"The LORD sends death,
and he brings to life.
He sends people to the grave,
and he raises them to life again.
7The LORD makes some people poor,
and others he makes rich.
He makes some people humble,
and others he makes great.
8The LORD raises the poor up from the dust,
and he lifts the needy from the ashes.
He lets the poor sit with princes
and receive a throne of honour.

"The foundations of the earth belong to the
LORD,
and the LORD set the world upon them.
9He protects those who are loyal to him,
but evil people will be silenced in darkness.
Power is not the key to success.
10The LORD destroys his enemies;
he will thunder in heaven against them.
The LORD will judge all the earth.
He will give power to his king
and make his appointed king strong."

Eli's Evil Sons

11Then Elkanah went home to Ramah, but the
boy continued to serve the LORD under Eli the
priest.
12Now Eli's sons were evil men; they did not
care about the LORD. 13This is what the priests
would normally do to the people: every time
someone brought a sacrifice, the meat would be
cooked in a pot. The priest's servant would then
come carrying a fork that had three prongs. 14He
would plunge the fork into the pot or the kettle.
Whatever the fork brought out of the pot be-
longed to the priest. But this is how they treated
all the Israelites who came to Shiloh to offer sac-
rifices. 15Even before the fat was burned, the
priest's servant would come to the person offer-
ing sacrifices and say, "Give the priest some meat
to roast. He won't accept boiled meat from you,
only raw meat."
16If the one who offered the sacrifice said, "Let
the fat be burned up first as usual, and then take
anything you want," the priest's servant would
answer, "No, give me the meat now. If you don't,
I'll take it by force."
17The LORD saw that the sin of the servants
was very great because they did not show respect
for the offerings made to the LORD.

Samuel Grows Up

18But Samuel obeyed the LORD. As a boy he
wore a linen holy robe.[d] 19Every year Samuel's
mother made a little coat for him and took it to
him when she went with her husband to Shiloh
for the sacrifice. 20When Eli blessed Elkanah and
his wife, he would say, "May the LORD repay you
with children through Hannah to take the place
of the boy Hannah prayed for and gave back to
the LORD." Then Elkanah and Hannah would go
home. 21The LORD was kind to Hannah, so she
became the mother of three sons and two daugh-
ters. And the boy Samuel grew up serving the
LORD.
22Now Eli was very old. He heard about every-
thing his sons were doing to all the Israelites
and how his sons had sexual relations with the
women who served at the entrance to the Meet-
ing Tent.[d] 23Eli said to his sons, "Why do you do
these evil things that the people tell me about?
24No, my sons. The LORD's people are spreading
a bad report about you. 25If you sin against some-
one, God can help you. But if you sin against the
LORD himself, no one can help you!" But Eli's sons
would not listen to him, because the LORD had
decided to put them to death.
26The boy Samuel grew physically. He pleased
the LORD and the people.
27A man of God came to Eli and said, "This is
what the LORD says: 'I clearly showed myself to
the family of your ancestor Aaron when they
were slaves to the king of Egypt. 28I chose them
from all the tribes[d] of Israel to be my priests. I
wanted them to go up to my altar, to burn
incense[d] and to wear the holy robe. I also let
the family of your ancestor have part of all the
offerings sacrificed by the Israelites. 29So why
don't you respect the sacrifices and gifts? You
honour your sons more than me. You grow fat
on the best parts of the meat the Israelites bring
to me.'
30"So the LORD, the God of Israel, says: 'I prom-
ised that your family and your ancestor's family
would serve me always.' But now the LORD says:
'This must stop! I will honour those who honour
me, but I will dishonour those who ignore me.
31The time is coming when I will destroy the
descendants[d] of both you and your ancestors.
No man will grow old in your family. 32You will see
trouble in my house. No matter what good things
happen to Israel, there will never be an old man
in your family. 33I will not totally cut off your
family from my altar. But your eyes will cry and
your heart be sad, because all your descendants
will die.
34" 'I will give you a sign. Both your sons,
Hophni and Phinehas, will die on the same day.
35I will choose a loyal priest for myself who will
listen to me and do what I want. I will make his
family continue, and he will always serve before
my appointed king. 36Then everyone left in your
family will come and bow down before him.

They will beg for a little money or a little food
and say, "Please give me a job as priest so I can
have food to eat."[1] "

God Calls Samuel

3 The boy Samuel served the LORD under Eli. In
those days the LORD did not speak directly to
people very often; there were very few visions.
2Eli's eyes were so weak he was almost blind.
One night he was lying in bed. 3Samuel was also
in bed in the LORD's house, where the Ark[d] of the
Agreement was. God's lamp was still burning.
4Then the LORD called Samuel, and Samuel an-
swered, "I am here!" 5He ran to Eli and said, "I
am here. You called me."
But Eli said, "I didn't call you. Go back to
bed." So Samuel went back to bed.
6The LORD called again, "Samuel!"
Samuel again went to Eli and said, "I am here.
You called me."
Again Eli said, "I didn't call you. Go back
to bed."
7Samuel did not yet know the LORD, and the
LORD had not spoken directly to him yet.
8The LORD called Samuel for the third time.
Samuel got up and went to Eli and said, "I am
here. You called me."
Then Eli realised the LORD was calling the boy.
9So he told Samuel, "Go to bed. If he calls you
again, say, 'Speak, LORD. I am your servant and I
am listening.' " So Samuel went and lay down in
bed.
10The LORD came and stood there and called
as he had before, "Samuel, Samuel!"
Samuel said, "Speak, LORD. I am your servant
and I am listening."

FOLLOWING GOD

Did Someone Call?

From the time she learned to play the flute, Jessica wanted to be a musician. She spent hours practising her flute for the school orchestra.

When Jessica wasn't practising her music, she was working on the school magazine. She hadn't planned on doing it, but her teacher had asked her to be magazine editor.

"I know you love music," her teacher told her, "but maybe you're overlooking your writing gifts."

Jessica dismissed the thought and kept concentrating on music. She regularly entered music competitions, hoping to get into a good music college. She did well in regional competitions, but never at national level. However, when the school magazine was entered in a national competition, it won first place.

"What's going on?" Jessica wondered, as she filled out applications for music schools. Her teacher's words came to mind: "Maybe you're overlooking your writing gifts."

Jessica went to music college, but didn't do well. She didn't enjoy all the theory and hours of practise. To lift her spirits, she went to work at the college newspaper. Now that was fun!

After the first term, she knew what she had to do. She dropped music and switched to English and communications.

"It took me a while to figure out what to do," she recalls. "I'm glad I finally paid attention to the gifts God gave me."

It took several years for Jessica to understand how God wanted her to use her gifts. Similarly, Samuel didn't recognise God's call right away in **1 Samuel 3:1–20**. But by listening to the advice of Eli the priest, Samuel heard and followed God's call.

- What signs did Jessica see that were similar to the calls Samuel heard?
- When have you, like Samuel, had trouble knowing what God wanted you to do?

Consider . . .

- silently listening for God's direction when you pray.
- asking someone you respect to help you figure out ways God might want you to follow him.

For more, see . . .

- Isaiah 6:1–8 (p.645)
- Acts 9:1–19 (p.1152)
- Mark 1:16–20 (p.997)

11The LORD said to Samuel, "Watch, I am going to do something in Israel that will shock those who hear about it. 12At that time I will do to Eli and his family everything I promised, from beginning to end. 13I told Eli I would punish his family always, because he knew his sons were evil. They acted without honour, but he did not stop them. 14So I swore to Eli's family, 'Your guilt will never be removed by sacrifice or offering.' "

15Samuel lay down until morning. Then he opened the doors of the house of the LORD. He was afraid to tell Eli about the vision, 16but Eli called to him, "Samuel, my son!"

Samuel answered, "I am here."

17Eli asked, "What did the LORD say to you? Don't hide it from me. May God punish you terribly if you hide from me anything he said to you." 18So Samuel told Eli everything and did not hide anything from him. Then Eli said, "He is the LORD. Let him do what he thinks is best."

19The LORD was with Samuel as he grew up; he did not let any of Samuel's messages fail to come true. 20Then all Israel, from Dan to Beersheba,[n] knew Samuel was a true prophet[d] of the LORD. 21And the LORD continued to show himself at Shiloh, and he showed himself to Samuel through his word.

4 So, news about Samuel spread through all of Israel.

The Philistines Capture the Ark of the Agreement

At that time the Israelites went out to fight the Philistines. The Israelites camped at Ebenezer and the Philistines at Aphek. 2The Philistines went to meet the Israelites in battle. And as the battle spread, they defeated the Israelites, killing about 4,000 soldiers on the battlefield. 3When some Israelite soldiers went back to their camp, the elders of Israel asked, "Why did the LORD let the Philistines defeat us? Let's bring the Ark[d] of the Agreement with the LORD here from Shiloh and take it with us into battle. Then God will save us from our enemies."

4So the people sent men to Shiloh. They brought back the Ark of the Agreement with the LORD All-powerful, who sits between the gold creatures with wings. Eli's two sons, Hophni and Phinehas, were there with the Ark.

5When the Ark of the Agreement with the LORD came into the camp, all the Israelites gave a great shout of joy that made the ground shake. 6When the Philistines heard Israel's shout, they asked, "What's all this shouting in the Hebrew camp?"

Then the Philistines found out that the Ark of the LORD had come into the Hebrew camp. 7They were afraid and said, "A god has come into the Hebrew camp! We're in trouble! This has never happened before! 8How terrible it will be for us! Who can save us from these powerful gods? They are the ones who struck the Egyptians with all kinds of disasters in the desert. 9Be brave, Philistines! Fight like men! In the past they were our slaves. So fight like men, or we will become their slaves."

10So the Philistines fought hard and defeated the Israelites, and every Israelite soldier ran away to his own home. It was a great defeat for Israel, because 30,000 Israelite soldiers were killed. 11The Ark of God was taken by the Philistines, and Eli's two sons, Hophni and Phinehas, died.

12That same day a man from the tribe[d] of Benjamin ran from the battle. He tore his clothes and put dust on his head to show his great sadness. 13When he arrived in Shiloh, Eli was by the side of the road. He was sitting there in a chair, watching, because he was worried about the Ark of God. When the Benjaminite entered Shiloh, he told the bad news. Then all the people in town cried loudly. 14Eli heard the crying and asked, "What's all this noise?"

The Benjaminite ran to Eli and told him what had happened. 15Eli was now 98 years old, and he was blind. 16The Benjaminite told him, "I have come from the battle. I ran all the way here today."

Eli asked, "What happened, my son?"

17The Benjaminite answered, "Israel ran away from the Philistines, and the Israelite army has lost many soldiers. Your two sons are both dead, and the Philistines have taken the Ark of God."

18When he mentioned the Ark of God, Eli fell backwards off his chair. He fell beside the gate, broke his neck, and died, because he was old and fat. He had led Israel for 40 years.

Sidelight

Have you ever been told not to lean back on your chair? You could fall over backwards. Eli did . . . and died (1 Samuel 4:18).

The Glory is Gone

19Eli's daughter-in-law, the wife of Phinehas, was pregnant and was about to give birth. When she heard the news that the Ark[d] of God had been taken and that Eli, her father-in-law, and Phinehas, her husband, were both dead, she

Dan to Beersheba Dan was the city farthest north in Israel, and Beersheba was the city farthest south. So this means all the people of Israel.

began to give birth to her child. The child was
born, but the mother had much trouble in giving
birth. [20]As she was dying, the women who helped
her said, "Don't worry! You've given birth to a
son!" But she did not answer or pay attention.
[21]She named the baby Ichabod,[n] saying, "Israel's
glory is gone." She said this because the Ark of
God had been taken and her father-in-law and
husband were dead. [22]She said, "Israel's glory is
gone, because the Ark of God has been taken
away."

Trouble for the Philistines

5 After the Philistines had captured the Ark[d]
of God, they took it from Ebenezer to Ash-
dod. [2]They carried it into Dagon's[d] temple and
put it next to Dagon. [3]When the people of Ash-
dod rose early the next morning, they found
that Dagon had fallen on his face on the ground
before the Ark of the LORD. So they put Dagon
back in his place. [4]The next morning when they
rose, they again found Dagon fallen on the
ground before the Ark of the LORD. His head and
hands had broken off and were lying in the
doorway. Only his body was still in one piece.
[5]So, even today, Dagon's priests and others who
enter his temple at Ashdod refuse to step on the
doorsill.

[6]The LORD was hard on the people of Ashdod
and their neighbours. He caused them to suffer
and gave them growths on their skin. [7]When the
people of Ashdod saw what was happening, they
said, "The Ark of the God of Israel can't stay with
us. God is punishing us and Dagon our god."
[8]The people of Ashdod called all five Philistine
kings together and asked them, "What should we
do with the Ark of the God of Israel?"

The rulers answered, "Move the Ark of the
God of Israel to Gath." So the Philistines moved
it to Gath.

[9]But after they moved it to Gath, there was a
great panic. The LORD was hard on that city also,
and he gave both old and young people in Gath
growths on their skin. [10]Then the Philistines sent
the Ark of God to Ekron.

But when it came into Ekron, the people of
Ekron yelled, "Why are you bringing the Ark of
the God of Israel to our city? Do you want to kill
us and our people?" [11]So they called all the kings
of the Philistines together and said, "Send the Ark
of the God of Israel back to its place before it kills
us and our people!" All the people in the city
were struck with terror because God was so hard
on them there. [12]The people who did not die
were troubled with growths on their skin. So the
people of Ekron cried loudly to heaven.

The Ark of God is Sent Home

6 The Philistines kept the Ark[d] of God in their
land seven months. [2]Then they called for
their priests and magicians and said, "What
should we do with the Ark of the LORD? Tell us
how to send it back home!"

[3]The priests and magicians answered, "If you
send back the Ark of the God of Israel, don't send
it back empty. You must give a penalty offering. If
you are then healed, you will know that it was
because of the Ark that you had such trouble."

[4]The Philistines asked, "What kind of penalty
offering should we send to Israel's God?"

They answered, "Make five gold models of
the growths on your skin and five gold models of
rats. The number of models must match the num-
ber of Philistine kings, because the same sickness
has come on you and your kings. [5]Make models
of the growths and the rats that are ruining the
country, and give honour to Israel's God. Then
maybe he will stop being so hard on you, your
gods and your land. [6]Don't be stubborn like the
king of Egypt and the Egyptians. God punished
them terribly until they let the Israelites leave
Egypt.

[7]"You must build a new cart and get two cows
that have just had calves. These must be cows
that have never had yokes[d] on their necks. Hitch
the cows to the cart, and take the calves home,
away from their mothers. [8]Put the Ark of the
LORD on the cart and the gold models for the
penalty offering in a box beside the Ark. Then
send the cart straight on its way. [9]Watch the cart.
If it goes towards Beth Shemesh in Israel's own
land, the LORD has given us this great sickness.
But if it doesn't, we will know that Israel's God
has not punished us. Our sickness just happened
by chance."

[10]The Philistines did what the priests and magi-
cians said. They took two cows that had just had
calves and hitched them to the cart, but they kept
their calves at home. [11]They put the Ark of the
LORD and the box with the gold rats and models
of growths on the cart. [12]Then the cows went
straight towards Beth Shemesh. They stayed on
the road, mooing all the way, and did not turn
right or left. The Philistine kings followed the
cows as far as the border of Beth Shemesh.

[13]Now the people of Beth Shemesh were har-
vesting their wheat in the valley. When they
looked up and saw the Ark of the LORD, they were
very happy. [14]The cart came to the field belonging
to Joshua of Beth Shemesh and stopped near
a large rock. The people of Beth Shemesh
chopped up the wood of the cart. Then they sac-
rificed the cows as burnt offerings to the LORD.

Ichabod This name means "no glory".

15The Levites took down the Ark of the LORD and the box that had the gold models, and they put both on the large rock. That day the people of Beth Shemesh offered whole burnt offerings and made sacrifices to the LORD. 16After the five Philistine kings saw this, they went back to Ekron the same day.

17The Philistines had sent these gold models of the growths as penalty offerings to the LORD. They sent one model for each Philistine town: Ashdod, Gaza, Ashkelon, Gath and Ekron. 18And the Philistines also sent gold models of rats. The number of rats matched the number of towns belonging to the Philistine kings, including both fortified cities and country villages. The large rock on which they put the Ark of the LORD is still there in the field of Joshua of Beth Shemesh.

19But some of the men of Beth Shemesh looked into the Ark of the LORD. So God killed 70 of them. The people of Beth Shemesh cried because the LORD had struck them down. 20They said, "Who can stand before the LORD, this holy God? Whom will he strike next?"

21Then they sent messengers to the people of Kiriath Jearim, saying, "The Philistines have brought back the Ark of the LORD. Come down and take it to your city."

7 The men of Kiriath Jearim came and took the Ark of the LORD to Abinadab's house on a hill. There they made Abinadab's son Eleazar holy for the LORD so he could guard the Ark of the LORD.

The LORD Saves the Israelites

2The Ark[d] stayed at Kiriath Jearim a long time—20 years in all. And the people of Israel began to follow the LORD again. 3Samuel spoke to the whole group of Israel, saying, "If you're turning back to the LORD with all your hearts, you must remove your foreign gods and your idols of Ashtoreth.[d] You must give yourselves fully to the LORD and serve only him. Then he will save you from the Philistines."

4So the Israelites put away their idols of Baal[d] and Ashtoreth, and they served only the LORD.

5Samuel said, "All Israel must meet at Mizpah, and I will pray to the LORD for you." 6So the Israelites met together at Mizpah. They drew water from the ground and poured it out before the LORD and did not eat that day. They confessed, "We have sinned against the LORD." And Samuel served as judge of Israel at Mizpah.

7The Philistines heard the Israelites were meeting at Mizpah, so the Philistine kings came up to attack them. When the Israelites heard they were coming, they were afraid. 8They said to Samuel, "Don't stop praying to the LORD our God for us! Ask him to save us from the Philistines!" 9Then Samuel took a baby lamb and offered it to the LORD as a whole burnt offering. He called to the LORD for Israel's sake, and the LORD answered him.

10While Samuel was burning the offering, the Philistines came near to attack Israel. But the LORD thundered against them with loud thunder. They were so frightened they became confused. So the Israelites defeated the Philistines in battle. 11The men of Israel ran out of Mizpah and chased the Philistines almost to Beth Car, killing the Philistines along the way.

Peace Comes to Israel

12After this happened Samuel took a stone and set it up between Mizpah and Shen. He named the stone Ebenezer,[n] saying, "The LORD has helped us to this point." 13So the Philistines were defeated and did not enter the Israelites' land again.

The LORD was against the Philistines all Samuel's life. 14Earlier the Philistines had taken towns from the Israelites, but the Israelites won them back, from Ekron to Gath. They also took back from the Philistines the lands near these towns. There was peace also between Israel and the Amorites.

15Samuel continued as judge of Israel all his life. 16Every year he went from Bethel to Gilgal to Mizpah and judged the Israelites in all these towns. 17But Samuel always went back to Ramah, where his home was. There he judged Israel and built an altar to the LORD.

Israel Asks for a King

8 When Samuel was old, he made his sons judges for Israel. 2His first son was named Joel, and his second son was named Abijah. Joel and Abijah were judges in Beersheba. 3But Samuel's sons did not live as he did. They tried to get money dishonestly, and they accepted money secretly to make wrong judgements.

4So all the elders came together and met Samuel at Ramah. 5They said to him, "You're old, and your sons don't live as you do. Give us a king to rule over us like all the other nations."

6When the elders said that, Samuel was not pleased. He prayed to the LORD, 7and the LORD told Samuel, "Listen to whatever the people say to you. They have not rejected you. They have rejected me from being their king. 8They are doing as they have always done. When I took them out of Egypt, they left me and served other gods. They are doing the same to you. 9Now listen to

Ebenezer This name means "stone of help".

the people, but warn them what the king who rules over them will do."

[10]So Samuel told those who had asked him for a king what the LORD had said. [11]Samuel said, "If you have a king ruling over you, this is what he will do: he will take your sons and make them serve with his chariots and his horses, and they will run in front of the king's chariot. [12]The king will make some of your sons commanders over thousands or over fifties. He will make some of your other sons plough his ground and reap his harvest. He will take others to make weapons of war and equipment for his chariots. [13]He will take your daughters to make perfume and cook and bake for him. [14]He will take your best fields, vineyards and olive groves and give them to his servants. [15]He will take one-tenth of your grain and grapes and give it to his officers and servants. [16]He will take your male and female servants, your best cattle and your donkeys and use them all for his own work. [17]He will take one-tenth of your flocks, and you yourselves will become his slaves. [18]When that time comes, you will cry out because of the king you chose. But the LORD will not answer you then."

[19]But the people would not listen to Samuel. They said, "No! We want a king to rule over us. [20]Then we will be the same as all the other nations. Our king will judge for us and go with us and fight our battles."

[21]After Samuel heard all that the people said, he repeated their words to the LORD. [22]The LORD answered, "You must listen to them. Give them a king."

Then Samuel told the people of Israel, "Go back to your towns."

Saul Looks for His Father's Donkeys

9 Kish, son of Abiel from the tribe[d] of Benjamin, was an important man. (Abiel was the son of Zeror, who was the son of Becorath, who was the son of Aphiah of Benjamin.) [2]Kish had a son named Saul, who was a fine young man. There was no Israelite better than he. Saul stood a head taller than any other man in Israel.

[3]Now the donkeys of Saul's father, Kish, were lost. So Kish said to Saul, his son, "Take one of the servants, and go and look for the donkeys." [4]Saul went through the mountains of Ephraim and the land of Shalisha, but he and the servant could not find the donkeys. They went into the land of Shaalim, but the donkeys were not there. They went through the land of Benjamin, but they still did not find them. [5]When they arrived in the area of Zuph, Saul said to his servant, "Let's go back or my father will stop thinking about the donkeys and will start worrying about us."

[6]But the servant answered, "A man of God is in this town. People respect him because everything he says comes true. Let's go into the town now. Maybe he can tell us something about the journey we have taken."

[7]Saul said to his servant, "If we go into the town, what can we give him? The food in our bags is gone. We have no gift to give him. Do we have anything?"

[8]Again the servant answered Saul. "Look, I have nearly a piece of silver. Give it to the man of God. Then he will tell us about our journey." [9](In the past, if someone in Israel wanted to ask something from God, he would say, "Let's go to the seer." [d] We call the person a prophet[d] today, but in the past he was called a seer.)

[10]Saul said to his servant, "That's a good idea. Come, let's go." So they went towards the town where the man of God was.

[11]As Saul and the servant were going up the hill to the town, they met some young women coming out to get water. Saul and the servant asked them, "Is the seer here?"

[12]The young women answered, "Yes, he's here. He's ahead of you. Hurry now. He has just come to our town today, because the people will offer a sacrifice at the place of worship. [13]As soon as you enter the town, you will find him before he goes up to the place of worship to eat. The people will not begin eating until the seer comes, because he must bless the sacrifice. After that, the guests will eat. Go now, and you should find him."

Saul Meets Samuel

[14]Saul and the servant went up to the town. Just as they entered it, they saw Samuel coming towards them on his way up to the place of worship.

[15]The day before Saul came, the LORD had told Samuel: [16]"About this time tomorrow I will send you a man from the land of Benjamin. Appoint him to lead my people Israel. He will save my people from the Philistines. I have seen the suffering of my people, and I have listened to their cry."

[17]When Samuel first saw Saul, the LORD said to Samuel, "This is the man I told you about. He will organise my people."

[18]Saul approached Samuel at the gate and said, "Please tell me where the seer's[d] house is."

[19]Samuel answered, "I am the seer. Go with me to the place of worship. Today you and your servant are to eat with me. Tomorrow morning I will answer all your questions and send you home. [20]Don't worry about the donkeys you lost three days ago, because they have been found.

Soon all the wealth of Israel will belong to you
and your family."
21Saul answered, "But I am from the tribe[d] of
Benjamin, the smallest tribe in Israel. And my
family group is the smallest in the tribe of Ben-
jamin. Why are you saying such things?"
22Then Samuel took Saul and his servant into
a large room and gave them a choice place at the
table. About 30 guests were there. 23Samuel said
to the cook, "Bring the meat I gave you, the por-
tion I told you to set aside."
24So the cook took the thigh and put it on the
table in front of Saul. Samuel said, "This is the
meat saved for you. Eat it, because it was set
aside for you for this special time. As I said, 'I had
invited the people.'" So Saul ate with Samuel
that day.
25After they finished eating, they came down
from the place of worship and went to the town.
Then Samuel talked with Saul on the roof[n] of his
house. 26At dawn they got up, and Samuel called
to Saul on the roof. He said, "Get up, and I will
send you on your way." So Saul got up and went
out of the house with Samuel. 27As Saul, his ser-
vant and Samuel were getting near the edge of
the city, Samuel said to Saul, "Tell the servant to
go on ahead of us, but you stay, because I have a
message from God for you."

Samuel Appoints Saul

10 Samuel took a jar of olive oil and poured
it on Saul's head. He kissed Saul and
said, "The LORD has appointed you to lead his
people. 2After you leave me today, you will meet
two men near Rachel's tomb on the border of
Benjamin at Zelzah. They will say to you, 'The
donkeys you were looking for have been found.
But now your father has stopped thinking about
his donkeys and is worrying about you. He is
asking, "What will I do about my son?"'
3"Then you will go on until you reach the big
tree at Tabor. Three men on their way to worship
God at Bethel will meet you there. One man will
be carrying three goats. Another will be carrying
three loaves of bread. And the third will have a
leather bag full of wine. 4They will greet you and
offer you two loaves of bread, which you must
accept. 5Then you will go to Gibeah of God,
where a Philistine camp is. When you approach
this town, a group of prophets[d] will come down
from the place of worship. They will be playing
harps, tambourines,[d] flutes and lyres,[d] and they
will be prophesying. 6Then the Spirit[d] of the LORD
will rush upon you with power. You will proph-
esy with these prophets, and you will be changed
into a different man. 7After these signs happen,
do whatever you find to do, because God is
with you.
8"Go ahead of me to Gilgal. I will come down
to you to offer whole burnt offerings and fellow-
ship offerings. But you must wait seven days.
Then I will come and tell you what to do."

Saul Made King

9When Saul turned to leave Samuel, God
changed Saul's heart. All these signs came true
that day. 10When Saul and his servant arrived
at Gibeah, Saul met a group of prophets.[d] The
Spirit[d] of God rushed upon him, and he prophe-
sied with the prophets. 11When people who had
known Saul before saw him prophesying with
the prophets, they asked each other, "What has
happened to Kish's son? Is even Saul one of the
prophets?"
12A man who lived there said, "Who is the
father of these prophets?" So this became a fa-
mous saying: "Is even Saul one of the prophets?"
13When Saul finished prophesying, he went to
the place of worship.
14Saul's uncle asked him and his servant,
"Where have you been?"
Saul said, "We were looking for the donkeys.
When we couldn't find them, we went to talk to
Samuel."
15Saul's uncle asked, "Please tell me. What did
Samuel say to you?"
16Saul answered, "He told us the donkeys had
already been found." But Saul did not tell his
uncle what Samuel had said about his becoming
king.
17Samuel called all the people of Israel to meet
with the LORD at Mizpah. 18He said, "This is what
the LORD, the God of Israel, says: 'I led Israel out
of Egypt. I saved you from Egypt's control and
from other kingdoms that were troubling you.'
19But now you have rejected your God. He saves
you from all your troubles and problems, but you
said, 'No! We want a king to rule over us.' Now
come, stand before the LORD in your tribes[d] and
family groups."
20When Samuel gathered all the tribes of Israel,
the tribe of Benjamin was picked. 21Samuel had
them pass by in family groups, and Matri's family
was picked. Then he had each man of Matri's
family pass by, and Saul son of Kish was picked.
But when they looked for Saul, they could not
find him. 22They asked the LORD, "Has Saul come
here yet?"
The LORD said, "Yes. He's hiding behind the
baggage."

roof In Bible times houses were built with flat roofs. The roof was used for drying things such as flax and fruit. And it was used as an extra room, as a place for worship and as a place to sleep in the summer.

23So they ran and brought him out. When Saul stood among the people, he was a head taller than anyone else. 24Then Samuel said to the people, "See the man the LORD has chosen. There is no one like him among all the people."

Then the people shouted, "Long live the king!"

Sidelight Even if you're shy, you could still hit the headlines. Saul, Israel's first king, was so shy that when the people tried to crown him, he hid behind some baggage (1 Samuel 10:20–24).

25Samuel explained the rights and duties of the king and then wrote them in a book and put it before the LORD. Then he told the people to go to their homes.

26Saul also went to his home in Gibeah. God touched the hearts of certain brave men who went along with him. 27But some troublemakers said, "How can this man save us?" They disapproved of Saul and refused to bring gifts to him. But Saul kept quiet.

Nahash Troubles Jabesh Gilead

11 About a month later Nahash the Ammonite and his army surrounded the city of Jabesh in Gilead. All the people of Jabesh said to Nahash, "Make a treaty with us, and we will serve you."

2But he answered, "I will make a treaty with you only if I'm allowed to tear out the right eye of each of you. Then all Israel will be ashamed!"

3The elders of Jabesh said to Nahash, "Give us seven days to send messengers through all Israel. If no one comes to help us, we will give ourselves up to you."

4When the messengers came to Gibeah where Saul lived and told the people the news, they cried loudly. 5Saul was coming home from ploughing the fields with his oxen when he heard the people crying. He asked, "What's wrong with the people that they are crying?" Then they told Saul what the messengers from Jabesh had said. 6When Saul heard their words, God's Spirit [d] rushed upon him with power, and he became very angry. 7So he took a pair of oxen and cut them into pieces. Then he gave the pieces of the oxen to messengers and ordered them to carry them through all the land of Israel.

The messengers said, "This is what will happen to the oxen of anyone who does not follow Saul and Samuel." So the people became very afraid of the LORD. They all came together as if they were one person. 8Saul gathered the people together at Bezek. There were 300,000 men from Israel and 30,000 men from Judah.

9They said to the messengers who had come, "Tell the people at Jabesh Gilead this: 'Before the day warms up tomorrow, you will be saved.' " So the messengers went and reported this to the people at Jabesh, and they were very happy. 10The people said to Nahash the Ammonite, "Tomorrow we will come out to meet you. Then you can do anything you want to us."

11The next morning Saul divided his soldiers into three groups. At dawn they entered the Ammonite camp and defeated them before the heat of the day. The Ammonites who escaped were scattered; no two of them were still together.

12Then the people said to Samuel, "Who didn't want Saul as king? Bring them here and we will kill them!"

13But Saul said, "No! No one will be put to death today. Today the LORD has saved Israel!"

14Then Samuel said to the people, "Come, let's go to Gilgal. There we will again promise to obey the king." 15So all the people went to Gilgal, and there, before the LORD, the people made Saul king. They offered fellowship offerings to the LORD, and Saul and all the Israelites had a great celebration.

Samuel's Farewell Speech

12 Samuel said to all Israel, "I have done everything you wanted me to do and have put a king over you. 2Now you have a king to lead you. I am old and grey, and my sons are here with you. I have been your leader since I was young. 3Here I am. If I have done anything wrong, you must testify against me before the LORD and his appointed king. Did I steal anyone's ox or donkey? Did I hurt or cheat anyone? Did I ever secretly accept money to pretend not to see something wrong? If I did any of these things, I will make it right."

4The Israelites answered, "You have not cheated us, or hurt us or taken anything unfairly from anyone."

5Samuel said to them, "The LORD is a witness to what you have said. His appointed king is also a witness today that you did not find anything wrong in me."

"He is our witness," they said.

6Then Samuel said to the people, "It is the LORD who chose Moses and Aaron and brought your ancestors out of Egypt. 7Now, stand there, and I will remind you of all the good things the LORD did for you and your ancestors.

8"After Jacob entered Egypt, his descendants[d] cried to the LORD for help. So the LORD sent Moses and Aaron, who took your ancestors out of Egypt and brought them to live in this place.

9"But they forgot the LORD their God. So he handed them over as slaves to Sisera, the commander of the army of Hazor, and as slaves to the Philistines and the king of Moab. They all fought against your ancestors. 10Then your ancestors cried to the LORD and said, 'We have sinned. We have left the LORD and served the Baals[d] and the Ashtoreths.[d] But now save us from our enemies, and we will serve you.' 11So the LORD sent Gideon,[n] Barak, Jephthah and Samuel. He saved you from your enemies around you, and you lived in safety. 12But when you saw Nahash king of the Ammonites coming against you, you said, 'No! We want a king to rule over us!'—even though the LORD your God was your king. 13Now here is the king you chose, the one you asked for. The LORD has put him over you. 14You must honour the LORD and serve him. You must obey his word and not turn against his commands. Both you and the king ruling over you must follow the LORD your God. If you do, it will be well with you. 15But if you don't obey the LORD, and if you turn against his commands, he will be against you. He will do to you what he did to your ancestors.

Sidelight The Israelites wanted to be like everyone else, so they chose a king to lead and fight for them. In asking for a king they chose to disobey God, who had promised to fight for them. Saul started well, and gave God the credit, but he later became disobedient (1 Samuel 13:1–23) and impatient. He was rejected from leadership to make way for David's success.

16"Now stand still and see the great thing the LORD will do before your eyes. 17It is now the time of the wheat harvest.[n] I will pray for the LORD to send thunder and rain. Then you will know what an evil thing you did against the LORD when you asked for a king."

18Then Samuel prayed to the LORD, and that same day the LORD sent thunder and rain. So the people were very afraid of the LORD and Samuel. 19They said to Samuel, "Pray to the LORD your God for us, your servants! Don't let us die! We've added to all our sins the evil of asking for a king."

20Samuel answered, "Don't be afraid. It's true that you did wrong, but don't turn away from the LORD. Serve the LORD with all your heart. 21Idols are of no use, so don't worship them. They can't help you or save you. They are useless! 22For his own sake, the LORD won't leave his people. Instead, he was pleased to make you his own people. 23I will surely not stop praying for you, because that would be sinning against the LORD. I will teach you what is good and right. 24You must honour the LORD and truly serve him with all your heart. Remember the wonderful things he did for you! 25But if you are stubborn and do evil, he will sweep you and your king away."

13

Saul was 30 years old when he became king, and he was king over Israel for 42 years.[n] 2Saul chose 3,000 men from Israel. 2,000 men stayed with him at Michmash in the mountains of Bethel, and 1,000 men stayed with Jonathan at Gibeah in Benjamin. Saul sent the other men in the army back home.

3Jonathan attacked the Philistine camp in Geba, and the other Philistines heard about it. Saul said, "Let the Hebrews hear what happened." So he told the men to blow trumpets through all the land of Israel. 4All the Israelites heard the news. The men said, "Saul has defeated the Philistine camp. Now the Philistines will really hate us!" Then the Israelites were called to join Saul at Gilgal.

5The Philistines gathered to fight Israel with 3,000[n] chariots and 6,000 men to ride in them. Their soldiers were as many as the grains of sand on the seashore. The Philistines went and camped at Michmash, which is east of Beth Aven. 6When the Israelites saw that they were in trouble, they went to hide in caves and bushes, among the rocks and in pits and wells. 7Some Hebrews even went across the Jordan River to the land of Gad and Gilead.

But Saul stayed at Gilgal, and all the men in his army were shaking with fear. 8Saul waited seven days, because Samuel had said he would meet him then. But Samuel did not come to Gilgal, and the soldiers began to leave.

9So Saul said, "Bring me the whole burnt offering and the fellowship offerings." Then Saul offered the whole burnt offering. 10Just as he finished, Samuel arrived, and Saul went to greet him.

11Samuel asked, "What have you done?"

Saul answered, "I saw the soldiers leaving me, and you were not here when you said you would

Gideon Also called Jerub-Baal.
time . . . harvest This was a dry time in the summer when no rains fell.
Saul . . . years This is how the verse is worded in some early Greek copies. The Hebrew is not clear here.
3,000 Some Greek copies say 3,000. The Hebrew copies say 30,000.

be. The Philistines were gathering at Michmash. 12Then I thought, 'The Philistines will come against me at Gilgal, and I haven't asked for the LORD's approval.' So I forced myself to offer the whole burnt offering."

13Samuel said, "You acted foolishly! You haven't obeyed the command of the LORD your God. If you had obeyed him, the LORD would have made your kingdom continue in Israel always, 14but now your kingdom will not continue. The LORD has looked for the kind of man he wants. He has appointed him to rule his people, because you haven't obeyed his command."

15Then Samuel left Gilgal and went to Gibeah in Benjamin. Saul counted the men who were still with him, and there were about 600.

Hard Times for Israel

16Saul and his son Jonathan and the soldiers with him stayed in Gibeah in the land of Benjamin. The Philistines made their camp at Michmash. 17Three groups went out from the Philistine camp to make attacks. One group went on the Ophrah road in the land of Shual. 18The second group went on the Beth Horon road. The third group went on the border road that overlooks the Valley of Zeboim towards the desert.

19The whole land of Israel had no blacksmith because the Philistines had said, "The Hebrews might make swords and spears." 20So all the Israelites had to go down to the Philistines to have their ploughs, hoes, axes and sickles sharpened. 21The Philistine blacksmiths charged about 8 grammes of silver for sharpening ploughs and hoes. And they charged 4 grammes of silver for sharpening picks, axes and the sticks used to guide oxen.

22So when the battle came, the soldiers with Saul and Jonathan had no swords or spears. Only Saul and his son Jonathan had them.

Sidelight The Philistines were such a threat to the Israelites partly because they were the only ones with iron weapons. Only Israelite royalty had swords (1 Samuel 13:19–22), and they were probably smuggled in from other countries.

Israel Defeats the Philistines

23A group from the Philistine army had gone out to the pass at Michmash.

14 One day Jonathan, Saul's son, said to the officer who carried his armour, "Come, let's go over to the Philistine camp on the other side." But Jonathan did not tell his father.

2Saul was sitting under a pomegranate[d] tree at the threshing[d] floor near Gibeah. He had about 600 men with him. 3One man was Ahijah who was wearing the holy robe.[d] (Ahijah was a son of Ichabod's brother Ahitub. Ichabod was the son of Phinehas, the son of Eli, the LORD's priest in Shiloh.) No one knew Jonathan had left.

4There was a steep slope on each side of the pass that Jonathan planned to go through to reach the Philistine camp. The cliff on one side was named Bozez, and the cliff on the other side was named Seneh. 5One cliff faced north towards Michmash. The other faced south towards Geba.

6Jonathan said to his officer who carried his armour, "Come. Let's go to the camp of those men who are not circumcised.[d] Maybe the LORD will help us. The LORD can give us victory if we have many people, or just a few."

7The officer who carried Jonathan's armour said to him, "Do whatever you think is best. Go ahead. I'm with you."

8Jonathan said, "Then come. We will cross over to the Philistines and let them see us. 9If they say to us, 'Stay there until we come to you,' we will stay where we are. We won't go up to them. 10But if they say, 'Come up to us,' we will climb up, and the LORD will let us defeat them. This will be the sign for us."

11When both Jonathan and his officer let the Philistines see them, the Philistines said, "Look! The Hebrews are crawling out of the holes they were hiding in!" 12The Philistines in the camp shouted to Jonathan and his officer, "Come up to us. We'll teach you a lesson!"

Jonathan said to his officer, "Climb up behind me, because the LORD has given the Philistines to Israel!" 13So Jonathan climbed up, using his hands and feet, and his officer climbed just behind him. Jonathan struck down the Philistines as he went, and his officer killed them as he followed behind him. 14In that first fight Jonathan and his officer killed about 20 Philistines over a fifth of a hectare of ground.

15All the Philistine soldiers panicked—those in the camp and those in the raiding party. The ground itself shook! God had caused the panic.

16Saul's guards were at Gibeah in the land of Benjamin when they saw the Philistine soldiers running in every direction. 17Saul said to his army, "Check to see who has left our camp." When they checked, they learned that Jonathan and his officer were gone.

18So Saul said to Ahijah the priest, "Bring the Ark[d] of God." (At that time it was with the Israelites.) 19While Saul was talking to the priest, the confusion in the Philistine camp was growing. Then Saul said to Ahijah, "Put your hand down!"

[20]Then Saul gathered his army and entered the battle. They found the Philistines confused, striking each other with their swords! [21]Earlier, there were Hebrews who had served the Philistines and had stayed in their camp, but now they joined the Israelites with Saul and Jonathan. [22]When all the Israelites hidden in the mountains of Ephraim heard that the Philistine soldiers were running away, they also joined the battle and chased the Philistines. [23]So the LORD saved the Israelites that day, and the battle moved on past Beth Aven.

Saul Makes Another Mistake

[24]The men of Israel were miserable that day because Saul had made an oath for all of them. He had said, "No one should eat food before evening and before I finish defeating my enemies. If he does, he will be cursed!" So no Israelite soldier ate food.

[25]Now the army went into the woods, where there was some honey on the ground. [26]They came upon some honey, but no one took any because they were afraid of the oath. [27]Jonathan had not heard the oath Saul had put on the army, so he dipped the end of his stick into the honey and lifted some out and ate it. Then he felt better. [28]Then one of the soldiers told Jonathan, "Your father made an oath for all the soldiers. He said any man who eats today will be cursed! That's why they are so weak."

[29]Jonathan said, "My father has made trouble for the land! See how much better I feel after just tasting a little of this honey! [30]It would have been much better for the men to eat the food they took from their enemies today. We could have killed many more Philistines!"

[31]That day the Israelites defeated the Philistines from Michmash to Aijalon. After that, they were very tired. [32]They had taken sheep, cattle and calves from the Philistines. Now they were so hungry they killed the animals on the ground and ate them, without draining the blood from them! [33]Someone said to Saul, "Look! The men are sinning against the LORD. They're eating meat without draining the blood from it!"

Saul said, "You have sinned! Roll a large stone over here now!" [34]Then he said, "Go to the men and tell them that each person must bring his ox and sheep to me and kill it here and eat it. Don't sin against the LORD by eating meat without draining the blood from it."

That night everyone brought his animals and killed them there. [35]Then Saul built an altar to the LORD. It was the first altar he had built to the LORD.

[36]Saul said, "Let's go after the Philistines tonight and rob them. We won't let any of them live!"

The men answered, "Do whatever you think is best."

But the priest said, "Let's ask God."

[37]So Saul asked God, "Should I chase the Philistines? Will you let us defeat them?" But God did not answer Saul at that time. [38]Then Saul said to all the leaders of his army, "Come here. Let's find out what sin has been done today. [39]As surely as the LORD lives who has saved Israel, even if my son Jonathan did the sin, he must die." But no one in the army spoke.

[40]Then Saul said to all the Israelites, "You stand on this side. I and my son Jonathan will stand on the other side."

The men answered, "Do whatever you think is best."

[41]Then Saul prayed to the LORD, the God of Israel, "Give me the right answer."

And Saul and Jonathan were picked; the other men went free. [42]Saul said, "Now let us discover if it is I or Jonathan my son who is guilty." And Jonathan was picked.

[43]Saul said to Jonathan, "Tell me what you have done."

So Jonathan told Saul, "I only tasted a little honey from the end of my stick. And must I die now?"

[44]Saul said, "Jonathan, if you don't die, may God punish me terribly."

[45]But the soldiers said to Saul, "Must Jonathan die? Never! He is responsible for saving Israel today! As surely as the LORD lives, not even a hair of his head will fall to the ground! Today Jonathan fought against the Philistines with God's help!" So the army saved Jonathan, and he did not die.

[46]Then Saul stopped chasing the Philistines, and they went back to their own land.

Saul Fights Israel's Enemies

[47]When Saul became king over Israel, he fought against Israel's enemies all around. He fought Moab, the Ammonites, Edom, the king of Zobah and the Philistines. Everywhere Saul went he defeated Israel's enemies. [48]He fought bravely and defeated the Amalekites. He saved the Israelites from their enemies who had robbed them.

[49]Saul's sons were Jonathan, Ishvi and Malki-Shua. His older daughter was named Merab, and his younger daughter was named Michal. [50]Saul's wife was Ahinoam, daughter of Ahimaaz. The commander of his army was Abner son of Ner, Saul's uncle. [51]Saul's father Kish and Abner's father Ner were sons of Abiel.

[52]All Saul's life he fought hard against the Philistines. When he saw strong or brave men, he took them into his army.

Saul Rejected as King

15 Samuel said to Saul, "The LORD sent
me to appoint you king over Israel. Now
listen to his message. 2This is what the LORD All-
powerful says: 'When the Israelites came out of
Egypt, the Amalekites tried to stop them from
going to Canaan. So I will punish them. 3Now go,
attack the Amalekites and destroy everything
they own as an offering to the LORD. Don't let
anything live. Put to death men and women, chil-
dren and small babies, cattle and sheep, camels
and donkeys.' "

4So Saul called the army together at Telaim.
There were 200,000 foot soldiers and 10,000
men from Judah. 5Then Saul went to the city of
Amalek and set up an ambush in the ravine. 6He
said to the Kenites, "Go away. Leave the Amalek-
ites so that I won't destroy you with them, be-
cause you showed kindness to the Israelites when
they came out of Egypt." So the Kenites moved
away from the Amalekites.

7Then Saul defeated the Amalekites. He fought
them all the way from Havilah to Shur, at
the border of Egypt. 8He took King Agag of the
Amalekites alive, but he killed all of Agag's army
with the sword. 9Saul and the army let Agag
live, along with the best sheep, fat cattle and
lambs. They let every good animal live, because
they did not want to destroy them. But when
they found an animal that was weak or useless,
they killed it.

10Then the LORD spoke his word to Samuel:
11"I am sorry I made Saul king, because he has
stopped following me and has not obeyed my
commands." Samuel was upset, and he cried out
to the LORD all night long.

12Early the next morning Samuel got up and
went to meet Saul. But the people told Samuel,
"Saul has gone to Carmel, where he has put up
a monument in his own honour. Now he has
gone down to Gilgal."

13When Samuel came to Saul, Saul said, "May
the LORD bless you! I have obeyed the LORD's
commands."

14But Samuel said, "Then why do I hear cattle
mooing and sheep bleating?"

15Saul answered, "The soldiers took them from
the Amalekites. They saved the best sheep and
cattle to offer as sacrifices to the LORD your God,
but we destroyed all the other animals."

16Samuel said to Saul, "Stop! Let me tell you
what the LORD said to me last night."

Saul answered, "Tell me."

17Samuel said, "Once you didn't think much of
yourself, but now you have become the leader
of the tribes[d] of Israel. The LORD appointed you
to be king over Israel. 18And he sent you on a
mission. He said, 'Go and destroy those evil
people, the Amalekites. Make war on them
until all of them are dead.' 19Why didn't you
obey the LORD? Why did you take the best
things? Why did you do what the LORD said was
wrong?"

20Saul said, "But I did obey the LORD. I did
what the LORD told me to do. I destroyed all
the Amalekites, and I brought back Agag their
king. 21The soldiers took the best sheep and
cattle to sacrifice to the LORD your God at
Gilgal."

22But Samuel answered,

"What pleases the LORD more:
  burnt offerings and sacrifices
  or obedience to his voice?
It is better to obey than to sacrifice.
  It is better to listen to God than to offer the
    fat of rams.
23Refusing to obey is as bad as the sin of sorcery.[d]
  Pride is as bad as the sin of worshipping idols.
You have rejected the LORD's command.
  Now he rejects you as king."

24Then Saul said to Samuel, "I have sinned. I
didn't obey the LORD's commands and your
words. I was afraid of the people, and I did what
they said. 25Now, I beg you, forgive my sin. Come
back with me so I may worship the LORD."

26But Samuel said to Saul, "I won't go back
with you. You rejected the LORD's command, and
now he rejects you as king of Israel."

27As Samuel turned to leave, Saul caught his
robe, and it tore. 28Samuel said to him, "The LORD
has torn the kingdom of Israel from you today and
has given it to one of your neighbours who is bet-
ter than you. 29The LORD is the Eternal One of Is-
rael. He does not lie or change his mind. He is not
a human being, so he does not change his mind.

30Saul answered, "I have sinned. But please
honour me in front of the elders of my people
and in front of the Israelites. Come back with me
so that I can worship the LORD your God." 31So
Samuel went back with Saul, and Saul worshipped
the LORD.

32Then Samuel said, "Bring me King Agag of
the Amalekites."

Agag came to Samuel in chains, but Agag
thought, "Surely the threat of death has passed."

33Samuel said to him, "Your sword made other
mothers lose their children. Now your mother
will have no children." And Samuel cut Agag to
pieces before the LORD at Gilgal.

34Then Samuel left and went to Ramah, but
Saul went up to his home in Gibeah. 35And
Samuel never saw Saul again for the rest of his
life, but he was sad for Saul. And the LORD was
very sorry he had made Saul king of Israel.

Samuel Goes to Bethlehem

16 The LORD said to Samuel, "How long
will you continue to feel sorry for Saul?
I have rejected him as king of Israel. Fill your
container with olive oil and go. I am sending you
to Jesse who lives in Bethlehem, because I have
chosen one of his sons to be king."
2But Samuel said, "If I go, Saul will hear the
news and will try to kill me."
The LORD said, "Take a young calf with you.
Say, 'I have come to offer a sacrifice to the LORD.'
3Invite Jesse to the sacrifice. Then I will tell you
what to do. You must appoint the one I show
you."
4Samuel did what the LORD told him to do.
When he arrived at Bethlehem, the elders of
Bethlehem shook with fear. They met him and
asked, "Are you coming in peace?"
5Samuel answered, "Yes, I come in peace.
I have come to make a sacrifice to the LORD. Set
yourselves apart to the LORD and come to the
sacrifice with me." Then he set Jesse and his sons
apart to the LORD, and he invited them to come
to the sacrifice.
6When they arrived, Samuel saw Eliab, and he
thought, "Surely the LORD has appointed this
person standing here before him."
7But the LORD said to Samuel, "Don't look
at how handsome Eliab is or how tall he is, be-
cause I have not chosen him. God does not
see the same way people see. People look at the
outside of a person, but the LORD looks at the
heart."
8Then Jesse called Abinadab and told him to
pass by Samuel. But Samuel said, "The LORD has
not chosen this man either." 9Then Jesse had
Shammah pass by. But Samuel said, "No, the
LORD has not chosen this one." 10Jesse had seven
of his sons pass by Samuel. But Samuel said to
him, "The LORD has not chosen any of these."

SELF-ESTEEM

Go For It!

At fifteen years old Matthew had the spelling age of a much younger person. He was seriously dyslexic and so had real trouble in reading, too. "Why not think about something like catering," the careers staff told him. "It's best to go for something you know you can achieve."

But then he had a session with a psychologist who was trying to get him extra time in exams. "What would you like to do?" the psychologist asked. Matthew replied that he would like to work professionally with people – perhaps be a psychologist himself. The psychologist was really encouraging. He knew that Matthew had a high IQ and could make it.

Matthew knew where he wanted to go. Even when he did poorly in his exams he still kept trying and his determination got him onto a good college course with fewer examinations – more course assessment. Sometimes, like David, Matthew was not sure how things would turn out and wondered if he should make other plans. Eventually he found one university which understood his problems and was willing to take him on. Today Matthew is close to the top of his class and well on target.

David knew what it was like to be put in his place. He wasn't the biggest, the strongest or the most heroic, but God still chose him. **1 Samuel 16:1–13** tells us why.

- What might have happened if Matthew and David had believed the negative things other people had said?
- What qualities did David have that you can see in yourself?

Consider . . .

- making a list of your good points that some people might overlook. Decide how you can use these gifts in serving God.
- talking to someone who is looked down upon at your school or church. Find out what areas they excel in, then encourage him or her to develop those skills even further.

For more, see . . .

- Psalm 147:10–11 (p.587)
- Ephesians 1:3–6 (p.1268)
- Galatians 2:6 (p.1258)

11Then he asked Jesse, "Are these all the sons
you have?"
Jesse answered, "I still have the youngest son.
He is out taking care of the sheep."
Samuel said, "Send for him. We will not sit
down to eat until he arrives."
12So Jesse sent and had his youngest son
brought in. He was a fine boy, tanned and hand-
some.
The LORD said to Samuel, "Go, appoint him,
because he is the one."
13So Samuel took the container of olive oil and
poured it on Jesse's youngest son to appoint him
in front of his brothers. From that day on, the
LORD's Spirit[d] worked in David. Samuel then
went back to Ramah.

David Serves Saul

14But the LORD's Spirit[d] had left Saul, and an
evil spirit from the LORD troubled him.
15Saul's servants said to him, "See, an evil spirit
from God is troubling you. 16Give us the com-
mand to look for someone who can play the harp.
When the evil spirit from God troubles you, he
will play, and you will feel better."
17So Saul said to his servants, "Find someone
who can play well and bring him to me."
18One of the servants said, "I have seen a son
of Jesse of Bethlehem play the harp. He is brave
and courageous. He is a good speaker and hand-
some, and the LORD is with him."
19Then Saul sent messengers to Jesse, saying,
"Send me your son David, who is with the
sheep." 20So Jesse loaded a donkey with bread, a
leather bag full of wine and a young goat, and he
sent them with his son David to Saul.
21When David came to Saul, he began to serve
him. Saul liked David and made him the officer
who carried his armour. 22Saul sent a message to
Jesse, saying, "Let David stay and serve me be-
cause I like him."
23When the evil spirit from God troubled Saul,
David would take his harp and play. Then the evil
spirit would leave him, and Saul would feel better.

David and Goliath

17 The Philistines gathered their armies for
war. They met at Socoh in Judah and
camped at Ephes Dammim between Socoh and

MUSIC

Musicianaries

One of the big bosses at MTV was quoted as saying, "We don't just influence this generation. We own this generation." And in some ways, he's right. Nothing has been as successful in recent times at shaping the minds and attitudes of the world's young people as music television. Nowadays, everyone wants to look, think and feel like a celebrity – even if it means "selling their soul to the devil" by compromising their faith in God.

However, there is a new breed of music missionaries – musicianaries – who refuse to believe that MTV owns this generation. They're the ones who allow Jesus to shape their destiny. Like young David in **1 Samuel 16:17–23**, they actually allow God to use their music to combat evil.

When confronted by sceptics who claimed that all rock music was evil, one famous Christian rocker wrote, "Why should the devil have all the good music?" Today, these musicianaries carry that same DNA. They'll use whatever style of music it takes to bring the message of Jesus' salvation to a broken, dying, celebrity-soaked world.

- Besides musical skills, what else did David have that made him so popular with King Saul?
- What skills have you been blessed with? Are you allowing God to use them to combat evil?

Consider . . .

- joining the ranks of musicianaries who would prefer to be shaped by the Word of God than by MTV.
- sponsoring a ministry you believe to be supporting true musicianaries. And don't forget to pray for them.

For more, see . . .

- 2 Chronicles 20:15–20 (p.414)
- Ephesians 6:10–20 (p.1277)
- 1 Corinthians 9:22–23 (p.1227)

Azekah. [2]Saul and the Israelites gathered in the Valley of Elah and camped there and took their positions to fight the Philistines. [3]The Philistines controlled one hill while the Israelites controlled another. The valley was between them.

[4]The Philistines had a champion fighter from Gath named Goliath. He was about 3 metres tall. He came out of the Philistine camp [5]with a bronze helmet on his head and a coat of bronze armour that weighed about 60 kilogrammes. [6]He wore bronze protectors on his legs, and he had a bronze spear on his back. [7]The wooden part of his larger spear was like a weaver's rod, and its blade weighed about 7 kilogrammes. The officer who carried his shield walked in front of him.

[8]Goliath stood and shouted to the Israelite soldiers, "Why have you taken positions for battle? I am a Philistine, and you are Saul's servants! Choose a man and send him to fight me. [9]If he can fight and kill me, we will be your servants. But if I can kill him, you will be our servants." [10]Then he said, "Today I stand and challenge the army of Israel! Send one of your men to fight me!" [11]When Saul and the Israelites heard the Philistine's words, they were very scared.

[12]Now David was the son of Jesse, an Ephrathite from Bethlehem in Judah. Jesse had eight sons. In Saul's time Jesse was an old man. [13]His three oldest sons followed Saul to the war. The first son was Eliab, the second was Abinadab, and the third was Shammah. [14]David was the youngest. Jesse's three oldest sons followed Saul, [15]but David went back and forth from Saul to Bethlehem, where he took care of his father's sheep.

[16]For 40 days the Philistine came out every morning and evening and stood before the Israelite army.

[17]Jesse said to his son David, "Take this 10 kilogrammes of cooked grain and ten loaves of bread to your brothers in the camp. [18]Also take ten pieces of cheese to the commander and to your brothers. See how your brothers are and bring back some proof to show me that they are all right. [19]Your brothers are with Saul and the army in the Valley of Elah, fighting against the Philistines."

[20]Early in the morning David left the sheep with another shepherd. He took the food and left as Jesse had told him. When David arrived at the camp, the army was going out to their battle positions, shouting their war cry. [21]The Israelites and Philistines were lining up their men to face each other in battle.

[22]David left the food with the man who kept the supplies and ran to the battle line to talk to his brothers. [23]While he was talking with them, Goliath, the Philistine champion from Gath, came out. He shouted things against Israel as usual, and David heard him. [24]When the Israelites saw Goliath, they were very much afraid and ran away.

[25]They said, "Look at this man! He keeps coming out to challenge Israel. The king will give much money to whoever kills him. He will also let whoever kills him marry his daughter. And his father's family will not have to pay taxes in Israel."

[26]David asked the men who stood near him, "What will be done to reward the man who kills this Philistine and takes away the shame from Israel? Who does this uncircumcised [d] Philistine think he is? Does he think he can speak against the armies of the living God?"

[27]The Israelites told David what would be done for the man who would kill Goliath.

[28]When David's oldest brother Eliab heard David talking with the soldiers, he was angry with David. He asked David, "Why did you come here? Who's taking care of those few sheep of yours in the desert? I know you are proud and wicked at heart. You came down here just to watch the battle."

[29]David asked, "Now what have I done wrong? Can't I even talk?" [30]When he turned to other people and asked the same questions, they gave him the same answer as before. [31]Yet what David said was told to Saul, and he sent for David.

[32]David said to Saul, "Don't let anyone be discouraged. I, your servant, will go and fight this Philistine!"

[33]Saul answered, "You can't go out against this Philistine and fight him. You're only a boy. Goliath has been a warrior since he was a young man."

[34]But David said to Saul, "I, your servant, have been keeping my father's sheep. When a lion or bear came and took a sheep from the flock, [35]then I would chase it. I would attack it and save the sheep from its mouth. When it attacked me, I caught it by its fur and hit it and killed it. [36]I, your servant, have killed both a lion and a bear! This uncircumcised Philistine will be like them, because he has spoken against the armies of the living God. [37]The LORD who saved me from a lion and a bear will save me from this Philistine."

Saul said to David, "Go, and may the LORD be with you." [38]Saul put his own clothes on David. He put a bronze helmet on his head and dressed him in armour. [39]David put on Saul's sword and tried to walk around, but he was not used to all the armour Saul had put on him.

He said to Saul, "I can't go in this, because I'm not used to it." Then David took it all off. [40]He took his stick in his hand and chose five smooth stones from a stream. He put them in his shepherd's bag. With his sling in his hand, he went to meet the Philistine.

41At the same time, the Philistine was coming closer to David. The man who held his shield walked in front of him. 42When Goliath looked at David and saw that he was only a boy, tanned and handsome, he looked down on David with disgust. 43He said, "Do you think I am a dog, that you come at me with a stick?" He used his gods' names to curse David. 44He said to David, "Come here. I'll feed your body to the birds of the air and the wild animals!"

45But David said to him, "You come to me using a sword and two spears. But I come to you in the name of the LORD All-powerful, the God of the armies of Israel! You have spoken against him. 46Today the LORD will hand you over to me, and I'll kill you and cut off your head. Today I'll feed the bodies of the Philistine soldiers to the birds of the air and the wild animals. Then all the world will know there is a God in Israel! 47Everyone gathered here will know the LORD does not need swords or spears to save people. The battle belongs to him, and he will hand you over to us."

Sidelight

Slam-dunking would have been easy for Goliath. At almost three metres tall he would have been just a few centimetres below the basketball rim. But he was no match for David who was good at "long shots" (1 Samuel 17:45–47).

48As Goliath came near to attack him, David ran quickly to meet him. 49He took a stone from his bag, put it into his sling, and slung it. The stone hit the Philistine and went deep into his forehead, and Goliath fell face down on the ground.

50So David defeated the Philistine with only a sling and a stone. He hit him and killed him. He did not even have a sword in his hand. 51Then David ran and stood beside him. He took Goliath's sword out of its holder and killed him by cutting off his head.

When the Philistines saw that their champion was dead, they turned and ran. 52The men of Israel and Judah shouted and chased the Philistines all the way to the entrance of the city of Gath and to the gates of Ekron.

The Philistines' bodies lay on the Shaaraim road as far as Gath and Ekron. 53The Israelites returned after chasing the Philistines and robbed their camp. 54David took Goliath's head to Jerusalem and put Goliath's weapons in his own tent.

55When Saul saw David go out to meet Goliath, Saul asked Abner, commander of the army, "Abner, who is that young man's father?"

Abner answered, "As surely as you live, my king, I don't know."

56The king said, "Find out whose son he is."

57When David came back from killing Goliath, Abner brought him to Saul. David was still holding Goliath's head.

58Saul asked him, "Young man, who is your father?"

David answered, "I am the son of your servant Jesse of Bethlehem."

Saul Fears David

18 When David finished talking with Saul, Jonathan felt very close to David. He loved David as much as he loved himself. 2Saul kept David with him from that day on and did not let him go home to his father's house. 3Jonathan made an agreement with David, because he loved David as much as himself. 4He took off his coat and gave it to David, along with his armour, including his sword, bow and belt.

5Saul sent David to fight in different battles, and David was very successful. Then Saul put David over the soldiers, which pleased Saul's officers and all the other people.

6After David had killed the Philistine, he and the men returned home. Women came out from all the towns of Israel to meet King Saul. They sang songs of joy, danced, and played tambourines[d] and stringed instruments. 7As they played, they sang,

"Saul has killed thousands of his enemies,
but David has killed tens of thousands."

8The women's song upset Saul, and he became very angry. He thought, "The women say David has killed tens of thousands, but they say I have killed only thousands. The only thing left for him to have is the kingdom!" 9So Saul watched David closely from then on, because he was jealous.

10The next day an evil spirit from God rushed upon Saul, and he prophesied[d] in his house. David was playing the harp as he usually did, but Saul had a spear in his hand. 11He threw the spear, thinking, "I'll pin David to the wall." But David escaped from him twice.

12The LORD was with David but had left Saul. So Saul was afraid of David. 13He sent David away and made him commander of 1,000 soldiers. So David led them in battle. 14He had great success in everything he did because the LORD was with him. 15When Saul saw that David was very successful, he feared David even more.

16But all the people of Israel and Judah loved
David because he led them well in battle.

Saul's Daughter Marries David

17Saul said to David, "Here is my older daugh-
ter Merab. I will let you marry her. All I ask is
that you remain brave and fight the LORD's bat-
tles." Saul thought, "I won't have to kill David.
The Philistines will do that."
18But David answered Saul, saying, "Who am
I? My family is not important enough for me
to become the king's son-in-law." 19So, when
the time came for Saul's daughter Merab to
marry David, Saul gave her instead to Adriel of
Meholah.
20Now Saul's other daughter, Michal, loved
David. When they told Saul, he was pleased. 21He
thought, "I will let her marry David. Then she
will be a trap for him, and the Philistines will
defeat him." So Saul said to David a second time,
"You may become my son-in-law."
22And Saul ordered his servants to talk with
David in private and say, "Look, the king likes
you. His servants love you. You should be his
son-in-law."
23Saul's servants said these words to David,
but David answered, "Do you think it is easy to
become the king's son-in-law? I am poor and
unimportant."
24When Saul's servants told him what David
had said, 25Saul said, "Tell David, 'The king
doesn't want money for the bride. All he wants
is 100 Philistine foreskins to get even with his
enemies.' " Saul planned to let the Philistines kill
David.
26When Saul's servants told this to David, he
was pleased to become the king's son-in-law.
27So he and his men went out and killed 200
Philistines. David brought all their foreskins to
Saul so he could be the king's son-in-law. Then
Saul gave him his daughter Michal for his wife.
28Saul saw that the LORD was with David and that
his daughter Michal loved David. 29So he grew
even more afraid of David, and he was David's
enemy all his life.
30The Philistine commanders continued to go
out to fight the Israelites, but every time, David
was more skilful than Saul's officers. So he be-
came famous.

Saul Tries to Kill David

19 Saul told his son Jonathan and all his
servants to kill David, but Jonathan liked
David very much. 2So he warned David, "My
father Saul is looking for a chance to kill you.
Watch out in the morning. Hide in a secret place.
3I will go out and stand with my father in the field
where you are hiding, and I'll talk to him about
you. Then I'll let you know what I find out."
4When Jonathan talked to Saul his father, he
said good things about David. Jonathan said,
"The king should do no wrong to your servant
David since he has done nothing wrong to you.
What he has done has helped you greatly. 5David
risked his life when he killed Goliath the Philis-
tine, and the LORD won a great victory for all
Israel. You saw it and were happy. Why would
you do wrong against David? He's innocent.
There's no reason to kill him!"
6Saul listened to Jonathan and then made this
promise: "As surely as the LORD lives, David won't
be put to death."
7So Jonathan called to David and told him
everything that had been said. He brought David
to Saul, and David was with Saul as before.
8When war broke out again, David went out
to fight the Philistines. He defeated them, and
they ran away from him.
9But once again an evil spirit from the LORD
rushed upon Saul as he was sitting in his house
with his spear in his hand. David was playing the
harp. 10Saul tried to pin David to the wall with his
spear, but David jumped out of the way. So Saul's
spear went into the wall, and David ran away
that night.
11Saul sent messengers to David's house to
watch him and to kill him in the morning. But
Michal, David's wife, warned him, saying, "To-
night you must run for your life. If you don't, you
will be dead in the morning." 12So she let David
down out of a window, and he ran away and
escaped. 13Then Michal took an idol, laid it on
the bed, covered it with clothes and put goats'
hair on its head.
14Saul sent messengers to take David prisoner,
but Michal said, "He is sick."
15Saul sent them back to see David, saying,
"Bring him to me on his bed so I can kill him."
16When the messengers entered David's house,
they found just an idol on the bed with goats'
hair on its head.
17Saul said to Michal, "Why did you trick me
this way? You let my enemy go so he could run
away!"
Michal answered Saul, "David told me if I did
not help him escape, he would kill me."
18After David had escaped from Saul, he went
to Samuel at Ramah and told him everything
Saul had done to him. Then David and Samuel
went to Naioth and stayed there. 19Saul heard
that David was in Naioth at Ramah. 20So he
sent messengers to capture him. But they
met a group of prophets[d] prophesying[d], with
Samuel standing there leading them. So the
Spirit[d] of God entered Saul's men, and they also
prophesied.

21When Saul heard the news, he sent more messengers, but they also prophesied. Then he sent messengers a third time, but they also prophesied. 22Finally, Saul himself went to Ramah, to the well at Secu. He asked, "Where are Samuel and David?"

The people answered, "In Naioth at Ramah."

23When Saul went to Naioth at Ramah, the Spirit of God also rushed upon him. And he walked on, prophesying until he came to Naioth at Ramah. 24He took off his robes and prophesied in front of Samuel. He lay that way all day and all night. That is why people ask, "Is even Saul one of the prophets?"

Jonathan Helps David

20 Then David ran away from Naioth in Ramah. He went to Jonathan and asked, "What have I done? What is my crime? How did I sin against your father? Why is he trying to kill me?"

2Jonathan answered, "No! You won't die! See, my father doesn't do anything great or small without first telling me. Why would he keep this from me? It's not true!"

3But David took an oath, saying, "Your father knows very well that you like me. He says to himself, 'Jonathan must not know about it, or he will tell David.' As surely as the LORD lives and as you live, I am only a step away from death!"

4Jonathan said to David, "I'll do anything you want me to do."

5So David said, "Look, tomorrow is the New Moon[d] festival. I am supposed to eat with the king, but let me hide in the field until the third evening. 6If your father notices I am gone, tell him, 'David begged me to let him go to his home town of Bethlehem. Every year at this time his family group offers a sacrifice.' 7If your father says, 'Fine,' I am safe. But if he becomes angry, you will know that he wants to hurt me. 8Jonathan, be loyal to me, your servant. You have made an agreement with me before the LORD. If I am guilty, you may kill me yourself! Why hand me over to your father?"

9Jonathan answered, "No, never! If I learn that my father plans to hurt you, I will warn you!"

10David asked, "Who will let me know if your father answers you unkindly?"

11Then Jonathan said, "Come, let's go out into the field." So the two of them went out into the field.

12Jonathan said to David, "I promise this before the LORD, the God of Israel: at this same time the day after tomorrow, I will find out how my father feels. If he feels good towards you, I will send word to you and let you know. 13But if my father plans to hurt you, I will let you know and send you away safely. May the LORD punish me terribly if I don't do this. And may the LORD be with you as he has been with my father. 14But show me the kindness of the LORD as long as I live so that I may not die. 15You must never stop showing your kindness to my family, even when the LORD has destroyed all your enemies from the earth."

16So Jonathan made an agreement with David. He said, "May the LORD hold David's enemies responsible." 17And Jonathan asked David to repeat his promise of love for him, because he loved David as much as he loved himself.

18Jonathan said to David, "Tomorrow is the New Moon festival. Your seat will be empty, so my father will miss you. 19On the third day go to the place where you hid when this trouble began. Wait by the rock Ezel. 20On the third day I will shoot three arrows to the side of the rock as if I am shooting at a target. 21Then I will send a boy to find the arrows. If I say to him, 'The arrows are near you; bring them here,' you may come out of hiding. You are safe. As the LORD lives, there is no danger. 22But if I say to the boy, 'Look, the arrows are beyond you,' you must go, because the LORD is sending you away. 23Remember what we talked about. The LORD is a witness between you and me for ever."

24So David hid in the field. When the New Moon festival came, the king sat down to eat. 25He sat where he always sat, near the wall. Jonathan sat across from him, and Abner sat next to Saul, but David's place was empty. 26That day Saul said nothing. He thought, "Maybe something has happened to David so that he is unclean."[d] 27But the next day was the second day of the month, and David's place was still empty. So Saul said to Jonathan, "Why hasn't the son of Jesse come to the feast yesterday or today?"

28Jonathan answered, "David begged me to let him go to Bethlehem. 29He said, 'Let me go, because our family has a sacrifice in the town, and my brother has ordered me to be there. Now if I am your friend, please let me go to see my brothers.' That is why he has not come to the king's table."

30Then Saul became very angry with Jonathan. He said, "You son of a wicked, worthless woman! I know you are on the side of David son of Jesse! You bring shame on yourself and on your mother who gave birth to you. 31As long as Jesse's son lives, you will never be king or have a kingdom. Now send for David and bring him to me. He must die!"

32Jonathan asked his father, "Why should David be killed? What wrong has he done?" 33Then Saul threw his spear at Jonathan, trying to kill him. So Jonathan knew that his father really wanted to kill David. 34Jonathan was very angry and left the table. That second day of the month he refused to eat. He was ashamed of his father and upset over David.

35The next morning Jonathan went out to the field to meet David as they had agreed. He had a young boy with him. 36Jonathan said to the boy, "Run and find the arrows I shoot." When he ran, Jonathan shot an arrow beyond him. 37The boy ran to the place where Jonathan's arrow fell, but Jonathan called, "The arrow is beyond you!" 38Then he shouted, "Hurry! Go quickly! Don't stop!" The boy picked up the arrow and brought it back to his master. 39(The boy knew nothing about what this meant; only Jonathan and David knew.) 40Then Jonathan gave his weapons to the boy and told him, "Go back to town."

41When the boy left, David came out from the south side of the rock. He bowed face down on the ground before Jonathan three times. Then David and Jonathan kissed each other and cried together, but David cried the most.

42Jonathan said to David, "Go in peace. We have promised by the LORD that we will be friends. We said, 'The LORD will be a witness between you and me, and between our descendants[d] always.'" Then David left, and Jonathan went back to town.

David Goes to See Ahimelech

21 David went to Nob to see Ahimelech the priest. Ahimelech shook with fear when he saw David, and he asked, "Why are you alone? Why is no one with you?"

2David answered him, "The king gave me a special order. He told me, 'No one must know what I am sending you to do or what I told you to do.' I told my men where to meet me. 3Now, what food do you have with you? Give me five loaves of bread or anything you find."

4The priest said to David, "I don't have any plain bread here, but I do have some holy bread.[n] You may eat it if your men have kept themselves from women."

5David answered, "No women have been near us for days. My men always keep themselves holy, even when we do ordinary work. And this is especially true when the work is holy."

6So the priest gave David the holy bread from the presence of God because there was no other. Each day the holy bread was replaced with hot bread.

7One of Saul's servants happened to be there that day. He had been held there before the LORD. He was Doeg the Edomite, the chief of Saul's shepherds.

8David asked Ahimelech, "Do you have a spear or sword here? The king's business was very important, so I left without my sword or any other weapon."

9The priest answered, "The sword of Goliath the Philistine, the one you killed in the Valley of Elah, is here. It is wrapped in a cloth behind the holy robe.[d] If you want it, you may take it. There's no other sword here but that one."

David said, "There is no other sword like it. Give it to me."

David Goes to Gath

10That day David ran away from Saul and went to Achish king of Gath. 11But the servants of Achish said to him, "This is David, the king of the Israelites. He's the man they dance and sing about, saying:

'Saul has killed thousands of his enemies,
but David has killed tens of thousands.'"

> **Sidelight** Most people know that David was a musician. Did you know he was an actor too? When he was afraid of being captured by the Philistine King Achish, he dribbled in his beard and acted crazy. He must have been good because the king let him go (1 Samuel 21:12–15).

12David paid attention to these words and was very much afraid of Achish king of Gath. 13So he pretended to be insane in front of Achish and his servants. While he was with them, he acted like a madman and made marks on the doors of the gate and let spit run down his beard.

14Achish said to his servants, "Look at the man! He's insane! Why do you bring him to me? 15I have enough madmen. I don't need you to bring him here to act like this in front of me! Don't let him in my house!"

David at Adullam and Mizpah

22 David left Gath and escaped to the cave of Adullam. When his brothers and other relatives heard that he was there, they went to see him. 2Everyone who was in trouble, or who owed money, or who was unsatisfied gathered around David, and he became their leader. About 400 men were with him.

3From there David went to Mizpah in Moab and spoke to the king of Moab. He said, "Please let my father and mother come and stay with you until I learn what God is going to do for me."

holy bread This was the bread that showed the people were in the presence of God. Normally only the priests ate this bread.

4So he left them with the king of Moab, and they stayed with him as long as David was hiding in the stronghold.[d]

5But the prophet[d] Gad said to David, "Don't stay in the stronghold. Go to the land of Judah." So David left and went to the forest of Hereth.

Saul Destroys Ahimelech's Family

6Saul heard that David and his men had been seen. Saul was sitting under the tamarisk tree on the hill at Gibeah, and all his officers were standing around him. He had a spear in his hand. 7Saul said to them, "Listen, men of Benjamin! Do you think the son of Jesse will give all of you fields and vineyards? Will David make you commanders over thousands of men or hundreds of men? 8You have all made plans against me! No one tells me when my son makes an agreement with the son of Jesse! No one cares about me! No one tells me when my son has encouraged my servant to ambush me this very day!"

9Doeg the Edomite, who was standing there with Saul's officers, said, "I saw the son of Jesse. He came to see Ahimelech son of Ahitub at Nob. 10Ahimelech prayed to the LORD for David and gave him food and gave him the sword of Goliath the Philistine."

11Then the king sent for the priest Ahimelech son of Ahitub and for all of Ahimelech's relatives who were priests at Nob. And they all came to the king. 12Saul said to Ahimelech, "Listen now, son of Ahitub."

Ahimelech answered, "Yes, master."

13Saul said, "Why are you and Jesse's son against me? You gave him bread and a sword! You prayed to God for him. David has turned against me and is waiting to attack me even now!"

14Ahimelech answered, "You have no other servant who is as loyal as David, your own son-in-law and captain of your bodyguards. Everyone in your house respects him. 15That was not the first time I prayed to God for David. Don't blame me or any of my relatives. I, your servant, know nothing about what is going on."

16But the king said, "Ahimelech, you and all your relatives must die!" 17Then he told the guards at his side, "Go and kill the priests of the LORD, because they are on David's side. They knew he was running away, but they didn't tell me."

But the king's officers refused to kill the priests of the LORD.

18Then the king ordered Doeg, "Go and kill the priests." So Doeg the Edomite went and killed the priests. That day he killed 85 men who wore the linen holy robe.[d] 19He also killed the people of Nob, the city of the priests. With the sword he killed men, women, children, babies, cattle, donkeys and sheep.

20But Abiathar, a son of Ahimelech, who was the son of Ahitub, escaped. He ran away and joined David. 21He told David that Saul had killed the LORD's priests. 22Then David told him, "Doeg the Edomite was there at Nob that day. I knew he would surely tell Saul. So I am responsible for the death of all your father's family. 23Stay with me. Don't be afraid. The man who wants to kill you also wants to kill me. You will be safe with me."

David Saves the People of Keilah

23 Someone told David, "Look, the Philistines are fighting against Keilah and stealing grain from the threshing[d] floors."

2David asked the LORD, "Should I go and fight these Philistines?"

The LORD answered him, "Go. Attack them, and save Keilah."

3But David's men said to him, "We're afraid here in Judah. We will be more afraid if we go to Keilah where the Philistine army is."

4David again asked the LORD, and the LORD answered, "Go down to Keilah. I will help you defeat the Philistines." 5So David and his men went to Keilah and fought the Philistines and took their cattle. David killed many Philistines and saved the people of Keilah. 6(Now Abiathar son of Ahimelech had brought the holy robe[d] with him when he came to David at Keilah.)

Saul Chases David

7Someone told Saul that David was now at Keilah. Saul said, "God has handed David over to me! He has trapped himself, because he has entered a town with gates and bars." 8Saul called all his army together for battle, and they prepared to go down to Keilah to attack David and his men.

9David learned Saul was making evil plans against him. So he said to Abiathar the priest, "Bring the holy robe."[d] 10David prayed, "LORD, God of Israel, I have heard that Saul plans to come to Keilah to destroy the town because of me. 11Will the leaders of Keilah hand me over to Saul? Will Saul come down to Keilah, as I heard? LORD, God of Israel, tell me, your servant!"

The LORD answered, "Saul will come down."

12Again David asked, "Will the leaders of Keilah hand me and my men over to Saul?"

The LORD answered, "They will."

13So David and his 600 men left Keilah and kept moving from place to place. When Saul found out that David had escaped from Keilah, he did not go there.

[14]David stayed in the desert hideouts and in the hills of the Desert of Ziph. Every day Saul looked for David, but the LORD did not surrender David to him.

[15]While David was at Horesh in the Desert of Ziph, he learned that Saul was coming to kill him. [16]But Saul's son Jonathan went to David at Horesh and strengthened his faith in God. [17]Jonathan told him, "Don't be afraid, because my father won't touch you. You will be king of Israel, and I will be second to you. Even my father Saul knows this." [18]The two of them made an agreement before the LORD. Then Jonathan went home, but David stayed at Horesh.

[19]The people from Ziph went to Saul at Gibeah and told him, "David is hiding in our land. He's at the protected places of Horesh, on the hill of Hakilah, south of Jeshimon. [20]Now, our king, come down any time you want. It's our duty to hand David over to you."

[21]Saul answered, "The LORD bless you for helping me. [22]Go and learn more about him. Find out where he is staying and who has seen him there. I have heard that he is clever. [23]Find all the hiding places he uses, and come back and tell me everything. Then I'll go with you. If David is in the area, I will track him down among all the families in Judah."

[24]So they went back to Ziph ahead of Saul. Now David and his men were in the Desert of Maon[n] in the desert area south of Jeshimon. [25]Saul and his men went to look for David, but David heard about it and went down to a rock and stayed in the Desert of Maon. When Saul heard that, he followed David into the Desert of Maon.

[26]Saul was going along one side of the mountain, and David and his men were on the other side. They were hurrying to get away from Saul, because Saul and his men were closing in on them. [27]But a messenger came to Saul, saying, "Come quickly! The Philistines are attacking our land!" [28]So Saul stopped chasing David and went to challenge the Philistines. That is why people call this place Rock of Parting. [29]David also left the Desert of Maon and stayed in the protected places of En Gedi.

David Shames Saul

24 After Saul returned from chasing the Philistines, he was told, "David is in the Desert of En Gedi." [2]So he took 3,000 chosen men from all Israel and began looking for David and his men near the Rocks of the Wild Goats.

[3]Saul came to the sheep pens beside the road. A cave was there, and he went in to relieve himself. Now David and his men were hiding far back in the cave. [4]The men said to David, "Today is the day the LORD spoke of when he said, 'I will give your enemy over to you. Do anything you want with him.' "

Then David crept up to Saul and quietly cut off a corner of Saul's robe. [5]Later David felt guilty because he had cut off a corner of Saul's robe. [6]He said to his men, "May the LORD keep me from doing such a thing to my master! Saul is the LORD's appointed king. I should not do anything against him, because he is the LORD's appointed king!" [7]David used these words to stop his men; he did not let them attack Saul. Then Saul left the cave and went on his way.

[8]When David came out of the cave, he shouted to Saul, "My master and king!" Saul looked back, and David bowed face down on the ground. [9]He said to Saul, "Why do you listen when people say, 'David wants to harm you'? [10]You have seen something with your own eyes today. The LORD put you in my power in the cave. They said I should kill you, but I was merciful. I said, 'I won't harm my master, because he is the LORD's appointed king.' [11]My father, look at this piece of your robe in my hand! I cut off the corner of your robe, but I didn't kill you. Now understand and know I am not planning any evil against you. I did nothing wrong to you, but you are hunting me to kill me. [12]May the LORD judge between us, and may he punish you for the wrong you have done to me! But I am not against you. [13]There is an old saying: 'Evil things come from evil people.' But I am not against you. [14]Whom is the king of Israel coming out against? Whom are you chasing? It's as if you are chasing a dead dog or a flea. [15]May the LORD be our judge and decide between you and me. May he support me and show that I am right. May he save me from you!"

[16]When David finished saying these words, Saul asked, "Is that your voice, David my son?" And he cried loudly. [17]He said, "You are a better man than I am. You have been good to me, but I have done wrong to you. [18]You told me what good things you did. The LORD handed me over to you, but you did not kill me. [19]If a person finds his enemy, he doesn't just send him on his way, does he? May the LORD reward you because you were good to me today. [20]I know you will surely be king, and you will rule the kingdom of Israel. [21]Now swear to me by the LORD that you will not kill my descendants[d] and that you won't wipe out my name from my father's family."

Maon Some early Greek copies say "Maon". The Hebrew copies say "Paran".

22So David made the promise to Saul. Then Saul went back home, and David and his men went up to their protected place.

Nabal Insults David

25 Now Samuel died, and all the Israelites met and had a time of sadness for him. Then they buried him at his home in Ramah.

David moved to the Desert of Maon. 2A man in Maon who had land at Carmel was very rich. He had 3,000 sheep and 1,000 goats. He was cutting the wool off his sheep at Carmel. 3His name was Nabal, and he was a descendant[d] of Caleb. His wife was named Abigail. She was wise and beautiful, but Nabal was cruel and mean.

4While David was in the desert, he heard that Nabal was cutting the wool from his sheep. 5So he sent ten young men and told them, "Go to Nabal at Carmel, and greet him for me. 6Say to Nabal, 'May you and your family and all who belong to you have good health! 7I have heard that you are cutting the wool from your sheep. When your shepherds were with us, we did not harm them. All the time your shepherds were at Carmel, we stole nothing from them. 8Ask your servants, and they will tell you. We come at a happy time, so be kind to my young men. Please give anything you can find for them and for your son David.' "

9When David's men arrived, they gave the message to Nabal, but Nabal insulted them. 10He answered them, "Who is David? Who is this son of Jesse? Many slaves are running away from their masters today! 11I have bread and water, and I have meat that I killed for my servants who cut the wool. But I won't give it to men I don't know."

12David's men went back and told him all Nabal had said. 13Then David said to them, "Put on your swords!" So they put on their swords, and David put on his also. About 400 men went with David, but 200 men stayed with the supplies.

14One of Nabal's servants said to Abigail, Nabal's wife, "David sent messengers from the desert to greet our master, but Nabal insulted them. 15These men were very good to us. They did not harm us. They stole nothing from us during all the time we were out in the field with them. 16Night and day they protected us. They were like a wall around us while we were with them caring for the sheep. 17Now think about it, and decide what you can do. Terrible trouble is coming to our master and all his family. Nabal is such a wicked man that no one can even talk to him."

18Abigail hurried. She took 200 loaves of bread, two leather bags full of wine, five cooked sheep, 15 kilogrammes of cooked grain, 100 cakes of raisins and 200 cakes of pressed figs and put all these on donkeys. 19Then she told her servants, "Go on. I'll follow you." But she did not tell her husband.

20Abigail rode her donkey and came down towards the mountain ravine. There she met David and his men coming down towards her.

21David had just said, "It's been useless! I watched over Nabal's property in the desert. I made sure none of his sheep was missing. I did good to him, but he has paid me back with evil. 22May God punish my enemies even more. I will not leave one of Nabal's men alive until morning."

23When Abigail saw David, she quickly got off her donkey and bowed face down on the ground before him. 24She fell at David's feet and said, "My master, let the blame be on me! Please let me talk to you. Listen to what I say. 25My master, don't pay attention to this worthless man Nabal. He is like his name. His name means 'fool', and he is truly a fool. But I, your servant, didn't see the men you sent. 26The LORD has kept you from killing and punishing anyone. As surely as the LORD lives and as surely as you live, may your enemies become like Nabal! 27I have brought a gift to you for the men who follow you. 28Please forgive my wrong. The LORD will certainly let your family have many kings, because you fight his battles. As long as you live, may you do nothing bad. 29Someone might chase you to kill you, but the LORD your God will keep you alive. He will throw away your enemies' lives as he would throw a stone from a sling. 30The LORD will keep all his promises of good things for you. He will make you leader over Israel. 31Then you won't feel guilty or troubled because you killed innocent people and punished them. Please remember me when the LORD brings you success."

32David answered Abigail, "Praise the LORD, the God of Israel, who sent you to meet me. 33May you be blessed for your wisdom. You have kept me from killing or punishing people today. 34As surely as the LORD, the God of Israel, lives, he has kept me from hurting you. If you hadn't come quickly to meet me, not one of Nabal's men would have lived until morning."

35Then David accepted Abigail's gifts. He told her, "Go home in peace. I have heard your words, and I will do what you have asked."

Nabal's Death

36When Abigail went back to Nabal, he was in the house, eating like a king. He was very drunk and in a good mood. So she told him nothing until the next morning. 37In the morning when he was not drunk, his wife told him everything. His heart stopped, and he became like stone. 38About ten days later the LORD struck Nabal and he died.

39When David heard that Nabal was dead, he said, "Praise the LORD! Nabal insulted me, but the LORD has supported me! He has kept me from doing wrong. The LORD has punished Nabal for his wrong."

Then David sent a message to Abigail, asking her to be his wife. 40His servants went to Carmel and said to Abigail, "David sent us to take you so you can become his wife."

41Abigail bowed face down on the ground and said, "I am your servant. I'm ready to serve you and to wash the feet of my master's servants." 42Abigail quickly got on a donkey and went with David's messengers, with her five maids following her. And she became David's wife.

43David also had married Ahinoam of Jezreel. So they were both David's wives. 44Saul's daughter Michal was also David's wife, but Saul had given her to Paltiel son of Laish, who was from Gallim.

David Shames Saul Again

26 The people of Ziph went to Saul at Gibeah and said to him, "David is hiding on the hill of Hakilah opposite Jeshimon."

2So Saul went down to the Desert of Ziph with 3,000 chosen men of Israel to look for David there. 3Saul made his camp beside the road on the hill of Hakilah opposite Jeshimon, but David stayed in the desert. When he heard Saul had followed him, 4he sent out spies and learned for certain that Saul had come to Hakilah.

5Then David went to the place where Saul had camped. He saw where Saul and Abner son of Ner, the commander of Saul's army, were sleeping. Saul was sleeping in the middle of the camp with all the army around him.

6David asked Ahimelech the Hittite and Abishai son of Zeruiah, Joab's brother, "Who will go down into Saul's camp with me?"

Abishai answered, "I'll go with you."

7So that night David and Abishai went into Saul's camp. Saul was asleep in the middle of the camp with his spear stuck in the ground near his head. Abner and the army were sleeping around Saul. 8Abishai said to David, "Today God has handed your enemy over to you. Let me pin Saul to the ground with my spear. I'll only have to do it once. I won't need to hit him twice."

9But David said to Abishai, "Don't kill Saul! No one can harm the LORD's appointed king and still be innocent! 10As surely as the LORD lives, the LORD himself will punish Saul. Maybe Saul will die naturally, or maybe he will go into battle and be killed. 11But may the LORD keep me from harming his appointed king! Take the spear and water jug that are near Saul's head. Then let's go."

12So David took the spear and water jug that were near Saul's head, and they left. No one saw them or knew about it or woke up, because the LORD had put them into a deep sleep.

13David crossed over to the other side of the hill and stood on top of the mountain far from Saul's camp. They were a long way away from each other. 14David shouted to the army and to Abner son of Ner, "Won't you answer me, Abner?"

Abner answered, "Who is calling for the king? Who are you?"

15David said. "You're the greatest man in Israel. Isn't that true? Why didn't you guard your master the king? Someone came into your camp to kill your master the king! 16You have not done well. As surely as the LORD lives, you and your men should die. You haven't guarded your master, the LORD's appointed king. Look! Where are the king's spear and water jug that were near his head?"

17Saul knew David's voice. He said, "Is that your voice, David my son?"

David answered, "Yes, it is, my master and king." 18David also said, "Why are you chasing me, my master? What wrong have I done? What evil am I guilty of? 19My master and king, listen to me. If the LORD made you angry with me, let him accept an offering. But if people did it, may the LORD curse them! They have made me leave the land the LORD gave me. They have told me, 'Go and serve other gods.' 20Now don't let me die far away from the LORD's presence. The king of Israel has come out looking for a flea! You're just hunting a bird in the mountains!"

21Then Saul said, "I have sinned. Come back, David my son. Today you respected my life, so I will not try to hurt you. I have been very stupid and foolish."

22David answered, "Here is your spear. Let one of your young men come here and get it. 23The LORD rewards us for the things we do right and for our loyalty to him. The LORD handed you over to me today, but I wouldn't harm the LORD's appointed king. 24As I respected your life today, may the LORD also respect my life and save me from all trouble."

25Then Saul said to David, "You are blessed, my son David. You will do great things and succeed."

So David went on his way, and Saul went back home.

David Lives with the Philistines

27 But David thought to himself, "Saul will catch me some day. The best thing I can do is escape to the land of the Philistines. Then he will give up looking for me in Israel, and I can get away from him."

2So David and his 600 men left Israel and went to Achish son of Maoch, king of Gath. 3David, his men and their families made their home in Gath with Achish. David had his two wives with him—Ahinoam of Jezreel and Abigail of Carmel, the widow of Nabal. 4When Saul heard that David had run away to Gath, he stopped looking for him.

5Then David said to Achish, "If you are pleased with me, give me a place in one of the country towns where I can live. I don't need to live in the royal city with you."

6That day Achish gave David the town of Ziklag, and Ziklag has belonged to the kings of Judah ever since. 7David lived in the Philistine land a year and four months.

8David and his men went to raid the people of Geshur, Girzi and Amalek. (These people had lived for a long time in the land that reached to Shur and Egypt.) 9When David fought them, he killed all the men and women and took their sheep, cattle, donkeys, camels and clothes. Then he returned to Achish.

10Achish would ask David, "Where did you go raiding today?" And David would tell him that he had gone to the southern part of Judah, or Jerahmeel, or to the land of the Kenites. 11David never brought a man or woman alive to Gath. He thought, "If we bring people alive, they may tell Achish, 'This is what David really did.' " David did this all the time he lived in the Philistine land. 12So Achish trusted David and said to himself, "David's own people, the Israelites, now hate him very much. He will serve me for ever."

Saul and the Witch of Endor

28 Later, the Philistines gathered their armies to fight against Israel. Achish said to David, "You understand that you and your men must join my army."

2David answered, "You will see for yourself what I, your servant, can do!"

Achish said, "Fine, I'll make you my bodyguard for life."

3Now Samuel was dead, and all the Israelites had shown their sadness for him. They had buried Samuel in his home town of Ramah.

And Saul had forced out the mediums[d] and fortune-tellers from the land.

4The Philistines came together and made camp at Shunem. Saul gathered all the Israelites and made camp at Gilboa. 5When he saw the Philistine army, he was afraid, and his heart pounded with fear. 6He prayed to the LORD, but the LORD did not answer him through dreams, Urim[d] or prophets.[d] 7Then Saul said to his servants, "Find me a woman who is a medium so I may go and ask her what will happen."

His servants answered, "There is a medium in Endor."

8Then Saul put on other clothes to disguise himself, and at night he and two of his men went to see the woman. Saul said to her, "Talk to a spirit for me. Bring up the person I name."

9But the woman said to him, "Surely you know what Saul has done. He has forced the mediums and fortune-tellers from the land. You are trying to trap me and get me killed."

10Saul made a promise to the woman in the name of the LORD. He said, "As surely as the LORD lives, you won't be punished for this."

11The woman asked, "Whom do you want me to bring up?"

He answered, "Bring up Samuel."

12When the woman saw Samuel, she screamed. She said, "Why have you tricked me? You are Saul!"

13The king said to the woman, "Don't be afraid! What do you see?"

The woman said, "I see a spirit coming up out of the ground."

14Saul asked, "What does he look like?"

The woman answered, "An old man wearing a coat is coming up."

Then Saul knew it was Samuel, and he bowed face down on the ground.

15Samuel asked Saul, "Why have you disturbed me by bringing me up?"

Saul said, "I am greatly troubled. The Philistines are fighting against me, and God has left me. He won't answer me any more, either by prophets or in dreams. That's why I called for you. Tell me what to do."

16Samuel said, "The LORD has left you and has become your enemy. So why do you call on me? 17He has done what he said he would do—the things he said through me. He has torn the kingdom out of your hands and given it to one of your neighbours, David. 18You did not obey the LORD; you did not show the Amalekites how angry he was with them. That's why he has done this to you today. 19The LORD will hand over both Israel and you to the Philistines. Tomorrow you and your sons will be with me. The LORD will hand over the army of Israel to the Philistines."

20Saul quickly fell flat on the ground and was afraid of what Samuel had said. He was also very weak because he had eaten nothing all that day and night.

21 Then the woman came to Saul and saw that he was really frightened. She said, "Look, I, your servant, have obeyed you. I have risked my life and done what you told me to do. 22 Now please listen to me. Let me give you some food so you may eat and have enough strength to go on your way."

23 But Saul refused, saying, "I won't eat."

His servants joined the woman in asking him to eat, and he listened to them. So he got up from the ground and sat on the bed.

24 At the house the woman had a fat calf, which she quickly killed. She took some flour and mixed dough with her hands. Then she baked some bread without yeast. 25 She put the food before them, and they ate. That same night they got up and left.

David Goes Back to Ziklag

29 The Philistines gathered all their soldiers at Aphek. Israel camped by the spring at Jezreel. 2 The Philistine kings were marching with their groups of 100 and 1,000 men. David and his men were marching behind Achish. 3 The Philistine commanders asked, "What are these Hebrews doing here?"

Achish told them, "This is David. He served Saul king of Israel, but he has been with me for over a year now. I have found nothing wrong in David since the time he left Saul."

4 But the Philistine commanders were angry with Achish and said, "Send David back to the city you gave him. He cannot go with us into battle. If he does, we'll have an enemy in our own camp. He could please his king by killing our own men. 5 David is the one the Israelites dance and sing about, saying:

'Saul has killed thousands of his enemies,
but David has killed tens of thousands.' "

6 So Achish called David and said to him, "As surely as the LORD lives, you are loyal. I would be pleased to have you serve in my army. Since the day you came to me, I have found no wrong in you. But the other kings don't trust you. 7 Go back in peace. Don't do anything to displease the Philistine kings."

8 David asked, "What wrong have I done? What evil have you found in me from the day I came to you until now? Why can't I go and fight your enemies, my lord and king?"

9 Achish answered, "I know you are as good as an angel from God. But the Philistine commanders have said, 'David must not go with us into battle.' 10 Early in the morning you and your master's servants should leave. Get up as soon as it is light and go."

11 So David and his men got up early in the morning and went back to the country of the Philistines. And the Philistines went up to Jezreel.

> **Sidelight** If you think it's not right to cry, read 1 Samuel 30:3–4. When David and his army found their town burned and their families carted off into captivity, they cried so much that they were too weak to cry any more.

David's War with the Amalekites

30 On the third day, when David and his men arrived at Ziklag, he found that the Amalekites had raided southern Judah and Ziklag, attacking Ziklag and burning it. 2 They captured the women and everyone, young and old, but they had not killed anyone. They had only taken them away.

3 When David and his men came to Ziklag, they found the town had been burned and their wives, sons and daughters had been taken as prisoners. 4 Then David and his army cried loudly until they were too weak to cry any more. 5 David's two wives had also been taken—Ahinoam of Jezreel and Abigail the widow of Nabal from Carmel. 6 The men in the army were threatening to kill David with stones, which greatly upset David. Each man was sad and angry because his sons and daughters had been captured, but David found strength in the LORD his God. 7 David said to Abiathar the priest, "Bring me the holy robe."[d]

8 Then David asked the LORD, "Should I chase the people who took our families? Will I catch them?"

The LORD answered, "Chase them. You will catch them, and you will succeed in saving your families."

9 David and the 600 men with him came to the Besor Ravine, where some of the men stayed. 10 David and 400 men kept up the chase. The other 200 men stayed behind because they were too tired to cross the ravine.

11 They found an Egyptian in a field and brought him to David. They gave the Egyptian some water to drink and some food to eat. 12 And they gave him a piece of a fig cake and two clusters of raisins. Then he felt better, because he had not eaten any food or drunk any water for three days and nights.

13 David asked him, "Who is your master? Where do you come from?"

He answered, "I'm an Egyptian, the slave of an Amalekite. Three days ago my master left me, because I was sick. 14We had attacked the southern area of the Kerethites, the land of Judah and the southern area of Caleb. We burned Ziklag, as well.

15David asked him, "Can you lead me to the people who took our families?"

He answered, "Yes, if you promise me before God that you won't kill me or give me back to my master. Then I will take you to them."

16So the Egyptian led David to the Amalekites. They were lying around on the ground, eating and drinking and celebrating with the things they had taken from the land of the Philistines and from Judah. 17David fought them from sunset until the evening of the next day. None of them escaped, except 400 young men who rode off on their camels. 18David got his two wives back and everything the Amalekites had taken. 19Nothing was missing. David brought back everyone, young and old, sons and daughters. He recovered the valuable things and everything the Amalekites had taken. 20David took all the sheep and cattle, and his men made these animals go in front, saying, "They are David's prize."

21Then David came to the 200 men who had been too tired to follow him, who had stayed at the Besor Ravine. They came out to meet David and the people with him. When he came near, David greeted the men at the ravine.

22But the evil men and troublemakers among those who followed David said, "Since these 200 men didn't go with us, we shouldn't give them any of the things we recovered. Just let each man take his wife and children and go."

23David answered, "No, my brothers. Don't do that after what the LORD has given us. He has protected us and given us the enemy who attacked us. 24Who will listen to what you say? The share will be the same for the one who stayed with the supplies as for the one who went into battle. All will share alike." 25David made this an order and rule for Israel, which continues even today.

26When David arrived in Ziklag, he sent some of the things he had taken from the Amalekites to his friends, the elders of Judah. He said, "Here is a present for you from the things we took from the LORD's enemies."

27David also sent some things to the leaders in Bethel, Ramoth in the southern part of Judah, Jattir, 28Aroer, Siphmoth, Eshtemoa, 29Racal, the cities of the Jerahmeelites and the Kenites, 30Hormah, Bor Ashan, Athach, 31Hebron and to the people in all the other places where he and his men had been.

The Death of Saul

31 The Philistines fought against Israel, and the Israelites ran away from them. Many Israelites were killed on Mount Gilboa. 2The Philistines fought hard against Saul and his sons, killing his sons Jonathan, Abinadab and Malki-Shua. 3The fighting was heavy around Saul. The archers shot him, and he was badly wounded. 4He said to the officer who carried his armour, "Pull out your sword and kill me. Then those uncircumcised [d] men won't make fun of me and kill me." But Saul's officer refused, because he was afraid. So Saul took his own sword and threw himself on it. 5When the officer saw that Saul was dead, he threw himself on his own sword, and he died with Saul. 6So Saul, his three sons and the officer who carried his armour died together that day.

7When the Israelites who lived across the Jezreel Valley and those who lived across the Jordan River saw how the Israelite army had run away, and that Saul and his sons were dead, they left their cities and ran away. Then the Philistines came and lived there.

8The next day when the Philistines came to take all the valuable things from the dead soldiers, they found Saul and his three sons dead on Mount Gilboa. 9They cut off Saul's head and took off his armour. Then they sent messengers through all the land of the Philistines to tell the news in the temple of their idols and to their people. 10They put Saul's armour in the temple of the Ashtoreths [d] and hung his body on the wall of Beth Shan.

11When the people living in Jabesh Gilead heard what the Philistines had done to Saul, 12the brave men of Jabesh marched all night and came to Beth Shan. They removed the bodies of Saul and his sons from the wall of Beth Shan and brought them to Jabesh. There they burned the bodies. 13They took their bones and buried them under the tamarisk tree in Jabesh. Then the people of Jabesh gave up eating for seven days.

2 Samuel

Why Read This Book:

- Learn how leaders can encourage people to follow God (2 Samuel 1—6).
- Discover how God can use people for good in spite of their faults (2 Samuel 7—12).
- See how family problems can hurt leaders (2 Samuel 13—20).

When?

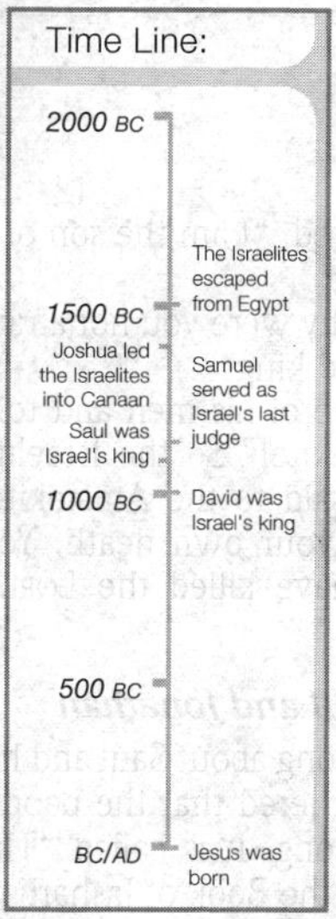

Behind the Scenes:

If 1 Samuel tells the story of David's youth (and it does), then 2 Samuel tells the story of his life as a king. David was first crowned as the king of Judah, and then later as the king of all Israel. He is without doubt one of the greatest role models in the Old Testament, and God himself referred to him as " . . . the kind of man I want. He will do all I want him to do" (Acts 13:22, p.1160).

But despite the fact that David achieved so much in his life, he wasn't perfect.

2 Samuel tells of his affair with Bathsheba, and then of the way that he had her husband murdered in order to try and cover up his sin. The book tells us about his struggle with family problems which led to the death of his precious son Absalom.

Yet throughout all these problems, hang-ups and sins, David never stopped trying to follow God. When God's prophet confronted the king about his sin, David repented without hesitation. When his family was falling apart, he cried out to God for help. ▷

Where?

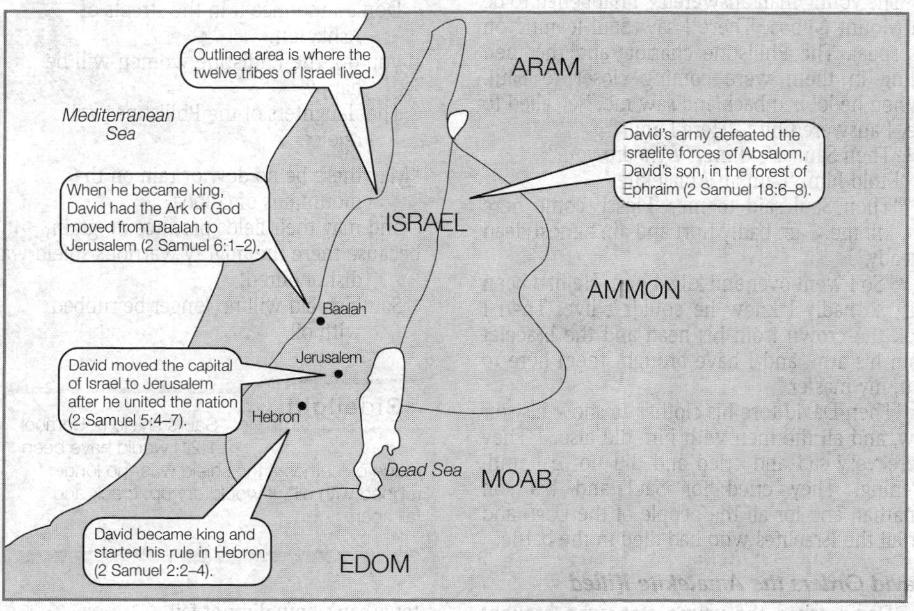

Behind the Scenes (cont.): Because David always relied on God, he became known as Israel's greatest king. He learned that God is a God of second chances, and that even when we fail, he is always prepared to pick us up, brush the dust from our clothes, and help us to continue following him.

David Learns About Saul's Death

1 Now Saul was dead. After David had de-
feated the Amalekites, he returned to Ziklag
and stayed there for two days. 2On the third day
a young man from Saul's camp came to Ziklag.
To show his sadness, his clothes were torn and
he had dust on his head. He came and bowed
face down on the ground before David.
3David asked him, "Where did you come
from?"
The man answered, "I escaped from the Israel-
ite camp."
4David asked him, "What happened? Please
tell me!"
The man answered, "The people have run
away from the battle, and many of them have
fallen and are dead. Saul and his son Jonathan
are dead also."
5David asked him, "How do you know Saul
and his son Jonathan are dead?"
6The young man answered, "I happened to be
on Mount Gilboa. There I saw Saul leaning on
his spear. The Philistine chariots and the men
riding in them were coming closer to Saul.
7When he looked back and saw me, he called to
me. I answered him, 'Here I am!'
8"Then Saul asked me, 'Who are you?'
"I told him, 'I am an Amalekite.'
9"Then Saul said to me, 'Please come here
and kill me. I am badly hurt and am almost dead
already.'
10"So I went over and killed him. He had been
hurt so badly I knew he couldn't live. Then I
took the crown from his head and the bracelet
from his arm, and I have brought them here to
you, my master."
11Then David tore his clothes to show his sor-
row, and all the men with him did also. 12They
were very sad and cried and did not eat until
evening. They cried for Saul and his son
Jonathan and for all the people of the LORD and
for all the Israelites who had died in the battle.

David Orders the Amalekite Killed

13David asked the young man who brought
the report, "Where are you from?"
The young man answered, "I am the son of a
foreigner, an Amalekite."
14David asked him, "Why were you not afraid
to kill the LORD's appointed king?"
15Then David called one of his men and told
him, "Go! Kill the Amalekite!" So the Israelite
killed him. 16David had said to the Amalekite,
"You are responsible for your own death. You
confessed by saying, 'I have killed the LORD's
appointed king.'"

David's Song About Saul and Jonathan

17David sang a funeral song about Saul and his
son Jonathan, 18and he ordered that the people
of Judah be taught this song. It is called "The
Bow", and it is written in the Book of Jashar:

19"Israel, your leaders have been killed on the
hills.
How the mighty have fallen in battle!
20Don't tell it in Gath.
Don't announce it in the streets of
Ashkelon.
If you do, the Philistine women will be
happy.
The daughters of the Philistines will
rejoice.

21"May there be no dew or rain on the
mountains of Gilboa,
and may their fields produce no grain,
because there the mighty warrior's shield was
dishonoured.
Saul's shield will no longer be rubbed
with oil.

Sidelight

Saul's shield (2 Samuel 1:21) would have been made of leather. If the shield was "no longer rubbed with oil", it would dry up, crack and fall apart.

22Jonathan's bow did not fail
to kill many soldiers.

Saul's sword did not fail
to wound many strong men.

23“We loved Saul and Jonathan
and enjoyed them while they lived.
They are together even in death.
They were faster than eagles.
They were stronger than lions.

24“You daughters of Israel, cry for Saul.
Saul clothed you with red dresses
and put gold decorations on them.

25“How the mighty have fallen in battle!
Jonathan is dead on Gilboa's hills.
26I cry for you, my brother Jonathan.
I enjoyed your friendship so much.
Your love to me was wonderful,
better than the love of women.
27“How the mighty have fallen!
The weapons of war are gone.”

David is Made King of Judah

2 Later, David prayed to the LORD, saying,
“Should I go up to any of the cities of
Judah?”

The LORD said to David, “Go.”

David asked, “Where should I go?”

The LORD answered, “To Hebron.”

2So David went up to Hebron with his two
wives: Ahinoam from Jezreel and Abigail, the
widow of Nabal from Carmel. 3David also
brought his men and their families, and they all
made their homes in the cities of Hebron. 4Then
the men of Judah came to Hebron and appointed
David king over Judah.

They told David that the men of Jabesh Gilead
had buried Saul. 5So David sent messengers to
the men of Jabesh Gilead and said to them, “The
LORD bless you. You have shown loyalty to your
master Saul by burying him. 6May the LORD now

DEATH

Goodbye England's Rose

The death of Diana, Princess of Wales, stunned our nation and the world. Everyone remembers where they were when they heard the news. Young and old, we joined together to grieve over a much loved lady. The three million flowers outside the palaces were a sign that people needed to do more than sit at home and mourn. They signed books, they threw bouquets into the path of the hearse as it made its way through England. It was obvious that something had to happen nationally to calm the people down and give them something to hold on to.

Elton John wrote a song for the funeral. Over thirty million people bought the record and felt strangely consoled by it.

When Saul and his son Jonathan died, David felt compelled to write a song. He saw the nation's grief and knew that he himself needed to do something. The funeral song that David wrote was given to the people of Judah. In fact, he ordered the nation to learn the song! There were no CDs in those days, so the song had to be taught.

Often we find it hard to express ourselves by speaking words alone, but to sing, to listen to music, to write it down maybe poetically is consolation itself.

Look at the words of David's song “The Bow” in **2 Samuel 1:17–27**, particularly the lines “We enjoyed them while they lived” and “I enjoyed your friendship so much”.

- Do you feel helped by remembering the good things?
- Have you ever lost anyone close to you? How did you cope?

Consider . . .

- writing things down when you are sad about the loss of someone you love and reading them later.
- telling the Lord how you feel, in a song or poem.

For more, see . . .

- Deuteronomy 34:1–12 (p.200)
- Matthew 5:4 (p.942)
- Isaiah 61:1–11 (p.705)

be loyal and true to you. I will also treat you well because you have done this. 7Now be strong and brave. Saul your master is dead, and the people of Judah have appointed me their king."

War Between Judah and Israel

8Abner son of Ner was the commander of Saul's army. Abner took Saul's son Ish-Bosheth to Mahanaim 9and made him king of Gilead, Ashuri, Jezreel, Ephraim, Benjamin and all Israel. 10Saul's son Ish-Bosheth was 40 years old when he became king over Israel, and he ruled two years. But the people of Judah followed David. 11David was king in Hebron for seven years and six months.

12Abner son of Ner and the servants of Ish-Bosheth son of Saul left Mahanaim and went to Gibeon. 13Joab son of Zeruiah and David's men also went there and met Abner and Ish-Bosheth's men at the pool of Gibeon. Abner's group sat on one side of the pool; Joab's group sat on the other.

14Abner said to Joab, "Let the young men have a contest here."

Joab said, "Yes, let them have a contest."

15Then the men got up and were counted—twelve from the people of Benjamin for Ish-Bosheth son of Saul, and twelve from David's men. 16Each man grabbed the one opposite him by the head and stabbed him in the side with a knife. So the men fell down together. For that reason, that place in Gibeon is called the Field of Knives. 17That day there was a terrible battle, and David's men defeated Abner and the Israelites.

Sidelight The pool of Gibeon – where Saul's and David's armies fought – was a huge well (2 Samuel 2:8–17). Archaeologists have discovered what was probably the pool. It is 11½ metres in diameter, and has a 79-step winding stairway down to the water level, which is roughly 10 metres below the ground.

Abner Kills Asahel

18Zeruiah's three sons, Joab, Abishai and Asahel, were there. Now Asahel was a fast runner, as fast as a deer in the field. 19Asahel chased Abner, going straight towards him. 20Abner looked back and asked, "Is that you, Asahel?"

Asahel said, "Yes, it is."

21Then Abner said to Asahel, "Turn to your right or left and catch one of the young men and take his armour." But Asahel refused to stop chasing him.

22Abner again said to Asahel, "Stop chasing me! If you don't stop, I'll have to kill you! Then I won't be able to face your brother Joab again!"

23But Asahel refused to stop chasing Abner. So using the back end of his spear, Abner stabbed Asahel in the stomach, and the spear came out of his back. Asahel died right there, and everyone stopped when they came to the place where Asahel's body lay.

24But Joab and Abishai continued chasing Abner. As the sun was going down, they arrived at the hill of Ammah, near Giah on the way to the desert near Gibeon. 25The men of Benjamin came to Abner, and all stood together at the top of the hill.

26Abner shouted to Joab, "Must the sword kill for ever? Surely you must know this will only end in sadness! Tell the people to stop chasing their own brothers!"

27Then Joab said, "As surely as God lives, if you had not said anything, the people would have chased their brothers until morning." 28Then Joab blew a trumpet, and his people stopped chasing the Israelites. They did not fight them any more.

29Abner and his men marched all night through the Jordan Valley. They crossed the Jordan River, and after marching all day, arrived at Mahanaim.

30After he had stopped chasing Abner, Joab came back and gathered the people together. Asahel and nineteen of David's men were missing. 31But David's men had killed 360 Benjaminites who had followed Abner. 32David's men took Asahel and buried him in the tomb of his father at Bethlehem. Then Joab and his men marched all night. The sun came up as they reached Hebron.

3 There was a long war between the people who supported Saul's family and those who supported David's family. The supporters of David's family became stronger and stronger, but the supporters of Saul's family became weaker and weaker.

David's Sons

2Sons were born to David at Hebron. The first was Amnon, whose mother was Ahinoam from Jezreel. 3The second son was Kileab, whose mother was Abigail, the widow of Nabal from Carmel. The third son was Absalom, whose mother was Maacah daughter of Talmai, the king of Geshur. 4The fourth son was Adonijah, whose mother was Haggith. The fifth son was Shephatiah, whose mother was Abital. 5The sixth son was Ithream, whose mother was Eglah, David's wife. These sons were born to David at Hebron.

Abner Joins David

6During the war between the supporters of Saul's family and the supporters of David's family, Abner made himself a main leader among the supporters of Saul.

7Saul once had a slave woman[d] named Rizpah, who was the daughter of Aiah. Ish-Bosheth said to Abner, "Why did you have sexual relations with my father's slave woman?"

8Abner was very angry because of what Ish-Bosheth said, and he replied, "I have been loyal to Saul and his family and friends! I didn't hand you over to David. I am not a traitor working for Judah! But now you are saying I did something wrong with this woman! 9May God help me if I don't join David! I will make sure that what the LORD promised does happen! 10I will take the kingdom from the family of Saul and make David king of Israel and Judah, from Dan to Beersheba!"[n]

11Ish-Bosheth couldn't say anything to Abner, because he was afraid of him.

12Then Abner sent messengers to ask David, "Who is going to rule the land? Make an agreement with me, and I will help you unite all Israel."

13David answered, "Good! I will make an agreement with you, but I ask you one thing. I will not meet with you unless you bring Saul's daughter Michal to me." 14Then David sent messengers to Saul's son Ish-Bosheth, saying, "Give me my wife Michal. She was promised to me, and I killed 100 Philistines to get her."

15So Ish-Bosheth sent men to take Michal from her husband Paltiel son of Laish. 16Michal's husband went with her, crying as he followed her to Bahurim. But Abner said to Paltiel, "Go back home." So he went home.

Sidelight Have you ever felt that your parents interfere with your choice of who to go out with? Think how David felt – he married Saul's daughter, Michal (1 Samuel 18:20–29, p.273) but when Saul fell out with David, he took his daughter away and gave her to someone else to marry (1 Samuel 25:44, p.279). Later, she was returned to David as part of a political bargain (2 Samuel 3:12–16).

17Abner sent this message to the elders of Israel: "You have been wanting to make David your king. 18Now do it! The LORD said of David, 'Through my servant David, I will save my people Israel from the Philistines and all their enemies.' "

19Abner also said these things to the people of Benjamin. He then went to Hebron to tell David what the Benjaminites and Israel wanted to do. 20Abner came with 20 men to David at Hebron. There David prepared a feast for them. 21Abner said to David, "My master and king, I will go and bring all the Israelites to you. Then they will make an agreement with you so you will rule over all Israel as you wanted." So David let Abner go, and he left in peace.

Abner's Death

22Just then Joab and David's men came from a battle, bringing many valuable things they had taken from the enemy. David had let Abner leave in peace, so he was not with David at Hebron. 23When Joab and all his army arrived at Hebron, the army said to Joab, "Abner son of Ner came to King David, and David let him leave in peace."

24Joab came to the king and said, "What have you done? Abner came to you. Why did you let him go? Now he's gone. 25You know Abner son of Ner! He came to trick you! He came to learn about everything you are doing!"

26After Joab left David, he sent messengers after Abner, and they brought him back from the well of Sirah. But David did not know this. 27When Abner arrived at Hebron, Joab took him aside into the gateway. He acted as though he wanted to talk with Abner in private, but Joab stabbed him in the stomach, and Abner died. Abner had killed Joab's brother Asahel, so Joab killed Abner to pay him back.

28Later when David heard the news, he said, "My kingdom and I are innocent for ever of the death of Abner son of Ner. The LORD knows this. 29Joab and his family are responsible for this. May his family always have someone with sores or with a skin disease. May they always have someone who must lean on a crutch. May some of his family be killed in war. May they always have someone without food to eat."

30(Joab and his brother Abishai killed Abner, because he had killed their brother Asahel in the battle at Gibeon.)

31Then David said to Joab and to all the people with Joab, "Tear your clothes and put on rough cloth to show how sad you are. Cry for Abner." King David himself followed the body of Abner. 32They buried Abner in Hebron, and David and all the people cried at Abner's grave.

33King David sang this funeral song for Abner.

"Did Abner die like a fool?

Dan to Beersheba Dan was the city farthest north in Israel, and Beersheba was the city farthest south. So this means all the people of Israel.

34 His hands were not tied.
His feet were not in chains.
He fell at the hands of evil men."

Then all the people cried again for Abner.
35 They came to encourage David to eat while it
was still day. But he made a promise, saying,
"May God punish me terribly if I eat bread or
anything else before the sun sets!"
36 All the people saw what happened, and they
agreed with what the king was doing, just as
they agreed with everything he did. 37 That day all
the people of Judah and Israel understood that
David did not order the killing of Abner son of Ner.
38 David said to his officers, "You know that a
great man died today in Israel. 39 Even though I
am the appointed king, I feel empty. These sons
of Zeruiah are too much for me. May the LORD
give them the punishment they should have."

Ish-Bosheth's Death

4 When Ish-Bosheth son of Saul heard that
Abner had died at Hebron, he was shocked
and all Israel became frightened. 2 Two men who
were captains in Saul's army came to Ish-
Bosheth. One was named Baanah, and the other
was named Recab. They were the sons of Rim-
mon of Beeroth, who was a Benjaminite. (The
town Beeroth belonged to the tribe[d] of Ben-
jamin. 3 The people of Beeroth ran away to Git-
taim, and they still live there as foreigners today.)
4 (Saul's son Jonathan had a son named Mephi-
bosheth, who was crippled in both feet. He was
five years old when the news came from Jezreel
that Saul and Jonathan were dead. Mephi-
bosheth's nurse had picked him up and run
away. But as she hurried to leave, she dropped
him, and now he was lame.)
5 Recab and Baanah, sons of Rimmon from
Beeroth, went to Ish-Bosheth's house in the af-
ternoon while he was having his midday rest.
6–7 They went into the middle of the house as if to
get some wheat. Ish-Bosheth was lying on his
bed in his bedroom. Then Recab and Baanah
stabbed him in the stomach, killed him, cut off
his head and took it with them. They escaped
and travelled all night through the Jordan Valley.
8 When they arrived at Hebron, they gave his
head to David and said to the king, "Here is the
head of Ish-Bosheth son of Saul, your enemy. He
tried to kill you! Today the LORD has paid back
Saul and his family for what they did to you!"
9 David answered Recab and his brother
Baanah, the sons of Rimmon of Beeroth, "As
surely as the LORD lives, he has saved me from all
trouble! 10 Once a man thought he was bringing
me good news. When he told me, 'Saul is dead!'
I seized him and killed him at Ziklag. That was
the reward I gave him for his news! 11 So even
more I must put you evil men to death because
you have killed an innocent man on his own bed
in his own house!"
12 So David commanded his men to kill Recab
and Baanah. They cut off the hands and feet of
Recab and Baanah and hung them over the pool
of Hebron. Then they took Ish-Bosheth's head
and buried it in Abner's tomb at Hebron.

David is Made King of Israel

5 Then all the tribes[d] of Israel came to David
at Hebron and said to him, "Look, we are
your own family. 2 Even when Saul was king, you
were the one who led Israel in battle. The LORD
said to you, 'You will be a shepherd for my peo-
ple Israel. You will be their leader.' "
3 So all the elders of Israel came to King David
at Hebron, and he made an agreement with
them in Hebron in the presence of the LORD.
Then they poured oil on David to make him king
over Israel.
4 David was 30 years old when he became
king, and he ruled 40 years. 5 He was king over
Judah in Hebron for seven years and six months,
and he was king over all Israel and Judah in
Jerusalem for 33 years.
6 When the king and his men went to
Jerusalem to attack the Jebusites who lived
there, the Jebusites said to David, "You can't get
inside our city. Even the blind and the crippled
can stop you." They thought David could not
enter their city. 7 But David did take the city of
Jerusalem with its strong walls, and it became
the City of David.
8 That day David said to his men, "To defeat the
Jebusites you must go through the water tunnel.
Then you can reach those 'crippled' and 'blind'
enemies. This is why people say, 'The blind and
the crippled may not enter the palace.' "
9 So David lived in the fortified city and called
it the City of David. David built more buildings
around it, beginning where the land was filled
in. He also built more buildings inside the city.
10 He became stronger and stronger, because the
LORD God All-powerful was with him.
11 Hiram king of the city of Tyre sent messen-
gers to David, along with cedar logs, carpenters
and stonecutters. They built a palace for David.

Sidelight Although Jerusalem wasn't very big by modern standards it was a well-protected fortress city. David captured it and became king of the nation, "because the LORD God All-powerful was with him" (2 Samuel 5:10).

12Then David knew that the LORD really had
made him king of Israel and that the LORD had
made his kingdom great because the LORD loved
his people Israel.
13After he came from Hebron, David took for
himself more slave women[d] and wives in Jeru-
salem. More sons and daughters were born to
David. 14These are the names of the sons born to
David in Jerusalem: Shammua, Shobab, Nathan,
Solomon, 15Ibhar, Elishua, Nepheg, Japhia,
16Elishama, Eliada and Eliphelet.

David Defeats the Philistines

17When the Philistines heard that David had
been made king over Israel, all the Philistines
went to look for him. But when David heard
the news, he went down to the stronghold.[d]
18The Philistines came and camped in the Valley
of Rephaim. 19David asked the LORD, "Should I
attack the Philistines? Will you hand them over
to me?"
The LORD said to David, "Go! I will certainly
hand them over to you."
20So David went to Baal Perazim and defeated
the Philistines there. David said, "Like a flood of
water, the LORD has broken through my enemies
in front of me." So David named the place Baal
Perazim.[n] 21The Philistines left their idols behind
at Baal Perazim, so David and his men carried
them away.
22Once again the Philistines came and camped
at the Valley of Rephaim. 23When David prayed
to the LORD, he answered, "Don't attack the Phi-
listines from the front. Instead, go around and at-
tack them in front of the balsam trees. 24When
you hear the sound of marching in the tops of the
balsam trees, act quickly. I, the LORD, will have
gone ahead of you to defeat the Philistine army."

Baal Perazim This name means "the LORD breaks through".

LEADERSHIP

Earned Respect

The other athletics team members didn't know what to think when Anne walked into the changing room. She was a first year, and everyone else on the team was in their second or third year at college. "How's everybody doing?" she said cheerfully.

Within weeks, Anne had become a star, beating the county record in the 400 metres. But when the local newspaper reporter asked her about it, she replied: "I'm glad the team did well. The whole team encouraged me in that race. We work hard together."

Anne would never take glory for her performance. And, gradually, the older girls began asking her for coaching. By the end of the season, the whole team had become one of the best in the county.

When it came to picking a captain for the next year, no one questioned whom to pick. She might only be in her second year, and usually a final-year student led the team, but Anne was the team's natural leader.

Like Anne, David had proved his leadership skills for years. So when it came time to find a new king, he was a natural choice, even though he was young. Read how the country chose him in **2 Samuel 5:1–5**.

- How did both Anne and David earn respect so that they were chosen as leaders? How did their humility help them both as leaders?
- How can you, like David, work to earn people's respect so that you can be a leader?

Consider . . .

- talking to a leader you respect about how he or she became a leader. Then put into practise one tip you have learned.
- working to be a team player at church, school and work, then watching to see what leadership role you might play.

For more, see . . .

- Jeremiah 1:4–10 (p.716)
- 1 Corinthians 3:5–9 (p.1216)
- Matthew 20:20–28 (p.976)

25So David did what the LORD commanded. He defeated the Philistines and chased them all the way from Gibeon to Gezer.

The Ark is Brought to Jerusalem

6 David again gathered all the chosen men of Israel—30,000 of them. 2Then he and all his people went to Baalah in Judah[n] to bring back the Ark[d] of God. The Ark is called by the Name, the name of the LORD All-powerful, whose throne is between the gold creatures with wings. 3They put the Ark of God on a new cart and brought it out of Abinadab's house on the hill. Uzzah and Ahio, sons of Abinadab, led the new cart 4which had the Ark of God on it. Ahio was walking in front of it. 5David and all the Israelites were celebrating in the presence of the LORD. They were playing wooden instruments: lyres,[d] harps, tambourines,[d] rattles and cymbals.

6When David's men came to the threshing[d] floor of Nacon, the oxen stumbled. So Uzzah reached out to steady the Ark of God. 7The LORD was angry with Uzzah and killed him because of what he did. So Uzzah died there beside the Ark of God. 8David was angry because the LORD had killed Uzzah. Now that place is called the Punishment of Uzzah.

9David was afraid of the LORD that day, and he said, "How can the Ark of the LORD come to me now?" 10So David would not move the Ark of the LORD to be with him in Jerusalem. Instead, he took it to the house of Obed-Edom, a man from Gath. 11The Ark of the LORD stayed in Obed-Edom's house for three months, and the LORD blessed Obed-Edom and all his family.

12The people told David, "The LORD has blessed the family of Obed-Edom and all that belongs to him, because the Ark of God is there." So David went and brought it up from Obed-Edom's house to Jerusalem with joy. 13When the men carrying the Ark of the LORD had walked six steps, David sacrificed a bull and a fat calf. 14Then David danced with all his might before the LORD. He had on a holy linen robe.[d] 15David and all the Israelites shouted with joy and blew the trumpets as they brought the Ark of the LORD to the city.

16As the Ark of the LORD came into the city, Saul's daughter Michal looked out of the window. When she saw David jumping and dancing in the presence of the LORD, she hated him.

17David put up a tent for the Ark of the LORD, and then the Israelites put it in its place inside the tent. David offered whole burnt offerings and fellowship offerings before the LORD. 18When David finished offering the whole burnt offerings and the fellowship offerings, he blessed the people in the name of the LORD All-powerful. 19David gave a loaf of bread, a cake of dates and a cake of raisins to every Israelite, both men and women. Then all the people went home.

20David went back to bless the people in his home, but Saul's daughter Michal came out to meet him. She said, "With what honour the king of Israel acted today! You took off your clothes in front of the servant girls of your officers like one who takes off his clothes without shame!"

21Then David said to Michal, "I did it in the presence of the LORD. The LORD chose me, not your father or anyone from Saul's family. The LORD appointed me to be over Israel. So I will celebrate in the presence of the LORD. 22Maybe I will lose even more honour, and maybe I will be brought down in my own opinion, but the girls you talk about will honour me!"

23And Saul's daughter Michal had no children to the day she died.

David Wants to Build a Temple

7 King David was living in his palace, and the LORD had given him peace from all his enemies around him. 2Then David said to Nathan the prophet,[d] "Look, I am living in a palace made of cedar wood, but the Ark[d] of God is in a tent!"

3Nathan said to the king, "Go and do what you really want to do, because the LORD is with you."

4But that night the LORD spoke his word to Nathan, 5"Go and tell my servant David, 'This is what the LORD says: will you build a house for me to live in? 6From the time I brought the Israelites out of Egypt until now I have not lived in a house. I have been moving around all this time with a tent as my home. 7As I have moved with the Israelites, I have never said to the tribes,[d] whom I commanded to take care of my people Israel, "Why haven't you built me a house of cedar?" '

8"You must tell my servant David, 'This is what the LORD All-powerful says: I took you from the pasture and from tending the sheep and made you leader of my people Israel. 9I have been with you everywhere you have gone and have defeated your enemies for you. I will make you as famous as any of the great people on the earth. 10Also I will choose a place for my people Israel, and I will plant them so they can live in their own homes. They will not be bothered any more. Wicked people will no longer bother them as they have in the past 11when I chose judges for my people Israel. But I will give you peace from all your enemies. I also tell you that I will make your descendants[d] kings of Israel after you.

Baalah in Judah Another name for Kiriath Jearim.

12“ ‘When you die and join your ancestors, I
will make one of your sons the next king, and I
will set up his kingdom. 13He will build a house
for me, and I will let his kingdom rule always. 14I
will be his father, and he will be my son. When
he sins, I will use other people to punish him.
They will be my whips. 15I took away my love
from Saul, whom I removed before you, but I
will never stop loving your son. 16But your fam-
ily and your kingdom will continue always be-
fore me. Your throne will last for ever.’ ”
17Nathan told David everything God had said
in this vision.

David Prays to God

18Then King David went in and sat in front of
the LORD. David said, “Lord GOD, who am I?
What is my family? Why did you bring me to
this point? 19But even this is not enough for
you, Lord GOD. You have also made promises
about my future family. This is not normal,
Lord GOD.
20“What more can I say to you, Lord GOD,
since you know me, your servant, so well! 21You
have done this great thing because you said you
would and because you wanted to, and you have
let me know about it. 22This is why you are
great, Lord GOD! There is no one like you. There
is no God except you. We have heard all this our-
selves! 23There is no nation like your people Is-
rael. They are the only people on earth that God
chose to be his own. You made your name well
known. You did great and wonderful miracles[d]
for them. You went ahead of them and forced
other nations and their gods out of the land. You
freed your people from slavery in Egypt. 24You
made the people of Israel your very own people
for ever, and, LORD, you are their God.
25“Now, LORD God, keep the promise for ever
that you made about my family and me, your ser-
vant. Do what you have said. 26Then you will be
honoured always, and people will say, ‘The LORD
All-powerful is God over Israel!’ And the family of
your servant David will continue before you.
27“LORD All-powerful, the God of Israel, you
have said to me, ‘I will make your family great.’
So I, your servant, am brave enough to pray to
you. 28Lord GOD, you are God, and your words

THANKFULNESS

Unnoticed Gifts

If you have trouble thinking of things to thank God for, start with this list of things:

- A defence against tiny bacteria and larger creatures such as fleas, wasps and jellyfish.
- A radiator to cool you.
- Padding that takes the shape of objects it touches.
- Half a million transmitters that send messages through your body.
- A unique pattern that identifies you.

All these things are in just one part of your body: your skin. Imagine how much else you have to be thankful for in your life and world! David recognised the gifts that God had given to him and his family. Read his prayer of thanksgiving in **2 Samuel 7:18–29**.

- Why does David say that God gives good things? What is David’s response?
- What has God given to you that reminds you of how important you are? How have you thanked God for that?

Consider . . .

- making a list of people and things for which you are most thankful. Thank God for each of these people or things this week, and write each person a thank-you message.
- tracing your family tree back as far as you can. Then talk to your parents about the strengths of each generation. Pray that God will guide and bless you and future generations.

For more, see . . .

- Psalm 98:1–9 (p.557)
- Colossians 1:9–13 (p.1289)
- Isaiah 63:7–9 (p.709)

are true. And you have promised these good things to me, your servant. [29]Please, bless my family. Let it continue before you always. Lord GOD, you have said so. With your blessing let my family always be blessed."

David Wins Many Wars

8 Later, David defeated the Philistines, conquered them, and took the city of Metheg Ammah.

[2]He also defeated the people of Moab. He made them lie on the ground, and then he used a rope to measure them. Those who were measured within two rope lengths were killed, but those who were within the next rope length were allowed to live. So the people of Moab became servants of David and gave him the payment he demanded.

[3]David also defeated Hadadezer son of Rehob, king of Zobah, as he went to take control again at the Euphrates River. [4]David captured 1,000 chariots, 7,000 men who rode in chariots, and 20,000 foot soldiers. He crippled all but 100 of the chariot horses.

[5]Arameans from Damascus came to help Hadadezer king of Zobah, but David killed 22,000 of them. [6]Then David put groups of soldiers in Damascus in Aram. The Arameans became David's servants and gave him the payment he demanded. The LORD gave David victory everywhere he went.

[7]David took the shields of gold that had belonged to Hadadezer's officers and brought them to Jerusalem. [8]David also took many things made of bronze from Tebah and Berothai, which had been cities under Hadadezer's control.

[9]Toi king of Hamath heard that David had defeated all the army of Hadadezer. [10]So Toi sent his son Joram to greet and congratulate King David for defeating Hadadezer. (Hadadezer had been at war with Toi.) Joram brought things made of silver, gold and bronze. [11]King David gave them to the LORD, along with the silver and gold he had taken from the other nations he had defeated. [12]These nations were Edom, Moab, Ammon, Philistia and Amalek. David also gave the LORD what he had taken from Hadadezer son of Rehob, king of Zobah.

[13]David was famous after he returned from defeating 18,000 Arameans in the Valley of Salt. [14]He put groups of soldiers all over Edom, and all the Edomites became his servants. The LORD gave David victory everywhere he went.

[15]David was king over all Israel, and he did what was fair and right for all his people. [16]Joab son of Zeruiah was commander over the army. Jehoshaphat son of Ahilud was the recorder. [17]Zadok son of Ahitub and Abiathar son of Ahimelech were priests. Seraiah was the royal secretary. [18]Benaiah son of Jehoiada was over the Kerethites and Pelethites.[n] And David's sons were priests.

David Helps Saul's Family

9 David asked, "Is anyone still left in Saul's family? I want to show kindness to that person for Jonathan's sake!"

[2]Now there was a servant named Ziba from Saul's family. So David's servants called Ziba to him. King David said to him, "Are you Ziba?"

He answered, "Yes, I am your servant."

[3]The king asked, "Is anyone left in Saul's family? I want to show God's kindness to that person."

Ziba answered the king, "Jonathan has a son still living who is crippled in both feet."

[4]The king asked Ziba, "Where is this son?"

Ziba answered, "He is at the house of Makir son of Ammiel in Lo Debar."

[5]Then King David had servants bring Jonathan's son from the house of Makir son of Ammiel in Lo Debar. [6]Mephibosheth, Jonathan's son, came before David and bowed face down on the floor.

David said, "Mephibosheth!"

Mephibosheth said, "I am your servant."

[7]David said to him, "Don't be afraid. I will be kind to you for your father Jonathan's sake. I will give you back all the land of your grandfather Saul, and you will always eat at my table."

[8]Mephibosheth bowed to David again and said, "You are being very kind to me, your servant! And I am no better than a dead dog!"

[9]Then King David called Saul's servant Ziba. David said to him, "I have given your master's grandson everything that belonged to Saul and his family. [10]You, your sons and your servants will farm the land and harvest the crops. Then your family will have food to eat. But Mephibosheth, your master's grandson, will always eat at my table."

(Now Ziba had fifteen sons and 20 servants.) [11]Ziba said to King David, "I, your servant, will do everything my master, the king, commands me."

So Mephibosheth ate at David's table as if he were one of the king's sons. [12]Mephibosheth had a young son named Mica. Everyone in Ziba's family became Mephibosheth's servants. [13]Mephibosheth lived in Jerusalem, because he always ate at the king's table. And he was crippled in both feet.

Kerethites and Pelethites These were probably special units of the army that were responsible for the king's safety, a kind of palace guard.

War with the Ammonites and Arameans

10 When Nahash king of the Ammonites died, his son Hanun became king after him. 2David said, "Nahash was loyal to me, so I will be loyal to his son Hanun." So David sent his messengers to comfort Hanun about his father's death.

David's officers went to the land of the Ammonites. 3But the Ammonite leaders said to Hanun, their master, "Do you think David wants to honour your father by sending men to comfort you? No! David sent them to study the city and spy it out and capture it!" 4So Hanun arrested David's officers. To shame them he shaved off half their beards and cut off their clothes at the hips. Then he sent them away.

5When the people told David, he sent messengers to meet his officers because they were very ashamed. King David said, "Stay in Jericho until your beards have grown back. Then come home."

6The Ammonites knew that they had insulted David. So they hired 20,000 Aramean foot soldiers from Beth Rehob and Zobah. They also hired the king of Maacah with 1,000 men and 12,000 men from Tob.

7When David heard about this, he sent Joab with the whole army. 8The Ammonites came out and prepared for battle at the city gate. The Arameans from Zobah and Rehob and the men from Tob and Maacah were out in the field by themselves.

9Joab saw that there were enemies both in front of him and behind him. So he chose some of the best soldiers of Israel and sent them out to fight the Arameans. 10Joab put the rest of the army under the command of Abishai, his brother. Then he sent them out to fight the Ammonites. 11Joab said to Abishai, "If the Arameans are too strong for me, you must help me. Or, if the Ammonites are too strong for you, I will help you. 12Be strong. We must fight bravely for our people and the cities of our God. The LORD will do what he thinks is right."

13Then Joab and the army with him went to attack the Arameans, and the Arameans ran away. 14When the Ammonites saw that the Arameans were running away, they also ran away from Abishai and went back to their city. So Joab returned from the battle with the Ammonites and came to Jerusalem.

15When the Arameans saw that Israel had defeated them, they came together into one big army. 16Hadadezer sent messengers to bring the Arameans from east of the Euphrates River, and they went to Helam. Their leader was Shobach, the commander of Hadadezer's army.

17When David heard about this, he gathered all the Israelites together. They crossed over the Jordan River and went to Helam. There the Arameans prepared for battle and attacked him. 18But the Arameans ran away from the Israelites. David killed 700 Aramean chariot drivers and 40,000 Aramean horsemen. He also killed Shobach, the commander of the Aramean army.

19When the kings who served Hadadezer saw that the Israelites had defeated them, they made peace with the Israelites and served them. And the Arameans were afraid to help the Ammonites again.

Sidelight If you wanted to shame a man in ancient Israel, you could shave off his beard. But if you did it, you had to be prepared for him to strike back in revenge. In 2 Samuel 10:1–19, such an act resulted in a war that took about 40,700 lives.

David Sins with Bathsheba

11 In the spring, when the kings normally went out to war, David sent out Joab, his servants and all the Israelites. They destroyed the Ammonites and attacked the city of Rabbah. But David stayed in Jerusalem. 2One evening David got up from his bed and walked around on the roof[n] of his palace. While he was on the roof, he saw a woman bathing. She was very beautiful. 3So David sent his servants to find out who she was. A servant answered, "That woman is Bathsheba daughter of Eliam. She is the wife of Uriah the Hittite." 4So David sent messengers to bring Bathsheba to him. When she came to him, he had sexual relations with her. (Now Bathsheba had purified herself from her monthly period.) Then she went back to her house. 5But Bathsheba became pregnant and sent word to David, saying, "I am pregnant."

6So David sent a message to Joab: "Send Uriah the Hittite to me." And Joab sent Uriah to David. 7When Uriah came to him, David asked him how Joab was, how the soldiers were and how the war was going. 8Then David said to Uriah, "Go home and rest."

So Uriah left the palace, and the king sent a gift to him. 9But Uriah did not go home. Instead, he slept outside the door of the palace as all the king's officers did.

roof In Bible times houses were built with flat roofs. The roof was used for drying things such as flax and fruit. And it was used as an extra room, as a place for worship and as a place to sleep in the summer.

10The officers told David, "Uriah did not go
home."
Then David said to Uriah, "You came from a
long trip. Why didn't you go home?"
11Uriah said to him, "The Ark[d] and the soldiers
of Israel and Judah are staying in tents. My mas-
ter Joab and his officers are camping out in the
fields. It isn't right for me to go home to eat and
drink and have sexual relations with my wife!"
12David said to Uriah, "Stay here today. To-
morrow I'll send you back to the battle." So
Uriah stayed in Jerusalem that day and the
next. 13Then David called Uriah to come to see
him, so Uriah ate and drank with David. David
made Uriah drunk, but he still did not go home.
That evening Uriah again slept with the king's
officers.
14The next morning David wrote a letter to
Joab and sent it by Uriah. 15In the letter David
wrote, "Put Uriah on the front lines where the
fighting is worst and leave him there alone. Let
him be killed in battle."
16Joab watched the city and saw where its
strongest defenders were and put Uriah there.
17When the men of the city came out to fight
against Joab, some of David's men were killed.
And Uriah the Hittite was one of them.
18Then Joab sent David a complete account of
the war. 19Joab told the messenger, "Tell King
David what happened in the war. 20After you
finish, the king may be angry and ask, 'Why
did you go so near the city to fight? Didn't you
know they would shoot arrows from the city
wall? 21Do you remember who killed Abimelech
son of Jerub-Besheth?[n] It was a woman on the
city wall. She threw a large stone for grinding
grain on Abimelech and killed him there in
Thebez. Why did you go so near the wall?' If

Jerub-Besheth Another name for Gideon.

SEXUALITY

Risking Everything

Something about Louise turned Alan's head. Perhaps it was her figure . . . or her playful smile . . . or her piercing eyes. Whatever it was, Alan couldn't get her out of his mind.

After two weeks of nervous planning, he finally found the courage to ask her out. He did everything he could to impress her. He polished his motorbike and took her to the best restaurant in town. He turned on his charm, making sure she knew how important she was.

After that first date, they kissed at the door. But over the next few weeks, Alan wanted more. Each time, he would try to go a little further. Each time she would resist.

As their dizzying romance continued, Alan became more aggressive. Louise continued to resist, but Alan applied even more pressure. "If you really loved me," he said, "you wouldn't make me stop."

"But I do love you, Alan," she replied.

"Well, I can't be sure unless you show me."

Frightened at the prospect of losing Alan, Louise finally gave in. Three months later, she discovered she was pregnant.

Like Louise, David risked everything to have Bathsheba. And it nearly cost him everything. Read **2 Samuel 11:1–15** to see what happened.

- How did Alan and David abuse their power? What choices did Louise and Bathsheba have?
- What would you have done if you had been in David's situation? What about Bathsheba's?

Consider . . .

- writing on a small card three things you could say to someone who pressures you to have sex. Keep the card in your wallet or purse.
- praying regularly that God will give you strength to resist sexual temptation.

For more, see . . .

- 2 Samuel 12:1–14 (p.295)
- 1 Thessalonians 4:3–8 (p.1298)
- Matthew 5:27–30 (p.944)

King David asks that, tell him, 'Your servant Uriah the Hittite also died.' "

22 The messenger left and went to David and told him everything Joab had told him to say. 23 The messenger told David, "The men of Ammon were winning. They came out and attacked us in the field, but we fought them back to the city gate. 24 The archers on the city wall shot at your servants, and some of your men were killed. Your servant Uriah the Hittite also died."

25 David said to the messenger, "Say this to Joab: 'Don't be upset about this. The sword kills everyone the same. Make a stronger attack against the city and capture it.' Encourage Joab with these words."

26 When Bathsheba heard that her husband was dead, she cried for him. 27 After she finished her time of sadness, David sent servants to bring her to his house. She became David's wife and gave birth to his son, but the LORD did not like what David had done.

David's Son Dies

12 The LORD sent Nathan to David. When he came to David, he said, "There were two men in a city. One was rich, but the other was poor. 2 The rich man had many sheep and cattle. 3 But the poor man had nothing except one little female lamb he had bought. The poor man fed the lamb, and it grew up with him and his children. It shared his food and drank from his cup and slept in his arms. The lamb was like a daughter to him.

4 "Then a traveller stopped to visit the rich man. The rich man wanted to feed the traveller, but he didn't want to take one of his own sheep or cattle. Instead, he took the lamb from the poor man and cooked it for his visitor."

5 David became very angry at the rich man. He said to Nathan, "As surely as the LORD lives, the man who did this should die! 6 He must pay for the lamb four times for doing such a thing. He had no mercy!"

SIN

Hidden Sins

- It wasn't a big crash. Just a little nudge in the car park. From what Trudy could see, just a rear light was broken. She would get it fixed before her parents returned from their weekend away, and they would never know she had taken the car without permission.
- When Justin Ball's parents asked him if he smoked, he was furious. "Of course not!" he shouted. "Don't you trust me?"
- It would be harmless. No one would know that Terri Walker's English test paper was just like Amy Woods's paper from four years ago. Amy had got an 'A' on it, so Terri figured she could too – with a lot less work.
- The lawn in front of the school looked like a moonscape. The tyres had torn the turf so badly that the whole lawn would have to be replaced. The head teacher demanded that anyone who knew what had happened report it. Almost everyone knew who it was. But no one said anything.

Just as people try to hide their sins today, David tried to hide his sin when he committed adultery with Bathsheba. But, as **2 Samuel 12:1–25** reveals, God saw the sin.

- What might the prophet Nathan say to the teenagers who tried to hide their sins?
- Just as David suffered the consequences of his sin, how have you suffered the consequences of something you've done wrong?

Consider . . .

- confessing to a parent or friend something you've done wrong but have kept hidden. Also confess it to God and accept his forgiveness.
- being honest and open next time you're confronted about something you did. See how the approach affects what happens.

For more, see . . .

- Psalm 51:1–13 (p.530)
- 1 John 1:8–10 (p.1371)
- Isaiah 29:15–16 (p.668)

7Then Nathan said to David, "You are the
man! This is what the LORD, the God of Israel,
says: 'I appointed you king of Israel and saved
you from Saul. 8I gave you his kingdom and his
wives. And I made you king of Israel and Judah.
And if that had not been enough, I would have
given you even more. 9So why did you ignore
the LORD's command? Why did you do what he
says is wrong? You killed Uriah the Hittite with
the sword of the Ammonites and took his wife to
be your wife! 10Now there will always be people
in your family who will die by a sword, because
you did not respect me; you took the wife of
Uriah the Hittite for yourself!'

11"This is what the LORD says: 'I am bringing
trouble to you from your own family. While you
watch, I will take your wives from you and give
them to someone who is very close to you. He
will have sexual relations with your wives, and
everyone will know it. 12You had sexual relations
with Bathsheba in secret, but I will do this so all
the people of Israel can see it.' "

13Then David said to Nathan, "I have sinned
against the LORD."

Nathan answered, "The LORD has taken away
your sin. You will not die. 14But what you did
caused the LORD's enemies to lose all respect for
him. For this reason the son who was born to
you will die."

15Then Nathan went home. And the LORD
caused the son of David and Bathsheba, Uriah's
widow, to be very sick. 16David prayed to God
for the baby. David refused to eat or drink. He
went into his house and stayed there, lying on
the ground all night. 17The elders of David's fam-
ily came to him and tried to pull him up from the
ground, but he refused to get up or to eat food
with them.

18On the seventh day the baby died. David's
servants were afraid to tell him that the baby was
dead. They said, "Look, we tried to talk to David
while the baby was alive, but he refused to listen
to us. If we tell him the baby is dead, he may do
something awful."

19When David saw his servants whispering,
he knew that the baby was dead. So he asked
them, "Is the baby dead?"

They answered, "Yes, he is dead."

20Then David got up from the floor, washed
himself, put lotions on and changed his clothes.
Then he went into the LORD's house to worship.
After that, he went home and asked for some-
thing to eat. His servants gave him some food,
and he ate.

21David's servants said to him, "Why are you
doing this? When the baby was still alive, you
refused to eat and you cried. Now that the baby
is dead, you get up and eat food."

22David said, "While the baby was still alive, I
refused to eat, and I cried. I thought, 'Who
knows? Maybe the LORD will feel sorry for me
and let the baby live.' 23But now that the baby is
dead, why should I go without food? I can't
bring him back to life. Some day I will go to him,
but he cannot come back to me."

24Then David comforted Bathsheba his wife.
He slept with her and had sexual relations
with her. She became pregnant again and had
another son, whom David named Solomon.
The LORD loved Solomon. 25The LORD sent
word through Nathan the prophet[d] to name
the baby Jedidiah,[n] because the LORD loved
the child.

David Captures Rabbah

26Joab fought against Rabbah, a royal city of
the Ammonites, and he was about to capture it.
27Joab sent messengers to David and said, "I
have fought against Rabbah and have captured
its water supply. 28Now bring the other soldiers
together and attack this city. Capture it before I
capture it myself and call it by my name!"

29So David gathered all the army and went to
Rabbah and fought against it and captured it.
30David took the crown off their king's head and
had it placed on his own head. That gold crown
weighed about 35 kilogrammes, and it had valu-
able gems in it. And David took many valuable
things from the city. 31He also brought out the
people of the city and forced them to work with
saws, iron picks and axes. He also made them
build with bricks. David did this to all the Am-
monite cities. Then David and all his army
returned to Jerusalem.

Amnon and Tamar

13 David had a son named Absalom and a
son named Amnon. Absalom had a beau-
tiful sister named Tamar, and Amnon loved her.
2Tamar was a virgin.[d] Amnon made himself sick
just thinking about her, because he could not
find any chance to be alone with her.

3Amnon had a friend named Jonadab son of
Shimeah, David's brother. Jonadab was a very
clever man. 4He asked Amnon, "Son of the king,
why do you look so sad day after day? Tell me
what's wrong!"

Amnon told him, "I love Tamar, the sister of
my half-brother Absalom."

5Jonadab said to Amnon, "Go to bed and act

Jedidiah This name means "loved by the Lord".

as if you are sick. Then your father will come to see you. Tell him, 'Please let my sister Tamar come in and give me food to eat. Let her make the food in front of me so I can watch and eat it from her hand.' "

[6]So Amnon went to bed and acted sick. When King David came in to see him, Amnon said to him, "Please let my sister Tamar come in. Let her make two of her special cakes for me while I watch. Then I will eat them from her hands."

[7]David sent for Tamar in the palace, saying, "Go to your brother Amnon's house and make some food for him." [8]So Tamar went to her brother Amnon's house, and he was in bed. Tamar took some dough and pressed it together with her hands. She made some special cakes while Amnon watched. Then she baked them. [9]Next she took the pan and served him, but he refused to eat.

He said to his servants, "All of you, leave me alone!" So they all left him alone. [10]Amnon said to Tamar, "Bring the food into the bedroom so I may eat from your hand."

Tamar took the cakes she had made and brought them to her brother Amnon in the bedroom. [11]She went to him so he could eat from her hands, but Amnon grabbed her. He said, "Sister, come to bed with me."

[12]Tamar said to him, "No, brother! Don't force me! This should never be done in Israel! Don't do this shameful thing! [13]I could never get rid of my shame! And you will be like the shameful fools in Israel! Please talk with the king, and he will let you marry me."

[14]But Amnon refused to listen to her. He was stronger than she was, so he forced her to have sexual relations with him. [15]After that, Amnon hated Tamar. He hated her more than he had loved her before. Amnon said to her, "Get up and leave!"

[16]Tamar said to him, "No! Sending me away would be worse than what you've already done!"

But he refused to listen to her. [17]He called his young servant back in and said, "Get this woman out of here and away from me! Lock the door after her." [18]So his servant led her out of the room and bolted the door after her.

Tamar was wearing a special robe with long sleeves, because the king's virgin daughters wore this kind of robe. [19]To show how upset she was, Tamar put ashes on her head and tore her special robe and put her hand on her head. Then she went away, crying loudly.

[20]Absalom, Tamar's brother, said to her, "Has Amnon, your brother, forced you to have sexual relations with him? For now, sister, be quiet. He is your half-brother. Don't let this upset you so much!" So Tamar lived in her brother Absalom's house and was sad and lonely.

[21]When King David heard the news, he was very angry. [22]Absalom did not say a word, good or bad, to Amnon. But he hated Amnon for disgracing his sister Tamar.

Absalom's Revenge

[23]Two years later Absalom had some men come to Baal Hazor, near Ephraim, to cut the wool from his sheep. Absalom invited all the king's sons to come also. [24]Absalom went to the king and said, "I have men coming to cut the wool. Please come with your officers and join me."

[25]King David said to Absalom, "No, my son. We won't all go, because it would be too much trouble for you." Although Absalom begged David, he would not go, but he did give his blessing.

[26]Absalom said, "If you don't want to come, then please let my brother Amnon come with us."

King David asked, "Why should he go with you?"

[27]Absalom kept begging David until he let Amnon and all the king's sons go with Absalom.

[28]Then Absalom commanded his servants, "Watch Amnon. When he is drunk, I will tell you, 'Kill Amnon.' Right then, kill him! Don't be afraid, because I have commanded you! Be strong and brave!" [29]So Absalom's young men killed Amnon as Absalom commanded, but all of David's other sons got on their mules and escaped.

[30]While the king's sons were on their way, the news came to David, "Absalom has killed all of the king's sons! Not one of them is left alive!" [31]King David tore his clothes and lay on the ground to show his sadness. All his servants standing nearby tore their clothes also.

[32]Jonadab son of Shimeah, David's brother, said to David, "Don't think all the young men, your sons, are killed. No, only Amnon is dead! Absalom has planned this ever since Amnon forced his sister Tamar to have sexual relations with him. [33]My master and king, don't think that all of the king's sons are dead. Only Amnon is dead!"

[34]In the meantime Absalom had run away.

A guard standing on the city wall saw many people coming from the other side of the hill. [35]So Jonadab said to King David, "Look, I was right! The king's sons are coming!"

[36]As soon as Jonadab had said this, the king's sons arrived, crying loudly. David and all his servants began crying also. [37]David cried for his son every day.

But Absalom ran away to Talmai[n] son of Ammihud, the king of Geshur. 38After Absalom ran away to Geshur, he stayed there for three years. 39When King David got over Amnon's death, he missed Absalom greatly.

Joab Sends a Wise Woman to David

14 Joab son of Zeruiah knew that King David missed Absalom very much. 2So Joab sent messengers to Tekoa to bring a wise woman from there. He said to her, "Pretend to be very sad. Put on funeral clothes and don't put lotion on yourself. Act like a woman who has been crying many days for someone who died. 3Then go to the king and say these words." Then Joab told her what to say.

4So the woman from Tekoa spoke to the king. She bowed face down on the ground to show respect and said, "My king, help me!"

5King David asked her, "What is the matter?"

The woman said, "I am a widow; my husband is dead. 6I had two sons. They were out in the field fighting, and no one was there to stop them. So one son killed the other son. 7Now all the family group is against me. They said to me, 'Bring the son who killed his brother so we may kill him for killing his brother. That way we will also get rid of the one who would receive what belonged to his father.' My son is like the last spark of a fire. He is all I have left. If they kill him, my husband's name and property will be gone from the earth."

8Then the king said to the woman, "Go home. I will take care of this for you."

9The woman of Tekoa said to him, "Let the blame be on me and my father's family. My master and king, you and your throne are innocent."

10King David said, "Bring me anyone who says anything bad to you. Then he won't bother you again."

11The woman said, "Please promise in the name of the LORD your God. Then my relative who has the duty of punishing a murderer won't add to the destruction by killing my son."

David said, "As surely as the LORD lives, no one will hurt your son. Not one hair from his head will fall to the ground."

12The woman said, "Let me say something to you, my master and king."

The king said, "Speak."

13Then the woman said, "Why have you decided this way against the people of God? When you judge this way, you show that you are guilty for not bringing back your son who was forced to leave home. 14We will all die some day. We're like water spilled on the ground; no one can gather it back. But God doesn't take away life. Instead, he plans ways that those who have been sent away will not have to stay away from him! 15My master and king, I came to say this to you because the people have made me afraid! I thought, 'Let me talk to the king. Maybe he will do what I ask. 16Maybe he will listen. Perhaps he will save me from those who want to keep both me and my son from getting what God gave us.'

17"Now I say, 'May the words of my master the king give me rest. Like an angel of God, you know what is good and what is bad. May the LORD your God be with you!' "

18Then King David said, "Do not hide the truth. Answer me one question."

The woman said, "My master the king, please ask your question."

19The king said, "Did Joab tell you to say all these things?"

The woman answered, "As you live, my master the king, no one could avoid that question. You are right. Your servant Joab did tell me to say these things. 20Joab did it so you would see things differently. My master, you are wise like an angel of God who knows everything that happens on earth."

Absalom Returns to Jerusalem

21The king said to Joab, "Look, I will do what I promised. Bring back the young man Absalom."

22Joab bowed face down on the ground and blessed the king. Then he said, "Today I know you are pleased with me, because you have done what I asked."

23Then Joab got up and went to Geshur and brought Absalom back to Jerusalem. 24But King David said, "Absalom must go to his own house. He may not come to see me." So Absalom went to his own house and did not go to see the king.

25Absalom was greatly praised for his handsome appearance. No man in Israel was as handsome as he. No blemish was on him from his head to his foot. 26At the end of every year, Absalom would cut his hair, because it became too heavy. When he weighed it, it would weigh about 2 kilogrammes by the royal measure.

27Absalom had three sons and one daughter. His daughter's name was also Tamar, and she was a beautiful woman.

28Absalom lived in Jerusalem for two full years without seeing King David. 29Then Absalom sent for Joab so he could send him to the king, but Joab would not come. Absalom sent a message a second time, but Joab still refused to come. 30Then Absalom said to his servants, "Look,

Talmai He was Absalom's grandfather.

Joab's field is next to mine, and he has barley
growing there. Go and burn it." So Absalom's
servants set fire to Joab's field.
31 Then Joab went to Absalom's house and said
to him, "Why did your servants burn my field?"
32 Absalom said to Joab, "I sent a message to
you, asking you to come here. I wanted to send
you to the king to ask him why he brought me
home from Geshur. It would have been better
for me to stay there! Now let me see the king. If
I have sinned, he can put me to death!"
33 So Joab went to the king and told him Absa-
lom's words. Then the king called for Absalom.
Absalom came and bowed face down on the
ground before the king, and the king kissed him.

Absalom Plans to Take David's Kingdom

15 After this, Absalom got a chariot and
horses for himself and 50 men to run
before him. 2 Absalom would get up early and
stand near the city gate.[n] Anyone who had a
problem for the king to settle would come here.
When someone came, Absalom would call out
and say, "What city are you from?"

The person would answer, "I'm from one of
the tribes[d] of Israel."
3 Then Absalom would say, "Look, your claims
are right, but the king has no one to listen to
you." 4 Absalom would also say, "I wish someone
would make me judge in this land! Then people
with problems could come to me, and I could
help them get justice."

> **Sidelight** Do you have a complaint about your local government? In ancient Israel, you wouldn't take your problem to the Town Hall. You would go to the city's gates, where people made business and legal deals. That's where Absalom took his complaints about his father, King David, and plotted to overthow him (2 Samuel 15:2–4).

5 People would come near Absalom to bow to
him. When they did, Absalom would reach out
his hand and take hold of them and kiss them.
6 Absalom did that to all the Israelites who came
to King David for decisions. In this way, Absalom
stole the hearts of all Israel.
7 After four years Absalom said to King David,
"Please let me go to Hebron. I want to carry out
my promise that I made to the LORD 8 while I was
living in Geshur in Aram. I said, 'If the LORD takes
me back to Jerusalem, I will worship him in
Hebron.' "
9 The king said, "Go in peace."

So Absalom went to Hebron. 10 But he sent se-
cret messengers through all the tribes of Israel.
They told the people, "When you hear the trum-
pets, say this: 'Absalom is the king at Hebron!' "
11 Absalom had invited 200 men to go with
him. So they went from Jerusalem with him, but
they didn't know what he was planning. 12 While
Absalom was offering sacrifices, he sent for
Ahithophel, one of the people who advised
David, to come from his home town of Giloh. So
Absalom's plans were working very well. More
and more people began to support him.
13 A messenger came to David, saying, "The
Israelites are giving their loyalty to Absalom."
14 Then David said to all his officers who were
with him in Jerusalem, "We must leave quickly!
If we don't, we won't be able to get away from
Absalom. We must hurry before he catches us
and destroys us and kills the people of Jeru-
salem."
15 The king's officers said to him, "We will do
anything you say."
16 The king set out with everyone in his house,
but he left ten slave women[d] to take care of the
palace. 17 The king left with all his people follow-
ing him, and they stopped at a house far away.
18 All the king's servants passed by him—the
Kerethites and Pelethites,[n] all those from Gath,
and the 600 men who had followed him.
19 The king said to Ittai, a man from Gath,
"Why are you also going with us? Turn back and
stay with King Absalom because you are a for-
eigner. This is not your homeland. 20 You joined
me only a short time ago. Should I make you
wander with us when I don't even know where
I'm going? Turn back and take your brothers with
you. May kindness and loyalty be shown to you."
21 But Ittai said to the king, "As surely as the
LORD lives and as you live, I will stay with you,
whether it means life or death."
22 David said to Ittai, "Go, march on." So Ittai
from Gath and all his people with their children
marched on. 23 All the people cried loudly as
everyone passed by. King David crossed the
Kidron Valley, and then all the people went on to
the desert. 24 Zadok and all the Levites with him
carried the Ark[d] of the Agreement with God.
They set it down, and Abiathar offered sacrifices
until all the people had left the city.
25 The king said to Zadok, "Take the Ark of
God back into the city. If the LORD is pleased

city gate People came here to conduct business. Public meetings and court cases were also held here.
Kerethites and Pelethites These were probably special units of the army that were responsible for the king's safety, a kind of palace guard.

with me, he will bring me back and will let me
see both it and Jerusalem again. 26But if the LORD
says he is not pleased with me, I am ready. He
can do what he wants with me."
27The king also said to Zadok the priest,
"Aren't you a seer? [d] Go back to the city in peace
and take your son Ahimaaz and Abiathar's son
Jonathan with you. 28I will wait near the cross-
ings into the desert until I hear from you." 29So
Zadok and Abiathar took the Ark of God back to
Jerusalem and stayed there.
30David went up the Mount of Olives, [d] crying
as he went. He covered his head and went bare-
foot. All the people with David covered their
heads also and cried as they went. 31Someone
told David, "Ahithophel is one of the people with
Absalom who made secret plans against you."
So David prayed, "LORD, please make Ahitho-
phel's advice foolish."
32When David reached the top of the moun-
tain where people used to worship God, Hushai
the Arkite came to meet him. Hushai's coat
was torn, and there was dust on his head to
show how sad he was. 33David said to Hushai, "If
you go with me, you will be just one more
person for me to take care of. 34But if you return
to the city, you can make Ahithophel's advice
useless. Tell Absalom, 'I am your servant, my
king. In the past I served your father, but now I
will serve you.' 35The priests Zadok and Abiathar
will be with you. Tell them everything you hear
in the royal palace. 36Zadok's son Ahimaaz and
Abiathar's son Jonathan are with them. Send
them to tell me everything you hear." 37So
David's friend Hushai entered Jerusalem just as
Absalom arrived.

Ziba Meets David

16 When David had passed a short way
over the top of the Mount of Olives, [d]
Ziba, Mephibosheth's servant, met him. Ziba had
a row of donkeys loaded with 200 loaves of
bread, 100 cakes of raisins, 100 cakes of figs and
leather bags full of wine. 2The king asked Ziba,
"What are these things for?"
Ziba answered, "The donkeys are for your
family to ride. The bread and cakes of figs are for
the servants to eat. And the wine is for anyone to
drink who might become weak in the desert."
3The king asked, "Where is Mephibosheth?"
Ziba answered him, "Mephibosheth is staying in
Jerusalem because he thinks, 'Today the Israelites
will give my father's kingdom back to me!' "
4Then the king said to Ziba, "All right. Every-
thing that belonged to Mephibosheth, I now give
to you!"
Ziba said, "I bow to you. I hope I will always
be able to please you."

Shimei Curses David

5As King David came to Bahurim, a man came
out and cursed him. He was from Saul's family
group, and his name was Shimei son of Gera.
6He threw stones at David and his officers, but
the people and soldiers gathered all around
David. 7Shimei cursed David, saying, "Get out,
get out, you murderer, you troublemaker. 8The
LORD is punishing you for the people in Saul's
family you killed! You took Saul's place as king,
but now the LORD has given the kingdom to your
son Absalom! Now you are ruined because you
are a murderer!"
9Abishai son of Zeruiah said to the king, "Why
should this dead dog curse you, the king? Let me
go over and cut off his head!"
10But the king answered, "This does not con-
cern you, sons of Zeruiah! If he is cursing me be-
cause the LORD told him to, who can question
him?"
11David also said to Abishai and all his officers,
"My own son is trying to kill me! This man is a
Benjaminite and has more right to kill me! Leave
him alone, and let him curse me because the
LORD told him to do this. 12Maybe the LORD will
see my misery and repay me with something
good for Shimei's curses today!"
13So David and his men went on down the
road, but Shimei followed on the nearby hillside.
He kept cursing David and throwing stones and
earth at him. 14When the king and all his people
arrived at the Jordan, they were very tired, so
they rested there.
15Meanwhile, Absalom, Ahithophel and all
the Israelites arrived at Jerusalem. 16David's
friend Hushai the Arkite came to Absalom and
said to him, "Long live the king! Long live the
king!"
17Absalom asked, "Why are you not loyal to
your friend David? Why didn't you leave
Jerusalem with your friend?"
18Hushai said, "I belong to the one chosen
by the LORD and by these people and everyone
in Israel. I will stay with you. 19In the past I
served your father. So whom should I serve
now? David's son! I will serve you as I served
him."

Ahithophel's Advice

20Absalom said to Ahithophel, "Tell us what
we should do."
21Ahithophel said, "Your father left behind
some of his slave women[d] to take care of the
palace. Have sexual relations with them. Then
all Israel will hear that your father is your enemy,
and all your people will be encouraged to give
you more support." 22So they put up a tent for

Absalom on the roof[n] of the palace where every-
one in Israel could see it. And Absalom had sex-
ual relations with his father's slave women.
23 At that time people thought Ahithophel's ad-
vice was as reliable as God's own word. Both
David and Absalom thought it was that reliable.

17 Ahithophel said to Absalom, "Let me
choose 12,000 men and chase David
tonight. 2 I'll catch him while he is tired and
weak, and I'll frighten him so all his people will
run away. But I'll kill only King David. 3 Then I'll
bring everyone back to you. If the man you are
looking for is dead, everyone else will return
safely." 4 This plan seemed good to Absalom and
to all the leaders of Israel.
5 But Absalom said, "Now call Hushai the
Arkite, so I can hear what he says." 6 When
Hushai came to Absalom, Absalom said to him,
"This is the plan Ahithophel gave. Should we fol-
low it? If not, tell us."
7 Hushai said to Absalom, "Ahithophel's advice
is not good this time." 8 Hushai added, "You
know your father and his men are strong. They
are as angry as a bear that is robbed of its cubs.
Your father is a skilled fighter. He won't stay all
night with the army. 9 He is probably already hid-
ing in a cave or some other place. If the first at-
tack fails, people will hear the news and think,
'Absalom's followers are losing!' 10 Then even the
men who are as brave as lions will be frightened,
because all the Israelites know your father is a
fighter. They know his men are brave!
11 "This is what I suggest: gather all the Is-
raelites from Dan to Beersheba.[n] There will be
as many people as grains of sand by the sea.
Then you yourself must go into the battle. 12 We
will go to David wherever he is hiding. We will
fall on him as dew falls on the ground. We will
kill him and all of his men so that no one will be
left alive. 13 If David escapes into a city, all the Is-
raelites will bring ropes to that city and pull it
into the valley. Not a stone will be left!"
14 Absalom and all the Israelites said, "The ad-
vice of Hushai the Arkite is better than that of
Ahithophel." (The LORD had planned to destroy
the good advice of Ahithophel so the LORD could
bring disaster on Absalom.)
15 Hushai told Zadok and Abiathar, the priests,
what Ahithophel had suggested to Absalom and
the elders of Israel. He also reported to them
what he himself had suggested. Hushai said,
16 "Quickly! Send a message to David. Tell him
not to stay tonight at the crossings into the
desert but to cross over the Jordan River at once.
If he crosses the river, he and all his people won't
be destroyed."
17 Jonathan and Ahimaaz were waiting at En
Rogel. They did not want to be seen going into
the city, so a servant girl would go out to them
and give them messages. Then Jonathan and
Ahimaaz would go and tell King David.
18 But a boy saw Jonathan and Ahimaaz and
told Absalom. So Jonathan and Ahimaaz left
quickly and went to a man's house in Bahurim.
He had a well in his courtyard, and they climbed
down into it. 19 The man's wife spread a sheet
over the opening of the well and covered it with
grain. No one could tell that anyone was hiding
there.
20 Absalom's servants came to the woman at
the house and asked, "Where are Ahimaaz and
Jonathan?"
She said to them, "They have already crossed
the brook."
Absalom's servants then went to look for
Jonathan and Ahimaaz, but they could not find
them. So they went back to Jerusalem.
21 After Absalom's servants left, Jonathan and
Ahimaaz climbed out of the well and went to tell
King David. They said, "Hurry, cross over the
river! Ahithophel has said these things against
you!" 22 So David and all his people crossed the
Jordan River. By dawn, everyone had crossed the
Jordan.
23 When Ahithophel saw that the Israelites did
not accept his advice, he saddled his donkey and
went to his home town. He left orders for his
family and property, and then he hanged himself.
He died and was buried in his father's tomb.

War Between David and Absalom

24 David arrived at Mahanaim. And Absalom
and all his Israelites crossed over the Jordan
River. 25 Absalom had made Amasa captain of the
army instead of Joab. Amasa was the son of a
man named Jether the Ishmaelite. Amasa's
mother was Abigail daughter of Nahash and sis-
ter of Zeruiah, Joab's mother. 26 Absalom and the
Israelites camped in the land of Gilead.
27 Shobi, Makir and Barzillai were at Ma-
hanaim when David arrived. Shobi son of Na-
hash was from the Ammonite town of Rabbah.
Makir son of Ammiel was from Lo Debar, and
Barzillai was from Rogelim in Gilead. 28 They
brought beds, bowls, clay pots, wheat, barley,
flour, roasted grain, beans, small peas, 29 honey,

roof In Bible times houses were built with flat roofs. The roof was used for drying things such as flax and fruit. And it was used as an extra room, as a place for worship and as a place to sleep in the summer.

Dan to Beersheba Dan was the city farthest north in Israel, and Beersheba was the city farthest south. So this means all the people of Israel.

milk curds, sheep and cheese made from cows' milk for David and his people. They said, "The people are hungry and tired and thirsty in the desert."

18 David counted his men and placed over them commanders of thousands and commanders of hundreds. 2He sent the troops out in three groups. Joab commanded one-third of the men. Joab's brother Abishai son of Zeruiah commanded another third. And Ittai from Gath commanded the last third. King David said to them, "I will also go with you."

3But the men said, "You must not go with us! If we run away in the battle, Absalom's men won't care. Even if half of us are killed, Absalom's men won't care. But you're worth 10,000 of us! You can help us most by staying in the city."

4The king said to his people, "I will do what you think is best." So the king stood at the side of the gate as the army went out in groups of 100 and 1,000.

5The king commanded Joab, Abishai and Ittai, "Be gentle with young Absalom for my sake." Everyone heard the king's orders to the commanders about Absalom.

6David's army went out into the field against Absalom's Israelites, and they fought in the forest of Ephraim. 7There David's army defeated the Israelites. Many died that day—20,000 men. 8The battle spread through all the country, but that day more men died in the forest than in the fighting.

Absalom Dies

9Then Absalom happened to meet David's troops. As Absalom was riding his mule, it went under the thick branches of a large oak tree. Absalom's head got caught in the tree, and his mule ran out from under him. So Absalom was left hanging above the ground.

10When one of the men saw it happen, he told Joab, "I saw Absalom hanging in an oak tree!"

11Joab said to him, "You saw him? Why didn't you kill him and let him fall to the ground? I would have given you a belt and ten pieces of silver!"

12The man answered, "I wouldn't touch the king's son even if you gave me 1,000 pieces of silver. We heard the king command you, Abishai and Ittai, 'Be careful not to hurt young Absalom.' 13If I had killed him, the king would have found out, and you would not have protected me!"

14Joab said, "I won't waste time here with you!" Absalom was still alive in the oak tree, so Joab took three spears and stabbed him in the heart. 15Ten young men who carried Joab's armour also gathered around Absalom and struck him and killed him.

16Then Joab blew the trumpet, so the troops stopped chasing the Israelites. 17Then Joab's men took Absalom's body and threw it into a large pit in the forest and filled the pit with many stones. All the Israelites ran away to their homes.

Sidelight If you haven't had your hair cut recently, take care – Absalom's long hair got caught in a tree when his mule walked under it, leaving Absalom hanging there. It's no wonder, either. He only cut it once a year when it became too heavy – weighing about $2^1/_2$ kilogrammes.

18When Absalom was alive, he had set up a pillar for himself in the King's Valley. He said, "I have no son to keep my name alive." So he named the pillar after himself, and it is called Absalom's Monument even today.

19Ahimaaz son of Zadok said to Joab, "Let me run and take the news to King David. I'll tell him the LORD has saved him from his enemies."

20Joab answered Ahimaaz, "No, you are not the one to take the news today. You may do it another time, but do not take it today, because the king's son is dead."

21Then Joab said to a man from Cush, "Go, tell the king what you have seen." The Cushite bowed to Joab and ran to tell David.

22But Ahimaaz son of Zadok begged Joab again, "No matter what happens, please let me go along with the Cushite!"

Joab said, "Son, why do you want to carry the news? You won't get any reward."

23Ahimaaz answered, "No matter what happens, I will run."

So Joab said to Ahimaaz, "Run!" Then Ahimaaz ran by way of the Jordan Valley and passed the Cushite.

24David was sitting between the inner and outer gates of the city. The watchman went up to the roof of the gate by the walls, and as he looked up, he saw a man running alone. 25He shouted the news to the king.

The king said, "If he is alone, he is bringing good news!"

The man came nearer and nearer to the city. 26Then the watchman saw another man running, and he called to the gatekeeper, "Look! Another man is running alone!"

The king said, "He is also bringing good news!"

27The watchman said, "I think the first man runs like Ahimaaz son of Zadok."

The king said, "Ahimaaz is a good man. He must be bringing good news!"

28Then Ahimaaz called a greeting to the king.
He bowed face down on the ground before the
king and said, "Praise the LORD your God! The
LORD has defeated those who were against you,
my king."
29The king asked, "Is young Absalom all
right?"
Ahimaaz answered, "When Joab sent me, I
saw some great excitement, but I don't know
what it was."
30The king said, "Step over here and wait." So
Ahimaaz stepped aside and stood there.
31Then the Cushite arrived. He said, "Master
and king, hear the good news! Today the LORD
has punished those who were against you!"
32The king asked the Cushite, "Is young Absa-
lom all right?"
The Cushite answered, "May your enemies
and all who come to hurt you be like that young
man!"
33Then the king was very upset, and he went
to the room over the city gate and cried. As
he went, he cried out, "My son Absalom, my
son Absalom! I wish I had died and not you.
Absalom, my son, my son!"

Joab Scolds David

19 People told Joab, "Look, the king is
sad and crying because of Absalom."
2David's army had won the battle that day. But it

REBELLION

Bad Boy

Pete and Julie wondered where a sick young man stopped and a stupid, self-destructive idiot started. It was especially painful for them as the sick young man was their son.

Tim had grown up in a happy family. He was a bright child, eager to learn and always laughing. He loved his brother and sister who were both doing fine at school and expected to go on to good universities.

But in his early teens, Tim turned into a rebel. He was rude to teachers and was regularly suspended from school. He did no homework. He fell in with a bad crowd.

Tim suffered from depression – although it was a while before it was properly diagnosed. His folks now knew that and wished they had taken action earlier. Everything seemed so clear with hindsight.

But now Tim, working in odd jobs here and there to make ends meet, regularly squandered his wages on alcohol and drugs. He lived in a succession of grimy squats. Sometimes he sneaked into the house and took money from his parents.

It was almost impossible to persuade him to see a doctor. Even when he did and got medication he forgot to take it, lost it or took drugs too which caused terrible mood swings as a side effect. How could Pete and Julie best show their love for their son?

2 Samuel 18:24–33 is about the immense human love between a father and son despite the son's dreadful rebellion.

- What do you think David hoped for as he waited for news of his son and the battle? How do you think he felt?
- Despite everything that Absalom had done, how did David react to the news of his death? Does this make sense to you?

Consider . . .

- praying for families that are torn apart by rebellion. Ask God to help the families to communicate and come back together.
- what you should do if you become aware of a friend's law breaking. Would it be better friendship to protect them or shop them?

For more, see . . .

- Hosea 11:1–11 (p.858)
- Romans 3:23 (p.1187)
- Luke 15:11–32 (p.1071)

became a very sad day for all the people, because they heard that the king was very sad for his son. [3]The people came into the city quietly that day. They were like an army that had been defeated in battle and had run away. [4]The king covered his face and cried loudly, "My son Absalom! Absalom, my son, my son!"

[5]Joab went into the king's house and said, "Today you have shamed all your men. They saved your life and the lives of your sons, daughters, wives and slave women.[d] [6]You have shamed them because you love those who hate you, and you hate those who love you. Today you have made it clear that your commanders and men mean nothing to you. What if Absalom had lived and all of us were dead? I can see you would be pleased. [7]Now go out and encourage your servants. I swear by the LORD that if you don't go out, no man will be left with you by tonight! That will be worse than all the troubles you have had from your youth until today."

[8]So the king went to the city gate.[n] When the news spread that the king was at the gate, everyone came to see him.

David Goes Back to Jerusalem

All the Israelites who had followed Absalom had run away to their homes. [9]People in all the tribes[d] of Israel began to argue, saying, "The king saved us from the Philistines and our other enemies, but he left the country because of Absalom. [10]We appointed Absalom to rule us, but now he has died in battle. We should make David the king again."

[11]King David sent a message to Zadok and Abiathar, the priests, that said, "Speak to the elders of Judah. Say, 'Even in my house I have heard what all the Israelites are saying. So why are you the last tribe to bring the king back to his palace? [12]You are my brothers, my own family. Why are you the last tribe to bring back the king?' [13]And say to Amasa, 'You are part of my own family. May God punish me terribly if I don't make you commander of the army in Joab's place!' "

[14]David touched the hearts of all the people of Judah at once. They sent a message to the king that said, "Return with all your men." [15]Then the king returned as far as the Jordan River. The men of Judah came to Gilgal to meet him and to bring him across the Jordan.

[16]Shimei son of Gera, a Benjaminite who lived in Bahurim, hurried down with the men of Judah to meet King David. [17]With Shimei came 1,000 Benjaminites. Ziba, the servant from Saul's family, also came, bringing his fifteen sons and 20 servants with him. They all hurried to the Jordan River to meet the king. [18]The people went across the Jordan to help bring the king's family back to Judah and to do whatever the king wanted. As the king was crossing the river, Shimei son of Gera came to him and bowed face down on the ground in front of the king. [19]He said to the king, "My master, don't hold me guilty. Don't remember the wrong I did when you left Jerusalem! Don't hold it against me. [20]I know I have sinned. That is why I am the first person from Joseph's family to come down and meet you today, my master and king!"

[21]But Abishai son of Zeruiah said, "Shimei should die because he cursed you, the LORD's appointed king!"

[22]David said, "This does not concern you, sons of Zeruiah! Today you're against me! No one will be put to death in Israel today. Today I know I am king over Israel!" [23]Then the king promised Shimei, "You won't die."

[24]Mephibosheth, Saul's grandson, also went down to meet King David. Mephibosheth had not cared for his feet, cut his beard or washed his clothes from the time the king had left Jerusalem until he returned safely. [25]When Mephibosheth came from Jerusalem to meet the king, the king asked him, "Mephibosheth, why didn't you go with me?"

[26]He answered, "My master, my servant Ziba tricked me! I said to Ziba, 'I am crippled, so saddle a donkey. Then I will ride it so I can go with the king.' [27]But he lied about me to you. You, my master and king, are like an angel from God. Do what you think is good. [28]You could have killed all my grandfather's family. Instead, you put me with those people who eat at your own table. So I don't have a right to ask anything more from the king!"

[29]The king said to him, "Don't say anything more. I have decided that you and Ziba will divide the land."

[30]Mephibosheth said to the king, "Let Ziba take all the land now that my master the king has arrived safely home."

[31]Barzillai of Gilead came down from Rogelim to cross the Jordan River with the king. [32]Barzillai was a very old man, 80 years old. He had taken care of the king when David was staying at Mahanaim, because Barzillai was a very rich man. [33]David said to Barzillai, "Cross the river with me. Come with me to Jerusalem, and I will take care of you."

[34]But Barzillai answered the king, "Do you know how old I am? Do you think I can go with you to Jerusalem? [35]I am 80 years old! I am too

city gate People came here to conduct business. Public meetings and court cases were also held here.

old to taste what I eat or drink. I am too old to hear the voices of men and women singers. Why should you be bothered with me? 36I am not worthy of a reward from you, but I will cross the Jordan River with you. 37Then let me go back so I may die in my own city near the grave of my father and mother. But here is Kimham, your servant. Let him go with you, my master and king. Do with him whatever you want."

38The king answered, "Kimham will go with me. I will do for him anything you wish, and I will do anything for you that you wish." 39The king kissed Barzillai and blessed him. Then Barzillai returned home, and the king and all the people crossed the Jordan.

40When the king crossed over to Gilgal, Kimham went with him. All the troops of Judah and half the troops of Israel led David across the river.

41Soon all the Israelites came to the king and said to him, "Why did our relatives, the people of Judah, steal you away? Why did they bring you and your family across the Jordan River with your men?"

42All the people of Judah answered the Israelites, "We did this because the king is our close relative. Why are you angry about it? We have not eaten food at the king's expense or taken anything for ourselves!"

43The Israelites answered the people of Judah, "We have ten tribes in the kingdom, so we have more right to David than you do! But you ignored us! We were the first ones to talk about bringing our king back!"

But the people of Judah spoke even more unkindly than the people of Israel.

Sheba Leads Israel Away from David

20 It happened that a troublemaker named Sheba son of Bicri from the tribe[d] of Benjamin was there. He blew the trumpet and said:

"We have no share in David!
We have no part in the son of Jesse!
People of Israel, let's go home!"

2So all the Israelites left David and followed Sheba son of Bicri. But the people of Judah stayed with their king all the way from the Jordan River to Jerusalem.

3David came back to his palace in Jerusalem. He had left ten of his slave women[d] there to take care of the palace. Now he put them in a locked house. He gave them food, but he did not have sexual relations with them. So they lived like widows until they died.

4The king said to Amasa, "Tell the men of Judah to meet with me in three days, and you must also be here." 5So Amasa went to call the men of Judah together, but he took more time than the king had said.

6David said to Abishai, "Sheba son of Bicri is more dangerous to us than Absalom was. Take my men and chase him before he finds walled cities and escapes from us." 7So Joab's men, the Kerethites and the Pelethites,[n] and all the soldiers went with Abishai. They went out from Jerusalem to chase Sheba son of Bicri.

8When Joab and the army came to the great rock at Gibeon, Amasa came out to meet them. Joab was wearing his uniform, and at his waist he wore a belt that held his sword in its case. As Joab stepped forwards, his sword fell out of its case. 9Joab asked Amasa, "Brother, is everything all right with you?" Then with his right hand he took Amasa by the beard to kiss him. 10Amasa was not watching the sword in Joab's hand. So Joab pushed the sword into Amasa's stomach, causing Amasa's insides to spill onto the ground. Joab did not have to stab Amasa again; he was already dead. Then Joab and his brother Abishai continued to chase Sheba son of Bicri.

11One of Joab's young men stood by Amasa's body and said, "Everyone who is for Joab and David should follow Joab!" 12Amasa lay in the middle of the road, covered with his own blood. When the young man saw that everyone was stopping to look at the body, he dragged it from the road, laid it in a field and put a cloth over it. 13After Amasa's body was taken off the road, all the men followed Joab to chase Sheba son of Bicri.

14Sheba went through all the tribes of Israel to Abel Beth Maacah. All the Berites also came together and followed him. 15So Joab and his men came to Abel Beth Maacah and surrounded it. They piled earth up against the city wall, and they began digging under the walls to bring them down.

16But a wise woman shouted out from the city, "Listen! Listen! Tell Joab to come here. I want to talk to him!"

17So Joab came near her. She asked him, "Are you Joab?"

He answered, "Yes, I am."

Then she said, "Listen to what I say."

Joab said, "I'm listening."

18Then the woman said, "In the past people would say, 'Ask for advice at Abel,' and the problem would be solved. 19I am one of the peaceful, loyal people of Israel. You are trying to destroy an important city of Israel. Why must you destroy what belongs to the LORD?"

Kerethites and Pelethites These were probably special units of the army that were responsible for the king's safety, a kind of palace guard.

[20]Joab answered, "I would prefer not to destroy or ruin anything! [21]That is not what I want. But there is a man here from the mountains of Ephraim, who is named Sheba son of Bicri. He has turned against King David. If you bring him to me, I will leave the city alone."

The woman said to Joab, "His head will be thrown over the wall to you."

[22]Then the woman spoke very wisely to all the people of the city. They cut off the head of Sheba son of Bicri and threw it over the wall to Joab. So he blew the trumpet, and the army left the city. Every man returned home, and Joab went back to the king in Jerusalem.

[23]Joab was commander of all the army of Israel. Benaiah son of Jehoiada led the Kerethites and Pelethites. [24]Adoniram was in charge of the men who were forced to do hard work. Jehoshaphat son of Ahilud was the recorder. [25]Sheba was the royal secretary. Zadok and Abiathar were the priests, [26]and Ira the Jairite was David's priest.

The Gibeonites Punish Saul's Family

21 During the time David was king, there was a shortage of food that lasted for three years. So David prayed to the LORD.

The LORD answered, "Saul and his family of murderers are the reason for this shortage, because he killed the Gibeonites." [2](Now the Gibeonites were not Israelites; they were a group of Amorites who were left alive. The Israelites had promised not to hurt the Gibeonites, but Saul had tried to kill them, because he was eager to help the people of Israel and Judah.)

King David called the Gibeonites together and spoke to them. [3]He asked, "What can I do for you? How can I make up for the harm done so you can bless the LORD's people?"

[4]The Gibeonites said to David, "We cannot demand silver or gold from Saul or his family. And we don't have the right to kill anyone in Israel."

Then David asked, "What do you want me to do for you?"

[5]The Gibeonites said, "Saul made plans against us and tried to destroy all our people who are left in the land of Israel. [6]So bring seven of his sons to us. Then we will kill them and hang them on stakes in the presence of the LORD at Gibeah, the home town of Saul, the LORD's chosen king."

The king said, "I will give them to you." [7]But the king protected Mephibosheth, the son of Jonathan, the son of Saul, because of the promise he had made to Jonathan in the LORD's name. [8]The king did take Armoni and Mephibosheth,[n] sons of Rizpah and Saul. (Rizpah was the daughter of Aiah.) And the king took the five sons of Saul's daughter Merab. (Adriel son of Barzillai the Meholathite was the father of Merab's five sons.) [9]David gave these seven sons to the Gibeonites. Then the Gibeonites killed them and hung them on stakes on a hill in the presence of the LORD. All seven sons died together. They were put to death during the first days of the harvest season at the beginning of barley harvest.

[10]Aiah's daughter Rizpah took the rough cloth that was worn to show sadness and put it on a rock for herself. She stayed there from the beginning of the harvest until the rain fell on her sons' bodies. During the day she did not let the birds of the sky touch her sons' bodies, and during the night she did not let the wild animals touch them.

[11]People told David what Aiah's daughter Rizpah, Saul's slave woman,[d] was doing. [12]Then David took the bones of Saul and Jonathan from the men of Jabesh Gilead. (The Philistines had hung the bodies of Saul and Jonathan in the public square of Beth Shan after they had killed Saul at Gilboa. Later the men of Jabesh Gilead had secretly taken them from there.) [13]David brought the bones of Saul and his son Jonathan from Gilead. Then the people gathered the bodies of Saul's seven sons who were hanged on stakes. [14]The people buried the bones of Saul and his son Jonathan at Zela in Benjamin in the tomb of Saul's father Kish. The people did everything the king commanded.

Then God answered the prayers for the land.

Wars with the Philistines

[15]Again there was war between the Philistines and Israel. David and his men went out to fight the Philistines, but David became tired. [16]Ishbi-Benob, one of the sons of Rapha,[d] had a bronze spearhead weighing about 3.5 kilogrammes and a new sword. He planned to kill David, [17]but Abishai son of Zeruiah killed the Philistine and saved David's life.

Then David's men made a promise to him, saying, "Never again will you go out with us to battle. If you were killed, Israel would lose its greatest leader."

[18]Later, at Gob, there was another battle with the Philistines. Sibbecai the Hushathite killed Saph, another one of the sons of Rapha.

[19]Later, there was another battle at Gob with the Philistines. Elhanan son of Jaare-Oregim from Bethlehem killed Goliath[n] from Gath. His spear was as large as a weaver's rod.

Mephibosheth This is not Jonathan's son but another man with the same name.
Goliath In 1 Chronicles 20:5 he is called Lahmi brother of Goliath.

[20]At Gath another battle took place. A very
large man was there; he had six fingers on each
hand and six toes on each foot—24 fingers and
toes in all. This man also was one of the sons of
Rapha. [21]When he challenged Israel, Jonathan
son of Shimeah, David's brother, killed him.

Sidelight David was again faced in battle by a giant, but he realised (probably with some sadness) that this was not his fight. He laid aside his armour and weaponry to allow Jonathan to bring the giant down (2 Samuel 21:21).

[22]These four sons of Rapha from Gath were
killed by David and his men.

David's Song of Praise

22 David sang this song to the LORD when
the LORD saved him from Saul and all his
other enemies. [2]He said:

"The LORD is my rock, my protection, my
Saviour.
[3]My God is my rock.
I can run to him for safety.
He is my shield and my saving strength,
my defender and my place of safety.
The LORD saves me from those who want to
harm me.
[4]I will call to the LORD, who is worthy of
praise,
and I will be saved from my enemies.
[5]"The waves of death came around me;
the deadly rivers overwhelmed me.
[6]The ropes of death wrapped around me.
The traps of death were before me.
[7]In my trouble I called to the LORD;
I cried out to my God.
From his temple he heard my voice;
my call for help reached his ears.
[8]"The earth trembled and shook.
The foundations of heaven began to shake.
They trembled because the LORD was angry.
[9]Smoke came out of his nose,
and burning fire came out of his mouth.
Burning coals went before him.
[10]He tore open the sky and came down
with dark clouds under his feet.
[11]He rode a creature with wings and flew.
He raced on the wings of the wind.
[12]He made darkness his shelter,
surrounded by fog and clouds.
[13]Out of the brightness of his presence
came flashes of lightning.
[14]The LORD thundered from heaven;
the Most High raised his voice.
[15]He shot his arrows and scattered his enemies.
His bolts of lightning confused them with
fear.
[16]The LORD spoke strongly.
The wind blew from his nose.
Then the valleys of the sea appeared,
and the foundations of the earth were seen.
[17]"The LORD reached down from above and
took me;
he pulled me from the deep water.
[18]He saved me from my powerful enemies,
from those who hated me, because they
were too strong for me.
[19]They attacked me at my time of trouble,
but the LORD supported me.
[20]He took me to a safe place.
Because he delights in me, he saved me.
[21]"The LORD spared me because I did what was
right.
Because I have not done evil, he has
rewarded me.
[22]I have followed the ways of the LORD;
I have not done evil by turning from
my God.
[23]I remember all his laws
and have not broken his rules.
[24]I am innocent before him;
I have kept myself from doing evil.
[25]The LORD rewarded me because I did what
was right,
because I did what the LORD said was right.
[26]"LORD, you are loyal to those who are loyal,
and you are good to those who are good.
[27]You are pure to those who are pure,
but you are against those who are evil.
[28]You save the humble,
but you bring down those who are proud.
[29]LORD, you give light to my lamp.
The LORD brightens the darkness
around me.
[30]With your help I can attack an army.
With God's help I can jump over a wall.
[31]"The ways of God are without fault;
the LORD's words are pure.
He is a shield to those who trust him.
[32]Who is God? Only the LORD.
Who is the Rock?[d] Only our God.
[33]God is my protection.
He makes my way free from fault.
[34]He makes me like a deer that does not
stumble;
he helps me stand on the steep mountains.
[35]He trains my hands for battle
so my arms can bend a bronze bow.
[36]You protect me with your saving shield.

You have stooped to make me great.
37You give me a better way to live,
so I live as you want me to.
38I chased my enemies and destroyed them.
I did not stop till they were destroyed.
39I destroyed and crushed them
so they couldn't rise up again.
They fell beneath my feet.
40You gave me strength in battle.
You made my enemies bow before me.
41You made my enemies turn back,
and I destroyed those who hated me.
42They called for help,
but no one came to save them.
They called to the LORD,
but he did not answer them.
43I beat my enemies into pieces,
like dust on the ground.
I poured them out and walked on them
like mud in the streets.

44"You saved me when my people attacked me.
You kept me as the leader of nations.
People I never knew serve me.
45Foreigners obey me.
As soon as they hear me, they obey me.
46They all become afraid
and tremble in their hiding places.

47"The LORD lives!
May my Rock be praised!
Praise God, the Rock, who saves me!
48God gives me victory over my enemies
and brings people under my rule.
49He frees me from my enemies.

"You set me over those who hate me.
You saved me from cruel men.
50So I will praise you, LORD, among the nations.
I will sing praises to your name.
51The LORD gives great victories to his king.
He is loyal to his appointed king,
to David and his descendants[d] for ever."

David's Last Words

23 These are the last words of David.

This is the message of David son of Jesse.
The man made great by the Most High
God speaks.
He is the appointed king of the God of Jacob;
he is the sweet singer of Israel:

2"The LORD's Spirit[d] spoke through me,
and his word was on my tongue.
3The God of Israel spoke;
the Rock[d] of Israel said to me:
'Whoever rules fairly over people,
who rules with respect for God,
4is like the morning light at dawn,
like a morning without clouds.
He is like sunshine after a rain
that makes the grass grow from the
ground.'

5"This is how God has cared for my family.
God made a lasting agreement with me,
right and sure in every way.
He will accomplish my salvation
and satisfy all my desires.

6"But all evil people will be thrown away like
thorns
that cannot be held in a hand.
7No one can touch them
except with a tool of iron or wood.
They will be thrown in the fire and burned
where they lie."

David's Army

8These are the names of David's warriors:
Josheb-Basshebeth, the Tahkemonite, was
head of the Three.[n] He killed 800 men at one
time.
9Next was Eleazar son of Dodai the Ahohite.
Eleazar was one of the three soldiers who were
with David when they challenged the Phili-
stines. The Philistines were gathered for battle,
and the Israelites drew back. 10But Eleazar
stayed where he was and fought the Philistines
until he was so tired his hand stuck to his sword.
The LORD gave a great victory for the Israelites
that day. The troops came back after Eleazar had
won the battle, but only to take weapons and ar-
mour from the enemy.
11Next there was Shammah son of Agee the
Hararite. The Philistines came together to fight
in a vegetable field. Israel's troops ran away from
the Philistines, 12but Shammah stood in the mid-
dle of the field and fought for it and killed the
Philistines. And the LORD gave a great victory.
13Once, three of the Thirty, David's chief sol-
diers, came down to him at the cave of Adullam
during harvest. The Philistine army had camped
in the Valley of Rephaim. 14At that time David
was in the stronghold,[d] and some of the
Philistines were in Bethlehem.
15David had a strong desire for some water. He
said, "Oh, I wish someone would get me water
from the well near the city gate of Bethlehem!"
16So the three warriors broke through the Philis-
tine army and took water from the well near the
city gate of Bethlehem. Then they brought it to
David, but he refused to drink it. He poured it
out before the LORD, 17saying, "May the LORD

Three, or maybe "Thirty" These were David's most powerful soldiers. See 1 Chronicles 11:11.

keep me from drinking this water! It would be
like drinking the blood of the men who risked
their lives!" So David refused to drink it. These
were the brave things that the three warriors did.
18Abishai, brother of Joab son of Zeruiah, was
captain of the Three. Abishai fought 300 soldiers
with his spear and killed them. He became as fa-
mous as the Three 19and was more honoured
than the Three. He became their commander
even though he was not one of them.
20Benaiah son of Jehoiada was a brave fighter
from Kabzeel who did mighty things. He killed
two of the best warriors from Moab. He also
went down into a pit and killed a lion on a
snowy day. 21Benaiah killed a large Egyptian
who had a spear in his hand. Benaiah had a club,
but he grabbed the spear from the Egyptian's
hand and killed him with his own spear. 22These
were the things Benaiah son of Jehoiada did. He
was as famous as the Three. 23He received more
honour than the Thirty, but he did not become a
member of the Three. David made him leader of
his bodyguards.

The Thirty Chief Soldiers

24The following men were among the Thirty:
Asahel brother of Joab;
Elhanan son of Dodo from Bethlehem;
25Shammah the Harodite;
Elika the Harodite;
26Helez the Paltite;
Ira son of Ikkesh from Tekoa;
27Abiezer the Anathothite;
Mebunnai the Hushathite;
28Zalmon the Ahohite;
Maharai the Netophathite;
29Heled son of Baanah the Netophathite;
Ithai son of Ribai from Gibeah in Benjamin;
30Benaiah the Pirathonite;
Hiddai from the ravines of Gaash;
31Abi-Albon the Arbathite;
Azmaveth the Barhumite;
32Eliahba the Shaalbonite;
the sons of Jashen;
Jonathan 33son of Shammah the Hararite;
Ahiam son of Sharar the Hararite;

GOVERNMENT

Respected Leaders

Bill Logue was a well-liked judge in the USA. He was respected by lawyers, by the police and convicted criminals alike. Even with his back-breaking load of court cases, Judge Logue found time to help underprivileged kids who had criminal records. He helped them start constructive lives so they wouldn't get into trouble again.

When Judge Logue was found to have throat cancer, cards, letters, flowers and presents swamped the hospital.

But nothing touched the judge as much as the fistful of letters he received from prisoners – prisoners he had sent to jail. "You helped me get my life back on track," they told him. "I'll never forget you. Thanks."

Judge Logue showed how God's followers can make a difference for good in government. When King David was dying, he celebrated how God had worked in his life for good. Read about it in **2 Samuel 23:1–7**.

- How do verses 3 and 4 describe Judge Logue and other Christians like him who serve in government?
- Do leaders today have the same opportunities to serve God as they did in David's time? How can you support and encourage them to do good?

Consider . . .

- praying that God will guide your country's leaders as they make important decisions.
- writing a letter to local leaders to express your opinion on an important issue they are confronting.

For more, see . . .

- Psalm 2:1–11 (p.500)
- 1 Timothy 2:1–3 (p.1308)
- Proverbs 16:10–15 (p.603)

34Eliphelet son of Ahasbai the Maacathite;
Eliam son of Ahithophel the Gilonite;
35Hezro the Carmelite;
Paarai the Arbite;
36Igal son of Nathan of Zobah;
the son of Hagri;
37Zelek the Ammonite;
Naharai the Beerothite, who carried the armour of Joab son of Zeruiah;
38Ira the Ithrite;
Gareb the Ithrite,
39and Uriah the Hittite.

There were 37 in all.

David Counts His Army

24 The LORD was angry with Israel again, and he caused David to turn against the Israelites. He said, "Go, count the people of Israel and Judah."

2So King David said to Joab, the commander of the army, "Go through all the tribes[d] of Israel, from Dan to Beersheba,[n] and count the people. Then I will know how many there are."

3But Joab said to the king, "May the LORD your God give you 100 times more people, and may my master the king live to see this happen. Why do you want to do this?"

4But the king commanded Joab and the commanders of the army, so they left the king to count the Israelites.

5After crossing the Jordan River, they camped near Aroer on the south side of the city in the ravine. They went through Gad and on to Jazer. 6Then they went to Gilead and the land of Tahtim Hodshi and to Dan Janai and around to Sidon. 7They went to the fortified city of Tyre and to all the cities of the Hivites and Canaanites. Finally, they went to southern Judah, to Beersheba. 8After nine months and 20 days, they had gone through all the land. Then they came back to Jerusalem.

9Joab gave the list of the people to the king. There were 800,000 men in Israel who could use the sword and 500,000 men in Judah.

10David felt ashamed after he had counted the people. He said to the LORD, "I have sinned greatly by what I have done. LORD, I beg you to forgive me, your servant, because I have been very foolish."

11When David got up in the morning, the LORD spoke his word to Gad, who was a prophet[d] and David's seer.[d] 12The LORD told Gad, "Go and tell David, 'This is what the LORD says: I offer you three choices. Choose one of them and I will do it to you.' "

13So Gad went to David and said to him, "Should three years of hunger come to you and your land? Or should your enemies chase you for three months? Or should there be three days of disease in your land? Think about it. Then decide which of these things I should tell the LORD who sent me."

14David said to Gad, "I am in great trouble. Let the LORD punish us, because the LORD is very merciful. Don't let my punishment come from human beings!"

15So the LORD sent a terrible disease on Israel. It began in the morning and continued until the chosen time to stop. From Dan to Beersheba 70,000 people died. 16When the angel raised his arm towards Jerusalem to destroy it, the LORD felt very sorry about the terrible things that had happened. He said to the angel who was destroying the people, "That is enough! Put down your arm!" The angel of the LORD was then by the threshing[d] floor of Araunah the Jebusite.

17When David saw the angel that killed the people, he said to the LORD, "I am the one who sinned and did wrong. These people only followed me like sheep. They did nothing wrong. Please punish me and my family."

18That day Gad came to David and said, "Go and build an altar to the LORD on the threshing floor of Araunah the Jebusite." 19So David did what Gad told him to do, just as the LORD commanded.

20Araunah looked and saw the king and his servants coming to him. So he went out and bowed face down on the ground before the king. 21He said, "Why has my master the king come to me?"

David answered, "To buy the threshing floor from you so I can build an altar to the LORD. Then the terrible disease will stop."

22Araunah said to David, "My master and king, you may take anything you want for a sacrifice. Here are some oxen for the whole burnt offering and the threshing boards and the yokes[d] for the wood. 23My king, I give everything to you." Araunah also said to the king, "May the LORD your God be pleased with you."

24But the king answered Araunah, "No, I will pay you for the land. I won't offer to the LORD my God burnt offerings that cost me nothing."

So David bought the threshing floor and the oxen for 50 pieces of silver. 25He built an altar to the LORD there and offered whole burnt offerings and fellowship offerings. Then the LORD answered his prayer for the country, and the disease in Israel stopped.

Dan to Beersheba Dan was the city farthest north in Israel, and Beersheba was the city farthest south. So this means all the people of Israel.

1 Kings

Why Read This Book:

- See how God blesses those who follow him (1 Kings 1—11).
- Recognise how faithfulness can help all parts of life (1 Kings 12—16).
- Discover what can happen to a country that turns away from God (1 Kings 17—22).

When?

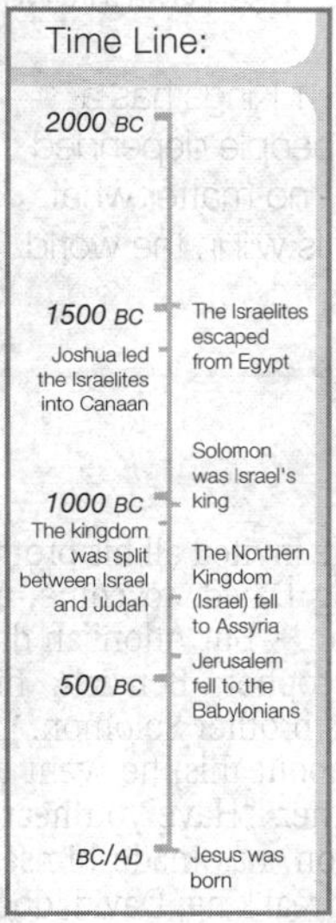

Behind the Scenes:

Imagine how different history books would be if they evaluated presidents and other world leaders on whether or not they followed God. Their political, economic and military feats would only be important when they showed obedience to God. Which presidents, kings and leaders would be judged good and which ones bad?

That's the kind of history we find in 1 and 2 Kings, which were one continuous book in the original text. The story begins with King David turning over the country to his son Solomon. Solomon inherited a strong and united nation, exploding with energy. Through political and economic manoeuvring, Solomon made the country – and himself – rich and powerful.

Solomon seemed headed for greatness. But in the end, the writer says, "Solomon did what the Lord said was wrong and did not follow the Lord completely as his father David had done" (1 Kings 11:6).

What happened? He began seeing the wealth and power as his own, not as gifts from God. Though he spent seven years building a beautiful temple for God (1 Kings 6), he spent thirteen years building his own palace. ▷

Where?

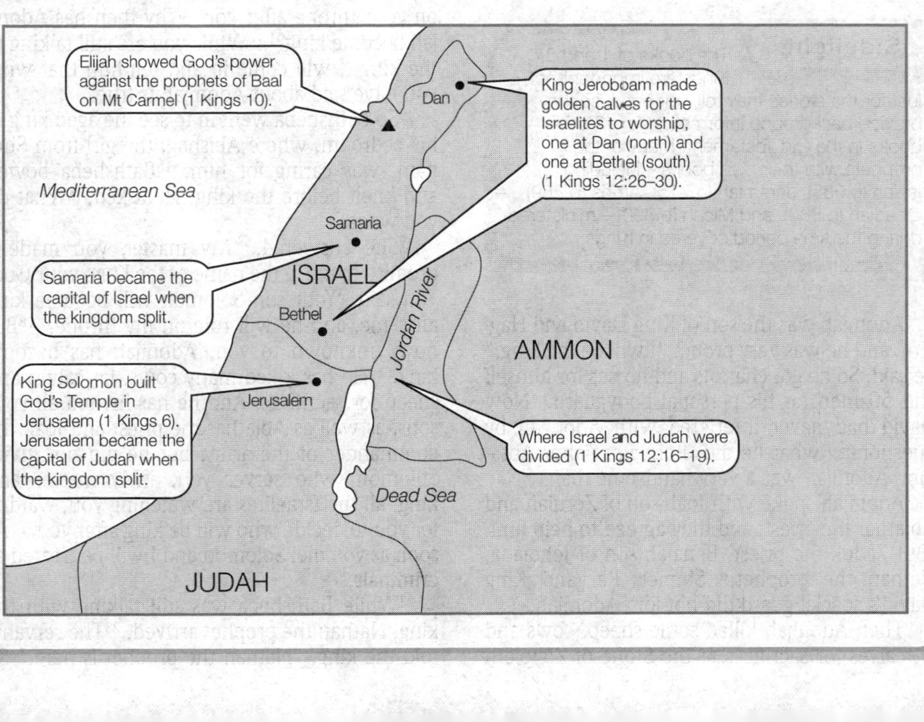

Behind the Scenes (cont.): Soon his power and prestige became more important than following God. He began worshipping false gods.

The kingdom started to crumble. First it split between Israel (in the north) and Judah (in the south). Then one king after another didn't follow God, and the people suffered as a result. When kings did follow God, the people prospered. But by the end of 2 Kings, both kingdoms had been overthrown and the people taken as slaves.

In telling about the rise and fall of good and bad kings, 1 Kings has a consistent theme: the long-term welfare of Israel and its people depended on obedience to God. And these stories remind us that – no matter what other forces are at play – God still works to accomplish his will in the world.

Adonijah Tries to Become King

1 At this time King David was very old, and although his servants covered him with blankets, he could not keep warm. 2They said to him, "We will look for a young woman to care for you. She will lie close to you and keep you warm." 3After searching everywhere in Israel for a beautiful young woman, they found a girl named Abishag from Shunam and brought her to the king. 4The girl was very beautiful, and she cared for the king and served him. But the king did not have sexual relations with her.

> **Sidelight** The books of 1 and 2 Kings are important not just for the stories they tell, but because they provide background information for 17 other books in the Old Testament. Many of the prophets with their own books – including Isaiah (p.638), Jeremiah (p.715), Amos (p.869), Obadiah (p.880), and Micah (p.890) – ministered during the time period covered in Kings.

5Adonijah was the son of King David and Haggith, and he was very proud. "I will be the king," he said. So he got chariots and horses for himself and 50 men for his personal bodyguard. 6Now David had never interfered with Adonijah by questioning what he did. Born next after Absalom, Adonijah was a very handsome man.

7Adonijah spoke with Joab son of Zeruiah and Abiathar the priest, and they agreed to help him. 8But Zadok the priest, Benaiah son of Jehoiada, Nathan the prophet,[d] Shimei, Rei and King David's special guard did not join Adonijah.

9Then Adonijah killed some sheep, cows and fat calves for sacrifices at the Stone of Zoheleth near the spring of Rogel. He invited all his brothers, the other sons of King David, to come, as well as all the men of Judah. 10But Adonijah did not invite Nathan the prophet, Benaiah, his father's special guard or his brother Solomon.

11When Nathan heard about this, he went to Bathsheba, Solomon's mother. "Have you heard that Adonijah, Haggith's son, has made himself king?" Nathan asked. "Our real king, David, does not know it. 12Let me tell you how you can save yourself and your sons. 13Go to King David and tell him, 'My master and king, you promised that my son Solomon would be king and would rule on your throne after you. Why then has Adonijah become king?' 14While you are still talking to the king, I will come in and tell him that what you have said about Adonijah is true."

15So Bathsheba went in to see the aged king in his bedroom, where Abishag, the girl from Shunam, was caring for him. 16Bathsheba bowed and knelt before the king. He asked, "What do you want?"

17She answered, "My master, you made a promise to me in the name of the LORD your God. You said, 'Your son Solomon will become king after me, and he will rule on my throne.' 18But now, unknown to you, Adonijah has become king. 19He has killed many cows, fat calves and sheep for sacrifices. And he has invited all your sons, as well as Abiathar the priest and Joab the commander of the army, but he did not invite Solomon, who serves you. 20My master and king, all the Israelites are watching you, waiting for you to decide who will be king after you. 21As soon as you die, Solomon and I will be treated as criminals."

22While Bathsheba was still talking with the king, Nathan the prophet arrived. 23The servants told the king, "Nathan the prophet is here." So

Nathan went to the king and bowed face down on the ground before him.

24 Nathan said, "My master and king, have you said that Adonijah will be the king after you and that he will rule on your throne? 25 Today he has sacrificed many cows, fat calves and sheep, and he has invited all your other sons, the commanders of the army, and Abiathar the priest. Right now they are eating and drinking with him. They are saying, 'Long live King Adonijah!' 26 But he did not invite me, your own servant, or Zadok the priest, or Benaiah son of Jehoiada or your son Solomon. 27 Did you do this? Since we are your servants, why didn't you tell us who should be king after you?"

David Makes Solomon King

28 Then the king said, "Tell Bathsheba to come in!" So she came in and stood before the king.

29 Then the king made this promise, "The LORD has saved me from all trouble. As surely as he lives, 30 I will do today what I have promised you in the name of the LORD, the God of Israel. I promised that your son Solomon would be king after me and rule on my throne in my place."

31 Then Bathsheba bowed face down on the ground and knelt before the king and said, "Long live my master King David!"

32 Then King David said, "Tell Zadok the priest, Nathan the prophet[d] and Benaiah son of Jehoiada to come in." When they came before the king, 33 he said to them, "Take my servants with you and put my son Solomon on my own mule. Take him down to the spring called Gihon. 34 There Zadok the priest and Nathan the prophet should pour olive oil on him and make him king over Israel. Blow the trumpet and shout, 'Long live King Solomon!' 35 Then come back up here with him. He will sit on my throne and rule in my place, because he is the one I have chosen to be the ruler over Israel and Judah."

36 Benaiah son of Jehoiada answered the king, "Amen! This is what the LORD, the God of my master, has declared! 37 The LORD has always helped you, our king. May he also help Solomon and make King Solomon's throne an even greater throne than yours."

38 So Zadok the priest, Nathan the prophet, and Benaiah son of Jehoiada left with the Kerethites and Pelethites.[n] They put Solomon on King David's mule and took him to the spring called Gihon. 39 Zadok the priest took the container of olive oil from the Holy Tent[d] and poured the oil on Solomon's head to show he was the king. Then they blew the trumpet, and all the people shouted, "Long live King Solomon!" 40 All the people followed Solomon into the city. Playing flutes and shouting for joy, they made so much noise the ground shook.

41 At this time Adonijah and all the guests with him were finishing their meal. When he heard the sound from the trumpet, Joab asked, "What does all that noise from the city mean?"

42 While Joab was speaking, Jonathan son of Abiathar the priest arrived. Adonijah said, "Come in! You are an important man, so you must be bringing good news."

43 But Jonathan answered, "No! Our master King David has made Solomon the new king. 44 King David sent Zadok the priest, Nathan the prophet, Benaiah son of Jehoiada, and all the king's bodyguards with him, and they have put Solomon on the king's own mule. 45 Then Zadok the priest and Nathan the prophet poured olive oil on Solomon at Gihon to make him king. After that they went into the city, shouting with joy. Now the whole city is excited, and that is the noise you hear. 46 Solomon has now become the king. 47 All the king's officers have come to tell King David that he has done a good thing. They are saying, 'May your God make Solomon even more famous than you and an even greater king than you.' " Jonathan continued, "And King David bowed down on his bed to worship God, 48 saying, 'Bless the LORD, the God of Israel. Today he has made one of my sons the king and allowed me to see it.' "

49 Then all of Adonijah's guests were afraid, and they left quickly and scattered. 50 Adonijah was also afraid of Solomon, so he went and took hold of the corners of the altar.[n] 51 Then someone told Solomon, "Adonijah is afraid of you, so he is at the altar, holding on to its corners. He says, 'Tell King Solomon to promise me today that he will not kill me.' "

52 So Solomon answered, "Adonijah must show that he is a man of honour. If he does that, I promise he will not lose even a single hair from his head. But if he does anything wrong, he will die." 53 Then King Solomon sent some men to get Adonijah. When he was brought from the altar, he came before King Solomon and bowed down. Solomon told him, "Go home."

Kerethites and Pelethites These were probably special units of the army that were responsible for the king's safety, a kind of palace guard.

corners of the altar If a person were innocent of a crime, he could run into the Holy Place where the altar was. If he held on to the corners of the altar, which looked like horns, he would be safe.

The Death of David

2 Since it was almost time for David to die, he
gave his son Solomon his last commands.
2David said, "My time to die is near. Be a good
and strong leader. 3Obey the LORD your God. Fol-
low him by obeying his demands, his commands,
his laws and his rules that are written in the
teachings of Moses. If you do these things, you
will be successful in all you do and wherever you
go. 4And if you obey the LORD, he will keep the
promise he made to me. He said: 'If your de-
scendants[d] live as I tell them and have complete
faith in me, a man from your family will always
be king over the people of Israel.'
5"Also, you remember what Joab son of Zeru-
iah did to me. He killed the two commanders of
Israel's armies: Abner son of Ner and Amasa son
of Jether. He did this as if he and they were at
war, although it was a time of peace. He put their
blood on the belt around his waist and on his
sandals on his feet. 6Punish him in the way you
think is wisest, but do not let him die peacefully
of old age.
7"Be kind to the children of Barzillai of Gilead,
and allow them to eat at your table. They wel-
comed me when I ran away from your brother
Absalom.
8"And remember, Shimei son of Gera, the
Benjaminite, is here with you. He cursed me the
day I went to Mahanaim. But when he came
down to meet me at the Jordan River, I promised
him before the LORD, 'Shimei, I will not kill
you.' 9But you should not leave him unpun-
ished. You are a wise man, and you will know
what to do to him, but you must be sure he is
killed."
10Then David died and was buried with his
ancestors in Jerusalem. 11He had ruled over

LEADERSHIP

The Mark of a Leader

Selwyn Hughes (who blessed millions through his *Everyday with Jesus* notes) was, like David, a Christian leader and was another man who knew how to die. He had cancer and, after ten years, when the doctors told him things didn't look great, he told people that he didn't know how long he had to live but asked them to pray that he would finish the work God wanted him to do and that he would die well.

He carried on writing and preaching until the cancer made it impossible and he went into a hospice. He was told that he had a matter of days to live and responded with eagerness and confidence by saying, "That's wonderful; I'm ready to meet Jesus."

Over those few days, his close friends and family visited him and he encouraged them by telling them he was ready for eternity. After a few days, he went into a peaceful sleep, with his friends praying at his bedside, and woke up in heaven.

Mick Brooks was one of Selwyn's friends. In the days that followed lots of people said to him, "Isn't it sad that Selwyn has died?" to which Mick answered, "Yes it is sad, but it's also joyful too; it's the best advert for dying that I've ever seen; it's great, it's orderly, it's godly. I hope I can do that."

Read **1 Kings 2:1–12**.

- How was what Selwyn did similar to what David says in the passage?
- How do you think you would have felt being an Israelite under David's leadership hearing those words?

Consider . . .

- what you would do for Jesus if you knew you only had a few days to live. Why not go ahead and do it anyway?
- what words of wisdom you would pass on to your friends. Write them down and keep them in your Bible.

For more, see . . .

- Psalm 132:11–18 (p.578)
- 2 Timothy 4:1–5 (p.1319)
- John 16:4–15 (p.1125)

Israel 40 years—seven years in Hebron and 33 years in Jerusalem.

Solomon Takes Control as King

[12]Solomon became king after David, his father, and he was in firm control of his kingdom.

[13]At this time Adonijah son of Haggith went to Bathsheba, Solomon's mother. "Do you come in peace?" Bathsheba asked.

"Yes. This is a peaceful visit," Adonijah answered. [14]"I have something to say to you."

"You may speak," she said.

[15]"You remember that at one time the kingdom was mine," Adonijah said. "All the people of Israel recognised me as their king, but things have changed. Now my brother is the king, because the LORD chose him. [16]Now I have one thing to ask you; please do not refuse me."

Bathsheba answered, "What do you want?"

[17]"I know King Solomon will do anything you ask him," Adonijah continued. "Please ask him to give me Abishag the Shunammite to be my wife."

[18]"Very well," she answered. "I will speak to the king for you."

[19]So Bathsheba went to King Solomon to speak to him for Adonijah. When Solomon saw her, he stood up to meet her, then bowed down and sat on the throne. He told some servants to bring another throne for his mother. Then she sat down at his right side.

[20]Bathsheba said, "I have one small thing to ask you. Please do not refuse me."

"Ask, mother," the king answered. "I will not refuse you."

[21]So she said, "Allow Abishag the Shunammite to marry your brother Adonijah."

[22]King Solomon answered his mother, "Why do you ask me to give him Abishag? Why don't you also ask for him to become the king since he is my older brother? Abiathar the priest and Joab son of Zeruiah would support him!"

[23]Then King Solomon swore by the name of the LORD, saying, "May God punish me terribly if this doesn't cost Adonijah his life! [24]By the LORD who has given me the throne that belonged to my father David and who has kept his promise and given the kingdom to me and my people, Adonijah will die today!" [25]Then King Solomon gave orders to Benaiah son of Jehoiada, and he went and killed Adonijah.

[26]King Solomon said to Abiathar the priest, "I should kill you too, but I will allow you to go back to your fields in Anathoth. I will not kill you at this time, because you helped carry the Ark[d] of the Lord GOD while marching with my father David. And I know you shared in all the hard times with him." [27]Then Solomon removed Abiathar from being the LORD's priest. This happened as the LORD had said it would, when he was speaking in Shiloh about the priest Eli and his descendants.[d]

[28]When Joab heard about what had happened, he was afraid. He had supported Adonijah but not Absalom. So Joab ran to the Tent[d] of the LORD and took hold of the corners of the altar.[n] [29]Someone told King Solomon that Joab had run to the Tent of the LORD and was beside the altar. Then Solomon ordered Benaiah to go and kill him.

[30]Benaiah went into the Tent of the LORD and said to Joab, "The king says, 'Come out!' "

But Joab answered, "No, I will die here."

So Benaiah went back to the king and told him what Joab had said. [31]Then the king ordered Benaiah, "Do as he says! Kill him there and bury him. Then my family and I will be free of the guilt of Joab, who has killed innocent people. [32]Without my father knowing it, he killed two men who were much better than he was—Abner son of Ner, the commander of Israel's army, and Amasa son of Jether, the commander of Judah's army. So the LORD will pay him back for those deaths. [33]Joab and his family will be for ever guilty of their deaths, but there will be peace from the LORD for David, his descendants, his family and his throne for ever."

[34]So Benaiah son of Jehoiada killed Joab, and he was buried near his home in the desert. [35]The king then made Benaiah son of Jehoiada commander of the army in Joab's place. He also made Zadok the new high priest in Abiathar's place.

[36]Next the king sent for Shimei. Solomon said to him, "Build a house for yourself in Jerusalem and live there. Don't leave the city. [37]The very day you leave and cross the Kidron Valley, someone will kill you, and it will be your own fault."

[38]So Shimei answered the king, "I agree with what you say. I will do what you say, my master and king." So Shimei lived in Jerusalem for a long time.

[39]But three years later two of Shimei's slaves ran away to Achish king of Gath, who was the son of Maacah. Shimei heard that his slaves were in Gath, [40]so he put his saddle on his donkey and went to Achish at Gath to find them. Then he brought them back from Gath.

corners of the altar If a person were innocent of a crime, he could run into the Holy Place where the altar was. If he held on to the corners of the altar, which looked like horns, he would be safe.

41Someone told Solomon that Shimei had gone from Jerusalem to Gath and had returned. 42So Solomon sent for Shimei and said, "I made you promise in the name of the LORD not to leave Jerusalem. I warned you if you went out anywhere you would die, and you agreed to what I said. 43Why did you break your promise to the LORD and disobey my command?" 44The king also said, "You know the many wrong things you did to my father David, so now the LORD will punish you for those wrongs. 45But the LORD will bless me and make the rule of David safe before the LORD for ever."

46Then the king ordered Benaiah to kill Shimei, and he did. Now Solomon was in full control of his kingdom.

Solomon Asks for Wisdom

3 Solomon made an agreement with the king of Egypt by marrying his daughter and bringing her to Jerusalem. At this time Solomon was still building his palace and the Temple[d] of the LORD, as well as a wall around Jerusalem. 2The Temple for the worship of the LORD had not yet been finished, so people were still sacrificing at altars in many places of worship. 3Solomon showed he loved the LORD by following the commands his father David had given him, except many other places of worship were still used to offer sacrifices and to burn incense.[d]

4King Solomon went to Gibeon to offer a sacrifice, because it was the most important place of worship. He offered a thousand burnt offerings on that altar. 5While he was at Gibeon, the LORD appeared to him in a dream during the night. God said, "Ask for whatever you want me to give you."

6Solomon answered, "You were very kind to your servant, my father David. He obeyed you, and he was honest and lived right. You showed great kindness to him when you allowed his son to be king after him. 7LORD my God, now you have made me, your servant, king in my father's place. But I am like a little child; I don't know how to do what must be done. 8I, your servant, am here among your chosen people, and there are too many of them to count. 9I ask that you give me an obedient heart so I can rule the people in the right way and will know the difference between right and wrong. Otherwise, it is impossible to rule this great people of yours."

10The Lord was pleased that Solomon had asked this. 11So God said to him, "You did not ask for a long life, or riches for yourself or the death of your enemies. Since you asked for wisdom to make the right decisions, 12I will do what you asked. I will give you wisdom and understanding that is greater than anyone has had in the past or will have in the future. 13I will also give you what you did not ask for: riches and honour. During your life no other king will be as great as you. 14If you follow me and obey my laws and commands as your father David did, I will also give you a long life."

15After Solomon woke up from the dream, he went to Jerusalem. He stood before the Ark[d] of the Agreement with the Lord, where he made burnt offerings and fellowship offerings. After that, he gave a feast for all his leaders and officers.

Solomon Makes a Wise Decision

16One day two women who were prostitutes[d] came to Solomon. As they stood before him, 17one of the women said, "My master, this woman and I live in the same house. I gave birth to a baby while she was there with me. 18Three days later this woman also gave birth to a baby. No one else was in the house with us; it was just the two of us. 19One night this woman rolled over on her baby, and he died. 20So she took my son from my bed during the night while I was asleep, and she carried him to her bed. Then she put the dead baby in my bed. 21The next morning when I got up to feed my baby, I saw that he was dead! When I looked at him more closely, I realised he was not my son."

22"No!" the other woman cried. "The living baby is my son, and the dead baby is yours!"

But the first woman said, "No! The dead baby is yours, and the living one is mine!" So the two women argued before the king.

23Then King Solomon said, "One of you says, 'My son is alive and your son is dead.' Then the other one says, 'No! Your son is dead and my son is alive.' "

24The king sent his servants to get a sword. When they brought it to him, 25he said, "Cut the living baby into two pieces, and give each woman half."

26The real mother of the living child was full of love for her son. So she said to the king, "Please, my master, don't kill him! Give the baby to her!"

But the other woman said, "Neither of us will have him. Cut him into two pieces!"

Sidelight Many people have half-brothers or half-sisters these days because of stepfamilies. But Solomon suggested another approach: settling a dispute by cutting the baby in half and giving each mother half (1 Kings 3:16–28). Scholars have found 22 similar stories of wisdom in other cultures of ancient times.

[27]Then King Solomon said, “Don’t kill him. Give the baby to the first woman, because she is the real mother.”

[28]When the people of Israel heard about King Solomon’s decision, they respected him very much. They saw he had wisdom from God to make the right decisions.

Solomon’s Officers

4 King Solomon ruled over all Israel. [2]These are the names of his leading officers:

Azariah son of Zadok was the priest;

[3]Elihoreph and Ahijah, sons of Shisha, recorded what happened in the courts;

Jehoshaphat son of Ahilud recorded the history of the people;

[4]Benaiah son of Jehoiada was commander of the army;

Zadok and Abiathar were priests;

[5]Azariah son of Nathan was in charge of the district governors;

Zabud son of Nathan was a priest and adviser to the king;

[6]Ahishar was responsible for everything in the palace;

Adoniram son of Abda was in charge of the slaves.

[7]Solomon placed twelve governors over the districts of Israel, who gathered food from their districts for the king and his family. Each governor was responsible for bringing food to the king for one month of each year. [8]These are the names of the twelve governors:

Ben-Hur was governor of the mountain country of Ephraim;

[9]Ben-Deker was governor of Makaz, Shaalbim, Beth Shemesh and Elon Bethhanan;

[10]Ben-Hesed was governor of Arubboth, Socoh and all the land of Hepher;

[11]Ben-Abinadab was governor of Naphoth Dor (he was married to Taphath, Solomon’s daughter);

[12]Baana son of Ahilud was governor of Taanach, Megiddo and all of Beth Shan next to Zarethan, this was below Jezreel from Beth Shan to Abel Meholah across from Jokmeam;

[13]Ben-Geber was governor of Ramoth in Gilead (he was governor of all the towns of Jair in Gilead—Jair was the son of Manasseh; Ben-Geber was also over the district of Argob in Bashan, which had 60 large, walled cities with bronze bars on their gates);

[14]Ahinadab son of Iddo was governor of Mahanaim;

[15]Ahimaaz was governor of Naphtali (he was married to Basemath, Solomon’s daughter);

[16]Baana son of Hushai was governor of Asher and Aloth;

[17]Jehoshaphat son of Paruah was governor of Issachar;

[18]Shimei son of Ela was governor of Benjamin;

[19]Geber son of Uri was governor of Gilead. Gilead had been the country of Sihon king of the Amorites and Og king of Bashan. But Geber was the only governor over this district.

Solomon’s Kingdom

[20]There were as many people in Judah and Israel as grains of sand on the seashore. The people ate, drank and were happy. [21]Solomon ruled over all the kingdoms from the Euphrates River to the land of the Philistines, as far as the border of Egypt. These countries brought Solomon the payments he demanded, and they were under his control all his life.

[22]Solomon needed much food each day to feed himself and all the people who ate at his table: 6,000 litres of fine flour, 12,000 litres of grain, [23]ten cows that were fed on good grain, 20 cows that were raised in the fields, 100 sheep, three kinds of deer, and fattened birds.

Sidelight

Each day it took 30 cattle (plus lots of other food) to feed all the people at Solomon’s table (1 Kings 4:23). That would be about 120,000 Big Macs a day.

[24]Solomon controlled all the countries west of the Euphrates River—the land from Tiphsah to Gaza. And he had peace on all sides of his kingdom. [25]During Solomon’s life Judah and Israel, from Dan to Beersheba,[n] also lived in peace; all of his people were able to sit under their own fig trees and grapevines.

[26]Solomon had 4,000 stalls for his chariot horses and 12,000 horses. [27]Each month one of the district governors gave King Solomon all the food he needed—enough for every person who ate at the king’s table. The governors made sure he had everything he needed. [28]They also brought enough barley and straw for Solomon’s chariot and work horses; each person brought this grain to the right place.

Dan to Beersheba Dan was the city farthest north in Israel, and Beersheba was the city farthest south. So this means all the people of Israel.

Solomon's Wisdom

29God gave Solomon great wisdom so he could
understand many things. His wisdom was as hard
to measure as the grains of sand on the seashore.
30His wisdom was greater than any wisdom of
the East, or any wisdom in Egypt. 31He was
wiser than anyone on earth. He was even wiser
than Ethan the Ezrahite, as well as Heman, Cal-
col and Darda—the three sons of Mahol. King
Solomon became famous in all the surrounding
countries. 32During his life he spoke 3,000 wise
sayings and also wrote 1,005 songs. 33He taught
about many kinds of plants—everything from
the great cedar trees of Lebanon to the weeds
that grow out of the walls. He also taught about
animals, birds, crawling things and fish. 34People
from all nations came to listen to King Solomon's
wisdom. The kings of all nations sent them
to him, because they had heard of Solomon's
wisdom.

Preparing to Build the Temple

5 Hiram, the king of Tyre, had always been
David's friend. When Hiram heard that Solo-
mon had been made king in David's place, he
sent his messengers to Solomon. 2Solomon sent
this message back to King Hiram: 3"You remem-
ber my father David had to fight many wars with
the countries around him, so he was never able
to build a temple for worshipping the LORD his
God. David was waiting until the LORD allowed
him to defeat all his enemies. 4But now the LORD
my God has given me peace on all sides of my
country. I have no enemies now, and no danger
threatens my people.

5"The LORD promised my father David, 'I will
make your son king after you, and he will
build a temple for worshipping me.' Now, I plan
to build that temple for worshipping the LORD
my God. 6So send your men to cut down cedar
trees for me from Lebanon. My servants will
work with yours, and I will pay them whatever
wages you decide. We don't have anyone who
can cut down trees as well as the people of
Sidon."

7When Hiram heard what Solomon asked, he
was very happy. He said, "Praise the LORD today!
He has given David a wise son to rule over this
great nation!" 8Then Hiram sent back this mes-
sage to Solomon: "I received the message you
sent, and I will give you all the cedar and pine
trees you want. 9My servants will bring them
down from Lebanon to the sea. There I will tie
them together and float them along the shore to
the place you choose. Then I will separate the
logs there, and you can take them away. In
return it is my wish that you give food to all
those who live with me." 10So Hiram gave
Solomon as much cedar and pine as he wanted.

Sidelight The cedars Solomon imported from Lebanon were in high demand as building materials (1 Kings 5:6–10). The wood is red and resists insects and decay, making it ideal for buildings, musical instruments, chests and household furnishings. Though these trees have almost become extinct, the Lebanese flag still features the pyramid-shaped tree.

11And Solomon gave Hiram about 2,000 tonnes
of wheat each year to feed the people who lived
with him. Solomon also gave him about 4,000
litres of pure olive oil every year.

12The LORD gave Solomon wisdom as he had
promised. And there was peace between Hiram
and Solomon; these two kings made a treaty be-
tween themselves.

13King Solomon forced 30,000 men of Israel
to help in this work. 14He sent a group of 10,000
men each month to Lebanon. Each group worked
in Lebanon for a month, then went home for two
months. A man named Adoniram was in charge.
15Solomon forced 80,000 men to work in the
hill country, cutting stone, and he had 70,000
men to carry the stones. 16There were also 3,300
men who directed the workers. 17King Solomon
commanded them to cut large blocks of fine
stone to be used for the foundation of the
Temple.[d] 18Solomon's and Hiram's builders and
the men from Byblos carved the stones and pre-
pared the stones and the logs for building the
Temple.

Solomon Builds the Temple

6 Solomon began to build the Temple[d] 480
years after the people of Israel had left
Egypt. This was during the fourth year of King
Solomon's rule over Israel. It was the second
month, the month of Ziv.

2The Temple was 30 metres long, 10 metres
wide and 15 metres high. 3The porch in front of
the main room of the Temple was 5 metres deep
and 10 metres wide. This room ran along the
front of the Temple itself. Its width was equal to
that of the Temple. 4The Temple also had win-
dows that opened and closed. 5Solomon also built
some side rooms against the walls of the main
room and the inner room of the Temple. He built
rooms all around. 6The rooms on the bottom
floor were 2.5 metres wide. Those on the middle
floor were 3 metres wide, and the rooms above
them were 3.5 metres wide. The Temple wall

that formed the side of each room was thinner than the wall in the room below. These rooms were pushed against the Temple wall, but they did not have their main beams built into this wall.

7The stones were prepared at the same place where they were cut from the ground. Since these stones were the only ones used to build the Temple, there was no noise of hammers, axes or any other iron tools at the Temple.

8The entrance to the ground floor beside the Temple was on the south side. From there, stairs went up to the first floor. And from there, stairs
went on to the second-floor rooms. 9Solomon
put a roof made from beams and cedar boards on the Temple. So he finished building the Temple
10as well as the ground floor that was beside the Temple. This ground floor was 2.5 metres high and was attached to the Temple by cedar beams.

Sidelight Solomon's Temple was one of the largest structures in Israel at the time, but it wasn't very big by today's standards. It only had about 250 square metres of floor space – smaller than a school gym (1 Kings 6:2–38).

11The LORD said to Solomon: 12"If you obey all my laws and commands, I will do for you what I promised your father David. 13I will live among the Israelites in this Temple, and I will never leave my people Israel."

14So Solomon finished building the Temple.
15The inside walls were covered from floor to ceiling with cedar boards. The floor was made
from pine boards. 16A room 10 metres long was built in the back part of the Temple. This room, called the Most Holy Place, was separated from the rest of the Temple by cedar boards which
reached from floor to ceiling. 17The main room, the one in front of the Most Holy Place, was
20 metres long. 18Everything inside the Temple was covered with cedar, which was carved with pictures of flowers and plants. A person could not see the stones of the wall, only the cedar.

19Solomon prepared the inner room at the back of the Temple to keep the Ark [d] of the Agreement
with the LORD. 20This inner room was 10 metres long, 10 metres wide and 10 metres high. He covered this room with pure gold, and he also
covered the altar of cedar. 21He covered the inside of the Temple with pure gold, placing gold chains across the front of the inner room, which
was also covered with gold. 22So all the inside of the Temple, as well as the altar of the Most Holy Place, was covered with gold.

23Solomon made two creatures from olive wood and placed them in the Most Holy Place.

Sidelight Building Solomon's Temple would ruin any church's budget (1 Kings 6:21). Just the gold overlay in the Temple would make it one of the most valuable buildings in the world if it were around today.

Each creature was 5 metres tall 24and had two wings. Each wing was 2.5 metres long, so it was 5 metres from the end of one wing to the end of the other. 25The creatures were the same
size and shape; 26each was 5 metres tall. 27These
creatures were put beside each other in the Most Holy Place with their wings spread out. One creature's wing touched one wall, and the other creature's wing touched the other wall with their wings touching each other in the middle of
the room. 28These two creatures were covered with gold.

29All the walls around the Temple were carved with pictures of creatures with wings, as well as palm trees and flowers. This was true for both
the main room and the inner room. 30The floors of both rooms were covered with gold.

31Doors made from olive wood were placed at the entrance to the Most Holy Place. These doors
had frames with five sides. 32Creatures with wings, as well as palm trees and flowers, were also carved on the two olive wood doors that were covered with gold. The creatures and the palm trees on the doors were covered with gold
as well. 33At the entrance to the main room there was a square door frame made of olive wood.
34Two doors were made from pine. Each door
had two parts so the doors folded. 35The doors
were covered with pictures of creatures with wings, as well as palm trees and flowers. All of the carvings were covered with gold, which was evenly spread over them.

36The inner courtyard was enclosed by walls, which were made of three rows of cut stones and one row of cedar boards.

37Work began on the Temple in Ziv, the second month, during the fourth year Solomon was
king over Israel. 38The Temple was finished during the eleventh year he was king, in the eighth month, the month of Bul. It was built exactly as it was planned. Solomon had spent seven years building it.

Solomon's Palace

7 King Solomon also built a palace for himself; it took him thirteen years to finish it. [2]Built of cedars from the Forest of Lebanon, it was 50 metres long, 25 metres wide and 15 metres high. It had four rows of cedar columns which supported the cedar beams. [3]There were 45 beams on the roof, with 15 beams in each row, and the ceiling was covered with cedar above the beams. [4]Windows were placed in three rows facing each other. [5]All the doors were square, and the three doors at each end faced each other.

[6]Solomon also built the porch that had pillars. This porch was 25 metres long and 15 metres wide. Along the front of the porch was a roof supported by pillars.

[7]Solomon also built a throne room where he judged people, called the Hall of Justice. This room was covered with cedar from the floor to the ceiling. [8]The palace where Solomon lived was built like the Hall of Justice, and it was behind this hall. Solomon also built the same kind of palace for his wife, who was the daughter of the king of Egypt.

[9]All these buildings were made with blocks of fine stone. First they were carefully cut. Then they were trimmed with a saw in the front and back. These fine stones went from the foundations of the buildings to the top of the walls. Even the courtyard was made with blocks of stone. [10]The foundations were made with large blocks of fine stone, some as long as 5 metres. Others were 4 metres long. [11]On top of these foundation stones were other blocks of fine stone and cedar beams. [12]The palace courtyard, the courtyard inside the Temple[d] and the porch of the Temple were surrounded by walls. All of these walls had three rows of stone blocks and one row of cedar beams.

The Temple is Completed Inside

[13]King Solomon sent to Tyre and had Huram brought to him. [14]Huram's mother was a widow from the tribe[d] of Naphtali. His father was from Tyre and had been skilled in making things from bronze. Huram was also very skilled and experienced in bronze work. So he came to King Solomon and did all the bronze work.

[15]He made two bronze pillars, each one 9 metres tall and 6 metres around. [16]He also made two bronze capitals[d] that were 2.5 metres tall, and he put them on top of the pillars. [17]Then he made a net of seven chains for each capital, which covered the capitals on top of the two pillars. [18]He made two rows of bronze pomegranates[d] to go on the nets. These covered the capitals at the top of the pillars. [19]The capitals on top of the pillars in the porch were shaped like lilies, and they were 2 metres tall. [20]The capitals were on top of both pillars, above the bowl-shaped section and next to the nets. At that place there were 200 pomegranates in rows all around the capitals. [21]Huram put these two bronze pillars at the porch of the Temple.[d] He named the south pillar He Establishes and the north pillar In Him Is Strength. [22]The capitals on top of the pillars were shaped like lilies. So the work on the pillars was finished.

[23]Then Huram made from bronze a large round bowl, which was called the Sea. It was 15 metres around, 5 metres across and 2.5 metres deep. [24]Around the outer edge of the bowl was a rim. Under this rim were two rows of bronze plants which surrounded the bowl. There were ten plants every 50 centimetres, and these plants were made in one piece with the bowl. [25]The bowl rested on the backs of twelve bronze bulls that faced outwards from the centre of the bowl. Three bulls faced north, three faced west, three faced south and three faced east. [26]The sides of the bowl were 10 centimetres thick, and it held about 40,000 litres. The rim of the bowl was like the rim of a cup or like a lily blossom.

[27]Then Huram made ten bronze stands, each one 2 metres long, 2 metres wide and 1.5 metres high. [28]The stands were made from square sides, which were put on frames. [29]On the sides were bronze lions, bulls and creatures with wings. On the frames above and below the lions and bulls were designs of flowers hammered into the bronze. [30]Each stand had four bronze wheels with bronze axles. At the corners there were bronze supports for a large bowl, and the supports had designs of flowers. [31]There was a frame on top of the bowls, 50 centimetres high above the bowls. The opening of the bowl was round, 75 centimetres deep. Designs were carved into the bronze on the frame, which was square, not round. [32]The four wheels, placed under the frame, were 75 centimetres high. The axles between the wheels were made as one piece with the stand. [33]The wheels were like a chariot's wheels. Everything on the wheels—the axles, rims, spokes and hubs—was made of bronze.

[34]The four supports were on the four corners of each stand. They were made as one piece with the stand. [35]A strip of bronze around the top of each stand was 25 centimetres deep. It was also made as one piece with the stand. [36]The sides of the stand and the frames were covered with carvings of creatures with wings, as well as lions, palm trees and flowers. [37]This is the way Huram made the ten stands. The bronze for each stand was melted and poured into a mould, so all the stands were the same size and shape.

38Huram also made ten bronze bowls, one
bowl for each of the ten stands. Each bowl was 2
metres across and could hold about 800 litres.
39Huram put five stands on the south side of the
Temple and five on the north side. He put the
large bowl in the south-east corner of the Tem-
ple. 40Huram also made bowls, shovels and small
bowls.

So Huram finished all his work for King Solo-
mon on the Temple of the LORD:

41two pillars;
two large bowls for the capitals on top
of the pillars;
two nets to cover the two large bowls
for the capitals on top of the pillars;
42400 pomegranates for the two nets
(there were two rows of pomegran-
ates for each net covering the bowls
for the capitals on top of the pillars);
43ten stands with a bowl on each stand;
44the large bowl with twelve bulls un-
der it;
45the pots, shovels, small bowls and all
the dishes for the Temple of the
LORD.

Huram made everything King Solomon wanted
from polished bronze. 46The king had these things
poured into clay moulds that were made in the
plain of the Jordan River between Succoth and
Zarethan. 47Solomon never weighed the bronze
used to make these things, because there was
too much to weigh. So the total weight of all the
bronze was never known.

48Solomon also made all the things for the
Temple of the LORD:

the golden altar;
the golden table which held the bread
that shows God's people are in his
presence;
49the lampstands of pure gold (five on
the right side and five on the left
side in front of the Most Holy Place);
the flowers, lamps and tongs of gold;
50the pure gold bowls, wick trimmers,
small bowls, pans and dishes used
to carry coals;
the gold hinges for the doors of the
Most Holy Place and the main room
of the Temple.

51Finally the work King Solomon did for the
Temple of the LORD was finished. Solomon
brought in everything his father David had set
apart for the Temple—silver, gold and other arti-
cles. He put everything in the treasuries of the
Temple of the LORD.

The Ark is Brought into the Temple

8 King Solomon called for the elders of Israel,
the heads of the tribes[d] and the leaders of
the families to come to him in Jerusalem. He
wanted them to bring the Ark[d] of the Agreement
with the LORD from the older part of the city. 2So
all the Israelites came together with King Solo-
mon during the festival in the month of Ethanim,
the seventh month.

3When all the elders of Israel arrived, the
priests lifted up the Ark. 4They carried the Ark of
the LORD, the Meeting Tent[d] and the holy things;
the priests and the Levites brought them up.
5King Solomon and all the Israelites gathered be-
fore the Ark and sacrificed so many sheep and
cattle no one could count them all. 6Then the
priests put the Ark of the Agreement with the
LORD in its place inside the Most Holy Place in
the Temple,[d] under the wings of the golden crea-
tures. 7The wings of these creatures were spread
out over the place for the Ark, covering it and its
carrying poles. 8The carrying poles were so long
that anyone standing in the Holy Place in front of
the Most Holy Place could see the ends of the
poles, but no one could see them from outside
the Holy Place. The poles are still there today.
9The only things inside the Ark were two stone
tablets[n] that Moses had put in the Ark at Mount
Sinai. That was where the LORD made his agree-
ment with the Israelites after they came out of
Egypt.

10When the priests left the Holy Place, a cloud
filled the Temple of the LORD. 11The priests could
not continue their work, because the Temple
was filled with the glory of the LORD.

Solomon Speaks to the People

12Then Solomon said, "The LORD said he would
live in a dark cloud. 13LORD, I have truly built a
wonderful Temple[d] for you—a place for you to
live for ever."

14While all the Israelites were standing there,
King Solomon turned to them and blessed them.
15Then he said, "Praise the LORD, the God of
Israel. He has done what he promised to my
father David. The LORD said, 16'Since the time I
brought my people Israel out of Egypt, I have not
chosen a city in any tribe[d] of Israel where a tem-
ple will be built for me. But I have chosen David
to lead my people Israel.'

17"My father David wanted to build a temple
for the LORD, the God of Israel. 18But the LORD said
to my father David, 'It was good that you wanted to
build a temple for me. 19But you are not the one
to build it. Your son, who comes from your own
body, is the one who will build my temple.'

stone tablets They were the two tablets on which God wrote the Ten Commandments.

20“Now the LORD has kept his promise. I am
the king now in place of David my father. Now I
rule Israel as the LORD promised, and I have built
the Temple for the LORD, the God of Israel. 21I
have made a place there for the Ark, in which is
the Agreement the LORD made with our ances-
tors when he brought them out of Egypt.”

Solomon's Prayer

22Then Solomon stood facing the LORD's altar,
and all the Israelites were standing behind him.
He spread out his hands towards the sky 23and
said:
“LORD, God of Israel, there is no god like you
in heaven above or on earth below. You keep
your agreement of love with your servants who
truly follow you. 24You have kept the promise
you made to your servant David, my father. You
spoke it with your own mouth and finished it
with your hands today. 25Now LORD, God of
Israel, keep the promise you made to your ser-
vant David, my father. You said, ‘If your sons are
careful to obey me as you have obeyed me, there
will always be someone from your family ruling
Israel.’ 26Now, God of Israel, please continue to
keep that promise you made to your servant
David, my father.
27“But, God, can you really live here on the
earth? The sky and the highest place in heaven
cannot contain you. Surely this house which

PRAYER

Praying About Real Life

When fifteen-year-old Linda and her mum talked about Linda's ex-boyfriend one evening, the conversation quickly escalated into a fight.

“Tony seems such a nice boy, Linda,” Mum complained. “I really think you handled the whole thing badly.”

“I didn't ask your opinion, Mum, but thanks anyway.” Linda's words dripped with sarcasm. She felt as if she were about to explode. “I'm tired of your constant meddling. I can't even put my shoes on without getting your approval first. I have a life, Mother. Why don't you let me live it by myself?”

Then Linda stormed away. She didn't know or care what her mother thought – she just wanted to leave.

Linda ended up at a nearby park for the next few hours. There, she discovered how much prayer can help. At first, she was angry with God. “Why does all this happen to me?” she asked God. “I shouldn't be having so much trouble with this! I'm a Christian.” Linda felt that she ought to be able to deal with her family problems. Soon, Linda asked God to help her. She spent some time worshipping and concentrating on God's power and goodness. Once she had calmed down, Linda asked God to help her to understand her mum's side of the argument.

Linda got home late, but in the morning, she and her mother apologised. That evening, they talked about how they could have dealt with their feelings better. And Linda decided to talk to Tony.

“It'll give me the chance to let him know I still care,” she told her mum, smiling.

Linda's relationship with her mum isn't perfect, but she knows that she can turn to God in prayer for real-life issues like this one.

King Solomon also turned to God and prayed about real-life issues. Read his prayer after God's Temple was built in **1 Kings 8:22–30**.

- What elements do Linda's prayer and King Solomon's prayer have in common? What's different?
- How does King Solomon's prayer compare with the kind of prayers you usually pray?

Consider . . .

- listing all the concerns of your life on paper and then talking to God about each one.
- offering to pray with others who are going through rough times.

For more, see . . .

- 2 Samuel 22:1–51 (p.307)
- John 17:20–26 (p.1128)
- Luke 1:46–55 (p.1037)

I have built cannot contain you. 28But please listen to my prayer and my request, because I am your servant. LORD my God, hear this prayer your servant prays to you today. 29Night and day please watch over this Temple[d] where you have said, 'I will be worshipped there.' Hear the prayer I pray facing this Temple. 30Hear my prayers and the prayers of your people Israel when we pray facing this place. Hear from your home in heaven, and when you hear, forgive us.

31"If someone wrongs another person, he will be brought to the altar in this Temple. If he swears an oath that he is not guilty, 32then hear in heaven. Judge the case, punish the guilty, but declare that the innocent person is not guilty.

33"When your people, the Israelites, sin against you, their enemies will defeat them. But if they come back to you and praise you and pray to you in this Temple, 34then hear them in heaven. Forgive the sins of your people Israel, and bring them back to the land you gave to their ancestors.

35"When they sin against you, you will stop the rain from falling on their land. Then they will pray, facing this place and praising you; they will stop sinning when you make them suffer. 36When this happens, please hear their prayer in heaven, and forgive the sins of your servants, the Israelites. Teach them to do what is right. Then please send rain to this land you have given particularly to them.

37"At times the land will become so dry that no food will grow, or a great sickness will spread among the people. Sometimes all the crops will be destroyed by locusts[d] or grasshoppers. Your people will be attacked in their cities by their enemy or will become sick. 38When any of these things happen, the people will become truly sorry. If your people spread their hands in prayer towards this Temple, 39then hear their prayers from your home in heaven. Forgive and treat each person as he should be treated because you know what is in a person's heart. Only you know what is in everyone's heart. 40Then your people will respect you as long as they live in this land you gave to our ancestors.

41–42"People who are not Israelites, foreigners from other lands, will hear about your greatness and power. They will come from far away to pray at this Temple. 43Then hear from your home in heaven, and do whatever they ask you. Then people everywhere will know you and respect you, just as your people in Israel do. Then everyone will know I built this Temple as a place to worship you.

44"When your people go out to fight their enemies along some road on which you send them, your people will pray to you, facing the city which you have chosen and the Temple I have built for you. 45Then hear in heaven their prayers, and do what is right.

46"Everyone sins, so your people will also sin against you. You will become angry with them and hand them over to their enemies. Their enemies will capture them and take them away to their countries far or near. 47Your people will be sorry for their sins when they are held as prisoners in another country. They will be sorry and pray to you in the land where they are held as prisoners, saying, 'We have sinned. We have done wrong and acted wickedly.' 48They will truly turn back to you in the land of their enemies. They will pray to you, facing this land you gave their ancestors, this city you have chosen and the Temple I have built for you. 49Then hear their prayers from your home in heaven, and do what is right. 50Forgive your people for all their sins and for turning against you. Make those who have captured them show them mercy. 51Remember, they are your special people. You brought them out of Egypt, as if you were pulling them out of a blazing furnace.

52"Give your attention to my prayers and the prayers of your people Israel. Listen to them whenever they ask you for help. 53You chose them from all the nations on earth to be your very own people. This is what you promised through Moses your servant when you brought our ancestors out of Egypt, Lord GOD."

54Solomon prayed this prayer to the LORD, kneeling in front of the altar with his arms raised towards heaven. When he finished praying, he got up. 55Then, in a loud voice, he stood and blessed all the people of Israel, saying: 56"Praise the LORD! He promised he would give rest to his people Israel, and he has given us rest. The LORD has kept all the good promises he gave through his servant Moses. 57May the LORD our God be with us as he was with our ancestors. May he never leave us, 58and may he turn us to himself so we will follow him. Let us obey all the laws and commands he gave our ancestors. 59May the LORD our God remember this prayer day and night and do what is right for his servant and his people Israel day by day. 60Then all the people of the world will know the LORD is the only true God. 61You must fully obey the LORD our God and follow all his laws and commands. Continue to obey in the future as you do now."

Sacrifices are Offered

62Then King Solomon and all Israel with him offered sacrifices to the LORD. 63Solomon killed 22,000 cattle and 120,000 sheep as fellowship

offerings. So the king and all the people gave the
Temple [d] to the LORD.
64 On that day King Solomon made holy the
middle part of the courtyard which is in front of
the Temple of the LORD. There he offered whole
burnt offerings, grain offerings and the fat of the
fellowship offerings. He offered them in the court-
yard, because the bronze altar before the LORD
was too small to hold all the burnt offerings,
the grain offerings and the fat of the fellowship
offerings.
65 Solomon and all the Israelites celebrated the
other festival that came at that time. People came
from as far away as Lebo Hamath and the brook
of Egypt. A great many people celebrated before
the LORD for seven days, then seven more days,
for a total of fourteen days. 66 On the following
day Solomon sent the people home. They blessed
the king as they went, happy because of all the
good things the LORD had done for his servant
David and his people Israel.

The LORD Appears to Solomon Again

9 Solomon finished building the Temple [d] of
the LORD and his royal palace and everything
he wanted to build. 2 Then the LORD appeared to
him again just as he had done before, in Gibeon.
3 The LORD said to him: "I have heard your prayer
and what you have asked me to do. You built this
Temple, and I have made it a holy place. I will be
worshipped there for ever and will watch over it
and protect it always.
4 "But you must serve me as your father David
did; he was fair and sincere. You must obey all
I have commanded and keep my laws and rules.
5 If you do, I will make your kingdom strong. This
is the promise I made to your father David—that
someone from his family would always rule
Israel.
6 "But you and your children must follow me
and obey the laws and commands I have given
you. You must not serve or worship other gods.
7 If you do, I will force Israel to leave the land I
have given them, and I will leave this Temple
that I have made holy. All the nations will make
fun of Israel and speak evil about them. 8 If the
Temple is destroyed, everyone who passes by
will be shocked. They will make fun of you and
ask, 'Why did the LORD do this terrible thing to
this land and this Temple?' 9 People will answer,
'This happened because they left the LORD their
God. This was the God who brought their ances-
tors out of Egypt, but they decided to follow
other gods. They worshipped and served those
gods, so the LORD brought all this disaster on
them.' "

Solomon's Other Achievements

10 By the end of 20 years, King Solomon had
built two buildings—the Temple [d] of the LORD
and the royal palace. 11 At that time King Solo-
mon gave 20 towns in Galilee to Hiram king of
Tyre, because Hiram had helped with the build-
ings. Hiram had given Solomon all the cedar,
pine and gold he wanted. 12 So Hiram travelled
from Tyre to see the towns Solomon had given
him, but when he saw them, he was not pleased.
13 He asked, "What good are these towns you
have given me, my brother?" So he named them
the Land of Cabul, [n] and they are still called that
today. 14 Hiram had sent Solomon about 4 tonnes
of gold.
15 This is the account of the forced labour Solo-
mon used to build the Temple and the palace. He
had them fill in the land and build the wall
around Jerusalem. He also had them rebuild the
cities of Hazor, Megiddo and Gezer. 16 (In the
past the king of Egypt had attacked and captured
Gezer. After burning it, he killed the Canaanites
who lived there. Then he gave it as a wedding
present to his daughter, who married Solomon.
17 So Solomon rebuilt it.) He also built the cities
of Lower Beth Horon 18 and Baalath, as well as
Tadmor, which is in the desert. 19 King Solomon
also built cities for storing grain and supplies and
cities for his chariots and horses. He built what-
ever he wanted in Jerusalem, Lebanon and every-
where he ruled.
20 There were other people in the land who
were not Israelites—Amorites, Hittites, Periz-
zites, Hivites and Jebusites. 21 They were descen-
dants [d] of people that the Israelites had not
destroyed. Solomon forced them to work for him
as slaves, as is still true today. 22 But Solomon did
not make slaves of the Israelites. They were his
soldiers, government leaders, officers, captains,
chariot commanders and drivers.
23 These were his most important officers over
the work. There were 550 supervisors over the
people who did the work on Solomon's projects.
24 The daughter of the king of Egypt moved
from the old part of Jerusalem to the palace that
Solomon had built for her. Then Solomon filled
in the surrounding land.
25 Three times each year Solomon offered whole
burnt offerings and fellowship offerings on the
altar he had built for the LORD. He also burned
incense [d] before the LORD. So he finished the
work on the Temple.
26 King Solomon also built ships at Ezion Geber,
a town near Elath on the shore of the Red Sea, in
the land of Edom. 27 Hiram had skilled sailors,
so he sent them to serve in these ships with

Cabul This name sounds like the Hebrew word for "worthless".

Solomon's men. 28The ships sailed to Ophir and brought back about 14 tonnes of gold to King Solomon.

The Queen of Sheba Visits Solomon

10 When the queen of Sheba heard about Solomon, she came to test him with hard questions. 2She travelled to Jerusalem with a large group of servants and camels carrying spices, jewels and much gold. When she came to Solomon, she talked with him about all she had in mind, 3and Solomon answered all her questions. Nothing was too hard for him to explain to her. 4The queen of Sheba learned that Solomon was very wise. She saw the palace he had built, 5the food on his table, his many officers, the palace servants and their good clothes. She saw the servants who served him at feasts and the whole burnt offerings he made in the Temple[d] of the LORD. All these things amazed her.

6So she said to King Solomon, "What I heard in my own country about your achievements and wisdom is true. 7I could not believe it then, but now I have come and seen it with my own eyes. I was not told even half of it! Your wisdom and wealth are much greater than I had heard. 8Your men and officers are very happy, because in always serving you, they are able to hear your wisdom. 9Praise the LORD your God, who was pleased to make you king of Israel. The LORD has constant love for Israel, so he made you king to keep justice and to rule fairly."

10Then she gave the king about 4 tonnes of gold and many spices and jewels. No one since that time has brought more spices than the queen of Sheba gave to King Solomon.

11(Hiram's ships brought gold from Ophir, as well as much juniper wood and jewels. 12Solomon used the juniper wood to build supports for the Temple of the LORD and the palace, and to make harps and lyres[d] for the musicians. Such fine juniper wood has not been brought in or been seen since that time.)

13King Solomon gave the queen of Sheba everything she wanted and asked for, in addition to what he had already given her of his wealth. Then she and her servants returned to her own country.

Solomon's Wealth

14Every year King Solomon received about 23 tonnes of gold. 15Besides that, he also received gold from the traders and merchants, as well as from the kings of Arabia and governors of the land.

16King Solomon made 200 large shields of hammered gold, each of which contained about 7 kilogrammes of gold. 17He also made 300 smaller shields of hammered gold, each of which contained about 2 kilogrammes of gold. The king put them in the Palace of the Forest of Lebanon.

18The king built a large throne of ivory and covered it with fine gold. 19The throne had six steps on it, and its back was round at the top. There were armrests on both sides of the chair, and each armrest had a lion beside it. 20Twelve lions stood on the six steps, one lion at each end of each step. Nothing like this had ever been made for any other kingdom. 21All of Solomon's drinking cups, as well as the dishes in the Palace of the Forest of Lebanon, were made of pure gold. Nothing was made from silver, because silver was not so valuable in Solomon's time.

22King Solomon also had many trading ships at sea, along with Hiram's ships. Every three years the ships returned, bringing back gold, silver, ivory, apes and baboons.

23So Solomon had more riches and wisdom than all the other kings on earth. 24People everywhere wanted to see King Solomon and listen to the wisdom God had given him. 25Every year those who came brought gifts of silver and gold, clothes, weapons, spices, horses and mules.

26Solomon had 1,400 chariots and 12,000 horses. He kept some in special cities for the chariots, and others he kept with him in Jerusalem. 27In Jerusalem Solomon made silver as common as stones and cedar trees as common as the fig trees on the western hills. 28He brought in horses from Egypt and Kue. His traders bought them in Kue. 29A chariot from Egypt cost about 600 pieces of silver, and a horse cost nearly 150 pieces of silver. Solomon's traders also sold horses and chariots to all the kings of the Hittites and the Arameans.

Solomon's Many Wives

11 King Solomon loved many women who were not from Israel. He loved the daughter of the king of Egypt, as well as women of the Moabites, Ammonites, Edomites, Sidonians and Hittites. 2The LORD had told the Israelites, "You must not marry people of other nations. If you do, they will cause you to follow their gods." But Solomon fell in love with these women. 3He had 700 wives who were from royal families and 300 slave women[d] who gave birth to his children. His wives caused him to turn away from God. 4As Solomon grew old, his wives caused him to follow other gods. He did not follow the LORD completely as his father David had done. 5Solomon worshipped Ashtoreth,[d] the goddess of the people of Sidon, and Molech,[d] the hated god of the Ammonites. 6So Solomon did what the LORD said was wrong and did not follow the LORD completely as his father David had done.

7 On a hill east of Jerusalem, Solomon built two places for worship. One was a place to worship Chemosh,[d] the hated god of the Moabites, and the other was a place to worship Molech, the hated god of the Ammonites. 8 Solomon did the same thing for all his foreign wives so they could burn incense[d] and offer sacrifices to their gods.

9 The LORD had appeared to Solomon twice, but the king turned away from following the LORD, the God of Israel. The LORD was angry with Solomon, 10 because he had commanded Solomon not to follow other gods. But Solomon did not obey the LORD's command. 11 So the LORD said to Solomon, "Because you have chosen to break your agreement with me and have not obeyed my commands, I will tear your kingdom away from you and give it to one of your officers. 12 But I will not take it away while you are alive because of my love for your father David. I will tear it away from your son when he becomes king. 13 I will not tear away all the kingdom from him, but I will leave him one tribe[d] to rule. I will do this because of David, my servant, and because of Jerusalem, the city I have chosen."

Solomon's Enemies

14 The LORD caused Hadad the Edomite, a member of the family of the king of Edom, to become Solomon's enemy. 15 Earlier, David had defeated Edom. When Joab, the commander of David's army, went into Edom to bury the dead, he killed all the males. 16 Joab and all the Israelites stayed in Edom for six months and killed every male in Edom. 17 At that time Hadad was only a young boy, so he ran away to Egypt with some of his father's officers. 18 They left Midian and went to Paran, where they were joined by other men. Then they all went to Egypt to see the king, who gave Hadad a house, some food and some land.

19 The king liked Hadad so much he gave Hadad a wife—the sister of Tahpenes, the king's wife. 20 They had a son named Genubath. Queen Tahpenes brought him up in the royal palace with the king's own children.

21 While he was in Egypt, Hadad heard that David had died and that Joab, the commander of the army, was dead also. So Hadad said to the king, "Let me go; I will return to my own country."

22 "Why do you want to go back to your own country?" the king asked. "What haven't I given you here?"

"Nothing," Hadad answered, "but please, let me go."

23 God also caused another man to be Solomon's enemy—Rezon son of Eliada. Rezon had run away from his master, Hadadezer king of Zobah. 24 After David defeated the army of Zobah, Rezon gathered some men and became the leader of a small army. They went to Damascus and settled there, and Rezon became king of Damascus. 25 Rezon ruled Aram, and he hated Israel. So he was an enemy of Israel all the time Solomon was alive. Both Rezon and Hadad made trouble for Israel.

26 Jeroboam son of Nebat was one of Solomon's officers. He was an Ephraimite from the town of Zeredah, and he was the son of a widow named Zeruah. Jeroboam turned against the king.

27 This is the story of how Jeroboam turned against the king. Solomon was filling in the land and repairing the wall of Jerusalem, the city of David, his father. 28 Jeroboam was a capable man, and Solomon saw that this young man was a good worker. So Solomon put him over all the workers from the tribes[d] of Ephraim and Manasseh.

29 One day as Jeroboam was leaving Jerusalem, Ahijah, the prophet[d] from Shiloh, who was wearing a new coat, met him on the road. The two men were alone out in the country. 30 Ahijah took his new coat and tore it into twelve pieces. 31 Then he said to Jeroboam, "Take ten pieces of this coat for yourself. The LORD, the God of Israel, says: 'I will tear the kingdom away from Solomon and give you ten tribes. 32 But I will allow him to control one tribe. I will do this for the sake of my servant David and for Jerusalem, the city I have chosen from all the tribes of Israel. 33 I will do this because Solomon has stopped following me and has worshipped the Sidonian god Ashtoreth,[d] the Moabite god Chemosh,[d] and the Ammonite god Molech. Solomon has not obeyed me by doing what I said is right and obeying my laws and commands, as his father David did.

34 " 'But I will not take all the kingdom away from Solomon. I will let him rule all his life because of my servant David, whom I chose, who obeyed all my commands and laws. 35 But I will take the kingdom away from his son, and I will allow you to rule over the ten tribes. 36 I will allow Solomon's son to continue to rule over one tribe so that there will always be a descendant of David, my servant, in Jerusalem, the city where I chose to be worshipped. 37 But I will make you rule over everything you want. You will rule over all of Israel, 38 and I will always be with you if you do what I say is right. You must obey all my commands. If you obey my laws and commands as David did, I will be with you. I will make your family a lasting family of kings, as I did for David, and give Israel to you. 39 I will punish David's children because of this, but I will not punish them for ever.' "

Solomon's Death

40Solomon tried to kill Jeroboam, but he ran
away to Egypt, to Shishak king of Egypt, where
he stayed until Solomon died.
41Everything else King Solomon did, and the
wisdom he showed, is written in the book of the
history of Solomon. 42Solomon ruled in Jerusalem
over all Israel for 40 years. 43Then he died and
was buried in Jerusalem, the city of David, his
father. And his son Rehoboam became king in
his place.

Israel Turns Against Rehoboam

12 Rehoboam went to Shechem, where all
the Israelites had gone to make him king.
2Jeroboam son of Nebat was still in Egypt, where
he had gone to escape from Solomon. When
Jeroboam heard about Rehoboam being made
king, he was living in Egypt. 3After the people
sent for him, he and the people went to Reho-
boam and said to him, 4"Your father forced us to
work very hard. Now, make it easier for us, and
don't make us work as hard as he did. Then we
will serve you."
5Rehoboam answered, "Go away for three
days, and then come back to me." So the people
left.
6King Rehoboam asked the elders who had ad-
vised Solomon during his lifetime, "How do you
think I should answer these people?"
7They said, "You should be like a servant to
them today. If you serve them and give them a
kind answer, they will serve you always."
8But Rehoboam rejected this advice. Instead,
he asked the young men who had grown up with
him and who served as his advisers. 9Rehoboam
asked them, "What is your advice? How should
we answer these people who said, 'Don't make
us work as hard as your father did'?"
10The young men who had grown up with
him answered, "Those people said to you, 'Your
father forced us to work very hard. Now make
our work easier.' You should tell them, 'My little
finger is bigger than my father's legs. 11He forced
you to work hard, but I will make you work
even harder. My father beat you with whips, but
I will beat you with whips that have sharp
points.' "
12Rehoboam had told the people, "Come back
to me in three days." So after three days Jero-
boam and all the people returned to Rehoboam.
13King Rehoboam spoke cruel words to them,
because he had rejected the advice the elders
had given him. 14He followed the advice of the
young men and said to the people, "My father
forced you to work hard, but I will make you
work even harder. My father beat you with
whips, but I will beat you with whips that have
sharp points." 15So the king did not listen to
the people. The LORD caused this to happen to
keep the promise he had made to Jeroboam
son of Nebat through Ahijah, a prophet[d] from
Shiloh.
16When all the Israelites saw that the new
king refused to listen to them, they said to the
king,

"We have no share in David!
    We have no part in the son of Jesse!
People of Israel, let's go to our own homes!
    Let David's son rule his own people!"

So the Israelites went home. 17But Rehoboam
still ruled over the Israelites who lived in the
towns of Judah.
18Adoniram was in charge of the people who
were forced to work. When Rehoboam sent him
to the people of Israel, they threw stones at him
until he died. But King Rehoboam ran to his char-
iot and escaped to Jerusalem. 19Since then, Israel
has been against the family of David.

> **Sidelight** When the kingdom was divided (1 Kings 12:16–19), Israel (the Northern Kingdom) was stronger economically, had more people, controlled major roads, and possessed the best land. Judah was smaller and had fewer resources. Yet Judah survived about 150 years longer than Israel. It didn't face as many attacks from hostile nations, and more of the kings followed God's leadership.

20When all the Israelites heard that Jeroboam
had returned, they called him to a meeting and
made him king over all Israel. Only the tribe[d] of
Judah continued to follow the family of David.
21When Rehoboam arrived in Jerusalem, he
gathered 180,000 of the best soldiers from the
tribes of Judah and Benjamin. As son of Solo-
mon, Rehoboam wanted to fight the people of
Israel to take back his kingdom.
22But God spoke his word to Shemaiah, a man
of God, saying, 23"Speak to Solomon's son Reho-
boam, the king of Judah, and to all the people of
Judah and Benjamin and the rest of the people.
Say to them, 24'The LORD says you must not go to
war against your brothers, the Israelites. Every
one of you should go home, because I made
all these things happen.' " So they obeyed the
LORD's command and went home as the LORD
had commanded.
25Then Jeroboam made Shechem in the moun-
tains of Ephraim a very strong city, and he lived
there. He also went to the city of Peniel and
made it stronger.

Jeroboam Builds Golden Calves

26Jeroboam said to himself, "The kingdom will probably go back to David's family. 27If the people continue going to the Temple[d] of the LORD in Jerusalem to offer sacrifices, they will want to be ruled again by Rehoboam. Then they will kill me and follow Rehoboam king of Judah."

28King Jeroboam asked for advice. Then he made two golden calves. "It is too long a journey for you to go to Jerusalem to worship," he said to the people. "Israel, here are your gods who brought you out of Egypt." 29Jeroboam put one golden calf in the city of Bethel and the other in the city of Dan. 30This became a very great sin, because the people travelled as far as Dan to worship the calf there.

31Jeroboam built temples on the places of worship. He also chose priests from all the people, not just from the tribe[d] of Levi. 32And he started a new festival on the fifteenth day of the eighth month, just like the festival in Judah. During that time the king offered sacrifices on the altar, along with sacrifices to the calves in Bethel he had made. He also chose priests in Bethel to serve at the places of worship he had made. 33So Jeroboam chose his own time for a festival for the Israelites—the fifteenth day of the eighth month. During that time he offered sacrifices on the altar he had built in Bethel. He set up a festival for the Israelites and offered sacrifices on the altar.

The Man of God Speaks Against Bethel

13 The LORD commanded a man of God from Judah to go to Bethel. When he arrived, Jeroboam was standing by the altar to offer a sacrifice. 2The LORD had commanded the man of God to speak against the altar. The man said, "Altar, altar, the LORD says to you: 'David's family will have a son named Josiah. The priests for the places of worship now make their sacrifices on you, but Josiah will sacrifice those priests on you. Human bones will be burned on you.' " 3That same day the man of God gave proof that these things would happen. "This is the LORD's sign that this will happen," he said. "This altar will break apart, and the ashes on it will fall to the ground."

4When King Jeroboam heard what the man of God said about the altar in Bethel, the king raised his hand from the altar and pointed at the man. "Take him!" he said. But when the king said this, his arm was paralysed, and he could not move it. 5The altar also broke into pieces, and its ashes fell to the ground. This was the sign the LORD had told the man of God to give.

6Then the king said to the man of God, "Please pray to the LORD your God for me, and ask him to heal my arm."

So the man of God prayed to the LORD, and the king's arm was healed, becoming as it was before.

7Then the king said to the man of God, "Please come home and eat with me, and I will give you a gift."

8But the man of God answered the king, "Even if you gave me half of your kingdom, I would not go with you. I will not eat or drink anything in this place. 9The LORD commanded me not to eat or drink anything nor to return on the same road by which I came." 10So he took a different road and did not return on the same road by which he had come to Bethel.

11Now an old prophet[d] was living in Bethel. His sons came and told him what the man of God had done there that day. They also told their father what he had said to King Jeroboam. 12The father asked, "Which road did he use when he left?" So his sons showed him the road the man of God from Judah had taken. 13Then the prophet told his sons to put a saddle on his donkey. So they saddled the donkey, and he left.

14He went after the man of God and found him sitting under an oak tree. The prophet asked, "Are you the man of God who came from Judah?"

The man answered, "Yes, I am."

15The prophet said, "Please come home and eat with me."

16"I can't go home with you," the man of God answered. "I can't eat or drink with you in this place. 17The LORD said to me, 'Don't eat or drink anything there or return on the same road by which you came.' "

18Then the old prophet said, "But I also am a prophet like you." Then he told a lie. He said, "An angel from the LORD came to me and told me to bring you to my home. He said you should eat and drink with me." 19So the man of God went to the old prophet's house, and he ate and drank with him there.

20While they were sitting at the table, the LORD spoke his word to the old prophet. 21The old prophet cried out to the man of God from Judah, "The LORD said you did not obey him! He said you did not do what the LORD your God commanded you. 22The LORD commanded you not to eat or drink anything in this place, but you came back and ate and drank. So your body will not be buried in your family grave."

23After the man of God finished eating and drinking, the prophet put a saddle on his donkey for him, and the man left. 24As he was travelling home, a lion attacked and killed him. His body lay on the road, with the donkey and the lion standing nearby. 25Some men who were travelling on that road saw the body and the lion standing nearby. So they went to the city where the old prophet lived and told what they had seen.

[26]The old prophet who had brought back the man of God heard what had happened. "It is the man of God who did not obey the LORD's command," he said. "So the LORD sent a lion to kill him, just as he said he would."

[27]Then the prophet said to his sons, "Put a saddle on my donkey," which they did. [28]The old prophet went out and found the body lying on the road, with the donkey and the lion still standing nearby. The lion had not eaten the body or hurt the donkey. [29]The prophet put the body on his donkey and carried it back to the city to have a time of sadness for him and to bury him. [30]The prophet buried the body in his own family grave, and they were sad for the man of God and said, "Oh, my brother."

[31]After the prophet buried the body, he said to his sons, "When I die, bury me in this same grave. Put my bones next to his. [32]Through him the LORD spoke against the altar at Bethel and against the places of worship in the towns of Samaria. What the LORD spoke through him will certainly come true."

[33]After this incident King Jeroboam did not stop doing evil. He continued to choose priests for the places of worship from among all the people. Anyone who wanted to be a priest for the places of worship was allowed to be one. [34]In this way the family of Jeroboam sinned, and this sin caused its ruin and destruction from the earth.

Jeroboam's Son Dies

14 At that time Jeroboam's son Abijah became very sick. [2]So Jeroboam said to his wife, "Go to Shiloh to see the prophet[d] Ahijah. He is the one who said I would become king of Israel. But dress yourself so people won't know you are my wife. [3]Take the prophet ten loaves of bread, some cakes and a jar of honey. Then ask him what will happen to our son, and he will tell you." [4]So the king's wife did as he said and went to Ahijah's home in Shiloh.

Now Ahijah was very old and blind. [5]The LORD said to him, "Jeroboam's son is sick, and Jeroboam's wife is coming to ask you about him. When she arrives, she will pretend to be someone else." Then the LORD told Ahijah what to say.

[6]When Ahijah heard her walking to the door, he said, "Come in, wife of Jeroboam. Why are you pretending to be someone else? I have bad news for you. [7]Go back and tell Jeroboam that this is what the LORD, the God of Israel, says: 'Jeroboam, I chose you from among all the people and made you the leader of my people Israel. [8]I tore the kingdom away from David's family, and I gave it to you. But you are not like my servant David, who always obeyed my commands and followed me with all his heart. He did only what I said was right. [9]But you have done more evil than anyone who ruled before you. You have stopped following me and have made other gods and idols of metal. This has made me very angry, [10]so I will soon bring disaster to your family. I will kill all the men in your family, both slaves and free men. I will destroy your family as completely as fire burns up manure. [11]Anyone from your family who dies in the city will be eaten by dogs, and those who die in the fields will be eaten by the birds. The LORD has spoken.' "

[12]Then Ahijah said to Jeroboam's wife, "Go home now. As soon as you enter your city, your son will die, [13]and all Israel will be sad for him and bury him. He is the only one of Jeroboam's family who will be buried, because he is the only one in the king's family who pleased the LORD, the God of Israel.

[14]"The LORD will put a new king over Israel, who will destroy Jeroboam's family, and this will happen soon. [15]Then the LORD will punish Israel, which will be like grass moving in the water. The LORD will pull up Israel from this good land, the land he gave their ancestors. He will scatter Israel beyond the Euphrates River, because he is angry with the people. They made the LORD angry when they set up idols to worship Asherah.[d] [16]Jeroboam sinned, and then he made the people of Israel sin. So the LORD will let the people of Israel be defeated."

[17]Then Jeroboam's wife left and returned to Tirzah. As soon as she entered her home, the boy died. [18]After they buried him, all Israel had a time of sadness for him, just as the LORD had said through his servant, the prophet Ahijah.

[19]Everything else Jeroboam did is written in the book of the history of the kings of Israel. He fought wars and continued to rule the people, [20]serving as king for 22 years. Then he died, and his son Nadab became king in his place.

The Death of Rehoboam

[21]Solomon's son Rehoboam was 41 years old when he became king of Judah. His mother was Naamah from Ammon. Rehoboam ruled in Jerusalem for seventeen years. (The LORD had chosen that city from all the land of Israel as the place where he would be worshipped.)

[22]The people of Judah did what the LORD said was wrong. Their sins made the LORD very angry, even more angry than he had been at their ancestors. [23]The people built stone pillars and places to worship gods and Asherah[d] idols on every high hill and under every green tree. [24]There were even male prostitutes[d] in the land. They acted

like the people who had lived in the land before the Israelites. They had done many evil things, and God had taken the land away from them.

[25]During the fifth year Rehoboam was king, Shishak king of Egypt attacked Jerusalem. [26]He took the treasures from the Temple[d] of the LORD and the king's palace. He took everything, even the gold shields Solomon had made. [27]So King Rehoboam made bronze shields to put in their place and gave them to the commanders of the guards for the palace gates. [28]Whenever the king went to the Temple of the LORD, the guards carried the shields. Later, they would put them back in the guardroom.

[29]Everything else King Rehoboam did is written in the book of the history of the kings of Judah. [30]There was hostility between Rehoboam and Jeroboam continually. [31]Rehoboam, son of Naamah from Ammon, died and was buried with his ancestors in Jerusalem, and his son Abijah became king in his place.

Abijah King of Judah

15 Abijah became king of Judah during the eighteenth year Jeroboam son of Nebat was king of Israel. [2]Abijah ruled in Jerusalem for three years. His mother was Maacah daughter of Abishalom. [3]He did all the same sins his father before him had done. Abijah was not faithful to the LORD his God as David, his great-grandfather, had been. [4]Because the LORD loved David, the LORD gave him a kingdom in Jerusalem and allowed him to have a son to be king after him. The LORD also kept Jerusalem safe. [5]David always did what the LORD said was right and obeyed his commands all his life, except the one time when David sinned against Uriah the Hittite.

[6]There was war between Abijah and Jeroboam during Abijah's lifetime. [7]Everything else Abijah did is written in the book of the history of the kings of Judah. During the time Abijah ruled, there was war between Abijah and Jeroboam. [8]Abijah died and was buried in Jerusalem, and his son Asa became king in his place.

Asa King of Judah

[9]During the twentieth year Jeroboam was king of Israel, Asa became king of Judah. [10]His grandmother's name was Maacah, the daughter of Abishalom. Asa ruled in Jerusalem for 41 years.

[11]Asa did what the LORD said was right, as his ancestor David had done. [12]He forced the male prostitutes[d] at the worship places to leave the country. He also took away the idols that his ancestors had made. [13]His grandmother Maacah had made a terrible Asherah[d] idol, so Asa removed her from being queen mother. He cut down that idol and burned it in the Kidron Valley. [14]The places of worship to gods were not removed. Even so, Asa was faithful to the LORD all his life. [15]Asa brought into the Temple[d] of the LORD the gifts he and his father had given: gold, silver and utensils.

[16]There was war between Asa and Baasha king of Israel all the time they were kings. [17]Baasha attacked Judah, and he made the town of Ramah strong so he could keep people from leaving or entering Judah, Asa's country.

[18]Asa took the rest of the silver and gold from the treasuries of the Temple of the LORD and his own palace and gave it to his officers. Then he sent them to Ben-Hadad son of Tabrimmon, who was the son of Hezion. Ben-Hadad was the king of Aram and ruled in the city of Damascus. Asa said, [19]"Let there be a treaty between you and me as there was between my father and your father. I am sending you a gift of silver and gold. Break your treaty with Baasha king of Israel so he will leave my land."

[20]Ben-Hadad agreed with King Asa, so he sent the commanders of his armies to attack the towns of Israel. They defeated the towns of Ijon, Dan and Abel Beth Maacah, as well as all Galilee and the area of Naphtali. [21]When Baasha heard about these attacks, he stopped building up Ramah and returned to Tirzah. [22]Then King Asa gave an order to all the people of Judah; everyone had to help. They carried away all the stones and wood Baasha had been using in Ramah, and they used them to build up Geba and Mizpah in the land of Benjamin.

[23]Everything else Asa did—his victories and the cities he built—is written in the book of the history of the kings of Judah. When he became old, he got a disease in his feet. [24]After Asa died, he was buried with his ancestors in Jerusalem, the city of David, his ancestor. Then Jehoshaphat, Asa's son, became king in his place.

Nadab King of Israel

[25]Nadab son of Jeroboam became king of Israel during the second year Asa was king of Judah. Nadab was king of Israel for two years, [26]and he did what the LORD said was wrong. Jeroboam had led the people of Israel to sin, and Nadab sinned in the same way as his father Jeroboam.

[27]Baasha son of Ahijah, from the tribe[d] of Issachar, made plans to kill Nadab. Nadab and all Israel were attacking the Philistine town of Gibbethon, so Baasha killed Nadab there. [28]This happened during Asa's third year as king of Judah, and Baasha became the next king of Israel.

Baasha King of Israel

[29]As soon as Baasha became king, he killed all of Jeroboam's family, leaving no one in Jeroboam's

family alive. He destroyed them all as the LORD had said would happen through his servant Ahijah from Shiloh. [30]King Jeroboam had sinned very much and had led the people of Israel to sin, so he made the LORD, the God of Israel, very angry.

[31]Everything else Nadab did is written in the book of the history of the kings of Israel. [32]There was war between Asa king of Judah and Baasha king of Israel all the time they ruled.

[33]Baasha son of Ahijah became king of Israel during Asa's third year as king of Judah. Baasha ruled in Tirzah for 24 years, [34]and he did what the LORD said was wrong. Jeroboam had led the people of Israel to sin, and Baasha sinned in the same way as Jeroboam.

16 Jehu son of Hanani spoke the word of the LORD against King Baasha. [2]The LORD said, "You were nothing, but I took you and made you a leader over my people Israel. But you have followed the ways of Jeroboam and have led my people Israel to sin. Their sins have made me angry, [3]so, Baasha, I will soon destroy you and your family. I will do to you what I did to the family of Jeroboam son of Nebat. [4]Anyone from your family who dies in the city will be eaten by dogs, and anyone from your family who dies in the fields will be eaten by birds."

[5]Everything else Baasha did and all his victories are written down in the book of the history of the kings of Israel. [6]So Baasha died and was buried in Tirzah, and his son Elah became king in his place.

[7]The LORD spoke his word against Baasha and his family through the prophet[d] Jehu son of Hanani. Baasha had done many things the LORD said were wrong, which made the LORD very angry. He did the same evil deeds that Jeroboam's family had done before him. The LORD also spoke against Baasha because he killed all of Jeroboam's family.

Elah King of Israel

[8]Elah son of Baasha became king of Israel during Asa's twenty-sixth year as king of Judah, and Elah ruled in Tirzah for two years.

[9]Zimri, one of Elah's officers, commanded half of Elah's chariots. Zimri made plans against Elah while the king was in Tirzah, getting drunk at Arza's home. (Arza was in charge of the palace at Tirzah.) [10]Zimri went into Arza's house and killed Elah during Asa's twenty-seventh year as king of Judah. Then Zimri became king of Israel in Elah's place.

Zimri King of Israel

[11]As soon as Zimri became king, he killed all of Baasha's family, not allowing any of Baasha's family or friends to live. [12]So Zimri destroyed all of Baasha's family just as the LORD had said it would happen through the prophet[d] Jehu. [13]Baasha and his son Elah sinned and led the people of Israel to sin, and they made the LORD, the God of Israel, angry because of their worthless idols.

[14]Everything else Elah did is written in the book of the history of the kings of Israel.

[15]So during Asa's twenty-seventh year as king of Judah, Zimri became king of Israel and ruled in Tirzah seven days.

The army of Israel was camped near Gibbethon, a Philistine town. [16]The men in the camp heard that Zimri had made secret plans against King Elah and had killed him. So that day in the camp they made Omri, the commander of the army, king over Israel. [17]So Omri and all the Israelite army left Gibbethon and attacked Tirzah. [18]When Zimri saw that the city had been captured, he went into the palace and set it on fire, burning the palace and himself with it. [19]So Zimri died because he had sinned by doing what the LORD said was wrong. Jeroboam had led the people of Israel to sin, and Zimri sinned in the same way as Jeroboam.

[20]Everything else Zimri did and the story of how he turned against King Elah are written down in the book of the history of the kings of Israel.

Omri King of Israel

[21]The people of Israel were divided into two groups. Half of the people wanted Tibni son of Ginath to be king, while the other half wanted Omri. [22]Omri's followers were stronger than the followers of Tibni son of Ginath, so Tibni died and Omri became king.

[23]Omri became king of Israel during the thirty-first year Asa was king of Judah. Omri ruled Israel for twelve years, six of those years in the city of Tirzah. [24]He bought the hill of Samaria from Shemer for about 6,000 pieces of silver. Omri built a city on that hill and called it Samaria after the name of its earlier owner, Shemer.

Sidelight King Omri doesn't get much press in the Bible (1 Kings 16:23–28), but he probably was one of the most powerful leaders of the Northern Kingdom. According to other sources, he established a strong rule and conquered the Moabites, long-term enemies. But, the Bible says, "he did more evil than all the kings who came before him".

[25]But Omri did what the LORD said was wrong; he did more evil than all the kings who came before him. [26]Jeroboam son of Nebat had led the people of Israel to sin, and Omri sinned in the

same way as Jeroboam. The Israelites made
the LORD, the God of Israel, very angry because
they worshipped worthless idols.
27Everything else Omri did and all his suc-
cesses are written in the book of the history of
the kings of Israel. 28So Omri died and was
buried in Samaria, and his son Ahab became
king in his place.

Ahab King of Israel

29Ahab son of Omri became king of Israel dur-
ing Asa's thirty-eighth year as king of Judah, and
Ahab ruled Israel in the city of Samaria for 22
years. 30More than any king before him, Ahab
son of Omri did many things the LORD said were
wrong. 31He sinned in the same ways as Jero-
boam son of Nebat, but he did even worse things.
He married Jezebel daughter of Ethbaal, the king
of Sidon. Then Ahab began to serve Baal[d] and
worship him. 32He built a temple in Samaria for
worshipping Baal and put an altar there for Baal.
33Ahab also made an idol for worshipping Ashe-
rah.[d] He did more things to make the LORD, the
God of Israel, angry than all the other kings be-
fore him.
34During the time of Ahab, Hiel from Bethel
rebuilt the city of Jericho. It cost Hiel the life of
Abiram, his oldest son, to begin work on the city,
and it cost the life of Segub, his youngest son, to
build the city gates.[n] This happened just as the
LORD, speaking through Joshua son of Nun, said
it would happen.[n]

Elijah Stops the Rain

17 Now Elijah the Tishbite was a prophet[d]
from the settlers in Gilead. "I serve the
LORD, the God of Israel," Elijah said to Ahab. "As
surely as the LORD lives, no rain or dew will fall
during the next few years unless I command it."
2Then the LORD spoke his word to Elijah:
3"Leave this place and go east and hide near
Kerith Ravine east of the Jordan River. 4You may
drink from the stream, and I have commanded
ravens to bring you food there." 5So Elijah did
what the LORD said; he went to Kerith Ravine,
east of the Jordan, and lived there. 6The birds
brought Elijah bread and meat every morning and
evening, and he drank water from the stream.
7After a while the stream dried up because
there was no rain. 8Then the LORD spoke his word
to Elijah, 9"Go to Zarephath in Sidon and live
there. I have commanded a widow there to take
care of you."
10So Elijah went to Zarephath. When he reached
the town gate, he saw a widow gathering wood
for a fire. Elijah asked her, "Would you bring me
a little water in a cup so I may have a drink."
11As she was going to get his water, Elijah said,
"Please bring me a piece of bread, too."
12The woman answered, "As surely as the LORD
your God lives, I have no bread. I have only a
handful of flour in a jar and only a little olive oil
in a jug. I came here to gather some wood so I
could go home and cook our last meal. My son
and I will eat it and then die from hunger."
13"Don't worry," Elijah said to her. "Go home
and cook your food as you have said. But first
make a small loaf of bread from the flour you
have, and bring it to me. Then cook something
for yourself and your son. 14The LORD, the God
of Israel, says, 'That jar of flour will never be
empty, and the jug will always have oil in it, until
the day the LORD sends rain to the land.' "
15So the woman went home and did what Eli-
jah told her to do. And the woman and her son
and Elijah had enough food every day. 16The jar
of flour and the jug of oil were never empty, just
as the LORD, through Elijah, had promised.

Elijah Brings a Boy Back to Life

17Some time later the son of the woman who
owned the house became sick. He grew worse
and worse and finally stopped breathing. 18The
woman said to Elijah, "Man of God, what have
you done to me? Did you come here to remind
me of my sin and to kill my son?"
19Elijah said to her, "Give me your son." Elijah
took the boy from her, carried him upstairs and
laid him on the bed in the room where he was
staying. 20Then he prayed to the LORD: "LORD my
God, this widow is letting me stay in her house.
Why have you done this terrible thing to her and
caused her son to die?" 21Then Elijah lay on top
of the boy three times. He prayed to the LORD,
"LORD my God, let this boy live again!"
22The LORD answered Elijah's prayer; the boy
began breathing again and was alive. 23Elijah car-
ried the boy downstairs and gave him to his
mother and said, "See! Your son is alive!"
24"Now I know you really are a man from
God," the woman said to Elijah. "I know that
the LORD truly speaks through you!"

Elijah Kills the Prophets of Baal

18 During the third year without rain, the
LORD spoke his word to Elijah: "Go and
meet King Ahab, and I will soon send rain." 2So
Elijah went to meet Ahab.

city gate People came here to conduct business. Public meetings and court cases were also held here.
the LORD . . . happen When Joshua destroyed Jericho, he said whoever rebuilt the city would lose his oldest and youngest sons. See Joshua 6:26.

By this time there was no food in Samaria.
3King Ahab sent for Obadiah, who was in charge
of the king's palace. (Obadiah was a true follower
of the LORD. 4When Jezebel was killing all the
LORD's prophets,[d] Obadiah hid 100 of them in
two caves, 50 in one cave and 50 in another. He
also brought them food and water.) 5Ahab said to
Obadiah, "Let's check every spring and valley in
the land. Maybe we can find enough grass to
keep our horses and mules alive and not have to
kill our animals." 6So each one chose a part of the
country to search; Ahab went in one direction
and Obadiah in another.
7While Obadiah was on his way, Elijah met
him. Obadiah recognised Elijah, so he bowed
down to the ground and said, "Elijah? Is it really
you, master?"
8"Yes," Elijah answered. "Go and tell your
master that I am here."
9Then Obadiah said, "What wrong have I
done for you to hand me over to Ahab like this?
He will put me to death. 10As surely as the LORD
your God lives, the king has sent people to every
country to search for you. If the ruler said you
were not there, Ahab forced the ruler to swear
you could not be found in his country. 11Now
you want me to go to my master and tell him,
'Elijah is here'? 12The Spirit[d] of the LORD may
carry you to some other place after I leave. If
I go and tell King Ahab you are here, and he
comes and doesn't find you, he will kill me! I
have followed the LORD since I was a boy.
13Haven't you been told what I did? When
Jezebel was killing the LORD's prophets, I hid 100
of them, 50 in one cave and 50 in another. I
brought them food and water. 14Now you want
me to go and tell my master you are here? He
will kill me!"

HUNGER AND POVERTY

Letting God Use You

John went to help at the rescue mission mainly because someone had asked him to go. He had never done anything like this before in all of his fifteen years. But a friend had asked him to help out this Sunday, and John couldn't think of any reason not to. So he went.

When they got there, John and his friends did simple tasks – preparing food, setting places, washing dishes, cleaning tables. They just helped where they were needed.

The rescue mission was run-down and dirty. The people they served were dirty from sleeping rough on the streets, and they didn't seem to appreciate what John and his friends were doing for them. Some of John's friends didn't go back when they were asked to help out again.

But John went back. And he would go again.

He felt that he was needed there, and it was rewarding to give to people when you knew that they couldn't pay you back.

John was impressed with the staff at the rescue mission, and with their attitude towards the people they served. Even though they acted hard at times, they really cared for the people who came there.

Hunger and poverty have existed in the world almost since the beginning of time. God wants Christians – every Christian – to offer help and God's love to the poor and hungry. God even used the great prophet Elijah to help a widow and her son in **1 Kings 17:8–16**.

- What's the difference between the widow in this passage and the people John helped? What motives did John have for helping the poor? What motives did Elijah have for helping the widow?
- How does God keep the "jars of flour and jugs of oil" full for poor and hungry people today? What role can you play in providing food for hungry people?

Consider . . .

- skipping dinner tonight and spending that time praying for poor and hungry people.
- following John's example by volunteering to work in a soup kitchen or a homeless shelter.

For more, see . . .

- Exodus 16:1–15 (p.74)
- John 6:30–35 (p.1105)
- Mark 6:34–44 (p.1007)

15 Elijah answered, "As surely as the LORD All-
powerful lives, whom I serve, I will be seen by
Ahab today."
16 So Obadiah went to Ahab and told him where
Elijah was. Then Ahab went to meet Elijah.
17 When he saw Elijah, he asked, "Is it you—
the biggest troublemaker in Israel?"
18 Elijah answered, "I have not made trouble
in Israel. You and your father's family have made
all this trouble by not obeying the LORD's com-
mands. You have gone after the Baals.[d] 19 Now tell
all Israel to meet me at Mount Carmel. Also bring
the 450 prophets of Baal and the 400 prophets of
Asherah,[d] who eat at Jezebel's table."
20 So Ahab called all the Israelites and those
prophets to Mount Carmel. 21 Elijah approached
the people and said, "How long will you not de-
cide between two choices? If the LORD is the true
God, follow him, but if Baal is the true God, fol-
low him!" But the people said nothing.
22 Elijah said, "I am the only prophet of the LORD
here, but there are 450 prophets of Baal. 23 Bring
two bulls. Let the prophets of Baal choose one
bull and kill it and cut it into pieces. Then let
them put the meat on the wood, but they are not
to set fire to it. I will prepare the other bull, put-
ting the meat on the wood but not setting fire to
it. 24 You prophets of Baal, pray to your god, and
I will pray to the LORD. The god who answers by
setting fire to his wood is the true God."
All the people agreed that this was a good idea.
25 Then Elijah said to the prophets of Baal,
"There are many of you, so you go first. Choose
a bull and prepare it. Pray to your god, but don't
start the fire."

Sidelight The 450 prophets of Baal had a home team advantage in the contest against Elijah and God (1 Kings 18:20–46). Baal was considered the god of Mt Carmel, and he was also the rain-giving god. When Elijah was the one who prayed and brought fire and ended the drought, the false prophets might have died of embarrassment if Elijah hadn't executed them first.

SUFFERING

What am I Doing Wrong?

For as long as she could remember, Louise had believed in God. Her whole family were very involved in the church, and at home God was a huge part of their lives.

Then, things began to change in Louise's house. Her parents started arguing, and eventually they told Louise and her brother they were getting a divorce. Louise was devastated; she didn't understand what was happening. The following month Louise's gran died and it felt like things couldn't get any worse. But soon Louise found out that her dad had a gambling problem and that they were thousands of pounds in debt. Her mum seemed to be getting sick all the time and Louise and her brother spent a lot of time visiting her in hospital.

Although the rest of her family didn't seem to care about God any more, Louise did. She still went to church and youth group; she really tried to read her Bible and she certainly prayed lots. Sometimes though, Louise couldn't help being angry with God. Why were all these awful things happening to her? Why had it all gone so wrong? Was it something she had done?

In **1 Kings 17:17–24** a widow was also going through a really hard time when her son fell ill and died.

- Why did the widow think her son was ill? Did Louise feel the same way?
- What did the widow learn from her son coming back to life?

Consider . . .

- whether there are any difficult situations in your life that you need to trust God with.
- keeping a journal and writing down all that is happening in your life. You'll be amazed, when you look back, at how much God was working in your life, even through the hard times.

For more, see . . .

- Isaiah 53 (p.697)
- Romans 5:1–5 (p.1190)
- John 9:1–7 (p.1111)

26So they took the bull that was given to them and prepared it. They prayed to Baal from morning until noon, shouting, "Baal, answer us!" But there was no sound, and no one answered. They danced around the altar they had built.

27At noon Elijah began to make fun of them. "Pray louder!" he said. "If Baal really is a god, maybe he is thinking, or busy, or travelling! Maybe he is sleeping so you will have to wake him!" 28The prophets prayed louder, cutting themselves with swords and spears until their blood flowed, which was the way they worshipped. 29The afternoon passed, and the prophets continued to act like this until it was time for the evening sacrifice. But no voice was heard; Baal did not answer, and no one paid attention.

30Then Elijah said to all the people, "Now come to me." So they gathered around him, and Elijah rebuilt the altar of the LORD, which had been torn down. 31He took twelve stones, one stone for each of the twelve tribes,[d] the number of Jacob's sons. (The LORD changed Jacob's name to Israel.) 32Elijah used these stones to rebuild the altar in honour of the LORD. Then he dug a ditch around the altar that was big enough to hold about 14 litres of seed. 33Elijah put the wood on the altar, cut the bull into pieces and laid the pieces on the wood. 34Then he said, "Fill four jars with water, and pour it on the meat and on the wood." Then Elijah said, "Do it again," and they did it again. Then he said, "Do it a third time," and they did it the third time. 35So the water ran off the altar and filled the ditch.

36At the time for the evening sacrifice, the prophet Elijah went near the altar. "LORD, you are the God of Abraham, Isaac and Israel," he prayed. "Prove that you are the God of Israel and that I am your servant. Show these people that you commanded me to do all these things. 37LORD, answer my prayer so these people will know that you, LORD, are God and that you will change their minds."

38Then fire from the LORD came down and burned the sacrifice, the wood, the stones and the ground around the altar. It also dried up the water in the ditch. 39When all the people saw this, they fell down to the ground, crying, "The LORD is God! The LORD is God!"

40Then Elijah said, "Capture the prophets of Baal! Don't let any of them run away!" The people captured all the prophets. Then Elijah led them down to the Kishon Valley, where he killed them.

The Rain Comes Again

41Then Elijah said to Ahab, "Now, go, eat and drink, because a heavy rain is coming." 42So King Ahab went to eat and drink. At the same time Elijah climbed to the top of Mount Carmel, where he bent down to the ground with his head between his knees.

43Then Elijah said to his servant, "Go and look towards the sea."

The servant went and looked. "I see nothing," he said.

Elijah told him to go and look again. This happened seven times. 44The seventh time, the servant said, "I see a small cloud, the size of a human fist, coming from the sea."

Elijah told the servant, "Go to Ahab and tell him to get his chariot ready and go home now. Otherwise, the rain will stop him."

Sidelight For a short time, Elijah may have been the fastest runner in the world. Fearing the rain would start while he was on the mountains, Elijah received God's power and ran from Mt Carmel to Jezreel – about ten miles – faster then the king's chariots (1 Kings 18:46). Some people will do anything to keep from getting their hair wet!

45After a short time the sky was covered with dark clouds. The wind began to blow, and soon a heavy rain began to fall. Ahab got in his chariot and started back to Jezreel. 46The LORD gave his power to Elijah, who tightened his clothes around him and ran ahead of King Ahab all the way to Jezreel.

Elijah Runs Away

19 King Ahab told Jezebel everything Elijah had done and how Elijah had killed all the prophets[d] with a sword. 2So Jezebel sent a messenger to Elijah, saying, "May the gods punish me terribly if by this time tomorrow I don't kill you just as you killed those prophets."

3When Elijah heard this, he was afraid and ran for his life, taking his servant with him. When they came to Beersheba in Judah, Elijah left his servant there. 4Then Elijah walked for a whole day into the desert. He sat down under a bush and asked to die. "I have had enough, LORD," he prayed. "Let me die. I am no better than my ancestors." 5Then he lay down under the tree and slept.

Suddenly an angel came to him and touched him. "Get up and eat," the angel said. 6Elijah saw near his head a loaf baked over coals and a jar of water, so he ate and drank. Then he went back to sleep.

7Later the LORD's angel came to him a second time. The angel touched him and said, "Get up and eat. If you don't, the journey will be too hard for you." 8So Elijah got up and ate and drank.

The food made him strong enough to walk for
40 days and nights to Mount Sinai, the mountain
of God. 9There Elijah went into a cave and stayed
all night.
Then the LORD spoke his word to him: "Elijah!
Why are you here?"
10He answered, "LORD God All-powerful, I
have always served you as well as I could. But the
people of Israel have broken their agreement with
you, destroyed your altars and killed your proph-
ets with swords. I am the only prophet left, and
now they are trying to kill me, too."
11The LORD said to Elijah, "Go, stand in front
of me on the mountain, and I will pass by you."
Then a very strong wind blew until it caused the
mountains to fall apart and large rocks to break
in front of the LORD. But the LORD was not in the
wind. After the wind, there was an earthquake,
but the LORD was not in the earthquake. 12After
the earthquake, there was a fire, but the LORD
was not in the fire. After the fire, there was a
quiet, gentle sound. 13When Elijah heard it, he
covered his face with his coat and went out and
stood at the entrance to the cave.
Then a voice said to him, "Elijah! Why are
you here?"
14He answered, "LORD God All-powerful, I have
always served you as well as I could. But the peo-
ple of Israel have broken their agreement with
you, destroyed your altars and killed your proph-
ets with swords. I am the only prophet left, and
now they are trying to kill me, too."

STRESS

I'll Get You For That!

Bullying is a terrible thing. It's more frightening than you can imagine. Let me tell you about Dan . . .

He was fourteen years old and went to the local secondary school. He wasn't particularly strong and his blond hair and blue eyes caught the attention of the tough guys. They started cornering him at break and asking for money. They threatened to beat him up if he didn't bring things to school for them. Dan was fearful, but also angry that people like them existed. But what could he do?

Most days he managed to get some money, or give them his lunch.

One day he had had enough.

A week later, one of his classmates called at his house and asked his mother if Dan was OK.

"What do you mean, 'How is he?'" she replied.

"Well, he hasn't been to school for most of the week and I assumed he was ill," stated his friend.

Dan's mother was shocked and when he came home that night, both his mother and father challenged him.

"Just tell us where you've been? We can't believe you've been playing truant."

Neither of them were angry, just very very concerned.

In the end, Dan explained, in tears, that he'd been standing on the corner of the High Street, trying to pluck up enough courage to jump in front of a car.

"My friend Matt had an accident a while back and it kept him off school for months," he explained.

Dan's parents had no idea of the stress put on an ordinary teenager. They were horrified and soon sorted the situation out.

Read **1 Kings 19:1–5** and see how Elijah was in a similar situation.

- Elijah was no weakling, but how did he cope with the stressful time in the passage?
- How is bullying approached at your school?

Consider . . .

- telling a close friend or respected teacher if you are being bullied.
- making a "loner" at school part of your close group of friends.

For more, see . . .

- Isaiah 51:12–16 (p.695)
- 2 Corinthians 12:8–10 (p.1252)

15The LORD said to him, "Go back on the road
that leads to the desert around Damascus. Enter
that city, and pour olive oil on Hazael to make
him king over Aram. 16Then pour oil on Jehu son
of Nimshi to make him king over Israel. Next,
pour oil on Elisha son of Shaphat from Abel
Meholah to make him a prophet in your place.
17Jehu will kill anyone who escapes from Haz-
ael's sword, and Elisha will kill anyone who
escapes from Jehu's sword. 18I have 7,000 peo-
ple left in Israel who have never bowed down
before Baal [d] and whose mouths have never
kissed his idol."

Elisha Becomes a Prophet

19So Elijah left that place and found Elisha son
of Shaphat ploughing a field with a team of oxen.
He owned twelve teams of oxen and was plough-
ing with the twelfth team. Elijah came up to Eli-
sha, took off his coat and put it on Elisha. 20Then
Elisha left his oxen and ran to follow Elijah. "Let
me kiss my father and my mother goodbye,"
Elisha said. "Then I will go with you."

Elijah answered, "Go back. It does not matter
to me."

21So Elisha went back and took his pair of
oxen and killed them. He used their wooden
yoke [d] for a fire. Then he cooked the meat and
gave it to the people. After they ate it, Elisha left
and followed Elijah and became his helper.

Ben-Hadad and Ahab Go to War

20 Ben-Hadad king of Aram gathered to-
gether all his army. There were 32 kings

LONELINESS

Better Do it Yourself

Struck by the constant news of suffering, poverty and ill health in Africa, Kerry and three of her mates decided that they should do something to help make a difference.

A national charity was holding a postcard campaign to petition the government to help the crisis. This would be the perfect opportunity to raise awareness in the school and do something productive at the same time. The four friends got together to divide up jobs and plan the event.

Kerry would contact the charity and get the info, posters and postcards. Mark would speak to the head teacher and ask permission to speak in assemblies, hand out postcards and put up collection points. Siobhan would organise student volunteers to hand out postcards around the school over the week. Dave would contact the local press to let the community know what was happening at the school and why.

With a week to go, Mark called Kerry and said he hadn't had time to speak to the head. Next was Dave – he hadn't called the paper. And, no surprise to Kerry, it soon came to light that Siobhan hadn't fulfilled her part of the bargain either.

Kerry had only been trying to do a good thing – putting herself out to make a difference. And her mates had just let her down, one by one. Why did no one else care? Frustration, betrayal, anger, but most of all, a total sense of loneliness came over Kerry as she struggled to work out what on earth to do now.

Take a look at **1 Kings 19:11–18**.

- Compare Kerry with Elijah. Why do you think Elijah felt let down and alone?
- God comforted Elijah – not with a big show of awesome power, but with a quiet, gentle sound. How often do you think of God as close and comforting?

Consider . . .

- writing a card of encouragement to someone who you've noticed doing a good job.
- spending time reading the Bible and praying about what God thinks about you. Look up every time God is called "Father" and what the Bible says about his children.

For more, see . . .

- Joshua 1:1–9 (p.202)
- Philippians 4:10–13 (p.1286)
- 2 Kings 6 13–17 (p.351)

with their horses and chariots who went with him and surrounded Samaria and attacked it. 2The king sent messengers into the city to Ahab king of Israel.

This was his message: "Ben-Hadad says, 3'Your silver and gold belong to me, as well as the best of your wives and children.' "

4Ahab king of Israel answered, "My master and king, I agree to what you say. I and everything I have belong to you."

5Then the messengers came to Ahab again. They said, "Ben-Hadad says, 'I told you before that you must give me your silver and gold, your wives and your children. 6About this time tomorrow I will send my men, who will search everywhere in your palace and in the homes of your officers. Whatever they want they will take and carry off.' "

7Then Ahab called a meeting of all the elders of his country. He said, "Ben-Hadad is looking for trouble. First he said I had to give him my wives, my children, my silver and my gold, and I have not refused him."

8The elders and all the people said, "Don't listen to him or agree to this."

9So Ahab said to Ben-Hadad's messengers, "Tell my master the king: 'I will do what you said at first, but I cannot allow this second command.' " And King Ben-Hadad's men carried the message back to him.

10Then Ben-Hadad sent another message to Ahab: "May the gods punish me terribly if I don't completely destroy Samaria. There won't be enough left for each of my men to get a handful of dust!"

11Ahab answered, "Tell Ben-Hadad, 'The man who puts on his armour should not boast. It's the man who lives to take it off who has the right to boast.' "

12Ben-Hadad was drinking in his tent with the other rulers when the message came from Ahab. Ben-Hadad commanded his men to prepare to attack the city, and they moved into place for battle.

13At the same time a prophet[d] came to Ahab king of Israel. The prophet said, "Ahab, the LORD says to you, 'Do you see that big army? I will hand it over to you today so you will know I am the LORD.' "

14Ahab asked, "Who will you use to defeat them?"

The prophet answered, "The LORD says, 'The young officers of the district governors will defeat them.' "

Then the king asked, "Who will command the main army?"

The prophet answered, "You will."

15So Ahab gathered the young officers of the district governors, 232 of them. Then he called together the army of Israel, about 7,000 people in all.

16They marched out at noon, while Ben-Hadad and the 32 rulers helping him were getting drunk in their tents. 17The young officers of the district governors attacked first. Ben-Hadad sent out scouts who told him that soldiers were coming from Samaria. 18Ben-Hadad said, "They may be coming to fight, or they may be coming to ask for peace. In either case capture them alive."

19The young officers of the district governors led the attack, followed by the army of Israel. 20Each officer of Israel killed the man who came against him. The men from Aram ran away as Israel chased them, but Ben-Hadad king of Aram escaped on a horse with some of his horsemen. 21Ahab king of Israel led the army and destroyed the Arameans' horses and chariots. King Ahab thoroughly defeated the Aramean army.

22Then the prophet went to Ahab king of Israel and said, "The king of Aram will attack you again next spring. So go home now and strengthen your army and see what you need to do."

23Meanwhile the officers of Ben-Hadad king of Aram said to him, "The gods of Israel are mountain gods. Since we fought in a mountain area, Israel won. Let's fight them on the flat land, and then we will win. 24This is what you should do. Don't allow the 32 rulers to command the armies, but put other commanders in their places. 25Gather an army like the one that was destroyed and as many horses and chariots as before. We will fight the Israelites on flat land, and then we will win." Ben-Hadad agreed with their advice and did what they said.

26The next spring Ben-Hadad gathered the army of Aram and went up to Aphek to fight against Israel.

27The Israelites also had prepared for war. They marched out to meet the Arameans and camped opposite them. The Israelites looked like two small flocks of goats, but the Arameans covered the area.

28A man of God came to the king of Israel with this message: "The LORD says, 'The people of Aram say that I, the LORD, am a god of the mountains, not a god of the valleys. So I will allow you to defeat this big army, and then you will know I am the LORD.' "

29The armies were camped across from each other for seven days. On the seventh day the battle began. The Israelites killed 100,000 Aramean soldiers in one day. 30The rest of them ran away to the city of Aphek, where a city wall fell on 27,000 of them. Ben-Hadad also ran away to the city and hid in a room.

31His officers said to him, "We have heard that the kings of Israel are trustworthy. Let's dress in rough cloth to show our sadness, and wear ropes on our heads. Then we will go to the king of Israel, and perhaps he will let you live."

32So they dressed in rough cloth and wore ropes on their heads and went to the king of Israel. They said, "Your servant Ben-Hadad says, 'Please let me live.' "

Ahab answered, "Is he still alive? He is my brother."

33Ben-Hadad's men had wanted a sign from Ahab. So when Ahab called Ben-Hadad his brother, they quickly said, "Yes! Ben-Hadad is your brother."

Ahab said, "Bring him to me." When Ben-Hadad came, Ahab asked him to join him in the chariot.

34Ben-Hadad said to him, "Ahab, I will give you back the cities my father took from your father. And you may put shops in Damascus, as my father did in Samaria."

Ahab said, "If you agree to this, I will allow you to go free." So the two kings made a peace agreement. Then Ahab let Ben-Hadad go free.

A Prophet Speaks Against Ahab

35One prophet from one of the groups of prophets[d] told another, "Hit me!" He said this because the LORD had commanded it, but the other man refused. 36The prophet said, "You did not obey the LORD's command, so a lion will kill you as soon as you leave me." When the man left, a lion found him and killed him.

Sidelight Outside the Bible, the earliest mention of any Israelite king refers to King Ahab (1 Kings 20:1–43). An Assyrian monument commemorating a battle says Ahab contributed 10,000 soldiers and 2,000 chariots to an alliance of countries that fought the Assyrians.

37The prophet went to another man and said, "Hit me, please!" So the man hit him and hurt him. 38The prophet wrapped his face in a cloth so no one could tell who he was. Then he went and waited by the road for the king. 39As Ahab king of Israel passed by, the prophet called out to him. "I went to fight in the battle," the prophet said. "One of our men brought an enemy soldier to me. Our man said, 'Guard this man. If he runs away, you will have to give your life in his place. Or, you will have to pay a fine of 3,000 pieces of silver.' 40But I was busy doing other things, so the man ran away."

The king of Israel answered, "You have already said what the punishment is. You must do what the man said."

41Then the prophet quickly took the cloth from his face. When the king of Israel saw him, he knew he was one of the prophets. 42The prophet said to the king, "This is what the LORD says: 'You freed the man I said should die, so your life will be taken instead of his. The lives of your people will also be taken instead of the lives of his people.' "

43Then King Ahab went back to his palace in Samaria, angry and upset.

Ahab Takes Naboth's Vineyard

21 After these things had happened, this is what followed. A man named Naboth owned a vineyard in Jezreel, near the palace of Ahab king of Israel. 2One day Ahab said to Naboth, "Give me your vineyard. It is near my palace, and I want to make it into a vegetable garden. I will give you a better vineyard in its place, or, if you prefer, I will pay you what it is worth."

3Naboth answered, "May the LORD keep me from ever giving my land to you. It belongs to my family."

4Ahab went home angry and upset, because he did not like what Naboth from Jezreel had said. (Naboth had said, "I will not give you my family's land.") Ahab lay down on his bed, turned his face to the wall and refused to eat.

5His wife, Jezebel, came in and asked him, "Why are you so upset that you refuse to eat?"

6Ahab answered, "I talked to Naboth, the man from Jezreel. I said, 'Sell me your vineyard, or, if you prefer, I will give you another vineyard for it.' But Naboth refused."

7Jezebel answered, "Is this how you rule as king over Israel? Get up, eat something, and cheer up. I will get Naboth's vineyard for you."

8So Jezebel wrote some letters, signed Ahab's name to them, and used his own seal[d] to seal them. Then she sent them to the elders and important men who lived in Naboth's town. 9The letter she wrote said: "Declare a day during which the people are to give up eating. Call the people together, and give Naboth a place of honour among them. 10Seat two troublemakers across from him, and have them say they heard Naboth speak against God and the king. Then take Naboth out of the city and kill him with stones."

11The elders and important men of Jezreel obeyed Jezebel's command, just as she wrote in the letters. 12They declared a special day on which the people were to give up eating. And they put Naboth in a place of honour before the people. 13Two troublemakers sat across from Naboth and said in front of everybody that they had heard him speak against God and the king. So the people carried Naboth out of the city and killed him with stones. 14Then the leaders sent a message to Jezebel, saying, "Naboth has been killed."

15When Jezebel heard that Naboth had been killed, she told Ahab, "Naboth of Jezreel is dead. Now you may go and take for yourself the vineyard he would not sell to you." 16When Ahab heard that Naboth of Jezreel was dead, he got up and went to the vineyard to take it for his own.

17At this time the LORD spoke his word to the prophet Elijah the Tishbite. The LORD said, 18"Go to Ahab king of Israel in Samaria. He is at Naboth's vineyard, where he has gone to take it as his own. 19Tell Ahab that I, the LORD, say to him, 'You have murdered Naboth and taken his land. So I tell you this: in the same place the dogs licked up Naboth's blood, they will also lick up your blood!' "

20When Ahab saw Elijah, he said, "So you have found me, my enemy!"

Elijah answered, "Yes, I have found you. You have always chosen to do what the LORD says is wrong. 21So the LORD says to you, 'I will soon destroy you. I will kill you and every male in your family, both slave and free. 22Your family will be like the family of King Jeroboam son of Nebat and like the family of King Baasha son of Ahijah. I will destroy you, because you have made me angry and have led the people of Israel to sin.'

23"And the LORD also says, 'Dogs will eat the body of Jezebel in the city of Jezreel.'

24"Anyone in your family who dies in the city will be eaten by dogs, and anyone who dies in the fields will be eaten by birds."

25There was no one like Ahab who had chosen so often to do what the LORD said was wrong, because his wife Jezebel influenced him to do evil. 26Ahab sinned terribly by worshipping idols, just as the Amorite people did. And the LORD had taken away their land and given it to the people of Israel.

27After Elijah finished speaking, Ahab tore his clothes. He put on rough cloth, refused to eat and even slept in the rough cloth to show how sad and upset he was.

28The LORD spoke his word to Elijah the Tishbite: 29"I see that Ahab is now sorry for what he has done. So I will not cause the trouble to come to him during his life, but I will wait until his son is king. Then I will bring this trouble to Ahab's family."

The Death of Ahab

22 For three years there was peace between Israel and Aram. 2During the third year Jehoshaphat king of Judah went to visit Ahab king of Israel.

3At that time Ahab asked his officers, "Do you remember that the king of Aram took Ramoth in Gilead from us? Why have we done nothing to get it back?" 4So Ahab asked King Jehoshaphat, "Will you go with me to fight at Ramoth in Gilead?"

"I will go with you," Jehoshaphat answered. "My soldiers are yours, and my horses are yours." 5Jehoshaphat also said to Ahab, "But first we should ask if this is the LORD's will."

6Ahab called about 400 prophets[d] together and asked them, "Should I go to war against Ramoth in Gilead or not?"

They answered, "Go, because the Lord will hand them over to you."

7But Jehoshaphat asked, "Isn't there a prophet of the LORD here? Let's ask him what we should do."

8Then King Ahab said to Jehoshaphat, "There is one other prophet. We could ask the LORD through him, but I hate him. He never prophesies anything good about me, but something bad. He is Micaiah son of Imlah."

Jehoshaphat said, "King Ahab, you shouldn't say that!"

9So Ahab king of Israel told one of his officers to bring Micaiah to him at once.

10Ahab king of Israel and Jehoshaphat king of Judah had on their royal robes and were sitting on their thrones at the threshing[d] floor, near the entrance to the gate of Samaria. All the prophets were standing before them, speaking their messages. 11Zedekiah son of Kenaanah had made some iron horns. He said to Ahab, "This is what the LORD says, 'You will use these horns to fight the Arameans until they are destroyed.' "

12All the other prophets said the same thing. "Attack Ramoth in Gilead and win, because the LORD will hand the Arameans over to you."

13The messenger who had gone to get Micaiah said to him, "All the other prophets are saying King Ahab will succeed. You should agree with them and give the king a good answer."

14But Micaiah answered, "As surely as the

LORD lives, I can tell him only what the LORD
tells me."
15 When Micaiah came to Ahab, the king
asked him, "Micaiah, should we attack Ramoth
in Gilead or not?"
Micaiah answered, "Attack and win! The LORD
will hand them over to you."
16 But Ahab said to Micaiah, "How many times
do I have to tell you to speak only the truth to me
in the name of the LORD?"
17 So Micaiah answered, "I saw the army of Is-
rael scattered over the hills like sheep without a
shepherd. The LORD said, 'They have no leaders.
They should go home and not fight.' "
18 Then Ahab king of Israel said to Jehoshaphat,
"I told you! He never prophesies anything good
about me, but only bad."
19 But Micaiah said, "Hear the message from
the LORD: I saw the LORD sitting on his throne
with his heavenly army standing near him on his
right and on his left. 20 The LORD said, 'Who will
trick Ahab into attacking Ramoth in Gilead where
he will be killed?'
"Some said one thing; some said another. 21 Then
one spirit came and stood before the LORD and
said, 'I will trick him.'
22 "The LORD asked, 'How will you do it?'
"The spirit answered, 'I will go to Ahab's
prophets and make them tell lies.'
"So the LORD said, 'You will succeed in tricking
him. Go and do it.' "
23 Micaiah said, "Ahab, the LORD has made your
prophets lie to you, and the LORD has decided
that disaster should come to you."
24 Then Zedekiah son of Kenaanah went up to
Micaiah and slapped him in the face. Zedekiah
said, "Has the LORD's spirit left me to speak
through you?"
25 Micaiah answered, "You will find out on the
day you go to hide in an inside room."
26 Then Ahab king of Israel ordered, "Take
Micaiah and send him to Amon, the governor of
the city, and to Joash, the king's son. 27 Tell them
I said to put this man in prison and give him only
bread and water until I return safely from the
battle."
28 Micaiah said, "Ahab, if you come back safely
from battle, the LORD has not spoken through
me. Remember my words, all you people!"
29 So Ahab king of Israel and Jehoshaphat king
of Judah went to Ramoth in Gilead. 30 King Ahab
said to Jehoshaphat, "I will go into battle, but I
will wear other clothes so no one will recognise
me. But you wear your royal clothes." So Ahab
wore other clothes and went into battle.
31 The king of Aram had ordered his 32 chariot
commanders, "Don't fight with anyone—impor-
tant or unimportant—except the king of Israel."
32 When these commanders saw Jehoshaphat,
they thought he was certainly the king of Israel,
so they turned to attack him. But Jehoshaphat
began shouting. 33 When they saw he was not
King Ahab, they stopped chasing him.
34 By chance, a soldier shot an arrow, but he
hit Ahab king of Israel between the pieces of his
armour. King Ahab said to his chariot driver,
"Turn round and get me out of the battle,
because I am hurt!" 35 The battle continued all
day. King Ahab was held up in his chariot and
faced the Arameans. His blood flowed down to
the bottom of the chariot. That evening he died.
36 Near sunset a cry went out through the army
of Israel: "Each man go back to his own city and
land."
37 In that way King Ahab died. His body was
carried to Samaria and buried there. 38 The men
cleaned Ahab's chariot at a pool in Samaria where
prostitutes [d] bathed, and the dogs licked his blood
from the chariot. These things happened as the
LORD had said they would.
39 Everything else Ahab did is written in the
book of the history of the kings of Israel. It tells
about the palace Ahab built and decorated with
ivory and the cities he built. 40 So Ahab died, and
his son Ahaziah became king in his place.

Jehoshaphat King of Judah

41 Jehoshaphat son of Asa became king of
Judah during Ahab's fourth year as king of Israel.
42 Jehoshaphat was 35 years old when he became
king, and he ruled in Jerusalem for 25 years. His
mother's name was Azubah daughter of Shilhi.
43 Jehoshaphat was good, like his father Asa, and
he did what the LORD said was right. But Jeho-
shaphat did not destroy the places where gods
were worshipped, so the people continued offer-
ing sacrifices and burning incense [d] there. 44 Jeho-
shaphat was at peace with the king of Israel.
45 Jehoshaphat fought many wars, and these wars
and his successes are written in the book of the
history of the kings of Judah. 46 There were male
prostitutes [d] still in the places of worship from
the days of his father, Asa. So Jehoshaphat forced
them to leave.
47 During this time the land of Edom had no
king; it was ruled by a governor.
48 King Jehoshaphat built trading ships to sail
to Ophir for gold. But the ships were destroyed
at Ezion Geber, so they never set sail. 49 Ahaziah
son of Ahab went to help Jehoshaphat, offering
to give Jehoshaphat some men to sail with his
men, but Jehoshaphat refused.
50 Jehoshaphat died and was buried with his an-
cestors in Jerusalem, the city of David, his ancestor.
Then his son Jehoram became king in his place.

Ahaziah King of Israel

51Ahaziah son of Ahab became king of Israel
in Samaria during Jehoshaphat's seventeenth
year as king over Judah. Ahaziah ruled Israel for
two years, 52and he did what the LORD said was
wrong. He did the same evil his father Ahab, his
mother Jezebel and Jeroboam son of Nebat had
done. All these rulers led the people of Israel into
more sin. 53Ahaziah worshipped and served the
god Baal,[d] and this made the LORD, the God of
Israel, very angry. In these ways Ahaziah did
what his father had done.

2 Kings

Why Read This Book:

- See how God uses leaders to encourage people to follow him (2 Kings 1–8).
- Learn how unfaithfulness to God can destroy a nation (2 Kings 9–17).
- Be encouraged that God keeps his promises even when people don't keep theirs (2 Kings 18–23).

When?

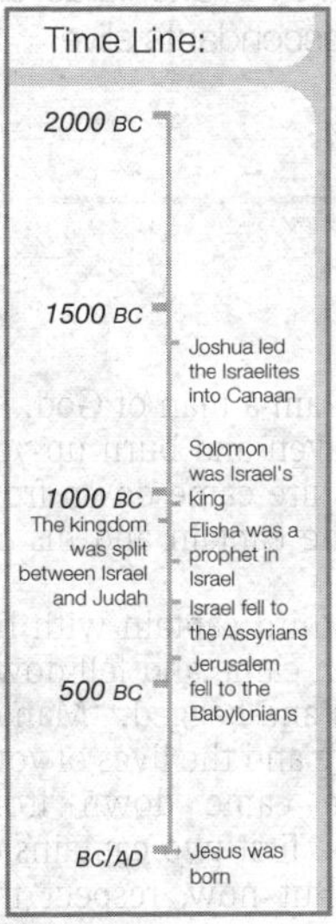

Behind the Scenes:

The land was in mess. The kingdom that David and Solomon built had split into Israel (in the north) and Judah (in the south), and both countries faced attack from the outside and unrest from within. Making matters worse, the people kept turning to the false god Baal for help, ignoring and forgetting the true God.

But even in this difficult situation, God hadn't forgotten his people. He sent the prophet Elisha to challenge them to turn back to God. Unlike his combative predecessor Elijah (1 Kings 16–19, p.331), Elisha was more of a healer and comforter. He performed numerous miracles to ease people's pain (2 Kings 4), and he also performed miracles on behalf of the nation (2 Kings 5). He showed that God hadn't given up on his people and would accept the Israelites if they would come back to him.

The Northern Kingdom did experience a brief revival under King Jeroboam II. But the overall decline continued, until Samaria – the northern capital – was destroyed and the people were taken into exile. ▷

Where?

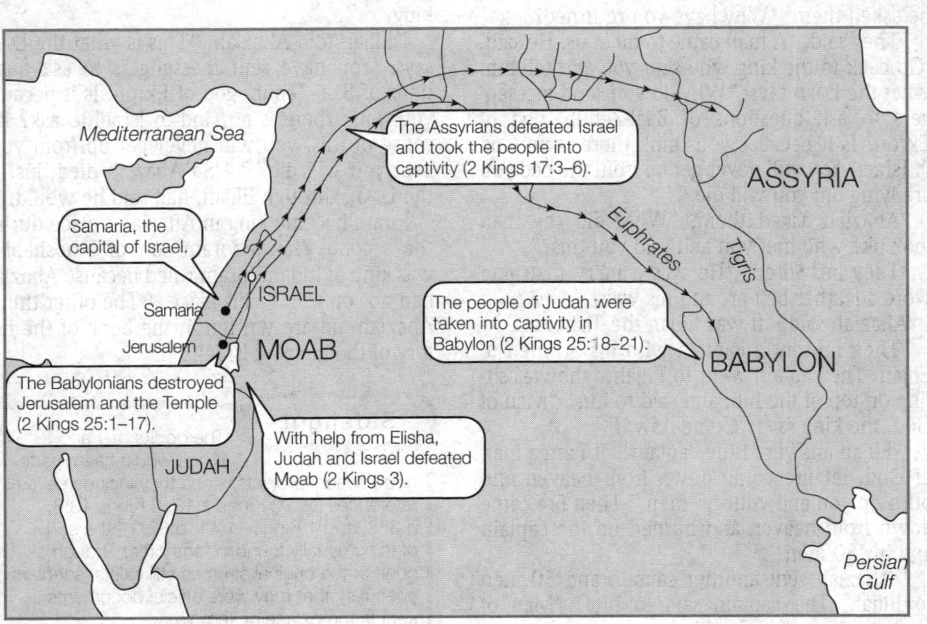

Behind the Scenes (cont.): The Southern Kingdom also experienced some good years – under King Josiah, who repaired the Temple and led a religious revival in Judah. But in the end, Judah fell, the Temple was destroyed, and the Babylonians took the people into exile.

Despite the Israelites' unfaithfulness, God remained faithful. During this time he sent great prophets to call the people back to himself. Even after Israel and Judah fell, God kept his promise to keep King David's descendants alive. And from those descendants eventually came Jesus.

Elijah and King Ahaziah

1 After Ahab died, Moab broke away from Israel's rule. 2Ahaziah fell down through the wooden bars in his upstairs room in Samaria and was badly hurt. He sent messengers and told them, "Go, ask Baal-Zebub, god of Ekron, if I will recover from my injuries."

3But the LORD's angel said to Elijah the Tishbite, "Go up and meet the messengers sent by the king of Samaria. Ask them, 'Why are you going to ask questions of Baal-Zebub, god of Ekron? Is it because you think there is no God in Israel?' 4This is what the LORD says: 'You will never get up from the bed you are lying on; you will die.' " Then Elijah left.

5When the messengers returned to Ahaziah, he asked them, "Why have you returned?"

6They said, "A man came to meet us. He said, 'Go back to the king who sent you and tell him what the LORD says: "Why do you send messengers to ask questions of Baal-Zebub, god of Ekron? Is it because you think there is no God in Israel? You will never get up from the bed you are lying on; you will die." ' "

7Ahaziah asked them, "What did the man look like who met you and told you this?"

8They answered, "He was a hairy man and wore a leather belt around his waist."

Ahaziah said, "It was Elijah the Tishbite."

9Then he sent a captain with his 50 men to Elijah. The captain went to Elijah, who was sitting on top of the hill, and said to him, "Man of God, the king says, 'Come down!' "

10Elijah answered the captain, "If I am a man of God, let fire come down from heaven and burn up you and your 50 men." Then fire came down from heaven and burned up the captain and his 50 men.

11Ahaziah sent another captain and 50 men to Elijah. The captain said to him, "Man of God, this is what the king says: 'Come down quickly!' "

12Elijah answered, "If I am a man of God, let fire come down from heaven and burn up you and your 50 men!" Then fire came down from heaven and burned up the captain and his 50 men.

13Ahaziah then sent a third captain with his 50 men. The third captain came and fell down on his knees before Elijah and begged, "Man of God, please respect my life and the lives of your 50 servants. 14See, fire came down from heaven and burned up the first two captains of 50 with all their men. But now, respect my life."

15The LORD's angel said to Elijah, "Go down with him and don't be afraid of him." So Elijah got up and went down with him to see the king.

16Elijah told Ahaziah, "This is what the LORD says: 'You have sent messengers to ask questions of Baal-Zebub, god of Ekron. Is it because you think there is no God in Israel to ask? Because of this, you will never get up from your bed; you will die.' " 17So Ahaziah died, just as the LORD, through Elijah, had said he would.

Joram became king in Ahaziah's place during the second year Jehoram son of Jehoshaphat was king of Judah. Joram ruled because Ahaziah had no son to take his place. 18The other things Ahaziah did are written in the book of the history of the kings of Israel.

Sidelight

The books of 1 and 2 Kings would have made good school projects, since they include several references (see 2 Kings 1:18, 2 Kings 13:8, p.358, and 1 Kings 11:41, p.327) – the sort of thing usually found in footnotes. Though none of the original sources still exists, scholars speculate that they were official documents kept in the palace or Temple.

Elijah is Taken to Heaven

2 It was almost time for the LORD to take
Elijah by a whirlwind up into heaven. While
Elijah and Elisha were leaving Gilgal, 2Elijah said
to Elisha, "Please stay here. The LORD has told
me to go to Bethel."
But Elisha said, "As the LORD lives, and as you
live, I won't leave you." So they went down to
Bethel. 3The groups of prophets at Bethel came
out to Elisha and said to him, "Do you know the
LORD will take your master away from you
today?"
Elisha said, "Yes, I know, but don't talk about it."
4Elijah said to him, "Stay here, Elisha, because
the LORD has sent me to Jericho."
But Elisha said, "As the LORD lives, and as you
live, I won't leave you."
So they went to Jericho. 5The groups of
prophets at Jericho came to Elisha and said, "Do
you know that the LORD will take your master
away from you today?"
Elisha answered, "Yes, I know, but don't talk
about it."
6Elijah said to Elisha, "Stay here. The LORD has
sent me to the Jordan River."

Sidelight The prophets Elijah and Elisha had similar names but different styles. Elijah – whose name means "the Lord is my God" – preached judgement and repentance, and lived alone. Elisha – whose name means "the Lord is salvation" – stressed hope and grace, and lived among the people, especially the poor. Yet God used these two different people to accomplish his work.

FRIENDS

Forever Friends

Steve and James had known each other for as long as they could remember. They lived across the street, went to the same primary school and would spend almost every waking moment together. On their first day at secondary school, the boys were given their new timetables. Steve, being brighter than James at most subjects, was placed in higher sets and as they read their timetables aloud they realised they had no classes together. James tried to pretend that it didn't matter, but he was gutted.

The first week went by and they still met up after school to walk home. Soon Steve started making new friends with people in his other classes and forgot to meet up with James. By the time the next school year came round, they had totally lost contact and didn't meet up at all.

One day after school, Steve was walking home with a group of his new friends when they started to shout abuse at a kid on the other side of the road. Steve thought it was really funny and began to join in until he realised that it was James, his old friend. James turned round to look at the gang of boys and saw that it was Steve and his new friends.

In that moment, Steve had a choice. Would he continue to pick on James and surely ruin their friendship forever or would he stand up for him? Steve chose to stand up for James, and told his friends to pack it in. Steve then walked home with James and they started hanging out again.

Read **2 Kings 2:1–12**.

- Elisha stuck by Elijah until he was taken to heaven, even when Elijah told him to leave him. What characteristics did it take for Elisha and Steve to stick with their friends?
- What were the rewards for Elisha and Steve for being faithful friends?

Consider . . .

- whether there are any situations when it isn't right to stand up for our friends.
- the reasons why we don't stand up for our friends when we should. Ask someone to pray with you to help you become a faithful friend.

For more, see . . .

- Ruth 1:14–18 (p.249)
- John 15:14–16 (p.1125)
- Job 42:7–10 (p.498)

Elisha answered, "As the LORD lives, and as
you live, I won't leave you."
So the two of them went on. 7Fifty men of the
groups of prophets came and stood at a distance
from where Elijah and Elisha were by the Jor-
dan. 8Elijah took off his coat, rolled it up, and hit
the water. The water divided to the right and to
the left, and Elijah and Elisha crossed over on
dry ground.
9After they had crossed over, Elijah said to
Elisha, "What can I do for you before I am taken
from you?"
Elisha said, "Leave me a double share of your
spirit."[n]
10Elijah said, "You have asked a hard thing.
But if you see me when I am taken from you, it
will be yours. If you don't, it won't happen."
11As they were walking and talking, a chariot
and horses of fire appeared and separated Elijah
from Elisha. Then Elijah went up to heaven in a

> **Sidelight** The prophet Elijah was whisked into heaven by a whirlwind, a chariot, and horses of fire – the first hot rod mentioned in the Bible (2 Kings 2:11). He is one of only two people mentioned in the Old Testament who never died. The other is Enoch (Genesis 5:24, p.8).

whirlwind. 12Elisha saw it and shouted, "My
father! My father! The chariots of Israel and their
horsemen!" And Elisha did not see him any
more. Then Elisha grabbed his own clothes and
tore them to show how sad he was.
13He picked up Elijah's coat that had fallen
from him. Then he returned and stood on the
bank of the Jordan. 14Elisha hit the water with
Elijah's coat and said, "Where is the LORD, the
God of Elijah?" When he hit the water, it divided
to the right and to the left, and Elisha crossed
over.
15The groups of prophets at Jericho were
watching and said, "Elisha now has the spirit Eli-
jah had." And they came to meet him, bowing
down to the ground before him. 16They said to
him, "There are 50 strong men with us. Please
let them go and look for your master. Maybe the
Spirit[d] of the LORD has taken Elijah up and set
him down on some mountain or in some valley."
But Elisha answered, "No, don't send them."
17When the groups of prophets had begged
Elisha until he couldn't refuse them any more,
he said, "Send them." So they sent 50 men who
looked for three days, but they could not find
him. 18Then they came back to Elisha at Jericho
where he was staying. He said to them, "I told
you not to go, didn't I?"

Elisha Makes the Water Pure

19The people of the city said to Elisha, "Look,
master, this city is a nice place to live as you can
see. But the water is so bad the land cannot grow
crops."
20Elisha said, "Bring me a new bowl and put
salt in it." So they brought it to him.
21Then he went out to the spring and threw
the salt in it. He said, "This is what the LORD
says: 'I have healed this water. From now on it
won't cause death, and it won't keep the land
from growing crops.'" 22So the water has been
healed to this day just as Elisha had said.

Boys Make Fun of Elisha

23From there Elisha went up to Bethel. On the
way some boys came out of the city and made
fun of him. They said to him, "Go up too, you
baldhead! Go up too, you baldhead!" 24Elisha
turned around, looked at them and put a curse
on them in the name of the LORD. Then two
mother bears came out of the woods and tore 42
of the boys to pieces. 25Elisha went to Mount
Carmel and from there he returned to Samaria.

> **Sidelight** If you like making fun of people, be careful. Some young men made fun of the prophet Elisha's baldness, and they got mauled by bears (2 Kings 2:23–25). Why was their teasing so bad? Elisha had shaved his head to show his role as a prophet of God, and they were jeering him to "go up" to heaven like Elijah. So they were really making fun of his faith.

War Between Israel and Moab

3 Joram son of Ahab became king over Israel
at Samaria in Jehoshaphat's eighteenth year
as king of Judah. And Joram ruled twelve years.
2He did what the LORD said was wrong, but he
was not like his father and mother; he removed
the stone pillars his father had made for Baal.[d]
3But he continued to sin like Jeroboam son of
Nebat who had led Israel to sin. Joram did not
stop doing these same sins.
4Mesha king of Moab raised sheep. He paid
the king of Israel 100,000 lambs and the wool of
100,000 sheep. 5But when Ahab died, the king

Leave . . . spirit By law, the first son in a family would inherit a double share of his father's possessions. Elisha is asking to inherit a share of his master's power as his follower. He is not asking for twice as much power as Elijah had.

of Moab turned against the king of Israel. 6So King Joram went out from Samaria and gathered Israel's army. 7He also sent messengers to Jehoshaphat king of Judah. "The king of Moab has turned against me," he said. "Will you go with me to fight Moab?"

Jehoshaphat replied, "I will go with you. My soldiers and my horses are yours."

8Jehoshaphat asked, "Which way should we attack?"

Joram answered, "Through the Desert of Edom."

9So the king of Israel went with the king of Judah and the king of Edom. After they had marched seven days, there was no more water for the army or for their animals that were with them. 10The king of Israel said, "This is terrible! The LORD has called us three kings together to hand us over to the Moabites!"

11But Jehoshaphat asked, "Is there a prophet[d] of the LORD here? We can ask the LORD through him."

An officer of the king of Israel answered, "Elisha son of Shaphat is here. He was Elijah's servant."

12Jehoshaphat said, "He speaks the LORD's truth." So the king of Israel and Jehoshaphat and the king of Edom went down to see Elisha.

13Elisha said to the king of Israel, "I have nothing to do with you. Go to the prophets of your father and to the prophets of your mother!"

The king of Israel said to Elisha, "No, the LORD has called us three kings together to hand us over to the Moabites."

14Elisha said, "As surely as the LORD All-powerful lives, whom I serve, I tell you the truth. I wouldn't even look at you or notice you if Jehoshaphat king of Judah were not here. I respect him. 15Now bring me someone who plays the harp."

While the harp was being played, the LORD gave Elisha power. 16Then Elisha said, "The LORD says to dig holes in the valley. 17The LORD says you won't see wind or rain, but the valley will be filled with water. Then you, your cattle and your other animals can drink. 18This is easy for the LORD to do; he will also hand Moab over to you. 19You will destroy every fortified city and every important town. You will cut down every good tree and stop up all springs. You will ruin every good field with rocks."

20The next morning, about the time the sacrifice was offered, water came from the direction of Edom and filled the valley.

21All the Moabites heard that the kings had come up to fight against them. So they gathered everyone old enough to put on armour and waited at the border. 22But when the Moabites got up early in the morning, the sun was shining on the water. They saw the water across from them, and it looked as red as blood. 23Then they said, "This is blood! The kings must have fought and killed each other! Come, Moabites, let's take the valuable things from the dead bodies!"

24When the Moabites came to the camp of Israel, the Israelites came out and fought them until they ran away. Then the Israelites went on into the land, killing the Moabites. 25They tore down the cities and threw rocks all over every good field. They stopped up all the springs and cut down all the good trees. Kir Hareseth was the only city with its stones still in place, but the men with slings surrounded it and conquered it too.

26When the king of Moab saw that the battle was too much for him, he took 700 men with swords to try to break through to the king of Edom. But they could not break through. 27Then the king of Moab took his oldest son, who would have been king after him, and offered him as a burnt offering on the wall. So there was great anger against the Israelites, who left and went back to their own land.

A Widow Asks Elisha for Help

4 The wife of a man from the groups of prophets[d] said to Elisha, "Your servant, my husband, is dead. You know he honoured the LORD. But now the man he owes money to is coming to take my two boys as his slaves!"

2Elisha answered, "How can I help you? Tell me, what do you have in your house?"

The woman said, "I don't have anything there except a pot of oil."

3Then Elisha said, "Go and get empty jars from all your neighbours. Don't ask for just a few. 4Then go into your house and shut the door behind you and your sons. Pour oil into all the jars, and set the full ones aside."

5So she left Elisha and shut the door behind her and her sons. As they brought the jars to her, she poured out the oil. 6When the jars were all full, she said to her son, "Bring me another jar."

But he said, "There are no more jars." Then the oil stopped flowing.

7She went and told Elisha. And the prophet said to her, "Go, sell the oil and pay what you owe. You and your sons can live on what is left."

The Shunammite Woman

8One day Elisha went to Shunem, where an important woman lived. She begged Elisha to stay and eat. So every time Elisha passed by, he stopped there to eat. 9The woman said to her husband, "I know that this is a holy man of God who passes by our house all the time. 10Let's make a small room on the roof[n] and put a bed in the room for him. We can put a table, a chair and a lampstand there. Then when he comes by, he can stay there."

> **Sidelight** If you judge prophets' power by the number of miracles they perform, Elisha was almost twice as powerful as his predecessor Elijah. The Bible tells of 13 miracles Elisha performed (see 2 Kings 4—6 for examples), but only 7 that Elijah performed. Miracles were important to show that God was more powerful than the false god Baal.

11One day Elisha came to the woman's house. After he went to his room and rested, 12he said to his servant Gehazi, "Call the Shunammite woman."

When the servant had called her, she stood in front of him. 13Elisha had told his servant, "Now say to her, 'You have gone to all this trouble for us. What can I do for you? Do you want me to speak to the king or the commander of the army for you?' "

She answered, "I live among my own people."

14Elisha said to Gehazi, "But what can we do for her?"

He answered, "She has no son, and her husband is old."

15Then Elisha said to Gehazi, "Call her." When he called her, she stood in the doorway. 16Then Elisha said, "About this time next year, you will hold a son in your arms."

The woman said, "No, master, man of God, don't lie to me, your servant!"

17But the woman became pregnant and gave birth to a son at that time the next year, just as Elisha had told her.

18The boy grew up and one day went out to his father, who was with the men harvesting grain. 19The boy said to his father, "My head! My head!"

The father said to his servant, "Take him to his mother!" 20The servant took him to his mother, and he lay on his mother's lap until noon. Then he died. 21So she took him up and laid him on Elisha's bed. Then she shut the door and left.

22She called to her husband, "Send me one of the servants and one of the donkeys. Then I can go quickly to the man of God and return."

23The husband said, "Why do you want to go to him today? It isn't the New Moon[d] or the Sabbath[d] day."

She said, "It will be all right."

24Then she saddled the donkey and said to her servant, "Lead on. Don't slow down for me unless I tell you." 25So she went to Elisha, the man of God, at Mount Carmel.

When he saw her coming from far away, he said to his servant Gehazi, "Look, there's the Shunammite woman! 26Run to meet her and ask, 'Are you all right? Is your husband all right? Is the boy all right?' "

She answered, "Everything is all right."

27Then she came to Elisha at the hill and grabbed his feet. Gehazi came near to pull her away, but Elisha said to him, "Leave her alone. She's very upset, and the LORD has not told me about it. He has hidden it from me."

28She said, "Master, did I ask you for a son? Didn't I tell you not to lie to me?"

29Then Elisha said to Gehazi, "Get ready. Take my walking stick in your hand and go quickly. If you meet anyone, don't say hello. If anyone greets you, don't answer. Lay my walking stick on the boy's face."

30The boy's mother said, "As surely as the LORD lives and as you live, I won't leave you!" So Elisha got up and followed her.

31Gehazi went on ahead and laid the walking stick on the boy's face, but the boy did not talk or move. Then Gehazi went back to meet Elisha. "The boy has not awakened," he said.

32When Elisha came into the house, the boy was lying dead on his bed. 33Elisha entered the room and shut the door, so only he and the boy were in the room. Then he prayed to the LORD. 34He went to the bed and lay on the boy, putting his mouth on the boy's mouth, his eyes on the boy's eyes, and his hands on the boy's hands. He stretched himself out on top of the boy. Soon the boy's skin became warm. 35Elisha turned away and walked around the room. Then he went back and put himself on the boy again. The boy sneezed seven times and opened his eyes.

36Elisha called Gehazi and said, "Call the Shunammite!" So he did. When she came, Elisha said, "Pick up your son." 37She came in and fell at Elisha's feet, bowing face down to the floor. Then she picked up her son and went out.

Elisha and the Stew

38When Elisha returned to Gilgal, there was a shortage of food in the land. While the groups of prophets[d] were sitting in front of him, he said to his servant, "Put the large pot on the fire, and boil some stew for these men."

39One of them went out into the field to gather plants. Finding a wild vine, he picked

roof In Bible times houses were built with flat roofs. The roof was used for drying things such as flax and fruit. And it was used as an extra room, as a place for worship and as a place to sleep in the summer.

fruit from the vine and filled his robe with it.
Then he came and cut up the fruit into the pot.
But they didn't know what kind of fruit it was.
40They poured out the stew for the others to eat.
When they began to eat it, they shouted, "Man
of God, there's death in the pot!" And they could
not eat it.
41Elisha told them to bring some flour. He
threw it into the pot and said, "Pour it out for the
people to eat." This time there was nothing
harmful in the pot.

Elisha Feeds the People

42A man from Baal Shalishah came to Elisha,
bringing him 20 loaves of barley bread from the
first harvest. He also brought fresh grain in his
sack. Elisha said, "Give it to the people to eat."
43Elisha's servant asked, "How can I feed 100
people with so little?"
"Give the bread to the people to eat," Elisha
said. "This is what the LORD says: 'They will eat
and will have food left over.' " 44After he gave it
to them, the people ate and had food left over, as
the LORD had said.

Naaman is Healed

5 Naaman was commander of the army of the
king of Aram. He was honoured by his mas-
ter, and he had much respect because the LORD
used him to give victory to Aram. He was a
mighty and brave man, but he had a skin disease.
2The Arameans had gone out to steal from the
Israelites and had taken a little girl as a captive.
This little girl served Naaman's wife. 3She said to
her mistress, "I wish my master would meet the
prophet[d] who lives in Samaria. He would cure
him of his disease."
4Naaman went to the king and told him what
the girl from Israel had said. 5The king of Aram
said, "Go ahead, and I will send a letter to the
king of Israel." So Naaman left and took with
him about 30,000 pieces of silver, as well as
6,000 pieces of gold and ten changes of clothes.
6He brought the letter to the king of Israel,

SICKNESS

Take Your Medicine

Although the lightweight brace could be worn under her clothes, Alison felt self-conscious about wearing it. She dreaded people's comments the first day she went to school with the "contraption". She thought that everyone would notice it and make fun.

But Alison knew that if she didn't wear the brace, she would probably need to have an operation. Alison had a curvature of the spine, a condition that could be stopped if she wore the back brace during her growing years. Without the brace, the curvature could have progressed so that she would not be able to stand up straight.

Alison wore the brace. And as it turned out, no one noticed. "No one even knew I had it," she recalls. That made the choice to wear the brace much easier. But it still seemed a nuisance. Every day over the next two years, Alison had to choose: should she wear her back brace or not?

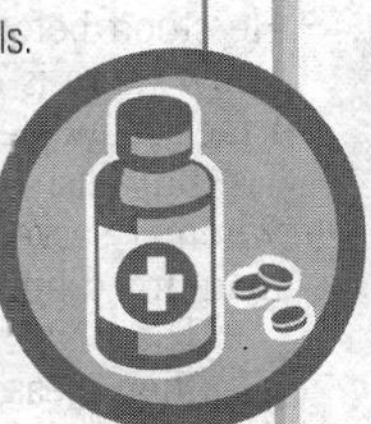

Sometimes, people avoid medical treatment just because it's strange or embarrassing. But people won't get better if they don't follow the doctor's – or God's – orders. That was Naaman's predicament in **2 Kings 5:1–14**.

- What does God have to do with Alison's and Naaman's medical treatments?
- What kinds of thing can keep God from working in our lives?

Consider . . .

- talking to someone at school who has to wear some kind of medical device and finding out how he or she feels about wearing it.
- encouraging someone you know to participate in God's healing processes by following doctor's orders.

For more, see . . .

- Psalm 41 (p.525)
- Acts 3:1–10 (p.1142)
- John 9:1–11 (p.1111)

which read, "I am sending my servant Naaman
to you so you can heal him of his skin disease."
7When the king of Israel read the letter, he
tore his clothes to show how upset he was. He
said, "I'm not God! I can't kill and make alive
again! Why does this man send someone with a
skin disease for me to heal? You can see that the
king of Aram is trying to start trouble with me."
8When Elisha, the man of God, heard that the
king of Israel had torn his clothes, he sent the
king this message: "Why have you torn your
clothes? Let Naaman come to me. Then he will
know there is a prophet in Israel." 9So Naaman
went with his horses and chariots to Elisha's
house and stood outside the door.
10Elisha sent Naaman a messenger who said,
"Go and wash in the Jordan River seven times.
Then your skin will be healed, and you will be
clean."
11Naaman became angry and left. He said, "I
thought Elisha would surely come out and stand
before me and call on the name of the LORD his
God. I thought he would wave his hand over the
place and heal the disease. 12The Abana and the
Pharpar, the rivers of Damascus, are better than all
the waters of Israel. Why can't I wash in them and
become clean?" So Naaman went away very angry.
13Naaman's servants came near and said to
him, "My father, if the prophet had told you to
do some great thing, wouldn't you have done it?
Doesn't it make more sense just to do it? After
all, he only told you, 'Wash, and you will be
clean.' " 14So Naaman went down and dipped in
the Jordan seven times, just as Elisha had said.
Then his skin became new again, like the skin of
a child. And he was clean.
15Naaman and all his group returned to Elisha.
He stood before Elisha and said, "Look, I now
know there is no God in all the earth except in
Israel. Now please accept a gift from me."
16But Elisha said, "As surely as the LORD lives
whom I serve, I won't accept anything." Naa-
man urged him to take the gift, but he refused.
17Then Naaman said, "If you won't take the
gift, then please give me some soil—as much as
two of my mules can carry. From now on I'll not
offer any burnt offering or sacrifice to any other
gods but the LORD. 18But let the LORD pardon me
for this: When my master goes into the temple of
Rimmon[n] to worship, he leans on my arm. Then
I must bow in that temple. May the LORD pardon
me when I do that."
19Elisha said to him, "Go in peace."
Naaman left Elisha and went a short way.
20Gehazi, the servant of Elisha the man of God,
thought, "My master has not accepted what
Naaman the Aramean brought. As surely as the
LORD lives, I'll run after him and get something
from him." 21So Gehazi went after Naaman.
When Naaman saw someone running after
him, he got off the chariot to meet Gehazi. He
asked, "Is everything all right?"
22Gehazi said, "Everything is all right. My
master has sent me. He said, 'Two young men
from the groups of prophets in the mountains of
Ephraim just came to me. Please give them 3,000
pieces of silver and two changes of clothes.' "
23Naaman said, "Please take 6,000 pieces,"
and he urged Gehazi to take it. He tied 68 kilo-
grammes of silver in two bags with two changes
of clothes. Then he gave them to two of his ser-
vants to carry for Gehazi. 24When they came to
the hill, Gehazi took these things from Naaman's
servants and put them in the house. Then he let
Naaman's servants go, and they left.
25When he came in and stood before his mas-
ter, Elisha said to him, "Where have you been,
Gehazi?"
"I didn't go anywhere," he answered.
26But Elisha said to him, "My spirit was with
you. I knew when the man turned from his char-
iot to meet you. This isn't a time to take money,
clothes, olives, grapes, sheep, oxen, male servants
or female servants. 27So Naaman's skin disease
will come on you and your children for ever."
When Gehazi left Elisha, he had the disease and
was as white as snow.

An Axehead Floats

6 The groups of prophets[d] said to Elisha, "The
place where we meet with you is too small for
us. 2Let's go to the Jordan River. There everyone
can get a log, and let's build a place there to live."
Elisha said, "Go."
3One of them said, "Please go with us."

Sidelight
Science says solid iron does not float. So does common sense. Get a lesson in how God can suspend the rules in 2 Kings 6:1–7.

Elisha answered, "I will go," 4so he went with
them. When they arrived at the Jordan, they cut
down some trees. 5As one man was cutting down
a tree, the head of his axe fell into the water. He
yelled, "Oh, my master! I borrowed that axe!"
6Elisha asked, "Where did it fall?" The man
showed him the place. Then Elisha cut down a
stick and threw it into the water, and it made the

temple of Rimmon The place where the Aramean people worshipped the god Rimmon.

iron head float. 7Elisha said, "Pick up the axe-head." Then the man reached out and took it.

Elisha and the Blinded Arameans

8The king of Aram was at war with Israel. He had a council meeting with his officers and said, "I will set up my camp in this place."

9Elisha, the man of God, sent a message to the king of Israel, saying, "Be careful! Don't pass that place, because the Arameans are going down there!"

10The king of Israel checked the place about which Elisha had warned him. Elisha warned him several times, so the king protected himself there.

11The king of Aram was angry about this. He called his officers together and demanded, "Tell me who of us is working for the king of Israel."

12One of the officers said, "None, my master and king. It's Elisha, the prophet[d] from Israel. He can tell you what you speak in your bedroom."

13The king said, "Go and find him so I can send men and catch him."

The servants came back and reported, "He is in Dothan."

14Then the king sent horses, chariots and many troops to Dothan. They arrived at night and surrounded the city.

15Elisha's servant got up early, and when he went out, he saw an army with horses and chariots all around the city. The servant said to Elisha, "Oh, my master, what can we do?"

16Elisha said, "Don't be afraid. The army that fights for us is larger than the one against us."

17Then Elisha prayed, "LORD, open my servant's eyes, and let him see."

The LORD opened the eyes of the young man, and he saw that the mountain was full of horses and chariots of fire all around Elisha.

18As the enemy came down towards Elisha, he prayed to the LORD, "Make these people blind." So he made the Aramean army blind, as Elisha had asked.

19Elisha said to them, "This is not the right road or the right city. Follow me and I'll take you to the man you are looking for." Then Elisha led them to Samaria.

20After they entered Samaria, Elisha said, "LORD, open these men's eyes so they can see." So the LORD opened their eyes, and the Aramean army saw that they were inside the city of Samaria!

21When the king of Israel saw the Aramean army, he said to Elisha, "My father, should I kill them? Should I kill them?"

22Elisha answered, "Don't kill them. You wouldn't kill people whom you captured with your sword and bow. Give them food and water, and let them eat and drink and then go home to their master." 23So he prepared a great feast for the Aramean army. After they ate and drank, the king sent them away, and they went home to their master. The soldiers of Aram did not come any more into the land of Israel.

A Shortage of Food

24Later, Ben-Hadad king of Aram gathered his whole army and surrounded and attacked Samaria. 25There was a shortage of food in Samaria. It was so bad that a donkey's head sold for about 80 pieces of silver, and 8 litres of dove's dung sold for about 5 pieces of silver.

26As the king of Israel was passing by on the wall, a woman yelled out to him, "Help me, my master and king!"

27The king said, "If the LORD doesn't help you, how can I? Can I get help from the threshing[d] floor or from the winepress?"[d] 28Then the king said to her, "What is your trouble?"

She answered, "This woman said to me, 'Give up your son so we can eat him today. Then we will eat my son tomorrow.' 29So we boiled my son and ate him. Then the next day I said to her, 'Give up your son so we can eat him.' But she had hidden him."

30When the king heard the woman's words, he tore his clothes in sadness. As he walked along the wall, the people looked and saw he had on rough cloth under his clothes to show his sadness. 31He said, "May God punish me terribly if the head of Elisha son of Shaphat isn't cut off from his body today!"

32The king sent a messenger to Elisha, who was sitting in his house with the elders. But before the messenger arrived, Elisha said to them, "See, this murderer is sending men to cut off my head. When the messenger arrives, shut the door and hold it; don't let him in. The sound of his master's feet is behind him."

33Elisha was still talking to the leaders when the messenger arrived. The king said, "This trouble has come from the LORD. Why should I wait for the LORD any longer?"

7 Elisha said, "Listen to the LORD's word. This is what the LORD says: 'About this time tomorrow 8 litres of fine flour will be sold for a piece of silver, and 6 kilogrammes of barley will be sold for a piece of silver. This will happen at the gate of Samaria.' "

2Then the officer who was close to the king answered Elisha, "Even if the LORD opened windows in the sky, that couldn't happen."

Elisha said, "You will see it with your eyes, but you will not eat any of it."

3There were four men with a skin disease at the entrance to the city gate. They said to each other, "Why should we sit here until we die? 4There is no food in the city. So if we go into the city, we will die there. If we stay here, we will die. So let's go to the Aramean camp. If they let us live, we will live. If they kill us, we die."

5So they got up at twilight and went to the Aramean camp, but when they arrived, no one was there. 6The Lord had caused the Aramean army to hear the sound of chariots, horses and a large army. They had said to each other, "The king of Israel has hired the Hittite and Egyptian kings to attack us!" 7So they got up and ran away in the twilight, leaving their tents, horses and donkeys. They left the camp standing and ran for their lives.

8When the men with the skin disease came to the edge of the camp, they went into one of the tents and ate and drank. They carried silver, gold and clothes out of the camp and hid them. Then they came back and entered another tent. They carried things from this tent and hid them, as well. 9Then they said to each other, "We're doing wrong. Today we have good news, but we are silent. If we wait until the sun comes up, we'll be discovered. Let's go right now and tell the people in the king's palace."

10So they went and called to the gatekeepers of the city. They said, "We went to the Aramean camp, but no one is there; we didn't hear anyone. The horses and donkeys were still tied up, and the tents were still standing." 11Then the gatekeepers shouted out and told the people in the palace.

12The king got up in the night and said to his officers, "I'll tell you what the Arameans are doing to us. They know we are starving. They have gone out of the camp to hide in the field. They're saying, 'When the Israelites come out of the city, we'll capture them alive. Then we'll enter the city.' "

13One of his officers answered, "Let some men take five of the horses that are still left in the city. These men are like all the Israelites who are left; they are also about to die. Let's send them to see what has happened."

14So the men took two chariots with horses. The king sent them after the Aramean army, saying, "Go and see what has happened." 15The men followed the Aramean army as far as the Jordan River. The road was full of clothes and equipment that the Arameans had thrown away as they had hurriedly left. So the messengers returned and told the king. 16Then the people went out and took valuable things from the Aramean camp. So 8 litres of fine flour were sold for a piece of silver, and 6 kilogrammes of barley were sold for a piece of silver, just as the LORD had said.

17The king chose the officer who was close to him to guard the gate, but the people trampled the officer to death. This happened just as Elisha had told the king when the king came to his house. 18He had said, "6 kilogrammes of barley and 8 litres of fine flour will each sell for a piece of silver about this time tomorrow at the gate of Samaria."

19But the officer had answered, "Even if the LORD opened windows in the sky, that couldn't happen." And Elisha had told him, "You will see it with your eyes, but you won't eat any of it." 20It happened to the officer just that way. The people trampled him in the gateway, and he died.

The Shunammite Regains Her Land

8 Elisha spoke to the woman whose son he had brought back to life. He said, "Get up and go with your family. Stay wherever you can, because the LORD has called for a time without food that will last seven years." 2So the woman got up and did as the man of God had said. She left with her family, and they stayed in the land of the Philistines for seven years. 3After seven years she returned from the land of the Philistines and went to beg the king for her house and land. 4The king was talking with Gehazi, the servant of the man of God. The king had said, "Please tell me all the great things Elisha has done." 5Gehazi was telling the king how Elisha had brought a dead boy back to life. Just then the woman whose son Elisha had brought back to life came and begged the king for her house and land.

Gehazi said, "My master and king, this is the woman, and this is the son Elisha brought back to life."

6The king asked the woman, and she told him about it. Then the king chose an officer to help her. "Give the woman everything that is hers," the king said. "Give her all the money made from her land from the day she left until now."

Ben-Hadad is Killed

7Then Elisha went to Damascus, where Ben-Hadad king of Aram was sick. Someone told him, "The man of God has arrived."

8The king said to Hazael, "Take a gift in your hand and go and meet him. Ask the LORD through him if I will recover from my sickness."

9So Hazael went to meet Elisha, taking with him a gift of 40 camels loaded with every good thing in Damascus. He came and stood before Elisha and said, "Your son Ben-Hadad king of Aram sent me to you. He asks if he will recover from his sickness."

10Elisha said to Hazael, "Go and tell Ben-Hadad, 'You will surely recover,' but the LORD has told me he will really die." [11]Hazael stared at Elisha until he felt ashamed. Then Elisha cried.

[12]Hazael asked, "Why are you crying, master?"

Elisha answered, "Because I know what evil you will do to the Israelites. You will burn their fortified cities with fire and kill their young men with swords. You will throw their babies to the ground and split open their pregnant women."

[13]Hazael said, "Am I a dog? How could I do such things?"

Elisha answered, "The LORD has shown me that you will be king over Aram."

[14]Then Hazael left Elisha and came to his master. Ben-Hadad said to him, "What did Elisha say to you?"

Hazael answered, "He told me that you will surely recover." [15]But the next day Hazael took a blanket and dipped it in water. Then he put it over Ben-Hadad's face, and he died. So Hazael became king in Ben-Hadad's place.

Jehoram King of Judah

[16]While Jehoshaphat was king in Judah, Jehoram son of Jehoshaphat became king of Judah. This was during the fifth year Joram son of Ahab was king of Israel. [17]Jehoram was 32 years old when he began to rule, and he ruled eight years in Jerusalem. [18]He followed the ways of the kings of Israel, just as the family of Ahab had done, because he married Ahab's daughter. Jehoram did what the LORD said was wrong. [19]But the LORD would not destroy Judah because of his servant David. The LORD had promised that one of David's descendants *d* would always rule.

[20]In Jehoram's time Edom broke away from Judah's rule and chose their own king. [21]So Jehoram and all his chariots went to Zair. The Edomites surrounded him and his chariot commanders. Jehoram got up and attacked the Edomites at night, but his army ran away to their tents. [22]From then until now the country of Edom has fought against the rule of Judah. At the same time Libnah also broke away from Judah's rule.

[23]The other acts of Jehoram and all the things he did are written in the book of the history of the kings of Judah. [24]Jehoram died and was buried with his ancestors in Jerusalem, and Jehoram's son Ahaziah ruled in his place.

[25]Ahaziah son of Jehoram became king of Judah during the twelfth year Joram son of Ahab was king of Israel. [26]Ahaziah was 22 years old when he became king, and he ruled one year in Jerusalem. His mother's name was Athaliah, a granddaughter of Omri king of Israel. [27]Ahaziah followed the ways of Ahab's family. He did what the LORD said was wrong, as Ahab's family had done, because he was a son-in-law to Ahab.

[28]Ahaziah went with Joram son of Ahab to Ramoth in Gilead, where they fought against Hazael king of Aram. The Arameans wounded Joram. [29]So King Joram returned to Jezreel to heal from the wound he had received from the Arameans at Ramoth when he fought Hazael king of Aram. Ahaziah son of Jehoram king of Judah went down to visit Joram son of Ahab at Jezreel, because he had been wounded.

Jehu is Chosen King

9 At the same time, Elisha the prophet *d* called a man from the groups of prophets. Elisha said, "Get ready, and take this small bottle of olive oil in your hand. Go to Ramoth in Gilead. [2]When you arrive, find Jehu son of Jehoshaphat, the son of Nimshi. Go in and make Jehu get up from among his brothers, and take him to an inner room. [3]Then take the bottle and pour the oil on Jehu's head and say, 'This is what the LORD says: I have appointed you king over Israel.' Then open the door and run away. Don't wait!"

[4]So the young man, the prophet, went to Ramoth in Gilead. [5]When he arrived, he saw the officers of the army sitting together. He said, "Commander, I have a message for you."

Jehu asked, "For which one of us?"

The young man said, "For you, commander."

[6]Jehu got up and went into the house. Then the young prophet poured the olive oil on Jehu's head and said to him, "This is what the LORD, the God of Israel says: 'I have appointed you king over the LORD's people Israel. [7]You must destroy the family of Ahab your master. I will punish Jezebel for the deaths of my servants the prophets and for all the LORD's servants who were murdered. [8]All of Ahab's family must die. I will not let any male child in Ahab's family live in Israel, whether slave or free. [9]I will make Ahab's family like the family of Jeroboam son of Nebat and like the family of Baasha son of Ahijah. [10]The dogs will eat Jezebel at Jezreel, and no one will bury her.' "

Then the young prophet opened the door and ran away.

[11]When Jehu went back to his master's officers, one of them said to Jehu, "Is everything all right? Why did this madman come to you?"

Jehu answered, "You know the man and how he talks."

[12]They answered, "That's not true. Tell us."

Jehu said, "He said to me, 'This is what the LORD says: I have appointed you to be king over Israel.' "

[13]Then the officers hurried, and each man took off his own coat and put it on the stairs for Jehu. They blew the trumpet and shouted, "Jehu is king!"

Joram and Ahaziah are Killed

14So Jehu son of Jehoshaphat, the son of Nimshi, made plans against Joram. Now Joram and all Israel had been defending Ramoth in Gilead from Hazael king of Aram. 15But King Joram had to return to Jezreel to heal from the injuries the Arameans had given him when he fought against Hazael king of Aram.

Jehu said, "If you agree with this, don't let anyone leave the city. They might tell the news in Jezreel." 16Then he got into his chariot and set out for Jezreel, where Joram was resting. Ahaziah king of Judah had gone down to see him.

17The look-out was standing on the watch-tower in Jezreel when he saw Jehu's troops coming. He said, "I see some soldiers!"

Joram said, "Take a horseman and send him to meet them. Tell him to ask, 'Is all in order?' "

18The horseman rode out to meet Jehu, and he said, "This is what the king says: 'Is all in order?' "

Jehu said, "Why bother yourself with order? Come along behind me."

The look-out reported, "The messenger reached them, but he is not coming back."

19Then Joram sent out a second horseman. This rider came to Jehu's group and said, "This is what the king says: 'Is all in order?' "

Jehu answered, "Why bother yourself with order? Come along behind me."

20The look-out reported, "The second man reached them, but he is not coming back. The man in the chariot is driving like Jehu son of Nimshi. He drives as if he were mad!"

> **Sidelight** The first record of bad driving in the Bible is in 2 Kings 9:20. King Jehu was such a bad driver that people could recognise his chariot driving from a distance. They said he drove "as if he were crazy". But since he was a king, nobody could complain.

21Joram said, "Get my chariot ready." Then the servant got Joram's chariot ready. Joram king of Israel and Ahaziah king of Judah went out, each in his own chariot, to meet Jehu at the property of Naboth the Jezreelite.

22When Joram saw Jehu, he said, "Is all in order, Jehu?"

Jehu answered, "There will never be any order as long as your mother Jezebel worships idols and uses witchcraft." [d]

23Joram turned the horses to run away and yelled to Ahaziah, "It's a trick, Ahaziah!"

24Then Jehu drew his bow and shot Joram between his shoulders. The arrow went through Joram's heart, and he fell down in his chariot.

25Jehu ordered Bidkar, his chariot officer, "Pick up Joram's body, and throw it into the field of Naboth the Jezreelite. Remember when you and I rode together with Joram's father Ahab. The LORD made this prophecy [d] against him: 26'Yesterday I saw the blood of Naboth and his sons, says the LORD, so I will punish Ahab in his field, says the LORD.' Take Joram's body and throw it into the field, as the LORD has said."

27When Ahaziah king of Judah saw this, he ran away towards Beth Haggan. Jehu chased him, saying, "Shoot Ahaziah, too!" Ahaziah was wounded in his chariot on the way up to Gur near Ibleam. He got as far as Megiddo but died there. 28Ahaziah's servants carried his body in a chariot to Jerusalem and buried him with his ancestors in his tomb in Jerusalem. 29(Ahaziah had become king over Judah in the eleventh year Joram son of Ahab was king.)

Death of Jezebel

30When Jehu came to Jezreel, Jezebel heard about it. She put on her eye paint and fixed her hair. Then she looked out of the window. 31When Jehu entered the city gate, Jezebel said, "Have you come in peace, you Zimri, [n] you who killed your master?"

32Jehu looked up at the window and said, "Who is on my side? Who?" Two or three servants looked out the window at Jehu. 33He said to them, "Throw her down." So they threw Jezebel down, and the horses ran over her. Some of her blood splashed on the wall and on the horses.

> **Sidelight** When wicked Queen Jezebel put on make-up (2 Kings 9:30–33), it was probably quite elaborate. Women in those days used black eyeliner, blue eyeshadow, red lipstick and nail polish, powders and perfume. None of it did much good, though, when she was thrown out of the window and trampled by horses.

34Jehu went into the house and ate and drank. Then he said, "Now see about this cursed woman. Bury her, because she is a king's daughter."

35The men went to bury Jezebel, but they could not find her. They found only her skull,

Zimri He was the man who killed Elah and the family of Baasha. Read 1 Kings 16:8–12.

feet and the palms of her hands. 36When they
came back and told Jehu, he said, "The LORD
said this through his servant Elijah the Tishbite:
'The dogs will eat Jezebel at Jezreel. 37Her body
will be like manure on the field in the land at
Jezreel. No one will be able to say that this is
Jezebel.' "

Families of Ahab and Ahaziah Killed

10 Ahab had 70 sons in Samaria. Jehu
wrote letters and sent them to Samaria
to the officers and elders of Jezreel and to the
guardians of the sons of Ahab. Jehu said, 2"You
have your master's sons with you, and you have
chariots, horses, a city with strong walls and
weapons. When you get this letter, 3choose the
best and most worthy person among your mas-
ter's sons, and make him king. Then fight for
your master's family."

4But the officers and leaders of Jezreel were
frightened. They said, "Two kings could not
stand up to Jehu, so how can we?"

5The palace manager, the city governor, the
elders and the guardians sent a message to
Jehu. "We are your servants," they said. "We
will do everything you tell us to do. We won't
make any man king, so do whatever you think
is best."

6Then Jehu wrote a second letter, saying, "If
you are on my side and will obey me, cut off
the heads of your master's sons and come to me
at Jezreel tomorrow about this time."

Now the 70 sons of the king's family were
with the leading men of the city who were
their guardians. 7When the leaders received the
letter, they took the king's sons and killed all 70
of them. They put their heads in baskets and
sent them to Jehu at Jezreel. 8The messenger
came to Jehu and told him, "They have brought
the heads of the king's sons."

Then Jehu said, "Lay the heads in two piles
at the city gate [n] until morning."

9In the morning, Jehu went out and stood be-
fore the people and said to them, "You are inno-
cent. Look, I made plans against my master and
killed him. But who killed all these? 10You
should know that everything the LORD said
about Ahab's family will come true. The LORD
has spoken through his servant Elijah, and the
LORD has done what he said." 11So Jehu killed
every one of Ahab's family in Jezreel who was
still alive. He also killed all Ahab's leading men,
close friends and priests. No one who had
helped Ahab was left alive.

12Then Jehu left and went to Samaria by way
of the road to Beth Eked of the Shepherds.
13There Jehu met some relatives of Ahaziah king
of Judah. Jehu asked, "Who are you?"

They answered, "We are relatives of Ahaziah.
We have come down to get revenge for the fam-
ilies of the king and the king's mother."

14Then Jehu said, "Take them alive!" So they
captured Ahaziah's relatives alive and killed
them at the well near Beth Eked—42 of them.
Jehu did not leave anyone alive.

15After Jehu left there, he met Jehonadab son
of Recab, who was also on his way to meet Jehu.
Jehu greeted him and said, "Are you as good a
friend to me as I am to you?"

Jehonadab answered, "Yes, I am."

Jehu said, "If you are, then give me your
hand." So Jehonadab gave him his hand, and
Jehu pulled him into the chariot. 16"Come with
me," Jehu said. "You can see how strong my feel-
ings are for the LORD." So Jehu had Jehonadab
ride in his chariot.

17When Jehu came to Samaria, he killed all of
Ahab's family in Samaria. He destroyed all those
who were left, just as the LORD had told Elijah it
would happen.

Baal Worshippers Killed

18Then Jehu gathered all the people together
and said to them, "Ahab served Baal [d] a little, but
Jehu will serve Baal much. 19Now call for me all
Baal's prophets and priests and all the people
who worship Baal. Don't let anyone miss this
meeting, because I have a great sacrifice for Baal.
Anyone who is not there will not live." But Jehu
was tricking them so he could destroy the wor-
shippers of Baal. 20He said, "Prepare a holy meet-
ing for Baal." So they announced the meeting.
21Then Jehu sent word through all Israel, and all
the worshippers of Baal came; not one stayed at
home. They came into the temple of Baal, and
the temple was filled from one side to the other.

22Jehu said to the man who kept the robes,
"Bring out robes for all the worshippers of Baal."
After he brought out robes for them, 23Jehu and
Jehonadab son of Recab went into the temple of
Baal. Jehu said to the worshippers of Baal, "Look
around, and make sure there are no servants of
the LORD with you. Be sure there are only wor-
shippers of Baal." 24Then the worshippers of Baal
went in to offer sacrifices and burnt offerings.

Jehu had 80 men waiting outside. He had told
them, "Don't let anyone escape. If you do, you
must pay with your own life."

25As soon as Jehu finished offering the burnt
offering, he ordered the guards and the captains,
"Go in and kill the worshippers of Baal. Don't let
anyone come out." So the guards and captains

city gate People came here to conduct business. Public meetings and court cases were also held here.

killed the worshippers of Baal with the sword
and threw their bodies out. Then they went to
the inner rooms of the temple 26and brought out
the pillars of the temple of Baal and burned
them. 27They tore down the stone pillar of Baal,
as well as the temple of Baal. And they made it
into a sewage pit, as it is today.
28So Jehu destroyed Baal worship in Israel,
29but he did not stop doing the sins Jeroboam
son of Nebat had done. Jeroboam had led Israel
to sin by worshipping the golden calves in Bethel
and Dan.
30The LORD said to Jehu, "You have done well
in obeying what I said was right. You have done
to the family of Ahab as I wanted. Because of
this, your descendants[d] as far as your great-great-
grandchildren will be kings of Israel." 31But Jehu
was not careful to follow the teachings of the
LORD, the God of Israel, with all his heart. He did
not stop doing the same sins Jeroboam had done,
by which he had led Israel to sin.
32At that time the LORD began to make Israel
smaller. Hazael defeated the Israelites in all the
land of Israel, 33taking all the land of the Jordan
known as the land of Gilead. (It was the region
of Gad, Reuben and Manasseh.) He took land
from Aroer by the Arnon Ravine through Gilead
to Bashan.
34The other things Jehu did—everything he
did and all his victories—are recorded in the
book of the history of the kings of Israel. 35Jehu
died and was buried in Samaria, and his son Je-
hoahaz became king in his place. 36Jehu was
king over Israel in Samaria for 28 years.

Athaliah and Joash

11 When Ahaziah's mother, Athaliah, saw
that her son was dead, she killed all the
royal family. 2But Jehosheba, King Jehoram's
daughter and Ahaziah's sister, took Joash, Ahaz-
iah's son. She stole him from among the other
sons of the king who were about to be mur-
dered. She put Joash and his nurse in a bedroom
to hide him from Athaliah, so he was not killed.
3He hid with her in the Temple[d] of the LORD for
six years. During that time Athaliah ruled the
land.
4In the seventh year Jehoiada sent for the
commanders of groups of 100 men, as well as
the Carites.[n] He brought them together in the
Temple of the LORD and made an agreement
with them. There, in the Temple of the LORD, he
made them promise loyalty, and then he showed
them the king's son. 5He commanded them,
"This is what you must do. A third of you who
go on duty on the Sabbath[d] will guard the king's
palace. 6A third of you will be at the Sur Gate,
and another third will be at the gate behind the
guard. This way you will guard the Temple. 7The
two groups who go off duty on the Sabbath must
protect the Temple of the LORD for the king. 8All
of you must stand around the king, each man
with his weapons in his hand. If anyone comes
near, kill him. Stay close to the king when he
goes out and when he comes in."
9The commanders of groups of 100 men
obeyed everything Jehoiada the priest had com-
manded. Each one took his men who came on
duty on the Sabbath and those who went off
duty on the Sabbath, and they came to Jehoiada
the priest. 10He gave the commanders the spears
and shields that had belonged to King David and
that were kept in the Temple of the LORD.

Joash Becomes King

11Then each guard took his place with his
weapons in his hand. There were guards from
the south side of the Temple[d] to the north side.
They stood by the altar and the Temple and
around the king. 12Jehoiada brought out the king's
son and put the crown on him and gave him a
copy of the agreement. They appointed him king
and poured olive oil on him. Then they clapped
their hands and said, "Long live the king!"
13When Athaliah heard the noise of the guards
and the people, she went to them at the Temple
of the LORD. 14She looked, and there was the
king, standing by the pillar, as the custom was.
The officers and trumpeters were standing be-
side him, and all the people of the land were
very happy and were blowing trumpets. Then
Athaliah tore her clothes and screamed, "Trai-
tors! Traitors!"
15Jehoiada the priest gave orders to the com-
manders of the groups of 100 men, who led the
army. He said, "Surround her with soldiers and
kill with a sword anyone who follows her." He
commanded this because he had said, "Don't
put Athaliah to death in the Temple of the
LORD." 16So they caught her when she came to
the horses' entrance near the palace. There she
was put to death.

Sidelight It may seem like a modern idea to have a woman as Prime Minister, but one woman, Athaliah, ruled Judah for seven years (2 Kings 11:1–3). She didn't get her position by popular vote!

Carites This was probably a special unit of the army that was responsible for the king's safety, a kind of palace guard similar to the Kerethites and the Pelethites.

17Then Jehoiada made an agreement between the LORD and the king and the people that they would be the LORD's special people. He also made an agreement between the king and the people. 18All the people of the land went to the temple of Baal[d] and tore it down, smashing the altars and idols. They also killed Mattan, the priest of Baal, in front of the altars.

Then Jehoiada the priest placed guards at the Temple of the LORD. 19He took with him the commanders of 100 men and the Carites, the royal bodyguards, as well as the guards and all the people of the land. Together they took the king out of the Temple of the LORD and went into the palace through the gate of the guards. Then the king sat on the royal throne. 20So all the people of the land were very happy, and Jerusalem had peace, because Athaliah had been put to death with the sword at the palace.

21Joash was seven years old when he became king.

Sidelight If anyone asked Joash if he had "grown up in the church" he could have easily said yes. In fact, he was hidden in the Temple for six years to keep from getting killed. At the age of seven, he became the youngest king in the Bible (2 Kings 11:1–3, 21).

12 Joash became king of Judah in Jehu's seventh year as king of Israel, and he ruled for 40 years in Jerusalem. His mother's name was Zibiah, and she was from Beersheba. 2Joash did what the LORD said was right as long as Jehoiada the priest taught him. 3But the places where gods were worshipped were not removed; the people still made sacrifices and burned incense[d] there.

Joash Repairs the Temple

4Joash said to the priests, "Take all the money brought as offerings to the Temple[d] of the LORD. This includes the money each person owes in taxes and the money each person promises or brings freely to the LORD. 5Each priest will take the money from the people he serves. Then the priests must repair any damage they find in the Temple."

6But by the twenty-third year Joash was king, the priests still had not repaired the Temple. 7So King Joash called for Jehoiada the priest and the other priests and said to them, "Why aren't you repairing the damage of the Temple? Don't take any more money from the people you serve, but hand over the money for the repair of the Temple." 8The priests agreed not to take any more money from the people and not to repair the Temple themselves.

9Jehoiada the priest took a box and made a hole in the top of it. Then he put it by the altar, on the right side as the people came into the Temple of the LORD. The priests guarding the doorway put all the money brought to the Temple of the LORD into the box.

10Each time the priests saw that the box was full of money, the king's royal secretary and the high priest came. They counted the money that had been brought to the Temple of the LORD, and they put it into bags. 11Next they weighed the money and gave it to the people in charge of the work on the Temple. With it they paid the carpenters and the builders who worked on the Temple of the LORD, 12as well as the bricklayers and stonecutters. They also used the money to buy timber and cut stone to repair the damage of the Temple of the LORD. It paid for everything.

13The money brought into the Temple of the LORD was not used to make silver cups, wick trimmers, bowls, trumpets, or gold or silver vessels. 14They paid the money to the workers, who used it to repair the Temple of the LORD. 15They did not demand to know how the money was spent, because the workers were honest. 16The money from the penalty offerings and sin offerings was not brought into the Temple of the LORD, because it belonged to the priests.

Joash Saves Jerusalem

17About this time Hazael king of Aram attacked Gath and captured it. Then he went to attack Jerusalem. 18Joash king of Judah took all the holy things given by his ancestors, the kings of Judah—Jehoshaphat, Jehoram and Ahaziah. He also took his own holy things as well as the gold that was found in the treasuries of the Temple[d] of the LORD and the gold from the palace. Joash sent all this treasure to Hazael king of Aram, who turned away from Jerusalem.

19Everything else Joash did is written in the book of the history of the kings of Judah. 20His officers made plans against him and killed him at Beth Millo on the road down to Silla. 21The officers who killed him were Jozabad son of Shimeath and Jehozabad son of Shomer. Joash was buried with his ancestors in Jerusalem, and Amaziah, his son, became king in his place.

Jehoahaz King of Israel

13 Jehoahaz son of Jehu became king over Israel in Samaria during the twenty-third year Joash son of Ahaziah was king of Judah.

Jehoahaz ruled for seventeen years, 2and he did
what the LORD said was wrong. Jehoahaz did the
same sins Jeroboam son of Nebat had done. Jer-
oboam had led Israel to sin, and Jehoahaz did
not stop doing these same sins. 3So the LORD was
angry with Israel and handed them over to Haz-
ael king of Aram and his son Ben-Hadad for a
long time.
4Then Jehoahaz begged the LORD, and the
LORD listened to him. The LORD had seen the
troubles of Israel; he saw how terribly the king
of Aram was treating them. 5He gave Israel a
man to save them, and they escaped from the
Arameans. The Israelites then lived in their
own homes as they had before, 6but they still
did not stop doing the same sins that the family
of Jeroboam had done. He had led Israel to sin,
and they continued doing those sins. The
Asherah [d] idol also was left standing in Samaria.
7Nothing was left of Jehoahaz's army except
50 horsemen, ten chariots and 10,000 foot sol-
diers. The king of Aram had destroyed them
and made them like chaff. [d]
8Everything else Jehoahaz did and all his vic-
tories are written in the book of the history of
the kings of Israel. 9Jehoahaz died and was
buried in Samaria, and his son Jehoash became
king in his place.

Jehoash King of Israel

10Jehoash son of Jehoahaz became king of Is-
rael in Samaria during Joash's thirty-seventh
year as king of Judah. Jehoash ruled for sixteen
years, 11and he did what the LORD said was
wrong. He did not stop doing the same sins Jer-
oboam son of Nebat had done. Jeroboam had
led Israel to sin, and Jehoash continued to do
the same thing. 12Everything else he did and all
his victories, including his war against Amaziah
king of Judah, are written in the book of the
history of the kings of Israel. 13Jehoash died,
and Jeroboam took his place on the throne. Je-
hoash was buried in Samaria with the kings of
Israel.

The Death of Elisha

14At this time Elisha became sick. Before he
died, Jehoash king of Israel went to Elisha and
cried for him. Jehoash said, "My father, my
father! The chariots of Israel and their horse-
men!"
15Elisha said to Jehoash, "Take a bow and ar-
rows." So he took a bow and arrows. 16Then
Elisha said to him, "Put your hand on the bow."
So Jehoash put his hand on the bow. Then Elisha
put his hands on the king's hands. 17Elisha said,
"Open the east window." So Jehoash opened the
window. Then Elisha said, "Shoot," and Jehoash
shot. Elisha said, "The LORD's arrow of victory
over Aram! You will defeat the Arameans at
Aphek until you destroy them."
18Elisha said, "Take the arrows." So Jehoash
took them. Then Elisha said to him, "Strike the
ground." So Jehoash struck the ground three
times and stopped. 19The man of God was angry
with him. "You should have struck five or six
times!" Elisha said. "Then you would have
struck Aram until you had completely destroyed
it. But now you will defeat it only three times."
20Then Elisha died and was buried.
At that time groups of Moabites would rob the
land in the springtime. 21Once as some Israelites
were burying a man, suddenly they saw a group
of Moabites coming. The Israelites threw the
dead man into Elisha's grave. When the man
touched Elisha's bones, the man came back to
life and stood on his feet.

War with Aram

22During all the days Jehoahaz was king,
Hazael king of Aram troubled Israel. 23But the
LORD was kind to the Israelites; he had mercy on
them and helped them because of his agreement
with Abraham, Isaac and Jacob. To this day he
has never wanted to destroy them or reject
them.
24When Hazael king of Aram died, his son
Ben-Hadad became king in his place. 25During a
war Hazael had taken some cities from Jehoa-
haz, Jehoash's father. Now Jehoash took back
those cities from Hazael's son Ben-Hadad. He de-
feated Ben-Hadad three times and took back the
cities of Israel.

Amaziah King of Judah

14 Amaziah son of Joash became king of
Judah during the second year Jehoash
son of Jehoahaz was king of Israel. 2Amaziah
was 25 years old when he became king, and he
ruled for 29 years in Jerusalem. His mother was
named Jehoaddin, and she was from Jerusalem.
3Amaziah did what the LORD said was right. He
did everything his father Joash had done, but he
did not do as his ancestor David had done. 4The
places where gods were worshipped were not re-
moved, so the people still sacrificed and burned
incense [d] there.
5As soon as Amaziah took control of the king-
dom, he put to death the officers who had mur-
dered his father the king. 6But he did not put to
death the children of the murderers because of
the rule written in the Book of the Teachings of
Moses. The LORD had commanded: "Parents
must not be put to death when their children do

wrong, and children must not be put to death when their parents do wrong. Each must die for his own sins."[n]

7In battle Amaziah killed 10,000 Edomites in the Valley of Salt. He also took the city of Sela. He called it Joktheel, as it is still called today.

8Amaziah sent messengers to Jehoash son of Jehoahaz, the son of Jehu, king of Israel. They said, "Come, let's meet face to face."

9Then Jehoash king of Israel answered Amaziah king of Judah, "A thornbush in Lebanon sent a message to a cedar tree in Lebanon. It said, 'Let your daughter marry my son.' But then a wild animal from Lebanon came by, walking on and crushing the thornbush. 10You have defeated Edom, but you have become proud. Stay at home and boast. Don't ask for trouble, or you and Judah will be defeated."

11But Amaziah would not listen, so Jehoash king of Israel went to attack. He and Amaziah king of Judah faced each other in battle at Beth Shemesh in Judah. 12Israel defeated Judah, and every man of Judah ran away to his home. 13At Beth Shemesh Jehoash king of Israel captured Amaziah king of Judah. (Amaziah was the son of Joash, who was the son of Ahaziah.) Jehoash went up to Jerusalem and broke down the wall of Jerusalem from the Gate of Ephraim to the Corner Gate, which was about 200 metres. 14He took all the gold and silver and everything in the Temple[d] of the LORD, and he took the treasuries of the palace and some hostages. Then he returned to Samaria.

15The other acts of Jehoash and his victories, including his war against Amaziah king of Judah, are written in the book of the history of the kings of Israel. 16Jehoash died and was buried in Samaria with the kings of Israel, and his son Jeroboam became king in his place.

17Amaziah son of Joash, the king of Judah, lived fifteen years after the death of Jehoash son of Jehoahaz, the king of Israel. 18The other things Amaziah did are written in the book of the history of the kings of Judah. 19The people in Jerusalem made plans against him. So he ran away to the town of Lachish, but they sent men after him to Lachish and killed him. 20They brought his body back on horses, and he was buried with his ancestors in Jerusalem, in the city of David.

21Then all the people of Judah made Uzziah[n] king in place of his father Amaziah. Uzziah was sixteen years old. 22He rebuilt the town of Elath and made it part of Judah again after Amaziah died.

Jeroboam King of Israel

23Jeroboam son of Jehoash became king of Israel in Samaria during the fifteenth year Amaziah was king of Judah. (Amaziah was the son of Joash.) Jeroboam ruled for 41 years, 24and he did what the LORD said was wrong. Jeroboam son of Nebat had led Israel to sin, and Jeroboam son of Jehoash did not stop doing the same sins. 25Jeroboam won back Israel's border from Lebo Hamath to the Dead Sea.[d] This happened as the LORD, the God of Israel, had said through his servant Jonah son of Amittai, the prophet[d] from Gath Hepher. 26The LORD had seen how the Israelites, both slave and free, were suffering terribly. No one was left who could help Israel. 27The LORD had not said he would completely destroy Israel from the world, so he saved the Israelites through Jeroboam son of Jehoash.

28Everything else Jeroboam did is written down—all his victories and how he won back from Judah the towns of Damascus and Hamath for Israel. All this is written in the book of the history of the kings of Israel. 29Jeroboam died and was buried with his ancestors, the kings of Israel. Jeroboam's son Zechariah became king in his place.

Uzziah King of Judah

15 Uzziah[n] son of Amaziah became king of Judah during Jeroboam's twenty-seventh year as king of Israel. 2Uzziah was sixteen years old when he became king, and he ruled for 52 years in Jerusalem. His mother was named Jecoliah, and she was from Jerusalem. 3He did what the LORD said was right, just as his father Amaziah had done. 4But the places where gods were worshipped were not removed, so the people still made sacrifices and burned incense[d] there.

5The LORD struck Uzziah with a skin disease, which he had until the day he died. So he had to live in a separate house. Jotham, the king's son, was in charge of the palace, and he governed the people of the land.

6All the other things Uzziah did are written in the book of the history of the kings of Judah. 7Uzziah died and was buried near his ancestors in Jerusalem, and his son Jotham became king in his place.

Zechariah King of Israel

8Zechariah son of Jeroboam was king over Israel in Samaria. He ruled for six months during Uzziah's[n] thirty-eighth year as king of Judah. 9Zechariah did what the LORD said was wrong, just as his ancestors had done. Jeroboam son of

"Parents . . . sins." See Deuteronomy 24:16.
Uzziah Also called Azariah.

Nebat had led the people of Israel to sin, and
Zechariah did not stop doing the same sins.
10 Shallum son of Jabesh made plans against
Zechariah and killed him in front of the people.
Then Shallum became king in his place. 11 The
other acts of Zechariah are written in the book of
the history of the kings of Israel. 12 The LORD had
told Jehu: "Your sons down to your great-great-
grandchildren will be kings of Israel," and the
LORD's word came true.

Shallum King of Israel

13 Shallum son of Jabesh became king during
Uzziah's[n] thirty-ninth year as king of Judah.
Shallum ruled for a month in Samaria. 14 Then
Menahem son of Gadi came up from Tirzah to
Samaria and attacked Shallum son of Jabesh in
Samaria. He killed him and became king in Shal-
lum's place.
15 The other acts of Shallum and his secret
plans are written in the book of the history of the
kings of Israel.

Menahem King of Israel

16 Menahem started out from Tirzah and at-
tacked Tiphsah, destroying the city and the area
nearby. This was because the people had refused
to open the city gate for him. He defeated them
and ripped open all their pregnant women.
17 Menahem son of Gadi became king over Is-
rael during Uzziah's thirty-ninth year as king of
Judah. Menahem ruled for ten years in Samaria,
18 and he did what the LORD said was wrong. Jer-
oboam son of Nebat had led Israel to sin, and all
the time Menahem was king, he did not stop
doing the same sins.
19 Pul king of Assyria came to attack the land.
Menahem gave him about 35 tonnes of silver so
Pul would support him and make his hold on the
kingdom stronger. 20 Menahem taxed Israel to
pay about 50 pieces of silver to each soldier of
the king of Assyria. So the king left and did not
stay in the land.
21 Everything else Menahem did is written in
the book of the history of the kings of Israel.
22 Then Menahem died, and his son Pekahiah be-
came king in his place.

Pekahiah King of Israel

23 Pekahiah son of Menahem became king over
Israel in Samaria during Uzziah's[n] fiftieth year as
king of Judah. Pekahiah ruled for two years,
24 and he did what the LORD said was wrong. Jer-
oboam son of Nebat had led Israel to sin, and
Pekahiah did not stop doing the same sins.
25 Pekah son of Remaliah was one of Pekahiah's
captains, and he made plans against Pekahiah.
He took 50 men of Gilead with him and killed
Pekahiah, as well as Argob and Arieh, in the
palace at Samaria. Then Pekah became king in
Pekahiah's place.
26 Everything else Pekahiah did is written in
the book of the history of the kings of Israel.

Pekah King of Israel

27 Pekah son of Remaliah became king over Is-
rael in Samaria during Uzziah's[n] fifty-second
year as king of Judah. Pekah ruled for 20 years,
28 and he did what the LORD said was wrong. Jer-
oboam son of Nebat had led Israel to sin, and
Pekah did not stop doing the same sins.
29 Tiglath-Pileser[n] was king of Assyria. He at-
tacked while Pekah was king of Israel, capturing
the cities of Ijon, Abel Beth Maacah, Janoah,
Kedesh and Hazor. He also captured Gilead and
Galilee and all the land of Naphtali and carried
the people away to Assyria. 30 Then Hoshea son
of Elah made plans against Pekah son of Re-
maliah and attacked and killed him. Then
Hoshea became king in Pekah's place during the
twentieth year Jotham son of Uzziah was king.
31 Everything else Pekah did is written in the
book of the history of the kings of Israel.

Jotham King of Judah

32 Jotham son of Uzziah became king of Judah
during the second year Pekah son of Remaliah
was king of Israel. 33 Jotham was 25 years old
when he became king, and he ruled for sixteen
years in Jerusalem. His mother's name was
Jerusha, daughter of Zadok. 34 Jotham did what
the LORD said was right, just as his father Uzziah
had done. 35 But the places where gods were
worshipped were not removed, and the people
still made sacrifices and burned incense[d] there.
Jotham rebuilt the Upper Gate of the Temple[d] of
the LORD.
36 The other things Jotham did while he was
king are written in the book of the history of the
kings of Judah. 37 At that time the LORD began to
send Rezin king of Aram and Pekah son of Re-
maliah against Judah. 38 Jotham died and was
buried with his ancestors in Jerusalem, the city
of David, his ancestor. Then Jotham's son Ahaz
became king in his place.

Ahaz King of Judah

16 Ahaz was the son of Jotham king of
Judah. Ahaz became king of Judah in the
seventeenth year Pekah son of Remaliah was

Uzziah Also called Azariah.
Tiglath-Pileser Also called Pul.

king of Israel. 2Ahaz was 20 years old when he
became king, and he ruled for sixteen years in
Jerusalem. Unlike his ancestor David, he did not
do what the LORD his God said was right. 3Ahaz
did the same things the kings of Israel had
done. He even made his son pass through fire.
He did the same hateful sins as the nations had
done whom the LORD had forced out of the land
ahead of the Israelites. 4Ahaz offered sacrifices
and burned incense[d] at the places where gods
were worshipped, on the hills and under every
green tree.

5Rezin king of Aram and Pekah son of
Remaliah, the king of Israel, came up to attack
Jerusalem. They surrounded Ahaz but could
not defeat him. 6At that time Rezin king of Aram
took back the city of Elath for Aram, and he
forced out all the people of Judah. Then Edomites
moved into Elath, and they still live there today.

7Ahaz sent messengers to Tiglath-Pileser[n] king
of Assyria, saying, "I am your servant and your
friend. Come and save me from the king of Aram
and the king of Israel, who are attacking me."
8Ahaz took the silver and gold that was in the
Temple[d] of the LORD and in the treasuries of the
palace, and he sent these as a gift to the king of
Assyria. 9So the king of Assyria listened to Ahaz.
He attacked Damascus and captured it and sent
all its people away to Kir. And he killed Rezin.

10Then King Ahaz went to Damascus to meet
Tiglath-Pileser king of Assyria. Ahaz saw an altar
at Damascus, and he sent plans and a pattern of
this altar to Uriah the priest. 11So Uriah the priest
built an altar, following the plans King Ahaz had
sent him from Damascus. Uriah finished the
altar before King Ahaz came back from Damas-
cus. 12When the king arrived from Damascus, he
saw the altar and went near and offered sacri-
fices on it. 13He burned his burnt offerings and
grain offerings and poured out his drink offering.
He also sprinkled the blood of his fellowship
offerings on the altar.

14Ahaz moved the bronze altar that was be-
fore the LORD at the front of the Temple. It was
between Ahaz's altar and the Temple of the
LORD, but he put it on the north side of his altar.
15King Ahaz commanded Uriah the priest, "On
the large altar burn the morning burnt offering,
the evening grain offering, the king's burnt offer-
ing and grain offering, and the whole burnt offer-
ing, the grain offering and the drink offering
for all the people of the land. Sprinkle on the
altar all the blood of the burnt offering and of the
sacrifice. But I will use the bronze altar to
ask questions of God." 16So Uriah the priest did
everything as King Ahaz commanded him.

17Then King Ahaz took off the side panels
from the bases and removed the washing bowls
from the top of the bases. He also took the large
bowl, which was called the Sea, off the bronze
bulls that held it up, and he put it on a stone
base. 18Ahaz took away the platform for the royal
throne, which had been built at the Temple of
the LORD. He also took away the outside en-
trance for the king. He did these things because
of the king of Assyria.

19The other things Ahaz did as king are writ-
ten in the book of the history of the kings of
Judah. 20Ahaz died and was buried with his an-
cestors in Jerusalem, and Ahaz's son Hezekiah
became king in his place.

Hoshea, Last King of Israel

17 Hoshea son of Elah became king over Is-
rael during Ahaz's twelfth year as king of
Judah. Hoshea ruled in Samaria for nine years.
2He did what the LORD said was wrong, but he
was not as bad as the kings of Israel who had
ruled before him.

3Shalmaneser king of Assyria came to attack
Hoshea. Hoshea had been Shalmaneser's servant
and had made the payments to Shalmaneser that
he had demanded. 4But the king of Assyria found
out that Hoshea had made plans against him by
sending messengers to So, the king of Egypt.
Hoshea had also stopped giving Shalmaneser the
payments, which he had paid every year in the
past. For that, the king put Hoshea in prison.
5Then the king of Assyria came and attacked all
the land of Israel. He surrounded Samaria and at-
tacked it for three years. 6He defeated Samaria in
the ninth year Hoshea was king, and he took the
Israelites away to Assyria. He settled them in
Halah, in Gozan on the Habor River and in the
cities of the Medes.

Israelites Punished for Sin

7All these things happened because the Israel-
ites had sinned against the LORD their God. He
had brought them out of Egypt and had rescued
them from the power of the king of Egypt, but
the Israelites had honoured other gods. 8They
lived like the nations the LORD had forced out of
the land ahead of them. They lived as their evil
kings had shown them, 9secretly sinning against
the LORD their God. They built places to worship
gods in all their cities, from the watchtower to
the fortified city. 10They put up stone pillars to
gods and Asherah[d] idols on every high hill and
under every green tree. 11The Israelites burned
incense[d] everywhere gods were worshipped,
just as the nations who lived there before them

Tiglath-Pileser Also called Pul.

had done, whom the LORD had forced out of the
land. The Israelites did wicked things that made
the LORD angry. 12They served idols when the
LORD had said, "You must not do this." 13The LORD
used every prophet[d] and seer[d] to warn Israel and
Judah. He said, "Stop your evil ways and obey my
commands and laws. Follow all the teachings that
I commanded your ancestors, the teachings that I
gave you through my servants the prophets."

14But the people would not listen. They were
stubborn, just as their ancestors had been who
did not believe in the LORD their God. 15They re-
jected the LORD's laws and the agreement he had
made with their ancestors. And they refused to
listen to his warnings. They worshipped useless
idols and became useless themselves. They did
what the nations around them did, which the
LORD had warned them not to do.

16The people rejected all the commands of the
LORD their God. They moulded statues of two
calves, and they made an Asherah idol. They
worshipped all the stars of the sky and served
Baal.[d] 17They made their sons and daughters
pass through fire and tried to find out the future
by magic and witchcraft.[d] They always chose to
do what the LORD said was wrong, which made
him angry. 18Because he was very angry with the
people of Israel, he removed them from his pres-
ence. Only the tribe[d] of Judah was left.

Judah is Also Guilty

19But even Judah did not obey the commands
of the LORD their God. They did what the Is-
raelites had done, 20so the LORD rejected all the
people of Israel. He punished them and let oth-
ers destroy them; he threw them out of his pres-
ence. 21When the LORD separated them from the
family of David, the Israelites made Jeroboam
son of Nebat their king. Jeroboam led the Is-
raelites away from the LORD and led them to sin
greatly. 22So they continued to do all the sins Jer-
oboam did. They did not stop doing these sins
23until the LORD removed the Israelites from his
presence, just as he had said through all his ser-
vants the prophets.[d] So the Israelites were taken
out of their land to Assyria, and they have been
there to this day.

The Beginning of the Samaritan People

24The king of Assyria brought people from
Babylon, Cuthah, Avva, Hamath and Sephar-
vaim and put them in the cities of Samaria to re-
place the Israelites. These people took over
Samaria and lived in the cities. 25At first they did
not worship the LORD, so he sent lions among
them which killed some of them. 26The king of
Assyria was told, "You sent foreigners into the
cities of Samaria who do not know the law of the
god of the land. This is why he has sent lions
among them. The lions are killing them because
they don't know what the god wants."

27Then the king of Assyria commanded, "Send
back one of the priests you took away. Let him live
there and teach the people what the god wants."
28So one of the priests who had been carried away
from Samaria returned to live in Bethel. And he
taught the people how to honour the LORD.

29But each nation made gods of its own and
put them in the cities where they lived and in
the temples where gods were worshipped.
These temples had been built by the Samaritans.
30The people from Babylon made Succoth
Benoth their god. The people from Cuthah wor-
shipped Nergal. The people of Hamath wor-
shipped Ashima. 31The Avvites worshipped
Nibhaz and Tartak. The Sepharvites burned their
children in the fire, sacrificing them to Adramm-
elech and Anammelech, the gods of Sepharvaim.
32They also honoured the LORD, but they chose
priests for the places where gods were wor-
shipped. The priests were chosen from among
themselves, and they made sacrifices for the peo-
ple. 33The people honoured the LORD but also
served their own gods, just as the nations did
from which they had been brought. 34Even
today they do as they did in the past. They do
not worship the LORD nor obey his rules and
commands. They do not obey the teachings or
the commands of the LORD, which he gave to the
children of Jacob, whom he had named Israel.
35The LORD had made an agreement with them
and had commanded them, "Do not honour
other gods. Do not bow down to them or wor-
ship them or offer sacrifices to them. 36Worship
the LORD who brought you up out of the land of
Egypt with great power and strength. Bow down
to him and offer sacrifices to him. 37Always obey
the rules, orders, teachings and commands he
wrote for you. Do not honour other gods. 38Do
not forget the agreement I made with you, and
do not honour other gods. 39Instead worship the
LORD your God, who will save you from all your
enemies."

40But the Israelites did not listen. They kept
on doing the same things they had done before.
41So these nations honoured the LORD but also
worshipped their idols, and their children and
grandchildren still do as their ancestors did.

Hezekiah King of Judah

18 Hezekiah son of Ahaz king of Judah be-
came king during the third year Hoshea
son of Elah was king of Israel. 2Hezekiah was 25
years old when he became king, and he ruled for
29 years in Jerusalem. His mother's name was
Abijah daughter of Zechariah. 3Hezekiah did

what the LORD said was right, just as his ancestor
David had done. 4He removed the places where
gods were worshipped. He smashed the stone
pillars and cut down the Asherah[d] idols. Also the
Israelites had been burning incense[d] to Nehush-
tan, the bronze snake Moses had made. But
Hezekiah broke it into pieces.
5Hezekiah trusted in the LORD, the God of Is-
rael. There was no one like him among all the
kings of Judah, either before him or after him.
6Hezekiah was loyal to the LORD and did not stop
following him; he obeyed the commands the
LORD had given Moses. 7And the LORD was with
Hezekiah, so he had success in everything he
did. He turned against the king of Assyria and
stopped serving him. 8Hezekiah defeated the
Philistines all the way to Gaza and its borders, in-
cluding the watchtowers and the fortified cities.

The Assyrians Capture Samaria

9Shalmaneser king of Assyria surrounded
Samaria and attacked it in the fourth year
Hezekiah was king. This was the seventh year
Hoshea son of Elah was king of Israel. 10After
three years the Assyrians captured Samaria. This
was in the sixth year Hezekiah was king, which
was Hoshea's ninth year as king of Israel. 11The
king of Assyria took the Israelites away to Assyria
and settled them in Halah, in Gozan on the
Habor River and in the cities of the Medes.
12This happened because they did not obey the
LORD their God. They broke his agreement and
did not obey all that Moses, the LORD's servant,
had commanded. They would not listen to the
commands or do them.

Assyria Attacks Judah

13During Hezekiah's fourteenth year as king,
Sennacherib king of Assyria attacked all the forti-
fied cities of Judah and captured them. 14Then
Hezekiah king of Judah sent a message to the
king of Assyria at Lachish. He said, "I have done
wrong. Leave me alone, and I will pay anything
you ask." So the king of Assyria made Hezekiah
pay about 10 tonnes of silver and 1 tonne of gold.
15Hezekiah gave him all the silver that was in the
Temple[d] of the LORD and in the palace treasuries.
16Hezekiah stripped all the gold that covered the
doors and doorposts of the Temple of the LORD.
Hezekiah had put gold on these doors himself,
but he gave it all to the king of Assyria.
17The king of Assyria sent out his supreme
commander, his chief officer and his field com-
mander. They went with a large army from
Lachish to King Hezekiah in Jerusalem. When
they came near the waterway from the upper
pool on the road where people do their laundry,
they stopped. 18They called for the king, so the
king sent Eliakim, Shebna and Joah out to meet
them. Eliakim son of Hilkiah was the palace
manager, Shebna was the royal secretary and
Joah son of Asaph was the recorder.
19The field commander said to them, "Tell
Hezekiah this:
" 'The great king, the king of Assyria, says:
What can you trust in now? 20You say you have
battle plans and power for war, but your words
mean nothing. Whom are you trusting for help
so that you turn against me? 21Look, you are de-
pending on Egypt to help you, but Egypt is like a
splintered walking stick. If you lean on it for
help, it will stab your hand and hurt you. The
king of Egypt will hurt all those who depend on
him. 22You might say, "We are depending on the
LORD our God," but Hezekiah destroyed the
LORD's altars and the places of worship.
Hezekiah told Judah and Jerusalem, "You must
worship only at this one altar in Jerusalem."
23" 'Now make an agreement with my master,
the king of Assyria: I will give you 2,000 horses
if you can find enough men to ride them. 24You
cannot defeat one of my master's least important
officers, so why do you depend on Egypt to give
you chariots and horsemen? 25I have not come
to attack and destroy this place without an order
from the LORD. The LORD himself told me to
come to this country and destroy it.' "
26Then Eliakim son of Hilkiah, Shebna and
Joah said to the field commander, "Please speak
to us in the Aramaic language. We understand it.
Don't speak to us in Hebrew, because the people
on the city wall can hear you."
27"No," the commander said, "my master did
not send me to tell these things only to you and
your king. He sent me to speak also to those
people sitting on the wall who will have to eat
their own dung and drink their own urine like
you."
28Then the commander stood and shouted
loudly in the Hebrew language, "Listen to what
the great king, the king of Assyria, says! 29The
king says you should not let Hezekiah fool you,
because he can't save you from my power.
30Don't let Hezekiah talk you into trusting the
LORD by saying, 'The LORD will surely save
us. This city won't be handed over to the king of
Assyria.'
31"Don't listen to Hezekiah. The king of As-
syria says, 'Make peace with me, and come out
of the city to me. Then everyone will be free to
eat the fruit from his own grapevine and fig tree
and to drink water from his own well. 32After
that I will come and take you to a land like your
own—a land with grain and new wine, bread
and vineyards, olives and honey. Choose to live
and not to die!'

"Don't listen to Hezekiah. He is fooling you when he says, 'The LORD will save us.' [33]Has a god of any other nation saved his people from the power of the king of Assyria? [34]Where are the gods of Hamath and Arpad? Where are the gods of Sepharvaim, Hena and Ivvah? They did not save Samaria from my power. [35]Not one of all the gods of these countries has saved his people from me. Neither can the LORD save Jerusalem from my power."

[36]The people were silent. They didn't answer the commander at all, because King Hezekiah had ordered, "Don't answer him."

[37]Then Eliakim, Shebna and Joah tore their clothes to show how upset they were. (Eliakim son of Hilkiah was the palace manager, Shebna was the royal secretary and Joah son of Asaph was the recorder.) The three men went to Hezekiah and told him what the field commander had said.

Sidelight The Assyrians' attack on Jerusalem led by Sennacherib isn't recorded only in the Bible (2 Kings 18:13–37). Archaeologists have found "Sennacherib's Prism", which gives the invaders' view of the situation. Another source tells how a plague of mice attacked Sennacherib's army to make the Assyrians retreat.

Jerusalem will Be Saved

19 When King Hezekiah heard the message, he tore his clothes and put on rough cloth to show how sad he was. Then he went into the Temple [d] of the LORD. [2]Hezekiah sent Eliakim, the palace manager and Shebna, the royal secretary, and the elders of the priests to Isaiah. They were all wearing rough cloth when they came to Isaiah the prophet, [d] the son of Amoz. [3]They told Isaiah, "This is what Hezekiah says: 'Today is a day of sorrow and punishment and disgrace, as when a child should be born, but the mother is not strong enough to give birth to it. [4]The king of Assyria sent his field commander to make fun of the living God. Maybe the LORD your God will hear what the commander said and will punish him for it. So pray for the few of us who are left alive.' "

[5]When Hezekiah's officers came to Isaiah, [6]he said to them, "Tell your master this: the LORD says, 'Don't be afraid of what you have heard. Don't be frightened by the words the servants of the king of Assyria have spoken against me. [7]Listen! I am going to put a spirit in the king of Assyria. He will hear a report that will make him return to his own country, and I will cause him to die by the sword there.' "

[8]The field commander heard that the king of Assyria had left Lachish. When he went back, he found the king fighting against the city of Libnah.

[9]The king received a report that Tirhakah, the Cushite king of Egypt, was coming to attack him. When the king of Assyria heard this, he sent messengers to Hezekiah, saying, [10]"Tell Hezekiah king of Judah: 'Don't be fooled by the god you trust. Don't believe him when he says Jerusalem will not be handed over to the king of Assyria. [11]You have heard what the kings of Assyria have done. They have completely defeated every country, so do not think you will be saved. [12]Did the gods of those people save them? My ancestors destroyed them, defeating the cities of Gozan, Haran and Rezeph, and the people of Eden living in Tel Assar. [13]Where are the kings of Hamath and Arpad? Where are the kings of Sepharvaim, Hena and Ivvah?' "

Hezekiah Prays to the LORD

[14]When Hezekiah received the letter from the messengers and read it, he went up to the Temple [d] of the LORD. He spread the letter out before the LORD [15]and prayed to the LORD: "LORD, God of Israel, whose throne is between the gold creatures with wings, only you are God of all the kingdoms of the earth. You made the heavens and the earth. [16]Hear, LORD, and listen. Open your eyes, LORD, and see. Listen to the words Sennacherib has said to insult the living God. [17]It is true, LORD, that the kings of Assyria have destroyed these countries and their lands. [18]They have thrown the gods of these nations into the fire, but they were only wood and rock statues that people made. So the kings have destroyed them. [19]Now, LORD our God, save us from the king's power so that all the kingdoms of the earth will know that you, LORD, are the only God."

God Answers Hezekiah

[20]Then Isaiah son of Amoz sent a message to Hezekiah that said, "This is what the LORD, the God of Israel, says: 'I have heard your prayer to me about Sennacherib king of Assyria.' [21]This is what the LORD has said against Sennacherib:

'The people of Jerusalem
    hate you and make fun of you.
The people of Jerusalem
    laugh at you as you run away.
[22]You have insulted me and spoken against me;
    you have raised your voice against me.
You have a proud look on your face,
    which is against me, the Holy One of
        Israel.

23 You have sent your messengers to insult the
Lord.
You have said, "With my many chariots
I have gone to the tops of the mountains,
to the highest mountains of Lebanon.
I have cut down its tallest cedars
and its best pine trees.
I have gone to its farthest places
and to its best forests.
24 I have dug wells in foreign countries
and drunk water there.
By the soles of my feet,
I have dried up all the rivers of Egypt."

25 " 'King of Assyria, surely you have heard.
Long ago I, the LORD, planned these
things.
Long ago I designed them,
and now I have made them happen.
I allowed you to turn those fortified cities
into piles of rocks.
26 The people in those cities were weak;
they were frightened and put to shame.
They were like grass in the field,
like tender, young grass,
like grass on the housetop
that is burned by the wind before it can
grow.

27 " 'I know when you rest,
when you come and go,
and how you rage against me.
28 Because you rage against me,
and because I have heard your proud
words,
I will put my hook in your nose
and my bit in your mouth.
Then I will force you to leave my country
the same way you came.'

29 "Then the LORD said, 'Hezekiah, I will give
you this sign:
This year you will eat the grain that grows
wild,
and the second year you will eat what
grows wild from that.
But in the third year, plant grain and
harvest it.
Plant vineyards and eat their fruit.
30 Some of the people in the family of Judah
will escape.
Like plants that take root,
they will grow strong and have many
children.
31 A few people will come out of Jerusalem
alive;
a few from Mount Zion [d] will live.
The strong love of the LORD All-powerful
will make this happen.'

32 "So this is what the LORD says about the king
of Assyria:
'He will not enter this city
or even shoot an arrow here.
He will not fight against it with shields
or build a ramp to attack the city walls.
33 He will return to his country the same way he
came,
and he will not enter this city,'
says the LORD.
34 'I will defend and save this city
for my sake and for the sake of David, my
servant.' "

35 That night the angel of the LORD went out
and killed 185,000 men in the Assyrian camp.
When the people got up early the next morning,
they saw all the dead bodies. 36 So Sennacherib
king of Assyria left and went back to Nineveh
and stayed there.
37 One day as Sennacherib was worshipping in
the temple of his god Nisroch, his sons Adramm-
elech and Sharezer killed him with a sword. Then
they escaped to the land of Ararat. So Sennach-
erib's son Esarhaddon became king of Assyria.

Hezekiah's Illness

20 At that time Hezekiah became so sick he
almost died. The prophet [d] Isaiah son of
Amoz went to see him and told him, "This is
what the LORD says: 'Make arrangements because
you are not going to live, but die.' "
2 Hezekiah turned towards the wall and
prayed to the LORD, 3 "LORD, please remember
that I have always obeyed you. I have given my-
self completely to you and have done what you
said was right." Then Hezekiah cried loudly.
4 Before Isaiah had left the middle courtyard,
the LORD spoke his word to Isaiah: 5 "Go back
and tell Hezekiah, the leader of my people: 'This
is what the LORD, the God of your ancestor
David, says: I have heard your prayer and seen
your tears, so I will heal you. Three days from
now you will go up to the Temple [d] of the LORD.
6 I will add fifteen years to your life. I will save
you and this city from the king of Assyria; I will
protect the city for my sake and for the sake of
my servant David.' "
7 Then Isaiah said, "Make a paste from figs."
So they made it and put it on Hezekiah's boil,
and he got well.
8 Hezekiah had asked Isaiah, "What will be
the sign that the LORD will heal me and that I
will go up to the Temple of the LORD on the third
day?"
9 Isaiah said, "The LORD will do what he says.
This is the sign from the LORD to show you: do
you want the shadow to go forwards ten steps or
back ten steps?"

10Hezekiah answered, "It's easy for the shadow to go forwards ten steps. Instead, let it go back ten steps."

11Then Isaiah the prophet called to the LORD, and the LORD brought the shadow ten steps back up the stairway of Ahaz that it had gone down.

Messengers from Babylon

12At that time Merodach-Baladan son of Baladan was king of Babylon. He sent letters and a gift to Hezekiah, because he had heard that Hezekiah was sick. 13Hezekiah listened to the messengers, so he showed them what was in his storehouses: the silver, gold, spices, expensive perfumes, his swords and shields, and all his wealth. He showed them everything in his palace and his kingdom.

14Then Isaiah the prophet[d] went to King Hezekiah and asked him, "What did these men say? Where did they come from?"

Hezekiah said, "They came from a faraway country—from Babylon."

15So Isaiah asked him, "What did they see in your palace?"

Hezekiah said, "They saw everything in my palace. I showed them all my wealth."

16Then Isaiah said to Hezekiah, "Listen to the words of the LORD: 17'In the future everything in your palace and everything your ancestors have stored up until this day will be taken away to Babylon. Nothing will be left,' says the LORD. 18'Some of your own children, those who will be born to you, will be taken away. And they will become servants in the palace of the king of Babylon.' "

19Hezekiah told Isaiah, "These words from the LORD are good." He said this because he thought, "There will be peace and security in my lifetime."

20Everything else Hezekiah did—all his victories, his work on the pool, his work on the tunnel to bring water into the city—is written in the book of the history of the kings of Judah. 21Then Hezekiah died, and his son Manasseh became king in his place.

Sidelight The tunnel King Hezekiah dug to provide water for Jerusalem during the Assyrian siege (2 Kings 20:20) was cut through 525 metres of solid limestone – a massive job completed without modern tunnelling machines. An inscription on "Hezekiah's Tunnel" says workers started digging at each end and met in the middle. People still walk through the tunnel today.

Manasseh King of Judah

21 Manasseh was twelve years old when he became king, and he was king for 55 years in Jerusalem. His mother's name was Hephzibah. 2He did what the LORD said was wrong. He did the hateful things the other nations had done—the nations that the LORD had forced out of the land ahead of the Israelites. 3Manasseh's father, Hezekiah, had destroyed the places where gods were worshipped, but Manasseh rebuilt them. He built altars for Baal,[d] and he made an Asherah[d] idol as Ahab king of Israel had done. Manasseh also worshipped all the stars of the sky and served them. 4The LORD had said about the Temple,[d] "I will be worshipped in Jerusalem," but Manasseh built altars in the Temple of the LORD. 5He built altars to worship the stars in the two courtyards of the Temple of the LORD. 6He made his own son pass through fire. He practised magic and told the future by explaining signs and dreams, and he got advice from mediums[d] and fortune-tellers. He did many things the LORD said were wrong, which made the LORD angry.

Sidelight The longest reign in the Bible was that of Manasseh. He reigned 55 years (2 Kings 21:1). Despite his long rule, Manasseh was considered one of the most evil kings of Judah (2 Chronicles 33:9, p.426). The king with the shortest reign was Zimri (1 Kings 16:15, p.331), who lasted only seven days!

7Manasseh carved an Asherah idol and put it in the Temple. The LORD had said to David and his son Solomon about the Temple, "I will be worshipped for ever in this Temple and in Jerusalem, which I have chosen from all the tribes[d] of Israel. 8I will never again make the Israelites wander out of the land I gave their ancestors. But they must obey everything I have commanded them and all the teachings my servant Moses gave them." 9But the people did not listen. Manasseh led them to do more evil than the nations the LORD had destroyed ahead of the Israelites.

10The LORD said through his servants the prophets,[d] 11"Manasseh king of Judah has done these hateful things. He has done more evil than the Amorites before him. He has also led Judah to sin with his idols. 12So this is what the LORD, the God of Israel, says: 'I will bring so much trouble on Jerusalem and Judah that anyone who hears about it will be shocked. 13I will stretch the

measuring line of Samaria over Jerusalem, and
the plumb line[d] used against Ahab's family will
be used on Jerusalem. I will wipe out Jerusalem
as a person wipes a dish and turns it upside
down. 14I will throw away the rest of my people
who are left. I will give them to their enemies,
and they will be robbed by all their enemies,
15because my people did what I said was wrong.
They have made me angry from the day their an-
cestors left Egypt until now.' "
16Manasseh also killed many innocent people,
filling Jerusalem from one end to the other with
their blood. This was besides the sin he led
Judah to do; he led Judah to do what the LORD
said was wrong.
17The other things Manasseh did as king, even
the sin he did, are written in the book of the his-
tory of the kings of Judah. 18Manasseh died and
was buried in the garden of his own palace, the
garden of Uzza. Then Manasseh's son Amon
became king in his place.

Amon King of Judah

19Amon was 22 years old when he became
king, and he was king for two years in Jerusalem.
His mother's name was Meshullemeth daughter
of Haruz, who was from Jotbah. 20Amon did
what the LORD said was wrong, as his father
Manasseh had done. 21He lived in the same way
his father had lived: he worshipped the idols his
father had worshipped, and he bowed down be-
fore them. 22Amon rejected the LORD, the God of
his ancestors, and did not follow the ways of the
LORD.
23Amon's officers made plans against him and
killed him in his palace. 24Then the people of the
land killed all those who had made plans to kill
King Amon, and they made his son Josiah king in
his place.
25Everything else Amon did is written in the
book of the history of the kings of Judah. 26He
was buried in his grave in the garden of Uzza,
and his son Josiah became king in his place.

Josiah King of Judah

22 Josiah was eight years old when he be-
came king, and he ruled for 31 years in
Jerusalem. His mother's name was Jedidah
daughter of Adaiah, who was from Bozkath.
2Josiah did what the LORD said was right. He
lived as his ancestor David had lived, and he did
not stop doing what was right.
3In Josiah's eighteenth year as king, he sent
Shaphan to the Temple[d] of the LORD. Shaphan
son of Azaliah, the son of Meshullam, was the
royal secretary. Josiah said, 4"Go up to Hilkiah
the high priest, and have him empty out the
money the gatekeepers have gathered from the
people. This is the money they have brought into
the Temple of the LORD. 5Have him give the
money to the supervisors of the work on the
Temple of the LORD. They must pay the workers
who repair the Temple of the LORD— 6the car-
penters, builders and bricklayers. Also use the
money to buy timber and cut stone to repair the
Temple. 7They do not need to report how they
use the money given to them, because they are
working honestly."

The Book of the Teachings is Found

8Hilkiah the high priest said to Shaphan the
royal secretary, "I've found the Book of the
Teachings in the Temple[d] of the LORD." He gave
it to Shaphan, who read it.
9Then Shaphan the royal secretary went to
the king and reported to Josiah, "Your officers
have paid out the money that was in the Temple
of the LORD. They have given it to the workers
and supervisors at the Temple." 10Then Shaphan
the royal secretary told the king, "Hilkiah the
priest has given me a book." And Shaphan read
from the book to the king.
11When the king heard the words of the Book
of the Teachings, he tore his clothes to show
how upset he was. 12He gave orders to Hilkiah
the priest, Ahikam son of Shaphan, Acbor son of
Micaiah, Shaphan the royal secretary and Asaiah
the king's servant. These were the orders: 13"Go
and ask the LORD about the words in the book
that was found. Ask for me, for all the people
and for all Judah. The LORD's anger is burning
against us, because our ancestors did not obey
the words of this book; they did not do all the
things written for us to do."
14So Hilkiah the priest, Ahikam, Acbor,
Shaphan and Asaiah went to talk to Huldah the
prophetess.[d] She was the wife of Shallum son of
Tikvah, the son of Harhas, who took care of the
king's clothes. Huldah lived in Jerusalem, in the
new area of the city.
15She said to them, "This is what the LORD,
the God of Israel, says: 'Tell the man who sent
you to me, 16"This is what the LORD says: 'I will
bring trouble to this place and to the people liv-
ing here, as it is written in the book which the
king of Judah has read. 17The people of Judah
have left me and have burned incense[d] to other
gods. They have made me angry by all that they
have done. My anger burns against this place
like a fire, and it will not be put out.' " 18Tell the
king of Judah, who sent you to ask the LORD,
"This is what the LORD, the God of Israel, says
about the words you heard: 19When you heard
my words against this place and its people, you
became sorry for what you had done and upset
yourself before me. I said they would be cursed

and would be destroyed. You tore your clothes to show how upset you were, and you cried in my presence. This is why I have heard you, says the LORD. 20So I will let you die, and you will be buried in peace. You won't see all the trouble I will bring to this place."'"

So they took her message back to the king.

The People Hear the Agreement

23 Then the king gathered all the elders of Judah and Jerusalem together. 2He went up to the Temple[d] of the LORD, and all the people from Judah and Jerusalem went with him. The priests, prophets[d] and all the people—from the least important to the most important—went with him. He read to them all the words of the Book of the Agreement that was found in the Temple of the LORD. 3The king stood by the pillar and made an agreement in the presence of the LORD to follow the LORD and obey his commands, rules and laws with his whole being, and to obey the words of the agreement written in this book. Then all the people promised to obey the agreement.

Josiah Destroys the Places for Idol Worship

4The king commanded Hilkiah the high priest and the priests of the next rank and the gatekeepers to bring out of the Temple[d] of the LORD everything made for Baal,[d] Asherah[d] and all the stars of the sky. Then Josiah burnt them outside Jerusalem in the open country of the Kidron Valley and carried their ashes to Bethel. 5The kings of Judah had chosen priests for these gods. These priests burnt incense[d] in the places where gods were worshipped in the cities of Judah and the towns around Jerusalem. They burnt incense to Baal, the sun, the moon, the planets and all the stars of the sky. But Josiah took those priests away. 6He removed the Asherah idol from the Temple of the LORD and took it outside Jerusalem to the Kidron Valley, where he burnt it and beat it into dust. Then he threw the ashes on the graves of the common people. 7He also tore down the houses of the male prostitutes[d] who were in the Temple of the LORD, where the women did weaving for Asherah.

8King Josiah brought all the false priests from the cities of Judah. He ruined the places where gods were worshipped, where the priests had burnt incense, from Geba to Beersheba. He destroyed the places of worship at the entrance to the Gate of Joshua, the ruler of the city, on the left side of the city gate. 9The priests at the places where gods were worshipped were not allowed to serve at the LORD's altar in Jerusalem. But they could eat bread made without yeast with their brothers.

10Josiah ruined Topheth, in the Valley of Ben Hinnom, so no one could sacrifice his son or daughter to Molech.[d] 11Judah's kings had placed horses at the front door of the Temple of the LORD in the courtyard near the room of Nathan-Melech, an officer. These horses were for the worship of the sun. So Josiah removed them and burnt the chariots that were for sun worship also.

12The kings of Judah had built altars on the roof[n] of the upstairs room of Ahaz. Josiah broke down these altars and the altars Manasseh had made in the two courtyards of the Temple of the LORD. Josiah smashed them to pieces and threw their dust into the Kidron Valley. 13King Josiah ruined the places where gods were worshipped east of Jerusalem, south of the Mount of Olives.[n] Solomon king of Israel had built these places. One was for Ashtoreth,[d] the hated goddess of the Sidonians. One was for Chemosh,[d] the hated god of Moab. And one was for Molech, the hated god of the Ammonites. 14Josiah smashed to pieces the stone pillars they worshipped, and he cut down the Asherah idols. Then he covered the places with human bones.

15Josiah also broke down the altar at Bethel—the place of worship made by Jeroboam son of Nebat, who had led Israel to sin. Josiah burnt that place, broke the stones of the altar into pieces, then beat them into dust. He also burnt the Asherah idol. 16When he turned round, he saw the graves on the mountain. He had the bones taken from the graves, and he burnt them on the altar to ruin it. This happened as the LORD had said it would through the man of God.

17Josiah asked, "What is that monument I see?"

The people of the city answered, "It's the grave of the man of God who came from Judah. This prophet announced the things you have done against the altar of Bethel."

18Josiah said, "Leave the grave alone. No one may move this man's bones." So they left his bones and the bones of the prophet who had come from Samaria.

19The kings of Israel had built temples for worshipping gods in the cities of Samaria, which had caused the LORD to be angry. Josiah removed all those temples and did the same things as he had done at Bethel. 20He killed all the priests of those

roof In Bible times houses were built with flat roofs. The roof was used for drying things such as flax and fruit. And it was used as an extra room, as a place for worship and as a place to sleep in the summer.

Mount of Olives Literally, "The Mountain of Ruin".

places of worship; he killed them on the altars
and burnt human bones on the altars. Then he
went back to Jerusalem.

Josiah Celebrates the Passover

21The king commanded all the people, "Cele-
brate the Passover[d] to the LORD your God as it is
written in this Book of the Agreement." 22The
Passover had not been celebrated like this since
the judges led Israel. Nor had one like it hap-
pened while there were kings of Israel and kings
of Judah. 23This Passover was celebrated to the
LORD in Jerusalem in the eighteenth year of King
Josiah's rule.
24Josiah destroyed the mediums,[d] fortune-
tellers, house gods and idols. He also destroyed
all the hated gods seen in the land of Judah and
Jerusalem. This was to obey the words of the
teachings written in the book Hilkiah the priest
had found in the Temple[d] of the LORD.
25There was no king like Josiah before or after
him. He obeyed the LORD with all his heart, soul
and strength, following all the Teachings of
Moses.
26Even so, the LORD did not stop his strong
and terrible anger. His anger burned against
Judah because of all Manasseh had done to make
him angry. 27The LORD said, "I will send Judah
out of my sight, as I have sent Israel away. I will
reject Jerusalem, which I chose. And I will take
away the Temple about which I said, 'I will be
worshipped there.' "
28Everything else Josiah did is written in the
book of the history of the kings of Judah.
29While Josiah was king, Neco king of Egypt
went to help the king of Assyria at the Euphrates
River. King Josiah marched out to fight against
Neco, but at Megiddo, Neco faced him and
killed him. 30Josiah's servants carried his body in
a chariot from Megiddo to Jerusalem and buried
him in his own grave. Then the people of Judah
chose Josiah's son Jehoahaz and poured olive oil
on him to make him king in his father's place.

Jehoahaz King of Judah

31Jehoahaz was 23 years old when he became
king, and he was king in Jerusalem for three
months. His mother's name was Hamutal, who
was the daughter of Jeremiah from Libnah. 32Je-
hoahaz did what the LORD said was wrong, just
as his ancestors had done.
33King Neco took Jehoahaz prisoner at Riblah
in the land of Hamath so that Jehoahaz could not
rule in Jerusalem. Neco made the people of
Judah pay about 3.5 tonnes of silver and about
35 kilogrammes of gold.
34King Neco made Josiah's son Eliakim the
king in place of Josiah his father. Then Neco
changed Eliakim's name to Jehoiakim. But Neco
took Jehoahaz to Egypt, where he died. 35Je-
hoiakim gave King Neco the silver and gold he
demanded. Jehoiakim taxed the land and took sil-
ver and gold from the people of the land to give
to King Neco. Each person had to pay his share.

Jehoiakim King of Judah

36Jehoiakim was 25 years old when he be-
came king, and he was king in Jerusalem for
eleven years. His mother's name was Zebidah
daughter of Pedaiah, who was from Rumah. 37Je-
hoiakim did what the LORD said was wrong, just
as his ancestors had done.

24 While Jehoiakim was king, Nebuchad-
nezzar king of Babylon attacked the land
of Judah. So Jehoiakim became Nebuchadnez-
zar's servant for three years. Then he turned
against Nebuchadnezzar and broke away from
his rule. 2The LORD sent raiding men from Bab-
ylon, Aram, Moab and Ammon against Je-
hoiakim to destroy Judah. This happened as the
LORD had said it would through his servants the
prophets.[d]
3The LORD commanded this to happen to the
people of Judah, to remove them from his pres-
ence, because of all the sins of Manasseh. 4He
had killed many innocent people and had filled
Jerusalem with their blood. And the LORD would
not forgive these sins.
5The other things that happened while Je-
hoiakim was king and all he did are written in
the book of the history of the kings of Judah. 6Je-
hoiakim died, and his son Jehoiachin became
king in his place.
7The king of Egypt did not leave his land
again, because the king of Babylon had captured
all that belonged to the king of Egypt, from the
brook of Egypt to the Euphrates River.

Jehoiachin King of Judah

8Jehoiachin was eighteen years old when he
became king, and he was king for three months
in Jerusalem. His mother's name was Nehushta
daughter of Elnathan from Jerusalem. 9Jehoiachin
did what the LORD said was wrong, just as his
father had done.
10At that time the officers of Nebuchadnezzar
king of Babylon came up to Jerusalem. When
they reached the city, they attacked it. 11Neb-
uchadnezzar himself came to the city while his
officers were attacking it. 12Jehoiachin king of
Judah surrendered to the king of Babylon, along
with Jehoiachin's mother, servants, elders and of-
ficers. So Nebuchadnezzar made Jehoiachin a
prisoner in the eighth year he was king of Bab-
ylon. 13Nebuchadnezzar took all the treasures
from the Temple[d] of the LORD and from the palace.

He cut up all the gold objects Solomon king
of Israel had made for the Temple of the LORD.
This happened as the LORD had said it would.
14Nebuchadnezzar took away all the people of
Jerusalem, including all the leaders, all the
wealthy people, and all the craftsmen and metal
workers. There were 10,000 prisoners in all.
Only the poorest people in the land were left.
15Nebuchadnezzar carried away Jehoiachin to
Babylon, as well as the king's mother and his
wives, the officers and the leading men of the
land. They were taken captive from Jerusalem to
Babylon. 16The king of Babylon also took all
7,000 soldiers, who were strong and able to fight
in war, and about 1,000 craftsmen and metal
workers. Nebuchadnezzar took them as prison-
ers to Babylon. 17Then he made Mattaniah,
Jehoiachin's uncle, king in Jehoiachin's place. He
also changed Mattaniah's name to Zedekiah.

Zedekiah King of Judah

18Zedekiah was 21 years old when he became
king, and he was king in Jerusalem for eleven
years. His mother's name was Hamutal daughter
of Jeremiah[n] from Libnah. 19Zedekiah did what
the LORD said was wrong, just as Jehoiakim had
done. 20All this happened in Jerusalem and
Judah because the LORD was angry with them.
Finally, he threw them out of his presence.

The Fall of Jerusalem

Zedekiah turned against the king of Babylon.
25 Nebuchadnezzar king of Babylon marched
against Jerusalem with his whole army
during Zedekiah's ninth year as king, on the
tenth day of the tenth month. He made a camp
around the city and piled earth against the city
walls to attack it. 2The city was under attack
until Zedekiah's eleventh year as king. 3By the
ninth day of the fourth month, the hunger was
terrible in the city. There was no food for the
people to eat. 4Then the city was broken into,
and the whole army ran away at night through
the gate between the two walls by the king's gar-
den. While the Babylonians were still surround-
ing the city, Zedekiah and his men ran away
towards the Jordan Valley. 5But the Babylonian
army chased King Zedekiah and caught up with
him in the plains of Jericho. All of his army was
scattered from him, 6so they captured Zedekiah
and took him to the king of Babylon at Riblah.
There he passed sentence on Zedekiah. 7They
killed Zedekiah's sons as he watched. Then they
put out his eyes and put bronze chains on him
and took him to Babylon.
8Nebuzaradan was the commander of the
king's special guards. This officer of the king of
Babylon came to Jerusalem on the seventh day
of the fifth month, in Nebuchadnezzar's nine-
teenth year as king of Babylon. 9Nebuzaradan set
fire to the Temple[d] of the LORD and the palace
and all the houses of Jerusalem. Every important
building was burned.
10The whole Babylonian army, led by the com-
mander of the king's special guards, broke down
the walls around Jerusalem. 11Nebuzaradan, the
commander of the guards, captured the people
left in Jerusalem, those who had surrendered to
the king of Babylon and the rest of the people.
12But the commander left behind some of the
poorest people of the land to take care of the
vineyards and fields.
13The Babylonians broke up the bronze pillars,
the bronze stands and the large bronze bowl,
which was called the Sea, in the Temple of the
LORD. Then they carried the bronze to Babylon.
14They also took the pots, shovels, wick trim-
mers, dishes and all the bronze objects used to
serve in the Temple. 15The commander of the
king's special guards took away the pans for
carrying hot coals, the bowls and everything
made of pure gold or silver. 16There were two pil-
lars and the large bronze bowl and the movable
stands which Solomon had made for the Temple
of the LORD. There was so much bronze that it
could not be weighed. 17Each pillar was about 9
metres high. The bronze capital[d] on top of the
pillar was about 1.5 metres high. It was deco-
rated with a net design and bronze pomegran-
ates[d] all around it. The other pillar also had a net
design and was like the first pillar.

Judah is Taken Prisoner

18The commander of the guards took some
prisoners—Seraiah the chief priest, Zephaniah
the priest next in rank, and the three doorkeep-
ers. 19Of the people who were still in the city, he
took the officer in charge of the fighting men, as
well as five people who advised the king. He
took the royal secretary who selected people for
the army and 60 other men who were in the
city. 20Nebuzaradan, the commander, took all
these people and brought them to the king of
Babylon at Riblah. 21There at Riblah, in the land
of Hamath, the king had them killed. So the peo-
ple of Judah were led away from their country as
captives.

Jeremiah This is not the prophet Jeremiah, but another man with the same name.

Gedaliah Becomes Governor

[22]Nebuchadnezzar king of Babylon left some people in the land of Judah. He appointed Gedaliah son of Ahikam, the son of Shaphan, as governor.

[23]The army captains and their men heard that the king of Babylon had made Gedaliah governor, so they came to Gedaliah at Mizpah. They were Ishmael son of Nethaniah, Johanan son of Kareah, Seraiah son of Tanhumeth the Netophathite, Jaazaniah son of the Maacathite, and their men. [24]Then Gedaliah promised these army captains and their men, "Don't be afraid of the Babylonian officers. Live in the land and serve the king of Babylon, and everything will go well for you."

[25]In the seventh month Ishmael son of Nethaniah, son of Elishama from the king's family, came with ten men and killed Gedaliah. They also killed the men of Judah and Babylon who were with Gedaliah at Mizpah. [26]Then all the people, from the least important to the most important, along with the army leaders, ran away to Egypt, because they were afraid of the Babylonians.

Jehoiachin is Set Free

[27]Jehoiachin king of Judah was held in Babylon for 37 years. In the thirty-seventh year Evil-Merodach became king of Babylon, and he let Jehoiachin out of prison on the twenty-seventh day of the twelfth month. [28]Evil-Merodach spoke kindly to Jehoiachin and gave him a seat of honour above the seats of the other kings who were with him in Babylon. [29]So Jehoiachin put away his prison clothes. For the rest of his life, he ate at the king's table. [30]Every day, for as long as Jehoiachin lived, the king gave him an allowance.

1 Chronicles

Why Read This Book:

- See God's faithfulness traced through history (1 Chronicles 1—9).
- Find out how David's relationship with God affected every area of his life (1 Chronicles 10—29).

When?

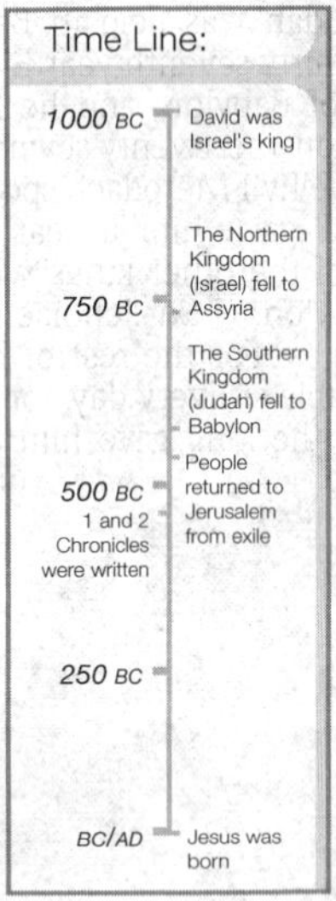

Behind the Scenes:

Most people – not just old people – like to understand about their "roots". They like to know which town their family came from and a little bit about their relatives and the way that older members of the family lived. Knowing about roots is less important for people who feel that they are part of a traditional society but, when life becomes a struggle, having something on which to base your feelings about yourself becomes a lifeline.

The books of 1 and 2 Chronicles (which were originally one book) are about roots. They were written hundreds of years after the events, to tell the Israelites where they had come from. The Israelites had been exiles – prisoners of war – in Babylon, where they had been taken because they did not follow God. They had returned to Jerusalem and were rebuilding their city, their history and their lives.

1 Chronicles was written to inspire these Israelites to return not only to Jerusalem but also to God. To do this, the author traced Israel's family roots and then told the story of the nation's greatest ruler, King David. Throughout the book one message is clear: the nation's success is directly linked to the people's relationship with God. ▷

Where?

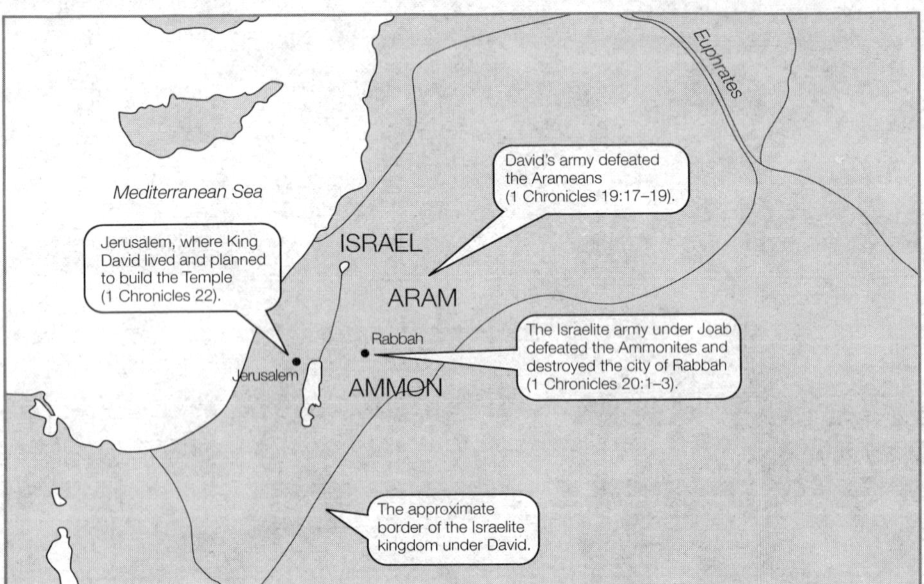

Behind the Scenes (cont.): The two books of Chronicles weren't written to give a precise history of the Israelites. For example, the stories of David and Solomon leave out some of the negative stories found in 1 and 2 Samuel (p.254 and p.283), and in 1 and 2 Kings (p.311 and p.343) which cover the same period.

Instead, 1 and 2 Chronicles were written to point out how God had guided people in the past and to remind readers of the importance of following God.

From Adam to Abraham

1 Adam was the father of Seth. Seth was the
father of Enosh. Enosh was the father of
Kenan. [2]Kenan was the father of Mahalalel.
Mahalalel was the father of Jared. Jared was
the father of Enoch. [3]Enoch was the father
of Methuselah. Methuselah was the father of
Lamech and Lamech was the father of Noah.

> **Sidelight** Genealogies – family histories – like the one in 1 Chronicles 1 – 9 are common in the Old Testament. In fact, there are about 24 of them in the Old Testament, with the Chronicles genealogy being the longest. Unlike modern genealogies, Old Testament lists included only important people, not everyone who descended from the original person.

[4]The sons of Noah were Shem, Ham and
Japheth.
[5]Japheth's sons were Gomer, Magog, Madai,
Javan, Tubal, Meshech and Tiras.
[6]Gomer's sons were Ashkenaz, Riphath and
Togarmah.
[7]Javan's sons were Elishah, Tarshish, Kittim [n]
and Rodanim.
[8]Ham's sons were Cush, Mizraim, [n] Put and
Canaan.
[9]Cush's sons were Seba, Havilah, Sabta,
Raamah and Sabteca.
Raamah's sons were Sheba and Dedan.
[10]Cush was the father of Nimrod, who grew up
to become a mighty warrior on the earth.
[11]Mizraim was the father of the Ludites, Anam-
ites, Lehabites and Naphtuhim,
[12]Pathrusites, Casluhites and Caphtorites. (The
Philistines came from the Casluhites.)
[13]Canaan's first child was Sidon. He was also
the father of the Hittites, [14]Jebusites, Amorites,
Girgashites, [15]Hivites, Arkites, Sinites, [16]Arvadites,
Zemarites and Hamathites.
[17]Shem's sons were Elam, Asshur, Arphaxad,
Lud and Aram.
Aram's sons were Uz, Hul, Gether and
Meshech.
[18]Arphaxad was the father of Shelah, who was
the father of Eber.
[19]Eber had two sons. One son was named
Peleg, [n] because the people on the earth were
divided into different languages during his life.
Peleg's brother was named Joktan.
[20]Joktan was the father of Almodad, Sheleph,
Hazarmaveth, Jerah, [21]Hadoram, Uzal, Diklah,

> **Sidelight** If you're looking for an easy Bible verse to memorise try 1 Chronicles 1:25. With just three words, it's the shortest verse in the Old Testament. But you might still have trouble remembering it: Eber, Peleg and Reu aren't common names.

[22]Obal, Abimael, Sheba, [23]Ophir, Havilah and
Jobab. All these were Joktan's sons. [24]The family
line included Shem, Arphaxad, Shelah, [25]Eber,
Peleg, Reu, [26]Serug, Nahor, Terah [27]and Abram,
who was called Abraham.

Abraham's Family

[28]Abraham's sons were Isaac and Ishmael.
[29]These were the sons of Isaac and Ishmael.
Ishmael's first son was Nebaioth. His other
sons were Kedar, Adbeel, Mibsam, [30]Mishma,
Dumah, Massa, Hadad, Tema, [31]Jetur, Naphish

Kittim His descendants were the people of Cyprus.
Mizraim This is another name for Egypt.
Peleg This name sounds like the Hebrew word for "divided".

and Kedemah. These were Ishmael's sons.
32Keturah, Abraham's slave woman,[d] gave birth
to Zimran, Jokshan, Medan, Midian, Ishbak
and Shuah.
Jokshan's sons were Sheba and Dedan.
33Midian's sons were Ephah, Epher, Hanoch,
Abida and Eldaah. All these were descendants[d] of
Keturah.
34Abraham was the father of Isaac and Isaac's
sons were Esau and Israel.
35Esau's sons were Eliphaz, Reuel, Jeush, Jalam
and Korah.
36Eliphaz's sons were Teman, Omar, Zepho,
Gatam, Kenaz, Timna and Amalek.
37Reuel's sons were Nahath, Zerah, Shammah
and Mizzah.

The Edomites from Seir

38Seir's sons were Lotan, Shobal, Zibeon,
Anah, Dishon, Ezer and Dishan.
39Lotan's sons were Hori, Homam and his sis-
ter was Timna.
40Shobal's sons were Alvan, Manahath, Ebal,
Shepho and Onam.
Zibeon's sons were Aiah and Anah.
41Anah's son was Dishon.
Dishon's sons were Hemdan, Eshban, Ithran
and Keran.
42Ezer's sons were Bilhan, Zaavan and Akan.
Dishan's sons were Uz and Aran.

The Kings of Edom

43These kings ruled in Edom before there were
kings in Israel. Bela son of Beor was king of
Edom, and his city was named Dinhabah.
44When Bela died, Jobab son of Zerah became
king. He was from Bozrah.
45When Jobab died, Husham became king. He
was from the land of the Temanites.
46When Husham died, Hadad son of Bedad be-
came king, and his city was named Avith. Hadad
defeated Midian in the country of Moab.
47When Hadad died, Samlah became king. He
was from Masrekah.
48When Samlah died, Shaul became king. He
was from Rehoboth by the river.
49When Shaul died, Baal-Hanan son of Acbor
became king.
50When Baal-Hanan died, Hadad became king,
and his city was named Pau. Hadad's wife was
named Mehetabel, and she was the daughter of
Matred, who was the daughter of Me-Zahab.
51Then Hadad died.
The leaders of the family groups of Edom were
Timna, Alvah, Jetheth, 52Oholibamah, Elah, Pinon,
53Kenaz, Teman, Mibzar, 54Magdiel and Iram.
These were the leaders of Edom.

Israel's Family

2 The sons of Israel[n] were Reuben, Simeon,
Levi, Judah, Issachar, Zebulun, 2Dan, Jo-
seph, Benjamin, Naphtali, Gad and Asher.

Judah's Family

3Judah's sons were Er, Onan and Shelah. A
Canaanite woman, the daughter of Shua, was
their mother. Judah's first son, Er, did what the
LORD said was wicked, so the LORD put him to
death. 4Judah's daughter-in-law Tamar gave birth
to Perez and Zerah. Judah was the father, so Ju-
dah had five sons.
5Perez's sons were Hezron and Hamul.
6Zerah had five sons: Zimri, Ethan, Heman,
Calcol and Darda.
7Carmi's son was Achan, who caused trouble
for Israel because he took things that had been
given to the LORD to be destroyed.
8Ethan's son was Azariah.
9Hezron's sons were Jerahmeel, Ram and
Caleb.
10Ram was Amminadab's father, and Ammina-
dab was Nahshon's father. Nahshon was the
leader of the people of Judah. 11Nahshon was the
father of Salmon, who was the father of Boaz.
12Boaz was the father of Obed, and Obed was the
father of Jesse.
13Jesse's first son was Eliab. His second son
was Abinadab, his third was Shimea, 14his fourth
was Nethanel, his fifth was Raddai, 15his sixth was
Ozem and his seventh son was David. 16Their
sisters were Zeruiah and Abigail. Zeruiah's three
sons were Abishai, Joab and Asahel. 17Abigail
was the mother of Amasa and his father was
Jether, an Ishmaelite.

Caleb's Family

18Caleb son of Hezron had children by his wife
Azubah and by Jerioth. Caleb and Azubah's sons
were Jesher, Shobab and Ardon. 19When Azubah
died, Caleb married Ephrath. They had a son
named Hur, 20who was the father of Uri, who
was the father of Bezalel.
21Later, when Hezron was 60 years old, he
married the daughter of Makir, Gilead's father.
Hezron had sexual relations with Makir's daugh-
ter, and she had a son named Segub. 22Segub was
the father of Jair. Jair controlled 23 cities in the
country of Gilead. 23(But Geshur and Aram cap-
tured the towns of Jair, as well as Kenath and
the small towns around it—60 towns in all.)

Israel Another name for Jacob.

All these were descendants[d] of Makir, the father
of Gilead.
24After Hezron died in Caleb Ephrathah, his
wife Abijah had his son, named Ashhur. Ashhur
became the father of Tekoa.

Jerahmeel's Family

25Hezron's first son was Jerahmeel. Jerah-
meel's sons were Ram, Bunah, Oren, Ozem and
Ahijah. Ram was Jerahmeel's first son. 26Jerah-
meel had another wife, named Atarah. She was
the mother of Onam.
27Jerahmeel's first son, Ram, had sons. They
were Maaz, Jamin and Eker.
28Onam's sons were Shammai and Jada.
Shammai's sons were Nadab and Abishur.
29Abishur's wife was named Abihail, and their
sons were Ahban and Molid.
30Nadab's sons were Seled and Appaim. Seled
died without having children.
31Appaim's son was Ishi, who became the
father of Sheshan.
Sheshan was the father of Ahlai.
32Jada was Shammai's brother, and Jada's sons
were Jether and Jonathan. Jether died without
having children.
33Jonathan's sons were Peleth and Zaza.
These were Jerahmeel's descendants.[d]
34Sheshan did not have any sons, only daugh-
ters. He had a servant from Egypt named Jarha.
35Sheshan let his daughter marry his servant
Jarha, and she had a son named Attai.
36Attai was the father of Nathan. Nathan was
the father of Zabad. 37Zabad was the father of
Ephlal. Ephlal was the father of Obed. 38Obed
was the father of Jehu. Jehu was the father of
Azariah. 39Azariah was the father of Helez.
Helez was the father of Eleasah. 40Eleasah was the
father of Sismai. Sismai was the father of Shallum.
41Shallum was the father of Jekamiah, and Jeka-
miah was the father of Elishama.

The Clans of Caleb

42Caleb was Jerahmeel's brother. Caleb's first
son was Mesha. Mesha was the father of Ziph,
and his son Mareshah was the father of Hebron.
43Hebron's sons were Korah, Tappuah, Rekem
and Shema. 44Shema was the father of Raham,
who was the father of Jorkeam. Rekem was the
father of Shammai. 45Shammai was the father of
Maon, and Maon was the father of Beth Zur.
46Caleb's slave woman[d] was named Ephah and
she was the mother of Haran, Moza and Gazez.
Haran was the father of Gazez.
47Jahdai's sons were Regem, Jotham, Geshan,
Pelet, Ephah and Shaaph.
48Caleb had another slave woman named Maa-
cah. She was the mother of Sheber, Tirhanah,
49Shaaph and Sheva. Shaaph was the father of
Madmannah. Sheva was the father of Macbenah
and Gibea. Caleb's daughter was Achsah.
50–51These were Caleb's descendants:[d] Caleb's
son Hur was the first son of his mother Ephra-
thah. Hur's sons were Shobal, Salma and Hareph.
Shobal was the father of Kiriath Jearim. Salma
was the father of Bethlehem. And Hareph was
the father of Beth Gader.
52Shobal was the father of Kiriath Jearim. Sho-
bal's descendants were Haroeh, half the Mana-
hathites, 53and the family groups of Kiriath
Jearim: the Ithrites, Puthites, Shumathites and
Mishraites. The Zorathites and the Eshtaolites
came from the Mishraite people.
54Salma's descendants were Bethlehem, the
Netophathites, Atroth Beth Joab, half the Mana-
hathites and the Zorites. 55His descendants in-
cluded the families who lived at Jabez, who
wrote and copied important papers. They were
called the Tirathites, Shimeathites and Su-
cathites and were from the Kenite family group
who came from Hammath. He was the father of
the people living in Recab.

David's Family

3 These are David's sons who were born in
Hebron. The first was Amnon, whose
mother was Ahinoam from Jezreel. The second
son was Daniel, whose mother was Abigail from
Carmel. 2The third son was Absalom, whose
mother was Maacah daughter of Talmai, the king
of Geshur. The fourth son was Adonijah, whose
mother was Haggith. 3The fifth son was Shepha-
tiah, whose mother was Abital. The sixth son
was Ithream, whose mother was Eglah. 4These
six sons of David were born to him in Hebron,
where David ruled for seven and a half years.
David ruled in Jerusalem for 33 years. 5These
were his children who were born in Jerusalem:
Shammua, Shobab, Nathan and Solomon—the
four children of David and Bathsheba, Ammiel's
daughter. 6–8David's other nine children were Ib-
har, Elishua, Eliphelet, Nogah; Nepheg, Japhia,
Elishama, Eliada and Eliphelet. 9These were all
of David's sons, except for those born to his slave
women.[d] David also had a daughter named
Tamar.

The Kings of Judah

10Solomon's son was Rehoboam. Rehoboam's
son was Abijah. Abijah's son was Asa. Asa's son
was Jehoshaphat. 11Jehoshaphat's son was Jeho-
ram. Jehoram's son was Ahaziah. Ahaziah's son
was Joash. 12Joash's son was Amaziah.
Amaziah's son was Azariah. Azariah's son was
Jotham. 13Jotham's son was Ahaz. Ahaz's son
was Hezekiah. Hezekiah's son was Manasseh.

14 Manasseh's son was Amon, and Amon's son
was Josiah.

15 These were Josiah's sons: his first son was
Johanan, his second was Jehoiakim, his third was
Zedekiah and his fourth was Shallum.

16 Jehoiakim was followed by Jehoiachin, and
he was followed by Zedekiah.

David's Descendants After the Babylonian Captivity

17 Jehoiachin was taken as a prisoner. His sons
were Shealtiel, 18 Malkiram, Pedaiah, Shenazzar,
Jekamiah, Hoshama and Nedabiah.

19 Pedaiah's sons were Zerubbabel and Shimei.

Zerubbabel's sons were Meshullam and Hana-
niah, and their sister was Shelomith. 20 Zerubbabel
also had five other sons: Hashubah, Ohel, Berekiah,
Hasadiah and Jushab-Hesed.

21 Hananiah's descendants[d] were Pelatiah and
Jeshaiah, and the sons of Rephaiah, Arnan, Obad-
iah and Shecaniah.

22 Shecaniah's son was Shemaiah. Shemaiah's
sons were Hattush, Igal, Bariah, Neariah and Sha-
phat. There were six in all.

23 Neariah had three sons: Elioenai, Hizkiah
and Azrikam.

24 Elioenai had seven sons: Hodaviah, Eliashib,
Pelaiah, Akkub, Johanan, Delaiah and Anani.

Other Family Groups of Judah

4 Judah's descendants[d] were Perez, Hezron,
Carmi, Hur and Shobal.

2 Reaiah was Shobal's son. Reaiah was the
father of Jahath, and Jahath was the father of
Ahumai and Lahad. They were the family groups
of the Zorathite people.

3–4 Hur was the oldest son of Caleb and his
wife Ephrathah. Hur was the leader of Bethle-
hem. His three sons were Etam, Penuel and
Ezer. Etam's sons were Jezreel, Ishma and
Idbash. They had a sister named Hazzelelponi.
Penuel was the father of Gedor and Ezer was the
father of Hushah.

5 Tekoa's father was Ashhur. Ashhur had two
wives named Helah and Naarah.

6 The sons of Ashhur and Naarah were Ahuz-
zam, Hepher, Temeni and Haahashtari. These
were the descendants of Naarah.

7 Helah's sons were Zereth, Zohar, Ethnan 8 and
Koz. Koz was the father of Anub, Hazzobebah
and the Aharhel family group. Aharhel was the
son of Harum.

9 There was a man named Jabez, who was
respected more than his brothers. His mother
named him Jabez[n] because she said, "I was in
much pain when I gave birth to him." 10 Jabez
prayed to the God of Israel, "Please do good
things for me and give me more land. Stay with
me, and don't let anyone hurt me. Then I won't
have any pain." And God did what Jabez had
asked.

11 Kelub, Shuhah's brother, was the father of
Mehir. Mehir was the father of Eshton. 12 Eshton
was the father of Beth Rapha, Paseah and Tehin-
nah. Tehinnah was the father of the people from
the town of Nahash. These people were from
Recah.

13 The sons of Kenaz were Othniel and Seraiah.

Othniel's sons were Hathath and Meonothai.
14 Meonothai was the father of Ophrah.

Seraiah was the father of Joab. Joab was the
ancestor of the people from Craftsmen's Valley,
named that because the people living there were
craftsmen.

Sidelight In Bible times most people worked from home and professions stuck together. One group lived in Craftsmen's Valley (1 Chronicles 4:14).

15 Caleb was Jephunneh's son. Caleb's sons
were Iru, Elah and Naam. Elah's son was Kenaz.

16 Jehallelel's sons were Ziph, Ziphah, Tiria and
Asarel.

17–18 Ezrah's sons were Jether, Mered, Epher
and Jalon. Mered married Bithiah, the daughter
of the king of Egypt. The children of Mered and
Bithiah were Miriam, Shammai and Ishbah. Ish-
bah was the father of Eshtemoa. Mered also had
a wife from Judah, who gave birth to Jered, Heber
and Jekuthiel. Jered became the father of Gedor.
Heber became the father of Soco. And Jekuthiel
became the father of Zanoah.

19 Hodiah's wife was Naham's sister. The sons
of Hodiah's wife were Eshtemoa and the father of
Keilah. Keilah was from the Garmite people, and
Eshtemoa was from the Maacathite people.

20 Shimon's sons were Amnon, Rinnah, Ben-
Hanan and Tilon.

Ishi's sons were Zoheth and Ben-Zoheth.

21–22 Shelah was Judah's son. Shelah's sons
were Er, Laadah, Jokim, the men from Cozeba,
Joash and Saraph. Er was the father of Lecah.
Laadah was the father of Mareshah and the fam-
ily groups of linen workers at Beth Ashbea. Joash
and Saraph ruled in Moab and Jashubi Lehem.
The writings about this family are very old.
23 These sons of Shelah were potters. They lived
in Netaim and Gederah and worked for the king.

Jabez This name in Hebrew sounds like the word for "pain".

Simeon's Children

24Simeon's sons were Nemuel, Jamin, Jarib,
Zerah and Shaul. 25Shaul's son was Shallum.
Shallum's son was Mibsam. Mibsam's son was
Mishma.

26Mishma's son was Hammuel. Hammuel's
son was Zaccur. Zaccur's son was Shimei.
27Shimei had sixteen sons and six daughters, but
his brothers did not have many children, so there
were not as many people in their family group as
there were in Judah.

28Shimei's children lived in Beersheba, Mola-
dah, Hazar Shual, 29Bilhah, Ezem, Tolad, 30Be-
thuel, Hormah, Ziklag, 31Beth Marcaboth, Hazar
Susim, Beth Biri and Shaaraim. They lived in
these cities until David became king. 32The five
villages near these cities were Etam, Ain, Rim-
mon, Token and Ashan. 33There were also other
villages as far away as Baalath. This is where they
lived. And they wrote the history of their family.

34–38The men in this list were leaders of their
family groups: Meshobab, Jamlech, Joshah son of
Amaziah, Joel, Jehu son of Joshibiah (Joshibiah
was the son of Seraiah, who was the son of Asiel),
Elioenai, Jaakobah, Jeshohaiah, Asaiah, Adiel,
Jesimiel, Benaiah and Ziza. (Ziza was the son of
Shiphi, who was the son of Allon. Allon was the
son of Jedaiah, who was the son of Shimri. And
Shimri was the son of Shemaiah.)

These families grew very large. 39They went
outside the city of Gedor to the east side of
the valley to look for pasture for their flocks.
40They found good pastures with plenty of grass,
and the land was open country and peaceful and
quiet. Ham's descendants [d] had lived there in the
past.

41These men who were listed came to Gedor
while Hezekiah was king of Judah. They fought
against the Hamite people, destroying their tents,
and also against the Meunites who lived there,
and completely destroyed them. So there are no
Meunites there even today. Then these men be-
gan to live there, because there was pasture for
their flocks. 42Ishi's sons, Pelatiah, Neariah, Re-
phaiah and Uzziel, led 500 of the Simeonites and
attacked the people living in the mountains of
Edom. 43They killed the few Amalekites who
were still alive. From that time until now these
Simeonites have lived in Edom.

Reuben's Children

5 Reuben was Israel's first son. Reuben should
have received the special privileges of the
oldest son, but he had sexual relations with his
father's slave woman. [d] So those special privileges
were given to Joseph's sons. (Joseph was a son of
Israel.) In the family history Reuben's name is not
listed as the first son. 2Judah became stronger
than his brothers, and a leader came from his
family. But Joseph's family received the privileges
that belonged to the oldest son. 3Reuben was
Israel's first son. Reuben's sons were Hanoch,
Pallu, Hezron and Carmi.

4These were the children of Joel: Shemaiah was
Joel's son. Gog was Shemaiah's son. Shimei
was Gog's son. 5Micah was Shimei's son. Reaiah
was Micah's son. Baal was Reaiah's son. 6Bee-
rah was Baal's son. Beerah was a leader of the
tribe [d] of Reuben. Tiglath-Pileser king of Assyria
captured him and took him away.

7Joel's brothers and all his family groups are
listed just as they are written in their family histo-
ries: Jeiel was the first, then Zechariah 8and Bela.
(Bela was the son of Azaz. Azaz was the son of
Shema, and Shema was the son of Joel.) They
lived in the area of Aroer all the way to Nebo and
Baal Meon. 9Bela's people lived to the east—as
far as the edge of the desert, which is beside the
Euphrates River—because they had too many
cattle for the land of Gilead.

10When Saul was king, Bela's people fought
a war against the Hagrite people and defeated
them. Then Bela's people lived in the tents that
had belonged to the Hagrites in all the area east
of Gilead.

Gad's Children

11The people from the tribe [d] of Gad lived near
the Reubenites. The Gadites lived in the area of
Bashan all the way to Salecah. 12Joel was the
main leader, Shapham was second, and then
Janai and Shaphat were leaders in Bashan.

13The seven relatives in their families were Mi-
chael, Meshullam, Sheba, Jorai, Jacan, Zia and
Eber. 14They were the descendants [d] of Abihail.
Abihail was Huri's son. Huri was Jaroah's son.
Jaroah was Gilead's son. Gilead was Michael's
son. Michael was Jeshishai's son. Jeshishai was
Jahdo's son, and Jahdo was the son of Buz. 15Ahi
was Abdiel's son, and Abdiel was Guni's son. Ahi
was the leader of their family.

16The Gadites lived in Gilead, Bashan and the
small towns around it, and on all the pasturelands
in the Plain of Sharon all the way to the borders.

17All these names were written in the family
history of Gad during the time Jotham was king
of Judah and Jeroboam was king of Israel.

Soldiers Skilled in War

18There were 44,760 soldiers from the tribes [d]
of Reuben and Gad and East Manasseh who car-
ried shields and swords and bows. They were
skilled in war. 19They started a war against the
Hagrites and the people of Jetur, Naphish and
Nodab. 20The men from the tribes of Manasseh,
Reuben and Gad prayed to God during the war,

asking him to help them. So he helped them because they trusted him. He handed over to them the Hagrites and all those who were with them. 21 They took the animals that belonged to the Hagrites: 50,000 camels, 250,000 sheep and 2,000 donkeys. They also captured 100,000 people. 22 Many Hagrites were killed because God helped the people of Reuben, Gad and Manasseh. Then they lived there until Babylon captured them and took them away.

East Manasseh

23 There were many people in East Manasseh, and they lived in the area of Bashan all the way to Baal Hermon, Senir and Mount Hermon.

24 These were the family leaders: Epher, Ishi, Eliel, Azriel, Jeremiah, Hodaviah and Jahdiel. They were all strong, brave and famous men, and leaders in their families. 25 But they sinned against the God that their ancestors had worshipped. They began worshipping the gods of the people in that land, and those were the people God was destroying. 26 So the God of Israel made Pul king of Assyria want to go to war. (Pul was also called Tiglath-Pileser.) He captured the people of Reuben, Gad and East Manasseh, and he took them away to Halah, Habor, Hara and near the Gozan River. They have lived there from that time until this day.

Levi's Children

6 Levi's sons were Gershon, Kohath and Merari.

2 Kohath's sons were Amram, Izhar, Hebron and Uzziel.

3 Amram's children were Aaron, Moses and Miriam.

Aaron's sons were Nadab, Abihu, Eleazar and Ithamar. 4 Eleazar was the father of Phinehas. Phinehas was the father of Abishua. 5 Abishua was the father of Bukki. Bukki was the father of Uzzi. 6 Uzzi was the father of Zerahiah. Zerahiah was the father of Meraioth. 7 Meraioth was the father of Amariah. Amariah was the father of Ahitub. 8 Ahitub was the father of Zadok. Zadok was the father of Ahimaaz. 9 Ahimaaz was the father of Azariah. Azariah was the father of Johanan. 10 Johanan was the father of Azariah. (Azariah was a priest in the Temple[d] Solomon built in Jerusalem.) 11 Azariah was the father of Amariah. Amariah was the father of Ahitub. 12 Ahitub was the father of Zadok. Zadok was the father of Shallum. 13 Shallum was the father of Hilkiah. Hilkiah was the father of Azariah. 14 Azariah was the father of Seraiah, and Seraiah was the father of Jehozadak.

15 Jehozadak was forced to leave his home when the LORD sent Judah and Jerusalem into captivity under the control of Nebuchadnezzar.

16 Levi's sons were Gershon, Kohath and Merari.

17 The names of Gershon's sons were Libni and Shimei.

18 Kohath's sons were Amram, Izhar, Hebron and Uzziel.

19 Merari's sons were Mahli and Mushi.

This is a list of the family groups of Levi, listed by the name of the father of each group.

20 Gershon's son was Libni. Libni's son was Jehath. Jehath's son was Zimmah. 21 Zimmah's son was Joah. Joah's son was Iddo. Iddo's son was Zerah. And Zerah's son was Jeatherai.

22 Kohath's son was Amminadab. Amminadab's son was Korah. Korah's son was Assir. 23 Assir's son was Elkanah. Elkanah's son was Ebiasaph. Ebiasaph's son was Assir. 24 Assir's son was Tahath. Tahath's son was Uriel. Uriel's son was Uzziah, and Uzziah's son was Shaul.

25 Elkanah's sons were Amasai and Ahimoth. 26 Ahimoth's son was Elkanah. Elkanah's son was Zophai. Zophai's son was Nahath. 27 Nahath's son was Eliab. Eliab's son was Jeroham. Jeroham's son was Elkanah, and Elkanah's son was Samuel.

28 Samuel's sons were Joel, the first son, and Abijah, the second son.

29 Merari's son was Mahli. Mahli's son was Libni. Libni's son was Shimei. Shimei's son was Uzzah. 30 Uzzah's son was Shimea. Shimea's son was Haggiah, and Haggiah's son was Asaiah.

The Temple Musicians

31 David chose some people to be in charge of the music in the house of the LORD. They began their work after the Ark[d] of the Agreement was put there. 32 They served by making music at the Holy Tent[d] (also called the Meeting Tent), and they served until Solomon built the Temple[d] of the LORD in Jerusalem. They followed the rules for their work.

Sidelight According to 1 Chronicles 6:31–32, King David may have started the first professional Jerusalem Philharmonic Orchestra and Chorus to lead music in the Temple. Today the musicians would probably go on strike: 1 Chronicles 9:33 (p.382) says they were on duty "day and night".

33 These are the musicians and their sons:

From Kohath's family there was Heman the singer. Heman was Joel's son. Joel was Samuel's son. 34 Samuel was Elkanah's son. Elkanah was Jeroham's son. Jeroham was Eliel's son. Eliel was Toah's son. 35 Toah was Zuph's son. Zuph was Elkanah's son. Elkanah was Mahath's son.

Mahath was Amasai's son. 36Amasai was Elka-
nah's son. Elkanah was Joel's son. Joel was Azariah's
son. Azariah was Zephaniah's son. 37Zephaniah
was Tahath's son. Tahath was Assir's son. Assir
was Ebiasaph's son. Ebiasaph was Korah's son.
38Korah was Izhar's son. Izhar was Kohath's son.
Kohath was Levi's son. Levi was Israel's son.

39There was Heman's helper Asaph, whose
group stood by Heman's right side. Asaph was
Berekiah's son. Berekiah was Shimea's son.
40Shimea was Michael's son. Michael was Baa-
seiah's son. Baaseiah was Malkijah's son. 41Malki-
jah was Ethni's son. Ethni was Zerah's son. Zerah
was Adaiah's son. 42Adaiah was Ethan's son. Ethan
was Zimmah's son. Zimmah was Shimei's son.
43Shimei was Jahath's son. Jahath was Gershon's
son, and Gershon was Levi's son.

44Merari's family were the helpers of Heman
and Asaph, and they stood by Heman's left side.
In this group was Ethan son of Kishi. Kishi was
Abdi's son. Abdi was Malluch's son. 45Malluch
was Hashabiah's son. Hashabiah was Amaziah's
son. Amaziah was Hilkiah's son. 46Hilkiah was
Amzi's son. Amzi was Bani's son. Bani was She-
mer's son. 47Shemer was Mahli's son. Mahli was
Mushi's son. Mushi was Merari's son, and Merari
was Levi's son.

48The other Levites served by doing their own
special work in the Holy Tent, the house of God.
49Aaron and his descendants [d] offered the sacrifi-
ces on the altar of burnt offering and burned the
incense on the altar of incense. They offered the
sacrifices that removed the Israelites' sins so they
could belong to God. They did all the work in the
Most Holy Place and followed all the laws that
Moses, God's servant, had commanded.

50These were Aaron's sons: Eleazar was
Aaron's son. Phinehas was Eleazar's son. Abishua
was Phinehas' son. 51Bukki was Abishua's son.
Uzzi was Bukki's son. Zerahiah was Uzzi's son.
52Meraioth was Zerahiah's son. Amariah was Me-
raioth's son. Ahitub was Amariah's son. 53Zadok
was Ahitub's son and Ahimaaz was Zadok's son.

Land for the Levites

54These are the places where Aaron's descen-
dants [d] lived. His descendants from the Kohath
family group received the first share of the land.

55They were given the city of Hebron in Judah
and the pastures around it, 56but the fields farther
from the city and the villages near Hebron were
given to Caleb son of Jephunneh. 57So the des-
cendants of Aaron were given Hebron, one of the
cities of safety. [n] They also received the towns
and pastures of Libnah, Jattir, Eshtemoa, 58Hilen,
Debir, 59Ashan, Juttah and Beth Shemesh. 60They
also received these towns and pastures from the
tribe of Benjamin: Gibeon, Geba, Alemeth and
Anathoth.

The Kohath family groups received a total of
thirteen towns.

61The rest of the Kohath family group was
given ten towns from the family groups of West
Manasseh. The towns were chosen by throwing
lots. [d]

62The Gershon family group received thir-
teen towns from the tribes of Issachar, Asher,
Naphtali and the part of Manasseh living in
Bashan.

63The Merari family group received twelve
towns from the tribes of Reuben, Gad and Zebu-
lun. Those towns were chosen by throwing lots.

64So the Israelites gave these towns and their
pastures to the Levites. 65The towns from the
tribes of Judah, Simeon and Benjamin, which
were named, were chosen by throwing lots.

66Some of the Kohath family groups received
towns and pastures from the tribe of Ephraim.
67They received Shechem, one of the cities of
safety, with its pastures in the mountains of
Ephraim. They also received the towns and pas-
tures of Gezer, 68Jokmeam, Beth Horon, 69Aijalon
and Gath Rimmon.

70The rest of the people in the Kohath family
group received the towns of Aner and Bileam and
their pastures from West Manasseh.

71From East Manasseh, the Gershon family re-
ceived the towns and pastures of Golan in Bashan
and Ashtaroth.

72–73From the tribe of Issachar, the Gershon
family received the towns and pastures of Ke-
desh, Daberath, Ramoth and Anem.

74–75From the tribe of Asher, the Gershon fam-
ily received the towns and pastures of Mashal,
Abdon, Hukok and Rehob.

76From the tribe of Naphtali, the Gershon fam-
ily received the towns and pastures of Kedesh in
Galilee, Hammon and Kiriathaim.

77The rest of the Levites, the people from the
Merari family, received from the tribe of Zebulun
the towns and pastures of Jokneam, Kartah, Rim-
mono and Tabor.

78–79From the tribe of Reuben, the Merari fam-
ily received the towns and pastures of Bezer in
the desert, Jahzah, Kedemoth and Mephaath.
(The tribe of Reuben lived east of the Jordan
River, across from Jericho.)

80–81From the tribe of Gad, the Merari family
received the towns and pastures of Ramoth in
Gilead, Mahanaim, Heshbon and Jazer.

cities of safety A person who had accidentally killed someone could go to one of the six cities of safety to receive protection and a fair trial.

Issachar's Children

7 Issachar had four sons: Tola, Puah, Jashub
and Shimron.
2Tola's sons were Uzzi, Rephaiah, Jeriel, Jah-
mai, Ibsam and Samuel, and they were leaders of
their families. In the family history of Tola's des-
cendants,[d] 22,600 men were listed as fighting
men during the time David was king.
3Uzzi's son was Izrahiah.
Izrahiah's sons were Michael, Obadiah, Joel
and Isshiah. All five of them were leaders. 4Their
family history shows they had 36,000 men ready
to serve in the army, because they had many
wives and children.
5The records of the family groups of Issachar
show there were 87,000 fighting men.

Benjamin's Children

6Benjamin had three sons: Bela, Beker and
Jediael.
7Bela had five sons: Ezbon, Uzzi, Uzziel, Jeri-
moth and Iri, and they were leaders of their famil-
ies. Their family history shows they had 22,034
fighting men.
8Beker's sons were Zemirah, Joash, Eliezer, Eli-
oenai, Omri, Jeremoth, Abijah, Anathoth and Ale-
meth. They all were Beker's sons. 9Their family
history listed the family leaders and 20,200 fight-
ing men.
10Jediael's son was Bilhan.
Bilhan's sons were Jeush, Benjamin, Ehud,
Kenaanah, Zethan, Tarshish and Ahishahar. 11All
these sons of Jediael were leaders of their famil-
ies. They had 17,200 fighting men ready to serve
in the army.
12The Shuppites and Huppites were descend-
ants[d] of Ir and the Hushites were descendants of
Aher.

Naphtali's Children

13Naphtali's sons were Jahziel, Guni, Jezer and
Shillem. They were Bilhah's grandsons.

Manasseh's Children

14These are Manasseh's descendants.[d] Manas-
seh had an Aramean slave woman,[d] who was the
mother of Asriel and Makir. Makir was Gilead's
father. 15Makir took a wife from the Huppites and
Shuppites. His sister was named Maacah. His sec-
ond son was named Zelophehad, and he had only
daughters. 16Makir's wife Maacah had a son
whom she named Peresh. Peresh's brother was
named Sheresh. Sheresh's sons were Ulam and
Rakem.
17Ulam's son was Bedan.
These were the sons of Gilead, who was the
son of Makir. Makir was Manasseh's son. 18Ma-
kir's sister Hammoleketh gave birth to Ishhod,
Abiezer and Mahlah.
19The sons of Shemida were Ahian, Shechem,
Likhi and Aniam.

Ephraim's Children

20These are the names of Ephraim's descend-
ants.[d] Ephraim's son was Shuthelah. Shuthelah's
son was Bered. Bered's son was Tahath. Tahath's
son was Eleadah. Eleadah's son was Tahath.
21Tahath's son was Zabad. Zabad's son was
Shuthelah.
Ezer and Elead went to Gath to steal cows and
sheep and were killed by some men who grew
up in that city. 22Their father Ephraim cried for them
many days, and his family came to comfort him.
23Then he had sexual relations with his wife
again. She became pregnant and gave birth to a
son whom Ephraim named Beriah[n] because of the
trouble that had happened to his family. 24Ephraim's
daughter was Sheerah. She built Lower Beth
Horon, Upper Beth Horon and Uzzen Sheerah.
25Rephah was Ephraim's son. Resheph was Re-
phah's son. Telah was Resheph's son. Tahan was
Telah's son. 26Ladan was Tahan's son. Ammihud
was Ladan's son. Elishama was Ammihud's son.
27Nun was Elishama's son, and Joshua was the
son of Nun.
28Ephraim's descendants lived in these lands
and towns: Bethel and the villages near it, Naaran
on the east, Gezer and the villages near it on the
west, and Shechem and the villages near it. These
villages went all the way to Ayyah and its villages.
29Along the borders of Manasseh's land were the
towns of Beth Shan, Taanach, Megiddo, Dor and
the villages near them. The descendants of Joseph
son of Israel lived in these towns.

Asher's Children

30Asher's sons were Imnah, Ishvah, Ishvi and
Beriah. Their sister was Serah.
31Beriah's sons were Heber and Malkiel. Mal-
kiel was Birzaith's father.
32Heber was the father of Japhlet, Shomer,
Hotham and their sister Shua.
33Japhlet's sons were Pasach, Bimhal and Ash-
vath. They were Japhlet's children.
34Japhlet's brother was Shomer. Shomer's sons
were Rohgah, Hubbah and Aram.
35Shomer's brother was Hotham. Hotham's
sons were Zophah, Imna, Shelesh and Amal.
36Zophah's sons were Suah, Harnepher, Shual,
Beri, Imrah, 37Bezer, Hod, Shamma, Shilshah,
Ithran and Beera.

Beriah This name sounds like the Hebrew word for "trouble".

38Jether's sons were Jephunneh, Pispah and Ara.
39Ulla's sons were Arah, Hanniel and Rizia.
40All these men were descendants of Asher and leaders of their families. They were powerful warriors and outstanding leaders. Their family history lists that they had 26,000 soldiers ready to serve in the army.

The Family History of King Saul

8 Benjamin was the father of Bela, his first son. Ashbel was his second son, Aharah was his third, 2Nohah was his fourth and Rapha was his fifth son.
3Bela's sons were Addar, Gera, Abihud, 4Abishua, Naaman, Ahoah, 5Gera, Shephuphan and Huram.
6These were the descendants[d] of Ehud and leaders of their families in Geba. They were forced to move to Manahath. 7Ehud's descendants were Naaman, Ahijah and Gera. Gera forced them to leave. He was the father of Uzza and Ahihud.
8–11Shaharaim and his wife Hushim had sons named Abitub and Elpaal. In Moab, Shaharaim divorced his wives Hushim and Baara. Shaharaim and his wife Hodesh had these sons: Jobab, Zibia, Mesha, Malcam, Jeuz, Sakia and Mirmah. They were leaders of their families.
12–13Elpaal's sons were Eber, Misham, Shemed, Beriah and Shema. Shemed built the towns of Ono and Lod and the villages around them. Beriah and Shema were leaders of the families living in Aijalon, and they forced out the people who lived in Gath.
14Beriah's sons were Ahio, Shashak, Jeremoth, 15Zebadiah, Arad, Eder, 16Michael, Ishpah and Joha.
17Elpaal's sons were Zebadiah, Meshullam, Hizki, Heber, 18Ishmerai, Izliah and Jobab.
19Shimei's sons were Jakim, Zicri, Zabdi, 20Elienai, Zillethai, Eliel, 21Adaiah, Beraiah and Shimrath.
22Shashak's sons were Ishpan, Eber, Eliel, 23Abdon, Zicri, Hanan, 24Hananiah, Elam, Anthothijah, 25Iphdeiah and Penuel.
26Jeroham's sons were Shamsherai, Shehariah, Athaliah, 27Jaareshiah, Elijah and Zicri.
28The family histories show that all these men were leaders of their families and lived in Jerusalem.
29Jeiel lived in the town of Gibeon, where he was the leader. His wife was named Maacah. 30Jeiel's first son was Abdon. His other sons were Zur, Kish, Baal, Ner, Nadab, 31Gedor, Ahio, Zeker 32and Mikloth. Mikloth was the father of Shimeah. These sons also lived near their relatives in Jerusalem.
33Ner was the father of Kish. Kish was the father of Saul, and Saul was the father of Jonathan, Malki-Shua, Abinadab and Esh-Baal.
34Jonathan's son was Merib-Baal, who was the father of Micah.
35Micah's sons were Pithon, Melech, Tarea and Ahaz. 36Ahaz was the father of Jehoaddah. Jehoaddah was the father of Alemeth, Azmaveth and Zimri. Zimri was the father of Moza. 37Moza was the father of Binea. Raphah was Binea's son. Eleasah was Raphah's son and Azel was Eleasah's son.
38Azel had six sons: Azrikam, Bokeru, Ishmael, Sheariah, Obadiah and Hanan. All these were Azel's sons.
39Azel's brother was Eshek. Eshek's first son was Ulam, his second was Jeush and Eliphelet was his third. 40Ulam's sons were mighty warriors and good archers. They had many sons and grandsons—150 of them in all.
All these men were Benjamin's descendants.

9 The names of all the people of Israel were listed in their family histories, and those family histories were put in the book of the kings of Israel.

The People in Jerusalem

The people of Judah were captured and forced to go to Babylon, because they were not faithful to God. 2The first people to come back and live in their own lands and towns were some Israelites, priests, Levites and Temple[d] servants.
3People from the tribes[d] of Judah, Benjamin, Ephraim and Manasseh lived in Jerusalem. This is a list of those people.
4There was Uthai son of Ammihud. (Ammihud was Omri's son. Omri was Imri's son. Imri was Bani's son. Bani was a descendant[d] of Perez, and Perez was Judah's son.)
5Of the Shilonite people there were Asaiah and his sons. Asaiah was the oldest son in his family.
6Of the Zerahite people there were Jeuel and other relatives of Zerah. There were 690 of them in all.
7From the tribe of Benjamin there was Sallu son of Meshullam. (Meshullam was Hodaviah's son, and Hodaviah was Hassenuah's son.) 8There was also Ibneiah son of Jeroham and Elah son of Uzzi. (Uzzi was Micri's son.) And there was Meshullam son of Shephatiah. (Shephatiah was Reuel's son, and Reuel was Ibnijah's son.) 9The family history of Benjamin lists 956 people living in Jerusalem, and all these were leaders of their families.
10Of the priests there were Jedaiah, Jehoiarib, Jakin and 11Azariah son of Hilkiah. (Hilkiah was Meshullam's son. Meshullam was Zadok's son.

Zadok was Meraioth's son. Meraioth was Ahitub's son. Ahitub was the officer responsible for the Temple of God.) [12]Also there was Adaiah son of Jeroham. (Jeroham was Pashhur's son, and Pashhur was Malkijah's son.) And there was Maasai son of Adiel. (Adiel was Jahzerah's son. Jahzerah was Meshullam's son. Meshullam was Meshillemith's son, and Meshillemith was Immer's son.) [13]There were 1,760 priests. They were leaders of their families, and they were responsible for serving in the Temple of God.

[14]Of the Levites there was Semaiah son of Hasshub. (Hasshub was Azrikam's son, and Azrikam was Hashabiah's son. Hashabiah was from the family of Merari.) [15]There were also Bakbakkar, Heresh, Galal and Mattaniah son of Mica. (Mica was Zicri's son, and Zicri was Asaph's son.) [16]There was also Obadiah son of Shemaiah. (Shemaiah was Galal's son and Galal was Jeduthun's son.) And there was Berekiah son of Asa. (Asa was the son of Elkanah, who lived in the villages of the Netophathites.)

[17]Of the gatekeepers there were Shallum, Akkub, Talmon, Ahiman and their relatives. Shallum was their leader. [18]These gatekeepers from the tribe of Levi still stand next to the King's Gate on the east side of the city. [19]Shallum was Kore's son. Kore was Ebiasaph's son, and Ebiasaph was Korah's son. Shallum and his relatives from the family of Korah were gatekeepers and were responsible for guarding the gates of the Temple. Their ancestors had also been responsible for guarding the entrance to the Temple of the LORD. [20]In the past Phinehas, Eleazar's son, was in charge of the gatekeepers, and the LORD was with Phinehas. [21]Zechariah son of Meshelemiah was the gatekeeper at the entrance to the Temple.

[22]In all, 212 men were chosen to guard the gates, and their names were written in their family histories in their villages. David and Samuel the seer[d] chose these men because they were dependable. [23]The gatekeepers and their descendants had to guard the gates of the Temple of the LORD. (The Temple took the place of the Holy Tent.[d]) [24]There were gatekeepers on all four sides of the Temple: east, west, north and south. [25]The gatekeepers' relatives who lived in the villages had to come and help them at times. Each time they came they helped the gatekeepers for seven days. [26]Because they were dependable, four gatekeepers were made the leaders of all the gatekeepers. They were Levites, and they were responsible for the rooms and treasures in the Temple of God. [27]They stayed up all night guarding the Temple of God, and they opened it every morning.

[28]Some of the gatekeepers were responsible for the dishes used in the Temple services. They counted these utensils when people took them out and when they brought them back. [29]Other gatekeepers were chosen to take care of the furniture and utensils in the Holy Place. They also took care of the flour, wine, oil, incense[d] and spices, [30]but some of the priests took care of mixing the spices. [31]There was a Levite named Mattithiah who was dependable and had the job of baking the bread used for the offerings. He was the first son of Shallum, who was from the family of Korah. [32]Some of the gatekeepers from the Kohath family had the job of preparing the special bread that was put on the table every Sabbath[d] day.

Sidelight If being a gatekeeper sounds like a cushy job, read 1 Chronicles 9:28–32 before applying. The Temple gatekeepers were probably priests who washed dishes, kept accounts, baked bread and mixed spices.

[33]Some of the Levites were musicians in the Temple. The leaders of these families stayed in the rooms of the Temple. Since they were on duty day and night, they did not do other work in the Temple.

[34]These are the leaders of the Levite families. Their names were listed in their family histories, and they lived in Jerusalem.

The Genealogy of King Saul

[35]Jeiel lived in the town of Gibeon, where he was the leader. His wife was named Maacah. [36]Jeiel's first son was Abdon. His other sons were Zur, Kish, Baal, Ner, Nadab, [37]Gedor, Ahio, Zechariah and Mikloth. [38]Mikloth was Shimeam's father. Jeiel's family lived near their relatives in Jerusalem.

[39]Ner was Kish's father. Kish was Saul's father. Saul was the father of Jonathan, Malki-Shua, Abinadab and Esh-Baal.

[40]Jonathan's son was Merib-Baal, who was the father of Micah.

[41]Micah's sons were Pithon, Melech, Tahrea and Ahaz. [42]Ahaz was Jadah's father. Jadah was the father of Alemeth, Azmaveth and Zimri. Zimri was Moza's father. [43]Moza was Binea's father. Rephaiah was Binea's son. Eleasah was Rephaiah's son, and Azel was Eleasah's son.

[44]Azel had six sons: Azrikam, Bokeru, Ishmael, Sheariah, Obadiah and Hanan. They were Azel's sons.

The Death of King Saul

10 The Philistines fought against Israel, and
the Israelites ran away from them. Many
Israelites were killed on Mount Gilboa. 2The Phi-
listines fought hard against Saul and his sons, kill-
ing his sons Jonathan, Abinadab and Malki-Shua.
3The fighting was heavy around Saul, and the
archers shot him with their arrows and
wounded him.
4Then Saul said to the officer who carried his
armour, "Pull out your sword and stab me. If you
don't, these Philistines who are not circumcised
will come and hurt me." But Saul's officer re-
fused, because he was afraid. So Saul took his
own sword and threw himself on it. 5When the
officer saw that Saul was dead, he threw himself
on his own sword and died. 6So Saul and three of
his sons died; all his family died together.
7When the Israelites living in the valley saw
that their army had run away and that Saul and
his sons were dead, they left their towns and ran
away. Then the Philistines came and settled in
them.
8The next day when the Philistines came to
strip the dead soldiers, they found Saul and his
sons dead on Mount Gilboa. 9The Philistines
stripped Saul's body and took his head and his
armour. Then they sent messengers through all
their country to tell the news to their idols and to
their people. 10The Philistines put Saul's armour
in the temple of their idols and hung his head in
the temple of Dagon. [d]
11All the people in Jabesh Gilead heard what
the Philistines had done to Saul. 12So the brave
men of Jabesh went and got the bodies of Saul
and his sons and brought them to Jabesh. They
buried their bones under the large tree in Jabesh.
Then the people of Jabesh gave up eating for
seven days.
13Saul died because he was not faithful to the
LORD and did not obey the LORD. He even went to
a medium [d] and asked her for advice 14instead of
asking the LORD. This is why the LORD put Saul to
death and gave the kingdom to Jesse's son David.

David Becomes King

11 Then the people of Israel came to David
at the town of Hebron and said, "Look,
we are your own family. 2Even when Saul was
king, you were the one who led Israel in battle.
The LORD your God said to you, 'You will be the
shepherd for my people Israel. You will be their
leader.' "
3So all the elders of Israel came to King David
at Hebron. He made an agreement with them in
Hebron in the presence of the LORD. Then they
poured oil on David to make him king over Israel.
The LORD had promised through Samuel that this
would happen.

David Captures Jerusalem

4David and all the Israelites went to the city
of Jerusalem. At that time Jerusalem was called
Jebus, and the people living there were named
Jebusites. 5They said to David, "You can't get in-
side our city." But David did take the city of
Jerusalem with its strong walls, and it became the
City of David.
6David had said, "The person who leads the
attack against the Jebusites will become the com-
mander over all my army." Joab son of Zeruiah
led the attack, so he became the commander of
the army.
7Then David made his home in the fortified
city, which is why it was named the City of Da-
vid. 8David rebuilt the city, beginning where the
land was filled in and going to the wall that was
around the city. Joab repaired the other parts of
the city. 9David became stronger and stronger,
and the LORD All-powerful was with him.

David's Mighty Warriors

10This is a list of the leaders over David's war-
riors who helped make David's kingdom strong.
All the people of Israel also supported David's
kingdom. These heroes and all the people of
Israel made David king, just as the LORD had
promised.
11This is a list of David's warriors:
Jashobeam was from the Hacmonite people.
He was the head of the Three, [n] David's most
powerful soldiers. He used his spear to fight 300
men at one time, and he killed them all.
12Next was Eleazar, one of the Three. Eleazar
was Dodai's son from the Ahohite people. 13Elea-
zar was with David at Pas-Dammim when the
Philistines came there to fight. There was a field
of barley at that place. The Israelites ran away
from the Philistines, 14but they stopped in the
middle of that field and fought for it and killed the
Philistines. The LORD gave them a great victory.
15Once, three of the Thirty, David's chief sol-
diers, came down to him at the rock by the cave
near Adullam. At the same time the Philistine
army had camped in the Valley of Rephaim.
16At that time David was in a stronghold, [d] and
some of the Philistines were in Bethlehem. 17Da-
vid had a strong desire for some water. He said,
"Oh, I wish someone would get me water from
the well near the city gate [n] of Bethlehem!" 18So

Three Or maybe "Thirty". These were David's most powerful soldiers. See 2 Samuel 23:8.
city gate People came here to conduct business. Public meetings and court cases were also held here.

the Three broke through the Philistine army and
took water from the well near the city gate in
Bethlehem. Then they brought it to David, but he
refused to drink it. He poured it out before the
LORD, 19saying, "May God keep me from drinking
this water! It would be like drinking the blood of
the men who risked their lives to bring it to me!"
So David refused to drink it.
These were the brave things that the three
warriors did.
20Abishai brother of Joab was the captain of the
Three. Abishai fought 300 soldiers with his spear
and killed them. He became as famous as the
Three 21and was more honoured than the Three.
He became their commander even though he
was not one of them.
22Benaiah son of Jehoiada was a brave fighter
from Kabzeel who did mighty things. He killed
two of the best warriors from Moab. He also went
down into a pit and killed a lion on a snowy day.
23Benaiah killed an Egyptian who was about 2.5
metres tall and had a spear as large as a weaver's
rod. Benaiah had a club, but he grabbed the spear
from the Egyptian's hand and killed him with his
own spear. 24These were the things Benaiah son
of Jehoiada did. He was as famous as the Three.
25He received more honour than the Thirty, but
he did not become a member of the Three. David
made him leader of his bodyguards.

The Thirty Chief Soldiers

26These were also mighty warriors:
Asahel brother of Joab;
Elhanan son of Dodo from Bethlehem;
27Shammoth the Harorite;
Helez the Pelonite;
28Ira son of Ikkesh from Tekoa;
Abiezer the Anathothite;
29Sibbecai the Hushathite;
Ilai the Ahohite;
30Maharai the Netophathite;
Heled son of Baanah the Netophathite;
31Ithai son of Ribai from Gibeah in
Benjamin;
Benaiah the Pirathonite;
32Hurai from the ravines of Gaash;
Abiel the Arbathite;
33Azmaveth the Baharumite;
Eliahba the Shaalbonite;
34the sons of Hashem the Gizonite;
Jonathan son of Shagee the Hararite;
35Ahiam son of Sacar the Hararite;
Eliphal son of Ur;
36Hepher the Mekerathite;
Ahijah the Pelonite;
37Hezro the Carmelite;
Naarai son of Ezbai;
38Joel brother of Nathan;
Mibhar son of Hagri;
39Zelek the Ammonite;
Naharai the Berothite, the officer who
carried the armour for Joab son of
Zeruiah;
40Ira the Ithrite;
Gareb the Ithrite;
41Uriah the Hittite;
Zabad son of Ahlai;
42Adina son of Shiza the Reubenite, who
was the leader of the Reubenites,
and his 30 soldiers;
43Hanan son of Maacah;
Joshaphat the Mithnite;
44Uzzia the Ashterathite;
Shama and Jeiel sons of Hotham the
Aroerite;
45Jediael son of Shimri;
Joha, Jediael's brother, the Tizite;
46Eliel the Mahavite;
Jeribai and Joshaviah, Elnaam's sons;
Ithmah the Moabite;
47Eliel, Obed and Jaasiel the Mezobaites.

Warriors Join David

12 These were the men who came to David
at Ziklag when David was hiding from
Saul son of Kish. They were among the warriors
who helped David in battle. 2They came with
bows for weapons and could use either their right
or left hands to shoot arrows or to sling rocks.
They were Saul's relatives from the tribe[d] of Ben-
jamin. 3Ahiezer was their leader, and there was
Joash. (Ahiezer and Joash were sons of Shemaah,
who was from the town of Gibeah.) There were
also Jeziel and Pelet, the sons of Azmaveth. There
were Beracah and Jehu from the town of Anath-
oth. 4And there was Ishmaiah from the town of
Gibeon; he was one of the Thirty. In fact, he was
the leader of the Thirty. There were Jeremiah,
Jahaziel, Johanan and Jozabad from Gederah.
5There were Eluzai, Jerimoth, Bealiah and Shem-
ariah. There was Shephatiah from Haruph.
6There were Elkanah, Isshiah, Azarel, Joezer and
Jashobeam from the family group of Korah. 7And
there were Joelah and Zebadiah, the sons of Jero-
ham, from the town of Gedor.
8Part of the people of Gad joined David at his
stronghold[d] in the desert. They were brave war-
riors trained for war and skilled with shields and
spears. They were as fierce as lions and as fast as
gazelles[d] over the hills.
9Ezer was the leader of Gad's army, and Oba-
diah was second in command. Eliab was third,
10Mishmannah was fourth, Jeremiah was fifth,
11Attai was sixth, Eliel was seventh, 12Johanan
was eighth, Elzabad was ninth, 13Jeremiah was
tenth and Macbannai was eleventh in command.

[14]They were the commanders of the army from Gad. The least of these leaders was in charge of 100 soldiers, and the greatest was in charge of 1,000. [15]They crossed the Jordan River and chased away the people living in the valleys, to the east and to the west. This happened in the first month of the year when the Jordan floods the valley.

[16]Other people from the tribes of Benjamin and Judah also came to David at his stronghold. [17]David went out to meet them and said to them, "If you have come peacefully to help me, I welcome you. Join me. But if you have come to turn me over to my enemies, even though I have done nothing wrong, the God of our fathers will see this and punish you."

[18]Then the Spirit[d] entered Amasai, the leader of the Thirty, and he said:

"We belong to you, David.
We are with you, son of Jesse.
Success, success to you.
Success to those who help you,
because your God helps you."

So David welcomed these men and made them leaders of his army.

[19]Some of the men from Manasseh also joined David when he went with the Philistines to fight Saul. But David and his men did not really help the Philistines. After talking about it, the Philistine leaders decided to send David away. They said, "If David goes back to his master Saul, we will be killed." [20]These are the men from Manasseh who joined David when he went to Ziklag: Adnah, Jozabad, Jediael, Michael, Jozabad, Elihu and Zillethai. Each of them was a leader of 1,000 men from Manasseh. [21]All these men of Manasseh were brave soldiers, and they helped David fight against groups of men who went around the country robbing people. These soldiers became commanders in David's army. [22]Every day more men joined David, and his army became large, like the army of God.

Others Join David at Hebron

[23]These are the numbers of the soldiers ready for battle who joined David at Hebron. They came to help turn the kingdom of Saul over to David, just as the LORD had said.

[24]There were 6,800 men with their weapons from Judah. They carried shields and spears.

[25]There were 7,100 men from Simeon. They were warriors ready for war.

[26]There were 4,600 men from Levi. [27]Jehoiada, a leader from Aaron's family, was in that group. There were 3,700 with him. [28]Zadok was also in that group. He was a strong young warrior, and with him came 22 leaders from his family.

[29]There were 3,000 men from Benjamin, who were Saul's relatives. Most of them had remained loyal to Saul's family until then.

[30]There were 20,800 men from Ephraim. They were brave warriors and were famous men in their own family groups.

[31]There were 18,000 men from West Manasseh. Each one was especially chosen to make David king.

[32]There were 200 leaders from Issachar. They knew what Israel should do, and they knew the right time to do it. Their relatives were with them and under their command.

[33]There were 50,000 men from Zebulun. They were trained soldiers and knew how to use every kind of weapon of war. They followed David completely.

[34]There were 1,000 officers from Naphtali. They had 37,000 soldiers with them who carried shields and spears.

[35]There were 28,600 men from Dan, who were ready for war.

[36]There were 40,000 trained soldiers from Asher, who were ready for war.

[37]There were 120,000 soldiers from the east side of the Jordan River from the people of Reuben, Gad and East Manasseh. They had every kind of weapon.

[38]All these fighting men were ready to go to war. They came to Hebron fully agreed to make David king of all Israel. All the other Israelites also agreed to make David king. [39]They spent three days there with David, eating and drinking, because their relatives had prepared food for them. [40]Also, their neighbours came from as far away as Issachar, Zebulun and Naphtali, bringing food on donkeys, camels, mules and oxen. They brought much flour, fig cakes, raisins, wine, oil, cows and sheep, because the people of Israel were very happy.

Bringing Back the Ark

13 David talked with all the officers of his army, the commanders of 100 men and the commanders of 1,000 men. [2]Then David called the people of Israel together and said, "If you think it is a good idea, and if it is what the LORD our God wants, let's send a message. Let's tell our fellow Israelites in all the areas of Israel and the priests and Levites living with them in their towns and pastures to come and join us. [3]Let's bring the Ark[d] of our God back to us. We did not use it to ask God for help while Saul was king." [4]All the people agreed with David, because they all thought it was the right thing to do.

[5]So David gathered all the Israelites, from the Shihor River in Egypt to Lebo Hamath, to bring the Ark of God back from the town of Kiriath

Jearim. 6David and all the Israelites with him
went to Baalah of Judah, which is Kiriath Jearim,
to get the Ark of God the LORD. God's throne is
between the golden, winged creatures on the
Ark, and the Ark is called by his name.
7The people carried the Ark of God from Abin-
adab's house on a new cart, and Uzzah and Ahio
guided it. 8David and all the Israelites were cele-
brating in the presence of God. With all their
strength they were singing and playing lyres,[d]
harps, tambourines,[d] cymbals and trumpets.
9When David's men came to the threshing[d]
floor of Kidon, the oxen stumbled, and Uzzah
reached out his hand to steady the Ark. 10The
LORD was angry with Uzzah and killed him, be-
cause he had touched the Ark. So Uzzah died
there in the presence of God.
11David was angry because the LORD had pun-
ished Uzzah in his anger. Now that place is called
The Punishment of Uzzah.
12David was afraid of God that day and asked,
"How can I bring the Ark of God home to me?"
13So David did not take the Ark with him to Jeru-
salem. Instead, he took it to the house of Obed-
Edom who was from Gath. 14The Ark of God
stayed with Obed-Edom's family in his house for
three months, and the LORD blessed Obed-Edom's
family and everything he owned.

David's Kingdom Grows

14 Hiram king of the city of Tyre sent mes-
sengers to David. He also sent cedar logs,
bricklayers and carpenters to build a palace for
David. 2Then David knew that the LORD really
had made him king of Israel and that he had
made his kingdom great. The LORD did this be-
cause he loved his people Israel.
3David married more women in Jerusalem and
had more sons and daughters. 4These are the
names of David's children born in Jerusalem:
Shammua, Shobab, Nathan, Solomon, 5Ibhar, Eli-
shua, Elpelet, 6Nogah, Nepheg, Japhia, 7Elish-
ama, Beeliada and Eliphelet.

David Defeats the Philistines

8When the Philistines heard that David had
been made king of all Israel, they went to look for
him. But David heard about it and went out to
fight them. 9The Philistines had attacked and
robbed the people in the Valley of Rephaim. 10Da-
vid asked God, "Should I go and attack the Philis-
tines? Will you hand them over to me?"
The LORD answered him, "Go, I will hand them
over to you."
11So David and his men went up to the town
of Baal Perazim and defeated the Philistines.
David said, "Like a flood of water, God has broken
through my enemies by using me." So that place
was named Baal Perazim.[n] 12The Philistines had
left their idols there, so David ordered his men to
burn them.
13Soon the Philistines attacked the people in
the valley again. 14David prayed to God again,
and God answered him, saying, "Don't attack the
Philistines from the front. Instead, go around
them and attack them in front of the balsam
trees. 15When you hear the sound of marching in
the tops of the balsam trees, then attack. I, God,
will have gone out before you to defeat the Philis-
tine army." 16David did as God commanded, and
he and his men defeated the Philistine army all
the way from Gibeon to Gezer.
17So David became famous in all the countries,
and the LORD made all nations afraid of him.

The Ark is Brought to Jerusalem

15 David built houses for himself in Jeru-
salem. Then he prepared a place for the
Ark[d] of God, and he set up a tent for it. 2David
said, "Only the Levites may carry the Ark of God.
The LORD chose them to carry the Ark of the LORD
and to serve him for ever."
3David called all the people of Israel to come
to Jerusalem. He wanted to bring the Ark of the
LORD to the place he had made for it. 4David
called together the descendants[d] of Aaron and
the Levites. 5There were 120 people from
Kohath's family group, with Uriel as their
leader. 6There were 220 people from Merari's
family group, with Asaiah as their leader. 7There
were 130 people from Gershon's family group,
with Joel as their leader. 8There were 200
people from Elizaphan's family group, with She-
maiah as their leader. 9There were 80 people
from Hebron's family group, with Eliel as their
leader. 10And there were 112 people from
Uzziel's family group, with Amminadab as their
leader.
11Then David asked the priests Zadok and Abi-
athar and these Levites to come to him: Uriel,
Asaiah, Joel, Shemaiah, Eliel and Amminadab.
12David said to them, "You are the leaders of the
families of Levi. You and the other Levites must
give yourselves for service to the LORD. Bring up
the Ark of the LORD, the God of Israel, to the place
I have made for it. 13The last time we did not ask
the LORD how to carry it. You Levites didn't carry
it, so the LORD our God punished us."
14Then the priests and Levites prepared them-
selves for service to the LORD so they could carry
the Ark of the LORD, the God of Israel. 15The Le-
vites used special poles to carry the Ark of God on

Baal Perazim This name means "the LORD breaks through".

their shoulders, as Moses had commanded, just
as the LORD had said they should.
16David told the leaders of the Levites to ap-
point their brothers as singers to play their lyres,[d]
harps and cymbals and to sing happy songs.
17So the Levites appointed Heman and his rel-
atives Asaph and Ethan. Heman was Joel's son.
Asaph was Berekiah's son. And Ethan, from the
Merari family group, was Kushaiah's son. 18There
was also a second group of Levites: Zechariah,
Jaaziel, Shemiramoth, Jehiel, Unni, Eliab, Bena-
iah, Maaseiah, Mattithiah, Eliphelehu, Mikneiah,
Obed-Edom and Jeiel. They were the Levite
guards.
19The singers Heman, Asaph and Ethan played
bronze cymbals. 20Zechariah, Jaaziel, Shemira-
moth, Jehiel, Unni, Eliab, Maaseiah and Benaiah
played the lyres. 21Mattithiah, Eliphelehu, Mikne-
iah, Obed-Edom, Jeiel and Azaziah played the
harps. 22The Levite leader Kenaniah was in
charge of the singing, because he was very good
at it.
23Berekiah and Elkanah were two of the guards
for the Ark of the Agreement. 24The priests Sheb-
aniah, Joshaphat, Nethanel, Amasai, Zechariah,
Benaiah and Eliezer had the job of blowing trum-
pets in front of the Ark of God. Obed-Edom and
Jehiah were also guards for the Ark.
25David, the elders of Israel, and the command-
ers of 1,000 soldiers went to get the Ark of the
Agreement with the LORD. They all went to bring
the Ark from Obed-Edom's house with great joy.
26Because God helped the Levites who carried
the Ark of the Agreement with the LORD, they
sacrificed seven bulls and seven rams. 27All the
Levites who carried the Ark, and Kenaniah, the
man in charge of the singing, and all the singers
wore robes of fine linen. David also wore a robe
of fine linen and a holy robe[d] of fine linen. 28So
all the people of Israel brought up the Ark of the
Agreement with the LORD. They shouted, blew
horns and trumpets and played cymbals, lyres
and harps.
29As the Ark of the Agreement with the LORD
entered Jerusalem, Saul's daughter Michal
watched from a window. When she saw King
David dancing and celebrating, she hated him.

16 They brought the Ark[d] of God and put it
inside the tent that David had set up for
it. Then they offered burnt offerings and fellow-
ship offerings to God. 2When David had finished
giving the burnt offerings and fellowship offer-
ings, he blessed the people in the name of the
LORD. 3He gave a loaf of bread, some dates and
raisins to every Israelite man and woman.
4Then David appointed some of the Levites to
serve before the Ark of the LORD. They had the job
of leading the worship and giving thanks and
praising the LORD, the God of Israel. 5Asaph, who
played the cymbals, was the leader. Zechariah
was second to him. The other Levites were Jaa-
ziel, Shemiramoth, Jehiel, Mattithiah, Eliab, Be-
naiah, Obed-Edom and Jeiel. They played the
lyres[d] and harps. 6Benaiah and Jahaziel were
priests who blew the trumpets regularly before
the Ark of the Agreement with God. 7That day
David first gave Asaph and his relatives the job of
singing praises to the LORD.

David's Song of Thanks

8Give thanks to the LORD and pray to him.
  Tell the nations what he has done.
9Sing to him; sing praises to him.
  Tell about all his miracles.[d]
10Be glad that you are his;
  let those who seek the LORD be happy.
11Depend on the LORD and his strength;
  always go to him for help.
12Remember the miracles he has done,
  his wonders, and his decisions.
13You are the descendants[d] of his servant,
    Israel;
  you are the children of Jacob, his chosen
    people.

14He is the LORD our God.
  His laws are for all the world.
15He will keep his agreement for ever;
  he will keep his promises always.
16He will keep the agreement he made with
    Abraham
  and the promise he made to Isaac.
17He made it a law for the people of Jacob;
  he made it an agreement with Israel to last
    for ever.
18He said, "I will give the land of Canaan
    to you,
  to belong to you."

19Then God's people were few in number,
  and they were strangers in the land.
20They went from one nation to another,
  from one kingdom to another.
21But he did not let anyone hurt them;
  he warned kings not to harm them.
22He said, "Don't touch my chosen people,
  and don't harm my prophets."[d]

23Sing to the LORD, all the earth.
  Every day tell how he saves us.
24Tell the nations about his glory;
  tell all peoples the miracles he does.
25The LORD is great; he should be praised.
  He should be respected more than all the
    gods.
26All the gods of the nations are only idols,
  but the LORD made the skies.

27He has glory and majesty;
he has power and joy in his Temple.[d]

28Praise the LORD, all nations on earth.
Praise the Lord's glory and power;
29 praise the glory of the LORD's name.
Bring an offering and come to him.
Worship the Lord because he is holy.
30Tremble before him, everyone on earth.
The earth is set, and it cannot be moved.
31Let the skies rejoice and the earth be glad.
Let people everywhere say, "The LORD is
king!"
32Let the sea and everything in it shout;
let the fields and everything in them
rejoice.
33Then the trees of the forest will sing
for joy before the LORD.
They will sing because he is coming to
judge the world.

34Thank the LORD because he is good.
His love continues for ever.
35Say to him, "Save us, God our Saviour,
and bring us back and save us from other
nations.
Then we will thank you
and will gladly praise you."
36Praise the LORD, the God of Israel.
He always was and always will be.

All the people said "Amen" and praised the Lord.
37Then David left Asaph and the other Levites
there in front of the Ark[d] of the Agreement with
the LORD. They were to serve there every day.
38David also left Obed-Edom and 68 other Le-
vites to serve with them. Hosah and Obed-Edom
son of Jeduthun were guards.
39David left Zadok the priest and the other
priests who served with him in front of the Tent
of the LORD at the place of worship in Gibeon.
40Every morning and evening they offered burnt
offerings on the altar of burnt offerings, following
the rules written in the Teachings of the LORD,
which he had given Israel. 41With them were He-
man and Jeduthun and other Levites. They were
chosen by name to sing praises to the LORD be-
cause his love continues for ever. 42Heman and
Jeduthun also had the job of playing the trumpets
and cymbals and other musical instruments when
songs were sung to God. Jeduthun's sons guarded
the gates.
43Then all the people left. Each person went
home, and David also went home to bless the
people in his home.

God's Promise to David

17 When David moved into his palace, he
said to Nathan the prophet, "Look, I am
living in a palace made of cedar, but the Ark[d] of
the Agreement with the LORD sits in a tent."
2Nathan said to David, "Do what you want to
do, because God is with you."
3But that night God spoke his word to Nathan,
saying, 4"Go and tell David my servant, 'This is
what the LORD says: You are not the person to
build a house for me to live in. 5From the time I
brought Israel out of Egypt until now I have not
lived in a house. I have moved from one tent site
to another and from one place to another. 6As I
have moved with the Israelites to different places,
I have never said to the leaders, whom I com-
manded to take care of my people, "Why haven't
you built me a house of cedar?" '
7"Now, tell my servant David: 'This is what
the LORD All-powerful says: I took you from the
pasture and from tending the sheep and made
you king of my people Israel. 8I have been with
you everywhere you have gone. I have defeated
your enemies for you. I will make you as famous
as any of the great people on the earth. 9I will
choose a place for my people Israel, and I will
plant them so they can live in their own homes.
They will not be bothered any more. Wicked peo-
ple will no longer hurt them as they have in the
past 10when I chose judges for my people Israel.
I will defeat all your enemies.
" 'I tell you that the LORD will make your des-
cendants[d] kings of Israel after you. 11When you
die and join your ancestors, I will make one of
your sons the new king, and I will set up his
kingdom. 12He will build a house for me, and I
will let his kingdom rule always. 13I will be his
father, and he will be my son. I took away my
love from Saul, who ruled before you, but I will
never stop loving your son. 14I will put him in
charge of my house and kingdom for ever. His
family will rule for ever.' "
15Nathan told David everything God had said
in this vision.

David Prays to God

16Then King David went in and sat in front of
the LORD. David said, "LORD God, who am I?
What is my family? Why did you bring me to this
point? 17But that was not enough for you, God.
You have also made promises about my future
family. LORD God, you have treated me like a very
important person.
18"What more can I say to you for honouring
me, your servant? You know me so well. 19LORD,
you have done this wonderful thing for my sake
and because you wanted to. You have made
known all these great things.
20"There is no one like you, LORD. There is
no God except you. We have heard all this
ourselves! 21There is no nation like your people

Israel. They are the only people on earth that God
chose to be his own. You made your name well
known by the great and wonderful things you did
for them. You went ahead of them and forced
other nations out of the land. You freed your peo-
ple from slavery in Egypt. 22You made the people
of Israel your very own people for ever, and,
LORD, you are their God.
23"LORD, keep the promise for ever that you
made about my family and me, your servant. Do
what you have said. 24Then you will be honoured
always, and people will say, 'The LORD All-
powerful, the God over Israel, is Israel's God!'
And the family of your servant David will con-
tinue before you.
25"My God, you have told me that you would
make my family great. So I, your servant, am
brave enough to pray to you. 26LORD, you are God,
and you have promised these good things to me,
your servant. 27You have chosen to bless my fam-
ily. Let it continue before you always. LORD, you
have blessed my family, so it will always be
blessed."

David Defeats Nations

18 Later, David defeated the Philistines,
conquered them, and took the city of
Gath and the small towns around it.
2He also defeated the people of Moab. So the
people of Moab became servants of David and
gave him the payment he demanded.
3David also defeated Hadadezer king of Zobah
all the way to the town of Hamath as he tried to
spread his kingdom to the Euphrates River. 4Da-
vid captured 1,000 of his chariots, 7,000 men
who rode in chariots and 20,000 foot soldiers. He
crippled all but 100 of the chariot horses.
5Arameans from Damascus came to help Had-
adezer king of Zobah, but David killed 22,000 of
them. 6Then David put groups of soldiers in Da-
mascus in Aram. The Arameans became David's
servants and gave him the payments he de-
manded. So the LORD gave David victory every-
where he went.
7David took the shields of gold that had be-
longed to Hadadezer's officers and brought them
to Jerusalem. 8David also took many things made
of bronze from Tebah and Cun, which had been
cities under Hadadezer's control. Later, Solomon
used this bronze to make things for the Temple:[d]
the large bronze bowl, which was called the Sea,
the pillars and other bronze utensils.
9Toi king of Hamath heard that David had de-
feated all the army of Hadadezer king of Zobah.
10So Toi sent his son Hadoram to greet and
congratulate King David for defeating Hadadezer.
(Hadadezer had been at war with Toi.) Hadoram
brought things made of gold, silver and bronze.
11King David gave them to the LORD, along with
the silver and gold he had taken from these na-
tions: Edom, Moab, the Ammonites, the Philis-
tines and Amalek.
12Abishai son of Zeruiah killed 18,000 Edom-
ites in the Valley of Salt. 13David put groups of
soldiers in Edom, and all the Edomites became
his servants. The LORD gave David victory every-
where he went.

David's Important Officers

14David was king over all of Israel, and he did
what was fair and right for all his people. 15Joab
son of Zeruiah was commander over the army.
Jehoshaphat son of Ahilud was the recorder. 16Za-
dok son of Ahitub and Abiathar son of Ahimelech
were priests. Shavsha was the royal secretary.
17Benaiah son of Jehoiada was over the Kerethites
and Pelethites.[n] And David's sons were impor-
tant officers who served at his side.

War with the Ammonites and Arameans

19 When Nahash king of the Ammonites
died, his son became king after him. 2Da-
vid said, "Nahash was loyal to me, so I will be
loyal to his son Hanun." So David sent messen-
gers to comfort Hanun about his father's death.
David's officers went to the land of the Am-
monites to comfort Hanun. 3But the Ammonite
leaders said to Hanun, "Do you think David
wants to honour your father by sending men to
comfort you? No! David sent them to study the
land and capture it and spy it out." 4So Hanun
arrested David's officers. To shame them he
shaved their beards and cut off their clothes at
the hips. Then he sent them away.
5When the people told David what had hap-
pened to his officers, he sent messengers to meet
them, because they were very ashamed. King Da-
vid said, "Stay in Jericho until your beards have
grown back. Then come home."
6The Ammonites knew that they had insulted
David. So Hanun and the Ammonites sent about
35 tonnes of silver to hire chariots and chariot
drivers from North West Mesopotamia, Aram
Maacah and Zobah. 7The Ammonites hired
32,000 chariots and the king of Maacah and his
army. So they came and set up camp near the
town of Medeba. The Ammonites themselves
came out of their towns and got ready for battle.
8When David heard about this, he sent Joab
with the whole army. 9The Ammonites came out

Kerethites and Pelethites These were probably special units of the army that were responsible for the king's safety, a kind of palace guard.

and prepared for battle at the city gate.[n] The
kings who had come to help were out in the field
by themselves.
10Joab saw that there were enemies both in
front of him and behind him. So he chose some
of the best soldiers of Israel and sent them out to
fight the Arameans. 11Joab put the rest of the
army under the command of Abishai, his brother.
Then they went out to fight the Ammonites.
12Joab said to Abishai, "If the Arameans are too
strong for me, you must help me. Or, if the Am-
monites are too strong for you, I will help you.
13Be strong. We must fight bravely for our people
and the cities of our God. The LORD will do what
he thinks is right."
14Then Joab and the army with him went
to attack the Arameans, and the Arameans ran
away. 15When the Ammonites saw that the
Arameans were running away, they also ran
away from Joab's brother Abishai and went back
to their city. So Joab went back to Jerusalem.
16When the Arameans saw that Israel had
defeated them, they sent messengers to bring
other Arameans from east of the Euphrates River.
Their leader was Shophach, the commander of
Hadadezer's army.
17When David heard about this, he gathered
all the Israelites, and they crossed over the Jor-
dan River. He prepared them for battle, facing
the Arameans. The Arameans fought with him,
18but they ran away from the Israelites. David
killed 7,000 Aramean chariot drivers and
40,000 Aramean foot soldiers. He also killed
Shophach, the commander of the Aramean
army.
19When those who served Hadadezer saw that
the Israelites had defeated them, they made
peace with David and served him. So the Arame-
ans refused to help the Ammonites again.

> **Sidelight** In the ancient world even war depended on the weather. Apparently the right time for war in the Old Testament was springtime (1 Chronicles 20:1). Kings would go to war right after the spring harvest when there wasn't much to do on the farm and when the soldiers could live off the land.

Joab Destroys the Ammonites

20 In the spring, the time of year when
kings normally went out to battle, Joab
led out the army of Israel. But David stayed in
Jerusalem. The army of Israel destroyed the land
of Ammon and went to the city of Rabbah and
attacked it. 2David took the crown off the head of
their king,[n] and had it placed on his own head.
That gold crown weighed about 35 kilogrammes,
and it had valuable gems in it. And David took
many valuable things from the city. 3He also
brought out the people of the city and forced
them to work with saws, iron picks and axes.
David did this to all the Ammonite cities. Then
David and all his army returned to Jerusalem.

Philistine Giants are Killed

4Later, at Gezer, war broke out with the Philis-
tines. Sibbecai the Hushathite killed Sippai, who
was one of the descendants[d] of the Rephaites.[d]
So those Philistines were defeated.
5Later, there was another battle with the Philis-
tines. Elhanan son of Jair killed Lahmi, the
brother of Goliath, who was from the town of
Gath. His spear was as large as a weaver's rod.
6At Gath another battle took place. A very
large man was there; he had six fingers on each
hand and six toes on each foot—24 fingers and
toes in all. This man also was one of the sons of
Rapha.[d] 7When he spoke against Israel, Jonathan
son of Shimea, David's brother, killed him.
8These descendants of Rapha from Gath were
killed by David and his men.

David Counts the Israelites

21 Satan was against Israel, and he caused
David to count the people of Israel. 2So
David said to Joab and the commanders of the
troops, "Go and count all the Israelites from Beer-
sheba to Dan.[n] Then tell me so I will know how
many there are."
3But Joab said, "May the LORD give the nation
a hundred times more people. My master the
king, all the Israelites are your servants. Why do
you want to do this, my master? You will make
Israel guilty of sin."
4But the king commanded Joab, so Joab left
and went through all Israel. Then he returned to
Jerusalem. 5Joab gave the list of the people to
David. There were 1,100,000 men in all of Israel
who could use the sword, and there were
470,000 men in Judah who could use the sword.
6But Joab did not count the tribes[d] of Levi and
Benjamin, because he disliked King David's or-
der. 7David had done something God had said
was wrong, so God punished Israel.

city gate People came here to conduct business. Public meetings and court cases were also held here.
their king Or, "Milcom", the god of the Ammonite people.
Beersheba to Dan Beersheba was the city farthest south in Israel, and Dan was the city farthest north. So this means all the people of Israel.

8Then David said to God, "I have sinned
greatly by what I have done! Now, I beg you to
forgive me, your servant, because I have been
very foolish."

9The LORD said to Gad, who was David's seer,[d]
10"Go and tell David, 'This is what the LORD says:
I offer you three choices. Choose one of them and
I will do it.' "

11So Gad went to David and said to him, "This
is what the LORD says: 'Choose for yourself 12three
years of hunger. Or choose three months of run-
ning from your enemies as they chase you with
their swords. Or choose three days of punishment
from the LORD, in which a terrible disease will
spread through the country. The angel of the
LORD will go through Israel destroying the peo-
ple.' Now, David, decide which of these things I
should tell the LORD who sent me."

13David said to Gad, "I am in great trouble. Let
the LORD punish me, because the LORD is very
merciful. Don't let my punishment come from
human beings."

14So the LORD sent a terrible disease on Israel,
and 70,000 people died. 15God sent an angel to
destroy Jerusalem, but when the angel started to
destroy it, the LORD saw it and felt very sorry
about the terrible things that had happened. So
he said to the angel who was destroying, "That is
enough! Put down your arm!" The angel of the
LORD was then standing at the threshing[d] floor of
Araunah the Jebusite.

16David looked up and saw the angel of the
LORD in the sky, holding his sword drawn and
pointed at Jerusalem. Then David and the elders
bowed face down on the ground. They were
wearing rough cloth to show their grief. 17David
said to God, "I am the one who sinned and did
wrong. I gave the order for the people to be coun-
ted. These people only followed me like sheep.
They did nothing wrong. LORD my God, please
punish me and my family, but stop the terrible
disease that is killing your people."

18Then the angel of the LORD told Gad to tell
David that he should build an altar to the LORD on
the threshing floor of Araunah the Jebusite. 19So
David did what Gad told him to do, in the name
of the LORD.

20Araunah was separating the wheat from the
straw. When he turned round, he saw the angel.
Araunah's four sons who were with him hid.
21David came to Araunah, and when Araunah
saw him, he left the threshing floor and bowed
face down on the ground before David.

22David said to him, "Sell me your threshing
floor so I can build an altar to the LORD here.
Then the terrible disease will stop. Sell it to me
for the full price."

23Araunah said to David, "Take this threshing
floor. My master the king, do anything you want.
Look, I will also give you oxen for the whole
burnt offerings, the threshing boards for the
wood, and wheat for the grain offering. I give
everything to you."

24But King David answered Araunah, "No,
I will pay the full price for the land. I won't
take anything that is yours and give it to the
LORD. I won't offer a burnt offering that costs me
nothing."

25So David paid Araunah about 7 kilogrammes
of gold for the place. 26David built an altar to the
LORD there and offered whole burnt offerings and
fellowship offerings. David prayed to the LORD,
and he answered him by sending down fire from
heaven on the altar of burnt offering. 27Then the
LORD commanded the angel to put his sword back
into its holder.

28When David saw that the LORD had answered
him on the threshing floor of Araunah, he offered
sacrifices there. 29The Holy Tent[d] that Moses
made while the Israelites were in the desert and
the altar of burnt offerings were in Gibeon at the
place of worship. 30But David could not go to the
Holy Tent to speak with God, because he was
afraid of the angel of the LORD and his sword.

22 David said, "The Temple[d] of the LORD
God and the altar for Israel's burnt offer-
ings will be built here."

David Makes Plans for the Temple

2So David ordered all foreigners living in Israel
to gather together. From that group David chose
stonecutters to cut stones to be used in building
the Temple[d] of God. 3David supplied a large
amount of iron to be used for making nails and
hinges for the gate doors. He also supplied more
bronze than could be weighed, 4and he supplied
more cedar logs than could be counted. Much of
the cedar had been brought to David by the peo-
ple from Sidon and Tyre.

5David said, "We should build a great Temple
for the LORD, which will be famous everywhere
for its greatness and beauty. But my son Solomon
is young. He hasn't yet learned what he needs to
know, so I will prepare for the building of it." So
David got many of the materials ready before he
died.

6Then David called for his son Solomon and
told him to build the Temple for the LORD, the
God of Israel. 7David said to him, "My son, I
wanted to build a temple for worshipping the
LORD my God. 8But the LORD spoke his word to
me, 'David, you have killed many people. You
have fought many wars. You cannot build a tem-
ple for worship to me, because you have killed
many people. 9But, you will have a son, a man of
peace and rest. I will give him rest from all his

enemies around him. His name will be Solo-
mon,[n] and I will give Israel peace and quiet
while he is king. 10Solomon will build a temple
for worship to me. He will be my son, and I will
be his father. I will make his kingdom strong;
someone from his family will rule Israel for
ever.' "
11David said, "Now, my son, may the LORD be
with you. May you build a temple for the LORD
your God, as he said you would. 12He will make
you the king of Israel. May the LORD give you
wisdom and understanding so you will be able to
obey the teachings of the LORD your God. 13Be
careful to obey the rules and laws the LORD gave
Moses for Israel. If you obey them, you will have
success. Be strong and brave. Don't be afraid or
discouraged.
14"Solomon, I have worked hard getting many
of the materials for building the Temple of the
LORD. I have supplied about 3,550 tonnes of gold,
about 35,000 tonnes of silver, so much bronze
and iron it cannot be weighed, and wood and
stone. You may add to them. 15You have many
workmen—stonecutters, bricklayers, carpenters
and people skilled in every kind of work. 16They
are skilled in working with gold, silver, bronze
and iron. You have more craftsmen than can be
counted. Now begin the work, and may the LORD
be with you."
17Then David ordered all the leaders of Israel
to help his son Solomon. 18David said to them,
"The LORD your God is with you. He has given
you rest from our enemies. He has handed over
to me the people living around us. The LORD and
his people are in control of this land. 19Now give
yourselves completely to obeying the LORD your
God. Build the holy place of the LORD God; build
the Temple for worship to the LORD. Then bring
the Ark[d] of the Agreement with the LORD and the
holy things that belong to God into the Temple."

The Levites

23 After David had lived long and was old,
he made his son Solomon the new king
of Israel. 2David gathered all the leaders of Israel,
along with the priests and Levites. 3He counted
the Levites who were 30 years old and older. In
all, there were 38,000 Levites. 4David said, "Of
these, 24,000 Levites will direct the work of the
Temple[d] of the LORD, 6,000 Levites will be offi-
cers and judges, 54,000 Levites will be gatekeep-
ers and 4,000 Levites will praise the LORD with
musical instruments I made for giving praise."
6David separated the Levites into three groups
that were led by Levi's three sons: Gershon,
Kohath and Merari.

The People of Gershon

7From the people of Gershon, there were La-
dan and Shimei.
8Ladan had three sons. His first son was Jehiel,
and his other sons were Zetham and Joel.
9Shimei's sons were Shelomoth, Haziel and
Haran. These three sons were leaders of Ladan's
families. 10Shimei had four sons: Jahath, Ziza, Je-
ush and Beriah. 11Jahath was the first son, and
Ziza was the second son. But Jeush and Beriah
did not have many children, so they were coun-
ted as if they were one family.

The People of Kohath

12Kohath had four sons: Amram, Izhar, Hebron
and Uzziel.
13Amram's sons were Aaron and Moses. Aaron
and his descendants[d] were chosen to be special
for ever. They were chosen to prepare the holy
things for the LORD's service, to offer sacrifices
before the LORD, and to serve him as priests. They
were to give blessings in his name for ever.
14Moses was the man of God, and his sons
were counted as part of the tribe[d] of Levi.
15Moses' sons were Gershom and Eliezer. 16Ger-
shom's first son was Shubael. 17Eliezer's first
son was Rehabiah. Eliezer had no other sons, but
Rehabiah had many sons.
18Izhar's first son was Shelomith.
19Hebron's first son was Jeriah, his second was
Amariah, his third was Jahaziel, and his fourth
was Jekameam.
20Uzziel's first son was Micah and his second
was Isshiah.

The People of Merari

21Merari's sons were Mahli and Mushi.
Mahli's sons were Eleazar and Kish. 22Eleazar
died without sons; he had only daughters. Ele-
azar's daughters married their cousins, the sons
of Kish. 23Mushi's three sons were Mahli, Eder
and Jerimoth.

The Levites' Work

24These were Levi's descendants[d] listed by
their families. They were the leaders of families.
Each person who was 20 years old or older was
listed. They served in the LORD's Temple.[d]
25David had said, "The LORD, the God of Israel,
has given rest to his people. He has come to live
in Jerusalem for ever. 26So the Levites don't need
to carry the Holy Tent[d] or any of the things used
in its services any more." 27David's last instruc-
tions were to count the Levites who were 20
years old and older.

Solomon This name sounds like the Hebrew word for "peace".

28The Levites had the job of helping Aaron's
descendants in the service of the Temple of the
LORD. They cared for the Temple courtyard and
side rooms, and they made all the holy things
pure. Their job was to serve in the Temple of
God. 29They were responsible for putting the
holy bread on the table, for the flour in the grain
offerings, for the bread made without yeast, for
the baking and mixing, and for the measuring.
30The Levites also stood every morning and gave
thanks and praise to the LORD. They also did this
every evening. 31The Levites offered all the burnt
offerings to the LORD on the special days of rest,
at the New Moon[d] festivals and at all appointed
feasts. They served before the LORD every day.
They were to follow the rules for how many
Levites should serve each time. 32So the Levites
took care of the Meeting Tent and the Holy
Place. And they helped their relatives, Aaron's
descendants, with the services at the Temple
of the LORD.

The Groups of the Priests

24 These were the groups of Aaron's sons:
Aaron's sons were Nadab, Abihu, Ele-
azar and Ithamar. 2But Nadab and Abihu died
before their father did, and they had no sons. So
Eleazar and Ithamar served as the priests. 3David,
with the help of Zadok, a descendant[d] of Eleazar,
and Ahimelech, a descendant of Ithamar, sepa-
rated their family groups into two different groups.
Each group had certain duties. 4There were
more leaders from Eleazar's family than from
Ithamar's—sixteen leaders from Eleazar's family
and eight leaders from Ithamar's family. 5Men were
chosen from Eleazar's and Ithamar's families by
throwing lots.[d] Some men from each family were
chosen to be in charge of the Holy Place, and
some were chosen to serve as priests.

6Shemaiah son of Nethanel, from the tribe[d] of
Levi, was the secretary. He recorded the names of
those descendants in front of King David, the offi-
cers, Zadok the priest, Ahimelech son of Abia-
thar, and the leaders of the families of the priests
and Levites. The work was divided by lots among
the families of Eleazar and Ithamar. The following
men with their groups were chosen.

7The first one chosen was Jehoiarib. The
second was Jedaiah. 8The third was Harim. The
fourth was Seorim. 9The fifth was Malkijah. The
sixth was Mijamin. 10The seventh was Hakkoz.
The eighth was Abijah. 11The ninth was Jeshua.
The tenth was Shecaniah. 12The eleventh was
Eliashib. The twelfth was Jakim. 13The thirteenth
was Huppah. The fourteenth was Jeshebeab.
14The fifteenth was Bilgah. The sixteenth was
Immer. 15The seventeenth was Hezir. The
eighteenth was Happizzez. 16The nineteenth
was Pethahiah. The twentieth was Jehezkel.
17The twenty-first was Jakin. The twenty-second
was Gamul. 18The twenty-third was Delaiah.
The twenty-fourth was Maaziah.

19These were the groups chosen to serve in the
Temple of the LORD. They obeyed the rules given
them by Aaron, just as the LORD, the God of Israel,
had commanded him.

The Other Levites

20These are the names of the rest of Levi's des-
cendants:[d]

Shubael was a descendant of Amram, and
Jehdeiah was a descendant of Shubael.

21Isshiah was the first son of Rehabiah.

22From the Izhar family group, there was
Shelomoth, and Jahath was a descendant of
Shelomoth.

23Hebron's first son was Jeriah, Amariah was
his second, Jahaziel was his third and Jekameam
was his fourth.

24Uzziel's son was Micah. Micah's son was
Shamir. 25Micah's brother was Isshiah and Is-
shiah's son was Zechariah.

26Merari's descendants were Mahli and Mushi.
Merari's son was Jaaziah. 27Jaaziah son of Merari
had sons named Shoham, Zaccur and Ibri.
28Mahli's son was Eleazar, but Eleazar did not
have any sons.

29Kish's son was Jerahmeel.

30Mushi's sons were Mahli, Eder and Jerimoth.

These are the Levites, listed by their families.
31They were chosen for special jobs by throwing
lots[d] in front of King David, Zadok, Ahimelech,
the leaders of the families of the priests and of the
Levites. They did this just as their relatives, the
priests, Aaron's descendants, had done. The fam-
ilies of the oldest brother and the youngest
brother were treated the same.

Sidelight It might seem strange if your minister started singing during a sermon. But 1 Chronicles 25:1 describes people who were chosen to preach – and play harps, lyres and cymbals. The cymbals must have helped if the sermon got boring.

The Music Groups

25 David and the commanders of the army
chose some of the sons of Asaph, Heman
and Jeduthun to preach and play harps, lyres[d]
and cymbals. Here is a list of the men who served
in this way:

2Asaph's sons who served were Zaccur, Jo-
seph, Nethaniah and Asarelah. King David chose
Asaph to preach, and Asaph directed his sons.

[3]Jeduthun's sons who served were Gedaliah,
Zeri, Jeshaiah, Shimei, Hashabiah and Mattithiah.
There were six of them, and Jeduthun directed
them. He preached and used a harp to give
thanks and praise to the LORD.
[4]Heman's sons who served were Bukkiah, Mat-
taniah, Uzziel, Shubael, Jerimoth, Hananiah,
Hanani, Eliathah, Giddalti, Romamti-Ezer, Josh-
bekashah, Mallothi, Hothir and Mahazioth. [5]All
these were sons of Heman, David's seer.[d] God
promised to make Heman strong, so Heman had
many sons. God gave him fourteen sons and three
daughters. [6]Heman directed all his sons in making
music for the Temple[d] of the LORD with cymbals,
lyres and harps; that was their way of serving in
the Temple of God. King David was in charge of
Asaph, Jeduthun and Heman. [7]These men and
their relatives were trained and skilled in making
music for the LORD. There were 288 of them.
[8]Everyone threw lots[d] to choose the time his fam-
ily was to serve at the Temple. The young and the
old, the teacher and the student, had to throw lots.
[9]First, the lot fell to Joseph, from the family of
Asaph.
Second, twelve men were chosen from Geda-
liah, his sons and relatives.
[10]Third, twelve men were chosen from Zaccur,
his sons and relatives.
[11]Fourth, twelve men were chosen from Izri,
his sons and relatives.
[12]Fifth, twelve men were chosen from Netha-
niah, his sons and relatives.
[13]Sixth, twelve men were chosen from Buk-
kiah, his sons and relatives.
[14]Seventh, twelve men were chosen from Jesa-
relah, his sons and relatives.

MUSIC

More Than Just a Song

Natalie was a very musical girl. She was one of those people who could just sit at a piano and play. Once she had heard a melody, she would play it straight back to you. When the youth pastor asked her if she would like to lead the worship at the Sunday evening service, she was flustered.

"Oh, I really don't think I could do that," she replied. "If you like, I could play along with the band, but I don't lead worship. You should ask Jason."

The youth pastor was puzzled. Natalie was far more musical than Jason. As far as he could remember, Jason didn't play anything, in fact, he could only recall him singing enthusiastically with his hands in the air. When he remarked on this to Natalie, she said:

"Oh but that's exactly what you want! To lead worship you have to have a ministry, you need to lead the people in praises to God. I can only play an instrument, but Jason could lead the people in worship."

The youth pastor was surprised at Natalie's insight into the situation and agreed to try Jason out. And she was right! Natalie took her place in the band and the music was wonderful, but the congregation followed Jason's lead and the worship was better than ever.

We all have gifts to use in our church, but there's a difference between playing music and leading worship. Natalie wisely understood this.

In **1 Chronicles 25:1–8** David chose some people who could play and some people who could preach to lead worship in the Temple.

- How did the men in verse 7 differ from Natalie?
- What gifts do you have that you've used in your church?

Consider . . .

- taking music lessons to develop any talents you have.
- approaching the church musicians and telling them you appreciate their help in worshipping the Lord.

For more, see . . .

- 1 Samuel 16:14–18 (p.270)
- Ephesians 5:19 (p.1275)
- Psalm 98:4–6 (p.558)

15Eighth, twelve men were chosen from Jesha-
iah, his sons and relatives.
16Ninth, twelve men were chosen from Matta-
niah, his sons and relatives.
17Tenth, twelve men were chosen from
Shimei, his sons and relatives.
18Eleventh, twelve men were chosen from Az-
arel, his sons and relatives.
19Twelfth, twelve men were chosen from
Hashabiah, his sons and relatives.
20Thirteenth, twelve men were chosen from
Shubael, his sons and relatives.
21Fourteenth, twelve men were chosen from
Mattithiah, his sons and relatives.
22Fifteenth, twelve men were chosen from Jeri-
moth, his sons and relatives.
23Sixteenth, twelve men were chosen from
Hananiah, his sons and relatives.
24Seventeenth, twelve men were chosen
from Joshbekashah, his sons and relatives.
25Eighteenth, twelve men were chosen from
Hanani, his sons and relatives.
26Nineteenth, twelve men were chosen from
Mallothi, his sons and relatives.
27Twentieth, twelve men were chosen from
Eliathah, his sons and relatives.
28Twenty-first, twelve men were chosen from
Hothir, his sons and relatives.
29Twenty-second, twelve men were chosen
from Giddalti, his sons and relatives.
30Twenty-third, twelve men were chosen from
Mahazioth, his sons and relatives.
31Twenty-fourth, twelve men were chosen
from Romamti-Ezer, his sons and relatives.

The Gatekeepers

26 These are the groups of the gatekeepers.
From the family of Korah, there was
Meshelemiah son of Kore, who was from
Asaph's family. 2Meshelemiah had sons.
Zechariah was his first son, Jediael was second,
Zebadiah was third, Jathniel was fourth, 3Elam
was fifth, Jehohanan was sixth and Eliehoenai
was seventh.
4Obed-Edom had sons. Shemaiah was his first
son, Jehozabad was second, Joah was third, Sacar
was fourth, Nethanel was fifth, 5Ammiel was
sixth, Issachar was seventh and Peullethai was
eighth. God blessed Obed-Edom with children.
6Obed-Edom's son Shemaiah also had sons.
They were leaders in their father's family be-
cause they were capable men. 7Shemaiah's sons
were Othni, Rephael, Obed, Elzabad, Elihu and
Semakiah. Elihu and Semakiah were skilled
workers. 8All these were Obed-Edom's descen-
dants.[d] They and their sons and relatives were
capable men and strong workers. Obed-Edom
had 62 descendants in all.
9Meshelemiah had sons and relatives who
were skilled workers. In all, there were eighteen.
10From the Merari family, Hosah had sons.
Shimri was chosen to be in charge. Although he
was not the oldest son, his father chose him to be
in charge. 11Hilkiah was his second son, Tabaliah
was third and Zechariah was fourth. In all, Hosah
had thirteen sons and relatives.
12These were the leaders of the groups of gate-
keepers, and they served in the Temple[d] of the
LORD. Their relatives also worked in the Temple.
13By throwing lots,[d] each family chose a gate to
guard. Young and old threw lots.
14Meshelemiah was chosen by lot to guard the
East Gate. Then lots were thrown for Meshele-
miah's son Zechariah. He was a wise counsellor
and was chosen for the North Gate. 15Obed-
Edom was chosen for the South Gate, and
Obed-Edom's sons were chosen to guard the
storehouse. 16Shuppim and Hosah were chosen
for the West Gate and the Shalleketh Gate on the
upper road.
Guards stood side by side with guards. 17Six
Levites stood guard every day at the East Gate;
four Levites stood guard every day at the North
Gate; four Levites stood guard every day at the
South Gate; and two Levites at a time guarded
the storehouse. 18There were two guards at the
western court and four guards on the road to the
court.
19These were the groups of the gatekeepers
from the families of Korah and Merari.

Other Leaders

20Other Levites were responsible for guarding
the treasuries of the Temple[d] of God and for the
places where the holy things were kept.
21Ladan was Gershon's son and the ancestor of
several family groups. Jehiel was a leader of one
of the family groups. 22His sons were Zetham and
Joel his brother, and they were responsible for the
treasuries of the Temple of the LORD.
23Other leaders were chosen from the family
groups of Amram, Izhar, Hebron and Uzziel.
24Shubael, the descendant[d] of Gershom, who
was Moses' son, was the leader responsible for
the treasuries. 25These were Shubael's relatives
from Eliezer: Eliezer's son Rehabiah, Rehabiah's
son Jeshaiah, Jeshaiah's son Joram, Joram's son
Zicri and Zicri's son Shelomith. 26Shelomith and
his relatives were responsible for everything that
had been collected for the Temple by King David,
by the heads of families, by the commanders of
1,000 men and of 100 men, and by other army
commanders. 27They also gave some of the things
they had taken in wars to be used in repairing the
Temple of the LORD. 28Shelomith and his relatives
took care of all the holy things. Some had been

given by Samuel the seer,[d] Saul son of Kish, Ab-
ner son of Ner and Joab son of Zeruiah.
[29]Kenaniah was from the Izhar family. He and
his sons worked outside the Temple as officers
and judges in different places in Israel.
[30]Hashabiah was from the Hebron family. He
and his relatives were responsible for the LORD's
work and the king's business in Israel west of the
Jordan River. There were 1,700 skilled men in
Hashabiah's group. [31]The history of the Hebron
family shows that Jeriah was their leader. In Da-
vid's fortieth year as king, the records were
searched, and some capable men of the Hebron
family were found living at Jazer in Gilead. [32]Je-
riah had 2,700 relatives who were skilled men
and leaders of families. King David gave them the
responsibility of directing the tribes[d] of Reuben,
Gad and East Manasseh in God's work and the
king's business.

Army Divisions

27 This is the list of the Israelites who
served the king in the army. Each di-
vision was on duty one month each year. There
were leaders of families, commanders of 100
men, commanders of 1,000 men, and other offi-
cers. Each division had 24,000 men.
[2]Jashobeam son of Zabdiel was in charge of the
first division for the first month. There were
24,000 men in his division. [3]Jashobeam, one of
the descendants[d] of Perez, was leader of all the
army officers for the first month.
[4]Dodai, from the Ahohites, was in charge of
the division for the second month. Mikloth was a
leader in the division. There were 24,000 men in
Dodai's division.
[5]The third commander, for the third month,
was Benaiah son of Jehoiada the priest. There
were 24,000 men in his division. [6]He was the Be-
naiah who was one of the Thirty[n] soldiers.
Benaiah was a brave warrior who led those men.
Benaiah's son Ammizabad was in charge of Bena-
iah's division.
[7]The fourth commander, for the fourth month,
was Asahel, the brother of Joab. Later, Asahel's
son Zebadiah took his place as commander.
There were 24,000 men in his division.
[8]The fifth commander, for the fifth month,
was Shamhuth, from Izrah's family. There were
24,000 men in his division.
[9]The sixth commander, for the sixth month,
was Ira son of Ikkesh from the town of Tekoa.
There were 24,000 men in his division.
[10]The seventh commander, for the seventh
month, was Helez. He was from the Pelonites
and a descendant of Ephraim. There were 24,000
men in his division.
[11]The eighth commander, for the eighth
month, was Sibbecai. He was from Hushah and
was from Zerah's family. There were 24,000 men
in his division.
[12]The ninth commander, for the ninth month,
was Abiezer. He was from Anathoth in Benjamin.
There were 24,000 men in his division.
[13]The tenth commander, for the tenth month,
was Maharai. He was from Netophah and was
from Zerah's family. There were 24,000 men in
his division.
[14]The eleventh commander, for the eleventh
month, was Benaiah. He was from Pirathon in
Ephraim. There were 24,000 men in his division.
[15]The twelfth commander, for the twelfth
month, was Heldai. He was from Netophah and
was from Othniel's family. There were 24,000
men in his division.

Leaders of the Tribes

[16]These were the leaders of the tribes[d] of Is-
rael. Eliezer son of Zicri was over the tribe of
Reuben. Shephatiah son of Maacah was over the
tribe of Simeon. [17]Hashabiah son of Kemuel was
over the tribe of Levi. Zadok was over the people
of Aaron. [18]Elihu, one of David's brothers, was
over the tribe of Judah. Omri son of Michael was
over the tribe of Issachar. [19]Ishmaiah son of Oba-
diah was over the tribe of Zebulun. Jerimoth son
of Azriel was over the tribe of Naphtali. [20]Hoshea
son of Azaziah was over the tribe of Ephraim. Joel
son of Pedaiah was over West Manasseh. [21]Iddo
son of Zechariah was over East Manasseh. Jaasiel
son of Abner was over the tribe of Benjamin.
[22]Azarel son of Jeroham was over the tribe of Dan.
These were the leaders of the tribes of Israel.
[23]The LORD had promised to make the Israelites
as many as the stars in the sky. So David only
counted the men who were 20 years old and
older. [24]Joab son of Zeruiah began to count the
people, but he did not finish. God became angry
with Israel for counting the people, so the num-
ber of the people was not put in the history book
about King David's rule.

The King's Directors

[25]Azmaveth son of Adiel was in charge of the
royal storehouses.
Jonathan son of Uzziah was in charge of the
storehouses in the country, towns, villages and
towers.
[26]Ezri son of Kelub was in charge of the field
workers who farmed the land.

Thirty These were David's most powerful soldiers. See 2 Samuel 23:20–39.

[27]Shimei, from the town of Ramah, was in
charge of the vineyards.
Zabdi, from Shapham, was in charge of storing
the wine that came from the vineyards.
[28]Baal-Hanan, from Geder, was in charge of
the olive trees and sycamore trees in the western
hills.
Joash was in charge of storing the olive oil.
[29]Shitrai, from Sharon, was in charge of the
herds that fed in the Plain of Sharon.
Shaphat son of Adlai was in charge of the herds
in the valleys.
[30]Obil, an Ishmaelite, was in charge of the
camels.
Jehdeiah, from Meronoth, was in charge of the
donkeys.
[31]Jaziz, from the Hagrites, was in charge of the
flocks.
All these men were the officers who took care
of King David's property.
[32]Jonathan was David's uncle, and he advised
David. Jonathan was a wise man and a teacher of
the law. Jehiel son of Hacmoni took care of the
king's sons. [33]Ahithophel advised the king. Hu-
shai, from the Arkite people, was the king's
friend. [34]Jehoiada and Abiathar later took Ahitho-
phel's place in advising the king. Jehoiada was
Benaiah's son. Joab was the commander of the
king's army.

David's Plans for the Temple

28 David commanded all the leaders of Is-
rael to come to Jerusalem. There were
the leaders of the tribes,[d] commanders of the di-
visions serving the king, commanders of 1,000
men and of 100 men, leaders who took care of
the property and animals that belonged to the
king and his sons, men over the palace, the pow-
erful men and all the brave warriors.
[2]King David stood up and said, "Listen to me,
my relatives and my people. I wanted to build a
place to keep the Ark[d] of the Agreement with the
LORD. I wanted it to be God's footstool. So I made
plans to build a temple. [3]But God said to me, 'You
must not build a temple for worshipping me, be-
cause you are a soldier and have killed many
people.'
[4]"But the LORD, the God of Israel, chose me
from my whole family to be king of Israel for
ever. He chose the tribe of Judah to lead, and
from the people of Judah, he chose my father's
family. From that family God was pleased to
make me king of Israel. [5]The LORD has given me
many sons, and from those sons he has chosen
Solomon to be the new king of Israel. Israel is the
LORD's kingdom. [6]The LORD said to me, 'Your son
Solomon will build my Temple[d] and its court-
yards. I have chosen Solomon to be my son, and
I will be his father. [7]He is obeying my laws and
commands now. If he continues to obey them, I
will make his kingdom strong for ever.' "
[8]David said, "Now, in front of all Israel, the
assembly of the LORD, and in the hearing of God,
I tell you these things: be careful to obey all the
commands of the LORD your God. Then you will
keep this good land and pass it on to your des-
cendants[d] for ever.
[9]"And you, my son Solomon, accept the God
of your father. Serve him completely and will-
ingly, because the LORD knows what is in every-
one's mind. He understands everything you
think. If you go to him for help, you will get an
answer. But if you turn away from him, he will
leave you for ever. [10]Solomon, you must under-
stand this. The LORD has chosen you to build the
Temple as his holy place. Be strong and finish
the job."
[11]Then David gave his son Solomon the plans
for building the Temple and the courtyard around
the Temple. They included its buildings, its store-
rooms, its upper rooms, its inside rooms and the
place where the people's sins were cancelled.
[12]David gave him plans for everything he had in
mind: the courtyards around the LORD's Temple
and all the rooms around it, the Temple treasuries
and the treasuries of the holy things used in the
Temple. [13]David gave Solomon directions for the
groups of the priests and Levites. David told him
about all the work of serving in the Temple of the
LORD and about the things to be used in the Tem-
ple service [14]that were made of gold or silver.
David told Solomon how much gold or silver
should be used to make each thing. [15]David told
him how much gold to use for each gold lamp-
stand and its lamps and how much silver to use
for each silver lampstand and its lamps. The dif-
ferent lampstands were to be used where needed.
[16]David told him how much gold should be used
for each table that held the holy bread and how
much silver should be used for the silver tables.
[17]He told how much pure gold should be used to
make the forks, bowls and pitchers and how
much gold should be used to make each gold
dish. He told how much silver should be used to
make each silver dish [18]and how much pure gold
should be used for the altar of incense.[d] He also
gave Solomon the plans for the chariot of the
golden creatures that spread their wings over the
Ark of the Agreement with the LORD.
[19]David said, "All these plans were written
with the LORD guiding me. He helped me under-
stand everything in the plans."
[20]David also said to his son Solomon, "Be
strong and brave, and do the work. Don't be
afraid or discouraged, because the LORD God, my
God, is with you. He will not fail you or leave you

until all the work for the Temple of the LORD is
finished. 21The groups of the priests and Levites
are ready for all the work on the Temple of God.
Every skilled worker is ready to help you with all
the work. The leaders and all the people will obey
every command you give."

Gifts for Building the Temple

29 King David said to all the Israelites who
were gathered, "God chose my son Solo-
mon, who is young and hasn't yet learned what
he needs to know, but the work is important.
This palace is not for people; it is for the LORD
God. 2I have done my best to prepare for building
the Temple[d] of God. I have given gold for the
things made of gold and silver for the things made
of silver. I have given bronze for the things made
of bronze and iron for the things made of iron. I
have given wood for the things made of wood
and onyx for the settings. I have given turquoise
gems of many different colours, valuable stones
and white marble. I have given much of all these
things. 3I have already given this for the Temple,
but now I am also giving my own treasures of
gold and silver, because I really want the Temple
of my God to be built. 4I have given about 100
tonnes of pure gold from Ophir and about 236
tonnes of pure silver. They will be used to cover the
walls of the buildings 5and for all the gold and silver
work. Skilled men may use the gold and silver to
make things for the Temple. Now, who is ready
to give himself to the service of the LORD today?"

ENVIRONMENT

Promises, Promises

The phone was ringing. This meant a couple of things to Harry. One, in his line of work it would be some stress-relating public relations problem. Two, he needed a cigarette. The two things went together. Ever since he'd joined the PR company he had this routine. Dealing with journalists and the media in general was hard work. He'd seen a lot of his colleagues turn to drink at the end of a rough day and he didn't want to go down the same road. So, if he had a cigarette he felt that it calmed him down and he could cope.

The trouble was, Harry was a Christian. He was very involved in his church and dedicated to helping his youth group.

On this particularly stressful day, Harry took time out to pray.

"Lord, help me to cope . . . " he said, and then lit up his cigarette and answered the phone.

As he finished the phone call, a workmate walked into the room.

"Phew, Harry it's like a fiery furnace in here with all that smoke!" he wafted his hands around. "Can't be good for you, and it's not doing me much good either." He started coughing. "Ugh, what are you putting in your body?"

It was only then that Harry remembered last week's Bible study. It was about the body being like a temple for the Holy Spirit, but he thought that it meant things like drugs and booze . . .

For the first time, he realised that God was telling him that he was polluting his body, the body that Jesus had bought with a price.

He made a firm promise to God there and then that he would never damage his body this way again. And he didn't.

1 Chronicles 28:4–8 talks of cleansing.

- How could Harry make himself ready, according to this passage?
- What impurities can you remove from your life to help you prepare for service?

Consider . . .

- embarking on a more healthy eating programme to help improve your physical well-being.
- writing down one thing that hinders your service to God. Ask God to help you put a stop to it.

For more, see . . .

- 1 Corinthians 3:16–17 (p.1218)
- Ephesians 5:26–27 (p.1276)
- 2 Corinthians 6:16—7:1 (p.1247)

6The family leaders and the leaders of the
tribes of Israel, the commanders of 1,000 men
and of 100 men, and the leaders responsible for
the king's work gave their valuable things. 7They
gave about 170 tonnes of gold, about 350 tonnes
of silver, about 600 tonnes of bronze and about
3,500 tonnes of iron to the Temple of God. 8Peo-
ple who had valuable gems gave them to the trea-
sury of the Temple of the LORD, and Jehiel, from
the Gershon family, took care of the valuable
gems. 9The leaders gave willingly and completely
to the LORD. The people rejoiced to see their lead-
ers give so gladly, and King David was also very
happy.

David's Prayer

10David praised the LORD in front of all the peo-
ple who were gathered. He said:

"We praise you, LORD,
God of our father Israel.
We praise you for ever and ever.
11LORD, you are great and powerful.
You have glory, victory and honour.
Everything in heaven and on earth belongs
to you.
The kingdom belongs to you, LORD;
you are the ruler over everything.
12Riches and honour come from you.
You rule everything.
You have the power and strength
to make anyone great and strong.
13Now, our God, we thank you
and praise your glorious name.

14"These things did not really come from me
and my people.
Everything comes from you;
we have given you back what you gave us.
15We are like foreigners and strangers,
as our ancestors were.
Our time on earth is like a shadow.
There is no hope.
16LORD our God, we have gathered all this
to build your Temple for worship of you.
But everything has come from you;
everything belongs to you.
17I know, my God, that you test people's
hearts.
You are happy when people do what is
right.

THANKFULNESS

A Letter to Dad

Amanda was twenty when she moved away from home to work for the summer. While she was away she wrote this letter.

"Lately I've thought of you often and wanted to thank you for many things!

I suppose I've started seeing the simple things that you and Mum taught us. The basics – like manners and respect – but also contentment with what we have, finding joy in each other, listening, forgiving and understanding. You taught us that those things not only make life flow more smoothly, but that they also show Jesus to the world. Now I understand!

Dad, I miss being able to share things with you. You always listen and understand. Thank you for all your time, love and care. You've planted many seeds. I know I'll be reaping from this garden for a lifetime!"

Amanda showed her appreciation for her father through a letter. In **1 Chronicles 29:10–13**, King David thanked his heavenly father for all he had done for Israel.

- How are Amanda's letter and David's prayer alike?
- How can you, like David, express your praise to God?

Consider . . .

- writing a poem expressing your thanks to God for something.
- sending a card to thank someone for something he or she has done for you.

For more, see . . .

- Psalm 100 (p.550)
- Revelation 7:9–12 (p.1393)
- Ephesians 1:15–16 (p.1269)

I was happy to give all these things,
and I gave with an honest heart.
Your people gathered here are happy to give
to you,
and I rejoice to see their giving.
18LORD, you are the God of our ancestors,
the God of Abraham, Isaac and Jacob.
Make your people want to serve you always,
and make them want to obey you.
19Give my son Solomon a desire to serve you.
Help him always obey your commands,
laws and rules.
Help him build the Temple
for which I have prepared."

20Then David said to all the people who were
gathered, "Praise the LORD your God." So they
all praised the LORD, the God of their ancestors,
and they bowed to the ground to give honour to
the LORD and the king.

Solomon Becomes King

21The next day the people sacrificed to the
LORD. They offered burnt offerings to him of
1,000 bulls, 1,000 rams and 1,000 male lambs.
They also brought drink offerings. Many sacrifices
were made for all the people of Israel. 22That day
the people ate and drank with much joy, and the
LORD was with them.

And they made David's son Solomon king for
the second time. They poured olive oil on Solo-
mon to appoint him king in the presence of the
LORD. And they poured oil on Zadok to appoint
him as priest. 23Then Solomon sat on the LORD's
throne as king and took his father David's place.
Solomon was very successful, and all the people
of Israel obeyed him. 24All the leaders and sol-
diers and King David's sons accepted Solomon
as king and promised to obey him. 25The LORD
made Solomon great before all the Israelites and
gave Solomon much honour. No king of Israel be-
fore Solomon had such honour.

David's Death

26David son of Jesse was king over all Israel.
27He had ruled over Israel 40 years—seven years
in Hebron and 33 years in Jerusalem. 28David
died when he was old. He had lived a good, long
life and had received many riches and honours.
His son Solomon became king after him.

29Everything David did as king, from beginning
to end, is recorded in the records of Samuel the
seer,[d] the records of Nathan the prophet and the
records of Gad the seer. 30Those writings tell
what David did as king of Israel. They tell about
his power and what happened to him and to
Israel and to all the kingdoms around them.

2 Chronicles

Why Read This Book:

- See how following God can unite people and help them to prosper (2 Chronicles 1—9).
- Learn what can happen when people turn away from God (2 Chronicles 10—36).

When?

Time Line:

- 1000 BC — David was Israel's king
- Solomon was Israel's king
- 750 BC — The Northern Kingdom (Israel) fell to Assyria
- The Southern Kingdom (Judah) fell to Babylon
- People returned to Jerusalem from exile
- 500 BC — 1 and 2 Chronicles were written
- 250 BC
- BC/AD — Jesus was born

Behind the Scenes:

If God offered to grant you a wish, what would you request? Popularity? Lots of money? Good looks? Fame? A new sports car?

When 2 Chronicles begins, Solomon had inherited Israel from his father, David, and God promised to give him whatever he asked for. Instead of asking for wealth or military power, Solomon requested wisdom to govern Israel the way that God wanted. His wish was granted. 2 Chronicles describes a glorious reign for Solomon. Central to Solomon's impact was the spectacular Temple that he built for God in Jerusalem. (See the introduction to 1 Kings for the rest of the story.)

Unfortunately, the nation struggled after Solomon's death. First, a civil war divided Israel into two kingdoms. The North – keeping the name Israel – rejected rule by David's descendants and chose its own king. The South – adopting the name Judah – kept David's descendants in power but had trouble maintaining a relationship with God.

2 Chronicles traces the history of the Israelites after King David, beginning with the united kingdom under Solomon and then focusing on Judah after the kingdom divided. The story is similar to the accounts in 1 and 2 Kings (p.311 and p.343).

2 Chronicles continues the message of 1 Chronicles, since they were originally one book (see 1 Chronicles introduction, p.372). The writer is retelling the history of Israel and Judah as a reminder and warning that the nation's success is directly linked to its relationship with God.

Where?

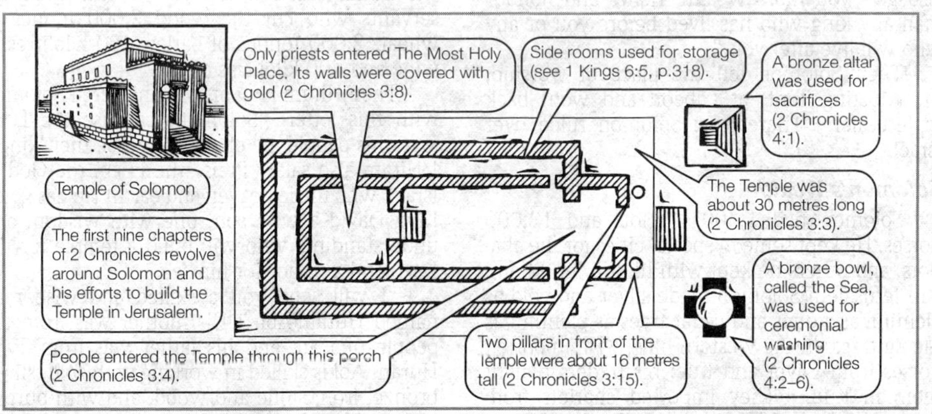

Solomon Asks for Wisdom

1 Solomon, David's son, became a powerful
king, because the LORD his God was with
him and made him very great.
2Solomon spoke to all the people of Israel—the
commanders of 100 men and of 1,000 men, the
judges, every leader in all Israel and the leaders of
the families. 3Then Solomon and all the people
with him went to the place of worship at the
town of Gibeon. God's Meeting Tent,[d] which
Moses the LORD's servant had made in the desert,
was there. 4David had brought the Ark[d] of God
from Kiriath Jearim to Jerusalem, where he had
made a place for it and had set up a tent for it.
5The bronze altar that Bezalel son of Uri, who
was the son of Hur, had made was in Gibeon in
front of the Holy Tent. So Solomon and the peo-
ple worshipped there. 6Solomon went up to the
bronze altar in the presence of the LORD at the
Meeting Tent and offered 1,000 burnt offerings
on it.
7That night God appeared to Solomon and said
to him, "Ask for whatever you want me to
give you."
8Solomon answered, "You have been very kind
to my father David, and you have made me king
in his place. 9Now, LORD God, may your promise
to my father David come true. You have made
me king of a people who are as many as the dust
of the earth. 10Now give me wisdom and know-
ledge so that I can lead these people in the right
way, because no one can rule them without your
help."
11God said to Solomon, "You have not asked
for wealth or riches or honour, or for the death of
your enemies, or for a long life. But since you
have asked for wisdom and knowledge to lead
my people, over whom I have made you king,
12I will give you wisdom and knowledge. I will
also give you more wealth, riches and honour
than any king who has lived before you or any
who will live after you."
13Then Solomon left the place of worship,
the Meeting Tent, at Gibeon and went back
to Jerusalem. There King Solomon ruled over
Israel.

Solomon's Wealth

14Solomon had 1,400 chariots and 12,000
horses. He kept some in special cities for the cha-
riots, and others he kept with him in Jerusalem.
15In Jerusalem Solomon made silver and gold as
plentiful as stones and cedar trees as plentiful as
the fig trees on the western hills. 16He imported
horses from Egypt and Kue; his traders bought
them in Kue. 17They imported chariots from
Egypt for about 600 pieces of silver each, and
horses cost nearly 150 pieces of silver apiece.
Then they sold the horses and chariots to all the
kings of the Hittites and the Arameans.

Solomon Prepares for the Temple

2 Solomon decided to build a temple[d] as a
place to worship the LORD and also a palace
for himself. 2He chose 70,000 men to carry loads,
80,000 men to cut stone in the hill country and
3,600 men to direct the workers.
3Solomon sent this message to Hiram king of
the city of Tyre: "Help me as you helped my
father David by sending him cedar logs so he
could build himself a palace to live in. 4I will
build a temple for worshipping the LORD my God,
and I will give this temple to him. There we will
burn sweet-smelling spices in his presence. We
will continually set out the holy bread in God's
presence. And we will burn sacrifices every
morning and evening, on Sabbath[d] days and New
Moons,[d] and on the other feast days commanded
by the LORD our God. This is a rule for Israel to
obey for ever.
5"The temple I build will be great, because our
God is greater than all gods. 6But no one can
really build a house for our God. Not even the
highest of heavens can hold him. How then can
I build a temple for him except as a place to burn
sacrifices to him?
7"Now send me a man skilled in working with
gold, silver, bronze and iron, and with purple, red
and blue thread. He must also know how to
make engravings. He will work with my skilled
craftsmen in Judah and Jerusalem, whom my
father David chose.
8"Also send me cedar, pine and juniper logs
from Lebanon. I know your servants are experi-
enced at cutting down the trees in Lebanon, and
my servants will help them. 9Send me a lot of
wood, because the temple I am going to build
will be large and wonderful. 10I will give your
servants who cut the wood 2,000 tonnes of
wheat, 2,000 tonnes of barley, 400 kilolitres of
wine and 400 kilolitres of oil."
11Then Hiram king of Tyre answered Solomon
with this letter: "Solomon, because the LORD
loves his people, he chose you to be their king."
12Hiram also said: "Praise the LORD, the God of
Israel, who made heaven and earth! He has given
King David a wise son, one with wisdom and
understanding, who will build a temple for the
LORD and a palace for himself.
13"I will send you a skilled and wise man
named Huram-Abi. 14His mother was from the
people of Dan, and his father was from Tyre.
Huram-Abi is skilled in working with gold, silver,
bronze, iron, stone and wood, and with purple,
blue and red thread, and expensive linen. He is
skilled in making engravings and can make any

design you show him. He will help your crafts-
men and the craftsmen of your father David.
15“Now send my servants the wheat, barley,
oil and wine you promised. 16We will cut as
much wood from Lebanon as you need and will
bring it on rafts by sea to Joppa. Then you may
carry it to Jerusalem.”
17Solomon counted all the foreigners living in
Israel. (This was after the time his father David
had counted the people.) There were 153,600
foreigners in the country. 18Solomon chose
70,000 of them to carry loads, 80,000 of them
to cut stone in the mountains and 3,600 of them
to direct the workers and to keep the people
working.

> **Sidelight** Mount Moriah, where Solomon built the Temple (2 Chronicles 3:1), is a highly sacred spot for modern-day Christians, Jews and Muslims. It is traditionally where Abraham offered his son Isaac as a sacrifice (Genesis 22:2, p.25) and where God came to David (2 Samuel 24:18, p.310). The Dome of the Rock, a Muslim shrine, has occupied this traditional spot since the seventh century AD.

Solomon Builds the Temple

3 Then Solomon began to build the Temple[d]
of the LORD in Jerusalem on Mount Moriah.
This was where the LORD had appeared to David,
Solomon's father. Solomon built the Temple on
the place David had prepared on the threshing[d]
floor of Araunah the Jebusite. 2Solomon began
building in the second month of the fourth year
he ruled Israel.
3Solomon used these measurements for build-
ing the Temple of God. It was 30 metres long and
10 metres wide, using the old measurement.
4The porch in front of the main room of the Tem-
ple was 10 metres long and 10 metres high.

He covered the inside of the porch with pure
gold. 5He put panels of pine on the walls of the
main room and covered them with pure gold.
Then he put designs of palm trees and chains in
the gold. 6He decorated the Temple with gems
and gold from Parvaim.[n] 7He put gold on the
Temple's ceiling beams, doorposts, walls and
doors, and he carved creatures with wings on the
walls.
8Then he made the Most Holy Place. It was 10
metres long and 10 metres wide, as wide as the
Temple. He covered its walls with over 20 tonnes
of pure gold. 9The gold nails weighed over 500
grammes. He also covered the upper rooms with
gold.
10He made two creatures with wings for the
Most Holy Place and covered them with gold.
11The wings of the gold creatures were 10 metres
across. One wing of one creature was 2.5 metres
long and touched the Temple wall. The crea-
ture's other wing was also 2.5 metres long, and
it touched a wing of the second creature. 12One
wing of the second creature touched the other
side of the room and was also 2.5 metres long.
The second creature's other wing touched the
first creature's wing, and it was also 2.5 metres
long. 13Together, the creatures' wings were 10
metres across. The creatures stood on their feet,
facing the main room.
14He made the curtain of blue, purple and red
thread, and expensive linen, and he put designs
of creatures with wings in it.
15He made two pillars to stand in front of the
Temple. They were about 16 metres tall, and the
capital[d] of each pillar was over 2 metres tall. 16He
made a net of chains and put them on the tops of
the pillars. He made 100 pomegranates[d] and put
them on the chains. 17Then he put the pillars up
in front of the Temple. One pillar stood on the
south side, the other on the north. He named the
south pillar He Establishes and the north pillar In
Him Is Strength.

Things for the Temple

4 He made a bronze altar 10 metres long, 10
metres wide and 5 metres tall. 2Then he
made from bronze a large round bowl, which was
called the Sea. It was 15 metres around, 5 metres
across and 2.5 metres deep. 3There were carvings
of bulls under the rim of the bowl—ten bulls
every 50 centimetres. They were in two rows
and were made in one piece with the bowl.
4The bowl rested on the backs of twelve
bronze bulls that faced outwards from the centre
of the bowl. Three bulls faced north, three faced
west, three faced south and three faced east. 5The
sides of the bowl were 8 centimetres thick, and
it held about 60,000 litres. The rim of the bowl
was like the rim of a cup or like a lily blossom.
6He made ten smaller bowls and put five on
the south side and five on the north. They were
for washing the animals for the burnt offerings,
but the large bowl was for the priests to wash in.
7He made ten lampstands of gold, following
the plans. He put them in the Temple,[d] five on
the south side and five on the north.
8He made ten tables and put them in the Tem-
ple, five on the south side and five on the north.
And he used gold to make 100 other bowls.

Parvaim There was a lot of gold there. It may have been in the country of Ophir.

9He also made the priests' courtyard and the
large courtyard. He made the doors that opened
to the courtyard and covered them with bronze.
10Then he put the large bowl in the south-east
corner of the Temple.

11Huram-Abi also made bowls, shovels and
small bowls. So he finished his work for King
Solomon on the Temple of God:

12two pillars;
two large bowls for the capitals on top of the pillars;
two nets to cover the two large bowls for the capitals on top of the pillars;
13400 pomegranates[d] for the two nets (there were two rows of pomegranates for each net covering the bowls for the capitals on top of the pillars);
14the stands with a bowl on each stand;
15the large bowl with twelve bulls under it;
16the pots, shovels, forks and all the objects to go with them.

All the things that Huram-Abi made for King
Solomon for the Temple of the LORD were made
of polished bronze. 17The king had these things
poured into clay moulds that were made in the
plain of the Jordan River between Succoth and
Zarethan. 18Solomon had so many things made
that the total weight of all the bronze was never
known.

19Solomon also made all the things for God's
Temple: the golden altar; tables which held the
bread that shows God's people are in his pres-
ence; 20the lampstands and their lamps of pure
gold, to burn in front of the Most Holy Place as
planned; 21the flowers, lamps and tongs of pure
gold; 22the pure gold wick trimmers, small bowls,
pans and dishes used to carry coals; the gold
doors for the Temple; and the inside doors of the
Most Holy Place and of the main room.

5 Finally all the work Solomon did for the
Temple[d] of the LORD was finished. He
brought in everything his father David had set
apart for the Temple—all the silver and gold and
everything. And he put everything in the treasur-
ies of God's Temple.

The Ark is Brought into the Temple

2Solomon called for the elders of Israel, the
heads of the tribes[d] and the leaders of the fami-
lies to come to him in Jerusalem. He wanted
them to bring the Ark[d] of the Agreement with
the LORD from the older part of the city. 3So all the
Israelites came together with the king during the
festival in the seventh month.

4When all the elders of Israel arrived, the Le-
vites lifted up the Ark. 5They carried the Ark of
the Agreement, the Meeting Tent[d] and the holy
utensils in it; the priests and the Levites brought
them up. 6King Solomon and all the Israelites
gathered before the Ark of the Agreement and
sacrificed so many sheep and bulls no one could
count them.

7Then the priests put the Ark of the Agreement
with the LORD in its place inside the Most Holy
Place in the Temple,[d] under the wings of the
golden creatures. 8The wings of these creatures
were spread out over the place for the Ark, cover-
ing it and its carrying poles. 9The carrying poles
were so long that anyone standing in the Holy
Place in front of the Most Holy Place could see
the ends of the poles. But no one could see them
from outside the Holy Place. The poles are still
there today. 10The only things inside the Ark
were two stone tablets[n] that Moses had put in
the Ark at Mount Sinai. That was where the LORD
made his agreement with the Israelites after they
came out of Egypt.

11Then all the priests left the Holy Place. (All
the priests from each group had made themselves
ready to serve the LORD.) 12All the Levite musi-
cians—Asaph, Heman, Jeduthun and all their
sons and relatives—stood on the east side of
the altar. They were dressed in white linen and
played cymbals, harps and lyres.[d] With them
were 120 priests who blew trumpets. 13Those
who blew the trumpets and those who sang to-
gether sounded like one person as they praised
and thanked the LORD. They sang as others played
their trumpets, cymbals and other instruments.
They praised the LORD with this song:

"He is good;
his love continues for ever."

Then the Temple of the LORD was filled with
a cloud. 14The priests could not continue their
work because of the cloud, because the LORD's
glory filled the Temple of God.

Sidelight Imagine having services in the street outside your church. That's what the ancient Israelites did. The Temple was considered God's house, which was symbolised by putting the Ark of the Agreement in it (2 Chronicles 5:2, 7). It wasn't really a place to gather for worship or study. They had meetings outside the Temple. But they had the weather for it too!

stone tablets They were the two stone tablets on which God wrote the Ten Commandments.

Solomon Speaks to the People

6 Then Solomon said, "The LORD said he
would live in the dark cloud. 2LORD, I have
built a wonderful Temple[d] for you—a place for
you to live for ever."
3While all the Israelites were standing there,
King Solomon turned to them and blessed them.
4Then he said, "Praise the LORD, the God of Israel.
He has done what he promised to my father
David. The LORD said, 5'Since the time I brought
my people out of Egypt, I have not chosen a city
in any tribe[d] of Israel where a temple will be
built for me. I did not choose a man to lead my
people Israel. 6But now I have chosen Jerusalem
as the place I am to be worshipped, and I have
chosen David to lead my people Israel.'
7"My father David wanted to build a temple
for the LORD, the God of Israel. 8But the LORD said
to my father David, 'It was good that you wanted
to build a temple for me. 9But you are not the one to
build it. Your son, who comes from your own
body, is the one who will build my temple.'
10"Now the LORD has kept his promise. I am
the king now in place of David my father. Now
I rule Israel as the LORD promised, and I have built
the Temple for the LORD, the God of Israel.
11There I have put the Ark,[d] in which is the
Agreement the LORD made with the Israelites."

Solomon's Prayer

12Then Solomon stood facing the LORD's altar,
and all the Israelites were standing behind him.
He spread out his hands. 13He had made a
bronze platform 2.5 metres long, 2.5 metres
wide and 1.5 metres high, and he had placed it
in the middle of the outer courtyard. Solomon
stood on the platform. Then he kneeled in front
of all the people of Israel gathered there, and he
spread out his hands towards the sky. 14He said,
"LORD, God of Israel, there is no god like you in
heaven or on earth. You keep your agreement of
love with your servants who truly follow you.
15You have kept the promise you made to your
servant David, my father. You spoke it with your
own mouth and finished it with your hands
today.
16"Now, LORD, God of Israel, keep the prom-
ise you made to your servant David, my father.
You said, 'If your sons are careful to obey my
teachings as you have obeyed, there will always
be someone from your family ruling Israel.'
17Now, LORD, God of Israel, please continue to
keep that promise you made to your servant.
18"But, God, can you really live here on the
earth with people? The sky and the highest
place in heaven cannot contain you. Surely this
house which I have built cannot contain you.
19But please listen to my prayer and my request,
because I am your servant. LORD my God, hear this
prayer your servant prays to you. 20Day and night
please watch over this Temple[d] where you have
said you would be worshipped. Hear the prayer I
pray facing this Temple. 21Hear my prayers and
the prayers of your people Israel when we pray
facing this place. Hear from your home in
heaven, and when you hear, forgive us.
22"If someone wrongs another person, he will
be brought to the altar in this Temple. If he
swears an oath that he is not guilty, 23then hear
in heaven. Judge the case, punish the guilty, but
declare that the innocent person is not guilty.
24"When your people, the Israelites, sin against
you, their enemies will defeat them. But if they
come back to you and praise you and pray to you
in this Temple, 25then listen from heaven. Forgive
the sin of your people Israel, and bring them back
to the land you gave to them and their ancestors.
26"When they sin against you, you will stop the
rain from falling on their land. Then they will
pray, facing this place and praising you; they
will stop sinning when you make them suf-
fer. 27When this happens, hear their prayer in
heaven, and forgive the sins of your servants, the
Israelites. Teach them to do what is right. Then
please send rain to this land you have given par-
ticularly to them.
28"At times the land will get so dry that no food
will grow, or a great sickness will spread among
the people. Sometimes the crops will be des-
troyed by locusts[d] or grasshoppers. Your people
will be attacked in their cities by their enemies, or
will become sick. 29When any of these things
happens, the people will become truly sorry. If
your people spread their hands in prayer towards
this Temple, 30then hear their prayers from your
home in heaven. Forgive and treat each person as
he should be treated because you know what is
in a person's heart. Only you know what is in
people's hearts. 31Then the people will respect
and obey you as long as they live in this land you
gave our ancestors.
32"People who are not Israelites, foreigners
from other lands, will hear about your greatness
and power. They will come from far away to pray
at this Temple. 33Then hear from your home in
heaven, and do whatever they ask you. Then peo-
ple everywhere will know you and respect you,
just as your people Israel do. Then everyone will
know that I built this Temple as a place to wor-
ship you.
34"When your people go out to fight their en-
emies along some road on which you send them,
your people will pray to you, facing this city
which you have chosen and the Temple I have
built for you. 35Then hear in heaven their prayers
and do what is right.

36“Everyone sins, so your people will also sin against you. You will become angry with them and will hand them over to their enemies. Their enemies will capture them and take them away to a country far or near. 37Your people will be sorry for their sins when they are held as prisoners in another country. They will be sorry and pray to you in the land where they are held as prisoners, saying, ‘We have sinned. We have done wrong and acted wickedly.’ 38They will truly turn back to you in the land where they are captives. They will pray, facing this land you gave their ancestors, this city you have chosen and the Temple I have built for you. 39Then hear their prayers from your home in heaven and do what is right. Forgive your people who have sinned against you.

40“Now, my God, look at us. Listen to the prayers we pray in this place.

41Now, rise, LORD God, and come to your
resting place.
Come with the Ark[d] of the Agreement that
shows your strength.
Let your priests receive your salvation,
LORD God,
and may your holy people be happy
because of your goodness.
42LORD God, do not reject your appointed one.
Remember your love for your servant
David.”

The Temple is Given to the LORD

7 When Solomon finished praying, fire came down from the sky and burned up the burnt offering and the sacrifices. The LORD’s glory filled the Temple.[d] 2The priests could not enter the Temple of the LORD, because the LORD’s glory filled it. 3When all the people of Israel saw the fire come down from heaven and the LORD’s glory on the Temple, they bowed down on the pavement with their faces to the ground. They worshipped and thanked the LORD, saying,

“He is good;
his love continues for ever.”

4Then King Solomon and all the people offered sacrifices to the LORD. 5King Solomon offered a sacrifice of 22,000 cattle and 120,000 sheep. So the king and all the people gave the Temple to God. 6The priests stood ready to do their work. The Levites also stood with the instruments of the LORD’s music that King David had made for praising the LORD. The priests and Levites were saying, “His love continues for ever.” The priests, who stood across from the Levites, blew their trumpets, and all the Israelites were standing.

7Solomon made holy the middle part of the courtyard, which is in front of the Temple of the LORD. There he offered whole burnt offerings and the fat of the fellowship offerings. He offered them in the courtyard, because the bronze altar he had made could not hold the burnt offerings, grain offerings and fat.

8Solomon and all the Israelites celebrated the festival for seven days. There were many people, and they came from as far away as Lebo Hamath and the brook of Egypt. 9For seven days they celebrated giving the altar for the worship of God. Then they celebrated the festival for seven days. On the eighth day they had a meeting. 10On the twenty-third day of the seventh month Solomon sent the people home, full of joy. They were happy because the LORD had been so good to David, Solomon and his people Israel.

The LORD Appears to Solomon

11Solomon finished the Temple[d] of the LORD and his royal palace. He had success in doing everything he planned in the Temple of the LORD and his own palace. 12Then the LORD appeared to Solomon at night and said to him, “I have heard your prayer and have chosen this place for myself to be a Temple for sacrifices.

13“I may stop the sky from sending rain. I may command the locusts[d] to destroy the land. I may send sicknesses to my people. 14Then if my people, who are called by my name, are sorry for what they have done, if they pray and obey me and stop their evil ways, I will hear them from heaven. I will forgive their sin, and I will heal their land. 15Now I will see them, and I will listen to the prayers prayed in this place. 16I have chosen this Temple and made it holy. So I will be worshipped there for ever. Yes, I will always watch over it and love it.

17“But you must serve me as your father David did. You must obey all I have commanded and keep my laws and rules. 18If you do, I will make your kingdom strong. This is the agreement I made with your father David, saying, ‘Someone from your family will always rule in Israel.’

19“But you must follow me and obey the laws and commands I have given you. You must not serve or worship other gods. 20If you do, I will take the Israelites out of my land, the land I have given them, and I will leave this Temple that I have made holy. All the nations will make fun of it and speak evil about it. 21This Temple is honoured now, but then, everyone who passes by will be shocked. They will ask, ‘Why did the LORD do this terrible thing to this land and this Temple?’ 22People will answer, ‘This happened because they left the LORD, the God of their ancestors, the God who brought them out of Egypt. They decided to follow other gods and worshipped and served them, so he brought all this disaster on them.’ ”

Solomon's Other Achievements

8 By the end of 20 years, Solomon had built
the Temple[d] of the LORD and the royal pal-
ace. 2Solomon rebuilt the towns that Hiram had
given him, and Solomon sent Israelites to live in
them. 3Then he went to Hamath Zobah and cap-
tured it. 4Solomon also built the town of Tadmor
in the desert, and he built all the towns in Ha-
math as towns for storing grain and supplies. 5He
rebuilt the towns of Upper Beth Horon and
Lower Beth Horon, protecting them with strong
walls, gates and bars in the gates. 6He also rebuilt
the town of Baalath. And he built all the other
towns for storage and all the cities for his chariots
and horses. He built all he wanted in Jerusalem,
Lebanon and everywhere he ruled.

7There were other people in the land who
were not Israelites—the Hittites, Amorites, Periz-
zites, Hivites and Jebusites. 8They were descend-
ants[d] of the people that the Israelites had not
destroyed. Solomon forced them to be slave
workers, as is still true today. 9But Solomon did
not make slaves of the Israelites. They were his
soldiers, chief captains, commanders of his cha-
riots and his chariot drivers. 10These were his
most important officers. There were 250 of them
to direct the people.

11Solomon brought the daughter of the king of
Egypt from the older part of Jerusalem to the pal-
ace he had built for her. Solomon said, "My wife
must not live in King David's palace, because the
places where the Ark[d] of the Agreement has been
are holy."

12Then Solomon offered burnt offerings to the
LORD on the altar he had built for the LORD in front
of the Temple porch. 13He offered sacrifices every
day as Moses had commanded. They were of-
fered on the Sabbath[d] days, New Moons[d] and the
three yearly feasts—the Feast[d] of Unleavened
Bread, the Feast of Weeks and the Feast of Shel-
ters. 14Solomon followed his father David's in-
structions and chose the groups of priests for their
service and the Levites to lead the praise and to
help the priests do their daily work. And he chose
the gatekeepers by their groups to serve at each
gate, as David, the man of God, had commanded.
15They obeyed all of Solomon's commands to the
priests and Levites, as well as his commands
about the treasuries.

16All Solomon's work was done as he had said
from the day the foundation of the Temple of the
LORD was begun, until it was finished. So the
Temple was finished.

17Then Solomon went to the towns of Ezion
Geber and Elath near the Red Sea[d] in the land of
Edom. 18Hiram sent ships to Solomon that were
commanded by his own men, who were skilled
sailors. Hiram's men went with Solomon's men
to Ophir and brought back about 15 tonnes of
gold to King Solomon.

The Queen of Sheba Visits

9 When the queen of Sheba heard about Solo-
mon's fame, she came to Jerusalem to test
him with hard questions. She had a large group
of servants with her and camels carrying spices,
jewels and much gold. When she came to
Solomon, she talked with him about all she had
in mind, 2and Solomon answered all her ques-
tions. Nothing was too hard for him to explain
to her. 3The queen of Sheba saw that Solomon
was very wise. She saw the palace he had built,
4the food on his table, his many officers, the
palace servants and their good clothes, the ser-
vants who served Solomon his wine and their
good clothes. She saw the whole burnt offerings
he made in the Temple[d] of the LORD. All these
things amazed her.

5So she said to King Solomon, "What I heard
in my own country about your achievements
and wisdom is true. 6I did not believe it then,
but now I have come and seen it with my own
eyes. I was not told even half of your great wis-
dom! You are much greater than I had heard.
7Your men and officers are very happy, because
in always serving you, they are able to hear your
wisdom. 8Praise the LORD your God who was
pleased to make you king. He has put you on his
throne to rule for the LORD your God, because
your God loves the people of Israel and supports
them for ever. He has made you king over them
to keep justice and to rule fairly."

9Then she gave the king about 4 tonnes of
gold and many spices and jewels. No one had
ever given such spices as the queen of Sheba
gave to King Solomon.

10Hiram's men and Solomon's men brought
gold from Ophir, juniper wood and jewels.
11King Solomon used the juniper wood to build
steps for the Temple of the LORD and the palace
and to make lyres[d] and harps for the musicians.
No one in Judah had ever seen such beautiful
things as these.

12King Solomon gave the queen of Sheba
everything she wanted and asked for, even more
than she had brought to him. Then she and her
servants returned to her own country.

Solomon's Wealth

13Every year King Solomon received about 23
tonnes of gold. 14Besides that, he also received
gold from traders and merchants. All the kings
of Arabia and the governors of the land also
brought gold and silver.

15King Solomon made 200 large shields of
hammered gold, each of which contained about

7 kilogrammes of hammered gold. 16He also made 300 smaller shields of hammered gold, each of which contained about 3 kilogrammes of gold. The king put them in the Palace of the Forest of Lebanon.

17The king built a large throne of ivory and covered it with pure gold. 18The throne had six steps on it and a gold footstool. There were armrests on both sides of the chair, and each armrest had a lion beside it. 19Twelve lions stood on the six steps, one lion at each end of each step. Nothing like this had ever been made for any other kingdom. 20All of Solomon's drinking cups, as well as the dishes in the Palace of the Forest of Lebanon, were made of pure gold. In Solomon's time people did not think silver was valuable.

21King Solomon had many ships that he sent out to trade, with Hiram's men as the crews. Every three years the ships returned, bringing back gold, silver, ivory, apes and baboons.

22King Solomon had more riches and wisdom than all the other kings on earth. 23All the kings of the earth wanted to see Solomon and listen to the wisdom God had given him. 24Year after year everyone who came brought gifts of silver and gold, clothes, weapons, spices, horses and mules.

25Solomon had 4,000 stalls for horses and chariots, and he had 12,000 horses. He kept some in special cities for the chariots, and others he kept with him in Jerusalem. 26Solomon ruled over all the kingdoms from the Euphrates River to the land of the Philistines, as far as the border of Egypt. 27In Jerusalem the king made silver as common as stones and cedar trees as plentiful as the fig trees on the western hills. 28Solomon imported horses from Egypt and all other countries.

Solomon's Death

29Everything else Solomon did, from the beginning to the end, is written in the records of Nathan the prophet,[d] and in the prophecy of Ahijah the Shilonite and in the visions of Iddo the seer,[d] who wrote about Jeroboam, Nebat's son. 30Solomon ruled in Jerusalem over all Israel for 40 years. 31Then Solomon died and was buried in Jerusalem, the city of David, his father. And Solomon's son Rehoboam became king in his place.

Israel Turns Against Rehoboam

10 Rehoboam went to Shechem, where all the Israelites had gone to make him king. 2Jeroboam son of Nebat was in Egypt, where he had gone to escape from King Solomon. When Jeroboam heard about Rehoboam being made king, he returned from Egypt. 3After the people sent for him, he and the people went to Rehoboam and said to him, 4"Your father forced us to work very hard. Now, make it easier for us, and don't make us work as he did. Then we will serve you."

> **Sidelight**
>
> 2 Chronicles 10—36 is a lot like a condensed version of 1 and 2 Kings (p.311 and p.343). In 2 Chronicles, the material on the divided kingdom takes up 27 chapters, but Kings devotes 36 chapters to the same period.

5Rehoboam answered, "Come back to me in three days." So the people left.

6King Rehoboam asked the elders who had advised Solomon during his lifetime, "How do you think I should answer these people?"

7They answered, "Be kind to these people. If you please them and give them a kind answer, they will serve you always."

8But Rehoboam rejected this advice. Instead, he asked the young men who had grown up with him and who served as his advisers. 9Rehoboam asked them, "What is your advice? How should we answer these people who said, 'Don't make us work as hard as your father did'?"

10The young men who had grown up with him answered, "The people said to you, 'Your father forced us to work very hard. Now make our work easier.' You should tell them, 'My little finger is bigger than my father's legs. 11He forced you to work hard, but I will make you work even harder. My father beat you with whips, but I will beat you with whips that have sharp points.' "

12Rehoboam had told the people, "Come back to me in three days." So after three days Jeroboam and all the people returned to Rehoboam. 13King Rehoboam spoke cruel words to them, because he had rejected the advice of the older leaders. 14He followed the advice of the young men and said, "My father forced you to work hard, but I will make you work even harder. My father beat you with whips, but I will beat you with whips that have sharp points." 15So the king did not listen to the people. God caused this to happen so that the LORD could keep the promise he had made to Jeroboam son of Nebat through Ahijah, a prophet[d] from Shiloh.

16When all the Israelites saw that the king refused to listen to them, they said to the king,

"We have no share in David!
  We have no part in the son of Jesse!
People of Israel, let's go to our own homes!
  Let David's son rule his own people."

So all the Israelites went home. 17But Rehoboam still ruled over the Israelites who lived in the towns of Judah.

18 Adoniram was in charge of the people who were forced to work. When Rehoboam sent him to the people, they threw stones at him until he died. But King Rehoboam ran to his chariot and escaped to Jerusalem. 19 Since then, Israel has been against the family of David.

11 When Rehoboam arrived in Jerusalem, he gathered 180,000 of the best soldiers from Judah and Benjamin. He wanted to fight Israel to take back his kingdom. 2 But the LORD spoke his word to Shemaiah, a man of God, saying, 3 "Speak to Solomon's son Rehoboam, the king of Judah, and to all the Israelites living in Judah and Benjamin. Say to them, 4 'The LORD says you must not go to war against your brothers. Every one of you should go home, because I made all these things happen.' " So they obeyed the LORD's command and turned back and did not attack Jeroboam.

Rehoboam Makes Judah Strong

5 Rehoboam lived in Jerusalem and built strong cities in Judah to defend it. 6 He built up the cities of Bethlehem, Etam, Tekoa, 7 Beth Zur, Soco, Adullam, 8 Gath, Mareshah, Ziph, 9 Adoraim, Lachish, Azekah, 10 Zorah, Aijalon and Hebron. These were fortified cities in Judah and Benjamin. 11 When Rehoboam made those cities strong, he put commanders and supplies of food, oil and wine in them. 12 Also, Rehoboam put shields and spears in all the cities and made them very strong. Rehoboam kept the people of Judah and Benjamin under his control.

13 The priests and the Levites from all over Israel joined Rehoboam. 14 The Levites even left their pasturelands and property and came to Judah and Jerusalem, because Jeroboam and his sons refused to let them serve as priests to the LORD. 15 Jeroboam chose his own priests for the places of worship and for the goat and calf idols he had made. 16 There were people from all the tribes [d] of Israel who wanted to obey the LORD, the God of Israel. So they went to Jerusalem with the Levites to sacrifice to the LORD, the God of their fathers. 17 These people made the kingdom of Judah strong, and they supported Solomon's son Rehoboam for three years. During this time they lived the way David and Solomon had lived.

Rehoboam's Family

18 Rehoboam married Mahalath, the daughter of Jerimoth and Abihail. Jerimoth was David's son, and Abihail was the daughter of Eliab, Jesse's son. 19 Mahalath gave Rehoboam these sons: Jeush, Shemariah and Zaham. 20 Then Rehoboam married Absalom's daughter Maacah, and she gave Rehoboam these children: Abijah, Attai, Ziza and Shelomith. 21 Rehoboam loved Maacah more than his other wives and slave women. [d] Rehoboam had eighteen wives and 60 slave women and was the father of 28 sons and 60 daughters.

22 Rehoboam chose Abijah son of Maacah to be the leader of his own brothers, because he planned to make Abijah king. 23 Rehoboam acted wisely. He spread his sons through all the areas of Judah and Benjamin, sending them to every fortified city. He gave plenty of supplies to his sons, and he also found wives for them.

Shishak Attacks Jerusalem

12 After Rehoboam's kingdom was set up and he became strong, he and the people of Judah stopped obeying the teachings of the LORD. 2 During the fifth year Rehoboam was king, Shishak king of Egypt attacked Jerusalem, because Rehoboam and the people were unfaithful to the LORD. 3 Shishak had 1,200 chariots and 60,000 horsemen. He brought troops of Libyans, Sukkites and Cushites from Egypt with him, so many they couldn't be counted. 4 Shishak captured the fortified cities of Judah and came as far as Jerusalem.

5 Then Shemaiah the prophet [d] came to Rehoboam and the leaders of Judah who had gathered in Jerusalem because they were afraid of Shishak. Shemaiah said to them, "This is what the LORD says: 'You have left me, so now I will leave you to face Shishak alone.' "

6 Then the leaders of Judah and King Rehoboam were sorry for what they had done. They said, "The LORD does what is right."

7 When the LORD saw they were sorry for what they had done, the LORD spoke his word to Shemaiah, saying, "The king and the leaders are sorry. So I will not destroy them but will save them soon. I will not use Shishak to punish Jerusalem in my anger. 8 But the people of Jerusalem will become Shishak's servants so they may learn that serving me is different from serving the kings of other nations."

9 Shishak king of Egypt attacked Jerusalem and took the treasures from the Temple [d] of the LORD and the king's palace. He took everything, even the gold shields Solomon had made. 10 So King Rehoboam made bronze shields to take their place and gave them to the commanders of the guards for the palace gates. 11 Whenever the king went to the Temple of the LORD, the guards went with him, carrying the shields. Later, they would put them back in the guardroom.

12 When Rehoboam was sorry for what he had done, the LORD held his anger back and did not fully destroy Rehoboam. There was some good in Judah.

13 King Rehoboam made himself a strong king in Jerusalem. He was 41 years old when he

became king, and he was king in Jerusalem for sev-
enteen years. Jerusalem is the city that the LORD
chose from all the tribes[d] of Israel in which he
was to be worshipped. Rehoboam's mother was
Naamah from the country of Ammon. 14Reho-
boam did evil because he did not want to obey
the LORD.
15The things Rehoboam did as king, from the
beginning to the end, are written in the records
of Shemaiah the prophet and Iddo the seer,[d] in
the family histories. There were wars between
Rehoboam and Jeroboam all the time they
ruled. 16Rehoboam died and was buried in
Jerusalem, and his son Abijah became king in
his place.

Abijah King of Judah

13 Abijah became the king of Judah during
the eighteenth year Jeroboam was king of
Israel. 2Abijah ruled in Jerusalem for three years.
His mother was Maacah daughter of Uriel from
the town of Gibeah.
And there was war between Abijah and Jero-
boam. 3Abijah led an army of 400,000 capable
soldiers into battle, and Jeroboam prepared to
fight him with 800,000 capable soldiers.
4Abijah stood on Mount Zemaraim in the
mountains of Ephraim and said, "Jeroboam and all
Israel, listen to me! 5You should know that the
LORD, the God of Israel, gave David and his sons
the right to rule Israel for ever by an agreement of
salt.[n] 6But Jeroboam son of Nebat, one of the
officers of Solomon, David's son, turned against
his master. 7Then worthless, evil men joined
Jeroboam against Rehoboam, Solomon's son. He
was young and didn't know what to do, so he
could not stop them.
8"Now you people are making plans against the
LORD's kingdom, which belongs to David's sons.
There are many of you, and you have the gold
calves Jeroboam made for you as gods. 9You have
thrown out the Levites and the LORD's priests,
Aaron's sons. You have chosen your own priests as
people in other countries do. Anyone who comes
with a young bull and seven rams can become a
priest of idols that are not gods.
10"But as for us, the LORD is our God; we have
not left him. The priests who serve the LORD are
Aaron's sons, and the Levites help them. 11They
offer burnt offerings and sweet-smelling incense[d]
to the LORD every morning and evening. They put
the bread on the special table in the Temple.[d] And
they light the lamps on the gold lampstand every
evening. We obey the command of the LORD our
God, but you have left him. 12God himself is with
us as our ruler. His priests blow the trumpet to call
us to war against you. Men of Israel, don't fight
against the LORD, the God of your ancestors, be-
cause you won't succeed."
13But Jeroboam had sent some troops to sneak
behind Judah's army. So while Jeroboam was in
front of Judah's army, Jeroboam's soldiers were be-
hind them. 14When the soldiers of Judah turned
around, they saw Jeroboam's army attacking both
in front and at the back. So they cried out to the
LORD, and the priests blew the trumpets. 15Then
the men of Judah gave a battle cry. When they
shouted, God caused Jeroboam and the army of
Israel to run away from Abijah and the army of
Judah. 16When the army of Israel ran away from
the men of Judah, God handed them over to
Judah. 17Abijah's army struck Israel so that
500,000 of Israel's best men were killed. 18So at
that time the people of Israel were defeated. And
the people of Judah won, because they depended
on the LORD, the God of their ancestors.
19Abijah's army chased Jeroboam's army and
captured from him the towns of Bethel, Jeshanah
and Ephron, and the small villages near them.
20Jeroboam never became strong again while Abi-
jah was alive. The LORD struck Jeroboam, and he
died.
21But Abijah became strong. He married four-
teen women and was the father of 22 sons and
sixteen daughters. 22Everything else Abijah did—
what he said and what he did—is recorded in the
writings of the prophet Iddo.
14 Abijah died and was buried in Jerusalem.
His son Asa became king in his place, and
there was peace in the country for ten years dur-
ing Asa's time.

Asa King of Judah

2Asa did what the LORD his God said was good
and right. 3He removed the foreign altars and the
places where gods were worshipped. He smashed
the stone pillars that honoured other gods, and he
tore down the Asherah[d] idols. 4Asa commanded
the people of Judah to follow the LORD, the God
of their ancestors, and to obey his teachings and
commandments. 5He also removed the places
where gods were worshipped and the incense al-
tars from every town in Judah. So the kingdom
had peace while Asa was king. 6Asa built fortified
cities in Judah during the time of peace. He had
no war in these years, because the LORD gave him
peace.
7Asa said to the people of Judah, "Let's build
up these towns and put walls around them. Let's
make towers, gates and bars in the gates. This
country is ours, because we have obeyed the LORD
our God. We have followed him, and he has

an agreement of salt An unbreakable agreement.

given us peace all around." So they built and had
success.
8Asa had an army of 300,000 men from Judah
and 280,000 men from Benjamin. The men from
Judah carried large shields and spears. The men
from Benjamin carried small shields and bows
and arrows. All of them were brave fighting men.
9Then Zerah from Cush came out to fight them
with an enormous army and 300 chariots. They
came as far as the town of Mareshah. 10So Asa

Sidelight Today, Zerah from Cush (2 Chronicles 14:9) would be "Zerah from Ethiopia", a country south-east of Egypt in Africa.

went out to fight Zerah and prepared for battle in
the Valley of Zephathah at Mareshah.
11Asa called out to the LORD his God, saying,
"LORD, only you can help weak people against the
strong. Help us, LORD our God, because we depend
on you. We fight against this enormous
army in your name. LORD, you are our God. Don't
let anyone win against you."
12So the LORD defeated the Cushites when
Asa's army from Judah attacked them, and the
Cushites ran away. 13Asa's army chased them as
far as the town of Gerar. So many Cushites were
killed that the army could not fight again; they
were crushed by the LORD and his army. Asa and
his army carried many valuable things away from
the enemy. 14They destroyed all the towns near
Gerar, because the people living in these towns
were afraid of the LORD. Since these towns had
many valuable things, Asa's army took them
away. 15Asa's army also attacked the camps
where the shepherds lived and took many sheep
and camels. Then they returned to Jerusalem.

Asa's Changes

15 The Spirit[d] of God entered Azariah son
of Oded. 2Azariah went to meet Asa and
said, "Listen to me, Asa and all you people of
Judah and Benjamin. The LORD is with you when
you are with him. If you obey him, you will find
him, but if you leave him, he will leave you. 3For
a long time Israel was without the true God and
without a priest to teach them and without the
teachings. 4But when they were in trouble, they
turned to the LORD, the God of Israel. They looked
for him and found him. 5In those days no one
could travel safely. There was much trouble in all
the nations. 6One nation would destroy another
nation, and one city would destroy another city,
because God troubled them with all kinds of
distress. 7But you should be strong. Don't give up,
because you will get a reward for your good
work."
8Asa felt brave when he heard these words
and the message from Azariah son of Oded the
prophet.[d] So he removed the hateful idols from
all of Judah and Benjamin and from the towns he
had captured in the hills of Ephraim. He repaired
the LORD's altar that was in front of the porch of
the Temple[d] of the LORD.
9Then Asa gathered all the people from Judah
and Benjamin and from the tribes[d] of Ephraim,
Manasseh and Simeon who were living in Judah.
Many people came to Asa even from Israel, because
they saw that the LORD, Asa's God, was
with him.
10Asa and these people gathered in Jerusalem
in the third month of the fifteenth year of Asa's
rule. 11At that time they sacrificed to the LORD
700 bulls and 7,000 sheep and goats from the
valuable things Asa's army had taken from their
enemies. 12Then they made an agreement to obey
the LORD, the God of their ancestors, with their
whole being. 13Anyone who refused to obey the
LORD, the God of Israel, was to be killed. It did not
matter if that person was important or unimportant,
a man or woman. 14Then Asa and the people
made a promise before the LORD, shouting
with a loud voice and blowing trumpets and
sheep's horns. 15All the people of Judah were
happy about the promise, because they had promised
with all their heart. They looked for God and
found him. So the LORD gave them peace in all the
country.
16King Asa also removed Maacah, his grandmother,
from being queen mother, because she
had made a terrible Asherah[d] idol. Asa cut down
that idol, smashed it into pieces and burned it in
the Kidron Valley. 17But the places of worship to
gods were not removed from Judah. Even so, Asa
was faithful all his life.
18Asa brought into the Temple of God the
gifts he and his father had given: silver, gold and
utensils.
19There was no more war until the thirty-fifth
year of Asa's rule.

Asa's Last Years

16 In the thirty-sixth year of Asa's rule,
Baasha king of Israel attacked Judah. He
made the town of Ramah strong so he could keep
people from leaving or entering Judah, Asa's
country.
2Asa took silver and gold from the treasuries of
the Temple[d] of the LORD and out of his own palace.
Then he sent it with messengers to Ben-Hadad
king of Aram, who lived in Damascus. Asa
said, 3"Let there be a treaty between you and me
as there was between my father and your father.

I am sending you silver and gold. Break your
treaty with Baasha king of Israel so he will leave
my land."
4Ben-Hadad agreed with King Asa and sent
the commanders of his armies to attack the
towns of Israel. They defeated the towns of Ijon,
Dan and Abel Beth Maacah, and all the towns in
Naphtali where treasures were stored. 5When
Baasha heard about this, he stopped building up
Ramah and left his work. 6Then King Asa
brought all the people of Judah to Ramah, and
they carried away the rocks and wood that
Baasha had used. And they used them to build
up Geba and Mizpah.
7At that time Hanani the seer[d] came to Asa
king of Judah and said to him, "You depended
on the king of Aram to help you and not on the
LORD your God. So the king of Aram's army
escaped from you. 8The Cushites and Libyans
had a large and powerful army and many chari-
ots and horsemen. But you depended on the
LORD to help you, so he handed them over to
you. 9The LORD searches all the earth for people
who have given themselves completely to him.
He wants to make them strong. Asa, you did
a foolish thing, so from now on you will have
wars."
10Asa was angry with Hanani the seer because
of what he had said; he was so angry that he put
Hanani in prison. And Asa was cruel to some of
the people at the same time.
11Everything Asa did as king, from the begin-
ning to the end, is written in the book of the
kings of Judah and Israel. 12In the thirty-ninth
year of his rule, Asa got a disease in his feet.
Though his disease was very bad, he did not ask

Sidelight

Did King Asa have one of the world's first cases of athlete's foot (2 Chronicles 16:12)? Probably not. He may have had dropsy, which makes the feet swell like a tumour. Or the phrase may be a polite way to say he had a sexually transmitted disease.

for help from the LORD, but only from the doc-
tors. 13Then Asa died in the forty-first year of his
rule. 14The people buried Asa in the tomb he had
made for himself in Jerusalem. They laid him on
a bed filled with spices and different kinds of
mixed perfumes, and they made a large fire to
honour him.

Jehoshaphat King of Judah

17 Jehoshaphat, Asa's son, became king of
Judah in his place. Jehoshaphat made
Judah strong so they could fight against Israel.
2He put troops in all the fortified cities of Judah,
in the land of Judah and in the towns of Ephraim
that his father Asa had captured.
3The LORD was with Jehoshaphat, because he
lived as his ancestor David had lived when he
first became king. Jehoshaphat did not ask for
help from the Baal[d] idols, 4but from the God of
his father. He obeyed God's commands and did
not live as the people of Israel lived. 5The LORD
made Jehoshaphat a strong king over Judah. All
the people of Judah brought gifts to Jehoshaphat,
so he had much wealth and honour. 6He wanted
very much to obey the LORD. He also removed
the places for worshipping gods and the Asherah[d]
idols from Judah.
7During the third year of his rule, Jehoshaphat
sent his officers to teach in the towns of Judah.
These officers were Ben-Hail, Obadiah, Zecha-
riah, Nethanel and Micaiah. 8Jehoshaphat sent
with them these Levites: Shemaiah, Nethaniah,
Zebadiah, Asahel, Shemiramoth, Jehonathan,
Adonijah, Tobijah and Tob-Adonijah. He also
sent the priests Elishama and Jehoram. 9These
leaders, Levites and priests taught the people in
Judah. They took the Book of the Teachings of
the LORD and went through all the towns of
Judah and taught the people.
10The nations near Judah were afraid of the
LORD, so they did not start a war against Jehosha-
phat. 11Some of the Philistines brought gifts and
silver to Jehoshaphat as he demanded. Some
Arabs brought him flocks: 7,700 rams and 7,700
goats.
12Jehoshaphat grew more and more powerful.
He built strong, walled cities and towns for
storing supplies in Judah. 13He kept many
supplies in the towns of Judah, and he kept
trained soldiers in Jerusalem. 14These soldiers
were listed by families. From the families of
Judah, these were the commanders of groups
of 1,000 men: Adnah was the commander
of 300,000 soldiers; 15Jehohanan was the
commander of 280,000 soldiers; 16Amasiah was
the commander of 200,000 soldiers. Amasiah
son of Zicri had volunteered to serve the LORD.
17These were the commanders from the famil-
ies of Benjamin: Eliada, a brave soldier, had
200,000 soldiers who used bows and shields.
18And Jehozabad had 180,000 men armed
for war.
19All these soldiers served King Jehoshaphat.
The king also put other men in the fortified cities
through all of Judah.

Micaiah Warns King Ahab

18 Jehoshaphat had much wealth and hon-
our, and he made an agreement with

King Ahab through marriage.[n] 2A few years later
Jehoshaphat went to visit Ahab in Samaria. Ahab
sacrificed many sheep and cattle at a great feast
to honour Jehoshaphat and the people with him.
He encouraged Jehoshaphat to attack Ramoth in
Gilead. 3Ahab king of Israel asked Jehoshaphat
king of Judah, "Will you go with me to attack
Ramoth in Gilead?"

Jehoshaphat answered, "I will go with you,
and my soldiers are yours. We will join you in the
battle." 4Jehoshaphat also said to Ahab, "But first
we should ask if this is the LORD's will."

5So King Ahab called 400 prophets[d] together
and asked them, "Should we go to war against
Ramoth in Gilead or not?"

They answered, "Go, because God will hand
them over to you."

6But Jehoshaphat asked, "Isn't there a prophet
of the LORD here? Let's ask him what we
should do."

7Then King Ahab said to Jehoshaphat, "There
is one other prophet. We could ask the LORD
through him, but I hate him. He never prophes-
ies[d] anything good about me, but always some-
thing bad. He is Micaiah son of Imlah."

Jehoshaphat said, "King Ahab, you shouldn't
say that!"

8So Ahab king of Israel told one of his officers
to bring Micaiah to him at once.

9Ahab king of Israel and Jehoshaphat king of
Judah had on their royal robes and were sitting
on their thrones at the threshing[d] floor, near the
entrance to the gate of Samaria. All the prophets
were standing before them speaking their mes-
sages. 10Zedekiah son of Kenaanah had made
some iron horns. He said to Ahab, "This is what
the LORD says: 'You will use these horns to fight
the Arameans until they are destroyed.' "

11All the other prophets said the same thing,
"Attack Ramoth in Gilead and win, because the
LORD will hand the Arameans over to you."

12The messenger who had gone to get Micaiah
said to him, "All the other prophets are saying
King Ahab will win. You should agree with them
and give the king a good answer."

13But Micaiah answered, "As surely as the
LORD lives, I can tell him only what my God says."

14When Micaiah came to Ahab, the king asked
him, "Micaiah, should we attack Ramoth in Gil-
ead or not?"

Micaiah answered, "Attack and win! They
will be handed over to you."

15But Ahab said to Micaiah, "How many times
do I have to tell you to speak only the truth to me
in the name of the LORD?"

16So Micaiah answered, "I saw the army of
Israel scattered over the hills like sheep without
a shepherd. The LORD said, 'They have no leaders.
They should go home and not fight.' "

17Then Ahab king of Israel said to Jehoshaphat,
"I told you! He never prophesies anything good
about me, but only bad."

18But Micaiah said, "Hear the message from
the LORD: I saw the LORD sitting on his throne with
his heavenly army standing on his right and on
his left. 19The LORD said, 'Who will trick King
Ahab of Israel into attacking Ramoth in Gilead
where he will be killed?'

"Some said one thing; some said another.
20Then one spirit came and stood before the LORD
and said, 'I will trick him.'

"The LORD asked, 'How will you do it?'

21"The spirit answered, 'I will go to Ahab's
prophets and make them tell lies.'

"So the LORD said, 'You will succeed in tricking
him. Go and do it.' "

22Micaiah said, "Ahab, the LORD has made your
prophets lie to you, and the LORD has decided that
disaster should come to you."

23Then Zedekiah son of Kenaanah went up to
Micaiah and slapped him in the face. Zedekiah
said, "Has the LORD's Spirit[d] left me to speak
through you?"

24Micaiah answered, "You will find out on the
day you go to hide in an inside room."

25Then Ahab king of Israel ordered, "Take Mi-
caiah and send him to Amon, the governor of the
city, and to Joash, the king's son. 26Tell them I said
to put this man in prison and give him only bread
and water until I return safely from the battle."

27Micaiah said, "Ahab, if you come back safely
from the battle, the LORD has not spoken through
me. Remember my words, all you people!"

Ahab is Killed

28So Ahab king of Israel and Jehoshaphat king
of Judah went to Ramoth in Gilead. 29King Ahab
said to Jehoshaphat, "I will go into battle, but I
will wear other clothes so no one will recognise
me. But you wear your royal clothes." So Ahab
wore other clothes and they went into battle.

30The king of Aram ordered his chariot com-
manders, "Don't fight with anyone—important or
unimportant—except the king of Israel." 31When
these commanders saw Jehoshaphat, they thought
he was the king of Israel, so they turned to attack
him. But Jehoshaphat began shouting and the LORD
helped him. God made the chariot commanders
turn away from Jehoshaphat. 32When they saw he
was not King Ahab, they stopped chasing him.

agreement . . . through marriage Jehoshaphat's son Jehoram married Athaliah, Ahab's daughter. See 2 Chronicles 21:6.

33By chance, a soldier shot an arrow which hit Ahab king of Israel between the pieces of his armour. King Ahab said to his chariot driver, "Turn around and get me out of the battle, because I am hurt!" 34The battle continued all day. King Ahab held himself up in his chariot and faced the Arameans until evening. Then he died at sunset.

19 Jehoshaphat king of Judah came back safely to his palace in Jerusalem. 2Jehu son of Hanani, a seer,[d] went out to meet him and said to the king, "Why did you help evil people? Why do you love those who hate the LORD? That is the reason the LORD is angry with you. 3But there is some good in you. You took the Asherah[d] idols out of this country, and you have tried to obey God."

Jehoshaphat Chooses Judges

4Jehoshaphat lived in Jerusalem. He went out again to be with the people, from Beersheba to the mountains of Ephraim, and he turned them back to the LORD, the God of their ancestors. 5Jehoshaphat appointed judges in all the land, in each of the strong, walled cities of Judah. 6Jehoshaphat said to them, "Watch what you do, because you are not judging for people but for the LORD. He will be with you when you make a decision. 7Now let each of you fear the LORD. Watch what you do, because the LORD our God wants people to be fair. He wants all people to be treated the same, and he doesn't want decisions influenced by money."

8And in Jerusalem Jehoshaphat appointed some of the Levites, priests and leaders of Israelite families to be judges. They were to decide cases about the law of the LORD and settle problems between the people who lived in Jerusalem. 9Jehoshaphat commanded them, "You must always serve the LORD completely, and you must fear him. 10Your people living in the cities will bring you cases about killing, about the teachings, commands, rules or some other law. In all these cases you must warn the people not to sin against the LORD. If you don't, he will be angry with you and your people. But if you warn them, you won't be guilty.

11"Amariah, the leading priest, will be over you in all cases about the LORD. Zebadiah son of Ishmael, a leader in the tribe[d] of Judah, will be over you in all cases about the king. Also, the Levites will serve as officers for you. Have courage. May the LORD be with those who do what is right."

Jehoshaphat Faces War

20 Later the Moabites, Ammonites and some Meunites came to start a war with Jehoshaphat. 2Messengers came and told Jehoshaphat, "A large army is coming against you from Edom, from the other side of the Dead Sea.[d] They are already in Hazazon Tamar!" (Hazazon Tamar is also called En Gedi.) 3Jehoshaphat was afraid, so he decided to ask the LORD what to do. He announced that no one in Judah should eat during this special time of prayer to God. 4The people of Judah came together to ask the LORD for help; they came from every town in Judah.

5The people of Judah and Jerusalem met in front of the new courtyard in the Temple[d] of the LORD. Then Jehoshaphat stood up, 6and he said, "LORD, God of our ancestors, you are the God in heaven. You rule over all the kingdoms of the nations. You have power and strength, so no one can stand against you. 7Our God, you forced out the people who lived in this land as your people Israel moved in. And you gave this land for ever to the descendants[d] of your friend Abraham. 8They lived in this land and built a Temple for you. They said, 9'If trouble comes upon us, or war, punishment, sickness or hunger, we will stand before you and before this Temple where you have chosen to be worshipped. We will cry out to you when we are in trouble. Then you will hear and save us.'

10"But now here are men from Ammon, Moab and Edom. You wouldn't let the Israelites enter their lands when the Israelites came from Egypt. So the Israelites turned away and did not destroy them. 11But see how they repay us for not destroying them! They have come to force us out of your land, which you gave us as our own. 12Our God, punish those people. We have no power against this large army that is attacking us. We don't know what to do, so we look to you for help."

13All the men of Judah stood before the LORD with their babies, wives and children. 14Then the Spirit[d] of the LORD entered Jahaziel. (Jahaziel was Zechariah's son. Zechariah was Benaiah's son. Benaiah was Jeiel's son and Jeiel was Mattaniah's son.) Jahaziel, a Levite and a descendant of Asaph, stood up in the meeting. 15He said, "Listen to me, King Jehoshaphat and all you people living in Judah and Jerusalem. The LORD says this to you: 'Don't be afraid or discouraged because of this large army. The battle is not your battle, it is God's. 16Tomorrow go down there and fight those people. They will come up through the Pass of Ziz. You will find them at the end of the ravine that leads to the Desert of Jeruel. 17You won't need to fight in this battle. Just stand strong in your places and you will see the LORD save you. Judah and Jerusalem, don't be afraid or discouraged because the LORD is with you. So go out against those people tomorrow.' "

18Jehoshaphat bowed face down on the ground. All the people of Judah and Jerusalem

bowed down before the LORD and worshipped
him. 19Then some Levites from the Kohathite and
Korahite people stood up and praised the LORD,
the God of Israel, with very loud voices.
20Jehoshaphat's army went out into the Desert
of Tekoa early in the morning. As they were start-
ing out, Jehoshaphat stood and said, "Listen to
me, people of Judah and Jerusalem. Have faith in
the LORD your God, and you will stand strong.
Have faith in his prophets,[d] and you will suc-
ceed." 21Jehoshaphat listened to the people's ad-
vice. Then he chose men to be singers to the
LORD, to praise him because he is holy and won-
derful. As they marched in front of the army, they
said,

"Thank the LORD,
because his love continues for ever."

22As they began to sing and praise God, the
LORD set ambushes for the people of Ammon,
Moab and Edom who had come to attack Judah.
And they were defeated. 23The Ammonites and
Moabites attacked the Edomites, destroying them
completely. After they had killed the Edomites,
they killed each other.
24When the men from Judah came to a place
where they could see the desert, they looked at
the enemy's large army. But they only saw dead
bodies lying on the ground; no one had escaped.
25When Jehoshaphat and his army came to take
their valuables, they found many supplies, much
clothing and other valuable things. There was
more than they could carry away; there was so
much it took three days to gather it all. 26On the
fourth day Jehoshaphat and his army met in the
Valley of Beracah and praised the LORD. That is
why that place has been called the Valley of Bera-
cah[n] to this day.
27Then Jehoshaphat led all the men from Judah
and Jerusalem back to Jerusalem. The LORD had
made them happy because their enemies were
defeated. 28They entered Jerusalem with harps,
lyres[d] and trumpets and went to the Temple of
the LORD.
29When all the kingdoms of the lands around
them heard how the LORD had fought Israel's en-
emies, they feared God. 30So Jehoshaphat's king-
dom was not at war. His God gave him peace
from all the countries around him.

Jehoshaphat's Rule Ends

31Jehoshaphat ruled over the country of Judah.
He was 35 years old when he became king, and
he ruled in Jerusalem for 25 years. His mother's
name was Azubah daughter of Shilhi. 32Jehosha-
phat was good like his father Asa, and he did
what the LORD said was right. 33But the places
where gods were worshipped were not removed,
and the people did not really want to follow the
God of their ancestors.
34The other things Jehoshaphat did as king,
from the beginning to the end, are written in the
records of Jehu son of Hanani, which are in the
book of the kings of Israel.
35Later, Jehoshaphat king of Judah made a
treaty with Ahaziah king of Israel, which was a
wrong thing to do. 36Jehoshaphat agreed with
Ahaziah to build trading ships, which they built
in the town of Ezion Geber. 37Then Eliezer son
of Dodavahu from the town of Mareshah spoke
against Jehoshaphat. He said, "Jehoshaphat, be-
cause you joined with Ahaziah, the LORD will
destroy what you have made." The ships were
wrecked so they could not sail out to trade.

21 Jehoshaphat died and was buried with
his ancestors in Jerusalem, the city of Da-
vid. Then his son Jehoram became king in his
place. 2Jehoram's brothers were Azariah, Jehiel,
Zechariah, Azariahu, Michael and Shephatiah.
They were the sons of Jehoshaphat king of Judah.
3Jehoshaphat gave his sons many gifts of silver,
gold and valuable things, and he gave them
fortified cities in Judah. But Jehoshaphat gave
the kingdom to Jehoram, because he was the
first son.

Jehoram King of Judah

4When Jehoram took control of his father's
kingdom, he killed all his brothers with a sword
and also killed some of the leaders of Judah. 5He
was 32 years old when he began to rule, and he
ruled eight years in Jerusalem. 6He followed in
the ways of the kings of Israel, just as the family
of Ahab had done, because he married Ahab's
daughter. Jehoram did what the LORD said was
wrong. 7But the LORD would not destroy David's
family because of the agreement he had made
with David. He had promised that one of David's
descendants[d] would always rule.
8In Jehoram's time, Edom broke away from
Judah's rule and chose their own king. 9So Jeho-
ram went to Edom with all his commanders
and chariots. The Edomites surrounded him and
his chariot commanders, but Jehoram got up
and attacked the Edomites at night. 10From then
until now the country of Edom has fought
against the rule of Judah. At the same time the
people of Libnah also broke away from Jehoram
because Jehoram left the LORD, the God of his
ancestors.
11Jehoram also built places to worship gods on
the hills in Judah. He led the people of Jerusalem
to sin, and he led the people of Judah away from

Beracah This name means "blessing" or "praise".

the LORD. 12Then Jehoram received this letter
from Elijah the prophet:

> This is what the LORD, the God of your
> ancestor David, says, "Jehoram, you have
> not lived as your father Jehoshaphat lived
> and as Asa king of Judah lived. 13But you
> have lived as the kings of Israel lived, lead-
> ing the people of Judah and Jerusalem to sin
> against God, as Ahab and his family did. You
> have killed your brothers and they were bet-
> ter than you. 14So now the LORD is about to
> punish your people, your children, wives
> and everything you own. 15You will have a
> terrible disease in your intestines that will
> become worse every day. Finally it will
> cause your intestines to come out."

Sidelight The "terrible disease in your intestines" that was prophesied for King Jehoram by Elijah (2 Chronicles 21:15) was probably dysentery, a common ailment in the Middle East and other parts of the world. The king's case may have been chronic, resulting in intestinal blockage and death.

16The LORD caused the Philistines and the
Arabs who lived near the Cushites to be angry
with Jehoram. 17So the Philistines and Arabs
attacked Judah and carried away all the wealth
of Jehoram's palace, as well as his sons and
wives. Only Jehoram's youngest son, Ahaziah,
was left.

18After these things happened, the LORD gave
Jehoram a disease in his intestines that could not
be cured. 19After he was sick for two years, Jeho-
ram's intestines came out because of the disease,
and he died in terrible pain. The people did not
make a fire to honour Jehoram as they had done
for his ancestors.

20Jehoram was 32 years old when he became
king, and he ruled for eight years in Jerusalem.
No one was sad when he died. He was buried in
Jerusalem, but not in the graves for the kings.

Ahaziah King of Judah

22 The people of Jerusalem chose Ahaziah,
Jehoram's youngest son, to be king in his
place. The robbers who had come with the Arabs
to attack Jehoram's camp had killed all of Jeho-
ram's older sons. So Ahaziah began to rule Judah.
2Ahaziah was 22 years old when he became king,
and he ruled for a year in Jerusalem. His mother's
name was Athaliah, a granddaughter of Omri.
3Ahaziah followed the ways of Ahab's family, be-
cause his mother encouraged him to do wrong.
4Ahaziah did what the LORD said was wrong, as
Ahab's family had done. They gave advice to
Ahaziah after his father died, and their bad advice
led to his death. 5Following their advice, Ahaziah
went with Joram son of Ahab to Ramoth in Gil-
ead, where they fought against Hazael king of
Aram. The Arameans wounded Joram. 6So Joram
returned to Jezreel to heal from the wounds he
received at Ramoth when he fought Hazael king
of Aram.

Ahaziah son of Jehoram and king of Judah
went down to visit Joram son of Ahab at Jezreel
because he had been wounded.

7God caused Ahaziah's death when he went to
visit Joram. Ahaziah arrived and went out with
Joram to meet Jehu son of Nimshi, whom the
LORD had appointed to destroy Ahab's family.
8While Jehu was punishing Ahab's family, he
found the leaders of Judah and the sons of Ahaz-
iah's relatives who served Ahaziah, and Jehu
killed them all. 9Then Jehu looked for Ahaziah.
Jehu's men caught him hiding in Samaria, so they
brought him to Jehu. Then they killed and buried
him. They said, "Ahaziah is a descendant [d] of
Jehoshaphat, and Jehoshaphat obeyed the LORD
with all his heart." No one in Ahaziah's family
had the power to take control of the kingdom of
Judah.

Athaliah and Joash

10When Ahaziah's mother, Athaliah, saw that
her son was dead, she killed all the royal family
in Judah. 11But Jehosheba, King Jehoram's daugh-
ter, took Joash, Ahaziah's son. She stole him from
among the other sons of the king who were going
to be murdered and put him and his nurse in a
bedroom. So Jehosheba, who was King Jehoram's
daughter and Ahaziah's sister and the wife of Je-
hoiada the priest, hid Joash so Athaliah could not
kill him. 12He hid with them in the Temple [d] of
God for six years. During that time Athaliah ruled
the land.

23 In the seventh year Jehoiada decided to
do something. He made an agreement
with the commanders of the groups of 100 men:
Azariah son of Jeroham, Ishmael son of Jehoha-
nan, Azariah son of Obed, Maaseiah son of Ada-
iah and Elishaphat son of Zicri. 2They went
around in Judah and gathered the Levites from all
the towns, and they gathered the leaders of the
families of Judah. Then they went to Jerusalem.
3All the people together made an agreement with
the king in the Temple [d] of God.

Jehoiada said to them, "The king's son will
rule, as the LORD promised about David's des-
cendants. [d] 4Now this is what you must do: you
priests and Levites go on duty on the Sabbath. [d] A
third of you will guard the doors. 5A third of you

will be at the king's palace, and a third of you will
be at the Foundation Gate. All the other people
will stay in the courtyards of the Temple of the
LORD. 6Don't let anyone come into the Temple
of the LORD except the priests and Levites who
serve. They may come because they have been
made ready to serve the LORD, but all the others
must do the job the LORD has given them. 7The
Levites must stay near the king, each man with
his weapon in his hand. If anyone tries to enter
the Temple, kill him. Stay close to the king when
he goes in and when he goes out."

Joash Becomes King

8The Levites and all the people of Judah
obeyed everything Jehoiada the priest had com-
manded. He did not excuse anyone from the
groups of the priests. So each commander took
his men who came on duty on the Sabbath [d] with
those who went off duty on the Sabbath. 9Jehoi-
ada gave the commanders of 100 men the spears
and the large and small shields that had belonged
to King David and that were kept in the Temple [d]
of God. 10Then Jehoiada told the men where to
stand, each man with his weapon in his hand.
There were guards from the south side of the
Temple to the north side. They stood by the altar
and the Temple and around the king.

11Jehoiada and his sons brought out the king's
son and put the crown on him and gave him a
copy of the agreement. Then they appointed him
king and poured olive oil on him and shouted,
"Long live the king!"

12When Athaliah heard the noise of the people
running and praising the king, she went to them
at the Temple of the LORD. 13She looked, and
there was the king standing by his pillar at the
entrance. The officers and the trumpeters were
standing beside him, and all the people of the
land were happy and blowing trumpets. The sing-
ers were playing musical instruments and leading
praises. Then Athaliah tore her clothes and
screamed, "Traitors! Traitors!"

14Jehoiada the priest sent out the commanders
of 100 men, who led the army. He said, "Sur-
round her with soldiers and take her out of the
Temple area. Kill with a sword anyone who fol-
lows her." He had said, "Don't put Athaliah to
death in the Temple of the LORD." 15So they
caught her when she came to the entrance of the
Horse Gate near the palace. There they put her to
death.

16Then Jehoiada made an agreement with the
people and the king that they would be the LORD's
special people. 17All the people went to the tem-
ple of Baal [d] and tore it down, smashing the altars
and idols. They killed Mattan, the priest of Baal,
in front of the altars.

18Then Jehoiada chose the priests, who were
Levites, to be responsible for the Temple of the
LORD. David had given them duties in the Temple
of the LORD. They were to offer the burnt offerings
to the LORD as the Teachings of Moses com-
manded, and they were to offer them with much
joy and singing as David had commanded. 19Je-
hoiada put guards at the gates of the Temple of
the LORD so that anyone who was unclean [d] in any
way could not enter.

20Jehoiada took with him the commanders of
100 men, the important men, the rulers of the
people, and all the people of the land to take the
king out of the Temple of the LORD. They went
through the Upper Gate into the palace, and then
they seated the king on the throne. 21So all the
people of the land were very happy, and Jeru-
salem had peace, because Athaliah had been put
to death with the sword.

Joash Repairs the Temple

24 Joash was seven years old when he be-
came king, and he ruled for 40 years in
Jerusalem. His mother's name was Zibiah, and
she was from Beersheba. 2Joash did what the
LORD said was right as long as Jehoiada the priest
was alive. 3Jehoiada chose two wives for Joash,
and Joash had sons and daughters.

4Later, Joash decided to repair the Temple [d] of
the LORD. 5He called the priests and the Levites
together and said to them, "Go to the towns of
Judah and gather the money all the Israelites have
to pay every year. Use it to repair the Temple of
your God. Do this now." But the Levites did not
hurry.

6So King Joash called for Jehoiada the leading
priest and said to him, "Why haven't you made
the Levites bring in from Judah and Jerusalem the
tax money that Moses, the LORD's servant, and
the people of Israel used for the Holy Tent?" [d]

7In the past the sons of wicked Athaliah had
broken into the Temple of God and used its holy
things for worshipping the Baal [d] idols.

8King Joash commanded that a box for contri-
butions be made. They put it outside, at the gate
of the Temple of the LORD. 9Then the Levites
made an announcement in Judah and Jerusalem,
telling people to bring to the LORD the tax money
Moses, the servant of God, had made the Israel-
ites give while they were in the desert. 10All the
officers and people were happy to bring their
money, and they put it in the box until the box
was full. 11When the Levites would take the box
to the king's officers, they would see that it was
full of money. Then the king's royal secretary and
the leading priest's officer would come and take
out the money and return the box to its place.
They did this often and gathered much money.

12King Joash and Jehoiada gave the money to the
people who worked on the Temple of the LORD.
And they hired stoneworkers and carpenters to
repair the Temple of the LORD. They also hired
people to work with iron and bronze to repair the
Temple.
13The people worked hard, and the work to
repair the Temple went well. They rebuilt the
Temple of God to be as it was before, but even
stronger. 14When the workers finished, they
brought the money that was left to King Joash
and Jehoiada. They used that money to make
utensils for the Temple of the LORD, utensils for
the service in the Temple and for the burnt offer-
ings, and bowls and other utensils from gold and
silver. Burnt offerings were given every day in the
Temple of the LORD while Jehoiada was alive.
15Jehoiada grew old and lived many years.
Then he died when he was 130 years old.
16Jehoiada was buried in Jerusalem with the
kings, because he had done much good in Judah
for God and his Temple.

Joash Does Evil

17After Jehoiada died, the officers of Judah
came and bowed down to King Joash, and he
listened to them. 18The king and these leaders
stopped worshipping in the Temple[d] of the LORD,
the God of their ancestors. Instead, they began to
worship the Asherah[d] idols and other idols. Be-
cause they did wrong, God was angry with the
people of Judah and Jerusalem. 19Even though
the LORD sent prophets[d] to the people to turn
them back to him and even though the prophets
warned them, they refused to listen.
20Then the Spirit[d] of God entered Zechariah
son of Jehoiada the priest. Zechariah stood before
the people and said, "This is what God says: 'Why

REBELLION

This is My Life

"Eleven p.m. But I'm seventeen! Everyone's going to laugh at me! No one has to be home that early!" Brian couldn't believe that his parents could be so unfair. Perhaps he had ignored their rules lately, but he was old enough to run his own life.

"I'm leaving!" he yelled and stormed out of the house.

After spending the night with a friend, he came home, hoping his parents would be really worried.

But his dad didn't yell or ask questions. He simply took away Brian's car keys.

Not to be beaten, Brian took out all his savings of £250 and bought an old car. It looked rough, but seemed to run OK, and he defiantly drove it home.

That night Brian decided to go cruising in his "new" car. Ten minutes away from home, the car ground to a painful halt – the clutch had gone. And Brian didn't have any money for repairs. He abandoned the car and walked home.

The car sat in the road until the police had it towed away.

Brian never saw his car or his £250 again. And he didn't drive the family car for two months.

By rebelling against his parents, Brian lost both money and privileges. Read **2 Chronicles 24:17–25** to learn how King Joash's rebellion against God affected his life.

- What were common factors in Brian's and Joash's rebellion?
- Joash's rebellion against God resulted in a murder. If you've ever rebelled against God, what has been a result of that rebellion?

Consider . . .

- evaluating your own life for signs of rebellion against God and then working on ways to get rid of the rebellion.
- visiting a prison or detention centre and sharing your experience of God's forgiveness.

For more, see . . .

- Proverbs 1:8–9 (p.590)
- 1 Peter 2:13–25 (p.1358)
- Romans 3:9–20 (p.1187)

do you disobey the LORD's commands? You will not be successful. Because you have left the LORD, he has also left you.' "

21But the king and his officers made plans against Zechariah. At the king's command they threw stones at him in the courtyard of the Temple of the LORD until he died. 22King Joash did not remember Jehoiada's kindness to him, so Joash killed Zechariah, Jehoiada's son. Before Zechariah died, he said, "May the LORD see what you are doing and punish you."

23At the end of the year, the Aramean army came against Joash. They attacked Judah and Jerusalem, killed all the leaders of the people, and sent all the valuable things to their king in Damascus. 24The Aramean army came with only a small group of men, but the LORD handed over to them a very large army from Judah, because the people of Judah had left the LORD, the God of their ancestors. So Joash was punished. 25When the Arameans left, Joash was badly wounded. His own officers made plans against him because he had killed Zechariah son of Jehoiada the priest. So they killed Joash in his own bed. He died and was buried in Jerusalem but not in the graves of the kings.

26The officers who made plans against Joash were Jozabad and Jehozabad. Jozabad was the son of Shimeath, a woman from Ammon. And Jehozabad was the son of Shimrith, a woman from Moab. 27The story of Joash's sons, the great prophecies[d] against him, and how he repaired the Temple of God are written in the book of the kings. Joash's son Amaziah became king in his place.

Amaziah King of Judah

25 Amaziah was 25 years old when he became king, and he ruled for 29 years in Jerusalem. His mother's name was Jehoaddin, and she was from Jerusalem. 2Amaziah did what the LORD said was right, but he did not really want to obey him. 3As soon as Amaziah took strong control of the kingdom, he put to death the officers who had murdered his father the king. 4But Amaziah did not put to death their children. He obeyed what was written in the Book of Moses, where the LORD commanded, "Parents must not be put to death when their children do wrong, and children must not be put to death when their parents do wrong. Each must die for his own sins." [n]

5Amaziah gathered the people of Judah together. He grouped all the people of Judah and Benjamin by families, and he put commanders over groups of 1,000 and over groups of 100. He counted the men who were 20 years old and older. In all there were 300,000 soldiers ready to fight and skilled with spears and shields. 6Amaziah also hired 100,000 soldiers from Israel for about 3.5 tonnes of silver. 7But a man of God came to Amaziah and said, "My king, don't let the army of Israel go with you. The LORD is not with Israel or the people from the tribe[d] of Ephraim. 8You can make yourself strong for war, but God will defeat you. He has the power to help you or to defeat you."

9Amaziah said to the man of God, "But what about the 3.5 tonnes of silver I paid to the Israelite army?"

The man of God answered, "The LORD can give you much more than that."

10So Amaziah sent the Israelite army back home to Ephraim. They were very angry with the people of Judah and went home angry.

11Then Amaziah became very brave and led his army to the Valley of Salt in the country of Edom. There Amaziah's army killed 10,000 Edomites. 12The army of Judah also captured 10,000 and took them to the top of a cliff and threw them off so that they split open.

13At the same time the Israelite troops that Amaziah had not allowed to fight in the war were robbing towns in Judah. From Samaria to Beth Horon they killed 3,000 people and took many valuable things.

14When Amaziah came home after defeating the Edomites, he brought back the idols they worshipped and started to worship them himself. He bowed down to them and offered sacrifices to them. 15The LORD was very angry with Amaziah, so he sent a prophet[d] to him who said, "Why have you asked their gods for help? They could not even save their own people from you!"

16As the prophet spoke, Amaziah said to him, "We never gave you the job of advising the king. Stop, or you will be killed."

The prophet stopped speaking except to say, "I know that God has decided to destroy you because you have done this. You did not listen to my advice."

17Amaziah king of Judah talked with those who advised him. Then he sent a message to Jehoash son of Jehoahaz, who was the son of Jehu king of Israel. Amaziah said to Jehoash, "Come, let's meet face to face."

18Then Jehoash king of Israel answered Amaziah king of Judah, "A thornbush in Lebanon sent a message to a cedar tree in Lebanon. It said, 'Let your daughter marry my son.' But then a wild animal from Lebanon came by, walking on and crushing the thornbush. 19You say to yourself that you have defeated Edom, but you have become proud and you boast. But stay at home! Don't ask for trouble, or you and Judah will be defeated."

"Parents . . . sins." See Deuteronomy 24:16.

20But Amaziah would not listen. God caused
this to happen so that Jehoash would defeat Ju-
dah, because Judah asked for help from the gods
of Edom. 21So Jehoash king of Israel went to at-
tack. He and Amaziah king of Judah faced each
other in battle at Beth Shemesh in Judah. 22Israel
defeated Judah, and every man of Judah ran away
to his home. 23At Beth Shemesh, Jehoash king of
Israel captured Amaziah king of Judah. (Amaziah
was the son of Joash, who was the son of Ahaz-
iah.) Then Jehoash brought him to Jerusalem. Je-
hoash broke down the wall of Jerusalem, from
the Gate of Ephraim to the Corner Gate, about
200 metres. 24He took all the gold and silver and
all the utensils from the Temple[d] of God that
Obed-Edom had taken care of. He also took the
treasures from the palace and some hostages.
Then he returned to Samaria.

25Amaziah son of Joash, the king of Judah,
lived fifteen years after the death of Jehoash son
of Jehoahaz, the king of Israel. 26The other things
Amaziah did as king, from the beginning to the
end, are written in the book of the kings of Judah
and Israel. 27When Amaziah stopped obeying the
LORD, the people in Jerusalem made plans against
him. So he ran away to the town of Lachish, but
they sent men after him to Lachish and killed
him. 28They brought his body back on horses, and
he was buried with his ancestors in Jerusalem,
the city of David.

Uzziah King of Judah

26 Then all the people of Judah made Uz-
ziah[n] king in place of his father Ama-
ziah. Uzziah was sixteen years old. 2He rebuilt
the town of Elath and made it part of Judah again
after Amaziah died.

3Uzziah was sixteen years old when he be-
came king, and he ruled for 52 years in Jeru-
salem. His mother's name was Jecoliah, and she
was from Jerusalem. 4He did what the LORD said
was right, just as his father Amaziah had done.
5Uzziah obeyed God while Zechariah was alive,
because he taught Uzziah how to respect and
obey God. And as long as Uzziah obeyed the
LORD, God gave him success.

Sidelight Wouldn't it be nice if everyone obeyed your slightest command? Uzziah must have felt that way when he became king at the age of sixteen (2 Chronicles 26:3). Do you suppose his first decree was to outlaw homework?

6Uzziah fought a war against the Philistines.
He tore down the walls around their towns of
Gath, Jabneh and Ashdod and built new towns
near Ashdod and in other places among the Phi-
listines. 7God helped Uzziah fight the Philistines,
the Arabs living in Gur Baal and the Meunites.
8Also, the Ammonites made the payments Uzziah
demanded. He was very powerful, so his name
became famous all the way to the border of
Egypt.

9Uzziah built towers in Jerusalem at the Cor-
ner Gate, the Valley Gate and where the wall
turned, and he made them strong. 10He also built
towers in the desert and dug many wells, because
he had many cattle on the western hills and in
the plains. He had people who worked his fields
and vineyards in the hills and in the fertile lands,
because he loved the land.

11Uzziah had an army of trained soldiers. They
were counted and put in groups by Jeiel the royal
secretary and Maaseiah the officer. Hananiah,
one of the king's commanders, was their leader.
12There were 2,600 leaders over the soldiers.
13They were in charge of an army of 307,500
men who fought with great power to help the
king against the enemy. 14Uzziah gave his army
shields, spears, helmets, armour, bows and stones
for their slings. 15In Jerusalem Uzziah made de-
vices that were invented by clever men. These
devices on the towers and corners of the city
walls were used to shoot arrows and large
rocks. So Uzziah became famous in faraway
places, because he had much help until he be-
came powerful.

Sidelight Modern military experts debate whether their weapons are offensive or defensive. But ancient city walls (2 Chronicles 26:15) served both purposes. Massive in size, the walls offered a strong defence against battering and invasion. They also gave people on the walls an offensive position from which to drop rocks, shoot arrows, or pour hot oil on attackers.

16But when Uzziah became powerful, his pride
led to his ruin. He was unfaithful to the LORD his
God; he went into the Temple[d] of the LORD to
burn incense[d] on the altar for incense. 17Azariah
and 80 other brave priests who served the LORD
followed Uzziah into the Temple. 18They told
him he was wrong and said to him, "You don't
have the right to burn incense to the LORD. Only
the priests, Aaron's descendants,[d] should burn

Uzziah Also called Azariah.

the incense, because they have been made holy.
Leave this holy place. You have been unfaithful,
and the LORD God will not honour you for this."
19Uzziah was standing beside the altar for in-
cense in the Temple of the LORD, and in his hand
was a pan for burning incense. He was very angry
with the priests. As he was standing in front of
the priests, a skin disease broke out on his fore-
head. 20Azariah, the leading priest, and all the
other priests looked at him and saw the skin dis-
ease on his forehead. So they hurried him out of
the Temple. Uzziah also rushed out, because the
LORD was punishing him. 21So King Uzziah had the
skin disease until the day he died. He had to live in
a separate house and could not enter the Temple of
the LORD. His son Jotham was in charge of the
palace, and he governed the people of the land.
22The other things Uzziah did as king, from
beginning to end, were written down by the
prophet Isaiah son of Amoz. 23Uzziah died and
was buried near his ancestors in a graveyard that
belonged to the kings. This was because people
said, "He had a skin disease." And his son Jotham
became king in his place.

Jotham King of Judah

27 Jotham was 25 years old when he be-
came king, and he ruled for sixteen years
in Jerusalem. His mother's name was Jerusha
daughter of Zadok. 2Jotham did what the LORD
said was right, just as his father Uzziah[n] had
done. (But Jotham did not enter the Temple[d] of
the LORD to burn incense[d] as his father had.) But
the people continued doing wrong. 3Jotham re-
built the Upper Gate of the Temple of the LORD
and he added greatly to the wall at Ophel. 4He
also built towns in the hill country of Judah, as
well as walled cities and towers in the forests.
5Jotham also fought the king of the Ammonites
and defeated them. So each year for three years
they gave Jotham about 3.5 tonnes of silver,
about 1,000 tonnes of wheat and about 1,000
tonnes of barley. 6Jotham became powerful, be-
cause he always obeyed the LORD his God.
7The other things Jotham did while he was
king and all his wars are written in the book of
the kings of Israel and Judah. 8Jotham was 25
years old when he became king, and he ruled for
sixteen years in Jerusalem. 9Jotham died and was
buried in Jerusalem, the city of David. Then Jo-
tham's son Ahaz became king in his place.

Ahaz King of Judah

28 Ahaz was 20 years old when he became
king, and he ruled for sixteen years in
Jerusalem. Unlike his ancestor David, he did not
do what the LORD said was right. 2Ahaz did the
same things the kings of Israel had done. He
made metal idols to worship Baal.[d] 3He burnt in-
cense[d] in the Valley of Ben Hinnom and made
his children pass[n] through the fire. He did the
same hateful sins as the nations had done whom
the LORD had forced out of the land ahead of the
Israelites. 4Ahaz offered sacrifices and burnt in-
cense at the places where gods were worshipped,
and on the hills and under every green tree.
5So the LORD his God handed over Ahaz to
the king of Aram. The Arameans defeated Ahaz
and took many people of Judah as prisoners to
Damascus.

He also handed over Ahaz to Pekah king of
Israel, and Pekah's army killed many soldiers of
Ahaz. 6The army of Pekah son of Remaliah killed
120,000 brave soldiers from Judah in one day.
Pekah defeated them because they had left the
LORD, the God of their ancestors. 7Zicri, a warrior
from Ephraim, killed King Ahaz's son Maaseiah.
He also killed Azrikam, the officer in charge of
the palace and Elkanah, who was second in com-
mand to the king. 8The Israelite army captured
200,000 of their own relatives. They took women,
sons and daughters and many valuable things
from Judah and carried them back to Samaria.
9But a prophet[d] of the LORD named Oded was
there. He met the Israelite army when it returned
to Samaria and said to them, "The LORD, the God
of your ancestors, handed Judah over to you, be-
cause he was angry with those people. But God
has seen the cruel way you killed them. 10Now you
plan to make the people of Judah and Jerusalem
your slaves, but you also have sinned against the
LORD your God. 11Now listen to me. Send back
your brothers and sisters whom you captured,
because the LORD is very angry with you."
12Then some of the leaders in Ephraim—
Azariah son of Jehohanan, Berekiah son of Meshil-
lemoth, Jehizkiah son of Shallum and Amasa son
of Hadlai—met the Israelite soldiers coming home
from war. 13They warned the soldiers, "Don't
bring the prisoners from Judah here. If you do,
we will be guilty of sin against the LORD, and that
will make our sin and guilt even worse. Our guilt
is already so great that he is angry with Israel."
14So the soldiers left the prisoners and valuable
things in front of the officers and people there.
15The leaders who were named took the prison-
ers and gave those who were naked the clothes
that the Israelite army had taken. They gave the
prisoners clothes, sandals, food, drink and medi-
cine. They put the weak prisoners on donkeys

Uzziah Also called Azariah.
pass This means that Ahaz sacrificed his children in the fire.

and took them back to their families in Jericho,
the city of palm trees. Then they returned home
to Samaria.
16–17At that time the Edomites came again and
attacked Judah and carried away prisoners. So
King Ahaz sent to the king of Assyria for help.
18The Philistines also robbed the towns in the
western hills and in southern Judah. They cap-
tured the towns of Beth Shemesh, Aijalon, Gede-
roth, Soco, Timnah and Gimzo, and the villages
around them. Then the Philistines lived in those
towns. 19The LORD brought trouble on Judah be-
cause Ahaz their king led the people of Judah to
sin, and he was unfaithful to the LORD. 20Tiglath-
Pileser king of Assyria came to Ahaz, but he gave
Ahaz trouble instead of help. 21Ahaz took some
valuable things from the Temple[d] of the LORD,
from the palace and from the princes, and he
gave them to the king of Assyria, but it did not
help.
22During Ahaz's troubles he was even more
unfaithful to the LORD. 23He offered sacrifices to
the gods of the people of Damascus, who had
defeated him. He thought, "The gods of the kings
of Aram helped them. If I offer sacrifices to them,
they will help me also." But this brought ruin to
Ahaz and all Israel.
24Ahaz gathered the things from the Temple of
God and broke them into pieces. Then he closed
the doors of the Temple of the LORD. He made
altars and put them on every street corner in Jeru-
salem. 25In every town in Judah, Ahaz made
places for burning sacrifices to worship other
gods. So he made the LORD, the God of his ances-
tors, very angry.
26The other things Ahaz did as king, from be-
ginning to end, are written in the book of the
kings of Judah and Israel. 27Ahaz died and was
buried in the city of Jerusalem, but not in the
graves of the kings of Israel. Ahaz's son Hezekiah
became king in his place.

Hezekiah Purifies the Temple

29 Hezekiah was 25 years old when he be-
came king, and he ruled for 29 years in
Jerusalem. His mother's name was Abijah daugh-
ter of Zechariah. 2Hezekiah did what the LORD
said was right, just as his ancestor David had
done.
3Hezekiah opened the doors of the Temple[d] of
the LORD and repaired them in the first month of
the first year he was king. 4Hezekiah brought in the
priests and Levites and gathered them in the
courtyard on the east side of the Temple. 5Heze-
kiah said, "Listen to me, Levites. Make your-
selves ready for the LORD's service, and make holy
the Temple of the LORD, the God of your ances-
tors. Remove from the Temple everything that
makes it impure. 6Our ancestors were unfaithful
to God and did what the LORD said was wrong.
They left the LORD and stopped worshipping at the
Temple where he lives. They rejected him. 7They
shut the doors of the porch of the Temple, and
they let the fire go out in the lamps. They stopped
burning incense[d] and offering burnt offerings in
the holy place to the God of Israel. 8So the LORD
became very angry with the people of Judah and
Jerusalem, and he punished them. Other people
are frightened and shocked by what he did to
them. So they insult the people of Judah. You
know these things are true. 9That is why our
ancestors were killed in battle and our sons,
daughters and wives were taken captive. 10Now
I, Hezekiah, have decided to make an agreement
with the LORD, the God of Israel, so he will not be
angry with us any more. 11My sons, don't waste
any more time. The LORD chose you to stand be-
fore him, to serve him, to be his servants and to
burn incense to him."
12These are the Levites who started to work.
From the Kohathite family there were Mahath
son of Amasai and Joel son of Azariah. From the
Merarite family there were Kish son of Abdi and
Azariah son of Jehallelel. From the Gershonite
family there were Joah son of Zimmah and Eden
son of Joah. 13From Elizaphan's family there were
Shimri and Jeiel. From Asaph's family there were
Zechariah and Mattaniah. 14From Heman's family
there were Jehiel and Shimei. From Jeduthun's
family there were Shemaiah and Uzziel.
15These Levites gathered their brothers to-
gether and made themselves holy for service in
the Temple. Then they went into the Temple of
the LORD to purify it. They obeyed the king's com-
mand that had come from the LORD. 16When the
priests went into the Temple of the LORD to purify
it, they took out all the unclean[d] things they
found in the Temple of the LORD and put them
in the Temple courtyard. Then the Levites took
these things out to the Kidron Valley. 17Beginning
on the first day of the first month, they made the
Temple holy for the LORD's service. On the eighth
day of the month, they came to the porch of the
Temple, and for eight more days they made the
Temple of the LORD holy. So they finished on
the sixteenth day of the first month.
18Then they went to King Hezekiah and said,
"We have purified the entire Temple of the LORD,
the altar for burnt offerings and its utensils, and
the table for the holy bread and all its utensils.
19When Ahaz was king, he was unfaithful to God
and removed some things from the Temple. But we
have put them back and made them holy for the
LORD. They are now in front of the LORD's altar."
20Early the next morning King Hezekiah gath-
ered the leaders of the city and went up to the

Temple of the LORD. 21They brought seven bulls,
seven rams, seven lambs and seven male goats.
These animals were an offering to remove the sin
of the people and the kingdom of Judah and to
make the Temple ready for service to God. King
Hezekiah commanded the priests, the descend-
ants[d] of Aaron, to offer these animals on the
LORD's altar. 22So the priests killed the bulls and
sprinkled their blood on the altar. They killed the
rams and sprinkled their blood on the altar. Then
they killed the lambs and sprinkled their blood on
the altar. 23Then the priests brought the male
goats for the sin offering before the king and the
people there. After the king and the people put
their hands on the goats, 24the priests killed them.
With the goats' blood they made an offering on
the altar to remove the sins of the Israelites so
they would belong to God. The king had said that
the burnt offering and sin offering should be
made for all Israel.
25King Hezekiah put the Levites in the Temple
of the LORD with cymbals, harps and lyres,[d] as
David, Gad and Nathan had commanded. (Gad
was the king's seer[d] and Nathan was a prophet.[d])
This command came from the LORD through his
prophets. 26So the Levites stood ready with Da-
vid's instruments of music, and the priests stood
ready with their trumpets.
27Then Hezekiah gave the order to sacrifice the
burnt offering on the altar. When the burnt offer-
ing began, the singing to the LORD also began. The
trumpets were blown and the musical instru-
ments of David king of Israel were played. 28All
the people worshipped, the singers sang and the
trumpeters blew their trumpets until the burnt
offering was finished.
29When the sacrifices were completed, King
Hezekiah and everyone with him bowed down
and worshipped. 30King Hezekiah and his officers
ordered the Levites to praise the LORD, using the
words David and Asaph the seer had used. So
they praised God with joy and bowed down and
worshipped.
31Then Hezekiah said, "Now that you people
of Judah have given yourselves to the LORD, come
near to the Temple of the LORD. Bring sacrifices
and offerings to show thanks to him." So the peo-
ple brought sacrifices and thank offerings, and
anyone who was willing also brought burnt offer-
ings. 32For burnt offerings they brought a total of
70 bulls, 100 rams and 200 lambs; all these ani-
mals were sacrificed as burnt offerings to the
LORD. 33The holy offerings totalled 600 bulls and
3,000 sheep and goats. 34There were not enough
priests to skin all the animals for the burnt offerings.
So their relatives the Levites helped them until
the work was finished and other priests could be
made holy. The Levites had been more careful to
make themselves holy for the LORD's service than
the priests. 35There were many burnt offerings
along with the fat of fellowship offerings and
drink offerings. So the service in the Temple of
the LORD began again. 36And Hezekiah and the
people were very happy that God had made it
happen so quickly for his people.

The Passover Celebration

30 King Hezekiah sent messages to all the
people of Israel and Judah, and he wrote
letters to the people of Ephraim and Manasseh.
Hezekiah invited all these people to come to the
Temple[d] of the LORD in Jerusalem to celebrate the
Passover[d] for the LORD, the God of Israel. 2King
Hezekiah, his officers and all the people in Jeru-
salem agreed to celebrate the Passover in the sec-
ond month. 3They could not celebrate it at the
normal time, because not enough priests had
made themselves ready to serve the LORD, and the
people had not yet gathered in Jerusalem. 4This
plan satisfied King Hezekiah and all the people.
5So they made an announcement everywhere in
Israel, from Beersheba to Dan,[n] telling the peo-
ple to come to Jerusalem to celebrate the Pass-
over for the LORD, the God of Israel. For a long
time most of the people had not celebrated the
Passover as the law commanded. 6At the king's
command, the messengers took letters from him
and his officers all through Israel and Judah. This
is what the letters said:

> People of Israel, return to the LORD, the
> God of Abraham, Isaac and Israel. Then God
> will return to you who are still alive, who
> have escaped from the kings of Assyria.
> 7Don't be like your ancestors or your relat-
> ives. They turned against the LORD, the God
> of their ancestors, so he caused other people
> to be disgusted with them. You know this is
> true. 8Don't be stubborn as your ancestors
> were, but obey the LORD willingly. Come to
> the Temple, which he has made holy for
> ever. Serve the LORD your God so he will not
> be angry with you. 9Come back to the LORD.
> Then the people who captured your relat-
> ives and children will be kind to them and
> will let them return to this land. The LORD
> your God is kind and merciful. He will not
> turn away from you if you return to him.

10The messengers went to every town in Eph-
raim and Manasseh, and all the way to Zebulun,

Beersheba to Dan Dan was the city farthest north in Israel, and Beersheba was the city farthest south. So this means all the people of Israel.

but the people laughed at them and made fun
of them. 11But some men from Asher, Manasseh
and Zebulun were sorry for what they had
done and went to Jerusalem. 12And God united
all the people of Judah in obeying King Hezekiah
and his officers, because their command had
come from the LORD.
13In the second month a large crowd came to-
gether in Jerusalem to celebrate the Feast[d] of Un-
leavened Bread. 14The people removed the altars
and incense[d] altars to gods in Jerusalem and
threw them into the Kidron Valley.
15They killed the Passover lamb on the four-
teenth day of the second month. The priests and
the Levites were ashamed, so they made them-
selves holy and brought burnt offerings into the
Temple of the LORD. 16They took their regular
places in the Temple as the Teachings of Moses,
the man of God, commanded. The Levites gave
the blood of the sacrifices to the priests, who
sprinkled it on the altar. 17Since many people in
the crowd had not made themselves holy, the
Levites killed the Passover lambs for everyone
who was not clean.[d] The Levites made each lamb
holy for the LORD. 18–19Although many people
from Ephraim, Manasseh, Issachar and Zebulun
had not purified themselves for the feast, they ate
the Passover even though it was against the law.
So Hezekiah prayed for them, saying, "LORD, you
are good. You are the LORD, the God of our ances-
tors. Please forgive all those who try to obey you
even if they did not make themselves clean as the
rules of the Temple command." 20The LORD lis-
tened to Hezekiah's prayer, and he healed the
people. 21The Israelites in Jerusalem celebrated
the Feast of Unleavened Bread for seven days
with great joy to the LORD. The Levites and priests
praised the LORD every day with loud music.
22Hezekiah encouraged all the Levites who
showed they understood well how to do their
service for the LORD. The people ate the feast
for seven days, offered fellowship offerings and
praised the LORD, the God of their ancestors.
23Then all the people agreed to stay seven
more days, so they celebrated with joy for seven
more days. 24Hezekiah king of Judah gave 1,000
bulls and 7,000 sheep to the people. The officers
gave 1,000 bulls and 10,000 sheep to the people.
Many priests made themselves holy. 25All the peo-
ple of Judah, the priests, the Levites, those who
came from Israel, the foreigners from Israel and the
foreigners living in Judah were very happy. 26There
was much joy in Jerusalem, because there had
not been a celebration like this since the time of
Solomon son of David and king of Israel. 27The
priests and Levites stood up and blessed the
people, and God heard them because their prayer
reached heaven, his holy home.

The Collection for the Priests

31 When the Passover[d] celebration was
finished, all the Israelites in Jerusalem
went out to the towns of Judah. There they
smashed the stone pillars used to worship gods.
They cut down the Asherah[d] idols and de-
stroyed the altars and places for worshipping
gods in all of Judah, Benjamin, Ephraim and
Manasseh. After they had destroyed all of them,
the Israelites returned to their own towns and
homes.
2King Hezekiah appointed groups of priests
and Levites for their special duties. They were to
offer burnt offerings and fellowship offerings, to
worship and to give thanks and praise at the
gates of the LORD's house. 3Hezekiah gave some
of his own animals for the burnt offerings, which
were given every morning and evening on Sab-
bath[d] days, during New Moons[d] and at other
feasts commanded in the LORD's Teachings.
4Hezekiah commanded the people living in
Jerusalem to give the priests and Levites the por-
tion that belonged to them. Then the priests and
Levites could give all their time to the LORD's
Teachings. 5As soon as the king's command
went out to the Israelites, they gave freely of the
first portion of their grain, new wine, oil, honey
and everything they grew in their fields. They
brought a large amount, one-tenth of every-
thing. 6The people of Israel and Judah who lived
in Judah also brought one-tenth of their cattle
and sheep and one-tenth of the holy things that
were given to the LORD their God, and they put
all of them in piles. 7The people began the piles
in the third month and finished in the seventh
month. 8When Hezekiah and his officers came
and saw the piles, they praised the LORD and his
people, the people of Israel. 9Hezekiah asked
the priests and Levites about the piles.
10Azariah, the leading priest from Zadok's fam-
ily, answered Hezekiah, "Since the people
began to bring their offerings to the Temple[d] of
the LORD, we have had plenty to eat and plenty
left over, because the LORD has blessed his peo-
ple. So we have all this left over."
11Then Hezekiah commanded the priests to
prepare the storerooms in the Temple of the
LORD. So this was done. 12Then the priests
brought in the offerings and the things given to
the LORD and a tenth of everything the people
had given. Conaniah the Levite was in charge of
these things, and his brother Shimei was second
to him. 13Conaniah and his brother Shimei were
over these supervisors: Jehiel, Azaziah, Nahath,
Asahel, Jerimoth, Jozabad, Eliel, Ismachiah, Ma-
hath and Benaiah. King Hezekiah and Azariah
the officer in charge of the Temple of God had
chosen them.

[14]Kore, son of Imnah the Levite, was in charge of the special gifts the people wanted to give to God. He was responsible for giving out the contributions made to the LORD and the holy gifts. Kore was the guard at the East Gate. [15]Eden, Miniamin, Jeshua, Shemaiah, Amariah and Shecaniah helped Kore in the towns where the priests lived. They gave from what was collected to the other groups of priests, both young and old.

[16]From what was collected, these men also gave to the males three years old and older who had their names in the Levite family histories. They were to enter the Temple of the LORD for their daily service, each group having its own responsibilities. [17]The priests were given their part of the collection, by families, as listed in the family histories. The Levites 20 years old and older were given their part of the collection, based on their responsibilities and their groups. [18]The Levites' babies, wives, sons and daughters also got part of the collection. This was done for all the Levites who were listed in the family histories, because they always kept themselves ready to serve the LORD.

[19]Some of Aaron's descendants,[d] the priests, lived on the farmlands near the towns or in the towns. Men were chosen by name to give part of the collection to these priests. All the males and those named in the family histories of the Levites received part of the collection.

[20]This is what King Hezekiah did in Judah. He did what was good and right and obedient before the LORD his God. [21]Hezekiah tried to obey God in his service of the Temple of God, and he tried to obey God's teachings and commands. He gave himself fully to his work for God. So he had success.

Assyria Attacks Judah

32 After Hezekiah did all these things to serve the LORD, Sennacherib king of Assyria came and attacked Judah. He and his army surrounded and attacked the fortified cities, hoping to take them for himself. [2]Hezekiah knew that Sennacherib had come to Jerusalem to attack it. [3]So Hezekiah and his officers and army commanders decided to cut off the water from the springs outside the city. So the officers and commanders helped Hezekiah. [4]Many people came and cut off all the springs and the stream that flowed through the land. They said, "The king of Assyria will not find much water when he comes here." [5]Then Hezekiah made Jerusalem stronger. He rebuilt all the broken parts of the wall and put towers on it. He also built another wall outside the first one and strengthened the area that was filled in on the east side of the old part of Jerusalem. He also made many weapons and shields.

[6]Hezekiah put army commanders over the people and met with them at the open place near the city gate. Hezekiah encouraged them, saying, [7]"Be strong and brave. Don't be afraid or worried because of the king of Assyria or his large army. There is a greater power with us than with him. [8]He only has men, but we have the LORD our God to help us and to fight our battles." The people were encouraged by the words of Hezekiah king of Judah.

[9]After this King Sennacherib of Assyria and all his army surrounded and attacked Lachish. Then he sent his officers to Jerusalem with this message for King Hezekiah of Judah and all the people of Judah in Jerusalem:

Sidelight The Assyrian attack on Lachish (2 Chronicles 32:9) was horrible for its citizens. Archaeologists have found the bones of 1,500 bodies in a pit there, a sign of the terrible siege.

> [10]Sennacherib king of Assyria says this: "You have nothing to trust in to help you. It is no use for you to stay in Jerusalem under attack. [11]Hezekiah says to you, 'The LORD our God will save us from the king of Assyria,' but he is fooling you. If you stay in Jerusalem, you will die from hunger and thirst. [12]Hezekiah himself removed your LORD's places of worship and altars. He told you people of Judah and Jerusalem that you must worship and burn incense[d] on only one altar.
>
> [13]"You know what my ancestors and I have done to all the people in other nations. The gods of those nations could not save their people from my power. [14]My ancestors destroyed those nations; none of their gods could save them from me. So your god cannot save you from my power. [15]Do not let Hezekiah fool you or trick you, and do not believe him. No god of any nation or kingdom has been able to save his people from me or my ancestors. Your god is even less able to save you from me."

[16]Sennacherib's officers said worse things against the LORD God and his servant Hezekiah. [17]King Sennacherib also wrote letters insulting the LORD, the God of Israel. They spoke against him, saying, "The gods of the other nations could not save their people from me. In the same way Hezekiah's God won't be able to save his people from me." [18]Then the king's officers shouted in Hebrew, calling out to the people of Jerusalem who were on the city wall. The officers wanted to scare the people away so they could capture

Jerusalem. 19They spoke about the God of Jerusalem as though he were like the gods the people of the world worshipped, which are made by human hands.

20King Hezekiah and the prophet[d] Isaiah son of Amoz prayed to heaven about this. 21Then the LORD sent an angel who killed all the soldiers, leaders and officers in the camp of the king of Assyria. So the king went back to his own country in disgrace. When he went into the temple of his god, some of his own sons killed him with a sword.

22So the LORD saved Hezekiah and the people in Jerusalem from Sennacherib king of Assyria and from all other people. He took care of them on every side. 23Many people brought gifts for the LORD to Jerusalem, and they also brought valuable gifts to King Hezekiah of Judah. From then on all the nations respected Hezekiah.

Hezekiah Dies

24At that time Hezekiah became so sick he almost died. When he prayed to the LORD, the LORD spoke to him and gave him a sign.[n] 25But Hezekiah did not thank God for his kindness, because he was so proud. So the LORD was angry with him and the people of Judah and Jerusalem. 26But later Hezekiah and the people of Jerusalem were sorry and stopped being proud, so the LORD did not punish them while Hezekiah was alive.

27Hezekiah had many riches and much honour. He made treasuries for his silver, gold, gems, spices, shields and other valuable things. 28He built storage buildings for grain, new wine and oil, stalls for all the cattle and pens for the sheep. 29He also built many towns. He had many flocks and herds, because God had given Hezekiah much wealth.

30It was Hezekiah who cut off the upper pool of the Gihon spring and made those waters flow straight down to the west side of the older part of Jerusalem. And Hezekiah was successful in everything he did. 31But once the leaders of Babylon sent messengers to Hezekiah, asking him about a strange sign[n] that had happened in the land. When they came, God left Hezekiah alone to test him so he could know everything that was in Hezekiah's heart.[n]

32Hezekiah's love for God and the other things he did as king are written in the vision of the prophet[d] Isaiah son of Amoz. This is in the book of the kings of Judah and Israel. 33Hezekiah died and was buried on a hill, where the graves of David's ancestors are. All the people of Judah and Jerusalem honoured Hezekiah when he died, and his son Manasseh became king in his place.

Manasseh King of Judah

33 Manasseh was twelve years old when he became king, and he was king for 55 years in Jerusalem. 2He did what the LORD said was wrong. He did the hateful things the nations had done—the nations that the LORD had forced out of the land ahead of the Israelites. 3Manasseh's father, Hezekiah, had torn down the places where gods were worshipped, but Manasseh rebuilt them. He also built altars for the Baal[d] gods, and he made Asherah[d] idols and worshipped all the stars of the sky and served them. 4The LORD had said about the Temple,[d] "I will be worshipped in Jerusalem for ever," but Manasseh built altars in the Temple of the LORD. 5He built altars to worship the stars in the two courtyards of the Temple of the LORD. 6He made his children pass through fire in the Valley of Ben Hinnom. He practised magic and witchcraft[d] and told the future by explaining signs and dreams. He got advice from mediums[d] and fortune-tellers. He did many things the LORD said were wrong, which made the LORD angry.

7Manasseh carved an idol and put it in the Temple of God. God had said to David and his son Solomon about the Temple, "I will be worshipped for ever in this Temple and in Jerusalem, which I have chosen from all the tribes[d] of Israel. 8I will never again make the Israelites leave the land I gave to their ancestors. But they must obey everything I have commanded them in all the teachings, rules and commands I gave them through Moses." 9But Manasseh led the people of Judah and Jerusalem to do wrong. They did more evil than the nations the LORD had destroyed ahead of the Israelites.

10The LORD spoke to Manasseh and his people, but they did not listen. 11So the LORD brought the king of Assyria's army commanders to attack Judah. They captured Manasseh, put hooks in him, placed bronze chains on his hands and took him to Babylon. 12As Manasseh suffered, he begged the LORD his God for help and humbled himself before the God of his ancestors. 13When Manasseh prayed, the LORD heard him and had pity on him. So the LORD let him return to Jerusalem and to his kingdom. Then Manasseh knew that the LORD is the true God.

14After that happened, Manasseh rebuilt the outer wall of Jerusalem and made it higher. It was in the valley on the west side of the Gihon spring and went to the entrance of the Fish Gate and around the hill of Ophel. Then he

sign See Isaiah 38:1–8. It tells the story about the sign and how the Lord gave Hezekiah fifteen more years to live.
God . . . heart See 2 Kings 20:12–19.

put commanders in all the fortified cities in Judah.

15Manasseh removed the idols of other nations, including the idol in the Temple of the LORD. He removed all the altars he had built on the Temple hill and in Jerusalem and threw them out of the city. 16Then he set up the LORD's altar and sacrificed on it fellowship offerings and offerings to show thanks to God. Manasseh commanded all the people of Judah to serve the LORD, the God of Israel. 17The people continued to offer sacrifices at the places of worship, but their sacrifices were only to the LORD their God. 18The other things Manasseh did as king, his prayer to his God, and what the seers[d] said to him in the name of the LORD, the God of Israel—all are recorded in the book of the history of the kings of Israel. 19Manasseh's prayer and God's pity for him, his sins, his unfaithfulness, the places he built for worshipping gods and the Asherah idols before he humbled himself—all are written in the book of the seers. 20Manasseh died and was buried in his palace. Then Manasseh's son Amon became king in his place.

Amon King of Judah

21Amon was 22 years old when he became king, and he was king for two years in Jerusalem. 22He did what the LORD said was wrong, as his father Manasseh had done. Amon worshipped and offered sacrifices to all the carved idols Manasseh had made. 23Amon did not humble himself before the LORD as his father Manasseh had done. Instead, Amon sinned even more.

24King Amon's officers made plans against him and killed him in his palace. 25Then the people of the land killed all those who had made plans to kill King Amon, and they made his son Josiah king in his place.

Josiah King of Judah

34 Josiah was eight years old when he became king, and he ruled for 31 years in Jerusalem. 2He did what the LORD said was right. He lived as his ancestor David had lived, and he did not stop doing what was right.

3In his eighth year as king while he was still young, Josiah began to obey the God of his ancestor David. In his twelfth year as king, Josiah began to remove from Judah and Jerusalem the gods, the places for worshipping gods, the Asherah[d] idols, and the wooden and metal idols. 4The people tore down the altars for the Baal[d] gods as Josiah directed. Then Josiah cut down the incense[d] altars that were above them. He broke up the Asherah idols and the wooden and metal idols and beat them into powder. Then he sprinkled the powder on the graves of the people who had offered sacrifices to these gods. 5He burned the bones of their priests on their own altars. So Josiah removed idol worship from Judah and Jerusalem, 6and from the towns in the areas of Manasseh, Ephraim and Simeon all the way to Naphtali, and in the ruins near these towns. 7Josiah broke down the altars and Asherah idols and beat the idols into powder. He cut down all the incense altars in all of Israel. Then he went back to Jerusalem.

8In Josiah's eighteenth year as king, he made Judah and the Temple[d] pure again. He sent Shaphan son of Azaliah, Maaseiah the city leader and Joah son of Joahaz the recorder to repair the Temple of the LORD, the God of Josiah. 9These men went to Hilkiah the high priest and gave him the money the Levite gatekeepers had gathered from the people of Manasseh, Ephraim and all the Israelites who were left alive, and also from all the people of Judah, Benjamin and Jerusalem. This is the money they had brought into the Temple of God. 10Then the Levites gave it to the supervisors of the work on the Temple of the LORD, and they paid the workers who rebuilt and repaired the Temple. 11They gave money to carpenters and builders to buy cut stone and wood. The wood was used to rebuild the buildings and to make beams for them, because the kings of Judah had let the buildings fall into ruin. 12The men did their work well. Their supervisors were Jahath and Obadiah, who were Levites from the family of Merari, and Zechariah and Meshullam, who were from the family of Kohath. These Levites were all skilled musicians. 13They were also in charge of the workers who carried loads and all the other workers. Some Levites worked as secretaries, officers and gatekeepers.

Sidelight The "places" or "high places" where people worshipped false gods weren't necessarily hills or mountains (2 Chronicles 34:3–7). They were sacred platforms on which idols stood. The only way to get people to stop worshipping at them was to destroy them completely as King Josiah did.

The Book of the Teachings is Found

14The Levites brought out the money that was in the Temple[d] of the LORD. As they were doing this, Hilkiah the priest found the Book of the LORD's Teachings that had been given through Moses. 15Hilkiah said to Shaphan the royal secretary, "I've found the Book of the Teachings in the Temple of the LORD!" Then he gave it to Shaphan.

16Shaphan took the book to the king and re-

Sidelight If you don't think secretaries are important, read 2 Chronicles 34:13, which tells that the Levites served as honoured secretaries in the Temple. Do you think they had to take a typing test?

ported to Josiah, "Your officers are doing everything you told them to do. 17They have paid out the money that was in the Temple of the LORD and have given it to the supervisors and the workers." 18Then Shaphan the royal secretary told the king, "Hilkiah the priest has given me a book." And Shaphan read from the book to the king.

19When the king heard the words of the Teachings, he tore his clothes to show how upset he was. 20He gave orders to Hilkiah, Ahikam son of Shaphan, Acbor son of Micaiah, Shaphan the royal secretary and Asaiah, the king's servant. These were the orders: 21"Go and ask the LORD about the words in the book that was found. Ask for me and for the people who are left alive in Israel and Judah. The LORD is very angry with us, because our ancestors did not obey the LORD's word; they did not do everything this book says to do."

22So Hilkiah and those the king sent with him went to talk to Huldah the prophetess.[d] She was the wife of Shallum son of Tikvah, the son of Harhas, who took care of the king's clothes. Huldah lived in Jerusalem, in the new area of the city.

23She said to them, "This is what the LORD, the God of Israel, says: Tell the man who sent you to me, 24'This is what the LORD says: I will bring trouble to this place and to the people living here. I will bring all the curses that are written in the book that was read to the king of Judah. 25The people of Judah have left me and have burned incense[d] to other gods. They have made me angry by all the evil things they have made. So I will punish them in my anger, which will not be put out.' 26Tell the king of Judah, who sent you to ask the LORD, 'This is what the LORD, the God of Israel, says about the words you heard: 27When you heard my words against this place and its people, you became sorry for what you had done and you upset yourself before me. You tore your clothes to show how upset you were, and you cried in my presence. This is why I have heard you, says the LORD. 28So I will let you die and be buried in peace. You won't see all the trouble I will bring to this place and the people living here.'"

So they took her message back to the king.

29Then the king gathered all the elders of Judah and Jerusalem together. 30He went up to the Temple of the LORD, and all the people from Judah and from Jerusalem went with him. The priests, the Levites and all the people—from the most important to the least important—went with him. He read to them all the words in the Book of the Agreement that was found in the Temple of the LORD. 31The king stood by his pillar and made an agreement in the presence of the LORD to follow the LORD and obey his commands, rules and laws with his whole being and to obey the words of the agreement written in this book. 32Then Josiah made all the people in Jerusalem and Benjamin promise to accept the agreement. So the people of Jerusalem obeyed the agreement of God, the God of their ancestors.

33And Josiah threw out the hateful idols from all the land that belonged to the Israelites. He led everyone in Israel to serve the LORD their God. While Josiah lived, the people obeyed the LORD, the God of their ancestors.

Josiah Celebrates the Passover

35 King Josiah celebrated the Passover[d] to the LORD in Jerusalem. The Passover lamb was killed on the fourteenth day of the first month. 2Josiah chose the priests to do their duties, and he encouraged them as they served in the Temple[d] of the LORD. 3The Levites taught the Israelites and were made holy for service to the LORD. Josiah said to them, "Put the Holy Ark[d] in the Temple that David's son Solomon, the king of Israel, built. Do not carry it from place to place on your shoulders any more. Now serve the LORD your God and his people Israel. 4Prepare yourselves by your family groups for service, and do the jobs that King David and his son Solomon gave you to do.

5"Stand in the holy place with a group of the Levites for each family group of the people. 6Kill the Passover lambs, and make yourselves holy to the LORD. Prepare the lambs for your relatives, the people of Israel, as the LORD through Moses commanded us to do."

7Josiah gave the Israelites 30,000 sheep and goats to kill for the Passover sacrifices, and he gave them 3,000 cattle. They were all his own animals.

8Josiah's officers also gave willingly to the people, the priests and the Levites. Hilkiah, Zechariah and Jehiel, the officers in charge of the Temple, gave the priests 2,600 lambs and goats and 300 cattle for Passover sacrifices. 9Conaniah, his brothers Shemaiah and Nethanel, and Hashabiah,

Jeiel and Jozabad gave the Levites 5,000 sheep and goats and 500 cattle for Passover sacrifices. These men were leaders of the Levites.

10When everything was ready for the Passover service, the priests and Levites went to their places, as the king had commanded. 11The Passover lambs were killed. Then the Levites skinned the animals and gave the blood to the priests, who sprinkled it on the altar. 12Then they gave the animals for the burnt offerings to the different family groups so the burnt offerings could be offered to the LORD as was written in the book of Moses. They also did this with the cattle. 13The Levites roasted the Passover sacrifices over the fire as they were commanded, and they boiled the holy offerings in pots, kettles and pans. Then they quickly gave the meat to the people. 14After this was finished, the Levites prepared meat for themselves and for the priests, the descendants[d] of Aaron. The priests worked until night, offering the burnt offerings and burning the fat of the sacrifices.

15The Levite singers from Asaph's family stood in the places chosen for them by King David, Asaph, Heman and Jeduthun, the king's seer.[d] The gatekeepers at each gate did not have to leave their places, because their fellow Levites had prepared everything for them for the Passover.

16So everything was done that day for the worship of the LORD, as King Josiah commanded. The Passover was celebrated, and the burnt offerings were offered on the LORD's altar. 17The Israelites who were there celebrated the Passover and the Feast[d] of Unleavened Bread for seven days. 18The Passover had not been celebrated like this in Israel since the prophet[d] Samuel was alive. None of the kings of Israel had ever celebrated a Passover as did King Josiah, the priests, the Levites, the people of Judah and Israel who were there, and the people of Jerusalem. 19This Passover was celebrated in the eighteenth year Josiah was king.

The Death of Josiah

20After Josiah did all this for the Temple,[d] Neco king of Egypt led an army to attack Carchemish, a town on the Euphrates River. And Josiah marched out to fight against Neco. 21But Neco sent messengers to Josiah, saying, "King Josiah, there should not be war between us. I did not come to fight you, but my enemies. God told me to hurry and he is on my side. So don't fight God, or he will destroy you."

22But Josiah did not go away. He wore different clothes so no one would know who he was. Refusing to listen to what Neco said at God's command, Josiah went to fight on the plain of Megiddo. 23In the battle King Josiah was shot by archers. He told his servants, "Take me away because I am badly wounded." 24So they took him out of his chariot and put him in another chariot and carried him to Jerusalem. There he died and was buried in the graves where his ancestors were buried. All the people of Judah and Jerusalem were very sad because he was dead.

> **Sidelight** If you want to buy a house on the plain of Megiddo (2 Chronicles 35:22), expect to pay high "war insurance". This plain may be one of the bloodiest battlegrounds in the world. Archaeologists have uncovered twenty cities – one on top of the other – that have been destroyed at this site.

25Jeremiah wrote some sad songs about Josiah. Even to this day all the men and women singers remember and honour Josiah with these songs. It became a custom in Israel to sing these songs that are written in the collection of sad songs.

26–27The other things Josiah did as king, from beginning to end, are written in the book of the kings of Israel and Judah. It tells how he loved what was written in the LORD's teachings.

Jehoahaz King of Judah

36 The people of Judah chose Josiah's son Jehoahaz and made him king in Jerusalem in his father's place.

2Jehoahaz was 23 years old when he became king, and he was king in Jerusalem for three months. 3Then King Neco of Egypt removed Jehoahaz from being king in Jerusalem. Neco made the people of Judah pay about 3.5 tonnes of silver and about 35 kilogrammes of gold. 4The king of Egypt made Jehoahaz's brother Eliakim the king of Judah and Jerusalem and changed his name to Jehoiakim. But Neco took his brother Jehoahaz to Egypt.

Jehoiakim King of Judah

5Jehoiakim was 25 years old when he became king, and he was king in Jerusalem for eleven years. He did what the LORD his God said was wrong. 6King Nebuchadnezzar of Babylon attacked Judah, captured Jehoiakim, put bronze chains on him and took him to Babylon. 7Nebuchadnezzar removed some of the things from the Temple[d] of the LORD, took them to Babylon and put them in his own palace.

8The other things Jehoiakim did as king, the hateful things he did and everything he was guilty of doing, are written in the book of the kings of

Israel and Judah. And Jehoiakim's son Jehoiachin
became king in his place.

Jehoiachin King of Judah

[9]Jehoiachin was eighteen years old when he
became king of Judah, and he was king in Jeru-
salem for three months and ten days. He did
what the LORD said was wrong. [10]In the spring
King Nebuchadnezzar sent for Jehoiachin and
brought him and some valuable treasures from
the Temple[d] of the LORD to Babylon. Then Nebu-
chadnezzar made Jehoiachin's uncle Zedekiah
the king of Judah and Jerusalem.

Zedekiah King of Judah

[11]Zedekiah was 21 years old when he became
king of Judah, and he was king in Jerusalem for
eleven years. [12]Zedekiah did what the LORD his
God said was wrong. The prophet[d] Jeremiah
spoke messages from the LORD, but Zedekiah did
not obey. [13]Zedekiah turned against King Nebu-
chadnezzar, who had forced him to swear in
God's name to be loyal to him. But Zedekiah
became stubborn and refused to obey the LORD,
the God of Israel. [14]Also, all the leaders of the
priests and the people of Judah became more
wicked, following the evil example of the other
nations. The LORD had made the Temple[d] in Jeru-
salem holy, but the leaders made it unholy.

The Fall of Jerusalem

[15]The LORD, the God of their ancestors, sent
prophets[d] again and again to warn his people,
because he had pity on them and on his Temple.[d]
[16]But they made fun of God's prophets and hated
God's messages. They refused to listen to the
prophets until, finally, the LORD became so angry
with his people that he could not be stopped. [17]So
God brought the king of Babylon to attack them.
The king killed the young men even when they
were in the Temple. He had no mercy on the
young men or women, the old men or those who
were sick. God handed all of them over to Nebu-
chadnezzar. [18]Nebuchadnezzar carried away to
Babylon all the things from the Temple of God,
both large and small, and all the treasures from
the Temple of the LORD and from the king and
his officers. [19]Nebuchadnezzar and his army set

ANGER

One Mad Mum

Cari Lightner was only thirteen years old when a drunk driver swerved and killed her.

When the police arrested the driver, they discovered he had been arrested many times before for drunk driving. Still, they told Cari's mother, Candy, that this man would probably go free. There were no laws in the USA at that time that could keep him in prison.

How could someone kill her daughter and go free? In her anger, Candy declared to friends, "I'm going to start an organisation." She created Mothers Against Drunk Drivers (MADD), a group that would work to pass tough laws that would punish drunk drivers. And the work paid off. Within five years, every state in the United States had made its drink-driving laws more strict.

MADD has made people aware of the problem of drinking and driving, and its efforts have saved lives.

Candy Lightner and the thousands of MADD members put their anger to work and brought about change. In **2 Chronicles 36:14–21**, you can see changes that occurred when God became angry with his people.

- What part did anger play in Candy's – and God's – actions?
- Based on this passage, what kinds of things make God angry?

Consider . . .

- writing to politicians about an issue you think needs to be changed.
- thinking of an issue that makes you angry and then doing three things to change the situation.

For more, see . . .

- Exodus 32:19–35 (p.91)
- Luke 19:45–48 (p.1083)
- Psalm 103:8 (p.559)

fire to God's Temple and broke down Jerusalem's
wall and burned all the palaces. They took or
destroyed every valuable thing in Jerusalem.

20Nebuchadnezzar took captive to Babylon the
people who were left alive, and he forced them to
be slaves for him and his descendants.[d] They re-
mained there as slaves until the Persian kingdom
defeated Babylon. 21And so what the LORD had
told Israel through the prophet Jeremiah hap-
pened: the country was an empty wasteland for
70 years to make up for the years of Sabbath
rest[n] that the people had not kept.

22In the first year Cyrus was king of Persia, the
LORD had Cyrus send an announcement to his
whole kingdom. This happened so the LORD's
message spoken by Jeremiah would come true.
He wrote:

23This is what Cyrus king of Persia says:
The Lord, the God of heaven, has given me all the kingdoms of the earth, and he has appointed me to build a Temple for him at Jerusalem in Judah. Now may the Lord your God be with all of you who are his people. You are free to go to Jerusalem.

Sabbath rest The Law said that every seventh year the land was not to be farmed. See Leviticus 25:1–7.

Ezra

Why Read This Book:

- See how God uses world events to help his people (Ezra 1).
- Learn how to trust God in the face of opposition (Ezra 4—6).
- Examine the cost of compromising beliefs (Ezra 7—10).

When?

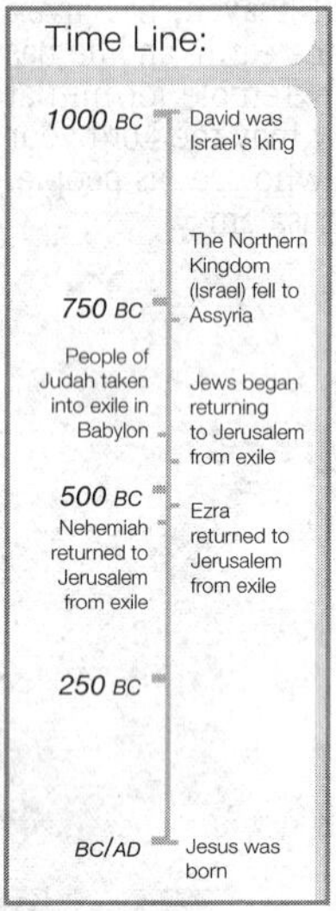

Behind the Scenes:

If you have moved from one community to another, you know what it's like to visit the old community. Nothing seems the same. Trees look larger, buildings older and people different. It's no longer home.

The people of Judah had been gone from Israel for many years, captives of the Babylonian Empire. The Persians had then conquered Babylon and let the captives go home. The Jews could return to Jerusalem and worship their God.

But things were different now. The people were different. Now they were called Jews, not Israelites. Many of them spoke primarily Aramaic, not the old Hebrew. They used to be rural people; now they lived in towns.

Instead of being an independent nation, the returning Jews were more like a religious community. The people who had stayed behind resented the exiles for wanting their land back. And Jerusalem, which the Babylonians had destroyed, lay in ruins. So, despite the excitement, home wasn't the way they had left it.

The books of Ezra and Nehemiah (p.443), which were originally one book, tell the story of these returning exiles. In general, the books focus on the rebuilding of the Temple (Ezra 1—7), the preserving of the faith (Ezra 8—10) and the rebuilding of Jerusalem's walls (Nehemiah).

Through it all, we often see people wanting to give up. We see leaders challenging them and renewing their energy. And we see the people's faithfulness even when the obstacles seem impossible. Their story can be a comfort and a challenge to help us to stick with our faith in tough times.

Where?

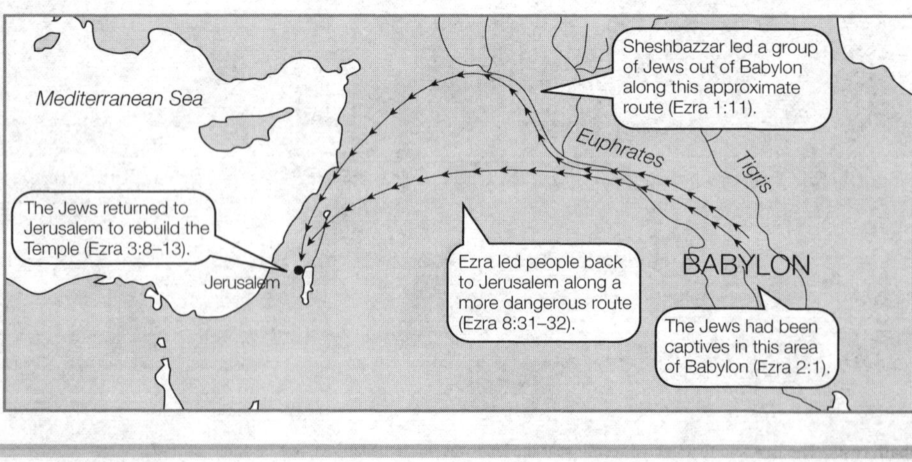

Cyrus Helps the Captives Return

1 In the first year Cyrus was king of Persia, the
LORD caused Cyrus to send an announce-
ment to his whole kingdom and to put it in writ-
ing. This happened so the LORD's message spoken
by Jeremiah would come true. He wrote:

2This is what Cyrus king of Persia says:
The LORD, the God of heaven, has given
all the kingdoms of the earth to me, and
he has appointed me to build a Temple[d]
for him at Jerusalem in Judah. 3May God
be with all of you who are his people.
You are free to go to Jerusalem in Judah
and build the Temple of the LORD, the
God of Israel, who is in Jerusalem. 4Those
who stay behind, wherever they live,
should support those who want to go.
Give them silver and gold, supplies and
cattle, and special gifts for the Temple of
God in Jerusalem.

Sidelight King Cyrus's decree granting religious freedom to the Jews apparently wasn't a special privilege for them alone (Ezra 1:4). Archaeologists have unearthed The Cyrus Cylinder, which reveals that Cyrus's policy extended to all people who had been taken captive by Babylon.

5Then the family leaders of Judah and Benja-
min and the priests and Levites got ready to go
to Jerusalem—everyone God had caused to
want to go to Jerusalem to build the Temple of
the LORD. 6All their neighbours helped them,
giving them things made of silver and gold,
along with supplies, cattle, valuable gifts and
special gifts for the Temple. 7Also, King Cyrus
brought out the bowls and pans that belonged
in the Temple of the LORD, which Nebuchadnez-
zar had taken from Jerusalem and put in the
temple of his own god. 8Cyrus king of Persia
had Mithredath the treasurer bring them and
count them out for Sheshbazzar, the prince of
Judah.
9He listed 30 gold dishes, 1,000 silver dishes,
29 pans, 10 30 gold bowls, 410 matching silver
bowls and 1,000 other pieces.
11There was a total of 5,400 pieces of gold
and silver. Sheshbazzar brought all these things
along when the captives went from Babylon to
Jerusalem.

Sidelight When Cyrus sent the Jews back to Jerusalem, he had them take 30 gold dishes, 1,000 silver dishes, 29 silver pans, 30 gold bowls and 410 silver bowls (Ezra 1:9) – valuables that had been taken from the Temple in Jerusalem by King Nebuchadnezzar when he destroyed it (2 Kings 25:8–17, p.370). Hope he sent a dishwasher too!

The Captives who Returned

2 These are the people of the area who re-
turned from captivity, whom Nebuchadnez-
zar king of Babylon had taken away to Babylon.
They returned to Jerusalem and Judah, each
going back to his own town. 2These people re-
turned with Zerubbabel, Jeshua, Nehemiah,
Seraiah, Reelaiah, Mordecai, Bilshan, Mispar,
Bigvai, Rehum and Baanah.

Sidelight Not all the Jews returned from exile when the Persians let them leave (Ezra 2:1–2). According to Babylonian records, some Jews had become prominent bankers, business people and government officials in Babylon.

These are the people from Israel: 3the
descendants[d] of Parosh—2,172; 4the descen-
dants of Shephatiah—372; 5the descendants of
Arah—775; 6the descendants of Pahath-Moab
(through the family of Jeshua and Joab)—2,812;
7the descendants of Elam—1,254; 8the descen-
dants of Zattu—945; 9the descendants of Zac-
cai—760; 10the descendants of Bani—642; 11the
descendants of Bebai—623; 12the descendants
of Azgad—1,222; 13the descendants of
Adonikam—666; 14the descendants of Bigvai—
2,056; 15the descendants of Adin—454; 16the
descendants of Ater (through the family of
Hezekiah)—98; 17the descendants of Bezai—
323; 18the descendants of Jorah—112; 19the de-
scendants of Hashum—223; 20the descendants
of Gibbar—95.
21These are the people from the towns:
of Bethlehem—123; 22of Netophah—56;
23of Anathoth—128; 24of Azmaveth—42; 25of
Kiriath Jearim, Kephirah and Beeroth—743; 26of
Ramah and Geba—621; 27of Michmash—122;
28of Bethel and Ai—223; 29of Nebo—52; 30of
Magbish—156; 31of the other town of Elam—
1,254; 32of Harim—320; 33of Lod, Hadid and
Ono—725; 34of Jericho—345; 35of Senaah—
3,630.
36These are the priests: the descendants of Je-
daiah (through the family of Jeshua)—973; 37the

descendants of Immer—1,052; 38 the descendants of Pashhur—1,247; 39 the descendants of Harim—1,017.

40 These are the Levites: the descendants of Jeshua and Kadmiel (through the family of Hodaviah)—74.

41 These are the singers: the descendants of Asaph—128.

42 These are the gatekeepers of the Temple:[d] the descendants of Shallum, Ater, Talmon, Akkub, Hatita and Shobai—139.

43 These are the Temple servants: the descendants of Ziha, Hasupha, Tabbaoth, 44 Keros, Siaha, Padon, 45 Lebanah, Hagabah, Akkub, 46 Hagab, Shalmai, Hanan, 47 Giddel, Gahar, Reaiah, 48 Rezin, Nekoda, Gazzam, 49 Uzza, Paseah, Besai, 50 Asnah, Meunim, Nephussim, 51 Bakbuk, Hakupha, Harhur, 52 Bazluth, Mehida, Harsha, 53 Barkos, Sisera, Temah, 54 Neziah and Hatipha.

55 These are the descendants of the servants of Solomon: the descendants of Sotai, Hassophereth, Peruda, 56 Jaala, Darkon, Giddel, 57 Shephatiah, Hattil, Pokereth-Hazzebaim and Ami.

58 The Temple servants and the descendants of the servants of Solomon numbered 392.

59 Some people came to Jerusalem from the towns of Tel Melah, Tel Harsha, Kerub, Addon and Immer, but they could not prove that their ancestors came from Israel. 60 They were the descendants of Delaiah, Tobiah and Nekoda—652.

61 Also these priests: the descendants of Hobaiah, Hakkoz and Barzillai, who had married a daughter of Barzillai from Gilead and was called by her family name.

62 These people searched for their family records but could not find them. So they could not be priests, because they were thought to be unclean. 63 The governor ordered them not to eat any of the food offered to God until a priest had settled this matter by using the Urim and Thummim.[d]

64 The total number of those who returned was 42,360. 65 This is not counting their 7,337 male and female servants and the 200 male and female singers they had with them. 66 They had 736 horses, 245 mules, 67 435 camels and 6,720 donkeys.

68 When they arrived at the Temple of the LORD in Jerusalem, some of the leaders of families gave offerings to rebuild the Temple of God on the same site as before. 69 They gave as much as they could to the treasury to rebuild the Temple—about 500 kilogrammes of gold, about 2,800 kilogrammes of silver and 100 pieces of clothing for the priests.

70 All the Israelites settled in their home towns. The priests, Levites, singers, gatekeepers and Temple servants, along with some of the other people, settled in their own towns as well.

Rebuilding the Altar

3 In the seventh month, after the Israelites were settled in their home towns, they met together in Jerusalem. 2 Then Jeshua son of Jozadak and his fellow priests joined Zerubbabel son of Shealtiel and began to build the altar of the God of Israel where they could offer burnt offerings, just as it is written in the Teachings of Moses, the man of God. 3 Even though they were afraid of the people living around them, they built the altar where it had been before. And they offered burnt offerings on it to the LORD morning and evening. 4 Then, to obey what was written, they celebrated the Feast[d] of Shelters. They offered the right number of sacrifices for each day of the festival. 5 After the Feast of Shelters, they had regular sacrifices every day, as well as sacrifices for the New Moon[d] and all the festivals commanded by the LORD. Also there were special offerings brought as gifts to the LORD. 6 On the first day of the seventh month they began to bring burnt offerings to the LORD, but the foundation of the LORD's Temple[d] had not yet been laid.

Rebuilding the Temple

7 Then they gave money to the bricklayers and carpenters. They also gave food, wine and oil to the cities of Sidon and Tyre so they would float cedar logs from Lebanon to the seacoast town of Joppa. Cyrus king of Persia had given permission for this.

8 In the second month of the second year after their arrival at the Temple[d] of God in Jerusalem, Zerubbabel son of Shealtiel, Jeshua son of Jozadak, their fellow priests and Levites, and all who had returned from captivity to Jerusalem began to work. They chose Levites 20 years old and older to be in charge of the building of the Temple of the LORD. 9 These men were in charge of the work of building the Temple of God: Jeshua and his sons and brothers; Kadmiel and his sons who were the descendants of Hodaviah; and the sons of Henadad and their sons and brothers. They were all Levites.

10 The builders finished laying the foundation of the Temple of the LORD. Then the priests, dressed in their robes, stood with their trumpets, and the Levites, the sons of Asaph, stood with their cymbals. They all took their places and praised the LORD just as David king of Israel had said to do. 11 With praise and thanksgiving, they sang to the LORD:

"He is good;
his love for Israel continues for ever."

And then all the people shouted loudly, "Praise the LORD! The foundation of his Temple has been laid." 12 But many of the older priests, Levites and

family leaders who had seen the first Temple
cried when they saw the foundation of this Tem-
ple. Most of the other people were shouting with
joy. 13The people made so much noise it could be
heard far away, and no one could tell the differ-
ence between the joyful shouting and the sad
crying.

Enemies of the Rebuilding

4 When the enemies of the people of Judah
and Benjamin heard that the returned
captives were building a Temple[d] for the LORD,
the God of Israel, 2they came to Zerubbabel and
the leaders of the families. The enemies said,
"Let us help you build, because we are like
you and want to worship your God. We have
been offering sacrifices to him since the time of
Esarhaddon king of Assyria, who brought us
here."
3But Zerubbabel, Jeshua and the leaders of Is-
rael answered, "You will not help us build a Tem-
ple to our God. We will build it ourselves for the
LORD, the God of Israel, as King Cyrus, the king of
Persia, commanded us to do."
4Then the people around them tried to discour-
age the people of Judah by making them afraid to
build. 5Their enemies hired others to delay the
building plans during the time Cyrus was king of
Persia. And it continued to the time Darius was
king of Persia.

More Problems for the Builders

6When Xerxes first became king, those enem-
ies wrote a letter against the people of Judah and
Jerusalem.
7When Artaxerxes became king of Persia, Bish-
lam, Mithredath, Tabeel and those with them
wrote a letter to Artaxerxes. It was written in the
Aramaic language and translated.
8Rehum the governor and Shimshai the gov-
ernor's secretary wrote a letter against Jerusalem
to Artaxerxes the king. It said:

Sidelight The Old Testament was originally written in Hebrew, right? Well, not all of it. Ezra 4:8—6:18 and 7:12–26 were written in Aramaic, which was the language Jesus would speak centuries later. Three other Old Testament passages were also written in Aramaic (Genesis 31:47, p.37; Jeremiah 10:11, p.729; and Daniel 2:4—7:28, p.834).

9This letter is from Rehum the governor,
Shimshai the secretary and their fellow
workers—the judges and important offi-
cers over the men who came from Tripolis,
Persia, Erech and Babylon, the Elamite
people of Susa, 10and those whom the
great and honourable Ashurbanipal forced
out of their countries and settled in the
city of Samaria and in other places of the
west of the Euphrates River.

11(This is a copy of the letter they sent to
Artaxerxes.)

To King Artaxerxes.
From your servants who live west of the
Euphrates River.

12King Artaxerxes, you should know that
the Jewish people who came to us from you
have gone to Jerusalem to rebuild that evil
city that refuses to obey. They are fixing the
walls and repairing the foundations of the
buildings.
13Now, King Artaxerxes, you should
know that if Jerusalem is built and its walls
are fixed, Jerusalem will not pay taxes of any
kind. Then the amount of money your gov-
ernment collects will be less. 14Since we
must be loyal to the government, we don't
want to see the king dishonoured. So we are
writing to let the king know. 15We suggest
you search the records of the kings who
ruled before you. You will find out that the
city of Jerusalem refuses to obey and makes
trouble for kings and areas controlled by Per-
sia. Since long ago it has been a place where
disobedience has started. That is why it was
destroyed. 16We want you to know, King
Artaxerxes, that if this city is rebuilt and its
walls fixed, you will be left with nothing
west of the Euphrates River.

17King Artaxerxes sent this answer:

To Rehum the governor and Shimshai the
secretary, to all their fellow workers living in
Samaria, and to those in other places west of
the Euphrates River.

Greetings.
18The letter you sent to us has been trans-
lated and read to me. 19I ordered the records
to be searched, and it was done. We found
that Jerusalem has a history of disobedience
to kings and has been a place of problems
and trouble. 20Jerusalem has had powerful
kings who have ruled over the whole area
west of the Euphrates River, and taxes of all
kinds have been paid to them. 21Now, give
an order for those men to stop work. The
city of Jerusalem will not be rebuilt until I
say so. 22Make sure you do this, because if
they continue, it will hurt the government.

[23]A copy of the letter that King Artaxerxes sent was read to Rehum and Shimshai the secretary and the others. Then they quickly went to the Jewish people in Jerusalem and forced them to stop building.

[24]So the work on the Temple[d] of God in Jerusalem stopped until the second year Darius was king of Persia.

Tattenai's Letter to Darius

5 The prophets Haggai and Zechariah, a descendant[d] of Iddo, prophesied[d] to the Jewish people in Judah and Jerusalem in the name of the God of Israel, who was over them. [2]Then Zerubbabel son of Shealtiel and Jeshua son of Jozadak started working again to rebuild the Temple[d] of God in Jerusalem. And the prophets of God were there, helping them.

[3]At that time Tattenai, who was the governor west of the Euphrates River, and Shethar-Bozenai and their fellow workers went to the Jewish people and asked, "Who gave you permission to rebuild this Temple and fix these walls?" [4]They also asked, "What are the names of the men working on this building?" [5]But their God was watching over the elders of the Jewish people. The builders were not stopped until a report could go to King Darius and his written answer could be received.

[6]This is a copy of the letter that was sent to King Darius by Tattenai, who was the governor of west of the Euphrates River, Shethar-Bozenai and the other important officers of west of the Euphrates River. [7]This is what was said in the report they sent to him:

To King Darius.

Greetings. May you have peace.

[8]King Darius, you should know that we went to the district of Judah where the Temple of the great God is. The people are building that Temple with large stones and they are putting timbers in the walls. They are working very hard and are building very fast.

[9]We asked their elders, "Who gave you permission to rebuild this Temple and these walls?" [10]We also asked for their names, and we wrote down the names of their leaders so you would know who they are.

[11]This is the answer they gave to us: "We are the servants of the God of heaven and earth. We are rebuilding the Temple that a great king of Israel built and finished many years ago. [12]But our ancestors made the God of heaven angry, so he handed them over to Nebuchadnezzar king of Babylon, who destroyed this Temple and took the people to Babylon as captives.

[13]"Later, in the first year Cyrus was king of Babylon, he gave a special order for this Temple to be rebuilt. [14]Cyrus brought out from the temple in Babylon the gold and silver bowls and pans that came from the Temple of God. Nebuchadnezzar had taken them from the Temple in Jerusalem and had put them in the temple in Babylon.

"Then King Cyrus gave them to Sheshbazzar, his appointed governor. [15]Cyrus said to him, 'Take these gold and silver bowls and pans, and put them back in the Temple in Jerusalem and rebuild the Temple of God where it was.' [16]So Sheshbazzar came and laid the foundations of the Temple of God in Jerusalem. From that day until now the work has been going on, but it is not yet finished."

[17]Now, if the king wishes, let a search be made in the royal records of Babylon. See if King Cyrus gave an order to rebuild this Temple in Jerusalem. Then let the king write to us and tell us what he has decided.

The Order of Darius

6 So King Darius gave an order to search the records kept in the treasury in Babylon. [2]A scroll was found in Ecbatana, the capital city of Media. This is what was written on it:

Note:

[3]King Cyrus gave an order about the Temple[d] of God in Jerusalem in the first year he was king. This was the order:

"Let the Temple be rebuilt as a place to present sacrifices. Let its foundations be laid; it should be 30 metres high and 30 metres wide. [4]It must have three layers of large stones and then one layer of timbers. The costs should be paid from the king's treasury. [5]The gold and silver utensils from the Temple of God should be put back in their places. Nebuchadnezzar took them from the Temple in Jerusalem and brought them to Babylon, but they are to be put back in the Temple of God in Jerusalem."

[6]Now then, Tattenai, governor of west of the Euphrates River, Shethar-Bozenai and all the officers of that area, stay away from there. [7]Do not bother the work on that Temple of God. Let the governor of the Jewish people and the Jewish elders rebuild this Temple where it was before.

[8]Also, I order you to do this for those elders of the Jewish people who are building this Temple: the cost of the building is to be fully paid from the royal treasury, from taxes collected from west of the Euphrates River.

Do this so the work will not stop. [9]Give
those people anything they need—young
bulls, rams or lambs for burnt offerings to
the God of heaven, or wheat, salt, wine or
olive oil. Give the priests in Jerusalem any-
thing they ask for every day without fail.
[10]Then they may offer sacrifices pleasing to
the God of heaven, and they may pray for
the life of the king and his sons.
[11]Also, I give this order: if anyone changes
this order, a wooden beam is to be pulled
from his house and driven through his body.
Because of his crime, make his house a pile

> **Sidelight** King Darius didn't like his orders to be questioned. If you changed what he said, a wooden beam was to be taken from your house and driven through your body (Ezra 6:11). According to other sources, Darius impaled 3,000 Babylonians when he captured their city.

of ruins. [12]God has chosen Jerusalem as the
place he is to be worshipped. May he punish
any king or person who tries to change this
order and destroy this Temple.

I, Darius, have given this order. Let it be
obeyed quickly and carefully.

Completion of the Temple

[13]So, Tattenai, the governor west of the Eu-
phrates River, Shethar-Bozenai and their fellow
workers carried out King Darius' order quickly
and carefully. [14]The Jewish elders continued to
build and were successful because of the preach-
ing of Haggai the prophet[d] and Zechariah, a des-
cendant of Iddo. They finished building the
Temple[d] as the God of Israel had commanded
and as kings Cyrus, Darius and Artaxerxes of
Persia had ordered. [15]The Temple was finished
on the third day of the month of Adar in the
sixth year Darius was king.
[16]Then the people of Israel celebrated and gave
the Temple to God to honour him. Everybody
was happy: the priests, the Levites and the rest of
the Jewish people who had returned from captiv-
ity. [17]They gave the Temple to God by offering
100 bulls, 200 rams and 400 lambs as sacrifices.
And as an offering to forgive the sins of all Israel,
they offered twelve male goats, one goat for each
tribe[d] in Israel. [18]Then they put the priests and
the Levites into their separate groups. Each group
had a certain time to serve God in the Temple at
Jerusalem as it is written in the Book of Moses.

The Passover is Celebrated

[19]The Jewish people who returned from capti-
vity celebrated the Passover[d] on the fourteenth
day of the first month. [20]The priests and Levites
had made themselves clean.[d] Then the Levites
killed the Passover lambs for all the people who
had returned from captivity, for their relatives
the priests and for themselves. [21]So all the people
of Israel who returned from captivity ate the
Passover lamb. So did the people who had given
up the unclean ways of their non-Jewish neigh-
bours in order to worship the LORD, the God of
Israel. [22]For seven days they celebrated the
Feast[d] of Unleavened Bread in a very joyful way.
The LORD had made them happy by changing the
mind of the king of Assyria so that he helped
them in the work on the Temple of the God of
Israel.

Ezra Comes to Jerusalem

7 After these things[n] during the rule of Artax-
erxes king of Persia, Ezra came up from Bab-
ylon. Ezra was the son of Seraiah, the son of
Azariah, the son of Hilkiah, [2]the son of Shallum,
the son of Zadok, the son of Ahitub, [3]the son of
Amariah, the son of Azariah, the son of Meraioth,
[4]the son of Zerahiah, the son of Uzzi, the son of
Bukki, [5]the son of Abishua, the son of Phinehas,
the son of Eleazar, the son of Aaron the high
priest. [6]This Ezra came to Jerusalem from Bab-
ylon. He was a teacher and knew well the Teach-
ings of Moses that had been given by the LORD,
the God of Israel. Ezra received everything he
asked for from the king, because the LORD his God
was helping him. [7]In the seventh year of King
Artaxerxes more Israelites came to Jerusalem.
Among them were priests, Levites, singers, gate-
keepers and Temple[d] servants.
[8]Ezra arrived in Jerusalem in the fifth month of
Artaxerxes' seventh year as king. [9]Ezra had left
Babylon on the first day of the first month, and he
arrived in Jerusalem on the first day of the fifth

> **Sidelight** Ezra's journey from Babylon to Jerusalem was about 1,440 km – about two days' driving. But because there were no motorways or cars, the trip took about four months (Ezra 7:9).

month, because God was helping him. [10]Ezra had
worked hard to know and obey the Teachings of
the LORD and to teach his rules and commands to
the Israelites.

After these things There is a time period of about 60 years between chapters six and seven.

Artaxerxes' Letter to Ezra

11King Artaxerxes had given a letter to Ezra, a
priest and teacher who taught about the com-
mands and laws the LORD gave Israel. This is a
copy of the letter:

Sidelight Ezra is known as the "Father of Judaism" for his role in preserving the faith (Ezra 7:10). Tradition credits him with dictating from memory 94 books (including 24 in the Old Testament) that might otherwise have been lost or burned during the Exile.

12From Artaxerxes, king of kings, to Ezra
the priest, a teacher of the Law of the God
of heaven.

Greetings.
13Now I give this order: Any Israelite in
my kingdom who wishes may go with you
to Jerusalem, including priests and
Levites. 14Ezra, you are sent by the king
and the seven people who advise him to
ask how Judah and Jerusalem are obeying
the Law of your God, which you are car-
rying with you. 15Also take with you the
silver and gold that the king and those
who advise him have given freely to the
God of Israel, whose Temple[d] is in
Jerusalem. 16Also take the silver and gold
you receive from the area of Babylon.
Take the offerings the Israelites and their
priests have given as gifts for the Temple
of your God in Jerusalem. 17With this
money buy bulls, rams and lambs, and the
grain offerings and drink offerings that go
with those sacrifices. Then sacrifice them
on the altar in the Temple of your God in
Jerusalem.
18You and your fellow Jews may spend
the silver and gold left over as you want
and as God wishes. 19Take to the God of
Jerusalem all the utensils for worship in
the Temple of your God, 20which we have
given you. Use the royal treasury to pay
for anything else you need for the Temple
of your God.
21Now I, King Artaxerxes, give this
order to all the men in charge of the treas-
ury of west of the Euphrates River: Give
Ezra, a priest and a teacher of the Law of
the God of heaven, whatever he asks for.
22Give him up to 3.5 tonnes of silver, 10
tonnes of wheat, 2,000 litres of wine and
2,000 litres of olive oil. And give him as
much salt as he wants. 23Carefully give
him whatever the God of heaven wants
for the Temple of the God of heaven. We
do not want God to be angry with the
king and his sons. 24Remember, you must
not make these people pay taxes of any
kind: priests, Levites, singers, gatekeep-
ers, Temple servants and other workers in
this Temple of God.
25And you, Ezra, use the wisdom you
have from your God to choose judges and
lawmakers to rule the Jewish people, west
of the Euphrates River. They know the
laws of your God, and you may teach any-
one who does not know them. 26Whoever
does not obey the law of your God or of
the king must be punished. He will be
killed, or sent away, or have his property
taken away, or be put in jail.

27Praise the LORD, the God of our ancestors. He
caused the king to want to honour the Temple of
the LORD in Jerusalem. 28The LORD has shown me,
Ezra, his love in the presence of the king, those
who advise the king and the royal officers. Be-
cause the LORD my God was helping me, I had
courage, and I gathered the leaders of Israel to
return with me.

Leaders Who Returned with Ezra

8 These are the leaders of the family groups
and those who were listed with them who
came back with me from Babylon during the rule
of King Artaxerxes.
2From the descendants[d] of Phinehas: Gershom.
From the descendants of Ithamar: Daniel.
From the descendants of David: Hattush 3of
the descendants of Shecaniah.
From the descendants of Parosh: Zechariah,
with 150 men.
4From the descendants of Pahath-Moab: Elie-
hoenai son of Zerahiah, with 200 men.
5From the descendants of Zattu: Shecaniah son
of Jahaziel, with 300 men.
6From the descendants of Adin: Ebed son of
Jonathan, with 50 men.
7From the descendants of Elam: Jeshaiah son of
Athaliah, with 70 men.
8From the descendants of Shephatiah: Zeba-
diah son of Michael, with 80 men.
9From the descendants of Joab: Obadiah son of
Jehiel, with 218 men.
10From the descendants of Bani: Shelomith son
of Josiphiah, with 160 men.
11From the descendants of Bebai: Zechariah
son of Bebai, with 28 men.
12From the descendants of Azgad: Johanan son
of Hakkatan, with 110 men.

13From the descendants of Adonikam, these
were the last ones: Eliphelet, Jeuel and Shemaiah,
with 60 men.
14From the descendants of Bigvai: Uthai and
Zaccur, with 70 men.

The Return to Jerusalem

15I called all those people together at the
canal that flows towards Ahava, where we
camped for three days. I checked all the people
and the priests, but I did not find any Levites.
16So I called these leaders: Eliezer, Ariel, Shema-
iah, Elnathan, Jarib, Elnathan, Nathan,
Zechariah and Meshullam. And I called Joiarib
and Elnathan, who were teachers. 17I sent these
men to Iddo, the leader at Casiphia, and told
them what to say to Iddo and his relatives, who
are the Temple[d] servants in Casiphia. I sent
them to bring servants to us for the Temple of
our God. 18Our God was helping us, so Iddo's
relatives gave us Sherebiah, a wise man from
the descendants of Mahli son of Levi, who was
the son of Israel. And they brought Sherebiah's
sons and brothers, for a total of eighteen men.
19And they brought to us Hashabiah and Jesha-
iah from the descendants of Merari, and his
brothers and nephews. In all there were 20
men. 20They also brought 220 of the Temple ser-
vants, a group David and the officers had set up
to help the Levites. All of those men were listed
by name.
21There by the Ahava Canal, I announced we
would all give up eating and humble ourselves
before our God. We would ask God for a safe
trip for ourselves, our children and all our pos-
sessions. 22I was ashamed to ask the king for sol-
diers and horsemen to protect us from enemies
on the road. We had said to the king, "Our God
helps everyone who obeys him, but he is very
angry with all who reject him." 23So we gave up
eating and prayed to our God about our trip,
and he answered our prayers.
24Then I chose twelve of the priests who
were leaders, Sherebiah, Hashabiah and ten of
their relatives. 25I weighed the offering of silver
and gold and the utensils given for the Temple
of our God, and I gave them to the twelve
priests I had chosen. The king, the people who
advised him, his officers and all the Israelites
there with us had given these things for the
Temple. 26I weighed out and gave them about
22 tonnes of silver, about 14 tonnes of silver ob-
jects and about 14 tonnes of gold. 27I gave them
20 gold bowls that weighed about 8.5 kilo-
grammes and two fine pieces of polished bronze
that were as valuable as gold.
28Then I said to the priests, "You and these
utensils belong to the LORD for his service. The
silver and gold are gifts to the LORD, the God of
your ancestors. 29Guard these things carefully.
In Jerusalem, weigh them in front of the leading
priests, Levites and the leaders of the family
groups of Israel in the rooms of the Temple of
the LORD." 30So the priests and Levites accepted
the silver, the gold and the utensils that had
been weighed to take them to the Temple of our
God in Jerusalem.
31On the twelfth day of the first month we left
the Ahava Canal and started towards Jerusalem.
Our God helped us and protected us from enem-
ies and robbers along the way. 32Finally we ar-
rived in Jerusalem where we rested three days.
33On the fourth day we weighed out the sil-
ver, the gold and the utensils in the Temple of
our God. We handed them to the priest Mere-
moth son of Uriah. Eleazar son of Phinehas was
with him, as were the Levites Jozabad son of
Jeshua and Noadiah son of Binnui. 34We
checked everything by number and by weight,
and the total weight was written down.
35Then the captives who returned made
burnt offerings to the God of Israel. They sacri-
ficed twelve bulls for all Israel, 96 rams and 77
lambs. For a sin offering there were twelve male
goats. All this was a burnt offering to the LORD.
36They took King Artaxerxes' orders to the royal
officers and to the governors, west of the Eu-
phrates River. Then these men gave help to the
people and the Temple of God.

Ezra's Prayer

9 After these things had been done, the lead-
ers came to me and said, "Ezra, the Israel-
ites, including the priests and Levites, have not
kept themselves separate from the people
around us. Those neighbours do evil things, as
the Canaanites, Hittites, Perizzites, Jebusites,
Ammonites, Moabites, Egyptians and Amorites
did. 2The Israelite men and their sons have mar-
ried these women. They have mixed the people
who belong to God with the people around
them. The leaders and officers of Israel have led
the rest of the Israelites to do this unfaithful
thing."
3When I heard this, I angrily tore my robe and
coat, pulled hair from my head and beard, and sat

Sidelight When Ezra got upset, he tore his clothes and pulled hair out of his head and beard – the only person to do that in the Bible (Ezra 9:3). Nehemiah had a less painful approach – for him, at least. He pulled out the hair of people at whom he was angry (Nehemiah 13:25, p.457).

down in shock. 4 Everyone who trembled in fear
at the word of the God of Israel gathered around
me because of the unfaithfulness of the captives
who had returned. I sat there in shock until the
evening sacrifice.
5 At the evening sacrifice I got up from where
I had shown my shame. My robe and coat were
torn, and I fell on my knees with my hands
spread out to the LORD my God. 6 I prayed, "My
God, I am too ashamed and embarrassed to lift up
my face to you, my God, because our sins are so
many. They are higher than our heads. Our guilt
even reaches up to the sky. 7 From the days of our
ancestors until now, our guilt has been great. Be-
cause of our sins, we, our kings and our priests
have been punished by the sword and captivity.
Foreign kings have taken away our things and
shamed us, even as it is today.
8 "But now, for a short time, the LORD our God
has been kind to us. He has let some of us come
back from captivity and has let us live in safety in
his holy place. And so our God gives us hope and
a little relief from our slavery. 9 Even though we
are slaves, our God has not left us. He caused the
kings of Persia to be kind to us and has given us
new life. We can rebuild the Temple[d] and repair
its ruins. And he has given us a wall to protect us
in Judah and Jerusalem.
10 "But now, our God, what can we say after
you have done all this? We have disobeyed your
commands 11 that you gave through your servants
the prophets.[d] You said, 'The land you are enter-
ing to own is ruined; the people living there have
spoiled it by the evil they do. Their evil filled the
land with uncleanness[d] from one end to the
other. 12 So do not let your daughters marry their
sons, and do not let their daughters marry your
sons. Do not wish for their peace or success.
Then you will be strong and eat the good things
of the land. Then you can leave this land to your
descendants[d] for ever.'
13 "What has happened to us is our own fault.
We have done evil things, and our guilt is great.
But you, our God, have punished us less than we
deserve; you have left a few of us alive. 14 We
should not again break your commands by allow-
ing marriages with these wicked people. If we
did, you would get angry enough to destroy us,

FORGIVENESS

An Unexpected Visitor

"The Pope has been shot!" These words echoed throughout the world on 13 May 1981. Pope John Paul II had been shot in the stomach by Mehmet Ali Agca.

It tooks hours of surgery and weeks of painful rehabilitation for the Pope to regain his health. Yet he survived and returned to his duties. The terrorist was captured and imprisoned. It seemed the end of a near-fatal story. But it wasn't.

Less than three years after the shooting, the Pope visited Agca in Rome's Rebibbia prison. Sitting in Agca's cell, John Paul held Agca's hand and spoke softly with him for twenty minutes.

What did the Pope say to the man who had tried to kill him? "I spoke to him as a brother whom I have pardoned, and who has my complete trust . . . I was able to meet my assailant and repeat to him the pardon I gave him immediately."

Pope John Paul II showed love to Mehmet Ali Agca by forgiving him. **Ezra 9:1–9** tells how God showed love to his people by forgiving them.

- Did Agca or the Israelites deserve the love and forgiveness they received? Why or why not?
- When has God forgiven you when you felt you didn't deserve it?

Consider . . .

- making a list of people who have offended you and then forgiving them in the same way that God has forgiven you.
- doing one loving thing for someone who it has been hard for you to love.

For more, see . . .

- Isaiah 1:18–20 (p.640)
- Romans 5:6–11 (p.1190)
- Matthew 6:9–15 (p.948)

and none of us would be left alive. 15LORD, God of
Israel, by your goodness a few of us are left alive
today. We admit that we are guilty and none of
us should be allowed to stand before you."

The People Confess Sin

10 As Ezra was praying and confessing and
crying and throwing himself down in
front of the Temple,[d] a large group of Israelite
men, women and children gathered around him
who were also crying loudly. 2Then Shecaniah
son of Jehiel the Elamite said to Ezra, "We have
been unfaithful to our God by marrying women
from the peoples around us. But even so, there is
still hope for Israel. 3Now let us make an agree-
ment before our God. We will send away all
these women and their children as you and those
who respect the commands of our God advise.
Let it be done to obey God's Teachings. 4Get up,
Ezra. You are in charge, and we will support you.
Have courage and do it."

5So Ezra got up and made the priests, Levites
and all the people of Israel promise to do what
was suggested; and they promised. 6Then
Ezra left the Temple and went to the room of
Jehohanan son of Eliashib. While Ezra was there,
he did not eat or drink, because he was still sad
about the unfaithfulness of the captives who had
returned.

7They sent out an order in Judah and Jeru-
salem for all the captives who had returned to
meet together in Jerusalem. 8Whoever did not
come to Jerusalem within three days would lose
his property and would no longer be a member of
the community of the returned captives. That
was the decision of the officers and elders.

9So within three days all the people of Judah
and Benjamin gathered in Jerusalem. It was the
twentieth day of the ninth month. All the people
were sitting in the open place in front of the Tem-
ple and were upset because of the meeting and
because it was raining. 10Ezra the priest stood up
and said to them, "You have been unfaithful and
have married non-Jewish women. You have
made Israel more guilty. 11Now, confess it to the
LORD, the God of your ancestors. Do his will and
separate yourselves from the people living around
you and from your non-Jewish wives."

12Then the whole group answered Ezra with a
loud voice, "Ezra, you're right! We must do what
you say. 13But there are many people here, and
it's the rainy season. We can't stand outside, and
this problem can't be solved in a day or two,
because we have sinned badly. 14Let our officers
make a decision for the whole group. Then
let everyone in our towns who has married a
non-Jewish woman meet with the elders and
judges of each town at a planned time, until the
hot anger of our God turns away from us."
15Only Jonathan son of Asahel, Jahzeiah son of
Tikvah, Meshullam and Shabbethai the Levite
were against the plan.

16So the returned captives did what was
suggested. Ezra the priest chose men who were
leaders of the family groups and named one
from each family division. On the first day of the
tenth month they sat down to study each case.
17By the first day of the first month, they dealt
with all the men who had married non-Jewish
women.

Those Guilty of Marrying Non-Jewish Women

18These are the descendants[d] of the priests
who had married foreign women:

From the descendants of Jeshua son of Jozadak
and Jeshua's brothers: Maaseiah, Eliezer, Jarib
and Gedaliah. 19(They all promised to divorce
their wives, and each one brought a ram from the
flock as a penalty offering.)

20From the descendants of Immer: Hanani and
Zebadiah.

21From the descendants of Harim: Maaseiah,
Elijah, Shemaiah, Jehiel and Uzziah.

22From the descendants of Pashhur: Elioenai,
Maaseiah, Ishmael, Nethanel, Jozabad and
Elasah.

23Among the Levites: Jozabad, Shimei, Kelaiah
(also called Kelita), Pethahiah, Judah and Eliezer.

24Among the singers: Eliashib.

Among the gatekeepers: Shallum, Telem and
Uri.

25And among the other Israelites, these mar-
ried non-Jewish women:

From the descendants of Parosh: Ramiah,
Izziah, Malkijah, Mijamin, Eleazar, Malkijah and
Benaiah.

26From the descendants of Elam: Mattaniah,
Zechariah, Jehiel, Abdi, Jeremoth and Elijah.

27From the descendants of Zattu: Elioenai, Elia-
shib, Mattaniah, Jeremoth, Zabad and Aziza.

28From the descendants of Bebai: Jehohanan,
Hananiah, Zabbai and Athlai.

29From the descendants of Bani: Meshullam,
Malluch, Adaiah, Jashub, Sheal and Jeremoth.

30From the descendants of Pahath-Moab: Adna,
Kelal, Benaiah, Maaseiah, Mattaniah, Bezalel,
Binnui and Manasseh.

31From the descendants of Harim: Eliezer, Ishi-
jah, Malkijah, Shemaiah, Shimeon, 32Benjamin,
Malluch and Shemariah.

33From the descendants of Hashum: Mattenai,
Mattattah, Zabad, Eliphelet, Jeremai, Manasseh
and Shimei.

34From the descendants of Bani: Maadai, Am-
ram, Uel, 35Benaiah, Bedeiah, Keluhi, 36Vaniah,

Meremoth, Eliashib, [37]Mattaniah, Mattenai and
Jaasu.
[38]From the descendants of Binnui: Shimei,
[39]Shelemiah, Nathan, Adaiah, [40]Macnadebai,
Shashai, Sharai, [41]Azarel, Shelemiah, Shemariah,
[42]Shallum, Amariah and Joseph.

[43]From the descendants of Nebo: Jeiel,
Mattithiah, Zabad, Zebina, Jaddai, Joel and
Benaiah.

[44]All these men had married non-Jewish
women, and some of them had children by these
wives.

Nehemiah

Why Read This Book:

- Understand the importance of acting on what you believe (Nehemiah 1—5).
- Recognise how serving God sometimes means standing against those who don't serve him (Nehemiah 6—7).
- See the life-changing effects of believing God's word (Nehemiah 8—13).

When?

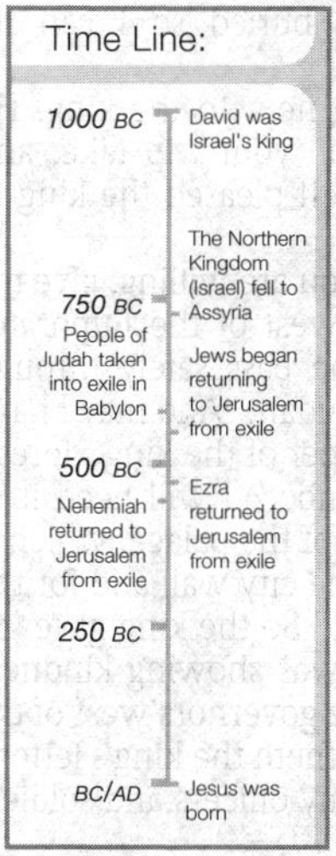

Behind the Scenes:

Can you imagine a member of the government resigning in order to walk across a desert and rebuild his home town? If you can, then you have a fairly good idea of what Nehemiah did.

He held a high office in the kingdom of Persia, which ruled almost all of the Near East. He had money and power.

Unlike many leaders in biblical times, whose positions led them away from God, Nehemiah was not really happy in his important position. The book of Nehemiah reads like a private diary. In it we learn that, although Nehemiah was a powerful leader, he had not let his position come between him and God.

In this book, we learn about what makes a good leader. We learn about Nehemiah's prayer life, organisational skills and dependence on God. We also learn that it isn't good enough for us to moan about how bad a situation is – we need to stand on our feet and take action. Only then will the world around us begin to change.

Where?

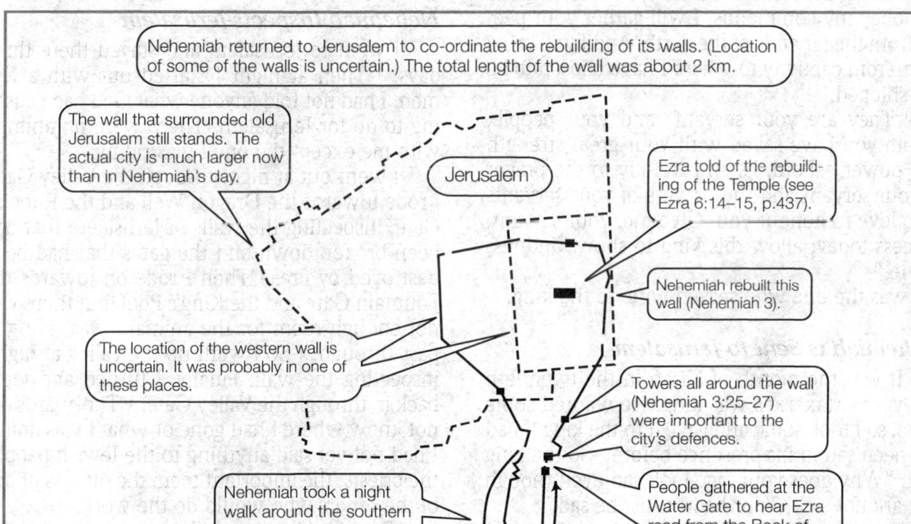

Nehemiah's Prayer

1 These are the words of Nehemiah son of Hacaliah.

In the month of Kislev in the twentieth year,[n] I, Nehemiah, was in the capital city of Susa. [2]One of my brothers named Hanani came with some other men from Judah. I asked them about Jerusalem and the Jewish people who lived through the captivity.

[3]They answered me, "Those who are left from the captivity are back in Judah, but they are in much trouble and are full of shame. The wall around Jerusalem is broken down, and its gates have been burnt."

[4]When I heard these things, I sat down and cried for several days. I was sad and ate nothing. I prayed to the God of heaven, [5]"LORD, God of heaven, you are the great God who is to be respected. You are loyal, and you keep your agreement with those who love you and obey your commands. [6]Look and listen carefully. Hear the prayer that I, your servant, am praying to you day and night for your servants, the Israelites. I confess the sins we Israelites have done against you. My father's family and I have sinned against you. [7]We have been wicked towards you and have not obeyed the commands, rules and laws you gave your servant Moses.

[8]"Remember what you taught your servant Moses, saying, 'If you are unfaithful, I will scatter you among the nations. [9]But if you return to me and obey my commands, I will gather your people from the far ends of the earth. And I will bring them from captivity to where I have chosen to be worshipped.'

[10]"They are your servants and your people, whom you have saved with your great strength and power. [11]Lord, listen carefully to the prayer of your servant and the prayers of your servants who love to honour you. Give me, your servant, success today; allow this king to show kindness to me."

I was the one who served wine to the king.

Nehemiah is Sent to Jerusalem

2 It was the month of Nisan in the twentieth year Artaxerxes was king. He wanted some wine, so I took some and gave it to the king. I had not been sad in his presence before. [2]So the king said, "Why does your face look sad even though you are not sick? Your heart must be sad."

Then I was very afraid. [3]I said to the king, "May the king live for ever! My face is sad because the city where my ancestors are buried lies in ruins, and its gates have been destroyed by fire."

[4]Then the king said to me, "What do you want?"

First I prayed to the God of heaven. [5]Then I answered the king, "If you are willing and if I have pleased you, send me to the city in Judah where my ancestors are buried so I can rebuild it."

[6]The queen was sitting next to the king. He asked me, "How long will your trip take, and when will you get back?" It pleased the king to send me, so I set a time.

[7]I also said to him, "If you are willing, give me letters for the governors west of the Euphrates River. Tell them to let me pass safely through their lands on my way to Judah. [8]And may I have a letter for Asaph, the keeper of the king's forest, telling him to give me timber? I will need it to make boards for the gates of the palace, which is by the Temple,[d] and for the city wall and for the house in which I will live." So the king gave me the letters, because God was showing kindness to me. [9]Then I went to the governors west of the Euphrates River and gave them the king's letters. The king had also sent army officers and soldiers on horses with me.

[10]When Sanballat the Horonite and Tobiah the Ammonite officer heard about this, they were upset that someone had come to help the Israelites.

Nehemiah Inspects Jerusalem

[11]I went to Jerusalem and stayed there three days. [12]Then at night I started out with a few men. I had not told anyone what God had caused me to do for Jerusalem. There were no animals with me except the one I was riding.

[13]I went out at night through the Valley Gate. I rode towards the Dragon Well and the Rubbish Gate, inspecting the walls of Jerusalem that had been broken down and the gates that had been destroyed by fire. [14]Then I rode on towards the Fountain Gate and the King's Pool, but there was not enough room for the animal I was riding to pass through. [15]So I went up the valley at night, inspecting the wall. Finally, I turned and went back in through the Valley Gate. [16]The guards did not know where I had gone or what I was doing. I had not yet said anything to the Jewish people, the priests, the important men, the officers or any of the others who would do the work.

[17]Then I said to them, "You can see the trouble we have here. Jerusalem is a pile of ruins, and its gates have been burned. Come, let's rebuild the

twentieth year This is probably referring to the twentieth year King Artaxerxes I ruled Persia.

wall of Jerusalem so we won't be full of shame
any longer." 18I also told them how God had been
kind to me and what the king had said to me.
Then they answered, "Let's start rebuilding."
So they began to work hard.
19But when Sanballat the Horonite, Tobiah the
Ammonite officer and Geshem the Arab heard
about it, they made fun of us and laughed at us.
They said, "What are you doing? Are you turning
against the king?"
20But I answered them, "The God of heaven
will give us success. We, his servants, will start
rebuilding, but you have no share, claim or me-
morial in Jerusalem."

Builders of the Wall

3 Eliashib the high priest and his fellow
priests went to work and rebuilt the Sheep
Gate. They gave it to the Lord's service and set
its doors in place. They worked as far as the
Tower of the Hundred and gave it to the Lord's
service. Then they went on to the Tower of
Hananel. 2Next to them, the men of Jericho
built part of the wall, and Zaccur son of Imri
built next to them.
3The sons of Hassenaah rebuilt the Fish Gate,
laying its boards and setting its doors, bolts and
bars in place. 4Meremoth son of Uriah, the son
of Hakkoz, made repairs next to them. Meshul-
lam son of Berekiah, the son of Meshezabel,
made repairs next to Meremoth. And Zadok son
of Baana made repairs next to Meshullam. 5The
men from Tekoa made repairs next to them, but
the leading men of Tekoa would not work under
their supervisors.
6Joiada son of Paseah and Meshullam son of
Besodeiah repaired the Old Gate. They laid
its boards and set its doors, bolts and bars
in place. 7Next to them, Melatiah from Gibeon,
other men from Gibeon and Mizpah, and Jadon
from Meronoth made repairs. These places
were ruled by the governor west of the
Euphrates River. 8Next to them, Uzziel son of
Harhaiah, a goldsmith, made repairs. And next
to him, Hananiah, a perfume maker, made
repairs. These men rebuilt Jerusalem as far as the
Broad Wall. 9The next part of the wall was
repaired by Rephaiah son of Hur, the ruler of half
of the district of Jerusalem. 10Next to him, Jeda-
iah son of Harumaph made repairs opposite his
own house. And next to him, Hattush son
of Hashabneiah made repairs. 11Malkijah son of
Harim and Hasshub son of Pahath-Moab
repaired another part of the wall and the Tower
of the Ovens. 12Next to them Shallum son of
Hallohesh, the ruler of half of the district of
Jerusalem, and his daughters made repairs.

Sidelight Did you know that women held building jobs in Bible times (Nehemiah 3:12)?

13Hanun and the people of Zanoah repaired
the Valley Gate, rebuilding it and setting its doors,
bolts and bars in place. They also repaired the
500 metres of the wall to the Rubbish Gate.
14Malkijah son of Recab, the ruler of the dis-
trict of Beth Hakkerem, repaired the Rubbish
Gate. He rebuilt that gate and set its doors, bolts
and bars in place.
15Shallun son of Col-Hozeh, the ruler of the
district of Mizpah, repaired the Fountain Gate.
He rebuilt it, put a roof over it and set its doors,
bolts and bars in place. He also repaired the wall
of the Pool of Siloam next to the King's Garden
all the way to the steps that went down from the
older part of the city. 16Next to Shallun was Ne-
hemiah[n] son of Azbuk, the ruler of half of the
district of Beth Zur. He made repairs opposite the
tombs of David and as far as the man-made pool
and the House of the Heroes.
17Next to him, the Levites made repairs,
working under Rehum son of Bani. Next to him,
Hashabiah, the ruler of half of the district of
Keilah, for his district. 18Next to him, Binnui
son of Henadad and his Levites made repairs.
Binnui was the ruler of the other half of the
district of Keilah. 19Next to them, Ezer son of
Jeshua, the ruler of Mizpah, repaired another
part of the wall. He worked across from the way
up to the storehouse for weapons, as far as the
bend. 20Next to him, Baruch son of Zabbai
worked hard on the wall that went from the
bend to the entrance to the house of Eliashib,
the high priest. 21Next to him, Meremoth son
of Uriah, the son of Hakkoz, repaired the
wall that went from the entrance to Eliashib's
house to the far end of it.
22Next to him worked the priests from the
surrounding area. 23Next to them, Benjamin and
Hasshub made repairs in front of their own
house. Next to them, Azariah son of Maaseiah,
the son of Ananiah, made repairs beside his own
house. 24Next to him, Binnui son of Henadad
repaired the wall that went from Azariah's house
to the bend and on to the corner. 25Palal son of
Uzai worked across from the bend and by the
tower on the upper palace, which is near the

Nehemiah This is a different Nehemiah from the one who wrote this book.

courtyard of the king's guard. Next to Palal,
Pedaiah son of Parosh made repairs. 26The Temple[d]
servants who lived on the hill of Ophel made
repairs as far as a point opposite the Water Gate.
They worked towards the east and the tower that
extends from the palace. 27Next to them, the peo-
ple of Tekoa repaired the wall from the great
tower that extends from the palace to the wall of
Ophel.
28The priests made repairs above the Horse
Gate, each working in front of his own house.
29Next to them, Zadok son of Immer made re-
pairs across from his own house. Next to him,
Shemaiah son of Shecaniah, the guard of the
East Gate, made repairs. 30Next to him, Hana-
niah son of Shelemiah, and Hanun, the sixth
son of Zalaph, made repairs on another part of
the wall. Next to them, Meshullam son of
Berekiah made repairs across from where he
lived. 31Next to him, Malkijah, one of the gold-
smiths, made repairs. He worked as far as the
house of the Temple servants and the traders,
which is across from the Inspection Gate, and as
far as the room above the corner of the wall.
32The goldsmiths and the traders made repairs
between the room above the corner of the wall
and the Sheep Gate.

Those Against the Rebuilding

4 When Sanballat heard we were rebuilding
the wall, he was very angry, even furious.
He made fun of the Jewish people. 2He said
to his friends and those with power in Samaria,
"What are these weak Jews doing? Will they
rebuild the wall? Will they offer sacrifices?
Can they finish it in one day? Can they bring
stones back to life from piles of rubbish and
ashes?"

Sidelight Rebuilding the walls may have seemed impossible to people who opposed the work (Nehemiah 4:2–3), partly because many of the stones had cracked when the city was burned by the Babylonians. The Jews did rebuild some existing walls with the old materials, but they had to build brand-new walls in some places.

3Tobiah the Ammonite, who was next to San-
ballat, said, "If a fox climbed up on the stone
wall they are building, it would break it down."
4I prayed, "Hear us, our God. We are hated.
Turn the insults of Sanballat and Tobiah back on
their own heads. Let them be captured and
stolen like valuables. 5Do not hide their guilt or
take away their sins so that you can't see them,
because they have insulted the builders."
6So we rebuilt the wall to half its height, be-
cause the people were willing to work.
7But Sanballat, Tobiah, the Arabs, the Ammon-
ites and the people from Ashdod were very angry
when they heard that the repairs to Jerusalem's
walls were continuing and that the holes in the
wall were being closed. 8So they all made plans to
come to Jerusalem and fight and stir up trouble.
9But we prayed to our God and appointed guards
to watch for them day and night.
10The people of Judah said, "The workers are
getting tired. There is so much rubbish we cannot
rebuild the wall."
11And our enemies said, "The Jews won't
know or see anything until we come among them
and kill them and stop the work."
12Then the Jewish people who lived near our
enemies came and told us ten times, "Every-
where you turn, the enemy will attack us." 13So
I put people behind the lowest places along the
wall—the open places—and I put families to-
gether with their swords, spears and bows.
14Then I looked around and stood up and said to
the important men, the leaders and the rest of the
people: "Don't be afraid of them. Remember the
Lord, who is great and powerful. Fight for your
brothers, your sons and daughters, your wives
and your homes."
15Then our enemies heard that we knew about
their plans and that God had ruined their plans.
So we all went back to the wall, each to his own
work.
16From that day on, half my people worked on
the wall. The other half was ready with spears,
shields, bows and armour. The officers stood be-
hind the people of Judah 17who were building the
wall. Those who carried materials did their work
with one hand and carried a weapon with the
other. 18Each builder wore his sword at his side
as he worked. The man who blew the trumpet to
warn the people stayed next to me.
19Then I said to the important men, the leaders
and the rest of the people, "This is a very big job.
We are spreading out along the wall so that we
are far apart. 20Wherever you hear the sound of
the trumpet, assemble there. Our God will fight
for us."
21So we continued to work with half the men
holding spears from sunrise till the stars came
out. 22At that time I also said to the people, "Let
every man and his helper stay inside Jerusalem at
night. They can be our guards at night and work-
men during the day." 23Neither I, my brothers,
my workers nor the guards with me ever took off
our clothes. Each person carried his weapon
even when he went for water.

Nehemiah Helps Poor People

5 The men and their wives complained loudly
against their fellow Jews. [2]Some of them were
saying, "We have many sons and daughters in
our families. To eat and stay alive, we need grain."
[3]Others were saying, "We are borrowing
money against our fields, vineyards and homes
to get grain because there is not much food."
[4]And still others were saying, "We are borrow-
ing money to pay the king's tax on our fields and
vineyards. [5]We are just like our fellow Jews, and
our sons are like their sons. But we have to sell
our sons and daughters as slaves. Some of our
daughters have already been sold. But there is
nothing we can do, because our fields and vine-
yards already belong to other people."
[6]When I heard their complaints about these
things, I was very angry. [7]After I thought about it,
I accused the important people and the leaders,
"You are charging your own brothers too much
interest." So I called a large meeting to deal with
them. [8]I said to them, "As much as possible, we
have bought freedom for our fellow Jews who
had been sold to foreigners. Now you are selling
your fellow Jews to us!" The leaders were quiet
and had nothing to say.
[9]Then I said, "What you are doing is not right.
Don't you fear God? Don't let our foreign enem-
ies shame us. [10]I, my brothers and my men are
also lending money and grain to the people. But
stop charging them so much for this. [11]Give back
their fields, vineyards, olive trees and houses
right now. Also give back the extra amount you
charged—the hundredth part of the money,
grain, new wine and oil."
[12]They said, "We will give it back and not
demand anything more from them. We will do
as you say."

HUNGER AND POVERTY

A Blanket of Love

Eleven-year-old Trevor Ferrell learned that there were people living on the streets of Philadelphia, in the USA – not far from his suburban home. Curious, he talked his parents into taking him there. Trevor got out of the car and gave a homeless person a blanket.

When Trevor returned home, he searched for extra blankets and clothing, and he convinced his parents to take him downtown again and again with deliveries.

He talked to people at his church, and they donated food, clothing and even a van to take things to the homeless.

Soon Trevor was in the newspapers, on television, even meeting the President of the USA! Trevor wanted to tell others what they could do to help.

Now there is a home in Philadelphia called "Trevor's Place". People can live and be fed there. Trevor Ferrell began by giving a little of himself and was able to challenge others to do the same. "One person can make a difference," Trevor says. "Just do what you can and follow your heart."

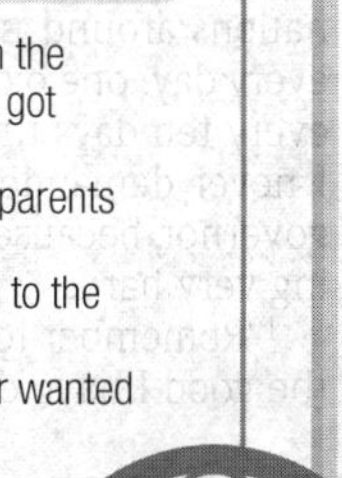

Nehemiah was also a person who made a difference for the poor. See how he helped them in **Nehemiah 5:1–11**.

- How did Nehemiah use his political power as governor of Judah to help the poor? How were Trevor's actions like Nehemiah's?
- How can you, like Trevor and Nehemiah, help people who are hungry?

Consider . . .

- helping low-income people in your community by giving non-perishable food to a food bank that distributes supplies to people in need.
- encouraging your government to take care of the needs of the poor by joining an organisation which speaks out for the poor.

For more, see . . .

- Doutoronomy 16:7 8 (p.170)
- James 2:1–9 (p.1348)
- Matthew 25:31–46 (p.987)

Then I called for the priests, and I made the important men and leaders take an oath to do what they had said. 13Also I shook out the folds of my robe and said, “In this way may God shake out everyone who does not keep his promise. May God shake him out of his house and out of the things that are his. Let that person be shaken out and emptied!”

Then the whole group said, “Amen,” and they praised the Lord. So the people did what they had promised.

14I was appointed governor in the land of Judah in the twentieth year of King Artaxerxes' rule. I was governor of Judah for twelve years, until his thirty-second year. During that time neither my brothers nor I ate the food that was allowed for a governor. 15But the governors before me had placed a heavy load on the people. They took about 40 pieces of silver from each person, along with food and wine. The governors' helpers before me also controlled the people, but I did not do that, because I feared God. 16I worked on the wall, as did all my men who were gathered there. We did not buy any fields.

17Also, I fed 150 Jewish people and officers at my table, as well as those who came from the nations around us. 18This is what was prepared every day: one ox, six good sheep, and birds. And every ten days there were all kinds of wine. But I never demanded the food that was allowed a governor, because the people were already working very hard.

19Remember to be kind to me, my God, for all the good I have done for these people.

More Problems for Nehemiah

6 Then Sanballat, Tobiah, Geshem the Arab and our other enemies heard that I had rebuilt the wall and that there was not one gap in it. But I had not yet set the doors in the gates. 2So Sanballat and Geshem sent me this message: “Come, Nehemiah, let's meet together in Kephirim on the plain of Ono.”

But they were planning to harm me. 3So I sent messengers to them with this answer: “I am doing a great work and I can't come down. I don't want the work to stop while I leave to meet you.” 4Sanballat and Geshem sent the same message to me four times, and each time I sent back the same answer.

5The fifth time Sanballat sent his helper to me with the message, and in his hand was an unsealed letter. 6This is what was written:

> A report is going around to all the nations, and Geshem says it is true, that you and the Jewish people are planning to turn against the king and that you are rebuilding the wall. They say you are going to be their king 7and that you have appointed prophets[d] to announce in Jerusalem: “There is a king of Judah!” The king will hear about this. So come, let's discuss this together.

8So I sent him back this answer: “Nothing you are saying is really happening. You are just making it up in your own mind.”

9Our enemies were trying to scare us, thinking, “They will get too weak to work. Then the wall will not be finished.”

But I prayed, “God, make me strong.”

10One day I went to the house of Shemaiah son of Delaiah, the son of Mehetabel. Shemaiah had to stay at home. He said, “Nehemiah, let's meet in the Temple[d] of God. Let's go inside the Temple and close the doors, because men are coming at night to kill you.”

11But I said, “Should a man like me run away? Should I run for my life into the Temple? I will not go.” 12I knew that God had not sent him but that Tobiah and Sanballat had paid him to prophesy[d] against me. 13They paid him to frighten me so I would do this and sin. Then they could give me a bad name to shame me.

14I prayed, “My God, remember Tobiah and Sanballat and what they have done. Also remember the prophetess Noadiah and the other prophets who have been trying to frighten me.”

Sidelight Building the wall around Jerusalem took 52 days (Nehemiah 6:15). Some archaeologists believe that the wall would have been more secure if Nehemiah had slowed the work down. Portions of the wall that have been uncovered show signs of the hasty construction. Nehemiah kept up the pace because his enemies were getting ready to attack (Nehemiah 4:11–24, p.446).

The Wall is Finished

15The wall of Jerusalem was completed on the twenty-fifth day of the month of Elul. It took 52 days to rebuild. 16When all our enemies heard about it and all the nations around us saw it, they were shamed. They then understood that the work had been done with the help of our God.

17Also in those days the important men of Judah sent many letters to Tobiah, and he answered them. 18Many Jewish people had promised to be faithful to Tobiah, because he was the son-in-law of Shecaniah son of Arah. And Tobiah's son

Jehohanan had married the daughter of Meshullam
son of Berekiah. 19These important men kept tell-
ing me about the good things Tobiah was doing,
and then they would tell Tobiah what I said
about him. So Tobiah sent letters to frighten me.
7 After the wall had been rebuilt and I had set
the doors in place, the gatekeepers, singers
and Levites were chosen. 2I put my brother Ha-
nani, along with Hananiah, the commander of
the palace, in charge of Jerusalem. Hananiah was
honest and feared God more than most people. 3I
said to them, "The gates of Jerusalem should not
be opened until the sun is hot. While the gate-
keepers are still on duty, have them shut and bolt
the doors. Appoint people who live in Jerusalem
as guards, and put some at guard posts and some
near their own houses."

Sidelight Though Nehemiah thought that Jerusalem was large (Nehemiah 7:4), by our standards it was very small – almost a village. The ancient city took up only 30 or 40 acres – only a short run around the perimeter.

The Captives Who Returned

4The city was large and roomy, but there were
few people in it, and the houses had not yet been
rebuilt. 5Then my God caused me to gather the
important men, the leaders and the common
people so I could register them by families. I
found the family history of those who had re-
turned first. This is what I found written there:
6These are the people of the area who returned
from captivity, whom Nebuchadnezzar king of
Babylon had taken away. They returned to Jeru-
salem and Judah, each going back to his own
town. 7These people returned with Zerubbabel,
Jeshua, Nehemiah, Azariah, Raamiah, Nahamani,
Mordecai, Bilshan, Mispereth, Bigvai, Nehum
and Baanah.
These are the people from Israel: 8the descend-
ants[d] of Parosh—2,172; 9the descendants of
Shephatiah—372; 10the descendants of Arah—
652; 11the descendants of Pahath-Moab (through
the family of Jeshua and Joab)—2,818; 12the des-
cendants of Elam—1,254; 13the descendants of
Zattu—845; 14the descendants of Zaccai—760;
15the descendants of Binnui—648; 16the des-
cendants of Bebai—628; 17the descendants of
Azgad—2,322; 18the descendants of Adoni-
kam—667; 19the descendants of Bigvai—2,067;
20the descendants of Adin—655; 21the descend-
ants of Ater (through Hezekiah)—98; 22the
descendants of Hashum—328; 23the descendants
of Bezai—324; 24the descendants of Hariph—
112; 25the descendants of Gibeon—95.
26These are the people from the towns of Beth-
lehem and Netophah—188; 27of Anathoth—
128; 28of Beth Azmaveth—42; 29of Kiriath Jea-
rim, Kephirah and Beeroth—743; 30of Ramah
and Geba—621; 31of Michmash—122; 32of
Bethel and Ai—123; 33of the other Nebo—52;
34of the other Elam—1,254; 35of Harim—320;
36of Jericho—345; 37of Lod, Hadid and Ono—
721; 38of Senaah—3,930.
39These are the priests: the descendants of Jed-
aiah (through the family of Jeshua)—973; 40the
descendants of Immer—1,052; 41the descend-
ants of Pashhur—1,247; 42the descendants of
Harim—1,017.
43These are the Levites: the descendants of
Jeshua (through Kadmiel through the family of
Hodaviah)—74.
44These are the singers: the descendants of
Asaph—148.
45These are the gatekeepers: the descendants
of Shallum, Ater, Talmon, Akkub, Hatita and
Shobai—138.
46These are the Temple[d] servants: the descend-
ants of Ziha, Hasupha, Tabbaoth, 47Keros, Sia,
Padon, 48Lebana, Hagaba, Shalmai, 49Hanan, Gid-
del, Gahar, 50Reaiah, Rezin, Nekoda, 51Gazzam,
Uzza, Paseah, 52Besai, Meunim, Nephussim,
53Bakbuk, Hakupha, Harhur, 54Bazluth, Mehida,
Harsha, 55Barkos, Sisera, Temah, 56Neziah and
Hatipha.
57These are the descendants of the servants of
Solomon: the descendants of Sotai, Sophereth,
Perida, 58Jaala, Darkon, Giddel, 59Shephatiah,
Hattil, Pokereth-Hazzebaim and Amon.
60The Temple servants and the descendants of
the servants of Solomon totalled 392 people.
61Some people came to Jerusalem from the
towns of Tel Melah, Tel Harsha, Kerub, Addon
and Immer, but they could not prove that their
ancestors came from Israel. Here are their names
and their number: 62the descendants of Delaiah,
Tobiah and Nekoda—642.
63And these priests could not prove that their
ancestors came from Israel: the descendants of
Hobaiah, Hakkoz and Barzillai. (He had married
a daughter of Barzillai from Gilead and was called
by her family name.)
64These people searched for their family
records, but they could not find them. So they
could not be priests, because they were thought
to be unclean.[d] 65The governor ordered them not
to eat any of the holy food until a priest settled
this matter by using the Urim and Thummim.[d]
66The total number of those who returned was
42,360. 67This is not counting their 7,337 male

and female servants and the 245 male and female
singers with them. 68They had 736 horses, 245
mules, 69435 camels and 6,720 donkeys.
70Some of the family leaders gave to the
work. The governor gave to the treasury about
8 kilogrammes of gold, 50 bowls and 530 pieces
of clothing for the priests. 71Some of the family
leaders gave about 170 kilogrammes of gold and
about 1.3 tonnes of silver to the treasury for the
work. 72The total of what the other people gave
was about 170 kilogrammes of gold, about a
tonne of silver and 67 pieces of clothing for the
priests. 73So these people all settled in their own
towns: the priests, the Levites, the gatekeepers,
the singers, the Temple servants and all the
other people of Israel.

Ezra Reads the Teachings

By the seventh month the Israelites were settled in their own towns.

8 All the people of Israel gathered together in
the square by the Water Gate. They asked
Ezra the teacher to bring out the Book of the
Teachings of Moses, which the LORD had given
to Israel.
2So on the first day of the seventh month,
Ezra the priest brought out the Teachings for the
crowd. Men, women and all who could listen
and understand had gathered. 3At the square by
the Water Gate Ezra read the Teachings out
loud from early morning until noon to the men,
women and everyone who could listen and understand. All the people listened carefully to the
Book of the Teachings.
4Ezra the teacher stood on a high wooden
platform that had been built just for this time.
On his right were Mattithiah, Shema, Anaiah,
Uriah, Hilkiah and Maaseiah. And on his left
were Pedaiah, Mishael, Malkijah, Hashum,
Hashbaddanah, Zechariah and Meshullam.
5Ezra opened the book in full view of everyone, because he was above them. As he opened
it, all the people stood up. 6Ezra praised the
LORD, the great God, and all the people held up
their hands and said, "Amen! Amen!" Then
they bowed down and worshipped the LORD
with their faces to the ground.
7These Levites explained the Teachings to the
people as they stood there: Jeshua, Bani, Sherebiah, Jamin, Akkub, Shabbethai, Hodiah, Maaseiah, Kelita, Azariah, Jozabad, Hanan and
Pelaiah. 8They read from the Book of the Teachings of God and explained what it meant so the
people understood what was being read.
9Then Nehemiah the governor, Ezra the priest
and teacher, and the Levites who were teaching
said to all the people, "This is a holy day to the
LORD your God. Don't be sad or cry." All the people had been crying as they listened to the words
of the Teachings.
10Nehemiah said, "Go and enjoy good food
and sweet drinks. Send some to people who
have none, because today is a holy day to the
Lord. Don't be sad, because the joy of the LORD
will make you strong."
11The Levites helped calm the people, saying,
"Be quiet, because this is a holy day. Don't
be sad."
12Then all the people went away to eat and
drink, to send some of their food to others and
to celebrate with great joy. They finally understood what they had been taught.
13On the second day of the month, the leaders of all the families, the priests and the Levites
met with Ezra the teacher. They gathered to
study the words of the Teachings. 14This is what
they found written in the Teachings: the LORD
commanded through Moses that the people of
Israel were to live in shelters during the feast of
the seventh month. 15The people were supposed to preach this message and spread it
through all their towns and in Jerusalem: "Go
out into the mountains, and bring back
branches from olive and wild olive trees, myrtle
trees, palms and shade trees. Make shelters
with them, as it is written."
16So the people went out and got tree
branches. They built shelters on their roofs,[n] in
their courtyards, in the courtyards of the Temple,[d] in the square by the Water Gate and in the
square next to the Gate of Ephraim. 17The
whole group that had come back from captivity
built shelters and lived in them. The Israelites
had not done this since the time of Joshua son of
Nun. And they were very happy.
18Ezra read to them every day from the Book
of the Teachings, from the first day to the last.
The people of Israel celebrated the feast for
seven days, and then on the eighth day the people gathered as the law said.

Israel Confesses Sins

9 On the twenty-fourth day of that same
month, the people of Israel gathered. They
did not eat, and they wore rough cloth and put
dust on their heads to show their sadness. 2Those
people whose ancestors were from Israel had separated themselves from all foreigners. They stood
and confessed their sins and their ancestors' sins.
3For a quarter of the day they stood where they

roofs In Bible times houses were built with flat roofs. The roof was used for drying things such as flax and fruit. And it was used as an extra room, as a place for worship and as a place to sleep in the summer.

were and read from the Book of the Teachings of
the LORD their God. For another quarter of the day
they confessed their sins and worshipped the
LORD their God. 4These Levites were standing
on the stairs: Jeshua, Bani, Kadmiel, Shebaniah,
Bunni, Sherebiah, Bani and Kanani. They called
out to the LORD their God with loud voices. 5Then
these Levites spoke: Jeshua, Kadmiel, Bani, Hash-
abneiah, Sherebiah, Hodiah, Shebaniah and Peth-
ahiah. They said, "Stand up and praise the LORD
your God, who lives for ever and ever."

The People's Prayer

"Blessed be your wonderful name.
It is more wonderful than all blessing and praise.
6You are the only LORD.
You made the heavens, even the highest heavens,
with all the stars.
You made the earth and everything on it,
the seas and everything in them;
you give life to everything.
The heavenly army worships you.

7"You are the LORD,
the God who chose Abram
and brought him out of Ur in Babylonia
and named him Abraham.
8You found him faithful to you,
so you made an agreement with him
to give his descendants *d* the land of the Canaanites,
Hittites, Amorites,
Perizzites, Jebusites and Girgashites.
You have kept your promise,
because you do what is right.

9"You saw our ancestors suffering in Egypt
and heard them cry out at the Red Sea.*d*
10You did signs and miracles*d* against the king of Egypt,
and against all his officers and all his people,
because you knew how proud they were.
You became as famous as you are today.
11You divided the sea in front of our ancestors;
they walked through on dry ground.
But you threw the people chasing them into the deep water,
like a stone thrown into mighty waters.
12You led our ancestors with a pillar of cloud by day
and with a pillar of fire at night.
It lit the way
they were supposed to go.
13You came down to Mount Sinai
and spoke from heaven to our ancestors.
You gave them fair rules and true teachings,
good orders and commands.
14You told them about your holy Sabbath*d*
and gave them commands, orders and teachings
through your servant Moses.
15When they were hungry, you gave them bread from heaven.
When they were thirsty, you brought them water from the rock.
You told them to enter and take over
the land you had promised to give them.

16"But our ancestors were proud and stubborn
and did not obey your commands.
17They refused to listen;
they forgot the miracles you did for them.
So they became stubborn and turned against you,
choosing a leader to take them back to slavery.
But you are a forgiving God.
You are kind and full of mercy.
You do not become angry quickly and you have great love.
So you did not leave them.
18Our ancestors even made an idol of a calf for themselves.
They said, 'This is your god, Israel,
who brought you up out of Egypt.'
They spoke against you.

19"You have great mercy,
so you did not leave them in the desert.
The pillar of cloud guided them by day,
and the pillar of fire led them at night,
lighting the way they were to go.
20You gave your good Spirit *d* to teach them.
You gave them manna *d* to eat
and water when they were thirsty.
21You took care of them for 40 years in the desert;
they needed nothing.
Their clothes did not wear out,
and their feet did not swell.

22"You gave them kingdoms and nations;
you gave them more land.
They took over the country of Sihon king of Heshbon
and the country of Og king of Bashan.
23You made their children as many as the stars in the sky,
and you brought them into the land
that you told their fathers to enter and take over.
24So their children went into the land and took over.
The Canaanites lived there, but you
defeated them for our ancestors.

You handed over to them the Canaanites,
their kings and the people of the land.
Our ancestors could do what they wanted
with them.
25They captured strong, walled cities and fertile
land.
They took over houses full of good things,
wells that were already dug,
vineyards, olive trees and many fruit trees.
They ate until they were full and grew fat;
they enjoyed your great goodness.

26"But they were disobedient and turned
against you
and ignored your teachings.
Your prophets [d] warned them to come back
to you,
but they killed those prophets
and spoke against you.
27So you handed them over to their enemies,
and their enemies treated them badly.
But in this time of trouble our ancestors cried
out to you,
and you heard from heaven.
You had great mercy
and gave them saviours who saved them
from the power of their enemies.
28But as soon as they had rest,
they again did what was evil.
So you left them to their enemies
who ruled over them.
When they cried out to you again,
you heard from heaven.
Because of your mercy, you saved them
again and again.
29You warned them to return to your
teachings,
but they were proud and did not obey your
commands.
If someone obeys your laws, he will live,
but they sinned against your laws.
They were stubborn, unwilling and
disobedient.
30You were patient with them for many years
and warned them by your Spirit through
the prophets,
but they did not pay attention.
So you handed them over to other
countries.
31But because your mercy is great, you did not
kill them all or leave them.
You are a kind and merciful God.

32"And so, our God, you are the great and
mighty and wonderful God.
You keep your agreement of love.
Do not let all our trouble seem unimportant
to you.
This trouble has come to us, to our kings and
our leaders,
to our priests and prophets,
to our ancestors and all your people
from the days of the kings of Assyria
until today.
33You have been fair in everything that has
happened to us;
you have been loyal, but we have been
wicked.
34Our kings, leaders, priests and ancestors did
not obey your teachings;
they did not pay attention to the commands
and warnings you gave them.
35Even when our ancestors were living in their
kingdom,
enjoying all the good things you had given
them,
enjoying the land that was fertile and full of
room,
they did not stop their evil ways.

36"Look, we are slaves today
in the land you gave our ancestors.
They were to enjoy its fruit and its good
things,
but look, we are slaves here.
37The land's great harvest belongs to the kings
you have put over us
because of our sins.
Those kings rule over us and our cattle as
they please,
so we are in much trouble.

The People's Agreement

38"Because of all this, we are making an agree-
ment in writing, and our leaders, Levites and
priests are putting their seals [d] on it."

10 These are the men who sealed the agree-
ment:
Nehemiah the governor, son of Hacaliah.
2Zedekiah, Seraiah, Azariah, Jeremiah, 3Pash-
hur, Amariah, Malkijah, 4Hattush, Shebaniah,
Malluch, 5Harim, Meremoth, Obadiah, 6Daniel,
Ginnethon, Baruch, 7Meshullam, Abijah, Mija-
min, 8Maaziah, Bilgai and Shemaiah. These are
the priests.
9These are the Levites who sealed it: Jeshua
son of Azaniah, Binnui of the sons of Henadad,
Kadmiel 10and their fellow Levites: Shebaniah,
Hodiah, Kelita, Pelaiah, Hanan, 11Mica, Rehob,
Hashabiah, 12Zaccur, Sherebiah, Shebaniah,
13Hodiah, Bani and Beninu.
14These are the leaders of the people who
sealed the agreement: Parosh, Pahath-Moab,
Elam, Zattu, Bani, 15Bunni, Azgad, Bebai, 16Ado-
nijah, Bigvai, Adin, 17Ater, Hezekiah, Azzur,
18Hodiah, Hashum, Bezai, 19Hariph, Anathoth,

Nebai, 20Magpiash, Meshullam, Hezir, 21Meshezabel, Zadok, Jaddua, 22Pelatiah, Hanan, Anaiah, 23Hoshea, Hananiah, Hasshub, 24Hallohesh, Pilha, Shobek, 25Rehum, Hashabnah, Maaseiah, 26Ahiah, Hanan, Anan, 27Malluch, Harim and Baanah.

28The rest of the people took an oath. They were the priests, Levites, gatekeepers, singers, Temple[d] servants, all those who separated themselves from foreigners to keep the Teachings of God and also their wives and their sons and daughters who could understand. 29They joined their fellow Israelites and their leading men in taking an oath, which was tied to a curse in case they broke the oath. They promised to follow the Teachings of God, which they had been given through Moses the servant of God, and to obey all the commands, rules and laws of the LORD our God.

30They said:

> We promise not to let our daughters marry foreigners nor to let our sons marry their daughters. 31Foreigners may bring goods or grain to sell on the Sabbath,[d] but we will not buy on the Sabbath or any holy day. Every seventh year we will not plant, and that year we will forget all that people owe us.
>
> 32We will be responsible for the commands to pay for the service of the Temple of our God. We will give 4 grammes of silver each year. 33It is for the bread that is set out on the table; the regular grain offerings and burnt offerings; the offerings on the Sabbaths, New Moon[d] festivals and special feasts; the holy offerings; the offerings to remove the sins of the Israelites so they will belong to God; and for the work of the Temple of our God.
>
> 34We, the priests, the Levites and the people, have thrown lots[d] to decide at what time of year each family must bring wood to the Temple. The wood is for burning on the altar of the LORD our God, and we will do this as it is written in the Teachings.
>
> 35We also will bring the first fruits from our crops and the first fruits[d] of every tree to the Temple each year.
>
> 36We will bring to the Temple our firstborn[d] sons and cattle and the firstborn of our herds and flocks, as it is written in the Teachings. We will bring them to the priests who are serving in the Temple.
>
> 37We will bring to the priests at the storerooms of the Temple the first of our ground meal, our offerings, the fruit from all our trees and our new wine and oil. And we will bring a tenth of our crops to the Levites, who will collect these things in all the towns where we work. 38A priest of Aaron's family must be with the Levites when they receive the tenth of the people's crops. The Levites must bring a tenth of all they receive to the Temple of our God to put in the storerooms of the treasury. 39The people of Israel and the Levites are to bring to the storerooms the gifts of grain, new wine and oil. That is where the utensils for the Temple are kept and where the priests who are serving, the gatekeepers and singers stay.
>
> We will not ignore the Temple of our God.

New People Move into Jerusalem

11 The leaders of Israel lived in Jerusalem. But the rest of the people threw lots[d] to choose one person out of every ten to come and live in Jerusalem, the holy city. The other nine could stay in their own cities. 2The people blessed those who volunteered to live in Jerusalem.

3These are the area leaders who lived in Jerusalem. (Some people lived on their own land in the cities of Judah. These included Israelites, priests, Levites, Temple[d] servants and descendants[d] of Solomon's servants. 4Others from the families of Judah and Benjamin lived in Jerusalem.)

These are the descendants of Judah who moved into Jerusalem. There was Athaiah son of Uzziah. (Uzziah was the son of Zechariah, the son of Amariah. Amariah was the son of Shephatiah, the son of Mahalalel. Mahalalel was a descendant of Perez.) 5There was also Maaseiah son of Baruch. (Baruch was the son of Col-Hozeh, the son of Hazaiah. Hazaiah was the son of Adaiah, the son of Joiarib. Joiarib was the son of Zechariah, a descendant of Shelah.) 6All the descendants of Perez who lived in Jerusalem totalled 468 men. They were soldiers.

7These are descendants of Benjamin who moved into Jerusalem. There was Sallu son of Meshullam. (Meshullam was the son of Joed, the son of Pedaiah. Pedaiah was the son of Kolaiah, the son of Maaseiah. Maaseiah was the son of Ithiel, the son of Jeshaiah.) 8Following him were Gabbai and Sallai, for a total of 928 men. 9Joel son of Zicri was appointed over them, and Judah son of Hassenuah was second in charge of the new area of the city.

10These are the priests who moved into Jerusalem. There was Jedaiah son of Joiarib, Jakin 11and Seraiah son of Hilkiah, the supervisor in the Temple. (Hilkiah was the son of Meshullam, the son of Zadok. Zadok was the son of Meraioth, the son of Ahitub.) 12And there were others with

them who did the work for the Temple. Alto-
gether there were 822 men. Also there was Ada-
iah son of Jeroham. (Jeroham was the son of
Pelaliah, the son of Amzi. Amzi was the son of
Zechariah, the son of Pashhur. Pashhur was the
son of Malkijah.) 13And there were family heads
with him. Altogether there were 242 men. Also
there was Amashsai son of Azarel. (Azarel was
the son of Ahzai, the son of Meshillemoth. Me-
shillemoth was the son of Immer.) 14And there
were brave men with Amashsai. Altogether there
were 128 men. Zabdiel son of Haggedolim was
appointed over them.

15These are the Levites who moved into Jeru-
salem. There was Shemaiah son of Hasshub.
(Hasshub was the son of Azrikam, the son of
Hashabiah. Hashabiah was the son of Bunni.)
16And there were Shabbethai and Jozabad, two of
the leaders of the Levites who were in charge of
the work outside the Temple. 17There was Matta-
niah son of Mica. (Mica was the son of Zabdi, the
son of Asaph.) Mattaniah was the director who
led the people in thanksgiving and prayer. There
was Bakbukiah, who was second in charge over
his fellow Levites. And there was Abda son of
Shammua. (Shammua was the son of Galal, the
son of Jeduthun.) 18Altogether 284 Levites lived
in the holy city of Jerusalem.

19The gatekeepers who moved into Jerusalem
were Akkub, Talmon and others with them.
There was a total of 172 men who guarded the
city gates.

20The other Israelites, priests and Levites lived
on their own land in all the cities of Judah.

21The Temple servants lived on the hill of
Ophel, and Ziha and Gishpa were in charge of
them.

22Uzzi son of Bani was appointed over the Le-
vites in Jerusalem. (Bani was the son of Hasha-
biah, the son of Mattaniah. Mattaniah was the
son of Mica.) Uzzi was one of Asaph's descen-
dants, who were the singers responsible for the
service of the Temple. 23The singers were under the
king's orders, which regulated them day by day.

24Pethahiah son of Meshezabel was the king's
spokesman. (Meshezabel was a descendant of
Zerah, the son of Judah.)

25Some of the people of Judah lived in villages
with their surrounding fields. They lived in Kiri-
ath Arba and its surroundings, in Dibon and its
surroundings, in Jekabzeel and its surroundings,
26in Jeshua, Moladah, Beth Pelet, 27Hazar Shual,
Beersheba and its surroundings, 28in Ziklag and
Meconah and its surroundings, 29in En Rimmon,
Zorah, Jarmuth, 30Zanoah, Adullam and their vil-
lages, in Lachish and the fields around it, and in
Azekah and its surroundings. So they settled from
Beersheba all the way to the Valley of Hinnom.

31The descendants of the Benjaminites from
Geba lived in Michmash, Aija, Bethel and its sur-
roundings, 32in Anathoth, Nob, Ananiah, 33Ha-
zor, Ramah, Gittaim, 34Hadid, Zeboim, Neballat,
35Lod, Ono and in the Valley of the Craftsmen.

36Some groups of the Levites from Judah set-
tled in the land of Benjamin.

Priests and Levites

12 These are the priests and Levites who
returned with Zerubbabel son of Sheal-
tiel and with Jeshua. There were Seraiah, Jeremiah,
Ezra, 2Amariah, Malluch, Hattush, 3Shecaniah,
Rehum, Meremoth, 4Iddo, Ginnethon, Abijah,
5Mijamin, Moadiah, Bilgah, 6Shemaiah, Joiarib,
Jedaiah, 7Sallu, Amok, Hilkiah and Jedaiah. They
were the leaders of the priests and their relatives
in the days of Jeshua.

8The Levites were Jeshua, Binnui, Kadmiel,
Sherebiah, Judah and Mattaniah. Mattaniah and
his relatives were in charge of the songs of
thanksgiving. 9Bakbukiah and Unni, their relat-
ives, stood across from them in the services.

10Jeshua was the father of Joiakim. Joiakim was
the father of Eliashib. Eliashib was the father of
Joiada. 11Joiada was the father of Jonathan and
Jonathan was the father of Jaddua.

12In the days of Joiakim, these priests were the
leaders of the families of priests: Meraiah, from
Seraiah's family; Hananiah, from Jeremiah's fam-
ily; 13Meshullam, from Ezra's family; Jehohanan,
from Amariah's family; 14Jonathan, from Mal-
luch's family; Joseph, from Shecaniah's family;
15Adna, from Harim's family; Helkai, from Mere-
moth's family; 16Zechariah, from Iddo's family;
Meshullam, from Ginnethon's family; 17Zicri,
from Abijah's family; Piltai, from Miniamin's and
Moadiah's families; 18Shammua, from Bilgah's
family; Jehonathan, from Shemaiah's family;
19Mattenai, from Joiarib's family; Uzzi, from Jeda-
iah's family; 20Kallai, from Sallu's family; Eber,
from Amok's family; 21Hashabiah, from Hilkiah's
family; and Nethanel, from Jedaiah's family.

22The leaders of the families of the Levites
and the priests were written down in the days of
Eliashib, Joiada, Johanan and Jaddua, while Dar-
ius the Persian was king. 23The family leaders
among the Levites were written down in the
history book, but only up to the time of Johanan
son of Eliashib. 24The leaders of the Levites
were Hashabiah, Sherebiah, Jeshua son of Kad-
miel and their relatives. Their relatives stood
across from them and gave praise and thanks-
giving to God. One group answered the other
group, as David, the man of God, had com-
manded.

25These were the gatekeepers who guarded
the storerooms next to the gates: Mattaniah,

Bakbukiah, Obadiah, Meshullam, Talmon and
Akkub. 26They served in the days of Joiakim son
of Jeshua, the son of Jozadak. They also served in
the days of Nehemiah the governor and Ezra the
priest and teacher.

The Wall of Jerusalem

27When the wall of Jerusalem was offered as a
gift to God, they asked the Levites to come from
wherever they lived to Jerusalem to celebrate
with joy the gift of the wall. They were to cele-
brate with songs of thanksgiving and with the
music of cymbals, harps and lyres. [d] 28They also
brought together singers from all around Jeru-
salem, from the Netophathite villages, 29from
Beth Gilgal and from the areas of Geba and Az-
maveth. The singers had built villages for them-
selves around Jerusalem. 30The priests and Levites
made themselves pure, and they also made the
people, the gates and the wall of Jerusalem pure.
31I had the leaders of Judah go up on top of the
wall, and I appointed two large choruses to give
thanks. One chorus went to the right on top of
the wall, towards the Rubbish Gate. 32Behind
them went Hoshaiah and half the leaders of Ju-
dah. 33Azariah, Ezra, Meshullam, 34Judah, Benja-
min, Shemaiah and Jeremiah also went. 35Some
priests with trumpets also went, along with Zech-
ariah son of Jonathan. (Jonathan was the son of
Shemaiah, the son of Mattaniah. Mattaniah was
the son of Micaiah, the son of Zaccur. Zaccur was
the son of Asaph.) 36Zechariah's relatives also
went. They were Shemaiah, Azarel, Milalai, Gila-
lai, Maai, Nethanel, Judah and Hanani. These
men played the musical instruments of David, the
man of God, and Ezra the teacher walked in front
of them. 37They went from the Fountain Gate
straight up the steps to the highest part of the wall
by the older part of the city. They went on above
the house of David to the Water Gate on the east.
38The second chorus went to the left, while I
followed them on top of the wall with half the
people. We went from the Tower of the Ovens to
the Broad Wall, 39over the Gate of Ephraim to the
Old Gate and the Fish Gate, to the Tower of
Hananel and the Tower of the Hundred. We
went as far as the Sheep Gate and stopped at the
Gate of the Guard.

MUSIC

Back of the Net

Jon was one of those quiet, unassuming kinds of guys who got on with life in his own way. But, even though Jon didn't say much, within a second of him walking into the room, you would notice something about him. Jon was a fanatic for his football team. Everyday he wore their scarf. He even wore their footy shirt under his school uniform, exposing it proudly at lunch during the daily kick around on the school field.

That wasn't all. Jon's most prized possession was his season ticket. Jon was a die-hard supporter and he'd be there, through thick and thin, rain or shine, home or away. This quiet guy, who rarely uttered a word, could be seen standing, hands raised, chest puffed out, singing at the top of his voice. And if they ever scored a goal (which wasn't that often), every fibre of his being exploded into jubilant adoration and ecstatic praise for those eleven men who had placed the ball in the back of the net.

Read **Nehemiah 12:27–43** and see how God's people celebrate what he's done for them.

- A wall doesn't sound that great, so why did the people go so crazy over a bunch of bricks?
- What's similar about Jon's footy enthusiasm and Israel with their new wall – and what's different?

Consider . . .

- making a list in five minutes of as many things as you can think of that God has done for you. Put the list in your Bible and take it with you next time you're going somewhere to sing songs to God. Get the list out and see how it fuels your worship.
- making up your own songs to praise God with.

For more, see . . .

- 1 Chronicles 13:8 (p.386)
- Romans 12:1–2 (p.1203)
- Psalm 98 (p.557)

40The two choruses took their places at the
Temple.[d] Half of the leaders and I did also.
41These priests were there with their trumpets:
Eliakim, Maaseiah, Miniamin, Micaiah, Elioenai,
Zechariah and Hananiah. 42These people were
also there: Maaseiah, Shemaiah, Eleazar, Uzzi,
Jehohanan, Malkijah, Elam and Ezer. The
choruses sang, led by Jezrahiah. 43The people
offered many sacrifices that day and were happy
because God had given them great joy. The
women and children were happy. The sound of
happiness in Jerusalem could be heard far away.

> **Sidelight** When the Jews dedicated the completed wall around Jerusalem (Nehemiah 12:27–43), they didn't cut a ribbon or break a bottle of champagne. They probably offered an animal sacrifice and sprinkled blood or holy water on the wall.

44At that time the leaders appointed men to be
in charge of the storerooms. These rooms were
for the gifts, the first fruits[d] and the tenth that the
people brought. The Teachings said they should
bring a share for the priests and Levites from the
fields around the towns. The people of Judah
were happy to do this for the priests and Levites
who served. 45They performed the service of their
God in making things pure. The singers and gate-
keepers also did their jobs, as David had com-
manded his son Solomon. 46Earlier, in the time of
David and Asaph, there was a leader of the sing-
ers and of the songs of praise and thanksgiving to
God. 47So it was in the days of Zerubbabel and
Nehemiah. All the people of Israel gave some-
thing to the singers and gatekeepers, and they
also set aside part for the Levites. Then the Le-
vites set aside part for the descendants[d] of Aaron.

Foreign People are Sent Away

13 On that day they read the Book of Moses
to the people, and they found that it said
no Ammonite or Moabite should ever be allowed
in the meeting to worship. 2The Ammonites and
Moabites had not welcomed the Israelites with
food and water. Instead, they had hired Balaam
to put a curse on Israel. (But our God turned the
curse into a blessing.) 3When the people heard
this teaching, they separated all foreigners from
Israel.

Nehemiah Returns to Jerusalem

4Before that happened, Eliashib the priest, who
was in charge of the Temple[d] storerooms, was
friendly with Tobiah. 5Eliashib let Tobiah use one
of the large storerooms. Earlier it had been used
for grain offerings, incense,[d] the utensils and the
tenth offerings of grain, new wine and olive oil
that belonged to the Levites, singers and gate-
keepers. It had also been used for gifts for the
priests.

6I was not in Jerusalem when this happened. I
had gone back to Artaxerxes king of Babylon in
the thirty-second year he was king. Finally I
asked the king to let me leave. 7When I returned
to Jerusalem, I found out the evil Eliashib had
done by letting Tobiah have a room in the Tem-
ple courtyard. 8I was very upset at this, so I threw
all of Tobiah's goods out of the room. 9I ordered
the rooms to be purified, and I brought back the
utensils for God's Temple, the grain offerings and
the incense.

10Then I found out the people were not giving
the Levites their shares. So the Levites and sing-
ers who served had gone back to their own farms.
11I argued with the officers, saying, "Why haven't
you taken care of the Temple?" Then I gathered
the Levites and singers and put them back at their
places.

12All the people of Judah then brought to the
storerooms a tenth of their crops, new wine and
olive oil. 13I put these men in charge of the store-
rooms: Shelemiah the priest, Zadok the teacher
and Pedaiah a Levite. I made Hanan son of Zac-
cur, the son of Mattaniah, their helper. Everyone
knew they were honest men. They gave out the
portions that went to their relatives.

14Remember me, my God, for this. Do not ig-
nore my love for the Temple and its service.

15In those days I saw people in Judah working
in the winepresses[d] on the Sabbath[d] day. They
were bringing in grain and loading it on donkeys.
And they were bringing loads of wine, grapes and
figs into Jerusalem on the Sabbath day. So I
warned them about selling food on that day.
16People from the city of Tyre who were living in
Jerusalem brought in fish and other things and
sold them there on the Sabbath day to the people
of Judah. 17I argued with the important men of
Judah and said to them, "What is this evil thing
you are doing? You are ruining the Sabbath day.
18This is just what your ancestors did. So our God
did terrible things to us and this city. Now you
are making him even more angry at Israel by ruin-
ing the Sabbath day."

19So I ordered that the doors be shut at sunset
before the Sabbath and not be opened until the
Sabbath was over. I put my servants at the gates
so no load could come in on the Sabbath. 20Once
or twice traders and sellers of all kinds of goods
spent the night outside Jerusalem. 21So I warned
them, "Why are you spending the night by the
wall? If you do it again, I will force you away."

After that, they did not come back on the Sab-
bath. 22Then I ordered the Levites to purify them-
selves and to guard the city gates to make sure
the Sabbath remained holy.

Remember me, my God, for this. Have mercy
on me because of your great love.

23In those days I saw men of Judah who had
married women from Ashdod, Ammon and
Moab. 24Half their children were speaking the
language of Ashdod or some other place, and they
couldn't speak the language of Judah. 25I argued
with those people, put curses on them, hit some
of them and pulled out their hair. I forced them
to make a promise to God, saying, "Do not let
your daughters marry the sons of foreigners, and
do not take the daughters of foreigners as wives
for your sons or yourselves. 26Foreign women
made King Solomon of Israel sin. There was
never a king like him in any of the nations. God
loved Solomon and made him king over all Israel,
but foreign women made him sin. 27And now you
are not obedient when you do this evil thing. You
are unfaithful to our God when you marry foreign
wives."

28Joiada was the son of Eliashib the high priest.
One of Joiada's sons married a daughter of San-
ballat the Horonite, so I sent him away from me.

29Remember them, my God, because they
made the priesthood unclean [d] and the agreement
of the priests and Levites unclean.

30So I purified them of everything that was for-
eign. I appointed duties for the priests and Le-
vites, giving each man his own job. 31I also made
sure wood was brought for the altar at regular
times and that the first fruits [d] were brought.

Remember me, my God; be kind to me.

Esther

Why Read This Book:

- Recognise God's work in life's circumstances (Esther 1—2)
- Discover how an obedient person can have a major impact in the world (Esther 4—10).

When?

Time Line:

1000 BC	David was Israel's king
	The Northern Kingdom (Israel) fell to Assyria
750 BC	
The Southern Kingdom (Judah) fell to Babylon	
500 BC	Jews began returning to Jerusalem from exile when Persia conquered Babylon
King Xerxes ruled Persia and the story of Esther took place during this time	
250 BC	
BC/AD	Jesus was born

Behind the Scenes:

How do you respond in a crisis? Does your fear make you freeze up so that you can't do anything to help? Or do you reveal far more strength than you would normally have?

Esther faced a tough situation. She might be able to save thousands of Jewish lives by stopping the decree of King Xerxes to exterminate all the Jews in the Persian Empire. But if she tried, she could lose her own life. Would she "freeze", or would she take heroic action? This book tells how Esther responded.

The story begins when King Xerxes got rid of Queen Vashti because she wouldn't obey him. Four years later, the king picked a new queen, Esther, not knowing that she was a Jew.

Then the plot thickens. Esther's cousin, Mordecai, refused to bow down to Haman, a court official. Haman became furious and convinced the king to order the killing of all the Jews. Through a messenger, Mordecai told Esther about the death decree and convinced her to use her influence to stop the order. Esther agreed, saying, "I will go to the king, even though it is against the law, and if I die, I die" (Esther 4:16). So she went to the king to plead for the Jews, including herself. She succeeded. Then Haman was executed and Mordecai honoured.

Esther is one of the most unusual books in the Bible. In some ways, it's a "secular" book; nowhere does it mention God, worship, prayer, or other religious practices. Yet God's protection is clear throughout. The number of "coincidences" in the book illustrate that God's hand is at work in events, even when we don't realise it.

Where?

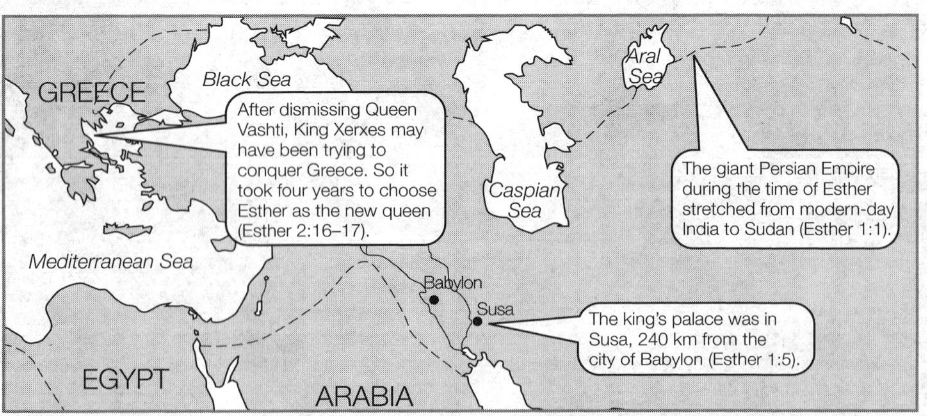

Queen Vashti Disobeys the King

1 This is what happened during the time of
King Xerxes, the king who ruled the 127
areas from India to Cush. 2In those days King
Xerxes ruled from his capital city of Susa. 3In the
third year of his rule, he gave a banquet for all his
important men and royal officers. The army lead-
ers from the countries of Persia and Media and the
important men from all Xerxes' empire were there.
4The banquet lasted 180 days. All during that
time King Xerxes was showing off the great
wealth of his kingdom and his own great riches
and glory. 5When the 180 days were over, the
king gave another banquet. It was held in the
courtyard of the palace garden for seven days,
and it was for everybody in the palace at Susa,
from the greatest to the least. 6The courtyard had
fine white curtains and purple linen that were

DRUGS AND ALCOHOL

Under the Influence

"I wonder what it's like to drown," Scott Walters mused aloud. He quietly exhaled, then slipped under the water in his backyard pool.

Scott was from a wealthy family and was about eleven when he began trying drinks from his father's drinks cabinet. No one in the family seemed to notice or care, so he continued to drink occasionally – in small amounts.

One afternoon several of Scott's friends came over to swim in the family pool.

"My family lets me drink whenever I want to," Scott claimed. "In fact, my dad and I drink together all the time."

"You're lying," scowled Brett, one of Scott's friends. "Your dad doesn't let you drink."

"What do you know?" countered Scott. "You've probably never had anything stronger than milk."

"OK, then," Brett said, "prove it. Prove to us that you drink."

Scott didn't really want to drink right then, because he never knew when his dad would come home. But after repeated dares from his friends, Scott went to the cabinet and poured a little from each bottle into a large glass. Then he drank it all. Scott's friends let out a big "Whoop!" impressed by Scott's ability to "handle his booze".

Scott didn't feel anything happen right away. He thought he was OK, so he jumped into the pool with his friends. But the longer his friends played, the more quiet and distant Scott became.

No one noticed when Scott slipped quietly under the water.

After a minute or two, Brett asked, "Hey, where's Scott?"

The boys saw Scott's form on the bottom. They frantically pulled him from the pool, laid him on the concrete on his side and tried to revive him. Scott soon came around and began to cough up water.

After a few minutes, Scott sat up on the edge of the pool, so drunk he didn't even realise he had almost died.

Alcohol and drugs keep us from thinking clearly. In **Esther 1:4–12**, read how King Xerxes reacted after drinking a large amount of wine.

- What effect did alcohol have on Scott and King Xerxes?
- What does this passage say about using drugs and alcohol?

Consider . . .

- writing reasons you choose not to use alcohol or other drugs, and keeping that list in your Bible as a reminder.
- scanning the newspaper for articles that involved drink driving or violence resulting from drug or alcohol use, then consider asking God to help the people in each of those situations.

For more, see . . .

- Proverbs 23:29–35 (p.610)
- Ephesians 5:15–18 (p.1275)
- Galatians 5:19–23 (p.1264)

tied to silver rings on marble pillars by white and
purple cords. And there were gold and silver
couches on a floor set with tiles of white marble,
shells and gems. 7Wine was served in gold cups
of various kinds. And there was plenty of the
king's wine, because he was very generous. 8The
king commanded that the guests be permitted to
drink as much as they wished. He told the wine
servers to serve each person what he wanted.

Sidelight Do you prefer sitting up or laying down? Did you realise that the very rich people in Esther's day spent their time lounged on gold and silver couches when they ate. Eating in bed was normal (Esther 1:4–8)! Ordinary folk had wooden beds with cord nets for mattresses and the poor slept on the ground covering themselves with their clothes.

9Queen Vashti also gave a banquet for the
women in the royal palace of King Xerxes.
10On the seventh day of the banquet, King
Xerxes was very happy, because he had been
drinking much wine. He gave a command to the
seven eunuchs[d] who served him—Mehuman,
Biztha, Harbona, Bigtha, Abagtha, Zethar and
Carcas. 11He commanded them to bring him
Queen Vashti, wearing her royal crown. She was
to come to show her beauty to the people and
important men, because she was very beautiful.
12The eunuchs told Queen Vashti about the
king's command, but she refused to come. Then
the king became very angry; his anger was like a
burning fire.

Sidelight Some people in ancient times really knew how to party. King Xerxes threw one that lasted six months. Herodotus, the Greek historian, noted the lengthy banquets where Xerxes may have made a plot to exterminate the Jews and a disastrous plan to invade Greece.

13It was a custom for the king to ask advice
from experts about law and order. So King Xerxes
spoke with the wise men who would know the
right thing to do. 14The wise men the king usually
talked to were Carshena, Shethar, Admatha,
Tarshish, Meres, Marsena and Memucan, seven
of the important men of Persia and Media. These
seven had special privileges to see the king and
had the highest rank in the kingdom. 15The king
asked them, "What does the law say must be
done to Queen Vashti? She has not obeyed the
command of King Xerxes, which the eunuchs
took to her."
16Then Memucan said to the king and the
other important men, "Queen Vashti has not
done wrong to the king alone. She has also done
wrong to all the important men and all the people
in all the empire of King Xerxes. 17All the wives
of the important men of Persia and Media will
hear about the queen's actions. Then they will no
longer honour their husbands. They will say,
'King Xerxes commanded Queen Vashti to be
brought to him, but she refused to come.' 18To-
day the wives of the important men of Persia and
Media have heard about the queen's actions. So
they will speak in the same way to their husbands,
and there will be no end to disrespect and anger.
19"So, our king, if it pleases you, give a royal
order, and let it be written in the laws of Persia
and Media, which cannot be changed. The law
should say Vashti is never again to enter the pres-
ence of King Xerxes. Also let the king give her
place as queen to someone who is better than she
is. 20And let the king's order be announced every-
where in his great kingdom. Then all the women
will respect their husbands, from the greatest to
the least."
21The king and his important men were happy
with this advice, so King Xerxes did as Memucan
suggested. 22He sent letters to all the areas of the
kingdom in the writing of each area and in the
language of each group of people. These letters
announced that each man was to be the ruler of
his own family.

Esther is Made Queen

2 Later, when King Xerxes was not so angry,
he remembered Vashti and what she had
done and his order about her. 2Then the king's
personal servants suggested, "Let a search be
made for beautiful young girls for the king. 3Let
the king choose supervisors in every area of his
kingdom to bring every beautiful young girl to
the palace at Susa. They should be taken to the
women's quarters and put under the care of
Hegai, the king's eunuch[d] in charge of the
women. And let beauty treatments be given to
them. 4Then let the girl who most pleases the
king become queen in place of Vashti." The king
liked this idea, so he did as they said.
5Now there was a Jewish man in the palace of
Susa whose name was Mordecai son of Jair. Jair
was the son of Shimei, the son of Kish. Mordecai
was from the tribe[d] of Benjamin, 6which had
been taken captive from Jerusalem by Nebuchad-
nezzar king of Babylon. They were part of the
group taken into captivity with Jehoiachin king of
Judah. 7Mordecai had a cousin named Hadassah,

who had no father or mother, so Mordecai took
care of her. Hadassah was also called Esther, and
she had a very pretty figure and face. Mordecai
had adopted her as his own daughter when her
father and mother died.
8When the king's command and order had
been heard, many girls had been brought to the
palace in Susa and put under the care of Hegai.
Esther was also taken to the king's palace and put
under the care of Hegai, who was in charge of the
women. 9Esther pleased Hegai, and he liked her.
So Hegai quickly began giving Esther her beauty
treatments and special food. He gave her seven
servant girls chosen from the king's palace. Then
he moved her and her seven servant girls to the
best part of the women's quarters.
10Esther did not tell anyone about her family or
who her people were, because Mordecai had told
her not to. 11Every day Mordecai walked back
and forth near the courtyard where the king's
women lived to find out how Esther was and
what was happening to her.
12Before a girl could take her turn with King
Xerxes, she had to complete twelve months of
beauty treatments that were ordered for the
women. For six months she was treated with oil
and myrrh [d] and for six months with perfumes
and cosmetics. 13Then she was ready to go to the
king. Anything she asked for was given to her to
take with her from the women's quarters to the
king's palace. 14In the evening she would go to
the king's palace, and in the morning she would
return to another part of the women's quarters.
There she would be placed under the care of
Shaashgaz, the king's eunuch in charge of the slave
women. [d] The girl would not go back to the king
again unless he was pleased with her and asked
for her by name.
15The time came for Esther daughter of Abihail,
Mordecai's uncle, who had been adopted by
Mordecai, to go to the king. She asked for only
what Hegai suggested she should take. (Hegai
was the king's eunuch who was in charge of the
women.) Everyone who saw Esther liked her.
16So Esther was taken to King Xerxes in the royal
palace in the tenth month, the month of Tebeth,
during Xerxes' seventh year as king.
17And the king was pleased with Esther more
than with any of the other girls. He liked her
more than any of the other girls, so he put a royal
crown on her head and made her queen in place
of Vashti. 18Then the king gave a great banquet
for Esther and invited all his important men and
royal officers. He announced a holiday for all the
empire and had the government give away gifts.

Sidelight If you think somebody at home takes too long in the bathroom, just be glad she isn't Esther. It took Esther a year of beauty treatments to get ready for the king (Esther 2:12–13).

Mordecai Discovers an Evil Plan

19Now Mordecai was sitting at the king's gate
when the girls were gathered the second time.
20Esther still had not told anyone about her family
or who her people were, just as Mordecai had
commanded her. She obeyed Mordecai just as
she had done when she was under his care.
21Now Bigthana and Teresh were two of the
king's officers who guarded the doorway. While
Mordecai was sitting at the king's gate, they be-
came angry and began to make plans to kill King
Xerxes. 22But Mordecai found out about their
plans and told Queen Esther. Then Esther told
the king how Mordecai had discovered the evil
plan. 23When the report was investigated, it was
found to be true, and the two officers who had
planned to kill the king were hanged. All this was
written down in the daily court record in the
king's presence.

Haman Plans to Destroy the Jewish People

3 After these things happened, King Xerxes
honoured Haman son of Hammedatha the
Agagite. He gave him a new rank that was higher
than all the important men. 2All the royal officers at
the king's gate would bow down and kneel before
Haman, as the king had ordered. But Mordecai
would not bow down or show him honour.
3Then the royal officers at the king's gate asked
Mordecai, "Why don't you obey the king's com-
mand?" 4And they said this to him every day.
When he did not listen to them, they told Haman
about it. They wanted to see if Haman would
accept Mordecai's behaviour because Mordecai
had told them he was Jewish.
5When Haman saw that Mordecai would not
bow down to him or honour him, he became
very angry. 6He thought of himself as too import-
ant to try to kill only Mordecai. He had been told
who the people of Mordecai were, so he looked
for a way to destroy all of Mordecai's people, the
Jews, in all of Xerxes' kingdom.
7It was in the first month of the twelfth year of
King Xerxes' rule—the month of Nisan. Pur (that
is, the lot [d]) was thrown before Haman to choose
a day and a month. So the twelfth month, the
month of Adar, was chosen.
8Then Haman said to King Xerxes, "There is a
certain group of people scattered among the other
people in all the areas of your kingdom. Their
customs are different from those of all the other

people, and they do not obey the king's laws. It
is not right for you to allow them to continue
living in your kingdom. 9If it pleases the king, let
an order be given to destroy those people. Then
I will pay 350 tonnes of silver to those who do
the king's business, and they will put it into the
royal treasury."
10So the king took his signet[d] ring off and gave
it to Haman son of Hammedatha, the Agagite, the
enemy of the Jewish people. 11Then the king said
to Haman, "The money and the people are yours.
Do with them as you please."
12On the thirteenth day of the first month, the
royal secretaries were called, and they wrote out
all of Haman's orders. They wrote to the king's
governors and to the captains of the soldiers in
each area and to the important men of each
group of people. The orders were written in the
writing of each area and in the language of each
people. They were written in the name of King
Xerxes and sealed with his signet ring. 13Letters
were sent by messengers to all the king's empire
ordering them to destroy, kill and completely
wipe out all the Jewish people. That meant young
and old, women and little children too. It was to
happen on a single day—the thirteenth day of
the twelfth month, which was Adar. And they
could take everything the Jewish people owned.
14A copy of the order was given out as a law in
every area so all the people would be ready for
that day.
15The messengers set out, hurried by the king's
command, as soon as the order was given in the
palace at Susa. The king and Haman sat down to
drink, but the city of Susa was in confusion.

Mordecai Asks Esther to Help

4 When Mordecai heard about all that had
been done, he tore his clothes, put on rough
cloth and ashes, and went out into the city crying
loudly and painfully. 2But Mordecai went only as
far as the king's gate, because no one was al-
lowed to enter that gate dressed in rough cloth.
3As the king's order reached every area, there
was great sadness and loud crying among the
Jewish people. They gave up eating and cried out
loudly, and many of them lay down on rough
cloth and ashes to show how sad they were.
4When Esther's servant girls and eunuchs[d]
came to her and told her about Mordecai, she
was very upset and afraid. She sent clothes for
Mordecai to put on instead of the rough cloth,
but he would not wear them. 5Then Esther called
for Hathach, one of the king's eunuchs chosen by
the king to serve her. Esther ordered him to find
out what was bothering Mordecai and why.
6So Hathach went to Mordecai, who was
in the city square in front of the king's gate.
7Mordecai told Hathach everything that had hap-
pened to him, and he told Hathach about the
amount of money Haman had promised to pay
into the king's treasury for the killing of the Jew-
ish people. 8Mordecai also gave him a copy of
the order to kill the Jewish people, which had
been given in Susa. He wanted Hathach to show
it to Esther and to tell her about it. And Mordecai
told him to order Esther to go into the king's
presence to beg for mercy and to plead with him
for her people.
9Hathach went back and reported to Esther
everything Mordecai had said. 10Then Esther told
Hathach to tell Mordecai, 11"All the royal officers
and people of the royal areas know that no man
or woman may go to the king in the inner court-
yard without being called. There is only one law
about this: anyone who enters must be put to
death unless the king holds out his gold sceptre.[d]
Then that person may live. And I have not been
called to go to the king for 30 days."
12Esther's message was given to Mordecai.
13Then Mordecai sent back word to Esther: "Just
because you live in the king's palace, don't think
that out of all the Jewish people you alone will
escape. 14If you keep quiet at this time, someone
else will help and save the Jewish people, but you
and your father's family will all die. And who
knows, you may have been chosen queen for just
such a time as this."
15Then Esther sent this answer to Mordecai:
16"Go and get all the Jewish people in Susa to-
gether. For my sake, give up eating; do not eat or
drink for three days, night and day. I and my
servant girls will also give up eating. Then I will
go to the king, even though it is against the law,
and if I die, I die."
17So Mordecai went away and did everything
Esther had told him to do.

Esther Speaks to the King

5 On the third day Esther put on her royal
robes and stood in the inner courtyard of the
king's palace, facing the king's hall. The king was
sitting on his royal throne in the hall, facing the
doorway. 2When the king saw Queen Esther
standing in the courtyard, he was pleased. He
held out to her the gold sceptre[d] that was in his
hand, so Esther went forwards and touched the
end of it.
3The king asked, "What is it, Queen Esther?
What do you want to ask me? I will give you as
much as half of my kingdom."
4Esther answered, "My king, if it pleases you,
come today with Haman to a banquet that I have
prepared for him."
5Then the king said, "Bring Haman quickly so
we may do what Esther asks."

So the king and Haman went to the banquet
Esther had prepared for them. 6As they were
drinking wine, the king said to Esther, "Now,
what are you asking for? I will give it to you.
What is it you want? I will give you as much as
half of my kingdom."

Sidelight Are you ever afraid to talk to someone in authority? Imagine how Esther must have felt when she approached the King. Frequent political assassinations at the time meant that security around King Xerxes was extremely tight, and anyone approaching the king without being invited was in danger of being killed!

7Esther answered, "This is what I want and
what I ask for. 8My king, if you are pleased with
me and if it pleases you, give me what I ask for
and do what I want. Come with Haman tomor-
row to the banquet I will prepare for you. Then
I will answer your question about what I want."

Haman's Plans Against Mordecai

9Haman left the king's palace that day happy
and content. But when he saw Mordecai at the
king's gate and saw that Mordecai did not stand
up or tremble with fear before him, Haman be-
came very angry with Mordecai. 10But he con-
trolled his anger and went home.
Then Haman called together his friends and his
wife, Zeresh. 11He told them how wealthy he was
and how many sons he had. He also told them all
the ways the king had honoured him and how
the king had placed him higher than his import-
ant men and his royal officers. 12He also said,
"I'm the only person Queen Esther invited to
come with the king to the banquet she gave. And
tomorrow also the queen has asked me to be her
guest with the king. 13But all this does not really

HEROES

Risky Business

"They were chasing a little boy of about ten years old. They caught up with him, and one of them took his gun and smashed the child's head in. They killed him."

Those are the words of Giorgio Perlasca, who witnessed this murder in Hungary in 1944. It was World War II, and the Nazis were killing the Jews, regardless of their age.

Although he was Italian, Perlasca was able to masquerade as a top Spanish diplomat and help to save the Jews.

For three months, Perlasca distributed letters to all the Jews he could find. The letters stated that the Jews had been granted the protection of the Spanish government. When he saw Jews being herded onto to trains, headed for death, he confronted the Nazis and ordered them to return the people to him. He housed more than 5,000 Jews in eleven apartment buildings where he hung Spain's flag to protect the occupants.

Historians estimate that Perlasca helped to save more than 10,000 people before his cover was blown when Spain cut off diplomatic relations with Hungary at the end of 1944.

Queen Esther also put her life on the line for the Jews. Read her story in **Esther 4:9–16**.

- What risks did both Perlasca and Esther take to save the Jews?
- We may not all have the chance to save thousands of people from dying, but we can still make a difference. How can you be a hero for God?

Consider . . .

- reading a biography of a Christian man or woman who made major inroads for others through their life.
- who your heroes are and how well they measure up to the standards of Esther. Then decide if you need to change heroes.

For more, see . . .

- Exodus 14:5–31 (p.71)
- Hebrews 11:29–40 (p.1342)
- Joshua 2:1–22 (p.203)

make me happy when I see that Jew Mordecai
sitting at the king's gate."
14Then Haman's wife, Zeresh, and all his
friends said, "Have a 25-metre-high platform
built, and in the morning ask the king to have
Mordecai hanged on it. Then go to the banquet
with the king and be happy." Haman liked this
suggestion, so he ordered the platform to be
built.

Mordecai is Honoured

6 That same night the king could not sleep. So
he gave an order for the daily court record to
be brought in and read to him. 2It was found
recorded that Mordecai had warned the king
about Bigthana and Teresh, two of the king's offi-
cers who guarded the doorway and who had
planned to kill the king.
3The king asked, "What honour and reward
have been given to Mordecai for this?"
The king's personal servants answered, "Noth-
ing has been done for Mordecai."
4The king said, "Who is in the courtyard?"
Now Haman had just entered the outer court of
the king's palace. He had come to ask the king
about hanging Mordecai on the platform he had
prepared.
5The king's personal servants said, "Haman is
standing in the courtyard."
The king said, "Bring him in."
6So Haman came in. And the king asked him,
"What should be done for a man whom the king
wants very much to honour?"
And Haman thought to himself, "Whom
would the king want to honour more than me?"
7So he answered the king, "This is what you
could do for the man you want very much to
honour. 8Have the servants bring a royal robe
that the king himself has worn. And also bring a
horse with a royal crown on its head, a horse
that the king himself has ridden. 9Let the robe
and the horse be given to one of the king's most
important men. Let the servants put the robe on
the man the king wants to honour, and let them
lead him on the horse through the city streets.
As they are leading him, let them announce:
'This is what is done for the man whom the king
wants to honour!' "
10The king commanded Haman, "Go quickly.
Take the robe and the horse just as you have said,
and do all this for Mordecai the Jew who sits at
the king's gate. Do not leave out anything you
have suggested."
11So Haman took the robe and the horse, and
he put the robe on Mordecai. Then he led him on
horseback through the city streets, announcing
before Mordecai: "This is what is done for the
man whom the king wants to honour!"
12Then Mordecai returned to the king's gate,
but Haman hurried home with his head covered,
because he was embarrassed and ashamed. 13He
told his wife, Zeresh, and all his friends every-
thing that had happened to him.
Haman's wife and the men who gave him
advice said, "You are starting to lose power to
Mordecai. Since he is a Jew, you cannot win
against him. You will surely be ruined." 14While
they were still talking, the king's eunuchs[d] came
to Haman's house and made him hurry to the
banquet Esther had prepared.

Haman is Hanged

7 So the king and Haman went in to eat with
Queen Esther. 2As they were drinking wine
on the second day, the king asked Esther again,
"What are you asking for? I will give it to you.
What is it you want? I will give you as much as
half of my kingdom."
3Then Queen Esther answered, "My king, if
you are pleased with me, and if it pleases you, let
me live. This is what I ask. And let my people
live, too. This is what I want. 4My people and I
have been sold to be destroyed, to be killed and
completely wiped out. If we had been sold as
male and female slaves, I would have kept quiet,
because that would not be enough of a problem
to bother the king."
5Then King Xerxes asked Queen Esther, "Who
is he, and where is he? Who has done such a
thing?"
6Esther said, "Our enemy and foe is this
wicked Haman!"
Then Haman was filled with terror before the
king and queen. 7The king was very angry, so he
got up, left his wine and went out into the palace
garden. But Haman stayed inside to beg Queen
Esther to save his life. He could see that the king
had already decided to kill him.

Sidelight Going to the palace garden to cool off was probably a good idea for the angry king (Esther 7:7). The palace at Susa was the king's winter palace because it was warmer than the government headquarters in Persepolis.

8When the king returned from the palace gar-
den to the banquet hall, he saw Haman falling
on the couch where Esther was lying. The king
said, "Will he even attack the queen while I am
in the house?"
As soon as the king said that, servants came in
and covered Haman's face. 9Harbona, one of the
eunuchs[d] there serving the king, said, "Look, a

25-metre-high platform stands near Haman's house. This is the one Haman had prepared for Mordecai, who gave the warning that saved the king."

The king said, "Hang Haman on it!" 10So they hanged Haman on the platform he had prepared for Mordecai. Then the king was not so angry any more.

Sidelight The execution planned by Haman for Mordecai, but carried out by the king on Haman (Esther 7:8–10), probably would not have been hanging in the modern sense, but may have involved impaling the victim on a sharp stake and then hanging the body in the city for display. Romans adapted this method to develop execution on crosses.

The King Helps the Jewish People

8 That same day King Xerxes gave Queen Esther everything Haman, the enemy of the Jewish people, had left when he died. And Mordecai came in to see the king, because Esther had told the king how he was related to her. 2Then the king took off his signet[d] ring that he had taken back from Haman, and he gave it to Mordecai. Esther put Mordecai in charge of everything Haman left when he died.

3Once again Esther spoke to the king. She fell at the king's feet and cried and begged him to stop the evil plan that Haman the Agagite had planned against the Jews. 4The king held out the gold sceptre[d] to Esther. So Esther got up and stood in front of him.

5She said, "My king, if you are pleased with me, and if it pleases you to do this, if you think it is the right thing to do, and if you are happy with me, let an order be written to cancel the letters Haman wrote. Haman the Agagite sent messages to destroy all the Jewish people in all of your kingdom. 6I could not stand to see that terrible thing happen to my people. I could not stand to see my family killed."

7King Xerxes answered Queen Esther and Mordecai the Jew, "Because Haman was against the Jewish people, I have given his things to Esther and my soldiers have hanged him. 8Now, in the king's name, write another order to the Jewish people as it seems best to you. Then seal the order with the king's signet ring, because no letter written in the king's name and sealed with his signet ring can be cancelled."

9At that time the king's secretaries were called. This was the twenty-third day of the third month, which is Sivan. The secretaries wrote out all of Mordecai's orders to the Jews, to the governors, to the captains of the soldiers in each area and to the important men of the 127 areas that reached from India to Cush. They wrote in the writing of each area and in the language of each people. They also wrote to the Jewish people in their own writing and language. 10Mordecai wrote orders in the name of King Xerxes and sealed the letters with the king's signet ring. Then he sent the king's orders by messengers on fast horses, horses that were raised just for the king.

Sidelight The longest verse in the Bible is Esther 8:9. It's 88 words long.

11These were the king's orders: the Jewish people in every city have the right to gather together to protect themselves. They may destroy, kill and completely wipe out the army of any area or people who attack them. And they are to do the same to the women and children of that army. They may also take by force the property of their enemies. 12The one day set for the Jewish people to do this in all the empire of King Xerxes was the thirteenth day of the twelfth month, the month of Adar. 13A copy of the king's order was to be sent out as a law in every area. It was to be made known to the people of every nation living in the kingdom so the Jewish people would be ready on that set day to strike back at their enemies.

Sidelight The Persians may not have had Royal Mail, but they had an excellent postal system to deliver Mordecai's letter (Esther 8:10). The Persian Empire was divided into 20 satrapies (or provinces), which were interconnected by an efficient postal service begun by King Cyrus around 535 BC.

14The messengers hurried out, riding on the royal horses, because the king commanded those messengers to hurry. And the order was also given in the palace at Susa.

15Mordecai left the king's presence wearing royal clothes of blue and white and a large gold crown. He also had a purple robe made of the best linen. And the people of Susa shouted for joy. 16It was a time of happiness, joy, gladness and honour for the Jewish people. 17As the king's order went to every area and city, there was joy and gladness among the Jewish people. In every area

and city to which the king's order went, they
were having feasts and celebrating. And many
people through all the empire became Jews,
because they were afraid of the Jewish people.

Victory for the Jewish People

9 The order the king had commanded was to
be done on the thirteenth day of the twelfth
month, the month of Adar. That was the day the
enemies of the Jewish people had hoped to defeat
them, but that was changed. So the Jewish peo-
ple themselves defeated those who hated them.
[2]The Jews met in their cities in all the empire of
King Xerxes in order to attack those who wanted
to harm them. No one was strong enough to fight
against them, because all the other people living
in the empire were afraid of them. [3]All the im-
portant men of the areas, the governors, captains
of the soldiers, and the king's officers helped
the Jewish people, because they were afraid of
Mordecai. [4]Mordecai was very important in the
king's palace. He was famous in all the empire,
because he was becoming a leader of more and
more people.

[5]And, with their swords, the Jewish people de-
feated all their enemies, killing and destroying
them. And they did what they wanted with
those people who hated them. [6]In the palace
at Susa, they killed and destroyed 500 men.
[7]They also killed: Parshandatha, Dalphon, Aspatha,
[8]Poratha, Adalia, Aridatha, [9]Parmashta, Arisai,
Aridai and Vaizatha, [10]the ten sons of Haman,
son of Hammedatha, the enemy of the Jewish
people. But the Jewish people did not take their
belongings.

[11]On that day the number killed in the palace
at Susa was reported to the king. [12]The king said
to Queen Esther, "The Jewish people have killed
and destroyed 500 people in the palace at Susa,
and they have also killed Haman's ten sons. What
have they done in the rest of the king's empire!
Now what else are you asking? I will do it! What
else do you want? It will be done!"

[13]Esther answered, "If it pleases the king, give
the Jewish people who are in Susa permission to
do again tomorrow what the king ordered for
today. And let the bodies of Haman's ten sons be
hanged on the platform."

[14]So the king ordered that it be done. A law
was given in Susa, and the bodies of the ten sons
of Haman were hanged. [15]The Jewish people in
Susa came together on the fourteenth day of the
month of Adar. They killed 300 people in Susa,
but they did not take their belongings.

[16]At that same time, all the Jewish people in
the king's empire also met to protect themselves
and get rid of their enemies. They killed 75,000
of those who hated them, but they did not take
their belongings. [17]This happened on the thir-
teenth day of the month of Adar. On the four-
teenth day they rested and made it a day of joyful
feasting.

The Feast of Purim

[18]But the Jewish people in Susa met on the
thirteenth and fourteenth days of the month of
Adar. Then they rested on the fifteenth day and
made it a day of joyful feasting.

[19]This is why the Jewish people who live in the
country and small villages celebrate on the four-
teenth day of the month of Adar. It is a day of
joyful feasting and a day for exchanging gifts.

[20]Mordecai wrote down everything that had
happened. Then he sent letters to all the Jewish
people in all the empire of King Xerxes, far and
near. [21]He told them to celebrate every year on
the fourteenth and fifteenth days of the month of
Adar, [22]because that was when the Jewish people
got rid of their enemies. They were also to cele-
brate it as the month their sadness was turned to
joy and their crying for the dead was turned into
celebration. He told them to celebrate those days
as days of joyful feasting and as a time for giving
food to each other and presents to the poor.

Sidelight The two despised Jews rose to become very important, but they never forgot their roots. Because of Esther and Mordecai's faithfulness, Jews celebrate each year in February or March with parties, gifts and aid to the poor as part of the joyous Feast of Purim (Esther 9:8–32).

[23]So the Jewish people agreed to do what
Mordecai had written to them, and they agreed to
hold the celebration every year. [24]Haman son of
Hammedatha, the Agagite, was the enemy of all
the Jewish people. He had made an evil plan
against the Jewish people to destroy them, and he
had thrown the Pur (that is, the lot[d]) to choose a
day to ruin and destroy them. [25]But when the
king learned of the evil plan, he sent out written
orders that the evil plans Haman had made
against the Jewish people would be used against
him. And those orders said that Haman and his
sons should be hanged on the platform. [26]So
these days were called Purim, which comes from
the word "Pur" (the lot). Because of everything
written in this letter and what they had seen and
what happened to them, [27]the Jewish people set
up this custom. They and their descendants[d] and
all those who join them are always to celebrate
these two days every year. They should do it
in the right way and at the time Mordecai had

ordered them in the letter. 28These two days should
be remembered and celebrated from now on in
every family, in every area and in every city.
These days of Purim should always be celebrated
by the Jewish people, and their descendants
should always remember to celebrate them too.
29So Queen Esther daughter of Abihail, along
with Mordecai the Jew, wrote this second letter
about Purim. Using the power they had, they
wrote to prove the first letter was true. 30And
Mordecai sent letters to all the Jewish people in
the 127 areas of the kingdom of Xerxes, writing
them a message of peace and truth. 31He wrote
to set up these days of Purim at the chosen
times. Mordecai the Jew and Queen Esther had
sent out the order for the Jewish people, just as
they had set up things for themselves and their
descendants: On these two days the people
should give up eating and cry loudly. 32Esther's
letter set up the rules for Purim and they were
written down in the records.

The Greatness of Mordecai

10 King Xerxes demanded taxes every-
where, even from the cities on the sea-
coast. 2And all the great things Xerxes did by his
power and strength are written in the record
books of the kings of Media and Persia. Also
written in those record books are all the things
done by Mordecai, whom the king made great.
3Mordecai the Jew was second in importance to
King Xerxes, and he was the most important
man among the Jewish people. His fellow Jews
respected him very much, because he worked
for the good of his people and spoke up for the
safety of all the Jewish people.

Job

Why Read This Book:

- Learn patience from someone who is suffering unfairly (Job 1:21—2:10; 16; 19).
- Realise it's OK to question God (Job 10, 13, 23).
- See how God is always there, even when he doesn't seem to be (Job 38—42).

When?

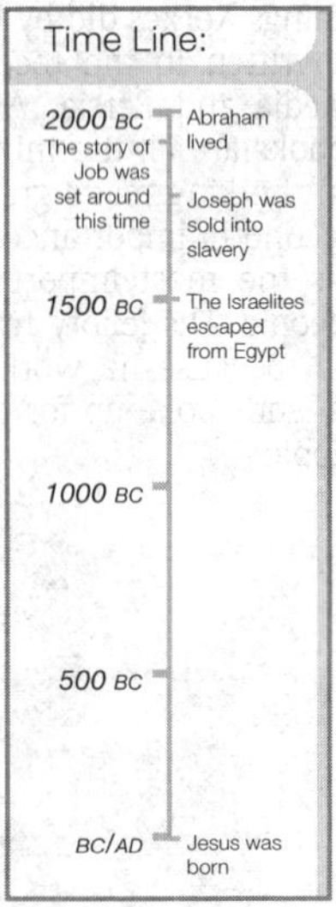

Behind the Scenes:

Why do good people suffer? Why do bad people seem to get away with everything? How can God love us if he lets bad things happen to us? If you have ever asked those questions, you are not alone. For centuries, people have asked them and struggled with them.

The book of Job addresses those questions as it tells about Job, an upright and wealthy man. Like others of his day, he believed that all his blessings were the result of his goodness. He accepted traditional answers to life's questions.

Then his life fell apart. He lost everything – his family, his health and his belongings. Life wasn't supposed to work out this way. In his pain, he cried out angrily to God, "Why do innocent people suffer?"

Four friends made matters worse by telling Job the same old thing: God rewards the righteous and punishes sinners (Job 3—37). Job sincerely believed he was innocent, but he couldn't explain the suffering. He felt betrayed by God. Yet patiently he kept his faith in God and waited for God's answers to his questions. ▷

Where?

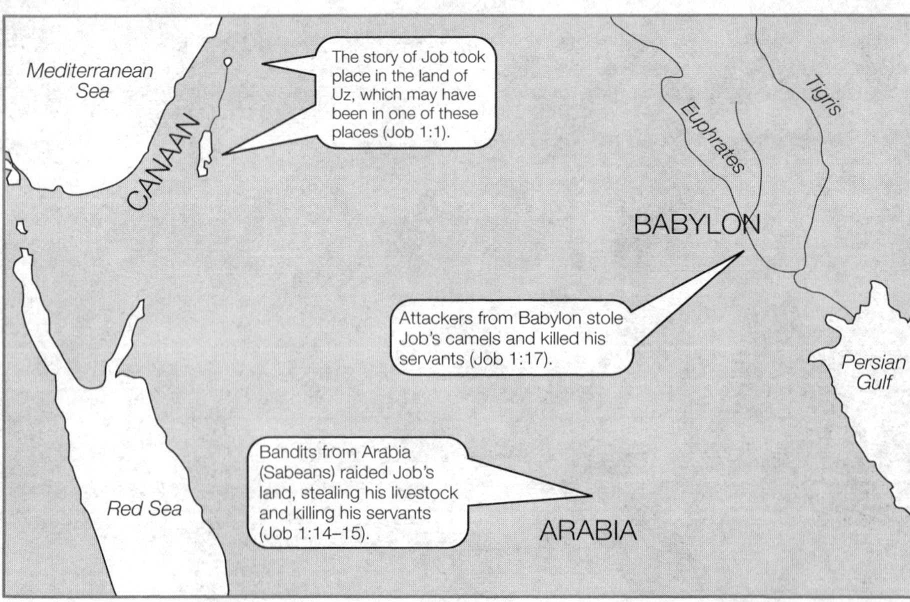

Behind the Scenes (cont.): Job and his friends never settled their debate. Suddenly God appeared on the scene through a storm, in chapters 38—41. He didn't answer Job, though he did speak to him. God reminded Job that his greatness and wisdom are beyond human understanding. Job then realised that it wasn't his place to try to understand God. Instead, he was to follow God faithfully no matter what happened.

People continue to struggle with why good people suffer. The book of Job tells us that it's OK to ask God tough questions. It also challenges us to remain faithful in spite of suffering. In the end, we can trust in God's goodness, justice and wisdom – even when we can't see it ourselves.

Job, the Good Man

1 A man named Job lived in the land of Uz. He
was an honest and innocent man; he hon-
oured God and stayed away from evil. 2Job had
seven sons and three daughters. 3He owned
7,000 sheep, 3,000 camels, 500 teams of oxen
and 500 female donkeys. He also had a large
number of servants. He was the greatest man
among all the people of the East.
4Job's sons took turns holding feasts in their
homes and invited their sisters to eat and drink
with them. 5After a feast was over, Job would
send and have them made clean.[d] Early in the
morning Job would offer a burnt offering for each
of them, because he thought, "My children may
have sinned and cursed God in their hearts." Job
did this every time.

Satan Appears Before the LORD

6One day the angels came to show themselves
before the LORD, and Satan was with them. 7The
LORD said to Satan, "Where have you come
from?"
Satan answered the LORD, "I have been wan-
dering around the earth, going back and forth
in it."
8Then the LORD said to Satan, "Have you no-
ticed my servant Job? No one else on earth is like
him. He is an honest and innocent man, honour-
ing God and staying away from evil."
9But Satan answered the LORD, "Job honours
God for a good reason. 10You have put a wall
around him, his family and everything he owns.
You have blessed the things he has done. His
flocks and herds are so large they almost cover
the land. 11But reach out your hand and destroy
everything he has, and he will curse you to your
face."
12The LORD said to Satan, "All right, then.
Everything Job has is in your power, but you
must not touch Job himself." Then Satan left the
LORD's presence.
13One day Job's sons and daughters were eat-
ing and drinking wine together at the oldest
brother's house. 14A messenger came to Job and
said, "The oxen were ploughing and the donkeys
were eating grass nearby, 15when the Sabeans at-
tacked and carried them away. They killed the
servants with swords, and I am the only one who
escaped to tell you!"
16The messenger was still speaking when an-
other messenger arrived and said, "Lightning
from God fell from the sky. It burned up the
sheep and the servants, and I am the only one
who escaped to tell you!"
17The second messenger was still speaking
when another messenger arrived and said, "The
Babylonians sent three groups of attackers that
swept down and stole your camels and killed the
servants. I am the only one who escaped to
tell you!"

Sidelight The theft of Job's camels is equivalent to stealing a Landrover today, as these amazing animals were prized for their swift and reliable transport abilities in the hot desert. A one-humped camel could reach a top speed of 16 kilometres an hour.

18The third messenger was still speaking when
another messenger arrived and said, "Your sons
and daughters were eating and drinking wine to-
gether at the oldest brother's house. 19Suddenly a
great wind came from the desert, hitting all four
corners of the house at once. The house fell in on
the young people, and they are all dead. I am the
only one who escaped to tell you!"
20When Job heard this, he got up and tore his
robe and shaved his head to show how sad he was.

Then he bowed down to the ground to worship
God. 21 He said:

"I was naked when I was born,
and I will be naked when I die.
The LORD gave these things to me,
and he has taken them away.
Praise the name of the LORD."

22 In all this Job did not sin or blame God.

Satan Appears Before the LORD Again

2 On another day the angels came to show
themselves before the LORD, and Satan was
with them again. 2 The LORD said to Satan,
"Where have you come from?"
Satan answered the LORD, "I have been wan-
dering around the earth, going back and forth
in it."
3 Then the LORD said to Satan, "Have you
noticed my servant Job? No one else on earth is
like him. He is an honest and innocent man,
honouring God and staying away from evil. You
caused me to ruin him for no good reason, but
he continues to be without blame."
4 "One skin for another!" Satan answered. "A
man will give all he has to save his own life. 5 But
reach out your hand and destroy his flesh and
bones, and he will curse you to your face."
6 The LORD said to Satan, "All right, then. Job is
in your power, but you may not take his life."
7 So Satan left the LORD's presence. He put
painful sores on Job's body, from the top of his
head to the soles of his feet. 8 Job took a piece of
broken pottery to scrape himself, and he sat in
ashes in misery.
9 Job's wife said to him, "Why are you trying to
stay innocent? Curse God and die!"
10 Job answered, "You are talking like a foolish
woman. Should we take only good things from
God and not trouble?" In spite of all this Job did
not sin in what he said.

DEATH

Praise Beyond the Grave

The bomb detonated. In milliseconds, a ball of heat and fire exploded, filling the train with debris, bits of metal and shards of glass. There were no survivors.

A hundred miles away was Abi. She'd stayed at home that day to do some exam revision before a mate's party. Her family had caught the train and gone out shopping. They'd caught the train that had blown up.

As time passed, Abi experienced a vast range of emotions. Sometimes she could do nothing but cry – cry until it hurt. Other times she felt guilty for not being on the train too. Some days just breathing seemed difficult; others were almost normal. Initially, her friends called round and tried to cheer her up. After a while though, they visited less often. They started to say things like, "It is time you got over it now" and "Try not to get angry at God" – but time was not making it better, and Abi was furious with God.

Job is struck by an incredible disaster. He is overwhelmed with grief and throws his whole self into mourning. He gets angry, and dares to ask why. Then he does an incredible thing. He bows down and worships the Lord, who is always in control, who rules our yesterday, our today and our tomorrow and who gives us life everlasting. Maybe Job's response in **Job 1:18–22** is not a bad one to copy.

- How does this passage affect your view of God?
- What would you say to Abi if you were one of her friends?

Consider . . .

- making a list of all that God has given you. Look at the list and give thanks to him, then tell him it is his if he needs it back again one day.
- visiting someone you know who has had someone close to them die. Let them know you read this and thought of them – it may be difficult, but they will really appreciate it.

For more, see . . .

- Psalm 23 (p.513)
- 1 Corinthians 15:35–58 (p.1236)
- Romans 5 (p.1190)
- Revelation 21 (p.1403)

Job's Three Friends Come to Help

11Now Job had three friends: Eliphaz the
Temanite, Bildad the Shuhite and Zophar the
Naamathite. When these friends heard about
Job's troubles, they agreed to meet and visit him.
They wanted to show their concern and to com-
fort him. 12They saw Job from far away, but he
looked so different they almost didn't recognise
him. They began to cry loudly and tore their
robes and put earth on their heads to show how
sad they were. 13Then they sat on the ground
with Job for seven days and seven nights. No one
said a word to him because they saw how much
he was suffering.

Job Curses His Birth

3 After seven days Job cried out and cursed
the day he had been born, 2saying:

3"Let the day I was born be destroyed,
and the night it was said, 'A boy is born!'
4Let that day turn to darkness.
Don't let God care about it.
Don't let light shine on it.
5Let darkness and gloom have that day.
Let a cloud hide it.
Let thick darkness cover its light.
6Let thick darkness capture that night.
Don't count it among the days of the year
or put it in any of the months.
7Let that night be empty,
with no shout of joy to be heard.
8Let those who curse days curse that day.
Let them prepare to wake up the sea
monster Leviathan. [d]
9Let that day's morning stars never appear;
let it wait for daylight that never comes.
Don't let it see the first light of dawn,
10because it allowed me to be born
and did not hide trouble from my eyes.

11"Why didn't I die as soon as I was born?
Why didn't I die when I came out of the
womb?
12Why did my mother's lap receive me,
and my mother's breasts feed me?
13If they had not been there,
I would be lying dead in peace;
I would be asleep and at rest
14with kings and wise men of the earth
who built places for themselves that are
now ruined.
15I would be asleep with rulers
who filled their houses with gold and silver.
16Why was I not buried like a child born dead,
like a baby who never saw the light of day?
17In the grave the wicked stop making trouble,
and the tired workers are at rest.
18In the grave there is rest for the captives
who no longer hear the shout of the slave
driver.
19People great and small are in the grave,
and the slave is freed from his master.

20"Why is light given to those in misery?
Why is life given to those who are so unhappy?
21They want to die, but death does not come.
They search for death more than for hidden
treasure.
22They are very happy
when they get to the grave.
23They cannot see where they are going.
God has hidden the road ahead.
24I make sad sounds as I eat;
my groans pour out like water.
25Everything I feared and dreaded
has happened to me.
26I have no peace or quietness.
I have no rest, only trouble."

Eliphaz Speaks

4 Then Eliphaz the Temanite answered:

2"If someone tried to speak with you, would
you be upset?
I cannot keep from speaking.
3Think about the many people you have taught
and the weak hands you have made strong.
4Your words have comforted those who fell,
and you have strengthened those who
could not stand.
5But now trouble comes to you, and you are
discouraged;
trouble hits you, and you are terrified.
6You should have confidence because you
respect God;
you should have hope because you are
innocent.

7"Remember that the innocent will not die;
honest people will never be destroyed.
8I have noticed that people who plough evil
and plant trouble, harvest it.
9God's breath destroys them,
and a blast of his anger kills them.
10Lions may roar and growl,
but when the teeth of a strong lion are
broken,
11that lion dies of hunger.
The cubs of the mother lion are scattered.

12"A word was brought to me in secret,
and my ears heard a whisper of it.
13It was during a troublesome dream
when people are in deep sleep.
14I was trembling with fear;
all my bones were shaking.

[15]A spirit glided past my face,
and the hair on my body stood on end.
[16]The spirit stopped,
but I could not see what it was.
A shape stood before my eyes,
and I heard a quiet voice.
[17]It said, 'Can a human be more right
than God?
Can a person be pure before his maker?
[18]God does not trust his angels;
he blames them for mistakes.
[19]So he puts even more blame on people who
live in clay houses,[n]
whose foundations are made of dust,
who can be crushed like a moth.
[20]Between dawn and sunset many people are
broken to pieces;
without being noticed, they die and are
gone for ever.
[21]The ropes of their tents are pulled up,
and they die without wisdom.'

5 "Call if you want to, Job, but no one will
answer you.
You can't turn to any of the holy ones.
[2]Anger kills the fool,
and jealousy kills the stupid.
[3]I have seen a fool succeed,
but I cursed his home immediately.
[4]His children are far from safety
and are crushed in court with no defence.
[5]The hungry eat his harvest,
even taking what grew among the thorns,
and thirsty people want his wealth.
[6]Hard times do not come up from the ground,
and trouble does not grow from the earth.
[7]People produce trouble
as surely as sparks fly upwards.

[8]"But if I were you, I would call on God
and bring my problem before him.
[9]God does wonders that cannot be understood;
he does so many miracles[d] they cannot be
counted.
[10]He gives rain to the earth
and sends water on the fields.
[11]He makes the humble person important
and lifts the sad to places of safety.
[12]He ruins the plans of those who trick others
so they have no success.
[13]He catches the wise in their own clever traps
and sweeps away the plans of those who try
to trick others.
[14]Darkness covers them up in the daytime;
even at noon they feel around in the dark.
[15]God saves the needy from their lies
and from the harm done by powerful people.
[16]So the poor have hope,
while those who are unfair are silenced.

[17]"The one whom God corrects is happy,
so do not hate being corrected by the
Almighty.
[18]God hurts, but he also bandages up;
he injures, but his hands also heal.
[19]He will save you from six troubles;
even seven troubles will not harm you.
[20]God will buy you back from death in times of
hunger,
and in battle he will save you from the
sword.
[21]You will be protected from the tongue that
strikes like a whip,
and you will not be afraid when destruction
comes.
[22]You will laugh at destruction and hunger,
and you will not fear the wild animals,
[23]because you will have an agreement with the
stones in the field,
and the wild animals will be at peace with you.
[24]You will know that your tent is safe,
because you will check the things you own
and find nothing missing.
[25]You will know that you will have many
children,
and your descendants[d] will be like the grass
on the earth.
[26]You will come to the grave with all your
strength,
like bundles of grain gathered at the right
time.

[27]"We have checked this, and it is true,
so hear it and decide what it means to you."

Job Answers Eliphaz

6 Then Job answered:

[2]"I wish my suffering could be weighed
and my misery put on scales.
[3]My sadness would be heavier than the sand
of the seas.
No wonder my words seem careless.
[4]The arrows of the Almighty are in me;
my spirit drinks in their poison;
God's terrors are gathered against me.

Sidelight There are many names for God throughout the Bible; the characters in Job referred to him as "God Almighty". The literal translation from Hebrew is "Lord of the Mountain" (Job 6:4).

clay houses This is probably talking about people's bodies.

5A wild donkey does not bray when it has
grass to eat,
and an ox is quiet when it has food.
6Tasteless food is not eaten without salt,
and there is no flavour in the white of
an egg.
7I refuse to touch it;
such food makes me sick.

8"How I wish that I might have what I ask for
and that God would give me what I
hope for.
9How I wish God would crush me
and reach out his hand to destroy me.
10Then I would have this comfort
and be glad even in this unending pain,
because I would know I did not reject the
words of the Holy One.

11"I do not have the strength to wait.
There is nothing to hope for,
so why should I be patient?
12I do not have the strength of stone;
my flesh is not bronze.
13I have no power to help myself,
because success has been taken away
from me.

14"They say, 'A man's friends should be kind to
him when he is in trouble,
even if he stops fearing the Almighty.'
15But my brothers cannot be counted on.
They are like streams that do not always
flow,
streams that sometimes run over.
16They are made dark by melting ice
and rise with melting snow.
17But they stop flowing in the dry season;
they disappear when it is hot.
18Travellers turn away from their paths
and go into the desert and die.
19The groups of travellers from Tema look for
water,
and the traders of Sheba look hopefully.
20They are upset because they had been sure;
when they arrive, they are disappointed.
21You also have been of no help.
You see something terrible, and you are
afraid.
22I have never said, 'Give me a gift.
Use your wealth to pay my debt.
23Save me from the enemy's power.
Buy me back from the clutches of cruel
people.'

24"Teach me, and I will be quiet.
Show me where I have been wrong.
25Honest words are painful,
but your arguments prove nothing.
26Do you mean to correct what I say?
Will you treat the words of a troubled man
as if they were only wind?
27You would even gamble for orphans
and would trade away your friend.

28"But now please look at me.
I would not lie to your face.
29Change your mind; do not be unfair;
think again, because my innocence is being
questioned.
30What I am saying is not wicked;
I can tell the difference between right and
wrong.

7 "People have a hard task on earth,
and their days are like those of a
hired man.
2They are like a slave wishing for the evening
shadows,
like a labourer waiting to be paid.
3But I am given months that are empty,
and nights of misery have been given to me.
4When I lie down, I think, 'How long until I
get up?'
The night is long, and I toss until dawn.
5My body is covered with worms and scabs,
and my skin is broken and full of sores.

6"My days go by faster than a weaver's tool,
and they come to an end without hope.
7Remember, God, that my life is only a breath.
My eyes will never see happy times again.
8Those who see me now will see me no more;
you will look for me, but I will be gone.
9As a cloud disappears and is gone,
people go to the grave and never return.
10They will never come back to their houses
again,
and their places will not know them any
more.

11"So I will not stay quiet;
I will speak out in the suffering of my spirit.
I will complain because I am so unhappy.
12I am not the sea or the sea monster.
So why have you set a guard over me?
13Sometimes I think my bed will comfort me
or that my couch will stop my complaint.
14Then you frighten me with dreams
and terrify me with visions.
15My throat prefers to be choked;
my bones welcome death.
16I hate my life; I don't want to live for ever.
Leave me alone, because my days have no
meaning.

17"Why do you make people so important
and give them so much attention?
18You examine them every morning
and test them every moment.

19Will you never look away from me
or leave me alone even long enough to
swallow?
20If I have sinned, what have I done to
you,
you watcher of men?
Why have you made me your target?
Have I become a heavy load for you?
21Why don't you pardon my wrongs
and forgive my sins?
I will soon lie down in the dust of death.
Then you will search for me, but I will be
no more."

Bildad Speaks to Job

8 Then Bildad the Shuhite answered:

2"How long will you say such things?
Your words are no more than wind.
3God does not twist justice;
the Almighty does not make wrong what is
right.
4Your children sinned against God,
and he punished them for their sins.
5But you should ask God for help
and pray to the Almighty for mercy.
6If you are good and honest,
he will stand up for you
and bring you back where you belong.
7Where you began will seem unimportant,
because your future will be so successful.

8"Ask old people;
find out what their ancestors learned,
9because we were only born yesterday and
know nothing.
Our days on earth are only a shadow.
10Those people will teach you and tell you
and speak about what they know.

DEPRESSION

Stirring Up Life

Mandy sat beside the swirling river that ran through town. Her fright and hurt had changed into a deadly heaviness. It stifled her. It dulled all hope.

Only last week everything had seemed all right. Then Stuart dumped her – just put his arm around her best friend and went off with her. It nearly killed Mandy. How could he . . . when he said he loved her? And how could Sheila?

Mandy tried to talk to her mum, but the whole house was a constant battlefield, with everyone yelling at each other. Her stepfather was out of work and there wasn't enough money to go round.

The water invited her into its depths. It offered an easy way out.

"Can I sit here with you?"

Mandy looked up at a tall girl. She had seen her a few times at school, always by herself, but self-assured, at ease.

"If you want."

"I'm nobody to you, but . . . I know what happened, and I care." The girl sat down. "I've been there. And even though it doesn't seem possible now, things will get better. Just hang on in there, OK?"

Mandy looked into the girl's brown eyes. Their sincerity stirred life inside Mandy.

Like Mandy, Job felt overwhelmed by a sense of loss and depression. Read his story in **Job 7:1–8**.

- How does Mandy's depression compare with Job's?
- When you feel the way Job did in verses 3 and 7, what do you need most?

Consider . . .

- talking to a trusted friend about a problem that's getting you down.
- organising a peer counselling programme at your church or school. Talk to your youth leader or school teacher for ideas.

For more, see . . .

- Psalm 139:1–24 (p.581)
- Philippians 2:1–4 (p.1282)
- 2 Corinthians 1:3–7 (p.1241)

11Papyrus[d] plants cannot grow where there is
no swamp,
and reeds cannot grow tall without water.
12While they are still growing and not yet cut,
they will dry up quicker than grass.
13That is what will happen to those who
forget God;
the hope of the wicked will be gone.
14What they hope in is easily broken;
what they trust is like a spider's web.
15They lean on the spider's web, but it breaks.
They hold on to it, but it does not hold up.
16They are like well-watered plants in the
sunshine
that spread their roots all through the
garden.
17They wrap their roots around a pile of rocks
and look for a place among the stones.
18But if a plant is torn from its place,
then that place rejects it and says, 'I never
saw you.'
19Now joy has gone away;
other plants grow up from the same earth.

20"Surely God does not reject the innocent
or give strength to those who do evil.
21God will yet fill your mouth with laughter
and your lips with shouts of joy.
22Your enemies will be covered with shame,
and the tents of the wicked will be gone."

Job Answers Bildad

9 Then Job answered:

2"Yes, I know that this is true,
but how can anyone be right in the
presence of God?
3Someone might want to argue with God,
but no one could answer God,
not even one out of a thousand.
4God's wisdom is deep, and his power
is great;
no one can fight him without getting hurt.
5God moves mountains without anyone
knowing it
and turns them over when he is angry.
6He shakes the earth out of its place
and makes its foundations tremble.
7He commands the sun not to shine
and shuts off the light of the stars.
8He alone stretches out the skies
and walks on the waves of the sea.
9It is God who made the Bear, Orion and the
Pleiades[n]
and the groups of stars in the southern sky.
10He does wonders that cannot be understood;
he does so many miracles[d] they cannot be
counted.
11When he passes me, I cannot see him;
when he goes by me, I do not
recognise him.
12If he snatches something away, no one can
stop him
or say to him, 'What are you doing?'
13God will not hold back his anger.
Even the helpers of the monster Rahab[d] lie
at his feet in fear.
14So how can I argue with God,
or even find words to argue with him?
15Even if I were right, I could not answer him;
I could only beg God, my Judge, for mercy.
16If I called to him and he answered,
I still don't believe he would listen to me.
17He would crush me with a storm
and multiply my wounds for no reason.
18He would not let me catch my breath
but would overwhelm me with misery.
19When it comes to strength, God is stronger
than I;
when it comes to justice, no one can
accuse him.
20Even if I were right, my own mouth would
say I was wrong;
if I were innocent, my mouth would say I
was guilty.

21"I am innocent,
but I don't care about myself.
I hate my own life.
22It is all the same. That is why I say,
'God destroys both the innocent and the
guilty.'
23If the whip brings sudden death,
God will laugh at the suffering of the
innocent.
24When the land falls into the hands of evil
people,
he covers the judges' faces so they can't
see it.
If it is not God who does this, then who is
it?

25"My days go by faster than a runner;
they fly away without my seeing any joy.
26They glide past like paper boats.
They attack like eagles swooping down to
feed.
27Even though I say, 'I will forget my
complaint;
I will change the look on my face and
smile,'

Bear . . . Pleiades Names of well-known groups of stars.

28I still dread all my suffering.
I know you will hold me guilty.
29I have already been found guilty,
so why should I struggle for no reason?
30I might wash myself with soap
and scrub my hands with strong soap,
31but you would push me into a dirty pit,
and even my clothes would hate me.

32"God is not a man like me, so I cannot answer him.
We cannot meet each other in court.
33I wish there were someone to make peace between us,
someone to decide our case.
34Maybe he could remove God's punishment
so his terror would no longer frighten me.
35Then I could speak without being afraid,
but I am not able to do that.

10 "I hate my life,
so I will complain without holding back;
I will speak because I am so unhappy.
2I will say to God: Do not hold me guilty,
but tell me what you have against me.
3Does it make you happy to trouble me?
Don't you care about me, the work of your hands?
Are you happy with the plans of evil people?
4Do you have human eyes
that see as we see?
5Are your days like the days of man,
and your years like our years?
6You look for the evil I have done
and search for my sin.
7You know I am not guilty,
but no one can save me from your power.

8"Your hands shaped and made me.
Do you now turn around and destroy me?
9Remember that you moulded me like a piece of clay.
Will you now turn me back into dust?
10You formed me inside my mother
like cheese formed from milk.
11You dressed me with skin and flesh;
you sewed me together with bones and muscles.
12You gave me life and showed me kindness,
and in your care you watched over my life.

13"But in your heart you hid other plans.
I know this was in your mind.
14If I sinned, you would watch me
and would not let my sin go unpunished.
15How terrible it will be for me if I am guilty!
Even if I am right, I cannot lift my head.
I am full of shame
and experience only pain.
16If I hold up my head, you hunt me like a lion
and again show your terrible power against me.
17You bring new witnesses against me
and increase your anger against me.
Your armies come against me.

18"So why did you allow me to be born?
I wish I had died before anyone saw me.
19I wish I had never lived,
but had been carried straight from birth to the grave.
20The few days of my life are almost over.
Leave me alone so I can have a moment of joy.
21Soon I will leave; I will not return
from the land of darkness and gloom,
22the land of darkest night,
from the land of gloom and confusion,
where even the light is darkness."

Zophar Speaks to Job

11 Then Zophar the Naamathite answered:
2"Should these words go unanswered?
Is this talker in the right?
3Your lies do not make people quiet;
people should correct you when you make fun of God.
4You say, 'My teachings are right,
and I am clean[d] in God's sight.'
5I wish God would speak
and open his lips against you
6and tell you the secrets of wisdom,
because wisdom has two sides.
Know this: God has even forgotten some of your sin.

7"Can you understand the secrets of God?
Can you search the limits of the Almighty?
8His limits are higher than the heavens;
you cannot reach them!
They are deeper than the grave;
you cannot understand them!
9His limits are longer than the earth
and wider than the sea.

10"If God comes along and puts you in prison
or calls you into court, no one can stop him.
11God knows who is evil,
and when he sees evil, he takes note of it.
12A fool cannot become wise
any more than a wild donkey can be born tame.

13"You must give your whole heart to him
and hold out your hands to him for help.

14Put away the sin that is in your hand;
let no evil remain in your tent.
15Then you can lift up your face without shame,
and you can stand strong without fear.
16You will forget your trouble
and remember it only as water gone by.
17Your life will be as bright as the
noonday sun,
and darkness will seem like morning.
18You will feel safe because there is hope;
you will look around and rest in safety.
19You will lie down and no one will scare you.
Many people will want favours from you.
20But the wicked will not be able to see,
so they will not escape.
Their only hope will be to die."

Job Answers Zophar

12 Then Job answered:
2"You really think you are the only wise people
and that when you die, wisdom will die
with you!
3But my mind is as good as yours;
you are not better than I am.
Everyone knows all these things.
4My friends all laugh at me
when I call on God and expect him to
answer me;
they laugh at me even though I am right
and innocent!
5Those who are comfortable don't care that
others have trouble;
they think it right that those people should
have troubles.
6The tents of robbers are not bothered,
and those who make God angry are safe.
They have their god in their pocket.

7"But ask the animals, and they will teach you,
or ask the birds of the air, and they will
tell you.
8Speak to the earth, and it will teach you,
or let the fish of the sea tell you.
9Every one of these knows
that the hand of the LORD has done this.
10The life of every creature
and the breath of all people are in God's
hand.
11The ear tests words
as the tongue tastes food.
12Older people are wise,
and long life brings understanding.

13"But only God has wisdom and power,
good advice and understanding.
14What he tears down cannot be rebuilt;
anyone he puts in prison cannot be let out.
15If God holds back the waters, there is no rain;
if he lets the waters go, they flood the land.
16He is strong and victorious;
both the one who fools others and the one
who is fooled belong to him.
17God leads the wise away as captives
and turns judges into fools.
18He takes off chains that kings put on
and puts a cloth on their bodies.
19He leads priests away naked
and destroys the powerful.
20He makes trusted people be silent
and takes away the wisdom of older leaders.
21He brings disgrace on important people
and takes away the weapons of the strong.
22He uncovers the deep things of darkness
and brings dark shadows into the light.
23He makes nations great and then destroys
them;
he makes nations large and then scatters
them.
24He takes understanding away from the
leaders of the earth
and makes them wander through a desert
without paths.
25They feel around in darkness with no light;
he makes them stumble like drunkards.

13 "Now my eyes have seen all this;
my ears have heard and
understood it.
2What you know, I also know.
You are not better than I am.
3But I want to speak to the Almighty
and to argue my case with God.
4But you smear me with lies.
You are worthless doctors, all of you!
5I wish you would just stop talking;
then you would really be wise!
6Listen to my argument,
and hear the pleading of my lips.
7You should not speak evil in the name of God;
you cannot speak God's truth by telling lies.
8You should not unfairly choose his side against
mine;
you should not argue the case for God.
9You will not do well if he examines you;
you cannot fool God as you might fool
humans.
10God would surely scold you
if you unfairly took one person's side.
11His bright glory would scare you,
and you would be very much afraid of him.
12Your wise sayings are worth no more than ashes,
and your arguments are as weak as clay.

13"Be quiet and let me speak.
Let things happen to me as they will.

14Why should I put myself in danger
and take my life in my own hands?
15Even if God kills me, I have hope in him;
I will still defend my ways to his face.
16This is my salvation.
The wicked cannot come before him.
17Listen carefully to my words;
let your ears hear what I say.
18See, I have prepared my case,
and I know I will be proved right.
19No one can accuse me of doing wrong.
If someone can, I will be quiet and die.

20"God, please just give me these two things,
and then I will not hide from you:
21Take your punishment away from me,
and stop frightening me with your terrors.
22Then call me, and I will answer,
or let me speak, and you answer.
23How many evil things and sins have I done?
Show me my wrong and my sin.
24Don't hide your face from me;
don't think of me as your enemy.
25Don't punish a leaf that is blown by the wind;
don't chase after straw.
26You write down cruel things against me
and make me suffer for my boyhood sins.
27You put my feet in chains
and keep close watch wherever I go.
You even mark the soles of my feet.

28"Everyone wears out like something rotten,
like clothing eaten by moths.

14 "All of us born to women
live only a few days and have lots of trouble.
2We grow up like flowers and then dry up and die.
We are like a passing shadow that does not last.
3Lord, do you need to watch me like this?
Must you bring me before you to be judged?
4No one can bring something clean from something dirty.
5Our time is limited.
You have given us only so many months to live
and have set limits we cannot go beyond.
6So look away from us and leave us alone
until we put in our time like a labourer.

7"If a tree is cut down,
there is hope that it will grow again
and will send out new branches.
8Even if its roots grow old in the ground,
and its stump dies in the earth,
9at the smell of water it will bud
and put out new shoots like a plant.
10But we die, and our bodies are laid in the ground;
we take our last breath and are gone.
11Water disappears from a lake,
and a river loses its water and dries up.
12In the same way, we lie down and do not rise again;
we will not get up or be awakened
until the heavens disappear.

13"I wish you would hide me in the grave;
hide me until your anger is gone.
I wish you would set a time
and then remember me!
14If a person dies, will he live again?
All my days are a struggle;
I will wait until things change for me.
15You will call, and I will answer you;
you will desire the creature your hands have made.
16Then you will count my steps,
but you will not keep track of my sin.
17My wrongs will be closed up in a bag,
and you will cover up my sin.

18"A mountain washes away and crumbles;
and a rock can be moved from its place.
19Water washes over stones and wears them down,
and rushing waters wash away the earth.
In the same way, you destroy my hope.
20You defeat a person for ever, and he is gone;
you change his appearance and send him away.
21His sons are honoured, but he does not know it;
his sons are disgraced, but he does not see it.
22He only feels the pain of his body
and feels sorry for himself."

Eliphaz Answers Job

15 Then Eliphaz the Temanite answered:
2"A wise person would not answer with empty words
or fill his stomach with the hot east wind.
3He would not argue with useless words
or make speeches that have no value.
4But you even destroy respect for God
and limit the worship of him.
5Your sin teaches your mouth what to say;
you use words to trick others.
6It is your own mouth, not mine, that shows you are wicked;
your own lips testify against you.

7"You are not the first man ever born;
you are not older than the hills.
8You did not listen in on God's secret advice.
But you limit wisdom to yourself.

9You don't know any more than we know.
You don't understand any more than we understand.
10Old people with grey hair are on our side;
they are even older than your father.

Sidelight Today many adults try to hide their age. In Old Testament times age was a mark of maturity, which required respect. That is why Eliphaz supported his arguments by saying that people with grey hair sided with him (Job 15:10).

11Is the comfort God gives you not enough for you,
even when words are spoken gently to you?
12Has your heart carried you away from God?
Why do your eyes flash with anger?
13Why do you speak out your anger against God?
Why do these words pour out of your mouth?

14"How can anyone be pure?
How can someone born to a woman be good?
15God places no trust in his holy ones,
and even the heavens are not pure in his eyes.
16How much less pure is one who is terrible and rotten
and drinks up evil as if it were water!

17"Listen to me, and I will tell you about it;
I will tell you what I have seen.
18These are things wise men have told;
their fathers told them, and they have hidden nothing.
19(The land was given to their fathers only,
and no foreigner lived among them.)
20The wicked suffer pain all their lives;
the cruel suffer during all the years saved up for them.
21Terrible sounds fill their ears,
and when things seem to be going well, robbers attack them.
22Evil people give up trying to escape from the darkness;
it has been decided that they will die by the sword.
23They wander around and will become food for vultures.
They know darkness will soon come.
24Worry and suffering terrify them;
they overwhelm them, like a king ready to attack,
25because they shake their fists at God
and try to get their own way against the Almighty.
26They stubbornly charge at God
with thick, strong shields.

27"Although the faces of the wicked are heavy with fat,
and their waists are fat with flesh,
28they will live in towns that are ruined,
in houses where no one lives,
which are crumbling into ruins.
29The wicked will no longer get rich,
and the riches they have will not last;
the things they own will no longer spread over the land.
30They will not escape the darkness.
A flame will dry up their branches;
God's breath will carry the wicked away.
31The wicked should not fool themselves by trusting what is useless.
If they do, they will get nothing in return.
32Their branches will dry up before they finish growing
and will never turn green.
33They will be like a vine whose grapes are pulled off before they are ripe,
like an olive tree that loses its blossoms.
34People without God can produce nothing.
Fire will destroy the tents of those who take money to do evil,
35who plan trouble and give birth to evil,
whose hearts plan ways to trick others."

Job Answers Eliphaz

16 Then Job answered:
2"I have heard many things like these.
You are all painful comforters!
3Will your long speeches never end?
What makes you keep on arguing?
4I also could speak as you do
if you were in my place.
I could make great speeches against you
and shake my head at you.
5But, instead, I would encourage you,
and my words would bring you relief.

6"Even if I speak, my pain is not less,
and if I don't speak, it still does not go away.
7God, you have surely taken away my strength
and destroyed my whole family.
8You have made me thin and weak,
and this shows I have done wrong.
9God attacks me and tears me with anger;
he grinds his teeth at me;
my enemy stares at me with his angry eyes.

[10]People open their mouths to make fun of me
and slap my cheeks to insult me.
They unite against me.
[11]God has turned me over to evil people
and has handed me over to the wicked.
[12]Everything was fine with me,
but God broke me into pieces;
he held me by the neck and crushed me.
He has made me his target;
[13] his archers surround me.
He stabs my kidneys without mercy;
he spills my blood on the ground.
[14]Again and again God attacks me;
he runs at me like a soldier.

[15]"I have sewed rough cloth over my skin to
show my sadness
and have buried my face in the dust.
[16]My face is red from crying;
I have dark circles around my eyes.
[17]Yet my hands have never done anything cruel,
and my prayer is pure.

[18]"Earth, please do not cover up my blood.
Don't let my cry ever stop being heard!
[19]Even now I have one who speaks for me in
heaven;
the one who is on my side is high above.
[20]The one who speaks for me is my friend.
My eyes pour out tears to God.
[21]He begs God on behalf of a human
as a person begs for his friend.

[22]"Only a few years will pass
before I go on the journey of no return.

17 My spirit is broken;
the days of my life are almost gone.
The grave is waiting for me.
[2]Those who laugh at me surround me;
I watch them insult me.

[3]"God, make me a promise.
No one will make a pledge for me.
[4]You have closed their minds to
understanding.
Do not let them win over me.
[5]A person might speak against his friends for
money,
but if he does, the eyes of his children go
blind.

[6]"God has made my name a curse word;
people spit in my face.
[7]My sight has grown weak because of my
sadness,
and my body is as thin as a shadow.
[8]Honest people are upset about this;
innocent people are upset with those who
do wrong.
[9]But those who do right will continue to do
right,
and those whose hands are not dirty with
sin will grow stronger.

[10]"But, all of you, come and try again!
I do not find a wise person among you.
[11]My days are gone, and my plans have been
destroyed,
along with the desires of my heart.
[12]These men think night is day;
when it is dark, they say, 'Light is near.'
[13]If the only home I hope for is the grave,
if I spread out my bed in darkness,
[14]if I say to the grave, 'You are my father,'
and to the worm, 'You are my mother' or
'You are my sister,'
[15]where, then, is my hope?
Who can see any hope for me?
[16]Will hope go down to the gates of death?
Will we go down together into the dust?"

Bildad Answers Job

18 Then Bildad the Shuhite answered:
[2]"When will you stop these speeches?
Be sensible, and then we can talk.
[3]You think of us as cattle,
as if we are stupid.
[4]You tear yourself to pieces in your anger.
Should the earth be vacant just for you?
Should the rocks move from their places?

[5]"The lamp of the wicked will be put out,
and the flame in their lamps will stop
burning.
[6]The light in their tents will grow dark,
and the lamps by their sides will go out.
[7]Their strong steps will grow weak;
they will fall into their own evil traps.
[8]Their feet will be caught in a net
when they walk into its web.
[9]A trap will catch them by the heel
and hold them tight.
[10]A trap for them is hidden on the ground,
right in their path.
[11]Terrible things startle them from every side
and chase them at every step.
[12]Hunger takes away their strength,
and disaster is at their side.
[13]Disease eats away parts of their skin;
death eats away at their arms and legs.
[14]They are torn from the safety of their tents
and dragged off to Death, the King of
Terrors.
[15]Their tents are set on fire,
and sulphur is scattered over their homes.
[16]Their roots dry up below ground,
and their branches die above ground.

17People on earth will not remember them;
their names will be forgotten in the land.
18They will be driven from light into darkness
and chased out of the world.
19They have no children or descendants[d]
among their people,
and no one will be left alive where they
once lived.
20People of the west will be shocked at what
has happened to them,
and people of the east will be very
frightened.
21Surely this is what will happen to the
wicked;
such is the place of one who does not
know God."

Job Answers Bildad

19 Then Job answered:
2"How long will you hurt me
and crush me with your words?
3You have insulted me ten times now
and attacked me without shame.
4Even if I have sinned,
it is my worry alone.
5If you want to make yourselves look better
than I,
you can blame me for my suffering.
6But know that God has wronged me
and pulled his net around me.

7"I shout, 'I have been wronged!'
But I get no answer.
I scream for help
but I get no justice.
8God has blocked my way so I cannot pass;
he has covered my paths with darkness.
9He has taken away my honour
and removed the crown from my head.
10He beats me down on every side until I am
gone;
he destroys my hope like a fallen tree.
11His anger burns against me,
and he treats me like an enemy.
12His armies gather;
they prepare to attack me.
They camp around my tent.

13"God has made my brothers my enemies,
and my friends have become strangers.
14My relatives have gone away,
and my friends have forgotten me.
15My guests and my female servants treat me
like a stranger;
they look at me as if I were a foreigner.
16I call for my servant, but he does not answer,
even when I beg him with my own mouth.
17My wife can't stand my breath,
and my own family dislikes me.
18Even the little boys hate me
and talk about me when I leave.
19All my close friends hate me;
even those I love have turned against me.
20I am nothing but skin and bones;
I have escaped by the skin of my teeth.
21Pity me, my friends, pity me,
because the hand of God has hit me.
22Why do you chase me as God does?
Haven't you hurt me enough?

23"How I wish my words were written down,
written on a scroll.
24I wish they were carved with an iron pen
into lead,
or carved into stone for ever.
25I know that my Defender lives,
and in the end he will stand upon the earth.
26Even after my skin has been destroyed,
in my flesh I will see God.
27I will see him myself;
I will see him with my very own eyes.
How my heart wants that to happen!

28"If you say, 'We will continue to trouble Job,
because the problem lies with him,'
29you should be afraid of the sword yourselves.
God's anger will bring punishment by the
sword.
Then you will know there is judgement."

Zophar Answers

20 Then Zophar the Naamathite answered:
2"My troubled thoughts cause me to answer,
because I am very upset.
3You correct me and I am insulted,
but I understand how to answer you.

4"You know how it has been for a long time,
ever since people were first put on the earth.
5The happiness of evil people is brief,
and the joy of the wicked lasts only a
moment.
6Their pride may be as high as the heavens,
and their heads may touch the clouds,
7but they will be gone for ever, like their own
dung.
People who knew them will say, 'Where are
they?'
8They will fly away like a dream
and not be found again;
they will be chased away like a vision in
the night.
9Those who saw them will not see them again;
the places where they lived will see them
no more.

10 Their children will have to pay back the poor,
and they will have to give up their wealth.
11 They had the strength of their youth in their
bones,
but it will lie with them in the dust of
death.
12 "Evil may taste sweet in their mouths,
and they may hide it under their tongues.
13 They cannot stand to let go of it;
they keep it in their mouths.
14 But their food will turn sour in their
stomachs,
like the poison of a snake inside them.
15 They have swallowed riches, but they will
spit them out;
God will make them vomit their riches up.
16 They will suck the poison of snakes,
and the snake's fangs will kill them.

Sidelight Snakes were dangerous desert residents in Bible times (Job 20:14–16). Numerous varieties of snake lived in the desert, and about half a dozen of the species were poisonous. In one instance, snakes invaded an Israelite camp (Numbers 21:6–8, p.148), and many of the Israelites died from the bites.

17 They will not admire the sparkling streams
or the rivers flowing with honey and cream.
18 They must give back what they worked for
without eating it;
they will not enjoy the money they made
from their trading,
19 because they troubled the poor and left them
with nothing.
They have taken houses they did not build.

20 "Evil people never lack an appetite,
and nothing escapes their selfishness.
21 But nothing will be left for them to eat;
their riches will not continue.
22 When they still have plenty, trouble will
catch up with them,
and great misery will come down on them.
23 When the wicked fill their stomachs,
God will send his burning anger against
them,
and blows of punishment will fall on them
like rain.
24 The wicked may run away from an iron
weapon,
but a bronze arrow will stab them.
25 They will pull the arrows out of their backs
and pull the points out of their livers.
Terrors will come over them;
26 total darkness waits for their treasure.
A fire not fanned by people will destroy
them
and burn up what is left of their tents.
27 The heavens will show their guilt,
and the earth will rise up against them.
28 A flood will carry their houses away,
swept away on the day of God's anger.
29 This is what God plans for evil people;
this is what he has decided they will
receive."

Job Answers Zophar

21 Then Job answered:
2 "Listen carefully to my words,
and let this be the way you comfort me.
3 Be patient while I speak.
After I have finished, you may continue to
make fun of me.

4 "My complaint is not just against people;
I have reason to be impatient.
5 Look at me and be shocked;
put your hand over your mouth in shock.
6 When I think about this, I am terribly afraid
and my body shakes.
7 Why do evil people live a long time?
They grow old and become more
powerful.
8 They see their children around them;
they watch them grow up.
9 Their homes are safe and without fear;
God does not punish them.
10 Their bulls never fail to mate;
their cows have healthy calves.
11 They send out their children like a flock;
their little ones dance about.
12 They sing to the music of tambourines[d] and
harps,
and the sound of the flute makes them
happy.
13 Evil people enjoy successful lives
and then go peacefully to the grave.
14 They say to God, 'Leave us alone!
We don't want to know your ways.
15 Who is the Almighty that we should
serve him?
What would we gain by praying to him?'
16 The success of the wicked is not their own
doing.
Their way of thinking is different from
mine.
17 Yet how often are the lamps of evil people
turned off?
How often does trouble come to them?
How often do they suffer God's angry
punishment?

18How often are they like straw in the wind
or like chaff[d] that is blown away by a
storm?
19It is said, 'God saves up a person's
punishment for his children.'
But God should punish the wicked
themselves so they will know it.
20Their eyes should see their own destruction,
and they should suffer the anger of the
Almighty.
21They do not care about the families they
leave behind
when their lives have come to an end.

22"No one can teach knowledge to God;
he is the one who judges even the most
important people.
23One person dies while he still has all his
strength,
feeling completely safe and comfortable.
24His body was well fed,
and his bones were strong and healthy.
25But another person dies with an unhappy
heart,
never enjoying any happiness.
26They are buried next to each other,
and worms cover them both.

27"I know very well your thoughts
and your plans to wrong me.
28You ask about me, 'Where is this great man's
house?
Where are the tents where the wicked
live?'
29Have you never asked those who travel?
Have you never listened to their stories?
30On the day of God's anger and punishment,
it is the wicked who are spared.
31Who will accuse them to their faces?
Who will pay them back for the evil they
have done?
32They are carried to their graves,
and someone keeps watch over their
tombs.
33The earth in the valley seems sweet
to them.
Everybody follows after them,
and many people go before them.

34"So how can you comfort me with this
nonsense?
Your answers are only lies!"

Eliphaz Answers

22 Then Eliphaz the Temanite answered:
2"Can anyone be of real use to God?
Can even a wise person do him good?
3Does it help the Almighty for you to be good?
Does he gain anything if you are innocent?
4Does God punish you for respecting him?
Does he bring you into court for this?
5No! It is because your evil is without limits
and your sins have no end.
6You took your brothers' things for a debt
they didn't owe;
you took clothes from people and left them
naked.
7You did not give water to tired people,
and you kept food from the hungry.
8You were a powerful man who owned land;
you were honoured and lived in the land.
9But you sent widows away empty-handed,
and you mistreated orphans.
10That is why traps are all around you
and sudden danger frightens you.
11That is why it is so dark you cannot see
and a flood of water covers you.

12"God is in the highest part of heaven.
See how high the highest stars are!
13But you ask, 'What does God know?
Can he judge us through the dark clouds?
14Thick clouds cover him so he cannot see us
as he walks around high up in the sky.'
15Are you going to stay on the old path
where evil people walk?
16They were carried away before their time
was up,
and their foundations were washed away
by a flood.
17They said to God, 'Leave us alone!
The Almighty can do nothing to us.'
18But it was God who filled their houses with
good things.
Their way of thinking is different from
mine.

19"Good people can watch and be glad;
the innocent can laugh at them and say,
20'Surely our enemies are destroyed,
and fire burns up their wealth.'

21"Obey God and be at peace with him;
this is the way to happiness.
22Accept teaching from his mouth,
and keep his words in your heart.
23If you return to the Almighty, you will be
blessed again.
So remove evil from your house.
24Throw your gold nuggets into the dust
and your fine gold among the rocks in the
ravines.
25Then the Almighty will be your gold
and the best silver for you.
26You will find pleasure in the Almighty,
and you will look up to him.

27You will pray to him, and he will hear you,
and you will keep your promises to him.
28Anything you decide will be done,
and light will shine on your ways.
29When people are made humble and you say,
'Have courage,'
then the humble will be saved.
30Even a guilty person will escape
and be saved because your hands are
clean." *d*

Job Answers

23 Then Job answered:
2"My complaint is still bitter today.
I am groaning because God's heavy hand is
on me.
3I wish I knew where to find God
so I could go to where he lives.
4I would present my case before him
and fill my mouth with arguments.
5I would learn how he would answer me
and would think about what he
would say.
6Would he not argue strongly against me?
No, he would really listen to me.
7Then an honest person could present his case
to God,
and I would be saved for ever by my judge.

8"If I go to the east, God is not there;
if I go to the west, I do not see him.
9When he is at work in the north, I catch no
sight of him;
when he turns to the south, I cannot
see him.
10But God knows the way that I take,
and when he has tested me, I will come
out like gold.
11My feet have closely followed his steps;
I have stayed in his way;
I did not turn aside.
12I have never left the commands he has
spoken;
I have treasured his words more than
my own.

13"But he is the only God.
Who can come against him?
He does anything he wants.
14He will do to me what he said he would do,
and he has many plans like this.
15That is why I am frightened of him;
when I think of this, I am afraid of him.
16God has made me afraid;
the Almighty terrifies me.
17But I am not hidden by the darkness,
by the thick darkness that covers my face.

24 "I wish the Almighty would set a time
for judging.
Those who know God do not see such
a day.
2Wicked people take other people's land;
they steal flocks and take them to new
pastures.
3They chase away the orphan's donkey
and take the widow's ox when she has no
money.
4They push needy people off the path;
all the poor of the land hide from them.
5The poor become like wild donkeys in the
desert
who go about their job of finding food.
The desert gives them food for their
children.
6They gather hay and straw in the fields
and pick up leftover grapes from the
vineyard of the wicked.
7They spend the night naked, because they
have no clothes,
nothing to cover themselves in the cold.
8They are soaked from mountain rains
and stay near the large rocks because they
have no shelter.
9The fatherless child is grabbed from its
mother's breast;
they take a poor mother's baby to pay for
what she owes.
10So the poor go around naked without any
clothes;
they carry bundles of grain but still go
hungry;
11they crush olives to get oil
and grapes to get wine, but they still go
thirsty.
12Dying people groan in the city,
and the injured cry out for help,
but God accuses no one of doing wrong.

13"Those who fight against the light
do not know God's ways
or stay in his paths.
14When the day is over, the murderers get up
to kill the poor and needy.
At night they go about like thieves.
15Those who are guilty of adultery *d* watch for
the night,
thinking, 'No one will see us,'
and they keep their faces covered.
16In the dark, evil people break into houses.
In the daytime they shut themselves up in
their own houses,
because they want nothing to do with the
light.
17Darkness is like morning to all these evil
people

who make friends with the terrors of
darkness.

18"They are like foam floating on the water.
Their part of the land is cursed;
no one uses the road that goes by their
vineyards.
19As heat and dryness quickly melt the snow,
so the grave quickly takes away the sinners.
20Their mothers forget them,
and worms will eat their bodies.
They will not be remembered,
so wickedness is broken in pieces like a
stick.
21These evil people abuse women who cannot
have children
and show no kindness to widows.
22But God drags away the strong by his power.
Even though they seem strong, they do not
know how long they will live.
23God may let these evil people feel safe,
but he is watching their ways.
24For a little while they are important, and
then they die;
they are laid low and buried like everyone
else;
they are cut off like the heads of grain.
25If this is not true, who can prove I am
wrong?
Who can show that my words are worth
nothing?"

Bildad Answers

25 Then Bildad the Shuhite answered:

2"God rules and he must be honoured;
he set up order in his high heaven.
3No one can count God's armies.
His light shines on all people.
4So no one can be good in the presence
of God,
and no one born to a woman can be pure.
5Even the moon is not bright
and the stars are not pure in his eyes.
6People are much less! They are like insects.
They are only worms!"

Job Answers Bildad

26 Then Job answered:

2"You are no help to the helpless!
You have not given help to the weak!
3Your advice lacks wisdom!
You have shown little understanding!
4Who has helped you say these words?
And where did you get these words?

5"The spirits of the dead tremble,
those who are beneath and in the waters.
6Death is naked before God;
destruction is uncovered before him.
7God stretches the northern sky out over
empty space
and hangs the earth on nothing.
8He wraps up the waters in his thick clouds,
but the clouds do not break under their
weight.
9He covers the face of the moon,
spreading his clouds over it.
10He draws the horizon like a circle on the
water
at the place where light and darkness meet.
11Heaven's foundations shake
when he thunders at them.
12With his power he controls the sea;
by his wisdom he destroys Rahab,[d] the sea
monster.
13He breathes, and the sky clears.
His hand stabs the fleeing snake.
14And these are only a small part of God's
works.
We only hear a small whisper of him.
Who could understand God's thundering
power?"

27 And Job continued speaking:

2"As surely as God lives, who has taken away
my rights,
the Almighty, who has made me unhappy,
3as long as I am alive
and God's breath of life is in my nose,
4my lips will not speak evil,
and my tongue will not tell a lie.
5I will never agree you are right;
until I die, I will never stop saying I am
innocent.
6I will insist that I am right; I will not back
down.
My sense of right and wrong will never
bother me.

7"Let my enemies be like evil people,
my foes like those who are wrong.
8What hope do the wicked have when
they die,
when God takes their life away?
9God will not listen to their cries
when trouble comes to them.
10They will not find joy in the Almighty,
even though they call out to God all the
time.

11"I will teach you about the power of God
and will not hide the ways of the Almighty.
12You have all seen this yourselves.
So why are we having all this talk that
means nothing?

13"Here is what God has planned for evil
people,
and what the Almighty will give to cruel
people:
14They may have many children, but the sword
will kill them.
Their children who are left will never have
enough to eat.
15Then they will die of disease and be buried,
and the widows will not even cry for them.
16The wicked may heap up silver like piles of
earth
and have so many clothes they are like piles
of clay.
17But good people will wear what evil people
have gathered,
and the innocent will divide up their silver.
18The houses the wicked build are like a
spider's web,
like a hut that a guard builds.
19The wicked are rich when they go to bed,
but they are rich for the last time;
when they open their eyes, everything is
gone.
20Fears come over them like a flood,
and a storm snatches them away in the
night.
21The east wind will carry them away, and then
they are gone,
because it sweeps them out of their place.
22The wind will hit them without mercy
as they try to run away from its power.
23It will be as if the wind is clapping its hands;
it will whistle at them as they run from
their place.

28 "There are mines where people dig
silver
and places where gold is made pure.
2Iron is taken from the ground,
and copper is melted out of rocks.
3Miners bring lights
and search deep into the mines
for metal in thick darkness.
4Miners dig a tunnel far from where people
live,
where no one has ever walked;
they work far from people, swinging and
swaying from ropes.
5Food grows on top of the earth,
but below ground things are changed as if
by fire.
6Sapphires are found in rocks,
and gold dust is also found there.
7No hawk knows that path;
the falcon has not seen it.
8Proud animals have not walked there,
and no lions cross over it.
9Miners hit the rocks of flint
and dig away at the bottom of the
mountains.
10They cut tunnels through the rock
and see all the treasures there.
11They search for places where rivers begin
and bring things hidden out into the light.

12"But where can wisdom be found,
and where does understanding live?
13People do not understand the value of
wisdom;
it cannot be found among those who are
alive.
14The deep ocean says, 'It's not in me;'
the sea says, 'It's not in me.'
15Wisdom cannot be bought with gold,
and its cost cannot be weighed in silver.
16Wisdom cannot be bought with fine gold
or with valuable onyx or sapphire gems.
17Gold and crystal are not as valuable as
wisdom,
and you cannot buy it with jewels of gold.
18Coral and jasper are not worth talking about,
and the price of wisdom is much greater
than rubies.
19The topaz from Cush cannot compare with
wisdom;
it cannot be bought with the purest gold.

20"So where does wisdom come from,
and where does understanding live?
21It is hidden from the eyes of every living
thing,
even from the birds of the air.
22The places of destruction and death say,
'We have heard reports about it.'
23Only God understands the way to wisdom,
and he alone knows where it lives,
24because he looks to the farthest parts of the
earth
and sees everything under the sky.
25When God gave power to the wind
and measured the water,
26when he made rules for the rain
and set a path for a thunderstorm to follow,
27then he looked at wisdom and decided its
worth;
he set wisdom up and tested it.
28Then he said to humans,
'The fear of the Lord is wisdom;
to stay away from evil is understanding.'"

Job Continues

29 Job continued to speak:
2"How I wish for the months that have passed
and the days when God watched over me.

3 God's lamp shone on my head,
and I walked through darkness by his light.
4 I wish for the days when I was strong,
when God's close friendship blessed my house.
5 The Almighty was still with me,
and my children were all around me.
6 It was as if my path were covered with cream
and the rocks poured out olive oil for me.
7 I would go to the city gate
and sit in the public square.
8 When the young men saw me, they would step aside,
and the old men would stand up in respect.
9 The leading men stopped speaking
and covered their mouths with their hands.
10 The voices of the important men were quiet,
as if their tongues stuck to the roof of their mouths.
11 Anyone who heard me spoke well of me,
and those who saw me praised me,
12 because I saved the poor who called out
and the orphan who had no one to help.
13 The dying person blessed me,
and I made the widow's heart sing.
14 I put on right living as if it were clothing;
I wore fairness like a robe and a turban.
15 I was eyes for the blind
and feet for the lame.
16 I was like a father to needy people,
and I took the side of strangers who were in trouble.
17 I broke the fangs of evil people
and snatched the captives from their teeth.

18 "I thought, 'I will live for as many days as there are grains of sand,
and I will die in my own house.

DECISION MAKING

To Fly or Not

Sixteen-year-old Neil stared at the model plane on his desk. He had loved planes all his life. Every penny he earned went on flying lessons, but now he wasn't sure.

The day before, Neil had watched helplessly as a friend's plane crashed before his eyes. He had rushed to the plane to try to help, but the crash was fatal. Neil could still remember cradling his friend's head in his lap; he remembered his dying breath.

What now? Should he go on with his own flying plans? He didn't want to die too.

For two days Neil sat in his bedroom. He analysed the risks, struggled through his fears and dreams, and recalled the conflicting advice given to him: "Follow your dream!" "Dreams are worthless when you're dead!" He didn't know what to do.

Then he took out an old Sunday school notebook he had made. On its cover was a picture of Jesus. Inside he had listed qualities of the Saviour: "He was sinless"; "He championed the poor"; "He was unselfish"; "He was close to God". Neil studied them closely and then closed his eyes in thanksgiving and made his choice.

"Mum," he said, "I hope you and Dad understand, but with God's help, I must go on flying."

Neil Armstrong's decision that day would eventually take him to the moon, to become the first human on its surface.

Neil learned that wisdom in making decisions is sometimes hard to find, as the writer said in **Job 28:20–28**.

- How did Neil and the writer of Job find wisdom?
- If wisdom is as difficult to find as verse 21 states, how do you find it?

Consider . . .

- asking God to give you wisdom concerning an important relationship in your life.
- listing the "fors" and "againsts" of decisions you must make soon. Pray that God will guide you.

For more, see . . .

- Deuteronomy 30:11–20 (p.192)
- Matthew 26:36–45 (p.990)
- Joshua 24:14–15 (p.222)

19My roots will reach down to the water.
The dew will lie on the branches all night.
20New honours will come to me continually,
and I will always have great strength.'

21"People listened to me carefully
and waited quietly for my advice.
22After I finished speaking, they spoke no more.
My words fell very gently on their ears.
23They waited for me as they would for rain
and drank in my words like spring rain.
24I smiled at them when they doubted,
and my approval was important to them.
25I chose the way for them and was their leader.
I lived like a king among his army,
like a person who comforts sad people.

30 "But now men who are younger than I make fun of me.
I would not even have let their fathers
sit with my sheep dogs.
2What use did I have for their strength
since they had lost their strength to work?
3They were thin from hunger
and wandered the dry and ruined land at night.
4They gathered desert plants among the brush
and ate the root of the broom tree.
5They were forced to live away from people;
people shouted at them as if they were thieves.
6They lived in dried up stream beds,
in caves and among the rocks.
7They howled like animals among the bushes
and huddled together in the brush.
8They are worthless people without names
and were forced to leave the land.

9"Now they make fun of me with songs;
my name is a joke among them.
10They hate me and stay far away from me,
but they do not mind spitting in my face.
11God has taken away my strength and made me suffer,
so they attack me with all their anger.
12On my right side they rise up like a mob.
They lay traps for my feet
and prepare to attack me.
13They break up my road
and work to destroy me,
and no one helps me.
14They come at me as if through a hole in the wall,
and they roll in among the ruins.
15Great fears overwhelm me.
They blow my honour away as if by a great wind,
and my safety disappears like a cloud.

16"Now my life is almost over;
my days are full of suffering.
17At night my bones ache;
gnawing pains never stop.
18In his great power God grabs hold of my clothing
and chokes me with the collar of my coat.
19He throws me into the mud,
and I become like earth and ashes.

20"I cry out to you, God, but you do not answer;
I stand up, but you just look at me.
21You have turned on me without mercy;
with your powerful hand you attacked me.
22You snatched me up and threw me into the wind
and tossed me about in the storm.
23I know you will bring me down to death,
to the place where all living people must go.

24"Surely no one would hurt a ruined man
when he cries for help in his time of trouble.
25I cried for those who were in trouble;
I have been very sad for poor people.
26But when I hoped for good, only evil came to me;
when I looked for light, darkness came.
27I never stop being upset;
days of suffering are ahead of me.
28I have turned black, but not by the sun.
I stand up in public and cry for help.
29I have become a brother to wild dogs
and a friend to ostriches.
30My skin has become black and peels off,
as my body burns with fever.
31My harp is tuned to sing a sad song,
and my flute is tuned to moaning.

31 "But I made an agreement with my eyes
not to look with desire at a girl.
2What has God above promised for people?
What has the Almighty planned from on high?
3It is ruin for evil people
and disaster for those who do wrong.
4God sees my ways
and counts every step I take.

5"If I have been dishonest
or lied to others,
6then let God weigh me on honest scales.
Then he will know I have done nothing wrong.
7If I have turned away from doing what is right,
or my heart has been led by my eyes to do wrong,
or my hands have been made unclean,[d]

8then let other people eat what I have planted,
and let my crops be ploughed up.

9"If I have desired another woman
or have waited at my neighbour's door for his wife,
10then let my wife grind another man's grain,
and let other men have sexual relations with her.
11That would be shameful,
a sin to be punished.
12It is like a fire that burns and destroys;
all I have done would be ploughed up.

13"If I have been unfair to my male and female slaves
when they had a complaint against me,
14how could I tell God what I did?
What will I answer when he asks me to explain what I've done?
15God made me in my mother's womb, and he also made them;
the same God formed both of us in our mothers' wombs.

16"I have never refused the appeals of the poor
or let widows give up hope while looking for help.
17I have not kept my food to myself
but have given it to the orphans.
18Since I was young, I have been like a father to the orphans.
From my birth I guided the widows.
19I have not let anyone die for lack of clothes
or let a needy person go without a coat.
20That person's heart blessed me,
because I warmed him with the wool of my sheep.
21I have never hurt an orphan
even when I knew I could win in court.
22If I have, then let my arm fall off my shoulder
and be broken at the joint.
23I fear destruction from God,
and I fear his majesty, so I could not do such things.

24"I have not put my trust in gold
or said to pure gold, 'You are my security.'
25I have not celebrated my great wealth
or the riches my hands had gained.
26I have not thought about worshipping the sun in its brightness
nor admired the moon moving in glory
27so that my heart was pulled away from God.
My hand has never offered the sun and moon a kiss of worship.
28If I had, these also would have been sins to be punished,
because I would have been unfaithful to God.

29"I have not been happy when my enemy fell
or laughed when he had trouble.
30I have not let my mouth sin
by cursing my enemy's life.
31The men of my house have always said,
'Everyone has eaten all he wants of Job's food.'
32No stranger ever had to spend the night in the street,
because I always let travellers stay in my home.
33I have not hidden my sin as others do,
secretly keeping my guilt to myself.
34I was not so afraid of the crowd
that I kept quiet and stayed inside
because I feared being hated by other families.

35("How I wish a court would hear my case!
Here I sign my name to show I have told the truth.
Now let the Almighty answer me;
let the one who accuses me write it down.
36I would wear the writing on my shoulder;
I would put it on like a crown.
37I would explain to God every step I took,
and I would come near to him like a prince.)

38"If my land cries out against me
and its ploughed rows are not wet with tears,
39if I have taken the land's harvest without paying
or have broken the spirit of those who worked the land,
40then let thorns come up instead of wheat,
and let weeds come up instead of barley."

The words of Job are finished.

Elihu Speaks

32 These three men stopped trying to an-
swer Job, because he was so sure he was
right. 2But Elihu son of Barakel the Buzite, from
the family of Ram, became very angry with Job,
because Job claimed he was right instead of God.
3Elihu was also angry with Job's three friends
who had no answer to show that Job was wrong,
yet continued to blame him. 4Elihu had waited
before speaking to Job, because the three friends
were older than he was. 5But when Elihu saw
that the three men had nothing more to say, he
became very angry.
6So Elihu son of Barakel the Buzite said this:

"I am young,
and you are old.
That is why I was afraid
to tell you what I know.

7I thought, 'Older people should speak,
and those who have lived many years
should teach wisdom.'
8But it is the spirit in a person,
the breath of the Almighty, that gives
understanding.
9It is not just older people who are wise;
they are not the only ones who understand
what is right.
10So I say, listen to me.
I too will tell you what I know.
11I waited while you three spoke,
and listened to your explanations.
While you looked for words to use,
12 I paid close attention to you.
But not one of you has proved Job wrong;
none of you has answered his arguments.
13Don't say, 'We have found wisdom;
only God will show Job to be wrong, not
people.'
14Job has not spoken his words against me,
so I will not use your arguments to
answer Job.

15"These three friends are defeated and have
no more to say;
words have failed them.
16Now they are standing there with no answers
for Job.
Now that they are quiet, must I wait to
speak?
17No, I too will speak
and tell what I know.
18I am full of words,
and the spirit in me causes me to speak.
19I am like wine that has been bottled up;
I am ready to burst like a new leather
wine bag.
20I must speak so I will feel relief;
I must open my mouth and answer.
21I will be fair to everyone
and not flatter anyone.
22I don't know how to flatter,
and if I did, my Maker would quickly take
me away.

33 "Now, Job, listen to my words.
Pay attention to everything I say.
2I open my mouth
and am ready to speak.
3My words come from an honest heart,
and I am sincere in saying what I know.
4The Spirit[d] of God created me,
and the breath of the Almighty gave me
life.
5Answer me if you can;
get yourself ready and stand before me.
6I am just like you before God;
I too am made out of clay.
7Don't be afraid of me;
I will not be hard on you.

8"But I heard what you have said;
I heard every word.
9You said, 'I am pure and without sin;
I am innocent and free from guilt.
10But God has found fault with me;
he considers me his enemy.
11He locks my feet in chains
and closely watches everywhere I go.'

12"But I tell you, you are not right in saying this,
because God is greater than we are.
13Why do you accuse God
of not answering anyone?
14God does speak—sometimes one way and
sometimes another—
even though people may not understand it.
15He speaks in a dream or a vision of the night
when people are in a deep sleep,
lying on their beds.
16He speaks in their ears
and frightens them with warnings
17to turn them away from doing wrong
and to keep them from being proud.
18God does this to save a person from death,
to keep him from dying.
19A person may be corrected while in bed in
great pain;
he may have continual pain in his very
bones.
20He may be in such pain that he even hates
food,
even the very best meal.
21His body becomes so thin there is almost
nothing left of it,
and his bones that were hidden now stick out.
22He is near death,
and his life is almost over.

23"But there may be an angel to speak for him,
one out of a thousand, who will tell him
what to do.
24The angel will beg for mercy and say:
'Save him from death.
I have found a way to pay for his life.'
25Then his body is made new like a child's.
It will return to the way it was when he
was young.
26That person will pray to God, and God will
listen to him.
He will see God's face and will shout with
happiness.
And God will set things right for him again.
27Then he will say to others,
'I sinned and twisted what was right,
but I did not receive the punishment I should
have received.

28God bought my life back from death,
and I will continue to enjoy life.'

29"God does all these things to a person
two or even three times
30so he won't die as punishment for his sins
and so he may still enjoy life.

31"Job, pay attention and listen to me;
be quiet, and I will speak.
32If you have anything to say, answer me;
speak up, because I want to prove you
right.
33But if you have nothing to say, then listen
to me;
be quiet, and I will teach you wisdom."

34 Then Elihu said:

2"Hear my words, you wise men;
listen to me, you who know a lot.
3The ear tests words
as the tongue tastes food.
4Let's decide for ourselves what is right,
and let's learn together what is good.

5"Job says, 'I am not guilty,
and God has refused me a fair trial.
6Instead of getting a fair trial,
I am called a liar.
I have been seriously hurt,
even though I have not sinned.'
7There is no other man like Job;
he takes insults as if he were drinking water.
8He keeps company with those who do evil
and spends time with wicked men,
9because he says, 'It is no use
trying to please God.'

10"So listen to me, you who can understand.
God can never do wrong!
It is impossible for the Almighty to do evil.

PERSISTENCE

Change of Plan

Sarah always knew that she wanted to be a doctor. At five years old, she'd play with stethoscopes. At eighteen, she was reading medical books instead of going to the cinema. While the rest of her friends had no idea what they wanted to be, Sarah passionately believed God had called her to be a doctor.

However, the summer just before Sarah was due to go to university, she got ill. She was in and out of hospital, yet the doctors had no idea what was wrong with her. Sarah managed to study whilst constantly trying new medication. But nothing worked. Finally, she got so ill that she had to move back in with her parents to be looked after.

Although never close to death, there were times when Sarah wanted to give up. She couldn't do the job that she loved, and although she still trusted God completely she had no idea why he was allowing her to go through this.

Then her church held a week of prayer. They committed themselves to pleading with God on her behalf, crying out to God to heal her. God answered their prayers and started to heal Sarah in his own time. She was able to start work with the benefit of seeing how much God used her when she thought she was useless. She could see how God was speaking to her in her suffering – teaching her, disciplining her and ultimately healing her.

Sarah still has days when she feels ill. But she no longer feels useless. She knows that our God is a God whose love and promises are constant, even when it may seem like there is no hope. Read **Job 33:14–24**.

- What hope do we see in this passage?
- What does this say about how God teaches and speaks to us?

Consider . . .

- whether you have ever felt you were in a hopeless situation. How did God work in that time?
- reading Ecclesiastes 3:1–11 to see what it says about God's sense of time compared to ours?

For more, see . . .

- Psalm 73:21–28 (p.544)
- Hebrews 12:4–12 (p.1343)

11God pays a person back for what he has done
and gives him what his actions deserve.
12Truly God will never do wrong;
the Almighty will never twist what is right.
13No one chose God to rule over the earth
or put him in charge of the whole world.
14If God should decide
to take away life and breath,
15then everyone would die together
and turn back into dust.

16"If you can understand, hear this;
listen to what I have to say.
17Can anyone govern who hates what is right?
How can you blame God who is both fair
and powerful?
18God is the one who says to kings, 'You are
worthless,'
or to important people, 'You are evil.'
19He is not nicer to princes than other people,
nor kinder to rich people than poor people,
because he made them all with his own
hands.
20They can die in a moment, in the middle of
the night.
They are struck down, and then they pass
away;
powerful people die without help.

21"God watches where people go;
he sees every step they take.
22There is no dark place or deep shadow
where those who do evil can hide from
him.
23He does not set a time
for people to come before him for judging.
24Without asking questions, God breaks
powerful people into pieces
and puts others in their place.
25Because God knows what people do,
he defeats them in the night, and they are
crushed.
26He punishes them for the evil they do
so that everyone else can watch,
27because they stopped following God
and did not care about any of his ways.
28The cry of the poor comes to God;
he hears the cry of the needy.
29But if God keeps quiet, who can blame him?
If he hides his face, who can see him?
God still rules over both nations and persons
alike.
30 He keeps the wicked from ruling
and from trapping others.

31"But suppose someone says to God,
'I am guilty, but I will not sin any more.
32Teach me what I cannot see.
If I have done wrong, I will not do it again.'
33So, Job, should God reward you as you want
when you refuse to change?
You must decide, not I,
so tell me what you know.

34"Those who understand speak,
and the wise who hear me say,
35'Job speaks without knowing what is true;
his words show he does not understand.'
36I wish Job would be tested completely,
because he answered like an evil man!
37Job now adds to his sin by turning
against God.
He claps his hands in protest,
speaking more and more against God."

35

Then Elihu said:

2"Do you think this is fair?
You say, 'God will show that I am right,'
3but you also ask, 'What's the use?
I don't gain anything by not sinning.'

4"I will answer you
and your friends who are with you.
5Look up at the sky
and see the clouds so high above you.
6If you sin, it does nothing to God;
even if your sins are many, they do nothing
to him.
7If you are good, you give nothing to God;
he receives nothing from your hand.
8Your evil ways only hurt a man like
yourself,
and the good you do only helps other
human beings.

9"People cry out when they are in trouble;
they beg for relief from powerful people.
10But no one asks, 'Where is God, my Maker,
who gives us songs in the night,
11who teaches more to us than the animals of
the earth
and wiser than the birds of the air?'
12God does not answer evil people when they
cry out,
because the wicked are proud.
13God does not listen to their useless
begging;
the Almighty pays no attention to them.
14He will listen to you even less
when you say that you do not see him,
that your case is before him,
that you must wait for him,
15 that his anger never punishes,
and that he doesn't notice evil.
16So Job is only speaking nonsense,
saying many words without knowing what
is true."

Elihu's Speech Continues

36 Elihu continued:
2"Listen to me a little longer, and I will show you
that there is more to be said for God.
3What I know comes from far away.
I will show that my Maker is right.
4You can be sure that my words are not false;
one who really knows is with you.

5"God is powerful, but he does not hate people;
he is powerful and sure of what he wants
to do.
6He will not keep evil people alive,
but he gives the poor their rights.
7He always watches over those who do right;
he sets them on thrones with kings
and they are honoured for ever.
8If people are bound in chains,
or if trouble, like ropes, ties them up,
9God tells them what they have done,
that they have sinned in their pride.
10God makes them listen to his warning
and commands them to change from doing
evil.
11If they obey and serve him,
the rest of their lives will be successful,
and the rest of their years will be happy.
12But if they do not listen,
they will die by the sword,
and they will die without knowing why.

13"Those who have wicked hearts hold on to
anger.
Even when God punishes them, they do
not cry for help.
14They die while they are still young,
and their lives end in disgrace.
15But God saves those who suffer through their
suffering;
he gets them to listen through their pain.

16"God is gently calling you from the jaws of
trouble
to an open place of freedom
where he has set your table full of the best
food.
17But now you are being punished like the
wicked;
you are getting justice.
18Be careful! Don't be led away from God by
riches;
don't let much money turn you away.
19Neither your wealth nor all your great strength
will keep you out of trouble.
20Don't wish for the night
when people are taken from their homes.
21Be careful not to turn to evil,
which you seem to want more than suffering.
22"God is great and powerful;
no other teacher is like him.
23No one has planned his ways for him;
no one can say to God, 'You have done
wrong.'
24Remember to praise his work,
about which people have sung.
25Everybody has seen it;
people look at it from far off.
26God is so great, greater than we can
understand!
No one knows how old he is.

27"He takes up the drops of water from the
earth
and turns them into rain.
28The rain then pours down from the clouds,
and showers fall on people.
29No one understands how God spreads out
the clouds
or how he sends thunder from where he
lives.
30Watch how God scatters his lightning
around him,
lighting up the deepest parts of the sea.
31This is the way God governs the nations;
this is how he gives us enough food.
32God fills his hands with lightning
and commands it to strike its target.
33His thunder announces the coming storm,
and even the cattle know it is near.

37 "At the sound of his thunder, my heart
pounds
as if it will jump out of my chest.
2Listen! Listen to the thunder of God's voice
and to the rumbling that comes from his
mouth.
3He turns his lightning loose under the
whole sky
and sends it to the farthest parts of the
earth.
4After that you can hear the roar
when he thunders with a great sound.
He does not hold back the flashing
when his voice is heard.
5God's voice thunders in wonderful ways;
he does great things we cannot understand.
6He says to the snow, 'Fall on the earth,'
and to the shower, 'Be a heavy rain.'
7With it, he stops everyone from working
so everyone knows it is the work of God.
8The animals take cover from the rain
and stay in their dens.
9The storm comes from where it was stored;
the cold comes with the strong winds.
10The breath of God makes ice,
and the wide waters become frozen.

11He fills the clouds with water
and scatters his lightning through them.
12At his command they swirl around
over the whole earth,
doing whatever he commands.
13He uses the clouds to punish people
or to water his earth and show his love.

14"Job, listen to this:
Stop and notice God's miracles. [d]
15Do you know how God controls the clouds
and makes his lightning flash?
16Do you know how the clouds hang in
the sky?
Do you know the miracles of God, who
knows everything?
17You suffer in your clothes
when the land is silenced by the hot, south
wind.
18You cannot stretch out the sky like God
and make it look as hard as polished bronze.
19Tell us what we should say to him;
we cannot get our arguments ready because
we do not have enough understanding.
20Should God be told that I want to speak?
Would a person ask to be swallowed up?
21No one can look at the sun
when it is bright in the sky
after the wind has blown all the clouds away.
22God comes out of the north in golden light,
in overwhelming greatness.
23The Almighty is too high for us to reach.
He has great strength;
he is always right and never punishes unfairly.
24That is why people honour him;
he does not respect those who say they are
wise."

The LORD Questions Job

38 Then the LORD answered Job from the
storm. He said:
2"Who is this that makes my purpose unclear
by saying things that are not true?
3Be strong like a man!
I will ask you questions,
and you must answer me.
4Where were you when I made the earth's
foundation?
Tell me, if you understand.
5Who marked off how big it should be?
Surely you know!
Who stretched a ruler across it?
6What were the earth's foundations set on,
or who put its cornerstone [d] in place
7while the morning stars sang together
and all the angels shouted with joy?

8"Who shut the doors to keep the sea in
when it broke through and was born,
9when I made the clouds like a coat for
the sea
and wrapped it in dark clouds,
10when I put limits on the sea

Sidelight Ancient cultures envisaged the earth resting on everything from pillars to sea turtles (Job 38:4–6). The fear and speculation has gone, since Newton discovered gravity.

and put its doors and bars in place,
11when I said to the sea, 'You may come this
far, but no farther;
this is where your proud waves must stop'?

12"Have you ever ordered the morning to begin,
or shown the dawn where its place was
13in order to take hold of the earth by its edges
and shake evil people out of it?
14At dawn the earth changes like clay being
pressed by a seal; [d]
the hills and valleys stand out like folds in
a coat.
15Light is not given to evil people;
their arm is raised to do harm, but it is
broken.

16"Have you ever gone to where the sea begins
or walked in the valleys under the sea?
17Have the gates of death been opened to you?
Have you seen the gates of the deep
darkness?
18Do you understand how wide the earth is?
Tell me, if you know all these things.

19"What is the path to the source of light,
and where does darkness live?
20Can you take them to their places?
Do you know the way to their homes?
21Surely you know, if you were already born
when all this happened!
Have you lived that many years?

22"Have you ever gone into the storehouse of
the snow
or seen the storehouses for hail,
23which I save for times of trouble,
for days of war and battle?
24Where is the place from which light comes?
Where is the place from which the east
winds blow over the earth?
25Who cuts a waterway for the heavy rains
and sets a path for the thunderstorm?
26Who waters the land where no one lives,
the desert that has no one in it?
27Who sends rain to satisfy the empty land
so the grass begins to grow?

28Does the rain have a father?
Who is father to the drops of dew?
29Who is the mother of the ice?
Who gives birth to the frost from the sky
30when the water becomes hard as stone,
and even the surface of the ocean is frozen?

31"Can you tie up the stars of the Pleiades
or loosen the ropes of the stars in Orion?
32Can you bring out the stars on time
or lead out the stars of the Bear with its cubs?
33Do you know the laws of the sky
and understand their rule over the earth?

34"Can you shout an order to the clouds
and cover yourself with a flood of water?
35Can you send lightning bolts on their way?
Do they come to you and say, 'Here we are'?
36Who put wisdom inside the mind
or understanding in the heart?
37Who has the wisdom to count the clouds?
Who can pour water from the jars of the sky
38when the dust becomes hard
and the clumps of earth stick together?

39"Do you hunt food for the female lion
to satisfy the hunger of the young lions
40while they lie in their dens
or hide in the bushes waiting to attack?
41Who gives food to the birds
when their young cry out to God
and wander about without food?

39 "Do you know when the mountain goats give birth?
Do you watch when the deer gives birth to her fawn?
2Do you count the months until they give birth
and know the right time for them to give birth?
3They lie down, their young are born,
and then the pain of giving birth is over.
4Their young ones grow big and strong in the wild country.
Then they leave their homes and do not return.

5"Who let the wild donkey go free?
Who untied its ropes?
6I am the one who gave the donkey the desert as its home;
I gave it the desert lands as a place to live.
7The wild donkey laughs at the confusion in the city,
and it does not hear the drivers shout.
8It roams the hills looking for pasture,
looking for anything green to eat.

9"Will the wild ox agree to serve you
and stay by your feeding box at night?
10Can you hold it to the ploughed row with a harness
so it will plough the valleys for you?
11Will you depend on the wild ox for its great strength
and leave your heavy work for it to do?
12Can you trust the ox to bring in your grain
and gather it to your threshing[d] floor?

13"The wings of the ostrich flap happily,
but they are not like the feathers of the stork.
14The ostrich lays its eggs on the ground
and lets them warm in the sand.
15It does not stop to think that a foot might step on them and crush them;
it does not care that some animal might walk on them.
16The ostrich is cruel to its young, as if they were not even its own.
It does not care that its work is for nothing,
17because God did not give the ostrich wisdom;
God did not give it a share of good sense.
18But when the ostrich gets up to run, it is so fast
that it laughs at the horse and its rider.

19"Job, are you the one who gives the horse its strength
or puts a flowing mane on its neck?
20Do you make the horse jump like a locust?[d]
It scares people with its proud snorting.
21It paws wildly, enjoying its strength,
and charges into battle.
22It laughs at fear and is afraid of nothing;
it does not run away from the sword.
23The bag of arrows rattles against the horse's side,
along with the flashing spears and swords.
24With great excitement, the horse races over the ground;
and it cannot stand still when it hears the trumpet.
25When the trumpet blows, the horse snorts, 'Aha!'
It smells the battle from far away;
it hears the shouts of commanders and the battle cry.

26"Is it through your wisdom that the hawk flies
and spreads its wings towards the south?

27Are you the one that commands the eagle
to fly
and build its nest so high?
28It lives on a high cliff and stays there at night;
the rocky peak is its protected place.
29From there it looks for its food;
its eyes can see it from far away.
30Its young eat blood,
and where there is something dead, the
eagle is there."

40 The LORD said to Job:
2"Will the person who argues with the
Almighty correct him?
Let the person who accuses God
answer him."

3Then Job answered the LORD:
4"I am not worthy; I cannot answer you
anything,
so I will put my hand over my mouth.
5I spoke once, but I will not answer again;
I even spoke twice, but I will say nothing
more."

6Then the LORD spoke to Job from the storm:
7"Be strong, like a man!
I will ask you questions,
and you must answer me.
8Would you say that I am unfair?
Would you blame me to make yourself look
right?
9Are you as strong as God?
Can your voice thunder like his?
10If so, then decorate yourself with glory and
beauty;
dress in honour and greatness as if they
were clothing.
11Let your great anger punish;
look at the proud and bring them down.
12Look at the proud and make them humble.
Crush the wicked wherever they are.
13Bury them all in the earth together;
cover their faces in the grave.
14If you can do that, then I myself will praise
you,
because you are strong enough to save
yourself.

15"Look at the behemoth,[n]
which I made just as I made you.
It eats grass like an ox.
16Look at the strength it has in its body;
the muscles of its stomach are powerful.
17Its tail moves like a cedar tree;
the muscles of its thighs are woven together.
18Its bones are like tubes of bronze;
its legs are like bars of iron.
19It is one of the first of God's works,
but its Maker can destroy it.
20The hills, where the wild animals play,
provide food for it.
21It lies under the lotus plants,
hidden by the tall grass in the swamp.
22The lotus plants hide it in their shadow;
the poplar trees by the streams surround it.
23If the river floods, it will not be afraid;
it is safe even if the Jordan River rushes to
its mouth.
24Can anyone blind its eyes and capture it?
Can anyone put hooks in its nose?

41 "Can you catch the leviathan[d] on a
fish-hook
or tie its tongue down with a rope?
2Can you put a cord through its nose
or a hook in its jaw?
3Will it keep begging you for mercy
and speak to you with gentle words?
4Will it make an agreement with you
and let you take it as your slave for life?
5Can you make a pet of the leviathan as you
would a bird
or put it on a leash for your girls?
6Will traders try to bargain with you for it?
Will they divide it up among the
merchants?
7Can you stick darts all over its skin
or fill its head with fishing spears?
8If you put one hand on it,
you will never forget the battle,
and you will never do it again!
9There is no hope of defeating it;
just seeing it overwhelms people.
10No one is brave enough to make it angry,
so who would be able to stand up
against me?
11No one has ever given me anything that I
must pay back,
because everything under the sky belongs
to me.

12"I will speak about Leviathan's arms and legs,
its great strength and well-formed body.
13No one can tear off its outer hide
or poke through its double armour.
14No one can force open its great jaws;
they are filled with frightening teeth.
15It has rows of shields on its back
that are tightly sealed together.
16Each shield is so close to the next one
that no air can go between them.

behemoth A large land animal, meaning obscure.

17They are joined strongly to one another;
they hold on to each other and cannot be separated.
18When it snorts, flashes of light are thrown out,
and its eyes look like the light at dawn.
19Flames blaze from its mouth;
sparks of fire shoot out.
20Smoke pours out of its nose,
as if coming from a large pot over a hot fire.
21Its breath sets coals on fire,
and flames come out of its mouth.
22There is great strength in its neck.
People are afraid and run away.
23The folds of its skin are tightly joined;
they are set and cannot be moved.
24Its chest is as hard as a rock,
even as hard as a grinding stone.
25The powerful fear its terrible looks
and draw back in fear as it moves.
26The sword that hits it does not hurt it,
nor the arrows, darts and spears.
27It treats iron as if it were straw
and bronze metal as if it were rotten wood.
28It does not run away from arrows;
stones from slings are like chaff[d] to it.
29Clubs feel like pieces of straw to it,
and it laughs when they shake a spear at it.
30The underside of its body is like broken pieces of pottery.
It leaves a trail in the mud like a threshing[d] board.

FOLLOWING GOD

His Presence

"There came into my soul . . . a sense of the glory of the divine being; a new sense, quite different from anything I had ever experienced before."

Jonathan Edwards (1703–1758)

Edwards followed God by devoting his life to proclaiming and defending the gospel as one of the leaders of the Great Awakening in New England in the USA.

"Down in my deep well, shrouded with blackness, feeling helpless and devoid of hope, I cried out for help. Now, at last, I was ready to go to any length to achieve sobriety. And God heard my cry and answered."

Michael

Michael felt God's presence in his time of need and began the long road to recovery from alcoholism through Alcoholics Anonymous. He follows God day by day as a minister who helps others to recover from alcoholism.

"At this moment I feel something 'let go' inside and lo, God is here! It is a heart-melting 'here-ness', a lovely whispering of father to child."

Frank Laubauch (1884–1970)

Laubauch became a missionary and developed a worldwide method of teaching people to read.

The experience of God's presence led these three to act on their faith. Job was also changed as he experienced God's presence. Read **Job 42:1–6**.

- How does Job's reaction to meeting God compare with these three people's sense of God's presence with them? How is it different?
- How would your faith change if you suddenly sensed God's presence, as in verses 4 and 5?

Consider . . .

- praying for God to give you a clear picture of what he wants you to do for him.
- writing down what you value most, why you value it, and how your feelings about it would change if you considered it as a loan from God.

For more, see . . .

- 1 Kings 19:11–13 (p.336)
- Acts 9:3–19 (p.1152)
- Psalm 63:1–8 (p.536)

31 It makes the deep sea bubble like a
boiling pot;
it stirs up the sea like a pot of oil.
32 When it swims, it leaves a shining path in the
water
that makes the sea look as if it had white
hair.
33 Nothing else on earth is equal to it;
it is a creature without fear.
34 It looks down on all those who are too proud;
it is king over all proud creatures."

Job Answers the LORD

42 Then Job answered the LORD:

2 "I know that you can do all things
and that no plan of yours can be ruined.
3 You asked, 'Who is this that made my
purpose unclear by saying things that
are not true?'
Surely I spoke of things I did not
understand;
I talked of things too wonderful for me to
know.

4 "You said, 'Listen now, and I will speak.
I will ask you questions,
and you must answer me.'
5 My ears had heard of you before,
but now my eyes have seen you.
6 So now I hate myself;
I will change my heart and life.
I will sit in the dust and ashes."

End of the Story

7 After the LORD had said these things to Job, he
said to Eliphaz the Temanite, "I am angry with
you and your two friends, because you have not
said what is right about me, as my servant Job
did. 8 Now take seven bulls and seven rams, and
go to my servant Job, and offer a burnt offering
for yourselves. My servant Job will pray for you,
and I will listen to his prayer. Then I will not
punish you for being foolish. You have not said
what is right about me, as my servant Job did."
9 So Eliphaz the Temanite, Bildad the Shuhite and
Zophar the Naamathite did as the LORD said, and
the LORD listened to Job's prayer.
10 After Job had prayed for his friends, the LORD
gave him success again. The LORD gave Job twice
as much as he had owned before. 11 Job's brothers
and sisters came to his house, along with every-
one who had known him before, and they all ate
with him there. They comforted him and made
him feel better about the trouble the LORD had
brought on him, and each one gave Job a piece of
silver and a gold ring.
12 The LORD blessed the last part of Job's life
even more than the first part. Job had 14,000
sheep, 6,000 camels, 1,000 teams of oxen and
1,000 female donkeys. 13 Job also had seven sons
and three daughters. 14 He named the first daugh-
ter Jemimah, the second daughter Keziah and the
third daughter Keren-Happuch. 15 There were no
other women in all the land as beautiful as Job's
daughters. And their father Job gave them land to
own along with their brothers.

Sidelight Unusual names were a source of pride in ancient times, and the names that Job gave his daughters were certainly unusual. Their Hebrew names translate as "dove", "cinnamon" and "container of eyeshadow" (Job 42:14).

16 After this, Job lived 140 years. He lived to see
his children, grandchildren, great-grandchildren
and great-great-grandchildren. 17 Then Job died;
he was old and had lived many years.

Psalms

When?

Time Line:

- 2000 BC
- The Israelites escaped from Egypt
- 1500 BC
- King David ruled Israel and almost half the psalms refer to him
- 1000 BC
- Judah fell to the Babylonians
- Jews began returning to Jerusalem from exile
- 500 BC
- Final collection of psalms was probably completed
- BC/AD Jesus was born

Why Read This Book:

- **Be inspired to express your feelings through songs about tough and joyful situations (such as Psalms 4, 27, 55, 147).**
- **Improve your prayer life by following the many models of prayer in the Psalms (such as Psalms 6, 32, 51, 102, 130, 143).**
- **Learn to praise and worship God through songs of praise (such as Psalms 8, 47, 81, 84, 108, 150).**

Behind the Scenes:

If you flip through a hymn book, you see some upbeat songs, some quiet, some well known and others that are rarely sung.

The book of Psalms was the hymn book for Jews and Christians for many centuries. Each psalm is really a song for worship. Like modern hymn books, Psalms contains songs that express joy, sadness, celebration, loneliness and many other emotions. Different psalms were written by different people over several centuries, so the book is rich with diversity. The New Testament quotes from Psalms more than any other book in the Old Testament, except Isaiah. Psalms is also the longest book of the Bible and contains some of the most popular reading in the Bible. Through these poetic words we can understand better our own hearts' longings to be close to God.

Where?

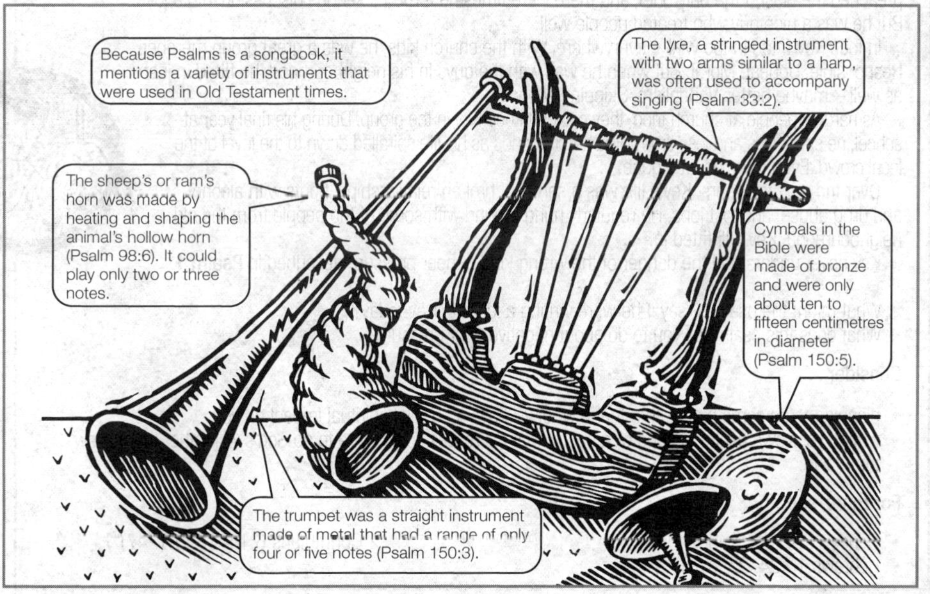

Book 1

Two Ways to Live

1 Happy are those who don't listen to the
wicked,
who don't go where sinners go,
who don't do what evil people do.
2They love the LORD's teachings,
and they think about those teachings day
and night.
3They are strong, like a tree planted by a river.
The tree produces fruit in season,
and its leaves don't die.
Everything they do will succeed.
4But wicked people are not like that.
They are like chaff[d] that the wind blows
away.
5So the wicked will not escape God's
punishment.
Sinners will not worship with God's people.
6This is because the LORD takes care of his
people,
but the wicked will be destroyed.

The LORD's Chosen King

2 Why are the nations so angry?
Why are the people making useless plans?
2The kings of the earth prepare to fight,
and their leaders make plans together
against the LORD
and his appointed one.
3They say, "Let's break the chains that hold us
back
and throw off the ropes that tie us down."

PEER PRESURE

The Laugh-a-Minute Kid

Kev Bennett was a riot. He could make more weird sounds, contort his face into more outrageous expressions and do more impressions than almost any other seventeen-year-old. He was so thin he could do tricks with his shoulder blades. People couldn't stop laughing when he tried playing "Chopsticks" on the piano with them!

And Kev was friendly. He seemed to relate to everyone. When he and his friends stopped at a fast food restaurant, in less than two minutes he would be charming the girl working the cash register and entertaining children three tables away.

Kev was great to have in the church youth group. Sure, he didn't always pay attention when the pastor preached (he wasn't the only one), and there were times he turned a serious discussion into a joke. But he was a nice guy who treated people well.

In fact, Kev fitted in too well – everywhere. With the church kids, he was a great group member. Responsible. Upbeat. Moral. But when he was with the guys in his neighbourhood, he fitted in just as well – maybe better. Vandalism. Skipping school.

As hard as people at church tried, they couldn't keep Kev in the group. During his final year at school, he spent less and less time with church friends as his life spiralled down to the level of the local crowd. Eventually, he was gone.

Over the next ten years, Kev's life was a series of broken relationships, bouts with alcohol and drug abuse, and lost jobs. He regularly hung around with some of the people from the old neighbourhood. Kev still fitted in.

Kev never understood the danger of the wrong kind of peer pressure described in **Psalm 1**.

- What might the psalmist say if he were writing a letter to Kev today?
- What does this psalm tell you to do about negative peer pressure?

Consider . . .

- planning to do something with a friend who will have a positive spiritual impact on you.
- writing your own psalm (a song or a poem) that expresses your desire to do God's will rather than follow the crowd.

For more, see . . .

- Genesis 26:1–11 (p.30)
- Hebrews 10:24–25 (p.1339)
- 2 Corinthians 6:14–18 (p.1247)

4But the one who sits in heaven laughs;
the Lord makes fun of them.
5Then the LORD warns them
and frightens them with his anger.

Sidelight The book of Psalms is actually made up of five separate books (see heading above Psalm 1). Psalms 1—41 are Book One. Psalms 42—72 are Book Two. Psalms 73—89 are Book Three. Psalms 90—106 are Book Four. And Psalms 107—150 are Book Five. Each "book" may have been collected at a different time.

6He says, "I have appointed my own king
to rule in Jerusalem on my holy mountain,
Zion."

7Now I will tell you what the LORD has
declared:

he said to me, "You are my son.
Today I have become your father.
8If you ask me,
I will give you the nations;
all the people on earth will be yours.
9You will rule over them with an iron rod.
You will break them into pieces like
pottery."

10So, kings, be wise;
rulers, learn this lesson.
11Obey the LORD with great fear.
Be happy, but tremble.
12Show that you are loyal to his son,
or you will be destroyed by his anger,
because he can quickly become angry.
But happy are those who trust him for
protection.

Sidelight The way citizens in Bible times showed their loyalty to royalty (Psalm 2:12) was by kissing the feet of the king or prince.

A Morning Prayer

David sang this when he ran away
from his son Absalom.

3 LORD, I have many enemies!
Many people have turned against me.
2Many are saying about me,
"God won't rescue him." *Selah*[d]

3But, LORD, you are my shield,
my wonderful God who gives me
courage.
4I will pray to the LORD,
and he will answer me from his holy
mountain. *Selah*

5I can lie down and go to sleep,
and I will wake up again,
because the LORD gives me strength.
6Thousands of troops may surround me,
but I am not afraid.

7LORD, rise up!
My God, come and save me!
You have struck my enemies on the cheek;
you have broken the teeth of the wicked.

8The LORD can save his people.
LORD, bless your people. *Selah*

An Evening Prayer

For the director of music. With stringed instruments.
A psalm of David.

4 Answer me when I pray to you,
my God who does what is right.
Make things easier for me when I am in
trouble.
Have mercy on me and hear my prayer.

2People, how long will you turn my honour
into shame?
How long will you love what is false and
look for new lies? *Selah*[d]
3You know that the LORD has chosen for
himself those who are loyal to him.
The LORD listens when I pray to him.

4When you are angry, do not sin.
Think about these things quietly
as you go to bed. *Selah*

5Do what is right as a sacrifice to the LORD
and trust the LORD.

6Many people ask,
"Who will give us anything good?"
LORD, be kind to us.
7But you have made me very happy,
happier than they are,
even with all their grain and new wine.
8I go to bed and sleep in peace,
because, LORD, only you keep me safe.

A Morning Prayer for Protection

For the director of music. For flutes. A psalm of David.

5 LORD, listen to my words.
Understand my sadness.

2Listen to my cry for help, my King and
my God,
because I pray to you.
3LORD, every morning you hear my voice.
Every morning, I tell you what I need,
and I wait for your answer.

4You are not a God who is pleased with the
wicked;
you do not live with those who do evil.
5Those people who make fun of you cannot
stand before you.
You hate all those who do evil.
6You destroy liars;
the LORD hates those who kill and trick
others.
7Because of your great love,
I can come into your Temple. [d]
Because I fear and respect you,
I can worship in your holy Temple.
8LORD, since I have many enemies,
show me the right thing to do.
Show me clearly how you want me to live.
9My enemies' mouths do not tell the truth;
in their hearts they want to destroy others.
Their throats are like open graves;
they use their tongues for telling lies.

ANGER

He Lost His Grip

The school paper's sports headline said it all: "Tom Harley Loses Tennis Tournament With a Smash".

Tom read the biting article and then let out a sigh. He had felt so stupid for letting his anger get to him at the tournament that day. But the deed was done. Nothing could repair his tennis racket. He had hurled the stringed beast at the fence in a spark of rage. And his brand new racket abruptly met the fence post. "Come on, Tom," his partner Jim had whispered intensely. "Relax. Your temper's going to lose this match for us."

"I'm fine," Tom had snapped. "Where's your extra racket?"

They probably would have lost anyway, but Tom was still furious about having to play with an unfamiliar racket. They only won three games in the next two sets.

The trainer didn't say a word that day, but Tom could tell he was furious. The next week at practise, he made Tom and Jim do extra "hate drills".

"Any doubles team with enough extra energy to waste on destroying tennis rackets," the coach said, "can surely handle a little extra running." So the twosome painfully ran the width of six tennis courts, forwards and backwards, again and again.

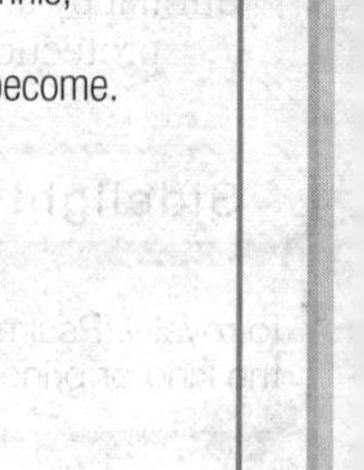

And then there was the teasing from Tom's team-mates.

"Hey, Tantrum Tom, fought off any marauding fence posts recently?"

"So, Tom, how many tennis rackets have you bought this month?"

Even with all this abuse, Tom hadn't learned his lesson. It took several more temper tantrums and broken rackets for him to learn the simple truth that anger wasn't going to make him play better tennis, or improve his life.

Anger can sometimes be constructive. But the psalmist reminds us how destructive anger can become. He warns us in **Psalm 4**, "When you are angry, do not sin." Hold on to the racket!

- Do you think throwing a tennis racket in a fit of anger is a sin? Why or why not?
- How can you avoid doing wrong things when you're angry?

Consider . . .

- seeking forgiveness from someone you've sinned against because of your anger.
- picturing the place or situation in which you get the angriest, and asking God to help you stay calm the next time you're there.

For more, see . . .

- Exodus 32 (p.90)
- Ephesians 4:26–27 (p.1274)
- Mark 11:15–19 (p.1020)

10God, declare them guilty!
Let them fall into their own traps.
Send them away because their sins are many;
they have turned against you.

11But let everyone who trusts you be happy;
let them sing glad songs for ever.
Protect those who love you
and who are happy because of you.
12LORD, you bless those who do what is right;
you protect them like a soldier's shield.

A Prayer for Mercy in Troubled Times

For the director of music. With stringed instruments.
Upon the sheminith. [d] A psalm of David.

6 LORD, don't punish me when you are angry;
don't punish me when you are very angry.
2LORD, have mercy on me because I am weak.
Heal me, LORD, because my bones ache.
3I am very upset.
LORD, how long will it be?

4LORD, return and save me;
save me because of your love.
5Dead people don't remember you;
those in the grave don't praise you.

6I am tired of crying to you.
Every night my bed is wet with tears;
my bed is soaked from my crying.
7My eyes are weak from so much crying;
they are weak from crying about my enemies.

8Get away from me, all you who do evil,
because the LORD has heard my crying.
9The LORD has heard my cry for help;
the LORD will answer my prayer.
10All my enemies will be ashamed and troubled.
They will turn and suddenly leave in shame.

A Prayer for Fairness

A shiggaion [d] of David which he sang to the LORD
about Cush, from the tribe of Benjamin.

7 LORD my God, I trust in you for protection.
Save me and rescue me
from those who are chasing me.
2Otherwise, like a lion they will tear me apart.
They will rip me to pieces, and no one can save me.

3LORD my God, what have I done?
Have my hands done something wrong?
4Have I done wrong to my friend
or stolen without reason from my enemy?
5If I have, let my enemy chase me and capture me.
Let him trample me into the dust
and bury me in the ground. *Selah* [d]

6LORD, rise up in your anger;
stand up against my enemies' anger.
Get up and demand fairness.
7Gather the nations around you
and rule them from above.
8LORD, judge the people.
LORD, defend me because I am right,
because I have done no wrong, God Most High.
9God, you do what is right.
You know our thoughts and feelings.
Stop those wicked actions done by evil people,
and help those who do what is right.

10God protects me like a shield;
he saves those whose hearts are right.
11God judges by what is right,
and God is always ready to punish the wicked.
12If they do not change their lives,
God will sharpen his sword;
he will string his bow and take aim.
13He has prepared his deadly weapons;
he has made his flaming arrows.

14There are people who think up evil
and plan trouble and tell lies.
15They dig a hole to trap others,
but they will fall into it themselves.
16They will get themselves into trouble;
the violence they cause will hurt only themselves.
17I praise the LORD because he does what is right.
I sing praises to the LORD Most High.

The LORD's Greatness

For the director of music. On the gittith. [d]
A psalm of David.

8 LORD our Lord,
your name is the most wonderful name
in all the earth!

It brings you praise in heaven above.
2You have taught children and babies
to sing praises to you
because of your enemies.
And so you silence your enemies
and destroy those who try to take revenge.

3I look at your heavens,
which you made with your fingers.

I see the moon and stars,
which you created.
4But why are people important to you?
Why do you take care of human beings?
5You made them a little lower than the angels
and crowned them with glory and honour.

6You put them in charge of everything you made.
You put all things under their control:
7all the sheep, the cattle
and the wild animals,
8the birds in the sky,
the fish in the sea
and everything that lives underwater.

9LORD our Lord,
your name is the most wonderful name in all the earth!

Thanksgiving for Victory

For the director of music. To the tune of "The Death of the Son". A psalm of David.

9 I will praise you, LORD, with all my heart.
I will tell of all the miracles [d] you have done.
2I will be happy because of you;
God Most High, I will sing praises to your name.

3My enemies turn back;

SELF-ESTEEM

A Speck?

When you look up in the sky at night, it's easy to see that the Earth is little more than a tiny speck in a giant universe. And within our solar system are nine planets, each of them unique and wonderful.

Mercury, the closest planet to the Sun, is still 58 million kilometres from the sun. Venus, the next closest planet, is just a little smaller than the Earth and is covered by a layer of clouds that hide its surface.

Beyond Earth is Mars, which is like a red desert of rock, sand and soil. Jupiter, the largest planet, comes next. Its diameter is eleven times that of Earth. Saturn is next and is the last planet we can see with the unaided eye. The next planet, Uranus is 2.9 billion kilometres from the sun. Beyond it are Neptune and Pluto, which have eccentric rotation patterns, so they sometimes switch places, making Pluto closer to the sun than Neptune.

Overwhelming, isn't it? It makes us seem so insignificant.

But wait! Mercury's temperature can reach 1,440 degrees. Clouds on Venus drip pure sulphuric acid. The atmosphere on Mars is like car exhaust. A mixture of sulphur and phosphorus make Jupiter like a giant match head, ready to ignite.

On Saturn, raindrops are liquefied methane gas. Uranus is covered in radioactive smog. One hemisphere of Neptune will not see sunlight until the year 2030. And Pluto is frozen solid.

Makes you think God cares specially for us on Earth, doesn't it?

When the psalmist looked to the heavens in **Psalm 8**, he, too, was overwhelmed and felt insignificant. But he recognised how special the Earth and its people are to God.

- How do these facts about the solar system relate to Psalm 8?
- Do you ever struggle with the thought that God values you and finds you important? What's the message of Psalm 8 for you?

Consider . . .

- listing the different ways in which you strive to feel important and comparing them to the reasons you believe that God truly values you. The Bible passages listed below can get you started.
- doing something special for yourself – such as going to a concert or buying yourself flowers – as a way of recognising how special you are to God!

For more, see . . .

- Genesis 1:26–31 (p.3)
- Romans 5:6–8 (p.1190)
- John 3:16–17 (p.1100)

they are overwhelmed and die because
of you.
4You have heard my complaint;
you sat on your throne and judged by what
was right.
5You spoke strongly against the foreign nations
and destroyed the wicked;
you wiped out their names for ever and
ever.
6The enemy is gone for ever.
You destroyed their cities;
no one even remembers them.

7But the LORD rules for ever.
He sits on his throne to judge,
8and he will judge the world in fairness;
he will decide what is fair for the nations.
9The LORD defends those who suffer;
he defends them in times of trouble.
10Those who know the LORD trust him,
because he will not leave those who come
to him.

11Sing praises to the LORD who is king on
Mount Zion.[d]
Tell the nations what he has done.
12He remembers who the murderers are;
he will not forget the cries of those who
suffer.

13LORD, have mercy on me.
See how my enemies hurt me.
Do not let me go through the gates of
death.
14Then, at the gates of Jerusalem, I will
praise you;
I will rejoice because you saved me.

15The nations have fallen into the pit they dug.
Their feet are caught in the nets they laid.
16The LORD has made himself known by his fair
decisions;
the wicked get trapped by what they do.
Higgaion.[d] *Selah*[d]
17Wicked people will go to the grave,
and so will all those who forget God.
18But those who have troubles will not be
forgotten.
The hopes of the poor will never die.

19LORD, rise up and judge the nations.
Don't let people think they are strong.
20Teach them to fear you, LORD.
The nations must learn that they are only
human. *Selah*

A Complaint About Evil People

10 LORD, why are you so far away?
Why do you hide when there is
trouble?
2Proudly the wicked chase down those who
suffer.
Let them be caught in their own traps.
3They boast about the things they want.
They bless the greedy but hate the LORD.
4The wicked people are too proud.
They do not look for God;
there is no room for God in their thoughts.
5They always succeed.
They are far from keeping your laws;
they make fun of their enemies.
6They say to themselves, "Nothing bad will
ever happen to me;
I will never be ruined."
7Their mouths are full of curses, lies and
threats;
they use their tongues for sin and evil.
8They hide near the villages.
They look for innocent people to kill;
they watch in secret for the helpless.
9They wait in hiding like a lion.
They wait to catch poor people;
they catch the poor in nets.
10The poor are thrown down and crushed;
they are defeated because the others are
stronger.
11The wicked think, "God has forgotten us.
He doesn't see what is happening."

12LORD, rise up and punish the wicked.
Don't forget those who need help.
13Why do wicked people hate God?
They say to themselves, "God won't
punish us."
14LORD, surely you see these cruel and evil
things;
look at them and do something.
People in trouble look to you for help.
You are the one who helps the orphans.
15Break the power of wicked people.
Punish them for the evil they have done.
16The LORD is King for ever and ever.
Destroy from your land those nations that
do not worship you.
17LORD, you have heard what the poor people
want.
Do what they ask, and listen to them.
18Protect the orphans and put an end to
suffering
so they will no longer be afraid of evil
people.

Trust in the LORD

For the director of music. Of David.

11 I trust in the LORD for protection.
So why do you say to me,
"Fly like a bird to your mountain.

2Like hunters, the wicked string their bows;
they set their arrows on the bowstrings.
They shoot from dark places
at those who are honest.
3When all that is good falls apart,
what can good people do?"

4The LORD is in his holy temple; [d]
the LORD sits on his throne in heaven.
He sees what people do;
he keeps his eye on them.
5The LORD tests those who do right,
but he hates the wicked and those who love to hurt others.
6He will send hot coals and burning sulphur on the wicked.
A whirlwind is what they will get.
7The LORD does what is right, and he loves justice,
so honest people will see his face.

Sidelight The psalmist refers to a whirlwind, which is all too common in the desert. The wind is called a sirocco and can last for many days, wreaking havoc and destruction.

A Prayer Against Liars

For the director of music. Upon the sheminith. [d]
A psalm of David.

12 Save me, LORD, because the good people are all gone;
no true believers are left on earth.
2Everyone lies to his neighbours;
they say one thing and mean another.

3The LORD will stop those flattering lips
and cut off those boasting tongues.
4They say, "Our tongues will help us win.
We can say what we wish; no one is our master."

5But the LORD says,
"I will now rise up,
because the poor are being hurt.
Because of the moans of the helpless,
I will give them the help they want."
6The LORD's words are pure,
like silver purified by fire,
like silver purified seven times over.

7LORD, you will keep us safe;
you will always protect us from such people.
8But the wicked are all around us;
everyone loves what is wrong.

A Prayer for God to be Near

For the director of music. A psalm of David.

13 How long will you forget me, LORD?
For ever?
How long will you hide from me?
2How long must I worry
and feel sad in my heart all day?
How long will my enemy win over me?

3LORD, look at me.
Answer me, my God;
tell me, or I will die.
4Otherwise my enemy will say, "I have won!"
Those against me will rejoice that I've been defeated.

5I trust in your love.
My heart is happy because you saved me.
6I sing to the LORD
because he has taken care of me.

The Unbelieving Fool

For the director of music. Of David.

14 Fools say to themselves,
"There is no God."
Fools are evil and do terrible things;
there is no one who does anything good.

2The LORD looked down from heaven on all people
to see if anyone understood,
if anyone was looking to God for help.
3But all have turned away.
Together, everyone has become evil.
There is no one who does anything good,
not even one.

4Don't the wicked understand?
They destroy my people as if they were eating bread.
They do not ask the LORD for help.
5But the wicked are filled with terror,
because God is with those who do what is right.
6The wicked upset the plans of the poor,
but the LORD will protect them.

7I pray that victory will come to Israel from Mount Zion! [d]
May the LORD bring them back.
Then the people of Jacob will rejoice,
and the people of Israel will be glad.

What the LORD Demands

A psalm of David.

15 LORD, who may enter your Holy Tent? [d]
Who may live on your holy mountain?

2 Only those who are innocent
and who do what is right.
Such people speak the truth from their hearts
3 and do not tell lies about others.
They do no wrong to their neighbours
and do not gossip.
4 They do not respect hateful people
but honour those who honour the
LORD.
They keep their promises to their
neighbours,
even when it hurts.
5 They do not charge interest on money they
lend
and do not take money to hurt innocent
people.
Whoever does all these things will never be
destroyed.

The LORD Takes Care of His People

A miktam[d] of David.

16 Protect me, God,
because I trust in you.

2 I said to the LORD, "You are my Lord.
Every good thing I have comes from you."
3 As for the godly people in the world,
they are the wonderful ones I enjoy.
4 But those who turn to idols
will have much pain.
I will not offer blood to those idols
or even speak their names.

5 No, the LORD is all I need.
He takes care of me.
6 My share in life has been pleasant;
my part has been beautiful.

DOUBT

Who Do You Believe?

The musicians that owned the studio were just about to go to bed when one of them decided to check downstairs again. He was thinking of making sure everything had been turned off. As soon as he walked down the stairs he gave a shout, and the rest of the guys ran towards the studio door. As they looked down the stairs they could see the water gushing in and flooding everything. It was rising fast and destroying keyboards and equipment as it went.

It actually took the Fire Brigade twenty-four hours to stem the flow. The culprit had been a burst water main just outside the studio.

The band that owned the studio sat and asked the Lord why this had happened.

Within a few days, many friends came around the studio with all kinds of advice . . . "Maybe God doesn't want you to have music in your house" . . . "The Lord is telling you that rock music is evil" . . . "He wants to bless you and start it up again" . . . "He wants you to see his provision."

The guys had many many doubts about the sense of it all, until the man from the water company came round and said:

"It is completely our fault. We will pay for all the instruments and for your studio to be completely rebuilt." The band were ecstatic!

In **Psalm 13** David didn't want the enemy to win over his doubts.

- What would the enemy have the band believe in this story? What was the truth?
- It's OK to doubt, but when was the last time you doubted God and what was the result?

Consider . . .

- sharing your doubts with a Christian leader that you respect. They may have been there and be able to help with some answers.
- visiting your local Christian bookshop to find a book that answers some of the difficult questions that Christians have to deal with.

For more, see . . .

- Jeremiah 1:4–10 (p.716)
- Romans 4:18–25 (p.1190)
- John 20:24–29 (p.1134)

7 I praise the LORD because he advises me.
Even at night, I feel his leading.
8 I keep the LORD before me always.
Because he is close by my side,
I will not be hurt.

9 So I rejoice and am glad.
Even my body has hope,
10 because you will not leave me in the grave.
You will not let your holy one rot.
11 You will teach me how to live a holy life.
Being with you will fill me with joy;
at your right hand I will find pleasure for ever.

A Prayer for Protection

A prayer of David.

17 LORD, hear me begging for fairness;
listen to my cry for help.
Pay attention to my prayer,
because I speak the truth.
2 You will judge that I am right;
your eyes can see what is true.

3 You have examined my heart;
you have tested me all night.
You questioned me without finding anything wrong;
I have not sinned with my mouth.
4 I have obeyed your commands,
so I have not done what evil people do.
5 I have done what you told me;
I have not failed.

6 I call to you, God,
and you answer me.
Listen to me now,
and hear what I say.
7 Your love is wonderful.
By your power you save those who trust you from their enemies.
8 Protect me as you would protect your own eye.
Hide me under the shadow of your wings.
9 Keep me from the wicked who attack me,
from my enemies who surround me.

10 They are selfish
and boast about themselves.
11 They have chased me until they have surrounded me.
They plan to throw me to the ground.

REVENGE

Hate Stealer

I can't remember his name. I'm really not sure how old he was. I can hardly remember his face. His broken English was difficult to understand. But I have never forgotten his story.

Before being baptised, this Vietnamese refugee stood before our church to tell how Jesus Christ had changed his life. He spoke of the horrors of war – of escape through jungles and rivers and over the border into Thailand, of hunger and near starvation in overcrowded camps, and of the joy of coming to America.

But above all his captivating stories, one part of his testimony left a lasting impression.

"Brothers and sisters," he said. "I came to America alone, and I came with much hatred in my heart. But when Jesus came into my heart, he stole my hate away. Now I can say that I love even my enemies."

David faced circumstances similar to this Vietnamese refugee. Read **Psalm 17** to find David's response to his enemies.

- What did David have in common with this Vietnamese refugee? How were their responses to their enemies different?
- How can you leave matters in God's hands – as David did – when you are treated unfairly?

Consider . . .

- praying for someone who has treated you unfairly and whom you consider to be an "enemy".
- listing ways in which the world would be different if people and nations would turn away from revenge. Then pray for world peace – starting in your own home and area.

For more, see . . .

- 1 Samuel 24 (p.277)
- Romans 12:14–21 (p.1205)
- Matthew 5:38–48 (p.946)

[12]They are like lions ready to kill;
like lions, they sit in hiding.

[13]LORD, rise up, face the enemy and throw them down.
Save me from the wicked with your sword.
[14]LORD, save me by your power
from those whose reward is in this life.

They have plenty of food.
They have many sons
and leave much money to their children.

[15]Because I have lived right, I will see your face.
When I wake up, I will see your likeness and be satisfied.

A Song of Victory

For the director of music. By the LORD's servant, David. David sang this song to the LORD when the LORD had saved him from Saul and all his other enemies.

18 I love you, LORD. You are my strength.
[2]The LORD is my rock, my protection, my Saviour.
My God is my rock.
I can run to him for safety.
He is my shield and my saving strength, my defender.
[3]I will call to the LORD, who is worthy of praise,
and I will be saved from my enemies.

[4]The ropes of death came around me;
the deadly rivers overwhelmed me.
[5]The ropes of death wrapped around me.
The traps of death were before me.
[6]In my trouble I called to the LORD.
I cried out to my God for help.
From his temple [d] he heard my voice;
my call for help reached his ears.

[7]The earth trembled and shook.
The foundations of the mountains began to shake.
They trembled because the LORD was angry.
[8]Smoke came out of his nose,
and burning fire came out of his mouth.
Burning coals went before him.
[9]He tore open the sky and came down
with dark clouds under his feet.
[10]He rode a creature with wings and flew.
He raced on the wings of the wind.
[11]He made darkness his covering, his shelter around him,
surrounded by fog and clouds.
[12]Out of the brightness of his presence came clouds
with hail and lightning.
[13]The LORD thundered from heaven;
the Most High raised his voice,
and there was hail and lightning.
[14]He shot his arrows and scattered his enemies.
His many bolts of lightning confused them with fear.
[15]LORD, you spoke strongly.
The wind blew from your nose.
Then the valleys of the sea appeared,
and the foundations of the earth were seen.

[16]The LORD reached down from above and took me;
he pulled me from the deep water.
[17]He saved me from my powerful enemies,
from those who hated me, because they were too strong for me.
[18]They attacked me at my time of trouble,
but the LORD supported me.
[19]He took me to a safe place.
Because he delights in me, he saved me.

[20]The LORD spared me because I did what was right.
Because I have not done evil, he has rewarded me.
[21]I have followed the ways of the LORD;
I have not done evil by turning away from my God.
[22]I remember all his laws
and have not broken his rules.
[23]I am innocent before him;
I have kept myself from doing evil.
[24]The LORD rewarded me because I did what was right,
because I did what the LORD said was right.

[25]LORD, you are loyal to those who are loyal,
and you are good to those who are good.
[26]You are pure to those who are pure,
but you are against those who are bad.
[27]You save the humble,
but you bring down those who are proud.
[28]LORD, you give light to my lamp.
My God brightens the darkness around me.
[29]With your help I can attack an army.
With God's help I can jump over a wall.

[30]The ways of God are without fault.
The LORD's words are pure.
He is a shield to those who trust him.
[31]Who is God? Only the LORD.
Who is the Rock? [d] Only our God.
[32]God is my protection.
He makes my way free from fault.
[33]He makes me like a deer that does not stumble;
he helps me stand on the steep mountains.
[34]He trains my hands for battle
so my arms can bend a bronze bow.

35You protect me with your saving shield.
You support me with your right hand.
You have stooped to make me great.
36You give me a better way to live,
so I live as you want me to.

37I chased my enemies and caught them.
I did not stop until they were destroyed.
38I crushed them so they couldn't rise up again.
They fell beneath my feet.
39You gave me strength in battle.
You made my enemies bow before me.
40You made my enemies turn back,
and I destroyed those who hated me.
41They called for help,
but no one came to save them.
They called to the LORD,
but he did not answer them.
42I beat my enemies into pieces, like dust in the wind.
I poured them out like mud in the streets.
43You saved me when the people attacked me.
You made me the leader of nations.
People I never knew serve me.
44As soon as they hear me, they obey me.
Foreigners obey me.
45They all become afraid
and tremble in their hiding places.

46The LORD lives!
May my Rock be praised.
Praise the God who saves me!
47God gives me victory over my enemies
and brings people under my rule.
48He saves me from my enemies.

You set me over those who hate me.
You saved me from cruel men.
49So I will praise you, LORD, among the nations.
I will sing praises to your name.
50The LORD gives great victories to his king.
He is loyal to his appointed king,
to David and his descendants [d] for ever.

God's Works and Word

For the director of music. A psalm of David.

19 The heavens tell the glory of God,
and the skies announce what his hands have made.
2Day after day they tell the story;
night after night they tell it again.
3They have no speech or words;
they have no voice to be heard.
4But their message goes out through all the world;
their words go everywhere on earth.
The sky is like a home for the sun.
5 The sun comes out like a bridegroom from his bedroom.
It rejoices like an athlete eager to run a race.
6The sun rises at one end of the sky
and follows its path to the other end.
Nothing hides from its heat.
7The teachings of the LORD are perfect;
they give new strength.
The LORD's rules can be trusted;
they make plain people wise.
8The orders of the LORD are right;
they make people happy.
The commands of the LORD are pure;
they light up the way.
9Respect for the LORD is good;
it will last for ever.
The judgements of the LORD are true;
they are completely right.
10They are worth more than gold,
even the purest gold.
They are sweeter than honey,
even the finest honey.
11By them your servant is warned.
Keeping them brings great reward.

12People cannot see their own mistakes.
Forgive me for my secret sins.
13Keep me from the sins of pride;
don't let them rule me.
Then I can be pure
and innocent of the greatest of sins.

14I hope my words and thoughts please you.
LORD, you are my Rock, [d] the one who saves me.

A Prayer for the King

For the director of music. A psalm of David.

20 May the LORD answer you in times of trouble.
May the God of Jacob protect you.
2May he send you help from his Temple [d]
and support you from Mount Zion. [d]
3May he remember all your offerings
and accept all your sacrifices. *Selah* [d]

4May he give you what you want
and make all your plans succeed,
5and we will shout for joy when you succeed,
and we will raise a flag in the name of our God.
May the LORD give you all that you ask for.

6Now I know the LORD helps his appointed king.
He answers him from his holy heaven

and saves him with his strong right hand.
7Some trust in chariots, others in horses,
but we trust the LORD our God.
8They are overwhelmed and defeated,
but we march forwards and win.

9LORD, save the king!
Answer us when we call for help.

Thanksgiving for the King

For the director of music. A psalm of David.

21 LORD, the king rejoices because of your strength;
he is so happy when you save him!
2You gave the king what he wanted
and did not refuse what he asked for. *Selah*[d]
3You put good things before him
and placed a gold crown on his head.
4He asked you for life,
and you gave it to him,
so his years go on and on.
5He has great glory because you gave him victories;
you gave him honour and praise.
6You always gave him blessings;
you made him glad because you were with him.
7The king truly trusts the LORD.
Because God Most High always loves him,
he will not be overwhelmed.

8Your hand is against all your enemies;
those who hate you will feel your power.
9When you appear,
you will burn them as in a furnace.
In your anger you will swallow them up,
and fire will burn them up.
10You will destroy their families from the earth;
their children will not live.
11They made evil plans against you,
but their traps won't work.
12You will make them turn their backs
when you aim your arrows at them.

BIBLE STUDY

What's the Use?

A Bible has many uses. You can get tiny versions that can be hung on a chain like a locket, and used for decoration. Many babies are presented with white Bibles to remind them of their Christening, as a memento. There are huge ones that lay open in big old churches.

On the other hand, you could use it as a doorstop. That what Sue's was for. It was a smallish black Bible with a gold pattern on it and it was just the right size to wedge in the bedroom door if you wanted some privacy. It was used this way for a number of years until one day everything changed.

Sue worked for a radio station and had been given a copy of the album *Jesus Christ Superstar* by its writer, Tim Rice. Sue immediately fell in love with the musical and played it for weeks on end. Then one day she was reading the lyric sheet and noticed that there was a text at the end of the last song. The song where Jesus was left dying on a cross. Out of curiosity, she picked up the Bible wedged in the door and started to read the account of Jesus' death. To her astonishment she read that when Jesus died, it wasn't the end of the story. She went on to read about the Resurrection, and soon afterwards Sue became a Christian.

She started to use the Bible as it was intended to be used, as a guideline for life.

Read in **Psalm 19** what the Bible is really for: that the Lord's teachings are perfect and give strength.

- What teachings in the psalm would help a young Christian?
- How can you use these truths in your life this week?

Consider . . .

- highlighting or underlining a verse in this psalm that has a special impact on you.
- finding a friend who will meet with you once a week to study the Bible.

For more, see . . .

- Psalm 119:1–48 (p.571)
- 2 Timothy 3:14–17 (p.1319)
- John 14:23–24 (p.1124)

13Be supreme, LORD, in your power.
We sing and praise your greatness.

The Prayer of a Suffering Man

For the director of music. To the tune of "The Doe of Dawn". A psalm of David.

22 My God, my God, why have you rejected me?
You seem far from saving me,
far from the words of my moans.
2My God, I call to you during the day,
but you do not answer.
I call at night;
I am not silent.

3You sit as the Holy One.
The praises of Israel are your throne.
4Our ancestors trusted you;
they trusted, and you saved them.
5They called to you for help
and were rescued.
They trusted you
and were not disappointed.

6But I am like a worm instead of a man.
People make fun of me and hate me.
7Those who look at me laugh.
They stick out their tongues and shake their heads.
8They say, "Turn to the LORD for help.
Maybe he will save you.
If he likes you,
maybe he will rescue you."

9You had my mother give birth to me.
You made me trust you
while I was just a baby.
10I have leaned on you since the day I was born;
you have been my God since my mother gave birth to me.
11So don't be far away from me.
Now trouble is near,
and there is no one to help.

12People have surrounded me like angry bulls.
Like the strong bulls of Bashan, they are on every side.
13Like hungry, roaring lions
they open their mouths at me.

Sidelight Travellers through the region of Bashan, north-east of Galilee, may have needed professional bodyguards. In addition to "strong bulls" (Psalm 22:12), Bashan was notorious for fierce lions and giant people.

14My strength is gone,
like water poured out onto the ground,
and my bones are out of joint.
My heart is like wax;
it has melted inside me.
15My strength has dried up like a clay pot,
and my tongue sticks to the top of my mouth.
You laid me in the dust of death.
16Evil people have surrounded me;
like dogs they have trapped me.
They have bitten my arms and legs.
17I can count all my bones;
people look and stare at me.
18They divided my clothes among them,
and they threw lots [d] for my clothing.

19But, LORD, don't be far away.
You are my strength; hurry to help me.
20Save me from the sword;
save my life from the dogs.
21Rescue me from the lion's mouth;
save me from the horns of the bulls.

22Then I will tell my fellow Israelites about you;
I will praise you in the public meeting.
23Praise the LORD, all you who respect him.
All you descendants [d] of Jacob, honour him;
fear him, all you Israelites.
24He does not ignore those in trouble.
He doesn't hide from them
but listens when they call out to him.

25LORD, I praise you in the great meeting of your people;
these worshippers will see me do what I promised.
26Poor people will eat until they are full;
those who look to the LORD will praise him.
May your hearts live for ever!
27People everywhere will remember
and will turn to the LORD.
All the families of the nations
will worship him
28because the LORD is King,
and he rules the nations.

29All the powerful people on earth will eat and worship.
Everyone will bow down to him,
all who will one day die.
30The people in the future will serve him;
they will always be told about the Lord.
31They will tell that he does what is right.
People who are not yet born
will hear what God has done.

The LORD the Shepherd

A psalm of David.

23 The LORD is my shepherd;
I have everything I need.
2He lets me rest in green pastures.
He leads me to calm water.
3He gives me new strength.
He leads me on paths that are right
for the good of his name.
4Even if I walk through a very dark valley,
I will not be afraid,
because you are with me.
Your rod and your staff[n] comfort me.

5You prepare a meal for me
in front of my enemies.
You pour oil on my head;[n]
you fill my cup to overflowing.
6Surely your goodness and love will be
with me
all my life,
and I will live in the house of the LORD for
ever.

Sidelight Psalm 23 has always been one of the favourite, most-quoted passages in the Old Testament. The early Christian church sang this song when people were baptised.

staff The stick a shepherd uses to guide and protect his sheep.
pour oil . . . head This can mean that God gave him great wealth and blessed him.

HAPPINESS

Full of Joy . . . Always

Frank Gamble grew up wanting to be a missionary. His path to London Bible College was part of fulfilling God's will for his life. Frank proved himself to be a friendly extrovert and keen on football.

Following his graduation he married Glenda and became assistant pastor at Roxeth Green Free Church, where his spiritual and musical gifts came to the fore.

From 1977, however, Frank became increasingly disabled. He had a disease called ankylosing spondylitis – a disease that slowly spreads and paralyses every joint in the body.

The years of ill health took a toll on Frank's body, but in contrast they made his radiant face that much more evident. Anyone who visited him to bring comfort came away with far more than they had been able to give.

Although the disease imprisoned his body, his mind and spirit were free and he left others laughing and relaxed.

Frank said, "God is good, and his love fills my heart with joy and hope. As a family we enjoy his presence and provision. One day I will walk and run again. But right now I can rejoice in my sufferings because I believe that he is producing good things in me."

Despite awful pain, Frank held on to the truth that David declared in **Psalm 23**.

- What phrase in Psalm 23 best describes the reason for Frank's happiness despite such terrible circumstances?
- How can you make the truths of Psalm 23 the foundation of your happiness?

Consider . . .

- taking a personal inventory of the sources of your happiness, by writing as many responses as you can to this phrase: "Happiness, for me, is . . ."
- going for a walk and talking to God about a "dark valley" you are going through at the moment.

For more, see . . .

- Psalm 100 (p.558)
- Philippians 4:4–7 (p.1285)
- Matthew 5:1–12 (p.942)

A Welcome for God into the Temple

A psalm of David.

24 The earth belongs to the LORD, and
everything in it—
the world and all its people.
2He built it on the waters
and set it on the rivers.

3Who may go up on the mountain of the
LORD?
Who may stand in his holy Temple? [d]
4Only those with clean hands and pure hearts,
who have not worshipped idols,
who have not made promises in the name
of a false god.
5They will receive a blessing from the LORD;
the God who saves them will declare them
right.
6They try to follow God;
they look to the God of Jacob for help.
Selah [d]

7Gates, open all the way.
Open wide, aged doors
so the glorious King will come in.
8Who is this glorious King?
The LORD, strong and mighty.
The LORD, the powerful warrior.
9Gates, open all the way.
Open wide, aged doors
so the glorious King will come in.
10Who is this glorious King?
The LORD All-powerful—
he is the glorious King. *Selah*

A Prayer for God to Guide

Of David.

25 LORD, I give myself to you;
2my God, I trust you.
Do not let me be disgraced;
do not let my enemies laugh at me.
3No one who trusts you will be disgraced,
but those who sin without excuse will be
disgraced.

4LORD, tell me your ways.
Show me how to live.
5Guide me in your truth,
and teach me, my God, my Saviour.
I trust you all day long.
6LORD, remember your mercy and love
that you have shown since long ago.
7Do not remember the sins
and wrong things I did when I was young.
But remember to love me always
because you are good, LORD.

8The LORD is good and right;
he points sinners to the right way.
9He shows those who are humble how to do
right,
and he teaches them his ways.
10All the LORD's ways are loving and true
for those who follow the demands of his
agreement.
11For the sake of your name, LORD,
forgive my many sins.
12Are there those who respect the LORD?
He will point them to the best way.
13They will enjoy a good life,
and their children will inherit the land.
14The LORD tells his secrets to those who
respect him;
he tells them about his agreement.
15My eyes are always looking to the LORD for
help.
He will keep me from any traps.

16Turn to me and have mercy on me,
because I am lonely and hurting.
17My troubles have grown larger;
free me from my problems.
18Look at my suffering and troubles,
and take away all my sins.
19Look at how many enemies I have!
See how much they hate me!
20Protect me and save me.
I trust you, so do not let me be disgraced.
21My hope is in you,
so may goodness and honesty guard me.
22God, save Israel from all their troubles!

The Prayer of an Innocent Believer

Of David.

26 LORD, defend me because I have lived
an innocent life.
I have trusted the LORD and never doubted.
2LORD, try me and test me;
look closely into my heart and mind.
3I see your love,
and I live by your truth.
4I do not spend time with liars,
nor do I make friends with those who hide
their sin.
5I hate the company of evil people,
and I won't sit with the wicked.
6I wash my hands to show I am innocent,
and I come to your altar, LORD.
7I raise my voice in praise
and tell of all the miracles [d] you have done.
8LORD, I love the Temple [d] where you live,
where your glory is.

9Do not kill me with those sinners
or take my life with those murderers.
10Evil is in their hands,
and they do wrong for money.

[11]But I have lived an innocent life,
so save me and have mercy on me.

[12]I stand in a safe place.
LORD, I praise you in the great meeting.

A Song of Trust in God

Of David.

27 The LORD is my light and the one who saves me.
I fear no one.
The LORD protects my life;
I am afraid of no one.
[2]Evil people may try to destroy my body.
My enemies and those who hate me attack me,
but they are overwhelmed and defeated.
[3]If an army surrounds me,
I will not be afraid.
If war breaks out,
I will trust the LORD.

[4]I ask only one thing from the LORD.
This is what I want:
let me live in the LORD's house
all my life.
Let me see the LORD's beauty
and look with my own eyes at his Temple.[d]
[5]During danger he will keep me safe in his shelter.
He will hide me in his Holy Tent,[d]
or he will keep me safe on a high mountain.

FEAR

Evacuation

The station was packed full of children looking nervously at the big train as it pulled into the platform, smoke pouring out of the funnel. Each child clutched a small bag of their belongings and a little cardboard box containing their gas mask, and each wore a label around their neck, as if they were parcels, saying who they were and where they were going. The whistle sounded and slowly, with tears in their eyes, the children got onto the train and waved goodbye to their parents.

This is the frightening situation that many children found themselves in during the Second World War, as they became evacuees. The British Government knew that big towns and cities would be the target for bombs, so encouraged people to send their children to the countryside where they would be safer. This was called the Evacuation.

The countryside was a big shock for many of the children who had never been out of the town or city – some were petrified because they had never seen (or heard or smelled) animals like cows before! When they arrived at their destination, the adults of the small towns and villages would sometimes pick which children they wanted to come and live with them, so lined the children up and chose them one by one.

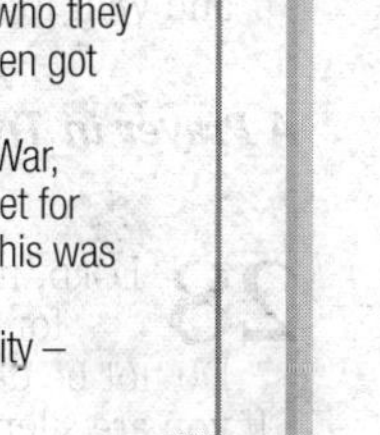

By the end of the Second World War, around 3.5 million people, mainly children, had experienced evacuation. At first, it must have been a terrifying experience, but it was much safer for them in the country, and many lives were saved.

Read **Psalm 27**.

- Imagine having to leave your family and go to live with strangers in another part of the country. How would that make you feel?
- Which verses in Psalm 27 would help you if you were an evacuee experiencing those feelings?

Consider . . .

- memorising the verse from Psalm 27 that you most want to remember next time you are afraid.
- circling in your Bible every time the word "will" is used in this psalm. What does that tell you about the confidence we can have in God when we are fearful?

For more, see . . .

- Joshua 1:1–9 (p.202)
- 1 John 4:18 (p.1374)
- Luke 8:22–25 (p.1053)

6My head is higher than my enemies
around me.
I will offer joyful sacrifices in his
Holy Tent.
I will sing and praise the LORD.

7LORD, hear me when I call;
have mercy and answer me.
8My heart said of you, "Go, worship him."
So I come to worship you, LORD.
9Do not turn away from me.
Do not turn your servant away in anger;
you have helped me.
Do not push me away or leave me alone,
God, my Saviour.
10If my father and mother leave me,
the LORD will take me in.
11LORD, teach me your ways,
and guide me to do what is right
because I have enemies.
12Do not hand me over to my enemies,
because they tell lies about me
and say they will hurt me.

13I truly believe
I will live to see the LORD's goodness.
14Wait for the LORD's help.
Be strong and brave,
and wait for the LORD's help.

A Prayer in Troubled Times

Of David.

28 LORD, my Rock, [d] I call out to you
for help.
Do not be deaf to me.
If you are silent,
I will be like those in the grave.
2Hear the sound of my prayer,
when I cry out to you for help.
I raise my hands
towards your Most Holy Place.

3Don't drag me away with the wicked,
with those who do evil.
They say "Peace" to their neighbours,
but evil is in their hearts.
4Pay them back for what they have done,
for their evil deeds.
Pay them back for what they have done;
give them their reward.
5They don't understand what the LORD has
done
or what he has made.
So he will knock them down
and not lift them up.

6Praise the LORD,
because he heard my prayer for help.

7The LORD is my strength and shield.
I trust him, and he helps me.
I am very happy,
and I praise him with my song.

8The LORD is powerful;
he gives victory to his chosen one.
9Save your people
and bless those who are your own.
Be their shepherd and carry them
for ever.

God in the Thunderstorm

A psalm of David.

29 Praise the LORD, you angels;
praise the LORD's glory and power.
2Praise the LORD for the glory of his
name;
worship the LORD because he is holy.

3The LORD's voice is heard over the sea.
The glorious God thunders;
the LORD thunders over the ocean.
4The LORD's voice is powerful;
the LORD's voice is majestic.
5The LORD's voice breaks the trees;
the LORD breaks the cedars of
Lebanon.

Sidelight God's power was indeed great to break the cedars of Lebanon (Psalm 29:5). These trees grew 20 to 25 metres tall, with trunks sometimes more than 4 metres in diameter. To cut them down and saw them up, even today, would be a mammoth task even with power saws.

6He makes the land of Lebanon dance like a
calf
and Mount Hermon jump like a baby
bull.
7The LORD's voice makes the lightning
flash.
8The LORD's voice shakes the desert;
the LORD shakes the Desert of Kadesh.
9The LORD's voice shakes the oaks
and strips the leaves off the trees.
In his Temple [d] everyone says, "Glory
to God!"

10The LORD controls the flood.
The LORD will be King for ever.
11The LORD gives strength to his people;
the LORD blesses his people with
peace.

Thanksgiving for Escaping Death

A psalm of David. A song for giving
the Temple[d] to the LORD.

30 I will praise you, LORD,
because you rescued me.
You did not let my enemies laugh at me.
2LORD, my God, I prayed to you,
and you healed me.
3You lifted me out of the grave;
you spared me from going down to the
place of the dead.

4Sing praises to the LORD, you who belong
to him;
praise his holy name.
5His anger lasts only a moment,
but his kindness lasts for a lifetime.
Crying may last for a night,
but joy comes in the morning.

6When I felt safe, I said,
"I will never fear."
7LORD, in your kindness you made my
mountain safe.
But when you turned away, I was
frightened.

8I called to you, LORD,
and asked you to have mercy on me.
9I said, "What good will it do if I die
or if I go down to the grave?

DEPRESSION

The Wall Came Tumbling Down

On 13 August 1961, at 2.30 a.m., with floodlights to illuminate their work and soldiers to ensure no interruptions, engineering crews began sinking posts in the pavement of Berlin. Then they attached massive sheets of barbed wire.

Many thought it was a farce, but from that middle-of-the-night beginning, the Berlin Wall was built. It divided families, friends and nations. About 10,000 East Germans attempted to cross the wall in the next 29 years, by tunnelling, flying, even blasting. At least 191 died trying.

The best-known defector, Peter Fechter, was shot down by border guards in front of photographers and TV crews in 1962. Others were imprisoned for trying to cross the wall.

Nothing portrayed the division of an entire country more dramatically than the Berlin Wall. And nothing else so well symbolised the broken people of this war-torn territory.

On 17 November 1989, Egon Krenz, the premier of East Germany, ordered that the wall be torn down. In no time, sledgehammers wielded by East and West Berliners broke through, opening the way for millions to cross back and forth in one joyous parade. No papers were checked. Even the border guards fought to keep from smiling.

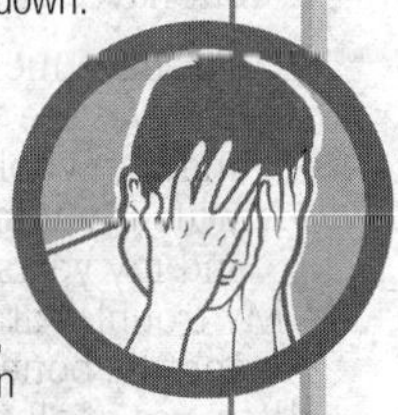

"The wall is gone!" the people chanted. "The wall is gone." From both sides of the city they climbed on top of undamaged portions of the three-metre structure, laughing, crying, embracing, singing and dancing.

When David was delivered from his enemies, he expressed the same joyous feeling in his prayer, "You changed my sorrow into dancing." Read **Psalm 30** to find out how your sorrow and depression can be turned to joy.

- How was the destruction of the Berlin Wall like David's deliverance?
- What "walls" of sorrow and depression need to be broken down by God in your life? What sorrow in your life would you like God to turn into dancing?

Consider . . .

- expressing thanks to people you turn to when you're depressed.
- planning a personal "party" complete with your favourite cake to celebrate a victory God has gained in your life.

For more, see . . .

- Isaiah 61.3 (p.705)
- Luke 15:11–32 (p.1071)
- Jonah 2 (p.885)

Dust cannot praise you;
it cannot speak about your truth.
10LORD, hear me and have mercy on me.
LORD, help me."

11You changed my sorrow into dancing.
You took away my clothes of sadness,
and clothed me in happiness.
12I will sing to you and not be silent.
LORD, my God, I will praise you for ever.

A Prayer of Faith in Troubled Times

For the director of music. A psalm of David.

31 LORD, I trust in you;
let me never be disgraced.
Save me because you do what is right.
2Listen to me
and save me quickly.
Be my rock of protection,
a strong city to save me.
3You are my rock and my protection.
For the good of your name, lead me and guide me.
4Set me free from the trap they set for me,
because you are my protection.
5I give you my life.
Save me, LORD, God of truth.

6I hate those who worship false gods.
I trust only in the LORD.
7I will be glad and rejoice in your love,
because you saw my suffering;
you knew my troubles.
8You have not handed me over to my enemies
but have set me in a safe place.

9LORD, have mercy, because I am in misery.
My eyes are weak from so much crying,
and my whole being is tired from grief.
10My life is ending in sadness,
and my years are spent in crying.
My troubles are using up my strength,
and my bones are getting weaker.
11Because of all my troubles, my enemies hate me,
and even my neighbours look down on me.
When my friends see me,
they are afraid and run.
12I am like a piece of a broken pot.
I am forgotten as if I were dead.
13I have heard many insults.
Terror is all around me.
They make plans against me
and want to kill me.

14LORD, I trust you.
I have said, "You are my God."
15My life is in your hands.
Save me from my enemies
and from those who are chasing me.
16Show your kindness to me, your servant.
Save me because of your love.
17LORD, I called to you,
so do not let me be disgraced.
Let the wicked be disgraced
and lie silent in the grave.
18With pride and hatred
they speak against those who do right.
So silence their lying lips.

19How great is your goodness
that you have stored up for those who fear you,
that you have given to those who trust you.
You do this for all to see.
20You protect them by your presence
from what people plan against them.
You shelter them from evil words.
21Praise the LORD.
His love to me was wonderful
when my city was attacked.
22In my distress, I said,
"God cannot see me!"
But you heard my prayer
when I cried out to you for help.

23Love the LORD, all you who belong to him.
The LORD protects those who truly believe,
but he punishes the proud as much as they have sinned.
24All you who put your hope in the LORD
be strong and brave.

It is Better to Confess Sin

A maskil[d] of David.

32 Happy is the person
whose sins are forgiven,
whose wrongs are pardoned.
2Happy is the person
whom the LORD does not consider guilty
and in whom there is nothing false.

3When I kept things to myself,
I felt weak deep inside me.
I moaned all day long.
4Day and night you punished me.
My strength was gone as in the summer heat. *Selah*[d]
5Then I confessed my sins to you
and didn't hide my guilt.
I said, "I will confess my sins to the LORD",
and you forgave my guilt. *Selah*

6For this reason, all who obey you
should pray to you while they still can.
When troubles rise like a flood,
they will not reach them.
7You are my hiding place.
You protect me from my troubles
and fill me with songs of salvation. *Selah*

8The LORD says, "I will make you wise and
show you where to go.
I will guide you and watch over you.
9So don't be like a horse or donkey
that doesn't understand.
They must be led with bits and reins,
or they will not come near you."
10Wicked people have many troubles,
but the LORD's love surrounds those who
trust him.
11Good people, rejoice and be happy in the LORD.
Sing all you whose hearts are right.

Praise God Who Creates and Saves

33 Sing to the LORD, you who do what is
right;
honest people should praise him.
2Praise the LORD on the harp;
make music for him on a ten-stringed lyre. [d]
3Sing a new song to him;
play well and joyfully.
4God's word is true,
and everything he does is right.
5He loves what is right and fair;
the LORD's love fills the earth.
6The sky was made at the LORD's command.
By the breath from his mouth, he made all
the stars.
7He gathered the water of the sea into a heap.
He made the great ocean stay in its place.
8All the earth should worship the LORD;
the whole world should fear him.
9He spoke, and it happened.
He commanded, and it appeared.
10The LORD upsets the plans of nations;
he ruins all their plans.
11But the LORD's plans will stand for ever;
his ideas will last from now on.
12Happy is the nation whose God is the LORD,
the people he chose for his very own.
13The LORD looks down from heaven
and sees every person.
14From his throne he watches
all who live on earth.
15He made their hearts
and understands everything they do.
16No king is saved by his great army.
No warrior escapes by his great strength.
17Horses can't bring victory;
they can't save by their strength.
18But the LORD looks after those who fear him,
those who put their hope in his love.
19He saves them from death
and spares their lives in times of hunger.
20So our hope is in the LORD.
He is our help, our shield to protect us.
21We rejoice in him,
because we trust his holy name.
22LORD, show your love to us
as we put our hope in you.

Praise God Who Judges and Saves

David's song from the time he pretended to be insane
so that Abimelech would send him away.

34 I will praise the LORD at all times;
his praise is always on my lips.
2My whole being praises the LORD.
The poor will hear and be glad.
3Praise the LORD with me,
and let us praise his name together.
4I asked the LORD for help, and he
answered me.
He saved me from all that I feared.
5Those who go to him for help are happy,
and they are never disgraced.
6This poor man called, and the LORD
heard him
and saved him from all his troubles.
7The angel of the LORD camps around those
who fear God,
and he saves them.
8Examine and see how good the LORD is.
Happy is the person who trusts him.
9You who belong to the LORD, fear him!
Those who fear him will have everything
they need.
10Even lions may get weak and hungry,
but those who look to the LORD will have
every good thing.
11Children, come and listen to me.
I will teach you to worship the LORD.
12You must do these things
to enjoy life and have many happy days.
13You must not say evil things,
and you must not tell lies.
14Stop doing evil and do good.
Look for peace and work for it.
15The LORD sees the good people
and listens to their prayers.
16But the LORD is against those who do evil;
he makes the world forget them.
17The LORD hears good people when they cry
out to him,
and he saves them from all their
troubles.
18The LORD is close to the broken-hearted,
and he saves those whose spirits have been
crushed.
19People who do what is right may have many
problems,
but the LORD will solve them all.

20He will protect their very bones;
not one of them will be broken.

21Evil will kill the wicked;
those who hate good people will be judged guilty.
22But the LORD saves his servants' lives;
no one who trusts him will be judged guilty.

Sidelight Have you ever made an acrostic in which you use each letter of a word to start a new word or phrase? Some psalms (such as Psalms 34, 37, 111 and 146) use this structure. In Hebrew, each unit of those psalms begins with a successive letter of the alphabet.

A Prayer for Help

Of David.

35 LORD, battle against those who battle with me.
Fight against those who fight against me.
2Pick up the shield and armour.
Rise up and help me.
3Lift up your spears, both large and small,
against those who chase me.
Tell me, "I will save you."

4Make those who want to kill me
be ashamed and disgraced.
Make those who plan to harm me
turn back and run away.
5Make them like chaff[d] blown by the wind
as the angel of the LORD forces them away.
6Let their road be dark and slippery
as the angel of the LORD chases them.
7For no reason they spread out their net to trap me;
for no reason they dug a pit for me.
8So let ruin strike them suddenly.
Let them be caught in their own nets;
let them fall into the pit and die.
9Then I will rejoice in the LORD;
I will be happy when he saves me.
10Even my bones will say,
"LORD, who is like you?
You save the weak from the strong,
the weak and poor from robbers."

11Men without mercy stand up to testify.
They ask me things I do not know.
12They repay me with evil for the good I have done,
and they make me very sad.
13Yet when they were sick, I put on clothes of sadness
and showed my sorrow by going without food.
But my prayers were not answered.
14 I acted as if they were my friends or brothers.
I bowed in sadness as if I were crying for my mother.
15But when I was in trouble, they gathered and laughed;
they gathered to attack before I knew it.
They insulted me without stopping.
16They made fun of me and were cruel to me
and ground their teeth at me in anger.
17Lord, how long will you watch this happen?
Save my life from their attacks;
save me from these people who are like lions.
18I will praise you in the great meeting.
I will praise you among crowds of people.

19Do not let my enemies laugh at me;
they hate me for no reason.
Do not let them make fun of me;
they have no cause to hate me.
20Their words are not friendly
but are lies about peace-loving people.
21They speak against me
and say, "Aha! We saw what you did!"

22LORD, you have been watching. Do not keep quiet.
Lord, do not leave me alone.
23Wake up! Come and defend me!
My God and Lord, fight for me!
24LORD my God, defend me with your justice.
Don't let them laugh at me.
25Don't let them think, "Aha! We got what we wanted!"
Don't let them say, "We destroyed him."

26Let them be ashamed and embarrassed,
because they were happy when I hurt.
Cover them with shame and disgrace,
because they thought they were better than I was.
27May my friends sing and shout for joy.
May they always say, "Praise the greatness of the LORD,
who loves to see his servants do well."
28I will tell of your goodness
and will praise you every day.

Wicked People and a Good God

For the director of music. Of David, the servant of the LORD.

36 Sin speaks to the wicked in their hearts.
They have no fear of God.

2They think too much of themselves
so they don't see their sin and hate it.
3Their words are wicked lies;
they are no longer wise or good.
4At night they make evil plans;
what they do leads to nothing good.
They don't refuse things that are evil.

5LORD, your love reaches to the heavens,
your loyalty to the skies.
6Your goodness is as high as the mountains.
Your justice is as deep as the great
ocean.
LORD, you protect both people and
animals.
7God, your love is so precious!
You protect people in the shadow of your
wings.
8They eat the rich food in your house,
and you let them drink from your river of
pleasure.
9You are the giver of life.
Your light lets us enjoy life.

10Continue to love those who know you
and to do good to those who are good.
11Don't let proud people attack me
and the wicked force me away.
12Those who do evil have been defeated.
They are overwhelmed;
they cannot do evil any longer.

God will Reward Fairly

Of David.

37 Don't be upset because of evil people.
Don't be jealous of those who do
wrong,
2because, like the grass, they will soon dry up.
Like green plants, they will soon die away.
3Trust the LORD and do good.
Live in the land and feed on truth.

JEALOUSY

Risky Business

Kevin was a thief – everyone knew that. After all, he didn't try to keep it much of a secret, did he? Every week he would boast that he had "done another job" with his elder brother – the same brother who had already been in jail.

But amazingly, his friends at school envied him. Oh no, they didn't envy the fact that if he got caught he would get a criminal record, but they did envy the fact that he could get anything.

Kevin would cycle to school on a brand new bike. He would always wear designer clothes and the latest trainers. His friends not only envied his bike and clothes, but also the fact that whatever he wanted was only another burglary away.

For days Kevin had been boasting that he was going to rob another house at the weekend, to get an MP3 player.

On Monday, Kevin wasn't at school. The expensive bike was not in the school shed. Someone had told the police which house was going to be robbed – and now he was at the police station facing charges that could ruin his entire life. All this, at the age of fourteen.

Now those who had envied Kevin laughed at him and enjoyed the fact that he was being punished. If these people had ever read **Psalm 37**, they wouldn't have been envious in the first place. Read it and see why.

- What does the psalm say our attitude should be towards people like Kevin?
- How does this psalm help you to stop feeling jealous of other people?

Consider . . .

- reading the psalm again and thinking of ten reasons why feeling jealous of someone is senseless.
- suggesting a group discussion about jealousy to your church youth leader.

For more, see . . .

- Proverbs 24:1–2 (p.610)
- James 1.9–11 (p.1348)
- Matthew 6:19–24 (p.948)

4Enjoy serving the LORD,
and he will give you what you want.

5Depend on the LORD;
trust him, and he will take care of you.
6Then your goodness will shine like the sun,
and your fairness like the noonday sun.

7Wait and trust the LORD.
Don't be upset when others get rich
or when someone else's plans succeed.

8Don't get angry.
Don't be upset; it only leads to trouble.
9Evil people will be sent away,
but those who trust the LORD will inherit
the land.

10In a little while the wicked will be no
more.
You may look for them, but they will be
gone.
11People who are not proud will inherit the
land
and will enjoy complete peace.

12The wicked make evil plans against good
people.
They grind their teeth at them in anger.
13But the Lord laughs at the wicked,
because he sees that their day is coming.
14The wicked draw their swords
and bend their bows
to kill the poor and helpless,
to kill those who are honest.
15But their swords will stab their own hearts,
and their bows will break.

16It is better to have little and be right
than to have much and be wrong.
17The power of the wicked will be broken,
but the LORD supports those who do right.
18The LORD watches over the lives of the
innocent,
and their reward will last for ever.
19They will not be ashamed when trouble
comes.
They will be full in times of hunger.

20But the wicked will die.
The LORD's enemies will be like the flowers
of the fields;
they will disappear like smoke.
21The wicked borrow and don't pay back,
but those who do right give freely to
others.
22Those whom the LORD blesses will inherit the
land,
but those he curses will be sent away.

23When a person's steps follow the LORD,
God is pleased with his ways.
24If he stumbles, he will not fall,
because the LORD holds his hand.

25I was young, and now I am old,
but I have never seen good people left
helpless
or their children begging for food.
26Good people always lend freely to others,
and their children are a blessing.

27Stop doing evil and do good,
so you will live for ever.
28The LORD loves justice
and will not leave those who worship him.
He will always protect them,
but the children of the wicked will die.
29Good people will inherit the land
and will live in it for ever.

30A good person speaks with wisdom,
and he says what is fair.
31The teachings of his God are in his heart,
so he does not fail to keep them.

32The wicked watch for good people
so that they may kill them.
33But the LORD will not take away his
protection
or let good people be judged guilty.

34Wait for the LORD's help
and follow him.
He will honour you and give you the land,
and you will see the wicked sent away.
35I saw a wicked and cruel man
who looked strong like a healthy tree in
good soil.
36But he died and was gone;
I looked for him, but he couldn't be found.

37Think of the innocent person,
and watch the honest one.
The man who has peace
will have children to live after him.
38But sinners will be destroyed;
in the end the wicked will die.

39The LORD saves good people;
he is their strength in times of trouble.
40The LORD helps them and saves them;
he saves them from the wicked,
because they trust in him for protection.

A Prayer in Time of Sickness

A psalm of David to remember.

38 LORD, don't punish me when you are
angry.
Don't punish me when you are furious.
2Your arrows have wounded me,
and your hand has come down on me.

3My body is sick from your punishment.
Even my bones are not healthy because of my sin.
4My guilt has overwhelmed me;
like a load it weighs me down.

5My sores stink and become infected
because I was foolish.
6I am bent over and bowed down;
I am sad all day long.
7I am burning with fever,
and my whole body is sore.
8I am weak and faint.
I moan from the pain I feel.

9Lord, you know everything I want;
my cries are not hidden from you.
10My heart pounds, and my strength is gone.
I am losing my sight.
11Because of my wounds, my friends and neighbours avoid me,
and my relatives stay far away.
12Some people set traps to kill me.
Those who want to hurt me plan trouble;
all day long they think up lies.

13I am like a deaf man; I cannot hear.
Like a mute, I cannot speak.
14I am like a person who does not hear,
who has no answer to give.
15I trust you, LORD.
You will answer, my Lord and God.
16I said, "Don't let them laugh at me
or boast when I am defeated."

17I am about to die,
and I cannot forget my pain.
18I confess my guilt;
I am troubled by my sin.
19My enemies are strong and healthy,
and many hate me for no reason.
20They repay me with evil for the good I did.
They lie about me because I try to do good.

21LORD, don't leave me;
my God, don't go away.
22Quickly come and help me,
my Lord and Saviour.

Life is Short

For the director of music. For Jeduthun.
A psalm of David.

39 I said, "I will be careful how I act
and will not sin by what I say.
I will be careful what I say
around wicked people."
2So I kept very quiet.
I didn't even say anything good,
but I became even more upset.
3I became very angry inside,
and as I thought about it, my anger burned.
So I spoke:
4"LORD, tell me when the end will come
and how long I will live.
Let me know how long I have.
5You have given me only a short life;
my lifetime is like nothing to you.
Everyone's life is only a breath. *Selah*[d]
6People are like shadows moving about.
All their work is for nothing;
they collect things but don't know who will get them.

7"So, Lord, what hope do I have?
You are my hope.
8Save me from all my sins.
Don't let wicked fools make fun of me.
9I am quiet; I do not open my mouth,
because you are the one who has done this.
10Stop punishing me;
your beating is about to kill me.
11You correct and punish people for their sins;
like a moth, you destroy what they love.
Everyone's life is only a breath. *Selah*

12"LORD, hear my prayer,
and listen to my cry.
Do not ignore my tears.
I am like a visitor with you.
Like my ancestors, I'm only here for a short time.
13Leave me alone so I can be happy
before I leave and am no more."

Praise and Prayer for Help

For the director of music. A psalm of David.

40 I waited patiently for the LORD.
He turned to me and heard my cry.
2He lifted me out of the pit of destruction,
out of the sticky mud.
He stood me on a rock
and made my feet steady.
3He put a new song in my mouth,
a song of praise to our God.
Many people will see this and worship him.
Then they will trust the LORD.

4Happy is the person
who trusts the LORD,
who doesn't turn to those who are proud
or to those who worship false gods.
5LORD my God, you have done many miracles.[d]
Your plans for us are many.
If I tried to tell them all,
there would be too many to count.

6You do not want sacrifices and offerings.
But you have made a hole in my ear
to show that my body and life are yours.

You do not ask for burnt offerings
and sacrifices to take away sins.
7Then I said, "Look, I have come.
It is written about me in the book.
8My God, I want to do what you want.
Your teachings are in my heart."

9I will tell about your goodness in the great meeting of your people.
LORD, you know my lips are not silent.
10I do not hide your goodness in my heart;
I speak about your loyalty and salvation.
I do not hide your love and truth
from the people in the great meeting.

11LORD, do not hold back your mercy from me;
let your love and truth always protect me.
12Troubles have surrounded me;
there are too many to count.
My sins have caught me
so that I cannot see a way to escape.
I have more sins than hairs on my head,
and I have lost my courage.

13Please, LORD, save me.
Hurry, LORD, to help me.
14People are trying to kill me.
Shame them and disgrace them.
People want to hurt me.
Let them run away in disgrace.
15People are making fun of me.
Let them be shamed into silence.
16But let those who follow you
be happy and glad.
They love you for saving them.
May they always say, "Praise the LORD!"

17Lord, because I am poor and helpless,
please remember me.

GOD'S POWER

Against All Odds

It was 18 June 1940, one of Britain's grimmest historical moments. Hitler's army had already wiped out the French army – one of the largest in the world – in forty days. Russia had signed a pact with Hitler. The United States was not involved. Britain stood alone.

Hitler's air force, the Luftwaffe, was mercilessly pounding English cities. Germany had more than eleven hundred fighter planes and fifteen hundred light bombers facing fewer than seven hundred British Spitfires and Hurricanes. Before the Battle of Britain was over, forty-five thousand in London alone were killed or injured.

Sir Winston Churchill – the wartime Prime Minister – was never known to be a particularly religious man. But during the darkest hours of the battle, something in him seemed to understand that only God could save his country from the Nazi pounding: "If the Almighty God in his mercy should lighten or shorten our labours and the torment of all mankind, all his servants will be thankful. Let God defend the right; heed the call of duty and honour, and see that our policy and conduct are upon the highest level, and that honour should be our guide."

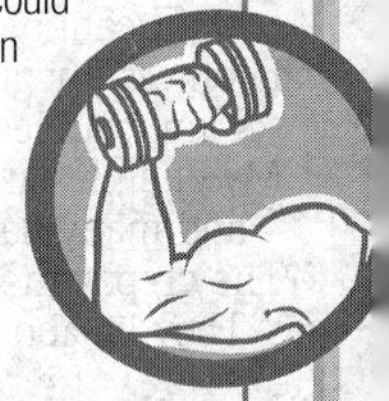

Against all odds, the British prevailed.

King David also called on God to save him from his enemies. Nowhere is David's cry for help expressed more strongly than in **Psalm 40**.

- How do you think Churchill would have responded to verses 1–3 if he had read them while Germany was bombing London?
- If you were writing a modern version of Psalm 40, what tough situations from your own life and the world would you include?

Consider . . .

- praying for God's deliverance in what you believe is the world's most pressing crisis.
- scanning news reports of current world crises and looking for references to dependence on God for help.

For more, see . . .

- Exodus 14:5–31 (p.71)
- 2 Peter 1:3–4 (p.1365)
- Daniel 6 (p.839)

You are my helper and saviour.
My God, do not wait.

A Prayer in Time of Sickness

For the director of music. A psalm of David.

41 Happy is the person who thinks about the poor.
When trouble comes, the LORD will save him.
2The LORD will protect him and spare his life
and will bless him in the land.
He will not let his enemies take him.
3The LORD will give him strength when he is sick,
and he will make him well again.

4I said, "LORD, have mercy on me.
Heal me, because I have sinned against you."
5My enemies are saying evil things about me.
They say, "When will he die and be forgotten?"
6Some people come to see me,
but they lie.
They just come to get bad news.
Then they go and gossip.

7All my enemies whisper about me
and think the worst about me.
8They say, "He has a terrible disease.
He will never get out of bed again."
9My best and truest friend, who ate at my table,
has even turned against me.

10LORD, have mercy on me.
Give me strength so I can pay them back.
11Because my enemies do not defeat me,
I know you are pleased with me.
12Because I am innocent, you support me
and will let me be with you for ever.

13Praise the LORD, the God of Israel.
He has always been,
and he will always be.
Amen and amen.

Book 2

Wishing to be Near God

For the director of music. A maskil [d] of the sons of Korah.

42 As a deer thirsts for streams of water,
so I thirst for you, God.
2I thirst for the living God.
When can I go to meet with him?
3Day and night, my tears have been my food.
People are always saying,
"Where is your God?"
4When I remember these things,
I speak with a broken heart.
I used to walk with the crowd
and lead them to God's Temple [d]
with songs of praise.

5Why am I so sad?
Why am I so upset?
I should put my hope in God
and keep praising him,
my Saviour and 6my God.

I am very sad.
So I remember you where the Jordan River begins,
near the peaks of Hermon and Mount Mizar.
7Troubles have come again and again,
sounding like waterfalls.
Your waves are crashing all around me.

8The LORD shows his true love every day.
At night I have a song,
and I pray to my living God.

9I say to God, my Rock, [d]
"Why have you forgotten me?
Why am I sad
and troubled by my enemies?"
10My enemies' insults make me feel
as if my bones were broken.
They are always saying,
"Where is your God?"

11Why am I so sad?
Why am I so upset?
I should put my hope in God
and keep praising him,
my Saviour and my God.

A Prayer for Protection

43 God, defend me.
Argue my case against those who don't follow you.
Save me from liars and those who do evil.
2God, you are my strength.
Why have you rejected me?
Why am I sad
and troubled by my enemies?
3Send me your light and truth
to guide me.
Let them lead me to your holy mountain,
to where you live.
4Then I will go to the altar of God,
to God who is my joy and happiness.
I will praise you with a harp,
God, my God.

5Why am I so sad?
Why am I so upset?
I should put my hope in God
and keep praising him,
my Saviour and my God.

A Prayer for Help

For the director of music. A maskil[d]
of the sons of Korah.

44 God, we have heard about you.
Our ancestors told us
what you did in their days,
in days long ago.
2With your power you forced the nations out
of the land
and placed our ancestors here.
You destroyed those other nations,
but you made our ancestors grow strong.
3It wasn't their swords that took the land.
It wasn't their power that gave them
victory.
But it was your great power and strength.
You were with them because you loved
them.

4My God, you are my King.
Your commands led Jacob's people to
victory.
5With your help we pushed back our
enemies.
In your name we trampled those who came
against us.
6I don't trust my bow to help me,
and my sword can't save me.
7You saved us from our foes,
and you made our enemies ashamed.
8We will praise God every day;
we will praise your name for ever. *Selah*[d]

9But you have rejected us and shamed us.
You don't march with our armies any
more.
10You let our enemies push us back,
and those who hate us have taken our
wealth.
11You gave us away like sheep to be eaten
and have scattered us among the nations.
12You sold your people for nothing
and made no profit on the sale.

13You made us a joke to our neighbours;
those around us laugh and make fun
of us.
14You made us a joke to the other nations;
people shake their heads.
15I am always in disgrace,
and I am covered with shame.
16My enemy is getting even
with insults and curses.

17All these things have happened to us,
but we have not forgotten you
or failed to keep our agreement with you.
18Our hearts haven't turned away from you,
and we haven't stopped following you.
19But you crushed us in this place where wild
dogs live,
and you covered us with deep darkness.
20If we had forgotten our God
or lifted our hands in prayer to foreign gods,
21God would have known,
because he knows what is in our hearts.
22But for you we are in danger of death all the
time.
People think we are worth no more than
sheep to be killed.

23Wake up, Lord! Why are you sleeping?
Get up! Don't reject us for ever.
24Why do you hide from us?
Have you forgotten our pain and troubles?
25We have been pushed down into the ground;
we are flat on the ground.
26Get up and help us.
Because of your love, save us.

A Song for the King's Wedding

For the director of music. To the tune of "Lilies".
A maskil. [d] A love song of the sons of Korah.

45 Beautiful words fill my mind.
I am speaking of royal things.
My tongue is like the pen of a skilled
writer.

2You are more handsome than anyone,
and you are an excellent speaker,
so God has blessed you for ever.
3Put on your sword, powerful warrior.
Show your glory and majesty.
4In your majesty win the victory
for what is true and right.
Your power will do amazing things.
5Your sharp arrows will enter
the hearts of the king's enemies.
Nations will be defeated before you.
6God, your throne will last for ever and ever.
You will rule your kingdom with fairness.
7You love right and hate evil,
so God has chosen you from among your
friends;
he has set you apart with much joy.
8Your clothes smell like myrrh, [d] aloes [d] and
cassia. [d]
From palaces of ivory
music comes to make you happy.
9Kings' daughters are among your honoured
women.
Your bride stands at your right side
wearing gold from Ophir.

10Listen to me, daughter; look and pay
attention.
Forget your people and your father's family.

11The king loves your beauty.
Because he is your master, you should obey him.

Sidelight With the rest of the psalms we can gain a unique understanding of all that God wants to share with us; he cares and delights to hear both our praise and our sorrows.

12People from the city of Tyre have brought a gift.
Wealthy people will want to meet you.
13The princess is very beautiful.
Her gown is woven with gold.
14In her beautiful clothes she is brought to the king.
Her bridesmaids follow behind her,
and they are also brought to him.
15They come with happiness and joy;
they enter the king's palace.

16You will have sons to replace your fathers.
You will make them rulers through all the land.
17I will make your name famous from now on,
so people will praise you for ever and ever.

God Protects His People

For the director of music. By alamoth.[d] A psalm of the sons of Korah.

46 God is our protection and our strength.
He always helps in times of trouble.
2So we will not be afraid even if the earth shakes,
or the mountains fall into the sea,
3even if the oceans roar and foam,
or the mountains shake at the raging sea. *Selah*[d]

4There is a river that brings joy to the city of God,
the holy place where God Most High lives.
5God is in that city, and so it will not be shaken.
God will help her at dawn.
6Nations tremble and kingdoms shake.
God shouts and the earth crumbles.
7The LORD All-powerful is with us;
the God of Jacob is our defender. *Selah*

8Come and see what the LORD has done,
the amazing things he has done on the earth.
9He stops wars everywhere on the earth.
He breaks all bows and spears
and burns up the chariots with fire.
10God says, "Be quiet and know that I am God.
I will be supreme over all the nations;
I will be supreme in the earth."
11The LORD All-powerful is with us;
the God of Jacob is our defender. *Selah*

God, the King of the World

For the director of music. A psalm of the sons of Korah.

47 Clap your hands, all you people.
Shout to God with joy.
2The LORD Most High is wonderful.
He is the great King over all the earth!
3He defeated nations for us
and put them under our control.
4He chose the land we would inherit.
We are the children of Jacob, whom he loved. *Selah*[d]
5God has risen with a shout of joy;
the LORD has risen as the trumpets sounded.
6Sing praises to God. Sing praises.
Sing praises to our King. Sing praises.
7God is King of all the earth,
so sing a song of praise to him.
8God is King over the nations.
God sits on his holy throne.
9The leaders of the nations meet
with the people of the God of Abraham,
because the leaders of the earth belong to God.
He is supreme.

Jerusalem, the City of God

A psalm of the sons of Korah.

48 The LORD is great; he should be praised
in the city of our God, on his holy mountain.
2It is high and beautiful
and brings joy to the whole world.
Mount Zion[d] is like the high mountains of the north;
it is the city of the Great King.
3God is within its palaces;
he is known as its defender.

4Kings joined together
and came to attack the city.
5But when they saw it, they were amazed.
They ran away in fear.
6Fear took hold of them;
they hurt like a woman having a baby.

7You destroyed the large trading ships
with an east wind.
8First we heard
and now we have seen
that God will always keep his city safe.
It is the city of the LORD All-powerful,
the city of our God. *Selah*[d]
9God, we come into your Temple[d]
to think about your love.
10God, your name is known everywhere;
all over the earth people praise you.
Your right hand is full of goodness.
11Mount Zion is happy
and all the towns of Judah rejoice,
because your decisions are fair.
12Walk around Jerusalem
and count its towers.
13Notice how strong they are.
Look at the palaces.
Then you can tell your children about them.
14This God is our God for ever and ever.
He will guide us from now on.

Trusting Money is Foolish

For the director of music. A psalm
of the sons of Korah.

49 Listen to this, all you nations;
listen, all you who live on earth.
2Listen, both great and small,
rich and poor together.

WORSHIP

With All Your Heart *or* With All Your Mind?

As Lester (or "Lecture" as he was affectionately known by the youth group) walked into church, he spotted the drum kit being set up. Without a second's hesitation, he turned on his heels, walked out the door and headed across town for a more "reverent" worship experience! Like a few of the middle-aged men at church, he couldn't stand modern songs, with their simple words and overly emotional "pop" music. After all, "They're not crammed full of rich biblical truths and majestic imagery like the good old hymns, are they?" "La la la la. La la la la (x8)" followed by "Jesus, you're great" never really seemed to give God the praise Lester felt he deserved.

Josh, the church's young drummer, was Lester's opposite! He loved the freedom and emotion of the modern songs and played his heart out to God. During the old hymns, he simply switched off, finding them "like a boring poetry lesson with all the passion and joy of a maths exam".

Do you have a Josh or Lester in your church? Maybe you relate to one of them yourself.

Take a look at **Psalm 47** and notice how rich the language is, describing in great detail and with beautiful imagery the awesome power of God, and yet all sung to the backdrop of shouts and cries of joy, clapping hands and trumpets. It involves both our minds *and* our emotions.

- If Josh and Lester were to read Psalm 47, what do you think they could both learn about worship?
- Notice how Psalm 47 is a command to *all* nations to worship the Lord. There are so many different styles of music and expressions of worship all across the world. What can we learn from other Christians in how they worship?

Consider . . .

- ways in which you can worship God this week apart from just singing. Worship is so much more than just singing; it should be a lifestyle.
- next time you go to church or youth group, asking God to help you worship him with all your heart *and* with all your mind, even when it's not easy and the style is not your first choice.

For more, see . . .

- Habakkuk 3 (p.907)
- Ephesians 5:19–20 (p.1275)
- Matthew 22:34–40 (p.980)

[3]What I say is wise,
and my heart speaks with understanding.
[4]I will pay attention to a wise saying;
I will explain my riddle on the harp.

[5]Why should I be afraid of bad days?
Why should I fear when evil men
surround me?
[6]They trust in their money
and boast about their riches.
[7]No one can buy back the life of another.
No one can pay God for his own life,
[8]because the price of a life is high.
No payment is ever enough.
[9]Do people live for ever?
Don't they all face death?

[10]See, even wise people die.
Fools and stupid people also die
and leave their wealth to others.
[11]Their graves will always be their homes.
They will live there from now on,
even though they named places after
themselves.

[12]Even rich people do not live for ever;
like the animals, people die.

[13]This is what will happen to those who trust
in themselves
and to their followers who believe them.
Selah[d]
[14]Like sheep, they must die,
and death will be their shepherd.
Honest people will rule over them in the
morning,
and their bodies will rot in a grave far from
home.
[15]But God will save my life
and will take me from the grave. *Selah*

[16]Don't be afraid of rich people
because their houses are more beautiful.
[17]They don't take anything to the grave;
their wealth won't go down with them.
[18]Even though they were praised when they
were alive—
and people may praise you when you
succeed—
[19]they will go to where their ancestors are.
They will never see light again.

[20]Rich people with no understanding
are just like animals that die.

God Wants True Worship

A psalm of Asaph.

50 The God of gods, the LORD, speaks.
He calls the earth from the rising to
the setting sun.
[2]God shines from Jerusalem,
whose beauty is perfect.
[3]Our God comes, and he will not be silent.
A fire burns in front of him,
and a powerful storm surrounds him.
[4]He calls to the sky above and to the earth
that he might judge his people.
[5]He says, "Gather around, you who
worship me,
who have made an agreement with me,
using a sacrifice."
[6]God is the judge,
and even the skies say he is right. *Selah*[d]

[7]God says, "My people, listen to me;
Israel, I will testify against you.
I am God, your God.
[8]I do not scold you for your sacrifices.
You always bring me your burnt
offerings.
[9]But I do not need bulls from your stalls
or goats from your pens,
[10]because every animal of the forest is already
mine.
The cattle on a thousand hills are mine.
[11]I know every bird on the mountains,
and every living thing in the fields
is mine.
[12]If I were hungry, I would not tell you,
because the earth and everything in it
are mine.
[13]I don't eat the meat of bulls
or drink the blood of goats.
[14]Give an offering to show thanks to God.
Give God Most High what you have
promised.

[15]Call to me in times of trouble.
I will save you, and you will
honour me."

[16]But God says to the wicked:

"Why do you talk about my laws?
Why do you mention my agreement?
[17]You hate my teachings
and turn your back on what I say.
[18]When you see a thief, you join him.
You take part in adultery.[d]
[19]You don't stop your mouth from
speaking evil,
and your tongue makes up lies.
[20]You speak against your brother
and lie about your mother's son.
[21]I have kept quiet while you did these
things,
so you thought I was just like you.
But I will scold you
and accuse you to your face.

22 "Think about this, you who forget God.
Otherwise, I will tear you apart,
and no one will save you.
23 Those people honour me
who bring me offerings to show thanks.
And I, God, will save those who do that."

A Prayer for Forgiveness

For the director of music. A psalm of David when the prophet[d] Nathan came to David after David's sin with Bathsheba.

51 God, be merciful to me
because you are loving.
Because you are always ready to be
merciful,
wipe out all my wrongs.
2 Wash away all my guilt
and make me clean again.

3 I know about my wrongs,
and I can't forget my sin.
4 You are the only one I have sinned
against;
I have done what you say is wrong.
You are right when you speak
and fair when you judge.
5 I was brought into this world in sin.
In sin my mother gave birth to me.

6 You want me to be completely truthful,
so teach me wisdom.

7 Take away my sin, and I will be clean.
Wash me, and I will be whiter than
snow.
8 Make me hear sounds of joy and gladness;
let the bones you crushed be happy
again.
9 Turn your face from my sins
and wipe out all my guilt.

10 Create in me a pure heart, God,
and make my spirit right again.

SEXUALITY

Fancy That

There was a family whose members always carried rucksacks. They lived in the strange belief that this was how normal people lived. They put a stone or pebble in their own rucksack every month if they felt they had been bad. After a while, the rucksacks became quite heavy, even though the load built up slowly.

Arriving at the especially self-conscious teenage years was often difficult: some covered up, choosing to wear baggy coats over their rucksacks; some just acted naturally, telling their friends it was something you could get used to or act as if it was not really there; others were paralysed with fear and never left their house.

Well that would be a bit stupid wouldn't it! No one carries their burdens round with them like that!
Or do they?

Some people seem to operate in that way with guilt. They carry regrets and self-loathing around with them all the time. Some are good at hiding it. Some manage to pretend it's not there. Some are crushed by it. And the guilt of sexual sin appears worse than the rest. It sort of lives with you; sticks to you; clings – like a rucksack full of rocks you have to carry around with you.

Psalm 51 is the psalm David wrote when he was convicted of his sins of adultery and murder. You can read the whole story of what David did in 2 Samuel 11:1 – 12:25.

- What does David do?
- How does he hope life will be different in the future?

Consider . . .

- what your natural tendency is when dealing with guilt. Do you pretend it's not there, get crushed by it, hide it, confess?
- asking God to give you the strength to stay away from sexual sin. He says he will. Do you trust him?

For more, see . . .

- Isaiah 43:25 (p.684)
- 1 John 1:8–10 (p.1371)
- Isaiah 44:22 (p.687)

11Do not send me away from you
or take your Holy Spirit[d] away from me.
12Give me back the joy of your salvation.
Keep me strong by giving me a willing spirit.
13Then I will teach your ways to those who do wrong,
and sinners will turn back to you.
14God, save me from the guilt of murder,
God of my salvation,
and I will sing about your goodness.
15Lord, let me speak
so I may praise you.
16You are not pleased by sacrifices, or I would give them.
You don't want burnt offerings.
17The sacrifice God wants is a broken spirit.
God, you will not reject a heart that is broken and sorry for sin.

18Do whatever good you wish for Jerusalem.
Rebuild the walls of Jerusalem.
19Then you will be pleased with right sacrifices
and whole burnt offerings,
and bulls will be offered on your altar.

God will Punish the Proud

For the director of music. A maskil[d] of David. When Doeg the Edomite came to Saul and said to him, "David is in Ahimelech's house."

52 Mighty warrior, why do you boast
about the evil you do?
God's love will continue for ever.
2You think up evil plans.
Your tongue is like a sharp razor,
making up lies.
3You love wrong more than right
and lies more than truth. *Selah*[d]
4You love words that bite
and tongues that lie.

5But God will ruin you for ever.
He will seize you and throw you out of your tent;
he will tear you away from the land of the living. *Selah*
6Those who do right will see this and fear God.
They will laugh at you and say,
7"Look what happened to the man
who did not depend on God
but depended on his money.
He grew strong by his evil plans."
8But I am like an olive tree
growing in God's Temple.[d]
I trust God's love
for ever and ever.
9God, I will thank you for ever for what you have done.
With those who worship you, I will trust you because you are good.

The Unbelieving Fool

For the director of music. By mahalath.[d] A maskil[d] of David.

53 Fools say to themselves,
"There is no God."
Fools are evil and do terrible things;
none of them does anything good.

2God looked down from heaven on all people
to see if anyone was wise,
if anyone was looking to God for help.
3But all have turned away.
Together, everyone has become evil;
none of them does anything good.
Not a single person.

4Don't the wicked understand?
They destroy my people as if they were eating bread.
They do not ask God for help.
5The wicked are filled with terror
where there had been nothing to fear.
God will scatter the bones of your enemies.
You will defeat them,
because God has rejected them.

6I pray that victory will come to Israel from Mount Zion![d]
May God bring them back.
Then the people of Jacob will rejoice,
and the people of Israel will be glad.

A Prayer for Help

For the director of music. With stringed instruments. A maskil[d] of David when the Ziphites went to Saul and said, "We think David is hiding among our people."

54 God, save me because of who you are.
By your strength show that I am innocent.

Sidelight Feeling down? Then praise God! That's the attitude of even the saddest psalms, which are called "laments". These laments (such as Psalms 54—61) show individuals and the nation of Israel praying in times of crisis. Of all the types of psalm, the lament is most common.

2Hear my prayer, God;
listen to what I say.

3Strangers turn against me,
and cruel men want to kill me.
They do not care about God. *Selah*[d]

4See, God will help me;
the Lord will support me.

5Let my enemies be punished with their own evil.
Destroy them because you are loyal to me.

6I will offer a sacrifice as a special gift to you.
I will thank you, LORD, because you are good.
7You have saved me from all my troubles,
and I have seen my enemies defeated.

A Prayer About a False Friend

For the director of music. With stringed instruments. A maskil[d] of David.

55 God, listen to my prayer
and do not ignore my cry for help.
2Pay attention to me and answer me.
I am troubled and upset
3by what the enemy says
and how the wicked look at me.
They bring troubles down on me,
and in anger they attack me.

4I am frightened inside;
the terror of death has attacked me.
5I am scared and shaking,
and terror grips me.
6I said, "I wish I had wings like a dove.
Then I would fly away and rest.
7I would wander far away
and stay in the desert. *Selah*[d]
8I would hurry to my place of escape,
far away from the wind and storm."

9Lord, destroy and confuse their words,
because I see violence and fighting in the city.
10Day and night they are all around its walls,
and evil and trouble are everywhere inside.
11Destruction is everywhere in the city;
trouble and lying never leave its streets.

12It was not an enemy insulting me.
I could stand that.
It was not someone who hated me.
I could hide from him.
13But it is you, a person like me,
my companion and good friend.
14We had a good friendship
and walked together to God's Temple.[d]
15Let death take away my enemies.
Let them die while they are still young
because evil lives with them.
16But I will call to God for help,
and the LORD will save me.
17Morning, noon and night I am troubled and upset,
but he will listen to me.
18Many are against me,
but he keeps me safe in battle.
19God who lives for ever
will hear me and punish them. *Selah*

But they will not change;
they do not fear God.

20The one who was my friend attacks his friends
and breaks his promises.
21His words are slippery like butter,
but war is in his heart.
His words are smoother than oil,
but they cut like knives.

22Give your worries to the LORD,
and he will take care of you.
He will never let good people down.
23But, God, you will bring down
the wicked to the grave.
Murderers and liars will live
only half a lifetime.

But I will trust in you.

Trusting God for Help

For the director of music. To the tune of "The Dove in the Distant Oak". A miktam[d] of David when the Philistines captured him in Gath.

56 God, be merciful to me because people are chasing me;
the battle has pressed me all day long.
2My enemies have chased me all day;
there are many proud people fighting me.

3When I am afraid,
I will trust you.
4I praise God for his word.
I trust God, so I am not afraid.
What can human beings do to me?

5All day long they twist my words;
all their evil plans are against me.
6They wait. They hide.
They watch my steps,
hoping to kill me.

7 God, do not let them escape;
punish the foreign nations in your anger.
8 You have recorded my troubles.
You have kept a list of my tears.
Aren't they in your records?

9 On the day I call for help, my enemies will be defeated.
I know that God is on my side.
10 I praise God for his word to me;
I praise the LORD for his word.
11 I trust in God. I will not be afraid.
What can people do to me?

12 God, I must keep my promises to you.
I will give you my offerings to thank you,
13 because you have saved me from death.
You have kept me from being defeated.
So I will walk with God
in the light among the living.

A Prayer in Troubled Times

For the director of music. To the tune of "Do Not Destroy". A miktam[d] of David when he escaped from Saul in the cave.

57 Be merciful to me, God; be merciful to me
because I come to you for protection.
Let me hide under the shadow of your wings
until the trouble has passed.

2 I cry out to God Most High,
to the God who does everything for me.
3 He sends help from heaven and saves me.
He punishes those who chase me. *Selah*[d]

God sends me his love and truth.

4 Enemies, like lions, are all around me;
I must lie down among them.
Their teeth are like spears and arrows,
their tongues as sharp as swords.

FRIENDS

Sisterly Love?

Vicky and her twin sister Sarah were like two peas in a pod to look at, but completely opposite in character. Vicky was the rebel, always staying out later than the deadline, up for the latest thrill, and into the latest extreme fashion or trend. Sarah, although not perfect, enjoyed school and studying, wasn't bothered about going to all the "cool" parties or being seen hanging around with the "right" group. In spite of their differences, Sarah and Vicky were close friends.

When she wasn't out shopping or hanging out with her sister, Vicky spent a lot of time with her boyfriend Blake, who had also become one of her best friends. After one particular spending spree, Vicky came home to find Blake and her sister, Sarah, kissing in the front room. Vicky couldn't believe her eyes and felt devastated, utterly betrayed by her two closest friends.

David was also betrayed by a close friend. Read **Psalm 55** to see how hurtful he found it.

- Why was the betrayal experienced by Vicky and David so hurtful?
- How can verse 22 help you deal with betrayal by a friend?

Consider . . .

- asking God to forgive you if you've betrayed a friend or allowing God to help you forgive a friend who has betrayed you.
- whether you can mend a friendship or relationship that has been broken by betrayal, by talking to the people concerned.

For more, see . . .

- Proverbs 17:9 (p.604)
- Luke 22:1–6 (p.1087)
- Matthew 26:69–75 (p.990)

5God is supreme over the skies;
his majesty covers the earth.

6They set a trap for me.
I am very worried.
They dug a pit in my path,
but they fell into it themselves. *Selah*

7My heart is steady, God; my heart is steady.
I will sing and praise you.
8Wake up, my soul.
Wake up, harp and lyre! *d*
I will wake up the dawn.

9Lord, I will praise you among the nations;
I will sing songs of praise about you to all the nations.
10Your great love reaches to the skies,
your truth to the clouds.
11God, you are supreme above the skies.
Let your glory be over all the earth.

Unfair Judges

For the director of music. To the tune of "Do Not Destroy". A miktam *d* of David.

58 Do you rulers really say what is right?
Do you judge people fairly?
2No, in your heart you plan evil;
you think up violent crimes in the land.
3From birth, evil people turn away from God;
they wander off and tell lies as soon as they are born.
4They are like poisonous snakes,
like deaf cobras that stop up their ears
5so they cannot hear the music of the snake charmer
no matter how well he plays.

6God, break the teeth in their mouths!
Tear out the fangs of those lions, LORD!
7Let them disappear like water that flows away.
Let them be cut short like a broken arrow.
8Let them be like snails that melt as they move.
Let them be like a child born dead who never saw the sun.
9His anger will blow them away alive
faster than burning thorns can heat a pot.
10Good people will be glad when they see him take revenge.
They will wash their feet in the blood of the wicked.
11Then people will say,
"There really are rewards for doing what is right.
There really is a God who judges the world."

A Prayer for Protection

For the director of music. To the tune of "Do Not Destroy". A miktam *d* of David when Saul sent men to watch David's house to kill him.

59 God, save me from my enemies.
Protect me from those who come against me.
2Save me from those who do evil
and from murderers.

3Look, men are waiting to ambush me.
Cruel men attack me,
but I have not sinned or done wrong, LORD.
4I have done nothing wrong, but they are ready to attack me.
Wake up to help me, and look.
5You are the LORD God All-powerful, the God of Israel.
Arise and punish those people.
Do not give those traitors any mercy. *Selah d*

6They come back at night.
Like dogs they growl and roam round the city.
7Notice what comes from their mouths.
Insults come from their lips,
because they say, "Who's listening?"
8But, LORD, you laugh at them;
you make fun of all of them.
9God, my strength, I am looking to you,
because God is my defender.
10My God loves me,
and he goes in front of me.

He will help me defeat my enemies.
11Lord, our protector, do not kill them, or my people will forget.
With your power scatter them and defeat them.
12They sin by what they say;
they sin with their words.
They curse and tell lies,
so let their pride trap them.
13Destroy them in your anger;
destroy them completely!
Then they will know
that God rules over Israel
and to the ends of the earth. *Selah*

14They come back at night.
Like dogs they growl
and roam round the city.
15They wander about looking for food,
and they howl if they do not find enough.

16But I will sing about your strength.
In the morning I will sing about your love.
You are my defender,
my place of safety in times of trouble.

17God, my strength, I will sing praises to you.
God, my defender, you are the God who loves me.

A Prayer After a Defeat

For the director of music. To the tune of "Lily of the Agreement". A miktam [d] of David. For teaching. When David fought the Arameans of North West Mesopotamia and Zobah, and when Joab returned and defeated 12,000 Edomites at the Valley of Salt.

60 God, you have rejected us and scattered us.
You have been angry, but please come back to us.
2You made the earth shake and crack.
Heal its breaks because it is shaking.
3You have given your people trouble.
You made us unable to walk straight, like people drunk with wine.

4You have raised a banner to gather those who fear you.
Now they can stand up against the enemy. *Selah* [d]

5Answer us and save us by your power
so the people you love will be rescued.
6God has said from his Temple, [d]
"When I win, I will divide Shechem
and measure off the Valley of Succoth.
7Gilead and Manasseh are mine.
Ephraim is like my helmet.
Judah holds my royal sceptre. [d]
8Moab is like my washbowl.
I throw my sandals at Edom.
I shout at Philistia."

9Who will bring me to the fortified city?
Who will lead me to Edom?
10God, surely you have rejected us;
you do not go out with our armies.
11Help us fight the enemy.
Human help is useless,
12but we can win with God's help.
He will defeat our enemies.

A Prayer for Protection

For the director of music. With stringed instruments. Of David.

61 God, hear my cry,
listen to my prayer.

2I call to you from the ends of the earth
when I am afraid.
Carry me away to a high mountain.
3You have been my protection,
like a strong tower against my enemies.

4Let me live in your Holy Tent [d] for ever.
Let me find safety in the shelter of your wings. *Selah* [d]
5God, you have heard my promises.
You have given me what belongs to those who fear you.

6Give the king a long life;
let him live many years.
7Let him rule in the presence of God for ever.
Protect him with your love and truth.

8Then I will praise your name for ever,
and every day I will keep my promises.

Trust Only in God

For the director of music. For Jeduthun. A psalm of David.

62 I find rest in God;
only he can save me.
2He is my rock and my salvation.
He is my defender;
I will not be defeated.

3How long will you attack someone?
Will all of you kill that person?
Who is like a leaning wall, like a fence ready to fall?
4They are planning to make that person fall.
They enjoy telling lies.
With their mouths they bless,
but in their hearts they curse. *Selah* [d]

5I find rest in God alone;
only he gives me hope.
6He is my rock and my salvation.
He is my defender;
I will not be defeated.
7My honour and salvation come from God.
He is my mighty rock and my protection.

8People, trust God all the time.
Tell him all your problems,
because God is our protection. *Selah*

9The least of people are only a breath,
and even the greatest are just a lie.
On the scales, they weigh nothing;
together they are only a breath.
10Do not trust in force.
Stealing is of no use.
Even if you gain more riches,
don't put your trust in them.

11God has said this,
and I have heard it over and over:

God is strong.
12 The Lord is loving.
You reward people for what they have
done.

Wishing to be Near God

A psalm of David when he was in the Desert of Judah.

63 God, you are my God.
I search for you.
I thirst for you
like someone in a dry, empty land
where there is no water.

2 I have seen you in the Temple [d]
and have seen your strength and glory.
3 Because your love is better than life,
I will praise you.
4 I will praise you as long as I live.
I will lift up my hands in prayer to your
name.
5 I will be content as if I had eaten the best
foods.
My lips will sing, and my mouth will
praise you.

6 I remember you while I'm lying in my
bed;
I think about you through the night.
7 You are my help.
Because of your protection, I sing.
8 I stay close to you;
you support me with your right hand.
9 Some people are trying to kill me,
but they will go down to the grave.
10 They will be killed with swords
and eaten by wild dogs.

11 But the king will rejoice in his God.
All who make promises in his name will
praise him,
but the mouths of liars will be shut.

WORRYING

Not in My Hands

Millie wasn't a happy person. She wasn't "glass is half empty" so much as not really having a glass at all! She was draining to be around because every little thing that happened was, to her, just something else that could go wrong. She was always worrying about things that were due to happen the next day, the next week, the next month. And her mind took her off on wild imaginings as she daydreamed about the terrible things that could be around the corner. Millie often got into bed at night and couldn't really remember much about the day.

Leo Buscaglia writes, "Worry never robs tomorrow of its sorrow, it only saps today of its joy."

Worry is assuming responsibilities you can't handle. The truth is that God never intended you to handle certain situations or problems on your own, because they were his to start with.

You can learn to control what goes on in your mind. How? By filling it with God's Word, applying it to each situation as it arises and leaning on it in the hard times, as David does in **Psalm 62**.

- David went through some really hard times. Why do you think he was able to write these words to God even though he was struggling?
- Why is it a sin to worry about situations?

Consider . . .

- all the situations that you worry about and pray that God will help you imagine a better scenario.
- every time you feel yourself worrying, saying out loud or in your head "I take captive those thoughts and make them obedient to you Lord" (2 Corinthians 10:5).

For more, see . . .

- Matthew 6:25 (p.948)
- Philippians 4:6–9 (p.1285)
- John 14:27 (p.1124)

A Prayer Against Enemies

For the director of music. A psalm of David.

64 God, listen to my complaint.
I am afraid of my enemies;
protect my life from them.
2Hide me from those who plan wicked things,
from that mob who does evil.

3They sharpen their tongues like swords
and shoot bitter words like arrows.
4From their hiding places they shoot at innocent people;
they shoot suddenly and are not afraid.

5They encourage each other to do wrong.
They talk about setting traps,
thinking no one will see them.
6They plan wicked things and say,
"We have a perfect plan."
The mind of human beings is hard to understand.

7But God will shoot them with arrows;
they will suddenly be struck down.
8Their own words will be used against them.
All who see them will shake their heads.

9Then everyone will fear God.
They will tell what God has done,
and they will learn from what he has done.
10Good people will be happy in the LORD
and will find protection in him.
Let everyone who is honest praise the LORD.

A Hymn of Thanksgiving

For the director of music. A psalm of David. A song.

65 God, you will be praised in Jerusalem.
We will keep our promises to you.
2You hear our prayers.
All people will come to you.
3Our guilt overwhelms us,
but you forgive our sins.
4Happy are the people you choose
and invite to stay in your court.
We are filled with good things in your house,
your holy Temple. *d*

5You answer us in amazing ways,
God our Saviour.
People everywhere on the earth
and beyond the sea trust you.
6You made the mountains by your strength;
you are dressed in power.
7You stopped the roaring seas,
the roaring waves,
and the uproar of the nations.
8Even those people at the ends of the earth
fear your miracles. *d*
You are praised from where the sun rises to where it sets.

9You take care of the land and water it;
you make it very fertile.
The rivers of God are full of water.
Grain grows because you make it grow.
10You send rain to the ploughed fields;
you fill the rows with water.
You soften the ground with rain,
and then you bless it with crops.
11You give the year a good harvest,
and you load the wagons with many crops.
12The desert is covered with grass
and the hills with happiness.
13The pastures are full of flocks,
and the valleys are covered with grain.
Everything shouts and sings for joy.

Praise God for What He Has Done

For the director of music. A song. A psalm.

66 Everything on earth, shout with joy to God!
2Sing about his glory!
Make his praise glorious!
3Say to God, "Your works are amazing!
Because your power is great,
your enemies fall before you.
4All the earth worships you
and sings praises to you.
They sing praises to your name." *Selah* *d*

5Come and see what God has done,
the amazing things he has done for people.
6He turned the sea into dry land.
The people crossed the river on foot.
So let us rejoice because of what he has done.
7He rules for ever with his power.
He keeps his eye on the nations,
so people should not turn against him. *Selah*

8You people, praise our God;
loudly sing his praise.
9He protects our lives
and does not let us be defeated.
10God, you have tested us;
you have purified us like silver.
11You let us be trapped
and put a heavy load on us.
12You let our enemies walk on our heads.

We went through fire and flood,
but you brought us to a place with good things.
13I will come to your Temple[d] with burnt offerings.
I will give you what I promised,
14 objects I promised to you when I was in trouble.
15I will bring you offerings of fat animals,
and I will offer rams, bulls and goats. *Selah*

16All of you who fear God, come and listen,
and I will tell you what he has done for me.
17I cried out to him with my mouth
and praised him with my tongue.
18If I had known of any sin in my heart,
the Lord would not have listened to me.
19But God has listened;
he has heard my prayer.
20Praise God,
who did not ignore my prayer
or hold back his love from me.

Everyone Should Praise God

For the director of music. With stringed instruments. A psalm. A song.

67 God, have mercy on us and bless us
and show us your kindness *Selah*[d]
2so the world will learn your ways,
and all nations will learn that you can save.

3God, the people should praise you;
all people should praise you.
4The nations should be glad and sing
because you judge people fairly.
You guide all the nations on earth. *Selah*
5God, the people should praise you;
all people should praise you.

6The land has given its crops.
God, our God, blesses us.
7God blesses us
so people all over the earth will fear him.

Praise God Who Saved the Nation

For the director of music. A psalm of David. A song.

68 Let God rise up and scatter his enemies;
let those who hate him run away from him.
2Blow them away as smoke
is driven away by the wind.
As wax melts before a fire,
let the wicked be destroyed before God.
3But those who do right should be glad
and should rejoice before God;
they should be happy and glad.

4Sing to God; sing praises to his name.
Prepare the way for him
who rides through the desert,
whose name is the LORD.
Rejoice before him.
5God is in his holy Temple.[d]
He is a father to orphans,
and he defends the widows.
6God gives the lonely a home.
He leads prisoners out with joy,
but those who turn against God will live in a dry land.

Sidelight
Israelite con men should have known better than to harass orphans and widows, two groups of people who had a special place in God's heart (Psalm 68:5). Look up the penalty for cheating the defenceless in Exodus 22:22–24, p.82.

7God, you led your people out
when you marched through the desert. *Selah*[d]
8The ground shook
and the sky poured down rain
before God, the God of Mount Sinai,
before God, the God of Israel.
9God, you sent much rain;
you refreshed your tired land.
10Your people settled there.
God, in your goodness
you took care of the poor.

11The Lord gave the command,
and a great army told the news:
12"Kings and their armies run away.
In camp they divide the wealth taken in war.
13Those who stayed by the campfires
will share the riches taken in battle."
14The Almighty scattered kings
like snow on Mount Zalmon.

15The mountains of Bashan are high;
the mountains of Bashan have many peaks.
16Why do you mountains with many peaks look with envy
on the mountain that God chose for his home?
The LORD will live there for ever.
17God comes with millions of chariots;

the Lord comes from Mount Sinai to his
holy place.
18When you went up to the heights,
you led a parade of captives.
You received gifts from the people,
even from those who turned against you.
And the LORD God will live there.

19Praise the Lord, God our Saviour,
who helps us every day. *Selah*
20Our God is a God who saves us;
the LORD God saves us from death.
21God will crush his enemies' heads,
the hairy skulls of those who continue to sin.
22The Lord said, "I will bring the enemy back
from Bashan;
I will bring them back from the depths of
the sea.
23Then you can stick your feet in their blood,
and your dogs can lick their share."
24God, people have seen your victory march;
God my King marched into the holy place.
25The singers are in front and the instruments
are behind.
In the middle are the girls with the
tambourines.[d]
26Praise God in the meeting place;
praise the LORD in the gathering of Israel.
27There is the smallest tribe,[d] Benjamin,
leading them.
And there are the leaders of Judah with
their group.
There also are the leaders of Zebulun and
of Naphtali.

28God, order up your power;
show the mighty power you have used for
us before.
29Kings will bring their wealth to you,
to your Temple in Jerusalem.
30Punish Egypt, the beast in the tall grass along
the river.
Punish the leaders of nations, those bulls
among the cows.
Defeated, they will bring you their silver.
Scatter those nations that love war.
31Messengers will come from Egypt;
the people of Cush will pray to God.

LONELINESS

On the Road Again

"Sometimes I think we're gypsies," Rebecca confesses, describing the way her family has moved seven times in four years. "When your father's in the army, you get used to it."

She laughs, but it sounds forced, and she looks away. There's a sadness in her voice, and she seems a little scared.

"You know, it's not that easy leaving friends and making new ones. When you're new, it helps a lot if people come up and introduce themselves," she says softly. "Or ask you to go to a club or church group meeting with them, or just to get a Coke. Loneliness must be one of the worst feelings in the world."

Everyone feels lonely sometimes. But, like Rebecca, we all have a home with God no matter how alone we may feel. Read **Psalm 68:1–10** to find God's assurance that he gives the lonely a place to belong.

- How do you think Rebecca would define the word "home" in this psalm?
- When you're feeling lonely, what sort of "home" do you think faith in God's love can help you to build?

Consider . . .

- organising a "welcome team" of kids to greet newcomers to your school or church.
- widening your circle of friends by making a list of talents that God has given you, including personality traits, such as a sense of humour, or the ability to listen, and using the list to guide you to new clubs and activities.

For more, see . . .

- Job 19:13–27 (p.481)
- 2 Timothy 4:16–18 (p.1321)
- Matthew 28:18–20 (p.995)

32Kingdoms of the earth, sing to God;
sing praises to the Lord. *Selah*
33Sing to the one who rides through the skies,
which are from long ago.
He speaks with a thundering voice.
34Announce that God is powerful.
He rules over Israel,
and his power is in the skies.
35God, you are wonderful in your Temple.
The God of Israel gives his people strength
and power.

Praise God!

A Cry for Help

For the director of music. To the tune of "Lilies".
A psalm of David.

69 God, save me,
because the water has risen to my
neck.
2I'm sinking down into the mud,
and there is nothing to stand on.
I am in deep water,
and the flood covers me.
3I am tired from calling for help;
my throat is sore.
My eyes are tired from waiting
for God to help me.
4There are more people who hate me for no
reason than hairs on my head;
powerful enemies want to destroy me for
no reason.
They make me pay back
what I did not steal.

5God, you know what I have done wrong;
I cannot hide my guilt from you.

6Lord GOD All-powerful,
do not let those who hope in you be
ashamed because of me.
God of Israel,
do not let your worshippers be disgraced
because of me.
7For you, I carry this shame,
and my face is covered with disgrace.
8I am like a stranger to my closest relatives
and a foreigner to my mother's children.
9My strong love for your Temple [d] completely
controls me.
When people insult you, it hurts me.
10When I cry and go without food,
they make fun of me.
11When I wear clothes of sadness,
they joke about me.
12They make fun of me in public places,
and the drunkards make up songs about me.

13But I pray to you, LORD, for favour.
God, because of your great love, answer me.
You are truly able to save.
14Pull me from the mud,
and do not let me sink.
Save me from those who hate me
and from the deep water.
15Do not let the flood drown me
or the deep water swallow me
or the grave close its mouth over me.
16LORD, answer me because your love is so good.
Because of your great kindness, turn to me.
17Do not hide from me, your servant.
I am in trouble. Hurry to help me!
18Come near and save me;
rescue me from my enemies.

19You see my shame and disgrace.
You know all my enemies and what they
have said.
20Insults have broken my heart
and left me weak.
I looked for sympathy, but there was none;
I found no one to comfort me.
21They put poison in my food
and gave me vinegar to drink.

22Let their own feasts cause their ruin;
let their feasts trap them and pay them back.
23Let their eyes be closed so they cannot see
and their backs be for ever weak from
troubles.
24Pour your anger out on them;
let your anger catch up with them.
25May their place be empty;
leave no one to live in their tents.
26They chase after those you have hurt,
and they talk about the pain of those you
have wounded.
27Charge them with crime after crime,
and do not let them have anything good.
28Wipe their names from the book of life,
and do not list them with those who do
what is right.

29I am sad and hurting.
God, save me and protect me.

30I will praise God in a song
and will honour him by giving thanks.
31That will please the LORD more than offering
him cattle,
more than sacrificing a bull with horns and
hoofs.
32Poor people will see this and be glad.
Be encouraged, you who worship God.
33The LORD listens to those in need
and does not look down on captives.

34Heaven and earth should praise him,
the seas and everything in them.
35God will save Jerusalem
and rebuild the cities of Judah.

Then people will live there and own the land.
36 The descendants[d] of his servants will
inherit that land,
and those who love him will live there.

A Cry for God to Help Quickly

For the director of music. A psalm of David. To help people remember.

70 God, come quickly and save me.
LORD, hurry to help me.
2Let those who are trying to kill me
be ashamed and disgraced.
Let those who want to hurt me
run away in disgrace.
3Let those who make fun of me
stop because of their shame.
4But let all those who worship you
rejoice and be glad.
Let those who love your salvation
always say, "Praise the greatness
of God."

5I am poor and helpless;
God, hurry to me.
You help me and save me.
LORD, do not wait.

An Old Person's Prayer

71 In you, LORD, is my protection.
Never let me be ashamed.
2Because you do what is right, save and
rescue me;
listen to me and save me.
3Be my place of safety
where I can always come.
Give the command to save me,

PERSISTENCE

Follow Your Dreams

Jane loved to dance. She had been doing it ever since she was little and now she was older she was starting to think that maybe she could make a career out of it. However, many of her school mates thought dancing was silly and would regularly make fun of her, her dancing and anything else they could in order to make her feel small. "It's a waste of time," they'd say, "you'll never be good enough." Though the comments really hurt Jane, she was determined to carry on because she knew how much fun dancing was for her and how good it was for keeping her fit.

After she finished school, she went to college to train as a dancer, and years later, after lots of hard work and dedication, she was asked to be the company's principal dancer. As the curtains opened on her first professional performance, she smiled with pride, knowing that all her hard work and perseverance had paid off. Thank goodness she hadn't given in to the taunts back in school, otherwise she would have missed out on all this.

Jane had to battle through people judging her and making fun of her because they didn't understand something that she was so passionate about.

- Jane's passion was dancing. What was it in **Psalm 69:6–15** that David was so passionate about?
- What is similar in the way that both Jane and King David coped with their situations?

Consider . . .

- how you'd feel if you were misunderstood and mocked by people around you because of something they didn't understand? Consider whether you've ever done the same to another person. If you have, go to them and say sorry.
- writing a list of things you are passionate about and that you would be prepared to persevere through difficult situations for.

For more, see . . .

- Romans 4:18–25 (p.1190)
- James 5:7–16 (p.1352)
- Hebrews 12:1–3 (p.1343)

because you are my rock and my fortified
city.
4My God, save me from the power of the
wicked
and from the hold of evil and cruel
people.
5LORD, you are my hope.
LORD, I have trusted you since I was
young.
6I have depended on you since I was born;
you helped me even on the day of my
birth.
I will always praise you.

7I am an example to many people,
because you are my strong protection.
8I am always praising you;
all day long I honour you.

9Do not reject me when I am old;
do not leave me when my strength
is gone.
10My enemies make plans against me,
and they meet together to kill me.
11They say, "God has left him.
Go after him and take him,
because no one will save him."
12God, don't be far off.
My God, hurry to help me.
13Let those who accuse me
be ashamed and destroyed.
Let those who are trying to hurt me
be covered with shame and disgrace.

14But I will always have hope
and will praise you more and more.
15I will tell how you do what is right.
I will tell about your salvation all day long,
even though it is more than I can tell.
16I will come and tell about your powerful
works, Lord GOD.
I will remind people that only you do what
is right.

17God, you have taught me since I was
young.
To this day I tell about the miracles [d]
you do.
18Even though I am old and grey,
do not leave me, God.
I will tell the children about your power;
I will tell those who live after me about
your might.

19God, your justice reaches to the skies.
You have done great things;
God, there is no one like you.
20You have given me many troubles and bad
times,
but you will give me life again.
When I am almost dead,
you will keep me alive.
21You will make me greater than ever,
and you will comfort me again.

22I will praise you with the harp.
I trust you, my God.
I will sing to you with the lyre, [d]
Holy One of Israel.
23I will shout for joy when I sing praises
to you.
You have saved me.
24I will tell about your justice all day long.
And those who want to hurt me
will be ashamed and disgraced.

A Prayer for the King

Of Solomon.

72 God, give the king your good
judgement
and the king's son your goodness.
2Help him judge your people fairly
and decide what is right for the poor.
3Let there be peace on the mountains
and goodness on the hills for the
people.
4Help him be fair to the poor
and save the needy
and punish those who hurt them.
5May they respect you as long as the sun
shines
and as long as the moon glows.
6Let him be like rain on the grass,
like showers that water the earth.
7Let goodness be plentiful while he lives.
Let peace continue as long as there is a
moon.
8Let his kingdom go from sea to sea,
and from the Euphrates River to the ends
of the earth.
9Let the people of the desert bow down
to him,
and make his enemies lick the dust.
10Let the kings of Tarshish and the faraway
lands
bring him gifts.
Let the kings of Sheba and Seba
bring their presents to him.
11Let all kings bow down to him
and all nations serve him.

12He will help the poor when they cry out
and will save the needy when no one else
will help.
13He will be kind to the weak and poor,
and he will save their lives.

14 He will save them from cruel people who try
to hurt them,
because their lives are precious to him.

15 Long live the king!
Let him receive gold from Sheba.
Let people always pray for him
and bless him all day long.
16 Let the fields grow plenty of grain
and the hills be covered with crops.
Let the land be as fertile as Lebanon,
and let the cities grow like the grass in a
field.
17 Let the king be famous for ever;
let him be remembered as long as the sun
shines.

Let the nations be blessed because of him,
and may they all bless him.

18 Praise the LORD God, the God of Israel,
who alone does such miracles.[d]

19 Praise his glorious name for ever.
Let his glory fill the whole world.
Amen and amen.

20 This ends the prayers of David son of Jesse.

Book 3

Should the Wicked Be Rich?

A psalm of Asaph.

73 God is truly good to Israel,
to those who have pure hearts.
2 But I had almost stopped believing;
I had almost lost my faith
3 because I was jealous of proud people.
I saw wicked people doing well.

4 They are not suffering;
they are healthy and strong.
5 They don't have troubles like the rest
of us;

HUNGER AND POVERTY

Making Apathy History

Bob Geldolf and Bono were the figureheads for the huge "Make Poverty History" campaign in 2005 which included the amazing "Live8" gigs and led rich governments to release billions in debt relief. There is a long way to go, but their actions have played a part in making the world a fairer place.

If you trace the campaign back to its roots, you will find a small group of nameless, praying Christians who met in a flat in London, inspired by words like those in **Psalm 72**: "decide what is right for the poor" and "be fair to the poor". They launched the "Jubilee 2000" campaign. Their prayers and their actions clearly touched the heart of God, and a worldwide movement for change was born. Millions wore wristbands, marched, petitioned and wrote to governments urging them to "be kind to the weak and poor".

Bob and Bono did a great job, but all their ranting would have come to nothing without the army of anonymous caring people who birthed the movement and maintained it through their efforts.

On one occasion, Mother Theresa, the remarkable nun who devoted her life to caring for the poorest of the poor in India, was asked by a cynical journalist, "Surely your work is just a drop in the ocean of need." Her wonderful answer was, "Yes, but the ocean is made up of tiny drops."

- What would it mean for you to "be fair to the poor" in the way you act?
- What good work by non-Christian companies or groups could you support in prayer?

Consider . . .

- praying for your youth leaders and parents that God would give them his heart to "do what is right for the poor".
- putting aside some of your money every week, specifically for work amongst the poor. Ask God to guide you as to where you should send it.

For more, see . . .

- Deuteronomy 14:22–29 (p.179)
- 2 Corinthians 9:6–11 (p.1248)
- Proverbs 14:31 (p.602)

they don't have problems like other
people.
6They wear pride like a necklace
and put on violence as their clothing.
7They are looking for profits
and do not control their selfish desires.
8They make fun of others and speak evil;
proudly they speak of hurting others.
9They boast to the sky.
They say that they own the earth.
10So their people turn to them
and give them whatever they want.
11They say, "How can God know?
What does God Most High know?"

12These people are wicked,
always at ease and getting richer.
13So why have I kept my heart pure?
Why have I kept my hands from doing
wrong?
14I have suffered all day long;
I have been punished every morning.

15God, if I had decided to talk like this,
I would have let your people down.
16I tried to understand all this,
but it was too hard for me to see
17until I went to the Temple [d] of God.
Then I understood what will happen to
them.

18You have put them in danger;
you cause them to be destroyed.
19They are destroyed in a moment;
they are swept away by terrors.
20It will be like waking from a dream.
Lord, when you rise up, they will
disappear.

21When my heart was sad
and I was angry,
22I was senseless and stupid.
I acted like an animal towards you.

23But I am always with you;
you have held my hand.
24You guide me with your advice,
and later you will receive me in honour.
25I have no one in heaven but you;
I want nothing on earth besides you.
26My body and my mind may become weak,
but God is my strength.
He is mine for ever.

27Those who are far from God will die;
you destroy those who are unfaithful.
28But I am close to God, and that is good.
The Lord GOD is my protection.
I will tell all that you have done.

A Nation in Trouble Prays

A maskil [d] of Asaph.

74 God, why have you rejected us for so
long?
Why are you angry with us, the sheep of
your pasture?
2Remember the people you bought long ago.
You saved us, and we are your very own.
After all, you live on Mount Zion. [d]
3Make your way through these old ruins;
the enemy wrecked everything in the
Temple. [d]

4Those who were against you shouted in your
meeting place
and raised their flags there.
5They came with axes raised
as if to cut down a forest of trees.
6They smashed the carved panels
with their axes and hatchets.
7They burned your Temple to the ground;
they have made the place where you live
unclean. [d]
8They thought, "We will completely crush
them!"
They burned every place where God was
worshipped in the land.
9We do not see any signs.
There are no more prophets, [d]
and no one knows how long this will last.

10God, how much longer will the enemy make
fun of you?
Will they insult you for ever?
11Why do you hold back your power?
Bring your power out in the open and
destroy them!

12God, you have been our king for a long time.
You bring salvation to the earth.
13You split open the sea by your power
and broke the heads of the sea monster.
14You smashed the heads of the monster
Leviathan [d]
and gave him to the desert creatures as
food.
15You opened up the springs and streams
and made the flowing rivers run dry.
16Both the day and the night are yours;
you made the sun and the moon.
17You set all the limits on the earth;
you created summer and winter.

18LORD, remember how the enemy insulted you.
Remember how those foolish people made
fun of you.
19Do not give us, your doves, to those wild
animals.
Never forget your poor people.

20Remember the agreement you made
with us,
because violence fills every dark corner of
this land.
21Do not let your suffering people be disgraced.
Let the poor and helpless praise you.

22God, arise and defend yourself.
Remember the insults that come from those
foolish people all day long.
23Don't forget what your enemies said;
don't forget their roar as they rise against
you always.

God the Judge

For the director of music. To the tune of "Do Not Destroy". A psalm of Asaph. A song.

75 God, we thank you;
we thank you because you are near.
We tell about the miracles[d] you do.

2You say, "I set the time for trial,
and I will judge fairly.
3The earth with all its people may shake,
but I am the one who holds it steady. *Selah*[d]
4I say to those who are proud, 'Don't boast,'
and to the wicked, 'Don't show your
power.
5Don't try to use your power against
heaven.
Don't be stubborn.' "

6No one from the east or the west
or the desert can judge you.
7God is the judge;
he judges one person as guilty and another
as innocent.
8The LORD holds a cup of anger in his hand;
it is full of wine mixed with spices.
He pours it out even to the last drop,
and the wicked drink it all.

9I will tell about this for ever;
I will sing praise to the God of Jacob.
10He will take all power away from the
wicked,
but the power of the good people will
grow.

The God Who Always Wins

For the director of music. With stringed instruments. A psalm of Asaph. A song.

76 People in Judah know God;
his fame is great in Israel.
2His Tent[d] is in Jerusalem;
his home is on Mount Zion.[d]
3There God broke the flaming arrows,
the shields, the swords and the weapons of
war. *Selah*[d]

4God, how wonderful you are!
You are more wonderful than the hills full
of animals.
5The brave soldiers were stripped
as they lay asleep in death.
Not one warrior
had the strength to stop it.
6God of Jacob, when you spoke strongly,
horses and riders fell dead.
7You are feared;
no one can stand against you when you are
angry.
8From heaven you gave the decision,
and the earth was afraid and silent.
9God, you stood up to judge
and to save the needy people of the earth.
Selah

10People praise you for your anger against evil.
Those who live through your anger are
stopped from doing more evil.

11Make and keep your promises to the LORD
your God.
From all around, gifts should come to the
God we worship.
12God breaks the spirits of great leaders;
the kings on earth fear him.

Remembering God's Help

For the director of music. For Jeduthun. A psalm of Asaph.

77 I cry out to God;
I call to God, and he will hear me.
2I look for the Lord on the day of trouble.
All night long I reach out my hands,
but I cannot be comforted.

3When I remember you God, I become
upset;
when I think, I become afraid. *Selah*[d]

4You keep my eyes from closing.
I am too upset to say anything.
5I keep thinking about the old days,
the years of long ago.
6At night I remember my songs.
I think and I ask myself:

7"Will the Lord reject us for ever?
Will he never be kind to us again?
8Is his love gone for ever?
Has he stopped speaking for all time?
9Has God forgotten mercy?
Is he too angry to pity us?" *Selah*

10Then I say, "This is what makes me sad:
for years the power of God Most High was
with us."

11I remember what the LORD did;
I remember the miracles[d] you did long ago.

12I think about all the things you did
and consider your deeds.

13God, your ways are holy.
No god is as great as our God.
14You are the God who does miracles;
you have shown people your power.
15By your great power you have saved your
people,
the descendants *d* of Jacob and Joseph. *Selah*

16God, the waters saw you;
they saw you and became afraid;
the deep waters shook with fear.
17The clouds poured down their rain.
The sky thundered.
Your lightning flashed back and forth like
arrows.
18Your thunder could be heard in the
whirlwind.
Lightning lit up the world.
The earth trembled and shook.
19You made a way through the sea
and paths through the deep waters,
but your footprints were not seen.

20You led your people like a flock
by using Moses and Aaron.

God Saved Israel from Egypt

A maskil *d* of Asaph.

78 My people, listen to my teaching;
listen to what I say.
2I will speak using stories;
I will tell secret things from long ago.
3We have heard them and known them
by what our ancestors have told us.
4We will not keep them from our children;
we will tell those who come later
about the praises of the LORD.
We will tell about his power
and the miracles *d* he has done.
5The LORD made an agreement with Jacob
and gave the Teachings to Israel,
which he commanded our ancestors
to teach to their children.
6Then their children would know them,
even their children not yet born.
And they would tell their children.
7So they would all trust God
and would not forget what he had done
but would obey his commands.
8They would not be like their ancestors
who were stubborn and disobedient.
Their hearts were not loyal to God,
and they were not true to him.

9The men of Ephraim had bows for weapons,
but they ran away on the day of battle.
10They didn't keep their agreement with God
and refused to live by his teachings.
11They forgot what he had done
and the miracles he had shown them.
12He did miracles while their ancestors
watched,
in the fields of Zoan in Egypt.
13He divided the Red Sea *d* and led them
through.
He made the water stand up like a wall.
14He led them with a cloud by day
and by the light of a fire by night.
15He split the rocks in the desert
and gave them more than enough water, as
if from the deep ocean.
16He brought streams out of the rock
and caused water to flow down like rivers.

17But the people continued to sin against him;
in the desert they turned against God Most
High.
18They decided to test God
by asking for the food they wanted.
19Then they spoke against God,
saying, "Can God prepare food in the
desert?
20When he hit the rock, water poured out
and rivers flowed down.
But can he give us bread also?
Will he provide his people with meat?"
21When the LORD heard them, he was very
angry.
His anger was like fire to the people of
Jacob;
his anger grew against the people of Israel.
22They had not believed God
and had not trusted him to save them.
23But he gave a command to the clouds above
and opened the doors of heaven.
24He rained manna *d* down on them to eat;
he gave them grain from heaven.
25So they ate the bread of angels.
He sent them all the food they could eat.
26He sent the east wind from heaven
and led the south wind by his power.
27He rained meat on them like dust.
The birds were as many as the sand of
the sea.
28He made the birds fall inside the camp,
all around the tents.
29So the people ate and became very full.
God had given them what they wanted.
30While they were still eating,
and while the food was still in their mouths,
31God became angry with them.
He killed some of the healthiest of them;
he struck down the best young men of
Israel.

32But they kept on sinning;
they did not believe even with the miracles.
33So he ended their days without meaning
and their years in terror.
34Any time he killed them, they would look to him for help;
they would come back to God and follow him.
35They would remember that God was their Rock, [d]
that God Most High had saved them.
36But their words were false,
and their tongues lied to him.
37Their hearts were not really loyal to God;
they did not keep his agreement.
38Still God was merciful.
He forgave their sins
and did not destroy them.
Many times he held back his anger
and did not stir up all his anger.
39He remembered that they were only human,
like a wind that blows and does not come back.
40They turned against God so often in the desert
and made him very sad there.
41Again and again they tested God
and brought pain to the Holy One of Israel.
42They did not remember his power
or the time he saved them from the enemy.
43They forgot the signs he did in Egypt
and his wonders in the fields of Zoan.
44He turned their rivers to blood
so no one could drink the water.
45He sent flies that bit the people.
He sent frogs that destroyed them.
46He gave their crops to grasshoppers
and what they worked for to locusts. [d]
47He destroyed their vines with hail
and their sycamore trees with sleet.
48He killed their animals with hail
and their cattle with lightning.
49He showed them his hot anger.
He sent his strong anger against them,
his destroying angels.
50He found a way to show his anger.
He did not keep them from dying
but let them die by a terrible disease.
51God killed all the firstborn [d] sons in Egypt,
the oldest son of each family of Ham. [n]
52But God led his people out like sheep
and he guided them like a flock through the desert.
53He led them to safety so they had nothing to fear,
but their enemies drowned in the sea.
54So God brought them to his holy land,
to the mountain country he took with his own power.
55He forced out the other nations,
and he had his people inherit the land.
He let the tribes [d] of Israel settle there in tents.

56But they tested God
and turned against God Most High;
they did not keep his rules.
57They turned away and were disloyal just like their ancestors.
They were like a crooked bow that does not shoot straight.
58They made God angry by building places to worship gods;
they made him jealous with their idols.
59When God heard them, he became very angry
and rejected the people of Israel completely.
60He left his dwelling at Shiloh,
the Tent where he lived among the people.
61He let the Ark, [d] his power, be captured;
he let the Ark, his glory, be taken by enemies.
62He let his people be killed;
he was very angry with his children.
63The young men died by fire,
and the young women had no one to marry.
64Their priests fell by the sword,
but their widows were not allowed to cry.

65Then the Lord got up as if he had been asleep;
he awoke like a man who had been drunk with wine.
66He struck down his enemies
and disgraced them for ever.
67But God rejected the family of Joseph;
he did not choose the tribe of Ephraim.
68Instead, he chose the tribe of Judah
and Mount Zion, [d] which he loves.
69And he built his Temple [d] high like the mountains.
Like the earth, he built it to last for ever.
70He chose David to be his servant
and took him from the sheep pens.

Ham The people in Egypt were descendants of Ham, one of Noah's sons. See Genesis 10:6.

[71]He brought him from tending the sheep
so he could lead the flock, the people of Jacob,
his own people, the people of Israel.
[72]And David led them with an innocent heart
and guided them with skilful hands.

The Nation Cries for Jerusalem

A psalm of Asaph.

79 God, nations have come against your chosen people.
They have ruined your holy Temple. [d]
They have turned Jerusalem into ruins.
[2]They have given the bodies of your servants as food to the wild birds.
They have given the bodies of those who worship you to the wild animals.
[3]They have spilled blood like water all around Jerusalem.
No one was left to bury the dead.
[4]We are a joke to the other nations;
they laugh and make fun of us.

[5]LORD, how long will this last?
Will you be angry for ever?
How long will your jealousy burn like a fire?
[6]Be angry with the nations that do not know you
and with the kingdoms that do not honour you.
[7]They have destroyed the people of Jacob
and destroyed their land.
[8]Don't punish us for our past sins.
Show your mercy to us soon,
because we are helpless!

[9]God our Saviour, help us
so people will praise you.
Save us and forgive our sins
so people will honour you.
[10]Why should the nations say,
"Where is their God?"
Tell the other nations in our presence
that you punish those who kill your servants.
[11]Hear the moans of the prisoners.
Use your great power
to save those sentenced to die.

[12]Repay those around us seven times over
for their insults to you, Lord.
[13]We are your people, the sheep of your flock.
We will thank you always;
for ever and ever we will praise you.

A Prayer to Bring Israel Back

For the director of music. To the tune of "Lilies of the Agreement". A psalm of Asaph.

80 Shepherd of Israel, listen to us.
You lead the people of Joseph like a flock.
You sit on your throne between the gold creatures with wings.
Show your greatness [2]to the people of Ephraim, Benjamin and Manasseh.
Use your strength,
and come to save us.

[3]God, take us back.
Show us your kindness so we can be saved.

[4]LORD God All-powerful,
how long will you be angry
at the prayers of your people?
[5]You have fed your people with tears;
you have made them drink many tears.
[6]You made those around us fight over us,
and our enemies make fun of us.

[7]God All-powerful, take us back.
Show us your kindness so we can be saved.

[8]You brought us out of Egypt as if we were a vine.
You forced out other nations and planted us in the land.
[9]You cleared the ground for us.
Like a vine, we took root and filled the land.
[10]We covered the mountains with our shade.
We had limbs like the mighty cedar tree.
[11]Our branches reached the Mediterranean Sea,
and our shoots went to the Euphrates River.

[12]So why did you pull down our walls?
Now everyone who passes by steals from us.
[13]Like wild pigs they walk over us;
like wild animals they feed on us.

[14]God All-powerful, come back.
Look down from heaven and see.
Take care of us, your vine.
[15] You planted this shoot with your own hands
and strengthened this child.

[16]Now it is cut down and burned with fire;
you destroyed us by your angry looks.
[17]With your hand,
strengthen the one you have chosen for yourself.
[18]Then we will not turn away from you.
Give us life again, and we will call to you for help.

19 LORD God All-powerful, take us back.
Show us your kindness so we can be saved.

A Song for a Holiday

For the director of music. By the gittith.[d] A psalm of Asaph.

81 Sing for joy to God, our strength;
shout out loud to the God of Jacob.
2 Begin the music. Play the tambourines.[d]
Play pleasant music on the harps and lyres.[d]

3 Blow the trumpet at the time of the New Moon,[d]
when the moon is full, when our feast begins.

Sidelight The sheep's horn was used like a trumpet (Psalm 81:3). It is the only ancient instrument mentioned in the Bible that's still used in Jewish synagogues. It's made by heating and shaping the animal's hollow horn.

4 This is the law for Israel;
it is the command of the God of Jacob.
5 He gave this rule to the people of Joseph
when they went out of the land of Egypt.

I heard a language I did not know, saying:
6 "I took the load off their shoulders;
I let them put down their baskets.
7 When you were in trouble, you called, and I saved you.
I answered you with thunder.
I tested you at the waters of Meribah. *Selah*[d]
8 My people, listen. I am warning you.
Israel, please listen to me!
9 You must not have foreign gods;
you must not worship any false god.
10 I, the LORD, am your God,
who brought you out of Egypt.
Open your mouth and I will feed you.

11 "But my people did not listen to me;
Israel did not want me.
12 So I let them go their stubborn way
and follow their own advice.

CELEBRATING

Shout Out Loud!

Imagine . . .

- Christmas without Christmas carols
- a wedding without the "Wedding March"
- the Trooping of the Colour without a band
- a party without music

Now for a really hard one. Imagine going for the rest of your life without a group of friends and relatives singing "Happy Birthday"!

It would be pretty miserable, wouldn't it?

People have used music to celebrate life's joys for centuries, dating all the way back to ancient writings such as the Psalms. **Psalm 81:1–10** calls people to shout and "sing for joy to God, our strength" for God's goodness and gifts.

- Why do you think the psalmist included a variety of methods for celebrating?
- What way of celebrating God do you enjoy most?

Consider . . .

- putting a simple prayer to music and singing it to God.
- learning a new song or joining a music group to find new ways to worship God.

For more, see . . .

- 1 Chronicles 13:6–8 (p.386)
- Ephesians 5:15–20 (p.1275)
- Psalm 149 (p.588)

13“I wish my people would listen to me;
I wish Israel would live my way.
14Then I would quickly defeat their enemies
and turn my hand against their foes.
15Those who hate the LORD would bow
before him.
Their punishment would continue for ever.
16But I would give you the finest wheat
and fill you with honey from the rocks.”

A Cry for Justice

A psalm of Asaph.

82 God is in charge of the great meeting;
he judges among the “gods”.
2He says, “How long will you defend evil
people?
How long will you show greater kindness
to the wicked? *Selah* [d]

3Defend the weak and the orphans;
defend the rights of the poor and suffering.
4Save the weak and helpless;
free them from the power of the wicked.

5“You know nothing. You don’t understand.
You walk in the dark,
while the world is falling apart.

6“I said, ‘You are “gods”.
You are all sons of God Most High.’
7But you will die like any other person;
you will fall like all the leaders.”

8God, come and judge the earth,
because you own all the nations.

A Prayer Against the Enemies

A song. A psalm of Asaph.

83 God, do not keep quiet;
God, do not be silent or still.
2Your enemies are making noises;
those who hate you are getting ready to
attack.
3They are making secret plans against your
people;
they plot against those you love.
4They say, “Come, let’s destroy them as a
nation.
Then no one will ever remember the name
‘Israel’.”

5They are united in their plan.
These have made an agreement against you:
6the families of Edom and the Ishmaelites,
Moab and the Hagrites,
7the people of Byblos, Ammon, Amalek,
Philistia and Tyre.
8Even Assyria has joined them
to help Ammon and Moab, the
descendants [d] of Lot. *Selah* [d]

9God, do to them what you did to Midian,
what you did to Sisera and Jabin at the
Kishon River.
10They died at Endor,
and their bodies rotted on the ground.
11Do to their important leaders what you did to
Oreb and Zeeb.
Do to their princes what you did to Zebah
and Zalmunna.
12They said, “Let’s take for ourselves
the pasturelands that belong to God.”

13My God, make them like tumbleweed,
like chaff [d] blown away by the wind.
14Be like a fire that burns a forest
or like flames that blaze through the
hills.
15Chase them with your storm,
and frighten them with your wind.
16Cover them with shame.
Then people will look for you, LORD.

17Make them afraid and ashamed for ever.
Disgrace them and destroy them.
18Then they will know that you are the
LORD,
that only you are God Most High over all
the earth.

Sidelight Psalms 84 and 122 – among others – are pilgrim songs, “songs for the road”. Three times a year, faithful Jews packed and got ready for the journey to Jerusalem – joining crowds of other “praise marchers” on the way.

Wishing to Be in the Temple

For the director of music. On the gittith. [d] A psalm of the sons of Korah.

84 LORD All-powerful,
how lovely is your Temple! [d]
2I want more than anything
to be in the courtyards of the LORD’s
Temple.
My whole being wants
to be with the living God.

3The sparrows have found a home,
and the swallows have nests.
They raise their young near your altars,
LORD All-powerful, my King and my God.
4Happy are the people who live at your
Temple;
they are always praising you. *Selah* [d]
5Happy are those whose strength comes
from you,
who want to travel to Jerusalem.

6As they pass through the Valley of Baca,
they make it like a spring.
The autumn rains fill it with pools of water.
7The people get stronger as they go,
and everyone meets with God in Jerusalem.

8LORD God All-powerful, hear my prayer;
God of Jacob, listen to me. *Selah*
9God, look at our shield;
be kind to your appointed king.

10One day in the courtyards of your Temple is better
than a thousand days anywhere else.
I would rather be a doorkeeper in the Temple of my God
than live in the homes of the wicked.
11The LORD God is like a sun and shield;
the LORD gives us kindness and honour.
He does not hold back anything good
from those whose lives are innocent.
12LORD All-powerful,
happy are the people who trust you!

A Prayer for the Nation

For the director of music. A psalm of the sons of Korah.

85 LORD, you have been kind to your land;
you brought back the people of Jacob.
2You forgave the guilt of the people
and covered all their sins. *Selah*[d]
3You stopped all your anger;
you turned back from your strong anger.

4God our Saviour, bring us back again.
Stop being angry with us.
5Will you be angry with us for ever?
Will you stay angry from now on?
6Won't you give us life again?
Your people would rejoice in you.

WORSHIP

Present of Presence

Natasha was known at the youth club for having a violent temper. If anyone annoyed her or said anything bad to her, she would fly off the handle. She was even known to lash out at people when she was in a rage.

One particular evening the talk was about spending time with God and being in his presence. This was new to Natasha, but it sounded good and she wanted to know more. The speaker said that when we are in God's presence he can change us from the inside out and make us new.

At the end of the talk, Natasha's heart was racing and she went to find the leader who had been speaking. "What is it that you want from God?" the leader asked.

"I don't know really," Natasha explained. "But I want to know more about his presence and to stop being so angry all the time!"

The youth leader explained that we can ask God to forgive us and he will fill us with his presence, then God can start changing us from the inside out. Natasha's heart was pounding really fast and she was excited and nervous at the same time. "I want that," she stammered . . . and they prayed together. As they did, Natasha felt a peace go through her body from the top of her head to the tips of her toes.

Since that day, whenever Natasha feels like she is going to get really angry and start going crazy, she starts to worship God and prays that his presence will fill her and help her be calm enough to sort out the situation. Read **Psalm 84**.

- Look at verse 10 and think about Natasha. What are the benefits of being with God?
- What are the things that stop us from being in God's presence and asking for his help?

Consider . . .

- encouraging your youth leader or minister when they help you worship God, by saying thank you to them.
- writing your own psalm to God telling him how he helps you and makes you feel.

For more, see . . .

- Luke 4:8 (p.1044)
- Romans 12:1 (p.1203)

7 LORD, show us your love,
and save us.

8 I will listen to God the LORD.
He has ordered peace for those who
worship him.
Don't let them go back to foolishness.
9 God will soon save those who respect him,
and his glory will be seen in our land.

10 Love and truth belong to God's people;
goodness and peace will be theirs.
11 On earth people will be loyal to God,
and God's goodness will shine down from
heaven.
12 The LORD will give his goodness,
and the land will give its crops.
13 Goodness will go before God
and prepare the way for him.

A Cry for Help

A prayer of David.

86 LORD, listen to me and answer me.
I am poor and helpless.
2 Protect me, because I worship you.
My God, save me, your servant who trusts
in you.
3 Lord, have mercy on me,
because I have called to you all day.
4 Give happiness to me, your servant,
because I give my life to you, Lord.

5 Lord, you are kind and forgiving
and have great love for those who call
to you.
6 LORD, hear my prayer,
and listen when I ask for mercy.
7 I call to you in times of trouble,
because you will answer me.

8 Lord, there is no god like you
and no works like yours.
9 Lord, all the nations you have made
will come and worship you.
They will honour you.
10 You are great and you do miracles.[d]
Only you are God.

11 LORD, teach me what you want me to do,
and I will live by your truth.
Teach me to respect you completely.
12 Lord, my God, I will praise you with all my
heart,
and I will honour your name for ever.
13 You have great love for me.
You have saved me from death.
14 God, proud men are attacking me;
a gang of cruel men is trying to kill me.
They do not respect you.
15 But Lord, you are a God who shows mercy
and is kind.
You don't become angry quickly.
You have great love and faithfulness.
16 Turn to me and have mercy.
Give me, your servant, strength.
Save me, the son of your female servant.
17 Show me a sign of your goodness.
When my enemies look, they will be
ashamed.
You, LORD, have helped me and
comforted me.

God Loves Jerusalem

A song. A psalm of the sons of Korah.

87 The LORD built Jerusalem on the holy
mountain.
2 He loves its gates
more than any other place in Israel.
3 City of God,
wonderful things are said about you. *Selah*[d]
4 God says, "I will put Egypt and Babylonia
on the list of nations that know me.
People from Philistia, Tyre and Cush
will be born there."

5 They will say about Jerusalem,
"This one and that one were born there.
God Most High will strengthen her."
6 The LORD will keep a list of the nations.
He will note, "This person was born there."
Selah

7 They will dance and sing,
"All good things come from Jerusalem."

A Sad Complaint

A song. A psalm of the sons of Korah. For the director of music. By the mahalath leannoth.[d] A maskil[d] of Heman the Ezrahite.

88 LORD, you are the God who saves me.
I cry out to you day and night.
2 Receive my prayer,
and listen to my cry.

3 My life is full of troubles,
and I am nearly dead.
4 They think I am on the way to my grave.
I am like a man with no strength.
5 I have been left as dead,
like a body lying in a grave
whom you don't remember any more,
cut off from your care.

6 You have brought me close to death;
I am almost in the dark place of the dead.
7 You have been very angry with me;
all your waves crush me. *Selah*[d]

8You have taken my friends away from me
and have made them hate me.
I am trapped and cannot escape.
9 My eyes are weak from crying.
LORD, I have prayed to you every day;
I have lifted my hands in prayer to you.

10Do you show your miracles [d] for the dead?
Do their spirits rise up and praise you? *Selah*
11Will your love be told in the grave?
Will your loyalty be told in the place of death?
12Will your miracles be known in the dark grave?
Will your goodness be known in the land of forgetfulness?
13But, LORD, I have called out to you for help;
every morning I pray to you.
14LORD, why do you reject me?
Why do you hide from me?

15I have been weak and dying since I was young.
I suffer from your terrors, and I am helpless.
16You have been angry with me,
and your terrors have destroyed me.
17They surround me daily like a flood;
they are all around me.
18You have taken away my loved ones and friends.
Darkness is my only friend.

A Song About God's Loyalty

A maskil [d] of Ethan the Ezrahite.

89 I will always sing about the LORD's love;
I will tell of his loyalty from now on.
2I will say, "Your love continues for ever;
your loyalty goes on and on like the sky."

3You said, "I made an agreement with the man of my choice;
I made a promise to my servant David.
4I told him, 'I will make your family continue for ever.
Your kingdom will go on and on.' " *Selah* [d]

5LORD, the heavens praise you for your miracles [d]
and for your loyalty in the meeting of your holy ones.
6Who in heaven is equal to the LORD?
None of the angels is like the LORD.
7When the holy ones meet, it is God they fear.
He is more frightening than all who surround him.
8Lord GOD All-powerful, who is like you?
LORD, you are powerful and completely trustworthy.

9You rule the mighty sea
and calm the stormy waves.
10You crushed the sea monster Rahab; [d]
by your power you scattered your enemies.
11The skies and the earth belong to you.
You made the world and everything in it.
12You created the north and the south.
Mount Tabor and Mount Hermon sing for joy at your name.
13Your arm has great power.
Your hand is strong; your right hand is lifted up.

14Your kingdom is built on what is right and fair.
Love and truth are in all you do.

15Happy are the people who know how to praise you.
LORD, let them live in the light of your presence.
16In your name they rejoice
and continually praise your goodness.
17You are their glorious strength,
and in your kindness you honour our king.
18Our king, our shield, belongs to the LORD,
to the Holy One of Israel.

19Once, in a vision, you spoke
to those who worship you.
You said, "I have given strength to a warrior;
I have raised up a young man from my people.
20I have found my servant David;
I appointed him by pouring holy oil on him.
21I will steady him with my hand
and strengthen him with my arm.
22No enemy will make him give forced payments,
and wicked people will not defeat him.
23I will crush his enemies in front of him;
I will defeat those who hate him.
24My loyalty and love will be with him.
Through me he will be strong.
25I will give him power over the sea
and control over the rivers.
26He will say to me, 'You are my father,
my God, the Rock, [d] my Saviour.'
27I will make him my firstborn [d] son,
the greatest king on earth.
28My love will watch over him for ever,
and my agreement with him will never end.
29I will make his family continue,
and his kingdom will last as long as the skies.

30"If his descendants [d] reject my teachings
and do not follow my laws,
31if they ignore my demands
and disobey my commands,
32then I will punish their sins with a rod
and their wrongs with a whip.

33But I will not hold back my love from David,
nor will I stop being loyal.
34I will not break my agreement
nor change what I have said.
35I have promised by my holiness,
I will not lie to David.
36His family will go on for ever.
His kingdom will last before me like the sun.
37It will continue for ever, like the moon,
like a dependable witness in the sky." *Selah*

38But now you have refused and rejected your appointed king.
You have been angry with him.
39You have abandoned the agreement with your servant
and thrown his crown to the ground.
40You have torn down all his city walls;
you have turned his strong cities into ruins.
41Everyone who passes by steals from him.
His neighbours insult him.
42You have given strength to his enemies
and have made them all happy.
43You have made his sword useless;
you did not help him stand in battle.
44You have kept him from winning
and have thrown his throne to the ground.
45You have cut his life short
and covered him with shame. *Selah*

46LORD, how long will this go on?
Will you ignore us for ever?
How long will your anger burn like a fire?
47Remember how short my life is.
Why did you create us? For nothing?
48What person alive will not die?
Who can escape the grave? *Selah*
49Lord, where is your love from times past,
which in your loyalty you promised to David?
50Lord, remember how they insulted your servant;
remember how I have suffered the insults of the nations.
51LORD, remember how your enemies insulted you
and how they insulted your appointed king wherever he went.

52Praise the LORD for ever!
Amen and amen.

Book 4

God is Eternal, and We are Not

A prayer of Moses, the man of God.

90 Lord, you have been our home
since the beginning.
2Before the mountains were born
and before you created the earth and the world,
you are God.
You have always been, and you will always be.
3You turn people back into dust.
You say, "Go back into dust, human beings."
4To you, a thousand years
is like the passing of a day,
or like a few hours in the night.
5While people sleep, you take their lives.
They are like grass that grows up in the morning.
6In the morning they are fresh and new,
but by evening they dry up and die.

7We are destroyed by your anger;
we are terrified by your hot anger.
8You have put the evil we have done right in front of you;
you clearly see our secret sins.
9All our days pass while you are angry.
Our years end with a moan.
10Our lifetime is 70 years
or, if we are strong, 80 years.
But the years are full of hard work and pain.
They pass quickly, and then we are gone.

11Who knows the full power of your anger?
Your anger is as great as our fear of you should be.
12Teach us how short our lives really are
so that we may be wise.

13LORD, how long before you return
and show kindness to your servants?
14Fill us with your love every morning.
Then we will sing and rejoice all our lives.
15We have seen years of trouble.
Now give us as much joy as you gave us sorrow.
16Show your servants the wonderful things you do;
show your greatness to their children.
17Lord our God, treat us well.
Give us success in what we do;
yes, give us success in what we do.

Safe in the LORD

91 Those who go to God Most High for safety
will be protected by the Almighty.
2I will say to the LORD, "You are my place of safety and protection.
You are my God and I trust you."
3God will save you from hidden traps
and from deadly diseases.

4He will cover you with his feathers,
and under his wings you can hide.
His truth will be your shield and protection.
5You will not fear any danger by night
or an arrow during the day.
6You will not be afraid of diseases that come
in the dark
or sickness that strikes at noon.
7At your side a thousand people may die,
or even ten thousand right beside you,
but you will not be hurt.
8You will only watch
and see the wicked punished.

9The LORD is your protection;
you have made God Most High your place
of safety.
10Nothing bad will happen to you;
no disaster will come to your home.
11He has put his angels in charge of you
to watch over you wherever you go.
12They will catch you in their hands
so that you will not hit your foot on a rock.
13You will walk on lions and cobras;
you will step on strong lions and snakes.
14The LORD says, "Whoever loves me, I will save.
I will protect those who know me.
15They will call to me, and I will answer them.
I will be with them in trouble;
I will rescue them and honour them.
16I will give them a long, full life,
and they will see how I can save."

Thanksgiving for God's Goodness

A psalm. A song for the Sabbath [d] day.

92 It is good to praise you, LORD,
to sing praises to God Most High.
2It is good to tell of your love in the morning
and of your loyalty at night.
3It is good to praise you with the ten-stringed
lyre [d]
and with the soft-sounding harp.
4LORD, you have made me happy by what you
have done;
I will sing for joy about what your hands
have done.
5LORD, you have done such great things!
How deep are your thoughts!
6Stupid people don't know these things,
and fools don't understand.
7Wicked people grow like the grass.
Evil people seem to do well,
but they will be destroyed for ever.

8But, LORD, you will be honoured for ever.

9LORD, surely your enemies,
surely your enemies will be destroyed,
and all who do evil will be scattered.
10But you have made me as strong as an ox.
You have poured fine oils on me.
11When I looked, I saw my enemies;
I heard the cries of those who are
against me.

12But good people will grow like palm trees;
they will be tall like the cedars of Lebanon.
13Like trees planted in the Temple of the
LORD,
they will grow strong in the courtyards of
our God.
14When they are old, they will still produce
fruit;
they will be healthy and fresh.
15They will say that the LORD is good.
He is my Rock, [d] and there is no wrong
in him.

The Majesty of the LORD

93 The LORD is king. He is clothed in
majesty.
The LORD is clothed in majesty
and armed with strength.
The world is set,
and it cannot be moved.
2LORD, your kingdom was set up long ago;
you are everlasting.

3LORD, the seas raise,
the seas raise their voice.
The seas raise up their pounding waves.
4The sound of the water is loud;
the ocean waves are powerful,
but the LORD above is much greater.

5LORD, your laws will stand for ever.
Your Temple [d] will be holy for ever.

God will Pay Back His Enemies

94 The LORD is a God who punishes.
God, show your greatness and
punish!
2Rise up, Judge of the earth,
and give the proud what they deserve.
3How long will the wicked be happy?
How long, LORD?
4They are full of proud words;
those who do evil boast about what they
have done.
5LORD, they crush your people
and make your children suffer.
6They kill widows and foreigners
and murder orphans.
7They say, "The LORD doesn't see;
the God of Jacob doesn't notice."

8You stupid ones among the people, pay
attention.
You fools, when will you understand?

9Can't the creator of ears hear?
Can't the maker of eyes see?
10Won't the one who corrects nations
punish you?
Doesn't the teacher of people know
everything?
11The LORD knows what people think.
He knows their thoughts are just a puff of
wind.

12LORD, those you correct are happy;
you teach them from your law.
13You give them rest from times of trouble
until a pit is dug for the wicked.
14The LORD won't leave his people
nor give up his children.
15Judgement will again be fair,
and all who are honest will follow it.

16Who will help me fight against the wicked?
Who will stand with me against those who
do evil?
17If the LORD had not helped me,
I would have died in a minute.
18I said, "I am about to fall,"
but, LORD, your love kept me safe.
19I was very worried,
but you comforted me and made me
happy.

20Crooked leaders cannot be friends with you.
They use the law to cause suffering.
21They join forces against people who do right
and sentence to death the innocent.
22But the LORD is my defender;
my God is the rock of my protection.
23God will pay them back for their sins
and will destroy them for their evil.
The LORD our God will destroy them.

A Call to Praise and Obedience

95 Come, let's sing for joy to the LORD.
Let's shout praises to the Rock [d] who
saves us.
2Let's come to him with thanksgiving.
Let's sing songs to him,

3because the LORD is the great God,
the great King over all gods.
4The deepest places on earth are his,
and the highest mountains belong to him.
5The sea is his because he made it,
and he created the land with his own
hands.

6Come, let's worship him and bow down.
Let's kneel before the LORD who
made us,
7because he is our God
and we are the people he takes care of
and the sheep that he tends.

Today listen to what he says:
8 "Do not be stubborn, as your ancestors were
at Meribah,
as they were that day at Massah in the
desert.
9There your ancestors tested me
and tried me even though they saw what
I did.
10I was angry with those people for forty years.
I said, 'They are not loyal to me
and have not understood my ways.'
11I was angry and made a promise,
'They will never enter my rest.' "

Praise for the LORD's Glory

96 Sing to the LORD a new song;
sing to the LORD, all the earth.
2Sing to the LORD and praise his name;
every day tell how he saves us.
3Tell the nations of his glory;
tell all peoples the miracles [d] he does,

4because the LORD is great; he should be
praised at all times.
He should be honoured more than all the
gods,
5because all the gods of the nations are only
idols,
but the LORD made the heavens.
6The LORD has glory and majesty;
he has power and beauty in his Temple. [d]

7Praise the LORD, all nations on earth;
praise the LORD's glory and power.
8Praise the glory of the LORD's name.
Bring an offering and come into his Temple
courtyards.
9Worship the LORD because he is holy.
Tremble before him, everyone on earth.

10Tell the nations, "The LORD is king."
The earth is set, and it cannot be moved.
He will judge the people fairly.
11Let the skies rejoice and the earth be glad;
let the sea and everything in it shout.
12 Let the fields and everything in them rejoice.
Then all the trees of the forest will sing
for joy
13 before the LORD, because he is coming.
He is coming to judge the world;
he will judge the world with fairness
and the peoples with truth.

A Hymn About the LORD's Power

97 The LORD is king. Let the earth rejoice;
faraway lands should be glad.

2Thick, dark clouds surround him.
His kingdom is built on what is right and
fair.

3 A fire goes before him
and burns up his enemies all around.
4 His lightning lights up the world;
when the people see it, they tremble.
5 The mountains melt like wax before
the LORD,
before the Lord of all the earth.
6 The heavens tell about his goodness,
and all the people see his glory.

7 Those who worship idols should be ashamed;
they boast about their gods.
All the gods should worship the LORD.

8 When Jerusalem hears this, she is glad,
and the towns of Judah rejoice.
They are happy because of your
judgements, LORD.
9 You are the LORD Most High over all the earth;
you are supreme over all gods.
10 People who love the LORD hate evil.
The LORD watches over those who follow him
and frees them from the power of the wicked.
11 Light shines on those who do right;
joy belongs to those who are honest.
12 Rejoice in the LORD, you who do right.
Praise his holy name.

The LORD of Power and Justice

A psalm.

98 Sing to the LORD a new song,
because he has done miracles.[d]
By his right hand and holy arm
he has won the victory.
2 The LORD has made known his power to save;
he has shown the other nations his victory
for his people.
3 He has remembered his love
and his loyalty to the people of Israel.

EVIL

The Prowling Lion

Steve was worried about the person who used to be his best friend. This friend, Jake, had previously been quite a normal guy, but he'd recently got interested in mysterious symbols and claimed to be a follower of Satan (or the devil). Steve, who wasn't religious at all, tried to persuade Jake that this was all total rubbish – a load of superstitious mumbo-jumbo.

The writer C.S. Lewis, author of the Narnia stories, once wrote that there are two wrong attitudes to evil: one is to take an unhealthy interest in it, like Jake; the other is to just dismiss it is as nonsense, like Steve.

The Bible makes it clear that evil is constantly near us – always attacking God's creation and particularly trying to influence us. And it's a destructive influence. The Old Testament pictures evil as waiting outside our door, wanting to grab us. The New Testament says that the devil is like a lion prowling around, looking for someone to eat. We can't just laugh the devil and evil off as unimportant.

But we have God on our side, the God who created the universe and who is far more powerful than anything inside it. Although the devil is incredibly strong compared to us, he is nothing compared to God. God has sent his Son Jesus to die on the cross to defeat the devil. The devil hoped that human beings would all die and be punished for committing sin, but God's plan all along was that Jesus would die for our sin. So the devil's hopes will come to nothing. And now God has given us power so we can stand up to the devil: if we're Christians, the Holy Spirit in us will give us strength to fight against the temptations that the devil tries to put in our minds. So we know that the devil exists, and that we should take him seriously – though not too seriously. **Read Psalm 97**.

- How can we know when we're being tempted to do evil?
- How can we stand up to the devil?

Consider . . .

- writing down specific moments in the last week when you feel the devil has tried to lead you astray.
- praying for strength to resist the devil when he tempts you to do evil.

For more, see . . .

- Genesis 4:7 (p.7)
- 1 John 4:4 (p.1374)
- 1 Peter 5:8 (p.1363)

All the ends of the earth have seen
God's power to save.
4Shout with joy to the LORD, all the earth;
burst into songs and make music.
5Make music to the LORD with harps,
with harps and the sound of singing.
6Blow the trumpets and the sheep's horns;
shout for joy to the LORD the King.
7Let the sea and everything in it shout;
let the world and everyone in it sing.
8Let the rivers clap their hands;
let the mountains sing together for joy.
9Let them sing before the LORD,
because he is coming to judge the world.
He will judge the world fairly;
he will judge the peoples with fairness.

The LORD, the Fair and Holy King

99 The LORD is king.
Let the peoples shake with fear.
He sits between the gold creatures with wings.
Let the earth shake.
2The LORD in Jerusalem is great;
he is supreme over all the peoples.
3Let them praise your name;
it is great, holy and to be feared.
4The King is powerful and loves justice.
LORD, you made things fair;
you have done what is fair and right
for the people of Jacob.
5Praise the LORD our God,
and worship at the Temple, [d] his footstool.
He is holy.
6Moses and Aaron were among his priests,
and Samuel was among his worshippers.
They called to the LORD,
and he answered them.
7He spoke to them from the pillar of cloud.
They kept the rules and laws he gave them.
8LORD our God, you answered them.
You showed them that you are a forgiving God,
but you punished them for their wrongs.
9Praise the LORD our God,
and worship at his holy mountain,
because the LORD our God is holy.

A Call to Praise the LORD

A psalm of thanks.

100 Shout to the LORD, all the earth.
2 Serve the LORD with joy;
come before him with singing.
3Know that the LORD is God.
He made us, and we belong to him;
we are his people, the sheep he tends.
4Come into his city with songs of thanksgiving
and into his courtyards with songs of praise.
Thank him and praise his name.
5The LORD is good. His love is for ever,
and his loyalty goes on and on.

A Promise to Rule Well

A psalm of David.

101 I will sing of your love and fairness;
LORD, I will sing praises to you.
2I will be careful to live an innocent life.
When will you come to me?

I will live an innocent life in my house.
3 I will not look at anything wicked.
I hate those who turn against you;
they will not be found near me.
4Let those who want to do wrong stay away from me;
I will have nothing to do with evil.
5If anyone secretly says things against his neighbour,
I will stop him.
I will not allow people
to be proud and look down on others.
6I will look for trustworthy people
so I can live with them in the land.
Only those who live innocent lives
will be my servants.
7No one who is dishonest will live in my house;
no liars will stay around me.

Sidelight If you repeat yourself too much, just tell people you're making up Hebrew poetry. One characteristic of this poetry – called parallelism – was that two consecutive lines would each say essentially the same thing in a different way. (For example, see Psalm 101:7.)

8Every morning I will destroy the wicked in the land.
I will rid the LORD's city of people who do evil.

A Cry for Help

A prayer of a person who is suffering when he is discouraged and tells the Lord his complaints.

102 LORD, listen to my prayer;
let my cry for help come to you.
2Do not hide from me
in my time of trouble.
Pay attention to me.
When I cry for help, answer me quickly.

3My life is passing away like smoke,
and my bones are burned up with fire.
4My heart is like grass
that has been cut and dried.
I forget to eat.
5Because of my grief,
my skin hangs on my bones.
6I am like a desert owl,
like an owl living among the ruins.
7I lie awake.
I am like a lonely bird on a housetop.
8All day long enemies insult me;
those who make fun of me use my name
as a curse.
9I eat ashes for food,
and my tears fall into my drink.
10Because of your great anger,
you have picked me up and thrown me away.
11My days are like a passing shadow;
I am like dried grass.

12But, LORD, you rule for ever,
and your fame goes on and on.
13You will come and have mercy on Jerusalem,
because the time has now come to be kind
to her;
the right time has come.
14Your servants love even her stones;
they even care about her dust.
15Nations will fear the name of the LORD,
and all the kings on earth will honour you.
16The LORD will rebuild Jerusalem;
there his glory will be seen.
17He will answer the prayers of the needy;
he will not reject their prayers.

18Write these things for the future
so that people who are not yet born will
praise the LORD.
19The LORD looked down from his holy place
above;
from heaven he looked down at the earth.
20He heard the moans of the prisoners,
and he freed those sentenced to die.
21The name of the LORD will be heard in
Jerusalem;
his praise will be heard there.
22People will come together,
and kingdoms will serve the LORD.

23God has made me tired of living;
he has cut short my life.
24So I said, "My God, do not take me in the
middle of my life.
Your years go on and on.
25In the beginning you made the earth,
and your hands made the skies.
26They will be destroyed, but you will remain.
They will all wear out like clothes.
And, like clothes, you will change them
and throw them away.
27But you never change,
and your life will never end.
28Our children will live in your presence,
and their children will remain with you."

Praise to the LORD of Love

Of David.

103 My whole being, praise the LORD;
all my being, praise his holy
name.
2My whole being, praise the LORD
and do not forget all his kindnesses.
3He forgives all my sins
and heals all my diseases.
4He saves my life from the grave
and loads me with love and mercy.
5He satisfies me with good things
and makes me young again, like the eagle.

6The LORD does what is right and fair
for all who are wronged by others.

7He showed his ways to Moses
and his deeds to the people of Israel.
8The LORD shows mercy and is kind.
He does not become angry quickly, and he
has great love.
9He will not always accuse us,
and he will not be angry for ever.
10He has not punished us as our sins should be
punished;
he has not repaid us for the evil we have
done.
11As high as the sky is above the earth,
so great is his love for those who
respect him.
12He has taken our sins away from us
as far as the east is from the west.
13The LORD has mercy on those who
respect him,
as a father has mercy on his children.
14He knows how we were made;
he remembers that we are dust.
15Human life is like grass;
we grow like a flower in the field.
16After the wind blows, the flower is gone,
and there is no sign of where it was.
17But the LORD's love for those who
respect him
continues for ever and ever,
and his goodness continues to their
grandchildren
18and to those who keep his agreement
and who remember to obey his orders.

19The LORD has set his throne in heaven,
and his kingdom rules over everything.

20 You who are his angels, praise the LORD.
You are the mighty warriors who do what he says
and who obey his voice.
21 You, his armies, praise the LORD;
you are his servants who do what he wants.
22 Everything the LORD has made
should praise him in all the places he rules.

My whole being, praise the LORD.

Praise to God Who Made the World

104 My whole being, praise the LORD.
LORD my God, you are very great.
You are clothed with glory and majesty;
2 you wear light like a robe.
You stretch out the skies like a tent.
3 You build your room above the clouds.
You make the clouds your chariot,
and you ride on the wings of the wind.
4 You make the winds your messengers,
and flames of fire are your servants.

5 You built the earth on its foundations
so it can never be moved.
6 You covered the earth with oceans;
the water was above the mountains.
7 But at your command, the water rushed away.
When you thundered your orders, it hurried away.
8 The mountains rose; the valleys sank.
The water went to the places you made for it.
9 You set borders for the seas that they cannot cross,
so water will never cover the earth again.

10 You make springs pour into the ravines;
they flow between the mountains.
11 They water all the wild animals;
the wild donkeys come there to drink.
12 Wild birds make nests by the water;
they sing among the tree branches.
13 You water the mountains from above.
The earth is full of the things you made.
14 You make the grass for cattle
and vegetables for the people.
You make food grow from the earth.
15 You give us wine that makes happy hearts
and olive oil that makes our faces shine.
You give us bread that gives us strength.

GOD'S LOVE

Easy to Take For Granted

It's invisible – easy to take for granted. Your hand will go right through it.

It combines with practically everything, and if it didn't, life couldn't exist. It's part of hundreds of thousands of things we use daily, and it makes up two-thirds of your body . . . nine-tenths of the oceans . . . one-fifth of the air you breathe.

Try living without it. You can't. Nothing can. It's invisible. You take it for granted and never think about it because it's everywhere.

You guessed it – it's oxygen.

In many ways, God's love is like oxygen. They're both invisible, and they're both everywhere.

But God's love is even more essential for life than oxygen. The writer of **Psalm 103** knew the importance of God's love for living.

- What phrases in this psalm reflect God's active, assertive love for us?
- How is God's love alive in the attitudes and actions of people you know?

Consider . . .

- thinking about what God has done in your life and writing two-word sentences combining the word "God . . ." and an action word, such as "God strengthens" or "God listens".
- choosing three ways in which you can become more active in showing God's love to others, starting this week.

For more, see . . .

- Genesis 1:26–31 (p.3)
- John 3:16–21 (p.1100)
- Proverbs 3:11–12 (p.592)

16The LORD's trees have plenty of water;
they are the cedars of Lebanon, which he planted.
17The birds make their nests there;
the stork's home is in the fir trees.
18The high mountains belong to the wild goats.
The rocks are hiding places for the badgers.

19You made the moon to mark the seasons,
and the sun always knows when to set.
20You make it dark, and it becomes night.
Then all the wild animals creep around.
21The lions roar as they attack.
They look to God for food.
22When the sun rises, they leave
and go back to their dens to lie down.
23Then people go to work
and work until evening.

24LORD, you have made many things;
with your wisdom you made them all.
The earth is full of your riches.
25Look at the sea, so big and wide,
with creatures large and small that cannot be counted.
26Ships travel over the ocean,
and there is the sea monster Leviathan, [d]
which you made to play there.

27All these things depend on you
to give them their food at the right time.
28When you give it to them,
they gather it up.
When you open your hand,
they are filled with good food.
29When you turn away from them,
they become frightened.
When you take away their breath,
they die and turn to dust.
30When you breathe on them,
they are created,
and you make the land new again.

31May the glory of the LORD be for ever.
May the LORD enjoy what he has made.
32He just looks at the earth, and it shakes.
He touches the mountains, and they smoke.

33I will sing to the LORD all my life;
I will sing praises to my God as long as I live.
34May my thoughts please him;
I am happy in the LORD.
35Let sinners be destroyed from the earth,
and let the wicked live no longer.

My whole being, praise the LORD.

Praise the LORD.

God's Love for Israel

105 Give thanks to the LORD and pray to him.
Tell the nations what he has done.
2Sing to him; sing praises to him.
Tell about all his miracles. [d]
3Be glad that you are his;
let those who seek the LORD be happy.
4Depend on the LORD and his strength;
always go to him for help.

5Remember the miracles he has done;
remember his wonders and his decisions.
6You are descendants [d] of his servant Abraham,
the children of Jacob, his chosen people.
7He is the LORD our God.
His laws are for all the world.

8He will keep his agreement for ever;
he will keep his promises always.
9He will keep the agreement he made with Abraham
and the promise he made to Isaac.
10He made it a law for the people of Jacob;
he made it an agreement with Israel to last for ever.
11The LORD said, "I will give you the land of Canaan,
and it will belong to you."

12Then God's people were few in number.
They were strangers in the land.
13They went from one nation to another,
from one kingdom to another.
14But the LORD did not let anyone hurt them;
he warned kings not to harm them.
15He said, "Don't touch my chosen people,
and don't harm my prophets." [d]

16God ordered a time of hunger in the land,
and he destroyed all the food.
17Then he sent a man ahead of them—
Joseph, who was sold as a slave.
18They put chains around his feet
and an iron ring around his neck.
19Then the time he had spoken of came,
and the LORD's words proved that Joseph was right.
20The king of Egypt sent for Joseph and freed him;
the ruler of the people set him free.
21He made him the master of his house;
Joseph was in charge of his riches.
22He could order the princes as he wished.
He taught the older men to be wise.

23Then his father Israel came to Egypt;
Jacob [n] lived in Egypt. [n]
24The LORD made his people grow in number,
and he made them stronger than their enemies.
25He caused the Egyptians to hate his people
and to make plans against his servants.
26Then he sent his servant Moses,
and Aaron, whom he had chosen.
27They did many signs among the Egyptians
and worked wonders in Egypt.
28The LORD sent darkness and made the land dark,
but the Egyptians turned against what he said.
29So he changed their water into blood
and made their fish die.
30Then their country was filled with frogs,
even in the bedrooms of their rulers.
31The LORD spoke and flies came,
and gnats were everywhere in the country.
32He made hail fall like rain
and sent lightning through their land.
33He struck down their grapevines and fig trees,
and he destroyed every tree in the country.
34He spoke and grasshoppers came;
the locusts [d] were too many to count.
35They ate all the plants in the land
and everything the earth produced.
36The LORD also killed all the firstborn [d] sons in the land,
the oldest son of each family.

37Then he brought his people out,
and they carried with them silver and gold.
Not one of his people stumbled.
38The Egyptians were glad when they left,
because the Egyptians were afraid of them.
39The LORD covered them with a cloud
and lit up the night with fire.
40When they asked, he brought them quail
and filled them with bread from heaven.
41God split the rock, and water flowed out;
it ran like a river through the desert.
42He remembered his holy promise
to his servant Abraham.

43So God brought his people out with joy,
his chosen ones with singing.
44He gave them the lands of other nations,
so they received what others had worked for.
45This was so they would keep his orders
and obey his teachings.

Praise the LORD!

Israel's Failure to Trust God

106 Praise the LORD!
Thank the LORD because he is good.
His love continues for ever.
2No one can tell all the mighty things the LORD has done;
no one can speak all his praise.
3Happy are those who do right,
who do what is fair at all times.

4LORD, remember me when you are kind to your people;
help me when you save them.
5Let me see the good things you do for your chosen people.
Let me be happy along with your happy nation;
let me join your own people in praising you.

6We have sinned just as our ancestors did.
We have done wrong; we have done evil.
7Our ancestors in Egypt
did not learn from your miracles. [d]
They did not remember all your kindnesses,
so they turned against you at the Red Sea. [d]
8But the LORD saved them for his own sake,
to show his great power.
9He commanded the Red Sea, and it dried up.
He led them through the deep sea as if it were a desert.
10He saved them from those who hated them.
He saved them from their enemies,
11and the water covered their foes.
Not one of them escaped.
12Then the people believed what the LORD said,
and they sang praises to him.

13But they quickly forgot what he had done;
they did not wait for his advice.
14They became greedy for food in the desert,
and they tested God there.
15So he gave them what they wanted,
but he also sent a terrible disease among them.

16The people in the camp were jealous of Moses
and of Aaron, the holy priest of the LORD.
17Then the ground opened up and swallowed Dathan
and closed over Abiram's group.
18A fire burned among their followers,
and flames burned up the wicked.

19The people made a gold calf at Mount Sinai
and worshipped a metal statue.

Jacob Also called Israel.
Egypt Literally, "the land of Ham". Also in verse 27. The people in Egypt were descendants of Ham, one of Noah's sons. See Genesis 10:6.

[20]They exchanged their glorious God
for a statue of a bull that eats grass.
[21]They forgot the God who saved them,
who had done great things in Egypt,[n]
[22]who had done miracles in Egypt
and amazing things by the Red Sea.
[23]So God said he would destroy them.
But Moses, his chosen one, stood
before him
and stopped God's anger from destroying
them.

[24]Then they refused to go into the beautiful
land of Canaan;
they did not believe what God promised.
[25]They grumbled in their tents
and did not obey the LORD.
[26]So he swore to them
that they would die in the desert.
[27]He said their children would be killed by
other nations
and that they would be scattered among
other countries.

[28]They joined in worshipping Baal[d] at Peor
and ate meat that had been sacrificed to
lifeless statues.
[29]They made the LORD angry by what they did,
so many people became sick with a terrible
disease.
[30]But Phinehas prayed to the LORD,
and the disease stopped.
[31]Phinehas did what was right,
and it will be remembered from now on.

[32]The people also made the LORD angry at
Meribah,
and Moses was in trouble because of them.
[33]The people turned against the Spirit[d]
of God,
so Moses spoke without stopping to think.

[34]The people did not destroy the other nations
as the LORD had told them to do.
[35]Instead, they mixed with the other nations
and learned their customs.
[36]They worshipped other nations' idols
and were trapped by them.
[37]They even killed their sons and daughters
as sacrifices to demons.[d]
[38]They killed innocent people,
their own sons and daughters,
as sacrifices to the idols of Canaan.
So the land was made unholy by their
blood.
[39]The people became unholy by their sins;
they were unfaithful to God in what
they did.

[40]So the LORD became angry with his
people
and hated his own children.
[41]He handed them over to other nations
and let their enemies rule over them.
[42]Their enemies were cruel to them
and kept them under their power.
[43]The LORD saved his people many times,
but they continued to turn against him.
So they became even more wicked.

[44]But God saw their misery
when he heard their cry.
[45]He remembered his agreement with them,
and he felt sorry for them because of his
great love.
[46]He caused them to be pitied
by those who held them captive.

[47]LORD our God, save us
and bring us back from other nations.
Then we will thank you
and will gladly praise you.

[48]Praise the LORD, the God of Israel.
He always was and always will be.
Let all the people say, "Amen!"

Praise the LORD!

Book 5

God Saves from Many Dangers

107 Thank the LORD because he is good.
His love continues for ever.
[2]That is what those whom the LORD has saved
should say.
He has saved them from the enemy
[3]and has gathered them from other lands,
from east and west, north and south.

[4]Some people had wandered in the desert
lands.
They found no city in which to live.
[5]They were hungry and thirsty,
and they were discouraged.
[6]In their misery they cried out to the
LORD,
and he saved them from their troubles.
[7]He led them on a straight road
to a city where they could live.
[8]Let them give thanks to the LORD for
his love
and for the miracles[d] he does for people.
[9]He satisfies the thirsty
and fills up the hungry.

[10]Some sat in gloom and darkness;
they were prisoners suffering in chains.

Egypt Literally, "the land of Ham". The people in Egypt were descendants of Ham, one of Noah's sons. See Genesis 10:6.

11They had turned against the words of God
and had refused the advice of God Most High.
12So he broke their pride by hard work.
They stumbled, and no one helped.
13In their misery they cried out to the LORD,
and he saved them from their troubles.
14He brought them out of their gloom and darkness
and broke their chains.
15Let them give thanks to the LORD for his love
and for the miracles he does for people.
16He breaks down bronze gates
and cuts apart iron bars.

17Some fools turned against God
and suffered for the evil they did.
18They refused to eat anything,
so they almost died.
19In their misery they cried out to the LORD,
and he saved them from their troubles.
20God gave the command and healed them,
so they were saved from dying.
21Let them give thanks to the LORD for his love
and for the miracles he does for people.
22Let them offer sacrifices to thank him.
With joy they should tell what he has done.

23Others went out to sea in ships
and did business on the great oceans.
24They saw what the LORD could do,
the miracles he did in the deep oceans.
25He spoke, and a storm came up,
which blew up high waves.
26The ships were tossed as high as the sky and fell low to the depths.
The storm was so bad that they lost their courage.
27They stumbled and fell like people who were drunk.
They did not know what to do.
28In their misery they cried out to the LORD,
and he saved them from their troubles.
29He stilled the storm
and calmed the waves.
30They were happy that it was quiet,
and God guided them to the port they wanted.
31Let them give thanks to the LORD for his love
and for the miracles he does for people.
32Let them praise his greatness in the meeting of the people;
let them praise him in the meeting of the elders.

33He changed rivers into a desert
and springs of water into dry ground.
34He made fertile land salty,
because the people there did evil.
35He changed the desert into pools of water
and dry ground into springs of water.
36He had the hungry settle there
so they could build a city in which to live.
37They planted seeds in the fields and vineyards,
and they had a good harvest.
38God blessed them, and they grew in number.
Their cattle did not become fewer.

39Because of disaster, troubles and sadness,
their families grew smaller and weaker.
40He showed he was displeased with their leaders
and made them wander in a pathless desert.
41But he lifted the poor out of their suffering
and made their families grow like flocks of sheep.
42Good people see this and are happy,
but the wicked say nothing.

43Whoever is wise will remember these things
and will think about the love of the LORD.

A Prayer for Victory

A song. A psalm of David.

108 God, my heart is steady.
I will sing and praise you with all my being.
2Wake up, harp and lyre! [d]
I will wake up the dawn.
3LORD, I will praise you among the nations;
I will sing songs of praise about you to all the nations.
4Your great love reaches to the skies,
your truth to the heavens.
5God, you are supreme above the skies.
Let your glory be over all the earth.

6Answer us and save us by your power
so the people you love will be rescued.
7God has said from his Temple, [d]
"When I win, I will divide Shechem
and measure off the Valley of Succoth.
8Gilead and Manasseh are mine.
Ephraim is like my helmet.
Judah holds my royal sceptre. [d]
9Moab is like my washbowl.
I throw my sandals at Edom.
I shout at Philistia."

10Who will bring me to the fortified city?
Who will lead me to Edom?
11God, surely you have rejected us;
you do not go out with our armies.
12Help us fight the enemy.
Human help is useless,

13but we can win with God's help.
He will defeat our enemies.

A Prayer Against an Enemy

For the director of music. A psalm of David.

109 God, I praise you.
Do not be silent.
2Wicked people and liars have spoken against me;
they have told lies about me.

> **Sidelight** Not all the psalms are positive and upbeat. Psalm 109, for example, sounds downright nasty. Verses 6–20 are written in the form of ancient Near Eastern curses, which were said to try to speed justice upon enemies and guilty people. A curse was intended to go into effect only if the person was guilty (see Numbers 5:18–28, p.134 and Deuteronomy 27:15–26, p.189).

3They have said hateful things about me
and attack me for no reason.
4They attacked me, even though I loved them
and prayed for them.
5I was good to them, but they repay me with evil.
I loved them, but they hated me in return.

6They say about me, "Have an evil person work against him,
and let an accuser stand against him.
7When he is judged, let him be found guilty,
and let even his prayers show his guilt.
8Let his life be cut short,
and let another man replace him as leader.
9Let his children become orphans
and his wife a widow.
10Make his children wander around, begging for food.
Let them be forced out of the ruins in which they live.
11Let the people to whom he owes money take everything he owns,
and let strangers steal everything he has worked for.
12Let no one show him love
or have mercy on his orphaned children.
13Let all his descendants[d] die
and be forgotten by those who live after him.
14LORD, remember how wicked his ancestors were,
and don't let the sins of his mother be wiped out.
15LORD, always remember their sins.
Then make people forget about them completely.

16"He did not remember to be loving.
He hurt the poor, the needy and those who were sad
until they were nearly dead.
17He loved to put curses on others,
so let those same curses fall on him.
He did not like to bless others,
so do not let good things happen to him.
18He cursed others as often as he wore clothes.
Cursing others filled his body and his life,
like drinking water and using olive oil.
19So let curses cover him like clothes
and wrap round him like a belt."
20May the LORD do these things to those who accuse me,
to those who speak evil against me.
21But you, Lord GOD,
be kind to me so others will know you are good.
Because your love is good, save me.
22I am poor and helpless
and very sad.
23I am dying like an evening shadow;
I am shaken off like a locust.[d]
24My knees are weak from hunger,
and I have grown thin.
25My enemies insult me;
they look at me and shake their heads.

26LORD my God, help me;
because you are loving, save me.
27Then they will know that your power has done this;
they will know that you have done it, LORD.
28They may curse me, but you bless me.
They may attack me, but they will be disgraced.
Then I, your servant, will be glad.
29Let those who accuse me be disgraced
and covered with shame like a coat.

30I will thank the LORD very much;
I will praise him in front of many people.
31He defends the helpless
and saves them from those who accuse them.

The LORD Appoints a King

A psalm of David.

110 The LORD said to my Lord,
"Sit by me at my right side
until I put your enemies under your control."

2The Lord will enlarge your kingdom beyond
Jerusalem,
and you will rule over your enemies.
3Your people will join you on your day of battle.
You have been dressed in holiness from
birth;
you have the freshness of a child.

4The Lord has made a promise
and will not change his mind.
He said, "You are a priest for ever,
a priest like Melchizedek."

5The Lord is beside you to help you.
When he becomes angry, he will crush kings.

ADDICTION

Every Other Word

James was a great DJ, one of the best and noted for his thorough professionalism. For Ben it was a fabulous opportunity to watch him at work. The young teenager had a great yearning to DJ for a living and took every chance that came his way to use his skills and watch others. But the opportunity to watch James in action was totally different. Ben had been asked along to the radio station by a neighbour who was engineering there.

When the day finally came and Ben walked into the studio, his eyes were everywhere, looking at the decks and the mixers, it was awe-inspiring.

James, his idol, came over and shook hands with him.

"So, you want to do this for a career eh? Then you'd better come and sit by me and I'll show you the tricks of the trade."

Ben couldn't believe it was happening. The show started live "on air" and James seemed to be able to do hundreds of things at once, changing jingles, cueing up newsflashes, sorting out the CDs, talking to his adoring public.

Then came the shock.

While the record was playing, the DJ took off his headphones to talk to the engineer and his producer. His sentences were absolutely littered with swear words! Not just one or two, but it seemed to Ben that it was every other word.

He was so taken aback that he said nothing and just carried on watching and listening to the programme. But there it was again, and again. Until finally during a break for the news, he dared to ask James about it.

"Oh my dear boy, it's nothing. Once you're on air you become a total professional, and off the air you are just yourself," he explained with a lazy smile.

"Aren't you afraid you're going to swear over the airwaves?" Ben asked, amazed.

"It's funny you should ask that, because I suppose once I'm doing the programme I'm concentrating, but once I'm off the air, I don't even notice I'm doing it!"

Ben went home with a totally different image in his head.

In **Psalm 109:17–21** David complains that people were trying to give him a false image, and one of the things they tried to do was to accuse him of the same sin as James in this story.

- According to Psalm 109:18, how natural can swearing become?
- Have you ever noticed some "habitual sin" in your life? What have you tried to do about it?

Consider . . .

- taking a deep breath the next time you're going to lose it . . . making sure you have control of your tongue, not the other way round!
- making a note of two things you struggle to control, then ask God to give you the power to control them.

For more, see . . .

- Psalm 141:3 (p.582)
- James 3:7–10 (p.1351)
- 1 Corinthians 10:12–13 (p.1228)

6 He will judge those nations, filling them with
dead bodies;
he will defeat rulers all over the world.
7 The king will drink from the brook on the way.
Then he will be strengthened.

Praise the LORD's Goodness

111

Praise the LORD!

I will thank the LORD with all my heart
in the meeting of his good people.

2 The LORD does great things;
those who enjoy them seek them.
3 What he does is glorious and splendid,
and his goodness continues for ever.
4 His miracles[d] are unforgettable.
The LORD is kind and merciful.
5 He gives food to those who fear him.
He remembers his agreement for ever.
6 He has shown his people his power
when he gave them the lands of other
nations.

7 Everything he does is good and fair;
all his orders can be trusted.
8 They will continue for ever.
They were made true and right.
9 He sets his people free.
He made his agreement everlasting.
He is holy and wonderful.

10 Wisdom begins with respect for the LORD;
those who obey his orders have good
understanding.
He should be praised for ever.

Honest People are Blessed

112

Praise the LORD!

Happy are those who respect the LORD,
who want what he commands.

2 Their descendants[d] will be powerful in the
land;
the children of honest people will be
blessed.
3 Their houses will be full of wealth and riches,
and their goodness will continue for ever.
4 A light shines in the dark for honest people,
for those who are merciful and kind and
good.

HONESTY

Slow But Sure

Almost everyone cheated in Mrs Young's algebra class. It was just so incredibly easy. The three class "brains" were generous with whispered answers on tests and would lend homework papers for copying. Mrs Young didn't seem to catch on, or else she ignored it, not knowing how to put a stop to it.

Robert didn't believe in cheating, though. He plodded along, doing his own work, scoring Cs or C+s. That's why everybody was surprised when he got the best maths results of anybody in the school – even better than the brains – and was accepted for university.

"How did you do it, Robert?" asked one of the brains from algebra.

"I just knew the stuff," Robert said with a smile. "I learned it, slowly but surely."

Honesty carries its own rewards today, just as it did in ancient times. **Psalm 112** talks about many of those rewards.

- How would the phrase "fair in their business" in verse 5 apply to Robert?
- In what ways can honesty keep you "steady" (verse 7) as you go about your business at school, work and home?

Consider . . .

- rewriting this psalm using your own words and applying it to your own circumstances.
- promising God never to cheat at school.

For more, see . . .

- 1 Samuel 12:1–5 (p.264)
- Colossians 3:9–10 (p.1292)
- Isaiah 33:15–17 (p.672)

5It is good to be merciful and generous.
Those who are fair in their business
6will never be defeated.
Good people will always be remembered.
7They won't be afraid of bad news;
their hearts are steady because they trust
the LORD.
8They are confident and will not be afraid;
they will look down on their enemies.
9They give freely to the poor.
The things they do are right and will
continue for ever.
They will be given great honour.

10The wicked will see this and become
angry;
they will grind their teeth in anger and
then disappear.
The wishes of the wicked will come to
nothing.

Praise for the LORD's Kindness

113 Praise the LORD!
Praise him, you servants of the LORD;
praise the name of the LORD.
2The LORD's name should be praised
now and for ever.
3The LORD's name should be praised
from where the sun rises to where
it sets.

4The LORD is supreme over all the nations;
his glory reaches to the skies.
5No one is like the LORD our God,
who rules from heaven,
6who bends down to look
at the skies and the earth.

7The LORD lifts the poor from the ground
and takes the helpless from the ashes.
8He seats them with princes,
the princes of his people.
9He gives children to the woman who has
none
and makes her a happy mother.

Praise the LORD!

Sidelight When Jesus and his disciples sang on the night Judas betrayed Jesus (Matthew 26:30, p.989), they probably sang Psalms 113—114 or Psalms 115—118. These songs were customarily sung during the Passover, which was being celebrated at the time.

God Brought Israel from Egypt

114 When the Israelites went out of
Egypt,
the people of Jacob left that foreign
country.
2Then Judah became God's holy place;
Israel became the land he ruled.

3The Red Sea [d] looked and ran away;
the Jordan River turned back.
4The mountains danced like rams
and the hills like little lambs.

5Sea, why did you run away?
Jordan, why did you turn back?
6Mountains, why did you dance like rams?
Hills, why did you dance like little lambs?

7Earth, shake with fear before the Lord,
before the God of Jacob.
8He turned a rock into a pool of water,
a hard rock into a spring of water.

The One True God

115 It does not belong to us, LORD.
The glory belongs to you
because of your love and loyalty.

2Why do the nations ask,
"Where is their God?"
3Our God is in heaven.
He does what he pleases.
4Their idols are made of silver and gold,
the work of human hands.
5They have mouths, but they cannot speak.
They have eyes, but they cannot see.
6They have ears, but they cannot hear.
They have noses, but they cannot smell.
7They have hands, but they cannot feel.
They have feet, but they cannot walk.
No sounds come from their throats.
8People who make idols will be like them,
and so will those who trust them.

9Family of Israel, trust the LORD;
he is your helper and your protection.
10Family of Aaron, trust the LORD;
he is your helper and your protection.
11You who respect the LORD should trust him;
he is your helper and your protection.

12The LORD remembers us and will bless us.
He will bless the family of Israel;
he will bless the family of Aaron.
13The LORD will bless those who respect him,
from the smallest to the greatest.

14May the LORD give you success,
and may he give you and your children
success.

15 May you be blessed by the LORD,
who made heaven and earth.

16 Heaven belongs to the LORD,
but he gave the earth to people.
17 Dead people do not praise the LORD;
those in the grave are silent.
18 But we will praise the LORD
now and for ever.

Praise the LORD!

Thanksgiving for Escaping Death

116 I love the LORD,
because he listens to my prayers
for help.
2 He paid attention to me,
so I will call to him for help as long as I live.

3 The ropes of death bound me,
and the fear of the grave took hold of me.
I was troubled and sad.
4 Then I called out the name of the LORD.
I said, "Please, LORD, save me!"

5 The LORD is kind and does what is right;
our God is merciful.
6 The LORD watches over the foolish;
when I was helpless, he saved me.

7 I said to myself, "Relax,
because the LORD takes care of you."

8 LORD, you saved me from death.
You stopped my eyes from crying;
you kept me from being defeated.
9 So I will walk with the LORD
in the land of the living.
10 I believed, so I said,
"I am completely ruined."
11 In my distress I said,
"All people are liars."

12 What can I give the LORD
for all the good things he has given to me?

THANKFULNESS

Showered With Blessings

Lily was brought up with good manners. She always said thank you for birthday presents and thanked God when she managed to get out of forgetting to do her homework.

However, Lily didn't feel like she had anything in common with the guy in **Psalm 116**. She'd never had armies approaching against her or been in a life-threatening situation where God had to save her from death. She knew that the Bible says Jesus is her rescuer but how could she be thankful when she'd never felt him save her like this? Lily knew she had it pretty good – so how could this psalm be relevant to her?

She found the answer in verse 7: "Relax, because the Lord takes care of you."

Whether she'd won a major battle or not, Lily realised her life has been showered with blessings. God was not only there for her in tough situations, but had promised her eternal life, happiness in heaven and she had an everlasting saviour in Jesus Christ. Like the writer in verses 1 and 2, Lily knew that God would hear and answer her every call and she should thank him for that, as well as everything else he gives her every day.

She made a vow to show her thankfulness to God in every situation, whether good or bad, for her favourite shoes or for strawberry milkshakes, for blessings that she never realised she had. She decided to live a life that made the most of the gifts God had given her, simply because she is his daughter.

- What does the psalm writer promise to give back to God to say thank you? Should we do the same?
- What do verses 14 and 18 mean? Does this say anything to us about how church should be?

Consider . . .

- whether you have felt like Lily did. Give thanks to God for all he has given you.
- making a list of all the things you love about God? Do you thank him for who he is as well as what he's given to you?

For more, see . . .

- John 3:16 (p.1100)
- 1 Thessalonians 5:16–18 (p.1301)
- Colossians 3:12–17 (p.1293)

13I will lift up the cup of salvation,
and I will pray to the LORD.
14I will give the LORD what I promised
in front of all his people.

15The death of one that belongs to the LORD
is precious in his sight.
16LORD, I am your servant;
I am your servant and the son of your
female servant.
You have freed me from my chains.

17I will give you an offering to show thanks
to you,
and I will pray to the LORD.
18I will give the LORD what I promised
in front of all his people,
19in the Temple [d] courtyards
in Jerusalem.

Praise the LORD!

Sidelight The shortest chapter in the Bible – Psalm 117 – is long on praise. The psalmist encourages the whole world to make music to God, which would make the Guinness Book of World Records for the Largest Community Sing-a-long.

A Hymn of Praise

117 All you nations, praise the LORD.
All you people, praise him
2because the LORD loves us very much,
and his truth is everlasting.

Praise the LORD!

Thanksgiving for Victory

118 Thank the LORD because he is good.
His love continues for ever.
2Let the people of Israel say,
"His love continues for ever."
3Let the family of Aaron say,
"His love continues for ever."
4Let those who respect the LORD say,
"His love continues for ever."
5I was in trouble, so I called to the LORD.
The LORD answered me and set me free.
6I will not be afraid, because the LORD is
with me.
People can't do anything to me.
7The LORD is with me to help me,
so I will see my enemies defeated.

8It is better to trust the LORD
than to trust people.
9It is better to trust the LORD
than to trust princes.

10All the nations surrounded me,
but I defeated them in the name of the
LORD.
11They surrounded me on every side,
but with the LORD's power I defeated them.
12They surrounded me like a swarm of bees,
but they died as quickly as thorns burn.
By the LORD's power, I defeated them.

13They chased me until I was almost defeated,
but the LORD helped me.
14The LORD gives me strength and a song.
He has saved me.

15Shouts of joy and victory
come from the tents of those who
do right:
"The LORD has done powerful things."
16The power of the LORD has won the victory;
with his power the LORD has done mighty
things.

17I will not die, but live,
and I will tell what the LORD has done.
18The LORD has taught me a hard lesson,
but he did not let me die.

19Open for me the Temple [d] gates.
Then I will come in and thank the LORD.
20This is the LORD's gate;
only those who are good may enter
through it.
21LORD, I thank you for answering me.
You have saved me.

22The stone that the builders rejected
became the cornerstone. [d]
23The LORD did this,
and it is wonderful to us.
24This is the day that the LORD has made.
Let us rejoice and be glad today!

25Please, LORD, save us;
please, LORD, give us success.
26God bless the one who comes in the name of
the LORD.
We bless all of you from the Temple of the
LORD.
27The LORD is God,
and he has shown kindness to us.
With branches in your hands, join the feast.
Come to the corners of the altar.

28You are my God, and I will thank you;
you are my God, and I will praise your
greatness.

29Thank the LORD because he is good.
His love continues for ever.

The Word of God

119 Happy are those who live pure
lives,
who follow the LORD's teachings.

Sidelight "Ah, your eyes, your lips, your regulations!" You've probably never written a love song to a book of laws, but the writer of Psalm 119 did. The longest chapter in the Bible serenades God's commandments – probably as written in Genesis through to Deuteronomy.

2Happy are those who keep his rules,
who try to obey him with their whole
heart.
3They don't do what is wrong;
they follow his ways.
4LORD, you gave your orders
to be obeyed completely.
5I wish I were more loyal
in obeying your demands.
6Then I would not be ashamed
when I study your commands.
7When I learned that your laws are fair,
I praised you with an honest heart.
8I will obey your demands,
so please don't ever leave me.

9How can a young person live a pure life?
By obeying your word.
10With all my heart I try to obey you.
Don't let me break your commands.
11I have taken your words to heart
so I would not sin against you.
12LORD, you should be praised.
Teach me your demands.
13My lips will tell about
all the laws you have spoken.
14I enjoy living by your rules
as people enjoy great riches.
15I think about your orders
and study your ways.
16I enjoy obeying your demands,
and I will not forget your word.

17Do good to me, your servant, so I can live,
so I can obey your word.
18Open my eyes to see
the miracles[d] in your teachings.
19I am a stranger on earth.
Do not hide your commands from me.
20I wear myself out with desire
for your laws all the time.
21You scold proud people;
those who ignore your commands are
cursed.
22Don't let me be insulted and hated
because I keep your rules.
23Even if princes speak against me,
I, your servant, will think about your
demands.
24Your rules give me pleasure;
they give me good advice.

25I am about to die.
Give me life, as you have promised.
26I told you about my life, and you
answered me.
Teach me your demands.
27Help me understand your orders.
Then I will think about your miracles.
28I am sad and tired.
Make me strong again as you have
promised.
29Don't let me be dishonest;
have mercy on me by helping me obey
your teachings.
30I have chosen the way of truth;
I have obeyed your laws.
31I hold on to your rules.
LORD, do not let me be disgraced.
32I will quickly obey your commands,
because you have made me happy.

33LORD, teach me your demands,
and I will keep them until the end.
34Help me understand, so I can keep your
teachings,
obeying them with all my heart.
35Lead me in the path of your commands,
because that makes me happy.
36Make me want to keep your rules
instead of wishing for riches.
37Keep me from looking at worthless things.
Let me live by your word.
38Keep your promise to me, your servant,
so you will be respected.
39Take away the shame I fear,
because your laws are good.
40How I want to follow your orders.
Give me life because of your goodness.

41LORD, show me your love,
and save me as you have promised.
42I have an answer for people who
insult me,
because I trust what you say.
43Never keep me from speaking your truth,
because I depend on your fair laws.
44I will obey your teachings
for ever and ever.
45So I will live in freedom,
because I want to follow your orders.
46I will discuss your rules with kings
and will not be ashamed.

47I enjoy obeying your commands,
which I love.
48I praise your commands, which I love,
and I think about your demands.

49Remember your promise to me, your servant;
it gives me hope.
50When I suffer, this comforts me:
your promise gives me life.
51Proud people always make fun of me,
but I do not reject your teachings.
52I remember your laws from long ago,
and they comfort me, LORD.
53I become angry with wicked people
who do not keep your teachings.
54I sing about your demands
wherever I live.
55LORD, I remember you at night,
and I will obey your teachings.
56This is what I do:
I follow your orders.

57LORD, you are my share in life;
I have promised to obey your words.
58I prayed to you with all my heart.
Have mercy on me as you have promised.
59I thought about my life,
and I decided to follow your rules.
60I hurried and did not wait
to obey your commands.
61Wicked people have tied me up,
but I have not forgotten your teachings.
62In the middle of the night, I get up to
thank you
because your laws are right.
63I am a friend to everyone who fears you,
to anyone who obeys your orders.
64LORD, your love fills the earth.
Teach me your demands.

65You have done good things for your servant,
as you have promised, LORD.
66Teach me wisdom and knowledge
because I trust your commands.
67Before I suffered, I did wrong,
but now I obey your word.
68You are good, and you do what is good.
Teach me your demands.
69Proud people have made up lies about me,
but I will follow your orders with all my
heart.

JUSTICE

To Live in Freedom

Reward posters offered large sums of money for her capture, dead or alive. She was just over 1.5 metres tall, and used to suffer from fainting spells because of a head injury inflicted by an owner when she was younger, but many people regarded her as extremely dangerous. Some even called her "the devil".

But others, many others, called her "Moses". She had, after all, led more than 200 men, women and children out of slavery to freedom in Canada via the Underground Railway.

Her real name was Harriet Tubman, and in the years just before America's Civil War in the 1800s, she risked her life time and time again, returning to the South to guide escaped slaves to freedom in the North.

In **Psalm 119:33–48**, the psalmist yearns for guidance to "live in freedom", as so many slaves did long ago. Just as the slaves depended on Harriet Tubman, so the psalmist depended on God to show him the way.

- Which verses of the passage would Harriet Tubman have identified with?
- According to this passage, how can God set you free?

Consider . . .

- writing down what total freedom means to you and what you think God would say it means.
- becoming a "Moses" to someone else by helping him or her to overcome an enslaving problem, such as drug abuse or a negative attitude.

For more, see . . .

- Joshua 1:8–9 (p.203)
- Romans 6:15–23 (p.1192)
- John 8:34–47 (p.1110)

70Those people have no feelings,
but I love your teachings.
71It was good for me to suffer
so I would learn your demands.
72Your teachings are worth more to me
than thousands of pieces of gold and silver.

73You made me and formed me with your hands.
Give me understanding so I can learn your commands.
74Let those who respect you rejoice when they see me,
because I put my hope in your word.
75LORD, I know that your laws are right
and that it was right for you to punish me.
76Comfort me with your love,
as you promised me, your servant.
77Have mercy on me so that I may live.
I love your teachings.
78Make proud people ashamed because they lied about me.
But I will think about your orders.
79Let those who respect you return to me,
those who know your rules.
80Let me obey your demands perfectly
so I will not be ashamed.

81I am weak from waiting for you to save me,
but I hope in your word.
82My eyes are tired from looking for your promise.
When will you comfort me?
83Even though I am like a wine bag going up in smoke,
I do not forget your demands.
84How long will I live?
When will you judge those who are hurting me?
85Proud people have dug pits to trap me.
They have nothing to do with your teachings.
86All of your commands can be trusted.
Liars are hurting me. Help me!
87They have almost put me in the grave,
but I have not rejected your orders.
88Give me life by your love
so I can obey your rules.

89LORD, your word is everlasting;
it continues for ever in heaven.
90Your loyalty will go on and on;
you made the earth, and it still stands.
91All things continue to this day because of your laws,
because all things serve you.
92If I had not loved your teachings,
I would have died from my sufferings.
93I will never forget your orders,
because you have given me life by them.
94I am yours. Save me.
I want to obey your orders.
95Wicked people are waiting to destroy me,
but I will think about your rules.
96Everything I see has its limits,
but your commands have none.

97How I love your teachings!
I think about them all day long.
98Your commands make me wiser than my enemies,
because they are mine for ever.
99I am wiser than all my teachers,
because I think about your rules.
100I have more understanding than the older leaders,
because I follow your orders.
101I have avoided every evil way
so I could obey your word.
102I haven't walked away from your laws,
because you yourself are my teacher.
103Your promises are sweet to me,
sweeter than honey in my mouth!
104Your orders give me understanding,
so I hate lying ways.

105Your word is like a lamp for my feet
and a light for my path.
106I will do what I have promised
and obey your fair laws.
107I have suffered for a long time.
LORD, give me life by your word.
108LORD, accept my willing praise
and teach me your laws.
109My life is always in danger,
but I haven't forgotten your teachings.
110Wicked people have set a trap for me,
but I haven't strayed from your orders.
111I will follow your rules for ever,
because they make me happy.
112I will try to do what you demand
for ever, until the end.

113I hate disloyal people,
but I love your teachings.
114You are my hiding place and my shield;
I hope in your word.
115Get away from me, you who do evil,
so I can keep my God's commands.
116Support me as you promised so I can live.
Don't let me be embarrassed because of my hopes.
117Help me, and I will be saved.
I will always respect your demands.
118You reject those who ignore your demands,
because their lies mislead them.
119You throw away the wicked of the world like rubbish.
So I will love your rules.
120I shake in fear of you;
I respect your laws.

121I have done what is fair and right.
Don't leave me to those who wrong me.
122Promise that you will help me, your servant.
Don't let proud people wrong me.
123My eyes are tired from looking for your
salvation
and for your good promise.
124Show your love to me, your servant,
and teach me your demands.
125I am your servant. Give me wisdom
so I can understand your rules.
126LORD, it is time for you to do something,
because people have disobeyed your
teachings.
127I love your commands
more than the purest gold.
128I respect all your orders,
so I hate lying ways.
129Your rules are wonderful.
That is why I keep them.
130Learning your words gives wisdom
and understanding for the foolish.
131I am nearly out of breath.
I really want to learn your commands.
132Look at me and have mercy on me
as you do for those who love you.
133Guide my steps as you promised;
don't let any sin control me.
134Save me from harmful people
so I can obey your orders.
135Show your kindness to me, your servant.
Teach me your demands.
136Tears stream from my eyes,
because people do not obey your teachings.
137LORD, you do what is right,
and your laws are fair.
138The rules you commanded are right
and completely trustworthy.
139I am so upset I am worn out,
because my enemies have forgotten your
words.
140Your promises are proven,
so I, your servant, love them.
141I am unimportant and hated,
but I have not forgotten your orders.
142Your goodness continues for ever,
and your teachings are true.
143I have had troubles and misery,
but I love your commands.
144Your rules are always good.
Help me understand so I can live.
145LORD, I call to you with all my heart.
Answer me, and I will keep your demands.
146I call to you.
Save me so I can obey your rules.
147I wake up early in the morning and cry out.
I hope in your word.
148I stay awake all night
so I can think about your promises.
149Listen to me because of your love;
LORD, give me life by your laws.
150Those who love evil are near,
but they are far from your teachings.
151But, LORD, you are also near,
and all your commands are true.
152Long ago I learned from your rules
that you made them to continue for ever.

153See my suffering and rescue me,
because I have not forgotten your
teachings.
154Argue my case and save me.
Let me live by your promises.
155Wicked people are far from being saved,
because they do not want your demands.
156LORD, you are very kind;
give me life by your laws.
157Many enemies are chasing me,
but I have not rejected your rules.
158I see those traitors, and I hate them,
because they do not obey what you say.
159See how I love your orders.
LORD, give me life by your love.
160Your words are true from the start,
and all your laws will be fair for ever.

161Leaders attack me for no reason,
but I fear your law in my heart.
162I am as happy over your promises
as if I had found a great treasure.
163I hate and despise lies,
but I love your teachings.
164Seven times a day I praise you
for your fair laws.
165Those who love your teachings will find true
peace,
and nothing will defeat them.
166I am waiting for you to save me, LORD.
I will obey your commands.
167I obey your rules,
and I love them very much.
168I obey your orders and rules,
because you know everything I do.

169Hear my cry to you, LORD.
Let your word help me understand.
170Listen to my prayer;
save me as you promised.
171Let me speak your praise,
because you have taught me your
demands.
172Let me sing about your promises,
because all your commands are fair.
173Give me your helping hand,
because I have chosen your commands.
174I want you to save me, LORD.
I love your teachings.

175Let me live so I can praise you,
and let your laws help me.
176I have wandered like a lost sheep.
Look for your servant, because I have not
forgotten your commands.

A Prayer of Someone Far from Home

A psalm for going up to worship.

120 When I was in trouble, I called to
the LORD,
and he answered me.
2LORD, save me from liars
and from those who plan evil.

3You who plan evil, what will God do to you?
How will he punish you?
4He will punish you with the sharp arrows of
a warrior
and with burning coals of wood.

5How terrible it is for me to live in the land of
Meshech,
to live among the people of Kedar.
6I have lived too long
with people who hate peace.
7When I talk peace,
they want war.

The LORD Guards His People

A song for going up to worship.

121 I look up to the hills,
but where does my help come
from?
2My help comes from the LORD,
who made heaven and earth.

3He will not let you be defeated.
He who guards you never sleeps.
4He who guards Israel
never rests or sleeps.
5The LORD guards you.

The LORD is the shade that protects you
from the sun.
6The sun cannot hurt you during the day,
and the moon cannot hurt you at night.

7The LORD will protect you from all dangers;
he will guard your life.
8The LORD will guard you as you come and go,
both now and for ever.

Happy People in Jerusalem

A song for going up to worship. Of David.

122 I was happy when they said to me,
"Let's go to the Temple [d] of the
LORD."
2Jerusalem, we are standing
at your gates.
3Jerusalem is built as a city
with the buildings close together.
4The tribes [d] go up there,
the tribes who belong to the LORD.
It is the rule in Israel
to praise the LORD at Jerusalem.
5There the descendants [d] of David
set their thrones to judge the people.
6Pray for peace in Jerusalem:
"May those who love her be safe.
7May there be peace within her walls
and safety within her strong towers."
8To help my relatives and friends,
I say, "Let Jerusalem have peace."
9For the sake of the Temple of the LORD
our God,
I wish good for her.

A Prayer for Mercy

A song for going up to worship.

123 LORD, I look upwards to you,
you who live in heaven.
2Slaves depend on their masters,
and a female servant depends on her
mistress.
In the same way, we depend on the LORD
our God;
we wait for him to show us mercy.
3Have mercy on us, LORD. Have mercy
on us,
because we have been insulted.
4We have suffered many insults from lazy
people
and much cruelty from the proud.

The LORD Saves His People

A song for going up to worship. Of David.

124 What if the LORD had not been on
our side?
(Let Israel repeat this.)
2What if the LORD had not been on our side
when we were attacked?
3When they were angry with us,
they would have swallowed us alive.
4They would have been like a flood
drowning us;
they would have poured over us like a
river.
5 They would have swept us away like a
mighty stream.

6Praise the LORD,
who did not let them chew us up.
7We escaped like a bird
from the hunter's trap.
The trap broke,
and we escaped.

8Our help comes from the LORD,
who made heaven and earth.

God Protects Those Who Trust Him

A song for going up to worship.

125 Those who trust the LORD are like Mount Zion,[d]
which sits unmoved for ever.
2As the mountains surround Jerusalem,
the LORD surrounds his people
now and for ever.
3The wicked will not rule
over those who do right.
If they did, the people who do right
might use their power to do evil.
4LORD, be good to those who are good,
whose hearts are honest.
5But, LORD, when you remove those who do evil,
also remove those who stop following you.
Let there be peace in Israel.

LORD, Bring Your People Back

A song for going up to worship.

126 When the LORD brought the prisoners back to Jerusalem,
it seemed as if we were dreaming.
2Then we were filled with laughter,
and we sang happy songs.
Then the other nations said,
"The LORD has done great things for them."
3The LORD has done great things for us,
and we are very glad.
4LORD, return our prisoners again,
as you bring streams to the desert.
5Those who cry as they plant crops
will sing at harvest time.
6Those who cry
as they carry out the seeds
will return singing
and carrying bundles of grain.

All Good Things Come from God

A song for going up to worship. Of Solomon.

127 If the LORD doesn't build the house,
the builders are working for nothing.
If the LORD doesn't guard the city,
the guards are watching for nothing.
2It is no use for you to get up early
and stay up late,
working for a living.
The LORD gives sleep to those he loves.
3Children are a gift from the LORD;
babies are a reward.
4Children who are born to a young man
are like arrows in the hand of a warrior.
5Happy is the man
who has his bag full of arrows.
They will not be defeated
when they fight their enemies at the city gate.

The Happy Home

A song for going up to worship.

128 Happy are those who respect the LORD
and obey him.
2You will enjoy what you work for,
and you will be blessed with good things.
3Your wife will give you many children,
like a vine that produces much fruit.
Your children will bring you much good,
like olive branches that produce many olives.
4This is how the man who respects the LORD
will be blessed.

5May the LORD bless you from Mount Zion;[d]
may you enjoy the good things of Jerusalem all your life.
6May you see your grandchildren.
Let there be peace in Israel.

A Prayer Against the Enemies

A song for going up to worship.

129 They have treated me badly all my life.
(Let Israel repeat this.)
2They have treated me badly all my life,
but they have not defeated me.
3Like farmers ploughing, they ploughed over my back,
making long wounds.
4But the LORD does what is right;
he has set me free from those wicked people.

5Let those who hate Jerusalem
be turned back in shame.
6Let them be like the grass on the roof
that dries up before it has grown.
7There is not enough of it to fill a hand
or to make into a bundle to fill one's arms.
8Let those who pass by them not say,
"May the LORD bless you.
We bless you by the power of the LORD."

A Prayer for Mercy

A song for going up to worship.

130 LORD, I am in great trouble,
so I call out to you.
2 Lord, hear my voice;
listen to my prayer for help.
3 LORD, if you punished people for all
their sins,
no one would be left, Lord.
4 But you forgive us,
so we respect you.

5 I wait for the LORD to help me,
and I trust his word.
6 I wait for the Lord to help me
more than night-watchmen wait for the
dawn,
more than night-watchmen wait for the
dawn.
7 People of Israel, put your hope in the
LORD
because he is loving
and able to save.
8 He will save Israel
from all their sins.

Childlike Trust in the LORD

A song for going up to worship. Of David.

131 LORD, my heart is not proud;
I don't look down on others.
I don't do great things,
and I can't do miracles.[d]
2 But I am calm and quiet,
like a baby with its mother.
I am at peace, like a baby with its
mother.

3 People of Israel, put your hope in the
LORD
now and for ever.

In Praise of the Temple

A song for going up to worship.

132 LORD, remember David
and all his suffering.
2 He made an oath to the LORD,
a promise to the Mighty God of Jacob.
3 He said, "I will not go home to my house,
or lie down on my bed,
4 or close my eyes,
or let myself sleep

FAMILY

Happy Families

Is there such thing as a normal family? Marriage, divorce, single parents, stepparents, adoption, living with the grandparents, fostering, alternative lifestyle – just as we individually are all unique, so too are our families. Normality, when it comes to families, is being different.

Families come in all sorts of shapes and sizes. However a family is put together, it is God's desire that we are supported and cared for by people who love us.

The writer of **Psalm 128** believes that children are a sign of blessing from God; that God uses families as a way of showing how he cares for each of us; and that if God is at the heart of the household, the house can become a home.

- Why do you think the writer of this psalm believes families are important?
- What parts of your family are similar to your friends'? How is it different? Is difference a good or bad thing?

Consider . . .

- collecting photos of your extended family or drawing pictures of them, building a collage of your family tree. Join each member together with thread, brothers and sisters, parents and children. See how you all connect. Thank God for the diversity in your family and pray for his blessing on it.
- making a prayer box filled with objects or photos to remind you of family members. Pray for one member of your family each day, asking God to be at the heart of their home.

For more, see . . .

- Joshua 24:14–15 (p.222)
- Ephesians 6:1–4 (p.1276)

5until I find a place for the LORD.
I want to provide a home for the Mighty
God of Jacob."
6We heard about the Ark[d] in Bethlehem.
We found it at Kiriath Jearim.
7Let's go to the LORD's house.
Let's worship at his footstool.
8Rise, LORD, and come to your resting place;
come with the Ark that shows your
strength.
9May your priests do what is right.
May your people sing for joy.
10For the sake of your servant David,
do not reject your appointed king.
11The LORD made a promise to David,
a sure promise that he will not
take back.
He promised, "I will make one of your
descendants[d]
rule as king after you.
12If your sons keep my agreement
and the rules that I teach them,
then their sons after them will rule
on your throne for ever and ever."
13The LORD has chosen Jerusalem;
he wants it for his home.
14He says, "This is my resting place for ever.
Here is where I want to stay.

SIN

What Harm?

Sarah knew it was stealing, in a way at least. But what choice did she have? Mr Walker, the Head of Music, had talked her into playing a solo, but her flute was old and unreliable. It sounded more like a tin pipe than a flute when she played it.

Ann, on the other hand, had a new, top-of-the-range flute that made each note sound like liquid silver. Ann didn't like other people playing her instrument, but what harm would it do if Sarah just switched the flutes in their cases the day before the contest?

For days Sarah agonised over her decision but finally decided, right or wrong, she just had to do it. She was nearly sick with nerves as she sneaked into the deserted music room the day before the contest, but the actual switch was easy. There was no one around to see her.

Sarah played her solo for the judges the next day. Ann's flute sounded lovely, but Sarah made lots of stupid mistakes. Her fingers felt like rubber. She couldn't concentrate.

Afterwards, she found Ann warming up for the band's contest number, using, of course, Sarah's old tin-pipe flute. As Sarah sat down in her own place beside Ann's first-flute spot, Ann stopped playing and turned to face her.

"Ann, I'm so sorry," Sarah whispered, her face burning. "I'm so ashamed. I just feel sick, and have all day."

Ann looked at Sarah for a long minute and then smiled. "Let's just forget it happened," she said. "It's OK, really."

But Sarah knew it wasn't OK. Not quite. Ann had forgiven her, but it would be harder for Sarah to forgive herself. She had let herself down.

People like Sarah have always faced temptation, and sometimes they've given in. **Psalm 130** shows the need for forgiveness of these sins.

- What might the psalmist advise Sarah to do next in her situation?
- What temptations do you face that you need to ask God to help you sort out?

Consider . . .

- writing on a slip of paper the main temptations you face today and then asking God each week to help you to overcome them.
- apologising to someone for something you did that hurt him or her.

For more, see . . .

- Isaiah 44:22–23 (p.687)
- 1 Corinthians 15:1–5 (p.1235)
- Jeremiah 31:31–34 (p.753)

15I will bless her with plenty;
I will fill her poor with food.
16I will cover her priests with salvation,
and those who worship me will really sing for joy.
17"I will make a king come from the family of David.
I will provide my appointed one descendants to rule after him.
18I will cover his enemies with shame,
but his crown will shine."

The Love of God's People

A song for going up to worship. Of David.

133 It is good and pleasant
when God's people live together in peace!
2It is like perfumed oil poured on the priest's head
and running down his beard.
It ran down Aaron's beard
and on to the collar of his robes.
3It is like the dew of Mount Hermon
falling on the hills of Jerusalem.
There the LORD gives his blessing
of life for ever.

Temple Guards, Praise the LORD

A song for going up to worship.

134 Praise the LORD, all you servants of the LORD,
you who serve at night in the Temple [d] of the LORD.
2Raise your hands in the Temple
and praise the LORD.
3May the LORD bless you from Mount Zion, [d]
he who made heaven and earth.

> **Sidelight** The night servants in the Temple (Psalm 134:1) were the security guards of their day. They kept the keys to the temple gates and made sure that no one walked off with the valuables stored there.

The LORD Saves, Idols do Not

135 Praise the LORD!
Praise the name of the LORD;
praise him, you servants of the LORD,
2you who stand in the LORD's Temple [d]
and in the Temple courtyards.
3Praise the LORD, because he is good;
sing praises to him, because it is pleasant.
4The LORD has chosen the people of Jacob for himself;
he has chosen the people of Israel for his very own.
5I know that the LORD is great.
Our Lord is greater than all the gods.
6The LORD does what he pleases,
in heaven and on earth,
in the seas and the deep oceans.
7He brings the clouds from the ends of the earth.
He sends the lightning with the rain.
He brings out the wind from his storehouses.
8He destroyed the firstborn [d] sons in Egypt
the firstborn of both people and animals.
9He did many signs and miracles [d] in Egypt
against the king and his servants.
10He defeated many nations
and killed powerful kings:
11Sihon king of the Amorites,
Og king of Bashan,
and all the kings of Canaan.
12Then he gave their land as a gift,
a gift to his people, the Israelites.
13LORD, your name is everlasting;
LORD, you will be remembered for ever.
14The LORD defends his people
and has mercy on his servants.
15The idols of other nations are made of silver and gold,
the work of human hands.
16They have mouths, but they cannot speak.
They have eyes, but they cannot see.
17They have ears, but they cannot hear.
They have no breath in their mouths.
18People who make idols will be like them,
and so will those who trust them.
19Family of Israel, praise the LORD.
Family of Aaron, praise the LORD.
20Family of Levi, praise the LORD.
You who respect the LORD should praise him.
21You people of Jerusalem, praise the LORD on Mount Zion. [d]

Praise the LORD!

God's Love Continues For Ever

136 Give thanks to the LORD because he is good.
His love continues for ever.
2Give thanks to the God of gods.
His love continues for ever.
3Give thanks to the Lord of lords.
His love continues for ever.

4Only he can do great miracles.[d]
His love continues for ever.
5With his wisdom he made the skies.
His love continues for ever.
6He spread out the earth on the seas.
His love continues for ever.
7He made the sun and the moon.
His love continues for ever.
8He made the sun to rule the day.
His love continues for ever.
9He made the moon and stars to rule the night.
His love continues for ever.

10He killed the firstborn[d] sons of the Egyptians.
His love continues for ever.
11He brought the people of Israel out of Egypt.
His love continues for ever.
12He did it with his great power and strength.
His love continues for ever.

13He parted the water of the Red Sea.[d]
His love continues for ever.
14He brought the Israelites through the middle of it.
His love continues for ever.
15But the king of Egypt and his army drowned in the Red Sea.
His love continues for ever.

16He led his people through the desert.
His love continues for ever.
17He defeated great kings.
His love continues for ever.
18He killed powerful kings.
His love continues for ever.
19He defeated Sihon king of the Amorites.
His love continues for ever.
20He defeated Og king of Bashan.
His love continues for ever.
21He gave their land as a gift.
His love continues for ever.
22It was a gift to his servants, the Israelites.
His love continues for ever.

23He remembered us when we were in trouble.
His love continues for ever.
24He freed us from our enemies.
His love continues for ever.
25He gives food to every living creature.
His love continues for ever.

26Give thanks to the God of heaven.
His love continues for ever.

Israelites in Captivity

137 By the rivers in Babylon we sat and cried
when we remembered Jerusalem.
2On the poplar trees nearby
we hung our harps.
3Those who captured us asked us to sing;
our enemies wanted happy songs.
They said, "Sing us a song about Jerusalem!"

4But we cannot sing songs about the LORD
while we are in this foreign country!
5Jerusalem, if I forget you,
let my right hand lose its skill.
6Let my tongue stick to the roof of my mouth
if I do not remember you,
if I do not think about Jerusalem
as my greatest joy.

7LORD, remember what the Edomites did
on the day Jerusalem fell.
They said, "Tear it down!
Tear it down to its foundations!"

8People of Babylon, you will be destroyed.
The people who pay you back for what you did to us will be happy.
9They will grab your babies
and throw them against the rocks.

A Hymn of Thanksgiving

A psalm of David.

138 LORD, I will thank you with all my heart;
I will sing to you before the gods.
2I will bow down facing your holy Temple,[d]
and I will thank you for your love and loyalty.
You have made your name and your word
greater than anything.
3On the day I called to you, you answered me.
You made me strong and brave.

4LORD, let all the kings of the earth praise you
when they hear the words you speak.
5They will sing about what the LORD has done,
because the LORD's glory is great.

6Though the LORD is supreme,
he takes care of those who are humble,
but he stays away from the proud.
7LORD, even when I have trouble all around me,
you will keep me alive.
When my enemies are angry,
you will reach down and save me by your power.
8LORD, you do everything for me.
LORD, your love continues for ever.
Do not leave us, whom you made.

God Knows Everything

For the director of music. A psalm of David.

139 LORD, you have examined me
and know all about me.
2You know when I sit down and when I
get up.
You know my thoughts before I think
them.
3You know where I go and where I lie down.
You know thoroughly everything I do.
4LORD, even before I say a word,
you already know it.

5You are all around me—in front and at the
back—
and have put your hand on me.
6Your knowledge is amazing to me;
it is more than I can understand.
7Where can I go to get away from your
Spirit?[d]
Where can I run from you?
8If I go up to the heavens, you are there.
If I lie down in the grave, you are there.
9If I rise with the sun in the east
and settle in the west beyond the sea,
10even there you would guide me.
With your right hand you would
hold me.

11I could say, "The darkness will hide me.
Let the light around me turn into night."
12But even the darkness is not dark to you.
The night is as light as the day;
darkness and light are the same to you.

13You made my whole being;
you formed me in my mother's body.

ABORTION

Precious

Chelsea had an abortion four years ago. She hadn't planned to, it just sort of happened. She hadn't planned to have sex with Ben or get pregnant either, that just sort of happened too. They were both shocked when they found out. It was too much to take in what with Ben's parents' divorce and their GCSEs. They split up three weeks later and Chelsea was advised to get rid of "It". She was told to move on with her life and forget it ever happened.

But it wasn't so easy to move on and forget. She began counselling sessions at a local church and, over the next two years, Chelsea began to deal with the pain and anger she felt. Each week she talked and prayed with her counsellor.

What did God think of her and what she had done to her baby? How could God forgive her? How could she ever forgive herself? One evening, as she was reading the words of Psalm 139 she felt an incredible sense of peace and it was then she knew: she belonged to God, she was his daughter. All the days of her life were precious and planned by her heavenly Father. She would never forget her past but she knew now that she had a future with the loving arms of God wrapped around her.

Take a look at **Psalm 139:13–16**.

- You're God's greatest invention! He put a lot of time and effort into you. Besides yourself, what's your other favourite invention of God's e.g. sand, guinea pigs, clouds?
- In verse 23, the psalm writer asks God to examine him to see if there is any bad thing in him. Do we make the most of God taking an interest in everything we do?

Consider . . .

- whether you know of anyone who thinks that their birth was "just an accident". How could you use this psalm to let them know they're precious to God?
- whether there are things in your life that you find hard to ask forgiveness for. Find someone in your church or youth group that you trust who will pray with you.

For more, see . . .

- Matthew 7:1–5 (p.949)
- Romans 8:38–39 (p.1197)

14I praise you because you made me in an
amazing and wonderful way.
What you have done is wonderful.
I know this very well.
15You saw my bones being formed
as I took shape in my mother's body.
When I was put together there,
16 you saw my body as it was formed.
All the days planned for me
were written in your book
before I was one day old.

17God, your thoughts are precious to me.
They are so many!
18If I could count them,
they would be more than all the grains of
sand.
When I wake up,
I am still with you.

19God, I wish you would kill the wicked!
Get away from me, you murderers!
20They say evil things about you.
Your enemies use your name
thoughtlessly.
21LORD, I hate those who hate you;
I hate those who rise up against you.
22I feel only hate for them;
they are my enemies.

23God, examine me and know my heart;
test me and know my nervous thoughts.
24See if there is any bad thing in me.
Lead me on the road to everlasting life.

A Prayer for Protection

For the director of music. A psalm of David.

140 LORD, rescue me from evil people;
protect me from cruel people
2who make evil plans,
who always start fights.
3They make their tongues sharp as a snake's;
their words are like snake poison. *Selah*[d]

4LORD, guard me from the power of wicked
people;
protect me from cruel people
who plan to trip me up.
5The proud hid a trap for me.
They spread out a net beside the road;
they set traps for me. *Selah*
6I said to the LORD, "You are my God."
LORD, listen to my prayer for help.
7LORD God, my mighty Saviour,
you protect me in battle.
8LORD, do not give the wicked what they
want.
Don't let their plans succeed,
or they will become proud. *Selah*

9Those around me have planned trouble.
Now let it come to them.
10Let burning coals fall on them.
Throw them into the fire
or into pits from which they cannot escape.
11Don't let liars settle in the land.
Let evil quickly hunt down cruel people.

12I know the LORD will get justice for the poor
and will defend the needy in court.
13Good people will praise his name;
honest people will live in his presence.

A Prayer Not to Sin

A psalm of David.

141 LORD, I call to you. Come quickly.
Listen to me when I call to you.
2Let my prayer be like incense[d] placed
before you,
and my praise like the evening sacrifice.

3LORD, help me control my tongue;
help me be careful about what I say.
4Take away my desire to do evil
or to join others in doing wrong.
Don't let me eat tasty food
with those who do evil.

5If a good person punished me, that would be
kind.
If he corrected me, that would be like
perfumed oil on my head.
I shouldn't refuse it.

But I pray against those who do evil.
6 Let their leaders be thrown down the cliffs.
Then people will know that I have spoken
correctly:
7"The ground is ploughed and broken up.
In the same way, our bones have been
scattered at the grave."

8GOD, I look to you for help.
I trust in you, LORD. Don't let me die.
9Protect me from the traps they set for me
and from the net that evil people have
spread.
10Let the wicked fall into their own nets,
but let me pass by safely.

A Prayer for Safety

A maskil[d] of David when he was in the cave.
A prayer.

142 I cry out to the LORD;
I pray to the LORD for mercy.
2I pour out my problems to him;
I tell him my troubles.

3When I am afraid,
you, LORD, know the way out.

In the path where I walk,
a trap is hidden for me.
4Look around me and see.
No one cares about me.
I have no place of safety;
no one cares if I live.

5LORD, I cry out to you.
I say, "You are my protection.
You are all I want in this life."
6Listen to my cry,
because I am helpless.
Save me from those who are chasing me,
because they are too strong for me.
7Free me from my prison,
and then I will praise your name.

Then good people will surround me,
because you have taken care of me.

A Prayer Not to be Killed

A psalm of David.

143 LORD, hear my prayer;
listen to my cry for mercy.
Answer me
because you are loyal and good.
2Don't judge me, your servant,
because no one alive is right before
you.

3My enemies are chasing me;
they crushed me to the ground.
They made me live in darkness
like those long dead.
4I am afraid;
my courage is gone.

5I remember what happened long ago;
I consider everything you have done.
I think about all you have made.
6I lift my hands to you in prayer.
As a dry land needs rain, I thirst for you.
Selah[d]

7LORD, answer me quickly,
because I am getting weak.
Don't turn away from me,
or I will be like those who are dead.
8Tell me in the morning about your love,
because I trust you.
Show me what I should do,
because my prayers go up to you.
9LORD, save me from my enemies;
I hide in you.
10Teach me to do what you want,
because you are my God.
Let your good Spirit[d]
lead me on level ground.

11LORD, let me live
so people will praise you.
In your goodness
save me from my troubles.
12In your love defeat my enemies.
Destroy all those who trouble me,
because I am your servant.

A Prayer for Victory

Of David.

144 Praise the LORD, my Rock,[d]
who trains me for war,
who trains me for battle.
2He protects me like a fortified city, and he
loves me.
He is my defender and my Saviour,
my shield and my protection.
He helps me keep my people under
control.

3LORD, why are people important to you?
Why do you even think about human
beings?
4People are like a breath;
their lives are like passing shadows.

5LORD, tear open the sky and come down.
Touch the mountains so they will smoke.
6Send the lightning and scatter my enemies.
Shoot your arrows and force them away.
7Reach down from above.
Save me and rescue me out of this sea of
enemies,
from these foreigners.
8They are liars;
they are dishonest.

9God, I will sing a new song to you;
I will play to you on the ten-stringed
harp.
10You give victory to kings.
You save your servant David from cruel
swords.
11Save me, rescue me from these foreigners.
They are liars; they are dishonest.
12Let our sons in their youth
grow like plants.
Let our daughters be
like the decorated stones in the Temple.[d]
13Let our barns be filled
with crops of all kinds.
Let our sheep in the fields have
thousands and tens of thousands of lambs.
14 Let our cattle be strong.
Let no one break in.
Let there be no war,
no screams in our streets.

15Happy are those who are like this;
happy are the people whose God is the
LORD.

Praise to God the King

A psalm of praise. Of David.

145 I praise your greatness, my God the King;
I will praise you for ever and ever.
2 I will praise you every day;
I will praise you for ever and ever.
3 The LORD is great and worthy of our praise;
no one can understand how great he is.

4 Parents will tell their children what you have done.
They will retell your mighty acts,
5 wonderful majesty and glory.
And I will think about your miracles.[d]
6 They will tell about the amazing things you do,
and I will tell how great you are.
7 They will remember your great goodness
and will sing about your fairness.

8 The LORD is kind and shows mercy.
He does not become angry quickly but is full of love.
9 The LORD is good to everyone;

ADDICTION

Burning Desire

Lisa and Paula were good friends at work. They shared the same interests and laughed at the same jokes. One day Lisa came in to the office waving two tickets in her hand.

"You'll never guess what!" she smiled at her friend. "I've won two seats for Wembley Arena on Thursday!"

Paula jumped out of her chair. "Oh that's fantastic! Who are you going to take?"

Lisa was waiting for this question, because she knew that the band who were playing at the arena, were one of Paula's favourites, and hers too.

"Well, I thought I might ask you . . . " she said lightly, knowing her friend would be thrilled.

The girls spent some time talking about what they were going to wear and then Lisa said, "The only thing is, it's a mid-week concert and we have to be back for work the next day, so I wondered if you should stay at our house for the night and then we could travel back to work together."

The plans were made, the concert was everything they dreamed of, and then the next morning . . .

Lisa found that waking her friend was a real problem. She shook her a few times and finally she roused from sleep.

"Paula! We're going to be late! Please get up!" cried a worried Lisa. Paula looked over the top of the duvet and said, "Give me a minute." With that she groped over the side of the bed and took a cigarette from her bag and lit it.

"Oh Paula! I can't believe you can do that!"

"Do what?" asked her friend.

"Put a cigarette in your mouth before you've even opened your eyes properly, or had a cup of tea or anything!" replied Lisa.

Paula looked at her friend wearily and said, "If you want me to get out of this bed, I need it. Believe me. I need it."

Read **Psalm 143:5–10** to find out what David needed.

- What is the difference between Paula's need and psalm writer David's need according to this passage?
- What are the likely outcomes of pursuing these two needs (addictions) for a long time?

Consider . . .

- Making a list of things you "need" and ask yourself if any of them have a harmful effect on your life.
- Asking the Lord to help you give up smoking, or help a friend who may wish to quit.

For more, see . . .

- Psalm 63:1–5 (p.536)
- 2 Peter 2:19 (p.1367)
- 1 Corinthians 3:16 (p.1218)

Sidelight If you're looking for something new to pray before each meal, try Psalm 145. This psalm is still recited in the morning, at noon and in the evening in Jewish synagogues. A fourth-century rabbi believed that reciting the psalm three times a day would assure one a place in the world to come.

he is merciful to all he has made.
10LORD, everything you have made will
praise you;
those who belong to you will bless you.
11They will tell about the glory of your
kingdom
and will speak about your power.
12Then everyone will know the mighty things
you do
and the glory and majesty of your kingdom.
13Your kingdom will go on and on,
and you will rule for ever.

The LORD will keep all his promises;
he is loyal to all he has made.
14The LORD helps those who have been
defeated
and takes care of those who are in trouble.
15All living things look to you for food,
and you give it to them at the right time.
16You open your hand,
and you satisfy all living things.
17Everything the LORD does is right.
He is loyal to all he has made.
18The LORD is close to everyone who prays
to him,
to all who truly pray to him.
19He gives those who respect him what they
want.
He listens when they cry, and he saves
them.

HUNGER AND POVERTY

Real Food

Linda's parents tell her that street beggars misuse money, spending it on drugs and alcohol. She sees the Big Issue seller outside the supermarket everyday on her way home from school. She doesn't like buying it, as she never has time to read it.

There is this one guy who sits in the underpass. He hardly looks up as he speaks. "Spare some change please," he says in a sickly, quiet voice. Linda tries to get eye contact.

"Sorry," she says, wanting to chat. She knows her parents would be cross if she gave the man money but perhaps she can make friends with him – bring him a sandwich or something.

After a few weeks, she does manage to sit by the man and chat for a few minutes. His name is Adam. He doesn't do drugs. He drinks sometimes as it makes him happier. He ran away from home aged fifteen when his stepfather threatened to kill him, and not for the first time. He shows Linda some sketches he has done of people who pass by. They are very good. He has a real eye for a mannerism. They are like cartoons. He shows her a picture he did of her. She has a halo round her head. She cries.

One day, at home by herself, Linda reads **Psalm 146**. She notices in particular verse 7 and wonders whether if God feeds the hungry perhaps she should stop worrying and leave it to him.

- What should Linda do?
- How does God feed the hungry today?

Consider . . .

- whether your prayer list is too local. How often do you pray for other parts of the world where there is terrible poverty?
- finding out whether there is a project for the homeless near you that you could volunteer to help with.

For more, see . . .

- Psalm 140:12–13 (p.582)
- Matthew 25:31–46 (p.987)
- Isaiah 61:1–3 (p.705)

20 The LORD protects everyone who loves him,
but he will destroy the wicked.

21 I will praise the LORD.
Let everyone praise his holy name for ever.

Praise God Who Helps the Weak

146 Praise the LORD!
My whole being, praise the LORD.
2 I will praise the LORD all my life;
I will sing praises to my God as long as I live.

3 Do not put your trust in princes
or other people, who cannot save you.
4 When people die, they are buried.
Then all of their plans come to an end.

5 Happy are those who are helped by the God
of Jacob.
Their hope is in the LORD their God.
6 He made heaven and earth,
the sea and everything in it.
He remains loyal for ever.
7 He does what is fair for those who have been
wronged.
He gives food to the hungry.
The LORD sets the prisoners free.
8 The LORD gives sight to the blind.
The LORD lifts up people who are in
trouble.
The LORD loves those who do right.
9 The LORD protects the foreigners.
He defends the orphans and widows,
but he blocks the way of the wicked.

10 The LORD will be King for ever.
Jerusalem, your God is everlasting.

Praise the LORD!

Praise God Who Helps His People

147 Praise the LORD!

It is good to sing praises to our God;
it is good and pleasant to praise him.

WORSHIP

Carrying a Rhythm of Praise

Phil was feeling like a fraud. He was starting to realise that when he was in church, he would sing songs declaring his love for God, making extravagant promises to read his Bible twenty-eight hours a day and to pray for five hours before he went to school. But then in the very next instant, he had forgotten all of his promises and abandoned all of his good intentions, his lifestyle not matching his words. Phil started to wonder if it was all worth it, because at the end of the day, he just felt guilty for not doing the things he said he would. Then a small phrase from a book Phil was reading really struck him: "Saving faith is the confidence that if you sell all you have and forsake all sinful pleasures, the hidden treasure of holy joy will satisfy your deepest desires" (John Piper – *Desiring God*).

Phil suddenly realised that Jesus is more amazing and more brilliant than anything he could pursue in this world. That's why, when he was in that place of worship, he just wanted to give it all – what else can you do when presented with such beauty? The journey for Phil became about carrying the rhythm of those moments into the rest of his life. When Phil forgot to read his Bible or pray, he didn't feel guilty, he was just gutted that he'd missed out on spending time with his mate, Jesus.

Read **Psalm 150** and see the response of the psalmist as he gets a glimpse of God.

- Have you ever felt like Phil, full of good intentions, but sadly lacking the lifestyle to match?
- How does Phil's story inspire you? Does the psalmist inspire you about what your reaction is when you're face to face with God?

Consider . . .

- your walk with Jesus so far. How much of it has been about you, your failings and issues? How much of it has been about him and who he is?
- making a list of things you're going to do this week to pursue Jesus – not because you have to, but because he's worth it!

For more, see . . .

- Psalm 96 (p.556)
- Isaiah 6:1–8 (p.645)

2 The LORD rebuilds Jerusalem;
he brings back the captured Israelites.
3 He heals the broken-hearted
and bandages their wounds.

4 He counts the stars
and names each one.
5 Our Lord is great and very powerful.
There is no limit to what he knows.
6 The LORD defends the humble,
but he throws the wicked to the ground.

7 Sing praises to the LORD;
praise our God with harps.
8 He fills the sky with clouds
and sends rain to the earth
and makes grass grow on the hills.
9 He gives food to cattle
and to the little birds that call.

10 He does not enjoy the strength of a horse
or the strength of a man.
11 The LORD is pleased with those who
respect him,
with those who trust his love.

12 Jerusalem, praise the LORD;
Jerusalem, praise your God.
13 He makes your city gates strong
and blesses your children inside.
14 He brings peace to your country
and fills you with the finest grain.

15 He gives a command to the earth,
and it quickly obeys him.
16 He spreads the snow like wool
and scatters the frost like ashes.
17 He throws down hail like rocks.
No one can stand the cold he sends.
18 Then he gives a command, and it melts.
He sends the breezes, and the waters flow.
19 He gave his word to Jacob,
his laws and demands to Israel.

MUSIC

Turn it Up Loud

Jenny did not believe in God. Her best friend Louise, however, was the complete opposite. She was a Christian and she was not shy about telling anyone. Jenny couldn't understand why Louise was so excited about her faith because when she thought of Christians all she could imagine was a bunch of old people, sitting in a huge church not being allowed to talk. Because of this, when Louise invited Jenny to a youth night run by her church Jenny said she'd go, but deep down wasn't looking forward to it. At 8 p.m. that night, Louise knocked on Jenny's door and together they drove to the church. Even before the girls walked through the doors, they could hear the loud music pumping out and the laughing and chattering coming from inside. Louise was smiling but Jenny looked confused.

"I thought churches were supposed to be quiet places where people go to pray," Jenny said.

"They can be," said Louise. "But that's not all church is. We believe we've got something to celebrate and you can't celebrate something that amazing in a quiet way all the time, can you! Imagine it was your birthday and instead of all your friends being upbeat and excited around you, they just handed you your presents with a quick handshake. How would you feel?"

Slowly it started to dawn on Jenny that the way in which Louise expressed her faith was very different to how she had first imagined, not all quiet and timid but actually using music and creating a great party atmosphere.

Louise was right in saying that Christians can praise God in all sorts of ways. Check out **Psalm 150**.

- There are many different ways to praise God. What are some of those mentioned in this psalm?
- When praising God, have you ever experienced the loud, party atmosphere described in this psalm?

Consider . . .

- looking at the way you thank God for things. Try to find new and exciting ways to express your praise.
- having a party with some friends in God's honour. Enjoy it and thank him with that same party atmosphere.

For more, see . . .

- Exodus 15:19–21 (p.73)
- John 12:3 (p.1116)
- Mark 11:8–10 (p.1019)

20He didn't do this for any other nation.
They don't know his laws.

Praise the LORD!

The World Should Praise the Lord

148 Praise the LORD!

Praise the LORD from the skies.
Praise him high above the earth.
2Praise him, all you angels.
Praise him, all you armies of heaven.
3Praise him, sun and moon.
Praise him, all you shining stars.
4Praise him, highest heavens
and you waters above the sky.
5Let them praise the LORD,
because they were created by his command.
6He put them in place for ever and ever;
he made a law that will never change.

7Praise the LORD from the earth,
you large sea animals and all the oceans,
8lightning and hail, snow and mist
and stormy winds that obey him,
9mountains and all hills,
fruit trees and all cedars,
10wild animals and all cattle,
crawling animals and birds,
11kings of the earth and all nations,
princes and all rulers of the earth,
12young men and women,
old people and children.

13Praise the LORD,
because he alone is great.
He is more wonderful than heaven and earth.
14God has given his people a king.
He should be praised by all who belong to him;
he should be praised by the Israelites, the people closest to his heart.

Praise the LORD!

Praise the God of Israel

149 Praise the LORD!

Sing a new song to the LORD;
sing his praise in the meeting of his people.

2Let the Israelites be happy because of God, their Maker.
Let the people of Jerusalem rejoice because of their King.
3They should praise him with dancing.
They should sing praises to him with tambourines[d] and harps.
4The LORD is pleased with his people;
he saves the humble.
5Let those who worship him rejoice in his glory.
Let them sing for joy even in bed!

6Let them shout his praise
with their two-edged swords in their hands.
7They will punish the nations
and defeat the people.
8They will put those kings in chains
and those important men in iron bands.
9They will punish them as God has written.
God is honoured by all who worship him.

Praise the LORD!

Praise the LORD with Music

150 Praise the LORD!

Praise God in his Temple;[d]
praise him in his mighty heaven.
2Praise him for his strength;
praise him for his greatness.
3Praise him with trumpet blasts;
praise him with harps and lyres.[d]
4Praise him with tambourines[d] and dancing;
praise him with stringed instruments and flutes.
5Praise him with loud cymbals;
praise him with crashing cymbals.
6Let everything that breathes praise the LORD.

Praise the LORD!

Proverbs

Why Read This Book:

- Discover life's basic goal (Proverbs 2:1–15).
- Find clear guidance on right and wrong (Proverbs 3, 10–23).
- Learn how to be wise instead of foolish (Proverbs 4, 6, 8, 9, 24).

When?

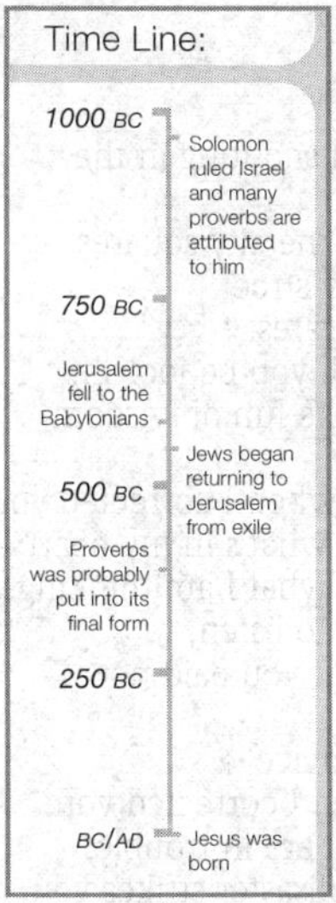

Behind the Scenes:

If you like "quotable quotes" or bumper sticker slogans, you'll love Proverbs. Unlike other books of the Bible, Proverbs is mostly a collection of one- and two-line sayings on various everyday subjects – family life, work, money, getting along with others, honesty and many more. These sayings represent the heart of important truths about life and relationships. This is the wisdom of God for every day.

The book is filled with sharp phrases, dramatic contrasts and vivid scenes from everyday life. A chapter may deal with dozens of different subjects (for example, see chapter 14). Because of their short, catchy style, these proverbs are easy to memorise. Other parts of Proverbs are longer, unified poems about wisdom, which is personified as a woman (see Proverbs 1:20–33).

Proverbs is divided into eight main sections. It begins with an introduction on wisdom (Proverbs 1–9), then has six collections of sayings by various "wise men" (Proverbs 10–31:9). It concludes with an acrostic poem on a perfect wife (Proverbs 31:10–31). Many scholars note that the perfect wife at the end of Proverbs is actually a fulfilment of all the virtues described in the rest of the book.

Collected hundreds of years ago to teach young people principles for life, Proverbs can still help guide us to make wise choices. And though many parts of Proverbs don't explicitly mention God, the sayings were gathered to help us to follow God in everything we do.

LIFE FILE LINKS

Investigate the Theme

To find a list of real life stories on this subject turn to the LIFE FILE GUIDE on pages 12 to 22 at the front of the Youth Bible.

PRIORITIES

The Importance of Proverbs

1 These are the wise words of Solomon son of David, king of Israel.

2They teach wisdom and self-control;
they will help you understand wise words.

Sidelight

Proverbs – short, catchy sayings – aren't found just in the book of Proverbs. They were a common type of writing in ancient times, and Jesus used them regularly in his teaching. See some examples in Matthew 6:21 (p.948) and Matthew 7:13 (p.950).

3They will teach you how to be wise and
self-controlled
and will teach you to do what is honest
and fair and right.
4They make the uneducated clever
and give knowledge and sense to the young.
5Wise people can also listen and learn;
even clever people can find good advice in
these words.
6Then anyone can understand wise words and
stories,
the words of the wise and their riddles.

7Knowledge begins with respect for the LORD,
but fools hate wisdom and self-control.

Warnings Against Evil

8My child, listen to your father's teaching
and do not forget your mother's advice.
9Their teaching will be like flowers in your
hair
or a necklace around your neck.

10My child, if sinners try to lead you into sin,
do not follow them.
11They will say, "Come with us.
Let's ambush and kill someone;
let's attack some innocent people just
for fun.
12Let's swallow them alive, as death does;
let's swallow them whole, as the grave
does.
13We will take all kinds of valuable things
and fill our houses with stolen goods.
14Come and join us,
and we will share with you stolen goods."
15My child, do not go along with them;
do not do what they do.
16They are eager to do evil
and are quick to kill.
17It is useless to spread out a net
right where the birds can see it.
18But sinners will fall into their own traps;
they will only catch themselves!
19All greedy people end up this way;
greed kills selfish people.

Wisdom Speaks

20Wisdom is like a woman shouting in the
street;
she raises her voice in the city squares.
21She cries out in the noisy street
and shouts at the city gates: *n*
22"You fools, how long will you be foolish?
How long will you make fun of wisdom
and hate knowledge?
23If only you had listened when I corrected you,
I would have told you what's in my heart;
I would have told you what I am thinking.
24I called, but you refused to listen;
I held out my hand, but you paid no
attention.
25You did not follow my advice
and did not listen when I corrected you.
26So I will laugh when you are in trouble.
I will make fun when disaster strikes you,
27when disaster comes over you like a storm,
when trouble strikes you like a whirlwind,
when pain and trouble overwhelm you.

28"Then you will call to me,
but I will not answer.
You will look for me,
but you will not find me.
29It is because you rejected knowledge
and did not choose to respect the LORD.
30You did not accept my advice,
and you rejected my correction.
31So you will get what you deserve;
you will get what you planned for others.
32Fools will die because they refuse to listen;
they will be destroyed because they do not
care.
33But those who listen to me will live in safety
and be at peace, without fear of injury."

Rewards of Wisdom

2 My child, listen to what I say
and remember what I command you.
2Listen carefully to wisdom;
set your mind on understanding.
3Cry out for wisdom,
and beg for understanding.

city gates People came here to conduct business. Public meetings and court cases were also held here.

4Search for it like silver,
and hunt for it like hidden treasure.
5Then you will understand respect for the LORD,
and you will find that you know God.
6Only the LORD gives wisdom;
he gives knowledge and understanding.
7He stores up wisdom for those who are
honest.
Like a shield he protects the innocent.
8He makes sure that justice is done,
and he protects those who are loyal
to him.

9Then you will understand what is honest and
fair
and what is the good and right thing to do.
10Wisdom will come into your mind,
and knowledge will be pleasing to you.
11Good sense will protect you;
understanding will guard you.
12It will keep you from the wicked,
from those whose words are bad,
13who don't do what is right
but what is evil.
14They enjoy doing wrong
and are happy to do what is crooked and
evil.
15What they do is wrong,
and their ways are dishonest.

16It will save you from the unfaithful wife
who tries to lead you into adultery[d] with
pleasing words.
17She leaves the husband she married when she
was young.
She ignores the promise she made before God.

SCHOOL

Wise Up!

At the end of year 7, Jason was top in his year in all subjects. His favourite subjects were maths and English, but he was also excellent in sports and music. Everyone liked him and would ask him the questions to the homework that no one else could answer! When he finished year 8, the teachers had high hopes that he'd go on to be one of the brightest pupils in the country.

However, by the time Jason reached year 9 he had started to MC with a crew that met near his house. Jason had a quick mind and was brilliant at writing lyrics for raps and soon he learnt how to battle other MCs. He began to make a name for himself with the crews around his area and started hanging out till the early hours of the morning and not going into school. By year 10, he had started getting involved in the drug culture too and began to get violent. His teachers started to get concerned when they saw that Jason's attendance at school was dropping and that his grades were slipping.

One teacher, Mr Mason, turned things around. He showed Jason that he could get into music after he had done his exams and that this was his only shot at the exams. Jason knew he was right and decided to go for it.

When Jason's exam results came through, he had come 10th in the country. Mr Mason came over to congratulate him and offer to help with his music career.

Jason replied, "I should be thanking you. I feel like I can do so much with my life now!"

Read **Proverbs 2:1–10**.

- What are the rewards of hard work and dedication, and what did Jason have to do to get them?
- Do these rewards apply to you? What rewards from learning and education do you want?

Consider . . .

- verse 1 which says – "remember what I command you". Write down some of the commands of God and ask him to help you keep them.
- asking a teacher, youth leader, family member or friend to give you extra help with the subjects at school that you find difficult.

For more, see . . .

- 1 Kings 3:4–15 (p.316)
- James 1:5 (p.1348)
- Colossians 2:1–4 (p.1291)

18Her house is on the way to death;
those who took that path are now all dead.
19No one who goes to her comes back
or walks the path of life again.

20But wisdom will help you be good
and do what is right.
21Those who are honest will live in the land,
and those who are innocent will remain
in it.
22But the wicked will be removed from the
land,
and the unfaithful will be thrown out of it.

Advice to Children

3 My child, do not forget my teaching,
but keep my commands in mind.
2Then you will live a long time,
and your life will be successful.

3Don't ever forget kindness and truth.
Wear them like a necklace.
Write them on your heart as if on a tablet.
4Then you will be respected
and will please both God and people.

5Trust the LORD with all your heart,
and don't depend on your own
understanding.
6Remember the LORD in all you do,
and he will give you success.

7Don't depend on your own wisdom.
Respect the LORD and refuse to do wrong.
8Then your body will be healthy,
and your bones will be strong.

9Honour the LORD with your wealth
and the first fruits[d] from all your crops.
10Then your barns will be full,
and your wine barrels will overflow with
new wine.

11My child, do not reject the LORD's discipline,
and don't get angry when he corrects you.
12The LORD corrects those he loves,
just as parents correct the child they
delight in.

13Happy is the person who finds wisdom,
the one who gets understanding.
14Wisdom is worth more than silver;
it brings more profit than gold.
15Wisdom is more precious than rubies;
nothing you could want is equal to it.
16With her right hand wisdom offers you a long
life,
and with her left hand she gives you riches
and honour.
17Wisdom will make your life pleasant
and will bring you peace.
18As a tree produces fruit, wisdom gives life to
those who use it,
and everyone who uses it will be happy.

19The LORD made the earth, using his wisdom.
He set the sky in place, using his
understanding.
20With his knowledge, he made springs flow
into rivers
and the clouds drop rain on the earth.

21My child, hold on to wisdom and
good sense.
Don't let them out of your sight.
22They will give you life
and beauty like a necklace around your
neck.
23Then you will go your way in safety,
and you will not get hurt.
24When you lie down, you won't be afraid;
when you lie down, you will sleep in peace.
25You won't be afraid of sudden trouble;
you won't fear the ruin that comes to the
wicked,
26because the LORD will keep you safe.
He will keep you from being trapped.

27Whenever you are able,
do good to people who need help.
28If you have what your neighbour asks for,
don't say, "Come back later.
I will give it to you tomorrow."
29Don't make plans to hurt your neighbour
who lives nearby and trusts you.
30Don't accuse a person for no good reason;
don't accuse someone who has not
harmed you.

31Don't be jealous of those who use violence,
and don't choose to be like them.
32The LORD hates those who do wrong,
but he is a friend to those who are honest.
33The LORD will curse the evil person's house,
but he will bless the home of those who do
right.
34The LORD laughs at those who laugh at him,
but he gives grace to those who are not
proud.
35Wise people will receive honour,
but fools will be disgraced.

Wisdom is Important

4 My children, listen to your father's
teaching;
pay attention so you will understand.
2What I am telling you is good,
so do not forget what I teach you.
3When I was a young boy in my father's house
and like an only child to my mother,

4my father taught me and said,
"Hold on to my words with all your heart.
Keep my commands and you will live.
5Get wisdom and understanding.
Don't forget or ignore my words.
6Hold on to wisdom, and it will take care
of you.
Love it, and it will keep you safe.
7Wisdom is the most important thing; so get
wisdom.
If it costs everything you have, get
understanding.
8Treasure wisdom, and it will make you great;
hold on to it, and it will bring you honour.
9It will be like flowers in your hair
and like a beautiful crown on your head."

10My child, listen and accept what I say.
Then you will have a long life.
11I am guiding you in the way of wisdom,
and I am leading you on the right path.
12Nothing will hold you back;
you will not be overwhelmed.
13Always remember what you have been taught,
and don't let go of it.
Keep all that you have learned;
it is the most important thing in life.
14Don't follow the ways of the wicked;
don't do what evil people do.
15Avoid their ways, and don't follow them.
Stay away from them and keep on going,
16because they cannot sleep until they do evil.
They cannot rest until they harm someone.
17They feast on wickedness and cruelty
as if they were eating bread and drinking
wine.

18The way of the good person is like the light
of dawn,
growing brighter and brighter until full
daylight.
19But the wicked walk around in the dark;
they can't even see what makes them
stumble.

20My child, pay attention to my words;
listen closely to what I say.
21Don't ever forget my words;
keep them always in mind.
22They are the key to life for those who find them;
they bring health to the whole body.
23Be careful what you think,
because your thoughts run your life.
24Don't use your mouth to tell lies;
don't ever say things that are not true.
25Keep your eyes focused on what is right,
and look straight ahead to what is good.
26Be careful what you do,
and always do what is right.
27Don't turn off the road of goodness;
keep away from evil paths.

Warning About Adultery

5 My son, pay attention to my wisdom;
listen to my words of understanding.
2Be careful to use good sense,
and watch what you say.
3The words of another man's wife may seem
sweet as honey;
they may be as smooth as olive oil.
4But in the end she will bring you sorrow,
causing you pain like a two-edged sword.
5She is on the way to death;
her steps are headed straight to the grave.
6She gives little thought to life.
She doesn't even know that her ways are
wrong.

7Now, my sons, listen to me,
and don't ignore what I say.
8Stay away from such a woman.
Don't even go near the door of her house,
9or you will give your riches to others,
and the best years of your life will be given
to someone cruel.
10Strangers will enjoy your wealth,
and what you worked so hard for will go to
someone else.
11You will groan at the end of your life
when your health is gone.
12Then you will say, "I hated being told what
to do!
I would not listen to correction!
13I would not listen to my teachers
or pay attention to my instructors.
14I came close to being completely ruined
in front of a whole group of people."

15Be faithful to your own wife,
just as you drink water from your own well.
16Don't pour your water in the streets;
don't give your love to just any woman.
17These things are yours alone
and shouldn't be shared with strangers.
18Be happy with the wife you married when
you were young.
She gives you joy, as your fountain gives
you water.
19She is as lovely and graceful as a deer.
Let her love always make you happy;
let her love always hold you captive.
20My son, don't be held captive by a woman
who takes part in adultery. [d]
Don't hold another man's wife.

21The LORD sees everything you do,
and he watches where you go.
22An evil man will be caught in his wicked ways;
the ropes of his sins will tie him up.

23He will die because he does not control
himself,
and he will be held captive by his
foolishness.

Dangers of Being Foolish

6 My child, be careful about giving a
guarantee for somebody else's loan,
about promising to pay what someone else
owes.
2You might get trapped by what you say;
you might be caught by your own words.
3My child, if you have done this and are under
your neighbour's control,
here is how to get free.
Don't be proud. Go to your neighbour
and beg to be free from your promise.
4Don't go to sleep
or even rest your eyes,
5but free yourself like a deer running from a
hunter,
like a bird flying away from a trapper.

6Go and watch the ants, you lazy person.
Watch what they do and be wise.
7Ants have no commander,
no leader or ruler,
8but they store up food in the summer
and gather their supplies at harvest.
9How long will you lie there, you lazy person?
When will you get up from sleeping?
10You sleep a little; you take a nap.
You fold your hands and lie down to rest.
11So you will be as poor as if you had been
robbed;
you will have as little as if you had been
held up.

Sidelight Sleeping until noon was not on for the writer of Proverbs (6:6–11). The book of Proverbs constantly blasts laziness and warns that lazy people will end up poor. He doesn't say that all the poor are lazy. Read the other side of the story in Proverbs 13:23 (p.601) and Proverbs 22:1–2, 22–23 (p.608).

12Some people are wicked and no good.
They go around telling lies,
13winking with their eyes, signalling with their
feet
and making signs with their fingers.
14They make evil plans in their hearts
and are always starting arguments.
15So trouble will strike them in an instant;
suddenly they will be so hurt no one can
help them.

16There are six things the LORD hates.
There are seven things he cannot stand:
17 a proud look,
a lying tongue,
hands that kill innocent people,
18 a mind that thinks up evil plans,
feet that are quick to do evil,
19 a witness who lies,
and someone who starts arguments
among families.

Warning About Adultery

20My son, keep your father's commands,
and don't forget your mother's
teaching.
21Keep their words in mind for ever
as though you had them tied around your
neck.
22They will guide you when you walk.
They will guard you when you sleep.
They will speak to you when you are
awake.
23These commands are like a lamp;
this teaching is like a light.
And the correction that comes from them
will help you have life.
24They will keep you from sinful women
and from the pleasing words of another
man's unfaithful wife.
25Don't desire her because she is beautiful.
Don't let her capture you by the way she
looks at you.
26A prostitute [d] will treat you like a loaf of
bread,
and a woman who takes part in adultery [d]
may cost you your life.
27You cannot carry hot coals against
your chest
without burning your clothes,
28and you cannot walk on hot coals
without burning your feet.
29The same is true if you have sexual relations
with another man's wife.
Anyone who does so will be punished.

30People don't hate a thief
when he steals because he is hungry.
31But if he is caught, he must pay back seven
times what he stole,
and it may cost him everything he owns.
32A man who takes part in adultery has no
sense;
he will destroy himself.
33He will be beaten up and disgraced,
and his shame will never go away.
34Jealousy makes a husband very angry,
and he will have no pity when he gets
revenge.

35He will accept no payment for the wrong;
he will take no amount of money.

The Woman of Adultery

7 My son, remember what I say,
and treasure my commands.
2Obey my commands, and you will live.
Guard my teachings as you would your own eyes.
3Remind yourself of them;
write them on your heart as if on a tablet.
4Treat wisdom as a sister,
and make understanding your closest friend.
5Wisdom and understanding will keep you away from adultery,[d]
away from the unfaithful wife and her pleasing words.

6Once while I was at the window of my house
I looked out through the shutters
7and saw some foolish young men.
I noticed one of them had no wisdom.
8He was walking down the street near the corner
on the road leading to her house.
9It was the twilight of the evening;
the darkness of the night was just beginning.
10Then the woman approached him,
dressed like a prostitute[d]
and planning to trick him.
11She was loud and stubborn
and never stayed at home.
12She was always out in the streets or in the city squares,
waiting around on the corners of the streets.
13She took hold of him and kissed him.
Without shame she said to him,
14"I made my fellowship offering and took some of the meat home.
Today I have kept my special promises.
15So I have come out to meet you;
I have been looking for you and have found you.
16I have covered my bed
with coloured sheets from Egypt.
17I have made my bed smell sweet
with myrrh,[d] aloes[d] and cinnamon.
18Come, let's make love until morning.
Let's enjoy each other's love.
19My husband is not home;
he has gone on a long trip.
20He took a lot of money with him
and won't be home for weeks."
21By her clever words she made him give in;
by her pleasing words she led him into doing wrong.
22All at once he followed her,
like an ox led to the butcher,
like a deer caught in a trap
23 and shot through the liver with an arrow.
Like a bird caught in a trap,
he didn't know what he did would kill him.

24Now, my sons, listen to me;
pay attention to what I say.
25Don't let yourself be tricked by such a woman;
don't go where she leads you.
26She has ruined many good men,
and many have died because of her.
27Her house is on the road to death,
the road that leads down to the grave.

Listen to Wisdom

8 Wisdom calls to you like someone shouting;
understanding raises her voice.
2On the hilltops along the road
and at the crossroads, she stands calling.
3Beside the city gates,[n]
at the entrances into the city, she calls out:
4"Listen, everyone, I'm calling out to you;
I am shouting to all people.
5You who are uneducated, be cleverer.
You who are foolish, get understanding.
6Listen, because I have important things to say,
and what I tell you is right.
7What I say is true,
I refuse to speak evil.
8Everything I say is honest;
nothing I say is crooked or false.
9People with good sense know what I say is true;
and those with knowledge know my words are right.
10Choose my teachings instead of silver,
and knowledge rather than the finest gold.
11Wisdom is more precious than rubies.
Nothing you could want is equal to it.

12"I am wisdom, and I am clever.
I also have knowledge and good sense.
13If you respect the LORD, you will also hate evil.
I hate pride and boasting,
evil ways and lies.

city gates People came here to conduct business. Public meetings and court cases were also held here.

14I have good sense and advice,
and I have understanding and power.
15I help kings to govern
and rulers to make fair laws.
16Princes use me to lead,
and so do all important people who judge fairly.
17I love those who love me,
and those who seek me find me.
18Riches and honour are mine to give.
So are wealth and lasting success.
19What I give is better than the finest gold,
better than the purest silver.
20I do what is right
and follow the path of justice.
21I give wealth to those who love me,
filling their houses with treasures.

22"I, wisdom, was with the LORD when he began his work,
long before he made anything else.
23I was created in the very beginning,
even before the world began.
24I was born before there were oceans,
or springs overflowing with water,
25before the hills were there,
before the mountains were put in place.
26God had not made the earth or fields,
not even the first dust of the earth.
27I was there when God put the skies in place,
when he stretched the horizon over the oceans,
28when he made the clouds above
and put the deep underground springs in place.
29I was there when he ordered the sea
not to go beyond the borders he had set.
I was there when he laid the earth's foundation.
30 I was like a child by his side.
I was delighted every day,
enjoying his presence all the time,
31enjoying the whole world,
and delighted with all its people.

32"Now, my children, listen to me,
because those who follow my ways are happy.

CREATION

Moment of Wonder

Waves rolled under Marty's canoe. One crested behind her and broke, spewing foam over her back. Panic gripped her. She leaned into the wind, paddling hard. Her muscles ached. Why had she taken this outdoor pursuits course?

The answer echoed within her, "to get back in touch with God." But where was he?

When she rounded the rocky point, stillness surrounded her. Sunlight broke through the clouds, sparkling into the blue depths of the protected cove. Marty rested her paddle and looked beneath her. Silver fish darted. She leaned back and gazed at the horizon. Sea birds skimmed inches above the water.

Suddenly the sea split beside her. A dolphin arched high, then dived, circling her. She sucked in her breath, overcome with wonder.

"Lord, oh Lord, you're everywhere!"

The voice of wisdom, in Proverbs, speaks about the joy in observing God's creation. Read about it in **Proverbs 8:22–31**.

- What might wisdom's voice say to Marty from this passage?
- Where do you most strongly sense God's presence? Why?

Consider . . .

- searching for the tiny forms of God's creation as you walk across a garden or open space, and thanking God for them.
- finding a special place in nature where you can go regularly to be with God.

For more, see . . .

- Psalm 104:1–35 (p.560)
- Revelation 4:11 (p.1391)
- Luke 8:22–26 (p.1053)

33 Listen to my teaching, and you will be wise;
do not ignore it.
34 Happy are those who listen to me,
watching at my door every day,
waiting at my open doorway.
35 Those who find me find life,
and the LORD will be pleased with them.
36 Those who do not find me hurt themselves.
Those who hate me love death."

Being Wise or Foolish

9 Wisdom has built her house;
she has made its seven columns.
2 She has prepared her food and wine;
she has set her table.
3 She has sent out her servant girls,
and she calls out from the highest place in
the city.
4 She says to those who are uneducated,
"Come in here, you foolish people!
5 Come and eat my food
and drink the wine I have prepared.
6 Stop your foolish ways, and you will live;
take the road of understanding.

7 "If you correct someone who makes fun of
wisdom, you will be insulted.
If you correct an evil person, you will get
hurt.
8 Do not correct those who make fun of
wisdom, or they will hate you.
But correct the wise, and they will love you.
9 Teach the wise, and they will become even
wiser;
teach good people, and they will learn even
more.

10 "Wisdom begins with respect for the LORD,
and understanding begins with knowing the
Holy One.
11 If you live wisely, you will live a long time;
wisdom will add years to your life.
12 The wise person is rewarded by wisdom,
but whoever makes fun of wisdom will
suffer for it."

SCHOOL

Crossroads

Paul's cane tapped from side to side, sweeping across the pavement. He approached a crossroad, but veered left. As his cane struck metal, he stopped.

"Mr Kennedy? Where am I?" he asked.

Paul's instructor from the school for the blind stood watching Paul's cane technique.

"What have you hit?" he asked. "Listen to the sound of it. Feel it."

Paul swung his cane again, turning his head as he listened to the metallic ring. "It's a car."

"Good. Get back on the pavement and cross the road." The instructor tensed. Would Paul follow what he had been taught? Or would he step into the path of an oncoming car?

Lorries passed in front of Paul. "I'm scared!"

"Listen for the traffic. You can do it," the instructor said.

Finally Paul stepped onto the crossing. The teacher let out a relieved breath; Paul had chosen the right time.

Proverbs 9:8–12 describes the rewards for a wise student who learns from a good teacher, as Paul did.

- According to this passage, where does the wisdom begin?
- Have you ever been regarded as wise, at school or otherwise as mentioned in verse 12?

Consider . . .

- telling a teacher whom you admire how he or she has helped you in life.
- offering to help classmates who are having trouble at school so that you can pass on to others what your teachers have taught you.

For more, see . . .

- Psalm 16:7–11 (p.508)
- John 7:14–18 (p.1108)
- Daniel 1:3–18 (p.833)

13Foolishness is like a loud woman;
she does not have wisdom or
knowledge.
14She sits at the door of her house
at the highest place in the city.
15She calls out to those who are passing by,
who are going along, minding their own
business.
16She says to those who are uneducated,
"Come in here, you foolish people!
17Stolen water is sweeter,
and food eaten in secret tastes better."
18But these people don't know that everyone
who goes there dies,
that her guests end up deep in the grave.

The Wise Words of Solomon

10 These are the wise words of Solomon:

A wise son makes his father happy,
but a foolish son makes his mother sad.

2Riches gained by doing wrong have no value,
but right living will save you from death.

3The LORD does not let good people go hungry,
but he keeps evil people from getting what
they want.

Sidelight

Two sections of Proverbs (Proverbs 10:1—22:16 and 25:1—29:27, p.611) are attributed to Solomon, the king who was said to have spoken 3,000 wise sayings (1 Kings 4:32–34, p.318).

4A lazy person will end up poor,
but a hard worker will become rich.

5Those who gather crops on time are wise,
but those who sleep through the harvest
are a disgrace.

6Good people will have rich blessings,
but the wicked will be overwhelmed by
violence.

7Good people will be remembered as a
blessing,
but evil people will soon be forgotten.

8The wise do what they are told,
but a talkative fool will be ruined.

9The honest person will live in safety,
but the dishonest will be caught.

10A wink may get you into trouble,
and foolish talk will lead to your ruin.

11The words of a good person give life, like a
fountain of water,
but the words of the wicked contain
nothing but violence.

12Hatred stirs up trouble,
but love forgives all wrongs.

13Clever people speak wisely,
but people without wisdom should be
punished.

14The wise don't tell everything they know,
but the foolish talk too much and are
ruined.

15Having lots of money protects the rich,
but having no money destroys the poor.

16Good people are rewarded with life,
but evil people are paid with punishment.

17Whoever accepts correction is on the way to
life,
but whoever ignores correction will lead
others away from life.

18Whoever hides hate is a liar.
Whoever tells lies is a fool.

19If you talk a lot, you are sure to sin;
if you are wise, you will keep quiet.

20The words of a good person are like pure
silver,
but an evil person's thoughts are worth
very little.

21Good people's words will help many others,
but fools will die because they don't have
wisdom.

22The LORD's blessing brings wealth,
and no sorrow comes with it.

23A foolish person enjoys doing wrong,
but a person with understanding enjoys
doing what is wise.

24Evil people will get what they fear most,
but good people will get what they want
most.

25A storm will blow the evil person away,
but a good person will always be safe.

26A lazy person bothers the one he works for
like vinegar on the teeth or smoke in the
eyes.

27Whoever respects the LORD will have a long
life,
but the life of an evil person will be cut
short.

28A good person can look forward to happiness,
but an evil person can expect nothing.

29The LORD will protect good people
but will ruin those who do evil.

30Good people will always be safe,
but evil people will not remain in the land.

31A good person says wise things,
but a liar's tongue will be stopped.

32Good people know the right thing to say,
but evil people only tell lies.

11 The LORD hates dishonest scales,
but he is pleased with honest weights.

2Pride leads only to shame;
it is wise to be humble.

3Good people will be guided by honesty;
dishonesty will destroy those who are not trustworthy.

4Riches will not help when it's time to die,
but right living will save you from death.

5The goodness of the innocent makes life easier,
but the wicked will be destroyed by their wickedness.

6Doing right brings freedom to honest people,
but those who are not trustworthy will be caught by their own desires.

Sidelight Because they didn't have digital scales in Bible times, people had to use stones and metal objects to work out how heavy something was before buying or selling it. They probably used hand-held scales and put the merchandise on one side and the weight on the other. Proverbs 11:1 warns against using inaccurate scales to cheat someone.

7When the wicked die, hope dies with them;
their hope in riches will come to nothing.

8The good person is saved from trouble;
it comes to the wicked instead.

9With words an evil person can destroy a neighbour,
but a good person will escape by being clever.

10When good people succeed, the city is happy.
When evil people die, there are shouts of joy.

11Good people bless and build up their city,
but the wicked can destroy it with their words.

12People without good sense find fault with their neighbours,
but those with understanding keep quiet.

13Gossips can't keep secrets,
but a trustworthy person can.

14Without leadership a nation falls,
but lots of good advice will save it.

15Whoever guarantees to pay somebody else's loan will suffer.
It is safer to avoid such promises.

16A kind woman gets respect,
but cruel men get only wealth.

17Kind people do themselves a favour,
but cruel people bring trouble on themselves.

18An evil person really earns nothing,
but a good person will surely be rewarded.

19Those who are truly good will live,
but those who chase after evil will die.

20The LORD hates those with evil hearts
but is pleased with those who are innocent.

21Evil people will certainly be punished,
but those who do right will be set free.

22A beautiful woman without good sense
is like a gold ring in a pig's snout.

23Those who do right only wish for good,
but the wicked can expect to be defeated by God's anger.

24Some people give much but get back even more.
Others don't give what they should and end up poor.

25Whoever gives to others will get richer;
those who help others will themselves be helped.

26People curse those who keep all the grain,
but they bless the one who is willing to sell it.

27Whoever looks for good will find kindness,
but whoever looks for evil will find trouble.

28Those who trust in riches will be ruined,
but a good person will be healthy like a green leaf.

29Whoever brings trouble to his family
will be left with nothing but the wind.
A fool will be a servant to the wise.

30A good person gives life to others;
the wise person teaches others how to live.

31Good people will be rewarded on earth,
and the wicked and the sinners will be punished.

12 Anyone who loves learning accepts correction,
but a person who hates being corrected is stupid.
2The LORD is pleased with a good person,
but he will punish anyone who plans evil.
3Doing evil brings no safety at all,
but a good person has safety and security.
4A good wife is like a crown for her husband,
but a disgraceful wife is like a disease in his bones.
5The plans that good people make are fair,
but the advice of the wicked will trick you.
6The wicked talk about killing people,
but the words of good people will save them.
7Wicked people die and they are no more,
but a good person's family continues.
8The wisdom of the wise wins praise,
but there is no respect for the stupid.
9A person who is not important but has a servant is better off
than someone who acts important but has no food.
10Good people take care of their animals,
but even the kindest acts of the wicked are cruel.
11Those who work their land will have plenty of food,
but the one who chases empty dreams is not wise.
12The wicked want what other evil people have stolen,
but good people want to give what they have to others.
13Evil people are trapped by their evil talk,
but good people stay out of trouble.
14People will be rewarded for what they say,
and they will also be rewarded for what they do.
15Fools think they are doing right,
but the wise listen to advice.
16Fools quickly show that they are upset,
but the wise ignore insults.
17An honest witness tells the truth,
but a dishonest witness tells lies.
18Careless words stab like a sword,
but wise words bring healing.
19Truth will continue for ever,
but lies are only for a moment.
20Those who plan evil are full of lies,
but those who plan peace are happy.
21No harm comes to a good person,
but an evil person's life is full of trouble.
22The LORD hates those who tell lies
but is pleased with those who keep their promises.
23Wise people keep what they know to themselves,
but fools can't keep from showing how foolish they are.
24Hard workers will become leaders,
but those who are lazy will be slaves.
25Worry is a heavy load,
but a kind word cheers you up.
26Good people take advice from their friends,
but an evil person is easily led to do wrong.
27The lazy catch no food to cook,
but a hard worker will have great wealth.
28Doing what is right is the way to life,
but there is another way that leads to death.

13 Wise children take their parents' advice,
but whoever makes fun of wisdom won't listen to correction.
2People will be rewarded for what they say,
but those who can't be trusted want only violence.
3Those who are careful about what they say protect their lives,
but whoever speaks without thinking will be ruined.
4The lazy will not get what they want,
but those who work hard will.
5Good people hate what is false,
but the wicked do shameful and disgraceful things.
6Doing what is right protects the honest person,
but doing evil ruins the sinner.
7Some people pretend to be rich but really have nothing.
Others pretend to be poor but really are wealthy.
8The rich may have to pay a ransom for their lives,
but the poor will face no such danger.

9Good people can look forward to a bright
future,
but the future of the wicked is like a flame
going out.

10Pride only leads to arguments,
but those who take advice are wise.

11Money that comes easily disappears quickly,
but money that is gathered little by little
will grow.

12It is sad not to get what you hoped for.
But wishes that come true are like eating
fruit from the tree of life.

13Those who reject what they are taught will
pay for it,
but those who obey what they are told will
be rewarded.

14The teaching of a wise person gives life.
It is like a fountain that can save people
from death.

15People with good understanding will be well
liked,
but the lives of those who are not
trustworthy are hard.

16Every wise person acts with good sense,
but fools show how foolish they are.

17A wicked messenger brings nothing but
trouble,
but a trustworthy one makes everything
right.

18A person who refuses correction will end up
poor and disgraced,
but the one who accepts correction will be
honoured.

19It is so good when wishes come true,
but fools hate to stop doing evil.

20Spend time with the wise and you will
become wise,
but the friends of fools will suffer.

21Trouble always comes to sinners,
but good people enjoy success.

22Good people leave their wealth to their
grandchildren,
but a sinner's wealth is stored up for good
people.

23A poor person's field might produce plenty of
food,
but others often steal it away.

24If you do not punish your children, you don't
love them,
but if you love your children, you will
correct them.

25Good people have enough to eat,
but the wicked will go hungry.

14

A wise woman strengthens her family,
but a foolish woman destroys hers by
what she does.

2People who live good lives respect the LORD,
but those who live evil lives don't.

3Fools will be punished for their proud words,
but the words of the wise will protect
them.

4When there are no oxen, there is no food in
the barn.
But with a strong ox, much grain can be
grown.

Sidelight In ancient times, oxen were more valuable to the Israelites than a music player is to a teenager (Proverbs 14:4). These great beasts were used to plough, tread corn, and pull carts. They even had a day off on the Sabbath (Exodus 23:12, p.83).

5A truthful witness does not lie,
but a false witness tells nothing but lies.

6Those who make fun of wisdom look for it
and do not find it,
but knowledge comes easily to those with
understanding.

7Stay away from fools,
because they can't teach you anything.

0A wise person will understand what to do,
but a foolish person is dishonest.

9Fools don't care if they sin,
but honest people work at being right.

10No one else can know your sadness,
and strangers cannot share your joy.

11The wicked person's house will be destroyed,
but a good person's tent will still be
standing.

12Some people think they are doing right,
but in the end it leads to death.

13Someone who is laughing may be sad inside,
and joy may end in sadness.

14Evil people will be paid back for their evil
ways,
and good people will be rewarded for their
good ones.

15Fools will believe anything,
but the wise think about what they do.

16Wise people are careful and stay out of trouble,
but fools are careless and quick to act.

17Someone with a quick temper does foolish things,
but someone with understanding remains calm.

18Fools are rewarded with nothing but more foolishness,
but the wise are rewarded with knowledge.

19Evil people will bow down to those who are good;
the wicked will bow down at the door of those who do right.

20The poor are rejected, even by their neighbours,
but the rich have many friends.

21It is a sin to hate your neighbour,
but being kind to the needy brings happiness.

22Those who make evil plans will be ruined,
but those who plan to do good will be loved and trusted.

23Those who work hard make a profit,
but those who only talk will be poor.

24Wise people are rewarded with wealth,
but fools only get more foolishness.

25A truthful witness saves lives,
but a false witness is a traitor.

26Those who respect the LORD will have security,
and their children will be protected.

27Respect for the LORD gives life.
It is like a fountain that can save people from death.

28A king is honoured when he has many people to rule,
but a prince is ruined if he has none.

29Patient people have great understanding,
but people with quick tempers show their foolishness.

30Peace of mind means a healthy body,
but jealousy will rot your bones.

31Whoever mistreats the poor insults their Maker,
but whoever is kind to the needy honours God.

32The wicked are ruined by their own evil,
but those who do right are protected even in death.

33Wisdom lives in those with understanding,
and even fools recognise it.

34Doing what is right makes a nation great,
but sin will bring disgrace to any people.

35A king is pleased with a wise servant,
but he will become angry with one who causes him shame.

15 A gentle answer will calm a person's anger,
but an unkind answer will cause more anger.

2Wise people use knowledge when they speak,
but fools pour out foolishness.

3The LORD's eyes see everything;
he watches both evil and good people.

4As a tree gives fruit, healing words give life,
but dishonest words crush the spirit.

5Fools reject their parents' correction,
but anyone who accepts correction is wise.

6Much wealth is in the houses of good people,
but evil people get nothing but trouble.

7Wise people use their words to spread knowledge,
but there is no knowledge in the thoughts of fools.

8The LORD hates the sacrifice that the wicked offer,
but he likes the prayers of honest people.

9The LORD hates what evil people do,
but he loves those who do what is right.

10The person who stops doing what is right will be punished,
and the one who hates to be corrected will die.

11The LORD knows what is happening in the world of the dead,
so he surely knows the thoughts of the living.

12Those who make fun of wisdom don't like to be corrected;
they will not ask the wise for advice.

13Happiness makes a person smile,
but sadness can break a person's spirit.

14People with understanding want more knowledge,
but fools just want more foolishness.

15Every day is hard for those who suffer,
but a happy heart is like a continual feast.

16It is better to be poor and respect the LORD
than to be wealthy and have much trouble.

17It is better to eat vegetables with those who love you
than to eat meat with those who hate you.

18People with quick tempers cause trouble,
but those who control their tempers stop a quarrel.

19A lazy person's life is like a patch of thorns,
but an honest person's life is like a smooth highway.

20A wise son makes his father happy,
but a foolish son hates his mother.

21A person without wisdom enjoys being foolish,
but someone with understanding does what is right.

22Plans fail without good advice,
but they succeed with the advice of many others.

23People enjoy giving good advice.
Saying the right word at the right time is so pleasing.

24Wise people's lives get better and better.
They avoid whatever would cause their death.

25The LORD will tear down the proud person's house,
but he will protect the widow's property.

26The LORD hates evil thoughts
but is pleased with kind words.

27Greedy people bring trouble to their families,
but the person who can't be paid to do wrong will live.

28Good people think before they answer,
but the wicked simply pour out evil.

29The LORD does not listen to the wicked,
but he hears the prayers of those who do right.

30Good news makes you feel better.
Your happiness will show in your eyes.

31If you listen to correction to improve your life,
you will live among the wise.

32Those who refuse correction hate themselves,
but those who accept correction gain understanding.

33Respect for the LORD will teach you wisdom.
If you want to be honoured, you must be humble.

16

People may make plans in their minds,
but only the LORD can make them come true.

2You may believe you are doing right,
but the LORD will judge your reasons.

3Depend on the LORD in whatever you do,
and your plans will succeed.

4The LORD makes everything go as he pleases.
He has even prepared a day of disaster for evil people.

5The LORD hates those who are proud.
They will surely be punished.

6Love and truth bring forgiveness of sin.
By respecting the LORD you will avoid evil.

7When people live so that they please the LORD,
even their enemies will make peace with them.

8It is better to be poor and right
than to be wealthy and dishonest.

9People may make plans in their minds,
but the LORD decides what they will do.

10The words of a king are like a message from God,
so his decisions should be fair.

11The LORD wants honest balances and scales;
all the weights are his work.

12Kings hate those who do wrong,
because governments only continue if they are fair.

13Kings like honest people;
they value someone who speaks the truth.

14An angry king can put someone to death,
so a wise person will try to make him happy.

15A smiling king can give people life;
his kindness is like a spring shower.

16It is better to get wisdom than gold,
and to choose understanding rather than silver!

17Good people stay away from evil.
By watching what they do, they protect their lives.

18Pride will destroy a person;
a proud attitude leads to ruin.

19It is better to be humble and be with those
who suffer
than to share stolen property with the
proud.
20Whoever listens to what is taught will
succeed,
and whoever trusts the LORD will be happy.
21The wise are known for their understanding.
Their pleasant words make them better
teachers.
22Understanding is like a fountain which gives
life to those who use it,
but foolishness brings punishment to fools.
23Wise people's minds tell them what to say,
and that helps them be better teachers.
24Pleasant words are like a honeycomb,
making people happy and healthy.
25Some people think they are doing right,
but in the end it leads to death.
26The workers' hunger helps them,
because their desire to eat makes them
work.
27Useless people make evil plans,
and their words are like a burning fire.
28A useless person causes trouble,
and a gossip ruins friendships.
29Cruel people trick their neighbours
and lead them to do wrong.
30Someone who winks is planning evil,
and the one who grins is planning
something wrong.
31Grey hair is like a crown of honour;
it is earned by living a good life.
32Patience is better than strength.
Controlling your temper is better than
capturing a city.
33People throw lots [d] to make a decision,
but the answer comes from the LORD.

17 It is better to eat a dry crust of bread
in peace
than to have a feast where there is
quarrelling.
2A wise servant will rule over the master's
disgraceful child
and will even inherit a share of what the
master leaves his children.
3A hot furnace tests silver and gold,
but the LORD tests hearts.
4Evil people listen to evil words.
Liars pay attention to cruel words.
5Whoever mistreats the poor insults their
Maker;
whoever enjoys someone's trouble will be
punished.
6Old people are proud of their
grandchildren,
and children are proud of their parents.
7Fools should not be proud,
and rulers should not be liars.
8Some people think they can pay others to do
anything they ask.
They think it will work every time.
9Whoever forgives someone's sin makes a
friend,
but telling about the sin breaks up
friendships.
10A wise person will learn more from a warning
than a fool will learn from a hundred
lashings.
11Disobedient people look only for trouble,
so a cruel messenger will be sent against
them.
12It is better to meet a bear robbed of her
cubs
than to meet a fool doing foolish things.
13Whoever gives evil in return for good
will always have trouble at home.
14Starting a quarrel is like a leak in a dam,
so stop it before a fight breaks out.
15The LORD hates both of these things:
freeing the guilty and punishing the
innocent.
16It won't do a fool any good to try to buy
wisdom,
because he doesn't have the ability to be
wise.
17A friend loves you all the time,
and a brother helps in time of trouble.
18It is not wise to promise
to pay what your neighbour owes.
19Whoever loves to argue loves to sin.
Whoever is proud a lot is asking for
trouble.
20A person with an evil heart will find no
success,
and the person whose words are evil will
get into trouble.
21It is sad to have a foolish child;
there is no joy in being the parent of a fool.
22A happy heart is like good medicine,
but a broken spirit drains your strength.

23When the wicked accept money to do wrong
there can be no justice.

24The person with understanding is always
looking for wisdom,
but the mind of a fool wanders everywhere.

25A foolish son makes his father sad
and causes his mother great sorrow.

26It is not good to punish the innocent
or to beat leaders for being honest.

27The clever person says very little,
and one with understanding stays calm.

28Even fools seem to be wise if they keep
quiet;
if they don't speak, they appear to
understand.

18 Unfriendly people are selfish
and hate all good sense.

2Fools do not want to understand anything.
They only want to tell others what they
think.

3Do something evil, and people won't
like you.
Do something shameful, and they will
make fun of you.

4Spoken words can be like deep water,
but wisdom is like a flowing stream.

5It is not good to honour the wicked
or to be unfair to the innocent.

6The words of fools start quarrels.
They make people want to beat them.

7The words of fools will ruin them;
their own words will trap them.

8The words of a gossip are like tasty bits of
food.
People like to take them all up.

9A person who doesn't work hard
is just like someone who destroys things.

10The LORD is like a strong tower;
those who do right can run to him for
safety.

11Rich people trust their wealth to protect
them.
They think it is like the high walls of a
city.

12Proud people will be ruined,
but the humble will be honoured.

13Anyone who answers without listening
is foolish and confused.

14The will to live can get you through sickness,
but no one can live with a broken spirit.

15The mind of a person with understanding
gets knowledge;
the wise person listens to learn more.

16Taking a gift to an important man
will help get you in to see him.

17The person who tells one side of a story
seems right,
until someone else comes and asks
questions.

18Throwing lots[d] can settle arguments
and keep the two sides from fighting.

19A brother who has been insulted is harder to
win back than a walled city,
and arguments separate people like the
barred gates of a palace.

20People will be rewarded for what they say;
they will be rewarded by how they speak.

21What you say can mean life or death.
Those who speak with care will be
rewarded.

22When a man finds a wife, he finds something
good.
It shows that the LORD is pleased
with him.

23The poor beg for mercy,
but the rich give rude answers.

24Some friends may ruin you,
but a real friend will be more loyal than a
brother.

19 It is better to be poor and honest
than to be foolish and tell lies.

2Enthusiasm without knowledge is not good.
If you act too quickly, you might make a
mistake.

3People's own foolishness ruins their lives,
but in their minds they blame the LORD.

4Wealthy people are always finding more
friends,
but the poor lose all theirs.

5A witness who lies will not go free;
liars will never escape.

6Many people want to please a leader,
and everyone is friends with those who
give gifts.

7Poor people's relatives avoid them;
even their friends stay far away.
They run after them, begging,
but they are gone.

8Those who get wisdom do themselves a
favour,
and those who love learning will succeed.

9A witness who lies will not go free;
liars will die.

10A fool should not live in luxury.
A slave should not rule over princes.

11Clever people are patient;
they will be honoured if they ignore insults.

12An angry king is like a roaring lion,
but his kindness is like the dew on the grass.

13A foolish son will ruin his father,
and a quarrelling wife is like dripping water.

Sidelight When we think of dripping water, we most often think of a dripping tap. But the dripping water of Proverbs 19:13 was much more annoying. It probably referred to a leaking roof. In Bible times, houses were made of mud and had flat roofs. With good care, roofs stayed pretty watertight, but leaky roofs were a common problem – and the source of many jokes.

14Houses and wealth are inherited from parents,
but a wise wife is a gift from the LORD.

15Lazy people sleep a lot,
and idle people will go hungry.

16Those who obey the commands protect themselves,
but those who are careless will die.

17Being kind to the poor is like lending to the LORD;
he will reward you for what you have done.

18Correct your children while there is still hope;
do not let them destroy themselves.

19People with quick tempers will have to pay for it.
If you help them out once, you will have to do it again.

20Listen to advice and accept correction,
and in the end you will be wise.

21People can make all kinds of plans,
but only the LORD's plan will happen.

22People want others to be loyal,
so it is better to be poor than to be a liar.

23Those who respect the LORD will live
and be satisfied, unbothered by trouble.

24Though the lazy person puts his hand in the dish,
he won't lift the food to his mouth.

25Whip those who make fun of wisdom, and perhaps foolish people will gain some wisdom.
Correct those with understanding, and they will gain knowledge.

26A son who robs his father and sends away his mother
brings shame and disgrace on himself.

27Don't stop listening to correction, my child,
or you will forget what you have already learned.

28An evil witness makes fun of fairness,
and wicked people love what is evil.

29People who make fun of wisdom will be punished,
and the backs of foolish people will be beaten.

20 Wine and beer make people loud and uncontrolled;
it is not wise to get drunk on them.

2An angry king is like a roaring lion.
Making him angry may cost you your life.

3Foolish people are always fighting,
but avoiding quarrels will bring you honour.

4Lazy farmers don't plough when they should;
they expect a harvest, but there is none.

5People's thoughts can be like a deep well,
but someone with understanding can find the wisdom there.

6Many people claim to be loyal,
but it is hard to find a trustworthy person.

7The good people who live honest lives
will be a blessing to their children.

8When a king sits on his throne to judge,
he knows evil when he sees it.

9No one can say, "I am innocent;
I have never done anything wrong."

10The LORD hates both these things:
dishonest weights and dishonest measures.

11Even children are known by their behaviour;
their actions show if they are innocent and good.

12The LORD has made both these things:
ears to hear and eyes to see.

13If you love to sleep, you will be poor.
If you stay awake, you will have plenty of food.

14Buyers say, "This is bad. It's no good."
Then they go away and boast about what they bought.

15There is gold and plenty of rubies,
but only a few people speak with knowledge.

16Take the coat of someone who promises to pay a stranger's debts,
and keep it until he pays what the stranger owes.

17Stolen food may taste sweet at first,
but later it will feel like a mouth full of gravel.

18Get advice if you want your plans to work.
If you go to war, get the advice of others.

19Gossips can't keep secrets,
so avoid people who talk too much.

20Those who curse their father or mother
will be like a light going out in darkness.

21Wealth inherited quickly in the beginning
will do you no good in the end.

22Don't say, "I'll pay you back for the wrong you did."
Wait for the LORD, and he will make things right.

23The LORD hates dishonest weights,
and dishonest scales do not please him.

24The LORD decides what a person will do;
no one understands what his life is all about.

25It's dangerous to promise something to God too quickly.
After you've thought about it, it may be too late.

26A wise king separates out the evil people,
and he drives the threshing wheel over them as they deserve.

27The LORD looks deep inside people
and searches through their thoughts.

28Loyalty and truth keep a king in power;
he continues to rule if he is loyal.

29Young men glory in their strength,
and old men are honoured for their grey hair.

30Hard punishment will get rid of evil,
and whippings can change an evil heart.

21

The LORD can control a king's mind as he controls a river;
he can direct it as he pleases.

2You may believe you are doing right,
but the LORD judges your reasons.

3Doing what is right and fair
is more important to the LORD than sacrifices.

4Proud looks, proud thoughts
and evil actions are sin.

5The plans of people who work hard earn a profit,
but those who act too quickly become poor.

6Wealth that comes from telling lies
vanishes like a mist and leads to death.

7The violence of the wicked will destroy them,
because they refuse to do what is right.

8Guilty people live dishonest lives,
but honest people do right.

9It is better to live in a corner on the roof*n*
than inside the house with a quarrelling wife.

10Evil people only want to harm others.
Their neighbours get no mercy from them.

11If you punish those who make fun of wisdom, a foolish person may gain some wisdom.
But if you teach the wise, they will get knowledge.

12God, who is always right, watches the house of the wicked
and brings ruin on every evil person.

roof In Bible times houses were built with flat roofs. The roof was used for drying things such as flax and fruit. And it was used as an extra room, as a place for worship and as a place to sleep in the summer.

13Whoever ignores the poor when they cry for help
will also cry for help and not be answered.

14A secret gift will calm an angry person;
a present given in secrecy will still great anger.

15When justice is done, good people are happy,
but evil people are ruined.

16Whoever does not use good sense
will end up among the dead.

17Whoever loves pleasure will become poor;
whoever loves wine and perfume will never be rich.

18Wicked people will suffer instead of good people,
and those who cannot be trusted will suffer instead of those who do right.

19It is better to live alone in the desert
than with a quarrelling and complaining wife.

20Wise people's houses are full of the best foods and olive oil,
but fools waste everything they have.

21Whoever tries to live right and be loyal
finds life, success and honour.

22A wise person can defeat a city full of warriors
and tear down the defences they trust in.

23Those who are careful about what they say
keep themselves out of trouble.

24People who act with stubborn pride
are called "proud", "boaster" and "mocker".

25Lazy people's desire for sleep will kill them,
because they refuse to work.
26All day long they wish for more,
but good people give without holding back.

27The LORD hates sacrifices brought by evil people,
particularly when they offer them for the wrong reasons.

28A lying witness will be forgotten,
but a truthful witness will speak on.

29Wicked people are stubborn,
but good people think carefully about what they do.

30There is no wisdom, understanding or advice
that can succeed against the LORD.

31You can get the horses ready for battle,
but it is the LORD who gives the victory.

22

Being respected is more important than having great riches.
To be well thought of is better than silver or gold.

2The rich and the poor are alike
in that the LORD made them all.

3The wise see danger ahead and avoid it,
but fools keep going and get into trouble.

4Respecting the LORD and not being proud
will bring you wealth, honour and life.

5Evil people's lives are like paths covered with thorns and traps.
People who guard themselves don't have such problems.

6Train children how to live right,
and when they are old, they will not change.

7The rich rule over the poor,
and borrowers are servants to those who lend.

8Those who plan evil will receive trouble.
Their cruel anger will come to an end.

9Generous people will be blessed,
because they share their food with the poor.

10Get rid of the one who makes fun of wisdom.
Then fighting, quarrels and insults will stop.

11Whoever loves pure thoughts and kind words
will have even the king as a friend.

12The LORD guards knowledge,
but he destroys false words.

13The lazy person says, "There's a lion outside!
I might get killed out in the street!"

14The words of an unfaithful wife are like a deep trap.
Those who make the LORD angry will get caught by them.

15Every child is full of foolishness,
but punishment can get rid of it.

16Whoever gets rich by mistreating the poor,
and gives presents to the wealthy, will become poor.

Other Wise Sayings

17Listen carefully to what wise people say;
pay attention to what I am teaching you.
18It will be good to keep these things in mind
so that you are ready to repeat them.

19 I am teaching them to you now
so that you will put your trust in
the LORD.
20 I have written thirty sayings for you,
which give knowledge and good advice.
21 I am teaching you true and reliable words
so that you can give true answers to
anyone who asks.

22 Do not abuse poor people because they are
poor,
and do not take away the rights of the
needy in court.
23 The LORD will defend them in court
and will take the life of those who take
away their rights.
24 Don't make friends with bad-tempered people
or spend time with those who have bad
tempers.
25 If you do, you will be like them.
Then you will be in real danger.

26 Don't promise to pay what someone else
owes,
and don't guarantee anyone's loan.
27 If you cannot pay the loan,
your own bed may be taken right out from
under you.

28 Don't move an old stone that marks a border,
because those stones were set up by your
ancestors.

FAMILY

Trust

The flashing of police lights reflected in the mirror of Eve's car. Oh no, not a speeding fine! At the worst possible time too. Eve pulled over and waited for the police officer to come to her car. Eve felt like crying. She had been planning to drive to an open-air concert at the weekend. However, getting a speeding fine would put her weekend plans at risk – if her parents found out. As the officer asked for her driving licence, she decided it would be better to tell her parents about the fine, after the concert. Then, she returned home and kept silent.

That night Eve tossed and turned. Her parents had always trusted her to tell the truth. Finally, at around midnight, she got up and went to her older brother to ask for his advice. He was still awake, listening to his music.

Eve told him what had happened and then asked what he thought.

"You had better tell them," he said. "They'll find out, and then you really will be in trouble!"

The next morning at breakfast, Eve spilled out the whole story to her parents. She told them about the fine and how sorry she was about it, and how she had struggled with telling them.

Disappointment clouded their eyes.

"I don't like the thought of you speeding," Dad said firmly.

"I know, Dad," Eve said. "I have learned the hard way."

Her parents left the room for a few mintues to talk together. Then they returned.

"You have to pay the fine," Mum said and then paused.

"And you can still go to the concert," Dad added with a smile.

Thrilled, Eve determined never to betray her parents' trust – and she is still keeping to that promise.

Read how **Proverbs 22:1–9** reflect Eve's family values of honesty and generosity.

- Which verse in the passage best summarises Eve's story?
- What would you pay to gain your family's respect and trust? As much as stated in verse 1?

Consider . . .

- talking to your parents about building trust in your relationship.
- writing on a card four things you can do to build your family's trust in you. Put it where only you can see it.

For more, see . . .

- Genesis 4:1–12 (p.7)
- 2 Timothy 3:14–15 (p.1319)
- Genesis 45:1–11 (p.51)

29Do you see people skilled in their work?
They will work for kings, not for ordinary people.

23 If you sit down to eat with a ruler,
notice the food that is in front of you.
2Control yourself
if you have a big appetite.
3Don't be greedy for his fine foods,
because that food might be a trick.

4Don't wear yourself out trying to get rich;
be wise enough to control yourself.
5Wealth can vanish in the wink of an eye.
It can seem to grow wings
and fly away like an eagle.

6Don't eat the food of selfish people;
don't be greedy for their fine foods.
7Selfish people are always worrying
about how much the food costs.
They tell you, "Eat and drink,"
but they don't really mean it.
8You will throw up the little you have eaten,
and you will have wasted your kind words.

9Don't speak to fools;
they will only ignore your wise words.

10Don't move an old stone that marks a border,
and don't take fields that belong to orphans.
11God, their defender, is strong;
he will take their side against you.

12Remember what you are taught,
and listen carefully to words of knowledge.

13Don't fail to punish children.
If you spank them, they won't die.
14If you spank them,
you will save them from death.

15My child, if you are wise,
then I will be happy.
16I will be so pleased
if you speak what is right.

17Don't envy sinners,
but always respect the LORD.
18Then you will have hope for the future,
and your wishes will come true.

19Listen, my child, and be wise.
Keep your mind on what is right.
20Don't drink too much wine
or eat too much food.
21Those who drink and eat too much become poor.
They sleep too much and end up wearing rags.

22Listen to your father, who gave you life,
and do not forget your mother when she is old.
23Learn the truth and never reject it.
Get wisdom, self-control and understanding.
24The father of a good child is very happy;
parents who have wise children are glad because of them.
25Make your father and mother happy;
give your mother a reason to be glad.

26My son, pay attention to me,
and watch closely what I do.
27A prostitute[d] is as dangerous as a deep pit,
and an unfaithful wife is like a narrow well.
28They ambush you like robbers
and cause many men to be unfaithful to their wives.

29Who has trouble? Who has pain?
Who fights? Who complains?
Who has unnecessary bruises?
Who has bloodshot eyes?
30It is people who drink too much wine,
who try out all different kinds of strong drinks.
31Don't stare at the wine when it is red,
when it sparkles in the cup,
when it goes down smoothly.
32Later it bites like a snake
with poison in its fangs.
33Your eyes will see strange sights,
and your mind will be confused.
34You will feel dizzy as if you're in a storm on the ocean,
as if you're on top of a ship's sails.
35You will think, "They hit me, but I'm not hurt.
They beat me up, but I don't remember it.
I wish I could wake up.
Then I would get another drink."

24 Don't envy evil people
or try to be friends with them.
2Their minds are always planning violence,
and they always talk about making trouble.

3It takes wisdom to have a good family,
and it takes understanding to make it strong.
4It takes knowledge to fill a home
with rare and beautiful treasures.

5Wise people have great power,
and those with knowledge have great strength.
6So you need advice when you go to war.
If you have lots of good advice, you will win.

7Foolish people cannot understand wisdom.
They have nothing to say in a discussion.

8Whoever makes evil plans
will be known as a troublemaker.
9Making foolish plans is sinful,
and making fun of wisdom is hateful.

10If you give up when trouble comes,
it shows that you are weak.

11Save those who are being led to their death;
rescue those who are about to be killed.
12If you say, "We don't know anything about this,"
God, who knows what's in your mind, will notice.
He is watching you, and he will know.
He will reward each person for what he has done.

13My child, eat honey because it is good.
Honey from the honeycomb tastes sweet.
14In the same way, wisdom is pleasing to you.
If you find it, you have hope for the future,
and your wishes will come true.

15Don't be wicked and attack a good family's house;
don't rob the place where they live.
16Even though good people may be bothered by trouble seven times, they are never defeated,
but the wicked are overwhelmed by trouble.

17Don't be happy when your enemy is defeated;
don't be glad when he is overwhelmed.
18The LORD will notice and be displeased.
He may not be angry with them any more.

19Don't envy evil people,
and don't be jealous of the wicked.
20An evil person has nothing to hope for;
the wicked will die like a flame that is put out.

21My child, respect the LORD and the king.
Don't join those people who refuse to obey them.
22The LORD and the king will quickly destroy such people.
Those two can cause great disaster!

More Words of Wisdom

23These are also sayings of the wise:

It is not good to take sides when you are the judge.
24Don't tell the wicked that they are innocent;
people will curse you, and nations will hate you.
25But things will go well if you punish the guilty,
and you will receive rich blessings.

26An honest answer is as pleasing
as a kiss on the lips.

27First, finish your outside work
and prepare your fields.
After that, you can build your house.

28Don't testify against your neighbour for no good reason.
Don't say things that are false.
29Don't say, "I'll get even;
I'll do to him what he did to me."

30I passed by a lazy person's field
and by the vineyard of someone with no sense.
31Thorns had grown up everywhere.
The ground was covered with weeds,
and the stone walls had fallen down.
32I thought about what I had seen;
I learned this lesson from what I saw.
33You sleep a little; you take a nap.
You fold your hands and lie down to rest.
34Soon you will be as poor as if you had been robbed;
you will have as little as if you had been held up.

More Wise Sayings of Solomon

25 These are more wise sayings of Solomon, copied by the men of Hezekiah king of Judah.
2God is honoured for what he keeps secret.
Kings are honoured for what they can discover.

3No one can measure the height of the skies or the depth of the earth.
So also no one can understand the mind of a king.

4Remove the scum from the silver,
so the silver can be used by the silversmith.

Sidelight

Do you need a good brain teaser to catch your friends out? Proverbs is filled with ancient riddles (see Proverbs 25:2–3). Unfortunately, the punchlines have lost some of their punch through translation, so they are not as much fun as they used to be.

5Remove wicked people from the king's
presence;
then his government will be honest and last
a long time.

6Don't boast to the king
and act as if you are great.
7It is better for him to give you a higher position
than to bring you down in front of the
prince.

Because of something you have seen,
8 do not quickly take someone to court.
What will you do later
when your neighbour proves you wrong?

9If you have an argument with your
neighbour,
don't tell other people what was said.
10Whoever hears it might shame you,
and you might not ever be respected
again.

11The right word spoken at the right time
is as beautiful as golden apples in a silver
bowl.

12A wise warning to someone who will listen
is as valuable as gold earrings or fine gold
jewellery.

13Trustworthy messengers refresh those who
send them,
like the coolness of snow in the summer-time.

14People who boast about gifts they never give
are like clouds and wind that give no rain.

15With patience you can convince a ruler,
and a gentle word can get through to the
hard-headed.

16If you find honey, don't eat too much,
or it will make you vomit.
17Don't go to your neighbour's house too often;
too much of you will make him hate you.

18When you lie about your neighbours,
it hurts them as much as a club, a sword
or a sharp arrow.

19Trusting unfaithful people when you are in
trouble
is like eating with a broken tooth or walking
with a crippled foot.

BOASTING

All Puffed Up

Porcupine puffer fish dart in and out of coral reefs as they feed. Their pale brown colour blends magically with the buff coral. But let a predator, such as a barracuda, threaten them, and they immediately become defensive. They pump water into themselves, almost doubling their size. They inflate into spine-covered balls. The attacker usually retreats, unwilling to swallow such large, thorny creatures.

However, when they puff up, predators can spot them. These floating curiosities are worth a lot of money. Once netted and brought to the surface, puffer fish inflate themselves with air. In that condition they die. Then they are dried and eventually hung on walls or heaped on shelves of coastal curio shops.

People who brag and boast are like spiny puffers. Take in what **Proverbs 25:6–7** says about puffed-up people.

- What are the puffer fish and the "boaster" in this passage trying to hide?
- In what situations are you tempted to exaggerate your knowledge, abilities, or material possessions? What might happen to you if you didn't pretend to be "great" as this passage directs?

Consider . . .

- writing on a ribbon three things you're tempted to boast about. Then tie the ribbon to your key-ring or purse as a reminder not to boast.
- writing a note to at least three people you admire for not being "people-pleasers", telling them how you admire that quality in them.

For more, see . . .

- Daniel 4:28–37 (p.837)
- Luke 18:9–14 (p.1078)
- Mark 9:33–35 (p.1015)

20Singing songs to someone who is sad
is like taking away his coat on a cold day
or pouring vinegar on soda.

21If your enemy is hungry, feed him.
If he is thirsty, give him a drink.
22Doing this will be like pouring burning coals
on his head,
and the LORD will reward you.

23As the north wind brings rain,
telling gossip brings angry looks.

24It is better to live in a corner on the roof[n]
than inside the house with a quarrelling
wife.

25Good news from a faraway place
is like a cool drink when you are tired.

26A good person who gives in to evil
is like a muddy spring or a dirty well.

27It is not good to eat too much honey,
nor does it bring you honour to boast about
yourself.

28Those who do not control themselves
are like a city whose walls are broken
down.

26

It shouldn't snow in summer or rain at
harvest.
Neither should a foolish person ever be
honoured.

2Curses will not harm someone who is
innocent;
they are like sparrows or swallows that fly
around and never land.

3Whips are for horses, and harnesses are for
donkeys,
so paddles are good for fools.

4Don't give fools a foolish answer,
or you will be just like them.

5But answer fools as they should be answered,
or they will think they are really wise.

6Sending a message by a foolish person
is like cutting off your feet or drinking
poison.

7A wise saying spoken by a fool
is as useless as the legs of a crippled
person.

8Giving honour to a foolish person
is like tying a stone in a catapult.

9A wise saying spoken by a fool
is like a thorn stuck in the hand of a
drunkard.

10Employing a foolish person or anyone just
passing by
is like an archer shooting at just anything.

11A fool who repeats his foolishness
is like a dog that goes back to what it has
vomited.

12There is more hope for a foolish person
than for those who think they are wise.

13The lazy person says, "There's a lion in the
road!
There's a lion in the streets!"

14Like a door turning back and forth on its
hinges,
the lazy person turns over and over in bed.

15Lazy people may put their hands in the dish,
but they are too tired to lift the food to
their mouths.

16The lazy person thinks he is wiser
than seven people who give sensible answers.

17Interfering in someone else's quarrel as you
pass by
is like grabbing a dog by the ears.

18Like a madman shooting
deadly, burning arrows
19is the one who tricks a neighbour
and then says, "I was just joking."

20Without wood, a fire will go out,
and without gossip, quarrelling will stop.

21Just as charcoal and wood keep a fire going,
a quarrelsome person keeps an argument
going.

22The words of a gossip are like tasty bits of
food;
people like to take them all up.

23Kind words from a wicked mind
are like a shiny coating on a clay pot.

24Those who hate you may try to fool you with
their words,
but in their minds they are planning evil.
25People's words may be kind, but don't
believe them,
because their minds are full of evil thoughts.
26Lies can hide hate,
but the evil will be plain to everyone.

roof In Bible times houses were built with flat roofs. The roof was used for drying things such as flax and fruit. And it was used as an extra room, as a place for worship and as a place to sleep in the summer.

27Whoever digs a pit for others will fall into it.
Whoever tries to roll a boulder down on
others will be crushed by it.

28Liars hate the people they hurt,
and false praise can ruin others.

27

Don't boast about tomorrow;
you don't know what may happen
then.

2Don't praise yourself. Let someone else do it.
Let the praise come from a stranger and
not from your own mouth.

3Stone is heavy, and sand is weighty,
but a complaining fool is worse than either.

4Anger is cruel and destroys like a flood,
but no one can put up with jealousy!

5It is better to correct someone openly
than to have love and not show it.

6The slap of a friend can be trusted to
help you,
but the kisses of an enemy are nothing but
lies.

7When you are full, not even honey tastes
good,
but when you are hungry, even something
bitter tastes sweet.

8A person who leaves his home
is like a bird that leaves its nest.

9The sweet smell of perfume and oils is
pleasant,
and so is good advice from a friend.

Sidelight If you don't like taking baths, slap on some extra aftershave or perfume. Water was usually scarce in Israel in Old Testament times, and that's what people did. No wonder putting on oil and perfume made people happy (Proverbs 27:9). It probably made everyone nearby even happier!

10Don't forget your friend or your parent's
friend.
Don't always go to your family for help
when trouble comes.
A neighbour close by is better than a family
far away.

11Be wise, my child, and make me happy.
Then I can respond to any insult.

12The wise see danger ahead and avoid it,
but fools keep going and get into trouble.

13Take the coat of someone who promises to
pay a stranger's loan,
and keep it until he pays what the stranger
owes.

14If you loudly greet your neighbour early in the
morning,
he will think of it as a curse.

15A quarrelling wife is as bothersome
as a continual dripping on a rainy day.
16Stopping her is like stopping the wind
or trying to hold oil in your hand.

17As iron sharpens iron,
so people can improve each other.

18Whoever tends a fig tree gets to eat its fruit,
and whoever takes care of his master will
receive honour.

19As water reflects your face,
so your mind shows what kind of person
you are.

20People will never stop dying and being
destroyed,
and they will never stop wanting more than
they have.

21A hot furnace tests silver and gold,
and people are tested by the praise they
receive.

22Even if you ground up a foolish person like
grain in a bowl,
you couldn't remove the foolishness.

23Be sure you know how your sheep are doing,
and pay attention to the condition of your
cattle.
24Riches will not go on for ever,
nor do governments go on for ever.
25Bring in the hay, and let the new grass appear.
Gather the grass from the hills.
26Make clothes from the lambs' wool,
and sell some goats to buy a field.
27There will be plenty of goat's milk
to feed you and your family
and to make your servant girls healthy.

28

Evil people run even though no one is
chasing them,
but good people are as brave as a lion.

2When a country is disobedient, it has one
ruler after another;
but when it is led by a man with
understanding and knowledge, it
continues strong.

3Rulers who mistreat the poor
are like a hard rain that destroys the crops.

4Those who disobey what they have been
taught praise the wicked,
but those who obey what they have been
taught are against them.

5Evil people do not understand justice,
but those who follow the LORD understand
it completely.

6It is better to be poor and innocent
than to be rich and wicked.

7Children who obey what they have been
taught are clever,
but friends of troublemakers disgrace their
parents.

8Some people get rich by overcharging others,
but their wealth will be given to those who
are kind to the poor.

9If you refuse to obey what you have been
taught,
your prayers will not be heard.

10Those who lead good people to do wrong
will be ruined by their own evil,
but the innocent will be rewarded with
good things.

11Rich people may think they are wise,
but the poor with understanding will prove
them wrong.

12When good people triumph, there is great
happiness,
but when the wicked get control,
everybody hides.

13If you hide your sins, you will not succeed.
If you confess and reject them, you will
receive mercy.

14Those who are always respectful will be happy,
but those who are stubborn will get into
trouble.

15A wicked ruler is as dangerous to poor people
as a roaring lion or a charging bear.

16A ruler without wisdom will be cruel,
but the one who refuses to take dishonest
money will rule a long time.

17Don't help those who are guilty of murder;
let them run until they die.

18Innocent people will be kept safe,
but those who are dishonest will suddenly
be ruined.

19Those who work their land will have plenty
of food,
but the ones who chase empty dreams
instead will end up poor.

20A truthful person will have many blessings,
but those eager to get rich will be
punished.

21It is not good for a judge to take sides,
but some will sin for only a piece of bread.

22Selfish people are in a hurry to get rich
and do not realise they soon will be poor.

23Those who correct others will later be liked
more than those who give false praise.

24Whoever robs his father or mother
and says, "It's not wrong,"
is just like someone who destroys things.

25A greedy person causes trouble,
but the one who trusts the LORD will
succeed.

26Those who trust in themselves are foolish,
but those who live wisely will be
kept safe.

27Whoever gives to the poor will have
everything he needs,
but the one who ignores the poor will
receive many curses.

28When the wicked get control, everybody
hides,
but when they die, good people do well.

29 Whoever is stubborn after being
corrected many times
will suddenly be hurt beyond cure.

2When good people do well, everyone is
happy,
but when evil people rule, everyone
groans.

3Those who love wisdom make their parents
happy,
but friends of prostitutes[d] waste their
money.

4If a king is fair, he makes his country strong,
but if he takes gifts dishonestly, he tears his
country down.

5Those who give false praise to their
neighbours
are setting a trap for them.

6Evil people are trapped by their own sin,
but good people can sing and be happy.

7Good people care about justice for the poor,
but the wicked are not concerned.

8People who make fun of wisdom cause
trouble in a city,
but wise people calm anger down.

9When a wise person takes a foolish person to
court,
the fool only shouts or laughs, and there is
no peace.

10Murderers hate an honest person
and try to kill those who do right.

11Foolish people lose their tempers,
but wise people control theirs.

12If a ruler pays attention to lies,
all his officers will become wicked.

13The poor person and the cruel person are
alike
in that the LORD gave eyes to both of them.

14If a king judges poor people fairly,
his government will continue for ever.

15Correction and punishment make children
wise,
but those left alone will disgrace their
mother.

16When there are many wicked people, there is
much sin,
but those who do right will see them
destroyed.

17Correct your children, and you will be proud;
they will give you satisfaction.

18Where there is no word from God, people are
uncontrolled,
but those who obey what they have been
taught are happy.

19Words alone cannot correct a servant,
because even if he understands, he won't
respond.

20Do you see people who speak too quickly?
There is more hope for a foolish person
than for them.

21If you spoil your servants when they are
young,
they will bring you grief later on.

22An angry person causes trouble;
a person with a quick temper sins a lot.

23Pride will ruin people,
but those who are humble will be
honoured.

24Partners of thieves are their own worst
enemies.
If they have to testify in court, they are
afraid to say anything.

25Being afraid of people can get you into trouble,
but if you trust the LORD, you will be safe.

26Many people want to speak to a ruler,
but justice comes only from the LORD.

27Good people hate those who are dishonest,
and the wicked hate those who are honest.

Wise Words from Agur

30 These are the words of Agur son of
Jakeh.

This is his message to Ithiel and Ucal:

2"I am the most stupid person there is,
and I have no understanding.
3I have not learned to be wise,
and I don't know much about God, the
Holy One.
4Who has gone up to heaven and come back
down?
Who can hold the wind in his hand?
Who can gather up the waters in his coat?
Who has set in place the ends of the
earth?
What is his name or his son's name?
Tell me, if you know!

5"Every word of God is true.
He guards those who come to him for
safety.
6Do not add to his words,
or he will correct you and prove you are a
liar.

7"I ask two things from you, LORD.
Don't refuse me before I die.
8Keep me from lying and being dishonest.
And don't make me either rich or poor;
just give me enough food for each day.
9If I have too much, I might reject you
and say, 'I don't know the LORD.'
If I am poor, I might steal
and disgrace the name of my God.

10"Do not say bad things about servants to
their masters,
or they will curse you, and you will suffer
for it.

11"Some people curse their fathers
and do not bless their mothers.
12Some people think they are pure,
but they are not really free from evil.
13Some people have such a proud look!
They look down on others.
14Some people have teeth like swords;
their jaws seem full of knives.
They want to remove the poor from the earth
and the needy from the land.

15"Greed has two daughters
named 'Give' and 'Give'.

There are three things that are never satisfied,
really four that never say, 'I've had enough!':
16the cemetery, the childless mother,
the land that never gets enough rain
and fire that never says, 'I've had enough!'

17"If you make fun of your father
and refuse to obey your mother,
the birds of the valley will peck out your eyes,
and the vultures will eat them.

18"There are three things that are too hard for me,
really four I don't understand:
19the way an eagle flies in the sky,
the way a snake slides over a rock,
the way a ship sails on the sea
and the way a man and a woman fall in love.

20"This is the way of a woman who takes part in adultery: [d]
she acts as if she had eaten and washed her face;
she says, 'I haven't done anything wrong.'

21"There are three things that make the earth tremble,
really four it cannot stand:
22a servant who becomes a king,
a foolish person who has plenty to eat,
23a hated woman who gets married
and a maid who replaces her mistress.

24"There are four things on earth that are small,
but they are very wise:
25Ants are not very strong,
but they store up food in the summer.
26Rock badgers are not very powerful,
but they can live among the rocks.
27Locusts [d] have no king,
but they all go forwards in formation.
28Lizards can be caught in the hand,
but they are found even in kings' palaces.

29"There are three things that strut proudly,
really four that walk as if they were important:

30a lion, the proudest animal,
which is strong and runs from nothing,
31a rooster, a male goat
and a king when his army is around him.

32"If you have been foolish and proud,
or if you have planned evil, shut your mouth.
33Just as stirring milk makes butter,
and twisting noses makes them bleed,
so stirring up anger causes trouble."

Wise Words of King Lemuel

31 These are the words of King Lemuel, the message his mother taught him:
2"My son, I gave birth to you.
You are the son I prayed for.
3Don't waste your strength on women
or your time on those who ruin kings.

4"Kings should not drink wine, Lemuel,
and rulers should not desire beer.
5If they drink, they might forget the law
and keep the needy from getting their rights.
6Give beer to people who are dying
and wine to those who are sad.
7Let them drink and forget their need
and remember their misery no more.

8"Speak up for those who cannot speak for themselves;
defend the rights of all those who have nothing.
9Speak up and judge fairly,
and defend the rights of the poor and needy."

The Good Wife

10It is hard to find a good wife,
because she is worth far more than rubies.
11Her husband trusts her completely.
With her, he has everything he needs.
12She does him good and not harm
for as long as she lives.
13She looks for wool and flax
and likes to work with her hands.
14She is like a trader's ship,
bringing food from far away.
15She gets up while it is still dark
and prepares food for her family
and feeds her servant girls.
16She inspects a field and buys it.
With money she earned, she plants a vineyard.
17She does her work with energy,
and her arms are strong.
18She knows that what she makes is good.
Her lamp burns late into the night.

Sidelight The "good wife" of Proverbs 31:10–31 would have been a "supermum" centuries before that term was invented. Not only did she do everything around the house, she also farmed (verse 16), worked in manufacturing (verse 24), and did volunteer work (verse 20). The question is, what did the men do?

19 She makes thread with her hands
and weaves her own cloth.
20 She welcomes the poor
and helps the needy.
21 She does not worry about her family when it
snows,
because they all have fine clothes to keep
them warm.
22 She makes coverings for herself;
her clothes are made of linen and other
expensive material.
23 Her husband is known at the city meetings,
where he makes decisions as one of the
elders of the land.
24 She makes linen clothes and sells them
and provides belts for the merchants.
25 She is strong and is respected by the people.
She looks forward to the future with joy.
26 She speaks wise words
and teaches others to be kind.
27 She watches over her family
and never wastes her time.
28 Her children speak well of her.
Her husband also praises her,
29 saying, "There are many fine women,
but you are better than all of them."
30 Charm can fool you, and beauty can trick you,
but a woman who respects the LORD should
be praised.
31 Give her the reward she has earned;
she should be praised in public for what she
has done.

MARRIAGE

Like Great-Grandmother

Sarah Walker stood in her great-grandmother's wedding dress, watching her mother fit the new sleeves into place. "I'm scared," she said.

"Of what, Sarah?"

"Marriage." Sarah stared into the mirror. "I'm scared of being an adult – of being responsible for building a new life with Ben."

"I know." Her mother pushed back her hair. "But follow your great-grandmother's example; she built a wonderful life for herself and her husband."

Her mother smiled, remembering. "She helped keep the house, bore the babies, worked in the woollen mill, set broken bones, canned and pickled hundreds of jars of food each year, sewed clothes and prayed beside her children's beds each night. And through it all she was a loving lady. She and grandpa really loved each other and they made a great team. As grandpa lay dying, after 66 years of marriage, he said she was still his angel."

"Funny, she seems more like a modern, working woman, besides being a wife and mother," Sarah said.

The good wife in Proverbs also possessed some of the great-grandmother's qualities. Read **Proverbs 31:10–31**.

- In what ways is the great-grandmother like the wife in this passage?
- Which qualities, listed here in these verses, do you most want in your life?

Consider . . .

- looking for qualities of a godly wife or husband at your church, then asking God to help you build these qualities in yourself so that you will be a godly spouse if you marry.
- asking couples you admire for their secret of a successful marriage.

For more, see . . .

- Ruth 3—4 (p.251)
- 1 Peter 3:1–7 (p.1360)
- Ephesians 5:21–33 (p.1275)

Ecclesiastes

Why Read This Book:

- See the results of living a variety of lifestyles (Ecclesiastes 1—2).
- Find companionship when bad things happen (Ecclesiastes 4—5).
- Explore the problem of injustice and the mystery of God (Ecclesiastes 9—10).
- Accept and enjoy life as God has given it (Ecclesiastes 3, 6, 11—12).

When?

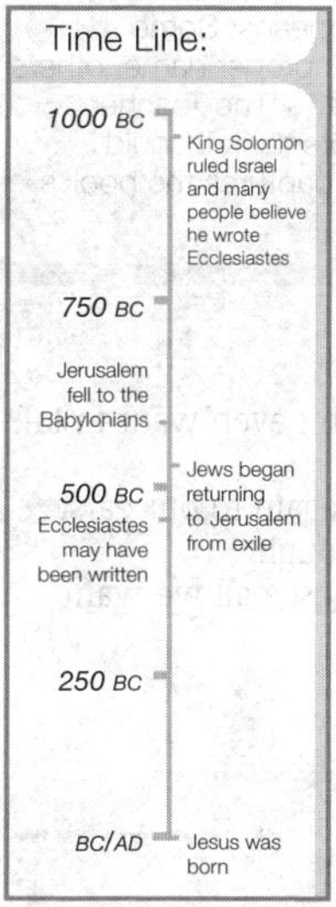

Behind the Scenes:

What brings happiness? What gives life meaning? People look in all kinds of places for answers to these questions.

Some people spend their lives making money to buy happiness. Then they die feeling empty and lonely.

Other people work hard at a career, hoping to find a way to leave a lasting impression on the world. Then they die, and people forget them.

Some people study and learn all they can in a quest for knowledge and understanding. Yet the world still holds mysteries they can't understand.

Other people spend all their time enjoying themselves, trying to have fun and feel good. But afterwards, life seems hollow and purposeless.

The writer of Ecclesiastes – often called the "Preacher" or the "Teacher" – walked down all these paths looking for happiness. Yet he never found it. Life was too complex and contradictory to understand through simple formulas. Good people suffered. Bad people prospered. It didn't make sense.

The book of Ecclesiastes contains the Teacher's thoughts about life and its meaning. Sometimes he seems cynical, because nothing in life seems meaningful (Ecclesiastes 1:2 and 12:8). Sometimes he says God is so distant we can't know him (Ecclesiastes 5:2).

Yet Ecclesiastes also gives insight and comfort on several levels.

- It is important to explore and reflect on what it means to follow God.
- It is all right to ask questions about life and our place in the universe. In fact, asking questions about ourselves and our relationship with God and the world can often help us to become stronger in our faith.
- We can see that despite having fame, fortune and wisdom, living without knowing God personally is empty and void of all meaning.
- The author believes life is worth living, even with its problems. He urges people to grab onto and enjoy the good things God gives us.
- Finally, God is in control – even when we can't see his work. "Honour God and obey his commands," he urges, "because this is all people must do" (Ecclesiastes 12:13).

1 These are the words of the Teacher, a son of
David, king in Jerusalem.
2 The Teacher says,
"Useless! Useless!
Completely useless!
Everything is useless."

3 What do people really gain
from all the hard work they do here on
earth?

Things Never Change

4 People live, and people die,
but the earth continues for ever.
5 The sun rises, the sun sets,
and then it hurries back to where it rises
again.
6 The wind blows to the south;
it blows to the north.
It blows from one direction and then
another.
Then it turns round and repeats the same
pattern, going nowhere.
7 All the rivers flow to the sea,
but the sea never becomes full.

Sidelight The title of Ecclesiastes is, itself, a mystery. It's translated from the Hebrew word "Qoheleth" but no one is sure what it means. Some scholars think it might be a proper name; others say it means "The Preacher", "The Teacher", or "Speaker". But still others think it could mean "The Arguer" which captures the book's contents well!

8 Everything is boring,
so boring that you don't even want to talk
about it.
Words come again and again to our ears,
but we never hear enough,
nor can we ever really see all we want
to see.

DISCOURAGEMENT

Nothing Changes Round Here

Sean lay on top of his bed. "I'm bored", he thought. "Nothing ever happens around here any more." He looked round his room and his eyes fell on his skateboard which he hadn't used since the skate park got shut – "lack of funds" is what the council had said.

"Its just pointless – nothing ever changes."

All of Sean's friends had just stopped hanging out when the skate park got locked up. Now they settled for playing skate games in their rooms, on their own.

Sean suddenly sat up. What if, just what if something could change? He began to scribble words into a notebook; he picked up his phone and sent texts to a couple of friends. And then he felt stupid. What was he thinking? Nothing could ever change. He couldn't make a difference. And so he threw his notebook aside, turned off his phone and went back to his PC skate game again.

Sean had a lot in common with the writer of Ecclesiastes. People at the time were pretty discouraged – they didn't think that anything could change. Take a look at **Ecclesiastes 1:2–11**.

- Which of these verses do you think Sean would have most identified with?
- Think about a time when you have felt like nothing will ever change. Which verses best describe how you felt?

Consider . . .

- looking in a local paper or on the Internet to find a story of someone choosing to make a difference.
- whether there is something you could get involved in that will change things where you live.

For more, see . . .

- Joshua 1:1–9 (p.202)
- Psalm 22 (p.512)
- Job 42:1–5 (p.498)

9All things continue the way they have been
since the beginning.
What has happened will happen again;
there is nothing new here on earth.
10Someone might say,
"Look, this is new,"
but really it has always been here.
It was here before we were.
11People don't remember what happened
long ago,
and in the future people will not remember
what happens now.
Even later, other people will not remember
what was done before them.

Does Wisdom Bring Happiness?

12I, the Teacher, was king over Israel in Jeru-
salem. 13I decided to use my wisdom to learn
about everything that happens on earth. I learned
that God has given us terrible things to face. 14I
looked at everything done on earth and saw that
it is all useless, like chasing the wind.

15If something is crooked,
you can't make it straight.
If something is missing,
you can't say it is there.

16I said to myself, "I have become very wise
and am now wiser than anyone who ruled
Jerusalem before me. I know what wisdom and
knowledge really are." 17So I decided to find out
about wisdom and knowledge and also about
foolish thinking, but this turned out to be like
chasing the wind.

18With much wisdom comes much
disappointment;
the person who gains more knowledge also
gains more sorrow.

Does "Having Fun" Bring Happiness?

2 I said to myself, "I will try having fun. I will
enjoy myself." But I found that this is also
useless. 2It is foolish to laugh all the time, and
having fun doesn't accomplish anything. 3I de-
cided to cheer myself up with wine while my
mind was still thinking wisely. I wanted to find a
way to enjoy myself and see what was good for
people to do during their few days of life.

Does Hard Work Bring Happiness?

4Then I did great things: I built houses and
planted vineyards for myself. 5I made gardens and
parks and I planted all kinds of fruit trees in them.
6I made pools of water for myself and used them
to water my growing trees. 7I bought male and
female slaves, and slaves were also born in my
house. I had large herds and flocks, more than
anyone in Jerusalem had ever had before. 8I also
gathered silver and gold for myself, treasures
from kings and other areas. I had male and female
singers and all the women a man could ever
want. 9I became very famous, even greater than
anyone who had lived in Jerusalem before me.
My wisdom helped me in all this.

10Anything I saw and wanted, I got for myself;
I did not miss any pleasure I desired.
I was pleased with everything I did,
and this pleasure was the reward for all my
hard work.
11But then I looked at what I had done,
and I thought about all the hard work.
Suddenly I realised it was useless, like
chasing the wind.
There is nothing to gain from anything we
do here on earth.

Sidelight The writer could have been thinking of people in the modern Western world. We suspect that there has to be more to life than work and a good time. There is. Our purpose can be found by following God.

Maybe Wisdom is the Answer

12Then I began to think again about being
wise,
and also about being foolish and doing mad
things.
But after all, what more can anyone do?
He can't do more than what the other king
has already done.
13I saw that being wise is certainly better than
being foolish,
just as light is better than darkness.
14Wise people see where they are going,
but fools walk around in the dark.
Yet I saw that
both wise and foolish people end the
same way.

15I thought to myself,
"What happens to a fool will happen to
me too,
so what is the reward for being wise?"
I said to myself,
"Being wise is also useless."
16The wise person and the fool
will both die,
and no one will remember either one for long.
In the future, both will be forgotten.

Is There Real Happiness in Life?

17So I hated life. It made me sad to think that
everything here on earth is useless, like chasing

the wind. [18]I hated all the things I had worked for
here on earth, because I must leave them to
someone who will live after me. [19]Someone else
will control everything for which I worked so
hard here on earth, and I don't know if he will be
wise or foolish. This is also useless. [20]So I became
sad about all the hard work I had done here on
earth. [21]People can work hard using all their wis-
dom, knowledge and skill, but they will die, and
other people will get the things for which they
worked. They did not do the work, but they will
get everything. This is also unfair and useless.
[22]What do people get for all their work and strug-
gling here on earth? [23]All of their lives their work
is full of pain and sorrow, and even at night their
minds don't rest. This is also useless.
[24]The best that people can do is eat, drink and
enjoy their work. I saw that even this comes from
God, [25]because no one can eat or enjoy life with-
out him. [26]If people please God, God will give
them wisdom, knowledge and joy. But sinners
will get only the work of gathering and storing
wealth that they will have to give to the ones
who please God. So all their work is useless, like
chasing the wind.

There is a Time for Everything

3 There is a time for everything,
and everything on earth has its special
season.

[2]There is a time to be born
and a time to die.
There is a time to plant
and a time to pull up plants.
[3]There is a time to kill
and a time to heal.
There is a time to destroy
and a time to build.
[4]There is a time to cry
and a time to laugh.
There is a time to be sad
and a time to dance.
[5]There is a time to throw away stones
and a time to gather them.

HAPPINESS

In the Here and Now

At the crack of dawn Rebecca lay in her bed, replaying the county trials in her head. She was running the 1,800 metres, pushing towards the finish. She had to get into the medal positions. She finished fourth.

"Rebecca, breakfast!" her mother called from the kitchen. Her mum had always been there for her, since her father had left. She crawled out of bed and ambled down the stairs.

As Rebecca sat down her mum joined her, saying, "Rebecca, I know you lost what was an important race for you, but then life isn't always fair. Just remember this: God has given you a gift and a body that enjoys it."

"Um," Rebecca grunted into her orange juice. "So?"

"I'm talking about enjoying the moment – the feel of your feet pounding the track, the tingle of adrenaline in your arms and legs, the sheer pleasure of being alive. It's good, even if you do lose a race or two."

Her mother's words fell on deaf ears then, but in the following years, those words helped Rebecca to really live life. Now she finds pleasure in the many things that God has given to her.

The writer of Ecclesiastes tried to find happiness in the middle of loss as well. Read **Ecclesiastes 2:18–26**.

- How does Rebecca's mum's advice compare with the advice in Ecclesiastes?
- How can you apply the advice in the passage to your life this week?

Consider . . .

- focusing only on your body sensations while washing the car, or eating or exercising.
- going for a walk in the woods and then writing in a diary all the good things that you noticed.

For more, see . . .

- Psalm 16:7–11 (p.508)
- 2 Corinthians 4:7–9 (p.1243)
- Luke 12:22–31 (p.1064)

There is a time to embrace
and a time to refrain.
6There is a time to look for something
and a time to stop looking for it.
There is a time to keep things
and a time to throw things away.
7There is a time to tear apart
and a time to sew together.
There is a time to be silent
and a time to speak.
8There is a time to love
and a time to hate.
There is a time for war
and a time for peace.

God Controls His World

9Do people really gain anything from their
work? 10I saw the hard work God has given peo-
ple to do. 11God has given them a desire to know
the future. He does everything just right and on
time, but people can never completely under-
stand what he is doing. 12So I realise that the best
thing for them is to be happy and enjoy them-
selves as long as they live. 13God wants all people
to eat and drink and be happy in their work,
which are gifts from God. 14I know that every-
thing God does will continue for ever. People
cannot add anything to what God has done, and
they cannot take anything away from it. God does
it this way to make people respect him.

15What happens now has happened in the past,
and what will happen in the future has
happened before.
God makes the same things happen again
and again.

Unfairness on Earth

16I also saw this here on earth:
where there should have been justice, there
was evil;

SADNESS

Death Watch

Derek's grandfather lay quietly in his bed at home, shrivelled to the bone by Parkinson's disease.

Derek held his calloused hand and whispered, "I love you, Grandad."

"I love you too," the old man whispered back, barely able to talk.

Tears sprang to Derek's eyes. "What will I do without you?"

"Remember our good times." The old man closed his eyes. "Enjoy your life . . . and follow God."

"I don't want to let you go," Derek began to cry.

"It's all right," Grandad said. "It's my time to go. God knows what he's doing."

Derek fought back tears as he watched his grandfather struggle to breathe.

"Will you play 'Take My Hand, Precious Lord'?" Grandad asked.

Derek sat at the piano in the next room and played the song Grandad had heard so many times before. Derek's heart broke with each note. But there was also a distant joy for the times he and Grandad had shared and the fact that the pain would finally end.

Even the sadness of death can be seen as a natural part of life, according to **Ecclesiastes 3:1–13**.

- Where in these verses are there words like the ones that Derek's grandfather spoke?
- How do these verses help you to cope with sadness?

Consider . . .

- writing an example for each of the times listed in the passage.
- looking through family photos and remembering times like those listed in Ecclesiastes.

For more, see . . .

- Psalm 88 (p.552)
- Philippians 3:4–7 (p.1283)
- Romans 5:3–5 (p.1190)

where there should have been right, there
was wrong.
17I said to myself,
God has planned a time for everything and
every action,
so he will judge both good people and bad.

18I decided that God leaves it the way it is to
test people and to show them they are just like
animals. 19The same thing happens to animals
and to people; they both have the same breath, so
they both die. People are no better off than the
animals, because everything is useless. 20Both
end up the same way; both came from dust and
both will go back to dust. 21Who can be sure that
the human spirit goes up to God and that the
spirit of an animal goes down into the ground?
22So I saw that the best thing people can do is to
enjoy their work, because that is all they have.
No one can help another person see what will
happen in the future.

Is It Better to be Dead?

4 Again I saw all the people who were mistreated here on earth.
I saw their tears
and that they had no one to comfort them.
Cruel people had all the power,
and there was no one to comfort those
they hurt.
2I decided that the dead
are better off than the living.
3But those who have never been born
are better off still;
they have not seen the evil
that is done here on earth.

Why Work So Hard?

4I realised the reason people work hard and try
to succeed: they are jealous of each other. This,
too, is useless, like chasing the wind.

5Some say it is foolish to fold your hands and
do nothing,
because you will starve to death.
6Maybe so, but I say it is better to be content
with what little you have.
Otherwise, you will always be struggling for
more,
and that is like chasing the wind.

7Again I saw something here on earth that
was useless:
8I saw a man who had no family,
no son or brother.
He always worked hard
but was never satisfied with what he had.
He never asked himself, "For whom am I
working so hard?
Why don't I let myself enjoy life?"
This also is very sad and useless.

Friends and Family Give Strength

9Two people are better than one,
because they get more done by working
together.
10If one falls down,
the other can help him up.
But it is bad for the person who is alone and
falls,
because no one is there to help.
11If two lie down together, they will be warm,
but a person alone will not be warm.
12An enemy might defeat one person,
but two people together can defend
themselves;
a rope that is woven of three strings is hard
to break.

Fame and Power are Useless

13A poor but wise boy is better than a foolish
but old king who doesn't listen to advice. 14A boy
became king. He had been born poor in the kingdom and had even gone to prison before becoming king. 15I watched all the people who live
on earth follow him and make him their king.
16Many followed him at first, but later, they did
not like him, either. So fame and power are useless, like chasing the wind.

Be Careful About Making Promises

5 Be careful when you go to worship at the
Temple. [d] It is better to listen than to offer
foolish sacrifices without even knowing you are
doing wrong.

2Think before you speak,
and be careful about what you say to God.
God is in heaven,
and you are on the earth,
so say only a few words to God.
3The saying is true: bad dreams come from
too much worrying,
and too many words come from foolish
people.

4If you make a promise to God, don't be slow
to keep it. God is not happy with fools, so give
God what you promised. 5It is better not to promise anything than to promise something and not
do it. 6Don't let your words cause you to sin, and
don't say to the priest at the Temple, "I didn't
mean what I promised." If you do, God will become angry with your words and will destroy
everything you have worked for. 7Many useless
promises are like so many dreams; they mean
nothing. You should respect God.

Officers Cheat Each Other

8 In some places you will see poor people mis-
treated. Don't be surprised when they are not
treated fairly or given their rights. One officer is

> **Sidelight** Making a promise in biblical times (Ecclesiastes 5:4–7) was more like signing an important legal contract (such as a marriage licence) today. Once you made a promise, you coudn't really get out of it.

cheated by a higher officer who in turn is cheated
by even higher officers. 9 The wealth of the coun-
try is divided up among them all. Even the king
makes sure he gets his share of the profits.

Wealth Cannot Buy Happiness

10 Whoever loves money
 will never have enough money;
Whoever loves wealth
 will not be satisfied with it.
 This is also useless.
11 The more wealth people have,
 the more friends they have to help spend it.
So what do people really gain?
 They gain nothing except to look at their riches.
12 Those who work hard sleep in peace;
 it is not important if they eat little or much.
But rich people worry about their wealth
 and cannot sleep.

13 I have seen real misery here on earth:
money saved is a curse to its owners.
14 They lose it all in a bad deal
and have nothing to give to their children.
15 People come into this world with nothing,
 and when they die they leave with nothing.
In spite of all their hard work,
 they leave just as they came.
16 This, too, is real misery:
they leave just as they came.
 So what do they gain from chasing the wind?
17 All they get are days full of sadness and sorrow,
 and they end up sick, defeated and angry.

Enjoy Your Life's Work

18 I have seen what is best for people here on
earth. They should eat and drink and enjoy their
work, because the life God has given them on
earth is short. 19 God gives some people the ability
to enjoy the wealth and property he gives them,
as well as the ability to accept their area in life
and enjoy their work. 20 They do not worry about
how short life is, because God keeps them busy
with what they love to do.

6 I have seen something else wrong here on
earth that causes serious problems for peo-
ple. 2 God gives great wealth, riches and honour
to some people; they have everything they want.
But God does not let them enjoy such things; a
stranger enjoys them instead. This is useless and
very wrong. 3 A man might have 100 children
and live a long time, but what good is it if he can't
enjoy the good God gives him or have a proper
burial? I say a baby born dead is better off than he
is. 4 A baby born dead is useless. It returns to
darkness without even a name. 5 That baby never
saw the sun and never knew anything, but it
finds more rest than that man. 6 Even if he lives
2,000 years, he doesn't enjoy the good God gives
him. Everyone is going to the same place.

7 People work just to feed themselves,
 but they never seem to get enough to eat.
8 In this way a wise person
 is no better off than a fool.
Then, too, it does a poor person little good
 to know how to get along in life.
9 It is better to see what you have
 than to want more.
Wanting more is useless—
 like chasing the wind.

Who Can Understand God's Plan?

10 Whatever happens was planned long ago.
 Everyone knows what people are like.
No one can argue with God,
 who is stronger than anyone.
11 The more you say,
 the more useless it is.
 What good does it do?

12 People have only a few useless days of life on
the earth; their short life passes like a shadow.
Who knows what is best for them while they
live? Who can tell them what the future will
bring?

Some Benefits of Serious Thinking

7 It is better to have respect than good perfume.
 The day of death is better than the day of birth.
2 It is better to go to a funeral
 than to a party.
We all must die,
 and everyone living should think about this.
3 Sorrow is better than laughter,
 and sadness has a good influence on you.

4A wise person thinks about death,
but a fool thinks only about having a good time.
5It is better to be criticised by a wise person
than to be praised by a fool.
6The laughter of fools
is like the burning of thorns in a cooking fire.
Both are useless.

7Even wise people are fools
if they let money change their thinking.

8It is better to finish something
than to start it.
It is better to be patient
than to be proud.
9Don't become angry quickly,
because getting angry is foolish.

10Don't ask, "Why was life better in the 'good old days?' "
It is not wise to ask such questions.

11Wisdom is better when it comes with money.
They both help those who are alive.
12Wisdom is like money:
they both help.
But wisdom is better,
because it can save whoever has it.

13Look at what God has done:
no one can straighten what he has made crooked.
14When life is good, enjoy it.
But when life is hard, remember:
God gives good times and hard times,
and no one knows what tomorrow will bring.

It is Impossible to be Truly Good

15In my useless life I have seen both of these:
I have seen good people die in spite of their goodness
and evil people live a long time in spite of their evil.
16Don't be too right,
and don't be too wise.
Why destroy yourself?
17Don't be too wicked,
and don't be foolish.
Why die before your time?
18It is good to grasp the one and not let go of the other;
those who honour God will hold them both.

19Wisdom makes a person stronger
than ten leaders in a city.

20Surely there is not a good person on earth
who always does good and never sins.
21Don't listen to everything people say,
or you might hear your servant insulting you.
22You know that many times
you have insulted others.

23I used wisdom to test all these things.
I wanted to be wise,
but it was too hard for me.
24I cannot understand why things are as they are.
It is too hard for anyone to understand.
25I studied and tried very hard to find wisdom,
to find some meaning for everything.
I learned that it is foolish to be evil,
and it is mad to act like a fool.

26I found that some women are worse than death
and are as dangerous as traps.
Their love is like a net,
and their arms hold men like chains.
A man who pleases God will be saved from them,
but a sinner will be caught by them.

27The Teacher says, "This is what I learned:
I added all these things together
to find some meaning for everything.
28While I was searching but not finding
I found one man among the thousands.
But not one woman among all these.
29One thing I have learned:
God made people good,
but they have found all kinds of ways to be bad."

Obey the King

8 No one is like the wise person
who can understand what things mean.
Wisdom brings happiness;
it makes sad faces happy.

2Obey the king's command, because you made
a promise to God. 3Don't be too quick to leave
the king. Don't support something that is wrong,
because the king does whatever he pleases.
4What the king says is law; no one tells him what
to do.

5Whoever obeys the king's command will be safe.
A wise person does the right thing at the right time.
6There is a right time and a right way for everything,
yet people often have many troubles.
7They do not know what the future holds,
and no one can tell them what will happen.

8No one can control the wind
or stop his own death.
No soldier is released in times of war,
and evil does not set free those who do
evil.

Justice, Rewards and Punishment

9I saw all of this as I considered all that is done
here on earth. Sometimes men harm those they
control. 10I saw the funerals of evil people who
used to go in and out of the holy place. They
were honoured in the same towns where they
had done evil. This is useless too.
11When evil people are not punished right
away, it makes others want to do evil too.
12Though a sinner might do 100 evil things and
might live a long time, I know it will be better for
those who honour God. 13I also know it will not
go well for evil people, because they do not hon-
our God. Like a shadow, they will not last.
14Sometimes something useless happens on
earth. Bad things happen to good people, and
good things happen to bad people. I say that this
is also useless. 15So I decided it was more impor-
tant to enjoy life. The best that people can do here
on earth is to eat, drink and enjoy life, because
these joys will help them do the hard work God
gives them here on earth.

We Cannot Understand All God Does

16I tried to understand all that happens on
earth. I saw how busy people are, working day
and night and hardly ever sleeping. 17I also saw
all that God has done. Nobody can understand
what God does here on earth. No matter how
hard people try to understand it, they cannot.
Even if wise people say they understand, they
cannot; no one can really understand it.

Is Death Fair?

9 I thought about all this and tried to under-
stand it. I saw that God controls good people
and wise people and what they do, but no one
knows if they will experience love or hate.

2Good and bad people end up the same—
those who are right and those who are
wrong,
those who are good and those who are evil,
those who are clean and those who are
unclean,
those who sacrifice and those who do not.
The same things happen to a good person
as happen to a sinner,
to a person who makes promises to God
and to one who does not.

3This is something wrong that happens here
on earth: what happens to one happens to all.
So people's minds are full of evil and foolish
thoughts while they live. After that, they join the
dead. 4But anyone still alive has hope; even a live
dog is better off than a dead lion!

5The living know they will die,
but the dead know nothing.
Dead people have no more reward,
and people forget them.
6After people are dead,
they can no longer love or hate
or envy.
They will never again share
in what happens here on earth.

Enjoy Life While You Can

7So go and eat your food and enjoy it;
drink your wine and be happy,
because that is what God wants you to do.
8Put on nice clothes
and make yourself look good.

9Enjoy life with the wife you love. Enjoy all the
useless days of this useless life God has given you
here on earth, because it is all you have. So enjoy
the work you do here on earth. 10Whatever work
you do, do your best, because you are going to
the grave, where there is no working, no plan-
ning, no knowledge and no wisdom.

> **Sidelight** Like most ancient Jews, the Teacher believed that death brought only "the grave" (Ecclesiastes 9:10). The Hebrew word "Sheol" referred to a silent gloomy, mysterious world where the early Jews believed that departed spirits went. The idea of heaven is more appealing, don't you think?

Time and Chance

11I also saw something else here on earth:
the fastest runner does not always win the
race,
the strongest soldier does not always win
the battle,
the wisest does not always have food,
the cleverest man does not always become
wealthy
and the talented one does not always
receive praise.
Time and chance happen to everyone.
12No one knows what will happen next.
Like a fish caught in a net,
or a bird caught in a trap,
people are trapped by evil
when it suddenly falls on them.

Wisdom Does Not Always Win

13I also saw something wise here on earth that
was very impressive to me. 14There was a small
town with only a few people in it. A great king
fought against it and put his armies all around it.
15Now there was a poor but wise man in the
town who used his wisdom to save his town. But
later on, everyone forgot about him. 16I still think
wisdom is better than strength. But those people
forgot about the poor man's wisdom and stopped
listening to what he said.

17The quiet words of a wise person
are better
than the shouts of a foolish ruler.
18Wisdom is better than weapons of war,
but one sinner can destroy much good.

10 Dead flies can make even perfume
stink.
In the same way, a little foolishness can
spoil wisdom.
2The heart of the wise leads to right,
but the heart of a fool leads to wrong.
3Even in the way fools walk along the road,
they show they are not wise;
they show everyone how stupid they are.
4Don't leave your job
just because your ruler is angry with you.
Remaining calm solves great problems.

5There is something else wrong that happens
here on earth.
It is the kind of mistake rulers make:
6fools are given important positions
while rich people are given lower ones;
7I have seen servants ride horses
while princes walk like servants on foot.
8Anyone who digs a pit might fall into it;
anyone who knocks down a wall might be
bitten by a snake;
9anyone who moves boulders might be hurt
by them;
and anyone who cuts logs might be harmed
by them.
10A dull axe means harder work.
Being wise will make it easier.
11If a snake bites the tamer before it is tamed,
what good is the tamer?

12The words of the wise bring them praise,
but the words of a fool will destroy them.
13A fool begins by saying foolish things
and ends by saying insane and wicked
things.
14A fool talks too much.
No one knows the future,
and no one can tell what will happen after
death.
15Work wears fools out;
they don't even know how to get home.

The Value of Work

16How terrible it is for a country whose king is
a child
and whose leaders eat all morning.
17How happy a country is whose king comes
from a good family,
whose leaders eat only at mealtimes
and for strength, not to get drunk.

18If someone is lazy, the roof will begin to fall.
If he doesn't fix it, the house will leak.

19A party makes you feel good,
wine makes you feel happy
and money buys anything.
20Don't make fun of the king,
and don't make fun of rich people, even in
your bedroom.
A little bird might carry your words;
a bird might fly and tell what you said.

Boldly Face the Future

11 Invest what you have,
because after a while you will get a
return.
2Invest what you have in several different
businesses,
because you don't know what disasters
might happen.

3If clouds are full of rain,
they will shower on the earth.
A tree can fall to the north or south,
but it will stay where it falls.
4Those who wait for perfect weather
will never plant seeds;
those who look at every cloud
will never harvest crops.

5You don't know where the wind will blow,
and you don't know how a baby grows
inside the mother.
In the same way, you don't know what God
is doing,
or how he created everything.
6Plant early in the morning,
and work until evening,
because you don't know if this or that will
succeed.
They might both do well.

Serve God While You are Young

7Sunshine is sweet;
it is good to see the light of day.
8People ought to enjoy every day of their lives,
no matter how long they live.

But they should also remember this:
you will be dead a long time.
Everything that happens then is useless.
9Young people, enjoy yourselves while you are young;
be happy while you are young.
Do whatever your heart desires,
whatever you want to do.
But remember that God will judge you
for everything you do.
10Don't worry,
and forget the troubles of your body,
because youth and childhood are useless.

The Problems of Old Age

12 Remember your Creator
while you are young,
before the days of trouble come
and the years when you say,
"I find no pleasure in them."
2When you get old,
the light from the sun, moon and stars will grow dark;
the rain clouds will never seem to go away.
3At that time your arms will shake
and your legs will become weak.
Your teeth will fall out so you cannot chew,
and your eyes will not see clearly.
4Your ears will be deaf to the noise in the streets,
and you will barely hear the millstone grinding grain.
You will wake up when a bird starts singing,
but you will barely hear the faint singing.
5You will fear high places
and will be afraid to go for a walk.
Your hair will become white like the flowers on an almond tree.
You will limp along like a grasshopper when you walk.
Your appetite will be gone.
Then you will go to your everlasting home,
and people will go to your funeral.
6Soon your life will snap like a silver chain
or break like a golden bowl.
You will be like a broken pitcher at a spring,
or a broken wheel at a well.
7You will turn back into the dust of the earth again,
but your spirit will return to God who gave it.

8Everything is useless!
The Teacher says that everything is useless.

Conclusion: Honour God

9The Teacher was very wise and taught the people what he knew. He very carefully thought about, studied and set in order many wise teachings. 10The Teacher looked for just the right words to write what is dependable and true.

11Words from wise people are like sharp sticks used to guide animals. They are like nails that have been driven in firmly. Altogether they are wise teachings that come from one Shepherd. 12So be careful, my son, about other teachings. People are always writing books, and too much study will make you tired.

Sidelight

When the homework piles up, quote the last part of Ecclesiastes 12:12. Maybe someone will take pity on you. The words "my son" were a common way for teachers to address pupils in Old Testament times.

13Now, everything has been heard,
so I give my final advice:
honour God and obey his commands,
because this is all people must do.
14God will judge everything,
even what is done in secret,
the good and the evil.

Song of Solomon

Why Read This Book:

- Identify with lovers' longing for each other (Song of Solomon 1–2).
- Celebrate true love and affection for a lover (Song of Solomon 3–5).
- Watch true love develop into commitment (Song of Solomon 6–8).

When?

Time Line:

- *1000 BC* – King Solomon ruled and may have written Song of Solomon
- *750 BC*
- Jerusalem fell to the Babylonians – Jews began returning to Jerusalem from exile
- *500 BC*
- *250 BC*
- *BC/AD* – Jesus was born

Behind the Scenes:

Romance. People read about it, dream about it and fantasise about it. We each hope that someone wonderful will meet us, marry us, share passionate, lasting love with us. But we don't expect to find much about this kind of romance in the Bible.

That's what's so surprising about the Song of Solomon, also known as Song of Songs. Using graphic imagery and language, this unusual book in the Bible celebrates God's gifts of love and sexuality. It appears to tell about a king and a shepherd both pursuing a beautiful peasant woman. Through poetry, the book shows admiration, yearning for love, physical attractiveness and dedicated commitment.

Scholars have debated the Song of Solomon for centuries – beginning before Jesus was born. They suggest several possible ways to interpret this unusual book:

- Symbolic – the book has a hidden or symbolic religious meaning about the relationship between God and Israel or between Christ and the church. Beneath the pictures of physical love lies the spiritual truth that God loves us completely.
- Literal – the book is what it appears to be: love songs about a beautiful courtship between a man and a woman. So these poems affirm a place for beautiful expressions of human love within our faith.
- Dramatic – the book is a drama about sexual love. The songs were written to be sung or performed by two to four actors and a chorus. The drama may have been performed as entertainment during weddings.

Whatever your view on the book's purpose, Song of Solomon should be treasured, because it gives beautiful images of committed love – both physical and spiritual – and celebrates human love as a gift from God.

LIFE FILE LINKS

Investigate the Theme

To find a list of real life stories on this subject turn to the LIFE FILE GUIDE on pages 12 to 22 at the front of the Youth Bible.

MARRIAGE

1 Solomon's Greatest Song.

The Woman Speaks to the Man She Loves

2Kiss me with the kisses of your mouth,
because your love is better than wine.

> **Sidelight** This book is the ultimate in marriage guidance counselling. The dramatic poetry pictures the love that Solomon has for his bride. In this we can see the importance of physical love within the boundaries of marriage.

3The smell of your perfume is pleasant,
and your name is pleasant like expensive perfume.
That's why the young women love you.
4Take me with you; let's run together.
The king takes me into his rooms.

Friends Speak to the Man

We will rejoice and be happy with you;
we praise your love more than wine.
With good reason, the young women love you.

The Woman Speaks

5I'm dark but lovely,
women of Jerusalem,
dark like the tents of Kedar,
like the curtains of Solomon.
6Don't look at how dark I am,
at how dark the sun has made me.
My brothers were angry with me
and made me tend the vineyards,
so I haven't tended my own vineyard!
7Tell me, you whom I love,
where do you feed your sheep?
Where do you let them rest at noon?
Why should I look for you near your friend's sheep,
like a woman who wears a veil? *n*

The Man Speaks to the Woman

8You are the most beautiful of women.
Surely you know to follow the sheep
and feed your young goats
near the shepherds' tents.
9My darling, you are like a mare
among the king's stallions.
10Your cheeks are beautiful with ornaments,
and your neck with jewels.
11We will make for you gold earrings
with silver hooks.

The Woman Speaks

12The smell of my perfume spreads out
to the king on his couch.
13My lover is like a bag of myrrh *d*
that lies all night between my breasts.
14My lover is like a bunch of flowers
from the vineyards at En Gedi.

> **Sidelight** Ancient lovers didn't have designer perfumes, but they were still into being attractive to others. Women wore sachets of fragrance around their necks (Song of Solomon 1:12–14), while men splashed perfume on their beards and robes.

The Man Speaks

15My darling, you are beautiful!
Oh, you are beautiful,
and your eyes are like doves.

The Woman Answers the Man

16You are so handsome, my lover,
and so pleasant!
Our bed is the grass.
17Cedar trees form our roof;
our ceiling is made of juniper wood.

The Woman Speaks Again

2 I am a rose in the Plain of Sharon,
a lily in the valleys.

The Man Speaks Again

2Among the young women, my darling
is like a lily among thorns!

The Woman Answers

3Among the young men, my lover
is like an apple tree in the woods!
I enjoy sitting in his shadow;
his fruit is sweet to my taste.
4He brought me to the banquet room,
and his banner over me is love.
5Strengthen me with raisins,
and refresh me with apples,
because I am weak with love.
6My lover's left hand is under my head,
and his right arm holds me tight.

The Woman Speaks to the Friends

7Women of Jerusalem, promise me
by the gazelles *d* and the deer
not to awaken
or excite my feelings of love
until it is ready.

veil This was the way a prostitute usually dressed.

The Woman Speaks Again

8I hear my lover's voice.
Here he comes jumping across the mountains,
skipping over the hills.
9My lover is like a gazelle[d] or a young deer.
Look, he stands behind our wall
looking through the windows,
looking through the blinds.
10My lover spoke and said to me,
"Get up, my darling;
let's go away, my beautiful one.
11Look, the winter is past;
the rains are over and gone.
12Blossoms appear through all the land.
The time has come to sing;
the cooing of doves is heard in our land.
13There are young figs on the fig trees,
and the blossoms on the vines smell sweet.
Get up, my darling;
let's go away, my beautiful one."

The Man Speaks

14My beloved is like a dove hiding in the cracks of the rock,
in the secret places of the cliff.
Show me your face,
and let me hear your voice.
Your voice is sweet,
and your face is lovely.

LOVE

Walk On By

Vicky would spend hours looking at the poster on her wall. What would it be like to meet him? If only she could, she knew that he would love her . . . they were made for each other . . . if only . . .

Then one day she managed to get tickets for his concert! She was so excited that she arrived hours too early and was rewarded by seeing the whole band arrive at the backstage area. She screamed with the other girls and the musicians politely came over and spoke to them through the wired fence. Vicky got his autograph and was overwhelmed when he smiled at her and said, "Will you be coming to Sheffield?" She nodded wildly and smiled back at him.

After the concert she went home and started to add up her savings. The Sheffield concert was hundreds of miles away from where she lived, but she was convinced that the pop star had personally invited her to be there.

She found out where they would be staying and managed to book a single room there as soon as she arrived. She was only fourteen years old but dressed herself up to look much older.

Then it happened. The dream of all dreams . . . she saw him outside his room and he beckoned her in. Deliriously happy, she allowed him to sleep with her but was a little confused when he wanted her to go. She told herself that it would be different when she saw him the next day. But when she saw him in the morning, he walked straight past her. No hint of recognition. Vicky was devastated as she began to realise what had happened. She'd used all her savings, lost respect . . . and her virginity. It wasn't love after all. It was just being used.

Read Song of **Solomon 2:10—3:4**, it talks of "never letting go" (3:4) and "My lover is mine and I am his" (2:16). Don't make Vicky's mistake.

- Where did Vicky go wrong, according to this passage?
- Could you look at the person you love and relate your feelings to this passage?

Consider . . .

- listing the things that you would feel, that would help to you know you are in love.
- talking to a couple you know who have a strong relationship, and asking them what makes their marriage so strong.

For more, see . . .

- Genesis 29:20 (p.34)
- 1 John 4:7–21 (p.1374)
- John 15:9–17 (p.1125)

15Catch the foxes for us—
the little foxes that ruin the vineyards
while they are in blossom.

The Woman Speaks

16My lover is mine, and I am his.
He feeds among the lilies
17until the day dawns
and the shadows disappear.
Turn, my lover.
Be like a gazelle*d* or a young deer
on the mountain valleys.

The Woman Dreams

3 At night on my bed,
I looked for the one I love;
I looked for him, but I could not find him.
2I got up and went around the city,
in the streets and squares,
looking for the one I love.
I looked for him, but I could not find him.
3The watchmen found me as they patrolled
the city,
so I asked, "Have you seen the one
I love?"
4As soon as I had left them,
I found the one I love.
I held him and would not let him go
until I brought him to my mother's house,
to the room where I was born.

The Woman Speaks to the Friends

5Women of Jerusalem, promise me
by the gazelles*d* and the deer
not to awaken
or excite my feelings of love
until it is ready.
6Who is this coming out of the desert
like a cloud of smoke?
Who is this that smells like myrrh,*d*
incense*d*
and other spices?
7Look, it's Solomon's couch*n*
with 60 soldiers around it,
the finest soldiers of Israel.
8These soldiers all carry swords
and have been trained in war.
Every man wears a sword at his side
and is ready for the dangers of the night.
9King Solomon had a couch made for himself
of wood from Lebanon.
10He made its posts of silver
and its braces of gold.
The seat was covered with purple cloth
that the women of Jerusalem wove with
love.

11Women of Jerusalem, go out and see King
Solomon.
He is wearing the crown his mother put on
his head
on his wedding day,
when his heart was happy!

The Man Speaks to the Woman

4 How beautiful you are, my darling!
Oh, you are beautiful!
Your eyes behind your veil are like doves.
Your hair is like a flock of goats streaming
down Mount Gilead.
2Your teeth are white like newly sheared
sheep
just coming from their bath.
Each one has a twin,
and none of them is missing.
3Your lips are like red silk thread,
and your mouth is lovely.
Your cheeks behind your veil
are like slices of a pomegranate.*d*
4Your neck is like David's tower,
built with rows of stones.
A thousand shields hang on its walls;
each shield belongs to a strong soldier.
5Your breasts are like two fawns,
like twins of a gazelle,*d*
feeding among the lilies.
6Until the day dawns
and the shadows disappear,
I will go to that mountain of myrrh*d*
and to that hill of incense.*d*
7My darling, everything about you is beautiful,
and there is nothing at all wrong with you.

Sidelight The poem in Song of Solomon 4:1–7 contains comparisons that may seem quite ridiculous to us today, but they were quite appealing in ancient times!

8Come with me from Lebanon, my bride.
Come with me from Lebanon,
from the top of Mount Amana,
from the tops of Mount Senir and Mount
Hermon.
Come from the lions' dens
and from the leopards' hills.
9My sister, my bride,
you have thrilled my heart;
you have thrilled my heart
with a glance of your eyes,
with one sparkle from your necklace.

couch Something like a bed carried by slaves on which the king lay or sat while travelling.

10Your love is so sweet, my sister, my bride.
Your love is better than wine,
and your perfume smells better than any spice.
11My bride, your lips drip honey;
honey and milk are under your tongue.
Your clothes smell like the cedars of Lebanon.
12My sister, my bride, you are like a garden
locked up,
like a walled-in spring, a closed fountain.
13Your limbs are like an orchard
of pomegranates with all the best fruit,
filled with flowers and nard,[d]
14nard and saffron,[d] calamus[d] and cinnamon,
with trees of incense, myrrh and aloes[d]—
all the best spices.
15You are like a garden fountain—
a well of fresh water
flowing down from the mountains of
Lebanon.

The Woman Speaks

16Awake, north wind.
Come, south wind.
Blow on my garden,
and let its sweet smells flow out.
Let my lover enter the garden
and eat its best fruits.

The Man Speaks

5 I have entered my garden, my sister, my
bride.
I have gathered my myrrh[d] with my
spice.
I have eaten my honeycomb and my honey.
I have drunk my wine and my milk.

The Friends Speak

Eat, friends, and drink;
yes, drink deeply, lovers.

SEXUALITY

Warning Signs

Matt had seen the warning signs. Rachel never really seemed that interested in praying with him and she had made some pretty bad choices in her past. Her insecurities had led her into a string of damaging relationships with non-Christian guys who had made her feel "loved" . . . as long as she gave them what they wanted. Matt knew that we all make bad choices and have to live with the consequences, and that God's grace offers forgiveness and a brand new start whatever we've done, but the problem was that Rachel never really seemed sorry for her past, so actually it was still a problem for the present. Was Rachel really the godly girl he had waited for, or was she just "playing at being a Christian" on Sundays?

Matt had only ever been interested in dating a girl who put Jesus first in her life. The trouble was things were getting complicated now – he had fallen in love! His heart was starting to make excuses. "Sure, Rachel isn't perfect, but none of us are, right?" "Maybe with my influence she'll put God first and deal with her past?" and "I'll never find another girl as nice as her!"

In the end, the decision to end the relationship was an easy one when Matt found out that Rachel had been cheating on him. Matt was devastated. In time, God healed his broken heart and Matt trusts that God has someone better for him.

God created the passion and excitement of falling in love. Check out the way it should be in **Song of Solomon 5:2–6**.

- What does this passage tell us about God's attitude to sex?
- Why does the Bible tell us that God's best for us is to marry a Christian and to wait until we're married before we have sex?

Consider . . .

- finding a Christian friend of the same sex to pray with and be accountable to in this area. It can be really great to pray together and help each other make good choices.
- any mistakes you may have made in this area. Ask God to forgive you and give you a new start.

For more, see . . .

- 1 Kings 11:1–13 (p.325)
- Proverbs 31:10–31 (p.617)
- Proverbs 7:1–27 (p.595)
- 2 Corinthians 6:14–18 (p.1247)

The Woman Dreams

2I sleep, but my heart is awake.
I hear my lover knocking.
"Open to me, my sister, my darling,
my dove, my perfect one.
My head is wet with dew,
and my hair with the dampness of the night."
3I have taken off my garment
and don't want to put it on again.
I have washed my feet
and don't want to get them dirty again.
4My lover put his hand through the opening,
and I felt excited inside.
5I got up to open the door for my lover.
Myrrh [d] was dripping from my hands
and flowing from my fingers,
onto the handles of the lock.
6I opened the door for my lover,
but my lover had left and was gone.
When he spoke, he took my breath away.
I looked for him, but I could not find him;
I called for him, but he did not answer.
7The watchmen found me
as they patrolled the city.
They hit me and hurt me;
the guards on the wall took away my veil.
8Promise me, women of Jerusalem,
if you find my lover,
tell him I am weak with love.

The Friends Answer the Woman

9How is your lover better than other lovers,
most beautiful of women?
How is your lover better than other lovers?
Why do you want us to promise this?

The Woman Answers the Friends

10My lover is healthy and tanned,
the best of ten thousand men.
11His head is like the finest gold;
his hair is wavy and black like a raven.
12His eyes are like doves
by springs of water.
They seem to be bathed in cream
and are set like jewels.
13His cheeks are like beds of spices;
they smell like mounds of perfume.
His lips are like lilies
flowing with myrrh. [d]
14His hands are like gold hinges,
filled with jewels.
His body is like shiny ivory
covered with sapphires.
15His legs are like large marble posts,
standing on bases of fine gold.
He is like a cedar of Lebanon,
like the finest of the trees.
16His mouth is sweet to kiss,
and I desire him very much.
Yes, daughters of Jerusalem,
this is my lover
and my friend.

The Friends Speak to the Woman

6 Where has your lover gone,
most beautiful of women?
Which way did your lover turn?
We will look for him with you.

The Woman Answers the Friends

2My lover has gone down to his garden,
to the beds of spices,
to feed in the gardens
and to gather lilies.
3I belong to my lover,
and my lover belongs to me.
He feeds among the lilies.

The Man Speaks to the Woman

4My darling, you are as beautiful as the city of Tirzah,
as lovely as the city of Jerusalem,
like an army flying flags.
5Turn your eyes from me,
because they excite me too much.
Your hair is like a flock of goats
streaming down Mount Gilead.
6Your teeth are white like sheep
just coming from their bath;
each one has a twin,
and none of them is missing.
7Your cheeks behind your veil
are like slices of a pomegranate. [d]

Sidelight You wouldn't usually say that your girlfriend has "fruity cheeks", but it was a compliment in Old Testament days! The pomegranate is a small, red fruit that's especially refreshing in a hot climate like Israel's (Song of Solomon 6:7). The round fruit is filled with pulp and seeds, somewhat like the inside of an orange in texture.

8There may be sixty queens and eighty slave women [d]
and so many girls you cannot count them,
9but there is only one like my dove, my perfect one.
She is her mother's only daughter,
the brightest of the one who gave her birth.
The young women saw her and called her happy;
the queens and the slave women also praised her.

The Young Women Praise the Woman

10Who is that young woman
that shines out like the dawn?
She is as pretty as the moon,
as bright as the sun,
as wonderful as an army flying flags.

The Man Speaks

11I went down into the orchard of nut trees
to see the blossoms of the valley,
to look for buds on the vines,
to see if the pomegranate[d] trees had bloomed.
12Before I realised it, my desire for you made me feel
like a prince in a chariot.

The Friends Call to the Woman

13Come back, come back, woman of Shulam.
Come back, come back,
so we may look at you!

The Woman Answers the Friends

Why do you want to look at the woman of Shulam
as you would at the dance of two armies?

The Man Speaks to the Woman

7 Your feet are beautiful in sandals,
you daughter of a prince.
Your round thighs are like jewels
shaped by an artist.
2Your navel is like a round drinking cup
always filled with wine.
Your stomach is like a pile of wheat
surrounded with lilies.
3Your breasts are like two fawns,
like twins of a gazelle.[d]
4Your neck is like an ivory tower.
Your eyes are like the pools in Heshbon
near the gate of Bath Rabbim.
Your nose is like the mountain of Lebanon
that looks down on Damascus.
5Your head is like Mount Carmel,
and your hair is like purple cloth;
the king is captured in its folds.
6You are beautiful and pleasant;
my love, you are full of delights.
7You are tall like a palm tree,
and your breasts are like its bunches of fruit.
8I said, "I will climb up the palm tree
and take hold of its fruit."
Let your breasts be like bunches of grapes,
the smell of your breath like apples,
9 and your mouth like the best wine.

The Woman Speaks to the Man

Let this wine go down sweetly for my lover;
may it flow gently past the lips and teeth.
10I belong to my lover,
and he desires only me.
11Come, my lover,
let's go out into the country
and spend the night in the fields.
12Let's go early to the vineyards
and see if the buds are on the vines.
Let's see if the blossoms have already opened
and if the pomegranates[d] have bloomed.
There I will give you my love.
13The mandrake flowers give their sweet smell,
and all the best fruits are at our gates.
I have saved them for you, my lover,
the old delights and the new.

Sidelight The mandrake flower (Song of Solomon 7:13) not only gave a sweet smell but was also thought to arouse sexual desire. The yellow-red fruit was also thought to increase fertility (see Genesis 30:14–16, p.35). No wonder it was called the "love apple"!

8 I wish you were like my brother
who fed at my mother's breasts.
If I found you outside,
I would kiss you,
and no one would look down on me.
2I would lead you and bring you
to my mother's house;
she is the one who taught me.
I would give you a drink of spiced wine
from my pomegranates.

The Woman Speaks to the Friends

3My lover's left hand is under my head,
and his right arm holds me tight.
4Women of Jerusalem,
promise not to awaken
or excite my feelings of love
until it is ready.

The Friends Speak

5Who is this coming out of the desert,
leaning on her lover?

The Man Speaks to the Woman

I woke you under the apple tree
where you were born;
there your mother gave birth to you.
6Put me like a seal on your heart,
like a seal on your arm.

Love is as strong as death;
jealousy is as strong as the grave.
Love bursts into flames
and burns like a hot fire.
7Even much water cannot put out the flame of love;
floods cannot drown love.
If a man offered everything in his house for love,
people would totally reject it.

The Woman's Brothers Speak

8We have a little sister,
and her breasts are not yet grown.
What should we do for our sister
on the day she becomes engaged?
9If she is a wall,
we will put silver towers on her.
If she is a door,
we will protect her with cedar boards.

The Woman Speaks

10I am a wall,
and my breasts are like towers.
So I was to him,
as one who brings happiness.
11Solomon had a vineyard at Baal Hamon.
He rented the vineyards for others to tend,
and everyone who rented had to pay
a thousand silver pieces for the fruit.
12But my own vineyard is mine to give.
Solomon, the thousand silver pieces are for you,
and two hundred pieces are for those who tend the fruit.

Sidelight If girls think their brothers are overprotective today, imagine how they would have felt in biblical times (Song of Solomon 8:8–9). Brothers were responsible for a sister until marriage, so they kept other men from taking advantage of her innocence. They would probably come with her on her dates today!

The Man Speaks to the Woman

13You who live in the gardens,
my friends are listening for your voice;
let me hear it.

The Woman Speaks to the Man

14Hurry, my lover,
be like a gazelle[d]
or a young deer
on the mountains where spices grow.

Isaiah

Why Read This Book:

- See how God works through world events to bring people to himself (Isaiah 1—35).
- Discover what can happen when people trust in things other than God (Isaiah 36—39).
- Be assured that God is working in the world, even when life seems hopeless (Isaiah 40—66).

When?

Behind the Scenes:

Isaiah could have had a simple life in Judah. He was probably well educated and may have been a priest. He knew the top people in Jerusalem, including the king.

But Isaiah saw trouble brewing, and the Lord called him to be a prophet. Though his country had been peaceful and prosperous under King Uzziah's leadership (see 2 Chronicles 26:1–23, p.420), Isaiah could tell that the good situation was changing. God wanted him to speak out!

First, he watched as the Assyrians conquered neighbouring Israel and threatened Judah. The king of Judah was tempted to form military alliances to protect the nation; Isaiah believed Judah should rely on God instead.

Second, while people paid lip service to God, they didn't really follow him. Instead, they took advantage of the poor.

The book of Isaiah has two distinct parts:

Chapters 1—39 deal with events in the eighth century before Christ, when Judah was independent but constantly threatened by the Assyrians. During this time, the prophet blasted the rich and powerful who neglected and oppressed the poor. And he challenged the nation not to rely on military power to defend itself, but to rely on God. ▷

Where?

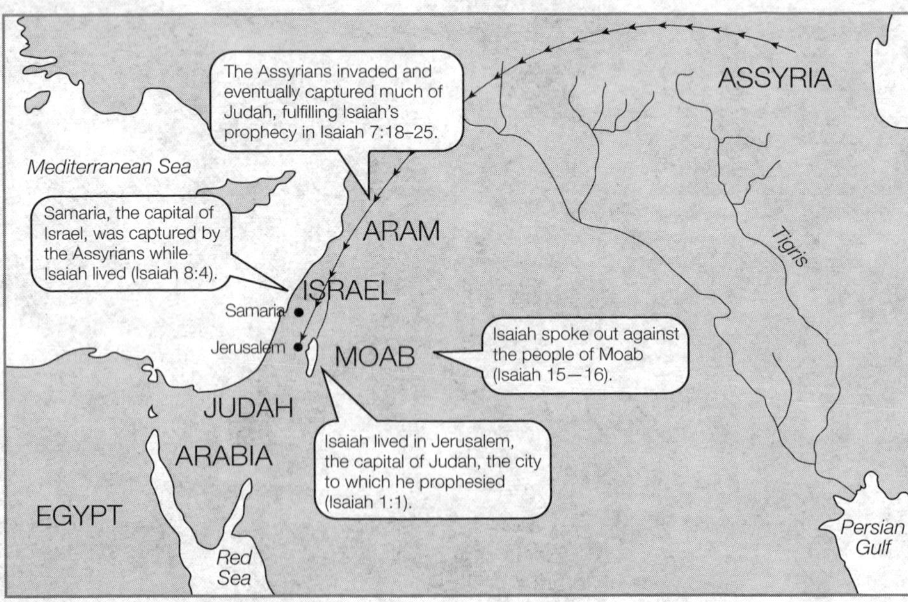

Behind the Scenes (cont.): Chapters 40—66 zoom forward to about two hundred years later, when the Persian Empire controlled Judah. After being in exile, the Jews were trying to rebuild their lives. Through this section, the prophet constantly comforts the people, assuring them that the past, present and future are all in God's hands. God's presence and love gave them hope.

Isaiah's message of hope points to a time when God would deliver his people through God's suffering servant (Isaiah 52—57). Since New Testament times, Christians have believed that these promises were fulfilled in the coming of Jesus Christ, who suffered and died for the sins of the world. (For example, see Isaiah 53.)

---

1 This is the vision Isaiah son of Amoz saw about what would happen to Judah and Jerusalem. Isaiah saw these things while Uzziah,[n] Jotham, Ahaz and Hezekiah were kings of Judah.

Sidelight The book of Isaiah is quoted more in the New Testament than any other book – and more than all the other prophetic books combined. The New Testament refers to Isaiah 150 times and actually quotes it 50 times.

God's Case Against His Children

2Heaven and earth, listen,
because the LORD is speaking:
"I raised my children and helped them grow up,
but they have turned against me.
3An ox knows its master,
and a donkey knows where its owner feeds it,
but the people of Israel do not know me;
my people do not understand."

4How terrible! Israel is a nation of sin,
a people loaded down with guilt,
a group of children doing evil,
children who are full of evil.
They have left the LORD;
they hate God, the Holy One of Israel,
and have turned away from him as if he were a stranger.
5Why should you continue to be punished?
Why do you continue to turn against him?
Your whole head is hurt,
and your whole heart is sick.
6There is no healthy spot
from the bottom of your foot to the top of your head;
you are covered with wounds, hurts and open sores
that are not cleaned and covered,
and no medicine takes away the pain.

7Your land is ruined;
your cities have been burnt with fire.
While you watch,
your enemies are stealing everything from your land;
it is ruined like a country destroyed by enemies.
8Jerusalem is left alone
like an empty shelter in a vineyard,
like a hut left in a field of melons,
like a city surrounded by enemies.
9The LORD All-powerful
allowed a few of our people to live.
Otherwise we would have been completely destroyed
like the cities of Sodom and Gomorrah.

10Jerusalem, your rulers are like those of Sodom,
and your people are like those of Gomorrah.
Hear the word of the LORD;
listen to the teaching of our God!
11The LORD says,
"I do not want all these sacrifices.
I have had enough of your burnt sacrifices
of rams and fat from fine animals.
I am not pleased
by the blood of bulls, lambs and goats.
12You come to meet with me,
but who asked you to do

Uzziah Also called Azariah.

all this running in and out of my Temple's [d]
rooms?
13Don't continue bringing me worthless
sacrifices!
I hate the incense [d] you burn.
I can't stand your New Moons, [d] Sabbaths [d]
and other feast days;
I can't stand the evil you do in your holy
meetings.
14I hate your New Moon feasts
and your other yearly feasts.
They have become a heavy weight
on me,
and I am tired of carrying it.
15When you raise your arms to me
in prayer,
I will refuse to look at you.
Even if you say many prayers,
I will not listen to you,
because your hands are full of blood.
16Wash yourselves and make yourselves
clean. [d]
Stop doing the evil things I see you do.
Stop doing wrong.
17 Learn to do good.
Seek justice.
Punish those who hurt others.
Help the orphans.
Stand up for the rights of widows."

18The LORD says,
"Come, let us talk about these things.
Though your sins are bright red,
they can be as white as snow.
Though your sins are deep red,
they can be white like wool.
19If you become willing and obey me,
you will eat good crops from the land.
20But if you refuse to obey and if you turn
against me,
you will be destroyed by your enemies'
swords."
The LORD himself said these things.

Jerusalem is Not Loyal to God

21The city of Jerusalem once followed
the LORD,
but she is no longer loyal to him.
She used to be filled with fairness;
people there lived the way God
wanted.
But now, murderers live there.
22Jerusalem, you have become like the scum
left when silver is purified;
you are like wine mixed with water.
23Your rulers are rebels
and friends of thieves.
They all accept money for doing wrong,
and they are paid to cheat people.
They don't seek justice for the orphans
or listen to the widows' needs.
24So the Lord GOD All-powerful,
the Mighty One of Israel, says:
"You, my enemies, will not cause me any
more trouble.
I will pay you back for what you did.
25I will turn against you
and clean away all your wrongs as if with
soap;
I will take all the worthless things out of
you.
26I will bring back judges as you had
long ago;
your counsellors will be like those you had
in the beginning.
Then you will be called the City That Is Right
with God,
the Loyal City."

27By doing what is fair,
Jerusalem will be free again.
By doing what is right,
her people who come back to the LORD will
have freedom.
28But sinners and those who turn against him
will be destroyed;
those who have left the LORD will die.

29"You will be ashamed,
because you have worshipped gods under
the oak trees.
You will be disgraced,
because you have worshipped idols in your
gardens.
30You will be like an oak whose leaves are
dying
or like a garden without water.
31Powerful people will be like small, dry pieces
of wood,
and their works will be like sparks.
They will burn together,
and no one will be able to put out that
fire."

The Message About Jerusalem

2 Isaiah son of Amoz saw this message about
Judah and Jerusalem:
2In the last days
the mountain on which the LORD's Temple [d]
stands
will become the most important of all
mountains.
It will be raised above the hills,
and people from all nations will come
streaming to it.

3 Many nations will come and say,
"Come, let us go up to the mountain of the LORD,
to the Temple of the God of Jacob.
Then God will teach us his ways,
and we will obey his teachings."
His teachings will go out from Jerusalem;
the message of the LORD will go out from Jerusalem.
4 He will settle arguments among the nations
and will make decisions for many nations.
Then they will make their swords into ploughs
and their spears into hooks for trimming trees.
Nations will no longer fight other nations,
nor will they train for war any more.

5 Come, family of Jacob,
and let us follow the way of the LORD.

A Terrible Day is Coming

6 LORD, you have left your people,
the family of Jacob,
because they have become filled with wrong ideas from people in the East.
They try to tell the future like the Philistines,
and they have completely accepted those foreign ideas.
7 Their land has been filled with silver and gold;
there are a great many treasures there.
Their land has been filled with horses;
there are many chariots there.
8 Their land is full of idols.
The people worship these idols they made with their own hands
and shaped with their own fingers.
9 People will not be proud any longer
but will bow low with shame.
God, do not forgive them.

PEACE

Peace at Any Price

The two boys pulled the cart behind them, up the street towards the depot. Occasionally bits of scrap would fall off and Danny, the smaller one, would have to stop and pile them back on top. They were very pleased with their haul.

They had an old stair rail that they had found in a bus shelter, some pots that they found in their father's shed, and some of his old garden tools too.

They were sure that the scrap metal they had collected would be enough to make a new gun for a soldier. They had seen the government film about turning ordinary objects into items that could be used for war, and they wanted to play their part. They thought that if they could just make enough weapons then Britain would win, and their father would be able to return home.

Sadly, that story from World War II did not bring peace. In fact most of the scrap metal collected was just left to rot – it was just an idea to make people feel like they were involved in the war effort.

The idea of turning ordinary things into weapons may have been one idea to win a war – but that is not God's plan for peace. In **Isaiah 2:1–5** God talks about doing the very opposite thing.

- Why do you think there will be no more war?
- According to this passage, what's the only way in which true peace – at home or in the world – can be achieved?

Consider . . .

- writing a list of what God will do in the last days.
- how we can learn from different countries and their wars in our relationships. Think about one situation that involves you, and one that is a world situation. Pray and ask God what you can do to stop the fighting in both of them.

For more, see . . .

- John 14:25–27 (p.1124)
- Philippians 4:7 (p.1286)
- Ephesians 4:26 (p.1274)

10Go into the caves of the cliffs;
dig holes and hide in the ground
from the anger of the LORD
and from his great power!
11Proud people will be made humble,
and they will bow low with shame.
At that time only the LORD will still be praised.

12The LORD All-powerful has a certain day planned
when he will punish the proud and those who boast,
and they will no longer be important.
13He will bring down the tall cedar trees from Lebanon
and the great oak trees of Bashan,
14all the tall mountains
and the high hills,
15every tall tower
and every high, strong wall,
16all the trading ships
and the beautiful ships.
17At that time proud people will be made humble,
and they will bow low with shame.
At that time only the LORD will be praised,
18 but all the idols will be gone.

19People will run to caves in the rocky cliffs
and will dig holes and hide in the ground
from the anger of the LORD
and his great power,
when he stands to shake the earth.
20At that time people will throw away
their gold and silver idols,
which they made for themselves to worship;
they will throw them away to the bats and moles.
21Then the people will hide in caves
and cracks in the rocks
from the anger of the LORD
and his great power,
when he stands to shake the earth.

22You should stop trusting in people to save you,
because people are only human;
they aren't able to help you.

God Will Punish Judah and Jerusalem

3 Understand this:
the Lord GOD All-powerful
will take away everything Judah and Jerusalem need—
all the food and water,
2the heroes and great soldiers,
the judges and prophets, [d]
people who do magic and older leaders,
3the military leaders and government leaders,
the counsellors, the skilled craftsmen and those who try to tell the future.
4The LORD says, "I will cause young boys to be your leaders,
and foolish children will rule over you.
5People will be against each other; everyone will be against his neighbour.
Young people will not respect older people,
and common people will not respect important people."
6At that time a man will seize one of his brothers
from his own family and say,
"You have a coat, so you will be our leader.
These ruins will be under your control."
7But that brother will stand up and say,
"I cannot help you,
because I do not have food or clothes in my house.
You will not make me your leader."
8This will happen because Jerusalem has stumbled,
and Judah has fallen.
The things they say and do are against the LORD;
they turn against him.
9The look on their faces shows they are guilty;
like the people of Sodom, they are proud of their sin.
They don't care who sees it.
How terrible it will be for them,
because they have brought much trouble on themselves.

10Tell those who do what is right that things will go well for them,
because they will receive a reward for what they do.
11But how terrible it will be for the wicked!
They will be punished for all the wrong they have done.
12Children treat my people cruelly,
and women rule over them.
My people, your guides lead you in the wrong way
and turn you away from what is right.

13The LORD takes his place in court
and stands to judge the people.
14The LORD presents his case
against the older leaders and other leaders of his people:
"You have burned the vineyard.
Your houses are full of what you took from the poor.

15 What gives you the right to crush my people
and grind the faces of the poor into the
ground?"
The Lord God All-powerful says this.

A Warning to Women of Jerusalem

16 The Lord says,
"The women of Jerusalem are proud.
They walk around with their heads held
high,
and they flirt with their eyes.
They take quick, short steps,
making noise with their ankle bracelets."

17 So the Lord will put sores on the heads of
those women in Jerusalem,
and he will make them lose their hair.

18 At that time the Lord will take away every-
thing that makes them proud: their beautiful an-
kle bracelets, their headbands, their necklaces
shaped like the moon, 19 their earrings, bracelets
and veils, 20 their scarves, ankle chains, the cloth
belts worn around their waists, their bottles of
perfume and charms, 21 their signet[d] rings, nose
rings, 22 their fine robes, capes, shawls and purses,
23 their mirrors, linen dresses, turbans and long
shawls.

IMAGE

Hold Your Head Up!

Thomas had an eye for the girls. He also had an eye for the mirror. Everywhere he went, you could be sure that he found the nearest piece of glass to check his appearance. His friends often teased him about it, but he didn't care.

One day, he was going to church with around half-a-dozen of his mates and when they arrived, the youth leader was unloading his car. He was bringing in all the spare boxes of drinks and crisps from the youth club down the road.

"Give us a hand lads!" he yelled as they went past him.

The boys started to lift the boxes from the car. Just then, a very pretty girl walked into the church. None of the lads could remember seeing her before and they all nudged each other. Thomas immediately started smoothing his hair and said to the youth leader:

"Ermm, which is the heaviest box?"

The leader pointed to a rather huge box in the corner, and Thomas picked it up.

"Be careful Tom" the leader warned. "You won't be able to see over the top properly."

"No problem," he yelled back.

Thomas started trudging up the aisle with his heavy box, feeling every inch the hero, and dying to walk past the new girl and make an impression. Suddenly, his feet seemed to be trudging even more, and he could hear sniggers. Then he felt something on his shins. Then he went head first up the aisle!

Somehow, when he'd walked into the church, he'd managed to catch his feet under the narrow carpet that led down the middle of the church. And as he walked along, it rolled along in front of him, until now it was a huge roll of carpet!

Lying on the floor, he grinned at his mates as he realised what a fool he'd made of himself. Holding your head high can sometimes ruin your image. And it's not only the guys that make a mess of it, look at what **Isaiah 3:16–23** says about some of the women of the day.

- What mistake did Thomas make, that was the same as the women in verse 16?
- What danger do we face by being preoccupied with our appearance?

Consider . . .

- making a spiritual list to challenge the image list in verses 18–22.
- taking a decision to keep your spiritual development and personal appearance on a par.

For more, see . . .

- Mark 10:31 (p.1017)
- 1 Corinthians 4:7 (p.1219)
- Mark 12:38–40 (p.1023)

[24]Instead of wearing sweet-smelling perfume,
they will stink.
Instead of fine cloth belts, they will wear
the ropes of captives.
Instead of having their hair fixed in fancy
ways, they will be bald.
Instead of fine clothes, they will wear
clothes of sadness.
Instead of being beautiful, they will wear
the brand of a captive.
[25]At that time your men will be killed with
swords,
and your heroes will die in war.
[26]There will be crying and sadness near the
city gates.
Jerusalem will be like a woman who has
lost everything and sits on the ground.

4 At that time seven women
will seize one man
and say, "We will eat our own bread
and make our own clothes,
but please marry us!
Please, take away our shame."

The Branch of the LORD

[2]At that time the LORD's branch will be very
beautiful and great. The people still living in Israel
will be proud of what the land grows. [3]Those
who are still living in Jerusalem will be called
holy; their names are recorded among the living
in Jerusalem. [4]The Lord will wash away the filth
from the women of Jerusalem. He will wash the
bloodstains out of Jerusalem and clean the city
with the spirit of fairness and the spirit of fire.
[5]Then the LORD will cover Mount Zion and the
people who meet there with a cloud of smoke
during the day and with a bright, flaming fire at
night. There will be a covering over every person.
[6]This covering will protect the people from the
heat of the sun and will provide a safe place to
hide from the storm and rain.

Israel, the LORD's Vineyard

5 Now I will sing for my friend a song about
his vineyard.
My friend had a vineyard
on a hill with very rich soil.
[2]He dug and cleared the field of stones
and planted the best grapevines there.
He built a tower in the middle of it
and cut out a winepress [d] as well.
He hoped good grapes would grow there,
but only bad ones grew.

[3]My friend says, "You people living in
Jerusalem,
and you people of Judah,
judge between me and my vineyard.
[4]What more could I have done for my
vineyard
than I have already done?
Although I expected good grapes to grow,
why were there only bad ones?
[5]Now I will tell you
what I will do to my vineyard:
I will remove the hedge,
and it will be burnt.
I will break down the stone wall,
and it will be walked on.
[6]I will ruin my field.
It will not be trimmed or hoed,
and weeds and thorns will grow there.
I will command the clouds
not to rain on it."

[7]The vineyard belonging to the LORD
All-powerful
is the nation of Israel;
the garden that he loves
is the people of Judah.
He looked for justice, but there was only
killing.
He hoped for right living, but there were
only cries of pain.

[8]How terrible it will be for you who add more
houses to your houses
and more fields to your fields
until there is no room left for other people.
Then you are left alone in the land.

[9]The LORD All-powerful said this to me:
"The fine houses will be destroyed;
the large and beautiful houses will be left
empty.
[10]At that time a 25-hectare vineyard will make
only 20 litres of wine,
and 200 litres of seed will grow only 20
litres of grain."

[11]How terrible it will be for people who rise
early in the morning
to look for strong drink,
who stay awake late at night,
becoming drunk with wine.
[12]At their parties they have lyres, [d] harps,
tambourines, [d] flutes and wine.
They don't see what the LORD has done
or notice the work of his hands.
[13]So my people will be captured and taken
away,
because they don't really know me.
All the great people will die of hunger,
and the common people will die of
thirst.
[14]So the place of the dead wants more and
more people,
and it opens wide its mouth.

Jerusalem's important people and common
people will go down into it,
with their happy and noisy ones.
15So the common people and the great people
will be brought down;
those who are proud will be humbled.
16The LORD All-powerful will receive glory by
judging fairly;
the holy God will show himself holy by
doing what is right.
17Then the sheep will go anywhere they want,
and lambs will feed on the land that rich
people once owned.

18How terrible it will be for those people!
They pull their guilt and sins behind them
as people pull wagons with ropes.
19They say, "Let God hurry;
let him do his work soon
so we may see it.
Let the plan of the Holy One of Israel happen
soon
so that we will know what it is."

20How terrible it will be for people who call
good things bad
and bad things good,
who think darkness is light
and light is darkness,
who think sour is sweet
and sweet is sour.

21How terrible it will be for people who think
they are wise
and believe they are clever.

22How terrible it will be for people who are
famous for drinking wine
and are champions at mixing drinks.
23They take money to set the guilty free
and don't allow good people to be judged
fairly.
24They will be destroyed
just as fire burns straw or dry grass.
They will be destroyed
like a plant whose roots rot
and whose flower dies and blows away like
dust.
They have refused to obey the teachings of
the LORD All-powerful
and have hated the message from the Holy
God of Israel.
25So the LORD has become very angry with his
people,
and he has raised his hand to punish
them.
Even the mountains are frightened.
Dead bodies lie in the streets like
rubbish.
But the LORD is still angry;
his hand is still raised to strike down the
people.

26He raises a banner for the nations far away.
He whistles to call those people from the
ends of the earth.
Look! The enemy comes quickly!
27Not one of them becomes tired or falls down.
Not one of them gets sleepy and falls asleep.
Their weapons are close at hand,
and their sandal straps are not broken.
28Their arrows are sharp,
and all of their bows are ready to shoot.
The horses' hoofs are as hard as rocks,
and their chariot wheels move like a
whirlwind.
29Their shout is like the roar of a lion;
it is loud like a young lion.
They growl as they capture their captives.
There is no one to stop them from taking
their captives away.
30On that day they will roar
like the waves of the sea.
And when people look at the land,
they will see only darkness and pain;
all light will become dark in this thick
cloud.

Isaiah Becomes a Prophet

6 In the year that King Uzziah died, I saw the
Lord sitting on a very high throne. His long
robe filled the Temple. [d] 2Heavenly creatures of
fire stood above him. Each creature had six
wings: it used two wings to cover its face, two
wings to cover its feet and two wings for flying.
3Each creature was calling to the others:
"Holy, holy, holy is the LORD All-powerful.
His glory fills the whole earth."
4Their calling caused the frame around the door
to shake, as the Temple filled with smoke.
5I said, "Oh, no! I will be destroyed. I am not
pure, and I live among people who are not pure,
but I have seen the King, the LORD All-powerful."
6One of the heavenly creatures used a pair of
tongs to take a hot coal from the altar. Then he
flew to me with the hot coal in his hand. 7The
creature touched my mouth with the hot coal
and said, "Look, your guilt is taken away, because
this hot coal has touched your lips. Your sin is
taken away."
8Then I heard the Lord's voice, saying, "Whom
can I send? Who will go for us?"
So I said, "Here I am. Send me!"
9Then the Lord said, "Go and tell this to the
people:
'You will listen and listen, but you will not
understand.

You will look and look, but you will not
learn.'
10Make the minds of these people dumb.
Shut their ears. Cover their eyes.
Otherwise, they might really understand
what they see with their eyes
and hear with their ears.
They might really understand in their minds
and come back to me and be healed."
11Then I asked, "Lord, how long should I do
this?"
He answered,
"Until the cities are destroyed
and the people are gone,
until there are no people left in the houses,
until the land is destroyed and left empty.
12The LORD will send the people
far away,
and the land will be left empty.
13One-tenth of the people will be left in the
land,

Sidelight Did you know that Isaiah included 32 references to fire? Throughout the Bible, fire is a common symbol of God's presence, action and judgement. For example, look up Genesis 15:17 (p.18), Exodus 13:21–22 (p.71), Acts 2:3 (p.1138), Hebrews 12:29 (p.1345) and Revelation 2:18 (p.1390).

WORSHIP

Understanding God's Heart

When John Wesley was rescued from a blazing house as a child, he was convinced that God had saved him for a purpose. As he grew up in eighteenth-century England, he applied all his energy towards accomplishing God's will for his life. While studying at Oxford University, John led a group of men known as the "Holy Club". They met for Bible study and prayer, and cared for the sick, poor and imprisoned. Not long after completing his work at the university, John and his brother, Charles, sailed to America to spread Christ's message.

John had good intentions but still felt like a failure. He knew God had given him a purpose in life, but he didn't seem able to carry it out. He needed to know and experience God's heart before he could offer it to anyone else. John returned to England discouraged and disillusioned. "I went to America to convert the Indians," John said. "But, oh, who shall convert me?"

Then something wonderful happened. On 24 May 1738, John attended a Christian meeting in London, and his life was changed. In his journal, John described what happened.

"I felt my heart strangely warmed," he wrote. "I felt I did trust in Christ, Christ alone for salvation; and an assurance was given to me that he had taken away my sins, even mine, and saved me from the law of sin and death."

John Wesley became one of the most influential men in the history of Christianity. During the 52 years following that experience in 1738, he preached over 40,000 sermons and travelled over 300,000 kilometres, sharing the message of Christ with hundreds of thousands.

John needed to understand and worship God before trying to serve him. The prophet Isaiah had a similar experience that launched his ministry. Read about Isaiah's encounter with God in **Isaiah 6:1–8**.

- Why did both John Wesley and Isaiah need to understand God's heart and worship him before they could adequately serve God?
- According to this passage, what do you know about God's character?

Consider . . .

- asking God to reveal himself to you the way he did to Isaiah or to John Wesley.
- writing a song to God, praising him for the qualities about him that you know are true.

For more, see . . .

- 2 Chronicles 29:18–36 (p.422)
- Revelation 19:1–9 (p.1401)
- Psalm 50 (p.529)

but it will be destroyed again.
These people will be like an oak tree
whose stump is left when the tree is
chopped down.
The people who remain will be like a
stump that will sprout again."

Trouble with Aram

7 Now Ahaz was the son of Jotham, who was
the son of Uzziah.[n] When Ahaz was king
of Judah, Rezin king of Aram and Pekah son of
Remaliah, the king of Israel, went up to Jerusalem
to fight against it. But they were not able to de-
feat the city.
2Ahaz king of Judah received a message saying,
"The armies of Aram and Israel[n] have joined
together."
When Ahaz heard this, he and the people were
frightened. They shook with fear like trees of the
forest blown by the wind.
3Then the LORD told Isaiah, "You and your son
Shear-Jashub[n] should go and meet Ahaz at the
place where the water flows into the upper pool,
on the road where people do their laundry. 4Tell
Ahaz, 'Be careful. Be calm and don't worry.
Don't let those two men, Rezin and Pekah son of
Remaliah, scare you. Don't be afraid of their an-
ger or Aram's anger, because they are like two
barely burning sticks that are ready to go out.
5They have made plans against you, saying,
6"Let's fight against Judah and tear it apart. We
will divide the land for ourselves and make the
son of Tabeel the new king of Judah." 7But I, the
Lord GOD, say,
" 'Their plan will not succeed;
it will not happen,
8because Aram is led by the city of Damascus,
and Damascus is led by its weak king,
Rezin.
Within 65 years Israel will no longer be a
nation.
9Israel is led by the city of Samaria,
and Samaria is led by its weak king, the son
of Remaliah.
If your faith is not strong,
you will not have strength enough to
last.' "

Immanuel—God is With Us

10Then the LORD spoke to Ahaz again, saying,
11"Ask for a sign from the LORD your God to prove
to yourself that these things are true. It may be a
sign from as deep as the place of the dead or as
high as the heavens."
12But Ahaz said, "I will not ask for a sign or test
the LORD."
13Then Isaiah said, "Ahaz, descendant[d] of
David, listen carefully! Isn't it bad enough that you
wear out the patience of people? Do you also
have to wear out the patience of my God? 14The
Lord himself will give you a sign: the virgin[n] will
be pregnant. She will have a son, and she will
name him Immanuel.[n] 15He will be eating milk
curds and honey when he learns to reject what is
evil and to choose what is good. 16You are afraid
of the kings of Israel and Aram now. But before
the child learns to choose good and reject evil,
the lands of Israel and Aram will be empty. 17The
LORD will bring troubled times to you, your people
and to the people of your father's family. They
will be worse than anything that has happened
since Israel separated from Judah. The LORD will
bring the king of Assyria to fight against you.
18"At that time the LORD will whistle for the
Egyptians, and they will come like flies from
Egypt's faraway streams. He will call for the
Assyrians, and they will come like bees. 19These
enemies will camp in the deep ravines and in the
cliffs, by the thorn-bushes and watering holes.
20The Lord will hire Assyria and use it like a razor
to punish Judah. It will be as if the Lord is shaving
the hair from Judah's head and legs and removing
Judah's beard.
21"At that time a person will be able to keep
only one young cow and two sheep alive. 22There
will be only enough milk for that person to eat
milk curds. All who remain in the land will go
back to eating just milk curds and honey. 23In this
land there are now vineyards that have 1,000
grapevines, which are worth about 1,000 pieces
of silver. But these fields will become full of
weeds and thorns. 24The land will become wild
and useful only as a hunting ground. 25People
once worked and grew food on these hills, but at
that time people will not go there, because the
land will be filled with weeds and thorns. Only
sheep and cattle will go to those places."

Assyria will Come Soon

8 The LORD told me, "Take a large scroll and
write on it with an ordinary pen: 'Maher-
Shalal-Hash-Baz'. 2I will gather some men to be

Uzziah Also called Azariah.
Israel Literally, "Ephraim". Isaiah often uses "Ephraim" to mean all of Israel.
Shear-Jashub This name means "a part of the people will come back".
virgin The Hebrew word means "a young woman". Often this meant a girl who was not married and had not yet had sexual relations with anyone.
Immanuel This name means "God is with us".

reliable witnesses: Uriah the priest and Zechariah
son of Jeberekiah."
3Then I went to the prophetess,[d] and she be-
came pregnant and had a son. The LORD told me,
"Name the boy Maher-Shalal-Hash-Baz,[n] 4be-
cause the king of Assyria will take away all the
wealth and possessions of Damascus and Samaria
before the boy learns to say 'my father' or 'my
mother'."
5Again the LORD spoke to me, saying,
6"These people refuse to accept
the slow-moving waters of the pool of
Shiloah
and are terrified of Rezin
and Pekah son of Remaliah.
7So I, the Lord, will bring
the king of Assyria and all his power
against them,
like a powerful flood of water from the
Euphrates River.
The Assyrians will be like water rising over
the banks of the river,
flowing over the land.
8That water will flow into Judah and pass
through it,
rising to Judah's throat.
Immanuel, this army will spread its wings
like a bird
until it covers your whole country."
9Be broken, all you nations,
and be smashed to pieces.
Listen, all you faraway countries.
Prepare for battle and be smashed to pieces!
Prepare for battle and be smashed to pieces!
10Make your plans for the fight,
but they will be defeated.
Give orders to your armies,
but they will be useless,
because God is with us.

Maher-Shalal-Hash-Baz This name means "there will soon be looting and stealing".

DOUBT

Having Confidence

Jon had a problem with talking to girls.

While it seemed that all Jon's friends in college had steady girlfriends, he couldn't even approach a girl without breaking out in a cold sweat. It was bad enough being a new student in a new college, without also having to suffer the embarrassment of a glistening forehead and sweaty palms.

One night, Jon sought comfort and advice from his older brother, Mike. "I don't suppose I'll ever have a girlfriend," Jon confessed. "I just don't know what to say to girls. I'm not like the others. They all have girlfriends."

"That's ridiculous," Mike said flatly. "They don't have anything you haven't got. You've just go to believe in yourself. Take a risk."

Jon went to his room to think and pray about what Mike said. That night, he asked God to help him to see himself the way God does. He prayed for God to help him to develop confidence.

Jon needed help from God to ease his doubts and build his confidence. In **Isaiah 7:10–16**, King Ahaz also needed God's help to ease his doubts.

- What do King Ahaz and Jon have in common?
- Why do you sometimes hesitate to ask God for something, even if you feel you really need it?

Consider . . .

- listing ways in which God could help you to ease your doubt about him or any situation in your life and then asking him to give you that help.
- asking your parent or youth leader about ways in which you can overcome specific doubts in your life.

For more, see . . .

- Judges 6:11–24 (p.231)
- James 1:6–8 (p.1348)
- Matthew 14:22–33 (p.966)

Warnings to Isaiah

11The LORD spoke to me with his great power and warned me not to follow the lead of the rest of the people. He said,

12"People are saying that others make plans against them,
but you should not believe them.
Don't be afraid of what they fear;
do not dread those things.
13But remember that the LORD All-powerful is holy.
He is the one you should fear;
he is the one you should dread.
14Then he will be a place of safety for you.
But for the two families of Israel,
he will be like a stone that causes people to stumble,
like a rock that makes them fall.
He will be like a trap for the people of Jerusalem,
and he will catch them in his trap.
15Many people will fall over this rock.
They will fall and be broken;
they will be trapped and caught."

16Make an agreement.
Seal up the teaching while my followers are watching.
17I will wait for the LORD to help us,
the LORD who is ashamed of the family of Israel.
I will wait for him.

18I am here, and with me are the children the LORD has given me. We are signs and proofs for the people of Israel from the LORD All-powerful, who lives on Mount Zion. [d]

19Some people say, "Ask the mediums [d] and fortune-tellers, who whisper and mutter, what to do." But I tell you that people should ask their God for help. Why should people who are still alive ask something from the dead? 20You should follow the teachings and the agreement with the LORD. The mediums and fortune-tellers do not speak the word of the LORD, so their words are worth nothing.

21People will wander through the land troubled and hungry. When they become hungry, they will become angry and will look up and curse their king and their God. 22They will look around them at their land and see only trouble, darkness and awful gloom. And they will be forced into the darkness.

A New Day is Coming

9 But suddenly there will be no more gloom for the land that suffered. In the past God made the lands of Zebulun and Naphtali hang their heads in shame, but in the future those lands will be made great. They will stretch from the road along the Mediterranean Sea to the land beyond the Jordan River and north to Galilee, the land of people who are not Israelites.

2Before those people lived in darkness,
but now they have seen a great light.
They lived in a dark land,
but a light has shone on them.
3God, you have caused the nation to grow
and made the people happy.
And they have shown their happiness to you,
like the joy during harvest time,
like the joy of people
taking what they have won in war.
4Like the time you defeated Midian,
you have taken away their heavy load
and the heavy pole from their backs
and the rod the enemy used to punish them.
5Every boot that marched in battle
and every uniform stained with blood
has been thrown into the fire.
6A child has been born to us;
God has given a son to us.
He will be responsible for leading the people.
His name will be Wonderful Counsellor,
Powerful God,
Father Who Lives For Ever, Prince of Peace.
7Power and peace will be in his kingdom
and will continue to grow for ever.
He will rule as king on David's throne
and over David's kingdom.
He will make it strong
by ruling with justice and goodness
from now on and for ever.
The LORD All-powerful will do this
because of his strong love for his people.

God Will Punish Israel

8The Lord sent a message against the people of Jacob;
it says that God will judge Israel.
9Then everyone in Israel, even the leaders in Samaria,
will know that God has sent it.
Those people are proud and boast by saying,
10"These bricks have fallen,
but we will build again with cut stones.
These small trees have been chopped down,
but we will put great cedars there."
11But the LORD has brought the enemies of Rezin against them;
he has stirred up their enemies against them.

12The Arameans came from the east
and the Philistines from the west,
and they ate up Israel with their armies.
But the LORD was still angry;
his hand was still raised to punish the people.

13But the people did not return to the one who
had struck them;
they did not follow the LORD All-powerful.
14So the LORD cut off Israel's head and tail,
taking away both the branch and stalk
in one day.
15The older leaders and important men were
the head,
and the prophets[d] who speak lies were the tail.
16Those who led the people led them in the
wrong direction,
and those who followed them were
destroyed.
17So the Lord is not happy with the young
people,
nor will he show mercy to the orphans and
widows.
All the people are separated from God and
are very evil;
they all speak lies.
But the LORD is still angry;
his hand is still raised to strike down the
people.

18Evil is like a small fire.
First, it burns weeds and thorns.
Next, it burns the larger bushes in the forest,
and they all go up in a column of smoke.
19The LORD All-powerful is angry,
so the land will be burnt.
The people are like fuel for the fire;
no one will try to save his brother or sister.

JUSTICE

Christmas Truce

The bombs had been falling for weeks now. Rain had soaked into the soil till it could take no more. Puddles had formed and grown until the whole battlefield was a mess of mud and wire. The noise, booming hour on hour and day on day left no one in any doubt – these were dark days.

And yet that night, as soldiers lay in their damp rooms, carved out from the clay soil, something had changed. At first, they didn't notice. The sound was so much part of their daily routine that the soldiers had blocked it out. It took a good couple of hours to really register that the bombing had stopped.

As the sun rose, there was no smoke to hide its power. Day dawned unimpeded for the first time in months. There was light.

Soldiers tentatively put their heads above the trench top and looked over the desolate no-man's-land.

And then they heard singing . . .

Early in World War I, soldiers on both sides stopped their fighting for Christmas – the day remembering the birth of Jesus.

While they stopped only for one day to remember the birth of the Prince of Peace, this passage (**Isaiah 9:1–7**) talks about what Jesus really came to do, making things as they were always supposed to be. It's what we call justice.

- God talks about bringing light to us individually and as a society. What areas of your life do you want God to bring light to (to change for good)?
- What things does the passage say will happen when God moves to bring justice?

Consider . . .

- how God has always used people to help him make the world right. What can you see around you that you think needs God's light? Make a note to pray every day for God to change things.
- what you can get involved in locally that will help make things better for people around you.

For more, see . . .

- Matthew 5:14–16 (p.942)
- John 12:46 (p.1119)
- John 1:1–5 (p.1096)

20People will grab something on the right,
but they will still be hungry.
They will eat something on the left,
but they will not be filled.
Then they will each turn and eat their own children.
21The people of Manasseh will fight against the people of Ephraim,
and Ephraim will fight against Manasseh.
Then both of them will turn against Judah.

But the LORD is still angry;
his hand is still raised to strike down the people.

10 How terrible it will be for those who make unfair laws,
and those who write laws that make life hard for people.
2They are not fair to the poor,
and they rob my people of their rights.
They allow people to steal from widows
and to take from orphans what really belongs to them.
3How will you explain the things you have done?
What will you do when your destruction comes from far away?
Where will you run for help?
Where will you hide your riches then?
4You will have to bow down among the captives
or fall down among the dead bodies.

But the LORD is still angry;
his hand is still raised to strike down the people.

God Will Punish Assyria

5God says, "How terrible it will be for the king of Assyria.
I use him like a rod to show my anger;
in anger I use Assyria like a club.
6I send it to fight against a nation that is separated from God.
I am angry with those people,
so I command Assyria to fight against them,
to take their wealth from them,
to trample them down like mud in the streets.
7But Assyria's king doesn't understand that I am using him;
he doesn't know he is a tool for me.
He only wants to destroy other people
and to defeat many nations.
8The king of Assyria says to himself,
'All of my commanders are like kings.
9The city Calno is like the city Carchemish.
The city Hamath is like the city Arpad.
The city Samaria is like the city Damascus.
10I defeated those kingdoms that worship idols,
and those idols were more than the idols of Jerusalem and Samaria.
11As I defeated Samaria and her idols,
I will also defeat Jerusalem and her idols.' "

12When the Lord finishes doing what he
planned to Mount Zion[d] and Jerusalem, he will
punish Assyria. The king of Assyria is very proud,
and his pride has made him do these evil things,
so God will punish him. 13The king of Assyria
says this:
"By my own power I have done these things;
by my wisdom I have defeated many nations.
I have taken their wealth,
and, like a mighty one, I have taken their people.
14I have taken the riches of all these people,
like a person reaching into a bird's nest.
I have taken these nations,
like a person taking eggs.
Not one raised a hand
or opened its mouth to stop me."

15An axe is not better than the person who swings it.
A saw is not better than the one who uses it.
A stick cannot control the person who picks it up.
A club cannot pick up the person!
16So the Lord GOD All-powerful
will send a terrible disease upon Assyria's soldiers.
The strength of Assyria will be burned up
like a fire burning until everything is gone.

Sidelight When the Assyrian army marched into town, the locals could count on problems (Isaiah 10:12–16). The Assyrians were known for flattening cities with battering rams, shooting defenders from mobile archery towers and skinning survivors alive.

17God, the Light of Israel, will be like a fire;
the Holy One will be like a flame.
He will be like a fire
that suddenly burns the weeds and thorns.
18The fire burns away the great trees and rich farmlands,
destroying everything.
It will be like a sick person who wastes away.
19The trees left standing will be so few
that even a child could count them.

20At that time some people will be left alive in Israel
from the family of Jacob.
They will not continue to depend
on the person who defeated them.
They will learn truly to depend on the LORD,
the Holy One of Israel.
21Those who are left alive in Jacob's family
will again follow the powerful God.
22Israel, your people are many,
like the grains of sand by the sea.
But only a few of them will be left alive to return to the LORD.
God has announced that he will destroy the land
completely and fairly.
23The Lord GOD All-powerful will certainly destroy this land
as he has announced.

24This is what the Lord GOD All-powerful says:
"My people living in Jerusalem,
don't be afraid of the Assyrians,
who beat you with a rod
and raise a stick against you, as Egypt did.
25After a short time my anger against you will stop,
and then I will turn my anger to destroying them."

26Then the LORD All-powerful will beat the Assyrians with a whip
as he defeated Midian at the rock of Oreb.
He will raise his stick over the waters
as he did in Egypt.
27Then the troubles that Assyria puts on you
will be removed,
and the load they make you carry
will be taken away.

Assyria Invades Israel

28The army of Assyria will enter near Aiath.
Its soldiers will walk through Migron.
They will store their food in Michmash.
29The army will go over the pass.
The soldiers will sleep at Geba.
The people of Ramah will be afraid,
and the people of Saul at Gibeah will run away.
30Cry out, Bath Gallim!
Laishah, listen!
Poor Anathoth!
31The people of Madmenah are running away;
the people of Gebim are hiding.
32This day the army will stop at Nob.
They will shake their fist at Mount Zion,[d]
at the hill of Jerusalem.
33Watch! The Lord GOD All-powerful
with his great power will chop them down
like a great tree.
Those who are great will be cut down;
those who are important will fall to the ground.
34He will cut them down
as a forest is cut down with an axe.
And the great trees of Lebanon
will fall by the power of the Mighty One.

The King of Peace is Coming

11 A new branch will grow
from a stump of a tree;
so a new king will come
from the family of Jesse.[n]
2The Spirit[d] of the LORD will rest upon that king.
The Spirit will give him wisdom and
understanding, guidance and power.
The Spirit will teach him to know and
respect the LORD.
3This king will be glad to obey the LORD.
He will not judge by the way things look
or decide by what he hears.
4But he will judge the poor honestly;
he will be fair in his decisions for the poor people of the land.
At his command evil people will be punished,
and by his words the wicked will be put to death.
5Goodness and fairness will give him strength,
like a belt around his waist.

6Then wolves will live in peace with lambs,
and leopards will lie down to rest with goats.
Calves, lions and young bulls will eat together,
and a little child will lead them.
7Cows and bears will eat together in peace.
Their young will lie down to rest together.
Lions will eat hay as oxen do.

Sidelight Until God fully sets up the peaceful, new kingdom, you'll want to steer clear of the cobra (Isaiah 11:8). Some varieties of this snake – which can grow up to six feet long – spit venom into their victim's eyes.

Jesse King David's father.

8A baby will be able to play near a cobra's
hole,
and a child will be able to put his hand into
the nest of a poisonous snake.
9They will not hurt or destroy each other
on all my holy mountain,
because the earth will be full of the
knowledge of the LORD,
as the sea is full of water.

10At that time the new king from the family of
Jesse[n] will stand as a banner for all peoples. The
nations will come together around him, and the
place where he lives will be filled with glory. 11At
that time the Lord will again reach out and take
his people who are left alive in Assyria, North
Egypt, South Egypt, Cush, Elam, Babylonia,
Hamath and all the islands of the sea.

12God will raise a banner as a sign for all
nations,
and he will gather the people of Israel who
were forced from their country.
He will gather the scattered people of Judah
from all parts of the earth.
13At that time Israel will not be jealous any
more,
and Judah will have no more enemies.
Israel will not be jealous of Judah,
and Judah will not hate Israel.
14But Israel and Judah will attack the
Philistines on the west.
Together they will take the riches from the
people of the east.
They will conquer Edom and Moab,
and the people of Ammon will be under
their control.
15The LORD will dry up
the Red Sea[d] of Egypt.
He will wave his arm over the Euphrates
River
and dry it up with a scorching wind.
He will divide it into seven small rivers
so that people can walk across them with
their sandals on.

Jesse King David's father.

FUTURE

Back Again?

Lydia had a life where everything seemed hopeless. Her father was absent – in prison for drugs offences. Her mother had too many boyfriends calling round. In fact both parents loved Lydia very much but not each other. They were simply unable to cope. They wanted to, but they had never quite managed to provide her with clean clothes, a safe home and regular meals. Lydia and her brothers had to leave home and be taken into care.

One summer, Lydia went on a holiday with some people from the local church. It painted a picture of another world – strange, weird and wonderful. Folks took an interest in her, looked out for her, listened to her, played with her and prayed for her. Someone made sure there were spare clothes if she got wet. Food arrived three times a day, exactly when the timetable said it would. Every evening someone told a story from the Bible about things Jesus did.

Read **Isaiah 11:1–10**. It's about how Isaiah saw hope in the future.

- What will this branch, this king, this new and special leader be like? What will he do?
- Why did the church holiday work for Lydia? Why is it so good to get away from a situation in order to reflect upon it?

Consider . . .

- what's going on in the news at the moment that would make you pray for justice and hope for the future.
- praying verse 2 for yourself. Ask God to give you wisdom, understanding, guidance and power. If you have hopes and dreams, let him edit them.

For more, see . . .

- Isaiah 9:2–7 (p.649)
- Isaiah 49:22–23 (p.693)

16So God's people who are left alive
will have a way to leave Assyria,
just like the time the Israelites
came out of Egypt.

A Song of Praise to God

12 At that time you will say:
"I praise you, LORD!
You were angry with me,
but you are not angry with me now!
You have comforted me.
2God is the one who saves me;
I will trust him and not be afraid.
The LORD, the LORD gives me strength and
makes me sing.
He has saved me."
3You will receive your salvation with joy
as you would draw water from a well.

4At that time you will say,
"Praise the LORD and worship him.
Tell everyone what he has done
and how great he is.
5Sing praise to the LORD, because he has done
great things.
Let all the world know what he has done.
6Shout and sing for joy, you people of
Jerusalem,
because the Holy One of Israel does great
things before your eyes."

God's Message to Babylon

13 God showed Isaiah son of Amoz this
message about Babylon:
2Raise a flag on the bare mountain.
Call out to the men.
Raise your hand to signal them
to enter through the gates for important
people.
3I myself have commanded those people
whom I have separated as mine.
I have called those warriors to carry out my
anger.
They rejoice and are glad to do my will.

4Listen to the loud noise in the mountains,
the sound of many people.
Listen to the noise among the kingdoms,
the sound of nations gathering
together.
The LORD All-powerful is calling
his army together for battle.

ETERNAL LIFE

Safe Under the Falls

From a distance, Niagara Falls is a spectacular sight. But close up, it can be terrifying. Millions of litres of water rush over the cliff, falling 50 metres with tremendous force. Anyone caught in the falls would die instantly from the crushing impact on the jagged rocks below.

But with the help of guides, visitors can put on rubber suits and carefully make their way behind the falls. With water roaring and spraying just a few metres away, they can stand in a particular spot known as the Cave of the Winds and be perfectly safe.

Sometimes life can seem like the crushing pressure of Niagara Falls. But, as **Isaiah 12** promises, we can trust God to save and protect us.

- What similarities are there between the Cave of the Winds and God's promise of eternal life?
- How does reading this passage give you assurance of God's gift when you are surrounded by troubles?

Consider . . .

- blowing up a balloon and writing on it reasons you have to celebrate God's gift of eternal life. Keep the balloon in your room as a reminder.
- following Isaiah 12:4 by telling a non-Christian friend about the joy you have found in God's love, comfort and salvation.

For more, see . . .

- Micah 7:7–9 (p.896)
- 2 Peter 1:3–11 (p.1365)
- John 3:1–16 (p.1099)

5This army is coming from a faraway land,
from the edge of the horizon.
In anger the LORD is using this army like a weapon
to destroy the whole country.
6Cry, because the LORD's day of judging is near;
the Almighty is sending destruction.
7People will be weak with fear,
and their courage will melt away.
8Everyone will be afraid.
Pain and hurt will grab them;
they will hurt like a woman giving birth to a baby.
They will look at each other in fear,
with their faces red like fire.

God's Judgement Against Babylon

9Look, the LORD's day of judging is coming—
a terrible day, a day of God's anger.
He will destroy the land
and the sinners who live in it.
10The stars will not show their light;
the skies will be dark.
The sun will grow dark as it rises,
and the moon will not give its light.

11The LORD says, "I will punish the world for its evil
and wicked people for their sins.
I will cause proud people to lose their pride,
and I will destroy the pride of those who are cruel to others.
12People will be harder to find than pure gold;
there will be fewer people than there is fine gold in Ophir.
13I will make the sky shake,
and the earth will be moved from its place
by the anger of the LORD All-powerful
at the time of his burning anger.

14"Then the people from Babylon *d* will run away like hunted deer
or like sheep who have no shepherd.
Everyone will turn back to his own people;
each will run back to his own land.
15Everyone who is captured will be killed;
everyone who is caught will be killed with a sword.
16Their little children will be beaten to death in front of them.
Their houses will be robbed
and their wives raped.

17"Look, I will cause the armies of Media to attack Babylon.
They do not care about silver
or delight in gold.
18Their soldiers will shoot the young men with arrows;
they will show no mercy on children,
nor will they feel sorry for little ones.
19Babylon is the most beautiful of all kingdoms,
and the Babylonians are very proud of it.
But God will destroy it
like Sodom *d* and Gomorrah. *d*
20No one will ever live there
or settle there again.
No Arab will put a tent there;
no shepherd will bring sheep there.
21Only desert animals will live there,
and their houses will be full of wild dogs.
Owls will live there,
and wild goats will leap about in the houses.
22Wolves will howl within the strong walls,
and wild dogs will bark in the beautiful buildings.
The end of Babylon is near;
its time is almost over."

Israel will Return Home

14 The LORD will show mercy to the people
of Jacob, and he will again choose the
people of Israel. He will settle them in their own
land. Then non-Israelite people will join the
Israelites and will become a part of the family of
Jacob. 2Nations will take the Israelites back to
their land. Then those men and women from the
other nations will become slaves to Israel in the
LORD's land. In the past the Israelites were their
slaves, but now the Israelites will defeat those
nations and rule over them.

The King of Babylon will Fall

3The LORD will take away the Israelites' hard
work and will comfort them. They will no longer
have to work hard as slaves. 4On that day Israel
will sing this song about the king of Babylon:
The cruel king who ruled us is finished;
his angry rule is finished!
5The LORD has broken the sceptre *d* of evil rulers
and taken away their power.
6The king of Babylon struck people in anger
again and again.
He ruled nations in anger
and continued to hurt them.
7But now, the whole world rests and is quiet.
Now the people begin to sing.
8Even the pine trees are happy,
and the cedar trees of Lebanon rejoice.
They say, "The king has fallen,
so no one will ever cut us down again."
9The place of the dead is excited
to meet you when you come.

It wakes the spirits of the dead,
the leaders of the world.
It makes kings of all nations
stand up from their thrones to greet you.
10 All these leaders will make fun of you
and will say,
"Now you are weak, as we are.
Now you are just like us."
11 Your pride has been sent down to the place
of the dead.
The music from your harps goes with it.
Flies are spread out like your bed
beneath you,
and worms cover your body like a
blanket.

12 King of Babylon, morning star, you have
fallen from heaven,
even though you were as bright as the
rising sun!
In the past all the nations on earth bowed
down before you,
but now you have been cut down.
13 You told yourself,
"I will go up to heaven.
I will put my throne
above God's stars.
I will sit on the mountain of the gods,
on the slopes of the sacred mountain.
14 I will go up above the tops of the clouds.
I will be like God Most High."
15 But you were brought down to the grave,
to the deep places where the dead are.

16 Those who see you stare at you.
They think about what has happened to you
and say, "Is this the same man who caused
great fear on earth,
who shook the kingdoms,
17 who turned the world into a desert,
who destroyed its cities,
who captured people in war
and would not let them go home?"

18 Every king of the earth has been buried with
honour,
each in his own grave.
19 But you are thrown out of your grave,
like an unwanted branch.
You are covered by bodies
that died in battle,
by bodies to be buried in a rocky pit.
You are like a dead body other soldiers
walk on.
20 You will not be buried with those bodies,
because you ruined your own country
and killed your own people.
The children of evil people
will never be mentioned again.
21 Prepare to kill his children,
because their father is guilty.
They will never again take control of the earth;
they will never again fill the world with
their cities.

22 The LORD All-powerful says this:
"I will fight against those people;
I will destroy Babylon and its people,
its children and their descendants," [d] says
the LORD.
23 "I will make Babylon fit only for owls
and for swamps.
I will sweep Babylon as with a broom of
destruction,"
says the LORD All-powerful.

God will Punish Assyria

24 The LORD All-powerful has made this promise:
"These things will happen exactly as I
planned them;
they will happen exactly as I set them up.
25 I will destroy the king of Assyria in my
country;
I will trample him on my mountains.
He placed a heavy load on my people,
but that weight will be removed.

26 "This is what I plan to do for all the earth.
And this is the hand that I have raised over
all nations."
27 When the LORD All-powerful makes a plan,
no one can stop it.
When the LORD raises his hand to punish
people,
no one can stop it.

God's Message to Philistia

28 This message was given in the year that King
Ahaz died:
29 Country of Philistia, don't be happy
that the king who struck you is now dead.
He is like a snake that will give birth to
another dangerous snake.
The new king will be like a quick,
dangerous snake to bite you.
30 Even the poorest of my people will be able to
eat safely,
and people in need will be able to lie down
in safety.
But I will kill your family with hunger,
and all your people who are left will die.

31 People near the city gates, [n] cry out!
Philistines, be frightened,

city gates People come here to conduct business. Public meetings and court cases were also held there.

because a cloud of dust comes from the north.
It is an army, full of men ready to fight.
32What shall we tell the messengers from Philistia?
Say that the LORD has made Jerusalem strong
and that his poor people will go there for safety.

God's Message to Moab

15 This is a message about Moab:
In one night armies took the wealth from Ar in Moab,
and it was destroyed.
In one night armies took the wealth from Kir in Moab,
and it was destroyed.

Sidelight Even though the Moabites (Isaiah 15:1) were distant cousins of the Israelites, the two groups had been enemies ever since Moses tried to enter Canaan about seven hundred years before Isaiah (Judges 11:17, p.238).

2The people of Dibon go to the places of worship to cry.
The people of Moab cry for the cities of Nebo and Medeba.
Every head and beard has been shaved to show how sad Moab is.
3In the streets they wear rough cloth to show their sadness.
On the roofs[n] and in the public squares,
they are crying loudly.
4People in the cities Heshbon and Elealeh cry out loud.
You can hear their voices far away in the city Jahaz.
Even the soldiers are frightened;
they are shaking with fear.

5My heart cries with sorrow for Moab.
Its people run away to Zoar for safety;
they run to Eglath Shelishiyah.
People are going up the mountain road to Luhith,
crying as they go.
People are going on the road to Horonaim,
crying over their destruction.
6But the water of Nimrim has dried up.
The grass has dried up,
and all the plants are dead;
nothing green is left.
7So the people gather up what they have saved
and carry it across the Ravine of the Poplars.
8Crying is heard everywhere in Moab.
Their crying is heard as far away as the city Eglaim;
it is heard as far away as Beer Elim.
9The water of the city Dibon is full of blood,
and I, the LORD, will bring even more troubles to Dibon.
A few people living in Moab have escaped the enemy,
but I will send lions to kill them.

16 Send the king of the land
the payment he demands.
Send a lamb from Sela through the desert
to the mountain of Jerusalem.
2The women of Moab
try to cross the river Arnon
like little birds
that have fallen from their nest.

3They say: "Help us.
Tell us what to do.
Protect us from our enemies
as shade protects us from the noon sun.
Hide us, because we are running for safety!
Don't give us to our enemies.
4Let those of us who were forced out of Moab live in your land.
Hide us from our enemies."
The robbing of Moab will stop.
The enemy will be defeated;
those who hurt others will disappear from the land.
5Then a new loyal king will come;
this faithful king will be from the family of David.
He will judge fairly
and do what is right.

6We have heard that the people of Moab are proud
and very conceited.
They are very proud and angry,
but their boasting means nothing.
7So the people of Moab will cry;
they will all be sad.

roofs In Bible times houses were built with flat roofs. The roof was used for drying things such as flax and fruit. And it was used as an extra room, as a place for worship and as a place to sleep in the summer.

They will moan and groan
for the raisin cakes they had in
Kir Hareseth.
8 But the fields of Heshbon and the vines of
Sibmah cannot grow grapes;
foreign rulers have destroyed the
grapevines.
The grapevines once spread as far as the city
of Jazer and into the desert;
they had spread as far as the sea.
9 I cry with the people of Jazer
for the grapevines of Sibmah.
I will cry with the people of Heshbon and
Elealeh.
There will be no shouts of joy,
because there will be no harvest or ripe
fruit.
10 There will be no joy and happiness in the
orchards
and no songs or shouts of joy in the
vineyards.
No one makes wine in the winepresses,[d]
because I have put an end to shouts
of joy.
11 My heart cries for Moab like a harp playing a
funeral song;
I am very sad for Kir Hareseth.
12 The people of Moab will go to their places of
worship
and will try to pray.
But when they go to their temple to pray,
they will not be able.

13 Earlier the LORD said these things about
Moab. 14 Now the LORD says, "In three years all
those people and what they take pride in will be
hated. (This is three years as a hired helper would
count time.) There will be a few people left, but
they will be weak."

God's Message to Aram

17 This is a message about Damascus:
"The city of Damascus will be
destroyed;
only ruins will remain.
2 People will leave the cities of Aroer.
Flocks will wander freely in those empty
towns,
and there will be no one to bother them.
3 The fortified cities of Israel will be
destroyed.
The government in Damascus will end.
Those left alive of Aram will be
like the glory of Israel," says the LORD
All-powerful.

4 "At that time Israel's wealth will all be gone.
Israel will be like someone who has lost
much weight from sickness.
5 That time will be like the grain harvest in the
Valley of Rephaim.
The workers cut the wheat.
Then they cut the heads of grain from the
plants
and collect the grain.
6 That time will also be like the olive
harvest,
when a few olives are left.
Two or three olives are left in the top
branches.
Four or five olives are left on full branches,"
says the LORD, the God of Israel.

7 At that time people will look to God, their
Maker;
their eyes will see the Holy One of
Israel.
8 They will not trust the altars they
have made,
nor will they trust what their hands have
made,
not even the Asherah[d] idols
and altars.

9 In that day all their strong cities will be empty.
They will be like the cities the Hivites and the
Amorites left when the Israelites came to take the
land. Everything will be ruined.

10 You have forgotten the God who
saves you;
you have not remembered that God is your
place of safety.
You plant the finest grapevines
and grapevines from faraway places.
11 You plant your grapevines one day and try to
make them grow,
and the next day you make them
blossom.
But at harvest time everything will
be dead;
a sickness will kill all the plants.

12 Listen to the many people!
Their crying is like the noise from
the sea.
Listen to the nations!
Their crying is like the crashing of great
waves.
13 The people roar like the waves,
but when God speaks harshly to them, they
will run away.
They will be like chaff[d] on the hills being
blown by the wind,
or like tumbleweeds blown away by a
storm.
14 At night the people will be very
frightened.
Before morning, no one will be left.

So our enemies will come to our land,
but they will become nothing.

God's Message to Cush

18 How terrible it will be for the land
beyond the rivers of Cush.
It is filled with the sound of wings.
2 That land sends messengers across the sea;
they go on the water in boats made of
reeds.

Go, quick messengers,
to a people who are tall and
smooth-skinned,
who are feared everywhere.
They are a powerful nation that defeats other
nations.
Their land is divided by rivers.

3 All you people of the world, look!
Everyone who lives in the world, look!
You will see a banner raised on a
mountain.
You will hear a trumpet sound.
4 The LORD said to me,
"I will quietly watch from where I live,
like heat in the sunshine,
like the dew in the heat of harvest time."
5 The time will come, after the flowers have
bloomed and before the harvest,
when new grapes will be budding and
growing.
The enemy will cut the plants with knives;
he will cut down the vines and take them
away.
6 They will be left for the birds of the
mountains
and for the wild animals.
Birds will feed on them all summer,
and wild animals will eat them that
winter."

7 At that time a gift will be brought to the
LORD All-powerful
from the people who are tall and
smooth-skinned,
who are feared everywhere.
They are a powerful nation that defeats other
nations.
Their land is divided by rivers.
These gifts will be brought to the place of the
LORD All-powerful,
to Mount Zion. *d*

God's Message to Egypt

19 This is a message about Egypt:
Look, the LORD is coming on a fast
cloud
to enter Egypt.
The idols of Egypt will tremble before him,
and Egypt's courage will melt away.

2 The LORD says, "I will cause the Egyptians to
fight against themselves.
People will fight with their relatives;
neighbours will fight neighbours;
cities will fight cities;
kingdoms will fight kingdoms.
3 The Egyptians will be afraid,
and I will ruin their plans.
They will ask advice from their idols and
spirits of the dead,
from their mediums *d* and fortune-tellers."
4 The Lord GOD All-powerful says,
"I will hand Egypt over to a hard master,
and a powerful king will rule over them."

5 The sea will become dry,
and the water will disappear from the Nile
River.
6 The canals will stink;
the streams of Egypt will decrease and
dry up.
All the water plants will rot;
7 all the plants along the banks of the Nile
will die.
Even the planted fields by the Nile
will dry up, blow away and disappear.
8 The fishermen, all those who catch fish from
the Nile,
will groan and cry;
those who fish in the Nile will be sad.
9 All the people who make cloth from flax will
be sad,
and those who weave linen will lose hope.
10 Those who weave cloth will be broken.
All those who work for money will be sad.

11 The officers of the city of Zoan are fools;
the wise men who advise the king of Egypt
give wrong advice.
How can you say to him, 'I am wise'?
How can you say, 'I am from the old family
of the kings'?
12 Egypt, where are your wise men?
Let them show you
what the LORD All-powerful has planned for
Egypt.
13 The officers of Zoan have been fooled;
the leaders of Memphis have believed false
things.
So the leaders of Egypt
lead that nation the wrong way.
14 The LORD has made the leaders confused.
They have led Egypt to wander in the
wrong ways,
like drunk people stumbling in their own
vomit.

15There is nothing Egypt can do;
no one there can help.

16In that day the Egyptians will be like women.
They will be afraid of the LORD All-powerful, be-
cause he will raise his hand to strike them down.
17The land of Judah will bring fear to Egypt. Any-
one there who hears the name Judah will be
afraid, because the LORD All-powerful has planned
terrible things for them. 18At that time five cities
in Egypt will speak Hebrew, the language of
Canaan, and they will promise to be loyal to the
LORD All-powerful. One of these cities will be
named the City of Destruction. 19At that time
there will be an altar for the LORD in the middle
of Egypt and a monument to the LORD at the bor-
der of Egypt. 20This will be a sign and a witness
to the LORD All-powerful in the land of Egypt.
When the people cry to the LORD for help, he will
send someone to save and defend them. He will
rescue them from those who hurt them.
21So the LORD will show himself to the Egyp-
tians, and then they will know he is the LORD.
They will worship God and offer many sacrifices.
They will make promises to the LORD and will
keep them. 22The LORD will punish the Egyptians,
but then he will heal them. They will come back
to the LORD, and he will listen to their prayers and
heal them.
23At that time there will be a highway from
Egypt to Assyria, and the Assyrians will go to
Egypt, and the Egyptians will go to Assyria. The
Egyptians and Assyrians will worship God to-
gether. 24At that time Israel, Assyria and Egypt
will join together, which will be a blessing for the
earth. 25The LORD All-powerful will bless them,
saying, "Egypt, you are my people. Assyria, I
made you. Israel, I own you. You are all blessed!"

Sidelight Sargon, an Assyrian king during Isaiah's time (Isaiah 20:1), was not only a powerful military leader, but must have also been quite a scholar. He built the oldest library archaeologists have discovered, where twenty-five hundred books were found. Of course, that's a small number compared with modern libraries, which can have several million books.

Assyria will Defeat Egypt and Cush

20 Sargon king of Assyria sent a military
commander to Ashdod to attack that
city. So the commander attacked and captured
it. 2Then the LORD spoke through Isaiah son of
Amoz, saying, "Take the rough cloth off your
body, and take your sandals off your feet." So
Isaiah obeyed and walked around naked and
barefoot.
3Then the LORD said, "Isaiah my servant has
walked around naked and barefoot for three
years as a sign against Egypt and Cush. 4The king
of Assyria will carry away prisoners from Egypt and
Cush. Old people and young people will be led
away naked and barefoot, with their buttocks
bare. So the Egyptians will be shamed. 5People
who looked to Cush for help will be afraid, and
those who were amazed by Egypt's glory will be
shamed. 6People who live near the sea will say,
'Look at those countries. We trusted them to help
us. We ran to them so they would save us from
the king of Assyria. So how will we be able to
escape?'"

God's Message to Babylon

21 This is a message about the Desert by
the Sea:[n]

Disaster is coming from the desert
like wind blowing in the south.
It is coming from a terrible country.
2I have seen a terrible vision.
I see traitors turning against you
and people taking your wealth.

Elam, attack the people!
Media, surround the city and attack it!
I will bring an end to the pain the city
causes.

3I saw those terrible things, and now I am in
pain;
my pains are like the pains of giving
birth.
What I hear makes me very afraid;
what I see causes me to shake with fear.
4I am worried,
and I am shaking with fear.
My pleasant evening
has become a night of fear.

5They set the table;
they spread the rugs;
they eat and drink.
Leaders, stand up.
Prepare the shields for battle!

6The Lord said to me,
"Go, place a lookout for the city
and have him report what he sees.
7If he sees chariots and teams of horses,
donkeys or camels,
he should pay very close attention."

Desert by the Sea Probably Babylon.

8Then the lookout called out,
"My master, each day I stand in the watchtower watching;
every night I have been on guard.
9Look, I see a man coming in a chariot
with a team of horses."
The man gives back the answer,
"Babylon has fallen. It has fallen!
All the statues of her gods
lie broken on the ground."

10My people are crushed like grain on the threshing[d] floor.
My people, I tell you what I have heard
from the LORD All-powerful,
from the God of Israel.

God's Message to Edom

11This is a message about Dumah:[n]
Someone calls to me from Edom,
"Watchman, how much of the night is left?
Watchman, how much longer will it be night?"
12The watchman answers,
"Morning is coming, but then night will come again.
If you have something to ask,
then come back and ask."

God's Message to Arabia

13This is a message about Arabia:
A group of traders from Dedan
spent the night near some trees in Arabia.
14 They gave water to thirsty travellers;
the people of Tema gave food
to those who were escaping.
15They were running from swords,
from swords ready to kill,
from bows ready to shoot,
from a hard battle.

16This is what the Lord said to me: "In one year all the glory of the country of Kedar will be gone. (This is a year as a hired helper counts time.) 17At that time only a few of the archers, the soldiers of Kedar, will be left alive." The LORD, the God of Israel, has spoken.

God's Message to Jerusalem

22 This is a message about the Valley of Vision:[n]
What is wrong with you people?
Why are you on your roofs?[n]
2This city was a very busy city,
full of noise and wild parties.
Now your people have been killed,
but not with swords,
nor did they die in battle.
3All your leaders ran away together,
but they have been captured without using a bow.
All you who were captured
tried to run away before the enemy came.
4So I say, "Don't look at me.
Let me cry loudly.
Don't hurry to comfort me
about the destruction of Jerusalem."
5The Lord GOD All-powerful has chosen a special day
of riots and confusion.
People will trample each other in the Valley of Vision.
The city walls will be knocked down,
and the people will cry out to the mountain.
6The soldiers from Elam will gather their arrows
and their chariots and men on horses.
Kir will prepare their shields.
7Your nicest valleys will be filled with chariots.
Horsemen will be ordered to guard the gates of the city.
8 The walls protecting Judah will fall.

At that time the people of Jerusalem depended on
the weapons kept at the Palace of the Forest.
9You saw that the walls of Jerusalem
had many cracks that needed repairing.
You stored up water in the lower pool.
10You counted the houses of Jerusalem,
and you tore down houses to repair the walls with their stones.
11You made a pool between the two walls
to save water from the old pool,
but you did not trust the God who made these things;
you did not respect the One who planned them long ago.

12The Lord GOD All-powerful told the people
to cry and be sad,
to shave their heads and wear rough cloth.
13But look, the people are happy
and are having wild parties.
They kill the cattle and the sheep;
they eat the food and drink the wine.

Dumah Another name for Edom.
Valley of Vision This probably means a valley near Jerusalem.
roofs In Bible times houses were built with flat roofs. The roof was used for drying things such as flax and fruit. And it was used as an extra room, as a place for worship and as a place to sleep in the summer.

They say, "Let us eat and drink,
because tomorrow we will die."

14The LORD All-powerful said to me: "You people will die before this guilt is forgiven." The Lord GOD All-powerful said this.

God's Message to Shebna

15This is what the Lord GOD All-powerful says:
"Go to this servant Shebna,
the manager of the palace.
16Say to him, 'What are you doing here?
Who said you could cut out a tomb for yourself here?
Why are you preparing your tomb in a high place?
Why are you carving out a tomb from the rock?
17Look, mighty one! The LORD will throw you away.
He will take firm hold of you
18and roll you tightly into a ball
and throw you into another country.
There you will die,
and there your fine chariots will remain.
You are a disgrace to your master's house.
19I will force you out of your important job,
and you will be thrown down from your important place.'

20"At that time I will call for my servant Eliakim
son of Hilkiah. 21I will take your robe and put it
on him and give him your belt. I will hand over
to him the important job you have, and he will be
like a father to the people of Jerusalem and the
family of Judah. 22I will put the key to the house
of David around his neck. If he opens a door, no
one will be able to close it; if he closes a door, no
one will be able to open it. 23He will be like an
honoured chair in his father's house. I will make
him strong like a peg that is hammered into a
strong board. 24All the honoured and important
things of his family will depend on him; all the
adults and little children will depend on him.
They will be like bowls and jars hanging on him.
25"At that time," says the LORD All-powerful,
"the peg hammered into the strong board will
weaken. It will break and fall, and everything
hanging on it will be destroyed." The LORD says
this.

God's Message to Lebanon

23 This is a message about Tyre:
You trading ships, cry!
The houses and harbour of Tyre are destroyed.
This news came to the ships
from the land of Cyprus.
2Be silent, you who live on the island of Tyre;
you merchants of Sidon, be silent.
Sailors have made you rich.
3They travelled the sea to bring grain from Egypt;
the sailors of Tyre brought grain from the Nile Valley
and sold it to other nations.

4Sidon, be ashamed.
Strong city of the sea, be ashamed, because the sea says:
"I have not felt the pain of giving birth;
I have not reared young men or women."
5Egypt will hear the news about Tyre,
and it will make Egypt hurt with sorrow.

6You ships should return to Tarshish.
You people living near the sea should be sad.
7Look at your once happy city!
Look at your old, old city!
People from that city have travelled
far away to live.
8Who planned Tyre's destruction?
Tyre made others rich.
Its merchants were treated like princes,
and its traders were greatly respected.
9It was the LORD All-powerful who planned this.
He decided to make these proud people unimportant;
he decided to disgrace those who were greatly respected.
10Go through your land, people of Tarshish,
like the Nile goes through Egypt.
There is no harbour for you now!
11The LORD has stretched his hand over the sea
and made its kingdoms tremble.
He commands that Canaan's
fortified cities be destroyed.
12He said, "Sidon, you will not rejoice any longer,
because you are destroyed.
Even if you cross the sea to Cyprus,
you will not find a place to rest."
13Look at the land of the Babylonians;
it is not a country now.
Assyria has made it a place for wild animals.
Assyria built towers to attack it;
the soldiers took all the treasures from its cities,
and they turned it into ruins.
14So be sad, you trading ships,
because your strong city is destroyed.
15At that time people will forget about Tyre for
70 years, which is the length of a king's life.

After 70 years, Tyre will be like the prostitute [d] in this song:

16"Oh woman, you are forgotten.
Take your harp and walk through the city.
Play your harp well. Sing your song often.
Then people will remember you."

17After 70 years the LORD will deal with Tyre, and it will again have trade. It will be like a prostitute for all the nations of the earth. 18The profits will be saved for the LORD. Tyre will not keep the money she earns but will give them to the people who serve the LORD, so they will have plenty of food and nice clothes.

The LORD will Punish the World

24 Look! The LORD will destroy the earth
and leave it empty;
he will ruin the surface of the land and
scatter its people.
2At that time the same thing will happen to
everyone:
to common people and priests,
to slaves and masters,
to women slaves and their women masters,
to buyers and sellers,
to those who borrow and those who lend,
to bankers and those who owe the bank.
3The earth will be completely empty.
The wealth will all be taken,
because the LORD has commanded it.
4The earth will dry up and die;
the world will grow weak and die;
the great leaders in this land will become
weak.
5The people of the earth have ruined it,
because they do not follow God's teachings
or obey God's laws
or keep their agreement with God that was
to last for ever.
6So a curse will destroy the earth.
The people of the world are guilty,
so they will be burned up;
only a few will be left.
7The new wine will be bad, and the
grapevines will die.
People who were happy will be sad.
8The happy music of the tambourines [d] will end.
The happy sounds of wild parties will stop.
The joyful music from the harps will end.
9People will no longer sing while they drink
their wine.
The beer will taste bitter to those who drink it.
10The ruined city will be empty,
and people will hide behind closed doors.
11People in the streets will ask for wine,
but joy will have turned to sadness;
all the happiness will have left.
12The city will be left in ruins,
and its gates will be smashed to pieces.
13This is what will happen all over the earth
and to all the nations.
The earth will be like an olive tree after the
harvest
or like the few grapes left on a vine after
harvest.

14The people shout for joy.
From the west they praise the greatness of
the LORD.
15People in the east, praise the LORD.
People in the islands of the sea,
praise the name of the LORD, the God of
Israel.
16We hear songs from every part of the earth
praising God, the Righteous One.

But I said, "I am dying! I am dying!
How terrible it will be for me!
Traitors turn against people;
with their dishonesty, they turn against
people."
17There are terrors, holes and traps
for the people of the earth.
18Anyone who tries to escape from the sound
of terror
will fall into a hole.
Anyone who climbs out of the hole
will be caught in a trap.
The clouds in the sky will pour out rain,
and the foundations of the earth will shake.
19The earth will be broken up;
the earth will split open;
the earth will shake violently.
20The earth will stumble around like someone
who is drunk;
it will shake like a hut in a storm.
Its sin is like a heavy weight on its back;
it will fall and never rise again.

21At that time the LORD will punish
the powers in the sky above
and the rulers on earth below.
22They will be gathered together
like prisoners thrown into a pit;
they will be shut up in prison.
After much time they will be punished.
23The moon will be embarrassed,
and the sun will be ashamed,
because the LORD All-powerful will rule as
king
on Mount Zion [d] in Jerusalem.
Jerusalem's leaders will see his greatness.

A Song of Praise to God

25 LORD, you are my God.
I honour you and praise you,

because you have done amazing things.
You have always done what you said you would do;
you have done what you planned long ago.
2You have made the city a pile of rocks
and have destroyed her walls.
The city our enemies built with strong walls is gone;
it will never be built again.
3People from powerful nations will honour you;
cruel people from strong cities will fear you.
4You protect the poor;
you protect the helpless when they are in danger.
You are like a shelter from storms,
like shade that protects them from the heat.
The cruel people attack
like a rainstorm beating against the wall,
5 like the heat in the desert.
But you, God, stop their violent attack.
As a cloud cools a hot day,
you silence the songs of those who have no mercy.

God's Banquet for His Servants

6The LORD All-powerful will prepare a feast
on this mountain for all people.
It will be a feast with all the best food and wine,
the finest meat and wine.
7On this mountain God will destroy
the veil that covers all nations,
the veil that stretches over all peoples;

DEATH

Welcomed Into Heaven

Anna and Drew were sitting by her bedside, watching, when it happened. They'd seen the moment on TV and in films loads of times before, but this was real, this they were seeing with their own eyes.

Anna's nan was old and had been getting increasingly ill over the last few weeks. The hospital called to say that they expected her to pass away in a matter of days, so Anna's family arranged a rota so that someone would be by Nan's bedside 24 hours a day.

Anna and Drew were on the first night shift. Squeezing Drew's hand tightly, Anna prayed that somehow, even now, Nan would meet Jesus before she died and left this world.

Slowly, Nan's face changed. She had seemed asleep, but now, her eyes opened, looking past Anna and Drew towards the end of the bed. She seemed brighter, and for a second they could only look and stare. They'd never felt God's presence as clearly as they did at that moment. Then Nan relaxed back into the bed, closed her eyes, and gently took her last breath. She died, and slowly the colour drained from her face.

Anna and Drew stayed silent for a moment – but the fear had gone. They had just seen Nan pass away – and it was so obvious that what they saw in the bed before them was now just an empty body . . . the shell of Nan. They prayed again, thanking God that Nan had died peacefully – and they were sure that she had met Jesus before she went.

Read **Isaiah 25:6–9**. When we are sad because someone has died, there are promises that God is still in charge and has everything under control.

- How do you feel about the idea of death?
- What do these verses tell us about how God deals with death?

Consider . . .

- an experience you've had of someone close to you dying. Take some time to thank God for that person and for what they meant to you.
- writing a list of all the happy memories you have of them and remind yourself of them each time you feel sad.

For more, see . . .

- Psalm 23 (p.513)
- 1 Thessalonians 4:13–18 (p.1299)
- 1 Corinthians 15:50–57 (p.1237)

8 he will destroy death for ever.
The Lord GOD will wipe away every tear from every face.
He will take away the shame of his people from the earth.
The LORD has spoken.

9At that time people will say,
"Our God is doing this!
We have waited for him, and he has come to save us.
This is the LORD. We waited for him,
so we will rejoice and be happy when he saves us."
10The LORD will protect Jerusalem,
but he will crush our enemy Moab
like straw that is trampled down in the manure.

Sidelight Lawn care treatments may be new, but fertiliser has been around for a long time. The ancient Israelite farmers would mix together straw and manure to make fertiliser (Isaiah 25:10). If they were around today, they could sell their produce to organic farmers.

11They will spread their arms in it
like a person who is swimming.
But God will bring down their pride,
and all the clever things they have made will mean nothing.
12Moab's high walls protect them,
but God will destroy these walls.
He will throw them down to the ground,
even to the dust.

A Song of Praise to God

26 At that time people will sing this song in Judah:
We have a strong city.
God protects us with its strong walls and defences.
2Open the gates,
and the good people will enter,
those who follow God.
3You, LORD, give true peace
to those who depend on you,
because they trust you.
4So, trust the LORD always,
because he is our Rock [d] for ever.
5He will destroy the proud city,
and he will punish the people living there.
He will bring that high city down to the ground
and throw it down into the dust.
6Then those who were hurt by the city will walk on its ruins;
those who were made poor by the city will trample it under their feet.

7The path of life is level for those who are right with God;
LORD, you make the way of life smooth for those people.
8But, LORD, we are waiting
for your way of justice.
Our souls want to remember
you and your name.
9My soul wants to be with you at night,
and my spirit wants to be with you at the dawn of every day.
When your way of justice comes to the land,
people of the world will learn the right way of living.
10Evil people will not learn to do good
even if you show them kindness.
They will continue doing evil, even if they live in a good world;
they never see the LORD's greatness.
11LORD, you are ready to punish those people,
but they do not see that.
Show them your strong love for your people.
Then those who are evil will be ashamed.
Burn them in the fire
you have prepared for your enemies.
12LORD, all our success is because of what you have done,
so give us peace.
13LORD, our God, other masters besides you have ruled us,
but we honour only you.
14Those masters are now dead;
their ghosts will not rise from death.
You punished and destroyed them
and destroyed any memory of them.
15LORD, you multiplied the number of your people;
you multiplied them and brought honour to yourself.
You made the borders of the land wide.
16LORD, people remember you when they are in trouble;
they say quiet prayers to you when you punish them.
17LORD, when we are with you,
we are like a woman giving birth to a baby;
she cries and has pain from the birth.
18In the same way, we had pain.
We gave birth, but only to wind.
We don't bring salvation to the land
or make new people for the world.

19Your people have died, but they will live
again;
their bodies will rise from death.
You who lie in the ground,
wake up and be happy!
The dew covering you is like the dew of a
new day;
the ground will give birth to the dead.

Judgement: Reward or Punishment

20My people, go into your rooms
and shut your doors behind you.
Hide in your rooms for a short time
until God's anger is finished.
21The LORD will leave his place
to punish the people of the world for their
sins.
The earth will show the blood of the people
who have been killed;
it will not cover the dead any longer.

27 At that time the LORD will punish
Leviathan, [d] the gliding snake.
He will punish Leviathan, the coiled snake,
with his great and hard and powerful
sword.
He will kill the monster in the sea.

2At that time
people will sing about the pleasant vineyard.
3"I, the LORD, will care for that vineyard;
I will water it at the right time.
No one will hurt it,
because I will guard it day and night.
4I am not angry.
If anyone builds a wall of thorn-bushes
in war,
I will march to it and burn it.
5But if anyone comes to me for safety
and wants to make peace with me,
he should come and make peace with me."
6In the days to come, the people of Jacob will
be like a plant with good roots;
Israel will grow like a plant beginning to
bloom.
Then the world will be filled with their
children.

The LORD will Send Israel Away

7The LORD has not hurt his people as he hurt
their enemies;
his people have not been killed like those
who tried to kill them.
8He will settle his argument with Israel by
sending it far away.
Like a hot desert wind, he will drive it
away.
9This is how Israel's guilt will be forgiven;
this is how its sins will be taken away:
Israel will crush the rocks of the altar
to dust,
and no statues or altars will be left standing
for the Asherah [d] idols.
10At that time the fortified city will be empty
like a desert.
Calves will eat grass there.
They will lie down there
and eat leaves from the branches.
11The limbs will become dry and break off,
so women will use them for firewood.
The people refuse to understand,
so God will not comfort them;
their Maker will not be kind to them.
12At that time the LORD will begin gathering his
people one by one from the Euphrates River to
the brook of Egypt. He will separate them from
others as grain is separated from chaff. [d] 13Many
of my people are now lost in Assyria. Some have
run away to Egypt. But at that time a great trum-
pet will be blown, and all those people will come
and worship the LORD on that holy mountain in
Jerusalem.

Warnings to Israel

28 How terrible it will be for Samaria, the
pride of Israel's drunken people!
That beautiful crown of flowers is just a
dying plant
set on a hill above a rich valley where
drunkards live.
2Look, the Lord has someone who is strong
and powerful.
Like a storm of hail and strong wind,
like a sudden flood of water pouring over the
country,
he will throw Samaria down to the ground.
3That city, the pride of Israel's drunken people,
will be trampled underfoot.
4That beautiful crown of flowers is just a
dying plant
set on a hill above a rich valley.
That city will be like the first fig of summer.
Anyone who sees it
quickly picks it and eats it.

5At that time the LORD All-powerful
will be like a beautiful crown,
like a wonderful crown of flowers
for his people who are left alive.
6Then he will give wisdom to the judges who
must decide cases
and strength to those who battle at the city
gate.
7But now those leaders are drunk with
wine;
they stumble from drinking too much
beer.

The priests and prophets[d] are drunk with
beer
and are filled with wine.
They stumble from too much beer.
The prophets are drunk when they see
their visions;
the judges stumble when they make their
decisions.
8Every table is covered with vomit,
so there is not a clean place anywhere.

9The LORD is trying to teach the people a
lesson;
he is trying to make them understand his
teachings.
But the people are like babies too old for
breast milk,
like those who no longer nurse at their
mother's breast.
10So they make fun of the LORD's prophet
and say:
"A command here, a command there.
A rule here, a rule there.
A little lesson here, a little lesson there."
11So the LORD will use strange words and
foreign languages
to speak to these people.
12God said to them,
"Here is a place of rest;
let the tired people come and rest.
This is the place of peace."
But the people would not listen.
13So the words of the LORD will be,
"A command here, a command there.
A rule here, a rule there.
A little lesson here, a little lesson there."
They will fall back and be defeated;
they will be trapped and captured.

14So listen to the LORD's message, you who
boast,
you leaders in Jerusalem.
15You say, "We have made an agreement with
death;
we have a contract with death.
When terrible punishment passes by,
it won't hurt us.
Our lies will keep us safe,
and our tricks will hide us."

16Because of these things, this is what the Lord
GOD says:
"I will put a stone in the ground in
Jerusalem,
a tested stone.
Everything will be built on this important and
precious rock.
Anyone who trusts in it will never be
disappointed.
17I will use justice as a measuring line
and goodness as the standard.
The lies you hide behind will be destroyed as
if by hail.
They will be washed away as if in a flood.
18Your agreement with death will be erased;
your contract with death will not help you.
When terrible punishment comes,
you will be crushed by it.
19Whenever punishment comes, it will take
you away.
It will come morning after morning;
it will defeat you by day and by night.
Those who understand this punishment will
be terrified."
20You will be like the person who tried to sleep
on a bed that was too short
and with a blanket that was too narrow
to wrap around himself.
21The LORD will fight as he did at Mount
Perazim.
He will be angry as he was in the Valley of
Gibeon.
He will do his work, his strange work.
He will finish his job, his strange job.
22Now, you must not make fun of these things,
or the ropes around you will become
tighter.
The Lord GOD All-powerful has told me
how the whole earth will be destroyed.

The LORD Punishes Fairly

23Listen closely to what I tell you;
listen carefully to what I say.
24A farmer does not plough his field all the
time;
he does not go on working the soil.
25He makes the ground flat and smooth.
Then he plants the dill and scatters the
cumin.
He plants the wheat in rows,
the barley in its special place
and other wheat as a border around the
field.
26His God teaches him
and shows him the right way.
27A farmer doesn't use heavy boards to crush
dill;
he doesn't use a wagon wheel to crush
cumin.
He uses a small stick to break open the dill,
and with a stick he opens the cumin.
28The grain is ground to make bread.
People do not ruin it by crushing it for
ever.
The farmer separates the wheat from the
chaff[d] with his cart,
but he does not let his horses grind it.

29This lesson also comes from the LORD
All-powerful,
who gives wonderful advice, who is very
wise.

Warnings to Jerusalem

29 How terrible it will be for you,
Jerusalem,
the city where David camped.
Your festivals have continued
year after year.
2I will attack Jerusalem,
and that city will be filled with sadness and
crying.
It will be like an altar to me.
3I will put armies all around you, Jerusalem;
I will surround you with towers
and with devices to attack you.
4You will be pulled down and will speak from
the ground;
I will hear your voice rising from the
ground.
It will sound like the voice of a ghost;
your words will come like a whisper from
the dust.

5Your many enemies will become like fine
dust;
the many cruel people will be like chaff[d]
that is blown away.
Everything will happen very quickly.
6 The LORD All-powerful will come
with thunder, earthquakes and great noises,
with storms, strong winds and a fire that
destroys.
7Then all the nations that fight against
Jerusalem
will be like a dream;
all the nations that attack her
will be like a vision in the night.
8They will be like a hungry man who dreams
he is eating,
but when he awakens, he is still hungry.
They will be like a thirsty man who dreams
he is drinking,
but when he awakens, he is still weak and
thirsty.
It will be the same way with all the nations
who fight against Mount Zion.[d]

9Be surprised and amazed.
Blind yourselves so that you cannot see.
Become drunk, but not from wine.
Trip and fall, but not from beer.
10The LORD has made you go into a deep sleep.
He has closed your eyes. (The prophets[d]
are your eyes.)
He has covered your heads. (The seers[d] are
your heads.)

11This vision is like the words of a book that is
closed and sealed. You may give the book to
someone who can read and tell that person to
read it. But he will say, "I can't read the book,
because it is sealed." 12Or you may give the book
to someone who cannot read and tell him to read
it. But he will say, "I don't know how to read."

13The Lord says:
"These people say they love me;
they show honour to me with words,
but their hearts are far from me.
The honour they show me
is nothing but human rules.
14So I will continue to amaze these people
by doing more and more miracles.[d]
Their wise men will lose their wisdom;
their wise men will not be able to
understand."

Warnings About Other Nations

15How terrible it will be for those who try
to hide things from the LORD
and who do their work in darkness.
They think no one will see them or know
what they do.
16You are confused.
You think the clay is equal to the
potter.
You think that an object can tell the one who
made it,
"You didn't make me."
This is like a pot telling its maker,
"You don't know anything."

A Better Time is Coming

17In a very short time, Lebanon will become
rich farmland,
and the rich farmland will seem like a
forest.
18At that time the deaf will hear the words in a
book.
Instead of having darkness and gloom, the
blind will see.
19The LORD will make the poor people
happy;
they will rejoice in the Holy One of
Israel.
20Then the people without mercy will come to
an end;
those who do not respect God will
disappear.
Those who enjoy doing evil will be
gone:
21those who lie about others in court,
those who trap people in court,
those who lie and take justice from
innocent people in court.

22 This is what the LORD who set Abraham free
says to the family of Jacob:
"Now the people of Jacob will not be
ashamed
or disgraced any longer.
23 When they see all their children,
the children I made with my hands,
they will say my name is holy.
They will agree that the Holy One of Jacob
is holy,
and they will respect the God of Israel.
24 People who do wrong will now understand.
Those who complain will accept being
taught."

Warnings to the Stubborn Nation

30 The LORD said,
"How terrible it will be for these
stubborn children.
They make plans, but they don't ask me to
help them.
They make agreements with other nations,
without asking my Spirit.[d]
They are adding more and more sins to
themselves.
2 They go down to Egypt for help
without asking me about it first.
They hope they will be saved by the king of
Egypt;
they want Egypt to protect them.
3 But hiding in Egypt will bring you only
shame;
Egypt's protection will only disappoint you.
4 Your officers have gone to Zoan,
and your messengers have gone to Hanes,
5 but they will be put to shame,
because Egypt is useless to them.
It will give no help and will be of no use;
it will cause them only shame and
embarrassment."

God's Message to Judah

6 This is a message about the animals in
southern Judah:
Southern Judah is a dangerous place
full of lions and lionesses,
poisonous snakes and darting snakes.
The messengers travel through there with
their wealth on the backs of donkeys
and their treasure on the backs of camels.
They carry them to a nation that cannot help
them,
7 to Egypt whose help is useless.
So I call that country Rahab[d] the
Do-Nothing.

8 Now write this on a sign for the people,
write this on a scroll,
so that for the days to come
this will be a witness for ever.
9 These people are like children who lie and
refuse to obey;
they refuse to listen to the LORD's teachings.
10 They tell the seers,[d]
"Don't see any more visions!"
They say to the prophets,[d]
"Don't tell us the truth!
Say things that will make us feel good;
see only good things for us.
11 Stop blocking our path.
Get out of our way.
Stop telling us
about God, the Holy One of Israel."

12 So this is what the Holy One of Israel says:
"You people have refused to accept this message
and have depended on cruelty and lies to
help you.
13 You are guilty of these things.
So you will be like a high wall with cracks
in it
that falls suddenly and breaks into small
pieces.
14 You will be like a clay jar that breaks,
smashed into many pieces.
Those pieces will be too small
to take coals from the fire
or to get water from a well."

15 This is what the Lord GOD, the Holy One of
Israel, says:
"If you come back to me and trust me, you
will be saved.
If you will be calm and trust me, you will
be strong."
But you don't want to do that.
16 You say, "No, we need horses to run
away on."
So you will run away on horses.
You say, "We will ride away on fast horses."
So those who chase you will be fast.
17 One enemy will make threats,
and 1,000 of your men will run away.
Five enemies will make threats,
and all of you will run from them.
You will be left alone like a flagpole on a
hilltop,
like a banner on a hill.
18 The LORD wants to show his mercy to you.
He wants to rise and comfort you.
The LORD is a fair God,
and everyone who waits for his help will
be happy.

The LORD will Help His People

19 You people who live on Mount Zion[d] in
Jerusalem will not cry any more. The LORD will

hear your crying, and he will comfort you. When
he hears you, he will help you. 20The Lord has
given you sorrow and hurt like the bread and water
you ate every day. He is your teacher; he will not
continue to hide from you, but you will see your
teacher with your own eyes. 21If you go the
wrong way—to the right or to the left—you will
hear a voice behind you saying, "This is the right
way. You should go this way." 22You have statues
covered with silver and gold, but you will ruin
them for further use. You will throw them away
like filthy rags and say, "Go away!"

23At that time the LORD will send rain for the
seeds you plant in the ground, and the ground
will grow food for you. The harvest will be rich
and great, and you will have plenty of food in the
fields for your animals. 24Your oxen and donkeys
that work the soil will have all the food they
need. You will have to use shovels and pitchforks
to spread all their food. 25Every mountain and hill
will have streams filled with water. These things
will happen after many people are killed and the
towers are pulled down. 26At that time the light
from the moon will be bright like the sun, and the
light from the sun will be seven times brighter
than now, like the light of seven days. These
things will happen when the LORD bandages his
broken people and heals the hurts he gave them.

27Look! The LORD comes from far away.
His anger is like a fire with thick clouds of smoke.
His mouth is filled with anger,
and his tongue is like a burning fire.
28His breath is like a rushing river,
which rises to the throat.
He will judge the nations as if he is sifting them through the strainer of destruction.
He will place in their mouths a bit that will lead them the wrong way.
29You will sing happy songs
as on the nights you begin a festival.
You will be happy like people listening to flutes
as they come to the mountain of the LORD,
to the Rock[d] of Israel.
30The LORD will cause all people to hear his great voice
and to see his powerful arm come down with anger,
like a great fire that burns everything,
like a great storm with much rain and hail.
31Assyria will be afraid when it hears the voice of the LORD,
because he will strike Assyria with a rod.
32When the LORD punishes Assyria with a rod,
he will beat them to the music of tambourines[d] and harps;
he will fight against them with his mighty weapons.

Sidelight About the only similarity between the flute mentioned in Isaiah 30:29 and the flutes people play today is that you blow into both. Many ancient flutes (or pipes) were made from two separate pipes, each with one hole in it to control pitch. These high-pitched instruments were used mostly for weddings and funerals.

33Topheth[n] has been made ready for a long time;
it is ready for the king.
It was made deep and wide
with much wood and fire.
And the LORD's breath will come
like a stream of burning sulphur and set it on fire.

Warnings About Relying on Egypt

31 How terrible it will be for those people who go down to Egypt for help.
They think horses will save them.
They think their many chariots
and strong horsemen will save them.
But they don't trust God, the Holy One of Israel,
or ask the LORD for help.
2But he is wise and can bring them disaster.
He does not change his warnings.
He will rise up and fight against the evil people
and against those who try to help evil people.
3The Egyptians are only people and are not God.
Their horses are only animals and are not spirit.
The LORD will stretch out his arm,
and the one who helps will stumble,
and the people who wanted help will fall.
All of them will be destroyed together.

4The LORD says this to me:
"When a lion or a lion's cub kills an animal to eat,
it stands over the dead animal and roars.
A band of shepherds
may be assembled against it,

Topheth Gehenna; the Valley of Hinnom. Here people burned the bodies of criminals and animals, along with rubbish.

but the lion will not be afraid of their yelling
or upset by their noise.
So the LORD All-powerful will come down
to fight on Mount Zion [d] and on its hill.
5The LORD All-powerful will defend Jerusalem
like birds flying over their nests.
He will defend and save it;
he will 'pass over' and save Jerusalem."

6You children of Israel, come back to the God
you fought against. 7The time is coming when
each of you will stop worshipping idols of gold
and silver, which you sinned by making.

8"Assyria will be defeated by a sword, but not
the sword of a person;
Assyria will be destroyed, but not by a
person's sword.
Assyria will run away from the sword
of God,
but its young men will be caught and made
slaves.
9They will panic, and their protection will be
destroyed.
Their commanders will be terrified when
they see God's battle flag,"
says the LORD,
whose fire is in Jerusalem
and whose furnace is in Jerusalem.

A Good Kingdom is Coming

32 A king will rule in a way that brings
justice,
and leaders will make fair decisions.
2Then each ruler will be like a shelter from
the wind,
like a safe place in a storm,
like streams of water in a dry land,
like a cool shadow from a large rock in a
hot land.

3People will look to the king for help,
and they will truly listen to what he says.
4People who are now worried will be able to
understand.
Those who cannot speak clearly now will
then be able to speak clearly and
quickly.
5Fools will not be called great,
and people will not respect the wicked.
6A fool says foolish things,
and in his mind he plans evil.
A fool does things that are wicked,
and he says wrong things about the LORD.
A fool does not feed the hungry
or let thirsty people drink water.
7The wicked person uses evil like a tool.
He plans ways to take everything from the
poor.
He destroys the poor with lies,
even when the poor person is in the right.
8But a good leader plans to do good,
and those good things make him a good
leader.

Hard Times are Coming

9You women who are calm now,
stand up and listen to me.
You women who feel safe now,
hear what I say.
10You women feel safe now,
but after one year you will be afraid.
There will be no grape harvest
and no summer fruit to gather.
11Women, you are calm now, but you should
shake with fear.
Women, you feel safe now, but you should
tremble.
Take off your nice clothes
and put rough cloth around your waist to
show your sadness.
12Beat your breasts in grief, because the fields
that were pleasant are now empty.
Cry, because the vines that once had fruit
now have no more grapes.
13Cry for the land of my people,
in which only thorns and weeds
now grow.
Cry for the city that once was happy
and for all the houses that once were filled
with joy.
14The palace will be empty;
people will leave the noisy city.
Strong cities and towers will be empty.
Wild donkeys will love to live there, and
sheep will go there to eat.

Things will Get Better

15This will continue until God pours his Spirit [d]
from above upon us.
Then the desert will be like a fertile field
and the fertile field like a forest.
16Justice will be found even in the desert,
and fairness will be found in the fertile
fields.
17That fairness will bring peace,
and it will bring calm and safety for ever.
18My people will live in peaceful places
and in safe homes
and in calm places of rest.
19Hail will destroy the forest,
and the city will be completely
destroyed.
20But you will be happy as you plant seeds
near every stream
and as you let your cattle and donkeys
wander freely.

Warnings to Assyria and Promises to God's People

33 How terrible it will be for you who
destroy others
but have not been destroyed yet.
How terrible it will be for you, traitor,
whom no one has turned against yet.
When you stop destroying,
others will destroy you.
When you stop turning against others,
they will turn against you.

2LORD, be kind to us.
We have waited for your help.
Give us strength every morning.
Save us when we are in trouble.
3Your powerful voice makes people run away
in fear;
your greatness causes the nations to run away.
4Like locusts, [d] your enemies will take away
the things you stole in war.
Like locusts rushing about, they will take
your wealth.
5The LORD is very great, and he lives in a high
place.
He fills Jerusalem with fairness and justice.
6He will be your safety.
He is full of salvation, wisdom and
knowledge.
Respect for the LORD is the greatest treasure.

7See, brave men are crying out in the streets;
those who tried to bring peace are crying
loudly.
8There is no one on the roads,
no one walking in the paths.
People have broken the agreements they
made.
They refuse to believe the proof from
witnesses.
No one respects other people.
9The land is sick and dying;
Lebanon is ashamed and dying.
The Plain of Sharon is dry like the desert,
and the trees of Bashan and Carmel are
dying.

10The LORD says, "Now, I will stand up
and show my greatness.
Now, I will become important to the
people.
11You people do useless things
that are like hay and straw.
A destructive wind will burn you
like fire.
12People will be burned until their bones
become like lime;
they will burn quickly like dry
thorn-bushes."
13You people in faraway lands, hear what I
have done.
You people who are near me, learn about
my power.
14The sinners in Jerusalem are afraid;
those who are separated from God shake
with fear.
They say, "Can any of us live through this
fire that destroys?
Who can live near this fire that burns on
and on?"
15A person who does what is right
and speaks what is right,
who refuses to take money unfairly,
who refuses to take money to hurt
others,
who does not listen to plans of murder,
who refuses to think about evil—
16this is the kind of person who will be safe.
He will be protected as he would be in a
high, walled city.
He will always have bread,
and he will not run out of water.
17Your eyes will see the king in his beauty.
You will see the land that stretches far away.
18You will think about the terror of the past:
"Where is that officer?
Where is the one who collected the
taxes?
Where is the officer in charge of our
defence towers?"
19No longer will you see those proud people
from other countries,
whose strange language you couldn't
understand.

God will Protect Jerusalem

20Look at Jerusalem, the city of our festivals.
Look at Jerusalem, that beautiful place of
rest.
It is like a tent that will never be moved;
the pegs that hold her in place will never
be pulled up,
and her ropes will never be broken.
21There the LORD will be our Mighty One.
That land is a place with streams and wide
rivers,
but there will be no enemy boats on those
rivers;
no powerful ship will sail on them.
22This is because the LORD is our judge.
The LORD makes our laws.
The LORD is our king.
He will save us.
23You sailors from other lands, hear:
The ropes on your boats hang loose.
The mast is not held firm.
The sails are not spread open.

Then your great wealth will be divided.
There will be so much wealth that even the crippled people will carry off a share.
24No one living in Jerusalem will say, "I am sick."
The people who live there will have their sins forgiven.

God will Punish His Enemies

34 All you nations, come near and listen.
Pay attention, you peoples!
The earth and all the people in it should listen,
the world and everything in it.
2The LORD is angry with all the nations;
he is angry with their armies.
He will destroy them and kill them all.
3Their bodies will be thrown outside.
The stink will rise from the bodies,
and the blood will flow down the mountains.
4The sun, moon and stars will dissolve,
and the sky will be rolled up like a scroll.
The stars will fall
like dead leaves from a vine
or dried-up figs from a fig tree.
5The LORD's sword in the sky is covered with blood.
It will cut through Edom
and destroy those people as an offering to the LORD.
6The LORD's sword will be covered with blood;
it will be covered with fat,
with the blood from lambs and goats,
with the fat from the kidneys of rams.
This is because the LORD decided there will be a sacrifice in Bozrah
and much killing in Edom.
7The oxen will be killed,
and the cattle and the strong bulls.
The land will be filled with their blood,
and the earth will be covered with their fat.

8The LORD has chosen a time for punishment.
He has chosen a year when people must pay for the wrongs they did to Jerusalem.
9Edom's rivers will be like hot tar.
Its earth will be like burning sulphur.
Its land will be like burning tar.
10The fires will burn night and day;
the smoke will rise from Edom for ever.
Year after year that land will be empty;
no one will ever travel through that land again.
11Birds and small animals will own that land,
and owls and ravens will live there.
God will make it an empty wasteland;
it will have nothing left in it.
12The important people will have no one left to rule them;
the leaders will all be gone.
13Thorns will take over the strong towers,
and wild bushes will grow in the walled cities.
It will be a home for wild dogs
and a place for owls to live.
14Desert animals will live with the hyenas,
and wild goats will call to their friends.
Night animals will live there
and find a place of rest.
15Owls will nest there and lay eggs.
When the eggs open, the owls will gather their young under their wings.
Hawks will gather
with their own kind.

16Look at the LORD's scroll and read what is
written there:
None of these will be missing;
none will be without its mate.
God has given the command,
so his Spirit[d] will gather them together.
17God has divided the land among them,
and he has given them each their portion.
So they will own that land for ever
and will live there year after year.

God will Comfort His People

35 The desert and dry land will become happy;
the desert will be glad and will produce flowers.
Like a flower, 2it will have many blooms.
It will show its happiness, as if it were shouting with joy.
It will be beautiful like the forest of Lebanon,
as beautiful as the hill of Carmel and the Plain of Sharon.
Everyone will see the glory of the LORD
and the splendour of our God.

3Make the weak hands strong
and the weak knees steady.
4Say to people who are frightened,
"Be strong. Don't be afraid.
Look, your God will come,
and he will punish your enemies.
He will make them pay for the wrongs they did,
but he will save you."

5Then the blind people will see again,
and the deaf will hear.
6Crippled people will jump like deer,
and those who can't talk now will shout with joy.
Water will flow in the desert,
and streams will flow in the dry land.
7The burning desert will have pools of water,
and the dry ground will have springs.
Where wild dogs once lived,
grass and water plants will grow.
8A road will be there;
this highway will be called "The Road to Being Holy".
Evil people will not be allowed to walk on that road;
only good people will walk on it.
No fools will go on it.
9No lions will be there,
nor will dangerous animals be on that road.
They will not be found there.
That road will be for the people God saves;
10 the people the LORD has freed will return there.
They will enter Jerusalem with joy,
and their happiness will last for ever.
Their gladness and joy will fill them completely,
and sorrow and sadness will go far away.

The Assyrians Invade Judah

36 During Hezekiah's fourteenth year as
king, Sennacherib king of Assyria at-
tacked all the fortified cities of Judah and cap-
tured them. 2The king of Assyria sent out his
field commander with a large army from
Lachish to King Hezekiah in Jerusalem. When
the commander came near the waterway from
the upper pool on the road where people do
their laundry, he stopped. 3Eliakim, Shebna and
Joah went out to meet him. Eliakim son of
Hilkiah was the palace manager, Shebna was the
royal secretary and Joah son of Asaph was the
recorder.

DEPRESSION

Positive

"Are you sure you did the test properly?" Jan asked as she gently coaxed the instruction sheet out of Nicola's trembling hand. "Each one of these home kits is different, and you have to make sure you follow the directions." Jan began to read the instructions.

Nicola stood shaking as the tears ran silently down her cheeks. She could barely speak.

"I've taken this test three times, and it's the same every time." Nicola's voice began to crack. "I'm pregnant. I'm going to have a baby. But I don't want a baby . . . not now. I'm only sixteen years old. Jan, I'm so afraid, and so sad. Why did this have to happen to me?"

Nicola walked across the room and collapsed into the old brown chair that had comforted her so many times when she was a little girl. But there was no comfort in that chair now. With no words left, Jan quietly sat down next to Nicola, put her arms round her and began to pray.

Nicola's pregnancy may cause her to face many bouts of depression, but God can help her. Read **Isaiah 35** to discover the comfort that God can bring for Nicola and others who turn to him.

- If you could talk to Nicola, which verses of Isaiah 35 would you use to encourage her?
- Think about how you feel when you're depressed. What does Isaiah 35 say to you about your depression?

Consider . . .

- suggesting that your youth leader put a box marked "Teenage Problems" in your church, and encouraging group members to submit, anonymously, any situations they are having problems with. Spend time each week discussing the problems and finding biblical solutions.
- talking to a trusted friend about the cause of your depression.

For more, see . . .

- Job 19:7–27 (p.481)
- 2 Corinthians 1:3–5 (p.1241)
- Psalm 88 (p.552)

4The field commander said to them, "Tell
Hezekiah this:
" 'The great king, the king of Assyria, says:
What can you trust in now? 5You say you have
battle plans and power for war, but your words
mean nothing. Whom are you trusting for help
so that you turn against me? 6Look, you are
depending on Egypt to help you, but Egypt is like
a splintered walking stick. If you lean on it for
help, it will stab your hand and hurt you. The
king of Egypt will hurt all those who depend
on him. 7You might say, "We are depending
on the LORD our God," but Hezekiah destroyed
the LORD's altars and the places of worship.
Hezekiah told Judah and Jerusalem, "You must
worship only at this one altar."
8" 'Now make an agreement with my master,
the king of Assyria: I will give you 2,000 horses
if you can find enough men to ride them. 9You
cannot defeat one of my master's least important
officers, so why do you depend on Egypt to give
you chariots and horsemen? 10I have not come to
attack and destroy this country without an order
from the LORD. The LORD himself told me to
come to this country and destroy it.' "
11Then Eliakim, Shebna and Joah said to the
field commander, "Please speak to us in the Ara-
maic language. We understand it. Don't speak to
us in Hebrew, because the people on the city
wall can hear you."
12But the commander said, "My master did
not send me to tell these things only to you and
your king. He sent me to speak also to those
people sitting on the wall who will have to eat
their own dung and drink their own urine like
you."
13Then the commander stood and shouted
loudly in the Hebrew language, "Listen to what
the great king, the king of Assyria says. 14The
king says you should not let Hezekiah fool you,
because he can't save you. 15Don't let Hezekiah
talk you into trusting the LORD by saying, "The
LORD will surely save us. This city won't be
handed over to the king of Assyria.'
16"Don't listen to Hezekiah. The king of Assyria
says, 'Make peace with me, and come out of the
city to me. Then everyone will be free to eat the
fruit from his own grapevine and fig tree and to
drink water from his own well. 17After that I will
come and take you to a land like your own—a
land with grain and new wine, bread and vine-
yards.'
18"Don't let Hezekiah fool you, saying, 'The
LORD will save us.' Has a god of any other nation
saved his people from the power of the king of
Assyria? 19Where are the gods of Hamath and
Arpad? Where are the gods of Sepharvaim? They
did not save Samaria from my power. 20Not one
of all the gods of these countries has saved his
people from me. Neither can the LORD save
Jerusalem from my power."
21The people were silent. They didn't answer
the commander at all, because King Hezekiah
had ordered, "Don't answer him."
22Then Eliakim, Shebna and Joah tore their
clothes to show how upset they were. (Eliakim
son of Hilkiah was the palace manager, Shebna
was the royal secretary and Joah son of Asaph
was the recorder.) The three men went to Heze-
kiah and told him what the field commander had
said.

Hezekiah Asks God to Help

37 When King Hezekiah heard the mes-
sage, he tore his clothes and put on
rough cloth to show how sad he was. Then he
went into the Temple[d] of the LORD. 2Hezekiah
sent Eliakim, the palace manager, and Shebna,
the royal secretary, and the older priests to Isa-
iah. They were all wearing rough cloth when
they came to Isaiah the prophet,[d] the son of
Amoz. 3They told Isaiah, "This is what Hezekiah
says: Today is a day of sorrow and punishment
and disgrace, as when a child should be born,
but the mother is not strong enough to give birth
to it. 4The king of Assyria sent his field com-
mander to make fun of the living God. Maybe
the LORD your God will hear what the com-
mander said and will punish him for it. So pray
for the few of us who are left alive."
5When Hezekiah's officers came to Isaiah, 6he
said to them, "Tell your master this: The LORD
says, 'Don't be afraid of what you have heard.
Don't be frightened by the words the servants of
the king of Assyria have spoken against me.
7Listen! I am going to put a spirit in the king of
Assyria. He will hear a report that will make
him return to his own country, and I will cause
him to die by the sword there.' "
8The field commander heard that the king of
Assyria had left Lachish. When he went back,
he found the king fighting against the city of
Libnah.
9The king received a report that Tirhakah, the
Cushite king of Egypt, was coming to attack
him. When the king of Assyria heard this, he
sent messengers to Hezekiah, saying, 10"Tell
Hezekiah king of Judah: don't be fooled by the
god you trust. Don't believe him when he says
Jerusalem will not be handed over to the king of
Assyria. 11You have heard what the kings of As-
syria have done. They have completely defeated
every country, so do not think you will be saved.
12Did the gods of those people save them? My
ancestors destroyed them, defeating the cities of
Gozan, Haran and Rezeph, and the people of

Eden living in Tel Assar. 13Where are the kings
of Hamath and Arpad? Where are the kings of
Sepharvaim, Hena and Ivvah?"

Hezekiah Prays to the LORD

14When Hezekiah received the letter from the
messengers and read it, he went up to the Tem-
ple[d] of the LORD. He spread the letter out before
the LORD 15and prayed to the LORD: 16"LORD All-
powerful, you are the God of Israel, whose throne
is between the gold creatures with wings, only
you are God of all the kingdoms of the earth. You
made the heavens and the earth. 17Hear, LORD,
and listen. Open your eyes, LORD, and see. Listen
to all the words Sennacherib has said to insult the
living God.

18"It is true, LORD, that the kings of Assyria
have destroyed all these countries and their
lands. 19They have thrown the gods of these na-
tions into the fire, but they were only wood and
rock statues that people made. So the kings have
destroyed them. 20Now, LORD our God, save us
from the king's power so that all the kingdoms
of the earth will know that you, LORD, are the
only God."

The LORD Answers Hezekiah

21Then Isaiah son of Amoz sent a message to
Hezekiah that said, "This is what the LORD, the
God of Israel, says: "You prayed to me about
Sennacherib king of Assyria. 22So this is what
the LORD has said against Sennacherib:

The people of Jerusalem
hate you and make fun of you;
the people of Jerusalem
laugh at you as you run away.
23You have insulted me and spoken against me;
you have raised your voice against me.
You have a proud look on your face,
which is against me, the Holy One of
Israel!
24You have sent your messengers to insult the
Lord.
You have said, "With my many chariots
I have gone to the tops of the mountains,
to the highest mountains of Lebanon.
I have cut down its tallest cedars
and its best pine trees.
I have gone to its greatest heights
and its best forests.
25I have dug wells in foreign countries
and drunk water there.
By the soles of my feet,
I have dried up all the rivers of Egypt."

26" 'King of Assyria, surely you have heard.
Long ago I, the LORD, planned these
things.
Long ago I designed them,
and now I have made them
happen.
I allowed you to turn those fortified cities
into piles of rocks.
27The people in those cities were weak;
they were frightened and put to shame.
They were like grass in the field,
like tender, young grass,
like grass on the housetop
that is burned by the wind before it can
grow.

28" 'I know when you rest,
when you come and go,
and how you rage against me.
29Because you rage against me,
and because I have heard your proud
words,
I will put my hook in your nose
and my bit in your mouth.
Then I will force you to leave my country
the same way you came.'

30"Then the LORD said, 'Hezekiah, I will give
you this sign:

This year you will eat the grain that grows
wild,
and the second year you will eat what
grows wild from that.
But in the third year, plant grain and
harvest it.
Plant vineyards and eat their fruit.
31Some of the people in the family of Judah
will escape.
Like plants that take root,
they will grow strong and have many
children.
32A few people will come out of Jerusalem
alive;
a few from Mount Zion[d] will live.
The strong love of the LORD All-powerful
will make this happen.'

33"So this is what the LORD says about the king
of Assyria:

'He will not enter this city
or even shoot an arrow here.
He will not fight against it with shields
or build a ramp to attack the city walls.
34He will return to his country the same way
he came,
and he will not enter this city,'
says the LORD.
35'I will defend and save this city
for my sake and for David, my servant.'"

36Then the angel of the LORD went out and
killed 185,000 men in the Assyrian camp. When

the people got up early the next morning, they
saw all the dead bodies. 37 So Sennacherib king
of Assyria left and went back to Nineveh and
stayed there.
38 One day as Sennacherib was worshipping in
the temple of his god Nisroch, his sons Adramme-
lech and Sharezer killed him with a sword. Then
they escaped to the land of Ararat. So Sennach-
erib's son Esarhaddon became king of Assyria.

Hezekiah's Illness

38 At that time Hezekiah became very sick;
he was almost dead. The prophet[d] Isaiah
son of Amoz went to see him and told him, "This
is what the LORD says: Make arrangements, be-
cause you are not going to live, but die."
2 Hezekiah turned towards the wall and prayed
to the LORD, 3 "LORD, please remember that I have
always obeyed you. I have given myself com-
pletely to you and have done what you said was
right." Then Hezekiah cried loudly.
4 Then the LORD spoke his word to Isaiah: 5 "Go
to Hezekiah and tell him: 'This is what the LORD,
the God of your ancestor David, says: I have
heard your prayer and seen your tears. So I will
add fifteen years to your life. 6 I will save you and
this city from the king of Assyria; I will defend
this city.
7 " 'The LORD will do what he says. This is the
sign from the LORD to show you: 8 the sun has
made a shadow go down the stairway of Ahaz,
but I will make it go back ten steps.' " So the
shadow made by the sun went back up the ten
steps it had gone down.
9 After Hezekiah king of Judah got well, he
wrote this song:

10 I said, "I am in the middle of my life.
Do I have to go through the gates of death?
Will I have the rest of my life taken away
from me?"
11 I said, "I will not see the LORD
in the land of the living again.

DEATH

Old Before I Die

"I hope I'm old before I die." So sang Robbie Williams in an effort to get away from the old rebel teenage thought of dying before you got too old.

In Isaiah 38:1–9 Hezekiah King of Judah had been having a bad time, he'd been really sick and thought he was about to die. But the Lord had other ideas and sent Isaiah to tell Hezekiah to "make other plans" because God was going to heal him! The king was so overjoyed, that once he was well again, he wrote a song!

There are always times when we feel that life is not worth living. Robbie, who went to numerous detox centres, must have felt the same. But when threatened with death, we cling on and on because we don't want to lose our life.

Hezekiah sang about people he loved, his home, and the fact that he was only in the middle of his life – this was no time to die!

For Robbie, death was a serious threat and to the King of Judah it was a foregone conclusion, but they both recovered.

And they both wanted to sing about it!

Read Hezekiah's lyrics in **Isaiah 38:9–20**.

- What did Hezekiah suggest we do about life, in Isaiah 38:19.
- What different ways can you think of to celebrate life?

Consider . . .

- visiting and giving some encouragement to someone who has a serious illness that may be making them depressed.
- giving some financial help to an organisation helping the desperate, such as the Samaritans.

For more, see . . .

- Proverbs 20:29 (p.607)
- 2 Corinthians 4:16–17 (p.1244)
- 2 Corinthians 1.8–10 (p.1241)

I will not again see the people
who live on the earth.
12Like a shepherd's tent,
my home has been pulled down and taken from me.
I am finished
like the cloth a weaver rolls up and cuts from the loom[n]
In one day you brought me to this end.
13All night I cried loudly.
Like a lion, he crushed all my bones.
In one day you brought me to this end.
14I cried like a bird
and moaned like a dove.
My eyes became tired as I looked to the heavens.
Lord, I have troubles. Please help me."
15What can I say?
The Lord told me what would happen and then made it happen.
I have had these troubles in my soul,
so now I will be humble all my life.
16Lord, because of you, people live.
Because of you, my spirit also lives;
you made me well and let me live.
17It was for my own good
that I had such troubles.
Because you love me very much,
you did not let me die
but threw my sins
far away.
18People in the place of the dead cannot praise you;
those who have died cannot sing praises to you;
those who die don't trust you
to help them.
19The people who are alive are the ones who praise you.
They praise you as I praise you today.
A father should tell his children
that you provide help.

20The LORD saved me,
so we will play songs on stringed instruments
in the Temple of the LORD
all the days of our lives.

21Then Isaiah said, "Make a paste from figs and
put it on Hezekiah's boil. Then he will get well."
22Hezekiah then asked Isaiah, "What will be the
sign? What will show that I will go up to the
Temple[d] of the LORD?"

Messengers from Babylon

39 At that time Merodach-Baladan son of
Baladan was king of Babylon. He sent
letters and a gift to Hezekiah, because he had
heard that Hezekiah had been sick and was now
well. 2Hezekiah was pleased and showed the
messengers what was in his storehouses: the silver, gold, spices, expensive perfumes, his swords
and shields, and all his wealth. He showed them
everything in his palace and in his kingdom.
3Then Isaiah the prophet[d] went to King Hezekiah and asked him, "What did these men say?
Where did they come from?"

Hezekiah said, "They came from a faraway
country—from Babylon."
4So Isaiah asked him, "What did they see in
your palace?"

Hezekiah said, "They saw everything in my palace. I showed them all my wealth."

Sidelight Isaiah's vocal challenges to the different kings of Judah didn't make him popular (see Isaiah 39:1–8, for example). According to tradition, the evil king Manasseh had Isaiah killed by tying him between two planks of wood and sawing him in half.

5Then Isaiah said to Hezekiah: "Listen to the
words of the LORD All-powerful: 6'In the future
everything in your palace and everything your
ancestors have stored up until this day will be
taken away to Babylon. Nothing will be left,' says
the LORD. 7Some of your own children, those who
will be born to you, will be taken away, and they
will become servants in the palace of the king of
Babylon."
8Hezekiah told Isaiah, "These words from the
LORD are good." He said this because he thought,
"There will be peace and security in my lifetime."

Sidelight There's an old saying "Every cloud has a silver lining". The "silver lining" in Isaiah begins at chapter 40 – good news after a long series of gloomy news bulletins.

Israel's Punishment will End

40 Your God says,
"Comfort, comfort my people.
2Speak kindly to the people of Jerusalem
and tell them
that their time of service is finished,
that they have paid for their sins,
that the LORD has punished Jerusalem
twice for every sin they did."

loom A machine for making cloth from thread.

3This is the voice of one who calls out:
"Prepare in the desert
the way for the LORD.
Make a straight road in the dry lands
for our God.
4Every valley should be raised up,
and every mountain and hill should be made flat.
The rough ground should be made level,
and the rugged ground should be made smooth.
5Then the glory of the LORD will be shown,
and all people together will see it.
The LORD himself said these things."

6A voice says, "Cry out!"
Then I said, "What shall I cry out?"

"Say all people are like the grass,
and all their glory is like the flowers of the field.
7The grass dies and the flowers fall
when the breath of the LORD blows on them.
Surely the people are like grass.
8The grass dies and the flowers fall,
but the word of our God will live for ever."
9Jerusalem, you have good news to tell.
Go up on a high mountain.
Jerusalem, you have good news to tell.
Shout out loud the good news.
Shout it out and don't be afraid.
Say to the towns of Judah,
"Here is your God."
10Look, the Lord GOD is coming with power
to rule all the people.
Look, he will bring reward for his people;
he will have their payment with him.
11He takes care of his people like a shepherd.
He gathers them like lambs in his arms
and carries them close to him.
He gently leads the mothers of the lambs.

CELEBRATING

Ha!

Need a reason to laugh? Consider these.

- It takes 72 muscles to frown, but only fourteen to smile.
- Laughing relieves stress. After you laugh, your blood pressure briefly falls below normal, breathing slows, and tension subsides.
- A Stanford University doctor says that laughing 100 times each day is about the same amount of exercise as ten minutes of rowing a boat.
- Laughing may release natural painkillers in your body that have been found to combat arthritis and other painful conditions.
- "Happy patients usually work harder to recover," says the humour co-ordinator at a hospital in New York. So the hospital has a "humour room" where patients can benefit from funny books, tapes and music.
- You could get in the *Guinness Book of Records* by smiling longer than the current world record of ten hours and five minutes.

Isaiah 40:1–11 gives an even better reason to celebrate, smile and laugh with joy. Read a promise that will bring a smile to your face!

- What parts of this passage give you a good reason to laugh – or shout – with joyful celebration?
- How does it make you feel to know the promise of God's comfort and love that this passage celebrates?

Consider . . .

- keeping a "celebration first-aid kit" where you can put reminders of God's goodness to you. When you are feeling down, look through the kit to remind yourself that you have something to celebrate every day.
- throwing a party for friends just to have fun together.

For more, see . . .

- Ezra 6:13–22 (p.437)
- Romans 15:8–13 (p.1208)
- Luke 15 (p.1070)

God is Supreme

12Who has measured the oceans in the palm of
his hand?
Who has used his hand to measure
the sky?
Who has used a bowl to measure all the dust
of the earth
and scales to weigh the mountains and hills?
13Who has known the mind of the LORD
or been able to give him advice?
14Whom did he ask for help?
Who taught him the right way?
Who taught him knowledge
and showed him the way to understanding?

15The nations are like one small drop in a bucket;
they are no more than the dust on his
measuring scales.
To him the islands are no more than fine
dust on his scales.
16All the trees in Lebanon are not enough for
the altar fires,
and all the animals in Lebanon are not
enough for burnt offerings.
17Compared to the LORD all the nations are
worth nothing;
to him they are less than nothing.

18Can you compare God to anything?
Can you compare him to an image of
anything?
19An idol is formed by a craftsman,
and a goldsmith covers it with gold
and makes silver chains for it.
20A poor person cannot buy those expensive
statues,
so he finds a tree that will not rot.
Then he finds a skilled craftsman
to make it into an idol that will not fall over.

21Surely you know. Surely you have heard.
Surely from the beginning someone told you.
Surely you understand how the earth was
created.
22God sits on his throne above the circle of the
earth,
and compared to him, people are like
grasshoppers.
He stretches out the skies like a piece of cloth
and spreads them out like a tent to sit
under.
23He makes rulers unimportant
and the judges of this world worth nothing.
24They are like plants that are placed in the
ground,
like seeds that are planted.
As soon as they begin to grow strong,
he blows on them and they die,
and the wind blows them away like chaff. [d]

25God, the Holy One, says, "Can you compare
me to anyone?
Is anyone equal to me?"
26Look up to the skies.
Who created all these stars?
He leads out the army of heaven one by one
and calls all the stars by name.
Because he is strong and powerful,
not one of them is missing.

27People of Jacob, why do you complain?
People of Israel, why do you say,
"The LORD does not see what happens to me;
he does not care if I am treated fairly"?
28Surely you know.
Surely you have heard.
The LORD is the God who lives for ever,
who created all the world.
He does not become tired or need to rest.
No one can understand how great his
wisdom is.
29He gives strength to those who are tired
and more power to those who are weak.
30Even children become tired and need to rest,
and young people trip and fall.
31But the people who trust the LORD will
become strong again.
They will rise up as an eagle in the sky;
they will run and not need rest;
they will walk and not become tired.

The LORD will Help Israel

41 The LORD says, "Faraway countries,
listen to me.
Let the nations become strong.
Come to me and speak;
we will meet together to decide who is
right.

2"Who caused the one to come from
the east?
Who gives him victories everywhere he
goes?
The one who brought him gives nations over
to him
and defeats kings.
He uses his sword, and kings become like
dust.
He uses his bow, and they are blown away
like chaff. [d]
3He chases them and is never hurt,
going places he has never been before.
4Who caused this to happen?
Who has controlled history since the
beginning?
I, the LORD, am the one. I was here at the
beginning,
and I will be here when all things are
finished."

5All you faraway places, look and be afraid;
all you places far away on the earth, shake with fear.
Come close and listen to me.
6 The workers help each other
and say to each other, "Be strong!"
7The craftsman encourages the goldsmith,
and the workman who smooths the metal with a hammer encourages the one who shapes the metal.
He says, "This metal work is good."
He nails the statue to a base so it can't fall over.

Only the LORD Can Save Us

8The LORD says, "People of Israel, you are my servants.
People of Jacob, I chose you.
You are from the family of my friend Abraham.
9I took you from places far away on the earth
and called you from a faraway country.
I said, 'You are my servants.'
I have chosen you and have not turned against you.
10So don't worry, because I am with you.
Don't be afraid, because I am your God.
I will make you strong and will help you;
I will support you with my right hand that saves you.

11"All those people who are angry with you
will be ashamed and disgraced.
Those who are against you
will disappear and be lost.
12You will look for your enemies,
but you will not find them.
Those who fought against you
will vanish completely.
13I am the LORD your God,
who holds your right hand,
and I tell you, 'Don't be afraid.
I will help you.'
14You few people of Israel who are left,
do not be afraid even though you are weak as a worm.
I myself will help you," says the LORD.
"The one who saves you is the Holy One of Israel.
15Look, I have made you like a new threshing[d] board
with many sharp teeth.
So you will walk on mountains and crush them;
you will make the hills like chaff.[d]
16You will throw them into the air, and the wind will carry them away;
a windstorm will scatter them.
Then you will be happy in the LORD;
you will be proud of the Holy One of Israel.

17"The poor and needy people look for water,
but they can't find any.
Their tongues are dry with thirst.
But I, the LORD, will answer their prayers;
I, the God of Israel, will not leave them to die.
18I will make rivers flow on the dry hills
and springs flow through the valleys.
I will change the desert into a lake of water
and the dry land into fountains of water.
19I will make trees grow in the desert—
cedars, acacia, myrtle and olive trees.
I will put pine, fir and cypress trees
growing together in the desert.
20People will see these things and understand;
they will think carefully about these things and learn
that the LORD's power did this,
that the Holy One of Israel made these things."

The LORD Challenges False Gods

21The LORD says, "Present your case."
The King of Jacob says, "Tell me your arguments.
22Bring in your idols to tell us
what is going to happen.
Have them tell us what happened in the beginning.
Then we will think about these things,
and we will know how they will turn out.
Or tell us what will happen in the future.
23 Tell us what is coming next
so we will believe that you are gods.
Do something, whether it is good or bad,
and make us afraid.
24You gods are less than nothing;
you can't do anything.
Those who worship you should be hated.

25"I have brought someone to come out of the north.[n]
I have called by name a man from the east,
and he knows me.
He walks on kings as if they were mud,
just as a potter walks on the clay.

someone . . . north This probably means Cyrus, a king of Persia.

26Who told us about this before it happened?
Who told us ahead of time so we could
say, 'He was right'?
None of you told us anything;
none of you told us before it happened;
no one heard you tell about it.
27I, the LORD, was the first one to tell Jerusalem
that the people were coming home.
I sent a messenger to Jerusalem with the
good news.
28I look at the idols, but there is not one that
can answer.
None of them can give advice;
none of them can answer my questions.
29Look, all these idols are false.
They cannot do anything;
they are worth nothing.

The LORD's Special Servant

42 "Here is my servant, the one I support.
He is the one I chose, and I am
pleased with him.
I have put my Spirit[d] upon him,
and he will bring justice to all
nations.
2He will not cry out or yell
or speak loudly in the streets.
3He will not break a crushed blade
of grass
or put out even a weak flame.
He will truly bring justice;
4 he will not lose hope or give up
until he brings justice to the world.
And people far away will trust his
teachings."

SERVICE

Called to Compassion

Claudia was blind, autistic and in pain. Put in an institution when she was young, Claudia was angry and withdrawn. She would scream, eat her clothes, and refuse to co-operate with others.

When Claudia was fifteen she was still blind, and she was still autistic. She still could not really communicate with people, but she was peaceful, loving and trusting.

What had changed?

When she was nine or ten, Claudia became part of a l'Arche community in Honduras. The love, compassion and care she experienced in this Christian community helped her to discover inner peace.

Founded by Canadian-born Jean Vanier, more than seventy l'Arche (which means "the Ark" in French) communities around the world are home to people with learning disabilities who are forgotten or rejected by their society. For about thirty years, Vanier has given his life to these "little people", as he calls them.

For Vanier, his work is his ministry in Christ's name. "When we love others," Vanier says, "we can walk with them and share their pain . . . I believe that Jesus is calling us to be men and women of compassion, to walk with people in their pain . . . And then we discover how the pain and the cross are intimately linked with the joy of the resurrection."

Through his work with people who have learning disabilities around the world, Jean Vanier lives a life that reflects the spirit of **Isaiah 42:1–9**, which promises a special servant who would lead the people – a promise that was fulfilled in Jesus Christ.

- What parallels are there between the ministry of Jean Vanier and the description in the passage?
- How can you follow in the footsteps of the special servant described in the passage?

Consider . . .

- giving a few hours of your free time to work with people who have learning disabilities in your community. Afterwards, talk to a parent, friend, or trusted adult about the experience.
- reaching out to someone in need even when it may be inconvenient for you.

For more, see . . .

- Deuteronomy 11:13–15 (p.176)
- 1 Corinthians 9:19–23 (p.1227)
- 1 Samuel 3:1–10 (p.258)

5God, the LORD, said these things.
He created the skies and stretched them out.
He spread out the earth and everything on it.
He gives life to all people on earth,
to everyone who walks on the earth.
6The LORD says, "I, the LORD, called you to do right,
and I will hold your hand
and protect you.
You will be the sign of my agreement with the people,
a light to shine for all people.
7You will help the blind to see.
You will free those who are in prison,
and you will lead those who live in darkness out of their prison.
8"I am the LORD. That is my name.
I will not give my glory to another;
I will not let idols take the praise that should be mine.
9The things I said would happen have happened,
and now I tell you about new things.
Before those things happen,
I tell you about them."

A Song of Praise to the LORD

10Sing a new song to the LORD;
sing his praise everywhere on the earth.
Praise him, you people who sail on the seas
and you animals who live in them.
Praise him, you people living in faraway places.
11The deserts and their cities should praise him.
The settlements of Kedar should praise him.
The people living in Sela should sing for joy;
they should shout from the mountain tops.
12They should give glory to the LORD.
People in faraway lands should praise him.
13The LORD will march out like a strong soldier;
he will be excited like a man ready to fight a war.
He will shout out the battle cry
and defeat his enemies.

14The LORD says, "For a long time I have said nothing;
I have been quiet and held myself back.
But now I will cry out
and strain like a woman giving birth to a child.
15I will destroy the hills and mountains
and dry up all their plants.
I will make the rivers become dry land
and dry up the pools of water.
16Then I will lead the blind along a way they never knew;
I will guide them along paths they have not known.
I will make the darkness become light for them,
and the rough ground smooth.
These are the things I will do;
I will not leave my people.
17But those who trust in idols,
who say to their statues,
'You are our gods'
will be rejected in disgrace.

Israel Refused to Listen to the LORD

18"You who are deaf, hear me.
You who are blind, look and see.
19No one is more blind than my servant Israel
or more deaf than the messenger I send.
No one is more blind than the person I own
or more blind than the servant of the LORD.
20Israel, you have seen much, but you have not obeyed.
You hear, but you refuse to listen."
21The LORD made his teachings wonderful,
because he is good.
22These people have been defeated and robbed.
They are trapped in pits
or locked up in prison.
Like robbers, enemies have taken them away,
and there is no one to save them.
Enemies carried them off,
and no one said, "Bring them back."
23Will any of you listen to this?
Will you listen carefully in the future?
24Who let the people of Jacob be carried off?
Who let robbers take Israel away?
The LORD allowed this to happen,
because we sinned against him.
We did not live the way he wanted us to live
and did not obey his teaching.
25So he became very angry with us
and brought terrible wars against us.
It was as if the people of Israel had fire all around them,
but they didn't know what was happening.
It was as if they were burning,
but they didn't pay any attention.

God is Always with His People

43 Now this is what the LORD says.
He created you, people of Jacob;
he formed you, people of Israel.
He says, "Don't be afraid, because I have saved you.
I have called you by name, and you are mine.
2When you pass through the waters, I will be with you.
When you cross rivers, you will not drown.

When you walk through fire, you will not be burnt,
nor will the flames hurt you.
3This is because I, the LORD, am your God,
the Holy One of Israel, your Saviour.
I gave Egypt to pay for you,
and I gave Cush and Seba to make you mine.
4Because you are precious to me,
because I give you honour and love you,
I will give other people in your place;
I will give other nations to save your life.
5Don't be afraid, because I am with you.
I will bring your children from the east
and gather you from the west.
6I will tell the north: give my people to me.
I will tell the south: don't keep my people in prison.
Bring my sons from far away
and my daughters from faraway places.
7Bring to me all the people who are mine,
whom I made for my glory,
whom I formed and made."

Judah is God's Witness

8Bring out the people who have eyes but don't see
and those who have ears but don't hear.
9All the nations gather together,
and all the people come together.
Which of their gods said this would happen?
Which of their gods can tell what happened in the beginning?
Let them bring their witnesses to prove they were right.
Then others will say, "It is true."
10The LORD says, "You are my witnesses
and the servant I chose.
I chose you so you would know and believe me,
so you would understand that I am the true God.
There was no God before me,
and there will be no God after me.
11I myself am the LORD;
I am the only Saviour.
12I myself have spoken to you, saved you and told you these things.
It was not some foreign god among you.
You are my witnesses, and I am God,"
says the LORD.
13 "I have always been God.
No one can save people from my power;
when I do something, no one can change it."

14This is what the LORD, who saves you,
the Holy One of Israel, says:
"I will send armies to Babylon for you,
and I will knock down all its locked gates.
The Babylonians will shout their cries of sorrow.
15I am the LORD, your Holy One,
the Creator of Israel, your King."

God will Save His People Again

16This is what the LORD says.
He is the one who made a road through the sea
and a path through rough waters.
17He is the one who defeated the chariots and horses
and the mighty armies.
They fell together and will never rise again.
They were destroyed as a flame is put out.
18The LORD says, "Forget what happened before,
and do not think about the past.
19Look at the new thing I am going to do.
It is already happening. Don't you see it?
I will make a road in the desert
and rivers in the dry land.
20Even the wild animals will be thankful to me—
the wild dogs and owls.
They will honour me when I put water in the desert
and rivers in the dry land
to give water to my people, the ones I chose.
21 The people I made
will sing songs to praise me.

22"People of Jacob, you have not called to me;
people of Israel, you have become tired of me.
23You have not brought me your sacrifices of sheep
nor honoured me with your sacrifices.
I did not weigh you down with sacrifices to offer
or make you tired with incense[d] to burn.
24So you did not buy incense for me;
you did not freely bring me fat from your sacrifices.
Instead you have weighed me down with your many sins;
you have made me tired of your many wrongs.

25"I, I am the One who forgives all your sins, for my sake;
I will not remember your sins.
26But you should remind me.
Let's meet and decide what is right.
Tell what you have done and show you are right.

27Your first father sinned,
and your leaders have turned against me.
28So I will make your holy rulers unholy.
I will bring destruction on the people of Jacob,
and I will let Israel be insulted."

The LORD is the Only God

44 The LORD says, "People of Jacob, you are my servants. Listen to me!
People of Israel, I chose you."
2This is what the LORD says, who made you,
who formed you in your mother's body,
who will help you:
"People of Jacob, my servants, don't be afraid.
Israel, I chose you.
3I will pour out water for the thirsty land
and make streams flow on dry land.
I will pour out my Spirit [d] into your children
and my blessing on your descendants.
4Your children will grow like a tree in the grass,
like poplar trees growing beside streams of water.
5One person will say, 'I belong to the LORD,'
and another will use the name Jacob.
Another will sign his name 'I am the LORD's,'
and another will use the name Israel."

6The LORD, the king of Israel,
is the LORD All-powerful, who saves Israel.
This is what he says: "I am the beginning and the end.
I am the only God.
7Who is a god like me?
That god should come and prove it.
Let him tell and explain all that has happened since I set up my ancient people.

SIN

Taking the Weight Off

Miriam didn't want to be in home group. Lately, she had felt distant from God. As she took her coat off, her home group leader handed her paper and a pencil.

"Write down whatever's bothering you," Sarah said, "mistakes you've made or worries you have."

Miriam watched other people working on their lists. She thought about the party she had gone to two weeks earlier. The whole experience had made her feel cheap: as though she wasn't worthy of anyone's respect. She started writing: "acting wild", "going further than I wanted to".

"When we give our problems to God, he makes the weight lighter," Sarah said, after everyone had finished. She passed a metal wastebasket around the circle, and Miriam dropped her list in quickly. Sarah struck a match and set fire to the lists. As Miriam watched her list of sins burning, she felt God's love within her "burn away" the hurt of the sins she had committed. She took a deep breath and felt relieved for the first time in days. She realised that by admitting her mistakes to God she felt closer to him. Perhaps she could make a new start now.

Sin keeps people from being what God wants them to be. **Isaiah 43:16–25** reminds us that God is willing to forgive sin so that we can be close to him.

- How would Miriam have reacted to reading this passage?
- Which verses in this passage help you to understand God's forgiveness of your sin?

Consider . . .

- making a list of sins you've committed recently. Ask God to forgive you for each sin. Then burn the list in a metal dustbin outside.
- giving God a thank-you present because he forgives you. Choose a gift God would appreciate, such as something for the needy or a time commitment from you.

For more, see . . .

- Psalm 32:1–7 (p.518)
- Romans 3:23–26 (p.1187)
- Micah 7:18–20 (p.897)

He should also tell what will happen in the
future.
8Don't be afraid! Don't worry!
I have always told you what will happen.
You are my witnesses.
There is no other God but me.
I know of no other Rock;[d] I am the
only One."

Idols are Useless

9Some people make idols, but they are worth
nothing.
People treasure them, but they are useless.
Those people are witnesses for the statues,
but those people cannot see.
They know nothing, so they will be
ashamed.
10Who made these gods?
Who made these useless idols?
11The workmen who made them will be
ashamed,
because they are only human.
If they all would come together,
they would all be ashamed and afraid.

12One workman uses tools to heat iron,
and he works over hot coals.
With his hammer he beats the metal and
makes a statue,
using his powerful arms.

SELF-ESTEEM

Chosen

Luke's self-confidence was low. To be honest, he was not a huge fan of how he looked and he really wished his hair did not do that odd frizzy thing. Though he had friends, he often felt nervous in a group and worried what other people thought of him. There were loads of things that he enjoyed, but he didn't think he was particularly good at any of them. He had never been chosen for anything, so never really volunteered for stuff either.

One thing that he loved was photography. It was something he could do on his own, and he enjoyed the craft of taking great pictures. His bedroom was covered in amazing photos and he had a real talent, though he doubted that was true.

One day his sister saw a leaflet advertising a competition for young photographers. She knew that Luke would never enter himself, so she copied some examples of his work and entered him without his knowledge.

Five weeks later Luke received a letter saying that he had been short-listed to win the competition and that he was invited to exhibit some of his work and attend an awards ceremony. He was deeply confused. Who had entered him, how had this happened and what would he do? His sister owned up and after much discussion, persuaded him to go for it.

The day of the exhibition came. Luke's work looked amazing professionally framed and displayed. There were many people there and he was very nervous. Incredibly, his name was read out as the winner. He was gobsmacked! For the first time in his life he had been chosen; he had won the prize. Instantly, Luke's confidence and belief in himself grew.

Read **Isaiah 44:1–8**. God has chosen his people. He has chosen you!

- Where do you get your confidence from? How you look? Maybe success at school or in sports?
- How does knowing that God has chosen you affect your belief in yourself?

Consider . . .

- flicking through the Bible and writing down as many verses as you can that speak of the fact that God has chosen us, that he loves us, that he delights in us. Pin this list up somewhere in your room.
- starting each day by thanking God that he has chosen you.

For more, see . . .

- Psalm 139 (p.581)
- Ephesians 2:10 (p.1271)
- Romans 8:15–17 (p.1195)

But when he becomes hungry, he loses his
power.
If he does not drink water, he becomes tired.

13Another workman uses a line and a
compass
to draw on the wood.
Then he uses his chisels to cut a statue
and his calipers to measure the statue.
In this way, the workman makes the wood
look exactly like a person,
and this statue of a person sits in the
house.
14He cuts down cedars
or cypress or oak trees.
Those trees grew by their own power in the
forest.
Or he plants a pine tree, and the rain
makes it grow.
15Then he burns the tree.
He uses some of the wood for a fire to
keep himself warm.
He also starts a fire to bake his bread.
But he uses part of the wood to make a god,
and then he worships it!
He makes the idol and bows down to it!
16The man burns half of the wood in the fire.
He uses the fire to cook his meat,
and he eats the meat until he is full.
He also burns the wood to keep himself
warm. He says,
"Good! Now I am warm. I can see because
of the fire's light."
17But he makes a statue from the wood that is
left and calls it his god.
He bows down to it and worships it.
He prays to it and says,
"You are my god. Save me!"
18Those people don't know what they are
doing. They don't understand!
It is as if their eyes are covered so they
can't see.
Their minds don't understand.
19They have not thought about these things;
they don't understand.
They have never thought to themselves,
"I burnt half of the wood in the fire
and used the hot coals to bake my bread.
I cooked and ate my meat.
And I used the wood that was left to make
this hateful thing.
I am worshipping a block of wood!"
20He doesn't know what he is doing;
his confused mind leads him the
wrong way.
He cannot save himself
or say, "This statue I am holding is a
false god."

The LORD is the True God

21"People of Jacob, remember these things!
People of Israel, remember you are my
servants.
I made you, and you are my servants.
So Israel, I will not forget you.
22I have swept away your sins like a big cloud;
I have removed your sins like a cloud that
disappears into the air.
Come back to me because I saved you."

23Skies, sing for joy because the LORD did great
things!
Earth, shout for joy, even in your deepest parts!
Sing, you mountains, with thanks to God.
Sing, too, you trees in the forest!
The LORD saved the people of Jacob!
He showed his glory when he saved Israel.
24This is what the LORD says, who saved you,
who formed you in your mother's body:
"I, the LORD, made everything,
stretching out the skies by myself
and spreading out the earth all alone.
25I show that the lying prophets' *d* signs
are false;
I make fools of those who do magic.
I confuse even wise men;
they think they know much, but I make
them look foolish.
26I make the messages of my servants come true;
I make the advice of my messengers come
true.
I say to Jerusalem,
'People will live in you again!'
I say to the towns of Judah,
'You will be built again!'
I say to Jerusalem's ruins,
'I will repair you.'
27I tell the deep waters, 'Become dry!
I will make your streams become dry!'
28I say of Cyrus,*n* 'He is my shepherd
and will do all that I want him to do.
He will say to Jerusalem, "You will be built
again!"
He will tell the Temple, *d* "Your foundations
will be rebuilt."'"

God Chooses Cyrus to Free Israel

45 This is what the LORD says to Cyrus,
his appointed king:
"I hold your right hand

Cyrus A king of Persia who ruled from about 550 to 530 BC.

and will help you defeat nations
and take away other kings' power.
I will open doors for you
so city gates will not stop you.
2I will go before you
and make the mountains flat.
I will break down the bronze gates of the cities
and cut through their iron bars.
3I will give you the wealth that is stored away
and the hidden riches
so you will know I am the LORD,
the God of Israel, who calls you by name.
4I do these things for my servants, the people of Jacob,
and for my chosen people, the Israelites.
Cyrus, I call you by name,
and I give you a title of honour even though you don't know me.
5I am the LORD. There is no other God;
I am the only God.
I will make you strong,
even though you don't know me,
6so that everyone will know
there is no other God.
From the east to the west they will know
I alone am the LORD.
7I made the light and the darkness.
I bring peace, and I cause troubles.
I, the LORD, do all these things.

8"Sky above, make victory fall like rain;
clouds, pour down victory.
Let the earth receive it,
and let salvation grow,
and let victory grow with it.
I, the LORD, have created it.

9"How terrible it will be for those who argue with the God who made them.
They are like a piece of broken pottery among many pieces.
The clay does not ask the potter,
'What are you doing?'
The thing that is made doesn't say to its maker,
'You have no hands.'
10How terrible it will be for the child who says to his father,
'Why are you giving me life?'
How terrible it will be for the child who says to his mother,
'Why are you giving birth to me?'"

11This is what the LORD,
the Holy One of Israel, and its Maker, says:
"You ask me about what will happen.
You question me about my children.
You give me orders about what I have made.
12I made the earth
and all the people living on it.
With my own hands I stretched out the skies,
and I commanded all the armies in the sky.
13I will bring Cyrus to do good things,
and I will make his work easy.
He will rebuild my city
and set my people free
without any payment or reward.
The LORD All-powerful says this."

14The LORD says,
"The goods made in Egypt and Cush
and the tall people of Seba
will come to you
and will become yours.
The Sabeans will walk behind you,
coming along in chains.
They will bow down before you
and pray to you, saying,
'God is with you,
and there is no other God.'"

15God and Saviour of Israel,
you are a God that people cannot see.
16All the people who make idols will be put to great shame;
they will go off together in disgrace.
17But Israel will be saved by the LORD,
and that salvation will continue for ever.
Never again will Israel be put to shame.

18The LORD created the heavens.
He is the God who formed the earth and made it.
He did not want it to be empty,
but he wanted life on the earth.
This is what the LORD says:
"I am the LORD. There is no other God.
19I did not speak in secret
or hide my words in some dark place.
I did not tell the family of Jacob
to look for me in empty places.
I am the LORD, and I speak the truth;
I say what is right.

20"You people who have escaped from other nations,
gather together and come before me;
come near together.
People who carry idols of wood don't know what they are doing.
They pray to a god who cannot save them.
21Tell these people to come to me.
Let them talk about these things together.
Who told you long ago that this would happen?
Who told about it long ago?
I, the LORD, said these things.
There is no other God besides me.

I am the only good God. I am the Saviour.
There is no other God.
22"All people everywhere,
follow me and be saved.
I am God. There is no other God.
23I will make a promise by my own power,
and my promise is true;
what I say will not be changed.
I promise that everyone will bow before me
and will promise to follow me.
24People will say about me, 'Goodness and power
come only from the LORD.'"
Everyone who has been angry with him
will come to him and be ashamed.
25But with the LORD's help, the people of Israel
will be found to be good,
and they will praise him.

False Gods are Useless

46 Bel[d] and Nebo[d] bow down.
Their idols are carried by animals.
The statues are only heavy loads that must be
carried;
they only make people tired.

Sidelight The god Bel wasn't nice (Isaiah 46:1). According to mythology, Bel killed a dragon-goddess named Tiamat, cut her up, and formed the universe from her remains.

2These gods will all bow down.
They cannot save themselves
but will all be carried away like prisoners.
3"Family of Jacob, listen to me!
All you people from Israel who are still
alive, listen!
I have carried you since you were born;
I have taken care of you from your birth.
4Even when you are old, I will be the same.
Even when your hair has turned grey, I will
take care of you.
I made you and will take care of you.
I will carry you and save you.
5"Can you compare me to anyone?
No one is equal to me or like me.
6Some people are rich with gold
and weigh their silver on the scales.
They hire a goldsmith, and he makes it into
a god.
Then they bow down and worship it.
7They put it on their shoulders and carry it.
They set it in its place, and there it stands;
it cannot move from its place.
People may yell at it, but it cannot answer.
It cannot save them from their troubles.

8"Remember this, and do not forget it!
Think about these things, you who turn
against God.
9Remember what happened long ago.
Remember that I am God, and there is no
other God.
I am God, and there is no one like me.
10From the beginning I told you what would
happen in the end.
A long time ago I told you things that have
not yet happened.
When I plan something, it happens.
What I want to do, I will do.
11I am calling a man from the east to carry out
my plan;
he will come like a hawk from a country
far away.
I will make what I have said come true;
I will do what I have planned.
12Listen to me, you stubborn people,
who are far from what is right.
13I will soon do the things that are right.
I will bring salvation soon.
I will save Jerusalem
and bring glory to Israel."

God will Destroy Babylon

47 The LORD says, "City of Babylon,
go down and sit in the earth.
People of Babylon, sit on the ground.
You are no longer the ruler.
You will no longer be called
tender or beautiful.
2 You must use large stones to grind grain
into flour.
Remove your veil and your nice skirts.
Uncover your legs and cross the rivers.
3People will see your nakedness;
they will see your shame.
I will punish you;
I will punish every one of you."
4Our Saviour is named the LORD All-powerful;
he is the Holy One of Israel.
5"Babylon, sit in darkness and say nothing.
You will no longer be called the queen of
kingdoms.
6I was angry with my people,
so I rejected those who belonged to me.
I gave them to you,
but you showed them no mercy.
You even made the old people
work very hard.
7You said, 'I will live for ever
as the queen.'
But you did not think about these things
or consider what would happen.

8"Now, listen, you lover of pleasure.
You think you are safe.
You tell yourself,
'I am the only important person.
I will never be a widow
or lose my children.'
9Two things will happen to you suddenly, in a single day.
You will lose your children and your husband.
These things will truly happen to you,
in spite of all your magic,
in spite of your powerful tricks.
10You do evil things, but you feel safe
and say, 'No one sees what I do.'
Your wisdom and knowledge
have fooled you.
You say to yourself,
'I am God, and no one is equal to me.'
11But troubles will come to you,
and you will not know how to stop them.
Disaster will fall on you,
and you will not be able to keep it away.
You will be destroyed quickly;
you will not even see it coming.

12"Keep on using your tricks
and doing all your magic
that you have used since you were young.
Maybe they will help you;
maybe you will be able to scare someone.
13You are tired of the advice you have received.
So let those who study the sky—
those who tell the future by looking at the stars and the new moons—
let them save you from what is about to happen to you.
14But they are like straw;
fire will quickly burn them up.
They cannot save themselves
from the power of the fire.
They are not like coals that give warmth
nor like a fire that you may sit beside.
15You have worked with these people,
and they have been with you since you were young,
but they will not be able to help you.
Everyone will go his own way,
and there will be no one left to save you."

God Controls the Future

48 The LORD says, "Family of Jacob, listen to me.
You are called Israel,
and you come from the family of Judah.
You swear by the LORD's name
and praise the God of Israel,
but you are not honest or sincere.
2You call yourselves people of the holy city,
and you depend on the God of Israel,
who is named the LORD All-powerful.
3Long ago I told you what would happen.
I said these things and made them known;
suddenly I acted, and these things happened.
4I knew you were stubborn;
your neck was like an iron muscle,
and your head was like bronze.
5So a long time ago I told you about these things;
I told you about them before they happened
so you couldn't say, 'My idols did this,
and my wooden and metal statues made these things happen.'
6"You heard and saw everything that happened,
so you should tell this news to others.
Now I will tell you about new things,
hidden things that you don't know yet.
7These things are happening now, not long ago;
you have not heard about them before today.
So you cannot say, 'We already knew about that.'
8But you have not heard me; you have not understood.
Even long ago you did not listen to me.
I knew you would surely turn against me;
you have fought against me since you were born.
9But for my own sake I will be patient.
People will praise me for not becoming angry
and destroying you.
10I have made you pure, but not by fire, as silver is made pure.
I have purified you by giving you troubles.
11I do this for myself, for my own sake.
I will not let people speak evil against me,
and I will not let some god take my glory.

Israel will be Free

12"People of Jacob, listen to me.
People of Israel, I have called you to be my people.
I am God;
I am the beginning and the end.
13I made the earth with my own hands.
With my right hand I spread out the skies.
When I call them,
they come together before me."
14All of you, come together and listen.
None of the gods said these things would happen.
The LORD has chosen someone
to attack the Babylonians;
he will carry out his wishes against Babylon.
15"I have spoken; I have called him.[n]
I have brought him, and I will make him successful.

him This probably refers to Cyrus king of Persia.

16 Come to me and listen to this.
From the beginning I have spoken openly.
From the time it began, I was there."

Now, the Lord GOD
has sent me with his Spirit. [d]

17 This is what the LORD, who saves you,
the Holy One of Israel, says:
"I am the LORD your God,
who teaches you to do what is good,
who leads you in the way you should go.
18 If you had obeyed me,
you would have had peace like a
full-flowing river.
Good things would have flowed to you like
the waves of the sea.
19 You would have had many children,
as many as the grains of sand.
They would never have died out
nor been destroyed."

20 My people, leave Babylon!
Run from the Babylonians!
Tell this news with shouts of joy to the
people;
spread it everywhere on earth.
Say, "The LORD has saved his servants, the
people of Jacob."
21 They did not become thirsty when he led
them through the deserts.
He made water flow from a rock
for them.
He split the rock,
and water flowed out.
22 "There is no peace for evil people," says the
LORD.

FOLLOWING GOD

On a Mission

Joan was always a little bit strange. She was pretty religious, and some of her friends thought she was a bit intense. When she started saying that God was talking to her, her friends were even more puzzled. This religious stuff was for older people, monks and nuns, not twelve-year-old girls.

But Joan carried on, saying that she knew what it was she had to do in life, and that she was going to do it. As time went on, her friends thought it was just rubbish – she didn't seem to be doing anything different to them. Until one day, she went missing. Rumours flew around the village.

Then one night a royal herald (messenger) turned up and they got news that Joan had done exactly what she had been saying for years. She had gone to the king and crowned him. She had led an army and was defending her country against attackers.

This story may sound crazy – a seventeen-year-old girl leading an army – but it's true! It's the story of Joan of Arc. She lived in the 1400s, and was convinced that God had given her a mission to defend France (her country) against the English who had invaded. By the age of seventeen, she had led an army, had reinstated a French king, and was widely respected. Two years later, she was burned at the stake by the church who didn't know what to make of her. They thought she was wrong – but later apologised and remembered her as a saint.

Look at **Isaiah 49:1–13**. It talks of a God who gives people a mission in life – to be "a light for all nations to show people all over the world the way to be saved".

- What are some of the things that God asks of his servant?
- What is the end result?

Consider . . .

- what it is specifically that God might want you to do. It may not be leading an army, but what might it be?
- writing a list of the things you care about and seeing how they compare with the things that God talks about in the passage.

For more, see . . .

- Isaiah: 61:1–4 (p.705)
- Matthew 28:18–20 (p.995)
- Jeremiah 29:11–14 (p.749)

God Calls His Special Servant

49 All of you people in faraway places,
listen to me.
Listen, all you nations far away.
Before I was born, the LORD called me to
serve him.
The LORD named me while I was still in my
mother's body.
2He made my tongue like a sharp sword.
He hid me in the shadow of his hand.
He made me like a sharp arrow.
He hid me in the holder for his arrows.
3He told me, "Israel, you are my servant.
I will show my glory through you."
4But I said, "I have worked hard for nothing;
I have used all my power, but I did nothing
useful.
But the LORD will decide what my work is
worth;
God will decide my reward."
5The LORD made me in the body of my mother
to be his servant,
to lead the people of Jacob back to him
so that Israel might be gathered to him.
The LORD will honour me,
and I will get my strength from my God.
6Now he told me,
"You are an important servant to me
to bring back the tribes[d] of Jacob,
to bring back the people of Israel who are
left alive.
But, more importantly, I will make you a
light for all nations
to show people all over the world the way
to be saved."

7The LORD who saves you
is the Holy One of Israel.
He speaks to the one who is hated by the
people,
to the servant of rulers.
This is what he says: "Kings will see you and
stand to honour you;
great leaders will bow down before you,
because the LORD can be trusted.
He is the Holy One of Israel, who has
chosen you."

The Day of Salvation

8This is what the LORD says:
"At the right time I will hear your prayers.
On the day of salvation I will help you.
I will protect you,
and you will be the sign of my agreement
with the people.
You will bring back the people to the land
and give the land that is now ruined back
to its owners.
9You will tell the prisoners, 'Come out of your
prison.'
You will tell those in darkness, 'Come into
the light.'
The people will eat beside the roads,
and they will find food even on bare hills.
10They will not be hungry or thirsty.
Neither the hot sun nor the desert wind
will hurt them.
The God who comforts them will lead them
and guide them by springs of water.
11I will make my mountains into roads,
and the roads will be raised up.
12Look, people are coming to me from far away,
from the north and from the west,
from Aswan in southern Egypt."

13Heavens and earth, be happy.
Mountains, shout with joy,
because the LORD comforts his people
and will have pity on those who suffer.

Jerusalem and Her Children

14But Jerusalem said, "The LORD has left me;
the Lord has forgotten me."

15The LORD answers, "Can a woman forget the
baby she nurses?
Can she feel no kindness for the child to
which she gave birth?
Even if she could forget her children,
I will not forget you.
16See, I have written your name on my hand.
Jerusalem, I always think about your walls.
17Your children will soon return to you,
and the people who defeated you and
destroyed you will leave.
18Look up and look around you.
All your children are gathering to return
to you."
The LORD says, "As surely as I live,
your children will be like jewels
that a bride wears proudly.

19"You were destroyed and defeated,
and your land was made useless.
But now you will have more people than the
land can hold,
and those people who destroyed you will be
far away.
20Children were born to you while you were sad,
but they will say to you,
'This place is too small for us.
Give us a bigger place to live.'
21Then you will say to yourself,
'Who gave me all these children?
I was sad and lonely,
defeated and separated from my people.
So who reared these children?

I was left all alone.
Where did all these children come from?'"

22This is what the Lord GOD says:
"See, I will lift my hand to signal the nations;
I will raise my banner for all the people to see.
Then they will bring your sons back to you in their arms,
and they will carry your daughters on their shoulders.
23Kings will teach your children,
and daughters of kings will take care of them.
They will bow down before you
and kiss the ground at your feet.
Then you will know I am the LORD.
Anyone who trusts in me will not be disappointed."

24Can the wealth a soldier wins in war be taken away from him?
Can a prisoner be freed from a powerful soldier?
25This is what the LORD says:
"The prisoners will be taken from the strong soldiers.
What the soldiers have taken will be saved.
I will fight your enemies,
and I will save your children.
26I will force those who trouble you to eat their own flesh.
Their own blood will be the wine that makes them drunk.
Then everyone will know
I, the LORD, am the One who saves you;
I am the Powerful One of Jacob who saves you."

Israel was Punished for Its Sin

50 This is what the LORD says:
"People of Israel, you say I divorced your mother.
Then where is the paper that proves it?
Or do you think I sold you
to pay a debt?
Because of the evil things you did, I sold you.
Because of the times she turned against me,
your mother was sent away.
2I came home and found no one there;
I called, but no one answered.
Do you think I am not able to save you?
Do I not have the power to save you?
Look, I need only to shout and the sea becomes dry.
I change rivers into a desert,
and their fish rot because there is no water;
they die of thirst.
3I can make the skies dark;
I can make them black like clothes of sadness."

God's Servant Obeys

4The Lord GOD gave me the ability to teach
so that I know what to say to make the weak strong.
Every morning he wakes me.
He teaches me to listen like a student.
5The Lord GOD helps me learn,
and I have not turned against him
nor stopped following him.
6I offered my back to those who beat me.
I offered my cheeks to those who pulled my beard.
I won't hide my face from them
when they make fun of me and spit at me.
7The Lord GOD helps me,
so I will not be ashamed.
I will be determined,
and I know I will not be disgraced.
8He shows that I am innocent, and he is close to me.
So who can accuse me?
If there is someone, let us go to court together.
If someone wants to prove I have done wrong,
he should come and tell me.
9Look! It is the Lord GOD who helps me.
So who can prove me guilty?
Look! All those who try will become useless like old clothes;
moths will eat them.

10Who among you fears the LORD
and obeys his servant?
That person may walk in the dark
and have no light.
Then let him trust in the LORD
and depend on his God.
11But instead, some of you want to light your own fires
and make your own light.
So, go, walk in the light of your fires,
and trust your own light to guide you.
But this is what you will receive from me:
you will lie down in a place of pain.

Jerusalem will be Saved

51 The LORD says, "Listen to me,
those of you who try to live right
and follow the LORD.
Look at the rock from which you were cut;
look at the stone quarry from which you were dug.
2Look at Abraham, your ancestor,
and Sarah, who gave birth to your ancestors.
Abraham had no children when I called him,
but I blessed him and gave him many descendants.[d]
3So the LORD will comfort Jerusalem;
he will show mercy to those who live in her ruins.

He will change her deserts into a garden like
Eden;
he will make her empty lands like the
garden of the LORD.
People there will be very happy;
they will give thanks and sing songs.

4"My people, listen to me;
my nation, pay attention to me.
I will give the people my teachings,
and my decisions will be like a light to all
people.
5I will soon show that I do what is right.
I will soon save you.
I will use my power and judge all nations.
All the faraway places are waiting for me;
they wait for my power to help them.
6Look up to the heavens.
Look around you at the earth below.
The skies will disappear like clouds of smoke.
The earth will become useless like old clothes,
and its people will die like flies.
But my salvation will continue for ever,
and my goodness will never end.

7"You people who know what is right should
listen to me;
you people who follow my teachings should
hear what I say.
Don't be afraid of the evil things people say,
and don't be upset by their insults.
8Moths will eat those people as if they were
clothes,
and worms will eat them as if they were wool.
But my goodness will continue for ever,
and my salvation will continue from now on."

9Wake up, wake up, and use your strength,
powerful LORD.
Wake up as you did in the old times,
as you did a long time ago.
With your own power, you cut Rahab[d] into
pieces
and killed that sea monster.

REVENGE

Payback

Gavin woke up in the morning and, as usual, in his imagination, devised some terrible ways for the Millhouse gang to meet their ends. He rather hoped giant flying rats might eat them very slowly, swooping down to pick off an ear here and a finger there until they were no more, having first cried out for help in immense pain. Gavin was pulled back to reality by his mum's call from downstairs that his breakfast was ready.

Isaiah 50:4–9 does not tell us how to deal with a big bully if we're small or a white bully if we're black. In those cases, you should tell the teacher. Revenge is a blind alley.

It is a good passage to encourage you if you are being bullied, mocked and accused falsely because of your faith. It tells you to be a student of God and to look to him for support. If you are being bullied because you are teaching God's word or a Christian, then you should expect that people may make fun of you, and in some parts of the world even beat you (verse 6).

It is one of the most important passages in the Old Testament about Jesus – a passage Jesus lived out. He offered himself and did not hide.

- To whom do you think this passage applies? The world in general? Teachers of the Word of God? Followers of Jesus?
- Does God speak to you each morning as verse 5 suggests? Let God open your ears every day. Let his voice be the first voice you hear.

Consider . . .

- whether there is anyone on whom you really want revenge. Are you prepared to leave that to God for the sake of the gospel?
- how you would defend your faith with words in the law court mentioned in verse 8. How well would you do?

For more, see . . .

- Leviticus 19:17–18 (p.119)
- Acts 18:5–6 (p.1169)
- Matthew 5:38–42 (p.946)

10You dried up the sea
and the waters of the deep ocean.
You made the deepest parts of the sea into a road
for your people to cross over and be saved.
11The people the LORD has freed will return
and enter Jerusalem with joy.
Their happiness will last for ever.
They will have joy and gladness,

Sidelight When Isaiah 51:9 talks about cutting Rahab into little pieces, it's not referring to a person named Rahab. Rather, it refers to a sea monster of chaos that, according to an old legend, God killed in battle when he created the world. That's why the name was a put-down when it was used to refer to Egypt in Isaiah 30:7 (p.669).

and all sadness and sorrow will be gone
far away.
12The LORD says, "I am the one who comforts you.
So why should you be afraid of people,
who die?
Why should you fear people who die like
the grass?
13Have you forgotten the LORD who made you,
who stretched out the skies
and made the earth?
Why are you always afraid
of those angry people who trouble you
and who want to destroy?
But where are those angry people now?
14 People in prison will soon be set free;
they will not die in prison,
and they will have enough food.
15I am the LORD your God,
who stirs the sea and makes the waves roar.
My name is the LORD All-powerful.
16I will give you the words I want you to say.
I will cover you with my hands and
protect you.
I made the heavens and the earth,
and I say to Jerusalem, 'You are my people.'"

God Punished Israel

17Awake! Awake!
Get up, Jerusalem.
The LORD was very angry with you;
your punishment was like wine in a cup.
The LORD made you drink that wine;
you drank the whole cup until you
stumbled.
18Jerusalem had many people,
but there was not one to lead her.
Of all the people who grew up there,
no one was there to guide her.
19Troubles came to you two by two,
but no one will feel sorry for you.
There was ruin and disaster, great hunger
and fighting.
No one can comfort you.
20Your people have become weak.
They fall down and lie on every street
corner,
like animals caught in a net.
They have felt the full anger of the LORD
and have heard God's angry shout.

21So listen to me, poor Jerusalem,
you who are drunk but not from wine.
22Your God will defend his people.
This is what the LORD your God says:
"The punishment I gave you is like a cup
of wine.
You drank it and could not walk straight.
But I am taking that cup of my anger away
from you,
and you will never be punished by my
anger again.
23I will now give that cup of punishment to
those who gave you pain,
who told you,
'Bow down so we can walk over you.'
They made your back like dirt for them to
walk on;
you were like a street for them to
travel on."

Jerusalem will be Saved

52 Wake up, wake up, Jerusalem!
Become strong!
Be beautiful again,
holy city of Jerusalem.
The people who do not worship God and
who are not pure
will not enter you again.
2Jerusalem, you once were a prisoner.
Now shake off the dust and stand up.
Jerusalem, you once were a prisoner.
Now free yourself from the chains around
your neck.
3This is what the LORD says:
"You were not sold for a price,
so you will be saved without cost."
4This is what the Lord GOD says:
"First my people went down to Egypt
to live.
Later Assyria made them slaves.

5"Now see what has happened," says the LORD.
"Another nation has taken away my people
for nothing.
This nation who rules them makes fun of
me," says the LORD.
"All day long they speak against me.

6This has happened so my people will know
who I am,
and so, on that future day, they will know
that I am the one speaking to them.
It will really be me."
7How beautiful is the person
who comes over the mountains to bring
good news,
who announces peace
and brings good news,
who announces salvation
and says to Jerusalem,
"Your God is King."
8Listen! Your guards are shouting.
They are all shouting for joy!
They all will see with their own eyes
when the LORD returns to Jerusalem.
9Jerusalem, your buildings are destroyed now,
but shout and rejoice together,
because the LORD has comforted his people.
He has saved Jerusalem.
10The LORD will show his holy power
to all the nations.
Then everyone on earth
will see the salvation of our God.

11You people, leave, leave; get out of Babylon!
Touch nothing that is unclean. [d]
You men who carry the LORD's things used in
worship,
leave there and make yourselves pure.
12You will not be forced to leave Babylon quickly;
you will not be forced to run away,
because the LORD will go before you,
and the God of Israel will guard you from
behind.

The LORD's Suffering Servant

13The LORD says, "See, my servant will act
wisely.
People will greatly honour and respect him.
14Many people were shocked when they
saw him.

FREEDOM

Chains

Katherine was a forty-year-old American woman, with a huge secret.

One day she threw a party and invited all her friends and relations, she even sent invitations to her husband and her children. Unbeknown to them, this was going to be the biggest day in Katherine's life.

When everyone arrived at the party they were puzzled. It wasn't her birthday, so what were they celebrating? Katherine stepped into the middle of them and began to confess to a horrendous story. She was on the FBI's most wanted list. She had been running from them for twenty-three years. She explained how she couldn't live with the terrible guilt any more. And then, to everyone's amazement, she picked up the phone and called the FBI and gave herself up.

The FBI came around to the house and in front of everyone she loved, Katherine gave herself up. Yet, in the newspaper the next day, there was a photograph of a woman grinning from ear to ear as she was being led away in handcuffs.

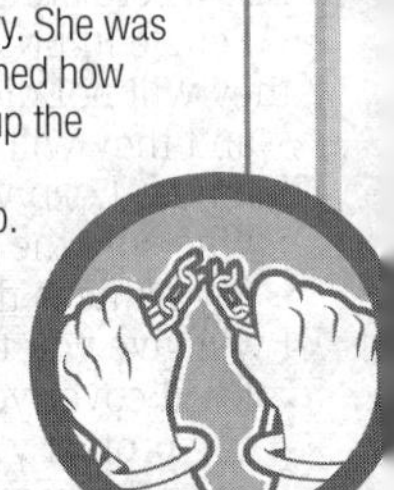

She was quoted saying, "I am now learning to live with openness and truth."

It was Katherine's first day of freedom in twenty-three years.

- Look at **Isaiah 52:2**. How does Katherine's story compare with Isaiah's?
- What are the "chains" that keep you from freedom?

Consider . . .

- writing down things in your life that make you feel guilty and stop you from following Jesus the way you really want to.
- taking a deep breath and confessing to a friend something that has made you feel bad. Then pray about it together.

For more, see . . .

- John 8:31–36 (p.1110)
- 1 John 1:9 (p.1371)
- Romans 6:15–23 (p.1192)

His appearance was so changed he did not
look like a man;
his form was changed so much they could
barely tell he was human.
15But now he will surprise many nations.
Kings will be amazed and shut their mouths.
They will see things they had not been told
about him,
and they will understand things they had
not heard."

53 Who would have believed what we
heard?
Who saw the LORD's power in this?
2He grew up like a small plant before the LORD,
like a root growing in a dry land.
He had no special beauty or form to make us
notice him;
there was nothing in his appearance to
make us desire him.
3He was hated and rejected by people.
He had much pain and suffering.
People would not even look at him.
He was hated, and we didn't even notice him.
4But he took our suffering on him
and felt our pain for us.
We saw his suffering
and thought God was punishing him.
5But he was wounded for the wrong we did;
he was crushed for the evil we did.
The punishment, which made us well, was
given to him,
and we are healed because of his wounds.
6We all have wandered away like sheep;
each of us has gone his own way.
But the LORD has put on him the
punishment
for all the evil we have done.

7He was beaten down and punished,
but he didn't say a word.
He was like a lamb being led to be killed.
He was quiet, as a sheep is quiet while its
wool is being cut;
he never opened his mouth.
8Men took him away roughly and unfairly.
He died without children to continue his
family.

JESUS CHRIST

What Love Looks Like

Robert was an "MK", a missionary kid; his parents served in South Asia. Sitting round a table with American friends one night, he and the others started talking about missions and how to know whether a person was "cut out" to be a missionary. Robert thought about his parents. He knew the commitment and love it took to be effective for Christ.

"It takes love to do missions," Robert stated. "And do you know what love looks like?

"Once I watched my dad hold a man's diseased feet in his hands," Robert continued. "The feet were swollen and full of pus, but he wasn't afraid to touch him, because he cared for that person. His only concern was loving that man like Jesus does. That's the kind of love I want to have."

Because of Jesus' deep love for us, he experienced extreme pain and suffering. **Isaiah 52:13—53:12** is a prophetic picture of this servant of God.

- How was the love of Robert's father for the sick man like the love of God's servant in this passage?
- What kind of suffering could you face as God's servant today?

Consider . . .

- writing a description of how Jesus might live today. What would he wear? How would he spend his time? With whom would he associate? Where would he go?
- adopting a person who serves God through mission work, ministry, or some kind of service by writing a note of appreciation, praying for the work he or she does, or offering your assistance.

For more, see . . .

- Isaiah 11:1–10 (p.652)
- Philippians 2:1–11 (p.1282)
- John 1:1–18 (p.1096)

He was put to death;
he was punished for the sins of my people.
9He was buried with wicked men,
and he died with the rich.
He had done nothing wrong,
and he had never lied.

10But it was the LORD who decided
to crush him and make him suffer.
The LORD made his life a penalty offering,
but he will still see his descendants [d] and live
a long life.
He will complete the things the LORD wants
him to do.
11"After his soul suffers many things,
he will see life and be satisfied.
My good servant will make many people
right with God;
he will carry away their sins.
12For this reason I will make him a great man
among people,
and he will share in all things with those
who are strong.
He willingly gave his life
and was treated like a criminal.
But he carried away the sins of many
people
and asked forgiveness for those who
sinned."

People will Return to Jerusalem

54 The LORD says, "Sing, Jerusalem.
You are like a woman who never
gave birth to children.
Start singing and shout for joy.
You never felt the pain of giving birth,
but you will have more children
than the woman who has a husband.
2Make your tent bigger;
stretch it out and make it wider.
Do not hold back.
Make the ropes longer
and its stakes stronger,
3because you will spread out to the right and
to the left.
Your children will take over other nations,
and they will again live in cities that once
were destroyed.

4"Don't be afraid, because you will not be
ashamed.
Don't be embarrassed, because you will not
be disgraced.
You will forget the shame you felt earlier;
you will not remember the shame you felt
when you lost your husband.
5The God who made you is like your
husband.
His name is the LORD All-powerful.
The Holy One of Israel is the one who
saves you.
He is called the God of all the earth.
6You were like a woman whose husband
left her,
and you were very sad.
You were like a wife who married young
and then her husband left her.
But the LORD called you to be his,"
says your God.
7God says, "I left you for a short time,
but with great kindness I will bring you
back again.
8I became very angry
and hid from you for a time,
but I will show you mercy with kindness for
ever,"
says the LORD who saves you.

9The LORD says, "This day is like the time of
Noah to me.
I promised then that I would never flood
the world again.
In the same way, I promise I will not be
angry with you
or punish you again.
10The mountains may disappear,
and the hills may come to an end,
but my love will never disappear;
my promise of peace will not come to
an end,"
says the LORD who shows mercy to you.

11"You poor city. Storms have hurt you,
and you have not been comforted.
But I will rebuild you with turquoise stones,
and I will build your foundations with
sapphires.
12I will use rubies to build your walls
and shining jewels for the gates
and precious jewels for all your outer walls.
13All your children will be taught by the LORD,
and they will have much peace.
14I will build you using fairness.
You will be safe from those who would
hurt you,
so you will have nothing to fear.
Nothing will come to make you afraid.
15I will not send anyone to attack you,
and you will defeat those who do
attack you.

16"See, I made the blacksmith.
He fans the fire to make it hotter,
and he makes the kind of tool he wants.
In the same way I have made the destroyer
to destroy.
17 So no weapon that is used against you will
defeat you.

You will show that those who speak against
you are wrong.
These are the good things my servants
receive.
Their victory comes from me," says the
LORD.

God Gives What is Good

55 The LORD says, "All you who are
thirsty,
come and drink.
Those of you who do not have money,
come, buy and eat!
Come buy wine and milk
without money and without cost.
2Why spend your money on something that is
not real food?
Why work for something that doesn't really
satisfy you?
Listen closely to me, and you will eat what is
good;
your soul will enjoy the rich food that
satisfies.
3Come to me and listen;
listen to me so you may live.
I will make an agreement with you that will
last for ever.
I will give you the blessings I promised to
David.
4I made David a witness of my power for all
nations,
a ruler and commander of many nations.
5You will call for nations that you don't yet
know.
And these nations that do not know you
will run to you
because of the LORD your God,
because of the Holy One of Israel who
honours you."
6So you should look for the LORD before it is
too late;
you should call to him while he is near.
7The wicked should stop doing wrong,
and they should stop their evil thoughts.
They should return to the LORD so he may
have mercy on them.
They should come to our God, because he
will freely forgive them.
8The LORD says, "My thoughts are not like
your thoughts.
Your ways are not like my ways.
9Just as the heavens are higher than the earth,
so are my ways higher than your ways
and my thoughts higher than your thoughts.
10Rain and snow fall from the sky
and don't return without watering the
ground.
They cause the plants to sprout and grow,
making seeds for the farmer
and bread for the people.
11The same thing is true of the words I speak.
They will not return to me empty.
They make the things happen that I want to
happen,
and they succeed in doing what I send
them to do.
12"So you will go out with joy
and be led out in peace.
The mountains and hills will burst into song
before you,
and all the trees in the fields will clap their
hands.
13Large cypress trees will grow where
thorn-bushes were.
Myrtle trees will grow where weeds were.
These things will be a reminder of the LORD's
promise,
and this reminder will never be destroyed."

Sidelight Replacing thorn-bushes with myrtle would require more than a little plant food (Isaiah 55:13). Thorn-bushes and weeds (or briars) are scraggly desert plants that survive with little nourishment. The myrtle is an evergreen shrub that grows along rivers and streams, and it symbolises peace, joy, generosity and justice – which fits the prophet's vision for the future.

All Nations will Obey the LORD

56 This is what the LORD says:
"Give justice to all people,
and do what is right,
because my salvation will come to you soon.
Soon everyone will know that I do what is
right.
2The person who obeys the law about the
Sabbath [d]
will be blessed,
and the person who does no evil
will be blessed."
3Foreigners who have joined the LORD should
not say,
"The LORD will not accept me with his
people."
The eunuch [d] should not say,
"Because I cannot have children, the LORD
will not accept me."
4This is what the LORD says:
"The eunuchs should obey the law about the
Sabbath

and do what I want
and keep my agreement.
5If they do, I will make their names
remembered
within my Temple[d] and its walls.
It will be better for them than children.
I will give them a name that will last for
ever,
that will never be forgotten.
6Foreigners will join the LORD
to worship him and love him,
to serve him,
to obey the law about the Sabbath,
and to keep my agreement.
7I will bring these people to my holy
mountain
and give them joy in my house of prayer.
The offerings and sacrifices
they place on my altar will please me,
because my Temple will be called
a house for prayer for people from all
nations."
8The Lord GOD says—
he who gathers the Israelites that were
forced to leave their country:
"I will bring together other people
to join those who are already gathered."

Israel's Leaders are Evil

9All you animals of the field,
all you animals of the forest, come to eat.
10The leaders who are to guard the people are
blind;
they don't know what they are doing.
All of them are like quiet dogs
that don't know how to bark.
They lie down and dream
and love to sleep.
11They are like hungry dogs
that are never satisfied.
They are like shepherds
who don't know what they are doing.
They all have gone their own way;
all they want to do is satisfy themselves.
12They say, "Come, let's drink some wine;
let's drink all the beer we want.
And tomorrow we will do this again,
or, maybe we will have an even better
time."

Israel Does Not Follow God

57 Those who are right with God
may die,
but no one pays attention.
Good people are taken away,
but no one understands.
Those who do right are being taken away
from evil
2and are given peace.
Those who live as God wants
find rest in death.

3"Come here, you magicians!
Come here, you sons of prostitutes[d] and
those who take part in adultery![d]
4Of whom are you making fun?
Whom are you insulting?
At whom do you stick out your tongue?
You turn against God,
and you are liars.
5You have sexual relations under every green
tree
to worship your gods.
You kill children in the ravines
and sacrifice them in the rocky places.
6You take the smooth rocks from the
ravines
as your portion.
You pour drink offerings on them to worship
them,
and you give grain offerings to them.
Do you think this makes me want to show
you mercy?
7You make your bed on every hill and
mountain,
and there you offer sacrifices.
8You have hidden your idols
behind your doors and doorposts.
You have left me, and you have uncovered
yourself.
You have pulled back the covers and
climbed into bed.
You have made an agreement with those
whose beds you love,
and you have looked at their nakedness.
9You use your oils and perfumes
to look nice for Molech.[d]
You have sent your messengers to faraway
lands;
you even tried to send them to the place of
the dead.
10You were tired from doing these things,
but you never gave up.
You found new strength,
so you did not stop.

11"Whom were you so afraid of
that you lied to me?
You have not remembered me
or even thought about me.
I have been quiet for a long time.
Is that why you are not afraid of me?
12I will tell about your 'goodness' and what
you do,
and those things will do you no good.
13When you cry out for help,
let the gods you have gathered help you.

The wind will blow them all away;
just a puff of wind will take them away.
But the person who depends on me will receive the land
and own my holy mountain."

The LORD will Save His People

14Someone will say, "Build a road! Build a road! Prepare the way!
Make the way clear for my people."
15And this is the reason: God lives for ever and is holy.
He is high and lifted up.
He says, "I live in a high and holy place,
but I also live with people who are sad and humble.
I give new life to those who are humble
and to those whose hearts are broken.
16I will not accuse for ever,
nor will I always be angry,
because then human life would grow weak.
Human beings, whom I created, would die.
17I was angry because they were dishonest in order to make money.
I punished them and turned away from them in anger,
but they continued to do evil.
18I have seen what they have done, but I will heal them.
I will guide them and comfort them and those who felt sad for them.
They will all praise me.
19I will give peace, real peace, to those far and near,
and I will heal them," says the LORD.
20But evil people are like the angry sea,
which cannot rest,
whose waves toss up waste and mud.
21"There is no peace for evil people," says my God.

How to Honour God

58 The LORD says, "Shout out loud. Don't hold back.
Shout out loud like a trumpet.
Tell my people what they have done against their God;
tell the family of Jacob about their sins.
2They still come every day looking for me
and want to learn my ways.
They act just like a nation that does what is right,
that obeys the commands of its God.
They ask me to judge them fairly.
They want God to be near them.
3They say, 'To honour you we had special days when we gave up eating,
but you didn't see.
We humbled ourselves to honour you,
but you didn't notice.' "

But the LORD says, "You do what pleases yourselves on these special days,
and you are unfair to your workers.
4On these special days when you do not eat,
you argue and fight
and hit each other with your fists.
You cannot do these things as you do now
and believe your prayers are heard in heaven.
5This kind of special day is not what I want.
This is not the way I want people to be sorry for what they have done.
I don't want people just to bow their heads like a plant
and wear rough cloth and lie in ashes to show their sadness.
This is what you do on your special days when you do not eat,
but do you think this is what the LORD wants?

6"I will tell you the kind of special day I want:
free the people you have put in prison unfairly
and undo their chains.
Free those to whom you are unfair
and stop their hard labour.
7Share your food with the hungry
and bring poor, homeless people into your own homes.
When you see someone who has no clothes,
give him yours,
and don't refuse to help your own relatives.
8Then your light will shine like the dawn,
and your wounds will quickly heal.
Your God will walk before you,
and the glory of the LORD will protect you from behind.
9Then you will call out, and the LORD will answer.
You will cry out, and he will say, 'Here I am.'

"If you stop making trouble for others,
if you stop using cruel words and pointing your finger at others,
10if you feed those who are hungry
and take care of the needs of those who are troubled,
then your light will shine in the darkness,
and you will be bright like sunshine at noon.
11The LORD will always lead you.
He will satisfy your needs in dry lands
and give strength to your bones.

You will be like a garden that has much water,
like a spring that never runs dry.
12Your people will rebuild the old cities that are now in ruins;
you will rebuild their foundations.
You will be known for repairing the broken places
and for rebuilding the roads and houses.
13"You must obey God's law about the Sabbath[d]
and not do what pleases yourselves on that holy day.
You should call the Sabbath a joyful day
and honour it as the LORD's holy day.
You should honour it by not doing whatever you please
nor saying whatever you please on that day.
14Then you will find joy in the LORD,
and I will carry you to the high places above the earth.
I will let you eat the crops of the land your ancestor Jacob had."
The LORD has said these things.

The Evil That People Do

59 Surely the LORD's power is enough to save you.
He can hear you when you ask him for help.
2It is your evil that has separated
you from your God.
Your sins cause him to turn away from you,
so he does not hear you.
3With your hands you have killed others,
and with your fingers you have done wrong.
With your lips you have lied,
and with your tongue you say evil things.
4People take each other to court unfairly,
and no one tells the truth in arguing his case.
They accuse each other falsely and tell lies.
They cause trouble and create more evil.

HYPOCRISY

Meaningless Acts

In the Minster there was a great procession at the start of the Easter Sunday morning communion service. They called it a Eucharist. Up the centre aisle came a line of people dressed in robes and finery – the good and the great. Minor canons, major canons, canons emeriti, archdeacons, deans, suffragan bishops and bishops. Everyone had been looking forward to this celebration for ages, even though most of the guests didn't understand most of the procession's titles.

The staff of the Minster, now processing in a dignified and orderly fashion along with their guests, had been at each other's throats that very morning. They had been arguing about the ceremony. They had been disputing the order of the procession. They had even squabbled about the sausage roll quality for the post-service buffet. Yet all the back-biting was put on hold for the procession. The organ boomed; the choir sang. "Everything is fine" said the service; "I hate your guts," said the people in their hearts.

In the congregation, the people sang the songs and hymns with gusto. They said, "Thanks be to God" at the end of readings, when prompted, affirming God's hatred of poverty and inequality. After a Bank Holiday relaxing, they went back to their regular jobs in the city and continued exploiting others for a little more cash.

Read **Isaiah 58:3–9a**.

- Why do some people pretend to be one way, then behave completely the opposite?
- How does God feel about those people? Is he like that?

Consider . . .

- becoming accountable to a friend for your behaviour as a Christian. Make a deal with each other that you will ask each other the hard questions about your behaviour, use of time and commitment to Jesus?
- whether members of your Christian youth group pretend they are more holy than they are.

For more, see . . .

- Hosea 6:1–10 (p.854)
- James 1:22–27 (p.1348)
- Matthew 7:1–5 (p.949)

5They hatch evil like eggs from poisonous
snakes.
If you eat one of those eggs, you will die,
and if you break one open, a poisonous
snake comes out.
People tell lies as they would spin a
spider's web.
6 The webs they make cannot be used for
clothes;
you can't cover yourself with those webs.
The things they do are evil,
and they use their hands to hurt others.
7They eagerly run to do evil,
and they are always ready to kill innocent
people.
They think evil thoughts.
Everywhere they go they cause ruin and
destruction.
8They don't know how to live in peace,
and there is no fairness in their lives.
They are dishonest.
Anyone who lives as they live will never
have peace.

Israel's Sin Brings Trouble

9Fairness has gone far away;
goodness is nowhere to be found.
We wait for the light, but there is only
darkness now.
We hope for a bright light, but all we have
is darkness.
10We are like the blind feeling our way along a
wall.
We feel our way as if we had no eyes.
In the brightness of day we trip as if it were
night.
We are like dead men among the strong.
11All of us growl like the bears.
We call out sadly like the doves.
We look for justice, but there isn't any.
We want to be saved, but salvation is far
away.

12We have done many wrong things against
our God;
our sins show we are wrong.
We know we have turned against God;
we know the evil things we have done:
13sinning and rejecting the LORD,
turning away from our God,
planning to hurt others and to disobey God,
planning and speaking lies.
14So we have driven away justice,
and we have kept away from what is
right.
Truth is not spoken in the streets;
what is honest is not allowed to enter the
city.
15Truth cannot be found anywhere,
and people who refuse to do evil are attacked.
The LORD looked and could not find any justice,
and he was displeased.
16He could not find anyone to help the people,
and he was surprised that there was no one
to help.
So he used his own power to save the
people;
his own goodness gave him strength.
17He covered himself with goodness like
armour.
He put the helmet of salvation on his head.
He put on the clothes of punishment
and wrapped himself in the coat of his
strong love.
18The LORD will pay back his enemies for what
they have done.
He will show his anger to those who were
against him;
he will punish the people in faraway places
as they deserve.
19Then people from the west will fear the LORD,
and people from the east will fear his glory.
The LORD will come quickly like a fast-flowing
river,
driven by the breath of the LORD.

20"Then a Saviour will come to Jerusalem
and to the people of Jacob who have
turned from sin,"
says the LORD.

21The LORD says, "This is my agreement with
these people: My Spirit [d] and my words that I give
you will never leave you or your children or your
grandchildren, now and for ever."

Jerusalem will be Great

60 "Jerusalem, get up and shine, because
your light has come,
and the glory of the LORD shines on you.
2Darkness now covers the earth;
deep darkness covers her people.
But the LORD shines on you,
and people see his glory around you.
3Nations will come to your light;
kings will come to the brightness of your
sunrise.

4"Look around you.
People are gathering and coming to you.
Your sons are coming from far away,
and your daughters are coming with
them.
5When you see them, you will shine with
happiness;
you will be excited and full of joy,

because the wealth of the nations across the
seas will be given to you;
the riches of the nations will come to you.
6Herds of camels will cover your land,
young camels from Midian and Ephah.
People will come from Sheba
bringing gold and incense,[d]
and they will sing praises to the LORD.
7All the sheep from Kedar will be given to you;
the rams from Nebaioth will be brought
to you.
They will be pleasing sacrifices on my altar,
and I will make my beautiful Temple[d] more
beautiful.

8"The people are returning to you like clouds,
like doves flying to their nests.
9People in faraway lands are waiting for me.
The great trading ships will come first,
bringing your children from faraway lands,
and with them silver and gold.
This will honour the LORD your God,
the Holy One of Israel,
who does wonderful things for you.

10"Jerusalem, foreigners will rebuild your walls,
and their kings will serve you.
When I was angry, I hurt you,
but now I want to be kind to you and
comfort you.

Sidelight The promise to Jerusalem that people from Sheba would come to Jerusalem to worship was quite an impressive promise (Isaiah 60:6). Sheba was over two thousand kilometres away – across the desert of present-day Saudia Arabia. Years earlier, the queen of Sheba had visited King Solomon and seen all his wealth (1 Kings 10:1–13, p.325).

SHARING FAITH

Take That Opportunity

Adam just didn't know how he was going to tell his friends about Jesus. He thought he'd done pretty well recently. All his friends knew he went to church, because he told them every Monday morning when they asked him what he'd got up to at the weekend. He'd even put his hand up in a religious studies lesson when the teacher asked if anyone in the room followed "the Christian religion". However, he knew that wasn't enough. He knew that Jesus wanted him to talk to his friends about the way he had changed Adam's life. Only problem was how to do it.

Adam decided his best bet was to start off by praying for his friends that they would become interested in Jesus. Imagine his surprise when a few weeks later one of his friends, Jay, started talking about Jesus. He said, "I saw this TV programme on Jesus last night and they said that he was a bit of a hippie and he probably took drugs. But that isn't right is it Adam? Tell me – what's the truth about this Jesus bloke."

Adam couldn't believe it – here was the perfect opportunity, so he took it. He had spent the last three weeks working out what he would say if someone did ask him about Jesus! Jay was really interested. He even started coming along to Adam's youth group to find out more.

Read **Isaiah 60:1–6** to see how God shines on Christians to make them a witness.

- Why do you think Adam wanted to talk about Jesus and not just his "Christian religion"?
- How can we be a light to people, like the one Isaiah talks about?

Consider . . .

- thinking and praying about two people you can show the "light of God" to over the next week. Plan how you can do it and then do it!
- what you would say to your friends if they asked you to talk about Jesus for five minutes.

For more, see . . .

- John 6:44 (p.1105)
- 2 Corinthians 5:11–21 (p.1245)
- 2 Corinthians 3:17–18 (p.1242)

11Your gates will always be open;
they will not be closed day or night
so the nations can bring their wealth to you,
and their kings will be led to you.
12The nation or kingdom that doesn't serve you
will be destroyed;
it will be completely ruined.

13"The great trees of Lebanon will be given
to you:
its pine, fir and cypress trees together.
You will use them to make my Temple
beautiful,
and I will give much honour to this place
where I rest my feet.
14The people who have hurt you will bow
down to you;
those who hated you will bow down at
your feet.
They will call you The City of the LORD,
Jerusalem, city of the Holy One of Israel.

15"You have been hated and left empty
with no one passing through.
But I will make you great from now on;
you will be a place of happiness for ever
and ever.
16You will be given what you need from the
nations,
like a child drinking milk from its mother.
Then you will know that it is I, the LORD,
who saves you.
You will know that the Powerful One of
Jacob protects you.
17I will bring you gold in place of bronze,
silver in place of iron,
bronze in place of wood,
iron in place of rocks.
I will change your punishment into peace,
and you will be ruled by what is right.
18There will be no more violence in your country;
it will not be ruined or destroyed.
You will name your walls Salvation
and your gates Praise.
19The sun will no longer be your light during
the day
nor will the brightness from the moon be
your light,
because the LORD will be your light for ever,
and your God will be your glory.
20Your sun will never set again,
and your moon will never be dark,
because the LORD will be your light for ever,
and your time of sadness will end.
21All of your people will do what is right.
They will receive the earth for ever.
They are the plant I have planted,
the work of my own hands
to show my greatness.
22The smallest family will grow to a thousand.
The least important of you will become a
powerful nation.
I am the LORD,
and when it is time, I will make these
things happen quickly."

The LORD's Message of Freedom

61 The Lord GOD has put his Spirit[d]
in me,
because the LORD has appointed me to tell
the good news to the poor.
He has sent me to comfort those whose
hearts are broken,
to tell the captives they are free
and to tell the prisoners they are released.
2He has sent me to announce the time when
the LORD will show his kindness
and the time when our God will punish
evil people.
He has sent me to comfort all those who
are sad
3 and to help the sorrowing people of
Jerusalem.
I will give them a crown to replace their ashes,
and the oil of gladness to replace their sorrow,
and clothes of praise to replace their spirit
of sadness.
Then they will be called Trees of Goodness,
trees planted by the LORD to show his
greatness.

4They will rebuild the old ruins
and restore the places destroyed long ago.
They will repair the ruined cities
that were destroyed for so long.
5My people, foreigners will come to tend your
sheep.
People from other countries will tend your
fields and vineyards.
6You will be called priests of the LORD;
you will be named the servants of our God.
You will have riches from all the nations on
earth,
and you will take pride in them.
7Instead of being ashamed, my people will
receive twice as much wealth.
Instead of being disgraced, they will be
happy because of what they receive.
They will receive a double share of the land,
so their happiness will continue for ever.
8"I, the LORD, love justice.
I hate stealing and everything that is wrong.
I will be fair and give my people what they
should have,
and I will make an agreement with them
that will continue for ever.

9Everyone in all nations will know the
children of my people,
and their children will be known among
the nations.
Anyone who sees them will know
that they are people the LORD has blessed."

10The LORD makes me very happy;
all that I am rejoices in my God.
He has covered me with clothes of
salvation
and wrapped me with a coat of goodness,
like a bridegroom dressed for his wedding,
like a bride dressed in jewels.
11The earth causes plants to grow,
and a garden causes the seeds planted in it
to grow.
In the same way the Lord GOD will make
goodness and praise
come from all the nations.

New Jerusalem

62 Because I love Jerusalem, I will
continue to speak for her;
for Jerusalem's sake I will not stop speaking
until her goodness shines like a bright light,
until her salvation burns bright like a flame.
2Jerusalem, the nations will see your goodness,
and all kings will see your glory.
Then you will have a new name,
which the LORD himself will give you.
3You will be like a beautiful crown in the
LORD's hand,
like a king's crown in your God's hand.

FREEDOM

The Last Word

The screams could be heard from miles around. Echoes bounced off the surrounding cliffs, as Jo's lungs emptied themselves in agony.

Somewhere in the darkness, the perpetrator scurried away back under a rock, as in an instant Jo discovered that, whilst they may not kill you, Portuguese scorpions cause a great deal of pain.

With a total abandonment of dignity, and tears streaming down her face, Jo floundered around desperately searching for a way to limit the pain searing through her body. Her friends struggled to remain calm in all the confusion and panic.

The situation was not looking good. The friends had been camping in the middle of nowhere. It was now the middle of the night and the mobile phones weren't working. How was help going to come? Jo couldn't focus on anything but the pain. She began to doubt that it would ever stop. Relief was a luxury that might never come.

But help did arrive. An ambulance drove her to the hospital. And with the administration of local anaesthetic and the antidote to the poison, she was freed from the pain, and peace and calm did indeed resume. And within a few weeks, although Jo could think of the pain, she couldn't remember the pain itself. She had been cured.

Isn't it amazing how pain never gets the last word? That even the memory of pain, can't seem to carry with it the pain within it? Peace lasts, pain doesn't.

Read **Isaiah 61:1–11**.

- How many promises does God make in the passage? What does he promise to bring freedom from?
- Have you ever felt like you're in one of those scenarios? What freedom does God promise you?

Consider . . .

- making a promise box full of pictures or objects that will remind you of the promises God makes us.
- how you can help someone who is bound up by one of the situations listed in the passage.

For more, see . . .

- Ezekiel 37:11–14 (p.820)
- Hebrews 2:14–15 (p.1331)
- Ephesians 3:14–21 (p.1271)

4You will never again be called the People that
God Left,
nor your land the Land that God
Destroyed.
You will be called the People God Loves,
and your land will be called the Bride
of God,
because the LORD loves you.
And your land will belong to him as a bride
belongs to her husband.
5As a young man marries a woman,
so your children will marry your
land.
As a man rejoices over his new wife,
so your God will rejoice over you.

6Jerusalem, I have put guards on the walls to
watch.
They must not be silent day or night.
You people who remind the LORD of your
needs in prayer
should never be quiet.
7You should not stop praying to him until he
builds up Jerusalem
and makes it a city all people will praise.

8The LORD has made a promise,
and by his power he will keep his promise.
He said, "I will never again give your grain
as food to your enemies.
I will not let your enemies drink the new
wine
that you have worked to make.
9The person who gathers food will eat it,
and he will praise the LORD.
The person who gathers the grapes will drink
the wine
in the courts of my Temple." [d]

10Go through, go through the gates!
Make the way ready for the people.
Build up, build up the road!
Move all the stones off the road.
Raise the banner as a sign for the people.

11The LORD is speaking
to all the faraway lands:
"Tell the people of Jerusalem,
'Look, your Saviour is coming.
He is bringing your reward to you;
he is bringing his payment with him.'"

PATIENCE

Wait On

Gilly is a new Christian. It is the first year of her Christian life. And now she is becoming impatient with her church, her prayer life (individual and at church) and the slow pace of change. She has grown quickly; they move slowly. Frustration follows.

At Gilly's church they don't sing the sort of songs they sang at the summer camp she attended. There are no guitarists in her church. It is full of older people who don't seem very enthusiastic.

One day Gilly talks to one of the older ladies over coffee after church. She discovers that they have been praying for someone like her to join them. Unbeknown to her, they have waited, watched, hoped and prayed for years. She is the answer to their prayers and they can't wait to see how God will use Gilly to bring new life to the church.

Read **Isaiah 62:1–12**.

- How might this passage encourage someone like Gilly?
- How much of this passage appears to be about the immediate (returning to Jerusalem) and how much about the distant future (your Saviour is coming)?

Consider . . .

- how patient you are. What things stretch your patience?
- what God is preparing you for. How is he doing that?

For more, see . . .

- Psalm 37:3–9 (p.521)
- Luke 18:1–8 (p.1078)
- Isaiah 40:3–11 (p.679)

12His people will be called the Holy People,
the Saved People of the LORD,
and Jerusalem will be called the City God
Wants,
the City God Has Not Rejected.

The LORD Judges His People

63 Who is this coming from Edom,
from the city of Bozrah, dressed
in red?
Who is this dressed in fine clothes
and marching forwards with his great
power?

He says, "I, the LORD, speak what is right.
I have the power to save you."

2Someone asks, "Why are your clothes
bright red
as if you had walked on the grapes to make
wine?"

3The LORD answers, "I have walked in the
winepress[d] alone,
and no one among the nations
helped me.
I was angry and walked on the nations
and crushed them because of
my anger.
Blood splashed on my clothes,
and I stained all my clothing.
4I chose a time to punish people,
and the time has come for me to save.
5I looked around, but I saw no one to
help me.
I was surprised that no one supported
me.
So I used my own power to save my
people;
my own anger supported me.
6While I was angry, I walked on the nations.
In my anger I punished them
and poured their blood on the ground."

SUFFERING

Feeling What You Feel

She woke in the middle of the night in excruciating pain. She knew something was wrong, very wrong. Emma struggled to get out of bed and downstairs to the phone to call the ambulance. It seemed to take an eternity for the ambulance to arrive and rush her off to hospital. She was in so much pain that she couldn't stand up straight; she was bent over in agony.

She woke up several hours later in a quiet hospital room on her own. A doctor walked past and noticed she was awake, so he came in to talk to her. Emma could tell by the expression on the doctor's face that something was wrong. The doctor sat down and started to tell Emma that there had been a complication with the pregnancy. They had tried everything they could to save the baby, but sadly it wasn't enough and the baby had died.

Emma was devastated. As she lay on her bed alone and in the silence, all she could think to do was to pray.

In the midst of all her sadness, she really felt Jesus alongside her. It was as if he was there with her, crying with her, with his arm around her shoulder.

Read **Isaiah 63:7–9**.

- Why do you think God chooses to feel the pain that we feel?
- When you are suffering how can you know God is there, like Emma did?

Consider . . .

- looking out for those people around you who are suffering and think of ways you can show them you care.
- praying for those Christians around the world who are tortured and suffer because of their faith.

For more, see . . .

- Jeremiah 31:12–13 (p.752)
- Hebrews 13:1–3 (p.1345)
- Romans 8:18 (p.1195)

The LORD's Kindness to His People

7I will tell about the LORD's kindness
and praise him for everything he has done.
I will praise the LORD for the many good things he has given us
and for his goodness to the people of Israel.
He has shown great mercy to us
and has been very kind to us.
8He said, "These are my people;
my children will not lie to me."
So he saved them.
9When they suffered, he suffered also.
He sent his own angel to save them.
Because of his love and kindness, he saved them.
Since long ago he has picked them up and carried them.
10But they turned against him
and made his Holy Spirit [d] very sad.
So he became their enemy,
and he fought against them.

11But then his people remembered what happened long ago,
in the days of Moses and the Israelites with him.
Where is the LORD who brought the people through the sea,
with the leaders of his people?
Where is the one
who put his Holy Spirit among them,
12who led Moses by the right hand
with his wonderful power,
who divided the water before them
to make his name famous for ever,
13who led the people through the deep waters?
Like a horse walking through a desert,
the people did not stumble.
14Like cattle that go down to the valley,
the Spirit of the LORD gave the people a place to rest.
LORD, that is the way you led your people,
and by this you won for yourself wonderful fame.

A Prayer for Help

15LORD, look down from the heavens and see;
look at us from your wonderful and holy home in heaven.
Where is your strong love and power?
Why are you keeping your love and mercy from us?
16You are our father.
Abraham doesn't know we are his children,
and Israel doesn't recognise us.
LORD, you are our father.
You are called "the one who has always saved us".
17LORD, why are you making us wander from your ways?
Why do you make us stubborn so that we don't honour you?
For our sake come back to us,
your servants, who belong to you.
18Your people had your Temple [d] for a while,
but now our enemies have walked on your holy place and crushed it.
19We have become like people you never ruled over,
like those who have never worn your name.

64 Tear open the skies and come down to earth
so that the mountains will tremble before you.
2Like a fire that burns twigs,
like a fire that makes water boil,
let your enemies know who you are.
Then all nations will shake with fear when they see you.
3You have done amazing things we did not expect.
You came down, and the mountains trembled before you.
4From long ago no one has ever heard of a God like you.
No one has ever seen a God besides you,
who helps the people who trust you.
5You help those who enjoy doing good,
who remember how you want them to live.
But you were angry because we sinned.
For a long time we disobeyed,
so how can we be saved?
6All of us are dirty with sin.
All the right things we have done are like filthy pieces of cloth.
All of us are like dead leaves,
and our sins, like the wind, have carried us away.
7No one worships you
or even asks you to help us.
That is because you have turned away from us
and have let our sins destroy us.
8But LORD, you are our father.
We are like clay, and you are the potter;
your hands made us all.
9LORD, don't continue to be angry with us;
don't remember our sins for ever.
Please, look at us,

because we are your people.
10 Your holy cities are empty like the desert.
Jerusalem is like a desert;
it is destroyed.
11 Our ancestors worshipped you
in our holy and wonderful Temple,
but now it has been burned with fire,
and all our precious things have been
destroyed.
12 When you see these things, will you hold
yourself back from helping us, LORD?
Will you be silent and punish us beyond
what we can stand?

All People will Learn About God

65 The LORD says, "I made myself known
to people who were not looking
for me.
I was found by those who were not asking
me for help.
I said, 'Here I am. Here I am,'
to a nation that was not praying to me.
2 All day long I stood ready to accept
people who turned against me,
but the way they continue to live is not
good;
they do anything they want to do.
3 Right in front of me
they continue to do things that make me angry.
They offer sacrifices to their gods in their
gardens,
and they burn incense [d] on altars of brick.
4 They sit among the graves
and spend their nights waiting to get
messages from the dead.
They eat the meat of pigs,
and their pots are full of soup made from
meat that is wrong to eat.
5 But they tell others, 'Stay away and don't
come near me.
I am too holy for you.'
These people are like smoke in my nose.

FOLLOWING GOD

No Wonder Your Breath Smells

Jack couldn't believe his eyes! He watched in horror as his dog was sick. A worrying sight for any eight-year-old who loves his pet, but what made it truly terrible was when, with a lick of her whiskers, Jack's dog slowly and very happily began to chew and chomp away at the vomit. Jack stood and screamed at her, "Stop it, it's gross, no wonder your breath smells!" But the dog paid no attention, she was simply thinking, "Great! Lunch . . . again."

God knows how disgusting sin is. He knows that it messes up our relationship with him, others and even ourselves. Much of what God said through prophets like Isaiah was, "Stop it, it's gross, it's going to mess your life up!" But like Jack's dog, Israel seemed to love doing the things that God hates. As a result, things had gone downhill. Isaiah was full of regret and disappointment. He could see how his people had stopped living God's way and were doing their own thing. Like a driver who has turned their Sat Nav off, Israel had stopped listening to God and had got themselves seriously lost.

Isaiah 63:16; 64:1–8 tells what it's like to be lost without God.

- How is being physically lost similar to wandering away from God's path for your life?
- According to Isaiah, his people wouldn't even ask for directions. Do you need to ask God for help?

Consider . . .

- the sins that you keep going back to. What could you do to make it more difficult for you to do that? Is there someone you could talk to each time that happens?
- listing the things that help you follow God such as people who help you, music, the Bible. Decide to have at least one of these things as part of your day, every day.

For more, see . . .

- Psalm 25 (p.514)
- James 1:21–25 (p.1348)
- Proverbs 26:11 (p.613)

Like a fire that burns all the time, they
continue to make me angry.

6"Look, it is written here before me.
I will not be quiet; instead, I will repay you
in full.
I will punish you for what you have done.
7I will punish you for your sins and your
ancestors' sins,"
says the LORD.
"They burned incense to gods on the
mountains
and shamed me on those hills.
So I will punish them as they should be
punished
for what they did."

8This is what the LORD says:
"When there is juice left in the grapes,
people do not destroy them,
because they know there is good left in
them.
So I will do the same thing to my servants—
I will not completely destroy them.
9I will leave some of the children of Jacob,
and some of the people of Judah will
receive my mountain.
I will choose the people who will live there;
my servants will live there.
10Then the Plain of Sharon will be a field for
flocks,
and the Valley of Achor will be a place for
herds to rest.
They will be for the people who want to
follow me.

11"But as for you who left the LORD,
who forgot about my holy mountain,
who worship the god Luck,
who hold religious feasts for the god Fate,
12I decide your fate, and I will punish you with
my sword.
You will all be killed,
because I called you, but you refused to
answer.
I spoke to you, but you wouldn't listen.
You did the things I said were evil
and chose to do things that displease me."

13So this is what the Lord GOD says:
"My servants will eat,
but you evil people will be hungry.
My servants will drink,
but you evil people will be thirsty.
My servants will be happy,
but you evil people will be shamed.
14My servants will shout for joy
because of the goodness of their hearts,
but you evil people will cry,
because you will be sad.
You will cry loudly, because your spirits will
be broken.
15Your names will be like curses to my servants,
and the Lord GOD will put you to death.
But he will call his servants by another
name.
16People in the land who ask for blessings
will ask for them from the faithful God.
And people in the land who make a
promise
will promise in the name of the
faithful God,
because the troubles of the past will be
forgotten.
I will make those troubles go away.

A New Time is Coming

17"Look, I will make new heavens and a new
earth,
and people will not remember the past
or think about those things.
18My people will be happy for ever
because of the things I will make.
I will make a Jerusalem that is full of joy,
and I will make her people a delight.
19Then I will rejoice over Jerusalem
and be delighted with my people.
There will never again be heard in
that city
the sounds of crying and sadness.
20There will never be a baby from that city
who lives only a few days.
And there will never be an older person
who doesn't have a long life.
A person who lives 100 years will be called
young,
and a person who dies before he is 100
will be thought of as a sinner.
21In that city those who build houses will live
there.
Those who plant vineyards will get to eat
their grapes.
22No more will one person build a house and
someone else live there.
One person will not plant a garden and
someone else eat its fruit.
My people will live a long time,
as trees live long.
My chosen people will live there
and enjoy the things they make.
23They will never again work for nothing.
They will never again give birth to children
who die young.
All my people will be blessed by the LORD;
they and their children will be blessed.
24I will provide for their needs before they
ask,

and I will help them while they are still
asking for help.
25 Wolves and lambs will eat together
in peace.
Lions will eat hay like oxen,
and a snake on the ground will not hurt
anyone.
They will not hurt or destroy each other
on all my holy mountain,"
says the LORD.

The LORD will Judge All Nations

66 This is what the LORD says:
"Heaven is my throne,
and the earth is my footstool.
So do you think you can build a house
for me?
Do I need a place to rest?
2 My hand made all things.
All things are here because I made them,"
says the LORD.

"These are the people I am pleased with:
those who are not proud or stubborn
and who fear my word.
3 But those people who kill bulls as a sacrifice
to me
are like those who kill people.
Those who kill sheep as a sacrifice
are like those who break the necks of
dogs.
Those who give me grain offerings
are like those who offer me the blood of
pigs. [n]

dogs . . . pigs God did not want his people to offer dogs and pigs as sacrifices because they were unclean animals.

EUTHANASIA

Playing God

Mike decided to get a part time job so he could start saving money towards his first car. It wasn't long before he found himself looking after grumpy old Charlie, a man in his mid-80s who lived just down the street from him. The job was relatively easy, a bit of gardening and tidying up around the house, so Mike set himself the task of spending quality time getting to know Charlie. He quickly discovered that beneath this rough, bitter exterior was a genuine, caring old man with tons of exciting stories from his experiences in the war.

A few months later, Charlie suffered a stroke which left him in a coma, unable to move or communicate. Mike was horrified when he overheard a few hushed conversations in which people kept using the term "euthanasia" (the process of painlessly ending the life of someone in Charlie's state). Surely that was up to God, wasn't it?

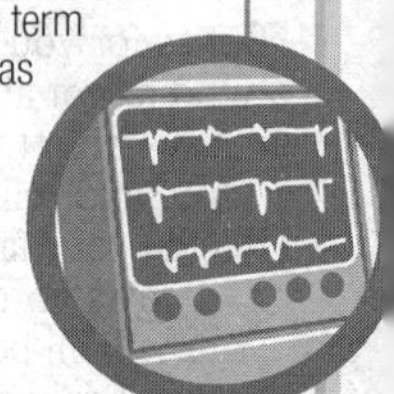

For those of us in the twenty-first century, euthanasia is a pretty hot topic, even among Christians. But **Isaiah 65:19–20** promises the people of God that a time is coming when even a 100-year-old will be called young!

- Where would you draw the line on the topic of euthanasia and "playing God"? What is that based upon?
- Do you have any close relationships with people you'd consider to be old? How might you benefit from such a friendship?

Consider . . .

- helping to shape your government's policies on euthanasia by writing to them. Your opinions count!
- taking time out to get to know an old person and even witness to them. They may be closer to their eternal home than you are.

For more, see . . .

- Genesis 21:1–7 (p.24)
- Proverbs 16:31 (p.604)
- Deuteronomy 5:16 (p.170)

Those who burn incense [d]
are like those who worship idols.
These people choose their own ways, not mine,
and they love the terrible things they do.
4So I will choose their punishments,
and I will punish them with what they fear most.
This is because I called to them, but they did not listen.
I spoke to them, but they did not hear me.
They did things I said were evil;
they chose to do things I did not like."

5You people who obey the words of the LORD,
listen to what he says:
"Your brothers hated you
and turned against you because you followed me.
Your brothers said, 'Let the LORD be honoured
so we may see you rejoice,'
but they will be punished.
6Listen to the loud noise coming from the city;
hear the noise from the Temple. [d]
It is the LORD punishing his enemies,
giving them the punishment they should have.

7"A woman does not give birth before she feels the pain;
she does not give birth to a son before the pain starts.
8No one has ever heard of that happening;
no one has ever seen that happen.
In the same way no one ever saw a country begin in one day;
no one has ever heard of a new nation beginning in one moment.
But Jerusalem will give birth to her children
just as soon as she feels the birth pains.
9In the same way I will not cause pain
without allowing something new to be born," says the LORD.
"If I cause you the pain,
I will not stop you from giving birth to your new nation," says your God.
10"Jerusalem, rejoice.
All you people who love Jerusalem, be happy.
Those of you who felt sad for Jerusalem
should now feel happy with her.
11You will take comfort from her and be satisfied,
as a child is nursed by its mother.
You will receive her good things
and enjoy her wealth."

12This is what the LORD says:

"I will give her peace that will flow to her like a river.
The wealth of the nations will come to her like a river overflowing its banks.
Like babies you will be nursed and held in my arms
and bounced on my knees.
13I will comfort you
as a mother comforts her child.
You will be comforted in Jerusalem."

14When you see these things, you will be happy
and you will grow like the grass.
The LORD's servants will see his power,
but his enemies will see his anger.
15Look, the LORD is coming with fire
and his armies with clouds of dust.
He will punish those people with his anger;
he will punish them with flames of fire.
16The LORD will judge the people with fire
and he will destroy many people with his sword;
he will kill many people.

17"These people make themselves holy and
pure to go to worship their gods in their gardens.

Sidelight Isaiah is the "Bible in miniature". It has sixty-six chapters – as compared with sixty-six biblical books. Both Isaiah and the Bible end with "new heavens and the new earth" (Isaiah 66:22 and Revelation 21:1, p.1403).

Following each other into their special gardens, they eat the meat of pigs and rats and other hateful things. But they will all be destroyed together," says the LORD.
18"I know they have evil thoughts and do evil
things, so I am coming to punish them. I will gather all nations and all people, and they will come together and see my glory.
19"I will put a mark on some of the people,
and I will send some of these saved people to the nations: to Tarshish, Libya, Lud (the land of archers), Tubal, Greece and all the faraway lands. These people have never heard about what I have done nor seen my glory. So the saved

people will tell the nations about my glory.
20And
they will bring all your fellow Israelites from all
nations to my holy mountain in Jerusalem. Your
fellow Israelites will come on horses, donkeys
and camels and in chariots and wagons. They
will be like the grain offerings that the people
bring in clean containers to the Temple," says
the LORD.
21"And I will choose even some of
these people to be priests and Levites," says the
LORD.

22"I will make new heavens and the new
earth, which will last for ever," says the LORD.
"In the same way, your names and your children
will always be with me.
23All people will come to
worship me every Sabbath[d] and every New
Moon,"[d] says the LORD.
24"They will go out and
see the dead bodies of the people who sinned
against me. The worms that eat them will never
die, and the fires that burn them will never stop,
and everyone will hate to see those bodies."

GOD'S LOVE

Like a Mother

She is frequently on the telephone. "Yes, nine-fifteen is fine," she might reply or "I'll try to get there tomorrow morning." Cots, blankets and beds fill her garage.

Susan directs unused and often unwanted clothing and furniture to those families and single parents who have touched "rock bottom". Often in their teens, many young mothers have nothing to put their babies in when they come home from hospital, or are being rapidly moved out of temporary hostel accommodation, with no furniture or money to create a home of their own.

Susan has her own family and home to run, and she often juggles meal-times with crisis callers, spending time and effort to provide basic supplies and a helping hand. Caring practically, she bubbles over with God's caring love and concern.

A new mother and desperate situations often need more than baby prams and furniture. They need the strength that comes from Christ. Susan makes that difference by offering those in need that kind of strength.

God loves his people as much as a mother loves her children. **Isaiah 66:10–14** describes God's love and care for us.

- How does Susan demonstrate the love that this passage describes?
- In what ways does God comfort and care for you?

Consider . . .

- writing a thank-you letter to someone who has shown you the kind of love that this passage describes.
- writing a description of the "perfect" parent and then thanking God for being a perfect parent to you.

For more, see . . .

- Deuteronomy 32:9–12 (p.195)
- 1 John 4:7–10 (p.1374)
- Hosea 11:1–4 (p.858)

Jeremiah

Why Read This Book:

- Learn the responsibilities that come with belonging to God (Jeremiah 1—25).
- See God's continuing love for people even when they have sinned (Jeremiah 26—36).
- Find hope even in times of suffering (Jeremiah 37—45).

When?

Behind the Scenes:

The nation of Judah was like somebody caught in the crossfire between warring inner-city gangs. Three world powers were fighting for control of the area we call the Near East. The Assyrians had been in control for quite a while, but the Egyptians and Babylonians would each take power within Jeremiah's lifetime. And Judah was caught in the middle.

But Judah was not like an innocent victim. Judah had stopped following God and was forming partnerships with pagan nations to try to protect itself. The people needed a word from God, and Jeremiah became the one whom God would use to proclaim that word – a word that Judah did not want to hear.

Jeremiah warned the people of Judah that they needed to obey God and rely on him. He condemned the false prophets and emphasised the need to repent and seek a personal relationship with God.

Jeremiah's tough message wasn't easy to accept – for Jeremiah or for the people of Judah. At first, Jeremiah was reluctant even to take the job (Jeremiah 1:6). He was abused, ridiculed, exiled to Egypt, and, in the end, possibly killed for what he said. ▷

Where?

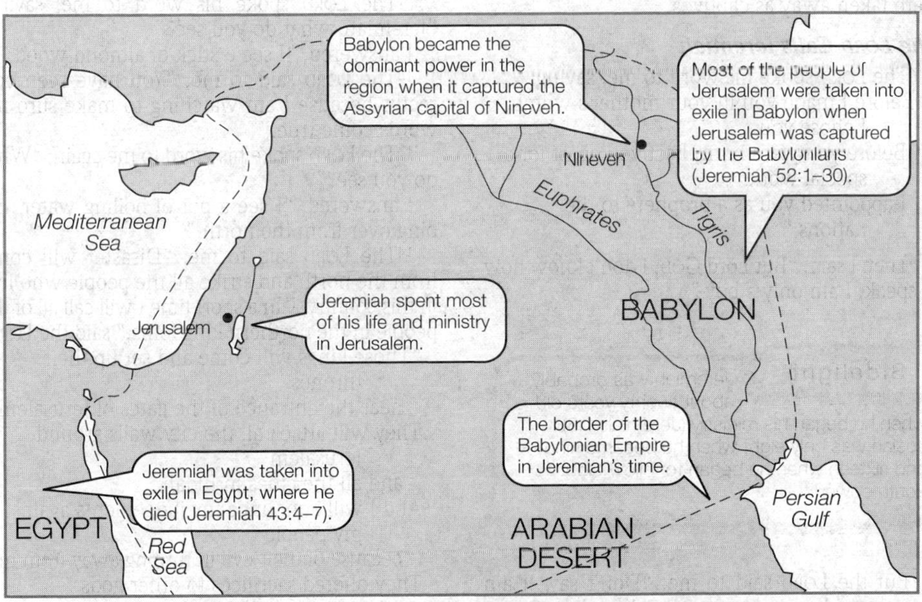

Behind the Scenes (cont.):

The pain he faced and the pain he saw his people experiencing saddened him.

His book – which was dictated to his secretary Baruch (Jeremiah 36:4) – is difficult to follow. The poems aren't arranged in logical order. Events jump back and forth in history. To get a better feel for the historical events surrounding the book, read either 2 Kings 23—24 (p.368) or 2 Chronicles 34—36 (p.427).

Through poems, stories, and object lessons, the book of Jeremiah shows the personal struggles, depression and anger Jeremiah experienced during his career. But through it all, Jeremiah continued doing the tough job he had been given. And even when he felt like giving up, he remembered that God would stand by him and comfort him.

Jeremiah was faithful to God's call – even when it was unpopular. And he was honest with God and faithful to God, even in the midst of his doubts, frustrations and anger. His life can be a valuable model for us today.

---

1 These are the words of Jeremiah son of
Hilkiah. He belonged to the family of priests
who lived in the town of Anathoth in the land of
Benjamin. 2The LORD spoke his word to Jeremiah
during the thirteenth year that Josiah son of
Amon was king of Judah. 3The LORD also spoke
to Jeremiah while Jehoiakim son of Josiah was
king of Judah and during the eleven years that
Zedekiah son of Josiah was king of Judah. In the
fifth month of his last year, the people of Jerusalem
were taken away as captives.

The LORD Calls Jeremiah

4The LORD spoke his word to me, saying:

5"Before I made you in your mother's womb,
I chose you.
Before you were born, I set you apart for a
special work.
I appointed you as a prophet[d] to the
nations."

6Then I said, "But Lord GOD, I don't know how
to speak. I am only a boy."

> **Sidelight** Jeremiah was probably about twenty years old when he began his ministry (Jeremiah 1:6). Josiah was only eight when he became king – and sixteen when he began to follow God. Youth power!

7But the LORD said to me, "Don't say, 'I am
only a boy.' You must go everywhere I send you,
and you must say everything I tell you to say.
8Don't be afraid of anyone, because I am with
you to protect you," says the LORD.
9Then the LORD reached out his hand and
touched my mouth. He said to me, "See, I am
putting my words in your mouth. 10Today I have
put you in charge of nations and kingdoms. You
will pull up and tear down, destroy and over-
throw, build up and plant."

Jeremiah Sees Two Visions

11The LORD spoke his word to me, saying:
"Jeremiah, what do you see?"
I answered, "I see a stick of almond wood."
12The LORD said to me, "You have seen cor-
rectly, because I am watching to make sure my
words come true."
13The LORD spoke his word to me again: "What
do you see?"
I answered, "I see a pot of boiling water, tip-
ping over from the north."
14The LORD said to me, "Disaster will come
from the north and strike all the people who live
in this country. 15In a short time I will call all of the
people in the northern kingdoms," said the LORD.

"Those kings will come and set up their
thrones
near the entrance of the gates of Jerusalem.
They will attack all the city walls around
Jerusalem
and all the cities in Judah.
16And I will announce my judgements against
my people
because of their evil in turning away from me.
They offered sacrifices to other gods
and worshipped idols they had made with
their own hands.

17“Jeremiah, get ready. Stand up and tell them
everything I command you to say. Don’t be afraid
of the people, or I will give you good reason to be
afraid of them. 18Today I am going to make you
a strong city, an iron pillar, a bronze wall. You
will be able to stand against everyone in the land:
Judah’s kings, officers, priests and the people of
the land. 19They will fight against you, but they
will not defeat you, because I am with you to
protect you!” says the LORD.

Israel Turns from God

2 The LORD spoke his word to me, saying: 2“Go
and speak to the people of Jerusalem, saying:
This is what the LORD says:

‘I remember how faithful you were to me
when you were a young nation.
You loved me like a young bride.
You followed me through the desert,
a land that had never been planted.
3The people of Israel were holy to the LORD,
like the first fruits from his harvest.
Those who tried to hurt Israel were judged
guilty.
Disasters struck them,’ ” says the LORD.

4Hear the word of the LORD, family of Jacob,
all you family groups of Israel.
5This is what the LORD says:
“I was fair to your ancestors,
so why did they turn away from me?
Your ancestors worshipped useless idols
and became useless themselves.
6Your ancestors didn’t say,
‘Where is the LORD who brought us out of
Egypt?
He led us through the desert,
through a dry and rocky land,
through a dark and dangerous land.
He led us where no one travels or lives.’

SELF-ESTEEM

The New Kid in the Group

As the newest member of the theatre group, Adam felt a little intimidated. There were good actors in the group. Also, Adam was afraid that friendships had already formed and that he would be an outsider.

On top of that, people in theatre learn to be very honest with their feelings. Adam feared that someone would tell him he was a hopeless actor. What if he didn’t measure up?

But Adam’s fears evaporated as he got involved. The group realised pretty quickly that Adam was a good actor. People accepted him at first because of his talent, and later they accepted him as a good friend too.

Adam was a little shy about sharing his friendship with God with his new-found friends. Before long, however, he found himself in deep conversations about faith with people who hadn’t really given God much thought. He invited them to church, and some went.

Although he started as an intimidated newcomer, with God’s help Adam discovered his own value to the group and to God.

Jeremiah was a young man when God first called him. Read how God responded to Jeremiah’s fears and lack of self-esteem, in **Jeremiah 1:4–10**.

- Why were both Adam and Jeremiah at first fearful of what they had to do?
- When you sense that God wants you to do something, how do your feelings and thoughts compare to those of young Jeremiah?

Consider . . .

- writing verses 6–8 on a piece of paper and carrying it with you for times when you need a confidence boost.
- giving three friends a self-esteem boost this week by telling them each a reason why you like or respect them.

For more, see . . .

- Isaiah 6:1–8 (p.645)
- 1 Timothy 4:12–16 (p.1311)
- Galatians 1:1–20 (p.1257)

7I brought you into a fertile land
so you could eat its fruit and produce.
But you came and made my land unclean; [d]
you made it a hateful place.
8The priests didn't ask,
'Where is the LORD?'
The people who know the teachings didn't know me.
The leaders turned against me.
The prophets [d] prophesied in the name of Baal [d]
and worshipped useless idols.

9"So now I will again tell what I have against you," says the LORD.
"And I will tell what I have against your grandchildren.
10Go across the sea to the island of Cyprus and see.
Send someone to the land of Kedar to look closely.
See if there has ever been anything like this.
11Has a nation ever exchanged its gods?
(Of course, its gods are not really gods at all.)
But my people have exchanged their glorious God
for idols worth nothing.
12Skies, be shocked at the things that have happened
and shake with great fear!" says the LORD.
13"My people have done two sins:
they have turned away from me,
the spring of living water.
And they have dug their own wells,
which are broken wells that cannot hold water.
14Have the people of Israel become slaves?
Have they become like someone who was born a slave?
Why were they taken captive?
15Enemies have roared like lions at Israel;
they have growled at Israel.
They have destroyed the land of Israel.
The cities of Israel lie in ruins,
and all the people have left.
16The men from the cities of Memphis and Tahpanhes
have disgraced you by shaving the top of your head.
17Haven't you brought this on yourselves
by turning away from the LORD your God
when he was leading you in the right way?
18It did not help to go to Egypt
and drink from the Shihor River.
It did not help to go to Assyria
and drink from the Euphrates River.
19Your evil will bring punishment to you,
and the wrong you have done will teach you a lesson.
Think about it and understand
that it is a terrible evil to turn away from the LORD your God.
It is wrong not to fear me,"
says the Lord GOD All-powerful.

20"Long ago you refused to obey me as an ox breaks its yoke. [d]
You broke the ropes I used to hold you
and said, 'I will not serve you!'
In fact, on every high hill
and under every green tree
you lay down as a prostitute. [d]
21But I planted you as a special vine,
as a very good seed.
How then did you turn
into a wild vine that grows bad fruit?
22Although you wash yourself with cleanser
and use much soap,
I can still see the stain of your guilt," says the Lord GOD.
23"How can you say to me, 'I am not guilty.
I have not worshipped the Baal [d] idols'?
Look at the things you did in the valley.
Think about what you have done.
You are like a she-camel in mating season
that runs from place to place.
24You are like a wild donkey that lives in the desert
and sniffs the wind at mating time.
At that time who can hold her back?
Any male who chases her will easily catch her;
at mating time, it is easy to find her.
25Don't run until your feet are bare
or until your throat is dry.
But you say, 'It's no use!
I love those other gods
and I must chase them!'

26"A thief is ashamed when someone catches him stealing.
In the same way, the family of Israel is ashamed—
they, their kings, their officers,
their priests and their prophets.
27They say to things of wood, 'You are my father,'
and to idols of stone, 'You gave birth to me.'
Those people won't look at me;
they have turned their backs to me.
But when they get into trouble, they say,
'Come and save us!'
28Where are the idols you made for yourselves?
Let them come and save you
when you are in trouble!

People of Judah, you have as many idols
as you have towns!
29"Why do you complain to me?
All of you have turned against me," says
the LORD.
30"I punished your people, but it did not
help.
They didn't come back when they were
punished.
With your swords you killed your
prophets
like a hungry lion.

31"People of Judah, pay attention to the word
of the LORD:
have I been like a desert to the people of
Israel
or like a dark and dangerous land?
Why do my people say, 'We are free to
wander.
We won't come to you any more'?
32A young woman does not forget her
jewellery,
and a bride does not forget the decorations
for her dress.
But my people have forgotten me
for more days than can be counted.
33You really know how to chase after love.
Even the worst women can learn evil ways
from you.
34Even on your clothes you have the blood
of poor and innocent people,
but they weren't thieves you caught
breaking in.
You do all these things,
35 but you say, 'I am innocent.
God is not angry with me.'
But I will judge you guilty of lying,
because you say, 'I have not sinned.'
36It is so easy for you to change your mind.
Even Egypt will let you down,
as Assyria let you down.
37You will eventually leave that place
with your hands on your head, like
captives.
You trusted those countries,
but you will not be helped by them,
because the LORD has rejected them.

Judah is Unfaithful

3 "If a man divorces his wife
and she leaves him and marries
another man,
should her first husband come back to her
again?
If he went back to her, wouldn't the land
become completely unclean? [d]
But you have acted like a prostitute [d] with
many lovers,
and now you want to come back to me?"
says the LORD.
2"Look up to the bare hilltops, Judah.
Is there any place where you have not
been a prostitute?
You have sat by the road waiting for lovers
like an Arab in the desert.
You made the land unclean,
because you did evil and were like a
prostitute.
3So the rain has not come,
and there have not been any spring
rains.
But your face still looks like the face of a
prostitute.
You refuse even to be ashamed of what
you did.

Sidelight In the Middle East, almost all of the rain falls during spring (May) and autumn (October). Since crops depend on this rain, the weather was often seen as a sign of God's blessing or cursing (see Jeremiah 3:3). No rain meant rejection by God, while a good period of rain meant God's blessing. Read 1 Kings 17:1–16 (p.332), 1 Kings 18:41–46 (p.335) and Isaiah 30:23–26 (p.670).

4Now you are calling to me,
'My father, you have been my friend since
I was young.
5Will you always be angry at me?
Will your anger last for ever?'
Judah, you said this,
but you did as much evil as you could!"

Judah and Israel are like Sisters

6When King Josiah was ruling Judah, the LORD
said to me, "Did you see what unfaithful Israel
did? She was like a prostitute [d] with her idols on
every hill and under every green tree. 7I said to
myself, 'Israel will come back to me after she
does this evil,' but she didn't come back. And
Israel's wicked sister Judah saw what she did.
8Judah saw that I divorced unfaithful Israel be-
cause of her adultery, [d] but that didn't make
Israel's wicked sister Judah afraid. She also went
out and acted like a prostitute! 9And she didn't
care that she was acting like a prostitute. So she
made her country unclean [d] and was guilty of
adultery, because she worshipped idols made of
stone and wood. 10Israel's wicked sister didn't
even come back to me with her whole heart, but
only pretended," says the LORD.

[11]The LORD said to me, "Unfaithful Israel had a
better excuse than wicked Judah. [12]Go and speak
this message towards the north:
'Come back, unfaithful people of Israel,' says
the LORD.
'I will stop being angry with you,
because I am full of mercy,' says the LORD.
'I will not be angry with you for ever.
[13]All you have to do is admit your sin—
that you turned against the LORD your God
and worshipped gods under every green tree
and didn't obey me,' " says the LORD.

[14]"Come back to me, you unfaithful children,"
says the LORD, "because I am your master. I will
take one person from every city and two from every
family group, and I will bring you to Jerusalem.
[15]Then I will give you new rulers who will be
faithful to me, who will lead you with know-
ledge and understanding. [16]In those days there
will be many of you in the land," says the LORD.
"At that time people will no longer say, 'I remem-
ber the Ark[d] of the Agreement.' They won't think
about it any more or remember it or miss it or
make another one. [17]At that time people will call
Jerusalem The Throne of the LORD, and all nations
will come together in Jerusalem to show respect
to the LORD. They will not follow their stubborn,
evil hearts any more. [18]In those days the family of
Judah will join the family of Israel. They will
come together from a land in the north to the
land I gave their ancestors.
[19]"I, the LORD, said,
'How happy I would be to treat you as my
own children
and give you a pleasant land,
a land more beautiful than that of any other
nation.'
I thought you would call me 'My Father'
and not turn away from me.
[20]But like a woman who is unfaithful to her
husband,
family of Israel, you have been unfaithful to
me," says the LORD.
[21]You can hear crying on the bare hilltops.
It is the people of Israel crying and praying
for mercy.
They have become very evil
and have forgotten the LORD their God.

[22]"Come back to me, you unfaithful children,
and I will forgive you for being unfaithful."

"Yes, we will come to you,
because you are the LORD our God.
[23]It was foolish to worship idols on the hills
and on the mountains.
Surely the salvation of Israel
comes from the LORD our God.
[24]Since our youth, shameful gods have eaten
up in sacrifice
everything our ancestors worked for—
their flocks and herds,
their sons and daughters.
[25]Let us lie down in our shame,
and let our disgrace cover us like a blanket.
We have sinned against the LORD our God,
both we and our ancestors.
From our youth until now,
we have not obeyed the LORD our God."

4 "If you will return, Israel,
then return to me," says the LORD.
"If you will throw away your idols that I
hate,
then don't wander away from me.
[2]If you say when you make a promise,
'As surely as the LORD lives,'
and you can say it in a truthful, honest and
right way,
then the nations will be blessed by him
and they will praise him for what he has
done."

[3]This is what the LORD says to the people of
Judah and to Jerusalem:
"Plough your unploughed fields,
and don't plant seeds among thorns.
[4]Give yourselves to the service of the LORD
and decide to obey him,
people of Judah and people of Jerusalem.
If you don't, my anger will spread among you
like a fire,
and no one will be able to put it out,
because of the evil you have done.

Trouble from the North

[5]"Announce this message in Judah and say it
in Jerusalem:
'Blow the trumpet throughout the country!'
Shout out loud and say,
'Come together!
Let's all escape to the fortified cities!'
[6]Raise the signal flag towards Jerusalem!
Run for your lives and don't wait,
because I am bringing disaster from the
north.
There will be terrible destruction."

[7]A lion has come out of his den;
a destroyer of nations has begun to march.
He has left his home
to destroy your land.
Your towns will be destroyed
with no one left to live in them.
[8]So put on rough cloth,
show how sad you are and cry loudly.
The terrible anger of the LORD
has not turned away from us.

9"When this happens," says the LORD,
"the king and officers will lose their courage.
The priests will be terribly afraid
and the prophets[d] will be shocked!"

10Then I said, "Lord GOD, you have tricked the
people of Judah and Jerusalem. You said, 'You
will have peace,' but now the sword is pointing
at our throats!"
11At that time this message will be given to
Judah and Jerusalem: "A hot wind blows from
the bare hilltops of the desert towards the LORD's
people. It is not a gentle wind to separate grain
from chaff.[d] 12I feel a stronger wind than that.
Now even I will announce judgements against
the people of Judah."

13Look! The enemy rises up like a cloud,
and his chariots come like a windstorm.
His horses are faster than eagles.
How terrible it will be for us! We are ruined!
14People of Jerusalem, clean the evil from your hearts so that you can be saved.
Don't continue making evil plans.
15A voice from Dan makes an announcement
and brings bad news from the mountains of Ephraim.
16"Report this to the nations.
Spread this news in Jerusalem:
'Invaders are coming from a faraway country,
shouting words of war against the cities of Judah.
17The enemy has surrounded Jerusalem as men guard a field,
because Judah turned against me,'" says the LORD.
18"The way you have lived and acted
has brought this trouble to you.
This is your punishment.
How terrible it is!
The pain stabs your heart!"

Jeremiah's Cry

19Oh, how I hurt! How I hurt!
I am bent over in pain.
Oh, the torture in my heart!
My heart is pounding inside me.
I cannot keep quiet,
because I have heard the sound of the trumpet.
I have heard the shouts of war.
20Disaster follows disaster;
the whole country has been destroyed.
My tents are destroyed in only a moment.
My curtains are torn down quickly.
21How long must I look at the war flag?
How long must I listen to the war trumpet?

22The LORD says, "My people are foolish.
They do not know me.
They are stupid children;
they don't understand.
They are skilful at doing evil,
but they don't know how to do good."

Disaster is Coming

23I looked at the earth
and it was empty and had no shape.
I looked at the sky
and its light was gone.
24I looked at the mountains
and they were shaking.
All the hills were trembling.
25I looked, and there were no people.
Every bird in the sky had flown away.
26I looked, and the good, rich land had become a desert.
All its towns had been destroyed
by the LORD and his great anger.

27This is what the LORD says:
"All the land will be ruined,
but I will not completely destroy it.
28So the people in the land will cry loudly
and the sky will grow dark,
because I have spoken and will not change my mind.
I have made a decision and I will not change it."
29At the sound of the horsemen and the archers,
all the people in the towns run away.
They hide in the thick bushes
and climb up into the rocks.
All of the cities of Judah are empty;
no one lives in them.
30Judah, you destroyed nation, what are you doing?
Why do you put on your finest dress
and decorate yourself with gold jewellery?
Why do you put colour around your eyes?
You make yourself beautiful, but it is all useless.
Your lovers hate you;
they want to kill you.

31I hear a cry like a woman having a baby,
distress like a woman having her first child.
It is the sound of Jerusalem gasping for breath.
She lifts her hands in prayer and says,
"Oh! I am about to faint
before my murderers!"

No One is Right

5 The LORD says, "Walk up and down the streets of Jerusalem.
Look around and discover these things.
Search the public squares of the city.
If you can find one person who does honest things,
who searches for the truth,
I will forgive this city.
2Although the people say, 'As surely as the LORD lives!'
they don't really mean it."
3LORD, don't you look for truth in people?
You struck the people of Judah,
but they didn't feel any pain.
You crushed them,
but they refused to learn what is right.
They became more stubborn than a rock;
they refused to turn back to God.
4But I thought,
"These are only the poor, foolish people.
They have not learned the way of the LORD
and what their God wants them to do.
5So I will go to the leaders of Judah
and talk to them.
Surely they understand the way of the LORD
and know what God wants them to do."
But even the leaders had all joined together to break away from the LORD;
they had broken their ties with him.
6So a lion from the forest will attack them.
A wolf from the desert will kill them.
A leopard is waiting for them near their towns.
It will tear to pieces anyone who comes out of the city,
because the people of Judah have sinned greatly.
They have wandered away from the LORD many times.

7The LORD said, "Tell me why I should forgive you.
Your children have left me
and have made promises to idols that are not gods at all.
I gave your children everything they needed,
but they still were like an unfaithful wife to me.
They spent much time in houses of prostitutes.[d]
8They are like well-fed horses filled with sexual desire;
each one wants another man's wife.
9Shouldn't I punish the people of Judah for doing these things?" says the LORD.
"Shouldn't I give a nation such as this the punishment it deserves?

10"Go along and cut down Judah's vineyards,
but do not completely destroy them.
Cut off all her people as if they were branches,
because they do not belong to the LORD.
11The families of Israel and Judah
have been completely unfaithful to me,"
says the LORD.

12Those people have lied about the LORD
and said, "He will not do anything to us!
Nothing bad will happen to us!
We will never see war or hunger!
13The prophets[d] are like an empty wind;
the word of God is not in them.
Let the bad things they say happen to them."

14So this is what the LORD God All-powerful
says:
"The people said I would not punish them.
So, the words I give you will be like fire,
and these people will be like wood that it burns up.
15Listen, family of Israel," says the LORD,
"I will soon bring a nation from far away to attack you.
It is an old nation that has lasted a long time.
The people there speak a language you do not know;
you cannot understand what they say.
16Their arrows bring death.
All their people are strong warriors.
17They will eat your crops and your food.
They will eat your sons and daughters.
They will eat your flocks and herds.
They will eat your grapes and figs.
They will destroy with their swords
the fortified cities you trust.

18"Yet even then," says the LORD, "I will not
destroy you completely. 19When the people of
Judah ask, "Why has the LORD our God done all
these terrible things to us?' then give them this
answer: 'You have left the LORD and served for-
eign idols in your own land. So now you will
serve foreigners in a land that does not belong
to you.'

20"Announce this message to the family of Jacob,
and tell it to the nation of Judah:
21hear this message, you foolish people who have no sense.
They have eyes, but they don't really see.
They have ears, but they don't really listen.
22Surely you are afraid of me," says the LORD.

"You should shake with fear in my
presence.
I am the one who made the beaches to be a
border for the sea,
a border the water can never go past.
The waves may pound the beach, but they
can't win over it.
They may roar, but they cannot go
beyond it.
23But the people of Judah are stubborn and
have turned against me.
They have turned aside and gone away
from me.
24They do not say to themselves,
'We should fear the LORD our God,
who gives us autumn and spring rains in
their seasons,
who makes sure we have the harvest at the
right time.'
25But your evil has kept away both rain and
harvest.
Your sins have kept you from enjoying good
things.
26There are wicked men among my people.
Like those who make nets for catching
birds,
they set their traps to catch people.
27Like cages full of birds,
their houses are full of lies.
They have become rich and powerful.
28 They have grown big and fat.
There is no end to the evil things they do.
They won't plead the case of the orphan
or help the poor be judged fairly.
29Shouldn't I punish the people of Judah for
doing these things?" says the LORD.
"Shouldn't I give a nation such as this the
punishment it deserves?

30"A terrible and shocking thing
has happened in the land of Judah:
31the prophets speak lies
and the priests take power into their own
hands,
and my people love it this way.
But what will you do when the end
comes?

Jerusalem is Surrounded

6 "Run for your lives, people of Benjamin!
Run away from Jerusalem!
Blow the war trumpet in the town of Tekoa!
Raise the warning flag over the town of
Beth Hakkerem!
Disaster is coming from the north;
terrible destruction is coming to you.
2Jerusalem, I will destroy you,
you who are fragile and gentle.
3Shepherds with their flocks will come against
Jerusalem.
They will set up their tents all around her,
each shepherd taking care of his own
section."
4They say, "Get ready to fight against
Jerusalem!
Get up! We will attack at noon!
But it is already getting late;
the evening shadows are growing long.
5So get up! We will attack at night.
We will destroy the strong towers of
Jerusalem!"

6This is what the LORD All-powerful says:
"Cut down the trees around Jerusalem
and build an attack ramp to the top of its
walls.
This city must be punished.
Inside it is nothing but slavery.
7Jerusalem pours out her evil
as a well pours out its water.
The sounds of violence and destruction are
heard within her.
I can see the sickness and hurts of
Jerusalem.
8Listen to this warning, Jerusalem,
or I will turn my back on you
and make your land an empty desert
where no one can live."

9This is what the LORD All-powerful says:
"Gather the few people of Israel who are left
alive,
as you would gather the last grapes on a
grapevine.
Check each vine again,
like someone who gathers grapes."

10To whom can I speak? Whom can I warn?
Who will listen to me?
The people of Israel have closed ears,
so they cannot hear my warnings.
They don't like the word of the LORD;
they don't want to listen to it!
11But I am full of the anger of the LORD
and I am tired of holding it in.

"Pour out my anger on the children who play
in the street
and on the young men gathered together.
A husband and his wife will both be caught
in his anger,
as will the very old.
12Their houses will be turned over to
others,
along with their fields and wives,
because I will raise my hand
and punish the people of Judah," says the
LORD.

13"Everyone, from the least important to the
greatest,
is greedy for money.
Even the prophets [d] and priests
all tell lies.
14They tried to heal my people's serious
injuries
as if they were small wounds.
They said, 'It's all right, it's all right.'
But really, it is not all right.
15They should be ashamed of the terrible way
they act,
but they are not ashamed at all.
They don't even know how to blush about
their sins.
So they will fall, along with everyone else.
They will be thrown to the ground when I
punish them," says the LORD.

16This is what the LORD says:
"Stand where the roads cross and look.
Ask where the old way is,
where the good way is, and walk on it.
If you do, you will find rest for yourselves.
But they have said, 'We will not walk on
the good way.'
17I set watchmen over you
and told you, 'Listen for the sound of the
war trumpet!'
But they said, 'We will not listen.'
18So listen, all you nations,
and pay attention, you witnesses.
Watch what I will do to the people of
Judah.
19Hear this, people of the earth:
I am going to bring disaster to the people
of Judah
because of the evil they plan.
They have not listened to my messages
and have rejected my teachings.
20Why do you bring me offerings of incense [d]
from the land of Sheba?
Why do you bring me sweet-smelling cane
from a faraway land?
Your burnt offerings will not be accepted;
your sacrifices do not please me."

21So this is what the LORD says:
"I will put problems in front of Judah.
Fathers and sons will stumble over them
together.
Neighbours and friends will die."

22This is what the LORD says:
"Look, an army is coming
from the land of the north;
a great nation is coming
from the far sides of the earth.
23The soldiers carry bows and spears.
They are cruel and show no mercy.
They sound like the roaring ocean
when they ride their horses.
That army is coming lined up for battle,
ready to attack you, Jerusalem."
24We have heard the news about that army
and are helpless from fear.
We are trapped by our pain,
like a woman having a baby.
25Don't go out into the fields
or walk down the roads,
because the enemy has swords.
There is terror on every side.
26My people, put on rough cloth
and roll in the ashes to show how sad
you are.
Cry loudly for those who are dead,
as if your only son were dead,
because the destroyer
will soon come against us.

27"Jeremiah, I have made you like a worker
who tests metal,
and my people are like the metal.
You must observe their ways
and test them.
28All my people have turned against me and
are stubborn.
They go around telling lies about others.
They are like bronze and iron
that became covered with rust.
They all act dishonestly.
29The fire is fanned to make it hotter,
but the lead does not melt.
The pure metal does not come out;
the evil is not removed from my people.
30My people will be called rejected silver,
because the LORD has rejected them."

Jeremiah's Temple Message

7 This is the word that the LORD spoke to
Jeremiah: 2"Stand at the gate of the Temple [d]
and preach this message there:
" 'Hear the word of the LORD, all you people of
the nation of Judah! All you who come through
these gates to worship the LORD, listen to this
message! 3This is what the LORD All-powerful, the
God of Israel, says: Change your lives and do
what is right! Then I will let you live in this place.
4Don't trust the lies of people who say, "This is
the Temple of the LORD. This is the Temple of the
LORD. This is the Temple of the LORD!" 5You must
change your lives and do what is right. Be fair to
each other. 6You must not oppress strangers,
orphans and widows. Don't kill innocent people
in this place! Don't follow other gods, or they
will ruin your lives. 7If you do these things, I will
let you live in this land that I gave to your ances-
tors to keep for ever.

8 " 'But look, you are trusting lies, which is use-
less. 9 Will you steal and murder and be guilty of
adultery?[d] Will you falsely accuse other people?
Will you burn incense[d] to the god Baal[d] and
follow other gods you have not known? 10 If you
do that, do you think you can come before me
and stand in this place where I have chosen to be
worshipped? Do you think you can say, "We
are safe!" when you do all these hateful things?
11 This place where I have chosen to be wor-
shipped is nothing more to you than a hideout for
robbers. I have been watching you, says the LORD.
12 " 'You people of Judah, go now to the town
of Shiloh, where I first made a place to be wor-
shipped. See what I did to it because of the evil
things the people of Israel had done. 13 You people
of Judah have done all these evil things too, says
the LORD. I spoke to you again and again, but you
did not listen to me. I called you, but you did not
answer. 14 So I will destroy the place where I have
chosen to be worshipped in Jerusalem. You trust
in that place, which I gave to you and your ances-
tors, but I will destroy it just as I destroyed
Shiloh. 15 I will push you away from me just as I
pushed away your relatives, the people of Israel!'
16 "As for you, Jeremiah, don't pray for these
people. Don't cry out for them or ask anything for
them or beg me to help them, because I will
not listen to you. 17 Don't you see what they are
doing in the towns of Judah and in the streets of
Jerusalem? 18 The children gather wood, and the
fathers use the wood to make a fire. The women
make the dough for cakes of bread, and they offer
them to the Queen Goddess.[d] They pour out drink
offerings to other gods to make me angry. 19 But I
am not the one the people of Judah are really hurt-
ing, says the LORD. They are only hurting them-
selves and bringing shame upon themselves.

FOLLOWING GOD

More Than Words

Daniel and Matt were brothers. Their dad was a very busy man. He ran his own business buying, renovating and selling houses, and Daniel and Matt spent many Saturdays working for their old man.

On one particular occasion, their dad was short-staffed and went to his sons to see if they could help. Daniel agreed. He didn't have any other plans so he thought, "Why not?" Matt did have other plans. He didn't want to spend his half-term covered in dust and paint, so he simply said, "No".

Half-term arrived, and Daniel and Matt's dad arrived at the job ready to get going. Unfortunately, Daniel was not there. 9.00 a.m., 10.00 a.m., 11.00 a.m., midday . . . still no Daniel. Though he had promised to turn up and help, he let his dad down and just didn't show. However, Matt was a different story. Though he had initially said no, he thought about it and decided he did want to help his dad. Matt arrived at 8.45 a.m. ready to work and spent the whole week covered in dust and paint.

Jesus tells a similar story to this in Matthew 21. It illustrates a famous phrase that says "actions speak louder than words". In **Jeremiah 7:1–15** the prophet warns the people that true worship is displayed, not by words or duty, but through our lives and in actions.

Following God means that we are more like Matt than Daniel. Daniel's actions did not back up his words. However, Matt's actions spoke much louder than his words.

- Can people see that you are a Christian by the way you live your life or are they left thinking, "You say one thing but do another!"
- If someone said to you, "Change your life and do what is right," what might you change?

Consider . . .

- spending a day making a note of every promise you make – from promising to help with the washing-up to arranging to meet a friend. How many of these commitments do you meet?
- whether there are things you could do (e.g. caring for people or giving to the poor) that demonstrate that your Christian life is more than words.

For more, see . . .

- 1 Kings 9:1–9 (p.324)
- Romans 12:1–2 (p.1203)
- Matthew 21.28–32 (p.978)

20"'So this is what the Lord GOD says: I will
pour out my anger on this place, on people and
animals, on the trees in the field and the crops in
the ground. My anger will be like a hot fire that
no one can put out.

Obedience is More than Sacrifice

21"'This is what the LORD All-powerful, the God
of Israel, says: Offer burnt offerings along with
your other sacrifices, and eat the meat yourselves!
22When I brought your ancestors out of Egypt, I
did not speak to them and give them commands
only about burnt offerings and sacrifices. 23I also
gave them this command: obey me, and I will be
your God and you will be my people. Do all that I
command so that good things will happen to you.
24But your ancestors did not listen or pay attention
to me. They were stubborn and did whatever their
evil hearts wanted. They went backwards, not for-
wards. 25Since the day your ancestors left Egypt, I
have sent my servants, the prophets, again and
again to you. 26But your ancestors did not listen or
pay attention to me. They were very stubborn and
did more evil than their ancestors.'

27"Jeremiah, you will tell all these things to the
people of Judah, but they will not listen to you.
You will call to them, but they will not answer
you. 28So say to them, 'This is the nation that has
not obeyed the LORD its God. These people do
nothing when I correct them. They do not tell the
truth; it has disappeared from their lips.

The Valley of Killing

29"'Cut off your hair and throw it away. Go up
to the bare hilltop and cry out, because the LORD
has rejected these people. He has turned his back
on them, and in his anger will punish them.
30The people of Judah have done what I said was
evil, says the LORD. They have set up their hateful
idols in the place where I have chosen to be wor-
shipped and have made it unclean.[d] 31The people
of Judah have built places of worship at Topheth
in the Valley of Ben Hinnom. There they burned
their own sons and daughters as sacrifices, some-
thing I never commanded. It never even entered
my mind. 32So, I warn you. The days are coming,
says the LORD, when people will not call this place
Topheth or the Valley of Ben Hinnom any more.
They will call it the Valley of Killing. They will
bury the dead in Topheth until there is no room
to bury anyone else. 33Then the bodies of the
dead will become food for the birds of the sky and
for the wild animals. There will be no one left
alive to chase them away. 34I will end the happy
sounds of the bride and bridegroom. There will
be no happy sounds in the cities of Judah or in the
streets of Jerusalem, because the land will be-
come an empty desert!

8 "'The LORD says: At that time they will re-
move from their tombs the bones of Judah's
kings and officers, priests and prophets,[d] and the
people of Jerusalem. 2The bones will be spread on
the ground under the sun, moon and stars that
the people loved and served and went after and
searched for and worshipped. No one will gather
up the bones and bury them. So they will be like
dung thrown on the ground. 3I will force the
people of Judah to leave their homes and their
land. Those of this evil family who are not dead
will wish they were, says the LORD All-powerful.'

Sin and Punishment

4"Say to the people of Judah: 'This is what the
LORD says:

When people fall down, don't they get up
again?
And when someone goes the wrong way,
doesn't he turn back?
5Why, then, have the people of Jerusalem gone
the wrong way
and not turned back?
They believe their own lies
and refuse to turn around and come back.
6I have listened to them very carefully,
but they do not say what is right.
They do not feel sorry about their wicked ways,
saying, "What have I done?"
Each person goes his own way,
like a horse charging into a battle.
7Even the birds in the sky
know the right times to do things.
The storks, doves, swifts and thrushes
know when it is time to migrate.
But my people don't know
what the LORD wants them to do.

8"'You keep saying, "We are wise,
because we have the teachings of the LORD."
But actually, those who explain the Scriptures
have written lies with their pens.
9These wise men refused to listen to the word
of the LORD,
so they are not really wise at all.
They will be ashamed.
They will be shocked and trapped.
10So I will give their wives to other men
and their fields to new owners.
Everyone, from the least important to the
greatest,
is greedy for money.
Even the prophets[d] and priests
all tell lies.
11They tried to heal my people's serious injuries
as if they were small wounds.
They said, "It's all right, it's all right."
But really, it is not all right.

12They should be ashamed of the terrible way
they act,
but they are not ashamed at all.
They don't even know how to blush about
their sins.
So they will fall, along with everyone else.
They will be thrown to the ground when I
punish them, says the LORD.
13" 'I will take away their crops, says the LORD.
There will be no grapes on the vine
and no figs on the fig tree.
Even the leaves will dry up and die.
I will take away what I gave them.' "
14"Why are we just sitting here?
Let's get together!
We have sinned against the LORD,
so he has given us poisoned water to drink.
Come, let's run to the fortified cities.
The LORD our God has decided that we
must die,
so let's die there.
15We hoped to have peace,
but nothing good has come.
We hoped for a time when he would heal us,
but only terror has come.
16From the land of Dan,
the snorting of the enemy's horses is heard.
The ground shakes from the neighing of
their large horses.
They have come and destroyed
the land and everything in it,
the city and all who live there."
17"Look! I am sending poisonous snakes to
attack you.
These snakes cannot be charmed,
and they will bite you," says the LORD.

Jeremiah's Sadness

18God, you are my comfort when I am very sad
and when I am afraid.
19Listen to the sound of my people.
They cry from a faraway land:
"Isn't the LORD still in Jerusalem?
Isn't Jerusalem's king still there?"
But God says, "Why did the people make me
angry by worshipping idols,
useless foreign idols?"
20And the people say, "Harvest time is over;
summer has ended,
and we have not been saved."
21Because my people are crushed, I am crushed.
I cry loudly and am afraid for them.
22Isn't there balm[d] in the land of Gilead?
Isn't there a doctor there?
So why aren't the hurts of my people healed?

9 I wish my head were like a spring of
water
and my eyes like a fountain of tears!
Then I could cry day and night
for my people who have been killed.
2I wish I had a place in the desert—
a house where travellers spend the night—
so I could leave my people.
I could go away from them,
because they are all unfaithful to God;
they are all turning against him.

Judah's Failures

3"They use their tongues like a bow,
shooting lies from their mouths like arrows.
Lies, not truth,
have grown strong in the land.
They go from one evil thing to another.
They do not know who I am," says the LORD.
4"Watch out for your friends
and don't trust your own relatives,
because every relative is a cheat
and every friend tells lies about you.
5Everyone lies to his friend
and no one speaks the truth.
The people of Judah have taught their
tongues to lie.
They have become tired from sinning.
6Jeremiah, you live in the middle of lies.
With their lies the people refuse to know
me," says the LORD.

7So this is what the LORD All-powerful says:
"I will test the people of Judah as a person
tests metal in a fire.
I have no other choice,
because my people have sinned.
8Their tongues are like sharp arrows.
Their mouths speak lies.
Everyone speaks nicely to his neighbour,
but he is secretly planning to attack him.
9Shouldn't I punish the people for doing this?"
says the LORD.
"Shouldn't I give a nation like this the
punishment it deserves?"

10I, Jeremiah, will cry loudly for the mountains
and sing a funeral song for the empty fields.
They are empty, and no one passes through.
The mooing of cattle cannot be heard.

Sidelight The "balm of Gilead" (Jeremiah 8:22) was a type of gum taken from aromatic bushes in an area east of the river Jordan. As early as Genesis 37:25 (p.44), when Joseph was sold to traders from Gilead, it was famous for its fragrant healing powers. We don't know whether it stung.

The birds have flown away,
and the animals are gone.

11"I, the LORD, will make the city of Jerusalem
a heap of ruins,
a home for wild dogs.
I will destroy the cities of Judah
so no one can live there."

12What person is wise enough to understand
these things? Is there someone who has been
taught by the LORD who can explain them? Why
was the land ruined? Why has it been made like
an empty desert where no one goes?
13The LORD answered, "It is because Judah has
stopped following my teachings that I gave them.
They have not obeyed me or done what I told
them to do. 14Instead, they were stubborn and
followed the Baals,[d] as their ancestors taught
them to do." 15So this is what the LORD All-
powerful, the God of Israel, says: "I will soon
make the people of Judah eat bitter food and
drink poisoned water. 16I will scatter them
through other nations that they and their ances-
tors never knew about. I will chase the people of
Judah with the sword until they are all killed."
17This is what the LORD All-powerful says:
"Now, think about these things!
Call for the women who cry at funerals to
come.
Send for those women who are good at
that job.
18Let them come quickly
and cry loudly for us.
Then our eyes will fill with tears
and streams of water will flow from our
eyelids.
19The sound of loud crying is heard from
Jerusalem:
'We are truly ruined!
We are truly ashamed!
We must leave our land,
because our houses are in ruins.' "
20Now, women of Judah, listen to the word of
the LORD;
open your ears to hear the words of his
mouth.
Teach your daughters how to cry loudly.
Teach one another a funeral song.
21Death has climbed in through our windows
and has entered our strong cities.
Death has taken away our children who play
in the streets
and the young men who meet in the city
squares.
22Say, "This is what the LORD says:
'The dead bodies of people will lie
in the open field like dung.
They will lie like grain a farmer has cut,
but there will be no one to gather them.' "
23This is what the LORD says:
"The wise must not boast about their
wisdom.
The strong must not boast about their
strength.
The rich must not boast about their money.
24But if someone wants to boast, let him boast
that he understands and knows me.
Let him boast that I am the LORD,
and that I am kind and fair,
and that I do things that are right on earth.
This kind of boasting pleases me," says the
LORD.

25The LORD says, "The time is coming when I
will punish all those who are circumcised[d] only
in the flesh: 26the people of Egypt, Judah, Edom,
Ammon and Moab and the desert people who cut
their hair short. The men in all those countries
are not circumcised. And the whole family of
Israel does not give itself to serving me."

The LORD and the Idols

10 Family of Israel, listen to what the LORD
says to you. 2This is what he says:
"Don't live like the people from other
nations,
and don't be afraid of special signs in
the sky,
even though the other nations are afraid of
them.
3The customs of other people are worth
nothing.
Their idols are just wood cut from the
forest,
shaped by a worker with his chisel.
4They decorate their idols with silver and
gold.
With hammers and nails they fasten them
down
so they won't fall over.
5Their idols are like scarecrows in melon
fields;
they cannot talk.
Since they cannot walk,
they must be carried.
Do not be afraid of those idols,
because they can't hurt you
and they can't help you either."

6LORD, there is no one like you.
You are great,
and your name is great and powerful.
7Everyone should respect you, King of the
nations;
you deserve respect.

Of all the wise people among the nations
and in all the kingdoms,
none of them is as wise as you.
8Those wise people are stupid and foolish.
Their teachings come from worthless wooden idols.
9Hammered silver is brought from Tarshish
and gold from Uphaz,
so the idols are made by craftsmen and goldsmiths.
They put blue and purple clothes on the idols.
All these things are made by skilled workers.
10But the LORD is the only true God.
He is the only living God, the King for ever.
The earth shakes when he is angry
and the nations cannot stand up to his anger.

11"Tell them this message: 'These gods did not make heaven and earth; they will be destroyed and disappear from heaven and earth.'"

12God made the earth by his power.
He used his wisdom to build the world
and his understanding to stretch out the skies.
13When he thunders, the waters in the skies roar.
He makes clouds rise in the sky all over the earth.
He sends lightning with the rain
and brings out the wind from his storehouses.

14People are so stupid and know so little.
Goldsmiths are made ashamed by their idols,
because those statues are only false gods.
They have no breath in them.
15They are worth nothing; people make fun of them.
When they are judged, they will be destroyed.
16But God, who is Jacob's Portion, [d] is not like the idols.
He made everything
and he chose Israel to be his special people.
The LORD All-powerful is his name.

Destruction is Coming

17Get everything you own and prepare to leave,
you people who are trapped by your enemies.
18This is what the LORD says:
"At this time I will throw out the people who live in this land.
I will bring trouble to them
so that they may be captured."
19How terrible it will be for me because of my injury.
My wound cannot be healed.
Yet I told myself,
"This is my sickness; I must suffer through it."
20My tent is ruined
and all its ropes are broken.
My children have gone away and left me.
No one is left to put up my tent again
or to set up a shelter for me.
21The shepherds are stupid
and don't ask the LORD for advice.
So they do not have success
and all their flocks are scattered and lost.
22Listen! The news is coming.
A loud noise comes from the north
to make the towns of Judah an empty desert
and a home for wild dogs!

Jeremiah's Prayer

23LORD, I know that a person's life doesn't really belong to him.
No one can control his own life.
24LORD, correct me, but be fair.
Don't punish me in your anger,
or you will destroy me.
25Pour out your anger on other nations
that do not know you
and do not pray to you.
Those nations have destroyed Jacob's family.
They have eaten him up completely
and destroyed his homeland.

The Agreement is Broken

11 These are the words that the LORD spoke
to Jeremiah: 2"Listen to the words of this
agreement and tell them to the people of Judah
and those living in Jerusalem. 3Tell them this is
what the LORD, the God of Israel, says: 'Cursed
is the person who does not obey the words of
this agreement 4that I made with your ancestors
when I brought them out of Egypt. Egypt was like
a furnace for melting iron!' I told them, 'Obey
me and do everything I command you. Then you
will be my people, and I will be your God. 5Then I
will keep the promise I made to your ancestors
to give them a fertile land.' And you are living in
that country today."

I answered, "Amen, LORD."

6The LORD said to me, "Announce [d] this mes-
sage in the towns of Judah and in the streets of
Jerusalem: 'Listen to the words of this agreement

and obey them. 7I warned your ancestors to obey
me when I brought them out of Egypt. I have
warned them again and again to this very day:
"Obey me!" 8But your ancestors did not listen to
me. They were stubborn and did what their own
evil hearts wanted. So I made all the curses of this
agreement come upon them. I commanded them
to obey the agreement, but they did not.' "

9Then the LORD said to me, "I know the people
of Judah and those living in Jerusalem have made
secret plans. 10They have gone back to the same
sins their ancestors did. Their ancestors refused
to listen to my message and followed and wor-
shipped other gods instead. The families of Israel
and Judah have broken the agreement I made
with their ancestors. 11So this is what the LORD
says: 'I will soon bring a disaster on the people of
Judah which they will not be able to escape. They
will cry to me for help, but I will not listen to
them. 12The people living in the towns of Judah
and the city of Jerusalem will pray to their idols
to whom they burn incense.[d] But those idols will
not be able to help when disaster comes. 13Look,
people of Judah, you have as many idols as there
are towns in Judah. You have built as many altars
to burn incense to that shameful god Baal[d] as
there are streets in Jerusalem.'

14"As for you, Jeremiah, don't pray for these
people or cry out for them or ask anything for
them. I will not listen when they call to me in the
time of their trouble.

15"What is my beloved Judah doing in my
Temple[d]
when she makes many evil plans?
Do you think animal sacrifices will stop your
punishment?
When you do your evil, then you are happy."
16The LORD called you "a leafy olive tree,
with beautiful fruit and shape."
But with the roar of a strong storm
he will set that tree on fire,
and its branches will be burned up.

17The LORD All-powerful, who planted you, has
announced that disaster will come to you. This is
because the families of Israel and Judah have
done evil and have made him angry by burning
incense to Baal.

Evil Plans Against Jeremiah

18The LORD showed me that men were making
plans against me. Because he showed me what
they were doing, I knew they were against me.
19Before this, I was like a gentle lamb waiting to
be slaughtered. I did not know they had made
plans against me, saying:
"Let us destroy the tree and its fruit.
Let's kill him so people will forget him."
20But, LORD All-powerful, you are a fair judge.
You know how to test people's hearts and
minds.
I have told you what I have against them.
So let me see you give them the
punishment they deserve.

21So the LORD speaks about the men from
Anathoth who plan to kill Jeremiah and say,
"Don't prophesy[d] in the name of the LORD, or we
will kill you!" 22So this is what the LORD All-
powerful says: "I will soon punish the men from
Anathoth. Their young men will die in war. Their
sons and daughters will die from hunger. 23No
one from the city of Anathoth will be left alive,
because I will cause a disaster to happen to them
that year."

Jeremiah's First Complaint

12 LORD, when I bring my case to you,
you are always right.
But I want to ask you about the justice you
give.
Why are evil people successful?
Why do dishonest people have such easy
lives?
2You have put the evil people here
like plants with strong roots.
They grow and produce fruit.
With their mouths they speak well of you,
but their hearts are really far away
from you.
3But you know my heart, LORD.
You see me and test my thoughts
about you.
Drag the evil people away like sheep to be
slaughtered.
Set them aside for the day of killing.
4How much longer will the land stay
dried up
and the grass in every field be dead?
The animals and birds in the land have died,
because the people are evil.
Yes, they are even saying,
"God does not see what happens to us."

Sidelight How would you like to have a complaint named after you? Jeremiah's protesting to God (Jeremiah 12:1–4) made its way into the dictionary as "jeremiad" – "a lamentation or tale of woe".

The LORD's Answer to Jeremiah

5"If you get tired while racing against people,
how can you race against horses?
If you stumble in a country that is safe,

what will you do in the thick thorn-bushes
along the Jordan River?
6Even your own brothers and members of your
own family
are making plans against you.
They are crying out against you.
Don't trust them,
even when they say nice things to you!

7"I have left Israel;
I have left my people.
I have given the people I love
over to their enemies.
8My people have become to me
like a lion in the forest.
They roar at me,
so I hate them.
9My people have become to me
like a speckled bird attacked on all sides by
hawks.
Go, gather the wild animals.
Bring them to get something to eat.
10Many shepherds have ruined my vineyards
and trampled the plants in my field.
They have turned my beautiful field
into an empty desert.
11They have turned my field into a desert
that is wilted and dead.
The whole country is an empty desert,
because no one who lives there cares.
12Many soldiers have marched over those
barren hills.
The LORD is using the armies to punish that
land
from one end to the other.
No one is safe.
13The people have planted wheat,
but they have harvested only thorns.
They have worked hard until they were very
tired,
but they have nothing for all their work.
They are ashamed of their poor harvest,
because the LORD's terrible anger has caused
this."

14This is what the LORD said to me: "Here is
what I will do to all my wicked neighbours who
take the land I gave my people Israel. I will pull
them up and throw them out of their land. And
I will pull up the people of Judah from among
them. 15But after I pull them up, I will feel sorry
for them again. I will bring each person back to
his own property and to his own land. 16I want
them to learn their lessons well. In the past they
taught my people to swear by Baal's*d* name. But
if they will now learn to swear by my name,
saying 'As surely as the LORD lives . . .' I will
allow them to rebuild among my people. 17But if
a nation will not listen to my message, I will pull
it up completely and destroy it," says the LORD.

Jeremiah's Linen Belt

13 This is what the LORD said to me: "Go
and buy a linen belt and put it around
your waist. Don't let the belt get wet."
2So I bought a linen belt, just as the LORD told
me, and put it around my waist. 3Then the LORD
spoke his word to me a second time: 4"Take
the belt you bought and are wearing, and go to
Perath. Hide the belt there in a crack in the
rocks." 5So I went to Perath and hid the belt
there, just as the LORD told me.
6Many days later the LORD said to me, "Now
go to Perath and get the belt I told you to hide
there." 7So I went to Perath and dug up the belt
and took it from where I had hidden it. But now
it was ruined; it was good for nothing.
8Then the LORD spoke his word to me. 9This
is what the LORD said: "In the same way I will
ruin the pride of the people of Judah and the
great pride of Jerusalem. 10These evil people
refuse to listen to my warnings. They stubbornly
do only what they want to do, and they follow
other gods to serve and worship them. So they
will become like this linen belt—good for noth-
ing. 11As a belt is wrapped tightly around a
person's waist, I wrapped the families of Israel
and Judah around me," says the LORD. "I did
that so they would be my people and bring
fame, praise and honour to me. But my people
would not listen.

Sidelight The Bible is full of people who taught in original ways. Elijah called down fire from heaven (1 Kings 18:20–39, p.363), and Jesus taught by parables (Matthew 13, p.961). Read how Jeremiah taught in Jeremiah 13:1–11 and 19:12–15 (p.738).

Warnings About Leather Wine Bags

12"Say to them: 'This is what the LORD, the God
of Israel, says: all leather bags for holding wine
should be filled with wine.' People will say to
you: 'Of course, we know all wine bags should be
filled with wine.' 13Then you will say to them,
'This is what the LORD says: I will make every-
one in this land like a drunken person—the
kings who sit on David's throne, the priests and
the prophets*d* and all the people who live in
Jerusalem. 14I will make them smash against one
another, fathers and sons alike, says the LORD. I
will not feel sorry or have pity on them or show

mercy that would stop me from destroying them.' "

Threat of Slavery

15Listen and pay attention.
Don't be too proud,
because the LORD has spoken to you.
16Give glory to the LORD your God
before he brings darkness
and before you slip and fall
on the dark hills.
You hope for light,
but he will turn it into thick darkness;
he will change it into deep gloom.
17If you don't listen to him,
I will cry secretly
because of your pride.
I will cry painfully,
and my eyes will overflow with tears,
because the LORD's people will be captured.

18Tell this to the king and the queen mother:
"Come down from your thrones,
because your beautiful crowns
have fallen from your heads."
19The cities of southern Judah are locked up
and no one can open them.
All Judah will be taken as captives to a foreign land;
they will be carried away completely.
20Jerusalem, look up and see
the people coming from the north.
Where is the flock God gave you to care for,
the flock you boasted about?
21What will you say when they appoint as your heads
those you had thought were your friends?
Won't you have much pain and trouble,
like a woman giving birth to a baby?
22You might ask yourself,
"Why has this happened to me?"
It happened because of your many sins.
Because of your sins, your skirt was torn off
and your body has been treated badly.
23Can a person from Cush change the colour of his skin?
Can a leopard change his spots?
In the same way, Jerusalem, you cannot change and do good,
because you are accustomed to doing evil.

24"I will scatter you like chaff [d] that is blown away by the desert wind.
25This is what will happen to you;
this is your part in my plans," says the LORD.
"Because you forgot me
and trusted in false gods,
26I will pull your skirts up over your face
so everyone will see your shame.
27I have seen the terrible things you have done:
your acts of adultery [d] and your snorting,
your prostitution, [d]
your hateful acts
on the hills and in the fields.
How terrible it will be for you, Jerusalem.
How long will you continue being unclean?" [d]

A Time Without Rain

14 These are the words that the LORD spoke
to Jeremiah about the time when there
was no rain:
2"The nation of Judah cries as if someone has died,
and her cities are very sad.
They are distressed over the land.
A cry goes up to God from Jerusalem.
3The important men send their servants to get water.
They go to the wells,
but they find no water.
So they return with empty jars.
They are ashamed and embarrassed
and cover their heads in shame.
4The ground is dry and cracked open,
because no rain falls on the land.
The farmers are upset and sad,
so they cover their heads in shame.
5Even the mother deer in the field
leaves her newborn fawn to die,
because there is no grass.
6Wild donkeys stand on the bare hills
and sniff the wind like wild dogs.
But their eyes go blind,
because there is no food."

7We know that we suffer because of our sins.
LORD, do something to help us for the good of your name.
We have left you many times;
we have sinned against you.
8God, the Hope of Israel,
you have saved Israel in times of trouble.
Why are you like a stranger in the land,
or like a traveller who only stays one night?
9Why are you like someone who has been attacked by surprise,
like a warrior who is not able to save anyone?
But you are among us, LORD,
and we are called by your name
so don't leave us without help!

10 This is what the LORD says about the people
of Judah:
"They really love to wander from me;
they don't stop themselves from
leaving me.
So now the LORD will not accept them.
He will now remember the evil they do
and will punish them for their sins."

11 Then the LORD said, "Don't pray for good
things to happen to the people of Judah. 12 Even
if they give up eating, I will not listen to their
prayers. Even if they offer burnt offerings and
grain offerings to me, I will not accept them. In-
stead, I will destroy the people of Judah with war,
hunger and terrible diseases."
13 But I said, "Oh, Lord GOD, the prophets[d]
keep telling the people, 'You will not suffer from
an enemy's sword or from hunger. I, the LORD,
will give you peace in this land.'"
14 Then the LORD said to me, "Those prophets
are prophesying lies in my name. I did not send
them or appoint them or speak to them. They
have been prophesying false visions, idolatries,
worthless magic and their own wishful thinking.
15 So this is what I say about the prophets who are
prophesying in my name. I did not send them.
They say, 'No enemy will attack this country
with swords. There will never be hunger in this
land.' So those prophets will die from hunger and
from an enemy's sword. 16 And the people to
whom the prophets speak will be thrown into the
streets of Jerusalem. There they will die from
hunger and from an enemy's sword. And no one
will be there to bury them, or their wives, or their
sons or their daughters. I will punish them.
17 "Jeremiah, speak this message to the people
of Judah:
'Let my eyes be filled with tears
night and day, without stopping.
My people have received a terrible blow;
they have been hurt badly.
18 If I go into the country,
I see people killed by swords.
If I go into the city,
I see much sickness, because the people
have no food.
Both the priests and the prophets
have been taken to a foreign land.'"

19 LORD, have you completely rejected the nation
of Judah?
Do you hate Jerusalem?
Why have you hurt us so badly
that we cannot be made well again?
We hoped for peace,
but nothing good has come.
We looked for a time of healing,
but only terror came.
20 LORD, we admit that we are wicked
and that our ancestors did evil things.
We have sinned against you.
21 For your sake, do not hate us.
Do not take away the honour from your
glorious throne.
Remember your agreement with us,
and do not break it.
22 Do foreign idols have the power to bring
rain?
Does the sky itself have the power to send
down showers?
No, it is you, LORD our God.
You are our only hope,
because you are the one who made all these
things.

15 Then the LORD said to me: "I would not
feel sorry for the people of Judah even if
Moses and Samuel prayed for them. Send them
away from me! Tell them to go! 2 When they ask
you, 'Where will we go?' tell them: 'This is what
the LORD says:
Those who are meant to die
will die.
Those who are meant to die in war
will die in war.
Those who are meant to die from hunger
will die from hunger.
Those who are meant to be taken captive
will be taken captive.'

3 "I will send four kinds of destroyers against
them," says the LORD. "I will send war to kill,
dogs to drag the bodies away, and the birds of the
air and wild animals to eat and destroy the bod-
ies. 4 I will make the people of Judah hated by
everyone on earth because of what Manasseh did
in Jerusalem. (Manasseh son of Hezekiah was
king of the nation of Judah.)

5 "Who will feel sorry for you, Jerusalem?
Who will be sad and cry for you?
Who will go out of his way to ask how
you are?
6 Jerusalem, you have left me," says the LORD.
"You keep going further and further away,
so I have taken hold of you and destroyed you.
I was tired of holding back my anger.
7 I have separated the people of Judah with my
pitchfork
and scattered them at the city gates of the
land.
My people haven't changed their ways.
So I have destroyed them
and taken away their children.
8 There are more widows than grains of sand
in the sea.
I brought a destroyer at noontime

against the mothers of the young men of
Judah.
I suddenly brought pain and fear
on the people of Judah.
9When the enemy attacked, a woman with
seven sons felt faint because they would
all die.
She became weak and unable to breathe.
Her bright day became dark from sadness.
She felt shame and disgrace.
And everyone else left alive in Judah
I will hand over to the enemies too!" says
the LORD.

Jeremiah's Second Complaint

10Mother, I am sorry that you gave birth to me
since I must accuse and criticise the whole
land.
I have not loaned or borrowed anything,
but everyone curses me.
11The LORD said,
"I have saved you for a good reason.
I have made your enemies beg you
in times of disaster and trouble.
12No one can smash a piece of iron or bronze
that comes from the north.
13Your wealth and treasures
I will give to others free of charge,
because the people of Judah have sinned
throughout the country.
14I will make you slaves to your enemies
in a land you have never known.
My anger is like a hot fire,
and it will burn against you."
15LORD, you understand.
Remember me and take care of me.
Punish for me those who are hurting me.
Don't destroy me while you remain patient
with them.
Think about the shame I suffer for you.
16Your words came to me and I listened
carefully to them.
Your words made me very happy,
because I am called by your name,
LORD God All-powerful.
17I never sat with the crowd
as they laughed and had fun.
I sat by myself, because you were there,
and you filled me with anger at the evil
around me.
18I don't understand why my pain has no end.
I don't understand why my injury is not
cured or healed.
Will you be like a brook that goes dry?
Will you be like a spring that stops flowing?

19So this is what the LORD says:
"If you change your heart and return to me, I
will take you back.
Then you may serve me.
And if you speak things that have worth,

Sidelight Reading Jeremiah is like stumbling into a room and finding someone crying (for example, see Jeremiah 15:10–18 and 20:7–18, p.739). No wonder Jeremiah became known as "the weeping prophet".

not useless words,
then you may speak for me.
Let the people of Judah turn to you,
but you must not change and be
like them.
20I will make you as strong as a wall to this
people,
as strong as a wall of bronze.
They will fight against you,
but they will not defeat you,
because I am with you.
I will rescue you and save you," says the
LORD.
21"I will save you from these wicked people
and rescue you from these cruel people."

The Day of Disaster

16 Then the LORD spoke his word to me:
2"You must not get married or have sons
or daughters in this place."
3The LORD says this about the sons and daugh-
ters born in this land and their mothers and fath-
ers: 4"They will die of terrible diseases, and no
one will cry for them or bury them. Their bodies
will lie on the ground like dung. They will die in
war, or they will starve to death. Their bodies will
be food for the birds of the sky and for the wild
animals."
5So this is what the LORD says: "Jeremiah, do
not go into a house where there is a funeral meal.
Do not go there to cry for the dead or to show
your sorrow for them, because I have taken back
my blessing, my love and my pity from these peo-
ple," says the LORD. 6"Important people and com-
mon people will die in the land of Judah. No one
will bury them or cry for them or cut himself or
shave his head to show sorrow for them. 7No one
will bring food to comfort those who are crying
for the dead. No one will offer a drink to comfort
someone whose mother or father has died.
8"Do not go into a house where the people are
having a feast to sit down to eat and drink, 9be-
cause this is what the LORD All-powerful, the God
of Israel, says: I will soon stop the sounds of joy

and gladness and the happy sounds of brides and
bridegrooms in this place. This will happen during your lifetime.
10"When you tell the people of Judah these
things, they will ask you, 'Why has the LORD said
these terrible things to us? What have we done
wrong? What sin have we done against the LORD
our God?'
11"Then say to them: 'This is because your
ancestors stopped following me,' says the LORD.
'And they followed other gods and served and
worshipped them. Your ancestors left me and
stopped obeying my teaching. 12But you have
done even more evil than your ancestors. You are
very stubborn and do only what you want to do;
you have not obeyed me. 13So I will throw you
out of this country and send you into a land that
you and your ancestors never knew. There you
can serve other gods day and night, because I will
not help you or show you any favours.'
14"People say, 'As surely as the LORD lives, who
brought the people of Israel out of Egypt . . .' But
the time is coming," says the LORD, "when people
will not say this any more. 15They will say instead, 'As surely as the LORD lives, who brought
the Israelites from the northern land and from all
the countries where he had sent them . . .' And I
will bring them back to the land I gave to their
ancestors.
16"I will soon send for many fishermen to
come to this land," says the LORD. "And they will
catch the people of Judah. After that, I will send
for many hunters to come to this land. And they
will hunt the people of Judah on every mountain
and hill and in the cracks of the rocks. 17I see
everything they do. They cannot hide from me
the things they do; their sin is not hidden from
my eyes. 18I will pay back the people of Judah
twice for every one of their sins, because they
have made my land unclean. [d] They have filled
my country with their hateful idols."

19LORD, you are my strength and my
protection,
my safe place in times of trouble.
The nations will come to you from all over
the world
and say, "Our ancestors had only false
gods,
useless idols that didn't help them.
20Can people make gods for themselves?
They will not really be gods!"

21The LORD says, "So I will teach those who
make idols.
This time I will teach them
about my power and my strength.
Then they will know
that my name is the LORD.

Judah's Guilty Heart

17 "The sin of the people of Judah is
written with an iron tool.
Their sins were cut with a hard point into
the stone that is their hearts.
Their sins were cut into the corners of their
altars.
2Even their children remember
their altars to idols and their Asherah [d]
idols
beside the green trees
and on the high hills.
3My mountain in the open country
and your wealth and treasures
I will give away to other people.
I will give away the places of worship in
your country,
because you sinned by worshipping there.
4You will lose the land I gave you
and it is your own fault.
I will let your enemies take you as their
slaves
to a land you have never known.
This is because you have made my anger
burn like a hot fire,
and it will burn for ever."

Trusting in Humans or God

5This is what the LORD says:
"A curse is placed on those who trust other
people,
who depend on humans for strength,
who have stopped trusting the LORD.
6They are like a bush in a desert
that grows in a land where no one lives,
a hot and dry land with bad soil.
They don't know about the good things God
can give.
7"But the person who trusts in the LORD will
be blessed.
The LORD will show him that he can be
trusted.
8He will be strong, like a tree planted near
water
that sends its roots by a stream.
It is not afraid when the days are hot;
its leaves are always green.
It does not worry in a year when no rain
comes;
it always produces fruit.
9"More than anything else, a person's mind is
evil
and cannot be healed.
No one truly understands it.
10But I, the LORD, look into a person's heart
and test the mind.
So I can decide what each one deserves;

I can give each one the right payment for
what he does."

11Like a bird hatching an egg it did not lay,
so are the people who get rich by cheating.
When their lives are half finished, they will
lose their riches.
At the end of their lives, it will be clear
they were fools.

12From the beginning, our Temple[d] has been
honoured
as a glorious throne for God.

13LORD, hope of Israel,
those who leave you will be shamed.
People who stop following the LORD will be
like a name written in the dust,
because they have left the LORD, the spring
of living water.

Jeremiah's Third Complaint

14LORD, heal me, and I will truly be healed.
Save me, and I will truly be saved.
You are the one I praise.

15The people of Judah keep asking me,
"Where is the word from the LORD?
Let's see that message come true!"

16LORD, I didn't run away from being the
shepherd you wanted.
I didn't want the terrible day to come.
You know everything I have said;
you see all that is happening.

17Don't be a terror to me.
I run to you for safety in times of trouble.

18Make those who are hurting me be ashamed,
but don't bring shame to me.
Let them be terrified,
but keep me from terror.
Bring the day of disaster on my enemies.
Destroy them, and destroy them again.

Keeping the Sabbath Holy

19This is what the LORD said to me: "Go and
stand at the People's Gate of Jerusalem, where
the kings of Judah go in and out. And then go to
all the other gates of Jerusalem. 20Say to them
there: 'Hear the word of the LORD, kings of
Judah, all you people of Judah, and all who live
in Jerusalem, who come through these gates into
the city. 21This is what the LORD says: be careful
not to carry a load on the Sabbath[d] day or bring it
through the gates of Jerusalem. 22Don't take a
load out of your houses on the Sabbath or do any

DECISION MAKING

What Do You Believe?

The book *Walden Two* tells about scientists who played a trick on some sheep. First, they fenced them in with an electrified wire. The sheep worked out pretty quickly that they should stay away from the wire.

Then the scientists replaced the wire with a piece of string. Not knowing the difference, the sheep stayed away from the string too. They even taught their young to stay away from the string. The young sheep believed that the string was dangerous because that's what the older sheep taught them.

People may not believe in electrified string, but we surely listen to a lot of things other people tell us. God warns us to put our trust in him, not in other people. He used Jeremiah to warn the people of Israel to trust in him and not be led astray by other people. Read about it in **Jeremiah 17:5–8**.

- How are the sheep in the experiment like the people in this passage?
- According to this passage, how should you evaluate others' advice?

Consider . . .

- listening to your favourite radio station and writing down the messages you hear in several songs. Do you trust those messages?
- keeping a list this week of the messages you hear about yourself from your friends (for example, "you're pretty", "you're a clown", "you're strange") and deciding if you agree with those messages.

For more, see . . .

- Exodus 32:1–35 (p.90)
- 2 Corinthians 11:12–15 (p.1251)
- Psalm 146:3–6 (p.586)

work on that day. But keep the Sabbath as a holy
day, as I commanded your ancestors. 23But your
ancestors did not listen or pay attention to me.
They were very stubborn and did not listen. I
punished them, but it didn't do any good. 24But
you must be careful to obey me, says the LORD.
You must not bring a load through the gates of
Jerusalem on the Sabbath, but you must keep the
Sabbath as a holy day and not do any work on
that day.

25" 'If you obey this command, kings who sit
on David's throne will come through the gates of
Jerusalem with their officers. They will come rid-
ing in chariots and on horses, along with the
people of Judah and Jerusalem. And the city of
Jerusalem will have people living in it for ever.
26People will come to Jerusalem from the villages
around it, from the towns of Judah, from the land
of Benjamin, from the western hills, from the
mountains and from southern Judah. They will all
bring to the Temple[d] of the LORD burnt offerings,
sacrifices, grain offerings, incense[d] and offerings
to show thanks to God. 27But you must obey me
and keep the Sabbath day as a holy day. You
must not carry any loads into Jerusalem on the
Sabbath. If you don't obey me, I will start a fire
at the gates of Jerusalem, and it will burn until it
burns even the strong towers. And it will not be
put out.' "

The Potter and the Clay

18 This is the word the LORD spoke to
Jeremiah: 2"Go down to the potter's
house, and I will give you my message there." 3So
I went down to the potter's house and saw him
working at the potter's wheel. 4He was using his
hands to make a pot from clay, but something
went wrong with it. So he used that clay to make
another pot the way he wanted it to be.

> **Sidelight** The potter (Jeremiah 18:1–4) had an important job in the ancient world. Pottery was preferred over leather or baskets, because it lasted longer, held liquids better, and protected things from animals and insects. Even broken pottery was useful. People etched notes on it because leather and papyrus – the paper of the day – were too expensive.

5Then the LORD spoke his word to me: 6"Family
of Israel, can't I do the same thing with you?"
says the LORD. "You are in my hands like the clay
in the potter's hands. 7There may come a time
when I will speak about a nation or a kingdom
that I will pull up by its roots or that I will pull
down to destroy it. 8But if the people of that na-
tion stop doing the evil they have done, I will
change my mind and not carry out my plans to
bring disaster to them. 9There may come another
time when I will speak about a nation that I will
build up and plant. 10But if I see it doing evil by
not obeying me, I will change my mind and not
carry out my plans to do good for them.

11"So, say this to the people of Judah and those
who live in Jerusalem: 'This is what the LORD
says: I am preparing disaster for you and making
plans against you. So stop doing evil. Change
your ways and do what is right.' 12But the people
of Judah will answer, 'It won't do any good to try!
We will continue to do what we want. Each of us
will do what his stubborn, evil heart wants!' "

13So this is what the LORD says:
"Ask the people in other nations this
question:
'Have you ever heard anything like this?'
The people of Israel have done a horrible
thing.
14The snow on the mountains of Lebanon
never melts from the rocks.
Its cool, flowing streams
do not dry up.
15But my people have forgotten me.
They burn incense to worthless idols
and have stumbled in what they do
and in the old ways of their ancestors.
They walk along back roads
and on poor highways.
16So Judah's country will become an empty
desert.
People will not stop making fun of it.
They will shake their heads as they pass by;
they will be shocked at how the country
was destroyed.
17Like a strong east wind,
I will scatter them before their enemies.
At that awful time they will not see me
coming to help them;
they will see me leaving."

Jeremiah's Fourth Complaint

18Then the people said, "Come, let's make
plans against Jeremiah. Surely the teaching of
the law by the priest will not be lost. We will still
have the advice from the wise men and the
words of the prophets.[d] So let's ruin him by
telling lies about him. We won't pay attention to
anything he says."

19LORD, listen to me.
Listen to what my accusers are saying!
20Good should not be paid back with evil,
but they have dug a pit in order to kill me.

Remember that I stood before you
and asked you to do good things for these
people
and to turn your anger away from them.
21So now, let their children starve,
and let their enemies kill them with
swords.
Let their wives lose their children and
husbands.
Let the men from Judah be put to death
and the young men be killed with swords
in battle.
22Let them cry out in their houses
when you bring an enemy against them
suddenly.
Let all this happen, because my enemies have
dug a pit to capture me
and have hidden traps for my feet.
23LORD, you know
about all their plans to kill me.
Don't forgive their crimes
or erase their sins from your mind.
Make them fall from their places;
punish them while you are angry.

Judah is like a Broken Jar

19 This is what the LORD said to me: "Go
and buy a clay jar from a potter. 2Take
some of the elders of the people and the priests,
and go out to the Valley of Ben Hinnom, near
the front of the Potsherd Gate. There speak the
words I tell you. 3Say, 'Kings of Judah and people
of Jerusalem, listen to this message from the LORD.
This is what the LORD All-powerful, the God of
Israel, says: I will soon bring a disaster on this
place that will amaze and frighten everyone who
hears about it. 4The people of Judah have stopped
following me. They have made this a place for
foreign gods. They have burnt sacrifices to other
gods that neither they, nor their ancestors, nor
the kings of Judah ever knew. They have filled
this place with the blood of innocent people.
5They have built places on hilltops to worship
Baal,[d] where they burn their children in the fire
to Baal. That is something I did not command or
speak about; it never even entered my mind.
6Now people call this place the Valley of Ben
Hinnom or Topheth, but the days are coming,
says the LORD, when people will call it the Valley
of Killing.
7" 'At this place I will ruin the plans of the
people of Judah and Jerusalem. The enemy will
chase them, and I will have them killed with
swords. I will make their dead bodies food for the
birds and wild animals. 8I will completely destroy
this city. People will make fun of it and shake
their heads when they pass by. They will be
shocked when they see how the city was des-
troyed. 9An enemy army will surround the city
and will not let anyone go out to get food. I will
make the people so hungry that they will eat the
bodies of their own sons and daughters, and then
they will begin to eat each other.'
10"While the people with you are watching,
break that jar. 11Then say this: 'The LORD All-
powerful says: I will break this nation and this
city just as someone breaks a clay jar that cannot
be put back together again. The dead people will
be buried here in Topheth, because there is no
other place for them. 12This is what I will do to
these people and to this place, says the LORD. I
will make this city like Topheth. 13The houses in
Jerusalem and the king's palaces will become as
unclean[d] as this place, Topheth, because the
people worshipped gods on the roofs[n] of their
houses. They worshipped the stars and burnt in-
cense[d] to honour them and gave drink offerings
to gods.' "
14When Jeremiah left Topheth where the LORD
had sent him to prophesy,[d] he went to the LORD's
Temple,[d] stood in the courtyard, and said to all
the people: 15"This is what the LORD All-powerful,
the God of Israel, says: 'I will soon bring disaster
to Jerusalem and the villages around it, as I said
I would. This will happen because the people are
very stubborn and do not listen at all to what
I say.' "

Pashhur will be Captured

20 Pashhur son of Immer was a priest and
the highest officer in the Temple[d] of the
LORD. When he heard Jeremiah prophesying[d] in
the Temple courtyard, 2he had Jeremiah the
prophet beaten. And he locked Jeremiah's hands
and feet between large blocks of wood at the
Upper Gate of Benjamin of the LORD's Temple.
3The next day when Pashhur took Jeremiah out
of the blocks of wood, Jeremiah said to him, "The
LORD's name for you is not Pashhur. Now his
name for you is Terror on Every Side. 4This is
what the LORD says: 'I will soon make you a terror
to yourself and to all your friends. You will watch
enemies killing your friends with swords. And I
will give all the people of Judah to the king of
Babylon, who will take them away as captives to
Babylon and then will kill them with swords. 5I
will give all the wealth of this city to its enemies—
its goods, its valuables and the treasures of the
kings of Judah. The enemies will carry all those
valuables off to Babylon. 6And Pashhur, you and

roofs In Bible times houses were built with flat roofs. The roof was used for drying things such as flax and fruit. And it was used as an extra room, as a place for worship and as a place to sleep in the summer.

everyone in your house will be taken captive. You will be forced to go to Babylon, where you will die and be buried, you and your friends to whom you have prophesied lies.' "

Jeremiah's Fifth Complaint

7LORD, you tricked me, and I was fooled.
You are stronger than I am, so you won.
I have become a joke;
everyone makes fun of me all day long.
8Every time I speak, I shout.
I am always shouting about violence and destruction.
I tell the people about the message I received from the LORD,
but this only brings me insults.
The people make fun of me all day long.
9Sometimes I say to myself,
"I will forget about the LORD.
I will not speak any more in his name."
But then his message becomes like a burning fire inside me,
deep within my bones.
I get tired of trying to hold it inside me,
and finally, I cannot hold it in.
10I hear many people whispering about me:
"Terror on every side!
Tell on him! Let's tell the rulers about him."
My friends are all just waiting for me to make some mistake.
They are saying,
"Maybe we can trick him
so we can defeat him
and pay him back."
11But the LORD is with me like a strong warrior,
so those who are chasing me will trip and fall;
they will not defeat me.
They will be ashamed because they have failed,
and their shame will never be forgotten.
12LORD All-powerful, you test good people;
you look deeply into the heart and mind of a person.
I have told you my arguments against these people,
so let me see you give them the punishment they deserve.

13Sing to the LORD!
Praise the LORD!
He saves the life of the poor
from the power of the wicked.

Jeremiah's Sixth Complaint

14Let there be a curse on the day I was born;
let there be no blessing on the day when my mother gave birth to me.
15Let there be a curse on the man
who brought my father the news:
"You have a son!"
This made my father very glad.
16Let that man be like the towns
the LORD destroyed without pity.
Let him hear loud crying in the morning
and battle cries at noon,
17because he did not kill me before I was born.
Then my mother would have been my grave;
she would have stayed pregnant for ever.
18Why did I have to come out of my mother's body?
All I have known is trouble and sorrow,
and my life will end in shame.

God Rejects King Zedekiah's Request

21 This is the word that the LORD spoke to
Jeremiah. It came when Zedekiah king
of Judah sent Pashhur son of Malkijah and the
priest Zephaniah son of Maaseiah to Jeremiah.
2They said, "Ask the LORD for us what will hap-
pen, because Nebuchadnezzar king of Babylon
is attacking us. Maybe the LORD will do mira-
cles[d] for us as he did in the past so Nebuchad-
nezzar will stop attacking us and leave."
3But Jeremiah answered them, "Tell King
Zedekiah this: 4'Here is what the LORD, the God
of Israel, says: you have weapons of war in your
hands to defend yourselves against the king of
Babylon and the Babylonians, who are all
around the city wall. But I will make those
weapons useless. Soon I will bring them into the
centre of this city. 5In my anger, my very great
anger, I myself will fight against you with my
great power and strength. 6I will kill everything
living in Jerusalem—both people and animals.
They will die from terrible diseases. 7Then, says
the LORD, I will hand over Zedekiah king of
Judah, his officers and the people in Jerusalem
who do not die from the terrible diseases or
battle or hunger, to Nebuchadnezzar king of
Babylon. I will let those win who want to kill
the people of Judah, so the people of Judah and
Jerusalem will be killed in war. Nebuchadnezzar
will not show any mercy or pity or feel sorry for
them!'
8"Also tell this to the people of Jerusalem:
'This is what the LORD says: I will let you choose
to live or die. 9Anyone who stays in Jerusalem
will die in war or from hunger or from a terrible
disease. But anyone who goes out of Jerusalem
and surrenders to the Babylonians who are
attacking you will live. Anyone who leaves the
city will save his life as if it were a prize won in
war. 10I have decided to make trouble for this

city and not to help it, says the LORD. I will give it to the king of Babylon, and he will burn it with fire.'

11"Say to Judah's royal family: 'Hear the word of the LORD. 12Family of David, this is what the LORD says:

You must judge people fairly every morning.
Save the person who has been robbed
from the power of his attacker.
If you don't, I will become very angry.
My anger will be like a fire that no one can put out,
because you have done evil things.

13" 'Jerusalem, I am against you,
you who live on top of the mountain
over this valley, says the LORD.
You say, "No one can attack us
or come into our strong city."
14But I will give you the punishment you deserve, says the LORD.
I will start a fire in your forests
that will burn up everything around you!' "

Judgement Against Evil Kings

22 This is what the LORD says: "Go down to
the palace of the king of Judah and
prophesy[d] this message there: 2'Hear the word of
the LORD, king of Judah, who rules from David's
throne. You and your officers, and your people
who come through these gates, listen! 3This is
what the LORD says: do what is fair and right. Save
the one who has been robbed from the power of
his attacker. Don't mistreat or hurt the foreigners,
orphans or widows. Don't kill innocent people
here. 4If you carefully obey these commands,
kings who sit on David's throne will come through
the gates of this palace with their officers and
people, riding in chariots and on horses. 5But if
you don't obey these commands, says the LORD,
I swear by my own name that this king's palace
will become a ruin.' "

6This is what the LORD says about the palace where the king of Judah lives:

"You are tall like the forests of Gilead,
like the mountain tops of Lebanon.
But I will truly make you into a desert,
into towns where no one lives.
7I will send men to destroy the palace,
each with his weapons.
They will cut up your strong, beautiful cedar beams
and throw them into the fire.

8"People from many nations will pass by this
city and ask each other, 'Why has the LORD done
such a terrible thing to Jerusalem, this great city?'
9And the answer will be: 'Because the people of
Judah stopped following the agreement with the
LORD their God. They worshipped and served
other gods.' "

Judgement Against Jehoahaz

10Don't cry for the dead king or be sad about him.
But cry painfully for the king who is being taken away,
because he will never return
or see his homeland again.

11This is what the LORD says about Jehoahaz
son of Josiah who became king of Judah after his
father died and who has left this place: "He will
never return. 12He will die where he has been
taken captive, and he will not see this land
again."

Judgement Against Jehoiakim

13"How terrible it will be for one who builds his palace by doing evil,
who cheats people so he can build its upper rooms.
He makes his own people work for nothing
and does not pay them.
14He says, 'I will build a great palace for myself
with large upper rooms.'
So he builds it with large windows
and uses cedar wood for the walls,
which he paints red.

15"Does having a lot of cedar in your house
make you a great king?
Your father was satisfied to have food and drink.
He did what was right and fair,
so everything went well for him.
16He helped those who were poor and needy,
so everything went well for him.
That is what it means to know God,"
says the LORD.
17"But you only look for and think about
what you can get dishonestly.
You are even willing to kill innocent people to get it.
You feel free to hurt people and to steal from them."

18So this is what the LORD says to Jehoiakim son
of Josiah king of Judah:

"The people of Judah will not cry when Jehoiakim dies,
saying: 'Oh, my brother,' or 'Oh, my sister.'
They will not cry for him, saying:
'Oh, master,' or 'Oh, my king.'
19They will bury him like a donkey,
dragging his body away
and throwing it outside the gates of Jerusalem.

[20]"Judah, go up to Lebanon and cry out.
Let your voice be heard in Bashan.
Cry out from Abarim,
because all your friends are destroyed!
[21]Judah, when you were successful, I warned you,
but you said, 'I won't listen.'
You have acted like this since you were young;
you have not obeyed me.
[22]Like a storm, my punishment will blow all your shepherds away
and send your friends into captivity.
Then you will really be ashamed and disgraced
because of all the wicked things you did.
[23]King, you live in your palace,
cosy in your rooms of cedar.
But when your punishment comes, how you will groan
like a woman giving birth to a baby!

Judgement Upon Jehoiachin

[24]"As surely as I live," says the LORD, "Je-
hoiachin son of Jehoiakim king of Judah, even if
you were a signet[d] ring on my right hand, I
would still pull you off. [25]I will hand you over to
Nebuchadnezzar king of Babylon and to the
Babylonians—those people you fear because
they want to kill you. [26]I will throw you and
your mother into another country. Neither of
you was born there, but both of you will die
there. [27]They will want to come back, but they
will never be able to return."

[28]Jehoiachin is like a broken pot someone threw away;
he is like something no one wants.
Why will Jehoiachin and his children be thrown out
and sent into a foreign land?
[29]Land, land, land of Judah,
hear the word of the LORD!
[30]This is what the LORD says:
"Write this down in the record about Jehoiachin:
He is a man without children,
a man who will not be successful in his lifetime.
And none of his descendants will be successful;
none will sit on the throne of David
or rule in Judah."

The Evil Leaders of Judah

23 "How terrible it will be for the leaders of
Judah, who are scattering and destroying
my people," says the LORD.

[2]They are responsible for the people, so the
LORD, the God of Israel, says to them: "You have
scattered my people and forced them away and
not taken care of them. So I will punish you for
the evil things you have done," says the LORD. [3]"I
sent my people to other countries, but I will
gather those who are left alive and bring them
back to their own country. Then they will have
many children and grow in number. [4]I will place
new leaders over my people, who will take care
of them. And my people will not be afraid or
terrified again, and none of them will be lost,"
says the LORD.

The Good Branch will Come

[5]"The days are coming," says the LORD,
"when I will raise up a good branch in David's family.
He will be a king who will rule in a wise way;
he will do what is fair and right in the land.
[6]In his time Judah will be saved
and Israel will live in safety.
This will be his name:
The LORD Does What Is Right.
[7]"So the days are coming," says the LORD, "when
people will not say again: 'As surely as the LORD
lives, who brought Israel out of Egypt . . .' [8]but
people will say something new: 'As surely as
the LORD lives, who brought the descendants of
Israel from the land of the north and from all the
countries where he had sent them away. . .' then
the people of Israel will live in their own land."

False Prophets will be Punished

[9]A message to the prophets:[d]
My heart is broken.
All my bones shake.
I'm like someone who is drunk,
like someone who has been overcome with wine.
This is because of the LORD
and his holy words.
[10]The land of Judah is full of people who are guilty of adultery.[d]
Because of this, the LORD cursed the land.
It has become a very sad place
and the pastures have dried up.
The people are evil
and use their power in the wrong way.

[11]"Both the prophets and the priests live as if there were no God.
I have found them doing evil things even in my own Temple,"[d] says the LORD.
[12]"So they will be in danger.
They will be forced into darkness
where they will be defeated.

I will bring disaster on them
in the year I punish them," says the LORD.

13"I saw the prophets of Samaria
do something wrong.
Those prophets prophesied by Baal[d]
and led my people Israel away.
14And I have seen the prophets of Jerusalem
do terrible things.
They are guilty of adultery
and live by lies.
They encourage evil people to keep on doing
evil,
so the people don't stop sinning.
All of those people are like the city of
Sodom.
The people of Jerusalem are like the city of
Gomorrah to me!"

15So this is what the LORD All-powerful says
about the prophets:
"I will make those prophets eat bitter food
and drink poisoned water,
because the prophets of Jerusalem spread
wickedness
through the whole country."

16This is what the LORD All-powerful says:
"Don't pay attention to what those prophets
are saying to you.
They are trying to fool you.
They talk about visions their own minds
made up,
not about visions from me.
17They say to those who hate me:
'The LORD says: you will have peace.'
They say to all those who are stubborn and do
as they please:
'Nothing bad will happen to you.'
18But none of these prophets has stood in the
meeting of angels
to see or hear the message of the LORD.
None of them has paid close attention to
his message.
19Look, the punishment from the LORD
will come like a storm.

LEADERSHIP

Who'll Pay For It?

Stephanie had nothing to do with the college "joke" that caused damages of about £1,000 to a small garden in the grounds. She didn't destroy the cherry tree, break the branches off another tree, or saw through the split-rail fence. But it was her picture that appeared on the front page of the local paper with the news story of the vandalism.

Why? Because as student union chair, Stephanie was responsible for answering to the press. She and the other union officers also had the responsibility to pay for the damage out of union funds. They had planned to donate those funds to the children's hospital.

Ironically, the garden had been constructed as a memorial to a student who died in 1974. The student's parents spent at least £7,000 of their own money to create the garden. This family, at the very least, deserved an apology. Whose responsibility was that?

Most student leaders consider that position to be an honour. But being a leader, Stephanie found out, also carries responsibility. In Judah, God held the leaders responsible for misguiding his people. See what God has to say to them in **Jeremiah 23:1–6**.

- Why do you think Stephanie and the leaders of Judah were held accountable for the things happening around them?
- What are some ways you can serve as a leader for God's people?

Consider . . .

- helping your family by taking responsibility for a household chore without being asked.
- offering your leadership in your school or church for a project that needs to be done, and then responsibly completing it.

For more, see . . .

- Micah 3:9–12 (p.892)
- 2 Peter 2:1–3 (p.1365)
- Matthew 23:13–36 (p.982)

His anger will be like a hurricane.
It will come swirling down on the heads of those wicked people.
20The LORD's anger will not stop
until he finishes what he plans to do.
When that day is over,
you will understand this clearly.
21I did not send those prophets,
but they ran to tell their message.
I did not speak to them,
but they prophesied anyway.
22But if they had stood in the meeting of angels,
they would have told my message to my people.
They would have turned the people from their evil ways
and from doing evil.

23"I am a God who is near," says the LORD.
"I am also a God who is far away."
24"No one can hide
where I cannot see him," says the LORD.
"I fill all of heaven and earth," says the LORD.

25"I have heard the prophets who prophesy lies
in my name. They say, 'I have had a dream! I
have had a dream!' 26How long will this continue
in the minds of these lying prophets? They proph-
esy from their own wishful thinking. 27They are
trying to make the people of Judah forget me by
telling each other these dreams. In the same way,
their ancestors forgot me and worshipped Baal.
28Is straw the same thing as wheat?" says the
LORD. "If a prophet wants to tell about his dreams,
let him! But let the person who hears my mes-
sage speak it truthfully! 29Isn't my message like a
fire?" says the LORD. "Isn't it like a hammer that
smashes a rock?
30"So I am against the false prophets," says
the LORD. "They keep stealing words from each
other and say they are from me. 31I am against the
false prophets," says the LORD. "They use their
own words and pretend it is a message from me.

HONESTY

Slow to Heal

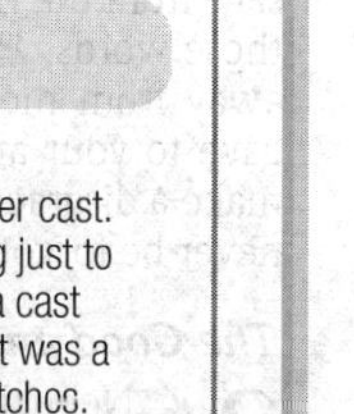

After coming second at the regional karate tournament, Dan McCarty got an invitation to a national competition. But one week before the trip, he tore the ligaments in his ankle and ended up in a plaster cast.

Still, nothing would stop Dan. He convinced his parents to let him make the trip anyway, promising just to watch the tournament. Once on his way, he told his karate instructor that the doctor had put him in a cast only as a precaution. He said he had both his doctor's and parents' permission to participate. Since it was a removable cast, he took it off when he got to the tournament and competed. He even won a few matches.

Although the cast was back on when he got home, his parents worked out what he had done by the way he talked about the competition. They felt betrayed!

Dan paid for his scheme: his ankle healed much more slowly than it would have otherwise. Luckily, the ankle wasn't permanently damaged.

Dan falsely used the authority of his doctor and parents to back up his lies to his instructor. In a similar way, false prophets appealed to God's authority to back up their lies in **Jeremiah 23:23–30**.

- Why were Dan's karate instructor and the people in the passage quick to accept lies?
- When people say, "Honest to God!" do you believe their story more than you would have otherwise? Why or why not?

Consider . . .

- tracking down a rumour you've heard at school and finding out how much is true.
- Mark Twain's comment on lying: "If you tell the truth you don't have to remember anything." Think of a time you've lied. Then make a list of all the other lies you had to tell to support it.

For more, see . . .

- Psalm 139:1–18 (p.581)
- 1 John 4:1–6 (p.1374)
- Matthew 5:33–37 (p.945)

32I am against the prophets who prophesy false
dreams," says the LORD. "They mislead my people
with their lies and false teachings! I did not send
them or command them to do anything for me.
They can't help the people of Judah at all," says
the LORD.

The Sad Message from the LORD

33"Suppose the people of Judah, a prophet[d] or
a priest asks you: 'Jeremiah, what is the message
from the LORD?' You will answer them and say,
'You are a heavy load to the LORD, and I will
throw you down, says the LORD.' 34A prophet or
a priest or one of the people might say, 'This is a
message from the LORD.' That person has lied, so
I will punish him and his whole family. 35This is
what you will say to each other: 'What did the
LORD answer?' or 'What did the LORD say?' 36But
you will never again say, 'The message of the
LORD', because the only message you speak is
your own words. You have changed the words of
our God, the living God, the LORD All-powerful.
37This is how you should speak to the prophets:
'What answer did the LORD give you?' or 'What
did the LORD say?' 38But don't say, 'The message
from the LORD'. If you use these words, this is
what the LORD says: because you called it a 'mes-
sage from the LORD', though I told you not to use
those words, 39I will pick you up and throw you
away from me, along with Jerusalem, which I
gave to your ancestors and to you. 40And I will
make a disgrace of you for ever; your shame will
never be forgotten."

The Good and Bad Figs

24 Nebuchadnezzar king of Babylon cap-
tured Jehoiachin son of Jehoiakim and
king of Judah, his officers and all the craftsmen
and metalworkers of Judah. He took them away
from Jerusalem and brought them to Babylon. It
was then that the LORD showed me two baskets of
figs arranged in front of the Temple[d] of the LORD.
2One of the baskets had very good figs in it, like
figs that ripen early in the season. But the other
basket had figs too rotten to eat.

3The LORD said to me, "What do you see,
Jeremiah?"

I answered, "I see figs. The good figs are very
good, but the rotten figs are too rotten to eat."

4Then the LORD spoke his word to me: 5"This
is what the LORD, the God of Israel, says: 'I sent
the people of Judah out of their country to live in
the country of Babylon. I think of those people as
good, like these good figs. 6I will look after them
and bring them back to the land of Judah. I will
not tear them down, but I will build them up. I
will not pull them up, but I will plant them so
they can grow. 7I will make them want to know
me, that I am the LORD. They will be my people,
and I will be their God, because they will return
to me with their whole hearts.

8" 'But the bad figs are too rotten to eat.' So this
is what the LORD says: 'Zedekiah king of Judah,
his officers and all the people from Jerusalem
who are left alive, even those who live in Egypt,
will be like those rotten figs. 9I will make those
people hated as an evil people by all the kingdoms
of the earth. People will make fun of them and
tell jokes about them and point fingers at them
and curse them everywhere I scatter them. 10I
will send war, hunger and disease against them.
I will attack them until they have all been killed.
Then they will no longer be in the land I gave to
them and their ancestors.' "

Sidelight Just as book reviews in newspapers give a summary of what each book is about, Jeremiah 25 was written as a summary of the prophet's ministry. So if you are feeling a little confused, Jeremiah 25 offers a brief review of the story so far . . .

A Summary of Jeremiah's Preaching

25 This is the message that came to Jeremiah
concerning all the people of Judah. It
came in the fourth year that Jehoiakim son of
Josiah was king of Judah and the first year
Nebuchadnezzar was king of Babylon. 2This is
the message Jeremiah the prophet[d] spoke to all
the people of Judah and Jerusalem:

3The LORD has spoken his word to me again
and again for these past 23 years. I have been a
prophet since the thirteenth year of Josiah son of
Amon king of Judah. I have spoken messages
from the LORD to you from that time until today,
but you have not listened.

4The LORD has sent all his servants the prophets
to you over and over again, but you have not
listened or paid any attention to them. 5Those
prophets have said, "Stop your evil ways. Stop
doing what is wrong so you can stay in the land
that the LORD gave to you and your ancestors to
live in for ever. 6Don't follow other gods to serve
them or to worship them. Don't make me, the
LORD, angry by worshipping idols that are the
work of your own hands, or I will punish you."

7"But you people of Judah did not listen to
me," says the LORD. "You made me angry by wor-
shipping idols that were the work of your own
hands, so I punished you."

8So this is what the LORD All-powerful says:
"Since you have not listened to my messages, 9I
will send for all the peoples of the north," says

the LORD, "along with my servant Nebuchadnezzar
king of Babylon. I will bring them all against
Judah, those who live there, and all the nations
around you, too. I will completely destroy all
those countries and leave them in ruins for ever.
People will be shocked when they see how badly
I have destroyed those countries. 10I will bring
an end to the sounds of joy and happiness, the
sounds of brides and bridegrooms, and the sound
of people grinding meal. And I will take away the
light of the lamp. 11That whole area will be an
empty desert, and these nations will be slaves of
the king of Babylon for 70 years.

12"But when the 70 years have passed, I will
punish the king of Babylon and his entire nation
for their evil," says the LORD. "I will make that
land a desert for ever. 13I will make happen all the
terrible things I said about Babylonia—everything
Jeremiah prophesied about all those foreign na-
tions, the warnings written in this book. 14Even
the Babylonians will have to serve many nations
and many great kings. I will give them the
punishment they deserve for all their own hands
have done."

Judgement on the Nations

15The LORD, the God of Israel, said this to me:
"My anger is like the wine in a cup. Take it from
my hand and make all the nations, to whom I am
sending you, drink all my anger from this cup.
16They will drink my anger and stumble about
and act like madmen because of the war I am
going to send among them."

17So I took the cup from the LORD's hand and
went to those nations and made them drink from
it. 18I served this wine to the people of Jerusalem
and the towns of Judah, and the kings and offi-
cers of Judah, so they would become a ruin. Then
people would be shocked and would insult them
and speak evil of them. And so it has been to this
day. 19I also made these people drink of the
LORD's anger: the king of Egypt, his servants, his
officers, all his people 20and all the foreigners
there; all the kings of the land of Uz; all the
kings of the Philistines (the kings of the cities of
Ashkelon, Gaza, Ekron and the people left at
Ashdod); 21the people of Edom, Moab and
Ammon; 22all the kings of Tyre and Sidon; all the
kings of the coastal countries to the west; 23the
people of Dedan and Tema and Buz; all who cut
their hair short; 24all the kings of Arabia; and the
kings of the people who live in the desert; 25all
the kings of Zimri, Elam and Media; 26and all the
kings of the north, near and far, one after the
other. I made all the kingdoms on earth drink
from the cup of the LORD's anger, but the king
of Babylon will drink from this cup after all the
others.

27"Then say to them, 'This is what the LORD
All-powerful, the God of Israel, says: drink this
cup of my anger. Get drunk from it and vomit.
Fall down and don't get up because of the war I
am sending among you!'

28"If they refuse to take the cup from your hand
and drink, say to them, 'The LORD All-powerful
says this: you must drink from this cup. 29Look! I
am already bringing disaster on Jerusalem, the
city that is called by my name. Do you think you
will not be punished? You will be punished! I am
sending war on all the people of the earth, says
the LORD All-powerful.'

30"You, Jeremiah, will prophesy[d] against them
with all these words. Say to them:

'The LORD will roar from heaven
and will shout from his Holy Temple.[d]
He will roar loudly against his land.
He will shout like people who walk on
grapes to make wine;
he will shout against all who live on the
earth.
31The noise will spread all over the earth,
because the LORD will accuse all the
nations.
He will judge and tell what is wrong with all
people,
and he will kill the evil people with a
sword,' " says the LORD.

32This is what the LORD All-powerful says:
"Disasters will soon spread
from nation to nation.
They will come like a powerful storm
from the faraway places on earth."

33At that time those killed by the LORD will reach
from one end of the earth to the other. No one
will cry for them or gather up their bodies and
bury them. They will be left lying on the ground
like dung.

34Cry, you leaders! Cry out loud!
Roll around in the dust, leaders of the
people!
It is now time for you to be killed.
You will fall and be scattered,
like pieces of a broken jar.
35There will be no place for the leaders to hide;
they will not escape.
36I hear the sound of the leaders shouting.
I hear the leaders of the people crying
loudly,
because the LORD is destroying their land.
37Those peaceful pastures will be like an empty
desert,
because the LORD is very angry.
38Like a lion, he has left his den.
Their land has been destroyed

because of the terrible war he brought,
because of his fierce anger.

Jeremiah's Lesson at the Temple

26 This message came from the LORD soon
after Jehoiakim son of Josiah became
king of Judah. 2This is what the LORD said:
"Jeremiah, stand in the courtyard of the Temple[d]
of the LORD. Give this message to all the people of
the towns of Judah who are coming to worship at
the Temple of the LORD. Tell them everything I
tell you to say; don't leave out a word. 3Perhaps
they will listen and stop their evil ways. If they
will, I will change my mind about bringing on
them the disaster that I am planning because of
the evil they have done. 4Say to them: 'This is
what the LORD says: you must obey me and follow
my teachings that I gave you. 5You must listen to
what my servants the prophets[d] say to you. I
have sent them to you again and again, but you
did not listen. 6If you don't obey me, I will destroy
my Temple in Jerusalem as I destroyed my Holy
Tent[d] at Shiloh. When I do, people all over the
world will curse Jerusalem.'"
7The priests, the prophets and all the people
heard Jeremiah speaking these words in the Tem-
ple of the LORD. 8When Jeremiah finished speak-
ing everything the LORD had commanded him
to say, the priests, prophets and all the people
grabbed Jeremiah. They said, "You must die!
9How dare you prophesy in the name of the LORD
that this Temple will be destroyed like the one at
Shiloh! How dare you say that Jerusalem will be-
come a desert without anyone to live in it!" And
all the people crowded around Jeremiah in the
Temple of the LORD.
10Now when the officers of Judah heard about
what was happening, they came out of the king's
palace and went up to the Temple of the LORD and
took their places at the entrance of the New Gate.
11Then the priests and prophets said to the offi-
cers and all the other people, "Jeremiah should

PEER PRESSURE

Quick Comeback

Tim's alcohol and drug abuse started as a simple desire to be "one of the lads". Tim wanted to fit in with his older brother and his brother's friends. Drinking and getting high were ways to do that.

Before long, Tim went from feeling peer pressure to delivering it. "I became the bad influence," he remembers. He would encourage friends to get drunk at parties, and he persuaded people who had never used drugs to get high.

One day, when Tim couldn't obtain any drugs or alcohol, he lost his temper and was beaten up in a fight. Then he saw himself in the mirror – and realised how desperate he was. Tim went for treatment for alcoholism and drug abuse. Thankfully, he's been able to stay clean and sober for ten months. And peer pressure hasn't deterred him.

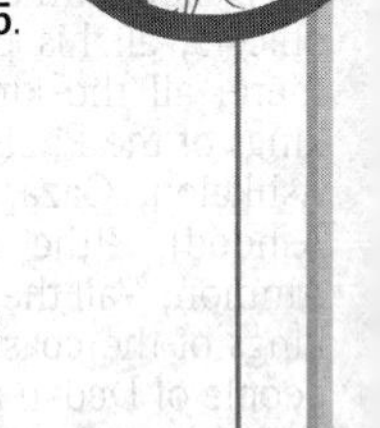

Tim still sees some of his old friends who drink. But they don't try to get Tim to drink. And if they did, Tim would know how to respond. "You've made your choice to use drugs or alcohol," he'd say. "Please respect my choice."

Jeremiah's peers wanted him to stop preaching God's word to them. They used the ultimate peer pressure threat: stop preaching, or we'll kill you. See how he responded in **Jeremiah 26:8–15**.

- What are the differences between Tim's friends and the people of Jeremiah's time?
- How is peer pressure today different from the peer pressure in this passage?

Consider . . .

- talking to a parent about the negative peer pressure he or she experiences – and how he or she deals with it.
- asking a close friend to form a partnership for positive peer pressure and perhaps writing a "contract" of specific ways you'll help each other.

For more, see . . .

- Daniel 3 (p.835)
- Acts 4:1–22 (p.1143)
- Matthew 5:10–12 (p.942)

be killed. He prophesied against Jerusalem, and
you heard him yourselves."
12Then Jeremiah spoke these words to all the
officers of Judah and all the other people: "The
LORD sent me to say everything you have heard
about this Temple and this city. 13Now change
your lives and start doing good and obey the LORD
your God. Then he will change his mind and not
bring on you the disaster he has told you about.
14As for me, I am in your power. Do to me what
you think is good and right. 15But be sure of one
thing. If you kill me, you will be guilty of killing
an innocent person. You will make this city and
everyone who lives in it guilty too! The LORD truly
sent me to you to give you this message."
16Then the officers and all the people said to
the priests and the prophets, "Jeremiah must not
be killed. What he told us comes from the LORD
our God."
17Then some of the elders of Judah stood up
and said to all the people, 18"Micah, from the
city of Moresheth, was a prophet during the time
Hezekiah was king of Judah. Micah said to all
the people of Judah, 'This is what the LORD All-
powerful says:

Jerusalem will be ploughed like a field.
It will become a pile of rocks,
and the hill where the Temple stands will
be covered with bushes.'

19"Hezekiah king of Judah and the people of
Judah did not kill Micah. You know that Hezekiah
feared the LORD and tried to please the LORD. So
the LORD changed his mind and did not bring
on Judah the disaster he had promised. If we
hurt Jeremiah, we will bring a terrible disaster
on ourselves!"
20(Now there was another man who prophes-
ied in the name of the LORD. His name was Uriah
son of Shemaiah from the city of Kiriath Jearim.
He preached the same things against Jerusalem
and the land of Judah that Jeremiah did. 21When
King Jehoiakim, all his army officers and all
the leaders of Judah heard Uriah preach, King
Jehoiakim wanted to kill Uriah. But Uriah heard
about it and was afraid. So he escaped to Egypt.
22Then King Jehoiakim sent Elnathan son of Acbor
and some other men to Egypt, 23and they brought
Uriah back from Egypt. Then they took him to
King Jehoiakim, who had Uriah killed with a
sword. His body was thrown into the burial place
where poor people are buried.)
24Ahikam son of Shaphan supported Jeremiah.
So Ahikam did not hand Jeremiah over to be
killed by the people.

Nebuchadnezzar is Made Ruler

27 The LORD spoke his word to Jeremiah
soon after Zedekiah son of Josiah was
made king of Judah. 2This is what the LORD said
to me: "Make a yoke[d] out of straps and poles,
and put it on the back of your neck. 3Then send
messages to the kings of Edom, Moab, Ammon,
Tyre and Sidon by their messengers who have
come to Jerusalem to see Zedekiah king of
Judah. 4Tell them to give this message to their
masters: 'The LORD All-powerful, the God of
Israel, says: "Tell your masters: 5I made the
earth, its people and all its animals with my great
power and strength. I can give the earth to any-
one I want. 6Now I have given all these lands to
Nebuchadnezzar king of Babylon, my servant. I
will make even the wild animals obey him. 7All
nations will serve Nebuchadnezzar and his son
and grandson. Then the time will come for Babylon
to be defeated, and many nations and great kings
will make Babylon their servant.
8" ' "But if some nations or kingdoms refuse to
serve Nebuchadnezzar king of Babylon and re-
fuse to be under his control, I will punish them
with war, hunger and terrible diseases, says the
LORD. I will use Nebuchadnezzar to destroy them.
9So don't listen to your false prophets,[d] those
who use magic to tell the future, those who ex-
plain dreams, the mediums[d] or magicians. They
all tell you, 'You will not be slaves to the king of
Babylon.' 10They are telling you lies that will
cause you to be taken far from your homeland. I
will force you to leave your homes, and you will die
in another land. 11But the nations who put them-
selves under the control of the king of Babylon
and serve him I will let stay in their own country,
says the LORD. The people from those nations
will live in their own land and farm it." ' "
12I gave the same message to Zedekiah king of
Judah. I said, "Put yourself under the control of the
king of Babylon and serve him, and you will live.
13Why should you and your people die from war,
hunger or disease, as the LORD said would happen
to those who do not serve the king of Babylon?
14But the false prophets are saying, 'You will never
be slaves to the king of Babylon.' Don't listen to
them because they are prophesying lies to you! 15'I
did not send them,' says the LORD. 'They are
prophesying lies and saying the message is from
me. So I will send you away, Judah. And you and
those prophets who prophesy to you will die.' "
16Then I, Jeremiah, said to the priests and all
the people, "This is what the LORD says: Those
false prophets are saying, 'The Babylonians will
soon return what they took from the Temple[d]
of the LORD.' Don't listen to them! They are
prophesying lies to you. 17Don't listen to those
prophets. But serve the king of Babylon, and you
will live. There is no reason for you to cause
Jerusalem to become a ruin. 18If they are prophets
and have the message from the LORD, let them

pray to the LORD All-powerful. Let them ask that the things which are still in the Temple of the LORD and in the king's palace and in Jerusalem not be taken away to Babylon.

19"This is what the LORD All-powerful says about those things left in Jerusalem, the pillars, the large bronze bowl, which is called the Sea, the stands that can be moved and other things. 20Nebuchadnezzar king of Babylon did not take these away when he took as captives Jehoiachin son of Jehoiakim king of Judah and all the other important people from Judah and Jerusalem to Babylon. 21This is what the LORD All-powerful, the God of Israel, says about the things left in the Temple of the LORD and in the king's palace and in Jerusalem: 22'All of them will also be taken to Babylon. And they will stay there until the day I go to get them,' says the LORD. 'Then I will bring them back and return them to this place.' "

The False Prophet Hananiah

28 It was in that same year, in the fifth month of Zedekiah's fourth year as king of Judah, soon after he began to rule. The prophet[d] Hananiah son of Azzur, from the town of Gibeon, spoke to me in the Temple[d] of the LORD in front of the priests and all the people. He said: 2"The LORD All-powerful, the God of Israel, says: 'I have broken the yoke[d] the king of Babylon has put on Judah. 3Before two years are over, I will bring back everything that Nebuchadnezzar king of Babylon took to Babylon from the LORD's Temple. 4I will also bring back Jehoiachin son of Jehoiakim king of Judah and all the other captives from Judah who went to Babylon,' says the LORD. 'So I will break the yoke the king of Babylon put on Judah.' "

5Then the prophet Jeremiah spoke to the prophet Hananiah in front of the priests and all the people who were standing in the Temple[d] of the LORD. 6He said, "Amen! Let the LORD really do that! May the LORD make the message you prophesy come true. May he bring back here everything from the LORD's Temple and all the people who were taken as captives to Babylon.

7"But listen to what I am going to say to you and all the people. 8There were prophets long before we became prophets, Hananiah. They prophesied that war, hunger and terrible diseases would come to many countries and great kingdoms. 9But if a prophet prophesies that we will have peace and that message comes true, he can be recognised as one truly sent by the LORD."

10Then the prophet Hananiah took the yoke off Jeremiah's neck and broke it. 11Hananiah said in front of all the people, "This is what the LORD says: 'In the same way I will break the yoke of Nebuchadnezzar king of Babylon. He put that yoke on all the nations of the world, but I will break it before two years are over.' " After Hananiah had said that, Jeremiah left the Temple.

12The LORD spoke his word to Jeremiah after the prophet Hananiah had broken the yoke off the prophet Jeremiah's neck. 13The LORD said, "Go and tell Hananiah, 'This is what the LORD says: You have broken a wooden yoke, but I will make a yoke of iron in its place! 14The LORD All-powerful, the God of Israel, says: I will put a yoke of iron on the necks of all these nations to make them serve Nebuchadnezzar king of Babylon, and they will be slaves to him. I will even give Nebuchadnezzar control over the wild animals.' "

15Then the prophet Jeremiah said to the prophet Hananiah, "Listen, Hananiah! The LORD did not send you, and you have made the people of Judah trust in lies. 16So this is what the LORD says: 'Soon I will remove you from the earth. You will die this year, because you taught the people to turn against the LORD.' "

17Hananiah died in the seventh month of that same year.

A Letter to the Captives in Babylon

29 This is the letter that Jeremiah the prophet[d] sent from Jerusalem to the elders who were among the captives, the priests and the prophets. He sent it to all the other people Nebuchadnezzar had taken as captives from Jerusalem to Babylon. 2(This letter was sent after all these people were taken away: Jehoiachin the king and the queen mother; the officers and leaders of Judah and Jerusalem; and the craftsmen and metalworkers from Jerusalem.) 3Zedekiah king of Judah sent Elasah son of Shaphan and Gemariah son of Hilkiah to Babylon to Nebuchadnezzar king of Babylon. So Jeremiah gave them this letter to carry to Babylon:

> 4This is what the LORD All-powerful, the God of Israel, says to all those people I sent away from Jerusalem as captives to Babylon: 5"Build houses and settle in the land. Plant gardens and eat the food they grow. 6Get married and have sons and daughters. Find wives for your sons, and let your daughters be married so they also may have sons and daughters. Have many children in Babylon; don't become fewer in number. 7Also do good things for the city where I sent you as captives. Pray to the LORD for the city where you are living, because if good things happen in the city, good things will happen to you also." 8The LORD All-powerful, the God of Israel, says: "Don't let the prophets among you and the people who do magic fool you. Don't listen to their dreams.

9They are prophesying lies to you, saying
that their message is from me. But I did
not send them," says the LORD.
10This is what the LORD says: "Babylon
will be powerful for 70 years. After that time
I will come to you, and I will keep my prom-
ise to bring you back to Jerusalem. 11I say
this because I know what I am planning for
you," says the LORD. "I have good plans for
you, not plans to hurt you. I will give you
hope and a good future. 12Then you will call
my name. You will come to me and pray
to me, and I will listen to you. 13You will
search for me. And when you search for me
with all your heart, you will find me! 14I will
let you find me," says the LORD. "And I will
bring you back from your captivity. I forced
you to leave this place, but I will gather you
from all the nations, from the places I have
sent you as captives," says the LORD. "And I
will bring you back to this place."
15You might say, "The LORD has given us
prophets here in Babylon."
16But the LORD says this about the king
who is sitting on David's throne now and all
the other people still in Jerusalem, your rel-
atives who did not go as captives to Babylon
with you. 17The LORD All-powerful says: "I
will soon send war, hunger and terrible dis-
eases against those still in Jerusalem. I will
make them like bad figs that are too rotten
to eat. 18I will chase them with war, hunger
and terrible diseases. I will make them hated
by all the kingdoms of the earth. People will
curse them and be shocked and will use
them as a shameful example wherever I
make them go. 19This is because they have
not listened to my message," says the LORD.
"I sent my message to them again and again
through my servants, the prophets, but they
did not listen," says the LORD.
20You captives, whom I forced to leave
Jerusalem and go to Babylon, listen to the
message from the LORD. 21The LORD All-
powerful, the God of Israel, says this about
Ahab son of Kolaiah and Zedekiah son of
Maaseiah: "These two men have been
prophesying lies to you, saying that their
message is from me. But soon I will hand
over those two prophets to Nebuchadnezzar
king of Babylon, and he will kill them in
front of you. 22Because of them, all the cap-
tives from Judah in Babylon will use this
curse: 'May the LORD treat you like Zedekiah
and Ahab, whom the king of Babylon
burned in the fire.' 23They have done evil
things among the people of Israel. They are
guilty of adultery[d] with their neighbours'
wives. They have also spoken lies and said
those lies were a message from me. I did not
tell them to do that. I know what they have
done; I am a witness to it," says the LORD.

24Also give a message to Shemaiah from the
Nehelamite family. 25The LORD All-powerful, the
God of Israel, says: "Shemaiah, you sent letters in
your name to all the people in Jerusalem, to the
priest Zephaniah son of Maaseiah, and to all the
priests. 26You said to Zephaniah, 'The LORD has
made you priest in place of Jehoiada. You are
to be in charge of the Temple[d] of the LORD.
You should arrest any madman who acts like
a prophet. Lock his hands and feet between
wooden blocks, and put iron rings around his
neck. 27Now Jeremiah from Anathoth is acting
like a prophet. So why haven't you arrested him?
28Jeremiah has sent this message to us in Babylon:
you will be there for a long time, so build houses
and settle down. Plant gardens and eat what they
grow.' "
29Zephaniah the priest read the letter to
Jeremiah the prophet. 30Then the LORD spoke his
word to Jeremiah: 31"Send this message to all the
captives in Babylon: 'This is what the LORD says
about Shemaiah the Nehelamite: Shemaiah has
prophesied to you, but I did not send him. He has
made you believe a lie. 32So the LORD says, I will
soon punish Shemaiah the Nehelamite and his
family. He will not see the good things I will do
for my people, says the LORD. None of his family
will be left alive among the people, because he
has taught the people to turn against me.' "

Sidelight

Jeremiah pulls no punches in telling the world exactly what God thinks. But at the same time he offers hope for his people (Jeremiah 30 and 33). Because of this, these two chapters have traditionally been called the "Book of Consolation" or the "Little Book of Comfort".

Promises of Hope

30 These are the words that the LORD spoke
to Jeremiah. 2The LORD, the God of Israel,
said: "Jeremiah, write in a book all the words I
have spoken to you. 3The days will come when
I will bring Israel and Judah back from captivity,"
says the LORD. "I will return them to the land I
gave their ancestors, and they will own it!" says
the LORD.
4The LORD spoke this message about the people
of Israel and Judah: 5this is what the LORD said:
"We hear people crying from fear.
They are afraid; there is no peace.

6Ask this question, and consider it:
a man cannot have a baby.
So why do I see every strong man
holding his stomach in pain like a woman
having a baby?
Why is everyone's face turning white like a
dead man's face?
7This will be a terrible day!
There will never be another time like this.
This is a time of great trouble for the people
of Jacob,
but they will be saved from it."

8The LORD All-powerful says, "At that time
I will break the yoke[d] from their necks
and tear off the ropes that hold them.
Foreign people will never again make my
people slaves.
9They will serve the LORD their God
and David their king,
whom I will send to them.

10"So people of Jacob, my servants, don't be
afraid.
Israel, don't be frightened," says the
LORD.
"I will soon save you from that faraway place
where you are captives.
I will save your family from that land.
The people of Jacob will be safe and have
peace again;
there will be no enemy to frighten them.
11I am with you and will save you,"
says the LORD.
"I will completely destroy all those nations
where I scattered you,
but I will not completely destroy you.
I will punish you fairly,
but I will still punish you."

12This is what the LORD says:
"You people have a wound that cannot be
cured;
your injury will not heal.
13There is no one to argue your case
and no cure for your sores.
So you will not be healed.
14All those nations who were your friends have
forgotten you.
They don't care about you.
I have hurt you as an enemy would.
I punished you very hard,
because your guilt was so great
and your sins were so many.
15Why are you crying out about your injury?
There is no cure for your pain.
I did these things to you because of your
great guilt,
because of your many sins.
16But all those nations that destroyed you will
now be destroyed.
All your enemies will become captives in
other lands.
Those who stole from you will have their
own things stolen.
Those who took things from you in war
will have their own things taken.
17I will bring back your health
and heal your injuries," says the LORD,
"because other people forced you away.
They said about you, 'No one cares for
Jerusalem!'"

18This is what the LORD says:
"I will soon make the tents of Jacob's people
as they used to be,
and I will have pity on Israel's houses.
The city will be rebuilt on its hill of ruins,
and the king's palace will stand in its
proper place.
19People in those places will sing songs of
praise.
There will be the sound of laughter.
I will give them many children
so their number will not be small.
I will bring honour to them
so no one will look down on them.
20Their descendants[d] will be as they were in
the old days.
I will set them up as a strong people
before me,
and I will punish the nations who have hurt
them.
21One of their own people will lead them;
their ruler will come from among them.
He will come near to me when I invite him.
Who would dare to come to me
uninvited?" says the LORD.
22"So you will be my people,
and I will be your God."

23Look! It is a storm from the LORD!
He is angry and has gone out to punish the
people.
Punishment will come like a storm
crashing down on the evil people.
24The LORD will stay angry
until he finishes punishing the people.
He will stay angry
until he finishes the punishment he
planned.
When that day comes,
you will understand this.

The New Israel

31 The LORD says, "At that time I will be
God of all Israel's family groups, and they
will be my people."

2This is what the LORD says:
"The people who were not killed by the
enemy's sword
found help in the desert.
I came to give rest to Israel."

3And from far away the LORD appeared to his
people and said,
"I love you people
with a love that will last for ever.
That is why I have continued
showing you kindness.
4People of Israel, I will build you up again
and you will be rebuilt.
You will pick up your tambourines [d]
again
and dance with those who are joyful.
5You will plant vineyards again
on the hills around Samaria.
The farmers will plant them
and enjoy their fruit.
6There will be a time when watchmen in the
mountains of Ephraim shout this
message:
'Come, let's go up to Jerusalem to worship
the LORD our God!' "

7This is what the LORD says:
"Be happy and sing for the people of Jacob.
Shout for Israel, the greatest of the nations.
Sing your praises and shout this:
'LORD, save your people,
those who are left alive from the nation of
Israel!'
8Look, I will soon bring Israel from the
country in the north,
and I will gather them from the faraway
places on earth.
Some of the people are blind and crippled.
Some of the women are pregnant, and
some are ready to give birth.
A great many people will come back.

CELEBRATING

Remembering Matt

Matt Floyd, seventeen, finished writing his talk for the retreat and attended a planning meeting on Sunday, but he never gave his talk. Three days later, while walking in the mountains, Matt lost his footing and fell to his death.

Matt's death shocked the other members of the youth group. But over the next few weeks, they pulled together and learned how to celebrate even in the face of tragedy. They attended Matt's funeral and celebrated the seventeen years of life God had granted him.

Then they went on with the retreat, introducing other teenagers to the God whom Matt knew. Matt's talk was read at the time he was supposed to give it. Kids cried as they listened to his words and remembered his voice. Some of the team members wore friendship bands to remind them of Matt's friendship. At the end of the weekend, they offered those bands to God.

"When Matt died we thought about cancelling the retreat," said one of the planning team members. "But I'm glad we didn't. God brought us closer together and helped us celebrate the blessings Matt had brought us."

Matt's friends learned that even in the midst of tragedies, we can celebrate God's goodness. Read how God encourages celebration – in hard times as well as good ones – in **Jeremiah 31:1–17**.

- What role does God play in the celebrations for Matt and the ones described in the passage?
- How do these celebrations compare to your ideas about celebrating?

Consider . . .

- celebrating what God has done for you the next time you are in a tough situation.
- writing your thoughts and memories of a relative or friend who has died, celebrating what that person meant to you.

For more, see . . .

- Nehemiah 8:9–12 (p.450)
- Luke 1:68–79 (p.1038)
- Psalm 150 (p.588)

9They will be crying as they come,
but they will pray as I bring them back.
I will lead those people by streams of water
on an even road where they will not stumble.
I am Israel's father,
and Israel is my firstborn[d] son.

10"Nations, listen to the message from the LORD.
Tell this message in the faraway lands by the sea:
'The one who scattered the people of Israel will bring them back,
and he will watch over his people like a shepherd.'
11The LORD will pay for the people of Jacob
and will buy them back from people stronger than they were.
12The people of Israel will come to the high points of Jerusalem
and shout for joy.
Their faces will shine with happiness about all the good things from the LORD:
the grain, new wine, oil, young sheep and young cows.
They will be like a garden that has plenty of water,
and they will not be troubled any more.
13Then young women of Israel will be happy and dance,
the young men and old men also.
I will change their sadness into happiness;
I will give them comfort and joy instead of sadness.
14The priests will have more than enough sacrifices,
and my people will be filled with the good things I give them!" says the LORD.

15This is what the LORD says:
"A voice was heard in Ramah
of painful crying and deep sadness:
Rachel crying for her children.
She refused to be comforted,
because her children are dead!"

16But this is what the LORD says:
"Stop crying;
don't let your eyes fill with tears.
You will be rewarded for your work!" says the LORD.
"The people will return from their enemy's land.
17So there is hope for you in the future," says the LORD.
"Your children will return to their own land.

18"I have heard Israel moaning:
'LORD, you punished me, and I have learned my lesson.
I was like a calf that had never been trained.
Take me back so that I may come back.
You truly are the LORD my God.
19LORD, after I wandered away from you,
I changed my heart and life.
After I understood,
I beat my breast with sorrow.
I was ashamed and disgraced,
because I suffered for the foolish things I did when I was young.'

20"You know that Israel is my dear son,
The child I love.
Yes, I often speak against Israel,
but I still remember him.
I love him very much
and I want to comfort him," says the LORD.

21"People of Israel, fix the road signs.
Put up signs to show you the way home.
Watch the road.
Pay attention to the road on which you travel.
People of Israel, come home,
come back to your towns.
22You are an unfaithful daughter.
How long will you wander before you come home?
The LORD has made something new happen in the land:
a woman will go seeking a man."

23The LORD All-powerful, the God of Israel,
says: "I will again do good things for the people
of Judah. At that time the people in the land of
Judah and its towns will again use these words:
'May the LORD bless you, home of what is good,
holy mountain.' 24People in all the towns of
Judah will live together in peace. Farmers and
those who move around with their flocks will live
together in peace. 25I will give rest and strength
to those who are weak and tired."
26After hearing that, I, Jeremiah, woke up and
looked around. My sleep had been very pleasant.
27The LORD says, "The time is coming when I
will help the families of Israel and Judah and their
children and animals to grow. 28In the past I
watched over Israel and Judah, to pull them up and
tear them down, to destroy them and bring them
disaster. But now I will watch over them to build
them up and make them strong," says the LORD.
29"At that time people will no longer say:
'The parents have eaten sour grapes,
and that caused the children to grind their teeth from the sour taste.'

30Instead, each person will die for his own sin;
the person who eats sour grapes will grind his
own teeth.

The New Agreement

31"Look, the time is coming," says the LORD,
"when I will make a new agreement
with the people of Israel
and the people of Judah.
32It will not be like the agreement
I made with their ancestors
when I took them by the hand
to bring them out of Egypt.
I was a husband to them,
but they broke that agreement," says the
LORD.
33"This is the agreement I will make
with the people of Israel at that time," says
the LORD:
"I will put my teachings in their minds
and write them on their hearts.
I will be their God,
and they will be my people.
34People will no longer have to teach their
neighbours and relatives
to know the LORD,
because all people will know me,
from the least to the most important," says
the LORD.
"I will forgive them for the wicked things
they did,
and I will not remember their sins any more."

The LORD will Never Leave Israel

35The LORD makes the sun shine in the day
and the moon and stars to shine at night.
He stirs up the sea so that its waves crash on
the shore.
The LORD All-powerful is his name.
This is what the LORD says:
36"Only if these laws should ever fail,"
says the LORD,

PROMISES

Changing Lives

Aristides Alvarado, twenty, is in his second year at university. But when he was in primary school, most people who knew him gave him less than a 50 per cent chance of passing any exams at all. Fortunately, "most people" didn't include Eugene M. Lang.

Lang is a wealthy businessman, in fact, a millionaire. A number of years ago, he returned to his primary school – one of the poorest schools in the United States. He promised 61 pupils, including Aristides, that if they passed the necessary exams he would pay for their college education.

Lang is keeping that promise. He helped those students through the final years of school, paying for trips and even tutors to help them stay on. About a half of the original 61 are in college, and their education is being paid for through Lang's "I Have a Dream" Foundation.

The students, who call themselves "Dreamers" are deeply grateful that Lang is keeping his promise.

"Mr Lang was one of the first people who took an interest in me," says Aristides. "I know I'm going to make it. And someday I'll be big – really big – and pay the tuition for my class of dreamers."

Lang and his friends aren't the only ones keeping promises these days. Read about God's promises in **Jeremiah 31:27–37**.

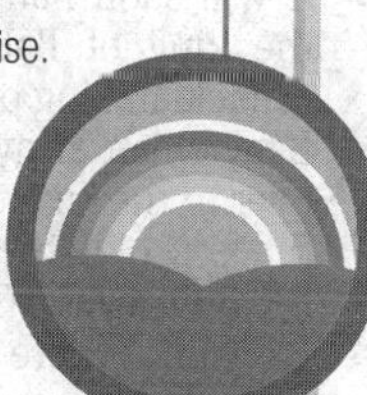

- What effects might Lang's or God's promises have on the people involved?
- What choices must you make to receive the benefit of God's promises?

Consider . . .

- reading Jesus' teaching in the Beatitudes (Matthew 5:1–12, p.942). Imagine Jesus using your name in his promises for believers.
- keeping a promise you've neglected.

For more, see . . .

- Lamentations 3:22–25 (p.783)
- John 2:18–22 (p.1098)
- Matthew 7:7–11 (p.950)

"will Israel's descendants[d] ever stop
being a nation before me."

37This is what the LORD says:
"Only if people can measure the sky above
and learn the secrets of the earth below,
will I reject all the descendants of Israel
because of what they have done," says the
LORD.

The New Jerusalem

38The LORD says, "The time is coming when
Jerusalem will be rebuilt for me—everything
from the Tower of Hananel to the Corner Gate.
39The measuring line will stretch from the Cor-
ner Gate straight to the hill of Gareb. Then it
will turn to the place named Goah. 40The whole
valley where dead bodies and ashes are thrown,
and all the terraces out to the Kidron Valley on
the east as far as the corner of the Horse Gate—
all that area will be holy to the LORD. The city
of Jerusalem will never again be torn down or
destroyed."

Jeremiah Buys a Field

32 This is the word the LORD spoke to
Jeremiah in the tenth year Zedekiah was
king of Judah, which was the eighteenth year of
Nebuchadnezzar. 2At that time the army of the
king of Babylon was surrounding Jerusalem. Je-
remiah the prophet was under arrest in the
courtyard of the guard, which was at the palace
of the king of Judah.
3Zedekiah king of Judah had put Jeremiah
in prison there. Zedekiah had asked, "Why
have you prophesied[d] the things you have?"
(Jeremiah had said, "This is what the LORD says:
'I will soon hand the city of Jerusalem over to
the king of Babylon, and he will capture it.
4Zedekiah king of Judah will not escape from the
Babylonian army, but he will surely be handed
over to the king of Babylon. And he will speak to
the king of Babylon face to face and see him with
his own eyes. 5The king will take Zedekiah to
Babylon, where he will stay until I have pun-
ished him,' says the LORD. 'If you fight against
the Babylonians, you will not succeed.' ")
6While Jeremiah was in prison, he said,
"The LORD spoke this word to me: 7Your cousin
Hanamel, son of your uncle Shallum, will come
to you soon. Hanamel will say to you, 'Jeremiah,
you are my nearest relative, so buy my field near
the town of Anathoth. It is your right and your
duty to buy that field.'
8"Then it happened just as the LORD had said.
My cousin Hanamel came to me in the courtyard
of the guard and said to me, 'Buy for yourself my
field near Anathoth in the land of Benjamin. It is
your right and duty to buy it and own it.' So I
knew this was a message from the LORD.
9"I bought the field at Anathoth from my
cousin Hanamel, weighing out 17 pieces of silver
for him. 10I signed the record and sealed it and
had some people witness it. I also weighed out
the silver on the scales. 11Then I took both copies
of the record of ownership—the one that was
sealed that had the demands and limits of owner-
ship, and the one that was not sealed. 12And I
gave them to Baruch son of Neriah, the son of
Mahseiah. My cousin Hanamel, the other wit-
nesses who signed the record of ownership, and
many Jews sitting in the courtyard of the guard
saw me give the record of ownership to Baruch.
13"With all the people watching, I told Baruch,
14'This is what the LORD All-powerful, the God of
Israel, says: Take both copies of the record of
ownership—the sealed copy and the copy that
was not sealed—and put them in a clay jar so
they will last a long time. 15This is what the LORD
All-powerful, the God of Israel, says: in the future
my people will once again buy houses and fields
for grain and vineyards in the land of Israel.'
16"After I gave the record of ownership to
Baruch son of Neriah, I prayed to the LORD, 17Oh,
Lord GOD, you made the skies and the earth with
your very great power. There is nothing too hard
for you to do. 18You show love and kindness to
thousands of people, but you also bring punish-
ment to children for their parents' sins. Great
and powerful God, your name is the LORD All-
powerful. 19You plan and do great things. You see
everything that people do, and you reward people
for the way they live and for what they do. 20You
did miracles[d] and wonderful things in the land of
Egypt. You have continued doing them in Israel
and among the other nations even until today. So
you have become well known. 21You brought
your people, the Israelites, out of Egypt using
signs and miracles and your great power and
strength. You brought great terror on everyone.
22You gave them this land that you promised to
their ancestors long ago, a fertile land. 23They
came into this land and took it for their own, but
they did not obey you or follow your teachings.
They did not do everything you commanded.
So you made all these terrible things happen to
them.
24"Look! The enemy has surrounded the city
and has built roads to the top of the walls to
capture it. Because of war, hunger and terrible
diseases, the city will be handed over to the
Babylonians who are attacking it. You said this
would happen and now you see it is happening.
25But now, Lord GOD, you tell me, 'Buy the field
with silver and call in witnesses.' You tell me this

while the Babylonian army is ready to capture the city."

26Then the LORD spoke this word to Jeremiah: 27"I am the LORD, the God of every person on the earth. Nothing is impossible for me. 28So this is what the LORD says: I will soon hand over the city of Jerusalem to the Babylonian army and to Nebuchadnezzar king of Babylon, who will capture it. 29The Babylonian army is already attacking the city of Jerusalem. They will soon enter it and start a fire to burn down the city and its houses. The people of Jerusalem offered sacrifices to Baal[d] on the roofs[n] of those same houses and poured out drink offerings to other idols to make me angry. 30From their youth, the people of Israel and Judah have done only the things I said were wrong. They have made me angry by worshipping idols made with their own hands," says the LORD. 31"From the day Jerusalem was built until now, this city has made me angry, so angry that I must remove it from my sight. 32I will destroy it, because of all the evil the people of Israel and Judah have done. The people, their kings and officers, their priests and prophets, all the people of Judah and the people of Jerusalem have made me angry. 33They turned their backs to me, not their faces. I tried to teach them again and again, but they wouldn't listen or learn. 34They put their hateful idols in the place where I have chosen to be worshipped, so they made it unclean.[d] 35In the Valley of Ben Hinnom they built places to worship Baal so they could burn their sons and daughters as sacrifices to Molech.[d] But I never commanded them to do such a hateful thing. It never entered my mind that they would do such a thing and cause Judah to sin.

36"You are saying, 'Because of war, hunger and terrible diseases, the city will be handed over to the king of Babylon.' But the LORD, the God of Israel, says about Jerusalem: 37I forced the people of Israel and Judah to leave their land, because I was furious and very angry with them. But soon I will gather them from all the lands where I forced them to go, and I will bring them back to this place, where they may live in safety. 38The people of Israel and Judah will be my people, and I will be their God. 39I will make them truly want to be one people with one goal. They will truly want to worship me all their lives, for their own good and for the good of their children after them.

40"I will make an agreement with them that will last for ever. I will never turn away from them; I will always do good to them. I will make them want to respect me so they will never turn away from me. 41I will enjoy doing good to them. And with my whole being I will surely plant them in this land and make them grow."

42This is what the LORD says: "I have brought this great disaster to the people of Israel and Judah. In the same way I will bring the good things that I promise to do for them. 43You are saying, 'This land is an empty desert, without people or animals. It has been handed over to the Babylonians.' But in the future, people will again buy fields in this land. 44They will use their money to buy fields. They will sign and seal their agreements and call in witnesses. They will again buy fields in the land of Benjamin, in the area around Jerusalem, in the towns of Judah and in the mountains, in the western hills and in southern Judah. I will make everything as good for them as it once was," says the LORD.

The Promise of the LORD

33 While Jeremiah was still locked up in the courtyard of the guards, the LORD spoke his word to him a second time: 2"These are the words of the LORD, who made the earth, shaped it and gave it order, whose name is the LORD: 3'Judah, pray to me, and I will answer you. I will tell you important secrets you have never heard before.' 4This is what the LORD, the God of Israel, says about the houses in Jerusalem and the royal palaces of Judah that have been torn down to be used in defence of the attack by the Babylonian army: 5'Some people will come to fight against the Babylonians. They will fill these houses with the bodies of people I killed in my hot anger. I have turned away from this city because of all the evil its people have done.

6" 'But then I will bring health and healing to the people there. I will heal them and let them enjoy great peace and safety. 7I will bring Judah and Israel back from captivity and make them strong countries as in the past. 8They sinned against me, but I will wash away that sin. They did evil and turned away from me, but I will forgive them. 9Then 'Jerusalem' will be to me a name that brings joy! And people from all nations of the earth will praise it when they hear about the good things I am doing there. They will be surprised and shocked at all the good things and the peace I will bring to Jerusalem.'

10"You are saying, 'Our country is an empty desert, without people or animals.' But this is what the LORD says: It is now quiet in the streets of Jerusalem and in the towns of Judah, without people or animals, but it will be noisy there soon! 11There will be sounds of joy and gladness and

roofs In Bible times houses were built with flat roofs. The roof was used for drying things such as flax and fruit. And it was used as an extra room, as a place for worship and as a place to sleep in the summer.

the happy sounds of brides and bridegrooms.
There will be the sounds of people bringing to the
Temple[d] of the LORD their offerings of thanks to
the LORD. They will say,

'Praise the LORD All-powerful,
because the LORD is good!
His love continues for ever!'

They will say this because I will again do good
things for Judah, as I did in the beginning," says
the Lord.
12This is what the LORD All-powerful says:
"This place is empty now, without people or ani-
mals. But there will be shepherds in all the towns
of Judah and pastures where they let their flocks
rest. 13Shepherds will again count their sheep as
the sheep walk in front of them. They will count
them in the mountains and in the western hills,
in southern Judah and the land of Benjamin, and
around Jerusalem and the other towns of Judah!"
says the LORD.

The Good Branch

14The LORD says, "The time is coming when I
will do the good thing I promised to the people of
Israel and Judah.

15In those days and at that time,
I will make a good branch sprout from
David's family.
He will do what is fair and right in the land.
16At that time Judah will be saved
and the people of Jerusalem will live in safety.
The branch will be named:
The LORD Does What Is Right."

17This is what the LORD says: "Someone from
David's family will always sit on the throne of the
family of Israel. 18And there will always be priests
from the family of Levi. They will always stand
before me to offer burnt offerings and grain offer-
ings and sacrifices to me."
19The LORD spoke his word to Jeremiah, saying:
20"This is what the LORD says: I have an agree-
ment with day and night that they will always
come at the right times. If you could change that
agreement, 21only then could you change my
agreement with David and Levi. Only then would
my servant David not have a descendant[d] ruling
as king on David's throne. And only then would
the family of Levi not be priests serving me in the
Temple.[d] 22But I will give many descendants to
my servant David and to the family group of Levi

FUTURE

Will Peace Ever Come?

"Nuclear weapons were described as a 'satanic weapon' that can cripple the total nervous system of civilisation." – *Die Zeit* (a German newspaper)

"The atomic age is here to stay – but are we?" – Bennett Cerf (publisher)

"Vast webs of advanced machinery pose danger enough . . . How much worse, then, when we consider another common trait of man: goofing up." – John Wesley White (author)

The future can seem uncertain and dangerous, and the spread of nuclear weapons adds to that uncertainty. But, even in difficult times, God keeps his promises. Read one of God's promises for the future in **Jeremiah 33:14–16**.

- God promises a Saviour in the passage. Do you think that promise includes being saved from nuclear weapons and war? Why or why not?
- How does your future look? How does faith in Christ affect the way you look at your future?

Consider . . .

- each day asking God to guide some part of your future. For example, Monday: Who will I marry? Tuesday: What career should I choose?
- writing one paragraph on how you would like to be remembered after your death. Choose one thing to do this week to help you towards your goals.

For more, see . . .

- Genesis 9:8–17 (p.11)
- Acts 1:6–11 (p.1137)
- Matthew 6:25–34 (p.948)

who serve me in the Temple. They will be as
many as the stars in the sky that no one can
count. They will be as many as the grains of sand
on the seashore that no one can measure."
23The LORD spoke his word to Jeremiah, saying:
24"Jeremiah, have you heard what the people are
saying? They say: 'The LORD turned away from
the two families of Israel and Judah that he
chose.' Now they don't think of my people as a
nation any more!"
25This is what the LORD says: "If I had not
made my agreement with day and night, and if I
had not made the laws for the sky and earth,
26only then would I turn away from Jacob's
descendants. And only then would I not let
the descendants of David my servant rule over the
descendants of Abraham, Isaac and Jacob. But I
will be kind to them and cause good things to
happen to them again."

A Warning to Zedekiah

34 The LORD spoke his word to Jeremiah
when Nebuchadnezzar king of Babylon
was fighting against Jerusalem and all the towns
around it. Nebuchadnezzar had with him all his
army and the armies of all the kingdoms and peo-
ples he ruled. 2This is what the LORD, the God of
Israel, said: "Jeremiah, go to Zedekiah king of
Judah and tell him: 'This is what the LORD says: I
will soon hand the city of Jerusalem over to the
king of Babylon, and he will burn it down! 3You
will not escape from the king of Babylon; you will
surely be captured and handed over to him. You
will see the king of Babylon with your own eyes,
and he will talk to you face to face. And you will
go to Babylon. 4But, Zedekiah king of Judah, lis-
ten to the promise of the LORD. This is what the
LORD says about you: You will not be killed with
a sword. 5You will die in a peaceful way. As peo-
ple made funeral fires to honour your ancestors,
the kings who ruled before you, so people will
make a funeral fire to honour you. They will cry
for you and sadly say, "Ah, master!" I myself
make this promise to you, says the LORD.' "
6So Jeremiah the prophet[d] gave this message to
Zedekiah in Jerusalem. 7This was while the army
of the king of Babylon was fighting against
Jerusalem and the cities of Judah that had not yet
been taken—Lachish and Azekah. These were
the only fortified cities left in the land of Judah.

Slaves are Mistreated

8The LORD spoke his word to Jeremiah. This
was after King Zedekiah had made an agreement
with all the people in Jerusalem to free all the
Hebrew slaves. 9Everyone was supposed to free
his Hebrew slaves, both male and female. No one
was to keep a fellow Jew as a slave. 10All the
officers and all the people accepted this agree-
ment; they agreed to free their male and female
slaves and no longer keep them as slaves. So all
the slaves were set free. 11But after that, the peo-
ple who had slaves changed their minds. So they
took back the people they had set free and made
them slaves again.
12Then the LORD spoke his word to Jeremiah:
13"This is what the LORD, the God of Israel, says:
I brought your ancestors out of Egypt where they
were slaves and made an agreement with them.
14I said to your ancestors: 'At the end of every
seven years, each one of you must set his He-
brew slaves free. If a fellow Hebrew has sold
himself to you, you must let him go free after he
has served you for six years.' But your ancestors
did not listen or pay attention to me. 15A short
time ago you changed your hearts and did what
I say is right. Each of you gave freedom to his
fellow Hebrews who were slaves. And you even
made an agreement before me in the place where
I have chosen to be worshipped. 16But now you
have changed your minds. You have shown you
do not honour me. Each of you has taken back
the male and female slaves you had set free, and
you have forced them to become your slaves
again.
17"So this is what the LORD says: You have not
obeyed me. You have not given freedom to your
fellow Hebrews, neither relatives nor friends. But
now I will give freedom, says the LORD, to war, to
terrible diseases and to hunger. I will make you
hated by all the kingdoms of the earth. 18I will
hand over the men who broke my agreement,
who have not kept the promises they made be-
fore me. They cut a calf into two pieces before me
and walked between the pieces.[n] 19These people
made the agreement before me by walking be-
tween the pieces of the calf: the leaders of Judah
and Jerusalem, the officers of the court, the
priests and all the people of the land. 20So I will
hand them over to their enemies and to everyone
who wants to kill them. Their bodies will become
food for the birds of the air and for the wild ani-
mals of the earth. 21I will hand Zedekiah king of
Judah and his officers over to their enemies and
to everyone who wants to kill them, and to the
army of the king of Babylon, even though they
have left Jerusalem. 22I will give the order, says
the LORD, to bring the Babylonian army back to
Jerusalem. It will fight against Jerusalem, capture
it, set it on fire and burn it down. I will destroy
the towns in Judah so that they become ruins
where no one lives!"

They . . . pieces. This showed that the men were willing to be killed, like this animal, if they did not keep their agreement.

The Recabite Family Obeys God

35 When Jehoiakim son of Josiah was king of Judah, the LORD spoke his word to Jeremiah, saying: [2]"Go to the family of Recab. Invite them to come to one of the side rooms of the Temple[d] of the LORD, and offer them wine to drink."

[3]So I went to get Jaazaniah son of Jeremiah,[n] the son of Habazziniah. And I gathered all of Jaazaniah's brothers and sons and the whole family of the Recabites together. [4]Then I brought them into the Temple of the LORD. We went into the room of the sons of Hanan son of Igdaliah, who was a man of God. The room was next to the one where the officers stay and above the room of Maaseiah son of Shallum, the doorkeeper in the Temple. [5]Then I put some bowls full of wine and some cups before the men of the Recabite family. And I said to them, "Drink some wine."

[6]But the Recabite men answered, "We never drink wine. Our ancestor Jonadab son of Recab gave us this command: 'You and your descendants[d] must never drink wine. [7]Also you must never build houses, plant seeds or plant vineyards, or do any of those things. You must live only in tents. Then you will live a long time in the land where you are wanderers.' [8]So we Recabites have obeyed everything Jonadab our ancestor commanded us. Neither we nor our wives, sons or daughters ever drink wine. [9]We never build houses in which to live, or own fields or vineyards, or plant crops. [10]We have lived in tents and have obeyed everything our ancestor Jonadab commanded us. [11]But when Nebuchadnezzar king of Babylon attacked Judah, we said to each other, 'Come, we must enter Jerusalem so we can escape the Babylonian army and the Aramean army.' So we have stayed in Jerusalem."

[12]Then the LORD spoke his word to Jeremiah: [13]"This is what the LORD All-powerful, the God of Israel, says: Jeremiah, go and tell the men of Judah and the people of Jerusalem: 'You should learn a lesson and obey my message,' says the LORD. [14]'Jonadab son of Recab ordered his descendants not to drink wine, and that command has been obeyed. Until today they have obeyed their ancestor's command; they do not drink wine. But I, the LORD, have given you messages again and again, but you did not obey me. [15]I sent all my servants the prophets to you again and again, saying, "Each of you must stop doing evil. You must change and be good. Do not follow other gods to serve them. If you obey me, you will live in the land I have given to you and your ancestors." But you have not listened to me or paid attention to my message. [16]The descendants of Jonadab son of Recab obeyed the commands their ancestor gave them, but the people of Judah have not obeyed me.'

[17]"So the LORD God All-powerful, the God of Israel, says: 'I will soon bring every disaster I said would come to Judah and to everyone living in Jerusalem. I spoke to those people, but they refused to listen. I called out to them, but they did not answer me.' "

[18]Then Jeremiah said to the Recabites, "This is what the LORD All-powerful, the God of Israel, says: 'You have obeyed the commands of your ancestor Jonadab and have followed all of his teachings; you have done everything he commanded.' [19]So this is what the LORD All-powerful, the God of Israel, says: 'There will always be a descendant of Jonadab son of Recab to serve me.' "

Jehoiakim Burns Jeremiah's Scroll

36 The LORD spoke this word to Jeremiah during the fourth year that Jehoiakim son of Josiah was king of Judah: [2]"Get a scroll. Write on it all the words I have spoken to you about Israel and Judah and all the nations. Write everything from when I first spoke to you, when Josiah was king, until now. [3]Perhaps the family of Judah will hear what disasters I am planning to bring on them and will stop doing wicked things. Then I would forgive them for the sins and the evil things they have done."

[4]So Jeremiah called for Baruch son of Neriah. Jeremiah spoke the messages the LORD had given him, and Baruch wrote those messages on the scroll. [5]Then Jeremiah commanded Baruch, "I cannot go to the Temple[d] of the LORD. I must stay here. [6]So I want you to go to the Temple of the LORD on a day when the people are giving up eating. Read from the scroll to all the people of Judah who come into Jerusalem from their towns. Read the messages from the LORD, which are the words you wrote on the scroll as I spoke them to you. [7]Perhaps they will ask the LORD to

> **Sidelight** Baruch was Jeremiah's secretary and friend who recorded the prophet's thoughts on scrolls made from treated animal skins (Jeremiah 36:4). Baruch was an important citizen of Jerusalem and probably served as a royal clerk. That made working with Jeremiah an occupational hazard, since Jeremiah was rarely in the king's good books.

Jeremiah Not the prophet Jeremiah, but a different man with the same name.

help them. Perhaps each one will stop doing
wicked things, because the LORD has announced
that he is very angry with them." 8So Baruch son
of Neriah did everything Jeremiah the prophet[d]
told him to do. In the LORD's Temple he read
aloud the scroll that had the LORD's messages
written on it.

9In the ninth month of the fifth year that
Jehoiakim son of Josiah was king, a special time
to give up eating was announced. All the people
of Jerusalem and everyone who had come into
Jerusalem from the towns of Judah were sup-
posed to give up eating to honour the LORD. 10At
that time Baruch read to all the people there the
scroll containing Jeremiah's words. He read the
scroll in the Temple of the LORD in the room of
Gemariah son of Shaphan, a royal secretary. That
room was in the upper courtyard at the entrance
of the New Gate of the Temple.

11Micaiah son of Gemariah, the son of
Shaphan, heard all the messages from the LORD
that were on the scroll. 12Micaiah went down to
the royal secretary's room in the king's palace
where all of the officers were sitting: Elishama the
royal secretary; Delaiah son of Shemaiah; Elnathan
son of Acbor; Gemariah son of Shaphan; Zedekiah
son of Hananiah; and all the other officers.
13Micaiah told those officers everything he had
heard Baruch read to the people from the scroll.

14Then the officers sent a man named Jehudi
son of Nethaniah to Baruch. (Nethaniah was the
son of Shelemiah, who was the son of Cushi.)
Jehudi said to Baruch, "Bring the scroll that you
read to the people and come with me."

So Baruch son of Neriah took the scroll and
went with Jehudi to the officers. 15Then the offi-
cers said to Baruch, "Please sit down and read
the scroll to us."

So Baruch read the scroll to them. 16When the
officers heard all the words, they became afraid
and looked at each other. They said to Baruch,
"We must certainly tell the king about these
words." 17Then the officers asked Baruch, "Tell
us, please, where did you get all these words you
wrote on the scroll? Did you write down what
Jeremiah said to you?"

18"Yes," Baruch answered. "Jeremiah spoke
them all to me, and I wrote them down with ink
on this scroll."

19Then the officers said to Baruch, "You and
Jeremiah must go and hide, and don't tell anyone
where you are."

20The officers put the scroll in the room of
Elishama the royal secretary. Then they went to
the king in the courtyard and told him all about
the scroll. 21So King Jehoiakim sent Jehudi to
get the scroll. Jehudi brought the scroll from the
room of Elishama the royal secretary and read it
to the king and to all the officers who stood
around the king. 22It was the ninth month of the
year, so King Jehoiakim was sitting in the winter
apartment. There was a fire burning in a small
firepot in front of him. 23After Jehudi had read
three or four columns, the king cut those columns
off of the scroll with a pen knife and threw them
into the firepot. Finally, the whole scroll was
burnt in the fire. 24King Jehoiakim and his ser-
vants heard everything that was said, but they
were not frightened! They did not tear their
clothes to show their sorrow. 25Elnathan, Delaiah
and Gemariah even tried to talk King Jehoiakim
out of burning the scroll, but he would not listen
to them. 26Instead, the king ordered Jerahmeel
son of the king, Seraiah son of Azriel and
Shelemiah son of Abdeel to arrest Baruch the
secretary and Jeremiah the prophet. But the LORD
had hidden them.

27So King Jehoiakim burnt the scroll where
Baruch had written all the words Jeremiah had
spoken to him. Then the LORD spoke his word to
Jeremiah: 28"Get another scroll. Write all the
words on it that were on the first scroll that
Jehoiakim king of Judah burnt up. 29Also say this to
Jehoiakim king of Judah: 'This is what the LORD
says: you burnt up that scroll and said, "Why,
Jeremiah, did you write on it 'the king of Babylon
will surely come and destroy this land and the
people and animals in it'?" 30So this is what
the LORD says about Jehoiakim king of Judah:
Jehoiakim's descendants[d] will not sit on David's
throne. When Jehoiakim dies, his body will
be thrown out on the ground. It will be left
out in the heat of the day and in the cold frost of
the night. 31I will punish Jehoiakim and his chil-
dren and his servants, because they have done
evil things. I will bring disasters upon them and
upon all the people in Jerusalem and Judah
everything I promised but which they refused to
hear.' "

Sidelight Imagine how you would feel if you'd spent hours working hard on an essay, only to have someone cut it up and burn it! That's what happened to Jeremiah when the king heard what he had written (Jeremiah 36:20–26). But Jeremiah didn't give up. He wrote an even longer book to replace the burnt one, which was still unpopular (Jeremiah 36:27–32)!

32So Jeremiah took another scroll and gave it to
Baruch son of Neriah, his secretary. As Jeremiah
spoke, Baruch wrote on the scroll the same
words that were on the scroll Jehoiakim king of

Judah had burnt in the fire. And many like words were added to the second scroll.

Jeremiah in Prison

37 Nebuchadnezzar king of Babylon had appointed Zedekiah son of Josiah to be king of Judah. Zedekiah took the place of Jehoiachin son of Jehoiakim. 2But Zedekiah, his servants and the people of Judah did not listen to the words the LORD had spoken through Jeremiah the prophet.[d]

3Now King Zedekiah sent Jehucal son of Shelemiah and the priest Zephaniah son of Maaseiah with a message to Jeremiah the prophet. This was the message: "Jeremiah, please pray to the LORD our God for us."

4At that time Jeremiah had not yet been put into prison. So he was free to go anywhere he wanted. 5The army of the king of Egypt had marched from Egypt towards Judah. Now the Babylonian army had surrounded the city of Jerusalem. When they heard about the Egyptian army marching towards them, the Babylonian army left Jerusalem.

6The LORD spoke his word to Jeremiah the prophet: 7"This is what the LORD, the God of Israel, says: Jehucal and Zephaniah, I know Zedekiah king of Judah sent you to seek my help. Tell this to King Zedekiah: 'The army of the king of Egypt came here to help you, but they will go back to Egypt. 8After that, the Babylonian army will return and attack Jerusalem and capture it and burn it down.'

9"This is what the LORD says: People of Jerusalem, do not fool yourselves. Don't say, 'The Babylonian army will surely leave us alone.' They will not! 10Even if you defeated all of the Babylonian army that is attacking you and there were only a few injured men left in their tents, they would come from their tents and burn down Jerusalem!"

11So the Babylonian army left Jerusalem to fight the army of the king of Egypt. 12Now Jeremiah tried to travel from Jerusalem to the land of Benjamin to get his share of the property that belonged to his family. 13When Jeremiah got to the Benjamin Gate of Jerusalem, the captain in charge of the guards arrested him. The captain's name was Irijah son of Shelemiah son of Hananiah. Irijah said, "You are leaving us to join the Babylonians!"

14But Jeremiah said to Irijah, "That's not true! I am not leaving to join the Babylonians." Irijah refused to listen to Jeremiah, so he arrested Jeremiah and took him to the officers of Jerusalem. 15Those rulers were very angry with Jeremiah and beat him. Then they put him in jail in the house of Jonathan the royal secretary, which had been made into a prison. 16So those people put Jeremiah into a cell in a dungeon, and Jeremiah was there for a long time.

17Then King Zedekiah sent for Jeremiah and had him brought to the palace. Zedekiah asked him in private, "Is there any message from the LORD?"

Jeremiah answered, "Yes, there is. Zedekiah, you will be handed over to the king of Babylon." 18Then Jeremiah said to King Zedekiah, "What crime have I done against you or your officers or the people of Jerusalem? Why have you thrown me into prison? 19Where are your prophets that prophesied this message to you: 'The king of Babylon will not attack you or this land of Judah?' 20But now, my master, king of Judah, please listen to me, and please do what I ask of you. Do not send me back to the house of Jonathan the royal secretary, or I will die there!"

21So King Zedekiah gave orders for Jeremiah to be put under guard in the courtyard of the guard and to be given bread each day from the street of the bakers until there was no more bread in the city. So he stayed under guard in the courtyard of the guard.

Jeremiah is Thrown into a Well

38 Shephatiah son of Mattan, Gedaliah son of Pashhur, Jehucal son of Shelemiah and Pashhur son of Malkijah heard what Jeremiah was telling all the people. He said: 2"This is what the LORD says: 'Everyone who stays in Jerusalem will die from war, or hunger or terrible diseases. But everyone who surrenders to the Babylonian army will live; they will escape with their lives and live.' 3And this is what the LORD says: 'This city of Jerusalem will surely be handed over to the army of the king of Babylon. He will capture this city!'"

4Then the officers said to the king, "Jeremiah must be put to death! He is discouraging the soldiers who are still in the city, and all the people, by what he is saying to them. He does not want good to happen to us; he wants to ruin us."

5King Zedekiah said to them, "Jeremiah is in your control. I cannot do anything to stop you."

6So the officers took Jeremiah and put him into the well of Malkijah, the king's son, which was in the courtyard of the guards. The officers used ropes to lower Jeremiah into the well, which did not have any water in it, only mud. And Jeremiah sank down into the mud.

7But Ebed-Melech, a Cushite and a servant in the palace, heard that the officers had put Jeremiah into the well. As King Zedekiah was sitting at the Benjamin Gate, 8Ebed-Melech left the palace and went to the king. Ebed-Melech said to him, 9"My master and king, these rulers have acted in an evil way. They have treated Jeremiah the prophet badly. They have thrown him into a well and left him there to die! When there is no more bread in the city, he will starve to death."

> **Sidelight** Originally used as a water supply, the well of Malkijah was used to imprison Jeremiah (Jeremiah 38:6). It was a muddy tank – a plastered hole in the ground – which could have been six metres deep.

10Then King Zedekiah commanded Ebed-Melech the Cushite, "Take 30 men from the palace and lift Jeremiah the prophet out of the well before he dies."

11So Ebed-Melech took the men with him and went to a room under the storeroom in the palace. He took some old rags and worn-out clothes from that room. Then he let those rags down with some ropes to Jeremiah in the well. 12Ebed-Melech the Cushite said to Jeremiah, "Put these old rags and worn-out clothes under your arms to be pads for the ropes." So Jeremiah did as Ebed-Melech said. 13The men pulled Jeremiah up with the ropes and lifted him out of the well. And Jeremiah stayed under guard in the courtyard of the guard.

Zedekiah Questions Jeremiah

14Then King Zedekiah sent someone to get Jeremiah the prophet[d] and bring him to the third entrance to the Temple[d] of the LORD. The king said to Jeremiah, "I am going to ask you something. Do not hide anything from me, but tell me everything honestly."

15Jeremiah said to Zedekiah, "If I give you an answer, you will surely kill me. And even if I give you advice, you will not listen to me."

16But King Zedekiah made a secret promise to Jeremiah, "As surely as the LORD lives who has given us breath and life, I will not kill you. And I promise not to hand you over to the officers who want to kill you."

17Then Jeremiah said to Zedekiah, "This is what the LORD God All-powerful, the God of Israel, says: 'If you surrender to the officers of the king of Babylon, your life will be saved. Jerusalem will not be burnt down, and you and your family will live. 18But if you refuse to surrender to the officers of the king of Babylon, Jerusalem will be handed over to the Babylonian army, and they will burn it down. And you yourself will not escape from them.' "

19Then King Zedekiah said to Jeremiah, "I'm afraid of some Jews who have already gone over to the side of the Babylonian army. If the Babylonians hand me over to them, they will treat me badly."

20But Jeremiah answered, "The Babylonians will not hand you over to the Jews. Obey the LORD by doing what I tell you. Then things will go well for you, and your life will be saved. 21But if you refuse to surrender to the Babylonians, the LORD has shown me what will happen. 22All the women left in the palace of the king of Judah will be brought out and taken to the important officers of the king of Babylon. Your women will make fun of you with this song:

'Your good friends misled you
 and were stronger than you.
While your feet were stuck in the mud,
 they left you.'

23"All your wives and children will be brought out and given to the Babylonian army. You yourself will not even escape from them. You will be taken prisoner by the king of Babylon, and Jerusalem will be burned down."

24Then Zedekiah said to Jeremiah, "Do not tell anyone that I have been talking to you, or you will die. 25If the officers find out I talked to you, they will come to you and say, 'Tell us what you said to King Zedekiah and what he said to you. Don't keep any secrets from us. If you don't tell us everything, we will kill you.' 26If they ask you, tell them, 'I was begging the king not to send me back to Jonathan's house to die.' "

27All the officers did come to question Jeremiah. So he told them everything the king had ordered him to say. Then the officers said no more to Jeremiah, because no one had heard what Jeremiah and the king had discussed.

28So Jeremiah stayed under guard in the courtyard of the guard until the day Jerusalem was captured.

The Fall of Jerusalem

39 This is how Jerusalem was captured: Nebuchadnezzar king of Babylon marched against Jerusalem with his whole army and surrounded the city to attack it. This was during the tenth month of the ninth year in which Zedekiah was king of Judah. 2This lasted until the ninth day of the fourth month in Zedekiah's eleventh year. Then the city wall was broken through. 3And all these officers of the king of Babylon came into Jerusalem and sat down at the Middle Gate: Nergal-Sharezer of the district of Samgar; Nebo-Sarsekim, a chief officer; Nergal-Sharezer, an important leader; and all the other important officers.

4When Zedekiah king of Judah and all his soldiers saw them, they ran away. They left Jerusalem at night and went out from the king's garden.

They went through the gate that was between the two walls and then headed towards the Jordan Valley. 5But the Babylonian army chased them and caught up with Zedekiah in the plains of Jericho. They captured him and took him to Nebuchadnezzar king of Babylon, who was at the town of Riblah in the land of Hamath. There Nebuchadnezzar passed his sentence on Zedekiah. 6At Riblah the king of Babylon killed Zedekiah's sons and all the important officers of Judah as Zedekiah watched. 7Then he put out Zedekiah's eyes. He put bronze chains on Zedekiah and took him to Babylon.

8The Babylonians set fire to the palace and to the houses of the people, and they broke down the walls around Jerusalem. 9Nebuzaradan, commander of the king's special guards, took the people left in Jerusalem, those captives who had surrendered to him earlier and the rest of the people of Jerusalem, and he took them all away to Babylon. 10But Nebuzaradan, commander of the guard, left some of the poorest people of Judah behind. They owned nothing, but that day he gave them vineyards and fields.

> **Sidelight** The eighteen-month siege of Jerusalem by the Babylonians was a gruelling experience for Jeremiah (Jeremiah 39:1–10). Lamentations 4 (p.784) describes the horrible conditions, including starvation and cannibalism.

11Nebuchadnezzar king of Babylon had given these orders about Jeremiah through Nebuzaradan, commander of the guard: 12"Find Jeremiah and take care of him. Do not hurt him, but do for him whatever he asks you." 13So Nebuchadnezzar sent these men for Jeremiah: Nebuzaradan, commander of the guards; Nebushazban, a chief officer; Nergal-Sharezer, an important leader; and all the other officers of the king of Babylon. 14They had Jeremiah taken out of the courtyard of the guard. Then they turned him over to Gedaliah son of Ahikam son of Shaphan, who had orders to take Jeremiah back home. So they took him home and he stayed among the people left in Judah.

15While Jeremiah was guarded in the courtyard, the LORD spoke his word to him: 16"Jeremiah, go and tell Ebed-Melech the Cushite this message: 'This is what the LORD All-powerful, the God of Israel, says: very soon I will make my words about Jerusalem come true through disaster, not through good times. You will see everything come true with your own eyes. 17But I will save you on that day, Ebed-Melech, says the LORD. You will not be handed over to the people you fear. 18I will surely save you, Ebed-Melech. You will not die from a sword, but you will escape and live. This will happen because you have trusted in me, says the LORD.' "

Jeremiah is Set Free

40 The LORD spoke his word to Jeremiah after Nebuzaradan, commander of the guards, had set Jeremiah free at the city of Ramah. He had found Jeremiah in Ramah bound in chains with all the captives from Jerusalem and Judah who were being taken away to Babylon. 2When commander Nebuzaradan found Jeremiah, Nebuzaradan said to him, "The LORD your God announced this disaster would come to this place. 3And now the LORD has done everything he said he would do. This disaster happened because the people of Judah sinned against the LORD and did not obey him. 4But today I am freeing you from the chains on your wrists. If you want to, come with me to Babylon and I will take good care of you. But if you don't want to come, then don't. Look, the whole country is open to you. Go wherever you wish." 5Before Jeremiah turned to leave, Nebuzaradan said, "Or go back to Gedaliah son of Ahikam, the son of Shaphan. The king of Babylon has chosen him to be governor over the towns of Judah. Go and live with Gedaliah among the people, or go anywhere you want."

Then Nebuzaradan gave Jeremiah some food and a present and let him go. 6So Jeremiah went to Gedaliah son of Ahikam at Mizpah and stayed with him there. He lived among the people who were left behind in Judah.

The Short Rule of Gedaliah

7Some officers and their men from the army of Judah were still out in the open country. They heard that the king of Babylon had put Gedaliah son of Ahikam in charge of the people who were left in the land: the men, women and children who were the poorest. They were the ones who were not taken to Babylon as captives. 8So these soldiers came to Gedaliah at Mizpah: Ishmael son of Nethaniah, Johanan and Jonathan sons of Kareah, Seraiah son of Tanhumeth, the sons of Ephai the Netophathite, Jaazaniah son of the Maacathite and their men.

9Gedaliah son of Ahikam, the son of Shaphan, made a promise to them, saying, "Do not be afraid to serve the Babylonians. Stay in the land and serve the king of Babylon. Then everything will go well for you. 10I myself will live in Mizpah and will speak for you before the Babylonians who come to us here. Harvest the wine, the summer fruit and the oil, and put what you harvest in your storage jars. Live in the towns you control."

11 The Jews in Moab, Ammon, Edom and other countries also heard that the king of Babylon had left a few Jews alive in the land. And they heard the king of Babylon had chosen Gedaliah as governor over them. (Gedaliah was the son of Ahikam, the son of Shaphan.) 12 When the people of Judah heard this news, they came back to Judah from all the countries where they had been scattered. They came to Gedaliah at Mizpah and gathered a large harvest of wine and summer fruit.

13 Johanan son of Kareah and all the army officers of Judah still in the open country came to Gedaliah at Mizpah. 14 They said to him, "Don't you know that Baalis king of the Ammonite people wants you dead? He has sent Ishmael son of Nethaniah to kill you." But Gedaliah son of Ahikam did not believe them.

15 Then Johanan son of Kareah spoke to Gedaliah in private at Mizpah. He said, "Let me go and kill Ishmael son of Nethaniah. No one will know anything about it. We should not let Ishmael kill you. Then all the Jews gathered around you would be scattered to different countries again, and the few people of Judah who are left alive would be lost."

16 But Gedaliah son of Ahikam said to Johanan son of Kareah, "Do not kill Ishmael! The things you are saying about Ishmael are not true."

41 In the seventh month Ishmael son of Nethaniah and ten of his men came to Gedaliah son of Ahikam at Mizpah. (Nethaniah was the son of Elishama.) Now Ishmael was a member of the king's family and had been one of the officers of the king of Judah. While they were eating a meal with Gedaliah at Mizpah, 2 Ishmael and his ten men got up and killed Gedaliah son of Ahikam, the son of Shaphan, with a sword. (Gedaliah was the man the king of Babylon had chosen as governor over Judah.) 3 Ishmael also killed all the Jews and the Babylonian soldiers who were there with Gedaliah at Mizpah.

4 The day after Gedaliah was murdered, before anyone knew about it, 5 80 men came to Mizpah bringing grain offerings and incense[d] to the Temple[d] of the LORD. Those men from Shechem, Shiloh and Samaria had shaved off their beards, torn their clothes and cut themselves.[n] 6 Ishmael son of Nethaniah went out from Mizpah to meet them, crying as he walked. When he met them, he said, "Come with me to meet Gedaliah son of Ahikam." 7 So they went into Mizpah. Then Ishmael son of Nethaniah and his men killed 70 of them and threw the bodies into a deep well. 8 But the ten men who were left alive said to Ishmael, "Don't kill us! We have wheat and barley and oil and honey that we have hidden in a field." So Ishmael let them live and did not kill them with the others. 9 Now the well where he had thrown all the bodies had been made by King Asa as a part of his defences against Baasha king of Israel. But Ishmael son of Nethaniah put dead bodies in it until it was full.

10 Ishmael captured all the other people in Mizpah: the king's daughters and all the other people who were left there. They were the ones whom Nebuzaradan, commander of the guard, had chosen Gedaliah son of Ahikam to take care of. So Ishmael son of Nethaniah captured those people, and he started to cross over to the country of the Ammonites.

11 Johanan son of Kareah and all his army officers with him heard about all the evil things Ishmael son of Nethaniah had done. 12 So they took their men and went to fight Ishmael son of Nethaniah and caught him near the big pool of water at Gibeon. 13 When the captives Ishmael had taken saw Johanan and the army officers, they were glad. 14 So all the people Ishmael had taken captive from Mizpah turned around and ran to Johanan son of Kareah. 15 But Ishmael son of Nethaniah and eight of his men escaped from Johanan and ran away to the Ammonites.

16 So Johanan son of Kareah and all his army officers saved the captives that Ishmael son of Nethaniah had taken from Mizpah after he murdered Gedaliah son of Ahikam. Among those left alive were soldiers, women, children and palace officers. And Johanan brought them back from the town of Gibeon.

The Escape to Egypt

17–18 Johanan and the other army officers were afraid of the Babylonians. Since the king of Babylon had chosen Gedaliah son of Ahikam to be governor of Judah and Ishmael son of Nethaniah had murdered him, Johanan was afraid that the Babylonians would be angry. So they decided to run away to Egypt. On the way they stayed at Geruth Kimham, near the town of Bethlehem.

42 While there, Johanan son of Kareah and Jezaniah son of Hoshaiah went to Jeremiah the prophet.[d] All the army officers and all the people, from the least important to the greatest, went along too. 2 They said to him, "Jeremiah, please listen to what we ask. Pray to the LORD your God for all the people left alive from the family of Judah. At one time there were many of us, but you can see that there are few of us now. 3 So pray that the LORD your God will tell us where we should go and what we should do."

shaved . . . themselves The men did this to show they were sad about the Temple in Jerusalem being destroyed.

4Then Jeremiah the prophet answered, "I un-
derstand what you want me to do. I will pray to
the LORD your God as you have asked. I will tell
you everything he says and not hide anything
from you."
5Then the people said to Jeremiah, "May the
LORD be a true and loyal witness against us if we
don't do everything the LORD your God sends you
to tell us. 6It does not matter if we like the mes-
sage or not. We will obey the LORD our God, to
whom we are sending you. We will obey what he
says so good things will happen to us."
7Ten days later the LORD spoke his word to
Jeremiah. 8Then Jeremiah called for Johanan son
of Kareah, the army officers with him and all the
other people, from the least important to the
greatest. 9Jeremiah said to them, "You sent me to
ask the LORD for what you wanted. This is what
the God of Israel says: 10'If you will stay in Judah,
I will build you up and not tear you down. I will
plant you and not pull you up, because I am sad
about the disaster I brought on you. 11Now you
fear the king of Babylon, but don't be afraid of
him. Don't be afraid of him,' says the LORD, 'be-
cause I am with you. I will save you and rescue
you from his power. 12I will be kind to you, and
he will also treat you with mercy and let you stay
in your land.'
13"But if you say, 'We will not stay in Judah,'
you will disobey the LORD your God. 14Or you
might say, 'No, we will go and live in Egypt.
There we will not see war, or hear the trumpets
of war or be hungry.' 15If you say that, listen to
the message of the LORD, you who are left alive
from Judah. This is what the LORD All-powerful,
the God of Israel, says: 'If you make up your mind
to go and live in Egypt, these things will happen:
16you are afraid of war, but it will find you in the
land of Egypt. And you are worried about hunger,
but it will follow you into Egypt, and you will die
there. 17Everyone who goes to live in Egypt will
die in war or from hunger or terrible disease. No
one who goes to Egypt will live; no one will es-
cape the terrible things I will bring to them.'
18"This is what the LORD All-powerful, the God
of Israel, says: 'I showed my anger against the
people of Jerusalem. In the same way I will show
my anger against you when you go to Egypt.
Other nations will speak evil of you. People will
be shocked by what will happen to you. You will
become a curse word, and people will insult you.
And you will never see Judah again.'
19"You who are left alive in Judah, the LORD has
told you, 'Don't go to Egypt.' Be sure you under-
stand this; I warn you today 20that you are mak-
ing a mistake that will cause your deaths. You
sent me to the LORD your God, saying, 'Pray to the
LORD our God for us. Tell us everything the LORD
our God says, and we will do it.' 21So today I have
told you, but you have not obeyed the LORD your
God in all that he sent me to tell you. 22So now
be sure you understand this: you want to go to
live in Egypt, but you will die there by war, hun-
ger or terrible diseases."

43 So Jeremiah finished telling the people
the message from the LORD their God; he
told them everything the LORD their God had sent
him to tell them.
2Azariah son of Hoshaiah, Johanan son of
Kareah, and some other men were too proud.
They said to Jeremiah, "You are lying! The LORD
our God did not send you to say, 'You must not go
to Egypt to live there.' 3Baruch son of Neriah is
causing you to be against us. He wants you to
hand us over to the Babylonians so they can kill
us or capture us and take us to Babylon."
4So Johanan, the army officers and all the peo-
ple disobeyed the LORD's command to stay in
Judah. 5But Johanan son of Kareah and the army
officers led away those who were left alive from
Judah. They were the people who had run away
from the Babylonians to other countries but
then had come back to live in Judah. 6They led
away the men, women and children, and the
king's daughters. Nebuzaradan commander of
the guard had put Gedaliah son of Ahikam son of
Shaphan in charge of those people. Johanan
also took Jeremiah the prophet[d] and Baruch son
of Neriah. 7These people did not listen to the
LORD. So they all went to Egypt to the city of
Tahpanhes.

Sidelight Tahpanhes (Jeremiah 43:7) was an Egyptian border fortress in the delta area of the Nile River. It would be the first city that refugees from Israel would reach when they entered Egypt.

8In Tahpanhes the LORD spoke his word to
Jeremiah: 9"Take some large stones. Bury them in
the clay in the brick pavement in front of the king
of Egypt's palace in Tahpanhes. Do this while the
Jews are watching you. 10Then say to them, 'This
is what the LORD All-powerful, the God of Israel,
says: I will soon send for my servant, Nebuchad-
nezzar king of Babylon. I will set his throne over
these stones I have buried, and he will spread his
covering for shade above them. 11He will come
here and attack Egypt. He will bring death to
those who are supposed to die. He will make
prisoners of those who are to be taken captive,
and he will bring war to those who are to
be killed with a sword. 12Nebuchadnezzar will
set fire to the temples of the gods of Egypt and

burn them. And he will take the idols away as
captives. As a shepherd wraps himself in his
clothes, so Nebuchadnezzar will wrap Egypt
around him. Then he will safely leave Egypt.
13He will destroy the stone pillars in the temple
of the sun god in Egypt, and he will burn down
the temples of the gods of Egypt.' "

Disaster in Egypt

44 Jeremiah received a message from the
LORD for all the Jews living in Egypt—in
the cities of Migdol, Tahpanhes, Memphis and in
southern Egypt. This was the message: 2"The
LORD All-powerful, the God of Israel, says: You
saw all the terrible things I brought on Jerusalem
and the towns of Judah, which are ruins today
with no one living in them. 3It is because the
people who lived there did evil. They made me
angry by burning incense [d] and worshipping other
gods that neither they nor you nor your ancestors
ever knew. 4I sent all my servants, the prophets, [d]
to you again and again. By them I said to you,
'Don't do this terrible thing that I hate.' 5But they
did not listen or pay attention. They did not stop
doing evil things and burning incense to other
gods. 6So I showed my great anger against them.
I poured out my anger in the towns of Judah and
the streets of Jerusalem so they are only ruins
and piles of stones today.
7"Now the LORD All-powerful, the God of
Israel, says: Why are you doing such great harm
to yourselves? You are cutting off the men and
women, children and babies from the family of
Judah, leaving yourselves without anyone from
the family of Judah. 8Why do you want to make
me angry by making idols? Why do you burn
incense to the gods of Egypt, where you have
come to live? You will destroy yourselves. Other
nations will speak evil of you and make fun of
you. 9Have you forgotten about the evil things
your ancestors did? And have you forgotten the
evil the kings and queens of Judah did? Have you
forgotten about the evil you and your wives did?
These things were done in the country of Judah
and in the streets of Jerusalem. 10Even to this day
the people of Judah are still too proud. They have
not learned to respect me or to follow my teach-
ings. They have not obeyed the laws I gave you
and your ancestors.
11"So this is what the LORD All-powerful, the
God of Israel, says: I am determined to bring dis-
asters on you. I will destroy the whole family of
Judah. 12The few who were left alive from Judah
were determined to go to Egypt and settle there,
but they will all die in Egypt. They will be killed
in war or die from hunger. From the least import-
ant to the greatest, they will be killed in war or
die from hunger. Other nations will speak evil
about them. People will be shocked by what has
happened to them. They will become a curse
word, and people will insult them. 13I will punish
those people who have gone to live in Egypt, just
as I punished Jerusalem, using swords, hunger
and terrible diseases. 14Of the people of Judah
who were left alive and have gone to live in
Egypt, none will escape my punishment. They
want to return to Judah and live there, but none
of them will live to return to Judah, except a few
people who will escape."
15A large group of the people of Judah who
lived in southern Egypt were meeting together.
Among them were many women of Judah who
were burning incense to other gods, and their
husbands knew it. All these people said to
Jeremiah, 16"We will not listen to the message from
the LORD that you spoke to us. 17We promised to
make sacrifices to the Queen Goddess, [d] and we
will certainly do everything we promised. We
will burn incense and pour out drink offerings to
worship her, just as we, our ancestors, kings and
officers did in the past. All of us did these things
in the towns of Judah and in the streets of
Jerusalem. At that time we had plenty of food
and were successful, and nothing bad happened
to us. 18But since we stopped making sacrifices to
the Queen Goddess and stopped pouring out drink
offerings to her, we have had great problems.
Our people have also been killed in war and by
hunger."
19The women said, "Our husbands knew what
we were doing. We had their permission to burn
incense to the Queen Goddess and to pour out
drink offerings to her. Our husbands knew we
were making cakes that looked like her and were
pouring out drink offerings to her."
20Then Jeremiah spoke to all the people—men
and women—who answered him. 21He said to
them, "The LORD remembered that you and your
ancestors, kings and officers, and the people of
the land burnt incense in the towns of Judah and
in the streets of Jerusalem. He remembered and
thought about it. 22Then he could not be patient
with you any longer. He hated the terrible things
you did. So he made your country an empty
desert, where no one lives. Other people curse
that country. And so it is today. 23All this hap-
pened because you burnt incense to other gods.
You sinned against the LORD. You did not obey
him or follow his teachings or the laws he gave
you. You did not keep your part of the agreement
with him. So this disaster has happened to you. It
is there for you to see."
24Then Jeremiah said to all those men and
women, "People of Judah who are now in Egypt,
hear the word of the LORD: 25The LORD All-
powerful, the God of Israel, says: you and your

wives did what you said you would do. You said,
'We will certainly keep the promises we made.
We promised to make sacrifices to the Queen
Goddess and to pour out drink offerings to her.'
So, go ahead. Do the things you promised, and
keep your promises. 26But hear the word of
the LORD. Listen, all you Jews living in Egypt.
The LORD says, 'I have sworn by my great name:
the people of Judah now living in Egypt will
never again use my name to make promises.
They will never again say in Egypt, "As surely as
the Lord GOD lives. . ." 27I am watching over
them, not to take care of them, but to hurt
them. The Jews who live in Egypt will die from
swords or hunger until they are all destroyed.
28A few will escape being killed by the sword
and will come back to Judah from Egypt. Then,
of the people of Judah who came to live in
Egypt, those who are left alive will know if my
word or their word came true. 29I will give you
a sign that I will punish you here in Egypt,' says
the LORD. 'When you see it happen, you will
know that my promises to hurt you will really
happen.' 30This is what the LORD says: 'Hophra
king of Egypt has enemies who want to kill him.
Soon I will hand him over to his enemies just as
I handed Zedekiah king of Judah over to Neb-
uchadnezzar king of Babylon, who wanted to
kill him.' "

A Message to Baruch

45 In the fourth year that Jehoiakim son of
Josiah was king of Judah. Jeremiah the
prophet[d] told these things to Baruch son of
Neriah, and Baruch wrote them on a scroll:
2"This is what the LORD, the God of Israel, says
to you, Baruch: 3You have said, 'How terrible it
is for me! The LORD has given me sorrow along
with my pain. I am tired because of my suffering
and cannot rest.' "
4The LORD said, "Say this to Baruch: 'This is
what the LORD says: I will soon tear down what
I have built, and I will pull up what I have
planted everywhere in Judah. 5Baruch, you are
looking for great things for yourself. Don't look
for them, because I will bring disaster on all the
people, says the LORD. You will have to go to
many places, but I will let you escape alive
wherever you go.' "

Messages to the Nations

46 The LORD spoke this word to Jeremiah
the prophet[d] about the nations:
2This message is to Egypt. It is about the army
of Neco king of Egypt, which was defeated at
the city of Carchemish on the Euphrates River
by Nebuchadnezzar king of Babylon. This was
in the fourth year that Jehoiakim son of Josiah
was king of Judah. This is the LORD's message to
Egypt:

3"Prepare your shields, large and small,
and march out for battle!
4Harness the horses
and get on them!
Go to your places for battle
and put on your helmets!
Polish your spears.
Put on your armour!
5What do I see?
That army is terrified,
and the soldiers are running away.
Their warriors are defeated.
They run away quickly
without looking back.
There is terror on every side!" says the LORD.
6"The fast runners cannot run away;
the strong soldiers cannot escape.
They stumble and fall
in the north, by the Euphrates River.
7Who is this, rising up like the Nile River,
like strong, fast rivers?
8Egypt rises up like the Nile River,
like strong, fast rivers.
Egypt says, 'I will rise up and cover the earth.
I will destroy cities and the people in them!'
9Horsemen, charge into battle!
Chariot drivers, drive hard!
March on, brave soldiers—
soldiers from the countries of Cush and Put
who carry shields,
soldiers from Lydia who use bows.

10"But that day belongs to the Lord GOD
All-powerful.
At that time he will give those people the
punishment they deserve.
The sword will kill until it is finished,
until it satisfies its thirst for their blood.
The Lord GOD All-powerful will offer a sacrifice
in the land of the north, by the Euphrates
River.

11"Go up to Gilead and get some balm,[d]
people of Egypt!
You have prepared many medicines,
but they will not work;
you will not be healed.
12The nations have heard of your shame,
and your cries fill all the earth.
One warrior has run into another;
both of them have fallen down together!"

13This is the message the LORD spoke to
Jeremiah the prophet[d] about Nebuchadnezzar
king of Babylon's coming to attack Egypt:
14"Announce this message in Egypt, and preach
it in Migdol.

Preach it also in the cities of Memphis and
Tahpanhes:
'Get ready for war,
because the battle is all around you.'
15Egypt, why were your warriors killed?
They could not stand because the LORD
pushed them down.
16They stumbled again and again
and fell over each other.
They said, 'Get up. Let's go back
to our own people and our homeland.
We must get away from our enemy's
sword!'
17In their homelands those soldiers called out,
'The king of Egypt is only a lot of noise.
He missed his chance for glory!' "
18The King's name is the LORD All-powerful.
He says, "As surely as I live,
a powerful leader will come.
He will be like Mount Tabor among the
mountains,
like Mount Carmel by the sea.
19People of Egypt, pack your things
to be taken away as captives,
because Memphis will be destroyed.
It will be a ruin, and no one will live
there.

20"Egypt is like a beautiful young cow,
but a horsefly is coming
from the north to attack her.
21The hired soldiers in Egypt's army
are like fat calves,
because even they all turn and run away
together;
they do not stand strong against the
attack.
Their time of destruction is coming;
they will soon be punished.
22Egypt is like a hissing snake that is trying to
escape.
The enemy comes closer and closer.
They come against Egypt with axes
like men who cut down trees.
23They will chop down Egypt's army
as if it were a great forest," says the LORD.
"There are more enemy soldiers than
locusts;[d]
there are too many to count.
24The people of Egypt will be ashamed.
They will be handed over to the enemy
from the north."

25The LORD All-powerful, the God of Israel,
says: "Very soon I will punish Amon, the god of
the city of Thebes. And I will punish Egypt, her
kings, her gods and the people who depend on
the king. 26I will hand those people over to their
enemies, who want to kill them. I will give them
to Nebuchadnezzar king of Babylon and his offi-
cers. But in the future, Egypt will live in peace as
it once did," says the LORD.

A Message to Israel

27"People of Jacob, my servants, don't be
afraid;
don't be frightened, Israel.
I will surely save you from those faraway
places
and your children from the lands where
they are captives.
The people of Jacob will have peace and
safety again,
and no one will make them afraid.
28People of Jacob, my servants, do not be
afraid,
because I am with you," says the LORD.
"I will completely destroy the many different
nations
where I scattered you.
But I will not completely destroy you.
I will punish you fairly,
but I will not let you escape your
punishment."

A Message to the Philistines

47 Before the king of Egypt attacked the city
of Gaza, the LORD spoke his word to
Jeremiah the prophet.[d] This message is to the
Philistine people.
2This is what the LORD says:
"See, the enemy is gathering in the north like
rising waters.
They will become like an overflowing
stream
and will cover the whole country like a flood,
even the towns and the people living in
them.
Everyone living in that country
will cry for help;
the people will cry painfully.
3They will hear the sound of the running
horses
and the noisy chariots
and the rumbling chariot wheels.
Parents will not help their children to safety,
because they will be too weak to help.
4The time has come
to destroy all the Philistines.
It is time to destroy all who are left alive
who could help the cities of Tyre and
Sidon.
The LORD will soon destroy the Philistines,
those left alive from the island of Crete.
5The people from the city of Gaza will be sad
and shave their heads.

The people from the city of Ashkelon will
be made silent.
Those left alive from the valley,
how long will you cut yourselves? [n]

6"You cry, 'Sword of the LORD,
how long will you keep fighting?
Return to your holder.
Stop and be still.'
7But how can his sword rest
when the LORD has given it a command?
He has ordered it
to attack Ashkelon and the seacoast."

A Message to Moab

48 This message is to the country of Moab. This is what the LORD All-powerful, the God of Israel, says:
"How terrible it will be for the city of Nebo,
because it will be ruined.
The town of Kiriathaim will be disgraced and
captured;
the strong city will be disgraced and
shattered.
2Moab will not be praised again.
Men in the town of Heshbon plan Moab's
defeat.
They say, 'Come, let us put an end to that
nation!'
Town of Madmen, [n] you will also be silenced.
The sword will chase you.
3Listen to the cries from the town of
Horonaim,
cries of much confusion and destruction.
4Moab will be broken up.
Her little children will cry for help.
5Moab's people go up the path to the town of
Luhith,
crying loudly as they go.
On the road down to Horonaim,
cries of pain and suffering can be heard.
6Run! Run for your lives!
Go like a bush being blown through the
desert.
7You trust in the things you do and in your
wealth,
so you also will be captured.
The god Chemosh [d] will go into captivity
and his priests and officers with him.
8The destroyer will come against every town;
not one town will escape.
The valley will be ruined,
and the high plain will be destroyed,
as the LORD has said.
9Give wings to Moab,
because she will surely leave her land.
Moab's towns will become empty,
with no one to live in them.
10A curse will be on anyone who doesn't do
what the LORD says,
and a curse will be on anyone who holds
back his sword from killing.

11"The people of Moab have never known
trouble.
They are like wine left to settle;
they have never been poured from one jar to
another.
They have not been taken into captivity.
So they taste as they did before,
and their smell has not changed.
12A time is coming," says the LORD,
"When I will send people to pour you from
your jars.
They will empty Moab's jars
and smash her jugs.
13The people of Israel trusted that god in the
town of Bethel,
and they were ashamed when there was no
help.
In the same way Moab will be ashamed of
their god Chemosh.

14"You cannot say, 'We are warriors!
We are brave men in battle!'
15The destroyer of Moab and her towns has
arrived.
Her best young men will be killed!" says
the King,
whose name is the LORD All-powerful.
16"The end of Moab is near,
and she will soon be destroyed.
17All you who live around Moab,
all you who know her, cry for her.
Say, 'The ruler's power is broken;
Moab's power and glory are gone.'

18"You people living in the town of Dibon,
come down from your place of
honour
and sit on the dry ground,
because the destroyer of Moab has come
against you.
And he has destroyed your fortified cities.
19You people living in the town of Aroer,
stand next to the road and watch.
See the man running away and the woman
escaping.
Ask them, 'What happened?'
20Moab is filled with shame, because she is
ruined.
Cry, Moab, cry out!

sad and . . . yourselves The people did these things to show their sadness.
Madmen This name sounds like the Hebrew word for "be silenced".

Announce at the Arnon River
that Moab is destroyed.
21 People on the high plain have been punished.
Judgement has come to these towns:
Holon, Jahzah and Mephaath;
22 Dibon, Nebo and Beth Diblathaim;
23 Kiriathaim, Beth Gamul and Beth Meon;
24 Kerioth and Bozrah.
Judgement has come to all the towns of Moab, far and near.
25 Moab's strength has been cut off,
and its arm broken!" says the LORD.

26 "The people of Moab thought they were greater than the LORD,
so punish them until they act as if they are drunk.
Moab will fall and roll around in its own vomit,
and people will even make fun of it.
27 Moab, you made fun of Israel.
Israel was caught in the middle of a gang of thieves.
When you spoke about Israel,
you shook your head and acted as if you were better than it.
28 People in Moab, leave your towns empty
and go and live among the rocks.
Be like a dove that makes its nest
at the entrance of a cave.

29 "We have heard that the people of Moab are proud,
very proud.
They are proud, very proud,
and in their hearts they think they are important."
30 The LORD says,
"I know Moab's great pride, but it is useless.
Moab's boasting accomplishes nothing.
31 So I cry sadly for Moab,
for everyone in Moab.
I moan for the people from the town of Kir Hareseth.
32 I cry with the people of the town of Jazer
for you, the grapevines of the town of Sibmah.
In the past your vines spread all the way to the sea,
as far as the sea of Jazer.
But the destroyer has taken over
your fruit and grapes.
33 Joy and happiness are gone
from the large, rich fields of Moab.
I have stopped the flow of wine from the winepresses. [d]
No one walks on the grapes with shouts of joy.
There are shouts,
but not shouts of joy.

34 "Their crying can be heard from Moabite towns,
from Heshbon to Elealeh and Jahaz.
It can be heard from Zoar as far away as Horonaim and Eglath Shelishiyah.
Even the waters of Nimrim are dried up.
35 I will stop Moab
from making burnt offerings at the places of worship
and from burning incense [d] to their gods,"
says the LORD.

36 "My heart cries sadly for Moab like a flute playing a funeral song.
It cries like a flute for the people from Kir Hareseth.
The money they made has all been taken away.
37 Every head has been shaved
and every beard cut off.
Everyone's hands are cut,
and everyone wears rough cloth around his waist. [n]

Sidelight If you wanted to show your sadness for those who had died in the time of Jeremiah 48:37, you would usually shave your head, cut your beard off and wear sackcloth around your waist. Today we simply wear black, but both approaches symbolise mourning.

38 People are crying on every roof [n] in Moab
and in every public square.
There is nothing but sadness,
because I have broken Moab
like a jar no one wants," says the LORD.
39 "Moab is shattered! The people are crying!
Moab turns away in shame!
People all around her make fun of her.
The things that happened fill them with great fear."

40 This is what the LORD says:
"Look! Someone is coming, like an eagle diving down from the sky
and spreading its wings over Moab.

Every head . . . waist. The people did these things to show their sadness for those who had died.
roof In Bible times houses were built with flat roofs. The roof was used for drying things such as flax and fruit. And it was used as an extra room, as a place for worship and as a place to sleep in the summer.

41The towns of Moab will be captured,
and the fortified cities will be defeated.
At that time Moab's warriors will be
frightened,
like a woman who is having a baby.
42The nation of Moab will be destroyed,
because they thought they were greater
than the LORD.
43Fear, deep pits and traps wait for you,
people of Moab," says the LORD.
44"People will run from fear,
but they will fall into the pits.
Anyone who climbs out of the pits
will be caught in the traps.
I will bring the year of punishment to Moab,"
says the LORD.

45"People have run from the powerful enemy
and have gone to Heshbon for safety.
But fire started in Heshbon;
a blaze has spread from the home town of
Sihon king of Moab.
It burnt up the leaders of Moab
and destroyed those proud people.
46How terrible it is for you, Moab!
The people who worship Chemosh have
been destroyed.
Your sons have been taken captive,
and your daughters have been taken away.

47"But in days to come,
I will make good things happen again to
Moab," says the LORD.

This ends the judgement on Moab.

A Message to Ammon

49 This message is to the Ammonite people.
This is what the LORD says:
"Do you think that Israel has no children?
Do you think there is no one to take the
land when the parents die?
If that were true, why did Molech[d] take
Gad's land
and why did Molech's people settle in
Gad's towns?"
2The LORD says,
"The time will come when I will make
Rabbah,
the capital city of the Ammonites, hear the
battle cry.
It will become a hill covered with ruins,
and the towns around it will be burnt.
Those people forced Israel out of that land,
but now Israel will force them out!" says
the LORD.
3"People in the town of Heshbon, cry sadly
because the town of Ai is destroyed!
Those who live in Rabbah, cry out!
Put on your rough cloth to show your
sadness, and cry loudly.
Run here and there for safety inside the
walls,
because Molech will be taken captive
and his priests and officers with him.
4You boast about your valleys
and about the fruit in your valleys.
You are like an unfaithful child
who believes his treasures will save him.
You think, 'Who would attack me?'
5I will soon bring terror on you
from everyone around you,"
says the Lord GOD All-powerful.
"You will all be forced to run away,
and no one will be able to gather you.

6"But the time will come
when I will make good things happen to
the Ammonites again,"
says the LORD.

A Message to Edom

7This message is to Edom. This is what the
LORD All-powerful says:
"Is there no more wisdom in the town of
Teman?
Can the wise men of Edom no longer give
good advice?
Have they lost their wisdom?
8You people living in the town of Dedan,
run away and hide in deep caves,
because I will bring disaster on the people of
Esau.
It is time for me to punish them.
9If workers came and picked the grapes from
your vines,
they would leave a few grapes behind.
If robbers came at night,
they would steal only enough for
themselves.
10But I will strip Edom bare.
I will find all their hiding places,
so they will not be able to hide
from me.
The children, relatives and neighbours
will die,
and Edom will be no more.
11Leave the orphans, and I will take care of
them.
Your widows also can trust in me."

12This is what the LORD says: "Some people did
not deserve to be punished, but they had to drink
from the cup of suffering anyway. People of
Edom, you deserve to be punished, so you will not
escape punishment. You must certainly drink from
the cup of suffering." 13The LORD says, "I swear

by my own name that the city of Bozrah will become a pile of ruins! People will be shocked by what happened there. They will insult that city and speak evil of it. And all the towns around it will become ruins for ever."

14 I have heard a message from the LORD.
A messenger has been sent among the nations, saying,
"Gather your armies to attack it!
Get ready for battle!"

15 "Soon I will make you the smallest of nations,
and you will be greatly hated by everyone.
16 Edom, you frightened other nations,
but your pride has fooled you.
You live in the hollow places of the cliff
and control the high places of the hills.
Even if you build your home as high as an eagle's nest,
I will bring you down from there," says the LORD.

17 "Edom will be destroyed.
People who pass by will be shocked to see the destroyed cities,
and they will be amazed at all her injuries.
18 Edom will be destroyed like the cities of Sodom and Gomorrah
and the towns around them," says the LORD.
"No one will live there!
No one will stay in Edom."

19 "Like a lion coming up from the thick bushes near the Jordan River
to attack a strong pen for sheep,
I will suddenly chase Edom from its land.
Who is the one I have chosen to do this?
There is no one like me,
no one who can take me to court.
None of their leaders can stand up against me."

20 So listen to what the LORD has planned to do against Edom.
Listen to what he has decided to do to the people in the town of Teman.
He will surely drag away the young ones of Edom.
Their home towns will surely be shocked at what happens to them.
21 At the sound of Edom's fall, the earth will shake.
Their cry will be heard all the way to the Red Sea.
22 The LORD is like an eagle swooping down
and spreading its wings over the city of Bozrah.
At that time Edom's soldiers will become very frightened,
like a woman having a baby.

A Message to Damascus

23 This message is to the city of Damascus:
"The towns of Hamath and Arpad are put to shame,
because they have heard bad news.
They are discouraged.
They are troubled like the tossing sea.
24 The city of Damascus has become weak.
The people want to run away;
they are ready to panic.
The people feel pain and suffering,
like a woman giving birth to a baby.
25 Damascus was a city of my joy.
Why have the people not left that famous city yet?
26 Surely the young men will die in the city squares,
and all her soldiers will be killed at that time," says the LORD All-powerful.
27 "I will set fire to the walls of Damascus,
and it will completely burn the strong cities of King Ben-Hadad."

A Message to Kedar and Hazor

28 This message is to the tribe[d] of Kedar and the kingdoms of Hazor, which Nebuchadnezzar king of Babylon defeated. This is what the LORD says:
"Go and attack the people of Kedar,
and destroy the people of the East.
29 Their tents and flocks will be taken away.
Their belongings will be carried off—
their tents, all their goods and their camels.
Men will shout to them,
'Terror on every side!'

30 "Run away quickly!
People in Hazor, find a good place to hide!" says the LORD.
"Nebuchadnezzar king of Babylon has made plans against you
and wants to defeat you.

31 "Get up! Attack the nation that is comfortable,
that is sure no one will defeat it," says the LORD.
"It does not have gates or fences to protect it.
Its people live alone.
32 The enemy will steal their camels
and their large herds of cattle as war prizes.
I will scatter the people who cut their hair short to every part of the earth,
and I will bring disaster on them from everywhere," says the LORD.

33"The city of Hazor will become a home for
wild dogs;
it will be an empty desert for ever.
No one will live there,
and no one will stay in it."

A Message to Elam

34Soon after Zedekiah became king of Judah,
the LORD spoke this word to Jeremiah the
prophet. [d] This message is to the nation of Elam.
35This is what the LORD All-powerful says:
"I will soon break Elam's bow,
its greatest strength.
36I will bring the four winds against Elam
from the four corners of the skies.
I will scatter its people everywhere the four
winds blow;
its captives will go to every nation.
37I will terrify Elam in front of their enemies,
who want to destroy them.
I will bring disaster to Elam
and show them how angry I am!" says the
LORD.
"I will send a sword to chase Elam
until I have killed them all.
38I will set up my throne in Elam to show that
I am king,
and I will destroy its king and its officers!"
says the LORD.
39"But I will make good things happen to Elam
again
in the future," says the LORD.

A Message to Babylon

50 This is the message the LORD spoke to
Babylon and the Babylonian people
through Jeremiah the prophet. [d]
2"Announce this to the nations.
Lift up a banner and tell them.
Speak the whole message and say:
'Babylon will be captured.
The god Bel [d] will be put to shame,
and the god Marduk [d] will be afraid.
Babylon's gods will be put to shame,
and her idols will be afraid!'
3A nation from the north will attack
Babylon
and make it like an empty desert.
No one will live there;
both people and animals will run away."

4The LORD says, "At that time
the people of Israel and Judah will come
together.
They will cry and look for the LORD
their God.
5Those people will ask how to go to Jerusalem
and will start in that direction.
They will come and join themselves to the
LORD.
They will make an agreement with him that
will last for ever,
an agreement that will never be forgotten.

6"My people have been like lost sheep.
Their leaders have led them in the
wrong way
and made them wander around in the
mountains and hills.
They forgot where their resting place was.
7Whoever saw my people hurt them.
And those enemies said, 'We did nothing
wrong.
Those people sinned against the LORD, their
true resting place,
the God their fathers trusted.'

8"Run away from Babylon,
and leave the land of the Babylonians.
Be like the goats that lead the flock.
9I will soon bring against Babylon
many great nations from the north.
They will take their places for war against it,
and it will be captured by people from the
north.
Their arrows are like trained soldiers
who do not return from war with empty
hands.
10The enemy will take all the wealth from the
Babylonians.
Those enemy soldiers will get all they
want," says the LORD.

11"Babylon, you are excited and happy,
because you took my land.
You dance around like a young cow in the grain.
Your laughter is like the neighing of male
horses.
12Your mother will be very ashamed;
the woman who gave birth to you will be
disgraced.
Soon Babylonia will be the least important of
all the nations.
She will be an empty, dry desert.
13Because of the LORD's anger,
no one will live there.
She will be completely empty.
Everyone who passes by Babylon will be
shocked.
They will shake their heads when they see
all her injuries.

14"Take your positions for war against Babylon,
all you soldiers with bows.
Shoot your arrows at Babylon! Do not save
any of them,
because Babylon has sinned against the
LORD.

[15]Soldiers around Babylon, shout the
war cry!
Babylon has surrendered, her towers have
fallen,
and her walls have been torn down.
The LORD is giving her people the punishment
they deserve.
You nations should give her what she
deserves;
do to her what she has done to others.
[16]Don't let the people from Babylon plant their
crops
or gather the harvest.
The soldiers treated their captives cruelly.
Now, let everyone go back home.
Let everyone run to his own country.

[17]"The people of Israel are like a flock of sheep
that are scattered
from being chased by lions.
The first lion to eat them up
was the king of Assyria.
The last lion to crush their bones
was Nebuchadnezzar king of Babylon."

[18]So this is what the LORD All-powerful, the
God of Israel, says:
"I will punish the king of Babylon and his
country
as I punished the king of Assyria.
[19]But I will bring the people of Israel back to
their own pasture.
They will eat on Mount Carmel and in
Bashan.
They will eat and be full
on the hills of Ephraim and Gilead."
[20]The LORD says,
"At that time people will try to find Israel's
guilt,
but there will be no guilt.
People will try to find Judah's sins,
but no sins will be found,
because I will leave a few people alive from
Israel and Judah,
and I will forgive their sins.

[21]"Attack the land of Merathaim.
Attack the people who live in Pekod.
Chase them, kill them, and completely
destroy them.
Do everything I commanded you!" says the
LORD.
[22]"The noise of battle can be heard all over the
country;
it is the noise of much destruction.
[23]Babylon was the hammer of the whole
earth,
but how broken and shattered that hammer
is now.
It is truly the most ruined
of all the nations.
[24]Babylon, I set a trap for you,
and you were caught before you knew it.
You fought against the LORD,
so you were found and taken prisoner.
[25]The LORD has opened up his storeroom
and brought out the weapons of his anger,
because the Lord GOD All-powerful has work
to do
in the land of the Babylonians.
[26]Come against Babylon from far away.
Break open her storehouses of grain.
Pile up her dead bodies like heaps of grain.
Completely destroy Babylon
and do not leave anyone alive.
[27]Kill all the young men in Babylon;
let them be killed like animals.
How terrible it will be for them, because the
time has come for their defeat;
it is time for them to be punished.
[28]Listen to the people running to escape the
country of Babylon!
They are telling Jerusalem
how the LORD our God is punishing Babylon
as it deserves
for destroying his Temple. [d]

[29]"Call for the archers
to come against Babylon.
Tell them to surround the city,
and let no one escape.
Pay her back for what she has done;
do to her what she has done to other
nations.
Babylon acted with pride against the LORD,
the Holy One of Israel.
[30]So her young men will be killed in her streets.
All her soldiers will die on that day," says
the LORD.
[31]"Babylon, you are too proud, and I am
against you,"
says the Lord GOD All-powerful.
"The time has come
for you to be punished.
[32]Proud Babylon will stumble and fall,
and no one will help her get up.
I will start a fire in her towns,
and it will burn up everything around her."

[33]This is what the LORD All-powerful says:
"The people of Israel
and Judah are slaves.
The enemy took them as prisoners
and won't let them go.
[34]But God is strong and will buy them back.
His name is the LORD All-powerful.
He will surely defend them with power
so he can give rest to their land.

But he will not give rest to those living in
Babylon."

35The LORD says,
"Let a sword kill the people living in
Babylon
and her officers and wise men!
36Let a sword kill her false prophets,[d]
and they will become fools.
Let a sword kill her warriors,
and they will be full of terror.
37Let a sword kill her horses and chariots
and all the soldiers hired from other
countries!
Then they will be like frightened women.
Let a sword attack her treasures,
so they will be taken away.
38Let a sword attack her waters
so they will be dried up.
She is a land of idols,
and the people go insane with fear over
them.
39"Desert animals and hyenas will live there,
and owls will live there,
but no people will ever live there again.
She will never be filled with people again.
40God completely destroyed the cities of Sodom
and Gomorrah
and the towns around them," says the
LORD.
"In the same way no people will live in
Babylon,
and no human being will stay there.
41"Look! An army is coming from the north.
A powerful nation and many kings
are coming together from all around the
world.
42Their armies have bows and spears.
The soldiers are cruel and have no
mercy.
As the soldiers come riding on their horses,
the sound is loud like the roaring sea.
They stand in their places, ready for battle.
They are ready to attack you, city of
Babylon.
43The king of Babylon heard about those
armies,
and he became helpless with fear.
Distress has gripped him.
His pain is like that of a woman giving
birth to a baby.

44"Like a lion coming up from the thick bushes
near the Jordan River
to attack a strong pen for sheep,
I will suddenly chase the people of Babylon
from their land.
Who is the one I have chosen to do this?
There is no one like me,
no one who can take me to court.
None of their leaders can stand up
against me."
45So listen to what the LORD has planned to do
against Babylon.
Listen to what he has decided to do to the
people in the city of Babylon.
He will surely drag away the young ones of
Babylon.
Their home towns will surely be shocked at
what happens to them.
46At the sound of Babylon's capture, the earth
will shake.
People in all nations will hear Babylon's cry
of distress.

51

This is what the LORD says:
"I will soon cause a destroying wind
to blow
against Babylon and the Babylonian people.
2I will send foreign people to destroy Babylon
like a wind that blows chaff[d] away.
They will destroy the land.
Armies will surround the city
when the day of disaster comes upon her.
3Don't let the Babylonian soldiers prepare their
bows to shoot.
Don't even let them put on their armour.
Don't feel sorry for the young men of Babylon,
but completely destroy her army.
4They will be killed in the land of the
Babylonians
and will die in her streets.
5The Lord GOD All-powerful
did not leave Israel and Judah,
even though they were completely guilty
in the presence of the Holy One of Israel.

6"Run away from Babylon
and save your lives!
Don't stay and be killed because of
Babylon's sins.
It is time for the LORD to punish Babylon;
he will give Babylon the punishment she
deserves.
7Babylon was like a gold cup in the LORD's
hand
that made the whole earth drunk.
The nations drank Babylon's wine,
and so they went mad.
8Babylon has suddenly fallen and been broken.
Cry for her!
Get balm[d] for her pain,
and perhaps she can be healed.

9"Foreigners in Babylon say, 'We tried to heal
Babylon,
but she cannot be healed.

So let us leave her and each go to his own
country.
Babylon's punishment is as high as the sky;
it reaches to the clouds.'

10"The people of Judah say, 'The LORD has
shown us to be right.
Come, let us tell in Jerusalem
what the LORD our God has done.'

11"Sharpen the arrows!
Pick up your shields!
The LORD has stirred up the kings of the
Medes,
because he wants to destroy Babylon.
The LORD will punish them as they deserve
for destroying his Temple. [d]
12Lift up a banner against the walls of
Babylon!
Bring more guards.
Put the watchmen in their places,
and get ready for a secret attack!
The LORD will certainly do what he has
planned
and what he said he would do against the
people of Babylon.
13People of Babylon, you live near much water
and are rich with many treasures,
but your end as a nation has come.
It is time to stop you from robbing other
nations.
14The LORD All-powerful has promised in his
own name:
'Babylon, I will surely fill you with so many
enemy soldiers they will be like a
swarm of locusts. [d]
They will stand over you and shout their
victory.'

15"The LORD made the earth by his power.
He used his wisdom to build the world
and his understanding to stretch out the
skies.
16When he thunders, the waters in the skies
roar.
He makes clouds rise in the sky all over the
earth.
He sends lightning with the rain
and brings out the wind from his
storehouses.

17"People are so stupid and know so little.
Goldsmiths are made ashamed by their
idols,
because those statues are only false gods.
They have no breath in them.
18They are worth nothing; people make fun of
them.
When they are judged, they will be
destroyed.
19But God, who is Jacob's Portion, [d] is not like
the idols.
He made everything,
and he chose Israel to be his special people.
The LORD All-powerful is his name.

20"You are my war club,
my battle weapon.
I use you to smash nations.
I use you to destroy kingdoms.
21I use you to smash horses and riders.
I use you to smash chariots and drivers.
22I use you to smash men and women.
I use you to smash old people and young
people.
I use you to smash young men and young
women.
23I use you to smash shepherds and flocks.
I use you to smash farmers and oxen.
I use you to smash governors and officers.

24"But I will pay back Babylon and all the
Babylonians for all the evil things they did to
Jerusalem in your sight," says the LORD.

25The LORD says,
"Babylon, you are a destroying mountain,
and I am against you.
You have destroyed the whole land.
I will put my hand out against you.
I will roll you off the cliffs,
and I will make you a burnt out mountain.
26People will not find any rocks in Babylon big
enough for cornerstones. [d]
People will not take any rocks from
Babylon to use for the foundation of a
building,
because your city will be just a pile of ruins
for ever," says the LORD.

27"Lift up a banner in the land!
Blow the trumpet among the nations!
Get the nations ready for battle against
Babylon.
Call these kingdoms of Ararat, Minni and
Ashkenaz to fight against her.
Choose a commander to lead the army
against Babylon.
Send so many horses that they are like a
swarm of locusts.
28Get the nations ready for battle against
Babylon—
the kings of the Medes,
their governors and all their officers,
and all the countries they rule.
29The land shakes and moves in pain,
because the LORD will do what he has
planned to Babylon.
He will make Babylon an empty desert,
where no one will live.

30Babylon's warriors have stopped fighting.
They stay in their protected cities.
Their strength is gone,
and they have become like frightened women.
Babylon's houses are burning.
The bars of her gates are broken.
31One messenger follows another;
messenger follows messenger.
They announce to the king of Babylon
that his whole city has been captured.
32The river crossings have been captured,
and the swamplands are burning.
All of Babylon's soldiers are terribly afraid."

33This is what the LORD All-powerful, the God of Israel, says:
"The city of Babylon is like a threshing[d] floor,
where people crush the grain at harvest time.
The time to harvest Babylon is coming soon."

34"Nebuchadnezzar king of Babylon has defeated and destroyed us.
In the past he took our people away,
and we became like an empty jar.
He was like a giant snake that swallowed us.
He filled his stomach with our best things.
Then he spat us out.
35Babylon did terrible things to hurt us.
Now let those things happen to Babylon,"
say the people of Jerusalem.
"The people of Babylon killed our people.
Now let them be punished for what they did," says Jerusalem.

36So this is what the LORD says:
"I will soon defend you, Judah,
and make sure that Babylon is punished.
I will dry up Babylon's sea
and make her springs become dry.
37Babylon will become a pile of ruins,
a home for wild dogs.
People will be shocked by what happened there.
No one will live there any more.
38Babylon's people roar like young lions;
they growl like baby lions.
39While they are stirred up,
I will give a feast for them
and make them drunk.
They will shout and laugh.
And they will sleep for ever and never wake up!" says the LORD.
40"I will take the people of Babylon to be killed.
They will be like lambs,
like rams and goats waiting to be killed.

41"How Babylon has been defeated!
The pride of the whole earth has been taken captive.
People from other nations are shocked at what happened to Babylon,
and the things they see make them afraid.
42The sea has risen over Babylon;
its roaring waves cover her.
43Babylon's towns are ruined and empty.
It has become a dry, desert land,
a land where no one lives.
People do not even travel through Babylon.
44I will punish the god Bel[d] in Babylon.
I will make him spit out what he has swallowed.
Nations will no longer come to Babylon;
even the wall around the city will fall.

45"Come out of Babylon, my people!
Run for your lives!
Run from the LORD's great anger.
46Don't lose courage;
rumours will spread through the land, but don't be afraid.
One rumour comes this year, and another comes the next year.
There will be rumours of terrible fighting in the country,
of rulers fighting against rulers.
47The time will surely come
when I will punish the idols of Babylon,
and the whole land will be disgraced.
There will be many dead people lying all around.
48Then heaven and earth and all that is in them
will shout for joy about Babylon.
They will shout because the army comes from the north
to destroy Babylon," says the LORD.

49"Babylon must fall, because she killed people from Israel.
She killed people from everywhere on earth.
50You who have escaped being killed with swords,
leave Babylon! Don't wait!
Remember the LORD in the faraway land
and think about Jerusalem."

51"We people of Judah are disgraced,
because we have been insulted.
We have been shamed,
because strangers have gone into
the holy places of the LORD's Temple!"[d]

52So the LORD says, "The time is coming soon
when I will punish the idols of Babylon.

Wounded people will cry with pain
all over that land.
53Even if Babylon grows until she touches
the sky,
and even if she makes her highest cities
strong,
I will send people to destroy her," says the
LORD.
54"Sounds of people crying are heard in
Babylon.
Sounds of people destroying things
are heard in the land of the Babylonians.
55The LORD is destroying Babylon
and making the loud sounds of the city
become silent.
Enemies come roaring in like ocean waves.
The roar of their voices is heard all
around.
56The army has come to destroy Babylon.
Her soldiers have been captured,
and their bows are broken,
because the LORD is a God who punishes
people for the evil they do.
He gives them the full punishment they
deserve.
57I will make Babylon's rulers and wise men
drunk,
and her governors, officers and soldiers too.
Then they will sleep for ever and never wake
up," says the King,
whose name is the LORD All-powerful.

58This is what the LORD All-powerful says:
"Babylon's thick wall will be completely
pulled down
and her high gates burnt.
The people will work hard, but it won't
help;
their work will only become fuel for the
flames!"

A Message to Babylon

59This is the message that Jeremiah the
prophet[d] gave to the officer Seraiah son of Neriah,
who was the son of Mahseiah. Seraiah went to
Babylon with Zedekiah king of Judah in the
fourth year of Zedekiah's reign. His duty was to
arrange the king's food and housing on the trip.
60Jeremiah had written on a scroll all the terrible
things that would happen to Babylon, all these
words about Babylon. 61Jeremiah said to Seraiah,
"As soon as you come to Babylon, be sure to read
this message so all the people can hear you.
62Then say, 'LORD, you have said that you will
destroy this place so that no people or animals
will live in it. It will be an empty ruin for ever.'
63After you finish reading this scroll, tie a stone to
it and throw it into the Euphrates River. 64Then
say, 'In the same way Babylon will sink and will
not rise again because of the terrible things I will
make happen here. Her people will fall.' "

The words of Jeremiah end here.

The Fall of Jerusalem

52 Zedekiah was 21 years old when he be-
came king, and he was king in Jerusalem
for eleven years. His mother's name was Hamutal
daughter of Jeremiah,[n] and she was from Libnah.
2Zedekiah did what the LORD said was wrong,
just as Jehoiakim had done. 3All this happened
in Jerusalem and Judah because the LORD was
angry with them. Finally, he threw them out of
his presence.

Zedekiah turned against the king of Babylon.
4Then Nebuchadnezzar king of Babylon marched
against Jerusalem with his whole army. They
made a camp around the city and built devices all
around the city walls to attack it. This happened
in Zedekiah's ninth year, tenth month and tenth
day as king. 5And the city was under attack until
Zedekiah's eleventh year as king.

6By the ninth day of the fourth month, the
hunger was terrible in the city; there was no food
for the people to eat. 7Then the city wall was
broken through, and the whole army of Judah ran
away at night. They left the city through the gate
between the two walls by the king's garden. Even
though the Babylonians were surrounding the
city, Zedekiah and his men headed towards the
Jordan Valley.

8But the Babylonian army chased King
Zedekiah and caught him in the plains of Jericho.
All of his army was scattered from him. 9So the
Babylonians captured Zedekiah and took him to
the king of Babylon at the town of Riblah in the
land of Hamath. There he passed sentence on
Zedekiah. 10At Riblah the king of Babylon killed
Zedekiah's sons as he watched. The king also
killed all the officers of Judah. 11Then he put
out Zedekiah's eyes, and put bronze chains
on him and took him to Babylon. And the king
kept Zedekiah in prison there until the day
he died.

12Nebuzaradan, commander of the king's spe-
cial guards and servant of the king of Babylon,
came to Jerusalem on the tenth day of the fifth
month. This was in Nebuchadnezzar's nine-
teenth year as king of Babylon. 13Nebuzaradan
set fire to the Temple[d] of the LORD, the palace
and all the houses of Jerusalem; every important
building was burnt. 14The whole Babylonian
army, led by the commander of the king's special

Jeremiah This is not the prophet Jeremiah but a different man with the same name.

guards, broke down all the walls around Jerusalem.
15 Nebuzaradan, the commander of the king's spe-
cial guards, took captive some of the poorest peo-
ple, those who were left in Jerusalem, those who
had surrendered to the king of Babylon and the
skilled craftsmen who were left in Jerusalem.
16 But Nebuzaradan left behind some of the poor-
est people of the land to take care of the vine-
yards and fields.

17 The Babylonians broke into pieces the bronze
pillars, the bronze stands and the large bronze
bowl, called the Sea, which were in the Temple
of the LORD. Then they carried all the bronze
pieces to Babylon. 18 They also took the pots,
shovels, wick trimmers, bowls, dishes and all the
bronze objects used to serve in the Temple. 19 The
commander of the king's special guards took
away bowls, pans for carrying hot coals, large
bowls, pots, lampstands, pans and bowls used
for drink offerings. He took everything that was
made of pure gold or silver.

20 There was so much bronze that it could not
be weighed: two pillars, the large bronze bowl
called the Sea with the twelve bronze bulls under
it and the movable stands, which King Solomon
had made for the Temple of the LORD.

21 Each of the pillars was about 9 metres high,
6 metres around and hollow inside. The wall of
each pillar was 8 centimetres thick. 22 The bronze
capital[d] on top of the one pillar was about 2.5
metres high. It was decorated with a net design
and bronze pomegranates[d] all around it. The
other pillar also had pomegranates and was like
the first pillar. 23 There were 96 pomegranates on
the sides of the pillars. There was a total of 100
pomegranates above the net design.

24 The commander of the king's special guards
took as prisoners Seraiah the chief priest,
Zephaniah the priest next in rank and the three
doorkeepers. 25 He also took from the city the of-
ficer in charge of the soldiers, seven people who
advised the king, the royal secretary who se-
lected people for the army and 60 other men
from Judah who were in the city when it fell.
26 Nebuzaradan, the commander, took these peo-
ple and brought them to the king of Babylon at
the town of Riblah. 27 There at Riblah, in the land
of Hamath, the king had them killed.

So the people of Judah were led away from
their country as captives. 28 This is the number
of the people Nebuchadnezzar took away as
captives: in the seventh year, 3,023 Jews; 29 in
Nebuchadnezzar's eighteenth year, 832 people
from Jerusalem; 30 in Nebuchadnezzar's twenty-
third year, Nebuzaradan, commander of the
king's special guards, took 745 Jews as captives.

In all 4,600 people were taken captive.

Jehoiachin is Set Free

31 Jehoiachin king of Judah was in prison in
Babylon for 37 years. The year Evil-Merodach
became king of Babylon he let Jehoiachin king of
Judah out of prison. He set Jehoiachin free on
the twenty-fifth day of the twelfth month. 32 Evil-
Merodach spoke kindly to Jehoiachin and gave
him a seat of honour above the seats of the
other kings who were with him in Babylon. 33 So
Jehoiachin put away his prison clothes, and for
the rest of his life, he ate at the king's table.
34 Every day the king of Babylon gave Jehoiachin
an allowance. This lasted as long as he lived,
until the day Jehoiachin died.

Lamentations

Why Read This Book:

- Find ways to express grief to God (Lamentations 1—2).
- Learn about taking responsibility for choices and consequences (Lamentations 3—4).
- Be encouraged to turn to God in times of trouble (Lamentations 5).

When?

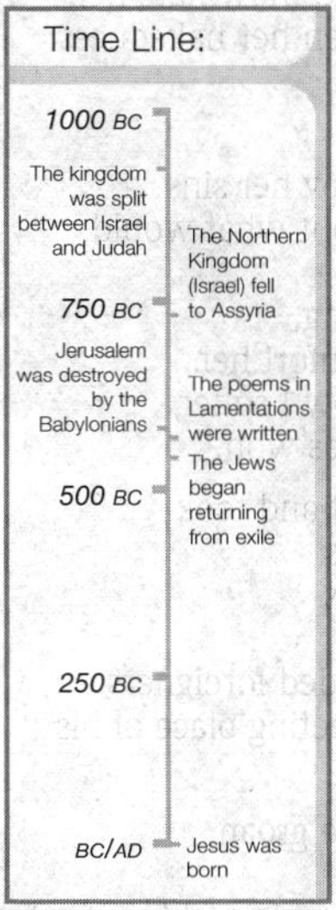

Behind the Scenes:

All of Jerusalem was in ruins.
Babylonians had surrounded the city and then burned it to the ground.
Children, women and men had been killed.
Desolation was everywhere.
Everything the Jews had known and loved was gone.
Full of sorrow, the five poems in Lamentations were written.
Grief is evident in each of the poems.
Hope shines through only towards the end of the book.
In future years, people read the book in times of sorrow.
Jews read it each year in August to remember the Temple's destruction and to repent of their sins.
Knowing God's love can help through times of crisis like this.

Like the lines you've just read, each part of the five poems in Lamentations begins with a different consecutive letter of the Hebrew alphabet – 22 letters in all. Of course, we can't see the structure in English, because the translated words are different. But the ancient Hebrews understood that the poems expressed their sorrow from beginning to end, "from A to Z".

Where?

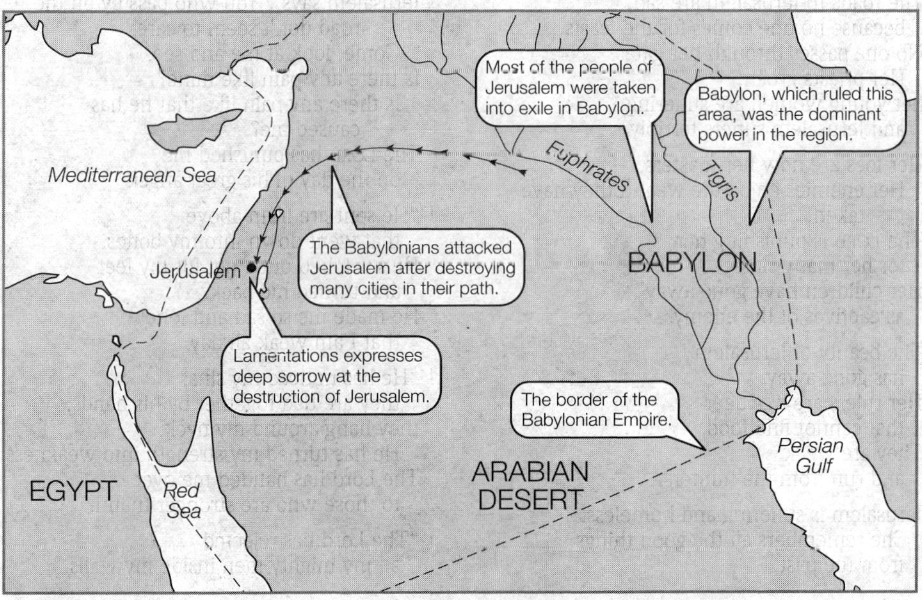

Jerusalem Cries over Her Loss

1 Jerusalem once was full of people,
but now the city is empty.
Jerusalem once was a great city among the nations,
but now she[n] is like a widow.
She was like a queen of all the other cities,
but now she is a slave.

2She cries loudly at night,
and tears are on her cheeks.
There is no one to comfort her;
all who loved her are gone.
All her friends have turned against her
and are now her enemies.

Sidelight The "blues" are nothing new. There are many books in the Bible which contain songs of sorrow (such as 2 Samuel 1:17–27, p.284, and Psalm 74, p.544), but the book of Lamentations is the only book of the Bible which is blue all through!

3Judah has gone into captivity
where she suffers and works hard.
She lives among other nations,
but she has found no rest.
Those who chased her caught her
when she was in trouble.

4The roads to Jerusalem are sad,
because no one comes for the feasts.
No one passes through her gates.
Her priests groan,
her young women are suffering,
and Jerusalem suffers terribly.

5Her foes are now her masters.
Her enemies enjoy the wealth they have taken.
The LORD is punishing her
for her many sins.
Her children have gone away
as captives of the enemy.

6The beauty of Jerusalem
has gone away.
Her rulers are like deer
that cannot find food.
They are weak
and run from the hunters.

7Jerusalem is suffering and homeless.
She remembers all the good things
from the past.
But her people were defeated by the enemy,
and there was no one to help her.
When her enemies saw her,
they laughed to see her ruined.

8Jerusalem sinned terribly,
so she has become unclean.[d]
Those who honoured her now hate her,
because they have seen her nakedness.
She groans
and turns away.

9She made herself dirty by her sins
and did not think about what would happen to her.
Her defeat was surprising,
and no one could comfort her.
She says, "LORD, see how I suffer,
because the enemy has won."

10The enemy reached out and took
all her precious things.
She even saw foreigners
enter her Temple.[d]
The LORD had commanded foreigners
never to enter the meeting place of his people.

11All of Jerusalem's people groan,
looking for bread.
They are trading their precious things for food
so they can stay alive.
The city says, "Look, LORD, and see.
I am hated."

12Jerusalem says, "You who pass by on the road don't seem to care.
Come, look at me and see.
Is there any pain like mine?
Is there any pain like that he has caused me?
The LORD has punished me
on the day of his great anger.

13"He sent fire from above
that went down into my bones.
He stretched out a net for my feet
and turned me back.
He made me so sad and lonely
that I am weak all day.

14"He has noticed my sins;
they are tied together by his hands;
they hang around my neck.
He has turned my strength into weakness.
The Lord has handed me over
to those who are stronger than I.

15"The Lord has rejected
all my mighty men inside my walls.

she In this poem the city of Jerusalem is described as a woman.

He brought an army against me
to destroy my young men.
As if in a winepress,[d] the Lord has crushed
the capital city of Judah.

16"I cry about these things;
my eyes overflow with tears.
There is no one near to comfort me,
no one who can give me strength again.
My children are left sad and lonely,
because the enemy has won."

17Jerusalem reaches out her hands,
but there is no one to comfort her.
The LORD commanded the people of Jacob
to be surrounded by their enemies.
Jerusalem is now unclean
like those around her.

18Jerusalem says, "The LORD is right,
but I refused to obey him.
Listen, all you people,
and look at my pain.
My young women and men
have gone into captivity.

19"I called out to my friends,
but they turned against me.
My priests and my elders
have died in the city
while looking for food
to stay alive.

20"Look at me, LORD. I am upset
and greatly troubled.
My heart is troubled,
because I have been so stubborn.
Out in the streets, the sword kills;
inside the houses, death destroys.

21"People have heard my groaning,
and there is no one to comfort me.
All my enemies have heard of my trouble,
and they are happy you have done this
to me.
Now bring that day you have announced
so that my enemies will be like me.

22"Look at all their evil.
Do to them what you have done to me
because of all my sins.
I groan over and over again,
and I am afraid."

The LORD Destroyed Jerusalem

2 Look how the Lord in his anger
has brought Jerusalem to shame.
He has thrown down the greatness of Israel
from the sky to the earth;
he did not remember the Temple,[d] his
footstool,
on the day of his anger.

2The Lord swallowed up without mercy
all the houses of the people of Jacob;
in his anger he pulled down
the strong places of Judah.
He threw her kingdom and its rulers
down to the ground in dishonour.

3In his anger he has removed
all the strength of Israel;
he took away his power from Israel
when the enemy came.
He burnt against the people of Jacob like a
flaming fire
that burns up everything around it.

4Like an enemy, he prepared to shoot
his bow,
and his hand was against us.
Like an enemy, he killed
all the good-looking people;
he poured out his anger like fire
on the tents of Jerusalem.

5The Lord was like an enemy;
he swallowed up Israel.
He swallowed up all her palaces
and destroyed all her strongholds.[d]
He has caused more moaning and groaning
for Judah.

6He cut down his Temple like a garden;
he destroyed the meeting-place.
The LORD has made Jerusalem forget
the set feasts and Sabbath[d] days.
He has rejected the king and the priest
in his great anger.

7The Lord has rejected his altar
and abandoned his Temple.
He has handed over to the enemy
the walls of Jerusalem's palaces.
Their uproar in the LORD's Temple
was like that of a feast day.

8The LORD planned to destroy
the wall around Jerusalem.
He measured the wall
and did not stop himself from destroying it.
He made the walls and defences sad;
together they have fallen.

9Jerusalem's gates have fallen to the ground;
he destroyed and smashed the bars of the
gates.
Her king and her princes are among the
nations.
The teaching of the LORD has stopped,
and the prophets[d] do not have
visions from the LORD.

10The elders of Jerusalem
sit on the ground in silence.

They throw dust on their heads
and put on rough cloth to show their sadness.
The young women of Jerusalem
bow their heads to the ground in sorrow.

11My eyes have no more tears,
and I am sick to my stomach.
I feel empty inside,
because my people have been destroyed.
Children and babies are fainting
in the streets of the city.

12They ask their mothers,
"Where is the grain and wine?"
They faint like wounded soldiers
in the streets of the city
and die in their mothers' arms.

13What can I say about you, Jerusalem?
What can I compare you to?
What can I say you are like?
How can I comfort you, Jerusalem?
Your ruin is as deep as the sea.
No one can heal you.

14Your prophets saw visions,
but they were false and worth nothing.
They did not point out your sins
to keep you from being captured.
They preached what was false
and led you wrongly.

15All who pass by on the road
clap their hands at you;
they make fun of Jerusalem
and shake their heads.
They ask, "Is this the city that people called
the most beautiful city,
the happiest place on earth?"

16All your enemies open their mouths
to speak against you.
They make fun and grind their teeth in anger.
They say, "We have swallowed you up.
This is the day we were waiting for!
We have finally seen it happen."

17The LORD has done what he planned;
he has kept his word
that he commanded long ago.
He has destroyed without mercy,
and he has let your enemies laugh at you.
He has strengthened your enemies.

18The people cry out to the Lord.
Wall of Jerusalem,
let your tears flow
like a river day and night.
Do not stop
or let your eyes rest.

19Get up, cry out in the night,
even as the night begins.
Pour out your heart like water
in prayer to the Lord.
Lift up your hands in prayer to him
for the life of your children
who are fainting with hunger
on every street corner.

20Jerusalem says: "Look, LORD, and see
to whom you have done this.
Women eat their own babies,
the children they have cared for.
Priests and prophets are killed
in the Temple of the Lord.

21"People young and old
lie outside on the ground.
My young women and young men
have been killed by the sword.
You killed them on the day of your anger;
you killed them without mercy.

22"You invited terrors to come against me on every side,
as if you were inviting them to a feast.
No one escaped or remained alive
on the day of the LORD's anger.
My enemy has killed
those I cared for and brought up."

The Meaning of Suffering

3 I am a man who has seen the suffering
that comes from the rod of the LORD's anger.
2He led me
into darkness, not light.
3He turned his hand against me
again and again, all day long.

4He wore out my flesh and skin
and broke my bones.
5He surrounded me with sadness
and attacked me with grief.
6He made me sit in the dark,
like those who have been dead a long time.

7He shut me in so I could not get out;
he put heavy chains on me.
8I cry out and beg for help,
but he ignores my prayer.
9He blocked my way with a stone wall
and led me in the wrong direction.

10He is like a bear ready to attack me,
like a lion in hiding.

11 He led me the wrong way and let me stray
and left me without help.
12 He prepared to shoot his bow
and made me the target for his arrows.
13 He shot me in the kidneys
with the arrows from his bag.
14 I was a joke to all my people,
who make fun of me with songs all day
long.
15 The LORD filled me with misery;
he made me drunk with suffering.
16 He broke my teeth with gravel
and trampled me into the ground.
17 I have no more peace.
I have forgotten what happiness is.
18 I said, "My strength is gone,
and I have no hope in the LORD."
19 LORD, remember my suffering and my
misery,
my sorrow and trouble.
20 Please remember me
and think about me.
21 But I have hope
when I think of this:
22 The LORD's love never ends;
his mercies never stop.
23 They are new every morning;
LORD, your loyalty is great.
24 I say to myself, "The LORD is mine,
so I hope in him."
25 The LORD is good to those who hope
in him,
to those who seek him.
26 It is good to wait quietly
for the LORD to save.
27 It is good for someone to work hard
while he is young.
28 He should sit alone and be quiet;
the LORD has given him hard work
to do.
29 He should bow down to the ground;
perhaps there is still hope.
30 He should let anyone slap his cheek;
he should be filled with shame.
31 The Lord will not reject
his people for ever.
32 Although he brings sorrow,
he also has mercy and great love.

SUFFERING

Letting it All Out

While lots of us go though hard times and difficult experiences, for the most part we don't have to deal with what Christians in other parts of the world go through. For them, being a Christian is a daily risk that may lead to attack, arrest, prison, torture – or worse. They live with suffering and stress that we can't even imagine. We are fortunate to be living in a place where we can express our Christian faith freely. It's important that we remember to pray for our brothers and sisters around the world. History shows us that people like them who stand up for God can find themselves experiencing serious suffering.

Read **Lamentations 3:1–24**, but be warned, it's not one of those bits of the Bible that will give you warm fuzzy feelings. You might have noticed that when it comes to dealing with suffering there are two kinds of people: those who suffer in silence and those who let it all out.

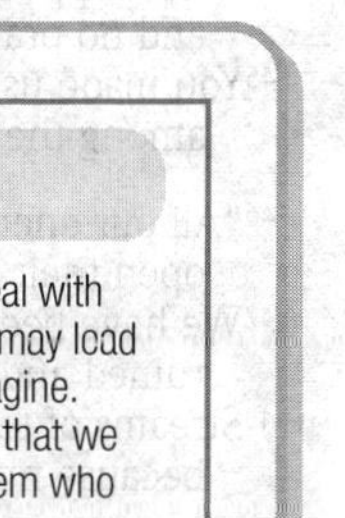

- Look at verses 22–24. What do the writer's thoughts lead him to do?
- What three top tips could you give, from this passage, to help someone who is suffering?

Consider . . .

- finding out more about organisations who work to help Christians around the world who are suffering persecution.
- sending an e-card to someone you know who is having a tough time at the moment.

For more, see . . .

- Isaiah 61:1–3 (p.705)
- 2 Corinthians 4:7–10 (p.1243)
- Romans 8:15–19 (p.1195)

33He does not like to punish people
or make them sad.

34He sees if any prisoner of the earth
is crushed under his feet;
35he sees if someone is treated unfairly
before the Most High God;
36the Lord sees
if someone is cheated in his case in court.

37Nobody can speak and have it happen
unless the Lord commands it.
38Both bad and good things
come by the command of the Most High God.
39No one should complain
when he is punished for his sins.

40Let us examine and see what we have done
and then return to the LORD.
41Let us lift up our hands and pray from our hearts
to God in heaven:
42"We have sinned and turned against you,
and you have not forgiven us.

43"You wrapped yourself in anger and chased us;
you killed us without mercy.
44You wrapped yourself in a cloud,
and no prayer could get through.
45You made us like scum and rubbish
among the other nations.

46"All our enemies
open their mouths and speak against us.
47We have been frightened and fearful,
ruined and destroyed."
48Streams of tears flow from my eyes,
because my people are destroyed.

49My tears flow continually,
without stopping,
50until the LORD looks down
and sees from heaven.
51I am sad when I see
what has happened to all the women of my city.

52Those who are my enemies for no reason
hunted me like a bird.
53They tried to kill me in a pit;
they threw stones at me.
54Water came up over my head,
and I said, "I am going to die."
55I called out to you, LORD,
from the bottom of the pit.
56You heard me calling, "Do not close your ears
and ignore my cry and shouts."
57You came near when I called to you;
you said, "Don't be afraid."

58Lord, you have taken my case
and given me back my life.
59LORD, you have seen how I have been wronged.
Now judge my case for me.
60You have seen how my enemies took revenge on me
and made evil plans against me.

61LORD, you have heard their insults
and all their evil plans against me.
62The words and thoughts of my enemies
are against me all the time.
63Look! In everything they do
they make fun of me with songs.

64Pay them back, LORD,
for what they have done.
65Make them stubborn,
and put your curse on them.
66Chase them in anger, LORD,
and destroy them from under your heavens.

The Attack on Jerusalem

4 See how the gold has lost its shine,
how the pure gold has lost its shine!
The stones of the Temple[d] are scattered
at every street corner.

2The precious people of Jerusalem
were more valuable than gold,
but now they are thought of as clay jars
made by the hands of a potter.

Sidelight Because only priests were allowed to enter the Most Holy Place in the Temple, the Babylonian trampling of the Temple (Lamentations 4:1) was difficult to cope with. In fact, the Temple's destruction was even more tragic to the devout Jew than the devastation in the rest of Jerusalem.

3Even wild dogs give their milk
to feed their young,
but my people are cruel
like ostriches in the desert.

4The babies are so thirsty
their tongues stick to the roofs of their mouths.
Children beg for bread,
but no one gives them any.

5Those who once ate fine foods
are now starving in the streets.
People who grew up wearing nice clothes
now pick through rubbish piles.

6My people have been punished
more than Sodom was.
Sodom was destroyed suddenly,
and no hands reached out to help her.

7Our princes were purer than snow
and whiter than milk.
Their bodies were redder than rubies;
they looked like sapphires.

8But now they are blacker than coal,
and no one recognises them in the streets.
Their skin hangs on their bones;
it is as dry as wood.

9Those who were killed in the war were
better off
than those killed by hunger.
They starve in pain and die,
because there is no food from the field.

10With their own hands kind women
cook their own children.
They became food
when my people were destroyed.

11The LORD turned loose all of his anger;
he poured out his strong anger.
He set fire to Jerusalem,
burning it down to the foundations.

12Kings of the earth and people of the world
could not believe
that enemies and foes
could enter the gates of Jerusalem.

13It happened because her prophets [d] sinned
and her priests did evil.
They killed in the city
those who did what was right.

14They wandered in the streets
as if they were blind.
They were dirty with blood,
so no one would touch their clothes.

15"Go away! You are unclean," [d] people
shouted at them.
"Get away! Get away! Don't touch us!"
So they ran away and wandered.
Even the other nations said, "Don't stay
here."

16The LORD himself scattered them
and did not look after them any more.
No one respects the priests
or honours the elders.

17Also, our eyes grew tired,
looking for help that never came.
We kept watch from our towers
for a nation to save us.

18Our enemies hunted us,
so we could not even walk in the
streets.
Our end is near. Our time is up.
Our end has come.

19Those who chased us
were faster than eagles in the sky.
They ran us into the mountains
and ambushed us in the desert.

20The LORD's appointed king, who was our very
breath,
was caught in their traps.
We had said about him, "We will be
protected by him
among the nations."

21Be happy and glad, people of Edom,
you who live in the land of Uz.
The cup of God's anger will come to you;
then you will get drunk and go naked.

22Your punishment is complete, Jerusalem.
He will not send you into captivity again.
But the LORD will punish the sins of Edom;
he will uncover your evil.

A Prayer to the LORD

5 Remember, LORD, what happened to us.
Look and see our disgrace.
2Our land has been turned over to strangers;
our houses have been given to foreigners.
3We are like orphans with no father;
our mothers are like widows.
4We have to buy the water we drink;
we must pay for the firewood.
5Those who chase after us want to catch us
by the neck.
We are tired and find no rest.
6We made an agreement with Egypt
and with Assyria to get enough food.
7Our ancestors sinned against you, but they
are gone;
now we suffer because of their sins.
8Slaves have become our rulers,
and no one can save us from them.
9We risk our lives to get our food;
we face death in the desert.
10Our skin is hot like an oven;
we burn with starvation.
11The enemy abused the women of
Jerusalem
and the girls in the cities of Judah.

12 Princes were hung by the hands;
they did not respect our elders.
13 The young men ground grain at the mill,
and boys stumbled under loads of wood.
14 The elders no longer sit at the city gates;
the young men no longer sing.
15 We have no more joy in our hearts;
our dancing has turned to sadness.
16 The crown has fallen from our head.
How terrible it is because we sinned.
17 Because of this we are afraid,
and now our eyes are dim.
18 Mount Zion [d] is empty,
and wild dogs wander around it.
19 But you rule for ever, LORD.
You will be King from now on.
20 Why have you forgotten us for so long?
Have you left us for ever?
21 Bring us back to you, LORD, and we will
return.
Make our days as they were before,
22 or have you completely rejected us?
Are you so angry with us?

Ezekiel

Why Read This Book:

- **Be encouraged by God's extraordinary efforts to call his people back to himself (Ezekiel 1—24).**
- **Take comfort in the promises God made through the prophet Ezekiel (Ezekiel 33—48).**

When?

Time Line:

- *1000 BC*
- The kingdom was split between Israel and Judah
- The Northern Kingdom (Israel) fell to Assyria
- *750 BC*
- Ezekiel began his ministry in exile in Babylon
- Jerusalem was totally destroyed by the Babylonians
- The Jews began returning from exile
- *500 BC*
- *250 BC*
- *BC/AD* Jesus was born.

Behind the Scenes:

"Prophet Sees UFO!" the headline would have screamed.

The story would reveal how Ezekiel, the prophet, saw the sky opening up, glowing lights in the sky, fire, and something like glowing metal in the middle of a cloud. Then, the story would continue, the prophet saw creatures – creatures who, the writer suggests, were probably aliens.

Finally – and this was the best part – a voice above the creatures boomed out. When Ezekiel looked up, he saw an amazing throne. It was all so powerful he was knocked off his feet.

But the prophet didn't see a UFO. The prophet saw a vision of God.

This unusual book is filled with such stories. Ezekiel lived during the most difficult time in the Old Testament. Jerusalem had been destroyed, and the people – including Ezekiel – had been taken into exile, mostly in Babylon. The people couldn't understand what had happened to their beloved city. Had God abandoned them?

Through visions, strange actions, and symbolic language, the prophet interpreted what had happened to the city and his people. ▷

Where?

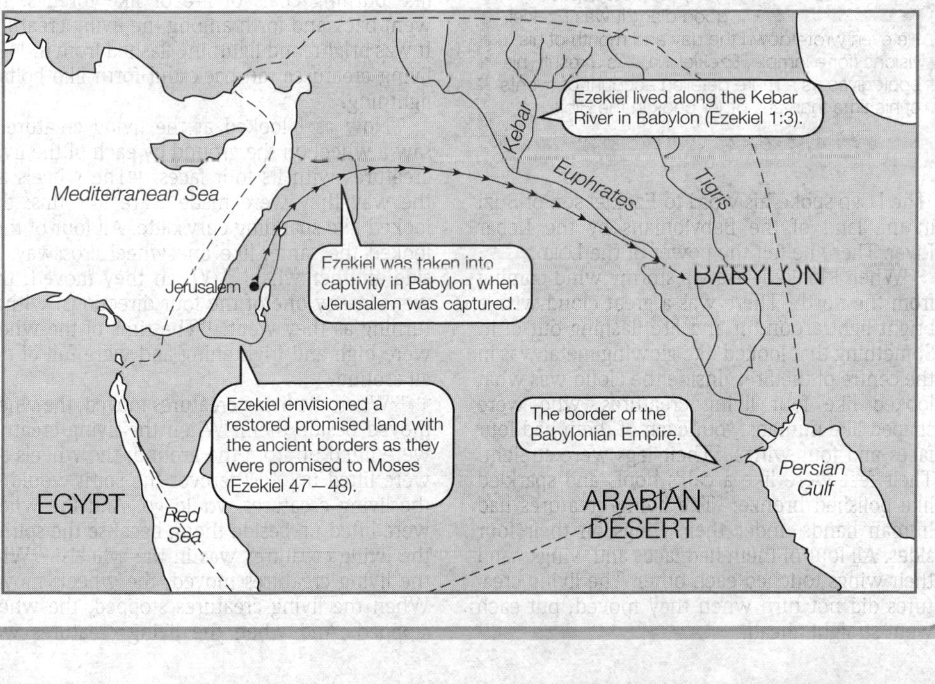

Behind the Scenes (cont.): First, he told how the people of Judah got themselves into trouble by refusing to listen to earlier prophets or to follow God. So God had used the invading Babylonians to punish the people.

Yet God had not abandoned his chosen people, Ezekiel insisted. Because of God's love and trustworthiness, he would restore the city to them and renew his relationship with them. They would respond to his gift by returning to him. At that point, God would again comfort his people.

As Ezekiel describes his dreams and visions, it's sometimes hard to understand the prophet's underlying message. In fact, from the beginning, scholars have been stumped by the specific meanings of passages.

But beneath all the unusual language, poetry, and imagery is a consistent message that still has meaning for us today: through everything, God wants people to "know that I am the Lord God" – a phrase that's repeated more than sixty times through the book.

Ezekiel's Vision of Living Creatures

1 It was the fifth day of the fourth month of
the thirtieth year of our captivity. I was by
the Kebar River among the people who had been
carried away as captives. The sky opened, and I
saw visions of God.
2It was the fifth day of the month of the fifth
year that King Jehoiachin had been a prisoner.

> **Sidelight** If any prophet kept a good diary, it was Ezekiel. He even wrote down the day and month of his visions (for example, Ezekiel 1:1). As a result, his book gives us a more detailed account of events of his time than any other book in the Bible.

3The LORD spoke his word to Ezekiel son of Buzi
in the land of the Babylonians by the Kebar
River. There he felt the power of the LORD.
4When I looked, I saw a stormy wind coming
from the north. There was a great cloud with a
bright light around it and fire flashing out of it.
Something that looked like glowing metal was in
the centre of the fire. 5Inside the cloud was what
looked like four living creatures, who were
shaped like humans, 6but each of them had four
faces and four wings. 7Their legs were straight.
Their feet were like a calf's hoofs and sparkled
like polished bronze. 8The living creatures had
human hands under their wings on their four
sides. All four of them had faces and wings, 9and
their wings touched each other. The living crea-
tures did not turn when they moved, but each
went straight ahead.
10Their faces looked like this: each living crea-
ture had a human face and the face of a lion
on the right side and the face of an ox on the
left side. And each one also had the face of an
eagle. 11That was what their faces looked like.
Their wings were spread out above. Each had
two wings that touched one of the other living
creatures and two wings that covered its body.
12Each went straight ahead. Wherever the spirit
would go, the living creatures would also go,
without turning. 13The living creatures looked
like burning coals of fire or like torches. Fire
went back and forth among the living creatures.
It was bright, and lightning flashed from it. 14The
living creatures ran back and forth like bolts of
lightning.
15Now as I looked at the living creatures, I
saw a wheel on the ground by each of the living
creatures with its four faces. 16The wheels and
the way they were made were like this: they
looked like sparkling chrysolite. All four of them
looked the same, like one wheel crossways in-
side another wheel. 17When they moved, they
went in any one of the four directions, without
turning as they went. 18The rims of the wheels
were high and frightening and were full of eyes
all around.
19When the living creatures moved, the wheels
moved beside them. When the living creatures
were lifted up from the ground, the wheels also
were lifted up. 20Wherever the spirit would go,
the living creatures would go. And the wheels
were lifted up beside them, because the spirit of
the living creatures was in the wheels. 21When
the living creatures moved, the wheels moved.
When the living creatures stopped, the wheels
stopped. And when the living creatures were

lifted from the ground, the wheels were lifted beside them, because the spirit of the living creatures was in the wheels.

22Now, over the heads of the living creatures was something like a dome that sparkled like ice and was frightening. 23And under the dome the wings of the living creatures were stretched out straight towards one another. Each living creature also had two wings covering its body. 24I heard the sound of their wings, like the roaring sound of the sea, as they moved. It was like the voice of God Almighty, a roaring sound like a noisy army. When the living creatures stopped, they lowered their wings.

25A voice came from above the dome over the heads of the living creatures. When the living creatures stopped, they lowered their wings. 26Now above the dome there was something that looked like a throne. It looked like a sapphire gem. And on the throne was a shape like a human. 27Then I noticed that from the waist up the shape looked like glowing metal with fire inside. From the waist down it looked like fire, and a bright light was all around. 28The surrounding glow looked like the rainbow in the clouds on a rainy day. It seemed to look like the glory of the LORD. So when I saw it, I bowed face down on the ground and heard a voice speaking.

The LORD Speaks to Ezekiel

2 He said to me, "Human, stand up on your feet so I may speak with you." 2While he spoke to me, the Spirit[d] entered me and put me on my feet. Then I heard the LORD speaking to me.

3He said, "Human, I am sending you to the people of Israel. That nation has turned against me and broken away from me. They and their ancestors have sinned against me until this very day. 4I am sending you to people who are stubborn and who do not obey. You will say to them, 'This is what the Lord GOD says.' 5They may listen, or they may not, since they are a people who have turned against me. But they will know that a prophet[d] has been among them. 6You, human, don't be afraid of the people or their words. Even though they may be like thorny branches and thorns all around you, and though you may feel as if you live with poisonous insects, don't be afraid. Don't be afraid of their words or their looks, because they are a people who rebel against me. 7But speak my words to them. They may listen, or they may not, because they turn against me. 8But you, human, listen to what I say to you. Don't turn against me as those people do. Open your mouth and eat what I am giving you."

9Then I looked and saw a hand stretched out to me, and a scroll was in it. 10He opened the scroll in front of me. Funeral songs, sad writings and words about troubles were written on the front and back.

3 Then the LORD said to me, "Human, eat what you find; eat this scroll. Then go and speak to the people of Israel." 2So I opened my mouth, and he gave me the scroll to eat.

3He said to me, "Human, eat this scroll which I am giving you, and fill your stomach with it." Then I ate it, and it was as sweet as honey in my mouth.

Sidelight Ever eaten something for a dare? Ezekiel ate stationery and said that it tasted like honey! When God told Ezekiel to eat the scroll (Ezekiel 3:1–3), it symbolised that the prophet had accepted God's mission to tell the news to the Jewish people. It would get people's attention on modern high streets, too.

4Then he said to me, "Human, go to the people of Israel, and speak my words to them. 5You are not being sent to people whose speech you can't understand, whose language is difficult. You are being sent to Israel. 6You are not being sent to many nations whose speech you can't understand and whose language is difficult and whose words you cannot understand. If I had sent you to them, they would have listened to you. 7But the people of Israel will not be willing to listen to you, because they are not willing to listen to me. Yes, all the people of Israel are stubborn and will not obey. 8See, I now make you as stubborn and as hard as they are. 9I am making you as hard as a diamond, harder than stone. Don't be afraid of them or be frightened by them, though they are a people who rebel against me."

10Also, he said to me, "Human, believe all the words I will speak to you, and listen carefully to them. 11Then go to the captives, your own people, and say to them, 'The Lord GOD says this.' Tell them this whether they listen or not."

12Then the Spirit lifted me up, and I heard a loud rumbling sound behind me, saying, "Praise the glory of the LORD in heaven." 13I heard the wings of the living creatures touching each other and the sound of the wheels by them. It was a loud rumbling sound. 14So the Spirit lifted me up and took me away. I was unhappy and angry, and I felt the great power of the LORD. 15I came to the captives from Judah, who lived by the Kebar River at Tel Abib. I sat there seven days where these people lived, feeling shocked.

Israel's Warning

16After seven days the LORD spoke his word to
me again. He said, 17"Human, I now make you a
watchman for Israel. Any time you hear a word
from my mouth, warn them for me. 18When I say
to the wicked, 'You will surely die,' you must
warn them so they may live. If you don't speak
out to warn the wicked to stop their evil ways,
they will die in their sin. But I will hold you
responsible for their death. 19If you warn the
wicked and they do not turn from their wicked-
ness or their evil ways, they will die because of
their sin. But you will have saved your life.
20"Again, those who do right may turn away
from doing good and do evil. If I make something
bad happen to them, they will die. Because you
have not warned them, they will die because of
their sin, and the good they did will not be re-
membered. But I will hold you responsible for
their deaths. 21But if you have warned those good
people not to sin, and they do not sin, they will
surely live, because they believed the warning.
And you will have saved your life."
22Then I felt the power of the LORD there.
He said to me, "Get up and go out to the plain.
There I will speak to you." 23So I got up and went
out to the plain. I saw the glory of the LORD
standing there, like the glory I saw by the Kebar
River, and I bowed face down on the ground.
24Then the Spirit[d] entered me and made me
stand on my feet. He spoke to me and said, "Go,
shut yourself up in your house. 25As for you,
human, the people will tie you up with ropes so
that you will not be able to go out among them.
26Also, I will make your tongue stick to the roof
of your mouth so you will be silent. You will not
be able to argue with the people, even though
they turn against me. 27But when I speak to you,
I will open your mouth, and you will say to
them, 'The Lord GOD says this.' Those who will
listen, let them listen. Those who refuse, let them
refuse, because they are a people who rebel
against me.

The Map of Jerusalem

4 "Now, human, get yourself a brick, put it in
front of you, and draw a map of Jerusalem
on it. 2Then surround it with an army. Build bat-
tle works against the city and a dirt road to the
top of the city walls. Set up camps around it, and

HONESTY

The Whole Truth

Jessica knew she was in trouble when the car skidded on the wet road, hitting the kerb hard enough to ruin a front wheel. Even though no one was hurt, the car would not move.

When she got home, Jessica told her parents what had happened. She admitted having seven people in her mini, and going over the speed limit.

"What I didn't tell them was that a friend was driving my car," she says.

Jessica's paying for the damage now with money from her Saturday job. She's afraid that if she tells her parents the whole truth, she will get into even more trouble. Jessica's parents might appreciate her honesty and not punish her more severely. God, too, appreciates honesty. He expects it even when it may cause more trouble than keeping silent. He demanded that Ezekiel tell the people the whole truth in **Ezekiel 3:16–21**.

- Why might it be difficult for Jessica or Ezekiel to be completely honest?
- How can you be honest with a friend who is doing something wrong and still preserve the friendship?

Consider . . .

- warning a friend about something he or she is doing that's wrong.
- discussing with your friends when, if ever, it's OK to tell white lies.

For more, see . . .

- Genesis 3:1–9 (p.5)
- Acts 5:1–11 (p.1145)
- 2 Samuel 12:1–14 (p.295)

put heavy logs in place to break down the walls.
3Then get yourself an iron plate and set it up like
an iron wall between you and the city. Turn your
face towards the city as if to attack it and then
attack. This is a sign to Israel.
4"Then lie down on your left side, and take
the guilt of Israel on yourself. Their guilt will be
on you for the number of days you lie on your
left side. 5I have given you the same number of
days as the years of the people's sin. So you will
have the guilt of Israel's sin on you for 390 days.
6"After you have finished these 390 days, lie
down for a second time, on your right side. You
will then have the guilt of Judah on you. I will
give it to you for 40 days, a day for each year of
their sin. 7Then you will look towards Jerusalem,
which is being attacked. With your arm bare,
you will prophesy[d] against Jerusalem. 8I will put
ropes on you so you cannot turn from one side to
the other until you have finished the days of your
attack on Jerusalem.

Sidelight To get God's message across, Ezekiel resorted to dramatic measures. Once he lay on his left side for 390 days to symbolise the siege of Jerusalem (Ezekiel 4:4–8). Another time he burned his hair (Ezekiel 5:1–3) to symbolise military defeat for Jerusalem. You won't see those drama sketches in church!

9"Take wheat, barley, beans, small peas and
millet seeds, put them in one bowl, and make
them into bread for yourself. You will eat it for
the 390 days you lie on your side. 10You will eat
220 grammes of food every day at set times.
11You will drink about ½ a litre of water every
day at set times. 12Eat your food as you would eat
a barley cake, baking it over human dung where
the people can see." 13Then the LORD said, "In the
same way Israel will eat unclean[d] food among the
nations where I force them to go."
14But I said, "No, Lord GOD! I have never been
made unclean. From the time I was young until
now I've never eaten anything that died by itself
or was torn by animals. Unclean meat has never
entered my mouth."

Sidelight When God told Ezekiel to cook his food over human excrement (Ezekiel 4:9–14), the prophet refused because human excrement was considered unclean (see Deuteronomy 23:12–14, p.186). But dried cow dung was – and still is – a common fuel in the Near East.

15"Very well," he said. "Then I will give you
cow's dung instead of human dung to use for
your fire to bake your bread."
16He also said to me, "Human, I am going to
cut off the supply of bread to Jerusalem. They will
eat the bread that is measured out to them, and
they will worry as they eat. They will drink water
that is measured out to them, and they will be in
shock as they drink it. 17This is because bread and
water will be hard to find. The people will be
shocked at the sight of each other, and they will
become weak because of their sin.

Ezekiel Cuts His Hair

5 "Now, human, take a sharp sword, and use
it like a barber's razor to shave your head
and beard. Then take scales and weigh and divide
the hair. 2Burn a third with fire in the middle of
the city when the days of the attack on Jerusalem
are over. Then take a third and cut it up with the
knife all around the city. And scatter a third to the
wind. This is how I will chase them with a sword.
3Also take a few of these hairs and tie them in
the folds of your clothes. 4Take a few more, throw
them into the fire and burn them up. From there
a fire will spread to all the people of Israel.
5"This is what the Lord GOD says: this is
Jerusalem. I have put her at the centre of the na-
tions with countries all around her. 6But she has
refused to obey my laws and has been more evil
than the nations. She has refused to obey my
rules, even more than nations around her. The
people of Jerusalem have rejected my laws and
have not lived by my rules.
7"So this is what the Lord GOD says: you have
caused more trouble than the nations around
you. You have not followed my rules or obeyed
my laws. You have not even obeyed the laws of
the nations around you.
8"So this is what the Lord GOD says: I myself
am against you, and I will punish you as the na-
tions watch. 9I will do things among you that I
have not done before and the like of which I will
never do again, because you do the things I hate.
10So parents among you will eat their children,
and children will eat their parents. I will punish
you and will scatter to the winds all who are left
alive. 11So the Lord GOD says: you have made my
Temple[d] unclean[d] with all your evil idols and the
hateful things you do. Because of this, as surely as
I live, I will cut you off. I will have no pity, and
I will show no mercy. 12A third of you will die by
disease or be destroyed by hunger inside your
walls. A third will fall dead by the sword outside
your walls. And a third I will scatter in every
direction as I chase them with a sword. 13Then my
anger will come to an end. I will use it up against
them, and then I will be satisfied. Then they will

know that I, the LORD, have spoken. After I have
carried out my anger against them, they will
know the strength of my feelings.
14"I will make you a ruin and a shame among
the nations around you, to be seen by all who
pass by. 15Then the nations around you will
shame you and make fun of you. You will be a
warning and a terror to them. This will happen
when I punish you in my great anger. I, the LORD,
have spoken. 16I will send a time of hunger to
destroy you, and then I will make your hunger
get even worse, and I will cut off your supply of
food. 17I will send a time of hunger and wild
animals against you, and they will kill your chil-
dren. Disease and death will sweep through your
people, and I will bring the sword against you to
kill you. I, the LORD, have spoken."

Prophecies Against the Mountains

6 Again the LORD spoke his word to me, saying:
2"Human, look towards the mountains of
Israel, and prophesy[d] against them. 3Say, 'Moun-
tains of Israel, listen to the word of the Lord GOD.
The Lord GOD says this to the mountains, the
hills, the ravines and the valleys: I will bring a
sword against you, and I will destroy your places
of idol worship. 4Your altars will be destroyed and
your incense[d] altars broken down. Your people
will be killed in front of your idols. 5I will lay the
dead bodies of the Israelites in front of their idols,
and I will scatter your bones around your altars.
6In all the places you live, cities will become
empty. The places of idol worship will be ruined;
your altars will become lonely ruins. Your idols
will be broken and brought to an end. Your in-
cense altars will be cut down, and the things you
made will be wiped out. 7Your people will be
killed and fall among you. Then you will know
that I am the LORD.
8" 'But I will leave some people alive; some
will not be killed by the nations when you are
scattered among the foreign lands. 9Then those
who have escaped will remember me, as they live
among the nations where they have been taken
as captives. They will remember how I was hurt
because they were unfaithful to me and turned
away from me and desired to worship their idols.
They will hate themselves because of the evil
things they did that I hate. 10Then they will know
that I am the LORD. I did not bring this terrible
thing on them for no reason.
11" 'This is what the Lord GOD says: clap your
hands, stamp your feet and groan because of all
the hateful, evil things the people of Israel have
done. They will die by war, hunger and disease.
12The person who is far away will die by disease.
The one who is nearby will die in war. The per-
son who is still alive and has escaped these will
die from hunger. So I will carry out my anger on
them. 13Their people will lie dead among their
idols around the altars, on every high hill, on all
the mountain tops and under every green tree
and leafy oak—all the places where they offered
sweet-smelling incense to their idols. Then you
will know that I am the LORD. 14I will use my
power against them to make the land empty and
wasted from the desert to Diblah, wherever they
live. Then they will know that I am the LORD.' "

Ezekiel Tells of the End

7 Again the LORD spoke his word to me, saying:
2"Human, the Lord GOD says this to the land
of Israel: an end! The end has come on the four

> **Sidelight** Why does God repeatedly address Ezekiel as "Human"? (See Ezekiel 7:2, for example.) It was simply to remind the people of the huge difference between God and people.

corners of the land. 3Now the end has come for
you, and I will send my anger against you. I will
judge you for the way you have lived, and I will
make you pay for all your actions that I hate. 4I
will have no pity on you; I will not hold back
punishment from you. Instead, I will make you
pay for the way you have lived and for your ac-
tions that I hate. Then you will know that I am
the LORD.
5"This is what the Lord GOD says: disaster on
top of disaster is coming. 6The end has come! The
end has come! It has stirred itself up against you!
Look! It has come! 7Disaster has come for you
who live in the land! The time has come; the day
of confusion is near. There will be no happy
shouting on the mountains. 8Soon I will pour out
my anger against you; I will carry out my anger
against you. I will judge you for the way you have
lived and will make you pay for everything you
have done that I hate. 9I will show no pity, and
I will not hold back punishment. I will pay you
back for the way you have lived and the things
you have done that I hate. Then you will know
that I am the LORD who punishes.
10"Look, the day is here. It has come. Disaster
has come, violence has grown and there is more
pride than ever. 11Violence has grown into a
weapon for punishing wickedness. None of the
people will be left—none of that crowd, none of
their wealth and nothing of value. 12The time has
come; the day has arrived. Don't let the buyer be
happy or the seller be sad, because my burning
anger is against the whole crowd. 13Sellers will
not return to the land they have sold as long as

they live, because the vision against all that
crowd will not be changed. Because of their sins,
they will not save their lives. 14They have blown
the trumpet, and everything is ready. But no one
is going to the battle, because my anger is against
all that crowd.

15"The sword is outside, and disease and hun-
ger are inside. Whoever is in the field will die by
the sword. Hunger and disease will destroy those
in the city. 16Those who are left alive and who
escape will be on the mountains, moaning like
doves of the valleys about their own sin. 17All
hands will hang weakly with fear, and all knees
will become weak as water. 18They will put on
rough cloth to show how sad they are. They will
tremble all over with fear. Their faces will show
their shame, and all their heads will be shaved.
19The people will throw their silver into the
streets, and their gold will be like rubbish. Their
silver and gold will not save them from the LORD's
anger. It will not satisfy their hunger or fill their
stomachs, because it caused them to fall into sin.
20They were proud of their beautiful jewellery
and used it to make their idols and their evil
statues, which I hate. So I will turn their wealth
into rubbish. 21I will give it to foreigners as trea-
sures from war and to the most evil people in the
world as treasure, and they will dishonour it. 22I
will also turn away from the people of Israel, and
they will dishonour my treasured place. Then
robbers will enter and dishonour it.

23"Make chains for captives, because the land
is full of bloody crimes and the city is full of viol-
ence. 24So I will bring the worst of the nations to
take over the people's houses. I will also end the
pride of the strong, and their holy places will be
dishonoured. 25When the people are suffering
greatly, they will look for peace, but there will be
none. 26Disaster will come on top of disaster, and
rumour will be added to rumour. Then they will
try to get a vision from a prophet;[d] the teachings
of God from the priest and the advice from the
older leaders will be lost. 27The king will cry
greatly, the prince will give up hope and the
hands of the people who own land will shake
with fear. I will punish them for the way they
have lived. The way they have judged others is
the way I will judge them. Then they will know
that I am the LORD."

Ezekiel's Vision of Jerusalem

8 It was the fifth day of the sixth month of the
sixth year of our captivity. I was sitting in my
house with the elders of Judah in front of me.
There I felt the power of the Lord GOD. 2I looked
and saw something that looked like a human.
From the waist down it looked like fire, and from
the waist up it looked like bright glowing metal.
3It stretched out the shape of a hand and caught
me by the hair on my head. The Spirit[d] lifted me
up between the earth and the sky. He took me in
visions of God to Jerusalem, to the entrance to
the north gate of the inner courtyard of the Tem-
ple.[d] In the courtyard was the idol that caused
God to be jealous. 4I saw the glory of the God of
Israel there, as I had seen on the plain.

5Then he said to me, "Human, now look to-
wards the north." So I looked up towards the
north, and in the entrance north of the gate of the
altar was the idol that caused God to be jealous.

6He said to me, "Human, do you see what they
are doing? Do you see how many hateful things
the people of Israel are doing here that drive me
far away from my Temple? But you will see
things more hateful than these."

7Then he brought me to the entry of the court-
yard. When I looked, I saw a hole in the wall. 8He
said to me, "Human, dig through the wall." So I
dug through the wall and saw an entrance.

9Then he said to me, "Go in and see the hate-
ful, evil things they are doing here." 10So I entered
and looked, and I saw every kind of crawling
thing and hateful beast and all the idols of the
people of Israel, carved on the wall all around.
11Standing in front of these carvings and idols
were 70 of the elders of Israel and Jaazaniah son
of Shaphan. Each man had his pan for burning
incense[d] in his hand, and a sweet-smelling cloud
of incense was rising.

12Then he said to me, "Human, have you seen
what the elders of Israel are doing in the dark?
Have you seen each man in the room of his own
idol? They say, 'The LORD doesn't see us. The
LORD has left the land.' " 13He also said to me,
"You will see them doing even more hateful
things."

14Then he brought me to the entrance of the
north gate of the Temple of the LORD, where I saw
women sitting and crying for Tammuz.[n] 15He
said to me, "Do you see, human? You will see
things even more hateful than these."

16Then he brought me into the inner courtyard
of the Temple. There I saw about 25 men at the
entrance to the Temple of the LORD, between the
porch and the altar. With their backs turned to
the Temple of the LORD, they faced east and were
worshipping the sun in the east.

17He said to me, "Do you see, human? Is it
unimportant that the people of Judah are doing
the hateful things they have done here? They have

Tammuz Tammuz was a god in Babylon. Every year people thought this god died when the plants died. After they cried for him, they believed he came back to life and the plants lived again.

filled the land with violence and made me con-
tinually angry. Look, they are insulting me in every
way they can. 18So I will act in anger. I will have
no pity, nor will I show mercy. Even if they shout
in my ears, I won't listen to them."

Vision of the Angels

9 Then he shouted with a loud voice in my
ears, "You who are chosen to punish this
city, come near with your weapon in your hand."
2Then six men came from the direction of the
upper gate, which faces north, each with his
powerful weapon in his hand. Among them was
a man dressed in linen with a writing case at his
side. The men went in and stood by the bronze
altar.

3Then the glory of the God of Israel went up
from above the creatures with wings, where it
had been, to the place in the Temple[d] where the
door opened. He called to the man dressed in
linen who had the writing case at his side. 4He
said to the man, "Go through Jerusalem and put
a mark on the foreheads of the people who groan
and cry about all the hateful things being done
among them."

Sidelight The "mark" in Ezekiel 9:4 was the taw – the last letter of the Hebrew alphabet – and was used to identify the righteous. Failure to have the mark on your forehead meant that you would be killed!

5As I listened, he said to the other men, "Go
through the city behind the man dressed in linen
and kill. Don't pity anyone, and don't show
mercy. 6Kill and destroy old men, young men and
women, little children and older women, but
don't touch any who have the mark on them.
Start at my Temple." So they started with the
elders who were in front of the Temple.

7Then he said to the men, "Make the Temple
unclean,[d] and fill the courtyards with those who
have been killed. Go out!" So the men went out
and killed the people in the city. 8While the men
were killing the people, I was left alone. I bowed
face down on the ground and I cried out, "Oh,
Lord God! Will you destroy everyone left alive
in Israel when you turn loose your anger on
Jerusalem?"

9Then he said to me, "The sin of the people of
Israel and Judah is very great. The land is filled
with people who murder, and the city is full of
people who are not fair. The people say, 'The
Lord has left the land, and the Lord does not see.'
10But I will have no pity, nor will I show mercy.
I will bring their evil back on their heads."

11Then the man dressed in linen with the writ-
ing case at his side reported, "I have done just as
you commanded me."

The Coals of Fire

10 Then I looked and saw in the dome
above the heads of the living creatures
something like a sapphire gem which looked like
a throne. 2The Lord said to the man dressed in
linen, "Go in between the wheels under the liv-
ing creatures, fill your hands with coals of fire
from between the living creatures, and scatter the
coals over the city."

As I watched, the man with linen clothes went
in. 3Now the living creatures were standing on
the south side of the Temple[d] when the man
went in. And a cloud filled the inner courtyard.
4Then the glory of the Lord went up from the
living creatures and stood over the door of the
Temple. The Temple was filled with the cloud,
and the courtyard was full of the brightness from
the glory of the Lord. 5The sound of the wings of
the living creatures was heard all the way to the
outer courtyard. It was like the voice of God
Almighty when he speaks.

6When the Lord commanded the man dressed
in linen, "Take fire from between the wheels,
from between the living creatures," the man
went in and stood by a wheel. 7One living crea-
ture put out his hand to the fire that was among
them, took some of the fire, and put it in the
hands of the man dressed in linen. Then the man
took the fire and went out.

The Wheels and the Creatures

8Something that looked like a human hand
could be seen under the wings of the living crea-
tures. 9I saw the four wheels by the living crea-
tures, one wheel by each living creature. The
wheels looked like shining chrysolite. 10All four
wheels looked alike: each looked like a wheel
crossways inside another wheel. 11When the
wheels moved, they went in any of the direc-
tions that the four living creatures faced. The
wheels did not turn about, and the living crea-
tures did not turn their bodies as they went. 12All
their bodies, their backs, their hands, their wings
and the wheels were full of eyes all over. Each of
the four living creatures had a wheel. 13I heard
the wheels being called "whirling wheels".
14Each living creature had four faces. The first
face was the face of a creature with wings. The
second face was a human face, the third was
the face of a lion and the fourth was the face of
an eagle.

15Then the living creatures flew up. They
were the same living creatures I had seen by the
Kebar River. 16When the living creatures moved,

the wheels moved beside them. When the living
creatures lifted their wings to fly up from the
ground, the wheels did not leave their place be-
side them. 17When the living creatures stopped,
the wheels stopped. When the creatures went
up, the wheels went up also, because the spirit of
the living creatures was in the wheels.
18Then the glory of the LORD left the door of the
Temple[d] and stood over the living creatures. 19As
I watched, the living creatures spread their wings
and flew up from the ground, with the wheels
beside them. They stood where the east gate of
the Temple of the LORD opened, and the glory of
the God of Israel was over them.
20These were the living creatures I had seen
under the God of Israel by the Kebar River. I
knew they were called cherubim.[d] 21Each one
had four faces and four wings, and under their
wings were things that looked like human hands.
22Their faces looked the same as the ones I had
seen by the Kebar River. They each went straight
ahead.

Prophecies Against Evil Leaders

11 The Spirit[d] lifted me up and brought me
to the front gate of the Temple[d] of the
LORD, which faces east. I saw 25 men where the
gate opens, among them Jaazaniah son of Azzur
and Pelatiah son of Benaiah, who were leaders of
the people. 2Then the LORD said to me, "Human,
these are the men who plan evil and give wicked
advice in this city of Jerusalem. 3They say, 'It
is almost time for us to build houses. This city
is like a cooking pot, and we are like the best
meat.' 4So prophesy[d] against them, prophesy,
human."
5Then the Spirit of the LORD entered me and
told me to say: "This is what the LORD says: you
have said these things, people of Israel, and I
know what you are thinking. 6You have killed
many people in this city, filling its streets with
their bodies.
7"So this is what the Lord GOD says: those peo-
ple you have killed and left in the middle of the
city are like the best meat, and this city is like the
cooking pot. But I will force you out of the city.
8You have feared the sword, but I will bring a
sword against you, says the Lord GOD. 9I will
force you out of the city and hand you over to
strangers and punish you. 10You will die by the
sword. I will punish you at the border of Israel so
you will know that I am the LORD. 11This city will
not be your cooking pot, and you will not be the
best meat in the middle of it. I will punish you at
the border of Israel. 12Then you will know that I
am the LORD. You did not live by my rules or obey
my laws. Instead, you did the same things as the
nations around you."

13As I prophesied, Pelatiah son of Benaiah died.
Then I bowed face down on the ground and
shouted with a loud voice, "Oh no, Lord GOD!
Will you completely destroy the Israelites who
are left alive?"

Promise to Those Remaining

14The LORD spoke his word to me, saying,
15"Human, the people still in Jerusalem have spo-
ken about your own relatives and all the people
of Israel who are captives with you, saying, 'They
are far from the LORD. This land has been given to
us as our property.'
16"So say, 'This is what the Lord GOD says: I
sent the people far away among the nations and
scattered them among the countries. But for a
little while I have become a Temple[d] to them in
the countries where they have gone.'
17"So say: 'This is what the Lord GOD says: I
will gather you from the nations and bring you
together from the countries where you have been
scattered. Then I will give you back the land of
Israel.'
18"When they come to this land, they will re-
move all the evil idols and all the hateful images.
19I will give them a desire to respect me com-
pletely, and I will put inside them a new way of
thinking. I will take out the stubborn heart of
stone from their bodies, and I will give them an
obedient heart of flesh. 20Then they will live by
my rules and obey my laws and keep them. They
will be my people, and I will be their God. 21But
those who want to serve their evil statues and
hateful idols, I will pay back for their evil ways,
says the Lord GOD."

Ezekiel's Vision Ends

22Then the living creatures lifted their wings
with the wheels beside them, and the glory of the
God of Israel was above them. 23The glory of the
LORD went up from inside Jerusalem and stopped
on the mountain on the east side of the city.
24The Spirit[d] lifted me up and brought me to
the captives who had been taken from Judah to
Babylonia. This happened in a vision given by
the Spirit of God, and then the vision I had seen
ended. 25And I told the captives from Judah all
the things the LORD had shown me.

Ezekiel Moves Out

12 Again the LORD spoke his word to me,
saying: 2"Human, you are living among a
people who refuse to obey. They have eyes to see,
but they do not see, and they have ears to hear,
but they do not hear, because they are a people
who refuse to obey.
3"So, human, pack your things as if you will be
taken away captive, and walk away like a captive

in the daytime with the people watching. Move
from your place to another with the people
watching. Perhaps they will understand, even
though they are a people who refuse to obey.
4During the day when the people are watching,
bring out the things you would pack as captive.
At evening, with the people watching, leave your
place like those who are taken away as captives
from their country. 5Dig a hole through the wall
while they watch, and bring your things out
through it. 6Lift them onto your shoulders with
the people watching, and carry them out in the
dark. Cover your face so you cannot see the
ground, because I have made you a sign to
the people of Israel."
7I did these things as I was commanded. In the
daytime I brought what I had packed as if I were
being taken away captive. Then in the evening I
dug through the wall with my hands. I brought
my things out in the dark and carried them on my
shoulders as the people watched.
8Then in the morning the LORD spoke his word
to me, saying: 9"Human, didn't Israel, who re-
fuses to obey, ask you, 'What are you doing?'
10"Say to them, 'This is what the Lord GOD
says: this message is about the king in Jerusalem
and all the people of Israel who live there.' 11Say,
'I am a sign to you.'
"The same things I have done will be done to
the people in Jerusalem. They will be taken away
from their country as captives. 12The king among
them will put his things on his shoulder in the
dark and will leave. The people will dig a hole
through the wall to bring him out. He will cover
his face so he cannot see the ground. 13But I will
spread my net over him, and he will be caught in
my trap. Then I will bring him to Babylon in the
land of the Babylonians. He will not see that land,
but he will die there. 14All who are around the
king—his helpers and all his army—I will scatter
in every direction, and I will chase them with a
sword.
15"They will know that I am the LORD when I
scatter them among the nations and spread them
among the countries. 16But I will save a few of
them from the sword and from hunger and dis-
ease. Then they can tell of their hateful actions
among the nations where they go. Then they
will know that I am the LORD."

The Lesson of Ezekiel's Shaking

17The LORD spoke his word to me, saying:
18"Human, tremble as you eat your food, and
shake with fear as you drink your water. 19Then
say to the people of the land: 'This is what the
Lord GOD says about the people who live in
Jerusalem in the land of Israel: they will eat their
food with fear and drink their water in shock,
because their land will be stripped bare because
of the violence of the people who live in it. 20The
cities where people live will become ruins, and
the land will become empty. Then you will know
that I am the LORD.' "

The Visions will Come True

21The LORD spoke his word to me, saying:
22"Human, what is this saying you have in the
land of Israel: 'The days go by and every vision
comes to nothing'? 23So say to them, 'This is
what the Lord GOD says: I will make them stop
saying this, and nobody in Israel will use this say-
ing any more.' But tell them, 'The time is near
when every vision will come true. 24There will be
no more false visions or pleasing prophecies[d] in-
side the nation of Israel, 25but I, the LORD, will
speak. What I say will be done, and it will not be
delayed. You refuse to obey, but in your time I
will say the word and do it, says the Lord GOD.' "
26The LORD spoke his word to me, saying:
27"Human, the people of Israel are saying, 'The
vision that Ezekiel sees is for a time many years
from now. He is prophesying about times far
away.'
28"So say to them: 'The Lord GOD says this:
none of my words will be delayed any more.
What I have said will be done, says the
Lord GOD.' "

Ezekiel Speaks Against False Prophets

13 The LORD spoke his word to me, saying:
2"Human, prophesy[d] against the proph-
ets[d] of Israel. Say to those who make up their
own prophecies: 'Listen to the word of the LORD.
3This is what the Lord GOD says: how terrible it
will be for the foolish prophets who follow their
own ideas and have not seen a vision from me!
4People of Israel, your prophets have been like
wild dogs hunting to kill and eat among ruins.
5Israel is like a house in ruins, but you have not
gone up into the broken places or repaired the
wall. So how can Israel hold back the enemy in
the battle on the LORD's day of judging? 6Your
prophets see false visions and prophesy lies. They
say, "This is the message of the LORD," when the
LORD has not sent them. But they still hope their
words will come true. 7You said, "This is the mes-
sage of the LORD," but that is a false vision. Your
prophecies are lies, because I have not spoken.
8" 'So this is what the Lord GOD says: because
you prophets spoke things that are false and saw
visions that do not come true, I am against you,
says the Lord GOD. 9I will punish the prophets
who see false visions and prophesy lies. They will
have no place among my people. Their names
will not be written on the list of the people of

Israel, and they will not enter the land of Israel.
Then you will know that I am the Lord GOD.
10“ ‘It is because they lead my people the
wrong way by saying, “Peace!” when there is no
peace. When the people build a weak wall, the
prophets cover it with whitewash to make it look
strong. 11So tell those who cover a weak wall
with whitewash that it will fall down. Rain will
pour down, hailstones will fall and a stormy wind
will break the wall down. 12When the wall has
fallen, people will ask you, “Where is the white-
wash you used on the wall?”
13“ ‘So this is what the Lord GOD says: I will
break the wall with a stormy wind. In my anger
rain will pour down, and hailstones will destroy
the wall. 14I will tear down the wall on which
you put whitewash. I will level it to the ground
so that people will see the wall's foundation.
And when the wall falls, you will be destroyed
under it. Then you will know that I am the LORD.
15So I will carry out my anger on the wall and
against those who covered it with whitewash.
Then I will tell you, “The wall is gone, and those
who covered it with whitewash are gone. 16The
prophets of Israel who prophesy to Jerusalem
and who see visions of peace for the city, when
there is no peace, will be gone, says the Lord
GOD.” ’

False Women Prophets

17“Now, human, look towards the women
among your people who make up their own
prophecies.[d] Prophesy against them. 18Say, ‘This
is what the Lord GOD says: how terrible it will
be for women who sew magic charms on their
wrists and make veils of every length to trap peo-
ple! You ruin the lives of my people but try to
save your own lives. 19For handfuls of barley and
pieces of bread, you have dishonoured me among
my people. By lying to my people, who listen to
lies, you have killed people who should not die,
and you have kept alive those who should not
live.
20“ ‘So this is what the Lord GOD says: I am
against your magic charms, by which you trap
people as if they were birds. I will tear those
charms off your arms, and I will free those people
you have trapped like birds. 21I will also tear off
your veils and save my people from your hands.
They will no longer be trapped by your power.
Then you will know that I am the LORD. 22By your
lies you have caused those who did right to be
sad, when I did not make them sad. And you
have encouraged the wicked not to stop being
wicked, and so save their lives. 23So you will not
see false visions or prophesy any more, and I will
save my people from your power so you will
know that I am the LORD.’ ”

Stop Worshipping Idols

14 Some of the elders of Israel came to me
and sat down in front of me. 2Then the
LORD spoke his word to me, saying: 3“Human,
these men want to worship idols. They put up
evil things that cause people to sin. Should I allow
them to ask me for help? 4So speak to them and
tell them, ‘This is what the Lord GOD says: when
any of the people of Israel want to worship idols
and put up evil things that cause people to sin
and then come to the prophet,[d] I, the LORD, will
answer them myself for worshipping idols. 5Then
I will win back my people Israel, who have left
me because of all their idols.’
6“So say to the people of Israel, ‘This is what
the Lord GOD says: Change your hearts and lives,
and stop worshipping idols. Stop doing all the
things I hate. 7Any of the Israelites or foreigners
in Israel can separate themselves from me by
wanting to worship idols or by putting up the
things that cause people to sin. Then if they come
to the prophet to ask me questions, I, the LORD,
will answer them myself. 8I will reject them. I
will make them a sign and an example, and I will
separate them from my people. Then you will
know that I am the LORD.
9“ ‘But if the prophet is tricked into giving a
prophecy, it is because I, the LORD, have tricked
that prophet to speak. Then I will use my power
against him and destroy him from among my peo-
ple Israel. 10The prophet will be as guilty as the
one who asks him for help; both will be respons-
ible for their guilt. 11Then the nation of Israel will
not leave me any more or make themselves
unclean[d] any more with all their sins. They will
be my people, and I will be their God, says the
Lord GOD.’ ”

Sidelight

If you wanted to listen to a “gentle” preacher in Bible times, you wouldn't have enjoyed hearing the prophet Ezekiel speak (Ezekiel 14:1–11). He pulled no punches, and might have been “bleeped” for referring to pagan idols as “dung balls” 39 times! This term is used elsewhere in the Old Testament, but only nine times.

Jerusalem will Not be Spared

12The LORD spoke his word to me, saying:
13“Human, if the people of a country sin against
me by not being loyal, I will use my power
against them. I will cut off their supply of food
and send a time of hunger, destroying both peo-
ple and animals. 14Even if three great men like
Noah, Daniel and Job were in that country, their

goodness could save only themselves, says the
Lord GOD.
15“Or I might send wild animals into that land,
leaving the land empty and without children.
Then no one would pass through it because of the
animals. 16As surely as I live, says the Lord GOD,
even if Noah, Daniel and Job were in the land,
they could not save their own sons or daughters.
They could save only themselves, but that coun-
try would become empty.
17“Or I might bring a war against that country.
I might say, ‘Let a war be fought in that land,’ in
this way destroying its people and its animals.
18As surely as I live, says the Lord GOD, even if
those three men were in the land, they could not
save their sons or daughters. They could save
only themselves.
19“Or I might cause a disease to spread in that
country. I might pour out my anger against it,
destroying and killing people and animals. 20As
surely as I live, says the Lord GOD, even if Noah,
Daniel and Job were in the land, they could not
save their son or daughter. They could save only
themselves because they did what was right.
21“This is what the Lord GOD says: my plans
for Jerusalem are much worse! I will send my
four terrible punishments against it—war,
hunger, wild animals and disease—to destroy its
people and animals. 22But some people will es-
cape; some sons and daughters will be led out.
They will come out to you, and you will see
what happens to people who live as they did.
Then you will be comforted after the disasters I
have brought against Jerusalem, after all the
things I have brought against it. 23You will be
comforted when you see what happens to them
for living as they did, because you will know
there was a good reason for what I did to
Jerusalem, says the Lord GOD.”

Story of the Vine

15 The LORD spoke his word to me, saying:
2“Human, is the wood of the vine better
than the wood of any tree in the forest? 3Can
wood be taken from the vine to make anything?
Can you use it to make a peg on which to hang
something? 4If the vine is thrown into the fire
for fuel, and the fire burns up both ends and
starts to burn the middle, is it useful for any-
thing? 5When the vine was whole, it couldn’t be
made into anything. When the fire has burnt it
completely, it certainly cannot be made into any-
thing.”
6So this is what the Lord GOD says: “Out of all
the trees in the forest, I have given the wood of
the vine as fuel for fire. In the same way I have
given up the people who live in Jerusalem 7and
will turn against them. Although they came
through one fire, fire will still destroy them.
When I turn against them, you will know that I
am the LORD. 8So I will make the land empty,
because the people have not been loyal, says the
Lord GOD.”

The LORD’s Kindness to Jerusalem

16 The LORD spoke his word to me, saying:
2“Human, tell Jerusalem about her hate-
ful actions. 3Say, ‘This is what the Lord GOD says
to Jerusalem: your beginnings and your ancestors
were in the land of the Canaanites. Your father
was an Amorite, and your mother was a Hittite.
4On the day you were born, your cord[n] was not
cut. You were not washed with water to clean
you. You were not rubbed with salt or wrapped
in cloths. 5No one felt sorry enough for you to do
any of these things for you. No, you were thrown
out into the open field, because you were hated
on the day you were born.

Sidelight In the time of Ezekiel 16:4, it was usual to rub a newborn baby with salt. This was believed to have had a medicinal purpose, and may also have symbolised purity (see 2 Kings 2:19–22, p.346).

6“ ‘When I passed by and saw you kicking
about in your blood, I said to you, “Live!” 7I made
you grow like a plant in the field. You grew up
and became tall and became like a beautiful
jewel. Your breasts formed, and your hair grew,
but you were naked and without clothes.
8“ ‘Later when I passed by you and looked at
you, I saw that you were old enough for love. So
I spread my robe over you and covered your
nakedness. I also made a promise to you and en-
tered into an agreement with you so that you
became mine, says the Lord GOD.
9“ ‘Then I bathed you with water, washed all
the blood off you, and put oil on you. 10I put
beautiful clothes made with needlework on you
and put sandals of fine leather on your feet. I
wrapped you in fine linen and covered you with
silk. 11I put jewellery on you: bracelets on your
arms, a necklace around your neck, 12a ring in
your nose, earrings in your ears and a beautiful
crown on your head. 13So you wore gold and
silver. Your clothes were made of fine linen, silk
and beautiful needlework. You ate fine flour,

cord The umbilical cord that gives the unborn baby food and air from its mother.

honey and olive oil. You were very beautiful and
became a queen. 14Then you became famous
among the nations, because you were so beauti-
ful. Your beauty was perfect, because of the glory
I gave you, says the Lord GOD.

Jerusalem Becomes a Prostitute

15" 'But you trusted in your beauty. You be-
came a prostitute,[d] because you were so famous.
You had sexual relations with anyone who passed
by. 16You took some of your clothes and made
your places of worship colourful. There you car-
ried on your prostitution. These things should not
happen; they should never occur. 17You also took
your beautiful jewellery, made from my gold and
silver I had given you, and you made for your-
selves male idols so you could be a prostitute
with them. 18Then you took your clothes with
beautiful needlework and covered the idols. You
gave my oil and incense[d] as an offering to them.
19Also, you took the bread I gave you, the fine
flour, oil and honey I gave you to eat, and you
offered them before the gods as a pleasing smell.
This is what happened, says the Lord GOD.
20" 'But your sexual sins were not enough for
you. You also took your sons and daughters who
were my children, and you sacrificed them to the
idols as food. 21You killed my children and offered
them up in fire to the idols. 22While you did all
your hateful acts and sexual sins, you did not
remember when you were young, when you
were naked and had no clothes and were left in
your blood.
23" 'How terrible! How terrible it will be for
you, says the Lord GOD. After you did all these
evil things, 24you built yourself a place to worship
gods. You made for yourself a place of worship in
every city square. 25You built a place of worship
at the beginning of every street. You made your
beauty hateful, offering your body for sex to any-
one who passed by, so your sexual sins became
worse and worse. 26You also had sexual relations
with the Egyptians, who were your neighbours
and partners in sexual sin. Your sexual sins be-
came even worse, and they caused me to be an-
gry. 27So then, I used my power against you and
took away some of your land. I let you be de-
feated by those who hate you, the Philistine
women, who were ashamed of your evil ways.
28Also, you had sexual relations with the Assyrians,
because you could not be satisfied. Even though
you had sexual relations with them, you still
were not satisfied. 29You did many more sexual
sins in Babylonia, the land of traders, but even
this did not satisfy you.
30" 'Truly your will is weak, says the Lord GOD.
You do all the things a stubborn prostitute does.
31You built your place to worship gods at the
beginning of every street, and you made places
of worship in every city square. But you were
not like a prostitute when you refused to accept
payment.
32" 'You are a wife who is guilty of adultery.[d]
You desire strangers instead of your husband.
33Men pay prostitutes, but you pay all your lovers
to come to you. And they come from all around
for sexual relations. 34So you are different from
other prostitutes. No man asks you to be a prosti-
tute, and you pay money instead of having money
paid to you. Yes, you are different.

The Prostitute is Judged

35" 'So, prostitute,[d] hear the word of the LORD.
36This is what the Lord GOD says: you showed
your nakedness to other countries. You uncov-
ered your body in your sexual sins with them as
your lovers and with all your hateful idols. You
killed your children and offered their blood to
your idols. 37So I will gather all your lovers with
whom you found pleasure. Yes, I will gather all
those you loved and those you hated. I will gather
them against you from all around, and I will strip
you naked in front of them so they can see your
nakedness. 38I will punish you as women guilty of
adultery[d] or as murderers are punished. I will put
you to death because I am angry and jealous. 39I
will also hand you over to your lovers. They will
tear down your places of worship and destroy
other places where you worship gods. They will
tear off your clothes and take away your jewel-
lery, leaving you naked and bare. 40They will
bring a crowd against you to throw stones at you
and cut you into pieces with their swords. 41They
will burn down your houses and will punish you
in front of many women. I will put an end to your
sexual sins, and you will no longer pay your lov-
ers. 42Then I will rest from my anger against you,
and I will stop being jealous. I will be quiet and
not angry any more.
43" 'Because you didn't remember when you
were young, but have made me angry in all these
ways, I will repay you for what you have done,
says the Lord GOD. Didn't you add sexual sins to
all your other acts which I hate?
44" 'Everyone who uses wise sayings will say
this about you: "The daughter is like her
mother." 45You are like your mother, who hated
her husband and children. You are also like your
sisters, who hated their husbands and children.
Your mother was a Hittite, and your father was
an Amorite. 46Your older sister is Samaria, who
lived north of you with her daughters; your youn-
ger sister is Sodom, who lived south of you with
her daughters. 47You not only followed their ways
and did the hateful things they did, but you were

soon worse than they were in all your ways. 48As
surely as I live, says the Lord GOD, this is true.
Your sister Sodom and her daughters never did
what you and your daughters have done.
49" 'This was the sin of your sister Sodom: she
and her daughters were proud and had plenty of
food and lived in great comfort, but she did not
help the poor and needy. 50So Sodom and her
daughters were proud and did things I hate in
front of me. So I got rid of them when I saw
what they did. 51Also, Samaria did not do half
the sins you do; you have done more hateful
things than they did. So you make your sisters
look good because of all the hateful things you
have done. 52You will suffer disgrace, because
you have provided an excuse for your sisters.
They are better than you are. Your sins were
even more terrible than theirs. Feel ashamed and
suffer disgrace, because you made your sisters
look good.
53" 'But I will give back to Sodom and her
daughters the good things they once had. I will
give back to Samaria and her daughters the good
things they once had. And with them I will also
give back the good things you once had 54so you
may suffer disgrace and feel ashamed for all the
things you have done. You even gave comfort to
your sisters in their sins. 55Your sisters, Sodom
with her daughters and Samaria with her daugh-
ters, will return to what they were before. You
and your daughters will also return to what you
were before. 56You humiliated your sister Sodom
when you were proud, 57before your evil was
uncovered. And now the Edomite women and
their neighbours say bad things about you. Even
the Philistine women humiliate you. Those
around you hate you. 58This is your punishment
for your terrible sins and for actions that I hate,
says the LORD.

God Keeps His Promises

59" 'This is what the Lord GOD says: I will do to
you what you have done. You hated and broke
the agreement you promised to keep. 60But I will
remember my agreement I made with you when
you were young, and I will make an agreement
that will continue for ever with you. 61Then you
will remember what you have done and feel
ashamed when you receive your sisters—both
your older and your younger sisters. I will give
them to you like daughters, but not because they
share in my agreement with you. 62I will set up
my agreement with you, and you will know that
I am the LORD. 63You will remember what you did
and feel ashamed. You will not open your mouth
again because of your shame, when I forgive
you for all the things you have done, says the
Lord GOD.' "

The Eagle and the Vine

17 The LORD spoke his word to me, saying:
2"Human, give a riddle and tell a story to
the people of Israel. 3Say, 'This is what the Lord
GOD says: a giant eagle with big wings and
long feathers of many different colours came to
Lebanon and took hold of the top of a cedar tree.
4He pulled off the top branch and brought it to a
land of traders, where he planted it in a city of
traders.
5" 'The eagle took some seed from the land
and planted it in a good field near plenty of water.
He planted it to grow like a willow tree. 6It grew
and became a low vine that spread over the
ground. The branches turned towards the eagle,
but the roots were under the eagle. So the seed
became a vine, and its branches grew, sending
out leaves.
7" 'But there was another giant eagle with big
wings and many feathers. The vine then bent its
roots towards this eagle. It sent out its branches
from the area where it was planted towards the
eagle so he could water it. 8It had been planted
in a good field by plenty of water so it could grow
branches and give fruit. It could have become a
fine vine.'
9"Say to them, 'This is what the Lord GOD says:
the vine will not continue to grow. The first eagle
will pull up the vine's roots and strip off its fruit.
Then the vine and all its new leaves will dry up
and die. It will not take a strong arm or many
people to pull the vine up by its roots. 10Even if it
is planted again, it will not continue to grow. It
will completely dry up and die when the east
wind hits it in the area where it grew.' "

Zedekiah Against Nebuchadnezzar

11Then the LORD spoke his word to me, saying:
12"Say now to the people who refuse to obey: 'Do
you know what these things mean?' Say: 'The
king of Babylon came to Jerusalem and took the
king and important men of Jerusalem and
brought them to Babylon. 13Then he took a mem-
ber of the family of the king of Judah and made
an agreement with him, forcing him to take an
oath. The king also took away the leaders of
Judah 14to make the kingdom weak so it would
not be strong again. Then the kingdom of Judah
could continue only by keeping its agreement
with the king of Babylon. 15But the king of Judah
turned against the king of Babylon by sending his
messengers to Egypt and asking them for horses
and many soldiers. Will the king of Judah suc-
ceed? Will the one who does such things escape?
He cannot break the agreement and escape.
16" 'As surely as I live, says the Lord GOD, he
will die in Babylon, in the land of the king who
made him king of Judah. The king of Judah hated

his promise to the king of Babylon and broke his
agreement with him. 17The king of Egypt with his
mighty army and many people will not help the
king of Judah in the war. The Babylonians will
build devices to attack the cities and to kill many
people. 18The king of Judah showed that he hated
the promise by breaking the agreement. He prom-
ised to support Babylon, but he did all these
things. So he will not escape.
19" 'So this is what the Lord GOD says: as surely
as I live, this is true: I will pay back the king of
Judah for hating my promise and breaking my
agreement. 20I will spread my net over him, and
he will be caught in my trap. Then I will bring
him to Babylon, where I will punish him for the
unfaithful acts he did against me. 21All the best of
his soldiers who escape will die by the sword,
and those who live will be scattered to every
wind. Then you will know that I, the LORD, have
spoken.
22" 'This is what the Lord GOD says: I myself
will also take a young branch from the top of a
cedar tree, and I will plant it. I will cut off a small
twig from the top of the tree's young branches,
and I will plant it on a very high mountain. 23I
will plant it on the high mountain of Israel. Then
it will grow branches and give fruit and become
a great cedar tree. Birds of every kind will build
nests in it and live in the shelter of the tree's
branches. 24Then all the trees in the countryside
will know that I am the LORD. I bring down the
high tree and make the low tree tall. I dry up
the green tree and make the dry tree grow. I am
the LORD. I have spoken, and I will do it.' "

God is Fair

18 The LORD spoke his word to me, saying:
2"What do you mean by using this saying
about the land of Israel:

'The parents have eaten sour grapes,
and that caused the children to grind their
teeth from the sour taste'?

3"As surely as I live, says the Lord GOD, this is
true: you will not use this saying in Israel any
more. 4Every living thing belongs to me. The life
of the parent is mine, and the life of the child is
mine. The person who sins is the one who
will die.
5"Suppose a person is good and does what is
fair and right. 6He does not eat at the mountain
places of worship. He does not look to the idols
of Israel for help. He does not have sexual rela-
tions with his neighbour's wife or with a woman
during her time of monthly bleeding. 7He does
not mistreat anyone but returns what was given
as a promise for a loan. He does not rob other
people. He gives bread to the hungry and clothes
to those who have none. 8He does not lend
money to get too much interest or profit. He
keeps his hand from doing wrong. He judges
fairly between one person and another. 9He lives
by my rules and obeys my laws faithfully. Who-
ever does these things is good and will surely
live, says the Lord GOD.
10"But suppose this person has a wild son
who murders people and who does any of these
other things. 11(Though the father himself has
not done any of these things.) This son eats at
the mountain places of worship. He has sexual
relations with his neighbour's wife. 12He mis-
treats the poor and needy. He steals and refuses
to return what was promised for a loan. He looks
to idols for help. He does things which I hate.
13He lends money for too much interest and
profit. Will this son live? No, he will not live! He
has done all these hateful things, so he will
surely be put to death. He will be responsible for
his own death.
14"Now suppose this son has a son who has
seen all his father's sins, but after seeing them
does not do those things. 15He does not eat at the
mountain places of worship. He does not look to
the idols of Israel for help. He does not have
sexual relations with his neighbour's wife. 16He
does not mistreat anyone or keep something
promised for a loan or steal. He gives bread to the
hungry and clothes to those who have none. 17He
keeps his hand from doing wrong. He does not
take too much interest or profit when he lends
money. He obeys my laws and lives by my rules.
He will not die for his father's sin; he will surely
live. 18But his father took other people's money
unfairly and robbed his brother and did what was
wrong among his people. So he will die for his
own sin.
19"But you ask, 'Why is the son not punished
for the father's sin?' The son has done what is fair
and right. He obeys all my rules, so he will surely
live. 20The person who sins is the one who will
die. A child will not be punished for a parent's
sin, and a parent will not be punished for a child's
sin. Those who do right will enjoy the results of
their own goodness; evil people will suffer the
results of their own evil.
21"But suppose the wicked stop doing all the
sins they have done and obey all my rules and do
what is fair and right. Then they will surely live;
they will not die. 22Their sins will be forgotten.
Because they have done what is right, they will
live. 23I do not really want the wicked to die, says
the Lord GOD. I want them to stop their bad ways
and live.
24"But suppose good people stop doing good
and do wrong and do the same hateful things the
wicked do. Will they live? All their good acts will
be forgotten, because they became unfaithful.

They have sinned, so they will die because of
their sins.
25“But you say, ‘What the Lord does isn't fair.’
Listen, people of Israel. I am fair. It is what you
do that is not fair! 26When good people stop doing
good and do wrong, they will die because of it.
They will die, because they did wrong. 27When
the wicked stop being wicked and do what is fair
and right, they will save their lives. 28Because
they thought about it and stopped doing all the
sins they had done, they will surely live; they will
not die. 29But the people of Israel still say, ‘What
the Lord does isn't fair.’ People of Israel, I am fair.
It is what you do that is not fair.
30“So I will judge you, people of Israel; I will
judge each of you by what you do, says the Lord
GOD. Change your hearts and stop all your sin-
ning so sin will not bring your ruin. 31Get rid of
all the sins you have done, and get for yourselves
a new heart and a new way of thinking. Why do
you want to die, people of Israel? 32I do not want
anyone to die, says the Lord GOD, so change your
hearts and lives so you may live.

A Sad Song for Israel

19 “Sing a funeral song for the leaders of
Israel. 2Say:
‘Your mother was like a female lion.
She lay down among the young lions.
She had many cubs.
3When she brought up one of her cubs,
he became a strong lion.
He learned to tear the animals he hunted,
and he ate people.
4The nations heard about him.
He was trapped in their pit,
and they brought him with hooks
to the land of Egypt.
5“ ‘The mother lion waited and saw
that there was no hope for her cub.
So she took another one of her cubs
and made him a strong lion.
6This cub roamed among the lions.
He was now a strong lion.
He learned to tear the animals he hunted,
and he ate people.
7He tore down their strong places
and destroyed their cities.
The land and everything in it
were terrified by the sound of his roar.
8Then the nations came against him
from areas all around,
and they spread their net over him.
He was trapped in their pit.
9Then they put him into a cage with chains
and brought him to the king of Babylon.
They put him into prison
so his roar could not be heard again
on the mountains of Israel.
10“ ‘Your mother was like a vine in your
vineyard,
planted beside the water.
The vine had many branches and gave much
fruit,
because there was plenty of water.
11The vine had strong branches,
good enough for a king's sceptre.[d]
The vine became tall
among the thick branches.
And it was seen, because it was tall
with many branches.
12But it was pulled up by its roots in anger
and thrown down to the ground.
The east wind dried it up.
Its fruit was torn off.
Its strong branches were broken off
and burned up.
13Now the vine is planted in the desert,
in a dry and thirsty land.
14Fire spread from the vine's main branch,
destroying its fruit.
There is not a strong branch left on it
that could become a sceptre for a king.’
This is a funeral song; it is to be used as a funeral
song.”

Israel Has Refused God

20 It was the tenth day of the fifth month of
the seventh year of our captivity. Some
of the elders of Israel came to ask about the LORD
and sat down in front of me.
2The LORD spoke his word to me, saying:
3“Human, speak to the elders of Israel and say to
them: ‘This is what the Lord GOD says: did you
come to ask me questions? As surely as I live, I
will not let you ask me questions.’
4“Will you judge them? Will you judge them,
human? Let them know the hateful things their
ancestors did. 5Say to them: ‘This is what the
Lord GOD says: When I chose Israel, I made a
promise to the descendants[d] of Jacob. I made my-
self known to them in Egypt, and I promised
them, “I am the LORD your God.” 6At that time I
promised them I would bring them out of Egypt
into a land I had found for them, a fertile land,
the best land in the world. 7I said to them, “Each
one of you must throw away the hateful idols
you have seen and liked. Don't make yourselves
unclean[d] with the idols of Egypt. I am the LORD
your God.”
8“ ‘But they turned against me and refused to
listen to me. They did not throw away the hateful
idols which they saw and liked; they did not give
up the idols of Egypt. Then I decided to pour out

my anger against them while they were still in
Egypt. 9But I acted for the sake of my name so it
would not be dishonoured in full view of the
nations where the Israelites lived. I made myself
known to the Israelites with a promise to bring
them out of Egypt while the nations were watch-
ing. 10So I took them out of Egypt and brought
them into the desert. 11I gave them my rules
and told them about my laws, by which people
will live if they obey them. 12I also gave them
my Sabbaths[d] to be a sign between us so they
would know that I am the LORD who made them
holy.

13" 'But in the desert Israel turned against me.
They did not follow my rules, and they rejected
my laws, by which people will live if they obey
them. They dishonoured my Sabbaths. Then I de-
cided to pour out my anger against them and
destroy them in the desert. 14But I acted for the
sake of my name so it would not be dishonoured
in full view of the nations who watched as I had
brought the Israelites out of Egypt. 15And in the
desert I swore to the Israelites that I would not
bring them into the land I had given them. It is
a fertile land, the best land in the world. 16This
was because they rejected my laws and did not
follow my rules. They dishonoured my Sabbaths
and wanted to worship their idols. 17But I had
pity on them. I did not destroy them or put an
end to them in the desert. 18I said to their chil-
dren in the desert, "Don't live by the rules of your
parents, or obey their laws. Don't make your-
selves unclean with their idols. 19I am the LORD
your God. Live by my rules, obey my laws and
follow them. 20Keep my Sabbaths holy, and they
will be a sign between me and you. Then you will
know that I am the LORD your God."

21" 'But the children turned against me. They
did not live by my rules, nor were they careful to
obey my laws, by which people will live if they
obey them. They dishonoured my Sabbaths. So I
decided to pour out my anger against them in the
desert. 22But I held back my anger. I acted for the
sake of my name so it would not be dishonoured
in full view of the nations who watched as I
brought the Israelites out. 23And in the desert I
swore to the Israelites that I would scatter them
among the nations and spread them among the
countries, 24because they had not obeyed my
laws. They had rejected my rules and dishon-
oured my Sabbaths and worshipped the idols of
their parents. 25I also allowed them to follow
rules that were not good and laws by which they
could not live. 26I let the Israelites make them-
selves unclean by the gifts they brought to their
gods when they sacrificed their first children in
the fire. I wanted to terrify them so they would
know that I am the LORD.'

27"So, human, speak to the people of Israel. Say
to them, 'This is what the Lord GOD says: your an-
cestors spoke against me by being unfaithful to me
in another way. 28When I had brought them into
the land I promised to give them, they saw every
high hill and every leafy tree. There they offered
their sacrifices to gods. They brought offerings
that made me angry and burned their incense[d]
and poured out their drink offerings. 29Then I said
to them: what is this high place where you go to
worship?' " (It is still called High Place today.)

30"So say to the people of Israel: 'This is what
the Lord GOD says: are you going to make your-
selves unclean as your ancestors did? Are you
going to be unfaithful and desire their hateful
idols? 31When you offer your children as gifts and
sacrifice them in the fire, you are making your-
selves unclean with all your idols even today. So,
people of Israel, should I let you ask me ques-
tions? As surely as I live, says the Lord GOD, I will
not accept questions from you.

32" 'What you want will not come true. You
say, "We want to be like the other nations, like
the people in other lands. We want to worship
idols made of wood and stone." 33As surely as I
live, says the Lord GOD, I will use my great power
and strength and anger to rule over you. 34I will
bring you out from the foreign nations. With my
great power and strength and anger I will gather
you from the lands where you are scattered. 35I
will bring you among the nations as I brought
your ancestors into the desert with Moses. There
I will judge you face to face. 36I will judge you the
same way I judged your ancestors in the desert of
the land of Egypt, says the Lord GOD. 37I will
count you like sheep and will bring you into line
with my agreement. 38I will get rid of those who
refuse to obey me and who turn against me. I will
bring them out of the land where they are now
living, but they will never enter the land of Israel.
Then you will know that I am the LORD.

39" 'This is what the Lord GOD says: people of
Israel, go and serve your idols for now. But later
you will listen to me; you will not continue to
dishonour my holy name with your gifts and
gods. 40On my holy mountain, the high mountain
of Israel, all Israel will serve me in the land, says
the Lord GOD. There I will accept you. There I
will expect your offerings, the first harvest of your
offerings, and all your holy gifts. 41I will accept
you like the pleasing smell of sacrifices when I
bring you out from the foreign nations and gather
you from the lands where you are scattered. Then
through you I will show how holy I am so the
nations will see. 42When I bring you into the land
of Israel, the land I promised your ancestors, you
will know that I am the LORD. 43There you will
remember everything you did that made you

unclean, and then you will hate yourselves for all
the evil things you have done. 44I will deal with
you for the sake of my name, not because of your
evil ways or unclean actions. Then you will
know I am the LORD, people of Israel, says the
Lord GOD.' "

Babylon, the LORD's Sword

45Now the LORD spoke his word to me, saying:
46"Human, look towards the south. Prophesy[d]
against the south and against the forest of the
southern area. 47Say to that forest: 'Hear the
word of the LORD. This is what the Lord GOD says:
I am ready to start a fire in you that will destroy
all your green trees and all your dry trees. The
flames that burn will not be put out. Every face
from south to north will feel their heat. 48Then all
the people will see that I, the LORD, have started
the fire. It will not be put out.' "

49Then I said, "Ah, Lord GOD! The people are
saying about me, 'He is only telling stories.' "

21 Then the LORD spoke his word to me,
saying: 2"Human, look towards Jerusalem
and speak against the holy place. Prophesy[d]
against the land of Israel. 3Say to Israel: 'This is
what the LORD says: I am against you. I will pull
my sword out of its holder, and I will cut off from
you both the wicked and those who do right.
4Because I am going to cut off the wicked and
those who do right, my sword will come out from
its holder and attack all people from south to
north. 5Then all people will know that I, the
LORD, have pulled my sword out from its holder.
My sword will not go back in again.'

6"So, human, groan with a breaking heart and
great sadness. Groan in front of the people.
7When they ask you, 'Why are you groaning?'
you will say, 'Because of what I have heard is
going to happen. When it happens, every heart
will melt with fear, and all hands will become
weak. Everyone will be afraid; all knees will be-
come weak as water. Look, it is coming, and it
will happen, says the Lord GOD.' "

8The LORD spoke his word to me, saying:
9"Human, prophesy and say, 'This is what the
Lord says:

A sword, a sword,
  made sharp and polished.
10It is made sharp for the killing.
  It is polished to flash like lightning.

" 'You are not happy about this horrible pun-
ishment by the sword. But my son Judah, you did
not change when you were only beaten with a
rod.

11The sword should be polished.
  It is meant to be held in the hand.
It is made sharp and polished,
  ready for the hand of a killer.
12Shout and yell, human,
  because the sword is meant for my people,
  for all the rulers of Israel.
They will be killed by the sword,
  along with my people.
  So beat your chest in sadness.

13" 'The test will come. And Judah, who is
hated by the armies of Babylon, will not last, says
the Lord GOD.'

14"So, human, prophesy
  and clap your hands.
Let the sword strike
  two or three times.
It is a sword meant for killing,
  a sword meant for much killing.
  This sword surrounds the people to be killed.
15Their hearts will melt with fear,
  and many people will die.
I have placed the killing sword
  at all their city gates.
Oh! The sword is made to flash like lightning.
  It is held, ready for killing.
16Sword, cut on the right side;
  then cut on the left side.
  Cut anywhere your blade is turned.
17I will also clap my hands
  and use up my anger.
I, the LORD, have spoken."

Jerusalem to be Destroyed

18The LORD spoke his word to me, saying:
19"Human, mark two roads that the king of
Babylon and his sword can follow. Both of these
roads will start from the same country. And make
signs where the road divides and one way goes
towards the city. 20Mark one sign to show the
road he can take with his sword to Rabbah in the
land of the Ammonites. Mark the other sign to
show the road to Judah and Jerusalem, which is
protected with strong walls. 21The king of Babylon
has come to where the road divides, and he is
using magic. He throws lots[d] with arrows and
asks questions of his family idols. He looks at the
liver of a sacrificed animal to learn where he

Sidelight Using arrows to predict the future (Ezekiel 21:21) was a favourite Babylonian divination (magic trick) to help make decisions – as some people use tarot cards, tea leaves and horoscopes today. The person would shake the arrows and throw them on the ground. The formation told the future. Occult tricks are always dangerous!

should go. 22The lot in his right hand tells him to
go to Jerusalem. It tells him to use logs to break
down the city gates, to shout the battle cry and
give the order to kill, and to build a dirt road to
the top of the walls and devices to attack the
walls. 23The people of Jerusalem have made
agreements with other nations to help them fight
Babylon. So they will think this prediction is
wrong, but it is really proof of their sin, and they
will be captured.
24"So this is what the Lord GOD says: 'You have
shown how sinful you are by turning against the
LORD. Your sins are seen in all the things you do.
Because of this proof against you, you will be
taken captive by the enemy.
25" 'You unclean[d] and evil leader of Israel, you
will be killed! The time of your final punishment
has come. 26This is what the Lord GOD says: take
off the royal turban and remove the crown.
Things will change. Those who are important
now will be made unimportant, and those who
are unimportant now will be made important. 27A
ruin! A ruin! I will make it a ruin! This place will
not be rebuilt until the one comes who has a right
to be king. Then I will give him that right.'

The Punishment of Ammon

28"And you, human, prophesy[d] and say: 'This
is what the Lord GOD says about the people of
Ammon and their insults:
a sword, a sword
is pulled out of its holder.
It is polished to kill and destroy,
to flash like lightning!
29Prophets[d] see false visions about you
and prophesy lies about you.
The sword will be put on the necks
of these unclean[d] and evil people.
Their day of judging has come;
the time of final punishment has come.
30Put the sword back in its holder.
I will judge you
in the place where you were created,
in the land where you were born.
31I will pour out my anger against you
and blast you with the fire of my anger.
I will hand you over to cruel men,
experts in destruction.
32You will be like fuel for the fire;
you will die in the land.
You will not be remembered,
because I, the LORD, have spoken.' "

The Sins of Jerusalem

22 The LORD spoke his word to me, saying:
2"And you, human, will you judge? Will
you judge the city of murderers? Then tell her
about all her hateful acts. 3You are to say: 'This is
what the Lord GOD says: you are a city that kills
those who come to live there. You make yourself
unclean[d] by making idols. 4You have become
guilty of murder and have become unclean by
your idols which you have made. So you have
brought your time of punishment near; you have
come to the end of your years. That is why I
have made you a shame to the nations and why
all lands laugh at you. 5Those near and those far
away laugh at you with your bad name, you city
full of confusion.
6" 'Jerusalem, see how each ruler of Israel in
you has been trying to kill people. 7The people in
you hate their fathers and mothers. They mistreat
the foreigners in you and wrong the orphans and
widows in you. 8You hate my holy things and
dishonour my Sabbaths.[d] 9The men in you tell
lies to cause the death of others. The people in
you eat food offered to idols at the mountain
places of worship, and they take part in sexual
sins. 10The men in you have sexual relations with
their fathers' wives and with women who are
unclean, during their time of monthly bleeding.
11One man in you does a hateful act with his
neighbour's wife, while another has shamefully
made his daughter-in-law unclean sexually. And
another forces his half-sister to have sexual
relations with him. 12The people in you take
money to kill others. You take unfair interest and
profits and make profits by mistreating your
neighbour. And you have forgotten me, says the
Lord GOD.
13" 'So, Jerusalem, I will shake my fist at you
for stealing money and for murdering people.
14Will you still be brave and strong when I punish
you? I, the LORD, have spoken, and I will act. 15I
will scatter you among the nations and spread
you through the countries. That is how I will get
rid of your uncleanness. 16But you, yourself, will
be dishonoured in the sight of the nations. Then
you will know that I am the LORD.' "

Israel is Worthless

17The LORD spoke his word to me, saying:
18"Human, the people of Israel have become use-
less like scum to me. They are like the copper,
tin, iron and lead left in the furnace when silver
is purified. 19So this is what the Lord GOD says:
'Because you have become useless like scum, I
am going to put you together inside Jerusalem.
20People put silver, copper, iron, lead and tin to-
gether inside a furnace to melt them down in a
blazing fire. In the same way I will gather you in
my hot anger and put you together in Jerusalem
and melt you down. 21I will put you together and
make you feel the heat of my anger. You will be
melted down inside Jerusalem. 22As silver is
melted in a furnace, you will be melted inside

the city. Then you will know that I, the LORD, have poured out my anger on you.' "

Sins of the People

23The LORD spoke his word to me, saying: 24"Human, say to the land, 'You are a land that has not had rain or showers when God is angry.' 25Like a roaring lion that tears the animal it has caught, Israel's rulers make evil plans. They have destroyed lives and have taken treasure and valuable things. They have caused many women to become widows. 26Israel's priests do cruel things to my teachings and do not honour my holy things. They make no difference between holy and unholy things, and they teach there is no difference between clean [d] and unclean things. They do not remember my Sabbaths, [d] so I am dishonoured by them. 27Like wolves tearing a dead animal, Jerusalem's leaders have killed people for profit. 28And the prophets [d] try to cover this up by false visions and by lying messages. They say, 'This is what the Lord GOD says' when the LORD has not spoken. 29The people cheat others and steal. They hurt people who are poor and needy. They cheat foreigners and do not treat them fairly.

30"I looked for someone to build up the walls and to stand before me where the walls are broken to defend these people, so I would not have to destroy them. But I could not find anyone. 31So I let them see my anger. I destroyed them with an anger that was like fire because of all the things they have done, says the Lord GOD."

Samaria and Jerusalem

23 The LORD spoke his word to me, saying: 2"Human, a woman had two daughters. 3While they were young, they went to Egypt and became prostitutes. [d] They let men touch and hold their breasts. 4The older girl was named Oholah, and her sister was named Oholibah. They became my wives and had sons and daughters. Oholah is Samaria, and Oholibah is Jerusalem. [n]

5"While still my wife, Samaria had sexual relations with other men. She had great sexual desire for her lovers, men from Assyria. The Assyrians were warriors and 6wore blue uniforms. They were all handsome young captains and commanders riding on horseback. 7Samaria became a prostitute for all the important men in Assyria and made herself unclean [d] with all the idols of everyone she desired. 8She continued the prostitution she began in Egypt. When she was young, she had slept with men, and they touched her breasts and had sexual relations with her.

9"So I handed her over to her lovers, the Assyrians, that she wanted so badly. 10They stripped her naked and took away her sons and daughters. Then they killed her with a sword. Women everywhere began talking about how she had been punished.

11"Her sister Jerusalem saw what happened, but she became worse than her sister in her sexual desire and prostitution. 12She also desired the Assyrians, who were all soldiers in beautiful uniforms—handsome young captains and commanders riding horses. 13I saw that both girls were alike; both were prostitutes.

14"But Jerusalem went even further. She saw carvings of Babylonian men on a wall. They wore red 15and had belts around their waists and turbans on their heads. They all looked like chariot officers born in Babylonia. 16When she saw them, she wanted to have sexual relations with them and sent messengers to them in Babylonia. 17So these Babylonian men came and had sexual relations with her and made her unclean. After that, she became sick of them. 18But she continued her prostitution so openly that everyone knew about it. And I finally became sick of her, as I had her sister. 19But she remembered how she was a young prostitute in Egypt, so she took part in even more prostitution. 20She wanted men who behaved like animals in their sexual desire. 21In the same way you desired to do the sinful things you had done in Egypt. There men touched and held your young breasts.

God's Judgement on Jerusalem

22"So, Jerusalem, this is what the Lord GOD says: you are tired of your lovers. So now I will make them angry with you and cause them to attack you from all sides. 23Men from Babylon and all Babylonia and men from Pekod, Shoa and Koa will attack you. All the Assyrians will attack you: handsome young captains and commanders, all of them important men and all riding horses. 24Those men will attack you with great armies and with their weapons, chariots and wagons. They will surround you with large and small shields and with helmets. And I will give them the right to punish you, and they will give you their own kind of punishment. 25Then you will see how strong my anger can be when they punish you in their anger. They will cut off your noses and ears. They will take away your sons and daughters, and those who are left will be burned. 26They will take off your clothes and steal

Oholah . . . Jerusalem Throughout this chapter Samaria is used in place of Oholah, and Jerusalem is used in place of Oholibah.

your jewellery. 27I will put a stop to the sinful life you began when you were in Egypt so that you will not desire it or remember Egypt any more.

28"This is what the Lord GOD says: you became tired of your lovers, but I am going to hand you over to those men you now hate. 29They will treat you with hate and take away everything you worked for, leaving you empty and naked. Everyone will know about the sinful things you did. Your sexual sins 30have brought this on you. You have had sexual relations with the nations and made yourselves unclean [d] by worshipping their idols. 31You did the same things your sister did, so you will get the same punishment, like a bitter cup to drink.

32"This is what the Lord GOD says:

you will drink the same cup your sister did,
 and that cup is deep and wide.
Everyone will make fun of you,
 because the cup is full.
33It will make you miserable and drunk.
 It is the cup of fear and ruin.
 It is the cup of your sister Samaria.
34You will drink everything in it,
 and then you will smash it
 and tear at your breasts.
I have spoken, says the Lord God.

35"So this is what the Lord GOD says: you have forgotten me and turned your back on me. So you will be punished for your sexual sins."

Judgement on Samaria and Jerusalem

36The LORD said to me: "Human, will you judge Samaria and Jerusalem, showing them their hateful acts? 37They are guilty of adultery [d] and murder. They have taken part in adultery with their idols. They even offered our children as sacrifices in the fire to be food for these idols. 38They have also done this to me: they made my Temple [d] unclean [d] and at the same time they dishonoured my Sabbaths. [d] 39They sacrificed their children to their idols. Then they entered my Temple at that very time to dishonour it. That is what they did inside my Temple!

40"They even sent for men from far away, who came after a messenger was sent to them. The two sisters bathed themselves for them, painted their eyes and put on jewellery. 41They sat on a fine bed with a table set before it, on which they put my incense [d] and my oil.

42"There was the noise of a reckless crowd in the city. Common people gathered, and drunkards were brought from the desert. They put bracelets on the wrists of the two sisters and beautiful crowns on their heads. 43Then I said about the one who was worn out by her acts of adultery, 'Let them continue their sexual sins with her. She is nothing but a prostitute.' [d] 44They kept going to her as they would go to a prostitute. So they continued to go to Samaria and Jerusalem, these shameful women. 45But men who do right will punish them as they punish women who take part in adultery and who murder people, because they are guilty of adultery and murder.

46"This is what the Lord GOD says: bring together a mob against Samaria and Jerusalem, and hand them over to be frightened and robbed. 47Let the mob kill them by throwing stones at them, and let them cut them down with their swords. Let them kill their sons and daughters and burn their houses down.

48"So I will put an end to sexual sins in the land. Then all women will be warned, and they will not do the sexual sins you have done. 49You will be punished for your sexual sins and the sin of worshipping idols. Then you will know that I am the Lord GOD."

The Pot and the Meat

24 The LORD spoke his word to me on the tenth day of the tenth month of the ninth year of our captivity. He said: 2"Human, write down today's date, this very date. The king of Babylon has surrounded Jerusalem this very day. 3And tell a story to the people who refuse to obey me. Say to them: 'This is what the Lord GOD says:

put on the pot; put it on
 and pour water in it.
4Put in the pieces of meat,
 the best pieces—the legs and the
 shoulders.
Fill it with the best bones.
5 Take the best of the flock,
and pile wood under the pot.
 Boil the pieces of meat
 until even the bones are cooked.

6" 'This is what the Lord GOD says:
how terrible it will be for the city of
 murderers!
 How terrible it will be for the rusty pot
 whose rust will not come off!
Take the meat out of it, piece by piece.
 Don't choose any special piece.

7" 'The blood from her killings is still in the
 city.
 She poured the blood on the bare rock.
She did not pour it on the ground
 where dust would cover it.
8To stir up my anger and revenge,
 I put the blood she spilled on the bare
 rock
 so it will not be covered.

9“ ‘So this is what the Lord GOD says:
How terrible it will be for the city of
murderers!
I myself will pile the wood high for
burning.
10Pile up the wood
and light the fire.
Finish cooking the meat.
Mix in the spices,
and let the bones burn.
11Then set the empty pot on the coals
so it may become hot and its copper sides
glow.
The dirty scum stuck inside it may then melt
and its rust burn away.
12But efforts to clean the pot have failed.
Its heavy rust cannot be removed,
even in the fire.

13“ ‘By your sinful action you have become un-
clean.[d] I wanted to cleanse you, but you are still
unclean. You will never be cleansed from your
sin until my anger against you is carried out.
14“ ‘I, the LORD, have spoken. The time has come
for me to act. I will not hold back punishment or
feel pity or change my mind. I will judge you by
your ways and actions, says the Lord GOD.’ ”

The Death of Ezekiel's Wife

15Then the LORD spoke his word to me, saying:
16“Human, I am going to take your wife from
you, the woman you look at with love. She will
die suddenly, but you must not be sad or cry
loudly for her or shed any tears. 17Groan silently;
do not cry loudly for the dead. Tie on your tur-
ban, and put your sandals on your feet. Do not
cover your face, and do not eat the food people
eat when they are sad about a death.”
18So I spoke to the people in the morning, and
my wife died in the evening. The next morning
I did as I had been commanded.
19Then the people asked me, “Tell us, what do
the things you are doing mean for us?”
20Then I said to them, “The LORD spoke his
word to me. He said, 21‘Say to the people of
Israel, this is what the Lord GOD says: I am going
to dishonour my Temple.[d] You think it gives you
strength. You are proud of it, and you look at it
with love and tenderness. But your sons and
daughters that you left behind in Jerusalem will
fall dead by the sword. 22When that happens,
you are to act as I have: you are not to cover
your face, and you are not to eat the food people
eat when they are sad about a death. 23Your tur-
bans must stay on your heads, and your sandals
on your feet. You must not cry loudly, but you
must rot away in your sins and groan to each
other. 24So Ezekiel is to be an example for you.
You must do all the same things he did. When all
this happens, you will know that I am the Lord
GOD.’
25“And as for you, human, this is how it will
be. I will take away the Temple that gives them
strength and joy, that makes them proud. They
look at it with love, and it makes them happy.
And I will take away their sons and daughters
also. 26At that time a person who escapes will
come to you with information for you to hear.
27At that very time your mouth will be opened.
You will speak and be silent no more. So you will
be a sign for them, and they will know that I am
the LORD.”

Sidelight If God had allowed Ezekiel to grieve for his wife, there would have been no flowers or nice funeral clothes. Under normal circumstances, the prophet would have gone barefoot, worn sackcloth, and sprinkled ashes on his head. To learn why he did none of them read Ezekiel 24:15–24.

Prophecy Against Ammon

25 The LORD spoke his word to me, saying:
2“Human, look towards the people of
Ammon and prophesy[d] against them. 3Say to
them, ‘Hear the word of the Lord GOD. This is
what the Lord GOD says: you were glad when
my Temple[d] was dishonoured, when the land of
Israel was ruined and when the people of Judah
were taken away as captives. 4So I am going to
give you to the people of the East to be theirs.
They will set up their camps among you and
make their homes among you. They will eat your
fruit and drink your milk. 5I will make the city of
Rabbah a pasture for camels and the land of
Ammon a resting place for sheep. Then you will
know that I am the LORD. 6This is what the Lord
GOD says: you have clapped your hands and
stamped your feet; you have laughed about all the
insults you made against the land of Israel. 7So I
will use my power against you. I will give you to
the nations as if you were treasures taken in war.
I will wipe you out of the lands so you will no
longer be a nation, and I will destroy you. Then
you will know that I am the LORD.’

Prophecy Against Moab and Edom

8“This is what the Lord GOD says: ‘Moab and
Edom say, “The people of Judah are like all the
other nations.” 9So I am going to take away the
cities that protect Moab's borders, the best cities
in that land: Beth Jeshimoth, Baal Meon and
Kiriathaim. 10Then I will give Moab, along with the

Ammonites, to the people of the East as their
possession. Then, along with the Ammonites,
Moab will not be a nation any more. 11So I will
punish the people of Moab, and they will know
that I am the LORD.'

Prophecy Against Edom

12"This is what the Lord GOD says: 'Edom took
revenge on the people of Judah, and the Edomites
became guilty because of it. 13So this is what the
Lord GOD says: I will use my power against Edom,
killing every human and animal in it. And I will
destroy Edom all the way from Teman to Dedan
as they die in battle. 14I will use my people Israel
to take revenge on Edom. So the Israelites will do
to Edom what my hot anger demands. Then the
Edomites will know what my revenge feels like,
says the Lord GOD.'

Prophecy Against Philistia

15"This is what the Lord GOD says: 'The Philis-
tines have taken revenge with hateful hearts. Be-
cause of their strong hatred, they have tried to
destroy Judah. 16So this is what the Lord GOD
says: I will use my power against the Philistines.
I will kill the Kerethites, and I will destroy those
people still alive on the coast of the Mediter-
ranean Sea. 17I will punish them in my anger and
do great acts of revenge to them. They will know
that I am the LORD when I take revenge on
them.' "

Prophecy Against Tyre

26 It was the eleventh year of our captivity,
on the first day of the month. The LORD
spoke his word to me, saying: 2"Human, the city
of Tyre has spoken against Jerusalem: 'The city
that traded with the nations is destroyed. Now
we can be the trading centre. Since the city of
Jerusalem is ruined, we can make money.' 3So
this is what the Lord GOD says: I am against you,
Tyre. I will bring many nations against you, like
the sea beating its waves on your island shores.
4They will destroy the walls of Tyre and pull
down her towers. I will also scrape away her
ruins and make her a bare rock. 5Tyre will be an
island where fishermen dry their nets. I have spo-
ken, says the Lord GOD. The nations will steal
treasures from Tyre. 6Also, her villages on the
shore across from the island will be destroyed by
war. Then they will know that I am the LORD.

Nebuchadnezzar to Attack Tyre

7"This is what the Lord GOD says: I will
bring a king from the north against Tyre. He is
Nebuchadnezzar king of Babylon, the greatest
king, with his horses, chariots, horsemen and a
great army. 8He will fight a battle and destroy your
villages on the shore across from the island. He
will set up devices to attack you. He will build a
road of earth to the top of the walls. He will raise
his shields against you. 9He will bring logs to
pound through your city walls, and he will break
down your towers with his iron bars. 10His horses
will be so many that they will cover you with
their dust. Your walls will shake at the noise of
horsemen, wagons and chariots. The king of
Babylon will enter your city gates as men enter a
city where the walls are broken through. 11The
hoofs of his horses will run over your streets.
He will kill your army with the sword, and your
strong pillars will fall down to the ground.
12Also, his men will take away your riches and
will steal the things you sell. They will break
down your walls and destroy your nice houses.
They will throw your stones, wood and rubbish
into the sea. 13So I will stop your songs; the
music of your harps will not be heard any more.
14I will make you a bare rock, and you will be a
place for drying fishing nets. You will not be built
again, because I, the LORD, have spoken, says the
Lord GOD.

15"This is what the Lord GOD says to Tyre: the
people who live along the sea coast will shake
with fear when they hear about your defeat.
Those of you who are injured and dying will
groan. 16Then all the leaders of the sea coast will
get down from their thrones, take off their beauti-
ful needlework clothes and show how afraid
they are. They will sit on the ground and tremble
all the time. When they see you, they will be
shocked. 17They will begin singing a funeral song
about you and will say to you:

'Tyre, you famous city, you have been
destroyed!
You have lost your sea power!
You and your people
had great power on the seas.
You made everyone around you
afraid of you.
18Now the people who live by the coast
tremble,
now that you have fallen.
The islands of the sea
are afraid because you have been defeated.'

19"This is what the Lord GOD says: I will make
you an empty city, like cities that have no people
living in them. I will bring the deep ocean waters
over you, and the Mediterranean Sea will cover
you. 20At that time I will send you down to the
place of the dead to join those who died long ago.
I will make you live with the dead below the
earth in places that are like old ruins. You will not
come back from there or have any place in the
world of the living again. 21Other people will be
afraid of what happened to you, and it will be the

end of you. People will look for you, but they
will never find you again, says the Lord GOD."

A Funeral Song for Tyre

27 The LORD spoke his word to me, saying:
2"Human, sing a funeral song for the city

> **Sidelight** The island city of Tyre (Ezekiel 27) was perhaps the major shipping city in the Middle East in Old Testament times. After the Babylonians had destroyed Jerusalem, they besieged Tyre for thirteen years, but didn't conquer it. Instead, the city and the empire reached a peaceful settlement.

of Tyre. 3Speak to Tyre, which has ports for the
Mediterranean Sea and is a place for trade for the
people of many lands along the sea coast. 'This is
what the Lord GOD says:

Tyre, you have said,
"I am like a beautiful ship."
4You were at home on the high seas.
Your builders made your beauty perfect.
5They made all your boards
of fir trees from Mount Hermon.
They took a cedar tree from Lebanon
to make a ship's mast for you.
6They made your oars
from oak trees from Bashan.
They made your deck
from cypress trees from the coast of Cyprus
and set ivory into it.
7Your sail of linen with designs sewed on it
came from Egypt
and became like a flag for you.
Your cloth shades over the deck were blue
and purple
and came from the island of Cyprus.
8Men from Sidon and Arvad used oars to
row you.
Tyre, your skilled men were the sailors on
your deck.
9Workers of Byblos were with you,
putting caulk[n] in your ship's seams.
All the ships of the sea and their sailors
came alongside to trade with you.

10" 'Men of Persia, Lydia and Put
were warriors in your army
and hung their shields and helmets on your
sides.
They made you look beautiful.
11Men of Arvad and Cilicia
guarded your city walls all around.
Men of Gammad
were in your watchtowers
and hung their shields around your walls.
They made your beauty perfect.

12" 'People of Tarshish became traders for you
because of your great wealth. They traded your
goods for silver, iron, tin and lead.
13" 'People of Greece, Tubal and Meshech be-
came merchants for you. They traded your goods
for slaves and things of bronze.
14" 'People of Beth Togarmah traded your
goods for work horses, war horses and mules.
15" 'People of Rhodes became merchants for
you, selling your goods on many coastal lands.
They brought back ivory tusks and valuable black
wood as your payment.
16" 'People of Aram became traders for you,
because you had so many good things to sell.
They traded your goods for turquoise, purple
cloth, cloth with designs sewed on, fine linen,
coral and rubies.
17" 'People of Judah and Israel became mer-
chants for you. They traded your goods for
wheat from Minnith, and for honey, olive oil and
balm.[d]
18–19" 'People of Damascus became traders for
you because you have many good things and great
wealth. They traded your goods for wine from
Helbon, wool from Zahar and barrels of wine from
Izal. They received wrought iron, cassia[d] and sugar
cane in payment for your good things.
20" 'People of Dedan became merchants for
you, trading saddle blankets for riding.
21" 'People of Arabia and all the rulers of
Kedar became traders for you. They received
lambs, rams and goats in payment for you.
22" 'The merchants of Sheba and Raamah be-
came merchants for you. They traded your goods
for all the best spices, valuable gems and gold.
23" 'People of Haran, Canneh and Eden and
the traders of Sheba, Asshur and Kilmad became
merchants for you. 24They were paid with the
best clothes, blue cloth, cloth with designs sewed
on, carpets of many colours and tightly wound
ropes.

25" 'Trading ships
carried the things you sold.
You were like a ship full of heavy cargo
in the middle of the sea.
26The men who rowed you
brought you out into the high seas,
but the east wind broke you to pieces
in the middle of the sea.
27Your wealth, your trade, your goods,
your seamen, your sailors, your workers,

caulk Something like tar put between the boards of a ship to make it waterproof.

your traders, your warriors
and everyone else on board
sank into the sea
on the day your ship was wrecked.
28The people on the shore shake with fear
when your sailors cry out.
29All the men who row
leave their ships;
the seamen and the sailors of other ships
stand on the shore.
30They cry loudly about you;
they cry very much.
They throw dust on their heads
and roll in ashes to show they are sad.
31They shave their heads for you,
and they put on rough cloth to show they
are upset.
They cry and sob for you;
they cry loudly.
32And in their loud crying
they sing a funeral song for you:
"No one was ever destroyed like Tyre,
surrounded by the sea."
33When the goods you traded went out over
the seas,
you met the needs of many nations.
With your great wealth and goods,
you made kings of the earth rich.
34But now you are broken by the sea
and have sunk to the bottom.
Your goods and all the people on board
have gone down with you.
35All those who live along the shore
are shocked by what happened to you.
Their kings are terribly afraid,
and their faces show their fear.
36The traders among the nations hiss at you.
You have come to a terrible end,
and you are gone for ever.' "

Prophecy Against the King of Tyre

28 The LORD spoke his word to me, saying:
2"Human, say to the ruler of Tyre: 'This
is what the Lord GOD says:
because you are proud,
you say, "I am a god.
I sit on the throne of a god
in the middle of the seas."
You think you are as wise as a god,
but you are a human, not a god.
3You think you are wiser than Daniel.
You think you can find out all secrets.
4Through your wisdom and understanding
you have made yourself rich.
You have gained gold and silver
and have saved it in your storerooms.
5Through your great skill in trading,
you have made your riches grow.
You are too proud
because of your riches.

6" 'So this is what the Lord GOD says:
you think you are wise
like a god,
7but I will bring foreign people against you,
the cruellest nation.
They will pull out their swords
and destroy all that your wisdom has built,
and they will dishonour your greatness.
8They will kill you;
you will die a terrible death
like those who are killed at sea.
9While they are killing you,
you will not be able to say any more, "I am
a god."
You will be only a human, not a god,
when your murderers kill you.
10You will die like an unclean [d] person;
foreigners will kill you.

I have spoken, says the Lord God.' "

11The LORD spoke his word to me, saying:
12"Human, sing a funeral song for the king of Tyre.
Say to him: 'This is what the Lord GOD says:
You were an example of what was perfect,
full of wisdom and perfect in beauty.
13You had a wonderful life,
as if you were in Eden, the garden of God.
Every valuable gem was on you:
ruby, topaz and emerald,
yellow quartz, onyx and jasper,
sapphire, turquoise and chrysolite.
Your jewellery was made of gold.
It was prepared on the day you were
created.
14I appointed a living creature to guard you.
I put you on the holy mountain of God.
You walked among the gems that shone
like fire.
15Your life was right and good
from the day you were created,
until evil was found in you.
16Because you traded with countries far away,
you learned to be cruel, and you sinned.
So I threw you down in disgrace from the
mountain of God.
And the living creature who guarded you
forced you out from among the gems that
shone like fire.
17You became too proud
because of your beauty.
You ruined your wisdom
because of your greatness.
I threw you down to the ground.
Your example taught a lesson to other
kings.

18You dishonoured your places of worship
through your many sins and dishonest
trade.
So I set on fire the place where you lived,
and the fire burned you up.
I turned you into ashes on the ground
for all those watching to see.
19All the nations who knew you
are shocked about you.
Your punishment was so terrible,
and you are gone for ever.' "

Prophecy Against Sidon

20The LORD spoke his word to me, saying:
21"Human, look towards the city of Sidon and
prophesy[d] against her. 22Say: 'This is what the
Lord GOD says:
I am against you, Sidon,
and I will show my glory among you.
People will know that I am the LORD
when I have punished Sidon;
I will show my holiness by defeating her.
23I will send diseases to Sidon,
and blood will flow in her streets.
Those who are wounded in Sidon will fall dead,
attacked from all sides.
Then they will know that I am the LORD.

God will Help Israel

24" 'No more will neighbouring nations be like
thorny branches or sharp thorns to hurt Israel.
Then they will know that I am the Lord GOD.
25" 'This is what the Lord GOD says: I will
gather the people of Israel from the nations where
they are scattered. I will show my holiness when
the nations see what I do for my people. Then
they will live in their own land—the land I gave
to my servant Jacob. 26They will live safely in the
land and will build houses and plant vineyards.
They will live in safety after I have punished all
the nations around who hate them. Then they
will know that I am the LORD their God.' "

Prophecy Against Egypt

29 It was the tenth year of our captivity, in
the tenth month, on the twelfth day of
the month. The LORD spoke his word to me,
saying: 2"Human, look towards the king of
Egypt, and prophesy[d] against him and all Egypt.
3Say: 'This is what the Lord GOD says:
I am against you, king of Egypt.
You are like a great crocodile that lies in
the Nile River.
You say, "The Nile is mine;
I made it for myself."
4But I will put hooks in your jaws,
and I will make the fish of the Nile stick to
your sides.
I will pull you up out of your rivers,
with all the fish sticking to your sides.
5I will leave you in the desert,
you and all the fish from your rivers.
You will fall onto the ground;
you will not be picked up or buried.
I have given you to the wild animals
and to the birds of the sky for food.
6Then all the people who live in Egypt will know
that I am the LORD.
" 'Israel tried to lean on you for help, but you
were like a crutch made out of a weak stalk of
grass. 7When their hands grabbed you, you splint-
ered and tore open their shoulders. When they
leaned on you, you broke and made all their
backs twist.
8" 'So this is what the Lord GOD says: I
will cause an enemy to attack you and kill your
people and animals. 9Egypt will become an
empty desert. Then they will know that I am the
LORD.
" 'Because you said, "The Nile River is mine,
and I have made it," 10I am against you and your
rivers. I will destroy the land of Egypt and make
it an empty desert from Migdol in the north to
Aswan in the south, all the way to the border of
Cush. 11No person or animal will walk through it,
and no one will live in Egypt for 40 years. 12I will
make the land of Egypt the most deserted country
of all. Her cities will be the most deserted of all
ruined cities for 40 years. I will scatter the Egyp-
tians among the nations, spreading them among
the countries.
13" 'This is what the Lord GOD says: after 40
years I will gather Egypt from the nations
where they have been scattered. 14I will bring
back the Egyptian captives and make them re-
turn to southern Egypt, to the land they came
from. They will become a weak kingdom there.
15It will be the weakest kingdom, and it will
never again rule other nations. I will make it so
weak it will never again rule over the nations.
16The Israelites will never again depend on
Egypt. Instead, Egypt's punishment will remind
the Israelites of their sin in turning to Egypt
for help. Then they will know that I am the
Lord GOD.' "

Egypt is Given to Babylon

17It was the first day of the first month of
the twenty-seventh year of our captivity. The
LORD spoke his word to me, saying: 18"Human,
Nebuchadnezzar king of Babylon made his army
fight hard against Tyre. Every soldier's head was
rubbed bare and every shoulder was rubbed raw.
But Nebuchadnezzar and his army gained noth-
ing from fighting Tyre. 19So this is what the
Lord GOD says: I will give the land of Egypt to

Nebuchadnezzar king of Babylon. He will take away Egypt's people and its wealth and its treasures as pay for his army. 20I am giving Nebuchadnezzar the land of Egypt as a reward for working hard for me, says the Lord GOD.

21"At that time I will make Israel grow strong again, and I will let you, Ezekiel, speak to them. Then they will know that I am the LORD."

Egypt will be Punished

30 The LORD spoke his word to me, saying: 2"Human, prophesy[d] and say, 'This is what the Lord GOD says:

Cry and say,
"The terrible day is coming."
3The day is near;
the LORD's day of judging is near.
It is a cloudy day
and a time when the nations will be judged.
4An enemy will attack Egypt,
and Cush will tremble with fear.
When the killing begins in Egypt,
her wealth will be taken away,
and her foundations will be torn down.

5Cush, Put, Lydia, Arabia, Libya and some of my people who had made an agreement with Egypt will fall dead in war.

6" 'This is what the LORD says:
those who fight on Egypt's side will fall.
The power she is proud of will be lost.
The people in Egypt will fall dead in war
from Migdol in the north to Aswan in the south,
says the Lord GOD.
7They will be the most deserted lands.
Egypt's cities will be the worst of cities that lie in ruins.
8Then they will know that I am the LORD
when I set fire to Egypt
and when all those nations on her side are crushed.

9" 'At that time I will send messengers in ships to frighten Cush, which now feels safe. The people of Cush will tremble with fear when Egypt is punished. And that time is sure to come.

10" 'This is what the Lord GOD says:
I will destroy great numbers of people in Egypt
through the power of Nebuchadnezzar king of Babylon.
11Nebuchadnezzar and his army,
the cruellest army of any nation,
will be brought in to destroy the land.
They will pull out their swords against Egypt
and will fill the land with those they kill.
12I will make the streams of the Nile River become dry land,
and then I will sell the land to evil people.
I will destroy the land and everything in it
through the power of foreigners.

I, the LORD, have spoken.

Egypt's Idols are Destroyed

13" 'This is what the Lord GOD says:
I will destroy the idols
and take away the statues of gods from the city of Memphis.
There will no longer be a leader in Egypt,
and I will spread fear through the land of Egypt.
14I will make southern Egypt empty
and start a fire in Zoan
and punish Thebes.
15And I will pour out my anger against Pelusium,
the stronghold of Egypt.
I will destroy great numbers of people in Thebes.
16I will set fire to Egypt.
Pelusium will be in great pain.
The walls of Thebes will be broken open,
and Memphis will have troubles every day.
17The young men of Heliopolis and Bubastis
will fall dead in war,
and the people will be taken away as captives.
18In Tahpanhes the day will be dark
when I break Egypt's power.
Then she will no longer be proud of her power.
A cloud will cover Egypt,
and her villages will be captured and taken away.
19So I will punish Egypt,
and they will know I am the LORD.' "

Egypt Becomes Weak

20It was in the eleventh year of our captivity, in the first month, on the seventh day of the month. The LORD spoke his word to me, saying: 21"Human, I have broken the powerful arm of the king of Egypt. It has not been tied up, so it will not get well. It has not been wrapped with a bandage, so it will not be strong enough to hold a sword in war. 22So this is what the Lord GOD says: I am against the king of Egypt. I will break his arms, both the strong arm and the broken arm, and I will make the sword fall from his hand. 23I will scatter the Egyptians among the nations, spreading them among the countries. 24I will make the arms of the king of Babylon strong and put my sword in his hand. But I will break the arms of

the king of Egypt. Then when he faces the king
of Babylon, he will cry out in pain like a dying
person. 25So I will make the arms of the king of
Babylon strong, but the arms of the king of Egypt
will fall. Then people will know that I am the
LORD when I put my sword into the hand of the
king of Babylon and he uses it in war against
Egypt. 26Then I will scatter the Egyptians among
the nations, spreading them among the countries.
Then they will know that I am the LORD."

A Cedar Tree

31 It was on the first day of the third month
of the eleventh year of our captivity. The
LORD spoke his word to me, saying: 2"Human, say
to the king of Egypt and his people:

'No one is like you in your greatness.
3Assyria was once like a cedar tree in Lebanon
with beautiful branches that shaded the
forest.
It was very tall;
its top was among the clouds.
4Much water made the tree grow;
the deep springs made it tall.
Rivers flowed
around the bottom of the tree
and sent their streams
to all other trees in the countryside.
5So the tree was taller
than all the other trees in the countryside.
Its limbs became long and big
because of so much water.
6All the birds of the sky
made their nests in the tree's limbs.
And all the wild animals
gave birth under its branches.
All great nations
lived in the tree's shade.
7So the tree was great and beautiful,
with its long branches,
because its roots reached down to much
water.
8The cedar trees in the garden of God
were not as great as it was.
The pine trees
did not have such great limbs.
The plane trees
did not have such branches.
No tree in the garden of God
was as beautiful as this tree.
9I made it beautiful
with many branches,
and all the trees of Eden in the garden
of God
wanted to be like it.

10" 'So this is what the Lord GOD says: the
tree grew tall. Its top reached the clouds, and it
became proud of its height. 11So I handed it over to
a mighty ruler of the nations for him to punish it.
Because it was evil, I got rid of it. 12The cruellest
foreign nation cut it down and left it. The tree's
branches fell on the mountains and in all the val-
leys, and its broken limbs were in all the ravines
of the land. All the nations of the earth left the
shade of that tree. 13The birds of the sky live on
the fallen tree. The wild animals live among the
tree's fallen branches. 14So the trees that grow by
the water will not be proud to be tall; they will
not put their tops among the clouds. None of the
trees that are watered well will grow that tall,
because they all are meant to die and go under
the ground. They will be with people who have
died and have gone down to the place of the
dead.

15" 'This is what the Lord GOD says: on the day
when the tree went down to the place of the
dead, I made the deep springs cry loudly. I cov-
ered them and held back their rivers, and the
great waters stopped flowing. I dressed Lebanon
in black to show her sadness about the great
tree, and all the trees in the countryside were
sad about it. 16I made the nations shake with fear
at the sound of the tree falling when I brought it
down to the place of the dead. It went to join
those who have gone down to the grave. Then all
the trees of Eden and the best trees of Lebanon,
all the well-watered trees, were comforted in the
place of the dead below the earth. 17These trees
had also gone down with the great tree to the
place of the dead. They joined those who were
killed in war and those among the nations who
had lived under the great tree's shade.

18" 'So no tree in Eden is equal to you, Egypt,
in greatness and honour, but you will go down to
join the trees of Eden in the place below the
earth. You will lie among unclean[d] people, with
those who were killed in war.

" 'This is about the king of Egypt and all his
people, says the Lord GOD.' "

A Funeral Song

32 It was on the first day of the twelfth
month of the twelfth year. The LORD
spoke his word to me, saying: 2"Human, sing a
funeral song about the king of Egypt. Say to him:

'You are like a young lion among the nations.
You are like a crocodile in the seas.
You splash around in your streams
and stir up the water with your feet,
making the rivers muddy.

3" 'This is what the Lord GOD says:
I will spread my net over you,
and I will use a large group of people
to pull you up in my net.

4Then I will throw you on the land
dropping you onto the ground.
I will let the birds of the sky rest on you
and all the animals of the earth eat you
until they are full.
5I will scatter your flesh on the mountains
and fill the valleys with what is left
of you.
6I will drench the land with your flowing
blood
as far as the mountains,
and the ravines will be full of your flesh.
7When I make you disappear,
I will cover the sky and make the stars
dark.
I will cover the sun with a cloud,
and the moon will not shine.
8I will make all the shining lights in the sky
become dark over you;
I will bring darkness over your land,
says the Lord GOD.
9I will cause many people to be afraid
when I bring you as a captive into other
nations,
to lands you have not known.
10I will cause many people to be shocked
about you.
Their kings will tremble with fear because
of you
when I swing my sword in front of them.
They will shake every moment
on the day you fall;
each king will be afraid for his own life.

11" 'So this is what the Lord GOD says:
the sword of the king of Babylon
will attack you.
12I will cause your people to fall
by the swords of mighty soldiers,
the most terrible in the world.
They will destroy the pride of Egypt
and all its people.
13I will also destroy all Egypt's cattle
which live alongside much water.
The foot of a human will not stir the water,
and the hoofs of cattle will not muddy it
any more.
14So I will let the Egyptians' water become
clear.
I will cause their rivers to run as smoothly
as olive oil,
says the Lord GOD.
15When I make the land of Egypt empty
and take everything that is in the land,
when I destroy all those who live in Egypt,
then they will know that I am the LORD.'

16"This is the funeral song people will sing for
Egypt. The women of the nations will sing it; they
will sing a funeral song for Egypt and all its peo-
ple, says the Lord GOD."

Egypt to be Destroyed

17It was in the twelfth year of our captivity, on
the fifteenth day of the month. The LORD spoke
his word to me, saying: 18"Human, cry for the
people of Egypt. Bring down Egypt, together with
the women of the powerful nations; bring them
down to the place of the dead below the earth to
join those who go to the place of the dead. 19Say
to them: 'Are you more beautiful than others?
Go and lie down in death with those who are un-
clean.' *d* 20The Egyptians will fall among those
killed in war. The sword is ready; the enemy will
drag Egypt and all her people away. 21From the
place of the dead the leaders of the mighty ones
will speak about the king of Egypt and the nations
which help him: 'The unclean, those killed in
war, have come down here and lie dead.'

22"Assyria and all its army lie dead there. The
graves of their soldiers are all around. All were
killed in war, 23and their graves were put in the
deepest parts of the place of the dead. Assyria's
army lies around its grave. When they lived on
earth, they frightened people, but now all of them
have been killed in war.

24"The nation of Elam is there with all its army
around its grave. All of them were killed in war.
They had frightened people on earth and were
unclean, so they went down to the lowest parts
of the place of the dead. They must carry their
shame with those who have gone down to the
place of the dead. 25A bed has been made for
Elam with all those killed in war. The graves of
her soldiers are all around her. All Elam's people
are unclean, killed in war. They frightened people
when they lived on earth, but now they must
carry their shame with those who have gone
down to the place of the dead. Their graves are
with the rest who were killed.

26"Meshech and Tubal are there with the
graves of all their soldiers around them. All of
them are unclean and have been killed in war.
They also frightened people when they lived on
earth. 27But they are not buried with the other
soldiers who were killed in battle long ago, those
who went with their weapons of war to the place
of the dead. These soldiers had their swords laid
under their heads and their shields on their bod-
ies. These mighty soldiers used to frighten people
when they lived on earth.

28"You, king of Egypt, will be broken and lie
among those who are unclean, who were killed
in war.

29"Edom is there also, with its kings and all its
leaders. They were mighty, but now they lie in
death with those killed in war, with those who

are unclean, with those who have gone down to
the place of the dead.
30“All the rulers of the north and all the
Sidonians are there. Their strength frightened
people, but they have gone down in shame with
those who were killed. They are unclean, lying
with those killed in war. They carry their shame
with those who have gone down to the place of
the dead.
31“The king of Egypt and his army will see
these who have been killed in war. Then he will
be comforted for all his soldiers killed in war, says
the Lord GOD. 32I made people afraid of the king
of Egypt while he lived on earth. But he and all
his people will lie among those who are unclean,
who were killed in war, says the Lord GOD.”

Ezekiel is Watchman for Israel

33 The LORD spoke his word to me, saying:
2“Human, speak to your people and say
to them: ‘Suppose I bring a war against a land.
The people of the land may choose one of their
men and make him their watchman. 3When he
sees the enemy coming to attack the land, he will
blow the trumpet and warn the people. 4If they
hear the sound of the trumpet but do nothing,
the enemy will come and kill them. They will be
responsible for their own deaths. 5They heard the
sound of the trumpet but didn’t do anything. So
they are to blame for their own deaths. If they
had done something, they would have saved
their own lives. 6But if the watchman sees the
enemy coming to attack and does not blow the
trumpet, the people will not be warned. Then if
the enemy comes and kills any of them, they
have died because of their own sin. But I will
punish the watchman for their deaths.’
7“You, human, are the one I have made a
watchman for Israel. If you hear a word from my
mouth, you must warn them for me. 8Suppose I
say to the wicked: ‘Wicked people, you will
surely die,’ but you don’t speak to warn the
wicked to stop doing evil. Then they will die be-
cause they were sinners, but I will punish you for
their deaths. 9But if you warn the wicked to stop
doing evil and they do not stop, they will die
because they were sinners. But you have saved
your life.
10“So you, human, say to Israel: ‘You have
said: surely our law-breaking and sins are hurting
us. They will kill us. What can we do so we will
live?’ 11Say to them: “The Lord GOD says: as surely
as I live, I do not want any who are wicked to die.
I want them to stop doing evil and live. Stop! Stop
your wicked ways! You don’t want to die, do
you, people of Israel?’
12“Human, say to your people: ‘The goodness
of those who do right will not save them when
they sin. The evil of wicked people will not
cause them to be punished if they stop doing it.
If good people sin, they will not be able to live by
the good they did earlier.’ 13If I tell good people,
“You will surely live,” they might think they
have done enough good and then do evil. Then
none of the good things they did will be remem-
bered. They will die because of the evil they
have done. 14Or, if I say to the wicked people,
“You will surely die,” they may stop sinning and
do what is right and honest. 15For example, they
may return what somebody gave them as a
promise to repay a loan, or pay back what they
stole. If they live by the rules that give life and do
not sin, then they will surely live, and they will
not die. 16They will not be punished for any of
their sins. They now do what is right and fair, so
they will surely live.
17“Your people say: ‘The way of the Lord is
not fair.’ But it is their own ways that are not fair.
18When the good people stop doing good and do
evil, they will die for their evil. 19But when the
wicked stop doing evil and do what is right and
fair, they will live. 20You still say: ‘The way of the
Lord is not fair.’ Israel, I will judge all of you by
your own ways.”

The Fall of Jerusalem Explained

21It was on the fifth day of the tenth month of
the twelfth year. A person who had escaped from
Jerusalem came to me and said, “Jerusalem has
been captured.” 22Now I had felt the power of
the LORD on me the evening before. He had made
me able to talk again before this person came to
me. I could speak; I was not without speech any
more.
23Then the LORD spoke his word to me, saying:
24“Human, people who live in the ruins in the
land of Israel are saying: ‘Abraham was only one
person, yet he was given the land as his own.
Surely the land has been given to us, who are
many, as our very own.’ 25So say to them: ‘This
is what the Lord GOD says: you eat meat with the
blood still in it, you ask your idols for help and
you murder people. Should you then have the
land as your very own? 26You depend on your
sword and do terrible things which I hate. Each
of you has sexual relations with his neighbour’s
wife. So should you have the land?’
27“Say to them: ‘This is what the Lord GOD
says: as surely as I live, those who are among the
city ruins in Israel will be killed in war. I will
cause those who live in the country to be eaten
by wild animals. People hiding in the strong-
holds[d] and caves will die of disease. 28I will make
the land an empty desert. The people’s pride in
the land’s power will end. The mountains of
Israel will become empty so that no one will pass

through them. 29They will know that I am the
LORD when I make the land an empty desert be-
cause of the things they have done that I hate.'
30"But as for you, human, your people are talk-
ing about you by the walls and in the doorways
of houses. They say to each other: 'Come now,
and hear the message from the LORD.' 31So they
come to you in crowds as if they were really
ready to listen. They sit in front of you as if they
were my people and hear your words, but they
will not obey them. With their mouths they tell
me they love me, but their hearts desire their
selfish profits. 32To your people you are nothing
more than a singer who sings love songs and has
a beautiful voice and plays a musical instrument
well. They hear your words, but they will not
obey them.

Sidelight If Ezekiel were a preacher today, he would probably have a big following. Ezekiel 33:32 tells how people were so attracted to his style and his beautiful voice that they didn't hear his challenging message.

33"When this comes true, and it surely will
happen, then the people will know that a
prophet[d] has been among them."

The Leaders are Like Shepherds

34 The LORD spoke his word to me, saying:
2"Human, prophesy[d] against the leaders
of Israel, who are like shepherds. Prophesy and
say to them: 'This is what the Lord GOD says: how
terrible it will be for the shepherds of Israel who
feed only themselves! Why don't the shepherds
feed the flock? 3You eat the milk curds, and you
clothe yourselves with the wool. You kill the fat
sheep, but you do not feed the flock. 4You have
not made the weak strong. You have not healed
the sick or put bandages on those that were hurt.
You have not brought back those who strayed
away or searched for the lost. But you have ruled
the sheep with cruel force. 5The sheep were scat-
tered, because there was no shepherd, and they
became food for every wild animal. 6My flock
wandered over all the mountains and on every
high hill. They were scattered all over the face of
the earth, and no one searched or looked for
them.
7" 'So, you shepherds, hear the word of the
LORD. This is what the Lord GOD says: 8As surely
as I live, my flock has been caught and eaten by
all the wild animals, because the flock has no
shepherd. The shepherds did not search for
my flock. No, they fed themselves instead of
my flock. 9So, you shepherds, hear the word of
the LORD. 10This is what the Lord GOD says: I am
against the shepherds. I will blame them for what
has happened to my sheep and will not let them
tend the flock any more. Then the shepherds will
stop feeding themselves, and I will take my flock
from their mouths so they will no longer be their
food.
11" 'This is what the Lord GOD says: I, myself,
will search for my sheep and take care of them.
12As a shepherd takes care of his scattered flock
when it is found, I will take care of my sheep. I
will save them from all the places where they
were scattered on a cloudy and dark day. 13I will
bring them out from the nations and gather
them from the countries. I will bring them to
their own land and pasture them on the moun-
tains of Israel, in the ravines and in all the places
where people live in the land. 14I will feed them
in a good pasture, and they will eat grass on the
high mountains of Israel. They will lie down
on good ground where they eat grass, and they
will eat in rich grassland on the mountains of
Israel. 15I will feed my flock and lead them to
rest, says the Lord GOD. 16I will search for the
lost, bring back those that strayed away, put
bandages on those that were hurt and make
the weak strong. But I will destroy those sheep
that are fat and strong. I will tend the sheep with
fairness.
17" 'This is what the Lord GOD says: as for you,
my flock, I will judge between one sheep and
another, between the rams and the male goats.
18Is it not enough for you to eat grass in the good
land? Must you crush the rest of the grass with
your feet? Is it not enough for you to drink clear
water? Must you make the rest of the water
muddy with your feet? 19Must my flock eat what
you crush, and must they drink what you make
muddy with your feet?
20" 'So this is what the Lord GOD says to them:
I, myself, will judge between the fat sheep and
the thin sheep. 21You push with your side and
with your shoulder, and you knock down all
the weak sheep with your horns until you have
forced them away. 22So I will save my flock; they
will not be hurt any more. I will judge between
one sheep and another. 23Then I will put over
them one shepherd, my servant David. He will
feed them and tend them and be their shepherd.
24Then I, the LORD, will be their God, and my
servant David will be a ruler among them. I, the
LORD, have spoken.
25" 'I will make an agreement of peace with
my sheep and will remove harmful animals from
the land. Then the sheep will live safely in the
desert and sleep in the woods. 26I will bless them
and let them live around my hill. I will cause the

rains to come when it is time; there will be show-
ers to bless them. 27Also the trees in the country-
side will give their fruit, and the land will give its
harvest. And the sheep will be safe on their land.
Then they will know that I am the LORD when I
break the bars of their captivity and save them
from the power of those who made them slaves.
28They will not be led captive by the nations
again. The wild animals will not eat them, but
they will live safely, and no one will make them
afraid. 29I will give them a place famous for its
good crops, so they will no longer suffer from
hunger in the land. They will not suffer the
insults of other nations any more. 30Then they
will know that I, the LORD their God, am with
them. The nation of Israel will know that they
are my people, says the Lord GOD. 31You, my
human sheep, are the sheep I care for, and I am
your God, says the Lord GOD.' "

Prophecy Against Edom

35 The LORD spoke his word to me, saying:
2"Human, look towards Edom and
prophesy[d] against it. 3Say to it: 'This is what the
Lord GOD says: I am against you, Edom. I will
stretch out my hand against you and make you an
empty desert. 4I will destroy your cities, and you
will become empty. Then you will know that I
am the LORD.
5" 'You have always been an enemy of Israel.
You let them be defeated in war when they were
in trouble at the time of their final punishment.
6So the Lord GOD says, as surely as I live, I will let
you be murdered. Murder will chase you. Since
you did not hate murdering people, murder will
chase you. 7I will make Edom an empty ruin and
destroy everyone who goes in or comes out of
it. 8I will fill its mountains with those who are
killed. Those killed in war will fall on your hills,

SCHOOL

Abused Privileges

Jenny felt honoured to be selected for the Vocal Ensemble, a special choir at her school. The group was invited to compete at a national music festival, held at a big concert hall. After the performance, the judges gave the group top marks. Jenny felt proud to be a member.

The choir's director gave the singers some free time before returning home. Many of them felt pretty rowdy. How could they have fun?

First, they tried monopolising the lifts and escalators. Jenny joined in.

They began disrupting others who had come for the festival. Jenny did too.

Some invaded the cafeteria, where one member was kicked out after fooling around with some trays. Others dumped ash trays on the floor.

Finally, the manager of the hall demanded to see the teacher in charge. When she learned what was going on, she disbanded the Vocal Ensemble on the spot. "I gave you free time as a reward for performing well," she said angrily, "but you selfishly violated my trust and other people's rights."

Now Jenny is not so proud to have been a part of the Ensemble. "It's a memory that you wish wasn't a memory," she says.

Like the members of the Vocal Ensemble, God's people receive special honours and privileges. When God promised special gifts for his people in **Ezekiel 34:11–24**, he also warned them not to abuse them selfishly.

- What do this passage and Jenny's story have to say about selfishness?
- What gifts has God given to you that you must be careful not to abuse?

Consider . . .

- drawing four circles on a sheet of paper, one each for family, time, money and friends. In each circle, list one way in which you can be less selfish this coming week, and then put all four ideas into action.
- asking forgiveness from someone whose trust you've broken or with whom you've acted selfishly.

For more, see . . .

- Exodus 16:11–21 (p.75)
- 1 Corinthians 11:20–22 (p.1229)
- Mark 12:1–12 (p.1021)

in your valleys and in all your ravines. 9I will make you a ruin for ever; no one will live in your cities. Then you will know that I am the LORD.

10" 'You said, "These two nations, Israel and Judah, and these two lands will be ours. We will take them for our own." But the LORD was there. 11So this is what the Lord GOD says: As surely as I live, I will treat you just as you treated them. You were angry and jealous because you hated them. So I will punish you and show the Israelites who I am. 12Then you will know that I, the LORD, have heard all your insults against the mountains of Israel. You said, "They have been ruined. They have been given to us to eat." 13You have not stopped your proud talk against me. I have heard you. 14This is what the Lord GOD says: all the earth will be happy when I make you an empty ruin. 15You were happy when the land of Israel was ruined, but I will do the same thing to you. Mount Seir and all Edom, you will become an empty ruin. Then you will know that I am the LORD.' "

Israel to Come Home

36 "Human, prophesy[d] to the mountains of Israel and say: 'Mountains of Israel, hear the word of the LORD. 2This is what the Lord GOD says: the enemy has said about you, "Now the old places to worship gods have become ours." ' 3So prophesy and say: "This is what the Lord GOD says: they have made you an empty ruin and have crushed you from all around. So you became a possession of the other nations. People have talked and whispered against you. 4So, mountains of Israel, hear the word of the Lord GOD. The Lord GOD speaks to the mountains, hills, ravines and valleys, to the empty ruins and abandoned cities that have been robbed and laughed at by the other nations. 5This is what the Lord GOD says: I speak in hot anger against the other nations. I speak against the people of Edom, who took my land for themselves with joy and with hate in their hearts. They forced out the people and took their pastureland.' 6So prophesy about the land of Israel and say to the mountains, hills, ravines and valleys: 'This is what the Lord GOD says: I speak in my jealous anger, because you have suffered the insults of the nations. 7So this is what the Lord GOD says: I promise that the nations around you will also have to suffer insults.

8" 'But you, mountains of Israel, will grow branches and fruit for my people, who will soon come home. 9I am concerned about you; I am on your side. You will be ploughed, and seed will be planted in you. 10I will increase the number of people who live on you, all the people of Israel. The cities will have people living in them, and the ruins will be rebuilt. 11I will increase the number of people and animals living on you. They will grow and have many young. You will have people living on you as you did before, and I will make you better off than at the beginning. Then you will know that I am the LORD. 12I will cause my people Israel to walk on you and own you, and you will belong to them. You will never again take their children away from them.

13" 'This is what the Lord GOD says: People say about you, "You eat people and take children from your nation." 14But you will not eat people any more or take away the children, says the Lord GOD. 15I will not make you listen to insults from the nations any more; you will not suffer shame from them any more. You will not cause your nation to fall any more, says the Lord GOD.' "

The LORD Acts for Himself

16The LORD spoke his word to me again, saying: 17"Human, when the nation of Israel was living in their own land, they made it unclean[d] by their ways and the things they did. Their ways were like a woman's uncleanness in her time of monthly bleeding. 18So I poured out my anger against them, because they murdered in the land and because they made the land unclean with their idols. 19I scattered them among the nations, and they were spread through the countries. I punished them for how they lived and what they did. 20They dishonoured my holy name in the nations where they went. The nations said about them: 'These are the people of the LORD, but they had to leave the land which he gave them.' 21But I had concern for my holy name, which the nation of Israel had dishonoured among the nations where they went.

22"So say to the people of Israel, 'This is what the Lord GOD says: Israel, I am going to act, but not for your sake. I will do something to help my holy name, which you have dishonoured among the nations where you went. 23I will prove the holiness of my great name, which has been dishonoured among the nations. You have dishonoured it among these nations, but the nations will know that I am the LORD when I prove myself holy before their eyes, says the Lord GOD.

24" 'I will take you from the nations and gather you out of all the lands and bring you back into your own land. 25Then I will sprinkle clean water on you, and you will be clean. I will cleanse you from all your uncleanness and your idols. 26Also, I will teach you to respect me completely, and I will put a new way of thinking inside you. I will take out the stubborn hearts of stone from your bodies, and I will give you obedient hearts of flesh. 27I will put my Spirit[d] inside you and help you live by my rules and carefully obey my laws.

28You will live in the land I gave to your ancestors, and you will be my people, and I will be your God. 29So I will save you from all your uncleanness. I will command the grain to come and grow; I will not allow a time of hunger to hurt you. 30I will increase the harvest of the field so you will never again suffer shame among the nations because of hunger. 31Then you will remember your evil ways and actions that were not good, and you will hate yourselves because of your sins and your terrible acts that I hate. 32I want you to know that I am not going to do this for your sake, says the Lord GOD. Be ashamed and embarrassed about your ways, Israel.

33" 'This is what the Lord GOD says: this is what will happen on the day I cleanse you from all your sins: I will cause the cities to have people living in them again, and the destroyed places will be rebuilt. 34The empty land will be ploughed so it will no longer be a ruin for everyone who passes by to see. 35They will say, "This land was ruined, but now it has become like the garden of Eden. The cities were destroyed, empty and ruined, but now they are protected and have people living in them." 36Then those nations still around you will know that I, the LORD, have rebuilt what was destroyed and have planted what was empty. I, the LORD, have spoken, and I will do it.'

37"This is what the Lord GOD says: I will let myself be asked by the people of Israel to do this for them again: I will make their people grow in number like a flock. 38They will be as many as the flocks brought to Jerusalem during her holy feasts. Her ruined cities will be filled with flocks of people. Then they will know that I am the LORD."

The Vision of Dry Bones

37 I felt the power of the LORD on me, and he brought me out by the Spirit[d] of the LORD and put me down in the middle of a valley. It was full of bones. 2He led me around among the bones, and I saw that there were many bones in the valley and that they were very dry. 3Then he asked me, "Human, can these bones live?"

I answered, "Lord GOD, only you know."

4He said to me, "Prophesy[d] to these bones and say to them, 'Dry bones, hear the word of the LORD. 5This is what the Lord GOD says to the bones: I will cause breath to enter you so you will come to life. 6I will put muscles on you and flesh on you and cover you with skin. Then I will put breath in you so you will come to life. Then you will know that I am the LORD.' "

7So I prophesied as I was commanded. While I prophesied, there was a noise and a rattling. The bones came together, bone to bone. 8I looked and saw muscles come on the bones, and flesh grew and skin covered the bones. But there was no breath in them.

9Then he said to me, "Prophesy to the wind.[n] Prophesy, human, and say to the wind, 'This is what the Lord GOD says: wind, come from the four winds, and breathe on these people who were killed so they can come back to life.' " 10So I prophesied as the LORD commanded me. And the breath came into them, and they came to life and stood on their feet, a very large army.

11Then he said to me, "Human, these bones are like all the people of Israel. They say, 'Our bones are dried up, and our hope has gone. We are destroyed.' 12So, prophesy and say to them, 'This is what the Lord GOD says: my people, I will open your graves and cause you to come up out of your graves. Then I will bring you into the land of Israel. 13My people, you will know that I am the LORD when I open your graves and cause you to come up from them. 14And I will put my Spirit inside you, and you will come to life. Then I will put you in your own land. And you will know that I, the LORD, have spoken and done it, says the LORD.' "

Judah and Israel Back Together

15The LORD spoke his word to me, saying, 16"Human, take a stick and write on it, 'For Judah and all the Israelites with him.' Then take another stick and write on it, 'The stick of Ephraim, for Joseph and all the Israelites with him.' 17Then join them together into one stick so they will be one in your hand.

18"When your people say to you, 'Explain to us what you mean by this,' 19say to them, 'This is what the Lord GOD says: I will take the stick for Joseph and the tribes[d] of Israel with him, which is in the hand of Ephraim, and I will put it with the stick of Judah. I will make them into one stick, and they will be one in my hand.' 20Hold the sticks on which you wrote these names in your hand so the people can see them. 21Say to the people, 'This is what the Lord GOD says: I am going to take the people of Israel from among the nations where they have gone. I will gather them from all around and bring them into their own land. 22I will make them one nation in the land, on the mountains of Israel. One king will rule all of them. They will never again be two nations; they will not be divided into two kingdoms any more. 23They will not continue to make themselves unclean[d] by their idols, their statues of gods which I hate, or by their sins. I will save them from all the ways they sin and turn against

wind This Hebrew word could also mean "breath" or "spirit".

me, and I will make them clean. Then they will be my people, and I will be their God.

24" 'My servant David will be their king, and they will all have one shepherd. They will live by my rules and obey my laws. 25They will live on the land I gave to my servant Jacob, the land in which your ancestors lived. They will all live on the land for ever: they, their children and their grandchildren. David my servant will be their king for ever. 26I will make an agreement of peace with them, an agreement that continues for ever. I will put them in their land and make them grow in number. Then I will put my Temple[d] among them for ever. 27The place where I live will be with them. I will be their God, and they will be my people. 28When my Temple is among them for ever, the nations will know that I, the LORD, make Israel holy.' "

Prophecy Against Gog

38 The LORD spoke his word to me, saying, 2"Human, look towards Gog of the land of Magog, the chief ruler of the nations of Meshech and Tubal. Prophesy[d] against him 3and say, 'The Lord GOD says this: I am against you, Gog, chief ruler of Meshech and Tubal. 4I will turn you around and put hooks in your jaws. And I will bring you out with all your army, horses and horsemen, all of whom will be dressed in beautiful uniforms. They will be a large army with large and small shields and all having swords. 5Persia, Cush and Put will be with them, all of them having shields and helmets. 6There will also be Gomer with all its troops and the nation of Togarmah from the far north with all its troops—many nations with you.

> **Sidelight** Ezekiel 38 and 39 give a prophecy about Gog and Magog, an unknown invading king and nation who will attack Israel. In Revelation 20:7–10 (p.1403), John continues this prophecy by telling of the ultimate defeat of this enemy.

7" 'Be prepared. Be prepared, you and all the armies that have come together to make you their commander. 8After a long time you will be called for service. After those years you will come into a land that has been rebuilt from war. The people in the land will have been gathered from many nations to the mountains of Israel, which were empty for a long time. These people were brought out from the nations, and they will all be living in safety. 9You will come like a storm. You, all your troops, and the many nations with you will be like a cloud covering the land.

10" 'This is what the Lord GOD says: at that time ideas will come into your mind, and you will think up an evil plan. 11You will say, "I will march against a land of towns without walls. I will attack those who are at rest and live in safety. All of them live without city walls or gate bars or gates. 12I will capture treasures and take valuable things. I will turn my power against the rebuilt ruins that now have people living in them. I will attack these people who have been gathered from the nations, who have become rich with farm animals and property, who live at the centre of the world." 13Sheba, Dedan and the traders of Tarshish, with all its villages, will say to you, "Did you come to capture treasure? Did you bring your troops together to take valuable things? Did you bring them to carry away silver and gold and to take away farm animals and property?" '

14"So prophesy, human, and say to Gog, 'This is what the Lord GOD says: now that my people Israel are living in safety, you will know about it. 15You will come with many people from your place in the far north. You will have a large group with you, a mighty army, all riding on horses. 16You will attack my people Israel like a cloud that covers the land. This will happen in the days to come when I bring you against my land. Gog, then the nations will know me when they see me prove how holy I am in what I do through you.

17" 'This is what the Lord GOD says: You are the one about whom I spoke in past days. I spoke through my servants, the prophets of Israel, who prophesied for many years that I would bring you against them. 18This is what will happen: on the day Gog attacks the land of Israel, I will become very angry, says the Lord GOD. 19With jealousy and great anger I tell you that at that time there will surely be a great earthquake in Israel. 20The fish of the sea, the birds of the sky, the wild animals, everything that crawls on the ground and all the people on the earth will shake with fear before me. Also, the mountains will be thrown down, the cliffs will fall and every wall will fall to the ground. 21Then I will call for a war against Gog on all my mountains, says the Lord GOD. Everyone's sword will attack the soldier next to him. 22I will punish Gog with disease and death. I will send a heavy rain with hailstones and burning sulphur on Gog, his army and the many nations with him. 23Then I will show how great I am. I will show my holiness, and I will make myself known to the many nations that watch. Then they will know that I am the LORD.'

The Death of Gog and His Army

39 "Human, prophesy[d] against Gog and say, 'This is what the Lord GOD says: I am against you, Gog, chief ruler of Meshech and Tubal.

2I will turn you around and lead you. I will bring
you from the far north and send you to attack the
mountains of Israel. 3I will knock your bow out
of your left hand and throw down your arrows
from your right hand. 4You, all your troops
and the nations with you will fall dead on the
mountains of Israel. I will let you be food for
every bird that eats meat and for every wild
animal. 5You will lie fallen on the ground, be-
cause I have spoken, says the Lord GOD. 6I will
send fire on Magog and those who live in safety
on the coastal lands. Then they will know that I
am the LORD.

7" 'I will make myself known among my peo-
ple Israel, and I will not let myself be dishonoured
any more. Then the nations will know that I am
the LORD, the Holy One in Israel. 8It is coming! It
will happen, says the Lord GOD. The time I talked
about is coming.

9" 'Then those who live in the cities of Israel
will come out and make fires with the enemy's
weapons. They will burn them, both large and
small shields, bows and arrows, war clubs and
spears. They will use the weapons to burn in their
fires for seven years. 10They will not need to take
wood from the field or chop firewood from the
forests, because they will make fires with the
weapons. In this way they will take the treasures
of those who took their treasures; they will take
the valuable things of those who took their valu-
able things, says the Lord GOD.

11" 'At that time I will give Gog a burial place
in Israel, in the Valley of the Travellers, east of
the Dead Sea.[d] It will block the road for trav-
ellers. Gog and all his army will be buried there,
so people will call it The Valley of Gog's Army.

12" 'The people of Israel will be burying them
for seven months to make the land clean[d] again.
13All the people in the land will bury them, and
they will be honoured on the day of my victory,
says the Lord GOD.

14" 'The people of Israel will choose men to
work through the land to make it clean. Along
with others, they will bury Gog's soldiers still lying
dead on the ground. After the seven months are
finished, they will still search. 15As they go
through the land, anyone who sees a human
bone is to put a marker by it. The sign will stay
there until the gravediggers bury the bone in The
Valley of Gog's Army. 16A city will be there
named Hamonah. So they will make the land
clean again.'

17"Human, this is what the Lord GOD says:
speak to every kind of bird and wild animal:
'Come together, come! Come together from all
around to my sacrifice, a great sacrifice which I
will prepare for you on the mountains of Israel.
Eat flesh and drink blood! 18You are to eat the
flesh of the mighty and drink the blood of the
rulers of the earth as if they were fat animals from
Bashan: rams, lambs, goats and bulls. 19You are
to eat and drink from my sacrifice which I have
prepared for you, eating fat until you are full and
drinking blood until you are drunk. 20At my table
you are to eat until you are full of horses and
riders, mighty men and all kinds of soldiers,' says
the Lord GOD.

21"I will show my glory among the nations. All
the nations will see my power when I punish
them. 22From that time onwards the people
of Israel will know that I am the LORD their
God. 23The nations will know Israel was taken
away captive because they turned against me.
So I turned away from them and handed them
over to their enemies until all of them died in
war. 24Because of their uncleanness[d] and their
sins, I punished them and turned away from
them.

25"So this is what the Lord GOD says: Now I
will bring the people of Jacob back from captiv-
ity, and I will have mercy on the whole nation of
Israel. I will not let them dishonour me. 26The
people will forget their shame and how they re-
jected me when they live again in safety on their
own land with no one to make them afraid. 27I
will bring the people back from other lands and
gather them from the lands of their enemies. So
I will use my people to show many nations that
I am holy. 28Then my people will know that I am
the LORD their God, because I sent them into cap-
tivity among the nations, but then I brought them
back to their own land, leaving no one behind. 29I
will not turn away from them any more, because
I will put my Spirit[d] into the people of Israel, says
the Lord GOD."

The New Temple

40 It was the twenty-fifth year of our captiv-
ity, at the beginning of the year, on the
tenth day of the month. It was in the fourteenth
year after Jerusalem was captured. On that same
day I felt the power of the LORD, and he brought
me to Jerusalem. 2In the visions of God he
brought me to the land of Israel and put me down
on a very high mountain. On the south of the
mountain there were some buildings that looked
like a city. 3He took me closer to the buildings,
and I saw a man who looked as if he were made
of bronze, standing in the gateway. He had a cord
made of linen and a stick in his hand, both for
measuring. 4The man said to me, "Human, look
with your eyes and hear with your ears. Pay at-
tention to all that I will show you, because that's
why you have been brought here. Tell the people
of Israel all that you see."

The East Gateway

5 I saw a wall that surrounded the Temple[d] area. The measuring stick in the man's hand was 3 metres long. So the man measured the wall, which was 3 metres thick and 3 metres high.

Sidelight Ezekiel's final vision is packed with measurements for a restored Temple in Jerusalem (Ezekiel 40–48). Its total floor space was about 80 square metres, which is less than the size of a basic swimming pool today.

6 Then the man went to the east gateway. He went up its steps and measured the opening of the gateway. It was 3 metres deep. 7 The rooms for the guards were 3 metres long and 3 metres wide. The walls that came out between the guards' rooms were about 2.5 metres thick. The opening of the gateway next to the porch that faced the Temple was 3 metres deep.

8 Then the man measured the porch of the gateway. 9 It was about 4.5 metres deep, and its side walls were a metre thick. The porch of the gateway faced the Temple.

10 On each side of the east gateway were three rooms, which measured the same on each side. The walls between each room were the same thickness. 11 The man measured the width of the entrance to the gateway, which was 5 metres wide. The width of the gate was about 6.5 metres. 12 And there was a low wall about 50 centimetres high in front of each room. The rooms were 3 metres on each side. 13 The man measured the gateway from the roof of one room to the roof of the opposite room. It was about 12.5 metres from one door to the opposite door. 14 The man also measured the porch, which was about 10 metres wide. The courtyard was around the porch. 15 From the front of the outer side of the gateway to the front of the porch of the inner side of the gateway was 25 metres. 16 The rooms and porch had small windows on both sides. The windows were narrower on the side facing the gateway. Carvings of palm trees were on each side wall of the rooms.

The Outer Courtyard

17 Then the man brought me into the outer courtyard where I saw rooms and a pavement of stones all around the court. Thirty rooms were along the edge of the paved walkway. 18 The pavement ran alongside the gates and was as deep as the gates were wide. This was the lower pavement. 19 Then the man measured from the outer wall to the inner wall. The outer court between these two walls was 50 metres on the east and on the north.

The North Gateway

20 The man measured the length and width of the north gateway leading to the outer courtyard. 21 Its three rooms on each side, its inner walls and its porch measured the same as the first gateway. It was 25 metres long and 12.5 metres wide. 22 Its windows, porch and carvings of palm trees measured the same as the east gateway. Seven steps went up to the gateway, and the gateway's porch was at the inner end. 23 The inner courtyard had a gateway across from the northern gateway like the one on the east. The man measured it and found it was 50 metres from inner gateway to outer gateway.

The South Gateway

24 Then the man led me south where I saw a gateway facing south. He measured its inner walls and its porch, and they measured the same as the other gateways. 25 The gateway and its porch had windows all around like the other gateways. It was 25 metres long and 12.5 metres wide. 26 Seven steps went up to this gateway. Its porch was at the inner end, and it had carvings of palm trees on its inner walls. 27 The inner courtyard had a gateway on its south side. The man measured from gate to gate on the south side, which was 50 metres.

The Inner Courtyard

28 Then the man brought me through the south gateway into the inner courtyard. The inner south gateway measured the same as the gateways in the outer wall. 29 The inner south gateway's rooms, inner walls and porch measured the same as the gateways in the outer wall. There were windows all around the gateway and its porch. The gateway was 25 metres long and 12.5 metres wide. 30 Each porch of each inner gateway was about 15 metres long and about 2.5 metres wide. 31 The inner south gateway's porch faced the outer courtyard. Carvings of palm trees were on its side walls, and its stairway had eight steps.

32 The man brought me into the inner courtyard on the east side. He measured the inner east gateway, and it was the same as the other gateways. 33 The inner east gateway's rooms, inside walls and porch measured the same as the other gateways. Windows were all around the gateway and its porch. The inner east gateway was 25 metres long and 12.5 metres wide. 34 Its porch faced the outer courtyard. Carvings of palm trees were on its inner walls on each side, and its stairway had eight steps.

35 Then the man brought me to the inner north gateway. He measured it, and it was the same as the other gateways. 36 Its rooms, inner walls and porch measured the same as the other gateways. There were windows all around the gateway, which was 25 metres long and 12.5 metres wide. 37 Its porch faced the outer courtyard. Carvings of palm trees were on its inner walls on each side, and its stairway had eight steps.

Rooms for Preparing Sacrifices

38 There was a room with a door that opened onto the porch of the inner north gateway. In this room the priests washed animals for the burnt offerings. 39 There were two tables on each side of the porch, on which animals for burnt offerings, sin offerings and penalty offerings were killed. 40 Outside, by each side wall of the porch, at the entrance to the north gateway, were two more tables. 41 So there were four tables inside the gateway, and four tables outside. In all there were eight tables on which the priests killed animals for sacrifices. 42 There were four tables made of cut stone for the burnt offering. These tables were about 75 centimetres long, 75 centimetres wide and about 50 centimetres high. On these tables the priests put their tools which they used to kill animals for burnt offerings and the other sacrifices. 43 Double shelves 8 centimetres wide were put up on all the walls. The flesh for the offering was put on the tables.

The Priests' Rooms

44 There were two rooms in the inner courtyard. One was beside the north gateway and faced south. The other room was beside the south gateway and faced north. 45 The man said to me, "The room which faces south is for the priests who serve in the Temple[d] area, 46 while the room that faces north is for the priests who serve at the altar. This second group of priests are descendants[d] of Zadok, the only descendants of Levi who can come near the LORD to serve him."

47 The man measured the inner courtyard. It was a square—50 metres long and 50 metres wide. The altar was in front of the Temple.

The Temple Porch

48 The man brought me to the porch of the Temple[d] and measured each side wall of the porch. Each was about 2.5 metres thick. The doorway was 7 metres wide. The side walls of the doorway were each about 1.5 metres wide. 49 The porch was 10 metres long and 6 metres wide, with ten steps leading up to it. Pillars were by the side walls, one on each side of the entrance.

The Holy Place of the Temple

41 The man brought me to the Holy Place and measured its side walls, which were each 3 metres thick. 2 The entrance was 5 metres wide. The walls alongside the entrance were each about 2.5 metres wide. The man measured the Holy Place, which was 25 metres long and 10 metres wide.

3 Then the man went inside and measured the side walls of the next doorway. Each was a metre thick. The doorway was 3 metres wide, and the walls next to it were each more than 3.5 metres thick. 4 Then the man measured the room at the end of the Holy Place. It was 10 metres long and 10 metres wide. The man said to me, "This is the Most Holy Place."

5 Then the man measured the wall of the Temple,[d] which was 3 metres thick. There were side rooms 2 metres wide all around the Temple. 6 The side rooms were on three different storeys, each above the other, with 30 rooms on each storey. All around the Temple walls there were ledges for the side rooms. The upper rooms rested on the ledges but were not attached to the Temple walls. 7 The side rooms around the Temple were wider on each higher storey, so rooms were wider on the top storey. A stairway went up from the lowest storey to the highest through the middle storey.

8 I also saw that the Temple had a raised base all around. Its edge was the foundation for the side rooms, and it was 3 metres thick. 9 The outer wall of the side rooms was about 2.5 metres thick. There was an open area between the side rooms of the Temple 10 and some other rooms. It was 10 metres wide and went all around the Temple. 11 The side rooms had doors which led to the open area around the outside of the Temple. One door faced north, and the other faced south. The open area was about 2.5 metres wide all around.

12 The building facing the private area at the west side was 35 metres wide. The wall around the building was about 2.5 metres thick and 45 metres long.

13 Then the man measured the Temple. It was 50 metres long. The private area, including the building and its walls, was in all 50 metres long. 14 Also the front of the Temple and the private area on its east side were 50 metres wide.

15 The man measured the length of the building facing the private area on the west side, and it was 50 metres from one wall to the other.

The Holy Place, the Most Holy Place and the outer porch 16 had wood panels on the walls. By the doorway, the Temple had wood panels on the walls. The wood covered all the walls from the floor up to the windows, 17up to the part of the wall above the entrance.

All the walls inside the Most Holy Place and the Holy Place, and on the outside, in the porch, 18had carvings of creatures with wings and palm trees. A palm tree was between each carved creature, and every creature had two faces. 19One was a human face looking towards the palm tree on one side. The other was a lion's face looking towards the palm tree on the other side. They were carved all around the Temple walls. 20From the floor to above the entrance, palm trees and creatures with wings were carved. The walls of the Holy Place 21had square doorposts. In front of the Most Holy Place was something that looked like 22an altar of wood. It was 1.5 metres high and 1 metre wide. Its corners, base and sides were wood. The man said to me, "This is the table that is in the presence of the LORD." 23Both the Holy Place and the Most Holy Place had double doors. 24Each of the doors had two pieces that would swing open. 25Carved on the doors of the Holy Place were palm trees and creatures with wings, like those carved on the walls. And there was a wooden roof over the front Temple porch. 26There were windows and palm trees on both side walls of the porch. The side rooms of the Temple were also covered by a roof over the stairway.

The Priests' Rooms

42 Then the man led me north out into the outer courtyard and to the rooms across from the private area and the building. 2These rooms on the north side were 50 metres long and 25 metres wide. 3There was 10 metres of the inner courtyard between them and the Temple. On the other side, they faced the stone pavement of the outer courtyard. The rooms were built in three storeys like steps and had balconies. 4There was a path on the north side of the rooms, which was 5 metres wide and 50 metres long. Doors led into the rooms from this path. 5The top rooms were narrower, because the balconies took more space from them. The rooms on the first and second storeys of the building were wider. 6The rooms were on three storeys. They did not have pillars like the pillars of the courtyards. So the top rooms were farther back than those on the first and second storeys. 7There was a wall outside parallel to the rooms and to the outer courtyard. It ran in front of the rooms for 25 metres. 8The row of rooms along the outer courtyard was 25 metres long, and the rooms that faced the Temple were about 50 metres long. 9The lower rooms had an entrance on the east side so a person could enter them from the outer courtyard, 10at the start of the wall beside the courtyard.

There were rooms on the south side, which were across from the private area and the building. 11These rooms had a path in front of them. They were like the rooms on the north with the same length and width and the same doors. 12The doors of the south rooms were like the doors of the north rooms. There was an entrance at the open end of a path beside the wall, so a person could enter at the east end.

13The man said to me, "The north and south rooms across from the private area are holy rooms. There the priests who go near the LORD will eat the most holy offerings. There they will put the most holy offerings—the grain offerings, sin offerings and penalty offerings—because the place is holy. 14The priests who enter the Holy Place must leave their serving clothes there before they go into the outer courtyard, because these clothes are holy. After they put on other clothes, they may go to the part of the Temple area which is for the people."

Outside the Temple Area

15When the man finished measuring inside the Temple[d] area, he brought me out through the east gateway. He measured the area all around. 16The man measured the east side with the measuring stick; it was 250 metres by the measuring stick. 17He measured the north side; it was 250 metres by the measuring stick. 18He measured the south side; it was 250 metres by the measuring stick. 19He went around to the west side; it measured 250 metres by the measuring stick. 20So he measured the Temple area on all four sides. The Temple area had a wall all around it that was 250 metres long and 250 metres wide. It separated what was holy from that which was not holy.

The LORD Among His People

43 Then the man led me to the outer east gateway, 2and I saw the glory of the God of Israel coming from the east. It sounded like the roar of rushing water, and its brightness made the earth shine. 3The vision I saw was like the vision I had seen when the LORD came to destroy the city and also like the vision I had seen by the Kebar River. I bowed face down on the ground. 4The glory of the LORD came into the Temple[d] area through the east gateway.

5Then the Spirit[d] picked me up and brought me into the inner courtyard. There I saw the LORD's glory filling the Temple. 6As the man stood at my side, I heard someone speaking to me from inside the Temple. 7The voice from the Temple said to me, "Human, this is my throne and the place where my feet rest. I will live here among the Israelites for ever. The people of Israel will not make my holy name unclean[d] again. Neither

the people nor their kings will make it unclean
with their sexual sins or with the dead bodies of
their kings. 8The kings made my name unclean
by putting their doorway next to my doorway,
and their doorpost next to my doorpost so only a
wall separated me from them. When they did
their acts that I hate, they made my holy name
unclean, and so I destroyed them in my anger.
9Now let them stop their sexual sins and take the
dead bodies of their kings far away from me.
Then I will live among them for ever.

10"Human, tell the people of Israel about the
Temple so they will be ashamed of their sins. Let
them think about the plan of the Temple. 11If
they are ashamed of all they have done, let them
know the design of the Temple and how it is
built. Show them its exits and entrances, all its
designs and also all its rules and teachings. Write
the rules as they watch so they will obey all the
teachings and rules about the Temple. 12This is
the teaching about the Temple: all the area
around the top of the mountain is most holy. This
is the teaching about the Temple.

The Altar

13"These are the measurements of the altar,
using the measuring stick. The altar's rim is 50
centimetres high and 50 centimetres wide, and
its rim is about 25 centimetres around its edge.
And the altar is this tall: 14from the ground up to
the lower ledge, it measures 1 metre. It is 50
centimetres wide. It measures 2 metres from
the smaller ledge to the larger ledge and is 50
centimetres wide. 15The place where the sacri-
fice is burned on the altar is 2 metres high, with
its four corners shaped like horns and reaching
up above it. 16It is square, 6 metres long and 6
metres wide. 17The upper ledge is also square, 7
metres long and 7 metres wide. The rim around
the altar is 25 centimetres wide, and its border is
50 centimetres wide all around. Its steps are on
the east side."

18Then the man said to me, "Human, this is
what the Lord GOD says: these are the rules for
the altar. When it is built, use these rules to offer
burnt offerings and to sprinkle blood on it. 19You
must give a young bull as a sin offering to the
priests, the Levites who are from the family of
Zadok and who come near me to serve me, says
the Lord GOD. 20Take some of the bull's blood
and put it on the four corners of the altar, on
the four corners of the ledge, and all around the
rim. This is how you will make the altar pure
and ready for God's service. 21Then take the bull
for the sin offering and burn it in the proper
place in the Temple[d] area, outside the Temple
building.

22"On the second day offer a male goat that has
nothing wrong with it for a sin offering. The priests
will make the altar pure and ready for God's serv-
ice as they did with the young bull. 23When you
finish making the altar pure and ready, offer a
young bull and a ram from the flock, both without
defect. 24You must offer them in the presence of
the LORD, and the priests are to throw salt on them
and offer them as a burnt offering to the LORD.

25"You must prepare a goat every day for seven
days as a sin offering. Also, the priests must pre-
pare a young bull and ram from the flock, both
without defect. 26For seven days the priests are to
make the altar pure and ready for God's service.
Then they will give the altar to God. 27After these
seven days, on the eighth day, the priests must
offer your burnt offerings and your fellowship
offerings on the altar. Then I will accept you,
says the Lord GOD."

The Outer East Gate

44 Then the man brought me back to the
outer east gateway of the Temple[d] area,
but the gate was shut. 2The LORD said to me,
"This gate will stay shut; it will not be opened.
No one may enter through it, because the LORD
God of Israel has entered through it. So it must
stay shut. 3Only the ruler himself may sit in the
gateway to eat a meal in the presence of the LORD.
He must enter through the porch of the gateway
and go out the same way."

4Then the man brought me through the outer
north gate to the front of the Temple. As I looked,
I saw the glory of the LORD filling the Temple of
the LORD, and I bowed face down on the ground.

5The LORD said to me, "Human, pay attention.
Use your eyes to see, and your ears to hear. See
and hear everything I tell you about all the rules
and teachings of the Temple of the LORD. Pay
attention to the entrance to the Temple and to all
the exits from the Temple area. 6Then speak to
those who refuse to obey. Say to the people of
Israel, 'This is what the Lord GOD says: Stop doing
all your acts that I hate, Israel! 7You brought
foreigners into my Holy Place who were not
circumcised[d] in the flesh and had not given
themselves to serving me. You dishonoured my
Temple when you offered me food, fat and
blood. You broke my agreement by all the things
you did that I hate. 8You did not take care of my
holy things yourselves but put foreigners in
charge of my Temple. 9This is what the Lord GOD
says: foreigners who are not circumcised in the
flesh and who do not give themselves to serving
me may not enter my Temple. Not even a
foreigner living among the people of Israel may
enter.

10" 'But the Levites who stopped obeying me
when Israel left me and who followed their idols
must be punished for their sin. 11These Levites
are to be servants in my Holy Place. They may
guard the gates of the Temple and serve in the
Temple area. They may kill the animals for the
burnt offering and the sacrifices for the people.
They may stand before the people to serve them.
12But these Levites helped the people worship
their idols and caused the people of Israel to fall,
so I make this promise: they will be punished for
their sin, says the Lord GOD. 13They will not come
near me to serve as priests, nor will they come
near any of my holy things or the most holy offer-
ings. But they will be made ashamed of the things
they did that I hate. 14I will put them in charge
of taking care of the Temple area, all the work
that must be done in it.

15" 'But the priests who are Levites and des-
cendants [d] of Zadok took care of my Holy Place
when Israel left me, so they may come near to
serve me. They may stand in my presence to offer
me the fat and blood of the animals they sacrifice,
says the Lord GOD. 16They are the only ones who
may enter my Holy Place. Only they may come
near my table to serve me and take care of the
things I gave them to do.

17" 'When they enter the gates of the inner
courtyard, they must wear linen robes. They
must not wear wool to serve at the gates of the
inner courtyard or in the Temple. 18They will
wear linen turbans on their heads and linen
underclothes. They will not wear anything that
makes them perspire. 19When they go out into
the outer courtyard to the people, they must take
off their serving clothes before they go. They
must leave these clothes in the holy rooms and
put on other clothes. Then they will not let their
holy clothes hurt the people.

20" 'They must not shave their heads or let
their hair grow long but must keep the hair of
their heads trimmed. 21None of the priests may
drink wine when they enter the inner courtyard.
22The priests must not marry widows or divorced
women. They may marry only virgins [d] from the
people of Israel or widows of priests. 23They must
teach my people the difference between what is
holy and what is not holy. They must help my
people know what is unclean [d] and what is clean.

24" 'In court they will act as judges. When they
judge, they will follow my teachings. They must
obey my laws and my rules at all my special feasts
and keep my Sabbaths [d] holy.

25" 'They must not go near a dead person,
making themselves unclean. [d] But they are al-
lowed to make themselves unclean if the dead
person is their father, mother, son, daughter,
brother or a sister who has not married. 26After a
priest has been made clean again, he must wait
seven days. 27Then he may go into the inner
courtyard to serve in the Temple, but he must
offer a sin offering for himself, says the Lord GOD.

28" 'These are the rules about the priests and
their property: they will have me instead of prop-
erty. You will not give them any land to own in
Israel; I am what they will own. 29They will eat
the grain offerings, sin offerings and penalty offer-
ings. Everything Israel gives to me will be theirs.
30The best fruits of all the first harvests and all the
special gifts offered to me will belong to the
priests. You will also give to the priests the first
part of your grain that you grind and so bring a
blessing on your family. 31The priests must not
eat any bird or animal that died a natural death or
one that has been torn by wild animals.

The Land is Divided

45 " 'When you divide the land for the
Israelite tribes [d] by throwing lots, [d] you
must give a part of the land to belong to the LORD.
It will be about 12 kilometres long and about 10
kilometres wide; all of this land will be holy.
2From this land, an area 250 metres square will
be for the Temple. [d] There will be an open space
around the Temple that is 250 metres wide. 3In
the holy area you will measure a part about 12
kilometres long and 5 kilometres wide, and in it
will be the Most Holy Place. 4This holy part of
the land will be for the priests who serve in the
Temple, who come near to the LORD to serve
him. It will be a place for the priests' houses and
for the Temple. 5Another area about 12 kilometres
long and more than 5 kilometres wide will be for
the Levites, who serve in the Temple area. It will
belong to them so they will have cities in which
to live.

6" 'You must give the city an area that is about
2.5 kilometres wide and about 12 kilometres
long, along the side of the holy area. It will belong
to all the people of Israel.

7" 'The ruler will have land on both sides of
the holy area and the city. On the west of the
holy area, his land will reach to the Mediter-
ranean Sea. On the east of the holy area, his land
will reach to the eastern border. It will be as long
as the land given to each tribe. 8Only this land
will be the ruler's property in Israel. So my rulers
will not be cruel to my people any more, but
they will let each tribe in the nation of Israel
have its share of the land.

9" 'This is what the Lord GOD says: You have
gone far enough, you rulers of Israel! Stop being
cruel and hurting people, and do what is right
and fair. Stop forcing my people out of their
homes, says the Lord GOD. 10You must have
honest scales, an honest dry measurement and

an honest liquid measurement. 11The dry meas-
ure and the liquid measure will be the same: the
liquid measure will always be a tenth of a
homer,[n] and the ephah will always be a tenth of
a homer. The measurement they follow will be
the homer. 12The shekel[n] will be worth 20 ger-
ahs, and a mina will be worth 60 shekels.

Offerings and Holy Days

13“ ‘This is the gift you should offer: one six-
tieth of your harvest of wheat, and one sixtieth
of your harvest of barley. 14The amount of oil you
are to offer is one-hundredth of your harvest.
(Ten baths make a homer and also make a cor.)
15You should give one sheep from each flock of
200 from the watering places of Israel. All these
are to be offered for the grain offerings, burnt
offerings and fellowship offerings to remove sins
so you will belong to God, says the Lord GOD.
16All people in the land will give this special offer-
ing to the ruler of Israel. 17It will be the ruler’s
responsibility to supply the burnt offerings, grain
offerings and drink offerings. These offerings will
be given at the feasts, at the New Moons,[d] on the
Sabbaths[d] and at all the other feasts of Israel.
The ruler will supply the sin offerings, grain offer-
ings and fellowship offerings to pay for the sins of
Israel.
18“ ‘This is what the Lord GOD says: on the first
day of the first month take a young bull without
defect. Use it to make the Temple[d] pure and
ready for God’s service. 19The priest will take
some of the blood from this sin offering and put
it on the doorposts of the Temple, on the four
corners of the ledge of the altar and on the posts
of the gate to the inner courtyard. 20You will do
the same thing on the seventh day of the month
for anyone who has sinned by accident or with-
out knowing it. This is how you make the Temple
pure and ready for God’s service.

Passover Feast Offerings

21“ ‘On the fourteenth day of the first month
you will celebrate the Feast[d] of Passover. It will
be a feast of seven days when you eat bread made
without yeast. 22On that day the ruler must offer
a bull for himself and for all the people of the land
as a sin offering. 23During the seven days of the
feast he must offer seven bulls and seven rams
that have nothing wrong with them. They will be
burnt offerings to the LORD, which the ruler will
offer every day of the seven days of the feast. He
must also offer a male goat every day as a sin
offering. 24The ruler must give as a grain offering
20 litres for each bull and 20 litres for each ram.
He must give 4 litres of olive oil for each 20 litres.
25“ ‘Beginning on the fifteenth day of the sev-
enth month, when you celebrate the Feast[d] of
Shelters, the ruler will supply the same things for
seven days: the sin offerings, burnt offerings,
grain offerings and the olive oil.

Rules for Worship

46 “ ‘This is what the Lord GOD says: the
east gate of the inner courtyard will stay
shut on the six working days, but it will be
opened on the Sabbath[d] day and on the day of
the New Moon.[d] 2The ruler will enter from out-
side through the porch of the gateway and stand
by the gatepost, while the priests offer the ruler’s
burnt offering and fellowship offering. The ruler
will worship at the entrance of the gateway, and
then he will go out. But the gate will not be shut
until evening. 3The people of the land will wor-
ship at the entrance of that gateway in the pres-
ence of the LORD on the Sabbaths and New
Moons. 4This is the burnt offering the ruler will
offer to the LORD on the Sabbath day: six male
lambs all without defect and a ram that has noth-
ing wrong with it. 5He must give a 20 litre grain
offering with the ram, but he may give as much
grain offering with the lambs as he pleases. He
must also give 4 litres of olive oil for each 20 litres
of grain. 6On the day of the New Moon he must
offer a young bull that has nothing wrong with it.
He must also offer six lambs and a ram that have
nothing wrong with them. 7The ruler must give
a 20 litre grain offering with the bull and 20 litres
with the ram. With the lambs, he may give
as much grain as he pleases. But he must give
4 litres of olive oil for each 20 litres of grain.
8When the ruler enters, he must go in through
the porch of the gateway, and he must go out the
same way.
9“ ‘When the people of the land come into the
LORD’s presence at the special feasts, those who
enter through the north gate to worship must go
out through the south gate. Those who enter
through the south gate must go out through the
north gate. They must not return the same way
they entered; everyone must go out the opposite
way. 10The ruler will go in with the people when
they go in and go out with them when they
go out.
11“ ‘At the feasts and regular times of worship
20 litres of grain must be offered with a young
bull, and 20 litres of grain must be offered with
a ram. But with an offering of lambs, the ruler

homer The Hebrew word means “donkey-load”. It measured about 200 litres. So an ephah was about 20 litres, and a bath was about 20 litres.
shekel In Ezekiel’s time a shekel weighed about 11 grammes.

may give as much grain as he pleases. He should
give 4 litres of olive oil for each 20 litres of grain.
12 The ruler may give an offering as a special gift
to the LORD; it may be a burnt offering or fellow-
ship offering. When he gives it to the LORD,
the inner east gate is to be opened for him. He
must offer his burnt offering or his fellowship
offering as he does on the Sabbath[d] day. Then he
will go out, and the gate will be shut after he
has left.
13 “ ‘Every day you will give a year-old lamb
that has nothing wrong with it for a burnt offer-
ing to the LORD. Do it every morning. 14 Also, you
must offer a grain offering with the lamb every
morning. For this you will give 3 litres of grain
and 1 litre of olive oil, to make the fine flour
moist, as a grain offering to the LORD. This is a rule
that must be kept from now on. 15 So you must
always give the lamb, together with the grain
offering and the olive oil, every morning as a
burnt offering.

Rules for the Ruler

16 “ ‘This is what the Lord GOD says: if the ruler
gives a gift from his land to any of his sons, that
land will belong to the son and then to the son’s
children. It is their property passed down from
their family. 17 But if the ruler gives a gift from
his land to any of his servants, that land will be-
long to the servant only until the year of free-
dom. Then the land will go back to the ruler.
Only the ruler’s sons may keep a gift of land from
the ruler. 18 The ruler must not take any of the
people’s land, forcing them out of their land. He
must give his sons some of his own land so
my people will not be scattered out of their own
land.’ ”

The Special Kitchens

19 The man led me through the entrance at the
side of the gateway to the priests’ holy rooms that
face north. There I saw a place at the west end.
20 The man said to me, “This is where the priests
will boil the meat of the penalty offering and sin
offering and bake the grain offering. Then they
will not need to bring these holy offerings into
the outer courtyard, because that would hurt the
people.”
21 Then the man brought me out into the outer
courtyard and led me to its four corners. In each
corner of the courtyard was a smaller courtyard.
22 Small courtyards were in the four corners of the
courtyard. Each small courtyard was the same
size, 20 metres long and 15 metres wide. 23 A
stone wall was around each of the four small
courtyards, and places for cooking were built in
each of the stone walls. 24 The man said to me,
“These are the kitchens where those who work
in the Temple[d] will boil the sacrifices offered by
the people.”

The River from the Temple

47 The man led me back to the door of the
Temple,[d] and I saw water coming out
from under the doorway and flowing east. (The
Temple faced east.) The water flowed down from
the south side wall of the Temple and then south
of the altar. 2 The man brought me out through
the outer north gate and led me around outside
to the outer east gate. I found the water coming
out on the south side of the gate.
3 The man went towards the east with a line in
his hand and measured about 500 metres. Then
he led me through water that came up to my
ankles. 4 The man measured about 500 metres
again and led me through water that came up to
my knees. Then he measured about 500 metres
again and led me through water up to my waist.
5 The man measured about 500 metres again, but
it was now a river that I could not cross. The
water had risen too high; it was deep enough for
swimming; it was a river that no one could cross.
6 The man asked me, “Human, do you see this?”
Then the man led me back to the bank of the
river. 7 As I went back, I saw many trees on both
sides of the river. 8 The man said to me, “This
water will flow towards the eastern areas and go
down into the Jordan Valley. When it enters the
Dead Sea,[d] it will become fresh. 9 Everywhere the
river goes, there will be many fish. Wherever this
water goes the Dead Sea will become fresh, and
so where the river goes there will be many living
things. 10 Fishermen will stand by the Dead Sea.

Sidelight In its current state, the Dead Sea is hardly a healthy habitat for the “many kinds of fish” that Ezekiel sees in his vision (Ezekiel 47:8–10). The surface of this body of water is about 400 metres below sea level, and 25 per cent of the sea is mineral, making it the saltiest and most uninhabitable sea in the world. It will take a true miracle for water to become fresh when it leaves the Dead Sea.

From En Gedi all the way to En Eglaim there will
be places to spread fishing nets. There will be
many kinds of fish in the Dead Sea, as many as in
the Mediterranean Sea. 11 But its swamps and
marshes will not become fresh; they will be left
for salt. 12 All kinds of fruit trees will grow on both
banks of the river, and their leaves will not dry
and die. The trees will have fruit every month,
because the water for them comes from the

Temple. The fruit from the trees will be used for
food, and their leaves for medicine."

Borders of the Land

13This is what the Lord GOD says: "These are
the borders of the land to be divided among the
twelve tribes[d] of Israel. Joseph will have two
parts of land. 14You will divide the land equally.
I promised to give it to your ancestors, so this
land will belong to you as family property.
15"This will be the border line of the land:
"On the north side it will start at the Mediter-
ranean Sea. It will go through Hethlon, towards
Lebo Hamath and on to the towns of Zedad,
16Berothah and Sibraim on the border between
Damascus and Hamath. Then it will go on to the
town of Hazer Hatticon on the border of the
country of Hauran. 17So the border line will go
from the Mediterranean Sea east to the town of
Hazar Enan, where the land belonging to Damas-
cus and Hamath lies on the north side. This will
be the north side of the land.
18"On the east side the border runs south from
a point between Hauran and Damascus. It will go
along the Jordan between Gilead and the land of
Israel and will continue to the town of Tamar on
the Dead Sea.[d] This will be the east side of the
land.
19"On the south side the border line will go east
from Tamar all the way to the waters of Meribah
Kadesh. Then it will run along the brook of Egypt
to the Mediterranean Sea. This will be the south
side of the land.
20"On the west side the Mediterranean Sea will
be the border line up to a place across from Lebo
Hamath. This will be the west side of your land.
21"You will divide this land among the tribes
of Israel. 22You will divide it as family property
for yourselves and for the foreigners who live
and have children among you. You are to treat
these foreigners in the same way as people born
in Israel; they are to share the land with the
tribes of Israel. 23In whatever tribe the foreigner
lives, you will give him some land," says the
Lord GOD.

Dividing the Land

48 "These are the areas of the tribes[d]
named here: Dan will have one share
at the northern border. It will go from the sea
through Hethlon to Lebo Hamath, all the way to
Hazar Enan, where Damascus lies to the north.
It will stop there next to Hamath. This will be
Dan's northern border from the east side to the
Mediterranean Sea on the west side.
2"South of Dan's border, Asher will have one
share. It will go from the east side to the west
side.
3"South of Asher's border, Naphtali will have
one share. It will go from the east side to the west
side.
4"South of Naphtali's border, Manasseh will
have one share. It will go from the east side to the
west side.
5"South of Manasseh's border, Ephraim will
have one share. It will go from the east side to the
west side.
6"South of Ephraim's border, Reuben will have
one share. It will go from the east side to the west
side.
7"South of Reuben's border, Judah will have
one share. It will go from the east side to the west
side.
8"South of Judah's border will be the holy area
which you are to give. It will be about 12 kilo-
metres wide and as long and wide as one of the
tribes' shares. It will run from the east side to the
west side. The Temple[d] will be in the middle of
this area.
9"The share which you will give the LORD will
be about 12 kilometres long and 10 kilometres
wide. 10The holy area will be divided among
these people. The priests will have land about 12
kilometres long on the north and south sides, and
10 kilometres wide on the west and east sides.
The Temple of the LORD will be in the middle of
it. 11This land is for the priests who are given the
holy duty of serving the LORD. They are the des-
cendants[d] of Zadok who did my work and did
not leave me when Israel and the Levites left me.
12They will have as their share a very holy part of
the holy portion of the land. It will be next to the
land of the Levites.
13"Alongside the land for the priests, the Levites
will have a share about 12 kilometres long and
5 kilometres wide; its full length will be about
12 kilometres and its full width about 10 kilo-
metres. 14The Levites are not to sell or trade any
of this land. They are not to let anyone else own
any of this best part of the land, because it be-
longs to the LORD.

City Property

15"The rest of the area will be about 2.5 kilo-
metres wide and 12 kilometres long. It will not
be holy but will belong to the city and be used for
homes and pastures. The city will be in the mid-
dle of it. 16These are the city's measurements: the
north side will be about 2 kilometres, the south
side about 2 kilometres, the east side about 2
kilometres and the west side about 2 kilometres.
17The city's land for pastures will be about 125
metres on the north, 125 metres on the south,
125 metres on the east and 125 metres on the
west. 18Along the long side of the holy area there
will be left 5 kilometres on the east and 5

kilometres on the west. It will be used to grow
food for the city workers. [19]The city workers
from all the tribes[d] of Israel will farm this land.
[20]This whole area will be square, 12 kilometres
by 12 kilometres. You shall give to the LORD the
holy share along with the city property.
[21]"Land that is left over on both sides of the
holy area and city property will belong to
the ruler. That land will extend east of the holy
area to the eastern border and west of it to the
Mediterranean Sea. Both of these areas run the
length of the lands of the tribes, and they belong
to the ruler. The holy area with the Holy Place
of the Temple[d] will be in the middle. [22]The
Levites' land and the city property will be in
the middle of the lands belonging to the ruler.
Those lands will be between Judah's border and
Benjamin's border.

The Other Tribes' Land

[23]"Here is what the rest of the tribes will re-
ceive: Benjamin will have one share. It will go
from the east side to the Mediterranean Sea on
the west side.
[24]"South of Benjamin's land, Simeon will have
one share. It will go from the east side to the west
side.
[25]"South of Simeon's land, Issachar will have
one share. It will go from the east side to the west
side.
[26]"South of Issachar's land, Zebulun will have
one share. It will go from the east side to the west
side.
[27]"South of Zebulun's land, Gad will have one
share. It will go from the east side to the west side.
[28]"The southern border of Gad's land will go
east from Tamar on the Dead Sea[d] to the waters
of Meribah Kadesh. Then it will run along the
brook of Egypt to the Mediterranean Sea.
[29]"This is the land you will divide among the
tribes of Israel to be their shares," says the
Lord GOD.

The Gates of the City

[30]"These will be the outside borders of the city:
the north side will measure more than 2 kilo-
metres. [31]There will be three gates facing north:
Reuben's Gate, Judah's Gate and Levi's Gate,
named after the tribes[d] of Israel.
[32]"The east side will measure more than 2
kilometres. There will be three gates facing east:
Joseph's Gate, Benjamin's Gate and Dan's Gate.
[33]"The south side will measure more than 2
kilometres. There will be three gates facing south:
Simeon's Gate, Issachar's Gate and Zebulun's Gate.
[34]"The west side will measure more than 2
kilometres. There will be three gates facing west:
Gad's Gate, Asher's Gate and Naphtali's Gate.
[35]"The city will measure about 12 kilometres
around. From then on the name of the city will
be The LORD Is There."

Daniel

Why Read This Book:

- Find courage to stand against pressure to compromise your beliefs (Daniel 1—6).
- Be assured that God works through history to fulfil his purposes (Daniel 7—12).

When?

Behind the Scenes:

After moving to a new town, he quickly became popular. People respected him. Then he started getting pressured to do things he knew were wrong. Saying no would have been easier if the people pressuring him weren't so important.

It sounds like something that could happen today, right? But it's a story set 2,500 years ago. Daniel had been dragged off to Babylon (modern-day Iraq) when the empire conquered Judah. Because of Daniel's ability to interpret dreams, the king chose him to be an important adviser.

But Daniel's career took a downward turn when he resisted the pressure to set aside his faith and worship the king. Because he wouldn't give in, he was sent to die in a den of lions, but God's power protected him. Through everything, Daniel remained faithful to God.

The book of Daniel has two parts. In the first part (chapters 1–6), we read the heroic story of Daniel and his friends. Then chapters 7–12 consist of Daniel's unusual visions that include symbols and heavenly messengers that proclaim God's Word. ▷

Where?

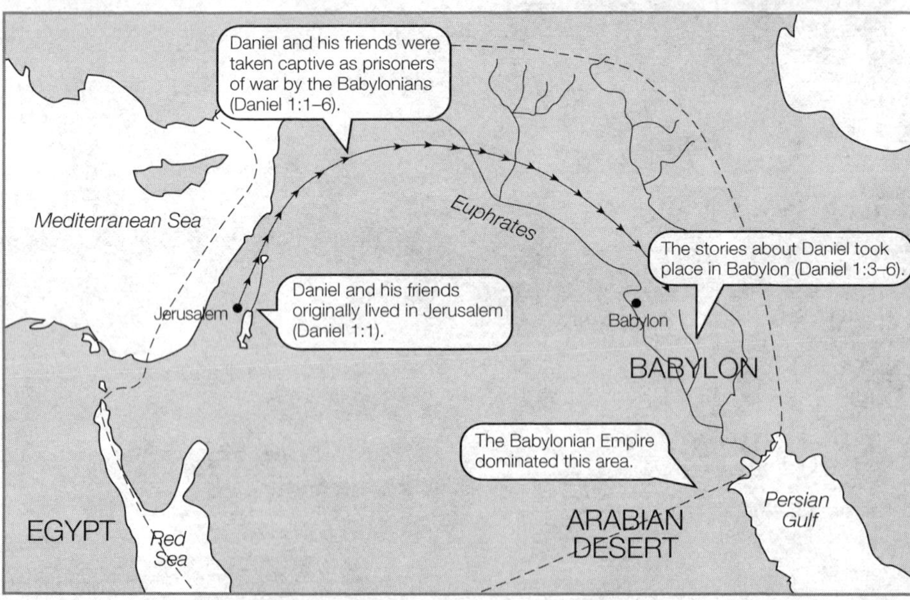

Behind the Scenes (cont.): Though parts of Daniel are difficult to understand, the book's underlying message is consistent: God is in control of history. Even when things get rough and we are under pressure, we can know that God is working to protect his people and advance his purposes in the world. We, like Daniel, should rely on God and remain faithful to God, no matter what happens.

Daniel Taken to Babylon

1 During the third year that Jehoiakim was king of Judah, Nebuchadnezzar king of Babylon came to Jerusalem and surrounded it with his army. [2]The Lord allowed Nebuchadnezzar to capture Jehoiakim king of Judah. Nebuchadnezzar also took some of the things from the Temple[d] of God, which he carried to Babylonia and put in the temple of his gods.

[3]Then King Nebuchadnezzar ordered Ashpenaz, his chief officer, to bring some of the Israelite men into his palace. He wanted them to be from important families, including the family of the king of Judah. [4]King Nebuchadnezzar wanted only young Israelite men who had nothing wrong with them. They were to be handsome and well educated, capable of learning and understanding and able to serve in his palace. Ashpenaz was to teach them the language and writings of the Babylonians. [5]The king gave the young men a certain amount of food and wine every day, just like the food he ate. The young men were to be trained for three years, and then they would become servants of the king of Babylon. [6]Among those young men were Daniel, Hananiah, Mishael and Azariah from the people of Judah.

> **Sidelight** In Old Testament times, names had important meanings. All four of the Israelites' names in Daniel 1:6 included syllables meaning God (El) or the Lord God (Yah). So these faithful men probably weren't excited when they were given Babylonian names, some of which included the names of false gods.

[7]Ashpenaz, the chief officer, gave them Babylonian names. Daniel's new name was Belteshazzar, Hananiah's was Shadrach, Mishael's was Meshach and Azariah's was Abednego.

[8]Daniel decided not to eat the king's food or drink his wine because that would make him unclean.[d] So he asked Ashpenaz for permission not to make himself unclean in this way.

[9]God made Ashpenaz, the chief officer, want to be kind and merciful to Daniel, [10]but Ashpenaz said to Daniel, "I am afraid of my master, the king. He ordered me to give you this food and drink. If you begin to look worse than other young men your age, the king will see this. Then he will cut off my head because of you."

[11]Ashpenaz had ordered a guard to watch Daniel, Hananiah, Mishael and Azariah. [12]Daniel said to the guard, "Please give us this test for ten days: don't give us anything but vegetables to eat and water to drink. [13]After ten days compare how we look with how the other young men look who eat the king's food. See for yourself and then decide how you want to treat us, your servants."

[14]So the guard agreed to test them for ten days. [15]After ten days they looked healthier and better fed than all the young men who ate the king's food. [16]So the guard took away the king's special food and wine, feeding them vegetables instead.

[17]God gave these four young men wisdom and the ability to learn many things that people had written and studied. Daniel could also understand visions and dreams.

[18]At the end of the time set for them by the king, Ashpenaz brought all the young men to King Nebuchadnezzar. [19]The king talked to them and found that none of the young men were as good as Daniel, Hananiah, Mishael and Azariah. So those four young men became the king's servants. [20]Every time the king asked them about something important, they showed much wisdom and understanding. They were ten times better than all the fortune-tellers and magicians in his kingdom! [21]So Daniel continued to be the king's servant until the first year Cyrus was king.

Nebuchadnezzar's Dream

2 During Nebuchadnezzar's second year as king, he had dreams that bothered him and kept him awake at night. [2]So the king called for his fortune-tellers, magicians, wizards and wise men, because he wanted them to tell him what he had dreamed. They came in and stood in front of the king.

3Then the king said to them, “I have had a
dream that bothers me, and I want to know what
it means.”
4The wise men answered the king in the
Aramaic language, “Our king, live for ever! Please
tell us, your servants, your dream. Then we will
tell you what it means.”
5King Nebuchadnezzar said to them, “I meant
what I said. You must tell me the dream and
what it means. If you don’t, I will have you torn
apart, and I will turn your houses into piles of
stones. 6But if you tell me my dream and its
meaning, I will reward you with gifts and great
honour. So tell me the dream and what it
means.”
7Again the wise men said to the king, “Tell us,
your servants, the dream, and we will tell you
what it means.”
8King Nebuchadnezzar answered, “I know you
are trying to get more time, because you know
that I meant what I said. 9If you don’t tell me my
dream, you will be punished. You have all agreed
to tell me lies and wicked things, hoping things
will change. Now, tell me the dream so that I will
know you can tell me what it really means!”
10The wise men answered the king, saying,
“No one on earth can do what the king asks!
No great and powerful king has ever asked the
fortune-tellers, magicians or wise men to do this;
11the king is asking something that is too hard.
Only the gods could tell the king this, but the
gods do not live among people.”
12When the king heard their answer, he became
very angry. He ordered that all the wise men of
Babylon be killed. 13So King Nebuchadnezzar’s
order to kill the wise men was announced, and
men were sent to look for Daniel and his friends
to kill them.
14Arioch, the commander of the king’s guards,
was going to kill the wise men of Babylon. But
Daniel spoke to him with wisdom and skill, 15say-
ing, “Why did the king order such a terrible pun-
ishment?” Then Arioch explained everything to
Daniel. 16So Daniel went to King Nebuchadnezzar
and asked for an appointment so that he could
tell the king what his dream meant.
17Then Daniel went to his house and explained
the whole story to his friends Hananiah, Mishael
and Azariah. 18Daniel asked his friends to pray
that the God of heaven would show them mercy
and help them understand this secret so he and
his friends would not be killed with the other
wise men of Babylon.
19During the night God explained the secret to
Daniel in a vision. Then Daniel praised the God
of heaven. 20Daniel said:

“Praise God for ever and ever,
because he has wisdom and power.
21He changes the times and seasons of the
year.
He takes away the power of kings
and gives their power to new kings.
He gives wisdom to those who are wise
and knowledge to those who understand.
22He makes known secrets that are deep and
hidden;
he knows what is hidden in darkness,
and light is all around him.
23I thank you and praise you, God of my
ancestors,
because you have given me wisdom and
power.
You told me what we asked of you;
you told us about the king’s dream.”

The Meaning of the Dream

24Then Daniel went to Arioch, the man King
Nebuchadnezzar had chosen to kill the wise
men of Babylon. Daniel said to him, “Don’t put the
wise men of Babylon to death. Take me to the
king, and I will tell him what his dream means.”
25Very quickly Arioch took Daniel to the king
and said, “I have found a man among the captives
from Judah who can tell the king what his dream
means.”
26The king asked Daniel, who was also called
Belteshazzar, “Are you able to tell me what I
dreamed and what it means?”
27Daniel answered, “No wise man, magician or
fortune-teller can explain to the king the secret
he has asked about. 28But there is a God in
heaven who explains secret things, and he has
shown King Nebuchadnezzar what will happen
at a later time. This is your dream, the vision you
saw while lying on your bed: 29our king, as you
were lying there, you thought about things to
come. God, who can tell people about secret
things, showed you what is going to happen.
30God also told this secret to me, not because I
have greater wisdom than any other living per-
son, but so that you may know what it means. In
that way you will understand what went through
your mind.
31“Our king, in your dream you saw a huge,
shiny and frightening statue in front of you. 32The
head of the statue was made of pure gold. Its
chest and arms were made of silver. Its stomach
and the upper part of its legs were made of
bronze. 33The lower part of the legs were made
of iron, while its feet were made partly of iron
and partly of baked clay. 34While you were look-
ing at the statue, you saw a rock cut free, but no
human being touched the rock. It hit the statue
on its feet of iron and clay and smashed them.
35Then the iron, clay, bronze, silver and gold
broke to pieces at the same time. They became

like chaff[d] on a threshing[d] floor in the summer
time; the wind blew them away and there was
nothing left. Then the rock that hit the statue
became a very large mountain that filled the
whole earth.
36“That was your dream. Now we will tell the
king what it means. 37Our king, you are the great-
est king. God of heaven has given you a kingdom,
power, strength and glory. 38Wherever people,
wild animals and birds live, God made you ruler
over them. King Nebuchadnezzar, you are the
head of gold on that statue.
39“Another kingdom will come after you, but
it will not be as great as yours. Next a third king-
dom, the bronze part, will rule over the earth.
40Then there will be a fourth kingdom, strong as
iron. In the same way that iron crushes and
smashes things to pieces, the fourth kingdom will
smash and crush all the other kingdoms.
41“You saw that the statue’s feet and toes were
partly baked clay and partly iron. That means the
fourth kingdom will be a divided kingdom. It will
have some of the strength of iron in it, just as you
saw iron was mixed with clay. 42The toes of the
statue were partly iron and partly clay. So the
fourth kingdom will be partly strong like iron and
partly breakable like clay. 43You saw the iron
mixed with clay, but iron and clay do not hold
together. In the same way the people of the
fourth kingdom will be a mixture, but they will
not be united as one people.
44“During the time of those kings, the God of
heaven will set up another kingdom that will
never be destroyed or given to another group of
people. This kingdom will crush all the other
kingdoms and bring them to an end, but it will
continue for ever.
45“King Nebuchadnezzar, you saw a rock cut
from a mountain, but no human being touched it.
The rock broke the iron, bronze, clay, silver and
gold to pieces. In this way the great God showed
you what will happen. The dream is true, and
you can trust this explanation.”
46Then King Nebuchadnezzar fell face down
on the ground in front of Daniel. The king hon-
oured him and commanded that an offering and
incense[d] be presented to him. 47Then the king
said to Daniel, “Truly I know your God is the
greatest of all gods, the Lord of all the kings. He
tells people about things they cannot know. I
know this is true, because you were able to tell
these secret things to me.”
48Then the king gave Daniel many gifts
plus an important position in his kingdom.
Nebuchadnezzar made him ruler over the whole
area of Babylon and put him in charge of all the
wise men of Babylon. 49Daniel asked the king to
make Shadrach, Meshach and Abednego leaders
over the area of Babylon, so the king did as Daniel
asked. Daniel himself became one of the people
who stayed at the royal court.

The Gold Idol and Blazing Furnace

3 King Nebuchadnezzar made a gold statue 30
metres high and 3 metres wide and set it up
on the plain of Dura in the area of Babylon. 2Then
he called for the leaders: the governors, assistant
governors, captains of the soldiers, people who
advised the king, keepers of the treasury, judges,
rulers and all other officers in his kingdom. He
wanted them to come to the special service for
the statue he had set up. 3So they all came for the
special service and stood in front of the statue
that King Nebuchadnezzar had set up. 4Then the
man who made announcements for the king
said in a loud voice, “People, nations and those
of every language, this is what you are com-
manded to do: 5when you hear the sound of the
horns, flutes, lyres,[d] zithers,[n] harps, pipes and
all the other musical instruments, you must bow
down and worship the gold statue that King
Nebuchadnezzar has set up. 6Anyone who doesn’t
bow down and worship will immediately be
thrown into a blazing furnace.”
7Now people, nations and those who spoke
every language were there. When they heard the
sound of the horns, flutes, lyres, zithers, pipes
and all the other musical instruments they bowed
down and worshipped the gold statue King
Nebuchadnezzar had set up.
8Then some Babylonians came up to the king
and began speaking against the men of Judah.
9They said to King Nebuchadnezzar, “Our king,
live for ever! 10Our king, you gave a command
that everyone who heard the horns, lyres, zithers,
harps, pipes and all the other musical instruments
would have to bow down and worship the gold
statue. 11Anyone who wouldn’t do this was to be
thrown into a blazing furnace. 12Our king, there
are some men of Judah whom you made officers
in the area of Babylon that did not pay attention
to your order. Their names are Shadrach, Meshach
and Abednego. They do not serve your gods
and do not worship the gold statue you have
set up.”
13Nebuchadnezzar became very angry and
called for Shadrach, Meshach and Abednego.
When they were brought to the king, 14Nebu-
chadnezzar said, “Shadrach, Meshach and
Abednego, is it true that you do not serve my
gods nor worship the gold statue I have set up?
15In a moment you will again hear the sound of

zithers Musical instruments with 30 to 40 strings.

the horns, flutes, lyres, zithers, harps, pipes and all the other musical instruments. If you bow down and worship the statue I made, that will be good. But if you do not worship it, you will immediately be thrown into the blazing furnace. What god will be able to save you from my power then?"

16Shadrach, Meshach and Abednego answered the king, saying, "Nebuchadnezzar, we do not need to defend ourselves to you. 17If you throw us into the blazing furnace, the God we serve is able to save us from the furnace. He will save us from your power, Our king. 18But even if God does not save us, we want you, Our king, to know this: we will not serve your gods or worship the gold statue you have set up."

19Then Nebuchadnezzar was furious with Shadrach, Meshach and Abednego, and he changed his mind. He ordered the furnace to be heated seven times hotter than usual. 20Then he commanded some of the strongest soldiers in his army to tie up Shadrach, Meshach and Abednego and throw them into the blazing furnace.

21So Shadrach, Meshach and Abednego were tied up and thrown into the blazing furnace while still wearing their robes, trousers, turbans and other clothes. 22The king's command was very strict, and the furnace was made so hot that the flames killed the strong soldiers who threw Shadrach, Meshach and Abednego into the furnace. 23Firmly tied, Shadrach, Meshach and Abednego fell into the blazing furnace.

24Then King Nebuchadnezzar was so surprised that he jumped to his feet. He asked the men who advised him, "Didn't we tie up only three men and throw them into the fire?"

They answered, "Yes, Our king."

25The king said, "Look! I see four men walking around in the fire. They are not tied up, and they are not burned. The fourth man looks like a son of the gods."

26Then Nebuchadnezzar went to the opening of the blazing furnace and shouted, "Shadrach, Meshach and Abednego, come out! Servants of the Most High God, come here!"

So Shadrach, Meshach and Abednego came out of the fire. 27When they came out, the governors, assistant governors, captains of the soldiers and royal advisers crowded around them and saw that the fire had not harmed their bodies. Their hair was not burned, their robes were not burned and they didn't even smell of smoke!

28Then Nebuchadnezzar said, "Praise the God of Shadrach, Meshach and Abednego. Their God has sent his angel and saved his servants from the fire! These three men trusted their God and refused to obey my command. They were willing to die rather than serve or worship any god other than their own. 29So I now give this command: anyone from any nation or language who says anything against the God of Shadrach, Meshach and Abednego will be torn apart and have his house turned into a pile of stones. No other god can save his people like this." 30Then the king promoted Shadrach, Meshach and Abednego in the area of Babylon.

Sidelight We can hope that Shadrach, Meshach and Abednego weren't wearing any jewellery when they were thrown into the blazing furnace (Daniel 3:16–27). The furnace would have been one used to smelt metals. Archaeologists have uncovered this kind of furnace, which is about two and a half metres in diameter.

Nebuchadnezzar's Dream of a Tree

4 King Nebuchadnezzar sent this letter to the people, nations and those who speak every language in all the world:

I wish you peace and great wealth!

2The Most High God has done miracles[d] and wonderful things for me that I am happy to tell you about.

3His wonderful acts are great,
and his miracles are mighty.
His kingdom goes on for ever,
and his rule continues from now on.

4I, Nebuchadnezzar, was happy and successful at my palace, 5but I had a dream that made me afraid. As I was lying on my bed, I saw pictures and visions in my mind that alarmed me. 6So I ordered all the wise men of Babylon to come to me and tell me what my dream meant. 7The fortune-tellers, magicians and wise men came, and I told them about the dream. But they could not tell me what it meant.

8Finally, Daniel came to me. (I called him Belteshazzar to honour my god, because the spirit of the holy gods is in him.) I told my dream to him. 9I said, "Belteshazzar, you are the most important of all the fortune-tellers. I know that the spirit of the holy gods is in you, so there is no secret that is too hard for you to understand. This was what I dreamed; tell me what it means. 10These are the visions I saw while I was lying in my bed: I looked, and there in front of me was a tree standing in the middle of the earth. And it was very tall. 11The tree grew large and strong. The top of the tree touched the

sky and could be seen from anywhere on
earth. 12The leaves of the tree were beauti-
ful. It had plenty of good fruit on it, enough
food for everyone. The wild animals found
shelter under the tree, and the birds lived
in its branches. Every animal ate from it.
13"As I was looking at those things in the
vision while lying on my bed, I saw an ob-
server, a holy angel coming down from
heaven. 14He spoke very loudly and said,
'Cut down the tree and cut off its branches.
Strip off its leaves and scatter its fruit. Let
the animals under the tree run away, and let
the birds in its branches fly away. 15But
leave the stump and its roots in the ground
with a band of iron and bronze around it; let
it stay in the field with the grass around it.
" 'Let the man become wet with dew,
and let him live among the animals and
plants of the earth. 16Let him not think like
a human any longer, but let him have the
mind of an animal for seven years.
17" 'The observers gave this command;
the holy ones declared the sentence. This is
so all people may know that the Most High
God [d] rules over every kingdom on earth.
God gives those kingdoms to anyone he
wants, and he chooses people to rule them
who are not proud.'
18"That is what I, King Nebuchadnezzar,
dreamed. Now Belteshazzar, [n] tell me what
the dream means. None of the wise men in
my kingdom can explain it to me, but you
can, because the spirit of the holy gods is
in you."

Daniel Explains the Dream

19Then Daniel, who was called Belteshaz-
zar, was very quiet for a while, because his
understanding of the dream frightened him.
So the king said, "Belteshazzar, do not let
the dream or its meaning make you afraid."
Then Belteshazzar answered, "My mas-
ter, I wish the dream were about your en-
emies, and I wish its meaning were for those
who are against you! 20You saw a tree in
your dream that grew large and strong. Its
top touched the sky, and it could be seen
from all over the earth. 21Its leaves were
beautiful, and it had plenty of fruit for every-
one to eat. It was a home for the wild ani-
mals, and its branches were nesting places
for the birds. 22Our king, you are that tree!
You have become great and powerful, like
the tall tree that touched the sky. Your
power reaches to the far parts of the earth.
23"Our king, you saw an observer, a holy
angel, coming down from heaven who said,
'Cut down the tree and destroy it. But leave
the stump and its roots in the ground with
a band of iron and bronze around it; leave it
in the field with the grass. Let him become
wet with dew and live like a wild animal for
seven years.'
24"This is the meaning of the dream, Our
king. The Most High God has commanded
these things to happen to my master the
king: 25you will be forced away from people
to live among the wild animals. People will
feed you grass like an ox, and dew from the
sky will make you wet. Seven years will
pass, and then you will learn this lesson: the
Most High God is ruler over every kingdom
on earth, and he gives those kingdoms to
anyone he chooses.
26"Since the stump of the tree and its
roots were left in the ground, your kingdom
will be given back to you when you learn
that one in heaven rules your kingdom.
27So, Our king, please accept my advice.
Stop sinning and do what is right. Stop
doing wicked things and be kind to the poor.
Then you might continue to be successful."

The King's Dream Comes True

28All these things happened to King
Nebuchadnezzar. 29Twelve months later as
he was walking on the roof [n] of his palace
in Babylon, 30he said, "I have built this great
Babylon as my royal home. I built it by my
power to show my glory and my majesty."
31The words were still in his mouth
when a voice from heaven said, "King
Nebuchadnezzar, these things will happen
to you: your royal power has been taken
away from you. 32You will be forced away
from people. You will live with the wild
animals and will be fed grass like an ox.
Seven years will pass before you learn this
lesson: the Most High God rules over every
kingdom on earth and gives those king-
doms to anyone he chooses."
33Immediately the words came true.
Nebuchadnezzar was forced to go away
from people, and he began eating grass like
an ox. He became wet from dew. His hair
grew long like the feathers of an eagle, and
his nails grew like the claws of a bird.

Belteshazzar Another name for Daniel.
roof In Bible times houses were built with flat roofs. The roof was used for drying things such as flax and fruit. And it was used as an extra room, as a place for worship and as a place to sleep in the summer.

34At the end of that time, I, Nebuchad-
nezzar, looked up towards heaven, and I
could think normally again! Then I gave
praise to the Most High God; I gave
honour and glory to him who lives for
ever.

Sidelight The power-hungry, grass-chomping King Nebuchadnezzar may have suffered from "pica", an unnatural craving for unusual objects (Daniel 4:33). It's the same word used for pregnant women who eat coal or paint!

God's rule is for ever,
and his kingdom continues for all
time.
35People on earth
are not truly important.
God does what he wants
with the powers of heaven
and the people on earth.
No one can stop his powerful hand
or question what he does.

36At that time I could think normally
again, and God gave back my great honour
and power and returned the glory to my
kingdom. The people who advised me and
the royal family came to me for help again.
I became king again and was even greater
and more powerful than before. 37Now I,
Nebuchadnezzar, give praise and honour
and glory to the King of heaven. Everything
he does is right and fair, and he is able to
make proud people humble.

The Writing on the Wall

5 King Belshazzar gave a big banquet for
1,000 royal guests and drank wine with
them. 2As Belshazzar was drinking his wine, he
gave orders to bring the gold and silver cups that
his ancestor Nebuchadnezzar had taken from
the Temple[d] in Jerusalem. This was so the king,
his royal guests, his wives and his slave women[d]
could drink from those cups. 3So they brought
the gold cups that had been taken from the Tem-
ple of God in Jerusalem. And the king and his
royal guests, his wives and his slave women
drank from them. 4As they were drinking, they
praised their gods, which were made from gold,
silver, bronze, iron, wood and stone.
5Suddenly the fingers of a person's hand ap-
peared and began writing on the plaster of the
wall, near the lampstand in the royal palace. The
king watched the hand as it wrote.
6King Belshazzar was very frightened. His face
turned white, his knees knocked together and he
could not stand up because his legs were too
weak. 7The king called for the magicians, wise
men and wizards of Babylon and said to them,
"Anyone who can read this writing and explain it
will receive purple clothes fit for a king and a gold
chain around his neck. And I will make that per-
son the third highest ruler in the kingdom."
8Then all the king's wise men came in, but
they could not read the writing or tell the king
what it meant. 9King Belshazzar became even
more afraid, and his face became even whiter.
His royal guests were confused.
10Then the king's mother, who had heard the
voices of the king and his royal guests, came into
the banquet room. She said, "Our king, live for
ever! Don't be afraid or let your face be white
with fear! 11There is a man in your kingdom who
has the spirit of the holy gods. In the days of your
father, this man showed understanding, know-
ledge and wisdom like the gods. Your father, King
Nebuchadnezzar, put this man in charge of all the
wise men, fortune-tellers, magicians and wizards.
12The man I am talking about is named Daniel,
whom the king named Belteshazzar. He was very
clever and had knowledge and understanding. He
could explain dreams and secrets and could
answer very hard problems. Call for Daniel. He
will tell you what the writing on the wall means."
13So they brought Daniel to the king, and the
king asked, "Is your name Daniel? Are you one of
the captives my father the king brought from
Judah? 14I have heard that the spirit of the gods is
in you, and that you are very clever and have
knowledge and extraordinary understanding.
15The wise men and magicians were brought to
me to read this writing and to explain what it
means, but they could not explain it. 16I have
heard that you are able to explain what things
mean and can find the answers to hard problems.
Read this writing on the wall and explain it to
me. If you can, I will give you purple clothes fit
for a king and a gold chain to wear around your
neck. And you will become the third highest ruler
in the kingdom."
17Then Daniel answered the king, "You may
keep your gifts for yourself, or you may give those
rewards to someone else. But I will read the
writing on the wall for you and will explain to
you what it means.
18"Our king, the Most High God made your
father Nebuchadnezzar a great, important and
powerful king. 19Because God made him impor-
tant, all the people, nations and those who
spoke every language were very frightened of
Nebuchadnezzar. If he wanted someone to die, he
killed that person. If he wanted someone to live,

he let that person live. Those he wanted to promote, he promoted. Those he wanted to be less important, he made less important.

20“But Nebuchadnezzar became too proud and stubborn, so he was taken off his royal throne. His glory was taken away. 21He was forced away from people, and his mind became like the mind of an animal. He lived with the wild donkeys and was fed grass like an ox and became wet with dew. These things happened to him until he learned his lesson: the Most High God rules over every kingdom on earth, and he sets anyone he chooses over those kingdoms.

22“Belshazzar, you already knew these things, because you are a descendant[d] of Nebuchadnezzar. Still you have not been sorry for what you have done. 23Instead, you have set yourself against the Lord of heaven. You ordered the drinking cups from the Temple of the Lord to be brought to you. Then you and your royal guests, your wives and your slave women drank wine from them. You praised the gods of silver, gold, bronze, iron, wood and stone that are not really gods; they cannot see or hear or understand anything. You did not honour God, who has power over your life and everything you do. 24So God sent the hand that wrote on the wall.

25“These are the words that were written on the wall: ‘Mene, mene, tekel, parsin’.

26“This is what the words mean: Mene: God has counted the days until your kingdom will end. 27Tekel: you have been weighed on the scales and found not good enough. 28Parsin: your kingdom is being divided and will be given to the Medes and the Persians.”

29Then Belshazzar gave an order for Daniel to be dressed in purple clothes and to have a gold chain put around his neck. And it was announced that Daniel was the third highest ruler in the kingdom. 30That very same night Belshazzar, king of the Babylonian people, was killed. 31So Darius the Mede became the new king when he was 62 years old.

Daniel and the Lions

6 Darius thought it would be a good idea to choose 120 governors who would rule his kingdom. 2He chose three men as supervisors over those governors, and Daniel was one of the supervisors. The supervisors were to ensure that the governors did not try to cheat the king. 3Daniel showed that he could do the work better than the other supervisors and governors, so the king planned to put Daniel in charge of the whole kingdom. 4Because of this, the other supervisors and governors tried to find reasons to accuse Daniel about his work in the government. But they could not find anything wrong with him or any reason to accuse him, because he was trustworthy and not lazy or dishonest. 5Finally these men said, “We will never find any reason to accuse Daniel unless it is about the law of his God.”

6So the supervisors and governors went as a group to the king and said: “King Darius, live for ever! 7The supervisors, assistant governors, governors, the people who advise you and the captains of the soldiers have all agreed that you should make a new law for everyone to obey: for the next 30 days no one should pray to any god or human except to you, Our king. Anyone who doesn’t obey will be thrown into the lions’ den. 8Now, Our king, make the law and sign your name to it so that it cannot be changed, because then it will be a law of the Medes and Persians and cannot be cancelled.” 9So King Darius signed the law.

10Even though Daniel knew that the new law had been written, he went to pray in an upstairs room in his house, which had windows that opened towards Jerusalem. Three times each day Daniel would kneel down to pray and thank God, just as he always had done.

Sidelight Daniel really wanted God’s attention when he dropped to his knees in prayer (Daniel 6:10). His fellow Jews normally stood when they addressed God.

11Then those men went as a group and found Daniel praying and asking God for help. 12So they went to the king and talked to him about the law he had made. They said, “Didn’t you sign a law that says no one may pray to any god or human except you, Our king? Doesn’t it say that anyone who disobeys during the next 30 days will be thrown into the lions’ den?”

The king answered, “Yes, that is the law, and the laws of the Medes and Persians cannot be cancelled.”

13Then they said to the king, “Daniel, one of the captives from Judah, is not paying attention to you, Our king, or to the law you signed. Daniel still prays to his God three times every day.” 14The king became very upset when he heard this. He wanted to save Daniel, and he worked hard until sunset trying to think of a way to save him.

15Then those men went as a group to the king. They said, “Remember, Our king, the law of the Medes and Persians says that no law or command given by the king can be changed.”

16So King Darius gave the order, and Daniel was brought in and thrown into the lions’ den.

The king said to Daniel, "May the God you serve
all the time save you!" 17A big stone was brought
and placed over the opening of the lions' den.
Then the king used his signet[d] ring and the rings
of his royal officers to put special seals[d] on the
rock. This showed that no one would move the
rock and bring Daniel out. 18Then King Darius
went back to his palace. He did not eat that night,
he did not have any entertainment brought to
him, and he could not sleep.

19The next morning King Darius got up at
dawn and hurried to the lions' den. 20As he came
near the den, he was worried. He called out to
Daniel, "Daniel, servant of the living God! Has
your God that you always worship been able to
save you from the lions?"

21Daniel answered, "Our king, live for ever!
22My God sent his angel to close the lions'
mouths. They have not hurt me, because my God
knows I am innocent. I never did anything wrong
to you, Our king."

23King Darius was very happy and told his ser-
vants to lift Daniel out of the lions' den. So they
lifted him out and did not find any injury on him,
because Daniel had trusted in his God.

24Then the king commanded that the men
who had accused Daniel be brought to the lions'
den. They, their wives and their children were
thrown into the den. The lions grabbed them be-
fore they hit the floor of the den and crushed
their bones.

25Then King Darius wrote a letter to all people
and all nations, to those who spoke every lan-
guage in the world:

I wish you great peace and wealth.

26I am making a new law for people in
every part of my kingdom. All of you must
fear and respect the God of Daniel.

Daniel's God is the living God;
he lives for ever.
His kingdom will never be destroyed,
and his rule will never end.
27God rescues and saves people
and does mighty miracles[d]
in heaven and on earth.
He is the one who saved Daniel
from the power of the lions.

28So Daniel was successful during the time
Darius was king and when Cyrus the Persian was
king.

Daniel's Dream About Four Animals

7 In Belshazzar's first year as king of Babylon,
Daniel had a dream. He saw visions as he
was lying on his bed, and he wrote down what he
had dreamed.

2Daniel said: "I saw my vision at night. In the
vision the wind was blowing from all four direc-
tions, which made the sea very rough. 3I saw four
huge animals come up from the sea, and each
animal was different from the others.

4"The first animal looked like a lion, but had
wings like an eagle. I watched this animal until its
wings were torn off. It was lifted from the ground
so that it stood up on two feet like a human, and
it was given the mind of a human.

5"Then I saw a second animal before me that
looked like a bear. It was raised up on one of its
sides and had three ribs in its mouth between its
teeth. It was told, 'Get up and eat all the meat
you want!'

6"After that, I looked, and there before me was
another animal. This animal looked like a leopard
with four wings on its back that looked like a
bird's wings. This animal had four heads and was
given power to rule.

7"After that, in my vision at night I saw in front
of me a fourth animal that was cruel, terrible and
very strong. It had large iron teeth. It crushed and
ate what it killed, and then it walked on what-
ever was left. This fourth animal was different
from any animal I had seen before, and it had ten
horns.

8"While I was thinking about the horns, an-
other horn grew up among them. It was a little
horn with eyes like a human's eyes. It also had a
mouth, and the mouth was boasting. The little
horn pulled out three of the other horns.

9"As I looked,
thrones were put in their places,
and God, who has been alive for ever, sat
on his throne.
His clothes were white like snow,
and the hair on his head was white like
wool.
His throne was made from fire,
and the wheels of his throne were blazing
with fire.
10A river of fire was flowing
from in front of him.
Many thousands of angels were serving him,
and millions of angels stood before him.
Court was ready to begin,
and the books were opened.

11"I kept on looking because the little horn was
boasting. I kept watching until finally the fourth
animal was killed. Its body was destroyed, and it
was thrown into the burning fire. 12(The power
and rule of the other animals had been taken
from them, but they were permitted to live for a
certain period of time.)

13"In my vision at night I saw in front of me
someone who looked like a human being coming
on the clouds in the sky. He came near God,

who has been alive for ever, and he was led to
God. [14]He was given authority, glory and the
strength of a king. People of every tribe,[d] nation
and language will serve him. His rule will last for
ever, and his kingdom will never be destroyed.

The Meaning of the Dream

[15]"I, Daniel, was worried. The visions that
went through my mind frightened me. [16]I came
near one of those standing there and asked what
all this meant.

"So he told me and explained to me what
these things meant: [17]'The four great animals are
four kingdoms that will come from the earth.
[18]But the holy people who belong to the Most
High God will receive the power to rule and will
have the power to rule for ever, from now on.'

[19]"Then I wanted to know what the fourth
animal meant, because it was different from all
the others. It was very terrible and had iron teeth
and bronze claws. It was the animal that crushed
and ate what it killed and then walked on what-
ever was left. [20]I also wanted to know about the
ten horns on its head and about the little horn
that grew there. It had pulled out three of the
other ten horns and looked greater than the oth-
ers. It had eyes and a mouth that kept boasting.
[21]As I watched, the little horn began making war
against God's holy people and was defeating
them [22]until God, who has been alive for ever,
came. He judged in favour of the holy people who
belong to the Most High God; then the time came
for them to receive the power to rule.

[23]"And he explained this to me: 'The fourth
animal is a fourth kingdom that will come on the
earth. It will be different from all the other king-
doms and will destroy people all over the world.
It will walk on and crush the whole earth. [24]The
ten horns are ten kings who will come from this
fourth kingdom. After those ten kings are gone,
another king will come. He will be different from
the kings who ruled before him, and he will

PERSISTENCE

What Do You See?

El Salvador suffered a devastating earthquake in 1986. Thousands of people were hurt and killed, and many buildings were destroyed. Carlos, Raphael and Cecilia, like most other people, were initially overwhelmed by the suffering and destruction. Soon, however, they organised their church's youth group to help. They began by sweeping and mopping floors at their church, which sheltered 300 refugees. Then they expanded into day care, tutoring, and health-care programmes. Seeing the amazing results of their work kept the young people going, even when they felt tired or overwhelmed.

They saw their work as the Christian challenge. Although the earthquake disaster eventually passed, they continued to help the victims of their country's civil war. Their belief in Jesus gave them strength to keep going.

"People must be involved together if progress is to be made," Cecilia explains. "We must be informed of needs in today's world and learn to see through the eyes of Jesus." That's where hope begins.

Daniel faced a similar situation that seemed overwhelming. Read about how he found hope in his vision in **Daniel 7:9–14**.

- How did visions of hope motivate the Salvadoran youth group and help Daniel in his troubles?
- Why might hope give you more strength to persist in difficult times?

Consider . . .

- drawing a symbol for one of the obstacles you face and then drawing a large cross through it. Tape it to your mirror to give you strength to persist.
- reading the newspaper and, for one week, asking God to give hope to those who are hurt or discouraged.

For more, see . . .

- Psalm 71 (p.541)
- Romans 8:18–25 (p.1195)
- Matthew 26:62–66 (p.990)

defeat three of the other kings. 25This king will
speak against the Most High God, and he will
hurt and kill God's holy people. He will try to
change times and laws that have already been set.
The holy people that belong to God will be in
that king's power for three and a half years.
26" 'But the court will decide what should hap-
pen. The power of the king will be taken away,
and his kingdom will be completely destroyed.
27Then the holy people who belong to the Most
High God will have the power to rule. They will
rule over all the kingdoms under heaven with
power and greatness, and their power to rule will
last for ever. People from all the other kingdoms
will respect and serve them.'
28"That was the end of the dream. I, Daniel,
was very afraid. My face became white from fear,
but I kept everything to myself."

Daniel's Vision

8 During the third year of King Belshazzar's
rule, I, Daniel, saw another vision, which
was like the first one. 2In this vision I saw myself
in the capital city of Susa, in the area of Elam. I
was standing by the Ulai Canal 3when I looked
up and saw a ram standing beside the canal. It
had two long horns, but one horn was longer and
newer than the other. 4I watched the ram charge
to the west, the north and the south. No animal
could stand before him, and none could save an-
other animal from his power. He did whatever he
wanted and became very powerful.
5While I was watching this, I saw a male goat
come from the west. This goat had one large horn
between his eyes that was easy to see. He crossed
over the whole earth so fast that his feet hardly
touched the ground.
6In his anger the goat charged the ram with the
two horns that I had seen standing by the canal. 7I
watched the angry goat attack the ram and break
the sheep's two horns. The ram was not strong
enough to stop it. The goat knocked the ram to the
ground and then walked all over him. No one was
able to save the ram from the goat, 8so the male
goat became very great. But when he was strong,
his big horn broke off and four horns grew in place
of the one big horn. Those four horns pointed in
four different directions and were easy to see.
9Then a little horn grew from one of those four
horns, and it became very big. It grew to the
south, the east and towards the beautiful land of
Judah. 10That little horn grew until it reached to
the sky. It even threw some of the army of heaven
to the ground and walked on them! 11That little
horn set itself up as equal to God, the Comman-
der of heaven's armies. It stopped the daily sacri-
fices that were offered to him, and the Temple,[d]
the place where people worshipped him, was
pulled down. 12Because there was a turning away
from God, the people stopped the daily sacrifices.
Truth was thrown down to the ground, and the
horn was successful in everything it did.
13Then I heard a holy angel speaking. Another
holy angel asked the first one, "How long will
the things in this vision last—the daily sacrifices,
the turning away from God that brings destruc-
tion, the Temple[d] being pulled down and the
army of heaven being walked on?"
14The angel said to me, "This will happen for
2,300 evenings and mornings. Then the holy
place will be repaired."
15I, Daniel, saw this vision and tried to under-
stand what it meant. In it I saw someone who
looked like a man standing near me. 16And I
heard a man's voice calling from the Ulai Canal:
"Gabriel, explain the vision to this man."
17Gabriel came to where I was standing. When
he came close to me, I was very afraid and bowed
face down on the ground. But Gabriel said to
me, "Human being, understand that this vision is
about the time of the end."
18While Gabriel was speaking, I fell into a deep
sleep with my face on the ground. Then he
touched me and lifted me to my feet. 19He said,
"Now, I will explain to you what will happen in
the time of God's anger. Your vision was about
the set time of the end.
20"You saw a ram with two horns, which are the
kings of Media and Persia. 21The male goat is the
king of Greece, and the big horn between its eyes is
the first king. 22The four horns that grew in the
place of the broken horn are four kingdoms. Those
four kingdoms will come from the nation of the first
king, but they will not be as strong as the first king.
23"When the end comes near for those king-
doms, a bold and cruel king who tells lies will
come. This will happen when many people have
turned against God. 24This king will be very pow-
erful, but his power will not come from himself.
He will cause terrible destruction and will be
successful in everything he does. He will destroy
powerful people and even God's holy people.
25This king will succeed by using lies and force.
He will think that he is very important. He will
destroy many people without warning; he will try
to fight even the Prince of princes! But that cruel
king will be destroyed, and not by human power.
26"The vision that has been shown to you
about these evenings and mornings is true. But
seal up the vision, because those things won't
happen for a long time."
27I, Daniel, became very weak and was sick for
several days after that vision. Then I got up and
went back to work for the king, but I was very
upset about the vision. I didn't understand what
it meant.

Daniel's Prayer

9 These things happened during the first year
Darius son of Xerxes was king over Babylon.
He was a descendant[d] of the Medes. 2During

> **Sidelight** When Daniel was told
> to seal the vision (Daniel
> 8:26), it probably involved writing it on a scroll,
> then rolling up the scroll, tying it shut, and
> fastening the ties with clay. The clay was then
> imprinted with a ring or stamp with a special seal
> or emblem on it. Then all the documents were
> placed in clay jars for safekeeping.

Darius' first year as king, I, Daniel, was reading
the Scriptures.[d] I saw that the LORD told Jeremiah
that Jerusalem would be empty ruins for 70
years.
3Then I turned to the Lord God and prayed
and asked him for help. I did not eat any food. To
show my sadness, I put on rough cloth and sat in
ashes. 4I prayed to the LORD my God and told him
about all of our sins. I said, "Lord, you are a great
God who causes fear and wonder. You keep your
agreement of love with all who love you and
obey your commands.
5"But we have sinned and done wrong. We
have been wicked and turned against you, your
commands and your laws. 6We did not listen to
your servants, the prophets, who spoke for you to
our kings, our leaders, our ancestors and all the
people of the land.
7"Lord, you are good and right, but we are
full of shame today—the people of Judah and
Jerusalem, all the people of Israel, those near and
far whom you scattered among many nations
because they were not loyal to you. 8LORD, we
are all ashamed. Our kings and leaders and our
fathers are ashamed, because we have sinned
against you.
9"But, Lord our God, you show us mercy and
forgive us even though we have turned against
you. 10We have not obeyed the LORD our God or
the teachings he gave us through his servants,
the prophets. 11All the people of Israel have dis-
obeyed your teachings and have turned away,
refusing to obey you. So you brought on us the
curses and promises of punishment written in the
Teachings of Moses, the servant of God, because
we sinned against you.
12"You said these things would happen to us
and our leaders, and you made them happen; you
brought on us a great disaster. Nothing has ever
been done on earth like what was done to
Jerusalem. 13All this disaster came to us just as it is
written in the Teachings of Moses. But we have
not pleaded with the LORD our God. We have not
stopped sinning. We have not paid attention to
your truth. 14The LORD was ready to bring the
disaster on us, and he did it because the LORD our
God is right in everything he does. But we still
did not obey him.
15"Lord our God, you used your power and
brought us out of Egypt. Because of that, your
name is known even today. But we have sinned
and have done wrong. 16Lord, you do what is
right, but please do not be angry with Jerusalem,
your city on your holy hill. Because of our sins
and the evil things done by our ancestors, people
all around insult and make fun of Jerusalem and
your people.
17"Now, our God, hear the prayers of your ser-
vant. Listen to my prayer for help, and for your
sake do good things for your holy place that is
in ruins. 18My God, pay attention and hear me.
Open your eyes and see all the terrible things that
have happened to us. See how our lives have
been ruined and what has happened to the city
that is called by your name. We do not ask these
things because we are good; instead, we ask be-
cause of your mercy. 19Lord, listen! Lord, forgive!
Lord, hear us and do something! For your sake,
don't wait, because your city and your people are
called by your name."

Gabriel's Explanation

20While I was saying these things in my prayer
to the LORD, my God, confessing my sins and the
sins of the people of Israel and praying for God's
holy hill, 21Gabriel came to me. (I had seen him
in my last vision.) He came flying quickly to me
about the time of the evening sacrifice, while I
was still praying. 22He taught me and said to me,
"Daniel, I have come to give you wisdom and to
help you understand. 23When you first started
praying, an answer was given, and I came to tell
you, because God loves you very much. So think
about the message and understand the vision.
24"God has ordered 490 years for your people
and your holy city for these reasons: to stop peo-
ple from turning against God; to put an end to
sin; to take away evil; to bring in goodness that
continues for ever; to bring about the vision and
prophecy;[d] and to appoint a most holy place.
25"Learn and understand these things. A com-
mand will come to rebuild Jerusalem. The time
from this command until the appointed leader
comes will be 49 years and 434 years. Jerusalem
will be rebuilt with streets and a trench filled
with water around it, but it will be built in times
of trouble. 26After the 434 years the appointed
leader will be killed; he will have nothing. The
people of the leader who is to come will destroy
the city and the holy place. The end of the city

will come like a flood, and war will continue until
the end. God has ordered that place to be com-
pletely destroyed. 27That leader will make firm an
agreement with many people for seven years. He
will stop the offerings and sacrifices after three
and a half years. A destroyer will do terrible
things until the ordered end comes to the des-
troyed city."

Daniel's Vision of a Man

10 During Cyrus' third year as king of Persia,
Daniel, whose name was Belteshazzar,
received a vision about a great war. It was a true
message that Daniel understood.
2At that time I, Daniel, had been very sad for
three weeks. 3I did not eat any fancy food or
meat, or drink any wine or use any perfumed oil
for three weeks.
4On the twenty-fourth day of the first month,
I was standing beside the great Tigris River.
5While standing there, I looked up and saw a
man dressed in linen clothes with a belt of fine
gold wrapped around his waist. 6His body was
like shiny yellow quartz. His face was bright like
lightning, and his eyes were like fire. His arms
and legs were shiny like polished bronze, and his
voice sounded like the roar of a crowd.
7I, Daniel, was the only person who saw the
vision. The men with me did not see it, because
they were so frightened that they ran away and
hid. 8So I was left alone, watching this great
vision. I lost my strength, my face turned white
like a dead person and I was helpless. 9Then I
heard the man in the vision speaking. As I
listened, I fell into a deep sleep with my face on
the ground.

GOD'S GRACE

Backstage Pass

Amber repeated the name of the band, the band that just happened to be Mark's favourite band in the whole world! He had known Amber for years but never realised her cousin who "played drums in a band" was in *that* band!

The following month, Amber sorted Mark out with free tickets. Mark watched the show from the VIP area and then made his way backstage. Hundreds of fans queued up at the stage doors, but their way was barred by two massive bouncers built like tanks. But Mark walked straight past them all with a simple wave of the laminated backstage pass hanging around his neck. Within minutes, he was chatting to the band and having his CD signed at the after-show party.

Mark was no more deserving than any of the other fans, so what made the difference? Grace. Undeserved favour, no strings attached, from someone who cared about him and had the power to help him.

Just like those fans left outside the concert with no way of getting in, none of us can gain entry to heaven without God's grace. All of us have fallen short of God's 100 per cent pass mark because of the wrong things that we've done, and that's enough to separate us from God forever. The fantastic news is that God offers us a free pass into heaven by grace alone, because Jesus has already paid the price for our sin on the cross. We never need to earn God's love – as if we ever could anyway!

Read **Daniel 9:17–19** to see how the writer knows that God is a God of grace and asks for his favour, even though he knows he doesn't deserve it.

- Why does the writer ask for God's forgiveness instead of simply asking God to ignore their sin?
- Why do so many non-Christians think that if God *does* exist, he'll let them into heaven if they've tried to live a good life, or tried to be a bit religious? How does this passage tell us this won't work?

Consider . . .

- ways that you can show grace to someone this week.
- whether you have asked Jesus for his free gift of forgiveness made possible by his death on the cross.

For more, see . . .

- Isaiah 53:4–6, 10–12 (p.697)
- Ephesians 2:1–10 (p.1270)
- Romans 3:21–26 (p.1187)
- Titus 3:3–7 (p.1324)

10Then a hand touched me and set me on my
hands and knees. I was so afraid that I was shak-
ing. 11The man in the vision said to me, “Daniel,
God loves you very much. Think carefully about
the words I will speak to you, and stand up, be-
cause I have been sent to you.” When he said
this, I stood up, but I was still shaking.
12Then the man said to me, “Daniel, do not be
afraid. Some time ago you decided to get under-
standing and to humble yourself before your God.
Since that time God has listened to you, and I have
come because of your prayers. 13But the prince of
Persia has been fighting against me for 21 days.
Then Michael, one of the most important angels,
came to help me, because I had been left there
with the king of Persia. 14Now I have come to
explain to you what will happen to your people,
because the vision is about a time in the future.”
15While he was speaking to me, I bowed face
down and could not speak. 16Then one who looked
like a man touched my lips, so I opened my mouth
and started to speak. I said to the one standing in
front of me, “Master, I am upset and afraid because
of what I saw in the vision. I feel helpless. 17Master,
how can I, your servant, talk with you? My
strength is gone, and it is hard for me to breathe.”
18The one who looked like a man touched me
again and gave me strength. 19He said, “Daniel,
don’t be afraid. God loves you very much. Peace
be with you. Be strong now; be courageous.”

When he spoke to me, I became stronger and said, “Master, speak, since you have given me strength.”

20Then he said, “Daniel, do you know why I
have come to you? Soon I must go back to fight
against the prince of Persia. When I go, the prince
of Greece will come, 21but I must first tell you
what is written in the Book of Truth. No one
stands with me against these enemies except
Michael, the angel ruling over your people.

11 In the first year that Darius the Mede was king, I stood up to support Michael in his fight against the prince of Persia.

Kingdoms of the South and North

2“Now then, Daniel, I tell you the truth: three
more kings will rule in Persia, and then a fourth
king will come. He will be much richer than all the
kings of Persia before him and will use his riches to
get power. He will stir up everyone against the
kingdom of Greece. 3Then a mighty king will
come, who will rule with great power and will do
anything he wants. 4After that king has come, his
kingdom will be broken up and divided out
towards the four parts of the world. His kingdom
will not go to his descendants,[d] and it will not
have the power that he had, because his kingdom
will be pulled up and given to other people.

5“The king of the South will become strong,
but one of his commanders will become even
stronger. He will begin to rule his own kingdom
with great power. 6Then after a few years, a new
friendship will develop. The daughter of the king
of the South will marry the king of the North in
order to bring peace. But she will not keep her
power, and his family will not last. She, her hus-
band, her child and those who brought her to
that country will be killed.
7“But a person from her family will become
king of the South and will attack the armies of the
king of the North. He will go into that king’s
strong, walled city and will fight and win. 8He
will take their gods, their metal idols and their
valuable things made of silver and gold back to
Egypt. Then he will not bother the king of the
North for a few years. 9Next, the king of the
North will attack the king of the South, but he
will be beaten back to his own country.
10“The sons of the king of the North will pre-
pare for war. They will get a large army together
that will move through the land very quickly, like
a powerful flood. Later, that army will come back
and fight all the way to the strong, walled city of
the king of the South. 11Then the king of the
South will become very angry and will march out
to fight against the king of the North. The king of
the North will have a large army, but he will lose
the battle, 12and the soldiers will be carried away.
The king of the South will then be very proud and
will kill thousands of soldiers from the northern
army, but he will not continue to be successful.
13The king of the North will gather another army,
larger than the first one. After several years he will
attack with a large army and many weapons.
14“In those times many people will be against
the king of the South. Some of your own people
who love to fight will turn against the king of the
South, thinking it is time for God’s promises to
come true. But they will fail. 15Then the king of
the North will come. He will build roads of earth
to the tops of the city walls and will capture a
strong, walled city. The southern army will not
have the power to fight back; even their best sol-
diers will not be strong enough to stop the north-
ern army. 16So the king of the North will do
whatever he wants; no one will be able to stand
against him. He will gain power and control in
the beautiful land of Israel and will have the
power to destroy it. 17The king of the North will
decide to use all his power to fight against the
king of the South, but he will make a peace agree-
ment with the king of the South. The king of the
North will give one of his daughters as a wife to
the king of the South so that he can defeat him. But
those plans will not succeed or help him. 18Then
the king of the North will turn his attention to

cities along the coast of the Mediterranean Sea and will capture them. But a commander will put an end to the pride of the king of the North, turning his pride back on him. 19After that happens the king of the North will go back to the strong, walled cities of his own country, but he will lose his power. That will be the end of him.

20"The next king of the North will send out a tax collector so he will have plenty of money. In a few years that ruler will be killed, although he will not die in anger or in a battle.

21"That ruler will be followed by a very cruel and hated man, who will not have the honour of being from a king's family. He will attack the kingdom when the people feel safe, and he will take power by lying to the people. 22He will sweep away in defeat large and powerful armies and even a prince who made an agreement. 23Many nations will make agreements with that cruel and hated ruler, but he will lie to them. He will gain much power, but only a few people will support him. 24The richest areas will feel safe, but that cruel and hated ruler will attack them. He will succeed where his ancestors did not. He will rob the countries he defeats and will give those things to his followers. He will plan to defeat and destroy strong cities, but he will be successful for only a short time.

25"That very cruel and hated ruler will have a large army that he will use to stir up his strength and courage. He will attack the king of the South. The king of the South will gather a large and very powerful army and prepare for war. But the people who are against him will make secret plans, and the king of the South will be defeated. 26People who were supposed to be his good friends will try to destroy him. His army will be swept away in defeat; many of his soldiers will be killed in battle. 27Those two kings will want to hurt each other. They will sit at the same table and lie to each other, but it will not do either one any good, because God has set a time for their end to come. 28The king of the North will go back to his own country with much wealth. Then he will decide to go against the holy agreement. He will take action and then return to his own country.

29"At the right time the king of the North will attack the king of the South again, but this time he will not be successful as he was before. 30Ships from the west will come and fight against the king of the North, so he will be afraid. Then he will return and show his anger against the holy agreement. He will be good to those who have stopped obeying the holy agreement.

31"The king of the North will send his army to make the Temple[d] in Jerusalem unclean.[d] They will stop the people from offering the daily sacrifice, and then they will set up the destroying terror. 32The king of the North will tell lies and cause those who have not obeyed God to be ruined. But those who know God and obey him will be strong and fight back.

33"Those who are wise will help the others understand what is happening. But they will be killed with swords or burned, or taken captive or robbed of their homes and possessions. These things will continue for many days. 34When the wise ones are suffering, they will get a little help, but many who join the wise ones will not help them in their time of need. 35Some of the wise ones will be killed. But the hard times must come so they can be made stronger and purer and without faults until the time of the end comes. Then, at the right time, the end will come.

The King Who Praises Himself

36"The king of the North will do whatever he wants. He will boast about himself and praise himself and think he is even better than a god. He will say things against the God of gods that no one has ever heard. And he will be successful until all the bad things have happened. Then what God has planned to happen will happen. 37The king of the North will not care about the gods his ancestors worshipped or the god that women worship. He won't care about any god. Instead, he will make himself more important than any god. 38The king of the North will worship power and strength, which his ancestors did not worship. He will honour the god of power with gold and silver, expensive jewels and gifts. 39That king will attack fortified cities with the help of a foreign god. He will give much honour to the people who join him, making them rulers in charge of many other people. And he will make them pay him for the land they rule.

40"At the time of the end, the king of the South will fight a battle against the king of the North. The king of the North will attack with chariots, soldiers on horses and many large ships. He will invade many countries and sweep through their lands like a flood. 41The king of the North will attack the beautiful land of Judah. He will defeat many countries, but Edom, Moab and the leaders of Ammon will be saved from him. 42The king of the North will show his power in many countries; Egypt will not escape. 43The king will get treasures of gold and silver and all the riches of Egypt. The Libyan and Nubian people will obey him. 44But the king of the North will hear news from the east and the north that will make him afraid and angry. He will go to destroy completely many nations. 45He will set up his royal tents between the sea and the beautiful mountain where the holy Temple[d] is built. But, finally, his end will come, and no one will help him.

The Time of the End

12 "At that time Michael, the great prince
who protects your people, will stand up.
There will be a time of much trouble, the worst
time since nations have been on earth, but your
people will be saved. Everyone whose name is
written in God's book will be saved. 2Many peo-
ple who have already died will live again. Some
of them will wake up to have life for ever, but
some will wake up to find shame and disgrace

> **Sidelight** Daniel 12:2 is the clearest reference in the Old Testament to the resurrection of the dead. Another possible reference is found in Isaiah 26:19 (p.666).

for ever. 3The wise people will shine like the
brightness of the sky. Those who teach others to
live right will shine like stars for ever and ever.
4"But you, Daniel, close up the book and seal
it. These things will happen at the time of the
end. Many people will go here and there to find
true knowledge."
5Then I, Daniel, looked, and saw two other
men. One was standing on my side of the river,
and the other was standing on the far side. 6The
man who was dressed in linen was standing over
the water in the river. One of the two men spoke
to him and asked, "How long will it be before
these amazing things come true?"
7The man dressed in linen, who stood over
the water, raised his hands towards heaven. And
I heard him swear by the name of God who lives
for ever, "It will be for three and a half years.

ETERNAL LIFE

Going the Distance

At the age of nineteen, Canadian Terry Fox lost his right leg to cancer. After the amputation, he became a discouraged and bitter young man. He assumed he was stuck in a wheelchair forever and felt cheated out of the "normal" things in life.

Trying to provide some motivation, Terry's former basketball coach showed him an article about a one-legged man who competed in the New York Marathon. The article ignited a sense of challenge in Terry. "If he can do it, so can I," Terry thought.

Gradually, Terry began to set goals for himself and decided to take more control of his life. He began to build his body and find ways to run with an artificial limb. He perfected the stride that came to be called the "Fox Trot". He was soon running frequently and feeling good about his life.

On April 12 1980, Terry started his "Marathon of Hope", a solo run across Canada to raise money for cancer research. Four and a half months later, after covering 5,300 miles and raising $24,000,000, he had to stop. The cancer had spread to his lungs. Terry was hospitalised, and pneumonia set in. He died at the age of twenty-two.

Terry remains a dramatic symbol of hope and courage to Canada and to the world. "I wanted to show people that just because they are disabled, it's not the end," he said.

All of us need more of that kind of hope and courage. Read about the rewards in **Daniel 12:1–3** for those who trust in God for strength to go the distance.

- What hope and encouragement would Terry have found in this passage as he struggled to complete his transcontinental trek?
- If you were to be remembered forever, how would you like to be remembered?

Consider . . .

- completing this sentence as many ways as possible: "When I think of eternal life, I imagine . . . "
- drawing a star and writing the name of a person you respect on it (see verse 3) and then thanking God for that person each day this week.

For more, see . . .

- Ezekiel 37:1–14 (p.820)
- 1 Corinthians 15:12–28 (p.1235)
- Mark 13:1 12 (p.1023)

The power of the holy people will finally be bro-
ken, and then all these things will come true."
8I heard the answer, but I did not really under-
stand, so I asked, "Master, what will happen
after all these things come true?"
9He answered, "Go your way, Daniel. The mes-
sage is closed up and sealed until the time of the
end. 10Many people will be made clean,[d] pure
and spotless, but the wicked will continue to be
wicked. Those wicked people will not understand
these things, but the wise will understand them.
11"The daily sacrifice will be stopped. Then,
1,290 days later, the destroying terror will be set
up. 12Those who wait for the end of the 1,335
days will be happy.
13"As for you, Daniel, go your way until the
end. You will get your rest, and at the end you
will rise to receive your reward."

Hosea

Why Read This Book:

- Discover how strong God's love is (Hosea 1 – 3).
- Learn what can happen when people turn from God (Hosea 6 – 10).
- Find assurance in God's love and forgiveness (Hosea 11 – 14).

When?

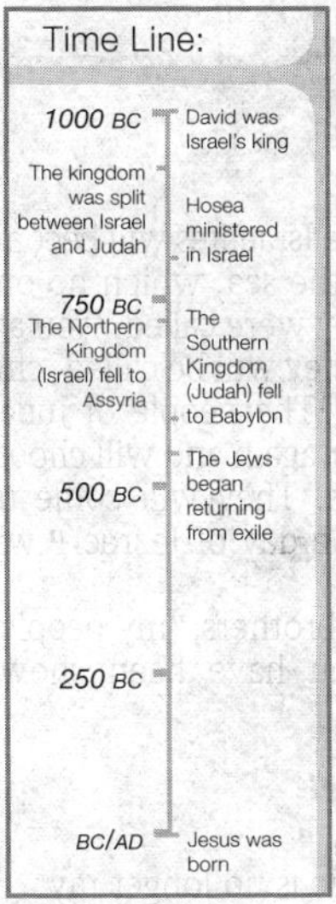

Behind the Scenes:

Imagine God telling someone to marry a prostitute. Then imagine that man remaining faithful to his bride even after she returned to her old job.

As improbable as that situation may sound, it is what happened in the book of Hosea. The prophet Hosea married Gomer, a prostitute. She was unfaithful to him, yet he continued to love her and forgive her. Even though her unfaithfulness hurt him, Hosea never stopped loving his unfaithful wife.

Hosea's life symbolised God's relationship to Israel. God had tried to build a relationship with the Israelites. But time after time, the Israelites had turned to other "lovers" – other gods. Yet God's love wouldn't let Israel go.

Hosea preached in the Northern Kingdom (Israel) in the eighth century BC. It was a time of prosperity, so the people didn't listen to him. But years of immorality and unfaithfulness followed, leading to Israel's destruction in 722 BC by the Assyrians. ▷

Where?

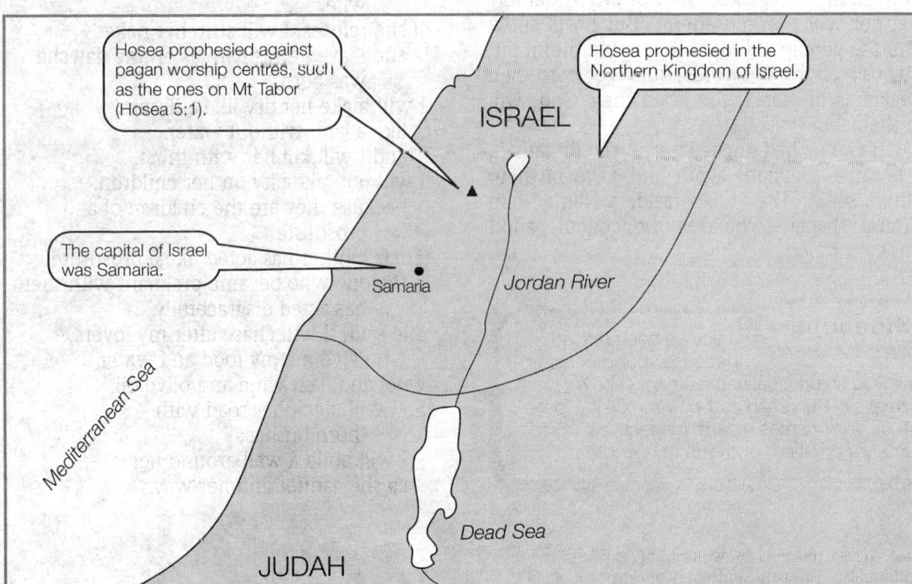

Behind the Scenes (cont.): The book of Hosea tells the story of a prophet's pleading with the people to stop turning away from God and to recognise God's everlasting and tender love. Through the prophet, God says, "I want faithful love . . . I want people to know me . . . " (Hosea 6:6). This central message in Hosea is a message for all time!

1 The LORD spoke his word to Hosea son of Beeri during the time that Uzziah, Jotham, Ahaz and Hezekiah were kings of Judah and Jeroboam son of Jehoash was king of Israel.

Hosea's Wife and Children

2When the LORD began speaking through
Hosea, the LORD said to him, "Go and marry an unfaithful woman and have unfaithful children, because the people in this country have been completely unfaithful to the LORD."
3So Hosea
married Gomer daughter of Diblaim, and she became pregnant and gave birth to Hosea's son.
4The LORD said to Hosea, "Name him Jezreel,[n] because soon I will punish the family of Jehu for the people they killed at Jezreel. In the future I will put an end to the kingdom of Israel
5and
break the power of Israel's army in the Valley of Jezreel."
6Gomer became pregnant again and gave birth to a daughter. The LORD said to Hosea, "Name her Lo-Ruhamah,[n] because I will not pity Israel any more, nor will I forgive them.
7But I will show
pity to the people of Judah. I will save them, but not by using bows or swords, horses or horsemen or weapons of war. I, the LORD their God, will save them."
8After Gomer had stopped nursing Lo-Ruhamah, she became pregnant again and gave birth to another son.
9The LORD said, "Name him
Lo-Ammi,[n] because you are not my people, and I am not your God.

Sidelight If you've been teased because your parents gave you an unusual name, imagine how Jezreel, Lo-Ruhamah and Lo-Ammi felt (Hosea 1:4–9). Their names meant, respectively, "God plants", "not pitied" and "not my people".

God's Promise to Israel

10"But the number of the Israelites will become like the grains of sand of the sea, which no one can measure or count. They were called, 'You are not my people', but later they will be called 'children of the living God'.
11The people of Judah
and Israel will join together again and will choose one leader for themselves. They will come up from the land, because the day of Jezreel[n] will be truly great.

2 "You are to call your brothers, 'my people', and your sisters, 'you have been shown pity'.

God Speaks About Israel

2"Plead with your mother.[n]
Accuse her, because she is no longer my wife,
and I am no longer her husband.
Tell her to stop acting like a prostitute,[d]
to stop behaving like an unfaithful wife.
3If she refuses, I will strip her naked
and leave her as bare as on the day she was born.
I will make her dry like a desert,
like a land without water,
and I will kill her with thirst.
4I will not take pity on her children,
because they are the children of a prostitute.
5Their mother has acted like a prostitute;
the one who became pregnant with them has acted disgracefully.
She said, 'I will chase after my lovers,[n]
who give me my food and water,
wool and flax, wine and olive oil.'
6So I will block her road with thorn-bushes;
I will build a wall around her
so she cannot find her way.

Jezreel This name in Hebrew means "God plants".
Lo-Ruhamah This name in Hebrew means "not pitied".
Lo-Ammi This name in Hebrew means "not my people".
mother Refers to the nation of Israel here.
lovers Refers to the nations surrounding Israel, who led Israel to worship false gods.

7She will run after her lovers,
but she won't catch them.
She will look for them,
but she won't find them.
Then she will say, 'I will go back to my first husband,[n]
because life was better then for me than it is now.'
8But she does not know that I was the one
who gave her grain, new wine and oil.
I gave her much silver and gold,
but she used it for Baal.[d]
9"So I will come back and take away my grain at harvest time
and my new wine when it is ready.
I will take back my wool and linen
that covered her nakedness.
10So I will show her nakedness to her lovers,
and no one will save her from me.
11I will put an end to all her celebrations:
her yearly festivals, her New Moon[d] festivals and her Sabbaths.[d]
I will stop all of her special feasts.
12I will destroy her vines and fig trees,
which she said were her pay from her lovers.
I will turn them into a forest,
and wild animals will eat them.
13I will punish her for all the times
she burned incense[d] to the Baals.
She put on her rings and jewellery
and went chasing after her lovers,
but she forgot me!"
says the LORD.
14"So I am going to attract her;
I will lead her into the desert
and speak tenderly to her.
15There I will give her back her vineyards,
and I will make the Valley of Trouble a door of hope.

husband Refers to God here.

FOLLOWING GOD

Going to the Wilderness

Sometimes it was so difficult to think clearly back home. Danny had grown up in the noise, clamour, and confusion of the inner city. Similar confusion filled his own life. Arrested for a series of minor crimes, Danny was sent to a detention centre.

Now here he was taking part in a survival challenge course – 19 days of mountain living. Feelings of frustration and anger from the inner city followed him. He had snapped at the leaders because of the cold and the rain, the long days of hiking and getting lost. Why couldn't he ever just relax? Why did he always feel angry and out of control?

Sitting out under the stars, Danny tried to sort out his feelings of failure with Bob, his group leader. They talked for a long time. Then Bob said, "If there were just one gift I could give you, it'd be the gift of peace – the peace that begins with accepting yourself as loved by God."

Sometimes following God requires us to leave our usual surroundings and go to a quiet place to hear his message. In **Hosea 2:14–20** read how God would become more real in the wilderness.

- How is God's message to Israel similar to the one that Danny heard?
- How does the passage's theme compare with your own ideas of what it means to follow God?

Consider . . .

- taking a long walk by yourself and listening for ways in which God wants you to serve him.
- serving God through a quiet act of kindness, such as listening to someone without interrupting, or donating your time and money to a ministry you support.

For more, see . . .

- Exodus 3:1–6 (p.61)
- Luke 9:28–36 (p.1055)
- Matthew 4:1–11 (p.941)

There she will respond as when she was
young,
as when she came out of Egypt."

16The LORD says, "In the future she will call me
'my husband';
no longer will she call me 'my baal'. *n*
17I will never let her say the names of Baal
again;
people won't use their names any more.
18At that time I will make an agreement for
them
with the wild animals, the birds and the
crawling things.
I will smash from the land
the bow and the sword and the weapons
of war,
so my people will live in safety.
19And I will make you my promised bride for
ever.
I will be good and fair;
I will show you my love and mercy.
20I will be true to you as my promised bride,
and you will know the LORD.

21"At that time I will speak to you," says the
LORD.
"I will speak to the skies,
and they will give rain to the earth.
22The earth will produce grain, new wine
and oil;
much will grow because my people are
called Jezreel. *n*
23I will plant my people in the land,
and I will show pity to the one I had called
'not shown pity'.
I will say, 'You are my people'
to those I had called 'not my people'.
And they will say to me, 'You are
our God.'"

Sidelight Hosea's wife Gomer (Hosea 3:1), was a prostitute, but God wanted Hosea to love her despite her past record of unfaithfulness. In the same way, God said that he loved his children despite the fact that they were unfaithful to him. This is what "unconditional love" really means.

Hosea Buys a Wife

3 The LORD said to me again, "Go and show
your love to a woman loved by someone
else, who has been unfaithful to you. In the same
way the LORD loves the people of Israel, even
though they worship other gods and love to eat
the raisin cakes." *n*
2So I bought her for 15 pieces of silver and 150
kilogrammes of barley. 3Then I told her, "You
must wait for me for many days. You must not be
a prostitute, *d* and you must not have sexual rela-
tions with any other man. I will act the same
way towards you."
4In the same way Israel will live many days
without a king or leader, without sacrifices or
holy stone pillars, and without the holy robe *d* or
an idol. 5After this, the people of Israel will return
to the LORD their God and follow him and the
king from David's family. In the last days they
will turn in fear to the LORD, and he will bless
them.

The LORD's Word Against Israel

4 People of Israel, listen to the LORD's
message.
The LORD has this
against you who live in the land:
"The people are not true, not loyal to God,
nor do those who live in the land even
know him.
2Cursing, lying, killing, stealing and adultery *d*
are everywhere.
One murder follows another.
3Because of this the land dries up,
and all its people are dying.
Even the wild animals and the birds of
the air
and the fish of the sea are dying.

God's Case Against the Priests

4"No one should accuse
or blame another person.
Don't blame the people, you priests,
when they quarrel with you.
5You will be ruined in the day,
and your prophets *d* will be ruined with you
in the night.
I will also destroy your mother. *n*
6My people will be destroyed,
because they have no knowledge.
You have refused to learn,
so I will refuse to let you be priests to me.
You have forgotten the teachings of your God,
so I will forget your children.
7The more priests there are,
the more they sin against me.

baal Another Hebrew word for husband, but it was the same word as the god Baal.
Jezreel This name in Hebrew means "God plants".
raisin cakes This food was eaten in the feasts that honoured false gods.
mother Here "mother" refers to the nation of Israel.

I will take away their honour
and give them shame.
8 Since the priests live off the sin offerings of
the people,
they want the people to sin more and
more.
9 The priests are as wrong as the people,
and I will punish them both for what they
have done.
I will repay them for the wrong they have
done.

10 "They will eat
but not have enough;
they will have sexual relations with the
prostitutes, [d]
but they will not have children,
because they have left the LORD
to give themselves to 11 prostitution,
to old and new wine,
which take away their ability to
understand.

God's Case Against the People

12 "My people ask wooden idols for advice;
they ask those sticks of wood to advise them!
Like prostitutes, they have chased after other
gods
and have left their own God.
13 They make sacrifices on the tops of the
mountains.
They burn offerings on the hills,
under oaks, poplars and other trees,
because their shade is nice.
So your daughters become prostitutes,
and your daughters-in-law are guilty of
adultery. [d]

14 "But I will not punish your daughters
for becoming prostitutes,
nor your daughters-in-law
for their sins of adultery.
I will not punish them,
because the men have sexual relations with
prostitutes

ADDICTION

Sold Out

- There is a boy in Liverpool who was christened with the names of every player in the Liverpool football team.
- There is a girl in Essex who buys tickets for every concert for her favourite artist, regardless of the amount of concerts on the tour, the countries or the expense involved.
- There are loads of people who have every *Star Trek* episode on video and go to every Star Trek Convention, dressed, of course, as their favourite character.
- There are grown male adults who take to the streets in stockings and suspender belts every time the *Rocky Horror Picture Show* comes to town.
- There are people who camp, complete with tents, outside the houses of famous film stars.

OK, some of these things are just fun, but unfortunately some of them are quite serious. The word stalker is defined in our dictionaries as someone who follows, shadows and creeps after people. They have taken their devotion to another level. An unacceptable one.

These are people who have left their own lives behind them, to take on someone else's. They have almost "sold" themselves. **Hosea 4:12–13** talks of people who have "prostituted themselves to another god".

- What does this passage say is missing in the lives of people such as these?
- What do people today have in common with those of Hosea's time?

Consider . . .

- write down how many things there are in your life that come higher on your list of priorities than your commitment to God.
- if there is anything taking God's place in your life, ask him to help and forgive you.

For more, see . . .

- Matthew 19:16–22 (p.974)
- 2 Peter 2:19 (p.1367)
- I Corinthians 6:12 (p.1221)

and offer sacrifices with the temple
prostitutes.
A foolish people will be ruined.
15"Israel, you act like a prostitute,
but do not be guilty towards the LORD.
Don't go to Gilgal
or go up to Beth Aven.[n]
Don't make promises,
saying, 'As surely as the LORD lives . . .'
16The people of Israel are stubborn
like a stubborn young cow.
Now the LORD will feed them
like lambs in the open country.
17The Israelites have chosen to worship idols,
so leave them alone.
18When they finish their drinking,
they completely give themselves to being
prostitutes;
they love these disgraceful ways.
19They will be swept away as if by a
whirlwind,
and their sacrifices will bring them only
shame.

God's Word Against the Leaders

5 "Listen, you priests.
Pay attention, people of Israel.
Listen, royal family,
because you will all be judged.
You have been like a trap at Mizpah
and like a net spread out at Mount Tabor.
2You have done many evil things,
so I will punish you all.
3I know all about the people of Israel;
what they have done is not hidden
from me.
Now that Israel acts like a prostitute,[d]
it has made itself unclean.[d]
4"They will not give up their deeds
and return to their God.
They are determined to be unfaithful
to me;
they do not know the LORD.
5Israel's pride testifies against them.
The people of Israel will stumble because of
their sin,
and the people of Judah will stumble with
them.
6They will come to worship the LORD,
bringing their flocks and herds,
but they will not be able to find him,
because he has left them.
7They have not been true to the LORD;
they are children who do not belong
to him.
So their false worship
will destroy them and their land.
8"Blow the horn in Gibeah
and the trumpet in Ramah.
Give the warning at Beth Aven,
and be first into battle, people of Benjamin.
9Israel will be ruined
on the day of punishment.
To the tribes[d] of Israel
I tell the truth.
10The leaders of Judah are like those
who steal other people's land.
I will pour my punishment over them
like a flood of water.
11Israel is crushed by the punishment,
because it decided to follow idols.
12I am like a moth to Israel,
like a rot to the people of Judah.
13"When Israel saw its wounds
and Judah saw its wounds,
Israel went to Assyria for help
and sent to the great king of Assyria.
But he cannot heal you
or cure your wounds.
14I will be like a lion to Israel,
like a young lion to Judah.
I will attack them
and tear them to pieces.
I will drag them off,
and no one will be able to save them.
15Then I will go back to my place
until they suffer for their guilt and turn
back to me.
In their trouble they will look for me."

The People are Not Faithful

6 "Come, let's go back to the LORD.
He has hurt us, but he will heal us.
He has wounded us, but he will bandage
our wounds.
2In two days he will put new life in us;
on the third day he will raise us up
so that we may live in his presence 3and
know him.
Let's try to learn about the LORD;
He will come to us as surely as the dawn
comes.
He will come to us like rain,
like the spring rain that waters the
ground."
4The LORD says, "Israel, what should I do
with you?
Judah, what should I do with you?
Your faithfulness is like a morning mist,
like the dew that goes away early in the day.

Gilgal . . . Beth Aven Cities in Israel where people worshipped false gods.

5I have warned you by my prophets[d]
that I will kill you and destroy you.
My justice comes out like bright light.
6I want faithful love
more than I want animal sacrifices.
I want people to know me
more than I want burnt offerings.
7But they have broken the agreement as
Adam did;
they have been unfaithful to me.
8Gilead is a city of people who do evil;
their footprints are bloody.
9The priests are like robbers waiting to attack
people;
they murder people on the road to
Shechem[n]
and do wicked things.
10I have seen horrible things in Israel.
Look at Israel's prostitution;[d]
Israel has become unclean.[d]

Shechem A city of safety where people could go for protection.

FOLLOWING GOD

Off Track

"Are you joking?" Richard asked.

The coach shook his head. "No, I'm not joking. You've been selected as a member of this year's national junior athletics team."

Richard took a deep breath to slow down the sudden surge of adrenaline that shot to his brain. Being selected for the national team had always been his ambition, but it had always seemed too far ahead to grasp. Nevertheless, he had trained hard and his ambition was now being fulfilled – he would be competing in the games which were only seven months away.

Curiously, Richard began to get lazy with his training. He began to enjoy talking more about his sport than he did practising it. Before long, he was regularly skipping training sessions in favour of posing in front of his friends.

"It's got to change, Richard," his coach told him four months before the big competition.

"What has?"

"Your attitude," the coach replied. "You're just not training hard enough for a national team member. There are a lot of athletes out there who would train all day long if they had to, just to be in your position."

Richard was shocked. He hadn't realised how much he had been neglecting his training.

This shock sent him back to his roots, back to the regular training which had earned him a position on the team in the first place. Gradually, his time improved, and eventually he was clocking faster times than ever before; but it had taken strong words of warning from the coach to shake him back into action.

In the same way, God is not satisfied with Christians who think they've done all they need to do and can relax until they get to heaven. Read about the burning enthusiasm which God expects in **Hosea 6:1–6**.

- Why did Richard's coach and God become angry with half-hearted efforts?
- How would your life change if you put everything you've got into following God? How could the church be different if every member got "on fire" for God? How would this affect the world?

Consider . . .

- comparing the activities of "routine" Christians with those of "committed" believers. Decide to become "committed" to God and put your decision into action.
- feeding your enthusiasm by getting to know God better through deeper times of daily prayer and studying the Bible.

For more, see . . .

- Micah 6:8 (p.896)
- Colossians 3:12–17 (p.1293)
- Matthew 22:34–40 (p.980)

11"Judah, I have set a harvest time for you
when I will make the lives of my people
good again.

7 When I heal Israel,
Israel's sin will go away,
and so will Samaria's evil.

"They cheat a lot!
Thieves break into houses,
and robbers are in the streets.
2It never enters their minds
that I remember all their evil deeds.
The bad things they do are all around
them;
they are right in front of me.

Israel's Evil Kings

3"They make the king happy with their
wickedness;
their rulers are glad with their lies.
4But all of them are traitors.
They are like an oven heated by a baker.
While he mixes the dough,
he does not need to stir up the fire.
5The kings get so drunk they get sick
every day.
The rulers become crazy with wine;
they make agreements with those who do
not know the true God.
6They burn like an oven;
their hearts burn inside them.
All night long their anger is low,
but when morning comes, it becomes a
roaring fire.
7All these people are as hot as an oven;
they burn up their rulers.
All their kings fall,
and no one calls on me.

Sidelight Political stability was something that the Israelites were lacking. In the space of just 25 years, the prophets saw the reign of six kings – four of whom were assassinated. This is probably what Hosea was referring to in Hosea 7:7.

Israel and the Other Nations

8"Israel mixes with other nations;
he is like a pancake cooked only on one
side.
9Foreign nations have eaten up his
strength,
but he doesn't know it.
Israel is weak and feeble, like an old man,
but he doesn't know it.
10Israel's pride will cause their defeat;
they will not turn back to the LORD
their God
or look to him for help in all this.
11Israel has become like a pigeon—
easy to fool and stupid.
First they call to Egypt for help.
Then they run to Assyria.
12When they go, I will catch them in a net,
I will bring them down like birds from
the sky;
I will punish them countless times for their
evil.
13How terrible for them because they left me!
They will be destroyed, because they
turned against me.
I want to save them,
but they have spoken lies against me.
14They do not call to me from their hearts.
They just lie on their beds and cry.
They come together to ask for grain and new
wine,
but they really turn away from me.
15Though I trained them and gave them
strength,
they have made evil plans against me.
16They did not turn to the Most High God.
They are like a loose bow that can't shoot.
Because their leaders boast about their
strength,
they will be killed with swords,
and the people in Egypt
will laugh at them.

Israel Has Trusted Wrong Things

8 "Put the trumpet to your lips and give the
warning!
The enemy swoops down on the LORD's
people like an eagle.
The Israelites have broken my agreement
and have turned against my teachings.
2They cry out to me,
'Our God, we in Israel know you!'
3But Israel has rejected what is good,
so the enemy will chase them.
4They chose their own kings
without asking my permission.
They chose their own leaders,
people I did not know.
They made their silver and gold into idols,
and for all this they will be destroyed.
5I hate the calf-shaped idol of Israel!
I am very angry with the people.
How long will they remain unclean? [d]
6The idol is something a craftsman made;
it is not God.
Israel's calf-shaped idol
will surely be smashed to pieces.

7"Israel's foolish plans are like planting the
wind,
but they will harvest a storm.
Like a stalk with no head of grain,
it produces nothing.
Even if it produced something,
other nations would eat it.
8Israel is eaten up;
the people are mixed among the other
nations
and have become useless to me.
9Israel is like a wild donkey all by itself.
They have run to Assyria;
They have hired other nations to protect
them.
10Although Israel is mixed among the nations,
I will gather them together.
They will become weaker and weaker
as they suffer under the great king of
Assyria.
11"Although Israel built more altars to
remove sin,
they have become altars for sinning.
12I have written many teachings for them,
but they think the teachings are strange
and foreign.
13The Israelites offer sacrifices to me as gifts
and eat the meat,
but the LORD is not pleased with them.
He remembers the evil they have done,
and he will punish them for their sins.
They will be slaves again as they were in
Egypt.
14Israel has forgotten their Maker and has built
palaces;
Judah has built many strong, walled cities.
But I will send fire on their cities
and destroy their strong buildings."

Israel's Punishment

9 Israel, do not rejoice;
don't shout for joy as the other
nations do.
You have been like a prostitute[d] against
your God.
You love the pay of prostitutes on every
threshing[d] floor.
2But the threshing floor and the winepress will
not feed the people,
and there won't be enough new wine.
3The people will not stay in the LORD's land.
Israel will return to being captives as they
were in Egypt,
and in Assyria they will eat food that they
are not allowed to eat.
4The Israelites will not give offerings of wine
to the LORD;
they will not give him sacrifices.
Their sacrifices will be like food that is eaten
at a funeral;
it is unclean,[d] and everyone who eats it
becomes unclean.
Their food will only satisfy their hunger;
they cannot sacrifice it in the Temple.[d]
5What will you do then on the day of feasts
and on the day of the LORD's festival?
6Even if the people are not destroyed,
Egypt will capture them;
Memphis[n] will bury them.
Weeds will grow over their silver treasures,
and thorns will drive them out of their
tents.
7The time of punishment has come,
the time to pay for sins.
Let Israel know this:
you think the prophet[d] is a fool,
and you say the spiritual person is mad.
You have sinned very much,
and your hatred is great.
8Is Israel a watchman?
Are God's people prophets?
Everywhere Israel goes, traps are set
for him.
He is an enemy in God's house.
9The people of Israel have gone deep into sin
as the people of Gibeah[n] did.
The Lord will remember the evil things they
have done
and he will punish their sins.
10"When I found Israel,
it was like finding grapes in the desert.
Your ancestors were like
finding the first figs on the fig tree.
But when they came to Baal Peor
they began worshipping an idol,
and they became as hateful as the thing
they worshipped.
11Israel's glory will fly away like a bird;
there will be no more pregnancy, no more
births, no more getting pregnant.
12But even if the Israelites bring up children,
I will take them all away.
How terrible it will be for them
when I go away from them!
13I have seen Israel, like Tyre,
given a pleasant place.
But the people of Israel will soon bring out
their children to be killed."
14LORD, give them what they should have.
What will you give them?

Memphis A city in Egypt famous for its tombs.
Gibeah The sins of the people of Gibeah caused a civil war. See Judges 19—21.

Make their women unable to have
children;
give them dried-up breasts that cannot feed
their babies.

15"The Israelites were very wicked in Gilgal,
so I have hated them there.
Because of the sinful things they have done,
I will force them to leave my land.
I will no longer love them;
their leaders have turned against me.
16Israel is beaten down;
its root is dying, and it has no fruit.
If they have more children,
I will kill the children they love."
17God will reject them,
because they have not obeyed him;
they will wander among the nations.

Israel will Pay for Sin

10 Israel is like a large vine
that produced plenty of fruit.
As the people became richer,
they built more altars for idols.
As their land became better,
they put up better stone pillars to honour
gods.
2Their heart was false,
and now they must pay for their guilt.
The LORD will break down their altars;
he will destroy their holy stone pillars.

3Then they will say, "We have no king,
because we didn't honour the LORD.
As for the king,
he couldn't do anything for us."
4They make many false promises
and agreements which they don't keep.
So people sue each other in court;
they are like poisonous weeds growing in a
ploughed field.
5The people from Israel are worried about
the calf-shaped idol at Beth Aven.
The people will cry about it,
and the priests will cry about it.
They used to shout for joy about its glory,
6but it will be carried off to Assyria
as a gift to the great king.
Israel will be disgraced,
and the people will be ashamed for not
obeying.
7Israel will be destroyed;
its king will be like a chip of wood floating
on the water.
8The places of false worship will be destroyed,
the places where Israel sinned.
Thorns and weeds will grow up
and cover their altars.
Then they will say to the mountains,
"Cover us!"
and to the hills, "Fall on us!"

9"Israel, you have sinned since the time of
Gibeah, *n*
and the people there have continued
sinning.
But war will surely overwhelm them in
Gibeah,
because of the evil they have done there.
10When I am ready,
I will come to punish them.
Nations will come together against them,
and they will be punished for their double
sins.
11Israel is like a well-trained young cow
that likes to thresh *d* grain.
I will put a yoke *d* on her neck
and make her work hard in the field.
Israel will plough,
and Judah will break up the ground.
12I said, 'Plant goodness,
harvest the fruit of loyalty,
plough the new ground of knowledge.
Look for the LORD until he comes
and pours goodness on you like water.'
13But you have ploughed evil
and harvested trouble;
you have eaten the fruit of your lies.
Because you have trusted in your own power
and your many soldiers,
14your people will hear the noise of battle,
and all your strong, walled cities will be
destroyed.
It will be like the time King Shalman
destroyed Beth Arbel in battle,
when mothers and their children were
crushed to death.
15The same will happen to you, people of
Bethel,
because you did so much evil.
When the sun comes up,
the king of Israel will die.

God's Love for Israel

11 "When Israel was a child, I loved him,
and I called my son out of Egypt.
2But when I called the people of Israel,
they went away from me.
They offered sacrifices to the Baals *d*
and burned incense *d* to the idols.
3It was I who taught Ephraim to walk,
and I took them by the arms,

Gibeah The sins of the people of Gibeah caused a civil war. See Judges 19—21.

but they did not understand
that I had healed them.
4I led them with cords of human kindness,
with ropes of love.
I lifted the yoke [d] from their neck
and bent down and fed them.

5"The Israelites will become captives again, as they were in Egypt,
and Assyria will become their king,
because they refuse to turn back to God.
6War will sweep through their cities
and will destroy them
and kill them because of their wicked plans.
7My people have made up their minds
to turn away from me.
The prophets [d] call them to turn to me,
but none of them honours me at all.
8"Israel, how can I give you up?
How can I give you away, Israel?
I don't want to make you like Admah
or treat you like Zeboiim. [n]
My heart beats for you,
and my love for you stirs up my pity.
9I won't punish you in my anger,
and I won't destroy Israel again.
I am God and not a human;
I am the Holy One, and I am among you.
I will not come against you in anger.
10They will go after the LORD,
and he will roar like a lion.
When he roars,
his children will hurry to him from the west.
11They will come swiftly
like birds from Egypt
and like doves from Assyria.
I will settle them again in their homes,"
says the LORD.

The LORD is Against Israel

12Israel has surrounded me with lies;
the people have made evil plans.
And Judah turns against God,
the faithful Holy One.

12 What Israel does is as useless as chasing the wind;
he chases the east wind all day.
They tell more and more lies
and do more and more violence.
They make agreements with Assyria,
and they send a gift of olive oil to Egypt.
2The LORD also has some things against Judah.
He will punish Israel for what they have done;
he will give them what they deserve.
3Their ancestor Jacob held on to his brother's heel
while the two of them were being born.
When he grew to be a man,
he wrestled with God.
4When Jacob wrestled with the angel and won,
he cried and asked for his blessing.
Later, God met with him at Bethel
and spoke with him there.
5It was the LORD God All-powerful;
the LORD is his great name.
6You must return to your God;
love him, do what is just,
and always trust in him as your God.

7The merchants use dishonest scales;
they like to cheat people.
8Israel said, "I am rich! I am someone with power!"
All their money will do them no good
because of the sins they have done.

9"But I am the LORD your God,
who brought you out of Egypt.
I will make you live in tents again
as you used to do on worship days.
10I spoke to the prophets [d]
and gave them many visions;
through them, I taught my lessons to you."

11The people of Gilead are evil,
worth nothing.
Though people sacrifice bulls at Gilgal,
their altars will become like piles of stone
in a ploughed field.
12Your ancestor Jacob fled to North West Mesopotamia
where he worked to get a wife;
he tended sheep to pay for her.
13Later the LORD used a prophet
to bring Jacob's descendants [d] out of Egypt;
he used a prophet
to take care of the Israelites.
14But the Israelites made the Lord angry when they killed other people,
and they deserve to die for their crimes.
The Lord will make them pay
for the disgraceful things they have done.

The Final Word Against Israel

13 People used to fear the tribe [d] of Ephraim;
they were important people in Israel.

Admah . . . Zeboiim Two other cities destroyed when God destroyed Sodom and Gomorrah.

But they sinned by worshipping Baal,[d]
so they must die.
2But they still keep on sinning more and more.
They make idols of their silver,
idols that are cleverly made,
the work of a craftsman.
Yet the people of Israel say to each other,
"Kiss those calf idols and sacrifice to them."
3So those people will be like the morning mist;
they will disappear like the morning dew.
They will be like chaff[d] blown from the threshing[d] floor,
like smoke going out of a window.

4"I, the LORD, have been your God
since you were in the land of Egypt.
You should have known no other God except me.
I am the only one who saves.
5I cared for them in the desert
where it was hot and dry.
6I gave them food, and they became full and satisfied.
But then they became too proud and forgot me.
7That is why I will be like a lion to them,
like a leopard waiting by the road.
8I will attack like a bear robbed of her cubs,
ripping their bodies open.
I will devour them like a lion
and tear them apart like a wild animal.

9"Israel, I will destroy you.
Who will be your helper then?
10What good is your king?
Can he save you in any of your towns?
What good are your leaders?
You said, 'Give us a king and leaders.'
11So I gave you a king, but only in anger,
and I took him away in my great anger.
12The sins of Israel are on record,
stored away, waiting for punishment.
13The pain of birth will come for him,
but he is like a foolish baby

Sidelight Childbirth was much more dangerous in Old Testament times than it is today in most places (Hosea 13:13). Many a woman died during childbirth because she couldn't deliver her child.

who won't come out of its mother's womb.
14Will I save them from the place of the dead?
Will I rescue them from death?
Where is your sickness, death?
Where is your pain, place of death?
I will show them no mercy.
15Israel is doing well among the nations,
but the LORD will send a wind from the east,
coming from the desert,
that will dry up his springs and wells of water.
It will destroy from their treasure houses
everything of value.
16The nation of Israel will be ruined,
because it fought against God.
The people of Israel will die in war;
their children will be torn to pieces,
and their pregnant women will be ripped open."

Israel Returns to God

14 Israel, return to the LORD your God,
because your sins have made you fall.
2Come back to the LORD
and say these words to him:
"Take away all our sin
and kindly receive us,
and we will keep the promises we made to you.
3Assyria cannot save us,
nor will we trust in our horses.
We will not say again, 'Our gods',
to the things our hands have made.
You show mercy to orphans."

4The LORD says,
"I will forgive them for leaving me
and will love them freely,
because I am not angry with them any more.
5I will be like the dew to Israel,
and they will blossom like a lily.
Like the cedar trees in Lebanon,
their roots will be firm.
6They will be like spreading branches,
like the beautiful olive trees
and the sweet-smelling cedars in Lebanon.
7The people of Israel will again live under my protection.
They will grow like the grain,
they will bloom like a vine,
and they will be as famous as the wine of Lebanon.
8Israel, have nothing to do with idols.

I, the LORD, am the one who answers your
prayers and watches over you.
I am like a green pine tree;
your blessings come from me."

9A wise person will know these things,
and an understanding person will take
them to heart.
The LORD's ways are right.
Good people live by following them,
but those who turn against God die
because of them.

Joel

Why Read This Book:

- **See how forgiveness begins with a change of heart (Joel 2).**
- **Hear Joel announce a new life for the faithful (Joel 3).**

When?

Time Line:

1000 BC	David was Israel's king
The kingdom was split between Israel and Judah	Possible time of Joel's life
750 BC	The Northern Kingdom (Israel) fell to Assyria
The Southern Kingdom (Judah) fell to Babylon	
500 BC	The Jews began returning from exile
250 BC	
BC/AD	Jesus was born

Behind the Scenes:

We seem to be living in an age of worldwide catastrophes.

- Economic recession has resulted in unemployment and homelessness.
- Disregard for God's environment has resulted in worldwide pollution.
- Greed for ornaments and fashion clothing, as well as the need for more land, has led to the extinction of rare animal species.
- Improved technology – whatever it costs – has led to a hole in the ozone layer.
- Selfishness and disobedience have resulted in Third World famines.
- "Easy sex" has led to a worldwide epidemic of AIDS, threatening the lives of millions.
- Modern wars make it easier to kill more people than ever before.

Judah was no stranger to catastrophes either, except that the land was attacked by locusts instead of AIDS. These insects destroyed everything in their paths, including crops of vegetables, fields, trees and vineyards. The swarms turned healthy farmland into barren wastelands. The people of Judah had never seen anything like it before.

In the book of Joel, the prophet saw what was happening as a sign of God's judgement of the people. He warned them that if they did not repent and turn back to God, a plague of locusts would be nothing compared with what would happen. If they repented, however, God would restore his people and bless them.

We don't know much about Joel himself, but the message which he preached is as relevant today as it was in his own time. God will bless those who follow him obediently, and judge those who oppose him.

LIFE FILE LINKS

Investigate the Theme

To find a list of real life stories on this subject turn to the LIFE FILE GUIDE on pages 12 to 22 at the front of the Youth Bible.

SIN

Locusts Destroy the Crops

1 The LORD spoke his word to Joel son of Pethuel:

2Elders, listen to this message.
Listen to me, all you who live in the land.
Nothing like this has ever happened during your lifetime
or during your ancestors' lifetimes.

> **Sidelight** The name Joel is common in the Old Testament (Joel 1:1). Twelve other people share this name (for examples, see 1 Samuel 8:2, p.261, and Nehemiah 11:9, p.453). The name means "The Lord is God" or "The Lord is my God".

3Tell your children about these things,
let your children tell their children,
and let your grandchildren tell their children.
4What the cutting locusts have left,
the swarming locusts have eaten;
what the swarming locusts have left,
the hopping locusts have eaten,
and what the hopping locusts have left,
the destroying locusts[n] have eaten.
5Drunkards, wake up and cry!
All you people who drink wine, cry!
Cry because your wine
has been taken away from your mouths.
6A powerful nation has come into my land
with too many soldiers to count.
It has teeth like a lion,
jaws like a female lion.
7It has made my grapevine a waste
and made my fig tree a stump.
It has stripped all the bark off my trees
and left the branches white.

> **Sidelight** The locust invasion described in Joel 1 wasn't a unique event. As recently as 1915 and 1930, the Middle East has been ravaged by plagues of these insects.

8Cry as a young woman cries
when the man she was going to marry has died.
9There will be no more grain or drink offerings
to offer in the Temple[d] of the LORD.
Because of this, the priests,
the servants of the LORD, are sad.
10The fields are ruined;
the ground is dried up.
The grain is destroyed,
the new wine is dried up,
and the olive oil runs out.
11Be sad, farmers.
Cry loudly, you who grow grapes.
Cry for the wheat and the barley.
Cry because the harvest of the field is lost.
12The vines have become dry,
and the fig trees are dried up.
The pomegranate[d] trees, the date palm trees,
the apple trees—
all the trees in the field have died.
And the happiness of the people has died, too.
13Priests, put on your rough cloth and cry to show your sadness.
Servants of the altar, cry out loud.
Servants of my God,
keep your rough cloth on all night to show your sadness.
Cry because there will be no more grain or drink offerings
to offer in the Temple of your God.
14Call for a day when no one eats food!
Tell everyone to stop work!
Bring the elders
and everyone who lives in the land
to the Temple of the LORD your God,
and cry out to the LORD.
15What a terrible day it will be!
The LORD's day of judging is near,
when punishment will come
like a destroying attack from the Almighty.
16Our food is taken away
while we watch.
Joy and happiness are gone
from the Temple of our God.
17Though we planted fig seeds,
they lie dry and dead in the earth.
The barns are empty and falling down.
The storerooms for grain have been broken down,
because the grain has dried up.
18The animals are groaning!
The herds of cattle wander around confused,

cutting . . . locusts These are different names for an insect like a large grasshopper. The locust can quickly destroy trees, plants and crops, and in this destruction, Joel sees a warning. God will cause this type of destruction when he punishes his people.

because they have no grass to eat;
even the flocks of sheep suffer.
19LORD, I am calling to you for help,
because fire has burned up the open pastures,
and flames have burned all the trees in the field.
20Wild animals also need your help.
The streams of water have dried up,
and fire has burned up the open pastures.

The Coming Day of Judgement

2 Blow the trumpet in Jerusalem;
shout a warning on my holy mountain.
Let all the people who live in the land shake with fear,
because the LORD's day of judging is coming;
it is near.
2It will be a dark, gloomy day,
cloudy and black.
Like the light at sunrise,
a great and powerful army will spread over the mountains.
There has never been anything like it before,
and there will never be anything like it again.

3In front of them a fire destroys;
behind them a flame burns.
The land in front of them is like the garden of Eden;
the land behind them is like an empty desert.
Nothing will escape from them.
4They look like horses,
and they run like war horses.
5It is like the noise of chariots
rumbling over the tops of the mountains,
like the noise of a roaring fire
burning dry stalks.

GOD'S POWER

The Big Blast

For 123 years Mount St Helens slept quietly. Whenever geologists looked down the throat of the volcano in Washington state, USA, all they found was ash and ice. Then, on 20 March 1980, earthquakes shook the area. Within a week the volcano became active

At first, people were frightened. But as weeks went by and nothing happened, they grew accustomed to living next to an active volcano. They got tired of hearing warnings of possible disaster. In fact, a carnival-like attitude prevailed, and the volcano's small eruptions became a source of entertainment.

On 18 May, Mount St Helens was rattled by another series of earthquakes. This time a huge section of the northern slope came crashing down the mountain. Two minutes later, the mountain exploded. The explosion, heard 300 kilometres away, was louder and more powerful than an atomic bomb. A billowing cloud of ash shot more than 20 kilometres into the air. Nearly 500 square kilometres of forest land were levelled. Hundreds of thousands of trees vaporised, clouds of grey ash filled the air, and the land was left barren.

The predicted eruption had come.

Like many of the people who scoffed at the predictions of Mount St Helens's eruption, most of the people in Joel's time paid little attention to the prophet's warnings that the Lord's judgement was soon to come. Read how the prophet describes God's warnings in **Joel 2:1–2**.

- Why do you think many of the people living near Mount St Helens and those who heard Joel's prophecy of God's power didn't believe the warnings?
- What warning signs should you be paying attention to?

Consider . . .

- going for a bike ride and viewing God's power in nature as you ride.
- reading Revelation (p.1388) and comparing John's visions with the ones in Joel.

For more, see . . .

- Psalm 98 (p.557)
- 2 Peter 3:1–13 (p.1367)
- Matthew 12:33–37 (p.961)

They are like a powerful army lined up for
battle.
6When they see them, nations shake with fear,
and everyone's face becomes pale.
7They charge like soldiers;
they climb over the wall like warriors.
They all march straight ahead
and do not move off their path.
8They do not run into each other,
because each walks in line.
They break through all efforts to stop them
and keep coming.
9They run into the city.
They run at the wall
and climb into the houses,
entering through windows like thieves.

Sidelight The Israelites couldn't keep the locusts out of their houses (Joel 2:9), because they didn't have glass windows or even shutters. Instead, they had wooden lattice-work built into the windows, but that didn't stop the "powerful army" (Joel 2:5) from "entering . . . like thieves".

10Before them, earth and sky shake.
The sun and the moon become dark,
and the stars stop shining.
11The LORD shouts out orders
to his army.
His army is very large!
Those who obey him are very strong!
The LORD's day of judging
is an overwhelming and terrible day.
No one can stand up against it!

Change Your Hearts

12The LORD says, "Even now, come back to me
with all your heart.
Go without food, and cry and be sad."
13Tearing your clothes is not enough to show
you are sad;
let your heart be broken.
Come back to the LORD your God,
because he is kind and shows mercy.
He doesn't become angry quickly,
and he has great love.
He can change his mind about doing harm.
14Who knows? Maybe he will turn back to you
and leave behind a blessing for you.
Grain and drink offerings belong to the LORD
your God.
15Blow the trumpet in Jerusalem;
call for a day when no one eats food.
Tell everyone to stop work.
16Bring the people together
and make the meeting holy for the LORD.
Bring together the elders,
as well as the children,
and even babies that still feed at their
mothers' breasts.
The bridegroom should come from his
room,
the bride from her bedroom.
17The priests, the LORD's servants, should cry
between the altar and the entrance to the
Temple.[d]
They should say, "LORD, have mercy on your
people.
Don't let them be put to shame;
don't let other nations make fun of
them.
Don't let people in other nations ask,
'Where is their God?' "

The LORD Restores the Land

18Then the LORD became concerned about his
land
and felt sorry for his people.
19He said to them:
"I will send you grain, new wine and
olive oil,
so that you will have plenty.
No more will I shame you
among the nations.
20I will force the army from the north to leave
your land
and go into a dry, empty land.
Their soldiers in front will be forced into the
Dead Sea,[a]
and those in the rear into the
Mediterranean Sea.
Their bodies will rot and stink.
The LORD has surely done a wonderful
thing!"
21Land, don't be afraid;
be happy and full of joy,
because the LORD has done a wonderful
thing.
22Wild animals, don't be afraid,
because the open pastures have grown
grass.
The trees have given fruit;
the fig trees and the grapevines have grown
much fruit.
23So be happy, people of Jerusalem;
be joyful in the LORD your God.
Because he does what is right,
he has brought you rain;
he has sent the autumn rain
and the spring rain for you, as before.

24And the threshing[d] floors will be full of grain;
the barrels will overflow with new wine
and olive oil.

The LORD Speaks

25"Though I sent my great army against you—
those swarming locusts and hopping
locusts,
the destroying locusts and the cutting
locusts[n] that ate your crops—
I will pay you back
for those years of trouble.
26Then you will have plenty to eat
and be full.
You will praise the name of the LORD your God,
who has done miracles[d] for you.
My people will never again be shamed.
27Then you will know that I am among the
people of Israel,
that I am the LORD your God,
and there is no other God.
My people will never be shamed again.

28"After this,
I will pour out my Spirit[d] on all kinds of
people.
Your sons and daughters will prophesy,[d]
your old men will dream dreams,
and your young men will see visions.
29At that time I will pour out my Spirit
also on male slaves and female slaves.
30I will show miracles
in the sky and on the earth:
blood, fire and thick smoke.

swarming . . . locusts These are different names for an insect like a large grasshopper. The locust can quickly destroy trees, plants and crops, and in this destruction, Joel sees a warning. God will cause this type of destruction when he punishes his people.

FORGIVENESS

Change of Heart

When their only son was killed by a drunk driver, Frank and Elizabeth Morris had just one wish: revenge. "We wanted him dead," Mrs Morris admits, talking about the killer.

Tommy Pigage pleaded guilty to the charge and was sent to prison. The Morrises were angry at the court for not giving him a longer sentence. In time, however, they realised their bitterness stopped them from getting on with their lives. They decided to visit Tommy.

Tommy expressed deep remorse for killing their son and admitted that he deserved his punishment. The Morrises were moved by his sensitivity and honesty. "I didn't want my son's death to be totally vain," Mrs Morris says. "And in my heart I know that if he could, my son would tell us to forgive Tommy."

The Morrises' decision to forgive not only freed them from their bitterness, but also started a change in Tommy's life. He quit drinking and turned to God. The Morrises continue to visit Tommy regularly and support him in his struggle with alcoholism. "The accident already wiped out one very special life. I don't want to see it waste Tommy's life, too," Mrs Morris says.

The giving and receiving of forgiveness is necessary for living in Christ. To change their lives, the Morrises needed to forgive – and Tommy needed their forgiveness. Read **Joel 2:12–19** for God's plea for people to change their hearts.

- How is the Morrises' (and Tommy's) change of heart similar to what God required of the people in Joel's time?
- Is forgiveness the same thing as fairness? Why or why not?

Consider . . .

- making a paper heart and listing on it people you need to forgive. Ask God to help you do it.
- taking the risk of asking forgiveness from someone you've hurt.

For more, see . . .

- Psalm 51 (p.530)
- Luke 13:1–5 (p.1066)
- Matthew 5:21–26 (p.943)

31 The sun will become dark,
the moon red as blood,
before the overwhelming and terrible day of
the LORD comes.
32 Then anyone who calls on the LORD
will be saved,
because on Mount Zion[d] and in Jerusalem
there will be people who will be saved,
just as the LORD has said.
Those left alive after the day of punishment
are the people whom the LORD called.

Punishment for Judah's Enemies

3 "In those days and at that time,
when I will make things better for Judah
and Jerusalem,
2 I will gather all the nations together
and bring them down into the Valley
Where the LORD Judges.
There I will judge them,
because those nations scattered my own
people Israel
and forced them to live in other nations.
They divided up my land
3 and threw lots[d] for my people.
They traded boys for prostitutes,[d]
and they sold girls to buy wine to drink.

4 "Tyre and Sidon and all of you regions of
Philistia! What did you have against me? Were you
punishing me for something I did, or were you
doing something to hurt me? I will very quickly
do to you what you have done to me. 5 You took
my silver and gold, and you put my precious trea-
sures in your temples. 6 You sold the people of
Judah and Jerusalem to the Greeks so that you
could send them far from their land.

7 "You sent my people to that faraway place,
but I will get them and bring them back, and I
will do to you what you have done to them. 8 I
will sell your sons and daughters to the people of

CREATION

A Load of Rubbish!

Marion Stoddart and her family watched their nice neighbourhood become a dumping ground for industrial waste and rubbish. Once beautiful, the river bank was scattered with litter, old furniture, and abandoned cars. The river smelled like a sewer.

Finally, Marion realised she could either move away or rescue the river, which was so polluted that people said it was "too thick to pour and too thin to plough". She organised other concerned residents in the community to reclaim the river.

They showed trade unions, business leaders, and politicians how everyone would benefit from making the river "fishable and swimmable". They even got one important politician's attention by giving him a bottle of filthy river water to keep on his desk until the river was clean again. Slowly, the various users of the river did their part to stop polluting and to clean up the mess, due in large part to Mrs Stoddart's group. Mrs Stoddart says it is possible for ordinary people to reclaim their world for good.

"You don't have to be really clever to make a difference," she says. "You just have to persuade the people with power, the people who care, and be really committed, persistent, and honest."

It is not God's will that we rubbish his creation. In **Joel 2:21–27** read of God's desire for the land's health and vitality.

- How does Mrs Stoddart's crusade compare to God's will for the land?
- From your reading of the passage, what do you think is God's will for the way we are to use the earth?

Consider . . .

- choosing one way today to show God's love for creation by reducing the amount of rubbish you create.
- leading a group from your school or church in cleaning up a river bank, a public park or a lake shore where you live.

For more, see . . .

- Genesis 1 (p.2)
- Luke 12:22–31 (p.1064)
- Psalm 104 (p.560)

Judah, and they will sell them to the Sabean people far away." The LORD said this.

God Judges the Nations

9Announce this among the nations:
Prepare for war!
Wake up the soldiers!
Let all the men of war come near and attack.
10Make swords from your ploughs,
and make spears from your hooks for trimming trees.
Let even the weak person say,
"I am a soldier."
11All of you nations, hurry,
and come together in that place.
LORD, send your soldiers
to gather the nations.
12"Wake up, nations,
and come to attack in the Valley Where the LORD Judges.
There I will sit to judge
all the nations on every side.
13Swing the cutting tool,
because the harvest is ripe.
Come, walk on them as you would walk on grapes to get their juice,
because the winepress[d] is full
and the barrels are spilling over,
because these people are so evil!"
14There are huge numbers of people
in the Valley of Decision,[n]
because the LORD's day of judging is near
in the Valley of Decision.
15The sun and the moon will become dark,
and the stars will stop shining.
16The LORD will roar like a lion from Jerusalem;
his loud voice will thunder from that city,
and the sky and the earth will shake.
But the LORD will be a safe place for his people,
a strong place of safety for the people of Israel.
17"Then you will know that I, the LORD your God,
live on my holy Mount Zion.[d]
Jerusalem will be a holy place,
and strangers will never even go through it again.

A New Life Promised for Judah

18"On that day wine will drip from the mountains,
milk will flow from the hills,
and water will run through all the ravines of Judah.
A fountain will flow from the Temple[d] of the LORD
and give water to the valley of acacia trees.
19But Egypt will become empty,
and Edom an empty desert,
because they were cruel to the people of Judah.
They killed innocent people in that land.
20But there will always be people living in Judah,
and people will live in Jerusalem from now on.
21Egypt and Edom killed my people,
so I will definitely punish them."

The LORD lives in Jerusalem!

Valley of Decision This is like the name Valley Where the LORD Judges in 3:2 and 3:12.

Amos

Why Read This Book:

- Read of the Lord's punishment for injustice (Amos 1—2).
- Be warned about vanity and self-centredness (Amos 6).
- See the Lord's reaction to those who oppress the poor (Amos 8).

When?

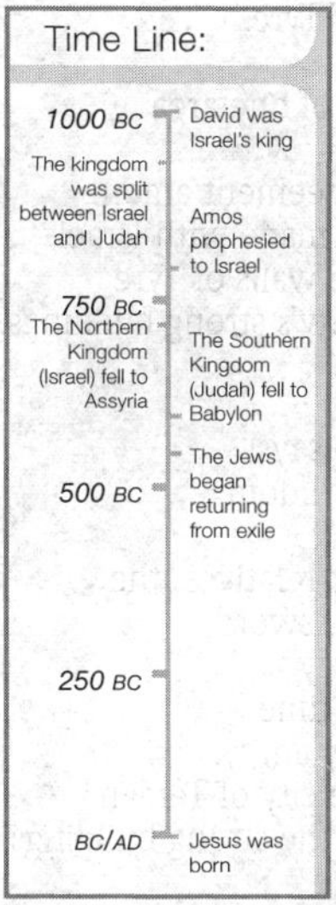

Behind the Scenes:

Amos was a very angry farmer! All around him were smug, satisfied people. The nation was prosperous. Surely God was on Israel's side. So why was Amos angry?

Underneath the prosperity was corruption. People had acquired their wealth by stepping on the poor. They relied on military power instead of God. Their worship was superficial. In short, they had forgotten what it meant to follow God.

Though he lived in the Southern Kingdom of Judah, Amos preached to the people of Israel in the Northern Kingdom. He took his uncompromising message straight to the religious authorities of his day. Instead of listening to him, they threw him out.

In the same way that Amos challenged the Israelites to reconsider their priorities, he challenges us. In the climax to his book, he reminds us what God wants: "Let justice flow like a river, and let goodness flow like a stream that never stops" (Amos 5:24).

Where?

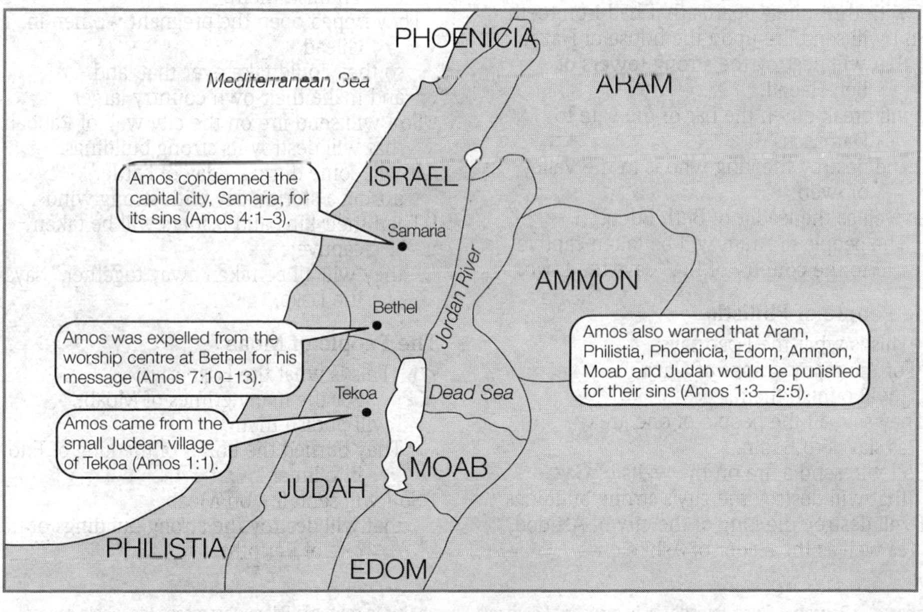

1 These are the words of Amos, one of the shepherds from the town of Tekoa. He saw this vision about Israel two years before the earthquake. It was at the time Uzziah was king of Judah and Jeroboam son of Jehoash was king of Israel.

2Amos said,
"The LORD will roar from Jerusalem;
he will send his voice from Jerusalem.
The pastures of the shepherds will become dry,
and even the top of Mount Carmel will dry up."

Sidelight The whole region of Israel was shaken by the earthquake mentioned in Amos 1:1. Though no one knows the exact date, it's probably the same earthquake mentioned in Zechariah 14:5 (p.926). Archaeologists believe the city of Hazor was destroyed by an earthquake about the same time.

Israel's Neighbours are Punished

The People of Aram

3This is what the LORD says:
"For the many crimes of Damascus,
I will punish them.
They drove over the people of Gilead
with threshing[d] boards that had iron teeth.
4So I will send fire upon the house of Hazael
that will destroy the strong towers of Ben-Hadad.
5I will break down the bar of the gate to Damascus
and destroy the king who is in the Valley of Aven,
as well as the leader of Beth Eden.
The people of Aram will be taken captive
to the country of Kir," says the LORD.

The People of Philistia

6This is what the LORD says:
"For the many crimes of Gaza,
I will punish them.
They sold all the people of one area
as slaves to Edom.
7So I will send a fire on the walls of Gaza
that will destroy the city's strong buildings.
8I will destroy the king of the city of Ashdod,
as well as the leader of Ashkelon.
Then I will turn against the people of the city of Ekron,
and the last of the Philistines will die," says the Lord GOD.

The People of Phoenicia

9This is what the LORD says:
"For the many crimes of Tyre,
I will punish them.
They sold all the people of one area
as slaves to Edom,
and they forgot the agreement among
relatives they had made with Israel.
10So I will send fire on the walls of Tyre
that will destroy the city's strong buildings."

The People of Edom

11This is what the LORD says:
"For the many crimes of Edom,
I will punish them.
They hunted down their relatives, the Israelites, with the sword,
showing them no mercy.
They were angry all the time
and kept on being very angry.
12So I will send fire on the city of Teman
that will even destroy the strong buildings of Bozrah." [n]

The People of Ammon

13This is what the LORD says:
"For the many crimes of Ammon,
I will punish them.
They ripped open the pregnant women in Gilead
so they could take over that land
and make their own country larger.
14So I will send fire on the city wall of Rabbah
that will destroy its strong buildings.
It will come during a day of battle,
during a stormy day with strong winds.
15Then their king and leaders will be taken captive;
they will all be taken away together," says the LORD.

The People of Moab

2 This is what the LORD says:
"For the many crimes of Moab,
I will punish them.
They burned the bones of the king of Edom into lime.
2So I will send fire on Moab
that will destroy the strong buildings of the city of Kerioth.

Teman . . . Bozrah Since Teman was in northern Edom and Bozrah was in southern Edom, this means the whole country will be destroyed.

The people of Moab will die in a great
noise,
in the middle of the sounds of war and
trumpets.
3So I will bring an end to the king of Moab,
and I will kill all its leaders with him," says
the LORD.

The People of Judah

4This is what the LORD says:
"For the many crimes of Judah,
I will punish them.
They rejected the teachings of the LORD
and did not keep his commands;
they followed the same gods
as their ancestors had followed.
5So I will send fire on Judah,
and it will destroy the strong buildings of
Jerusalem."

Israel is Punished

6This is what the LORD says:
"For the many crimes of Israel,
I will punish them.
For silver, they sell people who have done
nothing wrong;
they sell the poor to buy a pair of sandals.
7They walk on poor people as if they were
nothing,
and they refuse to be fair to those who are
suffering.
Fathers and sons have sexual relations with
the same woman,
and so they ruin my holy name.
8As they worship at their altars,
they lie down on clothes taken from the
poor.
They fine people,
and with that money they buy wine to
drink in the house of their god.

9"But it was I who destroyed the Amorites
before them,
who were tall like cedar trees and as strong
as oaks—
I destroyed them completely.
10It was I who brought you from the land of
Egypt
and led you for 40 years through the
desert
so I could give you the land of the
Amorites.
11I made some of your children prophets [d]
and some of your young people Nazirites. [d]
People of Israel, isn't this true?" says the
LORD.
12"But you made the Nazirites drink wine
and told the prophets not to prophesy.

13Now I will make you get stuck,
as a wagon loaded with grain gets stuck.
14No one will escape, not even the fastest
runner.
Strong people will not be strong enough;
warriors will not be able to save themselves.
15Soldiers with bows and arrows will not stand
and fight,
and even fast runners will not get away;
soldiers on horses will not escape alive.
16At that time even the bravest warriors
will run away without their armour," says
the LORD.

Warning to Israel

3 Listen to this word that the LORD has spoken
against you, people of Israel, against the
whole family he brought out of Egypt.
2"I have chosen only you
out of all the families of the earth,
so I will punish you
for all your sins."

3Two people will not walk together
unless they have agreed to do so.
4A lion in the forest does not roar
unless it has caught an animal;
it does not growl in its den
when it has caught nothing.
5A bird will not fall into a trap
where there is no bait;
the trap will not spring shut
if there is nothing to catch.
6When a trumpet blows a warning in a city,
the people tremble.
When trouble comes to a city,
the LORD has caused it.
7Before the Lord GOD does anything,
he tells his plans to his servants the
prophets. [d]
8The lion has roared!
Who wouldn't be afraid?
The Lord GOD has spoken.
Who will not prophesy?

9Announce this to the strong buildings of
Ashdod
and to the strong buildings of Egypt:
"Come to the mountains of Samaria,
where you will see great confusion
and people hurting others."

10"The people don't know how to do what is
right," says the LORD.
"Their strong buildings are filled with
treasures they took by force from
others."

11So this is what the Lord GOD says:
"An enemy will take over the land

and pull down your strongholds; [d]
he will take the treasures out of your strong buildings."

12This is what the LORD says:
"A shepherd might save from a lion's mouth
only two leg bones or a scrap of an ear of his sheep.
In the same way only a few Israelites in Samaria will be saved—
people who now sit on their beds
and on their couches."

13"Listen and be witnesses against the family of Jacob," says the Lord GOD, the God All-powerful.

14"When I punish Israel for their sins,
I will also destroy the altars at Bethel.
The corners of the altar will be cut off,
and they will fall to the ground.
15I will tear down the winter house,
together with the summer house.
The houses decorated with ivory will be destroyed,
and the great houses will come to an end,"
says the LORD.

Sidelight If rich people today built like the rich people in Amos's day, elephants would certainly be extinct. A great sign of wealth was to have ivory inlays in furniture and panelling in your house (Amos 3:15). Amos wasn't impressed.

Israel will Not Return

4 Listen to this message, you cows of Bashan [n] on the Mountain of Samaria.
You take things from the poor
and crush people who are in need.
Then you command your husbands,
"Bring us something to drink!"
2The Lord GOD has promised this:
"Just as surely as I am a holy God,
the time will come
when you will be taken away by hooks,
and what is left of you with fish-hooks.
3You will go straight out of the city
through holes in the walls,
and you will be thrown on the rubbish dump," says the LORD.

4"Come to the city of Bethel and sin;
come to Gilgal and sin even more.
Offer your sacrifices every morning,
and bring one-tenth of your crops every three days.
5Offer bread made with yeast as a sacrifice to show your thanks,
and boast about the special offerings you bring,
because this is what you love to do,
Israelites," says the Lord GOD.

6"I did not give you any food in your cities,
and there was not enough to eat in any of your towns,
but you did not come back to me," says the LORD.
7"I held back the rain from you
three months before harvest time.
Then I let it rain on one city
but not on another.
Rain fell on one field,
but another field got none and dried up.
8People weak from thirst went from town to town for water,
but they could not get enough to drink.
Still you did not come back to me," says the LORD.
9"I made your crops die from disease and mildew. [d]
When your gardens and your vineyards got larger,
locusts [d] ate your fig and olive trees.
But still you did not come back to me,"
says the LORD.
10"I sent disasters against you,
as I did to Egypt.
I killed your young men with swords,
and your horses were taken from you.
I made you smell the stink from all the dead bodies,
but still you did not come back to me,"
says the LORD.
11"I destroyed some of you
as I destroyed Sodom and Gomorrah.
You were like a burning stick pulled from a fire,
but still you did not come back to me,"
says the LORD.

12"So this is what I will do to you, Israel;
because I will do this to you,
get ready to meet your God, Israel."

13He is the one who makes the mountains
and creates the wind
and makes his thoughts known to people.
He changes the dawn into darkness
and walks over the mountains of the earth.
His name is the LORD God All-powerful.

Bashan Amos compares the rich, lazy women of Samaria to well-fed cows from Bashan, a place known for its rich animal pastures.

Israel Needs to Repent

5 Listen to this funeral song that I sing about you, people of Israel.
2"The young girl Israel has fallen,
and she will not rise up again.
She was left alone in her own land,
and there is no one to help her up."

3This is what the Lord GOD says:
"If 1,000 soldiers leave a city,
only 100 will return;
if 100 soldiers leave a city,
only ten will return."

4This is what the LORD says to the nation of
Israel:
"Come to me and live.
5 But do not look in Bethel
or go to Gilgal,
and do not go down to Beersheba.
The people of Gilgal will be taken away as captives,
and Bethel will become nothing."
6Come to the LORD and live,
or he will move like fire against the descendants[d] of Joseph.
The fire will burn Bethel,
and there will be no one to put it out.
7You turn justice upside down,
and you throw on the ground what is right.

8God is the one who made the star groups Pleiades and Orion;
he changes darkness into the morning light,
and the day into dark night.
He calls for the waters of the sea
to pour out on the earth.
The LORD is his name.
9He destroys the protected city;
he ruins the strong, walled city.
10You hate those who speak in court against evil,
and you can't stand those who tell the truth.
11You walk on poor people,
forcing them to give you grain.
You have built fancy houses of cut stone,
but you will not live in them.
You have planted beautiful vineyards,
but you will not drink the wine from them.
12I know your many crimes,
your terrible sins.
You hurt people who do right,
you take money to do wrong,
and you keep the poor from getting justice in court.

13In such times the wise person will keep quiet,
because it is a bad time.

14Try to do good, not evil,
so that you will live,
and the LORD God All-powerful will be with you
just as you say he is.
15Hate evil and love good;
be fair in the courts.
Perhaps the LORD God All-powerful will be kind
to the people of Joseph who are left alive.

16This is what the Lord, the LORD God All-
powerful, says:
"People will be crying in all the streets;
they will be saying, 'Oh, no!' in the public places.
They will call the farmers to come and weep
and will pay people to cry out loud for them.
17People will be crying in all the vineyards,
because I will pass among you to punish you," says the LORD.

Sidelight The people in Amos's time expected "the day of the LORD" to be a picnic. Amos painted a different picture – of inescapable terror. You can run but you can't hide!

The LORD's Day of Judging

18How terrible it will be for you who want
the LORD's day of judging to come.
Why do you want that day to come?
It will bring darkness for you, not light.
19It will be like someone who runs from a lion
and meets a bear,
or like someone who goes into his house
and puts his hand on the wall,
and then is bitten by a snake.
20So the LORD's day of judging will bring darkness, not light;
it will be very dark, not light at all.

21The LORD says, "I completely hate your feasts;
I cannot stand your religious meetings.
22If you offer me burnt offerings and grain offerings,
I won't accept them.
You bring your best fellowship offerings of fattened cattle,
but I will ignore them.

23Take the noise of your songs away from
me!
I won't listen to the music of your
harps.
24But let justice flow like a river,
and let goodness flow like a stream that
never stops.

25"People of Israel, you did not bring me
sacrifices and offerings
while you travelled in the desert for 40
years.
26You have carried with you
your king, the god Sakkuth
and Kaiwan your idol,
and the star gods you have made.
27So I will send you away as captives beyond
Damascus,"
says the LORD, whose name is the God
All-powerful.

Israel will be Destroyed

6 How terrible it will be for those who have
an easy life in Jerusalem,
for those who feel safe living on Mount
Samaria.
You think you are the important people of
the best nation in the world;
the Israelites come to you for help.
2Go and look at the city of Calneh,
and from there go to the great city Hamath;
then go down to Gath of the Philistines.
You are no better than these kingdoms.
Your land is no larger than theirs.
3You put off the day of punishment,
but you bring near the day when you can
do evil to others.
4You lie on beds decorated with ivory
and stretch out on your couches.
You eat tender lambs
and fattened calves.

HYPOCRISY

Empty Words

In her school, Elaine usually hung around with a close group of five or six girls. One of the fringe members of the group, Anne, was a common topic of conversation when she wasn't around. Even though Anne could be fun, the group didn't really like her.

When Anne was with the other girls, they were always friendly towards her. But after she had gone, they would go back to talking about her. "We all did it," Elaine says. "We were nice to her when she was around but destroyed her behind her back. It was sort of a habit to say bad things about her."

After a while, Elaine realised that the group was being hypocritical. "You really couldn't tell whether or not we liked Anne," she says. "I began to feel funny about the way we were treating her."

Elaine soon realised that she couldn't believe much of what the group said. Their words were often empty. So Elaine left the group. "What do they say about me now that I'm not around?" she wonders.

Just as Elaine's group was hypocritical in saying one thing but doing another, the people in Amos's time participated in Temple worship, but behaved in ways opposite to those that God desires. In **Amos 5:18–24**, the people of Israel are rebuked because their sinful actions didn't match their pious words.

- What was hypocritical about the way the group treated Anne and the way the people worshipped God in the passage?
- How do you think God's desire for justice, as expressed in the passage, applies to your own worship?

Consider . . .

- keeping a list of times when you have been hypocritical – when your actions were different from your beliefs. Pray for integrity and offer the list to God.
- calling your friends' attention to their mistreatment of someone else, but doing so in a Christian manner.

For more, see . . .

- Psalm 62 (p.535)
- Luke 13:10–17 (p.1067)
- Matthew 6:2–6 (p.947)

5You make up songs on your harps,
and, like David, you compose songs on
musical instruments.
6You drink wine by the bowlful
and use the best perfumed lotions.
But you are not sad over the ruin of
Israel,
7so you will be some of the first ones taken as
slaves.
Your feasting and lying around will come to
an end.

8The Lord GOD made this promise; the LORD
God All-powerful says:
"I hate the pride of the Israelites,
and I hate their strong buildings,
so I will let the enemy take the city
and everything in it."

SELF-ESTEEM

Hidden Talent

On the outside Nicolle was very ordinary. She lived on a council estate in the East End of London and had a thick Cockney accent. She was fourteen years old and had just started going to church. Everything was new to her and so she would comment on it.

"Cor! This Jesus stuff's good innit?" she would remark, and several people would raise an eyebrow at her rough approach to Christianity. In fact some members of the church treated her in a very condescending manner, almost as if her accent made her a second-class citizen.

Nicolle never really noticed this, and just went on blissfully enjoying her life as a very new Christian. She enjoyed the services and noticed that people often took part, giving a testimony, or singing a song.

"I wonder if I could do that?" she asked her friend one day, as they were walking to the bus stop.

"Do what?" asked Vicky.

"Well, I dunno. Sing a song I suppose. I think I only know 'Amazing Grace' . . . " she finished lamely.

Vicky looked alarmed . . . 'Amazing Grace' was a notoriously hard song to sing as a solo.

"Why not just give a testimony?" her friend suggested.

"'Cos I could never talk in front of all them people!" laughed Nicolle. Then she added, "But I could sing to 'em . . ."

Whilst waiting for the bus to arrive, Vicky found out that her new friend went to singing classes, and no ordinary singing classes. Nicolle was trained in Italian Opera . . . at the age of fourteen!

"I don't tell many people," she blushed. "Don't s'pose many people like that stuff."

Vicky couldn't wait for the service. When it finally arrived, she could see people looking uncomfortable as Nicolle took the platform. She watched as people nudged each other as her friend announced:

"I'm going to sing 'Amazing Grace'," and then nodded to the pianist.

The silence when she sang was almost as deafening as the applause afterwards!

She was outstanding!

Vicky hugged her friend as she took her seat.

Sometimes we think we are better than we are, and sometimes there is more to a person than we see. Read **Amos 6:1–7** to see why God rebuked Israel for their wrong attitudes.

- Look at verse 1. How are the people in the passage like some of the people in Nicolle's church?
- How close to your own views of materialism and feelings of security are those mentioned in this passage?

Consider . . .

- Listing the values – not the material things – that would improve your self-esteem.
- Joining a group to help others (and yourself) to grow in good self-esteem.

For more, see . . .

- Romans 12:3–16 (p.1204)
- James 4:1–6 (p.1351)
- Philippians 2:1–4 (p.1282)

9At that time there might be only ten people
left alive in just one house, but they will also die.
10When the relatives come to get the bodies to
take them outside, one of them will call to the
other and ask, "Are there any other dead bodies
with you?"
That person will answer, "No."
Then the one who asked will say, "Hush! We
must not say the name of the LORD."

11The LORD has given the command;
the large house will be broken into
pieces,
and the small house into bits.
12Horses do not run on rocks,
and people do not plough rocks with
oxen.
But you have changed fairness into poison;
you have changed what is right into a bitter
taste.
13You are happy that the town of Lo Debar
was captured,
and you say, "We have taken Karnaim [n] by
our own strength."

14The LORD God All-powerful says,
"Israel, I will bring a nation against you
that will make your people suffer from Lebo
Hamath in the north
to the valley south of the Dead Sea." [d]

The Vision of Locusts

7 This is what the Lord GOD showed me: he
was forming a swarm of locusts, [d] after the
king had taken his share of the first crop and the
second crop had just begun growing. 2When
the locusts ate all the crops in the country, I said,
"Lord GOD, forgive us. How could Israel live
through this? It is too small already!"
3So the LORD changed his mind about this. "It
will not happen," said the LORD.

The Vision of Fire

4This is what the Lord GOD showed me: the
Lord GOD was calling for fire to come down like
rain. It burned up the deep water and was going
to burn up the land. 5Then I cried out, "Lord
GOD, stop! How could Israel live through this? It
is too small already."
6So the LORD changed his mind about this too.
"It will not happen," said the Lord GOD.

The Vision of the Plumb Line

7This is what he showed me: the Lord stood
by a straight wall, with a plumb line [d] in his
hand. 8The LORD said to me, "Amos, what do you
see?"
I said, "A plumb line."
Then the Lord said, "See, I will put a plumb
line among my people Israel to show how
crooked they are. I will not look the other way
any longer.

9"The places where Isaac's descendants [d]
worship will be destroyed,
Israel's holy places will be turned into
ruins,
and I will attack King Jeroboam's family
with the sword."

Amaziah Speaks Against Amos

10Amaziah, a priest at Bethel, sent this message
to Jeroboam king of Israel: "Amos is making evil
plans against you with the people of Israel. He has
been speaking so much that this land can't hold
all his words. 11This is what Amos has said:
'Jeroboam will die by the sword,
and the people of Israel will be taken as
captives
out of their own country.'"

12Then Amaziah said to Amos, "Seer, [d] go back
right now to Judah. Do your prophesying [d] and
earn your living there, 13but don't prophesy any
more here at Bethel. This is the king's holy place,
and it is the nation's temple."
14Then Amos answered Amaziah, "I do not
make my living as a prophet, nor am I a member
of a group of prophets. I make my living as a

> **Sidelight** When Amos said that he took care of sycamore trees (Amos 7:14) – which bore figs – he did more than pick their fruit once a year. To ensure good fruit from these trees, the farmer had to slit the top of each fig as it grew.

shepherd, and I take care of sycamore trees.
15But the LORD took me away from tending the
flock and said to me, 'Go and prophesy to my
people Israel.' 16So listen to the LORD's word. You
tell me,
'Don't prophesy against Israel,
and stop prophesying against the
descendants of Isaac.'

17"Because you have said this, the LORD says:
'Your wife will become a prostitute [d] in the
city,
and your sons and daughters will be killed
with swords.

Lo Debar . . . Karnaim These were cities in Israel that the Israelites had captured in war.

Other people will measure your land and
divide it among themselves,
and you will die in a foreign country.
The people of Israel will definitely be taken
from their own land as captives.' "

The Vision of Ripe Fruit

8 This is what the Lord GOD showed me: a
basket of summer fruit. 2He said to me,
"Amos, what do you see?"

I said, "A basket of summer fruit."

Then the LORD said to me, "An end [n] has come
for my people Israel, because I will not overlook
their sins any more.

3"On that day the palace songs will become
funeral songs," says the Lord GOD. "There will be
dead bodies thrown everywhere! Silence!"

4Listen to me, you who walk on helpless
people,
you who are trying to destroy the poor
people of this country, saying,
5"When will the New Moon [d] festival be
over
so we can sell grain?
When will the Sabbath [d] be over
so we can bring out wheat to sell?
We can charge them more
and give them less,
and we can change the scales to cheat the
people.
6We will buy poor people for silver,
and needy people for the price of a pair of
sandals.
We will even sell the wheat that was swept
up from the floor."

7The LORD has sworn by his name, the Pride of
Jacob, "I will never forget everything that these
people did.
8The whole land will shake because of it,
and everyone who lives in the land will cry
for those who died.
The whole land will rise like the Nile;
it will be shaken, and then it will fall
like the Nile River in Egypt."

9The Lord GOD says:
"At that time I will cause the sun to go
down at noon
and make the earth dark on a bright day.
10I will change your festivals into days of crying
for the dead,
and all your songs will become songs of
sadness.
I will make all of you wear rough cloth to
show your sadness;
I will make you shave your heads
as well.
I will make it like a time of crying for the
death of an only son,
and its end like the end of an awful day."

11The Lord GOD says: "The days are coming
when I will cause a time of hunger in the
land.
The people will not be hungry for bread or
thirsty for water,
but they will be hungry for words from the
LORD.
12They will wander from the Mediterranean
Sea to the Dead Sea, [d]
from the north to the east.
They will search for the word of the LORD,
but they won't find it.
13At that time the beautiful young women and
the young men
will become weak from thirst.
14They make promises by the idol in Samaria
and say, 'As surely as the god of Dan
lives . . .'
and, 'As surely as the god of Beersheba [n]
lives, we promise . . .'
So they will fall
and never get up again."

Israel will be Destroyed

9 I saw the Lord standing by the altar, and he
said:
"Smash the top of the pillars
so that even the bottom of the doors will
shake.
Make the pillars fall on the people's
heads;
anyone left alive I will kill with a sword.
Not one person will get away;
no one will escape.
2If they dig down as deep as the place of the
dead,
I will pull them up from there.
If they climb up into heaven,
I will bring them down from there.
3If they hide at the top of Mount Carmel,
I will find them and take them away.
If they try to hide from me at the bottom of
the sea,
I will command a snake to bite them.
4If they are captured and taken away by their
enemies,

end The Hebrew word for "end" sounds like the Hebrew word for "summer fruit".
Dan . . . Beersheba Dan was the city farthest north in Israel, and Beersheba was the city farthest south. So this means all the people of Israel.

I will command the sword to kill them.
I will keep watch over them,

Sidelight Where do you go when you want to hide from God? Many people chose Mount Carmel, a wooded mountain overlooking the Mediterranean Sea and filled with vast caves. But even at the top of Carmel, God knew where they were . . .

but I will keep watch to give them trouble,
not to do them good."
5 The Lord GOD All-powerful touches the land,
and the land shakes.
Then everyone who lives in the land cries
for the dead.
The whole land rises like the Nile River
and falls like the river of Egypt.
6 The LORD builds his upper rooms above the
skies;
he sets their foundations on the earth.
He calls for the waters of the sea
and pours them out on the land.
The LORD is his name.

7 The LORD says,
"Israel, you are no different to me than the
people of Cush.
I brought Israel out of the land of Egypt,
the Philistines from Crete
and the Arameans from Kir.

JUSTICE

Dont Fake It

In the late seventies and eighties, a vicious civil war raged in the central American country of El Salvador. In 1980 alone, the war claimed the lives of 3,000 people every month. One man alone made a public appeal for the world to intervene. His name was Oscar Romero, the Catholic Archbishop of El Salvador.

Oscar Romero was not seen as political protestor. In fact he was appointed to such a high position because many of the bishops in El Salvador were wary of angering the government. They felt that Oscar, famous for being a "bookworm" would keep quiet. But something happened shortly after Oscar's appointment that meant he would stop at nothing to see the war end. The first priest Oscar ordained was ambushed by the army and killed for helping farmers stand up against the government.

On 24 March 1980, Archbishop Romero was shot dead by an army assassin during a mass where he was officiating. The day before his murder, he told a reporter:

"You can tell the people if they succeed in killing me, that I forgive and bless those who do it. Hopefully, they will realise they are wasting their time. A bishop will die, but the church of God, which is the people, will never perish."

God's voice throughout the Old and New Testament has always spoken out against injustice, as in **Amos 8:4–8**. His church and his prophets today still do.

- Would you be willing to speak up when you saw injustice, as Oscar Romero did?
- Look at verse 6. God pays attention to the cries of the poor. Do we pay enough attention to the impact our shopping choices have on poor people in the world?

Consider . . .

- taking time this week to allow God to speak to you through the injustice you see in your town and in the world.
- whether you and your family can buy more products that have been fairly traded, and so help those trying to earn a living in poorer countries.

For more, see . . .

- Psalm 146 (p.586)
- Luke 16:19–31 (p.1075)
- Luke 11:37–42 (p.1062)

8I, the Lord GOD, am watching the sinful
kingdom Israel.
I will destroy it
from off the earth,
but I will not completely destroy
Jacob's descendants," [d] says the LORD.
9"I am giving the command
to scatter the nation of Israel among all
nations.
It will be like someone shaking grain through
a strainer,
but not even a tiny stone falls through.
10All the sinners among my people
will die by the sword—
those who say,
'Nothing bad will happen to us.'

The LORD Promises to Restore Israel

11"The kingdom of David is like a fallen tent,
but in that day I will set it up again
and mend its broken places.
I will rebuild its ruins
as it was before.
12Then Israel will take over what is left of Edom
and the other nations that belong to me,"
says the LORD,
who will make it happen.

13The LORD says, "The time is coming when
there will be all kinds of food.
People will still be harvesting crops
when it's time to plough again.
People will still be taking the juice from grapes
when it's time to plant again.
Wine will drip from the mountains
and pour from the hills.
14I will bring my people Israel back from
captivity;
they will build the ruined cities again,
and they will live in them.
They will plant vineyards and drink the wine
from them;
they will plant gardens and eat their fruit.
15I will plant my people on their land,
and they will not be pulled out again
from the land which I have given them,"
says the LORD your God.

Obadiah

Why Read This Book:

- Learn what can happen to a nation that's filled with false pride (Obadiah 2—8).
- See how the righteous will be victorious (Obadiah 17—21).

When?

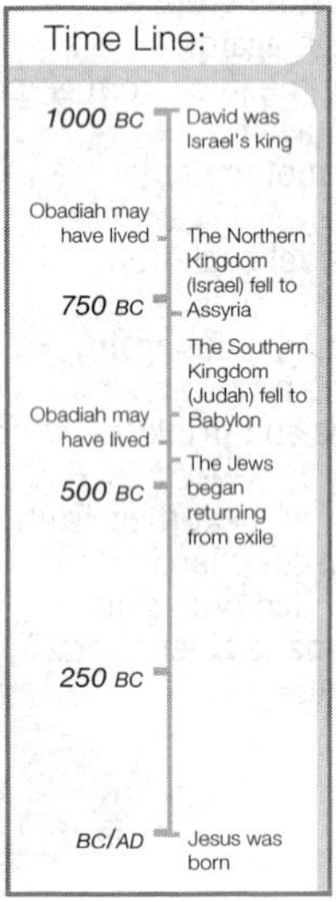

Behind the Scenes:

If you think you've seen real rivalries on the football pitch, "you ain't seen nothing yet!" Israel vs. Edom – now that's real rivalry!

Even though they were close neighbours, these two countries had been rivals for hundreds of years. They fought over control of trade routes. Then when Israel was raided by major empires, Edom not only didn't help, but actually shared the loot! All this from a nation of people who were actually related to Israel. Esau, the father of the Edomites, was the brother of Jacob (who was also called Israel). (See Genesis 25:30, p.30.)

Into the middle of this rivalry steps the prophet Obadiah. He describes God's anger at Edom for not helping oppressed people and for rejoicing over the Israelites' misfortune. And he predicts that Edom will be destroyed for its sinfulness, and that the nation of Israel will have the final victory.

Obadiah's message was more than a motivational talk at a rally for the Israelites. At times, it was harsh and full of revenge. God will correct the injustice by bringing down the Edomites, Obadiah said. His message reminds us to care for the weak around us and to keep hopeful even when we feel overwhelmed and beaten down. God will be victorious in the end!

Where?

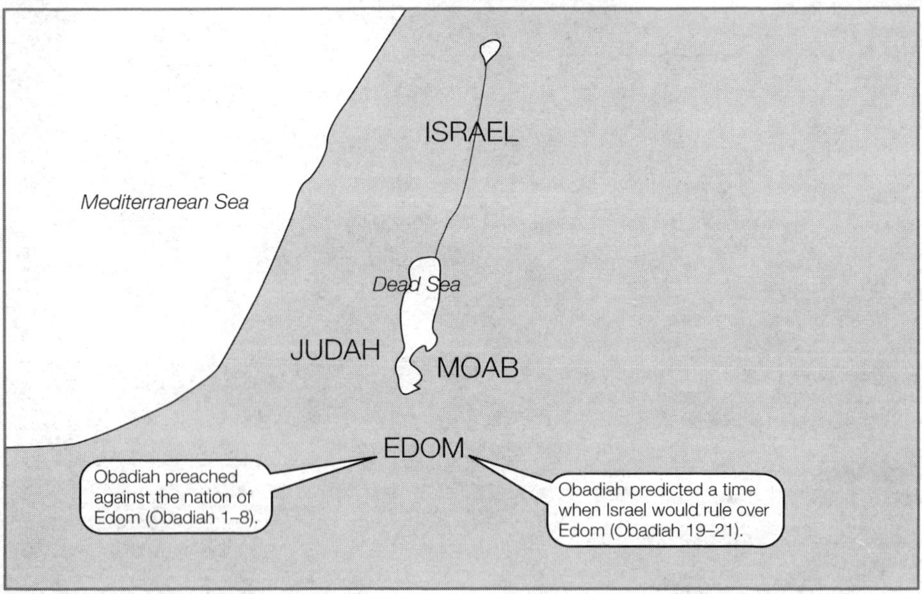

The LORD will Punish the Edomites

1This is the vision of Obadiah.

This is what the Lord GOD says about Edom: [n]

We have heard a message from the LORD.
A messenger has been sent among the nations, saying,
"Attack! Let's go and attack Edom!"

The Lord Speaks to the Edomites

2"Soon I will make you the smallest of nations.
You will be greatly hated by everyone.
3Your pride has fooled you,
you who live in the hollow places of the cliff.
Your home is up high,
you who say to yourself,
'No one can bring me down to the ground.'
4Even if you fly high like the eagle
and make your nest among the stars,
I will bring you down from there," says the LORD.
5"You will really be ruined!
If thieves came to you,
if robbers came by night,
they would steal only enough for themselves.
If workers came and picked the grapes from your vines,
they would leave a few behind.
6But you, Edom, will really lose everything!
People will find all your hidden treasures!

Sidelight Some people hide their money under mattresses, but the Edomites hoarded their wealth in the red cliffs, south of the Dead Sea where they lived (Obadiah 6). Obadiah mentions "treasures" on an average of once every seventh verse!

7All the people who are your friends
will force you out of the land.
The people who are at peace with you
will trick you and defeat you.
Those who eat your bread with you now
are planning a trap for you,
and you will not notice it."
8The LORD says, "On that day
I will surely destroy the wise people from Edom,
and those with understanding from the mountains of Edom.
9Then, city of Teman, your best warriors will be afraid
and everyone from the mountains of Edom will be killed.
10You did violence to your relatives, the Israelites,
so you will be covered with shame
and destroyed for ever.
11You stood aside without helping
while strangers carried Israel's treasures away.
When foreigners entered Israel's city gate
and threw lots [d] to decide what part of Jerusalem they would take,
you were like one of them.

Commands That Edom Broke

12"Edom, do not laugh at your brother Israel in his time of trouble
or be happy about the people of Judah when they are destroyed.
Do not boast when cruel things are done to them.
13Do not enter the city gate of my people
in their time of trouble
or laugh at their problems
in their time of trouble.
Do not take their treasures
in their time of trouble.
14Do not stand at the crossroads
to destroy those who are trying to escape.
Do not capture those who escape alive and turn them over to their enemy
in their time of trouble.

The Nations will be Judged

15"The LORD's day of judging is coming soon
to all the nations.
The same evil things you did to other people
will happen to you;
they will come back upon your own head.
16Because you drank in my Temple, [d]
all the nations will drink on and on.
They will drink and drink
until they disappear.

Edom The Edomites were the people who came from Esau, Jacob's twin brother. They were enemies of the Israelites.

17But on Mount Zion[d] some will escape the
judgement,
and it will be a holy place.
The people of Jacob will take back their
land
from those who took it from them.
18The people of Jacob will be like a fire
and the people of Joseph[n] like a flame.
But the people of Esau[n] will be like dry
stalks.
The people of Jacob will set them on fire
and burn them up.
There will be no one left of the people of
Esau."
This will happen because the LORD has said it.

19Then God's people will regain southern Judah
from Edom;
they will take back the mountains of Edom.
They will take back the western hills
from the Philistines.
They will regain the lands of Ephraim and
Samaria,
and Benjamin will take over Gilead.

people of Jacob . . . Joseph The people who came from Jacob and Joseph, or the Israelites.
people of Esau The people who came from Esau, or the Edomites.

SIN

What Are We Really Like?

What's the worst thing anyone can do? Kill someone? That's what people generally think.

Murder is probably the worst thing that can happen between human beings. But what about when God comes into the picture?

According to the Bible, sin is really serious. Often we can get away with things that our teachers and parents don't find out about, or we can talk our way out of trouble. But God always knows absolutely everything that we've done, and he knows our attitude to him.

He doesn't just see everything that we *do* – he knows what goes on in our heads as well. So he's well aware of what we're really like. Because God doesn't want his world to contain sin forever, eventually he will come in judgement and wipe it out. Where will we be when this happens? The truth is that we'll be in trouble, because we're all contaminated with this disease of sin. We will be in danger of what the Bible calls hell.

But God hasn't left us in this terrible situation. The good news, or the "Gospel", is that God has sent his son, Jesus, to rescue us. He can take away the sin that is such a massive part of our lives and which has such terrible results. On the cross, he died for our sin so we don't have to face the punishment for it. When we recognise that, we're brought into God's family. God never abandons us because of what we have done – he is much greater and more powerful than even the worst thing we can do. Jesus is always there and will never let us go.

Read **Obadiah 12–14**.

- What is sin against God?
- What happens if we sin even after we've asked God into our lives?

Consider . . .

- writing down everything you can remember doing wrong recently, praying for forgiveness, then tearing up the paper into the tiniest pieces possible!
- telling a friend if you find yourself thinking about your sins even after you've confessed them to God. Get them to pray with you that you would know and accept God's forgiveness and have the strength not to do these things again.

For more, see . . .

- Psalm 51:1–5 (p.530)
- Romans 3:23 (p.1187)
- Acts 2:38 (p.1140)
- Romans 6:23 (p.1193)

20People from Israel who once were forced to
leave their homes
will take the land of the Canaanites,
all the way to Zarephath.
People from Judah who once were forced
to leave Jerusalem and live in Sepharad
will take back the cities of southern Judah.
21Powerful warriors will go up on
Mount Zion,
where they will rule the people living on
Edom's mountains.
And the kingdom will belong to the LORD.

Jonah

Why Read This Book:

- Discover truth in a story of a prophet who was reluctant to do what God wanted him to do (Jonah 1—2).
- See that God's love and mercy are for all the world (Jonah 3—4).

When?

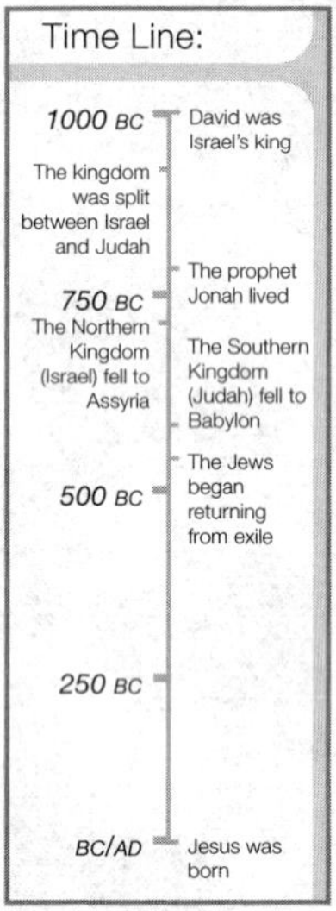

Behind the Scenes:

Being chosen to be a leader is always a great honour. But you probably wouldn't last long in the position if you simply basked in the glow of being chosen. You would have to fulfil the tasks – some you might not like – that come with the honour.

The Jews had been chosen by God to be his special people. Through history, God had guided and protected them. But what responsibilities for the rest of the world did that honour include? Should God's people shut off the world, focusing on their gifts from God? Or should they take the story of God's love to the rest of the world?

The story of Jonah addressed this dilemma. God called the prophet Jonah to go and preach at Nineveh, the heathen capital of Assyria. Not wanting to preach to non-Jewish people – especially pagans whose cruelty was widely known – Jonah went in the opposite direction. Like many Israelites, he enjoyed God's mercy on Israel but wanted all enemies to be destroyed.

God wouldn't let Jonah off from his mission, though. Through a storm and a big fish, God got Jonah's attention and turned him around. Reluctantly, Jonah went to Nineveh and preached, and the whole city turned to God. But Jonah wasn't happy. He went to sulk about God sparing the Ninevites from destruction.

God responded with a message that's at the heart of the book: "Shouldn't I show concern for the great city Nineveh, which has more than 120,000 people who do not know right from wrong . . .?" (Jonah 4:11). ▷

Where?

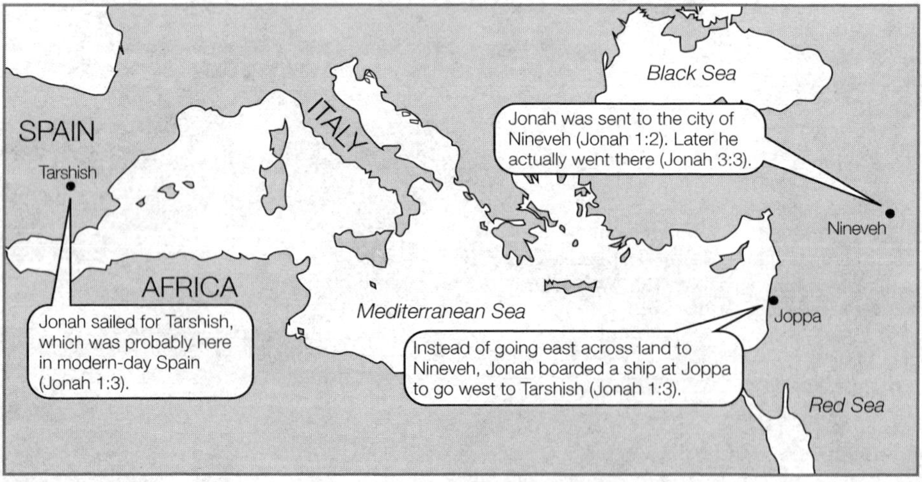

Behind the Scenes (cont.): Jonah's story reminds all God's followers that no one owns God. As Jesus said in Luke 5:32 (p.1047), "I have not come to invite good people but sinners to change their hearts and lives."

God Calls and Jonah Runs

1 The LORD spoke his word to Jonah son of
Amittai: 2"Get up and go to the great city of
Nineveh and preach against it, because I see the
evil things they do."
3But Jonah got up to run away from the LORD
by going to Tarshish. He went to the city of
Joppa, where he found a ship that was going to
the city of Tarshish. Jonah paid for the trip and
went aboard, planning to go to Tarshish to run
away from the LORD.

> **Sidelight** The name Jonah (Jonah 1:1) means "dove" which may be a traditional symbol for Israel (see Psalm 74:19–21, p.544).

4But the LORD sent a great wind on the sea,
which made the sea so stormy that the ship was
in danger of breaking apart. 5The sailors were
afraid, and each man cried to his own god. They
began throwing the cargo from the ship into the
sea to make the ship lighter.
But Jonah had gone down far inside the ship to
lie down, and he fell fast asleep. 6The captain of
the ship came and said, "Why are you sleeping?
Get up and pray to your god! Maybe your god
will pay attention to us, and we won't die!"
7Then the men said to each other, "Let's throw
lots [d] to see who caused these troubles to happen
to us."
When they threw lots, the lot showed that the
trouble had happened because of Jonah. 8Then
they said to him, "Tell us, who caused our trou-
ble? What is your job? Where do you come from?
What is your country? Who are your people?"
9Then Jonah said to them, "I am a Hebrew. I
fear the LORD, the God of heaven, who made the
sea and the land."
10The men were very afraid, and they asked
Jonah, "What terrible thing did you do?" (They
knew he was running away from the LORD be-
cause he had told them.)
11Since the wind and the waves of the sea
were becoming much stronger, they said to him,
"What should we do to you to make the sea
calm down for us?"
12Jonah said to them, "Pick me up and throw
me into the sea, and then it will calm down. I
know it is my fault that this great storm has come
on you."
13Instead, the men tried to row the ship back
to the land, but they could not, because the sea
was becoming more stormy.

Jonah's Punishment

14So the men cried to the LORD, "LORD, please
don't let us die because of this man's life; please
don't think we are guilty of killing an innocent
person. LORD, you have caused all this to happen;
you wanted it this way." 15So they picked up
Jonah and threw him into the sea, and the sea
became calm. 16Then they began to fear the LORD
very much; they offered a sacrifice to the LORD
and made promises to him.
17The LORD caused a big fish to swallow Jonah,
and Jonah was inside the fish for three days and
three nights.

> **Sidelight** Jonah spent three days and three nights in the belly of an enormous fish before it threw up (Jonah 1:7–2:10). Jesus used this incident to illustrate his own death and resurrection (see Matthew 12:40, p.961).

2 While Jonah was inside the fish, he prayed to
the LORD his God and said,

2"When I was in danger,
I called to the LORD,
and he answered me.
I was about to die,
so I cried to you
and you heard my voice.
3You threw me into the sea,
down, down into the deep sea.
The water was all around me,
and your powerful waves flowed
over me.
4I said, 'I was driven out of your presence,
but I hope to see your Holy Temple [d]
again.'
5The waters of the sea closed around my
throat.

The deep sea was all around me;
seaweed was wrapped around my head.
6When I went down to where the mountains
of the sea start to rise,
I thought I was locked in this prison
for ever,
but you saved me from the pit of death,
LORD my God.

7"When my life had almost gone,
I remembered the LORD.
I prayed to you,
and you heard my prayers in your Holy
Temple.

8"People who worship useless idols
give up their loyalty to you.
9But I will praise and thank you
while I give sacrifices to you,
and I will keep my promises to you.
Salvation comes from the LORD!"

10Then the LORD spoke to the fish, and the fish
threw up Jonah onto the dry land.

God Calls and Jonah Obeys

3 The LORD spoke his word to Jonah again
and said, 2"Get up and go to the great city
Nineveh and preach to it what I tell you to say."
3So Jonah obeyed the LORD and got up and
went to Nineveh. It was a very large city; just to
walk across it took a person three days. 4After
Jonah had entered the city and walked for one
day, he preached to the people, saying, "After 40
days, Nineveh will be destroyed!"
5The people of Nineveh believed God. They
announced that they would stop eating for a
while, and they put on rough cloth to show their
sadness. All the people in the city did this, from
the most important to the least important.
6When the king of Nineveh heard this news,
he got up from his throne, took off his robe and
covered himself with rough cloth and sat in
ashes to show how upset he was.
7He sent this announcement through Nineveh:

By command of the king and his important
men: no person or animal, herd or flock, will

THANKFULNESS

In All Circumstances

Lana came home from a wonderful weekend at her grandparents' to find that burglars had taken everything: camera, money, and a laptop with some really important work on it. Two windows were smashed, the whole place ransacked. She walked around the house and discovered more and more damage and mess.

This was when she became aware that she had a choice – she could look at the bad bits and enjoy the sympathy people would bring to her over the next few days, or she could celebrate in God that she and her family were safe, the house hadn't burned down, and that the insurance cover would enable them to replace the items that had been stolen. She realised that material possessions aren't actually that important. Her heart soared as she felt God's love flow through her, as she realised she'd passed one of God's biggest tests. She was learning what it means to praise God through the hard times!

Lana learnt that each time something bad happens, we can choose to be victims or we can choose to learn from it. We can choose to be negative or we can choose to be positive and look for the good. We can read about Jonah's thankful heart in **Jonah 2:2–9**.

- What did Lana have to do to be able to praise God through the hard times?
- What do you think now about praising God through the hard times?

Consider . . .

- writing a list or a poem about all the good things in your life you can thank God for.
- keeping greetings cards and stamps handy and sending thank-you letters when people do nice things for you.

For more, see . . .

- 1 Chronicles 29:10–20 (p.399)
- 1 Thessalonians 5:12–18 (p.1301)
- Isaiah 63:7–9 (p.709)

be allowed to taste anything. Do not let
them eat food or drink water. 8But every
person and animal should be covered with
rough cloth, and people should cry loudly to
God. Everyone must turn away from evil
living and stop doing harm all the time.
9Who knows? Maybe God will change his
mind. Maybe he will stop being angry and
then we will not die.

Sidelight The rough cloth the king put on when he heard about Nineveh's sins would make polyester feel like fine silk (Jonah 3:6). It was probably made of scratchy goat hair. Wearing it next to the skin virtually guaranteed discomfort. It was the common clothing to wear during times of repentance or mourning.

FORGIVENESS

Personal Peace

By 1938, when eighteen-year-old Joseph Mavsar left home to study for the ministry, he had heard many sermons about forgiveness. In a few years, however, he would know how hard it would become to live out those sermons.

In 1941, Italy invaded Yugoslavia and occupied Joseph's village.

The family's troubles increased when his father, a respected leader, refused to join the local communist resistance.

The family gathered for Christmas, 1942. Two days later, the communists attacked the house and killed Joseph's parents, four of his brothers and his only sister. Joseph and his twelve-year-old brother, Bill, jumped from a second-floor window and fled to the woods. The communists burned the others' bodies and stole the family's property.

Just two brothers of the large family survived the war.

Joseph went to the USA in 1948 as a minister. He amazed some and shocked others as he preached forgiveness for war crimes. Although he wanted the truth of the crimes against his family to be known, he still preached forgiveness.

As the 25th anniversary of his ordination approached, however, Joseph still struggled to forgive personally the people who had killed his family and taken all their possessions. Then a cousin in Yugoslavia wrote to Joseph, telling him that some of the killers were haunted by what they had done. "Come back and make peace with them," the cousin wrote.

Joseph returned to his village and found one of the communists living in his father's house.

"As I shook this man's hand and told him I forgave him," Joseph remembers, "he thanked me over and over, and said it was the best day of his life."

In his old age, Joseph continued to preach forgiveness. "In life we cannot be happy unless we're able to forgive," he said. "We must forgive, no matter how painful the hurt."

He knows what he's talking about.

Sometimes offences seem too great ever to be forgiven. Read in **Jonah 3:1–10** how the Lord forgives the people of Nineveh for their many sins.

- Jonah did not think Nineveh should be forgiven (Jonah 4:1). How do Joseph and Jonah differ in their willingness to forgive?
- Have you ever found it difficult to forgive someone, even though it was necessary for your own peace of mind?

Consider . . .

- forgiving someone who has hurt you, even though it's difficult to do.
- making the first move to restore a damaged relationship within your family or peers.

For more, see . . .

- Joel 2:12–19 (p.865)
- Acts 10:43 (p.1157)
- Luke 23:26–34 (p.1091)

10 When God saw what the people did, that
they stopped doing evil, he changed his mind and
did not do what he had warned. He did not pun-
ish them.

God's Mercy Makes Jonah Angry

4 But this made Jonah very unhappy, and he
became angry. 2 He prayed to the LORD,
"When I was still in my own country this is what
I said would happen, and that is why I quickly
ran away to Tarshish. I knew that you are a God
who is kind and shows mercy. You don't become
angry quickly, and you have great love. I knew
you would choose not to cause harm. 3 So now I
ask you, LORD, please kill me. It is better for me
to die than to live."

4 Then the LORD said, "Do you think it is right
for you to be angry?"

5 Jonah went out and sat down east of the city.
There he made a shelter for himself and sat in the
shade, waiting to see what would happen to the
city. 6 The LORD made a plant grow quickly up
over Jonah, which gave him shade and helped
him to be more comfortable. Jonah was very
pleased to have the plant. 7 But the next day
when the sun rose, God sent a worm to attack
the plant so that it died.

8 As the sun rose higher in the sky, God sent a
very hot east wind to blow, and the sun became
so hot on Jonah's head that he became very weak
and wished he were dead. He said, "It is better
for me to die than to live."

STRESS

Not Going My Way

Debbie was sweating – she had been dancing, singing and acting for the whole morning. She had worked so hard and really wanted that place at stage school. She'd prayed about it so much. She also wanted to stay in the area where she had so many friends.

They were announcing the numbers they had picked to go on to the next stage. Her number was 23 and the numbers went all the way to 50.

. . . 16, 19, 22, 27 . . . Number 23 wasn't called out. She sat with her heart still racing and looked at the floor. Why had it not worked out? Every one said she would make it. Why?

She started walking home, tears slowly rolling down her face. She was so stressed about her future and what to do next, she even wondered whether there was a point in living if she couldn't perform. Her friend Lucy was walking by and saw how upset Debbie was. They both sat on a bench and Lucy decided the best thing to do was pray.

After praying, Debbie felt a lot better and Lucy said to her, "God has got something better than you could ever think, he is in control, it's all good!" Debbie really hoped she was right.

Sometimes we need God to speak to us through a practical lesson in order for us to put our trust in him fully, and in Debbie's case God needed to close off an opportunity in order for her to see the greater plans he had for her.

Read **Jonah 4:5–9**.

- Have you ever felt like Jonah or Debbie?
- What do you think God was showing Jonah by sending the worm?

Consider . . .

- a time where you were really stressed about something. Think about what God taught you through that time.
- any exams or events that are coming up that may get you stressed and pray for wisdom in those circumstances.

For more, see . . .

- Matt 6:25–27 (p.948)
- Luke 10:38–42 (p.1058)
- Matt 10:29–31 (p.956)
- Romans 8:28 (p.1196)

9But God said to Jonah, "Do you think it is
right for you to be angry about the plant?"
Jonah answered, "It is right for me to be angry!
I am so angry I could die!"

10And the LORD said, "You are so concerned for
that plant even though you did nothing to make
it grow. It appeared one day, and the next day it
died. 11Then shouldn't I show concern for
the great city Nineveh, which has more than
120,000 people who do not know right from
wrong, and many animals too?"

Micah

Why Read This Book:

- See God's judgement on a nation that didn't follow him (Micah 1—2).
- Find out what happens when leaders' actions are unjust (Micah 3).
- Be encouraged by God's promise for the future (Micah 7).

When?

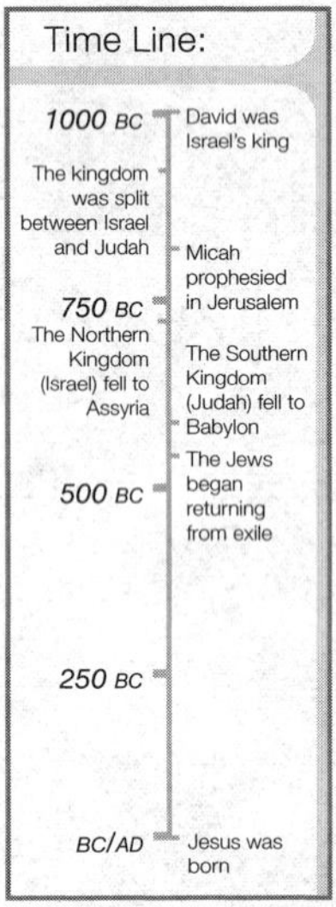

Behind the Scenes:

Everything was falling apart, but no one seemed to notice. And when people were confronted with their problems, they just yawned.

That was the prophet Micah's situation. When he started preaching in Judah, Israel was about to be conquered. And, he believed, the same fate awaited Judah because of its injustice to the poor and its immoral leadership.

Yet, Micah said, God would establish a kingdom of eternal peace.

The heart of Micah's message summarised what most of the prophets called people to do: "The Lord has told you, human, what is good; he has told you what he wants from you: to do what is right to other people, love being kind to others, and live humbly, obeying your God" (Micah 6:8). It's a message that's just as relevant today as it was more than 2,500 years ago.

Where?

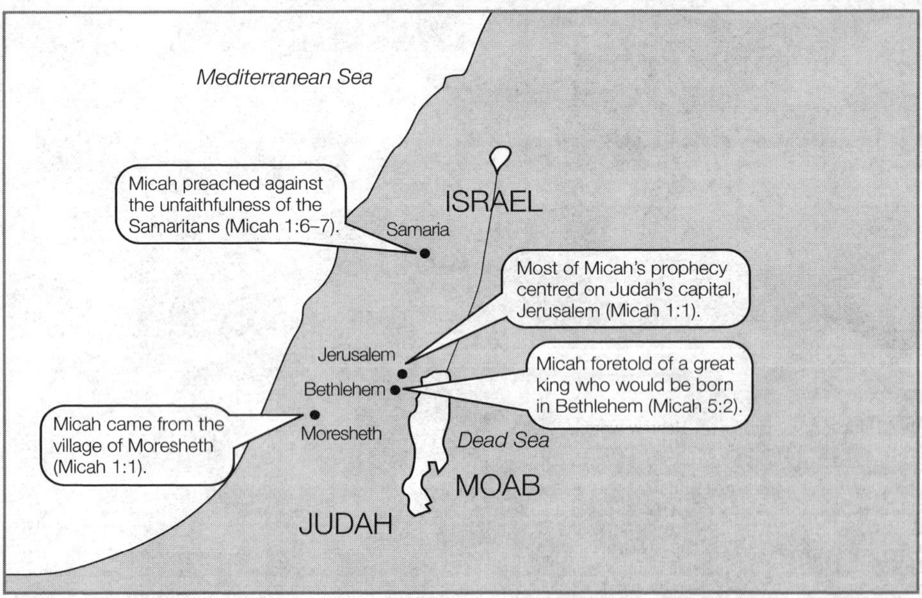

Samaria and Israel to Be Punished

1 During the time that Jotham, Ahaz and Hezekiah were kings of Judah, the word of the LORD came to Micah, who was from Moresheth. He saw these visions about Samaria and Jerusalem.

2Hear this, all you nations;
listen, earth and all you who live on it.
The Lord GOD will be a witness against you,
the Lord from his Holy Temple. [d]
3See, the LORD is coming out of his place;
he is coming down to walk on the tops of the mountains.
4The mountains will melt under him,
and the valleys will crack open,
like wax near a fire,
like water running down a hillside.
5All this is because of Jacob's sin,
because of the sins of the nation of Israel.
What is the place of Jacob's sin?
Isn't it Samaria?
What is Judah's place of idol worship?
Isn't it Jerusalem?

The LORD Speaks

6"So I will make Samaria a pile of ruins in the open country,
a place for planting vineyards.
I will pour her stones down into the valley
and strip her down to her foundations.
7All her idols will be broken into pieces;
all the gifts to her idols will be burned with fire.
I will destroy all her idols,
and because Samaria earned her money by being unfaithful to me,
this money will be carried off by others
who are not faithful to me."

Sidelight Micah has sometimes been called the "wailing prophet", based on Micah 1:8. He's not the only one who went "barefoot and naked" to make a point. Isaiah attracted attention the same way, in Isaiah 20:2–4 (p.660).

Micah's Great Sadness

8I will moan and cry because of this evil,
going around barefoot and naked.
I will cry loudly like the wild dogs
and make sad sounds like the owls do,
9because Samaria's wound cannot be healed.
It will spread to Judah;
it will reach the city gate of my people,
all the way to Jerusalem.
10Don't tell it in Gath. [n]
Don't cry in Acco. [n]
Roll in the dust
at Beth Ophrah. [n]
11Pass on your way, naked and ashamed,
you who live in Shaphir. [n]
Those who live in Zaanan [n]
won't come out.
The people in Beth Ezel [n] will cry,
but they will not give you any support.
12Those who live in Maroth [n]
will be anxious for good news to come,
because trouble will come from the LORD,
all the way to the gate of Jerusalem.
13You people living in Lachish, [n]
harness the fastest horse to the chariot.
Jerusalem's sins started in you;
yes, Israel's sins were found in you.
14So you must give farewell gifts
to Moresheth [n] in Gath.
The houses in Achzib [n] will be false help
to the kings of Israel.
15I will bring against you people who will take your land,
you who live in Mareshah. [n]
The glory of Israel
will go in to Adullam.
16Cut off your hair to show you are sad
for the children you love.
Make yourself bald like the eagle,
because your children will be taken away to a foreign land.

The Evil Plans of People

2 How terrible it will be for people who plan wickedness,
who lie on their beds and make evil plans.
When the morning light comes, they do what they planned,

Gath This name sounds like the Hebrew word for "tell".
Acco This name sounds like the Hebrew word for "cry".
Beth Ophrah This name means "house of dust".
Shaphir This name means "beautiful".
Zaanan This name sounds like the Hebrew word for "come out".
Beth Ezel This name means "house by the side of another", suggesting help or support.
Maroth This name sounds like the Hebrew word for "sad" or "miserable".
Lachish This name sounds like the Hebrew word for "horses".
Moresheth This may be a play on the word "engaged", referring to a farewell gift to a bride.
Achzib This name means "lie" or "trick".
Mareshah This name sounds like the Hebrew word for a person who captures other cities and lands.

because they have the power to do so.
2They want fields, so they take them;
they want houses, so they take them away.
They cheat people to get their houses;
they rob them even of their property.

3That is why the LORD says:
"Look, I am planning trouble against such people,
and you won't be able to save yourselves.
You will no longer walk proudly,
because it will be a terrible time.
4At that time people will make fun of you
and sing this sad song about you:
'We are completely ruined;
the LORD has taken away my people's land.
Yes, he has taken it away from me
and divided our fields among our enemies!'"
5So you will have no one from the LORD's people
to throw lots[d] to divide the land.

Micah is Asked Not to Prophesy

6The prophets say, "Don't prophesy[d] to us!
Don't prophesy about these things!
Nothing to make us feel bad will happen!"
7But I must say this, people of Jacob:
the LORD is becoming angry about what you have done.
My words are welcome
to the person who does what is right.
8But you are fighting against my people like an enemy.
You take the coats from people who pass by;
you rob them of their safety;
you plan war.
9You've forced the women of my people
from their nice houses;
you've taken my glory
from their children for ever.
10Get up and leave.
This is not your place of rest any more.
You have made this place unclean,[d]
and it is doomed to destruction.
11But you people want a false prophet
who will tell you nothing but lies.
You want one who promises to prophesy good things for you
if you give him wine and beer.
He's just the prophet for you.

The LORD Promises to Rescue His People

12"Yes, people of Jacob, I will bring all of you together;
I will bring together all those left alive in Israel.
I will put them together like sheep in a pen,
like a flock in its pasture;
the place will be filled with many people.
13Someone will open the way and lead the people out.
The people will break through the gate and leave the city where they were held captive.
Their king will go out in front of them,
and the LORD will lead them."

The Leaders of Israel are Guilty of Evil

3 Then I said,
"Listen, leaders of the people of Jacob;
listen, you rulers of the nation of Israel.
You should know how to decide cases fairly,
2 but you hate good and love evil.
You skin my people alive
and tear the flesh off their bones.
3You eat my people's flesh
and skin them and break their bones;
you chop them up like meat for the pot,
like meat in a cooking pan.
4They will cry to the LORD,
but he won't answer them.
At that time he will hide his face from them,
because what they have done is evil."

5The LORD says this about the prophets[d] who teach his people the wrong way of living:
"If these prophets are given food to eat,
they shout, 'Peace!'
But if someone doesn't give them what they ask for,
they call for a holy war against that person.
6So it will become like night for them,
without visions.
It will become dark for them, without any way to tell the future.
The sun is about to set for the prophets;
their day will become dark.
7The seers[d] will be ashamed;
the people who see the future will be embarrassed.
Yes, all of them will cover their mouths,
because there will be no answer from God."

Micah is an Honest Prophet of God

8But I am filled with power,
with the Spirit[d] of the LORD,
and with justice and strength,
to tell the people of Jacob how they have turned against God,
and the people of Israel how they have sinned.
9Leaders of Jacob and rulers of Israel,
listen to me,

you who hate fairness
and twist what is right.
10You build Jerusalem by murdering people;
you build it with evil.
11Its judges take money
to decide who wins in court.
Its priests only teach for pay,
and its prophets [d] only look into the future
when they get paid.
But they lean on the LORD and say,
"The LORD is here with us,
so nothing bad will happen to us."
12Because of you,
Jerusalem will be ploughed like a field.
The city will become a pile of rocks,
and the hill on which the Temple [d] stands
will be covered with bushes.

The Mountain of the LORD

4 In the last days
the mountain on which the LORD's
Temple [d] stands
will become the most important of all
mountains.
It will be raised above the hills,
and people from other nations will come
streaming to it.
2Many nations will come and say,
"Come, let us go up to the mountain of the
LORD,
to the Temple of the God of Jacob,
so that he can teach us his ways
and we can obey his teachings."
His teachings will go out from Jerusalem,
the word of the LORD from that city.
3The Lord will judge many nations;
he will make decisions about strong nations
that are far away.
They will hammer their swords into plough
blades
and their spears into hooks for trimming
trees.
Nations will no longer raise swords against
other nations;
they will not train for war any more.
4Everyone will sit under his own vine and fig
tree,
and no one will make them afraid,
because the LORD All-powerful has said it.
5All other nations may follow their own gods,
but we will follow the LORD our God for
ever and ever.

6The LORD says, "At that time,
I will gather the crippled;
I will bring together those who were sent
away,
those whom I caused to have trouble.
7I will keep alive those who were crippled,
and I will make a strong nation of those
who were sent away.
The LORD will be their king in Mount Zion [d]
from now on and for ever.
8And you, watchtower of the flocks, [n] hill of
Jerusalem,
to you will come the kingdom as in the
past.
Jerusalem, the right to rule will come again
to you."

Why the Israelites Must Go to Babylon

9Now, why do you cry so loudly?
Is your king gone?
Have you lost your helper,
so that you are in pain, like a woman
trying to give birth?
10People of Jerusalem, strain and be in pain.
Be like a woman trying to give birth,
because now you must leave the city
and live in the field.
You will go to Babylon,
but you will be saved from that place.
The LORD will go there
and buy you back from your enemies.

11But now many nations
have come to fight against you,
saying, "Let's destroy Jerusalem.
We will look at her and be glad we have
defeated her."
12But they don't know
what the LORD is thinking;
they don't understand his plan.
He has gathered them like bundles of grain
to the threshing [d] floor.
13"Get up and beat them, people of
Jerusalem.
I will make you strong as if you had horns
of iron
and hoofs of bronze.
You will beat many nations into small
pieces
and give their wealth to the LORD,
their treasure to the Lord of all the earth."

5 So, strong city, gather your soldiers
together,
because we are surrounded and attacked.
They will hit the leader of Israel
in the face with a club.

watchtower . . . flocks This probably means a part of Jerusalem. The leaders would be like shepherds in a tower watching their sheep.

The Ruler to Be Born in Bethlehem

2"But you, Bethlehem Ephrathah,
though you are too small to be among the army groups from Judah,
from you will come one who will rule Israel for me.
He comes from very old times,
from days long ago."

Sidelight The book of Micah has been important to Christians, partly because of Micah 5:2. Matthew 2:6 (p.937) says that this prophecy was fulfilled when Jesus was born in Bethlehem.

3The LORD will give up his people
until the one who is having a baby gives birth;
then the rest of his relatives will return
to the people of Israel.
4At that time the ruler of Israel will stand
and take care of his people
with the LORD's strength
and with the power of the name of the LORD his God.
The Israelites will live in safety,
because his greatness will reach all over the earth.
5 He will bring peace.

Rescue and Punishment

Assyria will surely come into our country
and walk over our large buildings.
We will set up seven shepherds,
eight leaders of the people.
6They will destroy the Assyrians with their swords;
they will conquer the land of Assyria with their swords drawn.
They will rescue us from the Assyrians when they come into our land,
when they walk over our borders.

7Then the people of Jacob who are left alive
will be to other people

LEADERSHIP

It's Not About How You Start . . .

Have you ever found yourself looking at other people and wishing you had their life? Maybe it's someone famous or just the person you sit next to in your maths class. We end up thinking that the rest of our life would be so much better if we had what they have. But your background doesn't have to dictate the rest of your life.

Agnes Gonxha Bojaxhiu was born in Macedonia in 1910. She had a relatively poor upbringing in an area that was being torn apart by religious intolerance and political upheaval. When she was seven, her father was killed. Not the greatest of starts in life! By the time Agnes was twelve she had decided that God wanted her to make a difference with her life and so six years later, when she was only eighteen, she moved into a convent in Ireland and became a nun.

Later, Agnes moved to India. She felt God telling her to "follow Jesus into the slums" and she started a work with the poor that would have a worldwide impact. Agnes became one of the greatest leaders the world has ever seen – motivating thousands of people to reach out to those others wouldn't touch. You might know her better as Mother Teresa.

Read **Micah 5:2–4**.

- What similarities are there between Jesus' background and Mother Teresa's?
- What makes someone like Mother Teresa want to make a difference in the world?

Consider . . .

- talking to God and asking him to show you where he wants you to lead.
- talking to your youth leader about ways in which you can begin to make a difference in your local area.

For more, see . . .

- Joshua 1:1–9 (p.202)
- Titus 1:5–9 (p.1323)
- 1 Timothy 4:12 (p.1311)

like dew from the LORD
or rain on the grass—
it does not wait for human beings;
it does not pause for any person.
8Those of Jacob's people who are left alive
will be scattered among many nations and peoples.
They will be like a lion among the animals of the forest,
like a young lion in a flock of sheep:
as it goes, it jumps on them
and tears them to pieces,
and no one can save them.
9So you will raise your fist in victory over your enemies,
and all your enemies will be destroyed.

10The LORD says, "At that time,
I will take your horses from you
and destroy your chariots.
11I will destroy the cities in your country
and tear down all your defences.
12I will take away the magic charms you use
so you will have no more fortune-tellers.
13I will destroy your statues of gods
and the stone pillars you worship
so that you will no longer worship
what your hands have made.
14I will tear down Asherah[d] idols from you
and destroy your cities.
15In my anger and rage,
I will pay back the nations that have not listened."

The LORD's Case

6 Now hear what the LORD says:
"Get up; plead your case in front of the mountains;
let the hills hear your story.
2Mountains, listen to the LORD's legal case.
Foundations of the earth, listen.
The LORD has a legal case against his people,
and he will accuse Israel."

SERVICE

Out of the Ordinary?

Mother Teresa once said, "Do ordinary things with extraordinary love."

How do you have an impact on the world? Have a huge hit album? Star in a blockbusting film? Score a hat trick in the World Cup?

Mother Teresa had a *massive* impact on our world. Not because she was rich, powerful or because she had celebrity status. She started out teaching at St Mary's High School in Calcutta but couldn't cope with seeing the poverty outside her classroom. She decided to do something about it.

In 1948, her decision meant she was to devote the rest of her life to working with the poorest of poor in the slums of Calcutta in India. Instead of teaching in a classroom, Mother Teresa opened up an open-air school for any homeless children no one else was prepared to care for.

Since 1948, her charity work has spread all round the world: into the former Soviet Union, Asia, Africa and South America. Literally millions of missionaries have been inspired by her example of doing "ordinary things with extraordinary love".

Read **Micah 6:1–8**.

- How is verse 8 of this passage similar to Mother Teresa's quote above?
- What ordinary things could you begin doing that might make a difference in your area?

Consider . . .

- asking God where he wants you serve in your church. Make a list of the ways you can begin to serve those around you.
- praying for those people in your church who serve others. Ask your church leader to give you a list. Think about writing these people a card thanking them for the way they serve.

For more, see . . .

- Mark 9:35 (p.1015)
- Philippians 2:1–11 (p.1282)
- Romans 12:15–17 (p.1205)

[3]He says, "My people, what did I do to you?
How did I make you tired of me?
Tell me.
[4]I brought you from the land of Egypt
and freed you from slavery;
I sent Moses, Aaron and Miriam to you.
[5]My people, remember
the evil plans of Balak king of Moab
and what Balaam son of Beor told Balak.
Remember what happened from Acacia to Gilgal
so that you will know the LORD does what is right!"

[6]You say, "What can I bring with me
when I come before the LORD,
when I bow before God on high?
Should I come before him with burnt offerings,
with year-old calves?
[7]Will the LORD be pleased with 1,000 rams?
Will he be pleased with 10,000 rivers of oil?
Should I give my first child for the evil I have done?
Should I give my very own child for my sin?"
[8]The LORD has told you, human, what is good;
he has told you what he wants from you:
to do what is right to other people,
love being kind to others,
and live humbly, obeying your God.

[9]The voice of the LORD calls to the city,
and the wise person honours him.
So pay attention to the rod of punishment;
pay attention to the One who threatens to punish.
[10]Are there still in the wicked house
wicked treasures
and the cursed false measure?
[11]Can I forgive people who cheat others
with wrong weights and scales?
[12]The rich people of the city
do cruel things.
Its people tell lies;
they do not tell the truth.
[13]As for me, I will make you sick.
I will attack you, ruining you because of your sins.
[14]You will eat, but you won't become full;
you will still be hungry and empty.
You will store up, but save nothing,
and what you store up, the sword will destroy.
[15]You will plant,
but you won't harvest.
You will step on your olives,
but you won't get any oil from them.
You will crush the grapes,
but you will not drink the new wine.
[16]This is because you obey the laws of King Omri
and do all the things that Ahab's family does;
you follow their advice.
So I will let you be destroyed.
The people in your city will be laughed at,
and other nations will make fun of you.

The Evil That People Do

7 Poor me! I am like a hungry man,
and all the summer fruit has been picked—
there are no grapes left to eat,
none of the early figs I love.
[2]All of the faithful people are gone;
there is not one good person left in this country.
Everyone is waiting to kill someone;
everyone is trying to trap someone else.
[3]With both hands they are doing evil.
Rulers ask for money,
and judges' decisions are bought for a price.
Rich people tell what they want,
and they get it.
[4]Even the best of them is like a thorn-bush;
the most honest of them is worse than a prickly thorn-bush.
The day that your watchmen[n] warned you about has come.
Now they will be confused.
[5]Don't believe your neighbour
or trust a friend.
Don't say anything,
even to your wife.
[6]A son will not honour his father,
a daughter will turn against her mother
and a daughter-in-law will be against her mother-in-law;
a person's enemies will be members of his own family.

The LORD's Kindness

[7]Israel says, "I will look to the LORD for help.
I will wait for God to save me;
my God will hear me.
[8]Enemy, don't laugh at me.

watchmen Another name for prophets. The prophets were like guards who stood on a city's wall and watched for trouble coming from far away.

I have fallen, but I will get up again.
I sit in the shadow of trouble now,
but the LORD will be a light for me.
9I sinned against the LORD,
so he was angry with me,
but he will defend my case in court.
He will bring about what is right for me.
Then he will bring me out into the light,
and I will see him set things right.
10Then my enemies will see this,
and they will be ashamed,
those who said to me,
'Where is the LORD your God?'
I will look down on them.
They will get walked on, like mud in the street."

Israel will Return

11The time will come when your walls will be built again,
when your country will grow.
12At that time your people will come back to you
from Assyria and the cities of Egypt,
and from Egypt to the Euphrates River,
and from sea to sea and mountain to mountain.
13The earth will be ruined for the people who live in it
because of their deeds.

A Prayer to God

14So shepherd your people with your stick;
tend the flock of people who belong to you.
That flock now lives alone in the forest
in the middle of a garden land.
Let them feed in Bashan and Gilead
as in days long ago.

15"As in the days when I brought you out of Egypt,
I will show them miracles." [d]

16When the nations see those miracles,
they will no longer boast about their power.
They will put their hands over their mouths,
refusing to listen.
17They will crawl in the dust like a snake,
like insects crawling on the ground.
They will come trembling from their holes to the LORD our God
and will turn in fear before you.
18There is no God like you.
You forgive those who are guilty of sin;
you don't look at the sins of your people
who are left alive.
You will not stay angry for ever,
because you enjoy being kind.
19You will have mercy on us again;
you will conquer our sins.
You will throw away all our sins
into the deepest part of the sea.

Sidelight Micah's name means, "Who is like God?" He answers the question in Micah 7:18–19. No one is. In fact, the Lord is so great that he tosses our darkest sins into the ocean. Since the Middle Ages, Orthodox Jews have visited a river or other body of water on the Jewish New Year and repeated verse 19 three times while tossing breadcrumbs on the water.

20You will be true to the people of Jacob,
and you will be kind to the people of Abraham
as you promised to our ancestors long ago.

Nahum

Why Read This Book:

- Discover how God can become angry when people don't follow him (Nahum 1).
- See how God's justice is victorious in the end (Nahum 2—3).

When?

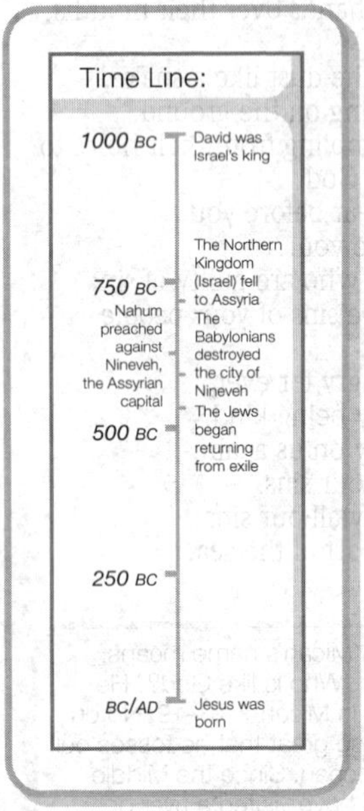

Behind the Scenes:

Think of the most powerful force in all the universe. Now imagine that force being angry. Scary, isn't it?

Nineveh – the capital of Assyria – heated God's anger to boiling point. The Assyrians had captured and destroyed Israel. For about 250 years, the brutal Assyrians had attacked and persecuted Israel and Judah. As a result, the city of Nineveh had come to symbolise everything evil.

The prophet Nahum announced the downfall of Nineveh, using a series of poems to convey his message. In these poems, we see God's anger at unrighteousness, and we see the wickedness of this city. Compare the book of Nahum with the book of Jonah (p.884), which also focuses on Nineveh. The comparison gives you a better sense of the many dimensions of God's personality. And in both books, we're reminded that God's strength extends to the whole world.

Where?

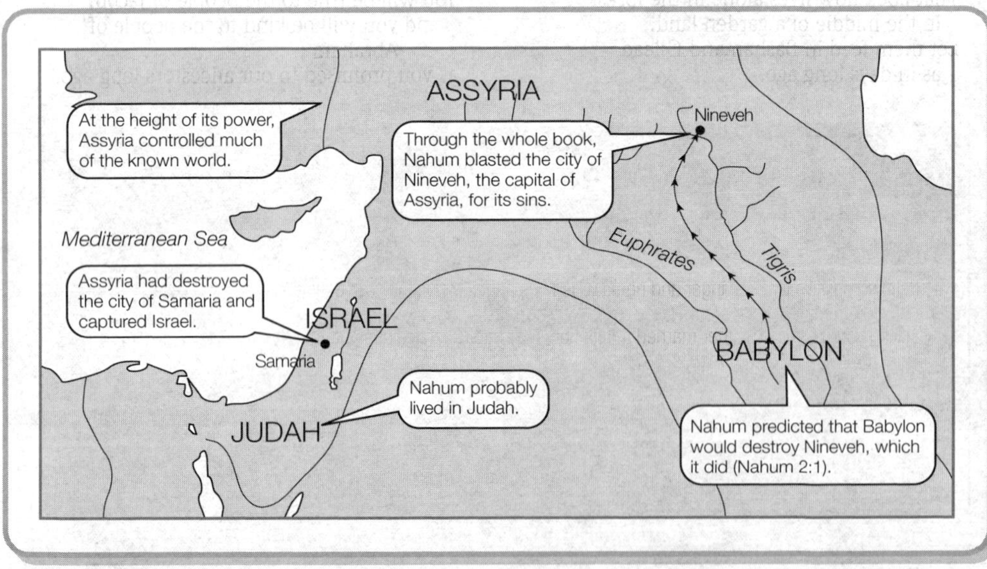

1 This is the message for the city of Nineveh.[n]
This is the book of the vision of Nahum, who
was from the town of Elkosh.

The LORD is Angry with Nineveh

2The LORD is a jealous God who punishes;
the LORD punishes and is filled with
anger.
The LORD punishes those who are
against him,
and he stays angry with his enemies.
3The LORD does not become angry quickly,
and his power is great.
The LORD will not let the guilty go
unpunished.
Where the LORD goes, there are whirlwinds
and storms,
and the clouds are the dust beneath his
feet.
4He speaks to the sea and makes it dry;
he dries up all the rivers.
The areas of Bashan and Carmel dry up,
and the flowers of Lebanon dry up.
5The mountains shake in front of him,
and the hills melt.
The earth trembles when he comes;

Nineveh The capital city of the country of Assyria. Nahum uses Nineveh to stand for all of Assyria.

JEALOUSY

Jealous Anger

After ten years of marriage and three children, David's commitment to his family began to wane. He started spending more time at the factory, and he was distant whenever he was home. Finally, he told his wife, Carol, that he had been having an affair for more than year. He was confused, he said, and guilt-ridden. He didn't expect Carol to forgive him, and even if she did, he wasn't sure he wanted the marriage to continue.

Carol was crushed. Their marriage had seemed so stable. Although they had fought more lately, David had always seemed to be a good father and husband.

Emotions flooded Carol. Sadness. Fear. Confusion. But, most of all, anger. She wanted to hurt the woman who had intruded into her family. "I hate her," Carol cried. "If I see her, I'll probably kill her – and maybe David too."

But Carol knew that wasn't the answer. So she prayed, and as she prayed, she believed that God wanted her to hold her family together. Carol channelled her anger into saving her family.

She told David that she loved him, she demanded that he cut off contact with the other woman; and she moved out until David could also decide that his family was worth fighting for.

One month later, David went to Carol. He told her that he wanted his family more than anything. He told her that he needed God back in his life. And he told her that the affair was over.

They have spent the past two years rebuilding their family with God's help.

God restored David and Carol's family because Carol channelled her jealous anger for good.

Read **Nahum 1:2–6** to find out how God uses his jealous anger against his enemies.

- How is God's jealous anger like Carol's? How is it different?
- What are some other ways in which jealous anger can have good results? What are its dangers?

Consider . . .

- defining positive jealous anger and negative jealous anger. Include in your definitions the difference between the two.
- asking your parents or other married adults how they have seen jealous anger in their relationship have positive or negative results.

For more, see . . .

- Hosea 11:1–11 (p.858)
- John 2:12–16 (p.1098)
- Jonah 4:1–11 (p.888)

the world and all who live in it shake with
fear.
6No one can stay alive when he is angry;
no one can survive his strong anger.
His anger is poured out like fire;
the rocks are smashed by him.

7The LORD is good,
giving protection in times of trouble.
He knows who trusts in him.
8But like a rushing flood,
he will completely destroy Nineveh;
he will chase his enemies until he kills
them.

Sidelight Nineveh was one of the oldest cities in Mesopotamia, and was situated next to the Tigris River, which is in what we now know as Iraq. It was a city of palaces and other beautiful buildings, and was looked upon as a powerful centre of trade and commerce. Today, however, Nineveh is only a vague memory – it has existed as nothing more than a pile of ruins ever since it was destroyed more than 2,500 years ago!

9The LORD will completely destroy
anyone making plans against him.
Trouble will not come a second time.
10Those people will be like tangled thorns
or like people drunk from their wine;
they will be burned up quickly like dry
weeds.
11Someone has come from Nineveh
who makes evil plans against the LORD
and gives wicked advice.

12This is what the LORD says:
"Although Assyria is strong and has many
people,
it will be defeated and brought to
an end.
Although I have made you suffer, Judah,
I will make you suffer no more.
13Now I will free you from their control
and tear away your chains."

14The LORD has given you this command,
Nineveh:
"You will not have descendants[d] to carry
on your name.
I will destroy the idols and metal images
that are in the temple of your gods.
I will make a grave for you,
because you are wicked."

15Look, there on the hills,
someone is bringing good news!
He is announcing peace!
Celebrate your feasts, people of Judah,
and give your promised sacrifices to God.
The wicked will not come to attack you
again;
they have been completely destroyed.

Nineveh will be Defeated

2 The destroyer[n] is coming to attack you,
Nineveh.
Guard the defences.
Watch the road.
Get ready.
Gather all your strength!
2Destroyers have destroyed God's people
and ruined their vines,
but the LORD will bring back Jacob's greatness
like Israel's greatness.

3The shields of his soldiers are red;
the army is dressed in red.
The metal on the chariots flashes like fire
when they are ready to attack;
their horses are excited.
4The chariots race through the streets
and rush back and forth through the city
squares.
They look like torches;
they run like lightning.
5He[n] calls his officers,
but they stumble on the way.
They hurry to the city wall,
and the shield is put into place.
6The river gates are thrown open,
and the palace is destroyed.
7It has been announced that the people of
Nineveh
will be captured and carried away.
The slave girls moan like doves
and beat their breasts, because they are sad.
8Nineveh is like a pool,
and now its water is draining away.
"Stop! Stop!" the people yell,
but no one turns back.
9Take the silver!
Take the gold!
There is no end to the treasure—
piles of wealth of every kind.
10Nineveh is robbed, ruined and destroyed.
The people lose their courage, and their
knees knock.
Stomachs ache, and everyone's face grows
pale.

destroyer The Babylonians, the Scythians and the Medes destroyed Nineveh.
He This probably means the king of Assyria.

11Where is the lions' [n] den
and the place where they feed their
young?
Where did the lion, lioness and cubs go
without being afraid?
12The lion killed enough for his cubs,
enough for his mate.
He filled his cave with the animals he caught;
he filled his den with meat he had killed.

13"I am against you, Nineveh,"
says the LORD All-powerful.
"I will burn up your chariots in smoke,
and the sword will kill your young lions.
I will stop you from hunting down others
on the earth,
and your messengers' voices
will no longer be heard."

It will be Terrible for Nineveh

3 How terrible it will be for the city that has
killed so many.
It is full of lies
and goods stolen from other countries.
It is always killing somebody.
2Hear the sound of whips
and the noise of the wheels.
Hear horses galloping
and chariots bouncing along!
3Horses are charging,
swords are shining,
spears are gleaming!
Many are dead;
their bodies are piled up—
too many to count.
People stumble over the dead bodies.

Sidelight The wartime cruelty of the Assyrians (Nahum 3:3) would have been similar to the terrible things that happened to the Jewish people in World War II. One Assyrian King boasted of building pyramids of chopped-off heads outside the enemy's city. Other kings stacked corpses like firewood near the conquered city's gates.

4The city was like a prostitute; [d]
she was charming and a lover of magic.
She made nations slaves with her
prostitution [d]
and her witchcraft. [d]

5"I am against you, Nineveh," says the LORD
All-powerful.
"I will pull your dress up over your face
and show the nations your nakedness
and the kingdoms your shame.
6I will throw filthy rubbish on you
and make a fool of you.
I will make people stare at you.
7Everyone who sees you will run away
and say,
'Nineveh is in ruins. Who will cry for her?'
Nineveh, where will I find anyone to
comfort you?"

8You are no better than Thebes, [n]
who sits by the Nile River
with water all around her.
The river was her defence;
the waters were like a wall around her.
9Cush and Egypt gave her endless strength;
Put and Libya supported her.
10But Thebes was captured
and went into captivity.
Her small children were beaten to death
at every street corner.
Lots [d] were thrown for her important men,
and all of her leaders were put in chains.

11Nineveh, you will be drunk too.
You will hide;
you will look for a place safe from the
enemy.
12All your defences are like fig trees with ripe
fruit.
When the tree is shaken, the figs fall into
the mouth of the eater.
13Look at your soldiers.
They are all women!
The gates of your land
are wide open for your enemies;
fire has burned the bars of your gates.

14Get enough water before the long war
begins.
Make your defences strong!
Get mud,
mix clay,
make bricks!
15There the fire will burn you up.
The sword will kill you;
like grasshoppers eating crops, the battle
will completely destroy you.
Grow in number like hopping locusts; [d]
grow in number like swarming locusts!
16Your traders are more than the stars in
the sky,
but like locusts, they strip the land and
then fly away.
17Your guards are like locusts.
Your officers are like swarms of locusts

lions' The symbol of Assyria was the lion.
Thebes A great city in Egypt.

that hang on the walls on a cold day.
When the sun comes up, they fly away,
and no one knows where they have gone.
18King of Assyria, your rulers are asleep;
your important men lie down to rest.
Your people have been scattered on the mountains,
and there is no one to bring them back.
19Nothing can heal your wound;
your injury will not heal.
Everyone who hears about you applauds,
because everyone has felt your endless cruelty.

Habakkuk

Why Read This Book:

- Listen to what God says about why wicked people prosper (Habakkuk 1—2).
- Learn the importance of waiting patiently for God (Habakkuk 3).

When?

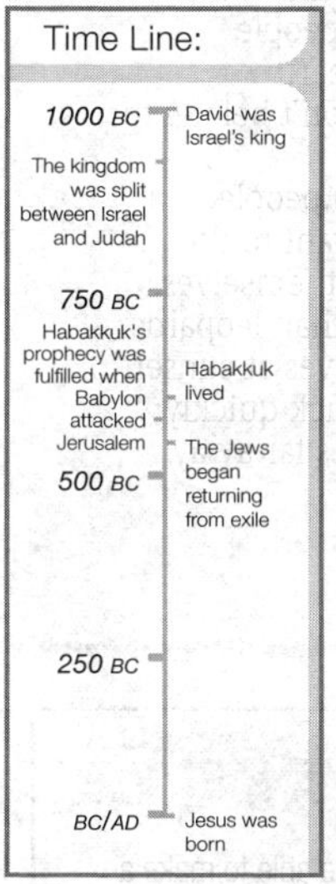

Behind the Scenes:

Sometimes it's hard to understand what God is doing in the world. Bad people seem to do well while good people suffer. Is God absent? Isn't he in control? Doesn't he have the power to control things? Or is God not a righteous God?

The prophet Habakkuk had those tough questions, and he wasn't afraid to ask them directly of God. His book takes the form of a question-and-answer session with God. Habakkuk asks the questions, and then God, through visions, gives answers:

Habakkuk: God, why don't you deliver your people from injustice?

God: Be patient. I've got it under control. The evil people will be punished.

Habakkuk: Why do you wait silently while wicked people destroy other people?

God: Justice will come. Live faithfully and you will be rewarded.

This short book is filled with comfort for people who suffer unjustly and for those who have trouble finding meaning in life. Not only does the prophet take honest questions to God, but the answers convince him that God is faithful and powerful.

"I will still be glad in the LORD," Habakkuk concludes. "I will rejoice in God my Saviour. The Lord God is my strength" (Habakkuk 3:18–19a). It's a reassuring message of faith and hope for all people who see life as meaningless or who suffer unjustly.

Where?

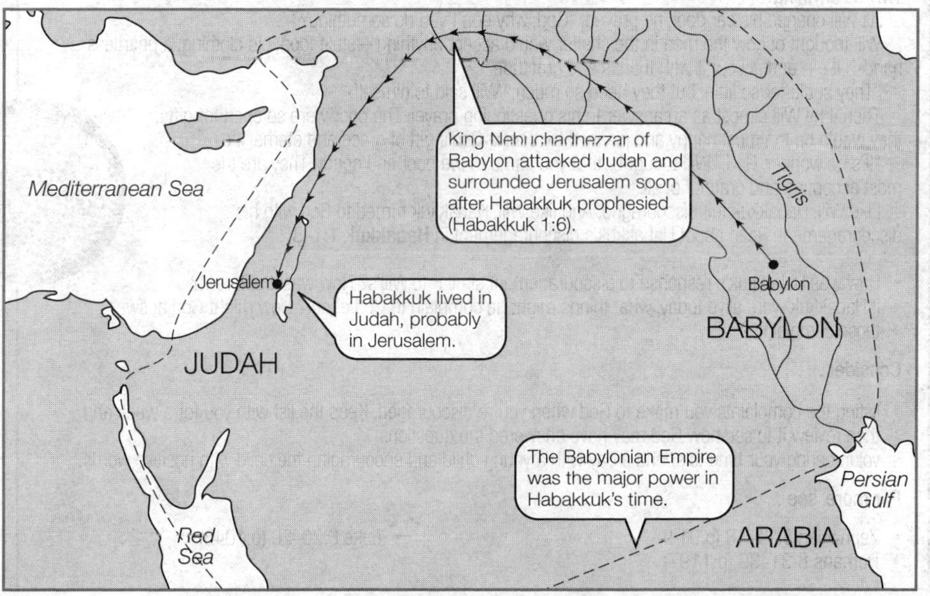

1 This is the message Habakkuk the prophet received.[d]

Habakkuk Complains

2 LORD, how long must I ask for help
and you ignore me?
I cry out to you about violence,
but you do not save us!
3 Why do you make me see wrong things
and make me look at trouble?
People are destroying things and hurting
others in front of me;
they are arguing and fighting.
4 So the teachings are weak,
and justice never comes.
Evil people gain while good people lose;
the judges no longer make fair
decisions.

The LORD Answers

5 "Look at the nations!
Watch them and be amazed and shocked.
I will do something in your lifetime
that you won't believe even when you are
told about it.
6 I will use the Babylonians,
those cruel and wild people
who march across the earth
and take lands that don't belong to
them.
7 They scare and frighten people.
They do what they want to do
and are good only to themselves.
8 Their horses are faster than leopards
and quicker than wolves at sunset.
Their horse soldiers attack quickly;
they come from places far away.

DISCOURAGEMENT

Is There Hope?

Will had volunteered to stay all night at the hostel for the homeless, hoping that he would be able to make a difference, hoping conditions might somehow change, hoping to feel needed and useful. The only thing that Will felt as he left the old building, though, was discouragement. As he left the shelter, he was glad to be free from the smell of old clothes, the sight of loneliness and the sounds of sadness.

He knew one thing: this type of service wasn't for him. He felt that he wasn't helpful and could do no good. Why do anything?

As Will opened his car door, he prayed, "God, why don't you do something?"

Will thought of how the men in the shelter would accept anything – stale food, old clothing, a heartless handshake – and accept it with thanks and gratitude.

"They settle for so little, but they need so much," Will said to himself.

Then it hit Will almost as an answer to his questioning prayer. The poor were so open for gifts; they would be the most happy and pleased to receive God's gift of grace and eternal life.

"It's no wonder, God," Will thought, "that you came to the poor and needy. They are the most accepting and grateful of all."

Like Will, Habakkuk felt discouraged. And like Will, Habakkuk turned to God with his discouragement. Read about Habakkuk's discouragement in **Habakkuk 1:1–3**.

- How was Habakkuk's response to discouragement similar to Will's? How was it different?
- If Habakkuk were alive today, what things might he complain to God about? How might God answer those complaints?

Consider . . .

- listing the complaints you make to God when you're discouraged. Keep the list with you for a week and then review it to see how God may have answered the questions.
- volunteering your time to spend a day with a young child and encouraging the child with positive words.

For more, see . . .

- Zephaniah 3:14–18 (p.914)
- Romans 8:31–39 (p.1197)
- Luke 6:20–26 (p.1048)

They attack quickly, like an eagle swooping
down for food.
9 They all come to fight.
Nothing can stop them.
Their prisoners are as many as the grains of
sand.
10They laugh at kings
and make fun of rulers.
They laugh at all the fortified cities
and build mounds of earth to the top of the
walls to capture them.
11Then they leave like the wind and
move on.
They are guilty of worshipping their own
strength."

Sidelight The name "Habakkuk" means "embracer" or "wrestler". This book of the Bible reads like a transcript of a telephone conversation – first Habakkuk complains to God, and then God responds. Read Habakkuk 1:1—2:17 for an example of this.

Habakkuk Complains Again

12LORD, you live for ever,
my God, my holy God.
We will not die.
LORD, you have chosen the Babylonians to
punish people;
our Rock,[d] you picked them to punish.
13Your eyes are too good to look at evil;
you cannot stand to see those who do
wrong.
So how can you put up with those evil
people?
How can you be quiet when the wicked
swallow up people who are better than
they are?
14You treat people like fish in the sea,
like sea creatures without a leader.
15The enemy brings them in with hooks.
He catches them in his net
and drags them in his nets.
So he rejoices and sings for joy.
16The enemy offers sacrifices to his net
and burns incense[d] to worship it,
because it lets him live like the rich
and enjoy the best food.
17Will he keep on taking riches with his
net?
Will he go on destroying people without
showing mercy?

2 I will stand like a guard to watch
and place myself at the tower.
I will wait to see what he will say to me;
I will wait to learn how God will answer
my complaint.

The LORD Answers

2The LORD answered me:
"Write down the vision;
write it clearly on clay tablets
so whoever reads it can run to tell
others.
3It is not yet time for the message to come
true,
but that time is coming soon;
the message will come true.
It may seem like a long time,
but be patient and wait for it,
because it will surely come;
it will not be delayed.
4The evil nation is very proud of itself;
it is not living as it should.
But those who are right with God will live
by trusting in him.

5"Just as wine can fool a person,
those who are too proud will not last,
because their desire is like a grave's desire for
death,
and like death they always want more.
They gather other nations for themselves
and collect for themselves all the
countries.
6But all the nations the Babylonians have hurt
will laugh at them.
They will make fun of the Babylonians
and say, 'How terrible it will be for the one
that steals many things.

Sidelight Wearing nose jewellery may be fashionable at different times, but people probably wouldn't be attracted to the "hooks" mentioned in Habakkuk 1:15. The verse may refer to the Assyrian practice of leading prisoners of war by rope that was attached to a hook pierced through the nose or lower lip.

How long will that nation get rich by
forcing others to pay them?'

7"One day the people from whom you have
taken money will turn against you.
They will realise what is happening and
make you shake with fear.
Then they will take everything you have.
8Because you have stolen from many
nations,

those who are left will take much
from you.
This is because you have killed many
people,
destroying countries and cities and
everyone in them.

9 “How terrible it will be for the nation that
becomes rich by doing wrong,
thinking they will live in a safe place
and escape harm.
10 Because you have made plans to destroy
many people,
you have made your own houses ashamed
of you.
Because of it, you will lose your lives.
11 The stones of the walls will cry out
against you,
and the boards that support the roof will
agree that you are wrong.

12 “How terrible it will be for the nation that
kills people to build a city,
that wrongs others just to start a town.
13 The LORD All-powerful will send fire
to destroy what those people have built;
all the nations' work will be for nothing.
14 Then, just as water covers the sea,
people everywhere will know the LORD's
glory.

15 “How terrible for the nation that makes its
neighbours drink,
pouring from the jug of wine until they are
drunk
so that it can look at their naked bodies.
16 You Babylonians will be filled with disgrace,
not respect.
It's your turn to drink and fall to the
ground like a drunk person.
The cup of anger from the LORD's right hand
is coming around to you.
You will receive disgrace, not respect.
17 You hurt many people in Lebanon,
but now you will be hurt.
You killed many animals there,

PATIENCE

I Want it Now!

It was easily the biggest and best film in the history of the universe. Or at least that is what the trailer, the magazines, film critics, and all the websites had said. Today was the premiere, and Mark was overcome with excitement.

He had rushed out of school on the “B of the bell” and got to the cinema in record time. Thirty minutes later and Mark was still alone in the room, even the adverts hadn't started. He began to get restless.

After a little while, Mark could take it no more. He stood, turned to face the projection room, and yelled out “HURRY UP!”

Read **Habakkuk 2:1–4**. In this passage, Habakkuk is learning to be patient. He finds out that God is in control and the best plan will happen, but in God's timing (which is perfect). Until then, he has to carry on being patient, and trusting in God.

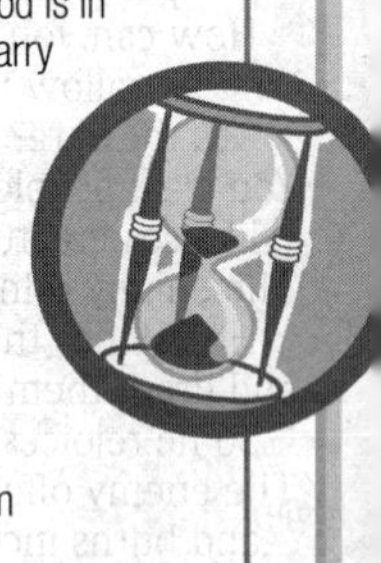

- What are the differences between the way the evil nation and the person right with God are described in verse 4?
- Read chapter 3. It's Habakkuk's final response. He remembers all that he has seen God do in the past. How might this help him to be patient and trust in God again for the future?

Consider . . .

- writing down all the wonderful things God has done in your past, and all the things you want him to do in your future. Thank him for the past and ask for help in trusting him for the future.
- talking to older people around you about things they have had to wait a long time for from God and learning from their experience.

For more, see . . .

- Psalm 37 (p.521)
- Hebrews 6:13–15 (p.1335)
- Galatians 5:22–23 (p.1264)

and now you must be afraid
because of what you did
to that land, those cities and the people
who lived in them.

The Message About Idols

18"An idol does no good, because a human
made it;
it is only a statue that teaches lies.
The one who made it expects his own work
to help him,
but he makes idols that can't even speak!
19How terrible it will be for the one who says
to a wooden statue, 'Come
to life!'
How terrible it will be for the one who
says to a silent stone, 'Get up!'
It cannot tell you what to do.
It is only a statue covered with gold and
silver;
there is no life in it.
20The LORD is in his Holy Temple; [d]
all the earth should be silent in his
presence."

Habakkuk's Prayer

3 This is the prayer of Habakkuk the prophet, [d]
on shigionoth. [d]

2LORD, I have heard the news about you;
I am amazed at what you have done.
LORD, do great things once again in our
time;
make those things happen again in our own
days.
Even when you are angry,
remember to be kind.

3God is coming from Teman;
the Holy One comes from Mount Paran. [n]
Selah [d]
His glory covers the skies,
and his praise fills the earth.
4He is like a bright light.
Rays of light shine from his hand,
and there he hides his power.
5Sickness goes before him,
and disease follows behind him.
6He stands and shakes the earth.
He looks, and the nations shake with fear.
The mountains, which stood for ages, break
into pieces;
the old hills fall down.
God has always done this.

7I saw that the tents of Cushan were in
trouble
and that the tents of Midian trembled.
8LORD, were you angry with the rivers,
or were you angry with the streams?
Were you angry with the sea
when you rode your horses and chariots of
victory? [n]
9You uncovered your bow
and commanded many arrows to be
brought to you. *Selah*
You split the earth with rivers.
10 The mountains saw you and shook with
fear.
The rushing water flowed.
The sea made a loud noise,
and its waves rose high.
11The sun and moon stood still in the sky;
they stopped when they saw the flash of
your flying arrows
and the gleam of your shining spear.
12In anger you marched on the earth;
in anger you punished the nations.
13You came out to save your people,
to save your chosen one.
You crushed the leader of the wicked
ones
and took everything he had, from head to
toe. *Selah*
14With the enemy's own spear you stabbed
the leader of his army.
His soldiers rushed out like a storm to
scatter us.
They were happy
as they were robbing the poor people in
secret.
15But you marched through the sea with your
horses,
stirring the great waters.

16I hear these things, and my body
trembles;
my lips tremble when I hear the
sound.
My bones feel weak,
and my legs shake.
But I will wait patiently for the day of
disaster
that will come to the people who
attack us.
17Fig trees may not grow figs,

Teman . . . Paran God is seen as again coming from the direction of Mount Sinai. He came from Sinai when he rescued his people from Egypt.
sea . . . victory This is probably talking about the Israelites crossing the Red Sea.

and there may be no grapes on the
vines.
There may be no olives growing
and no food growing in the
fields.
There may be no sheep in the pens
and no cattle in the barns.
18But I will still be glad in the LORD;
I will rejoice in God my Saviour.
19The Lord GOD is my strength.
He makes me like a deer that does not
stumble
so I can walk on the steep mountains.

For the director of music. On my stringed instruments.

Zephaniah

Why Read This Book:

- Discover what moral corruption can do to people (Zephaniah 1–2).
- Hear the promise of God's comfort for the faithful (Zephaniah 3).

When?

Behind the Scenes:

Have you ever had a really lousy day – so lousy that you were glad to go to bed to get it over with? When you woke up the next morning, you were determined to start out afresh, and you did everything to make sure the next day would be better.

In a sense, the people of Judah had just had a lousy hundred years. Their land had been controlled by the Assyrians. But now they had gained independence. They were ready to start a new day – to rebuild their nation and start again. King Josiah would lead them to new political strength.

But the people needed religious renewal as well. Domination by foreign powers had brought with it foreign customs and pagan gods. The Canaanite religion, Baalism, flourished in the country.

The prophet Zephaniah saw the corruption in the land and warned the people to change. As a prophet in Jerusalem, his ministry was probably influential in getting King Josiah to institute widespread religious reform based on the book of Deuteronomy (p.164).

Zephaniah's message to the people was that God would judge Judah for turning away from him. The book is filled with terrifying images of doom and punishment on "the Lord's day of judging" (Zephaniah 1:14). ▷

Where?

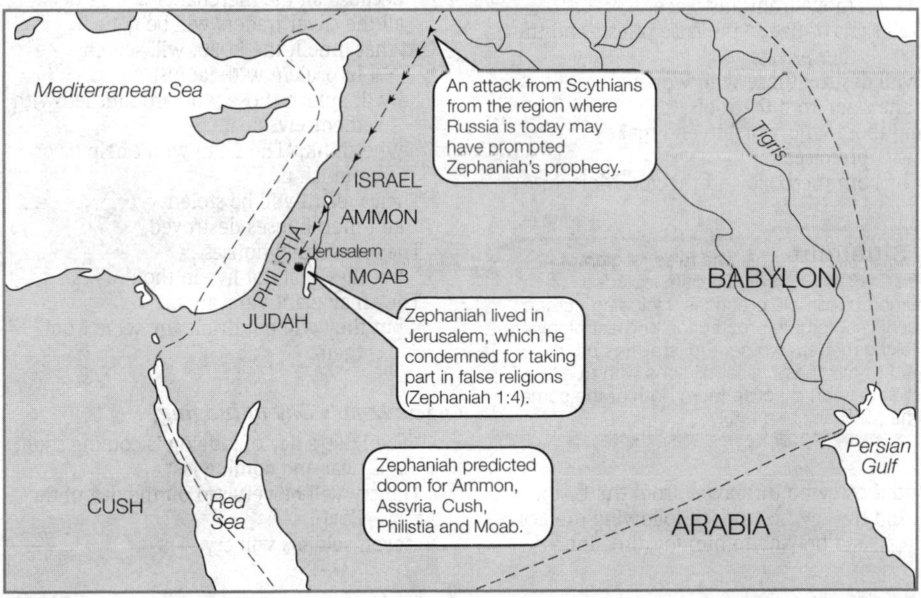

Behind the Scenes (cont.): But the book ends on a positive note, describing a time when people would return to God and the nation would be restored.

The book of Zephaniah has a message that's similar to that of many prophets: disaster will ultimately come for those who turn away from God. But God will build a new, lasting relationship with those who repent and serve him faithfully.

---

1 This is the word of the LORD that came through Zephaniah while Josiah son of Amon was king of Judah. Zephaniah was the son of Cushi, who was the son of Gedaliah. Gedaliah was the son of Amariah, who was the son of Hezekiah.

The LORD's Judgement

2"I will sweep away everything
from the earth," says the LORD.
3"I will sweep away the people and animals;
I will destroy the birds in the air
and the fish of the sea.
I will ruin the evil people,
and I will remove human beings from the earth," says the LORD.

The Future of Judah

4"I will punish Judah
and all the people living in Jerusalem.
I will remove from this place
all signs of Baal,[d] the false priests and the other priests.
5I will destroy those who worship
the stars from the roofs,[n]
and those who worship and make promises
by both the LORD and the god Molech,[d]

Sidelight The false religion of Baalism included numerous terrible practices, including human sacrifices, temple prostitution and astrology. Making matters worse, the Israelites often tried to mix these false religions with true religion – and practise them both at the same time (Zephaniah 1:4–5)!

6and those who turn away from the LORD,
and those who stopped following the LORD
and praying to him for direction.

7Be silent before the Lord GOD,
because the LORD's day for judging people is coming soon.
The LORD has prepared a sacrifice;
he has made holy his invited guests.
8On the day of the LORD's sacrifice,
I, the LORD, will punish the princes and the king's sons
and all those who wear foreign clothes.
9On that day I will punish those who worship Dagon,[d]
those who hurt others and tell lies in the temples of their gods.

10"On that day," says the LORD,
"a cry will be heard at the Fish Gate.
A wail will come from the new area of the city,
and a loud crash will echo from the hills.
11Cry, you people living in the market area,
because all the merchants will be dead;
all the silver traders will be gone.
12At that time I, the LORD, will search Jerusalem with lamps.
I will punish those who are satisfied with themselves,
who think, 'The LORD won't help us or punish us.'
13Their wealth will be stolen
and their houses destroyed.
They may build houses,
but they will not live in them.
They may plant vineyards,
but they will not drink any wine from them.

The LORD's Day of Judging

14"The LORD's day of judging is coming soon;
it is near and coming fast.
The cry will be very sad on the day of the LORD;
even soldiers will cry.

roofs In Bible times houses were built with flat roofs. The roof was used for drying things such as flax and fruit. And it was used as an extra room, as a place for worship and as a place to sleep in the summer.

15That day will be a day of anger,
a day of terror and trouble,
a day of destruction and ruin,
a day of darkness and gloom,
a day of clouds and blackness,
16a day of alarms and battle cries.
'Attack the strong, walled cities!
Attack the corner towers!'
17I will make life hard for the people;
they will walk around like the blind,
because they have sinned against the LORD.
Their blood will be poured out like dust,
and their insides will be dumped like
rubbish.
18On the day that God will show his anger,
neither their silver nor gold will save them.
The LORD's anger will be like a fire
that will burn up the whole world;
suddenly he will bring an end, yes, an end
to everyone on earth."

The LORD Asks People to Change

2 Gather together, gather,
you unwanted people.
2Do it before it's too late,
before you are blown away like chaff,[d]
before the LORD's terrible anger reaches
you,
before the day of the LORD's anger comes
to you.
3Come to the LORD, all you who are not
proud,
who obey his laws.
Do what is right. Learn to be humble.
Maybe you will escape
on the day the LORD shows his anger.

MONEY

Look Where it Got Them

Who, in 1923, was:

- president of the USA's largest steel company?
- president of the largest American gas company?
- president of the New York Stock Exchange?
- the greatest wheat speculator in America?
- the "Great Bear" of Wall Street?

In their day, these people made lots of money. They would have been considered the most successful men in the world. But look at what became of these successful moneybags:

- The president of the largest steel company, Charles Schwab, died penniless.
- The president of the largest gas company, Howard Hopson, went insane.
- The president of the New York Stock Exchange, Richard Whitney, was released from prison to die at home.
- Arthur Cutten, the greatest wheat speculator, died overseas – penniless and homeless.
- Mr C. Rivermore, the "Great Bear" of Wall Street, committed suicide.

Although these men had wealth and worldly success, their "kingdom" fell. They had based their lives and priorities on money, and money couldn't meet all their needs.

God wanted the people in Zephaniah's day to base their lives and priorities on much more than money. Read **Zephaniah 1:7–18** to learn more about God's directions and the limitations of money.

- How are the men in this story like the people in this passage?
- According to the Bible passage, what will happen to those who trust in money and riches?

Consider . . .

- giving some of your money and prized possessions to someone less fortunate.
- keeping track of the money you spend this week and evaluating whether your spending is pleasing to God.

For more, see . . .

- Ecclesiastes 7:11–12 (p.626)
- Mark 10:17–31 (p.1016)
- Matthew 6:19–34 (p.948)

Philistia will be Punished

4No one will be left in the city of Gaza,
and the city of Ashkelon will be destroyed.
Ashdod will be empty by noon,
and the people of Ekron will be chased away.
5How terrible it will be for you who live by the Mediterranean Sea,
you Philistines!
The word of the LORD is against you,
Canaan, land of the Philistines.

"I will destroy you
so that no one will be left."
6The land by the Mediterranean Sea, in which you live,
will become pastures, fields for shepherds and pens for sheep.
7It will belong to the descendants *d* of Judah who are left alive.
There they will let their sheep eat grass.
At night they will sleep
in the houses of Ashkelon.
The LORD their God will pay attention to them
and will make their life good again.

Moab and Ammon will be Punished

8"I have heard the insults of the country of Moab
and the threats of the people of Ammon.
They have insulted my people
and have taken their land."
9So the LORD All-powerful, the God of Israel, says,
"As surely as I live,
Moab will be destroyed like Sodom, *d*
and Ammon will be destroyed like Gomorrah *d*
a heap of weeds, a pit of salt
and a ruin for ever.
Those of my people who are left alive will take whatever they want from them;
those who are left from my nation will take their land."

10This is what Moab and Ammon get for being proud,
because they insulted and made fun of the people of the LORD All-powerful.
11The LORD will frighten them,
because he will destroy all the gods of the earth.
Then everyone in faraway places
will worship him wherever they are.

Cush and Assyria will be Destroyed

12"You Cushites also
will be killed by my sword."
13Then the LORD will turn against the north
and destroy Assyria.
He will make Nineveh
a ruin as dry as a desert.
14Flocks and herds will lie down there,
and all wild animals.
The owls and crows will sit
on the stone pillars.
The owl will call through the windows,
rubbish will be in the doorways,
and the wooden boards of the buildings will be gone.
15This is the happy and safe city
that thinks there is no one else as strong as it is.
But what a ruin it will be,
a place where wild animals live.
All those who pass by will make fun
and shake their fists.

Sidelight The nation of Cush (Zephaniah 2:12–14) is modern-day Ethiopia. By pairing Assyria and Cush in the passage, the prophet shows the broadness of God's judgement, since the two nations were in the extreme north and south of the known world at that time.

Jerusalem will be Punished

3 How terrible for the wicked, stubborn city of Jerusalem,
which hurts its own people.
2It obeys no voice;
it can't be taught to do right.
It doesn't trust the LORD;
it doesn't worship its God.
3Its officers are like roaring lions.
Its rulers are like hungry wolves that attack in the evening,
and in the morning nothing is left of those they attacked.
4Its prophets *d* are proud;
they are people who cannot be trusted.
Its priests don't respect holy things;
they break God's teachings.
5But the LORD is good, and he is there in that city.
He does no wrong.
Every morning he governs the people fairly;
every day he can be trusted.
But evil people are not ashamed of what they do.

6"I have destroyed nations;
their towers were ruined.

I made their streets empty
so no one goes there any more.
Their cities are ruined;
no one lives there at all.
7I said, 'Surely now Jerusalem will respect me
and will accept my teaching.'
Then the place where they lived would not
be destroyed,
and I would not have to punish them.
But they were still eager
to do evil in everything they did.
8Just wait," says the LORD.
"Some day I will stand up as a witness.
I have decided that I will gather nations
and assemble kingdoms.
I will pour out my anger on them,
all my strong anger.
My anger will be like fire
that will burn up the whole world.

A New Day for God's People

9"Then I will give the people of all nations
pure speech
so that all of them will speak the name of
the LORD
and worship me together.
10People will come from where the Nile River
begins;
my scattered people will come with gifts
for me.
11Then Jerusalem will not be ashamed
of the wrongs done against me,
because I will remove from this city
those who like to boast;

HAPPINESS

Singing Your Heart Out

Calvin loved footy and every week he would sing his heart out for his team. Chanting, clapping, singing – nothing gave Calvin a bigger buzz than watching his team win. And the songs didn't just stay in the stadium, everyone on the train and on his walk home would get to hear how happy Calvin and his mates were.

Calvin didn't just watch his team though – he played for them too. He had always been a talented player, but the turning point in Calvin's life was when he got signed at the age of twelve to play for the team he had always supported. It was a dream come true.

Over the years, Calvin worked hard playing for the youth teams and eventually, when he was eighteen, got to play for the reserves. Now Calvin was on the books a lot had changed. He was even getting up early in the mornings for training. One thing didn't change though – he still loved to watch his team play and would stand with thousands of others to sing and chant with joy at every goal.

When he was nineteen, Calvin played his first game for the first team. As he walked out of the tunnel and onto the pitch, the noise hit him. Looking up into the stands, Calvin slowly turned 360 degrees and absorbed the moment. Someone somewhere started a song and all the home fans joined in; it was deafening and the proudest day of Calvin's life. He had always been the one of the singers, celebrating and bigging up his team. Now the crowds were singing about him.

In **Zephaniah 3:14–18** the prophet tells Israel that they had got something to shout and sing about.

- What does the passage say that God's people should be celebrating?
- Like the crowd at Calvin's first game, verse 17 says that God will sing and be joyful about you. How does that make you feel?

Consider . . .

- re-reading the passage putting your own name in the place of "Jerusalem", "Israel" and "you".
- most football songs are famous tunes with the lyrics changed. Try rewriting one of your favourite songs with lyrics about God's love.

For more, see . . .

- Psalm 146 (p.586)
- 1 Peter 1:8 (p.1357)

there will never be any more proud people
on my holy mountain in Jerusalem.
12But I will leave in the city
the humble and those who are not proud,
and they will trust in the LORD.
13Those who are left alive in Israel won't do wrong
or tell lies;
they won't trick people with their words.
They will eat and lie down
with no one to make them afraid."

A Happy Song

14Sing, Jerusalem.
Israel, shout for joy!
Jerusalem, be happy
and rejoice with all your heart.
15The LORD has stopped punishing you;
he has sent your enemies away.
The King of Israel, the LORD, is with you;
you will never again be afraid of being harmed.
16On that day Jerusalem will be told,
"Don't be afraid, city of Jerusalem.
Don't give up.
17The LORD your God is with you;
the mighty One will save you.
He will rejoice over you.
You will rest in his love;
he will sing and be joyful about you."

18"I will take away the sadness planned for you,
which would have made you very ashamed.
19At that time I will punish
all those who harmed you.
I will save my people who cannot walk
and gather my people who have been thrown out.
I will give them praise and honour
in every place where they were shamed.
20At that time I will gather you;
at that time I will bring you back home.
I will give you honour and praise
from people everywhere
when I make things go well again for you,
as you will see with your own eyes," says the LORD.

Haggai

Why Read This Book:

- **Understand the importance of focusing on God's priorities instead of our own desires (Haggai 1).**
- **See the excitement of working together for God's glory (Haggai 2).**

When?

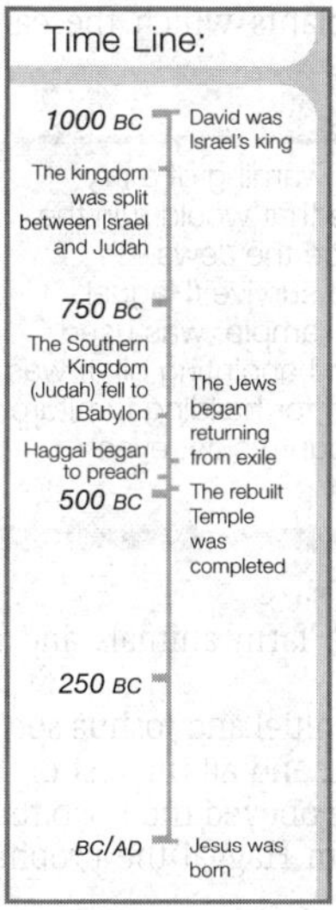

Behind the Scenes:

If you've ever moved, you know what it's like to get settled. You have to find your way around. You have to make new friends. You have to settle into a job or a school. In short, you are busy putting your new life together.

The Jewish people had just returned to Judah after being captives in Babylon. They were caught up in planting crops, repairing homes and earning a living.

But something was missing. While the Jews were enjoying their new freedom in their nice homes, God's Temple lay in ruins. God sent the prophet Haggai to show the Jews that their priorities were wrong: that they were being selfish and materialistic.

Building the Temple was important for the Jews, not so that they would have a place to worship, but as a symbol of God's leadership and lordship in the nation. It was the "place" of God's personal contact with his people. Haggai believed that the Temple would bring hope to a people who were depressed and struggling.

Haggai's ministry involved motivating people to complete God's Temple, which had been started almost twenty years earlier. Within three weeks, the people had started work on the Temple again. And four years later, the Temple was complete.

Though we don't face the challenge of building a Temple in Jerusalem, the book of Haggai still has important reminders for us. It reminds us to keep our priorities straight. And it reminds us to make God the centre of our lives – just as the Temple was the centre of life for the Jewish people.

Where?

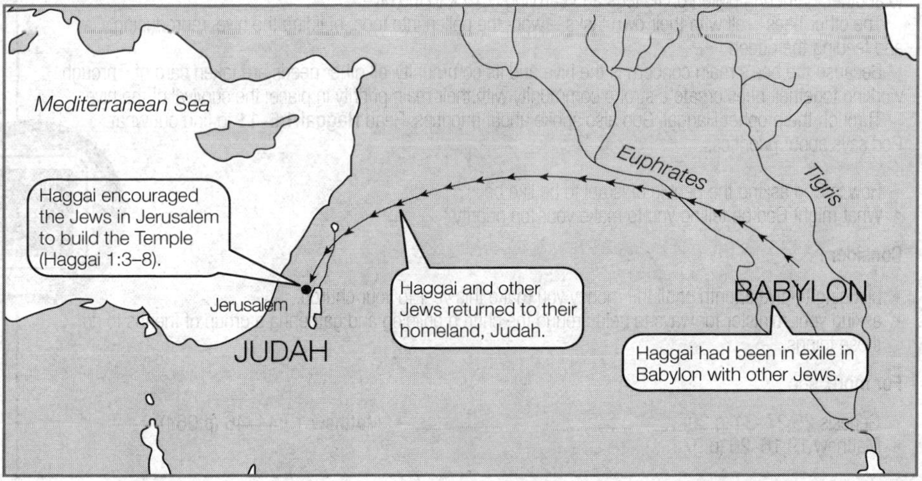

It is Time to Build the Temple

1 The prophet[d] Haggai spoke the word of the
LORD to Zerubbabel son of Shealtiel, the gov-
ernor of Judah, and to Joshua son of Jehozadak,
the high priest. This message came in the second
year that Darius was king, on the first day of the
sixth month:
2"This is what the LORD All-powerful says: 'The
people say the right time has not come to rebuild
the Temple[d] of the LORD.' "
3Then Haggai the prophet spoke the word of
the LORD: 4"Is it right for you to be living in fancy
houses while the Temple is still in ruins?"
5This is what the LORD All-powerful says:
"Think about what you have done. 6You have
planted much, but you harvest little. You eat, but
you do not become full. You drink, but you are
still thirsty. You put on clothes, but you are not
warm enough. You earn money, but then you
lose it all as if you had put it into a purse full of
holes."
7This is what the LORD All-powerful says:
"Think about what you have done. 8Go up to the
mountains, bring back wood and build the
Temple. Then I will be pleased with it and be
honoured," says the LORD. 9"You look for much,
but you find little. When you bring it home, I
destroy it. Why?" asks the LORD All-powerful.
"Because you all work hard for your own houses
while my house is still in ruins! 10Because of
what you have done, the sky holds back its rain
and the ground holds back its crops. 11I have
called for a time without rain on the land, and
on the mountains, and on the grain, the new
wine, the olive oil, the plants which the earth
produces, the people, the farm animals and all
the work of your hands."
12Zerubbabel son of Shealtiel and Joshua son of
Jehozadak, the high priest, and all the rest of the
people who were left alive obeyed the LORD their
God and the message from Haggai the prophet,

Sidelight The warning of a dry time that would ruin the harvest was alarming, since the Jews depended on the crops to survive (Haggai 1:11). The olive tree, for example, was used for food, fuel, medicine and anointing oil. It was also used in sacrifices and for building furniture. Olive trees covered the countryside, even growing on rocky hillsides.

PRIORITIES

The Way to Bee

It has no single home of its own. It makes nothing for itself. Yet the bee constantly works from one flower to another, gathering pollen on its legs and carrying it back to the hive.

The other bees – all with their own tasks – work the pollen into food, building the hive, reproducing, and feeding the queen.

Because the bee's main concern is the hive and its community, all other needs are taken care of. Through working together, bees create a strong community with their main priority in place: the survival of the hive.

Through the prophet Haggai, God also spoke about priorities. Read **Haggai 1:5–11** to find out what God says about priorities.

- How is God asking the people of Israel to be like bees?
- What might God be telling you to make your top priority?

1....
2....
3....

Consider . . .

- pledging to give a tenth of all the money you make this year to your church.
- asking your minister for ways to help around the church building and gathering a group of friends to do those things.

For more, see . . .

- Genesis 25:27–34 (p.30)
- Matthew 19:16–26 (p.974)
- Matthew 13:44–46 (p.964)

because the LORD their God had sent him. And
the people feared the LORD.
13Haggai, the LORD's messenger, gave the
LORD's message to the people, saying, "The LORD
says, 'I am with you.' " 14The LORD stirred up
Zerubbabel son of Shealtiel, the governor of
Judah, and Joshua son of Jehozadak, the high
priest, and all the rest of the people who were
left alive. So they came and worked on the Tem-
ple of their God, the LORD All-powerful. 15They
began on the twenty-fourth day of the sixth
month in the second year Darius was king.

The Beauty of the Temple

2 On the twenty-first day of the seventh month,
the LORD spoke his word through Haggai the
prophet,[d] saying, 2"Speak to Zerubbabel son of
Shealtiel, governor of Judah, and to Joshua son
of Jehozadak, the high priest, and to the rest of
the people who are left alive. Say, 3'Do any of you
remember how great the Temple[d] was before it
was destroyed? What does it look like now?
Doesn't it seem like nothing to you?' 4But the
LORD says, 'Zerubbabel, be brave. Also, Joshua
son of Jehozadak, the high priest, be brave. And
all you people who live in the land, be brave,'
says the LORD. 'Work, because I am with you,'
says the LORD All-powerful. 5'I made a promise to
you when you came out of Egypt, and my Spirit[d]
is still with you. So don't be afraid.'
6"This is what the LORD All-powerful says:
'In a short time I will once again shake the heav-
ens and the earth, the sea and the dry land. 7I
will shake all the nations, and they will bring
their wealth. Then I will fill this Temple with
glory,' says the LORD All-powerful. 8'The silver is
mine, and the gold is mine,' says the LORD All-
powerful. 9'The new Temple will be greater than
the one before,' says the LORD All-powerful. 'And
in this place I will give peace,' says the LORD
All-powerful."
10On the twenty-fourth day of the ninth
month in the second year Darius was king, the
LORD spoke his word to Haggai the prophet, say-
ing, 11"This is what the LORD All-powerful says:
'Ask the priests for a teaching. 12Suppose a
person carries in the fold of his clothes some
meat made holy for the LORD. If that fold touches
bread, cooked food, wine, olive oil or some other
food, will that be made holy?' "
The priests answered, "No."
13Then Haggai said, "A person who touches a
dead body will become unclean.[d] If he touches
any of these foods, will it become unclean, too?"
The priests answered, "Yes, it would become
unclean."
14Then Haggai answered, "The LORD says, 'This
is also true for the people of this nation. They are
unclean, and everything they do with their hands
is unclean to me. Whatever they offer at the altar
is also unclean.
15" 'Think about this from now on! Think about
how it was before you started laying stones on top
of stones to build the Temple of the LORD. 16A per-
son used to come to a pile of grain expecting to
find 20 basketfuls, but there were only ten. And a
person used to come to the wine vat to take out 50
jarfuls, but only 20 were there. 17I destroyed your
work with diseases, mildew[d] and hail, but you still
did not come back to me,' says the LORD. 18'It is
the twenty-fourth day of the ninth month, the day
in which the people finished working on the foun-
dation of the Temple of the LORD. From now on,
think about these things: 19Do you have seeds for
crops still in the barn? Your vines, fig trees, pome-
granates[d] and olive trees have not given fruit yet.
But from now on I will bless you!' "

The LORD Makes a Promise to Zerubbabel

20Then the LORD spoke his word a second time
to Haggai on the twenty-fourth day of the month.
He said, 21"Tell Zerubbabel, the governor of Judah,
'I am going to shake the heavens and the earth.
22I will destroy the foreign kingdoms and take
away the power of the kingdoms of the nations.
I will destroy the chariots and their riders. The
horses will fall with their riders, as people kill
each other with swords.' 23The LORD All-powerful
says, 'On that day I will take you, Zerubbabel son
of Shealtiel, my servant,' says the LORD, 'and I will
make you important like my signet[d] ring, because
I have chosen you!' says the LORD All-powerful."

Zechariah

Why Read This Book:

- **Be challenged to follow God and do his will (Zechariah 1–8).**
- **Find encouragement in knowing a glorious, peaceful future awaits God's people (Zechariah 9–14).**

When?

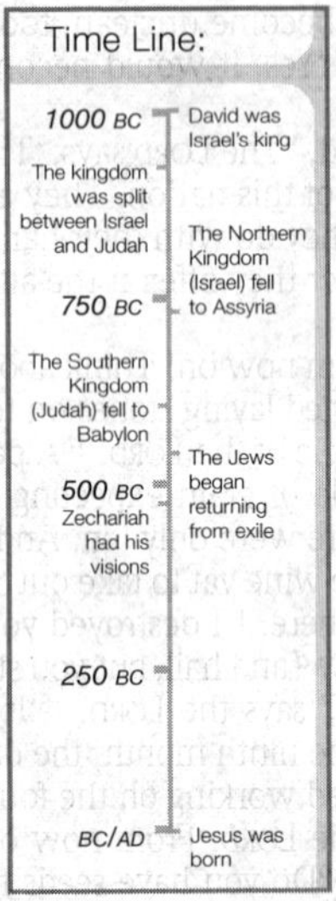

Behind the Scenes:

When you work on something, you like to see results. You want to know that your hard work will be worth the time and energy you've invested.

The people of Israel also wanted to see results when they started rebuilding their Temple. They wanted to know that they would be blessed for what they were doing.

The prophet Zechariah was there to assure them and encourage them. Like his colleague Haggai (p.915), who ministered at the same time, Zechariah believed that completing the Temple would be the first step towards bringing God's kingdom to earth.

Zechariah's encouragement came in a series of visions about the Temple (Zechariah 1:7–6:8). Each vision in the first part of the book shows activity between heaven and earth. They each show a world that's changing, and they have a universal theme – that God is bigger than the Temple or Judah. Through each vision, Zechariah encourages the people to rebuild the Temple and to focus on following God so that they will be ready for the coming of God's kingdom.

The second part of Zechariah (chapters 9–14) has a different focus. It concentrates on the coming kingdom of God instead of the Temple. In the coming age, the wicked will be destroyed and the righteous will be saved. This new kingdom will focus on justice, kindness and mercy rather than on rituals of religion.

The book of Zechariah has been treasured by Christians because many of its images of the Messiah (such as the Prince of Peace, Zechariah 9:9–10), foreshadow Jesus Christ's life and ministry. Just as Zechariah offered encouragement, hope and joy to the people of his day, so the book offers encouragement, hope and joy to us today.

LIFE FILE LINKS

Investigate the Theme

To find a list of real life stories on this subject turn to the LIFE FILE GUIDE on pages 12 to 22 at the front of the Youth Bible.

LEADERSHIP

The LORD *Calls His People Back*

1 In the eighth month of Darius' second year
as king, the LORD spoke his word to the
prophet[d] Zechariah son of Berekiah, who was the
son of Iddo. The LORD said, 2"The LORD was very
angry with your ancestors. 3So tell the people:
this is what the LORD All-powerful says: 'Return
to me, and I will return to you,' says the LORD
All-powerful. 4Don't be like your ancestors. In
the past the prophets said to them: this is what
the LORD All-powerful says: 'Stop your evil ways
and evil actions.' But they wouldn't listen or pay
attention to me, says the LORD. 5Your ancestors
are dead, and those prophets didn't live for ever.
6I commanded my words and laws to my ser-
vants the prophets, and they preached to your
ancestors, who returned to me. They said, 'The
LORD All-powerful did as he said he would. He
punished us for the way we lived and for what
we did.'"

Sidelight If you were to try and count the names in the phone book that begin with the letter "Z", the chances are that you wouldn't come up with many. But in the Bible, the name Zechariah alone (Zechariah 1:1) was used for more than 30 people! These included a gatekeeper (1 Chronicles 26:2, p.395), a harpist (1 Chronicles 15:20, p.387) and a trumpet-blowing priest (1 Chronicles 15:24, p.387). The Zechariah in this book was a prophet and probably also a priest.

The Vision of the Horses

7It was on the twenty-fourth day of the elev-
enth month, which is the month of Shebat, in
Darius' second year as king. The LORD spoke his
word to the prophet[d] Zechariah son of Berekiah,
who was the son of Iddo.
8During the night I had a vision. I saw a man
riding a red horse. He was standing among some
myrtle trees in a ravine, with red, brown and
white horses behind him.
9I asked, "What are these, sir?"
The angel who was talking with me answered,
"I'll show you what they are."
10Then the man standing among the myrtle
trees explained, "They are the ones the LORD sent
through all the earth."
11Then they spoke to the LORD's angel, who
was standing among the myrtle trees. They said,
"We have gone through all the earth, and every-
thing is calm and quiet."
12Then the LORD's angel asked, "LORD All-
powerful, how long will it be before you show
mercy to Jerusalem and the cities of Judah? You
have been angry with them for 70 years now."
13So the LORD answered the angel who was talk-
ing with me, and his words were comforting and
good.
14Then the angel who was talking to me said to
me, "Announce this: this is what the LORD All-
powerful says: 'I have a strong love for Jerusalem.
15And I am very angry with the nations that feel
so safe. I was only a little angry at them, but they
made things worse.'
16"So this is what the LORD says: 'I will return
to Jerusalem with mercy. My Temple[d] will be
rebuilt,' says the LORD All-powerful, 'and the mea-
suring line will be used to rebuild Jerusalem.'
17"Also announce: this is what the LORD All-
powerful says: 'My towns will be rich again. The
LORD will comfort Jerusalem again, and I will
again choose Jerusalem.'"

The Vision of the Horns

18Then I looked up and saw four animal horns.
19I asked the angel who was talking with me,
"What are these?"
He said, "These are the horns that scattered
the people of Judah, Israel and Jerusalem."
20Then the LORD showed me four craftsmen. 21I
asked, "What are they coming to do?"
He answered, "They have come to scare and
throw down the horns. These horns scattered
the people of Judah so that no one could even lift
up his head. These horns stand for the nations
that attacked the people of Judah and scattered
them."

The Vision of the Measuring Line

2 Then I looked up and saw a man holding a
line for measuring objects. 2I asked him,
"Where are you going?"
He said to me, "I am going to measure
Jerusalem, to see how wide and how long it is."
3Then the angel who was talking with me left,
and another angel came out to meet him. 4The
second angel said to him, "Run and tell that
young man, 'Jerusalem will become a city with-
out walls, because there will be so many people
and cattle in it. 5I will be a wall of fire around it,'
says the LORD. 'And I will be the glory within it.'
6"Oh no! Oh no! Run away from Babylon, be-
cause I have scattered you like the four winds of
heaven," says the LORD.
7"Oh no, Jerusalem! Escape, you who live right
in Babylon." 8This is what the LORD All-powerful
says: "After he has honoured me and sent me
against the nations who took your possessions—
because whoever touches you hurts what is
precious to me— 9I will shake my hand against
them so that their slaves will rob them."

Then you will know that the LORD All-powerful sent me.

10"Shout and be glad, Jerusalem. I am coming, and I will live among you," says the LORD. 11"At that time people from many nations will join with the LORD and will become my people. Then I will live among you, and you will know that the LORD All-powerful has sent me to you. 12The LORD will take Judah as his own part of the holy land, and Jerusalem will be his chosen city again. 13Be silent, everyone, in the presence of the LORD. He is coming out of the holy place where he lives."

The Vision of the High Priest

3 Then he showed me Joshua, the high priest, standing in front of the LORD's angel. And Satan was standing by Joshua's right side to accuse him. 2The LORD said to Satan, "The LORD says no to you, Satan! The LORD who has chosen Jerusalem says no to you! This man was like a burning stick pulled from the fire."

3Joshua was wearing dirty clothes and was standing in front of the angel. 4The angel said to those standing in front of him, "Take off those dirty clothes."

Then the angel said to Joshua, "Look, I have taken away your sin from you, and I am giving you beautiful, fine clothes."

5Then I said, "Put a clean turban on his head." So they put a clean turban on his head and dressed him while the LORD's angel stood there.

6Then the LORD's angel said to Joshua, 7"This is what the LORD All-powerful says: 'If you do as I tell you and serve me, you will be in charge of my Temple [d] and my courtyards. And I will let you be with these angels who are standing here.

8" 'Listen, Joshua, the high priest, and your friends who are sitting in front of you. They stand for what will happen. I am going to bring my servant called the Branch. 9Look, I put this stone in front of Joshua, a stone with seven sides. I will carve a message on it,' says the LORD All-powerful. 'And in one day I will take away the sin of this land.'

10"The LORD All-powerful says, 'In that day, each of you will invite your neighbour to sit under your own grapevine and under your own fig tree.' "

The Vision of the Lampstand

4 Then the angel who was talking with me returned and woke me up as if I had been asleep. 2He asked me, "What do you see?"

I said, "I see a solid gold lampstand with a bowl at the top. And there are seven lamps and also seven places for wicks. 3There are two olive trees by it, one on the right of the bowl and the other on the left."

4I asked the angel who talked with me, "Sir, what are these?"

5The angel said, "Don't you know what they are?"

"No, sir," I said.

6Then he told me, "This is the word of the LORD to Zerubbabel: 'You will not succeed by your own strength or power, but by my Spirit,' [d] says the LORD All-powerful.

7"Who are you, big mountain? In front of Zerubbabel you will become flat land, and he will bring out the topmost stone, shouting, 'It's beautiful! It's beautiful!' "

8Then the LORD spoke his word to me again, saying, 9"Zerubbabel has laid the foundation of this Temple, [d] and he will complete it. Then you will know that the LORD All-powerful has sent me to you.

10"The people should not think that small beginnings are unimportant. They will be happy when they see Zerubbabel with tools, building the Temple.

"(These are the seven eyes of the LORD, which look back and forth across the earth.)"

11Then I asked the angel, "What are the two olive trees on the right and left of the lampstand?"

12I also asked him, "What are the two olive branches beside the two gold pipes, from which the olive oil flows to the lamps?"

13He answered, "Don't you know what they are?"

"No, sir," I said.

14So he said, "They stand for the two who have been appointed to serve the LORD of all the earth."

Sidelight Though the flying scroll of Zechariah 5 had impressive dimensions, it doesn't hold the record. Archaeologists have discovered scrolls that would stretch almost half the length of a football field. Try fitting one of those textbooks into your locker!

The Vision of the Flying Scroll

5 I looked up again and saw a flying scroll.

2The angel asked me, "What do you see?"

I answered, "I see a flying scroll, 10 metres long and 5 metres wide."

3And he said to me, "This is the curse that will go all over the land. One side says every thief will be taken away. The other side says everyone who makes false promises will be taken away. 4The LORD All-powerful says, 'I will send it to the houses of thieves and to those who use my name to make false promises. The scroll will stay in that person's house and destroy it with its wood and stones.' "

The Vision of the Woman

[5]Then the angel who was talking with me came forwards and said to me, "Look up and see what is going out."

[6]"What is it?" I asked.

He answered, "It is a measuring basket going out." He also said, "It stands for the people's sins in all the land."

[7]Then the lid made of lead was raised, and there was a woman sitting inside the basket. [8]The angel said, "The woman stands for wickedness." Then he pushed her back into the basket and put the lid back down.

[9]Then I looked up and saw two women going out with the wind in their wings. Their wings were like those of a stork, and they lifted up the basket between earth and the sky.

[10]I asked the angel who was talking with me, "Where are they taking the basket?"

[11]"They are going to Babylonia to build a temple for it," he answered. "When the temple is ready, they will set the basket there in its place."

The Vision of the Four Chariots

6 I looked up again and saw four chariots going out between two mountains, mountains of bronze. [2]Red horses pulled the first chariot. Black horses pulled the second chariot. [3]White horses pulled the third chariot, and strong, spotted horses pulled the fourth chariot. [4]I asked the angel who was talking with me, "What are these, sir?"

[5]He said, "These are the four spirits of heaven. They have just come from the presence of the Lord of the whole world. [6]The chariot pulled by the black horses will go to the land of the north. The white horses will go to the land of the west, and the spotted horses will go to the land of the south."

[7]When the powerful horses went out, they were eager to go through all the earth. So he said, "Go through all the earth," and they did.

[8]Then he called to me, "Look, the horses that went north have caused my spirit to rest in the land of the north."

A Crown for Joshua

[9]The LORD spoke his word to me, saying, [10]"Take silver and gold from Heldai, Tobijah and Jedaiah, who were captives in Babylon. Go that same day to the house of Josiah son of Zephaniah, who came from Babylon. [11]Make the silver and gold into a crown, and put it on the head of Joshua son of Jehozadak, the high priest. [12]Tell him this is what the LORD All-powerful says: 'A man whose name is the Branch will branch out from where he is, and he will build the Temple[d] of the LORD. [13]One man[n] will build the Temple of the LORD, and the other[n] will receive honour. One man will sit on his throne and rule, and the other will be a priest on his throne. And these two men will work together in peace.' [14]The crown will be kept in the Temple of the LORD to remind Heldai, Tobijah, Jedaiah and Josiah son of Zephaniah. [15]People living far away will come and build the Temple of the LORD. Then you will know the LORD All-powerful has sent me to you. This will happen if you completely obey the LORD your God."

The People Should Show Mercy

7 In Darius' fourth year as king, on the fourth day of the ninth month, which is called Kislev, the LORD spoke his word to Zechariah. [2]The city of Bethel sent Sharezer, Regem-Melech and their men to ask the LORD a question. [3]They went to the prophets[d] and priests who were at the Temple[d] of the LORD All-powerful. The men said, "For years in the fifth month of each year we have shown our sadness and gone without food. Should we continue to do this?"

[4]The LORD All-powerful spoke his word to

Sidelight In Zechariah 7:4–10, God criticises the prophets and priests for fasting simply to make themselves feel better while failing to love and care for the people around them. Compare Zechariah 7:9–10 with James 1:26–27 (p.1348).

me, saying, [5]"Tell the priests and the people in the land: 'For 70 years you went without food and cried in the fifth and seventh months, but that was not really for me. [6]And when you ate and drank, it was really for yourselves. [7]The LORD used the earlier prophets to say the same thing, when Jerusalem and the surrounding towns were at peace and wealthy, and people settled in the southern area and the western hills.' "

[8]And the LORD spoke his word to Zechariah again, saying, [9]"This is what the LORD All-powerful says: 'Do what is right and true. Be kind

One man This probably refers to Zerubbabel.
other This probably refers to Joshua.

and merciful to each other. 10Don't hurt widows
and orphans, foreigners or the poor; don't even
think of doing evil to somebody else.'
11"But they refused to pay attention; they
were stubborn and did not want to listen any
more. 12They made their hearts as hard as rock
and would not listen to the teachings of the
LORD All-powerful. And they would not hear the
words he sent by his Spirit through the earlier
prophets. So the LORD All-powerful became very
angry.
13" 'When I called to them, they would not
listen. So when they called to me, I would not
listen,' says the LORD All-powerful. 14'I scattered
them like a hurricane to other countries which
they did not know. This good land was left so
ruined behind them that no one could live there.
They had made the desired land a ruin.' "

The LORD will Bless Jerusalem

8 The LORD All-powerful spoke his word, say-
ing, 2this is what the LORD All-powerful says:
"I have a very strong love for Jerusalem. My
strong love for her is like a fire burning in me."
3This is what the LORD says: "I will return to
Jerusalem and live in it. Then it will be called the
City of Truth, and the mountain of the LORD All-
powerful will be called the Holy Mountain."
4This is what the LORD All-powerful says:
"Old men and old women will again sit along
Jerusalem's streets, each carrying a cane because
of age. 5And the streets will be filled with boys
and girls playing."
6This is what the LORD All-powerful says:
"Those who are left alive then may think it is too
difficult to happen, but it is not too difficult for
me," says the LORD All-powerful. 7This is what
the LORD All-powerful says: "I will save my people
from countries in the east and west. 8I will bring
them back, and they will live in Jerusalem. They
will be my people, and I will be their good and
loyal God."
9This is what the LORD All-powerful says:
"Work hard, you who are hearing these words
today. The prophets spoke these words when the
foundation was laid for the house of the LORD
All-powerful, for the building of the Temple.[d]
10Before that time there was no money to hire
people or animals. People could not safely come
and go because of their enemies; I had turned
everyone against his neighbour. 11But I will not
do to these people who are left what I did in the
past," says the LORD All-powerful.
12"They will plant their seeds in peace, their
grapevines will have fruit, the ground will give
good crops, and the sky will send rain. I will give
all this to the people who are left alive. 13Judah
and Israel, your names have been used as curses
in other nations. But I will save you, and you will
become a blessing. So don't be afraid; work hard."
14This is what the LORD All-powerful says:
"When your ancestors made me angry, I planned
to punish you. I did not change my mind," says
the LORD All-powerful. 15"But now I will do some-
thing different. I am planning to do good to
Jerusalem and Judah. So don't be afraid. 16These
are the things you should do: tell each other the
truth. In the courts judge with truth and com-
plete fairness. 17Do not make plans to hurt your
neighbours, and don't love false promises. I hate
all these things," says the LORD.
18The LORD All-powerful spoke his word to me
again. 19This is what the LORD All-powerful says:
"The special days when you give up eating in the
fourth, fifth, seventh and tenth months will be-
come good, joyful, happy feasts in Judah. But you
must love truth and peace."
20This is what the LORD All-powerful says:
"Many people from many cities will still come to
Jerusalem. 21People from one city will go and say
to those from another city, 'We are going to pray
to the LORD and to ask the LORD All-powerful for
help. Come and go with us.' 22Many people and
powerful nations will come to worship the LORD
All-powerful in Jerusalem and to pray to the LORD
for help."
23This is what the LORD All-powerful says: "At
that time, ten men from different countries will
come and take hold of a Judean by his coat. They
will say to him, 'Let us go with you, because we
have heard that God is with you.' "

Punishment on Israel's Enemies

9 This message is the word of the LORD.

The message is against the land of Hadrach
and the city of Damascus.
The tribes[d] of Israel and all people
belong to the LORD.
2The message is also against the city of
Hamath, on the border,
and against Tyre and Sidon, with their skill.
3Tyre has built a strong wall for herself.
She has piled up silver like dust
and gold like the mud in the streets.
4But the Lord will take away all she has
and destroy her power on the sea.
That city will be destroyed by fire.
5The city of Ashkelon will see it and be afraid.
The people of Gaza will shake with fear,
and the people of Ekron will lose hope.
No king will be left in Gaza,
and no one will live in Ashkelon any more.
6Foreigners will live in Ashdod,
and I will destroy the pride of the
Philistines.

7I will stop them from drinking blood
and from eating forbidden food.
Those left alive will belong to God.
They will be leaders in Judah,
and Ekron will become like the Jebusites.
8I will protect my Temple[d]
from armies who would come or go.
No one will hurt my people again,
because now I am watching them.

Sidelight In times of peace, royalty would ride on a donkey, rather than on a white horse (which symbolised war). In Zechariah 9:9, the prophet pictures the future king of Jerusalem riding on a donkey, bringing peace and hope with him.

The King is Coming

9Rejoice greatly, people of Jerusalem!
Shout for joy, people of Jerusalem!
Your king is coming to you.
He does what is right, and he saves.
He is gentle and riding on a donkey,
on the colt of a donkey.
10I will take away the chariots from Ephraim
and the horses from Jerusalem.
The bows used in war will be broken.
The king will talk to the nations about peace.
His kingdom will go from sea to sea,
and from the Euphrates River to the ends of the earth.
11As for you, because of the blood of the agreement with you
I will set your prisoners free from the dry pit.
12You prisoners who have hope,
return to your place of safety.
Today I am telling you
that I will give you back twice as much as before.
13I will use Judah like a bow
and Ephraim like the arrows.
Jerusalem, I will use your men
to fight the men of Greece.
I will use you like a warrior's sword.

14Then the LORD will appear above them,
and his arrows will shoot like lightning.
The Lord GOD will blow the trumpet,
and he will march in the storms of the south.
15The LORD All-powerful will protect them;
they will destroy the enemy with catapults.
They will drink and shout like drunkards.
They will be filled like a bowl
used for sprinkling blood at the corners of the altar.
16On that day the LORD their God will save them
as if his people were sheep.
They will shine in his land
like jewels in a crown.
17They will be so pretty and beautiful.
The young men will grow strong on the grain
and the young women on new wine.

The LORD's Promises

10 Ask the LORD for rain during the springtime.
The LORD is the one who makes the clouds.
He sends the showers
and gives everyone green fields.
2Idols tell lies;
fortune-tellers see false visions
and tell about false dreams.
The comfort they give is worth nothing.
So the people are like lost sheep.
They are abused, because there is no shepherd.

3The LORD says, "I am angry with my shepherds,
and I will punish the leaders.
I, the LORD All-powerful, care
for my flock, the people of Judah.
I will make them like my proud war horses.
4From Judah will come the cornerstone,[d]
and the tent peg,
the battle bow,
and every ruler.
5Together they will be like soldiers
marching to battle through muddy streets.
The LORD is with them,
so they will fight and defeat the horsemen.

6"I will strengthen the people of Judah
and save the people of Joseph.
I will bring them back,
because I care about them.
It will be as though
I had never left them,
because I am the LORD their God,
and I will answer them.
7The people of Ephraim will be strong like soldiers;
they will be as glad as when they have drunk wine.
Their children will see it and rejoice;
they will be happy in the LORD.
8I will call my people
and gather them together.
I will save them,

and they will grow in number as they grew
in number before.
9 I have scattered them among the nations,
but in those faraway places, they will
remember me.
They and their children will live and
return.
10 I will bring them back from the land of
Egypt
and gather them from Assyria.
I will bring them to Gilead and Lebanon
until there isn't enough room for them all.
11 They will come through the sea of trouble.
The waves of the sea will be calm,
and the Nile River will dry up.
I will defeat Assyria's pride
and destroy Egypt's power over other
countries.
12 I will make my people strong,
and they will live as I say," says the LORD.

11 Lebanon, open your gates
so fire may burn your cedar trees.[n]
2 Cry, pine trees, because the cedar has fallen,
because the tall trees are ruined.
Cry, oaks in Bashan,
because the mighty forest has been cut
down.
3 Listen to the shepherds crying
because their rich pastures are destroyed.
Listen to the lions roaring
because the lovely land of the Jordan River
is ruined.

The Two Shepherds

4 This is what the LORD my God says: "Feed the flock that are about to be killed. 5 Their buyers kill them and are not punished. Those who sell them say, 'Praise the LORD, I am rich.' Even the shepherds don't feel sorry for their sheep. 6 I don't feel sorry any more for the people of this country," says the LORD. "I will let everyone be under the power of his neighbour and king. They will bring trouble to the country, and I will not save anyone from them."

7 So I fed the flock about to be killed, particularly the weakest ones. Then I took two sticks; I called one Pleasant and the other Union, and I fed the flock. 8 In one month I got rid of three shepherds. The flock did not pay attention to me, and I got impatient with them. 9 I said, "I will no longer take care of you like a shepherd. Let those that are dying die, and let those that are to be destroyed be destroyed. Let those that are left eat each other."

10 Then I broke the stick named Pleasant to break the agreement God made with all the nations. 11 That day it was broken. The weak ones in the flock who were watching me knew this message was from the LORD.

12 Then I said, "If you want to pay me, pay me. If not, then don't." So they paid me 30 pieces of silver.

13 The LORD said to me, "Throw the money to the potter." That is how little they thought I was worth.[n] So I took the 30 pieces of silver and threw them to the potter in the Temple[d] of the LORD.

14 Then I broke the second stick, named Union, to break the brotherhood between Judah and Israel.

15 Then the LORD said to me, "Get the things used by a foolish shepherd again, 16 because I am going to get a new shepherd for the country. He will not care for the dying sheep, or look for the young ones, or heal the injured ones or feed the healthy. But he will eat the best sheep and tear off their hoofs.

17 "How terrible it will be for the useless
shepherd
who abandoned the flock.
A sword will strike his arm and his right eye.
His arm will lose all its strength,
and his right eye will go blind."

Jerusalem will be Saved

12 This message is the word of the LORD to Israel. This is what the LORD says, who stretched out the skies, and laid the foundations of the earth, and put the human spirit within: 2 "I will make Jerusalem like a cup of poison to the nations around her. They will come and attack Jerusalem and Judah. 3 One day all the nations on earth will come together to attack Jerusalem, but I will make it like a heavy rock; anyone who tries to move it will get hurt. 4 At that time I will confuse every horse and cause its rider to go mad," says the LORD. "I will watch over Judah, but I will blind all the horses of the enemies. 5 Then the leaders of Judah will say to themselves, 'The people of Jerusalem are strong, because the LORD All-powerful is their God.'

6 "At that time I will make the leaders of Judah like a fire burning a stack of wood or like a fire burning straw. They will destroy all the people around them left and right. But the people of Jerusalem will remain safe.

7 "The LORD will save the homes of Judah first so that the honour given to David's family and to

trees In this poem, trees, bushes and animals stand for leaders of countries around Judah.
worth This was a small amount. It was about the price paid for a slave.

the people of Jerusalem won't be greater than the
honour given to Judah. 8At that time the LORD
will protect the people in Jerusalem. Then even
the weakest of them will be strong like David.
And the family of David will be like God, like an
angel of the LORD in front of them. 9At that time
I will go to destroy all the nations that attack
Jerusalem.

Crying for the One They Stabbed

10"I will pour out on David's family and the
people in Jerusalem a spirit of kindness and
mercy. They will look at me, the one they have
stabbed, and they will cry like someone crying
over the death of an only child. They will be as
sad as someone who has lost a firstborn[d] son.
11At that time there will be much crying in
Jerusalem, like the crying for Hadad Rimmon in
the plain of Megiddo. 12The land will cry, each
family by itself: the family of David by itself and
their wives by themselves, the family of Nathan
by itself and their wives by themselves, 13the fam-
ily of Levi by itself and their wives by themselves,
the family of Shimei by itself and their wives by
themselves, 14and all the rest of the families by
themselves and their wives by themselves.

13 "At that time a fountain will be open for
David's descendants[d] and for the people
of Jerusalem to cleanse them of their sin and
uncleanness."
2The LORD All-powerful says, "At that time I
will get rid of the names of the idols from the
land; no one will remember them any more. I
will also remove the prophets[d] and unclean[d] spir-
its from the land. 3If a person continues to proph-
esy, his own father and mother, the ones who
gave birth to him, will tell him, 'You have told
lies using the LORD's name, so you must die.'
When he prophesies, his own father and mother
who gave birth to him will stab him.
4"At that time the prophets will be ashamed of
their visions and prophecies. They won't try to
trick people by wearing the prophet's clothes
made of hair. 5Each of them will say, 'I am not a
prophet. I am a farmer and have been a farmer

SADNESS

Stabbed in the Back

Youth leader Hannah felt cheated and abused by her youth group. After returning from a recent retreat, she discovered that one of the older teenagers had bought and supplied beer and spirits for the younger kids on the trip.

When the group returned home, the word got out. Parents rang Hannah the next day, asking how such a thing could happen.

Hannah had no idea how it had happened. That was what made it so embarrassing. She thought she knew the group. Now she wasn't so sure. She had trusted the kids. Now she could make no promises.

Hannah spent the next month talking to all the kids who had been on the retreat. She shared her anger, pain and sadness. She also showed the group that she still loved them. Then she worked – against heavy opposition – to plan another youth retreat, one that could be done properly.

When the kids saw how much Hannah cared for them and how they had abused her trust in them, they felt sad and sorry. The sadness they felt was much like the sadness described in **Zechariah 12:7–10**.

- How did Hannah's youth group act like the people described in verse 10?
- According to this passage, how does God feel when we disobey?

Consider . . .

- listening carefully to a friend the next time he or she is sad.
- rewriting Zechariah 12:7–9, substituting your own name for "the people of Judah", "the people in Jerusalem" and "the family of David". Read the passage on bad days.

For more, see . . .

- Job 2:11–13 (p.471)
- Luke 19:41–44 (p.1083)
- Mark 15:33–34 (p.1030)

since I was young.' 6But someone will ask, 'What
are the deep cuts on your body?' And each will
answer, 'I was hurt at my friend's house.'

The Shepherd is Killed

7"Sword, hit the shepherd.
Attack the man who is my friend,"
says the LORD All-powerful.

> **Sidelight** If false prophets tried to get new jobs, they would have had trouble hiding their previous occupation. The deep cuts on their bodies (Zechariah 13:6) were probably self-inflicted while they were prophesying.

"Kill the shepherd,
and the sheep will scatter,
and I will punish the little ones."
8The LORD says, "Two-thirds of the people
through all the land will die. They will be
gone,
and one-third will be left.
9The third that is left I will test with fire,
purifying them like silver,
testing them like gold.
Then they will call on me,
and I will answer them.
I will say, 'You are my people,'
and they will say, 'The LORD is our God.' "

The Day of Punishment

14 The LORD's day of judging is coming
when the wealth you have taken will be
divided among you.
2I will bring all the nations together to fight
Jerusalem. They will capture the city and rob the
houses and attack the women. Half the people
will be taken away as captives, but the rest of the
people won't be taken from the city.
3Then the LORD will go to war against those
nations; he will fight as in a day of battle. 4On
that day he will stand on the Mount of Olives,[d]
east of Jerusalem. The Mount of Olives will split
in two, forming a deep valley that runs east and
west. Half the mountain will move towards the
north, and half will move towards the south.
5You will run through this mountain valley to
the other side, just as you ran from the earth-
quake when Uzziah was king of Judah. Then the
LORD my God will come and all the holy ones
with him.
6On that day there will be no light, cold or
frost. 7There will be no other day like it, and the
LORD knows when it will come. There will be no
day or night; even at evening it will still be light.
8At that time fresh water will flow from
Jerusalem. Half of it will flow east to the Dead Sea,[d]
and half will flow west to the Mediterranean
Sea. It will flow in summer and winter.
9Then the LORD will be king over the whole
world. At that time there will be only one LORD,
and his name will be the only name.
10All the land south of Jerusalem from Geba to
Rimmon will be turned into a plain. Jerusalem
will be raised up, but it will stay in the same
place. The city will reach from the Benjamin
Gate, to the First Gate, to the Corner Gate, and
from the Tower of Hananel to the king's wine-
presses.[d] 11People will live there, and it will
never be destroyed again. Jerusalem will be safe.
12But the LORD will bring a terrible disease on
the nations that fought against Jerusalem. Their
flesh will rot away while they are still standing
up. Their eyes will rot in their sockets, and their
tongues will rot in their mouths. 13At that time
the LORD will cause panic. Everybody will grab
his neighbour, and they will attack each other.
14The people of Judah will fight in Jerusalem. And
the wealth of the nations around them will be
collected—much gold, silver and clothes. 15A
similar disease will strike the horses, mules,
camels, donkeys and all the animals in the camps.
16All of those left alive of the people who came
to fight Jerusalem will come back to Jerusalem
year after year to worship the King, the LORD All-
powerful, and to celebrate the Feast[d] of Shelters.
17Anyone from the nations who does not go to
Jerusalem to worship the King, the LORD All-
powerful, will not have rain fall on his land. 18If
the Egyptians do not go to Jerusalem, they will
have no rain. Then the LORD will send them the
same terrible disease he sent the other nations
that did not celebrate the Feast of Shelters.
19This will be the punishment for Egypt and any
nation which does not go to celebrate the Feast
of Shelters.
20At that time the horses' bells will have writ-
ten on them: HOLY TO THE LORD. The cooking pots
in the Temple[d] of the LORD will be like the holy
altar bowls. 21Every pot in Jerusalem and Judah
will be holy to the LORD All-powerful, and every-
one who offers sacrifices will be able to take food
from them and cook in them. At that time there
will not be any buyers or sellers in the Temple of
the LORD All-powerful.

Malachi

Why Read This Book:

- Learn how to be loyal when things are tough (Malachi 1—2).
- Claim God's promise in the midst of discouragement (Malachi 3).

When?

Time Line:

- 1000 BC — David was Israel's king
- The kingdom was split between Israel and Judah
- The Northern Kingdom (Israel) fell to Assyria
- 750 BC
- The Southern Kingdom (Judah) fell to Babylon
- The Jews began returning from exile
- 500 BC
- Malachi ministered in Jerusalem
- 250 BC
- BC/AD — Jesus was born

Behind the Scenes:

Everything was supposed to be better now. The Jewish people returned to Jerusalem from exile, excited by the promises of Haggai (p.915) and Zechariah (p.918) about the coming of God's kingdom. But many years had passed, and life seemed about the same as it had always been – if not worse.

The community was still poor. Droughts and locusts continually ruined crops. Families were falling apart through divorce and adultery. The poor were being abused. And, worst of all, people had forgotten their faith. They just went through the motions of worshipping God.

In short, times were hard and God seemed far away. Why even try? the people seemed to say. They were upset and impatient. It seemed that God had not carried through his part of the agreement.

Enter Malachi, whose name means "my messenger". He pointed out how the country's priests were abusing or neglecting their God-given responsibilities. Their failure, the prophet said, was the main reason why things hadn't got any better. The prophet then challenged people to return to their faith. Then, at the time of judgement, the faithful would receive God's blessing.

When things don't go as we expect or hope, it's easy to think that God has let us down. And it's easy to relax our faith. But the book of Malachi urges us to stay strong. God loves us and is faithful, even when we can't see him working. We can have courage and hope in knowing that, in the end, God has a great future for all those that follow him.

LIFE FILE LINKS

Investigate the Theme

To find a list of real life stories on this subject turn to the LIFE FILE GUIDE on pages 12 to 22 at the front of the Youth Bible.

JUSTICE

1 This message is the word of the LORD given to Israel through Malachi.

God Loves Israel

2The LORD said, "I have loved you."

But you ask, "How have you loved us?"

The LORD said, "Esau and Jacob were brothers. I loved Jacob, 3but I hated Esau. I destroyed his mountain country and left his land to the wild dogs of the desert."

4The people of Edom might say, "We were destroyed, but we will go back and rebuild the ruins."

But the LORD All-powerful says, "If they rebuild them, I will destroy them. People will say, 'Edom is a wicked country. The LORD is always angry with the Edomites.' 5You will see these things with your own eyes. And you will say, 'The LORD is great, even outside the borders of Israel!' "

The Priests Don't Respect God

6The LORD All-powerful says, "A child honours his father, and a servant honours his master. I am a father, so why don't you honour me? I am a master, so why don't you respect me? You priests do not respect me.

"But you ask, 'How have we shown you disrespect?'

7"You have shown it by bringing unclean[d] food to my altar.

"But you ask, 'What makes it unclean?'

"It is unclean because you don't respect the altar of the LORD. 8When you bring blind animals as sacrifices, that is wrong. When you bring crippled and sick animals, that is wrong. Try giving them to your governor. Would he be pleased with you? He wouldn't accept you," says the LORD All-powerful.

9"Now ask God to be kind to you, but he won't accept you with such offerings," says the LORD All-powerful.

10"I wish one of you would close the Temple[d] doors so that you would not light useless fires on my altar! I am not pleased with you and will not accept your gifts," says the LORD All-powerful. 11"From the east to the west I will be honoured among the nations. Everywhere they will bring incense[d] and clean offerings to me, because I will be honoured among the nations," says the LORD All-powerful.

12"But you don't honour me. You say about the Lord's altar, 'It is unclean, and the food has no worth.' 13You say, 'We are tired of doing this,' and you sniff at it in disgust," says the LORD All-powerful.

"And you bring hurt, crippled and sick animals as gifts. You bring them as gifts, but I won't accept them from you," says the LORD. 14"The person who cheats will be cursed. He has a male animal in his flock and promises to offer it, but then he offers to the Lord an animal that has something wrong with it. I am a great king," says the LORD All-powerful, "and I am feared by all the nations.

Rules for Priests

2 "Priests, this command is for you. 2Listen to me. Pay attention to what I say. Honour my name," says the LORD All-powerful. "If you don't, I will send a curse on you and on your blessings. I have already cursed them, because you don't pay attention to what I say.

3"I will punish your descendants.[d] I will smear your faces with the animal insides left from your feasts, and you will be thrown away with it. 4Then you will know that I am giving you this command so my agreement with Levi will continue," says the LORD All-powerful. 5"My agreement for priests was with the tribe[d] of Levi. I promised them life and peace so they would honour me. And they did honour me and fear me. 6They taught the true teachings and spoke no lies. With peace and honesty they did what I said they should do, and they kept many people from sinning.

7"A priest should teach what he knows, and people should learn the teachings from him, because he is the messenger of the LORD All-powerful. 8But you priests have stopped obeying me. With your teachings you have caused many people to do wrong. You have broken the agreement with the tribe[d] of Levi!" says the LORD All-powerful. 9"You have not been careful to do what I say, but instead you take sides in court cases. So I have caused you to be hated and disgraced in front of everybody."

Judah was Not Loyal to God

10We all have the same father; the same God made us. So why do people break their promises to each other and show no respect for the agreement our ancestors made with God? 11The people of Judah have broken their promises. They have done something God hates in Israel and Jerusalem: the people of Judah did not respect the Temple[d] that the LORD loves, and the men of Judah married women who worship foreign gods. 12Whoever does this might bring offerings to the LORD All-powerful, but the LORD will still cut that person off from the community of Israel.

13This is another thing you do. You cover the LORD's altar with your tears. You cry and moan, because he does not accept your offerings and is not pleased with what you bring. 14You ask, "Why?" It is because the LORD sees how you treated the wife you married when you

were young. You broke your promise to her, even
though she was your partner and you had an agree-
ment with her. 15God made husbands and wives to
become one body and one spirit for his purpose—
so they would have children who are true to God.
So be careful, and do not break your promise
to the wife you married when you were young.
16The LORD God of Israel says, "I hate divorce.
And I hate people who do cruel things as easily as
they put on clothes," says the LORD All-powerful.
So be careful. And do not break your trust.

The Special Day of Judging

17You have tired the LORD with your words.
You ask, "How have we tired him?"
You did it by saying, "The LORD thinks anyone
who does evil is good, and he is pleased with
them." Or you asked, "Where is the God who is
fair?"

3 The LORD All-powerful says, "I will send my
messenger, who will prepare the way for
me. Suddenly, the Lord you are looking for will
come to his Temple; [d] the messenger of the agree-
ment, whom you want, will come." 2No one can
live through that time; no one can survive when
he comes. He will be like a purifying fire and like
laundry soap. 3Like someone who heats and puri-
fies silver, he will purify the Levites and make them
pure like gold and silver. Then they will bring offer-
ings to the LORD in the right way. 4And the LORD
will accept the offerings from Judah and Jerusalem,
as it was in the past. 5The LORD All-powerful says,
"Then I will come to you and judge you. I will be
quick to testify against those who take part in
evil magic, adultery [d] and lying under oath, those
who cheat workers of their pay and who cheat
widows and orphans, those who are unfair to
foreigners, and those who do not respect me.

GOD'S POWER

The Power of Right

Laura, the Head Girl, had a remarkable power over the school. The school hall could be full, and all Laura needed to do to quieten things down was to stand up, look out over the crowd and wait. Within a minute the whole hall would be quiet.

Where did Laura get her power?

Ask her fellow students:

"I trust her. If she says she's going to do something, she always does her best to do it."

Ask her teachers:

"She's truthful and honest. She owns up to her mistakes and will always try to do better. She even helps others through their mistakes."

Ask her friends' parents:

"I like her sincerity. Laura will listen to my daughter if she has a problem. She's a good friend who's there for others."

People had no reason to doubt Laura and countless reasons to admire her.

As you get to know God, you'll discover a God who has the ultimate powerful qualities of trust, honesty and sincerity. Read **Malachi 3:1–4** about the promised "messenger" of God whose power is like a purifying fire. This "messenger" is the promised Messiah, the Son of God.

- How much greater is God's power in Malachi than that of Laura?
- What area of your life needs the purifying power of God?

Consider . . .

- choosing one of the symbols of God's power from the passage (matches, laundry soap, silver or gold) and keeping it in your room as a reminder of God's power.
- wearing something gold or silver every day this week to remind you to pray for God's purifying power in your life.

For more, see . . .

- Psalm 51:10–13 (p.530)
- Revelation 21:1–8 (p.1403)
- Isaiah 25:1–5 (p.663)

Stealing from God

6"I the LORD do not change. So you descend-
ants[d] of Jacob have not been destroyed. 7Since
the time of your ancestors, you have disobeyed
my rules and have not kept them. Return to
me, and I will return to you," says the LORD
All-powerful.
"But you ask, 'How can we return?'
8"Should a person rob God? But you are rob-
bing me.
"You ask, 'How have we robbed you?'
"You have robbed me in your offerings and the
tenth of your crops. 9So a curse is on you, be-
cause the whole nation has robbed me. 10Bring to
the storehouse a full tenth of what you earn so
there will be food in my house. Test me in this,"
says the LORD All-powerful. "I will open the win-
dows of heaven for you and pour out all the bless-
ings you need. 11I will stop the insects so they
won't eat your crops. The grapes won't fall from
your vines before they are ready to pick," says the
LORD All-powerful. 12"All the nations will call you
blessed, because you will have a pleasant coun-
try," says the LORD All-powerful.

The LORD's Promise of Mercy

13The LORD says, "You have said terrible things
about me.

END TIMES

Don't Know When

Just because James had been on a couple of camping trips before, read a few books and seen countless "survival" programmes on TV, he thought he knew everything. He confidently set up the camp fire and threw enough wood on it to last him the night. But as the flames grew higher, a gust of wind suddenly scattered the hot embers and before he knew it, trees all around him were ablaze. He managed to escape and raise the alarm, but by now the damage was done and he could only watch in horror as the fire spread across the hillside.

It is estimated that over two-thirds of forest fires are started – accidentally or on purpose – by humans. Thousands and thousands of acres of forest are destroyed every year and when they burn out of control because of dry conditions and strong winds. Even people's houses caught in the path of the advancing flames go up in smoke too.

But not all wildfires are preventable. Many are inevitable – they will always happen somewhere, at some time because lightning is a common cause of fires, as well.

In such cases, most of the vegetation, trees and plants, is destroyed by the flames, but some animals manage to escape, relying on their instinct and abilities to survive. Every kind of animal has a different strategy. Deer, foxes and bears move quickly, so they can often escape the area affected. Other animals can't move as fast, so mice, snakes and lizards burrow deep into underground nests to escape the fire above.

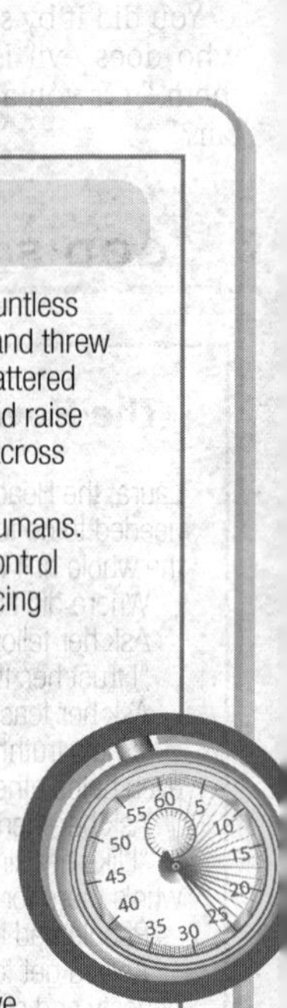

It's impossible to tell when forest fires are going to happen, but they will. And when they do, some things will be destroyed but some things will survive.

Read **Malachi 4:1–2**. It talks about a day when some people will be destroyed and others will live. But nobody knows when it will be.

- What day are the verses describing?
- How are those who "honour God" (verse 2) protected from the fire that will burn the "proud and evil people" (verse 1)?

Consider . . .

- ways in which you can honour God. Think of three practical things you can do, and share them with a friend so that they can help you do them.
- how you can talk to your non-Christian friends about the day of judgement.

For more, see . . .

- Psalm 68:1–4 (p.538)
- 1 Peter 4:4–5 (p.1360)
- Luke 3:7–9 (p.1042)

"But you ask, 'What have we said about you?'

Sidelight Malachi wanted every week to be like a Harvest Festival. Since food in Old Testament times was often as valuable as money is today, the people were called upon to give the first 10 per cent of their crops, and so show that they put God first (Malachi 3:6–10).

14"You have said, 'It is useless to serve God. It
did no good to obey his laws and to show the
LORD All-powerful that we were sorry for what
we did. 15So we say that proud people are happy.
Evil people succeed. They challenge God and get
away with it.' "
16Then those who honoured the LORD spoke
with each other, and the LORD listened and heard
them. The names of those who honoured the
LORD and respected him were written in his pres-
ence in a book to be remembered.
17The LORD All-powerful says, "They belong to
me; on that day they will be my very own. As a
parent shows mercy to his child who serves him,
I will show mercy to my people. 18You will again
see the difference between good and evil people,
between those who serve God and those who
don't.

The Day of the LORD's Judging

4 "There is a day coming that will burn like a
hot furnace, and all the proud and evil peo-
ple will be like straw. On that day they will be
completely burned up so that not a root or branch
will be left," says the LORD All-powerful. 2"But
for you who honour me, goodness will shine on
you like the sun, with healing in its rays. You
will jump around, like well-fed calves. 3Then
you will crush the wicked like ashes under your
feet on the day I will do this," says the LORD
All-powerful.
4"Remember the teaching of Moses my ser-
vant, those laws and rules I gave to him on
Mount Sinai for all the Israelites.
5"But I will send you Elijah the prophet[d] before
that great and terrifying day of the LORD's judging.
6Elijah will help parents love their children and
children love their parents. Otherwise, I will
come and put a curse on the land."

NEW
Testament

Matthew

When?

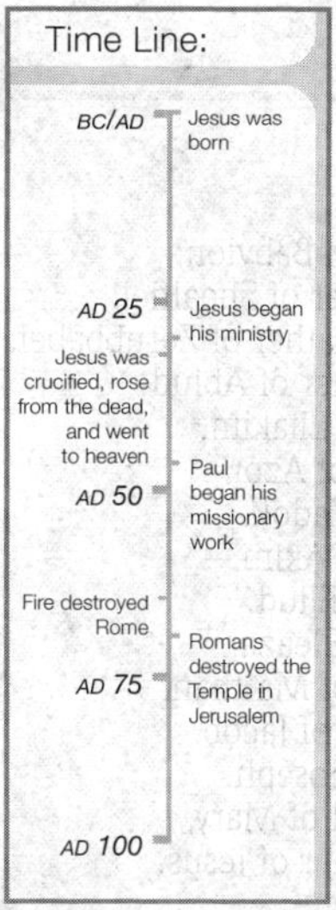

Why Read This Book:

- Learn how Jesus filled the role of the Messiah – the Saviour whose coming was anticipated in the Old Testament (Matthew 1—4).
- Find guidelines for living (Matthew 5—7).
- Understand Jesus' power as shown through many miracles and stories (Matthew 8—20).
- See what happened to Jesus that led to his death and resurrection (Matthew 21—28).

Behind the Scenes:

When you go for a job interview, your employers will want to know all about you, particularly if you are to be trusted with people's lives or their money. They will ask questions about your background. Where do you come from? Have you kept your word in the past? Are you honest? Are you reliable?

In the book of Matthew, the author digs into Jesus' background. He starts by listing Jesus' family tree – or genealogy – and then starts telling his life story in a simple yet dynamic style. Matthew quotes the Old Testament more than any of the other three gospels (he uses 53 actual quotations, and many more passing references) in order to prove to us that Jesus is God's promised Messiah to the Jews and Saviour of the Gentiles. Thanks to the author's linking Old Testament prophecies with the life of Jesus, this book acts as a "bridge" for us between the Old and New Testaments.

The Jews expected God to send a political Messiah who would set up a powerful kingdom here on earth, and were shocked that Jesus didn't seem to fit into the role that they had imagined. ▷

Where?

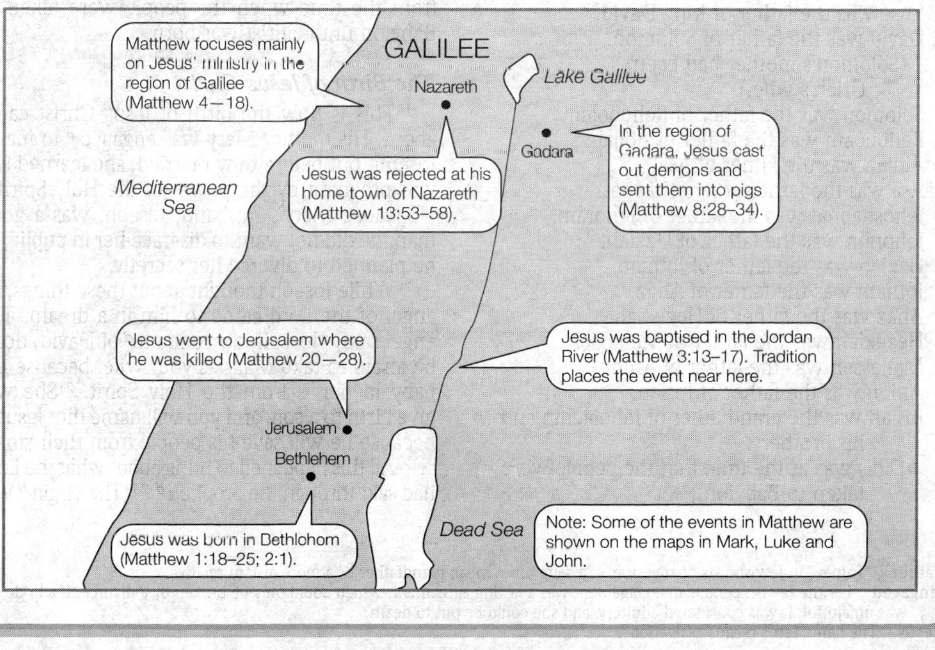

Behind the Scenes (cont.): Because of this, Matthew emphasises Jesus' teachings about what his kingdom would really be like, and proclaims him to be not only a king, but the King of Kings – the best of the best!

The grand finale of this book is a moving account of Jesus' last days on earth (Chapters 26–28), ending with his glorious resurrection and return to heaven.

The Family History of Jesus

1 This is the family history of Jesus Christ. He came from the family of David, and David came from the family of Abraham.
2Abraham was the father [n] of Isaac.
Isaac was the father of Jacob.
Jacob was the father of Judah and his brothers.
3Judah was the father of Perez and Zerah.
(Their mother was Tamar.)
Perez was the father of Hezron.
Hezron was the father of Ram.
4Ram was the father of Amminadab.
Amminadab was the father of Nahshon.
Nahshon was the father of Salmon.
5Salmon was the father of Boaz.
(Boaz's mother was Rahab.)
Boaz was the father of Obed.
(Obed's mother was Ruth.)
Obed was the father of Jesse.
6Jesse was the father of King David.
David was the father of Solomon.
(Solomon's mother had been Uriah's wife.)
7Solomon was the father of Rehoboam.
Rehoboam was the father of Abijah.
Abijah was the father of Asa.
8Asa was the father of Jehoshaphat.
Jehoshaphat was the father of Jehoram.
Jehoram was the father of Uzziah.
9Uzziah was the father of Jotham.
Jotham was the father of Ahaz.
Ahaz was the father of Hezekiah.
10Hezekiah was the father of Manasseh.
Manasseh was the father of Amon.
Amon was the father of Josiah.
11Josiah was the grandfather of Jehoiachin and his brothers.
(This was at the time that the people were taken to Babylon.)
12After they were taken to Babylon:
Jehoiachin was the father of Shealtiel.
Shealtiel was the grandfather of Zerubbabel.
13Zerubbabel was the father of Abiud.
Abiud was the father of Eliakim.
Eliakim was the father of Azor.
14Azor was the father of Zadok.
Zadok was the father of Akim.
Akim was the father of Eliud.
15Eliud was the father of Eleazar.
Eleazar was the father of Matthan.
Matthan was the father of Jacob.
16Jacob was the father of Joseph.
Joseph was the husband of Mary,
and Mary was the mother of Jesus.
Jesus is called the Christ. [d]
17So there were fourteen generations from
Abraham to David. And there were fourteen gen-
erations from David until the people were taken
to Babylon. And there were fourteen generations
from the time when the people were taken to
Babylon until Christ was born.

The Birth of Jesus Christ

18This is how the birth of Jesus Christ came
about. His mother Mary was engaged [n] to marry
Joseph, but before they married, she learned she
was pregnant by the power of the Holy Spirit. [d]
19Because Mary's husband, Joseph, was a good
man, he did not want to disgrace her in public, so
he planned to divorce her secretly.
20While Joseph thought about these things, an
angel of the Lord came to him in a dream. The
angel said, "Joseph, descendant [d] of David, don't
be afraid to take Mary as your wife, because the
baby in her is from the Holy Spirit. 21She will
give birth to a son, and you will name him Jesus, [n]
because he will save his people from their sins."
22All this happened to bring about what the Lord
had said through the prophet: [d] 23"The virgin [d] will

father "Father" in Jewish lists of ancestors can sometimes mean grandfather or a more distant relative.
engaged For the Jewish people an engagement was a lasting agreement, which could only be broken by a divorce. If a bride was unfaithful, it was considered adultery, and she could be put to death.
Jesus The name Jesus means "salvation".

be pregnant. She will have a son, and they will
name him Immanuel,"[n] which means "God is
with us".
24When Joseph woke up, he did what the
Lord's angel had told him to do. Joseph took
Mary as his wife, 25but he did not have sexual
relations with her until she gave birth to the son.
And Joseph named him Jesus.

Wise Men Come to Visit Jesus

2 Jesus was born in the town of Bethlehem in
Judea during the time when Herod was
king. When Jesus was born, some wise men from
the east came to Jerusalem. 2They asked, "Where
is the baby who was born to be the king of the
Jews? We saw his star in the east and have come
to worship him."
3When King Herod heard this, he was trou-
bled, as well as all the people in Jerusalem.
4Herod called a meeting of all the leading priests
and teachers of the law and asked them where
the Christ[d] would be born. 5They answered, "In
the town of Bethlehem in Judea. The prophet[d]
wrote about this in the Scriptures:[d]
6'But you, Bethlehem, in the land of Judah,
are important among the tribes[d] of
Judah.
A ruler will come from you
who will be like a shepherd for my people
Israel.' "
Micah 5:2

"The virgin . . . Immanuel," Quotation from Isaiah 7:14.

FOLLOWING GOD

What's Going On?

Jen had been acting strange for weeks. Up until now, Ian had really been enjoying going out with her, but recently things just hadn't felt right. She seemed to disappear without warning every now and then and Ian never really believed her excuses when she returned. Jen even stopped him from seeing her text messages and emails . . . but she'd never been bothered before.

It was getting Ian down. He still liked her – but why was she acting like this? Why couldn't they just relax with each other like before? She definitely had something on her mind. Maybe he should think about speaking to her, confronting her, perhaps even break up with her? He didn't want to make the wrong decision, so kept quiet and thought about it, to give himself some time.

One evening they were walking back to Ian's house when Jen suddenly suggested they walk a different route. Confused, but too preoccupied with his thoughts to argue, Ian followed. Before long, Jen stopped outside the community centre. "Let's go inside," she said. "But why?" Ian protested as he was dragged inside, "Why on earth do you want to come in here?"

"SURPRISE!" The room exploded into life – lights blinked on and music started up. The streamers finally settled and Ian looked round at the familiar faces. "Now do you understand why I've been acting a bit weird lately?" grinned Jen. "Hope it's worth it!"

Ian sighed and smiled. How had she kept it from him? How had he not guessed?

Read **Matthew 1:18–25**. Joseph, like Ian, was confused about what was going on with his relationship with his fiancée, Mary. And there was a surprise in store for him too!

- What difficult decisions did Joseph face?
- How might other people have viewed Joseph because of what he did?

Consider . . .

- whether you are confused by what God is doing in your life? Talk it through with an older Christian who may be able to advise and pray for you.
- taking time out to be with God and see what he says, before you make any big decisions in your life.

For more, see . . .

- Genesis 15:1–6 (p.16)
- 1 Timothy 4:7–10 (p.1311)

7Then Herod had a secret meeting with the
wise men and learned from them the exact time
they first saw the star. 8He sent the wise men to
Bethlehem, saying, "Look carefully for the child.
When you find him, come and tell me so I can
worship him too."
9After the wise men heard the king, they left.
The star that they had seen in the east went be-
fore them until it stopped above the place where
the child was. 10When the wise men saw the star,
they were filled with joy. 11They came to the
house where the child was and saw him with his
mother, Mary, and they bowed down and wor-
shipped him. They opened their gifts and gave
him treasures of gold, frankincense[d] and myrrh.[d]
12But God warned the wise men in a dream not
to go back to Herod, so they returned to their
own country by a different way.

Jesus' Parents Take Him to Egypt

13After they left, an angel of the Lord came to
Joseph in a dream and said, "Get up! Take the
child and his mother and escape to Egypt,
because Herod is starting to look for the child so
he can kill him. Stay in Egypt until I tell you to
return."
14So Joseph got up and left for Egypt during the
night with the child and his mother. 15And Joseph

WORSHIP

Enjoying God's Gifts

Sean hated Sunday mornings. "Sunday meant church, and that meant boring," he said. He felt boredom start with the first note of the organ, and he steadily suffered as worship went on. The best part to him was walking out of the church on the way home to lunch.

"Much of what happened there just didn't seem important," he said. "We sang a few old songs, read the Bible, listened to somebody talk for 30 minutes – how did any of that really worship God?"

The only thing that kept Sean's interest in church was the youth group. One Sunday evening, the group gathered at a nearby lake. They started a camp fire, and everyone watched a spectacular sunset. Sean sat in silence, enjoying the sunset's reflection on the still lake, until the last pink streak faded in the sky. "That's the most beautiful thing I've ever seen," he said.

Caroline overheard him. She had been sitting so quietly that he hadn't noticed her. She asked him, "Do you think God hears us when we say things like that? Do you think God likes it when we enjoy a sunset?"

"Yes," Sean replied. Then suddenly something "clicked" for Sean about worship. "Perhaps part of worship is enjoying something God has made," he said. "To watch a sunset, or the rain, and to be thankful that God had such good taste. Am I right?"

The next time he worshipped at church, he looked around at the people. Many of their faces wore the same expression of awe Sean had felt at the lake.

"Maybe this feeling of 'Wow!' is worship," he thought. "It isn't the motions you go through. It's when you see or hear or remember things so good that you have to catch your breath, and then thank and praise God for them."

In **Matthew 2:1–12**, read about the "Wow!" the wise men must have felt when they saw and worshipped the infant Jesus.

- In what ways might the wise men have felt as Sean did while he watched the sunset?
- When have you experienced a sense of "Wow!" in worship, either in or out of church?

Consider . . .

- noticing the ways that your church worships God and finding out the meaning of each part of the service.
- visiting a few other churches with your family or friends, and seeing what each church does differently.

For more, see . . .

- Psalm 19:1–6 (p.510)
- Revelation 4:1–11 (p.1391)
- Luke 9:28–36 (p.1055)

stayed in Egypt until Herod died. This happened to bring about what the Lord had said through the prophet:[d] "I called my son out of Egypt."[n]

Herod Kills the Baby Boys

16When Herod saw that the wise men had tricked him, he was furious. So he gave an order to kill all the baby boys in Bethlehem and in the surrounding area who were two years old
or younger. This was in keeping with the time
he learnt from the wise men. 17So what God
had said through the prophet[d] Jeremiah came
true:
18"A voice was heard in Ramah
of painful crying and deep sadness:
Rachel crying for her children.
She refused to be comforted,
because her children are dead." *Jeremiah 31:15*

"I called . . . Egypt." Quotation from Hosea 11:1.

FREEDOM

Going to a Safe Place

White journalist Donald Woods openly opposed the South African government's cruel policies towards its black people. In the early 1970s, Woods began to publish a newspaper that chronicled the government's repressive actions.

Woods befriended several leaders in the black liberation movement, including Steve Biko, and he grew even more committed to freedom for blacks. In spite of government and police warnings, Woods refused to turn his back on his friends.

The political situation soon worsened in South Africa. The police stepped up arrests of black leaders, who were later found tortured and often dead. In 1977, Steve Biko was arrested. Woods worked furiously for his friend's release, but faced unbending opposition from officials.

When Woods personally discovered the dead body of his tortured friend, he blasted the official explanation that Biko's death was accidental. While questioning the doctor, Woods heard him tearfully admit to falsifying the autopsy report. Woods, in his raging grief, openly accused the government of murdering Biko. South Africa's response was to arrest Woods.

After Woods had been held under house arrest for three months, his friends in the liberation movement devised a plan for him to escape from the country. After escaping the guards, he crossed the country disguised as a priest. Along the way, sympathisers risked their lives to see him safely along. But he finally made it to the bordering country of Lesotho.

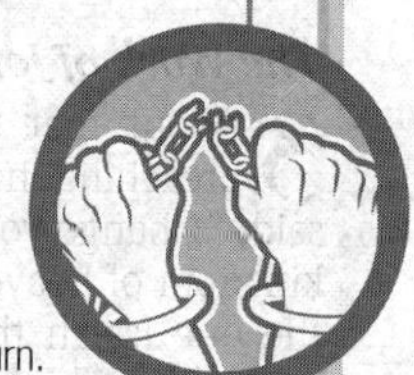

Woods' family also escaped and joined him in Lesotho. They moved to England, where Woods wrote the story of South Africa's cruelty. If he had not been able to escape, his story and Steve Biko's would not have been told. Because of changes in South Africa, Woods has been able to return. His story – and others like it – directly influenced these changes.

Joseph, Mary and Jesus also had to flee from their country so that Jesus could grow up and fulfil God's purpose for him. Read their story in **Matthew 2:13–23**.

- Why did Joseph and Mary and Donald Woods temporarily leave their homes instead of facing their persecution?
- Have you ever had to leave a "comfort zone" in your life to follow God? What happened?

Consider . . .

- watching the film *Cry Freedom* (about Donald Woods) and talking about whether God's freedom is similar or different, and why.
- looking up the word "freedom" in the dictionary, and then defining "Christian freedom" in your own words.

For more, see . . .

- Exodus 12:31–50 (p.70)
- Galatians 5:13–15 (p.1263)
- John 8:31–36 (p.1110)

Joseph and Mary Return

19 After Herod died, an angel of the Lord spoke
to Joseph in a dream while he was in Egypt.
20 The angel said, "Get up! Take the child and his
mother and go to the land of Israel, because the
people who were trying to kill the child are now
dead."

> **Sidelight** The "three kings" traditionally associated with Matthew 2:1–12 were probably neither "three" nor "kings". Some sources suggest that as many as a hundred of these philosophers, doctors and astrologers visited Jesus. Now that would make a Christmas play! The traditional idea of "three" comes from the three gifts they brought – gold, frankincense and myrrh.

21 So Joseph took the child and his mother
and went to Israel. 22 But he heard that Archelaus
was now king in Judea since his father Herod
had died. So Joseph was afraid to go there.
After being warned in a dream, he went to the
area of Galilee, 23 to a town called Nazareth, and
lived there. And so what God had said through
the prophets[d] came true: "He will be called a
Nazarene."[n]

The Work of John the Baptist

3 About that time John the Baptist[d] began
preaching in the desert area of Judea. 2 John
said, "Change your hearts and lives because the
kingdom of heaven is near." 3 John the Baptist is
the one Isaiah the prophet[d] was talking about
when he said:

"This is a voice of one
  who calls out in the desert:
'Prepare the way for the Lord.
  Make the road straight for him.'" *Isaiah 40:3*

4 John's clothes were made from camel's hair,
and he wore a leather belt around his waist. For
food, he ate locusts[d] and wild honey. 5 Many peo-
ple came from Jerusalem and Judea and all the
area around the Jordan River to hear John. 6 They
confessed their sins, and he baptised them in the
Jordan River.
7 Many of the Pharisees[d] and Sadducees[d] came
to the place where John was baptising people.
When John saw them, he said, "You are all
snakes! Who warned you to run away from God's
coming punishment? 8 Do the things that show
you really have changed your hearts and lives.
9 And don't think you can say to yourselves,
'Abraham is our father.' I tell you that God could
make children for Abraham from these rocks.
10 The axe is now ready to cut down the trees,

> **Sidelight** Many people today talk about eating "organic" foods, but John the Baptist was doing this almost 2,000 years ago! His diet of locusts and wild honey (Matthew 3:4) makes some people think that he might have been part of the desert Qumran community. These were people who lived in caves above the Dead Sea, and it was in these caves that the Dead Sea Scrolls – a selection of some of the earliest manuscripts of the Bible, and other writings – were discovered in 1947.

and every tree that does not produce good fruit
will be cut down and thrown into the fire.[n]
11 "I baptise you with water to show that your
hearts and lives have changed. But there is one
coming after me who is greater than I am, whose
sandals I am not good enough to carry. He
will baptise you with the Holy Spirit[d] and fire.
12 He will come ready to clean the grain, separat-
ing the good grain from the chaff.[d] He will put
the good part of the grain into his barn, but
he will burn the chaff with a fire that cannot be
put out."[n]

Jesus is Baptised by John

13 At that time Jesus came from Galilee to the
Jordan River and wanted John to baptise him.
14 But John tried to stop him, saying, "Why do you
come to me to be baptised? I need to be baptised
by you!"
15 Jesus answered, "Let it be this way for now.
We should do all things that are God's will." So
John agreed to baptise Jesus.
16 As soon as Jesus was baptised, he came up
out of the water. Then heaven opened, and he
saw God's Spirit[d] coming down on him like a
dove. 17 And a voice from heaven said, "This is
my Son, whom I love, and I am very pleased
with him."

Nazarene A person from the city of Nazareth, a name probably meaning "branch" (see Isaiah 11:1).
The axe . . . fire. This means that God is ready to punish his people who do not obey him.
He will . . . out. This means that Jesus will come to separate good people from bad people, saving the good and punishing the bad.

The Temptation of Jesus

4 Then the Spirit[d] led Jesus into the desert to
be tempted by the devil. 2Jesus ate nothing
for 40 days and nights. After this, he was very
hungry. 3The devil came to Jesus to tempt him,
saying, "If you are the Son of God, tell these rocks
to become bread."
4Jesus answered, "It is written in the Scrip-
tures,[d] 'A person does not live by eating only
bread, but by everything God says.' "[n]
5Then the devil led Jesus to the holy city of
Jerusalem and put him on a high place of the
Temple.[d] 6The devil said, "If you are the Son of
God, jump down, because it is written in the
Scriptures:

'He has put his angels in charge
of you.
They will catch you in their hands
so that you will not hit your foot on a
rock.' " *Psalm 91:11–12*

7Jesus answered him, "It also says in the Scrip-
tures, 'Do not test the Lord your God.' "[n]
8Then the devil led Jesus to the top of a very
high mountain and showed him all the kingdoms
of the world and all their splendour. 9The devil
said, "If you will bow down and worship me, I
will give you all these things."

'A person . . . says.' Quotation from Deuteronomy 8:3.
'Do . . . God.' Quotation from Deuteronomy 6:16.

GOD'S WILL

Are You Sure, Lord?

Jon sat in his supervisor's office discussing whether or not he should to stay for a second year as leader of his mission team. It was a hard decision. Jon had laid down his ambition of becoming a rock drummer to do this and the first year had been really tough. After praying about it and asking advice from friends and church leaders, he felt that despite the challenges, it *was* God's will for him to do a second year.

Then a few weeks later, Jon's friend Kate phoned him: "Amazing news, I've just met a band in America that needs a new drummer for their US tour. I told them about you and they want you to join! This *must* be from God! It's everything you've dreamed of!" Jon was stunned – this band was really famous. This was a once in a lifetime opportunity!

Jon knew God would never want him to do something that involved selfishness and broken promises, so he couldn't join the American band with any integrity, even though he wanted to so badly. Kate thought he was crazy to reject the offer, but Jon knew it was the only godly choice.

God really blessed his decision and used the situation to strengthen Jon's character. He and his team's ministry was really successful that year, leading many students to Christ. Years later, God even surprised him with better musical opportunities.

Read **Matthew 3:13–17** to see how John the Baptist also found God's will confusing and yet perfect. He was expecting Jesus to baptise *him* but Jesus insisted it should be the other way round!

- How can this passage help us when we see God act in a surprising way, contrary to what we were expecting?
- Why is it not always God's will for us to be happy and comfortable? Look at John the Baptist's lifestyle in the rest of chapter 3.

Consider . . .

- how you work out what God's will for you is. Do you just go by your feelings or do you also pray, read the Bible and ask for wisdom from older, wiser Christians?
- your ambitions, hopes and dreams? If God asked you to give them up for a different calling, could you?

For more, see . . .

- Isaiah 55:8–11 (p.699)
- Ephesians 2:10 (p.1271)
- Matthew 26:36–42 (p.990)
- 2 Peter 1:3–11 (p.1365)

10Jesus said to the devil, "Go away from me,
Satan! It is written in the Scriptures, 'You must
worship the Lord your God and serve only him.' "[n]
11So the devil left Jesus, and angels came and
took care of him.

Jesus Begins Work in Galilee

12When Jesus heard that John had been put in
prison, he went back to Galilee. 13He left Nazareth
and went to live in Capernaum, a town near Lake
Galilee, in the area near Zebulun and Naphtali.
14Jesus did this to bring about what the prophet[d]
Isaiah had said:
15"Land of Zebulun and land of Naphtali
along the sea,
beyond the Jordan River.
This is Galilee where the non-Jewish people
live.
16These people who live in darkness
will see a great light.
They live in a place covered with the
shadows of death,
but a light will shine on them." *Isaiah 9:1–2*

Jesus Chooses Some Followers

17From that time Jesus began to preach, saying,
"Change your hearts and lives, because the
kingdom of heaven is near."
18As Jesus was walking by Lake Galilee, he
saw two brothers, Simon (called Peter) and
his brother Andrew. They were throwing a net
into the lake because they were fishermen.
19Jesus said, "Come follow me, and I will make
you fish for people." 20So Simon and Andrew
immediately left their nets and followed him.
21As Jesus continued walking by Lake Galilee,
he saw two other brothers, James and John,
the sons of Zebedee. They were in a boat
with their father Zebedee, mending their nets.
Jesus told them to come with him. 22Immedi-
ately they left the boat and their father, and they
followed Jesus.

Jesus Teaches and Heals People

23Jesus went everywhere in Galilee, teaching
in the synagogues,[d] preaching the Good News[d]
about the kingdom of heaven, and healing all
the people's diseases and sicknesses. 24The news
about Jesus spread all over Syria, and people
brought all the sick to him. They were suffering
from different kinds of diseases. Some were in
great pain, some had demons,[d] some were
epileptics[n] and some were paralysed. Jesus
healed all of them. 25Many people from Galilee,
the Ten Towns,[n] Jerusalem, Judea and the land
across the Jordan River followed him.

Jesus Teaches the People

5 When Jesus saw the crowds, he went up on
a hill and sat down. His followers came to
him, 2and he began to teach them, saying:
3"Those people who know they have great
spiritual needs are happy,
because the kingdom of heaven belongs to
them.
4Those who are sad now are happy,
because God will comfort them.
5Those who are humble are happy,
because the earth will belong
to them.
6Those who want to do right more than
anything else are happy,
because God will fully satisfy them.
7Those who show mercy to others
are happy,
because God will show mercy to them.
8Those who are pure in their thinking are
happy,
because they will be with God.
9Those who work to bring peace are happy,
because God will call them his children.
10Those who are treated badly for doing good
are happy,
because the kingdom of heaven belongs to
them.
11"People will insult you and hurt you. They
will lie and say all kinds of evil things about you
because you follow me. But when they do, you
will be happy. 12Rejoice and be glad, because
you have a great reward waiting for you in
heaven. People did the same evil things to the
prophets[d] who lived before you.

You are like Salt and Light

13"You are the salt of the earth. But if the salt
loses its salty taste, it cannot be made salty again.
It is good for nothing, except to be thrown out
and walked on.
14"You are the light that gives light to the
world. A city that is built on a hill cannot be
hidden. 15And people don't hide a light under a
bowl. They put it on a lampstand so the light
shines for all the people in the house. 16In the
same way, you should be a light for other people.

'You . . . him.' Quotation from Deuteronomy 6:13.
epileptic A person with a disease that causes them sometimes to lose control of their body and perhaps faint, shake strongly or be unable to move.
Ten Towns In Greek, called "Decapolis". It was an area east of Lake Galilee that once had ten main towns.

Live so that they will see the good things you do and will praise your Father in heaven.

The Importance of the Law

[17]"Don't think that I have come to destroy the law of Moses or the teaching of the prophets.[d] I have not come to destroy them but to bring about what they said. [18]I tell you the truth, nothing will disappear from the law until heaven and earth are gone. Not even the smallest letter or the smallest part of a letter will be lost until everything has happened. [19]Whoever refuses to obey any command and teaches other people not to obey that command will be the least important in the kingdom of heaven. But whoever obeys the commands and teaches other people to obey them will be great in the kingdom of heaven. [20]I tell you that if you are no more obedient than the teachers of the law and the Pharisees,[d] you will never enter the kingdom of heaven.

Jesus Teaches About Anger

[21]"You have heard that it was said to our people long ago, 'You must not murder anyone.[n] Anyone who murders another will be judged.' [22]But I tell you, if you are angry with a brother or sister,[n] you will be judged. If you say bad things

You . . . anyone. Quotation from Exodus 20:13; Deuteronomy 5:17.
brother . . . sister Although the Greek text reads "brother" here and throughout this book, Jesus' words were meant for the entire church, including men and women.

HAPPINESS

Turning it on its Head

Lauren was in two minds about getting along to football practise. She loved the game and she was one of the best players at the club, but training was never much fun. That was down to the coach, David. His favourite thing to shout at the team was, "If you're smiling you're not training hard enough!" He was a football coach but he would never actually use footballs! David would have them doing endless laps of the training field, sit-ups and shuttle runs. Every week was the same, no variety . . . and no footballs! It just wasn't fun any more.

As she got to the ground, there was an unfamiliar figure standing in the middle of the team. Someone else was taking the training session. Lauren sat down with the rest of her team and the new coach introduced herself. Rachel was going to be taking the training from now on. David had moved to another team.

The next two hours were great! Lauren hadn't laughed so much in ages. They trained hard but Rachel made it fun. Relay races, piggyback races and mini competitions between the players . . . they even used footballs! Rachel explained that if the team was going to be a winning team they had to get on together. Next week was going to be a social at the ten-pin bowling alley. Rachel was turning everything they'd learnt about being a team on its head.

As Lauren cycled home, she had a huge smile on her face . . . she just felt sorry for the team that David was now training!

Read through **Matthew 5:1–12**.

- Have you ever had someone teach you in a new way that challenges how you think?
- In this passage, what do you think Jesus says to the crowd that's new?

Consider . . .

- making a list or drawing the things that make you happy. Compare your list to Matthew 5:1–12. What would Jesus' list look like?
- talking to God and asking him to help you understand what real happiness is.

For more, see . . .

- Psalm 1:1–3 (p.500)
- John 15:5–11 (p.1125)
- John 10:10 (p.1114)

to a brother or sister, you will be judged by the
council. And if you call someone a fool, you will
be in danger of the fire of hell.
23"So when you offer your gift to God at
the altar, and you remember that your brother
or sister has something against you, 24leave
your gift there at the altar. Go and make peace
with that person, and then come and offer your
gift.
25"If your enemy is taking you to court,
become friends quickly, before you go to court.
Otherwise, your enemy might turn you over to
the judge, and the judge might give you to a
guard to put you in jail. 26I tell you the truth, you
will not leave there until you have paid everything you owe.

Jesus Teaches About Sexual Sin

27"You have heard that it was said, 'You must
not be guilty of adultery.'[n] 28But I tell you that
if anyone looks at a woman and wants to sin
sexually with her, in his mind he has already
done that sin with the woman. 29If your right
eye causes you to sin, take it out and throw
it away. It is better to lose one part of your body
than to have your whole body thrown into hell.
30If your right hand causes you to sin, cut it
off and throw it away. It is better to lose one

'You . . . adultery.' Quotation from Exodus 20:14; Deuteronomy 5:18.

SHARING FAITH

Grain of Truth

Salt is used by humans in more than 14,000 ways. Did you know that:

- adding a pinch of salt to milk will keep it fresh longer.
- if you get stung by a bee, you should wet the spot with water immediately and cover it with salt to relieve the pain.
- sprinkling a little salt in canvas shoes occasionally will take up the moisture and help remove bad smells.

Read **Matthew 5:13–16** and see how Jesus uses salt as an example of how to be a Christian.

Salt used to have a much higher value than it does now. It was incredibly handy to have. Romans even got paid in salt rather than money sometimes! It had so many uses: it kept food fresh (in a time when there were no fridges), it purified food, stopped it from rotting and, just like with the bee sting, it was used for healing wounds.

When we understand how important salt was to the people Jesus was speaking to, we can begin to see what Jesus meant by saying that we should be like salt to the world. Jesus is saying that, as followers of him, we are to be like salt in our society: we are to purify it by our behaviour and keep the good things about it alive and fresh, to stop the rot, be examples of his kingdom, and bring God's healing.

- What do you think Jesus means about salt losing its saltiness?
- Can you think of a time when someone you know has been a really good light – where people have seen the good things they have done, and seen Jesus through them?

Consider . . .

- how you can make sure you don't lose your saltiness, so that you can always demonstrate God's love to people around you.
- getting a sachet of salt and sprinkling it somewhere where you want to be a light for God. As you do so, pray that God will help you as you live for him in that place.

For more, see . . .

- Isaiah 9:2–7 (p.649)
- 1 John 1:5–6 (p.1371)
- 1 Corinthians 13:1–7 (p.1232)

part of your body than for your whole body to
go into hell.

Jesus Teaches About Divorce

31"It was also said, 'Anyone who divorces his
wife must give her a written divorce paper.'[n]
32But I tell you that anyone who divorces his
wife forces her to be guilty of adultery.[d] The only
reason for a man to divorce his wife is if she has
sexual relations with another man. And anyone
who marries that divorced woman is guilty of
adultery.

Make Promises Carefully

33"You have heard that it was said to our
people long ago, 'Don't break your promises,
but keep the promises you make to the Lord.'[n]
34But I tell you, never swear an oath. Don't swear
an oath using the name of heaven, because heaven
is God's throne. 35Don't swear an oath using the

'Anyone . . . divorce paper.' Quotation from Deuteronomy 24:1.
'Don't . . . Lord.' This refers to Leviticus 19:12; Numbers 30:2; Deuteronomy 19:21.

ANGER

Beating the Bully

Life wasn't going well for twelve-year-old Carl. His parents had recently divorced, and he and his mum had moved from their farm to the city. Carl felt alone in his new school, which seemed huge. But now there was another problem. Another student, Darren, had threatened to beat Carl up after school. And he meant it.

After the last bell on Thursday, Carl tried to slip out of school without being seen. He wanted to get home quickly. As he turned a corner, Darren was waiting for him.

Carl's heart pounded with fear. Darren attacked and landed blow after blow. Carl tried to fight back, but Darren was several years older and much stronger. After a few minutes of a one-sided fight, Darren left his victim lying on the pavement. Carl got up slowly and walked the rest of the way home. At the front door, his mother saw his torn clothes, his bloody face and hands. Carl told her what had happened and asked, "Mum, why are people like that? Why does Darren like to hurt other people?"

"I don't know, darling," she answered. "It doesn't make sense. There must be something wrong with him." Carl knew that she was upset, although she was trying to hide her anger towards Darren.

Later that evening, Carl looked at his reflection in the hall mirror. His face was already puffy and purple. He looked at his mum and said, "I look peculiar, don't I?"

She laughed, and then he began to laugh. "You've certainly looked better," she said, with a sad smile. "How do you feel?"

"Sore," he said. "And a bit scared. But you know what? I'm not really cross with Darren. What you said about there being something wrong – I think there is. I thought I'd hate him. But I don't. I feel sort of sorry for him. I don't think anybody likes him. Perhaps that's why he does those things."

Jesus offers several ways for us to respond when we're angered and hurt by others. In **Matthew 5:17–26**, read how Jesus might have reacted.

- Did Carl react in the way Jesus commands? Why or why not?
- If Darren had beaten you up, how would you have handled your anger and hurt? What are some ways to handle the situation, according to the passage?

Consider . . .

- watching how some TV characters handle their anger. What would happen in the real world if people handled their anger in those ways?
- making peace with someone with whom you have a conflict before you next attend church.

For more, see . . .

- Proverbs 15:1 (p.602)
- Ephesians 4:17–32 (p.1273)
- Matthew 5:38–48 (p.946)

name of the earth, because the earth belongs to
God. Don't swear an oath using the name of
Jerusalem, because that is the city of the great
King. 36Don't even swear by your own head,
because you cannot make one hair on your head
become white or black. 37Say only yes if you
mean yes, and no if you mean no. If you say
more than yes or no, it is from the Evil One.

Don't Fight Back

38"You have heard that it was said, 'An eye for
an eye, and a tooth for a tooth.' [n] 39But I tell you,
don't stand up against an evil person. If someone
slaps you on the right cheek, turn to him the
other cheek as well. 40If someone wants to sue
you in court and take your shirt, let him have
your coat as well. 41If someone forces you to go
with him a kilometre, go with him 2 kilometres.
42If a person asks you for something, give it to
him. Don't refuse to give to someone who wants
to borrow from you.

Love All People

43"You have heard that it was said, 'Love your
neighbour [n] and hate your enemies.' 44But I say
to you, love your enemies. Pray for those
who hurt you. 45If you do this, you will be true
children of your Father in heaven. He causes

'An eye . . . tooth.' Quotation from Exodus 21:24; Leviticus 24:20; Deuteronomy 19:21.
Love your neighbour Quotation from Leviticus 19:18.

SEXUALITY

How Far's Too Far?

Unlike Gemma, Matt wasn't a Christian but early on in the relationship, Gemma had explained that as a Christian she didn't want to have sex before she got married. Unlike guys before him, Matt seemed to totally understand and told her that was fine.

During their 3-month relationship, Gemma and Matt had grown really close. He was sweet, caring and they were really open and shared everything in their lives. However, as they grew closer, so did their physical relationship. The line got pushed further and further forward.

Searching for answers, Gemma turned to the Bible. She needed to know how far was too far. It was obvious that God created sex for marriage but that just wasn't specific enough! She wanted details – a checklist of "OK" and "not OK". In a flash of revelation Gemma suddenly thought, "What if sex isn't just about my virginity?" In that moment, she understood that she and Matt had experienced things together that God intended for marriage. It all fell into place.

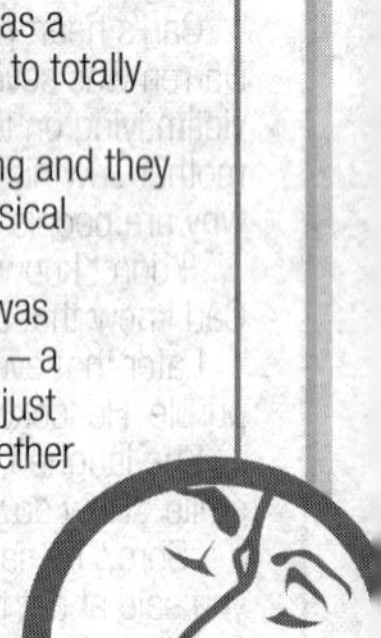

Gemma knew she'd sinned, but now she faced a decision. Did she stay with Matt and finish what she'd started or did she end the relationship and go back to God? This was the tougher option. It involved facing up to her actions, saying sorry, receiving forgiveness and changing the way she lived – with no Matt.

Read **Matthew 5:27–37**.

- Why do you think Jesus feels so strongly about sexual sin?
- Look at what Jesus says in verse 37. Does your body language matter as much as what you say?

Consider . . .

- how far is too far, and how this affects your current and future relationships.
- talking through these issues with someone wise who you trust. Be accountable to them and give them permission to ask how you're doing on your new rules.

For more, see . . .

- 1 Corinthians 6:12–13 (p.1221)
- Hebrews 13:4 (p.1345)
- 1 Thessalonians 4:3–4 (p.1298)

the sun to rise on good people and on evil
people, and he sends rain to those who do
right and to those who do wrong. 46If you love
only the people who love you, you will get no
reward. Even the tax collectors do that. 47And if
you are nice only to your friends, you are no
better than other people. Even those who don't
know God are nice to their friends. 48So you
must be perfect, just as your Father in heaven is
perfect.

Jesus Teaches About Giving

6 "Be careful! When you do good things, don't
do them in front of people to be seen by
them. If you do that, you will have no reward
from your Father in heaven.
2"When you give to the poor, don't be like the
hypocrites.[d] They blow trumpets in the
synagogues[d] and on the streets so that people
will see them and honour them. I tell you the
truth, those hypocrites already have their full

PEACE

The Second Mile

Tracy Collins pulled her car into the drive and groaned when she saw that the front door was ajar. "Not again!" she fumed. She knew her flat had been burgled for the third time.

When the police arrived, they helped her make a list of what was missing. "Not that there was much left to take," she said. "He really cleaned me out the first time."

The police were virtually positive who the thief was. After the previous burglary, one of the officers had let the name slip: Tim O'Conner. They recognised his style.

Tracy worked in an inner-city mission distributing food and clothing to needy people. Among the volunteers were adults placed on probation. Instead of going to prison, they were required to provide community service.

Several weeks after the third burglary, Tracy interviewed a new probationer, filling out a form that would record the hours worked. "What's your name?" she asked, her pen ready on the correct line.

"Tim O'Conner," he said.

Tracy choked, and looked into the young man's eyes. He sat calmly, waiting for the next question. He was well-dressed, well-groomed, and had good manners. She shook her head as if to clear it, and turned the document back to the first page, searching for the line that would tell her why he had been convicted. "Burglary," it read.

"Is something wrong?" he asked in a polite voice.

"He has no idea I'm one of his victims," she thought angrily. Then her anger turned into compassion as she wondered what made him break into other people's homes. "No," she answered. "Let's finish this form."

After they finished the interview, Tim was given a job. "Thanks," he said. "I'm glad the judge sent me here."

"So am I," Tracy said.

Tracy was surprised when she didn't feel like hitting back at Tim. Then she realised Jesus' words in **Matthew 5:38–48** must have helped her handle her anger in a peaceful manner.

- In light of the passage, do you think Tracy did the right thing?
- Does "turning the other cheek" mean that Jesus wants people to walk all over your rights? Why or why not?

Consider . . .

- listing the "normal" ways for handling conflicts, and then listing the "cheek-turning", peaceful ways next to them. Promise yourself to "turn the other cheek" the next time a conflict arises.
- walking away from a fight or keeping your cool in an argument in the future.

For more, see . . .

- Psalm 37 (p.521)
- Colossians 3:12–13 (p.1293)
- Luke 6:27–36 (p.1048)

Sidelight The coat (or robe) in Matthew 5:40 was a prized possession in Jesus' day. It was often the only protection that poor people had from cold nights. That's why the Old Testament protected it (Exodus 22:26–27, p.82). And rich people showed their wealth by the number and quality of coats or robes that they had (See James 5:1–2, p.1352).

reward. 3So when you give to the poor, don't
let anyone know what you are doing. 4Your
giving should be done in secret. Your Father
can see what is done in secret, and he will
reward you.

Jesus Teaches About Prayer

5"When you pray, don't be like the hypo-
crites.[d] They love to stand in the synagogues[d]
and on the street corners and pray so people will
see them. I tell you the truth, they already have
their full reward. 6When you pray, you should
go into your room and close the door and pray
to your Father who cannot be seen. Your Father
can see what is done in secret, and he will
reward you.

Sidelight Jews in Jesus' day had plenty of opportunities to give to people in need, which could lead to the problems that Jesus talked about in Matthew 6:1–4. Jerusalem had a "chamber of secrets" where people quietly left gifts. Then the needy could slip in unnoticed and claim goods without embarrassment.

7"And when you pray, don't be like those
people who don't know God. They continue say-
ing things that mean nothing, thinking that God
will hear them because of their many words.
8Don't be like them, because your Father knows
the things you need before you ask him. 9So
when you pray, you should pray like this:
'Our Father in heaven,
may your name always be kept holy.
10May your kingdom come
and what you want be done,
here on earth as it is in heaven.
11Give us the food we need for each day.
12Forgive us for our sins,
just as we have forgiven those who sinned
against us.
13And do not cause us to be tempted,
but save us from the Evil One.'
14Yes, if you forgive others for their sins, your
Father in heaven will also forgive you for your
sins. 15But if you don't forgive others, your Father
in heaven will not forgive your sins.

Jesus Teaches About Worship

16"When you give up eating,[n] don't put on a
sad face like the hypocrites.[d] They make their
faces look sad to show people they are giving up
eating. I tell you the truth, those hypocrites al-
ready have their full reward. 17So when you give
up eating, comb your hair and wash your face.
18Then people will not know that you are giving
up eating, but your Father, whom you cannot
see, will see you. Your Father sees what is done
in secret, and he will reward you.

God is More Important than Money

19"Don't store treasures for yourselves here on
earth where moths and rust will destroy them
and thieves can break in and steal them. 20But
store your treasures in heaven where they cannot
be destroyed by moths or rust and where thieves
cannot break in and steal them. 21Your heart will
be where your treasure is.
22"The eye is a light for the body. If your eyes
are good, your whole body will be full of light.
23But if your eyes are evil, your whole body
will be full of darkness. And if the only light you
have is really darkness, then you have the worst
darkness.
24"No one can serve two masters. The person
will hate one master and love the other, or
will follow one master and refuse to follow the
other. You cannot serve both God and worldly
riches.

Don't Worry

25"So I tell you, don't worry about the food or
drink you need to live, or about the clothes you
need for your body. Life is more than food, and
the body is more than clothes. 26Look at the birds
in the air. They don't plant or harvest or store
food in barns, but your heavenly Father feeds
them. And you know that you are worth much
more than the birds. 27You cannot add any time
to your life by worrying about it.
28"And why do you worry about clothes? Look
at how the lilies in the field grow. They don't

give up eating This is called "fasting". The people would give up eating for a special time of prayer and worship to God. It was also done to show sadness and disappointment.

work or make clothes for themselves. 29 But I tell
you that even Solomon with his riches was not
dressed as beautifully as one of these flowers.
30 God clothes the grass in the field, which is alive
today but tomorrow is thrown into the fire. So
you can be even more sure that God will clothe
you. Don't have so little faith! 31 Don't worry and
say, 'What will we eat?' or 'What will we drink?'
or 'What will we wear?' 32 The people who don't
know God keep trying to get these things, and
your Father in heaven knows you need them.
33 The thing you should want most is God's king-
dom and doing what God wants. Then all these
other things you need will be given to you. 34 So
don't worry about tomorrow, because tomorrow
will have its own worries. Each day has enough
trouble of its own.

Be Careful About Judging Others

7 "Don't judge other people, or you will be
judged. 2 You will be judged in the same way
that you judge others, and the amount you give
to others will be given to you.
3 "Why do you notice the little piece of dust in
your friend's eye, but you don't notice the big
piece of wood in your own eye? 4 How can you
say to your friend, "Let me take that little piece
of dust out of your eye'? Look at yourself! You
still have that big piece of wood in your own eye.
5 You hypocrite![d] First, take the wood out of your

PRIORITIES

Where's Your Heart?

Chris loved watching films – so much so that he tried to buy every one ever made. As soon as he had enough money, you'd find him in the local shop rummaging through the DVDs as if his life depended on it!

His films, known simply as "The Collection" took pride of place in Chris's bedroom. Sometimes they were organised alphabetically, sometimes in the order they were released and once, only once, in the order that Chris had bought them.

"The Collection" was the most important thing in Chris's life . . . until Helen started going to his youth group.

Helen was intelligent, funny, pretty and, most importantly, she had great taste in films. Helen was nice! On Thursday evenings, she volunteered at the old people's home and she gave all her old clothes to the local homeless shelter. She made friends with people that no one else liked and always helped out around the house.

The more time that Chris spent with Helen, the less time he spent watching films. He didn't even notice the change at first, until one day he bought a bunch of flowers for an old lady in his church that he hardly even knew. As he handed the florist his ten-pound note he thought about the DVDs he was giving up and "The Collection" sitting at home, sadly neglected . . . but he handed the money over anyway.

In **Matthew 6:19–21** Jesus is asking his disciples where their treasure is and what their priorities are. It wasn't a bad thing that Chris had lots of DVDs, the important thing was where his heart was.

- According to the passage, where should your treasure be?
- Where would making friends with people or giving clothes to a homeless shelter be described as storing treasure?

Consider . . .

- making a list of all the different "treasures" in your life. Make two columns, one for treasures that you can only enjoy here on earth and another for those that have heavenly and eternal value.
- where your treasure is. Ask God to be your treasure and to have your heart.

For more, see . . .

- 1 Corinthians 13:13 (p.1232)
- 1 Timothy 6:17–19 (p.1314)

own eye. Then you will see clearly to take the
dust out of your friend's eye.
6"Don't give holy things to dogs, and don't
throw your pearls before pigs. Pigs will only
trample on them, and dogs will turn to attack
you.

Ask God for What You Need

7"Ask, and God will give to you. Search, and
you will find. Knock, and the door will open for
you. 8Yes, everyone who asks will receive.
Everyone who searches will find. And everyone
who knocks will have the door opened.
9"If your children ask for bread, which of you
would give them a stone? 10Or if your children
ask for a fish, would you give them a snake?
11Even though you are bad, you know how to
give good gifts to your children. How much more
will your heavenly Father give good things to
those who ask him!
12"Do to others what you want them to do to
you. This is the meaning of the law of Moses and
the teaching of the prophets.[d]

The Way to Heaven is Hard

13"Enter through the narrow gate. The gate
is wide and the road is wide that leads to hell,
and many people enter through that gate. 14But
the gate is small and the road is narrow that
leads to true life. Only a few people find that
road.

People Know You by Your Actions

15"Be careful of false prophets.[d] They come to
you looking gentle like sheep, but they are really
dangerous like wolves. 16You will know these

WORRYING

Baby Blues

Tom's mum had just had another baby.

She'd spent the whole pregnancy worrying – "Will the nursery be ready in time?" "Will I be able to cope with another baby?" "Will we have enough money?" Tom could see she was excited about this new addition but at the same time was scared about the responsibility, about the worry that this new life would bring.

She needn't have worried. Grace was perfect. Unlike her mum, Grace simply didn't have the capacity to worry about anything. When she was cold, Tom put a blanket on her. When she needed feeding, Tom's mum fed her. When times were busy, people from church offered to baby-sit. Everything Grace needed was provided for her by those who loved her.

Even though Tom and his mum were grown up, both needed God in the same way. As children of God, just as they provided for Grace, God provides for their every need.

There was no need for Tom's mum to ever have worried because God has promised to look after them.

Somebody once said, "Worry is like a rocking chair. It gives you something to do but doesn't get you anywhere."

Read **Matthew 6:25–34**.

- What does this passage say we should think about when we are tempted to worry?
- Read Genesis 1:26 and 29–30. Here we are told that humans alone are made in his image and are "very good", when everything else is "good". How does that make you feel?

Consider . . .

- what you could do to help a friend cope with being stressed or worried.
- what you worry about most. Write it down and give it to God.

For more, see . . .

- Exodus 16 (p.74)
- Philippians 4:6 (p.1285)
- Psalm 46 (p.527)

people by what they do. Grapes don't come from
thorn-bushes, and figs don't come from thorny
weeds. 17In the same way, every good tree
produces good fruit, but a bad tree produces bad
fruit. 18A good tree cannot produce bad fruit, and
a bad tree cannot produce good fruit. 19Every tree
that does not produce good fruit is cut down and
thrown into the fire. 20In the same way, you will
know these false prophets by what they do.

21"Not all those who say that I am their Lord
will enter the kingdom of heaven. The only
people who will enter the kingdom of heaven
are those who do what my Father in heaven
wants. 22On the last day many people will say to
me, 'Lord, Lord, we spoke for you, and through
you we forced out demons [d] and did many mira-
cles.' [d] 23Then I will tell them clearly, "Get away
from me, you who do evil. I never knew you.'

Two Kinds of People

24"Everyone who hears my words and obeys
them is like a wise man who built his house on
rock. 25It rained hard, the floods came and the
winds blew and hit that house. But it did not fall,
because it was built on rock. 26Everyone who
hears my words and does not obey them is like a
foolish man who built his house on sand. 27It
rained hard, the floods came and the winds blew
and hit that house, and it fell with a big crash."

28When Jesus finished saying these things, the
people were amazed at his teaching, 29because
he did not teach like their teachers of the law.
He taught like a person who had authority.

Jesus Heals a Sick Man

8 When Jesus came down from the hill, great
crowds followed him. 2Then a man with a
skin disease came to Jesus. The man bowed
down before him and said, "Lord, you can heal
me if you will."

3Jesus reached out his hand and touched the
man and said, "I will. Be healed!" And immedi-
ately the man was healed of his disease. 4Then
Jesus said to him, "Don't tell anyone about this.

CULTS

Deadly Deception

Malaysia is home for a species of praying mantis that's made a career out of looking like a flower. But this "flower" kills unsuspecting bugs.

Pink, petal-like structures flank its spindly legs. Part of its green thorax simulates the stem of an orchid. A few brown markings here and there make it look slightly wilted. When a soft breeze blows, the mantis even simulates the flower's gentle swaying.

But this unusual insect is as deadly as it is beautiful. If a butterfly mistakes the mantis for an orchid, the mantis strikes with frightful speed and captures the butterfly in pink, vice-like forelegs.

Like butterflies, Christians need to be aware that not everything is as it appears. Many cults may look appealing, just as the praying mantis looks like an orchid to an unsuspecting butterfly. Learn how you can watch out for this kind of deception in **Matthew 7:15–29**.

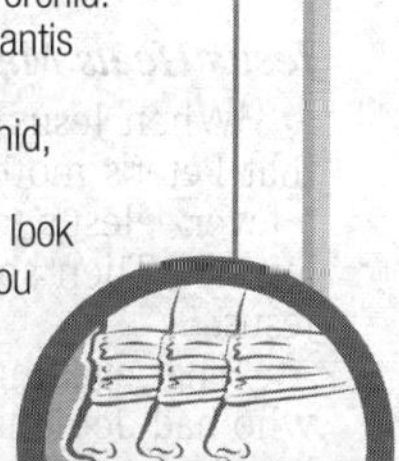

- How is a butterfly being captured by a praying mantis like those who build their houses on the sand?
- Who are some modern-day "false prophets" or groups you have heard of or have been contacted by? How might Jesus react to them?

Consider . . .

- praying for ways to resist the temptations of cults, and then investing time to grow in your faith in Christ.
- praying for those caught in cults, and sharing your faith with non-Christians.

For more, see . . .

- 1 Kings 18:1–40 (p.332)
- 2 Peter 2:1–22 (p.1305)
- Mark 13:14–23 (p.1024)

But go and show yourself to the priest[n] and offer
the gift Moses commanded[n] for people who are
made well. This will show the people what I
have done."

Jesus Heals a Soldier's Servant

5When Jesus entered the city of Capernaum,
an army officer came to him, begging for help.
6The officer said, "Lord, my servant is at home in
bed. He can't move his body and is in much
pain."
7Jesus said to the officer, "I will go and heal
him."
8The officer answered, "Lord, I am not worthy
for you to come into my house. You only need to
command it, and my servant will be healed. 9I,
too, am a man under the authority of others, and
I have soldiers under my command. I tell one
soldier, 'Go,' and he goes. I tell another soldier,
'Come,' and he comes. I say to my servant, 'Do
this,' and my servant does it."
10When Jesus heard this, he was amazed. He
said to those who were following him, "I tell you
the truth, this is the greatest faith I have found,
even in Israel. 11Many people will come from the
east and from the west and will sit and eat with
Abraham, Isaac and Jacob in the kingdom of
heaven. 12But those people who should be in the
kingdom will be thrown outside into the dark-
ness, where people will cry and grind their teeth
with pain."
13Then Jesus said to the officer, "Go home. Your
servant will be healed just as you believed he
would." And his servant was healed that same hour.

Jesus Heals Many People

14When Jesus went to Peter's house, he saw
that Peter's mother-in-law was sick in bed with
a fever. 15Jesus touched her hand, and the fever
left her. Then she stood up and began to serve
Jesus.
16That evening people brought to Jesus many
who had demons.[d] Jesus spoke and the demons
left them, and he healed all the sick. 17He did
these things to bring about what Isaiah the
prophet[d] had said:
"He took our suffering on him
and carried our diseases." *Isaiah 53:4*

People Want to Follow Jesus

18When Jesus saw the crowd around him, he
told his followers to go to the other side of the
lake. 19Then a teacher of the law came to Jesus
and said, "Teacher, I will follow you wherever
you go."
20Jesus said to him, "The foxes have holes to
live in, and the birds have nests, but the Son of
Man[d] has no place to rest his head."
21Another man, one of Jesus' followers, said
to him, "Lord, first let me go and bury my
father."
22But Jesus told him, "Follow me, and let the
people who are dead bury their own dead."

Jesus Calms a Storm

23Jesus got into a boat, and his followers
went with him. 24A great storm arose on the
lake so that waves covered the boat, but Jesus
was sleeping. 25His followers went to him and
woke him, saying, "Lord, save us! We will
drown!"
26Jesus answered, "Why are you afraid? You
don't have enough faith." Then Jesus got up and
gave a command to the wind and the waves, and
it became completely calm.
27The men were amazed and said, "What kind
of man is this? Even the wind and the waves
obey him!"

Jesus Heals Two Men with Demons

28When Jesus arrived at the other side of the
lake in the area of the Gadarene[n] people, two
men who had demons[d] in them met him. These
men lived in the burial caves and were so danger-
ous that people could not use the road by those
caves. 29They shouted, "What do you want with
us, Son of God? Did you come here to torture us
before the right time?"
30Near that place there was a large herd of pigs
feeding. 31The demons begged Jesus, "If you
make us leave these men, please send us into that
herd of pigs."
32Jesus said to them, "Go!" So the demons left
the men and went into the pigs. Then the whole
herd rushed down the hill into the lake and were
drowned. 33The herdsmen ran away and went
into the town, where they told about all of this
and what had happened to the men who had
demons. 34Then the whole town went out to see
Jesus. When they saw him, they begged him to
leave their area.

Jesus Heals a Paralysed Man

9 Jesus got into a boat and went back across
the lake to his own town. 2Some people
brought to Jesus a man who was paralysed and

show . . . priest The law of Moses said a priest must say when a Jewish person with a skin disease was well.
Moses commanded Read about this in Leviticus 14:1–32.
Gadarene From Gadara, an area south east of Lake Galilee.

lying on a mat. When Jesus saw the faith of these
people, he said to the paralysed man, "Be encour-
aged, young man. Your sins are forgiven."
3Some of the teachers of the law said to
themselves, "This man speaks as if he were God.
That is blasphemy!"[n]
4Knowing their thoughts, Jesus said, "Why are
you thinking evil thoughts? 5Which is easier: to
say, 'Your sins are forgiven,' or to tell him, 'Stand
up and walk'? 6But I will prove to you that the
Son of Man[d] has authority on earth to forgive
sins." Then Jesus said to the paralysed man,
"Stand up, take your mat and go home." 7And
the man stood up and went home. 8When the
people saw this, they were amazed and praised
God for giving power like this to human beings.

Jesus Chooses Matthew

9When Jesus was leaving, he saw a man
named Matthew sitting in the tax collector's
booth. Jesus said to him, "Follow me," and he
stood up and followed Jesus.

Sidelight Tax collectors in New Testament times were despised because they worked for the hated Roman invaders. Matthew was a tax collector when Jesus chose him (Matthew 9:9–13). Matthew's unpopularity rubbed off on Jesus.

10As Jesus was having dinner at Matthew's
house, many tax collectors and "sinners" came

blasphemy Saying things against God or not showing respect for God.

NON-CHRISTIANS

From the Problem to the Answer

Damien grew up in a very violent home in Manchester. His father was an abusive alcoholic who regularly beat him and his mother up.

Because he was bullied, he himself, as so often happens, became a bully. He displayed his anger and feelings of rejection through violence and crime. His life also slipped into a dangerous spiral of drugs and alcohol. Before too long, he was sentenced to six years in prison for armed robbery.

In prison, some Christians told him about the love of God and he had a powerful conversion. He came out of prison determined to change his ways, but without any support, he slipped back into his old destructive habits. It was only when some Christians moved into his area of inner-city Manchester and got alongside him that he received the encouragement and help he needed to make a go of his new Christian life.

Damien's life is now altogether different. He is a leader in the church, a positive role model to young people in the area and is bringing up his six-week-old son in a loving, Jesus-filled home. He has gone from being the problem to being the answer in that part of Manchester.

It is clear from reading **Matthew 9:9–13** that Jesus had a big heart for people like Damien. He chose to get alongside the "tax collectors and sinners" rather than condemning them, so that they would get the chance to be the people they were meant to be.

- What does Damien's story and these verses say to you about teaching those who don't know Jesus yet in your world?
- Why do you think the Pharisees were so upset with Jesus for associating with Matthew and his friends?

Consider . . .

- whether there is someone who God has spoken to you about who he wants you to pray for and share your faith with.
- how you could generally be more active in sharing Jesus' "invitation to sinners".

For more, see . . .

- Isaiah 56:1–8 (p.699)
- James 2:14–26 (p.1350)
- Luke 12:8–9 (p.1062)

and ate with Jesus and his followers. 11When the Pharisees[d] saw this, they asked Jesus' followers, "Why does your teacher eat with tax collectors and sinners?"

12When Jesus heard them, he said, "It is not the healthy people who need a doctor, but the sick. 13Go and learn what this means: 'I want kindness more than I want animal sacrifices.'[n] I did not come to invite good people but to invite sinners."

Jesus' Followers are Criticised

14Then the followers of John[n] came to Jesus and said, "Why do we and the Pharisees[d] often give up eating for a certain time,[n] but your followers don't?"

15Jesus answered, "The friends of the bridegroom are not sad while he is with them. But the time will come when the bridegroom will be taken from them, and then they will give up eating.

16"No one sews a patch of unshrunken cloth over a hole in an old coat. If he does, the patch will shrink and pull away from the coat, making the hole worse. 17Also, people never pour new wine into old leather bags. Otherwise, the bags will break, the wine will spill and the wine bags will be ruined. But people always pour new wine into new wine bags. Then both will continue to be good."

Jesus Gives Life to a Dead Girl and Heals a Sick Woman

18While Jesus was saying these things, a leader of the synagogue[d] came to him. He bowed down before Jesus and said, "My daughter has just died. But if you come and lay your hand on her, she will live again." 19So Jesus and his followers stood up and went with the leader.

20Then a woman who had been bleeding for twelve years came behind Jesus and touched the edge of his coat. 21She was thinking, "If I can just touch his clothes, I will be healed."

22Jesus turned and saw the woman and said, "Be encouraged, dear woman. You are made well because you believed." And the woman was healed from that moment on.

23Jesus continued along with the leader and went into his house. There he saw the funeral musicians and many people crying. 24Jesus said, "Go away. The girl is not dead, only asleep." But the people laughed at him. 25After the crowd had been thrown out of the house, Jesus went into the girl's room and took hold of her hand, and she stood up. 26The news about this spread all around the area.

Jesus Heals More People

27When Jesus was leaving there, two blind men followed him. They cried out, "Have mercy on us, Son of David!"[d]

28After Jesus went inside, the blind men went with him. He asked the men, "Do you believe that I can make you see again?"

They answered, "Yes, Lord."

29Then Jesus touched their eyes and said, "Because you believe I can make you see again, it will happen." 30Then the men were able to see. But Jesus warned them strongly, saying, "Don't tell anyone about this." 31But the blind men left and spread the news about Jesus all around that area.

32When the two men were leaving, some people brought another man to Jesus. This man could not talk because he had a demon[d] in him. 33After Jesus forced the demon to leave the man, he was able to speak. The crowd was amazed and said, "We have never seen anything like this in Israel."

34But the Pharisees[d] said, "The prince of demons is the one that gives him power to force demons out."

35Jesus travelled through all the towns and villages, teaching in their synagogues,[d] preaching the Good News[d] about the kingdom and healing all kinds of diseases and sicknesses. 36When he saw the crowds, he felt sorry for them because they were hurting and helpless, like sheep without a shepherd. 37Jesus said to his followers, "There are many people to harvest but only a few workers to help harvest them. 38Pray to the Lord, who owns the harvest, that he will send more workers to gather his harvest."[n]

Jesus Sends Out His Apostles

10 Jesus called his twelve followers together and gave them authority to drive out evil spirits and to heal every kind of disease and sickness. 2These are the names of the twelve apostles:[d] Simon (also called Peter) and his brother Andrew; James son of Zebedee, and his brother John; 3Philip and Bartholomew; Thomas and Matthew, the tax collector; James son of Alphaeus, and Thaddaeus; 4Simon the Zealot[d] and Judas Iscariot, who turned against Jesus.

5Jesus sent out these twelve men with the following order: "Don't go to the non-Jewish people or to any town where the Samaritans[d] live. 6But go to the people of Israel, who are like

'I want . . . sacrifices.' Quotation from Hosea 6:6.

John John the Baptist, who preached to people about Christ's coming (Matthew 3, Luke 3).

give up . . . time This is called "fasting". The people would give up eating for a special time of prayer and worship to God. It was also done to show sadness and disappointment.

"There are . . . harvest." As a farmer sends workers to harvest the grain, Jesus sends his followers to bring people to God.

lost sheep. [7]When you go, preach this: 'The
kingdom of heaven is near.' [8]Heal the sick, raise
the dead to life again, heal those who have skin
diseases and force demons[d] out of people. I give
you these powers freely, so help other people
freely. [9]Don't carry any money with you—gold
or silver or copper. [10]Don't carry a bag or extra
clothes or sandals or a walking stick. Workers
should be given what they need.
[11]"When you enter a city or town, find some
worthy person there and stay in that home until
you leave. [12]When you enter that home, say,
'Peace be with you.' [13]If the people there wel-
come you, let your peace stay there. But if they
don't welcome you, take back the peace you
wished for them. [14]And if a home or town
refuses to welcome you or listen to you, leave
that place and shake its dust off your feet.[n] [15]I
tell you the truth, on the Judgement Day it will
be better for the towns of Sodom[d] and Gomor-
rah[d] than for the people of that town.

Jesus Warns His Apostles

[16]"Listen, I am sending you out like sheep
among wolves. So be as clever as snakes and as
innocent as doves. [17]Be careful of people, because
they will arrest you and take you to court and
whip you in their synagogues.[d] [18]Because of me

shake . . . feet. A warning. It showed that they had rejected these people.

SICKNESS

Giving the World Friends

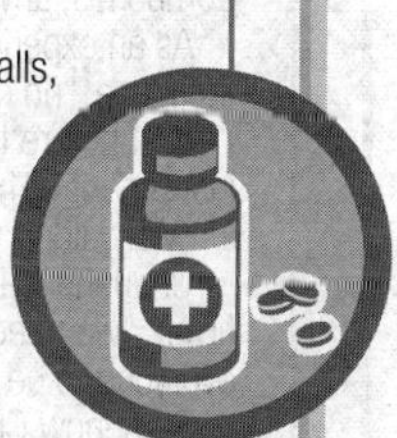

Rebecca, a high school student in the USA, can dance, walk and run. Not a huge achievement for most of us – but for Rebecca those abilities prove God's power. For not long ago, she was almost completely paralysed.

In the first year, Rebecca felt her muscles slowly becoming numb. She started avoiding PE lessons. Walking caused excruciating pain. Her mother finally took her to a doctor, and Rebecca was admitted to the hospital the same day.

A spinal tap confirmed that she had Guillain Barr Syndrome, a rare condition in which a virus attacks the nervous system, causing paralysis in all the motor functions. Although she began various drug and physical treatments, Rebecca's condition got worse. "The syndrome spread, and I could no longer sit upright in bed by myself," she recalls.

Doctors gave her little chance for recovery. But they did not count on God! "My spirits have been strengthened because of the love from family and friends," Rebecca says. "Daily I received phone calls, cards and flowers. My room was crowded with friends every day. It was a time for fellowship and support, not only for me, but also for my family and friends."

The doctors continued treatment, and Rebecca slowly recovered.

"Some people say the Lord doesn't give us answers we can see or touch, yet we all see and touch our family and friends," Rebecca says. "The Lord answered my prayers with a family who stroked my hair and sat next to me day and night while I lay motionless.

"The Lord brought me friends who told me, 'You will get better, because I'm praying for you.' I thank God for the answers he's given me."

Rebecca's doctors were amazed at her healing. Yet **Matthew 9:35 – 10:8** tells us how Jesus commissioned the disciples to heal the sick.

- How well did the people who prayed and stayed with Rebecca follow Jesus' commission to the apostles?
- How can you reach out in love and faith?

Consider . . .

- doing one activity this week to better your health and well-being.
- visiting someone in a hospital or nursing home and praying with him or her.

For more, see . . .

- 2 Kings 20:1–11 (p.365)
- Luke 18:35–43 (p.1080)
- Psalm 30:2–3 (p.517)

you will be taken to stand before governors and
kings, and you will tell them and the non-Jewish
people about me. 19When you are arrested, don't
worry about what to say or how to say it. At that
time you will be given the things to say. 20It will
not really be you speaking but the Spirit of your
Father speaking through you.
21"Brothers will give their own brothers to be
killed, and fathers will give their own children to
be killed. Children will fight against their own
parents and have them put to death. 22All people
will hate you because you follow me, but those
people who keep their faith until the end will be
saved. 23When you are treated badly in one city,
run to another city. I tell you the truth, you will
not finish going through all the cities of Israel
before the Son of Man [d] comes.
24"A student is not better than his teacher, and
a servant is not better than his master. 25A
student should be satisfied to become like his
teacher; a servant should be satisfied to become
like his master. If the head of the family is called
Beelzebul, [d] then the other members of the family
will be called worse names!

Fear God, Not People

26"So don't be afraid of those people, because
everything that is hidden will be shown. Every-
thing that is secret will be made known. 27I tell
you these things in the dark, but I want you to
tell them in the light. What you hear whispered
in your ear you should shout from the house-
tops. 28Don't be afraid of people, who can kill the
body but cannot kill the soul. The only one you
should fear is the one who can destroy the soul
and the body in hell. 29Two sparrows cost only a
penny, but not even one of them can die without
your Father's knowing it. 30God even knows how

SELF-ESTEEM

Playing Your Part

The second-period algebra test had been a disaster for Charlene Markham. Then she had slipped and fallen in the hallway in front of two dozen other students. As she sat in sixth-period band practise, her mind was everywhere except on the sheets of music.

"Sometimes I wonder if my being here at Springbrook High makes any difference at all," she thought as the music filled the room. "It's like the flautist's part in this medley. All you can hear are the trumpets and trombones, anyway."

As an experiment, Charlene raised the flute to her lips but only pretended to play. "See," she thought after the piece, "no one even noticed."

Just before the bell rang, Mr Westmore, the music teacher, instructed the students to put away their instruments. Then he asked Charlene to stay after the bell.

"Why didn't you play in the Sousa medley?" he asked.

Charlene was stunned that he knew. She didn't answer him. "Charlene," he said kindly, yet firmly, "we need every part in a piece of music to make it complete. The conductor looks for everyone to be playing his or her part."

Somehow Charlene felt better knowing she had been missed. "Maybe I have a part to play after all," she thought. Learn what Jesus says about your importance in **Matthew 10:24–33**.

- How does the Bible passage speak to Charlene's feelings of worthlessness?
- How does knowing that God loves you affect your feelings about yourself?

Consider . . .

- investing thirty minutes today in an activity for your own growth, health and well-being.
- listing all of the "sections" in God's "band" (the church) you can think of, such as musicians, leaders, helpers and so forth. Pick the one section that you're most interested in, and volunteer to "play" in it.

For more, see . . .

- Psalm 8:3–9 (p.503)
- 1 Corinthians 12:12–31 (p.1231)
- Romans 5:1–11 (p.1190)

many hairs are on your head. 31So don't be afraid.
You are worth much more than many sparrows.

Tell People About Your Faith

32"All those who stand before others and say
they believe in me, I will say before my Father in
heaven that they belong to me. 33But all who
stand before others and say they do not believe in
me, I will say before my Father in heaven that
they do not belong to me.
34"Don't think that I came to bring peace to
the earth. I did not come to bring peace, but a
sword. 35I have come so that
'a son will be against his father,
a daughter will be against her mother,
a daughter-in-law will be against her
mother-in-law.
36 A person's enemies will be members of his
own family.' *Micah 7:6*
37"Those who love their father or mother more
than they love me are not worthy to be my
followers. Those who love their son or daughter
more than they love me are not worthy to be my
followers. 38Whoever is not willing to carry the
cross and follow me is not worthy of me. 39Those
who try to hold on to their lives will give up true
life. Those who give up their lives for me will
hold on to true life. 40Whoever accepts you also
accepts me, and whoever accepts me also accepts
the One who sent me. 41Whoever meets a
prophet[d] and accepts him will receive the reward
of a prophet. And whoever accepts a good person
because that person is good will receive the re-
ward of a good person. 42Those who give one of

PRIORITIES

Who Comes First?

Jason was enthralled by every word Keith, his new pastor, spoke. He seemed to sell an attractive, yet challenging way of life that went the extra mile. He was getting some opposition within the church – people were beginning to feel uncomfortable because he was so radical – but he seemed to expect it and even thrive on it.

The church grew dramatically, doubling in size in a matter of months. Keith worked hard and seemed to be everywhere.

Jason followed Keith round learning about ministry, public speaking, evangelism and serving, by carrying bags and setting up equipment for meetings.

One day Keith took Jason aside. "You're special and I trust you," he said. "God is calling me to do something even more radical. I am being called to leave here and start a new community. Next week I'm going to move to a special place in the country that God has shown me. It will be a place where people trust God, live on the land and devote their time to worship, prayer and outreach. It will be a completely new type of society – a Jesus one. So are you in or out?"

Jason felt all sorts of objections going off in his head and wondered what his friends and family would say. But Keith suggested he read **Matthew 10:34–42**. He did. And as he read, he discovered that Keith was simply doing the Jesus thing. His pastor was calling people to follow Jesus more closely, not to follow him.

- What did Jesus mean when he said (verse 42) that he had not come to bring peace on the earth? Who did Jesus think he was?
- "Who is this man?" is the key question posed by the Gospels about Jesus. Was he mad, bad, good or God? In which direction does this passage point?

Consider . . .

- how you would feel if you were asked to give up everything and follow Jesus.
- what it means to carry Jesus' cross (verse 38).

For more, see . . .

- Luke 10:1–3 (p.1056)
- 1 John 3:1–3 (p.1373)

these little ones a cup of cold water because they
are my followers will truly get their reward."

Jesus and John the Baptist

11 After Jesus finished telling these things to
his twelve followers, he left there and
went to the towns in Galilee to teach and preach.
2John the Baptist[d] was in prison, but he heard
about what Christ was doing. So John sent some
of his followers to Jesus. 3They asked him, "Are
you the One who is to come, or should we wait
for someone else?"
4Jesus answered them, "Go and tell John what
you hear and see: 5the blind can see, the crippled
can walk and people with skin diseases are healed.
The deaf can hear, the dead are raised to life and
the Good News[d] is preached to the poor. 6Those
who do not stumble in their faith because of me
are blessed."
7As John's followers were leaving, Jesus began
talking to the people about John. Jesus said,
"What did you go out into the desert to see? A
reed[n] blown by the wind? 8What did you go out
to see? A man dressed in fine clothes? No, those
who wear fine clothes live in kings' palaces. 9So
why did you go out? To see a prophet?[d] Yes, and
I tell you, John is more than a prophet. 10This was
written about him:

'I will send my messenger ahead of you,
who will prepare the way for you.' *Malachi 3:1*

11I tell you the truth, John the Baptist is greater
than any other person ever born, but even
the least important person in the kingdom of
heaven is greater than John. 12Since the time

reed This means that John was not ordinary or weak like grass blown by the wind.

FAITH

The Faith Difference

Next time friends ask you, "Does your faith make a difference?" remember these statistics about teenagers:

1. Teenagers who have never used illegal drugs – 61% of regular churchgoers, versus 39% of non-churchgoers.
2. Teenagers who have never had sexual intercourse – 61% of regular churchgoers, versus 35% of non-churchgoers.
3. Teenagers who believe in a personal God – 87% of regular churchgoers, versus 64% of non-churchgoers.
4. Teenagers who read the Bible weekly – 58% of regular churchgoers, versus 17% of non-churchgoers.
5. Teenagers who plan to go to college – 57% of regular churchgoers, versus 33% of non-churchgoers.

Faith isn't an intellectual thing. As the statistics above illustrate, a committed faith makes a visible, real difference in the way we live. Perhaps it should make more. In **Matthew 11:2–11** the followers of John the Baptist asked Jesus whether he was the Christ. Read how he responded.

- Why is faith a powerful force in the miracles of Jesus as well as the behaviour of regular churchgoers?
- What difference does faith make in your own life? Have you seen the signs of God's work that are listed in the passage?

Consider . . .

- surveying your own behaviour in comparison to statistics. How well did you fit?
- drawing up your own survey and interviewing both churchgoers and non-churchgoers. Share your results with others at church and school.

For more, see . . .

- Judges 6:11–24 (p.231)
- James 5:13–18 (p.1353)
- Luke 13:1–9 (p.1066)

John the Baptist came until now, the kingdom of
heaven has been going forwards in strength,
and people have been trying to take it by force.
13All the prophets and the law of Moses told
about what would happen until the time John
came. 14And if you will believe what they said,
you will believe that John is Elijah, whom they
said would come. 15You people who can hear
me, listen!

16"What can I say about the people of this
time? What are they like? They are like children
sitting in the market place, who call out to each
other,

17'We played music for you, but you did not
dance;
we sang a sad song, but you did not cry.'
18John came and did not eat or drink like other
people. So people say, 'He has a demon.'[d] 19The
Son of Man[d] came, eating and drinking, and
people say, 'Look at him! He eats too much and
drinks too much wine, and he is a friend of tax
collectors and sinners.' But wisdom is proved to
be right by what it does."

Jesus Warns Unbelievers

20Then Jesus criticised the cities where he did
most of his miracles,[d] because the people did not
change their lives and stop sinning. 21He said,
"How terrible for you, Korazin! How terrible for
you, Bethsaida![n] If the same miracles I did in you

Korazin . . . Bethsaida Towns by Lake Galilee where Jesus preached to the people.

WORRYING

Driving You Crazy

"Watch out for that hedge! Get off of the pavement! Ellie the brake is the one in the middle!" barked Ellie's dad as he sat rigid with both hands gripping the sides of his passenger seat.

"You're not helping, Dad!" Ellie whined whilst steering back onto the road with a clunk and thud. "You keep shouting at me and telling me what to do – it's stressing me out!"

Later that night, Ellie explained the evening's lesson to her mum over a cup of tea.

Ellie's mum leaned forward across the kitchen table, "Don't worry, you can do it, you just need help. Listen darling, I know it will cost you, but I think you need to start learning with someone else. You need a professional who can help you feel more relaxed."

Ellie's new instructor, Pauline, was amazing. Ellie still found some things about driving difficult and scary but Pauline made it so much easier. She was gentle and fun. And soon Ellie began to believe that she could pass, with Pauline's help.

Many of the Jewish people had difficult lives. What made it worse was that the religious leaders told these people that their problems were because they weren't living right and keeping the rules. They thought God was angry and had abandoned them.

In **Matthew 11:25–30** Jesus turns everything upside down. When times are tough, he doesn't say that God is angry or list all their mistakes, instead he offers help, comfort and new ways of learning how to live.

- Compare Pauline with Jesus. What similarities can you think of?
- Ellie could give up or get help to get through. What are the things in your life that you feel "rubbish" about or want to give up on? Could you go to Jesus for help to get through them?

Consider . . .

- writing the things that are worrying you on separate bits of paper. Pray about each thing and find a different way each day throughout the week to destroy the paper (e.g. make into a paper aeroplane, throw on a fire, shred, paint over the words).
- buying a "well done, you passed" card. Graffiti/decorate the card's front with verses and pictures to help you remember that Jesus will help you. Frame the card.

For more, see . . .

- Psalm 4 (p.501)
- Jude 24–25 (p.1386)

had happened in Tyre and Sidon,[n] those people
would have changed their lives a long time ago.
They would have worn rough cloth and put
ashes on themselves to show they had changed.
22But I tell you, on the Judgement Day it will be
better for Tyre and Sidon than for you. 23And you,
Capernaum,[n] will you be lifted up to heaven?
No, you will be thrown down to the depths. If the
miracles I did in you had happened in Sodom,[d] its
people would have stopped sinning, and it would
still be a city today. 24But I tell you, on the Judge-
ment Day it will be better for Sodom than for you."

Jesus Offers Rest to People

25At that time Jesus said, "I praise you, Father,
Lord of heaven and earth, because you have hid-
den these things from the people who are wise
and clever. But you have shown them to those
who are like little children. 26Yes, Father, this is
what you really wanted.

27"My Father has given me all things. No one
knows the Son, except the Father. And no one
knows the Father, except the Son and those
whom the Son chooses to tell.

28"Come to me, all of you who are tired and
have heavy loads, and I will give you rest. 29Ac-
cept my teachings and learn from me, because I
am gentle and humble in spirit, and you will find
rest for your lives. 30The teaching that I ask you to
accept is easy; the load I give you to carry is light."

Jesus is Lord of the Sabbath

12 At that time Jesus was walking through
some fields of grain on a Sabbath[d] day.
His followers were hungry, so they began to pick
the grain and eat it. 2When the Pharisees[d] saw this,
they said to Jesus, "Look! Your followers are doing
what is unlawful to do on the Sabbath day."

3Jesus answered, "Have you not read what David
did when he and the people with him were hun-
gry? 4He went into God's house, and he and those
with him ate the holy bread, which was lawful
only for priests to eat. 5And have you not read in

> **Sidelight** If you think that today's society has a lot of rules and regulations, take a look at the Pharisees and think again (Matthew 12:1–8). On the Sabbath, no less than 39 major activities were forbidden, including putting a fire out, lifting something weighing more than two figs, writing and healing someone!

the law of Moses that on every Sabbath day the
priests in the Temple[d] break this law about the
Sabbath day? But the priests are not wrong for
doing that. 6I tell you that there is something here
that is greater than the Temple. 7The Scripture[d]
says, 'I want kindness more than I want animal
sacrifices.'[n] You don't really know what those
words mean. If you understood them, you would
not judge those who have done nothing wrong.

8"So the Son of Man[d] is Lord of the Sabbath day."

Jesus Heals a Man's Hand

9Jesus left there and went into their syn-
agogue,[d] 10where there was a man with a crippled
hand. They were looking for a reason to accuse
Jesus, so they asked him, "Is it right to heal on
the Sabbath[d] day?"[n]

11Jesus answered, "If any of you has a sheep,
and it falls into a ditch on the Sabbath day, you
will help it out of the ditch. 12Surely a human
being is more important than a sheep. So it is
lawful to do good things on the Sabbath day."

13Then Jesus said to the man with the crippled
hand, "Hold out your hand." The man held out
his hand, and it became well again, like the other
hand. 14But the Pharisees[d] left and made plans to
kill Jesus.

Jesus is God's Chosen Servant

15Jesus knew what the Pharisees[d] were doing,
so he left that place. Many people followed him,
and he healed all who were sick. 16But Jesus
warned the people not to tell who he was. 17He
did these things to bring about what Isaiah the
prophet[d] had said:

18"Here is my servant whom I have chosen.
I love him, and I am pleased with him.
I will put my Spirit[d] upon him,
and he will tell of my justice to all people.
19He will not argue or cry out;
no one will hear his voice in the streets.
20He will not break a crushed blade of grass
or put out even a weak flame
until he makes justice win the victory.
21 In him will the non-Jewish people find
hope." *Isaiah 42:1–4*

Jesus' Power is from God

22Then some people brought to Jesus a man
who was blind and could not talk, because he
had a demon.[d] Jesus healed the man so that he
could talk and see. 23All the people were amazed
and said, "Perhaps this man is the Son of David!"[d]

Tyre and Sidon Towns where wicked people lived.
Capernaum A town by Lake Galilee where Jesus preached to the people.
'I . . . sacrifices.' Quotation from Hosea 6:6.
"Is it right . . . day?" It was against Jewish law to work on the Sabbath day.

24When the Pharisees[d] heard this, they said, "Jesus uses the power of Beelzebul,[d] the ruler of demons, to force demons out of people."

25Jesus knew what the Pharisees were thinking, so he said to them, "Every kingdom that is divided against itself will be destroyed. And any city or family that is divided against itself will not continue. 26And if Satan forces out himself, then Satan is divided against himself, and his kingdom will not continue. 27You say that I use the power of Beelzebul to force out demons. If that is true, then what power do your people use to force out demons? So they will be your judges. 28But if I use the power of God's Spirit[d] to force out demons, then the kingdom of God has come to you.

29"If anyone wants to enter a strong person's house and steal his things, he must first tie up the strong person. Then he can steal the things from the house.

30"Whoever is not with me is against me. Whoever does not work with me is working against me. 31So I tell you, people can be forgiven for every sin and everything they say against God. But whoever speaks against the Holy Spirit will not be forgiven. 32Anyone who speaks against the Son of Man[d] can be forgiven, but anyone who speaks against the Holy Spirit will not be forgiven, now or in the future.

People Know You by Your Words

33"If you want good fruit, you must make the tree good. If your tree is not good, it will have bad fruit. A tree is known by the kind of fruit it produces. 34You snakes! You are evil people, so how can you say anything good? The mouth speaks the things that are in the heart. 35Good people have good things in their hearts, and so they say good things. But evil people have evil in their hearts, so they say evil things. 36And I tell you that on the Judgement Day people will be responsible for every careless thing they have said. 37The words you have said will be used to judge you. Some of your words will prove you right, but some of your words will prove you guilty."

The People Ask for a Miracle

38Then some of the Pharisees[d] and teachers of the law answered Jesus, saying, "Teacher, we want to see you work a miracle[d] as a sign."

39Jesus answered, "Evil and sinful people are the ones who want to see a miracle for a sign. But no sign will be given to them, except the sign of the prophet[d] Jonah. 40Jonah was in the stomach of the big fish for three days and three nights. In the same way, the Son of Man[d] will be in the grave three days and three nights. 41On the Judgement Day the people from Nineveh[n] will stand up with you people who live now, and they will show that you are guilty. When Jonah preached to them, they were sorry and changed their lives. And I tell you that someone greater than Jonah is here. 42On the Judgement Day, the Queen of the South[n] will stand up with you people who live today. She will show that you are guilty, because she came from far away to listen to Solomon's wise teaching. And I tell you that someone greater than Solomon is here.

People Today are Full of Evil

43"When an evil spirit comes out of a person, it travels through barren places, looking for a place to rest, but it doesn't find it. 44So the spirit says, 'I will go back to the house I left.' When the spirit comes back, it finds the house still empty, swept clean and made neat. 45Then the evil spirit goes out and brings seven other spirits even more evil than it is, and they go in and live there. So the person has even more trouble than before. It is the same way with the evil people who live today."

Jesus' True Family

46While Jesus was talking to the people, his mother and brothers stood outside, trying to find a way to talk to him. 47Someone told Jesus, "Your mother and brothers are standing outside, and they want to talk to you."

48He answered, "Who is my mother? Who are my brothers?" 49Then he pointed to his followers and said, "Here are my mother and my brothers. 50My true brother and sister and mother and father are those who do what my Father in heaven wants."

A Story About Planting Seed

13 That same day Jesus went out of the house and sat by the lake. 2Large crowds gathered around him, so he got into a boat and sat down, while the people stood on the shore. 3Then Jesus used stories to teach them many things. He said: "A farmer went out to plant his seed. 4While he was planting, some seed fell by the road, and the birds came and ate it all up. 5Some seed fell on rocky ground, where there wasn't much earth. That seed grew very fast, because the ground was not deep. 6But when the sun rose, the plants dried up, because they did not have deep roots. 7Some other seed fell among thorny weeds, which grew and choked the good

Nineveh The city where Jonah preached to warn the people. Read Jonah 3.
Queen of the South The Queen of Sheba. She travelled 1,600 kilometres to learn God's wisdom from Solomon. Read 1 Kings 10:1–13.

plants. 8 Some other seed fell on good ground
where it grew and produced a crop. Some plants
made 100 times more, some made 60 times
more and some made 30 times more. 9 You people
who can hear me, listen."

Why Jesus Used Stories to Teach

10 The followers came to Jesus and asked,
"Why do you use stories to teach the people?"
11 Jesus answered, "You have been chosen to
know the secrets about the kingdom of heaven,
but others cannot know these secrets. 12 Those
who have understanding will be given more,
and they will have all they need. But those who
do not have understanding, even what they have
will be taken away from them. 13 This is why I
use stories to teach the people: they see, but they
don't really see. They hear, but they don't really
hear or understand. 14 So they show that the
things Isaiah said about them are true:

'You will listen and listen, but you will not
understand.
You will look and look, but you will not learn.
15 For the minds of these people have become
stubborn.
They do not hear with their ears,
and they have closed their eyes.
Otherwise they might really understand
what they see with their eyes
and hear with their ears.
They might really understand in their minds
and come back to me and be healed.'

Isaiah 6:9–10

16 But you are blessed, because you see with your
eyes and hear with your ears. 17 I tell you the
truth, many prophets [d] and good people wanted

FOLLOWING GOD

The Secrets of the Kingdom

English cricket is a mystery to some and an absolute passion to others. What on earth is the strangely named "silly mid wicket", "square leg" or a "googly"? These and lots of other secrets are only made known to those who love the game of cricket and are keen enough to find out.

Even football, which may seem a far simpler game to cricket, has its hidden depths. How many of the millions who sit in the stadiums understand the "offside laws" or know what a "flat back 4" or the "spine" of a team is? Anyone, of course, can play the games but if you want to be exceptional, you need to know this stuff.

Jesus says to his followers (a very ordinary bunch of guys) in Matthew 13 that they have been chosen to know the secrets, not about some game or other, but about the very "kingdom of heaven". Those words, of course, are not just for the disciples but for us as well, two thousand years later. As we get passionate for God and put in the effort required in terms of prayer, Bible study, fellowship and reaching out to our friends, we'll find that more and more we are in tune with God and that he gives us eyes to see and ears to hear what the kingdom is all about.

Read **Matthew 13:1–23** and ask God to help you understand the "secrets of the kingdom".

- Why do you think Jesus compares following God to being the "good ground" for the seed of faith?
- How could you in your situation produce a crop of 30, 60, or 100 times what is being sown into you through the word of God?

Consider . . .

- giving God some extra time this week. Don't just storm in straight away with your requests, but listen and try to tune in to his way of thinking.
- people you know who started really well as Christians but have now stopped growing? Where do you think they have gone wrong? Pray for them and try gently encouraging them back to Jesus.

For more, see . . .

- Deuteronomy 31:11–13 (p.193)
- 2 Corinthians 13:8–13 (p.1254)
- 1 Samuel 3:1–21 (p.258)

to see the things that you now see, but they did
not see them. And they wanted to hear the things
that you now hear, but they did not hear them.

Jesus Explains the Seed Story

18"So listen to the meaning of that story about
the farmer. 19What is the seed that fell by the
road? That seed is like the person who hears the
message about the kingdom but does not under-
stand it. The Evil One comes and takes away
what was planted in that person's heart. 20And
what is the seed that fell on rocky ground? That
seed is like the person who hears the teaching
and quickly accepts it with joy. 21But he does not
let the teaching go deep into his life, so he keeps
it only a short time. When trouble or persecution
comes because of the teaching he accepted, he
quickly gives up. 22And what is the seed that fell
among the thorny weeds? That seed is like the
person who hears the teaching but lets worries
about this life and the temptation of wealth stop
that teaching from growing. So the teaching does
not produce fruit[n] in that person's life. 23But
what is the seed that fell on the good ground?
That seed is like the person who hears the teaching
and understands it. That person grows and pro-
duces fruit, sometimes 100 times more, sometimes
60 times more and sometimes 30 times more."

A Story About Wheat and Weeds

24Then Jesus told them another story: "The
kingdom of heaven is like a man who planted
good seed in his field. 25That night, when every-
one was asleep, his enemy came and planted
weeds among the wheat and then left. 26Later,
the wheat grew and the heads of grain grew, but
the weeds also grew. 27Then the man's servants
came to him and said, 'You planted good seed in
your field. Where did the weeds come from?'
28The man answered, 'An enemy planted weeds.'
The servants asked, 'Do you want us to pull up
the weeds?' 29The man answered, 'No, because
when you pull up the weeds, you might also pull
up the wheat. 30Let the weeds and the wheat

produce fruit To produce fruit means to have in your life the good things God wants.

SIN

A Crafty Enemy

Life in the Arctic would be pretty safe for the seal if it weren't for its enemy the polar bear.

This crafty predator probably uses more strategies than any other animal in capturing and killing its prey. It may spend 30 minutes in the water approaching a resting seal on an ice floe, surfacing silently to see where the prey is and then submerging again. It may drift like a small, harmless iceberg to within striking distance, and then explode from the water so suddenly and ferociously that the seal has no time to react.

When it's stalking on the ice, the polar bear slithers along on its chest and forelegs. It will build mounds of snow to hide behind while it waits at the edge of a breathing hole. It can surface in the seal's den and catch it sleeping there. Or it can dive so quickly into the den from above that the seal cannot escape.

We, too, must be wary of a crafty enemy. You can read about the enemy in Jesus' parable of the wheat and weeds in **Matthew 13:24–30.**

- How are the polar bear's tactics similar to the enemy's in the passage?
- How can you be prepared for the traps of the enemy in your life?

Consider . . .

- separating the forms of entertainment that you enjoy into categories of "wheat" and "weeds". Consider giving up one (or more) of the "weeds".
- looking up references to "Satan" and "devil" in the "Dictionary and Topical Concordance" at the back of this Bible (p.1406). Share what you learn with friends.

For more, see . . .

- Genesis 3:1–9 (p.5)
- 1 Peter 5:8–9 (p.1363)
- Hebrews 3:12–14 (p.1332)

grow together until the harvest time. At harvest
time I will tell the workers, "First gather the
weeds and tie them together to be burnt. Then
gather the wheat and bring it to my barn." ' "

Stories of Mustard Seed and Yeast

31Then Jesus told another story: "The king-
dom of heaven is like a mustard seed that a man
planted in his field. 32That seed is the smallest
of all seeds, but when it grows, it is one of the
largest garden plants. It becomes big enough
for the wild birds to come and build nests in its
branches."
33Then Jesus told another story: "The kingdom
of heaven is like yeast that a woman took and hid
in a large bowl of flour until it made all the dough
rise."
34Jesus used stories to tell all these things to the
people; he always used stories to teach them.
35This is as the prophet[d] said:

"I will speak using stories;
I will tell things that have been secret since
the world was made." *Psalm 78:2*

Jesus Explains About the Weeds

36Then Jesus left the crowd and went into the
house. His followers came to him and said, "Ex-
plain to us the meaning of the story about the
weeds in the field."
37Jesus answered, "The man who planted the
good seed in the field is the Son of Man.[d] 38The
field is the world, and the good seeds are all of
God's children who belong to the kingdom. The
weeds are those people who belong to the Evil
One. 39And the enemy who planted the bad seed
is the devil. The harvest time is the end of the world,
and the workers who gather are God's angels.
40"Just as the weeds are pulled up and burnt in
the fire, so it will be at the end of the world.
41The Son of Man will send out his angels, and

HAPPINESS

Real Treasure

When seventeen-year-old Derek bought his first car – a "previously owned" model – he expected to hit the road and leave his problems in the dust.

The car, Derek expected, would give him more time to do as he pleased. It would get him out of the house and away from his parents fighting all the time. It would surely improve his standing with girls.

But only a week later, the fan belt broke on the way to a football match.

One month later, he had to buy two new tyres.

Now he discovered, 30 kilometres from home, that the radiator was leaking. As the traffic swished past on the motorway, Derek and his friend Phil sat in the front seat of the car, watching the steam rise from under the bonnet.

"I always looked forward to owning my own car," Derek said. "But sometimes I feel as if the car owns me."

Derek learned an ageless truth that the more things we acquire, the more they use our time and energy. Possessions rarely bring the happiness expected, and often bring just the opposite. The Bible often talks about the spiritual kingdom and the only true happiness. Read three of Jesus' parables on the kingdom in **Matthew 13:44–52**.

- What are the differences between Derek's car and the "treasure hidden in a field" mentioned in the passage?
- What is the true value of the things you treasure?

Consider . . .

- praying that God will help you to value the things in life that truly last.
- interviewing an elderly Christian about what has meant most in his or her lifetime.

For more, see . . .

- Ecclesiastes 3:1–8 (p.622)
- Revelation 3:14–22 (p.1391)
- Philippians 4:4–9 (p.1285)

they will gather out of his kingdom all who cause
sin and all who do evil. 42The angels will throw
them into the blazing furnace, where the people
will cry and grind their teeth with pain. 43Then the
good people will shine like the sun in the kingdom
of their Father. You people who can hear me, listen.

Stories of a Treasure and a Pearl

44"The kingdom of heaven is like a treasure
hidden in a field. One day a man found the trea-
sure, and then he hid it in the field again. He was
so happy that he went and sold everything he
owned to buy that field.

45"Also, the kingdom of heaven is like a man
looking for fine pearls. 46When he found a very
valuable pearl, he went and sold everything he
had and bought it.

A Story of a Fishing Net

47"Also, the kingdom of heaven is like a net that
was put into the lake and caught many different
kinds of fish. 48When it was full, the fishermen
pulled the net to the shore. They sat down and put
all the good fish in baskets and threw away the bad
fish. 49It will be this way at the end of the world.
The angels will come and separate the evil people
from the good people. 50The angels will throw the
evil people into the blazing furnace, where people
will cry and grind their teeth with pain."

51Jesus asked his followers, "Do you under-
stand all these things?"

They answered, "Yes, we understand."

52Then Jesus said to them, "So every teacher of
the law who has been taught about the kingdom
of heaven is like the owner of a house. He brings
out both new things and old things he has saved."

Jesus Goes to His Home Town

53When Jesus finished teaching with these stor-
ies, he left there. 54He went to his home town
and taught the people in the synagogue,[d] and
they were amazed. They said, "Where did this
man get this wisdom and this power to do
miracles?[d] 55He is just the son of a carpenter. His
mother is Mary, and his brothers are James, Joseph,
Simon and Judas. 56And all his sisters are here
with us. Where then does this man get all these
things?" 57So the people were upset with Jesus.

But Jesus said to them, "A prophet[d] is hon-
oured everywhere except in his home town and
in his own home."

58So he did not do many miracles there
because they had no faith.

How John the Baptist Was Killed

14 At that time Herod, the ruler of Galilee,
heard the reports about Jesus. 2So he said
to his servants, "Jesus is John the Baptist,[d] who
has risen from the dead. That is why he can work
these miracles."[d]

3Some time before this, Herod had arrested
John, tied him up, and put him in prison. Herod
did this because of Herodias, who had been the
wife of Philip, Herod's brother. 4John had been
telling Herod, "It is not lawful for you to be mar-
ried to Herodias." 5Herod wanted to kill John,
but he was afraid of the people, because they
believed John was a prophet.[d]

6On Herod's birthday, the daughter of Hero-
dias danced for Herod and his guests, and she
pleased him. 7So he promised with an oath to
give her anything she wanted. 8Herodias told
her daughter what to ask for, so she said to
Herod, "Give me the head of John the Baptist
here on a dish." 9Although King Herod was very
sad, he had made a promise, and his dinner
guests had heard him. So Herod ordered that
what she asked for be done. 10He sent soldiers
to the prison to cut off John's head. 11And they
brought it on a dish and gave it to the girl, and
she took it to her mother. 12John's followers
came and got his body and buried it. Then they
went and told Jesus.

More than 5,000 Fed

13When Jesus heard what had happened to
John, he left in a boat and went to a lonely
place by himself. But the crowds heard about it
and followed him on foot from the towns.
14When he arrived, he saw a great crowd wait-
ing. He felt sorry for them and healed those who
were sick.

Sidelight The two fish which were brought to Jesus in Matthew 14:17–21 were probably sardine-sized fish which were plentiful in Lake Galilee. The poor usually ate this fish.

15When it was evening, his followers came to
him and said, "No one lives in this place, and it
is already late. Send the people away so they can
go to the towns and buy food for themselves."

16But Jesus answered, "They don't need to go
away. You give them something to eat."

17They said to him, "But we have only five
loaves of bread and two fish."

18Jesus said, "Bring the bread and the fish to
me." 19Then he told the people to sit down on the
grass. He took the five loaves and the two fish
and, looking up to heaven, he thanked God for
the food. Jesus divided the bread and gave it to
his followers, who gave it to the people. 20All the
people ate and were satisfied. Then the followers

filled twelve baskets with the leftover pieces of
food. 21There were about 5,000 men there who
ate, not counting women and children.

Jesus Walks on the Water

22Immediately Jesus told his followers to get
into the boat and go ahead of him across the
lake. He stayed there to send the people home.
23After he had sent them away, he went by him-
self up into the hills to pray. It was late, and Jesus
was there alone. 24By this time, the boat was al-
ready far away from land. It was being hit by
waves, because the wind was blowing against it.
25Between three and six o'clock in the morn-
ing, Jesus came to them, walking on the water.
26When his followers saw him walking on the
water, they were afraid. They said, "It's a ghost!"
and cried out in fear.
27But Jesus quickly spoke to them, "Have cour-
age! It is I. Do not be afraid."
28Peter said, "Lord, if it is really you, then com-
mand me to come to you on the water."
29Jesus said, "Come."
And Peter left the boat and walked on the
water to Jesus. 30But when Peter saw the wind
and the waves, he became afraid and began to
sink. He shouted, "Lord, save me!"
31Immediately Jesus reached out his hand and
caught Peter. Jesus said, "Your faith is small. Why
did you doubt?"

FEAR

The Handicap

Chris was "cool". Nothing seemed to unnerve him. That's why the youth group was surprised when he objected to the idea of a weekend service retreat at a home for mentally and physically disabled people.

"Why don't you like the idea?" someone asked.

"It's stupid, that's all!" Chris said.

"Are you scared, or what?" someone else asked.

"Yes, sure!" Chris responded sarcastically.

The group decided to go ahead, and planned the retreat. Chris grudgingly went along, and kept up his "cool" veneer. But inside, Chris was afraid of the people at the home. He coped with his fear by avoiding any contact with the residents.

But he couldn't avoid the dance. Chris walked in late and leaned against a wall in a dark corner. Sally, one of the residents, saw him and rushed up in her wheelchair. She tugged at his arm. "Dance with me," she pleaded.

He pretended he had not heard her.

"Please dance with me," she persisted. "Please?"

Reluctantly, Chris agreed. Although he felt awkward at first, Chris's fears soon faded. He discovered that Sally was fun. She had a sharp wit. Sally actually made Chris feel comfortable.

"I was scared," he admitted later. "I didn't know what to expect. Then I saw the love and care these people give. They are just like me. I am the one who was handicapped."

Like Chris's fear of the residents, Peter, one of Jesus' disciples, often suffered from fear. Read how he was afraid in **Matthew 14:22–33**.

- How are Chris's and Peter's reactions to fear similar?
- Would you have stayed in the boat or got out to walk on the water? Why?

Consider . . .

- dividing a piece of paper equally. On the left side list fears. On the right side list ways to overcome fears. Share your lists with a friend. Pray for one another.
- taking a step this week in overcoming one of your fears. For example, if you're shy, go up to someone at school or church and introduce yourself.

For more, see . . .

- Psalm 27 (p.515)
- 1 Corinthians 2:1–5 (p.1215)
- Mark 4:35–41 (p.1005)

32 After they got into the boat, the wind became
calm. 33 Then those who were in the boat worshipped
Jesus and said, "Truly you are the Son of God!"
34 When they had crossed the lake, they came
to shore at Gennesaret. 35 When the people there
recognised Jesus, they told people in the area
there that Jesus had come, and they brought all
their sick to him. 36 They begged Jesus to let them
touch just the edge of his coat, and all who
touched it were healed.

Obey God's Law

15 Then some Pharisees [d] and teachers of
the law came to Jesus from Jerusalem.
They asked him, 2 "Why don't your followers
obey the unwritten laws which have been
handed down to us? They don't wash their hands
before they eat."
3 Jesus answered, "And why do you refuse to
obey God's command so that you can follow
your own teachings? 4 God said, 'Honour your
father and your mother,' [n] and 'Anyone who says
cruel things to his father or mother must be put
to death.' [n] 5 But you say a person can tell his fa-
ther or mother, 'I have something I could use to
help you, but I have given it to God instead.'
6 You teach that person not to honour his father
or his mother. You rejected what God said for the
sake of your own rules. 7 You are hypocrites! [d]
Isaiah was right when he said about you:
8 'These people show honour to me with words,
but their hearts are far from me.
9 Their worship of me is worthless.
The things they teach are nothing but
human rules.' " *Isaiah 29:13*
10 After Jesus called the crowd to him, he said,
"Listen and understand what I am saying. 11 It is
not what people put into their mouths that makes
them unclean. [d] It is what comes out of their
mouths that makes them unclean."

'Honour . . . mother.' Quotation from Exodus 20:12; Deuteronomy 5:16.
'Anyone . . . death.' Quotation from Exodus 21:17.

PERSISTENCE

A Bible on Computer

Jayne Chenery wanted to develop a Bible that could be read by people like herself with cerebral palsy. Eventually she contacted the Bible Society and they agreed to start work. Jayne was determined to make sure that the project was completed. She would frequently ask her mother to telephone to check on progress – often with some new request.

Eventually the special computer edition of the books of Luke and Acts was completed and launched in December 1992. It had a speech synthesiser so that it could be understood by blind people. It also had enlarged type for those with sight problems and it could be operated by a person's head or fist or by blowing down a straw. It even included special helps and advice for people who were seriously disabled, all accessed by computer. Jayne was determined to make Luke's Story happen, even though, as a result of her disabilities, she died at sixteen years old – before it was finally launched.

In a way similar to Jayne's dedication to her dream, a woman pursued Jesus to heal her daughter. Read **Matthew 15:21–28** to see how.

- How is Jayne's persistence similar to the mother's in the passage?
- When have you been persistent like the mother? What happened?

Consider . . .

- looking for examples of persistent people on television. What qualities do they possess? Write five of those qualities on a card. Tape it to your mirror.
- taking a step this week in overcoming one of your fears. For example, if you're shy, go up to someone at school or church and introduce yourself.

For more, see . . .

- Ruth 1:1–18 (p.249)
- Ephesians 6:10–20 (p.1277)
- Mark 5:25–34 (p.1005)

12Then his followers came to him and asked, "Do you know that the Pharisees are angry because of what you said?"

13Jesus answered, "Every plant that my Father in heaven has not planted himself will be pulled up by the roots. 14Stay away from the Pharisees; they are blind leaders. And if a blind person leads a blind person, both will fall into a ditch."

15Peter said, "Explain the example to us."

16Jesus said, "Do you still not understand? 17Surely you know that all the food that enters the mouth goes into the stomach and then goes out of the body. 18But what people say with their mouths comes from the way they think; these are the things that make people unclean. 19Out of the mind come evil thoughts, murder, adultery,[d] sexual sins, stealing, lying and speaking evil of others. 20These things make people unclean; eating with unwashed hands does not make them unclean."

Jesus Helps a Non-Jewish Woman

21Jesus left that place and went to the area of Tyre and Sidon. 22A Canaanite woman from that area came to Jesus and cried out, "Lord, Son of David,[d] have mercy on me! My daughter has a demon,[d] and she is suffering very much."

23But Jesus did not answer the woman. So his followers came to Jesus and begged him, "Tell the woman to go away. She is following us and shouting."

24Jesus answered, "God sent me only to the lost sheep, the people of Israel."

25Then the woman came to Jesus again and bowed before him and said, "Lord, help me!"

26Jesus answered, "It is not right to take the children's bread and give it to the dogs."

27The woman said, "Yes, Lord, but even the dogs eat the crumbs that fall from their masters' table."

28Then Jesus answered, "Woman, you have great faith! I will do what you asked." And at that moment the woman's daughter was healed.

Jesus Heals Many People

29After leaving there, Jesus went along the shore of Lake Galilee. He went up on a hill and sat there.

30Great crowds came to Jesus, bringing with them the lame, the blind, the crippled, those who could not speak and many others. They put them at Jesus' feet, and he healed them. 31The crowd was amazed when they saw that people who could not speak before were now able to speak. The crippled were made strong. The lame could walk, and the blind could see. And they praised the God of Israel for this.

More than 4,000 Fed

32Jesus called his followers to him and said, "I feel sorry for these people, because they have already been with me three days, and they have nothing to eat. I don't want to send them away hungry. They might faint while going home."

33His followers asked him, "How can we get enough bread to feed all these people? We are far away from any town."

34Jesus asked, "How many loaves of bread do you have?"

They answered, "Seven, and a few small fish."

35Jesus told the people to sit on the ground. 36He took the seven loaves of bread and the fish and gave thanks to God. Then he divided the food and gave it to his followers, and they gave it to the people. 37All the people ate and were satisfied. Then his followers filled seven baskets with the leftover pieces of food. 38There were about 4,000 men there who ate, besides women and children. 39After sending the people home, Jesus got into the boat and went to the area of Magadan.

The Leaders Ask for a Miracle

16 The Pharisees[d] and Sadducees[d] came to Jesus, wanting to trick him. So they asked him to show them a miracle[d] from God.

2Jesus answered, "At sunset you say we will have good weather, because the sky is red. 3And in the morning you say that it will be a rainy day, because the sky is dark and red. You see these signs in the sky and know what they mean. In the same way, you see the things that I am doing now, but you don't know their meaning. 4Evil and sinful people ask for a miracle as a sign, but they will not be given any sign, except the sign of Jonah."[n] Then Jesus left them and went away.

Guard Against Wrong Teachings

5Jesus' followers went across the lake, but they had forgotten to bring bread. 6Jesus said to them, "Be careful! Beware of the yeast of the Pharisees[d] and the Sadducees."[d]

7His followers discussed the meaning of this, saying, "He said this because we forgot to bring bread."

8Knowing what they were talking about, Jesus asked them, "Why are you talking about not

Sidelight The city of Caesarea Philippi (Matthew 16:13) where Peter declared that Jesus was God's Son, was north of Lake Galilee in an area that wasn't Jewish. In fact, it had a pagan shrine to Pan, a Greek and Roman nature god.

sign of Jonah Jonah's three days in the fish are like Jesus' three days in the tomb. The story about Jonah is in the book of Jonah.

having bread? Your faith is small. 9Do you still not
understand? Remember the five loaves of bread
that fed the 5,000? And remember that you filled
many baskets with the leftovers? 10Or the seven
loaves of bread that fed the 4,000 and the many
baskets you then also filled? 11I was not talking to
you about bread. Why don't you understand that?
I am telling you to beware of the yeast of the
Pharisees and the Sadducees." 12Then the follow-
ers understood that Jesus was not telling them to
beware of the yeast used in bread but to beware of
the teaching of the Pharisees and the Sadducees.

Peter Says Jesus is the Christ

13When Jesus came to the area of Caesarea
Philippi, he asked his followers, "Who do people
say the Son of Man[d] is?"
14They answered, "Some say you are John the
Baptist.[d] Others say you are Elijah, and still others
say you are Jeremiah or one of the prophets."[d]
15Then Jesus asked them, "And who do you
say I am?"
16Simon Peter answered, "You are the Christ,[d]
the Son of the living God."
17Jesus answered, "You are blessed, Simon son
of Jonah, because no person taught you that. My
Father in heaven showed you who I am. 18So I
tell you, you are Peter.[n] On this rock I will build
my church, and the power of death will not be
able to defeat it. 19I will give you the keys of the
kingdom of heaven; the things you don't allow
on earth will be the things that God does not
allow, and the things you allow on earth will be
the things that God allows." 20Then Jesus warned
his followers not to tell anyone he was the Christ.

Jesus Says that He Must Die

21From that time on Jesus began telling his
followers that he must go to Jerusalem, where
the older Jewish leaders, the leading priests, and

Peter The Greek name "Peter", like the Aramaic name "Cephas", means "rock".

FAITH

T-e-a-c-h-e-r

A fever left Helen Keller blind and deaf at birth. She was imprisoned in a dark, silent world.

In 1887, when Helen was seven, Anne Sullivan, herself partially blind, became Helen's teacher. Anne had great vision and hope. She believed that Helen held untapped and unseen abilities. Months passed with very little progress, but Anne still believed.

Then, finally, Anne witnessed the results of faith. Helen was playing at the water pump. Anne finger-spelled "w-a-t-e-r" into her free hand. Anne wrote in her journal, "The word coming so close upon the sensation of cold water rushing over her hand seemed to startle her. A new light came into her face. She understood! Then turning around she asked my name. I spelled 'T-e-a-c-h-e-r'."

Thanks to Anne's faith, Helen's dark, lonely life opened wide to the light of communication and learning. Helen graduated with honours from Radcliffe College, and went on to a distinguished career as an educator, speaker and author. Helen and "Teacher" were lifelong companions.

Teacher's faith brought Helen out of darkness and into light. In **Matthew 16:13–20**, read how Jesus had faith in Peter, even when Peter wasn't sure of his own faith.

- How was Anne's and Helen's friendship similar to Jesus' and Peter's?
- Anne's faith enabled her to teach Helen. Peter's faith helped him to become a church leader. What does your faith help you to do?

Consider . . .

- helping young children to grow in their faith by volunteering to help one Sunday in the church crèche, Sunday school or holiday activity group.
- writing a Haiku poem that expresses faith. A Haiku poem has three lines. The first and third lines each have five syllables. The middle line has seven.

For more, see . . .

- Nehemiah 9:6–8 (p.451)
- Hebrews 11 (p.1341)
- Mark 8:27–38 (p.1012)

the teachers of the law would make him suffer many things. He told them he must be killed and then be raised from the dead on the third day.

22 Peter took Jesus aside and told him not to talk like that. He said, "God save you from those things, Lord! Those things will never happen to you!"

23 Then Jesus said to Peter, "Go away from me, Satan![n] You are not helping me! You don't care about the things of God, but only about the things people think are important."

24 Then Jesus said to his followers, "If people want to follow me, they must give up the things they want. They must be willing even to give up their lives to follow me. 25 Those who want to save their lives will give up true life, and those who give up their lives for me will have true life. 26 It is worth nothing for them to have the whole world if they lose their souls. They could never pay enough to buy back their souls. 27 The Son of Man[d] will come again with his Father's glory and with his angels. At that time, he will reward them for what they have done. 28 I tell you the truth, some people standing here will see the Son of Man coming with his kingdom before they die."

Jesus Talks with Moses and Elijah

17 Six days later, Jesus took Peter, James and John, the brother of James, up on a high mountain by themselves. 2 While they watched, Jesus' appearance was changed; his face became bright like the sun, and his clothes became white as light. 3 Then Moses and Elijah[n] appeared to them, talking with Jesus.

4 Peter said to Jesus, "Lord, it is good that we are here. If you want, I will put up three tents here—one for you, one for Moses and one for Elijah."

5 While Peter was talking, a bright cloud covered them. A voice came from the cloud and said, "This is my Son, whom I love, and I am very pleased with him. Listen to him!"

6 When his followers heard the voice, they were so frightened they fell to the ground. 7 But Jesus went to them and touched them and said, "Stand up. Don't be afraid." 8 When they looked up, they saw Jesus was now alone.

9 As they were coming down the mountain, Jesus commanded them not to tell anyone about what they had seen until the Son of Man[d] had risen from the dead.

10 Then his followers asked him, "Why do the teachers of the law say that Elijah must come first?"

11 Jesus answered, "They are right to say that Elijah is coming and that he will make everything the way it should be. 12 But I tell you that Elijah has already come, and they did not recognise him. They did to him whatever they wanted to do. It will be the same with the Son of Man; those same people will make the Son of Man suffer." 13 Then the followers understood that Jesus was talking about John the Baptist.[d]

> **Sidelight** When Peter suggested building three tents in Matthew 17:4, he may have been thinking about the annual Feast of Shelters. During this feast (which was like a harvest festival), Jews from everywhere would come to Jerusalem and build shelters in the streets and town square – anywhere with a little space.

Jesus Heals a Sick Boy

14 When Jesus and his followers came back to the crowd, a man came to Jesus and bowed before him. 15 The man said, "Lord, have mercy on my son. He has epilepsy[n] and is suffering very much, because he often falls into the fire or into the water. 16 I brought him to your followers, but they could not cure him."

17 Jesus answered, "You people have no faith, and your lives are all wrong. How long must I put up with you? How long must I continue to be patient with you? Bring the boy here." 18 Jesus gave a strong command to the demon[d] inside the boy. Then the demon came out, and the boy was healed from that time on.

19 The followers came to Jesus when he was alone and asked, "Why couldn't we force the demon out?"

20 Jesus answered, "Because your faith is too small. I tell you the truth, if your faith is as big as a mustard seed, you can say to this mountain, 'Move from here to there,' and it will move. All things will be possible for you." 21 [n]

Jesus Talks About His Death

22 While Jesus' followers were gathering in Galilee, he said to them, "The Son of Man[d] will be handed over to people, 23 and they will kill him. But on the third day he will be raised from the dead." And the followers were filled with sadness.

Jesus Talks About Paying Taxes

24 When Jesus and his followers came to Capernaum, the men who collected the Temple[d]

Satan Name for the devil, meaning "the enemy". Jesus means that Peter was talking like Satan.
Moses and Elijah Two of the most important Jewish leaders in the past. Moses had given them the law, and Elijah was an important prophet.
epilepsy A disease that causes a person sometimes to lose control of their body and perhaps faint, shake strongly or be unable to move.
Verse 21 Some Greek copies add verse 21: "That kind of spirit comes out only if you use prayer and give up eating."

tax came to Peter. They asked, "Does your teacher
pay the Temple tax?"
25Peter answered, "Yes, Jesus pays the tax."
Peter went into the house, but before he could
speak, Jesus said to him, "What do you think?
The kings of the earth collect different kinds of
taxes. But who pays the taxes—the king's
children or others?"
26Peter answered, "Other people pay the taxes."
Jesus said to Peter, "Then the children of the
king don't have to pay taxes. 27But we don't want
to upset these tax collectors. So go to the lake and
fish. After you catch the first fish, open its mouth
and you will find a coin. Take that coin and give
it to the tax collectors for you and me."

Who is the Greatest?

18 At that time the followers came to Jesus
and asked, "Who is greatest in the
kingdom of heaven?"
2Jesus called a little child to him and stood the
child before his followers. 3Then he said, "I tell
you the truth, you must change and become like
little children. Otherwise, you will never enter
the kingdom of heaven. 4The greatest person in
the kingdom of heaven is the one who makes
himself humble like this child.
5"Whoever accepts a child in my name accepts
me. 6If one of these little children believes in me,
and someone causes that child to sin, it would be
better for that person to have a large stone tied

FAITH

Speak Up

"Daddy, Daddy," whispered Nicki, "I need to say something!" Nicki's dad was about to lead an Easter Sunday service in the African village of Mwanza and was trying to listen to his translator – the last thing he needed was his five-year-old daughter interrupting.

"Be quiet," he replied.

Nicki was determined to be heard, so she went and bugged her mum until she listened. During one of the hymns before the sermon, Nicki's mum said to her husband, "I think you need to hear what she has to say."

So Nicki's dad relented. "Quickly Nicki, what is it you want to tell me?"

"Well . . . it's Easter Sunday and no one is smiling, I think someone should say something!"

So after being introduced to the 400 people Nicki stood up, fiddling with her dress and looking at the floor. After a few nervous moments, she looked up at the tall translator and said slowly, "Do you know that today is a very special day, because Jesus died on the cross and rose again for you and for me so we could have a place in heaven with him one day. So I don't really understand why no one is smiling. We should be really happy because Jesus loves us so much." As Nicki went to sit down you could hear a pin drop, and all you could see was a bunch of bright white smiles.

That morning there was no preaching because Nicki had said it all. People gave their lives to Jesus that day – people who went on to lead churches of their own.

Nicki was a little girl who had faith; God chose to use her on that day and the Holy Spirit really moved in that place.

Read **Matthew 17:14–20**.

- How do you think the disciples felt when they were told they could do anything if they had faith?
- Do you think you have faith that can move mountains?

Consider . . .

- next time someone tells you that they're unwell. Will your first thought be that they can be healed? If so, pray for them.
- chatting to someone you know who has been healed or someone who's prayed for another person and they've been healed. Ask them about their experience and about their faith.

For more, see . . .

- Matthew 21:18–22 (p.977)
- Luke 17:5–6 (p.1076)
- Luke 8:22–25 (p.1053)

around the neck and be drowned in the sea.
7How terrible for the people of the world because
of the things that cause them to sin. Such things
will happen, but how terrible for the one who
causes them to happen! 8If your hand or your foot
causes you to sin, cut it off and throw it away.
It is better for you to lose part of your body and
live for ever than to have two hands and two feet
and be thrown into the fire that burns for ever.
9If your eye causes you to sin, take it out and
throw it away. It is better for you to have only
one eye and live for ever than to have two eyes
and be thrown into the fire of hell.

A Lost Sheep

10"Be careful. Don't think these little children
are worth nothing. I tell you that they have
angels in heaven who are always with my Father
in heaven. 11 *n*
12"If a man has 100 sheep but one of the sheep
gets lost, he will leave the other 99 on the hill
and go to look for the lost sheep. 13I tell you the
truth, he is happier about that one sheep than
about the 99 that were never lost. 14In the same
way, your Father in heaven does not want any of
these little children to be lost.

When a Person Sins Against You

15"If your fellow believer sins against you, go
and tell him in private what he did wrong. If
he listens to you, you have helped that person to
be your brother or sister again. 16But if he refuses
to listen, go to him again and take one or two
other people with you. 'Every case may be

Verse 11 Some Greek copies add verse 11: "The Son of Man came to save lost people."

FRIENDS

Communication's What You Need

"I hate her. I can't believe she spoke to me like that, who does she think she is!" Kate had just come home and was livid with Gemma, her manager at work. Kate had been shouted at in front of everyone for taking five minutes extra on her lunch break. She felt embarrassed and hurt and wanted everyone to know how hard done by she was. She'd thought Gemma was a friend.

Kate's mum listened to her getting angrier and stopped her in mid-flow. "Have you spoken to Gemma about how she made you feel?"

Kate paused. "No, why would I do that? It would just bring up the bad situation again and she might even embarrass me further."

"But Gemma might just have had a bad day," explained Kate's mum, "or maybe what she said just came out wrong. You know she is a good friend and wouldn't want you to be unhappy. But you have to tell her what's up."

Kate calmed down and realised that perhaps she was blowing the situation out of proportion and decided to speak to Gemma to resolve the situation.

Read **Matthew 18:15–20** where it specifically talks about friendship in the church. It all comes down to communication.

- What does God promise to us in this passage?
- Do you think this approach works in every situation?

Consider . . .

- how you communicate that you appreciate your friends. Make a list of all your friends and write a letter or note saying something great about them, then send it to them.
- next time you have a conflict with a friend, talking it through with them properly rather than gossiping and complaining about them.

For more, see . . .

- Proverbs 11:13 (p.599)
- Matthew 6:14 (p.948)
- Proverbs 27:6 (p.614)
- Matthew 22:39 (p.980)

proved by two or three witnesses.'[n] [17]If he
refuses to listen to them, tell the church. If he
refuses to listen to the church, then treat him
like a person who does not believe in God or like
a tax collector.
[18]"I tell you the truth, the things you don't
allow on earth will be the things God does not
allow. And the things you allow on earth will be
the things that God allows.
[19]"Also, I tell you that if two of you on earth
agree about something and pray for it, it will be
done for you by my Father in heaven. [20]This is
true because if two or three people come
together in my name, I am there with them."

An Unforgiving Servant

[21]Then Peter came to Jesus and asked, "Lord,
when my fellow believer sins against me, how
many times must I forgive him? Should I forgive
him as many as seven times?"
[22]Jesus answered, "I tell you, you must forgive
him more than seven times. You must forgive
him even if he does wrong to you 77 times.
[23]"The kingdom of heaven is like a king
who decided to collect the money his servants
owed him. [24]When the king began to collect his
money, a servant who owed him several thou-
sand pounds was brought to him. [25]But the ser-
vant did not have enough money to pay his
master, the king. So the master ordered that
everything the servant owned should be sold,
even the servant's wife and children. Then the
money would be used to pay the king what the
servant owed.
[26]"But the servant fell on his knees and
begged, 'Be patient with me, and I will pay you

'Every . . . witnesses.' Quotation from Deuteronomy 19:15.

FORGIVENESS

So Sorry

Karen was in trouble and she knew it. She hadn't even started to look at the textbook, and the history exam would decide her grade.

She sat behind Mark, who was a bright student. He would help, she thought. "Psst, Mark," she whispered, poking him with her pencil. "Question five. Give me a clue."

Mark shrugged.

Karen poked him again with the pencil. Mark turned. "Stop it," he hissed.

"Mark, come up here and bring your paper," interrupted Ms Miller, the history teacher. As Mark walked to Ms Miller's desk, Karen pretended to work on her exam.

"I won't tolerate cheating," Ms Miller said quietly to Mark. She tossed the exam paper into the waste basket. Mark tried to explain what had happened, but she didn't believe him. "Take your seat and be quiet for the rest of the period," she snapped.

Karen saw Mark's face as he walked back towards his seat. His eyes showed his deep anger and hurt. "Why?" he whispered. Karen looked away.

As school ended, Karen saw Mark in the hall and tried to tell him how sorry she was. But Mark ignored her. At midnight, she still couldn't get Mark's hurt out of her mind. She knew what to do. "Tomorrow," she thought, "I'll tell Ms Miller what really happened, but will Mark ever forgive me?"

Both Karen and Mark could learn from **Matthew 18:21–35**.

- How is Karen's and Mark's struggle similar to the one in Jesus' story?
- Which character in Jesus' parable do you identify with most? Why?

Consider . . .

- listing the things you find difficult to forgive. Put them in order, from least to most difficult to forgive. What factors make forgiveness difficult?
- thinking of two people: one who has hurt you most, and one you have hurt the most. Pray for strength, and then do one thing to help bring forgiveness to both people.

For more, see . . .

- Jonah 3 (p.886)
- Luke 17:1–4 (p.1076)
- Micah 7:18–20 (p.897)

everything I owe.' [27]The master felt sorry for his
servant and told him he did not have to pay it
back. Then he let the servant go free.
[28]"Later, that same servant found another ser-
vant who owed him a few pounds. The servant
grabbed him around the neck and said, 'Pay me
the money you owe me!'
[29]"The other servant fell on his knees and
begged him, 'Be patient with me, and I will pay
you everything I owe.'
[30]"But the first servant refused to be patient.
He threw the other servant into prison until he
could pay everything he owed. [31]When the other
servants saw what had happened, they were
very sorry. So they went and told their master all
that had happened.
[32]"Then the master called his servant in and
said, 'You evil servant! Because you begged me
to forget what you owed, I told you that you did
not have to pay anything. [33]You should have
shown mercy to that other servant, just as I
showed mercy to you.' [34]The master was very
angry and put the servant in prison to be pun-
ished until he could pay everything he owed.
[35]"This king did what my heavenly Father will
do to you if you do not forgive your brother or
sister from your heart."

Jesus Teaches About Divorce

19 After Jesus said all these things, he left
Galilee and went into the area of Judea
on the other side of the Jordan River. [2]Large
crowds followed him, and he healed them there.
[3]Some Pharisees[d] came to Jesus and tried to
trick him. They asked, "Is it right for a man to
divorce his wife for any reason he chooses?"
[4]Jesus answered, "Surely you have read in
the Scriptures:[d] when God made the world,
'he made them male and female'.[n] [5]And God
said, 'So a man will leave his father and mother
and be united with his wife, and the two will
become one body.'[n] [6]So there are not two, but
one. God has joined the two together, so no one
should separate them."
[7]The Pharisees asked, "Why then did Moses
give a command for a man to divorce his wife by
giving her divorce papers?"
[8]Jesus answered, "Moses allowed you to di-
vorce your wives because you refused to accept
God's teaching, but divorce was not allowed in
the beginning. [9]I tell you that anyone who di-
vorces his wife and marries another woman is
guilty of adultery.[d] The only reason for a man to
divorce his wife is if his wife has sexual relations
with another man."
[10]The followers said to him, "If that is the only
reason a man can divorce his wife, it is better not
to marry."
[11]Jesus answered, "Not everyone can accept
this teaching, but God has made some able to
accept it. [12]There are different reasons why some
men cannot marry. Some men were born without
the ability to become fathers. Others were made
that way later in life by other people. And some
men have given up marriage because of the king-
dom of heaven. But the person who can marry
should accept this teaching about marriage."[n]

Jesus Welcomes Children

[13]Then the people brought their little children
to Jesus so he could put his hands on them[n] and
pray for them. His followers told them to stop,
[14]but Jesus said, "Let the little children come to
me. Don't stop them, because the kingdom of
heaven belongs to people who are like these chil-
dren." [15]After Jesus put his hands on the chil-
dren, he left that place.

A Rich Young Man's Question

[16]A man came to Jesus and asked, "Teacher,
what good thing must I do to have life for ever?"
[17]Jesus answered, "Why do you ask me about
what is good? Only God is good. But if you want
to have life for ever, obey the commands."
[18]The man asked, "Which commands?"
Jesus answered, " 'You must not murder
anyone; you must not be guilty of adultery;[d] you
must not steal; you must not tell lies about your
neighbour; [19]honour your father and mother;[n]
and love your neighbour as you love yourself.' "[n]
[20]The young man said, "I have obeyed all
these things. What else do I need to do?"
[21]Jesus answered, "If you want to be perfect,
then go and sell your possessions and give the

Sidelight Divorce has always been a controversial subject – even in Jesus' day. While some religious leaders said that someone could only get a divorce because of unfaithfulness, others argued that a husband could divorce a wife for burning supper, wearing the wrong thing in public, or even talking to another man. Jesus entered the debate in Matthew 19:1–12.

'he made . . . female' Quotation from Genesis 1:27 or 5:2.
'So . . . body.' Quotation from Genesis 2:24.
But . . . marriage. This may also mean, "The person who can accept this teaching about not marrying should accept it."
put his hands on them Showing that Jesus gave special blessings to these children.
'You . . . mother.' Quotation from Exodus 20:12–16; Deuteronomy 5:16–20.
'love . . . yourself.' Quotation from Leviticus 19:18.

money to the poor. If you do this, you will have
treasure in heaven. Then come and follow me."
[22]But when the young man heard this, he left
very sad, because he was rich.
[23]Then Jesus said to his followers, "I tell you
the truth, it will be hard for a rich person to
enter the kingdom of heaven. [24]Yes, I tell you
that it is easier for a camel to go through the eye
of a needle than for a rich person to enter the
kingdom of God."[25]When Jesus' followers heard
this, they were very surprised and asked, "Then
who can be saved?"
[26]Jesus looked at them and said, "This is
something people cannot do, but God can do all
things."
[27]Peter said to Jesus, "Look, we have left
everything and followed you. So what will we
have?"
[28]Jesus said to them, "I tell you the truth,
when the age to come has arrived, the Son of
Man[d] will sit on his great throne. All of you who
followed me will also sit on twelve thrones,
judging the twelve tribes[d] of Israel. [29]And all
those who have left houses, brothers, sisters,
father, mother, children or farms to follow me
will get much more than they left, and they will
have life for ever. [30]Many who have the highest
place now will have the lowest place in the
future. And many who have the lowest place
now will have the highest place in the future.

JUSTICE

It's Not Fair

The annual fun-run at Mount Farm had arrived at last. Hundreds of enthusiastic runners gathered at the starting line and prepared themselves for the three-mile race which lay ahead of them. They weren't running to win, but simply to take part. A medal was to be given to every competitor who completed the full three miles.

When the starting pistol was fired, feet pounded against the road in one thunderous roar. Many of the competitors had been sponsored, and were running in order to raise money for charity. Others were running to prove to their children and grandchildren that they were still fit. The children ran to prove that they were still fitter!

As the competitors approached the final half-mile of the race, a young boy of about twelve years of age joined in. He was wearing tracksuit bottoms and a white T-shirt. He ran more slowly than the rest of the runners, but when he finally reached the finishing line, he laughed out loud, thrilled with himself.

Then the medals were handed out. All the competitors who had gone the whole three miles were given their medals, and then the judge gave the young twelve-year-old boy a medal.

"You can't do that! He only ran half a mile!" some of the other competitors shouted.

The judge motioned for those who were making a fuss to come and take a look at something. Then he rolled the boy's trouser-leg up so that they could see his false foot.

"It may only be half a mile to you folks," the judge said, "but since young Robert here lost his foot in an accident, today was a half-mile marathon!"

Jesus tells a similar story in **Matthew 20:1–16**.

- How were the competitors' complaints similar to those of the vineyard workers?
- If you were amongst the first hired, how would you have felt? Would you have felt the same if you were one of the last hired? Why or why not?

Consider . . .

- watching the news on television or reading the newspapers and spotting items where justice is said to have been done. Ask yourself if justice, as taught by Jesus, really has been done.
- asking people that you meet what the word "justice" means. Compare their definitions with that of a dictionary, and then come up with your own definition.

For more, see . . .

- Job 8:3–6 (p.474)
- 2 Thessalonians 1:3–12 (p.1304)
- Luke 14:12–24 (p.1069)

A Story About Workers

20 "The kingdom of heaven is like a person
who owned some land. One morning,
he went out very early to hire some people to
work in his vineyard. 2The man agreed to pay
the workers a silver coin[n] for working on that
day. Then he sent them into the vineyard to
work. 3At about nine o'clock the man went to
the market-place and saw some other people
standing there, doing nothing. 4So he said to
them, 'If you go and work in my vineyard, I will
pay you what your work is worth.' 5So they
went to work in the vineyard. The man went out
again at about twelve o'clock and three o'clock
and did the same thing. 6At about five o'clock
the man went to the market-place again and saw
others standing there. He asked them, 'Why
have you stood here all day doing nothing?'
7They answered, 'No one has given us a job.'
The man said to them, 'Then you can go and
work in my vineyard.'
8"At the end of the day, the owner of the
vineyard said to the foreman of all the workers,
'Call the workers and pay them. Start with the
last people I hired and end with those I hired
first.'
9"When the workers who were hired at five
o'clock came to get their pay, each received a
silver coin. 10When the workers who were hired
first came to get their pay, they thought they
would be paid more than the others. But each
one of them also received a silver coin. 11When
they got their coin, they complained to the man
who owned the land. 12They said, 'Those people
were hired last and worked only one hour. But
you paid them the same as you paid us who
worked hard all day in the hot sun.' 13But the
man who owned the vineyard said to one of
those workers, 'Friend, I am being fair to you.
You agreed to work for a silver coin. 14So take
your pay and go. I want to give the man who
was hired last the same pay that I gave you. 15I
can do what I want with my own money. Are
you jealous because I am good to those people?'
16"So those who have the last place now will
have the first place in the future, and those who
have the first place now will have the last place
in the future."

Jesus Talks About His Own Death

17While Jesus was going to Jerusalem, he took
his twelve followers aside privately and said to
them, 18"Look, we are going to Jerusalem. The
Son of Man[d] will be turned over to the leading
priests and the teachers of the law, and they will
say that he must die. 19They will give the Son of
Man to the non-Jewish people to laugh at him
and beat him with whips and crucify him. But on
the third day, he will be raised to life again."

A Mother Asks Jesus a Favour

20Then the wife of Zebedee came to Jesus
with her sons. She bowed before him and asked
him to do something for her.

> **Sidelight** James and John, the sons of Zebedee, were nicknamed "the sons of thunder" (Matthew 20:20–24; see also Mark 3:17, p.1003). The nicknames may have come from their booming voices, or more probably, from the sort of behaviour they displayed in Luke 9:51–55 (p.1055)!

21Jesus asked, "What do you want?"
She said, "Promise that one of my sons will sit
at your right side and the other will sit at your
left side in your kingdom."
22But Jesus said, "You don't understand what
you are asking. Can you drink the cup that I am
about to drink?"[n]
The sons answered, "Yes, we can."
23Jesus said to them, "You will drink from my
cup. But I cannot choose who will sit at my right
or my left; those places belong to those for
whom my Father has prepared them."
24When the other ten followers heard this,
they were angry with the two brothers.
25Jesus called all the followers together and
said, "You know that the rulers of the non-Jewish
people love to show their power over the people.
And their important leaders love to use all their
authority. 26But it should not be that way among
you. Whoever wants to become great among you
must serve the rest of you like a servant. 27Who-
ever wants to become first among you must serve
the rest of you like a slave. 28In the same way, the
Son of Man[d] did not come to be served. He came
to serve others and to give his life as a ransom for
many people."

Jesus Heals Two Blind Men

29When Jesus and his followers were leaving
Jericho, a great many people followed him.
30Two blind men sitting by the road heard that
Jesus was going by, so they shouted, "Lord, Son
of David,[d] have mercy on us!"

coin Roman denarii. A silver coin was the average pay for one day's work.
drink . . . drink Jesus used the idea of drinking from a cup to ask if they could accept the same terrible things that would happen to him.

31 The people warned the blind men to be
quiet, but they shouted even more, "Lord, Son of
David, have mercy on us!"
32 Jesus stopped and said to the blind men,
"What do you want me to do for you?"
33 They answered, "Lord, we want to see."
34 Jesus felt sorry for the blind men and touched
their eyes, and at once they could see. Then they
followed Jesus.

Jesus Enters Jerusalem as a King

21 As Jesus and his followers were coming
closer to Jerusalem, they stopped at
Bethphage at the hill called the Mount of Olives.[d]
From there Jesus sent two of his followers 2 and
said to them, "Go to the town you can see ahead
of you. When you enter it, you will quickly find
a donkey tied there with its colt. Untie them and
bring them to me. 3 If anyone asks you why you
are taking the donkeys, say that the Master needs
them, and he will send them at once."
4 This was to bring about what the prophet[d]
had said:
5 "Tell the people of Jerusalem,
'Your king is coming to you.
He is gentle and riding on a donkey,
on the colt of a donkey.' " *Zechariah 9:9*
6 The followers went and did what Jesus told
them to do. 7 They brought the donkey and the
colt to Jesus and laid their coats on them, and
Jesus sat on them. 8 Many people spread their
coats on the road. Others cut branches from the
trees and spread them on the road. 9 The people
were walking ahead of Jesus and behind him,
shouting,
"Praise[n] to the Son of David![d]
God bless the One who comes in the name
of the Lord!
Praise to God in heaven!" *Psalm 118:26*
10 When Jesus entered Jerusalem, all the city
was filled with excitement. The people asked,
"Who is this man?"
11 The crowd answered, "This man is Jesus, the
prophet from the town of Nazareth in Galilee."

Jesus Goes to the Temple

12 Jesus went into the Temple[d] and threw out
all the people who were buying and selling there.
He turned over the tables of those who were ex-
changing different kinds of money, and he upset
the benches of those who were selling doves.
13 Jesus said to all the people there, "It is written
in the Scriptures,[d] 'My Temple will be called a
house for prayer.'[n] But you are changing it into
a 'hideout for robbers'."[n]
14 The blind and crippled people came to Jesus
in the Temple, and he healed them. 15 The leading
priests and the teachers of the law saw that Jesus
was doing wonderful things and that the children
were praising him in the Temple, saying,
"Praise[n] to the Son of David."[d] All these things
made the priests and the teachers of the law very
angry.
16 They asked Jesus, "Do you hear the things
these children are saying?"
Jesus answered, "Yes. Haven't you read in the
Scriptures, 'You have taught children and babies
to sing praises'?"[n]
17 Then Jesus left and went out of the city to
Bethany, where he spent the night.

The Power of Faith

18 Early the next morning, as Jesus was going
back to the city, he became hungry. 19 Seeing a fig
tree beside the road, Jesus went to it, but there
were no figs on the tree, only leaves. So Jesus said
to the tree, "You will never again have fruit." The
tree immediately dried up.
20 When his followers saw this, they were
amazed. They asked, "How did the fig tree dry up
so quickly?"
21 Jesus answered, "I tell you the truth, if you
have faith and do not doubt, you will be able to
do what I did to this tree and even more. You
will be able to say to this mountain, 'Go, fall into
the sea.' And if you have faith, it will happen. 22 If
you believe, you will get anything you ask for
in prayer."

Leaders Doubt Jesus' Authority

23 Jesus went to the Temple,[d] and while he was
teaching there, the leading priests and the older
leaders of the people came to him. They said,
"What authority do you have to do these things?
Who gave you this authority?"
24 Jesus answered, "I also will ask you a ques-
tion. If you answer me, then I will tell you what
authority I have to do these things. 25 Tell me:
when John baptised people, did that come from
God or just from other people?"
They argued about Jesus' question, saying, "If
we answer, 'John's baptism was from God', Jesus
will say, 'Then why didn't you believe him?'
26 But if we say, 'It was from people', we are afraid

Praise Literally, "Hosanna", a Hebrew word used at first in praying to God for help. At this time it was probably a shout of joy used in praising God or his Messiah.
'My Temple . . . prayer.' Quotation from Isaiah 56:7.
'hideout for robbers.' Quotation from Jeremiah 7:11.
'You . . . praises' Quotation from the Septuagint (Greek) version of Psalm 8:2.

of what the crowd will do because they all
believe that John was a prophet."[d]
27So they answered Jesus, "We don't know."
Jesus said to them, "Then I won't tell you what
authority I have to do these things.

A Story About Two Sons

28"Tell me what you think about this: a man
had two sons. He went to the first son and said,
'Son, go and work today in my vineyard.' 29The
son answered, 'I will not go.' But later the son
changed his mind and went. 30Then the father
went to the other son and said, 'Son, go and
work today in my vineyard.' The son answered,
'Yes, sir, I will go and work,' but he did not go.
31Which of the two sons obeyed his father?"
The priests and leaders answered, "The first
son."
Jesus said to them, "I tell you the truth, the tax
collectors and the prostitutes[d] will enter the
kingdom of God before you do. 32John came to
show you the right way to live. You did not
believe him, but the tax collectors and prostitutes
believed him. Even after seeing this, you still
refused to change your ways and believe him.

A Story About God's Son

33"Listen to this story: there was a man who
owned a vineyard. He put a wall around it and
dug a hole for a winepress[d] and built a tower.
Then he leased the land to some farmers and left
for a trip. 34When it was time for the grapes to be
picked, he sent his servants to the farmers to
get his share of the grapes. 35But the farmers
grabbed the servants, beat one, killed another
and then killed a third servant with stones. 36So
the man sent some other servants to the farmers,
even more than he sent the first time. But the
farmers did the same thing to the servants that
they had done before. 37So the man decided to
send his son to the farmers. He said, 'They will
respect my son.' 38But when the farmers saw

HYPOCRISY

Caught on Camera

If you read the little booklets that are inserted into the CD cases of some of the world's most famous music artists, you will often find messages of thanks to God. In fact, some pop celebrities make an even bigger deal out of publicly "giving God all the glory" when they are picking up awards or getting interviewed in magazines.

It's then really sad when a few weeks later they end up splashed all over the front page of the newspapers because they've been caught on camera looking bedraggled on a booze binge, or a having a shifty snog with somebody who isn't their partner! It's not our place to judge them – but we can learn from their mistakes.

Maybe you're not famous enough to have the paparazzi pouncing on you when you're up to no good, but you can ask your mates to watch your back instead. True friends will tell you when you're starting to go off the rails; they'll give you a hard time when you're starting to act like somebody different to the person God's made you to be.

Read **Matthew 21:28–32**.

- People say one thing and do another. Do you ever do that?
- Neither of the brothers in Jesus' story got it 100 per cent right. What would be the best way for them, and for you, to connect your words and actions?

Consider . . .

- asking a friend to point out your three greatest strengths and your three biggest weaknesses.
- writing a letter to yourself describing the kind of person you really want to be. Then sealing it in an envelope and opening it in a year's time.

For more, see . . .

- Genesis 3:8–12 (p.5)
- Matthew 7:4–5 (p.949)
- Psalm 26 (p.514)

the son, they said to each other, 'This son will
inherit the vineyard. If we kill him, it will be
ours!' [39]Then the farmers grabbed the son, threw
him out of the vineyard and killed him. [40]So
what will the owner of the vineyard do to these
farmers when he comes?"
[41]The priests and leaders said, "He will surely
kill those evil men. Then he will lease the
vineyard to some other farmers who will give
him his share of the crop at harvest time."
[42]Jesus said to them, "Surely you have read this
in the Scriptures: [d]

'The stone that the builders rejected
became the cornerstone. [d]
The Lord did this,
and it is wonderful to us.' *Psalm 118:22–23*

[43]"So I tell you that the kingdom of God will be
taken away from you and given to people who do
the things God wants in his kingdom. [44]The
person who falls on this stone will be broken,
and on whomsoever that stone falls, that person
will be crushed." [n]
[45]When the leading priests and the Pharisees [d]
heard these stories, they knew Jesus was
talking about them. [46]They wanted to arrest
him, but they were afraid of the people,
because the people believed that Jesus was a
prophet. [d]

Verse 44 Some copies do not have verse 44.

PRIORITIES

Top of the List

Lauren became a Christian after a wonderful week away at the church holiday club. Until then, she'd had no idea how much God loved her and that he wanted a relationship with her. It was incredible! She was thrilled when the leaders presented her with a Bible and she promised God she'd read it every day.

When she got home, Lauren volunteered to help out at Kids' Club and joined the youth group. Being a Christian meant so much to Lauren and she wanted to tell everyone and anyone about Jesus.

The following year Lauren started a new school, and over the next few years, things changed. Lauren made lots of friends and joined the drama group. She got the lead role in the school play but had to give up Kids' Club as she had too many rehearsals. Soon Lauren was missing church, as her boss at the restaurant wanted her to work Sundays. Even reading her Bible was difficult with all the homework she got.

In RE class one day, Lauren's teacher asked if anyone was a Christian. As Lauren raised her hand, her best friend Anna laughed. "Very funny," she said, "there's no way you're a Christian". Lauren was so shocked that she put her hand down and said nothing. She couldn't believe her closest friend had no idea she was a Christian.

At home that night, Lauren took out her Bible. Tears filled her eyes. She realised God wasn't her top priority any more; he wasn't even in the top ten. Friends, school, her job, the play – they had all taken the place that God once had in her life.

In **Matthew 22:1–14** Jesus tells a parable that helps us come to the same conclusions as Lauren: the most important thing in our lives is our relationship with God and how we live.

- How different were Lauren's priorities to that of the wedding guests?
- The king had a guest thrown out of the feast because he wasn't dressed properly. In what way do you think Lauren may not have looked like a Christian to her friends?

Consider . . .

- what your priorities are. Does God come first?
- how you can remind yourself that God is top priority. Try looking at how you spend your time each day. How much is spent on God?

For more, see . . .

- Matthew 22:37–38 (p.980)
- Colossians 3:1–17 (p.1292)
- Luke 10:38–42 (p.1058)

A Story About a Wedding Feast

22 Jesus again used stories to teach the people. He said, 2"The kingdom of heaven is like a king who prepared a wedding feast for his son. 3The king invited some people to the feast. When the feast was ready, the king sent his servants to tell the people, but they refused to come.

4"Then the king sent other servants, saying, 'Tell those who have been invited that my feast is ready. I have killed my best bulls and calves for the dinner, and everything is ready. Come to the wedding feast.'

5"But the people refused to listen to the servants and left to do other things. One went to work in his field, and another went to his business. 6Some of the other people grabbed the servants, beat them and killed them. 7The king was furious and sent his army to kill the murderers and burn their city.

8"After that, the king said to his servants, 'The wedding feast is ready. I invited those people, but they were not worthy to come. 9So go to the street corners and invite everyone you find to come to my feast.' 10So the servants went into the streets and gathered all the people they could find, both good and bad. And the wedding hall was filled with guests.

11"When the king came in to see the guests, he saw a man who was not dressed for a wedding. 12The king said, 'Friend, how were you allowed to come in here? You are not dressed for a wedding.' But the man said nothing. 13So the king told some servants, 'Tie this man's hands and feet. Throw him out into the darkness, where people will cry and grind their teeth with pain.'

14"Yes, many people are invited, but only a few are chosen."

Is It Right to Pay Taxes or Not?

15Then the Pharisees[d] left that place and made plans to trap Jesus into saying something wrong. 16They sent some of their own followers and some people from the group called Herodians.[n] They said, "Teacher, we know that you are an honest man and that you teach the truth about God's way. You are not afraid of what other people think about you, because you pay no attention to who they are. 17So tell us what you think. Is it right to pay taxes to Caesar[d] or not?"

18But knowing that these leaders were trying to trick him, Jesus said, "You hypocrites![d] Why are you trying to trap me? 19Show me a coin used for paying the tax." So the men showed him a coin.[n] 20Then Jesus asked, "Whose image and name are on the coin?"

21The men answered, "Caesar's."

Then Jesus said to them, "Give to Caesar the things that are Caesar's, and give to God the things that are God's."

22When the men heard what Jesus said, they were amazed and left him and went away.

Some Sadducees Try to Trick Jesus

23That same day some Sadducees[d] came to Jesus and asked him a question. (Sadducees believed that people would not rise from the dead.) 24They said, "Teacher, Moses said if a married man dies without having children, his brother must marry the widow and have children for him. 25Once there were seven brothers among us. The first one married and died. Since he had no children, his brother married the widow. 26Then the second brother also died. The same thing happened to the third brother and all the other brothers. 27Finally, the woman died. 28Since all seven men had married her, when people rise from the dead, whose wife will she be?"

29Jesus answered, "You don't understand, because you don't know what the Scriptures[d] say, and you don't know about the power of God. 30When people rise from the dead, they will not marry, nor will they be given to someone to marry. They will be like the angels in heaven. 31Surely you have read what God said to you about rising from the dead. 32God said, 'I am the God of Abraham, the God of Isaac and the God of Jacob.'[n] God is the God of the living, not the dead."

33When the people heard this, they were amazed at Jesus' teaching.

The Most Important Command

34When the Pharisees[d] learned that the Sadducees[d] could not argue with Jesus' answers to them, the Pharisees met together. 35One Pharisee, who was an expert on the law of Moses, asked Jesus this question to test him: 36"Teacher, which command in the law is the most important?"

37Jesus answered, " 'Love the Lord your God with all your heart, all your soul and all your mind.'[n] 38This is the first and most important command. 39And the second command is like

Herodians A political group that followed Herod and his family.
coin Roman denarii. A silver coin was the average pay for one day's work.
'I am . . . Jacob.' Quotation from Exodus 3:6.
'Love . . . mind.' Quotation from Deuteronomy 6:5.

the first: 'Love your neighbour as you love
yourself.'[n] 40All the law and the writings of the
prophets[d] depend on these two commands."

Jesus Questions the Pharisees

41While the Pharisees[d] were together, Jesus
asked them, 42"What do you think about the
Christ?[d] Whose son is he?"
They answered, "The Christ is the Son of
David."[d]
43Then Jesus said to them, "Then why did
David call him 'Lord'? David, speaking by the
power of the Holy Spirit,[d] said,
44'The LORD said to my Lord:
Sit by me at my right side,
until I put your enemies under your
control.' *Psalm 110:1*
45David calls the Christ 'Lord', so how can the
Christ be his son?"
46None of the Pharisees could answer Jesus'
question, and after that day no one was brave
enough to ask him any more questions.

Jesus Accuses Some Leaders

23 Then Jesus said to the crowds and to his
followers, 2"The teachers of the law and
the Pharisees[d] have the authority to tell you
what the law of Moses says. 3So you should
obey and follow whatever they tell you, but
their lives are not good examples for you to
follow. They tell you to do things, but they
themselves don't do them. 4They make strict
rules and try to force people to obey them, but
they are unwilling to help those who struggle

'Love . . . yourself.' Quotation from Leviticus 19:18.

HYPOCRISY

Watch Me

Matt was always doing something crazy to raise money for charity: sponsored mountain bike rides, shaving his eyebrows, or bungee jumping in a pair of Y-fronts.

"I'm just happy to help a hurting world. I really care about people who aren't as fortunate as me," he would tell the girls, who would all flutter their eyelids at him and tell him what a kind and generous person he was. Matt never seemed embarrassed by the attention.

Jon felt the pressure to be generous towards his classmate, Matt. Jon was a Christian, and felt others were watching him to see how he would react. "Matt is helping people," reasoned Jon, "and that's what Jesus told us to do."

Jon's church youth group were planning their mission week, when they would clean the local area and help people with their gardening and decorating to demonstrate God's love in a practical way. Jon decided to invite Matt to join in, as he always seemed so keen to help people.

But Jon was hurt by Matt's response: "Er no thanks! I don't want to waste my holiday doing the boring kind of work for other people that I usually try to get out of doing in my own home. But I do have a sponsored parachute jump coming up soon – it's going to be wicked fun, and it's for a good cause – maybe you can sponsor me for that?"

It's not a new thing for people's actions to say the opposite to their words. Jesus didn't like it. See what he had to say about it in **Matthew 23:1–12**.

- What are the similarities in behaviour between Matt and the Pharisees?
- What things were both Matt and the Pharisees getting right, and what things were they both getting wrong?

Consider . . .

- whether there are parts of your life where you need to bridge the gap between what you "preach" and what you "practise". What can you do about that this week?
- whether there is a situation where you could better demonstrate God's love through actions rather than words. Pray: "Lord Jesus, show me the situations in my life that require me to act like you, not just to talk like you."

For more, see . . .

- Mark 12:28–44 (p.1022)
- Luke 10:25–37 (p.1058)
- Luke 6:37–42 (p.1048)

under the weight of their rules.
5"They do good things so that other people
will see them. They make the boxes[n] of Scrip-
tures[d] that they wear bigger, and they make
their special prayer clothes very long. 6Those
Pharisees and teachers of the law love to have
the most important seats at feasts and in the
synagogues.[d] 7They love people to greet them
with respect in the market-places, and they love
to have people call them 'Teacher'.
8"But you must not be called 'Teacher', be-
cause you have only one Teacher, and you are all
brothers and sisters together. 9And don't call any
person on earth 'Father', because you have one
Father, who is in heaven. 10And you should not
be called 'Master', because you have only one
Master, the Christ.[d] 11Whoever is your servant is
the greatest among you. 12Whoever makes him-
self great will be made humble. Whoever makes
himself humble will be made great.
13"How terrible for you, teachers of the law
and Pharisees! You are hypocrites![d] You close the
door for people to enter the kingdom of heaven.
You yourselves don't enter, and you stop others
who are trying to enter. 14 [n]
15"How terrible for you, teachers of the law
and Pharisees! You are hypocrites! You travel
across land and sea to find one person who will
change to your ways. When you find that person,
you make him more fit for hell than you are.
16"How terrible for you! You guide the people,
but you are blind. You say, 'If people swear by
the Temple[d] when they make a promise, that
means nothing. But if they swear by the gold
that is in the Temple, they must keep that prom-
ise.' 17You are blind fools! Which is greater: the
gold or the Temple that makes that gold holy?
18And you say, 'If people swear by the altar when
they make a promise, that means nothing. But if
they swear by the gift on the altar, they must
keep that promise.' 19You are blind! Which is
greater: the gift or the altar that makes the gift
holy? 20The person who swears by the altar is
really using the altar and also everything on the
altar. 21And the person who swears by the
Temple is really using the Temple and also
everything in the Temple. 22The person who
swears by heaven is also using God's throne
and the One who sits on that throne.
23"How terrible for you, teachers of the law
and Pharisees! You are hypocrites! You give to
God one-tenth of everything you earn—even
your mint, dill and cumin.[n] But you don't obey
the really important teachings of the law—
justice, mercy and being loyal. These are the
things you should do, as well as those other
things. 24You guide the people, but you are blind!
You are like a person who picks a fly out of
a drink and then swallows a camel![n]
25"How terrible for you, teachers of the law
and Pharisees! You are hypocrites! You wash the
outside of your cups and dishes, but inside they
are full of things you got by cheating others and
by pleasing only yourselves. 26Pharisees, you are
blind! First make the inside of the cup clean, and
then the outside of the cup can be truly clean.
27"How terrible for you, teachers of the law
and Pharisees! You are hypocrites! You are like
tombs that are painted white. Outside, those
tombs look fine, but inside, they are full of the
bones of dead people and all kinds of unclean
things. 28It is the same with you. People look at
you and think you are good, but on the inside you
are full of hypocrisy and evil.
29"How terrible for you, teachers of the law
and Pharisees! You are hypocrites! You build
tombs for the prophets,[d] and you show honour to
the graves of those who lived good lives. 30You
say, 'If we had lived during the time of our ances-
tors, we would not have helped them kill the
prophets.' 31But you give proof that you are
children of those who murdered the prophets.
32And you will complete the sin that your ances-
tors started.
33"You are snakes! A family of poisonous
snakes! How are you going to escape God's
judgement? 34So I tell you this: I am sending to
you prophets and wise men and teachers. Some
of them you will kill and crucify. Some of them

Sidelight

When we come across the Pharisees we can guess that they are going to get it wrong. However, in Jesus' time the Pharisees were respected as being the most religious people around even if they weren't much fun to be with. They had the same sort of status as that highly respected group in your church or neighbourhood.

boxes Small leather boxes containing four important Scriptures. Some Jews tied these to the forehead and left arm, probably to show they were very religious.

Verse 14 Some Greek copies add verse 14: "How terrible for you, teachers of the law and Pharisees. You are hypocrites. You take away widows' houses, and you say long prayers so that people will notice you. So you will have a worse punishment."

mint, dill and cumin Herbs grown in gardens and used for spices. Only very religious people would be careful enough to give a tenth of these plants.

You . . . camel! Meaning, "You worry about the smallest mistakes but commit the biggest sin."

you will beat in your synagogues and chase from
town to town. 35So you will be guilty for the
death of all the good people who have been
killed on earth—from the murder of that good
man Abel to the murder of Zechariah[n] son of
Berakiah, whom you murdered between the
Temple and the altar. 36I tell you the truth, all of
these things will happen to you people who are
living now.

Jesus Feels Sorry for Jerusalem

37"Jerusalem, Jerusalem! You kill the prophets[d]
and stone to death those who are sent to you.
Many times I wanted to gather your people as a
hen gathers her chicks under her wings, but you
did not let me. 38Now your house will be left
completely empty. 39I tell you, you will not see me
again until that time when you will say, 'God bless
the One who comes in the name of the Lord.'"[n]

The Temple will Be Destroyed

24 As Jesus left the Temple[d] and was
walking away, his followers came up to
him to show him the Temple's buildings. 2Jesus
asked, "Do you see all these buildings? I tell
you the truth, not one stone will be left on
another. Every stone will be thrown down to the
ground."
3Later, as Jesus was sitting on the Mount of
Olives,[d] his followers came to be alone with him.
They said, "Tell us, when will these things
happen? And what will be the sign that it is time
for you to come again and for this age to end?"
4Jesus answered, "Be careful that no one fools

Abel . . . Zechariah In the order of the books of the Hebrew Old Testament, the first and last men to be murdered.
'God . . . Lord.' Quotation from Psalm 118:26.

LEADERSHIP

Leading a Just Cause

On 1 November 1872, Susan B. Anthony walked into a polling station, demanding to be registered to vote. She voted in the national election. Two weeks later a US marshal arrested her for "voting without lawful right". The judge wouldn't allow a jury trial. Her sentence was to pay a fine and the cost of the trial.

"Your Honour," declared Susan Anthony, "I shall never pay one dollar of your unjust penalty."

Susan had long been familiar with the controversy and conflict of reform movements. Years earlier, she had worked for the American Anti-Slavery Society. She regarded slavery as evil and un-Christian. She published the first women's newspaper and organised the first women's union. Now Susan was at the front of the National Women's Suffrage Movement, working tirelessly for women's voting rights.

The work was often discouraging. The press mocked her. She was denied entry into meetings. She was attacked by angry mobs. But these persecutions didn't stop her. She lectured, lobbied Congress and organised petitions.

In 1920, her efforts helped to change the law, making sure that everyone had the right to vote, regardless of their sex. But Susan never had the chance to vote. She had died fourteen years earlier.

Those who lead movements for justice usually suffer ridicule, persecution, and sometimes death. Read in **Matthew 23:34–39** what Jesus thinks about those who persecute the prophets of God.

- Why do you think people fear and persecute leaders such as Susan B. Anthony and the ones Jesus describes?
- When has your unpopular stance caused you to suffer persecution?

Consider . . .

- reading through one of the prophets of the Old Testament such as Amos (p.870), trying to understand why his messages were ridiculed and rejected.
- listening to leaders who have differing options, keeping your mind open for truth – even if it's uncomfortable.

For more, see . . .

- Jeremiah 3:11–13 (p.720)
- 2 Timothy 3:1–9 (p.1318)
- Ezekiel 20:13–20 (p.803)

you. 5 Many will come in my name, saying, 'I am
the Christ',[d] and they will fool many people.
6 You will hear about wars and stories of wars that
are coming, but don't be afraid. These things
must happen before the end comes. 7 Nations will
fight against other nations; kingdoms will fight
against other kingdoms. There will be times
when there is no food for people to eat, and there
will be earthquakes in different places. 8 These
things are like the first pains when something
new is about to be born.

9 "Then people will arrest you, hand you over
to be hurt and kill you. They will hate you be-
cause you believe in me. 10 At that time, many
will lose their faith, and they will turn against
each other and hate each other. 11 Many false
prophets[d] will come and cause many people to
believe lies. 12 There will be more and more evil
in the world, so most people will stop showing
their love for each other. 13 But those people who
keep their faith until the end will be saved. 14 The
Good News[d] about God's kingdom will be
preached in all the world, to every nation. Then
the end will come.

15 "Daniel the prophet spoke about 'the des-
troying terror'.[n] You will see this standing in the
holy place." (You who read this should under-
stand what it means.) 16 "At that time, the people
in Judea should run away to the mountains. 17 If
people are on the roofs[n] of their houses, they
must not go down to get anything out of their
houses. 18 If people are in the fields, they must not
go back to get their coats. 19 At that time, how
terrible it will be for women who are pregnant or
have nursing babies! 20 Pray that it will not be
winter or a Sabbath[d] day when these things hap-
pen and you have to run away, 21 because at that
time there will be much trouble. There will be
more trouble than there has ever been since the
beginning of the world until now, and nothing as
bad will ever happen again. 22 God has decided to
make that terrible time short. Otherwise, no one
would go on living. But God will make that time
short to help the people he has chosen. 23 At that
time, someone might say to you, 'Look, there is
the Christ!' Or another person might say, 'There
he is!' But don't believe them. 24 False Christs
and false prophets will come and perform
great wonders and miracles.[d] They will try to
fool even the people God has chosen, if that were
possible. 25 Now I have warned you about this
before it happens.

26 "If people tell you, 'The Christ is in the
desert', don't go there. If they say, 'The Christ is
in the inner room', don't believe it. 27 When the
Son of Man[d] comes, he will be seen by everyone,
like lightning flashing from the east to the west.
28 Wherever the dead body is, there the vultures
will gather.

29 "Soon after the trouble of those days,

'the sun will grow dark,
  and the moon will not give its light.
The stars will fall from the sky.
  And the powers of the heavens will be
    shaken.' *Isaiah 13:10; 34:4*

30 "At that time, the sign of the Son of Man will
appear in the sky. Then all the peoples of the
world will cry. They will see the Son of Man com-
ing on clouds in the sky with great power and
glory. 31 He will use a loud trumpet to send his an-
gels all around the earth, and they will gather his
chosen people from every part of the world.

32 "Learn a lesson from the fig tree: when its
branches become green and soft and new leaves
appear, you know summer is near. 33 In the same
way, when you see all these things happening,
you will know that the time is near, ready to
come. 34 I tell you the truth, all these things will
happen while the people of this time are still
living. 35 Earth and sky will be destroyed, but the
words I have said will never be destroyed.

When will Jesus Come Again?

36 "No one knows when that day or time will
be, not the angels in heaven, not even the Son.
Only the Father knows. 37 When the Son of Man[d]
comes, it will be like what happened during
Noah's time. 38 In those days before the flood,
people were eating and drinking, marrying and
giving their children to be married, until the day
Noah entered the ark. 39 They knew nothing
about what was happening until the flood came
and destroyed them. It will be the same when the
Son of Man comes. 40 Two men will be in the
field. One will be taken, and the other will be left.
41 Two women will be grinding grain with a
mill.[n] One will be taken, and the other will
be left.

42 "So always be ready, because you don't
know the day your Lord will come. 43 Remember
this: if the owner of the house knew what time
of night a thief was coming, the owner would
watch and not let the thief break in. 44 So you also
must be ready, because the Son of Man will come
at a time you don't expect him.

'the destroying terror' Mentioned in Daniel 9:27; 12:11 (see also Daniel 11:31).

roofs In Bible times houses were built with flat roofs. The roof was used for drying things such as flax and fruit. And it was used as an extra room, as a place for worship and as a place to sleep in the summer.

mill Two large, round, flat rocks used for grinding grain to make flour.

45“Who is the wise and loyal servant that
the master trusts to give the other servants
their food at the right time? 46When the master
comes and finds the servant doing his work,
the servant will be blessed. 47I tell you the
truth, the master will choose that servant to
take care of everything he owns. 48But suppose
that servant is evil, and thinks to himself,
‘My master will not come back soon,’ 49and he
begins to beat the other servants and eat and get
drunk with others like him? 50The master will
come when that servant is not ready and is not
expecting him. 51Then the master will cut him in
pieces and send him away to be with the
hypocrites,[d] where people will cry and grind
their teeth with pain.

A Story About Ten Bridesmaids

25 “At that time the kingdom of heaven will
be like ten bridesmaids who took their
lamps and went to wait for the bridegroom. 2Five
of them were foolish and five were wise. 3The
five foolish bridesmaids took their lamps, but they
did not take spare oil for the lamps to burn. 4The
wise bridesmaids took their lamps and more oil in
jars. 5Because the bridegroom was late, they
became sleepy and went to sleep.

6“At midnight someone cried out, ‘The
bridegroom is coming! Come and meet him!’
7Then all the bridesmaids woke up and got their
lamps ready. 8But the foolish ones said to the
wise, ‘Give us some of your oil, because our
lamps are going out.’ 9The wise bridesmaids
answered, ‘No, the oil we have might not be
enough for all of us. Go to the people who sell oil
and buy some for yourselves.’

10“So while the five foolish bridesmaids went
to buy oil, the bridegroom came. The bridesmaids
who were ready went in with the bridegroom to
the wedding feast. Then the door was closed
and locked.

FUTURE

The Rock

In San Francisco Bay, USA, an abandoned prison sits on Alcatraz Island. Its prisoners called it “The Rock”.

Whitey Thompson was a “hardened criminal”. He grew up in an abusive home. He ran away. Whitey seemed to have no future. After a failed bank robbery, Whitey was sent to jail, where he fought with guards and other prisoners. Being sent to “The Rock” seemed logical. It was the end of the line for those considered to be hopeless criminals.

Ironically, Whitey’s life turned around at Alcatraz. Whitey began to think about his future, which led him to find hope in Jesus.

Instead of killing time, he learned new skills, including painting. He painted beautiful landscapes. Guards, prisoners and visitors admired his art.

Whitey was released directly from Alcatraz to the streets. It wasn’t easy to keep looking towards the future and to build a new life. But Whitey finds strength in Jesus. Now Whitey can return to Alcatraz as a guest of the National Park Service, which runs the former prison as a tourist attraction. His eyes twinkle when tourists ask how he survived. “Here I was on The Rock,” he says. “Now I’ve found the true Rock.”

The future lies in Jesus. In **Matthew 24:36–44**, read Jesus’ promise to return. This promise not only gives hope for the future, but also a reason for living today, as Whitey discovered.

- What did Whitey discover in Jesus to help him to find hope for his future?
- How does knowing that Christ will return affect your view of your future?

Consider . . .

- making a list of the things you want to achieve. Keep the scripture in mind. If Jesus came tomorrow would you be ready?
- telling a cynical friend about the hope for the future you have in Jesus.

For more, see . . .

- Psalm 33:13–22 (p.519)
- 1 Thessalonians 5:1–11 (p.1300)
- Luke 12:35–40 (p.1064)

11“Later the others came back and said, ‘Sir, sir,
open the door to let us in.’ 12But the bridegroom
answered, ‘I tell you the truth, I don’t want to
know you.’
13“So always be ready, because you don’t know
the day or the hour the Son of Man[d] will come.

A Story About Three Servants

14“The kingdom of heaven is like a man who
was going to another place for a visit. Before he
left, he called for his servants and told them to
take care of his things while he was gone. 15He
gave one servant five bags of gold, another
servant two bags of gold and a third servant one
bag of gold, to each one as much as he could
manage. Then he left. 16The servant who got five
bags went quickly to invest the money and
earned five more bags. 17In the same way, the
servant who had two bags invested them and
earned two more. 18But the servant who got one
bag went out and dug a hole in the ground and
hid the master’s money.
19“After a long time the master came home
and asked the servants what they had done with
his money. 20The servant who was given five bags
of gold brought five more bags to the master and
said, ‘Master, you trusted me to care for five bags
of gold, so I used your five bags to earn five
more.’ 21The master answered, ‘You did well.
You are a good and loyal servant. Because you
were loyal with small things, I will let you care
for much greater things. Come and share my joy
with me.’
22“Then the servant who had been given two

DECISION MAKING

Watch the Time

Tim was so excited about the school trip to the theme park. Mrs Hill, his teacher, was always joking with Tim about how bad his timekeeping was, but on the afternoon before the trip, she called Tim to one side: “Tim, I know you’d be late for your own funeral but listen, we’ve GOT to leave on time tomorrow, so if you’re not here at 8.30 a.m., we’re leaving without you. OK?”

All the way home, Tim was telling himself over and over again what he needed to do: get everything ready before he went to bed, set the alarm, go to bed early and get a good night’s sleep. But as always, when Tim got into the house, he switched on his computer, and got engrossed in some games. Time flew by. When Tim finally fell into bed, he leant over and set his alarm clock for 7.00 a.m.

He woke with a start. Squinting, he looked at the clock – 8.23 a.m! Frantically, he jumped out of bed and raced to get his clothes on. He grabbed his bag and a couple of things he wished he’d got ready the night before and, still half-dressed, ran out of the front door and down the road.

Tim was back at his house just fifteen minutes later. He’d missed the coach. Just as Mrs Hill had warned, they had gone without him. How had it happened? How had he not been ready for something that was so important to him? It must have been a problem with the alarm clock.

Back in his room, Tim grabbed the clock to check he’d set it properly and slumped on his bed. It read 7.00 . . . p.m!

Read **Matthew 25:1–13**. It’s a story that Jesus told to explain how some people won’t be ready when he comes back.

- Both Tim and the bridesmaids in the story really wanted to be ready. What got in the way?
- Tim was disappointed at missing out on the trip. What did Jesus mean that the consequences were of the bridesmaids missing the wedding?

Consider . . .

- how we can be ready for when Jesus comes back. What does it mean?
- the things that distract you from being “watchful”.

For more, see . . .

- Mark 13:32–35 (p.1024)
- Romans 7:15–25 (p.1193)
- Luke 12:35–48 (p.1064)

bags of gold came to the master and said, 'Master,
you gave me two bags of gold to care for, so I used
your two bags to earn two more.' 23The master
answered, 'You did well. You are a good and loyal
servant. Because you were loyal with small
things, I will let you care for much greater things.
Come and share my joy with me.'
24"Then the servant who had been given one
bag of gold came to the master and said, 'Master,
I knew that you were a hard man. You harvest
things you did not plant. You gather crops where
you did not sow any seed. 25So I was afraid and
went and hid your money in the ground. Here is
your bag of gold.' 26The master answered, 'You
are a wicked and lazy servant! You say you knew
that I harvest things I did not plant and that I
gather crops where I did not sow any seed. 27So
you should have put my gold in the bank. Then,
when I came home, I would have received my
gold back with interest.'
28"So the master told his other servants, 'Take
the bag of gold from that servant and give it to the
servant who has ten bags of gold. 29Those who
have much will get more, and they will have
much more than they need. But those who do
not have much will have everything taken away
from them.' 30Then the master said, 'Throw that
useless servant outside, into the darkness where
people will cry and grind their teeth with pain.'

The King will Judge All People

31"The Son of Man[d] will come again in his
great glory, with all his angels. He will be King
and sit on his great throne. 32All the nations of the

SERVICE

Coffee For the Boss

Chris had, without doubt, managed to get the best work experience placement in the whole school. Chris was jammy like that. For the next three weeks, he was going to be the personal assistant to Sir James Mears, an incredibly rich, powerful and influential businessman. Everywhere he went, Chris would go too. So, whilst his classmates were serving customers in shops, Chris would be flying to New York in a private jet with Sir James to attend a meeting. OK, so he would be mainly making tea and coffee all day, but his mates would never know that! Besides, Chris thought he was making quite an impact, and was quietly hopeful he might be given a job at the end of it.

The final day arrived, and Chris was called into Sir James's office for his appraisal.

"Well Chris," began Sir James, "thank you for all you have done here. Although, I have to say I am a little disappointed. You have hardly made any cups of tea and coffee, and haven't done any of the other things I hoped you might."

Chris was stunned. "I made you loads of cups of coffee," he replied.

"Yes, you made me coffee," said Sir James, "but you never made a single cup for anyone else who works here. You ignored each and every one of them, even though you had to walk past them to get to the kitchen. You didn't think they were important enough to serve. In my company, we are all important, and we all serve each other. In fact, a measure of how good an employee you are is how much you serve the people around you, rather than just trying to impress the boss."

Read **Matthew 25:31–46**.

- How does verse 34 describe the reward Jesus has for people who serve others?
- Read the things that God regards as good service in verses 34–36. Do they sound hard things to do or are they things you could easily get involved in?

Consider . . .

- helping out in serving the needy with your church or a local charity.
- praying for people to cross your path who you can demonstrate Jesus' love to.

For more, see . . .

- Isaiah 1:11–17 (p.639)
- John 13:1–17 (p.1119)
- Matthew 20:25–28 (p.976)

world will be gathered before him, and he will
separate them into two groups as a shepherd sep-
arates the sheep from the goats. 33The Son of
Man will put the sheep on his right and the goats
on his left.
34"Then the King will say to the people on
his right, 'Come, my Father has given you his
blessing. Receive the kingdom God has prepared
for you since the world was made. 35I was
hungry, and you gave me food. I was thirsty,
and you gave me something to drink. I was alone
and away from home, and you invited me into
your house. 36I was without clothes, and you
gave me something to wear. I was sick, and
you cared for me. I was in prison, and you
visited me.'
37"Then the good people will answer, 'Lord,
when did we see you hungry and give you food,
or thirsty and give you something to drink?
38When did we see you alone and away from
home and invite you into our house? When did
we see you without clothes and give you
something to wear? 39When did we see you sick
or in prison and care for you?'
40"Then the King will answer, 'I tell you the
truth, anything you did for even the least of my
people here, you also did for me.'
41"Then the King will say to those on his left,
'Go away from me. You will be punished. Go
into the fire that burns for ever that was
prepared for the devil and his angels. 42I was
hungry, and you gave me nothing to eat. I was
thirsty, and you gave me nothing to drink. 43I was
alone and away from home, and you did not
invite me into your house. I was without
clothes, and you gave me nothing to wear. I
was sick and in prison, and you did not care
for me.'
44"Then those people will answer, 'Lord, when
did we see you hungry or thirsty or alone and
away from home or without clothes or sick or in
prison? When did we see these things and not
help you?'
45"Then the King will answer, 'I tell you
the truth, anything you refused to do for even
the least of my people here, you refused to do
for me.'
46"These people will go off to be punished for
ever, but the good people will go to live for ever."

The Plan to Kill Jesus

26 After Jesus finished saying all these
things, he told his followers, 2"You
know that the day after tomorrow is the day
of the Passover[d] Feast. On that day the Son
of Man[d] will be given to his enemies to be
crucified."
3Then the leading priests and the Jewish elders
had a meeting at the palace of the high priest,
named Caiaphas. 4At the meeting, they plan-
ned to set a trap to arrest Jesus and kill him.
5But they said, "We must not do it during
the feast, because the people might cause a riot."

Perfume for Jesus' Burial

6Jesus was in Bethany at the house of Simon,
who had a skin disease. 7While Jesus was there, a
woman approached him with an alabaster[d] jar
filled with expensive perfume. She poured this
perfume on Jesus' head while he was eating.
8His followers were upset when they saw
the woman do this. They asked, "Why waste that
perfume? 9It could have been sold for a great deal
of money and the money given to the poor."
10Knowing what had happened, Jesus said,
"Why are you troubling this woman? She did an
excellent thing for me. 11You will always have the
poor with you, but you will not always have me.
12This woman poured perfume on my body to
prepare me for burial. 13I tell you the truth, wher-
ever the Good News[d] is preached in all the
world, what this woman has done will be told,
and people will remember her."

Judas Becomes an Enemy of Jesus

14Then one of the twelve apostles, Judas
Iscariot, went to talk to the leading priests. 15He
said, "What will you pay me for giving Jesus to
you?" And they gave him 30 silver coins. 16After
that, Judas watched for the best time to turn
Jesus over.

Jesus Eats the Passover Meal

17On the first day of the Feast[d] of Unleavened
Bread, the followers came to Jesus. They said,
"Where do you want us to prepare for you to eat
the Passover[d] meal?"
18Jesus answered, "Go into the city to a certain
man and tell him, 'The Teacher says: the chosen
time is near. I will have the Passover with my
followers at your house.'" 19The followers did
what Jesus told them to do, and they prepared
the Passover meal.
20In the evening Jesus was sitting at the table
with his twelve followers. 21As they were eating,
Jesus said, "I tell you the truth, one of you will
turn against me."
22This made the followers very sad. Each one
began to say to Jesus, "Surely, Lord, I am not the
one who will turn against you, am I?"
23Jesus answered, "The man who has dipped
his hand with me into the bowl is the one who
will turn against me. 24The Son of Man[d] will die,
just as the Scriptures[d] say. But how terrible it will
be for the person who hands the Son of Man over
to be killed. It would be better for him if he had
never been born."

25 Then Judas, who would give Jesus to his
enemies, said to Jesus, "Teacher, surely I am not
the one, am I?"
Jesus answered, "Yes, it is you."

The Lord's Supper

26 While they were eating, Jesus took some
bread and thanked God for it and broke it. Then
he gave it to his followers and said, "Take this
bread and eat it; this is my body."
27 Then Jesus took a cup and thanked God for
it and gave it to the followers. He said, "Every
one of you drink this. 28 This is my blood which is
the new agreement that God makes with his
people. This blood is poured out for many to
forgive their sins. 29 I tell you this: I will not drink
of this fruit of the vine[n] again until that day
when I drink it new with you in my Father's
kingdom."
30 After singing a hymn, they went out to the
Mount of Olives.[d]

Jesus' Followers will Leave Him

31 Jesus told his followers, "Tonight you will all
stumble in your faith on account of me, because
it is written in the Scriptures:[d]
'I will kill the shepherd,
and the sheep will scatter.' *Zechariah 13:7*
32 But after I rise from the dead, I will go ahead of
you into Galilee."
33 Peter said, "Everyone else may stumble in
their faith because of you, but I will not."
34 Jesus said, "I tell you the truth, tonight before
the cockerel crows you will say three times that
you don't know me."
35 But Peter said, "I will never say that I don't
know you! I will even die with you!" And all the
other followers said the same thing.

fruit of the vine Product of the grapevine; this may also be translated "wine".

FRIENDS

Don't Drop Me

Have you ever played a trust game in a drama lesson? They're really simple – it's like playing a game of catch, only you're the ball. For example, you might be in a pair, standing in front of your partner. All you have to do is keep your feet still and fall backwards. Your partner promises to catch you. The question is, do you trust them enough to catch you or will you move your feet and catch yourself?

Trust is a tricky thing. You can't live your life without putting your trust in other people every single day: the bus driver not to crash the bus; the teacher to teach you the right information; a friend to keep a confidence. The problem with trust is that it makes us vulnerable. We don't want to have to rely on someone else. And we don't want to get hurt if they let us down.

Imagine someone catching you in a trust game and then, instead of tipping you forward so that you are upright again, they take a step back, dropping you to the floor. That is betrayal: putting your trust in someone and finding them to be unworthy of it; trusting someone who lets you down.

Read **Matthew 26:14–25**.

- Have you ever been betrayed? Have you ever betrayed someone else? How did it make you feel?
- Read on through the story (up to chapter 27:10). What do you think Jesus felt about Judas? How did the disciples feel about Judas? How did Judas feel about himself?

Consider . . .

- whether there is someone who has betrayed you. If so, write down what they did and how it made you feel. Ask Jesus to help you forgive that person and restore trust. Rip up the piece of paper, knowing that you don't hold anything against them anymore.
- whether there someone you have let down. Make them a card, asking them to forgive you.

For more, see . . .

- 2 Samuel 12:1–10 (p.295)
- Matthew 5:43–48 (p.946)
- Psalm 25:1–7 (p.514)

Jesus Prays Alone

36 Then Jesus went with his followers to a place called Gethsemane. He said to them, "Sit here while I go over there and pray." 37 He took Peter and the two sons of Zebedee with him, and he began to be very sad and troubled. 38 He said to them, "My heart is full of sorrow, to the point of death. Stay here and watch with me."

39 After walking a little farther away from them, Jesus fell to the ground and prayed, "My Father, if it is possible, do not give me this cup[n] of suffering. But do what you want, not what I want." 40 Then Jesus went back to his followers and found them asleep. He said to Peter, "You men, could you not stay awake with me for one hour? 41 Stay awake and pray for strength against temptation. The spirit wants to do what is right, but the body is weak."

42 Then Jesus went away a second time and prayed, "My Father, if it is not possible for this painful thing to be taken from me, and if I must do it, I pray that what you want will be done."

43 Then he went back to his followers, and again he found them asleep, because their eyes were heavy. 44 So Jesus left them and went away and prayed a third time, saying the same thing.

45 Then Jesus went back to his followers and said, "Are you still sleeping and resting? The time has come for the Son of Man[d] to be handed over to sinful people. 46 Get up, we must go. Look, here comes the man who has turned against me."

Jesus is Arrested

47 While Jesus was still speaking, Judas, one of the twelve apostles,[d] came up. With him were many people carrying swords and clubs who had been sent from the leading priests and the Jewish elders of the people. 48 Judas had planned to give them a signal, saying, "The man I kiss is Jesus. Arrest him." 49 At once Judas went to Jesus and said, "Greetings, Teacher!" and kissed him.

50 Jesus answered, "Friend, do what you came to do."

Then the people came and grabbed Jesus and arrested him. 51 When that happened, one of Jesus' followers reached for his sword and pulled it out. He struck the servant of the high priest and cut off his ear.

52 Jesus said to the man, "Put your sword back in its place. All who use swords will be killed with swords. 53 Surely you know I could ask my Father, and he would give me more than twelve armies of angels. 54 But it must happen this way to bring about what the Scriptures[d] say."

55 Then Jesus said to the crowd, "You came to get me with swords and clubs as if I were a criminal. Every day I sat in the Temple[d] teaching, and you did not arrest me there. 56 But all these things have happened so that it will come about as the prophets[d] wrote." Then all of Jesus' followers left him and ran away.

Jesus Before the Leaders

57 Those people who arrested Jesus led him to the house of Caiaphas, the high priest, where the teachers of the law and the Jewish elders were gathered. 58 Peter followed far behind to the courtyard of the high priest's house, and he sat down with the guards to see what would happen to Jesus.

59 The leading priests and the whole Jewish council tried to find something false against Jesus so they could kill him. 60 Many people came and told lies about him, but the council could find no real reason to kill him. Then two people came and said, 61 "This man said, 'I can destroy the Temple[d] of God and build it again in three days.' "

62 Then the high priest stood up and said to Jesus, "Aren't you going to answer? Don't you have something to say about their charges against you?" 63 But Jesus said nothing.

Again the high priest said to Jesus, "I command you by the power of the living God: tell us if you are the Christ,[d] the Son of God."

64 Jesus answered, "Those are your words. But I tell you, in the future you will see the Son of Man[d] sitting at the right hand of God, the Powerful One, and coming on clouds in the sky."

65 When the high priest heard this, he tore his clothes and said, "This man has said things that are against God! We don't need any more witnesses; you all heard him say these things against God. 66 What do you think?"

The people answered, "He should die."

67 Then the people there spat in Jesus' face and beat him with their fists. Others slapped him. 68 They said, "Prove to us that you are a prophet,[d] you Christ! Tell us who hit you!"

Peter Says He Doesn't Know Jesus

69 At that time, as Peter was sitting in the courtyard, a servant girl came to him and said, "You also were with Jesus of Galilee."

cup Jesus is talking about the terrible things that will happen to him. Accepting these things will be very hard, like drinking a cup of something bitter.

[70]But Peter said to all the people there that he
was never with Jesus. He said, "I don't know
what you are talking about."
[71]When he left the courtyard and was at the
gate, another girl saw him. She said to the people
there, "This man was with Jesus of Nazareth."
[72]Again, Peter said he was never with him,
saying, "I swear I don't know this man Jesus!"
[73]A short time later, some people standing
there went to Peter and said, "Surely you are
one of those who followed Jesus. The way you
talk proves it."
[74]Then Peter began to place a curse on him-
self and swear, "I don't know the man." At once,
a cockerel crowed. [75]And Peter remembered
what Jesus had told him: "Before the cockerel
crows, you will say three times that you don't
know me." Then Peter went outside and cried
bitterly.

Sidelight Practically every legal rule was broken to convict Jesus (Matthew 26:57–67). Jewish law prohibited trials at night, during Passover, and without legitimate witnesses – all of which happened in Jesus' trial. Any good judge today would throw out the verdict.

Jesus is Taken to Pilate

27 Early the next morning, all the leading
priests and elders of the people decided
that Jesus should die. [2]They tied him, led
him away, and turned him over to Pilate, the
governor.

Judas Kills Himself

[3]Judas, the one who had given Jesus to his
enemies, saw that they had decided to kill Jesus.
Then he was very sorry for what he had done. So
he took the 30 silver coins[n] back to the priests

coins Roman denarii. A silver coin was the average pay for one day's work.

STRESS

All Too Much

After school, there was a growing excitement. A steady crescendo of "Fight, fight, fight, FIGHT!" could be heard across the playground. Geoff heard the noise but wasn't interested. Then he heard the horrible half-cry/half-scream of "Geoff, help!"

Geoff's body froze as he turned his head through 180°. His eyes dilated as through the crowd he saw Tony, the new kid, his friend. Geoff gasped as he saw Tony fall under the blows of the bullies. Tony wouldn't hurt anyone but he was a little "different". People often felt threatened by that.

A younger kid began tugging at Geoff's jacket. It took a full five seconds for Geoff's awareness to register the annoyance. "You're Tony's mate, aren't you? Tony with the weird dress sense. Look, he's not even fighting back. He's soft," said the girl as she spat on the ground.

Geoff pulled free, "No, I don't know him. Sorry." Geoff looked back to the scene and held eye contact with Tony for the briefest of moments. In one movement, he turned and pressed play on his MP3 player to drown out the shouts. However, the music couldn't drown out the voice of guilt whispering in his mind. He started to pray.

Geoff knew that he should stand up for his friend, but in times of stress it's often difficult to make the right choices. Read how Peter coped under pressure in **Matthew 26:69–75**.

- Why do you think Peter didn't stand up for Jesus? How is this similar to Geoff's situation?
- In what situations do you find it difficult to make the right choices?

Consider . . .

- talking with a friend about how to make the right choices in times of stress.
- someone you know who needs a friend right now. Pray for an opportunity to show them friendship.

For more, see . . .

- Proverbs 28:13 (p.615)
- Luke 22:55 62 (p.1089)

and the leaders, 4saying, "I sinned; I handed over to you an innocent man."

The leaders answered, "What is that to us? That's your problem, not ours."

5So Judas threw the money into the Temple.[d] Then he went off and hanged himself.

6The leading priests picked up the silver coins in the Temple and said, "Our law does not allow us to keep this money with the Temple money, because it has paid for a man's death." 7So they decided to use the coins to buy Potter's Field as a place to bury strangers who died in Jerusalem. 8That is why that field is still called the Field of Blood. 9So what Jeremiah the prophet[d] had said came true: "They took 30 silver coins. That is how little the Israelites thought he was worth. 10They used those 30 silver coins to buy the potter's field, as the Lord commanded me."[n]

Pilate Questions Jesus

11Jesus stood before Pilate the governor, and Pilate asked him, "Are you the king of the Jews?"

Jesus answered, "Those are your words."

12When the leading priests and the elders accused Jesus, he said nothing.

13So Pilate said to Jesus, "Don't you hear them accusing you of all these things?"

14But Jesus said nothing in answer to Pilate, and Pilate was very surprised at this.

Pilate Tries to Free Jesus

15Every year at the time of Passover[d] the governor would free one prisoner whom the people chose. 16At that time there was a man in prison, named Barabbas, who was known to be very bad. 17When the people gathered at Pilate's house, Pilate said, "Whom do you want me to set free: Barabbas or Jesus who is called the Christ?"[d] 18Pilate knew that the people had turned Jesus over to him because they were jealous.

19While Pilate was sitting there on the judge's seat, his wife sent this message to him: "Don't have anything to do with that man, because he is innocent. Today I had a dream about him, and it troubled me very much."

20But the leading priests and elders convinced the crowd to ask for Barabbas to be freed and for Jesus to be killed.

21Pilate said, "I have Barabbas and Jesus. Which do you want me to set free for you?"

The people answered, "Barabbas."

22Pilate asked, "So what should I do with Jesus, the one called the Christ?"

They all answered, "Crucify him!"

23Pilate asked, "Why? What wrong has he done?"

But they shouted louder, "Crucify him!"

24When Pilate saw that he could do nothing about this and that a riot was starting, he took some water and washed his hands[n] in front of the crowd. Then he said, "I am not guilty of this man's death. You are the ones who are causing it!"

25All the people answered, "We and our children will be responsible for his death."

26Then he set Barabbas free. But Jesus was beaten with whips and handed over to the soldiers to be crucified.

27The governor's soldiers took Jesus into the governor's palace, and they all gathered around him. 28They took off his clothes and put a red robe on him. 29Using thorny branches, they made a crown, put it on his head, and put a stick in his right hand. Then the soldiers bowed before Jesus and made fun of him, saying, "Hail, King of the Jews!" 30They spat on Jesus. Then they took his stick and began to beat him on the head. 31After they finished, the soldiers took off the robe and put his own clothes on him again. Then they led him away to be crucified.

Jesus is Crucified

32As the soldiers were going out of the city with Jesus, they forced a man from Cyrene, named Simon, to carry the cross for Jesus. 33They all came to the place called Golgotha, which means the Place of the Skull. 34The soldiers gave Jesus wine mixed with gall[n] to drink. He tasted the wine but refused to drink it. 35When the soldiers had crucified him, they threw lots[d] to decide who would get his clothes. 36The soldiers sat there and continued watching him. 37They put a sign above Jesus' head with a charge against him. It said: THIS IS JESUS, THE KING OF THE JEWS. 38Two robbers were crucified beside Jesus, one on the right and the other on the left. 39People walked by and insulted Jesus and shook their heads, 40saying, "You said you could destroy the Temple[d] and build it again in three days. So save yourself! Come down from that cross if you are really the Son of God!"

"They . . . commanded me." See Zechariah 11:12–13 and Jeremiah 32:6–9.
washed his hands He did this as a sign to show that he wanted no part in what the people did.
gall Probably a drink of wine mixed with drugs to help a person feel less pain.

41The leading priests, the teachers of the law and the Jewish elders were also making fun of Jesus. 42They said, "He saved others, but he can't save himself! He says he is the king of Israel! If he is the king, let him come down now from the cross. Then we will believe in him. 43He trusts in God, so let God save him now, if God really wants him. He himself said, 'I am the Son of God.' "

44And in the same way, the robbers who were being crucified beside Jesus insulted him.

Jesus Dies

45At noon the whole country became dark, and the darkness lasted for three hours. 46At about three o'clock Jesus cried out in a loud voice, "Eli, Eli,[n] lama sabachthani?" This means, "My God, my God, why have you rejected me?"

47Some of the people standing there who heard this said, "He is calling Elijah."

48Quickly one of them ran and got a sponge and filled it with vinegar and tied it to a stick and gave it to Jesus to drink. 49But the others said, "Don't bother him. We want to see if Elijah will come to save him."

50But Jesus cried out again in a loud voice and died.

51Then the curtain in the Temple[n] was torn into two pieces, from the top to the bottom. Also, the earth shook and rocks broke apart. 52The graves opened, and many of God's people who had died were raised from the dead. 53They came out of the graves after Jesus was raised from the dead and went into the holy city, where they appeared to many people.

54When the army officer and the soldiers guarding Jesus saw this earthquake and everything else that happened, they were very frightened and said, "He really was the Son of God!"

55Many women who had followed Jesus from Galilee to help him were standing at a distance from the cross, watching. 56Mary Magdalene, and Mary the mother of James and Joseph, and the mother of James and John were there.

Jesus is Buried

57That evening a rich man named Joseph, a follower of Jesus from the town of Arimathea, came to Jerusalem. 58Joseph went to Pilate and asked to have Jesus' body. So Pilate gave orders for the soldiers to give it to Joseph. 59Then Joseph took the body and wrapped it in a clean linen cloth. 60He put Jesus' body in a new tomb that he had cut out of a wall of rock, and he rolled a very large stone to block the entrance of the tomb. Then Joseph went away. 61Mary Magdalene and the other woman named Mary were sitting near the tomb.

The Tomb of Jesus is Guarded

62The next day, the day after Preparation[d] Day, the leading priests and the Pharisees[d] went to Pilate. 63They said, "Sir, we remember that while that liar was still alive he said, 'After three days I will rise from the dead.' 64So give the order for the tomb to be guarded closely till the third day. Otherwise, his followers might come and steal the body and tell people that he has risen from the dead. That lie would be even worse than the first one."

65Pilate said, "Take some soldiers and go and guard the tomb the best way you know." 66So they all went to the tomb and made it safe from thieves by sealing the stone in the entrance and putting soldiers there to guard it.

Jesus Rises from the Dead

28 The day after the Sabbath[d] day was the first day of the week. At dawn on the first day, Mary Magdalene and another woman named Mary went to look at the tomb.

2At that time there was a strong earthquake. An angel of the Lord came down from heaven, went to the tomb and rolled the stone away from the entrance. Then he sat on the stone. 3He was shining as bright as lightning, and his clothes were white as snow. 4The soldiers guarding the tomb shook with fear because of the angel, and they became like dead men.

Sidelight The stones in front of tombs in Jesus' day were large, disc-shaped boulders (Matthew 28:2). They were placed in grooves so that they would roll down and block the entrance to the cave-like tombs, making them difficult to move.

5The angel said to the women, "Don't be afraid. I know that you are looking for Jesus, who has been crucified. 6He is not here. He has risen from the dead as he said he would. Come and see the place where his body was. 7And then go

Eli, Eli Some Bibles translate this as Eloi, Eloi.

curtain in the Temple A curtain divided the Most Holy Place from the other part of the Temple. That was the special building in Jerusalem where God commanded the Jewish people to worship him.

quickly and tell his followers, 'Jesus has risen
from the dead. He is going into Galilee ahead of
you, and you will see him there.'" Then the
angel said, "Now I have told you."
8The women left the tomb quickly. They
were afraid, but they were also very happy.
They ran to tell Jesus' followers what had
happened. 9Suddenly, Jesus met them and said,
"Greetings." The women came up to him, took
hold of his feet, and worshipped him. 10Then
Jesus said to them, "Don't be afraid. Go and tell
my followers to go on to Galilee, and they will
see me there."

The Soldiers Report to the Leaders

11While the women went to tell Jesus' followers,
some of the soldiers who had been guarding
the tomb went into the city to tell the leading
priests everything that had happened. 12Then
the priests met with the Jewish elders and
made a plan. They paid the soldiers a large
amount of money 13and said to them, "Tell the
people that Jesus' followers came during the
night and stole the body while you were asleep.
14If the governor hears about this, we will satisfy
him and save you from trouble." 15So the sol-
diers kept the money and did as they were told.
And that story is still spread among the Jewish
people even today.

Jesus Talks to His Followers

16The eleven followers went to Galilee to the
mountain where Jesus had told them to go. 17On
the mountain they saw Jesus and worshipped him,

SADNESS

Deeper Than Dewy Eyes

Being sad doesn't really mean what it used to. It can describe someone's dress sense or taste in music! But real sadness is a totally different thing, and it can't necessarily be seen on the outside. Yes, sometimes sadness is visible; we all shed a tear every now and again. But there is a kind of sadness that is much deeper than just getting dewy eyes during a slushy film.

The famous scientist Albert Einstein said, "Learn from yesterday, live for today, hope for tomorrow." Real sadness is the emotion that comes and fills the gap where hope used to live. It gives us the feeling that there's no point to tomorrow – it tells us that the best things in life are behind us and there's nothing left to look forward to.

At some time in our lives, we will all have to endure the bitter taste of this sadness. Some people seem to get off lightly; some people seem to get more than their fair share. Sadness can either creep or crash into our lives. Knowing how to deal with it will mean that we come out stronger instead of being paralysed by it.

Read **Matthew 27:57–61**.

- Think about the hopes and dreams Jesus' friends had in their hearts as they hung out with him. What kind of sadness would they be feeling at this time?
- The Bible talks about how Jesus understood the pain we go through at certain times in our life (see Isaiah 53:4). Isn't it amazing to know a God who shares our sadness as well as our joys?

Consider . . .

- asking your older relatives to tell you stories from their life. Listening is a great gift and they will appreciate your interest.
- whether something you've said or done has made someone else sad. Think about how you can make sure you don't do it again.

For more, see . . .

- Isaiah 35:10 (p.674)
- John 20:10–18 (p.1132)
- Isaiah 53:4–5 (p.697)
- Revelation 21:1–5 (p.1403)

but some of them did not believe it was really
Jesus. [18]Then Jesus came to them and said, "All
power in heaven and on earth is given to me. [19]So
go and make followers of all people in the world.
Baptise them in the name of the Father and the
Son and the Holy Spirit. [d] [20]Teach them to obey
everything that I have taught you, and I will be
with you always, even until the end of this age."

FOLLOWING GOD

Not Me, Lord!

"How do I know what God wants me to do?" Beth asked her minister. Beth was in her second year at college, struggling with her future. She was home for the Christmas break, thinking about the summer.

"Obviously, you want to follow God," Reverend Jones said. "Try listening. You'll be surprised at what you hear."

"I don't want to be a minister!" Beth shot back. "I'm not sure I feel called to do that."

"You don't have to be in full-time ministry to follow God," he said quietly. "Following God takes different paths. Why not explore other possibilities?"

Beth stayed open to God's calling. She was offered a job for the summer at a church camp. She accepted. She worked with children, led Bible studies, planned and led worship and music, and camped outdoors. She listened for God and learned what it meant to be a follower.

She returned to college ready for her final year. "I discovered that I'm good at things like teaching. I even like Bible studies," she wrote to Reverend Jones. "I still don't know what I'll do. But I'll keep finding ways to follow God."

Beth learned that following God may seem frightening at first. But after the initial "Yes, send me," serving God brings adventure, growth and true joy. Read **Matthew 28:16–20** to find Jesus' commission and promise for those who agree to follow him.

- What did Beth learn about following God? How is this similar to Jesus' command?
- How do you follow God? How do you seek to make others followers of God?

Consider . . .

- writing a scenario in which you befriend people who have never heard about Jesus. How will you teach them about faith?
- listing the ways in which the careers you're interested in could minister and spread God's kingdom.

For more, see . . .

- Exodus 3 (p.61)
- Acts 1:7–11 (p.1137)
- John 21 (p.1134)

Mark

Why Read This Book:

- Learn about the healings and miracles that Jesus performed (Mark 2—8).
- Listen to Jesus' teachings about following him (Mark 9—12).
- See how Jesus was victorious even though people killed him (Mark 14—16).

When?

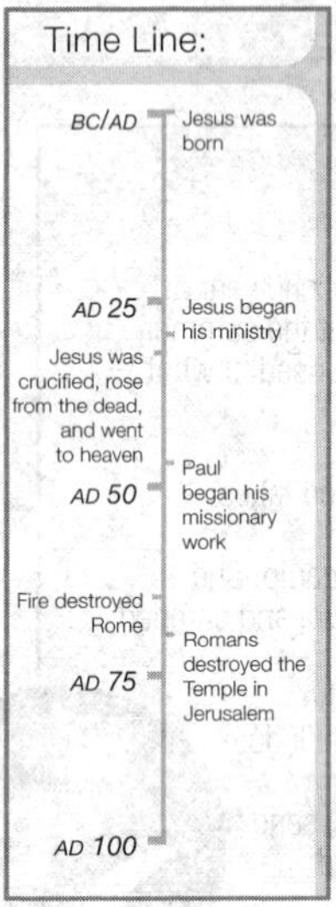

Behind the Scenes:

The Gospel of Mark is filled with short, quick "news items" about Jesus – moving quickly from scene to scene, and filled with action and drama.

It cuts quickly from one scene to the next – packed with simple, vivid stories. The Greek word translated "immediately" or "then" appears more than forty times in just sixteen chapters!

The book begins with a short section on John the Baptist, who announced Jesus' coming. Then it tells about Jesus' miracles and activities in the region of Lake Galilee. Finally, the action moves to Jerusalem, where Jesus was arrested and killed. Then he rose from the grave.

Unlike the other three gospels, this book was for people who weren't familiar with stories about Jesus, so it's a great place to begin learning the basics!

Where?

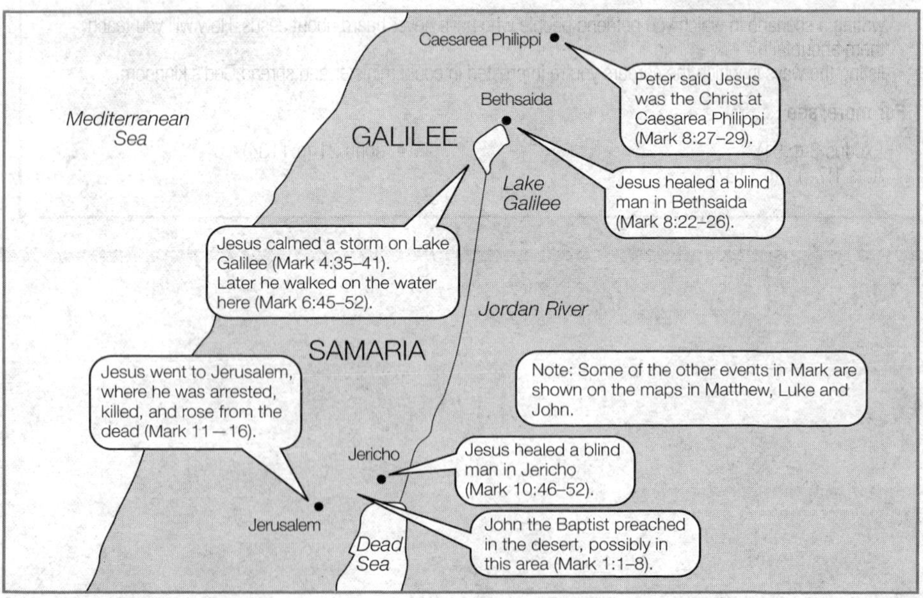

John Prepares for Jesus

1 This is the beginning of the Good News[d]
about Jesus Christ, the Son of God,[n] 2as the
prophet[d] Isaiah wrote:

"I will send my messenger ahead of you,
who will prepare your way." *Malachi 3:1*

3"This is a voice of one
who calls out in the desert:
'Prepare the way for the Lord.
Make the road straight for him.' " *Isaiah 40:3*

> **Sidelight** John the Baptist quoted from Isaiah about preparing the way for the Lord (Mark 1:2–3), a passage of scripture describing an ancient practice for travelling oriental kings. Whenever a ruler went to places without roads, a crew of workers went ahead to smooth out rough places for the king's chariot.

4John was baptising people in the desert and
preaching a baptism of changed hearts and lives
for the forgiveness of sins. 5All the people from
Judea and Jerusalem were going out to him. They
confessed their sins and were baptised by him in
the Jordan River. 6John wore clothes made from
camel's hair, had a leather belt around his waist
and ate locusts[d] and wild honey. 7This is what
John preached to the people: "There is one com-
ing after me who is greater than I; I am not good
enough even to kneel down and untie his san-
dals. 8I baptise you with water, but he will baptise
you with the Holy Spirit."[d]

Jesus is Baptised

9At that time Jesus came from the town of
Nazareth in Galilee and was baptised by John in
the Jordan River. 10Immediately, as Jesus was com-
ing up out of the water, he saw heaven open. The
Holy Spirit[d] came down on him like a dove, 11and
a voice came from heaven: "You are my Son,
whom I love, and I am very pleased with you."
12Then the Spirit sent Jesus into the desert.
13He was in the desert for 40 days and was
tempted by Satan. He was with the wild animals,
and the angels came and took care of him.

Jesus Chooses Some Followers

14After John was put in prison, Jesus went into
Galilee, preaching the Good News[d] from God.
15He said, "The right time has come. The king-
dom of God is near. Change your hearts and lives
and believe the Good News!"
16When Jesus was walking by Lake Galilee, he
saw Simon[n] and his brother Andrew throwing a
net into the lake because they were fishermen.
17Jesus said to them, "Come follow me, and I will
make you fish for people." 18So Simon and Andrew
immediately left their nets and followed him.
19Going a little farther, Jesus saw two more
brothers, James and John, the sons of Zebedee.
They were in a boat, mending their nets. 20Jesus
immediately called them, and they left their
father in the boat with the hired workers and
followed Jesus.

Jesus Forces Out an Evil Spirit

21Jesus and his followers went to Capernaum.
On the Sabbath[d] day he went to the synagogue[d]
and began to teach. 22The people were amazed
at his teaching, because he taught like a person
who had authority, not like their teachers of the
law. 23Just then, a man was there in the syna-
gogue who had an evil spirit in him. He shouted,
24"Jesus of Nazareth! What do you want with
us? Did you come to destroy us? I know who
you are—God's Holy One!"
25Jesus commanded the evil spirit, "Be quiet!
Come out of the man!" 26The evil spirit shook
the man violently, gave a loud cry and then came
out of him.
27The people were so amazed they asked each
other, "What is happening here? This man is
teaching something new, and with authority. He
even gives commands to evil spirits, and they
obey him." 28And the news about Jesus spread
quickly everywhere in the area of Galilee.

Jesus Heals Many People

29As soon as Jesus and his followers left the
synagogue,[d] they went with James and John to
the home of Simon[n] and Andrew. 30Simon's
mother-in-law was sick in bed with a fever, and
the people told Jesus about her. 31So Jesus went
to her bed, took her hand and helped her up. The
fever left her, and she began serving them.
32That evening, after the sun went down, the
people brought to Jesus all who were sick and had
demons[d] in them. 33The whole town gathered at
the door. 34Jesus healed many who had different
kinds of sicknesses, and he forced many demons to
leave people. But he would not allow the demons
to speak, because they knew who he was.
35Early the next morning, while it was still
dark, Jesus woke and left the house. He went to
a lonely place, where he prayed. 36Simon and his
friends went to look for Jesus. 37When they found
him, they said, "Everyone is looking for you!"

the Son of God Some Greek copies omit these words.
Simon Simon's other name was Peter.

38Jesus answered, "We should go to other towns
around here so I can preach there too. That is
the reason I came." 39So he went everywhere in
Galilee, preaching in the synagogues and forcing
out demons.

Jesus Heals a Sick Man

40A man with a skin disease came to Jesus. He
fell to his knees and begged Jesus, "You can heal
me if you will."
41Jesus felt sorry for the man, so he reached
out his hand and touched him and said, "I will.
Be healed!" 42Immediately the disease left the
man, and he was healed.
43Jesus told the man to go away at once, but he
warned him strongly, 44"Don't tell anyone about
this. But go and show yourself to the priest. And
offer the gift Moses commanded for people who
are made well.[n] This will show the people what
I have done." 45The man left there, but he began
to tell everyone that Jesus had healed him, and so
he spread the news about Jesus. As a result, Jesus
could not enter a town if people saw him. He
stayed in remote places [where nobody lived], but
people came to him from everywhere.

Jesus Heals a Paralysed Man

2 A few days later, when Jesus came back to
Capernaum, the news spread that he was at
home. 2Many people gathered together so that
there was no room in the house, not even outside
the door. And Jesus was teaching them God's
message. 3Four people came, carrying a paralysed
man. 4Since they could not get to Jesus because

Moses . . . well Read about this in Leviticus 14:1–32.

FOLLOWING GOD

Leaving Everything

Li Tang grew up in the Chinese capital of Beijing. All her life, Li's family and friends had taught her that God was not real. Li believed what others told her, but she hoped that some day she would find that there really is a God.

When Li was seventeen years old, she found a Bible in an old library. She opened it and began reading about God loving people and sending his Son to the world.

Li was amazed. Why had she never heard about this before? She wanted to know more about this God and follow him. How could she? She decided that she would leave everything – her family, her friends and even her country – to follow Jesus.

Her parents weren't thrilled with Li's decision to study Christianity, but they wanted her to be happy. Many of her friends couldn't understand why she wanted to leave.

Li moved to England to study and learn more about Jesus so that some day she could return to tell others about him. While in England, she met Christians who helped her to learn and to grow.

"You really experience the change in your life," Li reflected after she had decided to follow Jesus. "It's really a difference."

Jesus asked people to follow him. Often, following meant leaving many things behind. Yet following also meant gaining a friend like Jesus. Read about Jesus' first followers in **Mark 1:14–20**.

- How did what Li had to give up compare with what the disciples had to give up to follow Jesus?
- What have you had to give up to follow Jesus? What do you need to give up now to follow Jesus more fully?

Consider . . .

- making a small, wooden cross as a reminder of what it means to follow Jesus.
- interviewing two Christian friends about what it means to them to follow Jesus.

For more, see . . .

- Ruth 1:11–18 (p.249)
- John 1:35–42 (p.1097)
- Matthew 4:12–22 (p. 942)

of the crowd, they dug a hole in the roof right
above where he was speaking. When they got
through, they lowered the mat with the paralysed
man on it. 5When Jesus saw the faith of these
people, he said to the paralysed man, "Young
man, your sins are forgiven."
6Some of the teachers of the law were sitting
there, thinking to themselves, 7"Why does this
man say things like that? He is speaking as if he
were God. Only God can forgive sins."
8Jesus knew immediately what these teachers
of the law were thinking. So he said to them,
"Why are you thinking these things? 9Which
is easier: to tell this paralysed man, 'Your sins
are forgiven,' or to tell him, 'Stand up. Take your
mat and walk'? 10But I will prove to you that
the Son of Man[d] has authority on earth to forgive
sins." So Jesus said to the paralysed man, 11"I tell
you, stand up, take your mat, and go home."
12Immediately the paralysed man stood up, took
his mat and walked out while everyone was
watching him.

The people were amazed and praised God. They said, "We have never seen anything like this!"

Sidelight Most of Jesus' ministry took place around Lake Galilee (for example, see Mark 2:13–14). This lake is the world's lowest freshwater lake, with a surface 207 metres below sea level. Despite the lake's prominence in Jesus' ministry, it's only mentioned three times in the Old Testament (Numbers 34:11, p.161; Joshua 12:3, p.213; and Joshua 13:27, p.214).

FORGIVENESS

The Christmas Gift

"I can't stand him! He's the one who left us. Why should I have to ruin my Christmas by spending it with him?" Jessica shouted at her mother through sobs.

"Darling, that was three years ago," Helen said. She put her hand on her daughter's shoulder. "A lot has happened since then. We're different people now – and happier too."

"That doesn't make it right. He still left us," Jessica countered.

Helen sat down beside Jessica. "Your father needed work, and there was nothing here for him. He had to go somewhere he could feel useful and needed. I never believed he really wanted to leave us."

"But he did leave us," Jessica said. "And he never came back."

"You're right. But that doesn't mean he doesn't love you. Now he wants you to understand, to forgive him, and to get to know him again. Could you please forgive your father and go to his house for a few days for Christmas?" Helen asked sympathetically.

"I suppose I never really understood why he left, Mum." Jessica thought for a moment, then said, "I don't really want to, but I suppose I could spend part of my Christmas holiday with Dad."

As Jessica reached for the phone, Helen smiled and said quietly, "Perhaps forgiveness can be your Christmas gift to your dad."

Forgiveness can bring healing to people and relationships. Read **Mark 2:1–12** to see how Jesus' miracle resulted in forgiveness and healing.

- How did Jesus' and Jessica's forgiveness bring about healing?
- Who needs a healing word of forgiveness from you?

Consider . . .

- phoning someone you've not talked to for a long time because of a misunderstanding.
- listing people you need to forgive, forgiving each person and then performing an act of service for each one to bring about healing.

For more, see . . .

- Psalm 130 (p.577)
- Hebrews 12:14–15 (p.1344)
- Luke 5:17–26 (p.1047)

13 Jesus went to the lake again. The whole
crowd followed him there, and he taught them.
14 While he was walking along, he saw a man
named Levi [n] son of Alphaeus, sitting in the tax
collector's booth. Jesus said to him, "Follow me,"
and he stood up and followed Jesus.
15 Later, as Jesus was having dinner at Levi's
house, many tax collectors and "sinners" were
eating there with Jesus and his followers. Many
people like this followed Jesus. 16 When the
teachers of the law who were Pharisees [d] saw
Jesus eating with the tax collectors and "sinners",
they asked his followers, "Why does he eat with
tax collectors and sinners?"
17 Jesus heard this and said to them, "It is not
the healthy people who need a doctor, but the
sick. I did not come to invite good people but to
invite sinners."

Jesus' Followers are Criticised

18 Now the followers of John [n] and the Phar-
isees [d] often gave up eating for a certain time. [n]

Levi Also known as Matthew.
John John the Baptist, who preached to people about Christ's coming (Mark 1:4–8; Luke 3:1–22).
gave . . . time This is called "fasting". The people would give up eating for a special time of prayer and worship to God. It was also done to show sadness and disappointment.

CELEBRATING

Party Blues

Alison's graduation party really drew a crowd. She had invited all her friends, which came to around thirty. On top of that, her parents had invited several relatives and friends.

People filled every nook and corner in the house. A group of boys talked and joked on the patio. Several of the girls gathered in the kitchen and laughed at each other's stories. And a large assortment of other people crammed into the living room, talking about the degree ceremony and laughing at the antics of some of the students.

Everyone was having a great time. Everyone, that is, except Alison. She stood quietly in a corner of the kitchen, only half-listening to the girls' conversation.

"What's wrong, Al?" asked Christine, walking quietly over to Alison. "You seem far away."

"Yes, I suppose I am," Alison said with a weak smile. "It's just that now that I'm out of university, I don't know what's going to happen to my friendships. I love you all so much; it makes me sad to think of you not being in my life any more."

Christine touched Alison on the arm. "Hey, listen, none of us knows what's going to happen from one day to the next. We may all get to stay together for ever, or we may not. We just can't know for sure. But," she added with a smile, "we're here today. So let's go and join the others and have some fun, all right? After all, it is your party."

"OK, OK," Alison said jokingly. Then she reached out and grabbed Christine's hand. "Thanks, Chris. I needed to hear that."

Christine helped Alison to realise the importance of celebrating the good things that come along, even though they may not last. Jesus helped his disciples to understand the same truth. Read the story that Jesus used in **Mark 2:18–22**.

- How was Alison like the Pharisees' followers in this passage?
- How can you celebrate Jesus' presence in your life, as this passage directs?

Consider . . .

- writing down all the ways that Jesus reveals his presence in your life, and then thanking God for being so real to you.
- throwing a party to celebrate friendship and God's love.

For more, see . . .

- Isaiah 62:1–9 (p.706)
- John 3:25–30 (p.1101)
- Matthew 9:14–17 (p.954)

Some people came to Jesus and said, "Why do
John's followers and the followers of the Pharisees
often give up eating, but your followers don't?"
19Jesus answered, "The friends of the bridegroom
do not give up eating while the bridegroom is still
with them. As long as the bridegroom is with
them, they cannot give up eating. 20But the time
will come when the bridegroom will be taken
from them, and then they will give up eating.
21"No one sews a patch of unshrunken cloth
over a hole in an old coat. Otherwise, the patch
will shrink and pull away—the new patch will
pull away from the old coat. Then the hole will
be worse. 22Also, no one ever pours new wine
into old leather bags. Otherwise, the new wine
will break the bags, and the wine will be ruined
along with the bags. But new wine should be put
into new leather bags."

Jesus is Lord of the Sabbath

23One Sabbath[d] day, as Jesus was walking
through some fields of grain, his followers began
to pick some grain to eat. 24The Pharisees[d] said
to Jesus, "Why are your followers doing what is
not lawful on the Sabbath day?"
25Jesus answered, "Have you never read
what David did when he and those with him
were hungry and needed food? 26During the
time of Abiathar the high priest, David went into
God's house and ate the holy bread, which is
lawful only for priests to eat. And David also
gave some of the bread to those who were with
him."
27Then Jesus said to the Pharisees, "The
Sabbath day was made to help people; they were
not made to be ruled by the Sabbath day. 28So
then, the Son of Man[d] is Lord even of the
Sabbath day."

Jesus Heals a Man's Hand

3 Another time when Jesus went into a
synagogue,[d] a man with a crippled hand
was there. 2Some people watched Jesus closely
to see if he would heal the man on the

FREEDOM

Breathe Easy

Julia's heart was thumping. She was late home again and Dad would be cross. Dad had given her a curfew time of 9.30 p.m. but her watch now said 10.30 p.m. Julia had already been late home twice that week.

Julia wondered what she would say to her dad. She ran over the evening's events in her mind. She had been on her way home when she had heard crying. Her heart tightened and her fingernails cut into her palms. There before her was a boy of no more than six with terror-stricken, puffy eyes. "I'm lost," he said in dismay between sobs. Two thoughts struck her. Firstly, what about the curfew? Secondly, she had to help this poor, lost boy.

Julia reached into her handbag to find her phone and called the police, explaining where she was and who she had found. Julia held the small boy's hand until the police arrived. Mission accomplished.

Now Julia had to face her dad. The door of the house swung open and Julia saw him silhouetted in the entrance. His angry face softened into concern. "You did the right thing. We're so proud," he said.

Julia's dad set a curfew because he loved her but Julia was also given freedom to make her own choice. Read **Mark 2:23—3:6** to see how Jesus exercised freedom in love.

- Why do you think Jesus healed a man on the Sabbath day when it angered the religious leaders?
- Have you ever been guilty of having a judging attitude like the Pharisees?

Consider . . .

- the phrase "Love God and do what you please". Take some time to think about what that phrase means.
- praying that God will help you to understand when you judge people in the way the Pharisees judged Jesus. Ask him for forgiveness.

For more, see . . .

- Matthew 11:19 (p.959)
- Galatians 5:1 (p.1263)
- 2 Corinthians 3:17 (p.1242)

Sabbath[d] day so they could accuse him.
3Jesus said to the man with the crippled hand,
"Stand up here in the middle of everyone."
4Then Jesus asked the people, "Which is
lawful on the Sabbath day: to do good or to do
evil, to save a life or to kill?" But they said
nothing to answer him.
5Jesus was angry as he looked at the people,
and he felt very sad because they were stubborn.
Then he said to the man, "Hold out your hand."
The man held out his hand and it was healed.
6Then the Pharisees[d] left and began making plans
with the Herodians[n] about a way to kill Jesus.

Many People Follow Jesus

7Jesus left with his followers for the lake, and
a large crowd from Galilee followed him. 8Also
many people came from Judea, from Jerusalem,
from Idumea, from the lands across the Jordan
River and from the area of Tyre and Sidon.
When they heard what Jesus was doing, many
people came to him. 9When Jesus saw the
crowds, he told his followers to get a boat ready
for him to keep people from crowding against
him. 10He had healed many people, so all the
sick were pushing towards him to touch him.
11When evil spirits saw Jesus, they fell down

Herodians A political group that followed Herod and his family.

EVIL

Fearful Escape

Susan was small, tired and afraid. Her troubled eyes continually darted around the crowded bus stop. Everyone looked suspicious to Susan and made her want to run somewhere – anywhere – to get away from those who might find her and take her back.

Susan had a good reason to be afraid. Although she looked like any other teenager, Susan was different from most.

For the past six years, Susan had been involved in a coven that worshipped Satan. It had seemed fun when she started. Now, at eighteen, she wanted to get out.

Susan pulled at the sleeves of her sweater. Her arms must not be seen. They would expose her. Carved into her flesh were Satanic symbols to identify her as a devout Satanist. These marks were only an outward sign of the evil she had witnessed.

Susan had met some Christians a few years earlier. They had tried to tell her the truth about God's love and had offered to help her to escape to a new way of life. She had refused then, but now she was going to find them.

Seeing that no one was following her, she breathed a sigh of relief. As she climbed up the bus steps, Susan thought about how each step she took brought her closer to the freedom that Jesus offered.

Since the beginning of time, Satan has lied to people, telling them that his way is right and God's way is evil.

Mark 3:20–35 shows one instance when Satan convinced people that Jesus himself had an evil spirit.

- Why did Susan and the people in Jesus' day fear Satan?
- What promise do you see in this passage that helps you in the face of evil?

Consider . . .

- praying for your church and family to be united so that they can stand against evil.
- identifying an evil influence in your life and working to get rid of it.

For more, see . . .

- Genesis 3 (p.5)
- John 10:19–21 (p.1114)
- Matthew 9:32–34 (p.954)

before him and shouted, "You are the Son of
God!" 12But Jesus strongly warned them not to
tell who he was.

Jesus Chooses His Twelve Apostles

13Then Jesus went up on a mountain and
called to him the men he wanted, and they came
to him. 14Jesus chose twelve men and called them
apostles.[d] He wanted them to be with him, and
he wanted to send them out to preach 15and to
have the authority to force demons[d] out of peo-
ple. 16These are the twelve men he chose: Simon
(Jesus named him Peter), 17James and John, the
sons of Zebedee (Jesus named them Boanerges,
which means "Sons of Thunder"), 18Andrew,
Philip, Bartholomew, Matthew, Thomas, James
the son of Alphaeus, Thaddaeus, Simon the
Zealot[d] 19and Judas Iscariot, who later turned
against Jesus.

Some People Say Jesus Has a Devil

20Then Jesus went home, but again a crowd
gathered. There were so many people that Jesus
and his followers could not eat. 21When his
family heard this, they went to get him because
they thought he was out of his mind. 22But the
teachers of the law from Jerusalem were saying,
"Beelzebul[d] is living inside him! He uses power
from the ruler of demons[d] to force demons out
of people."
23So Jesus called the people together and
taught them with stories. He said, "Satan will
not force himself out of people. 24A kingdom that
is divided cannot continue, 25and a family that
is divided cannot continue. 26And if Satan is
against himself and fights against his own
people, he cannot continue; that is the end of
Satan. 27No one can enter a strong person's
house and steal his things unless he first ties up
the strong person. Then he can steal things from
the house. 28I tell you the truth, all sins that peo-
ple do and all the things people say against God
can be forgiven. 29But anyone who speaks
against the Holy Spirit[d] will never be forgiven;
he is guilty of a sin that continues for ever."
30Jesus said this because the teachers of the
law said that he had an evil spirit inside him.

Jesus' True Family

31Then Jesus' mother and brothers arrived.
Standing outside, they sent someone in to tell
him to come out. 32Many people were sitting
around Jesus, and they said to him, "Your mother
and brothers are waiting for you outside."
33Jesus asked, "Who are my mother and my
brothers?" 34Then he looked at those sitting
around him and said, "Here are my mother and
my brothers! 35My true brother and sister and
mother and father are those who do what God
wants."

A Story About Planting Seed

4 Again Jesus began teaching by the lake. A
great crowd gathered around him, so he sat
down in a boat near the shore. All the people
stayed on the shore close to the water. 2Jesus
taught them many things, using stories. He said,
3"Listen! A farmer went out to plant his seed.
4While he was planting, some seed fell by the
road, and the birds came and ate it up. 5Some
seed fell on rocky ground where there wasn't
much earth. That seed grew very fast, because
the ground was not deep. 6But when the sun
rose, the plants dried up because they did not
have deep roots. 7Some other seed fell among
thorny weeds, which grew and choked the good
plants. So those plants did not produce a crop.
8Some other seed fell on good ground and began
to grow. It got taller and produced a crop. Some
plants made 30 times more, some made 60 times
more, and some made 100 times more."
9Then Jesus said, "You people who can hear
me, listen!"

> **Sidelight**
> Jesus' story about planting seeds (Mark 4:1–9) not only has spiritual truth, but tells a lot about farming in those days. After ploughing a field, farmers would walk through the field scattering seeds around the field. Then they would go back over the field dragging branches across to cover the seeds and protect them from birds and strong winds.

Jesus Tells Why He Used Stories

10Later, when Jesus was alone, the twelve
apostles[d] and others around him asked him about
the stories.
11Jesus said, "You can know the secret about
the kingdom of God. But to other people I tell
everything by using stories 12so that:

'They will look and look, but they will not
learn.
They will listen and listen, but they will
not understand.
If they did learn and understand,
they would come back to me and be
forgiven.' " *Isaiah 6:9–10*

Jesus Explains the Seed Story

13Then Jesus said to his followers, "Don't you
understand this story? If you don't, how will you

understand any story? 14The farmer is like a
person who plants God's message in people.
15Sometimes the teaching falls on the road.
This is like the people who hear the teaching of
God, but Satan quickly comes and takes away
the teaching that was planted in them. 16Others
are like the seed planted on rocky ground. They
hear the teaching and quickly accept it with joy.
17But since they don't allow the teaching to go
deep into their lives, they keep it only a short
time. When trouble or persecution comes
because of the teaching they accepted, they
quickly give up. 18Others are like the seed
planted among the thorny weeds. They hear the
teaching, 19but the worries of this life, the
temptation of wealth and many other evil
desires keep the teaching from growing and
producing fruit[n] in their lives. 20Others are
like the seed planted in the good ground. They
hear the teaching and accept it. Then they grow
and produce fruit—sometimes 30 times more,
sometimes 60 times more and sometimes 100
times more."

Use What You Have

21Then Jesus said to them, "Do you hide a lamp
under a bowl or under a bed? No! You put the lamp
on a lampstand. 22Everything that is hidden will be
made clear and every secret thing will be made
known. 23You people who can hear me, listen!
24"Think carefully about what you hear. The
way you give to others is the way God will give
to you, but God will give you even more.
25Those who have understanding will be given
more. But those who do not have understand-
ing, even what they have will be taken away
from them."

Jesus Uses a Story About Seed

26Then Jesus said, "The kingdom of God is
like someone who plants seed in the ground.
27Night and day, whether the person is asleep or

producing fruit To produce fruit means to have in your life the good things God wants.

FAITH

It's Alive!

Witness, if you will, one of the most efficient, self-contained structures in nature. It possesses – on its own – almost everything it needs to survive and grow. It has its own coat, its own embryo and its own food supply.

It can even impregnate itself. That's right, each one has the male and female components it needs to create a fertilised egg.

The reproductive system is incredible, but it does need extra help to grow. After fertilisation, it remains dormant until warm, moist conditions promote germination.

Then its coat softens and the metabolism rate in the cells increases. It drinks water and even starts "breathing", while a simple digestion begins. The digested food travels to new areas of growth that emerge when cell division begins.

And congratulations, Mr and Mrs Seed, it's a plant!

The incredible seed is like the kingdom of God. Read **Mark 4:26–34** to see.

- How is a seed's reproductive system like faith's growth process in you?
- According to this passage, what benefits can come from faith's growth in you? What benefits can come from many people growing in faith?

Consider . . .

- working in a garden and drawing other parallels between the plant world and faith. Write your own parable to illustrate those parallels.
- choosing one quality from 2 Peter 1:5–9 (p.1365) to add to your faith. Create one project to help develop that quality.

For more, see . . .

- Ecclesiastes 11:1–6 (p.628)
- Luke 13:18–20 (p.1067)
- Matthew 13:24–32 (p.963)

awake, the seed still grows, but the person does not know how it grows. 28By itself the earth produces grain. First the plant grows, then the ear and then all the grain in the ear. 29When the grain is ready, the farmer cuts it, because the harvest time has come."

A Story About Mustard Seed

30Then Jesus said, "How can I show you what the kingdom of God is like? What story can I use to explain it? 31The kingdom of God is like a mustard seed, the smallest seed you plant in the ground. 32But when planted, this seed grows and becomes the largest of all garden plants. It produces large branches, and the wild birds can make nests in its shade."

33Jesus used many stories like these to teach the crowd God's message—as much as they could understand. 34He always used stories to teach them. But when he and his followers were alone, Jesus explained everything to them.

Jesus Calms a Storm

35That evening, Jesus said to his followers, "Let's go across the lake." 36Leaving the crowd behind, they took him in the boat just as he was. There were also other boats with them. 37A very strong wind came up on the lake. The waves came over the sides and into the boat so that it was already full of water. 38Jesus was at the back of the boat, sleeping with his head on a pillow. His followers woke him and said, "Teacher, don't you care that we are drowning!"

39Jesus stood up and commanded the wind and said to the waves, "Quiet! Be still!" Then the wind stopped, and it became completely calm.

40Jesus said to his followers, "Why are you afraid? Do you still have no faith?"

41The followers were very afraid and asked each other, "Who is this? Even the wind and the waves obey him!"

A Man with Demons Inside Him

5 Jesus and his followers went to the other side of the lake to the area of the Gerasene people. 2When Jesus got out of the boat, instantly a man with an evil spirit came to him from the burial caves. 3This man lived in the caves, and no one could tie him up, not even with a chain. 4Many times people had used chains to tie the man's hands and feet, but he always broke them off. No one was strong enough to control him. 5Day and night he would wander around the burial caves and on the hills, screaming and cutting himself with stones. 6While Jesus was still far away, the man saw him, ran to him and fell down before him.

7The man shouted in a loud voice, "What do you want with me, Jesus, Son of the Most High God? I command you in God's name not to torture me!" 8He said this because Jesus was saying to him, "You evil spirit, come out of the man."

9Then Jesus asked him, "What is your name?"

He answered, "My name is Legion,[n] because we are many spirits." 10He begged Jesus again and again not to send them out of that area.

11A large herd of pigs was feeding on a hill near there. 12The demons[d] begged Jesus, "Send us into the pigs; let us go into them." 13So Jesus allowed them to do this. The evil spirits left the man and went into the pigs. Then the herd of pigs—about 2,000 of them—rushed down the hill into the lake and were drowned.

14The herdsmen ran away and went to the town and to the countryside, telling everyone about this. So people went out to see what had happened. 15They came to Jesus and saw the man who used to have the many evil spirits, sitting, clothed and in his right mind. And they were frightened. 16The people who saw this told the others what had happened to the man who had the demons living in him, and they told about the pigs. 17Then the people began to beg Jesus to leave their area.

18As Jesus was getting back into the boat, the man who was freed from the demons begged to go with him.

19But Jesus would not let him. He said, "Go home to your family and tell them how much the Lord has done for you and how he has had mercy on you." 20So the man left and began to tell the people in the Ten Towns[n] about what Jesus had done for him. And everyone was amazed.

Jesus Gives Life to a Dead Girl and Heals a Sick Woman

21When Jesus went in the boat back to the other side of the lake, a large crowd gathered around him there. 22A leader of the synagogue,[d] named Jairus, came there, saw Jesus and fell at his feet. 23He begged Jesus, saying again and again, "My daughter is dying. Please come and put your hands on her so she will be healed and will live." 24So Jesus went with him.

A large crowd followed Jesus and pushed very close around him. 25Among them was a woman who had been bleeding for twelve years. 26She had suffered very much from many doctors and had spent all the money she had, but instead of improving, she was getting worse. 27When the woman heard about Jesus, she came up behind him in the

Legion Means very many. A legion was about 5,000 men in the Roman army.
Ten Towns In Greek, called "Decapolis". It was an area east of Lake Galilee that once had ten main towns.

crowd and touched his coat. 28She thought, "If
I can just touch his clothes, I will be healed."
29Instantly her bleeding stopped, and she felt in
her body that she was healed from her disease.
30At once Jesus felt power go out from him. So
he turned around in the crowd and asked, "Who
touched my clothes?"
31His followers said, "Look at how many peo-
ple are pushing against you! And you ask, 'Who
touched me?' "
32But Jesus continued looking around to see
who had touched him. 33The woman, knowing
that she was healed, came and fell at Jesus' feet.
Shaking with fear, she told him the whole truth.
34Jesus said to her, "Dear woman, you are made
well because you believed. Go in peace; be
healed of your disease."
35While Jesus was still speaking, some people
came from the house of the synagogue leader.
They said, "Your daughter is dead. There is no
need to bother the teacher any more."
36But Jesus paid no attention to what they
said. He told the synagogue leader, "Don't be
afraid; just believe."
37Jesus let only Peter, James and John the
brother of James go with him. 38When they
came to the house of the synagogue leader, Jesus
found many people there making lots of noise
and crying loudly. 39Jesus entered the house and
said to them, "Why are you crying and making
so much noise? The child is not dead, only asleep."
40But they laughed at him. So, after throwing
them out of the house, Jesus took the child's fa-
ther and mother and his three followers into the
room where the child was. 41Taking hold of the
girl's hand, he said to her, "Talitha, koum!" (This
means, "Young girl, I tell you to stand up!") 42At
once the girl stood right up and began walking.
(She was twelve years old.) Everyone was com-
pletely amazed. 43Jesus gave them strict orders
not to tell people about this. Then he told them
to give the girl something to eat.

Jesus Goes to His Home Town

6 Jesus left there and went to his home town,
and his followers went with him. 2On the
Sabbath [d] day he taught in the synagogue. [d] Many
people heard him and were amazed, saying,

SICKNESS

Miracles Happen

Doris's face was streaked with tears. "They say there's no hope," she sobbed, reaching for another tissue. "My granddaughter has a tumour the size of a tennis ball. It has completely surrounded her kidneys."

She continued haltingly, "The doctors aren't sure if other organs are involved. They don't think she'll live long."

Betty placed her hand on Doris's shoulder.

"Miracles do happen, Doris. We need to pray for a miracle."

"I've given up with God. Even he can't heal Wendy now. And besides, I don't think he's listening any more."

Doris was wrong. Even the doctors were wrong. A new medicine was added to Wendy's treatment, and she was healed.

God heals. He can use doctors, nurses and medicine to accomplish his purposes. Often he heals without their help, too – when people pray in faith. Read **Mark 5:21–43** to see how Jesus healed two people.

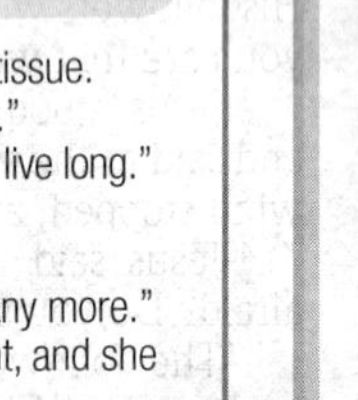

- How were the three healings – Wendy, the woman (verses 25–34) and the little girl – different from each other?
- Does God still heal in the way that Jesus did in this passage?

Consider . . .

- writing a letter as though you were going to send it to someone who has asked for healing and hasn't received it. Encourage that imaginary person.
- walking down the corridor of a local hospital and silently praying for God's healing for each patient.

For more, see . . .

- Psalm 103:1–5 (p.559)
- James 5:13–18 (p.1353)
- Matthew 9:1–26 (p.952)

"Where did this man get these teachings? What
is this wisdom that has been given to him? And
where did he get the power to do miracles?[d] 3He
is just the carpenter, the son of Mary and the
brother of James, Joseph, Judas and Simon. And
his sisters are here with us." So the people were
upset with Jesus.

4Jesus said to them, "A prophet[d] is honoured
everywhere except in his home town and with
his own people and in his own home." 5So Jesus
was not able to work any miracles there except
to heal a few sick people by putting his hands on
them. 6He was amazed at how many people had
no faith.

Then Jesus went to other villages in that area
and taught. 7He called his twelve followers to-
gether and got ready to send them out two by
two and gave them authority over evil spirits.
8This is what Jesus commanded them: "Take
nothing for your trip except a walking stick. Take
no bread, no bag and no money in your pockets.
9Wear sandals, but take only the clothes you are
wearing. 10When you enter a house, stay there
until you leave that town. 11If the people in a
certain place refuse to welcome you or listen to
you, leave that place. Shake its dust off your
feet[n] as a warning to them."

12So the followers went out and preached that
people should change their hearts and lives.
13They forced many demons[d] out and put olive
oil on many sick people and healed them.

How John the Baptist was Killed

14King Herod heard about Jesus, because he
was now well known. Some people said, "He is
John the Baptist,[d] who has risen from the dead.
That is why he can work these miracles."[d]

15Others said, "He is Elijah."[n]

Other people said, "Jesus is a prophet,[d] like
the prophets who lived long ago."

16When Herod heard this, he said, "I killed
John by cutting off his head. Now he has risen
from the dead!"

17Herod himself had ordered his soldiers to ar-
rest John and put him in prison in order to please
his wife, Herodias. She had been the wife of
Philip, Herod's brother, but then Herod had mar-
ried her. 18John had been telling Herod, "It is not
lawful for you to be married to your brother's
wife." 19So Herodias hated John and wanted to
kill him. But she couldn't, 20because Herod was
afraid of John and protected him. He knew John
was a good and holy man. Also, though John's
preaching always bothered him, he enjoyed
listening to John.

21Then the perfect time came for Herodias to
cause John's death. On Herod's birthday, he gave
a dinner party for the most important government
leaders, the commanders of his army and the
most important people in Galilee. 22When the
daughter of Herodias came in and danced, she
pleased Herod and the people eating with him.

So King Herod said to the girl, "Ask me for
anything you want, and I will give it to you."
23He promised her, "Anything you ask for I will
give to you—up to half of my kingdom."

24The girl went to her mother and asked,
"What should I ask for?"

Sidelight King Herod wasn't the sort of person who you would like to bump into on a dark night. He was responsible for beheading John the Baptist (Mark 6:14–29) and even murdering his own children!

Her mother answered, "Ask for the head of
John the Baptist."[d]

25At once the girl went back to the king and
said to him, "I want the head of John the Baptist
right now on a dish."

26Although the king was very sad, he had
made a promise, and his dinner guests had heard
it. So he did not want to refuse what she asked.
27Immediately the king sent a soldier to bring
John's head. The soldier went and cut off John's
head in the prison 28and brought it back on a
dish. He gave it to the girl, and the girl gave it to
her mother. 29When John's followers heard this,
they came and got John's body and put it in a
tomb.

More than 5,000 Fed

30The apostles[d] gathered around Jesus and told
him about all the things they had done and taught.
31Crowds of people were coming and going so
that Jesus and his followers did not even have
time to eat. He said to them, "Come away by
yourselves, and we will go to a lonely place to
get some rest."

32So they went in a boat by themselves to a
lonely place. 33But many people saw them leave
and recognised them. So from all the towns they
ran to the place where Jesus was going, and
they got there before him. 34When he arrived,
he saw a great crowd waiting. He felt sorry
for them, because they were like sheep without
a shepherd. So he began to teach them many
things.

Shake . . . feet A warning. It showed that they were rejecting these people.
Elijah A man who spoke for God and who lived hundreds of years before Christ. See 1 Kings 17.

[35]When it was late in the day, his followers
came to him and said, "No one lives in this
place, and it is already very late. [36]Send the
people away so they can go to the countryside
and towns around here to buy themselves some-
thing to eat."
[37]But Jesus answered, "You give them some-
thing to eat."
They said to him, "We would all have to work
a month to earn enough money to buy that much
bread!"
[38]Jesus asked them, "How many loaves of
bread do you have? Go and see."
When they found out, they said, "Five loaves
and two fish."
[39]Then Jesus told his followers to have the
people sit in groups on the green grass. [40]So they
sat in groups of 50 or 100. [41]Jesus took the five
loaves and two fish and, looking up to heaven,
he thanked God for the food. He divided the
bread and gave it to his followers for them to
give to the people. Then he divided the two fish
among them all. [42]All the people ate and were
satisfied. [43]The followers filled twelve baskets
with the leftover pieces of bread and fish. [44]There
were 5,000 men who ate.

HUNGER AND POVERTY

The Multiplication Principle

"We have only 3,000 tins. I wanted to collect 10,000," Kristen Green complained to Mr Rossetti, the Head of St Francis De Sales High School.

Mr Rossetti listened but didn't say much. Later that day during school assembly, he surprised Kristen by asking her to speak to the students about the food drive.

Kristen spoke about a man she had met at the local soup kitchen who each night asked for an extra plate of food for his dying wife. Kristen also told them about a hungry woman who shared her orange with the person sitting beside her. She continued, "We think of starving people being in Ethiopia, but these people live three blocks from this school." Kristen challenged the students to meet the goal of 10,000 tins of food in the next week.

After assembly, students asked Kristen how they could help. Suddenly everyone was mobilised. The football team went from door to door in the neighbourhood, asking for donations of tinned goods. The Fellowship of Christian Athletes collected $1,500 worth of food in one night. Kristen and a friend asked area grocers for food donations.

By Wednesday, the goal of 10,000 tins was met – a goal people had thought was unrealistic. (Only 4,000 tins had been collected the year before.) Kristen decided not to tell anyone that the goal had been reached before the deadline. On Friday, people cheered when she announced the total: 17,299 tins!

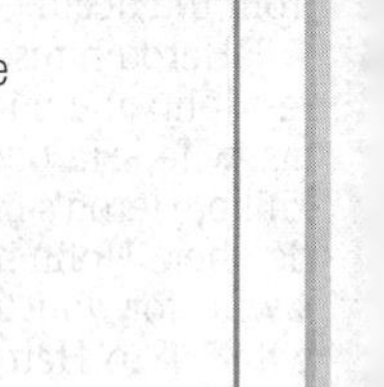

Kristen and others filled three school buses with the food. As they delivered the food to the soup kitchen, people standing in line thanked them and patted them on the back.

"We knew we were making a difference," Kristen says. "People were going to be able to eat."

Jesus and his disciples were also confronted with the challenge of feeding hungry people. Read **Mark 6:30–44** to see how Jesus fed a hungry mob.

- How is the multiplication of tinned food at De Sales High similar to Jesus' multiplying food for the multitude? How is it different?
- How have you seen Jesus increase your gifts or resources to help others?

Consider . . .

- giving up eating a meal and spending time in prayer for those who have less to eat than you do. Donate the money you would have spent on the meal to a Christian relief agency.
- organising a tinned food collection at your local church or school.

For more, see . . .

- 2 Kings 4:42–44 (p.349)
- John 6:1–15 (p.1104)
- Matthew 14:13–21 (p.965)

Jesus Walks on the Water

45 Immediately Jesus told his followers to get
into the boat and go ahead of him to Bethsaida
across the lake. He stayed behind to send the
people home. 46 After sending them away, he
went into the hills to pray.
47 That night, the boat was in the middle of the
lake, and Jesus was alone on the land. 48 He saw
his followers struggling hard to row the boat,
because the wind was blowing against them.
Between three and six o'clock in the morning,
Jesus came to them, walking on the water, and
he wanted to walk past the boat. 49 But when
they saw him walking on the water, they
thought he was a ghost and cried out. 50 They all
saw him and were afraid. But immediately Jesus
spoke to them and said, "Have courage! It is I.
Do not be afraid." 51 Then he got into the boat
with them, and the wind became calm. The
followers were greatly amazed. 52 They did not
understand about the miracle of the five loaves,
because their minds were closed.
53 When they had crossed the lake, they came
to shore at Gennesaret and tied the boat there.
54 When they got out of the boat, people immedi-
ately recognised Jesus. 55 They ran everywhere in
that area and began to bring sick people on mats
wherever they heard he was. 56 And everywhere
he went—into towns, cities or countryside—the
people brought the sick to the market-places.
They begged him to let them touch just the
edge of his coat, and all who touched it were
healed.

Obey God's Law

7 When some Pharisees[d] and some teachers
of the law came from Jerusalem, they gath-
ered around Jesus. 2 They saw some of Jesus'
followers eating food with hands that were not
clean,[d] that is, they hadn't washed them. 3 (The
Pharisees and all the Jews never eat before
washing their hands in a special way according
to their unwritten laws. 4 And when they buy
something in the market, they never eat it until

HYPOCRISY

An Open Letter to God

James was tired of seeing what he called "the Dr Jekyll and Mr Hyde" sides of his father. In his frustration, he wrote this letter to God.

Dear God,

There are a few things I just don't understand about people and the way they act.

Take my dad, for example. Don't get me wrong. He's a nice man; he goes to church with us and everything. But when it comes to his business, he really changes. Dad's always talking about how he really "got the best of that bloke" in a business deal or how he "beat her out of a contract." It just doesn't seem very Christian.

Oh, and another place is on the road. My dad gets really angry with other drivers and sometimes even yells at them.

And, oh well, I suppose I just don't understand. It just doesn't seem very Christian.

Can you help me to understand, God?

James

Hypocrisy is common. Even in Jesus' day, Jesus' followers were troubled by hypocrites. Read **Mark 7:1–23** to learn more about the situation.

- What was hypocritical about James's dad's actions and the Pharisees' actions?
- According to this passage, what's the cure for hypocrisy?

Consider . . .

- evaluating your own life for any hypocrisies and applying the "cure" to get rid of them.
- writing a letter to James that responds to his frustrations.

For more, see . . .

- Isaiah 29:13–14 (p.668)
- Romans 14:13–18 (p.1207)
- Matthew 15:1–20 (p.967)

they have washed themselves in a special way. They also follow many other unwritten laws, such as the washing of cups, pitchers and pots.)

5The Pharisees and the teachers of the law said to Jesus, "Why don't your followers obey the unwritten laws which have been handed down to us? Why do your followers eat their food with hands that are not clean?"

6Jesus answered, "Isaiah was right when he spoke about you hypocrites.[d] He wrote,

'These people show honour to me with words,
but their hearts are far from me.
7Their worship of me is worthless.
The things they teach are nothing but
human rules.' *Isaiah 29:13*

8You have stopped following the commands of God, and you follow only human teachings."

9Then Jesus said to them, "You cleverly ignore the commands of God so you can follow your own teachings. 10Moses said, 'Honour your father and your mother,'[n] and 'Anyone who says cruel things to his father or mother must be put to death.'[n] 11But you say a person can tell his father or mother, 'I have something I could use to help you, but it is Corban—a gift to God.' 12You no longer let that person use that money for his father or his mother. 13By your own rules, which you teach people, you are rejecting what God said. And you do many things like that."

14After Jesus called the crowd to him again, he said, "Every person should listen to me and understand what I am saying. 15There is nothing people put into their bodies that makes them unclean. People are made unclean by the things that come out of them." 16 [n]

17When Jesus left the people and went into the house, his followers asked him about this story. 18Jesus said, "Do you still not understand? Surely you know that nothing that enters someone from the outside can make that person unclean. 19It does not go into the heart, but into the stomach. Then it goes out of the body." (When Jesus said this, he meant that no longer was any food unclean for people to eat.)

20And Jesus said, "The things that come out of people are the things that make them unclean. 21All these evil things begin inside people, in the heart: evil thoughts, sexual sins, stealing, murder, adultery,[d] 22greed, evil actions, lying, doing sinful things, jealousy, speaking evil of others, pride and foolish living. 23All these evil things come from inside and make people unclean."

Jesus Helps a Non-Jewish Woman

24Jesus left that place and went to the area around Tyre. When he went into a house, he did not want anyone to know he was there, but he could not stay hidden. 25A woman whose daughter had an evil spirit in her heard that he was there. So she quickly came to Jesus and fell at his feet. 26She was Greek, born in Phoenicia, in Syria. She begged Jesus to force the demon[d] out of her daughter.

27Jesus told the woman, "It is not right to take the children's bread and give it to the dogs. First let the children eat all they want."

28But she answered, "Yes, Lord, but even the dogs under the table can eat the children's crumbs."

29Then Jesus said, "Because of your answer, you may go. The demon has left your daughter."

30The woman went home and found her daughter lying in bed; the demon was gone.

Jesus Heals a Deaf Man

31Then Jesus left the area around Tyre and went through Sidon to Lake Galilee, to the area of the Ten Towns.[n] 32While he was there, some people brought a man to him who was deaf and could not talk plainly. The people begged Jesus to put his hand on the man to heal him.

33Jesus led the man away from the crowd, by himself. He put his fingers in the man's ears and then spat and touched the man's tongue. 34Looking up to heaven, he sighed and said to the man, "Ephphatha!" (This means, "Be opened.") 35Instantly the man was able to hear and to use his tongue so that he spoke clearly.

36Jesus commanded the people not to tell anyone about what happened. But the more he commanded them, the more they told about it. 37They were completely amazed and said, "Jesus does everything well. He makes the deaf hear! And those who can't talk he makes able to speak."

More than 4,000 People Fed

8 Another time there was a great crowd with Jesus that had nothing to eat. So Jesus called his followers and said, 2"I feel sorry for these people, because they have already been with me for three days, and they have nothing to eat. 3If I send them home hungry, they will faint on the way. Some of them live a long way from here."

4Jesus' followers answered, "How can we get enough bread to feed all these people? We are far away from any town."

'Honour . . . mother' Quotation from Exodus 20:12; Deuteronomy 5:16.
'Anyone . . . death.' Quotation from Exodus 21:17.
Verse 16 Some Greek copies add verse 16: "You people who can hear me, listen!"
Ten Towns In Greek, called "Decapolis". It was an area east of Lake Galilee that once had ten main towns.

5Jesus asked, "How many loaves of bread do
you have?"
They answered, "Seven."
6Jesus told the people to sit on the ground.
Then he took the seven loaves, gave thanks to
God, and divided the bread. He gave the pieces to
his followers to give to the people, and they did
so. 7The followers also had a few small fish. After
Jesus gave thanks for the fish, he told his follow-
ers to give them to the people as well. 8All the
people ate and were satisfied. Then his followers
filled seven baskets with the leftover pieces of
food. 9There were about 4,000 people who ate.
After they had eaten, Jesus sent them home.
10Then right away he got into a boat with his
followers and went to the area of Dalmanutha.

The Leaders Ask for a Miracle

11The Pharisees[d] came to Jesus and began to
ask him questions. Hoping to trap him, they
asked Jesus for a miracle[d] from God. 12Jesus
sighed deeply and said, "Why do you people ask
for a miracle as a sign? I tell you the truth, no sign

Sidelight Jesus had conflicts with the Pharisees (Mark 8:11) throughout his ministry. These leaders were respected for their accurate interpretations of Jewish law. The historian Josephus estimates that 6,000 Pharisees lived in Palestine during Jesus' years.

SICKNESS

She Made a Difference

In the 1940s, more than 500,000 people in the city of Calcutta (5% of the city's population) literally lived and died in the streets. With even winter temperatures hovering in the upper 30s, the city could seem like hell on earth. It was there that the "poorest of the poor" lived, plagued by leprosy, tuberculosis, pneumonia and, most of all, poverty.

What hope was there in such a place? Surely no one could make a difference there. But Agnes thought differently. She believed that God was calling her to bring hope to these poor and downtrodden people.

In her journal, Agnes, better known as Mother Teresa, described her first day in the slums as a day of meeting Christ. She met Christ face to face there – the hungry Christ, the naked Christ, the sick Christ, the homeless Christ. She said that the touch of him in this distressing disguise gave her great joy, peace and strength.

So, clad in a white sari edged with blue, Mother Teresa began her work. She and a group of nuns taught the children of the poor. They provided care for lepers who could not get help anywhere else. They built shelters and hospitals so that the poor would have a place out of the streets. They fed the hungry and loved the unlovable. They literally changed the face of Calcutta.

Jesus' love flowed through Mother Teresa to touch people. Jesus' love always makes a difference. When Jesus touches sick people, their lives are never the same. Read **Mark 7:31–37** and imagine how the sick people who met Jesus must have felt.

- How is Mother Teresa's approach to ministry like Jesus' approach?
- Which of Jesus' actions are most important to people who are sick?

Consider . . .

- doing a task that you don't like to do (such as cleaning a bathroom) for a housebound member of your church.
- talking to your minister about how your church can minister to people with AIDS.

For more, see . . .

- Leviticus 13 (p.111)
- Luke 17:11–19 (p.1077)
- Matthew 8:1–4 (p.951)

will be given to you." 13Then Jesus left the Pharisees and went in the boat to the other side of the lake.

Guard Against Wrong Teachings

14His followers had only one loaf of bread with them in the boat; they had forgotten to bring more. 15Jesus warned them, "Be careful! Beware of the yeast of the Pharisees[d] and the yeast of Herod."

16His followers discussed the meaning of this, saying, "He said this because we have no bread."

17Knowing what they were talking about, Jesus asked them, "Why are you talking about not having bread? Do you still not see or understand? Are your minds closed? 18You have eyes, but you don't really see. You have ears, but you don't really listen. Remember when 19I divided five loaves of bread for the 5,000? How many baskets did you fill with leftover pieces of food?"

They answered, "Twelve."

20"And when I divided seven loaves of bread for the 4,000, how many baskets did you fill with leftover pieces of food?"

They answered, "Seven."

21Then Jesus said to them, "Don't you understand yet?"

Jesus Heals a Blind Man

22Jesus and his followers came to Bethsaida. There some people brought a blind man to Jesus and begged him to touch the man. 23So Jesus took the blind man's hand and led him out of the village. Then he spat on the man's eyes and put his hands on the man and asked, "Can you see now?"

24The man looked up and said, "Yes, I see people, but they look like trees walking around."

25Again Jesus put his hands on the man's eyes. Then the man opened his eyes wide and they were healed, and he was able to see everything clearly. 26Jesus told him to go home, saying, "Don't go into the town."

Peter Says Jesus is the Christ

27Jesus and his followers went to the towns around Caesarea Philippi. While they were travelling, Jesus asked them, "Who do people say I am?"

28They answered, "Some say you are John the Baptist.[d] Others say you are Elijah,[n] and others say you are one of the prophets."[d]

29Then Jesus asked, "But who do you say I am?"

Peter answered, "You are the Christ."[d]

30Jesus warned his followers not to tell anyone who he was.

31Then Jesus began to teach them that the Son of Man[d] must suffer many things and that he would be rejected by the Jewish elders, the leading priests and the teachers of the law. He told them that the Son of Man must be killed and then rise from the dead after three days. 32Jesus told them plainly what would happen. Then Peter took Jesus aside and began to tell him not to talk like that. 33But Jesus turned and looked at his followers. Then he told Peter not to talk in that way. He said, "Go away from me, Satan![n] You don't care about the things of God, but only about things people think are important."

34Then Jesus called the crowd to him, along with his followers. He said, "If people want to follow me, they must give up the things they want. They must be willing even to give up their lives to follow me. 35Those who want to save their lives will give up true life. But those who give up their lives for me and for the Good News[d] will have true life. 36It is worth nothing for them to have the whole world if they lose their souls. 37They could never pay enough to buy back their souls. 38The people who live now are living in a sinful and evil time. If people are ashamed of me and my teaching, the Son of Man[d] will be ashamed of them when he comes with his Father's glory and with the holy angels."

9 Then Jesus said to the people, "I tell you the truth, some people standing here will see the kingdom of God come with power before they die."

Jesus Talks with Moses and Elijah

2Six days later, Jesus took Peter, James and John up on a high mountain by themselves. While they watched, Jesus' appearance was changed. 3His clothes became shining white, whiter than any person could make them. 4Then Elijah and Moses[n] appeared to them, talking with Jesus.

5Peter said to Jesus, "Teacher, it is good that we are here. Let us make three tents—one for you, one for Moses and one for Elijah." 6Peter did not know what to say, because he and the others were so frightened.

7Then a cloud came and covered them, and a voice came from the cloud, saying, "This is my Son, whom I love. Listen to him!"

Elijah A man who spoke for God and who lived hundreds of years before Christ. See 1 Kings 17.
Satan Name for the devil meaning "the enemy". Jesus means that Peter was talking like Satan.
Elijah and Moses Two of the most important Jewish leaders in the past. Moses had given them the law, and Elijah was an important prophet.

8Suddenly Peter, James and John looked
around, but they saw only Jesus there alone with
them.
9As they were coming down the mountain,
Jesus commanded them not to tell anyone about
what they had seen until the Son of Man[d] had
risen from the dead.
10So the followers obeyed Jesus, but they dis-
cussed what he meant about rising from the dead.
11Then they asked Jesus, "Why do the teach-
ers of the law say that Elijah must come first?"
12Jesus answered, "They are right to say that
Elijah must come first and make everything the
way it should be. But why does the Scripture[d]
say that the Son of Man will suffer much and
that people will treat him as if he were nothing?
13I tell you that Elijah has already come. And
people did to him whatever they wanted to do,
just as the Scriptures said it would happen."

Jesus Heals a Sick Boy

14When Jesus, Peter, James and John came back
to the other followers, they saw a great crowd
around them and the teachers of the law arguing
with them. 15But as soon as the crowd saw Jesus,
the people were surprised and ran to welcome him.
16Jesus asked, "What are you arguing about?"
17A man answered, "Teacher, I brought my
son to you. He has an evil spirit in him that stops
him from talking. 18When the spirit attacks him,
it throws him on the ground. Then my son foams
at the mouth, grinds his teeth and becomes very
stiff. I asked your followers to force the evil spirit
out, but they couldn't."
19Jesus answered, "You people have no faith.
How long must I stay with you? How long must
I put up with you? Bring the boy to me."
20So the followers brought him to Jesus. As
soon as the evil spirit saw Jesus, it made the boy

FAITH

Are You Sure?

The debate had been fierce. After a GCSE Biology lesson, Esther and Livi had begun a discussion with Giles and Kat about how the world began. Esther and Livi were Christians and believed that there was a God behind all of creation and that there was a reason and purpose to it all. Giles and Kat were not Christians and believed that the world existed due to a random sequence of events and that there was no purpose behind it at all. The debate continued long into their lunch break.

Eventually, Mrs Lloyd, the biology teacher, interrupted the discussion and said something that took all four of them by surprise. She said, "Ultimately, even though you disagree, all four of you have some kind of faith."

What? Giles and Kat did not like this at all, so Giles responded, "No, they are making a statement of faith because they believe in religion. We are making a statement of fact because we believe in science."

Mrs Lloyd continued, "But Giles, none of what you are saying can be categorically proven, so the fact is, you have faith in what you are saying, even though your side of the argument does not have all the facts to back up your claim."

In **Mark 9:1–9**, Peter, James and John saw something that was almost beyond belief. Were they hallucinating? Were they dreaming? How could Jesus be standing with two people who were meant to be dead?

- If you were one of the disciples, it would be easier to have faith in Jesus, because you would have spoken and spent time with him. So what helps you have faith in Jesus?
- What things might you do to help build your faith?

Consider . . .

- making a list of all the things people have faith in: money, science, friendships, etc. What are the differences between having faith in these things and having faith in Jesus? How should these differences change your outlook on life?
- reading Hebrews 11:3 whilst staring at the stars. Give God the chance to speak to you whilst doing this.

For more, see . . .

- Mark 11:20–26 (p.1020)
- Hebrews 11:1–3 (p.1341)

lose control of himself, and he fell down and
rolled on the ground, foaming at the mouth.
21Jesus asked the boy's father, "How long has
this been happening?"
The father answered, "Since he was very
young. 22The spirit often throws him into a fire
or into water to kill him. If you can do anything
for him, please have pity on us and help us."
23Jesus said to the father, "You said, 'If you can!'
All things are possible for the one who believes."
24Immediately the father cried out, "I do be-
lieve! Help me to believe more!"
25When Jesus saw that a crowd was quickly
gathering, he ordered the evil spirit, saying, "You
spirit that makes people unable to hear or speak,
I command you to come out of this boy and never
enter him again!"
26The evil spirit screamed and caused the boy
to fall on the ground again. Then the spirit came
out. The boy looked as if he were dead, and many
people said, "He is dead!" 27But Jesus took hold
of the boy's hand and helped him to stand up.
28When Jesus went into the house, his follow-
ers began asking him privately, "Why couldn't
we force that evil spirit out?"
29Jesus answered, "That kind of spirit can only
be forced out by prayer."

Jesus Talks About His Death

30Then Jesus and his followers left that place
and went through Galilee. He didn't want
anyone to know where he was, 31because he was
teaching his followers. He said to them, "The
Son of Man[d] will be handed over to people, and
they will kill him. After three days, he will
rise from the dead." 32But the followers did not
understand what Jesus meant, and they were
afraid to ask him.

POPULARITY

Everyone is Going

Sam slammed his locker shut. It was Friday afternoon; the final bell had rung. He needed to catch Stuart and Justin before they got on their bus to check that they were all meeting at the football match that night.

As Sam turned from his locker, his foot caught on a wheel. It was Alex's wheelchair. Alex had broken his neck in a diving accident and was paralysed from the shoulders down.

"Hey, Sam, what are you lot doing tonight?" Alex asked.

"Well, er . . . " Sam hesitated as his eyes searched the cloakroom for the others, but Alex didn't wait for an answer.

"Would you like to come over to my house? My mum said she'd pick up some videos. Could you open my locker and put away the books in my rucksack, please?"

Sam impatiently unloaded the rucksack and deposited the books. As Sam closed the locker, Alex asked again, "Well? What about tonight?"

Sam glanced down the empty hall. The buses were pulling away. It was too late to make plans with Justin and Stuart. Alex needed a friend. But everyone would be going to the match.

Sam thought for a moment and then smiled at Alex. "What time do you want me to come over?"

The disciples also had to make a decision about what it meant to be popular. They were arguing about who was the greatest or the most popular. Read **Mark 9:30–37** to see how Jesus turned the tables on them.

- How would Sam's actions make him important in the kingdom of God?
- When have you had to decide between doing what's popular and what's right? How was that experience like the incident in this passage?

Consider . . .

- having lunch with an unpopular classmate.
- doing a household chore that everyone in your family dislikes doing.

For more, see . . .

- Proverbs 11:24–26 (p.599)
- Philippians 2:5–7 (p.1282)
- Matthew 18:1–5 (p.971)

Who is the Greatest?

33 Jesus and his followers went to Capernaum.
When they went into a house there, he asked
them, "What were you arguing about on the
road?" 34 But the followers did not answer, because
their argument on the road was about which one
of them was the greatest.
35 Jesus sat down and called the twelve apostles[d]
to him. He said, "Whoever wants to be the most
important must be last of all and servant of all."
36 Then Jesus took a small child and had him
stand among them. Taking the child in his arms,
he said, 37 "Whoever accepts a child like this in
my name accepts me. And whoever accepts me
accepts the One who sent me."

Anyone Not Against Us is For Us

38 Then John said, "Teacher, we saw someone
using your name to force demons[d] out of a person.
We told him to stop, because he does not belong
to our group."
39 But Jesus said, "Don't stop him, because any-
one who uses my name to do powerful things will
not easily say evil things about me. 40 Whoever is
not against us is with us. 41 I tell you the truth,
whoever gives you a drink of water because you
belong to the Christ[d] will truly get his reward.
42 "If one of these little children believes in
me, and someone causes that child to sin, it
would be better for that person to have a large
stone tied around his neck and be drowned in

ENVIRONMENT

Burning Bushes

Anya was on a wonderful holiday in Australia, and while she was there she stayed with some folk in Brisbane who owned land. The scenery was magnificent – everything she'd imagined and more. One very hot day, her host was taking her for a drive around the area and they came across some burnt forestry. It seemed to her that they drove for quite a way before they came across thriving bushland again.

"What happened there?" she asked Darryl. "Was it one of those bush fires we read about?"

He laughed and shook his head. "No, no," he said. "That was done deliberately."

"Deliberately?" she replied looking shocked.

"Yeah," he continued. "It's actually to stop bush fires. That's the reason it's done!"

Anya looked puzzled. "That doesn't make any sense. How can setting something on fire, stop a fire?"

Darryl explained. "When we have a really outrageous fire here, it spreads very quickly for miles and miles. Not just the trees and plants catch fire, but animals and birds as well. It's very sad to see. You know, a bird can be burnt and fly on for metres before it dies, so when it drops from the sky, it can start a fire there too."

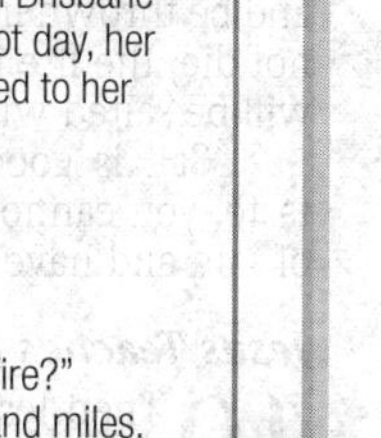

"So how does the deliberate fire help?" Anya was confused.

"Well," replied her host. "If you first burn everything in say, a mile radius, before any fires start, then if you do have a fire, it will automatically stop when it gets to the burnt-out spot. You'll see burnt-out places like this all over the country. Safety, see?"

"So, it's better to damage part of the land, to save the rest!" smiled Anya. "What a clever idea!"

"Bonzer!" laughed Darryl.

Read **Mark 9:42–48** and see how the same thing can apply to humans!

- How is Darryl's idea similar to this teaching?
- When have you had to cut something out of your life to bring you back to God?

Consider . . .

- volunteering to help at a local nature reserve, to make it a healthier environment for wildlife.
- writing down something you want to cut out of your life that affects your relationship with others. Then pray that God will help you to deal with it.

For more, see . . .

- John 15:1–2 (p.1124)
- 1 Corinthians 3:11–13 (p.1217)
- Romans 7:14–25 (p.1193)

the sea. [43]If your hand causes you to sin, cut it off. It is better for you to lose part of your body and live for ever than to have two hands and go to hell, where the fire never goes out. [44] [n] [45]If your foot causes you to sin, cut it off. It is better for you to lose part of your body and to live for ever than to have two feet and be thrown into hell. [46] [n] [47]If your eye causes you to sin, take it out. It is better for you to enter the kingdom of God with only one eye than to have two eyes and be thrown into hell. [48]In hell the worm does not die; the fire is never put out. [49]Every person will be salted with fire. [n]

> **Sidelight** The Greek word for "hell" (Mark 9:45–49) is Gehenna, and is based on the Hebrew name for the Hinnom Valley just outside Jerusalem. The valley, which was once used as a site for child sacrifices (see Jeremiah 32:35, p.755) later became a place to burn the bodies of animals and criminals. Jesus uses this word "hell" to describe the place of eternal punishment where all who reject the Good News will go (see also Matthew 13:40–42, p.964).

[50]"Salt is good, but if the salt loses its salty taste, you cannot make it salty again. So, be full of salt, and have peace with each other."

Jesus Teaches About Divorce

10 Then Jesus left that place and went into the area of Judea and across the Jordan River. Again, crowds came to him, and he taught them as he usually did.

[2]Some Pharisees [d] came to Jesus and tried to trick him. They asked, "Is it right for a man to divorce his wife?"

[3]Jesus answered, "What did Moses command you to do?"

[4]They said, "Moses allowed a man to write out divorce papers and send her away." [n]

[5]Jesus said, "Moses wrote that command for you because you were stubborn. [6]But when God made the world, 'he made them male and female'. [n] [7]'So a man will leave his father and mother and be united with his wife, [8]and the two will become one body.' [n] So there are not two, but one. [9]God has joined the two together, so no one should separate them."

[10]Later, in the house, his followers asked Jesus again about the question of divorce. [11]He answered, "Anyone who divorces his wife and marries another woman is guilty of adultery [d] against her. [12]And the woman who divorces her husband and marries another man is also guilty of adultery."

Jesus Accepts Children

[13]Some people brought their little children to Jesus so he could touch them, but his followers told them to stop. [14]When Jesus saw this, he was upset and said to them, "Let the little children come to me. Don't stop them, because the kingdom of God belongs to people who are like these children. [15]I tell you the truth, you must accept the kingdom of God as if you were a little child, or you will never enter it." [16]Then Jesus took the children in his arms, put his hands on them and blessed them.

A Rich Young Man's Question

[17]As Jesus started to leave, a man ran to him and fell on his knees before Jesus. The man asked, "Good teacher, what must I do to have life for ever?"

[18]Jesus answered, "Why do you call me good? Only God is good. [19]You know the commands: 'You must not murder anyone. You must not be guilty of adultery. [d] You must not steal. You must not tell lies about your neighbour. You must not cheat. Honour your father and mother.' " [n]

[20]The man said, "Teacher, I have obeyed all these things since I was a boy."

[21]Jesus, looking at the man, loved him and said, "There is one more thing you need to do. Go and sell everything you have, and give the money to the poor and you will have treasure in heaven. Then come and follow me."

[22]He was very sad to hear Jesus say this, and he left very sad, because he was rich.

[23]Then Jesus looked at his followers and said, "How hard it will be for the rich to enter the kingdom of God!"

[24]The followers were amazed at what Jesus said. But he said again, "My children, it is very hard to enter the kingdom of God! [25]It is easier for a camel to go through the eye of a needle than for a rich person to enter the kingdom of God."

[26]The followers were even more surprised and said to each other, "Then who can be saved?"

[27]Jesus looked at them and said, "This is something people cannot do, but God can. God can do all things."

Verse 44 Some Greek copies of Mark add verse 44, which is the same as verse 48.
Verse 46 Some Greek copies of Mark add verse 46, which is the same as verse 48.
Salted with fire Purified by fire as with the action of salt.
"Moses . . . away." Quotation from Deuteronomy 24:1.
'he made . . . female' Quotation from Genesis 1:27.
'So . . . body.' Quotation from Genesis 2:24.
'You . . . mother.' Quotation from Exodus 20:12–16; Deuteronomy 5:16–20.

28Peter said to Jesus, "Look, we have left
everything and followed you."
29Jesus said, "I tell you the truth, all those
who have left houses, brothers, sisters, mother,
father, children or farms for me and for the Good
News[d] 30will get more than they left. Here in
this world they will have a hundred times more
homes, brothers, sisters, mothers, children and
fields. And with those things, they will also suf-
fer for their belief. But in the age that is coming
they will have life for ever. 31Many who have the
highest place now will have the lowest place in
the future. And many who have the lowest place
now will have the highest place in the future."

Jesus Talks About His Death

32As Jesus and the people with him were on
the road to Jerusalem, he was leading the way.
His followers were amazed, but others in the
crowd who followed were afraid. Again Jesus
took the twelve apostles[d] aside and began to tell
them what was about to happen in Jerusalem.
33He said, "Look, we are going to Jerusalem. The
Son of Man[d] will be turned over to the leading
priests and the teachers of the law. They will say
that he must die, and they will turn him over to
the non-Jewish people, 34who will laugh at him
and spit on him. They will beat him with whips
and crucify him. But on the third day, he will rise
to life again."

Two Followers Ask Jesus a Favour

35Then James and John, sons of Zebedee, came
to Jesus and said, "Teacher, we want to ask you to
do something for us."
36Jesus asked, "What do you want me to do
for you?"
37They answered, "Let one of us sit at your
right side and one of us sit at your left side in
your glory in your kingdom."
38Jesus said, "You don't understand what you
are asking. Can you drink the cup that I must

FAITH

Christmas in June, July . . .

Corky is unique. He's a real trendsetter. For example, he always wears one red sock and one green sock to remind himself that every day is Christmas. His socks are a perfect reflection of the way he lives his Christian faith with others.

Corky often plays with children and talks with elderly people in his neighbourhood. Once he drove 200 miles to comfort someone whose friend had died suddenly. He is also a gifted photographer who captures the best of each person he photographs.

Corky is a joy to be with. His beaming smile lights up his cheeks as though he were Santa Claus himself. When friends see him, their natural reaction is to smile and give him a hug.

His faith is alive with wonder and joy – much like the excitement of a child who has just discovered that dirt and water make mud.

Jesus, himself, challenges us, no matter how old or young we are, to live the childlike faith and joy that Corky lives each day.

Read **Mark 10:13–16** to see how Jesus requires childlike faith.

- How does Corky reflect the kingdom of God in a childlike way?
- In what ways do you feel challenged to be more childlike in your own faith?

Consider . . .

- listing the questions you had about God as a child, then writing the answers you have discovered as you've grown.
- playing with a little child. Build with blocks, paint with your fingers, read stories. Notice the childlike qualities, such as curiosity, innocence and trust. Then work at applying those qualities to your faith.

For more, see . . .

- Isaiah 11:1–6 (p.652)
- Romans 8:14–17 (p.1195)
- Mark 9:33–37 (p.1015)

drink? And can you be baptised with the same
kind of baptism that I must go through?"[n]
39 They answered, "Yes, we can."
Jesus said to them, "You will drink the same
cup that I will drink, and you will be baptised
with the same baptism that I must go through.
40 But I cannot choose who will sit at my right
or my left; those places belong to those for
whom they have been prepared."
41 When the other ten followers heard this,
they began to be angry with James and John.
42 Jesus called them together and said, "The
non-Jewish people have rulers. You know that
those rulers love to show their power over the
people, and their important leaders love to use
all their authority. 43 But it should not be that
way among you. Whoever wants to become
great among you must serve the rest of you
like a servant. 44 Whoever wants to become the
first among you must serve all of you like a
slave. 45 In the same way, the Son of Man[d] did
not come to be served. He came to serve others
and to give his life as a ransom for many
people."

Jesus Heals a Blind Man

46 Then they came to the town of Jericho.
As Jesus was leaving there with his followers
and a great many people, a blind beggar named
Bartimaeus son of Timaeus was sitting by the
road. 47 When he heard that Jesus from
Nazareth was walking by, he began to shout,
"Jesus, Son of David,[d] have mercy on me!"
48 Many people warned the blind man to be
quiet, but he shouted even more, "Son of
David, have mercy on me!"
49 Jesus stopped and said, "Tell the man to
come here."
So they called the blind man, saying, "Cheer
up! Get to your feet. Jesus is calling you." 50 The
blind man jumped up, left his coat there, and
went to Jesus.
51 Jesus asked him, "What do you want me to
do for you?"
The blind man answered, "Teacher, I want to
see."
52 Jesus said, "Go, you are healed because
you believed." At once the man could see, and
he followed Jesus on the road.

Can you . . . through? Jesus was asking if they could suffer the same terrible things that would happen to him.

MONEY

What's Important?

"I have made many millions, but they have brought me no happiness. I would barter them all for the days I sat on an office stool in Cleveland and counted myself rich on $3 a week." – John Rockefeller, a multi-millionaire.

"The care of $200 million is too great a load for any brain or back to bear. It is enough to kill anyone. There is no pleasure in it." – W. H. Vanderbilt, who inherited a fortune.

"I am the most miserable man on earth." – John Jacob Astor, who died leaving $5 million.

"Millionaires seldom smile." – Andrew Carnegie, a millionaire.

Each of these people, who had lots of money, knew that other things were more important than money. Jesus tried to teach the same lesson to the young man in **Mark 10:17–30**. Read how he responded.

- How is what Jesus said similar to the quotes from these millionaires?
- How does your "wealth" help or hinder your faith?

Consider . . .

- drawing a treasure chest and "filling" it with all the things that are most valuable to you. Evaluate what Jesus would think of your treasure.
- giving someone £5 with no strings attached and for no particular reason – just for the fun of it. How does it make you feel?

For more, see . . .

- Deuteronomy 14:22–29 (p.179)
- Acts 3:1–10 (p.1142)
- Luke 21:1–4 (p.1085)

Jesus Enters Jerusalem as a King

11 As Jesus and his followers were coming
closer to Jerusalem, they came to the
towns of Bethphage and Bethany near the
Mount of Olives.[d] From there Jesus sent two of
his followers 2and said to them, "Go to the
town you can see there. When you enter it, you
will quickly find a colt tied, which no one has
ever ridden. Untie it and bring it here to me. 3If
anyone asks you why you are doing this, tell
him its Master needs the colt, and he will send
it at once."
4The followers went into the town, found a
colt tied in the street near the door of a house,
and untied it. 5Some people were standing
there and asked, "What are you doing? Why
are you untying that colt?" 6The followers
answered the way Jesus told them to answer,
and the people let them take the colt.
7They brought the colt to Jesus and put their
coats on it, and Jesus sat on it. 8Many people
spread their coats on the road. Others cut
branches in the fields and spread them on the
road. 9The people were walking ahead of Jesus
and behind him, shouting,

"Praise[n] God!
God bless the One who comes in the name
of the Lord! *Psalm 118:26*
10God bless the kingdom of our father David!
That kingdom is coming!
Praise to God in heaven!"

11Jesus entered Jerusalem and went into the
Temple.[d] After he had looked at everything, since
it was already late, he went out to Bethany with
the twelve apostles.[d]
12The next day as Jesus was leaving Bethany,
he became hungry. 13Seeing a fig tree in leaf
from far away, he went to see if it had any figs

Praise Literally, "Hosanna", a Hebrew word used at first in praying to God for help. At this time it was probably a shout of joy used in praising God or his Messiah.

SERVICE

The Small Things

Caleb was counting the days until he would be off to youth camp – the highlight of the year. Not only would he be playing guitar in the band on stage where everyone would see him, but he'd also get to hang out with his hero Zac, the youth leader. Caleb idolised Zac. He was generous, fun and always put the young people in the youth group first. To top it all, Zac was a fantastic guitarist who did gigs all over the country.

The day finally came when Caleb arrived at the youth camp complete with tent and rucksack. Excitedly, he went in search of Zac in the music tent, but Zac was nowhere to be found. Confused, Caleb started scouring the grounds. Just when he was about to give up, Caleb heard a rustling behind one of the tents. It was Zac, holding a black bin bag and sporting a cheerful smile.

"What are you doing?" exclaimed Caleb, disgusted to see someone like Zac picking up empty crisp packets so cheerfully. Zac beamed, "Well, someone's got to do it haven't they! The last group left rubbish everywhere. Fancy helping me out, Caleb?"

Caleb, like James and John, misunderstood what it meant to be a true servant. Read about James and John's encounter with Jesus in **Mark 10:35–45**.

- How is Zac's attitude similar to Jesus' attitude?
- What are the challenges of being a servant?

Consider . . .

- someone you know who is servant-hearted. Think of something special you could do for them today to show your appreciation.
- next time you're at youth group, looking out for the jobs which need doing and then take a couple of mates and do them.

For more, see . . .

- 1 Samuel 3:1–10 (p.258)
- John 13:1–17 (p.1119)
- Luke 22:24–27 (p.1087)

on it. But he found no figs, only leaves, because it was not the right season for figs. [14]So Jesus said to the tree, "May no one ever eat fruit from you again." And Jesus' followers heard him say this.

Jesus Goes to the Temple

[15]When Jesus returned to Jerusalem, he went into the Temple[d] and began to throw out those who were buying and selling there. He turned over the tables of those who were exchanging different kinds of money, and he upset the benches of those who were selling doves. [16]Jesus refused to allow anyone to carry goods through the Temple courts. [17]Then he taught the people, saying, "It is written in the Scriptures,[d] 'My Temple will be called a house for prayer for people from all nations.'[n] But you are changing God's house into a 'hideout for robbers'."[n]

[18]The leading priests and the teachers of the law heard all this and began trying to find a way to kill Jesus. They were afraid of him, because all the people were amazed at his teaching. [19]That evening, Jesus and his followers left the city.

The Power of Faith

[20]The next morning as Jesus was passing by with his followers, they saw the fig tree dry and dead, even to the roots. [21]Peter remembered the tree and said to Jesus, "Teacher, look! The fig tree you cursed is dry and dead!"

Sidelight

The people that Jesus threw out of the Temple were merchants who took advantage of those in Jerusalem on religious pilgrimages (Mark 11:15–17). They exchanged foreign currency for money to use in the Temple – with an extra charge, of course. Others sold doves to be used in Temple sacrifices.

'My Temple . . . nations.' Quotation from Isaiah 56:7.
'hideout for robbers'. Quotation from Jeremiah 7:11.

PERSISTENCE

The Long Run

"We don't know if your baby will live through the night," the doctors told Pat's new parents. She was born in 1966, weighing only one kilogramme, when few babies born three months premature survived.

But Pat was a fighter from the start.

By the time she reached secondary school, she was an excellent student and a local tennis star. She was also the area track champion in the 3,000 metres. When she finished eighth in her first county athletics meeting, everyone was confident that she had a great running future.

But then a back injury changed her plans. She could no longer run the way she used to. So she found a new way to give of herself – by becoming the track team's manager.

Pat explains why she perseveres: "My persistence comes from making the most of each opportunity I'm given. I wasn't expected to live in the first place, so now I just want to use the gifts I have to the best of my ability."

At one point in Jesus' ministry, he met a blind man who also exhibited Pat's perseverance. Read about the blind man in **Mark 10:46–52**.

- Why did Pat and the blind man persevere?
- How does your faith in Jesus help you to persevere in pursuing your goals?

Consider . . .

- making a plan of action to improve performance in one area of your life. Then spend the time needed to make progress. Evaluate your progress every month.
- setting short- and long-term goals. Write them in a diary, and keep the diary in your bag or wallet.

For more, see . . .

- Isaiah 35:1–10 (p.673)
- Hebrews 10:32–39 (p.1341)
- Luke 5:17–25 (p.1047)

22 Jesus answered, "Have faith in God. 23 I tell
you the truth, you can say to this mountain, 'Go,
fall into the sea.' And if you have no doubts in
your mind and believe that what you say will
happen, God will do it for you. 24 So I tell you to
believe that you have received the things you ask
for in prayer, and God will give them to you.
25 When you are praying, if you are angry with
someone, forgive him so that your Father in
heaven will also forgive your sins." 26 [n]

Leaders Doubt Jesus' Authority

27 Jesus and his followers went again to
Jerusalem. As Jesus was walking in the Temple,[d]
the leading priests, the teachers of the law and
the elders came to him. 28 They said to him,
"What authority do you have to do these things?
Who gave you this authority?"
29 Jesus answered, "I will ask you one question.
If you answer me, I will tell you what authority I
have to do these things. 30 Tell me: when John
baptised people, was that authority from God or
just from other people?"
31 They argued about Jesus' question, saying,
"If we answer, 'John's baptism was from God,'
Jesus will say, 'Then why didn't you believe
him?' 32 But if we say, 'It was from other people,'
the crowd will be against us." (These leaders
were afraid of the people, because all the people
believed that John was a prophet.[d])
33 So they answered Jesus, "We don't know."
Jesus said to them, "Then I won't tell you what
authority I have to do these things."

A Story About God's Son

12 Jesus began to use stories to teach the
people. He said, "A man planted a vine-
yard. He put a wall around it and dug a hole for

Verse 26 Some early Greek copies add verse 26: "But if you don't forgive other people, then your Father in heaven will not forgive your sins."

WORSHIP

1964

On 18 August 1964, the Beatles boarded a plane in London and flew to San Francisco to begin their first coast-to-coast concert tour of North America. The "Fab Four" expected to perform before more people in their 31-day tour than any other act in music history. What they didn't expect was "Beatlemania".

When the musicians arrived, they were greeted at the airport by 5,000 screaming fans. At the hotel where they stayed, they were greeted by 4,000 more. And that was just the beginning.

In the months that followed, the Beatles found themselves confronted by mobs raging with excitement. The foursome often had to travel in secret to avoid crowds. At their concerts, the music was often drowned out by excited, screaming fans.

Some people might think that the Beatles loved the attention. But they didn't.

"It wasn't as much fun for us as it was for all of you," commented George Harrison, the band's lead guitarist, when asked about Beatlemania. People worshipped the Beatles – even though they were just human beings and didn't really deserve that kind of adoration.

Everyone longs to worship something, to have a hero to look up to. That was true even in Jesus' time. **Mark 11:1–11** describes a worship scene that resembled Beatlemania – except Jesus actually deserves that much praise.

- How is the story in the passage like Beatlemania?
- If you had been in Jerusalem at the time of the passage, how would you have worshipped Jesus? How do you worship him today?

Consider . . .

- going to a Christian concert to discover a new way to worship.
- writing a song or poem of worship to Jesus, thanking him for what he's done for you.

For more, see . . .

- Psalm 66 (p.537)
- Luke 19:28–40 (p.1083)
- Matthew 21:1–11 (p.977)

a winepress[d] and built a tower. Then he leased
the land to some farmers and left for a trip.
2When it was time for the grapes to be picked,
he sent a servant to the farmers to get his share
of the grapes. 3But the farmers grabbed the ser-
vant and beat him and sent him away empty-
handed. 4Then the man sent another servant.
They hit him on the head and showed no respect
for him. 5So the man sent another servant,
whom they killed. The man sent many other ser-
vants; the farmers beat some of them and killed
others.
6"The man had one person left to send, his son
whom he loved. He sent him last of all, saying,
'They will respect my son.'
7"But the farmers said to each other, 'This son
will inherit the vineyard. If we kill him, it will be
ours.' 8So they took the son, killed him and
threw him out of the vineyard.
9"So what will the owner of the vineyard do?
He will come and kill those farmers and will give
the vineyard to other farmers. 10Surely you have
read this Scripture:[d]

'The stone that the builders rejected
became the cornerstone.[d]
11The Lord did this,
and it is wonderful to us.' " *Psalm 118:22–23*

12The Jewish leaders knew that the story was
about them. They wanted to find a way to arrest
Jesus, but they were afraid of the people. So the
leaders left him and went away.

Is It Right to Pay Taxes or Not?

13Later, the Jewish leaders sent some Pharisees[d]
and Herodians[n] to Jesus to trap him into saying
something wrong. 14They came to him and said,
"Teacher, we know that you are an honest man.
You are not afraid of what other people think about
you, because you pay no attention to who they
are. And you teach the truth about God's way. Tell
us: is it right to pay taxes to Caesar[d] or not?
15Should we pay them, or not?"
But knowing what these men were really trying
to do, Jesus said to them, "Why are you trying
to trap me? Bring me a coin to look at." 16They
gave Jesus a coin, and he asked, "Whose image
and name are on the coin?"
They answered, "Caesar's."
17Then Jesus said to them, "Give to Caesar the
things that are Caesar's, and give to God the
things that are God's." The men were amazed at
what Jesus said.

Some Sadducees Try to Trick Jesus

18Then some Sadducees[d] came to Jesus and
asked him a question. (Sadducees believed that
people would not rise from the dead.) 19They said,
"Teacher, Moses wrote that if a man's brother
dies, leaving a wife but no children, then that
man must marry the widow and have children
for his brother. 20Once there were seven broth-
ers. The first brother married and died, leaving
no children. 21So the second brother married the
widow, but he also died and had no children.
The same thing happened with the third brother.
22All seven brothers married her and died, and
none of the brothers had any children. Finally
the woman died too. 23Since all seven brothers
had married her, when people rise from the
dead, whose wife will she be?"
24Jesus answered, "Why don't you understand?
Don't you know what the Scriptures[d] say,
and don't you know about the power of God?
25When people rise from the dead, they will not
marry, nor will they be given to someone to
marry. They will be like the angels in heaven.
26Surely you have read what God said about peo-
ple rising from the dead. In the book in which
Moses wrote about the burning bush,[n] it says
that God told Moses, 'I am the God of Abraham,
the God of Isaac and the God of Jacob.'[n] 27God
is the God of the living, not the dead. You
Sadducees are wrong!"

The Most Important Command

28One of the teachers of the law came and
heard Jesus arguing with the Sadducees.[d] Seeing
that Jesus gave good answers to their questions,
he asked Jesus, "Which of the commands is most
important?"
29Jesus answered, "The most important com-
mand is this: 'Listen, people of Israel! The Lord our
God is the only Lord. 30Love the Lord your God
with all your heart, all your soul, all your mind and
all your strength.'[n] 31The second command is this:
'Love your neighbour as you love yourself.'[n] There
are no commands more important than these."
32The man answered, "That was a good an-
swer, Teacher. You were right when you said
God is the only Lord and there is no other God
besides him. 33One must love God with all his
heart, all his mind and all his strength. And one
must love his neighbour as he loves himself.
These commands are more important than all
the animals and sacrifices we offer to God."

Herodians A political group that followed Herod and his family.
burning bush Read Exodus 3:1–12 in the Old Testament.
'I am . . . Jacob.' Quotation from Exodus 3:6.
'Listen . . . strength.' Quotation from Deuteronomy 6:4–5.
'Love . . . yourself.' Quotation from Leviticus 19:18.

34When Jesus saw that the man answered him
wisely, Jesus said to him, "You are close to the
kingdom of God." And after that, no one was
brave enough to ask Jesus any more questions.
35As Jesus was teaching in the Temple,[d] he
asked, "Why do the teachers of the law say that
the Christ[d] is the son of David? 36David himself,
speaking by the Holy Spirit,[d] said:

'The LORD said to my Lord:
Sit by me at my right side,
until I put your enemies under your
control.' *Psalm 110:1*

37David himself calls the Christ 'Lord', so how
can the Christ be his son?" The large crowd
listened to Jesus with pleasure.
38Jesus continued teaching and said, "Beware
of the teachers of the law. They like to walk
around wearing fancy clothes, and they love
people to greet them with respect in the market-
places. 39They love to have the most important
seats in the synagogues[d] and at feasts. 40But they
cheat widows and steal their houses and then try
to make themselves look good by saying long
prayers. They will receive a greater punishment."

True Giving

41Jesus sat near the Temple[d] money box and
watched the people put in their money. Many
rich people gave large sums of money. 42Then a
poor widow came and put in two very small cop-
per coins, which were not even worth a penny.
43Calling his followers to him, Jesus said, "I tell
you the truth, this poor widow gave more than
all those rich people. 44They gave only what they
did not need. This woman is very poor, but she
gave all she had; she gave all she had to live on."

The Temple will Be Destroyed

13 As Jesus was leaving the Temple,[d] one of
his followers said to him, "Look, Teacher!

GIVING

Cough Up

The Dean of Murchester Cathedral strolls along the covered way to the almshouses. He has the court order in his hand and a solicitor with him. He wears his robes for emphasis; the solicitor wears a gown. In the houses, curtains twitch as people wonder what is going on.

These houses have been for the benefit of the local poor for many years. But now they are to be evicted. Even though some of the residents are very old and have lived in these houses for many years they will have to go. They will have to live in homes for the elderly from now on.

The well-to-do of Murchester, walking in the pretty, well-kept grounds of the Cathedral, see the thermometer marking the amount of money raised so far. They also write out cheques, feeling good that they have participated. Coming soon – new roof. The scaffolding will be ugly for a bit, but then there is always a price to pay for improvement.

Bekki likes popping into the Cathedral on the way home from school. She doesn't know why but it makes her feel peaceful. She sometimes wanders around the cool quiet covered corridors. Other times she sits in a side chapel and thinks for a bit. She feels sad that the roof needs repairing and as she leaves, she drops next week's dinner money into the box. "Hope Mum doesn't find out," she says to herself.

Read **Mark 12:38–44**.

- With which of the characters do you most identify? What should our attitude be towards giving?
- How do you feel about what Bekki did?

Consider . . .

- giving a percentage of your income to your church or charity.
- doing something for someone, without any benefit to yourself.

For more, see . . .

- Luke 18:9–14 (p.1078)
- Philippians 4:10–13 (p.1286)
- 2 Corinthians 8:1–3 (p.1248)

How beautiful the buildings are! How big the stones are!"

2Jesus said, "Do you see all these great buildings? Not one stone will be left on another. Every stone will be thrown down to the ground."

3Later, as Jesus was sitting on the Mount of Olives,[d] opposite the Temple, he was alone with Peter, James, John and Andrew. They asked Jesus, 4"Tell us, when will these things happen? And what will be the sign that they are going to happen?"

5Jesus began to answer them, "Be careful that no one fools you. 6Many people will come in my name, saying, 'I am the One,' and they will fool many people. 7When you hear about wars and stories of wars that are coming, don't be afraid. These things must happen before the end comes. 8Nations will fight against other nations, and kingdoms against other kingdoms. There will be earthquakes in different places, and there will be times when there is no food for people to eat. These things are like the first pains when something new is about to be born.

Sidelight Jesus' prediction that the Temple would be destroyed (Mark 13:1–2) came true within about 40 years. In AD 70, the Romans surrounded and sacked Jerusalem, burning the Temple to the ground. Today, the Muslim shrine called the "Dome of the Rock" stands on the Temple site.

9"You must be careful. People will arrest you and take you to court and beat you in their synagogues.[d] You will be forced to stand before kings and governors, to tell them about me. This will happen to you because you follow me. 10But before these things happen, the Good News[d] must be told to all people. 11When you are arrested and judged, don't worry ahead of time about what you should say. Say whatever is given you to say at that time, because it will not really be you speaking; it will be the Holy Spirit.[d]

12"Brothers will give their own brothers to be killed, and fathers will give their own children to be killed. Children will fight against their own parents and cause them to be put to death. 13All people will hate you because you follow me, but those people who keep their faith until the end will be saved.

14"You will see 'the destroying terror'[n] standing where it should not be." (You who read this should understand what it means.) "At that time, the people in Judea should run away to the mountains. 15If people are on the roofs[n] of their houses, they must not go down or go inside to get anything out of their houses. 16If people are in the fields, they must not go back to get their coats. 17At that time, how terrible it will be for women who are pregnant or have nursing babies! 18Pray that these things will not happen in winter, 19because those days will be full of trouble. There will be more trouble than there has ever been since the beginning, when God made the world, until now, and nothing as bad will ever happen again. 20God has decided to make that terrible time short. Otherwise, no one would go on living. But God will make that time short to help the people he has chosen. 21At that time, someone might say to you, 'Look, there is the Christ!'[d] Or another person might say, 'There he is!' But don't believe them. 22False Christs and false prophets[d] will come and perform great wonders and miracles.[d] They will try to fool even the people God has chosen, if that were possible. 23So be careful. I have warned you about all this before it happens.

24"During the days after this trouble comes,

'the sun will grow dark,
 and the moon will not give its light.
25The stars will fall from the sky.
 And the powers of the heavens will be
  shaken.' *Isaiah 13:10; 34:4*

26"Then people will see the Son of Man[d] coming in clouds with great power and glory. 27Then he will send his angels all around the earth to gather his chosen people from every part of the earth and from every part of heaven.

28"Learn a lesson from the fig tree: when its branches become green and soft and new leaves appear, you know summer is near. 29In the same way, when you see these things happening, you will know that the time is near, ready to come. 30I tell you the truth, all these things will happen while the people of this time are still living. 31Earth and sky will be destroyed, but the words I have said will never be destroyed.

32"No one knows when that day or time will be, not the angels in heaven, not even the Son. Only the Father knows. 33Be careful! Always be ready, because you don't know when that time will be. 34It is like a man who goes on a trip. He leaves his house and lets his servants take care of it, giving each one a special job to do. The man tells the servant guarding the door always to be watchful. 35So always be ready, because you don't know when the owner of the house will come back. It might be in the evening, or at midnight,

'the destroying terror' Mentioned in Daniel 9:27; 12:11 (cf. Daniel 11:31).
roofs In Bible times houses were built with flat roofs. The roof was used for drying things such as flax and fruit. And it was used as an extra room, as a place for worship and as a place to sleep in the summer.

or in the morning while it is still dark, or when the
sun rises. 36 Always be ready. Otherwise he might
come back suddenly and find you sleeping. 37 I tell
you this, and I say this to everyone: 'Be ready!' "

The Plan to Kill Jesus

14 It was now only two days before the
Passover [d] and the Feast [d] of Unleavened
Bread. The leading priests and teachers of the law
were trying to find a trick to arrest Jesus and kill
him. 2 But they said, "We must not do it during
the feast, because the people might cause a riot."

A Woman with Perfume for Jesus

3 Jesus was in Bethany at the house of Simon,
who had a skin disease. While Jesus was eating
there, a woman approached him with an alabas-
ter [d] jar filled with very expensive perfume, made
of pure nard. [d] She opened the jar and poured
the perfume on Jesus' head.
4 Some who were there became upset and said
to each other, "Why waste that perfume? 5 It was
worth a full year's work. It could have been sold
and the money given to the poor." And they got
very angry with the woman.
6 Jesus said, "Leave her alone. Why are you
troubling her? She did an excellent thing for me.
7 You will always have the poor with you,
and you can help them any time you want. But
you will not always have me. 8 This woman
did the only thing she could do for me; she
poured perfume on my body to prepare me for
burial. 9 I tell you the truth, wherever the Good
News [d] is preached in all the world, what this
woman has done will be told, and people will
remember her."

FUTURE

Be Prepared

In November 1990, grocery store shelves in New Madrid, Missouri, were cleared and boxes were packed with food, water, first-aid kits, torches and radios. People were frightened. Some people wouldn't even sleep in their own homes; they slept in their cars and pick-up trucks instead. Many even left the area.

"I'm terrified of this," resident Anna Harper said. "I feel like it's some terminal illness. I don't want to believe it, but there is so much talk about it."

Residents of this small town were preparing for the earthquake that Iben Browning, a business consultant from New Mexico, had predicted. He said that tidal forces were unusually high and could trigger an earthquake of 6.5 to 7.5 on the Richter scale 48 hours before or after 3 December, along the New Madrid fault.

While many residents of the small town scurried about to prepare for the catastrophe, others were calm about it. After all, these residents said, it's not as though they didn't already know they were living on a fault line.

The day in question came and went, and there was no earthquake.

In **Mark 13:24–33**, Jesus warns his followers of a certain day that they need to be prepared for in the future.

- According to this passage, no one knows when Jesus will return. To prepare for that day, which people should we be like – the people who prepared at the last minute or those who were ready at all times?
- If Jesus were to return today, would you be ready?

Consider . . .

- deciding what things you would put in an "emergency kit" for the end of the world, for example, faith or courage. Think about what you need to do to have those things ready.
- asking your minister or youth leader to teach on the "last days".

For more, see . . .

- Genesis 9:1–17 (p.10)
- 1 Thessalonians 4:13—5:11 (p.1299)
- Luke 21:25–36 (p.1087)

Sidelight The perfume that the woman poured on Jesus' feet at Bethany (Mark 14:3–9) might have made many modern perfumes seem cheap. Called "spikenard", it was taken from pink-blossomed plants in the Himalayan Mountains of northern India.

Judas Becomes an Enemy of Jesus

10One of the twelve apostles, Judas Iscariot,
went to talk to the leading priests to offer to
hand Jesus over to them. 11These priests were
pleased about this and promised to pay Judas
money. So he watched for the best time to turn
Jesus over.

Jesus Eats the Passover Meal

12It was now the first day of the Feast[d] of
Unleavened Bread when the Passover[d] lamb
was sacrificed. Jesus' followers said to him,
"Where do you want us to go and prepare for
you to eat the Passover meal?"
13Jesus sent two of his followers and said to
them, "Go into the city and a man carrying a jar
of water will meet you. Follow him. 14When he
goes into a house, tell the owner of the house,
'The Teacher says: where is my guest room in
which I can eat the Passover meal with my fol-
lowers?' 15The owner will show you a large
room upstairs that is furnished and ready. Pre-
pare the food for us there."
16So the followers left and went into the city.
Everything happened as Jesus had said, so they
prepared the Passover meal.
17In the evening, Jesus went to that house with
the twelve. 18While they were all eating, Jesus
said, "I tell you the truth, one of you will turn
against me—one of you eating with me now."
19The followers were very sad to hear this.
Each one began to say to Jesus, "I am not the
one, am I?"

DEATH

The Greatest Lesson

The common mayfly has a life expectancy of just one day, but is he miserable about it? Not one bit. He fills his day with the things he loves. He soars, he swoops, he savours every moment. Maybe there's a lesson in this for us longer-living creatures. Just think . . . if we embraced life like the mayfly, what a life that would be!

Many people think this is the best way life can be lived – being free with no responsibilities, taking each day as it comes and definitely never thinking about scary stuff like death. And yet we only have to watch the news for five minutes to be brought back down to earth with a bump – death is an unavoidable part of our lives. Similarly, Jesus' disciples had been living the dream. They'd heard him describe a new way of living life (see Matthew 6:25–34, p.948) and they'd watched him as he brought this life to impossible situations (see John 11:38–44, p.1116).

Read **Mark 14:12–26**. Jesus used this mealtime to introduce the greatest lesson he would ever teach. The lesson was this: only when you know that your eternity is secure can you really enjoy the time you have. Jesus knew that death had no power over him, so he could face it without fear. And the amazing thing is that the victory of his resurrection has enabled us to also share his prize – eternal life!

- Can you imagine why the disciples might find the things Jesus said around the meal table confusing?
- Was this Jesus' way of saying goodbye?

Consider . . .

- listening to a worship song about Jesus' death on the cross.
- what you would do with your life if you knew you only had one year left.

For more, see . . .

- Genesis 46:29–30 (p.53)
- Luke 2:28–32 (p.1040)
- Hebrews 2:9 (p.1330)

20Jesus answered, "It is one of the twelve—the
one who dips his bread into the bowl with me.
21The Son of Man[d] will die, just as the Scriptures[d]
say. But how terrible it will be for the person who
hands the Son of Man over to be killed. It would
be better for him if he had never been born."

The Lord's Supper

22While they were eating, Jesus took some
bread and thanked God for it and broke it. Then
he gave it to his followers and said, "Take it; this
is my body."
23Then Jesus took a cup and thanked God for
it and gave it to the followers, and they all drank
from the cup.
24Then Jesus said, "This is my blood which is
the new agreement that God makes with his
people. This blood is poured out for many. 25I tell
you the truth, I will not drink of this fruit of the
vine[n] again until that day when I drink it new in
the kingdom of God."
26After singing a hymn, they went out to the
Mount of Olives.[d]

Jesus' Followers Will Leave Him

27Then Jesus told the followers, "You will all
stumble in your faith, because it is written in the
Scriptures:[d]

'I will kill the shepherd,
and the sheep will scatter.' *Zechariah 13:7*

28But after I rise from the dead, I will go ahead of
you into Galilee."
29Peter said, "Everyone else may stumble in
their faith, but I will not."
30Jesus answered, "I tell you the truth, tonight
before the cockerel crows twice you will say
three times you don't know me."
31But Peter insisted, "I will never say that I
don't know you! I will even die with you!" And
all the other followers said the same thing.

Jesus Prays Alone

32Jesus and his followers went to a place called
Gethsemane. He said to them, "Sit here while I
pray." 33Jesus took Peter, James and John with
him, and he began to be very sad and troubled.
34He said to them, "My heart is full of sorrow, to
the point of death. Stay here and watch."
35After walking a little farther away from
them, Jesus fell to the ground and prayed that, if
possible, he would not have this time of suffer-
ing. 36He prayed, "Abba,[n] Father! You can do all
things. Take away this cup[n] of suffering. But do
what you want, not what I want."
37Then Jesus went back to his followers and
found them asleep. He said to Peter, "Simon, are
you sleeping? Couldn't you stay awake with me
for one hour? 38Stay awake and pray for strength
against temptation. The spirit wants to do what
is right, but the body is weak."
39Again Jesus went away and prayed the same
thing. 40Then he went back to his followers, and
again he found them asleep, because their eyes
were very heavy. And they did not know what to
say to him.
41After Jesus prayed a third time, he went back
to his followers and said to them, "Are you still
sleeping and resting? That's enough. The time has
come for the Son of Man[d] to be handed over to
sinful people. 42Get up, we must go. Look, here
comes the man who has turned against me."

Jesus is Arrested

43At once, while Jesus was still speaking, Judas,
one of the twelve apostles,[d] came up. With him
were many people carrying swords and clubs who
had been sent from the leading priests, the teach-
ers of the law and the Jewish elders.
44Judas had planned a signal for them, saying,
"The man I kiss is Jesus. Arrest him and guard
him while you lead him away." 45So Judas went
straight to Jesus and said, "Teacher!" and kissed
him. 46Then the people grabbed Jesus and
arrested him. 47One of his followers standing
nearby pulled out his sword and struck the ser-
vant of the high priest and cut off his ear.
48Then Jesus said, "You came to get me with
swords and clubs as if I were a criminal. 49Every
day I was with you teaching in the Temple,[d] and
you did not arrest me there. But all these things
have happened to make the Scriptures[d] come
true." 50Then all of Jesus' followers left him and
ran away.
51A young man, wearing only a linen cloth,
was following Jesus, and the people also grabbed
him. 52But the cloth he was wearing came off,
and he ran away naked.

Jesus Before the Leaders

53The people who arrested Jesus led him to the
house of the high priest, where all the leading
priests, the Jewish elders and the teachers of the
law were gathered. 54Peter followed far behind
and entered the courtyard of the high priest's
house. There he sat with the guards, warming
himself by the fire.
55The leading priests and the whole Jewish
council tried to find something that Jesus had

fruit of the vine Product of the grapevine; this may also be translated "wine".
Abba Name that a child called his father.
cup Jesus is talking about the terrible things that will happen to him. Accepting these things will be very hard, like drinking a cup of something bitter.

done wrong so they could kill him. But the council could find no proof of anything. [56]Many people came and told false things about him, but all said different things—none of them agreed.

[57]Then some people stood up and lied about Jesus, saying, [58]"We heard this man say, 'I will destroy this Temple[d] that people made. And three days later, I will build another Temple not made by people.' " [59]But even the things these people said did not agree.

[60]Then the high priest stood before them and asked Jesus, "Aren't you going to answer? Don't you have something to say about their charges against you?" [61]But Jesus said nothing; he did not answer.

The high priest asked Jesus another question: "Are you the Christ,[d] the Son of the blessed God?"

[62]Jesus answered, "I am. And in the future you will see the Son of Man[d] sitting at the right hand of God, the Powerful One, and coming on clouds in the sky."

[63]When the high priest heard this, he tore his clothes and said, "We don't need any more witnesses! [64]You all heard him say these things against God. What do you think?"

They all said that Jesus was guilty and should die. [65]Some of the people there began to spit at Jesus. They blindfolded him and beat him with their fists and said, "Prove you are a prophet!"[d] Then the guards led Jesus away and beat him.

Peter Says He Doesn't Know Jesus

[66]While Peter was in the courtyard, a servant girl of the high priest came there. [67]She saw Peter warming himself at the fire and looked closely at him.

Then she said, "You also were with Jesus, that man from Nazareth."

[68]But Peter said that he was never with Jesus. He said, "I don't know or understand what you are talking about." Then Peter left and went towards the entrance of the courtyard. And the cockerel crowed.[n]

[69]The servant girl saw Peter there, and again she said to the people who were standing nearby, "This man is one of those who followed Jesus." [70]Again Peter said that it was not true.

A short time later, some people were standing near Peter saying, "Surely you are one of those who followed Jesus, because you are from Galilee, too."

[71]Then Peter began to place a curse on himself and swear, "I don't know this man you're talking about!"

[72]At once, the cockerel crowed the second time. Then Peter remembered what Jesus had told him: "Before the cockerel crows twice, you will say three times that you don't know me." Then Peter lost control of himself and began to cry.

Pilate Questions Jesus

15 Very early in the morning, the leading priests, the older leaders, the teachers of the law and all the Jewish council decided what to do with Jesus. They tied him, led him away and turned him over to Pilate, the governor.

[2]Pilate asked Jesus, "Are you the king of the Jews?"

Jesus answered, "Those are your words."

[3]The leading priests accused Jesus of many things. [4]So Pilate asked Jesus another question, "You can see that they are accusing you of many things. Aren't you going to answer?"

[5]But Jesus still said nothing, so Pilate was very surprised.

Pilate Tries to Free Jesus

[6]Every year at the time of the Passover[d] the governor would free one prisoner whom the people chose. [7]At that time, there was a man named Barabbas in prison who was a rebel and had committed murder during a riot. [8]The crowd came to Pilate and began to ask him to free a prisoner as he always did.

[9]So Pilate asked them, "Do you want me to free the king of the Jews?" [10]Pilate knew that the leading priests had turned Jesus over to him because they were jealous. [11]But the leading priests had persuaded the people to ask Pilate to free Barabbas, not Jesus.

[12]Then Pilate asked the crowd again, "So what should I do with this man you call the king of the Jews?"

[13]They shouted, "Crucify him!"

[14]Pilate asked, "Why? What wrong has he done?"

But they shouted even louder, "Crucify him!"

[15]Pilate wanted to please the crowd, so he freed Barabbas for them. After having Jesus beaten with whips, he handed Jesus over to the soldiers to be crucified.

Sidelight The sort of beating that Jesus experienced (Mark 15:15) was a gruesome practice among the Romans. The whip was made of leather, lead and bone, and could tear out eyes, sever veins and rip open stomachs. It was a customary part of the death sentence.

And . . . crowed. A few, early Greek copies leave out this phrase.

16The soldiers took Jesus into the governor's
palace (called the Praetorium) and called all
the other soldiers together. 17They put a purple
robe on Jesus and used thorny branches to
make a crown for his head. 18They began to call
out to him, "Hail, King of the Jews!" 19The sol-
diers beat Jesus on the head many times with a
stick. They spat on him and made fun of him by
bowing on their knees and worshipping him.
20After they finished, the soldiers took off the
purple robe and put his own clothes on him
again. Then they led him out of the palace to be
crucified.

Jesus is Crucified

21A man named Simon from Cyrene, the
father of Alexander and Rufus, was coming
from the fields to the city. The soldiers forced
Simon to carry the cross for Jesus. 22They led
Jesus to the place called Golgotha, which means
the Place of the Skull. 23The soldiers tried to
give Jesus wine mixed with myrrh[d] to drink,
but he refused. 24The soldiers crucified Jesus
and divided his clothes among themselves,
throwing lots[d] to decide what each soldier
would get.

25It was nine o'clock in the morning when
they crucified Jesus. 26There was a sign with this
charge against Jesus written on it: THE KING OF
THE JEWS. 27They also put two robbers on crosses
beside Jesus, one on the right, and the other on
the left. 28 [n] 29People walked by and insulted
Jesus and shook their heads, saying, "You said
you could destroy the Temple[d] and build it again
in three days. 30So save yourself! Come down
from that cross!"

31The leading priests and the teachers of the
law were also making fun of Jesus. They said to
each other, "He saved other people, but he can't
save himself. 32If he is really the Christ,[d] the

Verse 28 Some Greek copies add verse 28: "And the Scripture came true that says, 'They put him with criminals.'"

PEER PRESSURE

Don't Give In!

Lee was considered the class geek and everyone had decided that this lunchtime they would pick on him. Half of Tom wanted to run in front of Lee and save him from this bullying, but the other half of him was scared that he would end up getting the same treatment. Then someone in the class shouted, "Oi Tom, what have you got to say?" There was a deafening silence as everyone looked at Tom to see whether he would stick up for his friend or join in with the group.

Without thinking, he shouted at Lee. He figured that the group would back off Lee if they thought they'd managed to turn his friend against him. But it didn't happen like that. As soon as Tom had finished shouting, the rest of the group carried on where they had left off and continued punching Lee, as Tom stood there watching helplessly. They only stopped when a teacher turned the corner, at which point they all ran off, Tom included.

Read **Mark 15:1–20.**

- Why did Tom and Pilate give in to pressure?
- Have you ever given in to pressure and then wished you hadn't?

Consider . . .

- times when you have given in to pressure and done something you've regretted. Ask God to forgive you and help you next time to withstand the urge to give in.
- whether the next time your friends are speaking against Jesus you will stand up for him.

For more, see . . .

- Proverbs 1:10–19 (p.590)
- Hebrews 12:1–3 (p.1343)
- Luke 6:22–23 (p.1048)

king of Israel, let him come down now from the
cross. When we see this, we will believe in
him." The robbers who were being crucified
beside Jesus also insulted him.

Jesus Dies

33At noon the whole country became dark,
and the darkness lasted for three hours. 34At three
o'clock Jesus cried in a loud voice, "Eli, Eli,[n]
lama sabachthani." This means, "My God, my
God, why have you rejected me?"
35When some of the people standing there
heard this, they said, "Listen! He is calling Elijah."
36Someone there ran and got a sponge, filled it
with vinegar, tied it to a stick, and gave it to Jesus
to drink. He said, "We want to see if Elijah will
come to take him down from the cross."
37Then Jesus cried in a loud voice and died.
38The curtain in the Temple[n] was torn into
two pieces, from the top to the bottom. 39When
the army officer who was standing in front of the
cross saw what happened when Jesus died, he
said, "This man really was the Son of God!"
40Some women were standing at a distance
from the cross, watching; among them were
Mary Magdalene, Salome and Mary the mother
of James and Joseph. (James was her youngest
son.) 41These women had followed Jesus in
Galilee and helped him. Many other women
were also there who had come with Jesus to
Jerusalem.

Jesus is Buried

42This was Preparation[d] Day. (That means the
day before the Sabbath[d] day.) That evening,
43Joseph from Arimathea was brave enough to go
to Pilate and ask for Jesus' body. Joseph, an import-
ant member of the Jewish council, was one of
the people who was waiting for the kingdom of
God to come. 44Pilate was amazed that Jesus

Eli, Eli Some Bibles translate this as Eloi, Eloi.
curtain in the Temple A curtain divided the Most Holy Place from the other part of the Temple. That was the special building in Jerusalem where God commanded the Jewish people to worship him.

JESUS CHRIST

Unexpected Saviour

Jesus painted no pictures. Yet some of the greatest artists were inspired by him to paint their greatest works.

Jesus wrote no poetry. Yet hundreds of the world's greatest poems pay tribute to him.

Jesus composed no music. Yet great musicians wrote some of their greatest music to praise him.

Jesus preached and taught for only three years. Socrates taught for 40 years, Plato for 50 years, and Aristotle for 40 years. Yet hundreds of millions more people follow Jesus than follow the three philosophers combined.

Jesus died on a cross as a criminal. Yet even a guard who helped to put him to death recognised that he was God's Son. Read **Mark 15:33–39** to see how Jesus showed that he was God's Son even in his death.

- What unexpected things do you see in Jesus' life as described by the passage and by the comparisons above?
- How does this passage strengthen your faith in Jesus as God's Son?

Consider . . .

- listing everything that you would expect a king to do. Then compare it to what you read in the Bible about Jesus. Identify similarities and differences.
- rereading the passage, putting yourself in the place of the officer. How would you have responded to this situation? What would you have said?

For more, see . . .

- Isaiah 53 (p.697)
- John 19:28–37 (p.1131)
- Matthew 16:21–28 (p.969)

was already dead, so he called the army officer
who had guarded Jesus and asked him if Jesus
had already died. 45The officer told Pilate that he
was dead, so Pilate told Joseph he could have the

Sidelight Most people who were crucified in Jesus' day were left on the cross or were simply discarded in a mass grave. By requesting Jesus' body for burial, Joseph saved Jesus from that final indignity (Mark 15:42–47).

body. 46Joseph bought some linen cloth, took the
body down from the cross, and wrapped it in the
linen. He put the body in a tomb that was cut
out of a wall of rock. Then he rolled a very large
stone to block the entrance of the tomb. 47And
Mary Magdalene and Mary the mother of Joseph
saw the place where Jesus was laid.

Jesus Rises from the Dead

16 The day after the Sabbath[d] day, Mary
Magdalene, Mary the mother of James,
and Salome bought some sweet-smelling spices
to put on Jesus' body. 2Very early on that day, the
first day of the week, soon after sunrise, the
women were on their way to the tomb. 3They
said to each other, "Who will roll away for us the
stone that covers the entrance of the tomb?"
4Then the women looked and saw that the
stone had already been rolled away, even though
it was very large. 5The women entered the tomb
and saw a young man wearing a white robe and
sitting on the right side, and they were afraid.

LIFE

A Light in the Darkness

Adam was heavily into drugs by the time he was fourteen. After being arrested for helping his friends to steal a radio, he was placed in a young offenders' unit. But he kept slipping further and further downhill.

He became more distant from his family and friends. And he started using drugs daily to try to escape the pain he felt inside.

One day Adam couldn't stand the pain any longer. He hated himself, and he didn't want to go on living. He felt trapped. The darkness was overwhelming, and he just couldn't see a way out.

Finally, he cried out to God. "Please," he pleaded, "please help me." Almost immediately he sensed a peace and calm inside, as if the darkness was replaced with a new hope.

In the following weeks, he began attending drug users' support meetings and joined a Christian fellowship. Adam had a new beginning.

"Turning my life over to God's direction is the toughest decision I've ever made," Adam later explained. "But my faith is beginning to pay off. I'm making new friends. I've found a job. I'm taking art classes. I feel alive. It's a day-to-day struggle to stay free of drugs, but I'm headed in the right direction for the first time in my life."

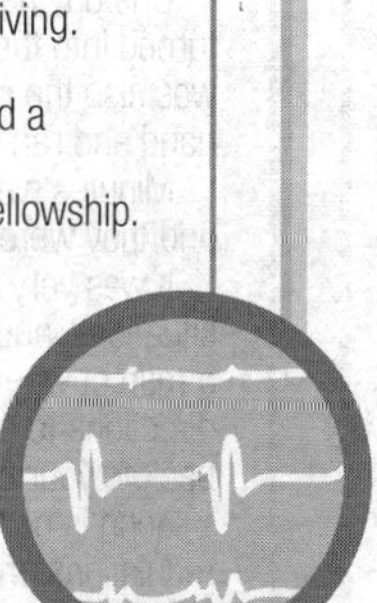

Adam was beginning to experience the life and power of Jesus' resurrection. Read about the resurrection in **Mark 16:1–8**.

- How was Adam's new life similar to Jesus' resurrection? How was it different?
- How is your response to Jesus' resurrection like or unlike the women's reactions?

Consider . . .

- asking God to "roll away" an obstacle in your life with his resurrection power.
- listing the ways in which you can "stop the pain" you may be experiencing, just as Adam stopped his pain. Ask others for help if you need to.

For more, see . . .

- Exodus 14 (p.71)
- John 20:1–18 (p.1132)
- Matthew 28:1–10 (p.993)

6But the man said, "Don't be afraid. You are
looking for Jesus from Nazareth, who has been
crucified. He has risen from the dead; he is not
here. Look, here is the place where they laid him.
7Now go and tell his followers and Peter, 'Jesus is
going into Galilee ahead of you, and you will see
him there as he told you before.' "
8The women were confused and shaking with
fear, so they left the tomb and ran away. They did
not tell anyone about what happened, because
they were afraid.

Verses 9–20 are not included in two of the best and oldest Greek copies of Mark.

Some Followers See Jesus

[9After Jesus rose from the dead early on the
first day of the week, he showed himself first to
Mary Magdalene. Once in the past, he had forced
seven demons[d] out of her. 10After Mary saw
Jesus, she went and told his followers, who were
very sad and were crying. 11But Mary told them
that Jesus was alive. She said that she had seen
him, but the followers did not believe her.
12Later, Jesus showed himself to two of his fol-
lowers while they were walking in the country,
but he did not look the same as before. 13These
followers went back to the others and told them
what had happened, but again, the followers did
not believe them.

Jesus Talks to the Apostles

14Later Jesus showed himself to the eleven
apostles while they were eating, and he criticised
them because they had no faith. They were stub-
born and refused to believe those who had seen
him after he had risen from the dead.

SHARING FAITH

Follow the Leader

As a young boy of five years old, John used to love to look in toyshops. He would daydream at a shop window and watch the working models going round and round.

One day he went out with his parents to a large shopping centre in Cardiff and was thrilled when they turned into the arcade. In actual fact, his mum and dad wanted to look at some furniture, but John knew this was also the place where his favourite toyshop was! So as soon as he had the chance, he let go of his mum's hand and ran off down the arcade to his shop window.

Minutes went by as John stood entranced. Then, thinking it was time to go, he looked up for his parents and they were nowhere to be seen. As a very small boy, all he could see were giants everywhere!

It was very frightening, and a situation we can all sympathise with. Many of us have been in similar situations, and when you are in a situation like that, you don't need some huge person to come up with a map of where you live, and try to explain how to get home. You don't want a list of bus stops, or directions to the nearest train station. You need a kind person to hold out their hand and lead you back to your parents.

John is now an evangelist, but he always remembers that people don't want a set of rules and regulations of "How to Become a Christian", they need someone to take them to Jesus.

When Jesus' followers first went out, they took this Good News everywhere. In **Mark 16:19–20** we see how the Lord helped his followers spread the Good News.

- How do people react when you tell them the Good News of Jesus Christ?
- What's the difference between a "map" and a "helping hand"?

Consider . . .

- telling a non-Christian friend about Jesus.
- asking your minister or youth leader to lead a training course on "How to Tell Others About Christ".

For more, see . . .

- Acts 1:1–14 (p.1137)
- 1 John 1:1–4 (p.1371)

[15]Jesus said to his followers, "Go everywhere
in the world, and tell the Good News[d] to every-
one. [16]Anyone who believes and is baptised
will be saved, but anyone who does not believe
will be punished. [17]And those who believe will
be able to do these things as proof: they will
use my name to force out demons.[d] They
will speak in new languages.[n] [18]They will pick
up snakes and drink poison without being hurt.
They will touch the sick, and the sick will be
healed."

[19]After the Lord Jesus said these things to his
followers, he was carried up into heaven, and he
sat at the right side of God. [20]The followers went
everywhere in the world and told the Good
News to people, and the Lord helped them. The
Lord proved that the Good News they told was
true by giving them power to work miracles.[d]]

languages This can also be translated "tongues".

Luke

Why Read This Book:

- Discover the Bible's only stories about Jesus' childhood (Luke 2).
- See how Jesus ministered to all people, especially the poor and the outcast (Luke 4—8).
- Enjoy some of Jesus' most famous stories (Luke 10, 15—16).
- Learn how Jesus gave his life for our sins (Luke 22—24).

When?

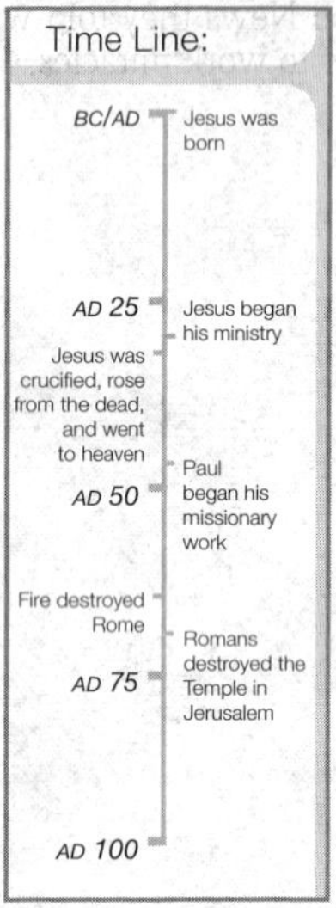

Behind the Scenes:

Imagine never hearing that Jesus was laid in a feeding box when he was born (Luke 2:7–11). Imagine not knowing the parable of the Good Samaritan (Luke 10:25–37). Or the parable of the son who left home, who is also known as the Prodigal Son (Luke 15:11–32). Imagine not knowing about Jesus' encounter with Zacchaeus (Luke 19:1–10).

We wouldn't have any of these stories without the Gospel of Luke.

Though the books of Matthew, Mark and John tell many stories about Jesus, they don't include about one-third of the material in Luke. Luke is the most complete account of Jesus' life. It's a detailed, organised picture of Jesus' life and ministry.

As you read the Gospel of Luke, you'll discover some important emphases. First, this book emphasises that Jesus came for all people, not just the Jews. You'll also see Jesus' particular concern for women, the poor and the outcasts of the world. Then the book shows Jesus as God's Spirit-led Son who came to offer eternal life to all people who follow him. ▷

Where?

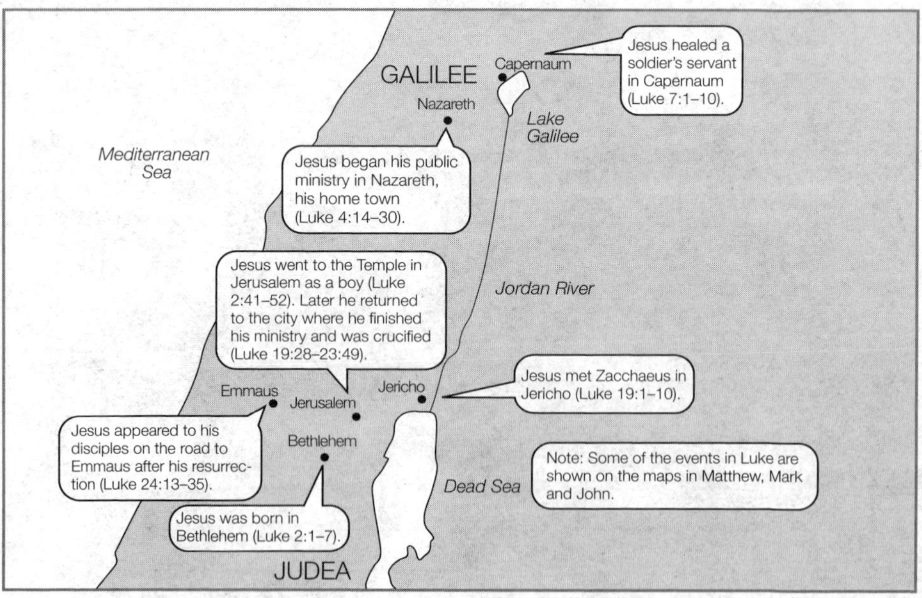

Behind the Scenes (cont.): Luke 19:10 says that "the Son of Man came to find lost people and save them". This book tells, in detail, the story of his coming. If you like the Gospel of Luke, try the sequel: the book of Acts (p.1136). It's written by the same author, and continues the story where Luke leaves off.

Luke Writes About Jesus' Life

1 Many have tried to report on the things that
happened among us. 2They have written
the same things that we learned from others—
the people who saw those things from the begin-
ning and served God by telling people his
message. 3Since I myself have studied everything
carefully from the beginning, most excellent[n]
Theophilus, it seemed good for me to write it out
for you. I arranged it in order 4to help you know
that what you have been taught is true.

Sidelight The Gospel of Luke is the longest New Testament book, with 1,151 verses. And the book of Acts – which Luke also wrote – isn't far behind. Since Luke was a doctor, a simple prescription probably took reams of paper!

Zechariah and Elizabeth

5During the time Herod ruled Judea, there
was a priest named Zechariah who belonged
to Abijah's group.[n] Zechariah's wife, Elizabeth,
came from the family of Aaron. 6Zechariah and
Elizabeth truly did what God said was good.
They did everything the Lord commanded
and were without fault in keeping his law. 7But
they had no children, because Elizabeth could
not have a baby, and both of them were very old.
8One day Zechariah was serving as a priest
before God, because his group was on duty.
9According to the custom of the priests, he was
chosen by lot[d] to go into the Temple of the Lord
and burn incense.[d] 10There were a great many
people outside praying at the time the incense
was offered. 11Then an angel of the Lord
appeared to Zechariah, standing on the right
side of the incense table. 12When he saw the
angel, Zechariah was startled and frightened.
13But the angel said to him, "Zechariah, don't
be afraid. God has heard your prayer. Your wife,
Elizabeth, will give birth to a son, and you will
name him John. 14He will bring you joy and
gladness, and many people will be happy be-
cause of his birth. 15John will be a great man for
the Lord. He will never drink wine or beer, and
even from birth, he will be filled with the Holy
Spirit.[d] 16He will help many people of Israel re-
turn to the Lord their God. 17He will go before
the Lord in spirit and power like Elijah. He will
make peace between parents and their children
and will bring those who are not obeying God
back to the right way of thinking, to make a
people ready for the coming of the Lord."
18Zechariah said to the angel, "How can I
know that what you say is true? I am an old
man, and my wife is old, too."
19The angel answered him, "I am Gabriel. I
stand before God, who sent me to talk to you
and to tell you this good news. 20Now, listen!
You will not be able to speak until the day these
things happen, because you did not believe
what I told you. But they will really happen."
21Outside, the people were still waiting for
Zechariah and were surprised that he was stay-
ing so long in the Temple. 22When Zechariah
came outside, he could not speak to them, and
they knew he had seen a vision in the Temple.
He could only make signs to them and
remained unable to speak. 23When his time of
service at the Temple was finished, he went
home.
24Later, Zechariah's wife, Elizabeth, became
pregnant and did not go out of her house for five
months. Elizabeth said, 25"Look what the Lord
has done for me! My people were ashamed[n] of
me, but now the Lord has taken away that
shame."

An Angel Appears to Mary

26During Elizabeth's sixth month of pregnancy,
God sent the angel Gabriel to Nazareth, a town
in Galilee, 27to a virgin.[d] She was engaged to
marry a man named Joseph from the family of

excellent This word was used to show respect to an important person like a king or ruler.
Abijah's group The Jewish priests were divided into 24 groups. See 1 Chronicles 24.
ashamed The Jewish people thought it was a disgrace for women not to have children.

David. Her name was Mary. 28The angel came to
her and said, "Greetings! The Lord has blessed
you and is with you."
29But Mary was very startled by what the
angel said and wondered what this greeting
might mean.
30The angel said to her, "Don't be afraid, Mary;
God has shown you his grace. 31Listen! You will
become pregnant and give birth to a son, and
you will name him Jesus. 32He will be great and
will be called the Son of the Most High. The
Lord God will give him the throne of King
David, his ancestor. 33He will rule over the peo-
ple of Jacob for ever, and his kingdom will never
end."
34Mary said to the angel, "How will this hap-
pen since I am a virgin?"
35The angel said to Mary, "The Holy Spirit[d]
will come upon you, and the power of the Most
High will cover you. For this reason the baby will
be holy and will be called the Son of God. 36Now
Elizabeth, your relative, is also pregnant with a
son though she is very old. Everyone thought she
could not have a baby, but she has been pregnant
for six months. 37God can do anything!"
38Mary said, "I am the servant of the Lord. Let
this happen to me as you say!" Then the angel
went away.

Mary Visits Elizabeth

39Mary got up and went quickly to a town
in the hills of Judea. 40She came to Zechariah's
house and greeted Elizabeth. 41When Elizabeth
heard Mary's greeting, the unborn baby inside
her jumped, and Elizabeth was filled with the
Holy Spirit.[d] 42She cried out in a loud voice, "God
has blessed you more than any other woman, and
he has blessed the baby to whom you will give
birth. 43Why has this good thing happened to
me, that the mother of my Lord comes to me?
44When I heard your voice, the baby inside
me jumped with joy. 45You are blessed because

GOD'S POWER

Power in Letting Go

Joni Eareckson loved to swim when she was young. She was an excellent diver too, and had even thought about trying out for the Olympics.

When she was seventeen, Joni and her friends went swimming in Chesapeake Bay. Joni dived into the unfamiliar waters, expecting to experience that cool, free-floating feeling she had come to love. Instead, she felt nothing. As her head struck the bottom, her spinal cord snapped – leaving her paralysed from the neck down.

Joni felt depressed and angry at the prospect of spending the rest of her life in a wheelchair. Most of her anger was aimed at God. "Oh God, how can you do this to me?" she prayed. "What have you done to me?"

Though God has never healed her physically, over the years she has grown into a beautiful free spirit. She sums it up like this: "When I had no choice but acceptance, trust and surrender . . . it was as if I had finally gained emotional independence – through complete dependence on God."

Read **Luke 1:26–38** to see how God brought forth life in another teenage girl because she was ready to accept, trust and surrender.

- How was Mary's response to God's actions different from or similar to Joni's?
- In what specific ways would you like to see God's power change your life?

Consider . . .

- underlining the verses in this passage that speak most to you, and memorising them.
- asking God to help you to understand his unlimited power and the ways that he chooses to use (or not to use) it.

For more, see . . .

- Psalm 31:14–24 (p.518)
- James 1:1–5 (p.1348)
- 2 Corinthians 12:7–10 (p.1252)

you believed that what the Lord said to you would really happen."

Mary Praises God

46 Then Mary said,
"My soul praises the Lord;
47 my heart rejoices in God my Saviour,
48 because he has shown his concern for his
humble servant girl.
From now on, all people will say that I am
blessed,
49 because the Powerful One has done great
things for me.
His name is holy.
50 God will show his mercy for ever and ever
to those who worship and serve him.
51 He has done mighty deeds by his power.
He has scattered the people who are proud
and think great things about themselves.
52 He has brought down rulers from their
thrones
and raised up the humble.
53 He has filled the hungry with good things
and sent the rich away with nothing.
54 He has helped his servant, the people of
Israel,
remembering to show them mercy
55 as he promised to our ancestors,
to Abraham and to his children for ever."
56 Mary stayed with Elizabeth for about three
months and then returned home.

The Birth of John

57 When it was time for Elizabeth to give birth,
she had a boy. 58 Her neighbours and relatives
heard how good the Lord was to her, and they
rejoiced with her.
59 When the baby was eight days old, they
came to circumcise[d] him. They wanted to name
him Zechariah because this was his father's
name, 60 but his mother said, "No! He will be
named John."
61 The people said to Elizabeth, "But no one in
your family has this name." 62 Then they made

BOASTING

A Tale of Two Teenagers

Ted and Ed were in their final year at school. One was voted most popular; the other most respected. Both passed their exams with excellent grades.

Ed never talked about himself. He never seemed to mind not being in the spotlight.

But Ted had to be the centre of attention. If he thought that others had missed the significance of his accomplishments, he quickly filled them in.

They were two of the county's best cross-country runners. Ted almost always finished first, and Ed almost always came in just behind him. They were both comfortable with that, and always managed to congratulate and praise each other after a race. In their final race meeting, however, Ed finished first. Ted couldn't congratulate or praise him, or even accept congratulations for himself. He was only comfortable with being Number One.

Ted boasted a lot to get attention, but Ed didn't. Read **Luke 1:39–56** to see how God blessed a young girl, who didn't boast or take credit for herself.

- If Mary were around today, what do you think she would be like?
- Are you more like Ed or Ted? How does Mary's prayer apply to you?

Consider . . .

- drawing a line with two endpoints labelled ED and TED. Place a pencil point where you think you fit on the line, and another where you would like to be on the line. Ask God to help you to reach your goal.
- thinking of someone you know who is like Ed, and spending more time with that person.

For more, see . . .

- Jeremiah 9:23–24 (p.728)
- Philippians 2:5–11 (p.1282)
- Romans 12:3–5 (p.1204)

signs to his father to find out what he would like
to name him.
63Zechariah asked for a writing tablet and
wrote, "His name is John," and everyone was
surprised. 64Immediately Zechariah could talk
again, and he began praising God. 65All their
neighbours became alarmed, and in all the moun-
tains of Judea people continued talking about all
these things. 66The people who heard about them
wondered, saying, "What will this child be?" be-
cause the Lord was with him.

Zechariah Praises God

67Then Zechariah, John's father, was filled
with the Holy Spirit and prophesied:[d]
68"Let us praise the Lord, the God of Israel,
because he has come to help his people
and has given them freedom.
69He has given us a powerful Saviour
from the family of God's servant David.
70He said that he would do this
through his holy prophets[d] who lived
long ago:
71He promised he would save us from our
enemies
and from the power of all those who
hate us.
72He said he would give mercy to our fathers
and that he would remember his holy
promise.
73God promised Abraham, our father,
74 that he would save us from the power of
our enemies
so we could serve him without fear,
75being holy and good before God as long as
we live.

WORSHIP

Humble Beginnings

He was born in a simple 2-bedroom house in Tupelo, Mississippi on 8 January 1935. His twin brother, Jesse Garon, was stillborn, leaving him to grow up as an only child. His early years were spent in poverty, with his mum, Gladys, working as a cotton picker and his dad, Vernon, drifting from one job to another.

When he was eleven, his parents couldn't afford the bicycle he really wanted, so his mum persuaded him to have a guitar instead. After he left school, he did a variety of jobs. He also went to night school and studied to be an electrician.

Doesn't sound like a life that would make many people stop and take notice – just a normal, average guy – a nobody. Who would have thought that he would achieve anything special, that he would become so famous that people would recognise him from just his first name?

His name was Elvis Presley. Adored by millions, he went on to star in 33 successful films and sold over one billion records across the world – more than any other artist. He is regarded as one of the most important figures of twentieth-century popular culture. That's quite some nobody!

Luke 2:8–21 tells of Jesus' birth in a very humble setting – when he was born he was put in an animal's feeding trough. And yet, some shepherds were being told about the very special man Jesus was going to grow up to be.

- Imagine you were one of the shepherds. How amazing must the experience have been for them to believe that this boy, born in such poverty would become the man they had been told about?
- Why was the news of Jesus – the Saviour – something to get so excited by?

Consider . . .

- expressing your worship to God for who Jesus is in whatever way you want – singing, dancing, doing some art, etc.
- what God might do with your life! Pray about what you would like to do, write your thoughts down, keep them in a safe place and read them again in a few years' time. See what God has done during that time.

For more, see . . .

- Psalm 98 (p.557)
- Philippians 2:5–11 (p.1282)
- Isaiah 9:6–7 (p.649)

76 “Now you, child, will be called a prophet of
the Most High God.
You will go before the Lord to prepare his way.
77 You will make his people know that they will
be saved
by having their sins forgiven.
78 With the loving mercy of our God,
a new day from heaven will dawn upon us.
79 It will shine on those who live in darkness,
in the shadow of death.
It will guide us into the path of peace.”
80 And so the child grew up and became
strong in spirit. John lived in the desert until the
time when he came out to preach to Israel.

The Birth of Jesus

2 At that time, Augustus Caesar[d] sent an
order that all people in the countries under
Roman rule must list their names in a register.
2 This was the first registration;[n] it was taken
while Quirinius was governor of Syria. 3 And all
went to their own towns to be registered.
4 So Joseph left Nazareth, a town in Galilee,
and went to the town of Bethlehem in Judea,
known as the town of David. Joseph went there
because he was from the family of David.
5 Joseph registered with Mary, to whom he was
engaged[n] and who was now pregnant. 6 While
they were in Bethlehem, the time came for
Mary to have the baby, 7 and she gave birth
to her first son. Because there were no rooms
left in the inn, she wrapped the baby with
pieces of cloth and laid him in a box where
animals are fed.

Sidelight When Mary wrapped Jesus with cloths (Luke 2:7), he probably couldn't move his arms because he was wrapped so tightly. In biblical times, people believed a good six-month “wrapping” prevented arms and legs from becoming crooked.

Shepherds Hear About Jesus

8 That night, some shepherds were in the fields
nearby watching their sheep. 9 Then an angel of
the Lord stood before them. The glory of the Lord
was shining around them, and they became very
frightened. 10 The angel said to them, “Do not be
afraid. I am bringing you good news that will be
a great joy to all the people. 11 Today your Saviour
was born in the town of David. He is Christ,[d] the
Lord. 12 This is how you will know him: you will
find a baby wrapped in pieces of cloth and lying
in a feeding box.”
13 Then a very large group of angels from
heaven joined the first angel, praising God and
saying:
14 “Give glory to God in heaven,
and on earth let there be peace among the
people who please God.”
15 When the angels left them and went back to
heaven, the shepherds said to each other, “Let's
go to Bethlehem. Let's see this thing that has
happened which the Lord has told us about.”
16 So the shepherds went quickly and found
Mary and Joseph and the baby, who was lying in
a feeding box. 17 When they had seen him, they
told what the angels had said about this child.
18 Everyone was amazed at what the shepherds
said to them. 19 But Mary treasured these things
and continued to think about them. 20 Then the
shepherds went back to their sheep, praising God
and thanking him for everything they had seen
and heard. It had been just as the angel had told
them.
21 When the baby was eight days old, he was
circumcised[d] and was named Jesus, the name
given by the angel before the baby began to grow
in Mary's womb.

Jesus is Presented in the Temple

22 When the time came for Mary and Joseph to
do what the law of Moses taught about being
made pure,[n] they took Jesus to Jerusalem to
present him to the Lord. 23 (It is written in the law
of the Lord: “Every first-born[d] male shall be given
to the Lord.”)[n] 24 Mary and Joseph also went
to offer a sacrifice, as the law of the Lord says:
“You must sacrifice two doves or two young
pigeons.”[n]

Simeon Sees Jesus

25 In Jerusalem lived a man named Simeon who
was a good man and godly. He was waiting for
the time when God would take away Israel's sor-
row, and the Holy Spirit[d] was in him. 26 Simeon
had been told by the Holy Spirit that he would
not die before he saw the Christ[d] promised by the
Lord. 27 The Spirit led Simeon to the Temple.[d]

registration Census. A counting of all the people and the things they own.
engaged For the Jewish people an engagement was a lasting agreement, which could only be broken by a divorce. If a bride was unfaithful it was considered adultery and she could be put to death.
pure The law of Moses said that 40 days after a Jewish woman gave birth to a son, she must be cleansed by a ceremony at the Temple. Read Leviticus 12:2–8.
“Every . . . Lord.” Quotation from Exodus 13:2.
“You . . . pigeons.” Quotation from Leviticus 12:8.

When Mary and Joseph brought the baby Jesus to
the Temple to do what the law said they must
do, 28Simeon took the baby in his arms and
thanked God:
29"Now, Lord, you can let me, your servant,
die in peace as you said.
30With my own eyes I have seen your
salvation,
31 which you prepared before all people.
32It is a light for the non-Jewish people to see
and an honour for your people, the
Israelites."
33Jesus' father and mother were amazed at
what Simeon had said about him. 34Then Simeon
blessed them and said to Mary, "God has chosen
this child to cause the fall and rise of many in
Israel. He will be a sign from God that many
people will not accept 35so that the thoughts of
many will be made known. And the things that
will happen will make your heart sad, too."

Anna Sees Jesus

36There was a prophetess,[d] Anna, from the
family of Phanuel in the tribe[d] of Asher. Anna
was very old. She had once been married for
seven years. 37Then her husband died, and she
was a widow for 84 years. Anna never left the
Temple but worshipped God, going without food
and praying day and night. 38Standing there at
that time, she thanked God and spoke about
Jesus to all who were waiting for God to free
Jerusalem.

Joseph and Mary Return Home

39When Joseph and Mary had done everything
the law of the Lord commanded, they went home

FAMILY

Faith 'n' Family

It was the last evening at the Christian camp and Ross had loved every minute of it. He had been playing footie, watching DVDs, having water fights and hanging out with his mates. During the camp, there had also been talks about God.

Each day he was getting more interested in what was being said. The final evening's talk was on "Being a Christian at Home". Ross started to realise that the main reason why he didn't want to be a Christian wasn't that he didn't believe in God and want to follow him, it was that he was that scared about what his family would say. He loved his family, and he and his big brothers were always having a laugh and getting into trouble.

One of the youth leaders came up to Ross at the end of the talk and they got chatting. The youth leader listened and then told him that although it might be hard when he got home, God would be with him and would help him.

Ross made a commitment that night to follow God and hasn't looked back since. As he had feared, his brothers teased him, but with God's help it wasn't as difficult as Ross thought it might be. His brothers even began to ask questions, wanting to know more about what he believed in. Ross realised that God was actually helping him love and look out for his family in a way he'd not done before.

Read **Luke 2:22–40**.

- Why did Jesus need his family? Why do we need our families?
- Who are the "Simeons" and "Annas" in your life who help you to see God's work in your life and your family? Why are these people important to you?

Consider . . .

- encouraging a family member, or someone who helps you get closer to God, by telling them why you think they are great and how they've helped you.
- when things get hard at home, finding someone in your church who can pray for you and for your family.

For more, see . . .

- Exodus 20:12 (p.79)
- 1 Timothy 5:8 (p.1311)
- Mark 5:19 (p.1005)

to Nazareth, their own town in Galilee. 40The
little child grew and became strong. He was filled
with wisdom, and God's goodness was upon him.

Jesus as a Boy

41Every year Jesus' parents went to Jerusalem
for the Passover[d] Feast. 42When he was twelve
years old, they went to the feast as they always
did. 43After the feast days were over, they started
home. The boy Jesus stayed behind in Jerusalem,
but his parents did not know it. 44Thinking that
Jesus was with them in the group, they travelled
for a whole day. Then they began to look for him
among their family and friends. 45When they did
not find him, they went back to Jerusalem to look
for him there. 46After three days they found Jesus
sitting in the Temple[d] with the teachers, listening
to them and asking them questions. 47All who
heard him were amazed at his understanding and
answers. 48When Jesus' parents saw him, they
were astonished. His mother said to him, "Son,
why did you do this to us? Your father and I were
very worried about you and have been looking
for you."

49Jesus said to them, "Why were you looking
for me? Didn't you know that I must be in my
Father's house?" 50But they did not understand
the meaning of what he said.

51Jesus went with them to Nazareth and was
obedient to them. But his mother kept in her
mind all that had happened. 52Jesus became wiser
and grew physically. People liked him, and he
pleased God.

The Preaching of John

3 It was the fifteenth year of the rule of Tiberius
Caesar.[d] These men were under Caesar:
Pontius Pilate, the ruler of Judea; Herod, the ruler

SPIRITUAL GROWTH

Who Am I?

When Brian was a boy, he used to love to make mud pies by the outdoor tap at the back of his house. His mum would give him old pie dishes, and he'd fill them with just the right mix of earth and water.

"You had to be careful to mix it properly," Brian recalls. "Too much earth, and your pie would crumble. Too much water, and it would ooze."

As Brian got older, he didn't make mud pies as often. But he still enjoyed working with his hands to create. In art class, Brian learned the basics of sculpture.

"I was hooked from then on," Brian says with a smile. "I loved the idea of taking an image in my head and making it a reality in the clay. It's been fun ever since!"

Brian now works as a sculptor part-time after school. He has already won several awards for his work and plans to attend an art school in London when he leaves school.

"I want to design the sort of sculptures that you see around the big office buildings," says Brian, "and have my own business."

Brian grins. "I never realised you could turn making mud pies into a career."

Brian's interest and skill in sculpting grew as he got older. In the same way, our ability to understand and appreciate God grows as we get older and expose ourselves to more of God's ways. Jesus also experienced this spiritual growth process. Read about it in **Luke 2:41–52**, especially verse 52.

- What do Jesus and Brian have in common based on the passage?
- Have you continued to learn more and more in the past year?

Consider . . .

- thinking about all the ways in which you have changed in the past year, and thanking God for helping you to grow spiritually.
- keeping a prayer journal to help you to log spiritual growth in your life.

For more, see . . .

- 1 Samuel 2:26 (p.257)
- Ephesians 4:4–16 (p.1272)
- 1 Corinthians 13:11–13 (p.1232)

of Galilee; Philip, Herod's brother, the ruler of
Iturea and Trachonitis; and Lysanias, the ruler
of Abilene. 2Annas and Caiaphas were the high
priests. At this time, the word of God came to
John son of Zechariah in the desert. 3He went all
over the area around the Jordan River preaching
a baptism of changed hearts and lives for the for-
giveness of sins. 4As it is written in the book of
Isaiah the prophet: [d]

This is the voice of one who calls out:
"Prepare in the desert
the way for the LORD.
Make a straight road in the dry lands
for our God.
5Every valley should be raised up,
and every mountain and hill should be
made flat.
The rough ground should be made level,
and the rugged ground should be made
smooth.
6Then the glory of the LORD will be shown,
and all people together will see it.
The LORD himself said these things."

Isaiah 40:3–5

7To the crowds of people who came to be bap-
tised by John, he said, "You are all snakes! Who
warned you to run away from God's coming
punishment? 8Do the things that show you really
have changed your hearts and lives. Don't begin
to say to yourselves, 'Abraham is our father.'
I tell you that God could make children for
Abraham from these rocks. 9The axe is now ready
to cut down the trees, and every tree that does
not produce good fruit will be cut down and
thrown into the fire." [n]

10The people asked John, "Then what should
we do?"

11John answered, "If you have two shirts,
share with the person who does not have one. If
you have food, share that also."

12Even tax collectors came to John to be bap-
tised. They said to him, "Teacher, what should
we do?"

13John said to them, "Don't take more taxes
from people than you have been ordered to take."

14The soldiers asked John, "What about us?
What should we do?"

John said to them, "Don't force people to give
you money, and don't lie about them. Be satisfied
with the pay you get."

15Since the people were hoping for the Christ [d]
to come, they wondered if John might be the one.

The axe . . . fire. This means that God is ready to punish his people who do not obey him.

JUSTICE

Your Fair Share

The saddest thing about poverty is that it can be stopped; there is enough money and enough resources in the world that everyone could afford to live and no one should have to die of starvation.

The great human rights campaigner, Nelson Mandela, once said, "Overcoming poverty is not a gesture of charity, it is an act of justice. It is the protection of a human right, the right to dignity and a decent life . . . Sometimes it falls on a generation to be great. You can be that great generation. Let your greatness blossom."

In **Luke 3:1–18** John urges the people to be satisfied with what they've got and give to the needy. He warns them that they shouldn't just be concerned with religion but with justice as well.

- What practical things does John suggest that the people do?
- If John were alive today, what do you think he'd say about the injustice in the world? What advice would he give us?

Consider . . .

- simple ways in which you can "let your greatness blossom". How could you help people that suffer from poverty?
- trying to remember the good things that God has given you and being quick to thank him for them.

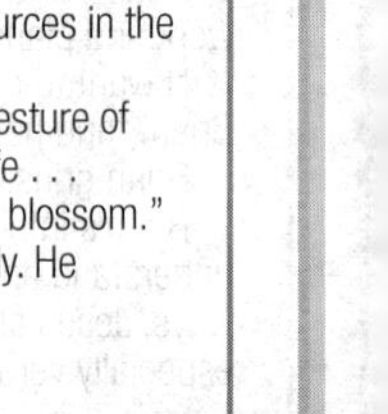

For more, see . . .

- Amos 5:24 (p.874)
- Matthew 6:1–4 (p.947)
- Micah 6:6–8 (p.896)

16 John answered everyone, "I baptise you with
water, but there is one coming who is greater than
I am. I am not good enough to untie his sandals.
He will baptise you with the Holy Spirit[d] and fire.
17 He will come ready to clean the grain, separating
the good grain from the chaff.[d] He will put the
good part of the grain into his barn, but he will
burn the chaff with a fire that cannot be put out."[n]
18 And John continued to preach the Good News,[d]
saying many other things to encourage the people.
19 But John spoke against Herod, the governor,
because of his sin with Herodias, the wife of
Herod's brother, and because of the many other
evil things Herod did. 20 So Herod did something
even worse: he put John in prison.

Jesus is Baptised by John

21 When all the people were being baptised by
John, Jesus also was baptised. While Jesus was
praying, heaven opened 22 and the Holy Spirit[d]
came down on him in the form of a dove. Then a
voice came from heaven, saying, "You are my Son,
whom I love, and I am very pleased with you."

The Family History of Jesus

23 When Jesus began his ministry, he was
about 30 years old. People thought that Jesus
was Joseph's son.

Joseph was the son[n] of Heli.
24 Heli was the son of Matthat.
Matthat was the son of Levi.
Levi was the son of Melki.[n]
Melki was the son of Jannai.
Jannai was the son of Joseph.
25 Joseph was the son of Mattathias.
Mattathias was the son of Amos.
Amos was the son of Nahum.
Nahum was the son of Esli.
Esli was the son of Naggai.
26 Naggai was the son of Maath.
Maath was the son of Mattathias.
Mattathias was the son of Semein.
Semein was the son of Josech.
Josech was the son of Joda.
27 Joda was the son of Joanan.
Joanan was the son of Rhesa.
Rhesa was the son of Zerubbabel.
Zerubbabel was the grandson of Shealtiel.
Shealtiel was the son of Neri.
28 Neri was the son of Melki.[n]
Melki was the son of Addi.
Addi was the son of Cosam.
Cosam was the son of Elmadam.
Elmadam was the son of Er.
29 Er was the son of Joshua.
Joshua was the son of Eliezer.
Eliezer was the son of Jorim.
Jorim was the son of Matthat.
Matthat was the son of Levi.
30 Levi was the son of Simeon.
Simeon was the son of Judah.
Judah was the son of Joseph.
Joseph was the son of Jonam.
Jonam was the son of Eliakim.
31 Eliakim was the son of Melea.
Melea was the son of Menna.
Menna was the son of Mattatha.
Mattatha was the son of Nathan.
Nathan was the son of David.
32 David was the son of Jesse.
Jesse was the son of Obed.
Obed was the son of Boaz.
Boaz was the son of Salmon.
Salmon was the son of Nahshon.
33 Nahshon was the son of Amminadab.
Amminadab was the son of Admin.[n]
Admin was the son of Arni.
Arni was the son of Hezron.
Hezron was the son of Perez.
Perez was the son of Judah.
34 Judah was the son of Jacob.
Jacob was the son of Isaac.
Isaac was the son of Abraham.
Abraham was the son of Terah.
Terah was the son of Nahor.
35 Nahor was the son of Serug.
Serug was the son of Reu.
Reu was the son of Peleg.
Peleg was the son of Eber.
Eber was the son of Shelah.
36 Shelah was the son of Cainan.
Cainan was the son of Arphaxad.
Arphaxad was the son of Shem.
Shem was the son of Noah.
Noah was the son of Lamech.
37 Lamech was the son of Methuselah.
Methuselah was the son of Enoch.
Enoch was the son of Jared.
Jared was the son of Mahalalel.
Mahalalel was the son of Kenan.
38 Kenan was the son of Enosh.
Enosh was the son of Seth.
Seth was the son of Adam.
Adam was the son of God.

He will . . . out. This means that Jesus will come to separate good people from bad people, saving the good and punishing the bad.
son "Son" in Jewish lists of ancestors can sometimes mean grandson or more distant relative.
Melki Some manuscripts spell Melki as Melchi.
Admin Some manuscripts say, "Amminadab, the son of Ram, the son of Hezron", other manuscripts vary widely.

Jesus is Tempted by the Devil

4 Jesus, filled with the Holy Spirit,[d] returned
from the Jordan River. The Spirit led Jesus
into the desert 2 where the devil tempted Jesus for
40 days. Jesus ate nothing during that time, and
when those days were ended, he was very hungry.
3 The devil said to Jesus, "If you are the Son of
God, tell this rock to become bread."
4 Jesus answered, "It is written in the Scrip-
tures:[d] 'A person does not live by eating only
bread.' "[n]
5 Then the devil took Jesus and showed him all
the kingdoms of the world in an instant. 6 The
devil said to Jesus, "I will give you all these king-
doms and all their power and glory. It has all been
given to me, and I can give it to anyone I wish.
7 If you worship me, then it will all be yours."
8 Jesus answered, "It is written in the Scrip-
tures: 'You must worship the Lord your God and
serve only him.' "[n]
9 Then the devil led Jesus to Jerusalem and put
him on a high place of the Temple.[d] He said to
Jesus, "If you are the Son of God, jump down. 10 It
is written in the Scriptures:

'He has put his angels in charge of you
to watch over you.' *Psalm 91:11*

11 It is also written:

'They will catch you in their hands
so that you will not hit your foot on a
rock.' " *Psalm 91:12*

12 Jesus answered, "But it also says in the Scrip-
tures: 'Do not test the Lord your God.' "[n]
13 After the devil had tempted Jesus in every
way, he left him to wait until a better time.

'A person . . . bread.' Quotation from Deuteronomy 8:3.
'You . . . him.' Quotation from Deuteronomy 6:13.
'Do . . . God.' Quotation from Deuteronomy 6:16.

SIN

Tempted?

Andrew and Sean were good friends. They went to the same church where they'd both been baptised. When they were a bit older, they started to help lead the youth club on a Friday night.

It was coming up to their eighteenth birthdays and the leaders invited them to go to Africa on a mission for three weeks. They jumped at the chance, and soon they were in Africa serving God. They saw hundreds become Christians and join the church. It was Christmas. Could life get any better?

When they came back from Africa, they started to celebrate their birthdays. Andrew went out for a posh meal with his family and planned to sample the nightlife of Manchester. Sean went to the pub with his mates and got drunk. Then he got a new job and started going out with a girl from work. Two weeks later, he moved in with her. He stopped going to church and seeing his Christian friends. He completely turned his back on God.

Andrew decided to make God the centre of his life. He goes to church and small group, and has nearly finished his college course. He hopes to go back to Africa again one day.

We've always got choices about how to live our lives. We're faced with temptation all the time. The question is, will we give in and be like Sean or resist it and be like Andrew? It is a hard thing to do, and in **Luke 4:1–13** Jesus is tempted by the devil but he doesn't give in for a second. Read it to see what happened.

- How did Jesus and Andrew have the strength to resist the devil and the temptation of sin?
- Do you think that God says it's OK to give in to temptation and sin? Why?

Consider . . .

- next time you're about to give in to sin, trying to stop and asking God to help you not to do it.
- praying for your friends who, like Sean, have given in to sin.

For more, see . . .

- Colossians 3:5–10 (p.1292)
- James 5:19–20 (p.1354)
- James 4:7–8 (p.1351)

Jesus Teaches the People

[14]Jesus returned to Galilee in the power of
the Holy Spirit, *d* and stories about him spread
throughout all the area. [15]He began to teach
in their synagogues, *d* and everyone praised
him.
[16]Jesus travelled to Nazareth, where he had
grown up. On the Sabbath *d* day he went to the
synagogue, as he always did, and stood up to
read. [17]The book of Isaiah the prophet *d* was given
to him. He opened the book and found the place
where this is written:
[18]"The Lord has put his Spirit in me,
because he appointed me to tell the Good
News *d* to the poor.
He has sent me to tell the captives they are free
and to tell the blind that they can see
again. *Isaiah 61:1*
God sent me to free those who have been
treated unfairly *Isaiah 58:6*
[19] and to announce the time when the Lord
will show his kindness." *Isaiah 61:2*
[20]Jesus closed the book, gave it back to the
assistant and sat down. Everyone in the syn-
agogue was watching Jesus closely. [21]He began
to say to them, "While you heard these words just
now, they were coming true!"
[22]All the people spoke well of Jesus and were
amazed at the words of grace he spoke. They
asked, "Isn't this Joseph's son?"

Sidelight If you don't like being noticed when you visit different churches, you wouldn't have visited many synagogues in Jesus' day. It was customary for the synagogue leader to invite visitors to address the congregation. Jesus took advantage of the opportunity to preach in Luke 4:14–19.

JUSTICE

I'm Not Part of the Problem!

When you look around the world today, it is pretty easy to see injustice. Millions of people die every year simply because they were born into poverty and don't have the same choices as people that live in richer countries. Millions of people are sold as slaves, to be exploited and worked until they are no longer physically able to endure the hardship. Rich countries force poor countries to open up their economies and spend their money paying back debts which drain their budgets dry so they can't spend money on things like health care and education. Where's the justice?

It's very easy to think that we aren't part of the problem. It's easy to blame injustice on people in power, like governments and the really, really rich. But realising justice requires all of us to understand that we all have a part to play. The reality is that every decision we make has an impact on other people. If we choose to buy clothes at the cheapest prices, then someone else will be forced to make those clothes for us and be paid very little for it. Is that fair? Is that justice? If we just sit silent and don't speak out on behalf of the billions of people in our world who are oppressed, can we really say we aren't part of the problem?

The world God created and intended us to live in was one of complete and perfect justice. Every time we make a decision, act or speak out in favour of people whose lives are destroyed by injustice, we bring our world back one step closer to the justice God wants for each and every person he created. Read **Luke 4:16–30**.

- What are some of the choices you make every day that affect the lives of other people?
- Do you react to injustice in the same way that the people Jesus was teaching did?

Consider . . .

- what changes you could make to your choices to ensure that you are not part of "the problem".
- making a commitment to choose to buy ethical and fair-trade products wherever possible.

For more, see . . .

- Exodus 23:1–9 (p.82)
- Amos 5 (p.873)
- Psalm 140:11–13 (p.582)

23Jesus said to them, "I know that you will tell
me the old saying: 'Doctor, heal yourself.' You
want to say, 'We heard about the things you did
in Capernaum. Do those things here in your own
town!' " 24Then Jesus said, "I tell you the truth,
a prophet is not accepted in his home town. 25But
I tell you the truth, there were many widows in
Israel during the time of Elijah. It did not rain in
Israel for three and a half years, and there was no
food anywhere in the whole country. 26But Elijah
was sent to none of those widows, only to a
widow in Zarephath, a town in Sidon. 27And
there were many with skin diseases living in
Israel during the time of the prophet Elisha. But
none of them were healed, only Naaman, who
was from the country of Syria."

28When all the people in the synagogue heard
these things, they became very angry. 29They got
up, forced Jesus out of town, and took him to the
edge of the cliff on which the town was built. They
planned to throw him off the edge, 30but Jesus
walked through the crowd and went on his way.

Jesus Forces Out an Evil Spirit

31Jesus went to Capernaum, a city in Galilee,
and on the Sabbath[d] day, he taught the people.
32They were amazed at his teaching, because he
spoke with authority. 33In the synagogue[d] a man
who had within him an evil spirit shouted in a
loud voice, 34"Jesus of Nazareth! What do you
want with us? Did you come to destroy us? I
know who you are—God's Holy One!"

35Jesus commanded the evil spirit, "Be quiet!
Come out of the man!" The evil spirit threw the
man down to the ground before all the people
and then left the man without hurting him.

36The people were amazed and said to each
other, "What does this mean? With authority and
power he commands evil spirits, and they come
out." 37And so the news about Jesus spread to
every place in the whole area.

Jesus Heals Many People

38Jesus left the synagogue[d] and went to the
home of Simon.[n] Simon's mother-in-law was
sick with a high fever, and they asked Jesus to
help her. 39He came to her side and commanded
the fever to leave. It left her, and immediately she
got up and began serving them.

40When the sun went down, the people brought
those who were sick to Jesus. Putting his hands on
each sick person, he healed every one of them.
41Demons[d] came out of many people, shouting,
"You are the Son of God." But Jesus commanded
the demons and would not allow them to speak,
because they knew Jesus was the Christ.[d]

42At daybreak, Jesus went to a lonely place, but
the people looked for him. When they found him,
they tried to keep him from leaving. 43But Jesus
said to them, "I must preach about God's king-
dom to other towns, too. This is why I was sent."

44Then he kept on preaching in the syna-
gogues[d] of Judea.

Jesus' First Followers

5 One day while Jesus was standing beside
Lake Galilee, many people were pressing all
around him to hear the word of God. 2Jesus saw
two boats at the shore of the lake. The fishermen
had left them and were washing their nets. 3Jesus
got into one of the boats, the one that belonged
to Simon,[n] and asked him to push off a little
from the land. Then Jesus sat down and contin-
ued to teach the people from the boat.

4When Jesus had finished speaking, he said to
Simon, "Take the boat into deep water, and put
your nets in the water to catch some fish."

5Simon answered, "Master, we worked hard all
night trying to catch fish, and we caught nothing.
But you say to put the nets in the water, so
I will." 6When the fishermen did as Jesus told
them, they caught so many fish that the nets began
to break. 7They called to their partners in the other
boat to come and help them. They came and filled
both boats so full that they were almost sinking.

8When Simon Peter saw what had happened,
he bowed down before Jesus and said, "Go away
from me, Lord. I am a sinful man!" 9He and the
other fishermen were amazed at the many fish
they caught, as were 10James and John, the sons
of Zebedee, Simon's partners.

Jesus said to Simon, "Don't be afraid. From
now on you will fish for people." 11When the
men brought their boats to the shore, they left
everything and followed Jesus.

Jesus Heals a Sick Man

12When Jesus was in one of the towns, there
was a man covered with a skin disease. When he
saw Jesus, he bowed before him and begged him,
"Lord, you can heal me if you will."

13Jesus reached out his hand and touched the
man and said, "I will. Be healed!" Immediately
the disease disappeared. 14Then Jesus said,
"Don't tell anyone about this, but go and show
yourself to the priest[n] and offer a gift for your
healing, as Moses commanded.[n] This will show
the people what I have done."

Simon Simon's other name was Peter.
show . . . priest The law of Moses said a priest must say when a Jewish person with a skin disease was well.
Moses commanded Read about this in Leviticus 14:1–32.

15But the news about Jesus spread even more.
Many people came to hear Jesus and to be healed
of their sicknesses, 16but Jesus often slipped away
to be alone so he could pray.

Jesus Heals a Paralysed Man

17One day as Jesus was teaching the people,
the Pharisees[d] and teachers of the law from
every town in Galilee and Judea and from
Jerusalem were there. The power of the Lord
was present for him to heal the sick. 18Just then,
some men were carrying on a mat a man who
was paralysed. They tried to bring him in and
put him down before Jesus. 19But because there
were so many people there, they could not find
a way in. So they went up on the roof and low-
ered the man on his mat through the ceiling into
the middle of the crowd right before Jesus. 20See-
ing their faith, Jesus said, "Friend, your sins are
forgiven."

Sidelight If you think access to buildings is a new problem for disabled people, read Luke 5:18–20. The friends probably had to dig through layers of clay, grass and branches to make a hole in the roof, since that's how most roofs were made in Jesus' time. The roofs were supported by wooden beams, which stretched from wall to wall.

21The Jewish teachers of the law and the
Pharisees thought to themselves, "Who is this
man who is speaking as if he were God? Only
God can forgive sins."
22But Jesus knew what they were thinking
and said, "Why are you thinking these things?
23Which is easier: to say, 'Your sins are forgiven,'
or to say, 'Stand up and walk'? 24But I will prove
to you that the Son of Man[d] has authority on
earth to forgive sins." So Jesus said to the paral-
ysed man, "I tell you, stand up, take your mat,
and go home."
25At once the man stood up before them,
picked up his mat and went home, praising God.
26All the people were completely amazed and
began to praise God. They were filled with much
respect and said, "Today we have seen amazing
things!"

Levi Follows Jesus

27After this, Jesus went out and saw a tax
collector named Levi[n] sitting in the tax collec-
tor's booth. Jesus said to him, "Follow me!" 28So
Levi got up, left everything and followed him.
29Then Levi gave a big dinner for Jesus at his
house. Many tax collectors and other people
were eating there, too. 30But the Pharisees[d] and
the men who taught the law for the Pharisees
began to complain to Jesus' followers, "Why do
you eat and drink with tax collectors and sin-
ners?"
31Jesus answered them, "It is not the healthy
people who need a doctor, but the sick. 32I have
not come to invite good people but sinners to
change their hearts and lives."

Jesus Answers a Question

33They said to Jesus, "John's followers often
give up eating[n] for a certain time and pray, just
as the Pharisees[d] do. But your followers eat and
drink all the time."
34Jesus said to them, "You cannot make the
friends of the bridegroom give up eating while
he is still with them. 35But the time will come
when the bridegroom will be taken away from
them, and then they will give up eating."
36Jesus told them this story: "No one takes
cloth off a new coat to cover a hole in an old
coat. Otherwise, he ruins the new coat, and the
cloth from the new coat will not be the same as
the old cloth. 37Also, no one ever pours new
wine into old leather bags. Otherwise, the new
wine will break the bags, the wine will spill out
and the leather bags will be ruined. 38New wine
must be put into new leather bags. 39No one
after drinking old wine wants new wine, be-
cause he says, 'The old wine is better.' "

Jesus is Lord over the Sabbath

6 One Sabbath[d] day Jesus was walking
through some fields of grain. His followers
picked the heads of grain, rubbed them in their
hands and ate them. 2Some Pharisees[d] said,
"Why do you do what is not lawful on the
Sabbath day?"
3Jesus answered, "Have you not read what
David did when he and those with him were
hungry? 4He went into God's house and took
and ate the holy bread, which is lawful only for
priests to eat. And he gave some to the people
who were with him." 5Then Jesus said to the
Pharisees, "The Son of Man[d] is Lord of the Sab-
bath day."

Jesus Heals a Man's Hand

6On another Sabbath[d] day Jesus went into the
synagogue[d] and was teaching, and a man with a
crippled right hand was there. 7The teachers of
the law and the Pharisees[d] were watching closely

Levi Also known as Matthew.
give up eating This is called "fasting". The people would give up eating for a special time of prayer and worship to God. It was also done to show sadness and disappointment.

to see if Jesus would heal on the Sabbath day so
they could accuse him. 8But he knew what they
were thinking, and he said to the man with the
crippled hand, "Stand up here in the middle of
everyone." The man got up and stood there.
9Then Jesus said to them, "I ask you, which is
lawful on the Sabbath day: to do good or to do
evil, to save a life or to destroy it?" 10Jesus looked
around at all of them and said to the man, "Hold
out your hand." The man held out his hand, and
it was healed.
11But the Pharisees and the teachers of the law
were very angry and discussed with each other
what they could do to Jesus.

Jesus Chooses His Apostles

12At that time Jesus went off to a mountain to
pray, and he spent the night praying to God.
13The next morning, Jesus called his followers to
him and chose twelve of them, whom he named
apostles:[d] 14Simon (Jesus named him Peter), his
brother Andrew, James, John, Philip, Bartholomew,
15Matthew, Thomas, James son of Alphaeus,
Simon (called the Zealot[d]), 16Judas son of James
and Judas Iscariot, who later turned Jesus over to
his enemies.

Jesus Teaches and Heals

17Jesus and the apostles[d] came down from the
mountain, and he stood on level ground. A large
group of his followers were there, as well as many
people from all around Judea, Jerusalem, and the
sea coast cities of Tyre and Sidon. 18They all came
to hear Jesus teach and to be healed of their sick-
nesses, and he healed those who were troubled
by evil spirits. 19All the people were trying to
touch Jesus, because power was coming from
him and healing them all.
20Jesus looked at his followers and said,
"Happy you people who are poor,
because the kingdom of God belongs to
you.
21Happy you people who are now hungry,
because you will be satisfied.
Happy you people who are now crying,
because you will laugh with joy.
22"People will hate you, shut you out, insult
you and say you are evil, because you follow the
Son of Man.[d] But when they do, you will be
happy. 23Be full of joy at that time, because you
have a great reward waiting for you in heaven.
Their ancestors did the same things to the
prophets.[d]
24"But how terrible it will be for you who are rich,
because you have had your easy life.
25How terrible it will be for you who are
full now,
because you will be hungry.
How terrible it will be for you who are
laughing now,
because you will be sad and cry.
26"How terrible when everyone says only good
things about you, because their ancestors said the
same things about the false prophets.

Love Your Enemies

27"But I say to you who are listening, love your
enemies. Do good to those who hate you, 28bless
those who curse you, pray for those who are
cruel to you. 29If anyone slaps you on one cheek,
offer him the other cheek, too. If someone takes
your coat, do not stop him from taking your shirt.
30Give to everyone who asks you, and when
someone takes something that is yours, don't ask
for it back. 31Do to others what you would want
them to do to you. 32If you love only the people
who love you, what praise should you get? Even
sinners love the people who love them. 33If you
do good only to those who do good to you, what
praise should you get? Even sinners do that! 34If
you lend things to people, always hoping to get
something back, what praise should you get?
Even sinners lend to other sinners so that they
can get back the same amount! 35But love your
enemies, do good to them, and lend to them
without hoping to get anything back. Then
you will have a great reward and you will be
children of the Most High God, because he is
kind even to people who are ungrateful and full
of sin. 36Show mercy, just as your Father shows
mercy.

Look at Yourselves

37"Don't judge other people, and you will not
be judged. Don't accuse others of being guilty,
and you will not be accused of being guilty. For-
give, and you will be forgiven. 38Give, and you
will receive. You will be given much. Pressed
down, shaken together and running over, it will
spill into your lap. The way you give to others is
the way God will give to you."
39Jesus told them this story: "Can a blind per-
son lead another blind person? No! Both of them
will fall into a ditch. 40A student is not better than
the teacher, but the student who has been fully
trained will be like the teacher.
41"Why do you notice the little piece of dust in
your friend's eye, but you don't notice the big
piece of wood in your own eye? 42How can you
say to your friend, 'Friend, let me take that little
piece of dust out of your eye' when you cannot
see that big piece of wood in your own eye! You
hypocrite![d] First, take the wood out of your own
eye. Then you will see clearly to take the dust out
of your friend's eye.

Two Kinds of Fruit

43"A good tree does not produce bad fruit, nor
does a bad tree produce good fruit. 44Each tree is
known by its own fruit. People don't gather figs
from thorn-bushes, and they don't get grapes
from bushes. 45Good people bring good things
out of the good stored in their hearts. But evil
people bring evil things out of the evil stored in
their hearts. People speak the things that are in
their hearts.

Two Kinds of People

46"Why do you call me, 'Lord, Lord,' but do
not do what I say? 47I will show you what every-
one is like who comes to me and hears my words
and obeys. 48That person is like a man building a
house who dug deep and laid the foundation on
rock. When the floods came, the water tried to
wash the house away, but it could not shake it,
because the house was built well. 49But the one
who hears my words and does not obey is like a
man who built his house on the ground without
a foundation. When the floods came, the house
quickly fell and was completely destroyed."

Jesus Heals a Soldier's Servant

7 When Jesus finished saying all these things
to the people, he went to Capernaum.
2There was an army officer who had a servant
who was very important to him. The servant
was so sick he was nearly dead. 3When the
officer heard about Jesus, he sent some Jewish
elders to him to ask Jesus to come and heal his
servant. 4The men went to Jesus and begged
him, saying, "This officer is worthy of your help.
5He loves our people, and he built us a syna-
gogue." [d]
6So Jesus went with the men. He was getting
near the officer's house when the officer sent
friends to say, "Lord, don't trouble yourself,
because I am not worthy to have you come into
my house. 7That is why I did not come to you
myself. But you only need to command it, and
my servant will be healed. 8I, too, am a man
under the authority of others, and I have soldiers
under my command. I tell one soldier, 'Go,' and
he goes. I tell another soldier, 'Come,' and he
comes. I say to my servant, 'Do this,' and my
servant does it."

LEADERSHIP

Fish Out of Water

Whales Commit Mass Suicide.

The 1986 newspaper headline alerted the community in Cape Cod to the baffling incident that had happened the night before. A herd, or "pod", of 94 whales had beached themselves on the shores of Cape Cod. They just swam up on to the sand . . . and died.

This wasn't the first or the last time that whales have committed this strange act around the world. Newspapers periodically report stories of whales beaching themselves.

Several theories try to explain why whales do this. One of them is that the whales are following a basic herd instinct. Every pod has a leader. If the leader becomes ill or disoriented, it might react by beaching itself. But since it's the leader, the other whales simply follow, even though it means death.

Sound ridiculous? Perhaps, but it's not so unlike the way that many people act. It's easy to follow leaders who say they have the right answers.

People who pretend to have life's answers but live destructively are called hypocrites. In **Luke 6:39–49**, Jesus was saddened and angered to find hypocrisy in the religious leaders around him.

- How is the lead whale like the blind leaders Jesus talks about in this passage?
- What leaders do young people follow, even though the leaders' lifestyles seem destructive?

Consider . . .

- listing the "good fruits" and "bad fruits" that you see in your own life, then asking God to take away the bad fruit.
- telling people you look to as leaders about the "good fruits" you see in their lives.

For more, see . . .

- Isaiah 29:13 (p.668)
- James 1:19–27 (p.1348)
- Amos 8:4–8 (p.877)

[9]When Jesus heard this, he was amazed. Turn-
ing to the crowd that was following him, he said,
"I tell you, this is the greatest faith I have found
anywhere, even in Israel."
[10]Those who had been sent to Jesus went back
to the house where they found the servant in
good health.

Jesus Brings a Man Back to Life

[11]Soon afterwards Jesus went to a town called
Nain, and his followers and a large crowd trav-
elled with him. [12]When he came near the town
gate, he saw a funeral. A mother, who was a
widow, had lost her only son. A large crowd
from the town was with the mother while her
son was being carried out. [13]When the Lord saw
her, he felt very sorry for her and said, "Don't
cry." [14]He went up and touched the coffin, and
the people who were carrying it stopped. Jesus
said, "Young man, I tell you, get up!" [15]And the
son sat up and began to talk. Then Jesus gave
him back to his mother.
[16]All the people were amazed and began prais-
ing God, saying, "A great prophet[d] has come to
us! God has come to help his people."

Sidelight The coffin where the boy lay when Jesus brought him back to life (Luke 7:11–15) wasn't like coffins today. In fact, it was probably just a board on which they laid the body. Just like today, wealthier people sometimes had more elaborate "funeral biers", as they were called.

[17]This news about Jesus spread through all
Judea and into all the places around there.

FAITH

To the Letter

"Do as I say to the letter and you'll be fine. Disobey and it could cost you your life!"

Those were the words which Ruth's parachute instructor had spoken to her at the beginning of her first lesson three weeks ago. Now, her training was almost complete. In minutes she would be leaping out of a plane thousands of feet in the air.

"Obedience," the instructor had continued, "is the essence of success in parachute jumping. Some people, eager to jump, ignore what they consider to be 'boring rules and regulations'. Sadly, a few of those folk have died."

As the plane settled into a steady path and her instructor motioned for her to go with him to the door, Ruth suddenly realised that talking about jumping from a plane and actually doing it were two very different things. But it was too late to go back now. She just had to step out in faith.

Ruth thought the fall was amazing – she couldn't put her excitement into words. The important thing was that she landed safely, just as her instructor had promised she would, and that she had raised over £500 for charity.

Ruth's instructor was teaching her to have faith in him and to obey his words if she wanted to succeed. In **Luke 7:1–10**, a soldier also understood this type of faith and became a success because of it.

- How is the soldier in this passage similar to Ruth? How is he different?
- Is your faith as strong as the officer's in this passage? Why or why not?

Consider . . .

- how your life would be different if you followed God's instructions to the letter. Why not choose to put your faith in him for every area of your life?
- memorising Hebrews 11:1 (p.1341) to learn God's definition of faith.

For more, see . . .

- Genesis 22:1–18 (p.25)
- Hebrews 11 (p.1341)
- Matthew 13:22–35 (p.963)

John Asks a Question

18John's followers told him about all these
things. He called for two of his followers 19and
sent them to the Lord to ask, "Are you the One
who is to come, or should we wait for someone
else?"
20When the men came to Jesus, they said,
"John the Baptist[d] sent us to you with this ques-
tion: 'Are you the One who is to come, or should
we wait for someone else?' "
21At that time, Jesus healed many people of
their sicknesses, diseases and evil spirits, and he
gave sight to many blind people. 22Then Jesus
answered John's followers, "Go and tell John
what you saw and heard here. The blind can see,
the crippled can walk and people with skin dis-
eases are healed. The deaf can hear, the dead are
raised to life and the Good News[d] is preached to
the poor. 23Those who do not stumble in their
faith because of me are blessed!"
24When John's followers left, Jesus began talk-
ing to the people about John: "What did you go
out into the desert to see? A reed[n] blown by the
wind? 25What did you go out to see? A man
dressed in fine clothes? No, people who have fine
clothes and much wealth live in kings' palaces.
26But what did you go out to see? A prophet?[d]
Yes, and I tell you, John is more than a prophet.
27This was written about him:

'I will send my messenger ahead of you,
who will prepare the way for you.' *Malachi 3:1*

28I tell you, John is greater than any other person
ever born, but even the least important person in
the kingdom of God is greater than John."
29(When the people, including the tax collec-
tors, heard this, they all agreed that God's teach-
ing was good, having been baptised by John.
30But the Pharisees[d] and experts on the law re-
fused to accept God's plan for themselves; they
did not let John baptise them.)
31Then Jesus said, "What shall I say about the
people of this time? What are they like? 32They
are like children sitting in the market-place, call-
ing to one another and saying,

'We played music for you, but you did not
dance;
we sang a sad song, but you did not cry.'

33John the Baptist came and did not eat bread or
drink wine, and you say, 'He has a demon[d] in
him.' 34The Son of Man[d] came eating and drink-
ing, and you say, 'Look at him! He eats too much
and drinks too much wine, and he is a friend of
tax collectors and sinners!' 35But wisdom is
proved to be right by what it does."

A Woman Washes Jesus' Feet

36One of the Pharisees[d] asked Jesus to eat with
him, so Jesus went into the Pharisee's house and
sat at the table. 37A sinful woman in the town
learnt that Jesus was eating at the Pharisee's
house. So she brought an alabaster[d] jar of per-
fume 38and stood behind Jesus at his feet, crying.
She began to wash his feet with her tears, and she
dried them with her hair, kissing them many
times and rubbing them with the perfume.
39When the Pharisee who asked Jesus to come to
his house saw this, he thought to himself, "If
Jesus were a prophet,[d] he would know that the
woman touching him is a sinner!"
40Jesus said to the Pharisee, "Simon, I have
something to say to you."
Simon said, "Teacher, tell me."
41Jesus said, "Two people owed money to the
same banker. One owed 500 silver coins[n] and
the other owed 50 silver coins. 42They had no
money to pay what they owed, but the banker
told both of them they did not have to pay him.
Which person will love the banker more?"
43Simon, the Pharisee, answered, "I think it
would be the one who owed him the most
money."
Jesus said to Simon, "You are right." 44Then
Jesus turned towards the woman and said to
Simon, "Do you see this woman? When I came
into your house, you gave me no water for my
feet, but she washed my feet with her tears and
dried them with her hair. 45You gave me no kiss
of greeting, but she has been kissing my feet since
I came in. 46You did not put oil on my head, but
she poured perfume on my feet. 47I tell you that
her many sins are forgiven, so she showed great
love. But the person who is forgiven only a little
will love only a little."
48Then Jesus said to her, "Your sins are for-
given."
49The people sitting at the table began to say
among themselves, "Who is this who even for-
gives sins?"
50Jesus said to the woman, "Because you be-
lieved, you are saved from your sins. Go in peace."

The Group with Jesus

8 After this, while Jesus was travelling through
some cities and small towns, he preached
and told the Good News[d] about God's kingdom.
The twelve apostles[d] were with him, 2and also
some women who had been healed of sicknesses
and evil spirits: Mary, called Magdalene, from
whom seven demons[d] had gone out; 3Joanna, the

reed It means that John was not ordinary or weak like grass blown by the wind.
coins Roman denarii. A silver coin was the average pay for one day's work.

wife of Chuza (the manager of Herod's house);
Susanna; and many others. These women used
their own money to help Jesus and his apostles.

A Story About Planting Seed

4When a great crowd was gathered, and peo-
ple were coming to Jesus from every town, he
told them this story:
5"A farmer went out to plant his seed. While
he was planting, some seed fell by the road. Peo-
ple walked on the seed, and the birds ate it up.
6Some seed fell on rock, and when it began to
grow, it died because it had no water. 7Some seed
fell among thorny weeds, but the weeds grew up
with it and choked the good plants. 8And some
seed fell on good ground and grew and made 100
times more."
As Jesus finished the story, he called out, "You
people who can hear me, listen!"
9Jesus' followers asked him what this story
meant.
10Jesus said, "You have been chosen to know
the secrets about the kingdom of God. But I use
stories to speak to other people so that:

'You will listen and listen, but you will not
understand.
You will look and look, but you will not
learn.' *Isaiah 6:9*

11"This is what the story means: the seed is
God's message. 12The seed that fell beside the road
is like the people who hear God's teaching, but the
devil comes and takes it away from them so they
cannot believe it and be saved. 13The seed that fell
on rock is like those who hear God's teaching and

NON-CHRISTIANS

The Kickflip Footballer

Carl was sitting in the back of the car listening to the radio. He was just about to drop off to sleep when he heard the DJ mention Carl's favourite football player, Justin Walker. The DJ was talking about a competition. The grand prize was Justin visiting the winner's house for tea. Within seconds Carl had typed the competition's answer into his mobile and was pressing send. Unbelievably, it was Carl's name that the DJ read out! Carl cheered, his mum clapped, narrowly missing a cyclist, and Carl's mates heard about nothing else all day.

Carl spent the next two weeks getting things organised for the visit of a lifetime, and his first job was to make sure his sister Amy stayed away! In Carl's eyes Amy was a complete "skater geek". She knew nothing about football and Carl thought that she would be an embarrassment – after all, he had a reputation to keep up. There was no way he wanted someone as cool as Justin to meet Amy.

Two weeks later, Justin Walker arrived, with a photographer and a producer from the radio station. Carl's mates looked impressed and everything was going well, until Amy walked in. Carl stared at her with anger and embarrassment. What was she doing here? Justin wouldn't want to talk to her?

Carl's train of thought was suddenly interrupted by Justin's laughter. Carl tuned in to Justin and Amy's conversation and couldn't believe what he was hearing.

"Yeah, yeah, he's an awesome skater isn't he," said Justin. "I've got an amazing DVD with him in. I'll send you one if you want." Justin Walker into skateboarding – NO WAY!

Read about the Pharisee that couldn't believe that Jesus would be interested in someone "sinful" in **Luke 7:36–50**.

- Both Jesus and Justin were interested in people that others had rejected. If Jesus was in your school or college, who do you think he would spend most of his time with?
- Carl was convinced that Justin wouldn't want to meet Amy, but he was wrong. Who have you thought wouldn't be interested in Jesus? Could you be wrong?

Consider . . .

- asking God to show you non-Christians that he wants you to spend more time with.
- asking your youth leader to do some sessions on how to tell your friends about Jesus.

For more, see . . .

- Isaiah 61:1–2 (p.705)
- Romans 1:16 (p.1185)

accept it gladly, but they don't allow the teaching
to go deep into their lives. They believe for a
while, but when trouble comes, they give up.
[14]The seed that fell among the thorny weeds is like
those who hear God's teaching, but they let the
worries, riches and pleasures of this life keep them
from growing and producing good fruit. [15]And the
seed that fell on the good ground is like those who
hear God's teaching with good, honest hearts and
obey it and patiently produce good fruit.

Use What You Have

[16]"No one after lighting a lamp covers it with
a bowl or hides it under a bed. Instead, the per-
son puts it on a lampstand so those who come in
will see the light. [17]Everything that is hidden will
become clear, and every secret thing will be
made known. [18]So be careful how you listen.
Those who have understanding will be given
more. But from those who do not have under-
standing, even what they think they have will be
taken away."

Jesus' True Family

[19]Jesus' mother and brothers came to see him,
but there was such a crowd they could not get to
him. [20]Someone said to Jesus, "Your mother and
your brothers are standing outside, wanting to
see you."

[21]Jesus answered them, "My mother and my
brothers are those who listen to God's teaching
and obey it!"

Jesus Calms a Storm

[22]One day Jesus and his followers got into a
boat, and he said to them, "Let's go across the
lake." And so they started across. [23]While they
were sailing, Jesus fell asleep. A very strong wind
blew up on the lake, causing the boat to fill with
water, and they were in danger.

[24]The followers went to Jesus and woke him,
saying, "Master! Master! We will drown!"

Jesus got up and gave a command to the wind
and the waves. They stopped, and it became
calm. [25]Jesus said to his followers, "Where is your
faith?"

The followers were afraid and amazed and said
to each other, "Who is this that commands even
the wind and the water, and they obey him?"

A Man with Demons Inside Him

[26]Jesus and his followers sailed across the lake
from Galilee to the area of the Gerasene people.
[27]When Jesus got out on the land, a man from the
town who had demons[d] inside him came to
Jesus. For a long time he had worn no clothes and
had lived in the burial caves, not in a house.
[28]When he saw Jesus, he cried out and fell down
before him. He said with a loud voice, "What do
you want with me, Jesus, Son of the Most High
God? I beg you, don't torture me!" [29]He said this
because Jesus was commanding the evil spirit to
come out of the man. Many times it had taken
hold of him. Though he had been kept under
guard and chained hand and foot, he had broken
his chains and had been forced by the demon out
into a lonely place.

[30]Jesus asked him, "What is your name?"

He answered, "Legion,"[n] because many de-
mons were in him. [31]The demons begged Jesus
not to send them into eternal darkness.[n] [32]A
large herd of pigs was feeding on a hill, and the
demons begged Jesus to allow them to go into the
pigs. So Jesus allowed them to do this. [33]When
the demons came out of the man, they went into
the pigs, and the herd ran down the hill into the
lake and was drowned.

[34]When the herdsmen saw what had hap-
pened, they ran away and reported this in the
town and the countryside. [35]And people went to
see what had happened. When they came to
Jesus, they found the man sitting at Jesus' feet,
clothed and in his right mind, because the de-
mons were gone. But the people were frightened.
[36]The people who saw this happen told the others
how Jesus had made the man well. [37]All the peo-
ple of the Gerasene country asked Jesus to leave,
because they were all very afraid. So Jesus got
into the boat and went back to Galilee.

[38]The man whom Jesus had healed begged to
go with him, but Jesus sent him away, saying,
[39]"Go back home and tell people how much God
has done for you." So the man went all over town
telling how much Jesus had done for him.

Jesus Gives Life to a Dead Girl and Heals a Sick Woman

[40]When Jesus got back to Galilee, a crowd wel-
comed him, because everyone was waiting for
him. [41]A man named Jairus, a leader of the syn-
agogue,[d] came to Jesus and fell at his feet, beg-
ging him to come to his house. [42]Jairus' only
daughter, about twelve years old, was dying.

While Jesus was on his way to Jairus' house,
the people were crowding all around him. [43]A
woman was in the crowd who had been bleeding
for twelve years, but no one was able to heal her.
[44]She came up behind Jesus and touched the
edge of his coat, and instantly her bleeding
stopped. [45]Then Jesus said, "Who touched me?"

"Legion" Means very many. A legion was about 5,000 men in the Roman army.
eternal darkness Literally, "the abyss", something like a pit or a hole that has no end.

When all the people said they had not touched him, Peter said, "Master, the people are all around you and are pushing against you."

46But Jesus said, "Someone did touch me, because I felt power go out from me." 47When the woman saw she could not hide, she came forwards, shaking, and fell down before Jesus. While all the people listened, she told why she had touched him and how she had been instantly healed. 48Jesus said to her, "Dear woman, you are made well because you believed. Go in peace."

49While Jesus was still speaking, someone came from the house of the synagogue leader and said to him, "Your daughter is dead. Don't bother the teacher any more."

50When Jesus heard this, he said to Jairus, "Don't be afraid. Just believe, and your daughter will be well."

51When Jesus went to the house, he let only Peter, John, James and the girl's father and mother go inside with him. 52All the people were crying and feeling sad because the girl was dead, but Jesus said, "Stop crying. She is not dead, only asleep."

53The people laughed at Jesus because they knew the girl was dead. 54But Jesus took hold of her hand and called to her, "My child, stand up!" 55Her spirit came back into her, and she stood up at once. Then Jesus ordered that she be given something to eat. 56The girl's parents were amazed, but Jesus told them not to tell anyone what had happened.

Jesus Sends Out the Apostles

9 Jesus called the twelve apostles[d] together and gave them power and authority over all demons[d] and the ability to heal sicknesses. 2He sent the apostles out to tell about God's kingdom and to heal the sick. 3He said to them, "Take nothing for your trip, neither a walking stick, bag, bread, money or extra clothes. 4When you enter a house, stay there until it is time to leave. 5If people do not welcome you, shake the dust off your feet[n] as you leave the town, as a warning to them."

6So the apostles went out and travelled through all the towns, preaching the Good News[d] and healing people everywhere.

Herod is Confused About Jesus

7Herod, the governor, heard about all the things that were happening and was confused, because some people said, "John the Baptist[d] has risen from the dead." 8Others said, "Elijah has come to us." And still others said, "One of the prophets[d] who lived long ago has risen from the dead." 9Herod said, "I cut off John's head, so who is this man I hear such things about?" And Herod kept trying to see Jesus.

More than 5,000 Fed

10When the apostles[d] returned, they told Jesus everything they had done. Then Jesus took them with him to a town called Bethsaida where they could be alone together. 11But the people learned where Jesus went and followed him. He welcomed them and talked with them about God's kingdom and healed those who needed to be healed.

12Late in the afternoon, the twelve apostles came to Jesus and said, "Send the people away. They need to go to the towns and countryside around here and find places to sleep and something to eat, because no one lives in this place."

13But Jesus said to them, "You give them something to eat."

They said, "We have only five loaves of bread and two fish, unless we go and buy food for all these people." 14(There were about 5,000 men there.)

Jesus said to his followers, "Tell the people to sit in groups of about 50 people."

15So the followers did this, and all the people sat down. 16Then Jesus took the five loaves of bread and two fish, and, looking up to heaven, he thanked God for the food. Then he divided the food and gave it to the followers to give to the people. 17They all ate and were satisfied, and what was left over was gathered up, filling twelve baskets.

Jesus is the Christ

18Once when Jesus was praying alone, his followers were with him, and he asked them, "Who do the people say I am?"

19They answered, "Some say you are John the Baptist.[d] Others say you are Elijah.[n] And others say you are one of the prophets[d] from long ago who has come back to life."

20Then Jesus asked, "But who do you say I am?"

Peter answered, "You are the Christ[d] from God."

21Jesus warned them not to tell anyone, saying, 22"The Son of Man[d] must suffer many things. He will be rejected by the Jewish elders, the leading priests, and the teachers of the law. He will be killed and after three days will be raised from the dead."

23Jesus said to all of them, "If people want to follow me, they must give up the things they want.

shake . . . feet A warning. It showed that they had rejected these people.
Elijah A man who spoke for God and who lived hundreds of years before Christ. See 1 Kings 17.

They must be willing to give up their lives daily
to follow me. 24Those who want to save their
lives will give up their lives. But those who give
up their lives for me will have true life. 25It is
worth nothing for them to have the whole world
if they themselves are destroyed or lost. 26If peo-
ple are ashamed of me and my teaching, then
the Son of Man[d] will be ashamed of them when
he comes in his glory and with the glory of the
Father and the holy angels. 27I tell you the truth,
some people standing here will see the kingdom
of God before they die."

Jesus Talks with Moses and Elijah

28About eight days after Jesus said these things,
he took Peter, John and James and went up on a
mountain to pray. 29While Jesus was praying, the
appearance of his face changed, and his clothes
became shining white. 30Then two men, Moses
and Elijah,[n] were talking with Jesus. 31They ap-
peared in heavenly glory, talking about his in-
tended departure which he would soon bring
about in Jerusalem. 32Peter and the others were
very sleepy, but when they awoke fully, they saw
the glory of Jesus and the two men standing with
him. 33When Moses and Elijah were about to
leave, Peter said to Jesus, "Master, it is good that
we are here. Let us make three tents—one for
you, one for Moses and one for Elijah." (Peter did
not know what he was talking about.)

34While he was saying these things, a cloud
came and covered them, and they became afraid
as the cloud covered them. 35A voice came from
the cloud, saying, "This is my Son, whom I have
chosen. Listen to him!"

36When the voice finished speaking, only Jesus
was there. Peter, John and James said nothing
and told no one at that time what they had seen.

Jesus Heals a Sick Boy

37The next day, when they came down from
the mountain, a large crowd met Jesus. 38A man
in the crowd shouted to him, "Teacher, please
come and look at my son, because he is my only
child. 39An evil spirit seizes my son, and suddenly
he screams. It causes him to lose control of him-
self and foam at the mouth. The evil spirit keeps
on hurting him and almost never leaves him. 40I
begged your followers to force the evil spirit out,
but they could not do it."

41Jesus answered, "You people have no faith,
and your lives are all wrong. How long must I
stay with you and put up with you? Bring your
son here."

42While the boy was coming, the demon[d]
threw him on the ground and made him lose
control of himself. But Jesus gave a strong com-
mand to the evil spirit and healed the boy and
gave him back to his father. 43All the people were
amazed at the great power of God.

Jesus Talks About His Death

While everyone was wondering about all that
Jesus did, he said to his followers, 44"Don't forget
what I tell you now: the Son of Man[d] will be
handed over to people." 45But the followers did
not understand what this meant; the meaning
was hidden from them so they could not under-
stand. But they were afraid to ask Jesus about it.

Who is the Greatest?

46Jesus' followers began to have an argument
about which one of them was the greatest.
47Jesus knew what they were thinking, so he took
a little child and stood the child beside him. 48Then
Jesus said, "Whoever accepts this little child in
my name accepts me. And whoever accepts me
accepts the One who sent me, because whoever
is least among you all is really the greatest."

Anyone Not Against Us is For Us

49John answered, "Master, we saw someone
using your name to force demons[d] out of people.
We told him to stop, because he does not belong
to our group."

50But Jesus said to him, "Don't stop him, be-
cause whoever is not against you is for you."

A Town Rejects Jesus

51When the time was coming near for Jesus to
depart, he was determined to go to Jerusalem.
52He sent some men ahead of him, who went
into a town in Samaria to make everything
ready for him. 53But the people there would not
welcome him, because he was set on going to
Jerusalem. 54When James and John, followers of
Jesus, saw this, they said, "Lord, do you want us
to call fire down from heaven and destroy those
people?"[n]

55But Jesus turned and scolded them. 56Then[n]
they went to another town.

Following Jesus

57As they were going along the road, someone
said to Jesus, "I will follow you anywhere you go."

Moses and Elijah Two of the most important Jewish leaders in the past. Moses had given them the law, and Elijah was an important prophet.

Verse 54 Here, some Greek copies add: ". . . as Elijah did."

Verses 55–56 Some copies read: "But Jesus turned and scolded them. And Jesus said, 'You don't know what kind of spirit you belong to. 56The Son of Man did not come to destroy the souls of people but to save them.' Then"

58Jesus said to them, "The foxes have holes to
live in, and the birds have nests, but the Son of
Man[d] has no place to rest his head."

Sidelight The disciples' reaction to Jesus' not being welcomed in a Samaritan town (Luke 9:51–56) would have been common in Jesus' day, given the hatred between the Jews and Samaritans at that time. A hundred years earlier, Jews had destroyed a Samaritan temple. Then, during the night, Samaritans had strewn human bones on the steps of the Jewish Temple in Jerusalem. To see Jesus' attitude towards the Samaritans, read John 4:5–10 (p.1101).

59Jesus said to another man, "Follow me!"
But he said, "Lord, first let me go and bury my
father."
60But Jesus said to him, "Let the people who
are dead bury their own dead. You must go and
tell about the kingdom of God."
61Another man said, "I will follow you, Lord,
but first let me go and say goodbye to my family."
62Jesus said, "Anyone who begins to plough a
field but keeps looking back is of no use in the
kingdom of God."

Jesus Sends Out the Seventy-two

10 After this, the Lord chose 72[n] others
and sent them out in pairs ahead of
him into every town and place where he planned

72 Many Greek copies read 70.

DECISION MAKING

Moving On

The family looked at each other. Murray's mum and sisters were smiling but he wasn't sure.

"Can we sleep on it?" Murray asked.

His dad smiled. "Of course," he said. "This is going to affect us all so I want the decision to be a family one and not just mine."

His father had been offered a chance of a new business, and that meant a bigger house and nicer cars, as well as his dad finally getting the job that he'd worked so hard for. The problem was that if his dad accepted the promotion, they'd have to live in Devon.

Murray sighed. All his friends were in Surrey.

On the other hand, his father would have the job of his dreams at last. The traffic was quieter and the sea was close by. It seemed that for every good point for staying in Surrey, there was a good point for moving to Devon.

Because of that, Murray thought that he had made up his mind, but he wanted to sleep on it before declaring his decision.

"Well?" his father asked the next morning. "I've already asked your mother and sisters and they've told me what they want. Now it all depends on you."

He took a deep breath. "I'd like to move to Devon!" he said nervously.

In **Luke 9:51–62** Jesus points out that important decisions can involve letting go of the past in order to get to a better place.

- How was Murray unlike those who asked about following Jesus?
- Have you decided to follow Jesus wherever he leads you? If not, why not?

Consider . . .

- the next time you have to make a decision, writing a list of points "for" and "against". Then take advice and pray about the decision before committing yourself.
- having a discussion with your youth group about difficult decisions you've each had to face.

For more, see . . .

- Joshua 24:14–15 (p.222)
- Acts 5:1–11 (p.1145)
- Proverbs 8 (p.595)

to go. [2]He said to them, "There are a great many people to harvest, but there are only a few workers. So pray to God, who owns the harvest, that he will send more workers to help gather his harvest. [3]Go now, but listen! I am sending you out like sheep among wolves. [4]Don't carry a purse, a bag or sandals, and don't waste time talking with people on the road. [5]Before you go into a house, say, 'Peace be with this house.' [6]If peaceful people live there, your blessing of peace will stay with them, but if not, then your blessing will come back to you. [7]Stay in the peaceful house, eating and drinking what the people there give you. A worker should be given his pay. Don't move from house to house. [8]If you go into a town and the people welcome you, eat what they give you. [9]Heal the sick who live there, and tell them, 'The kingdom of God is near you.' [10]But if you go into a town, and the people don't welcome you, then go into the streets and say, [11]'Even the dust from your town that sticks to our feet we wipe off against you.[n] But remember that the kingdom of God is near.' [12]I tell you, on the Judgement Day it will be better for the people of Sodom[d] than for the people of that town.

Jesus Warns Unbelievers

[13]"How terrible for you, Korazin! How terrible for you, Bethsaida! If the miracles[d] I did in you had happened in Tyre and Sidon,[n] those people would have changed their lives long ago. They would have worn rough cloth and put ashes on

dust . . . you A warning. It showed that they had rejected these people.
Tyre and Sidon Towns where wicked people lived.

SHARING FAITH

Inspiring Graffiti

In 1956, while working as a church caretaker, Arthur Stace, a former alcoholic and homeless man, heard a sermon preached at a church in Sydney, Australia, by a man called John Ridley. The preacher passionately expressed how he wished that the word "Eternity" could be written all over the streets and buildings of Sydney to encourage people to choose to live life in all its fullness, now and forever. Arthur was hugely impacted by the simple message, and after the service had finished took some chalk and wrote the word "Eternity" in neat, curved writing on the pavement outside.

For the next forty years, Arthur continued to write that same one-word sermon in chalk on pavements and walls all over Sydney. The word was often in the news, as various other people took the credit for the iconic graffiti. But Arthur didn't write the word for fame or fortune. He wrote it because his life was changed by the gift of eternity he received when he first accepted Christ. He couldn't preach amazing sermons but he could communicate this one life-changing word "Eternity"

In the year 2000, as the world celebrated the new millennium, fireworks exploded in amazing colours and patterns all over the Sydney Harbour Bridge. But the grand finale was the lighting of the word Eternity, written, this time in fire, in the same distinctive style that Arthur had used for decades. A life transformed by a simple message, that had been shared in a simple way to millions of people, was now broadcast to the entire world at one of the most significant celebrations in our modern history.

Read **Luke 10:1–12**.

- What is the one word that describes your life and all you live for?
- What can you do to share and show that word in the life you live?

Consider . . .

- asking God to help you find ways to share your faith everyday in the life that you live for him.
- making your own sign, poster or even T-shirt with the one word you feel God wants you to share with others.

For more, see . . .

- Mark 16:14–16 (p.1032)
- Acts 8:11–13 (p.1151)

themselves to show they had changed. 14But on the Judgement Day it will be better for Tyre and Sidon than for you. 15And you, Capernaum,[n] will you be lifted up to heaven? No! You will be thrown down to the depths!

16"Whoever listens to you listens to me, and whoever refuses to accept you refuses to accept me. And whoever refuses to accept me refuses to accept the One who sent me."

Satan Falls

17When the 72[n] came back, they were very happy and said, "Lord, even the demons[d] obeyed us when we used your name!"

18Jesus said, "I saw Satan fall like lightning from heaven. 19Listen, I have given you power to walk on snakes and scorpions, power that is greater than the enemy has. So nothing will hurt you. 20But you should not be happy because the spirits obey you but because your names are written in heaven."

Jesus Prays to the Father

21Then Jesus rejoiced in the Holy Spirit[d] and said, "I praise you, Father, Lord of heaven and earth, because you have hidden these things from the people who are wise and clever. But you have shown them to those who are like little children. Yes, Father, this is what you really wanted.

22"My Father has given me all things. No one knows who the Son is, except the Father. And no one knows who the Father is, except the Son and those whom the Son chooses to tell."

23Then Jesus turned to his followers and said privately, "You are blessed to see what you now see. 24I tell you, many prophets[d] and kings wanted to see what you now see, but they did not, and they wanted to hear what you now hear, but they did not."

The Good Samaritan

25Then an expert on the law stood up to test Jesus, saying, "Teacher, what must I do to get eternal life?"

26Jesus said, "What is written in the law? What do you read there?"

27The man answered, "Love the Lord your God with all your heart, all your soul, all your strength and all your mind."[n] Also, "Love your neighbour as you love yourself."[n]

28Jesus said to him, "Your answer is right. Do this and you will live."

29But the man, wanting to show the importance of his question, said to Jesus, "And who is my neighbour?"

30Jesus answered, "As a man was going down from Jerusalem to Jericho, some robbers attacked him. They tore off his clothes, beat him, and left him lying there, almost dead. 31It happened that a Jewish priest was going down that road. When he saw the man, he walked by on the other side.

Sidelight The Jerusalem-to-Jericho road where the man was robbed in Jesus' story (Luke 10:30) was notoriously dangerous. With a 1,097 metre drop in only 27 kilometres, this narrow, steep, twisting path – nicknamed "The Bloody Way" – was the notorious hangout of robbers.

32Next, a Levite[n] came there, and after he went over and looked at the man, he walked by on the other side of the road. 33Then a Samaritan[n] travelling down the road came to where the hurt man was. When he saw the man, he felt very sorry for him. 34The Samaritan went to him, poured olive oil and wine[n] on his wounds and bandaged them. Then he put the hurt man on his own donkey and took him to an inn where he cared for him. 35The next day, the Samaritan brought out two silver coins,[n] gave them to the innkeeper, and said, 'Take care of this man. If you spend more money on him, I will pay it back to you when I come again.' "

36Then Jesus said, "Which one of these three men do you think was a neighbour to the man who was attacked by the robbers?"

37The expert on the law answered, "The one who showed him mercy."

Jesus said to him, "Then go and do what he did."

Mary and Martha

38While Jesus and his followers were travelling, Jesus went into a town. A woman named Martha

Korazin . . . Bethsaida . . . Capernaum Towns by Lake Galilee where Jesus preached to the people.
72 Many Greek copies read 70.
"Love . . . mind." Quotation from Deuteronomy 6:5.
"Love . . . yourself." Quotation from Leviticus 19:18.
Levite Levites were members of the tribe of Levi who helped the Jewish priests with their work in the Temple. Read 1 Chronicles 23:24–32.
Samaritan Samaritans were people from Samaria. These people were part Jewish, but the Jews did not accept them as true Jews. Samaritans and Jews disliked each other.
olive oil and wine Oil and wine were used like medicine to soften and clean wounds.
coins Roman denarii. A silver coin was the average pay for one day's work.

let Jesus stay at her house. [39]Martha had a sister
named Mary, who was sitting at Jesus' feet and
listening to him teach. [40]But Martha was busy
with all the work to be done. She went in and said,
"Lord, don't you care that my sister has left me
alone to do all the work? Tell her to help me."
[41]But the Lord answered her, "Martha, Martha,
you are worried and upset about many things.
[42]Only one thing is important. Mary has chosen
the better thing, and it will never be taken away
from her."

Jesus Teaches About Prayer

11 Once Jesus was praying in a certain
place. When he finished, one of his
followers said to him, "Lord, teach us to pray as
John taught his followers."
[2]Jesus said to them, "When you pray, say:

'Father, may your name always be kept holy.
May your kingdom come.
[3]Give us the food we need for each day.
[4]Forgive us for our sins,
because we forgive everyone who has done
wrong to us.
And do not cause us to be tempted.' "

Continue to Ask

[5]Then Jesus said to them, "Suppose one of you
went to your friend's house at midnight and said
to him, 'Friend, loan me three loaves of bread. [6]A
friend of mine has come into town to visit me,
but I have nothing for him to eat.' [7]Your friend
inside the house answers, 'Don't bother me! The
door is already locked, and my children and I are
in bed. I cannot get up and give you anything.' [8]I
tell you, if friendship is not enough to make him

SERVICE

I Cannot Walk Away

In Rwanda in 1994, a massive civil war broke out between two different people groups in the country – it was between the Tutsis and the Hutus.

A Catholic priest called Vjeko Curic watched the horror unfold before his eyes; the situation was growing worse in the village where he lived. A Hutu mob was rising up and many Tutsi people were scared for their lives. He knew he had to do something to save his friends before it was too late. He began to shelter Tutsi families and smuggled others out of the country to safety. He helped provide meals, clothing and did anything he could to display God's love for them in this time of war and horror.

As the situation grew more and more dangerous, UN peacekeepers that were helping Father Curic began to leave the country. The Vatican also advised him to leave with them for his own safety, but Curic would not leave people in trouble, who he knew he could help.

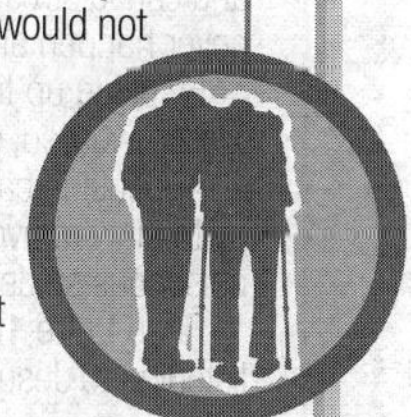

After several years, and a million deaths in Rwanda, the war ended. The country was shattered, but still Father Curic did not walk away. He helped people rebuild their lives, providing housing and medical supplies. He persevered in helping to bring peace back to the country, bringing Hutu and Tutsi people together.

Father Curic did all this in a country that he was not born in, with a people that spoke a different language, had a different skin colour and often saw him as an outsider.

Read **Luke 10:25–37**.

- How can you be like Father Curic where you live? Would you have walked away if you were in his position?
- What qualities do you see in Father Curic and the Good Samaritan? Do you have these?

Consider . . .

- helping someone where you live in a practical way, to show God's love to them, e.g. washing their car, tidying their garden.
- praying for people you know who work around the world helping people who are modern-day Good Samaritans.

For more, see . . .

- Matthew 25:31–46 (p.987)
- 1 John 3:10–23 (p.1374)
- James 2:14–18 (p.1350)

get up to give you the bread, your boldness will
make him get up and give you whatever you
need. 9So I tell you, ask, and God will give to you.
Search, and you will find. Knock, and the door
will open for you. 10Yes, everyone who asks will
receive. The one who searches will find. And
everyone who knocks will have the door opened.
11If your children ask for a fish, which of you
would give them a snake instead? 12Or, if your
children ask for an egg, would you give them a
scorpion? 13Even though you are bad, you know
how to give good things to your children. How
much more will your heavenly Father give the
Holy Spirit[d] to those who ask him!"

Jesus' Power is from God

14Once Jesus was sending out a demon[d] that
could not talk. When the demon came out, the
man who had been unable to speak, then spoke.
The people were amazed. 15But some of them
said, "Jesus uses the power of Beelzebul,[d] the
ruler of demons, to force demons out of people."
16Other people, wanting to test Jesus, asked
him to give them a sign from heaven. 17But
knowing their thoughts, he said to them, "Every
kingdom that is divided against itself will be des-
troyed. And a family that is divided against itself
will not continue. 18So if Satan is divided against
himself, his kingdom will not continue. You say

WORRYING

Fear in Disguise

Did you know that over 133,000 people every year are injured by doors? Apparently, over 400,000 people in the United States suffer injuries every year while relaxing or sleeping in bed!

Hearing statistics like that, does it make you worry about walking through a door or sleeping in bed? Probably not!

So why do we worry about some things and not about others?

Worrying is usually fear in disguise. Imagine someone who was scared about injuring themselves on a door – you can understand them worrying about whether it would happen or not. If you were scared that you were going to fall out of bed and hurt yourself, you'd probably worry about it.

Worrying is a state of mind and we can often find ourselves battling in our own minds, trying desperately not to worry – and yet we can't help it! But how often does what we're worrying about actually happen? One survey revealed that 92 per cent of our worries waste our time and energy and cause stress needlessly. The survey said that 40 per cent of our worries are over things that never happen and 30 per cent are over things in the past that cannot be changed or altered.

By using up time and energy worrying, we're unable to do other things. So next time you're feeling worried, stop, think and pray about how you could be using that time and energy positively.

And just in case you happen to be afraid of spiders or flying in planes – remember the following: by the law of averages, you are more likely to be killed by a flying champagne cork than by a poisonous spider and you have a higher chance of being killed by a donkey than dying in a plane crash.

Read **Luke 10:38–42**. When Jesus meets Mary and Martha, Martha is worried and it stops her from listening to Jesus.

- What do you think Martha might have been worrying about? What was she scared of?
- How does Jesus react to Martha's worrying?

Consider . . .

- whether there is anything you find yourself worrying about regularly. In the light of the passage, what is this worrying preventing you from doing?
- writing the words of Philippians 4:6–7 out on a piece of paper and putting it in a place where you can read it whenever you feel worried.

For more, see . . .

- Psalm 131 (p.577)
- 1 Peter 5:6–7 (p.1362)
- Philippians 4:6–7 (p.1285)

that I use the power of Beelzebul to force out
demons. 19But if I use the power of Beelzebul to
force out demons, what power do your people
use to force demons out? So they will be your
judges. 20But if I use the power of God to force
out demons, then the kingdom of God has come
to you.
21"When a strong person with many weapons
guards his own house, his possessions are safe.
22But when someone stronger comes and defeats
him, the stronger one will take away the weapons
the first man trusted and will give away the
possessions.
23"Anyone who is not with me is against me,
and anyone who does not work with me is working against me.

The Empty Person

24"When an evil spirit comes out of a person,
it travels through dry places, looking for a place to
rest. But when it finds no place, it says, 'I will go
back to the house I left.' 25And when it comes
back, it finds that house swept clean and made
neat. 26Then the evil spirit goes out and brings
seven other spirits more evil than it is, and they
go in and live there. So the person has even
more trouble than before."

People Who Are Truly Happy

27As Jesus was saying these things, a woman in
the crowd called out to Jesus, "Happy is the
mother who gave birth to you and nursed you."
28But Jesus said, "No, happy are those who
hear the teaching of God and obey it."

The People Want a Miracle

29As the crowd grew larger, Jesus said, "The
people who live today are evil. They want to see
a miracle[d] for a sign, but no sign will be given
them, except the sign of Jonah.[n] 30As Jonah was
a sign for those people who lived in Nineveh, the
Son of Man[d] will be a sign for the people of this

sign of Jonah Jonah's three days in the fish are like Jesus' three days in the tomb. See Matthew 12:40.

PRAYER

Countdown to Victory

"Oh, I'll never get it right. There's just no cure. It's hopeless."

That's probably what a lot of scientists were thinking in the first part of the twentieth century, when a disease called polio crippled and killed millions of people. Hundreds of researchers looked frantically for a cure. But it seemed like an impossible task. Then, in 1954, Dr Jonas Salk announced that after 200 attempts he had developed a vaccine. This terrible disease disappeared virtually overnight.

Later, a reporter asked Dr Salk how it felt to have had 200 failures and only one success. Salk replied that he had never experienced 200 failures. He had learned 200 lessons. And those lessons enabled him to create a usable vaccine. Rather than viewing each unsuccessful attempt as a tragedy, Dr Salk chose to see it as an opportunity to learn.

Dr Salk saw a need and didn't stop until the need was met. Similarly, persistent prayer is what Jesus recommends as one of the best ways to find answers in life. Read the story that Jesus told in **Luke 11:1–13**.

- How is Dr Salk like the man who needed bread in Jesus' story?
- How should you pray about problems you really care about?

Consider . . .

- writing about seven concerns that are important to you, and praying about a different concern each day this week.
- making a pact with a friend to become your "prayer partner" for the next month. Meet at least once a week to share requests and pray for each other.

For more, see . . .

- Psalm 130 (p.577)
- Luke 18:1–8 (p.1078)
- Matthew 6:1–15 (p.947)

time. 31On the Judgement Day the Queen of the
South[n] will stand up with the people who live
now. She will show they are guilty, because she
came from far away to listen to Solomon's wise
teaching. And I tell you that someone greater
than Solomon is here. 32On the Judgement Day
the people of Nineveh will stand up with the
people who live now, and they will show that
you are guilty. When Jonah preached to them,
they were sorry and changed their lives. And I
tell you that someone greater than Jonah is here.

Be a Light for the World

33"No one lights a lamp and puts it in a secret
place or under a bowl, but on a lampstand so the
people who come in can see. 34Your eye is a light
for the body. When your eyes are good, your
whole body will be full of light. But when your
eyes are evil, your whole body will be full of
darkness. 35So be careful not to let the light in
you become darkness. 36If your whole body is full
of light, and none of it is dark, then you will shine
bright, as when a lamp shines on you."

Jesus Accuses the Pharisees

37After Jesus had finished speaking, a Pharisee[d]
asked Jesus to eat with him. So Jesus went in and
sat at the table. 38But the Pharisee was surprised
when he saw that Jesus did not wash his hands[n]
before the meal. 39The Lord said to him, "You
Pharisees clean the outside of the cup and the
dish, but inside you are full of greed and evil.
40You foolish people! The same one who made
what is outside also made what is inside. 41So
give what is in your dishes to the poor, and then
you will be fully clean. 42How terrible for you
Pharisees! You give God one-tenth of even your
mint, your rue[d] and every other plant in your
garden. But you fail to be fair to others and to
love God. These are the things you should do
while continuing to do those other things. 43How
terrible for you Pharisees, because you love to
have the most important seats in the syn-
agogues,[d] and you love to be greeted with respect
in the market places. 44How terrible for you, be-
cause you are like hidden graves, which people
walk on without knowing."

Jesus Talks to Experts on the Law

45One of the experts on the law said to Jesus,
"Teacher, when you say these things, you are
insulting us, too."

46Jesus answered, "How terrible for you, you
experts on the law! You make strict rules that are
very hard for people to obey, but you yourselves
don't even try to follow those rules. 47How terri-
ble for you, because you build tombs for the
prophets[d] whom your ancestors killed! 48And
now you show that you approve of what your
ancestors did. They killed the prophets, and you
build tombs for them! 49This is why in his wis-
dom God said, 'I will send prophets and apostles[d]
to them. They will kill some, and they will treat
others cruelly.' 50So you who live now will be
punished for the deaths of all the prophets who
were killed since the beginning of the world—
51from the killing of Abel to the killing of
Zechariah,[n] who died between the altar and the
Temple.[d] Yes, I tell you that you who are alive
now will be punished for them all.

52"How terrible for you, you experts on the
law. You have taken away the key to learning
about God. You yourselves would not learn, and
you stopped others from learning, too."

53When Jesus left, the teachers of the law and
the Pharisees[d] began to give him trouble, asking
him questions about many things and 54trying to
catch him saying something wrong.

Don't Be Like the Pharisees

12 So many thousands of people had gath-
ered that they were stepping on each
other. Jesus spoke first to his followers, saying,
"Beware of the yeast of the Pharisees,[d] because
they are hypocrites.[d] 2Everything that is hidden
will be shown, and everything that is secret will
be made known. 3What you have said in the dark
will be heard in the light, and what you have
whispered in an inner room will be shouted from
the housetops.

4"I tell you, my friends, don't be afraid of peo-
ple who can kill the body but after that can do
nothing more to hurt you. 5I will show you the
one to fear. Fear the one who has the power to
kill you and also to throw you into hell. Yes, this
is the one you should fear.

6"Five sparrows are sold for only two pennies,
and God does not forget any of them. 7But God
even knows how many hairs you have on your
head. Don't be afraid. You are worth much more
than many sparrows.

Don't Be Ashamed of Jesus

8"I tell you, all those who stand before others
and say they believe in me, I, the Son of Man,[d]

Queen of the South The Queen of Sheba. She travelled 1,600 kilometres to learn God's wisdom from Solomon. Read 1 Kings 10:1–3.
wash his hands This was a Jewish religious custom that the Pharisees thought was very important.
Abel . . . Zechariah In the Hebrew Old Testament, the first and last men to be murdered.

will say before the angels of God that they belong
to me. 9But all who stand before others and say
they do not believe in me, I will say before the
angels of God that they do not belong to me.
10"Anyone who speaks against the Son of
Man[d] can be forgiven, but anyone who speaks
against the Holy Spirit[d] will not be forgiven.
11"When you are brought into the synagogues[d]
before the leaders and other powerful people,
don't worry about how to defend yourselves or
what to say. 12At that time the Holy Spirit will
teach you what you must say."

Jesus Warns Against Selfishness

13Someone in the crowd said to Jesus,
"Teacher, tell my brother to divide with me the
property our father left us."
14But Jesus said to him, "Who said I should
judge or decide between you?" 15Then Jesus said
to them, "Be careful and guard against all kinds
of greed. Life is not measured by how much one
owns."
16Then Jesus told this story: "There was a rich
man who had some land, which grew a good
crop. 17He thought to himself, 'What will I do?

ABORTION

What's it Worth?

The phone sounded urgent, even as it rang. Siobhan ran to answer it. She was used to urgent phone calls, as a minister's wife she got quite a few.

"Hello?"

There was silence and then a female voice started to whisper down the phone.

"You probably won't remember me. My name's Natalie, we met last year."

"Natalie? Oh yes, you were the girl I spoke to after the meeting at St Edmunds . . . " Siobhan was puzzled by the whispering voice, but tried not to let it bother her.

"I need to talk to you, but my dad's in the other room," Natalie carried on. "I can't let him hear me." By now it was obvious that the teenager was in considerable distress.

"What's happened? Just tell me," said the minister's wife.

"I'm pregnant and my dad's found out," she replied simply.

"Oh no." Siobhan's mind was racing. This girl was only fifteen.

"He came home tonight and told me that he has made an appointment for me to have an abortion. I have to go with him to hospital tomorrow." Natalie sounded terrified.

"Oh Natalie, my dear . . . " began Siobhan.

"The problem is," the teenage girl carried on, "the day after the abortion I have my exams! Will I be alright? Will I be able to go to school? You see, I must pass my exams, I've been working so hard."

Siobhan could hear Natalie starting to cry at the other end.

"But Natalie, this is really no time to worry about exams . . . " Siobhan started. "You are about to lose a baby!"

"I don't care about the baby," wailed Natalie. "I want to pass my exams!"

Luke 12:6–7 talks about values.

- What is the difference between Natalie's values and those of the passage?
- Take a moment to think about your own values. Is life the most precious thing to you?

Consider . . .

- making a list of the five most important things in your life. Now put them in the order you feel God would like them to be.
- supporting an organisation like "Care For The Family", that seeks to help young single parents.

For more, see . . .

- Psalm 121 (p.575)
- Luke 9:25 (p.1055)
- Matthew 6:25–27 (p.948)

I have no place to keep all my crops.' 18Then he said, 'This is what I will do: I will tear down my barns and build bigger ones, and there I will store all my grain and other goods. 19Then I can say to myself, "I have enough good things stored to last for many years. Rest, eat, drink and enjoy life!"'

20"But God said to him, 'Foolish man! Tonight your life will be taken from you. So who will get those things you have prepared for yourself?'

21"This is how it will be for those who store up things for themselves and are not rich towards God."

Sidelight The rich man in Jesus' story (Luke 12:16–21) would probably have been a millionaire today. Most farmers stored their food supply in clay jars of various sizes. To have a barn or grain silo would indicate extreme wealth. Archaeologists have discovered some underground grain silos that are over seven metres wide and more than six metres deep!

Don't Worry

22Jesus said to his followers, "So I tell you, don't worry about the food you need to live, or about the clothes you need in order for your body. 23Life is more than food, and the body is more than clothes. 24Look at the birds. They don't plant or harvest, they don't have storerooms or barns, but God feeds them. And you are worth much more than birds. 25You cannot add any time to your life by worrying about it. 26If you cannot do even the little things, then why worry about the big things? 27Consider how the lilies grow; they don't work or make clothes for themselves. But I tell you that even Solomon with his riches was not dressed as beautifully as one of these flowers. 28God clothes the grass in the field, which is alive today but tomorrow is thrown into the fire. So how much more will God clothe you? Don't have so little faith! 29Don't always think about what you will eat or what you will drink, and don't keep worrying. 30All the people in the world are trying to get these things, and your Father knows you need them. 31But seek God's kingdom, and all the other things you need will be given to you.

Don't Trust in Money

32"Don't fear, little flock, because your Father wants to give you the kingdom. 33Sell your possessions and give to the poor. Get for yourselves purses that will not wear out, the treasure in heaven that never runs out, where thieves can't steal and moths can't destroy. 34Your heart will be where your treasure is.

Always Be Ready

35"Be dressed, ready for service, and have your lamps shining. 36Be like servants who are waiting for their master to come home from a wedding party. When he comes and knocks, the servants immediately open the door for him. 37They will be blessed when their master comes home, because he sees that they were watching for him. I tell you the truth, the master will dress himself to serve and tell the servants to sit at the table, and he will serve them. 38Those servants will be happy when he comes in and finds them still waiting, even if it is midnight or later.

39"Remember this: if the owner of the house knew what time a thief was coming, he would not allow the thief to enter his house. 40So you also must be ready, because the Son of Man[d] will come at a time when you don't expect him!"

Who is the Trusted Servant?

41Peter said, "Lord, did you tell this story to us or to all people?"

42The Lord said, "Who is the wise and trusted servant that the master trusts to give the other servants their food at the right time? 43When the master comes and finds the servant doing his work, the servant will be blessed. 44I tell you the truth, the master will choose that servant to take care of everything he owns. 45But suppose the servant thinks to himself, 'My master will not come back soon,' and he begins to beat the other servants, men and women, and to eat and drink and get drunk. 46The master will come when that servant is not ready and is not expecting him. Then the master will cut him in pieces and send him away to be with the others who don't obey.

47"The servant who knows what his master wants but is not ready, or who does not do what the master wants, will be beaten with many blows! 48But the servant who does not know what his master wants and does things that should be punished will be beaten with few blows. From everyone who has been given much, much will be demanded. And from the one trusted with much, much more will be expected.

Jesus Causes Division

49"I came to set fire to the world, and I wish it were already burning! 50I have a baptism[n] to undergo and I feel very troubled until it is over. 51Do you think I came to give peace to the earth?

I . . . baptism Jesus was talking about the suffering he would soon go through.

No, I tell you, I came to divide it. 52From now
on, a family with five people will be divided, three
against two, and two against three. 53They will be
divided: father against son and son against father,
mother against daughter and daughter against
mother, mother-in-law against daughter-in-law
and daughter-in-law against mother-in-law."

Understanding the Times

54Then Jesus said to the people, "When you
see clouds coming up in the west, you say, 'It's
going to rain,' and it happens. 55When you feel
the wind begin to blow from the south, you say,
'It will be a hot day,' and it happens. 56Hypocrites![d]
You know how to understand the appearance of
the earth and sky. Why don't you understand
what is happening now?

Settle Your Problems

57"Why can't you decide for yourselves what is
right? 58If your enemy is taking you to court, try
hard to settle it on the way. If you don't, your

MONEY

It's Only Money

By the time he was thirty, Millard Fuller had achieved the American Dream. He was worth more than $1 million and lived a lifestyle that showed it. He drove a fancy car, lived in a huge house, owned lots of land, and generally enjoyed the things his money could buy. He and his wife Linda had just about anything that a young couple could want, except . . .

Except what? Well, they weren't sure. All Millard and Linda did know was that they weren't happy.

"We just thought there must be something more to life," Millard explains.

On the advice of a friend, Millard and Linda turned to God. They spent time reading the Bible and praying with other Christians at Koinonia Farms.

What could they do? What should they do?

"By seeing other Christians' lifestyles," explains Linda, "we quickly saw there was much more to life than the success money can bring. We realised God had a purpose for us. And we were determined to find out what it was."

Finally, they received the answer to their prayers. They believed that God wanted them to start something new. Something big. They believed God wanted them to make a new start.

So they did. They sold off their businesses and their big house, and gave the money away. They sold their land, their boats, their horses, their cattle. In fact, they got rid of just about everything.

After this, they didn't go on tour to boast about how kind they were, or how many points they had earned with God. Instead, they continued to pray about what God was calling them towards. For more than five years, they worked at various mission stations, continuing to pray. Finally, at God's prompting, they formed "Habitat for Humanity", a worldwide group that seeks to eliminate all substandard housing. Because the Fullers were able to give everything away and listen to God, thousands of families go to bed each night in safe, secure homes.

One of the passages that helped the Fullers to make their decision was **Luke 12:32–40**. Read it and see if you can understand their actions.

- How did these verses influence the Fullers?
- What can you do to apply Jesus' words in this passage?

Consider . . .

- deciding to give a specific portion of your money to your church charity.
- keeping a list of all the money you spend in a week. Sit down with your list and see who really determines how you spend it. Then pray for the freedom to give everything to God.

For more, see . . .

- Isaiah 58:6–11 (p.701)
- 2 Corinthians 9:6–9 (p.1248)
- Matthew 6:19–21 (p.948)

enemy might take you to the judge, and the
judge might turn you over to the officer, and the
officer might throw you into jail. 59I tell you, you
will not get out of there until you have paid
everything you owe."

Change Your Hearts

13 At that time some people were there
who told Jesus that Pilate[n] had killed
some people from Galilee while they were wor-
shipping. He mixed their blood with the blood of
the animals they were sacrificing to God. 2Jesus
answered, "Do you think this happened to them
because they were more sinful than all others
from Galilee? 3No, I tell you. But unless you
change your hearts and lives, you will be destroyed
as they were! 4What about those eighteen people
who died when the tower of Siloam fell on them?
Do you think they were more sinful than all the
others who live in Jerusalem? 5No, I tell you. But
unless you change your hearts and lives, you will
all be destroyed too!"

The Useless Tree

6Jesus told this story: "A man had a fig tree
planted in his vineyard. He came looking for
some fruit on the tree, but he found none. 7So the
man said to his gardener, 'I have been looking for
fruit on this tree for three years, but I never find
any. Cut it down. Why should it waste the
ground?' 8But the servant answered, 'Master,
let the tree have one more year to produce fruit.

Pilate Pontius Pilate was the Roman governor of Judea from AD 26 to AD 36.

END TIMES

Both Eyes Open

When Jade started working at the shop, everyone noticed the difference. Things were tidied away and everywhere looked brighter.

"It's not your job to dust and tidy." Alan, her boss, said to her one day. Jade smiled. "I know that, but I'm not doing anything else at the moment, so why not?"

Alan shrugged and let her get on with it. During the next few months, the shop almost changed shape. Layouts were rearranged, and orders kept up to date. He even came back from a holiday to find the shelves painted!

Then one day a customer came into the shop determined to cause trouble. Jade did her best to be nice to her, but nothing she did was going to be good enough for this cantankerous old woman.

"Get me the manager!" she yelled. "I demand to see the manager!"

By now, Alan had heard the rumpus at the other end of the shop and came over to see what was wrong. The lady complained bitterly that the "shop girl" was incompetent and should be sacked.

Alan very smoothly said, "I'm very sorry about this, but I stand by my staff. Jade is probably the best girl we've ever had here and is in no way incompetent. Perhaps you would let me serve you instead?"

Jade breathed a sigh of relief as she realised that her service to her boss had paid off at an awkward moment.

Luke 12:42–46 speaks about serving your master whether he's there or not.

- What might have happened to Jade if she hadn't been so watchful?
- What are the rewards for this kind of service, according to this passage?

Consider . . .

- Helping to prepare and clear up the room – or helping with refreshments – at your youth group.
- Ways to keep your life clean and tidy, ready for Christ.

For more see . . .

- Amos 4:12 (p.872)
- 1 Thessalonians 5:1–6 (p.1300)

Let me dig up the earth around it and put on
some manure. 9If the tree produces fruit next
year, good. But if not, you can cut it down.' "

Jesus Heals on the Sabbath

10Jesus was teaching in one of the synagogues [d]
on the Sabbath [d] day. 11A woman was there who,
for eighteen years, had an evil spirit in her that
made her crippled. Her back was always bent;
she could not stand up straight. 12When Jesus
saw her, he called her over and said, "Woman,
you are free from your sickness." 13Jesus put his
hands on her, and immediately she was able to
stand up straight and began praising God.
14The synagogue leader was angry because
Jesus healed on the Sabbath day. He said to the
people, "There are six days when one has to
work. So come to be healed on one of those days,
and not on the Sabbath day."
15The Lord answered, "You hypocrites! [d]
Doesn't each of you untie your work animals and
lead them to drink water every day—even on
the Sabbath day? 16This woman that I healed, a
daughter of Abraham, has been held by Satan for
eighteen years. Surely it is not wrong for her to
be freed from her sickness on a Sabbath day!"
17When Jesus said this, all of those who were
criticising him were ashamed, but the entire
crowd rejoiced at all the wonderful things Jesus
was doing.

Stories of Mustard Seed and Yeast

18Then Jesus said, "What is God's kingdom
like? What can I compare it with? 19It is like
a mustard seed that a man plants in his garden.

SPIRITUAL GROWTH

Every Day Counts

Tim was a friend of mine, in an unusual way. We met by accident and had very little in common. We liked different foods, different sports, different girls, and we each had our own definition of a "good time". We did share two things, though: we had the same birthday and we loved the same God. Sometimes this was all we could agree on, but we usually enjoyed our time together.

When we were eighteen, Tim died suddenly of a heart attack. He said that he wasn't feeling well, and he had passed out by the time the ambulance arrived. He was dead hours later. Through my tears, I realised that I didn't have anyone to share my birthday with. And I wasn't so sure about the God that I loved. Why did this happen? Everybody knows that teenagers aren't supposed to die, surely?

A few days later, Tim's family and friends got together to mourn his death. As we sat around talking, somebody told a story about Tim that brought a smile to our faces. Before long, all of Tim's old jokes were flying, along with stories of how his short life had touched each of us. In that conversation, we saw that Tim had tried to live each day as though it were an important chance to serve God.

I think of my friend Tim often, because his life challenged me. I realised that I don't know what will happen. So I must work to make each day count.

When people asked Jesus about their friends who had died, he gave them a challenge to use their days well. Read about it in **Luke 13:1–9**.

- How is Tim's story like the stories in the passage?
- What can you do to prepare yourself to "bear fruit" and so avoid being like the useless tree in the passage?

Consider . . .

- imagining that you have only two weeks to live. Decide what your priorities would be, then do them.
- buying two small potted plants and taking one to a person who is sick, elderly or shut-in. Keep the other in your room as a reminder to pray for your special friend – and as a reminder to always try to bear fruit for God's kingdom.

For more, see . . .

- Psalm 90 (p.554)
- Galatians 6:7–10 (p.1265)
- Matthew 7:15–23 (p.950)

The seed grows and becomes a tree, and the
wild birds build nests in its branches."
20 Jesus said again, "What can I compare God's
kingdom with? 21 It is like yeast that a woman
took and hid in a large bowl of flour until it made
all the dough rise."

The Narrow Door

22 Jesus was teaching in every town and village
as he travelled towards Jerusalem. 23 Someone said
to Jesus, "Lord, will only a few people be saved?"
Jesus said, 24 "Try hard to enter through the
narrow door, because many people will try to
enter there, but they will not be able. 25 When
the owner of the house gets up and closes the
door, you can stand outside and knock on the
door and say, 'Sir, open the door for us.' But he
will answer, 'I don't know you or where you
come from.' 26 Then you will say, 'We ate and
drank with you, and you taught in the streets of
our town.' 27 But he will say to you, 'I don't
know you or where you come from. Go away
from me, all you who do evil!' 28 You will cry and
grind your teeth with pain when you see Abraham, Isaac, Jacob and all the prophets[d] in God's
kingdom, but you yourselves thrown outside.

ETERNAL LIFE

Lollipop Ladies

It didn't matter whether it was blue sky or raining cats and dogs, whenever Hayley went to pick up her little sister Lucy from school, the lollipop lady was always there, standing in the middle of the road in her day-glo coat, waving a crocodile of tiny children across the road. Most of the traffic was driven by local people – and most of them were afraid of Mary. She ruled with a rod of iron! When she held up that baton, the vehicles came to a standstill.

One day Hayley got out of school earlier than usual and stood by the railings waiting for the bell to go. Mary came along, cheerful as ever:

"Hello darling, how are you today? Looks as if it will rain later, maybe even snow if it gets any colder . . . " The woman was a constant chatterbox.

Hayley smiled and said, "I hope not, our church has got its annual Fun Run tomorrow, we could do without snow!"

The lollipop lady turned towards her in amusement and said, "Well, now, I didn't take you for one of those Holy Joes!"

It was Hayley's turn to look puzzled as she said, "I'm suprised you're not a church-goer yourself, you seem to spend an awful lot of time helping other people."

"Ah well, that's where we are different," Mary replied confidently. "I don't need to go to church. I do my best, give help where it's needed. Look at all these little ones coming out now, yes, I'm sure God will shake my hand when I get to heaven . . . " And with that she ushered the children into single file and saw them safely across the road.

Hayley's heart was heavy as she made her way home. How sad that someone who was so eager to please had dismissed the God who had given her the helpful heart.

Listen to Jesus' words of warning in **Luke 13:22–30**.

- What did Jesus say about people like Mary who thought they were "good enough" to gain entrance to heaven?
- How can you keep on the narrow road to eternal life and avoid the obstacles?

Consider . . .

- taking a few minutes to write down what you imagine heaven to be like.
- selecting five goals that will help you walk the "narrow road". Write them down in your diary. Six months from now, see if you have achieved your goals.

For more, see . . .

- Matthew 7:13–23 (p.950)
- Hebrews 6:7–12 (p.1335)
- Ephesians 2:8–9 (p.1270)

29 People will come from the east, west, north
and south and will sit down at the table in the
kingdom of God. 30 There are those who have the
lowest place in life now who will have the high-
est place in the future. And there are those who
have the highest place now who will have the
lowest place in the future."

Jesus will Die in Jerusalem

31 At that time some Pharisees[d] came to Jesus
and said, "Go away from here! Herod wants to
kill you!"

32 Jesus said to them, "Go and tell that fox
Herod, 'Today and tomorrow I am forcing de-
mons[d] out and healing people. Then, on the
third day, I will reach my goal.' 33 Yet I must be
on my way today and tomorrow and the next
day. Surely it cannot be right for a prophet[d] to be
killed anywhere except in Jerusalem.

34 "Jerusalem, Jerusalem! You kill the prophets
and stone to death those who are sent to you.
Many times I wanted to gather your people as a
hen gathers her chicks under her wings, but you
would not let me. 35 Now your house is left com-
pletely empty. I tell you, you will not see me
until that time when you will say, 'God bless the
One who comes in the name of the Lord.' "[n]

Healing on the Sabbath

14 On a Sabbath[d] day, when Jesus went to
eat at the home of a leading Pharisee,[d]
the people were watching Jesus very closely.
2 And in front of him was a man with dropsy.[n]
3 Jesus said to the Pharisees and experts on the
law, "Is it right or wrong to heal on the Sabbath
day?" 4 But they would not answer his question.
So Jesus took the man, healed him and sent him
away. 5 Jesus said to the Pharisees and teachers of
the law, "If your child or ox falls into a well
on the Sabbath day, will you not pull him out
quickly?" 6 And they could not answer him.

Don't Make Yourself Important

7 When Jesus noticed that some of the guests
were choosing the best places to sit, he told this
story: 8 "When someone invites you to a wedding
feast, don't take the most important seat, be-
cause someone more important than you may
have been invited. 9 The host, who invited both
of you, will come to you and say, 'Give this per-
son your seat.' Then you will be embarrassed
and will have to move to the last place. 10 So
when you are invited, go and sit in a seat that is
not important. When the host comes to you, he
may say, 'Friend, move up here to a more impor-
tant place.' Then all the other guests will respect
you. 11 All who make themselves great will be
made humble, but those who make themselves
humble will be made great."

You will Be Rewarded

12 Then Jesus said to the man who had invited
him, "When you give a lunch or a dinner, don't
invite only your friends, your family, your other
relatives and your rich neighbours. At another
time they will invite you to eat with them, and
you will be repaid. 13 Instead, when you give a
feast, invite the poor, the crippled, the lame and
the blind. 14 Then you will be blessed, because
they have nothing and cannot pay you back. But
you will be repaid when the good people rise
from the dead."

A Story About a Big Banquet

15 One of those at the table with Jesus heard
these things and said to him, "Happy are the
people who will share in the meal in God's
kingdom."

16 Jesus said to him, "A man gave a big ban-
quet and invited many people. 17 When it was
time to eat, the man sent his servant to tell the
guests, 'Come. Everything is ready.'

18 "But all the guests made excuses. The first
one said, 'I have just bought a field, and I must
go and look at it. Please excuse me.' 19 Another
said, 'I have just bought five pairs of oxen; I must
go and try them. Please excuse me.' 20 A third
person said, 'I just got married; I can't come.'
21 So the servant returned and told his master
what had happened. Then the master became
angry and said, 'Go at once into the streets and
alleys of the town, and bring in the poor, the
crippled, the blind, and the lame.' 22 Later the
servant said to him, 'Master, I did what you com-
manded, but we still have room.' 23 The master
said to the servant, 'Go out to the roads and
country lanes, and tell the people there to come
so my house will be full. 24 I tell you, none of
those whom I invited first will eat with me.' "

Sidelight A party invitation in Jesus' day (Luke 14:15–24) included the day but never the hour. When the party was ready, slaves would go and get the guests. To reject an invitation you had earlier accepted was the ultimate insult – as this story illustrates!

'God . . . Lord.' Quotation from Psalm 118:26.
dropsy A sickness that causes the body to swell larger and larger.

The Cost of Being Jesus' Follower

25 Large crowds were travelling with Jesus,
and he turned and said to them, 26 "If anyone
comes to me but loves his father, mother, wife,
children, brothers or sisters—or even life—more
than me, he cannot be my follower. 27 Whoever
is not willing to carry the cross and follow me
cannot be my follower. 28 If you want to build a
tower, you first sit down and decide how much
it will cost, to see if you have enough money to
finish the job. 29 If you don't, you might lay the
foundation, but you would not be able to finish.
Then all who saw it would make fun of you,
30 saying, 'This person began to build but was not
able to finish.'

31 "If a king is going to fight another king, first
he will sit down and plan. He will decide if he
and his 10,000 soldiers can defeat the other king
who has 20,000 soldiers. 32 If he can't, then while
the other king is still far away, he will send some
people to speak to him and ask for peace. 33 In the
same way, you must give up everything you have
to be my follower.

Don't Lose Your Influence

34 "Salt is good, but if it loses its salty taste, you
cannot make it salty again. 35 It is no good for the
soil or for manure; it is thrown away.

"You people who can hear me, listen."

A Lost Sheep, a Lost Coin

15 The tax collectors and sinners all came to
listen to Jesus. 2 But the Pharisees[d] and
the teachers of the law began to complain: "Look,
this man welcomes sinners and even eats with
them."

3 Then Jesus told them this story: 4 "Suppose
one of you has 100 sheep but loses one of them.
Then he will leave the other 99 sheep in the open
field and go out and look for the lost sheep until

FRIENDS

No Such Thing as a Free Lunch?

Janice spent every Saturday cooking lunch for fifty old ladies and gentlemen.

She planned meticulously the week before, trying to add up how many carrots she would need, and borrowing pots and pans. On the day itself, she would get up at 6 a.m. to peel vegetables, heat the oven and lay tables like a 5-star restaurant.

Janice gave every Saturday for at least twenty years of her life to these old people. They were old and ill, she got no payment for cooking so many roast dinners, and very little help. So why did she do it?

Because she realised that God loved her and loved all these people that she cooked for. They had no family nearby, had probably not spoken to anyone that week or had the energy to cook themselves a decent meal. She wanted to show them love and friendship, so that they might see something of God's love for them on earth. She trusted in God and humbly gave her time and talents, knowing that the people she provided for would never be able to return the favour.

She knew that Jesus had died for her in order for her to be his friend, and she'd done nothing to deserve this friendship. So Janice will continue to wash potatoes and watch old ladies dribble, because she knows that for once in their week they feel loved and cared for; they'll know that they have a friend.

Read **Luke 14:7–14**.

- What does this passage tell us about people that we might not like to spend time with?
- What does it tell us about how to be a good friend? What is our reward for this friendship?

Consider . . .

- what friendship with Jesus really means. What does/should he get in return from us?
- making friends with someone who won't be able to repay you for your friendship.

For more, see . . .

- Matthew 25:34–40 (p.988)
- James 2:1–9 (p.1348)
- Philippians 2:1–11 (p.1282)

he finds it. [5]And when he finds it, he happily puts
it on his shoulders [6]and goes home. He calls to his
friends and neighbours and says, 'Be happy with
me because I found my lost sheep.' [7]In the same
way, I tell you there is more joy in heaven over
one sinner who changes his heart and life,
than over 99 good people who don't need to
change.
[8]"Suppose a woman has ten silver coins,[n] but
loses one. She will light a lamp, sweep the house
and look carefully for the coin until she finds it.
[9]And when she finds it, she will call her friends
and neighbours and say, 'Be happy with me be-
cause I have found the coin that I lost.' [10]In the
same way, there is joy in the presence of the
angels of God when one sinner changes his heart
and life."

The Son Who Left Home

[11]Then Jesus said, "A man had two sons. [12]The
younger son said to his father, 'Give me my share
of the property.' So the father divided the prop-
erty between his two sons. [13]Then the younger
son gathered up all that was his and travelled far
away to another country. There he wasted his
money in foolish living. [14]After he had spent
everything, a time came when there was no food
anywhere in the country, and the son was poor

coins Roman denarii. A silver coin was the average pay for one day's work.

PRIORITIES

Too Much to Do

Andrew Bolte is a likeable boy. He's athletic, funny, good-looking and charming. In fact, when Andrew joined the youth group at church, attendance went up. He was eager to learn more about following God and making friends.

Andrew was also eager to please others. So it wasn't long before he agreed to take part in Bible study, Sunday school and other activities. After a few years, you couldn't go to any youth group event without seeing Andrew or hearing how wonderful he was. And he was a great follower of God.

As time passed, Andrew stayed active in the group. But new things came up, too. He started playing sports at school. He joined a couple of academic clubs. He got a new girlfriend. He got a job and a car.

Andrew didn't want his friends to think he had forgotten them, so he kept volunteering for jobs in the group. He got so busy, though, that he began to do them poorly, or just forgot about them.

He still comes along to the youth group occasionally. Not long ago, he came to encourage the younger ones to keep active – "Just like I am," he said.

Afterwards, Michelle commented: "Andrew is all talk and no action. He never does what he says he will. It seems pretty useless to me."

Andrew wanted to follow God, but his overloaded lifestyle got in the way. When people asked Jesus what it takes to truly follow God, he had them make some hard choices. Read Jesus' requirements in **Luke 14:25–33**.

- How is Andrew's situation like that of the king mentioned in the passage?
- What does this passage say about your priorities and following God?

Consider . . .

- listing your top five priorities in life and taping the list to your mirror. Each day, pray for the chance to follow God in those areas of your life.
- keeping a daily diary for the coming week, writing down everything you do and how long it takes. At the end of the week, compare your daily diary with your priorities. What does it say?

For more, see . . .

- Psalm 119:105–115 (p.573)
- Philippians 3:8–11 (p.1283)
- Luke 9:23–26 (p.1054)

and hungry. 15So he got a job with one of the
citizens there who sent the son into the fields to
feed pigs. 16The son was so hungry that he
wanted to eat the food the pigs were eating, but
no one gave him anything. 17When he realised
what he was doing, he thought, 'All my father's
servants have plenty of food. But I am here, al-
most dying with hunger. 18I will leave and return
to my father and say to him, "Father, I have
sinned against God and have done wrong to you.
19I am no longer worthy to be called your son,
but let me be like one of your servants." ' 20So the
son left and went to his father.

"While the son was still a long way off, his
father saw him and felt sorry for his son. So the
father ran to him and hugged and kissed him.
21The son said, 'Father, I have sinned against God
and have done wrong to you. I am no longer
worthy to be called your son.' 22But the father
said to his servants, 'Hurry! Bring the best clothes
and put them on him. Also, put a ring on his
finger and sandals on his feet. 23And get our fat
calf and kill it so we can have a feast and cele-
brate. 24My son was dead, but now he is alive
again! He was lost, but now he is found!' So they
began to celebrate.

FAMILY

Stubborn Love

Stuart sat dumbfounded at the dining room table in Alan's house. For years Alan had told stories about how he hated his mum because she didn't really care about him. Alan had accused her of trying to control him, choose his friends for him, even choose his music.

He didn't really believe that his mother loved him.

Alan's mum had wanted him to stop smoking. She told him how hurtful and addictive it can be. But Alan claimed it was all a front – his mum just wanted to control him. She got her pleasure out of ruling his life, he thought.

But now, Stuart didn't know what to believe. He knew that at least some of Alan's stories must have been true, but a quick glance around the table told him that they weren't true any more. As Alan and his mum laughed and joked, it was obvious that something – no, everything, had changed.

Stuart didn't understand it, but he liked it. Later, when the others were outside working on Alan's eighteen-speed bike, Stuart asked what had changed.

"It was amazing," Alan said. "After one of our battles, Mum and I were both really upset. She started crying, and I yelled something like, 'What do you have to cry about?' She said she was crying because she loved me, and smoking was hurting me."

"At that moment I looked at her and realised she was telling the truth. I don't know how – something just clicked inside. I realised that she really does love me. So we decided to start all over again. It hasn't been easy, but I've given up smoking. Things have got a lot better!"

Alan discovered how God's love can change things for the better. Jesus told stories that show how God's love can change people's lives. Check them out in **Luke 15:1–10**.

- How do you think the love that Jesus talked about in this passage helped Alan's relationship with his mum to change?
- What can you do to help you to feel God's love for you?

Consider . . .

- writing what you think God's love is like, then comparing your ideas with 1 Corinthians 13:4–7 (p.1232).
- reading the words of "Amazing Grace" from a hymn book. Rewrite them to fit your own family. Then sing your own song of thanks to God for his love!

For more, see . . .

- Zephaniah 3:14–17 (p.914)
- 1 John 3:1–3 (p.1373)
- John 3:16 (p.1100)

25“The older son was in the field, and as he
came closer to the house, he heard the sound of
music and dancing. 26So he called to one of the
servants and asked what all this meant. 27The
servant said, ‘Your brother has come back, and
your father killed the fat calf, because your
brother came home safely.’ 28The older son was
angry and would not go in to the feast. So his
father went out and begged him to come in.
29But the older son said to his father, ‘I have
served you like a slave for many years and have
always obeyed your commands. But you never
gave me even a young goat to have at a feast
with my friends. 30But your other son, who
wasted all your money on prostitutes,[d] comes
home, and you kill the fat calf for him!’ 31The
father said to him, ‘Son, you are always with
me, and all that I have is yours. 32We had to
celebrate and be happy because your brother
was dead, but now he is alive. He was lost, but
now he is found.’ ”

True Wealth

16 Jesus also said to his followers, “Once
there was a rich man who had a manager to take care of his business. This manager
was accused of cheating him. 2So he called the
manager in and said to him, ‘What is this I hear
about you? Give me an account of what you
have done with my money, because you can’t be
my manager any longer.’ 3The manager thought
to himself, ‘What will I do since my master is
taking my job away from me? I am not strong
enough to dig ditches, and I am too proud to
beg. 4I know what I’ll do so that when I lose my
job people will welcome me into their homes.’

REBELLION

All is Forgiven

Many years ago in Spain there was a young man called José. He often disagreed with his father’s old-fashioned ways. The two had had their differences for some time, but one day it all came to a head and they had a huge row. With much bitterness and hurt, José stormed from the house and fled to Madrid.

Neither of them could stop thinking about the other, and after many years, both José and his father wished that they could see each other, to put aside their differences and start over again, but neither could pluck up the courage to get in contact. Until one day, the father could bear it no longer. Because he didn’t know where his son was, he arranged for an advert to go in the *El Liberal* newspaper. It said: “JOSÉ, MEET ME AT THE HOTEL MONTANA, NOON, TUESDAY. ALL IS FORGIVEN, PAPA.”

The father hoped desperately that his son would be there, but he couldn’t ever have imagined what he saw that day when he arrived. Not only was his son there, but there were 800 other young men waiting!

José is such a common name in Spain that hundreds of men called José had seen the advert in the newspaper and hoped it was for them; 800 young men were desperate for forgiveness and wanted to return home to a place where they knew they were accepted and loved.

Read **Luke 15:11–32**.

- When you have an argument with someone at home, how can you prevent it becoming so severe that you feel like leaving?
- What does the father in the passage teach us that God is like? Write a list of all the characteristics of God you can see through the story.

Consider . . .

- folding a piece of paper in half and making a list on one side of the ways in which you can sometimes be like the Prodigal Son in the story. Write some words on the other side that describe how you would like to behave.
- asking God to help you be more like Jesus in your reactions to conflict and hurt.

For more, see . . .

- Daniel 9:3–19 (p.843)
- 1 John 3:1 (p.1373)
- John 3:16–21 (p.1100)

5"So the manager called in everyone who
owed the master any money. He asked the first
one, 'How much do you owe?' 6He answered,
'3,000 litres of olive oil.' The manager said to
him, 'Take your bill, sit down quickly and write
1,500 litres.' 7Then the manager asked another
one, 'How much do you owe?' He answered, '18
tonnes of wheat.' Then the manager said to him,
'Take your bill and write 14 tonnes.' 8So, the
master praised the dishonest manager for being
clever. Yes, worldly people are more clever with
their own kind than spiritual people are.
9"I tell you, make friends for yourselves using
worldly riches so that when those riches are
gone, you will be welcomed in those homes that
continue for ever. 10Whoever can be trusted with
a little can also be trusted with a lot, and whoever
is dishonest with a little is dishonest with a lot.
11If you cannot be trusted with worldly riches,
then who will trust you with true riches? 12And
if you cannot be trusted with things that belong
to someone else, who will give you things of
your own?
13"No servant can serve two masters. The ser-
vant will hate one master and love the other, or
will follow one master and refuse to follow the
other. You cannot serve both God and worldly
riches."

God's Law Cannot Be Changed

14The Pharisees,[d] who loved money, were lis-
tening to all these things and made fun of Jesus.
15He said to them, "You make yourselves look
good in front of people, but God knows what is
really in your hearts. What is important to people
is hateful in God's sight.
16"The law of Moses and the writings of the
prophets[d] were preached until John[n] came.
Since then the Good News[d] about the kingdom
of God has been told, and everyone tries to enter

John John the Baptist, who preached to people about Christ's coming (Matthew 3, Luke 3).

MONEY

Tool or Master?

Money was tight for John Wesley. When he began his ministry in the 1700s, he had to budget to survive. After making careful calculations, he determined that he would need about £40 a year to live on. Remember, this was a long time ago! Because there was little inflation during that time, John stayed on that yearly budget for the rest of his life. When he first made that decision, his annual income was about £44. John was able to give away £4 that first year.

Later in his life, after he had written several books and become a famous minister, his income often exceeded £2,000 per year. But John still held to his budget and lived on £40. He gave the rest of the money to people who needed it or to charities that would help to tell others about God's love for them.

How could John do this? Was it hard? We don't know the answers to those questions. All we do know is that at an early age John Wesley decided to make sure that money would be his servant, not his master.

John Wesley, who started the Methodist Church, understood what Jesus talks about in **Luke 16:1–13**. Read the passage to learn Jesus' view on money.

- How did John Wesley apply Jesus' teaching in this passage to his own life?
- How would heeding these verses change your spending habits?

Consider . . .

- looking through the advertisements of two or three current magazines to see what they reveal about our society's view of money and material goods. How does society's view of money compare with Jesus'?
- making a commitment to give money to a worthwhile organisation, such as Christian Aid.

For more, see . . .

- Proverbs 30:7–9 (p.616)
- James 1:9–11 (p.1348)
- Luke 16:19–31 (p.1075)

it by force. 17It would be easier for heaven and
earth to pass away than for the smallest part of a
letter in the law to be changed.

Divorce and Remarriage

18"If a man divorces his wife and marries an-
other woman, he is guilty of adultery,[d] and the
man who marries a divorced woman is also guilty
of adultery."

The Rich Man and Lazarus

19Jesus said, "There was a rich man who al-
ways dressed in the finest clothes and lived in
luxury every day. 20And a very poor man named
Lazarus, whose body was covered with sores,
was laid at the rich man's gate. 21He wanted to
eat only the small pieces of food that fell from the
rich man's table. And the dogs would come
and lick his sores. 22Later, Lazarus died, and the
angels carried him to the arms of Abraham.[d] The
rich man died, too, and was buried. 23In the place
of the dead, he was in much pain. The rich man
saw Abraham far away with Lazarus at his side.

Sidelight To say that the rich man in Luke 16:19–31 wore "the finest clothes" would indicate that the man spent a lot of money on his wardrobe. The outer clothes were purple, a sign of true wealth and royalty. Some of his clothes might have been made out of an Egyptian yellowed flax that was so luxurious it was called "woven air".

24He called, 'Father Abraham, have mercy on me!
Send Lazarus to dip his finger in water and cool
my tongue, because I am suffering in this fire!'

DECISION MAKING

But I Didn't Think . . .

Sixteen-year-old Adam was in a daze as he walked out of Mr Lloyd's English class. His friends and classmates swirled by him in a rush to get to their final exam of the day.

"How was I supposed to know all that stuff?" he asked out loud.

"Oh, come on, Adam," said his friend Guy. "You've known for weeks that our whole exam would come from *Moby Dick*. Don't act surprised now."

"Yes, but it all seemed so complicated. There were so many details!"

"Tell the truth, Adam. Have you even read the book?" he asked.

He groaned. "Of course not! You know I watched the film. It's a stupid book anyway. What do I care about Ahab and the *Pequod* or whatever? I didn't have time. I thought all I'd need was the basic plot, not every little detail."

"You know whose fault that is," sighed Guy as he left Adam by the lockers. "See you later."

Adam did know whose fault it was. If only he could turn back the clock, he thought. If only he had made the right decision. Then he could have passed.

Adam made the wrong decision, and suffered for it. Fortunately, Adam's exam was not a life-or-death matter. **Luke 16:19–31** records a story about another man's test. But this man's test had eternal consequences.

- What similarities do you think exist between Adam and the rich man in the passage?
- How was the decision that the rich man faced like the decisions you face in life?

Consider . . .

- using a concordance to find times when Jesus talked about the importance of making wise choices. Look up "wisdom", "choice", "decide" or "decision".
- listing all the decisions you are facing right now, and asking your youth leader for advice on which choices would be best.

For more, see . . .

- Proverbs 8:10–11 (p.595)
- Romans 7:15–25 (p.1193)
- Isaiah 58:3–9 (p.701)

25But Abraham said, 'Child, remember when you
were alive you had the good things in life, but bad
things happened to Lazarus. Now he is comforted
here, and you are suffering. 26Besides, there is a
big pit between you and us, so no one can cross
over to you, and no one can leave there and come
here.' 27The rich man said, 'Father, then please
send Lazarus to my father's house. 28I have five
brothers, and Lazarus could warn them so that
they will not come to this place of pain.' 29But
Abraham said, 'They have the law of Moses and
the writings of the prophets;[d] let them learn from
them.' 30The rich man said, 'No, father Abraham!
If someone goes to them from the dead, they
would believe and change their hearts and lives.'
31But Abraham said to him, 'If they will not listen
to Moses and the prophets, they will not listen to
someone who comes back from the dead.' "

Sin and Forgiveness

17 Jesus said to his followers, "Things that
cause people to sin will happen, but how
terrible for the person who causes them to hap-
pen! 2It would be better for you to be thrown into
the sea with a large stone around your neck than
to cause one of these little ones to sin. 3So be
careful!

"If another follower sins, warn him, and if he
is sorry and stops sinning, forgive him. 4If he sins
against you seven times in one day and says that
he is sorry each time, forgive him."

How Big is Your Faith?

5The apostles[d] said to the Lord, "Give us more
faith!"

6The Lord said, "If your faith were the size of
a mustard seed, you could say to this mulberry

FRIENDS

For Better or For Worse

When a man and a woman get married, they make a lot of promises to each other. One of the toughest commitments in the marriage vows is the line "for better or for worse". This promise really takes friendship and relationships to a whole other level.

But is the for-better-or-for-worse approach to relationships just for married couples? This chunk of God's word suggests it isn't!

Great friends are not the mates who agree with everything you say and just let you get on and live your life. Great friends are the people who, even when it is really hard to say it, will challenge you on some of the bad decisions you make and then stick around to help you make the right choices as well.

Martin Luther King Jr once said, "In the end, we will remember not the words of our enemies, but the silence of our friends." If our friends are making bad choices and we say nothing, then we aren't a friend at all. If our friends turn on us and we don't forgive them, then maybe we weren't a friend to begin with.

A real friend will stick with you through the best and the worst life throws at you.

Read **Luke 17:1–10**.

- What are the character qualities you look for in a friend?
- Who are the friends that have challenged you about your choices as well as supported you in the good times?

Consider . . .

- becoming accountability partners with a friend you know you can trust and will ask you tough questions about the choices you make. Someone who you really respect as a strong Christian might be a good choice.
- making a deal to meet regularly and writing a list of challenging questions you can ask each other. Promise to get help from a trusted leader or parent if a situation it is too big for you to deal with on your own.

For more, see . . .

- 1 Samuel 20:1–42 (p.274)
- James 5:19–20 (p.1354)
- Romans 1:11–12 (p.1185)

tree, ‘Dig yourself up and plant yourself in the
sea,’ and it would obey you.

Be Good Servants

7“Suppose one of you has a servant who has
been ploughing the ground or caring for the
sheep. When the servant comes in from working
in the field, would you say, ‘Come in and sit
down to eat’? 8No, you would say to him, ‘Pre-
pare something for me to eat. Then get yourself
ready and serve me. After I finish eating and
drinking, you can eat.’ 9The servant does not get
any special thanks for doing what his master com-
manded. 10It is the same with you. When you
have done everything you are told to do, you
should say, ‘We are unworthy servants; we have
only done the work we should do.’ ”

Be Thankful

11While Jesus was on his way to Jerusalem, he
was going through the area between Samaria and
Galilee. 12As he came into a small town, ten men
who had a skin disease met him there. They did
not come close to Jesus 13but called to him,
“Jesus! Master! Have mercy on us!”
14When Jesus saw the men, he said, “Go and
show yourselves to the priests.” [n]
As the ten men were going, they were
healed. 15When one of them saw that he was
healed, he went back to Jesus, praising God in a
loud voice. 16Then he bowed down at Jesus’
feet and thanked him. (And this man was a
Samaritan. [d]) 17Jesus said, “Weren’t ten men
healed? Where are the other nine? 18Is this
Samaritan the only one who came back to

show . . . priests The law of Moses said a priest must say when a Jewish person with a skin disease became well.

THANKFULNESS

Attitude of Gratitude

Bruce’s father shook his head doubtfully. “I don’t see how we can do it, son,” he said.

Bruce knew his father was right, but it still hurt to think about missing the big trip. All of the players in the jazz orchestra were looking forward to that summer trip. But Bruce’s dad had been unemployed for a while, so money was tight – too tight to allow a seventeen-year-old to go touring round Europe for a month.

As Bruce left the room, he asked God to show him a way somehow. He continued to pray about it, and not long afterwards a family in his church asked him to do some gardening. Not much, but it was something. Soon more jobs came in, mostly from families who knew that Bruce was saving his money for the trip.

All spring, Bruce was busier than he had ever been. And that summer, he went to Europe with the band. The families he had worked for had provided the means to get there.

That was a long time ago, but Bruce hasn’t forgotten those families. He’s a youth minister now, committed to helping kids find their way out of rough spots. “I know I can’t go back and thank all those families who helped me,” Bruce says. “I don’t even remember some of their names. But I feel that I can express my thanks to God for all the good things in my life by helping others.”

Sometimes we only think of thankfulness when something really special happens to us. People like Bruce, though, understand what Jesus said about always being thankful. Read Jesus’ words in **Luke 17:11–19** to get the best advice on thankfulness.

- How is Bruce like the leper who returned to Jesus?
- What things in your life make you feel like running after Jesus just to say “thanks”?

Consider . . .

- writing a letter to God, thanking him for all the good things in your life.
- keeping stamps and blank postcards handy all the time. When people do something nice for you, send them a note of thanks.

For more, see . . .

- Psalm 100 (p.558)
- 1 Thessalonians 5:15–18 (p.1301)
- Acts 3:1–10 (p.1142)

thank God?" [19]Then Jesus said to him, "Stand up and go on your way. You were healed because you believed."

Sidelight The "skin disease" described in Luke 17:11–19 is often called leprosy. It was a dreaded disease, and people who had it were isolated from other people because they were unclean (see Leviticus 13:42–46, p.112). Leprosy in the Bible isn't the same disease that we call leprosy today. It must have been some sort of dermatitis.

God's Kingdom is Within You

[20]Some of the Pharisees[d] asked Jesus, "When will the kingdom of God come?"

Jesus answered, "God's kingdom is coming, but not in a way that you will be able to see with your eyes. [21]People will not say, 'Look, here it is!' or, 'There it is!' because God's kingdom is within[n] you."

[22]Then Jesus said to his followers, "The time will come when you will want very much to see one of the days of the Son of Man.[d] But you will not see it. [23]People will say to you, 'Look, there he is!' or, 'Look, here he is!' Stay where you are; don't go away and search.

When Jesus Comes Again

[24]"When the Son of Man[d] comes again, he will shine like lightning, which flashes across the sky and lights it up from one side to the other. [25]But first he must suffer many things and be rejected by the people of this time. [26]When the Son of Man comes again, it will be as it was when Noah lived. [27]People were eating, drinking, marrying and giving their children to be married until the day Noah entered the boat. Then the flood came and killed them all. [28]It will be the same as during the time of Lot. People were eating, drinking, buying, selling, planting and building. [29]But the day Lot left Sodom,[n] fire and sulphur rained down from the sky and killed them all. [30]This is how it will be when the Son of Man comes again.

[31]"On that day, a person who is on the roof and whose belongings are in the house should not go inside to get them. A person who is in the field should not go back home. [32]Remember Lot's wife.[n] [33]Those who try to keep their lives will lose them. But those who give up their lives will save them. [34]I tell you, on that night two people will be sleeping in one bed; one will be taken and the other will be left. [35]There will be two women grinding grain together; one will be taken, and the other will be left." [36][n]

[37]The followers asked Jesus, "Where will this be, Lord?"

Jesus answered, "Where there is a dead body, there the vultures will gather."

God will Answer His People

18 Then Jesus used this story to teach his followers that they should always pray and never lose hope. [2]"In a certain town there was a judge who did not respect God or care about people. [3]In that same town there was a widow who kept coming to this judge, saying, 'Give me my rights against my enemy.' [4]For a while the judge refused to help her. But afterwards, he thought to himself, 'Even though I don't respect God or care about people, [5]I will see that she gets her rights. Otherwise she will continue to bother me until I am worn out.' "

[6]The Lord said, "Listen to what the unfair judge said. [7]God will always give what is right to his people who cry to him night and day, and he will not be slow to answer them. [8]I tell you, God will help his people quickly. But when the Son of Man[d] comes again, will he find those on earth who believe in him?"

Being Right with God

[9]Jesus told this story to some people who thought they were very good and looked down on everyone else: [10]"A Pharisee[d] and a tax collector both went to the Temple[d] to pray. [11]The Pharisee stood alone and prayed, 'God, I thank you that I am not like other people who steal, cheat or take part in adultery,[d] or even like this tax collector. [12]I give up eating[n] twice a week, and I give one-tenth of everything I earn!'

[13]"The tax collector, standing at a distance, would not even look up to heaven. But he beat on his chest because he was so sad. He said, 'God, have mercy on me, a sinner.' [14]I tell you, when this man went home, he was right with God, but

within Or "among".
Sodom A city that God destroyed because the people were so evil.
Lot's wife A story about what happened to Lot's wife is found in Genesis 19:15–17, 26.
Verse 36 A few Greek copies add verse 36: "Two people will be in the field. One will be taken, and the other will be left."
give up eating This is called "fasting". The people would give up eating for a special time of prayer and worship to God. It was also done to show sadness and disappointment.

the Pharisee was not. All who make themselves
great will be made humble, but all who make
themselves humble will be made great."

Who will Enter God's Kingdom?

15Some people brought even their babies to
Jesus so he could touch them. When the follow-
ers saw this, they told them to stop. 16But Jesus
called for the children, saying, "Let the little chil-
dren come to me. Don't stop them, because the
kingdom of God belongs to people who are like
these children. 17I tell you the truth, you must
accept the kingdom of God as if you were a child,
or you will never enter it."

A Rich Man's Question

18A certain leader asked Jesus, "Good Teacher,
what must I do to have life for ever?"
19Jesus said to him, "Why do you call me
good? Only God is good. 20You know the com-
mands: 'You must not be guilty of adultery.[d] You
must not murder anyone. You must not steal.
You must not tell lies about your neighbour.
Honour your father and mother.' "[n]
21But the leader said, "I have obeyed all these
commands since I was a boy."
22When Jesus heard this, he said to him,
"There is still one more thing you need to do. Sell
everything you have and give it to the poor, and
you will have treasure in heaven. Then come and

'You . . . mother.' Quotation from Exodus 20:12–16; Deuteronomy 5:16–20.

END TIMES

If Only . . .

Doug was full of ideas, some of them very good. Unfortunately, most of his ideas stayed in his head and never made it to reality. So, when he had the terrific idea of an outdoor concert in the middle of the park as an outreach to the local people, it sounded great. He got the church youth together and they started making posters and sending letters to other churches asking them to join in. It was exciting. Of course, they needed good weather, but apart from that it was all systems go.

The local park had a great field that sloped, so the idea was that the bands would play in the "dip" end and the audience could then sit almost tiered up the slope end. Ideal.

On the day before the concert, Doug was told that you had to have permission to play in the park, you couldn't just wander in and start setting up stages and equipment all over the place. It was a panic because he hadn't thought of writing for permission. Amazingly, he managed to gain a permit on the day, just as the bands were arriving. He came running up to everyone, holding the important piece of paper in his hand.

"Phew, that was close wasn't it?" He grinned round at everyone and suddenly noticed their grim faces.

"What?" he asked confused. "What's the matter?"

"Doug . . . ?" started one musician.

"Yes?" replied Doug.

"Where's the electricity?"

Sometimes we are so busy planning and organising that we forget the vital things. Read **Luke 17:24–30** and see how the same things happened there.

- How is the lesson that Doug learned similar to one that happened in the time of Lot?

Consider . . .

- how you would change your lifestyle if you knew Christ's return was imminent.
- asking your youth leader to prepare a session on the events that point to Christ's return.

For more, see . . .

- Luke 21:34–36 (p.1087)
- 1 Thessalonians 5:1–6 (p.1300)
- Romans 13:1–14 (p.1206)

follow me." 23But when the man heard this, he
became very sad, because he was very rich.
24Jesus looked at him and said, "It is very hard
for rich people to enter the kingdom of God. 25It
is easier for a camel to go through the eye of a
needle than for a rich person to enter the king-
dom of God."

Who Can Be Saved?

26When the people heard this, they asked,
"Then who can be saved?"
27Jesus answered, "God can do things that are
not possible for people to do."
28Peter said, "Look, we have left everything
and followed you."
29Jesus said, "I tell you the truth, all those who
have left houses, wives, brothers, parents or chil-
dren for the kingdom of God 30will get much
more in this life. And in the age that is coming,
they will have life for ever."

Jesus will Rise from the Dead

31Then Jesus took the twelve apostles[d] aside
and said to them, "We are going to Jerusalem.
Everything the prophets[d] wrote about the Son of
Man[d] will happen. 32He will be turned over to
those who are not Jews. They will laugh at him,
insult him, spit on him, 33beat him with whips
and kill him. But on the third day, he will rise to
life again." 34The apostles did not understand
this; the meaning was hidden from them, and
they did not realise what was said.

Jesus Heals a Blind Man

35As Jesus came near the city of Jericho, a blind
man was sitting beside the road, begging. 36When

BOASTING

Maximum Ruler

In October 1989, pictures of General Manuel Noriega shaking his fist at the world made headlines everywhere. As dictator of the country of Panama, he'd just thwarted an attempt to remove him from power. Some reports suggested that he tortured and murdered as many as 75 rebel soldiers after the attempted coup.

Noriega controlled the Panamanian government arrogantly, as though he owned it. He held mock elections in which his people frightened voters away. He reportedly financed his lifestyle through illegal drug trafficking and commonly mocked and belittled his enemies.

In December, his arrogance reached its peak. He boasted that he was Panama's "maximum leader", daring anyone to disagree.

That month the USA invaded Panama and removed Noriega from power. Within days, he was on his way to face drugs charges in a Florida courtroom.

On New Year's Day, the world again saw Manuel Noriega's picture in the headlines. This time, though, the pictures showed a handcuffed man dressed in prison clothes being taken away to prison.

Jesus talked about how God views boastful and conceited people. Read what he said in **Luke 18:9–14**.

- What attitude did both General Noriega and the Pharisee display?
- How can pride interfere in your relationship with Christ?

Consider . . .

- finding "pride" in a dictionary and thinking about what part pride plays in boasting.
- writing the second half of Luke 18:14 on a postcard and placing it on your mirror as an encouragement to avoid arrogance.

For more, see . . .

- Jeremiah 9:23–24 (p.728)
- James 4:13–17 (p.1352)
- 1 Corinthians 4:6–7 (p.1219)

he heard the people coming down the road, he
asked, "What is happening?"
37They told him, "Jesus, from Nazareth, is go-
ing by."
38The blind man cried out, "Jesus, Son of
David, [d] have mercy on me!"
39The people leading the group warned the
blind man to be quiet. But the blind man shouted
even more, "Son of David, have mercy on me!"
40Jesus stopped and ordered the blind man to
be brought to him. When he came near, Jesus
asked him, 41"What do you want me to do for
you?"
He said, "Lord, I want to see."
42Jesus said to him, "Then see. You are healed
because you believed."
43At once the man was able to see, and he
followed Jesus, thanking God. All the people who
saw this praised God.

Zacchaeus Meets Jesus

19 Jesus was going through the city of
Jericho. 2A man was there named
Zacchaeus, who was a very important tax collec-
tor, and he was wealthy. 3He wanted to see who
Jesus was, but he was not able because he was
too short to see above the crowd. 4He ran ahead
to a place where Jesus would come, and he
climbed a sycamore tree so he could see him.
5When Jesus came to that place, he looked up
and said to him, "Zacchaeus, hurry and come
down! I must stay at your house today."

HOLY SPIRIT

Get Changed!

Christina grew up in a very tough and poor neighbourhood. From a young age, the hardship of her situation and the abuse she endured made Christina very vulnerable to anyone who offered her any kind of attention. In her late teens, she was offered attention by a guy who ended up forcing her to be a prostitute. Long after he had "got rid of her", Christina continued to work as a prostitute because her self-esteem was so low and she thought she didn't have any other way of earning a living. She had also tried to commit suicide and regularly wished she would die.

Then one day Christina met Jesus – "Jesus" in the form of a lady named Sarah. Sarah invited Christina to share a meal at the local café with her. When Christina spoke to her new friend she felt, for the first time, that she was loved and accepted for who she was, not what she could offer. Their friendship grew and Christina quickly realised that Sarah simply wanted to support and love her to a better life.

Christina asked Sarah a lot of questions about her faith and over time realised that Sarah's unconditional friendship was driven by her faith in God. Christina decided she wanted to get to know God as well and so, with Sarah's help, prayed a prayer asking God to change who she was from the inside out. Over time, the Holy Spirit transformed Christina into a woman who had deep confidence and real healing from all the hurts she had experienced.

Christina now teaches Sunday school at her church because she wants to help children to understand that God loves and cares for each of them and can change their lives into a life that is worth living.

Read **Luke 19:1–10**.

- What are the similarities between Zacchaeus and Christina?
- What are the similarities between Jesus and Sarah?

Consider . . .

- writing down some of the things that you do, think and say that you aren't so proud of. Ask the Holy Spirit to change you from the inside out and to help you live a life worth living, then tear up your list and throw it away.
- encouraging someone you know who is trying to change.

For more, see . . .

- Romans 12:1–3 (p.1203)
- Hebrews 11:1–3 (p.1341)
- 2 Corinthians 3:17–18 (p.1242)

Sidelight Asking to stay at Zacchaeus' house, as Jesus did in Luke 19:1–10, would have been seen as scandalous. As a tax collector, Zacchaeus was thought of as a thief or a swindler. Many tax collectors would charge more than the fair amount and keep the "profits" for themselves – a practice approved by the Roman government.

6Zacchaeus came down quickly and wel-
comed him gladly. 7All the people saw this and
began to complain, "Jesus is staying with a
sinner!"
8But Zacchaeus stood and said to the Lord, "I
will give half of my possessions to the poor. And
if I have cheated anyone, I will pay back four
times more."
9Jesus said to him, "Salvation has come to this
house today, because this man also belongs to
the family of Abraham. 10The Son of Man[d] came
to find lost people and save them."

A Story About Three Servants

11As the people were listening to this, Jesus
told them a story because he was near Jerusalem
and they thought God's kingdom would appear
immediately. 12He said: "A very important man
went to a country far away to be made a king and
then to return home. 13So he called ten of his
servants and gave a gold coin[n] to each servant.
He said, 'Do business with this money until I get
back.' 14But the people in the kingdom hated the

coin A Greek "mina". One mina was enough money to pay a person for three months work.

MONEY

Share and Share Alike

The minister had been giving his sermon as usual on Sunday. It was the story of the three servants, an amusing biblical incident in which a king distributed money to servants and then told them to go away and make more money with it. Graeme was waving his arms about, really getting into the story, happy that his congregation were "with him". They were nodding and agreeing in their seats as he expounded on the results of the servants' money-making escapades.

Then he looked up and said, "Now I would like all the church members to come forward." The members were used to his antics, and thought he was going to get them to act out part of the story. But instead, he came down from the pulpit and proceeded to go along the line giving them all a £10 note! They looked amazed and stupefied as he said,

"OK, now you have your money, I would like you to use it wisely over the next six months and we'll meet again and see how much money you have raised towards the new church building!"

It actually had a stunning effect on everyone, and when they did finally meet up again they had made a serious amount of money!

Some of the older ladies had bought fruit and sugar with their money, and made huge amounts of jam, which they sold in great quantities. Some teenagers had bought ladders, sponges and buckets between them and started up a window-cleaning business. And some of the men had bought shares and watched them go up!

Luke 19:11–27 shows us there is nothing wrong with making money. It's what we do with it that counts.

- What would you do if you had been given £10 in these circumstances?
- What does God expect you to do with the gifts he has given you, according to this passage?

Consider . . .

- evaluating how thoughtfully you spend your money.
- ways you can use what God has given you – be it money or talent – to make the best use of it.

For more, see . . .

- Ecclesiastes 5:10–17 (p.625)
- Acts 4:32–35 (p.1144)
- Matthew 6:31–33 (p.949)

man. So they sent a group to follow him and say, ‘We don’t want this man to be our king.’

15“But the man became king. When he returned home, he said, “Call those servants who have my money so I can know how much they earned with it.’

16“The first servant came and said, ‘Sir, I earned ten bags of money with the one you gave me.’ 17The king said to the servant, ‘Excellent! You are a good servant. Since I can trust you with small things, I will let you rule over ten of my cities.’

18“The second servant said, ‘Sir, I earned five bags of money with your one.’ 19The king said to this servant, ‘You can rule over five cities.’

20“Then another servant came in and said to the king, ‘Sir, here is your bag of money which I wrapped in a piece of cloth and hid. 21I was afraid of you, because you are a hard man. You even take money that you didn’t earn and gather food that you didn’t plant.’ 22Then the king said to the servant, ‘I will condemn you by your own words, you evil servant. You knew that I am a hard man, taking money that I didn’t earn and gathering food that I didn’t plant. 23Why then didn’t you put my money in the bank? Then when I came back, my money would have earned some interest.’

24“The king said to the men who were standing by, ‘Take the bag of money away from this servant and give it to the servant who earned ten bags of money.’ 25They said, ‘But sir, that servant already has ten bags of money.’ 26The king said, ‘Those who have will be given more, but those who do not have anything will have everything taken away from them. 27Now where are my enemies who didn’t want me to be king? Bring them here and kill them before me.’”

Jesus Enters Jerusalem as a King

28After Jesus said this, he went on towards Jerusalem. 29As Jesus came near Bethphage and Bethany, towns near the hill called the Mount of Olives,[d] he sent out two of his followers. 30He said, “Go to the town you can see there. When you enter it, you will find a colt tied there, which no one has ever ridden. Untie it and bring it here to me. 31If anyone asks you why you are untying it, say that the Master needs it.”

32The two followers went into town and found the colt just as Jesus had told them. 33As they were untying it, its owners came out and asked the followers, “Why are you untying our colt?”

34The followers answered, “The Master needs it.” 35So they brought it to Jesus, threw their coats on the colt’s back, and put Jesus on it. 36As Jesus rode towards Jerusalem, others spread their coats on the road before him.

37As he was coming close to Jerusalem, on the way down the Mount of Olives, the whole crowd of followers began joyfully shouting praise to God for all the miracles[d] they had seen. 38They said,

“God bless the king who comes in the name
of the Lord! *Psalm 118:26*
There is peace in heaven and glory to God!”

39Some of the Pharisees[d] in the crowd said to Jesus, “Teacher, tell your followers not to say these things.”

40But Jesus answered, “I tell you, if my followers didn’t say these things, then the stones would cry out.”

Jesus Cries for Jerusalem

41As Jesus came near Jerusalem, he saw the city and cried for it, 42saying, “I wish you knew today what would bring you peace. But now it is hidden from you. 43The time is coming when your enemies will build a wall around you and will hold you in on all sides. 44They will destroy you and all your people, and not one stone will be left on another. All this will happen because you did not recognise the time when God came to save you.”

Jesus Goes to the Temple

45Jesus went into the Temple[d] and began to throw out the people who were selling things there. 46He said, “It is written in the Scriptures,[d] ‘My Temple will be a house for prayer.’[n] But you have changed it into a ‘hideout for robbers’!”[n]

47Jesus taught in the Temple every day. The leading priests, the experts on the law and some of the leaders of the people wanted to kill Jesus. 48But they did not know how they could do it, because all the people were listening closely to him.

Jewish Leaders Question Jesus

20 One day Jesus was in the Temple,[d] teaching the people and telling them the Good News.[d] The leading priests, teachers of the law and Jewish elders came up to talk with him, 2saying, “Tell us what authority you have to do these things? Who gave you this authority?”

3Jesus answered, “I will also ask you a question. Tell me: 4when John baptised people, was that authority from God or just from other people?”

5They argued about this, saying, “If we answer, ‘John’s baptism was from God,’ Jesus will say, ‘Then why did you not believe him?’ 6But if we say, ‘It was from other people,’ all the people will stone us to death, because they believe John

‘My Temple . . . prayer.’ Quotation from Isaiah 56:7.
‘hideout for robbers’ Quotation from Jeremiah 7:11.

was a prophet." [d] 7So they answered that they
didn't know where it came from.
8Jesus said to them, "Then I won't tell you
what authority I have to do these things."

A Story About God's Son

9Then Jesus told the people this story: "A man
planted a vineyard and leased it to some farmers.
Then he went away for a long time. 10When it
was time for the grapes to be picked, he sent a ser-
vant to the farmers to get some of the grapes. But
they beat the servant and sent him away empty-
handed. 11Then he sent another servant. They
beat this servant also, and showed no respect for
him, and sent him away empty-handed. 12So the
man sent a third servant. The farmers wounded
him and threw him out. 13The owner of the vine-
yard said, 'What will I do now? I will send my son
whom I love. Maybe they will respect him.' 14But
when the farmers saw the son, they said to each
other, 'This son will inherit the vineyard. If we kill
him, it will be ours.' 15So the farmers threw the
son out of the vineyard and killed him.

"What will the owner of this vineyard do to
them? 16He will come and kill those farmers and
will give the vineyard to other farmers."

When the people heard this story, they said,
"Let this never happen!"
17But Jesus looked at them and said, "Then
what does this verse mean:

'The stone that the builders rejected
became the cornerstone'? [d] *Psalm 118:22*

18Everyone who falls on that stone will be bro-
ken, and the person on whom it falls, that person
will be crushed!"
19The teachers of the law and the leading
priests wanted to arrest Jesus at once, because
they knew the story was about them. But they
were afraid of what the people would do.

Is It Right to Pay Taxes or Not?

20So they watched Jesus and sent some spies
who acted as if they were sincere. They wanted to
trap Jesus into saying something wrong so they
could hand him over to the authority and power of
the governor. 21So the spies asked Jesus, "Teacher,

EVIL

Grim Snapshots

A three-year-old is taken from a shopping centre and murdered. Soon after, on the day before Mother's Day, another small child is killed in another shopping centre, this time by an IRA bomb . . .

A "joy rider" kills a ten-year-old girl delivering a birthday card . . .

When Colin discovered that he was adopted, he set about trying to locate his true parents. When at last he finally found his mother, she told him that she hated him and never wanted to see his face again . . .

When two teenage girls got bored, they broke into the home of an elderly lady, tortured and killed her . . .

Let's face it, evil happens. Many people try to sweep it under the rug and pretend that it doesn't exist – but it does.

Jesus never denied that the world is full of evil, but he always pointed out that God is triumphant over it. In **Luke 20:9–19**, Jesus tells a parable about the way God's triumph over evil will come about.

- What motivates people to abuse each other as they did both in the Bible story and in the snapshots above?
- How do you see God's power conquering evil in the passage that you have just read?

Consider . . .

- thanking God that he knows what the world is really like, and that he will one day get rid of evil for ever.
- praying about any situations that you come across which are obvious examples of evil in the world.

For more, see . . .

- Proverbs 24:19–20 (p.611)
- Romans 12:17–21 (p.1205)
- Matthew 21:33–43 (p.978)

we know that what you say and teach is true. You
pay no attention to who people are, and you al-
ways teach the truth about God's way. 22Tell us, is
it right for us to pay taxes to Caesar[d] or not?"
23But Jesus, knowing they were trying to trick
him, said, 24"Show me a silver coin.[n] Whose
image and name are on it?"
They said, "Caesar's."
25Jesus said to them, "Then give to Caesar the
things that are Caesar's, and give to God the
things that are God's."
26So they were not able to trap Jesus into any-
thing he said in the presence of the people. And
being amazed at his answer, they became silent.

Sidelight The Sadducees – who didn't believe in the resurrection of the dead (Luke 20:27) – were major rivals of the Pharisees in Jesus' time. In later years, the Sadducees were often considered heretics by other Jews.

Some Sadducees Try to Trick Jesus

27Some Sadducees,[d] who believed people
would not rise from the dead, came to Jesus.
28They asked, "Teacher, Moses wrote that if a
man's brother dies and leaves a wife but no chil-
dren, then that man must marry the widow and
have children for his brother. 29Once there were
seven brothers. The first brother married and
died, but had no children. 30Then the second
brother married the widow, and he died. 31And
the third brother married the widow, and he
died. The same thing happened with all seven
brothers; they died and had no children.
32Finally, the woman died also. 33Since all seven
brothers had married her, whose wife will she be
when people rise from the dead?"
34Jesus said to them, "On earth, people marry
and are given to someone to marry. 35But those
who will be worthy to be raised from the dead
and live again will not marry, nor will they
be given to someone to marry. 36In that life
they are like angels and cannot die. They are
children of God, because they have been raised
from the dead. 37Even Moses clearly showed
that the dead are raised to life. When he wrote
about the burning bush,[n] he said that the Lord
is 'the God of Abraham, the God of Isaac and
the God of Jacob.'[n] 38God is the God of the
living, not the dead, because all people are alive
to him."
39Some of the teachers of the law said,
"Teacher, your answer was good." 40No one was
brave enough to ask him another question.

Is the Christ the Son of David?

41Then Jesus said, "Why do people say that
the Christ[d] is the Son of David?[d] 42In the book of
Psalms, David himself says:

'The LORD said to my Lord:
Sit by me at my right side,
43 until I put your enemies under your
control.'[n] *Psalm 110:1*

44David calls the Christ 'Lord', so how can the
Christ be his son?"

Jesus Accuses Some Leaders

45While all the people were listening, Jesus said
to his followers, 46"Beware of the teachers of the
law. They like to walk around wearing fancy
clothes, and they love people to greet them with
respect in the market-places. They love to have
the most important seats in the synagogues[d] and
at feasts. 47But they cheat widows and steal their
houses and then try to make themselves look
good by saying long prayers. They will receive a
greater punishment."

True Giving

21 As Jesus looked up, he saw some rich
people putting their gifts into the Tem-
ple[d] money box.[n] 2Then he saw a poor widow
putting two small copper coins into the box. 3He
said, "I tell you the truth, this poor widow gave
more than all those rich people. 4They gave only
what they did not need. This woman is very poor,
but she gave all she had to live on."

The Temple will Be Destroyed

5Some people were talking about the Temple[d]
and how it was decorated with beautiful stones
and gifts offered to God.
But Jesus said, 6"As for these things you are
looking at, the time will come when not one
stone will be left on another. Every stone will be
thrown down."
7They asked Jesus, "Teacher, when will these
things happen? What will be the sign that they
are about to take place?"
8Jesus said, "Be careful so you are not fooled.
Many people will come in my name, saying, 'I am

coin Roman denarii. A silver coin was the average pay for one day's work.
burning bush Read Exodus 3:1–12 in the Old Testament.
'the God of . . . Jacob' These words are taken from Exodus 3:6.
until . . . control Literally, "until I make your enemies a footstool for your feet".
money box A special box in the Jewish place of worship where people put their gifts to God.

the One' and, 'The time has come!' But don't
follow them. 9When you hear about wars and
riots, don't be afraid, because these things must
happen first, but the end will come later."
10Then he said to them, "Nations will fight
against other nations, and kingdoms against other
kingdoms. 11In various places there will be great
earthquakes, sicknesses and a lack of food. Fear-
ful events and great signs will come from heaven.
12"But before all these things happen, people
will arrest you and treat you cruelly. They will
judge you in their synagogues[d] and put you in jail
and force you to stand before kings and governors,
because you follow me. 13But this will give you an
opportunity to tell about me. 14Make up your
minds not to worry ahead of time about what you
will say. 15I will give you the wisdom to say things
that none of your enemies will be able to stand
against or prove wrong. 16Even your parents,
brothers, relatives and friends will turn against
you, and they will kill some of you. 17All people
will hate you because you follow me. 18But none
of these things can really harm you. 19By continu-
ing to have faith you will save your lives.

Jerusalem will Be Destroyed

20"When you see armies all around Jerusalem,
you will know it will soon be destroyed. 21At
that time, the people in Judea should run away
to the mountains. The people in Jerusalem must
get out, and those who are near the city should
not go in. 22These are the days of punishment to
bring about all that is written in the Scriptures.[d]
23How terrible it will be for women who are
pregnant or have nursing babies! Great trouble
will come upon this land, and God will be angry
with these people. 24They will be killed by the
sword and taken as prisoners to all nations.
Jerusalem will be crushed by non-Jewish people
until their time is over.

PEER PRESSURE

Friends in Deed

Luke was studying for his exams when he learned that he had cancer. He was told that he would have to undergo painful chemotherapy.

For Luke the pain was even harder to take knowing that the treatment would make his hair fall out. Would he fit in at school? What would his friends say? Would they avoid him because they were embarrassed by his baldness? Would he be laughed at and mocked? He knew that his classmates' reactions could make having the awful disease even more unbearable.

What he didn't know – but soon discovered – was that his friends really cared. To make sure that Luke would fit in, his eight best friends all shaved their heads.

A stranger to the area might have wondered why nine students at the college had suddenly become skinheads. But one of those bald heads knew the power of positive peer pressure. That makes all the difference.

Peer pressure can be good or bad. The Bible talks about a negative sort of peer pressure that many Christians will face. Read **Luke 21:5–19**, especially verse 16, to find out more about it.

- Luke faced rejection at school. How will Christians face rejection by the world, according to this passage?
- What encouragement does this passage give you to stand up to pressure from people who try to get you to compromise what you believe?

Consider . . .

- making a list of pressures that challenge your relationships with God and your friends, then asking your youth leader for advice on how to overcome those pressures.
- making a pact with your friends always to encourage each other to follow God.

For more, see . . .

- 1 Samuel 20:28–42 (p.274)
- 1 Corinthians 15:33 (p.1236)
- Matthew 10:16–23 (p.955)

Don't Fear

25“There will be signs in the sun, moon
and stars. On earth, nations will be afraid and
confused because of the roar and fury of the sea.
26People will be so afraid they will faint, wonder-
ing what is happening to the world, because the
powers of the heavens will be shaken. 27Then peo-
ple will see the Son of Man[d] coming in a cloud
with power and great glory. 28When these things
begin to happen, look up and hold your heads high,
because the time when God will free you is near!”

Jesus' Words will Live for Ever

29Then Jesus told this story: “Look at the fig
tree and all the other trees. 30When their leaves
appear, you know that summer is near. 31In the
same way, when you see these things happening,
you will know that God's kingdom is near.

32“I tell you the truth, all these things will hap-
pen while the people of this time are still living.
33Earth and sky will be destroyed, but the words
I have spoken will never be destroyed.

Be Ready All the Time

34“Be careful not to spend your time feasting,
drinking or worrying about worldly things. If you
do, that day might come on you suddenly, 35like a
trap on all people on earth. 36So be ready all the
time. Pray that you will be strong enough to es-
cape all these things that will happen and that you
will be able to stand before the Son of Man.”[d]

37During the day, Jesus taught the people in
the Temple,[d] and at night he went out of the city
and stayed on the Mount of Olives.[d] 38Every
morning all the people got up early to go to the
Temple to listen to him.

Judas Becomes an Enemy of Jesus

22 It was almost time for the Feast[d] of Un-
leavened Bread, called the Passover[d]
Feast. 2The leading priests and teachers of the law
were trying to find a way to kill Jesus, because
they were afraid of the people.

3Satan entered Judas Iscariot, one of Jesus'
twelve apostles.[d] 4Judas went to the leading
priests and some of the soldiers who guarded the
Temple[d] and talked to them about a way to hand
Jesus over to them. 5They were pleased and
agreed to give Judas money. 6He agreed and
watched for the best time to hand Jesus over to
them when he was away from the crowd.

Jesus Eats the Passover Meal

7The Day of Unleavened[d] Bread came when
the Passover[d] lambs had to be sacrificed. 8Jesus
said to Peter and John, “Go and prepare the
Passover meal for us to eat.”

9They asked, “Where do you want us to pre-
pare it?” 10Jesus said to them, “After you go into
the city, a man carrying a jar of water will meet
you. Follow him into the house that he enters,
11and tell the owner of the house, ‘The Teacher
asks where is the guest room in which I may eat
the Passover meal with my followers?’ 12Then he
will show you a large, furnished room upstairs.
Prepare the Passover meal there.”

13So Peter and John left and found everything
as Jesus had said. And they prepared the Passover
meal.

The Lord's Supper

14When the time came, Jesus and the apostles[d]
were sitting at the table. 15He said to them, “I
wanted very much to eat this Passover[d] meal
with you before I suffer. 16I will not eat another
Passover meal until it is given its true meaning in
the kingdom of God.”

17Then Jesus took a cup, gave thanks and said,
“Take this cup and share it among yourselves. 18I
will not drink again from the fruit of the vine[n]
until God's kingdom comes.”

19Then Jesus took some bread, gave thanks,
broke it and gave it to the apostles, saying, “This
is my body, which I am giving for you. Do this to
remember me.” 20In the same way, after supper,
Jesus took the cup and said, “This cup is the new
agreement that God makes with his people. This
new agreement begins with my blood which is
poured out for you.

Who will Turn Against Jesus?

21“But one of you will turn against me, and his
hand is with mine on the table. 22What God has
planned for the Son of Man[d] will happen, but
how terrible it will be for that one who turns
against the Son of Man.”

23Then the apostles[d] asked each other which
one of them would do that.

Be like a Servant

24The apostles[d] also began to argue about which
one of them was the most important. 25But Jesus
said to them, “The kings of the non-Jewish people
rule over them, and those who have authority over
others like to be called ‘friends of the people’. 26But
you must not be like that. Instead, the greatest
among you should be like the youngest, and the
leader should be like the servant. 27Who is more
important: the one sitting at the table or the one
serving? You think the one at the table is more
important, but I am like a servant among you.

28“You have stayed with me through my strug-
gles. 29Just as my Father has given me a kingdom,

fruit of the vine Product of the grapevine; this may also be translated “wine”.

I also give you a kingdom 30 so you may eat and
drink at my table in my kingdom. And you will sit
on thrones, judging the twelve tribes [d] of Israel.

Don't Lose Your Faith!

31 "Simon, Simon, Satan has asked to test all
of you as a farmer tests his wheat. 32 I have prayed
that you will not lose your faith! Help your
brothers be stronger when you come back to me."
33 But Peter said to Jesus, "Lord, I am ready to
go with you to prison and even to die with you!"
34 But Jesus said, "Peter, before the cockerel
crows this day, you will say three times that you
don't know me."

Be Ready for Trouble

35 Then Jesus said to the apostles, [d] "When I
sent you out without a purse, a bag or sandals,
did you need anything?"
They said, "No."
36 He said to them, "But now if you have a
purse or a bag, carry that with you. If you don't
have a sword, sell your coat and buy one. 37 The
Scripture [d] says, 'He was treated like a criminal,' [n]
and I tell you this scripture must come true. It
was written about me, and it is happening now."
38 His followers said, "Look, Lord, here are
two swords."
He said to them, "That is enough."

Jesus Prays Alone

39 Jesus left the city and went to the Mount of
Olives, [d] as he often did, and his followers went
with him. 40 When he reached the place, he said
to them, "Pray for strength against temptation."
41 Then Jesus went about a stone's throw away
from them. He kneeled down and prayed,
42 "Father, if you are willing, take away this cup [n]
of suffering. But do what you want, not what I
want." 43 Then an angel from heaven appeared to

'He . . . criminal' Quotation from Isaiah 53:12.
cup Jesus is talking about the terrible things that will happen to him. Accepting these things will be hard, like drinking a cup of something bitter.

JEALOUSY

When Others Succeed

"Few men have the strength to honour a friend's success without envy." – Aeschylus

"Lots of people know a good thing the minute the other fellow sees it first." – Job E. Hedges

"The man who keeps busy helping the man below him won't have time to envy the man above him – and there may not be anybody above him anyway." – Henrietta C. Mears

"The greatest among you should be like the youngest, and the leader should be like the servant." – Jesus Christ

For more about what Jesus said to his jealous disciples – who were arguing about prestige – read **Luke 22:24–30**.

- What similarities and differences are there between what Jesus said and what these famous people said about jealousy?
- How are you like and unlike the disciples in the passage? What would Jesus say to you?

Consider . . .

- stopping yourself next time you feel jealous of someone. Instead, do an act of service for that person.
- setting three goals for the coming week that will help you to overcome jealous feelings you have towards someone you know.

For more, see . . .

- Genesis 37:2–28 (p.42)
- 1 Samuel 18:6–11 (p.272)
- 1 Peter 2:1 (p.1357)

him to strengthen him. 44Being full of pain, Jesus
prayed even harder. His sweat was like drops of
blood falling to the ground. 45When he finished
praying, he went to his followers and found them
asleep because of their sadness. 46Jesus said to
them, "Why are you sleeping? Get up and pray
for strength against temptation."

Jesus is Arrested

47While Jesus was speaking, a crowd came up,
and Judas, one of the twelve apostles,[d] was leading
them. He came close to Jesus so he could kiss him.
48But Jesus said to him, "Judas, are you using
a kiss to give the Son of Man[d] to his enemies?"
49When those who were standing around him
saw what was happening, they said, "Lord,
should we strike them with our swords?" 50And
one of them struck the servant of the high priest
and cut off his right ear.
51Jesus said, "Stop! No more of this." Then he
touched the servant's ear and healed him.
52Those who came to arrest Jesus were the
leading priests, the soldiers who guarded the
Temple[d] and the older Jewish leaders. Jesus said
to them, "You came out here with swords and
clubs as though I were a criminal. 53I was with
you every day in the Temple, and you didn't ar-
rest me there. But this is your time—the time
when darkness rules."

Peter Says He Doesn't Know Jesus

54They arrested Jesus, and led him away, and
brought him into the house of the high priest. Peter
followed far behind them. 55After the soldiers
started a fire in the middle of the courtyard and sat
together, Peter sat with them. 56A servant girl saw
Peter sitting there in the light, and looking closely
at him, she said, "This man was also with him."
57But Peter said this was not true; he said,
"Woman, I don't know him."
58A short time later, another person saw Peter
and said, "You are also one of them."

GOD'S WILL

Daring to Follow

Bruce Olson believed strongly that God wanted him to live with the savage Motilone Indians in the jungles of South America. So this shy boy set out to find them.

The Motilones were an isolated and fierce group. They hated white people and had killed or wounded all those who tried to contact them. Bruce's first encounter with them came when they shot an arrow through his thigh. Then they captured him and forced him to walk for hours to their village.

The months that followed were filled with pain, hunger and loneliness. But Bruce wouldn't give up. God had sent him. Eventually Bruce learned the Motilones' language and began communicating with his captors. They called him "Bruchko".

The Motilones have now come to love and respect Bruchko. Through him many people have met Jesus and have benefited from Bruchko's medical and agricultural expertise.

Bruce knew what God wanted him to do, and he wouldn't stop until he had accomplished it.

Jesus also refused to give up on God's will. Read about his experience in **Luke 22:39–46**, when he prayed the night before he was to suffer beatings and a cruel death.

- Knowing it would be hard, why do you think both Jesus and Bruchko insisted on following God's leadership?
- Jesus followed God's will all his life. What makes following God's will possible even when it's tough for you?

Consider . . .

- placing an object in your room that will remind you to seek God's desires.
- reading Bruce Olson's autobiography, entitled *Bruchko.*

For more, see . . .

- Psalm 143:8–11 (p.583)
- Mark 14:32–42 (p.1027)
- Matthew 26:36–46 (p.990)

But Peter said, "Man, I am not!"
59About an hour later, another man insisted,
"Certainly this man was with him, because he is
from Galilee, too."
60But Peter said, "Man, I don't know what you
are talking about!"
At once, while Peter was still speaking, a cock-
erel crowed. 61Then the Lord turned and looked
straight at Peter. And Peter remembered what
the Lord had said: "Before the cockerel crows this
day, you will say three times that you don't know
me." 62Then Peter went outside and cried bitterly.

The People Make Fun of Jesus

63The men who were guarding Jesus began
making fun of him and beating him.
64They blindfolded him and said, "Prove that
you are a prophet,[d] and tell us who hit you."
65They said many cruel things to Jesus.

Jesus Before the Leaders

66When day came, the council of the elders
of the people, both the leading priests and the
teachers of the law, came together and led Jesus
to their highest court. 67They said, "If you are
the Christ,[d] tell us."
Jesus said to them, "If I tell you, you will not
believe me. 68And if I ask you, you will not an-
swer. 69But from now on, the Son of Man[d] will
sit at the right hand of the powerful God."
70They all said, "Then are you the Son of God?"
Jesus said to them, "You say that I am."
71They said, "Why do we need witnesses
now? We ourselves heard him say this."

Pilate Questions Jesus

23 Then the whole group stood up and led
Jesus to Pilate.[n] 2They began to accuse
Jesus, saying, "We caught this man telling things

Pilate Pontius Pilate was the Roman governor of Judea from AD 26 to AD 36.

SUFFERING

The Price of Goals

In West Perrine, Florida, USA, Lee Lawrence had a dream.

"Can you imagine," he said, "all the churches in the neighbourhood . . . marching up Homestead Avenue to let the drug pushers know that we won't take it any more?"

The drug dealers didn't like Lee or his vision. Twice he was shot at while getting out of his car. The grocery shop he owned was vandalised; then someone tried to burn it down. Refusing to give up, Lee got several pushers arrested. His store became a drug-free haven for the neighbourhood kids.

In March 1989, Lee walked outside his shop and was met by a man firing a semi-automatic rifle. The first shot knocked Lee to the ground. A second man shot Lee again as he lay on the pavement. Minutes later he was dead. But his vision was not.

On Lee Lawrence's funeral day, more than 3,000 people from area churches linked arms and marched up Homestead Avenue singing, "We shall overcome: drugs and crime must go!"

It was a dream come true – and the start of big changes in West Perrine.

Lee was willing to face hardship – even death – to see his goal become a reality. Jesus also endured hardship because of his mission to reclaim humanity from sin. Read about it in **Luke 22:63–71**.

- What price were both Lee and Jesus willing to pay to see their goals become reality?
- How was Jesus' response in this passage like the way you respond when others attack your faith? How is your response different from Jesus'?

Consider . . .

- writing down three goals you would be willing to suffer for.
- looking through a newspaper to find three people who are suffering for doing right, and praying for them each day this week.

For more, see . . .

- Exodus 3:6–10 (p.61)
- 1 Peter 2:18–25 (p.1359)
- Mark 14:62–65 (p.1028)

that mislead our people. He says that we should not pay taxes to Caesar,[d] and he calls himself the Christ,[d] a king."

3Pilate asked Jesus, "Are you the king of the Jews?"

Jesus answered, "Those are your words."

4Pilate said to the leading priests and the people, "I find nothing against this man."

5They were insisting, saying, "But Jesus makes trouble with the people, teaching all around Judea. He began in Galilee, and now he is here."

Pilate Sends Jesus to Herod

6Pilate heard this and asked if Jesus was from Galilee. 7Since Jesus was under Herod's authority, Pilate sent Jesus to Herod, who was in Jerusalem at that time. 8When Herod saw Jesus, he was very glad, because he had heard about Jesus and had wanted to meet him for a long time. He was hoping to see Jesus work a miracle.[d] 9Herod asked Jesus many questions, but Jesus said nothing. 10The leading priests and teachers of the law were standing there, strongly accusing Jesus. 11After Herod and his soldiers had made fun of Jesus, they dressed him in a kingly robe and sent him back to Pilate. 12In the past, Pilate and Herod had always been enemies, but on that day they became friends.

Jesus Must Die

13Pilate called the people together with the leading priests and the Jewish leaders. 14He said to them, "You brought this man to me, saying he makes trouble among the people. But I have questioned him before you all, and I have not found him guilty of what you say. 15Also, Herod found nothing wrong with him; he sent him back to us. Look, he has done nothing for which he should die. 16So, after I punish him, I will let him go free." 17 [n]

18But the people shouted together, "Take this man away! Let Barabbas go free!" 19(Barabbas was a man who was in prison for his part in a riot in the city and for murder.)

20Pilate wanted to let Jesus go free and told this to the crowd. 21But they shouted again, "Crucify him! Crucify him!"

22A third time Pilate said to them, "Why? What wrong has he done? I can find no reason to kill him. So I will have him punished and set him free."

23But they continued to shout, demanding that Jesus be crucified. Their yelling became so loud that 24Pilate decided to give them what they wanted. 25He set free the man who was in jail for rioting and murder, and he handed Jesus over to them to do with him as they wished.

Jesus is Crucified

26As they led Jesus away, Simon, a man from Cyrene, was coming in from the fields. They forced him to carry Jesus' cross and to walk behind him.

27A large crowd of people was following Jesus, including some women who were sad and crying for him. 28But Jesus turned and said to them, "Women of Jerusalem, don't cry for me. Cry for yourselves and for your children. 29The time is coming when people will say, 'Happy are the women who cannot have children and who have no babies to nurse.' 30Then people will say to the mountains, 'Fall on us!' And they will say to the hills, 'Cover us!' 31If they act like this now when life is good, what will happen when bad times come?"[n]

32There were also two criminals led out with Jesus to be put to death. 33When they came to a place called the Skull, the soldiers crucified Jesus and the criminals—one on his right and the other on his left. 34Jesus said, "Father, forgive them, because they don't know what they are doing."[n]

> **Sidelight** If Jesus had been crucified the way most Roman prisoners were executed, he was probably nailed to a capital T-shaped (Roman) cross rather than the Italian cross that most churches now display (Luke 23:32–33).

The soldiers threw lots[d] to decide who would get his clothes. 35The people stood there watching. And the leaders made fun of Jesus, saying, "He saved others. Let him save himself if he is God's Chosen One, the Christ."[d]

36The soldiers also made fun of him, coming to Jesus and offering him some vinegar. 37They said, "If you are the king of the Jews, save yourself!" 38At the top of the cross these words were written: THIS IS THE KING OF THE JEWS.

39One of the criminals on a cross began to shout insults at Jesus: "Aren't you the Christ? Then save yourself and us."

40But the other criminal stopped him and said, "You should fear God! You are getting the same punishment as he is. 41We are punished justly, getting what we deserve for what we did. But this man has done nothing wrong." 42Then he said, "Jesus, remember me when you come into your kingdom."

Verse 17 A few Greek copies add verse 17: "Every year at the Passover Feast, Pilate had to release one prisoner to the people."
If . . . come? Literally, "If they do these things in the green tree, what will happen in the dry?"
Verse 34 Some early Greek copies do not have this part of the verse.

43Jesus said to him, "I tell you the truth, today
you will be with me in paradise."[n]

Jesus Dies

44It was about noon, and the whole land be-
came dark until three o'clock in the afternoon,
45because the sun did not shine. The curtain in
the Temple[n] was torn in two. 46Jesus cried out in
a loud voice, "Father, I give you my life." After
Jesus said this, he died.
47When the army officer there saw what hap-
pened, he praised God, saying, "Surely this was
a good man!"
48When all the people who had gathered there
to watch saw what happened, they returned
home, beating their chests because they were so
sad. 49But those who were close friends of Jesus,
including the women who had followed him
from Galilee, stood at a distance and watched.

Joseph Takes Jesus' Body

50There was a good and religious man named
Joseph who was a member of the Jewish council.
51But he had not agreed to the other leaders'
plans and actions against Jesus. He was from the
Jewish town of Arimathea and was waiting for
the kingdom of God to come. 52Joseph went to
Pilate to ask for the body of Jesus. 53He took the
body down from the cross, wrapped it in cloth,
and put it in a tomb that was cut out of a wall of
rock. This tomb had never been used before.
54This was late on Preparation[d] Day, and when
the sun went down, the Sabbath[d] day would
begin.

paradise A place where people who are obedient to God go when they die.
curtain in the Temple A curtain divided the Most Holy Place from the other part of the Temple. That was the special building in Jerusalem where God commanded the Jewish people to worship him.

NON-CHRISTIANS

Taking Every Opportunity

Steve and Lisa went on holiday to Indonesia and they were expecting it to be luxurious: sunbathing on the white sandy beach, snorkelling on the coral reef, eating lots of nice food and seeing all the sights. Things turned out very differently.

On the day they arrived, they were talking to some of the locals on the beach. They ended up talking about Jesus and, to their amazement, they all wanted to find out more. They asked Steve and Lisa to come back the next day and share from the Bible with them. They went back the next day and twenty people turned up!

Steve and Lisa spent every afternoon running a Bible study on the beach, and by the end of their holiday eight people had become Christians. They were also asked to speak at the local church in the shanty town. They got on so well that they were asked to return and run three weeks of mission.

Steve and Lisa returned several months later, and during the three weeks saw hundreds of people give their lives to God. They were absolutely blown away by what they saw – and all as a result of talking to people while on holiday!

Read **Luke 23:26–43**.

- How do you think Jesus would have felt about Steve and Lisa spending their holiday talking about him?
- Do you look for opportunities to talk about Jesus and then take them when they come?

Consider . . .

- being bold and talking to your friends about what Jesus has done in your life.
- meeting up with some Christian friends to pray for your other friends to become Christians and see what God does.

For more, see . . .

- Romans 1:16 (p.1185)
- 1 Peter 3:15–18 (p.1360)
- Ephesians 5:13–16 (p.1275)

55The women who had come from Galilee
with Jesus followed Joseph and saw the tomb and
how Jesus' body was laid. 56Then the women left
to prepare spices and perfumes.
On the Sabbath day they rested, as the law of
Moses commanded.

Jesus Rises from the Dead

24 Very early on the first day of the week,
at dawn, the women came to the tomb,
bringing the spices they had prepared. 2They
found the stone rolled away from the entrance of
the tomb, 3but when they went in, they did not
find the body of the Lord Jesus. 4While they were
wondering about this, two men in shining clothes
suddenly stood beside them. 5The women were
very afraid and bowed their heads to the ground.
The men said to them, "Why are you looking for
a living person in this place for the dead? 6He is
not here; he has risen from the dead. Do you
remember what he told you in Galilee? 7He said
the Son of Man[d] must be handed over to sinful
people, be crucified and rise from the dead on the
third day." 8Then the women remembered what
Jesus had said.
9The women left the tomb and told all these
things to the eleven apostles[d] and the other fol-
lowers. 10It was Mary Magdalene, Joanna, Mary
the mother of James, and some other women
who told the apostles everything that had hap-
pened at the tomb. 11But they did not believe the
women, because it sounded like nonsense. 12But
Peter got up and ran to the tomb. Bending down
and looking in, he saw only the cloth that Jesus'
body had been wrapped in. Peter went away to
his home, wondering about what had happened.

Jesus on the Road to Emmaus

13That same day two of Jesus' followers were
going to a town named Emmaus, about eleven
kilometres from Jerusalem. 14They were talking
about everything that had happened. 15While
they were talking and discussing, Jesus himself
came near and began walking with them, 16but
they were kept from recognising him. 17Then he
said, "What are these things you are talking about
while you walk?"
The two followers stopped, looking very sad.
18The one named Cleopas answered, "Are you
the only visitor in Jerusalem who does not know
what just happened there?"

LIFE

Good News

Bob Delker's family members mourned the day he died, but they also knew that others would live now because of him. Bob had decided to give his body to medicine. This meant that people who desperately needed organ donations would receive them. For these people, Bob's death brought new life.

A few received badly needed bone transplants. Critically injured burn victims received skin grafts. Corneas from Bob's eyes allowed two people to see.

In all, Bob's final gift helped 34 people. Countless others have been inspired to become organ donors because of Bob's example.

Bob's death brought new life to many people. Similarly, the sad news of Jesus' death meant the possibility of new life for all people everywhere. But unlike Bob Delker, Jesus didn't stay dead. Read **Luke 24:1–11** to discover what happened.

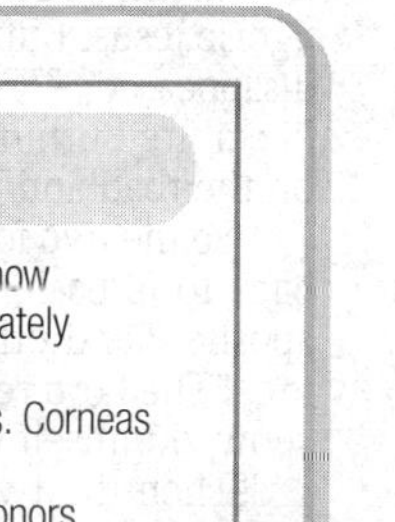

- How is an organ transplant a little like Jesus' coming back from the dead?
- How does Jesus' rising from the dead make a difference in your life?

Consider . . .

- listing the ways in which Christ's death has given you life.
- growing a plant in your room as a reminder of the spiritual life that Jesus gives you.

For more, see . . .

- Psalm 36:7–9 (p.521)
- John 20:1–18 (p.1132)
- Mark 16:1–8 (p.1031)

19 Jesus said to them, "What are you talking
about?"
They said, "About Jesus of Nazareth. He was a
prophet[d] who said and did many powerful things
before God and all the people. 20 Our leaders and
the leading priests handed him over to be sen-
tenced to death, and they crucified him. 21 But we
were hoping that he would free Israel. Besides
this, it is now the third day since this happened.
22 And today some women among us amazed us.
Early this morning they went to the tomb, 23 but
they did not find his body there. They came and
told us that they had seen a vision of angels who
said that Jesus was alive! 24 So some of our group
went to the tomb, too. They found it just as the
women said, but they did not see Jesus."
25 Then Jesus said to them, "You are foolish and
slow to believe everything the prophets said.
26 They said that the Christ[d] must suffer these
things before he enters his glory." 27 Then starting
with what Moses and all the prophets had said
about him, Jesus began to explain everything that
had been written about himself in the Scriptures.[d]
28 They came near the town of Emmaus, and
Jesus acted as if he were going farther. 29 But they
begged him, "Stay with us, because it is late; it is
almost night." So he went in to stay with them.
30 When Jesus was at the table with them, he
took some bread, gave thanks, divided it and gave
it to them. 31 And then they were allowed to rec-
ognise Jesus. But when they saw who he was, he
disappeared. 32 They said to each other, "It felt
like a fire burning in us when Jesus talked to us
on the road and explained the Scriptures to us."
33 So the two followers got up at once and went
back to Jerusalem. There they found the eleven
apostles[d] and others gathered. 34 They were say-
ing, "The Lord really has risen from the dead! He
showed himself to Simon."
35 Then the two followers told what had hap-
pened on the road and how they recognised Jesus
when he divided the bread.

Jesus Appears to His Followers

36 While the two followers were telling this,
Jesus himself stood right in the middle of them
and said, "Peace be with you."
37 They were fearful and terrified and thought
they were seeing a ghost. 38 But Jesus said, "Why
are you troubled? Why do you doubt what you
see? 39 Look at my hands and my feet. It is I my-
self! Touch me and see, because a ghost does not
have a living body as you see I have."
40 After Jesus said this, he showed them his
hands and feet. 41 While they still could not be-
lieve it because they were amazed and happy,
Jesus said to them, "Do you have any food here?"
42 They gave him a piece of grilled fish. 43 While
the followers watched, Jesus took the fish and
ate it.
44 He said to them, "Remember when I was
with you before? I said that everything written
about me must happen—everything in the law
of Moses, the books of the prophets[d] and the
Psalms."
45 Then Jesus opened their minds so they could
understand the Scriptures.[d] 46 He said to them, "It
is written that the Christ[d] would suffer and rise
from the dead on the third day 47 and that a
change of hearts and lives and forgiveness of sins
would be preached in his name to all nations,
starting at Jerusalem. 48 You are witnesses of these
things. 49 I will send you what my Father has
promised, but you must stay in Jerusalem until
you have received that power from heaven."

Jesus Goes Back to Heaven

50 Jesus led his followers as far as Bethany,
and he raised his hands and blessed them.
51 While he was blessing them, he was separated
from them and carried into heaven. 52 They wor-
shipped him and returned to Jerusalem very
happy. 53 They stayed in the Temple[d] all the time,
praising God.

John

Why Read This Book:

- Be reminded that Jesus Christ is fully human and fully divine (John 1).
- Find stories that reveal Jesus' glory as giver of eternal life (John 2—11).
- Learn the importance of Jesus' death and resurrection (John 13—21).

When?

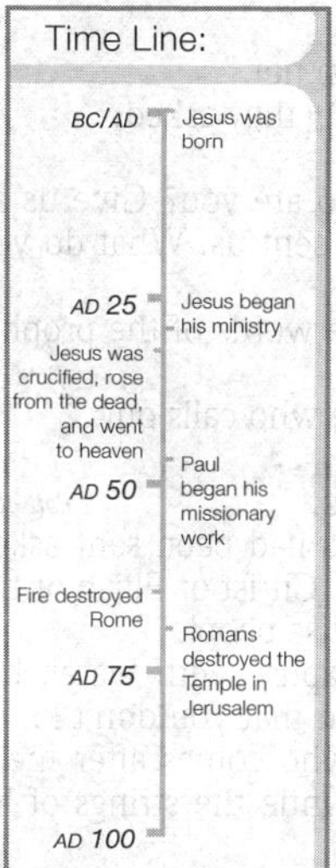

Behind the Scenes:

Imagine meeting someone for the first time. The conversation begins with "Hi, I'm Emma. I work in the Finance Department. I live down the road." You might go on to talk about hobbies, interests, background and other information.

But you still wouldn't really know that person. If you saw each other regularly, you would begin to understand each other's personality, values and uniqueness.

In some ways, the first three gospels (Matthew, p.935; Mark, p.996; and Luke, p.1034) are like the first part of a relationship with Jesus Christ. Through these books, we get to know stories about Jesus and what he did. But the Gospel of John digs deeper into who Jesus was, why he lived and the meaning of his life.

This fourth gospel is quite different from the other three. Like the others, it tells what Jesus said and did. But it goes a step further by interpreting Jesus' significance as God's Son.

Many new believers turn first to this gospel to discover what it means to be a Christian. That's not surprising, given the book's purpose as stated in John 20:31: "These [things] are written so that you may believe that Jesus is the Christ, the Son of God. Then, by believing, you may have life through his name."

Where?

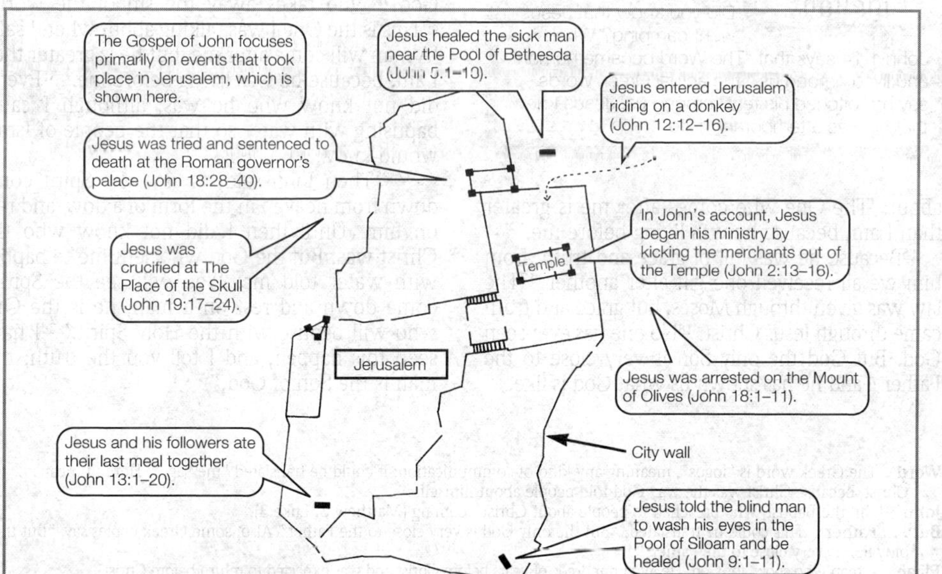

Christ Comes to the World

1 In the beginning there was the Word.[n] The Word was with God, and the Word was God. [2]He was with God in the beginning. [3]All things were made by him, and nothing was made without him. [4]In him there was life, and that life was the light of all people. [5]The Light shines in the darkness, and the darkness has not overpowered it.

[6]There was a man named John[n] who was sent by God. [7]He came to tell people the truth about the Light so that through him all people could hear about the Light and believe. [8]John was not the Light, but he came to tell people the truth about the Light. [9]The true Light that gives light to all was coming into the world!

[10]The Word was in the world, and the world was made by him, but the world did not know him. [11]He came to the world that was his own, but his own people did not accept him. [12]But to all who did accept him and believe in him he gave the right to become children of God. [13]They did not become his children in any human way—by any human parents or human desire. They were born of God.

[14]The Word became human and lived among us. We saw his glory—the glory that belongs to the only Son of the Father—and he was full of grace and truth. [15]John tells the truth about him and cries out, saying, "This is the One I told you about: 'The One who comes after me is greater than I am, because he was living before me.' "

[16]Because he was full of grace and truth, from him we all received one gift after another. [17]The law was given through Moses, but grace and truth came through Jesus Christ. [18]No one has ever seen God. But God the only Son is very close to the Father,[n] and he has shown us what God is like.

Sidelight Did you know that Jesus went camping? When John 1:14 says that "The Word became human and lived among us," the actual Greek words say he "pitched his tent" among us. Jesus knew that he was a temporary visitor.

John Tells People About Jesus

[19]Here is the truth John[n] told when the Jews in Jerusalem sent priests and Levites to ask him, "Who are you?"

[20]John spoke freely and did not refuse to answer. He said, "I am not the Christ."[d]

[21]So they asked him, "Then who are you? Are you Elijah?"[n]

He answered, "No, I am not."

"Are you the Prophet?"[n] they asked.

He answered, "No."

[22]Then they said, "Who are you? Give us an answer to tell those who sent us. What do you say about yourself?"

[23]John told them in the words of the prophet Isaiah:

"This is the voice of one who calls out:
'Prepare in the desert
the way for the LORD.' " *Isaiah 40:3*

[24]Some Pharisees[d] who had been sent asked John: [25]"If you are not the Christ or Elijah or the Prophet, why do you baptise people?"

[26]John answered, "I baptise with water, but there is one here with you that you don't know about. [27]He is the One who comes after me. I am not good enough to untie the strings of his sandals."

[28]This all happened at Bethany on the other side of the Jordan River, where John was baptising people.

[29]The next day John saw Jesus coming towards him. John said, "Look, the Lamb of God,[n] who takes away the sin of the world! [30]This is the One I was talking about when I said, 'A man will come after me, but he is greater than I am, because he was living before me.' [31]Even I did not know who he was, although I came baptising with water so that the people of Israel would know who he is."

[32-33]Then John said, "I saw the Spirit come down from heaven in the form of a dove and rest on him. Until then I did not know who the Christ was. But the God who sent me to baptise with water told me, 'You will see the Spirit[d] come down and rest on a man; he is the One who will baptise with the Holy Spirit.' [34]I have seen this happen, and I tell you the truth: this man is the Son of God."

Word The Greek word is "logos", meaning any kind of communication; it could be translated "message". Here, it means Christ, because Christ was the way God told people about himself.
John John the Baptist, who preached to people about Christ's coming (Matthew 3, Luke 3).
But . . . Father This could be translated, "But the only God is very close to the Father." Also, some Greek copies say, "But the only Son is very close to the Father."
Elijah A man who spoke for God. He lived hundreds of years before Christ and was expected to return before Christ (Malachi 4:5–6).
Prophet They probably meant the prophet that God told Moses he would send (Deuteronomy 18:15–19).
Lamb of God Name for Jesus. Jesus is like the lambs that were offered for a sacrifice to God.

The First Followers of Jesus

35The next day John[n] was there again with
two of his followers. 36When he saw Jesus walk-
ing by, he said, "Look, the Lamb of God!"[n]
37The two followers heard John say this, so
they followed Jesus. 38When Jesus turned and
saw them following him, he asked, "What are
you looking for?"
They said, "Rabbi, where are you staying?"
("Rabbi" means "Teacher".)
39He answered, "Come and see." So the two
men went with Jesus and saw where he was stay-
ing and stayed there with him that day. It was
about four o'clock in the afternoon.
40One of the two men who followed Jesus after
they heard John speak about him was Andrew,
Simon Peter's brother. 41The first thing Andrew
did was to find his brother Simon and say to him,
"We have found the Messiah." ("Messiah"
means "Christ".[d])

John John the Baptist, who preached to people about Christ's coming (Matthew 3, Luke 3).
Lamb of God Name for Jesus. Jesus is like the lambs that were offered for a sacrifice to God.

JESUS CHRIST

Where's the Party?

"Do you want to go to the party on Saturday, Annie?" Simon asked.

Annie looked at the floor and said, "No thanks, it's alright."

"What? Why don't you want to come? It'll be fun! It's only at Noel's and his parents will be there," he explained.

"I know, but no thanks," she replied sadly.

Simon could never understand Annie. She was a really nice-looking girl and he was sure she could be a lot of fun, but somehow it seemed that she never joined in anything. Almost as if she was afraid. He knew that she was a Christian, but failed to see how going to a party could be so terrible. He wasn't asking her to sleep with him or anything!

Annie could see that Simon was mystified, and one day she tried to explain her feelings to him.

"It's just that I don't want to be seen doing things that people might think are wrong . . ." she started.

Simon interrupted her straight away.

"No, Annie, you've got it wrong. If you want to be a good Christian then you've got to start being like Jesus. People never pointed at Jesus because he was doing things wrong, they pointed at him because he was doing things right!"

Annie was stunned. She'd never thought of it like that before.

But he was right! Jesus was known for the things he did, not the things he didn't do!

So she went to the party with Simon – taking Jesus with her – and had a great time. She danced and laughed and made new friends that she could influence for Christ, without ever having to compromise her position as a Christian. Gradually Annie became seen as a beautiful, fun-loving Christian girl.

Read **John 1:1–18** and see that John always pointed towards the glory of Jesus. He spoke of his grace and truth.

- How did Annie become like Jesus?
- Can you see your life as a way of pointing people to Jesus?

Consider . . .

- listing the things you can do with your friends without compromising your Christian beliefs.
- praying for a friend you would like to tell about Jesus and the way he has changed your life.

For more, see . . .

- Matthew 11:16–19 (p.959)
- Philippians 2:5–11 (p.1282)
- John 17:13–19 (p.1128)

42Then Andrew took Simon to Jesus. Jesus looked at him and said, "You are Simon son of John. You will be called Cephas." ("Cephas" means "Peter".[n])

43The next day Jesus decided to go to Galilee. He found Philip and said to him, "Follow me."

44Philip was from the town of Bethsaida, where Andrew and Peter lived. 45Philip found Nathanael and told him, "We have found the man that Moses wrote about in the law, and the prophets[d] also wrote about him. He is Jesus, the son of Joseph, from Nazareth."

46But Nathanael said to Philip, "Can anything good come from Nazareth?"

Philip answered, "Come and see."

47As Jesus saw Nathanael coming towards him, he said, "Here is truly an Israelite. There is nothing false in him."

48Nathanael asked, "How do you know me?"

Jesus answered, "I saw you when you were under the fig tree, before Philip told you about me."

49Then Nathanael said to Jesus, "Teacher, you are the Son of God; you are the King of Israel."

50Jesus said to Nathanael, "Do you believe simply because I told you I saw you under the fig tree? You will see greater things than that." 51And Jesus said to them, "I tell you the truth, you will all see heaven open and 'angels of God going up and coming down'[n] on the Son of Man."[d]

The Wedding at Cana

2 Two days later there was a wedding in the town of Cana in Galilee. Jesus' mother was there, 2and Jesus and his followers were also invited to the wedding. 3When all the wine was gone, Jesus' mother said to him, "They have no more wine."

4Jesus answered, "Dear woman, why come to me? My time has not yet come."

5His mother said to the servants, "Do whatever he tells you to do."

6In that place there were six stone water jars that the Jews used in their washing ceremony.[n] Each jar held about 100 litres.

7Jesus said to the servants, "Fill the jars with water." So they filled the jars to the top.

8Then he said to them, "Now take some out and give it to the master of the feast."

So they took the water to the master. 9When he tasted it, the water had become wine. He did not know where the wine came from, but the servants who had brought the water knew. The master of the wedding called the bridegroom 10and said to him, "People always serve the best wine first. Later, after the guests have been drinking awhile, they serve the cheaper wine. But you have saved the best wine till now."

11So in Cana of Galilee Jesus did his first miracle.[d] There he showed his glory, and his followers believed in him.

Sidelight The wedding at Cana (John 2:1–11) wouldn't have involved a short ceremony followed by a cold buffet reception. In Jesus' day, weddings usually lasted about a week. On the first day, the couple exchanged vows under a canopy. Then, for the next six days or more, the couple and all the guests celebrated with dancing, games, music, food and wine.

Jesus in the Temple

12After this, Jesus went to the town of Capernaum with his mother, brothers and followers. They stayed there for just a few days. 13When it was almost time for the Jewish Passover[d] Feast, Jesus went to Jerusalem. 14In the Temple[d] he found people selling cattle, sheep and doves. He saw others sitting at tables, exchanging different kinds of money. 15Jesus made a whip out of cords and forced all of them, both the sheep and cattle, to leave the Temple. He turned over the tables and scattered the money of those who were exchanging it. 16Then he said to those who were selling pigeons, "Take these things out of here! Don't make my Father's house a place for buying and selling!"

17When this happened, the followers remembered what was written in the Scriptures:[d] "My strong love for your Temple completely controls me."[n]

18The Jews said to Jesus, "Show us a miracle[d] to prove you have the right to do these things."

19Jesus answered them, "Destroy this temple, and I will build it again in three days."

Peter The Greek name "Peter", like the Aramaic name "Cephas", means "rock".
'angels . . . down' These words are from Genesis 28:12.
washing ceremony The Jewish people washed themselves in special ways before eating, before worshipping in the Temple and at other special times.
"My . . . me." Quotation from Psalm 69:9.

20 The Jews answered, "It took 46 years to
build this Temple! Do you really believe you can
build it again in three days?"
21 (But the temple Jesus meant was his own
body. 22 After Jesus was raised from the dead, his
followers remembered that Jesus had said this.
Then they believed the Scripture[d] and the words
Jesus had said.)
23 When Jesus was in Jerusalem for the Pass-
over Feast, many people believed in him because
they saw the miracles he did. 24 But Jesus did not
trust himself to them because he knew them all.
25 He did not need anyone to tell him about peo-
ple, because he knew what was in people's minds.

Nicodemus Comes to Jesus

3 There was a man named Nicodemus who
was one of the Pharisees[d] and an important
Jewish leader. 2 One night Nicodemus came to
Jesus and said, "Teacher, we know you are a
teacher sent from God, because no one can do
the miracles[d] you do unless God is with him."
3 Jesus answered, "I tell you the truth, unless
one is born again, he cannot be in God's kingdom."
4 Nicodemus said, "But if a person is already
old, how can he be born again? He cannot enter
his mother's body again. So how can a person be
born a second time?"
5 But Jesus answered, "I tell you the truth, un-
less one is born from water and the Spirit,[d] he
cannot enter God's kingdom. 6 Human life comes
from human parents, but spiritual life comes
from the Spirit. 7 Don't be surprised when I tell
you, 'You must all be born again.' 8 The wind
blows where it wants to and you hear the sound
of it, but you don't know where the wind comes
from or where it is going. It is the same with
every person who is born from the Spirit."

ANGER

Anger to Action

Ben and Caroline were students when they visited a township primary school in South Africa. The system of Apartheid had meant that the white minority lived much wealthier lives than the black majority. They saw black children sitting three to a desk and struggling to afford even basic pencils and notebooks. This made them angry when they thought of the school they had seen that morning, with its swimming pool, landscaped grounds and fantastic resources, which had been previously only for white children.

It would have been easy for them to feel bitter about the injustice they had seen, but instead Ben and Caroline felt that God was telling them to do something about the township children's situation.

The school had a brilliant choir, and Ben and Caroline thought that if they could bring them to the UK to perform, they would be able to raise money for their school.

They had never done anything like this before, and it took two years of hard fundraising and planning back in the UK to make this dream a reality, but it was their anger at the injustice that they had felt in South Africa that kept them going.

The choir came to the UK and performed around the country, selling CDs of their music and even meeting the Prime Minister. It was an amazing experience for Ben, Caroline and the children, but more importantly, the choir raised enough money to pay for a library and science building at the school in South Africa.

Jesus sometimes became angry too. Read what made him angry in **John 2:12–22**.

- What was the root cause of Jesus', and Ben and Caroline's anger?
- If Jesus and Ben and Caroline had not been angry, how might the outcomes have differed?

Consider . . .

- whether you feel angry about something at the moment. Is it righteous anger?
- asking God to show you how you can use your anger at an injustice to fuel you to demonstrate his love.

For more, see . . .

- Psalm 103:7–13 (p.559)
- James 1:19–20 (p.1348)
- Ephesians 4:26–27 (p.1274)

[9]Nicodemus asked, "How can this happen?"
[10]Jesus said, "You are an important teacher in
Israel, and you don't understand these things?
[11]I tell you the truth, we talk about what we
know, and we tell about what we have seen, but
you don't accept what we tell you. [12]I have told
you about things here on earth, and you do not
believe me. So you will not believe me if I tell
you about things of heaven. [13]The only one who
has ever gone up to heaven is the One who came
down from heaven—the Son of Man. [d]
[14]"Just as Moses lifted up the snake in the
desert, [n] the Son of Man must also be lifted up.
[15]So that everyone who believes can have eter-
nal life in him.
[16]"God loved the world so much that he
gave his one and only Son so that whoever be-
lieves in him may not be lost, but have eternal
life. [17]God did not send his Son into the world to
judge the world guilty, but to save the world
through him. [18]People who believe in God's Son
are not judged guilty. Those who do not believe
have already been judged guilty, because they
have not believed in God's one and only Son.
[19]They are judged by this fact: the Light has
come into the world, but they did not want light.
They wanted darkness, because they were doing
evil things. [20]All who do evil hate the light
and will not come to the light, because it will
show all the evil things they do. [21]But those
who follow the true way come to the light, and
it shows that the things they do were done
through God."

Jesus and John the Baptist

[22]After this, Jesus and his followers went into
the area of Judea, where he stayed with his
followers and baptised people. [23]John was also

Moses . . . desert When the Israelites were dying from snake bites, God told Moses to put a brass snake on a pole. The people who looked at the snake were healed (Numbers 21:4–9).

ETERNAL LIFE

The Ultimate Price

Tim had been in New York City before. He loved the annual trip that his family made from Provo, Utah, to watch the US Open together in New York, USA.

One Sunday during the 1990 tournament, Tim was waiting with his parents in a Manhattan underground station when a gang approached them. Surrounding the family, they robbed Tim's father and then attacked Tim's mother.

Tim fought back to defend his mother. The attackers turned from Tim's mother to Tim. In the struggle, one of the robbers pulled a knife and stabbed Tim to death.

Tim paid the ultimate price because he couldn't stand watching the ones he loved get hurt. Jesus, God's son, willingly paid the ultimate price for us because he doesn't want us to get hurt for ever.

In **John 3:1–21**, Jesus talks about the gift of eternal life that his death would provide.

- How were Tim's feelings for his parents like God's desires for us? How were they different?
- According to this passage (especially verses 16–18), what must we do to receive all that God desires for us?

Consider . . .

- writing John 3:16 on paper, putting it in a box, and gift-wrapping the box. Give the box to a friend as a reminder of God's gift of eternal life.
- asking your minister or youth leader what eternal life is, then comparing the answer with what Jesus said in this passage.

For more, see . . .

- Isaiah 12 (p.654)
- 1 John 5:1–12 (p.1375)
- 1 Timothy 1:12–17 (p.1308)

baptising in Aenon, near Salim, because there
was plenty of water there. People were going
there to be baptised. [24](This was before John was
put into prison.)
[25]Some of John's followers had an argument
with a Jew about religious washing.[n] [26]So they
came to John and said, "Teacher, remember the
man who was with you on the other side of
the Jordan River, the one you spoke about so
much? He is baptising, and everyone is going
to him."
[27]John answered, "A man can get only what
God gives him. [28]You yourselves heard me say,
'I am not the Christ,[d] but I am the one sent to
prepare the way for him.' [29]The bride belongs
only to the bridegroom. But the friend who helps
the bridegroom stands by and listens to him. He
is thrilled that he gets to hear the bridegroom's
voice. In the same way, I am really happy. [30]He
must become greater, and I must become less
important.

The One Who Comes from Heaven

[31]"The One who comes from above is greater
than all. The one who is from the earth belongs
to the earth and talks about things on the earth.
But the One who comes from heaven is greater
than all. [32]He tells what he has seen and heard,
but no one accepts what he says. [33]Whoever ac-
cepts what he says has proven that God is true.
[34]The One whom God sent speaks the words of
God, because God gives him the Spirit[d] fully.
[35]The Father loves the Son and has given him
power over everything. [36]Those who believe in
the Son have eternal life, but those who do not
obey the Son will never have life. God's anger
stays on them."

Jesus and a Samaritan Woman

4 The Pharisees[d] heard that Jesus was making
and baptising more followers than John, [2]al-
though Jesus himself did not baptise people, but
his followers did. [3]Jesus knew that the Pharisees
had heard about him, so he left Judea and went
back to Galilee. [4]But on the way he had to go
through the country of Samaria.
[5]In Samaria Jesus came to the town called
Sychar, which is near the field Jacob gave to his son
Joseph. [6]Jacob's well was there. Jesus was tired
from his long trip, so he sat down beside the well.
It was about twelve o'clock noon. [7]When a
Samaritan[d] woman came to the well to get some
water, Jesus said to her, "Please give me a drink."
[8](This happened while Jesus' followers were in
town buying some food.)
[9]The woman said, "I am surprised that you ask
me for a drink, since you are a Jewish man and I
am a Samaritan woman." (Jewish people are not
friends with Samaritans.[n])
[10]Jesus said, "If you only knew the free gift of
God and who it is that is asking you for water,
you would have asked him, and he would have
given you living water."
[11]The woman said, "Sir, where will you get
this living water? The well is very deep, and you
have nothing to get water with. [12]Are you greater
than Jacob, our father, who gave us this well and
drank from it himself along with his sons and
flocks?"
[13]Jesus answered, "Everyone who drinks this
water will be thirsty again, [14]but whoever drinks
the water I give will never be thirsty. The water
I give will become a spring of water flowing up
inside that person, giving eternal life."
[15]The woman said to him, "Sir, give me this
water so I will never be thirsty again and will not
have to come back here to get more water."
[16]Jesus told her, "Go and get your husband and
come back here."
[17]The woman answered, "I have no husband."
Jesus said to her, "You are right to say you
have no husband. [18]Really you have had five hus-
bands, and the man you live with now is not
your husband. You told the truth."
[19]The woman said, "Sir, I can see that you are
a prophet.[d] [20]Our ancestors worshipped on this
mountain, but you Jews say that Jerusalem is the
place where people must worship."
[21]Jesus said, "Believe me, woman. The time is
coming when neither in Jerusalem nor on this
mountain will you actually worship the Father.
[22]You Samaritans worship something you don't
understand. We understand what we worship,
because salvation comes from the Jews. [23]The
time is coming when the true worshippers will
worship the Father in spirit and truth, and that
time is here already. You see, the Father too is
actively seeking such people to worship him.
[24]God is spirit, and those who worship him must
worship in spirit and truth."
[25]The woman said, "I know that the Messiah
is coming." (Messiah is the One called Christ.[d])
"When the Messiah comes, he will explain every-
thing to us."
[26]Then Jesus said, "I am he—I, the one talking
to you."

religious washing The Jewish people washed themselves in special ways before eating, before worshipping in the Temple and at other special times.

Jewish people . . . Samaritans. This can also be translated "Jewish people don't use things that Samaritans have used."

27Just then his followers came back from town
and were surprised to see him talking with a
woman. But none of them asked, "What do you
want?" or "Why are you talking with her?"
28Then the woman left her water jar and went
back to town. She said to the people, 29"Come
and see a man who told me everything I ever
did. Do you think he might be the Christ?" 30So
the people left the town and went to see Jesus.
31Meanwhile, his followers were begging him,
"Teacher, eat something."
32But Jesus answered, "I have food to eat that
you know nothing about."
33So the followers asked themselves, "Has
somebody already brought him food?"
34Jesus said, "My food is to do what the One
who sent me wants me to do and to finish his
work. 35You have a saying, 'Four more months
till harvest.' But I tell you, open your eyes and look
at the fields ready for harvest now. 36Already, the

Sidelight Jesus risked getting into a lot of trouble when he spoke with the Samaritan woman (see John 4:1–30). The Jewish law made it illegal for teachers to speak to women, Jews to talk to Samaritans and the "righteous" to mingle with "sinners". Read what Jesus might have said to some of his critics in Matthew 9:10–12 (p.953).

STEREOTYPES

Prejudice

The bell rang. English was over for another day. Sam stared at his short story.

His classmates walked by, some commenting as they passed. "What an imagination you have in there!" Sam wasn't sure if it was a compliment or not. "I'd love to hear you try reading it yourself, spastic!" He was sure that wasn't a compliment.

Sam waited for the classroom to clear, then made his way to his next class: maths.

His teacher greeted him at the doorway. "Hello, Sam!" he yelled. "How are you today?"

Sam just nodded and wondered, once again, why people treated him as though he was deaf.

When Sam moved from his special school, one of the hardest adjustments was learning how to communicate with others. Some people were great. They shared Sam's interest in chess and science fiction, and made special efforts to make him their friend. Others, though, openly insulted him for being different.

Sam learned a lot about prejudice during his time at school. Because of his severe cerebral palsy, some people expected Sam to be stupid. He always took special pleasure in knocking down stereotypes by writing a creative short story or tackling the toughest maths problem.

Sam was different from others in some ways. His speech was often difficult to understand. He communicated by typing with touchsticks strapped to his hands. And he travelled by moving a joystick attached to his wheelchair.

But Sam had a lot more in common with those around him than many people thought. A lot of them refused to see beyond his wheelchair or his inability to speak as they did. And their prejudice was tough on Sam.

Jesus also had to overcome people's prejudice. Read **John 4:5–42** about how Jesus dealt with prejudice towards himself and others.

- How did Sam break down prejudice in the same way that Jesus did?
- What prejudices do you have? How would Jesus respond to those prejudices?

Consider . . .

- writing a letter to the editor of your school or local newspaper concerning a prejudice you see. Describe ways to combat that prejudice.
- regularly eating lunch at school with someone who has been hurt by prejudice.

For more, see . . .

- Psalm 9:7–10 (p.505)
- Galatians 3:26–29 (p.1261)
- Acts 10:1–33 (p.1154)

one who harvests is being paid and is gathering crops for eternal life. So the one who plants and the one who harvests celebrate at the same time. [37]Here the saying is true, 'One person plants, and another harvests.' [38]I sent you to harvest a crop that you did not work for. Others did the work, and you will finish their work." [n]

[39]Many of the Samaritans in that town believed in Jesus because of what the woman said: "He told me everything I ever did." [40]When the Samaritans came to Jesus, they begged him to stay with them, so he stayed there two more days. [41]And many more believed because of the things he said.

[42]They said to the woman, "First we believed in Jesus because of what you told us, but now we believe because we heard him ourselves. We know that this man really is the Saviour of the world."

Jesus Heals an Officer's Son

[43]Two days later, Jesus left and went to Galilee. [44](Jesus had said before that a prophet [d] is not respected in his own country.) [45]When Jesus arrived in Galilee, the people there welcomed him. They had seen all the things he did at the Passover [d] Feast in Jerusalem, because they had been there, too.

[46]Jesus went again to visit Cana in Galilee where he had changed the water into wine. One of the king's important officers lived in the city of Capernaum, and his son was sick. [47]When he heard that Jesus had come from Judea to Galilee, he went to Jesus and begged him to come to Capernaum and heal his son, because his son was almost dead. [48]Jesus said to him, "You people must see signs and miracles [d] before you will believe in me."

[49]The officer said, "Sir, come before my child dies."

[50]Jesus answered, "Go. Your son will live."

The man believed what Jesus told him and went home. [51]On the way the man's servants came and met him and told him, "Your son is alive."

[52]The man asked, "What time did my son begin to get well?"

They answered, "Yesterday at one o'clock the fever left him."

[53]The father knew that one o'clock was the exact time that Jesus had said, "Your son will live." So the man and all the people who lived in his house believed in Jesus.

[54]That was the second miracle Jesus did after coming from Judea to Galilee.

Jesus Heals a Man at a Pool

5 Later Jesus went to Jerusalem for a special Jewish feast. [2]In Jerusalem there is a pool with five covered porches, which is called Bethesda [n] in the Jewish language. [n] This pool is near the Sheep Gate. [3]Many sick people were lying on the porches beside the pool. Some were blind, some were crippled and some were paralysed. [n] [5]A man was lying there who had been sick for 38 years. [6]When Jesus saw the man and knew that he had been sick for such a long time, Jesus asked him, "Do you want to be well?"

[7]The sick man answered, "Sir, there is no one to help me get into the pool when the water starts moving. While I am coming to the water, someone else always gets in before me."

[8]Then Jesus said, "Stand up. Pick up your mat and walk." [9]And immediately the man was well; he picked up his mat and began to walk.

The day this happened was a Sabbath [d] day. [10]So the Jews said to the man who had been healed, "Today is the Sabbath. It is against our law for you to carry your mat on the Sabbath day."

[11]But he answered, "The man who made me well told me, 'Pick up your mat and walk.'"

[12]Then they asked him, "Who is the man who told you to pick up your mat and walk?"

[13]But the man who had been healed did not know who it was, because there were many people in that place, and Jesus had left.

[14]Later, Jesus found the man at the Temple [d] and said to him, "See, you are well now. Stop sinning so that something worse does not happen to you."

[15]Then the man left and told the Jews that Jesus was the one who had made him well.

[16]Because Jesus was doing this on the Sabbath day, the Jews began to persecute him. [17]But Jesus said to them, "My Father never stops working, and so I keep working, too."

[18]This made the Jews try still harder to kill him. They said, "First Jesus was breaking the law about the Sabbath day. Now he says that God is his own Father, making himself equal with God!"

But I . . . their work. As a farmer sends workers to harvest grain, Jesus sends his followers out to bring people to God.
Bethesda Also called Bethsaida or Bethzatha, a pool of water north of the Temple in Jerusalem.
Jewish language Hebrew or Aramaic, the languages of the Jewish people in the first century.
Verse 3 Some Greek copies add "and they waited for the water to move". A few later copies add verse 4: "Sometimes an angel of the Lord came down to the pool and stirred up the water. After the angel did this, the first person to go into the pool was healed from any sickness he had."

Jesus Has God's Authority

19But Jesus said, "I tell you the truth, the Son
can do nothing alone. The Son does only what
he sees the Father doing, because the Son does
whatever the Father does. 20The Father loves the
Son and shows the Son all the things he himself
does. But the Father will show the Son even
greater things than this so that you can all be
amazed. 21Just as the Father raises the dead and
gives them life, so also the Son gives life to those
he wants to. 22In fact, the Father judges no one,
but he has given the Son power to do all the
judging 23so that all people will honour the Son
as much as they honour the Father. Anyone who
does not honour the Son does not honour the
Father who sent him.

24"I tell you the truth, whoever hears what I
say and believes in the One who sent me has
eternal life. That person will not be judged guilty
but has already left death and entered life. 25I tell
you the truth, the time is coming and is already
here when the dead will hear the voice of the
Son of God, and those who hear will have life.
26Life comes from the Father himself, and he has
allowed the Son to have life in himself as well.
27And the Father has given the Son the power to
judge, because he is the Son of Man.[d] 28Don't
be surprised at this: a time is coming when all
who are dead and in their graves will hear his
voice. 29Then they will come out of their graves.
Those who did good will rise and have life for
ever, but those who did evil will rise to be judged
guilty.

Jesus is God's Son

30"I can do nothing alone. I judge only the
way I am told, so my judgement is fair. I don't try
to please myself, but I try to please the One who
sent me.

31"If only I tell people about myself, what I say
does not count. 32But there is another who tells
about me, and I know that the things he says
about me are true.

33"You have sent people to John, and he has
told you the truth. 34It is not that I accept such
human telling; I tell you this so you can be saved.
35John was like a burning and shining lamp, and
you were happy to enjoy his light for a while.

36"But I have a proof about myself that is
greater than that of John. The things I do, which
are the things my Father gave me to do, prove
that the Father sent me. 37And the Father him-
self who sent me has given proof about me. You
have never heard his voice or seen what he looks
like. 38His teaching does not live in you, because
you don't believe in the One the Father sent.
39You carefully study the Scriptures[d] because
you think they give you eternal life. They do in
fact tell about me, 40but you refuse to come to
me to have that life.

41"I don't need praise from people. 42But I
know you—I know that you don't have God's
love in you. 43I have come from my Father and
speak for him, but you don't accept me. But
when another person comes, speaking only for
himself, you will accept him. 44You try to get
praise from each other, but you do not try to get
the praise that comes from the only God. So
how can you believe? 45Don't think that I will
stand before the Father and say you are wrong.
The one who says you are wrong is Moses, the
one you hoped would save you. 46If you really
believed Moses, you would believe me, because
Moses wrote about me. 47But if you don't be-
lieve what Moses wrote, how can you believe
what I say?"

More than 5,000 Fed

6 After this, Jesus went across Lake Galilee (or,
Lake Tiberias). 2Many people followed him
because they saw the miracles[d] he did to heal the
sick. 3Jesus went up on a hill and sat down there
with his followers. 4It was almost the time for the
Jewish Passover[d] Feast.

5When Jesus looked up and saw a large crowd
coming towards him, he said to Philip, "Where
can we buy enough bread for all these people
to eat?" 6(Jesus asked Philip this question to test
him, because Jesus already knew what he planned
to do.)

7Philip answered, "We would all have to work
a month to buy enough bread for each person to
have only a little piece."

8Another one of his followers, Andrew, Simon
Peter's brother, said, 9"Here is a boy with five
loaves of barley bread and two little fish, but that
is not enough for so many people."

10Jesus said, "Tell the people to sit down." This
was a very grassy place, and about 5,000 men
sat down there. 11Then Jesus took the loaves of
bread, thanked God for them and gave them to
the people who were sitting there. He did the
same with the fish, giving as much as the people
wanted.

12When they had all had enough to eat, Jesus
said to his followers, "Gather the leftover pieces

Sidelight There were three types of bread in Jesus' day: small loaves (that would look similar to our rolls), round loaves (about the size of a football) and flat loaves (large, bread-like pancakes). The boy who gave loaves to Jesus (John 6:9) probably gave the first type, and they were made from barley, which suggests that he was poor.

of fish and bread so that nothing is wasted." 13So
they gathered up the pieces and filled twelve bas-
kets with the pieces left from the five barley
loaves.
14When the people saw this miracle[d] that Jesus
did, they said, "He must truly be the Prophet[n]
who is coming into the world."
15Jesus knew that the people planned to come
and take him by force and make him their king,
so he left and went into the hills alone.

Jesus Walks on the Water

16That evening Jesus' followers went down to
Lake Galilee. 17It was dark now, and Jesus had
not yet come to them. The followers got into a
boat and started across the lake to Capernaum.
18By now a strong wind was blowing, and the
waves on the lake were getting bigger. 19When
they had rowed the boat about five or six kilo-
metres, they saw Jesus walking on the water,
coming towards the boat. The followers were
afraid, 20but Jesus said to them, "It is I. Do not be
afraid." 21Then they were glad to take him into
the boat. At once the boat came to land at the
place where they wanted to go.

The People Seek Jesus

22The next day the people who had stayed on
the other side of the lake knew that Jesus had
not gone in the boat with his followers but that
they had left without him. And they knew that
only one boat had been there. 23But then some
boats came from Tiberias and landed near the
place where the people had eaten the bread after
the Lord had given thanks. 24When the people
saw that Jesus and his followers were not there
now, they got into boats and went to Capernaum
to find Jesus.

Jesus, the Bread of Life

25When the people found Jesus on the other
side of the lake, they asked him, "Teacher, when
did you come here?"
26Jesus answered, "I tell you the truth, you
aren't looking for me because you saw me do
miracles.[d] You are looking for me because you
ate the bread and were satisfied. 27Don't work for
the food that spoils. Work for the food that stays
good always and gives eternal life. The Son of
Man[d] will give you this food, because on him
God the Father has put his power."
28The people asked Jesus, "What are the
things God wants us to do?"
29Jesus answered, "The work God wants you
to do is this: believe the One he sent."
30So the people asked, "What miracle will you
do? If we see a miracle, we will believe you.
What will you do? 31Our fathers ate the manna[d]
in the desert. This is written in the Scriptures:[d]
'He rained manna[d] down on them to eat.'"[n]
32Jesus said, "I tell you the truth, it was not
Moses who gave you bread from heaven; it is my
Father who is giving you the true bread from
heaven. 33God's bread is the One who comes
down from heaven and gives life to the world."
34The people said, "Sir, give us this bread
always."
35Then Jesus said, "I am the bread that gives
life. Whoever comes to me will never be hungry,
and whoever believes in me will never be thirsty.
36But as I told you before, you have seen me and
still don't believe. 37The Father gives me my peo-
ple. Every one of them will come to me, and I
will always accept them. 38I came down from
heaven to do what God wants me to do, not
what I want to do. 39Here is what the One who
sent me wants me to do: I must not lose even
one whom God gave me, but I must raise them
all on the last day. 40Those who see the Son and
believe in him have eternal life, and I will raise
them on the last day. This is what my Father
wants."
41The Jews began to complain about Jesus
because he said, "I am the bread that comes
down from heaven." 42They said, "This is Jesus,
the son of Joseph. We know his father and
mother. How can he say, 'I came down from
heaven'?"
43But Jesus answered, "Stop complaining to
each other. 44The Father is the One who sent
me. No one can come to me unless the Father
draws him to me, and I will raise that person up
on the last day. 45It is written in the prophets,[d]
'They will all be taught by God.'[n] Everyone
who listens to the Father and learns from him
comes to me. 46No one has seen the Father ex-
cept the One who is from God; only he has seen
the Father. 47I tell you the truth, whoever
believes has eternal life. 48I am the bread that
gives life. 49Your ancestors ate the manna in the
desert, but still they died. 50Here is the bread
that comes down from heaven. Anyone who
eats this bread will never die. 51I am the living
bread that came down from heaven. Anyone
who eats this bread will live for ever. This bread
is my flesh, which I will give up so that the world
may have life."

Prophet They probably meant the prophet that God told Moses he would send (Deuteronomy 18:15–19).
'He gave . . . eat.' Quotation from Psalm 78:24.
'They . . . God.' Quotation from Isaiah 54:13.

52Then the Jews began to argue among them-
selves, saying, "How can this man give us his
flesh to eat?"
53Jesus said, "I tell you the truth, you must eat
the flesh of the Son of Man and drink his blood.
Otherwise, you won't have real life in you.
54Those who eat my flesh and drink my blood
have eternal life, and I will raise them up on the
last day. 55My flesh is true food, and my blood is
true drink. 56Those who eat my flesh and drink
my blood live in me, and I live in them. 57The
living Father sent me, and I live because of the
Father. So whoever eats me will live because of
me. 58I am not like the bread your ancestors ate.
They ate that bread and still died. I am the bread
that came down from heaven, and whoever eats
this bread will live for ever." 59Jesus said all these
things while he was teaching in the synagogue[d]
in Capernaum.

The Words of Eternal Life

60When the followers of Jesus heard this,
many of them said, "This teaching is hard. Who
can accept it?"
61Knowing that his followers were complain-
ing about this, Jesus said, "Does this teaching
bother you? 62Then will it also bother you to see
the Son of Man[d] going back to the place where
he came from? 63It is the Spirit that gives life.
The flesh doesn't give life. The words I told
you are spirit, and they give life. 64But some of
you don't believe." (Jesus knew from the begin-
ning who did not believe and who would turn
against him.) 65Jesus said, "That is the reason

PRIORITIES

One Man Down

"I'll do it!" one guy told Tony.

Tony looked at the volunteer and shook his head. "You're too fat."

"Then what about me?" another asked hopefully.

He shook his head again. "Too skinny."

"And me?" Yet another asked enthusiastically.

Tony shook his head again. "You must be joking! You're scared of the ball."

Tony was captain of the five-a-side indoor football team, and one player was ill. Some of the others had heard about the temporary vacancy and had volunteered to stand in for that evening. "Why weren't they any good?" Noel asked his friend. "We're one man down and there's less than two hours before the match! How can we play five-a-side with four men?"

Tony shrugged. "But they weren't what I was looking for. I want someone who's good, athletic . . . and fits with the image of my team!"

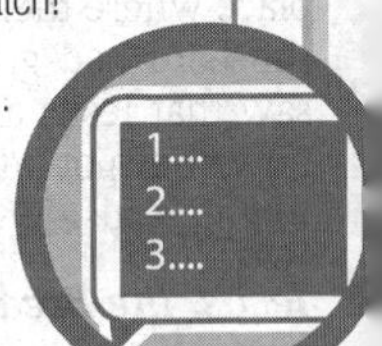

As the evening approached, Tony began to panic. In desperation, he located the boys who had earlier volunteered to play. "Do you still want to play?" he asked them – almost begged them.

"No thanks, Tony," they replied. "We've been asked to play on the basketball team tonight."

So with one man down, Tony's team played their five-a-side match. Predictably, they lost . . .

Tony placed more emphasis on how the boys looked than on finding a player. In **John 6:24–51**, some people put more emphasis on Jesus' miracles than on the Saviour himself.

- What similarities do you see between Tony and the people in this passage?
- What do you think this passage says about what God wants your priorities to be?

Consider . . .

- whether you are guilty of seeing people for what they are instead of who they are. How can you put this right?
- becoming friends with someone in your school that everyone else ignores. Show them that you are interested in their personality and not their looks.

For more, see . . .

- 1 Samuel 16:6–13 (p.269)
- James 2:1–9 (p.1348)
- Matthew 6:25–34 (p.948)

I said, 'If the Father does not bring a person to
me, that one cannot come.' "
66After Jesus said this, many of his followers
left him and stopped following him.
67Jesus asked the twelve followers, "Do you
want to leave, too?"
68Simon Peter answered him, "Lord, where
would we go? You have the words that give eter-
nal life. 69We believe and know that you are the
Holy One from God."
70Then Jesus answered, "I chose all twelve of
you, but one of you is a devil."
71Jesus was talking about Judas, the son of
Simon Iscariot. Judas was one of the twelve, but
later he was going to turn against Jesus.

Jesus' Brothers Don't Believe

7 After this, Jesus travelled around Galilee. He
did not want to travel in Judea, because
the Jews there wanted to kill him. 2It was time
for the Jewish Feast[d] of Shelters. 3So Jesus'
brothers said to him, "You should leave here
and go to Judea so your followers there can see
the miracles[d] you do. 4Anyone who wants to be
well known does not hide what he does. If you
are doing these things, show yourself to the
world." 5(Even Jesus' brothers did not believe
in him.)
6Jesus said to his brothers, "The right time
for me has not yet come, but any time is right
for you. 7The world cannot hate you, but it
hates me, because I tell it the evil things it
does. 8So you go to the feast. I will not go yet to
this feast, because the right time for me has not
yet come." 9After saying this, Jesus stayed in
Galilee.
10But after Jesus' brothers had gone to the
feast, Jesus went also. But he did not let people
see him. 11At the feast the Jews were looking for
him and saying, "Where is that man?"

LIFE

Along For the Ride

Amy had kept quiet about her heart problem for so long that even the memories of operations and long spells in hospital didn't seem real to her.

So when her youth group took a trip, Amy reluctantly delivered her mother's note to their group leader. The note said that Amy shouldn't go on the "white-knuckle" rides.

At first, Amy refused to join her boyfriend on one of the theme park's best rides. She kept quiet about her heart while he teased her about being chicken.

Amy finally gave in. The initial ride left her short of breath, but she wasn't feeling too bad at the end of it.

Just as her second attempt was beginning, Amy passed out. The ride operator stopped the ride, got Amy out, and called an ambulance.

Three hours later, Amy was having another heart operation. In the middle of surgery, her heart stopped for 20 seconds. Amy might have died if she had not been plugged into life-support equipment.

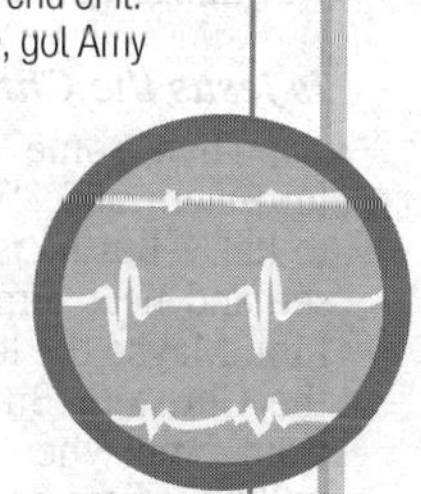

Amy has fully recovered, but her brush with death has made her more aware of how fragile life can be. And she's more open about her heart.

Life is a wonderful gift. Read **John 6:59–69** to see how Jesus said that he was the only one who could give life.

- What words of assurance would Amy find in the passage?
- What do you appreciate most about the life that Jesus has given you?

Consider . . .

- buying or picking a flower to display in your room as a reminder of the gift of life.
- spending an afternoon taking pictures of the things you enjoy most about life, then creating a photo arrangement.

For more, see . . .

- Leviticus 17:10–14 (p.116)
- Hebrews 9:11–15 (p.1337)
- Psalm 104:33–35 (p.561)

12Within the large crowd there, many people
were whispering to each other about Jesus.
Some said, "He is a good man."
Others said, "No, he fools the people." 13But
no one was brave enough to talk about Jesus
openly, because they were afraid of the Jews.

Jesus Teaches at the Feast

14When the feast was about half over, Jesus
went to the Temple[d] and began to teach. 15The
Jews were amazed and said, "This man has never
studied. How did he learn so much?"
16Jesus answered, "The things I teach are not
my own, but they come from him who sent me.
17If people choose to do what God wants, they
will know that my teaching comes from God and
not from me. 18Those who teach their own ideas
are trying to get honour for themselves. But those
who try to bring honour to the one who sent
them speak the truth, and there is nothing false
in them. 19Moses gave you the law,[n] but none
of you obeys that law. Why are you trying to
kill me?"
20The people answered, "A demon[d] has come
into you. We are not trying to kill you."
21Jesus said to them, "I did one miracle,[d]
and you are all amazed. 22Moses gave you the
law about circumcision.[d] (But really Moses did
not give you circumcision; it came from our an-
cestors.) And yet you circumcise a baby on a
Sabbath[d] day. 23If a baby can be circumcised on
a Sabbath day to obey the law of Moses, why are
you angry at me for healing a person's whole
body on the Sabbath day? 24Stop judging by the
way things look, but judge by what is really right."

Is Jesus the Christ?

25Then some of the people who lived in
Jerusalem said, "This is the man they are trying
to kill. 26But he is teaching where everyone can
see and hear him, and no one is trying to stop
him. Maybe the leaders have decided he really is
the Christ.[d] 27But we know where this man is
from. And when the real Christ comes, no one
will know where he comes from."
28Jesus, teaching in the Temple,[d] cried out,
"Yes, you know me, and you know where I am
from. But I have not come by my own authority.
I was sent by the One who is true, whom you
don't know. 29But I know him, because I am
from him, and he sent me."
30When Jesus said this, the people tried to take
him. But no one was able to touch him, because
it was not yet the right time. 31But many of the
people believed in Jesus. They said, "When the
Christ comes, will he do more miracles[d] than this
man has done?"

The Leaders Try to Arrest Jesus

32The Pharisees[d] heard the crowd whispering
these things about Jesus. So the leading priests
and the Pharisees sent some Temple[d] guards to
arrest him. 33Jesus said, "I will be with you a little
while longer. Then I will go back to the One who
sent me. 34You will look for me, but you will not
find me. And you cannot come where I am."
35The Jews said to each other, "Where will
this man go so we cannot find him? Will he go to
the Greek cities where our people live and teach
the Greek people there? 36What did he mean
when he said, 'You will look for me, but you
will not find me,' and 'You cannot come where
I am'?"

Jesus Talks About the Spirit

37On the last and most important day of the
feast Jesus stood up and said in a loud voice, "Let
anyone who is thirsty come to me and drink.
38If anyone believes in me, rivers of living water
will flow out from that person's heart, as the
Scripture[d] says." 39Jesus was talking about the
Holy Spirit.[d] The Spirit had not yet been given,
because Jesus had not yet been raised to glory.
But later, those who believed in Jesus would re-
ceive the Spirit.

The People Argue About Jesus

40When the people heard Jesus' words, some
of them said, "This man really is the Prophet."[n]
41Others said, "He is the Christ."[d]
Still others said, "The Christ will not come from
Galilee. 42The Scripture[d] says that the Christ will
come from David's family and from Bethlehem,
the town where David lived." 43So the people
did not agree with each other about Jesus. 44Some
of them wanted to arrest him, but no one was
able to touch him.

Some Leaders Won't Believe

45The Temple[d] guards went back to the lead-
ing priests and the Pharisees,[d] who asked, "Why
didn't you bring Jesus?"
46The guards answered, "The words he says
are greater than the words of any other person
who has ever spoken!"
47The Pharisees answered, "So Jesus has
fooled you also! 48Have any of the leaders or the
Pharisees believed in him? No! 49But these people,

law Moses gave God's people the law that God gave him on Mount Sinai (Exodus 34:29–32).
Prophet They probably meant the prophet God told Moses he would send (Deuteronomy 18:15–19).

who know nothing about the law, are under
God's curse."
50 Nicodemus, who had gone to see Jesus be-
fore, was in that group.[n] He said, 51 "Our law
does not judge a man without hearing him and
knowing what he has done."
52 They answered, "Are you from Galilee, too?
Study the Scriptures,[d] and you will learn that no
prophet[d] comes from Galilee."

Some early Greek manuscripts do not contain 7:53—8:11.

[53 And everyone left and went home.

The Woman Caught in Adultery

8 Jesus went to the Mount of Olives.[d] 2 But
early in the morning he went back to the
Temple,[d] and all the people came to him, and he
sat and taught them. 3 The teachers of the law
and the Pharisees[d] brought a woman who had
been caught in adultery.[d] They forced her to
stand before the people. 4 They said to Jesus,
"Teacher, this woman was caught having sexual
relations with a man who is not her husband.
5 The law of Moses commands that we stone to
death every woman who does this. What do you
say we should do?" 6 They were asking this to
trick Jesus so that they could have some charge
against him.

Nicodemus . . . group. The story about Nicodemus going and talking to Jesus is in John 3:1–21.

SEXUALITY

Once Forgiven, What Then?

Stephanie silently wept as Ross sat next to her on the settee, buttoning his shirt. The silence seemed to swallow them.

"Ross, we said we'd never do this again," she finally said through her tears.

"Well, we didn't mean to . . . It just happened," Ross responded.

"That's what you always say."

The two sat silently for a long time, and then Stephanie finally spoke, "I don't think we should see each other any more."

Ross didn't say anything. He just stared out of the window. But Stephanie knew by his sniffling that he was crying.

Stephanie reached across and touched his arm. "I'm sorry, Ross, but I just can't keep doing this to us – or to God. We just keep doing it and then asking God to forgive us."

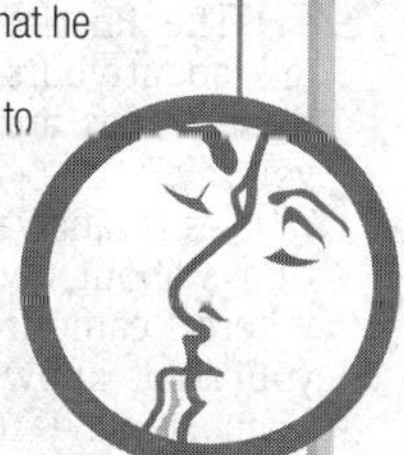

Ross jerked his head around and looked at Stephanie. "But God does forgive us, Steph," Ross argued. "We won't do it again."

Stephanie started crying even harder. "No, Ross, we say that every time. I'm serious this time. We can't keep sinning and expect God to forgive us. I love you, but this hurts too much. Please take me home."

In **John 8:1–11**, Jesus faced a woman caught in sexual sin. Read what he said to her.

- How are Ross and Stephanie similar to the woman caught in adultery? How are they different?
- What does this passage tell us about Jesus' perspective on sexual sin and the person who commits it? What is there in your life that needs to hear his "don't sin any more".

Consider . . .

- evaluating the videos you watch and deciding what view of sexuality they promote.
- acting on one area of your life where Jesus is telling you to go and not sin any more. Tell a friend or parent about it, and ask that person to support you in your decision.

For more, see . . .

- Psalm 51:1–19 (p.530)
- Ephesians 6:10–18 (p.1277)
- 1 Corinthians 6:12–20 (p.1221)

But Jesus bent down and started writing on
the ground with his finger. 7When they contin-
ued to ask Jesus their question, he rose up and
said, "Anyone here who has never sinned can
throw the first stone at her." 8Then Jesus bent
over again and wrote on the ground.
9Those who heard Jesus began to leave one by
one, first the older men and then the others.
Jesus was left there alone with the woman stand-
ing before him. 10Jesus rose up again and asked
her, "Woman, where are they? Has no one
judged you guilty?"
11She answered, "No one, sir."
Then Jesus said, "I also don't judge you guilty.
You may go now, but don't sin any more."]

> **Sidelight** When the teachers of the law and the Pharisees brought the woman caught in the act of adultery to Jesus (John 8:1–11), they weren't really concerned with doing what was right. What they were more interested in was trapping Jesus with their words so that they could "frame him" at a later date.

Jesus is the Light of the World

12Later, Jesus talked to the people again, say-
ing, "I am the light of the world. The person who
follows me will never live in darkness but will
have the light that gives life."
13The Pharisees[d] said to Jesus, "When you
talk about yourself, you are the only one to say
these things are true. We cannot accept what
you say."
14Jesus answered, "Yes, I am saying these
things about myself, but they are true. I know
where I came from and where I am going. But
you don't know where I came from or where
I am going. 15You judge by human standards.
I am not judging anyone. 16But when I do judge,
my judgement is true, because I am not alone.
The Father who sent me is with me. 17Your
own law says that when two witnesses say the
same thing, you must accept what they say. 18I
am one of the witnesses who speaks about
myself, and the Father who sent me is the other
witness."
19They asked, "Where is your father?"
Jesus answered, "You don't know me or
my Father. If you knew me, you would know
my Father, too." 20Jesus said these things while
he was teaching in the Temple,[d] near where
the money is kept. But no one arrested him,
because the right time for him had not yet
come.

The People Misunderstand Jesus

21Again, Jesus said to the people, "I will leave
you, and you will look for me, but you will die in
your sins. You cannot come where I am going."
22So the Jews asked, "Will Jesus kill himself?
Is that why he said, 'You cannot come where I
am going'?"
23Jesus said, "You people are from here below,
but I am from above. You belong to this world,
but I don't belong to this world. 24So I told you
that you would die in your sins. Yes, you will die
in your sins if you don't believe that I am he."
25They asked, "Then who are you?"
Jesus answered, "I am what I have told you
from the beginning. 26I have many things to say
and decide about you. But I tell people only the
things I have heard from the One who sent me,
and he speaks the truth."
27The people did not understand that he was
talking to them about the Father. 28So Jesus said
to them, "When you lift up the Son of Man,[d]
you will know that I am he. You will know that
these things I do are not by my own authority
but that I say only what the Father has taught
me. 29The One who sent me is with me. I always
do what is pleasing to him, so he has not left me
alone." 30While Jesus was saying these things,
many people believed in him.

Freedom from Sin

31So Jesus said to the Jews who believed in
him, "If you continue to obey my teaching, you
are truly my followers. 32Then you will know the
truth, and the truth will make you free."
33They answered, "We are Abraham's chil-
dren, and we have never been anyone's slaves.
So why do you say we will be free?"
34Jesus answered, "I tell you the truth, every-
one who lives in sin is a slave to sin. 35A slave
does not stay with a family for ever, but a son
belongs to the family for ever. 36So if the Son
makes you free, you will be truly free. 37I know
you are Abraham's children, but you want to
kill me because you don't accept my teaching.
38I am telling you what my Father has shown
me, but you do what your own father has
told you."
39They answered, "Our father is Abraham."
Jesus said, "If you were really Abraham's chil-
dren, you would do the things Abraham did. 40I
am a man who has told you the truth which I
heard from God, but you are trying to kill me.
Abraham did nothing like that. 41So you are
doing the things your own father did."
But they said, "We are not like children who
never knew who their father was. God is our
Father; he is the only Father we have."

42 Jesus said to them, "If God were really your Father, you would love me, because I came from God and now I am here. I did not come by my own authority; God sent me. 43 You don't understand what I say, because you cannot accept my teaching. 44 You belong to your father the devil, and you want to do what he wants. He was a murderer from the beginning and was against the truth, because there is no truth in him. When he tells a lie, he shows what he is really like, because he is a liar and the father of lies. 45 But because I speak the truth, you don't believe me. 46 Can any of you prove that I am guilty of sin? If I am telling the truth, why don't you believe me? 47 The person who belongs to God accepts what God says. But you don't accept what God says, because you don't belong to God."

Jesus is Greater than Abraham

48 The Jews answered, "We say you are a Samaritan[d] and have a demon[d] in you. Are we not right?"

49 Jesus answered, "I have no demon in me. I give honour to my Father, but you dishonour me. 50 I am not trying to get honour for myself. There is One who wants this honour for me, and he is the judge. 51 I tell you the truth, whoever obeys my teaching will never die."

52 The Jews said to Jesus, "Now we know that you have a demon in you! Even Abraham and the prophets[d] died. But you say, 'Whoever obeys my teaching will never die.' 53 Do you think you are greater than our father Abraham, who died? And the prophets died, too. Who do you think you are?"

54 Jesus answered, "If I give honour to myself, that honour is worth nothing. The One who gives me honour is my Father, and you say he is your God. 55 You don't really know him, but I know him. If I said I did not know him, I would be a liar like you. But I do know him, and I obey what he says. 56 Your father Abraham was very happy that he would see my day. He saw that day and was glad."

57 The Jews said to him, "You have never seen Abraham! You are not even 50 years old."

58 Jesus answered, "I tell you the truth, before Abraham was even born, I am!" 59 When Jesus said this, the people picked up stones to throw at him. But Jesus hid himself, and then he left the Temple.[d]

Jesus Heals a Man Born Blind

9 As Jesus was walking along, he saw a man who had been born blind. 2 His followers asked him, "Teacher, whose sin caused this man to be born blind—his own sin or his parents' sin?"

3 Jesus answered, "It is not this man's sin or his parents' sin that made him be blind. This man was born blind so that God's power could be shown in him. 4 While it is daytime, we must continue doing the work of the One who sent me. Night is coming, when no one can work. 5 While I am in the world, I am the light of the world."

6 After Jesus said this, he spat on the ground and made some mud with it and put the mud on the man's eyes. 7 Then he told the man, "Go and wash in the Pool of Siloam." (Siloam means Sent.) So the man went, washed and came back seeing.

Sidelight Sending the blind man to wash in the Pool of Siloam would clearly have been symbolic for the people in Jesus' day (John 9:7). This pool was the source of water used for religious ceremonies. It was also Jerusalem's main water supply.

8 The neighbours and some people who had earlier seen this man begging said, "Isn't this the same man who used to sit and beg?"

9 Some said, "He is the one," but others said, "No, he only looks like him."

The man himself said, "I am the man."

10 They asked, "How did you get your sight?"

11 He answered, "The man named Jesus made some mud and put it on my eyes. Then he told me to go to Siloam and wash. So I went and washed, and then I could see."

12 They asked him, "Where is this man?"

"I don't know," he answered.

Pharisees Question the Healing

13 Then the people took to the Pharisees[d] the man who had been blind. 14 The day Jesus had made mud and healed his eyes was a Sabbath[d] day. 15 So now the Pharisees asked the man, "How did you get your sight?"

He answered, "He put mud on my eyes, I washed, and now I see."

16 So some of the Pharisees were saying, "This man does not keep the Sabbath day, so he is not from God."

But others said, "A man who is a sinner can't do miracles[d] like these." So they could not agree with one another.

17 They asked the man again, "What do you say about him since it was your eyes he opened?"

The man answered, "He is a prophet."[d]

18The Jews did not believe that he had been
blind and could now see again. So they sent for
the man's parents 19and asked them, "Is this
your son who you say was born blind? Then
how does he now see?"
20His parents answered, "We know that this
is our son and that he was born blind. 21But
we don't know how he can now see. We don't
know who opened his eyes. Ask him. He is
old enough to speak for himself." 22His parents
said this because they were afraid of the Jews,
who had already decided that anyone who
said Jesus was the Christ[d] would be put out of
the synagogue.[d] 23That is why his parents said,
"He is old enough. Ask him."
24So for the second time, they called the man
who had been blind. They said, "You should give
God the glory by telling the truth. We know that
this man is a sinner."
25He answered, "I don't know if he is a sinner.
One thing I do know: I was blind, and now I see."
26They asked, "What did he do to you? How
did he make you see again?"
27He answered, "I have already told you, and
you didn't listen. Why do you want to hear it
again? Do you want to become his followers,
too?"
28Then they insulted him and said, "You are his
follower, but we are followers of Moses. 29We
know that God spoke to Moses, but as for this
man we don't even know where he comes from."
30The man answered, "This is a very strange
thing. You don't know where he comes from,
and yet he opened my eyes. 31We all know that
God does not listen to sinners, but he listens to
anyone who worships and obeys him. 32Nobody
has ever heard of anyone giving sight to a man
born blind. 33If this man were not from God, he
could do nothing."
34They answered, "You were born full of
sin! Are you trying to teach us?" And they threw
him out.

SIN

Blind Side

"I actually thought no one could tell I was drinking." Joe studied his hands for a moment before he looked up at the group. "I got caught the first time I got drunk. I thought about giving it up then. But my friends were into it, so I kept drinking with them."

Joe paused and took a deep breath. Then he continued, "Before long, I didn't need them as an excuse to drink. I enjoyed it so much, I drank whenever I got the chance." A few other teenagers in the group nodded knowingly. Joe relaxed a bit.

"I thought I was keeping up pretty well. I kept my position on the football team and my school results hadn't slipped too far. I tried to be careful with getting in on time and covering the alcohol on my breath.

"One day, my dad made some comment to me about how I was going to end up just like him. That shocked me! Dad's an alcoholic. And it scared me.

"So I talked to my youth leader, and he suggested that I join this support group," Joe said as his eyes swept over the teenagers seated in a circle. "I really thought I had everyone fooled. I suppose the only one blind to my drinking problem was me."

Jesus encountered blind people of all kinds. Read **John 9:1–41** to see the key to true sight.

- What are the similarities and differences between Joe's blindness and the Pharisees' blindness? Between Joe's blindness and that of the blind man?
- What does this Bible passage tell us about being blind to sin?

Consider . . .

- asking God to open your eyes to areas where you are blind to sin.
- asking a good friend to tell you about a blind spot in your life, then working to change it.

For more, see . . .

- Isaiah 6:9–10 (p.645)
- Ephesians 5:6–15 (p.1275)
- Matthew 15:1–20 (p.967)

Spiritual Blindness

35When Jesus heard that they had thrown him
out, Jesus found him and said, "Do you believe
in the Son of Man?"[d]
36He asked, "Who is the Son of Man, sir, so
that I can believe in him?"
37Jesus said to him, "You have seen him. The
Son of Man is the one talking with you."
38He said, "Lord, I believe!" Then the man
worshipped Jesus.
39Jesus said, "I came into this world so that
the world would be judged. I came so that the
blind[n] will see and so that those who see will be-
come blind."
40Some of the Pharisees[d] who were nearby
heard Jesus say this and asked, "Are you saying
we are blind, too?"
41Jesus said, "If you were blind, you would
not be guilty of sin. But since you keep saying
you see, your guilt remains."

The Shepherd and His Sheep

10 Jesus said, "I tell you the truth, the per-
son who does not enter the sheepfold by
the door, but climbs in by some other way, is a
thief and a robber. 2The one who enters by the
door is the shepherd of the sheep. 3The one who
guards the door opens it for him. And the sheep
listen to the voice of the shepherd. He calls his
own sheep by name and leads them out. 4When
he brings all his sheep out, he goes ahead of
them, and they follow him because they know
his voice. 5But they will never follow a stranger.
They will run away from him because they don't
know his voice." 6Jesus told the people this story,
but they did not understand what it meant.

Jesus is the Good Shepherd

7So Jesus said again, "I tell you the truth, I am
the door for the sheep. 8All the people who came
before me were thieves and robbers. The sheep

blind Jesus is talking about people who are spiritually blind, not physically blind.

JESUS CHRIST

Shepherds and Sheep

Shepherds have been around for thousands of years – and they're still going strong.

In Bible times, a shepherd could often be seen sitting alone on the hills, watching carefully for any wolves that might come and attack his flock.

Often, the shepherds of old would have a name for each of their sheep. They could tell the difference between each one and saw them as individual animals rather than just "one of my flock".

Even as night fell, the shepherds would remain with their sheep, and it wasn't unusual for them to sleep in the same field as their flock!

Occasionally, one of the sheep would get the idea of wandering away from the rest of the flock, and very often fell into a ditch or got its wool tangled in thorn bushes. In cases like this, the shepherd would leave the rest of his flock and go to help the one that had got itself into trouble.

Jesus seemed to know all about the shepherds of his day. In **John 10:1–30**, he identified himself as the Good Shepherd, and all his followers as his sheep.

- How is Jesus' care for his followers similar to the way that a shepherd takes care of his flock?
- How easily do you identify yourself as a sheep? Do you find it easy to follow Jesus the Shepherd or are you inclined to "wander off" and get into trouble?

Consider . . .

- why Jesus identified himself as the Good Shepherd, and ask yourself if you are a good sheep.
- identifying areas in your life where you tend to wander. How can you follow Jesus closely?

For more, see . . .

- Psalm 23 (p.513)
- Luke 15:1–7 (p.1070)
- Ezekiel 34:11–31 (p.817)

did not listen to them. 9I am the door, and the person who enters through me will be saved and will be able to come in and go out and find pasture. 10A thief comes to steal and kill and destroy, but I came to give life—life in all its fullness.

> **Sidelight** When Jesus describes a sheepfold in John 10:1–6 his listeners would have understood immediately, since sheep were the most common animals around. Sheepfolds were low buildings to protect the flock in bad weather with an outdoor pen and a wall. The wall was covered with thorny bushes to keep out wild animals.

11"I am the good shepherd. The good shepherd gives his life for the sheep. 12The worker who is paid to keep the sheep is different from the shepherd who owns them. When the worker sees a wolf coming, he runs away and leaves the sheep alone. Then the wolf attacks the sheep and scatters them. 13The man runs away because he is only a paid worker and does not really care about the sheep.

14–15"I am the good shepherd. I know my sheep, as the Father knows me. And my sheep know me, as I know the Father. I give my life for the sheep. 16I have other sheep that are not in this flock, and I must bring them also. They will listen to my voice, and there will be one flock and one shepherd. 17The Father loves me because I give my life so that I can take it back again. 18No one takes it away from me; I give my own life freely. I have the right to give my life, and I have the right to take it back. This is what my Father commanded me to do."

19Again the Jews did not agree with each other because of these words of Jesus. 20Many of them said, "A demon [d] has come into him and made him crazy. Why listen to him?"

21But others said, "A man who is crazy with a demon does not say things like this. Can a demon open the eyes of the blind?"

Jesus is Rejected

22The time came for the Feast [d] of Dedication at Jerusalem. It was winter, 23and Jesus was walking in the Temple [d] in Solomon's Porch. [d] 24The Jews gathered around him and said, "How long will you make us wonder about you? If you are the Christ, [d] tell us plainly."

25Jesus answered, "I have already told you, but you did not believe. The miracles [d] I do in my Father's name show who I am. 26But you don't believe, because you are not my sheep. 27My sheep listen to my voice; I know them, and they follow me. 28I give them eternal life, and they will never die, and no one can steal them out of my hand. 29My Father gave my sheep to me. He is greater than all, and no person can steal my sheep out of my Father's hand. 30The Father and I are one."

31Again the Jews picked up stones to kill Jesus. 32But he said to them, "I have done many good works from the Father. Which of these good works are you killing me for?"

33The Jews answered, "We are not killing you because of any good work you have done, but because you speak against God. You are only a human, but you say you are the same as God!"

34Jesus answered, "It is written in your law that God said, 'I said, you are gods.' [n] 35This Scripture [d] called those people gods who received God's message, and Scripture is always true. 36So why do you say that I speak against God because I said, 'I am God's Son'? I am the one God chose and sent into the world. 37If I don't do what my Father does, then don't believe me. 38But if I do what my Father does, even though you don't believe in me, believe what I do. Then you will know and understand that the Father is in me and I am in the Father."

39They tried to take Jesus again, but he escaped from them.

40Then he went back across the Jordan River to the place where John had first baptised. Jesus stayed there, 41and many people came to him and said, "John never did a miracle, but everything John said about this man is true." 42And in that place many believed in Jesus.

The Death of Lazarus

11 A man named Lazarus was sick. He lived in the town of Bethany, where Mary and her sister Martha lived. 2Mary was the woman who later put perfume on the Lord and wiped his feet with her hair. Mary's brother was Lazarus, the man who was now sick. 3So Mary and Martha sent someone to tell Jesus, "Lord, the one you love is sick."

4When Jesus heard this, he said, "This sickness will not end in death. It is for the glory of God, to bring glory to the Son of God." 5Jesus loved Martha and her sister and Lazarus. 6But when he heard that Lazarus was sick, he stayed where he was for two more days. 7Then Jesus said to his followers, "Let's go back to Judea."

'I . . . gods.' Quotation from Psalm 82:6.

8 The followers said, "But Teacher, the Jews
there tried to stone you to death only a short
time ago. Now you want to go back there?"
9 Jesus answered, "Are there not twelve hours
in the day? If anyone walks in the daylight, he
will not stumble, because he can see by this
world's light. 10 But if anyone walks at night,
he stumbles because there is no light to help
him see."
11 After Jesus said this, he added, "Our friend
Lazarus has fallen asleep, but I am going there to
wake him."
12 The followers said, "But Lord, if he is only
asleep, he will be all right."
13 Jesus meant that Lazarus was dead, but his
followers thought he meant Lazarus was really
sleeping. 14 So then Jesus said plainly, "Lazarus is
dead. 15 And I am glad for your sakes I was not
there so that you may believe. But let's go to him
now."
16 Then Thomas (the one called Didymus) said
to the other followers, "Let us also go so that we
can die with him."

Jesus in Bethany

17 When Jesus arrived, he learned that Lazarus
had already been dead and in the tomb for four
days. 18 Bethany was about three kilometres from
Jerusalem. 19 Many of the Jews had come there to
comfort Martha and Mary about their brother.
20 When Martha heard that Jesus was coming,
she went out to meet him, but Mary stayed at
home. 21 Martha said to Jesus, "Lord, if you had
been here, my brother would not have died.
22 But I know that even now God will give you
anything you ask."
23 Jesus said, "Your brother will rise and live
again."
24 Martha answered, "I know that he will rise
and live again in the resurrection [n] on the last day."

resurrection Being raised from the dead to live again.

DEATH

Sharing Sadness

They made their way through the church doors to a back pew. Neither of them knew Polly's father, but they had decided to go to his funeral because Polly was in their class.

It wasn't a comfortable situation for Stephen or Dan, but they couldn't begin to imagine how hard it must have been for Polly. As they followed the coffin out to the graveyard after the service, Polly looked round at them and sort of smiled and cried at the same time.

The next Thursday Polly came back to school and made a point of talking to Dan and Stephen before class. "I really want to thank you for being at my dad's funeral last Saturday. It means a lot to me," Polly said.

"We didn't know what else we could do to help," Dan offered.

"That was enough," Polly said. "Just knowing I had friends there made a difference. I didn't feel so alone. Your being around made the service easier to take. It was as if you were sharing some of the pain."

Jesus understood what it was like to grieve with friends. Read **John 11:1–45** to see how Jesus shared his friends' grief and how Jesus' presence made a difference.

- How did Stephen and Dan's actions compare with Jesus' actions?
- What does Jesus' reaction teach us about dealing with sadness?

Consider . . .

- telling a trusted friend about the death of someone who was important to you. Openly express your emotions.
- asking your minister or youth leader to help you and a group of friends to devise things that you can do when a friend's family member dies.

For more, see . . .

- Isaiah 61:1–3 (p.705)
- Revelation 21:1–4 (p.1403)
- Romans 12:9–15 (p.1205)

25Jesus said to her, "I am the resurrection and
the life. Those who believe in me will have life
even if they die. 26And everyone who lives and
believes in me will never die. Martha, do you
believe this?"
27Martha answered, "Yes, Lord. I believe that
you are the Christ,[d] the Son of God, the One who
was to come into the world."

Jesus Cries

28After Martha said this, she went back and
talked to her sister Mary alone. Martha said, "The
Teacher is here and he is asking for you." 29When
Mary heard this, she got up quickly and went to
Jesus. 30Jesus had not yet come into the town but
was still at the place where Martha had met him.
31The Jews were with Mary in the house, com-
forting her. When they saw her stand and leave
quickly, they followed her, thinking she was go-
ing to the tomb to cry there.
32But Mary went to the place where Jesus was.
When she saw him, she fell at his feet and said,
"Lord, if you had been here, my brother would
not have died."
33When Jesus saw Mary crying and the Jews
who came with her also crying, he was upset and
was deeply troubled. 34He asked, "Where did you
bury him?"
"Come and see, Lord," they said.
35Jesus cried.
36So the Jews said, "See how much he
loved him."
37But some of them said, "If Jesus opened the
eyes of the blind man, why couldn't he keep
Lazarus from dying?"

Jesus Raises Lazarus

38Again feeling very upset, Jesus came to the
tomb. It was a cave with a large stone covering the
entrance. 39Jesus said, "Move the stone away."
Martha, the sister of the dead man, said, "But,
Lord, it has been four days since he died. There
will be a bad smell."

Sidelight Lazarus had been dead four days before Jesus arrived (John 11:39). That would have made bringing him back to life particularly miraculous to people in Jesus' day. They believed that a soul stayed with a body for three days and then left.

40Then Jesus said to her, "Didn't I tell you that
if you believed you would see the glory of God?"
41So they moved the stone away from the en-
trance. Then Jesus looked up and said, "Father, I
thank you that you heard me. 42I know that you
always hear me, but I said these things because of
the people here around me. I want them to believe
that you sent me." 43After Jesus said this, he cried
out in a loud voice, "Lazarus, come out!" 44The
dead man came out, his hands and feet wrapped
with pieces of cloth, and a cloth around his face.
Jesus said to them, "Take the cloth off him
and let him go."

The Plan to Kill Jesus

45Many of the Jews, who had come to visit
Mary and saw what Jesus did, believed in him.
46But some of them went to the Pharisees[d] and
told them what Jesus had done. 47Then the lead-
ing priests and Pharisees called a meeting of the
Jewish council. They asked, "What should we
do? This man is doing many miracles.[d] 48If we let
him continue doing these things, everyone will
believe in him. Then the Romans will come and
take away our Temple[d] and our nation."
49One of the men there was Caiaphas, the
high priest that year. He said, "You people know
nothing! 50You don't realise that it is better for
one man to die for the people than for the whole
nation to be destroyed."
51Caiaphas did not think of this himself. As
high priest that year, he was really prophesying[d]
that Jesus would die for the Jewish nation 52and
for God's scattered children to bring them all to-
gether and make them one.
53That day they started planning to kill Jesus.
54So Jesus no longer travelled openly among the
Jews. He left there and went to a place near the
desert, to a town called Ephraim and stayed there
with his followers.
55It was almost time for the Jewish Passover[d]
Feast. Many from the country went up to
Jerusalem before the Passover to do the special
things to make themselves pure. 56The people
looked for Jesus and stood in the Temple asking
each other, "Is he coming to the Feast? What do
you think?" 57But the leading priests and the
Pharisees had given orders that if anyone knew
where Jesus was, he must tell them. Then they
could arrest him.

Jesus with Friends in Bethany

12 Six days before the Passover[d] Feast, Jesus
went to Bethany, where Lazarus lived,
whom Jesus had raised from the dead. 2There
they had a dinner for Jesus. Martha served
the food, and Lazarus was one of the people
eating with Jesus. 3Mary brought in half a litre
of very expensive perfume made from pure nard.[d]
She poured the perfume on Jesus' feet, and
then she wiped his feet with her hair. And
the sweet smell from the perfume filled the
whole house.

4Judas Iscariot, one of Jesus' followers, who
would later turn against him, was there. Judas
said, 5"This perfume was worth 300 silver
coins.[n] Why wasn't it sold and the money given
to the poor?" 6But Judas did not really care about
the poor; he said this because he was a thief. He
was the one who kept the money bag, and he
often stole from it.
7Jesus answered, "Leave her alone. It was right
for her to save this perfume for today, the day for
me to be prepared for burial. 8You will always
have the poor with you, but you will not always
have me."

The Plot Against Lazarus

9A large crowd of Jews heard that Jesus was
in Bethany. So they went there to see not only
Jesus but Lazarus, whom Jesus raised from the
dead. 10So the leading priests made plans to kill
Lazarus, too. 11Because of Lazarus many of the
Jews were leaving them and believing in Jesus.

Jesus Enters Jerusalem

12The next day a great crowd who had come to
Jerusalem for the Passover[d] Feast heard that Jesus
was coming there. 13So they took branches of
palm trees and went out to meet Jesus, shouting,

"Praise[n] God!
God bless the One who comes in the name
of the Lord!
God bless the King of Israel!" *Psalm 118:25–26*

14Jesus found a colt and sat on it. This was as
the Scripture[d] says,

15"Don't be afraid, people of Jerusalem!
Your king is coming,
sitting on the colt of a donkey." *Zechariah 9:9*

coins A silver Roman denarii coin was the average pay for one day's work.
Praise Literally, "Hosanna", a Hebrew word used at first in praying to God for help. At this time it was probably a shout of joy used in praising God or his Messiah.

SERVICE

Poured Out

On 9 October 2001, the BBC reported this story: "It's official – 'Jedi Knight' is ON the list of religions for the 2001 UK census." That year, in the lead up to the government census, emails were being excitedly passed around stating that if 10,000 people or more wrote in the census that their religious persuasion was Jedi Knight, it would become an official religion! How does a 1977 sci-fi B-movie influence over 10,000 people's supposed religious stance more than twenty-four years later? The reality is, sticking your name on a form doesn't make you a Jedi Knight, but at the same time, something caught the imagination of the country.

The struggle between good and evil is championed by heroes of courage, honour, dignity, courtesy and nobleness. We love those stories of old, with knights rescuing fair maidens, honouring their king, fighting for justice, taking up the charge to serve and protect the weak in humility, with no thought of reward. For these guys, to die for their king wasn't a matter of sacrifice, rather, it was considered an honour.

Mary of Bethany (the same Mary who sat at Jesus' feet and believed in him for the resurrection of her brother Lazarus) is someone who seems to have grasped the value of Jesus. She was ready to not only sign her name next to his, but to literally pour out an offering which was not just a sacrifice, but also an honour, because it was for Jesus. Check out **John 12:1–11**.

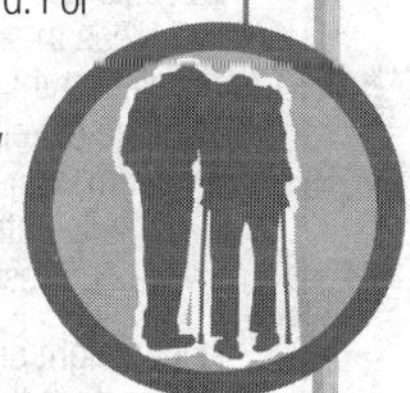

- Have you ever found yourself feeling a bit like Judas, as if things just aren't worth your time?
- If Jesus were in your house today, how might you serve him?

Consider . . .

- you and Jesus. Is he your king? Is he worth being poured out for?
- whether sometimes it can be as if we've shoved our name down to be a Christian, but not followed it through. Serving God is a privilege and begins with making a decision to become his constant student, to learn to serve the way he served. Is today the day to take things further?

For more, see . . .

- Genesis 22:1–19 (p.25)
- Luke 22:39–46 (p.1088)
- 2 Samuel 23:13–17 (p.308)
- Luke 23:26–46 (p.1091)

16 The followers of Jesus did not understand this at first. But after Jesus was raised to glory, they remembered that this had been written about him and that they had done these things to him.

People Tell About Jesus

17 There had been many people with Jesus when he raised Lazarus from the dead and told him to come out of the tomb. Now they were telling others about what Jesus did. 18 Many people went out to meet Jesus, because they had heard about this miracle.[d] 19 So the Pharisees[d] said to each other, "You can see that nothing is going right for us. Look! The whole world is following him."

Jesus Talks About His Death

20 There were some Greek people, too, who came to Jerusalem to worship at the Passover[d] Feast. 21 They went to Philip, who was from Bethsaida in Galilee, and said, "Sir, we would like to see Jesus." 22 Philip told Andrew, and then Andrew and Philip told Jesus.

23 Jesus said to them, "The time has come for the Son of Man[d] to receive his glory. 24 I tell you the truth, a grain of wheat must fall to the ground and die to make many seeds. But if it never dies, it remains only a single seed. 25 Those who love their lives will lose them, but those who hate their lives in this world will keep true life for ever. 26 Whoever serves me must follow me. Then my servant will be with me everywhere I am. My Father will honour anyone who serves me.

27 "Now I am very troubled. Should I say, 'Father, save me from this time'? No, I came to this time in order to suffer. 28 Father, bring glory to your name!"

Then a voice came from heaven, "I have brought glory to it, and I will do it again."

29 The crowd standing there, who heard the voice, said it was thunder.

But others said, "An angel has spoken to him."

30 Jesus said, "That voice was for your sake, not mine. 31 Now is the time for the world to be

LIFE

Life From the Ashes

In the summer of 1988, forest fires swept through nearly half of Yellowstone National Park's 1 million hectares in the USA. At first, it seemed as though life in the park could never be the same. The fire seemed to be a total disaster.

But it wasn't. Foresters pointed out that lodgepole pine trees had cones on them that would only open under intense heat – almost as though they were designed to respond to a forest fire. Yellowstone's dry climate kept dead wood from decaying quickly, so the ashes from the fire provided nutrients to the ground that could actually mean better growth for years to come. Bluebirds and woodpeckers would benefit from the open areas that the fire had created. Other animals would flourish with the nearly tenfold increase in plant species that the newly fortified and uncovered earth could offer.

No one at Yellowstone looks forward to forest fires. But it is known that fires, however devastating they seem, don't mean the end of things.

The devastation of death can be sudden and tragic – like the devastation of a forest fire. But new life can result. Read **John 12:20–36** to discover what Jesus said about life and new growth.

- How might an ecologist's attitude towards forest fires be like Jesus' attitude towards new life?
- What does the Bible passage say to you about life?

Consider . . .

- writing on a sheet of paper about an area of your life in which you need to give something up and then burying the paper in your garden. A week later, dig it up and evaluate your progress in letting go.
- walking through a park or forest to notice how death gives way to new growth.

For more, see . . .

- Ecclesiastes 3:1–8 (p.622)
- 1 John 1:5–7 (p.1371)
- 2 Corinthians 4:16–5:10 (p.1244)

judged; now the ruler of this world will be
thrown down. 32If I am lifted up from the earth,
I will draw all people towards me." 33Jesus said
this to show how he would die.
34The crowd said, "We have heard from the
law that the Christ[d] will live for ever. So why do
you say, 'The Son of Man must be lifted up'?
Who is this 'Son of Man'?"
35Then Jesus said, "The light will be with you
for a little longer, so walk while you have the
light. Then the darkness will not catch you. If
you walk in the darkness, you will not know
where you are going. 36Believe in the light while
you still have it so that you will become children
of light." When Jesus had said this, he left and
hid himself from them.

Some People Won't Believe in Jesus

37Though Jesus had done many miracles[d] in
front of the people, they still did not believe in
him. 38This was to bring about what Isaiah the
prophet[d] had said:

"Who would have believed what we heard?
Who saw the Lord's power in this?"

Isaiah 53:1

39This is why the people could not believe: Isaiah
had also said,
40Make the minds of these people dumb.
Shut their ears. Cover their eyes.
Otherwise, they might really understand
what they see with their eyes
and hear with their ears.
They might really understand in their
minds
and come back to me and be healed."

Isaiah 6:10

41Isaiah said this because he saw Jesus' glory and
spoke about him.
42But many believed in Jesus, even many
of the leaders. But because of the Pharisees,[d]
they did not say they believed in him for fear
they would be put out of the synagogue.[d] 43They
loved praise from people more than praise
from God.
44Then Jesus cried out, "Whoever believes
in me is really believing in the One who sent
me. 45Whoever sees me sees the One who
sent me. 46I have come as light into the world so
that whoever believes in me would not stay in
darkness.
47"Anyone who hears my words and does not
obey them, I do not judge, because I did not
come to judge the world, but to save the world.
48There is a judge for those who refuse to be-
lieve in me and do not accept my words. The
word I have taught will be their judge on the
last day. 49The things I taught were not from
myself. The Father who sent me told me what
to say and what to teach. 50And I know that
eternal life comes from what the Father com-
mands. So whatever I say is what the Father
told me to say."

Jesus Washes His Followers' Feet

13 It was almost time for the Jewish Pass-
over[d] Feast. Jesus knew that it was time
for him to leave this world and go back to the
Father. He had always loved those who were his
own in the world, and he loved them all the
way to the end.
2Jesus and his followers were at the evening
meal. The devil had already persuaded Judas
Iscariot, the son of Simon, to turn against Jesus.
3Jesus knew that the Father had given him
power over everything and that he had come
from God and was going back to God. 4So dur-
ing the meal Jesus stood up and took off his
outer clothing. Taking a towel, he wrapped it
around his waist. 5Then he poured water into a
bowl and began to wash the followers' feet, dry-
ing them with the towel that was wrapped
around him.
6Jesus came to Simon Peter, who said to him,
"Lord, are you going to wash my feet?"
7Jesus answered, "You don't understand now
what I am doing, but you will understand later."
8Peter said, "No, you will never wash my
feet."
Jesus answered, "If I don't wash your feet,
you are not one of my people."
9Simon Peter answered, "Lord, then wash
not only my feet, but wash my hands and my
head, too!"
10Jesus said, "After a person has had a bath,
his whole body is clean. He needs only to wash
his feet. And you men are clean,[d] but not all

> **Sidelight**
> Washing your hands before a meal is OK. But feet? They quickly became sore and dirty in New Testament times because people wore open sandals. Washing feet was an important sign of hospitality. Jesus washed the feet of his disciples as though he were a servant (John 13:1–20), showing his disciples how to serve one another. (See also Philippians 2:3–11,p.1282.)

of you." 11Jesus knew who would turn against
him, and that is why he said, "Not all of you
are clean."
12When he had finished washing their feet, he
put on his clothes and sat down again. He asked,
"Do you understand what I have just done for
you? 13You call me 'Teacher' and 'Lord', and you
are right, because that is what I am. 14If I, your

Lord and Teacher, have washed your feet, you
also should wash each other's feet. [15]I did this
as an example so that you should do as I have
done for you. [16]I tell you the truth, a servant
is not greater than his master. A messenger is
not greater than the one who sent him. [17]If
you know these things, you will be happy if you
do them.
[18]"I am not talking about all of you. I know
those I have chosen. But this is to bring about
what the Scripture [d] said: 'The man who ate at
my table has turned against me.' [n] [19]I am telling
you this now before it happens so that when it
happens, you will believe that I am he. [20]I tell
you the truth, whoever accepts anyone I send
also accepts me. And whoever accepts me also
accepts the One who sent me."

Jesus Talks About His Death

[21]After Jesus said this, he was very troubled.
He said openly, "I tell you the truth, one of you
will turn against me."
[22]The followers all looked at each other,
because they did not know whom Jesus was

'The man . . . me.' Quotation from Psalm 41:9.

CHURCH

Servants

Meet three men who each have 10 years of professional training behind them and yet are happy to do caretaking duties for no pay.

John is a Consultant Pathologist at a large hospital. He controls the work of a large department and often speaks at international conferences.

Alan is a manager and an engineer with responsibility for 300 staff and essential supplies to part of a large city.

Peter is an architect. He makes decisions involving millions of pounds and travels first-class to the sites where he is working.

Each man has responsibility, power and status, leading a large team. They are used to being in charge.

But each is part of another team, a serving team in their local church. They hire school halls for Sunday meetings, writing letters and making sure that they are posted. They stack chairs and sweep up afterwards. If somebody needs a lift to church, they make arrangements or do it themselves. They will even help church members with mowing the lawn or decorating if necessary.

Other people take the key management decisions in the church and not everybody in the church is happy to be involved in doing the humble tasks. But these men see their service as a way of meeting real needs.

John, Alan and Peter humble themselves without thinking too much about it, though the leaders of the church recognise their servant roles. They try to make sure that everyone in the church understands that in God's eyes setting out chairs is as important as preaching. In **John 13:1–17**, Jesus humbled himself and washed his disciples' feet.

- How is the men's help similar to Jesus' act of washing the feet of his disciples?
- The disciples felt uncomfortable as Jesus began to wash their feet. How would you have felt in their position and why?

Consider . . .

- how you could humble yourself and serve someone in your church.
- helping someone in church to do something which is boring but needs doing.

For more, see . . .

- Nehemiah 5:1–13 (p.447)
- Galatians 5:13–15 (p.1264)
- Matthew 20:20–28 (p.976)

talking about. 23One of the followers sitting[n] next
to Jesus was the follower Jesus loved. 24Simon
Peter made signs to him to ask Jesus whom he
was talking about.
25That follower leaned closer to Jesus and
asked, "Lord, who is it?"
26Jesus answered, "I will dip this bread into
the dish. The man I give it to is the man who will
turn against me." So Jesus took a piece of bread,
dipped it, and gave it to Judas Iscariot, the son of
Simon. 27As soon as Judas took the bread, Satan
entered him. Jesus said to him, "The thing that
you will do—do it quickly." 28No one at the table
understood why Jesus said this to Judas. 29Since
he was the one who kept the money bag, some
of the followers thought Jesus was telling him to
buy what was needed for the feast or to give
something to the poor.
30Judas took the bread Jesus gave him and im-
mediately went out. It was night.
31When Judas was gone, Jesus said, "Now
the Son of Man[d] receives his glory, and God re-
ceives glory through him. 32If God receives glory
through him, then God will give glory to the Son
through himself. And God will give him glory
quickly."
33Jesus said, "My children, I will be with you
only a little longer. You will look for me, and

sitting Literally, "lying". The people of that time ate lying down and leaning on one arm.

LOVE

Tough Love

Amie was furious. "But Dad, Rachel has the exact same skirt! And I know for a fact that her father doesn't think it's too short."

Amie's dad remained calm, yet firm. "Sweetheart, I simply cannot allow you to leave this house wearing that." Amie stomped back to her room and reluctantly changed into some jeans. Later on, at the party, she found Rachel surrounded by boys, all of them blatantly attracted by the skirt *she* should've been wearing. "My dad hates me," she thought . . .

In reality, Amie's dad didn't hate her at all. In fact, it was quite the opposite. Her father was simply exercising tough love. He knew, like Amie, that the skirt would achieve its purpose of grabbing all the guys' attention. Not only was he protecting her, but he also knew something that Amie wasn't ready to admit to herself yet. She really needed someone to like her for more than just the skirt she was wearing. Amie's dad was willing to trade his short-term discomfort for her long-term happiness.

Tough love is when your friend whispers, "You've got something between your teeth," without laughing at you. Tough love is when your teacher continues to show up for work each day, despite finding no respect in the classroom. It chooses honesty over popularity; sacrifice over fame.

In **John 13:31–35** Jesus showed his friends tough love when he told them, "Where I am going, you cannot come." He knew that the only way for them to truly understand how they should love each other, was if he exemplified the toughest love of all. Jesus *died* for his friends, and then he told them to do the same.

- How is Amie's dad's tough love for her like our Heavenly Father's tough love for us?
- Look at verse 34. Is Jesus' call to tough love a suggestion or a command? Would you be willing to die for your faith?

Consider . . .

- spending some time thinking about the people who show you tough love. Thank them, and show them the same kind of love.
- asking your heavenly dad for the same sacrificial heart Jesus had – one that was willing to die, in order that others could live.

For more, see . . .

- 1 Samuel 20 (p.274)
- John 15:12–17 (p.1125)
- Proverbs 27:6 (p.614)

what I told the Jews, I tell you now: where I am
going you cannot come.
34"I give you a new command: love each other.
You must love each other as I have loved you.
35All people will know that you are my followers
if you love each other."

Peter will Say He Doesn't Know Jesus

36Simon Peter asked Jesus, "Lord, where are
you going?"
Jesus answered, "Where I am going you can-
not follow now, but you will follow later."
37Peter asked, "Lord, why can't I follow you
now? I am ready to die for you!"
38Jesus answered, "Are you ready to die for
me? I tell you the truth, before the cockerel
crows, you will say three times that you don't
know me."

Jesus Comforts His Followers

14 Jesus said, "Don't let your hearts be
troubled. Trust in God, and trust in me.
2There are many rooms in my Father's house; I
would not tell you this if it were not true. I am
going there to prepare a place for you. 3After I go
and prepare a place for you, I will come back and
take you to be with me so that you may be where
I am. 4You know the way to the place where I am
going."
5Thomas said to Jesus, "Lord, we don't know
where you are going. So how can we know the
way?"
6Jesus answered, "I am the way, and the truth,
and the life. The only way to the Father is
through me. 7If you really knew me, you would
know my Father, too. But now you do know him,
and you have seen him."

DOUBT

Riding Out the Storm

Robin Graham is one of the youngest people in history to sail round the world alone. But success didn't come easily for him. He left on his three-year odyssey as a sixteen-year-old thrill-seeker. Adventure was like a drug to him.

His trip changed something deep inside him. A violent storm almost capsized his little sloop, the *Dove*. In the midst of the torrent, the *Dove's* mast snapped in two, and Robin barely survived a waterspout – a water-filled tornado.

But that wasn't the worst of it. When his boat entered the doldrums, a windless, currentless part of the ocean near the equator, Robin almost went mad with despair and doubt. At one point, he completely gave up hope that he would ever make it out of the doldrums, so he splashed paraffin all over his boat and set it on fire. Fortunately, Robin came to his senses and doused the fire before it did serious damage.

Three years after his departure, Robin sailed into the Los Angeles harbour to cheering crowds, honking cars and blasting steam whistles. He had made it. And, more importantly, he had wrestled with two great enemies – doubt and despair – and found himself stronger as a result.

Robin Graham is a courageous hero. But he had crippling doubts about himself, just like the "heroes of faith" in **John 14:1–14**.

- How were Robin's doubts like the doubts the disciples experienced after Jesus told them that he was leaving them?
- What doubts have you had that seem impossible for God to solve?

Consider . . .

- writing on paper, "The one thing I doubt the most is . . . " and finishing the sentence. Then ask a friend to pray with you about your doubt.
- writing out one nagging doubt you have about God. Then tape your "doubt" to a specific date on a calendar at least a week from today. Ask God to give you insight into your doubt by that date.

For more, see . . .

- Jonah (p.885)
- James 1:2–8 (p.1348)
- Matthew 14:22–33 (p.965)

8Philip said to him, "Lord, show us the Father.
That is all we need."
9Jesus answered, "I have been with you a long
time now. Do you still not know me, Philip?
Whoever has seen me has seen the Father. So
why do you say, 'Show us the Father'? 10Don't
you believe that I am in the Father and the Father
is in me? The words I say to you don't come from
me, but the Father lives in me and does his own
work. 11Believe me when I say that I am in the
Father and the Father is in me. Or believe
because of the miracles[d] I have done. 12I tell you
the truth, whoever believes in me will do the
same things that I do. Those who believe will do
even greater things than these, because I am
going to the Father. 13And if you ask for anything
in my name, I will do it for you so that the Fa-
ther's glory will be shown through the Son. 14If
you ask me for anything in my name, I will do it.

The Promise of the Holy Spirit

15"If you love me, you will obey my com-
mands. 16I will ask the Father, and he will give
you another Helper[n] to be with you for ever—
17the Spirit[d] of truth. The world cannot accept
him, because it does not see him or know him.
But you know him, because he lives with you and
he will be in you.

Helper "Counsellor" or "Comforter". Jesus is talking about the Holy Spirit.

PEACE

The True Champion

Four decades after his death, an obscure Scottish sprinter named Eric Liddell became a household name when the Oscar-winning film *Chariots of Fire* profiled his heroics in the 1924 Olympic Games. The film told of Liddell's strong Christian convictions and his decision to drop out of the Olympic 100-metre dash because the race was scheduled for Sunday, a day which he believed was to be a day of rest for Christians.

Later, Liddell shocked the sports world by competing in and winning the Olympic 400-metre race – an event he had not intended to enter. The actor who played Liddell in the film, Ian Charleson, said, "What I admired about him was his serenity. My whole personality changed during the time I was doing the part. I became very slow and laconic."

After his Olympic victory, Liddell returned to China where he continued his work as a Christian missionary. When war broke out, he and other Westerners were rounded up by Japanese troops and held as "civil internees". During Liddell's two years in the camp, he was cut off from his wife and children. Liddell worked long hours – with little complaint – to organise a sports and recreation programme for teenagers. He also helped people in any way he could and tutored students at night.

Towards the end of the war, Liddell died fighting a brain tumour. He died the same way he always ran – fighting for every inch but at peace inside.

Annie Buchan, a close friend, was with him when he died. Before slipping into a coma from which he would never recover, Eric told his friend, "Annie, it's complete surrender."

Eric Liddell knew by experience the sort of peace that Jesus promises to those who follow him. Read about that peace in **John 14:15–29**.

- Have you experienced the sort of peace that Eric Liddell knew and Jesus talked about?
- What does the passage tell you about how to know God's peace? What's one thing in your life that you feel you need peace about?

Consider . . .

- watching for times when you don't feel at peace, and stopping to pray for fifteen seconds.
- planning to take few hours or even a day or two for a "personal retreat" with God. Spend the time reading the Bible, praying and worshipping.

For more, see . . .

- Psalm 119:162–165 (p.574)
- James 3:13–18 (p.1351)
- Philippians 4:6–9 (p.1285)

18“I will not leave you all alone like orphans; I
will come back to you. 19In a little while the
world will not see me any more, but you will see
me. Because I live, you will live, too. 20On that
day you will know that I am in my Father, and
that you are in me and I am in you. 21Those who
know my commands and obey them are the
ones who love me, and my Father will love those
who love me. I will love them and will show my-
self to them.”
22Then Judas (not Judas Iscariot) said, “But,
Lord, why do you plan to show yourself to us
and not to the rest of the world?”
23Jesus answered, “If people love me, they will
obey my teaching. My Father will love them, and
we will come to them and make our home with
them. 24Those who do not love me do not obey
my teaching. This teaching that you hear is not
really mine; it is from my Father, who sent me.
25“I have told you all these things while I
am with you. 26But the Helper will teach you
everything and will cause you to remember all
that I told you. This Helper is the Holy Spirit
whom the Father will send in my name.
27“I leave you peace; my peace I give you. I do
not give it to you as the world does. So don't let
your hearts be troubled or afraid. 28You heard me
say to you, ‘I am going, but I am coming back to
you.’ If you loved me, you would be happy that
I am going back to the Father, because he is
greater than I am. 29I have told you this now,
before it happens, so that when it happens, you
will believe. 30I will not talk with you much
longer, because the ruler of this world is coming.
He has no power over me, 31but the world must
know that I love the Father, so I do exactly what
the Father told me to do.

“Come now, let us go.

Jesus is Like a Vine

15 “I am the true vine; my Father is the
gardener. 2He cuts off every branch of

SPIRITUAL GROWTH

Stick to Your Roots

Farzana's grandad was an avid gardener. He liked nothing better than going down to his allotment and tending to his award-winning roses. In fact, Farzana's grandma used to say that he liked plants more than people!

Farzana loved going to visit him and watch him care for his plants. He knew what was best for each and every one of them in order for them to reach their full potential. He faithfully visited each plant, as he knew that they would grow to be beautiful and all his hard work would be worthwhile.

In **John 15:1–17** we are told that the Lord is like a gardener, tending to us and giving us all we need. We are told that if we remain in him – if we learn about him, spend time with him and rely upon him for our every need – then God will give us everything we need in order to reach our full potential.

In Farzana's Christian life it sometimes felt like it was all too much hard work. She kept asking herself why she should cut off a bad habit if it wasn't harming anyone else, or why she should read the Bible when it seemed so out of date.

However, through her grandad's example, she could see how God was working with her, being a faithful gardener, having full confidence that she will produce beautiful fruit when she trusts in his way.

- Why does Jesus want to tell us this?
- We are told that, as part of the vine, God wants us to bear fruit. What do you think he means by this fruit (see also Galatians 5:22–23)?

Consider . . .

- which parts of your life need to be pruned in order for you to bear fruit.
- what practical things you think you need to do in order to remain in the vine and live in Jesus.

For more, see . . .

- Galatians 5:22–23 (p.1264)
- Hebrews 12:1 (p.1343)
- Philippians 1:6 (p.1280)

mine that does not produce fruit. And he trims and cleans every branch that produces fruit so that it will produce even more fruit. 3You are already clean[d] because of the words I have spoken to you. 4Remain in me, and I will remain in you. A branch cannot produce fruit alone but must remain in the vine. In the same way, you cannot produce fruit alone but must remain in me.

5"I am the vine, and you are the branches. If any remain in me and I remain in them, they produce much fruit. But without me they can do nothing. 6If any do not remain in me, they are like a branch that is thrown away and then dies. People pick up dead branches, throw them into the fire and burn them. 7If you remain in me and follow my teachings, you can ask anything you want, and it will be given to you. 8You should produce much fruit and show that you are my followers, which brings glory to my Father. 9I loved you as the Father loved me. Now remain in my love. 10I have obeyed my Father's commands, and I remain in his love. In the same way, if you obey my commands, you will remain in my love. 11I have told you these things so that you can have the same joy I have and so that your joy will be the fullest possible joy.

Sidelight Jesus' listeners would have immediately understood the comparison he made with himself and the vine in John 15:1–11. Vineyards were common in Israel, and people knew that to get a good harvest, the dead branches must be cut off from the vine and burned. This gave the other branches a better chance to grow and bear fruit. Without this painful care the grapes would be small and bitter.

12"This is my command: love each other as I have loved you. 13The greatest love a person can show is to die for his friends. 14You are my friends if you do what I command you. 15I no longer call you servants, because a servant does not know what his master is doing. But I call you friends, because I have made known to you everything I heard from my Father. 16You did not choose me; I chose you. And I gave you this work: to go and produce fruit, fruit that will last. Then the Father will give you anything you ask for in my name. 17This is my command: love each other.

Jesus Warns His Followers

18"If the world hates you, remember that it hated me first. 19If you belonged to the world, it would love you as it loves its own. But I have chosen you out of the world, so you don't belong to it. That is why the world hates you. 20Remember what I told you: a servant is not greater than his master. If people did wrong to me, they will do wrong to you, too. And if they obeyed my teaching, they will obey yours, too. 21They will do all this to you on account of me, because they do not know the One who sent me. 22If I had not come and spoken to them, they would not be guilty of sin, but now they have no excuse for their sin. 23Whoever hates me also hates my Father. 24I did works among them that no one else has ever done. If I had not done these works, they would not be guilty of sin. But now they have seen what I have done, and yet they have hated both me and my Father. 25But this happened so that what is written in their law would be true: 'They hated me for no reason.'[n]

26"I will send you the Helper[n] from the Father; he is the Spirit of truth who comes from the Father. When he comes, he will tell about me, 27and you also must tell people about me, because you have been with me from the beginning.

16 "I have told you these things to keep you from giving up. 2People will put you out of their synagogues.[d] Yes, the time is coming when those who kill you will think they are offering service to God. 3They will do this because they have not known the Father and they have not known me. 4I have told you these things now so that when the time comes you will remember that I warned you.

The Work of the Holy Spirit

"I did not tell you these things at the beginning, because I was with you then. 5Now I am going back to the One who sent me. But none of you asks me, 'Where are you going?' 6Your hearts are filled with sadness because I have told you these things. 7But I tell you the truth, it is better for you that I go away. When I go away, I will send the Helper[n] to you. If I do not go away, the Helper will not come. 8When the Helper comes, he will prove to the people of the world the truth about sin, about being right with God and about judgement. 9He will prove to them that sin is not believing in me. 10He will prove to them that being right with God comes through my going to the Father and not being seen by you any more. 11And the Helper will prove to them that judgement happened when the ruler of this world was judged.

12"I have many more things to say to you, but they are too much for you now. 13But when the Spirit[d] of truth comes, he will lead you into

'They . . . reason.' These words could be from Psalm 35:19 or Psalm 69:4.
Helper "Counsellor" or "Comforter". Jesus is talking about the Holy Spirit.

all truth. He will not speak his own words, but
he will speak only what he hears, and he will tell
you what is to come. 14The Spirit of truth will
bring glory to me, because he will take what I
have to say and tell it to you. 15All that the Father
has is mine. That is why I said that the Spirit will
take what I have to say and tell it to you.

Sadness will Become Happiness

16"After a little while you will not see me, and
then after a little while you will see me again."
17Some of the followers said to each other,
"What does Jesus mean when he says, 'After a
little while you will not see me, and then after a
little while you will see me again'? And what
does he mean when he says, 'Because I am going
to the Father'?" 18They also asked, "What does
he mean by 'a little while'? We don't understand
what he is saying."
19Jesus saw that the followers wanted to ask
him about this, so he said to them, "Are you ask-
ing each other what I meant when I said, 'After
a little while you will not see me, and then after
a little while you will see me again'? 20I tell you
the truth, you will cry and be sad, but the world
will be happy. You will be sad, but your sadness
will become joy. 21When a woman gives birth to
a baby, she has pain, because her time has come.
But when her baby is born, she forgets the pain,
because she is so happy that a child has been

HOLY SPIRIT

The Improbable Disciple

Nicky Cruz was a murderous, uncontrollable gang leader who had killed before and would probably kill again. Without overstating the truth, Cruz was the most unlikely prospect for Christian conversion. He was also one of the first gang members whom David Wilkerson, a rural minister, met on the rough streets of New York City.

Wilkerson left his comfortable surroundings and started a missionary outreach to gang members in New York during the late 1950s. He was idealistic, and sometimes his efforts to gain a foothold for Christ among the vicious gang culture failed miserably.

Time after time, Nicky rejected David's pleas to seek God's forgiveness – once threatening the thin, quaking minister with a knife to his throat. But David replied, "You can cut me to pieces, Nicky, but every piece will still cry out, 'I love you'."

David invited Nicky to attend a city-wide meeting he was organising for gang members. Impressed by the man's courage, Nicky told David that he and his gang would be there.

Nicky did show up, and David invited him to collect the offering. Nicky and his gang did and then headed for the backstage exit, sniggering at the gullible preacher.

But on the way out, Nicky felt a heavy, almost overpowering weight on his shoulders. He stopped. He couldn't escape the fearful truth: the Jesus about whom David had spoken required something of him. Nicky and his gang returned to meet David on stage. At the end of the meeting, Nicky told David, "I've given my heart to God."

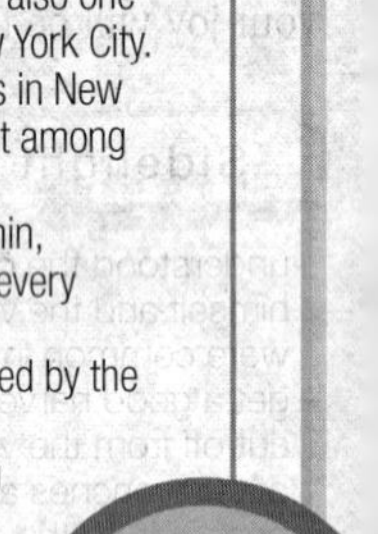

Today Nicky works with tough, inner-city teenagers. Jesus said one of the Holy Spirit's main responsibilities is to prove the truth to people who are like Nicky Cruz used to be. Read about the Holy Spirit in **John 16:4–15**.

- According to verse 8, how did the Holy Spirit influence Nicky Cruz?
- When have you felt the Holy Spirit working with you? Explain.

Consider . . .

- listing ten words that could replace the word "Holy" and ten words that could replace the word "Spirit". Mix and match the words to come up with combinations such as "Perfect Presence" or "Pure Companion".
- spending five minutes at the end of each day, thinking of ways in which the Holy Spirit was with you throughout the day.

For more, see . . .

- Psalm 51:10–13 (p.530)
- Acts 2:1–36 (p.1138)
- Luke 11:5–13 (p.1059)

born into the world. 22It is the same with you.
Now you are sad, but I will see you again and
you will be happy, and no one will take away
your joy. 23In that day you will not ask me for
anything. I tell you the truth, my Father will give
you anything you ask for in my name. 24Until
now you have not asked for anything in my name.
Ask and you will receive, so that your joy will be
the fullest possible joy.

Victory Over the World

25"I have told you these things, using stories
that hide the meaning. But the time will come
when I will not use stories like that to tell you
things; I will speak to you in plain words about
the Father. 26In that day you will ask the Father
for things in my name. I mean, I will not need to
ask the Father for you. 27The Father himself loves
you. He loves you because you have loved me
and believed that I came from God. 28I came from
the Father into the world. Now I am leaving the
world and going back to the Father."

29Then the followers of Jesus said, "You are
speaking clearly to us now and are not using
stories that are hard to understand. 30We can see
now that you know all things. You can answer a
person's question even before it is asked. This
makes us believe you came from God."

31Jesus answered, "So now you believe?
32Listen to me; a time is coming when you will
be scattered, each to his own home. That time is
now here. You will leave me alone, but I am never
really alone, because the Father is with me.

33"I told you these things so that you can have
peace in me. In this world you will have trouble,
but be brave! I have defeated the world."

PRAYER

God on the Streets

As I stood waiting, a Mancunian lad who looked familiar ran up to me with an excitement that belied his cool-bloke image. Clapping his hands together he blurted, "We've gotta get you to pray some stuff for us! You sorted Daz's hand right out so . . ."

"Where is he?" I interrupted. I *had* to see this . . . I'd prayed for Daz in the street two days before. He told me how he'd punched through a glass window because he lost his phone. Daz had severed two tendons in his hand, and his mate had then described in gruesome detail how the hand had been cut to the bone. Talking through it on the streets a few nights ago, Daz had been sceptical, but trusted enough to let me hold his hand in front of his mates and pray for him right there.

"It's tingling," he'd said, looking carefully at it. "I know there are some things in the world I don't understand."

"Daz!" his mate called him over. Daz wandered over looking a bit sheepish, a coy smile on his face. I reckon he was trying to work out how he was gonna explain himself. He looked down at his hand.

"I could move it a bit again," he showed me his wiggling little finger, "so I took the cast off and I could move it properly," he smiled. God had totally healed his hand.

This story is told by someone who had gone out of his way to offer to pray for people in the street. He is convinced that when we pray God does things. Are you?

John 17:1–26 gives us a record of some of the things Jesus prayed for his followers.

- What did Jesus pray?
- Why do you think he prayed for these things? How do they compare with your priorities in prayer?

Consider . . .

- getting some of your friends together regularly to pray for each other. You could set up a phone chain of people to pray.
- whether you have any friends like Daz. They may not know Jesus but you can be praying for them. Pick three or four friends to pray for – keep a note of what happens when you pray.

For more, see . . .

- Matthew 6.5–15 (p.948)
- Philippians 4:6 (p.1285)
- Ephesians 3:14–21 (p.1271)

Jesus Prays for His Followers

17 After Jesus said these things, he looked
towards heaven and prayed, "Father, the
time has come. Give glory to your Son so that
the Son can give glory to you. 2 You gave the Son
power over all people so that the Son could give
eternal life to all those you gave him. 3 And this is
eternal life: that people know you, the only true
God, and that they know Jesus Christ, the One
you sent. 4 Having finished the work you gave me
to do, I brought you glory on earth. 5 And now,
Father, give me glory with you; give me the glory
I had with you before the world was made.
6 "I showed what you are like to those you gave
me from the world. They belonged to you, and
you gave them to me, and they have obeyed your
teaching. 7 Now they know that everything you
gave me comes from you. 8 I gave them the teach-
ings you gave me, and they accepted them. They
knew that I truly came from you, and they be-
lieved that you sent me. 9 I am praying for them.
I am not praying for people in the world but for
those you gave me, because they are yours. 10 All
I have is yours, and all you have is mine. And my
glory is shown through them. 11 I am coming to
you; I will not stay in the world any longer. But
they are still in the world. Holy Father, keep
them safe by the power of your name, the name
you gave me, so that they will be one, just as you
and I are one. 12 While I was with them, I kept
them safe by the power of your name, the name
you gave me. I protected them, and only one of
them, the one worthy of destruction, was lost so
that the Scripture *d* would come true.
13 "I am coming to you now. But I pray these
things while I am still in the world so that these fol-
lowers can have all my joy in them. 14 I have given
them your teaching. And the world has hated
them, because they don't belong to the world, just
as I don't belong to the world. 15 I am not asking
you to take them out of the world but to keep them
safe from the Evil One. 16 They don't belong to the
world, just as I don't belong to the world. 17 Make
them ready for your service through your truth;
your teaching is truth. 18 I have sent them into the
world, just as you sent me into the world. 19 For
their sake, I am making myself ready to serve so
that they can be ready for their service of the truth.

> **Sidelight** Jesus' prayer in John 17 is the longest prayer in the New Testament. But Nehemiah holds the record for the longest Bible prayer with his prayer of praise, confession and covenant in Nehemiah 9:5–37 (p.451).

20 "I pray for these followers, but I am also pray-
ing for all those who will believe in me because of
their teaching. 21 Father, I pray that they can be one.
As you are in me and I am in you, I pray that they
can also be one in us. Then the world will believe
that you sent me. 22 I have given these people the
glory that you gave me so that they can be one, just
as you and I are one. 23 I will be in them and you
will be in me so that they will be completely one.
Then the world will know that you sent me and
that you loved them just as much as you loved me.
24 "Father, I want these people that you gave me
to be with me where I am. I want them to see my
glory, which you gave me because you loved me
before the world was made. 25 Father, you are the
One who is good. The world does not know you,
but I know you, and these people know you sent
me. 26 I showed them what you are like, and I will
show them again. Then they will have the same
love that you have for me, and I will live in them."

Jesus is Arrested

18 When Jesus finished praying, he went
with his followers across the Kidron Val-
ley. On the other side there was a garden, and
Jesus and his followers went into it.
2 Judas knew where this place was, because
Jesus often met his followers there. Judas was the
one who turned against Jesus. 3 So Judas came
there with a group of soldiers and some guards
from the leading priests and the Pharisees. *d* They
were carrying torches, lanterns and weapons.
4 Knowing everything that would happen to
him, Jesus went out and asked, "Who is it you are
looking for?"
5 They answered, "Jesus from Nazareth."
"I am he," Jesus said. (Judas, the one who
turned against Jesus, was standing there with
them.) 6 When Jesus said, "I am he," they moved
back and fell to the ground.
7 Jesus asked them again, "Who is it you are
looking for?"
They said, "Jesus of Nazareth."
8 "I told you that I am he," Jesus said. "So if you are
looking for me, let the others go." 9 This happened
so that the words Jesus said before would come
true: "I have not lost any of the ones you gave me."

> **Sidelight** The sword that Simon Peter used in John 18:10–11 was probably similar to a modern machete. Roman soldiers of this time used lightweight, well-balanced swords that were usually just over half a metre long for close-range combat. The sword is the most common weapon mentioned in the Bible, appearing more than 400 times from Genesis to Revelation.

[10]Simon Peter, who had a sword, pulled it out
and struck the servant of the high priest, cutting off
his right ear. (The servant's name was Malchus.)
[11]Jesus said to Peter, "Put your sword back.
Shouldn't I drink the cup[n] the Father gave me?"

Jesus is Brought Before Annas

[12]Then the soldiers with their commander and
the Jewish guards arrested Jesus. They tied him
[13]and led him first to Annas, the father-in-law of
Caiaphas, the high priest that year. [14]Caiaphas
was the one who had told the Jews that it would
be better if one man died for all the people.

Peter Says He Doesn't Know Jesus

[15]Simon Peter and another one of Jesus' fol-
lowers went along after Jesus. This follower
knew the high priest, so he went with Jesus into
the high priest's courtyard. [16]But Peter waited
outside near the door. The follower who knew
the high priest came back outside, spoke to the
girl at the door, and brought Peter inside. [17]The
girl at the door said to Peter, "Aren't you also one
of that man's followers?"

Peter answered, "No, I am not!"

[18]It was cold, so the servants and guards had
built a fire and were standing around it, warming

cup Jesus is talking about the terrible things that will happen to him. Accepting these things will be very hard, like drinking a cup of something bitter.

FEAR

All That You Can't Leave Behind

Nathan had developed a reputation for being a bad lad. He was proud of it because it meant that he got respect from his crew. Nathan and the guys were tight. What had been going round having a bit of a laugh in an attempt to evade boredom, had become carrying knives and looking for fights. Nathan was getting in deep.

Then something happened. The geeky Christians who ran the youth club had persuaded him to go along to a camp for the weekend, with the promise of abseiling, canoeing and some "God stuff" too. So Nathan went, thinking he'd do the activities, find a couple of girls to snog round the campfire, and catch forty winks while the Christians went on about God.

That weekend, he met God in a way that was inescapable and he found out that God loved him and accepted him – words that Nathan seldom heard. All the things he had been doing with his mates faded to grey when he held them against the promise of this new life with God.

It wasn't until the journey home in the minibus that his fears hit him. They approached his home town and Nathan saw the old streets where he lived out his old life. It had been so easy being a Christian away from home, away from his mates.

He worried that he would have no mates, no respect. What would his family say? He remembered what he used to call the Christians and dreaded to think what his mates would call him. As well as all this, he knew the dealers that supplied him wouldn't be happy about him pulling out of the game. As the minibus pulled up outside his house, he thought to himself, "Wouldn't it be easier if I just pretended this weekend had never happened?"

Read **John 18:1–27**.

- How is Peter's situation similar to Nathan's? How is it different?
- How do you think Jesus was able to overcome the fears he had about going to the cross?

Consider . . .

- writing down some of the things you would be fearful to give up so that you could follow Jesus. Pause and ask God what plans and adventures he has for your life as you choose to follow him.
- asking God to give you the strength to overcome your fears.

For more, see . . .

- Esther 4:1–17 (p.462)
- 1 John 4:18 (p.1374)
- Psalm 118:5–9 (p.570)

themselves. Peter also was standing with them,
warming himself.

The High Priest Questions Jesus

19 The high priest asked Jesus questions about
his followers and his teaching. 20 Jesus answered,
"I have spoken openly to everyone. I have always
taught in synagogues[d] and in the Temple,[d] where
all the Jews come together. I never said anything
in secret. 21 So why do you question me? Ask the
people who heard my teaching. They know
what I said."
22 When Jesus said this, one of the guards
standing there hit him. The guard said, "Is that
the way you answer the high priest?"
23 Jesus answered him, "If I said something
wrong, then say what it was. But if what I said is
true, why do you hit me?"
24 Then Annas sent Jesus, who was still tied, to
Caiaphas the high priest.

Peter Says Again He Doesn't Know Jesus

25 As Simon Peter was standing and warming
himself, they said to him, "Aren't you one of that
man's followers?"
Peter said it was not true; he said, "No, I
am not."
26 One of the servants of the high priest was
there. This servant was a relative of the man
whose ear Peter had cut off. The servant said,
"Didn't I see you with him in the garden?"
27 Again Peter said it wasn't true. At once a
cockerel crowed.

Jesus is Brought Before Pilate

28 Early in the morning they led Jesus from
Caiaphas' house to the Roman governor's palace.
They would not go inside the palace, because
they did not want to make themselves un-
clean;[n] they wanted to eat the Passover[d] meal.
29 So Pilate went outside to them and asked,
"What charges do you bring against this man?"
30 They answered, "If he were not a criminal,
we wouldn't have brought him to you."
31 Pilate said to them, "Take him yourselves
and judge him by your own law."
"But we are not allowed to put anyone to
death," the Jews answered. 32 (This happened so
that what Jesus said about how he would die
would come true.)
33 Then Pilate went back inside the palace and
called Jesus to him and asked, "Are you the king
of the Jews?"
34 Jesus said, "Is that your own question, or did
others tell you about me?"
35 Pilate answered, "I am not Jewish. It was
your own people and their leading priests who
handed you over to me. What have you done
wrong?"
36 Jesus answered, "My kingdom does not be-
long to this world. If it belonged to this world,
my servants would fight so that I would not be
given over to the Jews. But my kingdom is from
another place."
37 Pilate said, "So you are a king!"
Jesus answered, "You are the one saying I am
a king. This is why I was born and came into the
world: to tell people the truth. And everyone
who belongs to the truth listens to me."
38 Pilate said, "What is truth?" After he said
this, he went out to the Jews again and said to
them, "I find nothing against this man. 39 But it is
your custom that I free one prisoner to you at
Passover time. Do you want me to free the 'king
of the Jews'?"
40 They shouted back, "No, not him! Let
Barabbas go free!" (Barabbas was a robber.)

19 Then Pilate ordered that Jesus be taken
away and whipped. 2 The soldiers made a
crown from some thorny branches and put it on
Jesus' head and put a purple robe around him.
3 Then they came to him many times and said,
"Hail, King of the Jews!" and hit him in the face.
4 Again Pilate came out and said to them, "Look,
I am bringing Jesus out to you. I want you to know
that I find nothing against him." 5 So Jesus came
out, wearing the crown of thorns and the purple
robe. Pilate said to them, "Here is the man!"
6 When the leading priests and the guards saw
Jesus, they shouted, "Crucify him! Crucify him!"
But Pilate answered, "Crucify him yourselves,
because I find nothing against him."
7 The Jews answered, "We have a law that says
he should die, because he said he is the Son of
God."
8 When Pilate heard this, he was even more
afraid. 9 He went back inside the palace and asked
Jesus, "Where do you come from?" But Jesus did
not answer him. 10 Pilate said, "You refuse to
speak to me? Don't you know I have power to
set you free and power to have you crucified?"
11 Jesus answered, "The only power you have
over me is the power given to you by God. The
man who betrayed me to you is guilty of a
greater sin."
12 After this, Pilate tried to let Jesus go. But the
Jews cried out, "Anyone who makes himself
king is against Caesar. If you let this man go, you
are no friend of Caesar."
13 When Pilate heard what they were saying,
he brought Jesus out and sat down on the judge's

unclean Going into a non-Jewish place would make them unfit to eat the Passover Feast, according to Jewish law.

seat at the place called The Stone Pavement. (In the Jewish language[n] the name is Gabbatha.) [14]It was about noon on Preparation[d] Day of Passover[d] week. Pilate said to the Jews, "Here is your king!"

[15]They shouted, "Take him away! Take him away! Crucify him!"

Pilate asked them, "Do you want me to crucify your king?"

The leading priests answered, "The only king we have is Caesar."

[16]So Pilate handed Jesus over to them to be crucified.

Jesus is Crucified

The soldiers took charge of Jesus. [17]Carrying his own cross, Jesus went out to a place called The Place of the Skull, which in the Jewish language[n] is called Golgotha. [18]There they crucified Jesus. They also crucified two other men, one on each side, with Jesus in the middle. [19]Pilate wrote a sign and put it on the cross. It read: JESUS OF NAZARETH, THE KING OF THE JEWS. [20]The sign was written in the Jewish language, in Latin and in Greek. Many of the Jews read the sign, because the place where Jesus was crucified was near the city. [21]The leading Jewish priests said to Pilate, "Don't write, 'The King of the Jews'. But write, 'This man said, "I am the King of the Jews." ' "

[22]Pilate answered, "What I have written, I have written."

[23]After the soldiers crucified Jesus, they took his clothes and divided them into four parts, with each soldier getting one part. They also took his long shirt, which was all one piece of cloth, woven from top to bottom. [24]So the soldiers said to each other, "We should not tear this into parts. Let's throw lots[d] to see who will get it." This happened so that this Scripture would come true:[d]

> "They divided my clothes among them,
> and they threw lots[d] for my clothing."
>
> *Psalm 22:18*

So the soldiers did this.

[25]Standing near his cross were Jesus' mother, his mother's sister, Mary the wife of Clopas, and Mary Magdalene. [26]When Jesus saw his mother and the follower he loved standing nearby, he said to his mother, "Dear woman, here is your son." [27]Then he said to the follower, "Here is your mother." From that time on, the follower took her to live in his home.

Jesus Dies

[28]After this, Jesus knew that everything had been done. So that the Scripture[d] would come true, he said, "I am thirsty."[n] [29]There was a jar full of vinegar there, so the soldiers soaked a sponge in it, put the sponge on a branch of a hyssop plant and lifted it to Jesus' mouth. [30]When Jesus tasted the vinegar, he said, "It is finished." Then he bowed his head and died.

> **Sidelight** The "long shirt" that the soldiers gambled for (John 19:23–24) was, in reality, like Jesus' undergarment. Crucifixions were often done with the criminals naked to make the execution even more humiliating.

[31]This day was Preparation[d] Day, and the next day was a special Sabbath[d] day. Since the Jews did not want the bodies to stay on the cross on the Sabbath day, they asked Pilate to order that the legs of the men be broken[n] and the bodies be taken away. [32]So the soldiers came and broke the legs of the first man on the cross beside Jesus. Then they broke the legs of the man on the other cross beside Jesus. [33]But when the soldiers came to Jesus and saw that he was already dead, they did not break his legs. [34]But one of the soldiers stuck his spear into Jesus' side, and at once blood and water came out. [35](The one who saw this happen is the one who told us this, and whatever he says is true. And he knows that he tells the truth, and he tells it so that you might believe.) [36]These things happened to make the Scripture come true: "Not one of his bones will be broken."[n] [37]And another Scripture says, "They will look at the one they stabbed."[n]

Jesus is Buried

[38]Later, Joseph from Arimathea asked Pilate if he could take the body of Jesus. (Joseph was a secret follower of Jesus, because he was afraid of the Jews.) Pilate gave his permission, so Joseph came and took Jesus' body away. [39]Nicodemus, who earlier had come to Jesus at night, went with Joseph. He brought about 30 kilogrammes of myrrh[d] and aloes.[d] [40]These two men took Jesus' body and wrapped it with the spices in pieces of linen cloth, which is how the Jewish people bury the dead. [41]In the place where Jesus was crucified,

Jewish language Hebrew or Aramaic, the languages of the Jewish people in the first century.
"I am thirsty." Read Psalms 22:15; 69:21.
broken The breaking of their bones would make them die sooner.
"Not one . . . broken." Quotation from Psalm 34:20. The idea is from Exodus 12:46; Numbers 9:12.
"They . . . stabbed." Quotation from Zechariah 12:10.

there was a garden. In the garden was a new
tomb that had never been used before. 42The
men laid Jesus in that tomb because it was
nearby, and the Jews were preparing to start
their Sabbath[d] day.

Jesus' Tomb is Empty

20 Early on the first day of the week, Mary
Magdalene went to the tomb while it
was still dark. When she saw that the large stone
had been moved away from the tomb, 2she ran
to Simon Peter and the follower whom Jesus
loved. Mary said, "They have taken the Lord out
of the tomb, and we don't know where they
have put him."
3So Peter and the other follower started for the
tomb. 4They were both running, but the other
follower ran faster than Peter and reached the
tomb first. 5He bent down and looked in and saw
the strips of linen cloth lying there, but he did not
go in. 6Then, following him, Simon Peter arrived
and went into the tomb and saw the strips of
linen lying there. 7He also saw the cloth that had
been around Jesus' head, which was folded up
and laid in a different place from the strips of
linen. 8Then the other follower, who had reached
the tomb first, also went in. He saw and believed.
9(They did not yet understand from the Scrip-
tures[d] that Jesus must rise from the dead.)

Jesus Appears to Mary Magdalene

10Then the followers went back home. 11But
Mary stood outside the tomb, crying. As she
was crying, she bent down and looked inside

DEATH

Questions Unanswered

Jo was full of life. She'd been working for a Christian charity for several months now, but unlike the others, Jo didn't believe in God. At first, Jo was quiet; she kept her head down and found her new environment a bit strange. Naturally outgoing, it didn't take long before she was laughing, joking and having a ball with all her colleagues.

Without any faith in God, Jo found it amusing to see her new friends on their knees praying in the money for the bills. Much to her surprise, Jo witnessed the answers to the prayers, as every month every penny came in. Again and again she witnessed miracles as a God she didn't believe in kept doing amazing things!

Over a year down the line, Jo had seen God at work in her own life as well as all around her. Her colleagues challenged her. For the first time Jo was serious. She admitted she believed in God, she understood what Jesus did, but she wasn't ready to give up living the way she wanted, not just yet. Shortly after this, Jo got her dream job, one she'd always wanted. She'd regularly pop back to her old office, say hello and bring her enormous grin and even bigger personality!

A few weeks after one of these visits, the office received a phone call. Jo had been sent home from work ill. That night she had a pulmonary aneurysm, her heart stopped instantly, without warning; Jo had died. There was no way anyone could have known; she was only young. The whole office was shaken by the sad loss but more than that, one unspoken question hung in their minds, "Did she know Jesus?"

Read **John 19:38–42**.

- If you'd been there, how would you have reacted to the death of Jesus?
- What could Joseph of Arimathea have in common with Jo?

Consider . . .

- spending more time praying for those close to you who don't know Jesus.
- looking for ways to share Jesus with friends who don't know him – there's not always as much time as we think.

For more, see . . .

- John 14:6 (p.1122)
- Revelation 21:3–4 (p.1403)
- 2 Corinthians 5:1 (p.1244)

the tomb. 12 She saw two angels dressed in white,
sitting where Jesus' body had been, one at the
head and one at the feet.
13 They asked her, "Woman, why are you
crying?"
She answered, "They have taken away my
Lord, and I don't know where they have put
him." 14 When Mary said this, she turned around
and saw Jesus standing there, but she did not
know it was Jesus.
15 Jesus asked her, "Woman, why are you cry-
ing? Whom are you looking for?"
Thinking he was the gardener, she said to
him, "Did you take him away, sir? Tell me where
you put him, and I will get him."
16 Jesus said to her, "Mary."
Mary turned towards Jesus and said in the Jewish
language,[n] "Rabboni." (This means Teacher.)
17 Jesus said to her, "Don't hold on to me, be-
cause I have not yet gone up to the Father. But
go to my brothers and tell them, 'I am going back
to my Father and your Father, to my God and
your God.' "
18 Mary Magdalene went and said to the follow-
ers, "I saw the Lord!" And she told them what
Jesus had said to her.

Jesus Appears to His Followers

19 When it was evening on the first day of the
week, the followers were together. The doors

Jewish language Hebrew or Aramaic, the languages of the Jewish people in the first century.

DOUBT

The Death of Doubt

Rob and his brothers had fought with their dad through the years. He was a quiet man and a strong disciplinarian. He expected a lot from his four sons; his standards were high and generally inflexible. Going to church wasn't an option; it was expected.

Rob loved his dad, but it had always been a fearful, distant love. He had never really known, deep inside, whether his dad loved him. He saw God the same way – as a fearful, distant ruler he was forced to obey. So he wasn't sure if God loved him either. Until one cold November day.

Rob's dad had asked Rob to go for a walk with him – just the two of them. Rob didn't know what to think. What have I done? he wondered.

So Rob and his dad climbed up the hill together. They didn't say much and Rob could see that his dad had something important to tell him.

After a tense, awkward hour, his dad stopped, looked at Rob and said, "I know we haven't always seen eye to eye. And I know I've made life tough for you. But I don't ever want you to forget what I'm about to say to you. I love you as much as a father can love his son. And nothing will ever change that."

The words came with a power and a peace that enveloped Rob. Something changed between him and his dad in that moment. And something changed between Rob and God in that moment.

Rob felt, for the first time, the assurance of God's love for him.

Like Rob, the disciples sometimes had a hard time believing God. They doubted many of the promises Jesus had told them. And the chief doubter among them was Thomas. Read about Thomas's doubt in **John 20:19–31**.

- How did Rob's doubts about his father's love for him compare to Thomas's doubts about Jesus rising from the dead?
- When have you doubted the love of someone close to you?

Consider . . .

- taking a twenty-minute walk and asking God to demonstrate his love for you in something you see.
- reaffirming your love to a friend or family member who may be doubting your love.

For more, see . . .

- Job 40–41 (p.496)
- Romans 14:14–23 (p.1207)
- Luke 24:13–53 (p.1093)

were locked, because they were afraid of the Jews. Then Jesus came and stood right in the middle of them and said, "Peace be with you." 20After he said this, he showed them his hands and his side. The followers were thrilled when they saw the Lord.

21Then Jesus said again, "Peace be with you. As the Father sent me, I now send you." 22After he said this, he breathed on them and said, "Receive the Holy Spirit.[d] 23If you forgive anyone his sins, they are forgiven. If you don't forgive them, they are not forgiven."

Jesus Appears to Thomas

24Thomas (called Didymus), who was one of the twelve, was not with them when Jesus came. 25The other followers kept telling Thomas, "We saw the Lord."

But Thomas said, "I will not believe it until I see the nail marks in his hands and put my finger where the nails were and put my hand into his side."

26A week later the followers were in the house again, and Thomas was with them. The doors were locked, but Jesus came in and stood right in the middle of them. He said, "Peace be with you." 27Then he said to Thomas, "Put your finger here, and look at my hands. Put your hand here in my side. Stop being an unbeliever and believe."

28Thomas said to him, "My Lord and my God!"

29Then Jesus told him, "You believe because you see me. Those who believe without seeing me will be truly happy."

Why John Wrote this Book

30Jesus did many other miracles[d] in the presence of his followers that are not written in this book. 31But these are written so that you may believe that Jesus is the Christ,[d] the Son of God. Then, by believing, you may have life through his name.

Jesus Appears to Seven Followers

21 Later, Jesus showed himself to his followers again—this time at Lake Galilee.[n] This is how he showed himself: 2some of the followers were together—Simon Peter, Thomas (called Didymus), Nathanael from Cana in Galilee, the two sons of Zebedee and two other followers. 3Simon Peter said, "I am going out to fish."

The others said, "We will go with you." So they went out and got into the boat. They fished that night but caught nothing.

4Early the next morning Jesus stood on the shore, but the followers did not know it was Jesus. 5Then he said to them, "Friends, did you catch any fish?"

They answered, "No."

6He said, "Throw your net on the right side of the boat, and you will find some." So they did, and they caught so many fish they could not pull the net back into the boat.

7The follower whom Jesus loved said to Peter, "It is the Lord!" When Peter heard him say this, he wrapped his coat around himself. (Peter had taken his clothes off.) Then he jumped into the water. 8The other followers went ashore in the boat, dragging the net full of fish. They were not very far from shore, only about a hundred yards. 9When the followers stepped out of the boat and onto the shore, they saw a fire of hot coals. There were fish on the fire, and there was bread.

10Then Jesus said, "Bring some of the fish you have just caught."

11Simon Peter went into the boat and pulled the net to the shore. It was full of big fish, 153 in all, but even though there were so many, the net did not tear. 12Jesus said to them, "Come and eat." None of the followers dared ask him, "Who are you?" because they knew it was the Lord. 13Jesus came and took the bread and gave it to them, along with the fish.

14This was now the third time Jesus showed himself to his followers after he was raised from the dead.

Sidelight Barbecued fish for breakfast, anyone? That's what Jesus served when he appeared to his disciples (see John 21:4–13). Cooking fish on an open, charcoal fire was common in Jesus' day. He may have served them musht fish (now known as St Peter's fish), which is one of the most common fish in Lake Galilee.

Jesus Talks to Peter

15When they finished eating, Jesus said to Simon Peter, "Simon son of John, do you love me more than these?"

He answered, "Yes, Lord, you know that I love you."

Jesus said, "Feed my lambs."

16Again Jesus said, "Simon son of John, do you love me?"

He answered, "Yes, Lord, you know that I love you."

Jesus said, "Take care of my sheep."

Lake Galilee Literally, "Sea of Tiberias".

[17]A third time he said, "Simon son of John, do
you love me?"
Peter was hurt because Jesus asked him the
third time, "Do you love me?" Peter said, "Lord,
you know everything; you know that I love
you!"
He said to him, "Feed my sheep. [18]I tell you
the truth, when you were younger, you tied your
own belt and went where you wanted. But
when you are old, you will put out your hands
and someone else will tie you and take you
where you don't want to go." [19](Jesus said this to
show how Peter would die to give glory to God.)
Then Jesus said to Peter, "Follow me!"
[20]Peter turned and saw that the follower Jesus
loved was walking behind them. (This was the
follower who had leaned against Jesus at the
supper and had said, "Lord, who will turn against
you?") [21]When Peter saw him behind them, he
asked Jesus, "Lord, what about him?"
[22]Jesus answered, "If I want him to live until I
come back, that is not your business. You follow
me."
[23]So a story spread among the followers that
this one would not die. But Jesus did not say he
would not die. He only said, "If I want him to
live until I come back, that is not your business."
[24]That follower is the one who is telling these
things and who has now written them down.
We know that what he says is true.
[25]There are many other things Jesus did. If
every one of them were written down, I suppose
the whole world would not be big enough for all
the books that would be written.

CELEBRATING

Tears of Joy

Alison watched as her grandfather was carried into the ambulance. She had been with him when he had the heart attack, and now it was doubtful that she would ever see him alive again. As she watched the ambulance drive away with its sirens wailing and lights flashing, she began to sob.

Alison visited her grandfather that evening at the hospital. He was still alive, but only just. Alison was only allowed to see him for two minutes, and was then asked to leave him so he could try and recover in peace.

She telephoned the hospital several times each day to find out how her grandfather was getting on. Every time the answer was the same – stable but still critical.

Alison found herself imagining life without her grandfather. It would seem so empty. He had been her closest friend ever since she could remember, and now that friend was going to die.

It was one long, painful week later when the hospital telephoned Alison's house. Her mum was out, so Alison answered the phone.

It was the hospital. A lump rose in Alison's throat and threatened to explode. She almost knew what they were going to say . . .

"Your grandfather is now stable and out of danger," the nurse told her.

Alison replaced the telephone and sat down, stunned. She didn't know whether to laugh or cry, so she did both at the same time.

The disciples must have felt a similar sort of joyful relief when Jesus rose from the dead. You can read about their experience in **John 21:1–14**.

- How did Alison's up and down emotions compare with those of the disciples, both before and after they had heard the good news?
- Have you ever felt the sort of joy that the disciples experienced on the shores of Lake Galilee? When?

Consider . . .

- organising a special "celebration of Jesus" party with your church youth group. Why not make it a type of Christmas celebration?
- having a mini-celebration first thing every morning. Sing a song of praise and thank God that Jesus is alive!

For more, see . . .

- Psalm 126 (p.576)
- James 1:2–4 (p.1348)
- Luke 15:1–7 (p.1070)

Acts

Why Read This Book:

- Discover how the Christian church was born (Acts 1—9).
- Recognise that God wants all people to have faith in him (Acts 10—12).
- Be encouraged to tell others about your faith, as the early Christians did (Acts 13—28).

When?

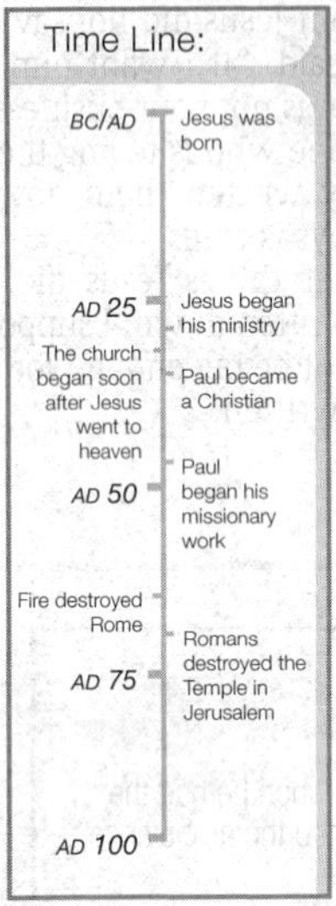

Behind the Scenes:

It looked like everything was over. Jesus was dead – executed by the Romans. After three years with Jesus, the disciples weren't sure what to do next. Maybe go back to fishing and tax-collecting and the other things they did before Jesus came along.

But three days later, Jesus rose from the dead, and the world has never been the same. The book of Acts tells how that event began changing the world.

Written by Luke, Acts picks up where the Gospel of Luke (p.1034) ends. It tells how Jesus went up into heaven, then sent his Holy Spirit fifty days later (Acts 2). The rest of the book tells how the Good News of Jesus Christ spread rapidly throughout the world. Most of the book focuses on two people: Peter and Paul. Peter had been Jesus' disciple, and his life was completely changed by the coming of the Spirit.

Unlike Peter, Paul began as an enemy of Christians. But through a miraculous conversion (Acts 9), he became a devout Christian and great church leader. Acts tells about his travels to spread the Good News and about many of the churches to which he later wrote letters.

Acts tells about a time Christians were in danger. Many churches had to meet in hiding, and Christian leaders were regularly thrown in jail – or killed – for what they believed and taught. Yet the early Christians didn't back down. Their determination can encourage us to live out our faith and tell others about it – even when we are tempted to hide it.

Where?

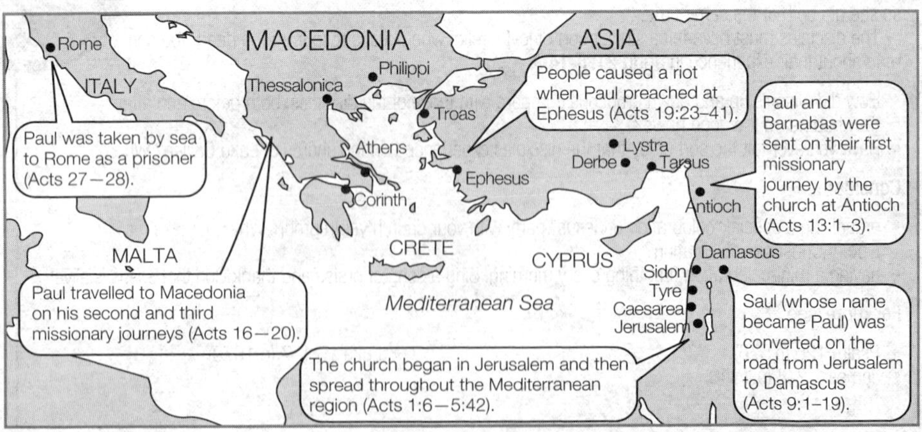

Luke Writes Another Book

1 To Theophilus.
The first book I wrote was about everything
Jesus began to do and teach 2until the day he
was taken up into heaven. Before this, with the help
of the Holy Spirit,[d] Jesus told the apostles[d] he had
chosen what they should do. 3After his death, he
showed himself to them and proved in many ways
that he was alive. The apostles saw Jesus during the
40 days after he was raised from the dead, and he
spoke to them about the kingdom of God. 4Once
when he was eating with them, he told them not to
leave Jerusalem. He said, "Wait here to receive the
promise from the Father which I told you about.
5John baptised people with water, but in a few days
you will be baptised with the Holy Spirit."

Jesus is Taken Up into Heaven

6When the apostles[d] were all together, they
asked Jesus, "Lord, are you now going to give the
kingdom back to Israel?"
7Jesus said to them, "The Father is the only One
who has the authority to decide dates and times.
These things are not for you to know. 8But when the
Holy Spirit[d] comes to you, you will receive power.
You will be my witnesses—in Jerusalem, in all of
Judea, in Samaria and in every part of the world."
9After he said this, as they were watching, he
was lifted up, and a cloud hid him from their
sight. 10As he was going, they were looking into
the sky. Suddenly, two men wearing white
clothes stood beside them. 11They said, "Men of
Galilee, why are you standing here looking into

SHARING FAITH

Taking to the Streets

In an effort to turn the youth weekend into a more practical event, the young people at the church in Kent were going to take a survey onto the high streets. They had spent most of their time inside the church building, having great fun with videos, music and Bible studies, but now it was time to "get real".

The survey was good, it was based on general questions like: Have you ever been to church? What do you think the church should be doing for young people? If you could get to know Jesus as a real person, would you be interested?

The 35-strong youth group had split up into small groups and were ready to go out.

"Who's going to ask the questions?" Lisa was talking to her group.

"Let's take it in turns," suggested Aaron.

"Now, remember . . . " began Hazel their youth leader, "as there are so many of you, it would be good to find groups of young people hanging around the town – shouldn't be too difficult on a Saturday afternoon! Right, you have exactly one hour. Go!"

Later when they came back, they were all talking and yelling excitedly.

"I can't believe you asked that bloke!" giggled Rosie.

"Well, what about the guys in McDonald's? They were a scream!" yelled Lisa.

"I just can't believe everyone was so great about it. I've filled in loads of surveys!" said Aaron.

"I've got at least six people who want to come back and watch the film tonight," related Jo.

Michael flopped into the nearest armchair. "Who would have thought talking about being a Christian could be so easy?"

Read **Acts 1:6–8** and see how the apostles were sent out.

- How does verse 8 compare to the youth weekend?
- How did the Holy Spirit help the apostles to witness?

Consider . . .

- praying seriously that the Holy Spirit would give you the power to be an effective witness.
- asking your minister or youth leader to plan a special event that can be used alongside a survey, as a witness in your area.

For more, see . . .

- Matthew 28:19–20 (p.995)
- Romans 10:13–15 (p.1200)
- Luke 24:46–49 (p.1094)

the sky? Jesus, whom you saw taken up from you
into heaven, will come back in the same way you
saw him go."

A New Apostle Is Chosen

12 Then they went back to Jerusalem from
the Mount of Olives.[d] (This mountain is about a
kilometre from Jerusalem.) 13 When they entered
the city, they went to the upstairs room where
they were staying. Peter, John, James, Andrew,
Philip, Thomas, Bartholomew, Matthew, James
son of Alphaeus, Simon (known as the Zealot[d])
and Judas son of James were there. 14 They all con-
tinued praying together with some women, in-
cluding Mary the mother of Jesus, and Jesus'
brothers.
15 During this time there was a meeting of the
believers (about 120 of them). Peter stood up and
said, 16–17 "Brothers and sisters,[n] in the Scrip-
tures[d] the Holy Spirit[d] said through David some-
thing that must happen involving Judas. He was
one of our own group and served together with
us. He led those who arrested Jesus." 18 (Judas
bought a field with the money he got for his evil
act. But he fell to his death, his body burst open,
and all his intestines poured out. 19 Everyone in
Jerusalem learned about this so they named this
place Akeldama. In their language Akeldama
means "Field of Blood".) 20 "In the Book of
Psalms," Peter said, "this is written:

'May his place be empty;
 leave no one to live in it.' *Psalm 69:25*

And it is also written:

'Let another man replace him as leader.'
Psalm 109:8

21–22 "So now a man must become a witness
with us of Jesus' being raised from the dead.
He must be one of the men who were part of our
group during all the time the Lord Jesus was
among us—from the time John was baptising
people until the day Jesus was taken up from us
to heaven."
23 They put the names of two men before
the group. One was Joseph Barsabbas, who was
also called Justus. The other was Matthias.
24–25 The apostles prayed, "Lord, you know the
thoughts of everyone. Show us which one of
these two you have chosen to do this work.
Show us who should be an apostle[d] in place of
Judas, who turned away and went where he
belongs." 26 Then they used lots[d] to choose
between them, and the lots showed that
Matthias was the one. So he became an apostle
with the other eleven.

The Coming of the Holy Spirit

2 When the day of Pentecost[d] came, they were
all together in one place. 2 Suddenly a noise
like a strong, blowing wind came from heaven
and filled the whole house where they were sit-
ting. 3 They saw something like flames of fire that
were separated and stood over each person
there. 4 They were all filled with the Holy Spirit,[d]
and they began to speak different languages[n] by
the power the Holy Spirit was giving them.

> **Sidelight** Before the birth of the church, Pentecost (Acts 2:1–4) was a major time of celebration among Jews. This festival celebrated the wheat harvest with religious ceremonies, eating, drinking, and music. The festivities surrounding the event may be why people thought the disciples were drunk (Acts 2:13).

5 There were some religious Jews staying in
Jerusalem who were from every country in
the world. 6 When they heard this noise, a crowd
came together. They were all surprised, because
each one heard them speaking in his own
language. 7 They were completely amazed at this.
They said, "Look! Aren't all these people that we
hear speaking from Galilee? 8 Then how is it poss-
ible that we each hear them in our own
languages? We are from different places: 9 Parthia,
Media, Elam, Mesopotamia, Judea, Cappadocia,
Pontus, Asia, 10 Phrygia, Pamphylia, Egypt, the
areas of Libya near Cyrene, Rome 11 (both Jews
and those who had become Jews), Crete and
Arabia. But we hear them telling in our own
languages about the great things God has done!"
12 They were all amazed and confused, asking
each other, "What does this mean?"
13 But others were making fun of them, saying,
"They have had too much wine."

Peter Speaks to the People

14 But Peter stood up with the eleven apostles,[d]
and in a loud voice he spoke to the crowd:
"My fellow Jews, and all of you who are in
Jerusalem, listen to me. Pay attention to what
I have to say. 15 These people are not drunk, as you
think; it is only nine o'clock in the morning!
16 But Joel the prophet[d] wrote about what is
happening here today:
17 'God says: In the last days
 I will pour out my Spirit[d] on all kinds of
  people.

Brothers and sisters Although the Greek text says "brothers" here and throughout this book, these words of the speakers were meant for the entire church, both men and women.
languages This can also be translated "tongues".

Your sons and daughters will prophesy.[d]
Your old men will dream dreams,
and your young men will see visions.
18At that time I will pour out my Spirit
also on my male slaves and female slaves.
19I will show miracles[d]
in the sky and on the earth:
blood, fire and thick smoke.
20The sun will become dark,
the moon red as blood,
before the overwhelming and terrible day of
the LORD comes.
21Then anyone who calls on the LORD
will be saved.' *Joel 2:28–32*

22"People of Israel, listen to these words: Jesus
from Nazareth was a very special man. God
clearly showed this to you by the miracles,
wonders and signs he did through Jesus. You all
know this, because it happened right here
among you. 23Jesus was given to you, and with
the help of those who don't know the law, you
put him to death by nailing him to a cross. But
this was God's plan which he had made long
ago; he knew all this would happen. 24God
raised Jesus from the dead and set him free from
the pain of death, because death could not hold
him. 25For David said this about him:

'I keep the LORD before me always.
Because he is close by my side,
I will not be hurt.
26So I rejoice and am glad.
Even my body has hope,
27because you will not leave me in the grave.
You will not let your holy one rot.
28You will teach me how to live a holy life.
Being with you will fill me with joy.'
Psalm 16:8–11

29"Brothers and sisters, I can tell you truly
that David, our ancestor, died and was buried.
His grave is still here with us today. 30He was
a prophet and knew God had promised him
that he would make a person from David's

HOLY SPIRIT

Power Up

On 15 June 1752, American politician and scientist, Benjamin Franklin went outside to fly a kite. Instead of choosing a nice, sunny afternoon, Franklin chose a stormy one in the hope that the dark clouds overhead could become a lightning storm. The scientist successfully extracted sparks from the clouds proving his theory that lightning was electricity. He survived his dangerous experiment unhurt, unlike other famous scientists who have since died from lightning strikes while performing similar experiments.

Electricity has immense power, capable of both lightning storms and boiling kettles, powering an entire city and giving light to a torch. Electrical power is everywhere – it's just there, meeting our every need, every time we turn on a light switch or open the fridge, use our mobile phone or watch a film. It's even there when we make a friend's hair stand on end with a balloon we've just rubbed on a jumper.

In **Acts 2:1–21** we read about the day of Pentecost when the Holy Spirit came and filled the disciples, giving them power, courage and amazing gifts. Just as electricity is everywhere, ready to power the things we need, so the Holy Spirit is with us whenever we need him as a source of power and comfort. As we invite the Holy Spirit into our lives, we are given the power we need to live the Christian life.

- Electricity powers many different things in different ways. How does the Holy Spirit give power to Christians?
- In what ways do we see the Holy Spirit's power in the passage?

Consider . . .

- asking God to fill you with his Holy Spirit and to use you.
- telling one person about Jesus. Depend on the Holy Spirit to help you communicate clearly.

For more, see . . .

- Joel 2:28 (p.866)
- 1 Corinthians 12:1–11 (p.1230)
- John 14:15–26 (p.1123)

family a king just as he was.[n] 31Knowing this
before it happened, David talked about the
Christ[d] rising from the dead. He said:

'He was not left in the grave.
His body did not rot.'

32So Jesus is the One whom God raised from the
dead. And we are all witnesses to this. 33Jesus
was lifted up to heaven and is now at God's
right side. The Father has given the Holy Spirit
to Jesus as he promised. So Jesus has poured out
that Spirit, and this is what you now see and
hear. 34David was not the one who was lifted up
to heaven, but he said:

'The LORD said to my Lord,
"Sit by me at my right side,
35 until I put your enemies under your
control."'[n] *Psalm 110:1*

36"So, all the people of Israel should know this
truly: God has made Jesus—the man you nailed
to the cross—both Lord and Christ."
37When the people heard this, they felt guilty
and asked Peter and the other apostles, "What
shall we do?"
38Peter said to them, "Change your hearts
and lives and be baptised,[d] each one of you, in
the name of Jesus Christ for the forgiveness of
your sins. And you will receive the gift of the
Holy Spirit. 39This promise is for you, for your

God . . . was See 2 Samuel 7:13; Psalm 132:11.
until . . . control Literally, "until I make your enemies a footstool for your feet".

SHARING FAITH

Say What You See

Toby turned up at youth group with a massive grin on his face. The other lads knew he would have some amazing news and were soon swarming round him with their questions.

"What was it like?"

"What did you see?"

"Did you get to demo stuff?"

Toby's dad worked for a magazine that reviewed computer games and consoles. Every year his dad would go to an international conference where the big companies launched their new games and hardware. This year, the magazine wanted to do an article about fathers and sons who both loved to game. So not only did Toby get to go to the conference but his dad interviewed him about everything they had seen and played.

"It was awesome," he told his mates. "Dad has been telling me about some of these games that have been in development for months but it was amazing to see them for myself." Then he started to explain everything he had seen, which games looked good, what the graphics were like, the playability . . . He went into every tiny detail and his mates were loving it.

A month or so later, he strolled in with his dad's magazine tucked under his arm, for the first time ever his words had been printed.

"How did you know what to say?" one of his friends asked.

"It was easy," Toby smiled, "I just said what I saw."

Read **Acts 2:29–32** to find out about someone else who "just said what he saw".

- What difference does it make that both Peter and Toby talked about things that they had seen for themselves?
- Do you like to hear about the things that have happened in people's lives? Why?

Consider . . .

- writing down what you have seen and know that God has done in your own life?
- ways that you can focus on your own story and personal experience of God when you talk to people about Christianity.

For more, see . . .

- 2 Peter 1:16–18 (p.1365)
- 1 John 1:1–3 (p.1371)

children and for all who are far away. It is for
everyone the Lord our God calls to himself."
40Peter warned them with many other words.
He begged them, "Save yourselves from the
evil of today's people!" 41Then those people who
accepted what Peter said were baptised. About
3,000 people were added to the number of
believers that day. 42They spent their time learning
the apostles' teaching, sharing, breaking bread[n]
and praying together.

The Believers Share

43The apostles[d] were doing many miracles[d] and
signs, and everyone felt great respect for God. 44All
the believers were together and shared every-
thing. 45They would sell their land and the things
they owned and then divide the money and give
it to anyone who needed it. 46The believers met to-
gether in the Temple[d] every day. They ate together
in their homes, happy to share their food with
joyful hearts. 47They praised God and were liked

breaking bread This may mean a meal as in verse 46, or the Lord's Supper, the special meal that Jesus told his followers to eat to remember him (Luke 22:14–20).

CHURCH

The Place to Belong

Rebecca longed to fit in. She wanted people to like her and be her friend. That's why she joined every organisation she could at school. She still didn't feel as though she fitted in, but at least she was busy.

During Science Club meeting one day, Lee invited Rebecca to church. She was not interested, remembering the church she had attended with her mother years before. Each service had been one long, boring sermon with her mum telling her to be quiet. That was not Rebecca's idea of fun. She was "busy", she lied to Lee.

But Lee persisted. Finally Rebecca agreed to endure one service – just to get him to leave her alone.

She didn't say much to him. When Lee and Rebecca arrived for church the next Sunday evening, the kids were standing around talking and laughing. Several of them recognised Rebecca and welcomed her. During the group time, people spoke to Rebecca and asked her opinion. Several people invited Rebecca to sit with them during the worship. And during the sermon, the minister told interesting stories. Rebecca never felt bored.

After church, all the kids went to Jason's house to complete plans for their fundraising project. Rebecca helped to make posters.

All the way home, Rebecca couldn't stop talking about how much she had liked Lee's church.

"It just seems as though I fit in there; know what I mean?" she commented.

"Yes, I know," Lee smiled. "So, I suppose we'll see you next week?"

Rebecca laughed and asked, "What do you think?"

People are attracted to places where people really care and teach God's Word. Read **Acts 2:36–47** to see how the first church attracted people by the way its people lived and worshipped together.

- How does the church in Acts compare with Lee's church?
- Which qualities does the Acts church have in common with your church and which qualities of this church are different from your church's?

Consider . . .

- befriending visitors who come to your church. Ask them to sit with you or invite them to other church activities.
- doing a specific job in your church, such as greeting visitors or writing for the newsletter. Become one of the people who makes church more of what God wants it to be.

For more, see . . .

- Isaiah 2:2–5 (p.640)
- Romans 12 (p.1203)
- Acts 4:32–35 (p.1144)

by all the people. Every day the Lord added those
who were being saved to the group of believers.

Peter Heals a Crippled Man

3 One day Peter and John went to the Temple[d]
at three o'clock, the time set each day for the
afternoon prayer service. 2There, at the Temple
gate called Beautiful Gate, was a man who had
been crippled all his life. Every day he was car-
ried to this gate to beg for money from the people
going into the Temple. 3The man saw Peter and
John going into the Temple and asked them for
money. 4Peter and John looked straight at him
and said, "Look at us!" 5The man looked at
them, thinking they were going to give him
some money. 6But Peter said, "I don't have any
silver or gold, but I do have something else I can
give you. By the power of Jesus Christ from
Nazareth, stand up and walk!" 7Then Peter
took the man's right hand and lifted him up.
Immediately the man's feet and ankles became
strong. 8He jumped up, stood on his feet and
began to walk. He went into the Temple with
them, walking and jumping and praising God.
9–10All the people recognised him as the crippled
man who always sat by the Beautiful Gate beg-
ging for money. Now they saw this same man
walking and praising God, and they were
amazed. They wondered how this could happen.

Peter Speaks to the People

11While the man was holding on to Peter and
John, all the people were amazed and ran to them
at Solomon's Porch.[d] 12When Peter saw this, he
said to them, "People of Israel, why are you sur-
prised? You are looking at us as if it were our own
power or goodness that made this man walk.
13The God of Abraham, Isaac and Jacob, the God
of our ancestors, gave glory to Jesus, his servant.
But you handed him over to be killed. Pilate

SICKNESS

The Hospital Proved It

"Dad . . . I was healed at one of the meetings," said the voice on the phone.

"Were you? Are you sure?"

Sue was sixteen years old – bright and popular. She was fit and working on her Silver Award for outdoor pursuits. Few people knew that she had a heart murmur which was picked up by the doctor's stethoscope. A hospital scanner showed that it was caused by a defective heart valve. The problem made little difference to her lifestyle but it was always in the background. Any infection – however small – had to be taken seriously and treated with antibiotics.

One week of the summer was spent at a Christian camp where a nationally known rock band – 65dba – led the youth work. High on the agenda was learning to respond to God in faith. During a time of worship, Ray – the leader – called for people with heart problems to go forward for prayer. Sue knew she had been healed and told her Christian parents. A month later she went for a regular hospital check up confident that she was now well.

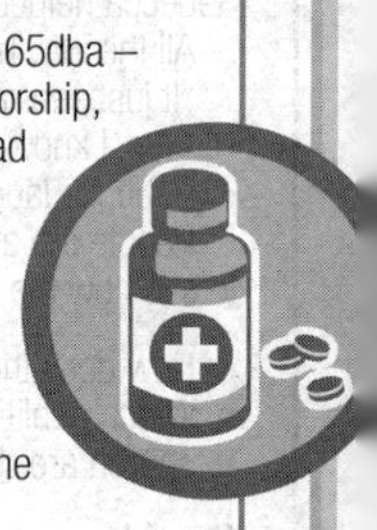

"That's funny," said the technician operating the echocardiogram. "I thought you had a bicuspid heart valve." She looked at the records. "We must have made a mistake."

Healings through the power of Jesus are often difficult to cope with. Read **Acts 3:11–19** to see.

- Why do you think Sue's father was uncertain about her healing? Should Sue have explained to the hospital staff about being prayed for?
- What does the passage say was the key factor in the man's healing?

Consider . . .

- talking to people who have been healed by faith in Jesus about how it happened.
- asking non-Christians about how they feel about healing through faith in Jesus.

For more, see . . .

- 2 Kings 4 (p.347)
- Luke 10:1–12 (p.1056)
- Mark 1:29–39 (p.997)

decided to let him go free, but you told Pilate you did not want Jesus. [14]You did not want the One who is holy and good but asked Pilate to give you a murderer[n] instead. [15]And so you killed the One who gives life, but God raised him from the dead. We are witnesses to this. [16]It was faith in Jesus that made this crippled man well. You can see this man, and you know him. He was made completely well because of trust in Jesus, and you all saw it happen!

[17]"Brothers and sisters,[n] I know you did those things to Jesus because neither you nor your leaders understood what you were doing. [18]God said through the prophets[d] that his Christ[d] would suffer and die. And now God has made these things come true in this way. [19]So you must change your hearts and lives! Come back to God, and he will forgive your sins. Then the Lord will give you times of spiritual rest. [20]And he will send Jesus, the One he chose to be the Christ. [21]But Jesus must stay in heaven until the time comes when all things will be made right again. God told about this time long ago when he spoke through his holy prophets. [22]Moses said, 'The Lord your God will give you a prophet like me, who is one of your own people. You must listen to everything he tells you. [23]Anyone who does not listen to that prophet will die, cut off from God's people.'[n] [24]Samuel, and all the other prophets who spoke for God after Samuel, told about this time now. [25]You are descendants[d] of the prophets. You have received the agreement God made with your ancestors. He said to your father Abraham, 'Through your descendants all the nations on the earth will be blessed.'[n] [26]God has raised up his servant Jesus and sent him to you first to bless you by turning each of you away from doing evil."

Peter and John at the Council

4 While Peter and John were speaking to the people, Jewish priests, the captain of the soldiers that guarded the Temple[d] and Sadducees[d] came up to them. [2]They were upset because the two apostles[d] were teaching the people and were preaching that people will rise from the dead through the power of Jesus. [3]The Jewish leaders grabbed Peter and John and put them in jail. Since it was already night, they kept them in jail until the next day. [4]But many of those who had heard Peter and John preach believed the things they said. There were now about 5,000 in the group of believers.

[5]The next day the Jewish rulers, the Jewish elders and the teachers of the law met in Jerusalem. [6]Annas the high priest, Caiaphas, John and Alexander were there, as well as everyone from the high priest's family. [7]They made Peter and John stand before them and then asked them, "By what power or authority did you do this?"

[8]Then Peter, filled with the Holy Spirit,[d] said to them, "Rulers of the people and you elders, [9]are you questioning us about a good thing that was done to a crippled man? Are you asking us who made him well? [10]We want all of you and all the Jewish people to know that this man was made well by the power of Jesus Christ from Nazareth. You crucified him, but God raised him from the dead. This man was crippled, but he is now well and able to stand here before you because of the power of Jesus. [11]Jesus is

'the stone[n] that you builders rejected,
which has become the cornerstone.'[d]

Psalm 118:22

[12]Jesus is the only One who can save people. His name is the only power in the world that has been given to save people. We must be saved through him."

[13]The Jewish leaders saw that Peter and John were not afraid to speak, and they understood that these men had no special training or education. So they were amazed. Then they realised that Peter and John had been with Jesus. [14]Because they saw the healed man standing there beside the two apostles, they could say nothing against them. [15]After the Jewish leaders ordered them to leave the meeting, they began to talk to each other. [16]They said, "What shall we do with these men? Everyone in Jerusalem knows they have done a great miracle,[d] and we cannot say it is not true. [17]But to keep it from spreading among the people, we must warn them not to talk to people any more using that name."

Sidelight The council before which Peter appeared in Acts 4:1–22 was the Sanhedrin, the Jewish High Court. It was composed of Jerusalem's religious and political leaders. Its main job was to protect Jewish life, custom, and law.

[18]So they called Peter and John in again and told them not to speak or to teach at all in the

murderer Barabbas, the man the crowd asked Pilate to set free instead of Jesus (Luke 23:18).
Brothers and sisters Although the Greek text says "brothers" here and throughout this book, Paul's words were meant for the entire church, including men and women.
'The Lord . . . people.' Quotation from Deuteronomy 18:15,19.
'Through . . . blessed.' Quotation from Genesis 22:18; 26:4.
stone A symbol meaning Jesus.

name of Jesus. 19But Peter and John answered
them, "You decide what God would want. Should
we obey you or God? 20We cannot keep quiet.
We must speak about what we have seen and
heard." 21The Jewish leaders warned the apos-
tles again and let them go free. They could not
find a way to punish them, because all the peo-
ple were praising God for what had been done.
22The man who received the miracle of healing
was more than 40 years old.

The Believers Pray

23After Peter and John left the meeting of Jew-
ish leaders, they went to their own group and
told them everything the leading priests and the
Jewish elders had said to them. 24When the be-
lievers heard this, they prayed to God together,
"Lord, you are the One who made the sky, the
earth, the sea and everything in them. 25By the
Holy Spirit,[d] through our father David your
servant, you said:

'Why are the nations so angry?
  Why are the people making useless plans?
26The kings of the earth prepare to fight,
  and their leaders make plans together
against the LORD
  and his appointed one.' *Psalm 2:1–2*

27These things really happened when Herod, Pon-
tius Pilate, those who are not Jews and the Jewish
people all came together against Jesus here in
Jerusalem. Jesus is your holy servant, the One you
made to be the Christ.[d] 28These people made
your plan happen because of your power and your
will. 29And now, Lord, listen to their threats. Lord,
help us, your servants, to speak your word with-
out fear. 30Help us to be brave by showing us your
power to heal. Give proofs and make miracles[d]
happen by the power of Jesus, your holy servant."
31After they had prayed, the place where they
were meeting was shaken. They were all filled
with the Holy Spirit, and they spoke God's word
without fear.

The Believers Share

32The group of believers were united in their
hearts and spirit. All those in the group acted as

SHARING FAITH

Responding to Opportunities

"Come on, Matt. Don't let me down! Mrs Reece trusts you," Sean pleaded. "She would let you into the classroom to use the lab at night, and you could copy the test answers while you're there. She'd never know."

"I can't abuse Mrs Reece's trust that way," Matt said. "And besides, it's wrong to cheat."

"Why can't you do it just this once? No one will know!" Sean persisted.

"I'll know and so will Jesus," Matt answered.

"But Jesus wants you to get good results, doesn't he?" Sean challenged.

"Yes, he does. This just isn't the way to get those good results."

Sean finally gave up pressuring Matt to compromise his faith. In fact, over time Sean even started asking about "this Jesus who runs your life".

Caught in a difficult situation, Matt shared his faith by showing how it influenced his actions. Read how Peter and John took advantage of an opportunity to talk about Jesus in **Acts 4:1–13**.

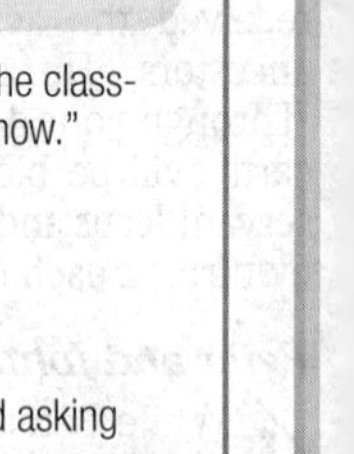

- What obstacles did Matt and Peter have to overcome to talk about their faith?
- What basic facts about Jesus did Peter consider essential in discussing his faith?

Consider . . .

- writing down ways in which you could share your faith with a non-Christian. Use one of these ways with someone this week.
- enlisting a friend to role-play faith-sharing situations, role-play talking to people who are sceptical, open, rebellious or interested.

For more, see . . .

- Daniel 1:3–16 (p.833)
- Colossians 4:5–6 (p.1294)
- Matthew 10:16–20 (p.955)

though their private property belonged to every-
one in the group. In fact, they shared everything.
[33]With great power the apostles[d] were telling
people that the Lord Jesus was truly raised from
the dead. And God blessed all the believers very
much. [34]No one in the group needed anything.
From time to time those who owned fields or
houses sold them, brought the money, [35]and gave
it to the apostles. Then the money was given to
anyone who needed it.
[36]One of the believers was named Joseph, a
Levite born in Cyprus. The apostles called him
Barnabas (which means "one who encourages").
[37]Joseph owned a field, sold it, brought the
money and gave it to the apostles.

Ananias and Sapphira Die

5 But a man named Ananias and his wife
Sapphira sold some land. [2]He kept back part
of the money for himself; his wife knew about this
and agreed to it. But he brought the rest of the
money and gave it to the apostles.[d] [3]Peter said,
"Ananias, why did you let Satan rule your
thoughts to lie to the Holy Spirit[d] and to keep for
yourself part of the money you received for the
land? [4]Before you sold the land, it belonged to
you. And even after you sold it, you could have
used the money in any way you wanted. Why did
you think of doing this? You lied to God, not to
us!" [5-6]When Ananias heard this, he fell down
and died. Some young men came in, wrapped up
his body, carried it out and buried it. And every-
one who heard about this was filled with fear.
[7]About three hours later his wife came in, but
she did not know what had happened. [8]Peter
said to her, "Tell me, was the money you got for
your field this much?"
Sapphira answered, "Yes, that was the price."
[9]Peter said to her, "Why did you and your hus-
band agree to test the Spirit of the Lord? Look! The
men who buried your husband are at the door, and
they will carry you out." [10]At that moment
Sapphira fell down by his feet and died. When the
young men came in and saw that she was dead,
they carried her out and buried her beside her hus-
band. [11]The whole church and all the others who
heard about these things were filled with fear.

The Apostles Heal Many

[12]The apostles[d] did many signs and miracles[d]
among the people. And they would all meet to-
gether on Solomon's Porch.[d] [13]None of the others
dared to join them, but all the people respected
them. [14]More and more men and women believed
in the Lord and were added to the group of believ-
ers. [15]The people placed their sick on beds and
mats in the streets, hoping that when Peter passed
by at least his shadow might fall on them. [16]Crowds
came from all the towns around Jerusalem, bring-
ing their sick and those who were bothered by evil
spirits, and all of them were healed.

Leaders Try to Stop the Apostles

[17]The high priest and all his friends (a group
called the Sadducees[d]) became very jealous.
[18]They took the apostles and put them in jail.
[19]But during the night, an angel of the Lord
opened the doors of the jail and led the apostles
outside. The angel said, [20]"Go and stand in the
Temple[d] and tell the people everything about
this new life." [21]When the apostles heard this,
they obeyed and went into the Temple early in
the morning and continued teaching.
When the high priest and his friends arrived,
they called a meeting of the Jewish leaders and
all the important Jewish elders. They sent some
men to the jail to bring the apostles to them.
[22]But, upon arriving, the officers could not find
the apostles. So they went back and reported to
the Jewish leaders. [23]They said, "The jail was
closed and locked, and the guards were standing
at the doors. But when we opened the doors, the
jail was empty!" [24]Hearing this, the captain of
the Temple guards and the leading priests were
confused and wondered what was happening.
[25]Then someone came and told them, "Listen!
The men you put in jail are standing in the Temple
teaching the people." [26]Then the captain and his
men went out and brought the apostles back. But
the soldiers did not use force, because they were
afraid the people would stone them to death.
[27]The soldiers brought the apostles to the
meeting and made them stand before the Jewish
leaders. The high priest questioned them, [28]say-
ing, "We gave you strict orders not to continue
teaching in that name. But look, you have filled
Jerusalem with your teaching and are trying to
make us responsible for this man's death."
[29]Peter and the other apostles answered, "We
must obey God, not human authority! [30]You killed
Jesus by hanging him on a cross. But God, the God
of our ancestors, raised Jesus up from the dead!
[31]Jesus is the One whom God raised to be on his
right side, as Leader and Saviour. Through him, all
Jewish people can change their hearts and lives and
have their sins forgiven. [32]We saw all these things
happen. The Holy Spirit,[d] whom God has given to
all who obey him, also proves these things are true."
[33]When the Jewish leaders heard this, they
became angry and wanted to kill them. [34]But a
Pharisee[d] named Gamaliel stood up in the
meeting. He was a teacher of the law, and all the
people respected him. He ordered the apostles to
leave the meeting for a little while. [35]Then he
said, "People of Israel, be careful what you are
planning to do to these men. [36]Remember when

Theudas appeared? He said he was a great man,
and about 400 men joined him. But he was
killed, and all his followers were scattered; they
were able to do nothing. 37Later, a man named
Judas came from Galilee at the time of the regis-
tration.[n] He also led a group of followers and
was killed, and all his followers were scattered.
38And so now I tell you: stay away from these
men, and leave them alone. If their plan comes
from human authority, it will fail. 39But if it is
from God, you will not be able to stop them. You
might even be fighting against God himself!"
The Jewish leaders agreed with what Gamaliel
said. 40They called the apostles in, beat them and

registration Census. A counting of all the people and the things they own.

PRIORITIES

Who's the Boss?

Richard Wurmbrand fidgeted in his chair as he listened to Gheorghe Gheorghiu-Dej, the Communist Party boss. Gheorghe promised the post-World War II clergy of Romania that his government would pay the clergy out of tax revenues if communism and Christianity would work together. Most of the audience cheered, and one church leader promised that the clergy would co-operate with the state.

But Richard didn't cheer. He had already been imprisoned and beaten several times for his faith. He knew that speaking out could again cost him his freedom.

Richard's wife, Sabina, sat beside him. "Go and wash this shame from the face of Christ!" she demanded.

Richard pleaded that he would be taken away if he spoke out against the communists.

"I don't need a coward," Sabina replied.

Gathering his courage, Richard asked permission to speak and was welcomed forward by the organisers, who apparently anticipated a unity speech. Instead, Richard began by saying it was the duty of ministers to glorify God, not earthly powers. He encouraged the clergy to support the eternal kingdom of God, not the powers of Romania.

As he continued, someone suddenly began to clap. And another person also clapped. Soon, the clapping erupted into waves of applause.

"Stop! Your right to speak has been withdrawn," ordered the Minister of Cults ("cults" included religious bodies of all kinds in Romania).

"My right to speak comes from God," Richard declared. He kept speaking until his microphone was disconnected.

Richard was imprisoned and the Ministry of Cults ran the church.

The situation has changed in Romania but in many other parts of the world, people face serious trouble if they stand up for Christ.

Like Richard, the apostles recognised the priority of obeying God and speaking out for him. Read **Acts 5:17–32** to see how they spoke out for Jesus even when threatened by imprisonment.

- Based on the story and the Bible passage, what were the top priorities for Richard Wurmbrand and the apostles?
- When have you faced opposition for your faith? How was that experience like and unlike the scripture passage?

Consider . . .

- making a poster of Acts 5:29 and writing around the border five priorities which you believe God wants you to follow. Then make a weekly schedule that reflects those priorities.
- talking to a friend about times when you have had to do something unpopular to make your faith your top priority.

For more, see . . .

- Psalm 119:17–24 (p.571)
- 2 Corinthians 11:23–29 (p.1252)
- Matthew 10:32–36 (p.957)

told them not to speak in the name of Jesus again. Then they let them go free. 41The apostles left the meeting full of joy because they were given the honour of suffering disgrace for Jesus. 42Every day in the Temple and in people's homes they continued teaching the people and telling the Good News[d]—that Jesus is the Christ.[d]

Seven Leaders are Chosen

6 The number of followers was growing. But during this same time, the Greek-speaking followers had an argument with the other Jewish followers. The Greek-speaking widows were not getting their share of the food that was given out every day. 2The twelve apostles[d] called the whole group of followers together and said, "It is not right for us to stop our work of teaching God's word in order to serve tables. 3So, brothers and sisters, choose seven of your own men who are good, full of the Spirit[d] and full of wisdom. We will put them in charge of this work. 4Then we can continue to pray and to teach the word of God."

> **Sidelight** Relationships between Jews and non-Jewish people were strained in Bible times. This prejudice shows up in Acts 6:1 where Greek (non-Jewish) Christians complained that their widows weren't receiving a fair share of the church's distributions. The book of Acts is filled with other stories that highlight the tensions between Jewish and non-Jewish Christians.

5The whole group liked the idea, so they chose these seven men: Stephen (a man with great faith and full of the Holy Spirit), Philip,[n] Procorus, Nicanor, Timon, Parmenas and Nicolas (a man from Antioch who had become a Jew). 6Then they put these men before the apostles, who prayed and laid their hands[n] on them.

7The word of God was continuing to spread. The group of followers in Jerusalem increased, and a great number of the Jewish priests believed and obeyed.

Stephen is Accused

8Stephen was richly blessed by God who gave him the power to do great miracles[d] and signs among the people. 9But some Jewish people were against him. They belonged to the synagogue[d] of Free Men[n] (as it was called), which included Jewish people from Cyrene, Alexandria, Cilicia and Asia. They all came and argued with Stephen.

10But the Spirit[d] was helping him to speak with wisdom, and his words were so strong that they could not argue with him. 11So they secretly urged some men to say, "We heard Stephen speak against Moses and against God."

12This upset the people, the Jewish elders and the teachers of the law. They came and grabbed Stephen and brought him to a meeting of the Jewish leaders. 13They brought in some people to tell lies about Stephen, saying, "This man is always speaking against this holy place and the law of Moses. 14We heard him say that Jesus from Nazareth will destroy this place and that Jesus will change the customs Moses gave us." 15All the people in the meeting were watching Stephen closely and saw that his face looked like the face of an angel.

Stephen's Speech

7 The high priest said to Stephen, "Are these things true?"

2Stephen answered, "Brothers and fathers, listen to me. Our glorious God appeared to Abraham, our ancestor, in Mesopotamia before he lived in Haran. 3God said to Abraham, 'Leave your country and your relatives, and go to the land I will show you.'[n] 4So Abraham left the country of Chaldea and went to live in Haran. After Abraham's father died, God sent him to this place where you now live. 5God did not give Abraham any of this land, not even a foot of it. But God promised that he would give this land to him and his descendants,[d] even before Abraham had a child. 6This is what God said to him: 'Your descendants will be strangers in a land they don't own. The people there will make them slaves and will mistreat them for 400 years. 7But I will punish the nation where they are slaves. Then your descendants will leave that land and will worship me in this place.'[n] 8God made an agreement with Abraham, the sign of which was circumcision.[d] And so when Abraham had his son, Isaac, Abraham circumcised him when he was eight days old. Isaac also circumcised his son, Jacob, and Jacob did the same for his sons, the twelve ancestors[n] of our people.

9"Jacob's sons became jealous of Joseph and sold him to be a slave in Egypt. But God was with

Philip Not the apostle named Philip.
laid their hands on The laying on of hands had many purposes, including the giving of a blessing, power or authority.
Free Men Jewish people who had been slaves or whose fathers had been slaves, but who were now free.
'Leave . . . you.' Quotation from Genesis 12:1.
'Your descendants . . . place.' Quotation from Genesis 15:13–14 and Exodus 3:12.
twelve ancestors Important ancestors of the Jewish people; the leaders of the twelve Jewish tribes.

him 10and saved him from all his troubles. The
king of Egypt liked Joseph and respected him be-
cause of the wisdom God gave him. The king
made him governor of Egypt and put him in
charge of all the people in his palace.
11"Then all the land of Egypt and Canaan be-
came so dry that nothing would grow, and the
people suffered very much. Jacob's sons, our an-
cestors, could not find anything to eat. 12But when
Jacob heard there was grain in Egypt, he sent his
sons there. This was their first trip to Egypt.
13When they went there a second time, Joseph
told his brothers who he was, and the king learned
about Joseph's family. 14Then Joseph sent messen-
gers to invite Jacob, his father, to come to Egypt
along with all his relatives (75 persons altogether).
15So Jacob went down to Egypt, where he and
his sons died. 16Later their bodies were moved to
Shechem and put in a grave there. (It was the
same grave Abraham had bought for a sum of
money from the sons of Hamor in Shechem.)
17"The promise God made to Abraham was
soon to come true, and the number of people in
Egypt grew large. 18Then a new king, who did
not know who Joseph was, began to rule Egypt.
19This king tricked our people and was cruel to
our ancestors, forcing them to leave their babies
outside to die. 20At this time Moses was born,
and he was very beautiful. For three months
Moses was cared for in his father's house.
21When they put Moses outside, the king's
daughter adopted him and raised him as if he

HONESTY

Rumours

"Shhhhh! There she is."

The girls at the back of the room stopped giggling and whispering when Zoë arrived for her history class on Monday morning.

"What's going on?" Zoë asked uncomfortably as she sat next to her best friend, Mary.

Mary shot a dirty look at the girls in the back of the room. "Someone is saying you're 'easy'," she said. "There's a note in the boys' toilets that says 'Zoë's fine, so get in line'."

Zoë couldn't believe it. She felt as though someone had just kicked her in the chest.

Just then, Mark leaned across the aisle and asked, "Hey, Zoë, can I be next in line?"

Zoë burst into tears and ran from the room. Her mind raced as she stumbled along the empty corridor. Where could such a false rumour have come from? Who could say such ugly things?

Then she remembered what Ben, her ex-boyfriend, had said. After begging her not to break up, he warned that she would be sorry if she did.

"This must be what he meant," Zoë thought as she leaned against a locker and slid down to sit on the floor.

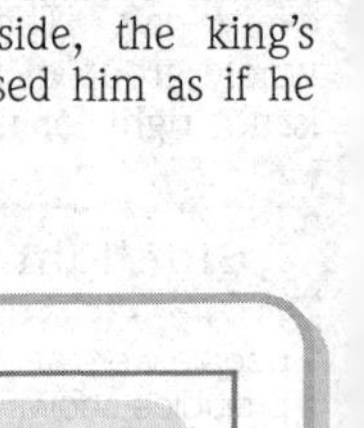

Zoë knew it would take a long time to clear her reputation. But she was determined that, no matter what, it would be cleared.

"Lord," she prayed, "help me to be strong." Zoë maintained her high standards in relationships with boys and in time the rumours died down.

Stephen was also a victim of lies and rumours, but he remained faithful to God, as we read in **Acts 6:8–15**.

- How could Zoë and Stephen be strong in the face of lies and rumours?
- When has someone told lies about you the way these people did about Stephen? How did you respond?

Consider . . .

- thinking of a tactful way to respond to people who spread rumours. Always talk to the person who is being talked about rather than spread rumours.
- what you would do to clear your reputation if someone spread dishonest rumours about you.

For more, see . . .

- Leviticus 19:16–19 (p.119)
- James 3:1–12 (p.1351)
- Matthew 26:57–68 (p.990)

were her own son. 22 The Egyptians taught Moses
everything they knew, and he was a powerful
man in what he said and did.
23 "When Moses was about 40 years old,
he thought it would be good to visit his own
people, the people of Israel. 24 Moses saw an
Egyptian mistreating an Israelite, so he defended
the Israelite and punished the Egyptian by
killing him. 25 Moses thought his own people
would understand that God was using him to
save them, but they did not. 26 The next day
when Moses saw two men of Israel fighting, he
tried to make peace between them. He said,
'Men, you are brothers. Why are you hurting
each other?' 27 The man who was hurting the
other pushed Moses away and said, 'Who made
you our ruler and judge? 28 Are you going to kill
me as you killed the Egyptian yesterday?'[n]
29 When Moses heard him say this, he left Egypt
and went to live in the land of Midian where he
was a stranger. While Moses lived in Midian, he
had two sons.
30 "Forty years later an angel appeared to
Moses in the flames of a burning bush as he was
in the desert near Mount Sinai. 31 When Moses
saw this, he was amazed and went near to look
closer. Moses heard the Lord's voice say, 32 'I am
the God of your ancestors, the God of Abraham,
Isaac and Jacob.'[n] Moses began to shake with
fear and was afraid to look. 33 The Lord said to
him, 'Take off your sandals, because you are
standing on holy ground. 34 I have seen the trou-
bles my people have suffered in Egypt. I have
heard their cries and have come down to save
them. And now, Moses, I am sending you back
to Egypt.'[n]
35 "This Moses was the same man the two
men of Israel rejected, saying, 'Who made you a
ruler and judge?'[n] Moses is the same man God
sent to be a ruler and saviour, with the help of
the angel that Moses saw in the burning bush.
36 So Moses led the people out of Egypt. He
worked miracles[d] and signs in Egypt, at the Red
Sea[d] and then in the desert for 40 years. 37 This is
the same Moses that said to the people of Israel,
'God will give you a prophet[d] like me, who is
one of your own people.'[n] 38 This is the Moses
who was with the gathering of the Israelites in
the desert. He was with the angel that spoke to
him at Mount Sinai, and he was with our ances-
tors. He received commands from God that give
life, and he gave those commands to us.

39 "But our ancestors did not want to obey
Moses. They rejected him and wanted to go back
to Egypt. 40 They said to Aaron, 'Make us gods
who will lead us. Moses led us out of Egypt, but
we don't know what has happened to him.'[n]
41 So the people made an idol that looked like a
calf. Then they brought sacrifices to it and were
proud of what they had made with their own
hands. 42 But God turned against them and did
not try to stop them from worshipping the sun,
moon and stars. This is what is written in the
book of the prophets: God says,

'People of Israel, you did not bring me
sacrifices and offerings
while you travelled in the desert for 40
years.
43 You have carried with you
your king, the god Sakkuth,
and Kaiwan your idol
and the star gods you have made.
So I will send you away as captives beyond
Damascus.'
Amos 5:25–27

44 "The Holy Tent[d] where God spoke to our
ancestors was with them in the desert. God told
Moses how to make this Tent, and he made it
like the plan God showed him. 45 Later, Joshua
led our ancestors to capture the lands of the
other nations. Our people went in, and God
forced the other people out. When our people
went into this new land, they took with them
this same Tent they had received from their
ancestors. They kept it until the time of David,
46 who pleased God and asked God to let him
build a house for him, the God of Jacob. 47 But
Solomon was the one who built the Temple.[d]
48 "But the Most High does not live in houses
that people build with their hands. As the
prophet says:

49 'Heaven is my throne,
and the earth is my footstool.
So do you think you can build a house for
me? says the Lord.
Do I need a place to rest?
50 Remember, my hand made all these things!' "
Isaiah 66:1–2

51 Stephen continued speaking: "You stubborn
people! You have not given your hearts to God,
nor will you listen to him! You are always against
what the Holy Spirit[d] is trying to tell you, just
as your ancestors were. 52 Your ancestors tried
to hurt every prophet who ever lived. Those
prophets said long ago that the One who is good

'Who . . . yesterday?' Quotation from Exodus 2:14.
'I am . . . Jacob.' Quotation from Exodus 3:6.
'Take . . . Egypt.' Quotation from Exodus 3:5–10.
'Who . . . judge?' Quotation from Exodus 2:14.
'God . . . people.' Quotation from Deuteronomy 18:15.
'Make . . . him.' Quotation from Exodus 32:1.

would come, but your ancestors killed them. And
now you have turned against and killed the One
who is good. 53You received the law of Moses,
which God gave you through his angels, but you
haven't obeyed it."

Stephen is Killed

54When the leaders heard this, they became
furious. They were so cross they were grinding
their teeth at Stephen. 55But Stephen was full of
the Holy Spirit.[d] He looked up to heaven and saw
the glory of God and Jesus standing at God's right
side. 56He said, "Look! I see heaven open and
the Son of Man[d] standing at God's right side."
57Then they shouted loudly and covered their
ears and all ran at Stephen. 58They took him out
of the city and began to throw stones at him to
kill him. And those who told lies against Stephen
left their coats with a young man named Saul.
59While they were throwing stones, Stephen
prayed, "Lord Jesus, receive my spirit." 60He fell
on his knees and cried in a loud voice, "Lord, do
not hold this sin against them." After Stephen
said this, he died.

8 Saul agreed that the killing of Stephen was
good.

Troubles for the Believers

On that day the church of Jerusalem began to
be persecuted,[d] and all the believers, except the
apostles,[d] were scattered throughout Judea and
Samaria.
2And some religious people buried Stephen
and cried loudly for him. 3Saul was also trying to
destroy the church, going from house to house,
dragging out men and women and putting them
in jail. 4And wherever they were scattered, they
told people the Good News.[d]

Philip Preaches in Samaria

5Philip[n] went to the city of Samaria and
preached about the Christ.[d] 6When the people

Philip Not the apostle named Philip.

ANGER

Rage

Ann, thirteen, appeared to be a model student and a devoted daughter. But one night, Ann brought two boys into her bedroom and called her father to come upstairs. Using a knife and a length of pipe, the three teenagers slashed and beat him to death. Ann had been psychologically abused by her father.

Alan, fourteen, was the school punchbag. Gangling and clumsy, with few friends, he was the target of daily harassment and beatings. One morning in late January, Alan headed for school carrying one of his father's high-power rifles and ammunition. When he got there, he opened fire, killing the school's headmaster and wounding two teachers and one student. He thought his actions might win his harsh father's approval.

A group of Jewish leaders, religious and proper, faithfully practised the regulations of their faith. When Stephen, a Christian disciple, started preaching about Jesus, the Jewish leaders went berserk. They carried Stephen out of the city and hurled stones at him until he was dead.

Read **Acts 7:51–60** to get the full story of how these Jewish leaders let their anger lead to destruction.

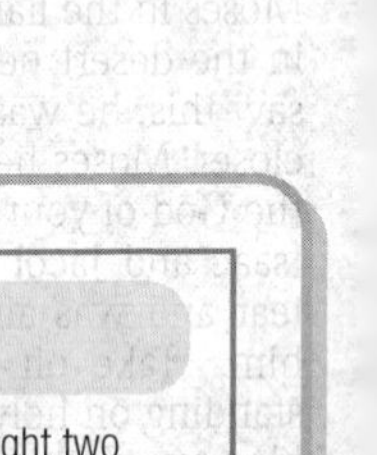

- What caused Ann's, Alan's and the Jewish leaders' rage?
- Why was Stephen able to respond to his killers the way he did?

Consider . . .

- praying before expressing your anger so that you won't do something you'll regret later.
- seeking help from Christian friends if your anger turns to rage. Protect yourself and others by learning how to handle anger.

For more, see . . .

- Deuteronomy 13:6–11 (p.178)
- James 1:19–20 (p.1348)
- Ephesians 4:26–32 (p.1274)

there heard Philip and saw the miracles[d] he was
doing, they all listened carefully to what he said.
7Many of these people had evil spirits in them,
but Philip made the evil spirits leave. The spirits
made a loud noise when they came out. Philip
also healed many weak and crippled people
there. 8So the people in that city were very
happy.

9But there was a man named Simon in that
city. Before Philip came there, Simon had prac-
tised magic and amazed all the people of
Samaria. He boasted and called himself a great
man. 10All the people—the least important to
the most important—paid attention to Simon,
saying, "This man has the power of God, called
'the Great Power!' " 11Simon had amazed them
with his magic so long that the people became
his followers. 12But when Philip told them the
Good News[d] about the kingdom of God and the
power of Jesus Christ, men and women believed
Philip and were baptised.[d] 13Simon himself
believed, and after he was baptised, he stayed
very close to Philip. When he saw the miracles
and the powerful things Philip did, Simon was
amazed.

14When the apostles[d] who were still in
Jerusalem heard that the people of Samaria had
accepted the word of God, they sent Peter and
John to them. 15When Peter and John arrived,
they prayed that the Samaritan believers might
receive the Holy Spirit.[d] 16These people had
been baptised in the name of the Lord Jesus, but
the Holy Spirit had not yet come upon any of
them. 17Then, when the two apostles began
laying their hands on[n] the people, they received
the Holy Spirit.

18Simon saw that the Spirit was given to peo-
ple when the apostles laid their hands on them.
So he offered the apostles money, 19saying,
"Give me also this power so that anyone on
whom I lay my hands will receive the Holy
Spirit."

20Peter said to him, "You and your money
should both be destroyed, because you thought
you could buy God's gift with money. 21You can-
not share with us in this work since your heart
is not right before God. 22Change your heart!
Turn away from this evil thing you have done,
and pray to the Lord. Maybe he will forgive you
for thinking this. 23I see that you are full of
bitter jealousy and ruled by sin."

24Simon answered, "Both of you pray for me
to the Lord so the things you have said will not
happen to me."

25After Peter and John told the people what
they had seen Jesus do and after they had spoken
the message of the Lord, they went back to
Jerusalem. On the way, they went through many
Samaritan towns and preached the Good News to
the people.

Philip Teaches an Ethiopian

26An angel of the Lord said to Philip,[n] "Get
ready and go south to the road that leads down
to Gaza from Jerusalem—the desert road." 27So
Philip got ready and went. On the road he saw a
man from Ethiopia, a eunuch.[d] He was an im-
portant officer in the service of Candace, the
queen of the Ethiopians; he was responsible for
taking care of all her money. He had gone to
Jerusalem to worship. 28Now, as he was on his
way home, he was sitting in his chariot reading
from the Book of Isaiah, the prophet.[d] 29The
Spirit[d] said to Philip, "Go to that chariot and stay
near it."

30So when Philip ran towards the chariot, he
heard the man reading from Isaiah the prophet.
Philip asked, "Do you understand what you are
reading?"

31He answered, "How can I understand unless
someone explains it to me?" Then he invited
Philip to climb in and sit with him. 32The portion
of Scripture[d] he was reading was this:

"He was like a sheep being led to be killed.
He was quiet, as a lamb is quiet while its
wool is being cut;
he never opened his mouth.
33 He was shamed and was treated unfairly.
He died without children to continue his
family.
His life on earth has ended." *Isaiah 53:7–8*

34The officer said to Philip, "Please tell me,
who is the prophet talking about—himself or
someone else?" 35Philip began to speak, and start-
ing with this same Scripture, he told the man the
Good News[d] about Jesus.

> **Sidelight** Acts 8:26–40 tells of what is probably the conversion of the first African. He came from an area south of Egypt called Nubia. Philip had travelled about 80 kilometres from Jerusalem to witness to this man.

36While they were travelling down the road,
they came to some water. The officer said, "Look,
here is water. Why shouldn't I be baptised?"[d]

laying their hands on The laying on of hands had many purposes, including the giving of a blessing, power or authority.
Philip Not the apostle named Philip.

37 [n] 38 Then the officer commanded the chariot to
stop. Both Philip and the officer went down into
the water, and Philip baptised him. 39 When they
came up out of the water, the Spirit of the Lord
took Philip away; the officer never saw him again.
And the officer continued on his way home, full
of joy. 40 But Philip appeared in a city called
Azotus and preached the Good News in all the
towns on the way from Azotus to Caesarea.

Saul is Converted

9 In Jerusalem Saul was still threatening the
followers of the Lord by saying he would kill
them. So he went to the high priest 2 and asked
him to write letters to the synagogues[d] in the city
of Damascus. Then if Saul found any followers of
Christ's Way, men or women, he would arrest
them and bring them back to Jerusalem.
3 So Saul headed towards Damascus. As he
came near the city, a bright light from heaven
suddenly flashed around him. 4 Saul fell to the
ground and heard a voice saying to him, "Saul,
Saul! Why are you persecuting[d] me?"
5 Saul said, "Who are you, Lord?"
The voice answered, "I am Jesus, whom you
are persecuting. 6 Get up now and go into the city.
Someone there will tell you what you must do."
7 The people travelling with Saul stood there
but said nothing. They heard the voice, but they
saw no one. 8 Saul got up from the ground
and opened his eyes, but he could not see. So
those with Saul took his hand and led him into

Verse 37 Some late copies of Acts add verse 37: "Philip answered, 'If you believe with all your heart, you can.' The officer said, 'I believe that Jesus Christ is the Son of God.' "

BIBLE STUDY

Creative Questions

"I've begun wondering if there really is a God," Kevin said and looked down at his shoes. "I mean, how do I know Christianity isn't just wishful thinking?"

Kevin looked round the room. Everyone was silent.

Finally, Jeremy spoke up. "I like to tackle it from the opposite point of view. I try to prove that there isn't a God."

Then everyone started talking at once.

"That leads to even harder questions," said someone in the corner. "How can you explain everything in this world if there isn't a Creator?"

"And why do people get angry at things like murder and child abuse if there isn't a God who shows the difference between right and wrong?"

"Yes! And what about people's need for religion? Why should they want to worship God if there is no God?"

The questions went on and on. Finally, the kids were silent. Jeremy looked round and smiled. "Believing there is no God takes more faith than realising there is one," he said. "Thanks for stretching my faith."

There's nothing wrong with sincere questions because they lead to real answers. An Ethiopian asked questions that led to faith in Jesus in **Acts 8:26–40**.

- How do you think his questions led Kevin to deeper faith? How did the Ethiopian's questions lead him to God's salvation?
- What questions would you ask about the passage which the Ethiopian had read?

Consider . . .

- listing the questions you have about God and searching for answers to those questions.
- writing down questions as you read the Bible. Ask these questions during youth group.

For more, see . . .

- Isaiah 53:7–8 (p.697)
- Hebrews 6:1–3 (p.1335)
- John 20:24–29 (p.1134)

Damascus. 9 For three days Saul could not see and
did not eat or drink.
10 There was a follower of Jesus in Damascus
named Ananias. The Lord spoke to Ananias in a
vision, "Ananias!"
Ananias answered, "Here I am, Lord."
11 The Lord said to him, "Get up and go to
Straight Street. Find the house of Judas,[n] and ask
for a man named Saul from the city of Tarsus. He is
there now, praying. 12 Saul has seen a vision in which
a man named Ananias comes to him and lays his
hands on him. Then he is able to see again."
13 But Ananias answered, "Lord, many people
have told me about this man and the terrible
things he did to your holy people in Jerusalem.
14 Now he has come here to Damascus, and the
leading priests have given him the power to arrest
everyone who worships you."
15 But the Lord said to Ananias, "Go! I have
chosen Saul for an important work. He must tell
about me to those who are not Jews, to kings and
to the people of Israel. 16 I will show him how
much he must suffer for my name."
17 So Ananias went to the house of Judas. He laid
his hands on[n] Saul and said, "Brother Saul, the
Lord Jesus sent me. He is the one you saw on the
road on your way here. He sent me so that you can
see again and be filled with the Holy Spirit."[d]
18 Immediately, something that looked like fish
scales fell from Saul's eyes, and he was able to see
again! Then Saul got up and was baptised.[d] 19 After
he ate some food, his strength returned.

Saul Preaches in Damascus

Saul stayed with the followers of Jesus in
Damascus for a few days. 20 Soon he began to

Judas This is not either of the apostles named Judas.
laid his hands on The laying on of hands had many purposes, including the giving of a blessing, power or authority.

NON-CHRISTIANS

Show and Tell

Charles Blondin stretched a 330-metre tightrope across Niagara Falls on 30 June 1859. About 25,000 spectators gathered to watch the incredible stunt. Charles stood in front of the crowd and asked, "How many believe I can walk across Niagara Falls?"

"We believe," the crowd roared. And Charles walked safely across Niagara Falls, 50 metres up.

Five days later, he asked, "How many believe I can walk across Niagara Falls blindfolded and pushing a wheelbarrow?"

The crowd cheered. And Charles did it again.

Two weeks later, the crowd gathered again. "How many believe I can walk across with a person on my back?" he asked.

The crowd screamed: "Of course! We believe!"

Charles looked straight at a person in the front. "You, sir. Climb on!" The man refused.

There's a big difference between talking about faith and acting on that faith. In **Acts 9:1–20**, Saul and Ananias both learned what it meant to act on their faith.

- Which was most difficult to act on: Charles's challenge or Jesus' instructions to Saul and Ananias? Why?
- What did Ananias's actions communicate to Saul?

Consider . . .

- becoming an "Ananias" to a friend who is struggling with his or her faith. Provide encouragement and support as that person searches for what it means to follow God.
- writing the story of a time when you have experienced God's love. Then tell your story to a friend.

For more, see . . .

- Exodus 4.1–17 (p.63)
- James 2:14–18 (p.1350)
- Acts 22:1–16 (p.1174)

preach about Jesus in the synagogues,[d] saying,
"Jesus is the Son of God."
21All the people who heard him were amazed.
They said, "This is the man who was in Jerusalem
trying to destroy those who trust in this name! He
came here to arrest the followers of Jesus and
take them back to the leading priests."
22But Saul grew more powerful. His proofs that
Jesus is the Christ[d] were so strong that the Jewish
people in Damascus could not argue with him.
23After many days, some Jewish people made
plans to kill Saul. 24They were watching the city
gates day and night, but Saul learned about their
plan. 25One night some followers of Saul helped
him leave the city by lowering him in a basket
through an opening in the city wall.

Saul Preaches in Jerusalem

26When Saul went to Jerusalem, he tried to join
the group of followers, but they were all afraid of
him. They did not believe he was really a follower.
27But Barnabas accepted Saul and took him to the
apostles.[d] Barnabas explained to them that Saul
had seen the Lord on the road and the Lord had
spoken to Saul. Then he told them how boldly Saul
had preached in the name of Jesus in Damascus.
28And so Saul stayed with the followers, going
everywhere in Jerusalem, preaching boldly in the
name of the Lord. 29He would often talk and ar-
gue with the Jewish people who spoke Greek, but
they were trying to kill him. 30When the follow-
ers learned about this, they took Saul to Caesarea
and from there sent him to Tarsus.
31The church everywhere in Judea, Galilee and
Samaria had a time of peace and became stron-
ger. Respecting the Lord by the way they lived,
and being encouraged by the Holy Spirit,[d] the
group of believers continued to grow.

Peter Heals Aeneas

32As Peter was travelling through all the area,
he visited God's people who lived in Lydda.
33There he met a man named Aeneas, who was
paralysed and had not been able to leave his
bed for the past eight years. 34Peter said to him,
"Aeneas, Jesus Christ heals you. Stand up and
make your bed." Aeneas stood up immediately.
35All the people living in Lydda and on the Plain
of Sharon saw him and turned to the Lord.

Peter Heals Tabitha

36In the city of Joppa there was a follower
named Tabitha (whose Greek name was Dorcas).
She was always doing good deeds and kind acts.
37While Peter was in Lydda, Tabitha became sick
and died. Her body was washed and put in a
room upstairs. 38Since Lydda is near Joppa and
the followers in Joppa heard that Peter was in
Lydda, they sent two messengers to Peter. They
begged him, "Hurry, please come to us!" 39So
Peter got ready and went with them. When he
arrived, they took him to the upstairs room
where all the widows stood around Peter, crying.
They showed him the shirts and coats Tabitha
had made when she was still alive. 40Peter sent
everyone out of the room and kneeled and prayed.
Then he turned to the body and said, "Tabitha,
stand up." She opened her eyes, and when she
saw Peter, she sat up. 41He gave her his hand and
helped her up. Then he called the saints[d] and the
widows into the room and showed them that
Tabitha was alive. 42People everywhere in Joppa
learned about this, and many believed in the
Lord. 43Peter stayed in Joppa for many days with a
man named Simon who was a leatherworker.

Peter Teaches Cornelius

10 At Caesarea there was a man named
Cornelius, an officer in the Italian group
of the Roman army. 2Cornelius was a religious
man. He and all the other people who lived in
his house worshipped the true God. He gave
much of his money to the poor and prayed to
God often. 3One afternoon about three o'clock,
Cornelius clearly saw a vision. An angel of God
came to him and said, "Cornelius!"
4Cornelius stared at the angel. He became
afraid and said, "What do you want, Lord?"
The angel said, "God has heard your prayers.
He has seen that you give to the poor, and he
remembers you. 5Send some men now to Joppa
to bring back a man named Simon who is also
called Peter. 6He is staying with a man, also
named Simon, who is a leatherworker and has a
house beside the sea." 7When the angel who
spoke to Cornelius left, Cornelius called two of
his servants and a soldier, a religious man who
worked for him. 8Cornelius explained everything
to them and sent them to Joppa.
9About noon the next day as they came near
Joppa, Peter was going up to the roof[n] to pray.
10He was hungry and wanted to eat, but while
the food was being prepared, he had a vision.
11He saw heaven opened and something coming
down that looked like a big sheet being lowered
to earth by its four corners. 12In it were all kinds
of animals, reptiles and birds. 13Then a voice said
to Peter, "Get up, Peter; kill and eat."
14But Peter said, "No, Lord! I have never eaten
food that is unholy or unclean."[d]

roof In Bible times houses were built with flat roofs. The roof was used for drying things such as flax and fruit. And it was used as an extra room, as a place for worship and as a place to sleep in the summer.

15 But the voice said to him again, "God has made
these things clean so don't call them 'unholy'!"
16 This happened three times, and at once the sheet
was taken back to heaven.
17 While Peter was wondering what this vision
meant, the men Cornelius sent had found Simon's
house and were standing at the gate. 18 They asked,
"Is Simon Peter staying here?"
19 While Peter was still thinking about the vi-
sion, the Spirit[d] said to him, "Listen, three men
are looking for you. 20 Get up and go downstairs.
Go with them without doubting, because I have
sent them to you."
21 So Peter went down to the men and said, "I
am the one you are looking for. Why did you
come here?"
22 They said, "A holy angel spoke to Cornelius,
an army officer and a good man; he worships
God. All the Jewish people respect him. The
angel told Cornelius to ask you to come to his
house so that he can hear what you have to say."
23 So Peter asked the men to come in and spend
the night.
The next day Peter got ready and went with
them, and some of the followers from Joppa
joined him. 24 On the following day they came to
Caesarea. Cornelius was waiting for them and
had called together his relatives and close friends.
25 When Peter entered, Cornelius met him, fell at
his feet and worshipped him. 26 But Peter helped
him up, saying, "Stand up. I too am only a hu-
man." 27 As he talked with Cornelius, Peter went
inside where he saw many people gathered. 28 He
said, "You people understand that it is against
our Jewish law for Jewish people to associate
with or visit anyone who is not Jewish. But God
has shown me that I should not call any person
'unholy' or 'unclean'. 29 That is why I did not
argue when I was asked to come here. Now,
please tell me why you sent for me."

EUTHANASIA

I'm Coming Home

Geoff's life stretched out in front of him. Young, intelligent, handsome, popular, he had everything going for him. To look at him you would never have thought that something was wrong. But a whisper began to circulate the church. Geoff had been diagnosed with cancer.

It was almost as if the diagnosis made him sick. Over the course of a few short weeks, Geoff turned from a young, healthy, active teenager, to someone greying and old before his time. His weight dropped dramatically, his hair thinned. His body looked all out of proportion. Although nobody wanted to say it, everybody knew that Geoff was dying.

The prospect of death raises a whole host of uneasy questions and emotions. Will God heal him? What should we do about watching him suffer? When do we pray, comfort, act? How do we do any of these things?

Out of all those involved in Geoff's last few months, it was he who led everyone through the maze of knowing what to do. His wisdom: God is in control; if God wants to change this he can do, but he will take me home when he wants.

Read **Acts 9:36–42**.

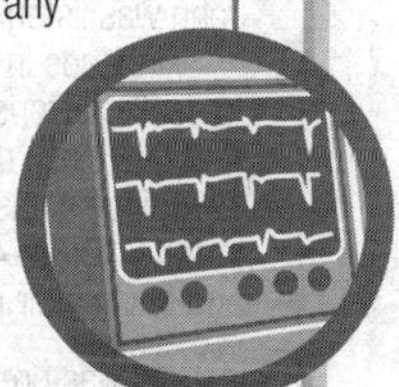

- How could Geoff trust that God knew best?
- How would this passage be an encouragement to Geoff?

Consider . . .

- making a list of things you find it hard to trust God with. Things that you like to be in control of. Put them in a box and bury them in the ground. Hold a funeral service as the things you are in control of die, so God can take control.
- prayer-walking around your local park. Look at how God looks after everything growing around you. God is in control of the natural world. Ask God to be in control of your life too.

For more see . . .

- Ecclesiastes 3:1–8 (p.622)
- Hebrews 12:1–3 (p.1343)
- Daniel 3:13–27 (p.835)

30Cornelius said, "Four days ago, I was praying
in my house at this same time—three o'clock in
the afternoon. Suddenly, there was a man stand-
ing before me wearing shining clothes. 31He said,
'Cornelius, God has heard your prayer and has
seen that you give to the poor and remembers
you. 32So send some men to Joppa and ask Simon
Peter to come. Peter is staying in the house of a
man, also named Simon, who is a leatherworker
and has a house beside the sea.' 33So I sent for
you immediately, and it was very good of you to
come. Now we are all here before God to hear
everything the Lord has commanded you to
tell us."
34Peter began to speak: "I really understand
now that to God every person is the same. 35In
every country God accepts anyone who wor-
ships him and does what is right. 36You know the
message that God has sent to the people of Israel
is the Good News[d] that peace has come through
Jesus Christ. Jesus is the Lord of all people! 37You
know what has happened all over Judea, begin-
ning in Galilee after John[n] preached to the peo-
ple about baptism. 38You know about Jesus from
Nazareth, that God gave him the Holy Spirit[d]
and power. You know how Jesus went every-
where doing good and healing those who were
ruled by the devil, because God was with him.
39We saw what Jesus did in Judea and in
Jerusalem, but the Jews in Jerusalem killed him
by hanging him on a cross. 40Yet, on the third
day, God raised Jesus to life and caused him to be
seen, 41not by all the people, but only by the wit-
nesses God had already chosen. And we are
those witnesses who ate and drank with him
after he was raised from the dead. 42He told us to

John John the Baptist, who preached to people about Christ's coming (Matthew 3, Luke 3).

STEREOTYPES

The Colour of Hatred

"It's not that blacks are bad," John says. "There are quite a few, well, not quite a few, but a sizeable number of non-whites who are intelligent."

John is a racist. He believes that whites are the "chosen people" – that all non-white races should live in their own territories, away from whites. He is also a leader of the Aryan Youth Movement.

John doesn't look like a skinhead. His blond hair is cut conservatively. He has a respectable job and dresses like most people his age.

But John's racist beliefs are deeply ingrained. His father leads a group of adult racists called the White Aryan Resistance. When other children were growing up with stories about Goldilocks and the three bears, John was listening to stories of hatred and prejudice.

Skinheads in John's Aryan Youth Movement have been linked to such brutalities as beating people to death, terrorising people of non-white origin, and even nailing a former skinhead to a cross. And they have done all these things in the name of preserving their race.

Prejudice has blinded John and other racists to the fact that God loves all people the same. In **Acts 10:34–48**, Peter challenges the people of his day to see others from God's perspective and to lay their prejudices aside.

- How was prejudice in Peter's day different from John's prejudice? How was it similar?
- According to this passage, what is the cure for prejudice?

Consider . . .

- observing people in a shopping centre. Evaluate which people you do or don't have prejudices towards. Then ask God to remove your prejudices.
- getting to know someone you have prejudged. Think about the ways in which that person is different from what you had expected.

For more, see . . .

- Genesis 3:20 (p.7)
- Acts 11:1–18 (p.1157)
- John 4:1–27 (p.1101)

preach to the people and to tell them that he is
the one whom God chose to be the judge of the
living and the dead. 43All the prophets say it is
true that all who believe in Jesus will be forgiven
their sins through Jesus' name."
44While Peter was still saying this, the Holy
Spirit[d] came down on all those who were listen-
ing. 45The Jewish believers who came with Peter
were amazed that the gift of the Holy Spirit had
been given even to those who were not Jews.
46These Jewish believers heard them speaking in
different languages[n] and praising God. Then Peter
said, 47"Can anyone keep these people from being
baptised[d] with water? They have received the
Holy Spirit just as we did!" 48So Peter ordered that
they be baptised in the name of Jesus Christ. Then
they asked Peter to stay with them for a few days.

Peter Returns to Jerusalem

11 The apostles[d] and the believers in Judea
heard that some who were not Jewish
had accepted God's teaching too. 2But when
Peter came to Jerusalem, some Jewish believers
argued with him. 3They said, "You went into the
homes of people who are not circumcised[d] and
ate with them!"
4So Peter explained the whole story to them.
5He said, "I was in the city of Joppa, and while I
was praying, I had a vision. I saw something
that looked like a big sheet being lowered from
heaven by its four corners. It came very close to
me. 6I looked inside it and saw animals, wild
beasts, reptiles and birds. 7I heard a voice say to
me, 'Get up, Peter; kill and eat.' 8But I said, 'No,
Lord! I have never eaten anything that is unholy
or unclean.'[d] 9But the voice from heaven spoke
again, 'God has made these things clean, so don't
call them unholy.' 10This happened three times.
Then the whole thing was taken back to heaven.
11Just then three men who were sent to me from
Caesarea came to the house where I was staying.
12The Spirit[d] told me to go with them without
doubting. These six believers here also went with
me, and we entered the house of Cornelius. 13He
told us about the angel he saw standing in his
house. The angel said to him, 'Send some men to
Joppa and invite Simon Peter to come. 14By the
words he will say to you, you and all your family
will be saved.' 15When I began my speech, the
Holy Spirit came upon them just as he came
upon us at the beginning. 16Then I remembered
the words of the Lord. He said, 'John baptised[d]
with water, but you will be baptised with the
Holy Spirit.' 17Since God gave them the same gift
he gave us who believed in the Lord Jesus
Christ, how could I stop the work of God?"
18When the Jewish believers heard this, they
stopped arguing. They praised God and said, "So
God is allowing even those who are not Jewish to
turn to him and live."

The Good News Comes to Antioch

19Many of the believers were scattered when
they were persecuted[d] after Stephen was killed.
Some of them went as far as Phoenicia, Cyprus
and Antioch telling the message to others, but
only to Jews. 20Some of these believers were peo-
ple from Cyprus and Cyrene. When they came to
Antioch, they spoke also to Greeks, telling them
the Good News[d] about the Lord Jesus. 21The
Lord was helping the believers, and a large group
of people believed and turned to the Lord.
22The church in Jerusalem heard about all
of this, so they sent Barnabas to Antioch.
23–24Barnabas was a good man, full of the Holy
Spirit[d] and full of faith. When he reached Antioch
and saw how God had blessed the people, he was
glad. He encouraged all the believers in Antioch
always to obey the Lord with all their hearts, and
many people became followers of the Lord.
25Then Barnabas went to the city of Tarsus to
look for Saul, 26and when he found Saul, he
brought him to Antioch. For a whole year Saul
and Barnabas met with the church and taught
many people there. In Antioch the followers
were called Christians for the first time.

Sidelight The name "Christian" (Acts 11:26) may have originally been an insult. It meant "devotees of the Anointed One" or "followers of Christ". The term was widely used by the end of the first century.

27About that time some prophets[d] came from
Jerusalem to Antioch. 28One of them, named
Agabus, stood up and spoke with the help of the
Holy Spirit. He said, "A very hard time is coming
to the whole world. There will be no food to eat."
(This happened when Claudius ruled.) 29The be-
lievers all decided to help the followers who lived
in Judea, as much as each one could. 30They gath-
ered the money and gave it to Barnabas and Saul,
who brought it to the elders[d] in Judea.

Herod Agrippa Hurts the Church

12 During that same time King Herod began
to mistreat some who belonged to the
church. 2He ordered James, the brother of John,
to be killed by the sword. 3Herod saw that the

languages This can also be translated "tongues".

Jewish people liked this, so he decided to arrest Peter, too. (This happened during the time of the Feast[d] of Unleavened Bread.)

4After Herod arrested Peter, he put him in jail and handed him over to be guarded by sixteen soldiers. Herod planned to bring Peter before the people for trial after the Passover[d] Feast. 5So Peter was kept in jail, but the church prayed earnestly to God for him.

Peter Leaves the Jail

6The night before Herod was to bring him to trial, Peter was sleeping between two soldiers, bound with two chains. Other soldiers were guarding the door of the jail. 7Suddenly, an angel of the Lord stood there, and a light shone in the cell. The angel struck Peter on the side and woke him up. "Hurry! Get up!" the angel said. And the chains fell off Peter's hands. 8Then the angel told him, "Get dressed and put on your sandals." And Peter did. Then the angel said, "Put on your coat and follow me." 9So Peter followed him out, but he did not know if what the angel was doing was real; he thought he might be seeing a vision. 10They went past the first and second guards and came to the iron gate that separated them from the city. The gate opened by itself for them, and they went through it. When they had walked down one street, the angel suddenly left him.

11Then Peter realised what had happened. He thought, "Now I know that the Lord really sent his angel to me. He rescued me from Herod and from all the things the Jewish people thought would happen."

12When he considered this, he went to the home of Mary, the mother of John Mark. Many people were gathered there, praying. 13Peter knocked on the outside door, and a servant girl named Rhoda came to answer it. 14When she recognised Peter's voice, she was so happy she forgot to open the door. Instead, she ran inside and told the group, "Peter is at the door!"

15They said to her, "You are mad!" But she kept on saying it was true, so they said, "It must be Peter's angel."

16Peter continued to knock, and when they opened the door, they saw him and were amazed. 17Peter made a sign with his hand to tell them to be quiet. He explained how the Lord led him out of the jail, and he said, "Tell James and the other believers what happened." Then he left to go to another place.

18The next day the soldiers were very upset and wondered what had happened to Peter. 19Herod looked everywhere for him but could not find him. So he questioned the guards and ordered that they be killed.

The Death of Herod Agrippa

Later Herod moved from Judea and went to the city of Caesarea, where he stayed. 20Herod was very angry with the people of Tyre and Sidon, but the people of those cities all came in a group to him. After convincing Blastus, the king's personal servant, to be on their side, they asked Herod for peace, because their country got its food from his country.

21On a chosen day Herod put on his royal robes, sat on his throne and made a speech to the people. 22They shouted, "This is the voice of a god, not a human!" 23Because Herod did not give the glory to God, an angel of the Lord immediately caused him to become sick, and he was eaten by worms and died.

24God's message continued to spread and reach people.

25After Barnabas and Saul finished their task in Jerusalem, they returned to Antioch, taking John Mark with them.

Barnabas and Saul are Chosen

13 In the church at Antioch there were these prophets[d] and teachers: Barnabas, Simeon (also called Niger), Lucius (from the city of Cyrene), Manaen (who had grown up with Herod, the ruler) and Saul. 2They were all worshipping the Lord and gave up eating for a certain time.[n] During this time the Holy Spirit[d] said to them, "Set apart for me Barnabas and Saul to do a special work for which I have chosen them."

3So after they had given up eating and prayed, they laid their hands on[n] Barnabas and Saul and sent them out.

Barnabas and Saul in Cyprus

4Barnabas and Saul, sent out by the Holy Spirit,[d] went to the city of Seleucia. From there they sailed to the island of Cyprus. 5When they came to Salamis, they preached the Good News[d] of God in the Jewish synagogues.[d] John Mark was with them to help.

6They went across the whole island to Paphos where they met a Jewish magician named Bar-Jesus. He was a false prophet[d] 7who always stayed close to Sergius Paulus, the governor and a clever man. He asked Barnabas and Saul to come to him, because he wanted to hear the message of God. 8But Elymas, the magician, was against them. (Elymas is the name for Bar-Jesus

gave up . . . time This is called "fasting". The people would give up eating for a special time of prayer and worship to God. It was also done to show sadness and disappointment.

laid their hands on The laying on of hands had many purposes, including the giving of a blessing, power or authority.

in the Greek language.) He tried to stop the gov-
ernor from believing in Jesus. 9But Saul, who
was also called Paul, was filled with the Holy
Spirit. He looked straight at Elymas 10and said,
"You son of the devil! You are an enemy of every-
thing that is right! You are full of evil tricks and
lies, always trying to change the Lord's truths
into lies. 11Now the Lord will touch you, and you
will be blind. For a time you will not be able to
see anything—not even the light from the sun."
Then everything became dark for Elymas, and
he walked around, trying to find someone to lead
him by the hand. 12When the governor saw this,
he believed because he was amazed at the teach-
ing about the Lord.

Paul and Barnabas Leave Cyprus

13Paul and those with him sailed from Paphos
and came to Perga, in Pamphylia. There John
Mark left them to return to Jerusalem. 14They
continued their trip from Perga and went to
Antioch, a city in Pisidia. On the Sabbath[d] day
they went into the synagogue[d] and sat down.
15After the law of Moses and the writings of the
prophets[d] were read, the leaders of the syna-
gogue sent a message to Paul and Barnabas:
"Brothers, if you have any message that will en-
courage the people, please speak."
16Paul stood up, raised his hand and said, "You
Israelites and you who worship God, please
listen! 17The God of the Israelites chose our
ancestors. He made the people great during the
time they lived in Egypt, and he brought them
out of that country with great power. 18And he
was patient with them for 40 years in the desert.
19God destroyed seven nations in the land of
Canaan and gave the land to his people. 20All this
happened in about 450 years.
"After this, God gave them judges until the time
of Samuel the prophet. 21Then the people asked for

BIBLE STUDY

The Maker's Instructions

As Luke ripped open the packaging to his new laptop, he knew that his dad was going to say it. Even as he held it in his hands and grappled with the power lead to plug it in, he was just waiting for his dad to say those same words that he said every time he got something new . . . "Don't lose the instructions!"

"Luke, don't rush. Take your time. Sit down. Let me read the instructions through with you. You'll only regret it later when you don't know how to use it properly!"

Luke hated it! It was always the same. His dad always seemed to be putting a downer on getting something new. It was same when he got his new phone, and his new sound system. Luke even remembered his dad doing the same when he got his first bike! It had 3 wheels – what could go wrong?

No one reads the instructions to anything! His dad was so frustrating. And what annoyed him most was that Luke knew his dad was right! Luke took a deep breath and let his dad help him. They read through how to set up the laptop. An hour later they had got on the Internet, set up some user profiles and found out how to make it secure online.

Read through **Acts 13:22–33**.

- In this passage, Paul shows that he really knows his stuff when it comes to Jesus. How easy do you find it to understand the Bible? When we take time to understand the Bible we will understand more about Jesus.
- Have you ever taken the time to make sure you really understood something you were trying to do? Did you get more out of it?

Consider . . .

- chatting with someone in your church about how they can help you understand the Bible better.
- setting yourself a challenge to spend a week researching different ways to read the Bible and understand it better. At the end of the week, decide on your strategy to get into the Bible.

For more, see . . .

- Psalm 119:105 (p.573)
- 2 Timothy 3:13–17 (p.1319)
- John 8:31–32 (p.1110)

a king, so God gave them Saul son of Kish. Saul was from the tribe[d] of Benjamin and was king for 40 years. 22After God took him away, God made David their king. God said about him: 'I have found in David son of Jesse the kind of man I want. He will do all I want him to do.' 23So God has brought Jesus, one of David's descendants,[d] to Israel to be its Saviour,[d] as he promised. 24Before Jesus came, John[n] preached to all the people of Israel about a baptism[d] of changed hearts and lives. 25When he was finishing his work, he said, 'Who do you think I am? I am not the Christ.[d] He is coming later, and I am not worthy to untie his sandals.'

26"Brothers, sons of the family of Abraham, and those of you who are not Jews who worship God, listen! The news about this salvation has been sent to us. 27Those who live in Jerusalem and their leaders did not realise that Jesus was the Saviour. They did not understand the words that the prophets wrote, which are read every Sabbath day. But they made them come true when they said Jesus was guilty. 28They could not find any real reason for Jesus to be put to death, but they asked Pilate to have him killed. 29When they had done to him all that the Scriptures[d] had said, they took him down from the cross and laid him in a tomb. 30But God raised him up from the dead! 31After this, for many days, those who had gone with Jesus from Galilee to Jerusalem saw him. They are now his witnesses to the people. 32We tell you the Good News[d] about the promise God made to our ancestors. 33God has made this promise come true for us, his children, by raising Jesus from the dead. We read about this also in Psalm 2:

'You are my son.
Today I have become your father.' *Psalm 2:7*

34God raised Jesus from the dead, and he will never go back to the grave and become dust. So God said:

'I will give you the blessings
I promised to David.' *Isaiah 55:3*

35But in another place God says:

'You will not let your holy one rot.' *Psalm 16:10*

36David did God's will during his lifetime. Then he died and was buried beside his ancestors, and his body did rot in the grave. 37But the One God raised from the dead did not rot in the grave. 38–39Brothers, understand what we are telling you: you can have forgiveness of your sins through Jesus. The law of Moses could not free you from your sins. But through Jesus everyone who believes is free from all sins. 40Be careful! Don't let what the prophets said happen to you:

41'Look at the nations!
Watch them and be amazed and shocked.
I will do something in your lifetime
that you won't believe even when you are
told about it.' " *Habakkuk 1:5*

42While Paul and Barnabas were leaving the synagogue, the people asked them to tell them more about these things on the next Sabbath. 43When the meeting was over, many Jews and those who had changed to the Jewish religion and who worshipped God followed Paul and Barnabas from that place. Paul and Barnabas were persuading them to continue trusting in God's grace.

44On the next Sabbath day, almost everyone in the city came to hear the word of the Lord. 45Seeing the crowd, the Jewish people became very jealous and said insulting things and argued against what Paul said. 46But Paul and Barnabas spoke very boldly, saying, "We must speak the message of God to you first. But you refuse to listen. You are judging yourselves not worthy of having eternal life! So we will now go to the people of other nations. 47This is what the Lord told us to do, saying:

'I have made you a light for the nations;
you will show people all over the world the
way to be saved.' " *Isaiah 49:6*

48When those who were not Jewish heard Paul say this, they were happy and gave honour to the message of the Lord. And the people who were chosen to have life for ever believed the message.

49So the message of the Lord was spreading through the whole country. 50But the Jewish people stirred up some of the important religious women and the leaders of the city. They started trouble against Paul and Barnabas and forced them out of their area. 51So Paul and Barnabas shook the dust off their feet[n] and went to Iconium. 52But the followers were filled with joy and the Holy Spirit.[d]

Paul and Barnabas in Iconium

14 In Iconium, Paul and Barnabas went as usual to the Jewish synagogue.[d] They spoke so well that a great many Jews and Greeks believed. 2But some of the Jews who did not believe excited the non-Jewish people and turned them against the believers. 3Paul and Barnabas stayed in Iconium a long time and spoke bravely for the Lord. He showed that their message about his grace was true by giving them the power to work miracles[d] and signs. 4But the city was divided. Some of the people agreed with the Jews, and others believed the apostles.[d]

5Some who were not Jews, some Jews and some of their rulers wanted to mistreat Paul and Barnabas and to stone them to death. 6When Paul and Barnabas learned about this, they ran away to Lystra and Derbe, cities in Lycaonia, and

John John the Baptist, who preached to people about Christ's coming (Matthew 3, Luke 3).
shook . . . feet A warning. It showed that they had rejected these people.

to the areas around those cities. 7They announced
the Good News[d] there, too.

Paul in Lystra and Derbe

8In Lystra there sat a man who had been born
crippled; he had never walked. 9As this man was
listening to Paul speak, Paul looked straight at him
and saw that he believed God could heal him. 10So
he cried out, "Stand up on your feet!" The man
jumped up and began walking around. 11When
the crowds saw what Paul did, they shouted in
the Lycaonian language, "The gods have become
like humans and have come down to us!" 12Then
the people began to call Barnabas "Zeus"[n] and
Paul "Hermes",[n] because he was the main speaker.
13The priest in the temple of Zeus, which was near
the city, brought some bulls and flowers to the
city gates. He and the people wanted to offer a
sacrifice to Paul and Barnabas. 14But when the
apostles,[d] Barnabas and Paul, heard about it, they
tore their clothes. They ran in among the people,
shouting, 15"Friends, why are you doing these
things? We are only human beings like you. We
are bringing you the Good News[d] and are telling
you to turn away from these worthless things and
turn to the living God. He is the One who made
the sky, the earth, the sea and everything in them.
16In the past, God let all the nations do what they
wanted. 17Yet he proved he is real by showing
kindness, by giving you rain from heaven and

"Zeus" The Greeks believed in many gods, of whom Zeus was the most important.
"Hermes" The Greeks believed he was a messenger for the other gods.

JEALOUSY

A Door to Greater Evil

School report day. David dreaded walking into his house. He reckoned that his parents had already seen Sarah's report, and he knew that his would never compare to hers.

"They'll probably give her a new CD or something for every A," David thought.

As David opened the front door, he heard his parents talking in the living room.

"Sarah, this is an outstanding report – as usual," his dad gushed.

"We're so proud of you, darling. You've worked so hard," his mother added.

David tried to sneak past his parents, but just as he turned the corner his mother called out, "David, come here. Let's see how you did this term."

"Oh great," David thought, "here comes World War III." David walked into the living room and handed his mother his crumpled report from his back pocket.

She unfolded it and said, "Well, these are good grades, David."

"Hmmm," his dad mused. "You seem to have improved your grade in biology. Good work."

"Yes, right," David fumed. "I know it's not as good as Sarah's. Nothing I do is ever as good as her."

He stormed out of the room, leaving his family in shock.

David let his jealousy of Sarah affect his response to his parents. In **Acts 13:44–52**, some Jewish leaders allowed their jealousy to affect the way they treated Paul and Barnabas.

- Why were David and the Jewish leaders jealous? What were the consequences of David's and the Jewish leaders' jealousy?
- When have you been jealous of someone? What were the consequences?

Consider . . .

- making a list of your talents and things you are good at, then reading the list when you are tempted to be jealous of someone else.
- thanking God for someone you are jealous of. Be excited when that person does well.

For more, see . . .

- Genesis 37 (p.42)
- Acts 17:5–9 (p.1167)
- Psalm 37:1–8 (p.521)

crops at the right times, by giving you food and fill-
ing your hearts with joy." 18Even with these words,
they were barely able to keep the crowd from
offering sacrifices to them.
19Then some Jewish people came from Antioch
and Iconium and persuaded the people to turn
against Paul. So they threw stones at him and
dragged him out of town, thinking they had
killed him. 20But the followers gathered around
him, and he got up and went back into the town.
The next day he and Barnabas left and went to
the city of Derbe.

Sidelight Paul and Barnabas faced a real case of mistaken identity when they visited Lystra, a town in the centre of modern-day Turkey (Acts 14:8–18). The people in the region believed a myth that the Greek gods Zeus and Hermes had previously visited the area. When Paul and Barnabas healed a cripple, the people thought the gods had returned, putting the Christian missionaries in an awkward situation.

The Return to Antioch in Syria

21Paul and Barnabas told the Good News[d] in
Derbe, and many became followers. Paul and
Barnabas returned to Lystra, Iconium and Antioch,
22making the followers of Jesus stronger and
helping them stay in the faith. They said, "We
must suffer many things to enter God's king-
dom." 23They chose elders[d] for each church, by
praying and giving up eating for a certain time.[n]
These elders had trusted the Lord, so Paul and
Barnabas put them in the Lord's care.
24Then they went through Pisidia and came
to Pamphylia. 25When they had preached the

giving up . . . time This is called "fasting". The people would give up eating for a special time of prayer and worship to God. It was also done to show sadness and disappointment.

HEROES

Admire, Don't Worship

Mandy admired everything about her minister. When he first came to her church, she was immediately drawn to his dynamic personality, his warm smile and his genuine concern for people.

The minister always had time to listen. He always talked about how great the young people of the church were. Mandy believed that God must be just like her minister.

Whenever the youth group had a controversial discussion, Mandy would go to her minister later and ask what he thought. Mandy would explain what he said in the next meeting.

Eleven months after coming to Mandy's church, her minister left suddenly to go to another church. He never answered any of Mandy's letters, and didn't return her phone calls. He never even said goodbye.

Mandy was crushed and heartbroken. How could he treat her church like this? How could he treat her like this when she had respected him so much? Mandy felt betrayed. Could she ever trust a minister again?

Worshipping a person always leads to disappointment. Her minister turned out to be human – with human faults and inconsistencies. In **Acts 14:8–18**, God used Paul and Barnabas to work miracles, but even they weren't worthy of worship.

- What led Mandy to worship her minister, and the people to worship Paul and Barnabas?
- Based on Paul and Barnabas's words, what are appropriate ways to treat spiritual leaders?

Consider . . .

- thanking God for the good qualities of people you admire. Ask God to help you to keep your admiration in proper perspective.
- getting to know someone you admire and learning about his or her human and less admirable qualities as well.

For more, see . . .

- Exodus 20:2–6 (p.79)
- 1 Corinthians 4:1–7 (p.1218)
- Daniel 3 (p.835)

message in Perga, they went down to Attalia. 26And
from there they sailed away to Antioch where
the believers had put them into God's care and
had sent them out to do this work. Now they
had finished.
27When they arrived in Antioch, Paul and
Barnabas gathered the church together. They
told the church all about what God had done
with them and how God had made it possible for
those who were not Jewish to believe. 28And
they stayed there a long time with the followers.

The Meeting at Jerusalem

15 Then some people came to Antioch from
Judea and began teaching the non-Jewish
believers: "You cannot be saved if you are not
circumcised[d] as Moses taught us." 2Paul and
Barnabas were against this teaching and argued
with them about it. So the church decided to
send Paul, Barnabas and some others to Jerusalem
where they could talk more about this with the
apostles[d] and elders.[d]
3The church helped them leave on the trip, and
they went through the countries of Phoenicia and
Samaria, telling all about how those who were
not Jewish had turned to God. This made all the
believers very happy. 4When they arrived in
Jerusalem, they were welcomed by the apostles,
the elders and the church. Paul, Barnabas and the
others told about everything God had done with
them. 5But some of the believers who belonged to
the Pharisee[d] group came forwards and said,
"The non-Jewish believers must be circumcised.
They must be told to obey the law of Moses."
6The apostles and the elders gathered to con-
sider this problem. 7After a long debate, Peter
stood up and said to them, "Brothers, you know
that in the early days God chose me from among
you to preach the Good News[d] to those who are
not Jewish. They heard the Good News from me,
and they believed. 8God, who knows the thoughts
of everyone, accepted them. He showed this to
us by giving them the Holy Spirit,[d] just as he did
to us. 9To God, those people are not different from
us. When they believed, he made their hearts
pure. 10So now why are you testing God by put-
ting a heavy load around the necks of the non-
Jewish believers? It is a load that neither we nor
our ancestors were able to carry. 11But we be-
lieve that we and they too will be saved by the
grace of the Lord Jesus."
12Then the whole group became quiet. They
listened to Paul and Barnabas tell about all the
miracles[d] and signs that God did through them
among the non-Jewish people. 13After they fin-
ished speaking, James said, "Brothers, listen to
me. 14Simon has told us how God showed his
love for the non-Jewish people. For the first time
he is accepting from among them a people to be
his own. 15The words of the prophets[d] agree with
this too:
16'After these things I will return.
The kingdom of David is like a fallen tent.
But I will rebuild its ruins,
and I will set it up.
17Then those people who are left alive may ask
the Lord for help,
and the other nations that belong to me,
says the Lord,
who will make it happen.
18 And these things have been known for a
long time.' *Amos 9:11–12*
19"So I think we should not bother the non-
Jewish people who are turning to God. 20Instead,
we should write a letter to them telling them
these things: stay away from food that has been
offered to idols (which makes it unclean[d]), any
kind of sexual sin, eating animals that have been
strangled, and blood. 21They should do these
things, because for a long time in every city the
law of Moses has been taught. And it is still read
in the synagogue[d] every Sabbath[d] day."

Letter to Non-Jewish Believers

22The apostles,[d] the elders[d] and the whole
church decided to send some of their men with
Paul and Barnabas to Antioch. They chose Judas
Barsabbas and Silas, who were respected by the
believers. 23They sent the following letter with
them:

From the apostles and elders, your
brothers.
To all the non-Jewish believers in Antioch,
Syria and Cilicia:
Greetings!
24We have heard that some of our group
have come to you and said things that trou-
ble and upset you. But we did not tell them
to do this. 25We have all agreed to choose
some messengers and send them to you
with our dear friends Barnabas and Paul—
26people who have given their lives to serve
our Lord Jesus Christ. 27So we are sending
Judas and Silas, who will tell you the same
things. 28It has pleased the Holy Spirit[d] that
you should not have a heavy load to carry,
and we agree. You need to do only these
things: 29stay away from any food that has
been offered to idols, any animals that have
been strangled, blood and any kind of sexual
sin. If you stay away from these things, you
will do well.
Goodbye.

30So they left Jerusalem and went to Antioch
where they gathered the church and gave them

the letter. 31When they read it, they were very happy because of the encouraging message. 32Judas and Silas, who were also prophets,[d] said many things to encourage the believers and make them stronger. 33After some time Judas and Silas were sent off in peace by the believers, and they went back to those who had sent them. 34[n]

35But Paul and Barnabas stayed in Antioch and, along with many others, preached the Good News[d] and taught the people the message of the Lord.

Paul and Barnabas Separate

36After some time, Paul said to Barnabas, "We should go back to all those towns where we preached the message of the Lord. Let's visit the believers and see how they are doing."

37Barnabas wanted to take John Mark with them, 38but he had left them at Pamphylia; he did not continue with them in the work. So Paul did not think it was a good idea to take him. 39Paul and Barnabas had such a serious argument about this that they separated and went different ways. Barnabas took Mark and sailed to Cyprus, 40but Paul chose Silas and left. The believers in Antioch put Paul into the Lord's care, 41and he went through Syria and Cilicia, giving strength to the churches.

Timothy Goes with Paul

16 Paul came to Derbe and Lystra, where a follower named Timothy lived. Timothy's mother was Jewish and a believer, but his father was a Greek.

2The believers in Lystra and Iconium respected Timothy and said good things about him. 3Paul wanted Timothy to travel with him, but all the Jews living in that area knew that Timothy's father was Greek. So Paul circumcised[d] Timothy to please the Jews. 4Paul and those with him travelled from town to town and gave the decisions made by the apostles[d] and elders[d] in Jerusalem for the people to obey. 5So the churches became stronger in the faith and grew larger every day.

Paul is Called Out of Asia

6Paul and those with him went through the areas of Phrygia and Galatia since the Holy Spirit[d] did not let them preach the Good News[d] in the country of Asia. 7When they came near the country of Mysia, they tried to go into Bithynia, but the Spirit of Jesus did not let them. 8So they passed by Mysia and went to Troas. 9That night Paul saw in a vision a man from Macedonia. The man stood and begged, "Come over to Macedonia and help us." 10After Paul had seen the vision, we immediately prepared to leave for Macedonia, understanding that God had called us to tell the Good News to those people.

Lydia Becomes a Christian

11We left Troas and sailed straight to the island of Samothrace. The next day we sailed to Neapolis.[n] 12Then we went by land to Philippi, a Roman colony[n] and the leading city in that part of Macedonia. We stayed there for several days.

13On the Sabbath[d] day we went outside the city gate to the river where we thought we would find a special place for prayer. Some women had gathered there, so we sat down and talked with them. 14One of the listeners was a woman named Lydia from the city of Thyatira whose job was selling purple cloth. She worshipped God, and he opened her mind to pay attention to what Paul was saying. 15She and all the people in her house were baptised.[d] Then she invited us to her home, saying, "If you think I am truly a believer in the Lord, then come and stay in my house." And she persuaded us to stay with her.

Paul and Silas in Jail

16Once, while we were going to the place for prayer, a servant girl met us. She had a special spirit[n] in her, and she earned a lot of money for her owners by telling fortunes. 17This girl followed Paul and us, shouting, "These men are servants of the Most High God. They are telling you how you can be saved."

18She kept this up for many days. This bothered Paul, so he turned and said to the spirit, "By the power of Jesus Christ, I command you to come out of her!" Immediately, the spirit came out.

19When the owners of the servant girl saw this, they knew that now they could not use her to make money. So they grabbed Paul and Silas and dragged them before the city rulers in the market place. 20They brought Paul and Silas to the Roman rulers and said, "These men are Jews and are making trouble in our city. 21They are teaching things that are not right for us as Romans to do."

22The crowd joined the attack against them. The Roman officers tore the clothes of Paul and

Verse 34 Some Greek copies add verse 34: ". . . but Silas decided to remain there."
Neapolis City in Macedonia. It was the first city Paul visited on the continent of Europe.
Roman colony A town begun by Romans with Roman laws, customs and privileges.
spirit This was a spirit from the devil, which caused her to have special knowledge.

Silas and had them beaten with rods. 23Then Paul
and Silas were thrown into jail, and the jailer was
ordered to guard them carefully. 24When he
heard this order, he put them far inside the jail
and pinned their feet down between large blocks
of wood.
25About midnight Paul and Silas were praying
and singing songs to God as the other prisoners
listened. 26Suddenly, there was a strong earth-
quake that shook the foundation of the jail. Then
all the doors of the jail broke open, and all the
prisoners were freed from their chains. 27The
jailer woke up and saw that the jail doors were
open. Thinking that the prisoners had already
escaped, he got his sword and was about to kill
himself.[n] 28But Paul shouted, "Don't hurt your-
self! We are all here."
29The jailer told someone to bring a light.
Then he ran inside and, shaking with fear, fell
down before Paul and Silas. 30He brought them
outside and said, "Men, what must I do to be
saved?"

kill himself He thought the leaders would kill him for letting the prisoners escape.

GOD'S WILL

Close to Your Heart

Sandra Graham was one term away from leaving school and she had no idea what she would do with her life. She had been praying for God to show her his will, but still there were no answers.

One Sunday after church, Ted Holt, the youth leader, asked Sandra to come home with his family of eight for dinner.

All through the meal, they talked about Sandra's plans after school.

"What do you think God wants you to do, Sandra?" Ted asked as they picked up their coffee cups.

"I've been praying about it, but God just doesn't seem to answer," Sandra lamented.

Ted's voice softened. "What do you want to do?" he asked.

"God's will," she answered.

Again, Ted asked, "But what do you want to do?"

Sandra was confused. "That's it. I want to do God's will."

Ted smiled. "Sandra, I have six kids, and I want nothing more than for each of my kids to be happy. I'll do almost anything to make that happen."

Sandra nodded, not sure what this had to do with her decision.

Ted laughed heartily when he saw her confusion. "Sandra, God is your father, and he wants you to be happy. He's probably been showing you all the time what his will is."

"He has?" Sandra asked incredulously.

"Yes, he has. Look into your heart. I'll bet your desires will point you towards God's will."

Sandra did find God's will. She went to college and after she graduated, she used her love for drama to teach others how to communicate their faith. In **Acts 16:6–10**, Paul also found God's will.

- What was Ted trying to help Sandra learn about finding God's will? In the passage, how did God show his will to Paul and the others?
- Do you think God still reveals his will to people as he did in the passage? In what other ways do people learn God's will?

Consider . . .

- keeping track of what happens to you in the coming week. See if any patterns emerge that show God leading you in a particular direction.
- interviewing an older person in your church about discovering God's will.

For more, see . . .

- Psalm 32:6–11 (p.518)
- Luke 22:41–43 (p.1088)
- Matthew 6:9–13 (p.948)

31They said to him, "Believe in the Lord Jesus
and you will be saved—you and all the people in
your house." 32So Paul and Silas told the mes-
sage of the Lord to the jailer and all the people in
his house. 33At that hour of the night the jailer
took Paul and Silas and washed their wounds.
Then he and all his people were baptised[d] imme-
diately. 34After this the jailer took Paul and Silas
home and gave them food. He and his family
were very happy because they now believed
in God.
35The next morning, the Roman officers sent
the police to tell the jailer, "Let these men go
free."
36The jailer said to Paul, "The officers have
sent an order to let you go free. You can leave
now. Go in peace."
37But Paul said to the police, "They beat us in
public without a trial, even though we are
Roman citizens.[n] And they threw us in jail. Now
they want to make us go away quietly. No! Let
them come themselves and bring us out."
38The police told the Roman officers what
Paul said. When the officers heard that Paul and
Silas were Roman citizens, they were afraid. 39So
they came and told Paul and Silas they were
sorry and took them out of jail and asked them to
leave the city. 40So when they came out of the jail,

Roman citizens Roman law said that Roman citizens must not be beaten before they had a trial.

SHARING FAITH

Take Me Instead

Maximilian Kolbe was born in Poland in 1894 and ordained as a priest in 1918. In 1941, he was transported in a trainload of prisoners to the Nazi concentration camp in Auschwitz.

During his time in the camp, one of the prisoners escaped from his block and as a deterrent, the commandant sentenced ten prisoners to death by starvation. No food, no water, no hope, no return.

One of the prisoners sentenced to death was Francis Gajowniczek. When he heard he had been picked to be the tenth man to die, he exclaimed in a panic-stricken voice, "I have a wife and family, please don't take me!"

When Maximilian Kolbe heard Francis, he spoke loudly and clearly, "I will die in his place. I am old, and as a younger man, Francis can be more useful. He has a wife and child. I have no family. Take me instead of him."

This was unheard of, but his request was granted. Maximilian Kolbe spent the rest of his time in Auschwitz praying for the other prisoners and talking to them about God. He was eventually killed by lethal injection.

Francis was later freed and dedicated his life to telling the story of Maximilian Kolbe.

Read **Acts 16:25–34** which is an account of how Paul and disciples acted as God's witnesses whilst in prison, just like Maximilian Kolbe.

- Why do you think Paul and the disciples weren't afraid to share their faith in Jesus whilst they were in prison?
- What things stop you from telling others about Jesus?

Consider . . .

- writing down the names of two friends who you want to speak to about Jesus in the next month. Meet with a friend to pray for them.
- asking your youth leader to recommend some books about inspiring figures from history who have shared their faith in Jesus.

For more, see . . .

- Luke 12:8–9 (p.1062)
- 1 John 4:13–18 (p.1374)
- Romans 10:9–11 (p.1200)

they went to Lydia's house where they saw some
of the believers and encouraged them. Then
they left.

Paul and Silas in Thessalonica

17 Paul and Silas travelled through Amphipo-
lis and Apollonia and came to Thessalonica
where there was a Jewish synagogue.[d] 2Paul
went into the synagogue as he always did, and
on each Sabbath[d] day for three weeks, he talked
with the Jews about the Scriptures.[d] 3He ex-
plained and proved that the Christ[d] must die
and then rise from the dead. He said, "This Jesus
I am telling you about is the Christ." 4Some of
the Jews were convinced and joined Paul and
Silas, along with many of the Greeks who wor-
shipped God and many of the important women.
5But the Jews became jealous. So they got
some evil men from the market-place, formed a
mob and started a riot. They ran to Jason's
house, looking for Paul and Silas, wanting to
bring them out to the people. 6But when they
did not find them, they dragged Jason and some
other believers to the leaders of the city. The peo-
ple were yelling, "These people have made trou-
ble everywhere in the world, and now they have
come here too! 7Jason is keeping them in his
house. All of them do things against the laws of
Caesar,[d] saying there is another king, called
Jesus."
8When the people and the leaders of the city
heard these things, they became very upset.
9They made Jason and the others put up a sum of
money. Then they let the believers go free.

FRIENDS

Loyalty Card

Joe and Dan were really good friends. Dan was clever, but had very bad dyslexia. Joe understood. His eldest brother Steve had had similar problems. Besides, nothing would stop Joe and Dan being friends.

One day a new family came to live in the flat upstairs from Dan. Almost immediately, there was trouble. Billy was big for his age and started making his presence felt in the estate. He took to calling Dan names and trying to get other kids to gang up on him. Joe consistently stood up for him, and one night stood in front of Dan as if to protect him and confronted Billy.

"I want you to leave Dan alone," he shouted. "He's done nothing to you."

"But he can't even spell his own name," laughed back Billy cruelly.

Dan went red and kept silent. Joe's brother Steve came out of the flat at that moment. He was a rugby player, a big guy, and glared at Billy.

"I don't think we've met," Steve said to Billy without a smile. "But like our Joe said, if you mess with Dan here, I won't be too pleased. I have dyslexia too and it's not stopped me doing anything I've set my mind to. Stay away from him, yeah!"

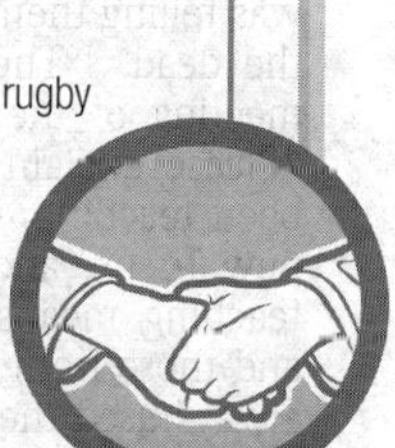

Billy was stunned and quickly made his way home.

Steve smiled at Dan, "Come on mate, let's have a go on that computer of yours and see if I can beat you again!"

Take a look at **Acts 17:1–15**.

- How is Steve like Jason in the Bible passage?
- Paul and Silas had each other for encouragement when they had a tough time – how do you think Dan felt about having Joe (and Steve) standing up for him?

Consider . . .

- what makes a friendship great. Can you think of a few ways that you could show your friends this week what they mean to you?
- encouraging a Christian friend who is in a difficult situation to be strong and keep going.

For more, see . . .

- Proverbs 17:9 (p.604)
- John 15:13 (p.1125)
- Proverbs 18:24 (p.605)

Paul and Silas Go to Berea

10That same night the believers sent Paul and Silas to Berea where they went to the Jewish synagogue.[d] 11These Jews were more willing to listen than the Jews in Thessalonica. The Jews in Berea were eager to hear what Paul and Silas said and studied the Scriptures[d] every day to find out if these things were true. 12So, many of them believed, as well as many important Greek women and men. 13But the Jews in Thessalonica learned that Paul was preaching the word of God in Berea, too. So they came there, upsetting the people and making trouble. 14The believers quickly sent Paul away to the coast, but Silas and Timothy stayed in Berea. 15The people leading Paul went with him to Athens. Then they carried a message from Paul back to Silas and Timothy for them to come to him as soon as they could.

Paul Preaches in Athens

16While Paul was waiting for Silas and Timothy in Athens, he was troubled because he saw that the city was full of idols. 17In the synagogue,[d] he talked with the Jews and the Greeks who worshipped God. He also talked every day with people in the market-place.

18Some of the Epicurean and Stoic philosophers[n] argued with him, saying, "This man doesn't know what he is talking about. What is he trying to say?" Others said, "He seems to be telling us about some other gods," because Paul was telling them about Jesus and his rising from the dead. 19They got Paul and took him to a meeting of the Areopagus,[n] where they said, "Please explain to us this new idea you have been teaching. 20The things you are saying are new to us, and we want to know what this teaching means." 21(All the people of Athens and those from other countries who lived there always used their time to talk about the newest ideas.)

22Then Paul stood before the meeting of the Areopagus and said, "People of Athens, I can see you are very religious in all things. 23As I was going through your city, I saw the objects you worship. I found an altar that had these words written on it: TO A GOD WHO IS NOT KNOWN. You worship a god that you don't know, and this is the God I am telling you about! 24The God who made the whole world and everything in it is the Lord of the land and the sky. He does not live in temples[d] built by human hands. 25This God is the One who gives life, breath and everything else to people. He does not need any help from them; he has everything he needs. 26God began by making one person, and from him came all the different people who live everywhere in the world. God decided exactly when and where they must live. 27God wanted them to look for him and perhaps search all around for him and find him, though he is not far from any of us: 28'We live in him. We walk in him. We are in him.' Some of your own poets have said: 'For we are his children.' 29Since we are God's children, you must not think that God is like something that people imagine or make from gold, silver or rock. 30In the past, people did not understand God, and he ignored this. But now, God tells all people in the world to change their hearts and lives. 31God has set a day that he will judge all the world with fairness, by the man he chose long ago. And God has proved this to everyone by raising that man from the dead!"

32When the people heard about Jesus being raised from the dead, some of them laughed. But others said, "We will hear more about this from you later." 33So Paul went away from them. 34But some of the people believed Paul and joined him. Among those who believed was Dionysius, a member of the Areopagus, a woman named Damaris and some others.

Paul in Corinth

18 Later Paul left Athens and went to Corinth. 2Here he met a Jew named Aquila who had been born in the country of Pontus. But Aquila and his wife, Priscilla, had recently moved to Corinth from Italy, because Claudius[n] commanded that all Jews must leave Rome. Paul went to visit Aquila and Priscilla. 3Because they were tentmakers, just as he was, he stayed with them and worked with them. 4Every Sabbath[d] day he talked with the Jews and Greeks in the synagogue,[d] trying to persuade

Sidelight Claudius (Acts 18:2) ruled Rome for thirteen years and was partially paralysed. He kicked Christians out of Rome for allegedly starting riots that threatened the Roman peace – a common charge against early Christians.

Epicurean and Stoic philosophers Philosophers were those who searched for truth. Epicureans believed that pleasures, especially pleasures of the mind, were the goal of life. Stoics believed that life should be without feelings of joy or grief.
Areopagus A council or group of important leaders in Athens. They were like judges.
Claudius The emperor (ruler) of Rome, AD 41–54.

them to believe in Jesus.
5Silas and Timothy came from Macedonia
and joined Paul in Corinth. After this, Paul spent
all his time telling people the Good News,[d]
showing the Jews that Jesus is the Christ.[d]
6But they would not accept Paul's teaching and
said some evil things. So he shook off the dust
from his clothes[n] and said to them, "If you
are not saved, it will be your own fault! I have
done all I can do! After this, I will go only to
those who are not Jewish." 7Paul left the syna-
gogue and moved into the home of Titius Justus,
next to the synagogue. This man worshipped
God. 8Crispus was the leader of that synagogue,
and he and all the people living in his house
believed in the Lord. Many others in Corinth
also listened to Paul and believed and were
baptised.[d]
9During the night, the Lord told Paul in a
vision: "Don't be afraid. Continue talking to peo-
ple and don't be quiet. 10I am with you, and no
one will hurt you because many of my people are
in this city." 11Paul stayed there for a year and a
half, teaching God's word to the people.

Paul is Brought Before Gallio

12When Gallio was the governor of the coun-
try of Southern Greece, some of the Jews came
together against Paul and took him to the court.
13They said, "This man is teaching people to
worship God in a way that is against our law."
14Paul was about to say something, but Gallio
spoke to the Jews, saying, "I would listen to you
Jews if you were complaining about a crime or some
wrong. 15But the things you are saying are only
questions about words and names—arguments
about your own law. So you must solve this prob-
lem yourselves. I don't want to be a judge of these
things." 16And Gallio made them leave the court.
17Then they all grabbed Sosthenes, the leader
of the synagogue,[d] and beat him there before the
court. But this did not bother Gallio.

Paul Returns to Antioch

18Paul stayed with the believers for many
more days. Then he left and sailed for Syria, with
Priscilla and Aquila. At Cenchrea Paul cut off his
hair,[n] because he had made a promise to God.
19Then they went to Ephesus, where Paul left

shook . . . clothes This was a warning to show that Paul would no longer talk to the Jews in that city.
cut . . . hair Jews did this to show that the time of a special promise to God was finished.

NON-CHRISTIANS

A Starting Place

Jay Dugan is a talented musician. His friend explained God as a director who "conducts" every element of life to move in harmony.

Amanda Reddy has moved nine times in eleven years. Her friend explained God as the friend who goes with us no matter where we move or what new situation we face.

Jason Gaddy is a soccer star. His friend explained God as a coach who insists on practise, works to tone our life muscles, teaches strategy for difficult experiences, and cheers every games from the sidelines.

Some Greek leaders thought there must be a god they did not know. In **Acts 17:22–31**, Paul focused on their understanding of that god to guide them to a full knowledge of the true God.

- Why is it effective to explain God by using things people already understand?
- What images did Paul use to describe God in this passage?

Consider . . .

- underlining phrases about God in Acts 17:22–31 that someone who has never been in church could understand. Use these phrases to explain God to your non-Christian friends.
- thinking of a way to explain Jesus to a non-Christian friend. Begin with an image your friend will relate to.

For more, see . . .

- Exodus 3:12–15 (p.61)
- 1 Corinthians 9:19–23 (p.1227)
- John 4:5–25 (p.1101)

Priscilla and Aquila. While Paul was there, he went into the synagogue[d] and talked with the Jews. [20]When they asked him to stay with them longer, he refused. [21]But as he left, he said, "I will come back to you again if God wants me to." And so he sailed away from Ephesus.

[22]When Paul landed at Caesarea, he went and gave greetings to the church in Jerusalem. After that, Paul went to Antioch. [23]He stayed there for a while and then left and went through the regions of Galatia and Phrygia. He travelled from town to town in these regions, giving strength to all the followers.

Apollos in Ephesus and Corinth

[24]A Jew named Apollos came to Ephesus. He was born in the city of Alexandria and was a good speaker who knew the Scriptures[d] well. [25]He had been taught about the way of the Lord and was always very excited when he spoke and taught the truth about Jesus. But the only baptism[d] Apollos knew about was the baptism that John[n] taught. [26]Apollos began to speak very boldly in the synagogue,[d] and when Priscilla and Aquila heard him, they took him to their home and helped him better understand the way of God. [27]Now Apollos wanted to go to the country of Southern Greece. So the believers helped him and wrote a letter to the followers there, asking them to accept him. These followers had believed in Jesus because of God's grace, and when Apollos arrived, he helped them very much. [28]He argued very strongly with the Jews before all the people, clearly proving with the Scriptures that Jesus is the Christ.[d]

Paul in Ephesus

19 While Apollos was in Corinth, Paul was visiting some places on the way to Ephesus. There he found some followers [2]and asked them, "Did you receive the Holy Spirit[d] when you believed?"

They said, "We have never even heard of a Holy Spirit."

[3]So he asked, "What kind of baptism did you have?"

They said, "It was the baptism[d] that John[n] taught."

[4]Paul said, "John's baptism was a baptism of changed hearts and lives. He told people to believe in the One who would come after him, and that One is Jesus."

[5]When they heard this, they were baptised in the name of the Lord Jesus. [6]Then Paul laid his hands on them,[n] and the Holy Spirit came upon them. They began speaking different languages[n] and prophesying.[d] [7]There were about twelve people in this group.

[8]Paul went into the synagogue[d] and spoke out boldly for three months. He talked with the Jews and persuaded them to accept the things he said about the kingdom of God. [9]But some of the Jews became stubborn. They refused to believe and said evil things about the Way of Jesus before all the people. So Paul left them, and, taking the followers with him, he went to the school of a man named Tyrannus. There Paul talked with people every day [10]for two years. Because of his work, every Jew and Greek in the country of Asia heard the word of the Lord.

The Sons of Sceva

[11]God used Paul to do some very special miracles.[d] [12]Some people took handkerchiefs and clothes that Paul had used and put them on the sick. When they did this, the sick were healed and evil spirits left them.

[13]But some Jews also were travelling around and making evil spirits go out of people. They tried to use the name of the Lord Jesus to force the evil spirits out. They would say, "By the same Jesus that Paul talks about, I order you to come out!" [14]Seven sons of Sceva, a leading Jewish priest, were doing this.

[15]But on one occasion an evil spirit said to them, "I know Jesus, and I know about Paul, but who are you?"

[16]Then the man who had the evil spirit jumped on them. Because he was so much stronger than all of them, they ran away from the house naked and hurt. [17]All the people in Ephesus—Jews and Greeks—learned about this and were filled with fear and gave great honour to the Lord Jesus. [18]Many of the believers began to confess openly and tell all the evil things they had done. [19]Some of them who had used magic brought their magic books and burned them before everyone. Those books were worth about 50,000 silver coins.[n]

[20]So in a powerful way the word of the Lord kept spreading and growing.

[21]After these things, Paul decided to go to Jerusalem, planning to go through the countries of Macedonia and Southern Greece and then on to Jerusalem. He said, "After I have been to Jerusalem, I must also visit Rome." [22]Paul sent

John John the Baptist, who preached to people about Christ's coming (Matthew 3, Luke 3).
laid his hands on them The laying on of hands had many purposes, including the giving of a blessing, power or authority.
languages This can also be translated "tongues".
50,000 silver coins Probably drachmas. A silver coin was enough to pay a worker for one day's labour.

Timothy and Erastus, two of his helpers, ahead
to Macedonia, but he himself stayed in Asia for
a while.

Trouble in Ephesus

23And during that time, there was some seri-
ous trouble in Ephesus about the Way of Jesus.
24A man named Demetrius, who worked with sil-
ver, made little silver models that looked like the
temple[d] of the goddess Artemis.[n] Those who did
this work made much money. 25Demetrius had a
meeting with them and some others who did the
same kind of work. He told them, "Men, you
know that we make a lot of money from our
business. 26But look at what this man Paul is
doing. He has convinced and turned away many
people in Ephesus and in almost all of Asia! He
says the gods made by human hands are not real.
27There is a danger that our business will lose its
good name, but there is also another danger: peo-
ple will begin to think that the temple of the great
goddess Artemis is not important. Her greatness
will be destroyed, but Artemis is the goddess that
everyone in Asia and the whole world worships."
28When the others heard this, they became very
angry and shouted, "Artemis, the goddess of
Ephesus, is great!" 29The whole city became con-
fused. The people grabbed Gaius and Aristarchus,

Artemis A Greek goddess that the people of Asia Minor worshipped.

FAITH

Growing Up

Tick the items that are true of your relationship with God.

☐ I understand God better now than when I first started learning about him. ☐ I genuinely enjoy being involved in activities related to my faith. ☐ God helps me to love and care for people. ☐ My relationships are better as a result of my faith in God. ☐ I understand scripture better than I used to. ☐ I ask God to help me to solve problems. ☐ My friends and family know that I'm a Christian. ☐ I take time each day to pray. ☐ I know that God loves me. ☐ I ask God to forgive me when I have done something wrong. ☐ I am honest with God about my feelings. ☐ I tell people about Jesus. ☐ My relationship with God deeply influences my actions.

Now rate yourself:

- 6 to 13 ticks – Your faith is definitely growing. You are experiencing the type of growth described in Acts 19:1–7.
- 3 to 5 ticks – Be careful that your faith is not stagnating. Read the items you didn't tick, and begin building those things into your life. Be encouraged by Acts 19:1–7.
- 0 to 2 ticks – Your faith is wilting. Water it with the Word of God and get involved with other Christians soon – before your faith withers.

In **Acts 19:1–7**, Paul explained truth that the followers did not know. When they heard all that God had done for them, they were changed – and their faith could grow.

- How did Paul help people's faith to grow? What items in the checklist would be true for the people in the passage?
- How did the people in this passage express their faith?

Consider . . .

- pretending it's New Year resolution time. Write a letter to Jesus describing ways your relationship has grown, what you appreciate about him and how you hope your relationship will grow in the next year.
- choosing one item from the list to begin building into your life.

For more, see . . .

- Psalm 15 (p.506)
- Colossians 1:9–14 (p.1289)
- 1 Corinthians 3:1–9 (p.1216)

who were from Macedonia and were travelling
with Paul, and ran to the theatre. 30Paul wanted to
go in and talk to the crowd, but the followers did
not let him. 31Also, some leaders of Asia who were
friends of Paul sent him a message, begging him
not to go into the theatre. 32Some people were
shouting one thing, and some were shouting an-
other. The meeting was completely confused; most
of them did not know why they had come together.
33The Jews put a man named Alexander in front of
the people, and some of them told him what to do.
Alexander waved his hand so he could explain
things to the people. 34But when they saw that
Alexander was a Jew, they all shouted the same
thing for two hours: "Great is Artemis of Ephesus!"

35Then the city clerk made the crowd be quiet.
He said, "People of Ephesus, everyone knows that
Ephesus is the city that keeps the temple of the
great goddess Artemis and her holy stone[n] that fell
from heaven. 36Since no one can say this is not
true, you should be quiet. Stop and think before
you do anything. 37You brought these men here,
but they have not said anything evil against our
goddess or stolen anything from her temple. 38If
Demetrius and those who work with him have a
charge against anyone they should go to the courts
and judges where they can argue with each other.
39If there is something else you want to talk about,
it can be decided at the legal town meeting of the
people. 40I say this because some people might see
this trouble today and say that we are rioting. We
could not explain this, because there is no real
reason for this meeting." 41After the city clerk said
these things, he told the people to go home.

Paul in Macedonia and Greece

20 When the trouble stopped, Paul sent for
the followers to come to him. After he had
encouraged them and said goodbye, he left and
went to the country of Macedonia. 2He said many
things to strengthen the followers in the different
places on his way through Macedonia. Then he
went to Greece, 3where he stayed for three
months. He was ready to sail for Syria, but some
Jews were planning something against him. So
Paul decided to go back through Macedonia to
Syria. 4The men who went with him were Sopater
son of Pyrrhus, from the city of Berea; Aristarchus
and Secundus, from the city of Thessalonica;
Gaius, from Derbe; Timothy; and Tychicus and
Trophimus, two men from the country of Asia.
5These men went on ahead and waited for us at
Troas. 6We sailed from Philippi after the Feast[d] of
Unleavened Bread. Five days later we met them in
Troas, where we stayed for seven days.

Paul's Last Visit to Troas

7On the first day of the week,[n] we all met to-
gether to break bread,[n] and Paul spoke to the
group. Because he was planning to leave the next
day, he kept on talking until midnight. 8We were
all together in a room upstairs, and there were
many lamps in the room. 9A young man named
Eutychus was sitting in the window. As Paul con-
tinued talking, Eutychus was falling into a deep
sleep. Finally, he went sound asleep and fell to the
ground from the third floor. When they picked
him up, he was dead. 10Paul went down to Euty-
chus, knelt down and put his arms around him.
He said, "Don't worry. He is alive now." 11Then
Paul went upstairs again, broke bread and ate. He
spoke to them for a long time, until it was early
morning, and then he left. 12They took the young
man home alive and were greatly comforted.

The Trip from Troas to Miletus

13We went on ahead of Paul and sailed for the
city of Assos, where he wanted to join us on the
ship. Paul had planned this because he wanted to
go to Assos by land. 14When he met us there,
we took him aboard and went to Mitylene. 15We
sailed from Mitylene and the next day came to a
place near Chios. The following day we sailed to
Samos, and the next day we reached Miletus.
16Paul had already decided not to stop at Ephesus,
because he did not want to stay too long in the
country of Asia. He was hurrying to be in Jerusalem
on the day of Pentecost,[d] if that were possible.

The Elders from Ephesus

17Now from Miletus Paul sent to Ephesus and
called for the elders[d] of the church. 18When they
came to him, he said, "You know about my life
from the first day I came to Asia. You know the
way I lived all the time I was with you. 19The
Jews made plans against me, which troubled me
very much. But you know I always served the
Lord unselfishly, and I often cried. 20You know I
preached to you and did not hold back anything
that would help you. You know that I taught you
in public and in your homes. 21I warned both
Jews and Greeks to change their lives and turn to
God and believe in our Lord Jesus. 22But now I
must obey the Holy Spirit[d] and go to Jerusalem. I
don't know what will happen to me there. 23I
know only that in every city the Holy Spirit tells

holy stone Probably a meteorite or stone that the people thought looked like Artemis.
first day of the week Sunday, which for the Jews began at sunset on our last day of the week. But if in this part of Asia a different system of time was used, then the meeting was on our Sunday night.
break bread Probably the Lord's Supper, the special meal that Jesus told his followers to eat to remember him (Luke 22:14–20).

me that troubles and even jail wait for me. 24I
don't care about my own life. The most impor-
tant thing is that I complete my mission, the
work that the Lord Jesus gave me—to tell people
the Good News[d] about God's grace.
25"And now, I know that none of you among
whom I was preaching the kingdom of God will
ever see me again. 26So today I tell you that if any
of you should be lost, I am not responsible, 27be-
cause I have told you everything God wants you
to know. 28Be careful for yourselves and for all
the people the Holy Spirit has given to you to
care for. You must be like shepherds to the
church of God,[n] which he bought with the
death of his own Son. 29I know that after I leave,
some people will come like wild wolves and try
to destroy the flock. 30Also, some from your own
group will rise up and twist the truth and will
lead away followers after them. 31So be careful!
Always remember that for three years, day and
night, I never stopped warning each of you, and
I often cried over you.
32"Now I am putting you in the care of God
and the message about his grace. It is able to give
you strength, and it will give you the blessings
God has for all his holy people. 33When I was
with you, I never wanted anyone's money or fine
clothes. 34You know I always worked to take
care of my own needs and the needs of those
who were with me. 35I showed you in all things
that you should work as I did and help the weak.
I taught you to remember the words Jesus said:
'It is more blessed to give than to receive.'"
36When Paul had said this, he knelt down with
all of them and prayed. 37–38And they all cried be-
cause Paul had said they would never see him
again. They put their arms around him and
kissed him. Then they went with him to the ship.

Paul Goes to Jerusalem

21 After we all said goodbye to them, we
sailed straight to the island of Cos. The
next day we reached Rhodes, and from there we
went to Patara. 2There we found a ship going to
Phoenicia, so we went aboard and sailed away.
3We sailed near the island of Cyprus, seeing it to
the north, but we sailed on to Syria. We stopped
at Tyre because the ship needed to unload its
cargo there. 4We found some followers in Tyre
and stayed with them for seven days. Through
the Holy Spirit[d] they warned Paul not to go
to Jerusalem. 5When we finished our visit, we left
and continued our trip. All the followers, even
the women and children, came outside the city
with us. After we all knelt on the beach and
prayed, 6we said goodbye and got on the ship,
and the followers went back home.
7We continued our trip from Tyre and arrived
at Ptolemais, where we greeted the believers
and stayed with them for a day. 8The next day
we left Ptolemais and went to the city of Caesarea.
There we went into the home of Philip the
preacher,[d] one of the seven helpers,[n] and stayed
with him. 9He had four unmarried daughters
who had the gift of prophesying.[d] 10After we had
been there for some time, a prophet named
Agabus arrived from Judea. 11He came to us and
borrowed Paul's belt and used it to tie his own
hands and feet. He said, "The Holy Spirit says,
'This is how the Jews in Jerusalem will tie up the
man who wears this belt. Then they will give
him to those who are not Jews.'"
12When we all heard this, we and the people
there begged Paul not to go to Jerusalem. 13But
he said, "Why are you crying and making me
so sad? I am not only ready to be tied up in
Jerusalem, I am ready to die for the Lord Jesus!"
14We could not persuade him to stay away from
Jerusalem. So we stopped begging him and said,
"We pray that what the Lord wants will be done."
15After this, we got ready and started on our
way to Jerusalem. 16Some of the followers from
Caesarea went with us and took us to the home
of Mnason, where we would stay. He was from
Cyprus and was one of the first followers.

Paul Visits James

17In Jerusalem the believers were glad to see
us. 18The next day Paul went with us to visit
James, and all the elders[d] were there. 19Paul
greeted them and told them everything God had
done among the non-Jewish people through him.
20When they heard this, they praised God. Then
they said to Paul, "Brother, you can see that
many thousands of Jews have become believers.
And they think it is very important to obey the
law of Moses. 21They have heard about your
teaching, that you tell the Jews who live among
those who are not Jews to leave the law of
Moses. They have heard that you tell them not to
circumcise[d] their children and not to obey Jewish
customs. 22What should we do? They will learn
that you have come. 23So we will tell you what
to do: four of our men have made a promise
to God. 24Take these men with you and share in
their cleansing ceremony.[n] Pay their expenses so
they can shave their heads.[n] Then it will prove
to everyone that what they have heard about

of God Some Greek copies say, "of the Lord".
helpers The seven men chosen for a special work described in Acts 6:1–6.
cleansing ceremony The special things Jews did to end the Nazirite promise.
shave their heads The Jews did this to show that their promise was finished.

you is not true and that you follow the law of Moses in your own life. 25We have already sent a letter to the non-Jewish believers. The letter said: 'Do not eat food that has been offered to idols, or blood or animals that have been strangled. Do not take part in sexual sin.' "

26The next day Paul took the four men and shared in the cleansing ceremony with them. Then he went to the Temple[d] and announced the time when the days of the cleansing ceremony would be finished. On the last day an offering would be given for each of the men.

27When the seven days were almost over, some Jews from Asia saw Paul at the Temple. They upset all the people and grabbed Paul. 28They shouted, "People of Israel, help us! This is the man who goes everywhere teaching against the law of Moses, against our people and against this Temple. Now he has brought some Greeks into the Temple and has made this holy place unclean!"[d] 29(The Jews said this because they had seen Trophimus, a man from Ephesus, with Paul in Jerusalem. The Jews thought that Paul had brought him into the Temple.)

Sidelight When Paul was accused of making the Temple unclean, he was being accused of a crime punishable by death (Acts 21:28). Archaeologists have found a temple inscription that says: "No foreigner is to enter . . . Whoever is caught will render himself liable to the consequent penalty of death."

30All the people in Jerusalem became upset. Together they ran, took Paul and dragged him out of the Temple. The Temple doors were closed immediately. 31While they were trying to kill Paul, the commander of the Roman army in Jerusalem learned that there was trouble in the whole city. 32Immediately he took some officers and soldiers and ran to the place where the crowd was gathered. When the people saw them, they stopped beating Paul. 33The commander went to Paul and arrested him. He told his soldiers to tie Paul with two chains. Then he asked who he was and what he had done wrong. 34Some in the crowd were yelling one thing, and some were yelling another. Because of all this confusion and shouting, the commander could not learn what had happened. So he ordered the soldiers to take Paul to the army building. 35When Paul came to the steps, the soldiers had to carry him because the people were ready to hurt him. 36The whole mob was following them, shouting, "Kill him!"

37As the soldiers were about to take Paul into the army building, he spoke to the commander, "May I say something to you?"

The commander said, "Do you speak Greek? 38I thought you were the Egyptian who started some trouble against the government not long ago and led 4,000 killers out to the desert."

39Paul said, "No, I am a Jew from Tarsus in the country of Cilicia. I am a citizen of that important city. Please, let me speak to the people."

40The commander gave permission, so Paul stood on the steps and waved his hand to quiet the people. When there was silence, he spoke to them in the Jewish language.[n]

Paul Speaks to the People

22 Paul said, "Friends, fellow Jews, listen to my defence to you." 2When the Jews heard him speaking the Jewish language,[n] they became very quiet. Paul said, 3"I am a Jew, born in Tarsus in the country of Cilicia, but I grew up in this city. I was a student of Gamaliel,[n] who carefully taught me everything about the law of our ancestors. I was very serious about serving God, just as are all of you here today. 4I persecuted the people who followed the Way of Jesus, and some of them were even killed. I arrested men and women and put them in jail. 5The high priest and the whole council of Jewish elders can tell you this is true. They gave me letters to the Jewish brothers in Damascus. So I was going there to arrest these people and bring them back to Jerusalem to be punished.

6"At about noon when I came near Damascus, a bright light from heaven suddenly flashed all around me. 7I fell to the ground and heard a voice saying, 'Saul, Saul, why are you persecuting me?' 8I asked, 'Who are you, Lord?' The voice said, 'I am Jesus from Nazareth whom you are persecuting.' 9Those who were with me did not hear the voice, but they saw the light. 10I said, 'What shall I do, Lord?' The Lord answered, 'Get up and go to Damascus. There you will be told about all the things I have planned for you to do.' 11I could not see, because the bright light had made me blind. So my companions led me into Damascus.

12"There a man named Ananias came to me. He was a religious man; he obeyed the law of Moses, and all the Jews who lived there respected him. 13He stood by me and said, 'Brother

Jewish language Hebrew or Aramaic, the languages of the Jews in the first century.
Gamaliel A very important teacher of the Pharisees, a Jewish religious group (Acts 5:34).

Saul, see again!' Immediately I was able to see
him. 14He said, 'The God of our ancestors chose
you long ago to know his plan, to see the
Righteous One and to hear words from him.
15You will be his witness to all people, telling
them about what you have seen and heard.
16Now, why wait any longer? Get up, be
baptised[d] and wash your sins away, trusting in
him to save you.'
17"Later, when I returned to Jerusalem, I
was praying in the Temple,[d] and I saw a vision.
18I saw the Lord saying to me, 'Hurry! Leave
Jerusalem now! The people here will not accept
the truth about me.' 19But I said, 'Lord, they
know that in every synagogue[d] I put the
believers in jail and beat them. 20They also know
I was there when Stephen, your witness, was
killed. I stood there agreeing and holding the
coats of those who were killing him!' 21But
the Lord said to me, 'Leave now. I will send
you far away to the non-Jewish people.' "
22The crowd listened to Paul until he said
this. Then they began shouting, "Kill him!
Get him out of the world! He should not be
allowed to live!" 23They shouted, threw off
their coats[n] and threw dust into the air.[n]

threw off their coats This showed that the Jews were very angry with Paul.
threw dust into the air This showed even greater anger.

SHARING FAITH

It Happened to Me

Did you know that it is against the law to go into a school and tell kids that they should become Christians? There is a good reason for it, you see kids have to be in school, they don't have an option, therefore anyone could go in and tell them anything and they would have to accept it as the truth. Schools would be wide open to people preaching all sorts of weird and perverted ideas, so this law is in place to prevent that happening.

However, Christians are welcomed in to many Religious Education lessons to give a testimony – basically, the story of their life and how they became Christians. That way, you are saying "This is what happened to me," and that's fine.

When Joel was asked to give his testimony at his local school (it was only two years after leaving!) he was very nervous, especially as his Christian testimony was only one year old! He was known at his school for all the bad things he did. But as his old teacher gave him a warm introduction with reminders of his wayward escapades, he began to relax.

He told the students how he'd left school with not much hope of a job, even though he was good at woodwork, and how he'd met up with a girl who was a Christian. She introduced him to her church and he gradually started to do odd jobs for them. He was soon indispensable and the more time he spent with these "Christians" the more he listened and liked what he heard. He told the pupils how he had asked questions about the life of Jesus, and how people at the church had explained things to him.

He didn't realise how excited and interesting his talk was, until kids started to ask questions at the end. He answered everything by starting off with, "I can only tell you what happened to me, but . . ."

Read **Acts 22:12–16** to see how important a testimony is.

- How were Joel's actions like the instructions given to Paul in this passage?
- What did Paul need to do before telling others about Jesus?

Consider . . .

- asking your minister to approach a local headmaster to see if he would let your church help with Christian assemblies.
- being baptised or confirmed, as a public witness to others of your Christian beliefs.

For more see . . .

- Isaiah 43:10 (p.684)
- 2 Peter 1:16 (p.1365)
- Acts 10:39–42 (p.1156)

24 Then the commander ordered the soldiers
to take Paul into the army building and beat him.
He wanted to make Paul tell why the people
were shouting against him like this. 25 But as the
soldiers were tying him up, preparing to beat
him, Paul said to an officer nearby, "Do you have
the right to beat a Roman citizen[n] who has not
been proven guilty?"

26 When the officer heard this, he went to the
commander and reported it. The officer said,
"Do you know what you are doing? This man is
a Roman citizen."

27 The commander came to Paul and said, "Tell
me, are you really a Roman citizen?"

He answered, "Yes."

28 The commander said, "I paid a lot of money
to become a Roman citizen."

But Paul said, "I was born a citizen."

29 The men who were preparing to question
Paul moved away from him immediately. The
commander was frightened because he had al-
ready tied Paul, and Paul was a Roman citizen.

Paul Speaks to Jewish Leaders

30 The next day the commander decided to
learn why the Jews were accusing Paul. So he or-
dered the leading priests and the Jewish council
to meet. The commander took Paul's chains off.
Then he brought Paul out and stood him before
their meeting.

23 Paul looked at the Jewish council and
said, "Brothers, I have lived my life with
a clear conscience before God up to this day."
2 Ananias,[n] the high priest, heard this and told
the men who were standing near Paul to hit him
on the mouth. 3 Paul said to Ananias, "God will
hit you, too! You are like a wall that has been
painted white. You sit there and judge me, using
the law of Moses, but you are telling them to hit
me, and that is against the law."

4 The men standing near Paul said to him,
"You cannot insult God's high priest like that!"

5 Paul said, "Brothers, I did not know this
man was the high priest. It is written in the
Scriptures,[d] 'You must not curse a leader of your
people.'"[n]

6 Some of the men in the meeting were
Sadducees,[d] and others were Pharisees.[d] Know-
ing this, Paul shouted to them, "My brothers, I am
a Pharisee, and my father was a Pharisee. I am on
trial here because I believe that people will rise
from the dead."

7 When Paul said this, there was an argument
between the Pharisees and the Sadducees, and
the group was divided. 8 (The Sadducees do not
believe in angels or spirits or that people will
rise from the dead. But the Pharisees believe in
them all.) 9 So there was a great uproar. Some of
the teachers of the law, who were Pharisees,
stood up and argued, "We find nothing wrong
with this man. Maybe an angel or a spirit did
speak to him."

10 The argument was beginning to turn into
such a fight that the commander was afraid the
Jews would tear Paul to pieces. So he told the
soldiers to go down and take Paul away and put
him in the army building.

11 The next night the Lord came and stood by
Paul. He said, "Be brave! You have told people in
Jerusalem about me. You must do the same in
Rome."

12 In the morning some of the Jews made a
plan to kill Paul, and they took an oath not to eat
or drink anything until they had killed him.
13 There were more than 40 Jews who made this
plan. 14 They went to the leading priests and the
Jewish elders and said, "We have taken an oath
not to eat or drink until we have killed Paul. 15 So
this is what we want you to do: send a message
to the commander to bring Paul out to you as
though you want to ask him more questions.
We will be waiting to kill him while he is on the
way here."

16 But Paul's nephew heard about this plan and
went to the army building and told Paul. 17 Then
Paul called one of the officers and said, "Take this
young man to the commander. He has a message
for him."

18 So the officer brought Paul's nephew to the
commander and said, "The prisoner, Paul, asked
me to bring this young man to you. He wants to
tell you something."

19 The commander took the young man's hand
and led him to a place where they could be
alone. He asked, "What do you want to tell
me?"

20 The young man said, "The Jews have
decided to ask you to bring Paul down to their
council meeting tomorrow. They want you to
think they are going to ask him more questions.
21 But don't believe them! More than 40 men
are hiding and waiting to kill Paul. They have
all taken an oath not to eat or drink until they
have killed him. Now they are waiting for you
to agree."

22 The commander sent the young man away,
ordering him, "Don't tell anyone that you have
told me about their plan."

Roman citizen Roman law said that Roman citizens must not be beaten before they had a trial.
Ananias This is not the man named Ananias in Acts 22:12.
'You . . . people.' Quotation from Exodus 22:28.

Paul is Sent to Caesarea

[23]Then the commander called two officers and
said, "I need some men to go to Caesarea. Get
200 soldiers, 70 horsemen and 200 men with
spears ready to leave at nine o'clock tonight.
[24]Get some horses for Paul to ride so he can be
taken to Governor Felix safely." [25]And he wrote
a letter that said:

> [26]From Claudius Lysias.
> To the Most Excellent Governor Felix:
> Greetings.
> [27]The Jews had taken this man and
> planned to kill him. But I learned that he is
> a Roman citizen, so I went with my soldiers
> and saved him. [28]I wanted to know why
> they were accusing him, so I brought him
> before their council meeting. [29]I learned
> that the Jews said Paul did some things
> that were wrong by their own laws, but no
> charge was worthy of jail or death. [30]When
> I was told that some of the Jews were plan-
> ning to kill Paul, I sent him to you at once.
> I also told those Jews to tell you what they
> have against him.

[31]So the soldiers did what they were told and
took Paul and brought him to the city of Antipatris
that night. [32]The next day the horsemen went
with Paul to Caesarea, but the other soldiers went
back to the army building in Jerusalem. [33]When
the horsemen came to Caesarea and gave the let-
ter to the governor, they turned Paul over to him.
[34]The governor read the letter and asked Paul,
"What area are you from?" When he learned that
Paul was from Cilicia, [35]he said, "I will hear your
case when those who are against you come here,
too." Then the governor gave orders for Paul to be
kept under guard in Herod's palace.

Paul is Accused

24 Five days later Ananias, the high priest,
went to the city of Caesarea with some
of the Jewish elders and a lawyer named Tertullus.
They had come to make charges against Paul
before the governor. [2]Paul was called into the
meeting, and Tertullus began to accuse him, say-
ing, "Most Excellent Felix! Our people enjoy
much peace because of you, and many wrong
things in our country are being made right
through your wise help. [3]We accept these things
always and in every place, and we are thankful
for them. [4]But not wanting to take any more of
your time, I beg you to be kind and listen to our
few words. [5]We have found this man to be a
troublemaker, stirring up the Jews everywhere in
the world. He is a leader of the Nazarene[d]
group. [6]Also, he was trying to make the Temple[d]
unclean,[d] but we stopped him.[n] [8]By asking him
questions yourself, you can decide if all these
things are true." [9]The other Jews agreed and said
that all of this was true.

[10]When the governor made a sign for Paul to
speak, Paul said, "Governor Felix, I know you
have been a judge over this nation for a long
time. So I am happy to defend myself before you.
[11]You can learn for yourself that I went to wor-
ship in Jerusalem only twelve days ago. [12]Those
who are accusing me did not find me arguing
with anyone in the Temple or stirring up the peo-
ple in the synagogues[d] or in the city. [13]They can-
not prove the things they are saying against me
now. [14]But I will tell you this: I worship the God
of our ancestors as a follower of the Way of Jesus.
The Jews say that the Way of Jesus is not the
right way. But I believe everything that is taught
in the law of Moses and that is written in the
books of the Prophets.[d] [15]I have the same hope
in God that they have—the hope that all people,
good and bad, will surely be raised from the
dead. [16]This is why I always try to do what I
believe is right before God and people.

[17]"After being away from Jerusalem for several
years, I went back to bring money to my people
and to offer sacrifices. [18]I was doing this when
they found me in the Temple. I had finished the
cleansing ceremony and had not made any trou-
ble; no people were gathering around me. [19]But
there were some Jews from the country of Asia
who should be here, standing before you. If I
have really done anything wrong, they are the
ones who should accuse me. [20]Or ask these Jews
here if they found any wrong in me when I stood
before the Jewish council in Jerusalem. [21]But I
did shout one thing when I stood before them:
'You are judging me today because I believe that
people will rise from the dead!' "

[22]Felix already understood much about the
Way of Jesus. He stopped the trial and said,
"When commander Lysias comes here, I will de-
cide your case." [23]Felix told the officer to keep
Paul guarded but to give him some freedom and
to let his friends bring what he needed.

Paul Speaks to Felix and His Wife

[24]After some days Felix came with his wife,
Drusilla, who was Jewish, and asked for Paul to
be brought to him. He listened to Paul talk about
believing in Christ Jesus. [25]But Felix became
afraid when Paul spoke about living right, self-
control and the time when God will judge the

Verse 6 Some Greek copies add verses 6b–8a: "And we wanted to judge him by our own law. [7]But the officer Lysias came and used much force to take him from us. [8]And Lysias commanded those who wanted to accuse Paul to come to you."

world. He said, "Go away now. When I have more time, I will call for you." [26]At the same time Felix hoped that Paul would give him some money, so he often sent for Paul and talked with him.

[27]But after two years, Felix was replaced by Porcius Festus as governor. But Felix had left Paul in prison to please the Jews.

Paul Asks to See Caesar

25 Three days after Festus became governor, he went from Caesarea to Jerusalem.

> **Sidelight** The Judean governor Felix was greedy, brutal and incompetent. He once killed 400 men suspected of terrorist activities – without a trial. When Paul wouldn't pay him a bribe, Felix left the apostle in jail for two years, until Felix was succeeded in office (Acts 24:1–27).

[2]There the leading priests and the important Jewish leaders made charges against Paul before Festus. [3]They asked Festus to do them a favour. They wanted him to send Paul back to Jerusalem, because they had a plan to kill him on the way. [4]But Festus answered that Paul would be kept in Caesarea and that he himself was returning there soon. [5]He said, "Some of your leaders should go with me. They can accuse the man there in Caesarea, if he has really done something wrong."

[6]Festus stayed in Jerusalem another eight or ten days and then went back to Caesarea. The next day he told the soldiers to bring Paul before him. Festus was seated on the judge's seat [7]when Paul came into the room. The Jewish people who had come from Jerusalem stood around him, making serious charges against him, which they could not prove. [8]This is what Paul said to defend himself: "I have done nothing wrong against the Jewish law, against the Temple[d] or against Caesar."[d]

[9]But Festus wanted to please the Jews. So he asked Paul, "Do you want to go to Jerusalem for me to judge you there on these charges?"

[10]Paul said, "I am standing at Caesar's judgement seat now, where I should be judged. I have done nothing wrong to the Jews; you know this is true. [11]If I have done something wrong and the law says I must die, I do not ask to be saved from death. But if these charges are not true, then no one can give me to them. I want Caesar to hear my case!"

[12]Festus talked about this with his advisors. Then he said, "You have asked to see Caesar, so you will go to Caesar!"

Paul Before King Agrippa

[13]A few days later King Agrippa and Bernice came to Caesarea to visit Festus. [14]They stayed there for some time, and Festus told the king about Paul's case. Festus said, "There is a man that Felix left in prison. [15]When I went to Jerusalem, the leading priests and the Jewish elders there made charges against him, asking me to sentence him to death. [16]But I answered, 'When a man is accused of a crime, Romans do not hand him over until he has been allowed to face his accusers and defend himself against their charges.' [17]So when these Jews came here to Caesarea for the trial, I did not waste time. The next day I sat on the judge's seat and commanded that the man be brought in. [18]The Jews stood up and accused him, but not of any serious crime as I thought they would. [19]The things they said were about their own religion and about a man named Jesus who died. But Paul said that he is still alive. [20]Not knowing how to find out about these questions, I asked Paul, 'Do you want to go to Jerusalem and be judged there?' [21]But he asked to be kept in Caesarea. He wants a decision from the emperor.[n] So I ordered that he be held until I could send him to Caesar."[d]

[22]Agrippa said to Festus, "I would also like to hear this man myself."

Festus said, "Tomorrow you will hear him."

[23]The next day Agrippa and Bernice appeared with great show, acting like very important people. They went into the judgement room with the army leaders and the important men of Caesarea. Then Festus ordered the soldiers to bring Paul in. [24]Festus said, "King Agrippa and all who are gathered here with us, you see this man. All the Jewish people, here and in Jerusalem, have complained to me about him, shouting that he should not live any longer. [25]When I judged him, I found no reason to order his death. But since he asked to be judged by Caesar, I decided to send him. [26]But I have nothing definite to write to the emperor about him. So I have brought him before all of you—especially you, King Agrippa. I hope you can question him and give me something to write. [27]I think it is foolish to send a prisoner to Caesar without telling what charges are against him."

emperor The ruler of the Roman Empire, which was almost all the known world.

Paul Defends Himself

26 Agrippa said to Paul, "You may now speak to defend yourself."

Then Paul raised his hand and began to speak. 2He said, "King Agrippa, I am very happy to stand before you and will answer all the charges the Jewish people make against me. 3You know so much about all the Jewish customs and the things the Jews argue about, so please listen to me patiently.

4"All the Jewish people know about my whole life, how I lived from the beginning in my own country and later in Jerusalem. 5They have known me for a long time. If they want to, they can tell you that I was a good Pharisee.[d] And the Pharisees obey the laws of the Jewish religion more carefully than any other group. 6Now I am on trial because I hope for the promise that God made to our ancestors. 7This is the promise that the twelve tribes[d] of our people hope to receive as they serve God day and night. My king, the Jews have accused me because I hope for this same promise! 8Why do any of you people think it is impossible for God to raise people from the dead?

9"I, too, thought I ought to do many things against Jesus from Nazareth. 10And that is what I did in Jerusalem. The leading priests gave me the power to put many of God's people in jail, and when they were being killed, I agreed it was a good thing. 11In every synagogue,[d] I often punished them and tried to make them speak against Jesus. I was so angry against them I even went to other cities to find them and punish them.

12"On one occasion the leading priests gave me permission and the power to go to Damascus. 13On the way there, at noon, I saw a light from heaven. It was brighter than the sun and flashed all around me and those who were travelling with me. 14We all fell to the ground. Then I heard a voice speaking to me in the Jewish language,[n] saying, 'Saul, Saul, why are you persecuting me? You are only hurting yourself by fighting me.' 15I said, 'Who are you, Lord?' The Lord said, 'I am Jesus, the one you are persecuting. 16Stand up! I have chosen you to be my servant and my witness—you will tell people the things that you have seen and the things that I will show you. This is why I have come to you today. 17I will keep you safe from your own people and also from those who are not Jewish. I am sending you to them 18to open their eyes so that they may turn away from darkness to the light, away from the power of Satan and to God. Then their sins can be forgiven, and they can have a place with those people who have been made holy by believing in me.'

19"King Agrippa, after I had this vision from heaven, I obeyed it. 20I began telling people that they should change their hearts and lives and turn to God and do things to show they really had changed. I told this first to those in Damascus, then in Jerusalem and in every part of Judea, and also to those who are not Jewish. 21This is why the Jews took me and were trying to kill me in the Temple.[d] 22But God has helped me, and so I stand here today, telling all people, small and great, what I have seen. But I am saying only what Moses and the prophets[d] said would happen— 23that the Christ[d] would die, and as the first to rise from the dead, he would bring light to the Jewish and non-Jewish people."

Paul Tries to Persuade Agrippa

24While Paul was saying these things to defend himself, Festus said loudly, "Paul, you are out of your mind! Too much study has driven you insane!"

25Paul said, "Most excellent Festus, I am not mad. My words are true and sensible. 26King Agrippa knows about these things, and I can speak freely to him. I know he has heard about all these things, because they did not happen in a corner. 27King Agrippa, do you believe what the prophets[d] wrote? I know you believe."

28King Agrippa said to Paul, "Do you think you can persuade me to become a Christian in such a short time?"

29Paul said, "Whether it is a short or a long time, I pray to God that not only you but every person listening to me today would be saved and be like me—except for these chains I have."

30Then King Agrippa, Governor Festus, Bernice and all the people sitting with them stood up 31and left the room. Talking to each other, they said, "There is no reason why this man should die or be put in jail." 32And Agrippa said to Festus, "We could let this man go free, but he has asked Caesar[d] to hear his case."

Paul Sails for Rome

27 It was decided that we would sail for Italy. An officer named Julius, who served in the emperor's[n] army, guarded Paul and some other prisoners. 2We got on a ship that was from the city of Adramyttium and was about to sail to different ports in the country of Asia. Aristarchus, a man from the city of Thessalonica in Macedonia, went with us. 3The next day we came to Sidon. Julius was very good to Paul and

Jewish language Hebrew or Aramaic, the languages of the Jews in the first century.
emperor The ruler of the Roman Empire, which was almost all the known world.

gave him freedom to go and visit his friends, who took care of his needs. 4We left Sidon and sailed close to the island of Cyprus, because the wind was blowing against us. 5We went across the sea by Cilicia and Pamphylia and landed at the city of Myra, in Lycia. 6There the officer found a ship from Alexandria that was going to Italy, so he put us on it.

7We sailed slowly for many days. We had a hard time reaching Cnidus because the wind was blowing against us, and we could not go any further. So we sailed by the south side of the island of Crete near Salmone. 8Sailing past it was hard. Then we came to a place called Fair Havens, near the city of Lasea.

9We had lost much time, and it was now dangerous to sail, because it was already after the Day of Cleansing.[n] So Paul warned them, 10"Men, I can see there will be a lot of trouble on this trip. The ship, the cargo and even our lives may be lost." 11But the captain and the owner of the ship did not agree with Paul, and the officer believed what the captain and owner of the ship said. 12Since that harbour was not a good place for the ship to stay for the winter, most of the men decided that the ship should leave. They hoped we could go to Phoenix and stay there for the winter. Phoenix, a city on the island of Crete, had a harbour which faced south-west and north-west.

The Storm

13When a good wind began to blow from the south, the men on the ship thought, "This is the wind we wanted, and now we have it." So they pulled up the anchor, and we sailed very close to the island of Crete. 14But then a very strong wind named the "northeaster" came from the island. 15The ship was caught in it and could not sail against it. So we stopped trying and let the wind carry us. 16When we went below a small island named Cauda, we were barely able to bring in the lifeboat. 17After the men took the lifeboat in, they tied ropes around the ship to hold it together. The men were afraid that the ship would hit the sandbanks of Syrtis,[n] so they lowered the sail and let the wind carry the ship. 18The next day the storm was blowing us so hard that the men threw out some of the cargo. 19A day later with their own hands they threw out the ship's equipment. 20When we could not see the sun or the stars for many days, and the storm was very bad, we lost all hope of being saved.

21After the men had gone without food for a long time, Paul stood up before them and said, "Men, you should have listened to me. You should not have sailed from Crete. Then you would not have had all this trouble and loss. 22But now I tell you to cheer up because none of you will die. Only the ship will be lost. 23Last night an angel came to me from the God I belong to and worship. 24The angel said, 'Paul, do not be afraid. You must stand before Caesar.[d] And God has promised you that he will save the lives of everyone sailing with you.' 25So men, have courage. I trust in God that everything will happen as his angel told me. 26But we will run aground on an island."

27On the fourteenth night we were still being carried around in the Adriatic Sea.[n] About midnight the sailors thought we were close to land, 28so they lowered a rope with a weight on the end of it into the water. They found that the water was 20 fathoms deep. They went a little further and lowered the rope again. It was 15 fathoms deep. 29The sailors were afraid that we would hit the rocks, so they threw four anchors into the water and prayed for daylight to come. 30Some of the sailors wanted to leave the ship, and they lowered the lifeboat, pretending they were throwing more anchors from the front of the ship. 31But Paul told the officer and the other soldiers, "If these men do not stay in the ship, your lives cannot be saved." 32So the soldiers cut the ropes and let the lifeboat fall into the water.

33Just before dawn Paul began persuading all the people to eat something. He said, "For the past fourteen days you have been waiting and watching and not eating. 34Now I beg you to eat something. You need it to stay alive. None of you will lose even one hair of your heads." 35After he said this, Paul took some bread and thanked God for it before all of them. He broke off a piece and began eating. 36They all felt better and started eating, too. 37There were 276 people on the ship. 38When they had eaten all they wanted, they began making the ship lighter by throwing the grain into the sea.

The Ship is Destroyed

39When daylight came, the sailors saw land. They did not know what land it was, but they saw a bay with a beach and wanted to sail the ship to the beach if they could. 40So they cut the ropes to the anchors and left the anchors in the sea. At the same time, they untied the ropes that were holding the rudders. Then they raised the front sail into the wind and sailed towards

Day of Cleansing An important Jewish holy day in the autumn of the year. Bad storms arose on the sea at this time of year.
Syrtis Shallow area in the sea near the Libyan coast.
Adriatic Sea The sea between Greece and Italy, including the central Mediterranean.

the beach. 41But the ship hit a sandbank. The
front of the ship stuck there and could not move,
but the back of the ship began to break up from
the big waves.
42The soldiers decided to kill the prisoners so
none of them could swim away and escape.
43But Julius, the officer, wanted to let Paul live
and did not allow the soldiers to kill the prison-
ers. Instead he ordered everyone who could
swim to jump into the water first and swim to
land. 44The rest were to follow using wooden
boards or pieces of the ship. And this is how all
the people made it safely to land.

Sidelight Paul often experienced rough waters while sailing (Acts 27:13–44). Storms, a common occurrence in the Mediterranean Sea, made travel hazardous for wooden trading ships. Today, one Greek island, only fourteen and a half kilometres long, has 400 churches that were built by sailors who were fulfilling vows they made to God in the midst of perilous storms.

Paul on the Island of Malta

28 When we were safe on land, we learned
that the island was called Malta. 2The
people who lived there were very good to us.
Because it was raining and very cold, they made
a fire and welcomed all of us. 3Paul gathered a
pile of sticks and was putting them on the fire
when a poisonous snake came out because of the
heat and bit him on the hand. 4The people living
on the island saw the snake hanging from Paul's
hand and said to each other, "This man must be a
murderer! He did not die in the sea, but Justice[n]
does not want him to live." 5But Paul shook the
snake off into the fire and was not hurt. 6The peo-
ple thought that Paul would swell up or fall down
dead. They waited and watched him for a long
time, but nothing bad happened to him. So they
changed their minds and said, "He is a god!"
7There were some fields around there owned
by Publius, an important man on the island. He
welcomed us into his home and was very good
to us for three days. 8Publius' father was sick with
a fever and dysentery.[n] Paul went to him, prayed
and put his hands on the man and healed him.
9After this, all the other sick people on the island
came to Paul, and he healed them, too. 10–11The
people on the island gave us many honours.
When we were ready to leave, three months
later, they gave us the things we needed.

Paul Goes to Rome

We got on a ship from Alexandria that had
stayed on the island during the winter. On the
front of the ship was the sign of the twin gods.[n]
12We stopped at Syracuse for three days. 13From
there we sailed to Rhegium. The next day a
wind began to blow from the south, and a day
later we came to Puteoli. 14We found some be-
lievers there who asked us to stay with them for
a week. Finally, we came to Rome. 15The believ-
ers in Rome heard that we were there and came
out as far as the Market of Appius[n] and the
Three Inns[n] to meet us. When Paul saw them,
he was encouraged and thanked God.

Paul in Rome

16When we arrived at Rome, Paul was allowed
to live alone, with the soldier who guarded him.
17Three days later Paul sent for the Jewish
leaders there. When they came together, he said,
"Brothers, I have done nothing against our
people or the customs of our ancestors. But I was
arrested in Jerusalem and given to the Romans.
18After they asked me many questions, they
could find no reason why I should be killed.
They wanted to let me go free, 19but the Jewish
people there argued against that. So I had to
ask to come to Rome to have my trial before
Caesar.[d] But I have no charge to bring against
my own people. 20That is why I wanted to see
you and talk with you. I am bound with this
chain because I believe in the hope of Israel."
21They answered Paul, "We have received no
letters from Judea about you. None of our Jewish
brothers who have come from there brought
news or told us anything bad about you. 22But
we want to hear your ideas, because we know
that people everywhere are speaking against this
religious group."
23Paul and the Jewish people chose a day for a
meeting and on that day many more of the Jews
met with Paul at the place he was staying. He
spoke to them all day long. Using the law of
Moses and the prophets'[d] writings, he explained
the kingdom of God, and he tried to persuade
them to believe these things about Jesus. 24Some
believed what Paul said, but others did not. 25So
they argued and began leaving after Paul said one

Justice The people thought there was a god named Justice who would punish bad people.
dysentery A sickness like diarrhoea.
twin gods Statues of Castor and Pollux, gods in old Greek tales.
Market of Appius A town about 44 kilometres from Rome.
Three Inns A town about 48 kilometres from Rome.

more thing to them: "The Holy Spirit[d] spoke
the truth to your ancestors through Isaiah the
prophet, saying,
26'Go and tell this people:
You will listen and listen, but you will not
understand.
You will look and look, but you will not learn.
27Make the minds of these people dumb.
Shut their ears. Cover their eyes.
Otherwise, they might really understand
what they see with their eyes
and hear with their ears.
They might really understand in their
minds
and come back to me and be healed.'

Isaiah 6:9–10

28"I want you to know that God has also sent
his salvation to those who are not Jewish, and
they will listen!" 29 [n]
30Paul stayed two full years in his own rented
house and welcomed all people who came to visit
him. 31He boldly preached about the kingdom of
God and taught about the Lord Jesus Christ, and
no one tried to stop him.

Verse 29 Some late Greek copies add verse 29: "After Paul said this, the Jews left. They were arguing very much with one another."

Romans

Why Read This Book:

- Understand that all people have sinned (Romans 1—3).
- Learn how Jesus Christ pays for our sins (Romans 4—8).
- Be challenged to live the Christian life (Romans 12—15).

When?

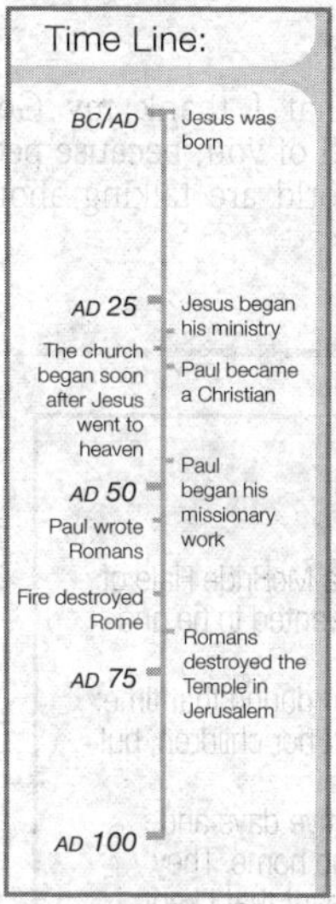

Behind the Scenes:

Suppose a friend sat down with you at lunchtime and asked, out of the blue, "What do you believe?" What would you say?

Romans is the apostle Paul's answer to that question: What do you believe? For more than twenty years, he had been a missionary, spreading the good news about Jesus Christ. He wanted to visit the Roman church, but before he went, he wanted the Roman Christians to understand what he believed.

So he wrote them this letter, which many people believe is the best, most powerful summary of Christian beliefs in the Bible. It reads like a text book as it sets out to explain important principles. The letter explains how all people have sinned and how God sent Jesus to pay for those sins and make people right with God (Romans 3:22–28).

But don't think that Romans is all theory. Right from the beginning Paul highlights the real-life impact of the principles. Later in the book he deals with issues like:

- baptism
- overcoming sin
- spiritual gifts
- government
- relating to unbelievers

Romans is packed with powerful statements about God and faith. From this book we can learn how God's love for us overcomes the power of sin in our lives and how we can live lives that please God.

Where?

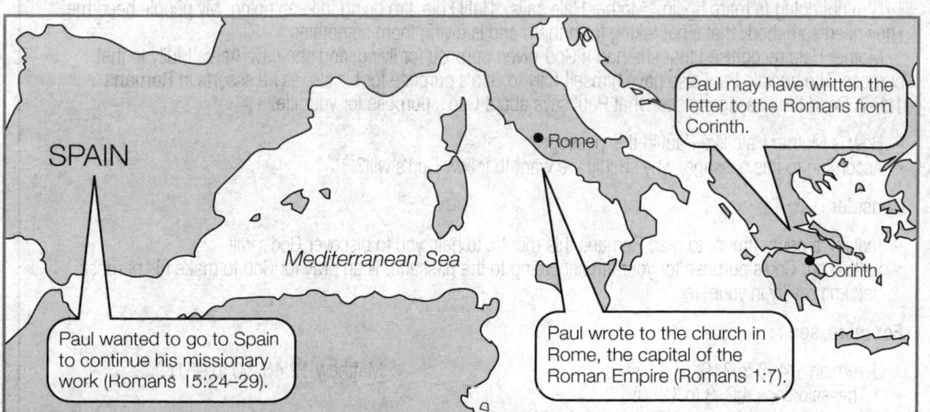

1 From Paul, a servant of Christ Jesus. God
called me to be an apostle[d] and chose me to
tell the Good News.[d]
2God promised this Good News long ago
through his prophets,[d] as it is written in the Holy
Scriptures.[d] 3–4The Good News is about God's
Son, Jesus Christ our Lord. As a man, he was
born from the family of David. But through the
Spirit[d] of holiness he was appointed to be God's
Son with great power by rising from the dead.
5Through Christ, God gave me the special work
of an apostle, which was to lead people of all
nations to believe and obey. I do this work for
him. 6And you who are in Rome are also called
to belong to Jesus Christ.
7To all of you in Rome whom God loves and
has called to be his holy people:
Grace and peace to you from God our Father
and the Lord Jesus Christ.

A Prayer of Thanks

8First I want to say that I thank my God
through Jesus Christ for all of you, because peo-
ple everywhere in the world are talking about

GOD'S WILL

Mother Hale

"My husband and I had dreams of what we were going to do with our children," recalls Clara McBride Hale of her life in the early part of the 1900s. "We dreamed that they'd grow up and be what they wanted to be and have a good life."

But Clara's husband died when their children, Lorraine and Nathan, were five and six. And during that time, untrained women could only do domestic jobs, such as house cleaning. Clara had to support her children, but she didn't want to leave them alone while she went to work.

"So I decided to take in other people's children," Clara continues. "They were coming for five days and going home on Saturday and Sunday. But then they started saying that they didn't want to go home. They wanted to stay with me all the time. So the parents would give me extra money, and that meant that I kept them all the time."

What started as a "survival" business bloomed into a lifetime ministry for Clara, who came to be known by the children and their parents as "Mother Hale".

"I raised 40," Mother Hale recalls. "Every one of them went to college, every one of them graduated, and they all have lovely jobs. I have singers, dancers, preachers and things like that. No big names or anything, but they're happy."

In 1969, when Mother Hale was 64 years old, she decided to retire. She had raised 40 children and felt ready for someone else to take over.

"Then my daughter sent me a girl with an addict baby. Within two months, I had 22 babies living in a five-room flat. My decision to stop didn't mean anything. It seemed as though God wanted them. He kept sending them, and he kept making a way for me to make it.

"I'm not going to retire again," Mother Hale says. "Until I die, I'm going to keep doing. My people need me. They need somebody that's not taking from them and is giving them something."

Mother Hale recognised that she had a God-given purpose for living, and she gave herself fully to that purpose. The apostle Paul also gave himself fully to God's purpose for his life, as he asserts in **Romans 1:1–7**. Read the passage to see what Paul says about God's purpose for your life.

- How is Mother Hale like Paul in this passage?
- According to this passage, why should we want to follow God's will?

Consider . . .

- making a commitment to read Romans this month, to help you to discover God's will.
- writing out God's purpose for your life according to the passage. Then pray for God to make his purpose become reality in your life.

For more, see . . .

- Jeremiah 1:4–8 (p.716)
- 1 Thessalonians 4:3–8 (p.1298)
- Matthew 12:46–50 (p.961)

your faith. 9God, whom I serve with my whole
heart by telling the Good News[d] about his Son,
knows that I always mention you 10every time I
pray. I pray that I will be allowed to come to you,

Sidelight The recipients of the letter to the Romans lived in the capital of the giant, powerful Roman Empire (Romans 1:7). The Romans built a 400,000-kilometre long complex of roads that would have circled the equator ten times if it had been one long road.

and this will happen if God wants it. 11I want
very much to see you, to give you some spiritual
gift to make you strong. 12I mean that I want us
to help each other with the faith we have. Your
faith will help me, and my faith will help you.
13Brothers and sisters,[n] I want you to know that
I planned many times to come to you, but this
has not been possible. I wanted to come so that
I could help you grow spiritually as I have helped
the other non-Jewish people.
14I have a duty to all people—Greeks and
those who are not Greeks, the wise and the fool-
ish. 15That is why I want so much to preach the
Good News to you in Rome.
16I am proud of the Good News, because it is
the power God uses to save everyone who be-
lieves—to save the Jews first, and also to save
those who are not Jews. 17The Good News
shows how God makes people right with him-
self—that it begins and ends with faith. As the
Scripture[d] says, "But those who are right with
God will live by trusting in him."[n]

All People Have Done Wrong

18God's anger is shown from heaven against
all the evil and wrong things people do. By their
own evil lives they hide the truth. 19God shows
his anger because some knowledge of him has
been made clear to them. Yes, God has shown
himself to them. 20There are things about him
that people cannot see—his eternal power and all
the things that make him God. But since the be-
ginning of the world those things have been easy
to understand by what God has made. So people
have no excuse for the bad things they do. 21They
knew God, but they did not give glory to God or
thank him. Their thinking became useless. Their
foolish minds were filled with darkness. 22They
said they were wise, but they became fools.
23They traded the glory of God who lives for ever
for the worship of idols made to look like earthly
people, birds, animals and snakes.
24Because they did these things, God left them
and let them go their sinful way, wanting only to
do evil. As a result, they became full of sexual
sin, using their bodies wrongly with each other.
25They traded the truth of God for a lie. They
worshipped and served what had been created
instead of the God who created those things, who
should be praised for ever. Amen.
26Because people did those things, God left
them and let them do the shameful things they
wanted to do. Women stopped having natural
sex and started having sex with other women.
27In the same way, men stopped having natural
sex and began wanting each other. Men did
shameful things with other men, and in their
bodies they received the punishment for those
wrongs.
28People did not think it was important to
have a true knowledge of God. So God left them
and allowed them to have their own worthless
thinking and to do things they should not do.
29They are filled with every kind of sin, evil, self-
ishness and hatred. They are full of jealousy,
murder, fighting, lying and thinking the worst
about each other. They gossip 30and say evil
things about each other. They hate God. They
are rude and conceited and boast about them-
selves. They invent ways of doing evil. They do
not obey their parents. 31They are foolish, they
do not keep their promises, and they show no
kindness or mercy to others. 32They know God's
law says that those who live like this should die.
But they themselves not only continue to do
these evil things, they applaud others who do
them.

You People Also are Sinful

2 If you think you can judge others, you are
wrong. When you judge them, you are really
judging yourself guilty, because you do the same
things they do. 2God judges those who do wrong
things, and we know that his judging is right.
3You judge those who do wrong, but you do
wrong yourselves. Do you think you will be able
to escape the judgement of God? 4He has been
very kind and patient, waiting for you to change,
but you think nothing of his kindness. Perhaps
you do not understand that God's kindness is
meant to lead you to change your hearts and
lives. 5But you are stubborn and refuse to change,

Brothers and sisters Although the Greek text says "brothers" here and throughout this book, Paul's words were meant for the entire church, both men and women.
"But those . . . him." Quotation from Habakkuk 2:4.

so you are making your own punishment even
greater on the day he shows his anger. On that
day everyone will see God's right judgements.
6God will reward or punish every person for
what that person has done. 7Some people, by al-
ways continuing to do good, live for God's glory,
for honour and for life that has no end. God will
give them life for ever. 8But other people are self-
ish. They refuse to follow truth and, instead, fol-
low evil. God will give them his punishment and
anger. 9He will give trouble and suffering to every-
one who does evil—to the Jews first and also to
those who are not Jews. 10But he will give glory,
honour and peace to everyone who does good—
to the Jews first and also to those who are not
Jews. 11For God judges all people in the same way.
12People who do not have the law [d] and who
are sinners will be lost, although they do not
have the law. And, in the same way, those who
have the law and are sinners will be judged by
the law. 13Hearing the law does not make people
right with God. It is those who obey the law
who will be right with him. 14(Those who are
not Jews do not have the law, but when they
freely do what the law commands, they are the
law for themselves. This is true even though
they do not have the law. 15They show that in
their hearts they know what is right and wrong,
just as the law commands. And they show
this by their thoughts. Sometimes their thoughts
tell them they did wrong, and sometimes
their thoughts tell them they did right.) 16All
these things will happen on the day when
God, through Christ Jesus, will judge people's
secret thoughts. The Good News [d] that I preach
says this.

PARENTS

Funny Folks

Tom needed an excuse to use his parents' car to take his friends for a spin. "Dad, can I borrow your car to pick up some school notes from my mate's house?"

His dad said no, so he moved on to his mum but, "Sorry son, your dad said no so I need to stand by his decision."

Furious that he didn't get his own way, Tom waited until his mum and dad were settled in front of the TV, then sneaked out, took the car and picked up his friends.

Later, there was a knock on the door. As Tom's parents looked into the face of a policeman they learned that he'd pulled Tom over for reckless driving and wanted to confirm that the car wasn't stolen. Tom was in BIG trouble!

Looking back on it, Tom admitted he had known his parents were right to say no, and he wished he'd listened. Instead of resenting the way they made decisions together, he became happy and relieved that they were a team he could trust in.

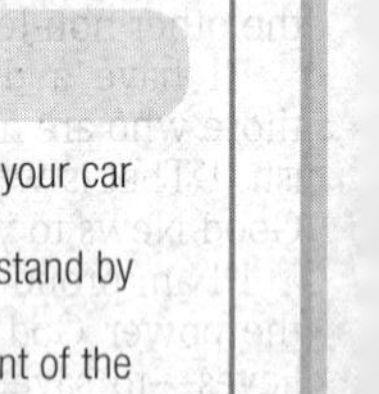

Tom learned a big lesson about obeying your parents even if you're angry at their decision. If they love you, they want the best for you, and you don't need to keep questioning or fighting against their decisions.

Read **Romans 1:28–32.**

- How could Tom have better dealt with the dilemma he faced?
- Why does the Bible tell us that we should obey our parents?

Consider . . .

- talking to your parents about taking on a little more responsibility in certain areas, for example, managing your money or time.
- your reactions towards your parents and try making a bigger effort to listen to their point of view.

For more see . . .

- Exodus 20:12 (p.79)
- Colossians 3:20 (p.1294)
- Ephesians 6:1 (p.1276)

The Jews and the Law

17What about you? You call yourself a Jew. You trust in the law of Moses and boast that you are close to God. 18You know what he wants you to do and what is important, because you have learned the law. 19You think you are a guide for the blind and a light for those who are in darkness. 20You think you can show foolish people what is right and teach those who know nothing. You have the law; so you think you know everything and have all truth. 21You teach others, so why don't you teach yourself? You tell others not to steal, but you steal. 22You say that others must not take part in adultery,[d] but you are guilty of that sin. You hate idols, but you steal from temples. 23You boast about having God's law, but you bring shame to God by breaking his law, 24just as the Scriptures[d] say: "Those who are not Jews speak against God's name because of you."[n]

25If you follow the law, your circumcision[d] has meaning. But if you break the law, it is as if you were never circumcised. 26People who are not Jews are not circumcised, but if they do what the law says, it is as if they were circumcised. 27You Jews have the written law and circumcision, but you break the law. So those who are not circumcised in their bodies, but still obey the law, will show that you are guilty. 28They can do this because a person is not a true Jew if he is only a Jew in his physical body; true circumcision is not only on the outside of the body. 29A person is a Jew only if he is a Jew inside; true circumcision is done in the heart by the Spirit,[d] not by the works of the written law. Such a person gets praise from God rather than from people.

3 So, do Jews have anything that other people do not have? Is there anything special about being circumcised?[d] 2Yes, of course, there is in every way. The most important thing is this: God trusted the Jews with his teachings. 3If some Jews were not faithful to him, will that stop God from doing what he promised? 4No! God will continue to be true even when every person is false. As the Scriptures[d] say:

"So you will be shown to be right when you
speak,
and you will win your case." *Psalm 51:4*

5When we do wrong, that shows more clearly that God is right. So can we say that God is wrong to punish us? (I am talking as people might talk.) 6No! If God could not punish us, he could not judge the world.

7A person might say, "When I lie, it really gives him glory, because my lie shows God's truth. So why am I judged a sinner?" 8It would be the same to say, "We should do evil so that good will come." Some people find fault with us and say we teach this, but they are wrong and deserve the punishment they will receive.

All People are Guilty

9So are we Jews better than others? No! We have already said that Jews and those who are not Jews are all guilty of sin. 10As the Scriptures[d] say:

"There is no one who always does what is
right,
not even one.
11 There is no one who understands.
There is no one who looks to God for help.
12All have turned away.
Together, everyone has become useless.
There is no one who does anything good;
there is not even one." *Psalm 14:1–3*
13"Their throats are like open graves;
they use their tongues for telling lies."
Psalm 5:9
"Their words are like snake poison." *Psalm 140:3*
14 "Their mouths are full of cursing and hate."
Psalm 10:7
15"They are always ready to kill people.
16 Everywhere they go they cause ruin and
misery.
17They don't know how to live in peace."
Isaiah 59:7–8
18 "They have no fear of God." *Psalm 36:1*

19We know that the law's commands are for those who have the law.[d] This stops all excuses and brings the whole world under God's judgement, 20because no one can be made right with God by following the law. The law only shows us our sin.

How God Makes People Right

21But God has a way to make people right with him without the law, and he has now shown us that way which the law and the prophets[d] told us about. 22God makes people right with himself through their faith in Jesus Christ. This is true for all who believe in Christ, because all people are the same: 23all have sinned and are not good enough for God's glory, 24and all need to be made right with God by his grace, which is a free gift. They need to be made free from sin through Jesus Christ. 25God gave him as a way to forgive sin through faith in the blood of Jesus' death. This showed that God always does what is right and fair, as in the past when he was patient and did not punish people for their sins. 26And God gave Jesus to show today that he does what is right. God did this so he could judge rightly and so he could make right any person who has faith in Jesus.

"Those . . . you." Quotation from Isaiah 52:5; Ezekiel 36:20.

27So do we have a reason to boast about our-
selves? No! And why not? It is the way of faith
that stops all boasting, not the way of trying to
obey the law. 28A person is made right with God
through faith, not through obeying the law. 29Is
God only the God of the Jews? Is he not also the
God of those who are not Jews? 30Of course he is,
because there is only one God. He will make Jews
right with him by their faith, and he will also
make those who are not Jews right with him
through their faith. 31So do we destroy the law by
following the way of faith? No! Faith causes us to
be what the law truly wants.

The Example of Abraham

4 So what can we say that Abraham,[n] the
father of our people, learned about faith? 2If
Abraham was made right by the things he did, he
had a reason to boast. But this is not God's view,
3because the Scripture[d] says, "Abraham believed
God, and God accepted Abraham's faith, and that
faith made him right with God."[n]
4When people work, their pay is not given as a
gift, but as something earned. 5But people cannot
do any work that will make them right with God.
So they must trust in him, who makes even evil
people right in his sight. Then God accepts their
faith, and that makes them right with him. 6David
said the same thing. He said that people are truly
blessed when God, without paying attention to
good deeds, makes people right with himself.
7"Happy are they
whose sins are forgiven,
whose wrongs are pardoned.

Abraham Most respected ancestor of the Jews. Every Jew hoped to see Abraham.
"Abraham . . . God." Quotation from Genesis 15:6.

FORGIVENESS

Only a Car

Uncle Charles let Dean borrow his new, red Mazda MX5 for the New Year Disco. It was less than two weeks old.

The magical night ended much too early for Dean, about 3 a.m., when he dropped off his partner at her house and started the long drive across town to home. The next thing he knew, he was waking up, skidding madly across the deserted suburban road, scraping the side of the car against a crash barrier before he could come to a stop.

He drove home, parked the car against the kerb, and sat on the front steps, waiting for morning to come. His stomach was in a knot. He didn't even try to sleep.

At 8 a.m., Dean stood next to his uncle as he silently examined the wide scar that now marred the door of his new car. Uncle Charles's breathing was slow and measured. The silence seemed to go on for ever.

How could Dean ever make this up to him? How could he pay for the damage or heal the hurt he saw in his face?

Finally, the older man placed his hand on Dean's shoulder and gave it a reassuring squeeze. He shrugged, smiled and said, "It's only a car."

At that moment, Dean knew something of the sort of forgiveness Paul was talking about when he wrote **Romans 3:21–28**.

- How is Uncle Charles's act of forgiveness like the forgiveness that Paul talks about in this passage?
- According to the passage, how do we receive God's forgiveness?

Consider . . .

- writing about a way someone has hurt you recently and then tearing up the paper and forgiving the hurt.
- talking to a friend you've hurt and asking for forgiveness.

For more, see . . .

- Psalm 103:10–13 (p.559)
- Hebrews 8:10–13 (p.1337)
- Luke 6:27–36 (1048)

8Happy is the person
whom the Lord does not consider guilty."
Psalm 32:1–2
9Is this blessing only for those who are circum-
cised[d] or also for those who are not circumcised?
We have already said that God accepted Abraham's
faith and that faith made him right with God. 10So
how did this happen? Did God accept Abraham
before or after he was circumcised? It was before
his circumcision. 11Abraham was circumcised to
show that he was right with God through faith before
he was circumcised. So Abraham is the father of all
those who believe but are not circumcised; he is
the father of all believers who are accepted as being
right with God. 12And Abraham is also the father of
those who have been circumcised and who live
following the faith that our father Abraham had
before he was circumcised.

God Keeps His Promise

13Abraham[n] and his descendants[d] received the
promise that they would get the whole world.

Abraham Most respected ancestor of the Jews. Every Jew hoped to see Abraham.

FAITH

Free Approval

Ed really liked Julie. In fact, he was totally crazy about her.

Julie was funny, clever, beautiful – everything Ed wanted in a girl. For weeks, Ed watched Julie as she went from office to office. He watched her while she ate lunch. He watched her as she walked home from work.

Finally, after weeks of planning, he worked up the courage to ask her out.

"Hello, Ed. What's up?" Julie asked with that smile Ed loved so much.

"Er, I was wondering . . ." he said, clearing his throat. "I was wondering if you'd like to go out on Friday night." Ed couldn't believe that his heart could pound so hard.

"Certainly, I'd love to," Julie responded without missing a beat.

That was the first of many evenings together. Julie really liked Ed. He was funny and sensitive. And, of course, Ed liked Julie, but he couldn't believe that she could be interested in him.

As they continued to go out together, Ed kept doing things for Julie to keep her interested. He bought her gifts. He offered to run errands for her. One day, he even offered her his car so that she wouldn't have to walk to work.

"Ed, I don't want your car," Julie said.

"It's OK, really," Ed assured her. "I want you to have it."

"No, Ed, you don't understand." Julie took a deep breath. "You don't need to try so hard. I already like you. You really don't need to do anything to win my love. So just relax, all right? You're starting to drive me mad."

Ed felt embarrassed. "It's just that it's hard to believe," he said.

"Well, believe it," Julie said, grinning, and she kissed him.

Ed had a difficult time believing that Julie could love him unless he did things to earn her affection.

Romans 4:1–12 tells a similar story about Abraham, who discovered that God's favour is also based on believing. Read the passage to see why we can't earn God's approval through our actions.

- How does Ed's response to Julie differ from Abraham's response to God?
- According to the passage, what does God require for you to have a relationship with him?

Consider . . .

- thinking of ways in which you might try to earn God's love and then asking God to help you to accept his love by faith.
- writing out how you think God sees you, and having your youth leader do the same. Compare the two descriptions, and ask God to increase your faith to believe the truth about how he sees you.

For more, see . . .

- Genesis 15:1–6 (p.16)
- Ephesians 2:8–9 (p.1270)
- Galatians 3:6–27 (p.1260)

He did not receive that promise through the law, [d]
but through being right with God by his faith.
14If people could receive what God promised
by following the law, then faith is worthless.
And God's promise to Abraham is worthless,
15because the law can only bring God's anger.
But if there is no law, there is nothing to disobey.
16So people receive God's promise by having
faith. This happens so the promise can be a free
gift. Then all of Abraham's children can have that
promise. It is not only for those who live under
the law of Moses but for anyone who lives with
faith like that of Abraham, who is the father of us
all. 17As it is written in the Scriptures: [d] "I am
making you a father of many nations." [n] This is
true before God, the God Abraham believed, the
God who gives life to the dead and who creates
something out of nothing.
18There was no hope that Abraham would
have children. But Abraham believed God and
continued hoping, and so he became the father of
many nations. As God told him, "Your descend-
ants also will be too many to count." [n] 19Abraham
was almost 100 years old, much past the age for
having children, and Sarah could not have chil-
dren. Abraham thought about all this, but his
faith in God did not become weak. 20He never
doubted that God would keep his promise, and
he never stopped believing. He grew stronger in
his faith and gave praise to God. 21Abraham felt
sure that God was able to do what he had prom-
ised. 22So, "God accepted Abraham's faith, and
that faith made him right with God." [n] 23Those
words ("God accepted Abraham's faith") were
written not only for Abraham 24but also for us.
God will accept us also because we believe in the
One who raised Jesus our Lord from the dead.
25Jesus was given to die for our sins, and he was
raised from the dead to make us right with God.

Right with God

5 Since we have been made right with God by
our faith, we have peace with God. This hap-
pened through our Lord Jesus Christ, 2who has
brought us into that blessing of God's grace that
we now enjoy. And we are happy because of the
hope we have of sharing God's glory. 3We also
have joy with our troubles, because we know
that these troubles produce patience. 4And pa-
tience produces character, and character pro-
duces hope. 5And this hope will never disappoint
us, because God has poured out his love to fill
our hearts. He gave us his love through the Holy
Spirit, [d] whom God has given to us.
6When we were unable to help ourselves, at
the moment of our need, Christ died for us, al-
though we were living against God. 7Very few
people will die to save the life of someone else
although perhaps for a good person someone
might possibly die. 8But God shows his great love
for us in this way: Christ died for us while we
were still sinners.
9So through Christ we will surely be saved
from God's anger, because we have been made
right with God by the blood of Christ's death.
10While we were God's enemies, he made friends
with us through the death of his Son. Surely,
now that we are his friends, he will save us
through his Son's life. 11And not only that, now
we are also very happy in God through our Lord
Jesus Christ. Through him we are now God's
friends again.

Adam and Christ Compared

12Sin came into the world because of what one
man did, and with sin came death. This is why
everyone must die—because everyone sinned.
13Sin was in the world before the law of Moses, [d]
but sin is not counted against us as breaking a
command when there is no law. 14But from the
time of Adam to the time of Moses, everyone
had to die, even those who had not sinned by
breaking a command, as Adam had.
Adam was like the One who was coming in
the future. 15But God's free gift is not like Adam's
sin. Many people died because of the sin of that
one man. But the grace from God was much
greater; many people received God's gift of life
by the grace of the one man, Jesus Christ. 16After
Adam sinned once, he was judged guilty. But the
gift of God is different. God's free gift came after
many sins, and it makes people right with God.
17One man sinned, and so death ruled all people
because of that one man. But now those people
who accept God's full grace and the great gift of
being made right with him will surely have true
life and rule through the one man, Jesus Christ.
18So as one sin of Adam brought the punish-
ment of death to all people, one good act that

Sidelight Adam – the man in the Garden of Eden (Genesis 1–4, p.2) – seems to get blamed for more than his share of sin in Romans 5:12–21. But don't feel too sorry for him. Paul uses Adam to represent all people. That's not surprising when you know that "adam" means "human".

"I . . . nations." Quotation from Genesis 17:5.
"Your . . . count." Quotation from Genesis 15:5.
"God . . . God." Quotation from Genesis 15:6.

Christ did makes all people right with God. And
that brings true life for all. 19One man disobeyed
God, and many became sinners. In the same way,
one man obeyed God, and many will be made
right. 20The law came to make sin worse. But
when sin grew worse, God's grace increased.
21Sin once used death to rule us, but God gave
people more of his grace so that grace could rule
by making people right with him. And this brings
life for ever through Jesus Christ our Lord.

Dead to Sin but Alive in Christ

6 So do you think we should continue sinning
so that God will give us even more grace?
2No! We died to our old sinful lives, so how can
we continue living with sin? 3Did you forget that
all of us became part of Christ when we were
baptised?[d] We shared his death in our baptism.
4When we were baptised, we were buried with
Christ and shared his death. So, just as Christ was
raised from the dead by the wonderful power of
the Father, we also can live a new life.
5Christ died, and we have been joined with
him by dying too. So we will also be joined with
him by rising from the dead as he did. 6We know
that our old life died with Christ on the cross so
that our sinful selves would have no power over
us and we would not be slaves to sin. 7Anyone
who has died is made free from sin's control.
8If we died with Christ, we know we will also
live with him. 9Christ was raised from the dead,
and we know that he cannot die again. Death has
no power over him now. 10Yes, when Christ died,
he died to defeat the power of sin just once—
enough for all time. He now has a new life, and
his new life is with God. 11In the same way, you
should see yourselves as being dead to the power
of sin and alive with God through Christ Jesus.
12So, do not let sin control your life here on
earth so that you do what your sinful self wants

FRIENDS

What Are Friends For?

Sometimes Liz got frustrated with her friends. It seemed as though she was always having to bail them out of something.

Take Christine for example. She was bottom in algebra. And Nancy had just broken up with her boyfriend and was depressed all the time. Linda was gaining weight like mad, and all she did was complain about it and go on eating.

As if that weren't enough, last week all three of these friends had gone to a party and had got drunk. Liz had to drive them home to make sure that they got home safely.

Sometimes it seemed as though Liz's friends were trying to cause her problems. It was all getting to be too much. Too much concern, too much pain.

Perhaps she should just find new friends. It would certainly make her life easier. But . . .

"Hello, Liz!" Christine said, setting her tray down beside Liz's at the cafeteria table. "This algebra is impossible. Can you help me?"

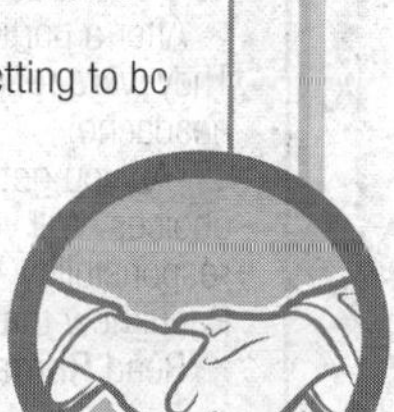

This was it. The true test. Was Liz strong enough? She gathered her courage, took a deep breath, paused and said, "Sure, Christine. What are friends for?" And she meant it.

Liz learned that friendship means commitment, even when friends disappoint you.

Romans 5:1–19 calls God our friend. Read the passage to discover how committed he is to us.

- How is Liz's friendship with her friends like God's friendship with us in Jesus Christ?
- How can you model your friendship with God in human friendships?

Consider . . .

- writing down the names of three friends and praying for them each day this week.
- writing a card, buying flowers or doing a favour for a friend, just to say "I'm committed to you".

For more, see . . .

- Job 2:11–13 (p.471)
- John 15:13–16 (p.1125)
- Proverbs 17:17 (p.604)

to do. 13Do not offer the parts of your body to
serve sin, as things to be used in doing evil. In-
stead, offer yourselves to God as people who have
died and now live. Offer the parts of your body to
God to be used in doing good. 14Sin will not be
your master, because you are not under law but
under God's grace.

Be Slaves of Righteousness

15So what should we do? Should we sin be-
cause we are under grace and not under law? No!
16Surely you know that when you give yourselves
like slaves to obey someone, then you are really
slaves of that person. The person you obey is your
master. You can follow sin, which brings spiritual
death, or you can obey God, which makes you
right with him. 17In the past you were slaves to
sin—sin controlled you. But thank God, you
fully obeyed the things that you were taught.
18You were made free from sin, and now you are
slaves to goodness. 19I use this example because
this is hard for you to understand. In the past you
offered the parts of your body to be slaves to sin
and evil; you lived only for evil. In the same way
now you must give yourselves to be slaves of
goodness. Then you will live only for God.
20In the past you were slaves to sin, and good-
ness did not control you. 21You did evil things,
and now you are ashamed of them. Those things
only bring death. 22But now you are free from sin

FREEDOM

With Freedom Comes Responsibility

It seemed like every time something good came along Paul's parents would tell him he couldn't do it, as he was "too young". He was too young to stay out late, too young to drink at parties, too young to have a girlfriend. But as Paul got older, his parents were running out of excuses to tell him what he could and couldn't do.

Opportunities were coming his way – parties every weekend where alcohol was on tap. If he dressed right, Paul found he could pass for eighteen and get into a nightclub. Some of his mates were driving now – they didn't have to leave early for parents to pick them up or even get the last bus home – they could stay out all night!

If he was honest, Paul knew that his parents didn't like the way he was living. And he also knew that people at his church would struggle with it too. But he'd decided to get the most out of life – he'd show his mates that being a Christian meant he could still do everything they did!

After a particularly heavy session, Paul was struggling to stay awake at his youth group. They were reading through Romans and his youth leader said something that got through his headache.

"As you get older you will get more freedom from your parents and you're going to face choices. Will you decide to push the boundaries God has given us? With freedom comes responsibility. Will you abuse the freedom you get or will you take responsibility for how you live?" Paul knew that he needed to decide.

Read **Romans 6:1–12**.

- What does this passage say about the freedom God has given us? What responsibilities do Christians have?
- What decision has Paul got to make?

Consider . . .

- writing the words "I AM FREE TO DO GOOD" right across the middle of a piece of paper. Around it write about the freedom that you're going to get as you get older – driving, drinking, staying out later, college, etc. With a different-coloured pen, write next to each freedom how you can use it for some good, e.g. drinking responsibly to set an example for your mates.
- making a promise with a friend to pray for each other that as you get older you'll take your responsibilities seriously and live life God's way.

For more, see . . .

- Proverbs 4:20–27 (p.593)
- Romans 12:2 (p.1204)

and have become slaves of God. This brings you
a life that is only for God, and this gives you life
for ever. 23 When people sin, they earn what sin
pays—death. But God gives us a free gift—life
for ever in Christ Jesus our Lord.

An Example from Marriage

7 Brothers and sisters, all of you understand
the law of Moses.[d] So surely you know that
the law rules over people only while they are
alive. 2 For example, a woman must stay married
to her husband as long as he is alive. But if her
husband dies, she is free from the law of mar-
riage. 3 But if she marries another man while her
husband is still alive, the law says she is guilty of
adultery.[d] But if her husband dies, she is free
from the law of marriage. Then if she marries
another man, she is not guilty of adultery.

4 In the same way, my brothers and sisters,
your old selves died, and you became free from
the law through the body of Christ. This hap-
pened so that you might belong to someone
else—the One who was raised from the dead—
and so that we might be used in service to God.
5 In the past, we were ruled by our sinful selves.
The law made us want to do sinful things that
controlled our bodies, so the things we did were
bringing us death. 6 In the past, the law held us
like prisoners, but our old selves died and we
were made free from the law. So now we serve
God in a new way with the Spirit,[d] and not in the
old way with written rules.

Our Fight Against Sin

7 You might think I am saying that sin and the
law[d] are the same thing. That is not true. But the
law was the only way I could learn what sin
meant. I would never have known what it means
to want to take something belonging to someone
else if the law had not said, "You must not want
to take your neighbour's things."[n] 8 And sin
found a way to use that command and cause me
to want all kinds of things I should not want. But
without the law, sin has no power. 9 I was alive
before I knew the law. But when the law's com-
mand came to me, then sin began to live, 10 and
I died. The command was meant to bring life,
but for me it brought death. 11 Sin found a way to
fool me by using the command to make me die.

12 So the law is holy, and the command is holy
and right and good. 13 Does this mean that some-
thing that is good brought death to me? No! Sin
used something that is good to bring death to me.
This happened so that I could see what sin is
really like; the command was used to show that
sin is very evil.

The War Within Us

14 We know that the law is spiritual, but I am
not spiritual since sin rules me as if I were its slave.
15 I do not understand the things I do. I do not do
what I want to do, and I do the things I hate.
16 And if I do not want to do the hated things I
do, that means I agree that the law is good. 17 But
I am not really the one who is doing these hated
things; it is sin living in me that does them. 18 Yes,
I know that nothing good lives in me—I mean
nothing good lives in the part of me that is earthly
and sinful. I want to do the things that are good,
but I do not do them. 19 I do not do the good things
I want to do, but I do the bad things I do not want
to do. 20 So if I do things I do not want to do, then
I am not the one doing them. It is sin living in
me that does those things.

21 So I have learned this rule: when I want to
do good, evil is there with me. 22 In my mind, I
am happy with God's law. 23 But I see another law
working in my body, which makes war against
the law that my mind accepts. That other law
working in my body is the law of sin, and it
makes me its prisoner. 24 What a miserable man I
am! Who will save me from this body that brings
me death? 25 I thank God for saving me through
Jesus Christ our Lord!

So in my mind I am a slave to God's law, but
in my sinful self I am a slave to the law of sin.

Be Ruled by the Spirit

8 So now, those who are in Christ Jesus are
not judged guilty. 2 Through Christ Jesus the
law of the Spirit[d] that brings life made me free
from the law that brings sin and death. 3 The law
was without power, because the law was made
weak by our sinful selves. But God did what the
law could not do. He sent his own Son to earth
with the same human life that others use for sin.
By sending his Son to be an offering to pay for
sin, God used a human life to destroy sin. 4 He did
this so that we could be the kind of people the
law correctly wants us to be. Now we do not live
following our sinful selves, but we live following
the Spirit.

5 Those who live following their sinful selves
think only about things that their sinful selves
want. But those who live following the Spirit are
thinking about the things the Spirit wants them
to do. 6 If people's thinking is controlled by the
sinful self, there is death. But if their thinking is
controlled by the Spirit, there is life and peace.
7 When people's thinking is controlled by the sin-
ful self, they are against God, because they refuse
to obey God's law and really are not even able to

"You . . . things." Quotation from Exodus 20:17.

obey God's law. 8Those people who are ruled by
their sinful selves cannot please God.
9But you are not ruled by your sinful selves.
You are ruled by the Spirit, if that Spirit of God
really lives in you. But the person who does not
have the Spirit of Christ does not belong to
Christ. 10Your body will always be dead because
of sin. But if Christ is in you, then the Spirit gives
you life, because Christ made you right with God.
11God raised Jesus from the dead, and if God's
Spirit is living in you, he will also give life to your
bodies that die. God is the One who raised Christ
from the dead, and he will give life through his
Spirit that lives in you.
12So, my brothers and sisters, we must not be
ruled by our sinful selves or live the way our
sinful selves want. 13If you use your lives to do
the wrong things your sinful selves want, you

DRUGS AND ALCOHOL

Not Alone . . .

Seven years, five months, three days. That's how long Sharon had been sober. Counting today. And she didn't mind talking about it to her fellow Alcoholics Anonymous members. It helped her to stick at recovering.

"I started drinking when I was still at school," she explained. "But I didn't start abusing it until I was in college. By the time I was out of education and starting a career, I was an alcoholic."

Sharon went on to tell how a marriage and the addition of two children didn't change her drinking habits much. "I managed to keep up with my responsibilities, both at home and at work," she said. "As long as I did that, I convinced myself that I had it under control."

But then things changed. A messy divorce. Trouble at work. And a daughter who almost died from rheumatic fever.

"I began to drink more often – for comfort, and sometimes, to forget. Eventually, events in my life began to blur together. I was never sober.

"And the worse I felt about myself the more I drank. Finally, I just wanted to die. So I tried to drink myself to death. Five days later I woke up in a hospital room attached to a load of machines. The doctors say that I didn't even know who I was. I lay there and cried. I couldn't eat. I couldn't sleep. I was a failure. I couldn't even kill myself properly." Sharon pulled a tissue from the box beside her. The session leader motioned her to continue.

"Then," she went on, "the hospital chaplain walked in, and there was this woman with him. They both just sat down. And the woman asked, 'Do you want to give up drinking?'"

Now Sharon's tears came in full flood. "I just cried like a baby. I wanted to give up, but I didn't know how! Then she said, 'You don't have to do it alone. You've got me and the chaplain here and a whole flock of people willing to help. And you've got God, too, love. Don't forget about God'."

Sharon blew her nose on a tissue and looked around at the faces of her friends. "For the first time I realised that I wasn't alone. And I haven't had a drink since that day – all because you, and God, are keeping me sober."

Sharon learned that she wasn't alone in her struggle. And God made a difference in her life. The apostle Paul made a similar discovery. Read about it in **Romans 7:14–25**.

- How is Sharon's addiction like the "battle" that Paul describes?
- In what ways does God show that he is with you when you're pressured to use alcohol or drugs?

Consider . . .

- encouraging a friend who is dealing with issues like Sharon's to seek skilled help.
- finding an appropriate support group in your community if you struggle with a drinking or drug problem. Your minister or a church leader can help you.

For more, see . . .

- Proverbs 23:29–32 (p.610)
- Luke 21:34–36 (p.1087)
- Isaiah 5:11–12 (p.644)

will die spiritually. But if you use the Spirit's help to stop doing the wrong things you do with your body, you will have true life.

[14]The true children of God are those who let God's Spirit lead them. [15]The Spirit we received does not make us slaves again to fear: it makes us children of God. With that Spirit we cry out, "Father".[n] [16]And the Spirit himself joins with our spirits to say we are God's children. [17]If we are God's children, we will receive blessings from God together with Christ. But we must suffer as Christ suffered so that we will have glory as Christ has glory.

Our Future Glory

[18]The sufferings we have now are nothing compared to the great glory that will be shown to us. [19]Everything God made is waiting with excitement for God to show his children's glory completely. [20]Everything God made was changed to become useless, not by its own wish but because God wanted it and because all along there was this hope: [21]that everything God made would be set free from ruin to have the freedom and glory that belong to God's children.

[22]We know that everything God made has been waiting until now in pain, like a woman

"Father" Literally, "Abba, Father". Jewish children called their fathers "Abba".

SPIRITUAL GROWTH

Power to Change

Rick was a young guy who had always been self-centred and rude. Many people found him hard to get on with and even a little scary. He hung around with friends who encouraged him to be a bully and together they would torment the other pupils at their school. He even terrified members of his own family, who walked on eggshells to keep the peace.

One day his parents sent him on a Christian camp. He was furious at having to go and threatened to leave home and never come back again. But despite all the threats, he went to the camp, as they wanted. At least, he thought, he didn't have to be with his family for a whole week . . . and who knows what trouble he could get himself into without them around!

Whilst Rick was at the camp, he was surprised to meet people who loved Jesus but were still funny, cool and interesting. One night, he went to one of the meetings and a huge transformation occurred. He gave his life to God. Rick instantly felt different on the inside – all the hate and anger he'd felt for so long suddenly weren't there!

When he came home, his family couldn't believe the immediate change in him. They could even see that something was different about him before he'd got down the garden path! At school he was sometimes tempted to fall back into old habits and behave in ways he knew were wrong. But he could feel something had altered inside and he knew that everything that was happening in him was good.

Read **Romans 8:6–17**. The passage explains how – just like Rick – when we become Christians, some amazing changes can take place in our lives.

- According to the passage, what changes take place in us when we become Christians?
- Can you tell when other people have the Spirit of God "living" in them (verse 11) as people could with Rick?

Consider . . .

- what changes you have noticed in yourself or in other people since you or they became Christians.
- what areas of your life still need the Holy Spirit's work. If you don't already pray regularly with someone, ask someone to be a prayer partner with you so you can help each other be changed by God's power.

For more, see . . .

- Psalm 1:1–3 (p.500)
- Hebrews 12:1–13 (p.1343)
- Colossians 3:1–10 (p.1292)

ready to give birth. 23Not only the world, but we
also have been waiting with pain inside us. We
have the Spirit[d] as the first part of God's promise.
So we are waiting for God to finish making us his
own children, which means our bodies will be
made free. 24We were saved, and we have this
hope. If we see what we are waiting for, that is
not really hope. People do not hope for something they already have. 25But we are hoping for
something we do not have yet, and we are waiting for it patiently.
26Also, the Spirit helps us with our weakness.
We do not know how to pray as we should. But
the Spirit himself speaks to God for us, even begs
God for us with deep feelings that words cannot
explain. 27God can see what is in people's hearts.
And he knows what is in the mind of the Spirit,
because the Spirit speaks to God for his people in
the way God wants.
28We know that in everything God works for
the good of those who love him. They are the
people he called, because that was his plan.
29God knew them before he made the world,
and he decided that they would be like his
Son so that Jesus would be the firstborn[n] of
many brothers. 30God planned for them to be like

firstborn Here this probably means that Christ was the first in God's family to share God's glory.

PATIENCE

Looking Back

Patrick had been a Christian for about six months before the problems started.

What problems? "Well, I lost my job," Patrick recalls. "Then the transmission on my car packed up, and I had no money to repair it. But that wasn't the real problem. My girlfriend broke up with me. I really wanted to marry this girl, but she said that I wasn't what she wanted in a husband. That really hurt."

Before he had become a Christian at the age of eighteen, Patrick had lived a wild lifestyle, filled with drinking and taking drugs and sleeping with girlfriends.

"I came to Christ to get away from all that," he recalls. "But when all these problems started, I began to feel really insecure. It was all I could do not to go out and get drunk or call up one of my old girlfriends. I felt gross inside. I began to wonder whether I was really a Christian."

But Patrick didn't go back to his old lifestyle. Even though he didn't understand why all these things were happening to him, he knew that God was in control. So he waited.

"Things didn't get better right away," Patrick says, "but I knew I had made the right decision. And that helped me to believe even more that, if I was patient, God would come through for me. And he did!"

Patrick and his girlfriend got back together, and he got a new job – better than the other one. Now Patrick knows the value of obeying God even when you don't know what God is doing.

Patrick learned that becoming like Christ takes patience. Paul talked about how all creation is waiting patiently for us to become like Christ. Read why in **Romans 8:22–30**.

- How does Patrick demonstrate the patience that the passage describes?
- According to the passage, what is God's ultimate purpose for you? Why do we need patience to wait for his purpose to be fulfilled?

Consider . . .

- dreaming about the kind of person you want to be ten years from now, then asking God to give you the patience to let him make you into the person he wants you to be.
- working on a project that takes a long time to finish, such as a quilt or a model ship. Use the experience to learn more about patience.

For more, see . . .

- Lamentations 3:25–26 (p.783)
- James 5:7–11 (p.1352)
- Hebrews 11:8–16 (p.1342)

his Son; and those he planned to be like his Son,
he also called; and those he called, he also made
right with him; and those he made right, he also
glorified.

God's Love in Christ Jesus

31So what should we say about this? If God is
with us, no one can defeat us. 32He did not spare
his own Son but gave him for us all. So with
Jesus, God will surely give us all things. 33Who
can accuse the people God has chosen? No one,
because God is the One who makes them right.
34Who can say God's people are guilty? No one,
because Christ Jesus died, but he was also raised
from the dead, and now he is on God's right side,
begging God for us. 35Can anything separate us
from the love Christ has for us? Can troubles or
problems or sufferings or hunger or nakedness or
danger or violent death? 36As it is written in the
Scriptures:[d]

"For you we are in danger of death all the
time.
People think we are worth no more than
sheep to be killed." *Psalm 44:22*

37But in all these things we have full victory
through God who showed his love for us. 38Yes,
I am sure that neither death, nor life, nor angels,
nor ruling spirits, nothing now, nothing in the
future, nor powers, 39nothing above us, nothing
below us, nor anything else in the whole world
will ever be able to separate us from the love of
God that is in Christ Jesus our Lord.

LOVE

You Can't Break the Unbreakable

Gary had listened to his parents arguing for many months. He knew they were going through a tough patch, and he'd even heard the "D" word mentioned. But surely not – *his* parents wouldn't end their marriage, would they?

When Gary's parents divorced in 2004, they were one of 167,116 divorces granted in the UK. That's 334,232 individuals choosing to break off a relationship they had been committed to. How many children and family members would have been affected by those broken relationships too?

We're not used to relationships that are completely permanent. Thousands of people promise to stay with each other forever but marriages frequently break up, and even the strongest friendships sometimes fade away. Pop group members who seem inseparable often try their luck with a solo career.

It's very easy for us to think of our relationship with God in the same way. At times, we may feel really close to him, but during tough times we may feel that the relationship is breaking. Sometimes, when people attack us for our belief and trust in God, we can feel threatened and distanced from God, as if our relationship has become fragile and could break any minute.

But we need to think of our relationship with God as being like concrete. Once you mix sand, water and cement powder together to make concrete, there's no way of getting it back to its component parts. Not your bare hands, a hammer, nor even a pneumatic drill will be able to break concrete up and turn it back into sand, water and cement. When we become Christians there's *nothing* that can separate us from God! **Romans 8:31–39** explains how we should trust that our relationship with God is unbreakable.

- Is there anything that can separate us from the love of God?
- What role does Jesus play in our unbreakable relationship with God?

Consider . . .

- writing out this passage and putting it up on your bedroom wall as a reminder that even when you *feel* distant from God, you'll never be separated from him.
- telling God that you intend to stick with him through all circumstances.

For more, see . . .

- Matthew 6:25–34 (p.948)
- Ephesians 6:10–18 (p.1277)
- Ephesians 2:1–10 (p.1270)

God and the Jewish People

9 I am in Christ, and I am telling you the truth;
I do not lie. My feelings are ruled by the
Holy Spirit,[d] and they tell me I am not lying. 2I
have great sorrow and always feel much sadness.
3I wish I could help my Jewish brothers and
sisters, my people. I would even wish that I were
cursed and cut off from Christ if that would help
them. 4They are the people of Israel, God's
chosen children. They have seen the glory of
God, and they have the agreements that God
made between himself and his people. God gave
them the law of Moses[d] and the right way of
worship and his promises. 5They are the descen-
dants[d] of our great ancestors, and they are the
earthly family into which Christ was born, who
is God over all. Praise him for ever![n] Amen.
6It is not that God failed to keep his promise
to them. But only some of the people of Israel
are truly God's people,[n] 7and only some of
Abraham's[n] descendants are true children of
Abraham. But God said to Abraham: "The
descendants I promised you will be from Isaac."[n]
8This means that not all of Abraham's descen-
dants are God's true children. Abraham's true
children are those who become God's children
because of the promise God made to Abraham.
9God's promise to Abraham was this: "At the
right time I will return, and Sarah will have a
son."[n] 10And that is not all. Rebekah's sons had

born . . . for ever! This can also mean, "born. May God, who rules over all things, be praised for ever!"
God's people Literally, "Israel", the people God chose to bring his blessings to the world.
Abraham Most respected ancestor of the Jews. Every Jew hoped to see Abraham.
"The descendants . . . Isaac." Quotation from Genesis 21:12.
"At . . . son." Quotation from Genesis 18:10,14.

GOD'S GRACE

Undeserving

There were only 14 places on the trip and everyone wanted to go. The school football team had been invited to go on a two-week tour to play other school teams in France and Germany.

The day came to announce the squad and there was no surprise when Tom Bannister's name was read out first. He was the Captain and everyone knew that he was bound to be chosen. One by one the names were read out and, to be honest, the list was as everyone had expected.

Eventually the coach came to read out the 14th member of the squad. There were three possibilities for this final place and everyone waited in eager anticipation to see which one of three were in. But something then happened that shocked the listening crowd that had gathered. A complete outsider, Will Arnold, got the place.

Will Arnold! Nobody could believe it. Why him? He didn't deserve a place in the squad. He had never played for the first team and he hadn't even turned up to one of the trials. There was uproar and disbelief as the coach stood by his decision and said it was *his* choice and his choice was Will Arnold.

The story sounds hard to believe. But in **Romans 9:10–16** we have a similar situation.

The passage talks about the fact that God chose Jacob because "he was the one God wanted to call, not because of anything he did" (verse 12). It goes on to say that God chooses who he wants to choose and it is not based on what we want or try to do. This is grace!

- Do you still think that you need to do things in order to earn God's approval?
- God chose Jacob because Jacob was the one that he wanted to call. What might God be calling you to?

Consider . . .

- how God includes us even though we don't deserve it. How might this affect how you include other people and give them a second chance?
- starting each day by thanking God that he has shown kindness to you even though you don't deserve it.

For more, see . . .

- Jeremiah 1:4–10 (p.716)
- 1 Timothy 1:12–14 (p.1308)
- 1 Corinthians 1:26–31 (p.1215)

Sidelight Some Jewish Christians argued about what was required to be a Christian (Romans 9:1–33). They wanted the non-Jewish Christians to follow a whole list of rules. If they had won, every male would have been circumcised on becoming a Christian (see Galatians 5, p.1263).

the same father, our father Isaac. 11–12But before
the two boys were born, God told Rebekah, "The
older will serve the younger."[n] This was before
the boys had done anything good or bad. God
said this so that the one chosen would be chosen
because of God's own plan. He was chosen be-
cause he was the one God wanted to call, not be-
cause of anything he did. 13As the Scripture[d]
says, "I loved Jacob, but I hated Esau."[n]
14So what should we say about this? Is God un-
fair? In no way. 15God said to Moses, "I will show
kindness to anyone to whom I want to show kind-
ness, and I will show mercy to anyone to whom I
want to show mercy."[n] 16So God will choose the
one to whom he decides to show mercy; his
choice does not depend on what people want or
try to do. 17The Scripture says to the king of Egypt:
"I made you king for this reason: to show my
power in you so that my name will be talked
about in all the earth."[n] 18So God shows mercy
where he wants to show mercy, and he makes
stubborn the people he wants to make stubborn.
19So one of you will ask me: "Then why does
God blame us for our sins? Who can fight his
will?" 20You are only human, and human beings
have no right to question God. An object should
not ask the person who made it, "Why did you
make me like this?" 21The potter can make any-
thing he wants to make. He can use the same clay
to make one thing for special use and another
thing for daily use.
22It is the same way with God. He wanted to
show his anger and to let people see his power.
But he patiently stayed with those people he was
angry with—people who were due to be des-
troyed. 23He waited with patience so that he
could make known his rich glory to the people
who receive his mercy. He has prepared these
people to have his glory, 24and we are those
people whom God called. He called us not from
the Jews only but also from those who are not
Jews. 25As the Scripture says in Hosea:

"I will say, 'You are my people'
to those I had called 'not my people'.
And I will show my love
to those people I did not love." *Hosea 2:1, 23*
26"They were called,
'You are not my people',
but later they will be called
'children of the living God'." *Hosea 1:10*

27And Isaiah cries out about Israel:

"Israel, your people are many,
like the grains of sand by the sea.
But only a few of them will be left alive to
return to the LORD.
28 God has announced that he will destroy the
land completely and fairly." *Isaiah 10:22*

29It is as Isaiah said:

"The Lord All-powerful
allowed a few of our people to live.
Otherwise we would have been completely
destroyed
like the cities of Sodom[d] and Gomorrah."[d] *Isaiah 1:9*

30So what does all this mean? Those who are
not Jews were not trying to make themselves
right with God, but they were made right with
God because of their faith. 31The people of Israel
tried to follow a law to make themselves right with
God. But they did not succeed, 32because they tried
to make themselves right by the things they did
instead of trusting in God to make them right.
They stumbled over the stone that causes people
to stumble. 33As it is written in the Scripture:

"I will put in Jerusalem a stone that causes
people to stumble,
a rock that makes them fall.
Anyone who trusts in it will never be
disappointed." *Isaiah 8:14; 28:16*

10 Brothers and sisters, the thing I want
most is for all the Jews to be saved. That
is my prayer to God. 2I can say this about them:
they really try to follow God, but they do not
know the right way. 3Because they did not know
the way that God makes people right with him,
they tried to make themselves right in their
own way. So they did not accept God's way of
making people right. 4Christ ended the law[d] so
that everyone who believes in him may be right
with God.
5Moses describes how to be made right by fol-
lowing the law. He says, "A person who obeys
these things will live because of them."[n] 6But this
is what the Scripture says about being made
right through faith: "Don't say to yourself, 'Who
will go up into heaven?' " (That means, "Who

"The older . . . younger." Quotation from Genesis 25:23.
"I . . . Esau." Quotation from Malachi 1:2–3.
"I . . . mercy." Quotation from Exodus 33:19.
"I . . . earth." Quotation from Exodus 9:16.
"A person . . . them." Quotation from Leviticus 18:5.

will go up to heaven and bring Christ down to
earth?”) 7“And do not say, ‘Who will go down
into the world below?’ ” (That means, “Who will
go down and bring Christ up from the dead?”)
8This is what the Scripture says: “The word is
near you; it is in your mouth and in your heart.” [n]
That is the teaching of faith that we are telling.
9If you use your mouth to say, “Jesus is Lord,” and
if you believe in your heart that God raised Jesus
from the dead, you will be saved. 10We believe
with our hearts, and so we are made right with God.
And we use our mouths to say that we believe and
so we are saved. 11As the Scripture says, “Anyone
who trusts in him will never be disappointed.” [n]
12That Scripture says “anyone” because there
is no difference between those who are Jews
and those who are not. The same Lord is the
Lord of all and gives many blessings to all who
trust in him, 13as the Scripture says, “Anyone
who calls on the Lord will be saved.” [n]
14But before people can ask the Lord for help,
they must believe in him; and before they can
believe in him, they must hear about him; and
for them to hear about the Lord, someone must
tell them; 15and before someone can go and tell
them, that person must be sent. It is written,
“How beautiful is the person who comes to
bring good news.” [n]

Verses 6–8 Quotations from Deuteronomy 30:12–14.
“Anyone . . . disappointed.” Quotation from Isaiah 28:16.
“Anyone . . . saved.” Quotation from Joel 2:32.
“How . . . news.” Quotation from Isaiah 52:7.

SHARING FAITH

You Don’t Say

Every Monday at school, Olivia’s best friend Hannah would ask her about her weekend.

“Um, just saw some friends, spent some time with the family,” she’d reply, even though she had been at youth group, heard about some amazing miracles, prayed, worshipped and then had a fantastic time at a church picnic which had felt like a big family party.

Hannah felt sorry for Olivia. She knew she went to church at weekends, but Olivia never seemed to have anything very exciting happen in her life. Week after week, the pattern was the same. Olivia felt as if she came alive during her “God time” at the weekends, and yet the best thing in her life was the hardest thing in her life to share with her friend.

Hannah started to feel that Olivia was losing interest in their friendship. Hannah didn’t keep any secrets from her mates, but she felt that Olivia was keeping a lot back from her. One Monday Hannah confronted Olivia.

“Liv, I was really fed up this weekend and texted you to see if we could meet up. You didn’t get back to me, and then I saw you with a gang of other guys having a great time playing rounders in the park . . . but you’d said you didn’t have anything much planned for the weekend.” Tears welled up in Hannah’s eyes.

Olivia didn’t know what to say. She had been afraid to share the biggest and best part of her life with a friend who really cared about her.

Read **Romans 10:8–18** which explains the importance of telling others of your faith in Christ, and not assuming that they won’t want to know.

- Why was Olivia so afraid of sharing her faith, and were her fears justified?
- In the Bible passage, why are you told to tell others about your faith in Jesus?

Consider . . .

- how you would explain to someone what being a Christian means. Try writing your response down.
- praying for someone you know who doesn’t know the good news of Jesus. Ask God for wisdom to know how to share your faith with them.

For more, see . . .

- Matthew 5:13–16 (p.942)
- Acts 2 (p.1138)
- Matthew 10:32–33 (p.957)

16But not all the Jews accepted the good
news. As Isaiah said, "LORD, who believed what
we told them?" [n] 17So faith comes from hearing
the Good News, [d] and people hear the Good News
when someone tells them about Christ.
18But I ask: Didn't people hear the Good News?
Yes, they heard—as the Scripture says:

"Their message went out through all the
world;
their words go everywhere on earth."
Psalm 19:4

19Again I ask: Didn't the people of Israel
understand? Yes, they did understand. First,
Moses says:

"So I will use those who are not a nation to
make them jealous;
I will use a nation that does not understand
to make them angry." *Deuteronomy 32:21*

20Then Isaiah is bold enough to say:

"I was found by those who were not asking
me for help.
I said, 'Here I am. Here I am,' to a nation
that was not praying to me." *Isaiah 65:1*

"Lord, . . . them?" Quotation from Isaiah 53:1.

GOD'S GRACE

Pockets of People

Everywhere they looked, it seemed to Paul and Katie that people were building empires. The Christians they knew were all part of some organisation, and even their church had a sister building.

"How come we're not part of someone's set up?" asked Paul one day.

"I don't really know," said Katie. "It's never felt right has it? We've always been here by ourselves."

They had a ministry with young people and it was growing, but every time someone asked them to join their organisation, they felt that God was saying "No".

"It's just the opposite to what everyone else is doing . . . can it be right?" they kept asking themselves. But the more offers they had, the more they felt adamant about turning them down. Even a chance to become pastors in a massive youth church in America didn't sway them.

After one particularly enticing offer, they decided to go and talk the situation over with a well-respected national leader.

"Do you think we should come and join you?" they asked him, knowing that he would like the idea.

"No," came the bold reply.

Paul and Katie were quite shocked. They expected to be ushered into the Christian Ministry team with open arms.

"Why ever not?" they asked in unison.

"Because," replied the leader, "I firmly believe that God has pockets of people all over the world, and he wants them on their own, in that place. You are two of those people."

The couple were so pleased with his honest reply. It would have been so easy for him to use them, and yet he saw God's grace at work in them and realised it was a "no-go" area.

The leader knew that God had chosen Paul and Katie. Read **Romans 11:1–6** to see how God sets people aside by his grace.

- How important was the couple's own ability according to this passage?
- According to this passage, how important is it to prepare yourself should God choose you?

Consider . . .

- where you place your trust. Is it in your own abilities or in God's strength?
- listing a few Christians in places of influence (politicians, musicians . . .). Pray regularly that God will give them grace and strength to make a stand for Christian values.

For more, see . . .

- Romans 5:15 (p.1190)
- Titus 3:5–7 (p.1324)
- Romans 9:10–16 (p.1198)

21But about Israel God says,
"All day long I stood ready to accept
people who turned against me." *Isaiah 65:2*

God Shows Mercy to All People

11 So I ask: Did God throw out his people?
No! I myself am an Israelite from the
family of Abraham, from the tribe[d] of Benjamin.
2God chose the Israelites to be his people before
they were born, and he has not thrown his people
out. Surely you know what the Scripture[d] says
about Elijah, how he prayed to God against the
people of Israel. 3"Lord," he said, "they have
killed your prophets,[d] and they have destroyed
your altars. I am the only prophet left, and now
they are trying to kill me too."[n] 4But what an-
swer did God give Elijah? He said, "But I have left
7,000 people in Israel who have never bowed
down before Baal."[n] 5It is the same now. There
are a few people that God has chosen by his
grace. 6And if he chose them by grace, it is not for
the things they have done. If they could be made
God's people by what they did, God's gift of grace
would not really be a gift.
7So this is what has happened: although the
Israelites tried to be right with God, they did not
succeed, but the ones God chose did become right
with him. The others were made stubborn and
refused to listen to God. 8As it is written in the
Scriptures:
"God gave the people a dull mind so they
could not understand." *Isaiah 29:10*
"But to this day the LORD has not given you a
mind that understands;
you don't really understand what you see
with your eyes or hear with your ears."
Deuteronomy 29:4
9And David says:
"Let their own feasts trap them and cause
their ruin;
let their feasts cause them to stumble and
be paid back.
10Let their eyes be closed so they cannot see
and their backs be for ever weak from
troubles." *Psalm 69:22–23*
11So I ask: when the Jews fell, did that fall
destroy them? No! But their mistake brought
salvation to those who are not Jews, in order to
make the Jews jealous. 12The Jews' mistake
brought rich blessings for the world, and the
Jews' loss brought rich blessings for the non-
Jewish people. So surely the world will receive
much richer blessings when enough Jews
become the kind of people God wants.
13Now I am speaking to you who are not Jews.
I am an apostle[d] to those who are not Jews, and
since I have that work, I will make the most of it.
14I hope I can make my own people jealous and,
in that way, help some of them to be saved.
15When God turned away from the Jews, he be-
came friends with other people in the world. So
when God accepts the Jews, surely that will
bring them life after death.
16If the first piece of bread is offered to God,
then the whole loaf is made holy. If the roots
of a tree are holy, then the tree's branches are
holy too.
17It is as if some of the branches from an olive
tree have been broken off. You non-Jewish peo-
ple are like the branch of a wild olive tree that
has been joined to that first tree. You now share
the strength and life of the first tree, the Jews.
18So do not boast about those branches that were
broken off. If you boast, remember that you do
not support the root, but the root supports you.
19You will say, "Branches were broken off so that
I could be joined to their tree." 20That is true.
But those branches were broken off because they
did not believe, and you continue to be part of
the tree only because you believe. Do not be
proud, but be afraid. 21If God did not let the
natural branches of that tree stay, then he will
not let you stay if you don't believe.
22So you see that God is kind and also very
strict. He punishes those who stop following
him. But God is kind to you, if you continue fol-
lowing in his kindness. If you do not, you will be
cut off from the tree. 23And if the Jews will
believe in God again, he will accept them back.
God is able to put them back where they were.
24It is not natural for a wild branch to be part
of a good tree. And you who are not Jews are like
a branch cut from a wild olive tree and joined
to a good olive tree. But since those Jews are like
a branch that grew from the good tree, surely
they can be joined to their own tree again.
25I want you to understand this secret, brothers
and sisters, so you will understand that you do not
know everything: part of Israel has been made
stubborn, but that will change when many who are
not Jews have come to God. 26And that is how all
Israel will be saved. It is written in the Scriptures:
"Then a Saviour will come to Jerusalem
and to the people of Jacob[n] who have
turned from sin.
27This is how Israel's guilt will be forgiven;
this is how its sins will be taken away."
Isaiah 59:20–21; 27:9
28The Jews refuse to accept the Good News,[d]
so they are God's enemies. This has happened
to help you who are not Jews. But the Jews are

"Lord . . . too." Quotation from 1 Kings 19:10,14.
"But . . . Baal." Quotation from 1 Kings 19:18.
Jacob Father of the twelve family groups of Israel, the people God chose to be his own.

still God's chosen people, and he loves them
very much because of the promises he made to
their ancestors. 29God never changes his mind
about the people he calls and the things he gives
them. 30At one time you refused to obey God.
But now you have received mercy, because those
people refused to obey. 31And now the Jews
refuse to obey, because God showed mercy to
you. But this happened so that they also can
receive mercy from him. 32God has given all
people over to their stubborn ways so that he can
show mercy to all.

Praise to God

33Yes, God's riches are very great, and his
wisdom and knowledge have no end! No one
can explain the things God decides or under-
stand his ways. 34As the Scripture[d] says,

"Who has known the mind of the Lord
or been able to give him
advice?" *Isaiah 40:13*
35"No one has ever given God anything
that he must pay back." *Job 41:11*
36Yes, God made all things, and everything
continues through him and for him. To him be
the glory for ever! Amen.

Give Your Lives to God

12 So brothers and sisters, since God has
shown us great mercy, I beg you to offer
your lives as a living sacrifice to him. Your
offering must be only for God and pleasing to
him, which is the spiritual way for you to
worship. 2Do not change yourselves to be like
the people of this world, but be changed within
by a new way of thinking. Then you will be able

GOD'S LOVE

Free Gifts

James volunteered to help in an inner-city community shop, where he sorted used clothing and helped people to pick out things they needed for free.

One Friday, while James was walking to the bus stop near the shop, he passed a market stall. He recognised one of the kids as the child of a woman who often came to the free shop. After a few moments of talking to the child, he began to recognise more than just the little boy.

There, piled on the old card tables, were stacks of blue jeans, sweatshirts, socks, shoes and mittens that James had seen earlier that week at the free shop. He was outraged! These people didn't take the clothing from the shop because they needed it. They took it so that they could sell it! What a rip-off!

"It just doesn't seem right," James complained to Jim, the shop manager. "We gave them those clothes so that they'd have something to wear, not so that they could sell them."

"Well, it seems they needed the clothes either way," responded Jim. "They needed the clothes to sell for cash so that they could buy other things. Besides, we help these people because we care about them, not because they always respond the way we want them to."

"It sounds risky," James said.

"Love always is," answered Jim.

Jim helped James to see that their love wasn't something people should have to earn. God's love is like that too. Read **Romans 11:29–36** to find a description of God's merciful gift of love for us.

- How is the free shop like God's love for us?
- What would happen to your relationship with God if his love depended on your doing what he wanted?

Consider . . .

- writing down five reasons why God's love can never be taken away from you. Read Romans 8:31–39 (p.1197) for a few hints.
- giving a pound to someone you meet who is in need – without knowing how that person will use the money.

For more, see . . .

- Psalm 103:6–14 (p.559)
- 1 John 4:7–12 (p.1374)
- Ephesians 2:4–7 (p.1270)

to decide what God wants for you; you will
know what is good and pleasing to him and
what is perfect. 3Because God has given me a
special gift, I have something to say to everyone
among you. Do not think you are better than
you are. You must decide what you really are by
the amount of faith God has given you. 4Each
one of us has a body with many parts, and these
parts all have different uses. 5In the same way,
we are many, but in Christ we are all one body.
Each one is a part of that body, and each part
belongs to all the other parts. 6We all have
different gifts, each of which came because of
the grace God gave us. The person who has the
gift of prophecy[d] should use that gift in agree-
ment with the faith. 7Anyone who has the gift
of serving should serve. Anyone who has the
gift of teaching should teach. 8Whoever has the
gift of encouraging others should encourage.
Whoever has the gift of giving to others should
give freely. Anyone who has the gift of being a
leader should try hard when he leads. Whoever
has the gift of showing mercy to others should
do so with joy.

FOLLOWING GOD

Bouncing Betties

The Bouncing Betty was the worst sort of land mine in the Vietnam War. It was loaded with a spring so that when you stepped on it, it flew into the air, about waist high, and then exploded. It was designed to blow people apart and to strike terror into the hearts of young soldiers.

The plan worked on Craig.

He was on patrol one day with five other soldiers and a Vietnamese man who was supposed to be their guide. They had been out for about three hours, walking quietly through the bush, just looking and listening and trying not to get shot.

Then they came to a clearing, perhaps thirty metres across. The situation had "Bouncing Betty" written all over it. And Craig just knew that snipers were hiding in the jungle on the other side, waiting for him and his buddies to step into that clearing. But the bush was too thick to go around the clearing, so they had no choice but to go through.

The Vietnamese guide signalled for quiet and pointed to his feet, then spread his fingers on both hands. "Stay quiet," he whispered. "Follow me. Put your feet where I put mine. Stay ten metres behind the man in front of you."

Craig had never been so scared in his life. The guide went ten metres out into the clearing and then motioned for Craig to follow. Slowly now, despite his fears, he managed to keep putting his feet in the impressions left by the guide. He kept his head down, waiting for a sniper's bullet.

And then it was over. He took a deep breath and realised that he had made it across. Shaking violently, he looked up and saw the Vietnamese guide smiling at him. It was nice to have someone in whose steps you could walk.

Craig learned that to get through rough times he had to deny his own desires and follow someone he could trust, someone who knew the way. **Romans 12:1–16** talks about God as the one who knows the way for our lives. Read the passage to see how we can walk in his steps.

- How is the way that Craig followed the guide similar to the way that you follow God?
- According to the passage, why should you follow God (see verses 1–2)?

Consider . . .

- asking your youth leader to read Romans 12:6–8. Ask the leader to tell you which gifts he thinks you have. Then ask God to give you more opportunities to use your gifts.
- writing down how your life would change if you walked each day in Christ's steps by following his instructions in this passage.

For more, see . . .

- Psalm 119:9–16 (p.571)
- Luke 14:25–33 (p.1070)
- Luke 9:23–26 (p.1054)

9Your love must be real. Hate what is evil,
and hold on to what is good. 10Love each other
like brothers and sisters. Give each other more
honour than you want for yourselves. 11Do not
be lazy but work hard, serving the Lord with
all your heart. 12Be joyful because you have hope.
Be patient when trouble comes, and pray at all
times. 13Share with God's people who need help.
Bring strangers in need into your homes.

14Wish good for those who harm you; wish
them well and do not curse them. 15Be happy
with those who are happy, and be sad with those
who are sad. 16Live in peace with each other.
Do not be proud, but make friends with those
who seem unimportant. Do not think how
clever you are.

17If someone does wrong to you, do not pay
him back by doing wrong to him. Try to do what

GOVERNMENT

An Inch is as Good as a Mile

Daniel used to write a column for his school newspaper. It wasn't a big column, but it was fun. He wrote humorously about school food, class workload, or the latest bungle of the notoriously bad football team. He had been given the job because his best friend, Sam, was the editor. And much to their surprise, the column had become one of the paper's most popular features, even among kids who attended other schools.

One Monday on the way to class, Daniel saw a student in a wheelchair and an older woman trying – unsuccessfully – to push the wheelchair over the kerb.

When Daniel stopped to help, he noticed a wheelchair ramp cut into the kerb just a few yards away. But the yellow paint that marked it off had faded, and someone had parked in front of it.

"Unbelievable," Daniel said, shaking his head.

"Believe it," said the student in the wheelchair, whose name was Bruce. "It happens all the time. That's why my mum has to come with me. More than half the ramps haven't been painted for five years. People just ignore them."

Daniel smelled a story. He agreed to meet Bruce and his mum the next day. They would bring their extra wheelchair, and Daniel would spend the day trying to get around school in it.

That's how Daniel discovered that the main lift stopped two inches below the floor level (as good as two miles when you're in a wheelchair). He had trouble negotiating the super-narrow doors in the music room. And he discovered high water fountains everywhere and over a hundred obstacles all over the school. And that was in just six hours!

The next day, Daniel wrote about his experiences, but somehow that just didn't seem enough. He also attended student council meetings and talked to the headmaster about it.

A few months later, Daniel talked to Bruce again. But this time his mum wasn't with him. "She doesn't need to come with me any more," he said. "For some reason, the head just seemed to wake up."

"Perhaps somebody tapped him on the shoulder," Daniel said.

Romans 13:1–10 encourages us to do what's right in serving our government. In Paul's day, that meant carefully following the laws laid out by Rome. But in today's democracy, it can mean helping to shape policy – just as Daniel did. Read the passage to see what else Paul said about your relationship with the government.

- Would Paul have approved of Daniel's actions? Why or why not?
- What's one thing that you can do to apply this passage to your situation?

Consider . . .

- standing for a place on your school or college's student council.
- writing a letter to your member of parliament, relating your concerns about the disabled, education, or some other issue that you care about.

For more, see . . .

- 1 Samuel 8:1–22 (p.261)
- 1 Peter 2:13–17 (p.1358)
- Matthew 22:17–21 (p.980)

everyone thinks is right. [18]Do your best to live in
peace with everyone. [19]My friends, do not try to
punish others when they wrong you, but wait
for God to punish them with his anger. It is
written: "I will punish those who do wrong; I
will repay them,"[n] says the Lord. [20]But you
should do this:

"If your enemy is hungry, feed him.
If he is thirsty, give him a drink.
Doing this will be like pouring burning coals
on his head." *Proverbs 25:21–22*

[21]Do not let evil defeat you, but defeat evil by
doing good.

Christians Should Obey the Law

13 All of you must yield to the government
rulers. No one rules unless God has given
him the power to rule, and no one rules now
without that power from God. [2]So those who are
against the government are really against what
God has commanded. And they will bring pun-
ishment on themselves. [3]Those who do right do
not have to fear the rulers; only those who do
wrong fear them. Do you want to be unafraid of
the rulers? Then do what is right, and they will
praise you. [4]The ruler is God's servant to help
you. But if you do wrong, then be afraid. He has
the power to punish; he is God's servant to
punish those who do wrong. [5]So you must yield
to the government, not only because you might
be punished, but because you know it is right.

[6]This is also why you pay taxes. Rulers are
working for God and give their time to their
work. [7]Pay everyone, then, what you owe. If
you owe any kind of tax, pay it. Show respect
and honour to them all.

"I . . . them," Quotation from Deuteronomy 32:35.

DRUGS AND ALCOHOL

Just Trying to Fit In?

Despite hearing horror stories about drugs, Carly thought she thought could handle it. When she moved schools in year 9 she didn't want to get bullied again and tried her hardest to fit in with the popular crowd at her new school. At first she thought it was just a bit of fun, she thought she could get away with it. Just as long as she didn't take any "really bad" drugs, she thought she'd be OK. Carly thought wrong. Her life went completely downhill. She hit rock bottom and even attempted suicide.

Talking to a friend some time later Carly said, "I tried everything just to be popular. I only wanted to be liked. Since then God has come into my life and shown me that he loves me. And if the creator of the universe loves me then I don't need to do anything to fit in, I already fit in to God's amazing family."

It's unbelievable to see how much the people we hang around with can influence us. You can choose to be influenced by them or let God influence your life.

Romans 13:11–14 talks about leaving the world of darkness and living in God's light instead. If you know and have accepted what Jesus has done for you it means you can and should live in God's light, not in the darkness of sin.

- How do you think Carly's life changed?
- Are there any areas of your life you're living in darkness? If so, ask God to help you live for him.

Consider . . .

- if you haven't done already or you feel you need to again, asking God to forgive you and come into your life and help you to live in the light.
- praying for any friends you have who are living in darkness and ask God to show you a way of bringing them to his light.

For more, see . . .

- Proverbs 23:31–35 (p.610)
- Ephesians 5:17–18 (p.1275)
- Ephesians 2:1–4 (p.1270)
- 1 Peter 4:2–5 (p.1360)

Loving Others

8Do not owe people anything, except always
owe love to each other, because the person
who loves others has obeyed all the law. 9The
law says, "You must not be guilty of adultery.[d]
You must not murder anyone. You must not
steal. You must not want to take your neigh-
bour's things."[n] All these commands and all
others are really only one rule: "Love your
neighbour as you love yourself."[n] 10Love never
hurts a neighbour, so loving is obeying all
the law.

11Do this because we live in an important
time. It is now time for you to wake up from
your sleep, because our salvation is nearer now
than when we first believed. 12The "night"[n] is
almost finished, and the "day"[n] is almost here.
So we should stop doing things that belong
to darkness and take up the weapons used for
fighting in the light. 13Let us live in a right
way, like people who belong to the day. We
should not have wild parties or get drunk. There
should be no sexual sins of any kind, no fighting
or jealousy. 14But clothe yourselves with the
Lord Jesus Christ and forget about satisfying your
sinful self.

Do Not Criticise Other People

14 Accept into your group someone who is
weak in faith, and do not argue about
opinions. 2One person believes it is right to eat
all kinds of food.[n] But another, who is weak, be-
lieves it is right to eat only vegetables. 3The one
who knows that it is right to eat any kind of food
must not reject the one who eats only vegeta-
bles. And the person who eats only vegetables
must not think that the one who eats all foods is
wrong, because God has accepted that person.
4You cannot judge another person's servant. The
master decides if the servant is doing well or not.
And the Lord's servant will do well because the
Lord helps him do well.

5Some think that one day is more important
than another, and others think that every day is
the same. Let all be sure in their own mind.
6Those who think one day is more important
than other days are doing that for the Lord. And
those who eat all kinds of food are doing that for
the Lord, and they give thanks to God. Others
who refuse to eat some foods do that for the
Lord, and they give thanks to God. 7We do not
live or die for ourselves. 8If we live, we are living
for the Lord, and if we die, we are dying for the
Lord. So living or dying, we belong to the Lord.

> **Sidelight** Relations with the government were important to Roman Christians, since they lived in the capital city. When Paul wrote Romans 13:1–7, about obeying the government, Christians were tolerated – sometimes even protected – by the state. Within a few years, though, Christians would face the constant threat of torture and execution.

9The reason Christ died and rose from the dead
to live again was so he would be Lord over both
the dead and the living. 10So why do you judge
your brothers or sisters in Christ? And why do
you think you are better than they are? We will
all stand before God to be judged, 11because it is
written in the Scriptures:[d]

> " 'As surely as I live,' says the Lord,
> 'Everyone will bow before me and will
> promise to follow me.' " *Isaiah 45:23*

12So each of us will have to answer to God.

Do Not Cause Others to Sin

13For that reason we should stop judging
each other. We must make up our minds not to
do anything that will make another Christian
sin. 14I am in the Lord Jesus, and I know that
there is no food that is wrong to eat. But if a
person believes something is wrong, that thing
is wrong for him. 15If you hurt your brother's
or sister's faith because of something you eat,
you are not really following the way of love.
Do not destroy someone's faith by eating food
he thinks is wrong, because Christ died for
him. 16Do not allow what you think is good
to become what others say is evil. 17In the
kingdom of God, eating and drinking are not
important. The important things are living right
with God, peace, and joy in the Holy Spirit.[d]
18Anyone who serves Christ by living this way
is pleasing God and will be accepted by other
people.

19So let us try to do what makes for peace and
help one another. 20Do not let the eating of food
destroy the work of God. All foods are all right to

"You . . . things." Quotation from Exodus 20:13–15,17.
"Love . . . yourself." Quotation from Leviticus 19:18.
"night" This is used as a symbol of the sinful world we live in. This world will soon end.
"day" This is used as a symbol of the good time that is coming, when we will be with God.
all . . . food The Jewish law said there were some foods Jews should not eat. When Jews became Christians, some of them did not understand they could now eat all foods.

eat, but it is wrong to eat food that causes
someone else to sin. 21It is better not to eat meat
or drink wine or do anything that will cause your
brother or sister to sin.
22Your beliefs about these things should be
kept secret between you and God. People are
happy if they can do what they think is right
without feeling guilty. 23But those who eat
something without being sure it is right are
wrong because they did not believe it was right.
Anything that is done without believing it is
right is a sin.
15 We who are strong in faith should help
the weak with their weaknesses, and
not please only ourselves. 2Let each of us please
our neighbours for their good, to help them
be stronger in faith. 3Even Christ did not live
to please himself. It was as the Scriptures[d] said:
"When people insult you, it hurts me."[n]
4Everything that was written in the past
was written to teach us. The Scriptures give
us patience and encouragement so that we
can have hope. 5Patience and encouragement
come from God. And I pray that God will
help you all agree with each other the
way Christ Jesus wants. 6Then you will all be
joined together, and you will give glory to God
the Father of our Lord Jesus Christ. 7Christ
accepted you, so you should accept each other,
which will bring glory to God. 8I tell you that
Christ became a servant of the Jews to show
that God's promises to the Jewish ancestors

"When . . . me." Quotation from Psalm 69:9.

DECISION MAKING

Different is OK!

Katie studied languages at university, so when she got married just after graduating she and her new husband, Rob, chose to go to Italy for their honeymoon. On Sunday they managed to find a church much like their own back home.

Once the service started Rob and Katie enjoyed themselves, even though Katie noticed that one or two women were looking at her quite oddly. After the service, the questioning began to find out whether Katie and Rob were Christians, what church they came from and whether they believed the Bible was God's Word. Eventually their new Italian friends were satisfied, even though they still looked puzzled.

"Tell us," they asked, "do many Christian women wear trousers and make-up in Britain?"

"Yes. It's not a problem," said Katie, surprised but glad to know what the issue had been.

Later that week Katie, Rob and their new friends had a meal together and laughed over the misunderstanding, as they passed around several bottles of wine and discussed differences between Christian groups they each knew.

"Did you know," teased Rob, "that there are some Christians in Britain and North America who believe that you can't be a Christian and drink wine."

"No," said the Italians. "That's impossible. How could anybody believe that?" Eventually they agreed that each person should make honest decisions based on their own convictions, even if others would disagree.

Romans 14:5–12 challenges us all to make decisions based on our faith.

- How are the Christians Rob and Katie met like the people in the passage?
- How might this passage affect the way you make comparisons between groups of Christians?

Consider . . .

- talking to your youth leader about your church's beliefs. Ask how your church came to believe the things it does.
- making lifestyle decisions based on what the Bible teaches. Work towards making sure that your lifestyle matches your beliefs.

For more, see . . .

- 1 Kings 12:1–20 (p.327)
- Acts 5:12–32 (p.1145)
- Matthew 7:13–14 (p.950)

are true. 9And he also did this so that those
who are not Jews could give glory to God for
the mercy he gives to them. It is written in the
Scriptures:

"So I will praise you, LORD, among the
nations.
I will sing praises to your name." *Psalm 18:49*

10The Scripture also says,

"Be happy, you who are not Jews, together
with his people." *Deuteronomy 32:43*

11Again the Scripture says,

"All you nations, praise the LORD.
All you people, praise him." *Psalm 117:1*

12And Isaiah says,

"The new king from the family of Jesse[n]
will stand as a banner for all peoples;

Jesse Jesse was the father of David, king of Israel. Jesus was from their family.

FRIENDS

Hey Grunge!

It was on a cold Sunday morning in December that Peter first came to church. He arrived halfway through the pastor's message and sat quietly at the back. He felt more than a little out of place, to say the least. What made him feel even more uncomfortable was the fact that everyone seemed to be staring at him ...

"I wonder who that is?" Belinda asked her mum when she saw the visitor.

"I'd have nothing to do with him if I were you, Belinda," her mum said.

Belinda looked at Peter's haircut and the many earrings he wore – and the stud in his nose. "Well, I know he doesn't look like the usual sort of person who comes to church, but shouldn't we make him feel welcome anyway?"

Belinda's mum shook her head. "His name's Peter," she said. "His dad's in prison for beating up a security guard and his sister's a prostitute, or so they say."

"What difference does that make? Jesus became a friend of prostitutes didn't he?"

"You're not Jesus," her mum replied.

Belinda soon discovered that a lot of other people in the church felt the same way. It wasn't that they were trying to be nasty, but they were careful not to talk to him.

Peter continued to visit the church for several weeks, but still no one had spoken to him. He began to feel as though he wasn't welcome, despite the fact that he'd accepted Jesus as his Lord and Saviour just a few weeks ago.

Belinda had been praying for Peter every day since she had first seen him. She had resisted the urge to go and say "Hello", but now that seemed to be ridiculous. How could the church claim to be a true representative of Jesus Christ if it didn't make a guy like Peter feel welcome? Surely Jesus would have been the first to go and sit next to him?

Although she knew her mum wouldn't approve, Belinda approached Peter after the service and invited him to tea.

Belinda's mum soon got to know Peter for the person he was, rather than for the reputation he had been branded with. Within weeks, Belinda's family were good friends of Peter, and before long his mum was coming to church and discovering the good news of Jesus!

Belinda started the ball rolling by accepting Peter when everyone else was too scared to go near him. Read what the apostle Paul said about accepting others in **Romans 15:4–13**.

- Based on this passage, what might Paul have said to Belinda?
- How does the fact that Christ has accepted someone help you to accept them too?

Consider ...

- getting to know someone who is often neglected because of the way he or she dresses.
- asking God to help you to accept others just as he has accepted them – unconditionally.

For more, see ...

- 1 Samuel 18:1–4 (p.272)
- John 13:20 (p.1120)
- Job 2:11–13 (p.471)

the nations will come together
around him
and the place where he lives will be filled
with glory." *Isaiah 11:10*

[13]I pray that the God who gives hope will fill
you with much joy and peace while you trust in
him. Then your hope will overflow by the
power of the Holy Spirit.[d]

Paul Talks About His Work

[14]My brothers and sisters, I am sure that
you are full of goodness. I know that you have
all the knowledge you need and that you are
able to teach each other. [15]But I have written to
you very openly about some things I wanted
you to remember. I did this because God gave
me this special gift: [16]to be a minister of Christ
Jesus to those who are not Jews. I served God
by teaching his Good News,[d] so that the non-
Jewish people could be an offering that God
would accept—an offering made holy by the
Holy Spirit.[d]

[17]So I am proud of what I have done for
God in Christ Jesus. [18]I will not talk about any-
thing except what Christ has done through
me in leading those who are not Jews to obey
God. They have obeyed God because of what I
have said and done, [19]because of the power of
miracles[d] and the great things they saw, and be-
cause of the power of the Holy Spirit. I preached
the Good News from Jerusalem all the way
around to Illyricum, and so I have finished that
part of my work. [20]I always want to preach the
Good News in places where people have never
heard of Christ, because I do not want to build
on the work someone else has already started.
[21]But it is written in the Scriptures:[d]

"Those who were not told about him
will see,
and those who have not heard about him
will understand." *Isaiah 52:15*

Paul's Plan to Visit Rome

[22]This is the reason I was stopped many times
from coming to you. [23]Now I have finished my
work here. Since for many years I have wanted
to come to you, [24]I hope to visit you on my way
to Spain. After I enjoy being with you for a
while, I hope you can help me on my trip.
[25]Now I am going to Jerusalem to help God's
people. [26]The believers in Macedonia and
Southern Greece were happy to give their
money to help the poor among God's people at
Jerusalem. [27]They were happy to do this, and
really they owe it to them. These who are not
Jews have shared in the Jews' spiritual blessings,
so they should use their material possessions to
help the Jews. [28]After I am sure the poor in
Jerusalem get the money that has been given for
them, I will leave for Spain and visit you on the
way. [29]I know that when I come to you I will
bring Christ's full blessing.

[30]Brothers and sisters, I beg you to help me in
my work by praying to God for me. Do this be-
cause of our Lord Jesus and the love that the
Holy Spirit[d] gives us. [31]Pray that I will be saved
from the non-believers in Judea and that this
help I bring to Jerusalem will please God's peo-
ple there. [32]Then, if God wants me to, I will
come to you with joy, and together you and I
will have a time of rest. [33]The God who gives
peace be with you all. Amen.

Greetings to the Christians

16 I recommend to you our sister Phoebe,
who is a helper[n] in the church in
Cenchrea. [2]I ask you to accept her in the Lord
in the way God's people should. Help her with
anything she needs, because she has helped me
and many other people also.

[3]Give my greetings to Priscilla and Aquila,
who work together with me in Christ Jesus
[4]and who risked their own lives to save my life.
I am thankful to them, and all the non-Jewish
churches are thankful as well. [5]Also, greet for
me the church that meets at their house.

Greetings to my dear friend Epenetus, who
was the first person in the country of Asia to
follow Christ. [6]Greetings to Mary, who worked
very hard for you. [7]Greetings to Andronicus
and Junias, my relatives, who were in prison
with me. They are very important apostles.[d]
They were believers in Christ before I was.
[8]Greetings to Ampliatus, my dear friend in the
Lord. [9]Greetings to Urbanus, a worker together
with me for Christ. And greetings to my dear
friend Stachys. [10]Greetings to Apelles, who was

Sidelight Since the early Christians didn't have any church buildings, they usually met in each others' homes (Romans 16:3–5). Priscilla and Aquila were quite wealthy and they had a large house where Christians could gather for worship. Even today, meeting in a house has a different atmosphere from a church meeting!

helper Literally, "deaconess". This might mean the same as one of the special women helpers in 1 Timothy 3:11.

tested and proved that he truly loves Christ.
Greetings to all those who are in the family
of Aristobulus. 11 Greetings to Herodion, my
fellow citizen. Greetings to all those in the fam-
ily of Narcissus who belong to the Lord.
12 Greetings to Tryphena and Tryphosa, women
who work very hard for the Lord. Greetings to
my dear friend Persis, who also has worked
very hard for the Lord. 13 Greetings to Rufus,
who is a special person in the Lord, and to his
mother, who has been like a mother to me also.
14 Greetings to Asyncritus, Phlegon, Hermes, Pa-
trobas, Hermas and all the brothers who are
with them. 15 Greetings to Philologus and Julia,
Nereus and his sister, and Olympas, and to all
God's people with them. 16 Greet each other
with a holy kiss. All of Christ's churches send
greetings to you.

BIBLE STUDY

Recipe

Chas had baked bread before. Hundreds of times.

Well, twice, anyway.

"It's a simple loaf of white bread. That shouldn't be too hard," Chas thought aloud. "A little yeast, a little oil, a little flour – nothing to it."

Chas put all the ingredients into the big bowl that his mother always used, added more flour until the mixture was a big ball, and then dumped it on to the worktop.

As Chas kneaded the dough he imagined how surprised his parents would be when he presented his bread for breakfast the next morning. It was their 25th wedding anniversary.

Chas covered the big ball of dough with a light coating of butter, flipped it into the bowl, covered it with clingfilm, and set it aside in a warm corner of the room to rise.

"See, nothing to it," he said smugly. "Didn't even have to look at the recipe."

Now all he had to do was wait for it to rise. Thirty minutes. Nothing. An hour. Nothing.

"It's just sitting there in the bowl like a . . . like a big lump of dough. Why isn't it rising?" Chas asked himself.

He checked the expiry date on the yeast packed. No problem – it wouldn't expire for another three months. So what could it be?

Reluctantly, he went to the cookery book.

"Let's see," he mused. "Flour, oil, yeast, sugar . . .

"Sugar! Of course!"

Without sugar, the yeast couldn't do its job. No wonder the bread wasn't rising! He had left out a small but vital ingredient.

Chas's bread couldn't rise without sugar. In the same way, Paul says that a Christian can't reach a mature faith without having the right ingredients in his or her life. Read **Romans 16:22–27** to see what those ingredients are.

- What, according to Paul, is the effect of God's message on people's lives?
- According to this passage, what ingredients might you be lacking to bring you to Christian maturity?

Consider . . .

- asking your parent or youth leader to give you a recipe for Bible study. Ask what steps you should follow in studying the Bible.
- regularly attending your youth group's weekly Bible study. If you don't have one, ask your youth leader to start one.

For more, see . . .

- Joshua 1:8 (p.203)
- Revelation 1:1–3 (p.1388)
- Psalm 19:7–11 (p.510)

17 Brothers and sisters, I ask you to look out for those who cause people to be against each other and who upset other people's faith. They are against the true teaching you learned, so stay away from them. 18 Such people are not serving our Lord Christ but are only doing what pleases themselves. They use fancy talk and fine words to fool the minds of those who do not know about evil. 19 All the believers have heard that you obey, so I am very happy because of you. But I want you to be wise in what is good and innocent in what is evil.

20 The God who brings peace will soon defeat Satan and give you power over him.

The grace of our Lord Jesus be with you.

21 Timothy, a worker together with me, sends greetings, as well as Lucius, Jason and Sosipater, my relatives.

22 I am Tertius, and I am writing this letter from Paul. I send greetings to you in the Lord.

23 Gaius is letting me and the whole church here use his home. He also sends greetings to you, as do Erastus, the city treasurer, and our brother Quartus. 24 [n]

25 Glory to God who can make you strong in faith by the Good News [d] that I tell people and by the message about Jesus Christ. The message about Christ is the secret that was hidden for long ages past but is now made known. 26 It has been made clear through the writings of the prophets. [d] And by the command of the eternal God it is made known to all nations that they might believe and obey.

27 To the only wise God be glory for ever through Jesus Christ! Amen.

Verse 24 Some Greek copies add verse 24: "The grace of our Lord Jesus Christ be with all of you. Amen."

1 Corinthians

Why Read This Book:

- Hear down-to-earth advice about dealing with church problems (1 Corinthians 1—10).
- Learn the importance of working together as Christians (1 Corinthians 11—13).
- Discover the promise of Christ's victory over death (1 Corinthians 14—16).

When?

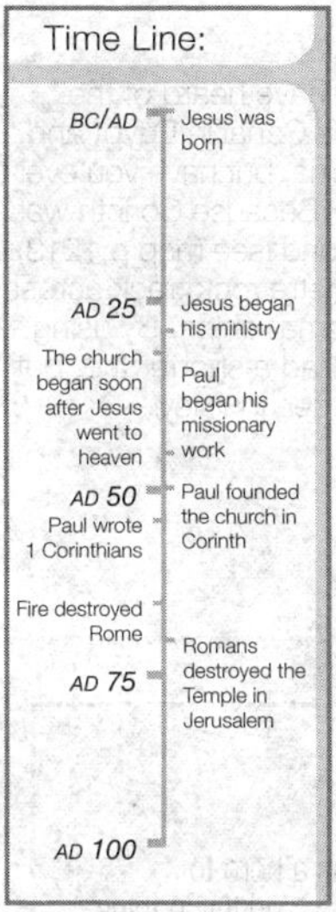

Behind the Scenes:

When Bob went on a trip with his friends, he thought that it would be a riot with no adults around.

For the first few days everything was great. But as the week wore on, everyone got on everyone else's nerves. With no set regulations to keep everyone in line, chaos ruled. By the end of the week Bob couldn't wait to get home and return to a normal routine.

The Corinthian church faced a similar situation. It was made up of people from a whole variety of backgrounds and income levels, and appears to have been weak on leadership. They began arguing about sex, marriage, leaders and worship, and before long, the church was divided.

That's where the apostle Paul comes in. He had started the church himself around two years before these problems arose and so, naturally, he was concerned that it was destroying itself. He wrote 1 Corinthians, and made a point of answering the major questions that had started the arguments in the church – marriage and being single, food offered to idols, what life in the church should be like, the role of spiritual gifts including tongues. Then he challenged the church to follow Christ in everything.

Maybe you think that the problems we face nowadays are unique and that life nearly 2,000 years ago was vastly different? Read 1 Corinthians and think again.

Where?

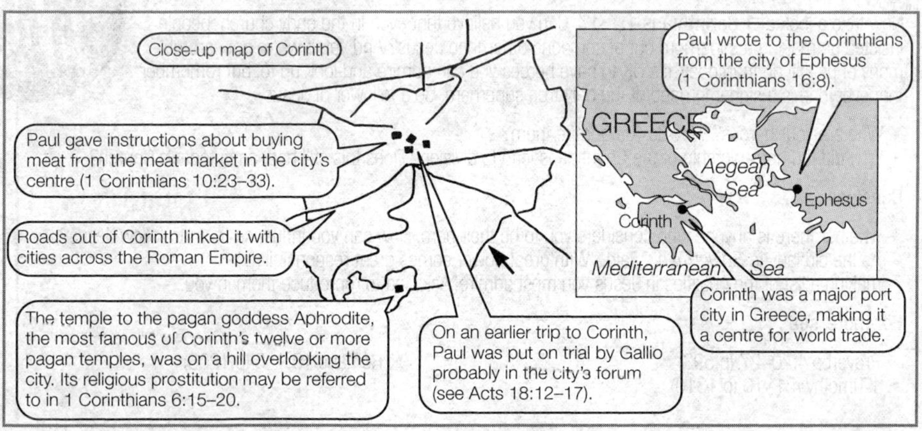

1 From Paul. God called me to be an apostle[d] of
Christ Jesus because that is what God wanted.
Also from Sosthenes, our brother in Christ.
[2]To the church of God in Corinth, to you who
have been made holy in Christ Jesus. You were
called to be God's holy people with all people
everywhere who pray in the name of the Lord
Jesus Christ—their Lord and ours:
[3]Grace and peace to you from God our Father
and the Lord Jesus Christ.

Paul Gives Thanks to God

[4]I always thank my God for you because of
the grace God has given you in Christ Jesus. [5]I
thank God because in Christ you have been
made rich in every way, in all your speaking and
in all your knowledge. [6]Just as our witness
about Christ has been proved to you, [7]so you
have every gift from God while you wait for our
Lord Jesus Christ to come again. [8]Jesus will
keep you strong until the end so that there will
be no wrong in you on the day our Lord Jesus
Christ comes again. [9]God, who has called you to
share everything with his Son, Jesus Christ our
Lord, is faithful.

Sidelight You have heard of the Suez Canal in Egypt and the Panama Canal in Panama, but have you ever heard of the Corinth Track? Because Corinth was located on a small strip of land (see map p.1213), the city built an eight-kilometre rock track across the land to roll cargo and small ships. By using this track, sailors not only had a shorter trip, but they avoided a dangerous sea journey.

HEROES

Superhero

The Bible is full of heroes. Moses was a hero to Joshua, Elijah was a hero to Elisha, Paul was a hero to Timothy, and David was a hero to his entire nation. But there is really only one true superhero, and if you think about it long enough, you'll know exactly who that is. Philippians 2:8–9 tells us that God the Father was so impressed with his Son's humility, that he raised him to the highest place, and made his name greater than any other name. Let's take a minute to consider some of Jesus' superhero qualities:

- He controlled the weather (Matthew 8:23–27, p.952)
- He forgave sins (Matthew 9:1–8, p.952)
- He multiplied stuff (Mark 6:30–44, p.1007)
- He walked on water (Mark 6:45–51, p. 1009)
- He healed people (Mark 6:53–56, p.1009)
- He raised the dead (John 11:1–44, p.1114)
- He rose from the dead (John 20:1–9, p.1132)
- He flew (Acts 1:9–11, p.1137)

Now take a look at **1 Corinthians 1:1–17**. Can you believe that even in the early church, people insisted on making a superhero out of someone other than Jesus? And yet, if we're not careful, many of us still do that today. It's OK to have heroes you can admire and look up to, but remember that everyone is a sinner in need of the only true superhero. Be a follower of Jesus.

- Who are your heroes? Why do you admire them?
- Why did the hero-worship of the Corinthians lead to division? Does this still happen in today's Church?

Consider . . .

- whether there is anyone who considers you to be their hero. How can you influence them to follow Jesus? As the old lady in *Spiderman 2* said, "With great power comes great responsibility."
- making a list of the qualities in Jesus you most admire. Ask God to reproduce them in you.

For more, see . . .

- Proverbs 4:20–27 (p.593)
- 1 Timothy 4:1–16 (p.1310)
- Romans 15:1–6 (p.1208)

Problems in the Church

10I beg you, brothers and sisters,[n] by the name of our Lord Jesus Christ that all of you agree with each other and not be split into groups. I beg that you be completely joined together by having the same kind of thinking and the same purpose. 11My brothers and sisters, some people from Chloe's family have told me quite plainly that there are quarrels among you. 12This is what I mean: one of you says, "I follow Paul"; another says, "I follow Apollos"; another says, "I follow Peter"; and another says, "I follow Christ." 13Christ has been divided up into different groups! Did Paul die on the cross for you? No! Were you baptised[d] in the name of Paul? No! 14I thank God I did not baptise any of you except Crispus and Gaius 15so that now no one can say you were baptised in my name. 16(I also baptised the family of Stephanas, but I do not remember that I baptised anyone else.) 17Christ did not send me to baptise people but to preach the Good News.[d] And he sent me to preach the Good News without using words of human wisdom so that the cross of Christ[n] would not lose its power.

Christ is God's Power and Wisdom

18The teaching about the cross is foolishness to those who are being lost, but to us who are being saved it is the power of God. 19It is written in the Scriptures:[d]

"Their wise men will lose their wisdom;
their wise men will not be able to
understand." *Isaiah 29:14*

20Where is the wise person? Where is the educated person? Where is the skilled talker of this world? God has made the wisdom of the world foolish. 21Because of the wisdom of God the world did not know God through its own wisdom. So God chose to use the message that sounds foolish to save those who believe. 22The Jews ask for miracles,[d] and the Greeks want wisdom. 23But we preach a crucified Christ. This is a big problem to the Jews, and it is foolishness to those who are not Jews. 24But Christ is the power of God and the wisdom of God to those people God has called—Jews and Greeks. 25Even the foolishness of God is wiser than human wisdom, and the weakness of God is stronger than human strength.

26Brothers and sisters, look at what you were when God called you. Not many of you were wise in the way the world judges wisdom. Not many of you had great influence. Not many of you came from important families. 27But God chose the foolish things of the world to shame the wise, and he chose the weak things of the world to shame the strong. 28He chose what the world thinks is unimportant and what the world looks down on and thinks is nothing in order to destroy what the world thinks is important. 29God did this so that no one can boast in his presence. 30Because of God you are in Christ Jesus, who has become for us wisdom from God. In Christ we are put right with God, and have been made holy, and have been set free from sin. 31So, as the Scripture says, "If someone wants to boast, he should boast only about the Lord."[n]

The Message of Christ's Death

2 Dear brothers and sisters, when I came to you, I did not come preaching God's secret with fancy words or a show of human wisdom. 2I decided that while I was with you I would forget about everything except Jesus Christ and his death on the cross. 3So when I came to you, I was weak and fearful and trembling. 4My teaching and preaching were not with words of human wisdom that persuade people but with proof of the power that the Spirit[d] gives. 5This was so that your faith would be in God's power and not in human wisdom.

God's Wisdom

6However, I speak a wisdom to those who are mature. But this wisdom is not from this world or from the rulers of this world, who are losing their power. 7I speak God's secret wisdom, which he has kept hidden. Before the world began, God planned this wisdom for our glory. 8None of the rulers of this world understood it. If they had, they would not have crucified the Lord of glory. 9But as it is written in the Scriptures:[d]

"From long ago no one
has ever heard of a God like you.
No one has ever seen
a God besides you,
who helps the people who trust you."
Isaiah 64:4

10But God has shown us these things through the Spirit.[d]

The Spirit searches out all things, even the deep secrets of God. 11Who knows the thoughts

brothers and sisters Although the Greek text says "brothers" here and throughout this book, Paul's words were meant for the entire church, both men and women.
cross of Christ Paul uses the cross as a picture of the gospel, the story of Christ's death and rising from the dead to pay for our sins. The cross, or Christ's death, was God's way to save us.
"If . . . Lord." Quotation from Jeremiah 9:24.

that another person has? Only a person's spirit
that lives within him knows his thoughts. It is
the same with God. No one knows the thoughts
of God except the Spirit of God. 12Now we did
not receive the spirit of the world, but we
received the Spirit that is from God so that we
can know all that God has given us. 13And we
speak about these things, not with words taught
us by human wisdom but with words taught us
by the Spirit. And so we explain spiritual truths
to spiritual people. 14A person who does not
have the Spirit does not accept the truths that
come from the Spirit of God. That person thinks
they are foolish and cannot understand them,
because they can only be judged to be true
by the Spirit. 15The spiritual person is able to
judge all things, but no one can judge him. The
Scripture says:

16"Who has known the mind of the LORD
or been able to give him advice?" *Isaiah 40:13*

But we have the mind of Christ.

Following People is Wrong

3 Brothers and sisters, in the past I could not
talk to you as I talk to spiritual people.
I had to talk to you as I would to people without
the Spirit[d]—babies in Christ. 2The teaching
I gave you was like milk, not solid food,
because you were not able to take solid food.
And even now you are not ready. 3You are still
not spiritual, because there is jealousy and
quarrelling among you, and this shows that you
are not spiritual. You are acting like people of the
world. 4One of you says, "I belong to Paul," and
another says, "I belong to Apollos." When you
say things like this, you are acting like people of
the world.

5Is Apollos important? No! Is Paul important?
No! We are only servants of God who helped
you believe. Each one of us did the work God
gave us to do. 6I planted the seed, and Apollos
watered it. But God is the One who made it
grow. 7So the one who plants is not important,

PRIORITIES

Is This All There Is?

When Howard Hughes was 45, he was one of the most glamorous men in America. He owned an airline and hotels around the world. He dated actresses, flew exotic test aircraft, and worked on top-secret CIA contracts.

Twenty years later, Howard Hughes was the world's richest man – with $2.3 billion. But he was also one of the world's most pathetic. He lived in small, dark rooms in his hotels. He preferred to keep his life without sun and without joy. He had a straggly beard down to his waist and two-inch-long fingernails. His body had wasted away to a mere 50 kilogrammes.

He spent most of his time watching films over and over again – sometimes watching the same film 150 times. He lay naked in bed, deathly afraid of germs. Life had lost its meaning for him.

Finally, hooked on drugs, Howard Hughes died at the age of 67, because he didn't have a medical device his company had helped to develop.

Howard Hughes had it all – worldly wisdom, wealth, power, fame. He had all the things the world considers important. But they weren't enough. Read **1 Corinthians 1:18–31** to see what Paul says is really important in life.

- How was Howard Hughes's life an illustration of this passage?
- According to this passage, what does God say is the most important thing for Christians?

Consider . . .

- doing something "foolish" – such as helping someone who doesn't deserve it – as a sign of your faith.
- tearing out words and pictures from a magazine that show what the world says is important and what God says is important. Make a separate pile for each category.

For more, see . . .

- Psalm 139:1–18 (p.581)
- 1 John 3:1–3 (p.1373)
- 2 Corinthians 11:16–31 (p.1251)

and the one who waters is not important. Only
God, who makes things grow, is important. 8The
one who plants and the one who waters have
the same purpose, and each will be rewarded
for his own work. 9We are God's workers, work-
ing together; you are like God's farm, God's
house.
10Using the gift God gave me, I laid the
foundation of that house like an expert builder.
Others are building on that foundation, but all
people should be careful how they build on it.
11The foundation that has already been laid
is Jesus Christ, and no one can lay down any
other foundation. 12But if people build on that
foundation, using gold, silver, jewels, wood,
grass or straw, 13their work will be clearly seen,
because the Day of Judgement[n] will make it
seen. That Day will appear with fire, and the fire
will test everyone's work to show what sort of
work it was. 14If the building that has been put

Sidelight Even though Apollos isn't mentioned much in the Bible, he appears to have been an influential church leader. For a while he was a leader in Corinth, and may have been a better preacher than Paul (1 Corinthians 3:1–9).

Day of Judgement The day Christ will come to judge all people and take his people to live with him.

SCHOOL

The Powerful Way

It was disgusting! While Scott was at the evening soccer practise, someone had smeared animal guts all over his bike. Scott just stood in the car park looking shocked.

Things had not been the same since he had seriously committed his life to Christ. Many of his friends didn't understand. They thought that Scott was snubbing them when he wouldn't go drinking with them. The abuse came first. Then a few flattened tyres. Then rumours.

But this? This was sick!

Scott's best friend, Geoff, walked up behind him. When he saw the bike, Geoff blew up.

"I can't believe . . . the nerve of those . . . " Geoff was so angry that he couldn't even finish his sentences. "We know who's behind this," he fumed. "Let's go and kick some heads!"

Scott shook his head and began to smile. "No way. Two quid and some elbow grease, and we'll never know it happened. Besides, aren't we supposed to act more like Jesus? Do you think Jesus would bash heads now?"

Geoff looked at his friend and began to smile. "You're something else. You're also right. OK. To the jet wash we go!"

Scott had plenty of reasons to take revenge. But, instead, Scott prayed for those people and treated them as he would anyone else. People noticed. During his final months at school, people who knew what Scott had been through asked what his secret was.

It was hard for Scott to live the Christian life at school. But because he didn't fight back, Scott's actions demonstrated God's power. To find out more about demonstrating God's power at school, read **1 Corinthians 2:1–11**.

- How do Scott's actions show the difference between God's wisdom and the world's wisdom?
- According to this passage, what should our attitude be as we talk about and demonstrate our faith?

Consider . . .

- imagining that you were with Paul when he was experiencing some of the feelings he talks about in this passage. Write what you would say to encourage him.
- demonstrating God's power at school by not getting angry if people ridicule your faith.

For more, see . . .

- Joshua 6 (p.205)
- 2 Timothy 1:6–8 (p.1316)
- Ephesians 3:14–21 (p.1271)

on the foundation still stands, the builder will get
a reward. 15But if the building is burned up, the
builder will suffer loss. The builder will be saved,
but it will be as one who escaped from a fire.
16Don't you know that you are God's temple
and that God's Spirit lives in you? 17If anyone
destroys God's temple, God will destroy that
person, because God's temple is holy and you are
that temple.
18Do not fool yourselves. If you think you are
wise in this world, you should become a fool so
that you can become truly wise, 19because the
wisdom of this world is foolishness with God. It
is written in the Scriptures,[d] "He catches those
who are wise in their own clever traps."[n] 20It is
also written in the Scriptures, "The Lord knows
what wise people think. He knows their thoughts
are just a puff of wind."[n] 21So you should not
boast about human leaders. All things belong to
you: 22Paul, Apollos and Peter; the world, life,
death, the present and the future—all these be-
long to you. 23And you belong to Christ, and
Christ belongs to God.

Apostles are Servants of Christ

4 People should think of us as servants of
Christ, the ones God has trusted with his
secrets. 2Now in this way those who are trusted
with something valuable must show they are
worthy of that trust. 3As for myself, I do not care
if I am judged by you or by any human court. I do
not even judge myself. 4I know of no wrong I

"He . . . traps." Quotation from Job 5:13.
"The Lord . . . wind." Quotation from Psalm 94:11.

POPULARITY

Pop Idols and Popularity

Mark was a pretty average kid at school and had lots of friends, but like so many people, he wanted to be one of the "in crowd". The popular kids had it so easy – everyone wanted to be *like* them and the opposite sex wanted to be *with* them! Never was this truer than for the lads in the year 11 rock band as they sang the classic rock song "It's so easy, when everybody's tryin' to please me" to a star-struck crowd of teenage girls. So Mark did what any self-respecting wannabe would do – he learned to play the electric guitar and joined a band!

After a few years, he had become a fine guitarist, graduated from music college and enjoyed the popularity and prestige of touring the UK with a band. At his peak, God challenged Mark to serve him with his music and give up his ambitions of fame and fortune. Over the next few years, Mark took the Gospel into schools, colleges and universities all over Europe as part of a band who gave their testimonies and preached the Gospel at shows.

Mark never earned much money, never achieved the fame he'd once dreamt of and never gained any critical acclaim for his music, but had the far greater joy of knowing that God had used him to bring many young people to Jesus and encouraged countless others in their faith.

Read **1 Corinthians 3:1–23.**

- The Corinthians were arguing over who was a better leader and evangelist, Paul or Apollos. How does this passage show us that this is foolish?
- What does this passage tell us is more important than popularity?

Consider . . .

- whether you have any special talents or skills that you could use for God rather than your own popularity. Why not chat to a church leader or youth leader about how you could use them in church?
- whether you try hard to be popular. Ask God to show you that he created you to be uniquely you, not to try and be someone you're not.

For more, see . . .

- Proverbs 23:15–21 (p.610)
- 1 Corinthians 12:12–27 (p.1231)
- Daniel 1:1–21 (p.833)
- Philippians 2:1–11 (p.1282)

have done, but this does not make me right
before the Lord. The Lord is the One who judges
me. 5So do not judge before the right time; wait
until the Lord comes. He will bring to light things
that are now hidden in darkness, and will make
known the secret purposes of people's hearts.
Then God will praise each one of them.
6Brothers and sisters, I have used Apollos and
myself as examples so you could learn through
us the meaning of the saying, "Follow only what
is written in the Scriptures." [d] Then you will not
be more proud of one person than another.
7Who says you are better than others? What do
you have that was not given to you? And if it was
given to you, why do you boast as if you did not
receive it as a gift?
8You think you already have everything you
need. You think you are rich. You think you have
become kings without us. I wish you really were
kings so we could be kings together with you. 9But
it seems to me that God has put us apostles [d] in last
place, like those sentenced to die. We are like a
show for the whole world to see—angels and peo-
ple. 10We are fools for Christ's sake, but you are
very wise in Christ. We are weak, but you are
strong. You receive honour, but we are shamed.
11Even to this very hour we do not have enough to
eat or drink or to wear. We are often beaten, and
we have no homes in which to live. 12We work
hard with our own hands for our food. When peo-
ple curse us, we bless them. When they hurt us,
we put up with it. 13When they tell evil lies about

SERVICE

Worthy of the Trust

"Son, please don't go."

Bill Dukes's eyes met his father's. "Dad, I believe God wants me in Brazil this year. We've been waiting on the missionary board for a long time. Now the appointment is here. I've got to go."

Bill nearly broke down as he watched his dad's eyes fill with tears. The doctors didn't think Bill's dad had long to live. If Bill left for Brazil, his father might die before Bill could come home.

"Look, Dad, I know you want me to stay. I want to be with you too. But I have to ask what God wants. And as far as I can tell now, he wants me in Brazil."

As Bill drove away from his parents' house, his mind replayed doubts that others had expressed about his decision.

"A wife, one boy, and a baby on the way. You're crazy!"

"Do you really think God would call you away from your father now?"

"We need priests in this country. Why don't you stay?"

Bill weighed his options.

For eight years, Bill and his family worked in South America. And, against all predictions by doctors and the expectations of Bill's family, Bill's father was alive to welcome him home.

"I'm convinced that God is faithful," Bill says, "especially in those times when someone has to make a hard choice to be faithful in serving God."

The Corinthian Christians needed to be reminded of the same thing. Read how Paul makes the point clear in **1 Corinthians 4:1–5**.

- How would Bill's feelings about his life compare with Paul's feelings?
- How do you feel about God knowing and judging the secrets of your heart?

Consider . . .

- thanking God for a servant whose faithfulness has helped you in some way. Ask God to help you to do the same for someone else.
- evaluating any commitments to serve that you have made and haven't kept. Begin fulfilling those commitments this week.

For more, see . . .

- Joshua 24:14–15 (p.222)
- Ephesians 4:11–16 (p.1273)
- Luke 16:10–12 (p.1074)

us, we speak nice words about them. Even today,
we are treated as though we were the rubbish of
the world—the scum of the earth.
14I am not trying to make you feel ashamed. I
am writing this to give you a warning as my
own dear children. 15For though you may have
10,000 teachers in Christ, you do not have
many fathers. Through the Good News[d] I be-
came your father in Christ Jesus, 16so I beg you,
please follow my example. 17That is why I am
sending to you Timothy, my son in the Lord. I
love Timothy, and he is faithful. He will help you
remember my way of life in Christ Jesus, just as
I teach it in all the churches everywhere.
18Some of you have become proud, thinking
that I will not come to you again. 19But I will
come to you very soon if the Lord wishes. Then
I will know what the proud ones do, not what
they say, 20because the kingdom of God is pres-
ent not in talk but in power. 21Which do you
want: that I come to you with punishment or
with love and gentleness?

Wickedness in the Church

5 It is actually being said that there is sexual
sin among you. And it is a kind that does not
happen even among people who do not know
God. A man there has his father's wife. 2And you
are proud! You should have been filled with sad-
ness so that the man who did this should be put
out of your group. 3I am not there with you in
person, but I am with you in spirit. And I have
already judged the man who did that sin as if I
were really there. 4When you meet together in
the name of our Lord Jesus, and I meet with you
in spirit with the power of our Lord Jesus, 5then
hand this man over to Satan. So his sinful self[n]
will be destroyed, and his spirit will be saved on
the day of the Lord.
6Your boasting is not good. You know the say-
ing, "Just a little yeast makes the whole batch of
dough rise." 7Take out all the old yeast so that
you will be a new batch of dough without yeast,
which you really are. For Christ, our Passover[d]
lamb, has been sacrificed. 8So let us celebrate this
feast, but not with the bread that has the old
yeast—the yeast of sin and wickedness. Let us
celebrate this feast with the bread that has no
yeast—the bread of goodness and truth.
9I wrote to you in my earlier letter not to asso-
ciate with those who sin sexually. 10But I did not
mean you should not associate with those of this
world who sin sexually, or with the greedy, or
robbers, or those who worship idols. To get away
from them you would have to leave this world.
11I am writing to tell you that you must not asso-
ciate with those who call themselves believers in
Christ but who sin sexually, or are greedy, or wor-
ship idols, or abuse others with words, or get
drunk, or cheat people. Do not even eat with
people like that.
12–13It is not my business to judge those who
are not part of the church. God will judge them.
But you must judge the people who are part of
the church. The Scripture[d] says, "You must get
rid of the evil person among you."[n]

Sidelight Corinth was known for lawsuits (1 Corinthians 6:1). Trials were social events, and sitting on the jury was a privilege. One record tells of a jury with 6,000 people on it.

Judging Problems Among Christians

6 When you have something against another
Christian, how can you bring yourself to go
before judges who are not right with God? Why
do you not let God's people decide who is right?
2Surely you know that God's people will judge
the world. So if you are to judge the world, are
you not able to judge small cases as well? 3You
know that in the future we will judge angels, so
surely we can judge the ordinary things of this
life. 4If you have ordinary cases that must be
judged, are you going to appoint people as judges
who mean nothing to the church? 5I say this to
shame you. Surely there is someone among you
wise enough to judge a complaint between be-
lievers. 6But now one believer goes to court
against another believer—and you do this in
front of unbelievers!
7The fact that you have lawsuits against each
other shows that you are already defeated. Why
not let yourselves be wronged? Why not let your-
selves be cheated? 8But you yourselves do wrong
and cheat, and you do this to other believers!
9–10Surely you know that the people who do
wrong will not inherit God's kingdom. Do not be
fooled. Those who sin sexually, worship idols,
take part in adultery,[d] those who are male pros-
titutes[d] or men who have sexual relations with
other men, those who steal, are greedy, get
drunk, lie about others or rob—these people will
not inherit God's kingdom. 11In the past, some of
you were like that, but you were washed clean.
You were made holy, and you were made right
with God in the name of the Lord Jesus Christ
and in the Spirit[d] of our God.

sinful self Literally, "flesh". This could also mean his body.
"You . . . you." Quotation from Deuteronomy 17:7; 19:19; 22:21,24; 24:7.

Use Your Bodies for God's Glory

12"I am allowed to do all things," but all things
are not good for me to do. "I am allowed to do all
things," but I will not let anything make me its
slave. 13"Food is for the stomach, and the stomach
for food," but God will destroy them both. The
body is not for sexual sin but for the Lord, and the
Lord is for the body. 14By his power God has raised
the Lord from the dead and will also raise us from
the dead. 15Surely you know that your bodies are
parts of Christ himself. So I must never take the
parts of Christ and join them to a prostitute![d] 16It
is written in the Scriptures,[d] "The two will be-
come one body."[n] So you should know that any-
one who joins with a prostitute becomes one body
with the prostitute. 17But the one who joins with
the Lord is one spirit with the Lord.
18So run away from sexual sin. Every other sin
people do is outside their bodies, but those who sin
sexually sin against their own bodies. 19You should
know that your body is a temple for the Holy
Spirit[d] who is in you. You have received the Holy
Spirit from God. So you do not belong to your-
selves, 20because you were bought by God for a
price. So honour God with your bodies.

About Marriage

7 Now I will discuss the things you wrote to
me about. It is good for a man not to have
sexual relations with a woman. 2But because
sexual sin is a danger, each man should have his
own wife, and each woman should have her own
husband. 3The husband should give his wife all
that he owes her as his wife. And the wife should
give her husband all that she owes him as her hus-
band. 4The wife does not have full rights over her
own body; her husband shares them. And the hus-
band does not have full rights over his own body;
his wife shares them. 5Do not refuse to give your
bodies to each other, unless you both agree to stay

"The two . . . body." Quotation from Genesis 2:24.

BOASTING

Honest to God!

Nothing ordinary ever seemed to happen to Rob. His stories of extravagant family holidays, chance meetings with famous people and doing unbelievable feats were too amazing to be true. When Tim McCormick questioned the facts of his stories, Rob would get defensive. He would insist he was being truthful by saying, "Honest to God!"

Finally, Tim caught Rob in a blatant lie. One Saturday morning he phoned to tell Tim that he had got a ticket to a rock concert that had been sold out for more than two months. He wouldn't show Tim the ticket for fear of losing it, he said, nor would he explain how he got it. Yet he tried to make Tim believe that he had an "inside" source. He promised to tell him all about the concert the next day.

But that night, during the very hour of the concert, Tim spotted Rob with his family at a superstore more than fifty kilometres from the concert site! Tim confronted Rob the next day, and he still insisted that he had been at the concert. When Tim told him he had seen him at the superstore, he finally admitted that he had exaggerated a little – but he had bought the group's latest album, he said.

Tim's friendship with Rob crumbled after that. Read **1 Corinthians 5:6–8** to see what Paul thought about boasting.

- How was Rob's boasting like the yeast that Paul writes about?
- What effects has boasting had in your relationships?

Consider . . .

- listing specific ways in which people can keep themselves from boasting.
- asking God to show you if you have been boasting. If so, tell the modest truth to the people you boasted to.

For more, see . . .

- Isaiah 10:8–15 (p.651)
- Jeremiah 9:23–24 (p.728)
- James 4:13–17 (p.1352)

away from sexual relations for a time so you can
give your time to prayer. Then come together
again so Satan cannot tempt you because of a lack
of self-control. 6I say this to give you permission to
stay away from sexual relations for a time. It is not
a command to do so. 7I wish that everyone were
like me, but each person has his own gift from
God. One has one gift, another has another gift.
8Now for those who are not married and for
the widows I say this: it is good for them to stay
unmarried as I am. 9But if they cannot control
themselves, they should marry. It is better to
marry than to burn with sexual desire.
10Now I give this command for the married
people. (The command is not from me; it is from
the Lord.) A wife should not leave her husband.
11But if she does leave, she must not marry
again, or she should make up with her husband.
Also the husband should not divorce his wife.
12For all the others I say this (I am saying
this, not the Lord): if a Christian man has a wife
who is not a believer, and she is happy to live
with him, he must not divorce her. 13And if a
Christian woman has a husband who is not a
believer, and he is happy to live with her, she
must not divorce him. 14The husband who is not
a believer is made holy through his believing
wife. And the wife who is not a believer is made
holy through her believing husband. If this were
not true, your children would not be clean, [d] but
now your children are holy.
15But if those who are not believers decide to
leave, let them leave. When this happens, the
Christian man or woman is free. But God called
us to live in peace. 16Wife, you don't know;
maybe you will save your husband. And hus-
band, you don't know; maybe you will save
your wife.

HOMOSEXUALITY

Step Up For the Prize

The moment of truth had arrived. After months of exhausting rehearsals and fierce competitions, the final ten contestants stood before the judges. Only five of them would be chosen to make the band, the others would be sent home empty-handed. As they stood waiting silently, their hearts seemed to beat very loudly.

Five names were called out. One by one, the judges gave a list of reasons why each one of them would not be in the band. They were sent home. And the other five then stepped up and claimed their prize.

Read **1 Corinthians 6:9–11**. In this passage, Paul, like the competition judges, gives us a list of some of the characteristics of people who will not win the prize of inheriting God's kingdom.

It causes arguments today, but homosexuality is clearly stated here as something that does not please God. Homosexuality has been around for ages, it is found in Genesis, but people are still unsure as to what makes a person "gay" (is it in the genes or is it a conscious decision?). Despite its history and mystery, it's on the list.

If, as you read this, you are thinking that you may be gay, you need first to know that Jesus loves you. Then you need to spend some time with him, working out how you can live the life you were created to live, walking with Jesus the whole time.

- How do you react to people who fail God's test for levels of sexual purity? How does Jesus react to them? Read John 8:1–11 (p.1109) to find out more.
- "If I follow what Paul is saying, I am able to do whatever I want, because I will just be forgiven again, right?" Read Paul's answer in Romans 6:1–14 (p.1191).

Consider . . .

- whether your attitude towards homosexuality is one that might not please Jesus? Maybe you could spend some time saying sorry to God and asking him to change your attitude.
- making a list of characteristics you want to display in your life. For help, check out Matthew 5:1–12 (p.942).

For more, see . . .

- Genesis 2:4–25 (p.3)
- John 8:1–11 (p.1109)
- Genesis 19:1–29 (p.23)

Live as God Called You

17But in any case each one of you should con-
tinue to live the way God has given you to live—
the way you were when God called you. This is
a rule I make in all the churches. 18If a man was
already circumcised[d] when he was called, he
should not undo his circumcision. If a man was
without circumcision when he was called, he
should not be circumcised. 19It is not important if
a man is circumcised or not. The important thing
is obeying God's commands. 20Each one of you
should stay the way you were when God called
you. 21If you were a slave when God called you,
do not let that bother you. But if you can be free,
then make good use of your freedom. 22Those
who were slaves when the Lord called them are
free persons who belong to the Lord. In the same
way, those who were free when they were called
are now Christ's slaves. 23You all were bought at
a great price, so do not become slaves of people.
24Brothers and sisters, each of you should stay as
you were when you were called, and stay there
with God.

Questions About Getting Married

25Now I write about people who are not mar-
ried. I have no command from the Lord about this;
I give my opinion. But I can be trusted, because
the Lord has shown me mercy. 26The present time
is a time of trouble, so I think it is good for you to

DRUGS AND ALCOHOL

God's Temple is Your Body!

Penny went to a party on a Friday night with a whole load of her mates. After a while, some of the group got bored and decided to go to the corner shop to see if they would get served if they tried to buy a bottle of vodka. A little bit later, they came back with two bottles which were quickly opened and passed around. Penny didn't really feel comfortable about this and at first managed to ignore the bottle and carry on her conversation. However, after a while, some of the group started teasing her about not drinking and she gave in and had a large swig. While not really liking the taste, she felt pressured and carried on drinking throughout the evening. She ended up feeling really dizzy and was sick in the toilet. The next morning she felt rather ill and embarrassed.

It is easy to come into contact with illegal substances. A survey of over 9,000 English school pupils aged eleven to fifteen found that:

- 11 per cent had taken drugs in the last month
- 19 per cent had taken drugs in the last year
- 9 per cent were regular smokers (10 per cent of girls, compared with 7 per cent of boys)
- 22 per cent had drunk alcohol in the last week

How do Penny's actions and the statistics of school pupils compare with people you know of that age?

Read **1 Corinthians 6:12–20**. Paul warns of the dangers of becoming focused on or addicted to worldly things. In our culture these might include food, sex, computer gaming, drugs and alcohol.

- Why should you listen to what the Bible says about these temptations?
- What are the things that you do that damage your "temple for the Holy Spirit" (verse 19)?

Consider . . .

- thinking about everything linked to parties you go to. Write them down on a piece of paper under three columns: things which God would take delight in; things which are not wrong in themselves but open to abuse; things which God would forbid.
- developing an accountability group with a couple of your mates where you check up on each other, including how you act on a party night.

For more, see . . .

- Proverbs 1:10 (p.590)
- Romans 12:2 (p.1203)
- Proverbs 23:29–35 (p.610)

stay the way you are. 27If you have a wife, do not
try to become free from her. If you are not married,
do not try to find a wife. 28But if you decide to
marry, you have not sinned. And if a girl who has
never married decides to marry, she has not
sinned. But those who marry will have trouble in
this life, and I want you to be free from trouble.
29Brothers and sisters, this is what I mean: we
do not have much time left. So starting now,
those who have wives should live as if they had
no wives. 30Those who are crying should live as
if they were not crying. Those who are happy
should live as if they were not happy. Those who
buy things should live as if they own nothing.
31Those who use the things of the world should
live as if they were not using them, because this
world in its present form will soon be gone.
32I want you to be free from worry. A man
who is not married is busy with the Lord's work,
trying to please the Lord. 33But a man who is
married is busy with things of the world, trying
to please his wife. 34He must think about two
things—pleasing his wife and pleasing the Lord.
A woman who is not married or a girl who has
never married is busy with the Lord's work. She
wants to be holy in body and spirit. But a mar-
ried woman is busy with things of the world,
as to how she can please her husband. 35I am
saying this to help you, not to limit you. But
I want you to live in the right way, to give
yourselves fully to the Lord without concern for
other things.
36If a man thinks he is not doing the right
thing with the girl he is engaged to, if she is al-
most past the best age to marry and he feels he
should marry her, he should do what he wants.
They should get married. It is no sin. 37But if a
man is sure in his mind that there is no need for
marriage, and has his own desires under control,
and has decided not to marry the one to whom
he is engaged, he is doing the right thing. 38So
the man who marries his girl does right, but the
man who does not marry will do better.
39A woman must stay with her husband as
long as he lives. But if her husband dies, she is
free to marry any man she wants, but she must

LOVE

Give God the No.1 Spot

Dave first saw Dawn when he was leaving church and she was in a coffee shop opposite. He knew her from school, and had always liked her, but for the first time their eyes met and she smiled! Instantly, Dave melted.

As time went by, they got to know each other better. To begin with, Dave was worried that Dawn wasn't a Christian, but he thought that maybe if he prayed hard enough it would only be a matter of time before she met God. Time went by and whilst they got to know each other much better – and fell in love – Dawn had not yet met God. Dave still really wanted to be involved in the church and help run the percussion group he'd set up, but increasingly he found himself phoning at the last minute to say he couldn't come. He knew he was putting Dawn before God.

However much he tried, he couldn't seem to change the priorities in his life. The love he had for Dawn was really strong, and he knew deep down that it was pulling him further from a deeper love, the love of his Father God.

Read **1 Corinthians 7:29–35**. Paul gives some advice about people in this kind of situation.

- What do you think Paul would say to Dave?
- What are the things in verse 35 that Paul says we should do?

Consider . . .

- spending some time thinking and praying about how you can live for God fully and not let other things get in the way.
- whether you have asked Jesus into your life. If not, why not ask him to forgive you and give you new life today.

For more, see . . .

- Matthew 10:37 (p.957)
- 1 John 5:1–5 (p.1375)
- 1 John 3:16 (p.1374)

marry in the Lord. 40The woman is happier if she
does not marry again. This is my opinion, but I
believe I also have God's Spirit.[d]

About Food Offered to Idols

8 Now I will write about meat that is sacri-
ficed to idols. We know that "we all have
knowledge." Knowledge puffs you up with
pride, but love builds up. 2If you think you know
something, you do not yet know anything as you
should. 3But if any person loves God, that person
is known by God.
4So this is what I say about eating meat
sacrificed to idols: we know that an idol is really
nothing in the world, and we know there is only
one God. 5Even though there are things called
gods, in heaven or on earth (and there are many
"gods" and "lords"), 6for us there is only one
God—our Father. All things came from him, and
we live for him. And there is only one Lord—
Jesus Christ. All things were made through him,
and we also were made through him.
7But not all people know this. Some people
are still so used to idols that when they eat meat,
they still think of it as being sacrificed to an idol.
Because their conscience is weak, when they eat
it, they feel guilty. 8But food will not bring us
closer to God. Refusing to eat does not make us
less pleasing to God, and eating does not make
us better in God's sight.
9But be careful that your freedom does not
cause those who are weak in faith to fall into sin.
10You have "knowledge", so you have freedom
to eat in an idol's temple.[n] But someone who is
weak in faith might see you eating there and be
encouraged to eat meat sacrificed to idols while
thinking it is wrong to do so. 11This weak be-
liever for whom Christ died is ruined because of
your "knowledge". 12When you sin against your
brothers and sisters in Christ like this and cause
them to do what they feel is wrong, you are also
sinning against Christ. 13So if the food I eat
causes them to fall into sin, I will never eat meat
again so that I will not cause any of them to sin.

idol's temple Building where a god is worshipped.

FREEDOM

Free to Do Good

Holly was overweight. All the kids made fun of her when she tried to play games with them. And when refreshments were served, they would say things such as "Quick! Hide the food. Here comes Holly."

One night after youth group, youth leader Max found Holly crying in an empty room. She told Max about how much it hurt when the others made fun of her, and how she wanted to lose weight but couldn't. Max couldn't relate to Holly's weight problem; he was a runner and never seemed to put on weight. But he could empathise with the pain that she felt.

"I'll tell you what, Holly," he offered. "You give up sweets and so will I. And why don't you start running with me?"

Holly agreed. The two ran together three times a week. And at youth group meetings, while the kids were eating biscuits and sweets, Max and Holly chewed on raw carrot.

In four months, Holly had lost 15 kilogrammes. She felt better about herself. Holly told Max that she couldn't have done it without him.

Max could have eaten whatever he wanted, but he gave up his freedom to help Holly. Read **1 Corinthians 8:1–13** to see how Paul encourages Christians to use their freedom to help others.

- How do Max's actions demonstrate the principles of this passage?
- How would your friends describe your use of the freedom you have in Jesus?

Consider . . .

- changing an area of your life if your freedom is hurting others.
- talking to a new Christian and asking what he or she thinks about how Christians use their freedom.

For more, see . . .

- Deuteronomy 30:11–20 (p.192)
- 1 Timothy 4:10–12 (p.1311)
- 1 Corinthians 10:23–24 (p.1228)

Paul is like the Other Apostles

9 I am a free man. I am an apostle.[d] I have seen
Jesus our Lord. You people are all an example
of my work in the Lord. 2If others do not accept
me as an apostle, surely you do, because you are
proof that I am an apostle in the Lord.
3This is the answer I give people who want to
judge me: 4do we not have the right to eat and
drink? 5Do we not have the right to bring a
believing wife with us when we travel as do the
other apostles and the Lord's brothers and Peter?
6Are Barnabas and I the only ones who must
work to earn our living? 7No soldier ever serves
in the army and pays his own salary. No one ever
plants a vineyard without eating some of the
grapes. No person takes care of a flock without
drinking some of the milk.
8I do not say this by human authority; God's
law also says the same thing. 9It is written in the
law of Moses: "When an ox is working in the grain,
do not cover its mouth to keep it from eating."[n]
When God said this, was he thinking only about
oxen? No. 10He was really talking about us. Yes,
that Scripture[d] was written for us, because it
goes on to say: "The one who ploughs and the
one who works in the grain should hope to get
some of the grain for their work." 11Since we
planted spiritual seed among you, is it too much
if we should harvest from you some things for
this life? 12If others have the right to get something from you, surely we have this right, too.
But we do not use it. No, we put up with everything ourselves so that we will not keep anyone
from believing the Good News[d] of Christ.
13Surely you know that those who work at the
Temple[d] get their food from the Temple, and

"When an ox . . . eating." Quotation from Deuteronomy 25:4.

SHARING FAITH

Just Doin' My Job Sir

A paperboy drops a newspaper outside a house on one of his regular rounds. The homeowner opens the door and calls after him, "Thanks for bringing me my paper this morning!"

"Just doin' my job, sir."

A doctor finishes a routine check-up with one of his oldest patients. Before leaving the room, the old lady turns and says, "Thank you for fitting me into your busy schedule."

"Just doin' my job, ma'am."

A missionary is mocked and ridiculed by the very people he's sacrificed everything for. His family is kidnapped, his home is torched, and he's beaten to within an inch of his life and left bleeding in the gutter.

"Just doin' my job, sir."

In **1 Corinthians 9:16–27**, the apostle Paul reminds us that as Christians it is our *duty* to share our faith. We're *all* meant to be missionaries – people willing to set aside our own precious ambitions for the most important job entrusted to mankind this side of heaven – telling the Good News. And if we're doing it properly, we will definitely face tough times. We want health, wealth and happiness, but the Bible promises trials, tests and temptations! Like a good athlete, we must grow stronger through these difficult situations, using self-control to win the prize.

- Read verse 22. Who have you become like, in order to win them to Christ? How much effort did that take?
- When was the last time you were mocked for sharing your faith in Jesus? How much of a threat to the devil are you?

Consider . . .

- disciplining yourself to memorise Bible verses that will come in handy when you're sharing your faith.
- teaming up with other young Christians for the purpose of going out and witnessing together. Why not do it right now?

For more, see . . .

- Isaiah 61:1–3 (p.705)
- Matthew 10:1–15 (p.954)

those who serve at the altar get part of what is
offered at the altar. [14]In the same way, the Lord
has commanded that those who tell the Good
News should get their living from this work.
[15]But I have not used any of these rights. And
I am not writing this now to get anything from
you. I would rather die than have my reason for
boasting taken away. [16]Telling the Good News
does not give me any reason for boasting. Telling
the Good News is my duty—something I must
do. And how terrible it will be for me if I do not
tell the Good News. [17]If I preach because it is my
own choice, I have a reward. But if I preach and
it is not my choice to do so, I am only doing the
duty that was given to me. [18]So what reward do I
get? This is my reward: that when I tell the Good
News I can offer it freely. I do not use my full
rights in my work of preaching the Good News.
[19]I am free and belong to no one. But I make
myself a slave to all people to win as many as I
can. [20]To the Jews I became like a Jew to win the
Jews. I myself am not ruled by the law. But to
those who are ruled by the law I became like a
person who is ruled by the law. I did this to win
those who are ruled by the law. [21]To those who
are without the law I became like a person who
is without the law. I did this to win those people
who are without the law. (But really, I am not
without God's law—I am ruled by Christ's law.)
[22]To those who are weak, I became weak so I
could win the weak. I have become all things to
all people so I could save some of them in any
way possible. [23]I do all this because of the Good
News and so I can share in its blessings.
[24]You know that in a race all the runners run,
but only one gets the prize. So run to win! [25]All
those who compete in the games use self-control
so they can win a crown. That crown is an
earthly thing that lasts only a short time, but our
crown will never be destroyed. [26]So I do not run
without a goal. I fight like a boxer who is hitting
something—not just the air. [27]I treat my body
hard and make it my slave so that I myself will
not be rejected after I have preached to others.

Warnings from Israel's Past

10 Brothers and sisters, I want you to know
what happened to our ancestors who
followed Moses. They were all under the cloud
and all went through the sea. [2]They were all

SEXUALITY

Exit Strategy

There were a few battered chairs and a dartboard in the corner. A group of lads Alex recognised from school were huddled together on one of the sofas in the youth club, flicking through a magazine and laughing. As Alex and Joe approached them, Alex could see they were looking at a "top-shelf" magazine. One of the guys looked up, "Here you go Alex, I found a pile of these in a skip." And he chucked one at him.

"Nah mate, not interested," said Alex. "Come on Joe, let's go and play some pool." But Joe wanted to hang around with the guys. "Come on Joe, let's go."

"It's alright *little boy,* we know you're not quite grown up enough for this yet?" teased one of the boys. Alex could tell that Joe wanted to stay and join in with them. Alex nearly gave in. He was about to sit down and look at the mags when he realised the pool table had just become free.

"Come on Joe, let's see who the little boy is! See if you can beat me at pool, best out of five."

"All right," said Joe, "you're on!"

Read **1 Corinthians 10:1–13**.

- Why is Paul keen to warn the Corinthians not to sin sexually?
- What are the best ways of avoiding temptation to sin sexually?

Consider . . .

- designing an "exit strategy" for times when you are tempted by sexual sin.
- listing situations when you might be tempted sexually. Then decide how you will avoid them.

For more, see . . .

- John 8:31–38 (p.1110)
- Ephesians 5:1–5 (p.1274)
- Galatians 6:7–10 (p.1265)

Sidelight Paul's reference to "running the race" in 1 Corinthians 9:24–27 would have reminded the Corinthians of the Isthmian Games, held every two years in Corinth's coliseum. These games were the most famous athletic competition of their time except for the ancient Olympics. The games might have included wrestling, boxing, chariot races and foot races.

baptised[d] as followers of Moses in the cloud and
in the sea. 3They all ate the same spiritual food,
4and all drank the same spiritual drink. They
drank from that spiritual rock that followed
them, and that rock was Christ. 5But God was
not pleased with most of them, so they died in
the desert.
6And these things happened as examples for us,
to stop us from wanting evil things as those people
did. 7Do not worship idols, as some of them did.
Just as it is written in the Scriptures:[d] "They sat
down to eat and drink, and then they got up and
sinned sexually."[n] 8We must not take part in sex-
ual sins, as some of them did. In one day 23,000
of them died because of their sins. 9We must not
test Christ as some of them did; they were killed
by snakes. 10Do not complain as some of them
did; they were killed by the angel that destroys.
11The things that happened to those people are
examples. They were written down to teach us,
because we live in a time when all these things of
the past have reached their goal. 12If you think you
are strong, you should be careful not to fall. 13The
only temptation that has come to you is that which
everyone has. But you can trust God, who will not
let you be tempted more than you can stand. But
when you are tempted, he will also give you a way
to escape so that you will be able to stand it.
14So, my dear friends, run away from the wor-
ship of idols. 15I am speaking to you as to intelligent
people; judge for yourselves what I say. 16We give
thanks for the cup of blessing,[n] which is a sharing
in the blood of Christ. And the bread that we
break is a sharing in the body of Christ. 17Because
there is one loaf of bread, we who are many are
one body, because we all share that one loaf.
18Think about the Israelites: do not those who
eat the sacrifices share in the altar? 19I do not
mean that the food sacrificed to an idol is impor-
tant. I do not mean that an idol is anything at all.
20But I say that what is sacrificed to idols is offered
to demons,[d] not to God. And I do not want you to
share anything with demons. 21You cannot drink
the cup of the Lord and the cup of demons also.
You cannot share in the Lord's table and the table
of demons. 22Are we trying to make the Lord jeal-
ous? We are not stronger than he is, are we?

How to Use Christian Freedom

23"We are allowed to do all things," but all
things are not good for us to do. "We are allowed
to do all things," but not all things help others
grow stronger. 24Do not look out only for your-
selves. Look out for the good of others also.
25Eat any meat that is sold in the meat market.
Do not ask questions to see if it is meat you think
is wrong to eat. 26You may eat it, "because the
earth belongs to the Lord, and everything in it."[n]
27Those who are not believers may invite you to
eat with them. If you want to go, eat anything that
is put before you. Do not ask questions to see if you
think it might be wrong to eat. 28But if anyone says
to you, "That food was offered to idols," do not eat
it. Do not eat it because of that person who told you
and because eating it might be thought to be
wrong. 29I don't mean you think it is wrong, but the
other person might. But why, you ask, should my
freedom be judged by someone else's conscience?
30If I eat the meal with thankfulness, why am I crit-
icised because of something for which I thank God?
31The answer is, if you eat or drink, or if you do
anything, do it all for the glory of God. 32Never do
anything that might hurt others—Jews, Greeks
or God's church— 33just as I, also, try to please
everybody in every way. I am not trying to do
what is good for me but what is good for most
people so they can be saved.
11 Follow my example, as I follow the
example of Christ.

Being Under Authority

2I praise you because you remember me in
everything, and you follow closely the teachings
just as I gave them to you. 3But I want you to un-
derstand this: the head of every man is Christ, the
head of a woman is the man[n] and the head of Christ
is God. 4Every man who prays or prophesies[d]
with his head covered brings shame to his head.
5But every woman who prays or prophesies with
her head uncovered brings shame to her head.
She is the same as a woman who has her head
shaved. 6If a woman does not cover her head, she
should have her hair cut off. But since it is shame-
ful for a woman to cut off her hair or to shave her
head, she should cover her head. 7But a man
should not cover his head, because he is the

"They . . . sexually." Quotation from Exodus 32:6.
cup of blessing The cup of the fruit of the vine that Christians thank God for and drink at the Lord's Supper.
"because . . . it." Quotation from Psalms 24:1; 50:12; 89:11.
the man This could also mean "her husband".

likeness and glory of God. But woman is man's
glory. 8Man did not come from woman, but
woman came from man. 9And man was not
made for woman, but woman was made for man.
10So that is why a woman should have a symbol
of authority on her head, because of the angels.
11But in the Lord women are not independent
of men, and men are not independent of women.
12This is true because woman came from man,
but also man is born from woman. But everything
comes from God. 13Decide this for yourselves: is it
right for a woman to pray to God with her head
uncovered? 14Even nature itself teaches you that
wearing long hair is shameful for a man. 15But
long hair is a woman's glory. Long hair is given to
her as a covering. 16Some people may still want to
argue about this, but I would add that neither we
nor the churches of God have any other practice.

The Lord's Supper

17In the things I tell you now I do not praise you,
because when you come together you do more
harm than good. 18First, I hear that when you
meet together as a church you are divided, and I
believe some of this. 19(It is necessary to have dif-
ferences among you so that it may be clear which
of you really have God's approval.) 20When you
come together, you are not really eating the Lord's
Supper. [n] 21This is because when you eat, each per-
son eats without waiting for the others. Some peo-
ple do not get enough to eat, while others have too
much to drink. 22You can eat and drink in your
own homes! You seem to think God's church is
not important, and you embarrass those who are
poor. What should I tell you? Should I praise you?
I do not praise you for doing this.

Lord's Supper The special meal that Jesus told his followers to eat to remember him (Luke 22:14–20).

WORSHIP

Remember Me?

The second Sunday in March is a special day for Sharon's family. Each year on this date, her family gathers for a meal. When the table has been cleared, the family photo albums are brought out and passed round.

Everyone smiles to see how each family member has changed from picture to picture over the years. The giggles sometimes erupt into laughter when the pictures prompt funny stories. Sharon's favourite is the one about her dad being chased by a bull when he was a teenager.

And there are always tears when the family sees the photos of its absent members. No eye is dry when photos of Jonathan, Sharon's younger brother, are passed around. He died of cystic fibrosis when he was five.

Some of Sharon's friends think her family's habit is a bit strange. A few have even wondered if it isn't like worshipping the dead.

But Sharon shrugs off their comments. "It's just how we remember the people who've been important to our family. I never met my grandparents, but I feel as if I know them. I've seen their pictures and heard stories about them at least once a year for as long as I can remember," she explains. "I don't think we worship our dead relatives; we just celebrate their lives."

As Christians, we don't worship the dead. But we do worship one who died and rose from the dead. Read **1 Corinthians 11:23–26** to see how Paul explains one way in which Christians can celebrate Jesus' life and work.

- How is the celebration which Paul describes similar to the celebration in Sharon's family? How is it different?
- What do you do in your church and life to remember Jesus?

Consider . . .

- creating other celebrations to remember Jesus. For example, a candlelit dinner could remind you that Jesus is the light of the world.
- talking to your minister about the ways in which your church follows this scripture.

For more, see . . .

- Exodus 12:14–20 (p.70)
- Luke 22:14–20 (p.1087)
- Exodus 16:31–36 (p.75)

23The teaching I gave you is the same teaching
I received from the Lord: on the night when the
Lord Jesus was handed over to be killed, he took
bread 24and gave thanks for it. Then he broke the
bread and said, "This is my body; it is for you. Do
this to remember me." 25In the same way, after
they ate, Jesus took the cup. He said, "This cup
is the new agreement that is sealed with the
blood of my death. When you drink this, do it to
remember me." 26Every time you eat this bread
and drink this cup you are telling others about
the Lord's death until he comes.
27So a person who eats the bread or drinks the
cup of the Lord in a way that is not worthy of it will
be guilty of sinning against the body and the blood
of the Lord. 28Look into your own hearts before you
eat the bread and drink the cup, 29because all who
eat the bread and drink the cup without recognis-
ing the body eat and drink judgement against them-
selves. 30That is why many in your group are sick
and weak, and many have died. 31But if we judged
ourselves in the right way, God would not judge us.
32But when the Lord judges us, he punishes us so
that we will not be destroyed along with the world.
33So my brothers and sisters, when you come
together to eat, wait for each other. 34Anyone
who is too hungry should eat at home so that in
meeting together you will not bring God's judge-
ment on yourselves. I will tell you what to do
about the other things when I come.

Gifts from the Holy Spirit

12 Now, brothers and sisters, I want you to
understand about spiritual gifts. 2You know

SELF-ESTEEM

A Reassuring Gift

People have differing views about spiritual gifts today. This true story shows how important the issue was for one person.

Debbie was a normal twelve-year-old, apart from one invisible but serious problem. She suffered from dyslexia. People like Debbie lack the ability to work out how words should be spelled and often have poor handwriting, as well as finding difficulty with reading and spelling – even when they are very intelligent. Debbie's problem meant that she often felt left out – that God had not given her one very important gift and that she was worth less than other people.

One day Debbie was in a church meeting where people of her age were asked whether they wanted to know the Holy Spirit's power in their lives. During that meeting as she prayed, Debbie received the gift of speaking in different languages – that have never been learned. It is sometimes called the "gift of tongues". The best thing about it was that this new gift made her feel so much closer to her Heavenly Father. Now she felt that God had included her and that she was just as important as everybody else.

Debbie still uses her prayer language to speak to God and still finds spelling a problem. But she found the confidence to apply to university when she was about twenty-two years old. The course was ideal for her because she was sometimes allowed to present her work audiovisually instead of writing essays.

Today Debbie is a qualified social worker, helping families who feel worthless and unwanted.

Read **1 Corinthians 12:1–11** to find out what Paul says about gifts.

- According to the passage what are the important things about spiritual gifts? Are they different from natural abilities?
- How do you feel about gifts like tongues, prophecy and healing?

Consider . . .

- meeting with friends to discuss how you each feel about spiritual gifts (including those mentioned in other parts of the Bible).
- identifying people like Debbie and reassuring them that they are important to God and to you.

For more, see . . .

- 1 Samuel 16:1–13 (p.269)
- 1 Corinthians 14:1–5 (p.1232)
- Romans 12:1–8 (p.1203)

the way you lived before you were believers. You
let yourselves be influenced and led away to
worship idols—things that could not speak. 3 So I
want you to understand that no one who is
speaking with the help of God's Spirit[d] says,
"Jesus be cursed." And no one can say, "Jesus is
Lord," without the help of the Holy Spirit.
4 There are different kinds of gifts, but they are
all from the same Spirit. 5 There are different
ways to serve but the same Lord to serve. 6 And
there are different ways that God works through
people but the same God. God works in all of us
in everything we do. 7 Something from the Spirit
can be seen in each person, for the common
good. 8 The Spirit gives one person the ability to
speak with wisdom, and the same Spirit gives an-
other the ability to speak with knowledge. 9 The
same Spirit gives faith to one person. And, to
another, that one Spirit gives gifts of healing.
10 The Spirit gives to another person the power to
do miracles,[d] to another the ability to prophesy.[d]
And he gives to another the ability to know the
difference between good and evil spirits. The
Spirit gives one person the ability to speak in dif-
ferent kinds of languages[n] and to another the
ability to interpret those languages. 11 One Spirit,
the same Spirit, does all these things, and the
Spirit decides what to give each person.

The Body of Christ Works Together

12 A person's body is only one thing, but it has
many parts. Though there are many parts to a
body, all those parts make only one body. Christ
is like that also. 13 Some of us are Jews, and some
are Greeks. Some of us are slaves, and some are
free. But we were all baptised[d] into one body

languages This can also be translated "tongues".

CHURCH

Watching Every Detail

Michelangelo spent four years painting the 40-metre-long by 13-metre-wide ceiling of the Sistine Chapel. Every day for hours, Michelangelo would lie on his back on the scaffolding, perfecting the details of hundreds of figures from the book of Genesis.

The colour. The curves of the lines. The facial expressions. The shadows. The hair. The noses. The fingers. Every detail was important.

But the ceiling was nearly twenty metres from the floor. Those admiring Michelangelo's work could see the mastery of his work, but they couldn't see the details from so far away.

One day one of Michelangelo's friends asked Michelangelo why he spent so many hours painstakingly perfecting each detail – details no one would ever be able to see. "After all, who will know whether it is perfect or not?" he asked.

"I shall," Michelangelo replied.

Michelangelo saw the many possibilities of detail for the ceiling of the Sistine Chapel. And he knew that when all those details came together, they would make a masterpiece.

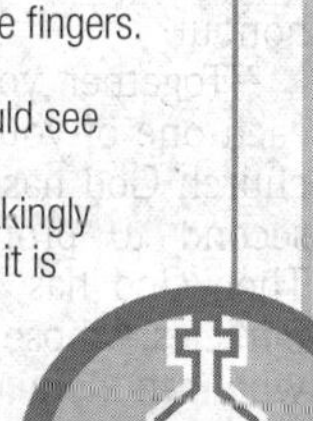

That's what **1 Corinthians 12:12–27** is all about. Read what Paul says about the importance of many parts making one body – the church.

- According to the passage, why are details so important?
- How can this passage help you see to the important gifts that each person brings to your church?

Consider . . .

- asking a teenager, a middle-aged adult, and a senior citizen about the ways in which they contribute to church and why those contributions are important. Then evaluate your own contributions.
- getting involved in the church and using your talents. If you sing, join the choir. If you're good at art, make posters to publicise events.

For more, see . . .

- 1 Kings 5:5–18 (p.318)
- 1 Peter 4:7–11 (p.1360)
- Colossians 3:11–17 (p.1292)

through one Spirit.[d] And we were all made to
share in the one Spirit.
[14]The human body has many parts. [15]The foot
might say, "Because I am not a hand, I am not
part of the body." But saying this would not stop
the foot from being a part of the body. [16]The ear
might say, "Because I am not an eye, I am not
part of the body." But saying this would not stop
the ear from being a part of the body. [17]If the
whole body were an eye, it would not be able to
hear. If the whole body were an ear, it would not
be able to smell. [18–19]If each part of the body
were the same part, there would be no body. But
truly God put all the parts, each one of them, in
the body as he wanted them. [20]So then there are
many parts, but only one body.
[21]The eye cannot say to the hand, "I don't
need you!" And the head cannot say to the foot,
"I don't need you!" [22]No! Those parts of the
body that seem to be the weaker are really
necessary. [23]And the parts of the body we think
are less are the parts to which we give the most
honour. We give special respect to the parts we
want to hide. [24]The more beautiful parts of our
body need no special care. But God put the body
together and gave more honour to the parts that
need it [25]so our body would not be divided. God
wanted the different parts to care the same for
each other. [26]If one part of the body suffers, all
the other parts suffer with it. Or if one part of
our body is honoured, all the other parts share its
honour.
[27]Together you are the body of Christ, and
each one of you is a part of that body. [28]In the
church God has given a place first to apostles,[d]
second to prophets[d] and third to teachers.
Then God has given a place to those who do
miracles,[d] those who have gifts of healing, those
who can help others, those who are able to
govern, and those who can speak in different
languages.[n] [29]Not all are apostles. Not all are
prophets. Not all are teachers. Not all do mira-
cles. [30]Not all have gifts of healing. Not all speak
in different languages. Not all interpret those
languages. [31]But you should truly want to have
the greater gifts.

Love is the Greatest Gift

And now I will show you the best way of all.
13 I may speak in different languages[n] of
people or even angels. But if I do not
have love, I am only a noisy bell or a crashing
cymbal. [2]I may have the gift of prophecy.[d] I may
understand all the secret things of God and have
all knowledge, and I may have faith so great I
can move mountains. But even with all these
things, if I do not have love, then I am nothing.
[3]I may give away everything I have, and I may
even give my body as an offering to be burnt.[n]
But I gain nothing if I do not have love.
[4]Love is patient and kind. Love is not jealous,
it does not boast, and it is not proud. [5]Love is not
rude, is not selfish, and does not get upset with
others. Love does not count up wrongs that have
been done. [6]Love is not happy with evil but is
happy with the truth. [7]Love patiently accepts
all things. It always trusts, always hopes, and
always remains strong.
[8]Love never ends. There are gifts of prophecy,
but they will be ended. There are gifts of speak-
ing in different languages, but those gifts will
stop. There is the gift of knowledge, but it will
come to an end. [9]The reason is that our knowl-
edge and our ability to prophesy are not perfect.
[10]But when perfection comes, the things that are
not perfect will end. [11]When I was a child, I
talked like a child, I thought like a child, I
reasoned like a child. When I became a man, I
stopped those childish ways. [12]It is the same
with us. Now we see a dim reflection, as if we
were looking into a mirror, but then we shall see
clearly. Now I know only a part, but then I will
know fully, as God has known me. [13]So these
three things continue for ever: faith, hope and
love. And the greatest of these is love.

Sidelight The Bible's famous "love chapter" (1 Corinthians 13) stands in sharp contrast to the kind of "love" for which Corinth was infamous. Above Corinth on the hill of Acropolis was the temple of Aphrodite, who was the Greek goddess of love. Prostitute-priestesses worked in that temple, supposedly "cleansing" men of sin through weird sexual acts.

Desire Spiritual Gifts

14 You should seek after love, and you
should truly want to have the spiritual
gifts, especially the gift of prophecy.[d] [2]I will ex-
plain why. Those who have the gift of speaking
in different languages[n] are not speaking to peo-
ple; they are speaking to God. No one under-
stands them; they are speaking secret things
through the Spirit.[d] [3]But those who prophesy

languages This can also be translated "tongues".
Verse 3 Other Greek copies read: "hand over my body in order that I may boast."

are speaking to people to give them strength, encouragement and comfort. 4The ones who speak in different languages are helping only themselves, but those who prophesy are helping the whole church. 5I wish all of you had the gift of speaking in different kinds of languages, but more, I wish you would prophesy. Those who prophesy are greater than those who can only speak in different languages—unless someone is there who can explain what is said so that the whole church can be helped.

6Brothers and sisters, will it help you if I come to you speaking in different languages? No! It will help you only if I bring you a new truth or some new knowledge, or prophecy, or teaching. 7It is the same as with lifeless things that make sounds—like a flute or a harp. If they do not make clear musical notes, you will not know what is being played. 8And in a war, if the trumpet does not give a clear sound, who will prepare for battle? 9It is the same with you. Unless you speak clearly with your tongue, no one can understand what you are saying. You will be talking into the air! 10It may be true that there are all kinds of sounds in the world, and none is without meaning. 11But unless I understand the meaning of what someone says to me, I will be a foreigner to him, and he will be a foreigner to me. 12It is the same with you. Since you want spiritual gifts very much, seek most of all to have the gifts that help the church grow stronger.

13The one who has the gift of speaking in a different language should pray for the gift to interpret what is spoken. 14If I pray in a different language, my spirit is praying, but my mind does

LOVE

All or Nothing?

Scott and Charlotte were Christians. They went to the same church youth group. They both really liked each other and eventually Scott asked her out on a date.

Charlotte's friends came round to help her get ready and soon it came to 7.30 p.m., when Scott would be arriving to pick her up.

When the doorbell rang, Charlotte ran down the stairs and flung the door open . . . all she could see was roses. Scott had brought her a dozen red roses and a box of her favourite chocolates!

"I just want everything to be perfect tonight," Scott explained. They left for the date and Charlotte was continually surprised by Scott's generosity. He gave her compliments all night and paid for a lovely meal and for tickets to a film she really wanted to see.

On the way out of the cinema, Charlotte thanked Scott for such a great time.

"It wasn't difficult," Scott said, "you're easy to do nice things for. I really like you!"

Just as he said that, they passed a homeless man on the street who was asking for money.

"Should we give him anything?" Charlotte asked Scott.

Begrudgingly, Scott said, "Er, well I guess we ought to give him a little something because we're Christians."

Read **1 Corinthians 13:1–13**.

- Why was it easy for Scott to be loving towards Charlotte but not the homeless man?
- Verses 4–8 talk about the gifts or qualities of love that we should show. Which ones do you find the easiest and which are the hardest?

Consider . . .

- making a list of the people you find difficult to love and copy out verses 4–8 alongside it. Pray for them each week that God would help you to love them more and to show it.
- hanging on with a friend or relative you are about to give up on. Keep loving this person through a difficult time.

For more, see . . .

- Matthew 5:43–48 (p.946)
- Luke 6:27–36 (p.1048)

nothing. 15So what should I do? I will pray with
my spirit, but I will also pray with my mind.
I will sing with my spirit, but I will also sing
with my mind. 16If you praise God with your
spirit, those persons there without understanding
cannot say amen[n] to your prayer of thanks, be-
cause they do not know what you are saying.
17You may be thanking God in a good way, but
the other person is not helped.
18I thank God that I speak in different kinds
of languages more than all of you. 19But in the
church meetings I would rather speak five words
I understand in order to teach others than thou-
sands of words in a different language.
20Brothers and sisters, do not think like chil-
dren. In evil things be like babies, but in your
thinking you should be like adults. 21It is written
in the Scriptures:[d]

"With people who use strange words and
foreign languages
The LORD will speak to these people.
But people would not listen to me,"
Isaiah 28:11–12

says the Lord.
22So the gift of speaking in different kinds of
languages is a proof for those who do not be-
lieve, not for those who do believe. And
prophecy is for people who believe, not for those
who do not believe. 23Suppose the whole church
meets together and everyone speaks in different
languages. If some people come in who do not
understand or do not believe, they will say you
are mad. 24But suppose everyone is prophesying
and some people come in who do not believe or
do not understand. If everyone is prophesying,
their sin will be shown to them, and they will be
judged by all that they hear. 25The secret things
in their hearts will be made known. So they will
bow down and worship God saying, "Truly, God
is with you."

amen To say amen means to agree with the things that were said.

HOLY SPIRIT

A New Dimension

Knowing how to pray can sometimes be a real problem.

Richard was at his church prayer meeting and was praying quietly for each of the people in the college Christian group where he was one of the student leaders.

Even though he was just an average teenage Christian he did want to see each of the people he was involved with developing their relationship with God. Prayer was going well until he came to one particular girl – Sarah. Was she a Christian or was she not? She probably was but he was unsure. How should he pray?

Richard chose to pray in different languages (or tongues) as Paul suggested in **1 Corinthians 14:13–20**.

Richard prayed quietly for some minutes and stopped when he knew that God had answered his prayers, even though he did not understand what he was praying.

Several days later, at a special meeting attended by the college group, Sarah decided to become a Christian. As she explained to her friends, "I knew that I needed to be sure." Richard was glad that the Holy Spirit had helped him pray effectively.

- According to this passage, what does Paul think about speaking in different languages given by the Spirit?
- Are there the same dangers with other spiritual gifts?

Consider . . .

- getting together with your friends and discussing ways in which you need the Holy Spirit's help in praying.
- thumbing through your address book and asking the Holy Spirit how you might pray for each person listed.

For more, see . . .

- Jonah 4 (p.888)
- Romans 8:26–27 (p.1196)
- Matthew 6:5–15 (p.948)
- 1 Timothy 2:1–4 (p.1308)

Meetings Should Help the Church

26So, brothers and sisters, what should you
do? When you meet together, one person has a
song, and another has a teaching. Another has
a new truth from God. Another speaks in a
different language,[n] and another person inter-
prets that language. The purpose of all these
things should be to help the church grow
strong. 27When you meet together, if anyone
speaks in a different language, it should be
only two, or not more than three, who speak.
They should speak one after the other, and
someone else should interpret. 28But if there
is no interpreter, then those who speak in a
different language should be quiet in the church
meeting. They should speak only to themselves
and to God.
29Only two or three prophets[d] should speak,
and the others should judge what they say. 30If a
message from God comes to another person
who is sitting, the first speaker should stop.
31You can all prophesy one after the other. In
this way all the people can be taught and en-
couraged. 32The spirits of prophets are under
the control of the prophets themselves. 33God is
not a God of confusion but a God of peace.
As is true in all the churches of God's people,
34women should keep quiet in the church meet-
ings. They are not allowed to speak, but they
must yield to this rule as the law says. 35If they
want to learn something, they should ask their
own husbands at home. It is shameful for a
woman to speak in the church meeting. 36Did
God's teaching come from you? Or are you the
only ones to whom it has come?
37Those who think they are prophets or spiri-
tual persons should understand that what I am
writing to you is the Lord's command. 38Those
who ignore this will be ignored by God.
39So my brothers and sisters, you should truly
want to prophesy. But do not stop people from
using the gift of speaking in different kinds of
languages. 40But let everything be done in a
right and orderly way.

The Good News About Christ

15 Now, brothers and sisters, I want you to
remember the Good News[d] I brought to
you. You received this Good News and continue
strong in it. 2And you are being saved by it if you
continue believing what I told you. If you do
not, then you believed for nothing.
3I passed on to you what I received, of which
this was most important: that Christ died for our
sins, as the Scriptures[d] say; 4that he was buried
and was raised to life on the third day as
the Scriptures say; 5and that he was seen by
Peter and then by the twelve apostles.[d] 6After
that, Jesus was seen by more than 500 of the
believers at the same time. Most of them are still
living today, but some have died. 7Then he was
seen by James and later by all the apostles. 8Last
of all he was seen by me—as by a person not
born at the normal time. 9All the other apostles
are greater than I am. I am not even good
enough to be called an apostle, because I perse-
cuted the church of God. 10But God's grace has
made me what I am, and his grace to me was not
wasted. I worked harder than all the other apos-
tles. (But it was not I really; it was God's grace
that was with me.) 11So if I preached to you or
the other apostles preached to you, we all preach
the same thing, and this is what you believed.

We will be Raised from the Dead

12Now since we preached that Christ was
raised from the dead, why do some of you say
that people will not be raised from the dead? 13If
no one is ever raised from the dead, then Christ
has not been raised. 14And if Christ has not been
raised, then our preaching is worth nothing,
and your faith is worth nothing. 15And also,
we are guilty of lying about God, because we
testified of him that he raised Christ from the
dead. But if people are not raised from the dead,
then God never raised Christ. 16If the dead are
not raised, Christ has not been raised either.
17And if Christ has not been raised, then your
faith has nothing to it; you are still guilty of your
sins. 18And those in Christ who have already
died are lost. 19If our hope in Christ is for this life
only, we should be pitied more than anyone else
in the world.
20But Christ has truly been raised from the
dead—the first one, and proof that those who
sleep in death will also be raised. 21Death has
come because of what one man did, but the ris-
ing from death also comes because of one man.
22In Adam all of us die. In the same way, in
Christ all of us will be made alive again. 23But
everyone will be raised to life in the right order.
Christ was first to be raised. When Christ comes
again, those who belong to him will be raised to
life, 24and then the end will come. At that time
Christ will destroy all rulers, authorities and
powers, and he will hand over the kingdom to
God the Father. 25Christ must rule until he puts
all enemies under his control. 26The last enemy
to be destroyed will be death. 27The Scripture[d]
says that God put all things under his control.[n]

language This can also be translated "tongue".
God put . . . control. From Psalm 8:6.

When it says "all things" are under him, it is clear
this does not include God himself. God is the
One who put everything under his control.
28After everything has been put under the Son,
then he will put himself under God, who had
put all things under him. Then God will be the
complete ruler over everything.
29If the dead are never raised, what will peo-
ple do who are being baptised[d] for the dead? If
the dead are not raised at all, why are people
being baptised for them?
30And what about us? Why do we put our-
selves in danger every hour? 31I die every day.
That is true, brothers and sisters, just as it is true
that I boast about you in Christ Jesus our Lord.
32If I fought wild animals in Ephesus only with
human hopes, I have gained nothing. If the dead
are not raised, "Let us eat and drink, because
tomorrow we will die."[n]
33Do not be fooled: "Bad friends will ruin
good habits." 34Come back to your right way of
thinking and stop sinning. Some of you do not
know God—I say this to shame you.

What Kind of Body will We Have?

35But someone may ask, "How are the dead
raised? What kind of body will they have?"
36Foolish person! When you sow a seed, it must

Sidelight Though Paul probably didn't fight wild animals himself (1 Corinthians 15:32), he is probably referring to the Roman "sport" of putting prisoners in an arena, then releasing wild animals to maul the prisoners while huge crowds watched. Animals used in this activity included lions, bears, leopards, rhinoceroses, crocodiles, tigers and elephants. A decade after Paul wrote this letter, Christians faced this kind of persecution.

"Let us . . . die." Quotation from Isaiah 22:13; 56:12.

FAITH

Stick With It

It's not easy to become an emperor moth. To emerge into the world, the moth must force its way through the neck of a flask-shaped cocoon. Getting through this opening takes hours of intense struggle. The insect must squirm and wriggle to push its way through.

If you watched an emperor moth's struggle, you might feel sorry for the struggling insect and snip the confining threads to make an easier exit. But if you did, the moth would never develop its wings. Instead, it would spend most of its life crawling, never able to spread its wings and fly.

Scientists who study this moth believe that the pressure on the insect's body forces the essential juices into the wings, thus preparing the wings for flight. Without the pressure, the wings would never become strong.

Sometimes having faith is difficult. Like the emperor moth, we struggle. We feel overwhelmed – tested. And we wish someone would step in and take the struggle away.

But our faith grows through those struggles, as Paul reminds us in **1 Corinthians 15:1–11**.

- According to this passage, what are we to continue to believe in?
- How can the example of the people's faith in this passage encourage you when you struggle with your faith?

Consider . . .

- phoning an older person in your congregation to ask about his or her journey of faith – including the ups and downs.
- talking to a friend about the ways in which you have grown after a difficult time.

For more, see . . .

- Genesis 22 (p.25)
- Hebrews 11 (p.1341)
- Daniel 3 (p.835)

die in the ground before it can live and grow.
37And when you sow it, it does not have the same
"body" it will have later. What you sow is only a
bare seed, maybe wheat or something else. 38But
God gives it a body that he has planned for it, and
God gives each kind of seed its own body. 39All
things made of flesh are not the same: people
have one kind of flesh, animals have another,
birds have another and fish have another. 40Also
there are heavenly bodies and earthly bodies. But
the beauty of the heavenly bodies is one kind,
and the beauty of the earthly bodies is another.
41The sun has one kind of beauty, the moon has
another beauty and the stars have another. And
each star is different in its beauty.

42It is the same with the dead who are raised to
life. The body that is "planted" will ruin and
decay, but it is raised to a life that cannot be
destroyed. 43When the body is "planted", it is
without honour, but it is raised in glory. When
the body is "planted", it is weak, but when it is
raised, it is powerful. 44The body that is "planted"
is a physical body. When it is raised, it is a
spiritual body.

There is a physical body, and there is also a
spiritual body. 45It is written in the Scriptures: [d]
"The first man, Adam, became a living person." [n]
But the last Adam became a spirit that gives life.
46The spiritual did not come first, but the physical
and then the spiritual. 47The first man came from
the dust of the earth. The second man came from
heaven. 48People who belong to the earth are like
the first man of earth. But those people who be-
long to heaven are like the man of heaven. 49Just
as we were made like the man of earth, so we
will also be made like the man of heaven.

50I tell you this, brothers and sisters: flesh and
blood cannot have a part in the kingdom of God.
Something that will ruin cannot have a part in
something that never ruins. 51But look! I tell you
this secret: we will not all sleep in death, but we
will all be changed. 52It will take only a second—
as quickly as an eye blinks—when the last trum-
pet sounds. The trumpet will sound, and those
who have died will be raised to live for ever, and
we will all be changed. 53This body that can be
destroyed must clothe itself with something that
can never be destroyed. And this body that dies

"The first . . . person." Quotation from Genesis 2:7.

DEATH

Life After Death

What do teenagers think about death? According to a Gallup poll, two-thirds of teenagers believe in life after death. But while most teenagers believe in life after death, most teenagers also fear death. According to a Youth Monitor poll:

- Three out of four teenagers worry that one of their parents will die.
- Half worry about themselves dying.
- Two other major worries – being in a car accident or a plane crash – also hint at this fear of death.

Fearing death is natural for most people. But Paul says that death isn't final for Christians. Read about the other side of death in **1 Corinthians 15:12–28**.

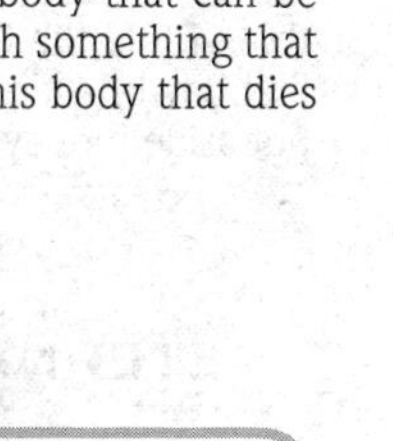

- Why does Paul talk about Christ when explaining being raised from the dead?
- How does this passage help you to deal with your fears about death?

Consider . . .

- going to a church cemetery and reading the epitaphs on gravestones. Decide how you can develop the faith and hope indicated by the sayings.
- having coffee with your youth leader and talking about your fears concerning death.

For more, see . . .

- Isaiah 57:1–2 (p.700)
- Hebrews 2:14–15 (p.1331)
- John 5:24–29 (p.1104)

must clothe itself with something that can never
die. 54So this body that can be destroyed will
clothe itself with that which can never be
destroyed, and this body that dies will clothe
itself with that which can never die. When this
happens, this Scripture will be made true:
"Death is destroyed for ever." *Isaiah 25:8*
55"Death, where is your victory?
Where is your pain, place of death?"
Hosea 13:14
56Death's power to hurt is sin, and the power of
sin is the law. [d] 57But we thank God! He gives us
the victory through our Lord Jesus Christ.
58So my dear brothers and sisters, stand
strong. Do not let anything change you. Always
give yourselves fully to the work of the Lord, be-
cause you know that your work in the Lord is
never wasted.

The Gift for Other Believers

16 Now I will write about the collection of
money for God's people. Do the same
thing I told the Galatian churches to do: 2on the
first day of every week, each one of you should
put aside money as you have been blessed. Save
it up so you will not have to collect money after
I come. 3When I arrive, I will send whomever
you approve to take your gift to Jerusalem. I will
send them with letters of introduction, 4and if it
seems good for me to go also, they will go along
with me.

Paul's Plans

5I plan to go through Macedonia, so I will
come to you after I go through there. 6Perhaps I
will stay with you for a time or even all winter.
Then you can help me on my trip, wherever
I go. 7I do not want to see you now just in pass-
ing. I hope to stay a longer time with you if the
Lord allows it. 8But I will stay at Ephesus until
Pentecost, [d] 9because a good opportunity for a
great and growing work has been given to me
now. And there are many people working
against me.
10If Timothy comes to you, see to it that he has
nothing to fear with you, because he is working
for the Lord just as I am. 11So none of you should
treat Timothy as unimportant, but help him on
his way in peace so that he can come back to me.
I am expecting him to come with the brothers.

ETERNAL LIFE

We Shall All Be Changed

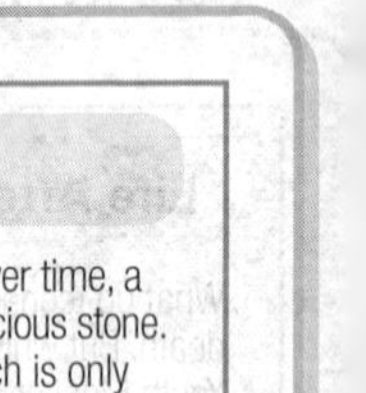

Coal, buried deep within the earth, sometimes encounters intense pressure and heat. When it does, over time, a diamond results. Under the right conditions, the mineral beryl transforms into an emerald, another precious stone. But if beryl contains impurities and undergoes the same conditions, the result is aquamarine – which is only a semi-precious stone. When rocks with specks of gold are melted, the weighty gold deposits sink to the bottom, and the impurities are scraped from the top. After the process has been repeated several times, only pure gold remains.

Just as minerals change under the right conditions, so our bodies will change at death. In **1 Corinthians 15:35–58**, Paul talks about the transformation and refining that will occur in our bodies.

- How will the change in our bodies be similar to what happens to rocks? How will it be different?
- How does the value of eternal life compare with the value of precious stones?

Consider . . .

- drawing a picture of what you think heaven will be like.
- hanging a "We Shall All Be Changed" sign in your wardrobe to remind you of how our earthly bodies will change.

For more, see . . .

- Job 19:25–27 (p.481)
- Revelation 22:1–5 (p.1404)
- Psalm 73:23–28 (p.544)

12Now about our brother Apollos: I strongly
encouraged him to visit you with the other
brothers. He did not at all want to come now; he
will come when he has the opportunity.

Paul Ends His Letter

13Be careful. Continue strong in the faith. Have
courage, and be strong. 14Do everything in love.
15You know that the family of Stephanas
were the first believers in Southern Greece and
that they have given themselves to the service of
God's people. I ask you, brothers and sisters, 16to
follow the leading of people like these and
anyone else who works and serves with them.
17I am happy that Stephanas, Fortunatus and
Achaicus have come. You are not here, but they
have filled your place. 18They have refreshed my
spirit and yours. You should recognise the value
of people like these.
19The churches in the country of Asia send
greetings to you. Aquila and Priscilla greet you
in the Lord, as does the church that meets in
their house. 20All the brothers and sisters here
send greetings. Give each other a holy kiss
when you meet.
21I, Paul, am writing this greeting with my
own hand.
22If anyone does not love the Lord, let him be
separated from God—lost for ever!

Come, O Lord!

23The grace of the Lord Jesus be with you.
24My love be with all of you in Christ Jesus.

2 Corinthians

Why Read This Book:

- Explore what it means to be a minister for Christ (2 Corinthians 1—7).
- Be challenged to give generously to God's work (2 Corinthians 8—9).
- See what Christians have to brag about (2 Corinthians 10—13).

When?

Time Line:

- BC/AD — Jesus was born
- AD 25 — Jesus began his ministry
- The church began soon after Jesus went to heaven
- Paul began his missionary work
- AD 50 — Paul founded the church in Corinth
- Paul wrote 2 Corinthians
- Fire destroyed Rome
- Romans destroyed the Temple in Jerusalem
- AD 75
- AD 100

Behind the Scenes:

Paul frequently had to handle people problems. In 1 Corinthians, Paul urged the Christians of Corinth to stop arguing and start working together as they followed Christ. They listened, and the divisions in the church were healed. But then, about a year later, word gets back to him that they are heading for trouble once again . . .

The problem was that some people had started spreading rumours about Paul. They said that he was unqualified, unstable, boastful and a liar. Even worse, the Corinthians believed these lies, and turned to false teachers for guidance.

Paul was obviously upset that the people he loved were turning against him, but he was more concerned with the fact that they were being led away from following Jesus by these false teachers. He had been forced into defending his ministry, and he did so by writing a blunt letter to the Corinthians (which unfortunately has been lost), being careful not to pull any punches (see 2 Corinthians 2:3–4). In this letter, he demanded that the people stop following the false teachers and turn back to Christ. The church followed his advice and told him how much they cared for him. Paul breathed a sigh of relief and thanked God that the crisis was over.

In 2 Corinthians, Paul begins to rebuild his damaged relationship with the Corinthians by explaining why he wrote the letter (see 2 Corinthians 7:6–16), and telling them how much he loves them (see 2 Corinthians 12:11–21).

This letter shows us that being a Christian leader isn't easy. Leaders are just as human as the next person, and they have feelings that can be hurt. Read 2 Corinthians and see for yourself how a Christian leader feels when faced with difficulties in the church.

Where?

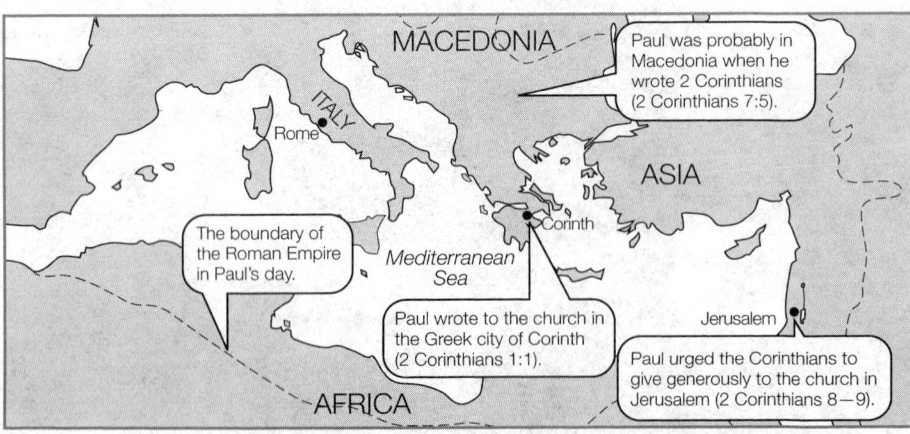

1 From Paul, an apostle[d] of Christ Jesus. I
am an apostle because that is what God
wanted. Also from Timothy our brother in
Christ.
To the church of God in Corinth, and to all of
God's people everywhere in Southern Greece:
[2]Grace and peace to you from God our Father
and the Lord Jesus Christ.

Sidelight The Corinthian church was made up of a varied group of people who came to this major city from around the world. Paul hints at this when he addresses them in 2 Corinthians 1:2 with "grace", a Greek greeting, and "peace", a Hebrew greeting.

Paul Gives Thanks to God

[3]Praise be to the God and Father of our Lord
Jesus Christ. God is the Father who is full of
mercy and all comfort. [4]He comforts us every
time we have trouble, so when others have
trouble, we can comfort them with the same
comfort God gives us. [5]We share in the many
sufferings of Christ. In the same way, much
comfort comes to us through Christ. [6]If we have
troubles, it is for your comfort and salvation,
and if we have comfort, you also have comfort.
This helps you to accept patiently the same suf-
ferings we have. [7]Our hope for you is strong,
knowing that you share in our sufferings and
also in the comfort we receive.
[8]Brothers and sisters,[n] we want you to know
about the trouble we suffered in Asia. We had
great burdens there that were beyond our own
strength. We even gave up hope of living.
[9]Truly, in our own hearts we believed we would
die. But this happened so we would not trust in
ourselves but in God, who raises people from
the dead. [10]God saved us from these great dan-
gers of death, and he will continue to save us.
We have put our hope in him, and he will save
us again. [11]And you can help us with your
prayers. Then many people will give thanks for
us—that God blessed us because of their many
prayers.

The Change in Paul's Plans

[12]This is what we are proud of, and I can say
it with a clear heart: in everything we have done
in the world, and especially with you, we have
had an honest and sincere heart from God. We
did this by God's grace, not by the kind of wis-
dom the world has. [13–14]We write to you only
what you can read and understand. And I hope
that as you have understood some things about
us, you may come to know everything about us.
Then you can be proud of us, as we will be proud
of you on the day our Lord Jesus Christ comes
again.
[15]I was so sure of all this that I made plans to
visit you first so you could be blessed twice. [16]I
planned to visit you on my way to Macedonia and
again on my way back. I wanted to get help from
you for my trip to Judea. [17]Do you think that I
made these plans without really meaning it? Or
maybe you think I make plans as the world does,
so that I say "yes, yes" and at the same time
"no, no."
[18]But if you can believe God, you can believe
that what we tell you is never both "yes" and
"no". [19]The Son of God, Jesus Christ, that Silas
and Timothy and I preached to you, was not
"yes" and "no". In Christ it has always been
"yes". [20]The "yes" to all of God's promises is in
Christ, and through Christ we say "yes" to the
glory of God. [21]Remember, God is the One who
makes you and us strong in Christ. God made
us his chosen people. [22]He put his mark on us
to show that we are his, and he put his Spirit[d]
in our hearts to be a guarantee for all he has
promised.
[23]I tell you this, and I ask God to be my witness
that this is true: the reason I did not come back
to Corinth was to keep you from being punished
or hurt. [24]We are not trying to control your faith.
You are strong in faith. But we are workers with
you for your own joy.
2 So I decided that my next visit to you would
not be another one to make you sad. [2]If I
make you sad, who will make me glad? Only
you can make me glad—particularly the person
whom I made sad. [3]I wrote you a letter for this
reason: that when I came to you I would not be
made sad by the people who should make me
happy. I felt sure of all of you, that you would
share my joy. [4]When I wrote to you before, I was
very troubled and unhappy in my heart, and I
wrote with many tears. I did not write to make
you sad, but to let you know how much I
love you.

Forgive the Sinner

[5]Someone there among you has caused sad-
ness, not to me, but to all of you. I mean he

Brothers and sisters Although the Greek text says "brothers" here and throughout this book, Paul's words were meant for the entire church, both men and women.

caused sadness to all in some way. (I do not want to make it sound worse than it really is.) 6The punishment that most of you gave him is enough for him. 7But now you should forgive him and comfort him to keep him from having too much sadness and giving up completely. 8So I beg you to show that you love him. 9I wrote to you to test you and to see if you obey in everything. 10If you forgive someone, I also forgive him. And what I have forgiven—if I had anything to forgive—I forgave it for you, as if Christ were with me. 11I did this so that Satan would not win anything from us, because we know very well what Satan's plans are.

Paul's Concern in Troas

12When I came to Troas to preach the Good News[d] of Christ, the Lord gave me a good opportunity there. 13But I had no peace, because I did not find my brother Titus. So I said goodbye to them at Troas and went to Macedonia.

Victory Through Christ

14But thanks be to God, who always leads us in victory through Christ. God uses us to spread his knowledge everywhere like a sweet-smelling perfume. 15Our offering to God is this: we are the sweet smell of Christ among those who are being saved and among those who are being lost. 16To those who are lost, we are the smell of death that brings death, but to those who are being saved, we are the smell of life that brings life. So who is able to do this work? 17We do not sell the word of God for a profit as many other people do. But in Christ we speak the truth before God, as messengers of God.

Servants of the New Agreement

3 Are we starting to boast about ourselves again? Do we need letters of introduction to you or from you, like some other people? 2You yourselves are our letter, written on our hearts, known and read by everyone. 3You show that you are a letter from Christ sent through us. This letter is not written with ink but with the Spirit[d] of the living God. It is not written on stone tablets[n] but on human hearts.

4We can say this, because through Christ we feel certain before God. 5We are not saying that we can do this work ourselves. It is God who makes us able to do all that we do. 6He made us able to be servants of a new agreement from himself to his people. This new agreement is not a written law, but it is of the Spirit. The written law brings death, but the Spirit gives life.

7The law that brought death was written in words on stone. It came with God's glory, which made Moses' face so bright that the Israelites could not continue to look at it. But that glory later disappeared. 8So surely the new way that brings the Spirit has even more glory. 9If the law that judged people guilty of sin had glory, surely the new way that makes people right with God has much greater glory. 10That old law had glory, but it really loses its glory when it is compared to the much greater glory of this new way. 11If that law which disappeared came with glory, then this new way which continues for ever has much greater glory.

12We have this hope, so we are very bold. 13We are not like Moses, who put a covering over his face so the Israelites would not see it. The glory was disappearing, and Moses did not want them to see it fade. 14But their minds were closed, and even today that same covering hides the meaning when they read the old agreement. That covering is taken away only through Christ. 15Even today, when they read the law of Moses, there is a covering over their minds. 16But when a person changes and follows the Lord, that covering is taken away. 17The Lord is the Spirit, and where the Spirit of the Lord is, there is freedom. 18Our faces, then, are not covered. We all show the Lord's glory, and we are being changed to be like him. This change in us brings ever greater glory, which comes from the Lord, who is the Spirit.

Preaching the Good News

4 God, with his mercy, gave us this work to do, so we don't give up. 2But we have turned away from secret and shameful ways. We use no trickery, and we do not change the teaching of God. We teach the truth plainly, showing everyone who we are. Then they can know in their hearts what kind of people we are in God's sight. 3If the Good News[d] that we preach is hidden, it is hidden only to those who are lost. 4The devil who rules this world has blinded the minds of those who do not believe. They cannot see the light of the Good News—the Good News about the glory of Christ, who is exactly like God. 5We do not preach about ourselves, but we preach

stone tablets Meaning the law of Moses that was written on stone tablets (Exodus 24:12; 32:16).

that Jesus Christ is Lord and that we are your
servants for Jesus. 6God once said, "Let the
light shine out of the darkness!" This is the
same God who made his light shine in our
hearts by letting us know the glory of God that
is in the face of Christ.

Spiritual Treasure in Clay Jars

7We have this treasure from God, but we are
like clay jars that hold the treasure. This shows
that the great power is from God, not from us.
8We have troubles all around us, but we are not
defeated. We do not know what to do, but we
do not give up the hope of living. 9We are

> **Sidelight** Hiding treasures in clay jars was a common practice in biblical times, because people didn't suspect anything valuable would be kept in such a container (2 Corinthians 4:7). It's like hiding your money in a sock.

NON-CHRISTIANS

Trying Too Hard

David tried to live a perfect life. He went to church and was active in his youth group. He faithfully read the Bible and shared his faith with others.

David's problem was that he got carried away.

At school David constantly talked about his beliefs. In history lessons he challenged everything his teacher said. In science lessons he blasted theories and ideas as un-Christian. During lunch he commented on other people's food, telling them that God wanted them to treat their bodies like a temple. Between classes he witnessed in the halls.

At first, teachers and students listened to him. But soon, people around him grew irritated. Teachers began to cut him off, and students just laughed. The more they laughed or ignored him the harder he tried. Finally, even other Christians began to sneer. They started calling him "the preacher" and "super Christian".

Holly was also a Christian. Although she, too, was tired of David's style, she felt sorry when others put him down. One day David complained to Holly that no one ever listened.

"Perhaps you're trying too hard," Holly suggested. "After all, we don't have to be preaching all the time. We just need to let God's love shine through."

Over the next few weeks, whenever Holly saw David she just smiled. For a long time David didn't seem to have heard her. He just kept on preaching and witnessing, and students kept on making fun of him.

Slowly, David began following Holly's advice. He still lived out his faith, but instead of being obnoxious, he expressed it with a smile, a kind word or an offer of help. And, for the first time, people began responding positively to David's efforts.

Sometimes we get so tied up in trying to convert others that we don't let God's love show through us to non-Christians. Read **2 Corinthians 4:3–12** to discover more about the treasure of God's love and how to share your faith with the world.

- How does David's discovery relate to Paul's belief that we are clay jars holding the treasure of God's love?
- How have you shared God's treasure with a non-Christian?

Consider . . .

- asking God to teach you how to respect others while you share your beliefs with them.
- inviting a friend who doesn't go to church to come with you to worship. Introduce him or her to your Christian friends.

For more, see . . .

- Genesis 18:16–33 (p.21)
- Colossians 3:12–17 (p.1293)
- Matthew 28:16–20 (p.994)

persecuted, but God does not leave us. We are
hurt sometimes, but we are not destroyed. 10 We
carry the death of Jesus in our own bodies
so that the life of Jesus can also be seen in our
bodies. 11 We are alive, but for Jesus we are
always in danger of death so that the life of
Jesus can be seen in our bodies that die. 12 So
death is working in us, but life is working in
you.
13 It is written in the Scriptures,[d] "I believed,
so I spoke."[n] Our faith is like this too. We
believe, and so we speak. 14 God raised the Lord
Jesus from the dead, and we know that God
will also raise us with Jesus. God will bring us
together with you, and we will stand before
him. 15 All these things are for you. And so the
grace of God that is being given to more and
more people will bring increasing thanks to
God for his glory.

Living by Faith

16 So we do not give up. Our physical body is
becoming older and weaker, but our spirit in-
side us is made new every day. 17 We have small
troubles for a while now, but they are helping
us gain an eternal glory that is much greater
than the troubles. 18 We set our eyes not on
what we see but on what we cannot see. What
we see will last only a short time, but what we
cannot see will last for ever.

5 We know that our body—the tent we live
in here on earth—will be destroyed. But when

"I . . . spoke." Quotation from Psalm 116:10.

FAITH

Unseen Water

Frank Zeigler's ranch in Wyoming, USA, had been in his family for years, but had never been used. It was full of cacti and rocks. Surely the land could be used for something, Frank thought. He thought of raising sheep, but sheep couldn't live there without water. He thought of mining the minerals that had been discovered long ago, but there was no water to process the ore.

"I know there is more," he told his wife. "I just know there is. God is always giving us gifts, but half the time we don't see them."

One day as he rode across the barren range, he suddenly stopped. He piled up five or six rocks then went home and phoned a drilling company. Frank told them to drill a deep water well where he had piled the rocks.

At first the owners laughed. "There's no water on that land. You know that," they teased.

But he insisted. "I just have a feeling it's there," he said. Finally they agreed to drill. Months later, they hit water almost one mile underground.

Astonished, the drilling crew asked how he knew water was down there. Frank shrugged. "I guess I had the faith that there was more there than my eyes could see."

As Frank did, it's important for us to have faith not just in things seen but in things unseen as well.

To learn more, read **2 Corinthians 4:13–18**.

- How does Frank's search for water parallel the faith described in the passage? How does it differ?
- Which part of this passage gives you the greatest sense of hope in your faith?

Consider . . .

- thinking about things that you know exist even though you can't see them, such as air and electricity. List ways in which you know that God exists even though you can't see him.
- stepping out in faith in an area where you may not have all the "facts" but still believe that what you're doing is God's will.

For more, see . . .

- Psalm 116 (p.569)
- Colossians 3:1–4 (p.1292)
- Romans 8:18–28 (p.1195)

that happens, God will have a house for us. It will not be a house made by human hands; instead, it will be a home in heaven that will last for ever. 2But now we groan in this tent. We want God to give us our heavenly home, 3because it will clothe us so we will not be naked. 4While we live in this body, we have burdens, and we groan. We do not want to be naked, but we want to be clothed with our heavenly home. Then this body that dies will be fully covered with life. 5This is what God made us for, and he has given us the Spirit[d] to be a guarantee for this new life.

6So we always have courage. We know that while we live in this body, we are away from the Lord. 7We live by what we believe, not by what we can see. 8So I say that we have courage. We really want to be away from this body and be at home with the Lord. 9Our only goal is to please God whether we live here or there, 10because we must all stand before Christ to be judged. Each of us will receive what we should get—good or bad—for the things we did in the earthly body.

Becoming Friends with God

11Since we know what it means to fear the Lord, we try to help people accept the truth about us. God knows what we really are, and I hope that in your hearts you know too. 12We are not trying to prove ourselves to you again, but we are telling you about ourselves so you will be proud of us. Then you will have an answer for those who are proud about things that can be seen rather than what is in the heart. 13If we are out of our minds, it is for God. If we have our right

FOLLOWING GOD

Daring to Believe

Christopher Wren's big opportunity as an architect came after the Great Fire of London in 1666. It was the chance of a lifetime: still in his twenties, he was commissioned to rebuild not only 51 churches but also St Paul's Cathedral. He prayed and worked to design a cathedral with a magnificently arched ceiling stretching towards heaven.

But when the church was almost finished, other architects in London claimed that the building was flawed. They said that six additional pillars were needed or else the roof would fall.

Wren genuinely believed that God was guiding him in building the cathedral. Still, the other architects were older and more experienced. So, instead of reacting angrily, he listened and prayed. After much discussion he agreed to add the pillars.

At least that's what everyone thought.

After the cathedral was finished in 1710, Wren left London. Fifty years later, after his death, workers were repainting the ceiling when they discovered something strange. Each of the six additional pillars was a few inches short of the vaulted ceiling.

Like Christopher Wren we are called to follow God as best we know how, which often requires courage and creativity.

To learn more about following God read **2 Corinthians 5:6–17**.

- How does Christopher Wren's decision to follow God's call in his heart relate to Paul's advice to live by believing in Christ?
- How have you made choices that reflect the challenge of verse 9? What happened?

Consider . . .

- choosing a creative way to follow God this week, such as writing, drawing or singing.
- interviewing your minister, a teacher, or a friend about times when he or she struggled with decisions to follow God, and what happened.

For more, see . . .

- Isaiah 65:17–25 (p.711)
- Philippians 1:19–20 (p.1281)
- John 14:1–7 (p.1122)

minds, it is for you. 14 The love of Christ controls
us, because we know that One died for all, so all
have died. 15 Christ died for all so that those who
live would not continue to live for themselves.
He died for them and was raised from the dead so
that they would live for him.
16 From this time on we do not think of any-
one as the world does. In the past we thought
of Christ as the world thinks, but we no longer
think of him in that way. 17 If anyone belongs
to Christ, there begins a new creation. The old
things have gone: everything is made new!
18 All this is from God. Through Christ, God
made peace between us and himself, and God
gave us the work of telling everyone about the
peace we can have with him. 19 God was in
Christ, making peace between the world and
himself. In Christ, God did not hold the world
guilty of its sins. And he gave us this message of
peace. 20 So we have been sent to speak for
Christ. It is as if God is calling to you through
us. We speak for Christ when we beg you to be
at peace with God. 21 Christ had no sin, but God
made him become sin so that in Christ we
could become right with God.

6 We are workers together with God, so
we beg you: do not let the grace that
you received from God be for nothing. 2 God
says,

"At the right time I will hear your prayers.
On the day of salvation I will help you."

Isaiah 49:8

I tell you that the "right time" is now, and the
"day of salvation" is now.
3 We do not want anyone to find fault with
our work, so nothing we do will be a problem
for anyone. 4 But in every way we show we
are servants of God: in accepting many hard
things, in troubles, in difficulties and in great
problems. 5 We are beaten and thrown into

SUFFERING

Trying to Stand Strong

Sanjeev, a church minister working in Gampaha district in Sri Lanka, had to suspend church services because he was in fear of physical attack on his church members.

One Sunday, as the congregation attempted to gather at their church in Yakkala in Gampaha, a group of at least fifty people blocked the road leading to the church. The mob was armed with clubs and hurled verbal abuse at the Christians. They had also put up posters featuring anti-Christian slogans around the town.

Sanjeev was warned to stop holding services and told that Yakkala had no need of a Christian church. He was also accused of doing and saying certain things – all of which were lies – in an attempt to ruin his reputation.

The church had been attacked just a few weeks before. He had asked for police protection but no action had been taken. So this second incident led Sanjeev to make the reluctant decision to cancel services so as not to endanger his people and risk a riot and the destruction of the church.

Paul faced similar persecution all his life. Read **2 Corinthians 6:3–10** and see Paul's attitude to what was happening.

- Not all persecution stories have a happy ending. How might Sanjeev apply what Paul writes in Corinthians to his own situation?
- What gave Paul such hope despite all the attacks and opposition he faced?

Consider . . .

- whether you have ever been persecuted because you are a Christian. How did it make you feel?
- how many people around the world suffer merely because of their faith in Jesus. Why not find an organisation that supports persecuted Christians and commit to praying regularly for God's protection and peace.

For more, see . . .

- Psalm 57 (p.533)
- 1 Peter 5:8–11 (p.1363)
- Jeremiah 1:4–8 (p.716)

prison. We meet those who become upset
with us and start riots. We work hard, and
sometimes we get no sleep or food. 6We show
we are servants of God by our pure lives, our
understanding, patience and kindness, by the
Holy Spirit,[d] by true love, 7by speaking the
truth and by God's power. We use our right
living to defend ourselves against everything.
8Some people honour us, but others blame us.
Some people say evil things about us, but

Sidelight Paul knew what the inside of a prison looked like and not just as a visitor. He was beaten up and thrown into prison for his faith (2 Corinthians 6:5) at least seven times in places like Jerusalem, Philippi and Rome before being executed by the Roman government (see 2 Timothy 4:6–8, p.1320).

others say good things. Some people say we are
liars, but we speak the truth. 9We are not
known, yet we are well known. We seem to be
dying, but we continue to live. We are pun-
ished, but we are not killed. 10We have much
sadness, but we are always rejoicing. We are
poor, but we are making many people rich in
faith. We have nothing, but really we have
everything.
11We have spoken freely to you in Corinth
and have opened our hearts to you. 12Our
feelings of love for you have not stopped, but
you have stopped your feelings of love for
us. 13I speak to you as if you were my children.
Do to us as we have done—open your hearts
to us.

Warning About Those Who Do Not Believe

14You are not the same as those who do not
believe. So do not join yourselves to them. Good
and bad do not belong together. Light and dark-
ness cannot share together. 15How can Christ and
Belial, the devil, have any agreement? What can
a believer have together with a non-believer?
16The temple of God cannot have any agreement
with idols, and we are the temple of the living
God. As God said: "I will live with them and walk
with them. And I will be their God, and they will
be my people."[n]

17"You people, leave, leave,
get out of Babylon!
Touch nothing that is unclean."[d] *Isaiah 52:11; Ezekiel 20:34,41*

18"I will be your father,
and you will be my sons and daughters,
says the Lord Almighty." *2 Samuel 7:14; 7:8*

7 Dear friends, we have these promises from
God, so we should make ourselves pure—
free from anything that makes body or soul un-
clean. We should try to become holy in the way
we live, because we respect God.

Paul's Joy

2Open your hearts to us. We have not done
wrong to anyone, we have not ruined the faith of
anyone, and we have not cheated anyone. 3I do
not say this to blame you. I told you before that
we love you so much we would live or die with
you. 4I feel very sure of you and am very proud
of you. You give me much comfort, and in all of
our troubles I have great joy.
5When we came into Macedonia, we had no
rest. We found trouble all around us. We had
fighting on the outside and fear on the inside.
6But God, who comforts those who are troubled,
comforted us when Titus came. 7We were com-
forted, not only by his coming but also by the
comfort you gave him. Titus told us about your
wish to see me and that you are very sorry for
what you did. He also told me about your great
care for me, and when I heard this, I was much
happier.
8Even if my letter made you sad, I am not
sorry I wrote it. At first I was sorry, because
it made you sad, but you were sad only for a
short time. 9Now I am happy, not because you
were made sad, but because your sorrow
made you change your lives. You became sad
in the way God wanted you to, so you were not
hurt by us in any way. 10The kind of sorrow God
wants makes people change their hearts and
lives. This leads to salvation, and you cannot be
sorry for that. But the kind of sorrow the world
has brings death. 11See what this sorrow—the
sorrow God wanted you to have—has done to
you: it has made you very serious. It made you
want to prove you were not wrong. It made you
angry and afraid. It made you want to see me. It
made you care. It made you want the right thing
to be done. You proved you were innocent in
the problem. 12I wrote that letter, not because of
the one who did the wrong or because of the
person who was hurt. I wrote the letter so you
could see, before God, the great care you have
for us. 13That is why we were comforted.
Not only were we very comforted, we were
even happier to see that Titus was so happy.

"I . . . people." Quotation from Leviticus 26:11–12; Jeremiah 32:38; Ezekiel 37:27.

All of you made him feel much better. [14]I
boasted to Titus about you, and you showed
that I was right. Everything we said to you was
true, and you have proved that what we
boasted about to Titus is true. [15]And his love
for you is stronger when he remembers that
you were all ready to obey. You welcomed him
with respect and fear. [16]I am very happy that I
can trust you fully.

Christian Giving

8 And now, brothers and sisters, we want
you to know about the grace God gave the
churches in Macedonia. [2]They have been
tested by great troubles, and they are very poor.
But they gave much because of their great
joy. [3]I can tell you that they gave as much as
they were able and even more than they could
afford. No one told them to do it. [4]But they
begged and pleaded with us to let them
share in this service for God's people. [5]And they
gave in a way we did not expect: they first gave
themselves to the Lord and to us. This is what
God wants. [6]So we asked Titus to help you
finish this special work of grace since he is the
one who started it. [7]You are rich in every-
thing—in faith, in speaking, in knowledge, in
truly wanting to help, and in the love you
learned from us. In the same way, be strong
also in the grace of giving.

[8]I am not commanding you to give. But I
want to see if your love is true by comparing
you with others that really want to help. [9]You
know the grace of our Lord Jesus Christ. You
know that Christ was rich, but for you he
became poor so that by his becoming poor you
might become rich.

[10]This is what I think you should do: last year
you were the first to want to give, and you
were the first who gave. [11]So now finish the
work you started. Then your "doing" will be
equal to your "wanting to do". Give from what
you have. [12]If you want to give, your gift will
be accepted. It will be judged by what you
have, not by what you do not have. [13]We do
not want you to have troubles while other
people are at ease, but we want everything to
be equal. [14]At this time you have plenty. What
you have can help others who are in need.
Then later, when they have plenty, they can
help you when you are in need, and all will be
equal. [15]As it is written in the Scriptures, [d] "The
person who gathered more did not have too
much, nor did the person who gathered less
have too little." [n]

Titus and His Companions Help

[16]I thank God because he gave Titus the
same love for you that I have. [17]Titus accepted
what we asked him to do. He wanted very
much to go to you, and this was his own
idea. [18]We are sending with him the brother
who is praised by all the churches because of
his service in preaching the Good News. [d]
[19]Also, this brother was chosen by the churches
to go with us when we deliver this gift of
money. We are doing this service to bring
glory to the Lord and to show that we really
want to help.

[20]We are being careful so that no one will
criticise us for the way we are handling this
large gift. [21]We are trying hard to do what the
Lord accepts as right and also what people
think is right.

[22]Also, we are sending with them our
brother, who is always ready to help. He has
proved this to us in many ways, and he wants
to help even more now, because he has much
faith in you.

[23]Now about Titus—he is my partner who is
working with me to help you. And about the
other brothers—they are sent from the
churches, and they bring glory to Christ. [24]So
show these men the proof of your love and the
reason we are proud of you. Then all the
churches can see it.

Help for Fellow Christians

9 I really do not need to write to you about
this help for God's people. [2]I know you
want to help. I have been boasting about
this to the people in Macedonia, telling them
that you in Southern Greece have been ready
to give since last year. And your desire to give
has made most of them ready to give also. [3]But
I am sending the brothers to you so that
our boasting about you in this will not be
empty words. I want you to be ready, as I said
you would be. [4]If any of the people from
Macedonia come with me and find that you are
not ready, we will be ashamed that we were
so sure of you. (And you will be ashamed
too!) [5]So I thought I should ask these brothers
to go to you before we do. They will finish
getting in order the generous gift you promised
so it will be ready when we come. And it will
be a generous gift—not one that you did not
want to give.

[6]Remember this: the person who plants a lit-
tle will have a small harvest, but the person
who plants a lot will have a big harvest. [7]Each

"The person . . . little." Quotation from Exodus 16:18.

one should give as he has decided in his heart
to give. You should not be sad when you
give, and you should not give because you
feel forced to give. God loves the person who
gives happily. 8And God can give you more
blessings than you need. Then you will always
have plenty of everything—enough to give
to every good work. 9It is written in the
Scriptures:[d]

"He gives freely to the poor.
The things he does are right and will
continue for ever." *Psalm 112:9*

10God is the One who gives seed to the farmer
and bread for food. He will give you all the seed
you need and make it grow so there will be a
great harvest from your goodness. 11He will
make you rich in every way so that you can
always give freely. And your giving through us

GIVING

Just For the Record

When Amanda started her new job, she found some of the staff at the shop a little difficult to get on with. One boy called Luke particularly shied away from her.

Then one day during a coffee break, they were all discussing their musical tastes.

"I don't think rock music will ever die," remarked one lad.

"Personally, I prefer dance stuff," replied Amanda.

A scoffing noise came from Luke, who said: "You've just got no taste! You've got to go back to the sixties and pure Bob Dylan to hear anything really decent."

The rest of the staff were surprised to hear that Luke, who probably wasn't born when Dylan was around, was such a big fan. It turned out that he had a huge collection of his vinyl records.

At this point, Amanda remarked, "Strange, because I have a rare Bob Dylan record in my collection."

Luke hooted with laughter. "You? You've got a rare record? No you haven't!" he carried on. "You can't have!"

Amanda started to look puzzled. "OK, maybe it's not. But I used to work for a record company and I got it from there. I'll bring it in tomorrow."

The next day she walked into the shop carrying a brown paper bag.

"Here you are Luke," she said.

He opened the bag slowly, and inside was one of the rarest of all Bob Dylan vinyls. He was shocked to the core and started to turn very pale.

"You have got a rare record . . ." he whispered, stating the obvious. Then he cleared his throat. "Um. OK . . . so how much will you sell it for?"

"Oh, I don't want to sell it . . . have it," she said simply.

"You can't give this away!" yelled Luke. "Have you any idea what it's worth?"

"Luke. You're the fan. I have something that means more to you than me, so it makes sense that you should have it," she replied.

There was a silence, then Luke looked at her and said very seriously: "I know you're a Christian. I'll come and try your church out this Sunday."

Amanda laughed. "It's not a bribe! You don't have to do that!"

But he did.

In a world that gives to receive, Amanda showed kindness. She took **2 Corinthians 8:5–15** to heart.

- Why did Amanda give away a collector's item?
- In what way does this passage challenge you to give to others?

Consider . . .

- doing an unexpected task around the house as a way of giving of yourself.
- organising a fundraising event to help a Christian mission or Third World project.

For more, see . . .

- Acts 20:32–35 (p.1173)
- Philippians 2:5–7 (p.1282)

will cause many to give thanks to God. 12This
service you do not only helps the needs of
God's people, it also brings much more thanks
to God. 13It is a proof of your faith. Many
people will praise God because you obey the
Good News [d] of Christ—the gospel you say you
believe—and because you freely share with
them and with all others. 14And when they pray,
they will wish they could be with you because
of the great grace that God has given you.
15Thanks be to God for his gift that is too won-
derful for words.

Paul Defends His Ministry

10 I, Paul, am begging you with the gentle-
ness and the kindness of Christ. Some
people say that I am easy on you when I am
with you and bold when I am away. 2They
think we live in a worldly way, and I plan to be
very bold with them when I come. I beg you
that when I come I will not need to use that
same boldness with you. 3We do live in the
world, but we do not fight in the same way the
world fights. 4We fight with weapons that are
different from those the world uses. Our
weapons have power from God that can
destroy the enemy's strong places. We destroy
people's arguments 5and every proud thing that
raises itself against the knowledge of God. We
capture every thought and make it give up and
obey Christ. 6We are ready to punish anyone
there who does not obey, but first we want you
to obey fully.

7You must look at the facts before you. If you
feel sure that you belong to Christ, you must
remember that we belong to Christ just as you
do. 8It is true that we boast freely about the
authority the Lord gave us. But this authority is

SHARING FAITH

Doing the Right Thing

Indra was always aware of the homeless people she saw on the street, huddled in shop doorways, as she walked home on cold winter nights. She didn't want to stare, but occasionally she glanced over the scarf tightly wrapped round her neck to catch a glimpse of their faces.

There was one person in particular that grabbed her attention – a girl who couldn't have been much older than her. Indra remembered this girl and prayed for her often, though she didn't see her again for some time.

One day, Indra was walking home with a couple of friends when up ahead she saw some of the homeless people, and instantly recognised the girl she had seen before. She felt a nudge deep in her heart to do something for this girl, and as they got closer, Indra was already reaching into her bag to get some money. But she stopped to think and pray, and asked God to show her the best way to help the girl.

The girl looked nervously at Indra. Never before had someone actually stopped to talk to her – at most, people threw the odd coin in her direction as they went past. Indra introduced herself and asked the girl if she was hungry. Then she invited her to come with her to a café to have something to eat.

At first, the other people in the café gave Indra and the girl funny looks, thinking they were going to cause trouble. But when everyone saw what Indra was doing, most people smiled warmly, knowing that she was doing a very kind thing.

Read **2 Corinthians 8:20–21**. Paul and Titus knew that it took a lot of effort to do what was good in God's eyes as well as the eyes of those around them.

- How had Indra been careful to do what was right?
- What effect do you think it had on the people in the café to see what Indra had done?

Consider . . .

- how you can make sure that what you decide to do in your life is seen as good by God *and* other people.
- praying that people would see God through your actions.

For more, see . . .

- Romans 14:13–23 (p.1207)
- 1 Peter 2:11–12 (p.1358)

to build you up, not to tear you down. So I will
not be ashamed. 9I do not want you to think I am
trying to scare you with my letters. 10Some peo-
ple say, "Paul's letters are powerful and sound
important, but when he is with us, he is weak.
And his speaking is nothing." 11They should
know this: we are not there with you now, so we
say these things in letters. But when we are
there with you, we will show the same authority
that we show in our letters.

12We do not dare to compare ourselves with
those who think they are very important. They
use themselves to measure themselves, and
they judge themselves by what they themselves
are. This shows that they know nothing. 13But
we will not boast about things outside the work
that was given us to do. We will limit our boast-
ing to the work that God gave us, and this in-
cludes our work with you. 14We are not
boasting too much, as we would be if we had
not already come to you. But we have come to
you with the Good News[d] of Christ. 15We limit
our boasting to the work that is ours, not what
others have done. We hope that as your faith
continues to grow, you will help our work to
grow much larger. 16We want to tell the Good
News in the areas beyond your city. We do not
want to boast about work that has already been
done in another person's area. 17But, "If some-
one wants to boast, he should boast only about
the Lord."[n] 18It is not those who say they are
good who are accepted but those who the Lord
thinks are good.

Sidelight Paul may have been a superstar missionary but he would never have made it to the front cover of a fashion magazine. A book, around at the same time as the New Testament was written, described him as "a man small of stature, with bald head and crooked legs . . . with eyebrows meeting and nose somewhat hooked". His critics described him as " . . . weak. And his speaking is nothing" (2 Corinthians 10:10).

Paul and the False Apostles

11 I wish you would be patient with me
even when I am a little foolish, but you
are already doing that. 2I am jealous over you
with a jealousy that comes from God. I promised
to give you to Christ, as your only husband. I
want to give you as his pure bride. 3But I am
afraid that your minds will be led away from
your true and pure following of Christ just
as Eve was tricked by the snake with his evil
ways. 4You are very patient with anyone who
comes to you and preaches a different Jesus
from the one we preached. You are very willing
to accept a spirit or good news that is different
from the Spirit[d] and Good News[d] you received
from us.

5I do not think that those "great apostles" are
any better than I am. 6I may not be a trained
speaker, but I do have knowledge. We have
shown this to you clearly in every way.

7I preached God's Good News to you with-
out pay. I made myself unimportant to make
you important. Do you think that was wrong?
8I accepted pay from other churches, taking
their money so I could serve you. 9If I needed
something when I was with you, I did not trou-
ble any of you. The brothers who came from
Macedonia gave me all that I needed. I did not
allow myself to depend on you in any way, and
I will never depend on you. 10No one in
Southern Greece will stop me from boasting
about that. I say this with the truth of Christ in
me. 11And why do I not depend on you? Do
you think it is because I do not love you? God
knows that I love you.

12And I will continue doing what I am doing
now, because I want to stop those people from
having a reason to boast. They would like to
say that the work they boast about is the same
as ours. 13Such men are not true apostles[d]
but are workers who lie. They change them-
selves to look like apostles of Christ. 14This
does not surprise us. Even Satan changes him-
self to look like an angel of light.[n] 15So it does
not surprise us if Satan's servants also make
themselves look like servants who work for
what is right. But in the end they will be
punished for what they do.

Paul Tells About His Sufferings

16I tell you again: no one should think I am a
fool. But if you think so, accept me as you would
accept a fool. Then I can boast a little, too.
17When I boast because I feel sure of myself, I
am not talking as the Lord would talk but as a
fool. 18Many people are boasting about their lives
in the world. So I will boast too. 19You are wise,
so you will gladly be patient with fools! 20You are

"If . . . Lord." Quotation from Jeremiah 9:24.
angel of light Messenger from God. The devil fools people so that they think he is from God.

even patient with those who order you around, or use you, or trick you, or think they are better than you, or hit you in the face. [21]It is shameful to me to say this, but we were too "weak" to do those things to you!

But if anyone else is brave enough to boast, then I also will be brave and boast. (I am talking as a fool.) [22]Are they Hebrews?[n] So am I. Are they Israelites? So am I. Are they from Abraham's family? So am I. [23]Are they serving Christ? I am serving him more. (I am mad to talk like this.) I have worked much harder than they. I have been in prison more often. I have been hurt more in beatings. I have been near death many times. [24]Five times the Jews have given me their punishment of 39 lashes with a whip. [25]Three different times I was beaten with rods. One time I was almost stoned to death. Three times I was in ships that were wrecked, and one of those times I spent a night and a day in the sea. [26]I have gone on many travels and have been in danger from rivers, thieves, my own people, the Jews and those who are not Jews. I have been in danger in cities, in places where no one lives and on the sea. And I have been in danger with false Christians. [27]I have done hard and tiring work, and many times I did not sleep. I have been hungry and thirsty, and many times I have been without food. I have been cold and without clothes. [28]Besides all this, there is on me every day the load of my concern for all the churches. [29]I feel weak every time someone is weak, and I feel upset every time someone is led into sin.

[30]If I must boast, I will boast about the things that show I am weak. [31]God knows I am not lying. He is the God and Father of the Lord Jesus Christ, and he is to be praised for ever. [32]When I was in Damascus, the governor under King Aretas wanted to arrest me, so he put guards around the city. [33]But my friends lowered me in a basket through a hole in the city wall. So I escaped from the governor.

A Special Blessing in Paul's Life

12 I must continue to boast. It will do no good, but I will talk now about visions and revelations[n] from the Lord. [2]I know a man in Christ who was taken up to the third heaven fourteen years ago. I do not know whether the man was in his body or out of his body, but God knows. [3–4]And I know that this man was taken up to paradise.[n] I don't know if he was in his body or away from his body, but God knows. He heard things he is not able to explain, things that no human is allowed to tell. [5]I will boast about a man like that, but I will not boast about myself, except about my weaknesses. [6]But if I wanted to boast about myself, I would not be a fool, because I would be telling the truth. But I will not boast about myself. I do not want people to think more of me than what they see me do or hear me say.

[7]So that I would not become too proud of the wonderful things that were shown to me, a painful problem[n] was given to me. This problem was a messenger from Satan, sent to beat me and keep me from being too proud. [8]I begged the Lord three times to take this problem away from me. [9]But he said to me, "My grace is enough for you. When you are weak, my power is made perfect in you." So I am very happy to boast about my weaknesses. Then Christ's power can live in me. [10]For this reason I am happy when I have weaknesses, insults, hard times, sufferings and all kinds of troubles for Christ. Because when I am weak, then I am truly strong.

Paul's Love for the Christians

[11]I have been talking like a fool, but you made me do it. You are the ones who should say good things about me. I am worth nothing, but those "great apostles" are not worth any more than I am! [12]When I was with you, I patiently did the things that prove I am an apostle[d]—signs, wonders and miracles.[d] [13]So you received everything that the other churches have received. Only one thing was different: I was not a burden to you. Forgive me for this!

[14]I am now ready to visit you the third time, and I will not be a burden to you. I want nothing from you, except you. Children should not have to save up to give to their parents. Parents should save to give to their children. [15]So I am happy to give everything I have for you, even myself. If I love you more, will you love me less?

[16]It is clear I was not a burden to you, but you think I was sly and lied to catch you. [17]Did I cheat you by using any of the messengers I sent to you? No, you know I did not. [18]I asked Titus to go to you, and I sent our brother with him. Titus did not cheat you, did he? No, you know

Hebrews A name for the Jews that some Jews were very proud of.
revelation Making known truth that has been hidden.
paradise A place where good people go when they die.
painful problem Literally, "thorn in the flesh".

that Titus and I did the same thing and with the
same spirit.
[19]Do you think we have been defending
ourselves to you all this time? We have been
speaking in Christ and before God. You are our
dear friends, and everything we do is to make
you stronger. [20]I am afraid that when I come,
you will not be what I want you to be, and
I will not be what you want me to be. I am
afraid that among you there may be arguing,
jealousy, anger, selfish fighting, evil talk, gossip,
pride and confusion. [21]I am afraid that when
I come to you again, my God will make me
ashamed before you. I may be saddened by
many of those who have sinned because they
have not changed their hearts or turned from
their sexual sins and the shameful things they
have done.

Final Warnings and Greetings

13 I will come to you for the third time.
"Every case must be proved by two or
three witnesses." [n] [2]When I was with you the
second time, I gave a warning to those who had
sinned. Now I am away from you, and I give a
warning to all the others. When I come to you

"Every . . . witnesses." Quotation from Deuteronomy 19:15.

PARENTS

Open House

Any night of the week you would find friends around Joel's house. Weekends were a speciality.

"It's so much better round here than at my place," remarked Andy, one of his best friends.

"Why's that?" asked Joel.

"Well, your mum's so cool. Here we are up in your room, making a noise, playing music and the only thing your mum does is bring us food!" He grinned as he tucked into his third cake.

"Why? What does your mum do?" asked Joel, puzzled.

"She'd kick us all out for a start!" he replied. "There's no way she'd let me have my friends upstairs – and absolutely no way she'd make food for them!"

Joel thought about this after his friend had left, and later spoke to his parents about what Andy had said.

"I thought all parents were like you," he smiled. "So, why do you do all these things for me?"

His mother Cheryl laughed.

"Joel, you're our son, we love seeing you happy and having fun. If your friends want to come round that's great. We get to meet them and talk to them, and the house is full of life, what could be better? Plus of course, we know where you are and who you are with."

"Yes," put in his father. "So, if you go to a football game with Andy, we know he's the one with dyed orange hair who likes chocolate cake and computer games!"

Joel pondered this for a while and then asked, "But things get spilt on the carpet and sometimes you have to come and remind us of the time; don't you mind?"

"I can easily clean things up," his mother replied. "So, you'd better get it through your head that we like having you around, it's your house too you know."

2 Corinthians 12:14–15 reminds us that children are not the providers of a household.

- Why, according to these verses, does the system of parents providing work so well?
- What does Paul ask for in return for his visit?

Consider . . .

- getting up early one Saturday morning and treating your parents to a cooked breakfast in bed!
- asking God to help you to be patient during times of family tension.

For more, see . . .

- Luke 15:20 (p.1072)
- 2 Timothy 1:5 (p.1316)
- Ephesians 6:4 (p.1276)

again, I will not be easy with them. 3You want
proof that Christ is speaking through me. My
proof is that he is not weak among you, but he is
powerful. 4It is true that he was weak when he
was killed on the cross, but he lives now by
God's power. It is true that we are weak in
Christ, but for you we will be alive in Christ by
God's power.
5Look closely at yourselves. Test yourselves
to see if you are living in the faith. You know
that Jesus Christ is in you—unless you fail the
test. 6But I hope you will see that we ourselves
have not failed the test. 7We pray to God that
you will not do anything wrong. It is not impor-
tant to see that we have passed the test, but
it is important that you do what is right, even
if it seems we have failed. 8We cannot do
anything against the truth, but only for the
truth. 9We are happy to be weak, if you are
strong, and we pray that you will become
complete. 10I am writing this while I am away
from you so that when I come I will not have to
be harsh in my use of authority. The Lord gave
me this authority to build you up, not to tear
you down.
11Now, brothers and sisters, I say goodbye.

IMAGE

On a Personal Level

Joe went into church humming cheerfully to himself. The older man at the door muttered "Good morning" to him and Joe responded by patting his back.

Joe quickly found his friends and waved at them as he made his way across to where they were sitting.

"How's it going everyone?" he grinned as he took his seat.

During the service it was noticeable that Joe always gave it his all. He sang with great gusto and prayed seriously. His friends always felt encouraged when he was around.

After the service, he was stopped by the usher at the door.

"Young man," he said. "Do you think your clothes are appropriate for the House of God?"

Joe blinked twice and smiled. "How do you mean?" He looked down at himself, at his scruffy T-shirt and his favourite jeans.

"Well . . . ." started the usher. "If you were going to meet the Queen, would you wear those clothes?"

"No," stated Joe.

"And why not?" asked the old man.

"Because I don't know her and I've never been to Buckingham Palace. I'd probably have to spruce up a bit," he explained.

"Then don't you think that Jesus deserves the same treatment?" the usher asked cunningly.

"Not on your life mate!" came the shocked reply. "Jesus is my friend, a really good friend. I know him really well, just like I know my mates here," Joe said, pointing to them. "If I went round my mates' houses all done up like that, they'd think I'd gone mad!"

And with that Joe left the church, still humming happily.

Paul's advice to the people in **2 Corinthians 13:5–10** was to test themselves, to see if Jesus was living in them.

- How can you know if your image as a Christian is right, according to 2 Corinthians 13:7?
- If you look closely at yourself – beyond the clothes – what do you find?

Consider . . .

- whether you are ever guilty of judging people on the clothes that they wear, rather than the person they are.
- discussing with your youth group what sort of statement your clothes make to other people.

For more, see . . .

- 1 Samuel 16:7 (p.269)
- 1 John 2:5 (p.1372)
- 2 Corinthians 5:12 (p.1245)

Sidelight The custom of kissing other Christians in the early church (2 Corinthians 13:12) later became a regular part of worship, and is still practised in some Near Eastern cultures. Today, Christians in the Western world greet each other in a variety of ways, from a simple handshake to a big hug!

Try to be perfect. Do what I have asked you to
do. Agree with each other, and live in peace.
Then the God of love and peace will be with
you.
12 Greet each other with a holy kiss. 13 All of
God's holy people send greetings to you.
14 The grace of the Lord Jesus Christ, the love
of God, and the fellowship of the Holy Spirit[d]
be with you all.

Galatians

Why Read This Book:

- See the dangers of listening to false teachers (Galatians 1—2).
- Discover the freedom we have through faith in Christ (Galatians 3).
- Find out how Christians should use their freedom (Galatians 5—6).

When?

Time Line:

	BC/AD	Jesus was born
	AD 20	
	AD 30	Jesus began his ministry
Paul became a Christian		The church began soon after Jesus went to heaven
	AD 40	
	AD 50	Paul started churches in Galatia
Paul wrote Galatians		
	AD 60	
Fire destroyed Rome		Romans destroyed the Temple in Jerusalem
	AD 70	

Behind the Scenes:

What do you have to do to be a Christian? Do you have to practise certain rituals? Do you have to follow certain rules?

Those were controversial questions in the early church, as we discover in Paul's letter to the Galatians. Not long before, Paul had started the churches in Galatia. But soon after he left, people began questioning his beliefs and authority. They said that non-Jewish people who became Christians also had to follow Jewish laws and rituals to be true Christians – a view that was splitting the early church (see Acts 15, p.1163).

When Paul heard what was happening, he wrote this letter to confront the problem. "You have already accepted the Good News. If anyone is preaching something different to you, he should be judged guilty!" he blasts in Galatians 1:9. Then Paul gets to the heart of the Christian faith. He explains that people can't do anything to earn God's promises. Those promises are free gifts for all people, to be received by faith in Christ. Instead of being the law's prisoners, Christians live in freedom.

Someone always seems to be telling us that serving God means following a long list of dos and don'ts. Paul's letter to the Galatians reminds us that being a Christian isn't a matter of what we do or don't do; it's a matter of accepting what Jesus Christ did for us. Now that's Good News!

Where?

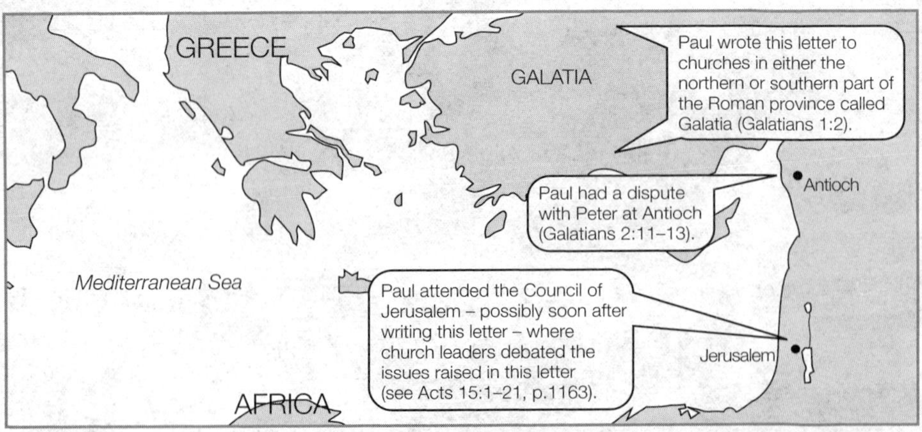

1 From Paul, an apostle.[d] I was not chosen to
be an apostle by human beings, nor was I
sent from human beings. I was made an apostle
through Jesus Christ and God the Father who
raised Jesus from the dead. 2This letter is also
from all those of God's family[n] who are
with me.

To the churches in Galatia:[n]

3Grace and peace to you from God our Father
and the Lord Jesus Christ. 4Jesus gave himself for
our sins to free us from this evil world we live in,
as God the Father planned. 5The glory belongs to
God for ever and ever. Amen.

The Only Good News

6God, by his grace through Christ, called you
to become his people. So I am amazed that you
are turning away so quickly and believing some-
thing different from the Good News.[d] 7Really,
there is no other Good News. But some people

those . . . family The Greek text says "brothers".
Galatia Probably the same country where Paul preached and began churches on his first missionary trip. Read the book of Acts, chapters 13 and 14.

CULTS

Good News, Bad News

Daniel had gone to church on and off since he was little, but he had never felt that he really needed God. That is, until last summer. Nearly everything Daniel did seemed to go wrong. He was fired from his summer job, and then he wrote his car off. Now his dad had moved out. Daniel began to think that perhaps he needed some help with his life.

He immediately thought of Phil. Nothing seemed to throw him. He seemed to be into the supernatural.

So Daniel started talking to Phil during lunch. Phil had an answer for every question Daniel asked. He made everything seem so simple and clear-cut. Phil talked about what it took to be one of the "Chosen Ones" – a new religious group that he was involved with. "Wow," Daniel thought, "he really knows his stuff!"

Of course, Phil explained the Bible differently from anything Daniel had ever heard, but Phil seemed to know what he was talking about. It all seemed so simple. All you had to do was follow a list of rules and requirements, and you would be fine.

The more Daniel talked to Phil and read Phil's books, the more he began to feel as if he, too, might finally be on the home straight to God. After all, wasn't he learning new things every day? Wasn't he trying to do everything he was supposed to do to be one of the Chosen Ones?

But still Daniel wondered. Sometimes he would wake up in the middle of the night, afraid he had not done everything he was supposed to do. He would thumb through the books, studying the requirements and trying to shake the feeling that he wasn't good enough. Daniel wanted to talk to Phil about his doubts, but he was afraid that if he said anything, he might lose his place among the Chosen Ones.

Daniel wished he could know that he was right with God. Read **Galatians 1:1–10** to see how the Galatians made the same mistake.

- According to this passage (especially verses 4–6), how is the Good News very different from the requirements of groups like the Chosen Ones?
- Have you ever found yourself being attracted by the promises of a cult? What made the promises attractive? How did you resist the pull?

Consider . . .

- asking God to teach you how to respect others while you share your beliefs with them.
- inviting a friend who doesn't go to church to come with you to worship. Introduce him or her to your Christian friends.

For more, see . . .

- Deuteronomy 13:1–4 (p.178)
- 1 John 4:1–6 (p.1374)
- Matthew 7:13–20 (p.950)

are confusing you; they want to change the Good
News of Christ. 8We preached to you the Good
News. So if we ourselves, or even an angel from
heaven, should preach to you something differ-
ent, we should be judged guilty! 9I said this be-
fore, and now I say it again: you have already
accepted the Good News. If anyone is preaching
something different to you, he should be judged
guilty!

> **Sidelight** If Paul wrote Galatians early in his career – as some scholars believe – it may have been the first New Testament book written, dated less than 20 years after Jesus lived. Other scholars think that either 1 Thessalonians (p.1295) or James (p.1347) was the first book to be written.

10Do you think I am trying to make people
accept me? No, God is the One I am trying to
please. Am I trying to please people? If I still
wanted to please people, I would not be a servant
of Christ.

Paul's Authority is from God

11Brothers and sisters,[n] I want you to know
that the Good News[d] I preached to you was not
made up by human beings. 12I did not get it from
humans, nor did anyone teach it to me, but Jesus
Christ showed it to me.

13You have heard about my past life in the
Jewish religion. I attacked the church of God and
tried to destroy it. 14I was becoming a leader in
the Jewish religion, doing better than most other
Jews of my age. I tried harder than anyone else
to follow the teachings handed down by our
ancestors.

15But God had special plans for me and set me
apart for his work even before I was born. He
called me through his grace 16and showed his Son
to me so that I might tell the Good News about
him to those who are not Jewish. When God
called me, I did not get advice or help from any
person. 17I did not go to Jerusalem to see those
who were apostles[d] before I was. But, without
waiting, I went away to Arabia and later went
back to Damascus.

18After three years I went to Jerusalem to meet
Peter and stayed with him for fifteen days. 19I met
no other apostles, except James, the brother of
the Lord. 20God knows that these things I write
are not lies. 21Later, I went to the areas of Syria
and Cilicia.

22In Judea the churches in Christ had never
met me. 23They had only heard it said, "This man
who was attacking us is now preaching the same
faith that he once tried to destroy." 24And these
believers praised God because of me.

Other Apostles Accepted Paul

2 After fourteen years I went to Jerusalem
again, this time with Barnabas. I also took
Titus with me. 2I went because God showed me
I should go. I met with the believers there, and
in private I told their leaders the Good News[d]
that I preach to the non-Jewish people. I did not
want my past work and the work I am now
doing to be wasted. 3Titus was with me, but he
was not forced to be circumcised,[d] even though
he was a Greek. 4We talked about this problem
because some false believers had come into our
group secretly. They came in like spies to over-
turn the freedom we have in Christ Jesus. They
wanted to make us slaves. 5But we did not give
in to those false believers for a minute. We
wanted the truth of the Good News to continue
for you.

6Those leaders who seemed to be important
did not change the Good News that I preach.
(It doesn't matter to me if they were "important"
or not. To God everyone is the same.) 7But these
leaders saw that I had been given the work of
telling the Good News to those who are not
Jewish, just as Peter had the work of telling
the Jews. 8God gave Peter the power to work as
an apostle[d] for the Jewish people. But he also
gave me the power to work as an apostle for
those who are not Jews. 9James, Peter and John,
who seemed to be the leaders, understood that
God had given me this special grace, so they
accepted Barnabas and me. They agreed that
they would go to the Jewish people and that
we should go to those who are not Jewish.
10The only thing they asked us was to remember
to help the poor—something I really wanted
to do.

Paul Shows that Peter was Wrong

11When Peter came to Antioch, I challenged
him to his face, because he was wrong. 12Peter
ate with the non-Jewish people until some Jewish
people sent from James came to Antioch. When
they arrived, Peter stopped eating with those

Brothers and sisters Although the Greek text says "brothers" here and throughout this book, Paul's words were meant for the entire church, both men and women.

who weren't Jewish, and he separated himself
from them. He was afraid of the Jews. 13So Peter
was a hypocrite,[d] as were the other Jewish be-
lievers who joined with him. Even Barnabas was
influenced by what these Jewish believers did.
14When I saw they were not following the truth
of the Good News,[d] I spoke to Peter in front of
them all. I said, "Peter, you are a Jew, but you
are not living like a Jew. You are living like those
who are not Jewish. So why do you now try
to force those who are not Jewish to live like
Jews?"
15We were not born as non-Jewish "sinners",
but as Jews. 16Yet we know that a person is made
right with God not by following the law,[d] but by
trusting in Jesus Christ. So we, too, have put our
faith in Christ Jesus, that we might be made right
with God because we trusted in Christ. It is
not because we followed the law, because no
one can be made right with God by following
the law.
17We Jews came to Christ, trying to be made
right with God, and it became clear that we are
sinners too. Does this mean that Christ encour-
ages sin? No! 18But I would really be wrong to
begin teaching again those things that I gave up.
19It was the law that put me to death, and I died
to the law so that I can now live for God. 20I was
put to death on the cross with Christ, and I do
not live any more—it is Christ who lives in me.
I still live in my body, but I live by faith in the
Son of God who loved me and gave himself to
save me. 21By saying these things I am not going
against God's grace. Just the opposite, if the law
could make us right with God, then Christ's
death would be useless.

FAITH

It's Not About Rules

Hassan cannot believe the stories his father tells him, Hassan's life is so different to his dad's childhood. Hassan's father speaks of being forced to pray many times in the day, not being allowed to listen to music or the radio, eating only certain food and everyone wearing white robes to show they are all equal in the sight of Allah.

Hassan's life is very different. He comes home, listens to the music charts and, generally, he wears what he likes.

Hassan is confused as to why some people live under such strict rules.

Hassan's father tells of the first time he watched the film telling the story of Jesus. After moving to England, he became friends with a Christian who explained Jesus' love – how Jesus loved him regardless of whether he kept certain rules and laws. Hassan's father found this difficult to understand; he had been brought up to believe that only people who kept all the rules of their religion would enter paradise. He was amazed by this man Jesus – his love, his death and his words of freedom. Could this story be true, that Jesus died to set him free, that there was nothing he could do to earn his place in God's family? Later that night Hassan's father said a short prayer and felt for the first time an overwhelming sense of peace.

Read **Galatians 2:11–21**.

- Hassan's dad and Peter were confused when they heard that salvation is by faith and cannot be earned. How do you understand this?
- How did Hassan's father change when he understood that faith in Jesus is important?

Consider . . .

- writing a "Faith" list of all the things that you need faith to believe in.
- reading more about religions where they believe you have to earn salvation. Pray for the people you read about that, like Hassan's dad, they would hear about Jesus.

For more, see . . .

- Romans 3:21–31 (p.1187)
- Hebrews 11 (p.1341)
- Ephesians 2:4–10 (p.1270)

Sidelight The Greek word translated "guardian" in Galatians 3:24 could almost be translated "babysitter". It refers to the person – usually a slave – who was responsible for taking care of young children (see also Galatians 4:1–7, p.1261). Possibly half of the population of the Roman Empire were slaves during the New Testament times.

Blessing Comes Through Faith

3 You people in Galatia were told very clearly
about the death of Jesus Christ on the cross.
But you were foolish; you let someone trick you.
[2]Tell me this one thing: how did you receive the
Holy Spirit?[d] Did you receive the Spirit by fol-
lowing the law?[d] No, you received the Spirit be-
cause you heard the Good News[d] and believed
it. [3]You began your life in Christ by the Spirit.
Now are you trying to make it complete by your
own power? That is foolish. [4]Were all your expe-
riences wasted? I hope not! [5]Does God give you
the Spirit and work miracles[d] among you be-
cause you follow the law? No, he does these
things because you heard the Good News and
believed it.

[6]The Scriptures[d] say the same thing about
Abraham: "Abraham believed God, and God ac-
cepted Abraham's faith, and that faith made him
right with God."[n] [7]So you should know that the
true children of Abraham are those who have
faith. [8]The Scriptures, telling what would hap-
pen in the future, said that God would make the
non-Jewish people right through their faith. This
Good News was told to Abraham beforehand, as
the Scripture says: "All nations will be blessed
through you."[n] [9]So all who believe as Abraham
believed are blessed just as Abraham was. [10]But
those who depend on following the law to
make them right are under a curse, because the
Scriptures say, "Anyone will be cursed who does
not always obey what is written in the Book of
the Law."[n] [11]Now it is clear that no one can be
made right with God by the law, because the
Scriptures say, "Those who are right with God
will live by trusting in him."[n] [12]The law is not
based on faith. It says, "A person who obeys
these things will live because of them."[n] [13]Christ
took away the curse the law put on us. He
changed places with us and put himself under
that curse. It is written in the Scriptures, "Any-
one whose body is displayed on a tree[n] is cursed."
[14]Christ did this so that God's blessing promised
to Abraham might come through Jesus Christ to
those who are not Jews. Jesus died so that by our
believing we could receive the Spirit that God
promised.

The Law and the Promise

[15]Brothers and sisters,[n] let us think in human
terms: even an agreement made between two
persons is firm. After that agreement is accepted
by both people, no one can stop it or add any-
thing to it. [16]God made promises both to Abraham
and to his descendant.[d] God did not say, "and to
your descendants". That would mean many
people. But God said, "and to your descendant".
That means only one person; that person is
Christ. [17]This is what I mean: God had an agree-
ment with Abraham and promised to keep it.
The law, which came 430 years later, cannot
change that agreement and so destroy God's
promise to Abraham. [18]If the law could give us
Abraham's blessing, then the promise would not
be necessary. But that is not possible, because
God freely gave his blessings to Abraham through
the promise he had made.

[19]So what was the law for? It was given to
show that the wrong things people do are against
God's will. And it continued until the special de-
scendant, who had been promised, came. The
law was given through angels who used Moses
for a mediator[n] to give the law to people. [20]But a
mediator is not needed when there is only one
side, and God is only one.

The Purpose of the Law of Moses

[21]Does this mean that the law is against
God's promises? Never! That would be true
only if the law could make us right. But God did
not give a law that can bring life. [22]Instead, the
Scriptures[d] showed that the whole world is

"Abraham . . . God." Quotation from Genesis 15:6.
"All . . . you." Quotation from Genesis 12:3; 18:18.
"Anyone . . . Law." Quotation from Deuteronomy 27:26.
"Those . . . him." Quotation from Habakkuk 2:4.
"A person . . . them." Quotation from Leviticus 18:5.
displayed on a tree Deuteronomy 21:22–23 says that when a person was killed for doing wrong, the body was hung on a tree to show shame. Paul means that the cross of Jesus was like that.
brothers and sisters Although the Greek text says "brothers" here and throughout this book, the words of Paul were meant for the entire church, both men and women.
mediator A person who helps one person talk to or give something to another person.

bound by sin. This was so the promise would be
given through faith to people who believe in
Jesus Christ.
23 Before this faith came, we were all held
prisoners by the law. We had no freedom until
God showed us the way of faith that was com-
ing. 24 In other words, the law was our guardian
leading us to Christ so that we could be made
right with God through faith. 25 Now the way of
faith has come, and we no longer live under a
guardian.
26–27 You were all baptised[d] into Christ, and so
you were all clothed with Christ. This means
that you are all children of God through faith in
Christ Jesus. 28 In Christ, there is no difference
between Jew and Greek, slave and free person,
male and female. You are all the same in Christ
Jesus. 29 You belong to Christ, so you are Abraham's
descendants. You will inherit all of God's bless-
ings because of the promise God made to
Abraham.
4 I want to tell you this: while those who
will inherit their fathers' property are
still children, they are no different from slaves. It
does not matter that the children own every-
thing. 2 While they are children, they must obey
those who are chosen to care for them. But
when the children reach the age set by their
fathers, they are free. 3 It is the same for us.
We were once like children, slaves to the

STEREOTYPES

Inside Out

In this corner: Harold, church warden, board member, businessman. Grey suit and tie, starched shirt, thick glasses.

In that corner: Josh, would-be radical, always off on some wild project to save the world, usually involving loud music. Out of date mohican haircut, ripped jeans, T-shirt, earring.

Mohican sizes up Suit: "He'll turn me down before I even ask. Old people are like that. Narrow-minded, afraid of anything new."

Suit sizes up Mohican: "Oh dear. Here we go. Another daft idea. And if I say no, he'll call me old-fashioned."

"Hello, Josh. What's up?"

"We want to fix up the old scout hut for a place to have a weekly Bible study." Suit frowns.

So does Mohican. "I knew it," he thinks. "You think we can't be trusted."

"Hmmm," Suit muses. "These kids' clothes are certainly peculiar, but their hearts are in the right place."

"Sounds like an excellent idea to me," Suit finally says. "What's your first topic?"

Mohican is down for the count. "Er, the importance of prayer," he manages to get out.

"Now that's a subject I always need help with," Suit says.

"Well," Mohican grins, "why don't you join us some time?"

Though people may be different on the outside, they are the same in Jesus Christ. Read this truth in **Galatians 3:23–29**.

- How are Suit and Mohican – or as it says in this passage, a Jew and a Greek – no different in Christ?
- What criteria have you used to judge another Christian?

Consider . . .

- tearing out pictures of five different types of people from a magazine. On each picture, write five ideas that you have about people like that person. Check your ideas by getting to know people in each category.
- visiting a church with a different culture. For example, if you are from an Anglican church, visit a Pentecostal church.

For more, see . . .

- 1 Samuel 16:1–13 (p.269)
- 2 Corinthians 5:11–12 (p.1245)
- Romans 2:28–29 (p.1187)

useless rules of this world. 4But when the
right time came, God sent his Son who was
born of a woman and lived under the law. 5God
did this so he could buy freedom for those who
were under the law and so we could become
his children.

6Since you are God's children, God sent the
Spirit of his Son into your hearts, and the Spirit[d]
cries out, "Father".[n] 7So now you are not a
slave; you are God's child, and God will give you
the blessing he promised, because you are his
child.

Paul's Love for the Christians

8In the past you did not know God. You were
slaves to gods that were not real. 9But now you
know the true God. Really, it is God who knows
you. So why do you turn back to those weak and
useless rules you followed before? Do you want
to be slaves to those things again? 10You still
follow teachings about special days, months,
seasons and years. 11I am afraid for you, that my
work for you has been wasted.

12Brothers and sisters, I became like you, so I
beg you to become like me. You were very good

"Father" Literally, "Abba, Father". Jewish children called their fathers "Abba".

GOD'S LOVE

Too Good to be True?

"Yours Free! Just Ring and Claim Your Prize! No Obligation!" It was a once-in-a-lifetime offer that Jackie couldn't refuse when it arrived in the post.

Of course, Jackie had heard that some of these offers were cons. But this one looked like a safe bet. It guaranteed that she would get "a luxurious fur coat" or a "limited edition Mercedes sports car with all the extras".

"Everyone's a winner," the card boasted. "Ring now to learn what you have won!"

"What harm can it do," Jackie thought to herself, picking up the phone.

Sure enough, she had won! The fur coat was being packed for her. And the contest's agent asked if she would also consider another special offer. For only £99 (on credit card, if you like), she could receive beauty tips from "the nation's foremost beauty experts" in an exclusive newsletter for teenage girls called "Looking Good".

In addition, she would have access to a freephone "Looks Line". She could ring the number at any time, day or night, and receive personal consultations on anything from shoes to eye shadow – for the rest of her life. It was just a one-off fee, Jackie told herself. And it was good for a lifetime. So she placed her order with her mum's credit card.

Jackie's excitement turned to displeasure when she received the genuine dyed rabbit fur coat. She knew she had been taken in when the one-page "Looking Good" newsletter arrived, complete with revolutionary beauty tips such as "wash your face thoroughly each night before going to bed".

Something that had seemed like a dream just a few days earlier now seemed like a nightmare. It had sounded too good to be true. And it was.

Galatians 4:4–7 tells about an offer of God's love that seems too good to be true, but really is true!

- What differences do you see between the once-in-a-lifetime offer that Jackie fell for and the once-for-all-times offer of God's love that's described in the passage?
- What parts of God's offer of love are most appealing to you? How have you responded to that offer?

Consider . . .

- using the form and style of a direct-mail offer to write a postcard about God's offer of love. Send it to a friend who needs some encouragement.
- talking to a friend who was adopted about what it feels like to be specially chosen by parents. Discuss similarities between that and the experience of being a child of God.

For more, see . . .

- Isaiah 64:8–9 (p.709)
- Romans 8:31–39 (p.1197)
- Matthew 7:7–11 (p.950)

to me before. 13You remember that it was because of sickness that I came to you the first time, preaching the Good News.[d] 14Though my sickness was a trouble for you, you did not hate me or make me leave. But you welcomed me as an angel from God, as if I were Jesus Christ himself! 15You were very happy then, but where is that joy now? I am ready to testify that you would have taken out your eyes and given them to me if that were possible. 16Now am I your enemy because I tell you the truth?

17Those people[n] are working hard to persuade you, but this is not good for you. They want to persuade you to turn against us and follow only them. 18It is good for people to show interest in you, but only if their purpose is good. This is always true, not just when I am with you. 19My little children, again I feel the pain of childbirth for you until you truly become like Christ. 20I wish I could be with you now and could change the way I am talking to you, because I do not know what to think about you.

The Example of Hagar and Sarah

21Some of you still want to be under the law. Tell me, do you know what the law says? 22The Scriptures[d] say that Abraham had two sons. The mother of one son was a slave woman, and the mother of the other son was a free woman. 23Abraham's son from the slave woman was born in the normal human way. But the son from the free woman was born because of the promise God made to Abraham.

24This story teaches something else: the two women are like the two agreements between God and his people. One agreement is the law that God made on Mount Sinai,[n] and the people who are under this agreement are like slaves. The mother named Hagar is like that agreement. 25She is like Mount Sinai in Arabia and is a picture of the earthly Jewish city of Jerusalem. This city and its people, the Jews, are slaves to the law. 26But the heavenly Jerusalem, which is above, is like the free woman. She is our mother. 27It is written in the Scriptures:

"Be happy, Jerusalem.
  You are like a woman who never gave
    birth to children.
Start singing and shout for joy.
  You never felt the pain of giving birth,
but you will have more children
  than the woman who has a husband."

Isaiah 54:1

28My brothers and sisters, you are God's children because of his promise, as Isaac was then. 29The son who was born in the normal way treated the other son badly. It is the same today. 30But what does the Scripture say? "Throw out the slave woman and her son. The son of the slave woman should not inherit anything. The son of the free woman should receive it all."[n] 31So, my brothers and sisters, we are not children of the slave woman, but of the free woman.

Keep Your Freedom

5 We have freedom now, because Christ made us free. So stand strong. Do not change and go back into the slavery of the law.[d] 2Listen, I, Paul, tell you that if you go back to the law by being circumcised,[d] Christ does you no good. 3Again, I warn every man: if you allow yourselves to be circumcised, you must follow all the law. 4If you try to be made right with God through the law, your life with Christ is over—you have left God's grace. 5But we have the true hope that comes from being made right with God, and by the Spirit[d] we wait eagerly for this hope. 6When we are in Christ Jesus, it is not important if we are circumcised or not. The important thing is faith—the kind of faith that works through love.

7You were running a good race. Who stopped you from following the true way? 8This change did not come from the One who chose you. 9Be careful! "Just a little yeast makes the whole batch of dough rise." 10But I trust in the Lord that you will not believe those different ideas. Whoever is confusing you with such ideas will be punished.

Sidelight Circumcision (Galatians 5:2–6) was an important ritual for Jews, symbolising bringing a baby boy into God's family. A festive occasion marked each circumcision, which was usually performed by the boy's father.

11My brothers and sisters, I do not teach that a man must be circumcised. If I teach circumcision, why am I still being attacked? If I still taught circumcision, my preaching about the cross would not be a problem. 12I wish the people who are bothering you would castrate[n] themselves!

13My brothers and sisters, God called you to be free, but do not use your freedom as an excuse to do what pleases your sinful self. Serve each other

Those people They are the false teachers who were bothering the believers in Galatia (Galatians 1:7).
Mount Sinai Mountain in Arabia where God gave his laws to Moses (Exodus 19 and 20).
"Throw . . . all." Quotation from Genesis 21:10.
castrate To cut off part of the male sex organ. Paul wanted to show that he was very upset with the false teachers.

with love. 14 The whole law is made complete in
this one command: "Love your neighbour as you
love yourself."[n] 15 If you go on hurting each other
and tearing each other apart, be careful, or you
will completely destroy each other.

The Spirit and Human Nature

16 So I tell you: live by following the Spirit.[d]
Then you will not do what your sinful selves
want. 17 Our sinful selves want what is against the
Spirit, and the Spirit wants what is against our
sinful selves. The two are against each other, so
you cannot do just what you please. 18 But if the
Spirit is leading you, you are not under the law.
19 The wrong things the sinful self does are
clear: being sexually unfaithful, not being pure,
taking part in sexual sins, 20 worshipping gods,
doing witchcraft,[d] hating, making trouble, being
jealous, being angry, being selfish, making people
angry with each other, causing divisions among
people, 21 feeling envy, being drunk, having wild
and wasteful parties, and doing other things like
these. I warn you now as I warned you before:
those who do these things will not inherit God's
kingdom. 22 But the Spirit produces the fruit of
love, joy, peace, patience, kindness, goodness,
faithfulness, 23 gentleness, self-control. There is
no law that says these things are wrong. 24 Those
who belong to Christ Jesus have crucified their
own sinful selves. They have given up their old

"Love . . . yourself." Quotation from Leviticus 19:18.

SERVICE

Free to Serve

The 1970s. Afro hair, flares, the Bee Gees.

And Watergate.

The scandal of Watergate led to the first resignation by an American president since the nation was founded. It was a turbulent time, full of suspicion, intrigue, distrust and power-hungry leaders. In the middle of it was Charles W. Colson.

Chuck Colson was a presidential aide for Richard Nixon. He was one of several White House staff who were put in prison for the Watergate scandal. Colson served seven months.

Before he was sent to prison, Colson became a Christian. And while in prison, he saw at first hand the tremendous obstacles facing prisoners, ex-prisoners and their families. "Rather than rehabilitating, prisons have become breeding grounds for crime," he says.

After his release from prison, Colson could have done like many people. He could have forgotten about his prison experience and got on with his life. But he chose not to forget. He founded Prison Fellowship, a Christian outreach to inmates. Today, Colson regularly visits prisons and works for prison reform in countries around the world, including Britain.

Because of Colson's organisation, nearly 40,000 volunteers work in more than 600 prisons in the USA alone. His dedicated concern has resulted in the changed lives of thousands of inmates and families.

Chuck Colson turned his freedom into an opportunity to help those in prison. **Galatians 5:13–26** talks about the relationship between freedom and service. Read the passage to discover why God sets people free.

- How does Colson's choice to serve prisoners reflect this passage?
- How have you used your freedom in Christ as an avenue to serve others?

Consider . . .

- using some of your "free time" to serve other people.
- becoming a pen pal with a prison inmate, or contacting Prison Fellowship whose address can be obtained through your church.

For more, see . . .

- Leviticus 19:17–18 (p.119)
- Philippians 2:4–7 (p.1282)
- 1 Corinthians 10:23–24 (p.1228)

selfish feelings and the evil things they wanted to
do. 25We get our new life from the Spirit, so we
should follow the Spirit. 26We must not be proud
or make trouble with each other or be jealous of
each other.

Help Each Other

6 Brothers and sisters, if someone in your
group does something wrong, you who are
spiritual should go to that person and gently help
make him right again. But be careful, because
you might be tempted to sin too. 2By helping each
other with your troubles, you truly obey the
law of Christ. 3If anyone thinks he is important
when he really is not, he is only fooling himself.
4Each person should judge his own actions and
not compare himself with others. Then he can
be proud for what he himself has done. 5Each
person must be responsible for himself.
6Anyone who is learning the teaching of God
should share all the good things he has with his
teacher.

Life is like Planting a Field

7Do not be fooled: you cannot cheat God. Peo-
ple harvest only what they plant. 8If they plant to
satisfy their sinful selves, their sinful selves will
bring them ruin. But if they plant to please the
Spirit,*d* they will receive eternal life from the
Spirit. 9We must not become tired of doing good.
We will receive our harvest of eternal life at the
right time if we do not give up. 10When we have
the opportunity to help anyone, we should do it.
But we should give special attention to those
who are in the family of believers.

Paul Ends His Letter

11See what large letters I use to write this my-
self. 12Some people are trying to force you to be
circumcised*d* so the Jews will accept them. They

FRIENDS

Bringing Someone Back

Dan and Josh had been best mates since they were little. They'd gone to the same school and were in the same church youth group.

Just lately, Dan had started hanging around with a group of his other friends from school. He'd started going to their parties instead of youth group. Then he started going out with a girl from school and slowly stopped coming to church.

Josh was gutted. He and Dan had been such strong Christians and they did everything together. But now things had changed. Dan didn't seem to want to be around Josh any more. It was as if Dan knew that what he was doing was wrong and didn't want to be around Josh because he felt guilty or ashamed.

Josh had a choice to make. He could either be like some of the others in the youth group who bad-mouthed Dan and said things like, "I always knew he wasn't really a Christian," or he could choose to remain friends with Dan and try to show him the way back to Jesus.

It wasn't always easy, and often Josh felt like giving up, but after years of patiently praying and putting up with him, Dan re-committed his life to God.

Galatians 6:1–10 reminds us that none of us is immune to struggling as a Christian and gives us some great advice on how to deal with our friends who are finding it hard to follow Jesus.

- How do you think Josh would have felt seeing Dan turn his back on God?
- How do you react to Christian friends who are finding it hard to stay on the right track?

Consider . . .

- whether there is one of your friends who has turned away from God. Perhaps you could meet up regularly with other friends to pray for them until they come back to Jesus.
- meeting up with another Christian regularly so that they can challenge you when you go in the wrong direction.

For more, see . . .

- Colossians 2:6–10 (p.1292)
- James 5:19–20 (p.1354)
- Hebrews 10:24–25 (p.1339)

are afraid they will be attacked if they follow only
the cross of Christ.[n] 13 Those who are circum-
cised do not obey the law themselves, but they
want you to be circumcised so they can boast
about what they forced you to do. 14 I hope I will
never boast about things like that. The cross
of our Lord Jesus Christ is my only reason for
boasting. Through the cross of Jesus my world
was crucified, and I died to the world. 15 It is not
important if a man is circumcised or uncircum-
cised. The important thing is being the new peo-
ple God has made. 16 Peace and mercy to those
who follow this rule—and to all of God's people.
17 So do not give me any more trouble. I have
scars on my body that show[n] I belong to Christ
Jesus.
18 My brothers and sisters, the grace of our
Lord Jesus Christ be with your spirit. Amen.

Sidelight The apostle Paul usually dictated his letters to a friend who would write down his words as he spoke. In Galatians 6:11, however, Paul makes it clear that in this case he is writing the letter with his own hand and comments on the different handwriting! Some scholars think Paul might have had poor eyesight.

cross of Christ Paul uses the cross as a picture of the gospel, the story of Christ's death and rising from the dead to pay for our sins. The cross, or Christ's death, was God's way to save us.

that show Many times Paul was beaten and whipped by people who were against him because he was teaching about Christ. The scars were from these beatings.

Ephesians

Why Read This Book:

- Discover the blessings we have because we belong to Christ (Ephesians 1–3).
- Learn how to be united in our relationships with others (Ephesians 4–6:4).
- Gather the armour that you need to follow God (Ephesians 6:10–20).

When?

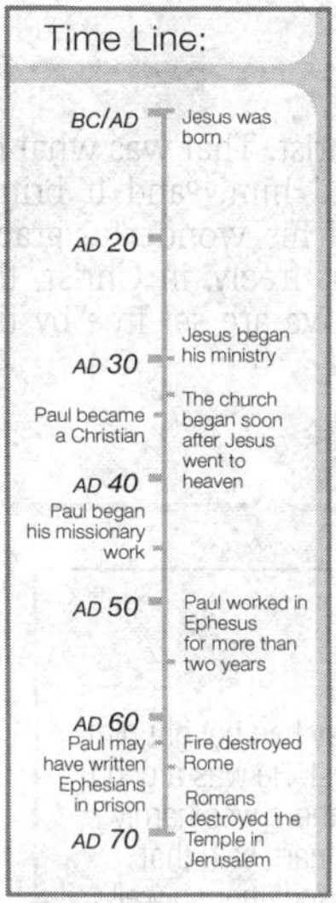

Behind the Scenes:

Sometimes it's easy to forget exactly where we fit into God's plan.

- "What is the meaning of my life?"
- "What am I meant to be doing with it?"
- "Where is the world going?"

This letter (addressed to the Ephesian church but passed around several Asian churches) answers such questions. It tells us about the spiritual blessings that Christians have in Jesus, about the fact that we have a brand new life, and how all Christians form one gigantic, powerful, united church.

The letter goes on to give us some guidelines as to how we should live our lives to God's glory. The writer talks about why we should always tell the truth, and he even includes sections about how children and parents, wives and husbands, and slaves and masters should relate to each other.

The final section of Ephesians tells us that we are involved in a very real spiritual battle against the powers of darkness, and describes the armour of God that we can wear at all times.

So there you have it – as Christians, we are brand new people who have been chosen to follow God and stand against evil. Read Ephesians for quick-start instructions on living the life you were made for!

Where?

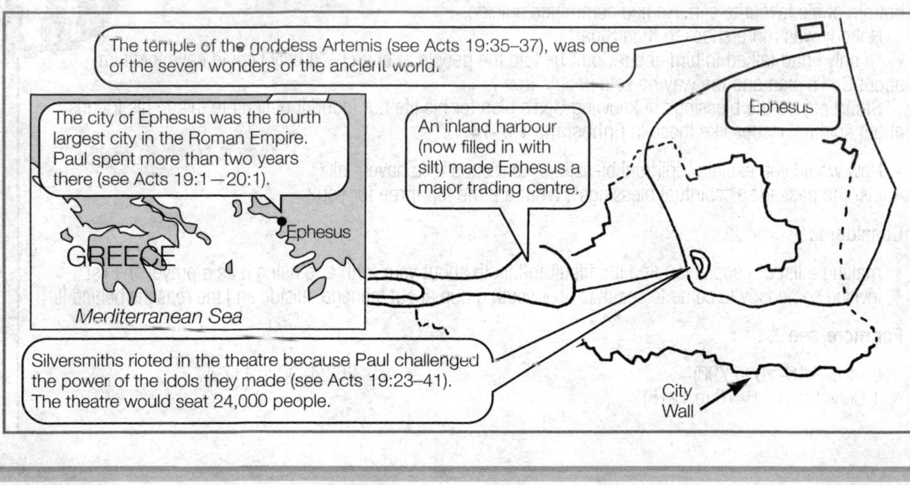

1 From Paul, an apostle[d] of Christ Jesus. I am
an apostle because that is what God wanted.
To God's holy people living in Ephesus, believ-
ers in Christ Jesus:
2Grace and peace to you from God our Father
and the Lord Jesus Christ.

Spiritual Blessings in Christ

3Praise be to the God and Father of our Lord
Jesus Christ. In Christ, God has given us every
spiritual blessing in the heavenly world. 4That is,
in Christ, he chose us before the world was made
so that we would be his holy people—people
without blame before him. 5Because of his love,
God had already decided to make us his own
children through Jesus Christ. That was what he
wanted and what pleased him, 6and it brings
praise to God because of his wonderful grace.
God gave that grace to us freely, in Christ, the
One he loves. 7In Christ we are set free by the

Sidelight Many scholars believe that this letter was originally circulated among many churches, since the earliest manuscripts do not include the words "in Ephesus" in Ephesians 1:1. In the second century AD, one source called this letter the "letter to the Laodiceans" – citizens of another city in Asia Minor.

NON-CHRISTIANS

I May be Gone Some Time

Gary had everything going for him. Money was no problem. His parents had pots of it. They had bought him a car – a convertible with a good turn of speed – as soon as he had passed his driving test. He was a good sportsman and was heavily into outdoor pursuits. Potholing, mountaineering, canoeing – there was hardly a weekend when he didn't have some breathtaking project on. His one Christian friend, Stuart, said that Gary was somebody who was difficult to talk to about needing God because he had got it together so well.

One morning Gary was missing from class. He was due to be playing in a match that afternoon so Stuart tried to ring his home. It was strange that there was no answer to the call. If he was ill why wasn't he answering? However, Gary's whereabouts were soon forgotten in the panic to put the team together.

Late that evening, Steve, Gary's older brother, had gone into his room wondering why Gary had not come in. On his bed was a note which said, "I've gone to our favourite place. I may be gone some time."

The favourite place was a cliff near their home. But it was the last sentence of the note which filled Steve with fear. Both Steve and Gary had often heard the story of Scott's fatal expedition to the South Pole. They both knew that a note which said, "I may be gone some time", had been left by Captain Oates, who had purposely walked out to die in a sub-zero blizzard.

The next morning Steve's worst fears were realised when he discovered Gary's body at the bottom of his favourite cliff. He had committed suicide.

Nobody was more shocked than Stuart.

"If only I had talked to him about God," he told the people at church. "If only I could have told him about God's plan and the way he sets people free."

Stuart enjoys the blessings of knowing God's plan for his life but found it difficult to talk to his friends about spiritual issues like those in **Ephesians 1:3–14**.

- How would you explain "spiritual blessings" to friends who have it all?
- List the passage's "spiritual blessings". What are the top three for you?

Consider . . .

- making a list of people you find it difficult to talk to about your faith and using it as a prayer "hit list".
- inviting somebody to come to speak to your youth group about teenage suicide and the reasons behind it.

For more, see . . .

- Ezekiel 3:16–20 (p.790)
- 1 Corinthians 2:6–16 (p.1215)
- Acts 26:24–32 (p.1179)

blood of his death, and so we have forgiveness of
sins. How rich is God's grace, [8]which he has
given to us so fully and freely. God, with full wis-
dom and understanding, [9]let us know his secret
purpose. This was what God wanted, and he
planned to do it through Christ. [10]His goal was to
carry out his plan, when the right time came,
that all things in heaven and on earth would be
joined together in Christ as the head.
[11]In Christ we were chosen to be God's peo-
ple, because from the very beginning God had de-
cided this in keeping with his plan. And he is the
One who makes everything agree with what he
decides and wants. [12]We are the first people who
hoped in Christ, and we were chosen so that we
would bring praise to God's glory. [13]So it is with
you. When you heard the true teaching—the
Good News [d] about your salvation—you believed
in Christ. And in Christ, God put his special mark
of ownership on you by giving you the Holy Spir-
it [d] that he had promised. [14]That Holy Spirit is the
guarantee that we will receive what God prom-
ised for his people until God gives full freedom to
those who are his—to bring praise to God's glory.

Paul's Prayer

[15]That is why since I heard about your faith in
the Lord Jesus and your love for all God's people,
[16]I have not stopped giving thanks to God for you.
I always remember you in my prayers, [17]asking
the God of our Lord Jesus Christ, the glorious
Father, to give you a spirit of wisdom and revela-
tion [d] so that you will know him better. [18]I pray
also that you will have greater understanding in
your heart so you will know the hope to which
he has called us and that you will know how rich

GOD'S POWER

Touch From Heaven

Maria stepped onto the stage. She shared how she was born deaf. The preacher asked if he could pray for her. He did, then spoke into one ear, "Do you hear me?"

"Yes!" she replied.

He spoke into the other ear. Again she replied, "Yes!" the excitement in her voice growing.

He returned to the first ear, "Do you hear me now?" he asked in a whisper barely audible to others around.

She whispered back, "Yes!"

As the crowd laughed at the amazing events unfolding, Maria couldn't contain her excitement any more. She jumped up and down declaring, "God has healed me; Jesus has healed me!"

This story is an incredible testimony of God's power but it doesn't stop there. Maria actually has a twin sister who was also born deaf. That night the preacher felt God telling him to pray out loud for the sister too, and a day or two later he received a call to say that the sister's ears had also suddenly popped open and she also could hear for the first time!

God is a powerful God. He can bring change in many ways to many people at the same time. He chooses when to visit people, sometimes when we least expect it, and even if our prayers seem to go unanswered, God actually has a way of using our struggles to help others in need.

We are a bit like a vacuum cleaner, if we are not plugged in to the power source we are useless; without God's power we will never see the kind of changes in our lives that we dream of. This power is available to all who ask for it as we read in **Ephesians 1:15–23**.

- How is God's power different from earthly power?
- Are there any areas in your life where you'd like to see more of God's power?

Consider . . .

- making a list of names of people or things in your life you want to see changed by God's power, then commit to praying for them.
- praying for people in other parts of the world who need to depend on God in their struggles.

For more, see . . .

- 1 Chronicles 29:11–12 (p.399)
- 2 Peter 1:3–4 (p.1365)
- Acts 1:7–8 (p.1137)

and glorious are the blessings God has promised
his holy people. [19]And you will know that God's
power is very great for us who believe. That
power is the same as the great strength [20]God
used to raise Christ from the dead and put him at
his right side in the heavenly world. [21]God has
put Christ over all rulers, authorities, powers and
kings, not only in this world but also in the next.
[22]God put everything under his power and made
him the head over everything for the church,
[23]which is Christ's body. The church is filled with
Christ, and Christ fills everything in every way.

We Now Have Life

2 In the past you were spiritually dead because
of your sins and the things you did against
God. [2]Yes, in the past you lived the way the
world lives, following the ruler of the evil powers
that are above the earth. That same spirit is now
working in those who refuse to obey God. [3]In the
past all of us lived like them, trying to please our
sinful selves and doing all the things our bodies
and minds wanted. We should have suffered
God's anger because of the way we were. We
were the same as all other people.

[4]But God's mercy is great, and he loved us very
much. [5]Though we were spiritually dead because
of the things we did against God, he gave us new
life with Christ. You have been saved by God's
grace. [6]And he raised us up with Christ and gave
us a seat with him in the heavens. He did this for
those in Christ Jesus [7]so that for all future time he
could show the very great riches of his grace by
being kind to us in Christ Jesus. [8]I mean that you

PEACE

Enemy in My House

Elaine and her father were best friends. She had always run to him when she was hurt. But as Elaine got older, everything changed. Her father spent more time away from home. And when he was at home, he and Elaine's mother fought all the time.

One day after school, Elaine found her mother lying across her bed, crying. The wardrobe doors were open, and her father's clothes had gone. Elaine's father had been having an affair and had moved out. Elaine couldn't believe it. How could her dad walk out on her like this?

Within three months, Elaine's parents were together, trying to restore their marriage. But Elaine couldn't see herself loving her father again. She avoided him. She even put a "No Men Allowed" sign on her bedroom door.

When Elaine went away to university, she was relieved to get away from the tense relationship with her dad. But during her first year, she heard the gospel and decided to follow Christ.

Her life began to change. She realised that God wanted to rebuild her relationship with her dad. While home one weekend, Elaine cried as she told her dad she forgave him and asked him to forgive her.

From that point on, there was peace in Elaine's home – the kind of peace that made her homesick for time with her father.

God's love brought peace between Elaine and her dad. Read **Ephesians 2:4–22** to see how Christ also broke down the walls and established peace between the Jews and those who were not Jews.

- How was Elaine's broken relationship with her dad like the broken relationship between Jewish and non-Jewish people? How was it different?
- How can Christ break down walls of hatred between you and other people that you know?

Consider . . .

- asking God to reveal any walls in your relationships that need to be broken down.
- making peace with someone from whom you feel separated by giving that person a brick or rock and explaining that you want to break down the "wall" between you.

For more, see . . .

- Psalm 120:6–7 (p.575)
- Hebrews 12:14–15 (p.1344)
- Romans 9 (p.1198)

have been saved by grace through believing. You did not save yourselves: it was a gift from God. 9It was not the result of your own work, so you cannot boast about it. 10God has made us what we are. In Christ Jesus, God made us to do good works, which God planned in advance for us to live our lives doing.

One in Christ

11You were not born Jewish. You are the people the Jews call "uncircumcised". Those who call you "uncircumcised" call themselves "circumcised". (Their circumcision is only something they themselves do on their bodies.) 12Remember that in the past you were without Christ. You were not citizens of Israel, and you had no part in the agreements[n] with the promise that God made to his people. You had no hope, and you did not know God. 13But now in Christ Jesus, you who were far away from God are brought near through the blood of Christ's death. 14Christ himself is our peace. He made both Jewish people and those who are not Jews one people. They were separated as if there were a wall between them, but Christ broke down that wall of hate by giving his own body. 15The Jewish law had many commands and rules, but Christ ended that law. His purpose was to make the two groups of people become one new people in him and in this way make peace. 16It was also Christ's purpose to end the hatred between the two groups, to make them into one body, and to bring them back to God. Christ did all this with his death on the cross. 17Christ came and preached peace to you who were far away from God, and to those who were near to God. 18Yes, it is through Christ we all have the right to come to the Father in one Spirit.[d]

19Now you who are not Jewish are not foreigners or strangers any longer, but are citizens together with God's holy people. You belong to God's family. 20You are like a building that was built on the foundation of the apostles[d] and prophets.[d] Christ Jesus himself is the most important stone[n] in that building, 21and that whole building is joined together in Christ. He makes it grow and become a holy temple in the Lord. 22And in Christ you, too, are being built together with the Jews into a place where God lives through the Spirit.

Sidelight

To describe Jesus as the "most important stone" or cornerstone (Ephesians 2:20) makes him essential for the "building". When workers started building, they would first place one stone – the cornerstone – and then line up all the walls based on this stone to make sure everything was straight.

Paul's Work in Telling the Good News

3 So I, Paul, am a prisoner of Christ Jesus for you who are not Jews. 2Surely you have heard that God gave me this work through his grace to help you. 3He let me know his secret by showing it to me. I have already written a little about this. 4If you read what I wrote then, you can see that I truly understand the secret about the Christ.[d] 5People who lived in other times were not told that secret. But now, through the Spirit,[d] God has shown that secret to his holy apostles[d] and prophets.[d] 6This is that secret: that through the Good News[d] those who are not Jews will share with the Jews in God's blessing. They belong to the same body, and they share together in the promise that God made in Christ Jesus.

7By God's special gift of grace given to me through his power, I became a servant to tell that Good News. 8I am the least important of all God's people, but God gave me this gift—to tell those who are not Jews the Good News about the riches of Christ, which are too great to understand fully. 9And God gave me the work of telling all people about the plan for his secret, which has been hidden in him since the beginning of time. He is the One who created everything. 10His purpose was that through the church all the rulers and powers in the heavenly world will now know God's wisdom, which has so many forms. 11This agrees with the purpose God had since the beginning of time, and he carried out his plan through Christ Jesus our Lord. 12In Christ we can come before God with freedom and without fear. We can do this through faith in Christ. 13So I ask you not to become discouraged because of the sufferings I am having for you. My sufferings are for your glory.

The Love of Christ

14So I bow in prayer before the Father 15from whom every family in heaven and on earth gets its true name. 16I ask the Father in his great glory to give you the power to be strong inwardly through his Spirit.[d] 17I pray that Christ will live in your hearts by faith and that your lives will be strong in love and be built on love. 18And I pray that you and all God's holy people will have the power to understand the greatness of Christ's love—how wide and how long and how high

agreements The agreements that God gave to his people in the Old Testament.
most important stone Literally, "cornerstone". The first and most important stone in a building.

and how deep that love is. 19Christ's love is
greater than anyone can ever know, but I pray
that you will be able to know that love. Then you
can be filled with the fullness of God.
20With God's power working in us, God can do
much, much more than anything we can ask or
imagine. 21To him be glory in the church and in
Christ Jesus for all time, for ever and ever. Amen.

The Unity of the Body

4 I am in prison because I belong to the Lord.
God chose you to be his people, so I tell you
now to live the life to which God called you.
2Always be humble, gentle and patient, accepting
each other in love. 3You are joined together with
peace through the Spirit, [d] so do all you can to
continue together in this way. 4There is one body
and one Spirit, and God called you to have one
hope. 5There is one Lord, one faith and one bap-
tism. [d] 6There is one God and Father of every-
thing. He rules everything and is everywhere and
is in everything.
7Christ gave each one of us the special gift of
grace, showing how generous he is. 8That is why
it says in the Scriptures, [d]

"When he went up to the heights,
he led a parade of captives,
and he gave gifts to all peoples." *Psalm 68:18*

GOD'S LOVE

Can You Feel It?

Katie was seventeen years old and thought she was a bad witness for Jesus. It wasn't that she didn't try, it was just that she was never quite sure that she was doing the right thing.

One day she had the opportunity to talk to a TV personality (her father worked for a large TV station and sometimes she was allowed to go and watch a show). This particular day, she found herself drinking coffee in the hospitality suite with her father and the show's host, Peter. He was politely asking her questions and she was so engrossed in her answers that she didn't notice her dad slip away.

Somehow, she'd managed to tell Peter that she was a Christian and how it had totally changed her life. Unknown to her, Peter was very impressed.

Three months later, Katie found herself back in her dad's TV studio watching the rehearsals for a new programme. Her eyebrows lifted in surprise when she saw Peter walk in. He'd been working on another "set" and dropped in unexpectedly. She turned and smiled at him, not in the least expecting him to acknowedge her, but he grinned and walked over.

"Hi Katie!" he said.

"Oh! I didn't think you'd remember me!" she gasped.

Peter laughed and said, "Oh I would always remember you. I meet thousands and thousands of people, but rarely do I meet anyone who has such strong convictions as you." Katie was taken aback as he continued:

"I don't know what it is about you Christians . . . but you always bring a fantastic sense of peace with you. I can honestly say that I don't find it with anyone else." He looked at her earnestly and said, "Do you know, I can almost feel it?"

It reminded Katie that God's love in her life was much stronger than she realised.

Read **Ephesians 3:14–21** to see that God's great love and power is at work in Christians.

- What ways do you show God's love in your life?
- Verse 20 says that God's power works in us. What ways does God work in your life?

Consider . . .

- making a sign about God's love for you. Hang it where you can see it each morning, and remember that God's love for you has no limits.
- thanking God for a way in which he has shown his love for you.

For more, see . . .

- Psalm 36:5–10 (p.521)
- Romans 8:35–39 (p.1197)
- John 13:34–35 (p.1122)

9 When it says, "He went up," what does it mean? It means that he first came down to the earth. 10 So Jesus came down, and he is the same One who went up above all the sky. Christ did that to fill everything with his presence. 11 And Christ gave gifts to people—he made some to be apostles,[d] some to be prophets,[d] some to go and tell the Good News,[d] and some to have the work of caring for and teaching God's people. 12 Christ gave those gifts to prepare God's holy people for the work of serving, to make the body of Christ stronger. 13 This work must continue until we are all joined together in the same faith and in the same knowledge of the Son of God. We must become like a mature person, growing until we become like Christ and have his perfection.

Sidelight As Christians, we belong to the family of Christ, and as the family of Christ, we belong together. This is the point which Paul makes in Ephesians 4:1–13.

14 Then we will no longer be babies. We will not be tossed about like a ship that the waves carry one way and then another. We will not be influenced by every new teaching we hear from people who are trying to fool us. They make plans and try any kind of trick to fool people into following the wrong path. 15 No! Speaking the truth with love, we will grow up in every way into Christ, who is the head. 16 The whole body depends on Christ, and all the parts of the body are joined and held together. Each part does its own work to make the whole body grow and be strong with love.

The Way You Should Live

17 In the Lord's name, I tell you this. Do not continue living like those who do not believe. Their thoughts are worth nothing. 18 They do not understand, and they know nothing, because they refuse to listen. So they cannot have the life that God gives. 19 They have lost all feeling of

CHURCH

Friends or Foes?

After several months of fighting among Westside Church members, the "get-rid-of-the-minister" side won. The Reverend Howard fought back tears as he announced his resignation on Sunday morning. He moved away within a month.

Many church members on the "keep-the-minister" side were angry and disillusioned; most of them left the Westside Church within six months. Some went to other churches. But some stayed away from the church for years.

Those who stayed at Westside Church chose a new minister – one they were sure they would like much better than the Reverend Howard. But in less than two years, the church members were fighting again.

After watching the church destroy itself for the second time, one of the young people commented, "I don't think you can even call this place a church – anyway, I don't think it's what God meant the church to be."

This teenager's perception fits the description of the church in **Ephesians 4:1–6**. Read this scripture to see what God wants the church to be like.

- If Westside Church members had applied these verses to their situation, how would the outcome have been different?
- How can you use this passage to promote unity within your church?

Consider . . .

- encouraging your youth group to pray weekly for your church to be united.
- talking to your minister about creating an annual "Unity Award" for church members who consistently promote unity in your church.

For more, see . . .

- Psalm 133 (p.579)
- 1 Peter 3:8–12 (p.1360)
- Titus 3:9–11 (p.1324)

shame, and they use their lives for doing evil. They
continually want to do all kinds of evil. 20But
what you learned in Christ was not like this. 21I
know that you heard about him, and you are in
him, so you were taught the truth that is in
Jesus. 22You were taught to leave your old self—
to stop living the evil way you lived before. That
old self becomes worse, because people are fooled
by the evil things they want to do. 23But you
were taught to be made new in your hearts, 24to
become a new person. That new person is made
to be like God—made to be truly good and holy.
25So you must stop telling lies. "Tell each
other the truth,"[n] because we all belong to each
other in the same body. 26When you are angry,
do not sin, and be sure to stop being angry before
the end of the day. 27Do not give the devil a way
to defeat you. 28Those who are stealing must
stop stealing and start working. They should
earn an honest living for themselves. Then they
will have something to share with those who are
poor.
29When you talk, do not say harmful things,
but say what people need—words that will help
others become stronger. Then what you say will
do good to those who listen to you. 30And do not
make the Holy Spirit[d] sad. The Spirit is God's
proof that you belong to him. God gave you the
Spirit to show that God will make you free when
the final day comes. 31Do not be bitter or angry
or cross. Never shout angrily or say things to
hurt others. Never do anything evil. 32Be kind
and loving to each other, and forgive each other
just as God forgave you in Christ.

Living in the Light

5 You are God's children whom he loves, so
try to be like him. 2Live a life of love just as
Christ loved us and gave himself for us as a
sweet-smelling offering and sacrifice to God.

"Tell . . . truth," Quotation from Zechariah 8:16.

CULTS

Hazardous to Your Health

Jim Jones was an ordained minister who thought he was the Messiah. Jones demanded total allegiance from his followers, telling them that he was going to create the perfect society – free from hate, crime, and lack of anything.

People sold everything they had and gave it to Jones. Nearly 1,000 people followed Jones to Guyana in South America, where he established a settlement called Jonestown.

In 1978, Leo Ryan, a US representative from California, travelled to Jonestown to investigate rumours that Jones was holding some people against their will. In fear of being caught, Jones had Ryan and three journalists who accompanied Ryan killed. Then, to destroy all evidence of his lies and deceit, Jones ordered his followers to take poison in a religious ceremony. More than 900 people – including Jones himself – died in what is now called the "Jonestown Massacre".

The people in Jonestown didn't recognise Jim Jones's lies. **Ephesians 4:11–16** warns us to be mature so that we can recognise false teachings.

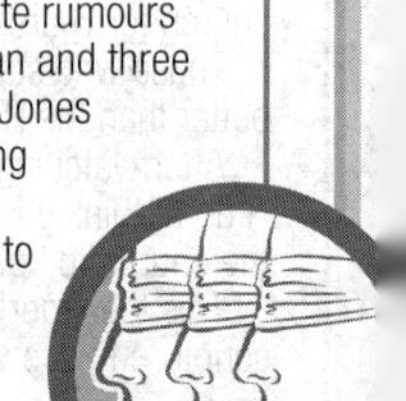

- How were the people in Jim Jones's church like the babies described here?
- Has anyone ever tried to lead you down the wrong path? How did the truth help you to stay on God's path?

Consider . . .

- talking to your minister or other church leader about the elements of truth that your own church emphasises.
- asking your minister or youth leader to lead a study on a new "religious movement" to discover whether or not it is founded on the truth.

For more, see . . .

- Proverbs 4 (p.592)
- Philippians 4:8–9 (p.1286)
- Romans 1:18–32 (p.1185)

3But there must be no sexual sin among you,
or any kind of evil or greed. Those things are not
right for God's holy people. 4Also, there must be
no evil talk among you, and you must not speak
foolishly or tell evil jokes. These things are not
right for you. Instead, you should be giving
thanks to God. 5You can be sure of this: no one
will have a place in the kingdom of Christ and of
God who sins sexually, or does evil things, or
is greedy. Anyone who is greedy is serving a
false god.
6Do not let anyone fool you by telling you
things that are not true, because these things will
bring God's anger on those who do not obey him.
7So have nothing to do with them. 8In the past
you were full of darkness, but now you are full of
light in the Lord. So live like children who belong
to the light. 9Light brings every kind of goodness,
right living and truth. 10Try to learn what pleases
the Lord. 11Have nothing to do with the things
done in darkness, which are not worth anything.
But show that they are wrong. 12It is shameful
even to talk about what those people do in secret.
13But the light makes all things easy to see, 14and
everything that is made easy to see can become
light. This is why it is said:

"Wake up, sleeper!
Rise from death,
and Christ will shine on you."

15So be very careful how you live. Do not live
like those who are not wise, but live wisely.
16Use every chance you have for doing good, be-
cause these are evil times. 17So do not be foolish
but learn what the Lord wants you to do. 18Do
not be drunk with wine, which will ruin you,
but be filled with the Spirit.[d] 19Speak to each
other with psalms, hymns and spiritual songs,
singing and making music in your hearts to the
Lord. 20Always give thanks to God the Father for
everything, in the name of our Lord Jesus Christ.

Wives and Husbands

21Yield to obey each other because you respect
Christ.
22Wives, yield to your husbands, as you do to
the Lord, 23because the husband is the head of the
wife, as Christ is the head of the church. And he
is the Saviour[d] of the body, which is the church.

ANGER

Handle With Care

Clare wasn't having a good day. Her boyfriend broke up with her before her first lesson. She got her maths exam back and knew that her parents would not be pleased with her marks. She missed lunch. And then she mouthed off at her PE teacher.

She shook her head as she recalled the incident.

"Come on, Clare," Mrs Eaton had yelled. "You can't do press-ups with your bottom in the air. Try 50 more, and do them properly this time!"

"I'd like to see you do 50 press-ups, you fat slob," Clare mumbled – a little louder than she intended.

Now she was sitting in the detention room while everyone else in the school was on their way home.

"If only I'd kept my mouth shut," Clare moaned.

Sometimes our anger can get us into trouble. Read the warning about anger in **Ephesians 4:25–5:2**.

- According to this passage, did Clare's anger lead to sin or not?
- How can you be angry, and yet not sin?

Consider . . .

- listing three things that make you angry. Beside each one, write a brief description of how you can handle the situation without sinning.
- resolving to deal quickly with things that make you angry.

For more, see . . .

- Psalm 4 (p.501)
- James 1:19–20 (p.1348)
- Proverbs 22:24–25 (p.609)

24As the church yields to Christ, so you wives
should yield to your husbands in everything.
25Husbands, love your wives as Christ loved
the church and gave himself for it 26to make it
belong to God. Christ used the word to make the
church clean by washing it with water. 27He died
so that he could give the church to himself like a
bride in all her beauty. He died so that the
church could be pure and without fault, with no
evil or sin or any other wrong thing in it. 28In the
same way, husbands should love their wives as
they love their own bodies. The man who loves
his wife loves himself. 29No one ever hates his
own body, but feeds and takes care of it. And
that is what Christ does for the church, 30be-
cause we are parts of his body. 31The Scripture
says, "So a man will leave his father and mother
and be united with his wife, and the two
will become one body." *n* 32That secret is very
important—I am talking about Christ and the
church. 33But each one of you must love his wife
as he loves himself, and a wife must respect her
husband.

Children and Parents

6 Children, obey your parents as the Lord
wants, because this is the right thing to do.
2The command says, "Honour your father and
mother." *n* This is the first command that has a
promise with it— 3"Then everything will be well
with you, and you will have a long life on the
earth." *n*
4Fathers, do not make your children angry,
but raise them with the training and teaching of
the Lord.

Slaves and Masters

5Slaves, obey your masters here on earth with
fear and respect and from a sincere heart, just as
you obey Christ. 6You must do this not only while
they are watching you, to please them. With all
your heart you must do what God wants as peo-
ple who are obeying Christ. 7Do your work with
enthusiasm. Work as if you were serving the
Lord, not as if you were serving only men and
women. 8Remember that the Lord will give a re-
ward to everyone, slave or free, for doing good.

"So . . . body." Quotation from Genesis 2:24.
"Honour . . . mother." Quotation from Exodus 20:12; Deuteronomy 5:16.
"Then . . . earth." Quotation from Exodus 20:12; Deuteronomy 5:16.

DECISION MAKING

Who's Going to Know?

Rob was having the time of his life on tour in Germany with his community orchestra – and no parents! There were adults, of course, but Rob was making his own decisions and loving every minute of it.

On Saturday night, Rob's friends went out to get their first taste of Germany. Most band members wanted to take advantage of Germany's sex shows.

Rob wasn't sure. He didn't feel quite right about going but it seemed to be something everybody did when they were away from home.

He thought, "Anyway. Who's going to know?"

"I'd know," Rob finally told himself, after remembering the advice in **Ephesians 5:6–20**. See how this passage can help you to make difficult decisions.

- What principles do you find in this passage that Rob may have used in making his decision?
- How can you use the passage's advice in a decision that you face now?

Consider . . .

- praying and writing about what God wants you to do with your life.
- writing a letter to a friend who's facing a difficult decision. Include the passage's advice on decision making.

For more, see . . .

- 1 Kings 18:1–40 (p.332)
- James 1:5–8 (p.1348)
- Romans 12:1–2 (p.1203)

9 Masters, in the same way, be good to your
slaves. Do not threaten them. Remember that
the One who is your Master and their Master is
in heaven, and he treats everyone alike.

Wear the Full Armour of God

10 Finally, be strong in the Lord and in his great
power. 11 Put on the full armour of God so that
you can fight against the devil's evil tricks. 12 Our
fight is not against people on earth but against
the rulers and authorities and the powers of this
world's darkness, against the spiritual powers of
evil in the heavenly world. 13 That is why you
need to put on God's full armour. Then on the
day of evil you will be able to stand strong. And
when you have finished the whole fight, you will
still be standing. 14 So stand strong, with the belt
of truth tied around your waist and the protection
of right living on your chest. 15 On your feet wear
the Good News[d] of peace to help you stand
strong. 16 And also use the shield of faith with
which you can stop all the burning arrows of the
Evil One. 17 Accept God's salvation as your hel-
met, and take the sword of the Spirit,[d] which is
the word of God. 18 Pray in the Spirit at all times
with all kinds of prayers, asking for everything you
need. To do this you must always be ready and
never give up. Always pray for all God's people.
19 Also pray for me that when I speak, God
will give me words so that I can tell the secret
of the Good News without fear. 20 I have been
sent to preach this Good News, and I am doing

Sidelight The "shield of faith" in Ephesians 6:16 is a comparison to the large Roman shield used by heavily armed soldiers. This shield was designed to protect against burning darts, one of the most dangerous weapons of the time. When the dart hit the shield, it sank into wood, and the flame was extinguished.

WORSHIP

Guitar Man

Matthew bought his first guitar at a junk sale. Once he could play three chords without looking at his hands, he sometimes played with a rock band – the others in the band were just a little better than him. They really enjoyed themselves, practising, writing songs and playing at parties and school events. They may not have been good – but they were loud and their audiences loved them. Matthew took lessons from a professional rock guitarist and over the next year his skills improved immensely. He practised hard, playing and singing along to CDs in his room.

When he went to university, with all his books and clothes, Matthew took an amplifier and brand new solid guitar. He was hoping to find a place in a college rock band.

But Matthew got deeply involved in the growing Christian Union and soon found himself playing in worship meetings and outreach events – needing to practise every week and learn a lot of new material.

He still enjoys playing rock music and jamming with friends whenever he gets a chance. But now his priority is making music to the Lord and he realises that to lead others into the freedom of real worship requires more than skill on the guitar. Read about it in **Ephesians 5:15–20**.

- What is the difference between playing music and "making music in your hearts to the Lord"?
- Look at the things mentioned in the passage. How might they affect the way you do music?

Consider . . .

- making a list of songs which are important to you and asking your worship leader if they can be included on the church programme.
- starting to collect Christian contemporary or praise music and using it to help you praise God.

For more, see . . .

- 1 Chronicles 25:1–8 (p.393)
- Colossians 3:15–17 (p.1293)
- Psalm 33 (p.519)

that now, here in prison. Pray that when I preach
the Good News I will speak without fear, as I
should.

Final Greetings

21 I am sending to you Tychicus, our brother
whom we love and a faithful servant of the
Lord's work. He will tell you everything that is
happening with me. Then you will know how I
am and what I am doing. 22 I am sending him to
you for this reason—so that you will know how
we are, and he can encourage you.
23 Peace and love with faith to you from God
the Father and the Lord Jesus Christ. 24 Grace to
all of you who love our Lord Jesus Christ with
love that never ends.

HOLY SPIRIT

A New Super-Power

Should I do what my friends want me to? Why should I bother with God? Why care what my family says?

Every day we make decisions – dozens of them – and try to work things out for the best, even though it's a struggle. But there's another even bigger struggle going on: we're caught up in a spiritual war with all the forces of evil in the world. This is terrifying when we realise what it involves – evil spiritual powers trying to influence us to do what we often know is wrong. They help us convince ourselves that we should do something even though it's going to be a bad move. But how can we stop ourselves?

If we believe in Jesus, God gives us the most amazing power that we could have – a power much stronger than the spiritual forces which talk us into doing evil. This power from God is called the "Holy Spirit". Unfortunately, we often think that the Holy Spirit is a bit of a weird, ghostly thing, but that's all wrong. The Holy Spirit is a person: he is God, alongside God the Father and God the Son, Jesus. Although this is a really deep mystery that it's hard to get our heads round, it's true. He's a person who we can know and have a relationship with. When we do things that he doesn't like, the Bible says we upset him. But when we put our trust in God, he leads us and shows us the way we should live.

Often our lives are full of doubts and confused ideas – but if we pray to God, the Holy Spirit will show us what to do. **Ephesians 6:10–20** teaches about the spiritual armour God has given us to help us.

- What wrong ideas might we have about the Holy Spirit?
- What does this passage tell us the Holy Spirit does?

Consider . . .

- how there's much more to life than what we see. Ask God that you would be able to "pray in the Spirit" and know him leading you.
- as you read your Bible, being aware of how the Holy Spirit is speaking to you through it. Share what you feel with someone who has been a Christian for a while.

For more, see . . .

- John 14:26 (p.1124)
- Romans 8:26 (p.1196)
- Acts 2:38 (p.1140)
- Galatians 5:16–26 (p.1264)

Philippians

Why Read This Book:

- Discover how serving other people serves Christ (Philippians 1—2).
- Learn why growing in faith is so important (Philippians 3).
- Learn Paul's secret of having joy amidst suffering (Philippians 4).

When?

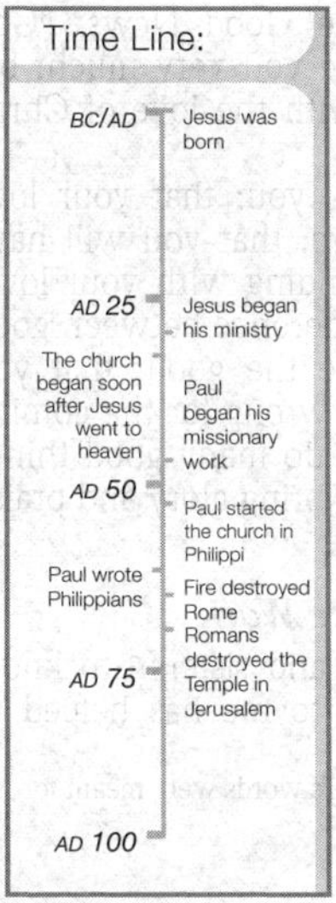

Behind the Scenes:

Paul spent his life telling the Good News of Jesus Christ and starting new churches. But what did he get for it? He was put on trial, run out of town, stoned, beaten with rods and thrown in prison several times. In addition, other Christians misunderstood and opposed him.

In short, Paul had plenty of reasons to be gloomy and depressed. But, as we learn in Philippians, Paul felt just the opposite. In fact, this short letter from Paul is probably the most upbeat, cheerful book in the Bible.

Part of the reason he was happy was that the Christians in Philippi had heard about his imprisonment and had taken up a collection for him. Their love and concern made Paul deeply grateful, and Paul thanks them in this letter.

But the most important reason for Paul's happiness is clear in the letter. "To me the only important thing about living is Christ," he writes, "and dying would be profit for me" (Philippians 1:21).

The Romans could chain Paul's body, but they couldn't chain Paul's heart. And in this letter to his friends at Philippi, the apostle shares his secret for facing difficult circumstances with a song on his lips and joy in his heart.

Where?

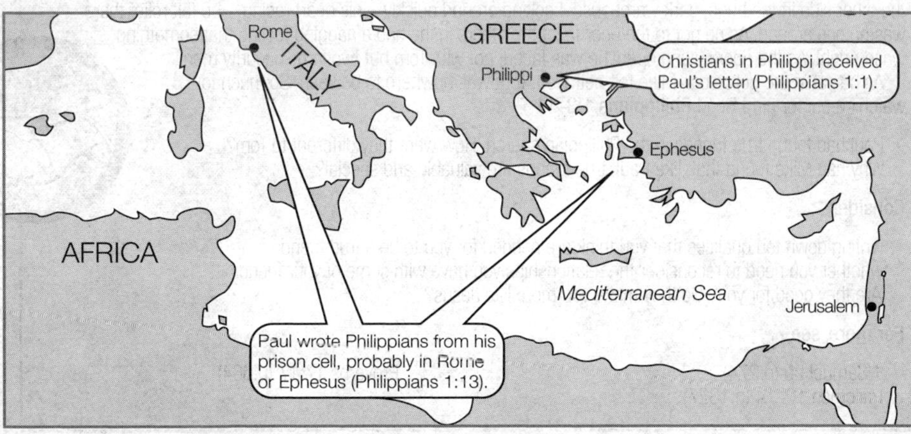

1 From Paul and Timothy, servants of Christ
Jesus.
To all of God's holy people in Christ Jesus who
live in Philippi, including your elders[d] and
deacons:[d]
2Grace and peace to you from God our Father
and the Lord Jesus Christ.

Sidelight A woman, Lydia, was the first person baptised in Europe. She was probably a leader in the early Philippian church (see Acts 16:11–15, p.1164), but she may not have stayed there long, since she made a living as a travelling merchant who sold purple-dyed cloth.

Paul's Prayer

3I thank my God every time I remember you,
4always praying with joy for all of you. 5I thank
God for the help you gave me while I preached
the Good News[d]—help you gave from the first
day you believed until now. 6God began doing a
good work in you, and I am sure he will
continue it until it is finished when Jesus Christ
comes again.
7And I know that I am right to think like this
about all of you, because I have you in my heart.
All of you share in God's grace with me while I
am in prison and while I am defending and
proving the truth of the Good News. 8God
knows that I want to see you very much, be-
cause I love all of you with the love of Christ
Jesus.
9This is my prayer for you: that your love
will grow more and more; that you will have
knowledge and understanding with your love;
10that you will see the difference between good
and bad and will choose the good; that you
will be pure and without wrong for the coming
of Christ; 11that you will do many good things
with the help of Christ to bring glory and praise
to God.

Paul's Troubles Help the Work

12I want you brothers and sisters[n] to know
that what has happened to me has helped to

brothers and sisters Although the Greek text says "brothers" here and throughout this book, Paul's words were meant for the entire church, both men and women.

FRIENDS

Pick Your Friends Carefully

Mike was smaller than other kids in his class. This made him a bit insecure and he found himself getting into fights. That's when he got friendly with Tom. Tom was someone who everyone feared and it made Mike feel good inside when Tom had asked him to join his gang.

The night was perfect, no one was about and Mike felt a kind of buzz that he would be getting hold of some much-needed cash. He managed to squeeze himself through the window without any problem. He landed on the other side in the huge, dark warehouse. Looking around quickly – his heart racing – he felt relief there was no one around. As he got to the door to let the others in, he had a nagging feeling that something wasn't right. As the door swung open, he was faced, not with Tom but two large security men.

As he sat in the police car, Mike felt betrayed. Tom was nowhere to be seen. So much for watching out for him! Read **Philippians 1:3–11**.

- Paul had found true friends in the Philippian church. How were they different to Tom?
- Why had Mike found that, like Paul, true friends are valuable and special?

Consider . . .

- writing down ten qualities that you think are needed for you to be a true friend.
- whether you need to reconsider the relationships you have with some of your friends. Are they good for you? Do they make you more like Jesus?

For more, see . . .

- 1 Samuel 20 (p.274)
- Philemon 10–14 (p.1327)
- Proverbs 17:17 (p.604)

spread the Good News.[d] 13All the palace guards
and everyone else knows that I am in prison be-
cause I am a believer in Christ. 14Because I am in
prison, most of the believers have become more
bold in Christ and are not afraid to speak the
word of God.
15It is true that some preach about Christ be-
cause they are jealous and ambitious, but
others preach about Christ because they want
to help. 16They preach because they have love,
and they know that God gave me the work
of defending the Good News. 17But the others
preach about Christ for selfish and wrong
reasons, wanting to make trouble for me in
prison.
18But it doesn't matter. The important thing
is that in every way, whether for right or
wrong reasons, they are preaching about
Christ. So I am happy, and I will continue to
be happy. 19Because you are praying for me and
the Spirit of Jesus Christ is helping me, I know
this trouble will bring my freedom. 20I expect
and hope that I will not fail Christ in any-
thing but that I will have the courage now, as

DEATH

After AIDS

For Daniel, a childhood filled with rejection became a life of rejection. His parents' failed marriage contributed to his own broken marriages.

A need to escape problems led to drug and alcohol addictions. A desire for some kind of acceptance led to homosexuality. And homosexuality led to AIDS.

Abandoned by family and friends, Daniel faced death alone. He was ready to end his life when Jean, a Christian friend, invited Daniel into her home. Through Jean's caring, Daniel eventually decided to follow Christ.

What changes occurred in the heart of this beaten, lonely man! He experienced the release of forgiveness from his past. For the first time in his life, he felt genuine acceptance and unconditional love. And he had a place to belong, with people who cared for him.

As his body weakened, Daniel's spirit grew stronger and stronger. He was revitalised by his new-found hope in Christ.

Daniel directed his energy to reaching out with the love of Jesus to those who needed it most. He visited AIDS patients at a local hospital and shared his story with many dying people who had also been rejected. He spoke at churches and support groups, and he explained how God's love reaches even those whom some find unlovable. He spent his time eagerly giving and receiving love.

"I don't know how long I'm going to live, but I want to live the rest of my days for the Lord," Daniel told his friends.

After several months, Daniel died. Those who were touched by Daniel's life felt a tremendous loss. But at the same time, they rejoiced because they knew Daniel was at peace and happy to be with Jesus.

Paul faced death peacefully under different circumstances. Read **Philippians 1:21–27** to see Paul's attitude towards living and dying.

- How were Daniel's and Paul's attitudes about life affected by what they thought about death?
- According to this passage, what is the purpose of life and death?

Consider . . .

- thinking of the top reason you have to live, then putting more energy into that activity.
- discussing your feelings about death with a Christian friend. Think about the way your priorities look from a heavenly perspective.

For more, see . . .

- Psalm 42 (p.525)
- Galatians 2:20–21 (p.1259)
- Romans 14:7–8 (p.1207)

always, to show the greatness of Christ in
my life here on earth, whether I live or die. 21To
me the only important thing about living is
Christ, and dying would be profit for me. 22If I
continue living in my body, I will be able to
work for the Lord. I do not know what to
choose—living or dying. 23It is hard to choose
between the two. I want to leave this life and
be with Christ, which is much better, 24but you
need me here in my body. 25Since I am sure of
this, I know I will stay with you to help you
grow and have joy in your faith. 26You will be
very happy in Christ Jesus when I am with
you again.

27Only one thing concerns me: be sure
that you live in a way that brings honour to
the Good News of Christ. Then whether I
come and visit you or am away from you, I
will hear that you are standing strong with one
purpose, that you work together as one for
the faith of the Good News, 28and that you are
not afraid of those who are against you. All of
this is proof that your enemies will be de-
stroyed but that you will be saved by God.
29God gave you the honour not only of believ-
ing in Christ but also of suffering for him, both
of which bring glory to Christ. 30When I was
with you, you saw the struggles I had, and
you hear about the struggles I am having now.
You yourselves are having the same kind of
struggles.

2 Does your life in Christ give you strength?
Does his love comfort you? Do we share
together in the Spirit? Do you have mercy and
kindness? 2If so, make me very happy by having
the same thoughts, sharing the same love, and
having one mind and purpose. 3When you do
things, do not let selfishness or pride be your
guide. Instead, be humble and give more honour
to others than to yourselves. 4Do not be inter-
ested only in your own life, but be interested in
the lives of others.

Be Unselfish like Christ

5In your lives you must think and act like
Christ Jesus.

6Christ himself was like God in everything.
  But he did not think that being equal with
    God was something to be used for his
    own benefit.
7But he gave up his place with God and made
    himself nothing.

CHURCH

Sticking Together

When a flock of geese fly south for the winter, they fly in a V-shaped formation. If they didn't, they would never reach their destination.

Researchers have found that the V-shaped formation helps geese to fly at least 71 per cent further than they could fly alone, because each bird creates an updraught for the one behind it, making flying easier.

If one goose falls out of formation, the wind resistance slows the bird down. If it doesn't act quickly, it will not be able to keep up with its flock. So, it quickly gets back into formation.

Like geese, Christians need to work together in the church. Read **Philippians 2:1–11** to learn how.

- How is the geese's V-shaped formation like the passage's description of Christians working together?
- How does being with other Christians encourage you in your faith?

Consider . . .

- writing your name and the names of other people in a V-shaped pattern to symbolise how you support each other. Thank God for people in the church who lead and support you.
- talking to your youth leader or a Sunday school teacher about how you can create an"updraught" to support and encourage others in your church.

For more, see . . .

- Psalm 133:1–3 (p.579)
- Acts 2:44–47 (p.1141)
- Mark 9:33–37 (p.1015)

He was born to be a man
and became like a servant.
8And when he was living as a man,
he humbled himself and was fully obedient
to God,
even when that caused his death—death
on a cross.
9So God raised him to the highest place.
God made his name greater than every
other name
10so that every knee will bow to the name of
Jesus—
everyone in heaven, on earth and under
the earth.
11And everyone will confess that Jesus Christ is
Lord
and bring glory to God the Father.

Be the People God Wants You to Be

12My dear friends, you have always obeyed
God when I was with you. It is even more im-
portant that you obey now while I am away from
you. Keep on working to complete your salvation
with fear and trembling, 13because God is work-
ing in you to help you want to do and be able to
do what pleases him.
14Do everything without complaining or argu-
ing. 15Then you will be innocent and without any
wrong. You will be God's children without fault.
But you are living with crooked and evil people
all around you, among whom you shine like stars
in the dark world. 16You offer the teaching that
gives life. So when Christ comes again, I can be
happy because my work was not wasted. I ran
the race and won.
17Your faith makes you offer your lives as a
sacrifice in serving God. If I have to offer my own
blood with your sacrifice, I will be happy and full
of joy with all of you. 18You also should be happy
and full of joy with me.

Timothy and Epaphroditus

19I hope in the Lord Jesus to send Timothy to
you soon. I will be happy to learn how you are.
20I have no one else like Timothy, who truly cares
for you. 21Other people are interested only in
their own lives, not in the work of Jesus Christ.
22You know the kind of person Timothy is. You
know he has served with me in telling the Good
News,[d] as a son serves his father. 23I plan to send
him to you quickly when I know what will hap-
pen to me. 24I am sure that the Lord will help me
to come to you soon.
25Epaphroditus, my brother in Christ, works
and serves with me in the army of Christ. When
I needed help, you sent him to me. I think now
that I must send him back to you, 26because he
wants very much to see all of you. He is worried
because you heard that he was sick. 27Yes, he was
sick, and nearly died, but God had mercy on him
and me too so that I would not have more
sadness. 28I want very much to send him to you
so that when you see him you can be happy, and

Sidelight If the sickness that Epaphroditus suffered from had been a fever (see Philippians 2:26–27), the common treatment in New Testament times would have been to hang a bag around his neck. The bag would have contained, among other items, seven hairs from seven old dogs!

I can stop worrying about you. 29Welcome him
in the Lord with much joy. Give honour to peo-
ple like him, 30because he almost died for the
work of Christ. He risked his life to give me the
help you could not give in your service to me.

The Importance of Christ

3 My brothers and sisters, be full of joy in the
Lord. It is no trouble for me to write the
same things to you again, and it will help you to
be more ready. 2Watch out for those who do
evil, who are like dogs, who insist on cutting[n]
the body. 3We are the ones who are truly
circumcised.[d] We worship God through his
Spirit,[d] and our pride is in Christ Jesus. We do
not put trust in ourselves or anything we can
do, 4although I might be able to put trust in my-
self. If anyone thinks he has a reason to trust in
himself, he should know that I have greater rea-
son for trusting in myself. 5I was circumcised
eight days after my birth. I am from the people
of Israel and the tribe[d] of Benjamin. I am a
Hebrew,[n] and my parents were Hebrews. I
had a strict view of the law, which is why I be-
came a Pharisee.[d] 6I was so enthusiastic I tried
to hurt the church. No one could find fault
with the way I obeyed the law of Moses.
7Those things were important to me, but now I
think they are worth nothing because of Christ.
8Not only those things, but I think that all
things are worth nothing compared with the
greatness of knowing Christ Jesus my Lord.
Because of him, I have lost all those things, and
now I know they are worthless rubbish. This al-
lows me to have Christ 9and to belong to him.

cutting The word in Greek is like the word "circumcise", but it means "to cut completely off".
Hebrew A name for the Jews that some Jews were very proud of.

Now I am right with God, not because I fol-
lowed the law, but because I believed in Christ.
God uses my faith to make me right with him.
10I want to know Christ and the power that
raised him from the dead. I want to share in his
sufferings and become like him in his death.
11Then I have hope that I myself will be raised
from the dead.

Continuing Towards Our Goal

12I do not mean that I am already as God
wants me to be. I have not yet reached that
goal, but I continue trying to reach it and to
make it mine. Christ wants me to do that,
which is the reason he made me his. 13Brothers
and sisters, I know that I have not yet reached
that goal, but there is one thing I always do.
Forgetting the past and straining towards what
is ahead, 14I keep trying to reach the goal and
get the prize for which God called me through
Christ to the life above.

15All of us who are spiritually mature should
think this way too. And if there are things you do
not agree with, God will make them clear to you.
16But we should continue following the truth we
already have.

17Brothers and sisters, all of you should try
to follow my example and to copy those who
live the way we showed you. 18Many peo-
ple live like enemies of the cross of Christ. I
have often told you about them, and it makes
me cry to tell you about them now. 19In the
end, they will be destroyed. They do whatever
their bodies want, they are proud of their shame-
ful acts, and they think only about earthly
things. 20But our homeland is in heaven, and
we are waiting for our Saviour,[d] the Lord Jesus
Christ, to come from heaven. 21By his power

POPULARITY

The Right Thing

Michelle had two passions in life: singing and people! As a youth worker, she'd spent the last year working really hard to start a youth club that was now flourishing. She loved the fact that she was able to build up great friendships with those who came.

In her spare time she practised her other passion, singing, in a band. When her band started to get gigs all over the country, she loved it.

Over the next few years, she got to experience many different countries and cultures with the band, and they built up a large fan base. They'd get letters from people all over the world saying how cool their songs were and how they couldn't wait to see the band in concert.

With all the touring that was going on Michelle was spending more and more time away from home, her family and the youth club that she led. Deep down she knew that she wasn't giving as much time and attention to those things as she felt she should be. How could she lead a youth club without being there? The dilemma played on her mind for months before she finally made a decision. In the end, she felt that the calling on her life for the youth project was so strong that she needed to give up the band and concentrate more on those relationships that God had blessed her with back home.

Michelle considered doing what God wanted of her to be more important than the enticing fame and fortune that came with being in a successful band. In **Philippians 3:8–11** Paul is describing a similar situation.

- What was it that Paul gave up in order to focus his attention fully on God?
- Why do you think Paul is so passionate about being right with God?

Consider . . .

- what you would be prepared to give up if God asked you to. Is there anything you wouldn't give up?
- writing a list of priorities in your life and chatting to a friend about them.

For more, see . . .

- Genesis 22:6–13 (p.25)
- Philippians 2:3–11 (p.1282)

to rule all things, he will change our simple bodies and make them like his own glorious body.

Sidelight When Paul said our "homeland is in heaven" (Philippians 3:20), he literally said that Christians live in a colony of heaven. The Philippian Christians would have seen this as a great privilege, since Philippi was a colony of the Roman Empire (see Acts 16:12, p.1164). Being a colony meant that Philippi had special privileges, including self-government, exemption from control by regional governments, and exemption from many taxes.

What the Christians are to Do

4 My dear brothers and sisters, I love you and
want to see you. You bring me joy and make
me proud of you, so stand strong in the Lord as
I have told you.
2 I ask Euodia and Syntyche to agree in the
Lord. 3 And I ask you, my faithful friend, to help
these women. They served with me in telling the
Good News,[d] together with Clement and others
who worked with me, whose names are written
in the book of life.[n]
4 Be full of joy in the Lord always. I will say
again, be full of joy.
5 Let everyone see that you are gentle and kind.
The Lord is coming soon. 6 Do not worry about
anything, but pray and ask God for everything

book of life God's book that has the names of all God's chosen people (Revelation 3:5; 21:27).

PERSISTENCE

Sticking With It

Wilma Rudolph dreamed of competing in the Olympics. But she had everything stacked against her.

She was born prematurely in a Tennessee shack, weighing only 2 kilogrammes. Scarlet fever and polio struck, forcing her to wear a steel brace on her leg.

Wilma remembers: "My father was the one who sort of babied me and was sympathetic . . . my mother was the one who made me work, made me believe that one day it would be possible for me to walk without braces." Wilma's mother told her that, with persistence, she could follow her dreams in life.

So at the age of nine, Wilma did away with the braces. Four years later she developed a rhythmic stride and entered her first race. She came in last. But she didn't give up.

"I worked very hard for the next four years," Wilma recalls. "I was self-motivated and motivated by my family. It took sheer determination to be able to run 100 metres and remember all of the mechanics that go along with it. It takes steady nerves and being a fighter to stay out there."

In the 1960 Olympics, Wilma Rudolph set the world record in the 100-metre dash. She also won the 200-metre sprint and ran the anchor leg for the US 400-metre relay team. She was the first American woman to win three gold medals in track and field at a single Olympiad.

Wilma Rudolph learned the lesson of **Philippians 3:12–21**. Read the passage to discover the key to persistence.

- In the light of the passage, why was Wilma persistent?
- What was Paul's spiritual goal, according to this passage? How can this passage help you to persist in reaching such a goal?

Consider . . .

- watching part of a sports event on television. Look for evidences of persistence, then apply what you learn to a challenge you face.
- setting a specific goal to help you to grow in your faith and persisting to meet that goal this week.

For more, see . . .

- Psalm 37:23–24 (p.522)
- 1 Timothy 6:11–16 (p.1313)
- Luke 9:57–62 (p.1055)

you need, always giving thanks. 7And God's
peace, which is so great we cannot understand
it, will keep your hearts and minds in Christ
Jesus.
8Brothers and sisters, think about the things
that are good and worthy of praise. Think about
the things that are true and honourable and right
and pure and beautiful and respected. 9Do what
you learned and received from me, what I told
you, and what you saw me do. And the God who
gives peace will be with you.

Paul Thanks the Christians

10I am very happy in the Lord that you have
shown your care for me again. You continued to
care about me, but there was no way for you to
show it. 11I am not telling you this because I need
anything. I have learned to be satisfied with the
things I have and with everything that happens.
12I know how to live when I am poor, and I know
how to live when I have plenty. I have learned
the secret of being happy at any time in every-
thing that happens, when I have enough to eat
and when I go hungry, when I have more than I
need and when I do not have enough. 13I can do
all things through Christ, because he gives me
strength.
14But it was good that you helped me when I
needed it. 15You Philippians remember when I
first preached the Good News *d* there. When I left

PEACE

Beyond Understanding

The ringing telephone pierced the night. "Hello, Mrs Gibson? This is the police."

Naomi's throat tightened, but she managed to gulp, "Yes, what is it?"

"It's your daughter, Caroline. There's been an accident." Shocked, Naomi sobbed uncontrollably and dropped the phone. Her husband, Neil, grabbed it and learned that Caroline was still alive, but that she had extensive head injuries and was unconscious. A police helicopter was flying her to hospital.

When Neil and Naomi arrived at the hospital, Caroline was in a coma. Her head was bruised and swollen. Her back was broken, and her body lay lifeless. Her heart had stopped once in the helicopter, but the paramedics had restarted it. Surgeons were inserting a catheter into Caroline's skull to relieve the pressure on her brain.

During the operation, Naomi prayed in the hospital chapel. As she read her Bible, an overwhelming peace filled her. She couldn't explain what she felt, especially with her daughter so close to death. All she knew was that God seemed near and that he would take care of Caroline.

For days, Neil and Naomi rarely left Caroline's side. Naomi's prayers surprised even her, because they were filled with thanksgiving rather than questioning or pleading. Her heart was filled with God's peace.

It took a long time for Caroline to recover, and much of what happened in the weeks after the accident is now a blur to her. But every hour is vivid to Neil and Naomi. They were joyful that their daughter was alive.

In **Philippians 4:1–9**, Paul describes the secret of having a joy that is greater than life's difficulties. Read it to understand Naomi's experience.

- Which actions or attitudes from this passage did Naomi have that resulted in peace?
- Which ones can most help you to experience God's peace?

Consider . . .

- listing the nine steps to peace – one step from each verse in this passage. Choose one step which you can take to experience God's peace.
- planning with a friend to pray together during difficult times.

For more, see . . .

- Psalm 25 (p.514)
- John 14:27–29 (p.1124)
- Luke 6:17–23 (p.1048)

Macedonia, you were the only church that gave
me help. 16Several times you sent me things I
needed when I was in Thessalonica. 17Really, it is
not that I want to receive gifts from you, but I
want you to have the good that comes from
giving. 18And now I have everything, and more.

Sidelight The words "joy" and "rejoice" occur in some form sixteen times in Philippians (for example, Philippians 4:4). Even in prison, Paul's thoughts were focused on joy!

I have all I need, because Epaphroditus brought
your gift to me. It is like a sweet-smelling sacrifice
offered to God, who accepts that sacrifice and is
pleased with it. 19My God will use his wonderful
riches in Christ Jesus to give you everything you
need. 20Glory to our God and Father for ever and
ever! Amen.

21Greet each of God's people in Christ. Those
who are with me send greetings to you. 22All of
God's people greet you, particularly those from
the palace of Caesar. [d]

23The grace of the Lord Jesus Christ be with
you all.

Colossians

Why Read This Book:

- Learn the importance of following only Jesus Christ (Colossians 1).
- Discover how to respond to false teachers (Colossians 2).
- Find guidelines for living a Christian life (Colossians 3—4).

When?

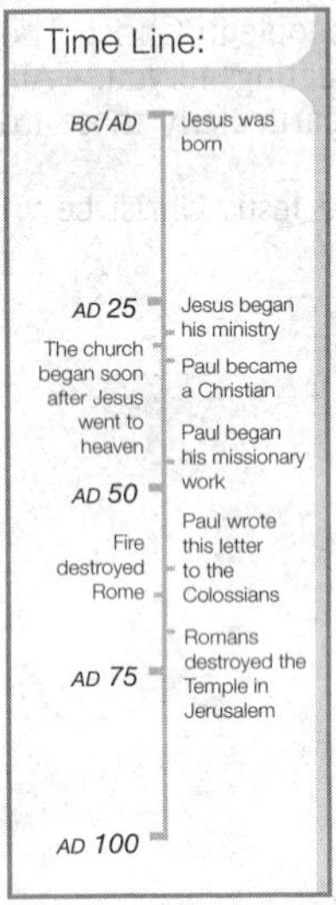

Behind the Scenes:

Astrology. Witchcraft. Ghosts. UFOs. Tarot cards. Ouija boards. The Loch Ness monster. Mysterious things can intrigue and attract us.

We are not the only people who can be fascinated with these kinds of things. Early Christians in Colosse were attracted to the same kinds of mysterious or supernatural things. Someone apparently came into the church and began teaching people to worship angels and cosmic powers. Jesus is fine, they argued, but these other mysterious powers controlled human destiny and gave secret knowledge (Colossians 2:16–23).

This letter to the Colossians challenges these false teachers. But instead of picking apart their arguments, the letter goes on the offensive, telling the Colossians the truth about Jesus Christ. "He ranks higher than everything that has been made," the letter states. "Christ is all that is important" (Colossians 1:15; 3:11).

The letter's advice to the Colossians is good advice for today, too. When we feel tempted to look for power in other, mysterious things, this book reminds us of the source of true power. And when someone suggests that we need to do something else for salvation, Colossians assures us that Jesus is all we need.

Where?

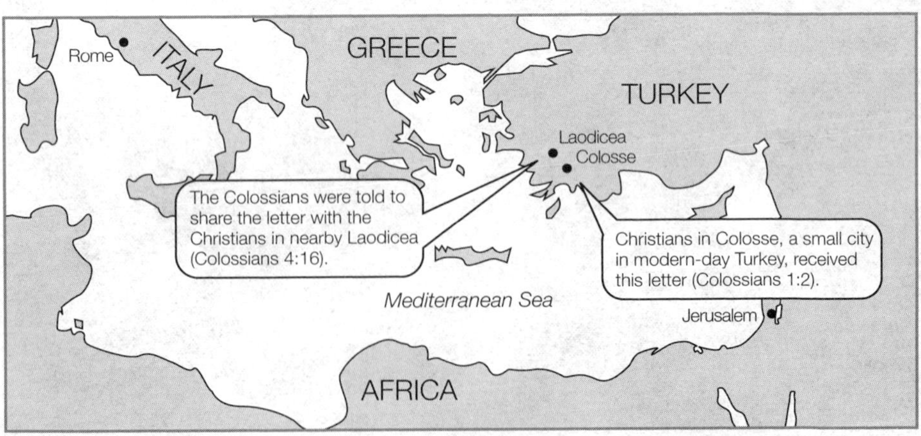

1 From Paul, an apostle[d] of Christ Jesus. I am
an apostle because that is what God wanted.
Also from Timothy, our brother.
2To the holy and faithful brothers and sisters[n]
in Christ that live in Colosse:
Grace and peace to you from God our Father.
3In our prayers for you we always thank God,
the Father of our Lord Jesus Christ, 4because we
have heard about the faith you have in Christ
Jesus and the love you have for all of God's peo-
ple. 5You have this faith and love because of your
hope, and what you hope for is kept safe for you
in heaven. You learned about this hope when
you heard the message about the truth, the
Good News[d] 6that was told to you. Everywhere
in the world that Good News is bringing bless-
ings and is growing. This has happened with you
too, since you heard the Good News and under-
stood the truth about the grace of God. 7You
learned about God's grace from Epaphras, whom
we love. He works together with us and is a
faithful servant of Christ for us. 8He also told us
about the love you have from the Holy Spirit.[d]
9Because of this, since the day we heard about
you, we have continued praying for you, asking
God that you will know fully what he wants. We
pray that you will also have great wisdom and
understanding in spiritual things 10so that you
will live the kind of life that honours and pleases
the Lord in every way. You will produce fruit in

brothers and sisters Although the Greek text says "brothers" here and throughout this book, Paul's words were meant for the entire church, both men and women.

GOD'S WILL

A Life Pleasing God

From childhood, Robert Beck knew that he wanted to be a missionary to Africa. Every day he kept his goal foremost in his mind. He read magazine articles and books and watched TV news reports and documentaries on Africa. At school he wrote stories and reports about the African people.

After leaving school, Robert studied for a theology degree, then completed a course at theological college.

After almost 20 years of education, Robert was finally ready to start on his goal. He started a church in Africa.

Robert preached regularly at the mission church. He taught children about God's love. He befriended the people when they were sick and lonely, and cheerfully devoted all his time to his vision of God's will.

But after only one year in Africa, Robert contracted malaria and died of complications.

Some of Robert's friends and relatives wondered if he had wasted his life. "How can it be fair that this should happen to such a promising young man?" they asked bitterly. "Can this really be God's will?"

Back at Robert's college, the news of his death shocked and saddened the whole community. The tutors asked whether any graduating student would consider serving the church that Robert had started.

Eight signed up to serve.

Although Robert died young, he lived "the kind of life that honours and pleases the Lord in every way" and produced "fruit in every good work" (Colossians 1:10). He followed God's will, just as Paul urged his readers to do in **Colossians 1:1–14**.

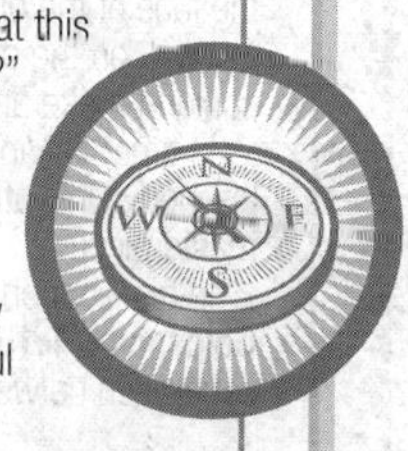

- In the light of this passage, how was God's will accomplished with Robert?
- How can this passage help you to discover God's will for your life?

Consider . . .

- praying that God will let you "know fully what he wants" for your future (Colossians 1:9).
- keeping a journal about God's will for your life. Read Bible verses about God's will (see below) and write your thoughts as you apply those verses to decisions that you are facing.

For more, see . . .

- Psalm 40:8–10 (p.524)
- Mark 3:31–35 (p.1003)
- Matthew 6:9–13 (p.948)

every good work and grow in the knowledge of
God. 11God will strengthen you with his own
great power so that you will not give up when
troubles come, but you will be patient. 12And you

> **Sidelight** The city of Colosse (Colossians 1:2) was once a major mill town, known for its wool-working and cloth-dying industries. In fact, a widely used dark red wool cloth was known as colossinum. However, the city had declined by the time this letter was written, and may have been devastated by a major earthquake in AD 60 or 61.

will joyfully give thanks to the Father who has
made you able to have a share in all that he has
prepared for his people in the kingdom of light.
13God has freed us from the power of darkness
and brought us into the kingdom of his dear Son.
14The Son paid for our sins, and in him we have
forgiveness.

The Importance of Christ

15No one can see God, but Jesus Christ is exactly
like him. He ranks higher than everything that has
been made. 16Through his power all things were
made—things in heaven and on earth, things seen
and unseen, all powers, authorities, lords and
rulers. All things were made through Christ and for
Christ. 17He was there before anything was made,
and all things continue because of him. 18He is the
head of the body, which is the church. Everything
comes from him. He is the first one who was raised
from the dead. So in all things Jesus has first place.
19God was pleased for all of himself to live in
Christ. 20And through Christ, God has brought all
things back to himself again—things on earth and
things in heaven. God made peace through the
blood of Christ's death on the cross.
21At one time you were separated from God.
You were his enemies in your minds, and the evil

FORGIVENESS

The Face of Hatred

Just before Leonardo da Vinci began painting "The Last Supper", he argued bitterly with a fellow painter. Da Vinci was so enraged that he decided to paint the face of his enemy as the face of Judas Iscariot. In this way the hated painter's face would be preserved for ages in the face of the disciple who betrayed Jesus.

Da Vinci painted the face of Judas quickly. At first he took delight as everyone who came past recognised the face of the other painter in Judas.

Work on the other disciples' portraits continued. Da Vinci tried several times to start Jesus' face, but couldn't make any progress. Something seemed to baffle him, frustrating his best efforts.

In time, da Vinci saw his hatred of the other painter as the problem holding him back from finishing his work. Only after repainting the face of Judas was he able to paint Jesus' face and complete his masterpiece.

In his work on "The Last Supper", da Vinci learned something important about forgiveness. **Colossians 1:15–29** has a similar lesson as it explains how Christ came to forgive – to end the separation between God and people.

- How was Leonardo da Vinci's separation from his fellow painter like humanity's separation from God as described in the passage?
- How do you feel when you are forgiven? How do you feel when you forgive someone else?

Consider . . .

- confessing your sin to God, and if you can, to an adult you trust. It may help you to feel God's forgiveness.
- closing your eyes and thinking about the face of someone that you need to forgive. Then imagine the face of Jesus next to that person's, and ask God to help you to forgive them.

For more, see . . .

- Psalm 79:8–9 (p.548)
- Romans 5:1–11 (p.1190)
- Luke 6:37–38 (p.1048)

things you did were against God. 22But now God
has made you his friends again. He did this through
Christ's death in the body so that he might bring
you into God's presence as people who are holy,
with no wrong, and with nothing of which God
can judge you guilty. 23This will happen if you con-
tinue strong and sure in your faith. You must not
be moved away from the hope brought to you by
the Good News *d* that you heard. That same Good
News has been told to everyone in the world, and
I, Paul, help in preaching that Good News.

Paul's Work for the Church

24I am happy in my sufferings for you. There
are things that Christ must still suffer through his
body, the church. I am accepting, in my body,
my part of these things that must be suffered.
25I became a servant of the church because God
gave me a special work to do that helps you, and
that work is to tell fully the message of God.
26This message is the secret that was hidden from
everyone since the beginning of time, but now it
is made known to God's holy people. 27God de-
cided to let his people know this rich and glorious
secret which he has for all people. This secret is
Christ himself, who is in you. He is our only hope
for glory. 28So we continue to preach Christ to
each person, using all wisdom to warn and to
teach everyone, in order to bring each one into
God's presence as a mature person in Christ. 29To
do this, I work and struggle, using Christ's great
strength that works so powerfully in me.

2 I want you to know how hard I work for
you, those in Laodicea, and others who have

CULTS

Fatal Attraction

Anne was an average schoolgirl. Her grades were average: Bs and Cs in most subjects. Her interest in school was average: she thought school was OK, but she would much rather play tennis or watch television. Her social life was average: an occasional date or evening out with some friends.

Anne couldn't wait to leave school and get on with life. She didn't know what she wanted, but she knew that it had to be more interesting than what she was doing.

One day after school, Anne went to the shops. There, some members of a religious group approached her. Anne had never heard of the group. But because they offered her a chance to belong, to take part in something greater than herself, she joined them.

After two years, Anne decided that the cult had manipulated her for its own ends. The group had offered "answers" to tough questions, but then told her to stop asking questions – to "just believe". It used her to raise money by selling flowers, sweets, and other things, but when she asked where all the money was going, she was told it wasn't her concern.

Finally, she dropped out. She felt sick about the two years she had wasted. "Why was I attracted to that group?" she later asked herself. "I was a typical youngster with a comfortable lifestyle. Why did I change my life so drastically? I wasn't that unhappy."

The Colossian Christians experienced a similar attraction to false beliefs. **Colossians 2:1–15** warns the early Christians not to be fooled by empty teachings.

- How might Anne's response to the cult have been different if she had listened to the warnings in this passage?
- How can you recognise false teachers today, according to the passage?

Consider . . .

- making a list of Paul's warnings about false teachers. Refer to it when someone offers you quick, appealing answers to tough questions.
- asking your minister or youth leader to get literature from cult groups and asking for his help in evaluating the groups' claims in the light of scripture.

For more, see . . .

- Deuteronomy 13:1–5 (p.178)
- 2 Peter 2:17–22 (p.1367)
- Matthew 24:23–25 (p.984)

never seen me. 2I want them to be strengthened
and joined together with love so that they may
be rich in their understanding. This leads to their
knowing fully God's secret, that is, Christ him-
self. 3In him all the treasures of wisdom and
knowledge are safely kept.
4I say this so that no one can fool you by argu-
ments that seem good, but are false. 5Though I
am absent from you in my body, my heart is with
you, and I am happy to see your good lives and
your strong faith in Christ.

Sidelight Although Paul never visited the Colossian church, it is believed that the fellowship was started by people who heard the gospel in Ephesus (see Acts 19:10, p.1170). Because the population of Colosse was largely a "mixed bag" of different races and creeds, it was easy for crazy (and dangerous) ideas to spring up.

Continue to Live in Christ

6As you received Christ Jesus the Lord, so con-
tinue to live in him. 7Keep your roots deep in
him and have your lives built on him. Be strong
in the faith, just as you were taught, and always
be thankful.
8Be sure that no one leads you away with false
and empty teaching that is only human, which
comes from the ruling spirits of this world, and
not from Christ. 9All of God lives in Christ fully
(even when Christ was on earth), 10and you
have a full and true life in Christ, who is ruler
over all rulers and powers.
11Also in Christ you had a different kind of cir-
cumcision,[d] a circumcision not done by hands.
It was through Christ's circumcision, that is, his
death, that you were made free from the power
of your sinful self. 12When you were baptised,[d]
you were buried with Christ, and you were
raised up with him through your faith in God's
power that was shown when he raised Christ
from the dead. 13When you were spiritually dead
because of your sins and because you were not
free from the power of your sinful self, God
made you alive with Christ, and he forgave all
our sins. 14He cancelled the debt, which listed
all the rules we failed to follow. He took away
that record with its rules and nailed it to the
cross. 15God stripped the spiritual rulers and
powers of their authority. With the cross, he
won the victory and showed the world that they
were powerless.

Don't Follow People's Rules

16So do not let anyone make rules for you
about eating and drinking or about a religious
feast, a New Moon[d] Festival or a Sabbath[d] day.
17These things were like a shadow of what was
to come. But what is true and real has come and
is found in Christ. 18Do not let anyone disqualify
you by making you humiliate yourself and wor-
ship angels. Such people enter into visions,
which fill them with foolish pride because of
their human way of thinking. 19They do not hold
tightly to Christ, the head. It is from him that all
the parts of the body are cared for and held to-
gether. So it grows in the way God wants it to
grow.
20Since you died with Christ and were made
free from the ruling spirits of the world, why do
you act as if you still belong to this world by fol-
lowing rules like these: 21"Don't eat this",
"Don't taste that", "Don't even touch that
thing"? 22These rules refer to earthly things that
are gone as soon as they are used. They are only
man-made commands and teachings. 23They
seem to be wise, but they are only part of a man-
made religion. They make people pretend not to
be proud and make them punish their bodies,
but they do not really control the evil desires of
the sinful self.

Your New Life in Christ

3 Since you were raised from the dead with
Christ, aim at what is in heaven, where
Christ is sitting at the right hand of God. 2Think
only about the things in heaven, not the things
on earth. 3Your old sinful self has died, and your
new life is kept with Christ in God. 4Christ is our
life, and when he comes again, you will share in
his glory.
5So put all evil things out of your life: sexual
sinning, doing evil, letting evil thoughts control
you, wanting things that are evil and greed. This
is really serving a false god. 6These things make
God angry.[n] 7In your past, evil life you also did
these things.
8But now also put these things out of your
life: anger, bad temper, doing or saying things
to hurt others and using evil words when you
talk. 9Do not lie to each other. You have left your
old sinful life and the things you did before.
10You have begun to live the new life, in which
you are being made new and are becoming like
the One who made you. This new life brings you
the true knowledge of God. 11In the new life
there is no difference between Greeks and Jews,
those who are circumcised[d] and those who are
not circumcised, or people who are foreigners,

These . . . angry Some Greek copies add: "against the people who do not obey God".

or Scythians.[n] There is no difference between
slaves and free people. But Christ is in all believ-
ers, and Christ is all that is important.
12God has chosen you and made you his holy
people. He loves you. So always do these things:
show mercy to others, be kind, humble, gentle
and patient. 13Get along with each other, and
forgive each other. If someone does wrong to
you, forgive that person because the Lord forgave
you. 14Do all these things; but most important,
love each other. Love is what holds you all to-
gether in perfect unity. 15Let the peace that Christ
gives control your thinking, because you were all
called together in one body[n] to have peace. Al-
ways be thankful. 16Let the teaching of Christ
live in you richly. Use all wisdom to teach and
instruct each other by singing psalms, hymns
and spiritual songs with thankfulness in your
hearts to God. 17Everything you do or say should
be done to obey Jesus your Lord. And in all you
do, give thanks to God the Father through Jesus.

Sidelight If you feel as though you have read some of Colossians somewhere else, you might be right. The book is filled with passages that closely parallel Ephesians (for example, compare Colossians 3:16–17 with Ephesians 5:19–20, p.1275). In fact, about half of Ephesians' 155 verses also have similarities to verses in Colossians.

Scythians The Scythians were known as very wild and cruel people.
body The spiritual body of Christ, meaning the church or his people.

FOLLOWING GOD

Wake Up!

At school, George shyly kept to himself. His few friends thought he was nice enough, but nobody, including himself, thought he had much talent or potential. In fact, they rarely seemed to think anything of him. That was all right with George, since he rarely thought about anything anyway. He was content just to exist without any goals, dreams, or ideas.

About the only thing George enjoyed was driving around town in his car. It seemed a way to pass empty hours. But one day another car slammed into George's, sending his car off the road towards a tree. George was thrown from the car just before it smashed into the tree.

When George regained consciousness, he kept hearing the police say how lucky he was. George suffered minor injuries, but the car was a write-off.

George's near tragedy awakened him to the reality of his empty life. Deciding that he wanted to live for more than driving his car, he poured himself into many new interests, including film-making. A few years after his accident, George Lucas entertained millions with *American Graffiti*, the *Star Wars* trilogy, and the *Indiana Jones* films.

George Lucas was lucky: he lost his car, but gained a new purpose in life. **Colossians 3:1–10** tells Christians to "wake up" to a whole, new life that is far more important than any new career.

- How does George Lucas's awakening to life illustrate Paul's challenge to live a different way in Christ? How is it different?
- In the light of this passage, how is your "old life" different from your "new life in Christ"?

Consider . . .

- writing on one side of a sheet of paper things that are different because of your "new life in Christ". On the other side, write out temptations that you can avoid because of this new life. Thank God for giving you strength.
- trying a new skill or interest that might help you to follow God's will. Focus your attention on the gifts that you believe God has given to you.

For more, see . . .

- Habakkuk 3:2 (p.907)
- Revelation 21:1–5 (p.1403)
- Luke 9:24 (p.1055)

Your New Life with Other People

[18]Wives, yield to the authority of your hus-
bands, because this is the right thing to do in the
Lord.
[19]Husbands, love your wives and be gentle
with them.
[20]Children, obey your parents in all things, be-
cause this pleases the Lord.
[21]Fathers, do not nag your children. If you are
too hard to please, they may want to stop trying.
[22]Slaves, obey your masters in all things. Do
not obey just when they are watching you, to
gain their favour, but serve them honestly, be-
cause you respect the Lord. [23]In all the work you
are doing, work the best you can. Work as if you
were doing it for the Lord, not for people.
[24]Remember that you will receive your reward
from the Lord, which he promised to his people.
You are serving the Lord Christ. [25]But remember
that anyone who does wrong will be punished for
that wrong, and the Lord treats everyone the same.

4 Masters, give what is good and fair to your
slaves. Remember that you have a Master in
heaven.

What the Christians are to Do

[2]Continue praying, keeping alert and always
thanking God. [3]Also pray for us that God will give
us an opportunity to tell people his message. Pray
that we can preach the secret that God has made
known about Christ. This is why I am in prison.
[4]Pray that I can speak in a way that will make it
clear, as I should.
[5]Be wise in the way you act with people who
are not believers, making the most of every op-
portunity. [6]When you talk, you should always be
kind and pleasant so you will be able to answer
everyone in the way you should.

News About the People with Paul

[7]Tychicus is my dear brother in Christ and a
faithful minister and servant with me in the
Lord. He will tell you all the things that are hap-
pening to me. [8]This is why I am sending him: so
you may know how we are and he may encour-
age you. [9]I send him with Onesimus, a faithful
and dear brother in Christ, and one of your
group. They will tell you all that has happened
here.
[10]Aristarchus, a prisoner with me, and Mark,
the cousin of Barnabas, greet you. (I have al-
ready told you what to do about Mark. If he
comes, welcome him.) [11]Jesus, who is called
Justus, also greets you. These are the only Jewish
believers who work with me for the kingdom of
God, and they have been a comfort to me.
[12]Epaphras, a servant of Jesus Christ, from
your group, also greets you. He always prays for
you that you will grow to be spiritually mature
and have everything God wants for you. [13]I
know he has worked hard for you and the peo-
ple in Laodicea and in Hierapolis. [14]Demas and
our dear friend Luke, the doctor, greet you.
[15]Greet the brothers in Laodicea. And greet
Nympha and the church that meets in her house.
[16]After this letter is read to you, be sure it is also
read to the church in Laodicea. And you read the
letter that I wrote to Laodicea. [17]Tell Archippus,
"Be sure to finish the work the Lord gave you."
[18]I, Paul, greet you and write this with my
own hand. Remember me in prison. Grace be
with you.

1 Thessalonians

Why Read This Book:

- **Be encouraged to stand up for your faith even when those around you make fun of you (1 Thessalonians 2—3).**
- **See the importance of growing strong in faith (1 Thessalonians 4—5).**

When?

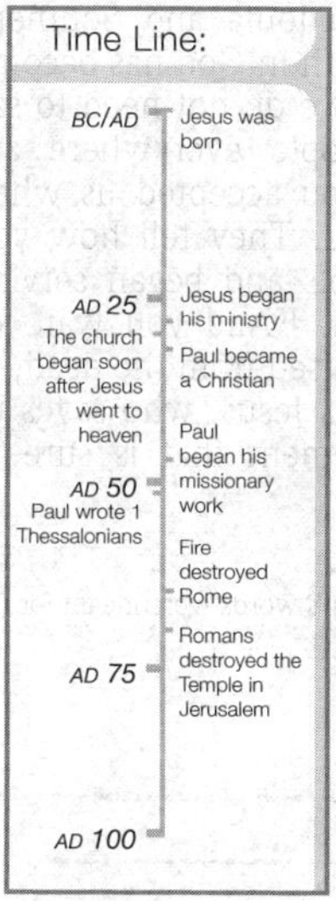

Behind the Scenes:

Remember what it was like when you first decided to follow Jesus? You may have thought that all your troubles would be over. You probably felt really good on the inside, and if anyone had warned you that life was still going to be difficult, you might have laughed.

But then it happens. It's Monday morning and you feel bad. Where did that happy feeling get to? Why don't I feel wonderful like I did last week? Will I be able to live out my new faith now that I'm back in the "real world"?

The Thessalonians might have felt the same way. They had just been visited by the apostle Paul, and after listening to him preach, they had become Christians. But now Paul had been forced to leave town, and they were left alone – new Christians in an unfriendly city with nobody to care for them.

Paul wrote this letter to the people of Thessalonica and encouraged them to "hang on in there" and develop their new faith despite their situation. He explained why he had to leave town so suddenly, and then told them to look forward to the day when Christ would return.

Being a Christian isn't easy – no one ever said it would be. This letter was made for new Christians. It can encourage you just as it did the Thessalonians. Read it as if Paul were speaking directly to you, then take up his challenge and decide to develop your faith whatever the world throws at you! Then fix your eyes on Jesus and stay with it because he is coming back again.

Where?

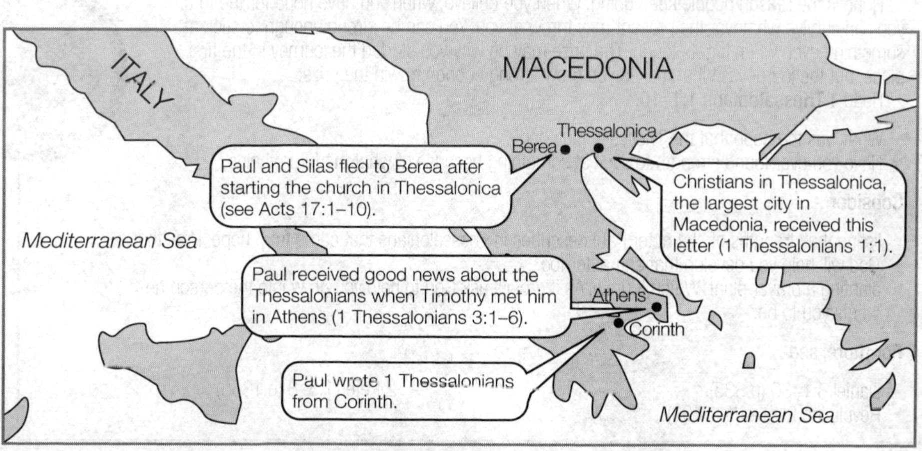

1 From Paul, Silas and Timothy.
To the church in Thessalonica, the church
in God the Father and the Lord Jesus Christ:
Grace and peace to you.

The Faith of the Thessalonians

2We always thank God for all of you and men-
tion you when we pray. 3We continually recall
before God our Father the things you have done
because of your faith and the work you have
done because of your love. And we thank him
that you continue to be strong because of your
hope in our Lord Jesus Christ.
4Brothers and sisters,[n] God loves you, and
we know he has chosen you, 5because the
Good News[d] we brought to you came not
only with words, but with power, with the
Holy Spirit[d] and with sure knowledge that it is
true. Also you know how we lived when we
were with you in order to help you. 6And
you became like us and like the Lord. You
suffered much, but still you accepted the
teaching with the joy that comes from the Holy
Spirit. 7So you became an example to all
the believers in Macedonia and Southern
Greece. 8And the Lord's teaching spread from
you not only into Macedonia and Southern
Greece, but now your faith in God has become
known everywhere. So we do not need to say
anything about it. 9People everywhere are
telling about the way you accepted us when
we were there with you. They tell how you
stopped worshipping idols and began serving
the living and true God. 10And you wait for
God's Son, whom God raised from the dead, to
come from heaven. He is Jesus, who saves us
from God's angry judgement that is sure to
come.

Brothers and sisters Although the Greek text says "brothers" here and throughout this book, Paul's words were meant for the entire church, both men and women.

SPIRITUAL GROWTH

Those Who Wait

Why do people go on reality TV shows? Fame? Fortune? The dream job? The perfect partner? Just to get on the telly?

Whatever the prize they are competing for, they will go through anything to achieve it.

The prize may be the reason why people go on the show, but it's the drama itself that keeps the viewers watching. These shows make good television because they reveal what a person is really like. The prize is the incentive; the journey is the drama. How much do they want the prize on offer? Will they fight for it? How will they handle setbacks, failures, unforeseen challenges? Will they last the distance? Do they truly believe that the prize is theirs for the taking? "Can they win?" becomes "Will they win?"

Hope is the reason people keep going. When you believe, when you have hope for the future you can survive whatever the present may throw at you. You can be strong enough to stick at something even when it gets tough. The prize may be why you started the journey in the first place, but the journey is what makes you grow strong enough to win the prize.

Read **1 Thessalonians 1:1–10**.

- What was the hope that the Thessalonians had?
- Have you ever found strength to stick at something because of what the future holds?

Consider . . .

- listing the strengths of character Paul describes in Thessalonians that come from hope. Pray that God will help you develop that character too.
- planting a prayer plant. Watch it grow. As it grows, ask God to help you grow into the person he wants you to be.

For more, see . . .

- Daniel 3:1–30 (p.835)
- Revelation 21:1–4 (p.1403)
- 2 Peter 1:3–8 (p.1365)

Paul's Work in Thessalonica

2 Brothers and sisters, you know our visit to
you was not a failure. [2]Before we came
to you, we suffered in Philippi. People there
insulted us, as you know, and many people were
against us. But our God helped us to be brave
and to tell you his Good News.[d] [3]Our appeal
does not come from lies or wrong reasons, nor
were we trying to trick you. [4]But we speak
the Good News because God tested us and
trusted us to do it. When we speak, we are not
trying to please people, but God, who tests our
hearts. [5]You know that we never tried to influ-
ence you by saying nice things about you. We
were not trying to get your money; we had no
selfishness to hide from you. God knows that
this is true. [6]We were not looking for human
praise, from you or anyone else, [7]even though

Sidelight If all the New Testament books were to appear in the Bible in the order in which they were actually written, 1 Thessalonians might come first (with the possible exception of Galatians, p.1256 or James, p.1347). It is believed to have been written only twenty years after Jesus was crucified and rose from the dead.

Sidelight Most Christian leaders are not in it for the money. Paul certainly wasn't (1 Thessalonians 2:5–9). To support himself, Paul worked as a tent-maker (see Acts 18:3, p.1168) so that he wouldn't have to take any money away from the churches he started.

LEADERSHIP

Single Minded

Smith Wigglesworth was an amazing man, often referred to as "The Apostle of Faith". He was born in Yorkshire in 1859 and, initially, had a career as a plumber. He did not have great wealth or education and for many years was unable to read. When he was forty-eight he began preaching, and over the next forty years, he achieved awesome things for God around the world. He preached hundreds of times and saw many people saved and many people healed.

His methods were, at times, unconventional and many established Christians, churches and leaders rejected him as being too controversial and, to be honest, slightly odd. But other people's opinions did not seem to bother him – he was completely single-minded. He was only interested in doing what God wanted him to do and because of this, his identity was not based on what other people thought of him. Once, when receiving criticism for what he was doing he simply said, "You people that are judging me, please leave your judgement outside, for I obey God."

What amazing leadership!

In **1 Thessalonians 2:1–13** Paul talks about some of his experiences of leadership. Leadership is not an easy task. It's full of hard work and self-sacrifice and may mean that, at times, you are unpopular. But what is more important – doing what God wants or what other people want?

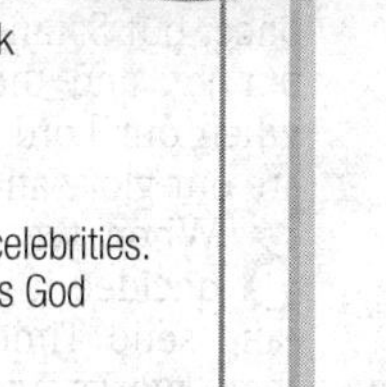

- What are the leadership qualities that Paul describes in these verses?
- What matters most to you: what God thinks of you and wants you to do or what other people think of you and want you to do?

Consider . . .

- making a list of all the people who influence the decisions you make: teachers, friends, parents, celebrities. Put them in order of those who have most influence through to those who have least. Where does God come in the list?
- how you could display in your life some of the character traits that Paul lists in these verses.

For more, see . . .

- John 13:1–17 (p.1119)
- Philippians 2:1–13 (p.1282)
- 2 Corinthians 6:3–11 (p.1246)

as apostles[d] of Christ we could have used our
authority over you.
But we were very gentle with you, like a
mother caring for her little children. 8Because
we loved you, we were happy to share not
only God's Good News with you, but even our
own lives. You had become so dear to us!
9Brothers and sisters, I know you remember
our hard work and difficulties. We worked
night and day so we would not burden any of
you while we preached God's Good News to
you.
10When we were with you, we lived in a
holy and honest way, without fault. You know
this is true, and so does God. 11You know
that we treated each of you as a father treats
his own children. 12We encouraged you, we
told you and we insisted that you live good
lives for God, who calls you to his glorious
kingdom.
13Also, we always thank God because when
you heard his message from us, you
accepted it as the word of God, not the words of
humans. And it really is God's message which
works in you who believe. 14Brothers and sis-
ters, your experiences have been like those of
God's churches in Christ that are in Judea.[n] You
suffered from the people of your own country,
as they suffered from the Jews, 15who kill-
ed both the Lord Jesus and the prophets[d] and
forced us to leave that country. They do not
please God and are against all people. 16They try
to stop us from teaching those who are not Jews
so they may be saved. By doing this, they are in-
creasing their sins to the limit. The anger of God
has come to them at last.

Paul Wants to Visit Them Again

17Brothers and sisters, though we were sepa-
rated from you for a short time, our thoughts
were still with you. We wanted very much to see
you and tried hard to do so. 18We wanted to
come to you. I, Paul, tried to come more than
once, but Satan stopped us. 19You are our hope,
our joy and the crown we will take pride in
when our Lord Jesus Christ comes. 20Truly you
are our glory and our joy.
3 When we could not wait any longer, we
decided it was best to stay in Athens alone
2and send Timothy to you. Timothy, our bro-
ther, works with us for God and helps us
tell people the Good News[d] about Christ.
We sent him to strengthen and encourage you
in your faith 3so none of you would be upset
by these troubles. You yourselves know that
we must face these troubles. 4Even when we
were with you, we told you we all would have
to suffer, and you know it has happened. 5Be-
cause of this, when I could wait no longer, I
sent Timothy to you so I could learn about your
faith. I was afraid the devil had tempted you,
and then our hard work would have been
wasted.
6But Timothy now has come back to us from
you and has brought us good news about your
faith and love. He told us that you always re-
member us in a good way and that you want to
see us just as much as we want to see you. 7So,
brothers and sisters, while we have much trou-
ble and suffering, we are encouraged about
you because of your faith. 8Our life is really full
if you stand strong in the Lord. 9We have so
much joy before our God because of you. We
cannot thank him enough for all the joy we feel.
10Night and day we continue praying with all
our heart that we can see you again and give
you all the things you need to make your faith
strong.
11Now may our God and Father himself and
our Lord Jesus prepare the way for us to come to
you. 12May the Lord make your love grow more
and multiply for each other and for all people so
that you will love others as we love you. 13May
your hearts be made strong so that you will be
holy and without fault before our God and
Father when our Lord Jesus comes with all his
holy ones.

A Life that Pleases God

4 Brothers and sisters, we taught you how to
live in a way that will please God, and
you are living that way. Now we ask and
encourage you in the Lord Jesus to live that
way even more. 2You know what we told you
to do by the authority of the Lord Jesus. 3God
wants you to be holy and to stay away from
sexual sins. 4He wants each of you to learn to
control your own body[n] in a way that is holy
and honourable. 5Don't use your body for
sexual sin like the people who do not know
God. 6Also, do not wrong or cheat another
Christian in this way. The Lord will punish peo-
ple who do those things as we have already told
you and warned you. 7God called us to be holy
and does not want us to live in sin. 8So the
person who refuses to obey this teaching is

Judea The Jewish land where Jesus lived and taught and where the church first began.
learn . . . body This might also mean "learn to live with your own wife."

disobeying God, not simply a human teaching.
And God is the One who gives us his Holy
Spirit.[d]
9We do not need to write to you about having
love for your Christian family, because God has
already taught you to love each other. 10And truly
you do love the Christians in all of Macedonia.
Brothers and sisters, now we encourage you to
love them even more.
11Do all you can to live a peaceful life. Take
care of your own business, and do your own
work as we have already told you. 12If you do,
then people who are not believers will respect
you, and you will not have to depend on others
for what you need.

Sidelight The church in Thessalonica would have been in an excellent position to love all the "Christians in all of Macedonia" (1 Thessalonians 4:10). The city was the capital of its province, so its residents had contact with people from all over the province.

The Lord's Coming

13Brothers and sisters, we want you to
know about those Christians who have died
so you will not be sad, as others who have
no hope. 14We believe that Jesus died and that

HAPPINESS

Piece of Cake

Amy sat in a busy teashop with her mum in Belfast munching on a delicious cake full of cream and chocolate. She watched the many people go by the shop window, while she was nice and warm, away from the cold outside. She loved this teashop, it was her favourite, and spending time with her mum was always special.

After a while, Amy's attention was drawn to a little girl outside the shop, her nose pressed up to the glass of the window, looking in at the lovely cakes. Amy noticed that the little girl did not have any shoes on. On such a cold winter's day, she wore a ragged dress and looked very thin and cold. The little girl licked her lips – she was dreaming of having one of the cakes that Amy was busy munching on. Amy's happiness turned to a feeling of deep sadness.

Sitting by the fire, Amy wrote in large letters on a scrap of paper, "When I grow up and money I have,
I know what I will do, I'll build a great big lovely palace, for little girls like you."

Years later, what Amy had written in that short poem came true. Amy Carmichael went on to help hundreds of children in India. She built an orphanage that housed hundreds of children who had no homes or future. The orphanages were not palaces, as she wrote in her childhood poem, but for the children she rescued they were more than palaces – they were homes. Many of the children she rescued were hungry, ill and had nothing, yet in Amy's care experienced a happiness they had only dreamt of.

Read **1 Thessalonians 3:9–13**.

- How was Amy affected by seeing someone who did not have a happy life like she had? Would you have reacted like this?
- Paul states that his true happiness is found in helping others. How is that true of Amy in this story? Do you think this is true for you?

Consider . . .

- asking God to fill you with that deep joy, happiness and security that can only be found in him.
- writing a "Happy" list of ways you can make others happy this week. Make someone else smile!

For more, see . . .

- Psalm 126:1–6 (p.576)
- Proverbs 14:21 (p.602)
- Proverbs 3:1–18 (p.592)

he rose again. So, because of him, God will raise
with Jesus those who have died. [15]What we tell
you now is the Lord's own message. We who are
living when the Lord comes again will not go be-
fore those who have already died. [16]The Lord
himself will come down from heaven with a
loud command, with the voice of the archangel[n]
and with the trumpet call of God. And those
who have died believing in Christ will rise first.
[17]After that, we who are still alive will be gath-
ered up with them in the clouds to meet the
Lord in the air. And we will be with the Lord
for ever. [18]So encourage each other with these
words.

Be Ready for the Lord's Coming

5 Now, brothers and sisters, we do not need
to write to you about times and dates. [2]You
know very well that the day the Lord comes
again will be a surprise, like a thief that comes
in the night. [3]While people are saying, "We
have peace and we are safe," they will be de-
stroyed quickly. It is like pains that come
quickly to a woman having a baby. Those peo-
ple will not escape. [4]But you, brothers and sis-
ters, are not living in darkness, and so that day
will not surprise you like a thief. [5]You are all
people who belong to the light and to the day.
We do not belong to the night or to darkness.
[6]So we should not be like other people who are
sleeping, but we should be awake and have
self-control. [7]Those who sleep, sleep at night.
Those who get drunk, get drunk at night. [8]But
we belong to the day, so we should control our-
selves. We should wear faith and love to pro-
tect us, and the hope of salvation should be our
helmet. [9]God did not choose us to suffer his
anger but to have salvation through our Lord

archangel The leader among God's angels or messengers.

DEATH

We Have Hope

Jonathan Harwell was thirteen when his parents had a baby girl. The birth was a major cause for celebration, because Jonathan's parents had wanted another child since he was four years old. Years of trying, years of crying, years of suffering through three miscarriages, had finally produced Jonathan's baby sister, whom they named Sarah.

Jonathan and his parents were overjoyed with the new addition to their family. They redecorated one bedroom as a nursery and designed a playroom. They planned a special outing each weekend. They thoroughly enjoyed their new family member.

Their joy lasted six short months. One morning they woke up to discover that Sarah had died in her sleep. The doctors labelled the cause of death as sudden infant death syndrome – a cot death. They told the family not to blame themselves – it was virtually impossible to prevent a cot death at that time.

Although Jonathan and his parents felt a bit comforted by the doctors, they were still devastated by Sarah's death.

As Jonathan tried to work through his grief, he read **1 Thessalonians 4:13–14**. Jonathan shared the passage with his parents, and they were all comforted by its words of hope.

- How were Jonathan and his family comforted by this passage?
- How does it feel to know that some day you will see Christian loved ones who have died?

Consider . . .

- writing a memorial letter to someone you loved who has died. Keep the letter as a reminder.
- thinking of someone who has recently lost a loved one. Phone, write to, or visit that person, or take them out for a meal. Offer a little comfort.

For more, see . . .

- Isaiah 25:7–8 (p.664)
- 2 Timothy 1:9–10 (p.1316)
- Romans 8:37–39 (p.1197)

Jesus Christ. 10Jesus died for us so that we can
live together with him, whether we are alive or
dead when he comes. 11So encourage each
other and give each other strength, just as you
are doing now.

Final Instructions and Greetings

12Now, brothers and sisters, we ask you to ap-
preciate those who work hard among you, who
lead you in the Lord and teach you. 13Respect
them with a very special love because of the work
they do.
Live in peace with each other. 14We ask you,
brothers and sisters, to warn those who do not
work. Encourage the people who are afraid. Help
those who are weak. Be patient with everyone.
15Be sure that no one pays back wrong for wrong,
but always try to do what is good for each other
and for all people.
16Always be joyful. 17Pray continually, 18and
give thanks whatever happens. That is what God
wants for you in Christ Jesus.
19Do not hold back the work of the Holy
Spirit.[d] 20Do not treat prophecy[d] as if it were
unimportant. 21But test everything. Keep what is
good, 22and stay away from everything that is evil.
23Now may God himself, the God of peace,
make you pure, belonging only to him. May your

ETERNAL LIFE

Be Prepared!

Pete is an evangelist. He's stayed with people in just about every country in the world. Sometimes he's dined with princes, other times he's sat on the ground and eaten rice with his hands. His life is a whirlwind of planes, boats and cars. It doesn't matter to him what the circumstance is, he's just happy preaching. But he also loves to get home and spend some time relaxing with his friends. Going out for meals, listening to music and laughing.

His life "on the road" has given him a great understanding for people in similar situations. He knows what it's like to arrive at someone's house and find that they haven't prepared a meal for him. Or to come in from an exhausting journey and have his hosts talk to him into the early hours, when all he wanted to do was go to bed.

So Pete decided this would never happen to anyone who came to stay with him!

He enjoyed having guests at his house, especially fellow-itinerants (people who spent all their time travelling up and down the country telling people the Good News of Jesus Christ). He had a real understanding of the needs of folk in this situation. So, he made sure that his guest room had everything he could think of.

A very comfortable bed, a TV, books, writing material . . . even a well-stocked fridge!

Regardless of whether he know there was anyone coming to stay or not, the fridge was full of coke, chocolate bars and other snacks. The date wasn't important to him, if he wasn't home then he knew that a neighbour had the key and could let anyone in.

He was just ready! Ready for anyone at any time. Some people laughed at him for this, but Pete knew how important it was to be prepared.

1 Thessalonians 5:1–11 is all about being prepared and ready for the Lord's coming.

- What qualities did Pete have that are written about in this passage?
- What can you do to "be prepared" for the Lord's return?

Consider . . .

- going through your day's activities as if it were the day Jesus were coming back. Did you act differently or the same?
- hanging a "Maybe Today" sign in your room, to remind you to live each day to the fullest and be ready for Christ's return.

For more, see . . .

- Daniel 12:1–13 (p.847)
- 2 Peter 3:8–13 (p.1368)
- Matthew 21:1–14 (p.977)

whole self—spirit, soul and body—be kept safe
and without fault when our Lord Jesus Christ
comes. 24You can trust the One who calls you to
do that for you.
25Brothers and sisters, pray for us.

26Give each other a holy kiss when you meet.
27I tell you by the authority of the Lord to read
this letter to all the believers.
28The grace of our Lord Jesus Christ be with
you.

2 Thessalonians

Why Read This Book:

- Learn how God is with us now and in the future (2 Thessalonians 1).
- Find hope and comfort in God's love in the midst of life's tough times (2 Thessalonians 2—3).

When?

Time Line:

- BC/AD — Jesus was born
- AD 25 — Jesus began his ministry
- The church began soon after Jesus went to heaven
- Paul began his missionary work
- AD 50 — 2 Thessalonians may have been written
- Fire destroyed Rome
- Romans destroyed the Temple in Jerusalem
- AD 75
- AD 100

Behind the Scenes:

You are about to graduate. You have passed all your exams, but you still have one final test left to go. You don't think the test will make any difference to your grade or the job you will get. How hard will you study?

The Thessalonian Christians were in a similar situation. They had been told that "the day of the Lord" (Christ's Second Coming) had already come, and some believed it. As a result, they didn't think they had anything to worry about, since they would all go to heaven soon. So they left work, sat around doing nothing, interfered in other people's business, and depended on the church for charity. Worst of all, people decided they didn't really have to worry about growing spiritually.

2 Thessalonians challenged this outlook, saying the day of the Lord had not come and would not come for some time. Instead of sitting around, waiting for the end, Christians should be working hard and seeking to grow in their faith.

Sometimes we can be so excited about God's gift of eternal life that it makes everything else seem like a waste of time. 2 Thessalonians reminds us that God has a purpose for us on earth, and we are called to do God's work in this world. We are called to keep growing in our faith whatever happens.

LIFE FILE LINKS

Investigate the Theme

To find a list of real life stories on this subject turn to the LIFE FILE GUIDE on pages 12 to 22 at the front of the Youth Bible.

FAITH

1 From Paul, Silas and Timothy.
To the church in Thessalonica in God our
Father and the Lord Jesus Christ:
2 Grace and peace to you from God the Father
and the Lord Jesus Christ.

Paul Talks About God's Judgement

3 We must always thank God for you, brothers
and sisters.[n] This is only right, because your
faith is growing more and more, and the love
that every one of you has for each other is in-
creasing. 4 So we boast about you to the other
churches of God. We tell them about the way
you continue to be strong and have faith even
though you are being treated badly and are suf-
fering many troubles.
5 This is proof that God is right in his judge-
ment. He wants you to be counted worthy of his
kingdom for which you are suffering. 6 God will
do what is right. He will give trouble to those
who trouble you. 7 And he will give rest to you
who are troubled and to us also when the Lord
Jesus appears with burning fire from heaven with
his powerful angels. 8 Then he will punish those
who do not know God and who do not obey
the Good News[d] about our Lord Jesus Christ.

brothers and sisters Although the Greek text says "brothers" here and throughout this book, Paul's words were meant for the entire church, both men and women.

SUFFERING

When Silence Falls

Susie had been a Christian most of her life. She had a lovely family and home, and a great relationship with God. She was the kind of girl that everyone loved to be around. She was funny, sweet, very loving and caring and the best friend you could ask for. As Susie grew older, she was desperate for more of God, more wisdom, more love and more understanding.

Unlike her friends, Susie had a daily quiet time. God always met with her, until one day.

"That's strange," she thought. "Must be me."

On the days that followed, God seemed to stay quiet. She had no words, no pictures, no good thoughts, no tingle down her spine and no joy. Her days got dryer, so she tried even harder.

Around the same time, Susie realised her boyfriend was acting very strangely towards her. She confronted him and he told her he'd realised he no longer loved her. Susie was devastated and turned to God for comfort, but still he appeared to stay silent.

Shortly afterwards, Susie received a phone call. Her best friend had been in a serious accident, she was lying in intensive care.

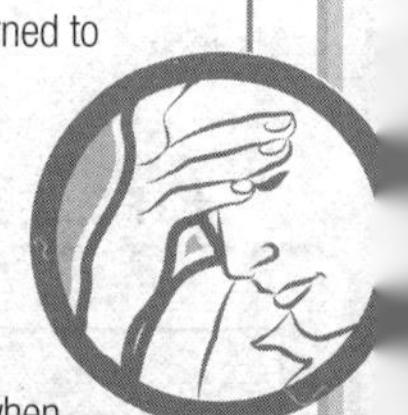

Lost and alone, Susie opened her Bible. Desperate, and crying out to God, her quiet time became a very loud time – but still she heard nothing.

Susie began to blame God. "Why are you doing this? Why are you ignoring me? Do you care? Are you even there?" As Susie cried, she remembered in the past telling God that no matter what the circumstances he was still God and deserved her worship. She realised that it's easy to pray when God feels really close and things are good, but as soon as he'd tested her to see if she really meant it about worshipping him in *all* circumstances, she had struggled. Read **2 Thessalonians 1:1–12**.

- What should our response be when suffering comes our way?
- How might knowing that you will have peace with God in the future help you through troubles right now?

Consider . . .

- the troubles you may be experiencing at the moment. Think about what God may be teaching you.
- getting hold of some books by people who have suffered for Jesus. How did they keep going?

For more, see . . .

- Romans 8:17–18 (p.1195)
- 1 Peter 3:8–22 (p.1360)
- 2 Corinthians 1:3–7 (p.1241)

9Those people will be punished with a destruc-
tion that continues for ever. They will be kept
away from the Lord and from his great power.
10This will happen on the day when the Lord
Jesus comes to receive glory because of his
holy people. And all the people who have be-
lieved will be amazed at Jesus. You will be
in that group, because you believed what we
told you.

Sidelight Being a Christian in the first century could be dangerous (2 Thessalonians 1:4). The Roman Emperor Nero was notorious for torturing Christians by covering them with tar and setting them on fire, then holding chariot races as they burned.

11That is why we always pray for you, asking
our God to help you live the kind of life he
called you to live. We pray that with his power
God will help you do the good things you want
and perform the works that come from your
faith. 12We pray all this so that the name of our
Lord Jesus Christ will have glory in you, and
you will have glory in him. That glory comes
from the grace of our God and the Lord Jesus
Christ.

Evil Things will Happen

2 Brothers and sisters, we have something to
say about the coming of our Lord Jesus
Christ and the time when we will meet together
with him. 2Do not become easily upset in your
thinking or afraid if you hear that the day of the
Lord has already come. Someone may say this in
a prophecy[d] or in a message or in a letter as if it
came from us. 3Do not let anyone fool you in
any way. That day of the Lord will not come
until the turning away[n] from God happens and
the Man of Evil, who is on his way to hell, ap-
pears. 4He will be against and put himself above
anything called God or anything that people
worship. And that Man of Evil will even go
into God's Temple[d] and sit there and say that he
is God.
5I told you when I was with you that all this
would happen. Do you not remember? 6And
now you know what is stopping that Man of Evil
so he will appear at the right time. 7The secret
power of evil is already working in the world,
but there is one who is stopping that power. And
he will continue to stop it until he is taken out of
the way. 8Then that Man of Evil will appear, and
the Lord Jesus will kill him with the breath that
comes from his mouth and will destroy him with
the glory of his coming. 9The Man of Evil will
come by the power of Satan. He will have great
power, and he will do many different false mir-
acles,[d] signs and wonders. 10He will use every
kind of evil to trick those who are lost. They will
die, because they refused to love the truth. (If
they loved the truth, they would be saved.) 11For
this reason God sends them something powerful
that leads them away from the truth so they will
believe a lie. 12So all those will be judged guilty
who did not believe the truth, but enjoyed doing
evil.

You are Chosen for Salvation

13Brothers and sisters, whom the Lord loves,
God chose you from the beginning to be saved.
So we must always thank God for you. You are
saved by the Spirit[d] that makes you holy and by
your faith in the truth. 14God used the Good
News[d] that we preached to call you to be saved
so you can share in the glory of our Lord Jesus
Christ. 15So, brothers and sisters, stand strong
and continue to believe the teachings we gave
you in our speaking and in our letter.
16–17May our Lord Jesus Christ himself and
God our Father encourage you and strengthen
you in every good thing you do and say. God
loved us, and through his grace he gave us a
good hope and encouragement that continues for
ever.

Pray for Us

3 And now, brothers and sisters, pray for us
that the Lord's teaching will continue to
spread quickly and that people will give honour
to that teaching, just as you did. 2And pray that
we will be protected from stubborn and evil peo-
ple, because not all people believe.
3But the Lord is faithful and will give you
strength and will protect you from the Evil One.
4The Lord makes us feel sure that you are doing
and will continue to do the things we told you.
5May the Lord lead your hearts into God's love
and Christ's patience.

The Duty to Work

6Brothers and sisters, by the authority of our
Lord Jesus Christ we command you to stay away
from any believer who refuses to work and does
not follow the teaching we gave you. 7You your-
selves know that you should live as we live. We
were not lazy when we were with you. 8And
when we ate another person's food, we always

turning away Or "the rebellion".

paid for it. We worked very hard night and day
so we would not be an expense to any of you.
[9]We had the right to ask you to help us, but we
worked to take care of ourselves so we would be
an example for you to follow. [10]When we were
with you, we gave you this rule: "Anyone who
refuses to work should not eat."
[11]We hear that some people in your group re-
fuse to work. They do nothing but busy them-
selves in other people's lives. [12]We command
those people and beg them in the Lord Jesus
Christ to work quietly and earn their own food.
[13]But you, brothers and sisters, never become
tired of doing good.
[14]If some people do not obey what we tell you
in this letter, then take note of them. Have noth-
ing to do with them so they will feel ashamed.
[15]But do not treat them as enemies. Warn them
as fellow believers.

Final Words

[16]Now may the Lord of peace give you peace
at all times and in every way. The Lord be with
all of you.
[17]I, Paul, end this letter now in my own hand-
writing. All my letters have this to show they are
from me. This is the way I write.

[18]The grace of our Lord Jesus Christ be with
you all.

Sidelight Lazy people spent their time interfering in other people's lives instead of working, so Paul told them that if someone didn't work when he was capable of doing so, he shouldn't eat either (2 Thessalonians 3:11–13)! This principle is also taught in Proverbs 19:15 (p.606).

GOD'S LOVE

Difficult Times

The Smith family experienced the pits of despair. Mr Smith, a fantastic engineer, loving husband and father, was killed in a car accident. He left a wife, an eighteen-year-old daughter, and a sixteen-year-old son. How would the family survive this difficult time?

Their church rallied round them. People volunteered to mow their lawn and repair their house. Church members cooked and served meals every day right after the death and once a week throughout the following year. The church collected a special offering for their immediate expenses and found a job for Mrs Smith. Church friends supported the family throughout that difficult first year with phone calls, visits, cards and gifts.

The Smiths wrote this thank-you to their congregation: "Through your prayers, dear friends, we have been comforted. Through your kind acts we have been soothed. We experienced God's love through you and your love. You made an unbearable experience bearable."

As the church comforted the Smiths, **2 Thessalonians 2:13—3:5** promises that God's love will comfort Christians who suffer.

- How is the love shown to the Smiths by their congregation like the love that comforted the early Christians?
- How does God's love comfort you through tough times?

Consider . . .

- circling the word "love" each time you read your Bible over the next several days. Count the number of "loves". Notice how God's love for you is stressed throughout the Bible. Start with the passages listed below.
- letting God's love shine through you. Think of someone who is sad or lonely (for example, a new person at school or an elderly church member who has lost a spouse). Surprise that person with a present or a card.

For more, see . . .

- Psalm 89:1–2 (p.553)
- Romans 5:6–8 (p.1190)
- Matthew 11:28–30 (p.960)

1 Timothy

Why Read This Book:

- Learn how to guard against false teaching (1 Timothy 1).
- Find out what to look for in a good church leader (1 Timothy 2—5).
- See what is really important in life (1 Timothy 6).

When?

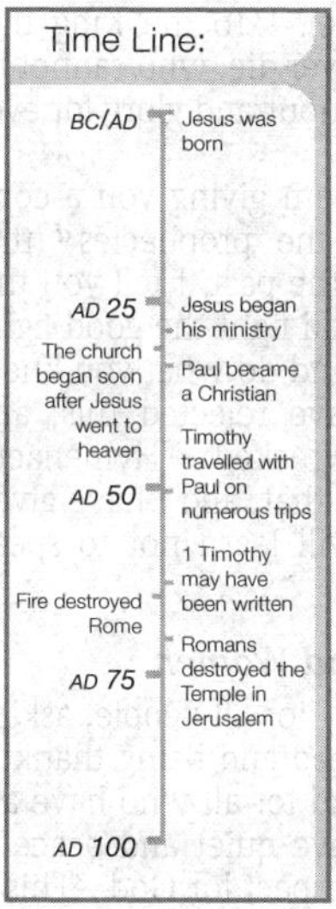

Behind the Scenes:

When you begin using a computer, you could just turn it on and start pressing keys, hoping you will hit the right ones to make something happen. But some people begin by reading the machine's manual. There you will find step-by-step things to do to use the machine correctly.

The first Christians didn't have experience of running a church. Many times they tried different things, hoping they were right. But they also needed a "practical handbook".

1 Timothy was just what they needed. It gives church leaders specific guidance on running a church: choosing leaders, dealing with false teachings, and order in worship, for example. It's called a "pastoral letter" because it focuses on the work of pastors. The two other pastoral letters in the Bible are 2 Timothy (p.1315) and Titus (p.1322).

Just because 1 Timothy was originally written about church leaders doesn't mean they are the only ones who can benefit from reading it. The book helps all Christians to learn the differences between true and false teachings. And it gives practical guidance on how to live as Christians.

Where?

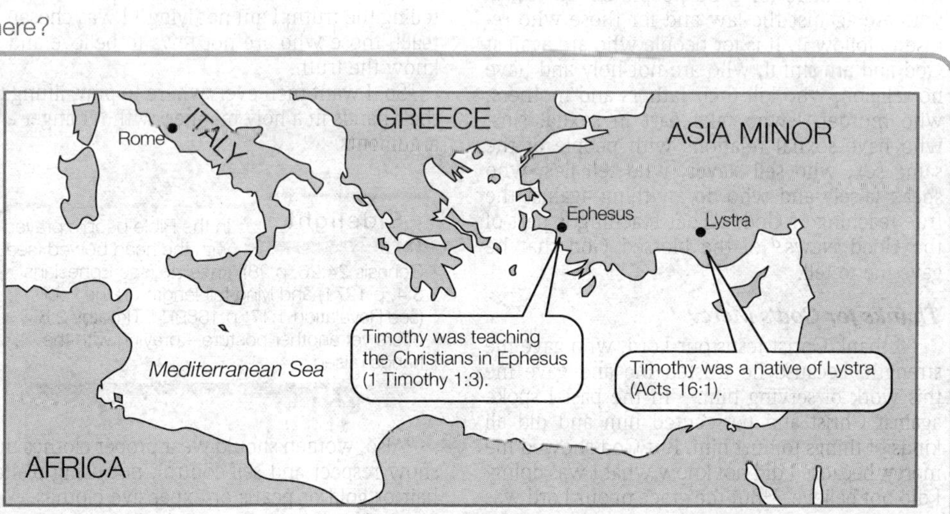

1 From Paul, an apostle[d] of Christ Jesus, by the command of God our Saviour[d] and Christ Jesus our hope.

2To Timothy, a true child to me because you believe:

Grace, mercy and peace from God the Father and Christ Jesus our Lord.

Warning Against False Teaching

3I asked you to stay longer in Ephesus when I went into Macedonia so you could command some people there to stop teaching false things. 4Tell them not to spend their time on stories that are not true and on long lists of names in family histories. These things only bring arguments; they do not help God's work, which is done in faith. 5The purpose of this command is for people to have love, a love that comes from a pure heart and a good conscience and a true faith. 6Some people have missed these things and turned to useless talk. 7They want to be teachers of the law, but they do not understand either what they are talking about or what they are sure about.

> **Sidelight** Genealogies were popular in Bible times (1 Timothy 1:4). Even Alexander the Great made up his own family tree, and linked himself with the Greek gods Hercules and Achilles!

8But we know that the law is good if someone uses it correctly. 9We also know that the law is not made for good people but for those who are against the law and for those who refuse to follow it. It is for people who are against God and are sinful, who are not holy and have no religion, who kill their fathers and mothers, who murder, 10who take part in sexual sins, who have sexual relations with people of the same sex, who sell slaves, who tell lies, who speak falsely and who do anything against the true teaching of God. 11That teaching is part of the Good News[d] of the blessed God that he gave me to tell.

Thanks for God's Mercy

12I thank Christ Jesus our Lord, who gave me strength, because he trusted me and gave me this work of serving him. 13In the past I spoke against Christ and persecuted him and did all kinds of things to hurt him. But God showed me mercy, because I did not know what I was doing. I did not believe. 14But the grace of our Lord was fully given to me, and with that grace came the faith and love that are in Christ Jesus.

15What I say is true, and you should fully accept it: Christ Jesus came into the world to save sinners, of whom I am the worst. 16But I was given mercy so that in me, the worst of all sinners, Christ Jesus could show that he has patience without limit. His patience with me made me an example for those who would believe in him and have life for ever. 17To the King that rules for ever, who will never die, who cannot be seen, the only God, be honour and glory for ever and ever. Amen.

18Timothy, my child, I am giving you a command that agrees with the prophecies[d] that were given about you in the past. I tell you this so you can follow them and fight the good fight. 19Continue to have faith and do what you know is right. Some people have rejected this, and their faith has been shipwrecked. 20Hymenaeus and Alexander have done that, and I have given them to Satan so they will learn not to speak against God.

Some Rules for Men and Women

2 First, I tell you to pray for all people, asking God for what they need and being thankful to him. 2Pray for rulers and for all who have authority so that we can have quiet and peaceful lives full of worship and respect for God. 3This is good, and it pleases God our Saviour, 4who wants all people to be saved and to know the truth. 5There is one God and one way human beings can reach God. That way is through Christ Jesus, who is himself human. 6He gave himself as a payment to free all people. He is proof that came at the right time. 7That is why I was chosen to tell the Good News[d] and to be an apostle.[d] (I am telling the truth; I am not lying.) I was chosen to teach those who are not Jews to believe and to know the truth.

8So, I want men everywhere to pray, lifting up their hands in a holy manner, without anger and arguments.

> **Sidelight** In the Bible people prayed with the head bowed (see Genesis 24:26, p.28), kneeling (see Ephesians 3:4, p.1271) and lying full-length on the floor (see Revelation 1:17, p.1389). 1 Timothy 2:8 offers yet another posture – praying with the hands raised.

9Also, women should wear proper clothes that show respect and self-control, not using plaited hair or gold or pearls or expensive clothes. 10Instead, they should do good deeds, which is right for women who say they worship God.

11Let a woman learn by listening quietly and
being ready to co-operate in everything. 12But I
do not allow a woman to teach or to have author-
ity over a man, but to listen quietly, 13because
Adam was formed first and then Eve. 14And Adam
was not tricked, but the woman was tricked and
became a sinner. 15But she will be saved through
having children if they continue in faith, love and
holiness, with self-control.

Elders in the Church

3 What I say is true: anyone wanting to become
an elder[d] desires a good work. 2An elder
must not give people a reason to criticise him,
and he must have only one wife. He must be self-
controlled, wise, respected by others, ready to
welcome guests and able to teach. 3He must not
drink too much wine or like to fight, but rather be
gentle and peaceful, not loving money. 4He must
be a good family leader, having children who co-
operate with full respect. 5(If someone does not
know how to lead the family, how can that person
take care of God's church?) 6But an elder must not
be a new believer, or he might be too proud of
himself and be judged guilty just as the devil was.
7An elder must also have the respect of people
who are not in the church so he will not be criti-
cised by others and caught in the devil's trap.

FORGIVENESS

Oops!

Jon had cycled home from school since the age of twelve. Every day he sped out of the school gates and along the road. He passed the butchers and the newsagents, then turned a corner and continued until the driveway of his house was in sight.

After all these years, Jon didn't really need to think about cycling home – it seemed to take care of itself almost automatically. He'd become quite skilful at swerving into the drive and avoiding his father's small saloon car by inches. Fortunately, his dad always parked the car in the same place, so Jon had no trouble in navigating his way around it.

But today he did and it was too late to do anything by the time he realised that the saloon car had been replaced with a brand new estate. He crashed into the side of the car then sat, dazed, staring at the spinning wheel of his bicycle.

"What have you done?" he heard his dad cry in pain. "My car!"

"Oops!" Jon sighed to himself.

"Sorry Dad, I haven't done any damage, have I?"

His dad inspected the door of his new pride and joy and saw a long, deep scratch in the paintwork. "Yes," he murmured.

Jon felt sick. "I didn't expect it," he said.

"I bought it this afternoon. I've been planning to surprise the family for weeks with it . . . It looks like I certainly surprised you."

"I'm sorry," Jon said again.

His dad nodded. "Apology accepted. Just remember to be a bit more careful in future, eh?"

Jon sighed with relief. He didn't expect to be forgiven as easily as that, but he was glad that he had been.

Jon's dad showed mercy towards his son. **1 Timothy 1:12–17** also talks about mercy.

- Why were Jon and the writer of 1 Timothy thankful for the forgiveness they received?
- How might God's forgiveness help you to deal with the sins you've committed?

Consider . . .

- asking God to forgive you for anything you have done wrong.
- showing someone mercy the next time they do something wrong to you. Tell them that you have forgiven them and don't bear any grudge.

For more, see . . .

- Genesis 50:15–21 (p.57)
- 2 Corinthians 2:5–10 (p.1241)
- Matthew 6:14–15 (p.948)

Deacons in the Church

[8]In the same way, deacons[d] must be respected
by others, not saying things they do not mean.
They must not drink too much wine or try to get
rich by cheating others. [9]With a clear conscience
they must follow the secret of the faith that God
made known to us. [10]Test them first. Then let
them serve as deacons if you find nothing wrong
in them. [11]In the same way, women[n] must be
respected by others. They must not speak evil of
others. They must be self-controlled and trust-
worthy in everything. [12]Deacons must have only
one wife and be good leaders of their children
and their own families. [13]Those who serve well
as deacons are making an honourable place for
themselves, and they will be very bold in their
faith in Christ Jesus.

The Secret of Our Life

[14]Although I hope I can come to you soon, I
am writing these things to you now. [15]Then,
even if I am delayed, you will know how to live
in the family of God. That family is the church of
the living God, the support and foundation of the
truth. [16]Without doubt, the secret of our life of
worship is great:

He was shown to us in a human body,
  proved right in spirit,[d]
and seen by angels.
  He was preached to those who are not
    Jews,
believed in by the world,
  and taken up in glory.

A Warning About False Teachers

4 Now the Holy Spirit[d] clearly says that in the
later times some people will stop believing
the faith. They will follow spirits that lie and
teachings of demons.[d] [2]Such teachings come
from the false words of liars whose understanding
is destroyed as if by a hot iron. [3]They forbid peo-
ple to marry and tell them not to eat certain foods

women This might mean the wives of the deacons, or it might mean women who serve in the same way as deacons.

PRAYER

Pray For All People

"I'm sailing tonight to Saudi Arabia. I'll see you when I get back."

Diane put the phone down. Saudi Arabia? Her boyfriend Gary was going to Saudi Arabia with the army. She didn't even really know where Saudi Arabia was!

She said a quick prayer, asking God to keep Gary safe.

Diane swallowed the lump in her throat and searched for a world atlas. She was terrified that something could happen to Gary, but she at least wanted to know where he was going.

During the worship service on Sunday, her minister said, "Let's pray for all people," and then listed different parts of the world, including Saudi Arabia. Diane's mind usually wandered during those prayers, since the places seemed so far away and irrelevant to her life. But this time she paid attention.

What happened in Saudi Arabia really did affect her life.

When Diane's boyfriend suddenly went overseas, she understood the importance of praying for all people. **1 Timothy 2:1–4** expands our prayer concerns beyond ourselves and reminds us that God cares for the whole world.

- How does praying for a country such as Saudi Arabia fit the message?
- Which countries and rulers should you pray for today?

Consider . . .

- reading the international section of your newspaper. Ask members of your church to pray for the people mentioned there.
- looking at a world atlas, and praying for people in different parts of the world. Pray for them each evening.

For more, see . . .

- Psalm 46 (p.527)
- James 5:13–18 (p.1353)
- Ephesians 6:18–20 (p.1277)

which God created to be eaten with thanks by people who believe and know the truth. 4Everything God made is good, and nothing should be refused if it is accepted with thanks, 5because it is made holy by what God has said and by prayer.

Be a Good Servant of Christ

6By telling these things to the brothers and sisters,[n] you will be a good servant of Christ Jesus. You will be made strong by the words of the faith and the good teaching which you have been following. 7But do not follow foolish stories that disagree with God's truth, but train yourself to serve God. 8Training your body helps you in some ways, but serving God helps you in every way by bringing you blessings in this life and in the future life too. 9What I say is true, and you should fully accept it. 10This is why we work and struggle: we hope in the living God who is the Saviour[d] of all people, especially of those who believe.

> **Sidelight** Since the Olympics started in Ancient Greece, most people in Bible times knew about training the body – gladiators were often seen "working out" for their next competition. 1 Timothy 4:8 tells us that, while physical exercise is profitable, spiritual exercise is even more so!

11Command and teach these things. 12Do not let anyone treat you as if you are unimportant because you are young. Instead, be an example to the believers with your words, your actions, your love, your faith, and your pure life. 13Until I come, continue to read the Scriptures[d] to the people, strengthen them, and teach them. 14Use the gift you have, which was given to you through prophecy[d] when the group of elders[d] laid their hands on[n] you. 15Continue to do those things; give your life to doing them so your progress may be seen by everyone. 16Be careful in your life and in your teaching. If you continue to live and teach rightly, you will save both yourself and those who listen to you.

Rules for Living with Others

5 Do not speak angrily to an older man, but plead with him as if he were your father. Treat younger men like brothers, 2older women like mothers and younger women like sisters. Always treat them in a pure way.

3Take care of widows who are truly widows. 4But if a widow has children or grandchildren, let them first learn to do their duty to their own family and to repay their parents or grandparents. That pleases God. 5The true widow, who is all alone, puts her hope in God and continues to pray night and day for God's help. 6But the widow who uses her life to please herself is really dead while she is alive. 7Tell the believers to do these things so that no one can criticise them. 8Whoever does not care for his own relatives, especially his own family members, has turned against the faith and is worse than someone who does not believe in God.

9To be on the list of widows, a woman must be at least 60 years old. She must have been faithful to her husband. 10She must be known for her good works—works such as raising her children, accepting strangers, washing the feet of God's people, helping those in trouble and giving her life to do all kinds of good deeds.

11But do not put younger widows on that list. After they give themselves to Christ, they may be pulled away from him by their physical needs, and then they will want to marry again. 12They will be judged for not doing what they first promised to do. 13Besides that, they would learn to waste their time, going from house to house. And they not only waste their time but also may begin to gossip and busy themselves with other people's lives, saying things they should not say. 14So I want the younger widows to marry, have children and take care of their homes. Then no enemy will have any reason to criticise them. 15But some have already turned away to follow Satan.

16If any woman who is a believer has widows in her family, she should care for them herself. The church should not have to care for them. Then it will be able to take care of those who are truly widows.

17The elders[d] who lead the church well should receive double honour, especially those who work hard by speaking and teaching, 18because the Scripture[d] says: "When an ox is working in the grain, do not cover its mouth to keep it from eating,"[n] and "A worker should be given his pay."[n]

brothers and sisters Although the Greek text says "brothers" here and throughout this book, Paul's words were meant for the entire church, both men and women.
laid their hands on The laying on of hands had many purposes, including the giving of a blessing, power or authority.
"When . . . eating," Quotation from Deuteronomy 25:4.
"A worker . . . pay." Quoted in Luke 10:7.

19Do not listen to someone who accuses an
elder, without two or three witnesses. 20Tell
those who continue sinning that they are wrong.
Do this in front of the whole church so that the
others will have a warning.
21Before God and Christ Jesus and the chosen
angels, I command you to do these things with-
out showing favour of any kind to anyone.
22Think carefully before you lay your hands
on[n] anyone, and don't share in the sins of oth-
ers. Keep yourself pure.
23Stop drinking only water, but drink a little
wine to help your stomach and your frequent
sicknesses.
24The sins of some people are easy to see even
before they are judged, but the sins of others are
seen only later. 25So also good deeds are easy to
see, but even those that are not easily seen can-
not stay hidden.

6 All who are slaves under a yoke[d] should
show full respect to their masters so no one
will speak against God's name and our teaching.
2The slaves whose masters are believers should
not show their masters any less respect because
they are believers. They should serve their mas-
ters even better, because they are helping believ-
ers they love.
You must teach and preach these things.

False Teaching and True Riches

3Anyone who has a different teaching does
not agree with the true teaching of our Lord
Jesus Christ and the teaching that shows the true
way to serve God. 4This person is full of pride
and understands nothing, but is sick with a love
for arguing and fighting about words. This brings
jealousy, fighting, speaking against others, evil
mistrust 5and constant quarrels from those who

lay your hands on The laying on of hands had many purposes, including the giving of a blessing, power or authority.

MONEY

The Root of All Evil

We can do whatever we want with our own money, can't we? That's what we usually think. If anyone steals money from us, we want it back. If someone asks us for money on the street, we feel that we should keep the cash deep in our pockets. If we go to church and the collection comes to us, we might put some change in to make sure that people see it and possibly hear a clinking of coins, but we're not going to put much in – it would be like throwing it away.

But God has a totally different view of our money. Like everything else we have, it really belongs to him. Because it's really his, we should be careful about how we spend it. It hasn't just come to us because we've got it as a present from a relative, as an allowance, or because we've earned it – it's actually a gift from God.

A little bit of money can go a long way when God uses it. It could be used to feed hungry people in the Third World. Or it might end up buying Bibles for a country where there's a shortage of them. Or it could be used to buy a Christian book that would help us to follow Jesus better.

God cares about our money: he can use it to change people's lives. Let's ask God to help us resist the temptation just to buy another DVD or pair of trainers or computer game, and think about something different we can do with our cash instead.

Read **1 Timothy 6:6–16**.

- What makes us spend our money as we do?
- What do verses 10 and 11 tell us we should be concentrating on?

Consider . . .

- ways of using some of your money to help people who need it more than you do.
- buying something for yourself that will help you follow Jesus better.

For more, see . . .

- Psalm 24:1 (p.514)
- 1 Corinthians 4:7 (p.1219)
- Luke 21:1–4 (p.1085)

have evil minds and have lost the truth. They
think that serving God is a way to get rich.
6Serving God does make us very rich, if we are
satisfied with what we have. 7We brought nothing
into the world, so we can take nothing out. 8But,
if we have food and clothes, we will be satisfied
with that. 9Those who want to become rich bring
temptation to themselves and are caught in a trap.
They want many foolish and harmful things that
ruin and destroy people. 10The love of money
causes all kinds of evil. Some people have left the
faith, because they wanted to get more money,
but they have caused themselves much sorrow.

Some Things to Remember

11But you, man of God, run away from all
those things. Instead, live in the right way,
serve God, have faith, love, patience and gen-
tleness. 12Fight the good fight of faith, grabbing
hold of the life that continues for ever. You
were called to have that life when you con-
fessed the good confession before many wit-
nesses. 13In the sight of God, who gives life to
everything, and of Christ Jesus, I give you a
command. Christ Jesus made the good confes-
sion when he stood before Pontius Pilate. 14Do
what you were commanded to do without
wrong or blame until our Lord Jesus Christ
comes again. 15God will make that happen
at the right time. He is the blessed and only
Ruler, the King of all kings and the Lord of all
lords. 16He is the only One who never dies.
He lives in light so bright no one can go near
it. No one has ever seen God, or can see him.

FAITH

Knowing it All

Professor Cooper was a very intelligent man. His academic work had won him many awards and prizes. The professor was greatly respected in his community, which was why the local primary school asked him if he would come to speak at one of their morning assemblies.

The professor gave a talk about how important it was to study hard at school, and told the children how hard he had worked and the great things that had happened in his life because of his successful studying. He finished his talk by asking the children what the best thing was that they had ever learnt.

A little boy from the youngest class put his hand up. In a squeaky, yet confident voice the boy said, "Jesus loves me and Jesus loves you."

The professor was stunned; tears welled in his eyes. It was something that he had last heard many years ago at Sunday school when he himself was little; it was something that he had once believed, and yet had ignored for all these years. Suddenly everything that he had learnt and achieved seemed worthless compared to this wonderful faith of a six-year-old.

In the early days of the church, some people were losing sight of the simple message that Jesus had brought, and were being sucked into a false religion called "Gnosticism". This told people that the way to be saved by God was to gain lots of knowledge. Read **1 Timothy 6:20–21** to see what advice Paul gave to the Christians.

- What does this story and the Bible passage tell us is the most important thing to understand?
- According to both the passage and the story, what is in our care that needs to be "looked after" or it will be lost?

Consider . . .

- asking God to make clearer those parts of the gospel that you find difficult to understand, and if you can, ask a good Christian friend to help you too.
- praying that as you learn more about Jesus, you will never lose sight of the very simple message of love that he brought.

For more, see . . .

- 2 Chronicles 1:7–12 (p.402)
- Ephesians 3:16–19 (p.1271)
- Matthew 25:14–30 (p.986)

May honour and power belong to God for ever.
Amen.
17 Command those who are rich with things
of this world not to be proud. Tell them to hope
in God, not in their uncertain riches. God richly
gives us everything to enjoy. 18 Tell the rich peo-
ple to do good, to be rich in doing good deeds,
to be generous and ready to share. 19 By doing
that, they will be saving a treasure for them-
selves as a strong foundation for the future.
Then they will be able to have the life that is
true life.
20 Timothy, guard what God has trusted to you.
Stay away from foolish, useless talk and from the
arguments of what is falsely called "knowledge".
21 By saying they have that "knowledge", some
have missed the true faith.
Grace be with you.

Sidelight

Saying that Jesus Christ is "King of all kings and the Lord of all lords" (1Timothy 6:15) was a bold statement in the midst of the persecution that the early Christians faced. Near the end of the first century, the Roman emperor Domitian demanded that his subjects address him as "Lord and God". Christians who refused were threatened, exiled and put to death.

2 Timothy

Why Read This Book:

- **Be encouraged to keep following God, even when you face danger for doing it (2 Timothy 1—2).**
- **Find out how to make it through tough times (2 Timothy 3—4).**

When?

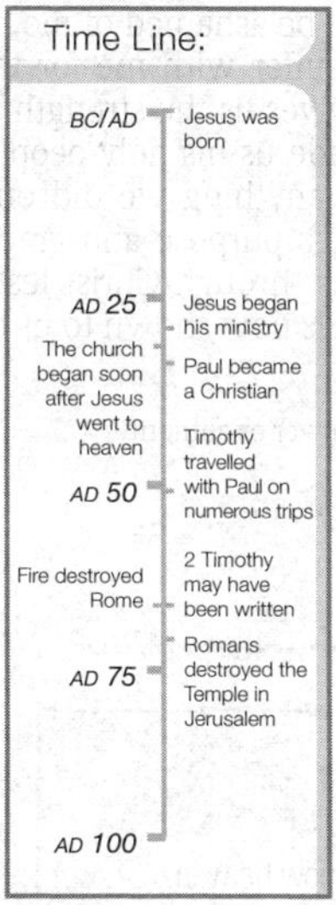

Behind the Scenes:

People who know they are soon to die often divide up their belongings and ask those around them to finish the jobs they have started. Paul knew he was facing death (2 Timothy 4:6–8), so – just like a relay runner – he wrote this letter to hand over the baton of ministry for Timothy to carry on.

2 Timothy captures what a retiring leader would say to a new leader. It gives lots of encouragement. It gives advice on how to become a leader. And it says that the road will be rocky and rough at times, but that we should remain strong anyway.

While 1 Timothy gives instructions on how to run a church, 2 Timothy is a personal letter – like one you would write to a close friend. It encourages Christians facing tough times, since the Roman government was persecuting Christians. And it can encourage us to stick to our faith today, even when people try to pull us away.

Where?

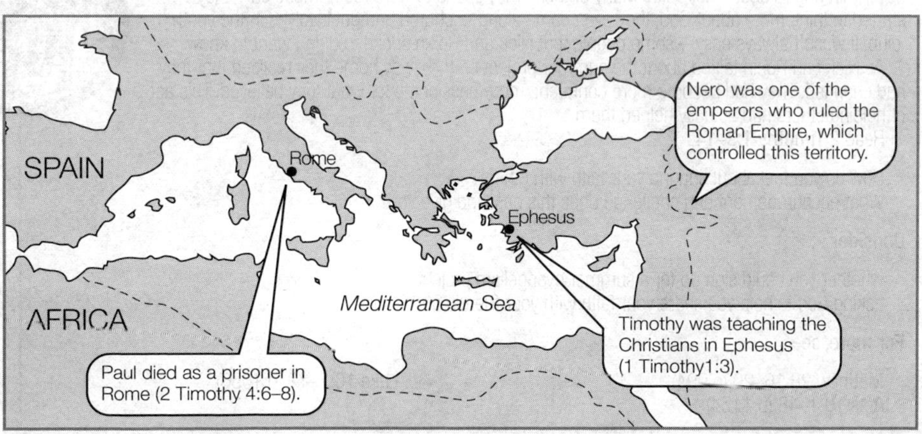

1 From Paul, an apostle [d] of Christ Jesus by the
will of God. God sent me to tell about the
promise of life that is in Christ Jesus.
[2]To Timothy, a dear child to me:
Grace, mercy and peace to you from God the
Father and Christ Jesus our Lord.

Encouragement for Timothy

[3]I thank God as I always mention you in my
prayers, day and night. I serve him, doing what I
know is right as my ancestors did. [4]Remembering
that you cried for me, I want very much to see
you so I can be filled with joy. [5]I remember your
true faith. That faith first lived in your grand-
mother Lois and in your mother Eunice, and I
know you now have that same faith. [6]This is why
I remind you to keep using the gift God gave you
when I laid my hands on [n] you. Now let it grow,
as a small flame grows into a fire. [7]God did not
give us a spirit that makes us afraid but a spirit of
power and love and self-control.
[8]So do not be ashamed to tell people about
our Lord Jesus, and do not be ashamed of me, in
prison for the Lord. But suffer with me for the
Good News. [d] God, who gives us the strength to
do that, [9]saved us and made us his holy people.
That was not because of anything we did our-
selves but because of God's purpose and grace.
That grace was given to us through Christ Jesus
before time began, [10]but it is now shown to us by

laid my hands on The laying on of hands had many purposes, including the giving of a blessing, power or authority.

SHARING FAITH

Stand Out or Sit Down?

Nick signed up to a summer evangelism project. It seemed like a good idea at the time, but now he was beginning to question whether it was "him" or not. Nick was quite a shy person, he didn't want to stand out in the crowd, he just wanted to be like everybody else. People would often say that to be a Christian was to be distinctive, to be different. This was the last thing that Nick wanted – he wanted to be normal. Just as Nick was about to pull out of the summer team, Robin, a friend from his youth group told Nick how he had encouraged him to think about sharing his faith too. Robin wanted to sign up to go on the summer team with Nick. What was Nick to do now? He could pull out and let Robin go on his own, or they could both go together.

It seemed a bit easier for Nick, knowing that Robin was going to be with him for this summer project. The two friends talked about what they expected to happen over the summer, they shared their hopes and their fears together. Nick was glad that Robin was going on the team – he wouldn't have made it otherwise.

The two friends went off on their summer project. It was a great time: challenging at times, fun at times and also terrifying at times. Nick and Robin found themselves talking to people they had never met before about their faith. Many of those they spoke to were really impacted – they started to think more about God, they even came along to church and got involved in the youth club. It wasn't always easy – some people that Nick and Robin spoke to didn't want to know.

As Nick and Robin talked about the summer project on their way home they realised that they had changed. They had become more confident, more passionate for what they believed. This act of helping others had actually helped them.

Read **2 Timothy 1:3–14**.

- How do you feel about sharing your faith with others?
- What encouragement and challenge does this passage give you?

Consider . . .

- whether you could sign up for a summer evangelism project.
- asking God to help you share your faith with your friends and family.

For more, see . . .

- Matthew 28:16–20 (p.994)
- Acts 10:1–48 (p.1154)
- Luke 10:1–12 (p.1056)

the coming of our Saviour [d] Christ Jesus. He de-
stroyed death, and through the Good News he
showed us the way to have life that cannot be
destroyed. 11I was chosen to tell that Good News
and to be an apostle and a teacher. 12I am suffer-
ing now because I tell the Good News, but I am
not ashamed, because I know Jesus, the One in
whom I have believed. And I am sure he is able
to protect what he has trusted me with until that
day. [n] 13Follow the pattern of true teachings that
you heard from me in faith and love, which are
in Christ Jesus. 14Protect the truth that you were
given; protect it with the help of the Holy Spirit [d]
who lives in us.

15You know that everyone in the country of
Asia has left me, even Phygelus and Hermo-
genes. 16May the Lord show mercy to the family
of Onesiphorus, who has often helped me and
was not ashamed that I was in prison. 17When
he came to Rome, he looked eagerly for me until
he found me. 18May the Lord allow him to find
mercy from the Lord on that day. You know how
many ways he helped me in Ephesus.

> **Sidelight** Like his friend Paul (2 Timothy 1:8), Timothy also experienced persecution for his faith, according to Hebrews 13:23 (p.1346). He was imprisoned but released. While the Bible does not tell us so, Paul was apparently executed while a prisoner in Rome.

A Loyal Soldier of Christ Jesus

2 You then, Timothy, my child, be strong in
the grace we have in Christ Jesus. 2You
should teach people whom you can trust the
things you and many others have heard me say.
Then they will be able to teach others. 3Share in
the troubles we have like a good soldier of Christ
Jesus. 4A soldier wants to please the enlisting offi-
cer, so no one serving in the army wastes time
with everyday matters. 5Also an athlete who
takes part in a contest must obey all the rules in
order to win. 6The farmer who works hard
should be the first person to get some of the food
that was grown. 7Think about what I am saying,
because the Lord will give you the ability to
understand everything.

8Remember Jesus Christ, who was raised from
the dead, who is from the family of David. This
is the Good News [d] I preach, 9and I am suffering
because of it to the point of being bound with
chains like a criminal. But God's teaching is not
in chains. 10So I patiently accept all these trou-
bles so that those whom God has chosen can
have the salvation that is in Christ Jesus. With
that salvation comes glory that never ends.

11This teaching is true:

If we died with him, we will also live
with him.
12 If we accept suffering, we will also rule
with him.
If we refuse to accept him, he will refuse
to accept us.
13 If we are not faithful, he will still be
faithful,
because he cannot be false to himself.

A Worker Pleasing to God

14Continue teaching these things, warning
people in God's presence not to argue about
words. It does not help anyone, and it ruins those
who listen. 15Do the best you can to give yourself
to God as the kind of person he will accept. Be a
worker who is not ashamed and who uses the
true teaching in the right way. 16Stay away from
foolish, useless talk, because that will lead peo-
ple further away from God. 17Their evil teaching
will spread like a sickness inside the body.
Hymenaeus and Philetus are like that. 18They
have left the true teaching, saying that the rising
from the dead has already taken place, and so
they are destroying the faith of some people. 19But
God's strong foundation continues to stand. These
words are written on the seal: "The Lord knows
those who belong to him," [n] and "Everyone who
wants to belong to the Lord must stop doing
wrong."

20In a large house there are not only things
made of gold and silver, but also things made of
wood and clay. Some things are used for special
purposes, and others are made for ordinary jobs.
21All who make themselves clean [d] from evil will
be used for special purposes. They will be made
holy, useful to the Master, ready to do any good
work.

22But run away from the evil young people like
to do. Try hard to live right and to have faith, love
and peace, together with those who trust in the
Lord from pure hearts. 23Stay away from foolish
and stupid arguments, because you know they
grow into quarrels. 24And a servant of the Lord
must not quarrel but must be kind to everyone,
a good teacher and patient. 25The Lord's servant
must gently teach those who disagree. Then
maybe God will let them change their minds so
they can accept the truth. 26And they may wake

day The day Christ will come to judge all people and take his people to live with him.
"The Lord . . . him", Quotation from Numbers 16:5.

up and escape from the trap of the devil, who
catches them to do what he wants.

The Last Days

3 Remember this! In the last days there will be
many troubles, 2because people will love
themselves, love money, boast and be proud.
They will say evil things against others and will
not obey their parents or be thankful or be the
kind of people God wants. 3They will not love
others, will refuse to forgive, will gossip and will
not control themselves. They will be cruel, will
hate what is good, 4will turn against their friends
and will do foolish things without thinking. They
will be conceited, will love pleasure instead of
God, 5and will act as if they serve God but will
not have his power. Stay away from those people.
6Some of them go into homes and get control of
weak women who are full of sin and are led
by many evil desires. 7These women are always
learning new teachings, but they are never able
to understand the truth fully. 8Just as Jannes and

Sidelight When 2 Timothy 3:2 cautions Timothy about people who love only themselves and money, it targets the culture of Ephesus, where Timothy worked. Nicknamed the treasure house of the ancient world, the major seaport city of Ephesus was famous for selfish, materialistic living.

PATIENCE

Worth the Wait

For 30 years, Rosa Parks bristled at the inequalities all around her. Because she was black, she had to ride at the back of the bus. Her skin colour made everything more difficult for her in the segregated South of the USA.

On her way home from work in 1955, in Montgomery, Alabama, Rosa boarded a bus and filled a vacant seat. She was exhausted. Her neck, shoulders and back ached from sewing alterations all day. A few white people boarded the bus after Rosa, and they all found seats, except for one white man.

The bus driver asked someone to give up a seat, meaning that a black person was to give up a seat for the white person. Since Rosa was sitting in a seat closest to the front and closest to the aisle, everyone looked at her. But Rosa would not budge. Finally, two police officers arrested her.

Rosa's arrest stirred an uproar in the black community. People were furious at the unfairness of forcing a black woman to give up her seat on a bus to a white man just because of her skin colour.

People gathered at Dexter Avenue Baptist Church to organise a bus boycott that made history and brought Martin Luther King Jr to national attention. The 381-day boycott required intense patience and endurance as the organisers set up car pools to take workers who relied on the buses. The boycott succeeded when Montgomery buses were made desegregated in 1956. No longer would blacks be forced to give up their seats for whites.

Because of Rosa Parks's patience and the patience of the boycott leaders, the civil rights movement of the 1950s and 1960s was born. By refusing to budge, Rosa showed the patience reflected in **2 Timothy 2:8–13**.

- How are the patience and suffering mentioned in this passage like the patience and suffering of blacks in the boycott?
- How could this passage help you to be more patient during difficult times?

Consider . . .

- asking God for patience to deal with a problem that you are facing, and then being patient.
- talking with your family about creating a rule for silently counting to fifteen when someone tries a family member's patience.

For more, see . . .

- Numbers 11:4–20 (p.139)
- 1 Peter 4:12–19 (p.1361)
- Romans 8:16–18 (p.1195)

Jambres were against Moses, these people are
against the truth. Their thinking has been ruined,
and they have failed in trying to follow the faith.
9But they will not be successful in what they do,
because as with Jannes and Jambres, everyone
will see that they are foolish.

Obey the Teachings

10But you have followed what I teach, the
way I live, my goal, faith, patience and love. You
know I never give up. 11You know how I have
been hurt and have suffered, as in Antioch, Ico-
nium and Lystra. I have suffered, but the Lord
saved me from all those troubles. 12Everyone who
wants to live as God desires, in Christ Jesus, will
be hurt. 13But people who are evil and cheat oth-
ers will go from bad to worse. They will fool
others, but they will also be fooling themselves.
14But you should continue following the
teachings you learned. You know they are true,
because you trust those who taught you. 15Since
you were a child you have known the Holy Scrip-
tures[d] which are able to make you wise. And that
wisdom leads to salvation through faith in Christ
Jesus. 16All Scripture is given by God and is useful
for teaching, for showing people what is wrong in
their lives, for correcting faults and for teaching
how to live right. 17Using the Scriptures, the per-
son who serves God will be capable, having all
that is needed to do every good work.

4 I give you a command in the presence of
God and Christ Jesus, the One who will
judge the living and the dead, and by his coming
and his kingdom: 2preach the Good News.[d] Be
ready at all times, and tell people what they need
to do. Tell them when they are wrong. Encour-
age them with great patience and careful teach-
ing, 3because the time will come when people
will not listen to the true teaching but will find
many more teachers who please them by saying

BIBLE STUDY

Take Time to Learn

Reading the Bible is important, isn't it? But do you do it? Many American Christian teenagers don't, said *Teenage* magazine:

- 13 per cent of Christian teenagers say they never read their Bible.
- Only 8 per cent say they read the Bible every day.
- 44 per cent say they read the Bible only when they feel like it.
- And the rest, 35 per cent, read the Bible a few times a week, or less.

The evidence shows that the same is probably true for Britain and Australia as well.
Teenagers say the top five reasons for not reading the Bible are:

1. They are too busy.
2. They would rather do something else.
3. They think the Bible is boring.
4. They don't know how to study the Bible.
5. They forget to read it.

The Bible has been called the most printed and the least read of all books. Teenagers might get a lot from the Bible if they read it knowing the value of Scripture as described in **2 Timothy 3:14–4:5**.

- According to this passage, of what value is Bible study to the Christian's life?
- What can you do to make Bible study an important part of your life?

Consider . . .

- asking your youth minister or pastor for tips on how to make Bible study easier and more effective.
- spending one week reading through one of the Gospels (Matthew, Mark, Luke or John) with a friend, meeting every day at lunch to discuss what you have learned in your reading.

For more, see . . .

- Psalm 119:97–104 (p.573)
- 2 Timothy 1:13–14 (p.1317)
- John 5:39 (p.1104)

the things they want to hear. 4They will stop
listening to the truth and will begin to follow
false stories. 5But you should control yourself at
all times, accept troubles, do the work of telling
the Good News and complete all the duties of a
servant of God.
6My life is being given as an offering to God,
and the time has come for me to leave this life. 7I
have fought the good fight, I have finished the
race, I have kept the faith. 8Now, a crown is
being held for me—a crown for being right with
God. The Lord, the judge who judges rightly,
will give the crown to me on that day[n]—not
only to me but to all those who have waited with
love for him to come again.

Personal Words

9Do your best to come to me as soon as you
can, 10because Demas, who loved this world, left
me and went to Thessalonica. Crescens went to
Galatia, and Titus went to Dalmatia. 11Luke is
the only one still with me. Get Mark and bring
him with you when you come, because he can
help me in my work here. 12I sent Tychicus to
Ephesus. 13When I was in Troas, I left my coat
there with Carpus. So when you come, bring it
to me, along with my books, particularly the
ones written on parchment.[n]
14Alexander the metalworker did many harm-
ful things against me. The Lord will punish him
for what he did. 15You also should be careful that

day The day Christ will come to judge all people and take his people to live with him.
parchment A writing paper made from the skins of sheep.

PERSISTENCE

Practise Makes Perfect

Jeff often went to a big Christian festival and loved the times of worship. He dreamed of one day being able to play in a worship band but there was just one problem – he couldn't play!

But on his fourteenth birthday, sporting a big red bow, tied neatly round the neck was his first guitar. For hours, Jeff strutted around his bedroom, imagining he was playing at a huge venue – thousands of people gasping in awe as he thumped out his guitar solos.

Jeff, like every other person when they start playing an instrument, was . . . rubbish. His music teacher told him he would probably fail his GCSE music and shouldn't bother. Without much subtlety, his parents bought him a pair of headphones, and Jeff started to wonder if he was really cut out to be a musician.

One thing kept him going. Every lunchtime, he met up with the other bad guitarists in Room 3, which was always empty, and played each other the "riff of the week", the thing they'd been pouring over every night in their rooms with their guitars, amps . . . and headphones. It was like a kind of self-help group!

After some time, this group became a band. The band did gigs at school, played at the youth club . . . and Jeff got an A for GCSE music.

There was far more at stake for Paul as he considered what it meant to persist through hard times to reach his life goal. Check it out in **2 Timothy 4:6–18**.

- How does Paul's persistence inspire us?
- What was the thing that kept him going?

Consider . . .

- whether there's stuff you're dealing with right now that seems impossible. Ask God to inspire you and give you the strength to persist.
- whether you know anyone who is struggling at the moment. Encourage them to hang in there and keep going.

For more, see . . .

- Daniel 6 (p.839)
- Philippians 3:12–21 (p.1284)
- Romans 5:1–5 (p.1190)

he does not hurt you, because he fought strongly
against our teaching.
16The first time I defended myself, no one
helped me; everyone left me. May they be
forgiven. 17But the Lord stayed with me and
gave me strength so I could fully tell the Good
News[d] to all those who are not Jews. So I was
saved from the lion's mouth. 18The Lord will
save me when anyone tries to hurt me, and he
will bring me safely to his heavenly kingdom.
Glory for ever and ever be the Lord's. Amen.

Final Greetings

19Greet Priscilla and Aquila and the family of
Onesiphorus. 20Erastus stayed in Corinth, and I
left Trophimus sick in Miletus. 21Try as hard as
you can to come to me before winter.
Eubulus sends greetings to you. Also Pudens,
Linus, Claudia and all the brothers and sisters in
Christ greet you.
22The Lord be with your spirit. Grace be
with you.

Sidelight Have trouble misplacing things? Take heart. So did the apostle Paul. He left his coat in Troas (2 Timothy 4:13), which was more than a hundred miles from Ephesus, and close to a thousand miles from Rome – the two places he might have been when he asked the people to send the coat to him. This coat was probably a heavy cloak that would have kept Paul warmer in a damp prison cell.

Titus

Why Read This Book:

- Find out what it takes to be a Christian leader (Titus 1).
- Discover how to live as a Christian (Titus 2–3).

When?

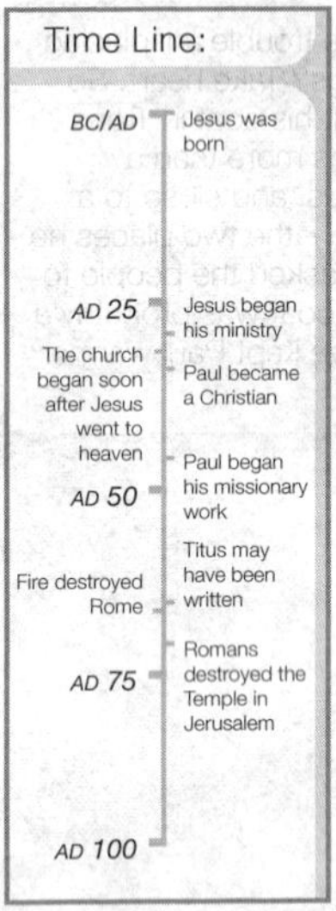

Behind the Scenes:

Hypocrites – everyone has met them at some time or another. Imagine meeting someone who tells you that they are a Christian, then goes around stealing, cheating other people and spreading lies and rumours about someone. How would you react? Chances are that you wouldn't have anything to do with them if you could possibly help it!

Titus encountered the same sort of people during his visit to Crete. The locals had a reputation for being lazy, telling lies and doing nothing but eating (Titus 1:2). Instead of writing them off, however, he went to work with them, and helped them to grow as Christians.

As you can imagine, it wasn't an easy job, particularly for somebody who was quite young. So Paul encourages Titus to keep up the good work, and gives him some tips about how he can help the Cretans to overcome their past way of life and launch out into living brand new Christian lives.

This letter to Titus is jam-packed with practical, down-to-earth advice, including how Christians should relate to political leaders, those who quarrel about the law and people who start arguments. Like 1 Timothy (p.1307) this letter includes all sorts of practical instructions about Christian leadership mixed in with the basics of belief and help for quality living.

Where?

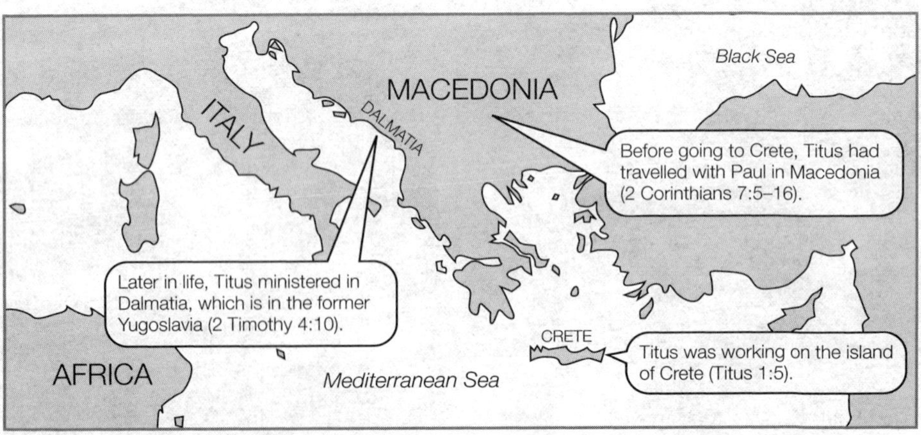

1 From Paul, a servant of God and an apostle[d] of Jesus Christ. I was sent to help the faith of God's chosen people and to help them know the truth that shows people how to serve God. [2]That faith and that knowledge come from the hope of life for ever, which God promised to us before time began. And God cannot lie. [3]At the right time God let the world know about that life through preaching. He trusted me with that work, and I preached by the command of God our Saviour.

[4]To Titus, my true child in the faith which we share:

Grace and peace from God the Father and Christ Jesus our Saviour.

Titus' Work in Crete

[5]I left you in Crete so you could finish doing the things that still needed to be done and so you could appoint elders[d] in every town, as I directed you. [6]An elder must not be guilty of doing wrong, must have only one wife, and must have believing children. They must not be known as children who are wild and do not obey. [7]As a manager of God's work, an elder must not be guilty of doing wrong, being selfish or becoming angry quickly. He must not drink too much wine, like to fight or try to get rich by cheating others. [8]An elder must be ready to welcome guests, love what is good, be wise, live right and be holy and self-controlled. [9]By holding on to the trustworthy word just as we teach it, an elder can help people by using true teaching, and he can show those who are against the true teaching that they are wrong.

Sidelight When Titus 1:8 says that elders must accept others into their homes, it means more than just giving them a cup of tea. If a stranger stopped at the door, a hospitable person was expected to feed, lodge, protect and clothe the stranger, if necessary. The Greek word for hospitality literally means "lover of strangers".

[10]There are many people who refuse to obey, who talk about worthless things and lead others into the wrong way—mainly those who say all who are not Jews must be circumcised.[d] [11]These people must be stopped, because they are upsetting whole families by teaching things they should not teach, which they do to get rich by cheating people. [12]Even one of their own prophets said, "Cretan people are always liars, evil animals and lazy people who do nothing but eat." [13]The words that prophet said are true. So firmly tell those people they are wrong so they may become strong in the faith, [14]not accepting Jewish false stories and the commands of people who reject the truth. [15]To those who are pure, all things are pure, but to those who are full of sin and do not believe, nothing is pure. Both their minds and their thinking have been ruined. [16]They say they know God, but their actions show they do not accept him. They are hateful people, they refuse to obey and they are useless for doing anything good.

Following the True Teaching

2 But you must tell everyone what to do to follow the true teaching. [2]Teach older men to be self-controlled, serious, wise, strong in faith, in love and in patience.

[3]In the same way, teach older women to be holy in their behaviour, not speaking against others or having the habit of too much wine, but teaching what is good. [4]Then they can teach the young women to love their husbands, to love their children, [5]to be wise and pure, to be good workers at home, to be kind and to yield to their husbands. Then no one will be able to criticise the teaching God gave us.

[6]In the same way, encourage young men to be wise. [7]In every way be an example of doing good deeds. When you teach, do it with honesty and seriousness. [8]Speak the truth so that you cannot be criticised. Then those who are against you will be ashamed because there is nothing bad to say about us.

[9]Slaves should yield to their own masters at all times, trying to please them and not arguing with them. [10]They should not steal from them but should show their masters they can be fully trusted so that in everything they do they will make the teaching of God our Saviour attractive.

[11]That is the way we should live, because God's grace that can save everyone has come. [12]It teaches us not to live against God nor to do the evil things the world wants to do. Instead, that grace teaches us to live now in a wise and right way and in a way that shows we serve God. [13]We should live like that while we wait for our great hope and the coming of the glory of our great God and Saviour Jesus Christ. [14]He gave himself for us so he might pay the price to free us from all evil and to make us pure people who belong only to him—people who are always wanting to do good deeds.

[15]Say these things and encourage the people and tell them what is wrong in their lives, with all authority. Do not let anyone treat you as if you were unimportant.

The Right Way to Live

3 Remind the believers to yield to the author-
ity of rulers and government leaders, to obey
them, to be ready to do good, 2to speak no evil
about anyone, to live in peace and to be gentle
and polite to all people.
3In the past we also were foolish. We did not
obey, we were wrong, and we were slaves to
many things our bodies wanted and enjoyed.
We spent our lives doing evil and being jealous.
People hated us, and we hated each other. 4But
when the kindness and love of God our Saviour
was shown, 5he saved us because of his mercy.
It was not because of good deeds we did to be
right with him. He saved us through the wash-
ing that made us new people through the Holy
Spirit.[d] 6God poured out richly upon us that
Holy Spirit through Jesus Christ our Saviour.
7Being made right with God by his grace, we
could have the hope of receiving the life that
never ends.
8This teaching is true, and I want you to be
sure the people understand these things. Then
those who believe in God will be careful to use
their lives for doing good. These things are good
and will help everyone.
9But stay away from those who have foolish
arguments and talk about useless family histories
and argue and quarrel about the law.[d] Those
things are worth nothing and will not help any-
one. 10After a first and second warning, avoid
someone who causes arguments. 11You can know
that such people are evil and sinful; their own
sins prove them wrong.

NON-CHRISTIANS

The Wonder Drug

Alexander Fleming was a brilliant but careless scientific researcher, whose lab was scattered with unfinished experiments. After a long holiday, he found that one of his experiments which had been sitting in the sunlight had gone mouldy. He started experimenting with the mould and found that it could cure illnesses such as meningitis and pneumonia. He had discovered penicillin.

At first, no one took any notice of this remarkable invention, but we now know it as a miracle drug which has saved millions of lives.

Imagine that was you. You've been searching all your life for this cure, and then one day, all of a sudden, it appears. You've done nothing to discover it – it's just been given to you. This drug has the potential to save thousands of lives and cure millions of people – you'd tell the world!

Now imagine it's gone one step further – this drug gives eternal life. It ends unhappiness, it's an invitation to the biggest party ever known, it's a relationship with a guy who loves you so much he died for you, it's a chance to escape all the things that hurt us and make us feel ashamed. It's a fresh start, a new beginning, a cure for every illness and a chance to become perfect. It urges you to practise godliness, to have a pure heart and a desire to do right – qualities that are really attractive to people around you. And the even better news – it's available to everyone.

Despite the initial rebukes and statements of disbelief, you know that people need this drug – and without you, they will never hear about it. Like Alexander Fleming's discovery, only a thousand times better, this is good news! We need to shout it from the rooftops – we've found Jesus!

Read **Titus 2:11–3:7**.

- What practical things does this passage tell us about following Jesus?
- How would we respond to those who think this passage implies that God is a killjoy?

Consider . . .

- what we find hard about telling people about Jesus. Why not practise in your head, ways of telling people the Good News, then write them down so that you don't forget them.
- whether you realise how important it is to be open about your faith.

For more, see . . .

- Matthew 28:19–20 (p.995)
- 1 Peter 3:14–16 (p.1360)

Some Things to Remember

[12]When I send Artemas or Tychicus to you, try hard to come to me at Nicopolis, because I have decided to stay there this winter. [13]Do all you can to help Zenas the lawyer and Apollos on their journey so that they have everything they need. [14]Our people must learn to use their lives for doing good deeds to provide what is necessary so that their lives will not be useless.

[15]All who are with me greet you. Greet those who love us in the faith.

Grace be with you all.

Sidelight The reason Paul says he plans to spend the winter in Nicopolis (Titus 3:12) was that ships stopped sailing during the stormy winter months. It made it difficult to get home for Christmas!

Philemon

Why Read This Book:

- Learn how to treat fellow Christians (Philemon 4–7).
- Discover how to see others as friends in Christ (Philemon 8–21).

When?

Behind the Scenes:

Life in Roman times could be very hard. Although the Romans were very clever planners and builders and had good laws for the upper classes, they could be very cruel. Onesimus was not one of the privileged people. He was a slave and could be executed. He had stolen from his master, then run away. Under Roman law, a runaway slave had no rights. Disobedience meant possible beatings, branding on the face with a red hot iron and even crucifixion.

But something had happened since Onesimus had left his master. He had become a Christian through Paul's influence. And, making the matter even more complicated, his master Philemon was also a Christian. Onesimus knew he should return to his master, but he also knew that he could die if he went back.

So Paul wrote this letter to persuade Philemon to forgive Onesimus and welcome him back as a Christian friend. Instead of telling Philemon to punish Onesimus, Paul asked that the wrongdoing be charged to Paul.

Though we no longer live with slavery, we, like Philemon, may be tempted to look down on people because of the colour of their skin, the amount of money they have, or what they wear. And we may treat them as second class citizens and think we are first class. In Philemon, Paul challenges all of us to rethink those prejudices.

Where?

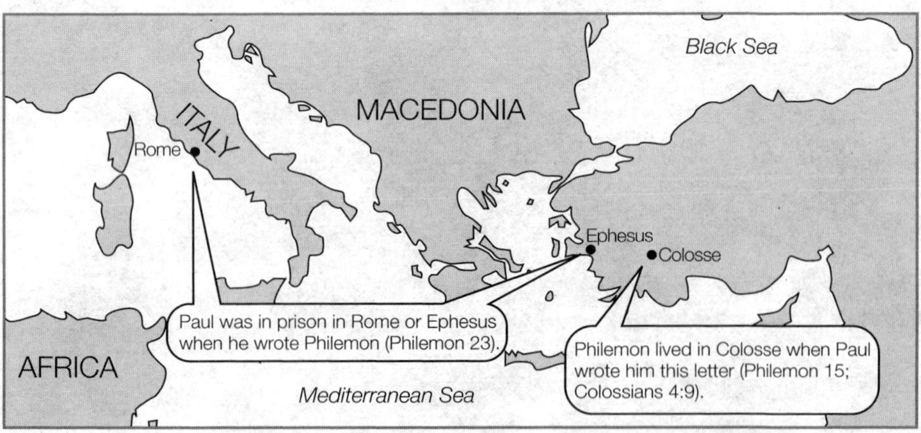

1From Paul, a prisoner of Christ Jesus, and
from Timothy, our brother.
To Philemon, our dear friend and worker with
us; 2to Apphia, our sister; to Archippus, a worker
with us; and to the church that meets in your
home:
3Grace and peace to you from God our Father
and the Lord Jesus Christ.

Philemon's Love and Faith

4I always thank my God when I mention you
in my prayers, 5because I hear about the love
you have for all God's holy people and the faith
you have in the Lord Jesus. 6I pray that the faith
you share may make you understand every
blessing we have in Christ. 7I have great joy
and comfort, my brother, because the love
you have shown to God's people has refreshed
them.

Accept Onesimus as a Brother

8So, in Christ, I could be bold and order you to
do what is right. 9But because I love you, I am
pleading with you instead. I, Paul, an old man
now and also a prisoner for Christ Jesus, 10am
pleading with you for my child Onesimus, who
became my child while I was in prison. 11In the
past he was useless to you, but now he has become useful for both you and me.
12I am sending him back to you, and with him
I am sending my own heart. 13I wanted to keep
him with me so that in your place he might help
me while I am in prison for the Good News.[d]
14But I did not want to do anything without asking you first so that any good you do for me will
be because you want to do it, not because I
forced you. 15Maybe Onesimus was separated
from you for a short time so you could have him
back for ever— 16no longer as a slave, but better

FRIENDS

When Friends Let You Down

Mr Green was one of those cool teachers that everyone loved. Every term he would set an assignment that involved a presentation in front of the class. For most students, this was the highlight of the term. Everyone wanted to do well. Everyone except Simon.

Simon, Jess and Ryan were best friends, and thought it would be great to work together on Mr Green's project. Unfortunately, Simon suffered from an extreme case of full-on laziness. If he could avoid work of any kind, he would.

Jess and Ryan worked hard, preparing their bits of the presentation, doing extra work at home and giving up their lunchtimes to do research. But rather than gathering materials, Simon played football; instead of researching . . . well, who knows what he did!

As Jess and Ryan realised that Simon hadn't done any of the things he'd said he was going to do for the project, their relationship got more and more strained and they stopped hanging out with him.

With one day to go, Jess and Ryan went to Simon and explained to him how what he had done had made them feel. He was gutted, but determined to make amends. They stayed up all night and finished the presentation.

The next day, they did the presentation and Mr Green was amazed, it was so good. Simon got the chance to redeem himself – an A grade won, a friendship restored.

Read **Philemon 4–21** and see what Paul says to Philemon after Onesimus has let him down.

- How does Paul prepare a way for Onesimus and Philemon's friendship?
- How easy would you find it to be a friend to the friendless?

Consider . . .

- whether a friend has ever let you down. How did you deal with it?
- whether there is anyone you know who could do with a friend right now?

For more, see . . .

- Job 42:7–12 (p.498)
- Romans 3:23–24 (p.1187)
- John 21:15–19 (p.1134)

than a slave, as a loved brother. I love him very much, but you will love him even more, both as a person and as a believer in the Lord.
17So if you consider me your partner, welcome Onesimus as you would welcome me. 18If he has
done anything wrong to you or if he owes you
anything, charge that to me. 19I, Paul, am writing
this with my own hand. I will pay it back, and I will say nothing about what you owe me for your own life. 20So, my brother, I ask that you do this
for me in the Lord: refresh my heart in Christ. 21I
write this letter, knowing that you will do what I ask you and even more.
22One more thing—prepare a room for me in which to stay, because I hope God will answer your prayers and I will be able to come to you.

Sidelight

Slavery was common in the Roman Empire in Paul's day. According to some estimates, there were about sixty million slaves in the Empire – up to half the total population.

Final Greetings

23Epaphras, a prisoner with me for Christ Jesus, sends greetings to you. 24And also Mark,
Aristarchus, Demas and Luke, workers together with me, send greetings.
25The grace of our Lord Jesus Christ be with your spirit.

Hebrews

Why Read This Book:

- Discover how Jesus Christ fulfilled God's promises (Hebrews 1—7).
- Learn about the sacrifice Jesus made for us (Hebrews 8—10).
- Be challenged to stay strong in your faith (Hebrews 11—13).

When?

Time Line:

BC/AD	Jesus was born
AD 25	Jesus began his ministry
The church began soon after Jesus went to heaven	Paul became a Christian
AD 50	Paul began his missionary work
Fire destroyed Rome	Hebrews was written
AD 75	Romans destroyed the Temple in Jerusalem
AD 100	

Behind the Scenes:

Imagine a courtroom scene. The jury has heard persuasive testimony from many different people. Now the jury is about to go behind closed doors to come to a verdict about whether Christianity does hold the truth. But first the lawyers will present their closing arguments.

The book of Hebrews is like a closing argument in defence of Christianity. Using careful logic and referring often to testimony, the writer shows that Jesus Christ is the Son of God and worthy of our faith. The book compares and contrasts Jesus with all of Old Testament history and argues that Jesus is the climax of everything in the past.

So, the author concludes, "Let us look only to Jesus, the One who began our faith and who makes it perfect. . . . Think about Jesus' example. . . . So do not get tired and stop trying" (Hebrews 12:2–3).

We don't know how the original readers responded to the convincing argument in Hebrews. But we do know that the book has become a treasured source of encouragement and hope for Christians through the centuries. Just as this letter encouraged its first readers to hold strong to their faith, it can do the same for us today.

LIFE FILE LINKS

Investigate the Theme

To find a list of real life stories on this subject turn to the LIFE FILE GUIDE on pages 12 to 22 at the front of the Youth Bible.

JESUS CHRIST

God Spoke Through His Son

1 In the past God spoke to our ancestors
through the prophets[d] many times and in
many different ways. 2But now in these last days
God has spoken to us through his Son. God has
chosen his Son to own all things, and through
him he made the world. 3The Son reflects the
glory of God and shows exactly what God is
like. He holds everything together with his
powerful word. When the Son made people
clean from their sins, he sat down at the right
side of God, the Great One in heaven. 4The
Son became much greater than the angels, and
God gave him a name that is much greater
than theirs.

Sidelight We don't know who wrote Hebrews. Its goal was to show Christ's superiority to the Old Testament laws. Because of this, many people find it useful to read Hebrews alongside Leviticus, because of the connections (for example, read Hebrews 9:11 — 10:18, p.1337, alongside Leviticus 4, p.103).

5This is because God never said to any of the
angels,

"You are my Son.
Today I have become your Father." *Psalm 2:7*

Nor did God say of any angel,

"I will be his father,
and he will be my son." *2 Samuel 7:14*

6And when God brings his firstborn Son into the
world, he says,

"All the gods should worship him."[n] *Psalm 97:7*

7This is what God said about the angels:

"God makes his angels become like winds.
He makes his servants become like flames
of fire." *Psalm 104:4*

8But God said this about his Son:

"God, your throne will last for ever and
ever.
You will rule your kingdom with fairness.
9You love right and hate evil,
so God has chosen you from among your
friends;
he has set you apart with much joy."
Psalm 45:6–7

10God also says,

"In the beginning you made the earth,
and your hands made the skies.
11They will be destroyed, but you will remain.
They will all wear out like clothes.
12And, like clothes, you will change them and
throw them away.
But you never change,
and your life will never end." *Psalm 102:25–27*

13And God never said this to an angel:

"Sit by me at my right side
until I put your enemies under your
control."[n] *Psalm 110:1*

14All the angels are spirits who serve God and
are sent to help those who will receive salvation.

Our Salvation is Great

2 So we must be more careful to follow what
we were taught. Then we will not stray away
from the truth. 2The teaching God spoke through
angels was shown to be true, and anyone who did
not follow it or obey it received the punishment
that was earned. 3So surely we also will be pun-
ished if we ignore this great salvation. The Lord
himself first told about this salvation, and it was
proven true to us by those who heard him. 4God
also proved it by using wonders, great signs,
many kinds of miracles[d] and by giving people
gifts through the Holy Spirit,[d] just as he wanted.

Christ Became like Humans

5God did not choose angels to be the rulers of
the new world that was coming, which is what
we have been talking about. 6It is written in the
Scriptures,[d]

"But why are people important to you?
Why do you take care of human beings?
7You made them a little lower than the angels
and crowned them with glory and honour.
You put them in charge of everything
you made.
8 You put all things under their control."
Psalm 8:4–6

When God put everything under their control,
there was nothing left that they did not rule.
Still, we do not yet see them ruling over every-
thing. 9But we see Jesus, who for a short time
was made lower than the angels. And now he is
wearing a crown of glory and honour because he
suffered and died. And by God's grace, he died
for everyone.

10God is the One who made all things, and all
things are for his glory. He wanted to have many
children share his glory, so he made the One
who leads people to salvation perfect through
suffering.

"All . . . him." These words are found in Deuteronomy 32:43 in the Septuagint, the Greek version of the Old Testament, and in a Hebrew copy among the Dead Sea Scrolls.

until . . . control Literally, "until I make your enemies a footstool for your feet."

11 Jesus, who makes people holy, and those
who are made holy are from the same family. So
he is not ashamed to call them his brothers and
sisters. *n* 12 He says,
"Then, I will tell my fellow Israelites
about you;
I will praise you in the public meeting."
Psalm 22:22
13 He also says,
"I will trust in God." *Isaiah 8:17*
And he also says,
"I am here, and with me are the children
God has given me." *Isaiah 8:18*
14 Since these children are people with physical
bodies, Jesus himself became like them. He did
this so that, by dying, he could destroy the one
who has the power of death—the devil— 15 and
free those who were like slaves all their lives
because of their fear of death. 16 Clearly, it is not an-
gels that Jesus helps, but the people who are from
Abraham. *n* 17 For this reason Jesus had to be made
like his brothers in every way so he could be their
merciful and faithful high priest in service to God.
Then Jesus could bring forgiveness for their sins.
18 And now he can help those who are tempted,
because he himself suffered and was tempted.

Jesus is Greater than Moses

3 So all of you holy brothers and sisters, who
were called by God, think about Jesus, who
was sent to us and is the high priest of our faith.
2 Jesus was faithful to God as Moses was in God's
family. 3 Jesus has more honour than Moses, just
as the builder of a house has more honour
than the house itself. 4 Every house is built by
someone, but the builder of everything is God
himself. 5 Moses was faithful in God's family as a
servant, and he told what God would say in the
future. 6 But Christ is faithful as a Son over God's
house. And we are God's house if we keep on

brothers and sisters Although the Greek text says "brothers" here and throughout this book, the writer's words refer to the entire church, both men and women.
Abraham Most respected ancestor of the Jews. Every Jew hoped to see Abraham.

IMAGE

Created by Design

Michael loved designer labels. It was his thing. He really enjoyed going out on a Saturday with his hard-earned cash and coming back home with carrier bags with designer names on them. And like he always said, there's nothing wrong with that, it was his money.

The only trouble was, that Michael worked in a place where oil and grease were the order of the day. He would spend many hours beneath leaking engines and machinery. The firm he worked for provided overalls, but there was no way Michael was ever going to be seen in them! So, each day he dressed for work in designer shirts, trousers and shoes. And each night he would come home with his clothes covered in dirt. When this was pointed out to him, he would shrug his shoulders and say, "It's OK, I'll get some more at the end of the month." His friends thought he was crazy, but that's just the way he was. He couldn't bear to be caught in plain clothes.

Hebrews 1:10–14 talks about how throw-away our lifestyle is.

- What is the difference between God and the "disposable" world?
- How is Michael's attitude to clothes similar to God's view of creation? How is it different?

Consider . . .

- taking care over your appearance just as God took care in creating a beautiful world.
- your financial priorities, is there a good balance in the way you use your money?

For more, see . . .

- Esther 8:15–17 (p.465)
- Matthew 6:28–33 (p.948)
- Psalm 45 (p.526)

being very sure about our great hope.

We Must Continue to Follow God

7So it is as the Holy Spirit[d] says:
"Today listen to what he says.
8Do not be stubborn as in the past
when you turned against God,
when you tested God in the desert.
9There your ancestors tried me and tested me
and saw the things I did for 40 years.
10I was angry with them.
I said, 'They are not loyal to me
and have not understood my ways.'
11I was angry and made a promise,
'They will never enter my rest.'"[n]
Psalm 95:7–11

12So brothers and sisters, be careful that none
of you has an evil, unbelieving heart that will turn
you away from the living God. 13But encourage
each other every day while it is "today".[n] Help
each other so none of you will become hardened
because sin has tricked you. 14We all share in
Christ if we keep till the end the sure faith we had
in the beginning. 15This is what the Scripture[d] says:
"Today listen to what he says.
Do not be stubborn as in the past
when you turned against God." *Psalm 95:7–8*

Sidelight If Hebrews had been submitted as a project, it would probably have been given top marks for research and documentation. The book quotes from the Old Testament more than 80 times, including Psalm 95:7–11 (p.556), in Hebrews 3:7–11.

16Who heard God's voice and was against him?
It was all those people Moses led out of Egypt.
17And with whom was God angry for 40 years?

rest A place in which to rest that God promised to give his people.
"today" This word is taken from verse 7. It means that it is important to do these things now.

SHARING FAITH

Can You Tell the Difference?

When she graduated from college, Bev Johnson became a short-term missionary at a school in Japan. Each day she led a Bible study and taught English to the Japanese.

Each day an elderly woman came to the Bible study. She sat quietly at the back of the room and rushed out when the study ended. And each day Bev grew more curious.

One day after the Bible study, Bev walked quickly to the woman and began a conversation. The woman spoke excellent English. She told Bev that she had heard of Jesus since she was a young girl. The woman owned a Bible and knew much of it by heart.

"Are you a Christian?" Bev asked.

"No, no I'm not," the woman said, "but I've seen Christians, and I'm watching to see if Jesus makes any difference in their lives."

From that incident, Bev learned how people need to see Jesus in Christians. Read how Jesus can shine through us in **Hebrews 2:9–18**.

- How does the older woman's statement to Bev relate to this passage?
- Why do you think God, in Jesus, became a person for us to know?

Consider . . .

- listing all the ways in which Jesus showed what God is like, such as loving all people, and so on. Choose one of those ways to show how you follow Christ.
- letting at least one other person know this week how Christ has made a difference to you.

For more, see . . .

- Isaiah 57:14–21 (p.701)
- John 11:28–43 (p.1116)
- Matthew 20:29–34 (p.976)

He was angry with those who sinned, who died in
the desert. 18And to whom was God talking when
he promised that they would never enter his rest?
He was talking to those who did not obey him.
19So we see they were not allowed to enter and
have God's rest, because they did not believe.

4 Now, since God has left us the promise that
we may enter his rest, let us be very careful
so none of you will fail to enter. 2The Good
News [d] was preached to us just as it was to them.
But the teaching they heard did not help them,
because they heard it but did not accept it with
faith. 3We who have believed are able to enter
and have God's rest. As God has said,

"I was angry and made a promise,
'They will never enter my rest.'" *Psalm 95:11*

But God's work was finished from the time he
made the world. 4In the Scriptures he talked
about the seventh day of the week: "And on the
seventh day God rested from all his works." [n]
5And again in the Scripture God said, "They will
never enter my rest."

6It is still true that some people will enter
God's rest, but those who first heard the way
to be saved did not enter, because they did
not obey. 7So God planned another day, called
"today". He spoke about that day through
David a long time later in the same Scripture
used before:

"Today listen to what he says.

"And . . . works." Quotation from Genesis 2:2.

FOLLOWING GOD

When the Going Gets Tough . . .

Isabella Baumfree was an American slave born to a Dutch owner in Ulster County, New York, USA, about 1797. She was separated from her family and sold twice before she was twelve. Even after she was set free in 1827, she barely survived as a servant in New York City.

After the Civil War began, Isabella left New York to "travel up an' down the land showin' the people their sins an' bein' a sign unto them." She even changed her name to Sojourner Truth.

Sojourner Truth became famous for her unique style of preaching. Although she couldn't read or write, she preached a message of freedom for slaves, women and the poor. She spoke in a heavy Dutch accent, knew the Bible well, and drew stares wearing a turban.

Because blacks – especially black women – were routinely oppressed, Sojourner Truth found the going difficult. But she kept at it, hardened by her life of slavery and struggle. Her fame spread; she even met President Lincoln in 1864.

Fame doesn't always equal popularity, as Sojourner Truth found out. She often preached and lectured before hostile audiences. Many times she was told her mission was hopeless. "I don't care any more for your talk than I do for the bite of a flea," someone told her.

"Perhaps not," she replied, "but the Lord willing, I'll keep you scratchin'."

Sojourner Truth knew that following God requires commitment and endurance. So did the writer of Hebrews. And, in **Hebrews 4:1–13**, the writer promises that endurance and commitment will not go unrewarded.

- How was Sojourner Truth's persistence in her mission like the challenge of the passage to stay obedient to God? How did she embody the theme of verses 12–13?
- What does the passage say about those who truly follow God versus those who just say they do?

Consider . . .

- taking an unpopular stand on an issue because you believe it's what God wants you to do.
- listing things that you would honestly die for. Decide how to follow those priorities better this week.

For more, see . . .

- Deuteronomy 33:26–29 (p.200)
- Acts 7:51–60 (p.1149)
- Luke 10:25–37 (p.1058)

Do not be stubborn." *Psalm 95:7–8*
8We know that Joshua[n] did not lead the people
into that rest,[n] because God spoke later about
another day. 9This shows that the rest for God's
people is still coming. 10Anyone who enters
God's rest will rest from his work as God did.
11Let us try as hard as we can to enter God's rest
so that no one will fail by following the example
of those who refused to obey.
12God's word is alive and working and is
sharper than a double-edged sword. It cuts all
the way into us, where the soul and the spirit are
joined, to the centre of our joints and bones. And
it judges the thoughts and feelings in our hearts.
13Nothing in all the world can be hidden from
God. Everything is clear and lies open before
him, and to him we must explain the way we
have lived.

Jesus is Our High Priest

14Since we have a great high priest, Jesus the
Son of God, who has gone into heaven, let us hold

Joshua After Moses died, Joshua became leader of the Jewish people and led them into the land that God promised to give them.
rest Literally, "sabbath rest", meaning a sharing in the rest that God began after he created the world.

GOD'S LOVE

Mayday!

"Mayday! Mayday!" The international distress message crackled on the coastguard's radio.

The crew, all volunteers, left their day jobs, and leapt onto bicycles and into cars as the siren on the lifeboat house went off. They quickly climbed into their waterproof overalls and lifejackets as the coxswain listened to the coastguard. Within minutes, the doors of the lifeboat house rattled open and the lifeboat was sliding down the ramps into the foaming waves.

The weather was terrible. Torrential rain beat against the surface of the writhing ocean, making visibility a very dangerous problem. The small fishing boat which had sent out the Mayday call had struck rocks in the storm, and the lifeboat crew had to be careful not to do the same thing.

When the crew had located the floundering fishing boat, they managed to get a line across the heaving water and helped the two relieved fishermen onto their lifeboat.

"The skipper's in the water!" one of the fishermen told them.

Without hesitating, one of the crew sent a distress flare into the sky.

By now, an RAF helicopter was hovering over the waters. The pilot managed to find the floating man and sent a winch down to rescue him. For a while it seemed as though the airman on the end of the line would drown, too. But eventually he was able to grab the shivering sailor.

Thirty minutes later the three fishermen were safely ashore. They couldn't thank the sea rescue team enough for saving their lives.

The lifeboat crew are not paid – they are volunteers. Yet many times a year they risk their own lives to save those of others. Jesus Christ carried out an even deadlier mission – he *gave* his life in order to pay for our sins! Read about this amazing love in **Hebrews 4:14—5:10**.

- How does the sea rescue team illustrate the kind of self-sacrificing love that this passage describes?
- How does knowing about God's endless love for you affect your everyday life?

Consider . . .

- looking for examples of sacrificial love in the news and on television. Let their stories remind you of Christ's love for mankind.
- thanking God for sending his Son to die for you, then share this good news with those around you.

For more, see . . .

- Daniel 9:1–9 (p.843)
- Romans 3:21–26 (p.1187)
- Matthew 7:7–11 (p.950)

on to the faith we have. 15For our high priest is able to understand our weaknesses. When he lived on earth, he was tempted in every way that we are, but he did not sin. 16Let us, then, feel very sure that we can come before God's throne where there is grace. There we can receive mercy and grace to help us when we need it.

5 Every high priest is chosen from among other people. He is given the work of going before God for them to offer gifts and sacrifices for sins. 2Since he himself is weak, he is able to be gentle with those who do not understand and who are doing wrong things. 3Because he is weak, the high priest must offer sacrifices for his own sins and also for the sins of the people.

4To be a high priest is an honour, but no one chooses himself for this work. He must be called by God as Aaron [n] was. 5So also Christ did not choose himself to have the honour of being a high priest, but God chose him. God said to him,

"You are my Son.
Today I have become your Father." *Psalm 2:7*

6And in another Scripture [d] God says,

"You are a priest for ever,
a priest like Melchizedek." [n] *Psalm 110:4*

7While Jesus lived on earth, he prayed to God and asked God for help. He prayed with loud cries and tears to the One who could save him from death, and his prayer was heard because he trusted God. 8Even though Jesus was the Son of God, he learned obedience by what he suffered. 9And because his obedience was perfect, he was able to give eternal salvation to all who obey him. 10In this way God made Jesus a high priest, a priest like Melchizedek.

Warning Against Falling Away

11We have much to say about this, but it is hard to explain because you are so slow to understand. 12By now you should be teachers, but you need someone to teach you again the first lessons of God's message. You still need the teaching that is like milk. You are not ready for solid food. 13Anyone who lives on milk is still a baby and knows nothing about right teaching. 14But solid food is for those who are grown up. They have practised in order to know the difference between good and evil.

6 So let us go on to grown-up teaching. Let us not go back over the beginning lessons we learned about Christ. We should not again start teaching about faith in God and about turning away from those acts that lead to death. 2We should not return to the teaching about baptisms, [n] about laying on of hands, [n] about the raising of the dead and eternal judgement. 3And we will go on to grown-up teaching if God allows.

4Some people cannot be brought back again to a changed life. They were once in God's light, and enjoyed heaven's gift, and shared in the Holy Spirit. [d] 5They found out how good God's word is, and they received the powers of his new world. 6But they fell away from Christ. It is impossible to bring them back to a changed life again, because they are nailing the Son of God to a cross again and are shaming him in front of others.

7Some people are like land that gets plenty of rain. The land produces a good crop for those who work it, and it receives God's blessings. 8Other people are like land that grows thorns and weeds and is worthless. It is in danger of being cursed by God and will be destroyed by fire.

9Dear friends, we are saying this to you, but we really expect better things from you that will lead to your salvation. 10God is fair; he will not forget the work you did and the love you showed for him by helping his people. And he will remember that you are still helping them. 11We want each of you to go on with the same hard work all your lives so you will surely get what you hope for. 12We do not want you to become lazy. Be like those who through faith and patience will receive what God has promised.

13God made a promise to Abraham. [n] And as there is no one greater than God, he used himself when he swore to Abraham, 14saying, "I will

> **Sidelight** Many scholars believe that the book of Hebrews may have originally been a sermon, partly because the author mentions speaking in several places (for example, in Hebrews 6:9). If it was originally a sermon, it would have taken about 50 minutes to read aloud. The services often included "breaking of bread" (communion), teaching, preaching, singing, praying, prophesying and reading letters.

Aaron Aaron was Moses' brother and the first Jewish high priest.
Melchizedek A priest and king who lived in the time of Abraham. (Read Genesis 14:17–24.)
baptisms The word here may refer to Christian baptism, or it may refer to the Jewish ceremonial washings.
laying on of hands The laying on of hands had many purposes, including the giving of a blessing, power or authority.
Abraham Most respected ancestor of the Jews. Every Jew hoped to see Abraham.

surely bless you and give you many descen-
dants." [n] [15]Abraham waited patiently for this to
happen, and he received what God promised.
[16]People always use the name of someone
greater than themselves when they swear. The
oath proves that what they say is true, and this
ends all arguing. [17]God wanted to prove that his
promise was true to those who would get what
he promised. And he wanted them to under-
stand clearly that his purposes never change, so
he made an oath. [18]These two things cannot
change: God cannot lie when he makes a prom-
ise, and he cannot lie when he makes an oath.
These things encourage us who came to God for
safety. They give us strength to hold on to the
hope we have been given. [19]We have this hope
as an anchor for the soul, sure and strong. It en-
ters behind the curtain in the Most Holy Place in
heaven, [20]where Jesus has gone ahead of us and
for us. He has become the high priest for ever, a
priest like Melchizedek. [n]

Sidelight If you think Melchizedek (Hebrews 7:1) is a hard name to say, try the Bible's longest name: Maher-Shalal-Hash-Baz, the name of Isaiah's son (Isaiah 8:1, p.647).

The Priest Melchizedek

7 Melchizedek [n] was the king of Salem and a
priest for God Most High. He met Abraham
when Abraham was coming back after defeating
the kings. When they met, Melchizedek blessed
Abraham, [2]and Abraham gave him a tenth of every-
thing he had brought back from the battle. First,
Melchizedek's name means "king of goodness",
and he is king of Salem, which means "king of
peace". [3]No one knows who Melchizedek's
father or mother was, [n] where he came from, when
he was born, or when he died. Melchizedek is like
the Son of God; he continues being a priest for ever.
[4]You can see how great Melchizedek was.
Abraham, the great father, gave him a tenth of
everything that he won in battle. [5]Now the law
says that those in the tribe [d] of Levi who become
priests must collect a tenth from the people—
their own people—even though the priests and
the people are from the family of Abraham.
[6]Melchizedek was not from the tribe of Levi, but
he collected a tenth from Abraham. And he
blessed Abraham, the man who had God's prom-
ises. [7]Now everyone knows that the more impor-
tant person blesses the less important person.
[8]Priests receive a tenth, even though they are only
men who live and then die. But Melchizedek,
who received a tenth from Abraham, continues
living, as the Scripture [d] says. [9]We might even say
that Levi, who receives a tenth, also paid it when
Abraham paid Melchizedek a tenth. [10]Levi was
not yet born, but he was in the body of his ances-
tor when Melchizedek met Abraham.
[11]The people were given the law [n] based on a
system of priests from the tribe of Levi, but they
could not be made perfect through that system.
So there was a need for another priest to come,
a priest like Melchizedek, not Aaron. [12]And when
a different kind of priest comes, the law must be
changed, too. [13]We are saying these things about
Christ, who belonged to a different tribe. No one
from that tribe ever served as a priest at the altar.
[14]It is clear that our Lord came from the tribe of
Judah, and Moses said nothing about priests be-
longing to that tribe.

Jesus is like Melchizedek

[15]And this becomes even more clear when
we see that another priest comes who is like
Melchizedek. [16]He was not made a priest by
human rules and laws but through the power of his
life, which continues for ever. [17]It is said about him,
"You are a priest for ever,
a priest like Melchizedek." *Psalm 110:4*
[18]The old rule is now set aside, because it was
weak and useless. [19]The law of Moses could not
make anything perfect. But now a better hope
has been given to us, and with this hope we can
come near to God. [20]It is important that God did
this with an oath. Others became priests without
an oath, [21]but Christ became a priest with God's
oath. God said:
"The Lord has made a promise
and will not change his mind.
'You are a priest for ever.' " *Psalm 110:4*
[22]This means that Jesus is the guarantee of a bet-
ter agreement [n] from God to his people.
[23]When one of the other priests died, he could
not continue being a priest. So there were many
priests. [24]But because Jesus lives for ever, he will
never stop serving as priest. [25]So he is able always
to save those who come to God through him be-
cause he always lives, asking God to help them.

"I . . . descendants." Quotation from Genesis 22:17.
Melchizedek A priest and king who lived in the time of Abraham. (Read Genesis 14:17–24.)
No one . . . was Literally, "Melchizedek was without father, without mother, without genealogy."
The . . . law This refers to the people of Israel who were given the law of Moses.
agreement God gives a contract or agreement to his people. For the Jews, this agreement was the law of Moses. But now God has given a better agreement to his people through Christ.

26Jesus is the kind of high priest we need. He
is holy, sinless, pure, not influenced by sinners
and he is raised above the heavens. 27He is not
like the other priests who had to offer sacrifices
every day, first for their own sins, and then for
the sins of the people. Christ offered his sacrifice
only once and for all time when he offered him-
self. 28The law chooses high priests who are peo-
ple with weaknesses, but the word of God's oath
came later than the law. It made God's Son to be
the high priest, and that Son has been made per-
fect for ever.

Jesus is Our High Priest

8 Here is the point of what we are saying: we
have a high priest who sits on the right side
of God's throne in heaven. 2Our high priest
serves in the Most Holy Place, the true place of
worship that was made by God, not by humans.
3Every high priest has the work of offering gifts
and sacrifices to God. So our high priest must also
offer something to God. 4If our high priest were
now living on earth, he would not be a priest,
because there are already priests here who follow
the law by offering gifts to God. 5The work they
do as priests is only a copy and a shadow of what
is in heaven. This is why God warned Moses
when he was ready to build the Holy Tent:[d] "Be
very careful to make everything by the plan I
showed you on the mountain."[n] 6But the priestly
work that has been given to Jesus is much greater
than the work that was given to the other priests.
In the same way, the new agreement that Jesus
brought from God to his people is much greater
than the old one. And the new agreement is
based on promises of better things.
7If there had been nothing wrong with the first
agreement,[n] there would have been no need for
a second agreement. 8But God found something
wrong with his people. He says:

"Look, the time is coming, says the LORD,
when I will make a new agreement
with the people of Israel
and the people of Judah.
9It will not be like the agreement
I made with their ancestors
when I took them by the hand
to bring them out of Egypt.
But they broke that agreement,
and I turned away from them, says the
LORD.
10This is the agreement I will make
with the people of Israel at that time, says
the LORD.
I will put my Teachings in their minds
and write them on their hearts.
I will be their God,
and they will be my people.
11People will no longer have to teach their
neighbours and relatives
to know the LORD,
because all people will know me,
from the least to the most important.
12I will forgive them for the wicked things
they did,
and I will not remember their sins any
more." *Jeremiah 31:31–34*

13God called this a new agreement, and so he
has made the first agreement old. And anything
that is old and worn out is ready to disappear.

The Old Agreement

9 The first agreement[n] had rules for worship
and a man-made place for worship. 2The
Holy Tent[d] was set up for this. The first area in
the Tent was called the Holy Place. In it were the
lamp and the table with the bread that was made
holy for God. 3Behind the second curtain was a
room called the Most Holy Place. 4In it was a
golden altar for burning incense[d] and the Ark[d]
covered with gold that held the old agreement.
Inside this Ark was a golden jar of manna,[d]
Aaron's rod that once grew leaves, and the stone
tablets[n] of the old agreement. 5Above the Ark
were the creatures that showed God's glory,
whose wings reached over the lid. But we cannot
tell everything about these things now.
6When everything in the Tent was made ready
in this way, the priests went into the first room
every day to worship. 7But only the high priest
could go into the second room, and he did that
only once a year. He could never enter the inner
room without taking blood with him, which he
offered to God for himself and for sins the people
did without knowing they did them. 8The Holy
Spirit[d] uses this to show that the way into the
Most Holy Place was not open while the system of
the old Holy Tent was still being used. 9This is an
example for the present time. It shows that the
gifts and sacrifices offered cannot make the con-
science of the worshipper perfect. 10These gifts
and sacrifices were only about food and drink and
special washings. They were rules for the body, to
be followed until the time of God's new way.

The New Agreement

11But when Christ came as the high priest of
the good things we now have, he entered the

"Be . . . mountain." Quotation from Exodus 25:40.
first agreement The contract God gave the Jewish people when he gave them the law of Moses.
stone tablets They were the two stone tablets on which God wrote the Ten Commandments.

greater and more perfect tent. It is not made
by humans and does not belong to this world.
12Christ entered the Most Holy Place only
once—and for all time. He did not take with him
the blood of goats and calves. His sacrifice was
his own blood, and by it he set us free from sin
for ever. 13The blood of goats and bulls and the
ashes of a cow are sprinkled on the people who
are unclean,[d] and this makes their bodies clean
again. 14How much more is done by the blood of
Christ! He offered himself through the eternal
Spirit[n] as a perfect sacrifice to God. His blood
will make our consciences pure from useless acts
so we may serve the living God.
15For this reason Christ brings a new agree-
ment from God to his people. Those who are
called by God can now receive the blessings he
has promised, blessings that will last for ever.
They can have those things because Christ died
so that the people who lived under the first agree-
ment could be set free from sin.
16When there is a will,[n] it must be proven that
the one who wrote that will is dead. 17A will
means nothing while the person is alive; it can be
used only after the person dies. 18This is why
even the first agreement could not begin without
blood to show death. 19First, Moses told all the
people every command in the law. Next he took
the blood of calves and mixed it with water. Then
he used red wool and a branch of the hyssop
plant to sprinkle it on the Book of the law and on
all the people. 20He said, "This is the blood that
begins the Agreement that God commanded you
to obey."[n] 21In the same way, Moses sprinkled

Spirit This refers to the Holy Spirit, to Christ's own spirit, or to the spiritual and eternal nature of his sacrifice.
will A legal document that shows how a person's money and property are to be distributed at the time of death. This is the same word in Greek as "agreement" in verse 15.
"This . . . obey." Quotation from Exodus 24:8.

SIN

Unexpected Forgiveness

Diane and Chris had been going out for about a year. Both were sixteen. When Diane stopped coming to youth group meetings, Donna, her youth leader, dropped by after school to see if she was OK.

Diane confessed that her relationship with Chris had got very physical. "I think I'm pregnant," she said. She and Chris had had sex on a date four weeks earlier. "It just happened. We didn't plan it," she kept saying.

"Have you told your parents?" Donna asked.

"No!" she screamed. "They would absolutely die if they knew!"

"That's not the main issue," Donna said. "They need to know, and you need their help."

Donna promised to stay with Diane until her parents came home from work. When Diane told them the news, they were upset at first, but they assured Diane that they loved her. What she had done was wrong, but it didn't change the way they felt about her. She was their daughter.

Diane learned a hard lesson about sex before marriage. She also learned a lot about the kind of forgiveness and acceptance written about in **Hebrews 9:11–28**.

- How was forgiveness by Diane's parents like and unlike the forgiveness described in this passage? How did the price that Diane's parents paid in the story differ from the price that Christ paid in the passage?
- How are our sins forgiven, according to the passage?

Consider . . .

- talking to a trusted adult about a sin that you're struggling with.
- defining the word "sin", using this passage and the ones listed in "For More, See . . ." for guidance. Find out whether your friends and minister agree with your definition.

For more, see . . .

- Genesis 4:1–12 (p.7)
- Romans 6:12–14 (p.1191)
- Romans 3:21–26 (p.1187)

the blood on the Holy Tent[d] and over all the things used in worship. 22The law says that almost everything must be made clean by blood, and sins cannot be forgiven without blood to show death.

Christ's Death Takes Away Sins

23So the copies of the real things in heaven had to be made clean[d] by animal sacrifices. But the real things in heaven need much better sacrifices. 24Christ did not go into the Most Holy Place made by humans, which is only a copy of the real one. He went into heaven itself and is there now before God to help us. 25The high priest enters the Most Holy Place once every year with blood that is not his own. But Christ did not offer himself many times. 26Then he would have had to suffer many times since the world was made. But Christ came only once and for all time at just the right time to take away all sin by sacrificing himself. 27Just as everyone must die once and be judged, 28so Christ was offered as a sacrifice once to take away the sins of many people. And he will come a second time, not to offer himself for sin, but to bring salvation to those who are waiting for him.

10 The law is only an unclear picture of the good things coming in the future; it is not the real thing. The people under the law offer the same sacrifices every year, but these sacrifices can never make perfect those who come near to worship God. 2If the law could make them perfect, the sacrifices would have already stopped. The worshippers would be made clean, and they would no longer have a sense of sin. 3But these sacrifices remind them of their sins every year, 4because it is impossible for the blood of bulls and goats to take away sins.

> **Sidelight**
> When Hebrews 10:1 talks about making "the same sacrifices every year", it refers to the annual Jewish holiday of Yom Kippur. On this day, the high priest would symbolically transfer the sins of Israel to a goat (known as a scapegoat). Then the goat would be carried away to the desert where it – along with the sins – would be lost and forgotten (see Leviticus 16:7–10, 20–22, p.115).

5So when Christ came into the world, he said:
"You do not want sacrifices and offerings,
but you have prepared a body for me.
6You do not ask for burnt offerings
and sacrifices to take away sins.
7Then I said, 'Look, I have come.
It is written about me in the book.
My God, I want to do what you want.'"
Psalm 40:6–8

8In this Scripture[d] he first said, "You do not want sacrifices and offerings. You do not ask for burnt offerings and offerings to take away sins." (These are all sacrifices that the law commands.) 9Then he said, "Look, I have come to do what you want." God ends the first system of sacrifices so he can set up the new system. 10And because of this, we are made holy through the sacrifice Christ made in his body once and for all time.

11Every day the priests stand and do their religious service, often offering the same sacrifices. Those sacrifices can never take away sins. 12But after Christ offered one sacrifice for sins, for ever, he sat down at the right side of God. 13And now Christ waits there for his enemies to be put under his power. 14With one sacrifice he made perfect for ever those who are being made holy.

15The Holy Spirit[d] also tells us about this. First he says:
16"This is the agreement[n] I will make
with them at that time, says the LORD.
I will put my teachings in their minds
and write them on their hearts." *Jeremiah 31:33*
17Then he says:
"Their sins and the evil things they do—
I will not remember any more." *Jeremiah 31:34*
18Now when these have been forgiven, there is no more need for a sacrifice for sins.

Continue to Trust God

19So, brothers and sisters, we are completely free to enter the Most Holy Place without fear because of the blood of Jesus' death. 20We can enter through a new and living way that Jesus opened for us. It leads us through the curtain[d]—Christ's body. 21And since we have a great priest over God's house, 22let us come near to God with a sincere heart and a sure faith, because we have been made free from a guilty conscience, and our bodies have been washed with pure water. 23Let us hold firmly to the hope that we have confessed, because we can trust God to do what he promised.

24Let us think about each other and help each other to show love and do good deeds. 25You should not stay away from the church meetings, as some are doing, but you should meet together

agreement God gives a contract or agreement to his people. For the Jews, this agreement was the law of Moses. But now God has given a better agreement to his people through Christ.

and encourage each other. Do this even more as
you see the day[n] coming.
26 If we decide to go on sinning after we have
learnt the truth, there is no longer any sacrifice
for sins. 27 There is nothing but fear in waiting for
the judgement and the terrible fire that will des-
troy all those who live against God. 28 Anyone
who refused to obey the law of Moses was found
guilty from the proof given by two or three wit-
nesses. He was put to death without mercy. 29 So
what do you think should be done to those who
do not respect the Son of God, who look at the
blood of the agreement that made them holy as
no different from others' blood, who insult the
Spirit[d] of God's grace? Surely they should have a
much worse punishment. 30 We know that God
said, "I will punish those who do wrong; I will
repay them."[n] And he also said, "The Lord will
judge his people."[n] 31 It is a terrible thing to fall
into the hands of the living God.

day The day Christ will come to judge all people and take his people to live with him.
"I . . . them." Quotation from Deuteronomy 32:35.
"The Lord . . . people." Quotation from Deuteronomy 32:36; Psalm 135:14.

CHURCH

Family of Friends

Jeremy had had a rough life. His parents were divorced, and he had bounced between one parent and the other. When he signed up for summer youth camp, everyone was surprised, since he had shown little interest in church until then.

When they arrived at the camp, the campers were split into groups of ten, each including an adult leader. The group would stay together for a week.

Jeremy started acting up immediately. His leader and the other campers tried to include him, but he ignored their kind gestures. His behaviour was rude and selfish.

Finally the camp leader, Cheryl, sat down with him after supper. When she asked Jeremy what he didn't like, he said, "All they do is sit around and talk about their problems. I'm bored."

Cheryl explained to Jeremy that they were trying to build relationships, and that he was choosing not to be a part. "You don't have to participate, but you must respect other people's feelings," she said.

Jeremy spent the next day listening. He watched the group care for each other. Before he knew it, he was telling the group about his family and how much he hated moving back and forth between parents.

The group listened. Then one of the boys spoke. "We will be family for you, if you'll let us," he offered Jeremy, and the others agreed.

Jeremy couldn't believe it at first. But through the week, the campers' concern and their openness to him convinced him.

On the last day of camp, Jeremy thanked the group. "I've never known what it meant to have a real family, until this week," he said. "I know things still won't be easy at home, but I know at least ten people who care."

Fortunately for Jeremy, he experienced the love of a group of committed Christians who wouldn't give up on him. In **Hebrews 10:19–39**, the writer talks about this kind of commitment to the family of God.

- How well did Jeremy's group live up to this passage's message?
- According to this passage, why do we need the church?

Consider . . .

- praying for someone at church who you think is incredibly rude or obnoxious. Then pray for help in understanding that person.
- accepting the care and concern of others if they invite you to church youth group meetings or outings. You may find new friends there.

For more, see . . .

- Isaiah 65:1–2 (p.710)
- Acts 2:43–47 (p.1141)
- Matthew 16:13–20 (p.969)

32 Remember those days in the past when you
first learnt the truth. You had a hard struggle with
many sufferings, but you continued strong.
33 Sometimes you were hurt and attacked before
crowds of people, and sometimes you shared
with those who were being treated that way.
34 You helped the prisoners. You even had joy
when all that you owned was taken from you,
because you knew you had something better and
more lasting.
35 So do not lose the courage you had in the
past, which has a great reward. 36 You must hold
on, so you can do what God wants and receive
what he has promised. 37 For in a very short time,

"The One who is coming will come
and will not be delayed.
38 The person who is right with me
will live by trusting in me.
But if he turns back with fear,
I will not be pleased with him." *Habakkuk 2:3–4*

39 But we are not those who turn back and are
lost. We are people who have faith and are saved.

What is Faith?

11 Faith means being sure of the things we
hope for and knowing that something
is real even if we do not see it. 2 Faith is the rea-
son we remember great people who lived in the
past.
3 It is by faith we understand that the whole
world was made by God's command so what we
see was made by something that cannot be seen.
4 It was by faith that Abel offered God a better
sacrifice than Cain did. God said he was pleased
with the gifts Abel offered and called Abel a good
man because of his faith. Abel died, but through
his faith he is still speaking.
5 It was by faith that Enoch was taken to
heaven so he would not die. He could not be
found, because God had taken him away. Before
he was taken, the Scripture[d] says that he was a
man who truly pleased God. 6 Without faith no
one can please God. Anyone who comes to God
must believe that he is real and that he rewards
those who truly want to find him.

FAITH

Not by Sight

After living with perfect sight for twelve years, Michelle became blind in a matter of seconds. A bad fall caused her to knock the back of her head and her sight was lost forever.

Suddenly, Michelle found herself in a strange world where images of her surroundings didn't exist. She had to learn to read Braille with her fingertips and to get around the house largely by memory.

Then the clinic told Michelle that they were going to give her a guide dog. When they did so, it took her a long time to get used to following an animal instead of her own two eyes.

"It was weird," she says. "All my life I'd been so independent, and now I have to walk not by sight, but by putting my faith in Elli, my guide dog."

In a similar way, the writer of Hebrews wanted Christians to understand how faith sometimes requires us to believe in things that we can't see or hear. He goes on to give some examples of people who lived not by sight, but by faith, in **Hebrews 11:1–16**.

- How is Michelle like the people that the writer of Hebrews uses as examples?
- When have you ever trusted God in "blind faith"? What happened? How would you describe your experience to others?

Consider . . .

- developing an area of your faith that you know is weak, such as witnessing, or serving others.
- how you often trust other people even when you don't realise it (such as having faith in the bus driver to get you safely to a destination), then compare how often you put your faith in God alone.

For more, see . . .

- Genesis 12:1–5 (p.14)
- Romans 4:13–25 (p.1189)
- Mark 4:35–41 (p.1005)

[7]It was by faith that Noah heard God's warnings about things he could not yet see. He obeyed God and built a large boat to save his family. By his faith, Noah showed that the world was wrong, and he became one of those who are made right with God through faith.

[8]It was by faith Abraham obeyed God's call to go to another place God promised to give him. He left his own country, not knowing where he was to go. [9]It was by faith that he lived like a foreigner in the country God promised to give him. He lived in tents with Isaac and Jacob, who had received that same promise from God. [10]Abraham was waiting for the city[n] that has real foundations—the city planned and built by God.

[11]He was too old to have children, and Sarah could not have children. It was by faith that Abraham was made able to become a father, because he trusted God to do what he had promised. [12]This man was so old he was almost dead, but from him came as many descendants[d] as there are stars in the sky. Like the sand on the seashore, they could not be counted.

[13]All these great people died in faith. They did not get the things that God promised his people, but they saw them coming far in the future and were glad. They said they were like visitors and strangers on earth. [14]When people say such things, they show they are looking for a country that will be their own. [15]If they had been thinking about the country they had left, they could have gone back. [16]But they were waiting for a better country—a heavenly country. So God is not ashamed to be called their God, because he has prepared a city for them.

[17]It was by faith that Abraham, when God tested him, offered his son Isaac as a sacrifice. God made the promises to Abraham, but Abraham was ready to offer his own son as a sacrifice. [18]God had said, "The descendants I promised you will be from Isaac."[n] [19]Abraham believed that God could raise the dead, and really, it was as if Abraham got Isaac back from death.

[20]It was by faith that Isaac blessed the future of Jacob and Esau. [21]It was by faith that Jacob, as he was dying, blessed each one of Joseph's sons. Then he worshipped as he leaned on the top of his walking stick.

[22]It was by faith that Joseph, while he was dying, spoke about the Israelites leaving Egypt and told about what to do with his body.

[23]It was by faith that Moses' parents hid him for three months after he was born. They saw that Moses was a beautiful baby, and they were not afraid to disobey the king's order.

[24]It was by faith that Moses, when he grew up, refused to be called the son of the king of Egypt's daughter. [25]He chose to suffer with God's people instead of enjoying sin for a short time. [26]He thought it was better to suffer for the Christ[d] than to have all the treasures of Egypt, because he was looking for God's reward. [27]It was by faith that Moses left Egypt and was not afraid of the king's anger. Moses continued strong as if he could see the God that no one can see. [28]It was by faith that Moses prepared the Passover[d] and spread the blood on the doors so the one who brings death would not kill the firstborn[d] sons of Israel.

[29]It was by faith that the people crossed the Red Sea as if it were dry land. But when the Egyptians tried it, they were drowned.

[30]It was by faith that the walls of Jericho fell after the people had marched around them for seven days.

[31]It was by faith that Rahab, the prostitute,[d] welcomed the spies and was not killed with those who refused to obey God.

[32]Do I need to give more examples? I do not have time to tell you about Gideon, Barak, Samson, Jephthah, David, Samuel and the prophets.[d] [33]Through their faith they defeated kingdoms. They did what was right, received God's promises and shut the mouths of lions. [34]They stopped great fires and were saved from being killed with swords. They were weak, and yet were made strong. They were powerful in battle and defeated other armies. [35]Women received their dead relatives raised back to life. Others were tortured and refused to accept their freedom so they could be raised from the dead to a better life. [36]Some were laughed at and beaten. Others were put in chains and thrown into prison. [37]They were stoned to death, they were cut in half and they were killed with swords. Some wore the skins of sheep and goats. They were poor, abused and treated badly. [38]The world was not good enough for them! They wandered in deserts

Sidelight If you think you have had a hard life, read Hebrews 11:32–38. When verse 37 talks about being "cut in half", it may refer to the prophet Isaiah (p.638), who, according to tradition, met this fate.

city The spiritual "city" where God's people live with him. Also called "the heavenly Jerusalem". (See Hebrews 12:22.)
"The descendants . . . Isaac." Quotation from Genesis 21:12.

and mountains, living in caves and holes in the
earth.
39All these people are known for their faith, but
none of them received what God had promised.
40God planned to give us something better so that
they would be made perfect, along with us.

Follow Jesus' Example

12 We have around us many people whose
lives tell us what faith means. So let us
run the race that is before us and never give up.
We should remove from our lives anything that
would get in the way and the sin that so easily
holds us back. 2Let us look only to Jesus, the One
who began our faith and who makes it perfect.
He suffered death on the cross. But he accepted
the shame as if it were nothing because of the joy
that God put before him. And now he is sitting
at the right side of God's throne. 3Think about
Jesus' example. He held on while wicked people
were doing evil things to him. So do not get tired
and stop trying.

God is Like a Father

4You are struggling against sin, but your
struggles have not yet caused you to be killed.

PERSISTENCE

Worth the Effort

They'd been told that the "Adventure Breaks" were tough, but this weekend was more than they had bargained for.

In order to reach the small huts where they were staying for the weekend, the small group of adventurers had hiked for five miles in the simmering, humid heat of a July heatwave. They'd been given an hour to unpack their rucksacks and have something to eat, then they went canoeing for three hours.

They returned to their huts tired and wet. After just two hours of free time, the group again ventured into the wilderness and spent that first Friday evening learning a little about how to survive in the wild.

Saturday morning had seen the group on the assault course. The various obstacles were designed to push the young teenagers to the limit . . . and beyond.

Having completed the gruelling course, the 30 youngsters were now hiking back to their huts for a brief rest.

"I can't go on!" Tony wheezed as he climbed the hill.

Will knew what his friend meant. It was only Saturday lunchtime and they still had almost a day and a half to go. The rest of the programme included cross country running, climbing, abseiling and various other strenuous activities.

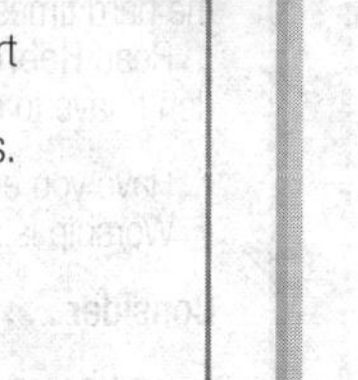

Tony stopped to catch his breath. "I wish I'd never come."

Will smiled. "You'll feel different when it's over," he said. "The key to making the whole weekend worthwhile is *persistence*."

Tony shook his head and continued.

On Sunday afternoon, Tony had decided that Will was right. The weekend *had* been worth the effort after all. The simple fact that he'd managed to stick out the whole course made him feel good.

Read **Hebrews 12:1–13** and discover the importance of being persistent in our lives as Christians.

- Why is persistence important according to the passage?
- Have you ever felt like Tony and wanted to give up? What made you feel that way?

Consider . . .

- completing a project which you have started and put to one side.
- being persistent where your Bible reading is concerned. Set yourself a target for the coming week and stick with it.

For more, see . . .

- Isaiah 42:1–4 (p.682)
- Ephesians 6:10–18 (p.1277)
- Luke 18:1–5 (p.1078)

5 You have forgotten the encouraging words that
call you his children:

"My child, don't think the Lord's discipline is
worth nothing,
and don't get angry when he corrects you.
6 The Lord corrects those he loves,
and he punishes everyone he accepts as his
child." *Proverbs 3:11–12*

7 So hold on through your sufferings, because
they are like a father's discipline. God is treating
you as children. All children are disciplined by their
fathers. 8 If you are never disciplined (and every
child must be disciplined), you are not true chil-
dren. 9 We have all had fathers here on earth who
disciplined us, and we respected them. So it is even
more important that we accept discipline from the
Father of our spirits so we will have life. 10 Our
fathers on earth disciplined us for a short time in
the way they thought was best. But God disciplines
us to help us, so we can become holy as he is. 11 We
do not enjoy being disciplined. It is painful, but
later, after we have learned from it, we have peace,
because we start living in the right way.

Be Careful How You Live

12 You have become weak, so make yourselves
strong again. 13 Live in the right way so that you
will be saved and your weakness will not cause
you to be lost.
14 Try to live in peace with all people, and try to
live free from sin. Anyone whose life is not holy
will never see the Lord. 15 Be careful that no one
fails to receive God's grace and begins to cause
trouble among you. A person like that can ruin
many of you. 16 Be careful that no one takes part
in sexual sin or is like Esau and never thinks

WORSHIP

No Matter What

On Wednesday evening, Kerrie and Sam went for a meal to catch up on each other's news. Sam was really enjoying uni life, doing whatever she wanted – sleeping with loads of guys, getting drunk, smoking and having a good time. Kerrie was listening to all of her stories thinking what a change had taken place. The girls used to pray for their school and pray for people who were making the kind of choices Sam was making.

Confused by what she heard, Kerrie asked Sam how her walk with God was going. Sam's reply was simple: "Look I've done so much stuff in my life that's wrong, how can I worship God or even talk to him? I've sinned so many times that I can't get my life back to what it was before."

Kerrie explained to Sam that we don't need to come to God with our lives totally sorted. We need to go to him and be in his presence and ask him about our lives, ask him to forgive us. Running away from God and looking to things that don't give us true joy and even harm us is not the answer.

As time went on, Sam got back into a real relationship with God and worked through the habits of her daily life. She discovered that God doesn't want perfect people, he wants people with broken hearts, confused lives and with imperfections to come to him and to worship him through the hard times as well as the good.

Read **Hebrews 12:18–25**. It talks of the complete forgiveness Jesus has to offer and that we don't have to come to him perfect, but with a heart that lifts him up no matter what.

- Have you ever felt that it's too hard or that you are unworthy to worship God?
- Worship is so much more than just singing. What ways other than singing can we worship God?

Consider . . .

- whether you are feeling that you've sinned beyond repair. It is not uncommon. Remember that God loves you and forgives everything that you've done if you just ask him. You have been saved from your sins by Jesus' death on the cross.
- whether you know anyone who is trying to run away from God. Rather than telling them what they're doing wrong, remind them of his never-ending love and forgiveness.

For more, see . . .

- Psalm 24:3–5 (p.514)
- Luke 15:11–32 (p.1071)
- Psalm 51:10–17 (p.530)

about God. As the elder son, Esau would have re-
ceived everything from his father, but he sold all
that for a single meal. 17You remember that after
Esau did this, he wanted to get his father's bless-
ing, but his father refused. Esau could find no
way to change what he had done, even though
he wanted the blessing so much that he cried.

18You have not come to a mountain that can
be touched and that is burning with fire. You
have not come to darkness, sadness and storms.
19You have not come to the noise of a trumpet or
to the sound of a voice like the one the people of
Israel heard and begged not to hear another
word. 20They did not want to hear the com-
mand: "If anything, even an animal, touches the
mountain, it must be put to death with stones."[n]
21What they saw was so terrible that Moses said,
"I am shaking with fear."[n]

22But you have come to Mount Zion, to the
city of the living God, the heavenly Jerusalem.
You have come to thousands of angels gathered
together with joy. 23You have come to the meet-
ing of God's first-born[n] children whose names
are written in heaven. You have come to God,
the judge of all people, and to the spirits of good
people who have been made perfect. 24You have
come to Jesus, the One who brought the new
agreement from God to his people, and you have
come to the sprinkled blood[n] that has a better
message than the blood of Abel.[n]

25So be careful and do not refuse to listen
when God speaks. Others refused to listen to him
when he warned them on earth, and they did not
escape. So it will be worse for us if we refuse to
listen to God who warns us from heaven. 26When
he spoke before, his voice shook the earth, but
now he has promised, "Once again I will shake
not only the earth but also the heavens."[n] 27The
words "once again" clearly show us that every-
thing that was made—things that can be
shaken—will be destroyed. Only the things that
cannot be shaken will remain.

28So let us be thankful, because we have a
kingdom that cannot be shaken. We should wor-
ship God in a way that pleases him with respect
and fear, 29because our God is like a fire that
burns things up.

13 Keep on loving each other as brothers and
sisters. 2Remember to welcome strangers,
because some who have done this have welcomed
angels without knowing it. 3Remember those who
are in prison as if you were in prison with them.
Remember those who are suffering as if you
were suffering with them.

4Marriage should be honoured by everyone,
and husband and wife should keep their mar-
riage pure. God will judge as guilty those who
take part in sexual sins. 5Keep your lives free
from the love of money, and be satisfied with
what you have. God has said,

"I will never leave you;
I will never forget you." *Deuteronomy 31:6*

6So we can be sure when we say,

"I will not be afraid, because the Lord is my
helper.
People can't do anything to me." *Psalm 118:6*

7Remember your leaders who taught God's
message to you. Remember how they lived and
died, and copy their faith. 8Jesus Christ is the
same yesterday, today and for ever.

9Do not let all kinds of strange teachings lead
you into the wrong way. Your hearts should be
strengthened by God's grace, not by obeying
rules about foods, which do not help those who
obey them.

10We have a sacrifice, but the priests who serve
in the Holy Tent[d] cannot eat from it. 11The high
priest carries the blood of animals into the Most
Holy Place where he offers this blood for sins. But
the bodies of the animals are burnt outside the
camp. 12So Jesus also suffered outside the city to
make his people holy with his own blood. 13So let
us go to Jesus outside the camp, holding on as he
did when he bore our disgrace.

14Here on earth we do not have a city that lasts
for ever, but we are looking for the city that we
will have in the future. 15So through Jesus let us
always offer to God our sacrifice of praise, coming
from lips that speak his name. 16Do not forget to
do good to others, and share with them, because
such sacrifices please God.

17Obey your leaders and act under their au-
thority. They are watching over you, because
they are responsible for your souls. Obey them so
that they will do this work with joy, not sadness.
It will not help you to make their work hard.

18Pray for us. We are sure that we have a clear
conscience, because we always want to do the
right thing. 19I especially beg you to pray so that
God will send me back to you soon.

"If . . . stones." Quotation from Exodus 19:12–13.
"I . . . fear." Quotation from Deuteronomy 9:19.
first-born The first son born in a Jewish family was given the most important place in the family and received special blessings. All of God's children are like that.
sprinkled blood The blood of Jesus' death.
Abel The son of Adam and Eve, who was killed by his brother Cain (Genesis 4:8).
"Once . . . heavens." Quotation from Haggai 2:6,21.

20-21I pray that the God of peace will give you
every good thing you need so you can do what
he wants. God raised from the dead our Lord
Jesus, the Great Shepherd of the sheep, because
of the blood of his death. His blood began the
eternal agreement that God made with his peo-
ple. I pray that God will do in us what pleases
him, through Jesus Christ, and to him be glory
for ever and ever. Amen.

22My brothers and sisters, I beg you to listen
patiently to this message I have written to en-
courage you, because it is not very long. 23I want
you to know that our brother Timothy has been
let out of prison. If he arrives soon, we will both
come to see you.

24Greet all your leaders and all of God's people.
Those from Italy send greetings to you.

25Grace be with you all.

SERVICE

Seeing is Believing

James and Lucy were just married. They didn't have their own place, but were renting half of a house. They didn't have a lot, but were thrilled with the carpet and furnishings provided by their friends.

One day they came home to find the lounge flooded. Water was pouring through the ceiling where the people upstairs had left a tap on. The new carpet was ruined and they just stood in despair. A Christian friend chose that moment to call round and see how they were doing. He took one look at the situation and said, "Get your coats, we're going out for a meal!"

"We can't leave this mess!" they both wailed. But he insisted, and took them to a good restaurant and they gradually relaxed in his company. By the time he paid the bill, they were feeling much better.

He turned to them and said, "OK, let's go and tackle the problem!"

Between the three of them, they dragged the carpet onto the lawn outside and dried it out.

Afterwards, James said to Lucy, "I think we've just seen a sermon in action!"

Hebrews 13:1–8 reminds us to care for each other in many different ways.

- How did the Christian friend's attitude compare with this passage?
- Which of these teachings apply to your own life?

Consider . . .

- phoning someone who has done something for you lately to let them know you appreciate what they have done.
- doing something for someone in need, such as gardening, or running an errand.

For more, see . . .

- Matthew 6:1–4 (p.947)
- Acts 4:32–35 (p.1144)
- Luke 7:1–10 (p.1049)

James

Why Read This Book:

- Learn how to handle temptation, testing and trouble (James 1).
- Understand the connection between what you believe and what you do (James 2—3).
- See what can happen when you let God be in charge of your life (James 4—5).

When?

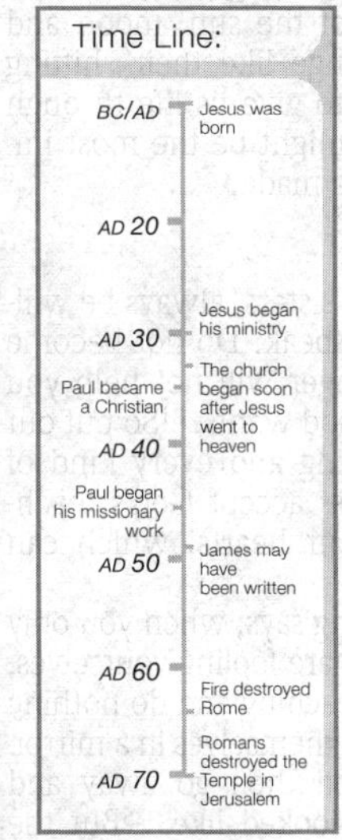

Behind the Scenes:

If someone says, "Would you mind taking out the rubbish?" it's easy to forget or find some excuse for not doing it. But suppose someone says, "Take out the rubbish!" It's hard to ignore the demand or find an excuse not to do it.

The book of James is like the second example. Its guidance is so clear that it is hard to ignore. "Do not become angry easily" (James 1:19). "Never think some people are more important than others (James 2:1). "Do not tell evil lies about each other" (James 4:11). In fact, James has more than 50 direct commands in just five chapters!

While much of the New Testament focuses on what Christians believe, James focuses on how Christians behave. Some early Christians apparently thought they could do whatever they wanted because God would forgive them anyway. But James warns them that "if people say they have faith, but do nothing, their faith is worth nothing" (James 2:14).

This short book is loaded with advice on putting our faith into action. It covers many areas of life that we continue to struggle with: handling money, relations between the rich and poor, boasting, judging others, being patient. The book is as practical today as when it was written almost 2,000 years ago.

Where?

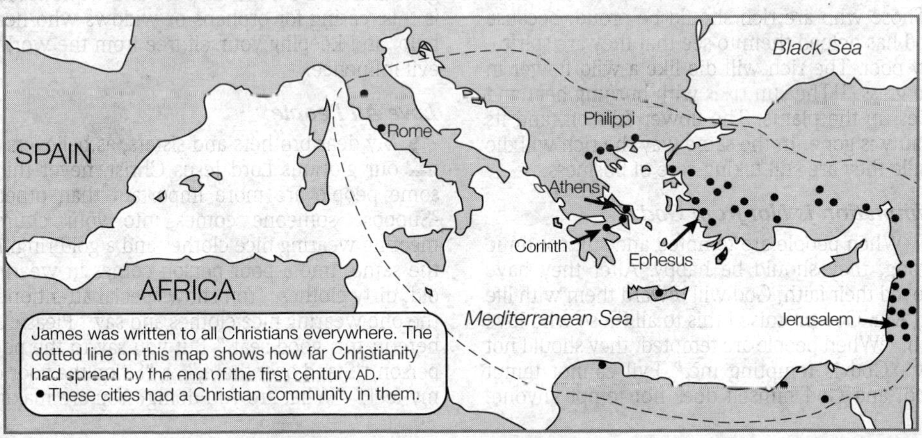

James was written to all Christians everywhere. The dotted line on this map shows how far Christianity had spread by the end of the first century AD.
• These cities had a Christian community in them.

1 From James, a servant of God and of the
Lord Jesus Christ.
To all of God's people who are scattered every-
where in the world:

Greetings.

Faith and Wisdom

2My brothers and sisters,[n] when you have
many kinds of troubles, you should be full of joy,
3because you know that these troubles test your

> **Sidelight** James was a common name in the first century, so we are not sure who wrote this letter. One theory is that the author was a brother of Jesus. This James became the leader of the Jerusalem church and later was put to death because of his faith.

faith, and this will give you patience. 4Let your
patience show itself perfectly in what you do.
Then you will be perfect and complete and will
have everything you need. 5But if any of you
needs wisdom, you should ask God for it. He is
generous and enjoys giving to all people, so he
will give you wisdom. 6But when you ask God,
you must believe and not doubt. Anyone who
doubts is like a wave in the sea, blown up and
down by the wind. 7–8Such who doubt are think-
ing two different things at the same time, and
they cannot decide about anything they do. They
should not think they will receive anything from
the Lord.

True Riches

9Believers who are poor should be proud, be-
cause God has made them spiritually rich.
10Those who are rich should be proud, because
God has helped them to see that they are spiritu-
ally poor. The rich will die like a wild flower in
the grass. 11The sun rises with burning heat and
dries up the plants. The flower falls off, and its
beauty is gone. In the same way the rich will die
while they are still taking care of business.

Temptation is Not from God

12When people are tempted and still continue
strong, they should be happy. After they have
proved their faith, God will reward them with life
for ever. God promised this to all those who love
him. 13When people are tempted, they should not
say, "God is tempting me." Evil cannot tempt
God, and God himself does not tempt anyone.
14But people are tempted when their own evil
desire leads them away and traps them. 15This
desire leads to sin, and then the sin grows and
brings death.
16My dear brothers and sisters, do not be
fooled about this. 17Every good action and every
perfect gift is from God. These good gifts come
down from the Creator of the sun, moon and
stars, who does not change like their shifting
shadows. 18God decided to give us life through
the word of truth so we might be the most im-
portant of all the things he made.

Listening and Obeying

19My dear brothers and sisters, always be will-
ing to listen and slow to speak. Do not become
angry easily, 20because anger will not help you
live the right kind of life God wants. 21So put out
of your life every evil thing and every kind of
wrong. Then in gentleness accept God's teach-
ing that is planted in your hearts, which can
save you.
22Do what God's teaching says; when you only
listen and do nothing, you are fooling yourselves.
23Those who hear God's teaching and do nothing
are like people who look at themselves in a mirror.
24They see their faces and then go away and
quickly forget what they looked like. 25But the
truly happy people are those who carefully study
God's perfect law that makes people free, and
they continue to study it. They do not forget what
they heard, but they obey what God's teaching
says. Those who do this will be made happy.

The True Way to Worship God

26People who think they are religious but say
things they should not say are just fooling them-
selves. Their "religion" is worth nothing. 27Reli-
gion that God accepts as pure and without fault
is this: caring for orphans or widows who need
help, and keeping yourself free from the world's
evil influence.

Love All People

2 My dear brothers and sisters, as believers in
our glorious Lord Jesus Christ, never think
some people are more important than others.
2Suppose someone comes into your church
meeting wearing nice clothes and a gold ring. At
the same time a poor person comes in wearing
old, dirty clothes. 3You show special attention to
the one wearing nice clothes and say, "Please, sit
here in this good seat." But you say to the poor
person, "Stand over there," or, "Sit on the floor by
my feet." 4What are you doing? You are making

brothers and sisters Although the Greek text says "brothers" here and throughout this book, James' words were meant for the entire church, both men and women.

some people more important than others, and
with evil thoughts you are deciding that one per-
son is better.
[5]Listen, my dear brothers and sisters! God
chose the poor in the world to be rich with faith
and to receive the kingdom God promised to
those who love him. [6]But you show no respect
to the poor. The rich are always trying to control
your lives. They are the ones who take you to
court. [7]And they are the ones who speak against
Jesus, who owns you.
[8]This royal law is found in the Scriptures:[d]
"Love your neighbour as you love yourself."[n] If
you obey this law, you are doing right. [9]But if you
treat one person as being more important than
another, you are sinning. You are guilty of break-
ing God's law. [10]A person who follows all of

"Love . . . yourself." Quotation from Leviticus 19:18.

Sidelight Wearing a gold ring (James 2:2) was a sign of great wealth in New Testament times. People who wanted to show off their wealth would cover their fingers with rings, often several on each finger. They would even rent rings when they particularly wanted to impress people. Imagine the car they would hire to go to the prom!

BIBLE STUDY

Happy People

How many times have you been listening to someone talk and then realised that your mind has been a thousand miles away? And just how embarrassed have you felt when someone has asked you a question relating to that talk? Sometimes it's not even that you didn't want to hear it, but your mind just wandered!

James 1:25 tells us that people who remember what they heard are "happy people" – but it also says that they studied and memorised too!

Here's something to think about:

- You remember 10 per cent of what you hear.
- You remember 30 per cent of what you write down.
- You remember 45 per cent of what you study . . . and . . .
- 100 per cent of what you memorise!

When Ruth went on a youth weekend, she was told that there would be a big prize for whoever could memorise the most of part of the Bible. Some kids were going for 50 words (that's three or four verses), some decided to get together and test each other on a whole parable (word perfect!). Ruth went for Genesis chapter 1. On the final night of the holiday, ten kids had learnt more scripture than they'd ever learnt before. The guy that came third had learnt 230 words! The guy that came second could remember 340 words! Ruth won, she doggedly kept going until she could recite over 500 words of the story of creation!

Sometimes we just need a little incentive, but each of these kids was thrilled to realise that God's word could be fun to learn and then easy to use!

Read **James 1:17–27** to discover what James says about studying the Bible.

- What happens if you hear and do nothing?
- How might your life change if you accepted James's challenge?

Consider . . .

- memorising a few important verses of scripture and repeating them daily.
- taking notes the next time you hear a sermon in church. You'll be amazed how much you will remember.

For more, see . . .

- Psalm 119:9–16 (p.571)
- Acts 17:11 (p.1168)
- Luke 11:27–28 (p.1061)

God's law but fails to obey even one command is
guilty of breaking all the commands in that law.
11The same God who said, "You must not be guilty
of adultery,"[d,n] also said, "You must not murder
anyone."[n] So if you do not take part in adultery
but you murder someone, you are guilty of break-
ing all of God's law. 12In everything you say and
do, remember that you will be judged by the law
that makes people free. 13So you must show mercy
to others, or God will not show mercy to you
when he judges you. But the person who shows
mercy can stand without fear at the judgement.

Faith and Good Works

14My brothers and sisters, if people say they have
faith, but do nothing, their faith is worth nothing.
Can faith like that save them? 15A brother or sis-
ter in Christ might need clothes or food. 16If you
say to that person, "God be with you! I hope you
stay warm and get plenty to eat," but you do not
give what that person needs, your words are
worth nothing. 17In the same way, faith that is
alone—that does nothing—is dead.

18Someone might say, "You have faith, but I
have deeds." Show me your faith without doing
anything, and I will show you my faith by what I
do. 19You believe there is one God. Good! But
the demons[d] believe that too, and they tremble
with fear.

20You foolish person! Must you be shown that
faith that does nothing is worth nothing? 21Abra-
ham, our ancestor, was made right with God by

"You . . . adultery," Quotation from Exodus 20:14; Deuteronomy 5:18.
"You . . . anyone." Quotation from Exodus 20:13; Deuteronomy 5:17.

STEREOTYPES

A Perfect Ten?

Pat and her friends moved down the food queue. Two boys serving food watched Pat and the other girls, and grinned. When she got near them, they reached under the counter, pulled out two cardboard signs with numbers, and put them on a high ledge behind them. "9" and "5", Pat thought, reading the cards. "I wonder what they mean?"

When Pat's friend Mary got to the same place in the queue, the boys changed the numbers to an "8" and a "6". By now everybody had stopped eating to watch. When the next girl in the queue received a "9" and a "7", people cheered. "They're rating us," Pat suddenly realised. Her face turned red.

Pat and her friends laughed uncomfortably as the two boys continued to rate girls as they passed in line. Then Debbie joined the queue. She wasn't "perfect-looking" and was a bit overweight. Pat dreaded how the boys might rate Debbie. But as she passed along the queue, the boys just ignored her. They didn't rate her at all. Then, when other "better-looking" girls came up in the line, the boys resumed their rating game. But the game wasn't funny to Pat. She felt judged, and imagined how hurt Debbie probably felt.

Sometimes it may seem like fun to judge other people, but being judged is rarely funny. Read in **James 2:1–17** what James wrote about treating people as though they are more important than others.

- What does James say is wrong with judging people the way the boys were rating the girls in the food queue?
- When have you judged someone unfairly because of clothes or grades or skill at sports? What makes us fall into doing things like that?

Consider . . .

- thinking about one person that you have judged. The next time you see this person, say, "Hello".
- watching this week how often you put people down. Whenever you realise that you have put someone down, quickly say something that builds the person up too.

For more, see . . .

- 1 Samuel 16:7 (p.269)
- Romans 12:14–16 (p.1205)
- Matthew 7:1–5 (p.949)

what he did when he offered his son Isaac on the
altar. 22So you see that Abraham's faith and the
things he did worked together. His faith was
made perfect by what he did. 23This shows the
full meaning of the Scripture[d] that says: "Abraham
believed God, and God accepted Abraham's
faith, and that faith made him right with God."[n]
And Abraham was called God's friend.[n] 24So you
see that people are made right with God by what
they do, not by faith only.

25Another example is Rahab, a prostitute,[d]
who was made right with God by something she
did. She welcomed the spies into her home and
helped them escape by a different road.
26Just as a person's body that does not have a
spirit is dead, so faith that does nothing is dead!

Controlling the Things We Say

3 My brothers and sisters, not many of you
should become teachers, because you know
that we who teach will be judged more strictly.
2We all make many mistakes. If people never said
anything wrong, they would be perfect and able
to control their entire selves too. 3When we put
bits into the mouths of horses to make them obey
us, we can control their whole bodies. 4Also a
ship is very big, and it is pushed by strong winds.
But a very small rudder controls that big ship,
making it go wherever the person wants. 5It is the
same with the tongue. It is a small part of the
body, but it boasts about great things.

A big forest fire can be started with only a little
flame. 6And the tongue is like a fire. It is a whole
world of evil among the parts of our bodies. The
tongue spreads its evil through the whole body.
The tongue is set on fire by hell, and it starts a fire
that influences all of life. 7People can tame every
kind of wild animal, bird, reptile and fish, and
they have tamed them, 8but no one can tame the
tongue. It is wild and evil and full of deadly
poison. 9We use our tongues to praise our Lord
and Father, but then we curse people, whom
God made like himself. 10Praises and curses come
from the same mouth! My brothers and sisters,
this should not happen. 11Do good and bad water
flow from the same spring? 12My brothers and
sisters, can a fig tree make olives, or can a grape-
vine make figs? No! And a well full of salty water
cannot give good water.

True Wisdom

13Are there those among you who are truly
wise and understanding? Then they should show
it by living right and doing good things with a
gentleness that comes from wisdom. 14But if you
are selfish and have bitter jealousy in your hearts,
do not boast. Your boasting is a lie that hides the
truth. 15That kind of "wisdom" does not come
from God but from the world. It is not spiritual;
it is from the devil. 16Where jealousy and selfish-
ness are, there will be confusion and every kind
of evil. 17But the wisdom that comes from God is
first of all pure, then peaceful, gentle and easy to
please. This wisdom is always ready to help those
who are troubled and to do good for others. It is
always fair and honest. 18People who work for
peace in a peaceful way plant a good crop of good
living.

Give Yourselves to God

4 Do you know where your fights and argu-
ments come from? They come from the self-
ish desires that war within you. 2You want
things, but you do not have them. So you are
ready to kill and are jealous of other people, but
you still cannot get what you want. So you argue
and fight. You do not get what you want, because
you do not ask God. 3Or when you ask, you do
not receive because the reason you ask is wrong.
You want things so you can use them for your
own pleasures.

4So, you are not loyal to God! You should
know that loving the world is the same as hating
God. Anyone who wants to be a friend of the
world becomes God's enemy. 5Do you think the
Scripture[d] means nothing that says, "The Spirit[d]
that God made to live in us wants us for himself
alone."[n] 6But God gives us even more grace, as
the Scripture says,

"God is against the proud,
but he gives grace to the humble."

Proverbs 3:34

7So give yourselves completely to God. Stand
against the devil, and the devil will run from
you. 8Come near to God, and God will come
near to you. You sinners, clean sin out of your
lives. You who are trying to follow God and the
world at the same time, make your thinking
pure. 9Be sad, cry and weep! Change your laugh-
ter into crying and your joy into sadness. 10Don't
be too proud in the Lord's presence, and he will
make you great.

You Are Not the Judge

11Brothers and sisters, do not tell evil lies about
each other. If you speak against your fellow be-
lievers or judge them, you are judging and speak-
ing against the law they follow. And when you
are judging the law, you are no longer a follower
of the law. You have become a judge. 12God is

"Abraham . . . God." Quotation from Genesis 15:6.
God's friend These words about Abraham are found in 2 Chronicles 20:7 and Isaiah 41:8.
"The Spirit . . . alone." These words may be from Exodus 20:5.

the only Lawmaker and Judge. He is the only
One who can save and destroy. So it is not right
for you to judge your neighbour.

Let God Plan Your Life

[13]Some of you say, "Today or tomorrow we
will go to some city. We will stay there a year, do
business and make money." [14]But you do not
know what will happen tomorrow! Your life is
like a mist. You can see it for a short time, but
then it goes away. [15]So you should say, "If the
Lord wants, we will live and do this or that."
[16]But now you are proud and you boast. All of
this boasting is wrong. [17]Anyone who knows the
right thing to do, but does not do it, is sinning.

A Warning to the Rich

5 You rich people, listen! Cry and be very sad
because of the troubles that are coming to
you. [2]Your riches have rotted, and your clothes
have been eaten by moths. [3]Your gold and silver
have rusted, and that rust will be a proof that you
were wrong. It will eat your bodies like fire. You
saved your treasure for the last days. [4]The pay
you did not give the workers who harvested
your fields cries out against you, and the cries of
the workers have been heard by the Lord All-
powerful. [5]Your life on earth was full of rich liv-
ing and pleasing yourselves with everything you
wanted. You made yourselves fat, like an animal
ready to be killed. [6]You have judged guilty and
then murdered innocent people, who were not
against you.

Be Patient

[7]Brothers and sisters, be patient until the Lord
comes again. A farmer patiently waits for his
valuable crop to grow from the earth and for it to
receive the autumn and spring rains. [8]You, too,
must be patient. Do not give up hope, because
the Lord is coming soon. [9]Brothers and sisters,
do not complain against each other or you will
be judged guilty. And the Judge is ready to come!
[10]Brothers and sisters, follow the example of the
prophets[d] who spoke for the Lord. They suffered
many hard things, but they were patient. [11]We
say they are happy because they did not give up.
You have heard about Job's patience, and you

BOASTING

Spain's Greatest Matador . . . Almost

Though only twenty-one years old, José Cubero had leaped to fame as one of Spain's most spectacular matadors. In bullfight after bullfight, he had dodged his way to triumph.

It was no surprise, then, when he made especially quick work of a bull during a routine bullfight. Thrusting his sword one last time, José watched the bull collapse on to the dirt of the arena. José had performed well, and he knew it. He turned to bask in the applause.

Enjoying the roaring cheers, José was unaware that the bull behind him was not dead. The bull suddenly rose and lunged, one of its horns piercing the matador from the back. José Cubero, a rising young star, was dead.

When we have done well, we like to get people's attention. We like to listen to the cheers. But James reminds us in **James 3:13–18** to do "good things with a gentleness that comes from wisdom." Boasting of our actions is a dangerous practice.

- What else might James have told José Cubero about boasting?
- What makes people eager to boast? Why might Christians have less need to boast?

Consider . . .

- noticing, as you watch television today, which characters boast. How do you feel about these characters?
- writing on a card this saying: "There's no limit to the amount of good you can do if you don't care who gets the credit." Place it where you will see it.

For more, see . . .

- Daniel 4:28–37 (p.837)
- Philippians 2:3–11 (p.1282)
- Luke 14:7–11 (p.1069)

know the Lord's purpose for him in the end. You know the Lord is full of mercy and is kind.

Be Careful What You Say

12My brothers and sisters, above all, do not
use an oath when you make a promise. Don't
use the name of heaven, earth or anything else
to prove what you say. When you mean yes, say
only "yes", and when you mean no, say only
"no" so you will not be judged guilty.

The Power of Prayer

13Anyone who is having troubles should
pray. Anyone who is happy should sing praises.
14Anyone who is sick should call the church's
elders.[d] They should pray for and pour oil on
the person[n] in the name of the Lord. 15And the
prayer that is said with faith will make the

Sidelight Using oil as medicine was a common practice in Bible times (James 5:14). The good Samaritan in Jesus' parable poured oil on the victim's wounds (Luke 10:34, p.1058). People who had headaches probably had the greasiest heads in town!

pour oil on the person Oil was used in the name of the Lord as a sign that the person was now set apart for God's special attention and care.

GOD'S WILL

Thy Will be Done

It's so easy to fantasise about what you would do if you were all of a sudden struck down by some fatal disease. How you would react, how you would be a martyr and accept it. But most of us know that deep down, we would be terrified and yell at God about the unfairness of it all.

Mark was twenty-one years old. Good looking, athletic, he had a host of admirers. One day he had a headache, and by the evening he was feeling really bad. By the next morning he was in intensive care with a suspected brain tumour. His close friends came to see him at the hospital and nobody knew what to say.

"Don't worry lads," he said. "God knows what he's doing."

His friends left the ward devastated. These things just didn't happen to someone like him.

Mark was released from hospital after an operation that was only half-successful. It left him knowing that he had maybe only a few months to live. His mother wanted him to stay at home and be looked after. His church wanted to help him. His friends wanted him to do whatever he felt he should do.

So Mark went into schools, telling kids about his faith in Jesus and the fact that life was precious. He told them about his own life and how it would shortly end, but he knew that God had planned it this way, and he was adamant about it.

Finally, Mark became paralysed and his friends rushed to his bedside where he asked to take communion with them.

As the wine was held to his lips, he whispered, "Isn't it wonderful what Jesus did for us?" and smiled.

He died shortly afterwards.

James 4:13–17 reminds us that our future is in God's hands.

- How was Mark's faith relevant to this passage?
- What plans have you got for your future? How does God fit in to them?

Consider . . .

- evaluating your dreams for the future in the light of this passage on God's will.
- having an "In God's Hands" file. Write down those things that you have to face in the future that you cannot control . . . and commit them to God.

For more, see . . .

- Psalm 139 (p.581)
- Matthew 6:25–34 (p.948)
- Proverbs 16:1–9 (p.603)

sick person well; the Lord will heal that person.
And if the person has sinned, the sins will be
forgiven. 16Confess your sins to each other and
pray for each other so God can heal you. When a
believing person prays, great things happen. 17Eli-
jah was a human being just like us. He prayed
that it would not rain, and it did not
rain on the land for three and a half years! 18Then
Elijah prayed again, and the rain came down
from the sky, and the land produced crops again.

Saving a Soul

19My brothers and sisters, if one of you
wanders away from the truth, and someone
helps that person come back, 20remember this:
anyone who brings a sinner back from the wrong
way will save that sinner's soul from death and
will cause many sins to be forgiven.

PATIENCE

What Are You Waiting For?

Connor and Gaz had been friends since year 7. They were both really into skateboarding and spent many hours at the local skate park hanging out with the older lads, perfecting their moves.

Gaz emailed Connor to say that they should meet up back at the skate park. The meeting was set and Gaz arrived early. It was a hot day, so he plonked himself down on a bench and waited for his friend. An hour went by and still Connor didn't show.

Gaz began to walk round the park to check other areas: maybe Connor had forgotten where to go. Just then, he got a text from Connor. "Sorry I'm late. Took the wrong bus. Wait by the skate park. I'll be there soon." Gaz smiled to himself. Connor had never been great at timekeeping, but he was happy to wait. He knew Connor would arrive soon.

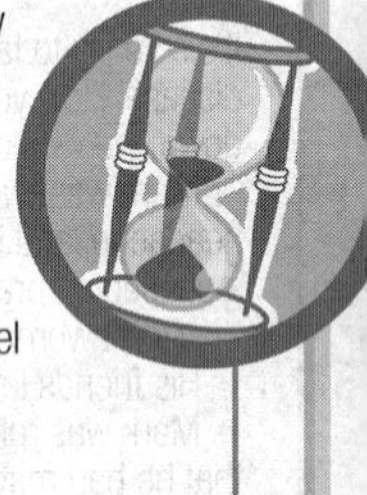

Read **James 5:7–11**.

- Gaz was beginning to lose hope that Connor would ever show up. Have you ever felt that you had to wait a long time for God to answer your prayer? Why do you think this is?
- Can you think of someone who has persevered in the face of suffering but who, when the time of pain and difficulty was over, praised God for being good to them? How does that make you feel about issues you're facing?

Consider . . .

- what things you are *really* waiting for. Why don't you pray for God to give you patience?
- how we often have to be patient when we're trying to get good at something – we're not usually great straight away! Why not try learning a new skill to teach you patience and perseverance?

For more, see . . .

- 2 Corinthians 4:16–18 (p.1244)
- Hebrews 10:35–39 (p.1341)
- Galatians 5:22 (p.1264)

1 Peter

Why Read This Book:

- See the benefits of the salvation that God offers you (1 Peter 1:3—2:10).
- Discover how Christians should live (1 Peter 2:11—4:11).
- Learn how to grow even when suffering (1 Peter 4:12—5:11).

When?

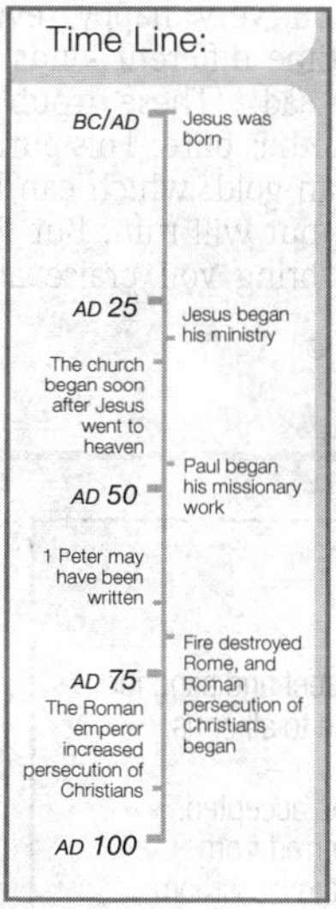

Behind the Scenes:

Living the Christian life at school or work doesn't always make us popular. Our friends might laugh at us, or make fun of us because of what we believe. Let's face it, living it out in the real world can be tough sometimes. It was certainly tough for the Christians of Asia Minor (modern-day Turkey). They lived in a pagan society, and were laughed at and even beaten and killed because of their faith. Some of them might have felt that living the Christian life was too difficult, or too painful. Some may even have been tempted to get rid of their Christian "label" altogether, and return to living comfortable lives as pagans.

It was to these people that the apostle Peter wrote this letter. It encouraged the Christians of Asia Minor to stick with their faith, despite the suffering to which they were being subjected. It offered practical advice about how they could cope with the pressures they faced and how to live with the pain – reminding them that in everything, no matter how bad things got, God was still in control, and he cared for them with all of his heart.

Maybe you are having a tough time as a Christian. Maybe those around you are making your life uncomfortable, or even painful. Maybe you too are tempted to shake off your Christian "label". Don't give up! Read 1 Peter and apply what he says to your life, and no matter what your life's circumstances are, you too can feel good about the fact that God is in control, and that he will make sure that you are on the winning side in the long term.

Where?

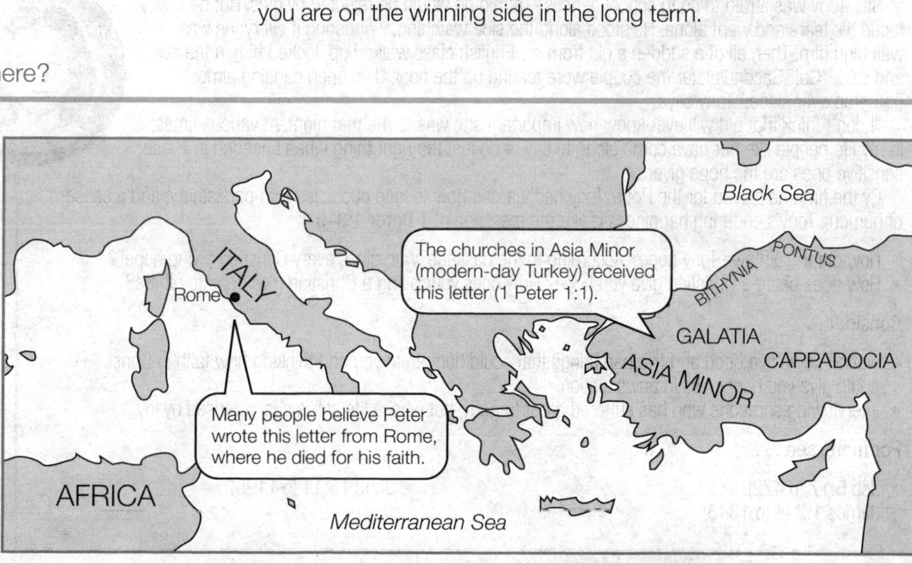

1 From Peter, an apostle[d] of Jesus Christ.
To God's chosen people who are away
from their homes and are scattered all around the
countries of Pontus, Galatia, Cappadocia, Asia
and Bithynia. 2God planned long ago to choose
you by making you his holy people, which is the
Spirit's[d] work. God wanted you to obey him and
to be made clean by the blood of the death of
Jesus Christ.
Grace and peace be yours more and more.

We Have a Living Hope

3Praise be to the God and Father of our Lord
Jesus Christ. In God's great mercy he has caused
us to be born again into a living hope, because
Jesus Christ rose from the dead. 4Now we hope
for the blessings God has for his children. These
blessings, which cannot be destroyed or be
spoiled or lose their beauty, are kept in heaven for
you. 5God's power protects you through your
faith until salvation[d] is shown to you at the end
of time. 6This makes you very happy, even
though now for a short time different kinds of
troubles may make you sad. 7These troubles
come to prove that your faith is pure. This purity
of faith is worth more than gold, which can be
proved to be pure by fire but will ruin. But the
purity of your faith will bring you praise and

HAPPINESS

The Hope Giver

Tony Melendez amazed 100 million US TV viewers in 1987 as he played the guitar with his feet and sang for Pope John Paul II. "Tony," the Pope said, after embracing the performer, "you are giving hope to all of us. My wish to you is to continue giving this hope to all the people."

Born without arms, Tony is normal in every other way. But he had struggled for years to be accepted.

Without persistence, Tony might never have graduated from high school. When he transferred from special education into a "normal" English class, all eyes watched him when he walked into the classroom. He shrugged off his rucksack, pulled out a notebook with his toes and put it on the floor. Then he grabbed a pencil between his two biggest toes and began taking notes. Even the teacher had stopped the discussion of *Moby Dick* to watch. Everyone stared in silence.

"Somebody had to break the silence," Tony recalled. "Hope the floor is clean," he said with a grin. "If it isn't, I'll have to turn in a dirty paper." The students and teacher laughed, and then the lesson continued. It was one of the many awkward times when he had to show his strength.

Still, Tony was afraid to go to school dances – afraid he would be rejected by girls. But he finally faced his fears and went alone. He stood along the side watching, wondering if everyone was watching him. Then all of a sudden a girl from his English class walked up, looked him in the eye, and said, "Go!" Seconds later the couple were tearing up the floor. "I've been dancing almost non-stop ever since," Tony says.

"I don't think that girl will ever know how important she was to me that night. At various times in my life people like her have come along to say or do just the right thing when I needed it. These sensitive ones are the hope givers."

By the time he played for the Pope, Tony had learned how to face obstacles with persistence and a sense of humour. Tony's enduring happiness is like the message of **1 Peter 1:3–9**.

- How did the girl give Tony hope? According to the passage, who gives every Christian "living hope"?
- How does being a Christian give you hope? How does your being a Christian give hope to others?

Consider . . .

- writing down five good and five bad things that could happen to you and thinking how faith in Christ could give you happiness in any situation.
- interviewing someone who has suffered great tragedy, but whose life still is characterised by joy.

For more, see . . .

- Job 5:17 (p.472)
- James 1:2–4 (p.1348)
- John 15:11 (p.1125)

glory and honour when Jesus Christ is shown to
you. 8You have not seen Christ, but still you love
him. You cannot see him now, but you believe in
him. So you are filled with a joy that cannot be
explained, a joy full of glory. 9And you are receiv-
ing the goal of your faith—the salvation of your
souls.

10The prophets[d] searched carefully and tried to
learn about this salvation. They prophesied about
the grace that was coming to you. 11The Spirit[d] of
Christ was in the prophets, telling in advance
about the sufferings of Christ and about the glory
that would follow those sufferings. The prophets
tried to learn about what the Spirit was showing
them, when those things would happen, and
what the world would be like at that time. 12It
was shown them that their service was not for
themselves but for you, when they told about the
truths you have now heard. Those who preached
the Good News[d] to you told you those things
with the help of the Holy Spirit who was sent
from heaven—things into which angels desire to
look.

A Call to Holy Living

13So prepare your minds for service and have
self-control. All your hope should be for the gift
of grace that will be yours when Jesus Christ is
shown to you. 14Now that you are obedient chil-
dren of God do not live as you did in the past.
You did not understand, so you did the evil things
you wanted. 15But be holy in all you do, just as
God, the One who called you, is holy. 16It is writ-
ten in the Scriptures:[d] "You must be holy, be-
cause I am holy."[n]

17You pray to God and call him Father, and
he judges each person's work equally. So while
you are here on earth, you should live with re-
spect for God. 18You know that in the past you
were living in a worthless way, a way passed
down from the people who lived before you.
But you were saved from that useless life. You
were bought, not with something that ruins
like gold or silver, 19but with the precious blood
of Christ, who was like a pure and perfect
lamb. 20Christ was chosen before the world
was made, but he was shown to the world in
these last times for your sake. 21Through Christ
you believe in God, who raised Christ from the
dead and gave him glory. So your faith and your
hope are in God.

22Now that you have made your souls pure by
obeying the truth, you can have true love for your
Christian brothers and sisters.[n] So love each
other deeply with all your heart. 23You have been
born again, and this new life did not come from
something that dies, but from something that
cannot die. You were born again through God's
living message that continues for ever. 24The
Scripture says,

"All people are like the grass,
and all their glory is like the flowers of the
field.
The grass dies and the flowers fall,
25 but the word of the Lord will live for
ever." *Isaiah 40:6–8*

And this is the word that was preached to
you.

Jesus is the Living Stone

2 So then, rid yourselves of all evil, all lying,
hypocrisy,[d] jealousy and evil speech. 2As
newborn babies want milk, you should want the
pure and simple teaching. By it you can grow up
and be saved, 3because you have already exam-
ined and seen how good the Lord is.

4Come to the Lord Jesus, the "stone"[n] that
lives. The people of the world did not want this
stone, but he was the stone God chose, and he
was precious. 5You also are like living stones, so
let yourselves be used to build a spiritual temple—
to be holy priests who offer spiritual sacrifices to
God. He will accept those sacrifices through
Jesus Christ. 6The Scripture[d] says:

"I will put a stone in the ground in
Jerusalem.
Everything will be built on this important
and precious rock.
Anyone who trusts in him
will never be disappointed." *Isaiah 28:16*

7This stone is worth much to you who believe.
But to the people who do not believe,

"the stone that the builders rejected
has become the cornerstone."[d] *Psalm 118:22*

8Also, he is

"a stone that causes people to stumble,
a rock that makes them fall." *Isaiah 8:14*

They stumble because they do not obey what
God says, which is what God planned to happen
to them.

9But you are a chosen people, royal priests, a
holy nation, a people for God's own possession.
You were chosen to tell about the wonderful acts
of God, who called you out of darkness into his
wonderful light. 10At one time you were not a
people, but now you are God's people. In the

"You must be . . . holy." Quotation from Leviticus 11:45; 19:2; 20:7.
brothers and sisters Although the Greek text says "brothers" here and throughout this book, Peter's words refer to the entire church, both men and women.
"stone" The most important stone in God's spiritual temple or house (his people).

past you had never received mercy, but now you
have received God's mercy.

Live for God

11 Dear friends, you are like foreigners and
strangers in this world. I beg you to avoid the evil
things your bodies want to do that fight against
your soul. 12 People who do not believe are living
all around you and might say that you are doing
wrong. Live such good lives that they will see the
good things you do and will give glory to God on
the day when Christ comes again.

Yield to Every Human Authority

13 For the Lord's sake, yield to the people who
have authority in this world: the king, who is the
highest authority, 14 and the leaders who are sent
by him to punish those who do wrong and to
praise those who do right. 15 It is God's desire that
by doing good you should stop foolish people
from saying stupid things about you. 16 Live as free
people, but do not use your freedom as an excuse
to do evil. Live as servants of God. 17 Show respect
for all people: love the brothers and sisters of
God's family, respect God, honour the king.

LOVE

Given, Not Earned

The argument was brutal. Rachel's parents didn't want her to go to the party. They didn't know the boy throwing it, didn't know his parents, didn't know who was going to be there, and didn't know what the teenagers would be doing.

"You're eighteen years old, Rachel," her father said. "We won't forbid you to go. But if you ignore our wishes on this, don't expect us to honour your wishes on other things . . . including the use of the car."

They thought that withholding the car would stop her.

But it didn't. "I'm tired of you using the car to force me to do what you want," she shot back. "Just keep the car! I don't need it! I've got friends who'll take me to parties!"

With that, she stormed out, called her friends, and headed for the party. Rachel savoured her apparent victory.

But then she arrived at the party. It was wild. Heavy drinking. Too many people. No adults around.

She wanted to leave but her "friends" had left without her. She was left to walk 10 kilometres home.

She stood alone outside, wondering what to do.

"Hey, Beautiful! Want a lift?" a voice said from a car pulling up behind her. Rachel felt a surge of fear, and looked for somewhere to run. But when she glanced over her shoulder at the car, she saw her dad's smiling face.

She got in. Dad spoke first. "Diana phoned," he explained. "She said that they tried to find you before they left but it was too crowded. They wanted to get out of there before their car got blocked in."

"I didn't think you'd be willing to come and get me," Rachel said. "Not after the things I said and did."

Dad pulled the car over and turned to look at her. "Hey," he said. "You're my daughter. I love you. Nothing you say or do can ever change that."

Rachel learned something about true love that night. **1 Peter 1:17–23** talks about the kind of love that Rachel felt from her dad.

- According to the passage, how is Rachel's dad's love for her like God's love?
- How might your life change if you trusted and accepted God's love as described in 1 Peter?

Consider . . .

- comparing your parents' love with God's love. Share your observations with your mum or dad.
- talking with a grandparent, aunt, or uncle about times when someone had to discipline your mum or dad. How was that person's love like God's love for you?

For more, see . . .

- Deuteronomy 7:7–9 (p.172)
- 1 John 4:7–10 (p.1374)
- Romans 4:1–8 (p.1188)

Follow Christ's Example

18 Slaves, yield to the authority of your mas-
ters with all respect, not only those who are
good and kind, but also those who are dishon-
est. 19 A person might have to suffer even when
it is unfair, but if he thinks of God and stands the
pain, God is pleased. 20 If you are beaten for
doing wrong, there is no reason to praise you for
being patient in your punishment. But if you suf-
fer for doing good, and you are patient, then
God is pleased. 21 This is what you were called to
do, because Christ suffered for you and gave
you an example to follow. So you should do as
he did.
22 "He had never sinned,
and he had never lied." *Isaiah 53:9*
23 People insulted Christ, but he did not insult
them in return. Christ suffered, but he did not
threaten. He let God, the One who judges
rightly, take care of him. 24 Christ carried our sins
in his body on the cross so we would stop living
for sin and start living for what is right. And you
are healed because of his wounds. 25 You were
like sheep that wandered away, but now you
have come back to the Shepherd and Protector
of your souls.

Sidelight Because the early Christians were viewed suspiciously, 1 Peter 2:12 urges them to "live good lives" so that people would not accuse them of wrongdoing. Among other things, early Christians were falsely accused of eating children because they followed Jesus' command to eat his body and drink his blood in the Communion (also called the Lord's Supper). You can read about this in 1 Corinthians 11:23–26, p.1230).

SELF-ESTEEM

Bully Boy

For as long as he could remember, Ben had been teased because he was thin. The other boys of his age who were more muscular enjoyed shoving him around and making him feel small, and if there was one thing that Ben hated, it was feeling small.

Like many people who get bullied, instead of doing something positive to deal with the problem, Ben became a bully too.

Obviously, he couldn't bully the boys who were the same age as him because he was the smallest, so he decided to pick on the boys who were younger. He would wait for them to come out of school and then begin to tease them for being so young and weak. Bullying other people made him feel strong and powerful, and that's how he had always wanted to feel.

As the months passed, the boys that Den bullied decided to continue the chain and bully those who were even younger. Before long there weren't many boys in the school who weren't being bullied by someone or other, and that was all because Ben had decided to try and build his self-esteem at any cost.

1 Peter 2:2–10 tells how Jesus offers a different foundation for building self-esteem.

- If Ben had read this passage, how might he have reacted differently in the situation?
- Whenever your self-esteem takes a knock, how can this passage help you to regain it?

Consider . . .

- what lengths you would go to in order to gain your self-esteem. How do these lengths compare with the teaching contained in this passage?
- making a list of five people you know who have a poor self-esteem.

For more, see . . .

- Isaiah 8:12–14 (p.649)
- 2 Corinthians 6:3–10 (p.1246)
- Hosea 2:23 (p.852)

Wives and Husbands

3 In the same way, you wives should yield to your husbands. Then, if some husbands do not obey God's teaching, they will be persuaded to believe without anyone saying a word to them. They will be persuaded by the way their wives live. 2Your husbands will see the pure lives you live with your respect for God. 3It is not fancy hair, gold jewellery or fine clothes that should make you beautiful. 4No, your beauty should come from within you—the beauty of a gentle and quiet spirit that will never be destroyed and is very precious to God. 5In this same way the holy women who lived long ago and followed God made themselves beautiful, yielding to their own husbands. 6Sarah obeyed Abraham, her husband, and called him her master. And you women are true children of Sarah if you always do what is right and are not afraid.

Sidelight When 1 Peter 3:3–4 says true beauty comes from the inside, it would not have made the jewellery merchants happy. In those times, women would decorate their hair with elaborate combs and hairpins, some of which were made of gold and all of which were expensive to buy.

7In the same way, you husbands should live with your wives in an understanding way, since being answered they are weaker than you. But show them respect, because God gives them the same blessing he gives to you—the grace that gives true life. Do this so that nothing will stop your prayer.

Suffering for Doing Right

8Finally, all of you should be in agreement, understanding each other, loving each other as family, being kind and humble. 9Do not do wrong to repay a wrong, and do not insult to repay an insult. But repay with a blessing, because you yourselves were called to do this so that you might receive a blessing. 10The Scripture[d] says,

"You must do these things
  to enjoy life and have many happy days.
You must not say evil things,
  and you must not tell lies.
11Stop doing evil and do good.
  Look for peace and work for it.
12The Lord sees the good people
  and listens to their prayers.
But the Lord is against
  those who do evil." *Psalm 34:12–16*

13If you are trying hard to do good, no one can really hurt you. 14But even if you suffer for doing right, you are blessed.

"Don't be afraid of what they fear;
  do not dread those things." *Isaiah 8:12–13*

15But respect Christ as the holy Lord in your hearts. Always be ready to answer everyone who asks you to explain about the hope you have, 16but answer in a gentle way and with respect. Keep a clear conscience so that those who speak evil of your good life in Christ will be made ashamed. 17It is better to suffer for doing good than for doing wrong if that is what God wants. 18Christ himself suffered for sins once. He was not guilty, but he suffered for those who are guilty to bring you to God. His body was killed, but he was made alive in the spirit. 19And in the spirit he went and preached to the spirits in prison 20who refused to obey God long ago in the time of Noah. God was waiting patiently for them while Noah was building the boat. Only a few people—eight in all—were saved by water. 21And that water is like baptism[d] that now saves you—not the washing of dirt from the body, but the promise made to God from a good conscience. And this is because Jesus Christ was raised from the dead. 22Now Jesus has gone into heaven and is at God's right side ruling over angels, authorities and powers.

Change Your Lives

4 Since Christ suffered while he was in his body, strengthen yourselves with the same way of thinking Christ had. The person who has suffered in the body is finished with sin. 2Strengthen yourselves so that you will live here on earth doing what God wants, not the evil things people want. 3In the past you wasted too much time doing what non-believers enjoy. You were guilty of sexual sins, evil desires, getting drunk, wild and drunken parties, and hateful idol worship. 4Non-believers think it is strange that you do not do the many wild and wasteful things they do, so they insult you. 5But they will have to explain this to God, who is ready to judge the living and the dead. 6For this reason the Good News[d] was preached to those who are now dead. Even though they were judged like all people, the Good News was preached to them so they could live in the spirit as God lives.

Use God's Gifts Wisely

7The time is near when all things will end. So think clearly and control yourselves so that you will be able to pray. 8Most importantly, love each other deeply, because love will cause

many sins to be forgiven. 9Open your homes to
each other, without complaining. 10Each of you
has received a gift to use to serve others. Be
good servants of God's various gifts of grace.
11Anyone who speaks should speak words from
God. Anyone who serves should serve with
the strength God gives so that in everything
God will be praised through Jesus Christ.
Power and glory belong to him for ever and
ever. Amen.

Suffering as a Christian

12My friends, do not be surprised at the terri-
ble trouble which now comes to test you. Do
not think that something strange is happening
to you. 13But be happy that you are sharing in
Christ's sufferings so that you will be happy and
full of joy when Christ comes again in glory.
14When people insult you because you follow
Christ, you are blessed, because the glorious
Spirit,[d] the Spirit of God, is with you. 15Do not
suffer for murder, theft or any other crime, nor
because you trouble other people. 16But if you
suffer because you are a Christian, do not be
ashamed. Praise God because you wear that
name. 17It is time for judgement to begin with
God's family. And if that judging begins with us,
what will happen to those people who do not
obey the Good News[d] of God?
18"If it is very hard for a good person to be
saved,
the wicked person and the sinner will
surely be lost!"[n]
19So those who suffer as God wants should
trust their souls to the faithful Creator as they
continue to do what is right.

"If . . . lost!" Quotation from Proverbs 11:31 in the Septuagint, the Greek version of the Old Testament.

SUFFERING

The Cost of Faith

"Listen," said Jason to his friend Baz. "I don't want to hear about your Jesus! Leave me alone!"

The words broke Baz's heart. Jason had been his best friend since they moved up to middle school. But now, three years later, their friendship was in jeopardy because Baz had become a Christian and had let his friends know.

Jason had confronted Baz at a friend's party, accusing him of "thinking you're better than everyone else" because Baz had chosen not to drink any more.

"Let me know when you get over this religion stuff," Jason had said. "Maybe then we can be friends again."

At that, Jason left Baz standing alone. Baz feared that he had just lost his best friend.

"No one ever told me that being a Christian could hurt like this or cost so much," Baz muttered to himself as he went home. "Perhaps it's just not worth it. I thought being a Christian meant that life got better, not more painful."

As we grow in faith, we change. Sometimes friends change with us. Sometimes they don't. This change may cause some pain. **1 Peter 4:12–19** reminds us that being a Christian does not insulate us from pain and suffering. In fact, Peter lets us know that we can expect it as we grow in Christ. He also reminds us that some things are worth suffering for.

- What comfort or understanding might this passage give to Baz in the loss of his friendship with Jason?
- When have you paid for your faith? How did you grow from that experience?

Consider . . .

- praying for a friend that you know is suffering at present.
- reading about the life of a Christian martyr. Your minister can help you to find such a story.

For more, see . . .

- Psalm 56:1–4 (p.532)
- 1 Peter 2:19–25 (p.1359)
- John 15:18–21 (p.1125)

The Flock of God

5 Now I have something to say to the elders[d]
in your group. I also am an elder. I have seen
Christ's sufferings, and I will share in the glory
that will be shown to us. I beg you to 2shepherd
God's flock, for whom you are responsible.
Watch over them because you want to, not be-
cause you are forced. That is how God wants it.
Do it because you are happy to serve, not be-
cause you want money. 3Do not be like a ruler
over people you are responsible for, but be good
examples to them. 4Then when Christ, the Chief
Shepherd, comes, you will get a glorious crown
that will never lose its beauty.
5In the same way, younger people should be
willing to be under older people. And all of you
should be very humble with each other.

> **Sidelight** If you were a star athlete in Peter's day, you might receive a palm branch (suitable for hanging) and a wreath of olive leaves, parsley, celery leaves or ivy. These wreaths were a source of great pride, but, like a bouquet of roses, they didn't last long. Maybe that is one reason 1 Peter 5:4 urges chasing crowns that would not need watering!

"God is against the proud,
but he gives grace to the humble."
Proverbs 3:34

6Be humble under God's powerful hand so
he will lift you up when the right time comes.
7Give all your worries to him, because he cares
about you.

DRUGS AND ALCOHOL

Out of Control

Sue worried a lot about Mandy. She was such a great outgoing sort of girl, but always on the lookout for something new to try. She got bored fairly easily and was always suggesting outrageous things to do. When she got her first job in the West End of London, she soon found a crowd of friends who smoked pot. She came home on the train with wide empty eyes, to tell Sue of her new-found hobby.

"It's just great, and it doesn't do you any harm at all!" she laughed.

Sue was not so sure. She'd seen people on drugs before and it hadn't looked so great to her.

"Mandy, are you sure about this?" she asked. "Be careful!"

Over the next few months, Mandy progressed from pot to pills. Uppers, downers and speed.

"Hey Sue, take some of these, but be sure not to fall asleep, OK?" she would say.

Her friend always refused, and when Mandy asked why, she would always say, "I don't like being out of control." Mandy would just shrug her shoulders and carry on regardless.

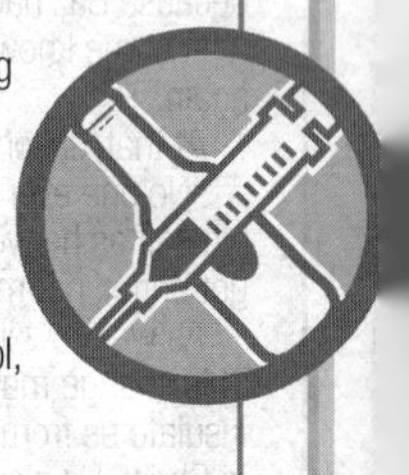

Then one day Sue came across Mandy surrounded by a group of "friends". They seemed to be looking closely at something.

"What is it?" asked Sue, breaking through the group.

Mandy held out her arm. "It's my very first track!" She gave a slightly dazed smile. There on the inside of her arm was a small red vein. Mandy was shooting stuff. Very soon, she was out of control, no turning back. Sue watched two of Mandy's best friends die from overdoses.

1 Peter 5:6–11 states very boldy that if you're out of control, then you're the devil's fodder.

- How was Sue's behaviour like verse 9?
- How could this passage help people you know who may be into drugs?

Consider . . .

- praying seriously for any friends you know who are into drugs.
- being totally honest with yourself if you have a drugs or alcohol problem, and then seeking help from your church or local substance abuse programme.

For more, see . . .

- Psalm 10:6 (p.505)
- 2 Peter 2:18–20 (p.1367)
- Proverbs 5:21–23 (p.593)

[8]Control yourselves and be careful! The devil,
your enemy, goes around like a roaring lion look-
ing for someone to eat. [9]Refuse to give in to him,
by standing strong in your faith. You know that
your Christian family all over the world is having
the same kinds of suffering.

[10]And after you suffer for a short time, God,
who gives all grace, will make everything right.
He will make you strong and support you
and keep you from falling. He called you to share
in his glory in Christ, a glory that will continue
for ever. [11]All power is his for ever and ever.
Amen.

Final Greetings

[12]I wrote this short letter with the help of
Silas, who I know is a faithful brother in Christ.
I wrote to encourage you and to tell you that
this is the true grace of God. Stand strong in that
grace.

Sidelight When 1 Peter 5:13 mentions Babylon, it probably refers to Rome, the capital of the Roman Empire. (The comparison comes from the common practice of using Babylon as a "code name" for Rome.) By the time 1 Peter was written, the historic city of Babylon was just a small, insignificant village.

[13]The church in Babylon, chosen like you,
sends you greetings. Mark, my son in Christ,
also greets you. [14]Give each other a kiss of
Christian love when you meet.

Peace to all of you who are in Christ.

2 Peter

Why Read This Book:

- Be certain that the Christian faith is true (2 Peter 1).
- Learn how to respond to false teaching (2 Peter 2).
- Anticipate Christ's return (2 Peter 3).

When?

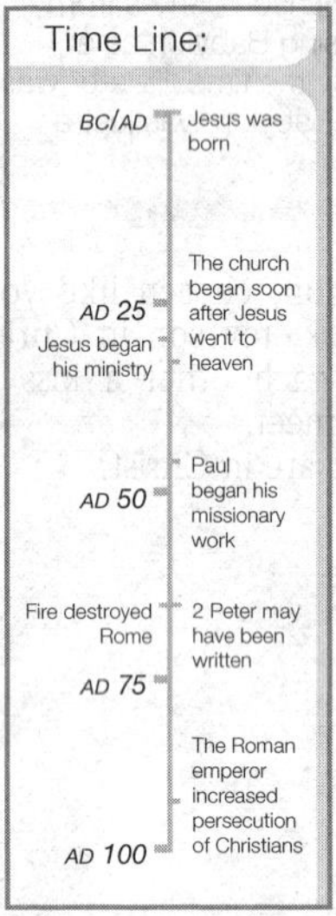

Behind the Scenes:

Opinions! Everybody has them and many Christians find it hard to sort them out, but in today's society, it's an issue that crops up again and again. The fact is that there are a lot of different voices in the world telling us entirely different things. Some people claim that Christianity is out of date and useless in the twenty-first century. Others tell us that *they* have a better way of life. A lot of people think that any one religion is as good as another. When it comes down to the bottom line, many Christians ask themselves, "How do I know that I'm right when there are so many other faiths in the world?"

The early Christians probably asked themselves the same thing when false teachers started entering the church. They knew that society had its false teachers, but now they were coming to church! How could they know once and for all that theirs was the true faith?

In 2 Peter, the writer puts their minds at rest. He assures them that the Christian faith is true, and then goes on to tell them all about false teachers, and how they operate. Having said all of that, and having settled any doubts which the Christians had, Peter ends his short letter by reminding them that Christ will come again, and encourages them to concentrate on building up their faith in preparation.

Most Christians have doubts at one time or another. If you have doubts about the Christian faith, read 2 Peter and be certain that the faith is true. If you are already certain, then read 2 Peter and help someone you know who is having doubts.

LIFE FILE LINKS

Investigate the Theme

To find a list of real life stories on this subject turn to the LIFE FILE GUIDE on pages 12 to 22 at the front of the Youth Bible.

FUTURE

1 From Simon Peter, a servant and apostle[d] of
Jesus Christ.
To you who have received a faith as valuable
as ours, because our God and Saviour[d] Jesus
Christ does what is right.
2Grace and peace be given to you more and
more, because you truly know God and Jesus our
Lord.

> **Sidelight** If you want to read a short version of 2 Peter, look at Jude (p.1384). About nineteen of the twenty-five verses in Jude are similar to verses in 2 Peter.

God Has Given Us Blessings

3Jesus has the power of God, by which he has
given us everything we need to live and to serve
God. We have these things because we know
him. Jesus called us by his glory and goodness.
4Through these he gave us the very great and
precious promises. With these gifts you can share
in being like God, and the world will not ruin you
with its evil desires.
5Because you have these blessings, do your
best to add these things to your lives: to your
faith, add goodness; and to your goodness, add
knowledge; 6and to your knowledge, add self-
control; and to your self-control, add patience;
and to your patience, add service for God; 7and to
your service for God, add kindness for your broth-
ers and sisters[n] in Christ; and to this kindness,
add love. 8If all these things are in you and are
growing, they will help you to be useful and
productive in your knowledge of our Lord Jesus
Christ. 9But anyone who does not have these
things cannot see clearly. He is blind and has
forgotten that he was made clean from his past
sins.
10My brothers and sisters, try hard to be certain
that you really are called and chosen by God. If
you do all these things, you will never fall. 11And
you will be given a very great welcome into the
eternal kingdom of our Lord and Saviour Jesus
Christ.
12You know these things, and you are very
strong in the truth, but I will always help you
remember them. 13I think it is right for me to
help you remember as long as I am in this body.
14I know I must soon leave this body, as our Lord
Jesus Christ has shown me. 15I will try my best so
that you may be able to remember these things
even after I am gone.

We Saw Christ's Glory

16When we told you about the powerful com-
ing of our Lord Jesus Christ, we were not telling
just clever stories that someone invented. But we
saw the greatness of Jesus with our own eyes.
17Jesus heard the voice of God, the Greatest
Glory, when he received honour and glory from
God the Father. The voice said, "This is my Son,
whom I love, and I am very pleased with him."
18We heard that voice from heaven while we
were with Jesus on the holy mountain.
19This makes us more sure about the message
the prophets[d] gave. It is good for you to follow
closely what they said as you would follow
a light shining in a dark place, until the day be-
gins and the morning star rises in your hearts.
20Most of all, you must understand this: no
prophecy in the Scriptures[d] ever comes from the
prophet's own interpretation. 21No prophecy
ever comes from what a person wanted to say,
but people led by the Holy Spirit[d] spoke words
from God.

False Teachers

2 There used to be false prophets[d] among
God's people, just as you will have some
false teachers in your group. They will secretly
teach things that are wrong—teachings that will
cause people to be lost. They will even refuse to
accept the Master, Jesus, who bought their free-
dom. So they will bring quick ruin on themselves.
2Many will follow their evil ways and say evil
things about the way of truth. 3Those false teach-
ers only want your money, so they will use you
by telling you lies. Their judgement spoken
against them long ago is still coming, and their
ruin is certain.
4When angels sinned, God did not let them go
free without punishment. He sent them to hell
and put them in caves of darkness where they are
being held for judgement. 5And God punished
the world long ago when he brought a flood to
the world that was full of people who were
against him. But God saved Noah, who preached
about being right with God, and seven other peo-
ple with him. 6And God also destroyed the evil
cities of Sodom[d] and Gomorrah by burning them
until they were ashes. He made those cities an
example of what will happen to those who are
against God. 7But he saved Lot from those cities.
Lot, a good man, was troubled because of the
dirty lives of evil people. 8(Lot was a good man,
but because he lived with evil people every day,
his good heart was hurt by the evil things he saw
and heard.) 9So the Lord knows how to save

brothers and sisters Although the Greek text says "brothers" here and throughout this book, Peter's words were meant for the entire church, both men and women.

those who serve him when troubles come. He
will hold evil people and punish them, while
waiting for the Judgement Day. 10 That punish-
ment is especially for those who live by doing the
evil things their sinful selves want and who hate
authority.

These false teachers are bold and do anything
they want. They are not afraid to speak against
the angels. 11 But even the angels, who are much
stronger and more powerful than false teachers,
do not accuse them with insults before the Lord.
12 But these people speak against things they do
not understand. They are like animals that act
without thinking, animals born to be caught and
killed. And, like animals, these false teachers will
be destroyed. 13 They have caused many people
to suffer, so they themselves will suffer. That is
their pay for what they have done. They take
pleasure in openly doing evil, so they are like
dirty spots and stains among you. They delight in
trickery while eating meals with you. 14 Every
time they look at a woman they want her, and
their desire for sin is never satisfied. They lead
weak people into the trap of sin, and they have
taught their hearts to be greedy. God will punish
them! 15 These false teachers left the right road
and lost their way, following the way Balaam
went. Balaam was the son of Beor, who loved
being paid for doing wrong. 16 But a donkey,
which cannot talk, told Balaam he was sinning.

ADDICTION

Twice is Enough

When Caroline saw she was putting on weight she was mortified. This was the kind of thing that happened to her friends. She'd heard them talking about diets and waistlines but had never taken much notice.

So, at the age of eighteen, she decided to go to the gym. It was a great place, not how she'd imagined it at all. The instructors were quite jolly and gave her a good fitness test before they let her do any exercises.

"You're not overweight, Caroline," one of them told her. "You just need to keep fit. If you just tone your muscles up, you'll look and feel loads better."

The first week, she went to the gym on Tuesday and Thursday. The second and third week she did the same. Already Caroline was beginning to see the difference in her appearance, and she liked it!

"Maybe if I went to the gym more often, I'd look even better!" she thought. And so stepped it up to three times a week. By the end of a few months, Caroline was going to the gym every day. Her physique was terrific, but she found she had little time for anything else.

Then one day she was too busy to go. She felt a small panic inside her and the next day she tried to do her fitness programme twice, to make up for it. Suddenly, she felt light-headed and the next thing she knew, she was coming round after fainting.

"Caroline, you're doing far too much," her instructor told her. "You're not an athlete, you're not in training, so twice a week at a gym is sufficient."

"But I was looking so good!" she wailed.

"There won't be much difference in how you look, but if you carry on like this you'll get addicted. We've seen it happen to people and trust me, you're on your way to all sorts of problems," the instructor warned.

Caroline learned a big lesson just in time. Many people become obsessed with exercising and dieting, when all they need is to control their lifestyle. Read **2 Peter 2:19** where we are warned about getting too involved with any one thing.

- What words of warning could Caroline have paid attention to from this passage?
- Why does this passage use the word "slave"?

Consider . . .

- listing some advertisements you have seen that trap you with false words.
- seeking help from your youth leader if you feel addicted or enslaved.

For more, see . . .

- John 8:34–36 (p.1110)
- 1 Peter 2:16 (p.1358)

It spoke with a man's voice and stopped the
prophet's mad thinking.
17 Those false teachers are like springs without
water and clouds blown by a storm. A place in
the blackest darkness has been kept for them.
18 They boast with words that mean nothing.
By their evil desires they lead people into the
trap of sin—people who are just beginning to es-
cape from others who live in error. 19 They prom-
ise them freedom, but they themselves are not
free. They are slaves of things that will be de-
stroyed. For people are slaves of anything that
controls them. 20 They were made free from the
evil in the world by knowing our Lord and
Saviour[d] Jesus Christ. But if they return to evil
things and those things control them, then it is
worse for them than it was before. 21 Yes, it
would be better for them to have never known
the right way than to know it and to turn away
from the holy teaching that was given to them.
22 What they did is like this true saying: "A dog
goes back to what it has thrown up,"[n] and,
"After a pig is washed, it goes back and rolls in
the mud."

Jesus will Come Again

3 My friends, this is the second letter I have
written you to help your honest minds re-
member. 2 I want you to think about the words
the holy prophets[d] spoke in the past, and re-
member the command our Lord and Saviour[d]
gave us through your apostles.[d] 3 It is most

"A dog . . . up" Quotation from Proverbs 26:11.

IMAGE

Who Do You Think You Are?

Luis Palau was enjoying a very successful mission in Cardiff. The mission posters were on all the buses, and his face had been on TV.

The week had gone well, and the evenings at Cardiff Castle were tremendous. Thousands of people came along to hear him preach, and on this particular night, several local VIPs and famous faces too.

Then the thunderstorm started. The sky turned a thick black and the lightning streaked across the castle grounds. The peacocks in the grounds started screaming, and the thunder crashed through the PA.

The singers kept on singing and Luis kept on preaching. He finally reached his appeal, and people started to flock forward, wanting to know more about this Jesus. Wanting him in their lives.

Suddenly, a man appeared from nowhere. He stood in the middle of the swelling crowd at the front of the grounds. He walked until he stood just a few feet from the preacher and he started to laugh. The sound was evil, and the man stood there, wearing a grey raincoat and a crown of thorns. He laughed and he jeered and he pointed to his head.

The platform party started to pray and Luis prayed for the crowd.

The man disappeared as suddenly as he had arrived.

2 Peter 3:3 says we should expect such things.

- Why is it important that we understand these things, according to this passage?
- How can looking forward to Jesus coming back help you in an image crisis?

Consider . . .

- what positive things you might say the next time your faith is challenged or ridiculed.
- planning with your youth group some projects that will improve the image of Christianity in your school or college, such as the Christian Union organising the Christmas party, or fundraising for Third World issues.

For more, see . . .

- Luke 16:14–15 (p.1074)
- Acts 17:32 (p.1168)
- Acts 2:12–13 (p.1138)

important for you to understand what will
happen in the last days. People will laugh at you.
They will live doing the evil things they want to
do. [4]They will say, "Jesus promised to come
again. Where is he? Our fathers have died, but
the world continues the way it has been since it
was made." [5]But they do not want to remember
what happened long ago. By the word of God
heaven was made, and the earth was made from
water and with water. [6]Then the world was
flooded and destroyed with water. [7]And that
same word of God is keeping heaven and earth
that we now have in order to be destroyed
by fire. They are being kept for the Judgement
Day and the destruction of all who are against
God.
[8]But do not forget this one thing, dear friends:
to the Lord one day is as a thousand years, and a
thousand years is as one day. [9]The Lord is not
slow in doing what he promised—the way some
people understand slowness. But God is being
patient with you. He does not want anyone to be
lost, but he wants all people to change their
hearts and lives.
[10]But the day of the Lord will come like a
thief. The skies will disappear with a loud noise.
Everything in them will be destroyed by fire, and
the earth and everything in it will be burnt up. [n]

will be burnt up Many Greek copies say, "will be found". One copy says, "will disappear".

END TIMES

School's Out

The school caretaker was annoyed. This was nothing new, he always found something to complain about, but today he was doubly upset. He was opening the top windows during assembly when he heard a man talking to the pupils about Jesus. The pupils listened attentively to the Christian and applauded at the end of his entertaining talk. Fuming, the caretaker went to the headmaster's office and said, "If you are going to allow Christians into your school, then you should invite other people to share their beliefs in assembly."

"Who were you thinking of?" asked the head.

"Me," he replied. "I think I have the right to stand up there and tell them about MY faith!"

The headmaster realised he was being put on the spot and made a snap decision.

"Alright, Harry. You can take assembly next week, it'll do the children good to hear someone they know."

Unfortunately, the head didn't check up on the caretaker's faith and forgot all about it until the day of his assembly.

The caretaker stood on the stage and told the children in no uncertain terms that the world was going to end tomorrow. He told them of signs in the sky and many mathematical equations. He waved his arms about and spoke extremely loudly.

The next day . . . hardly any pupils came to school.

This is a true story, and a sad one. We can be easily led and look whichever way people point. **2 Peter 3:14–18** warns about people such as these.

- How is the school caretaker like the ignorant people Peter writes about?
- How is it best to keep away from false teachings?

Consider . . .

- getting involved in a course such as "Alpha", which would help you to understand the Christian faith better.
- discussing any doubts you may have about the Christian faith with a trusted Christian friend.

For more, see . . .

- Matthew 24:26–31 (p.984)
- Revelation 3:11 (p.1390)
- Colossians 2:6–8 (p.1292)

[11]In that way everything will be destroyed. So
what kind of people should you be? You should
live holy lives and serve God, [12]as you wait for
and look forward to the coming of the day of
God. When that day comes, the skies will be de-
stroyed with fire, and everything in them will
melt with heat. [13]But God made a promise to us,
and we are waiting for a new heaven and a new
earth where goodness lives.

Sidelight According to 2 Peter 3:15–16, you are in good company if you sometimes have trouble understanding Romans (p.1183) or other books that Paul wrote. Peter did too. This passage is a rare example of a New Testament author giving another New Testament book the authority of scripture.

[14]Dear friends, since you are waiting for this
to happen, do your best to be without sin
and without fault. Try to be at peace with God.
[15]Remember that we are saved because our Lord
is patient. Our dear brother Paul told you the
same thing when he wrote to you with the
wisdom that God gave him. [16]He writes about
this in all his letters. Some things in Paul's letters
are hard to understand, and people who are
ignorant and weak in faith explain these
things falsely. They also falsely explain the other
Scriptures,[d] but they are destroying themselves
by doing this.

[17]Dear friends, since you already know about
this, be careful. Do not let those evil people lead
you away by the wrong they do. Be careful so
you will not fall from your strong faith. [18]But
grow in the grace and knowledge of our Lord
and Saviour Jesus Christ. Glory be to him now
and for ever! Amen.

1 John

Why Read This Book:

- Find out how to grow closer to God (1 John 1—2).
- See what it's like to be part of God's family (1 John 3—4).
- Be certain of life with God after death (1 John 5).

When?

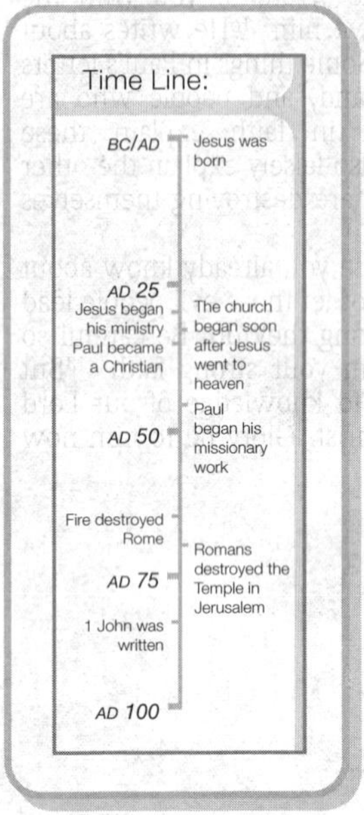

Behind the Scenes:

When you read the book of 1 John, you almost have the feeling that a grandfather has gathered his grandchildren around a fire to talk. You can see his love for them and you know from the way they look at him that they respect him a great deal.

As he talks to his "children", as he calls them, you can feel the warmth. He reassures them of God's love for them. He gently coaxes them to believe in and follow God.

But he also has another purpose. He is worried that the younger Christians are hearing mixed messages about Jesus Christ. People – known as gnostics – are saying that Jesus wasn't really human, he was only divine. Furthermore, they were arguing that they could do whatever they wanted to do with their bodies, because the physical body was separate from the spiritual nature.

The grandfather knows that these ideas are wrong. Jesus was both fully human and fully divine. And what the body does certainly affects the spirit – for better or worse. So the grandfather challenges the false teaching and urges his children to stick to the truth.

Of course, 1 John isn't really a fireside chat between a grandfather and his grandchildren. It's a letter or sermon written to Christians to help them to grow in their faith and to counteract the false teaching that was gaining influence.

Yet the true spirit of the letter comes through when we imagine the love and warmth that comes when we sit around a fireplace, listening to the advice of a wise grandfather. Not only did the words encourage and challenge the original hearers to keep following God, but they challenge and encourage us today.

Where?

1 We write to you now about what has always
existed, which we have heard, we have seen
with our own eyes, we have looked at, and we
have touched with our hands. We write to you
about the Word[n] that gives life. 2He who gives
life was shown to us. We saw him and can give
proof about it. And now we announce to you that
he has life that continues for ever. He was with
God the Father and was shown to us. 3We an-
nounce to you what we have seen and heard,
because we want you also to have fellowship
with us. Our fellowship is with God the Father
and with his Son, Jesus Christ. 4We write this to
you so you can be full of joy with us.

God Forgives our Sins

5Here is the message we have heard from
Christ and now announce to you: God is light,[n]
and in him there is no darkness at all. 6So if we
say we have fellowship with God, but we con-
tinue living in darkness, we are liars and do not
follow the truth. 7But if we live in the light, as
God is in the light, we can share fellowship with
each other. Then the blood of Jesus, God's Son,
cleanses us from every sin.
8If we say we have no sin, we are fooling
ourselves, and the truth is not in us. 9But if we
confess our sins, he will forgive our sins, because
we can trust God to do what is right. He will

Word The Greek word is "logos", meaning any kind of communication. Here, it means Christ, who was the way God told people about himself.
light Here, this word is used as a symbol of God's goodness or truth.

HONESTY

No Excuses

Laura remembers the first time that she lied to her mum about where she was going. "Janet, Kate and I are going to see a film," she lied without looking straight into her mum's eyes.

Could her mum tell she was lying? Laura couldn't tell, so she quickly left the house.

The party was well underway when the three girls arrived.

"See, it wasn't so hard to fool your mum," Janet teased Laura.

Still, Laura was tense the whole evening. When she got home, her mum asked about the film.

"It was OK," Laura replied. "Well, good night."

Laura felt relieved as she closed her bedroom door. "I got away with it," she thought.

Each lie became easier. Soon Laura lied with ease. "What Mum doesn't know won't hurt her," she reasoned.

One evening she came home and found her mum waiting for her.

"Your life's a lie!" her mum shouted.

"It's not my fault," Laura cried. "You never let me out of the house unless I lie. Besides, other kids do it. It's no big deal."

"I don't think I know you now," Mum said. "And I can't trust you any more. What has happened to you . . . to us?"

Laura didn't know the answer. Instead, she blamed her mum for her lies and excused her behaviour by comparing herself to her friends. Yet **1 John 1:1–2:2** shows that excuses don't eliminate sin.

- How is Laura's situation similar to the sin described in these verses?
- Why do you think John so strongly emphasises confessing sin?

Consider . . .

- apologising to someone who has been hurt by your sins.
- selecting a verse from the passage that conveys the "no excuses" idea. Write the verse on a small card and memorise it.

For more, see . . .

- Genesis 3:1–13 (p.5)
- Luke 15:11–24 (p.1071)
- Psalm 51:1–13 (p.530)

cleanse us from all the wrongs we have done.
10If we say we have not sinned, we make God a
liar, and we do not accept God's teaching.

Jesus is our Helper

2 My dear children, I write this letter to you so
you will not sin. But if anyone does sin, we
have a helper in the presence of the Father—
Jesus Christ, the One who does what is right. 2He
is the way our sins are taken away, and not only
our sins but the sins of all people.

> **Sidelight** Perhaps the biggest heresy (wrong doctrine) that the early church faced involved the gnostic understanding of evil. Gnostics – whose name came from the word for "knowledge" – believed evil was simply an error that grew out of ignorance; the person who did wrong was not really responsible. There are lots of people around today who think the same way. 1 John responded that people are responsible for their sins and must be forgiven to be right with God (1 John 1:9; 2:2).

3We can be sure that we know God if we obey
his commands. 4Anyone who says, "I know God,"
but does not obey God's commands is a liar, and
the truth is not in that person. 5But if someone
obeys God's teaching, then in that person God's
love has truly reached its goal. This is how we
can be sure we are living in God: 6whoever says
that he lives in God must live as Jesus lived.

The Command to Love Others

7My dear friends, I am not writing a new com-
mand to you but an old command you have had
from the beginning. It is the teaching you have
already heard. 8But also I am writing a new com-
mand to you, and you can see its truth in Jesus
and in you, because the darkness is passing away,
and the true light is already shining.
9Anyone who says, "I am in the light,"[n] but
hates a brother or sister,[n] is still in the darkness.
10Whoever loves a brother or sister lives in the
light and will not cause anyone to stumble in
their faith. 11But whoever hates a brother or sister
is in darkness, lives in darkness and does not
know where to go, because the darkness has
made that person blind.
12I write to you, dear children,
because your sins are forgiven through Christ.
13I write to you, parents,
because you know the One who existed
from the beginning.
I write to you, young people,
because you have defeated the Evil One.
14I write to you, children,
because you know the Father.
I write to you, parents,
because you know the One who existed
from the beginning.
I write to you, young people,
because you are strong;
the teaching of God lives in you,
and you have defeated the Evil One.
15Do not love the world or the things in
the world. If you love the world, the love of the
Father is not in you. 16These are the ways of the
world: wanting to please our sinful selves, want-
ing the sinful things we see and being too proud
of what we have. None of these come from the
Father, but all of them come from the world.
17The world and everything that people want in
it are passing away, but the person who does
what God wants lives for ever.

Reject the Enemies of Christ

18My dear children, these are the last days. You
have heard that the enemy of Christ[d] is coming,
and now many enemies of Christ are already
here. This is how we know that these are the last
days. 19These enemies of Christ were in our fel-
lowship, but they left us. They never really be-
longed to us; if they had been a part of us, they
would have stayed with us. But they left, and this
shows that none of them really belonged to us.
20You have the gift[n] that the Holy One gave
you, so you all know the truth. 21I do not write
to you because you do not know the truth but
because you do know the truth. And you know
that no lie comes from the truth.
22Who is the liar? It is the person who does
not accept Jesus as the Christ. This is the enemy
of Christ: the person who does not accept the
Father and his Son. 23Whoever does not accept
the Son does not have the Father. But whoever
confesses the Son has the Father, too.
24Be sure you continue to follow the teaching
you heard from the beginning. If you continue to
follow what you heard from the beginning, you
will stay in the Son and in the Father. 25And this
is what the Son promised to us—life for ever.
26I am writing this letter about those people
who are trying to lead you the wrong way.
27Christ gave you a special gift that is still in you,

light Here, this word is used as a symbol of God's goodness or truth.
brother or sister Although the Greek text says "brother" here and throughout this book, John's words were meant for the entire church, both men and women.
gift This might mean the Holy Spirit, or it might mean teaching or truth as in verse 24.

so you do not need any other teacher. His gift
teaches you about everything, and it is true, not
false. So continue to live in Christ, as his gift
taught you.
28Yes, my dear children, live in him so that
when Christ comes back, we can be without fear
and not be ashamed in his presence. 29If you
know that Christ is all that is right, you know that
all who do right are God's children.

We are God's Children

3 The Father has loved us so much that we are
called children of God. And we really are his
children. The reason the people in the world do
not know us is that they have not known him.
2Dear friends, now we are children of God, and
we have not yet been shown what we will be in
the future. But we know that when Christ comes
again, we will be like him, because we will see
him as he really is. 3Christ is pure, and all who
have this hope in Christ keep themselves pure
like Christ.
4The person who sins breaks God's law. Yes,
sin is living against God's law. 5You know that
Christ came to take away sins and that there is no
sin in Christ. 6So anyone who lives in Christ does
not go on sinning. Anyone who goes on sinning
has never really understood Christ and has never
known him.
7Dear children, do not let anyone lead you the
wrong way. Christ is all that is right. So to be like
Christ a person must do what is right. 8The devil
has been sinning since the beginning, so anyone
who continues to sin belongs to the devil. The
Son of God came for this purpose: to destroy the
devil's work.
9Those who are God's children do not
continue sinning, because the new life from God

FOLLOWING GOD

Life at the Top

Lynn Hill has always been at the top of everything. When she was a child, she was at the top of trees, telegraph poles, even street lights. Now she is on top of cliffs and mountains as one of the world's leading rock climbers. She is one of the few people who has defied gravity and scaled cliffs that are "steeper" than vertical.

Lynn has become so good because she dedicates her life to her climbing. A picture taken the day after her wedding shows how important climbing is to her. It shows her and her new husband – also a climber, of course – in full wedding dress hanging from a rope.

Lynn knows how important it is not to become lax in her climbing techniques. Once she fell more than twenty metres down a cliff because she had forgotten to tie a simple knot on her safety rope. A tree branch slowed her fall and saved her life, although she was injured.

"The rock is a tool for learning and understanding," she says. "When you get to the top, you've conquered something inside as well."

Lynn's dedication to climbing illustrates the kind of dedication that Christians should have in following God. **1 John 3:1–24** encourages Christians not to be distracted from following God.

- What parallels do you see between Lynn's dedication to rock climbing and the passage's guidance about being a Christian?
- How have other Christians encouraged and kept you following God?

Consider . . .

- thinking about everything you have done in the past 24 hours. Decide which things helped you to follow God and which ones did not.
- asking a Christian friend to help you overcome a sin that keeps you from following God, with the kind of dedication Lynn has for rock climbing.

For more, see . . .

- Psalm 95:1–11 (p.556)
- Ephesians 5:1–11 (p.1274)
- Romans 7:14–25 (p.1193)

remains in them. They are not able to go on sin-
ning, because they have become children of
God. 10So we can see who God's children are
and who the devil's children are: those who do
not do what is right are not God's children, and
those who do not love their brothers and sisters
are not God's children.

We Must Love Each Other

11This is the teaching you have heard from the
beginning: we must love each other. 12Do not be
like Cain who belonged to the Evil One and killed
his brother. And why did he kill him? Because
the things Cain did were evil, and the things his
brother did were good.
13Brothers and sisters, do not be surprised
when the people of the world hate you. 14We
know we have left death and have come into life
because we love each other. Whoever does not
love is still dead. 15Everyone who hates a brother
or sister is a murderer,[n] and you know that no
murderers have eternal life in them. 16This is how
we know what real love is: Jesus gave his life for
us. So we should give our lives for our brothers

> **Sidelight** When 1 John 3:13 told believers not to be surprised that the world hates them, it was speaking to an everyday reality for Christians at that time in Asia Minor. Even the Roman historian Tacitus, who lived during that time, wrote that Romans hated the Christians.

and sisters. 17Suppose someone has enough to
live on and sees a brother or sister in need, but
does not help. Then God's love is not living in
that person. 18My children, we should love peo-
ple not only with words and talk, but by our
actions and true caring.
19–20This is the way we know that we belong
to the way of truth. When our hearts make us
feel guilty, we can still have peace before God.
God is greater than our hearts, and he knows
everything. 21My dear friends, if our hearts do
not make us feel guilty, we can come without
fear into God's presence. 22And God gives us
what we ask for because we obey God's com-
mands and do what pleases him. 23This is what
God commands: that we believe in his Son, Jesus
Christ, and that we love each other, just as he
commanded. 24The people who obey God's
commands live in God, and God lives in them.
We know that God lives in us because of the
Spirit[d] God gave us.

Warning Against False Teachers

4 My dear friends, many false prophets[d] have
gone out into the world. So do not believe
every spirit, but test the spirits to see if they are
from God. 2This is how you can know God's
Spirit:[d] every spirit who confesses that Jesus
Christ came to earth as a human is from God.
3And every spirit who refuses to say this about
Jesus is not from God. It is the spirit of the enemy
of Christ,[d] which you have heard is coming, and
now he is already in the world.
4My dear children, you belong to God and
have defeated them, because God's Spirit, who is
in you, is greater than the devil, who is in the
world. 5And they belong to the world, so what
they say is from the world, and the world listens
to them. 6But we belong to God, and those who
know God listen to us. But those who are not
from God do not listen to us. That is how we
know the Spirit that is true and the spirit that is
false.

Love Comes from God

7Dear friends, we should love each other, be-
cause love comes from God. Everyone who loves
has become God's child and knows God. 8Who-
ever does not love does not know God, because
God is love. 9This is how God showed his love to
us: he sent his one and only Son into the world
so that we could have life through him. 10This is
what real love is: it is not our love for God; it is
God's love for us in sending his Son to be the way
to take away our sins.
11Dear friends, if God loved us that much we
also should love each other. 12No one has ever
seen God, but if we love each other, God lives in
us, and his love is made perfect in us.
13We know that we live in God and he lives in
us, because he gave us his Spirit.[d] 14We have
seen and can testify that the Father sent his Son
to be the Saviour[d] of the world. 15Whoever con-
fesses that Jesus is the Son of God has God living
inside, and that person lives in God. 16And so we
know the love that God has for us, and we trust
that love.
God is love. Those who live in love live in
God, and God lives in them. 17This is how love is
made perfect in us: that we can be without
fear on the day God judges us, because in this
world we are like him. 18Where God's love is,
there is no fear, because God's perfect love drives

Everyone . . . murderer If one person hates a brother or sister, then in the heart that person has killed that brother or sister. Jesus taught about this sin to his followers (Matthew 5:21–26).

out fear. It is punishment that makes a person
fear, so love is not made perfect in the person
who fears.
19We love because God first loved us. 20If peo-
ple say, "I love God," but hate their brothers or
sisters, they are liars. Those who do not love
their brothers and sisters, whom they have
seen, cannot love God, whom they have never
seen. 21And God gave us this command: those
who love God must also love their brothers and
sisters.

Faith in the Son of God

5 Everyone who believes that Jesus is the
Christ[d] is God's child, and whoever loves
the Father also loves the Father's children. 2This is
how we know we love God's children: when we
love God and obey his commands. 3Loving God
means obeying his commands. And God's com-
mands are not too hard for us, 4because every-
one who is a child of God conquers the world.
And this is the victory that conquers the world—
our faith. 5So the one who wins against the
world is the person who believes that Jesus is the
Son of God.
6Jesus Christ is the One who came by water[n]
and blood.[n] He did not come by water only, but
by water and blood. And the Spirit[d] says that this
is true, because the Spirit is the truth. 7So there
are three witnesses that tell us about Jesus: 8the
Spirit, the water and the blood; and these three
witnesses agree. 9We believe people when they

water This probably means the water of Jesus' baptism.
blood This probably means the blood of Jesus' death.

LOVE

Called to the Streets

Kelly had grown up in a nice home and had always struggled with "poor" people. She had been taught to get a job, work hard, and keep a nice home. But Kelly was obedient to God when he called her to move long-term onto an infamous deprived inner-city estate. Kelly believed that if God had called her to work with the poor, he would give her a heart for them.

After a number of weeks, Kelly was beginning to worry. God hadn't changed her heart – in fact, she hated it! She desperately wanted to love these people, but she simply didn't. She continued to pray about the situation.

A few days later, Kelly was sitting on a bench watching the world go by as, with a huge cheeky grin, one of her little neighbours came towards her.

Ruby had filthy hands, disgusting clothes, dirt all over her face and a single finger wedged up her nose. Trying not to pull a face, Kelly forced a smile at Ruby. Reacting to the smile, Ruby walked up to Kelly, went around behind her, pulled her finger out of her nose and went to play with Kelly's flowing hair. Kelly's first reaction was to jump up screaming, "Get your hands off me you disgusting child!" However, she didn't. In that moment, something inside Kelly broke. In an instant, she was filled with the love of Jesus for Ruby. She saw her through a new pair of eyes.

From that day on, Kelly was transformed – her heart was changed and a deep love for the people of the estate flowed through her veins.

Read **1 John 4:7–12**.

- What does the passage teach us about how we should feel about other people?
- Did Kelly do the right thing, according to the passage?

Consider . . .

- how much love you have for people. Make a list of things you could do to increase that love.
- whether there are any people who you're struggling to love. Ask God to change your heart towards them.

For more, see . . .

- Matthew 10:42 (p.957)
- 1 Corinthians 13:4–7 (p.1232)
- John 13:34–35 (p.1122)

say something is true. But what God says is more
important, and he has told us the truth about his
own Son. 10 Anyone who believes in the Son of
God has the truth that God told us. Anyone who
does not believe makes God a liar, because that
person does not believe what God told us about
his Son. 11 This is what God told us: God has
given us eternal life, and this life is in his Son.
12 Whoever has the Son has life, but whoever
does not have the Son of God does not have life.

We Have Eternal Life Now

13 I write this letter to you who believe in the
Son of God so you will know you have eternal
life. 14 And this is the boldness we have in God's
presence: that if we ask God for anything that
agrees with what he wants, he hears us. 15 If we
know he hears us every time we ask him, we
know we have what we ask from him.
16 If anyone sees a brother or sister sinning (sin
that does not lead to eternal death), that person

DISCOURAGEMENT

Hope Breakers and Makers

Have you ever had a day when everything went wrong? Sometimes the day seems to consist of one disappointing event after another. These disappointments can be called "hope breakers". Hope breakers can lead to outright discouragement if they persist. Which of these hope breakers seem familiar to you?

- threats of war in the world
- fights with your parents
- an accident in the family car
- breaking up with a girlfriend/boyfriend
- getting a poor result in an exam
- doubting your Christian beliefs
- too much homework
- criticism from others
- feeling alone

Hope can overcome discouragement. Hope reminds you of a brighter future. Which of the events below are "hope makers" for you?

- feeling good about your life
- getting good marks in a difficult exam
- giving and receiving Christian love from others
- getting into the team
- enjoying a beautiful day
- knowing that God loves you
- getting a fantastic job
- having a great time with friends
- renewing a broken friendship

John offered reassurance and hope to Christians who had experienced too many hope breakers. Read John's hope-making ideas in **1 John 5:1–15**.

- How do the breakers and makers above compare with the passage?
- What phrases in this passage offer you the most hope?

Consider . . .

- writing out the promises and assurances in this passage. Stick the list up on your door.
- acting as a hope maker to a discouraged friend by offering encouragement, time or help.

For more, see . . .

- Psalm 42 (p.525)
- Romans 8:35–39 (p.1197)
- John 15:18–27 (p.1125)

should pray, and God will give the sinner life. I
am talking about people whose sin does not lead
to eternal death. There is sin that leads to death.
I do not mean that a person should pray about
that sin. 17Doing wrong is always sin, but there is
sin that does not lead to eternal death.

18We know that those who are God's children
do not continue to sin. The Son of God keeps
them safe, and the Evil One cannot touch them.
19We know that we belong to God, but the Evil
One controls the whole world. 20We also know
that the Son of God has come and has given us
understanding so that we can know the True
One. And our lives are in the True One and in his
Son, Jesus Christ. He is the true God and the
eternal life.

21So, dear children, keep yourselves away from
gods.

2 John

Why Read This Book:

- Learn ways to show Christian love (2 John 1–6).
- Examine the danger of listening to false teachers (2 John 7–11).

When?

Time Line:

BC/AD	Jesus was born
AD 25 Jesus began his ministry; Paul became a Christian	The church began soon after Jesus went to heaven
AD 50	Paul began his missionary work
Fire destroyed Rome	
AD 75	Romans destroyed the Temple in Jerusalem
2 John was written	
AD 100	

Behind the Scenes:

Salesmen use every trick they can to con us into buying things that we don't need. Television advertisements try and tell us that a certain soft drink will make us more popular and will generate friends out of thin air. Newspapers twist facts when reporting stories so that they fit in with their viewpoint. It seems as if there is always someone who is out to pull the wool over our eyes.

The early Christians also knew what it was like to be tricked. Because of their famous generosity and hospitality towards strangers, some false teachers took advantage of them and began teaching false doctrine in the church.

2 John was written to warn churches to be on their guard. It encouraged the Christians to continue being loving towards one another, but told them to make sure that what was taught in the churches didn't contradict the gospel they had first heard. They should stay as far away from false teachers as possible.

While 2 John urges Christians to be on their guard, 3 John reminds them that they shouldn't stop being hospitable to others. In short, the message of 2 John is, "Don't believe the hype!"

LIFE FILE LINKS

Investigate the Theme

To find a list of real life stories on this subject turn to the LIFE FILE GUIDE on pages 12 to 22 at the front of the Youth Bible.

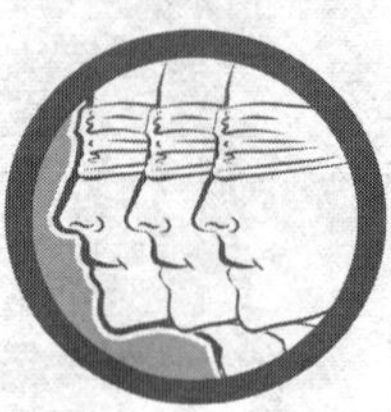

CULTS

[1]From the Elder.[n]
To the chosen lady[n] and her children:
I love all of you in the truth,[n] and all those
who know the truth love you. [2]We love you be-
cause of the truth that lives in us and will be with
us for ever.
[3]Grace, mercy and peace from God the Father
and his Son, Jesus Christ, will be with us in truth
and love.
[4]I was very happy to learn that some of your
children are following the way of truth, as the
Father commanded us. [5]And now, dear lady, this
is not a new command but is the same command
we have had from the beginning. I ask you that
we all love each other. [6]And love means living
the way God commanded us to live. As you have
heard from the beginning, his command is this:
live a life of love.
[7]Many false teachers are in the world now
who do not confess that Jesus Christ came to
earth as a human. Anyone who does not confess

Sidelight If other books in the New Testament are letters (such as 1 Corinthians, p.1213), then 2 John is more like a postcard. With only thirteen verses, it is the shortest book in the Bible. One reason why it may have been short is so that it could fit on a single sheet of papyrus, the paper of the day (2 John 12).

Elder "Elder" means an older person. It can also mean a special leader in the church (as in Titus 1:5).
lady This might mean a woman, or in this letter it might mean a church. If it is a church, then "her children" would be the people of the church.
truth The truth or "Good News" about Jesus Christ that joins all believers together.

CULTS

Knock Knock . . .

They're just weird, aren't they? This probably sums up what we really think about cults and what's wrong with them. We don't really bother with what they actually think because it's easy to write them off, just like everyone else does. But what do they think?

The most well known of the "cults" are probably the Jehovah's Witnesses. Like Christians, they believe that the Bible is the inspired word of God. So if they believe in the Bible, then what's the problem with them? The Jehovah's Witnesses' big mistake is that they don't think Jesus is God. This is a complete misunderstanding of the Bible. After all, it calls Jesus "God", and says that he forgives people's sins – something only God can do.

Another group, known as the Mormons, also believes in the Bible. But they get Jesus wrong as well. They teach that we need both Jesus *and* the "new revelation" about God that came in America in the 1800s. But Christians have always believed that Jesus is enough for our salvation. We just need to believe in him – we don't need anything extra. So we don't need "Another Testament of Jesus Christ", as the *Book of Mormon* calls itself on the front cover.

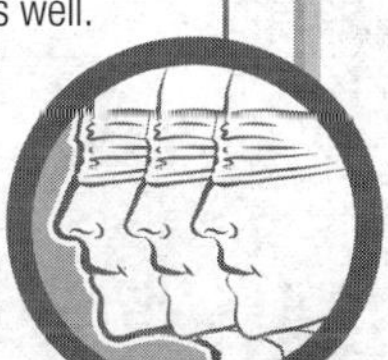

People may get Christianity and these kinds of cults mixed up, but **2 John:7–11** tells us how we can recognise false teaching.

- What attitude does Jesus want us to have to cults?
- How can we be ready to answer their questions?

Consider . . .

- seeking to understand more of Christ's teachings so that you will know when a false teacher "goes beyond" them (verse 9).
- becoming aware of cults operating in your area and learning more about what they believe. Make a list, comparing your findings with Christianity.

For more, see . . .

- John 1.1 (p.1096)
- 2 Timothy 4:3–4 (p.1319)
- John 14:5–7 (p.1122)

this is a false teacher and an enemy of Christ.[d]
8Be careful yourselves that you do not lose everything you have worked for, but that you receive your full reward.
9Anyone who goes beyond Christ's teaching and does not continue to follow only his teaching does not have God. But whoever continues to follow the teaching of Christ has both the Father and the Son. 10If someone comes to you and does not bring this teaching, do not welcome or accept that person into your house. 11If you welcome such a person, you share in the evil work.

12I have many things to write to you, but I do not want to use paper and ink. Instead, I hope to come to you and talk face to face so we can be full of joy.

13The children of your chosen sister[n] greet you.

sister Sister of the "lady" in verse 1. This might be another woman or another church.

3 John

Why Read This Book:

- **Consider how Christians can support one another (3 John 1–8).**
- **See how much damage one negative leader can do (3 John 9–11).**

When?

Time Line:

- BC/AD – Jesus was born
- AD 25 – Jesus began his ministry
- The church began soon after Jesus went to heaven
- Paul became a Christian
- Paul began his missionary work
- AD 50
- Fire destroyed Rome
- Romans destroyed the Temple in Jerusalem
- AD 75
- 3 John was written
- AD 100

Behind the Scenes:

Suppose a visitor walked into your church. Would you welcome him or her? Would you invite the visitor home for dinner? And suppose the visitor expressed different views from yours during discussion. Would you be open to those views? Or would you cut the person off?

The two central characters in 3 John would answer those questions quite differently. Gaius (3 John 1) would probably welcome the visitor and listen closely to his or her views. Diotrephes (3 John 9) would probably shun the visitor and squelch his or her opinions.

The situation in 3 John was different from your church, of course. Gaius was welcoming missionaries sent by "the Elder" (3 John 1), and the writer thanks him for it. Diotrephes refused to welcome these missionaries. In fact, he tried to kick out of the church anyone who did welcome them.

Like 2 John (p.1378), 3 John focuses on welcoming and showing love to fellow Christians. Taken together, these two letters tell a lot about the church. Christians are called to love, accept and serve one another in Christ. But at the same time, Christians are to be on guard against false teachers. These two themes are as relevant to Christians today as they were back then.

LIFE FILE LINKS

Investigate the Theme

To find a list of real life stories on this subject turn to the LIFE FILE GUIDE on pages 12 to 22 at the front of the Youth Bible.

CHURCH

1From the Elder.[n]
To my dear friend Gaius, whom I love in the
truth:[n]
2My dear friend, I know your soul is doing
fine, and I pray that you are doing well in every
way and that your health is good. 3I was very
happy when some brothers and sisters[n] came
and told me about the truth in your life and how
you are following the way of truth. 4Nothing
gives me greater joy than to hear that my chil-
dren are following the way of truth.
5My dear friend, it is good that you help
the brothers and sisters, even those you do
not know. 6They told the church about your
love. Please help them to continue their trip
in a way worthy of God. 7They started out
in service to Christ, and they have been accept-
ing nothing from non-believers. 8So we should
help such people; when we do, we share in

Sidelight The early Christians showed their love for one another by being hospitable (3 John 5–8). They would invite Christian travellers to stay at their homes regardless of whether they knew them personally or not.

Elder "Elder" means an older person. It can also mean a special leader in the church (as in Titus 1:5).
truth The truth or "Good News" about Jesus Christ that joins all believers together.
brothers and sisters Although the Greek text says "brothers" here and throughout this book, John's words were meant for the entire church, both men and women.

SERVICE

Every Little Helps

Helena and Darren were fairly new to their church.

One Sunday, an appeal was made from the front that if anyone had specific prayer requests they should make them known. They looked at each other, smiled, and agreed it was time to bite the bullet and let the church know that they had been trying for a baby for years, without success.

From that Sunday onwards, Helena and Darren were astounded by how supportive the church were – praying for them and encouraging them to remain positive.

When, finally, their prayers were answered and they were able to introduce new baby Elizabeth to everyone in the congregation, Helena and Darren were beaming with excitement.

Very soon, both Helena and Darren became increasingly tired because of the sleepless nights. One night, as they slouched exhausted on the couch at the end of another long day, they heard a knock at the door. It was a young couple from their church holding a piping hot casserole dish. Some friends from church had decided to take it in turns to cook and deliver the new parents evening meals for the next month.

Helena and Darren were so grateful for the support their church was giving them that they told friends in other parts of the country all about it. As a result, churches all over the country did similar things for new parents in their church families.

Read **3 John:5–8**.

- Would you be prepared to help anyone – even someone you didn't know?
- What does John consider as the privilege of helping others that makes serving so rewarding?

Consider . . .

- helping out more around the house or helping out someone at your church who is struggling to cope.
- praying that God would open your eyes to the needs of people around you and that you'd know how to respond.

For more, see . . .

- Matthew 25:35–40 (p.988)
- John 13:12–17 (p.1119)
- Luke 10:27–37 (p.1058)

their work for the truth.
[9]I wrote something to the church, but Diotrephes, who loves to be their leader, will not listen to us.
[10]So if I come, I will talk about what Diotrephes is doing, about how he lies and says evil things about us. But more than that, he refuses to accept the other brothers and sisters; he even stops those who do want to accept them and puts them out of the church.
[11]My dear friend, do not follow what is bad; follow what is good. The one who does good belongs to God. But the one who does evil has never known God.
[12]Everyone says good things about Demetrius, and the truth agrees with what they say. We also speak well of him, and you know what we say is true.
[13]I have many things I want to write you, but I do not want to use pen and ink.
[14]I hope to see you soon and talk face to face.
[15]Peace to you. The friends here greet you. Please greet each friend there by name.

Jude

When?

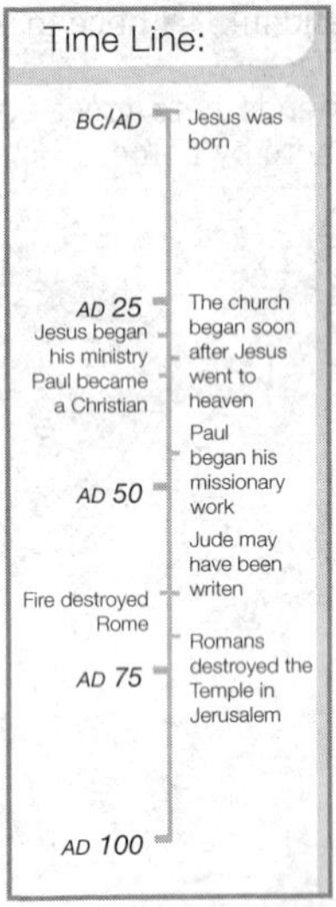

Why Read This Book:

- Test others' beliefs against the truth of Jesus Christ (Jude 1—4).
- Focus on the dangers of listening to false teachers (Jude 5—16).
- Be challenged to stay strong in your faith (Jude 17—24).

Behind the Scenes:

Not many people enjoy visiting the dentist, but the fact is that it's necessary. Eating sugary foods can create small holes in the surface of teeth, and if they aren't dealt with, the tooth will eventually go rotten and start to hurt. At that point, it's too late to do anything about it – you either have the tooth filled or pulled out! Eat less sugar and your teeth are less likely to rot.

The early church had to deal with another type of rotting. False teachers had sneaked into the church and started telling lies about Jesus and how to be saved. If the false teachers were allowed to stay then, like a tooth, the whole church would soon be rotten – eaten away by false teaching.

Jude wrote this letter to the Christians and urged them to get rid of the false teachers before the whole church rotted! Their false teaching and low standards were infecting the church and threatening its existence.

Jude encourages the Christians to grow strong in their own faith, so that they won't be influenced by any false teachers who appear on the scene in the future. He tells them to pray, to keep their eyes fixed on God's love for them, and to continue preaching the Good News of Jesus to non-Christians.

LIFE FILE LINKS

Investigate the Theme

To find a list of real life stories on this subject turn to the LIFE FILE GUIDE on pages 12 to 22 at the front of the Youth Bible.

NON-CHRISTIANS

1From Jude, a servant of Jesus Christ and a
brother of James.
To all who have been called by God. God the
Father loves you, and you have been kept safe in
Jesus Christ:
2Mercy, peace and love be yours richly.

God will Punish Sinners

3Dear friends, I wanted very much to write to
you about the salvation[d] we all share. But I felt
the need to write to you about something else: I
want to encourage you to fight hard for the faith
that was given the holy people of God once and
for all time. 4Some people have secretly entered
your group. Long ago the prophets[d] wrote about
these people who will be judged guilty. They are
against God and have changed the grace of our
God into a reason for sexual sin. They also refuse
to accept Jesus Christ, our only Master and Lord.
5I want to remind you of some things you al-
ready know: remember that the Lord saved his
people by bringing them out of the land of Egypt.
But later he destroyed all those who did not be-
lieve. 6And remember the angels who did not
keep their place of power but left their proper
home. The Lord has kept these angels in dark-
ness, bound with everlasting chains, to be judged
on the great day. 7Also remember the cities of

PERSISTENCE

In the Swim

Charlie had been an asthmatic since birth. He often had to sit out of school sports because he would get out of breath very quickly.

As he sat on the sidelines watching the other kids enjoy themselves, he felt sad. If only there was something that he could do that might make him feel better. If only there was some sport which he could excel in.

On the next visit to his doctor, Charlie asked if there was any sport which he could concentrate on without damaging his health. The doctor suggested swimming as one of the best sports and so within a week Charlie was in his local pool.

At first he could only manage a few strokes before he got breathless, but he persevered and soon he was able to swim from one side of the pool to the other. By now he had decided that his goal was to compete in a 100-metre breaststroke race – and win.

Every day he could be found in the pool, either swimming or exercising his legs or arms on their own. He figured that the stronger his limbs were, the less his body would have to fight for breath.

His theory proved right. Over several months Charlie developed his muscles and felt fitter than ever before. When the date of the 100-metre breaststroke race was announced, Charlie was the first to enter his name.

On the day of the race, his friends came to the pool to cheer him on. None of them really expected Charlie to win; they simply admired his guts and determination.

But the determination paid off, and when Charlie left the pool that day, he was holding a medal for coming first.

It's this kind of determination and faith that **Jude 17–25** urges all Christians to have as they follow God.

- How does Charlie's brave determination compare with the sort that Jude advised Christians to have?
- How can this passage encourage you to "keep going" when the going gets tough?

Consider . . .

- what are the weakest points of your faith? Be determined to strengthen them and so be able to follow God without "losing your breath".
- practising sharing your faith with a Christian friend, then sharing it with a non-Christian friend.

For more, see . . .

- Psalm 113 (p.568)
- 1 Peter 2:4–10 (p.1357)
- 1 Thessalonians 5:12–22 (p.1301)

Sodom[d] and Gomorrah[d] and the other towns
around them. In the same way they were full of
sexual sin and people who desired sexual rela-
tions that God does not allow. They suffer the
punishment of eternal fire, as an example for all
to see.
8It is the same with these people who have
entered your group. They are guided by dreams
and make themselves dirty with sin. They reject
God's authority and speak against the angels.
9Not even the archangel[n] Michael, when he ar-
gued with the devil about who would have the
body of Moses, dared to judge the devil guilty.
Instead, he said, "The Lord punish you." 10But
these people speak against things they do not un-
derstand. And what they do know, by feeling, as
dumb animals know things, are the very things
that destroy them. 11It will be terrible for them.
They have followed the way of Cain, and for
money they have given themselves to doing the
wrong that Balaam did. They have fought against
God as Korah did, and like Korah, they surely will
be destroyed. 12They are like dirty spots in your
special Christian meals you share. They eat with
you and have no fear, caring only for themselves.
They are clouds without rain, which the wind
blows around. They are autumn trees without
fruit that are pulled out of the ground. So they are
twice dead. 13They are like wild waves of the sea,
tossing up their own shameful actions like foam.
They are like stars that wander in the sky. A place
in the blackest darkness has been kept for them
for ever.
14Enoch, the seventh descendant[d] from Adam,
said about these people: "Look, the Lord is com-
ing with many thousands of his holy angels to
15judge every person. He is coming to punish all
who are against God for all the evil they have
done against him. And he will punish the sinners
who are against God for all the evil they have said
against him."
16These people complain and blame others, do-
ing the evil things they want to do. They boast
about themselves, and they flatter others to get
what they want.

Sidelight Don't look for the quotation by Enoch in the Old Testament (Jude 14–15). This is a direct quote from a book known as 1 Enoch, which is part of the 65 documents known as the Pseudepigrapha. Christians don't consider these books part of scripture, but the books were widely read and quoted in New Testament times.

A Warning and Things to Do

17Dear friends, remember what the apostles[d]
of our Lord Jesus Christ said before. 18They said
to you, "In the last times there will be people
who laugh about God, following their own evil
desires which are against God." 19These are the
people who divide you, people whose thoughts
are only of this world, who do not have the
Spirit.[d]
20But dear friends, use your most holy faith to
build yourselves up, praying in the Holy Spirit.
21Keep yourselves in God's love as you wait for
the Lord Jesus Christ with his mercy to give you
life for ever.
22Show mercy to people who have doubts.
23Take others out of the fire, and save them.
Show mercy mixed with fear to others, hating
even their clothes which are dirty from sin.

Praise God

24God is strong and can keep you from falling.
He can bring you before his glory without any
wrong in you and can give you great joy. 25He is
the only God, the One who saves us. To him be
glory, greatness, power and authority through
Jesus Christ our Lord for all time past, now and
for ever. Amen.

archangel The leader among God's angels or messengers.

Revelation

Why Read This Book:

- Hear warnings about problems in churches (Revelation 1—3).
- See God's power against the forces of evil (Revelation 4—11).
- Be comforted by God's promise of hope for all his people (Revelation 12—22).

When?

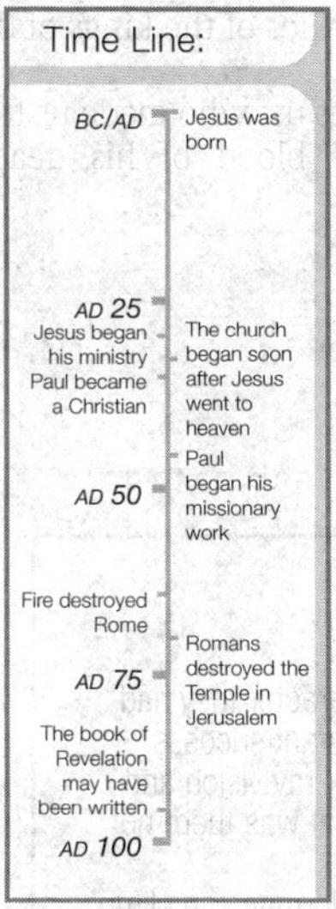

Behind the Scenes:

A blood-red moon. A lamb with seven horns and seven eyes. Locusts with golden crowns. White, red, black and pale horses. A giant, red dragon. A sea of glass mixed with fire. All straight out of a science-fiction movie? No! They are from the book of Revelation, the last book of the Bible – exciting, mysterious . . . and confusing.

This book can be so difficult to understand because it is "apocalyptic". Most often, this kind of literature was written during tough times, when the church was being persecuted. One reason for using the images was to have symbols that Christians would understand, but others would not.

That's certainly true of the book of Revelation. At the time, Christians were under attack by the Roman authorities who demanded that all people worship the emperor. Many Christians refused, and many were executed.

Scholars view the symbols, events and visions in Revelation in different ways. Some of the major views include:

- The book describes the first-century situation, and all the events described in it have taken place.
- The book predicts a long chain of events, concluding with Christ's Second Coming.
- The visions describe the final days before the end of the world, and do not relate directly to biblical times.
- The book does not predict the future; rather it uses symbolic language to teach religious truth about God's victory over evil.

Whatever your viewpoint, the main themes are clear. God is powerful. Jesus Christ reigns forever. Those who suffer for Christ will ultimately share his victory.

Where?

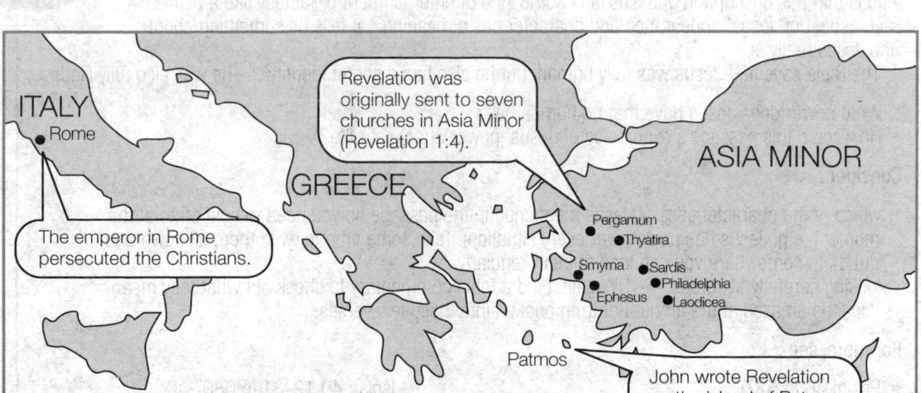

John Tells About this Book

1 This is the revelation[n] of Jesus Christ,
which God gave to him, to show his servants
what must soon happen. And Jesus sent his angel
to show it to his servant John, 2who has told
everything he has seen. It is the word of God; it
is the message from Jesus Christ. 3Happy is the
one who reads the words of God's message, and
happy are the people who hear this message and
do what is written in it. The time is near when all
of this will happen.

Jesus' Message to the Churches

4From John.
To the seven churches in the country of Asia:
Grace and peace to you from the One who is
and was and is coming, and from the seven spirits
before his throne, 5and from Jesus Christ. Jesus is
the faithful witness, the first among those raised
from the dead. He is the ruler of the kings of the
earth.

He is the One who loves us, who made us free
from our sins with the blood of his death.

revelation A making known of truth that has been hidden.

GOD'S POWER

Is It a Bird?

In a comic book in 1938, writer Jerry Siegel and illustrator Joe Shuster introduced a character they had created when they were growing up together. He was called "Superman" and was an instant success. With a secret identity (he was really called Clark Kent), super-human powers (including x-ray vision and amazing strength), plus a colourful costume (pants on the outside of his trousers?) – what was there not to admire?!

If you could be a superhero and have super-human powers, what would you be? Spiderman can climb up walls and swing through cities . . . Batman has a sidekick, Robin, and the Batmobile. Would you want to have the ability to become invisible or have a special weapon of some kind? And what would your costume be?

Everyone loves a hero.

The reason Superman was so popular was because he did amazing things that no other person could, and he fought evil to make the world a better place. The comic-book readers could easily engross themselves in the story and imagine what it would be like to be the superhero or be rescued by him.

Read **Revelation 1:4–18**. It's an amazing description of Jesus which John saw in a vision that makes Jesus seem like a comic-book superhero. But what we need to remember as we read is that this description of Jesus isn't some kind of entertainment or fantasy like a comic. Each aspect of Jesus' appearance and character has a meaning – it tells us something about who Jesus really is.

The Bible says that Jesus was fully human, but he also had a secret identity . . . he was also fully God!

- What power does Jesus have that no human has?
- How could this passage's expression of Jesus' power affect your life?

Consider . . .

- which of the characteristics of Jesus mentioned in the passage do you need to hold on to at the moment (e.g. Jesus has power over every situation). Take some time to write them all down and put them somewhere you can look at them regularly.
- looking carefully at verses 12–15 again. Find a Bible commentary to check out what they mean. You'll be amazed at the amount of truth packed into these few verses.

For more, see . . .

- Psalm 46 (p.527)
- Luke 18:27–39 (p.1080)
- Isaiah 40:12–31 (p.680)

6He made us to be a kingdom of priests who
serve God his Father. To Jesus Christ be glory
and power for ever and ever! Amen.
7Look, Jesus is coming with the clouds, and
everyone will see him, even those who stabbed
him. And all peoples of the earth will cry loudly
because of him. Yes, this will happen! Amen.
8The Lord God says, “I am the Alpha and the
Omega.[n] I am the One who is and was and is
coming. I am the Almighty.”
9I, John, am your brother. All of us share with
Christ in suffering, in the kingdom and in pa-
tience to continue. I was on the island of Patmos,[n]
because I had preached the word of God and the
message about Jesus. 10On the Lord’s day I was in
the Spirit,[d] and I heard a loud voice behind me
that sounded like a trumpet. 11The voice said,
“Write what you see in a book and send it to the
seven churches: to Ephesus, Smyrna, Pergamum,
Thyatira, Sardis, Philadelphia and Laodicea.”
12I turned to see who was talking to me. When I
turned, I saw seven golden lampstands 13and
someone among the lampstands who was “like a
Son of Man”.[n] He was dressed in a long robe and
had a gold band around his chest. 14His head
and hair were white like wool, as white as snow,
and his eyes were like flames of fire. 15His feet
were like bronze that glows hot in a furnace, and
his voice was like the noise of flooding water.
16He held seven stars in his right hand, and a
sharp two-edged sword came out of his mouth.
He looked like the sun shining at its brightest time.
17When I saw him, I fell down at his feet like
a dead man. He put his right hand on me and
said, “Do not be afraid. I am the First and the
Last. 18I am the One who lives; I was dead, but
look, I am alive for ever and ever! And I hold the
keys to death and to the place of the dead. 19So
write the things you see, what is now and what
will happen later. 20Here is the secret of the seven
stars that you saw in my right hand and the seven
golden lampstands: the seven lampstands are the
seven churches, and the seven stars are the
angels of the seven churches.

> **Sidelight** The island of Patmos, where John wrote Revelation (Revelation 1:9), was the Alcatraz of the Roman Empire. Religious and political prisoners were banished to this island “prison”, which is only about sixteen kilometres long.

To the Church in Ephesus

2 “Write this to the angel of the church in
Ephesus:
“The One who holds the seven stars in his
right hand and walks among the seven golden
lampstands says this: 2I know what you do, how
you work hard and never give up. I know you do
not put up with the false teachings of evil people.
You have tested those who say they are apostles[d]
but really are not, and you found they are liars.
3You have patience and have suffered troubles for
my name and have not given up.
4“But I have this against you: you have left the
love you had in the beginning. 5So remember
where you were before you fell. Change your
hearts and do what you did at first. If you do not
change, I will come to you and will take away
your lampstand from its place. 6But there is some-
thing you do that is right: you hate what the
Nicolaitans[n] do, as much as I.
7“Every person who has ears should listen to
what the Spirit[d] says to the churches. To those
who win the victory I will give the right to eat the
fruit from the tree of life, which is in the garden
of God.

To the Church in Smyrna

8“Write this to the angel of the church in
Smyrna:
“The One who is the First and the Last, who
died and came to life again, says this: 9I know
your troubles and that you are poor, but really
you are rich! I know the bad things some people
say about you. They say they are Jews, but they
are not true Jews. They are a synagogue[d] that
belongs to Satan. 10Do not be afraid of what you
are about to suffer. I tell you, the devil will put
some of you in prison to test you, and you will
suffer for ten days. But be faithful, even if you
have to die, and I will give you the crown of life.
11“Everyone who has ears should listen to what
the Spirit[d] says to the churches. Those who win
the victory will not be hurt by the second death.

To the Church in Pergamum

12“Write this to the angel of the church in
Pergamum:
“The One who has the sharp, two-edged sword
says this: 13I know where you live. It is where
Satan has his throne. But you are true to me. You
did not refuse to tell about your faith in me even
during the time of Antipas, my faithful witness
who was killed in your city, where Satan lives.

Alpha and the Omega The first and last letters of the Greek alphabet. This means “the beginning and the end”.
Patmos A small island in the Aegean Sea, near the coast of Asia Minor (modern Turkey).
“like . . . Man” “Son of Man” is a name Jesus called himself. See dictionary.
Nicolaitans This is the name of a religious group that followed false beliefs and ideas.

14“But I have a few things against you: you
have some there who follow the teaching of
Balaam. He taught Balak how to cause the people
of Israel to sin by eating food offered to idols and by
taking part in sexual sins. 15You also have some
who follow the teaching of the Nicolaitans.[n]
16So change your hearts and lives. If you do not,
I will come to you quickly and fight against them
with the sword that comes out of my mouth.
17“Everyone who has ears should listen to
what the Spirit[d] says to the churches.
“I will give some of the hidden manna[d] to
everyone who wins the victory. I will also give to
each one who wins the victory a white stone
with a new name written on it. No one knows
this new name except the one who receives it.

To the Church in Thyatira

18“Write this to the angel of the church in
Thyatira:
“The Son of God, who has eyes that blaze like
fire and feet like shining bronze, says this: 19I
know what you do. I know about your love, your
faith, your service and your patience. I know that
you are doing more now than you did at first.
20“But I have this against you: you let that
woman Jezebel spread false teachings. She says
she is a prophetess,[d] but by her teaching she leads
my people to take part in sexual sins and to eat
food that is offered to idols. 21I have given her
time to change her heart and turn away from her
sin, but she does not want to change. 22So I will
throw her on a bed of suffering. And all those
who take part in adultery[d] with her will suffer
greatly if they do not turn away from the wrongs
she does. 23I will also kill her followers. Then
all the churches will know I am the One who
searches hearts and minds, and I will repay each
of you for what you have done.
24“But others of you in Thyatira have not fol-
lowed her teaching and have not learned what
some call Satan's deep secrets. I say to you that
I will not put any other load on you. 25Only con-
tinue in your loyalty until I come.
26“I will give power over the nations to every-
one who wins the victory and continues to be
obedient to me until the end.
27‘You will rule over them with an iron rod,
as when pottery is broken into pieces.’

Psalm 2:9

28This is the same power I received from my Fa-
ther. I will also give him the morning star.
29Everyone who has ears should listen to what
the Spirit[d] says to the churches.

Sidelight Mathematicians, arise! Numbers have an important role in Revelation, with many having symbolic significance. For example, seven (Revelation 3:1) symbolises completeness; four signifies the created universe (Revelation 7:1, p.1393); and twelve symbolises the church or Israel (Revelation 21:12–14, p.1404).

To the Church in Sardis

3 “Write this to the angel of the church in
Sardis:
“The One who has the seven spirits and the
seven stars says this: I know what you do. People
say that you are alive, but really you are dead.
2Wake up! Make yourselves stronger before what
you have left dies completely. I have found that
what you are doing is less than what my God
wants. 3So do not forget what you have received
and heard. Obey it, and change your hearts and
lives. So you must wake up, or I will come like a
thief, and you will not know when I will come to
you. 4But you have a few there in Sardis who
have kept their clothes clean, so they will walk
with me and will wear white clothes, because
they are worthy. 5Those who win the victory will
be dressed in white clothes like them. And I will
not erase their names from the book of life, but I
will say they belong to me before my Father and
before his angels. 6Everyone who has ears should
listen to what the Spirit[d] says to the churches.

To the Church in Philadelphia

7“Write this to the angel of the church in
Philadelphia:
“This is what the One who is holy and true,
who holds the key of David, says. When he opens
a door, no one can close it. And when he closes it,
no one can open it. 8I know what you do. I have
put an open door before you, which no one can
close. I know you have a little strength, but you
have obeyed my teaching and were not afraid to
speak my name. 9Those in the synagogue[d] that be-
longs to Satan say they are Jews, but they are not
true Jews; they are liars. I will make them come
before you and bow at your feet, and they will
know that I have loved you. 10You have obeyed my
teaching about not giving up your faith. So I will
keep you from the time of trouble that will come to
the whole world to test those who live on earth.
11“I am coming soon. Continue strong in your
faith so no one will take away your crown. 12I will

Nicolaitans This is the name of a religious group that followed false beliefs and ideas.

make those who win the victory to become pil-
lars in the temple of my God, and they will never
have to leave it. I will write on them the name of
my God and the name of the city of my God, the
new Jerusalem,[n] that comes down out of heaven
from my God. I will also write on them my new
name. 13Everyone who has ears should listen to
what the Spirit[d] says to the churches.

To the Church in Laodicea

14"Write this to the angel of the church in
Laodicea:
"The Amen,[n] the faithful and true witness,
the beginning of all God has made, says this: 15I
know what you do, that you are neither hot nor
cold. I wish that you were either hot or cold!
16But because you are warm—neither hot, nor
cold—I am ready to spit you out of my mouth.
17You say, 'I am rich, and I have become wealthy
and do not need anything.' But you do not know
that you are really miserable, pitiful, poor, blind
and naked. 18I advise you to buy from me gold
made pure in fire so you can be truly rich. Buy
from me white clothes so you can be clothed and
so you can cover your shameful nakedness. Buy
from me medicine to put on your eyes so you
can truly see.
19"I correct and punish those whom I love. So
be eager to do right, and change your hearts and
lives. 20Here I am! I stand at the door and knock. If
you hear my voice and open the door, I will come
in and eat with you, and you will eat with me.
21"Those who win the victory will sit with me
on my throne in the same way that I won the
victory and sat down with my Father on his
throne. 22Everyone who has ears should listen to
what the Spirit[d] says to the churches."

John Sees Heaven

4 After the vision of these things I looked, and
there before me was an open door in heaven.
And the same voice that spoke to me before, that
sounded like a trumpet, said, "Come up here,
and I will show you what must happen after
this." 2Immediately I was in the Spirit,[d] and be-
fore me was a throne in heaven, and someone
was sitting on it. 3The One who sat on the
throne looked like precious stones, like jasper
and carnelian. All around the throne was a rain-
bow the colour of an emerald. 4Around the
throne there were 24 other thrones with 24 eld-
ers sitting on them. They were dressed in white
and had golden crowns on their heads. 5Light-
ning flashes and noises and thundering came
from the throne. Before the throne seven lamps
were burning, which are the seven spirits of God.
6Also before the throne there was something that
looked like a sea of glass, clear like crystal.
In the centre and around the throne were four
living creatures with eyes all over them, in front
and behind. 7The first living creature was like a
lion. The second was like a calf. The third had a
face like a man. The fourth was like a flying eagle.
8Each of these four living creatures had six wings
and was covered all over with eyes, inside and
out. Day and night they never stop saying:
"Holy, holy, holy is the Lord God Almighty.
He was, he is, and he is coming."
9These living creatures give glory, honour and
thanks to the One who sits on the throne, who
lives for ever and ever. 10Then the 24 elders bow
down before the One who sits on the throne, and
they worship him who lives for ever and ever.
They put their crowns down before the throne
and say:
11"You are worthy, our Lord and God,
to receive glory and honour and power,
because you made all things.
Everything existed and was made,
because you wanted it."

5 Then I saw a scroll in the right hand of the
One sitting on the throne. The scroll had
writing on both sides and was kept closed with
seven seals. 2And I saw a powerful angel calling
in a loud voice, "Who is worthy to break the seals
and open the scroll?" 3But there was no one in
heaven or on earth or under the earth who could
open the scroll or look inside it. 4I cried hard
because there was no one who was worthy to
open the scroll or look inside. 5But one of the
elders said to me, "Do not cry! The Lion[n] from the
tribe[d] of Judah, David's descendant,[d] has won
the victory so that he is able to open the scroll
and its seven seals."
6Then I saw a Lamb standing in the centre of
the throne and in the middle of the four living
creatures and the elders. The Lamb looked as if

Sidelight Ancient scrolls (Revelation 5:1) were created by beating papyrus (a reed found in the Nile River) into sheets (often about 20 cm x 25 cm) and sewing them together. A scroll of Revelation – written on both sides to save money – would have been about 4½ metres long!

Jerusalem This name is used to mean the spiritual city God built for his people. See Revelation 21—22.
Amen Used here as a name for Jesus; it means to agree fully that something is true.
Lion Here refers to Christ.

he had been killed. He had seven horns and seven
eyes, which are the seven spirits of God that were
sent into all the world. 7The Lamb came and
took the scroll from the right hand of the One sit-
ting on the throne. 8When he took the scroll, the
four living creatures and the 24 elders bowed
down before the Lamb. Each one of them had a
harp and golden bowls full of incense,[d] which
are the prayers of God's holy people. 9And they
all sang a new song to the Lamb:

"You are worthy to take the scroll
and to open its seals,
because you were killed,
and with the blood of your death you
bought people for God
from every tribe, language, people and
nation.
10You made them to be a kingdom of priests
for our God,
and they will rule on the earth."

11Then I looked, and I heard the voices of many
angels around the throne, and the four living
creatures, and the elders. There were thousands
and thousands of angels, 12saying in a loud voice:

"The Lamb who was killed is worthy
to receive power, wealth, wisdom and strength,
honour, glory and praise!"

13Then I heard all creatures in heaven and on
earth and under the earth and in the sea saying:

"To the One who sits on the throne
and to the Lamb
be praise and honour and glory and power
for ever and ever."

14The four living creatures said, "Amen," and
the elders bowed down and worshipped.

6 Then I watched while the Lamb opened the
first of the seven seals. I heard one of the
four living creatures say with a voice like thun-
der, "Come!" 2I looked, and there before me was
a white horse. The rider on the horse held a bow,
and he was given a crown, and he rode out, de-
termined to win the victory.

3When the Lamb opened the second seal, I
heard the second living creature say, "Come!"

WORSHIP

Heaven Download

Nathan removed his headphones and handed them back to his friend Isaac. "That last song you downloaded had a weird ending."

"I know," Isaac replied. "But hey, maybe that's just the music of tomorrow!" They both proceeded to play air guitars and scrunch their faces.

"Rock and roll, baby, yeah!"

Strangely, the last book of the Bible is full of all sorts of weird things. Living creatures that talk and sing, a lamb with seven horns and seven eyes, periodic bursts of huge crowds shouting and then remaining completely silent . . . and that's just a handful of them! The reason is because the whole book was "downloaded" to the world thousands of years ago through a man who could only describe his glimpse of heaven in images he was familiar with.

Revelation 5:11–14 paints a beautiful picture of all God's creation worshipping him together in perfect unison. The elders are so overloaded by this incredible insight into the character of God, that (like Isaac's computer) they literally "crash" down to their knees, bowing before him.

- What are some ways that you really connect with God?
- What was the last thing you "downloaded" from heaven while spending time worshipping God? When will you tap into eternity again?

Consider . . .

- meditating and thinking about the characteristics of God mentioned in this passage.
- taking the time to find a secret place to connect with God. Let him even give you *new* expressions of worship.

For more, see . . .

- Psalm 100 (p.558)
- Ezekiel 1:1–28 (p.788)
- Isaiah 6:1–8 (p.645)
- Revelation 22:1–5 (p.1404)

4Then another horse came out, a red one. Its
rider was given power to take away peace from
the earth and to make people kill each other, and
he was given a big sword.

5When the Lamb opened the third seal, I
heard the third living creature say, "Come!" I
looked, and there before me was a black horse,
and its rider held a pair of scales in his hand.
6Then I heard something that sounded like a
voice coming from the middle of the four living
creatures. The voice said, "A litre of wheat for a
day's pay, and 3 litres of barley for a day's pay,
and do not damage the olive oil and wine!"

7When the Lamb opened the fourth seal, I
heard the voice of the fourth living creature say,
"Come!" 8I looked, and there before me was a
pale horse. Its rider was named death, and Hades[n]
was following close behind him. They were given
power over a quarter of the earth to kill people
by war, by starvation, by disease and by the wild
animals of the earth.

9When the Lamb opened the fifth seal, I saw
under the altar the souls of those who had been
killed because they were faithful to the word of
God and to the message they had received. 10These
souls shouted in a loud voice, "Holy and true Lord,
how long until you judge the people of the earth
and punish them for killing us?" 11Then each one
of them was given a white robe and was told to
wait a short time longer. There were still some of
their fellow servants and brothers and sisters[n] in
the service of Christ who must be killed as they
were. They had to wait until all of this was finished.

12Then I watched while the Lamb opened the
sixth seal, and there was a great earthquake. The
sun became black like rough black cloth, and
the whole moon became red like blood. 13And the
stars in the sky fell to the earth like figs falling from
a fig tree when the wind blows. 14The sky disap-
peared as a scroll when it is rolled up, and every
mountain and island was moved from its place.

15Then the kings of the earth, the rulers, the
generals, the rich people, the powerful people,
the slaves and the free people hid themselves in
caves and in the rocks on the mountains. 16They
called to the mountains and the rocks, "Fall on
us. Hide us from the face of the One who sits on
the throne and from the anger of the Lamb!
17The great day for their anger has come, and
who can stand against it?"

The 144,000 People of Israel

7 After the vision of these things I saw four
angels standing at the four corners of the
earth. The angels were holding the four winds of
the earth to keep them from blowing on the land
or on the sea or on any tree. 2Then I saw another
angel coming up from the east who had the seal of
the living God. And he called out in a loud voice
to the four angels to whom God had given power
to harm the earth and the sea. 3He said to them,
"Do not harm the land or the sea or the trees until
we mark with a sign the foreheads of the people
who serve our God." 4Then I heard how many
people were marked with the sign. There were
144,000 from every tribe[d] of the people of Israel.

5From the tribe of Judah 12,000 were
marked with the sign,
from the tribe of Reuben 12,000,
from the tribe of Gad 12,000,
6from the tribe of Asher 12,000,
from the tribe of Naphtali 12,000,
from the tribe of Manasseh 12,000,
7from the tribe of Simeon 12,000,
from the tribe of Levi 12,000,
from the tribe of Issachar 12,000,
8from the tribe of Zebulun 12,000,
from the tribe of Joseph 12,000,
and from the tribe of Benjamin 12,000 were
marked with the sign.

The Great Crowd Worships God

9After the vision of these things I looked, and
there was a great number of people, so many that
no one could count them. They were from every
nation, tribe,[d] people and language of the earth.
They were all standing before the throne and be-
fore the Lamb, wearing white robes and holding
palm branches in their hands. 10They were shout-
ing in a loud voice, "Salvation belongs to our God,
who sits on the throne, and to the Lamb." 11All
the angels were standing around the throne and
the elders and the four living creatures. They all
bowed down on their faces before the throne and
worshipped God, 12saying, "Amen! Praise, glory,
wisdom, thanks, honour, power and strength be-
long to our God for ever and ever. Amen!"

13Then one of the elders asked me, "Who are
these people dressed in white robes? Where did
they come from?"

14I answered, "You know who they are, sir."

And the elder said to me, "These are the people
who have come out of the great distress. They
have washed their robes and made them white
in the blood of the Lamb.[n] 15Because of this,
they are before the throne of God. They worship
him day and night in his temple.[d] And the One
who sits on the throne will be present with them.

Hades The unseen world of the dead.
brothers and sisters Although the Greek text says "brothers" here and throughout this book, John's words refer to the entire church, both men and women.
washed . . . Lamb This means they believed in Jesus so that their sins could be forgiven through Christ's blood.

[16]Those people will never be hungry again, and
they will never be thirsty again. The sun will not
hurt them, and no heat will burn them, [17]be-
cause the Lamb at the centre of the throne will
be their shepherd. He will lead them to springs
of water that give life. And God will wipe away
every tear from their eyes."

The Seventh Seal

8 When the Lamb opened the seventh seal,
there was silence in heaven for about half an
hour. [2]And I saw the seven angels who stand be-
fore God and to whom were given seven trumpets.
[3]Another angel came and stood at the altar,
holding a golden pan for incense. [d] He was given

Sidelight The seals which secured the documents in Revelation (see Revelation 8:1) meant: that the message was one of authority, that it belonged to the person named on the seal (in this case God) and that the message was not a fake. The seal also served to make sure that the documents were secure – a kind of biblical "For Your Eyes Only" message!

SADNESS

The Worst Year of Her Life

Lisa had looked forward to her first year in college. She did not know it would be her life's worst.

Early in the autumn her mother was diagnosed as having cancer. Her dad gave up his job to help care for her mum. Money, time and energy were scarce. And Lisa was carrying a heavy workload at college.

"I had to take care of the house, feed everyone, and plough through my work," she recalls. "It was tough, but I got along somehow."

One day, however, her mother entered the hospital for one final, risky operation to fight the cancer. "When the surgeons came out of the operating theatre, I could tell by the way they looked at me that she was gone," she says.

After the funeral, Lisa's life changed dramatically. Her father, in deep grief, wandered about the house. One day Lisa found a "For Sale" sign in their front garden. "It's too painful for me to live here," her father said.

Unable to find work and desperately lonely, her father returned to his home town. Lisa faced the difficult choice: either live with her older sister or go with her father. Even though she missed her dad, Lisa stayed with her sister.

What sustained her through this sad time? "Christian friends and a caring church got me through the experience," she says. "I couldn't pray, because I was mad at God. All I'd do was cry. These friends just kept loving me, even when I was unlovely."

Lisa carried on with college, studying engineering. Her father, in time, overcame his grief and went on with his life.

"My world fell apart when I was sixteen," Lisa reflects. "Our family suffered a lot. But with God's help, we got through it all, and that's what matters."

Everyone experiences pain, disappointment and uncontrollable events. When those sad times seem overwhelming, Christians can turn to passages such as **Revelation 7:9–17** for a message of hope.

- What hope could Lisa gain from these verses?
- How could these verses help you to deal with sadness in your life?

Consider . . .

- doing something positive to help get you out of the blues. Try visiting a friend, watching a comedy film or exercising.
- visiting someone who is having a sad time. Take a small gift to show you care.

For more, see . . .

- Psalm 40:1–3 (p.523)
- Hebrews 10:23–25 (p.1339)
- Ecclesiastes 3:1–8 (p.622)

much incense to offer with the prayers of all God's
holy people. The angel put this offering on the
golden altar before the throne. [4]The smoke from
the incense went up from the angel's hand to
God with the prayers of God's people. [5]Then the
angel filled the incense pan with fire from the
altar and threw it on the earth, and there were
flashes of lightning, thunder and loud noises, and
an earthquake.

The Seven Angels and Trumpets

[6]Then the seven angels who had the seven
trumpets prepared to blow them.
[7]The first angel blew his trumpet, and hail and
fire mixed with blood were poured down on the
earth. And a third of the earth, and all the green
grass, and a third of the trees were burnt up.
[8]Then the second angel blew his trumpet, and
something that looked like a big mountain, burn-
ing with fire, was thrown into the sea. And a
third of the sea became blood, [9]a third of the
living things in the sea died, and a third of the
ships were destroyed.
[10]Then the third angel blew his trumpet, and a
large star, burning like a torch, fell from the sky. It
fell on a third of the rivers and on the springs of
water. [11]The name of the star is Wormwood.[n] And
a third of all the water became bitter, and many
people died from drinking the water that was bitter.
[12]Then the fourth angel blew his trumpet, and
a third of the sun, and a third of the moon, and a
third of the stars were struck. So a third of them
became dark, and a third of the day was without
light, and also the night.
[13]While I watched, I heard an eagle that was fly-
ing high in the air cry out in a loud voice, "Trouble!
Trouble! Trouble for those who live on the earth
because of the remaining sounds of the trumpets
that the other three angels are about to blow!"

9 Then the fifth angel blew his trumpet, and I
saw a star fall from the sky to the earth. The
star was given the key to the deep hole that leads
to the bottomless pit. [2]Then it opened up the
hole that leads to the bottomless pit, and smoke
came up from the hole like smoke from a big
furnace. Then the sun and sky became dark be-
cause of the smoke from the hole. [3]Then locusts[d]
came down to the earth out of the smoke, and
they were given the power to sting like scorpi-
ons.[n] [4]They were told not to harm the grass on
the earth or any plant or tree. They could harm
only the people who did not have the sign of God
on their foreheads. [5]These locusts were not given
the power to kill anyone, but to cause pain to the
people for five months. And the pain they felt was
like the pain a scorpion gives when it stings some-
one. [6]During those days people will look for a
way to die, but they will not find it. They will
want to die, but death will run away from them.
[7]The locusts looked like horses prepared for
battle. On their heads they wore what looked like
crowns of gold, and their faces looked like human
faces. [8]Their hair was like women's hair, and their
teeth were like lions' teeth. [9]Their chests looked
like iron breastplates, and the sound of their wings
was like the noise of many horses and chariots
hurrying into battle. [10]The locusts had tails with
stingers like scorpions, and in their tails was their
power to hurt people for five months. [11]The
locusts had a king who was the angel of the bot-
tomless pit. His name in the Hebrew language is
Abaddon and in the Greek language is Apollyon.[n]
[12]The first trouble is past; there are still two
other troubles that will come.
[13]Then the sixth angel blew his trumpet, and I
heard a voice coming from the horns on the
golden altar that is before God. [14]The voice said to
the sixth angel who had the trumpet, "Free the
four angels who are tied at the great river
Euphrates." [15]And they let loose the four angels
who had been kept ready for this hour and day
and month and year so they could kill a third of all
people on the earth. [16]I heard how many troops
on horses were in their army—200,000,000.
[17]The horses and their riders I saw in the vision
looked like this: they had breastplates that were
fiery red, dark blue and yellow like sulphur. The
heads of the horses looked like heads of lions,
with fire, smoke and sulphur coming out of their
mouths. [18]A third of all the people on earth were
killed by these three terrible disasters coming out
of the horses' mouths: the fire, the smoke and the
sulphur. [19]The horses' power was in their mouths
and in their tails; their tails were like snakes with
heads, and with them they hurt people.
[20]The other people who were not killed by
these terrible disasters still did not change their
hearts and turn away from what they had made
with their own hands. They did not stop wor-
shipping demons[d] and idols made of gold, silver,
bronze, stone and wood—things that cannot see
or hear or walk. [21]These people did not change
their hearts and turn away from murder or evil
magic, from their sexual sins or stealing.

The Angel and the Small Scroll

10 Then I saw another powerful angel com-
ing down from heaven dressed in a cloud

Wormwood Name of a very bitter plant; used here to give the idea of bitter sorrow.
scorpions A scorpion is an insect-like creature with a poisonous sting.
Abaddon, Apollyon Both names mean "Destroyer".

with a rainbow over his head. His face was like
the sun, and his legs were like pillars of fire. [2]The
angel was holding a small scroll open in his hand.
He put his right foot on the sea and his left foot on
the land. [3]Then he shouted loudly like the roaring
of a lion. And when he shouted, the voices of
seven thunders spoke. [4]When the seven thunders
spoke, I started to write. But I heard a voice from
heaven say, "Keep hidden what the seven thun-
ders said, and do not write them down."

[5]Then the angel I saw standing on the sea and
on the land raised his right hand to heaven, [6]and
he made a promise by the power of the One who
lives for ever and ever. He is the One who made
the skies and all that is in them, the earth and all
that is in it, and the sea and all that is in it. The
angel promised, "There will be no more waiting!
[7]In the days when the seventh angel is ready to
blow his trumpet, God's secret will be finished.
This secret is the Good News[d] God told to his
servants, the prophets."[d]

[8]Then I heard the same voice from heaven
again, saying to me: "Go and take the open scroll
that is in the hand of the angel that is standing
on the sea and on the land."

[9]So I went to the angel and told him to give me
the small scroll. And he said to me, "Take the
scroll and eat it. It will be sour in your stomach,
but in your mouth it will be sweet as honey." [10]So
I took the small scroll from the angel's hand and
ate it. In my mouth it tasted sweet as honey, but
after I ate it, it was sour in my stomach. [11]Then I
was told, "You must prophesy[d] again about many
peoples, nations, languages and kings."

The Two Witnesses

11 I was given a measuring stick like a rod,
and I was told, "Go and measure the
temple[d] of God and the altar, and count the peo-
ple worshipping there. [2]But do not measure
the yard outside the temple. Leave it alone, be-
cause it has been given to those who are not
God's people. And they will trample on the holy
city for 42 months. [3]And I will give power to my
two witnesses to prophesy[d] for 1,260 days, and
they will be dressed in rough cloth to show their
sadness."

[4]These two witnesses are the two olive trees
and the two lampstands that stand before the Lord
of the earth. [5]And if anyone tries to hurt them, fire
comes from their mouths and kills their enemies.
And if anyone tries to hurt them in whatever way,
in that same way that person will die. [6]These wit-
nesses have the power to stop the sky from rain-
ing during the time they are prophesying. And
they have power to make the waters become
blood, and they have power to send every kind of
trouble to the earth as many times as they want.

[7]When the two witnesses have finished telling
their message, the beast that comes up from the
bottomless pit will fight a war against them. He
will defeat them and kill them. [8]The bodies of
the two witnesses will lie in the street of the great
city where the Lord was killed. This city is named
Sodom[n] and Egypt, which has a spiritual mean-
ing. [9]Those from every race of people, tribe,[d]
language and nation will look at the bodies of the
two witnesses for three and a half days, and they
will refuse to bury them. [10]People who live on
the earth will rejoice and be happy because these
two are dead. They will send each other gifts, be-
cause these two prophets brought much suffer-
ing to those who live on the earth.

[11]But after three and a half days, God put the
breath of life into the two prophets again. They
stood on their feet, and everyone who saw them
became very afraid. [12]Then the two prophets
heard a loud voice from heaven saying, "Come
up here!" And they went up into heaven in a
cloud as their enemies watched.

[13]In the same hour there was a great earth-
quake, and a tenth of the city was destroyed.
7,000 people were killed in the earthquake, and
those who did not die were very afraid and gave
glory to the God of heaven.

[14]The second trouble is finished. Pay atten-
tion: the third trouble is coming soon.

The Seventh Trumpet

[15]Then the seventh angel blew his trumpet.
And there were loud voices in heaven, saying:

"The power to rule the world
now belongs to our Lord and his Christ,[d]
and he will rule for ever and ever."

[16]Then the 24 elders, who sit on their thrones
before God, bowed down on their faces and wor-
shipped God. [17]They said:

"We give thanks to you, Lord God Almighty,
who is and who was,
because you have used your great power
and have begun to rule!
[18]The people of the world were angry,
but your anger has come.
The time has come to judge the dead
and to reward your servants the prophets[d]
and your holy people,
all who respect you, great and small.
The time has come to destroy those who
destroy the earth!"

[19]Then God's temple[d] in heaven was opened.
The Ark[d] that holds the agreement God gave to
his people could be seen in his temple. Then there

Sodom City that God destroyed because the people were so evil.

were flashes of lightning, noises, thunder, an
earthquake and a great hailstorm.

The Woman and the Dragon

12 And then a great wonder appeared in
heaven: a woman was clothed with the
sun, and the moon was under her feet, and a
crown of twelve stars was on her head. 2She was
pregnant and cried out with pain, because she was
about to give birth. 3Then another wonder ap-
peared in heaven: there was a giant red dragon
with seven heads and seven crowns on each head.
He also had ten horns. 4His tail swept a third of the
stars out of the sky and threw them down to the
earth. He stood in front of the woman who was
ready to give birth so he could eat her baby as soon
as it was born. 5Then the woman gave birth to a
son who will rule all the nations with an iron rod.
And her child was taken up to God and to his
throne. 6The woman ran away into the desert to a
place God prepared for her where she would be
taken care of for 1,260 days.
7Then there was a war in heaven. Michael[n]
and his angels fought against the dragon, and the
dragon and his angels fought back. 8But the
dragon was not strong enough, and he and his
angels lost their place in heaven. 9The giant
dragon was thrown down out of heaven. (He is
that old snake called the devil or Satan, who
tricks the whole world.) The dragon with his
angels was thrown down to the earth.
10Then I heard a loud voice in heaven saying:
"The salvation and the power and the
kingdom of our God
and the authority of his Christ[d] have now
come.
The accuser of our brothers and sisters,
who accused them day and night before
our God,
has been thrown down.
11And our brothers and sisters defeated him
by the blood of the Lamb's death
and by the message they preached.
They did not love their lives so much
that they were afraid of death.
12So rejoice, you heavens
and all who live there!
But it will be terrible for the earth and the sea,
because the devil has come down to you!
He is filled with anger,
because he knows he does not have much
time."
13When the dragon saw he had been thrown
down to the earth, he hunted for the woman who
had given birth to the son. 14But the woman was
given the two wings of a great eagle so she could
fly to the place prepared for her in the desert.
There she would be taken care of for three and a
half years, away from the snake. 15Then the snake
poured water out of its mouth like a river towards
the woman so the flood would carry her away.
16But the earth helped the woman by opening its
mouth and swallowing the river that came from
the mouth of the dragon. 17Then the dragon was
very angry at the woman, and he went off to
make war against all her other children—those
who obey God's commands and who have the
message Jesus taught.
18And the dragon stood on the seashore.

The Two Beasts

13 Then I saw a beast coming up out of the
sea. It had ten horns and seven heads,
and there was a crown on each horn. A name
against God was written on each head. 2This
beast looked like a leopard, with feet like a bear's
feet and a mouth like a lion's mouth. And the
dragon gave the beast all of his power and his
throne and great authority. 3One of the heads of
the beast looked as if it had been killed by a
wound, but this death wound was healed. Then
the whole world was amazed and followed the
beast. 4People worshipped the dragon because
he had given his power to the beast. And they
also worshipped the beast, asking, "Who is like
the beast? Who can make war against it?"

Sidelight The reign of the Roman Emperor Nero (often paralleled with the first beast in Revelation 13) was marked by terrible crimes, destruction, and persecution of Christians. When he sent someone to murder his own mother, she bared her body and cried, "Strike my womb because it bore a Nero!"

5The beast was allowed to say proud words and
words against God, and it was allowed to use its
power for 42 months. 6It used its mouth to speak
against God, against God's name, against the place
where God lives, and against all those who live in
heaven. 7It was given power to make war against
God's holy people and to defeat them. It was given
power over every tribe,[d] people, language and na-
tion. 8And all who live on earth will worship the
beast—all the people since the beginning of the
world whose names are not written in the Lamb's
book of life. The Lamb is the One who was killed.
9Anyone who has ears should listen:
10If you are to be a prisoner,
then you will be a prisoner.

Michael The archangel – leader among God's angels or messengers (Jude 9).

If you are to be killed with the sword,
then you will be killed with the sword.
This means that God's holy people must have
patience and faith.
11Then I saw another beast coming up out of
the earth. It had two horns like a lamb, but it
spoke like a dragon. 12This beast stands before the
first beast and uses the same power the first beast
has. By this power it makes everyone living on
earth worship the first beast, who had the death
wound that was healed. 13And the second beast
does great miracles[d] so that it even makes fire
come down from heaven to earth while people
are watching. 14It fools those who live on earth by
the miracles it has been given the power to do. It
does these miracles to serve the first beast. The
second beast orders people to make an idol to
honour the first beast, the one that was wounded
by the deadly sword but sprang to life again.
15The second beast was given power to give life
to the idol of the first one so that the idol could
speak. And the second beast was given power to
command all who will not worship the image of
the beast to be killed. 16The second beast also
forced all people, small and great, rich and poor,
free and slave, to have a mark on their right hand
or on their forehead. 17No one could buy or sell
without this mark, which is the name of the beast
or the number of its name. 18This takes wisdom.
Let the one who has understanding find the
meaning of the number, which is the number of
a person. Its number is 666.

The Song of the Saved

14 Then I looked, and there before me was
the Lamb standing on Mount Zion.[n]
With him were 144,000 people who had his
name and his Father's name written on their
foreheads. 2And I heard a sound from heaven
like the noise of flooding water and like the
sound of loud thunder. The sound I heard was
like people playing harps. 3And they sang a new
song before the throne and before the four living
creatures and the elders. No one could learn the
new song except the 144,000 who had been
bought from the earth. 4These are the ones
who did not do sinful things with women, be-
cause they kept themselves pure. They follow
the Lamb everywhere he goes. These 144,000
were bought from among the people of the earth
as people to be offered to God and the Lamb.
5They were not guilty of telling lies; they are
without fault.

The Three Angels

6Then I saw another angel flying high in the
air. He had the eternal Good News[d] to preach to
those who live on earth—to every nation, tribe,[d]
language and people. 7He preached in a loud
voice, "Fear God and give him praise, because
the time has come for God to judge all people. So
worship God who made the heavens, and the
earth, and the sea, and the springs of water."
8Then the second angel followed the first
angel and said, "Ruined, ruined is the great city
of Babylon! She made all the nations drink the
wine of the anger of her adultery."[d]
9Then a third angel followed the first two
angels, saying in a loud voice: "If anyone
worships the beast and his idol and gets the
beast's mark on the forehead or on the hand,
10that one also will drink the wine of God's
anger, which is prepared with all its strength in
the cup of his anger. And that person will be put
in pain with burning sulphur before the holy
angels and the Lamb. 11And the smoke from
their burning pain will rise for ever and ever.
There will be no rest, day or night, for those who
worship the beast and his idol or who get the
mark of his name." 12This means God's holy
people must be patient. They must obey God's
commands and keep their faith in Jesus.
13Then I heard a voice from heaven saying,
"Write this: happy are the dead who die from
now on in the Lord."
The Spirit[d] says, "Yes, they will rest from their
hard work, and the reward of all they have done
stays with them."

The Earth is Harvested

14Then I looked, and there before me was a
white cloud, and sitting on the white cloud was
One who looked like a Son of Man.[n] He had a
gold crown on his head and a sharp sickle[n] in his
hand. 15Then another angel came out of the tem-
ple[d] and called out in a loud voice to the One who
was sitting on the cloud, "Take your sickle and
harvest the earth, because the time to harvest has
come, and the fruit of the earth is ripe." 16So the
One who was sitting on the cloud swung his
sickle over the earth, and the earth was harvested.
17Then another angel came out of the temple
in heaven, and he also had a sharp sickle. 18And
then another angel, who has power over the fire,
came from the altar. This angel called to the angel
with the sharp sickle, saying, "Take your sharp
sickle and gather the bunches of grapes from the

Mount Zion Another name for Jerusalem; here meaning the spiritual city of God's people.
Son of Man "Son of Man" is a name Jesus called himself. See dictionary.
sickle A farming tool with a curved blade. It was used to harvest grain.

earth's vine, because its grapes are ripe." 19 Then
the angel swung his sickle over the earth. He
gathered the earth's grapes and threw them
into the great winepress [d] of God's anger. 20 They
were trampled in the winepress outside the
city, and blood flowed out of the winepress as
high as horses' bridles for a distance of about
300 kilometres.

The Last Troubles

15 Then I saw another wonder in heaven
that was great and amazing. There were
seven angels bringing seven disasters. These are
the last disasters, because after them, God's anger
is finished.
2 I saw what looked like a sea of glass mixed
with fire. All of those who had won the victory
over the beast and his idol and over the number
of his name were standing by the sea of glass.
They had harps that God had given them. 3 They
sang the song of Moses, the servant of God, and
the song of the Lamb:

"You do great and wonderful things, *Psalm 111:2*
Lord God Almighty. *Amos 3:13*
Everything the LORD does is right and true, *Psalm 145:17*
King of the nations.
4 Everyone will respect you, Lord, *Jeremiah 10:7*
and will honour you.
Only you are holy.
All the nations will come
and worship you, *Psalm 86:9–10*
because the right things you have
done
are now made known." *Deuteronomy 32:4*

5 After this I saw that the temple [d] (the Tent [d] of
the Agreement) in heaven was opened. 6 And the
seven angels bringing the seven disasters came
out of the temple. They were dressed in clean,
shining linen and wore golden bands tied around
their chests. 7 Then one of the four living crea-
tures gave to the seven angels seven golden
bowls filled with the anger of God, who lives for
ever and ever. 8 The temple was filled with smoke
from the glory and the power of God, and no one
could enter the temple until the seven disasters of
the seven angels were finished.

The Bowls of God's Anger

16 Then I heard a loud voice from the tem-
ple saying to the seven angels, "Go and
pour out the seven bowls of God's anger on the
earth."
2 The first angel left and poured out his bowl
on the land. Then ugly and painful sores came
upon all those who had the mark of the beast
and who worshipped his idol.
3 The second angel poured out his bowl on the
sea, and it became blood like that of a dead man,
and every living thing in the sea died.
4 The third angel poured out his bowl on the
rivers and the springs of water, and they became
blood. 5 Then I heard the angel of the waters saying:

"Holy One, you are the One who is and
who was.
You are right to decide to punish these evil
people.
6 They have poured out the blood of your holy
people and your prophets. [d]
So now you have given them blood to drink
as they deserve."

7 And I heard a voice coming from the altar
saying:

"Yes, Lord God Almighty,
the way you punish evil people is right and
fair."

8 The fourth angel poured out his bowl on the
sun, and he was given power to burn the people
with fire. 9 They were burned by the great heat,
and they cursed the name of God, who had con-
trol over these disasters. But the people refused
to change their hearts and lives and give glory
to God.
10 The fifth angel poured out his bowl on the
throne of the beast, and darkness covered its
kingdom. People bit their tongues because of the
pain. 11 They also cursed the God of heaven
because of their pain and the sores they had, but
they refused to change their hearts and turn away
from the evil things they did.
12 The sixth angel poured out his bowl on the
great river Euphrates so that the water in the river
was dried up to prepare the way for the kings
from the east to come. 13 Then I saw three evil
spirits that looked like frogs coming out of the
mouth of the dragon, out of the mouth of the
beast and out of the mouth of the false prophet.
14 These evil spirits are the spirits of demons, [d]
which have power to do miracles. [d] They go out
to the kings of the whole world to gather them
together for the battle on the great day of God
Almighty.
15 "Listen! I will come as a thief comes! Happy
are those who stay awake and keep their clothes
on so that they will not walk around naked and
have people see their shame."
16 Then the evil spirits gathered the kings to-
gether to the place that is called Armageddon in
the Hebrew language.
17 The seventh angel poured out his bowl into
the air. Then a loud voice came out of the tem-
ple [d] from the throne, saying, "It is finished!"
18 Then there were flashes of lightning, noises,
thunder, and a big earthquake—the worst earth-
quake that has ever happened since people have

been on earth. 19The great city split into three
parts, and the cities of the nations were des-
troyed. And God remembered the sins of Babylon
the Great, so he gave that city the cup filled with
the wine of his terrible anger. 20Then every island
ran away, and mountains disappeared. 21Giant
hailstones, each weighing up to 50 kilogrammes,
fell from the sky upon people. People cursed
God for the disaster of the hail, because this
disaster was so terrible.

> **Sidelight** Revelation 16:15 isn't a warning to wear pyjamas in bed. According to Jewish laws of the time, the captain of the Temple would check up on the Temple police at night. If someone was asleep on duty, his clothes were taken off and burned, and he was sent away naked and disgraced. Anyone want an extra cup of coffee or something else to keep them awake?

The Woman on the Animal

17 Then one of the seven angels who had
the seven bowls came and spoke to me.
He said, "Come, and I will show you the punish-
ment that will be given to the great prostitute,[d]
the one sitting over many waters. 2The kings of
the earth sinned sexually with her, and the peo-
ple of the earth became drunk from the wine of
her sexual sin."

3Then the angel carried me away by the Spirit[d]
to the desert. There I saw a woman sitting on a
red beast. It was covered with names insulting to
God written on it, and it had seven heads and
ten horns. 4The woman was dressed in purple
and red and was shining with the gold, precious
jewels and pearls she was wearing. She had a
golden cup in her hand, a cup filled with evil
things and the uncleanness of her sexual sin.
5On her forehead a title was written that was
secret. This is what was written:

THE GREAT BABYLON
MOTHER OF PROSTITUTES
AND OF THE EVIL THINGS OF THE EARTH

6Then I saw that the woman was drunk with
the blood of God's holy people and with the
blood of those who were killed because of their
faith in Jesus.

When I saw the woman, I was very amazed.
7Then the angel said to me, "Why are you
amazed? I will tell you the secret of this woman
and the beast she rides—the one with seven
heads and ten horns. 8The beast you saw was
once alive but is not alive now. But soon it will
come up out of the bottomless pit and go away to
be destroyed. There are people who live on earth
whose names have not been written in the book
of life since the beginning of the world. They will
be amazed when they see the beast, because he
was once alive, is not alive now, but will come
again.

9"You need a wise mind to understand this.
The seven heads on the beast are seven moun-
tains where the woman sits. 10And they are seven
kings. Five of the kings have already been de-
stroyed, one of the kings lives now, and another
has not yet come. When he comes, he must stay
a short time. 11The beast that was once alive, but
is not alive now, is also an eighth king. He be-
longs to the first seven kings, and he will go
away to be destroyed.

12"The ten horns you saw are ten kings who
have not yet begun to rule, but they will receive
power to rule with the beast for one hour. 13All
ten of these kings have the same purpose, and
they will give their power and authority to
the beast. 14They will make war against the
Lamb, but the Lamb will defeat them, because
he is Lord of lords and King of kings. He will
defeat them with his called, chosen and faithful
followers."

15Then the angel said to me, "The waters that
you saw, where the prostitute sits, are peoples,
races, nations and languages. 16The ten horns and
the beast you saw will hate the prostitute. They
will take everything she has and leave her naked.
They will eat her body and burn her with fire.
17God made the ten horns want to carry out his
purpose by agreeing to give the beast their power
to rule, until what God has said comes about.
18The woman you saw is the great city that rules
over the kings of the earth."

Babylon is Destroyed

18 After the vision of these things, I saw
another angel coming down from
heaven. This angel had great power, and his glory
made the earth bright. 2He shouted in a powerful
voice:

"Ruined, ruined is the great city of
Babylon!
She has become a home for demons[d]
and a prison for every evil spirit,
and a prison for every unclean[d] bird and
unclean beast.
3She has been ruined, because all the peoples
of the earth
have drunk the wine of the desire of her
sexual sin.
She has been ruined also because the kings of
the earth
have sinned sexually with her,

and the merchants of the earth
have grown rich from the great wealth of her luxury."

4Then I heard another voice from heaven saying:
"Come out of that city, my people,
so that you will not share in her sins,
so that you will not receive the disasters that will come to her.
5Her sins have piled up as high as the sky,
and God has not forgotten the wrongs she has done.
6Give that city the same as she gave to others.
Pay her back twice as much as she did.
Prepare wine for her that is twice as strong
as the wine she prepared for others.
7She gave herself much glory and rich living.
Give her the same amount of suffering and sadness.
She says to herself, 'I am a queen sitting on my throne.
I am not a widow; I will never be sad.'
8So these disasters will come to her in one day:
death, and crying, and great hunger,
and she will be destroyed by fire,
because the Lord God who judges her is powerful."

9The kings of the earth who sinned sexually
with her and shared her wealth will see the
smoke from her burning. Then they will cry and
be sad because of her death. 10They will be afraid
of her suffering and stand far away and say:
"Terrible! How terrible for you, great city,
powerful city of Babylon,
because your punishment has come in one hour!"

11And the merchants of the earth will cry and
be sad about her, because now there is no one to
buy their cargoes— 12cargoes of gold, silver, jewels,
pearls; fine linen, purple cloth, silk, red cloth;
all kinds of citron wood and all kinds of things
made from ivory, expensive wood, bronze, iron
and marble; 13cinnamon, spice, incense, *d* myrrh, *d*
frankincense; *d* wine, olive oil, fine flour, wheat;
cattle, sheep, horses, carriages; slaves and human
lives.

14The merchants will say,
"Babylon, the good things you wanted are gone from you.
All your rich and fancy things have disappeared.
You will never have them again."
15The merchants who became rich from selling
to her will be afraid of her suffering and will
stand far away. They will cry and be sad 16and
say:
"Terrible! How terrible for the great city!
She was dressed in fine linen, purple and red cloth,
and she was shining with gold, precious jewels and pearls!
17All these riches have been destroyed in one hour!"

Every sea captain, all those who travel, the
sailors, and all those who earn their living from
the sea stood far away from Babylon. 18As they
saw the smoke from her burning, they cried out
loudly, "There was never a city like this great
city!" 19And they threw dirt on their heads and
cried, weeping and were sad. They said:
"Terrible! How terrible for the great city!
All the people who had ships on the sea
became rich because of her wealth!
But she has been destroyed in one hour!
20Be happy because of this, heaven!
Be happy, God's holy people and apostles *d*
and prophets! *d*
God has punished her because of what she did to you."

21Then a powerful angel picked up a large stone,
like one used for grinding grain, and threw it
into the sea. He said:
"In the same way, the great city of Babylon will be thrown down,
and it will never be found again.
22The music of people playing harps and other instruments, flutes and trumpets,
will never be heard in you again.
No workman doing any job
will ever be found in you again.
The sound of grinding grain
will never be heard in you again.
23The light of a lamp
will never shine in you again,
and the voices of a bridegroom and bride
will never be heard in you again.
Your merchants were the world's great people,
and all the nations were tricked by your magic.
24You are guilty of the death of the prophets and God's holy people
and all who have been killed on earth."

People in Heaven Praise God

19 After this vision and announcement I
heard what sounded like a great many
people in heaven saying:
"Hallelujah! *n*
Salvation, glory and power belong to our God,

Hallelujah This means "praise God!"

2 because his judgements are true and right.
He has punished the prostitute[d]
who made the earth evil with her
sexual sin.
He has paid her back for the death of his
servants."
3Again they said:
"Hallelujah!
She is burning, and her smoke will rise for
ever and ever."
4Then the 24 elders and the four living crea-
tures bowed down and worshipped God, who
sits on the throne. They said:
"Amen, Hallelujah!"

Sidelight In the same way that we shake hands today to greet someone, in Bible times people would bow (Revelation 19:4). Depending on whom you were greeting, you would either nod your head politely or give a more elaborate bend-at-the waist bow.

5Then a voice came from the throne, saying:
"Praise our God, all you who serve him
and all you who honour him, both small
and great!"
6Then I heard what sounded like a great
many people, like the noise of flooding water
and like the noise of loud thunder. The people
were saying:
"Hallelujah!
Our Lord God, the Almighty, rules.
7Let us rejoice and be happy
and give God glory,
because the wedding of the Lamb has come,
and the Lamb's bride has made herself
ready.
8Fine linen, bright and clean, was given to her
to wear."
(The fine linen means the good things done by
God's holy people.)
9And the angel said to me, "Write this: happy
are those who have been invited to the wedding
meal of the Lamb!" And the angel said, "These
are the true words of God."
10Then I bowed down at the angel's feet to
worship him, but he said to me, "Do not wor-
ship me! I am a servant like you and your broth-
ers and sisters who have the message of Jesus.
Worship God, because the message about Jesus
is the spirit that gives all prophecy."[d]

The Rider on the White Horse

11Then I saw heaven opened, and there before
me was a white horse. The rider on the horse is
called Faithful and True, and he is right when he
judges and makes war. 12His eyes are like burning
fire, and on his head are many crowns. He has a
name written on him, which no one but himself
knows. 13He is dressed in a robe dipped in blood,
and his name is the Word of God. 14The armies
of heaven, dressed in fine linen, white and clean,
were following him on white horses. 15Out of the
rider's mouth comes a sharp sword that he will
use to defeat the nations, and he will rule them
with a rod of iron. He will crush out the wine in
the winepress[d] of the terrible anger of God the
Almighty. 16On his robe and on his upper leg was
written this name: KING OF KINGS AND LORD OF LORDS.
17Then I saw an angel standing in the sun, and
he called with a loud voice to all the birds flying
in the sky: "Come and gather together for the
great feast of God 18so that you can eat the bod-
ies of kings, generals, mighty people, horses and
their riders, and the bodies of all people—free,
slave, small and great."
19Then I saw the beast and the kings of the
earth. Their armies were gathered together to
make war against the rider on the horse and his
army. 20But the beast was captured and with him
the false prophet[d] who did the miracles[d] for the
beast. The false prophet had used these miracles
to trick those who had the mark of the beast and
worshipped his idol. The false prophet and the
beast were thrown alive into the lake of fire that
burns with sulphur. 21And their armies were
killed with the sword that came out of the mouth
of the rider on the horse, and all the birds ate the
bodies until they were full.

The 1,000 Years

20 I saw an angel coming down from
heaven. He had the key to the bottom-
less pit and a large chain in his hand. 2The angel
grabbed the dragon, that old snake who is the
devil and Satan, and tied him up for 1,000 years.
3Then he threw him into the bottomless pit,
closed it and locked it over him. The angel did
this so he could not trick the people of the earth
any more until the 1,000 years were ended. After
1,000 years he must be set free for a short time.
4Then I saw some thrones and people sitting
on them who had been given the power to judge.
And I saw the souls of those who had been killed
because they were faithful to the message of Jesus
and the message from God. They had not wor-
shipped the beast or his idol, and they had not
received the mark of the beast on their foreheads
or on their hands. They came back to life and ruled
with Christ for 1,000 years. 5(The others that were
dead did not live again until the 1,000 years
were ended.) This is the first raising of the dead.
6Happy and holy are those who share in this first
raising of the dead. The second death has no power

over them. They will be priests for God and for
Christ and will rule with him for 1,000 years.
7 When the 1,000 years are over, Satan will be
set free from his prison. 8 Then he will go out to
trick the nations in all the earth—Gog and
Magog—to gather them for battle. There are so
many people they will be like sand on the seashore.
9 And Satan's army marched across the earth and
gathered around the camp of God's people and the
city God loves. But fire came down from heaven
and burnt them up. 10 And Satan, who tricked
them, was thrown into the lake of burning sulphur
with the beast and the false prophet.[d] There they
will be punished day and night for ever and ever.

People of the World are Judged

11 Then I saw a great white throne and the One
who was sitting on it. Earth and sky ran away
from him and disappeared. 12 And I saw the dead,
great and small, standing before the throne. Then
books were opened, and the book of life was
opened. The dead were judged by what they had
done, which was written in the books. 13 The sea
gave up the dead who were in it, and Death and
Hades[n] gave up the dead who were in them.
Each person was judged by what he had done.
14 And Death and Hades were thrown into the
lake of fire. The lake of fire is the second death.
15 And anyone whose name was not found written
in the book of life was thrown into the lake of fire.

The New Jerusalem

21 Then I saw a new heaven and a new
earth. The first heaven and the first earth
had disappeared, and there was no sea any more.
2 And I saw the holy city, the new Jerusalem,[n]
coming down out of heaven from God. It was
prepared like a bride dressed for her husband.
3 And I heard a loud voice from the throne, say-
ing, "Now God's presence is with people, and he
will live with them, and they will be his people.
God himself will be with them and will be their
God. 4 He will wipe away every tear from their
eyes, and there will be no more death, sadness,

Hades The unseen world of the dead.
new Jerusalem The spiritual city where God's people live with him.

DEATH

Fear of Dying

"Thank you for flying with us," crackled the steward's voice over the intercom after the jet had landed. "And we encourage you to be extra careful on the most dangerous part of your journey: driving to your final destination in a car."

Many people fear flying, yet the odds of dying in a commercial aeroplane crash are only about 1 in 800,000. You're more likely to die by choking on food than in a plane crash.

In fact, all of the following are more dangerous than flying, based on the number of fatalities for each: car accidents, falls, fires and burns, drownings, shootings, poisonings.

Many people fear the way they will die more than they fear death itself.

The Biblo, however, promises Christians that God has overcome death. **Revelation 21:1–6** offers a description of life with God beyond death.

- What does this picture of heaven say to people's many fears about dying?
- How does the passage speak to your own fears about death?

Consider . . .

- selecting a story about death from the newspaper and using it to discuss your feelings about death with a friend or trusted adult.
- imagining what someone who has died might be experiencing in heaven. Thank God for his gift of eternal life that overcomes death.

For more, see . . .

- Psalm 23 (p.513)
- 1 Corinthians 15:12–23 (p.1235)
- Luke 23:32–43 (p.1091)

crying or pain, because all the old ways are gone."

5The One who was sitting on the throne said, "Look! I am making everything new!" Then he said, "Write this, because these words are true and can be trusted."

> **Sidelight** Weddings have always been expensive! In Bible times (see Revelation 21:2), the bride's face was made to look glossy and shiny with cosmetics. Her hair was dressed in gold and pearls, and she wore valuable pieces of family jewellery. People borrowed what they couldn't afford, but the bride always looked stunning.

6The One on the throne said to me, "It is finished. I am the Alpha and the Omega,[n] the Beginning and the End. I will give free water from the spring of the water of life to anyone who is thirsty. 7Those who win the victory will receive this, and I will be their God, and they will be my children. 8But cowards, those who refuse to believe, who do evil things, who kill, who sin sexually, who do evil magic, who worship idols and who tell lies—all these will have a place in the lake of burning sulphur. This is the second death."

9Then one of the seven angels who had the seven bowls full of the seven last troubles came to me, saying, "Come with me, and I will show you the bride, the wife of the Lamb." 10And the angel carried me away by the Spirit[d] to a very large and high mountain. He showed me the holy city, Jerusalem, coming down out of heaven from God. 11It was shining with the glory of God and was bright like a very expensive jewel, like a jasper, clear as crystal. 12The city had a great high wall with twelve gates with twelve angels at the gates, and on each gate was written the name of one of the twelve tribes[d] of Israel. 13There were three gates on the east, three on the north, three on the south and three on the west. 14The walls of the city were built on twelve foundation stones, and on the stones were written the names of the twelve apostles[d] of the Lamb.

15The angel who talked with me had a measuring rod made of gold to measure the city, its gates and its wall. 16The city was built in a square, and its length was equal to its width. The angel measured the city with the rod. The city was 2,200 kilometres long, 2,200 kilometres wide and 2,200 kilometres high. 17The angel also measured the wall. It was 80 metres high, by human measurements, which the angel was using. 18The wall was made of jasper, and the city was made of pure gold, as pure as glass. 19The foundation stones of the city walls were decorated with every kind of jewel. The first foundation was jasper, the second was sapphire, the third was chalcedony, the fourth was emerald, 20the fifth was onyx, the sixth was carnelian, the seventh was chrysolite, the eighth was beryl, the ninth was topaz, the tenth was chrysoprase, the eleventh was jacinth, and the twelfth was amethyst. 21The twelve gates were twelve pearls, each gate having been made from a single pearl. And the street of the city was made of pure gold as clear as glass.

22I did not see a temple[d] in the city, because the Lord God Almighty and the Lamb are the city's temple. 23The city does not need the sun or the moon to shine on it, because the glory of God is its light, and the Lamb is the city's lamp. 24By its light the people of the world will walk, and the kings of the earth will bring their glory into it. 25The city's gates will never be shut on any day, because there is no night there. 26The glory and the honour of the nations will be brought into it. 27Nothing unclean[d] and no one who does shameful things or tells lies will ever go into it. Only those whose names are written in the Lamb's book of life will enter the city.

22 Then the angel showed me the river of the water of life. It was shining like crystal and was flowing from the throne of God and of the Lamb 2down the middle of the street of the city. The tree of life was on each side of the river. It produces fruit twelve times a year, once each month. The leaves of the tree are for the healing of all the nations. 3Nothing that God judges guilty will be in that city. The throne of God and of the Lamb will be there, and God's servants will worship him. 4They will see his face, and his name will be written on their foreheads. 5There will never be night again. They will not need the light of a lamp or the light of the sun, because the Lord God will give them light. And they will rule as kings for ever and ever.

6The angel said to me, "These words can be trusted and are true." The Lord, the God of the spirits of the prophets,[d] sent his angel to show his servants the things that must happen soon.

7"Listen! I am coming soon! Happy is the one who obeys the words of prophecy in this book."

8I, John, am the one who heard and saw these things. When I heard and saw them, I bowed down to worship at the feet of the angel who showed these things to me. 9But the angel said to me, "Do not worship me! I am a servant like you,

Alpha and the Omega The first and last letters of the Greek alphabet. This means "the beginning and the end".

your brothers the prophets and all those who
obey the words in this book. Worship God!"
10Then the angel told me, "Do not keep secret
the words of prophecy in this book, because the
time is near for all this to happen. 11Let whoever
is doing evil continue to do evil. Let whoever
is unclean continue to be unclean. Let whoever is
doing right continue to do right. Let whoever is
holy continue to be holy."
12"Listen! I am coming soon! I will bring my
reward with me, and I will repay each one of
you for what you have done. 13I am the Alpha
and the Omega,[n] the First and the Last, the Be-
ginning and the End.
14"Happy are those who wash their robes[n] so
that they will receive the right to eat the fruit from
the tree of life and may go through the gates into
the city. 15Outside the city are the evil people, those
who do evil magic, who sin sexually, who murder,
who worship idols, and who love lies and tell lies.
16"I, Jesus, have sent my angel to tell you
these things for the churches. I am the descen-
dant[d] from the family of David, and I am the
bright morning star."
17The Spirit[d] and the bride say, "Come!" Let
the one who hears this say, "Come!" Let who-
ever is thirsty come; whoever wishes may have
the water of life as a free gift.
18I warn everyone who hears the words of the
prophecy of this book: if anyone adds anything
to these words, God will add to that person the
disasters written about in this book. 19And if any-
one takes away from the words of this book of
prophecy, God will take away that one's share of
the tree of life and of the holy city, which are
written about in this book.
20Jesus, the One who says these things are
true, says, "Yes, I am coming soon."
Amen. Come, Lord Jesus!
21The grace of the Lord Jesus be with all. Amen.

Alpha and the Omega The first and last letters of the Greek alphabet. This means "the beginning and the end".
wash their robes This means they believed in Jesus so that their sins could be forgiven through Christ's blood.

ETERNAL LIFE

A Bit of Heaven

Three hundred teenage tourists gathered in the Swiss Alps, 2,200 metres above sea level. Rising even higher on one side were craggy, snow-capped peaks. A huge glacier stretched out on the other side, seemingly unaffected by the warm July day.

The group gathered for outdoor worship, which began with a trio of alpine horns echoing hymns across the valley. The minister shared the Good News of Christ. Then voices joined together to close the service with familiar choruses of praise to God.

The day passed quickly, filled with hugs, songs, shouts of pleasure, helping hands, huge smiles and incredible sights. As the teenagers waited to return to Grindelwald on Europe's longest chair lift, several girls talked.

"I hope heaven's like this," said one of the girls.

"Heaven's going to be even better!" said another.

God's promise of eternal life in heaven is even better! Read the promise in **Revelation 22:12–21**.

- What do you think made the girls think of heaven during their outing in Switzerland? How do you think the mountain experience compares with heaven itself?
- What difference does God's promise of eternal life make in your everyday living?

Consider . . .

- remembering a time when you felt overwhelmed by nature as a reminder of God's greatness.
- asking yourself what you need to do to respond to the invitation in verse 17: "Let whoever is thirsty come; whoever wishes may have the water of life as a free gift."

For more, see . . .

- Psalm 16:9–11 (p.508)
- John 4:5–42 (p.1101)
- Matthew 19:16–30 (p.974)

A

Aaron (AIR-on) *older brother of Moses.*
- before the king of Egypt, Exodus 4:14–16; 5:1–5; 7:1–2
- death of, Numbers 20:22–29

Abba (AB-uh) *word for "father" in Aramaic.*
- Jesus called God "Abba", Mark 14:36
- we can call God "Abba", Romans 8:15; Galatians 4:6

Abednego (a-BED-nee-go) *one of the three friends of Daniel whom God protected from the fiery furnace.*
- refused the king of Babylon's food, Daniel 1:3–17
- thrown into the fiery furnace, Daniel 3

Abel (AY-bul) *the second son of Adam and Eve.*
- born to Adam and Eve, Genesis 4:2
- approved by God, Genesis 4:3–4; Hebrews 11:4
- murdered by Cain, Genesis 4:8; 1 John 3:12

Abib (ah-BEEB) *first month of the Jewish calendar, about the same time of year as our March or April; also called "Nisan"; means "young ears of grain".*
- the time the Israelites left Egypt, Exodus 13:3–4
- the time for the feast of Unleavened Bread, Exodus 23:15; 34:18

Abigail, sister of David (AB-ee-gale) 1 Chronicles 2:13–17

Abigail, wife of Nabal
- brought food to David, 1 Samuel 25:14–35
- became David's wife, 1 Samuel 25:36–42

Abijah, king of Judah (a-BY-jah) 1 Kings 15:1–8; 2 Chronicles 13:1 — 14:1

Abijah, son of Jeroboam
- death of, 1 Kings 14:1–18

Abijah, son of Samuel, 1 Samuel 8:1–3

ability
- given by God, 2 Corinthians 3:5–6
- through Christ, Philippians 4:13
- differing abilities, 1 Corinthians 12:7–11

Abimelech, king of Gerar (a-BIM-eh-lek)
- tried to take Sarah as his wife, Genesis 20

Abimelech, king of the Philistines
- tried to take Rebekah as his wife, Genesis 26:6–11

Abimelech, son of Gideon
- birth of, Judges 8:29–31
- murdered his brothers, Judges 9:1–6
- defeated the people of Shechem, Judges 9:22–45
- burned the Tower of Shechem, Judges 9:46–49
- death of, Judges 9:50–55

Abishai (a-BISH-eye) *nephew of King David.*
- served in David's army, 2 Samuel 23:18–19; 1 Chronicles 18:12–13
- saved David's life, 2 Samuel 21:15–17

Abner (AB-nur) *commander of Saul's army.*
- at Goliath's defeat, 1 Samuel 17:55–57
- made Ish-Bosheth king of Israel, 2 Samuel 2:8–10
- later loyal to David, 2 Samuel 3:6–21
- killed by Joab, 2 Samuel 3:22–27

Abraham (AY-bra-ham) *father of the Jewish nation.*
- called from Ur by God, Genesis 12:1–4
- lied about Sarai, Genesis 12:10–20
- separated from Lot, Genesis 13
- God's agreement with, Genesis 15; 17
- name changed, Genesis 17:3–6
- father of Isaac, Genesis 21:1–7
- offered Isaac as a sacrifice, Genesis 22:1–19
- father of the faithful, Romans 4
- God's friend, James 2:23

Absalom (AB-suh-lum) *one of David's sons.*
- turned against David, 2 Samuel 15 — 18:8
- killed by Joab, 2 Samuel 18:9–15

abstain (ab-STAIN) *to keep from doing something.*
- from food offered to idols, Acts 15:20
- from evil, 1 Thessalonians 5:22
- from lust, 1 Peter 2:11

abyss (uh-BISS) See "bottomless pit".

accept
- a prophet not accepted, Luke 4:24
- accepted by God, Acts 10:35; 15:7–8; Romans 14:3
- each other, Romans 14:1; 15:7
- Jesus, John 12:48

accuse
- Jesus accused by the Jews, Matthew 27:12–13; Mark 15:3; Luke 6:7
- Paul accused by the Jews, Acts 23:27–29; 26:7
- the devil, as the accuser, Revelation 12:10

Achaia (a-KA-yuh) See "Greece".

Achan (AY-can) *an Israelite who disobeyed God during the battle of Jericho,* Joshua 7

Achish (AY-kish) *king of the Philistine city of Gath.*
- David pretends to be insane, 1 Samuel 21:10–15
- David in his army, 1 Samuel 27; 29

actions
- judged by, Proverbs 20:11; Matthew 11:19; Galatians 6:4
- of love, 1 John 3:18
- of goodness, Matthew 5:16

Adam (AD-um) *the first man.*
- created by God, Genesis 1:26 — 2:25
- disobeyed God, Genesis 3
- compared to Christ, 1 Corinthians 15:21–22,45–49

adder, *a poisonous snake.* See "snake".

Adonijah (ad-oh-NY-jah) *David's fourth son.*
- son of Haggith, 2 Samuel 3:4
- tried to become king, 1 Kings 1
- killed by Solomon, 1 Kings 2:12–25

Adoni-Zedek (a-DOH-ny-ZEE-dek) *an Amorite king of Jerusalem.*
- defeated by Joshua, Joshua 10:1–28

Adullam (a-DULL-am) *a city about twenty-one kilometres from Bethlehem.*
- David hid in a cave there, 2 Samuel 23:13

adultery (ah DULL-ter-ee) *breaking a marriage promise by having sexual relations with someone other than your husband or wife.*
- "You must not be guilty of adultery", Exodus 20:14
- Christ teaches about, Matthew 5:27–32; Luke 16:18
- woman caught in adultery, John 8:1–11

advice
- given by Ahithophel, 2 Samuel 15:30 — 17:23
- given to Rehoboam, 1 Kings 12:1–15

- teachings about, Proverbs 11:14; 12:5,15; 19:20

Agabus (AG-uh-bus) *a Christian prophet.*
- warned the people, Acts 11:27–30
- warned Paul about going to Jerusalem, Acts 21:10–11

Agag (AY-gag) *king of the Amalekites.*
- captured by Saul, 1 Samuel 15

agreement *a contract, promise, or covenant.*
- with Noah, Genesis 9:1–17
- with Abraham, Genesis 15; 17:1–14
- Ark of the Agreement, Exodus 25:10–22; 1 Samuel 4—5; 2 Samuel 6:1–15
- with the Israelites, Exodus 19:3–8,24; Deuteronomy 29
- new agreement, 2 Corinthians 2:12—3:18
- difference between the old and new agreements, Hebrews 8—10

Agrippa (uh-GRIP-pah) See "Herod Agrippa".

Ahab (AY-hab) *evil king of Israel who was married to Jezebel.*
- worshipped Baal, 1 Kings 16:29–33
- had Naboth killed, 1 Kings 21
- death of, 1 Kings 22:1–40

Ahasuerus (ah-HAZ-oo-rus) *Hebrew word for the Greek name Xerxes.* See "Xerxes".

Ahaz (AY-haz) *twelfth king of Judah,* 2 Kings 16; 2 Chronicles 28

Ahaziah, king of Judah (ay-ha-ZY-uh) 2 Chronicles 22:1–9

Ahaziah, son of Ahab
- king of Israel, 1 Kings 22:40–53

Ahijah, great-grandson of Eli (a-HY-jah) 1 Samuel 14:1–23

Ahijah, the prophet
- told Jeroboam the kingdom would be divided, 1 Kings 11:29–39
- told that Jeroboam's son would die, 1 Kings 14:1–18

Ahimelech, the high priest (a-HIM-eh-lek)
- helped David, 1 Samuel 21:1–9

Ahimelech, the Hittite warrior, 1 Samuel 26:6

Ahithophel (a-HITH-oh-fel) *gave advice to King David.*
- helped Absalom rebel against David, 1 Samuel 15:31; 16:15—17:23

Ai (AY-eye) *a city completely destroyed by the Israelites,* Joshua 7—8:28

Akeldama (a-KEL-dah-mah) *field bought with the money Judas received for betraying Jesus,* Matthew 27:3–10; Acts 1:18–19

alabaster (ala-BAS-ter) *light-coloured stone with streaks or stripes through it,* Matthew 26:7; Mark 14:3; Luke 7:37

alamoth (AL-a-moth) *a musical word, which may mean "like a flute" or "high-pitched",* Psalm 46

All-Powerful, *a name for God,* 1 Chronicles 11:9; Psalm 24:10; Isaiah 6:3–5; Malachi 3:1–17

Almighty, *a name for God.*
- "I am God Almighty", Genesis 17:1
- "I appeared to Abraham . . . by the name, God Almighty", Exodus 6:3
- "Holy, holy, holy is the Lord God Almighty", Revelation 4:8

almond
- design of the lampstands in Holy Tent, Exodus 25:31–36
- Aaron's stick produced, Numbers 17:8

aloes (AL-ohs) *oils from sweet-smelling sap of certain trees; used to make perfume and medicine and to prepare bodies for burial,* Psalm 45:8; Proverbs 7:17
- used to prepare Jesus' body for burial, John 19:39

Alpha and Omega (AL-fah and oh-MAY-guh) *the first and last letters of the Greek alphabet, like our A and Z.*
- used to describe Jesus, Revelation 1:8; 21:6; 22:13

altar (ALL-ter) *a place where sacrifices, gifts, or prayers were offered to a god.*
- built by Noah, Genesis 8:20
- built by Abraham, Genesis 22:9
- for burnt offerings, Exodus 27:1–8
- for incense, Exodus 30:1–10
- corners of, Exodus 27:2; 30:10; 1 Kings 1:50
- for the Temple, 2 Chronicles 4:1

Amalekites (a-MAL-ek-ites) *fierce, fighting people who descended from Esau; they were enemies of Israel and were finally wiped out during the time of Hezekiah.*
- enemies of Israel, Exodus 17:8–16; 1 Samuel 15
- destroyed by King Hezekiah, 1 Chronicles 4:43

Amasa (AM-a-sa) *leader of Absalom's army when he rebelled against David,* 2 Samuel 17:25
- made leader of David's army, 2 Samuel 19:13
- killed by Joab, 2 Samuel 20:1–10

Amaziah (am-ay-ZY-uh) *the ninth king of Judah,* 2 Kings 14; 2 Chronicles 25

amen (AH-MEN) *Hebrew word for "that is right",* 1 Chronicles 16:36; Psalm 106:48; 1 Corinthians 14:16
- "Amen Come, Lord Jesus!" Revelation 22:20

Ammonites (AM-on-ites) *descendants of Lot's son, Ben-Ammi,* Genesis 19:36–38
- enemies of Israel, Judges 10:6—11:33; 1 Samuel 11; 2 Samuel 10:1–14
- worshipped Molech, 1 Kings 11:5

Amon (AM-on) *the fifteenth king of Judah,* 2 Kings 21:18–26; 2 Chronicles 33:20–25
- an ancestor of Jesus, Matthew 1:10

Amorites (AM-or-ites) *a group of wicked people who worshipped false gods and lived in Canaan when the Israelites arrived.*
- defeated by Israel, Numbers 21:21–32; Joshua 10:1—11:14

Amos (AY-mos) *a prophet who warned Israel of God's punishment for disobedience.*
- a shepherd from Tekoa, Amos 1:1
- his visions, Amos 7—9:10

Anak/Anakites (A-nak/AN-uh-kites) *a group of large, fighting people who lived in Canaan when the Israelites arrived.*
- feared by the twelve spies, Numbers 13:22,28,33; Deuteronomy 1:26–28
- defeated by Joshua, Joshua 11:21–23

Ananias, husband of Sapphira (an-uh-NY-us)
- killed for lying to the Holy Spirit, Acts 5:1–6

Ananias, a Christian in Damascus
- helped Saul of Tarsus, Acts 9:10–19; 22:12–16

Ananias, the high priest
- at Paul's trial, Acts 23:1–5

Andrew, *a fisherman and brother of the apostle Peter.*
- chosen by Jesus to be an apostle, Mark 1:16–18; 3:13–19

- brought Peter to Jesus, John 1:40–42
- waited with the apostles in Jerusalem, Acts 1:13

angel (AIN-jel) *a heavenly being.*
- rescued Lot from Sodom, Genesis 19:1–22
- led Israel to Canaan, Exodus 23:20–23; 32:34
- announced Jesus' birth, Matthew 1:20–21; Luke 1:26–37; 2:8–15
- helped Jesus, Matthew 4:11; Luke 22:43
- helped the apostles, Acts 5:19–20; 12:6–10
- will bring judgement, Matthew 13:24–50; 24:31
- archangel, 1 Thessalonians 4:16; Jude 9
- less than Christ, Hebrews 1:4–14; 1 Peter 3:22
- rebellious angels, 2 Peter 2:4; Jude 6
- serving in heaven, Revelation 7—10

anger, *wrath.*
- of God toward people, John 3:36; Romans 1:18; 2:5–6; Colossians 3:5–6
- saved from God's anger by Christ, Romans 5:9; 1 Thessalonians 1:10; 5:9
- warnings against, Matthew 5:21–22; Ephesians 4:26,31; James 1:19–20

animal
- created by God, Genesis 1:20–25
- to be ruled by people, Genesis 1:26
- named by Adam, Genesis 2:19–20
- saved by Noah, Genesis 6:19–20
- clean, Leviticus 11:1–3,9; Deuteronomy 14:3–6
- unclean, Leviticus 11:4–8,10–12,26–44; Deuteronomy 14:7–8

Annas (AN-us) *a high priest of the Jews during Jesus' lifetime,* Luke 3:2; John 18:13
- questioned Peter and John, Acts 4:5–22

anoint (a-NOINT) *to pour oil on.*
- to appoint a priest, Exodus 28:41; 40:13
- to appoint a king, 1 Samuel 10:1; 16:12–13; 2 Kings 9:6
- the Holy Tent, Numbers 7:1
- to heal sickness, Mark 6:13; James 5:14

Anti-Christ (AN-tee KRYST) See "enemy of Christ".

Antioch in Pisidia (AN-tee-ok) *a small city in the country of Pisidia.*
- Paul preached there, Acts 13:14–15

Antioch in Syria, *third largest city in the Roman Empire.*
- Saul and Barnabas preached there, Acts 11:19–26
- followers first called "Christians" there, Acts 11:26
- Peter in Antioch, Galatians 2:11–12
- Paul preached there, Acts 13:14–15

Antipas (AN-ti-pas) *the father of Herod the great and the ruler of Judea 55–43 BC,* Revelation 2:13

Apollos (a-POL-us) *an educated Jew from Alexandria.*
- taught by Aquila and Priscilla, Acts 18:24–28
- preached to the Corinthians, 1 Corinthians 1:12; 3:4–6
- friend of Paul, Titus 3:13

apostle (uh-POS-'l) *someone who is sent off. Jesus chose these twelve special followers and sent them to tell the Good News about him to the whole world.*
- twelve chosen by Jesus, Mark 3:14–19
- Matthias chosen, Acts 1:12–26
- Paul chosen, 1 Corinthians 15:3–11; 2 Corinthians 12:11–12
- duties and powers of, Luke 9:1–6; Acts 5:12–16; 8:18
- leaders of the church, Acts 15; 16:4; 1 Corinthians 12:28
- false apostles, 2 Corinthians 11:13; Revelation 2:2

appearance
- not to judge by, 1 Samuel 16:7; John 7:24
- deceiving, Matthew 23:27–28
- of Jesus, Isaiah 53:2; Philippians 2:7

Aquila (AK-wi-lah) *a Jewish Christian from Rome.*
- friend of Paul, Acts 18:2–3; Romans 16:3–5
- taught Apollos, Acts 18:24–28

Arabah (AR-uh-bah) *the Hebrew word for the Jordan Valley.* See "Jordan Valley".

Arabah, Sea of, See "Dead Sea".

Aram (AR-um) *a country northeast of Israel,* 1 Kings 11:25; 15:18; 2 Kings 5:1; Isaiah 7:1
- known as "Syria" in the New Testament, Matthew 4:24; Acts 15:23

Aramaic (AR-uh-MAY-ik) *the language of the people in the nation of Aram.*
- common language of the Jews, 2 Kings 18:26; John 19:13,17,20; Acts 21:40

Ararat (AR-uh-rat) *a group of mountains located in what is now Turkey and the Soviet Union.*
- Noah's boat landed there, Genesis 8:14

Araunah (a-RAW-nah) *a Jebusite who was also called Oman.*
- sold his threshing floor to King David, 2 Samuel 24:15–25; 1 Chronicles 21:18–28

archangel (ark-AIN-jel) *the leader of God's angels,* 1 Thessalonians 4:16; Jude 9

Areopagus (AR-ee-OP-uh-gus) *a council or group of important leaders in Athens.*
- Paul spoke there, Acts 17:16–34

argue
- the apostles argued, Mark 9:33–37; Luke 9:46–48
- avoid arguments, Philippians 2:14; 2 Timothy 2:23–26; Titus 3:9
- Michael argued with the devil, Jude 9

Aristarchus (ar-i-STAR-kus) *a man from Thessalonica who often travelled with Paul,* Acts 27:2; Colossians 4:10; Philemon 24

ark, Noah's, *the huge boat that Noah built to save his family from the flood God sent to cover the earth.* See "boat".

Ark of the Agreement, *a special box made of acacia wood and gold. Inside were the stone tablets on which the Ten Commandments were written. Later, a pot of manna and Aaron's walking stick were also put into the Ark. It was to remind the people of Israel of God's promise to be with them.*
- building of, Exodus, 25:10–22; 37:1–9
- crossing the Jordan River, Joshua 3:1–17
- captured by the Philistines, 1 Samuel 4—7:1
- touched by Uzzah, 2 Samuel 6:1–8; 1 Chronicles 13
- placed in the Temple, 2 Chronicles 5:2–10
- contents of, Hebrews 9:4–5

Ark of the Covenant, See "Ark of the Agreement".

armour
- of Saul, 1 Samuel 17:38–39; 31:9–10
- of God, Ephesians 6:10–17

arrest
- John the Baptist arrested, Matthew 14:3; Mark 6:17
- Jesus arrested, Matthew 26:50–57; Mark 14:44–50; John 18:1–14
- Peter arrested, Acts 12:1–4
- Paul arrested, Acts 28:17–20

Artaxerxes (ar-tah-ZERK-sees) *the title or name of Persian kings,* Ezra 4:7; Nehemiah 2:1
- letter to Ezra, Ezra 7:11–26

Artemis (AR-tuh-mis) *a goddess that many Greeks worshipped,* Acts 19:23–41

Asa (AY-sah) *the third king of Judah,* 1 Kings 15:9–24; 2 Chronicles 14—16

Asaph (AY-saf) *a leader of singers when David was king,* 1 Chronicles 16:5,7; 25:1–2; 2 Chronicles 5:12
- songs of, Psalms 73—83

ascension (uh-SEN-shun) *lifted up; used to describe Jesus' return to heaven,* Acts 1:2–11; 2:32–33

ashamed
- of Jesus, Mark 8:38; Luke 9:26; 2 Timothy 1:8
- for suffering as a Christian, 1 Peter 4:16

Ashdod (ASH-dod) *one of the five strong, walled cities of the Philistines; called Azotus in the New Testament.*
- Ark of the Agreement there, 1 Samuel 5:1–8
- later called "Azotus", Acts 8:40

Asherah (ah-SHIR-ah) *a Canaanite goddess thought to be the wife of the god Baal.*
- worshipped by Israelites, 1 Kings 14:14–15,22–23; 15:13
- worship forbidden, Exodus 34:13–14; Deuteronomy 16:21–22

Ashkelon (ASH-keh-lon) *one of the five important cities of the Philistines,* Judges 1:18; Zephaniah 2:4,7
- thirty of its men killed by Samson, Judges 14:19

Ashtoreth (ASH-toh-reth) *a goddess of the people of Assyria and Canaan. At times the Israelites forgot God and built idols to worship her.* Judges 2:13; 1 Samuel 7:3–4; 12:10
- worshipped by Solomon, 1 Kings 11:5,33

Asia (AY-zhuh) *the western part of the country now called "Turkey".*
- Paul preached there, Acts 19:10,26
- seven churches of, Revelation 1:4

assembly (a-SEM-blee) *a meeting; a group of people gathered for a purpose.*
- of the church, Hebrews 10:24–25
- conduct in, James 2:1–4

assurance (uh-SHURE-ans) *with confidence; without doubts.*
- about the Gospel, 1 Thessalonians 1:5
- before God, Hebrews 10:22–23; 1 John 5:14–15
- faith as, Hebrews 11:1

Assyria (a-SEER-ee-uh) *a powerful nation north and east of Israel.*
- enemy of Israel, 2 Kings 15:19–20; 17:3–6
- enemy of Judah, 2 Kings 18:13—19:36; Isaiah 36—37:37

Astarte (ah-STAR-tay) *another name for the goddess Ashtoreth.* See "Ashtoreth".

Athaliah (ath-uh-LY-uh) *the only woman who ruled over Judah,* 2 Kings 11; 2 Chronicles 22:10—23:21

Athens (ATH-enz) *the leading city of the country of Greece.*
- Paul preached there, Acts 17:16–34

atonement (a-TONE-ment) *to remove or forgive sins.*
- through animal sacrifices, Exodus 30:10; Leviticus 17:11; Numbers 25:13
- through faith in the blood of Jesus' death, Romans 3:25; Hebrews 2:17; 9:22; 10:11–12

Atonement, Day of, See "Cleansing, Day of".

Augustus (aw-GUS-tus) *the title meaning "honoured" that the Romans gave to Octavian when he began ruling the Roman world in 27 BC. He was Emperor when Jesus was born,* Luke 2:1

Augustus Caesar (aw-GUS-tus SEE-zer) *or Caesar Augustus, the first Roman emperor,* Luke 2:1

authority (aw-THOR-ee-tee) *power or right to control.*
- proper use of, Matthew 20:25–26; Luke 22:24–30; Titus 2:15
- respect for, Luke 20:20–26; Romans 13:1–7; 1 Timothy 2:2; 1 Peter 2:13–17; Hebrews 13:17
- Jesus' authority, Matthew 7:29; 9:6; Mark 11:27–33; Luke 5:24; John 5:19–29

B

Baal (BAY-el) *a god of the Canaanites; "Baal" was the common word for "master, lord". He was known as the son of Dagon, or the son of El, who was known as the father of the false gods.*
- worshipped by Israelites, Judges 2:10–11; Jeremiah 11:13
- Elijah defeated prophets of Baal, 1 Kings 18:1–40
- Baal worship destroyed by Jehu, 2 Kings 10:18–28

Baal-Zebub, See "Beelzebul".

Baasha (Baa-shah) *the third king of Israel,* 1 Kings 15:27—16:7; 2 Chronicles 16:1–6; Jeremiah 41:9

Babel (BAY-bel) *a tower built to reach the sky,* Genesis 11:1–9

baby
- Moses as, Exodus 2:1–10
- Solomon determined mother of, 1 Kings 3:16–28
- Elizabeth's, Luke 1:39–44
- Jesus as, Luke 2:6–21
- as a symbol of new Christians, 1 Peter 2:2

Babylon (BAB-ee-lon) *city on the Euphrates River; capital of Babylonia.*
- captives in Babylon, Psalm 137:1; Jeremiah 29:10
- destruction predicted, Jeremiah 51:36–37
- as a symbol of evil, Revelation 14:8; 17.5

Babylonians (bab-e-LONE-e-unz) *people of the country Babylonia. Also called "Chaldeans".*
- capture warned by Jeremiah, Jeremiah 21; 25
- captured the people of Judah, 2 Kings 20:12–18; 24—25; Jeremiah 39:1–10
- Daniel in Babylon, Daniel 1—4
- released Israelite captives, Ezra 2

Balaam (BAY-lum) *a prophet from Midian.*
- asked by Balak to prophesy, Numbers 22—24; 2 Peter 2:15–16; Revelation 2:14
- death of, Numbers 31:8

balm, *oil from a plant used as medicine,* Genesis 37:25; Jeremiah 8:22; 51:8; Ezekiel 27:17

Baptist, John the (BAP-tist) *someone who baptises. John, a relative of Jesus, was called this because he baptised many people.* Matthew 3:1–6
- condemned Pharisees and Sadducees, Matthew 3:7–10
- preached about Jesus, Matthew 3:11–12
- baptised Jesus, Matthew 3:13–17
- in prison, Matthew 11:1–6; Luke 7:18–23
- described by Jesus, Matthew 11:7–12; 17:10–13; Luke 7:24–28
- death of, Matthew 14:1–12; Mark 6:14–29

- baptism of, Matthew 21:25–26; Acts 10:37; 18:25; 19:3–4
- Jesus mistaken for, Matthew 16:13–14; Mark 8:27–28; Luke 9:18–19

baptism (BAP-tiz-em) *dipping or immersing.*

- by John, Matthew 3:6; Mark 1:4; Luke 3; Acts 19:3
- of Jesus, Matthew 3:13–17
- examples of, Acts 2:38–41; 8:36–38; 16:15,33
- with fire, Matthew 3:11; Luke 3:16
- with the Holy Spirit, Mark 1:8; Acts 1:5; 11:16

Barabbas (bah-RAB-us) *a robber who had murdered someone in Jerusalem. He was freed instead of Jesus.* Matthew 27:15–26; Mark 15:6–11

Barak (BA-rak) *a leader of Israel's army when Deborah was judge,* Judges 4—5

Bar-Jesus, See "Elymas".

barley (BAR-lee) *a type of grain used to make bread.*

- harvest of, Ruth 1:22; 2:17,23; 2 Samuel 21:9
- loaves of, John 6:9–13

barn

- storing in, Matthew 6:26
- rich man's, Luke 12:16–20

Barnabas (BAR-nah-bus) *an encourager who helped the apostles,* Acts 4:36; 11:23

- worked with Paul, Acts 11:26; 13—15
- influenced by hypocrites, Galatians 2:13

Bartholomew (bar-THOL-oh-mew) *one of the twelve apostles of Jesus,* Matthew 10:3; Mark 3:18; Luke 6:14; Acts 1:13

Bartimaeus (bar-teh-MAY-us) *a blind man who was healed by Jesus,* Mark 10:46–52

Baruch (BAH-rook) *a friend of the prophet Jeremiah,* Jeremiah 36

Bathsheba (bath-SHE-buh) *the mother of Solomon and wife of David,* 2 Samuel 11—12:25; 1 Kings 1—2:22

beatitude (bee-A-ti-tyood) *blessed or happy; often used for Jesus' teaching in Matthew 5:3–12; Luke 6:20–22*

Beelzebul (bee-EL-ze-bull) *false god of the Philistines; in the New Testament it often refers to the devil.*

- name for Satan, Matthew 12:24; Mark 3:22; Luke 11:15

Beersheba (beer-SHE-buh) *the town farthest south in the land of Judah,* 2 Samuel 3:10; 2 Chronicles 30:5

- Abraham made an agreement there, Genesis 21:14–34

beg

- Jesus begged by demons, Matthew 8:28–34; Mark 5:1–13; Luke 8:26–33
- Jesus begged by people, Matthew 14:36; Mark 7:24–26,32; 8:22

beggar

- Bartimaeus, Mark 10:46–52
- Lazarus, Luke 16:19–31
- at Beautiful Gate, Acts 3:1–10
- man born blind, John 9:1–12

Bel, *a false god of the Babylonians,* Jeremiah 50:2; 51:44

believe

- in God, Acts 16:34; Romans 4:24
- in Jesus, Matthew 18:6; John 12:44; 14:11–12; 1 John 5:10
- in the Good News, Mark 1:15; 11:24; Acts 15:7
- rewards of believing, Matthew 21:22; John 20:31; 1 Thessalonians 2:13
- a lie, 2 Thessalonians 2:11

believers (be-LEE-vers) *the followers of Jesus,* John 3:16; Acts 4:32; 5:14; Galatians 6:10

Belshazzar (bell-SHAZ-er) *a ruler of Babylon,* Daniel 5

Belteshazzar (BELL-teh-SHAZ-er) *the Babylonian name that Nebuchadnezzar gave to Daniel,* Daniel 4:8; 5:12

Benaiah (bee-NAY-uh) *the captain of David's bodyguard,* 2 Samuel 23:20–23

- commander of Solomon's army, 1 Kings 2:34–35

Ben-Hadad (ben-HAY-dad) *two or three Syrian kings who often fought against Israel,* 1 Kings 20:1–34; 2 Kings 6:24—8:15

Benjamin (BEN-jah-min) *the youngest son of Jacob and Rachel.*

- birth of, Genesis 35:16–20
- reunited with Joseph, Genesis 42—45

Bernice (Bur-nees) *the oldest daughter of Herod Agrippa I,* Acts 25:13—26:32

Bethany (BETH-a-nee) *a small town about three kilometres from Jerusalem.*

- home of Mary, Martha, and Lazarus, John 11:1; 12:1
- home of Simon, Mark 14:3

Bethel (BETH-el) *a town about nineteen kilometres north of Jerusalem.*

- named by Jacob, Genesis 28:10–19
- Jeroboam built idols there, 1 Kings 12:26–33

Bethesda (be-THES-da) See "Bethzatha, pool of".

Bethlehem (BETH-le-hem) *a small town eight kilometres from Jerusalem.*

- hometown of King David, 1 Samuel 16:1,13
- birthplace of Jesus, Matthew 2:1; Luke 2:15–17

Bethsaida (beth-SAY-ih-duh) *a city in Galilee and home of Peter, Andrew, and Philip,* John 1:44; 12:21

- rejected Jesus, Matthew 11:20–21; Luke 10:13

Bethzatha, pool of (beth-ZA-tha) *a pool in Jerusalem near the Sheep Gate.*

- Jesus healed a man there, John 5:1–18

betray (be-TRAY) *to turn against.*

- families against each other, Mark 13:12–13
- Jesus betrayed, Matthew 26:20–25; Mark 14:18–46; John 13:2–30

birds

- created by God, Genesis 1:20–21
- saved by Noah, Genesis 6:19–20; 7:1–3
- unclean, Leviticus 11:13–19
- cared for by God, Matthew 6:25–27; Luke 12:24

birth

- spiritual birth, John 1:13; 3:3–8; 1 Peter 1:23

bishop, See "elder".

bitter

- water, Exodus 15:22–25; Numbers 5:18–27; Revelation 8:11
- herbs, Exodus 12:8

bitterness (BIT-er-nes) *sorrow or pain; anger or hatred.*

- warning against, Acts 8:23; Ephesians 4:31; James 3:14

blasphemy (BLAS-feh-mee) *saying things against God or not showing respect for God.*

- examples of, 1 Timothy 1:13; Revelation 13:6
- warnings against, Matthew 12:31–32; Mark 3:28–29
- Jesus accused of, Matthew 9:3; 26:65; Mark 2:6–7; John 10:36

blessing (BLES-ing) *a gift from God; asking God's favour on.*
- promised to Abraham, Genesis 12:1–3
- Isaac blessed Jacob, Genesis 27:1–41
- from God, Acts 3:25; Romans 10:12; 15:27; Hebrews 6:7
- by Jesus, Mark 10:16; Luke 24:50; John 1:16
- by each other, Luke 6:28; 1 Corinthians 4:12; 1 Peter 3:9

blind
- the blind healed, Matthew 9:27–31; 15:30; Mark 8:22–26; John 9
- Saul struck blind, Acts 9:8–9
- spiritually blind, Matthew 23:16–26; John 9:35–41; 2 Peter 1:5–9

blood, *sometimes used to mean "death".*
- water turned into, Exodus 7:14–24
- used in the Passover, Exodus 12:13–23
- not to be eaten, Leviticus 3:17; Deuteronomy 12:16; 1 Samuel 14:31–34
- of animal sacrifices, Leviticus 1; 3; 4; Hebrews 9:12–13; 10:4
- of Christ, Matthew 26:28; Romans 5:9; Hebrews 9:14; 1 John 1:7

boasting
- warnings against, Proverbs 27:1; 2 Corinthians 10:12–18; James 4:16; Jude 16
- about the Lord, 1 Corinthians 1:31; 2 Corinthians 10:17; Galatians 6:14

boat, *ark.*
- built by Noah, Genesis 6:11–21
- of the apostles, Matthew 4:21–22; John 21:3–11
- used by Jesus, Matthew 8:23; 13:2; 14:13–34

body
- made of dust, Genesis 2:7; 3:19
- health of, Proverbs 3:7–8; 4:20–22; 14:30
- attitudes toward, Matthew 6:25; Romans 6:13; Ephesians 5:29
- warnings against misuse, Romans 8:13; 1 Corinthians 6:18–20; 1 Thessalonians 4:5

body of Christ, *sometimes means Jesus' human body; also a way of describing Christians.*
- Christ's physical body, John 2:19–21; 19:38; Acts 2:31; 1 Corinthians 11:24; 1 Timothy 3:16; 1 Peter 3:18
- the Church as Christ's spiritual body, Romans 12:5; 1 Corinthians 12:12–31; Ephesians 1:23; 4:4; 5:23

bone
- "whose bones came from my bones", Genesis 2:23
- Ezekiel's vision of, Ezekiel 37:1–14
- none of Jesus' bones to be broken, John 19:36

book, *parchments, scroll.*
- Book of the Jashar, *a book of songs celebrating the glory of Israel,* Joshua 10:13; 2 Samuel 1:18
- Book of the Teachings, Deuteronomy 30:10; Joshua 1:8; 2 Chronicles 34:14–32; Ezra 8
- book of life, Philippians 4:3; Revelation 3:5; 13:8; 20:12; 21:27
- "Jesus did many other miracles . . . not written in this book", John 20:30
- "the whole world would not be big enough for all the books", John 21:25

bottomless pit, *the place where the devil and his demons live,* Luke 8:31; Revelation 9:1–11; 11:7; 17:8; 20:1–3

box of Scriptures, *small leather boxes that some Jews tied to their foreheads and left arms; also called "phylacteries" or "frontlets".*
- held the Law of Moses, Deuteronomy 6:6–8
- Jesus criticised misuse of, Matthew 23:5

bread, *the most important food in New Testament times; usually made of barley or wheat.*
- to feed 5,000 people, Matthew 14:13–21; Mark 6:30–44; Luke 9:10–17; John 6:1–13
- to feed 4,000 people, Matthew 15:32–39; Mark 8:1–10
- Jesus, the bread of life, John 6:25–59
- "A person does not live by eating only bread", Matthew 4:4; Luke 4:4
- "Give us the food we need for each day", Luke 11:3
- in the Lord's Supper, Luke 22:19; Acts 20:7; 1 Corinthians 10:16; 11:17–34

bread that shows we are in God's presence, *twelve loaves of bread that were kept on the table in the Holy Tent and later in the Temple; also called "Bread of the Presence" or "showbread",* Leviticus 24:5–9
- eaten by David, Matthew 12:3–4; Mark 2:25–26; Luke 6:4

bride, Song of Solomon 4:8–12
- belongs to the bridegroom, John 3:29
- of Christ, Revelation 21:2,9

bridegroom
- sun compared to, Psalm 19:5
- Jesus compared to, Matthew 9:15; Mark 2:19–20; Luke 5:34
- Jesus' story of, Matthew 25:1–13
- at Jesus' first miracle, John 2:9

brother, *a family member; people from the same country; or Christians.*
- physical brothers, Proverbs 18:24; Matthew 19:29; Mark 12:18–23
- Jesus' brothers, Matthew 13:55; Mark 3:31; John 2:12; 7:3; Acts 1:14; 1 Corinthians 9:5
- spiritual brothers, Romans 8:29; 12:10; 1 Timothy 6:2; Hebrews 2:11; 1 Peter 2:17

burn
- sacrifices, Exodus 29:10–42; Leviticus 1—4
- incense, Exodus 30:7–8; Numbers 16:40; Jeremiah 48:35; Luke 1:9
- Jericho burned by Israelites, Joshua 6:24
- idols burned by Josiah, 2 Kings 23:4–20
- jealousy like a fire, Psalm 79:5
- chaff, Matthew 3:12; Luke 3:17
- lake of burning sulphur, Revelation 21:8

burnt offerings, *a whole animal sacrificed as a gift to God.*
- rules about, Leviticus 1; 6:8–13; Numbers 28—29
- less important than obedience, 1 Samuel 15:22; Psalm 51:16–19
- less important than love, Hosea 6:6; Mark 12:32–33

bury, Matthew 8:21–22; Luke 9:59–60
- Abraham buried Sarah, Genesis 23
- Jacob not to be buried in Egypt, Genesis 47:29–30; 50:1–14
- strangers, Matthew 27:7
- in baptism, Romans 6:4

C

Caesar (SEE-zer) *a famous Roman family; used as the title of the Roman emperors.*
- Augustus, Luke 2:1
- Tiberius, Luke 3:1; 20:22; John 19:12
- Claudius, Acts 11:28; 17:7; 18:2
- Nero, Acts 25:8; 27:24; Philippians 4:22

Caesarea (SES-uh-REE-uh) *a city on the Mediterranean Sea,* Acts 10:1; 21:8; 23:32

Caesarea Philippi (SES-uh-REE-uh fih-LIP-eye) *a city at the base of Mount Hermon,* Matthew 16:13; Mark 8:27

Caiaphas (KAY-uh-fus) *the Jewish high priest from AD 18 to 36.*
- plotted to kill Jesus, Matthew 26:3–5; John 11:45–54
- father-in-law to Annas, John 18:13
- at Jesus' trial, Matthew 26:57–67
- questioned Peter and John, Acts 4:5–22

Cain, *the first son of Adam and Eve.*
- killed his brother Abel, Genesis 4:1–24; 1 John 3:12

Caleb (KAY-leb) *one of the twelve men Moses sent to spy out Canaan.*
- explored Canaan, Numbers 13—14
- given the city of Hebron, Joshua 14:6–15

calf
- gold idol, Exodus 32:1–20; 1 Kings 12:26–30; 2 Kings 10:28–29
- fatted, Luke 15:23,27,30

camel, Genesis 37:25; 1 Samuel 30:17; 1 Kings 10:2
- Rebekah watered Abraham's camels, Genesis 24:10–20
- "easier for a camel to go through the eye of a needle", Matthew 19:24; Mark 10:25; Luke 18:25
- "swallows a camel", Matthew 23:24

Cana (KAY-nah) *a small town near the city of Nazareth in Galilee.*
- place of Jesus' first miracle, John 2:1–11

Canaan (KAY-nan) *land God promised to the Israelites,* Leviticus 25:38; Numbers 13:2; 33:51; Psalm 105:11

Capernaum (kay-PUR-nee-um) *a city on the western shore of Lake Galilee.*
- Jesus lived there, Matthew 4:12–13
- Jesus healed there, Matthew 8:5–13; Luke 4:31–41
- rejected Jesus, Matthew 11:23–24

capital, *the top of a pillar, usually decorated with beautiful carvings.*
- in the Temple, 1 Kings 7:16–20; 2 Kings 25:17

captive
- Israelites as captives, Deuteronomy 28:41; 2 Kings 25:21; Jeremiah 30:3

cassia (cass-EE-uh) *a pleasant-smelling powder. Its odour is like the bark of the cinnamon plant,* Exodus 30:23–24; Psalm 45:8

census (SEN-sus) *a count of the number of people who live in an area.*
- the Israelites counted, Numbers 1:2; 26:2
- ordered by David, 1 Chronicles 21:1–2
- ordered by Augustus Caesar, Luke 2:1–3

centurion (sen-TYUR-ree-un) *a Roman army officer who commanded a hundred soldiers.*
- centurion's servant healed by Jesus, Matthew 8:5–13; Luke 7:1–10
- at Jesus' death, Matthew 27:54; Mark 15:39; Luke 23:47
- Cornelius, Acts 10

Cephas (SEE-fuss) *the Aramaic word for "rock"; in Greek, "Peter". Jesus gave this name to the apostle Simon.* John 1:42

chaff (CHAF) *the husk of a head of grain. Farmers would toss the grain and chaff into the air. Since the chaff is lighter, the wind would blow it away, and the good grain would fall back to the threshing floor.*
- sinners to be destroyed like chaff, Psalms 1:4; 35:5; Matthew 3:12; Luke 3:17

Chaldeans, See "Babylonians".

change of heart and life, *repentance.*
- commanded, Matthew 3:2; Mark 1:15; Luke 13:3; Acts 3:19; 17:30
- causes of, Romans 2:4; 2 Corinthians 7:9–10
- examples of, Matthew 12:41; Luke 11:32

chariot
- Egyptians' chariots destroyed, Exodus 14:5–28
- of fire, 2 Kings 2:11; 6:17
- Ethiopian taught in a chariot, Acts 8:27–31

Chemosh (KEE-mosh) *a god of the Moabites,* Jeremiah 48:13
- worshipped by Solomon, 1 Kings 11:7

cherubim (CHAIR-uh-bim) *heavenly beings with wings and the faces of men and animals.*
- guarded the garden of Eden, Genesis 3:24
- on the Ark of the Agreement, Exodus 25:18–22; 1 Kings 6:23–28
- seen by Ezekiel, Ezekiel 10:1–20

children
- of God, John 1:12; Romans 8:14; 1 Peter 1:14; 1 John 3:1–10
- training of, Ephesians 6:4; Colossians 3:21
- obedience of, Ephesians 6:1; Colossians 3:20; 1 Timothy 3:4
- become like, Matthew 18:3–4
- "Let the little children come to me", Matthew 19:14; Mark 10:14; Luke 18:16

chosen
- Israelites chosen by God, Deuteronomy 7:7–8; 9:4–5; Isaiah 44:1
- people chosen by God, Romans 8:33; Ephesians 1:4–5; 2 Timothy 2:10; 1 Peter 1:2; 2:9
- Jesus chosen by God, Hebrews 1:2; 1 Peter 2:4

Christ (KRYST) *anointed (or chosen) one. Jesus is the Christ, chosen by God to save people from their sins.*
- active in creation, John 1:1–3; Colossians 1:15–17; Hebrews 1:2,10
- equal with God, John 5:23; 10:30; Philippians 2:6; Colossians 2:9; Hebrews 1:3
- purpose of his death, Romans 5:6; 14:9; Hebrews 9:28; 1 Peter 3:18
- gives life, John 5:21; 6:35; 10:28; 11:25; 14:6
- as Saviour, Matthew 1:21; John 12:47
- as judge, Matthew 10:32–33; 25:31–46; John 5:22; Acts 17:31
- living in Christians, John 17:23; Romans 8:10; 2 Corinthians 1:21; Ephesians 3:17
- his return, Acts 1:11; 1 Thessalonians 5:1–11; Hebrews 9:28; 2 Peter 3:10
- enemy of, 1 John 2:18,22; 4:3; 2 John 7

Christians (KRIS-chuns) *Christ's followers,* Acts 11:26; 26:28; 1 Peter 4:16

church
- established by Christ, Matthew 16:18
- Christ as its head, Ephesians 1:22; 5:23; Colossians 1:18
- Christ died for, Ephesians 5:25
- activities of, Acts 12:5; 1 Corinthians 14:26–40; 1 Timothy 5:16; Hebrews 10:24–25

circumcision (SIR-kum-SIH-zhun) *the cutting off of the foreskin of the male sex organ; each Jewish boy was circumcised on the eighth day after he was born; this was done as a sign of the agreement God had made with his people, the Jews.*
- commanded by God, Genesis 17; Leviticus 12:1–3
- spiritual circumcision, Philippians 3:3; Colossians 2:11

city of refuge, See "safety, city of".

Claudius (CLAW-dee-us) *the fourth Roman emperor. He ruled from AD 41 to 54.* Acts 11:28; 17:7; 18:2

clean, *the state of a person, animal, or action that is pleasing to God. Under the Teachings of Moses, unclean animals could not be eaten. People who were considered clean could live and serve God normally.*
- clean and unclean animals, Deuteronomy 14:1–21; Mark 7:19; Acts 10
- clean and unclean people, Leviticus 13
- spiritually clean, Ephesians 5:26; Hebrews 9:14; 2 Peter 1:9

Cleansing, Day of, *the Day of Atonement; the most special day of the year for the Israelites when the high priest could go into the Most Holy Place. Animals were sacrificed for the sins of the people as a sign that people were cleansed of their sins for a year.*
- rules about, Leviticus 23:26–32; 25:9

cloud
- Israel led by pillar of cloud, Exodus 13:21
- cloud as small as a fist, 1 Kings 18:44
- Jesus leaves and will return in clouds, Luke 21:27; Acts 1:9; 1 Thessalonians 4:17; Revelation 1:7

Colossae (kol-OSS-ee) *a city in the country of Turkey,* Colossians 1:1–2

comfort, *to help ease someone's pain, grief, or trouble.*
- bad comforters, Job 16:2
- by shepherd's rod, Psalm 23:4
- from God, Isaiah 49:13; Matthew 5:4; 2 Corinthians 1:3–4
- from the Holy Spirit, John 14:16–18

commands
- to be taught, Deuteronomy 6:1–7; Matthew 5:19
- to be obeyed, Deuteronomy 8:6; Proverbs 19:16; John 15:10
- a new command, John 13:34
- to love, Galatians 5:14; 1 Timothy 1:5; 2 John 6

communion (KUH-myu-nyun) See "Lord's Supper".

complain
- Pharisees complained, Luke 5:30
- disciples complained, John 6:61
- warnings against, Philippians 2:14

concubine (KON-kyu-bine) See "slave woman".

condemn (kon-DEM) *to judge someone guilty of doing wrong,* John 3:16–18; Romans 2:1; 8:1

coney, See "rock badger".

confess
- admitting sin, Psalm 32:5, Proverbs 28:13; James 5:16; 1 John 1:9
- admitting Christ is Lord, Romans 10:9–10; Philippians 2:11; 1 Timothy 6:12; 1 John 4:2–3

confidence (KON-fih-dens) *a feeling of assurance; trust.*
- from the Lord, 2 Thessalonians 3:4; 2 Timothy 1:7
- in Christ, Philippians 4:13
- before God, 1 John 3:21

conscience (KON-shunts) *a person's belief about what is right and wrong.*
- Paul's good conscience, Acts 23:1
- commanded to have a good conscience, 1 Timothy 3:9; Hebrews 9:14
- a troubled conscience, Hebrews 10:22; 1 John 3:20
- a corrupt conscience, 1 Timothy 4:2; Titus 1:15

contentment, *satisfaction.*
- Paul learned, Philippians 4:11
- with possessions, Luke 3:14; 1 Timothy 6:6; Hebrews 13:5

conversion (kon-VER-zhun) *a person's turning toward God and becoming a Christian.*
- examples of, Acts 9:1–22; 11:19–21; 1 Thessalonians 1:9

coral (KOR-al) *a type of limestone that forms in the ocean,* Job 28:18; Ezekiel 27:16

Corinth (KOR-inth) *a large seaport in the country of Greece.*
- Paul preached there, Acts 18:1–11
- Paul's letters to the church there, 1 and 2 Corinthians

Cornelius (kor-NEEL-yus) *a Roman army officer in charge of a hundred soldiers,* Acts 10

cornerstone, *the most important stone at the corner of the base of a building; Jesus is called the cornerstone of the new law.*
- Christ as the cornerstone, Ephesians 2:20; 1 Peter 2:4–8

council (KOWN-s'l) *or meeting; the highest Jewish court in the days of the Jesus.*
- Jesus before the council, Matthew 26:57–68; Mark 14:53–65
- apostles before the council, Acts 4:1–22; 22:30 — 23:10
- Stephen before the council, Acts 6:8–7

courage
- need for, Joshua 1:6–9; Psalm 27:14; 1 Corinthians 16:13; Philippians 1:20
- examples of, Acts 4:13; 5:17–32; 20:22–24

court, courtyard, *part of a building that has walls, but no roof. The Temple had four courts:*
- the Court of the Non-Jews (Gentiles), a large open area just inside the walls of Herod's Temple, Mark 11:15–17; John 10:23; Acts 3:11
- the Court of Women, the next area, where both men and women were allowed, Mark 12:41–44
- the Court of Israel, the inner area of the Temple, where only Jewish men were allowed
- the Court of the Priests, the innermost court in the Temple, where only priests were allowed, Matthew 23:35

covenant (KUV-eh-nant) See "agreement".

covet (KUV-et) *to want strongly something that belongs to someone else.*
- forbidden by God, Exodus 20:17; Romans 13:9; Hebrews 13:5

creation
- of the world, Genesis 1 — 2; Job 38 — 41; Psalm 8; Isaiah 40:21–26; John 1:1–3; Hebrews 11:3

creator, *one who makes something out of nothing.*
- God as our Maker, Deuteronomy 32:6
- "Remember your Creator", Ecclesiastes 12:1

Crete (KREET) *an island in the Mediterranean Sea.*
- Paul visited there, Acts 27:7; Titus 1:5

cross, *two rough beams of wood nailed together, criminals were killed on crosses.*

- Jesus died on a cross, Matthew 27:31–50; Mark 15:20–37; Luke 23:26–46; John 19:16–30
- importance of, 1 Corinthians 1:18; 2:2; Galatians 6:14; Ephesians 2:16; Colossians 2:13–14
- as a symbol of death to oneself, Matthew 10:38; Luke 9:23; Romans 6:6; Galatians 5:24

crown, *a special band worn around the head.*
- a king's crown, Psalm 21:2–3; Song of Solomon 3:11; Revelation 12:3
- of thorns, Matthew 27:29; Mark 15:17; John 19:2
- of victory, 1 Corinthians 9:25; 2 Timothy 4:8; 1 Peter 5:4

crucifixion (kroo-see-FIK-shun) *to be killed on a cross.* See "cross".

cubit (KU-bit) *a measurement in Bible times; about forty centimetres,* Revelation 21:17

cud, *an animal's food that is chewed slightly, swallowed, brought up, then chewed more completely a second time,* Leviticus 11; Deuteronomy 14

cumin (QU-min) *a plant with small seeds used for seasoning food,* Matthew 23:23

cup
- of the king of Egypt, Genesis 40:11
- of Joseph, Genesis 44:1–17
- of Lord's Supper, Matthew 26:27–29; Mark 14:22–25; Luke 22:17–20; 1 Corinthians 11:25–29
- of anger, Isaiah 51:17–23
- of water, Matthew 10:42; Mark 9:41

cupbearer, *the officer who tasted and served the king his wine.*
- to the king of Egypt, Genesis 40
- Nehemiah, cupbearer to Artaxerxes, Nehemiah 1:11

curse
- from God, Deuteronomy 11:26–29; John 7:49; Galatians 3:10–13
- forbidden to people, Matthew 15:4; Romans 12:14; James 3:9–10
- response to, Luke 6:28; 1 Corinthians 4:12

curtain
- of the Holy Tent, Exodus 26:1–2; 36:9
- of the Temple, Matthew 27:51; Mark 15:38; Luke 23:45

Cush, a country in Africa, Genesis 2:13; Psalm 68:31; Isaiah 18; 20

Cush, grandson of Noah, Genesis 10

Cyprus (SY-prus) *an island in the Mediterranean Sea,* Acts 11:19–20; 13:4; 15:39

Cyrene (sy-REE-nee) *a city in North Africa,* Acts 2:10; 6:9
- Simon of, Matthew 27:32; Mark 15:21; Luke 23:26

Cyrus (SY-rus) *a king of Persia,* Daniel 1:21
- sent captives home, Ezra 1; 6
- chosen by God, Isaiah 44:28 — 45:13

D

Dagon (DAY-gon) *a false god of the Philistines,* Judges 16:23; 1 Samuel 5:2–7; 1 Chronicles 10:10

Damascus (dah-MAS-kus) *a city sixty-four kilometres east of Lake Galilee.*
- a chief city of Syria, 1 Kings 15:18; 2 Chronicles 24:23
- condemned by Amos, Amos 1:3,5
- Paul converted there, Acts 9:1–22

Dan, a city
- Israel's most northern city, Judges 20:1; 2 Samuel 16:11

Dan, son of Jacob, Genesis 30:6; 49:16–17; Joshua 19:40–48

Daniel (DAN-yel) *a Hebrew captive taken to Babylon as a young man.*
- taken to Babylon, Daniel 1:1–6
- became king's servant, Daniel 1:7–21
- explained Nebuchadnezzar's dreams, Daniel 2; 4
- read the writing on the wall, Daniel 5
- thrown into lion's den, Daniel 6
- his visions, Daniel 7; 8; 10
- a prophet, Matthew 24:15

Darius Hystaspes (dah-REE-us his-TAHS-peez) *a ruler of Persia who allowed the Jews to finish rebuilding the Temple,* Ezra 5 — 6

Darius the Mede, *the king of Persia who made Daniel an important ruler under him,* Daniel 5:31 — 6:28; Haggai 1:1; Zechariah 1:1

darkness, *having no light; a symbol of evil.*
- before creation, Genesis 1:2
- as a plague, Exodus 10:21–23
- at Jesus' death, Matthew 27:45; Mark 15:33; Luke 23:44–45
- spiritual, John 1:5; Romans 13:12; Colossians 1:13
- as punishment, Matthew 8:12; 2 Peter 2:17; Jude 6,13

David (DAY-vid) *Israel's greatest king.*
- son of Jesse, 1 Samuel 16:13–23
- played harp for Saul, 1 Samuel 16:14–23
- killed Goliath, 1 Samuel 17
- friend of Jonathan, 1 Samuel 18:1–4; 19:1–7; 20
- chased by Saul, 1 Samuel 18 — 19; 23:7–29
- protected Saul, 1 Samuel 24; 26
- became king, 2 Samuel 2:1–7; 5:1–14
- married Bathsheba, 2 Samuel 11 — 12:25
- reign of, 2 Samuel 5 — 1 Kings 1
- not allowed to build the Temple, 2 Samuel 7:1–17
- death of, 1 Kings 2:1–11
- Jesus as son of David, Matthew 22:42–45; Luke 1:27; 20:41–44

deacon (DEE-kun) *a person chosen to serve the church in special ways,* Philippians 1:1; 1 Timothy 3:8–13

Dead Sea, *large lake at the south end of the Jordan River. Several small streams flow into it, but it has no outlet. It is so salty that nothing lives in it. It is also called the "Sea of Arabah", "Salt Sea", and the "Eastern Sea".* Genesis 14:3; Numbers 34:3,12; Joshua 3:16

deaf, *unable or unwilling to hear.*
- healed, Matthew 11:5; Luke 7:22
- and dumb spirit, Mark 9:25

death
- a result of sin, Genesis 2:16–17; Romans 5:12; 6:23; 1 Corinthians 15:21
- Christ's victory over, 1 Corinthians 15:24–26,54–57; 2 Timothy 1:10; Hebrews 2:14; Revelation 1:18
- spiritual death, Ephesians 2:1; Colossians 2:13

Deborah (DEB-oh-rah) *the only woman judge over Israel,* Judges 4 — 5

Decapolis (dee-KAP-oh-lis) *ten towns in an area southeast of Lake Galilee,* Matthew 4:25; Mark 5:20; 7:31

Delilah (dee-LYE-luh) *an evil Philistine woman whom Samson loved,* Judges 16:4–20

Demas (DEE-mus) *a Christian who helped the apostle Paul when Paul was in prison.*

- worked with Paul, Colossians 4:14; Philemon 24
- left Paul, 2 Timothy 4:10

Demetrius (deh-MEE-tree-us) *a silver worker in Ephesus,* Acts 19:23–27,38

demon, *an evil spirit from the devil. Sometimes demons lived in people, but Jesus could force them out.*

- people possessed by, Matthew 8:28–32; 9:32–33; Mark 7:24–30; 9:17–29
- Jesus accused of demon possession, Mark 3:22; John 7:20; 8:48; 10:20–21
- demons recognised Jesus, Mark 1:23–26; 3:11–12; 5:7–8; Acts 19:15; James 2:19

deny (di-NY) *refusing to believe the truth.*

- denying Christ, Matthew 10:32–33; 2 Timothy 2:12; 1 John 2:22–23
- Peter denied Christ, Matthew 26:34–35,69–75

descendants (de-SEN-dants) *family members who are born to a person or his children; grandchildren, great-grandchildren, great-great-grandchildren and so on,* Genesis 13:14–16; 15:12–16

devil (DEV-'l) *Satan; a spirit and the enemy of God and humans.*

- Jesus tempted by, Matthew 4:1–11; Luke 4:1–13
- children of, John 8:41–44; Acts 13:10; 1 John 3:7–10
- people to oppose, Ephesians 4:27; 6:11; James 4:7

Didymus (DID-ee-mus) *another name for Thomas, one of Jesus' apostles,* John 11:16; 20:24; 21:2

disciple (dih-SYE-p'l) See "follower".

disease

- a result of sin, Exodus 15:26; Deuteronomy 7:15; 28:60–61
- healed by Jesus, Matthew 4:23–24; 15:30–31; 21:14; Luke 7:21
- healed by apostles, Acts 5:12–16; 9:32–35; 14:8–10; 19:11–12; 28:8–9

disobedience

- brought sin, Romans 5:19
- to be punished, 2 Corinthians 10:6; Hebrews 4:11

divide

- heavens and earth, Genesis 1:6–8
- Red Sea, Exodus 14:16,21
- family against itself, Matthew 12:25; Mark 3:25; Luke 11:17

divorce

- teachings about, Deuteronomy 22:13–19,28–29; 24:1–4; Matthew 5:31–32; 19:1–12; 1 Corinthians 7:10–16

dog

- drinking water like a dog, Judges 7:5–6
- returns to its vomit, Proverbs 26:11; 2 Peter 2:22
- licked Ahab's blood, 1 Kings 22:38
- licked Lazarus's sores, Luke 16:20–21

door

- Jesus at the door, John 10:1
- "Knock, and the door will open", Luke 11:9–10
- "I stand at the door and knock", Revelation 3:20

donkey

- Balaam's, Numbers 22:21–30
- jawbone of, Judges 15:15–17
- ridden by Jesus, Matthew 21:1–7

Dorcas (DOR-kus) *Tabitha; a Christian woman known for helping the poor.*

- raised from the dead, Acts 9:36–43

dove, *a small bird similar to a pigeon; often a symbol for love, peace, and the Holy Spirit.*

- sent out by Noah, Genesis 8:8–12
- form taken by the Spirit of God, Matthew 3:16; Mark 1:10
- sellers of, John 2:14–16

dreams

- Joseph's, Genesis 37:1–11
- the king of Egypt's, Genesis 41:1–36
- Nebuchadnezzar's, Daniel 2; 4
- angel appeared to Joseph, Matthew 1:20–21; 2:13,19
- "your old men will dream dreams", Acts 2:17

drunkenness

- Noah became drunk, Genesis 9:20–23
- warnings against, Romans 13:13; 1 Corinthians 6:10; Ephesians 5:18; 1 Peter 4:3

E

eagle

- "to rise up as an eagle", Isaiah 40:31

earth

- creation of, Genesis 1:9–10; Jeremiah 51:15
- belongs to God, Exodus 19:5; Psalm 24:1

earthquake

- experienced by Elijah, 1 Kings 19:11–12
- at the death of Jesus, Matthew 27:51–54
- at Jesus' resurrection, Matthew 28:2
- experienced by Paul and Silas, Acts 16:25–26

Ebal (EE-buhl) *a mountain in Samaria next to Mount Gerizim.*

- place to announce curses, Deuteronomy 11:29; 27:12–13; Joshua 8:30–35

Eden, garden of (EE-den) *the home God created for Adam and Eve,* Genesis 2:8 — 3:24; Ezekiel 36:35; Joel 2:3

Edom (EE-dum) *Esau; the land where Esau's descendants lived.*

- the land of Esau, Genesis 36:8–9
- refused to let Israelites pass through, Numbers 20:14–21; Judges 1:17–18
- broke away from Judah, 2 Kings 8:20–22
- to be punished, Jeremiah 49:7–22; Ezekiel 25:12–14; Obadiah

education

- of Moses, Acts 7:22
- of children, Deuteronomy 6:1–7
- brings wisdom, Proverbs 8:33; 22:6

Eglon (EGG-lon) *a king of Moab,* Judges 3:12–25

Egypt (EE-jipt) *a country in the northeast part of Africa.*

- Joseph there, Genesis 39 — 50
- Israelites there, Genesis 46:5–34; Exodus 1; Acts 7:9–38
- Israelites left, Exodus 12:31–51
- Jesus there, Matthew 2:13–15

Ehud (EE-hud) *the second judge of Israel,* Judges 3:12–30

elder (EL-der) *older men who led God's people; appointed leaders in the church.*

- leaders of the Jews, Numbers 11:16–25; Deuteronomy 19:11–12; Matthew 21:23; Acts 4:5–7
- leaders of the church, Acts 11:30; 14:23; 15:2; 16:4
- duties and qualities, Acts 20:28; 1 Timothy 3:1–7; Titus 1:6–9; 1 Peter 5:1–3

Eleazar (el-ee-AY-zar) *son of Aaron.*

- birth of, Exodus 6:23–25
- Moses became angry with, Leviticus 10:16–20
- a high priest, Numbers 3:32
- divided the promised land, Numbers 34:17

election, *process of selecting.* See "chosen".

Eli (EE-lye) *a priest and the next-to-last judge of Israel.*
- trained Samuel, 1 Samuel 1:9–28; 2:11; 3
- didn't discipline his sons, 1 Samuel 2:12–36
- death of, 1 Samuel 4:1–18

Elihu (ee-LYE-hew) *the fourth of Job's friends to try to explain Job's troubles,* Job 32–37

Elijah (ee-LIE-juh) *a prophet who spoke for God.*
- fed by ravens, 1 Kings 17:1–6
- brought boy to life, 1 Kings 17:7–24
- against prophets of Baal, 1 Kings 18:1–40
- condemned Ahab, 1 Kings 21:17–29
- taken to heaven, 2 Kings 2:1–12
- appeared with Jesus, Matthew 17:1–13; Mark 9:2–13; Luke 9:28–36

Elisha (ee-LYE-shuh) *the prophet who took Elijah's place as God's messenger.*
- received Elijah's spirit, 2 Kings 2:9–14
- helped a Shunammite woman, 2 Kings 4:1–36
- miracles of, 2 Kings 2:19–22; 4:38–44; 6:1–7
- healed Naaman, 2 Kings 5
- death of, 2 Kings 13:14–20

Elizabeth (ee-LIZ-uh-beth) *the wife of Zechariah, a priest.*
- mother of John the Baptist, Luke 1:5–25,57–66
- visited by Mary, Luke 1:39–45

Elkanah (el-KAY-nuh) *the father of Samuel,* 1 Samuel 1—2:11

Elymas (EL-ih-mus) *Bar-Jesus; a magician in the city of Paphos in Cyprus,* Acts 13:4–12

Emmaus (ee-MAY-us) *a town twelve kilometres from Jerusalem.*
- Jesus appeared to disciples near there, Luke 24:13–39

encourage
- encouragement from God, Romans 15:4–5
- Christians to encourage each other, 1 Thessalonians 5:14; 2 Timothy 4:2; Hebrews 3:13; 10:24–25
- examples of encouragement, Acts 11:23; 13:15; 15:31–32

endurance, See "patience".

enemy
- attitude toward, Exodus 23:4–5; Matthew 5:43–48; Luke 6:27–36; Romans 12:20
- God's enemies, Romans 5:10; Philippians 3:18–19; James 4:4

enemy of Christ, *the anti-Christ,* 1 John 2:18,22; 4:3; 2 John 7

Enoch (EE-nok) *a man who walked with God,* Genesis 5:21–24; Hebrews 11:5

enrolment, See "census".

envy, See "jealousy".

Epaphras (EP-ah-fruss) *a Christian who started the church at Colossae,* Colossians 1:7–8; 4:12–13; Philemon 23

Epaphroditus (ee-PAF-ro-DYE-tus) *a Christian in the church at Philippi,* Philippians 2:25–30; 4:18

ephah (EE-fah) *a common measurement for dry materials, about twenty litres,* Exodus 16:36

Ephesus (EF-eh-sus) *the capital city in the Roman state of Asia.*
- Paul's work there, Acts 18:18–20; 1 Corinthians 16:8–9
- church there, Ephesians 1:1; Revelation 2:1–7

ephod (EF-ahd) See "robe, holy".

Ephraim (EE-frah-im) *Joseph's younger son,* Genesis 41:50–52; 48:8–20
- descendants of, Numbers 26:35; Joshua 16:5–10

Epicureans (EPI-cure-ee-ans) *people who followed the teachings of a man named Epicurus, who taught that happiness should be a person's goal in life,* Acts 17:18

equality (ee-KWOL-eh-tee) *being identical in value.*
- in death, Ecclesiastes 3:19–20
- of Jewish and non-Jewish people, Romans 10:12
- in Christ, Galatians 3:26–28

Esau (EE-saw) See "Edom".

Esther (ES-ter) *a Jewish girl who became the wife of Ahasuerus, King of Persia,* Esther 1—10
- became queen, Esther 1—2:18
- learned of the plan to kill the Jews, Esther 3—4
- saved the Jews, Esther 5—8

eternal, See "forever".

eternal life, *the new kind of life promised to those who follow Jesus, and which never ends.*
- conditions for, Mark 10:17–31; John 3:14–15; 12:25; 17:3; Galatians 6:7–8
- source of, John 6:27–29; 10:28; Titus 1:2; 1 John 5:11–12

Ethiopia (EE-thee-o-pee-uh) *earlier called "Cush".* See "Cush".

eunuch (YOU-nuk) *a man who cannot have sexual relations. In Bible times, eunuchs were often high officers in royal palaces or armies.* 2 Kings 9:32; Esther 2:3; Isaiah 56:3–5; Acts 8:26–40

Euphrates (you-FRAY-teez) *a long, important river in Bible lands.*
- in the garden of Eden, Genesis 2:10–14
- a boundary, Genesis 15:18; 1 Kings 4:21,24; 2 Kings 24:7

Eutychus (YOU-ti-cus) *a young man in the city of Troas who was brought back to life,* Acts 20:7–12

evangelist (ee-VAN-juh-list) *someone who tells the Good News.*
- Philip, the evangelist, Acts 21:8
- as a gift from Christ, Ephesians 4:11

Eve (EEV) *the first woman.*
- created by God, Genesis 2:18–25
- tricked by Satan, Genesis 3; 2 Corinthians 11:3; 1 Timothy 2:13–14

everlasting, *living forever, eternal.*
- God, Genesis 21:33; Nehemiah 9:5; Isaiah 40:28
- Christ, Isaiah 9:6
- kingdom, Daniel 4:3; 2 Peter 1:11
- fire, Matthew 18:8,25,41
- gospel, Revelation 14:6

evil
- warnings against, Amos 5:15; Romans 12:9; 1 Thessalonians 5:22
- to be punished, Proverbs 24:20; Isaiah 13:11

evil spirit, See "demon".

eye
- "eye for eye", Exodus 21:23–24; Matthew 5:38

forty-eight kilometres north of Jerusalem.
- blessings announced from there, Deuteronomy 11:29; 27:12; Joshua 8:33

Gethsemane (geth-SEM-uh-nee) *a garden of olive trees just outside Jerusalem.*
- Jesus arrested there, Matthew 26:36–56; Mark 14:32–50

Gibeah (GIB-ee-uh) *a city about four kilometres north of Jerusalem,* Judges 19:12 — 20:43; 1 Samuel 10:26

Gibeon (GIB-ee-uhn) *a town about ten kilometres northwest of Jerusalem.*
- Joshua defeated Amorites there, Joshua 9 — 10

Gideon (GID-ee-on) *the judge who led Israel to defeat the Midianites,* Judges 6:1 — 8:35
- angel appeared to, Judges 6:11–24
- destroyed Baal idol, Judges 6:25–32
- defeated Midianites, Judges 6:33 — 8:21
- the sign of the fleece, Judges 6:36–40
- built an idol, Judges 8:22–27
- death of, Judges 8:28–32
- hero of faith, Hebrews 11:32–34

gifts, *talents or abilities.*
- spiritual, Romans 12:6–8; 1 Corinthians 7:7; 12; 14:1–25; Ephesians 4:7

Gihon (GYE-hohn) *a spring outside the walls of Jerusalem,* 1 Kings 1:38–39; 2 Chronicles 32:30; 33:14

Gilead (GIL-ee-ad) *the area that Israel owned east of the Jordan River,* Numbers 32; Deuteronomy 3:10–16

Gilgal (GIL-gal) *the first place the Israelites camped after entering the promised land,* Joshua 4:19 — 5:12

gittith (GIT-tith) *probably a musical word and a musical instrument,* Psalms 8; 81; 84

giving
- examples of generous giving, Mark 12:43; Acts 10:2; 11:29–30; 2 Corinthians 8:3–5
- proper attitude towards, Matthew 6:3–4; Romans 12:8; 1 Corinthians 13:3; 2 Corinthians 9:7

gleaning (GLEEN-ing) *to gather grain left in the field after harvest,* Ruth 2

glory, *visible sign of God's greatness.*
- appeared in a cloud, Exodus 16:10; 24:16–17
- seen by Moses, Exodus 33:18–23
- "The heavens tell the glory of God", Psalm 19:1
- seen by Ezekiel, Ezekiel 1:26–28; 3:23; 8:4
- at Jesus' birth, Luke 2:8–14
- of Jesus, Luke 9:28–32
- seen by Stephen, Acts 7:55
- in the temple in heaven, Revelation 15:8

gluttony (GLUH-tun-ee) *eating too much.*
- warnings against, Deuteronomy 21:20; Proverbs 23:20–21
- Jesus accused of, Matthew 11:19; Luke 7:34

goat
- for a sin offering, Leviticus 9:3
- divided from sheep, Matthew 25:32–33
- blood of, Hebrews 9:12–13; 10:4

God, *the One who made the world and everything in it.* See also "glory".
- the creator, Genesis 1; Acts 17:24; Romans 1:25
- nearness of, Acts 17:27–28; James 4:8
- goodness of, Matthew 19:17; Acts 14:17; Romans 2:4; 1 John 4:7–11
- eternal nature of, Psalm 102:24–28; 1 Timothy 1:17; 6:16
- names of, Exodus 3:13–14; 1 Timothy 6:15; Hebrews 12:9; James 1:17; 5:4
- power of, Job 9:4–19; Isaiah 40:12–31; Matthew 19:26
- mercy of, Exodus 20:6; Numbers 14:18; Ephesians 2:4
- justice of, Psalm 67:4; Acts 17:31; Romans 2:2

golden calf, *an idol made to worship false gods.*
- made by Aaron, Exodus 32:1–24
- made by Jeroboam, 1 Kings 12:26–33

golden rule, *a name often used for Jesus' command: "Do to others what you want them to do to you",* Matthew 7:12; Luke 6:31

Golgotha (GOL-goh-thuh) *Calvary; the hill where Jesus was crucified,* Matthew 27:33; Mark 15:22; John 19:17

Goliath (go-LYE-eth) *the giant from Gath whom David killed,* 1 Samuel 17

Gomorrah (goh-MOR-ruh) *an evil city near Sodom.*
- destroyed by God, Genesis 18:17 — 19:29; Matthew 10:11–15; 2 Peter 2:6

Good News, *also called the "gospel". Jesus died on the cross, was buried, and came back to life so people can be saved.* Mark 1:1; Acts 5:42; 13:26–39
- power of, Romans 1:16–17; Colossians 1:5–6; 1 Corinthians 15:2
- preached by the apostles, Luke 9:6; Acts 8:25; Philippians 1:5,12–14

Goshen (GO-shen) *an area in the Nile delta of Egypt.*
- home for Joseph's family, Genesis 45:9–10; 47:1–6,27

gospel (GOS-p'l) *"good news". The first four books of the New Testament are called the gospels because they tell the good news of what Jesus has done for us.* See "Good News".

gossip
- to be avoided, Romans 1:28–32; 2 Corinthians 12:20; 1 Timothy 5:13

government (GUV-ern-ment) *group of people in charge of managing and making laws for people in a country or city.*
- to be obeyed, Matthew 22:15–21; Romans 13:1–7; Titus 3:1; 1 Peter 2:13–17

governor
- Joseph, governor of Egypt, Genesis 42:6
- Nehemiah, governor of Judah, Nehemiah 5:14
- Pilate, governor of Judea, Matthew 27:2
- Felix, governor of Judea, Acts 23:26

grace, *God's kindness and love shown to us, even though we do not deserve them.*
- source of, Ephesians 3:7; Hebrews 4:14–16
- saved by, Acts 15:11, Romans 3:24; Ephesians 2:5–8; 2 Timothy 1:9
- misuse of, Romans 6; Galatians 5:4; Jude 4

grandchildren
- a blessing, Ruth 4:15; Proverbs 17:6
- inherit grandparents' wealth, Proverbs 13:22

grave, See "tomb".

Great Sea, See "Mediterranean Sea".

Greece, *once the most powerful nation in southeast Europe. Northern Greece was called "Macedonia". Southern Greece was called "Achaia".*
- Paul preached there, Acts 16:11–12; 20:1–6

greed, *selfish desire for more than one's share of something.*
- never satisfied, Proverbs 27:20
- beware of, Luke 12:15
- love of money, 1 Timothy 6:10

Greek, *the language of the New Testament.*
- the language of Greece, John 19:20; Acts 21:37; Revelation 9:11
- the people from Greece, Acts 14:1; 16:1; Colossians 3:11

grief
- of David for Absalom, 2 Samuel 18:33
- of the disciples, Matthew 17:23; John 16:6

guidance (GYD-ns) *direction.*
- by God, Exodus 13:21
- of the humble, Psalm 25:9
- of the Holy Spirit, John 16:15

guilt, *fact of having done wrong; regret, shame.*
- for improper worship, 1 Corinthians 11:27
- for breaking the Law, James 2:10
- cleansed of, Job 33:9; Isaiah 6:7; Hebrews 10:22

H

Habakkuk (HA-ba-kuk) *a prophet who wrote about the same time as Jeremiah,* Habakkuk 1 — 3

Hades (HAY-deez) *the world of the dead,* Revelation 6:8; 20:13–14

Hagar (HAY-gar) *Sarah's slave-girl.*
- gave birth to Ishmael, Genesis 16
- sent away by Sarah, Genesis 21:8–21

Haggai (HAG-ay-eye) *a prophet in Jerusalem when the Israelites came back from Babylon,* Ezra 5:1, 6:14; Haggai 1 — 2

half-tribe, *one of the two parts of the tribe of Manasseh. One half-tribe settled east of the Jordan and the other settled west of the Jordan.* Joshua 1:12–15; 13:8–9; 22

Ham, *the son of Noah,* Genesis 6:10; 9:18–19; 10:6

Haman (HAY-man) *the chief officer under Ahasuerus, King of Persia.*
- planned to kill the Jews, Esther 3 — 6
- hanged, Esther 7

hands, laying on, *a ceremony where a person places his hands upon another.*
- for healing, Mark 5:23; 6:5; Luke 4:40
- to receive the Holy Spirit, Acts 8:17–19; 19:6
- for blessing, Mark 10:16; Acts 13:3

Hannah (HAN-uh) *the mother of Samuel,* 1 Samuel 1 — 2:21

happiness
- of the people of God, Psalms 144:15; 146:5; Proverbs 16:20; Matthew 5:3–12
- comes from wisdom, Proverbs 3:13

Haran (HA-ran)
- Abraham's brother, Genesis 11:26–31
- home of Abraham, Genesis 11:31 — 12:5

harlot, See "prostitute".

harp, *the favourite musical instrument of the Jews.*
- first played, Genesis 4:21
- played by David, 1 Samuel 16:23; 18:10–11
- to praise God, Psalms 33:2; 71:22; 150:3

harvest
- of the poor, Ruth 2
- as a symbol, Matthew 9:37–38; 13:24–30,39; Revelation 14:14–16

hate
- seven things God hates, Proverbs 6:16–19
- a time to, Ecclesiastes 3:8
- of the world toward Jesus, John 15:18
- equal to murder, 1 John 3:15
- commands against, Galatians 5:19–21; 1 John 4:19–21

head
- a part of the body, Genesis 3:15; Psalm 23:5; Matthew 8:20; 1 Corinthians 12:21; Revelation 14:14
- a leader, Ephesians 1:22; Colossians 1:18

heal
- a time to, Ecclesiastes 3:3
- by faith, Matthew 9:21–22; James 5:15
- "Doctor, heal yourself." Luke 4:23

heart, *the mind or feelings; not the physical heart that pumps blood,* Deuteronomy 6:5; Matthew 22:37

heaven
- the home of God, Matthew 5:34; Mark 16:19; John 3:13; Revelation 4
- angel spoke from, Genesis 21:17; 22:11
- opened, Matthew 3:16; Acts 7:56; 10:11
- fire from, 2 Kings 1:10–14; 1 Chronicles 21:26
- third heaven, 2 Corinthians 12:2
- the new heaven, Revelation 21:1–4
- kingdom of, Matthew 3:2; 5:3,19–20

Hebrew (HEE-broo) *the language used by the people of Israel and for the writing of most of the Old Testament,* Acts 21:40

Hebrews (HEE-brooz) *another name for the Jewish people,* Exodus 7:16; 2 Corinthians 11:22; Philippians 3:5

Hebron (HEH-bron) *a city about thirty-three kilometres southwest of Jerusalem,* Genesis 13:18; Numbers 13:22; 2 Samuel 2:1–11

heir (AIR) *the person who inherits what belongs to a relative. Because through Christ we can be adopted children of God, Christians are heirs to God's riches*
- Abraham's heir, Genesis 15:3–4
- heir of God, Romans 8:17; Galatians 4:7

hell
- home of the devil and his angels, 2 Peter 2:4
- future home of sinners, Matthew 10:28; 23:33; Revelation 21:8
- descriptions of, Matthew 13:42; Mark 9:47–48; James 3:6; Revelation 14:11

helmet
- worn in battle, 1 Samuel 17:5; Ezekiel 23:24
- a symbol of salvation, Isaiah 59:17; Ephesians 6:17; 1 Thessalonians 5:8

help
- the stone of help, 1 Samuel 7:12
- the Holy Spirit as helper, Romans 8:26; Philippians 1:19
- from God, Psalms 46:1; 121:1–2; Isaiah 41:10

- commanded, 1 Thessalonians 5:14; Hebrews 6:10

Hermes (HER-meez) *the Greek god of skilful speaking and the messenger of the other Greek gods,* Romans 16:14

Herod I (HEH-rud) *"Herod the Great"; king of Palestine from 40 to 4 BC,* Matthew 2:1; Luke 1:5

Herod Agrippa I (uh-GRIP-a) *king of Palestine from AD 41 to 44,* Acts 12:1

Herod Agrippa II, *king of Palestine from AD 52 to 70,* Acts 25:13—26:32

Herod Antipas (AN-ti-pus) *king of Palestine from 4 BC to about AD 39,* Matthew 14:1; Mark 6:14; Luke 23:7

Herodias (heh-ROW-dee-us) *the granddaughter of Herod I.*
- asked for John's head, Matthew 14:3–12; Mark 6:17–28; Luke 3:19

Hezekiah (hez-eh-KY-uh) *one of the good kings of Judah.*
- destroyed idols, 2 Kings 18:1–8; 2 Chronicles 29—31
- attacked by Assyria, 2 Kings 18:9—19:37; 2 Chronicles 32:1–23; Isaiah 36—37
- life extended by God, 2 Kings 20:1–11; Isaiah 38
- death of, 2 Kings 20:12–21; 2 Chronicles 32:24–33

higgaion (hig-GI-on) *probably a time to think quietly during a song,* Psalm 9:16

high place, *a place to worship gods,* 1 Kings 14:23; 2 Chronicles 31:1; 33:3

high priest, *the most important religious leader of the Jewish people.*
- rules for, Leviticus 21:10–15
- of the Jews, Exodus 29:30; Numbers 35:25; Matthew 26:3; Acts 23:2
- Jesus as, Hebrews 2:17; 3:1; 4:14—5:10; 8:1–6

Hilkiah (hil-KY-ah) *high priest when Josiah was King,* 2 Kings 22—23; 2 Chronicles 34

Hinnom, Valley of (HIN-num) *an area where rubbish was burned just outside of Jerusalem; also called "Gehenna",* Joshua 15:8; 18:16; Nehemiah 11:30

Hiram (HY-rum) *king of Tyre when David and Solomon were kings over Israel*
- supplied trees for Solomon's Temple, 2 Samuel 5:11; 1 Kings 5:1–18; 9:11–27; 10:22

Hittites (HIT-tites) *people who lived in what is now Turkey,* Genesis 23:1–16; Exodus 3:8; Joshua 1:4; 1 Samuel 11:3

Holy (HO-lee) *pure, belonging to and willing to serve God.*
- holiness of God, Leviticus 11:45; Isaiah 6:3; Hebrews 12:10; Revelation 4:8
- holy kiss, Romans 16:16
- people to be holy, Ephesians 1:4; Colossians 1:22–23; 3:2; 1 Peter 1:15–16

Holy of Holies, See "Most Holy Place".

Holy Place, *a room in the Holy Tent and the Temple,* Exodus 26:31–35; 28:29; Leviticus 6:30; 1 Kings 8:10–11

Holy Spirit (HO-lee SPIH-rit) *one of the three persons of God. The Holy Spirit helped the apostles do miracles and led men to write God's word; he lives in Christians today.*
- in creation, Genesis 1:2
- living in Christians, John 14:15–17; 1 Corinthians 6:19; Galatians 4:6
- as a helper, John 14:25–26; 16:7–15; Romans 8:1–27; Galatians 5:22–25
- filled with, Luke 1:15; Acts 2:4; 7:55; 11:23–24
- sin against, Matthew 12:31; Acts 5:3; 1 Thessalonians 5:19; Hebrews 10:29

Holy Tent, See "Meeting Tent".

honest (ON-ist)
- heart, Luke 8:15
- people, 2 Kings 12:15
- answer, Proverbs 24:26
- commanded, Mark 10:19; Philippians 4:8

honour (ON-uh)
- for the old, Leviticus 19:32
- from God, 1 Samuel 2:30
- comes from humility, Proverbs 15:33
- to the deserving, Romans 13:7
- shown to parents, Exodus 20:12; Matthew 15:4
- shown to God, Proverbs 3:9; John 5:23; Revelation 4:9
- not shown to a prophet in his own town, Matthew 13:57

hope, *looking forward to something you really expect to happen.*
- reason for, Romans 5:3–5; 15:4; 2 Thessalonians 2:16; 1 Peter 1:13
- nature of, Romans 8:24–25
- results of, Colossians 1:5; Hebrews 6:18

Hophni (HOF-nee) *an evil son of Eli the priest,* 1 Samuel 2:12–34; 3:11—4:18

Horeb, Mount, (HOR-rebb) See "Sinai".

horses, Exodus 14:9; 1 Kings 10:26–29; Psalm 33:16–17; James 3:3

Hosanna (ho-ZAN-ah) *a shout of joy in praising God,* Matthew 21:9,15; Mark 11:9; John 12:13

Hosea (ho-ZEE-uh) *a prophet who lived about seven hundred years before Christ.*
- his unfaithful wife, Hosea 1
- his warnings to Israel, Hosea 2:4–14

hospitality
- of Abraham, Genesis 18:1–16
- teachings about, Romans 12:13; 1 Timothy 3:2; 5:9–10; 1 Peter 4:9

hosts, *armies; God is called the "Lord of hosts".* See "Lord of hosts".

Huldah (HUL-duh) *a woman prophet,* 2 Kings 22:14–20; 2 Chronicles 34:22–28

humble (HUM-bul) *not boasting or calling attention to yourself.*
- Moses as example of, Numbers 12:3
- humility commanded, Luke 14:7–11; 22:24–27; Ephesians 4:2; Philippians 2:3
- Jesus' humility, Philippians 2:5–8

hunger
- feeding the hungry, Matthew 25:34–35; Romans 12:20
- spiritual, John 6:35; 1 Peter 2:2

husband
- responsibilities of, 1 Corinthians 7:3–5; Ephesians 5:25–33; Colossians 3:19; 1 Peter 3:7

hymn (HIM) *a song that teaches us about God or praises him,* Matthew 26:30; Ephesians 5:19; Colossians 3:16
- Jesus and apostles sang, Matthew 26:30; Mark 14:26
- teachings about, Ephesians 5:19; Colossians 3:16

hypocrisy (hi-POK-ri-see) *acting as if one is good when that is not true,* Matthew 23:28; 1 Peter 2:1

hypocrite (HIP-oh-krit) *a person who acts as if he is good but isn't.*
- warnings about, Matthew 6:2,5,16; 7:3–5; Luke 13:15–17
- Pharisees as hypocrites, Matthew 15:1–9; 23:13–32

hyssop (HIS-op) *a small bushy plant; marjoram,* Exodus 12:22; Leviticus 14:4,6; John 19:29

I

Iconium (eye-KOH-nee-um) *a city in Galatia where Paul preached,* Acts 14:1–7,19–23

idol (EYE-d'l) *a statue of a false god.* See also "Baal", "Chemosh", "Molech".
- worship of, 2 Kings 17:12–17; Acts 17:16–23; 19:24; Romans 1:25
- warnings against worship of, Leviticus 19:4; Deuteronomy 6:14–15; 1 Corinthians 5:10–11; 6:9–10
- Baal, 1 Kings 18:17–40
- Chemosh, Numbers 21:29
- Molech, Jeremiah 32:35

ignorance (IG-nor-rance) *a lack of knowledge.*
- not an excuse, Leviticus 5:17

image, *likeness.*
- God's, Genesis 1:26–27
- Caesar's, Luke 20:24
- the Lord's, 2 Corinthians 3:18
- Jesus in God's image, Hebrews 1:3

immorality (IM-mor-RAL-i-tee) *evil; sinfulness.* See also "sin".
- warnings against, 1 Corinthians 5:9–11; 6:9–10; Galatians 5:19–21; Ephesians 5:5

immortality (IM-mor-TAL-i-tee) *life after death,* Job 14:1–14; Daniel 12:1–2; 1 Corinthians 15:12–58; 2 Timothy 1:10 See also "eternal life".

impossible
- people cannot do, Matthew 19:26
- for God to lie, Hebrews 6:18
- without faith to please God, Hebrews 11:6

incense (IN-sense) *a spice burned to make a sweet smell.*
- altar of, Exodus 30:1–10,34–38; Revelation 8:3–5
- used in worship, Psalm 141:2
- as a gift, Matthew 2:11

inheritance (in-HEH-ri-tence) *something valuable that is handed down within a family.*
- of land, Numbers 36:8; Deuteronomy 3:28; Psalm 25:13

iniquity, (in-I-kwi-tee) See "sin".

inn, *a place for travellers to spend the night,* Luke 2:7; 10:34

innocence (IN-oh-sense) *not guilty of sin.*
- of Adam and Eve, Genesis 2:25
- declared by Job, Job 34:5
- declared by Pilate, Matthew 27:24

inspiration (IN-spi-RAY-shun) *"God-breathed". It is used to mean that the Bible writers wrote what God wanted them to write.* 2 Timothy 3:16; 2 Peter 1:20–21

Isaac (EYE-zak) *the son of Abraham and Sarah.*
- birth of, Genesis 21:1–4
- offered as a sacrifice, Genesis 22:1–19
- married Rebekah, Genesis 24
- tricked by Jacob, Genesis 27
- hero of faith, Hebrews 11:20

Isaiah (eye-ZY-uh) *prophet who lived about seven hundred years before Christ.*
- became a prophet, Isaiah 6:1–8
- prophesied to Hezekiah, 2 Kings 19—20
- prophecies fulfilled, Matthew 3:3; 4:14; 13:14–15

Ish-Bosheth (ish-BOW-sheth) *son of Saul,* 2 Samuel 2:8–4

Ishmael (ISH-may-el) *son of Abraham and Hagar.*
- birth of, Genesis 16:2–16
- sent away from Abraham's camp, Genesis 21:8–21

Israel, kingdom of (IZ-ray-el) *the northern kingdom which had ten tribes.*
- beginning of, 1 Kings 11:27–12
- fall of, 2 Kings 17:1–18
- rulers of, 1 Kings 15:25–16; 22:51–53; 2 Kings 13; 14:23—17:6

Israel, son of Isaac, *Hebrew for "he who wrestles with God". Jacob's name was changed to Israel when he struggled with an angel at Bethel.* Genesis 32:22–28; 35:9–10. See also "Jacob".
- name given to Jacob's descendants, Genesis 49:28; Exodus 4:22; Psalm 22:23; Romans 9:3–5

Issachar (IS-uh-car) *a son of Jacob and Leah,* Genesis 30:18
- his descendants, Numbers 1:28–29; 26:23

ivory (EYE-voh-ree) *a creamy white bone that comes from elephant tusks,* 1 Kings 10:18; 22:39; Psalm 45:8

J

Jabbok River (JAB-ok) *a stream about eighty kilometres long that runs into the Jordan River,* Numbers 21:24; Joshua 12:2; Judges 11:13

Jabesh Gilead (JAY-besh GIL-ee-ad) *a small town on the east side of the Jordan River,* Judges 21:6–14; 2 Samuel 2:4–7

Jabin, king of Hazor (JAY-bin) *led a group of kings against the Israelites,* Joshua 11:1–11

Jabin, king of Canaan, *defeated by Israel when Deborah was judge,* Judges 4

Jacob (JAY-cub) *one of the sons of Isaac.*
- cheated Esau, Genesis 25:29–34
- tricked Isaac, Genesis 27:1–29
- his dream of a ladder to heaven, Genesis 28:10–22
- tricked by his sons, Genesis 37:10–22
- moved to Egypt, Genesis 45:25—47:12
- hero of faith, Hebrews 11:20–21

Jacob's Portion (JAY-cubs POR-shun) *a name for God, meaning he cares for Jacob's people,* Jeremiah 10:16; 51:19

jailer, *a keeper of a jail.*
- Paul and Silas, Acts 16:23

Jairus (JEYE-rus) *a ruler of the synagogue.*
- Jesus brought his daughter back to life, Matthew 9:18–26; Mark 5:21–43; Luke 8:40–56

James, brother of Jesus, Matthew 13:55; Acts 12:17; 21:18
- later an apostle, Galatians 1:19

James, son of Alphaeus, *an apostle,* Matthew 10:3; Mark 3:18; Luke 6:15; Acts 1:13

James, son of Zebedee, *an apostle of Jesus and a brother of the apostle John,* Matthew 10:2; Mark 10:35; Acts 12:2

Japheth (JAY-fith) *one of Noah's three sons,* Genesis 5:32; 7:13; 9:18–27; 10:1–5

Jashar, Book of (JA-shar) *a book mentioned in the Bible, but not part of it,* Joshua 10:12–13; 2 Samuel 1:17–27

Jason (JAY-son) *a Christian in Thessalonica,* Acts 17:5–9

jealousy (JEH-luh-see)
- to describe God, Exodus 20:5; 34:14; Deuteronomy 5:9
- examples of, Genesis 37:11; 1 Samuel 18:19; Matthew 27:18; Acts 5:17
- warnings against, Romans 13:13; 1 Corinthians 13:4; 1 Timothy 6:4; 1 Peter 2:1

Jebusites (JEB-you-sites) *people who lived around Jerusalem before the time of David,* Joshua 15:63; Judges 19:10–11; 2 Samuel 4:6–8

Jehoahaz, son of Jehu (jeh-HO-uh-haz) *king of Israel who lived about eight hundred years before Christ,* 2 Kings 13:1–9

Jehoahaz, son of Josiah, *king of Judah for only three months,* 2 Kings 23:31–34; 2 Chronicles 36:1–4

Jehoash (jeh-HO-ash) *a king of Israel,* 2 Kings 13:10 — 14:16

Jehoiachin (jeh-HO-uh-kin) *the next-to-last king of Judah.*
- surrendered to Babylon, 2 Kings 24:8–17
- in Babylon, 2 Kings 25:27–30

Jehoiada (jah-HO-yah-duh) *the chief priest in Jerusalem during Joash's rule,* 2 Kings 11 — 12; 2 Chronicles 22:11–24

Jehoiakim (jeh-HO-uh-kim) *king of Judah about 600 BC,* 2 Kings 23:34 — 24:6
- tried to kill Jeremiah, Jeremiah 26:1–23
- burned Jeremiah's scroll, Jeremiah 36:1–23

Jehoram (jeh-HOR-am) *or "Joram"; the fifth king of Judah,* 2 Kings 8:16-29; 2 Chronicles 21:4–20

Jehoshaphat (jeh-HOSH-uh-fat) *one of the good kings of Judah.*
- faithful to God, Chronicles 17:1–9
- appointed judges, 2 Chronicles 19:4–11
- defeated Moab and Ammon, 2 Chronicles 20

Jehovah (jeh-HOVE-uh) *a name for God; also translated "Lord",* Exodus 3:15; 6:3; Deuteronomy 28:58; Psalm 83:18

Jehu (JAY-hew) *an army captain who became king of Israel.*
- appointed as king, 2 Kings 9:1–13
- killed Joram and Ahaziah, 2 Kings 9:14–29
- stopped Baal worship, 2 Kings 10:18–35

Jephthah (JEF-thuh) *one of the judges of Israel.*
- fought the Ammonites, Judges 11:1–29,32–33
- his vow, Judges 11:30–31,34–39
- fought the people of Ephraim, Judges 12:2–7

Jeremiah (jer-eh-MY-ah) *a prophet who warned the people of Judah,* Jeremiah 1 — 52
- became a prophet, Jeremiah 1:1–10
- songs of, 2 Chronicles 35:25
- his prophecies fulfilled, 2 Chronicles 36:21–22; Matthew 2:17; 27:9
- wrote a scroll, Jeremiah 36

Jericho (JEHR-ih-ko) *probably the oldest city in the world,* Mark 10:46; Luke 10:30; 19:1
- fall of, Joshua 2 — 6
- rebuilt, 1 Kings 16:34

Jeroboam, son of Jehoash (jeh-ro-BO-am) *a king of Israel,* 2 Kings 14:23–29; Amos 7:7–17

Jeroboam, son of Nebat, *first ruler of the northern kingdom of Israel.*
- given ten tribes by God, 1 Kings 11:26–40
- built idols, 1 Kings 12:26–33
- warned by God, 1 Kings 13:1–34
- death of his son, 1 Kings 14:1–20

Jerusalem (jeh-ROO-suh-lem) *"Zion" or "City of David"; the greatest city of Palestine.*
- the City of David, 2 Samuel 5:6–7
- captured by Babylonians, 2 Chronicles 36:15–23
- Jews returned to, Ezra 1 — 2
- the new Jerusalem, Galatians 4:26; Hebrews 12:22; Revelation 3:12; 21 — 22

Jesse (JEH-see) *father of King David,* 1 Samuel 16 — 17; 1 Chronicles 2:13–15; Luke 3:32; Romans 15:12

Jesus (JEE-zus) *"Saviour"; the son of God.* See also "Christ", "Son of David", "Son of Man".
- birth and childhood of, Matthew 1 — 2; Luke 1 — 2
- temptation of, Matthew 4:1–11; Mark 1:12–13; Luke 4:1–13
- miracles of, Matthew 8 — 9; Mark 6:30–56; Luke 17:11; 22:50–51; John 2:1; 11
- appeared with Moses and Elijah, Matthew 17:1–13; Mark 9:2–13; Luke 9:28–36
- forced men from the Temple, Matthew 21:12–13; John 2:13–17
- the Last Supper, Matthew 26:17–30; Luke 22:1–20; John 13
- trial and death of, Matthew 26:57 — 27:66; Mark 15; Luke 22:66 — 23:56; John 18 — 19
- appearances after resurrection, Matthew 28; Mark 16; Luke 24; John 20 — 21; 1 Corinthians 15:5–8
- Son of God, Matthew 3:16–17; 26:63–64; John 1:14

Jethro (JETH-row) *father of Moses' wife,* Exodus 2:16–21
- advised Moses, Exodus 18

Jews (JOOZ) *first, the tribe of Judah; later, any of the twelve tribes,* Ezra 4:12; Esther 3 — 10; Acts 2:5
- against Jesus, John 5:16–18; 7:1,32–36; 10:25–42
- Jesus, king of, Matthew 2:2; 27:11–14,29; John 19:17–22
- and non-Jewish people, 1 Corinthians 12:13; Galatians 3:28; Colossians 3:11

Jezebel (JEZ-eh-bell) *the evil wife of King Ahab.*
- married Ahab, 1 Kings 16:31
- killed the Lord's prophets, 1 Kings 18:4–14
- killed Naboth, 1 Kings 21:1–23
- death of, 2 Kings 9:30–37

Jezreel (JEZ-reel) *the name of a town and a valley near the Jordan River,* Judges 6:33; 1 Kings 21:1; 2 Kings 8:29

Joab (JO-ab) *the commander of King David's army,* 2 Samuel 2:12 — 3; 10 — 11; 14; 18 — 20; 24; 1 Kings 1 — 2

Joanna (jo-ANN-uh) *a woman Jesus healed,* Luke 8:2–3; 23:55 — 24:11

Joash, Gideon's father (JO-ash)
- protected Gideon, Judges 6:28–32

Joash, son of Ahaziah, *became king of Judah when he was seven,* 2 Kings 11 — 12; 2 Chronicles 22:10–14

Job (JOBE) *a wealthy man who honoured God.*
- ruined by Satan, Job 1 — 2:10
- wealth restored, Job 42:7
- example of patience, James 5:11

Joel (JO-el) *a prophet who wrote the book of Joel,* Joel 1 — 3; Acts 2:16

Johanan (jo-HAN-an) *a Jewish army captain,* Jeremiah 40:8—43

John, the apostle, *one of the sons of Zebedee.*
- called by Jesus, Mark 1:19–20
- at Jesus' transfiguration, Mark 9:2
- with Jesus in Gethsemane, Mark 14:33–42
- in the early church, Acts 3—4
- writer of Revelation, Revelation 1:1–4,9

John the Baptist, *Jesus' relative and the son of Elizabeth and Zechariah the priest.*
- birth of, Luke 1:5–25,57–80
- preached at the Jordan River, Matthew 3:1–12
- baptised Jesus, Matthew 3:13–17
- killed by Herod, Matthew 14:1–12

John Mark, See "Mark".

Jonah (JO-nah) *a prophet whom God told to preach to the city of Nineveh.*
- ran from God, Jonah 1:1–3
- swallowed by a fish, Jonah 1:4—2:10
- went to Nineveh, Jonah 3
- complained to God, Jonah 4
- the sign of, Matthew 12:38–41; 16:4; Luke 11:29–32

Jonathan (JON-a-thun) *the oldest son of King Saul.*
- David's friend, 1 Samuel 18:1–4
- saved David's life, 1 Samuel 19:1–7; 20
- death of, 1 Samuel 31:2

Joppa (JOP-uh) *a city on the coast of Palestine,* Jonah 1:3
- Peter preached there, Acts 9:36–42; 10:9–36

Joram (JO-ram) *son of Ahab; also a king of Israel,* 2 Kings 3:1–3; 8:29; 9:14–29

Jordan (JOR-d'n) *the only large river in Palestine.*
- Israelites crossed, Joshua 3
- Jesus baptised in, Matthew 3:13–17; Mark 1:9–11

Jordan Valley, *the valley along the Jordan River,* Deuteronomy 1:1; 3:17; Joshua 11:2

Joseph of Arimathea (JOZ-if) *took the body of Jesus down from the cross and buried it in a tomb Joseph had dug for himself,* Matthew 27:57–60; Mark 15:42–46; Luke 23:50–54

Joseph of Nazareth, *husband of Mary, Jesus' mother.*
- angel appeared to, Matthew 1:18–24
- went to register in Bethlehem, Luke 2:4–7
- took Jesus to the Temple, Luke 2:21–52

Joseph, son of Jacob, *one of the twelve sons of Israel.*
- sold into slavery, Genesis 37
- put into prison, Genesis 39
- interpreted dreams, Genesis 40—41
- reunited with family, Genesis 42—50

Joshua (JOSH-yoo-ah) *leader of the Israelites into the promised land.*
- spied out Canaan, Numbers 13
- chosen to replace Moses, Numbers 27:12–23; Deuteronomy 34:9–10
- conquered Canaan, Joshua 1; 3—12
- death of Joshua 23—24

Josiah (jo-SY-uh) *king of Judah about 640 to 609 BC*
- became king, 2 Kings 22:1–2
- found the lost laws of God, 2 Kings 22:3–20
- gave the law to the people, 2 Kings 23:1–30

Jothan, youngest son of Gideon (JO-than) Judges 9:1–21,57

Jothan, son of Uzziah, *a king of Judah,* 2 Kings 15:32–38; 2 Chronicles 27

joy, Psalm 43:4; John 15:11; 17:13; 1 Thessalonians 1:6
- a fruit of the Holy Spirit, Galatians 5:22
- God as the source, Psalms 43:4; 45:7; Romans 15:13
- joy from the Holy Spirit, Luke 10:21; Romans 14:17; Galatians 5:22; 1 Thessalonians 1:6

Jubilee (JOO-bih-lee) *a Jewish celebration that took place once every fifty years. Israelites were to let the soil rest, to free their slaves, and to return land and houses to their first owners or their descendants.* Leviticus 25; 27:17–24; Numbers 36:4

Judah, son of Jacob (JOO-dah) Genesis 29:35
- saved Joseph, Genesis 37:26–27
- deceived by Tamar, Genesis 38
- reunited with Joseph, Genesis 43—44
- tribe of, Numbers 1:26–27; 26:20–22; Joshua 15
- Jesus, a descendant of, Matthew 1:2–3; Luke 3:33–34; Revelation 5:5

Judah, kingdom of, *the southern kingdom when Israel split in two.*
- beginning of, 1 Kings 11:27—12:20
- rules of, 1 Kings 14:21—15:24; 22:41–50; 2 Kings 8:16–29; 11—12; 14—16; 18—24
- fall of, 2 Kings, 24:18—25:22

Judas Iscariot (JOO-dus is-KA-ree-ut) *apostle who handed Jesus over to be killed.*
- chosen by Jesus, Matthew 10:4; Mark 3:19
- apostles' treasurer, John 12:4–6; 13:27–29
- betrayed Jesus, Matthew 26:14–16, 47–50; Luke 22:1–6; John 6:70–71; 13:2,21–30
- death of, Matthew 27:3–5

Judas, brother of Jesus, Matthew 13:55; Mark 6:3

Judas, son of James
- an apostle, Luke 6:16; Acts 1:13

Jude (JOOD) *brother of James,* Jude 1

Judea (joo-DEE-uh) *the land of the Jews,* Matthew 2:1; 3:1; Luke 1:5; 3:1; Acts 1:8

judges (JUJ-ez) *leaders of Israel after Joshua and before the kings,* Judges 2:16–19; 3:7–4; 10—12; 1 Samuel 8:1–5

judging
- warnings against, Matthew 7:1–5; 1 Corinthians 4:5; James 4:11–12
- good kinds of judging, 1 Corinthians 5:12; 6:2; 10:15
- God's judging of people, Matthew 11:22; Acts 17:31; 2 Peter 2:9; 3:7

Judgement Day (JUJ-ment) *the day Christ will judge all people,* Matthew 11:20–24; 12:33–37; 2 Peter 2:9–10; 3:7–13

Julius (JOOL-yus) *a Roman soldier in charge of Paul while Paul was taken to Rome,* Acts 27:1–3

justify (JUS-teh-fy) *to make someone right with God,* Romans 3:24; 5:1; Galatians 2:16; Titus 3:7

K

Kadesh/Kadesh Barnea (KAY-desh BAR-nee-uh) *a town in the Desert of Zin,* Numbers 20:1–21; Joshua 10:41

Kenites (KEN-ites) *a tribe of early metal workers,* Genesis 15:19; Judges 1:16; 4:11; 1 Samuel 27:10

Kerethites (KAIR-uh-thites) *King David's bodyguards,* 2 Samuel 8:18; 1 Kings 1:38

Keturah (keh-TOO-rah) *Abraham's second wife,* Genesis 25:1–4; 1 Chronicles 1:32–33

key, *something that solves or explains.*
- to God's kingdom, Matthew 16:19
- to death, Revelation 1:18

Kidron Valley (KID-ron) *a valley between Jerusalem and the Mount of Olives,* 2 Samuel 15:23; John 18:1
- idols burned there, 1 Kings 15:13; 2 Kings 23:4

kill
- Cain killed, Genesis 4:10–11
- laws against, Exodus 20:13
- of baby boys, Exodus 1:16; Matthew 2:16
- Jesus killed, Matthew 27:31–50; Mark 15:20–37; Luke 23:25–46; John 19:16–30

kindness
- of God, Exodus 34:6–7; Jeremiah 9:24; Romans 2:4; Ephesians 2:4–7
- commanded, 2 Corinthians 6:6; Ephesians 4:32; Colossians 3:12; 2 Peter 1:5–7

king
- King of kings, 1 Timothy 6:15; Revelation 17:14

Kingdom (KING-d'm) *the kingdom of heaven is God ruling in the lives of his people.*
- the nature of, Matthew 5:19–20; 19:14; Luke 17:20–21; Romans 14:17
- parables of, Matthew 13:24–52; 18:23–35; 20:1–16; 25:1-30; Mark 4:30–33; Luke 13:18–21
- belongs to, Matthew 5:3,10; 19:14

Kiriath Jearim (KEER-yath JEE-ah-rim) *a town in the hills about nineteen kilometres west of Jerusalem,* 1 Samuel 6:20—7:20; 1 Chronicles 13:5–6; 2 Chronicles 1:4

Kish, *father of Saul,* 1 Samuel 9:1–2

Kishon (KI-shon) *the name of a valley and a stream,* Judges 4:13; 5:21; Kings 18:40

kiss, *a greeting of friendship, love, or respect.*
- of Judas, Matthew 26:48–49; Mark 14:44–45; Luke 22:47–48
- holy kiss, Romans 16:16; 1 Corinthians 16:20; 1 Peter 5:14

Kittim (KIH-tim) *the island of Cyprus,* Genesis 10:4; Numbers 24:24; 1 Chronicles 1:7; Isaiah 23:1,12

kneel (NEEL)
- Solomon kneeled before God, 1 Kings 8:54
- Daniel kneeled before God, Daniel 6:10
- everyone to kneel before Jesus, Philippians 2:10

knock (NOK)
- "knock, and the door will open", Matthew 7:7
- at the door, Luke 13:25
- Peter knocked, Acts 12:13,16
- Jesus knocks, Revelation 3:20

knowledge (NOHL-ij)
- tree of, Genesis 2:9,17
- value of, Proverbs 1:7; 8:10; 18:15; 24:5; 2 Peter 1:5–6
- lack of, Hosea 4:6; Romans 1:28
- limitations of, 1 Corinthians 8:1–2; 13:2, 8–10

Kohath (KO-hath) *a son of Levi,* Exodus 6:16–20; Numbers 3:17–19

Kohathites (KO-hath-ites) *descendants of Kohath.*
- worked in the Holy Tent and Temple, Numbers 3:27–31; 4:1–20; 1 Chronicles 9:17–32

Korah (KO-rah) *the musician,* Psalms 42; 44—49; 84

Korah, son of Izhar, *rebelled against Moses,* Numbers 16:1–40

L

Laban (LAY-ban) *father of Leah and Rachel.*
- Jacob worked for, Genesis 29:13–30
- divided his flocks with Jacob, Genesis 30:29–43
- chased Jacob, Genesis 31:19–55

Lachish (LAK-ish) *a city about fifty kilometres southwest of Jerusalem*
- Joshua defeated, Joshua 10

lake
- of Galilee, Luke 5:1–2; 8:22–23,33
- of fire, Revelation 19:20
- of sulphur, Revelation 20:10; 21:8

lamb (LAM) *an animal that the Jews often offered as a gift to God.*
- as sacrifice, Genesis 4:4; Exodus 12:3–10; Leviticus 3:6–11; 4:32–35; 5:6; 14:24–25
- Jesus, the lamb of God, John 1:29,36; 1 Corinthians 5:7; 1 Peter 1:19; Revelation 5—7

Lamech, a descendant of Cain (LAY-mek) Genesis 4:18–24

Lamech, son of Methuselah, *the father of Noah,* Genesis 5:28–31

lamp, *a small bowl that held a wick and burned olive oil, thus giving light,* Matthew 25:1–13; Luke 8:16–18
- "Your word is like a lamp for my feet", Psalm 119:105

lampstand, *a holder for a lamp.*
- in the Holy Tent, Exodus 25:31–40; Numbers 8:1–4
- in the Temple, 1 Kings 7:49
- symbol of the church, Revelation 1:12–13,20

language (LAN-gwij)
- world spoke only one, Genesis 11:1,6
- confused at Babel, Genesis 11:7,9
- Aramaic, 2 Kings 18:26; Ezra 4:7; John 19:20
- Latin, John 19:20
- Greek, John 19:20; Acts 21:37

Laodicea (lay-oh-dih-SEE-uh) *a town in what is now Turkey,* Colossians 4:13–16; Revelation 3:14–22

Last Supper, *the meal Jesus ate with his followers the night before his death,* Matthew 26:17–30; Mark 14:12–26; Luke 22:7–20; 1 Corinthians 11:23–26

Latin (LAT-in) *the language spoken by the Romans during New Testament times,* John 19:20

laughter (LARF-ter)
- Sarah laughed, Genesis 18:12
- mouths filled with, Psalm 126:2
- sorrow better than, Ecclesiastes 7:3
- changed into crying, James 4:9

law
- as rules, Romans 4:15; 6:14–15; Galatians 5:18
- as God's rules or teachings, Psalm 119; Romans 7:22; 8:7; James 1:25; 1 John 3:4

Law of Moses, See "Teachings of Moses".

laying on of hands, See "hands, laying on".

- Matthias chosen by, Acts 1:26

love, *a strong feeling of affection, loyalty and concern for someone.*
- love of God commanded, Deuteronomy 6:5; 11:1; Matthew 22:36–38
- of God for people, Psalm 36; John 3:16; Romans 5:8; 8:39; Ephesians 1:4; 1 John 4:10–11
- of people for God, 1 Corinthians 8:3; 1 John 5:3
- of Christ for people, John 13:1; 15:9; Romans 8:35; Galatians 2:20; 1 John 3:16
- of people for Christ, Matthew 10:37; 1 Corinthians 16:22; 1 Peter 1:8
- of people for each other, Leviticus 19:18; Luke 6:27–35; John 13:34–35; 1 Corinthians 13; 1 John 4:7

Luke, *a non-Jewish doctor who often travelled with the apostle Paul,* Colossians 4:14; 2 Timothy 4:11

lust, *wanting something evil.*
- to be avoided, Proverbs 6:25; Matthew 5:28; Colossians 3:5; 1 Thessalonians 4:5
- typical of the ungodly, Romans 1:26; 1 Peter 4:3

Lydia (LID-ee-uh) *a woman from the city of Thyatira who sold purple cloth,* Acts 16:13–15,40

lying
- warnings against, Ephesians 4:25; Colossians 3:9; Revelation 21:8
- devil as a liar, John 8:44
- to the Holy Spirit, Acts 5:1–6

lyre (LIRE) *a musical instrument with strings, similar to a harp,* 1 Chronicles 15:16; Psalms 33:2; 81:2

Lystra (LIS-tra) *a city of Lycaonia.*
- Paul preached there, Acts 14:6–20; 16:1; 2 Timothy 3:11

M

Macedonia (mas-eh-DOH-nee-uh) *the northern part of Greece.*
- Paul preached there, Acts 16:6–10; 20:1–6; 1 Corinthians 16:5–9; Philippians 4:15

Machpelah (mack-PEE-luh) *the land Abraham bought from Ephron, the Hittite.*
- Sarah buried there, Genesis 23:7–19
- Abraham buried there, Genesis 25:7–10
- Jacob buried there, Genesis 49:29–33; 50:12–13

magic (MAJ-ik) *trying to use the power of evil spirits to make unnatural things happen.*
- magicians of Egypt, Genesis 41:8; Exodus 7:11–12
- condemned, Leviticus 19:26; 20:27; Deuteronomy 18:10–12
- Simon the magician, Acts 8:9–24
- Elymas the magician, Acts 13:6–11
- Ephesian magicians burn their books, Acts 19:17–19

mahalath (mah-HAY-lath) *probably a musical word; may be the name of a tune or may mean to dance and shout,* Psalms 53; 88

Malachi (MAL-uh-ky) *a prophet who lived about the time of Nehemiah. He wrote the last book of the Old Testament.* Malachi 1:1

man, *humankind; a male.*
- created by God, Genesis 1:26–27; 2:7–23
- born of woman, Job 14:1
- important to God, Psalm 8:4–8
- woman created for, 1 Corinthians 11:9

Manasseh, son of Hezekiah (mah-NASS-uh) *a king of Judah for fifty-five years,* 2 Kings 21:1–17; 2 Chronicles 33:1–20

Manasseh, son of Joseph, *older brother of Ephraim. His descendants were the tribe of Manasseh.* Genesis 41:51; 46:20; 48:1–20
- descendants of, Numbers 1:34; 26:29–34; Joshua 13:8–13; 17
- eastern half-tribe, Joshua 1:12–17; 22
- western half-tribe, Joshua 21:5,25; 22:7

manger (MAIN-jur) *a box where animals are fed,* Luke 2:6–17

manna (MAN-uh) *the white, sweet-tasting food God gave the people of Israel in the wilderness. It appeared on the ground during the night so they could gather it in the morning.*
- God sent to Israel, Exodus 16:11–36; Joshua 5:10–12
- kept in the Ark, Exodus 16:31–34; Hebrews 9:1–4

Manoah (man-NO-uh) *the father of Samson,* Judges 13

Marduk (MAR-dook) *a god of the Babylonians. The Babylonians believed that people were evil because Marduk had created them from the blood of an evil god.* Jeremiah 50:2

Mark, *John Mark; a cousin to Barnabas; travelled with Paul and Barnabas and wrote the Gospel of Mark,* Acts 12:12,25; 13:5; Colossians 4:10; 2 Timothy 4:11
- left Paul, Acts 13:13
- travelled with Barnabas, Acts 15:36–41

marketplace, *usually a large open area inside a city where people came to buy and sell goods,* Matthew 20:3; Mark 7:4; 12:38; Luke 7:32; Acts 16:19

marriage
- teachings about, Mark 10:6–9; 1 Corinthians 7:1–16; Hebrews 13:4; 1 Timothy 5:14
- authority in, Ephesians 5:21; Colossians 3:18

Mars Hill, See "Areopagus".

Martha (MAR-thuh) *the sister of Mary and Lazarus who lived in Bethany.*
- criticised Mary, Luke 10:38–42
- at death of Lazarus, John 11:17–44

martyr (MAR-ter) *"witness"; one who knows about something. Later, martyr came to mean a person who was killed for being a witness.*
- Stephen, first Christian martyr, Acts 7:54–60
- James killed, Acts 12:2
- heroes of faith killed, Hebrews 11:32–37

Mary Magdalene (MAG-duh-lin) *a follower of Jesus from the town of Magdala; the first person to see Jesus after he came back to life.*
- at Jesus' death, Matthew 27:55–56,61
- saw Jesus after his resurrection, Matthew 28:1–10; Mark 16:1–11; John 20:10–18

Mary, mother of Jesus
- engaged to marry Joseph, Matthew 1:18–25; Luke 2:4–5
- angel appeared to, Luke 1:26–45
- birth of Jesus, Luke 2:6–21
- with Jesus in Jerusalem, Luke 2:41–52
- at wedding in Cana, John 2:1–10
- at Jesus' death, John 19:25–27
- with the apostles, Acts 1:14

Mary of Bethany, *sisters of Martha and Lazarus, and a friend of Jesus.*
- sat at Jesus' feet, Luke 10:38–42
- at death of Lazarus, John 11:1–45
- poured oil on Jesus' feet, John 12:1–8

maskil (MAS-kil) *probably a description of the kind of song that some of the Psalms were,* Psalms 32; 42; 44; 45

master, *lord; ruler.*
- "No one can serve two masters." Matthew 6:24
- not to be called, Matthew 23:10
- to be obeyed, Ephesians 6:5
- how to treat slaves, Ephesians 6:9
- in heaven, Ephesians 6:9; Colossians 4:1
- Jesus as, Luke 5:5; 8:24; 17:13

Matthew (MATH-you) *also called Levi; a tax collector; wrote the Gospel of Matthew,* Matthew 9:9–10; 10:3; Acts 1:13

Matthias (ma-THY-us) *chosen to be an apostle after Judas Iscariot killed himself,* Acts 1:15–26

meat
- given by God in the wilderness, Exodus 16:1–15; Numbers 11:4–34; Psalm 78:27
- eating meat sacrificed to idols, Acts 15:20; 1 Corinthians 8; 10:25–32

Medes (MEEDS) *the people who lived in Media, which is called "Iran" today,* 2 Kings 17:6; Ezra 6:2; Esther 1:3–19; Daniel 5:28; 6:8–15

mediator (MEE-dee-ay-ter) *a go-between.*
- Jesus as, 1 Timothy 2:5

medicine
- happy heart as, Proverbs 17:22

Mediterranean Sea (med-ih-teh-RANE-ee-un) *a large sea west of Canaan; also called the "Great Sea" or the "Western Sea",* Numbers 34:6–7; Joshua 1:4

medium (MEED-ee-um) *a person who tries to help living people talk to the spirits of the dead.*
- condemned, Leviticus 19:31; Deuteronomy 18:11–13; Isaiah 8:19–20
- of Endor, 1 Samuel 28
- Josiah destroyed mediums, 2 Kings 23:24

Meeting Tent, *"Tabernacle" or "Holy Tent"; a special tent where the Israelites worshipped God. It was used from the time they left Egypt until Solomon built the Temple in Jerusalem.*
- description of, Exodus 25—27
- set up, Exodus 39:32—40:36

Megiddo (meh-GID-oh) *important town in northern Israel where many battles were fought. The book of Revelation tells about a great battle between good and evil at "Armageddon", which means "the hill of Megiddo".* Joshua 12:8–21; 2 Kings 23:29–30; Revelation 16:16

Melchizedek (mel-KIZ-ih-dek) *priest and king who worshipped God in the time of Abraham,* Genesis 14:17–24
- Christ compared to, Hebrews 5:4–10; 7

Mene, mene, tekel, parsin (MEE-nee, TEH-kul, PAR-sun) *the words written on the wall by a mysterious hand at Belshazzar's feast,* Daniel 5

Mephibosheth (me-FIB-o-sheth) *crippled son of Jonathan,* 2 Samuel 4:4
- David's agreement with, 2 Samuel 9
- tricked by Ziba, 2 Samuel 16:1–4; 19:24–30

Merab (ME-rab) *daughter of King Saul,* 1 Samuel 14:49; 18:17–19

Merarites (meh-RA-rites) *descendants of Merari, a son of Levi; they were responsible for caring for the frame of the Holy Tent,* Numbers 3:17,33–37; 4:29–33

mercy (MUR-see) *kindness and forgiveness.*
- God's mercy to people, Exodus 34:6; Deuteronomy 4:31; Luke 1:50; Ephesians 2:4
- people's mercy to each other, Matthew 5:7; James 2:13

mercy seat, See "lid on the Ark of the Agreement".

Mesha (MEE-shuh) *an evil king of Moab,* 2 Kings 3:4–27

Meshach (MEE-shack) *friend of Daniel who was put in the fiery furnace,* Daniel 1—3

messenger, 1 Samuel 23:27; 1 Kings 19:2
- John the Baptist as, Matthew 11:10; Mark 1:2; Luke 7:27
- of Satan, 2 Corinthians 12:7

Messiah (meh-SYE-uh) *"anointed one"; the Greek word for Messiah is "Christ". Christians believe that Jesus is the Messiah or the Christ.* John 1:40–41; 4:25–26

Methuselah (meh-THOO-zeh-lah) *lived 969 years, longer than anyone else in the Bible; the son of Enoch and the grandfather of Noah,* Genesis 5:21–27

Micah (MY-cuh) *a prophet who told the people of Israel and Judah about their sins,* Micah 1—7

Micaiah (my-KAY-uh) *a prophet of God,* 1 Kings 22:8–28; 2 Chronicles 18

Michael (MY-kul) *the archangel of God,* Jude 9; Revelation 12:7

Michal (MY-kul) *a daughter of Saul and wife of David,* 1 Samuel 18:20–29; 19:11–17; 2 Samuel 3:13–16
- criticised David, 2 Samuel 6:16–23

Michmash (MIK-mash) *a hilly area about ten kilometres northeast of Jerusalem,* 1 Samuel 13:23—14:23; Isaiah 10:28

Midian (MID-ee-un) *a son of Abraham; his descendants were called "Midianites",* Genesis 25:1–6
- Joseph sold to, Genesis 37:18–36
- Jethro, a descendant of, Exodus 2:15–21
- enemy of Israel, Judges 6—7

midnight
- when the firstborn of Egypt died, Exodus 12:29
- Paul and Silas freed from jail, Acts 16:25–26
- Paul preached until, Acts 20:7

miktam (MIK-tam) *a kind of song that may describe some of the Psalms. It may mean that it is a sad song or a song about danger.* Psalms 16; 56—60

mildew (MIL-dyu) *a growth that appears on things that have been damp for a long time,* Leviticus 13:47–59; 14:33–54

milk, 1 Peter 2:2

millstones, *huge stones used for grinding grain into flour or meal,* Deuteronomy 24:6; Matthew 18:6; Luke 17:1–2
- used to kill Abimelech, Judges 9:53; 2 Samuel 11:21

minister (MIN-i-ster) *servant; one who lives serving God and others,* Romans 15:15–16; Colossians 4:7

miracle (MIR-ik-'l) *"wonderful thing"; a great event which can be done only by God's help. Miracles are special signs to show God's power.*
- purpose of, Exodus 10:1–2; Mark 2:8–12; John 2:11; Acts 3:1–10
- over nature, Exodus 14:21–22; Joshua 10:12–13; Matthew 8:23–27; 14:22–32; 21:18–22
- of healing, Matthew 8:14–17; 9:27–31; Mark 7:31–37; Acts 14:3
- of bringing people back to life, Mark 5:21–43; John 11:1–44; Acts 9:36–43

Miriam (MIR-ee-um) *the sister of Moses and Aaron.*
- watched over Moses, Exodus 2:1–8
- song of, Exodus 15:19–21
- punished, Numbers 12:1–15
- death of, Numbers 20:1

mistress (MISS-tres) *a female head of the household,* Proverbs 30:21–23
- Hagar as, Genesis 16:4–9

Mizpah (MIZ-par) *the place where Jacob and Laban made a pile of stones to remind them of their agreement not to be angry with each other,* Genesis 31:44–49

Mizpah, the city, *a few kilometres north of Jerusalem,* Judges 11:29–34; 1 Samuel 7:5–16; 2 Kings 25:23

Moab (MO-ab) *the country on the east side of the Dead Sea.*
- fought with Israel, Numbers 22:1 — 25:9; Judges 3:12–30
- home of Ruth, Ruth 1:2,4
- rebelled against Israel, 2 Kings 3:4–27

mob
- against Paul, Acts 17:5; 21:30–36

Molech (MO-lek) *a god of the Canaanite people. Those who worshipped Molech often sacrificed their own children to him by burning them on altars.* Leviticus 18:21; 20:1–5; 2 Kings 23:10; Jeremiah 32:35

money, *many kinds of money were used in Bible days – gold, silver and copper.*
- proper attitudes toward, Luke 16:13; Hebrews 13:5; 1 Timothy 3:3; 6:10

moneychangers, *people who traded money from other countries for Jewish money.*
- of the Temple, Matthew 21:12–13; Mark 11:15–17; Luke 19:45–46; John 2:13–16

Mordecai (MOR-deh-kay-eye) *a man who helped Esther to save the Jews from death.*
- discovered a plot, Esther 2:19–23
- asked Esther to help, Esther 4
- honoured by the king, Esther 6

Moriah (moh-RYE-uh) *the land where Abraham went to sacrifice Isaac,* Genesis 22:2
- site of the Temple, 2 Chronicles 3:1

mortar (MORE-tar) *a stone bowl where grain is ground into flour by pounding; also, the stick material that holds bricks together,* Genesis 11:3; Exodus 1:14

Moses (MO-zez) *the man who led God's people out of the land of Egypt; the author of the first five books of the Old Testament.*
- birth of, Exodus 2:1–10
- in Midian, Exodus 2:11 — 4:17
- led Israel out of Egypt, Exodus 4:18 — 12:51; 13:17–31
- received the law, Exodus 20 — 31
- struck the rock, Numbers 20:1–13
- death of, Deuteronomy 31:14 — 34:12

Most High God, *translation for the name of the one true God, maker of Heaven and Earth,* Daniel 4:17

Most Holy Place, *the inner and most special room in the Holy Tent and the Temple.*
- rules about, Leviticus 16:2–20
- in the Temple, 1 Kings 6:16–35
- entered by Christ, Hebrews 9:3–25

mother-in-law
- law about, Deuteronomy 27:23
- of Ruth, Ruth 1:3–4
- Peter's, Matthew 8:14–15; Luke 4:38–39
- family against, Matthew 10:35; Luke 12:53

mothers
- treatment of, Exodus 20:12; 21:15,17; Leviticus 19:3; Proverbs 1:8; 13:1; 23:22,25; Matthew 15:4; 1 Timothy 5:2,4

Mount of Olives, *a hill covered with olive trees near Jerusalem; site of the garden of Gethsemane,* Matthew 21:1; 24:3; John 8:1
- David cried there, 2 Samuel 15:30
- Jesus prayed there, Luke 22:39–53
- Jesus ascended from there, Acts 1:6–12

Mount Sinai (SYE-nee-eye) *a mountain in the Sinai Peninsula.*
- Lord spoke with Moses there, Exodus 24:16; Acts 7:30,38
- law given on, Exodus 31:18

Mount Zion (ZY-on) *one of the hills on which Jerusalem was built; later it became another name for the whole city of Jerusalem; also a name for heaven.*
- hill of Jerusalem, 2 Kings 19:31; Psalm 48:2,11; Isaiah 24:23
- as heaven, Hebrews 12:22; Revelation 14:1

mourning (MORN-ing) *showing sadness, especially when someone has died.*
- examples of, Genesis 50:3; Deuteronomy 34:8; 1 Samuel 31:11–13

murder
- laws against, Exodus 20:13; Deuteronomy 5:17; Matthew 5:21
- committed by Barabbas, Mark 15:7
- devil as a murderer, John 8:44
- full of, Romans 1:29

music
- to the Lord, Judges 5:3; Ephesians 5:19
- in the Temple, 1 Chronicles 25:6–7

myrrh (MUR) *sweet-smelling liquid taken from certain trees and shrubs; used as a perfume and a painkiller,* Genesis 37:25; 43:11; Proverbs 7:17
- given to Jesus, Matthew 2:11; Mark 15:23
- used in Jesus' burial, John 19:39–40

mystery (MIH-ster-ee) *a secret.*
- revealed by God, Daniel 2:28
- of the message of Christ, Romans 16:25–26; Colossians 2:2; 4:3
- of Gentiles also being saved, Ephesians 3:1–6; Colossians 1:25–27
- of life after death, 1 Corinthians 15:51

N

Naaman (NAY-uh-mun) *a commander of the Aramean army; healed by Elisha of a skin disease,* 2 Kings 5; Luke 4:27

Nabal (NAY-bal) *husband of Abigail.*
- refused to help David, 1 Samuel 25:2–13
- saved by Abigail, 1 Samuel 25:14–35
- death of, 1 Samuel 25:36–38

Naboth (NAY-both) *killed by Jezebel so she could steal his vineyard,* 1 Kings 21

Nadab (NAY-dab) *son of Aaron.*
- saw God, Exodus 24:1–11
- death of, Leviticus 10:1; Numbers 3:4; 26:61

Nahum (NAY-hum) *a prophet of God; wrote the book of Nahum,* Nahum 1—3

naked

- Adam and Eve, Genesis 2:25
- realisation of nakedness, Genesis 3:7–10
- born, Job 1:21

Naomi (nay-OH-mee) *mother-in-law of Ruth,* Ruth 1:1–5

- returned to Bethlehem, Ruth 1:6–22
- encouraged Ruth, Ruth 2:19—3:4
- became a grandmother, Ruth 4:13–17

Naphtali (NAF-tah-lee) *the sixth son of Jacob; his descendants were the tribe of Naphtali,* Genesis 30:7–8; Numbers 26:48–50; Joshua 19:32–39

nard, *an expensive perfume which was imported from India,* Song of Solomon 4:13; Mark 14:3; John 12:3

Nathan (NAY-thun) *a prophet during the time of David and Solomon,* 1 Kings 1

- told David not to build the Temple, 2 Samuel 7:1–17
- told David the parable of the lamb, 2 Samuel 12:1–25

Nathanael (nuh-THAN-yul) *one of Jesus' twelve apostles; probably also called "Bartholomew",* John 1:43–51

nation

- formed and spread, Genesis 10:32
- against nation, Mark 13:8
- Good News preached to every one, Revelation 14:6

Nazarene (NAZ-uh-reen) *a person from the town of Nazareth. Jesus was called a Nazarene, so his followers sometimes were also called Nazarenes.* Matthew 2:21–23; Acts 24:5

Nazareth (NAZ-uh-reth) *the city in Galilee where Jesus grew up,* Matthew 2:21–23; Luke 4:16–30; John 1:45–46

Nazirite (NAZ-e-rite) *a special promise made to God, which had rules about eating certain foods and cutting the hair.*

- rules for, Numbers 6:1–21
- made by Samson, Judges 13:2–7; 16:17

Nebo, god of the Babylonians (NEE-boh) Isaiah 46:1

Nebo, the mountain

- Moses died there, Deuteronomy 34:1–5

Nebuchadnezzar (neb-you-kud-NEZ-zur) *a Babylonian king.*

- conquered Jerusalem, 2 Kings 24—25; 2 Chronicles 36
- his dreams, Daniel 2; 4
- and fiery furnace, Daniel 3

Nebuzaradan (NEB-you-ZAR-ah-dan) *the commander of Nebuchadnezzar's army.*

- captured Jerusalem, 2 Kings 25:8–12; Jeremiah 39:8–14; 40:1–6

Neco (NECK-o) *king of Egypt from 609 to 594 BC.*

- killed King Josiah, 2 Kings 23:29–37; 2 Chronicles 35:20–27
- captured Jehoahaz, 2 Chronicles 36:1–4
- defeated by Nebuchadnezzar, Jeremiah 46:2

Nehemiah (NEE-uh-MY-uh) *led the first group of Israelites back to Jerusalem from Babylon.*

- sent to Jerusalem, Nehemiah 2
- rebuilt walls of Jerusalem, Nehemiah 3—4; 6
- as governor, Nehemiah 8:9; 10:1

neighbour (NAY-bur)

- teachings about, Exodus 20:16–17; Leviticus 19:13–18; Proverbs 3:27–29; Matthew 19:19; Luke 10:25–37

Nephilim (NEF-eh-lim) *people who were famous for being large and strong. The ten spies who were afraid to enter Canaan had seen the Nephilim who lived there.* Genesis 6:4; Numbers 13:30–33

Ner (NUR) *father of Kish,* 1 Chronicles 8:33; 9:36,39

net

- fishing with, Matthew 4:18; Luke 5:5,6; John 21:6–11
- kingdom of heaven like, Matthew 13:47

new

- a new song, Psalms 40:3; 98:1
- a new name, Isaiah 62:2; Revelation 2:17
- new mercies every morning, Lamentations 3:22–23
- a new heart, Ezekiel 18:31; 36:26
- a new life, Romans 6:4; Ephesians 4:23–24; Colossians 3:10; 1 Peter 1:3
- a new agreement, Jeremiah 31:31; 1 Corinthians 11:25; Hebrews 8:8; 9:15; 12:24
- a new heaven and earth, 2 Peter 3:13; Revelation 21:1

New Moon, *a Jewish feast held on the first day of the month. It was celebrated with animal sacrifices and the blowing of trumpets. It was to dedicate the month to the Lord.* Numbers 10:10; 2 Chronicles 2:4; 8:13; Psalm 81:3; Isaiah 1:11–17

Nicodemus (nick-oh-DEE-mus) *an important Jewish ruler and teacher. Jesus taught him about spiritual life.* John 3:1–21; 7:45–53; 19:38–42

night, *can refer to ordinary darkness or be a symbol of distress, judgement, or evil.*

- created by God, Genesis 1:5; Psalm 19:1–2
- time of distress, Psalms 30:5; 42:8; 77:6
- time of judgement, John 9:4
- symbol of evil, 1 Thessalonians 5:5
- no night in heaven, Revelation 21:25

Nile River, *a river in Africa more than four thousand kilometres long.*

- baby Moses placed there, Exodus 2:1–10
- turned to blood, Exodus 7:14–25
- produced plague of frogs, Exodus 8:1–15

Nineveh (NIN-eh-vuh) *one of the oldest and most important cities in the world. For many years it was the capital of Assyria.* Genesis 10:8–11

- Jonah preached there, Jonah 1:1–2; 3—4; Matthew 12:41
- Nahum prophesied against, Nahum 1—3

Noah (NO-uh) *saved his family and the animals from the flood.*

- built the boat, Genesis 6:8–22
- saved from the flood, Genesis 7—8
- agreement with God, Genesis 9:1–17

Nob, *a town where priests lived during the days of King Saul,* 1 Samuel 21:1

noise

- joyful, Psalm 66:1
- of many people, Isaiah 17:12
- skies will disappear with, 2 Peter 3:10

noon

- sun to go down at, Amos 8:9
- bright light at, Acts 22:6

O

oath, *a promise or vow.*
- rules about, Matthew 5:33–37; 23:16–22; James 5:12
- God's oath, Hebrews 6:16–18
- examples of, 1 Samuel 14:24–28; 1 Kings 1:29–30; Psalm 132:1–12

Obadiah (oh-bah-DYE-uh) *a prophet of God who warned the Edomites they would be punished,* Obadiah 1–21

obedience
- to God, Leviticus 25:18; Deuteronomy 27:10; Acts 5:29
- to parents, Ephesians 6:1; Colossians 3:20
- to government, Romans 13:1–7; Titus 3:1–2; Matthew 22:17–21
- punishment for disobedience, Ephesians 5:6; 2 Thessalonians 1:8; 1 Timothy 1:9

offering *a gift or sacrifice.* See "sacrifice".
- brought by Cain, Genesis 4:3–5
- of non-Jewish people, Romans 15:16
- of Christ, Hebrews 10:5–18

Og (OHG) *the king of Bashan who was defeated by the Israelites,* Numbers 21:33–35; Deuteronomy 3:1–11

oil, *in Bible times usually means olive oil; used for cooking, medicine, burning in lamps, and anointing.* See "anoint".
- for lamps, Exodus 25:5–6; Matthew 25:1–10
- as medicine, Luke 10:34
- in offerings, Leviticus 2; 14:12–31
- in cooking, 1 Kings 17:10–16

ointment, See "perfume".

olive (OL-iv) *a small fruit; its oil was used in anointing ceremonies and as medicine.* See "oil".
- leaf, Genesis 8:11
- trees, Deuteronomy 6:11; 1 Samuel 8:14; Habakkuk 3:17; John 18:1

Omega, See "Alpha and Omega".

Omri (OM-ree) *an evil king of Israel,* 1 Kings 16:15–28

Onesimus (oh-NES-ih-mus) *the slave of a Christian named Philemon,* Colossians 4:9; Philemon

Onesiphorus (OH-nes-if-FOR-us) *a Christian friend of Paul who lived in Ephesus,* 2 Timothy 1:16–18; 4:19

onyx (ON-ix) *a precious stone with layers of black and white running through it,* Genesis 2:12; Job 28:16
- used in the holy vest, Exodus 25:7; 28:9–14; 39:6–7,13

Orpah (OR-pah) *the sister-in-law of Ruth,* Ruth 1:3–14

Ophir (OH-fur) *a land known for its gold and beautiful trees. Its location is uncertain.* Psalm 45:9; Isaiah 13:12
- Solomon traded with Ophir, 1 Kings 9:28; 10:11; 1 Chronicles 29:4

oven, *fire was built in the bottom of a clay barrel to bake bread,* Exodus 8:3; Leviticus 2:4; Hosea 7:4

oxen
- not to be coveted, Exodus 20:17
- as offering, Numbers 7:12–83
- not to be denied food, Deuteronomy 25:4; 1 Corinthians 9:9
- Elisha ploughed with, 1 Kings 19:19–21
- pulled the cart containing the Ark, 1 Chronicles 13:9

P

pain
- of a woman in childbirth, Genesis 3:16; Isaiah 13:8; Romans 8:22; Galatians 4:19,27
- not found in the new Jerusalem, Revelation 21:4

palace
- of David, 2 Samuel 5:11–12
- of Solomon, 1 Kings 7:1–12

palm tree, *a tall tree with long, fan-shaped branches growing out of the top; gives dates for food and wood for building,* Exodus 15:27; Nehemiah 8:15
- Jericho, city of, Deuteronomy 34:3; Judges 1:16; 3:13
- branches spread before Jesus, John 12:12–13

papyrus (pa-PY-rus) *a tall reed that grows in swampy places; used to make paper,* Job 8:11; 9:26

parable (PAR-uh-b'l) *a story that teaches a lesson by comparing two things.*
- of the kingdom of God, Matthew 13; 20:1–16
- of the lost sheep, coin, and son, Luke 15:1–31
- of the Judgement Day, Matthew 25

Paradise (PAR-uh-dice) *"garden"; a place where God's people go when they die,* Luke 23:43; 2 Corinthians 12:3–4

Paran (PAH-ran) *a desert area between Egypt and Canaan,* Genesis 21:20; Numbers 10:12; 12:16; 13:1–26

parchment (PARCH-ment) *a writing material made from the skin of sheep or goats,* 2 Timothy 4:13

parents
- responsibilities of, Ephesians 6:4; Colossians 3:21

Passover Feast (PASS-o-ver FEEST) *an important holy day for the Jews in the spring of each year. They ate a special meal on this day to remind them that God had freed them from being slaves in Egypt.*
- first Passover, Exodus 12:1–30
- commanded, Numbers 9:1–14
- celebrated by Jesus, Matthew 26:2, 17–19

patience (PAY-shentz) *to handle pain or difficult times calmly and without complaining.*
- of God, Romans 2:4; 2 Peter 3:9
- teachings about, 1 Corinthians 13:4,7; Hebrews 6:12
- comes from the Holy Spirit, Galatians 5:22
- commanded, Romans 12:12; Ephesians 4:2; 1 Thessalonians 5:14; James 5:7–8

Patmos (PAT-moss) *a small, rocky island in the Aegean Sea between Greece and Turkey,* Revelation 1:9

Paul, *the Roman name for "Saul". Saul was a Jew, born in the city of Tarsus. He became an apostle and a great servant of God.*
- conversion of, Acts 9:1–22
- name changed from "Saul", Acts 13:9
- healings by, Acts 14:8–10; 19:11–12; 20:7–12; 28:1–11
- imprisoned, Acts 23:35–28:31
- death of, 2 Timothy 4:6–8

peace
- from God, Psalm 29:11; John 14:27; Romans 5:1
- commanded, Romans 12:18; 14:17–19; Colossians 3:15
- Prince of Peace, Isaiah 9:6
- from the Holy Spirit, Galatians 5:22

pearl (PURL), Matthew 7:6; 1 Timothy 2:9; Revelation 21:21

- parable of, Matthew 13:45–46

Pekah (PEE-kuh) *an evil king of Israel,* 2 Kings 15:25–16:9; Isaiah 7:1–10

Pekahiah (peck-uh-HI-uh) *an evil king of Israel,* 2 Kings 15:22–26

Pelethites (PELL-eh-thites) *King David's bodyguards,* 2 Samuel 15:18; 20:6–7,23

Peninnah (pe-NIN-uh) *a wife of Elkanah,* 1 Samuel 1:2–6

Pentecost (PEN-tee-cost) *a Jewish feast day celebrating the summer harvest. The apostles began telling the Good News on Pentecost after Jesus died.* Acts 2:1–41; 20:16; 1 Corinthians 16:8

perfect
- describing Jesus, Hebrews 2:10; 5:9; 7:28
- describing God, Psalm 18:30; Matthew 5:48
- God's perfect law, James 1:25
- will of God, Romans 12:2
- love, 1 John 4:18
- people made perfect, 2 Corinthians 13:11; Hebrews 10:1–14; 11:40; 12:23

perfume
- used in idol worship, Isaiah 57:9
- poured on Jesus' feet, Mark 14:3–9; Luke 7:36–39; John 12:3

Pergamum (PER-guh-mum) *a town in the Roman province of Asia in what is now Turkey,* Revelation 2:12–17

Persecution (PUR-seh-CUE-shun) *trying to hurt people. Christians in the New Testament times were often persecuted by being put in jail or killed.*
- blessings with, Matthew 5:11–12; 1 Peter 3:8–17
- examples of, Acts 8:1–4; 1 Peter 3:13–15
- response to, Matthew 5:44; Romans 12:14; 1 Corinthians 4:12; 2 Corinthians 12:2
- of Christians, Matthew 13:21; 2 Timothy 3:12

Persia (PUR-zhuh) *a powerful country during the last years of the Old Testament; now called "Iran".*
- defeated Babylon, 2 Chronicles 36:20–23
- let captives return to Jerusalem, Ezra 1:1–11

Peter, *a fisherman; he and his brother, Andrew, were the first two apostles Jesus chose. First called "Simon", Jesus changed his name to "Cephas" or "Peter", which means "rock".*
- called to follow Jesus, Matthew 4:18–20
- walked on water, Matthew 14:22–33
- at the Last Supper, John 13:1–11
- defended Jesus, John 18:10–11
- denied Jesus, Mark 14:66–72; Luke 22:54–62
- preached the Good News, Acts 2:14–40
- an elder in the church, 1 Peter 5:1

pharaoh (FAIR-row) *the title given to the kings of Egypt.*
- made Joseph ruler of Egypt, Genesis 40—47
- made Israelites slaves, Exodus 1—14

Pharisees (FA-rih-seez) *"the separate people"; they followed the Jewish religious laws and customs very strictly. Jesus often spoke against them for their religious teachings and traditions.*
- practices of, Matthew 9:14; 15:1–9; Mark 7:1–13; Luke 7:30
- against Jesus, Matthew 12:14; 22:15; John 8:1–6
- criticised by Jesus, Matthew 5:20; Matthew 23

Philadelphia (fill-uh-DEL-fee-uh) *a city in the country now called "Turkey",* Revelation 3:7–13

Philemon (fy-LEE-mun) *a Christian in the city of Colossae,* Philemon 1–25

Philip, the apostle (FIL-ip) *friend of Peter and Andrew.*
- called by Jesus, John 1:43
- brought Nathanael to Jesus, John 1:44–50
- brought Greeks to Jesus, John 12:21–22

Philip, *the evangelist, a Greek-speaking Jew chosen to serve in the church in Jerusalem.*
- preached in Samaria, Acts 8:5–13
- preached to the Ethiopian, Acts 8:26–39
- his daughters prophesied, Acts 21:8–9

Philip, the tetrarch, *son of Herod I and Cleopatra.*
- ruler of Iturea and Trachonitis, Luke 3:1

Philippi (FIL-ip-eye) *a city in northeastern Greece,* Philippians 1:1; 4:15
- Paul in jail there, Acts 16:11–40

Philistines (FIL-ih-steyens) *people who were Israel's enemy for many years; worshipped false gods.*
- Samson defeated, Judges 15—16
- captured the Ark of the Agreement, 1 Samuel 4—6
- David defeated, 1 Samuel 17—18; 2 Samuel 5:17–25; 21:15–22

Phinehas, son of Eleazar (FIN-ee-us) *a priest and grandson of Aaron,* Numbers 25:1–13

Phinehas, son of Eli, *an evil priest,* 1 Samuel 1:3; 2:34; 4:4–11

Phoebe (FEE-bee) *a woman in the church in Cenchrea,* Romans 16:1

Phoenicia (foh-NEE-shuh) *an early name for the land on the east coast of the Mediterranean Sea; called "Lebanon" today,* Mark 7:26; Acts 11:19; 15:3

phylactery (fil-LAK-tur-ee) See "box of Scriptures".

pigs
- considered unclean, Leviticus 11:7
- snout of, Proverbs 11:22
- "don't throw your pearls before pigs", Matthew 7:6
- demons sent into, Matthew 8:30–33; Mark 5:11–13; Luke 8:32–33
- fed by prodigal son, Luke 15:15–16

Pilate, Pontius (PIE-lut, PON-shus) *the Roman governor of Judea from AD 26 to 36,* Luke 3:1; 13:1
- handed Jesus over to be killed, Matthew 27; Mark 15; Luke 23; John 18:28—19:38

pillar (PILL-ur) *a large stone that is set upright; also a tall column of stone that supports the roof of a building.*
- of Jacob, Genesis 28:18–22
- to worship false gods, 2 Kings 17:9–12
- in the Temple, 1 Kings 7:6,15–22
- of cloud and fire, Exodus 13:21–22; 14:19–24; 33:8–10

Pisgah, Mount (PIS-guh) *one of the high spots on Mount Nebo where Moses stood to see into the promised land,* Numbers 23:14; Deuteronomy 3:27; 34:1

plague (PLAYG) *a disaster. God sent ten plagues on the land of Egypt so the Egyptians would set the Israelites free.*
- on the Egyptians, Exodus 7—11
- on the Israelites, Exodus 32:35; Numbers 11:31–33; 16:41–50; 25:1–9

plumb line (PLUM LINE) *a string with a rock or other weight on*

one end. People used it to see if a wall was straight.
- symbol for God's judging, 2 Kings 21:10–13; Amos 7:7–8

pomegranate (POM-ee-gran-it) *a reddish fruit about the size of an apple,* Numbers 13:23; Joel 1:12
- design on priests' clothing, Exodus 28:33–34
- design of Temple decorations, 1 Kings 7:18–20

poor
- God's care for, Psalm 140:12; Proverbs 22:22–23; Matthew 11:5; James 2:5
- treatment of, Leviticus 19:9–10; Matthew 25:34–36; Luke 14:12–14

possessions
- promised land given to Israelites, Genesis 17:8; Numbers 32:22; Joshua 1:11
- proper attitudes toward, Ecclesiastes 5:10 — 6:6; Luke 12:13–21; Acts 2:45; 1 John 3:17
- danger of, Matthew 19:22
- sold by Christians, Acts 2:45

Potiphar (POT-ih-fur) *an officer for the king of Egypt. He put Joseph in charge of his household.* Genesis 39

pottage (POT-edge) *a thick vegetable soup or stew,* Genesis 25:29–34; 2 Kings 4:38–41

potter (POT-ur) *a person who makes pots and dishes out of clay.*
- as a symbol of God, Jeremiah 18:1–6

power
- of Jesus, Matthew 24:30; 28:18; Luke 6:19
- of the Spirit, Luke 4:14; Acts 1:8; Romans 15:19
- of Satan, Acts 26:18
- of the apostles, Luke 9:1; Acts 4:33

praetorium (pray-TORE-ee-um) *the governor's palace in New Testament times,* Matthew 27:27; Acts 23:35

praise (PRAYZ) *to say good things about someone or something. God's people can praise him by singing, praying, and by living the way he tells us to live.* 1 Chronicles 16:4–7; Psalms 103; 104; 145 — 150

prayer
- teachings about, Matthew 5:44–45; 21:18–22; Philippians 4:6; James 5:15–16
- Jesus' model prayer, Matthew 6:5–15

preach, *to give a talk on a religious subject; to tell the Good News.*
- Jonah preached to Nineveh, Jonah 3:2–4
- John preached, Matthew 3:1; Mark 1:4; Luke 3:3
- Jesus preached, Matthew 4:17; Mark 2:2; Luke 4:43–44
- Good News preached, Acts 8:25,40; Galatians 2:7; 1 Thessalonians 2:9
- preaching commanded, 2 Timothy 4:2

Preparation Day (prep-a-RAY-shun DAY) *the day before the Sabbath day. On that day the Jews prepared for the Sabbath.* Luke 23:54; John 19:14,31

pride
- warnings against, Romans 12:3; 1 Corinthians 13:4; Philippians 2:3; James 4:6

priest (PREEST) *in the Old Testament, a servant of God who worked in the Holy Tent or Temple.* See also "high priest".
- clothes for, Exodus 28
- appointing of, Exodus 29:1–37
- rules for, Leviticus 21 — 22:16

Priscilla (prih-SIL-uh) *a friend of Paul,* Acts 18:1–4,18–19; Romans 16:3–4
- taught Apollos, Acts 18:24–26

prison
- Joseph in prison, Genesis 39:20 — 41:40
- Peter in prison, Acts 5:17–20
- Paul in prison, Acts 16:23–34

prodigal (PROD-ee-gul) *careless and wasteful.*
- the prodigal son, Luke 15:11–32

promise
- from God, Joshua 1:3; 1 Kings 8:20; Galatians 3:14; Ephesians 3:6
- first commandment with, Ephesians 6:2
- Lord is not slow in keeping, 2 Peter 2:9

prophecy (PROF-es-see) *a message; God speaking through chosen people called "prophets",* Ezekiel 14:9; 1 Thessalonians 5:20; 2 Peter 1:20–21

prophesy (PROF-es-sy) *to speak a prophecy,* Acts 2:17–18. See "prophecy".
- a spiritual gift, 1 Corinthians 14:1–5

prophet (PROF-it) *a messenger; one who is able, with God's help, to tell God's message correctly. Sometimes prophets told what would happen in the future.* Matthew 11:13–14
- how to judge, Deuteronomy 13:1–5; 18:21–22
- examples of, Ezra 5:1; Jeremiah 1:1–9; Matthew 3:3
- false prophets, Deuteronomy 13:1–5

prophetess (prof-it-ESS) *a female prophet,* Exodus 15:20; Judges 4:4; 2 Kings 22:14; Luke 2:36. See "prophet".

prostitute (PROSS-ti-tyoot) *a person who sells his or her body for sex.*
- warnings against, 1 Corinthians 6:15
- examples of, Genesis 38:15–16; Jeremiah 3:1–3; Hosea 3:2–3; Matthew 21:32

proverbs (PROV-erbs) *wise sayings. The book of Proverbs contains many wise sayings that tell how to live a good and happy life.* 1 Kings 4:32; Proverbs

psalm (SAHM) *a song. The book of Psalms is like a songbook.* Ephesians 5:19; Colossians 3:16

publican (PUB-leh-kun) *See "tax collector".*

Publius (PUB-lee-uss) *an important man of the island of Malta,* Acts 28:7–8

Pul (PULL) See "Tiglath-Pileser".

punishment
- of Cain, Genesis 4:13
- everlasting, Matthew 25:46; 2 Thessalonians 1:8–9
- for rejecting Jesus, Hebrews 10:29
- by government, Romans 13:4; 1 Peter 2:14

pure
- gold, Exodus 25:11–39; 37; 1 Kings 6:20–21
- heart, Psalm 51:10; Matthew 5:8
- describing Jesus, Hebrews 7:26
- describing people, Job 4:17; 15:14; Philippians 1:10; Titus 1:15
- water, Hebrews 10:22

Purim, See "Feast of Purim".

purple, *a colour that, in Bible times, was worn by kings, queens, and other rich people. Purple cloth was expensive because the purple dye came from special shellfish.* Exodus 25:1–4; Judges 8:26; Mark 15:17; Acts 16:14

Q

quail (KWAYL) *a brownish-white bird.*
- given by God to Israel, Exodus 16:11–13; Numbers 11:31–34; Psalm 105:40

quarrel
- Israelites quarrelled with Moses, Exodus 17:1–7

Queen Goddess, *Ishtar; a goddess of the Babylonians,* Jeremiah 7:18; 44:15–29

Queen of Heaven, See "Queen Goddess".

queen of Sheba, See "Sheba, queen of".

question
- Solomon questioned by queen of Sheba, 1 Kings 10:1–3
- Jesus questioned, Mark 8:11; Luke 23:9; John 8:6
- asked by Jesus, Matthew 21:24
- apostles questioned by Jews, Acts 4:7; 5:27

quiet
- words, Ecclesiastes 9:17
- riot quieted, Acts 19:35–36
- life, 1 Thessalonians 4:11; 1 Timothy 2:2

Quirinius (kwy-RIN-ee-us) *the Roman governor of Syria when Jesus was born,* Luke 2:1–3

quiver (KWIH-vur) *a bag to hold arrows,* Psalm 127:5; Isaiah 49:2

R

Rabbah (RAB-ah) *the capital city of the Ammonites,* 2 Samuel 11:1; 12:26–29; Ezekiel 25:5

rabbi/rabboni (RAB-eye/rah-BONE-eye) *teacher. Jesus' followers often called him "rabbi" as a sign of respect.* John 1:38; 20:16

Rachel (RAY-chel) *a wife of Jacob and the mother of Benjamin and Joseph.*
- married Jacob, Genesis 29:1–30
- gave birth to Joseph, Genesis 30:22–24
- stole Laban's idols, Genesis 31:19–35
- death of, Genesis 35:16–20

Rahab, the dragon (RAY-hab) *In a well-known story, Rahab was defeated. Egypt was sometimes called Rahab to show that it would be defeated.* Job 9:13; Isaiah 30:7

Rahab, the prostitute, *a woman in Jericho. She hid the Israelite spies and helped them escape.*
- hid the spies, Joshua 2:1–21
- rescued from Jericho, Joshua 6:16–25
- an example of faith, Hebrews 11:31; James 2:25

rainbow
- a sign of God's agreement with people, Genesis 9:8–17

raisin, 1 Samuel 25:18; 30:12; 1 Chronicles 12:40

ram, *a male sheep.*
- offered instead of Isaac, Genesis 22:13
- used for burnt offerings, Exodus 29; Leviticus 8:18–29; Numbers 28:11 — 29:37
- with two horns, Daniel 8:3–22

Ramah (RAY-muh) *a town about eight kilometres north of Jerusalem,* Jeremiah 31:15; Matthew 2:18

Rameses (RAM-eh-seez) *one of the cities built by the Israelites when they were slaves in Egypt,* Exodus 1:11; 12:37; Numbers 33:3

Ramoth Gilead (RAY-moth GIL-ee-ad) *one of the cities of safety on the east side of the Jordan River,* Joshua 20:8; 1 Kings 4:13; 2 Kings 8:28—9:14

ransom, *payment that frees a captive.*
- Jesus as a ransom for sins, Matthew 20:28; 1 Timothy 2:6; Hebrews 9:15

Rapha (RAY-fa) *a leader of a group of people in Canaan who may have been giants. The descendants of Rapha are called "Rephaites".* 2 Samuel 21:15–22; Joshua 13:12

raven, *a large black bird similar to a crow which eats dead things.*
- sent out by Noah, Genesis 8:7
- fed Elijah, 1 Kings 17:4–6

read
- the Book of the Teachings, Joshua 8:34–35; Nehemiah 8:2–9
- reading the teachings commanded, Deuteronomy 17:18–19; 31:9–13
- brings happiness, Revelation 1:3

Rebekah (ree-BEK-uh) *the wife of Isaac and the mother of Jacob and Esau.*
- married Isaac, Genesis 24
- gave birth to Jacob and Esau, Genesis 25:19–26
- helped deceive Isaac, Genesis 27
- buried at Machpelah, Genesis 49:31

redeem (ree-DEEM) *to buy something back or to buy a slave's freedom.*
- property, Leviticus 25:23–34; Ruth 4:3–6
- slave, Leviticus 25:47–49
- redeemed by God, 1 Corinthians 6:20; Galatians 4:5; Titus 2:14

Red Sea, *Sea of Reeds; a large body of water between Africa and Arabia.*
- Israelites crossed, Exodus 13:17 — 14:31

refuge, *a place of safety or protection.*
- God as our refuge, Deuteronomy 33:27; 2 Samuel 22:3; Psalms 18:2; 31:2; 71:3; 91:2
- city of, Numbers 35:6–34; Joshua 20

Rehoboam (ree-ho-BO-um) *son of Solomon who took his place as king.*
- became king, 1 Kings 11:41–43
- Israel rebelled against, 1 Kings 12:1–24
- strengthened Judah, 2 Chronicles 11:5–17
- disobeyed God, 2 Chronicles 12

rejoice
- commanded to, Matthew 5:11–12; Romans 12:15; Philippians 4:4; 1 Peter 4:13
- examples of, 1 Samuel 6:13; Nehemiah 12:43

remissions (rih-MISH-un) See "forgiveness".

remnant (REM-nant) *a small part that is left; a name used for the Jews who were left alive after their captivity in Babylon.*
- of Israelites who returned to Jerusalem, Ezra 9:15; Nehemiah 1:2; Isaiah 10:20–22

repent (ree-PENT) *being sorry for doing something wrong and not continuing to do that wrong.* See "change of heart and life".

Rephaites, See "Rapha".

respect
- to parents, Leviticus 19:3; 1 Timothy 3:4
- between husbands and wives, Ephesians 5:33; 1 Peter 3:7
- to all people, 1 Peter 2:17; 3:16

rest
- on the seventh day, Genesis 2:2; Exodus 31:15; Hebrews 4:4
- given by the Lord, Psalm 95:11; Jeremiah 6:16; Matthew 11:28
- heaven as a place of rest, Revelation 14:13

resurrection (REZ-uh-REK-shun) *a dead person's coming back to life.*
- of Jesus, Matthew 28:1–10; Mark 16; Luke 24; John 20—21; Acts 2:24–32; Romans 1:4
- of God's people, John 6:39; Acts 24:15; 1 Corinthians 15; Philippians 3:10–11; Hebrews 11:35

Reuben (ROO-ben) *oldest of Jacob's twelve sons.*
- birth of, Genesis 29:32
- tried to save Joseph, Genesis 37:18–29
- descendants of, Exodus 6:14; Numbers 1:20; Joshua 13:15–23

revelation (rev-uh-LAY-shun) *showing plainly something that has been hidden,* 2 Corinthians 12:1; Revelation 1:1–3

revenge
- warnings against, Leviticus 19:18; Romans 12:19; 1 Thessalonians 5:15; 1 Peter 3:9

reward
- in heaven, Matthew 5:12
- for obedience, Psalm 19:11
- for what a person does, Matthew 6:1–18; 10:42; 16:27; Colossians 3:24
- children as a reward, Psalm 127:3

Rhoda (ROAD-uh) *a servant girl in the home of John Mark's mother,* Acts 12:6–17

righteousness (RY-chuss-ness) *being right with God and doing what is right.*
- explained, Romans 3:19–26; 2 Corinthians 5:21; 6:4–7; Philippians 3:8–9
- Abraham as an example of, Romans 4:3
- right living, 2 Corinthians 6:7; Ephesians 5:9; 1 Timothy 6:11; 1 Peter 2:24

robber
- Temple as a hideout for, Jeremiah 7:11; Matthew 21:13
- attacked man on road to Jericho, Luke 10:30
- killed with Jesus, Matthew 27:38–44; John 18:40

robe, holy, *"ephod"; a special type of clothing for the priests in the Old Testament. The holy robe for the high priest had gold and gems on it.*
- description of, Exodus 25:7; 28:6–14; 39:2–7
- one made by Micah, Judges 17:1–5; 18:14–20
- worn by David, 2 Samuel 6:14

Rock, *often used as a name for God. As a large rock is strong and provides a hiding place, so God is strong and protects us from our enemies.* Genesis 49:24; 2 Samuel 22:32–49; Psalm 19:14

rock badger (ROK-BAD-jur) *a coney; a small, tailless animal like a rabbit that hides among the mountain gorges and rocky areas of Arabia,* Psalm 104:18; Proverbs 30:26

Rome, *the capital city of the Roman Empire at the time of Christ,* Acts 2:10; 18:2; Romans 1:7
- Paul sent there, Acts 23:11; 28:14–15

roof
- spies hid there, Joshua 2:6
- David saw Bathsheba from there, 2 Samuel 11:2
- built room for Elisha there, 2 Kings 4:8–10
- man lowered through, Mark 2:3–4
- Peter prayed there, Acts 10:9

rue (roo) *a garden plant used for seasoning and medicine,* Luke 11:42

Ruth (ROOTH) *a widow from Moab.*
- moved to Judah, Ruth 1
- worked in Boaz's field, Ruth 2
- married Boaz, Ruth 3—4
- birth of Obed, Ruth 4:13–22

S

Sabbath (SAB-uth) *means "rest"; the seventh day of the Jewish week; the Jews' day to worship God. They were not allowed to work on this day.*
- commands about, Exodus 20:8–11; 31:12–17
- Jesus is Lord of, Matthew 12:1–13; Mark 2:23–28; Luke 6:1–11

sackcloth (SAK-cloth) *a type of clothing made from rough cloth; worn by people to show their sadness,* Genesis 37:33–35; Esther 4:1; Matthew 11:21

sacrifice (SAK-rih-fice) *to give something valuable to God.*
- burnt sacrifices, Leviticus 6:8–13
- drink sacrifices, Leviticus 23:13; Numbers 15:5; 28:7
- penalty sacrifices, Leviticus 7:1–10
- fellowship sacrifices, Leviticus 3; 7:11–27
- sin sacrifices, Leviticus 4
- limits of, Hebrews 9; 10
- living sacrifice, Romans 12:1

Saducees (SAD-you-seez) *a Jewish religious group that didn't believe in angels or resurrection; they believed only the first five books of the Old Testament were true.*
- challenged Jesus, Matthew 22:23–33
- arrested Peter and John, Acts 4:1–3
- arrested the apostles, Acts 5:17–42
- Paul spoke to the council, Acts 23:1–9

safety, city of, *city of refuge. In Bible times, someone who had accidentally killed another person could go to a city of safety for protection. As long as he was there, the dead person's relative could not punish him.*
- rules about, Numbers 35:6–34; Joshua 20

saffron (SAF-ron) *a purple flower; parts of it are used as a spice,* Song of Solomon 4:14

saint, *holy person; another word for "Christian",* Acts 9:41, Romans 1:7; 1 Corinthians 14:33

Salem (SAY-lem) *means "peace"; an old name for Jerusalem.*
- home of Melchizedek, Genesis 14:18; Hebrews 7:1–2

Salome, daughter of Herodias (sah-LU-mee)
- had John the Baptist killed, Matthew 14:3–12; Mark 6:17–29

Salome, wife of Zebedee, *the mother of the apostles James and John,* Mark 15:40; 16:1

salt
- used to preserve foods, Job 6:6; Mark 9:50
- Lot's wife turned into salt, Genesis 19:15–26
- "You are the salt of the earth", Matthew 5:13

Salt Sea, See "Dead Sea".

salvation (sal-VAY-shun) *being rescued from danger; being saved from sin and its punishment.*
- as God's gift, John 3:16; Ephesians 2:8; Titus 2:11
- through Christ, Acts 4:12; 1 Thessalonians 5:9; 1 Timothy 1:15; Hebrews 5:7–9

- as a helmet, Ephesians 6:17; 1 Thessalonians 5:8
- urgency of, 2 Corinthians 6:2; Hebrews 2:3
- rejoice in, Psalms 9:14; 13:5; 51:12; Isaiah 25:9

Samaritan (sah-MAH-rih-tun) *a person from the area of Samaria in Palestine. These people were only partly Jewish, so the Jews hated them.* John 4:9
- Jesus taught a Samaritan woman, John 4:1–42
- story of the good Samaritan, Luke 10:25–37

Samson (SAM-son) *one of Israel's judges; he was famous for his great strength.*
- birth of, Judges 13
- married a Philistine, Judges 14—15
- tricked by Delilah, Judges 16:4–22
- death of, Judges 16:23–31
- hero of faith, Hebrews 11:32

Samuel (SAM-u-el) *the last judge in Israel.*
- birth of, 1 Samuel 1:1–20
- worked in the Temple, 1 Samuel 1:21—2:26
- became a prophet, 1 Samuel 3
- appointed Saul as king, 1 Samuel 10
- appointed David as king, 1 Samuel 16:1–13
- death of, 1 Samuel 25:1

Sanballat (san-BAL-lat) *governor of Samaria who tried to stop Nehemiah from rebuilding the walls of Jerusalem,* Nehemiah 4—6

sanctify (SANK-teh-fy) *to make holy or ready for service to God,* John 17:17–19; 1 Corinthians 6:11; 1 Peter 1:2

sanctuary (SANK-choo-air-ee) See "Holy Place".

sand
- Abraham's descendants as numerous as, Genesis 22:17; 32:12
- Job's days as numerous as, Job 29:18
- house built on, Matthew 7:26–27

Sanhedrin (san-HEE-drin) See "council".

Sapphira (sah-FY-ruh) *wife of Ananias.*
- lied to the Holy Spirit, Acts 5:1–11

Sarah (SAIR-uh) *wife of Abraham,* Genesis 11:29–30
- gave Hagar to Abraham, Genesis 16:1–6
- name changed from "Sarai", Genesis 17:15–16
- gave birth to Isaac, Genesis 21:1–7
- death of, Genesis 23

Satan (SAY-tun) *means "enemy"; the devil; the enemy of God and man.*
- encouraged David to sin, 1 Chronicles 21:1
- tested Job, Job 1:6–12; 2:1–7
- tempted Jesus, Luke 4:1–13
- a fallen angel, Luke 10:18–19
- to be thrown into lake of fire, Revelation 20:10

Saul, king of Israel
- appointed king, 1 Samuel 9—10
- disobeyed God, 1 Samuel 15
- tried to kill David, 1 Samuel 19; 23:7–29
- death of, 1 Samuel 31

Saul of Tarsus, Acts 13:9. See "Paul".

saviour, (SAY-vee-ur) *a rescuer*
- God as Saviour, Psalm 25:5; Isaiah 45:21; Luke 1:47; 1 Timothy 1:1
- Christ as Saviour, Luke 2:11; John 4:42; Ephesians 5:23; Titus 2:13

scarlet (SCAR-let) *a bright red colour,* Exodus 26:1; Joshua 2:18; Isaiah 1:18; Matthew 27:28

sceptre (SEP-tur) *a wand or a rod that the king holds; a sign of his power,* Esther 4:11; Psalm 60:7

scourge (SKURJ) *to beat someone with a whip or stick,* 1 Kings 12:11
- Jesus scourged, Matthew 27:26; Mark 15:15
- Paul scourged, Acts 21:32; 2 Corinthians 11:24

scribe, *to write, to count, and to put in order. In New Testament times scribes were men who wrote copies of the Scriptures.*
- Ezra as scribe, Nehemiah 8:1
- against Jesus, Matthew 15:1–9
- condemned by Jesus, Matthew 23:13–36

Scriptures (SCRIP-churs) *special writings of God's word for people. When the word Scriptures is used in the New Testament, it usually means the Old Testament. Later, it came to mean the whole Bible.*
- fulfilled, Matthew 26:52–54; John 19:24,28,36
- given by God, 2 Timothy 3:16

scroll, *a long roll of paper used for writing,* Deuteronomy 17:18; Jeremiah 36; Revelation 5:1–5

Scythians (SITH-ee-unz) *a group of wandering people who lived near the Black Sea,* Colossians 3:11

Sea of Galilee, See "Galilee, Lake".

Sea of Reeds, See "Red Sea".

seal, *a tool with a design or picture carved on it. Kings pressed this seal into wax and used it like a signature. Sometimes these seals were worn as rings.*
- examples of, 1 Kings 21:8; Esther 8:8

seed
- created by God, Genesis 1:11,12,29
- parables of, Matthew 13:1–43

seer, *another name for prophet.* See "prophet".

selah (SEE-lah) *probably a musical direction; used in the Psalms. It may mean to pause. The word was not intended to be spoken when reading the psalm.* Psalms 3:2,4,8;89:4,37,45,48

Sennacherib (sen-AK-ur-ib) *king of Assyria from 705 to 681 BC*
- attacked Jerusalem, 2 Kings 18:13–19; 2 Chronicles 32:1–23; Isaiah 36—37

Sermon on the Mount, *a sermon Jesus preached as he was sitting on the side of a mountain near Lake Galilee,* Matthew 5—7

serpent, See "snake".

servant
- of the Lord, Deuteronomy 34:5; Joshua 2:8; 1 Kings 11:32; Luke 1:38
- Jesus as a, Philippians 2:7
- parable of, Matthew 25:14–30
- Jesus' followers to be, Matthew 20:25–27

Seth, *the third son of Adam and Eve,* Genesis 4:25–26; 5:6–8; Luke 3:38

Shadrach (SHAD-rak) *a friend of Daniel.*
- taken into captivity, Daniel 1
- became a leader, Daniel 2:49

- saved from the furnace, Daniel 3

Shallum (SHAL-um) *king of Israel who ruled for only one month in 752 BC,* 2 Kings 15:10–15

Shalmaneser (shal-mah-NEE-zer) *a king of Assyria,* 2 Kings 17:1–6; 18:9

Shaphan (SHAY-fan) *an assistant to King Josiah,* 2 Kings 22:3–14; 2 Chronicles 34:8–21

sharing
- commanded, Luke 3:11; Romans 12:13; 1 Timothy 6:18
- examples of, Acts 2:42–47; 4:32; 2 Corinthians 8:1–4

Sharon (SHAR-un) *the plain in Palestine along the coast of the Mediterranean Sea,* 1 Chronicles 5:16; 27:29; Song of Solomon 2:1; Isaiah 33:9

sheaf (SHEEF) *a bundle of grain stalks that have been cut and tied together,* Genesis 37:7; Leviticus 23:10; Job 24:10

Sheba, queen of (SHE-buh) *a queen who came to visit Solomon and see his wealth,* 1 Kings 10:1–13

Shebna (SHEB-nuh) *the manager of the palace for King Hezekiah,* 2 Kings 18:17—19:4; Isaiah 36:1—37:4

sheep
- God's people compared to, Ezekiel 34; John 10:1–18; 1 Peter 2:25
- parable of, Luke 15:1–7

Shem, *Noah's oldest son,* Genesis 6:10; 7:13; 10:21–31

sheminith (SHEM-ih-nith) *a musical term in the Psalms that means an octave (eight notes); may mean to use an instrument with eight strings,* Psalms 6; 12

shepherd
- David as, 1 Samuel 17:15,34–36
- Lord as, Psalm 23
- Jesus, the good shepherd, John 10:1–18
- elders as, 1 Peter 5:1–4

Sheshbazzar (shesh-BAZ-ur) *governor of the Jews in 538 BC,* Ezra 1:7–11; 5:13–16

shiggaion (shi-GY-on) *probably a musical term; used in the Psalms; may mean that the psalm is a sad song,* Psalm 7

shigionoth (shi-GY-o-noth) *probably a musical term,* Habakkuk 3:1

Shiloh (SHY-low) *a town north of Jerusalem.*
- location of the Holy Tent, Joshua 18:1,8; Judges 18:31; Jeremiah 7:12

Shimei (SHIM-ee-eye) *a relative of King Saul.*
- cursed David, 2 Samuel 16:5–14
- asked forgiveness, 2 Samuel 19:16–23
- death of, 1 Kings 2:36–46

ship, 1 Kings 9:26–28; 22:48; Acts 27

Shishak (SHY-shak) *king of Egypt during the time of Solomon and Rehoboam.*
- attacked Jerusalem, 1 Kings 14:25–28; 2 Chronicles 12:1–9

showbread, See "bread that shows we are in God's presence".

Shunammite (SHOO-nah-mite) *a person from Shunem, a town in northern Israel.*
- Shunammite woman took care of Elisha, 2 Kings 4:8–17
- her son raised from the dead, 2 Kings 4:18–37
- given back her land, 2 Kings 8:1–6

sickle (SICK-ul) *a tool for cutting grain,* Revelation 14:14–19

Sidon (SY-don) *a Phoenician city on the coast of the Mediterranean Sea,* Genesis 10:19; Matthew 11:21–22; Mark 7:31; Acts 27:3–4

siege mound (SEEJ) *earth piled against a city wall to make it easier for attackers to climb up and attack the city,* 2 Samuel 20:15; Isaiah 37:33; Jeremiah 6:6

signet ring (SIG-net RING) *a ring worn by a king or other important person. It had his seal on it.* Genesis 41:42; Esther 3:10; 8:2–10; Daniel 6:17. See "seal".

Sihon (SY-hon) *a king of the Amorites when the Israelites came out of Egypt.*
- refused to let Israelites pass, Numbers 21:21–31; Deuteronomy 2:24–37

Silas (SY-lus) *also "Silvanus"; a teacher in the church in Jerusalem, who often travelled with Paul.*
- sent to the Gentiles, Acts 15:22–23; 17:16
- joined Paul in Corinth, Acts 18:5
- helped with Peter's letter, 1 Peter 5:12

Siloam, pool of (sy-LO-um) *a pool of water in Jerusalem,* John 9:1–12

Silvanus (sil-VAN-us) See "Silas".

Simeon of Jerusalem (SIM-ee-un) *a godly man who saw baby Jesus in the Temple,* Luke 2:25–35

Simeon of Israel, *one of the twelve sons of Israel,* Genesis 29:33; 42:23–36
- descendants of, Numbers 1:22–23; 26:12–14

Simon, brother of Jesus (SY-mun) Matthew 13:55

Simon of Cyrene (sy-REE-nee) *carried the cross of Jesus,* Matthew 27:32; Mark 15:21; Luke 23:26

Simon Peter, See "Peter".

Simon, the magician, *tried to buy the power of the Holy Spirit,* Acts 8:9–24

Simon, the Zealot, *an apostle of Jesus,* Matthew 10:4; Mark 3:18; Luke 6:15; Acts 1:13

sin, *a word, thought, or act against the law of God.*
- offering for, Leviticus 4; 6:24–30; Hebrews 7:27, 10:4–12
- committed by everyone, Romans 3:23; 1 John 1:8–10
- Christ died for, Romans 4:25; 1 Corinthians 15:3; 1 Peter 2:24; 1 John 2:2; 3:5
- results of, Isaiah 59:2; Romans 6:23; Ephesians 2:1; Hebrews 12:1

Sinai (SYE-nee-eye) *a mountain in the desert between Egypt and Canaan.*
- Moses received the Ten Commandments there, Exodus 19–20

singing, *a way of praising God and teaching each other,* Judges 5:3; Psalm 30:4; Ephesians 5:19; Colossians 3:16

Sisera (SIS-er-uh) *captain of a Canaanite army,* Judges 4

slave
- rules about, Exodus 21:1–11,16,26–32; Ephesians 6:5–9; 1 Timothy 6:1–2

slave woman, *concubine; she bore children for her master, but was not considered equal to a wife.*
- Hagar as, Genesis 16:1–3
- of Solomon, 1 Kings 11:2–3

sleep
- God never sleeps, Psalm 121:4
- danger of, Proverbs 6:10–11
- Eutychus fell asleep, Acts 20:9
- to awake from, Romans 13:11
- a gift from the Lord, Psalm 127:2

sling, *a weapon for throwing rocks,* Judges 20:16; 1 Samuel 17:39–50; 2 Kings 3:24–25

slothful (SLOTH-ful) *lazy and undependable,* Proverbs 6:6–11; 13:4; Matthew 25:26; Hebrews 6:12

sluggard, See "slothful".

snake
- sticks became snakes, Exodus 7:8–13
- bronze snake made by Moses, Numbers 21:4–9; John 3:14
- Paul bitten by, Acts 28:1–6

Sodom (SOD-um) *a town known for its evil people.*
- destroyed, Genesis 18:17—19:29
- symbol of evil, Matthew 10:11–15; 11:20–24; Revelation 11:8

soldier
- arrested Jesus, John 18:12–13
- made fun of Jesus, Matthew 27:27–31; Luke 23:11
- at Jesus' death, Matthew 27:32–37; Luke 23:26–38,47; John 19:1–3,16–24,28–35
- lied about Jesus' resurrection, Matthew 28:11–15
- Cornelius, Acts 10:1
- guarded Peter, Acts 12:6
- Christian compared to, 2 Timothy 2:3–4

Solomon (SOL-o-mon) *a son of David; famous for his wisdom.*
- became king, 1 Kings 1:28–53
- wisdom of, 1 Kings 3:1–15; 4:29–34
- made a wise decision, 1 Kings 3:16–28
- built the Temple, 1 Kings 6; 7:13–51
- visited by the queen of Sheba, 1 Kings 10:1–13; Matthew 12:42
- married many women, 1 Kings 11:1–8
- death of, 1 Kings 11:40–41

Solomon's Porch (SOL-o-mon's PORCH) *a covered courtyard on the east side of the Temple,* 1 Kings 7:6; John 10:23; Acts 3:11; 5:12

Son of David, *a name the Jews used for the Christ because the Saviour was to come from the family of King David,* Matthew 1:1; 9:27; 15:22; 21:9

Son of Man, *a name Jesus called himself. It showed that he was God's Son, but he was also a human being.* Matthew 24:30; Mark 13:26; Luke 21:27; 22:69–70

sorcery (SOR-sir-ee) *trying to put magical spells on people or harming them by magic,* Acts 8:9–25; 19:18–19
- warnings against, Leviticus 19:26; Deuteronomy 18:14–15; 2 Kings 17:17

soul (SOLE) *what makes a person alive. Sometimes the Bible writers used words like "heart" and "soul" to mean a person's whole being or the person himself.*
- "destroy the soul and the body", Matthew 10:28
- losing, Matthew 16:26
- "all your heart and all your soul", Matthew 22:37
- joined with the spirit, Hebrews 4:12

sower, *someone who plants seeds to grow into crops,* Matthew 13:1–43; 2 Corinthians 9:6

Spirit (SPIH-rit) See "Holy Spirit".

spirit, *the part of humans that was made to be like God because God is spirit. The New Testament also talks about evil spirits.* Isaiah 26:9; 1 Thessalonians 5:23; James 2:26
- evil spirit, Matthew 12:43; Mark 1:23; 5:2; Luke 4:33

spiritual gifts, *special talents or abilities that God gives his people,* Romans 12:6–8; 1 Corinthians 12:1–11; 14; Ephesians 4:7–13

spring, *a natural fountain,* Genesis 7:11; Exodus 15:27

staff, *a shepherd's walking stick,* Exodus 4:1–5; 7:8–12; Numbers 20:6–11; Psalm 23:4

steal, See also "robber".
- commands against, Exodus 20:15; Matthew 19:18; Romans 13:9; Ephesians 4:28

Stephen (STEE-ven) *one of the seven men chosen to serve the church in Jerusalem; the first martyr for Christ.*
- chosen to serve the church, Acts 6:5–6
- killed by the Jews, Acts 6:8—7:60

Stoics (STOW-ics) *followers of a man named Zero, who believed that nature was controlled by the gods and who taught that people should learn self-control,* Acts 17:18

stoning, *a way of killing someone by throwing rocks at him.*
- commanded, Deuteronomy 17:2–7
- Naboth stoned, 1 Kings 21:13
- Stephen stoned, Acts 7:54–60
- Paul stoned, Acts 14:19

strength
- love God with all your strength, Deuteronomy 6:5; Mark 12:30
- God as the source, Psalms 18:1; 73:26; Philippians 4:13; 1 Peter 4:11

stronghold, *a fortress, a well protected place,* 1 Samuel 22:4; 2 Samuel 5:17

suffering
- proper attitude toward, 2 Corinthians 1:3–7; James 5:10
- value of, Romans 8:17–18; 1 Peter 3:8–17
- of Jesus, Isaiah 53:3–10; Luke 24:26,46; Philippians 3:10; Hebrews 2:18

swaddling clothes, *pieces of cloth that were wrapped around a newborn baby in Jesus' time,* Luke 2:7–12

sword
- of fire, Genesis 3:24
- a weapon, Joshua 5:13; 1 Samuel 17:45; Matthew 26:51–52
- the word of God, Ephesians 6:17; Hebrews 4:12

Sychar (SY-kar) *a small town in Samaria near Jacob's well,* John 4:5–6

synagogue (SIN-uh-gog) *"a meeting". By the first century, the Jews met in synagogues to read and study the Scriptures. The building was also used as the Jewish court and as a school.*
- Jesus taught in, Matthew 4:23; Mark 1:21; Luke 4:16–17
- Paul spoke there, Acts 17:1,10

Syria (SEER-ee-uh) *an area north of Galilee and east of the Mediterranean Sea; called "Aram" in Old Testament times.* See "Aram".
- enemy of Israel, 1 Kings 11:25; 20:1–34; 2 Kings 13:22–25
- learned about Jesus, Matthew 4:24

T

tabernacle (TAB-er-NAK-'l) See "Meeting Tent".

tablets of the agreement, *two flat stones on which God wrote the Ten Commandments.*
- given to Moses, Exodus 19—20; 24:12–18
- broken by Moses, Exodus 32:15–19
- the second tablets, Exodus 34:1–4
- in the Most Holy Place, Hebrews 9:4

Tabitha (TAB-eh-thuh) See "Dorcas".

Tabor, Mount (TAY-bor) *in the Valley of Jezreel about twenty kilometres from Lake Galilee,* Judges 4:6–16; Psalm 89:12

tambourine (tam-bah-REEN) *a musical instrument that is beaten to keep rhythm,* Exodus 15:20; 1 Samuel 18:6; Psalm 81:2

Tarshish (TAR-shish) *a city somewhere on the western side of the Mediterranean Sea,* Jonah 1:3; 4:2

Tarsus (TAR-sus) *the most important city in Cilicia, which is now the country of Turkey,* Acts 9:30; 11:25–26
- home of Paul, Acts 9:11; 21:39; 22:3

tax collector, *a Jew hired by the Romans to collect taxes,* Matthew 9:10–11
- Matthew, Matthew 10:3; Luke 5:27
- Zacchaeus, Luke 19:1–10

teacher
- Jesus called a, Matthew 8:19; Mark 10:17; John 1:38; 3:2
- in the church, Romans 12:7; Ephesians 4:11; 1 Timothy 4:13
- false, 1 Timothy 4:1–5; 2 Peter 2:1
- to be judged more strictly, James 3:1

teaching
- commanded, Deuteronomy 6:1–7; Matthew 28:20; 2 Timothy 2:2,14–15; Titus 2

Teachings of Moses, *or the "Law of Moses",* Deuteronomy 31:24–26; Joshua 23:6; Nehemiah 8
- purpose of, Romans 3:20; 5:20; Galatians 3:21–25
- limitations of, Romans 8:3; Galatians 2:19; Hebrews 10:1

temple (TEM-p'l) *a building where people worship. God told the Jewish people to worship him at the Temple in Jerusalem.*
- Solomon's Temple, 1 Kings 6—8; 2 Chronicles 2—7
- the Temple rebuilt, Ezra 3
- the body as a temple, John 2:19–22; 1 Corinthians 3:16–17; 6:19–20; 2 Corinthians 6:16

temptation (temp-TAY-shun) *the devil's attempt to get us to do something wrong.*
- Jesus tempted, Matthew 4:1–11; Luke 4:1–13; Hebrews 4:15–16
- a way of escape from, 1 Corinthians 10:13
- source of, James 1:13–15

Ten Commandments, *the rules God gave Moses on Mount Sinai,* Exodus 20:1–20; 31:18; 34:1–28; Deteronomy 5:1–22

tent
- Abram's tents, Genesis 13:18
- peg, Judges 4:21–22
- makers of, Acts 18:3

Tent, See "Meeting Tent".

Thaddaeus (THAD-ee-us) *one of the twelve apostles,* Matthew 10:3; Mark 3:18

thankfulness, Psalm 107:1; 1 Thessalonians 5:8; Hebrews 12:28

Theophilus (thee-OFF-ih-lus) *the person to whom the books of Luke and Acts were written,* Luke 1:1–4; Acts 1:1

Thessalonica (THES-ah-loh-nik-ah) *the capital of the country of Macedonia, which is now northern Greece,* 1 Thessalonians 1:1; 2 Thessalonians 1:1
- Paul preached there, Acts 17:1–9

Thomas (TOM-us) *Didymus; one of the twelve apostles,* Matthew 10:2–3
- questioned Jesus, John 14:5–7
- saw Jesus after resurrection, John 20:24–29; 21:2

thorn, *sharp points on a branch or stem of a plant.*
- as a curse on Adam, Genesis 3:17–18
- crown of, Matthew 27:29; Mark 15:17; John 19:2–5

threshing floor, *a place where farmers separated grain from chaff. This was done by beating the stalks on the hard ground, throwing them in the air, and letting the wind blow the chaff away.*
- angel visited Gideon there, Judges 6:11
- David bought, 2 Samuel 24:16–25

throne
- king's throne, 1 Kings 10:18–19
- God's throne, Matthew 5:34; Hebrews 4:16; Revelation 3:21; 4

Thummim (THUM-im) *the Urim and Thummim may have been gems. They were attached to the holy robe of the high priest and were used to learn God's will.* Exodus 28:29–30; Leviticus 8:8; Deuteronomy 33:8

Thyatira (THY-ah-TY-rah) *an important city in Asia famous for its purple cloth,* Acts 16:13–14; Revelation 1:11; 2:18–29

Tiberius Caesar (tie-BEER-ee-us SEE-zur) *Roman emperor during the last half of Jesus' life,* Luke 3:1

Tiglath-Pileser (TIG-lath-peh-LEE-zur) *king of Assyria who helped Ahaz; also called "Pul".*
- attacked Israel, 2 Kings 15:19–20
- rescued Ahaz, 2 Kings 16:7–10

Tigris (TY-gris) *a great river in the eastern part of the Bible lands,* Genesis 2:14; Daniel 10:4

Timothy (TIM-oh-thee) *close friend and helper of the apostle Paul.*
- helped Paul, Acts 16:1–3; 17:13–16; 1 Corinthians 4:17; 2 Corinthians 1:19
- instructed by Paul, 1 and 2 Timothy

tithe (TYTH) *"tenth". The Jews were told to give one tenth of what they earned to God.* Leviticus 27:30–32; Deuteronomy 12:1–6; Luke 11:42; 18:12

Titus (TY-tus) *trusted friend and helper of the apostle Paul.*
- helped Corinthians, 2 Corinthians 7:6–7,13–15;8:6,16,23
- appointed elders, Titus 1:4–5
- Paul's instructions to, Titus 1—3

Tobiah (toe-BY-uh) *tried to keep Nehemiah from rebuilding the walls of Jerusalem,* Nehemiah 2:10–20; 6:10–19; 13:4–9

tomb (TOOM)
- of Lazarus, John 11:38–44
- of Jesus, Matthew 27:57—28:15; Mark 15:42—16:30; Luke 23:50—24:12; John 19:38—20:9

tongue (TUNG)
- lying tongue hated by God, Proverbs 6:16–17
- cannot be tamed, James 3:2–12

tower of Babel, See "Babel".

transfiguration (tranz-fig-you-RAY-shun) *"to change". Jesus was transfigured in front of Peter, James, and John when his face and clothes began to shine brightly.* Matthew 17:1–9; Mark 9:2–9; Luke 9:28–36

tree
- of knowledge of good and evil, Genesis 2:9; 3:3
- of life, Genesis 2:9; Revelation 2:7; 22:2,14
- people compared to, Psalms 1:3; 92:12; Jeremiah 17:8; Matthew 3:10; 12:33
- cross described as a tree, Galatians 3:13

trespass, (TRESS-pass) See "sin".

tribe, *all descendants of a certain person. The twelve tribes of Israel were descendants of the twelve sons of Jacob, who was later named "Israel".* Numbers 1—2
- Canaan divided among, Joshua 13:7–33; 15—19

triumphal entry (try-UM-ful) *the time Jesus entered Jerusalem just before his death,* Matthew 21:1–11; Mark 11:1–19; Luke 19:28–44; John 12:12–15

Troas (TRO-az) *one of the most important cities in northwest Asia,* Acts 16:8–10; 20:5–12; 2 Corinthians 2:12

Trophimus (TROF-eh-mus) *non-Jewish Christian who travelled with Paul,* Acts 20:3–4; 21:27–29; 2 Timothy 4:20

trumpet (TRUM-pet) *in Bible times it was made from animal horns; used to call an army together or announce something important,* Numbers 10:2–10; Joshua 6:4–20; 1 Corinthians 15:52

trust
- a duty, Luke 16:11; 1 Corinthians 4:2; Titus 2:10
- in God, Psalm 20:7; Proverbs 3:5; 16:20; Romans 4:5;10:11; 1 Peter 2:6
- in lesser things, Psalms 49:13–14; 118:9; Proverbs 11:28; Isaiah 2:22

truth
- speaking honestly, Psalm 15:2; Proverbs 16:13
- God's message, John 17:17; Romans 1:25; Ephesians 1:13; 1 John 1:6

tunic (TYOU-nik) *a kind of coat,* Exodus 28:39–40; John 19:23

Tychicus (TYK-ih-kus) *Christian from Asia who did important jobs for Paul,* Acts 20:4; Ephesians 6:21–22; Colossians 4:7–9

Tyre (TIRE) *large, important city in Phoenicia, which is now part of the country of Lebanon,* Mark 7:24–31; Acts 12:20
- Hiram, king of, 2 Samuel 5:11; 1 Kings 9:10–14; 2 Chronicles 2
- a wicked city, Matthew 11:21–22; Luke 10:13–14

U

uncircumcised, See "circumcision".

unclean, *the state of a person, animal or action that was not pleasing to God. In the Old Testament God said certain animals were unclean and were not to be eaten. If a person disobeyed the rules about being clean, he was called unclean and could not serve God until he was made clean again.* See "clean".
- unclean animals, Leviticus 11; Acts 10:9–15
- unclean people, Leviticus 12—15
- God declared everyone to be clean, Acts 10

unleavened bread (un-LEV-'nd BREAD) *bread made without yeast.*
- used in the Passover Feast, Exodus 12:20; Deuteronomy 16:1–4

Unleavened Bread, Day of, *the first day of the Feast of Unleavened Bread or Passover,* Matthew 26:17; Luke 22:7

upper room, *upstairs room in a house.*
- Jesus and his followers met there, Mark 14:14–15; Luke 22:9–12

Ur (ERR) *a great city thousands of years ago; today in the country of Iraq.*
- home of Abram, Genesis 11:28–31

Uriah (you-RY-uh) *a soldier in King David's army.*
- killed by David, 2 Samuel 11

Urim (YOUR-im) See "Thummim".

Uzzah (UZ-uh) *touched the Ark of the Agreement and died,* 2 Samuel 6:1–8; 1 Chronicles 13:1–14

Uzziah (uh-ZY-uh) *a king of Judah,* 2 Kings 15:13–15; 2 Chronicles 26; Isaiah 6:1

V

Vashti (VASH-tee) *the wife of Ahasuerus, king of Persia,* Esther 1:1–20

veil (VALE) *a head covering usually worn by women; also, a curtain in the Temple.*
- worn by women, Genesis 24:65; Song of Solomon 4:1; Isaiah 3:19
- the Temple veil, Matthew 27:51; Mark 15:38; Luke 23:45

vine
- fruit of the, Matthew 26:29; Mark 14:25; Luke 22:18
- Jesus as the, John 15:1–11

vineyard (VIN-yard)
- Naboth's, 1 Kings 21
- parables of, Matthew 20:1–16; 28:46; Mark 12:1–12; Luke 20:9–19

virgin (VUR-jin) *person who has not had sexual relations,* Deuteronomy 22:13–29; Isaiah 7:14; Matthew 1:23; Luke 1:34

vision (VIH-shun) *like a dream. God often spoke to his people in visions.*
- of Abram, Genesis 15:1
- of Daniel, Daniel 2:19
- of Peter and Cornelius, Acts 10:1–16
- of Paul, Acts 16:9

vow, *a special and serious promise often made to God.*
- rules about, Numbers 30; Deuteronomy 23:21–23
- the Nazirite, Numbers 6:1–21
- of Jephthah, Judges 11:29–40
- of Paul, Acts 18:18

W

war
- rumours of, Matthew 24:6–7; Mark 13:7–8; Luke 21:9–10
- spiritual, 2 Corinthians 10:3–4
- will end, Micah 4:1–3

watchman
- examples of, 2 Samuel 18:24–27; Psalm 130:6
- prophets as watchmen, Ezekiel 3:17; Micah 7:4

water
- in creation, Genesis 1:1–2,6–10
- bitter, Exodus 15:22–27
- from a rock, Exodus 17:1–7

- for David, 2 Samuel 23:15–17
- drink of, Matthew 10:42; Mark 9:41
- Jesus walked on, Matthew 14:22–36
- turned to wine, John 2:1–11
- living water, John 4:1–15

"Way, the", *one of the earliest names given to Christians. Jesus said he was "the way" to reach God.* Acts 9:1–2; 19:9,23; 22:4; 24:14,22

wedding, Matthew 22:1–14; Luke 14:8; John 2:1–11

Western Sea, See "Mediterranean Sea".

widow

- examples of, Ruth 4:10; 1 Kings 17:8–24; Luke 21:2–4
- care for, Deuteronomy 24:17–22; 1 Timothy 5:3–16; James 1:27

wife

- man united with, Genesis 2:24
- the good wife, Proverbs 31:10–31
- teachings about, 1 Corinthians 7:1–16
- responsibility of, Ephesians 5:21–24,33; Colossians 3:18; 1 Peter 3:1

wine

- danger of, Proverbs 20:1; Ephesians 5:18
- at wedding in Cana, John 2:1–11
- for the stomach, 1 Timothy 5:23

winepress, *a pit where grapes were mashed to get the juice out. The winepress is sometimes used to describe how enemy armies will defeat people as if they were grapes crushed in a winepress.*

- examples of, Judges 6:11; Matthew 21:33
- as a symbol of punishment, Lamentations 1:15; Revelation 14:19–20; 19:15

wisdom (WIZ-d'm) *understanding what is really important in life. This wisdom comes from God.* Proverbs 1:1–2,7; 2; 4

- Solomon asked for, 1 Kings 4:29–34
- source of, James 1:5
- a parable about, Matthew 25:1–13

wise men, *"magi"; men who studied the stars,* Genesis 41:8; Exodus 7:11; Matthew 2:1–12

witchcraft, *using the power of the devil to do magic.*

- warnings against, Deuteronomy 18:10–12; Galatians 5:19–21
- examples of, 2 Kings 9:22; 2 Chronicles 33:6

witness, Acts 1:8,22; 2:32; 22:14–15

woman

- created by God, Genesis 2:22–23
- how to treat a, 1 Timothy 5:2,14

word, *in the Bible often means God's message to us in the Scriptures. Jesus is called the "Word" because he shows us what God is like.*

- like a lamp, Psalm 119:105
- like a sword, Hebrews 4:12
- living in God's people, John 15:7; Colossians 3:16; 1 John 2:14
- lasts forever, Matthew 24:35; 1 Peter 1:25
- people's words, Proverbs 12:25; 25:11; Matthew 12:36–37
- as a message, 1 Peter 1:24–25; 1 John 2:14
- Jesus as the "Word", John 1:1–5,14; 1 John 1:1–2

world, *the planet Earth; also the people on this earth who follow Satan.*

- as the Earth, 2 Samuel 22:16; Psalm 18:15
- as a symbol of wickedness, Romans 12:2; Ephesians 2:2

worship, *to praise and serve God.*

- commanded, Exodus 34:14; Luke 4:8; John 4:20–24

X-Y

Xerxes (ZERK-sees) *a king of Persia; also called "Ahasuerus",* Esther 1 — 10

yeast *an ingredient used to make breads and cakes rise; used in the New Testament to stand for a person's influence over others.* See also "unleavened bread".

- as a symbol for influence, Mark 8:15; Luke 13:21

yoke, *a wooden frame that fits on the necks of animals to hold them together while working.*

- examples of, Deuteronomy 21:3; 1 Kings 19:19–21

youth

- "Remember your Creator", Ecclesiastes 12:1
- teachings about, 1 Timothy 4:12

Z

Zacchaeus (za-KEE-us) *Jewish tax collector in the city of Jericho,* Luke 19:1–8

Zadok (ZAY-dok) *priest who helped King David, 2 Samuel 15:24–36; 17:15–21; 1 Kings 1:18–45*

Zarephath (ZA-reh-fath) *a Canaanite town where the prophet Elijah helped a widow,* 1 Kings 17:8–24; Luke 4:25–26

Zealots (ZEL-ots) *a group of Jewish men also called "Enthusiasts". They hated the Romans for controlling their home country, and they planned to force the Romans out.*

- Simon, the Zealot, Matthew 10:4; Mark 3:18; Luke 6:15; Acts 1:13

Zebedee (ZEB-uh-dee) *a fisherman on Lake Galilee,* Matthew 4:21–22; 20:20; Mark 1:19–20; Luke 5:10; John 21:2

Zechariah, father of John the Baptist (ZEK-uh-RY-uh) *a Jewish priest,* Luke 1:5–25,57–80.

Zechariah, king of Israel, *ruled for only six months; killed by Shallum,* 2 Kings 14:29; 15:8–11

Zechariah, son of Berekiah, *a prophet who wrote the next-to-last book in the Old Testament,* Ezra 5:1; Zechariah 1 — 14

Zechariah, son of Jehoiada, *a priest who taught the people to serve God,* 2 Chronicles 24:20–25

Zedekiah, son of Josiah, (zed-eh-KY-uh) *the last king of Judah,* 2 Kings 24:16 — 25:7

Zedekiah, son of Kenaanah, *a false prophet during the time of King Ahab,* 1 Kings 22:1–24

Zedekiah, son of Maaseiah, *a false prophet in Babylon during the time of Jeremiah,* Jeremiah 29:21–23

Zephaniah (zef-uh-NY-uh) *a prophet who lived when Josiah was king of Judah; wrote the short book of Zephaniah,* Zephaniah 1:1

Zerubbabel (zeh-RUB-uh-bull) *governor of Jerusalem after the Jews had been in captivity in Babylon for seventy years.*

- returned from exile, Ezra 2:2
- built the altar of God, Ezra 3:1–6
- rebuilt the Temple, Ezra 3:7–10; 5:2

Zeus (ZOOSS) *the chief of the Greek gods,* Acts 14:12–14

Ziba (ZY-buh) *a servant of Saul,* 2 Samuel 9:1–11; 16:1–4; 19:24–30

Zimri (ZIM-rye) *a king of Israel,* 1 Kings 16:11–20

Zion (ZY-on) *a hill inside the city of Jerusalem.* See "Mount Zion".

Ziph (ZIF) *a city about forty kilometres south of Jerusalem,* 1 Samuel 23:14–28; 26:1–25

Zipporah (zih-POR-uh) *the wife of Moses,* Exodus 2:15–22; 4:24–26; 18:1–3

zither (ZITH-ur) *a type of musical instrument that had about forty strings on it,* Ezekiel 3:5,7,10,15